第1巻 和文法令名

1. 会社法（第1編から第8編） ・kaishahou
   - Companies Act (Part I, Part II, Part III and Part IV, Part V, Part VI, Part VII and Part VIII)
2. 会社法施行令 ・kaishahou sikou rei ……………………………… 2
   - Order for Enforcement of the Companies Act
9. 財務諸表等の監査証明に関する内閣府令 …………… 1183
   - zaimu shohyoutou no kansashoumeini kansuru naikakufu rei
   - Cabinet Office Ordinance on Audit Certification of Financial Statements, etc.
14. 資金移動業者に関する内閣府令 ・sikin idougyousha ni kansuru naikaku-fu rei ……………………………………………………………… 1345
    - Cabinet Office Ordinance on Funds Transfer Service Providers
10. 四半期財務諸表等の用語・様式及び作成方法に関する規則 ……… 1199
    - shihanki zaimu syohyoutou no yougo-yousiki oyobi sakuseihouhou ni kansuru kisoku
    - Ordinance on Terminology, Forms, and Preparation Methods of Quarterly Financial Statements, etc.
12. 社債、株式等の振替に関する法律施行令 ……………… 1345
    - shasai, kabusikitou no furikaeni kansuru houritu sikou rei
    - Order for Enforcement of the Act on Book-Entry of Company Bonds, Shares, etc.
8. 商業登記法 ・shouygyou touki hou ……………………… 1273
   - Commercial Registration Act
13. 証券情報等の提供又は公表に関する内閣府令 ………… 1139
    - shouken jouhoutou no teikyou matawa kouhyou ni kansuru naikakufu rei
    - Cabinet Office Ordinance on the Provision and Publication of Information on Securities
4. 信託業法 ・shintaku gyou hou ……………………………… 1325
   - Trust Business Act
3. 信託法 ・shintakuhou ……………………………………… 483
   - Trust Act
6. 保険業法 ・hokengyou hou ………………………………… 381
   - Insurance Business Act
7. 保険業法施行令 ・hokengyou hou sikou rei ……………… 539
   - Order for Enforcement of the Insurance Business Act
5. 保険法 ・hoken hou ……………………………………… 未完成
   - Insurance Act
11. 連結財務諸表の用語・様式及び作成方法に関する規則 …… 1227
    - renketu zaimu shohyou no yougo-yousiki oyobi sakuseihouhou ni kansuru kisoku
    - Ordinance on Terminology, Forms, and Preparation Methods of Consolidated Financial Statements

1st ed.2014.10   JSB英文六法

Kashiwagi Noboru
柏木 昇 監修

JSB英文六法
JAPANESE STATUTE BOOK

Vol. 1 *PART I*
Companies Act ;
Commercial Law
第 1 巻
Ⅰ 会社法・商法編

2015

信山社
SHINZANSHA
1431-4

はしがき

　本書は，法務省の「**日本法令外国語訳データベースシステム**」(http://www.japaneselawtranslation.go.jp/) に掲載された法令の英訳を編集し，収録したものである。法令外国語訳は，司法制度改革の一環として，日本法令の信頼できる整合性のある外国語訳を提供するという目的のために平成17（2005）年にスタートした。そのためには日本の法令用語の訳語を確定する必要がある。「株式会社」は "business corporation", "corporation", "company", "joint stock company", "kabushiki-kaisya" 等と，訳者の好みに応じて訳されていた。これでは読者は混乱するばかりである。名古屋大学の協力を得て「**法令用語日英標準対訳辞書**」を作成した。しかし，このような辞書は一朝一夕にできるものではない。この辞書はいまだに改善の途上にある。法令の翻訳も，なんども専門家の校閲を経てから公開されている。法令の翻訳は完全な翻訳はありえない。原文が常に正しい。法令に曖昧な表現があったとしたならば，翻訳も原文の通りに曖昧に翻訳しなければならない。翻訳者が解釈を加えることは望ましくない。法令の翻訳はたいへん根気のいる仕事である。しかし，**法務省「法令外国語訳推進会議」**のメンバーの弁護士や学者が計算を度外視して協力してくださっている。また，英文表現に関しては法務省のネイティブ・アドバイザー Ms. Solana Sawyer が適切な意見を提供してくれている。これらの人々の協力を得て前述の「日本法令外国語訳データベースシステム」には広く世界中から**毎日約8万件から10万件のアクセス**がなされている。法令の翻訳は，毎年新法と改正法が成立することと，より適切な訳語と表現を検討する必要があるという理由で **never ending story** である。しかし，より適切な訳語と表現を探すことはおもしろくやりがいのある仕事である。

　このたび，信山社がこれらの法令外国語訳を紙媒体で出版してくださることになった。紙媒体には電子媒体とは異なった使いやすさがある。より多くの人に英語版日本法令が読まれ，新版を重ねることを期待したい。

　2014年2月27日

柏木　昇

PREFACE

This book contains English translations of statutes published on the web site of the Ministry of Justice (http://www.japaneselawtranslation.go.jp/). The Government started in 2005 translations of Japanese statutes for the purpose of providing reliable and consistent translation. This is a project of the Justice System Reform commenced in 2001.

Before publications of our English translations, even basic legal words were translated inconsistently at the discretion of translators. For example, "*kabushiki kaisya*" is a company corresponding to business corporation, company limited by share, société anonyme or sociedad anónima. This term was translated, according to the taste of translators, as business corporation, corporation, company, joint stock company or *kabushiki-kaisha*. Foreign readers of the translation were much confused. In order to avoid such a confusion which may arise due to inconsistency, we created the Standard Legal Terms Dictionary with a great assistance of professors at the University of Nagoya (http://www.japaneselawtranslation.go.jp/dict/?re=01). The dictionary, however, is still tentative, and it will take a long time to be completed. The dictionary is revised and improved every year.

There is no perfect translation of statutes, although the translations mentioned above are reviewed by several experts. The difficulty lies in the fact that the original text is always authentic. A statute which contains ambiguity should be expressed in English with the ambiguity. No translation of statutes should have a priority over the original text. The translator may not add any intentional interpretation into the translation. The work of quality control and review of the translation is a patient and meticulous work, and therefore I want to express a deep gratitude to members of Japanese Law Translation Council (professors and attorneys) who devoted their precious time and energy. The Advisor, Ms. Solana Sawyer, whose mother language is English, greatly helped us and my gratitude should be extended to him too.

Every day, 80,000 to 100,000 accesses are made to the above mentioned web site from all over the world. Translation work of statutes is not an ending story. Every year, new statutes or amendments are promulgated. This project, quite challenging and interesting, requires a continuous work and need help of readers in order to make the translation better and more understandable.

Before concluding this preface, I express also my thanks to *Shinzan-sha*. *Shinzan-sha* kindly offered to publish the translations in a hard copy form. Publication in paper has its own advantage over the digital one. I hope that many people will not only use this book but also assist us to improve our translations.

June 12, 2014   Noboru Kashiwagi

英文六法を利用するに当たっての注意事項

1．本書に収録された法令は，**法務省の「日本法令外国語訳データベースシステム」に掲載されたものであるが，最新の現行法令ではない場合がある**。その理由は，第1に英訳に時間がかかる。第2に出来上がった翻訳の質を担保するため法務省のネイティブ・アドバイザーと「法務省法令外国語訳推進会議」のメンバーがチェックするためにまた時間がかかる。訳語の確定には著名な学者のグループに検討を依頼することもある。したがって，残念ながら，ある法令の英訳がインターネットの日本法令外国語訳データベースシステムに掲載されたときは，すでに改正法が成立していることがある。したがって，本英文六法の利用に当たってはすでに改正がなされていないかということを必ず確認する必要がある。

2．すべての日本法令用語は，正確な英語の対応語はない。「法律行為」のように似た概念すらない場合がある。法令の英訳にあたっては，英訳された日本法令が，英語圏の人達にとって最も近いイメージを生み出すような訳とした。たとえば，抵当権は "mortgage" と訳してある。抵当権では所有権は抵当権者に移転しないが，"mortgage" では title が mortgagee に移転するから，これは誤訳だ，という人もいる。そのような人は抵当権を "hypothec" と訳すべきだと主張する。しかし，私が打診した範囲では，コモン・ローのローヤーで，"hypothec" という言葉を聞いたことがない，という人が多かった。翻訳を利用する人達の分からない言葉に置き換えても，翻訳をしたことにはならない。以前は，株式会社を "kabushiki-kaisha" とローマ字に置き換えて翻訳をしていた人がいたが，ローマ字に置き換えても日本語を知らない英語圏の人達のための翻訳にはならない。そこで，「**日本法令外国語訳データベース」ではローマ字は使っていない**。重要なことは，翻訳はあくまで翻訳にすぎず，原文は日本語であることである。

3．整合性のとれた法令の英訳を目指しているが，法令用語の訳語についても，表現方法についても，ほぼ毎月1回開催される「法令外国語訳推進会議」で改良されている。法令外国語訳のプロジェクトはまだ発展途上にある。収録英文法令の中には整合性の取れていない訳語や訳し方が見られる。訳語や訳文の改良を重ねる内に訳語の不統一が少なくなって行くと予想される。たとえば，まだ本書には **he/she** のような表現が残っている。しかし，英語圏の立法ルールでは，このような gender を意識した表現は避けることが一般的である。新しい翻訳では **he/she, his/her** のようなを避けている。**shall** の使い方にも統一性がない。ここに収録した英文法令ではまだ他にも修正すべき点が沢山残ってしまっている。これらは鋭意修正し，よりよい英訳とすることで努力中である。

2014年2月27日

柏 木　昇

Warning for the Use of This Book

1. Statutes in English contained in this book are those published at the web site of Japanese Law Translation Database System. The contained translated statutes may not be the current statutes but be of older version. It is because; first, it takes some time to translate a newly published statute into English. Second, in order to ensure the accuracy and consistency of the translation, the translation is reviewed by native advisors of the Ministry of Justice and a member of Japanese Law Translation Council that takes time again. Sometimes, when the translation is up on the website, the translated statute may have already been modified by a subsequent statute. Therefore, it is absolutely necessary to confirm if a translated statute contained in this book has been modified by any subsequent statute.

2. Without exception, legal terms in Japanese language do not have corresponding English term of exact match. Even there is a case where there is no English word similar to the Japanese legal term. An example is the word "*horitsu-koi*" that corresponds by and large to "*Rechtsgeschäft*" in German and "*acte juridique*" in French. When we review the translation, our aim is to create an idea in the mind of readers most similar to the meaning of the original word. In order to do that, the translated word must be understandable to people who understand English but not Japanese. For example, some people argue that the word "*teito-ken*" should be translated into "hypothec." I asked several friends of mine who are grown up in the United States, Australia and UK. Many of them told me that they have not heard of the word. The word hypothec seems to have been derived from German word "*Hypotek*" and French word "*hypothèque.*" Even though "*teito-ken*" is much more similar to "*Hypotek*" and "*hypothèque,*" the English word "hypothec" is useless in our translation because many readers do not understand the meaning. Instead we translated "*teito-ken*" as mortgage. By the word "mortgage", readers will at least imagine a security right on real property created by an agreement. Just replacing a Japanese word into an un-understandable English word is not translation.

We also do not use Japanese expressed in the Roman alphabet. For example, in the past, some translator translated "*kabushiki-kaisha*" that corresponds to a business corporation, as "*kabushiki-kaisha.*" It is not translation. Our aim of translation is to convey an idea in English similar to the original Japanese word, to people who do not understand Japanese language. Expressing a Japanese word with phonetic alphabet expression is not translation.

3. We are trying hard to keep consistency. Every month, a meeting of Japanese Law Translation Council discusses the better translation of Japanese legal words used in statutes and the style of translation. Translation of Japanese statutes with accuracy and consistency is a formidable work. Still we are in the development stage. There remain many inconsistencies and rooms for improvements. We hope that these inconsistencies and rooms for improvements will be less and less. We are going to avoid the expression "he/she." Still there are many of "he/she" in the translated statutes. The use of the word "shall" is not consistent through the translation. We will continue to improve the quality of the translation of Japanese statutes.

第 1 巻 目 次

第 1 巻欧文・和文目次 ……………………………………………… (前見返)
    欧文法令名索引 (前見返 ii)
    和文法令名索引 (前見返 iii)
    新着情報のお知らせ (五十音順) (前見返し iv)

はしがき …………………………………………………………………… 2

PREFACE …………………………………………………………………… 3

英文六法を利用するに当たっての注意事項 ……………………… 4

Warning for the Use of This Book …………………………………… 5

●アクセス頻度順目次 ………………………………………………… **7**

法令用語日英標準対訳辞書〔前付〕
（平成 26 年 3 月改訂版）はしがき Preface ………………… 19

平成 22 年版はしがき Preface ……………………………………… 22

日本法令外国語訳推進会議構成員 ……………………… 20〜21, 25〜27

法令用語日英標準対訳辞書目次 …………………………………… 28
  I 翻訳の基本スタンス (29)
    凡　例 (33)
    特別編 (39)
      法令の形式 (39)
      法令の題名等 (40)
      法令番号 (42)
      法令の慣用的表現 (43)

第 1 巻～第 5 巻 アクセス頻度順目次

	〈第 1 巻〉第 Ⅰ 部　会社法・商法編　頁	翻訳法令年月日	翻訳日	最新改正法年月日
1	・Companies Act (Part Ⅰ, Part Ⅱ, Part Ⅲ and Part Ⅳ, Part Ⅴ, Part Ⅵ, Part Ⅶ and Part Ⅷ)·················· 1 ・kaishahou (dai1hen kara dai8hen) ・会社法（第 1 編から第 8 編）		2009 (H21).4.1	
2	・Order for Enforcement of the Companies Act ·················· 359 ・kaishahou sikou rei ・会社法施行令		2010 (H22).3.24	
3	・Trust Act ·················· 381 ・shintakuhou ・信託法		2009 (H21).11.2	
4	・Trust Business Act ·················· 483 ・shintaku gyou hou ・信託業法		0000 (H00).0.00	
5	・Insurance Act ·················· 000 ・hoken hou ・保険法		（未完）	
6	・Insurance Business Act ·················· 539 ・hokengyou hou ・保険業法		2010 (H22).6.2	
7	・Order for Enforcement of the Insurance Business Act ·················· 1013 ・hokengyou hou sikou rei ・保険業法施行令		2010 (H22).6.3	
8	・Commercial Registration Act ·················· 1139 ・shougyou touki hou ・商業登記法		2009 (H21).6.11	
9	・Cabinet Office Ordinance on Audit Certification of Financial Statements, etc. ·················· 1183 ・zaimu shohyoutou no kansashoumeini kansuru naikakufu rei ・財務諸表等の監査証明に関する内閣府令		2011 (H23).5.10	

1st ed.2014.10　　　7　　　JSB英文六法

第1巻～第5巻 アクセス頻度順目次

		翻訳法令年月日	翻訳日	最新改正法年月日
10	・Ordinance on Terminology, Forms, and Preparation Methods of Quarterly Financial Statements, etc.············1199 ・shihanki zaimu syohyoutou no yougo-yousiki oyobi sakuseihouhou ni kansuru kisoku ・四半期財務諸表等の用語・様式及び作成方法に関する規則	2011 (H23).5.9		
11	・Ordinance on Terminology, Forms, and Preparation Methods of Consolidated Financial Statements············1227 ・renketu zaimu shohyou no yougo-yousiki oyobi sakuseihouhou ni kansuru kisoku ・連結財務諸表の用語・様式及び作成方法に関する規則	2011 (H23).4.22		
12	・Order for Enforcement of the Act on Book-Entry of Company Bonds, Shares, etc.············1273 ・shasai, kabusikitou no furikaeni kansuru houritu sikou rei ・社債，株式等の振替に関する法律施行令	2010 (H22).11.26		
13	・Cabinet Office Ordinance on the Provision and Publication of Information on Securities············1325 ・shouken jouhoutou no teikyou matawa kouhyou ni kansuru naikakufu rei ・証券情報等の提供又は公表に関する内閣府令	2010 (H22).6.2		
14	・Cabinet Office Ordinance on Funds Transfer Service Providers············13445 ・sikin idougyousha ni kansuru naikakufu rei ・資金移動業者に関する内閣府令	2010 (H22).11.26		

	〈第2巻〉第Ⅱ部　民法編	翻訳法令年月日	翻訳日	最新改正法年月日
15	・Civil Code (Part Ⅰ, Part Ⅱ, and Part Ⅲ, Part Ⅳ and Part Ⅴ) ・minpou (dai1hen kara dai5hen) ・民法（第1編から第5編）	2009 (H21).4.1		
16	・Product Liability Act ・seizoubutu sekinin hou ・製造物責任法	2009 (H21).4.1		

第 1 巻～第 5 巻 アクセス頻度順目次

17	・Act on Land and Building Leases ・shakuti shakuya hou ・借地借家法	2010 (H22).7.23	
18	・Act on Special Provisions, etc. of the Civil Code Concerning the Perfection Requirements for the Assignment of Movables and Claims ・dousan oyobi saiken no jouto no taikou youken ni kansuru minpou no tokurei ni kansuru houritu ・動産及び債権の譲渡の対抗要件に関する民法の特例に関する法律	2009 (H21).5.21	
19	・Real Property Registration Act ・fudousan touki hou ・不動産登記法	2009 (H21).10.14	
20	・Order for Enforcement of the Installment Sales Act（割賦販売法自体は未掲載） ・kappu hanbai hou sikou rei ・割賦販売法施行令	2009 (H21).12.1	
21	・Limited Partnership Act for Investment ・toushi jigyou yugen sekinin kumiai keiyaku ni kansuru houritu ・投資事業有限責任組合契約に関する法律	2009 (H21).4.1	
22	・Enforcement Order of the Limited Partnership Act for Investment ・toushi jigyou yugen sekinin kumiai keiyaku ni kansuru houritu sikou rei ・投資事業有限責任組合契約に関する法律施行令	2009 (H21).4.1	
23	・Limited Liability Partnership Act ・yugen sekinin jigyou kumiai keiyaku ni kansuru houritu ・有限責任事業組合契約に関する法律	2009 (H21).4.1	
24	・Act on Securitization of Assets ・shisan no ryudouka ni kansuru houritu ・資産の流動化に関する法律	2009 (H21).11.11	
25	・Electronically Recorded Monetary Claims Act ・densi kiroku saiken hou ・電子記録債権法	2009 (H21).4.1	
26	・Order for Enforcement of the Electronically Recorded Monetary Claims Act ・densi kiroku saiken hou sikou rei ・電子記録債権法施行令	2010 (H22).11.26	

目次

1st ed.2014.10　　　　　　　　　　JSB英文六法

第1巻〜第5巻 アクセス頻度順目次

		翻訳法令年月日	翻訳日	最新改正法年月日
27	・Ordinance for Enforcement of the Electronically Recorded Monetary Claims Act ・denshi kiroku saiken hou shikou kisoku ・電子記録債権法施行規則		2010 (H22).11.26	
28	・Basic Consumer Act ・shouhisha kihon hou ・消費者基本法		2011 (H23).1.4	
29	・Consumer Contract Act ・shouhisha keiyaku hou ・消費者契約法		2011 (H23).1.4	
30	・Ordinance for Enforcement of the Consumer Contract Act ・shouhisha keiyaku sikou kisoku ・消費者契約施行規則		2011 (H23).1.4	
31	・Consumer Safety Act ・shouhisha anzen hou ・消費者安全法		2011 (H23).4.22	
32	・Act on Specified Commercial Transactions ・tokutei syoutorihiki ni kansuru houritu ・特定商取引に関する法律		2009 (H21).12.1	
33	・Order for Enforcement of the Act on Specified Commercial Transactions ・tokutei shoutorihiki ni kansuru houritu sikou rei ・特定商取引に関する法律施行令		2009 (H21).12.1	
34	・Regulations for Enforcement of the Act on Specified Commercial Transactions ・tokutei shoutorihiki ni kansuru houritu sikou kisoku ・特定商取引に関する法律施行規則		2009 (H21).4.1	
35	・Act on the Deposit, etc. Transaction Agreements of Specified Commodities, etc. ・tokutei shouhin no yotakutou torihiki ni kansuru houritu ・特定商品等の預託等取引契約に関する法律		2009 (H21).12.1	
〈第2巻〉第Ⅲ部　倒産法編		翻訳法令年月日	翻訳日	最新改正法年月日
36	・Bankruptcy Act ・hasan hou ・破産法		2009 (H21).10.20	
37	・Civil Rehabilitation Act ・minji saisei hou ・民事再生法		2009 (H21).4.1	

第1巻～第5巻 アクセス頻度順目次

38	・kaisha kousei hou ・会社更生法		(未完成)	
39	・Act on Recognition of and Assistance for Foreign Insolvency Proceedings ・gaikoku tousan no shounin enjo ni kansuru houritu ・外国倒産の承認援助に関する法律		2010 (H22).11.18	

〈第3巻〉第Ⅳ部　民事手続法編	翻訳法令年月日	翻訳日	最新改正法年月日
40	・Code of Civil Procedure ・minji soshou hou ・民事訴訟法		2009 (H21).4.1	
41	・Act on the Civil Jurisdiction of Japan with respect to a Foreign State, etc. ・gaikokutou ni taisuru wagakuni no minji saiban ni kansuru houritu ・外国等に対する我が国の民事裁判権に関する法律		2010 (H22).3.23	
42	・Civil Provisional Remedies Act ・minji hozen hou ・民事保全法		2012 (H24).3.22	
43	・Civil Execution Act ・minji sikkou hou ・民事執行法		2009 (H21).4.1	
44	・Act on Costs of Civil Procedure ・minji soshou hiyou ni kansuru houritu ・民事訴訟費用に関する法律		2009 (H21).11.18	
45	・Rules of Civil Procedure ・minji soshou kisoku ・民事訴訟規則		2009 (H21).4.1	
46	・Act on General Rules for Application of Laws ・hou no tekiyou ni kansuru tusoku hou ・法の適用に関する通則法		2011 (H23).4.27	

〈第3巻〉第Ⅴ部　国籍法・移民法編	翻訳法令年月日	翻訳日	最新改正法年月日
47	・Nationality Act ・kokuseki hou ・国籍法		2009 (H21).5.21	
48	・Immigration Control and Refugee Recognition Act ・shutunyukoku kanri oyobi nanmin nintei hou ・出入国管理及び難民認定法		2009 (H21).12.21	

49	· Ordinance for Enforcement of the Immigration Control and Refugee Recognition Act · shutsunyukoku kanri oyobi nanmin nintei hou shikou kisoku · 出入国管理及び難民認定法施行規則	2009 (H21).6.5	
50	· Ministerial Ordinance to Provide for Criteria Pursuant to Article 7, paragraph (1), item (ii) of the Immigration Control and Refugee Recognition Act · shutsunyukoku kanri oyobi nanmin nintei hou dai7jyou dai1kou dai2gou no kijyunwo sadameru syourei · 出入国管理及び難民認定法第7条第1項第2号の基準を定める省令	2009 (H21).10.7	

〈第3巻〉第Ⅵ部　金融商品取引編	翻訳法令年月日	翻訳日	最新改正法年月日
51 · Financial Instruments and Exchange Act · kinyu shouhintorihiki hou · 金融商品取引法		2009 (H21).6.16	
52 · Cabinet Office Ordinance on Definitions under Article 2 of the Financial Instruments and Exchange Act · kinyu syouhintorihiki dai2jyou ni kiteisuru teigi ni kansuru naikakufu rei · 金融商品取引法第2条に規定する定義に関する内閣府令		2010 (H22).6.25	
53 · Order Providing for the Categories, etc. Prescribed in Article 26, Paragraph (2) of the Banking Act · ginkou hou dai26jyou dai2kou ni kiteisuru kubun touwo sadameru meirei · 銀行法第26条第2項に規定する区分等を定める命令		2010 (H22).5.10	
54 · Act Regulating the Receipt of Contributions, the Receipt of Deposits, and Interest Rates · shussi no ukeire, azukarikin oyobi kinritou no torisimari ni kansuru houritu · 出資の受入れ、預り金及び金利等の取締りに関する法律		2011 (H23).11.11	
55 · Money Lending Business Act · kashikingyou hou · 貸金業法		2009 (H21).11.11	

第1巻～第5巻 アクセス頻度順目次

56	・Order for Enforcement of the Money Lending Act ・kashikingyou hou sikou rei ・貸金業法施行令		2010 (H22).6.3	
57	・Act on Sales, etc. of Financial Instruments ・kinyu syouhin no hanbaitou ni kansuru houritu ・金融商品の販売等に関する法律		2010 (H22).6.25	
58	・Order for Enforcement of the Act on the Sale, etc. of Financial Instruments ・kinyusyouhin no hanbaitou ni kansuru houritu sikou rei ・金融商品の販売等に関する法律施行令		2010 (H22).11.26	
59	・Order for Enforcement of the Act on Engagement in Trust Business by a Financial Institution ・kinyukikan no sintakugyoumu no keneitou ni kansuru houritu sikou rei ・金融機関の信託業務の兼営等に関する法律施行令		2010 (H22).11.26	
60	・Ordinance for Enforcement of the Act on Engagement in Trust Business by a Financial Institution ・kinyukikan no sintakugyoumu no keneitou ni kansuru houritu sikou kisoku ・金融機関の信託業務の兼営等に関する法律施行規則		2010 (H22).11.26	
61	・Act on Investment Trusts and Investment Corporations ・tousi sintaku oyobi tousihoujin ni kansuru houritu ・投資信託及び投資法人に関する法律		2009 (H21).10.12	
62	・Order for Enforcement of the Act on Investment Trusts and Investment Corporations ・tousi sintaku oyobi tousihoujin ni kansuru houritu sikou rei ・投資信託及び投資法人に関する法律施行令		2010 (H22).6.3	
〈第4巻〉第Ⅶ部　知的財産法編		翻訳法令年月日	翻訳日	最新改正法年月日
63	・Patent Act ・tokkyo hou ・特許法		2009 (H21).4.1	
64	・Trademark Act ・shouhyou hou ・商標法		2009 (H21).4.1	

1st ed.2014.10　　　　　13　　　　　JSB英文六法

65	· Trademark Act · chosakuken hou 　ちょさくけんほう · 著作権法		2009 (H21).4.1	
66	· Design Act · ishou hou 　いしょうほう · 意匠法		2009 (H21).4.1	
67	· Utility Model Act · jituyou sinan hou 　じつようしんあんほう · 実用新案法		2009 (H21).4.1	
	〈第4巻〉第Ⅷ部　税法編	翻訳法令 年月日	翻訳日	最新改正法 年月日
68	· National Tax Collection Act（Extract） · kokuzei choushu hou (syou) 　こくぜいちょうしゅうほう · 国税徴収法（抄）		2009 (H21).10.26	
69	· Act on General Rules for National Taxes (Extract) · kokuzei tusoku hou (syou) 　こくぜいつうそくほう · 国税通則法（抄）		2009 (H21).10.26	
70	· Income Tax Act · syotokuzei hou (hikyojusha, gaikoku houjin kanren) 　しょとくぜいほう · 所得税法（非居住者，外国法人関連）		2009 (H21).4.1	
71	· Order for Enforcement of the Income Tax Act（Limited to the provisions related to nonresidents and foreign corporations） · syotokuzei hou sikou rei (hikyojusha, gaikoku houjin kanren) 　しょとくぜいほうしこうれい · 所得税法施行令（非居住者，外国法人関連）		2009 (H21).8.18	
72	· Ordinance for Enforcement of the Income Tax Act (Limited to the provisions related to nonresidents and foreign corporations) · syotokuzei hou sikou kisoku (hikyojusha, gaikoku houjin kanren) 　しょとくぜいほうしこうきそく · 所得税法施行規則（非居住者，外国法人関連）		2010 (H22).7.9	
73	· Act on Special Measures Concerning Taxation · sozei tokubetu soti hou (hikyojusha, gaikoku houjin kanren) 　そぜいとくべつそちほう · 租税特別措置法（非居住者，外国法人関連）		2009 (H21).4.1	

第1巻〜第5巻 アクセス頻度順目次

74	・Order for Enforcement of the Act on Special Measures Concerning Taxation (Limited to the provisions related to nonresidents and foreign corporations) ・sozei tokubetu soti hou sikou rei (hikyojusha, gaikoku houjin kanren) ・租税特別措置法施行令（非居住者，外国法人関連）		2010 (H22).7.9	
75	・Corporation Tax Act ・houjinzei hou (gaikoku houjin kanren bubun) ・法人税法（外国法人関連部分）		2009 (H21).4.1	
76	・Order for Enforcement of the Corporation Tax Act（Limited to the provisions related to foreign corporations） ・houjinzei hou shikou rei (gaikoku houjin kanren bubun) ・法人税法施行令（外国法人関連部分）		2009 (H21).8.18	
77	・Ordinance for Enforcement of the Corporation Tax Act (Limited to the provisions related to foreign corporations) ・houjinzei hou shikou kisoku (gaikoku houjin kanren bubun) ・法人税法施行規則（外国法人関連部分）		2009 (H21).10.26	
	〈第4巻〉第Ⅸ部　銀行編	翻訳法令年月日	翻訳日	最新改正法年月日
78	・Banking Act ・ginkou hou ・銀行法		2010 (H22).6.2	
79	・Bank of Japan Act ・nihon ginkou hou ・日本銀行法		2009 (H21).4.1	
80	・Deposit Insurance Act (Tentative translation) ・yokin hoken hou (zanteiban) ・預金保険法（暫定版）			
81	・Ordinance for Enforcement of the Deposit Insurance Act ・yokin hoken hou shikou kisoku ・預金保険法施行規則		2010 (H22).11.26	
	〈第4巻〉第Ⅹ部　労働法編	翻訳法令年月日	翻訳日	最新改正法年月日
82	・Labor Standards Act ・roudou kijyun hou ・労働基準法		2009 (H21).4.1	

1st ed.2014.10　　　　　　　　　15　　　　　　　　　JSB英文六法

83	· Ordinance for Enforcement of the Labor Standards Act · roudou kijyun hou sikou kisoku · 労働基準法施行規則	2009 (H21).4.1	
84	· Industrial Safety and Health Act · roudou anzen eisei hou · 労働安全衛生法	2009 (H21).4.1	
85	· Labor Union Act · roudou kumiai hou · 労働組合法	2009 (H21).4.1	
86	· Labor Relations Adjustment Act · roudou kankei chousei hou · 労働関係調整法	2009 (H21).6.16	
87	· Industrial Accident Compensation Insurance Act · roudousha saigai hosyou hoken hou · 労働者災害補償保険法	2009 (H21).9.11	
88	· Labor Contract Act · roudou keiyaku hou · 労働契約法	(H22).11.5	
89	· Act on the Collection, etc. of Insurance Premiums of Labor Insurance · roudou hoken no hokenryou no chousyutou ni kansuru houritu · 労働保険の保険料の徴収等に関する法律	2009 (H21).4.1	
	〈第4巻〉第XI部　外国為替編	翻訳法令 年月日	翻訳日	最新改正法 年月日
90	· Foreign Exchange and Foreign Trade Act · gaikoku kawase oyobi gaikoku boueki hou · 外国為替及び外国貿易法	2009 (H21).12.1	
91	· Foreign Exchange Order · gaikou kawase rei · 外国為替令	2009 (H21).5.22	
92	· Ministerial Ordinance on Trade Relation Invisible Trade, etc. · boueki kankei bouekigai torihiki ni kansuru syourei · 貿易関係貿易外取引に関する省令	2009 (H21).5.22	
93	· Import Trade Control Order · yunyu boueki kanri rei · 輸入貿易管理令	2009 (H21).4.1	

94	· Export Trade Control Order (Tentative translation) · yushutu boueki kanri rei · 輸出貿易管理令	2009 (H21).6.16	
95	· Ordinance of the Ministry Specifying Goods and Technologies Pursuant to Provisions of the Appended Table 1 of the Export Control Order and the Appended Table of the Foreign Exchange Order · yushutu boueki kanrirei beppyou dai1 oyobi gaikoku kawaserei beppyou no kitei ni motoduki kamotu mataha gijutu wo sadameru syourei · 輸出貿易管理令別表第一及外国為替令別表の規定に基づき貨物又は技術を定める省令		
96	· Export Trade Control Ordinance (Tentative translation) · yushutu boueki kanri kisoku · 輸出貿易管理規則	2009 (H21).5.27	
97	· Cabinet Order on Inward Direct Investment, etc. · tainai chokusetu toushitou ni kansuru seirei · 対内直接投資等に関する政令	2011 (H23).2.19	
98	· Order on Inward Direct Investment, etc. · tainai chokusetu toushitou ni kansuru meirei · 対内直接投資等に関する命令	2011 (H23).2.19	
99	· Trade Insurance and Investment Act · boueki hoken hou · 貿易保険法	2011 (H23).1.20	
100	· Public Announcement on the Items of Goods Subject to Import Quotas, the Places of Origin or Places of Shipment of Goods Requiring Approval for Import, and Other Necessary Matters Concerning Import of Goods · yunyu wariate wo ukerubeki kamotu no hinmoku, yunyu no syounin woukerubeki kamotu no gensanti mataha funadumi tiiki sonota kamotu no yunyu ni tuite hituyouna jikou no kouhyou · 輸入割当てを受けるべき貨物の品目，輸入の承認を受けるべき貨物の原産地又は船積地域その他貨物の輸入について必要な事項の公表	英文だけ データ無， 和英交互の HTML 66枚	

	〈第 4 巻〉第 XII 部　独占禁止法関係	翻訳法令年月日	翻訳日	最新改正法年月日
101	・Act on Prohibition of Private Monopolization and Maintenance of Fair Trade ・shiteki dokusen no kinshi oyobi kousei torihiki no kakuho ni kansuru houritu ・私的独占の禁止及び公正取引の確保に関する法律		2010 (H22).10.15	
102	・Unfair Competition Prevention Act (Tentative translation) ・fusei kyousou boushi hou ・不正競争防止法		2009 (H21).12.1	
103	・Act against Delay in Payment of Subcontract Proceeds, Etc. to Subcontractors ・shitauke daikin tien boushi hou ・下請代金遅延防止法		2009 (H21).4.1	
104	・Designation of Unfair Trade Practices ・fukousei na torihiki hou ・不公正な取引方法		2009 (H21).4.1	
105	・Rules on Applications for Approval, Reporting, Notification, etc. Pursuant to the Provisions of Articles 9 to 16 of the Act on Prohibition of Private Monopolization and Maintenance of Fair Trade ・shiteki dokusen no kinshi oyobi kousei torihiki no kakuho ni kansuru houritu dai9jyou kara dai16jyou madeno kiteiniyoru ninkano shinsei, houkoku oyobi todokedetou ni kansuru kisoku ・私的独占の禁止及び公正取引の確保に関する法律第9条から第16条までの規定による認可の申請，報告及び届出等に関する規則		2010 (H22).10.19	
106	・Designation of Specific Unfair Trade Practices by Large-Scale Retailers Relating to Trade with Suppliers ・daikibo kourigyousha niyoru nounyugyousha tono torihikiniokeru tokuteino fuseina torihiki houhou ・大規模小売業者による納入業者との取引における特定の不公正な取引方法		2009 (H21).4.1	

107	・Act on Elimination and Prevention of Involvement in Bid Rigging, etc. and Punishments for Acts by Employees that Harm Fairness of Bidding, etc. ・nyusatu dangou kanyo koui no haijo oyobi bousi narabi ni syokuin niyoru nyusatutou no kouseiwo gaisubeki kouitou no syobatu ni kansuru houritu ・入札談合等関与行為の排除及び防止並びに職員による入札等の公正を害すべき行為等の処罰に関する法律	2009 (H21).4.1	
108	・Rules on Hearings by the Fair Trade Commission ・kousei torihiki iinkai no shinpan ni kansuru kisoku ・公正取引委員会の審判に関する規則	2010 (H22).9.3	
109	・Rules on Reporting and the Submission of Supporting Materials in Relation to Immunity from or Reduction of Surcharges ・kachoukin no genmen ni kakaru houkoku oyobi shiryou no teisyutu ni kansuru kisoku ・課徴金の減免に係る報告及び資料の提出に関する規則	2011 (H23).1.14	
110	・Act against Unjustifiable Premiums and Misleading Representations ・futou keihinrui oyobi futou hyouji bousi hou ・不当景品類及び不当表示防止法	2009 (H21).4.1	
〈第5巻〉第XIII部　法令用語和英辞書 （最新版＝平成25年3月改訂版）		翻訳法令 年月日	改訂日	最新改正法 年月日
111	・Standard Legal Terms Dictionary ・hourei yougo nichiei hyoujyun taiyaku jisho ・法令用語日英標準対訳辞書	2014 (H26.3)	

A 《ABC順法令一覧》25年7月19日現在

A 《ABC順法令一覧》25年7月19日現在

法外訳 SYS	法令名	所管庁	PDFデータ頁数	○:済 △:未完 →備考
118	下請代金支払遅延等防止法	公正取引委員会	14	○
265	不当景品類及び不当表示防止法	消費者庁	13	○
205	知的財産高等裁判所設置法	法務省	3	○
7	運輸安全委員会設置法	国土交通省	24	○
234	特定機器に係る適合性評価手続の結果の外国との相互承認の実施に関する法律	総務省	43	○
314	労働者派遣事業の適正な運営の確保及び派遣労働者の就業条件の整備等に関する法律	厚生労働省	77	○
243	逃亡犯罪人引渡法	法務省	22	○
50	行政機関の保有する情報の公開に関する法律	総務省	22	○
4	石綿による健康被害の救済に関する法律	環境省	66	○
77	公益社団法人及び公益財団法人の認定等に関する法律	内閣府	55	○
199	建物の区分所有等に関する法律	法務省	57	○
227	特定化学物質の環境への排出量の把握等及び管理の改善の促進に関する法律	経済産業省	25	○
296	有害物質を含有する家庭用品の規制に関する法律	厚生労働省	6	○
268	文化財の不法な輸出入等の規制等に関する法律	文部科学省	4	○
291	民事訴訟費用等に関する法律	法務省	50	○

A 《ABC 順法令一覧》25 年 7 月 19 日現在

＊S＝昭和、H＝平成

翻訳（英訳）	法令番号	改正	辞書 ver	翻訳日	法なび
Act against Delay in Payment of Subcontract Proceeds, Etc. to Subcontractors	S31 法律第 120 号	H17 法律第 87 号	1.0	H21.4.1	76
Act against Unjustifiable Premiums and Misleading Representations	S37 法律第 134 号	H17 法律第 35 号	1.0	H21.4.1	185
Act for Establishment of the Intellectual Property High Court	H16 法律第 119 号		2.0	H21.4.1	138
Act for Establishment of the Japan Transport Safety Board	S48 法律第 113 号	H20 法律第 26 号	3.0	H22.5.27	
Act for Implementation of the Mutual Recognition between Japan and Foreign States in Relation to Results of Conformity Assessment Procedures of Specified Equipment	H13 法律第 111 号	H19 法律第 92 号	3.0	H21.4.1	159
Act for Securing the Proper Operation of Worker Dispatching Undertakings and Improved Working Conditions for Dispatched Workers	S60 法律第 88 号	H18 法律第 82 号	2.0	H21.4.1	218
Act of Extradition	S28 法律第 68 号	H19 法律第 37 号	3.0	H22.2.19	167
Act on Access to Information Held by Administrative Organs	H11 法律第 42 号	H16 法律第 84 号	1.0	H21.4.1	35
Act on Asbestos Health Damage Relief	H18 法律第 4 号		2.0	H21.4.1	3
Act on Authorization of Public Interest Incorporated Associations and Public Interest Incorporated Foundation	H18 法律第 49 号		2.0	H21.4.1	48
Act on Building Unit Ownership, etc.	S37 法律第 69 号	H20 法律第 203 号	5.0	H23.3.2	
Act on Confirmation, etc. of Release Amounts of Specific Chemical Substances in the Environment and Promotion of Improvements to the Management Thereof	H11 法律第 86 号	H14 法律第 152 号	1.0	H21.4.1	155
Act on Control of Household Products Containing Harmful Substances	S48 法律第 112 号	H21 法律第 49 号	4.0	H22.2.17	
Act on Controls on the Illicit Export and Import and other matters of Cultural Property	H14 法律第 81 号		1.0	H21.4.1	189
Act on Costs of Civil Procedure	S46 法律第 40 号	H19 法律第 113 号	4.0	H21.11.18	

日本法令外国語訳データベースシステム　最終１覧データ収集日：H25.7.19

ABC 順目次

1st ed.2014.10　　　JSB英文六法

A《ABC順法令一覧》25年7月19日現在

法外訳SYS	法令名	所管庁	PDFデータ頁数	○:済 △:未完 →備考
32	家畜伝染病予防法	農林水産省	69	○
137	地震保険に関する法律	財務省	24	○
210	電子署名及び認証業務に関する法律	経済産業省	30	○
245	入札談合等関与行為の排除及び防止並びに職員による入札等の公正を害すべき行為の処罰に関する法律	公正取引委員会	10	○
42	企業立地の促進等による地域における産業集積の形成及び活性化に関する法律	経済産業省	48	○
278	法の適用に関する通則法	法務省	22	○
89	国税通則法（抄）	財務省	26	○
69	携帯音声通信事業者による契約者等の本人確認等及び携帯音声通信役務の不正な利用の防止に関する法律	総務省	21	○
200	短時間労働者の雇用管理の改善等に関する法律	厚生労働省	25	○
92	国際捜査共助等に関する法律	法務省	17	○
224	投資信託及び投資法人に関する法律	金融庁	268	○
124	借地借家法	法務省	30	○
184	船舶油濁損害賠償保障法	国土交通省	43	○
36	海難審判法	国土交通省	18	○
251	日本電信電話株式会社等に関する法律	総務省	52	○
61	刑事収容施設及び被収容者等の処遇に関する法律	法務省	204	○
97	港則法	国土交通省	20	○
35	海洋生物資源の保存及び管理に関する法律	農林水産省	34	○

A 《ABC 順法令一覧》25 年 7 月 19 日現在

翻訳（英訳）	法令番号	改正	辞書 ver	翻訳日	法なび
Act on Domestic Animal Infectious Diseases Control	S26 法律第 166 号	H16 法律第 68 号	1.0	H21.4.1	25
Act on Earthquake Insurance	S41 法律第 73 号	H11 法律第 160 号	3.0	H22.3.9	90
Act on Electronic Signatures and Certification Business	H12 法律第 102 号	H18 法律第 10 号	1.0	H21.4.1	142
Act on Elimination and Prevention of Involvement in Bid Rigging, etc. and Punishments for Acts by Employees that Harm Fairness of Bidding, etc.	H14 法律第 101 号	H18 法律第 110 号	2.0	H21.4.1	169
Act on Formation and Development of Regional Industrial Clusters through Promotion of Establishment of New Business Facilities, etc.	H19 法律第 40 号	H20 法律第 37 号	3.0	H21.4.1	29
Act on General Rules for Application of Laws	H18 法律第 78 号		5.0	H23.4.27	
Act on General Rules for National Taxes (Extract)	S37 法律第 66 号	H19 法律第 6 号	4.0	H21.10.26	
Act on Identification, etc. by Mobile Voice Communications Carriers of their Subscribers, etc. and for Prevention of Improper Use of Mobile Voice Communications Services	H17 法律第 31 号		2.0	H21.4.1	41
Act on Improvement, etc. of Employment Management for Part-Time Workers	H5 法律第 76 号	H19 法律第 72 号	2.0	H21.4.1	134
Act on International Assistance in Investigation and Other Related Matters	S55 法律第 69 号	H18 法律第 58 号	2.0	H21.4.1	58
Act on Investment Trusts and Investment Corporations	S26 法律第 198 号	H20 法律第 65 号	3.0	H21.10.12	154
Act on Land and Building Leases	H3 法律第 90 号	H19 法律第 132 号	4.0	H22.7.23	
Act on Liability for Oil Pollution Damage	S50 法律第 95 号	H16 法律第 37 号	2.0	H21.4.1	123
Act on Marine Accident Inquiry	S22 法律第 135 号	H20 法律第 26 号	3.0	H21.6.16	28
Act on Nippon Telegraph and Telephone Corporation, etc.	S59 法律第 85 号	H17 法律第 87 号	1.0	H21.4.1	175
Act on Penal Detention Facilities and Treatment of Inmates and Detainees	H17 法律第 50 号	H19 法律第 37 号	2.0	H21.4.1	38
Act on Port Regulations	S23 法律第 174 号	H18 法律第 68 号	2.0	H21.4.1	62
Act on Preservation and Control of Living Marine Resources	H8 法律第 77 号	H19 法律第 77 号	4.0	H21.4.1	27

A《ABC順法令一覧》25年7月19日現在

法外訳 SYS	法令名	所管庁	PDF データ 頁数	○:済 △:未完 →備考
161	私的独占の禁止及び公正取引の確保に関する法律	公正取引委員会	133	○
74	個別労働関係紛争の解決の促進に関する法律	厚生労働省	10	○
203	地球温暖化対策の推進に関する法律	環境省	39	○
294	民間資金等の活用による公共施設等の整備等の促進に関する法律	内閣府	23	○
113	裁判外紛争解決手続の利用の促進に関する法律	法務省	28	○
273	保健師助産師看護師法	厚生労働省	55	○
126	児童買春、児童ポルノに係る行為等の処罰及び児童の保護等に関する法律	法務省	11	○
24	外国倒産処理手続の承認援助に関する法律	法務省	54	○
121	使用済自動車の再資源化等に関する法律	経済産業省	136	○
22	外国人漁業の規制に関する法律	農林水産省	8	○
260	ヒトに関するクローン技術等の規制に関する法律	文部科学省	19	○
236	特定電子メールの送信の適正化等に関する法律	総務省	21	○
235	特定特殊自動車排出ガスの規制等に関する法律	環境省	32	○
52	金融商品の販売等に関する法律	金融庁	14	○
103	雇用の分野における男女の均等な機会及び待遇の確保等に関する法律	厚生労働省	21	○
170	資産の流動化に関する法律	金融庁	313	○
319	老人福祉法	厚生労働省	52	○
93	国際連合安全保障理事会決議第1874号等を踏まえ我が国が実施する貨物検査等に関する特別措置法	外務省	13	○

JSB英文六法　　1st ed. 2014.10

A 《ABC 順法令一覧》25 年 7 月 19 日現在

翻訳（英訳）	法令番号	改正	辞書 ver	翻訳日	法なび
Act on Prohibition of Private Monopolization and Maintenance of Fair Trade	S22 法律第 54 号	H21 法律第 51 号	4.0	H22.10.15	104
Act on Promoting the Resolution of Individual Labor-Related Disputes	H13 法律第 112 号	H16 法律第 140 号	1.0	H21.4.1	47
Act on Promotion of Global Warming Countermeasures	H10 法律第 117 号	H18 法律第 57 号	1.0	H21.4.1	136
Act on Promotion of Private Finance Initiative	H11 法律第 117 号	H18 法律第 53 号	3.0	H21.4.1	204
Act on Promotion of Use of Alternative Dispute Resolution	H16 法律第 151 号	H18 法律第 50 号	1.0	H21.4.1	72
Act on Public Health Nurses, Midwives, and Nurses	S23 法律第 203 号	H21 法律第 78 号	6.0	H24.10.31	
Act on Punishment of Activities Relating to Child Prostitution and Child Pornography, and the Protection of Children	H11 法律第 52 号	H16 法律第 106 号	1.0	H21.4.1	80
Act on Recognition of and Assistance for Foreign Insolvency Proceedings	H12 法律第 129 号	H18 法律第 50 号	3.0	H22.11.18	
Act on Recycling, etc. of End-of-Life Vehicles	H14 法律第 87 号	H18 法律第 50 号	2.0	H21.4.1	78
Act on Regulation of Fishing Operation by Foreign Nationals	S42 法律第 60 号	H13 法律第 92 号	1.0	H21.4.1	16
Act on Regulation of Human Cloning Techniques	H12 法律第 146 号		1.0	H21.4.1	181
Act on Regulation of Transmission of Specified Electronic Mail	H14 法律第 26 号	H17 法律第 87 号	1.0	H21.4.1	161
Act on Regulation, Etc. of Emissions from Non-road Special Motor Vehicles	H17 法律第 51 号		1.0	H21.4.1	160
Act on Sales, etc. of Financial Instruments	H12 法律第 101 号	H18 法律第 66 号	3.0	H22.6.25	
Act on Securing, Etc. of Equal Opportunity and Treatment between Men and Women in Employment	S47 法律第 113 号	H18 法律第 82 号	1.0	H21.4.1	66
Act on Securitization of Assets	H10 法律第 105 号	H20 法律第 65 号	3.0	H21.11.11	
Act on Social Welfare for the Elderly	S38 法律第 133 号	H20 法律第 42 号	4.0	H22.10.6	
Act on Special Measures concerning Cargo Inspections etc. Conducted by the Government Taking into Consideration United Nations Security Council Resolution 1874, etc.	H22 法律第 43 号		5.0	H24.6.29	

日本法令外国語訳データベースシステム 最終1覧データ収集日：H25.7.19

ABC順目次

1st ed. 2014.10　　　25　　　JSB 英文六法

A《ABC順法令一覧》25年7月19日現在

法外訳 SYS	法令名	所管庁	PDFデータ頁数	○:済 △:未完 →備考
108	債権管理回収業に関する特別措置法（H18.法律第115号による改正のうち，H22.6月18日施行分（第18条第5項）については未反映）	法務省	29	○
215	電気事業者による新エネルギー等の利用に関する特別措置法（第2条第2項第6号改正未施行）	経済産業省	11	○
68	原子力災害対策特別措置法	経済産業省	58	○
187	租税特別措置法（非居住者、外国法人関連部分）	財務省	226	○
26	外国弁護士による法律事務の取扱いに関する特別措置法	法務省	44	○
246	日本国とアメリカ合衆国との間の相互協力及び安全保障条約第6条に基づく施設及び区域並びに日本国における合衆国軍隊の地位に関する協定の実施に伴う郵便法の特例に関する法律	総務省	4	○
247	日本国とアメリカ合衆国との間の相互協力及び安全保障条約第6条に基づく施設及び区域並びに日本国における合衆国軍隊の地位に関する協定の実施に伴う電波法の特例に関する法律	総務省	2	○
248	日本国とアメリカ合衆国との間の相互協力及び安全保障条約第6条に基づく施設及び区域並びに日本国における合衆国軍隊の地位に関する協定等の実施に伴う電気通信事業法等の特例に関する法律	総務省	4	○
209	電子消費者契約及び電子承諾通知に関する民法の特例に関する法律	経済産業省	4	○

A《ABC 順法令一覧》25 年 7 月 19 日現在

翻訳（英訳）	日本法令外国語訳データベースシステム 最終1覧データ収集日：H25.7.19					法なび
	法令番号	改正	辞書ver	翻訳日	
Act on Special Measures Concerning Claim Management and Collection Businesses	H10 法律第 126 号	H20 法律第 74 号	3.0	H21.12.25	
Act on Special Measures Concerning New Energy Use by operators of electric utilities (The revision of Article 2, paragraph (2), item (vi) has not come into force.)	H14 法律第 62 号	H21 法律第 70 号	4.0	H21.12.15	145
Act on Special Measures Concerning Nuclear Emergency Preparedness	H11 法律第 156 号	H18 法律第 118 号	2.0	H21.4.1	45
Act on Special Measures Concerning Taxation (Limited to the provisions related to nonresidents and foreign corporations)	S32 法律第 26 号	H19 法律第 6 号	2.0	H21.4.1	126
Act on Special Measures concerning the Handling of Legal Services by Foreign Lawyers	S61 法律第 66 号	H15 法律第 128 号	1.0	H21.4.1	19
Act on Special Provisions of the Postal Act attendant upon the Enforcement of the "Agreement under Article VI of the Treaty of Mutual Cooperation and Security between Japan and the United States of America regarding Facilities and Areas and the Status of United States Armed Forces in Japan"	S27 法律第 122 号	H17 法律第 102 号	1.0	H21.4.1	170
Act on Special Provisions of the Radio Law Attendant upon the Enforcement of the "Agreement under Article VI of the Treaty of Mutual Cooperation and Security between Japan and the United States of America regarding Facilities and Areas and the Status of United States Armed Forces in Japan"	S27 法律第 108 号	S35 法律第 102 号	2.0	H21.4.1	171
Act on Special Provisions of the Telecommunications Business Law, etc. Attendant upon the Enforcement of the "Agreement under ARTICLE VI of the Treaty of Mutual Cooperation and Security between Japan and the United States of America regarding Facilities and Areas and the Status of United States Armed Forces in Japan"	S27 法律第 107 号	S59 法律第 87 号	2.0	H21.4.1	172
Act on Special Provisions to the Civil Code Concerning Electronic Consumer Contracts and Electronic Acceptance Notice	H13 法律第 95 号		1.0	H21.4.1	141

1st ed.2014.10 27 JSB 英文六法

A 《ABC順法令一覧》25年7月19日現在

法外訳 SYS	法令名	所管庁	PDFデータ頁数	○:済 △:未完 →:備考
219	動産及び債権の譲渡の対抗要件に関する民法の特例等に関する法律	法務省	20	○
230	特定商取引に関する法律	消費者庁	160	○
253	農林物資の規格化及び品質表示の適正化に関する法律	農林水産省	49	○
254	半導体集積回路の回路配置に関する法律	経済産業省	48	○
30	外国等に対する我が国の民事裁判権に関する法律	法務省	15	○
307	労働保険の保険料の徴収等に関する法律	厚生労働省	123	○
6	遺伝子組換え生物等の使用等の規制による生物の多様性の確保に関する法律	環境省	37	○
233	特定商品等の預託等取引契約に関する法律	消費者庁	12	○
20	化学物質の審査及び製造等の規制に関する法律（附則第4条未施行 等）	経済産業省	77	○
255	排他的経済水域における漁業等に関する主権的権利の行使等に関する法律	農林水産省	19	○
112	裁判の迅速化に関する法律	法務省	4	○
303	遺言の方式の準拠法に関する法律	法務省	3	○
267	扶養義務の準拠法に関する法律	法務省	3	○
237	特定電気通信役務提供者の損害賠償責任の制限及び発信者情報の開示に関する法律	総務省	6	○
193	大規模小売店舗立地法	経済産業省	20	○
240	独立行政法人産業技術総合研究所法	経済産業省	17	○

ABC順目次

JSB英文六法　　　　1st ed.2014.10

A 《ABC 順法令一覧》25 年 7 月 19 日現在

翻訳（英訳）	日本法令外国語訳データベースシステム 最終1覧データ収集日：H25.7.19					法なび
	法令番号	改正	辞書ver	翻訳日	
Act on Special Provisions, etc. of the Civil Code Concerning the Perfection Requirements for the Assignment of Movables and Claims	H1 法律第 104 号	H19 法律第 23 号	3.0	H21.5.21	149
Act on Specified Commercial Transactions	S51 法律第 57 号	H21 法律第 49 号	4.0	H21.12.1	156
Act on Standardization and Proper Quality Labeling of Agricultural and Forestry Products	S25 法律第 175 号	H21 法律第 49 号	4.0	H21.4.1	
Act on the Circuit Layout of a Semiconductor Integrated Circuits	S60 法律第 43 号	H18 法律第 50 号	3.0	H21.4.1	177
Act on the Civil Jurisdiction of Japan with respect to a Foreign State, etc.	H21 法律第 24 号		4.0	H22.3.23	
Act on the Collection, etc. of Insurance Premiums of Labor Insurance	S44 法律第 84 号	H19 法律第 110 号	3.0	H21.4.1	213
Act on the Conservation and Sustainable Use of Biological Diversity through Regulations on the Use of Living Modified Organisms	H15 法律第 97 号	H19 法律第 8 号	2.0	H21.4.1	5
Act on the Deposit, etc. Transaction Agreements of Specified Commodities, etc.	S61 法律第 62 号	H21 法律第 49 号	4.0	H21.12.1	
Act on the Evaluation of Chemical Substances and Regulation of Their Manufacture, etc. (Article 4 of the Supplementary Provisions unenforced, etc.)	S48 法律第 117 号	H21 法律第 39 号	4.0	H21.12.1	14
Act on the Exercise of the Sovereign Right for Fishery, etc. in the Exclusive Economic Zone	H8 法律第 76 号	H13 法律第 91 号	2.0	H21.4.1	178
Act on the Expediting of Trials	H15 法律第 107 号		2.0	H21.4.1	71
Act on the Law Applicable to the Form of Wills	S39 法律第 100 号	H18 法律第 78 号	5.0	H22.12.21	
Act on the Law Applicable to the Obligation of Support	S61 法律第 84 号	H18 法律第 78 号	5.0	H22.12.21	
Act on the Limitation of Liability for Damages of Specified Telecommunications Service Providers and the Right to Demand Disclosure of Identification Information of the Senders	H13 法律第 137 号		2.0	H21.4.1	162
Act on the Measures by Large-Scale Retail Stores for Preservation of Living Environment	H10 法律第 91 号	H12 法律第 91 号	3.0	H21.4.24	130
Act on the National Institute of Advanced Industrial Science and Technology	H11 法律第 203 号	H19 法律第 36 号	3.0	H21.12.10	

A 《ABC順法令一覧》25年7月19日現在

ABC順目次

法外訳 SYS	法令名	所管庁	PDFデータ頁数	○:済 △:未完 →備考
239	独立行政法人新エネルギー・産業技術総合開発機構法（第2条未施行 等）	経済産業省	50	○
107	高齢者虐待の防止、高齢者の養護者に対する支援等に関する法律	厚生労働省	18	○
259	配偶者からの暴力の防止及び被害者の保護に関する法律	内閣府	29	○
1	アイヌ文化の振興並びにアイヌの伝統等に関する知識の普及及び啓発に関する法律	国土交通省		△
169	資源の有効な利用の促進に関する法律	経済産業省	40	○
147	新エネルギー利用等の促進に関する特別措置法	経済産業省	15	○
226	特定先端大型研究施設の共用の促進に関する法律	文部科学省	24	○
304	容器包装に係る分別収集及び再商品化の促進等に関する法律	経済産業省	49	○
191	大学等における技術に関する研究成果の民間事業者への移転の促進に関する法律	経済産業省	32	○
180	水産資源保護法	農林水産省	46	○
73	個人情報の保護に関する法律	内閣府	35	○
49	行政機関の保有する個人情報の保護に関する法律	総務省	45	○
8	エネルギーの使用の合理化に関する法律	経済産業省	111	○
33	核原料物質、核燃料物質及び原子炉の規制に関する法律	経済産業省	233	○
269	武力攻撃事態における外国軍用品等の海上輸送の規制に関する法律	防衛省	33	○
14	会社分割に伴う労働契約の承継等に関する法律	厚生労働省	7	○
91	国際受刑者移送法	法務省	32	○
270	武力攻撃事態における捕虜等の取扱いに関する法律	防衛省	105	○

A 《ABC 順法令一覧》25 年 7 月 19 日現在

翻訳（英訳）	法令番号	改正	辞書 ver	翻訳日	法なび
Act on the New Energy and Industrial Technology Development Organization (Article 2 unenforced, etc.)	H14 法律第 145 号	H21 法律第 70 号	4.0	H21.12.1	164
Act on the Prevention of Elder Abuse, Support for Caregivers of Elderly Persons and Other Related Matters	H17 法律第 124 号	H20 法律第 42 号	4.0	H22.10.6	
Act on the Prevention of Spousal Violence and the Protection of Victims	H13 法律第 31 号	H19 法律第 113 号	2.0	H21.4.1	180
Act on the Promotion of Ainu Culture, and Dissemination and Enlightenment of Knowledge about Ainu Tradition, etc.	H9 法律第 52 号	H18 法律第 50 号	2.0	H21.4.1	1
Act on the Promotion of Effective Utilization of Resources	H3 法律第 48 号	H14 法律第 1 号	1.0	H21.4.1	111
Act on the Promotion of New Energy Usage	H9 法律第 37 号	H17 法律第 87 号	2.0	H21.11.2	96
Act on the Promotion of Public Utilization of the Specific Advanced Large Research Facilities	H6 法律第 78 号	H18 法律第 37 号	3.0	H22.5.27	
Act on the Promotion of Sorted Collection and Recycling of Containers and Packaging	H7 法律第 112 号	H18 法律第 76 号	1.0	H21.4.1	212
Act on the Promotion of Technology Transfer from Universities to Private Business Operators	H10 法律第 52 号	H17 法律第 87 号	2.0	H21.4.1	129
Act on the Protection of Fishery Resources	S26 法律第 313 号	H19 法律第 77 号	2.0	H21.4.1	120
Act on the Protection of Personal Information	H15 法律第 57 号	H15 法律第 119 号	1.0	H21.4.1	46
Act on the Protection of Personal Information Held by Administrative Organs	H15 法律第 58 号	H17 法律第 102 号	2.0	H21.4.1	34
Act on the Rational Use of Energy	S54 法律第 49 号	H20 法律第 47 号	3.0	H21.4.24	6
Act on the Regulation of Nuclear Source Material, Nuclear Fuel Material and Reactors	S32 法律第 166 号	H19 法律第 84 号	3.0	H21.4.9	42
Act on the Restriction of Maritime Transportation of Foreign Military Supplies, etc. in Armed Attack Situations	H16 法律第 116 号	H18 法律第 118 号	4.0	H21.9.1	187
Act on the Succession to Labor Contracts upon Company Split	H12 法律第 103 号	H17 法律第 87 号	2.0	H21.4.1	12
Act on the Transnational Transfer of Sentenced Persons	H14 法律第 66 号	H22 法律第 29 号	1.0	H23.12.15	57
Act on the Treatment of Prisoners of War and Other Detainees in Armed Attack Situations	H16 法律第 117 号	H20 法律第 5 号	3.0	H21.7.16	188

A《ABC順法令一覧》25年7月19日現在

法外訳 SYS	法令名	所管庁	PDF データ 頁数	○:済 △:未完 →備考
5	育児休業、介護休業等育児又は家族介護を行う労働者の福祉に関する法律	厚生労働省	62	○
218	動物の愛護及び管理に関する法律	環境省	29	○
130	出資の受入れ、預り金及び金利等の取締りに関する法律	法務省	12	○
46	行政事件訴訟法	法務省	39	○
51	行政相談委員法	総務省	4	○
47	行政手続法	総務省	39	○
23	外国人登録法	法務省	30	○
272	弁護士法	法務省	107	○
250	日本銀行法	財務省	62	○
58	銀行法	金融庁	298	○
59	銀行法	金融庁	239	○
258	破産法	法務省	218	○
120	住生活基本法	国土交通省		△
220	土地基本法	国土交通省	8	○
182	生物多様性基本法	環境省	17	○
256	犯罪被害者等基本法	内閣府	12	○
9	エネルギー政策基本法	経済産業省	7	○
141	循環型社会形成推進基本法	環境省	20	○
37	肝炎対策基本法	厚生労働省	12	○
34	海洋基本法	内閣官房	16	○

A 《ABC 順法令一覧》25 年 7 月 19 日現在

翻訳（英訳）	法令番号	改正	辞書 ver	翻訳日	法なび
Act on the Welfare of Workers Who Take Care of Children or Other Family Members Including Child Care and Family Care Leave	H3 法律第 76 号	H16 法律第 160 号	1.0	H21.4.1	4
Act on Welfare and Management of Animals	S48 法律第 105 号	H17 法律第 68 号	2.0	H21.4.1	148
Act Regulating the Receipt of Contributions, the Receipt of Deposits, and Interest Rates	S29 法律第 195 号	H19 法律第 85 号	6.0	H23.11.11	84
Administrative Case Litigation Act	S37 法律第 139 号	H19 法律第 109 号	4.0	H22.9.14	
Administrative Counselors Act	S41 法律第 99 号	H11 法律第 160 号	1.0	H21.4.1	36
Administrative Procedure Act	H5 法律第 88 号	H17 法律第 73 号	1.0	H21.4.1	32
Alien Registration Act	S27 法律第 125 号	H16 法律第 152 号	2.0	H21.4.1	17
Attorney Act	S24 法律第 205 号	H17 法律第 87 号	3.0	H22.3.12	191
Bank of Japan Act	H9 法律第 89 号	H19 法律第 102 号	2.0	H21.4.1	174
Banking Act	S56 法律第 59 号	H21 法律第 59 号	4.0	H22.6.2	37
Banking Act	S56 法律第 59 号	H18 法律第 109 号	3.0	H21.6.16	37
Bankruptcy Act	H16 法律第 75 号	H18 法律第 109 号	3.0	H21.10.20	179
Basic Act for Housing	H18 法律第 61 号		2.0	H21.4.1	77
Basic Act for Land	H 元法律第 84 号	H11 法律第 160 号	1.0	H21.4.1	150
Basic Act on Biodiversity	H20 法律第 58 号		3.0	H22.5.27	
Basic Act on Crime Victims	H16 法律第 161 号		2.0	H21.4.1	182
Basic Act on Energy Policy	H14 法律第 71 号		1.0	H21.4.1	7
Basic Act on Establishing a Sound Material-Cycle Society	H12 法律第 110 号		3.0	H21.4.1	92
Basic Act on Hepatitis Measures	H21 法律第 97 号		5.0	H22.10.15	
Basic Act on Ocean Policy	H19 法律第 33 号		2.0	H21.4.1	26

ABC 順目次

1st ed.2014.10　　　　33　　　　JSB 英文六法

A 《ABC順法令一覧》25年7月19日現在

法外訳 SYS	法令名	所管庁	PDF データ 頁数	○:済 △:未完 →備考
106	高度情報通信ネットワーク社会形成基本法	内閣官房	15	○
295	ものづくり基盤技術振興基本法	経済産業省	10	○
154	消費者基本法	消費者庁	17	○
1-9 117	**財務諸表等の監査証明に関する内閣府令**	金融庁	32	○
55	金融商品取引法第2条に規定する定義に関する内閣府令	金融庁	114	○
1-14 171	**資金移動業者に関する内閣府令**	金融庁	47	○
1-13 168	**証券情報等の提供又は公表に関する内閣府令**	金融庁	39	○
190	総合科学技術会議令	内閣府	2	○
75	公正取引委員会の審判費用等に関する政令	公正取引委員会	4	○
198	対内直接投資等に関する政令	経済産業省	42	○
79	公認会計士法	金融庁	137	○
125	児童福祉法	厚生労働省	136	○
244	都市計画法	国土交通省	149	○
100	航空法	国土交通省	146	○
292	民法（第1編第2編第3編）	法務省	232	○
293	民法（第4編第5編）	法務省	106	○
287	民事執行法	法務省	154	○
284	民事保全法	法務省	36	○
286	民事再生法	法務省	253	○

A 《**ABC 順法令一覧**》25 年 7 月 19 日現在

翻訳（英訳）	法令番号	改正	辞書 ver	翻訳日	法なび
Basic Act on the Formation of an Advanced Information and Telecommunications Network Society	H12 法律第 144 号		2.0	H21.4.1	69
Basic Act on the Promotion of Core Manufacturing Technology	H11 法律第 2 号		2.0	H21.4.1	205
Basic Consumer Act	S43 法律第 78 号	H21 法律第 49 号	3.0	H23.1.4	
Cabinet Office Ordinance on Audit Certification of Financial Statements, etc.	S32 大蔵省令第 12 号	H21 内閣府令第 73 号	5.0	H23.5.10	
Cabinet Office Ordinance on Definitions under Article 2 of the Financial Instruments and Exchange Act	H5 大蔵省令第 14 号	H21 内閣府令第 78 号	3.0	H22.6.25	
Cabinet Office Ordinance on Funds Transfer Service Providers	H22 内閣府令第 4 号		5.0	H22.11.26	
Cabinet Office Ordinance on the Provision and Publication of Information on Securities	H20 内閣府令第 78 号	H21 内閣府令第 78 号	4.0	H22.6.2	
Cabinet Order for the Council for Science and Technology Policy	H12 政令第 258 号		3.0	H21.5.27	128
Cabinet Order on Expenses, etc. for Hearings by the Japan Fair Trade Commission	S23 政令第 332 号	H16 政令第 201 号	4.0	H22.10.28	
Cabinet Order on Inward Direct Investment, etc.	S55 政令第 261 号	H22 政令第 19 号	5.0	H23.2.19	133
Certified Public Accountants Act	S23 法律第 103 号	H19 法律第 99 号	3.0	H22.4.28	50
Child Welfare Act	S22 法律第 164 号	H19 法律第 73 号	2.0	H21.4.1	79
City Planning Act	S43 法律第 100 号	H20 法律第 40 号	3.0	H21.6.11	168
Civil Aeronautics Act	S27 法律第 231 号	H18 法律第 118 号	2.0	H21.4.1	64
Civil Code (Part I, Part II, and Part III)	明治 29 法律第 89 号	H18 法律第 78 号	2.0	H21.4.1	202
Civil Code (Part IV and Part V)	明治 29 法律第 89 号	H18 法律第 78 号	2.0	H21.4.1	203
Civil Execution Act	S54 法律第 4 号	H19 法律第 95 号	3.0	H21.4.1	199
Civil Provisional Remedies Act	H 元法律第 91 号	H23 法律第 36 号	6.0	H24.3.22	197
Civil Rehabilitation Act	H11 法律第 225 号	H17 法律第 87 号	3.0	H21.4.1	198

A《ABC 順法令一覧》25 年 7 月 19 日現在

法外訳 SYS	法令名	所管庁	PDF データ 頁数	○:済 △:未定 →備考
289	民事訴訟法（暫定版）	法務省	195	○
62	刑事訴訟法（第1編第2編）	法務省	143	○
63	刑事訴訟法（第3編以降）	法務省	42	○
1-8 134	**商業登記法**	**法務省**	92	○
132	商品取引所法	経済産業省	380	○
1-1 15	**会社法**（第1編第2編第3編第4編）	**法務省**	539	○
1-1 16	**会社法**（第5編第6編第7編第8編）	**法務省**	269	○
189	総合法律支援法	法務省	52	○
38	貨物利用運送事業法	国土交通省	41	○
155	消費者契約法	消費者庁	60	○
153	消費生活用製品安全法	経済産業省	92	○
157	消費者安全法	消費者庁	25	○
206	著作権法	文部科学省	127	○
279	法人税法（外国法人関連部分）	財務省	27	○
116	裁判所法	法務省	53	○
138	執行官法	法務省	12	○
323	預金保険法（暫定版）	金融庁	177	○
3	意匠法	経済産業省	57	○
195	大規模小売業者による納入業者との取引における特定の不公正な取引方法	公正取引委員会		△
261	不公正な取引方法	公正取引委員会		△

JSB英文六法　　1st ed.2014.10

Ⓐ《ABC 順法令一覧》25 年 7 月 19 日現在

翻訳（英訳）	法令番号	改正	辞書 ver	翻訳日	法なび
Code of Civil Procedure (Tentative translation)	H8 法律第 109 号	H23 法律第 36 号	6.0	H24.3.22	200
Code of Criminal Procedure (Part I and Part II)	S23 法律第 131 号	H18 法律第 36 号	2.0	H21.4.1	39
Code of Criminal Procedure (Part III 〜)	S23 法律第 131 号	H19 法律第 95 号	3.0	H21.4.1	
Commercial Registration Act	S38 法律第 125 号	H17 法律第 87 号	3.0	H21.6.11	88
Commodity Exchange Act	S25 法律第 239 号	H18 法律第 65 号	3.0	H21.8.18	85
Companies Act (Part I, Part II, Part III and Part IV)	H17 法律第 86 号	H18 法律第 109 号	2.0	H21.4.1	13
Companies Act (Part V, Part VI, Part VII and Part VIII)	H17 法律第 86 号	H18 法律第 109 号	3.0	H21.4.1	13
Comprehensive Legal Support Act	H16 法律第 74 号	H20 法律第 19 号	3.0	H21.4.1	127
Consigned Freight Forwarding Business Act	H 元法律第 82 号	H14 法律第 77 号	2.0	H22.8.10	
Consumer Contract Act	H12 法律第 61 号	H21 法律第 49 号	3.0	H23.1.4	102
Consumer Product Safety Act	S48 法律第 31 号	H19 法律第 117 号	3.0	H21.4.1	101
Consumer Safety Act	H21 法律第 50 号		6.0	H23.4.22	
Copyright Act	S45 法律第 48 号	H18 法律第 121 号	2.0	H21.4.1	139
Corporation Tax Act（Limited to the provisions related to foreign corporations）	S40 法律第 34 号	H19 法律第 6 号	2.0	H21.4.1	195
Court Act	S22 法律第 59 号	H18 法律第 36 号	2.0	H21.4.1	75
Court Enforcement Officer Act	S41 法律第 111 号	H19 法律第 18 号	5.0	H22.7.6	
Deposit Insurance Act (Tentative translation)	S46 法律第 34 号	H20 法律第 65 号	5.0	H22.11.26	
Design Act	S34 法律第 125 号	H18 法律第 55 号	1.0	H21.4.1	2
Designation of Specific Unfair Trade Practices by Large-Scale Retailers Relating to Trade with Suppliers	H17 公正取引委員会告示第 11 号		2.0	H21.4.1	131
Designation of Unfair Trade Practices	S57 公正取引委員会告示第 15 号		1.0	H21.4.1	183

A 《ABC順法令一覧》25年7月19日現在

法外訳 SYS	法令名	所管庁	PDFデータ頁数	○:済 △:未完 →備考
216	電気用品安全法	経済産業省	63	○
214	電気事業法	経済産業省	191	○
208	電子公告規則	法務省	21	○
211	電子記録債権法	金融庁	76	○
104	雇用保険法	厚生労働省	116	○
164	職業安定法	厚生労働省	58	○
223	投資事業有限責任組合契約に関する法律施行令	経済産業省	13	○
242	統計調査に用いる産業分類並びに疾病、傷害及び死因分類を定める政令の規定に基づき、産業に関する分類の名称及び分類表を定める等の件	総務省		△
300	輸出貿易管理令（暫定版）	経済産業省	114	○
302	輸出貿易管理規則（暫定版）	経済産業省	24	○
54	金融商品取引法	金融庁	834	○
158	消防法	総務省	189	○
179	水産基本法	農林水産省	19	○
45	漁業法	農林水産省	133	○
173	食品安全基本法	内閣府	22	○
174	食品安全委員会令	内閣府	2	○
175	食品衛生法	厚生労働省	60	○
178	食料・農業・農村基本法	農林水産省	21	○
29	外国為替及び外国貿易法（第515条の1未施行 等）	経済産業省	119	○

[A] 《ABC 順法令一覧》25 年 7 月 19 日現在

翻訳（英訳）	日本法令外国語訳データベースシステム　最終1覧データ収集日：H25.7.19				法なび
	法令番号	改正	辞書ver	翻訳日	
Electrical Appliances and Materials Safety Act	S36 法律第 234 号	H19 法律第 116 号	3.0	H21.10.14	146
Electricity Business Act	S39 法律第 170 号	H17 法律第 87 号	1.0	H21.4.1	144
Electronic Public Notice Rules	H18 法務省令第 14 号	H21 法務省令第 5 号	4.0	H22.3.26	
Electronically Recorded Monetary Claims Act	H19 法律第 102 号		3.0	H21.4.1	143
Employment Insurance Act	S49 法律第 116 号	H19 法律第 30 号	2.0	H22.6.1	67
Employment Security Act	S22 法律第 141 号	H19 法律第 79 号	2.0	H21.4.1	107
Enforcement Order of the Limited Partnership Act for Investment	H10 政令第 235 号	H16 政令第 173 号	1.0	H21.4.1	153
Establishment of the nomenclature and classification table concerning industries pursuant to the provision of the Cabinet Order Providing for Industrial Classification and Classification of Diseases, Injuries and Death to be used for Statistical Surveys	H14 総務省告示第 139 号	改正：	1.0	H21.4.1	166
Export Trade Control Order (Tentative translation)	S24 政令第 378 号	H23 政令第 141 号	6.0	H24.4.19	209
Export Trade Control Ordinance (Tentative translation)	S24 通商産業省令第 64 号	H22 経済産業省令第 6 号	6.0	H24.4.19	211
Financial Instruments and Exchange Act	S23 法律第 25 号	H18 法律第 109 号	3.0	H21.6.16	
Fire Service Act	S23 法律第 186 号	H20 法律第 41 号	3.0	H21.3.30	103
Fisheries Basic Act	H13 法律第 819 号	H17 法律第 819 号	1.0	H21.4.1	119
Fishery Act	S24 法律第 267 号	H19 法律第 77 号	3.0	H21.6.16	31
Food Safety Basic Act	H15 法律第 48 号	H19 法律第 8 号	3.0	H21.4.1	113
Food Safety Commission Order	H15 政令第 273 号	H15 政令第 505 号	3.0	H21.4.1	114
Food Sanitation Act	S22 法律第 233 号	H18 法律第 53 号	2.0	H21.4.1	115
Food, Agriculture and Rural Areas Basic Act	H11 法律第 106 号	H17 法律第 819 号	1.0	H21.4.1	118
Foreign Exchange and Foreign Trade Act	S24 法律第 228 号	H21 法律第 59 号	4.0	H21.12.1	22

ABC 順目次

1st ed.2014.10　　　39　　　JSB 英文六法

A 《ABC順法令一覧》25年7月19日現在

法外訳 SYS	法令名	所管庁	PDFデータ頁数	○:済 △:未完 →備考
28	外国為替令	経済産業省	114	○
151	森林・林業基本法	農林水産省	14	○
12	ガス事業法	経済産業省	160	○
48	行政機関が行う政策の評価に関する法律	総務省	17	○
252	熱供給事業法	経済産業省	22	○
105	高圧ガス保安法	経済産業省	171	○
277	北海道開発法	国土交通省	2	○
31	家庭用品品質表示法	消費者庁	17	○
166	職業能力開発促進法	厚生労働省	90	○
127	出入国管理及び難民認定法	法務省	130	○
299	輸入貿易管理令	経済産業省	26	○
142	所得税法（非居住者、外国法人関連部分）	財務省	35	○
317	労働者災害補償保険法	厚生労働省	86	○
311	労働安全衛生法	厚生労働省	242	○
94	工業標準化法	経済産業省	43	○
110	産業技術力強化法	経済産業省	23	○
1-6 275	**保険業法**	**金融庁**	1019	△
204	知的財産基本法	内閣官房	16	○
140	少年法	法務省	48	○
310	労働契約法	厚生労働省	7	○
318	労働関係調整法	厚生労働省	17	○

JSB英文六法　　　　　　　　　　1st ed.2014.10

A 《ABC 順法令一覧》25 年 7 月 19 日現在

翻訳（英訳）	法令番号	改正	辞書 ver	翻訳日	法なび
Foreign Exchange Order	S55 政令第 260 号	H20 政令第 237 号	3.0	H21.5.22	21
Forest and Forestry Basic Act	S39 法律第 161 号	H15 法律第 119 号	1.0	H21.4.1	99
Gas Business Act	S29 法律第 51 号	H17 法律第 87 号	1.0	H21.4.1	10
Government Policy Evaluations Act	H13 法律第 86 号	H15 法律第 23 号	1.0	H21.4.1	33
Heat Supply Business Act	S47 法律第 88 号	H16 法律第 94 号	2.0	H21.4.1	176
High Pressure Gas Safety Act	S26 法律第 204 号	H17 法律第 73 号	3.0	H21.4.1	68
Hokkaido Development Act	S25 法律第 126 号	H11 法律第 117 号	1.0	H21.4.1	193
Household Goods Quality Labeling Act	S37 法律第 104 号	H11 法律第 204 号	2.0	H21.4.1	24
Human Resources Development Promotion Act	S44 法律第 64 号	H18 法律第 81 号	3.0	H21.5.19	109
Immigration Control and Refugee Recognition Act	S26 政令第 319 号	H21 法律第 79 号	1.0	H21.12.21	81
Import Trade Control Order	S24 政令第 414 号	H15 政令第 248 号	1.0	H21.4.1	208
Income Tax Act（Limited to the provisions related to nonresidents and foreign corporations）	S40 法律第 33 号	H19 法律第 6 号	2.0	H21.4.1	94
Industrial Accident Compensation Insurance Act	S22 法律第 50 号	H19 法律第 111 号	3.0	H21.9.11	
Industrial Safety and Health Act	S47 法律第 57 号	H18 法律第 25 号	1.0	H21.4.1	216
Industrial Standardization Act	S24 法律第 185 号	H17 法律第 87 号	2.0	H21.4.1	59
Industrial Technology Enhancement Act	H12 法律第 44 号	H19 法律第 36 号	2.0	H21.4.1	70
Insurance Business Act	H7 法律第 105 号	H21 法律第 59 号	3.0	H22.6.2	
Intellectual Property Basic Act	H14 法律第 122 号		1.0	H21.4.1	137
Juvenile Act	S23 法律第 168 号	H20 法律第 71 号	4.0	H22.3.31	
Labor Contract Act	H19 法律第 128 号		5.0	H22.11.5	
Labor Relations Adjustment Act	S21 法律第 25 号	H16 法律第 140 号	3.0	H21.6.16	221

A《ABC順法令一覧》25年7月19日現在

法外訳 SYS	法令名	所管庁	PDFデータ頁数	○:済 △:未完 備考
308	労働基準法	厚生労働省	66	○
313	労働組合法	厚生労働省	46	○
25	外国医師等が行う臨床修練に係る医師法第17条等の特例等に関する法律	厚生労働省	24	○
297	有限責任事業組合契約に関する法律	経済産業省	35	○
222	投資事業有限責任組合契約に関する法律	経済産業省	21	○
13	介護保険法	厚生労働省	377	○
72	計量法	経済産業省	176	○
2	医師法	厚生労働省	23	○
44	気象業務法	国土交通省	59	○
102	鉱業法	経済産業省	103	○
98	港湾の施設の技術上の基準を定める省令	国土交通省	31	○
283	貿易関係貿易外取引等に関する省令	経済産業省	28	○
146	指定化学物質等の性状及び取扱いに関する情報の提供の方法等を定める省令	経済産業省	6	○
129	出入国管理及び難民認定法第7条第1項第2号の基準を定める省令	法務省	34	○
40	貸金業法	金融庁	157	○
39	貨物自動車運送事業法	国土交通省	53	○
86	国家行政組織法	総務省	15	○
82	国土利用計画法	国土交通省		△

ABC順目次

JSB英文六法　　　　　　1st ed.2014.10

A 《ABC順法令一覧》25年7月19日現在

翻訳（英訳）	日本法令外国語訳データベースシステム　最終1覧データ収集日：H25.7.19					法なび
	法令番号	改正	辞書ver	翻訳日	
Labor Standards Act	S22法律第49号	H16法律第147号	1.0	H21.4.1	214
Labor Union Act	S24法律第174号	H17法律第87号	1.0	H21.4.1	217
Law concerning the Exceptional Cases of the Medical Practitioners' Act, Article 17, on the Advanced Clinical Training of Foreign Medical Practitioners, etc.	S62法律第29号	H18法律第84号	2.0	H21.4.1	18
Limited Liability Partnership Act	H17法律第40号	H17法律第87号	1.0	H21.4.1	206
Limited Partnership Act for Investment	H10法律第90号	H16法律第34号	1.0	H21.4.1	152
Long-Term Care Insurance Act	H9法律第123号	H19法律第110号	2.0	H21.4.1	11
Measurement Act	H4法律第51号	H18法律第10号	2.0	H21.4.1	44
Medical Practitioners' Act	S23法律第201号	H19法律第96号	4.0	H23.1.24	
Meteorological Service Act	S27法律第165号	H19法律第115号	3.0	H21.4.15	
Mining Act	S25法律第289号	H16法律第94号	3.0	H21.4.1	65
Ministerial Ordinance for the Technical Standards for Port and Harbor Facilities	H19国土交通省令第15号		3.0	H22.6.18	
Ministerial Ordinance on Trade Relation Invisible Trade, etc.	H10通商産業省令第8号	H19経済産業省令第67号	3.0	H21.5.22	196
Ministerial Ordinance Specifying the Method of Provision of Information on the Properties and Handling of Designated Chemical Substances, etc.	H12通商産業省令第401号	H21経済産業省令第27号	6.0	H24.4.10	
Ministerial Ordinance to Provide for Criteria Pursuant to Article 7, paragraph (1), item (ii) of the Immigration Control and Refugee Recognition Act	H2法務省令第16号	H21法務省令第18号	2.0	H21.10.7	83
Money Lending Business Act	S58法律第32号	H20法律第74号	3.0	H21.11.11	
Motor Truck Transportation Business Act	H元法律第83号	H18法律第50号	2.0	H22.8.10	
National Government Organization Act	S23法律第120号	H18法律第118号	2.0	H21.4.1	54
National Land Use Planning Act	S49法律第92号		3.0	H23.2.25	

A 《ABC順法令一覧》25 年 7 月 19 日現在

法外訳 SYS	法令名	所管庁	PDFデータ頁数	○:済 △:未完 →備考
85	国家公務員法	人事院	71	○
84	国家公務員倫理法	総務省	30	○
83	国土形成計画法	国土交通省	16	○
88	国税徴収法（抄）	財務省	3	○
90	国籍法	法務省	19	○
66	原子力損害賠償支援機構法	内閣府	42	○
96	更生保護法	法務省	63	○
95	更生保護事業法	法務省	39	○
183	石油の備蓄の確保等に関する法律	経済産業省	28	○
315	労働者派遣事業の適正な運営の確保及び派遣労働者の就業条件の整備等に関する法律施行令	厚生労働省	34	○
1-12 160	**社債、株式等の振替に関する法律施行令**	金融庁	107	○
228	特定化学物質の環境への排出量の把握等及び管理の改善の促進に関する法律施行令	経済産業省	45	○
56	金融機関の信託業務の兼営等に関する法律施行令	金融庁	31	○
225	投資信託及び投資法人に関する法律施行令	金融庁	158	○
114	裁判外紛争解決手続の利用の促進に関する法律施行令	法務省	2	○
188	租税特別措置法施行令（非居住者,外国法人関連部分）	財務省	379	○

A 《ABC 順法令一覧》25 年 7 月 19 日現在

翻訳（英訳）	法令番号	改正	辞書 ver	翻訳日	法なび
National Public Service Act	S22 法律第 120 号	H17 法律第 50 号	1.0	H21.4.1	53
National Public Service Ethics Act	H11 法律第 129 号	H17 法律第 102 号	2.0	H21.4.1	52
National Spatial Planning Act	S25 法律第 205 号	H17 法律第 89 号	1.0	H21.4.1	51
National Tax Collection Act（Extract）	S34 法律第 147 号	H19 法律第 102 号	4.0	H21.10.26	55
Nationality Act	S25 法律第 147 号	H20 法律第 88 号	3.0	H21.5.21	56
Nuclear Damage Compensation Facilitation Corporation Act	H23 法律第 94 号		6.0	H24.5.7	
Offenders Rehabilitation Act	H19 法律第 88 号		3.0	H21.4.1	61
Offenders Rehabilitation Services Act	H7 法律第 86 号	H17 法律第 87 号	2.0	H21.4.1	60
Oil Stockpiling Act	S50 法律第 96 号		2.0	H21.4.1	122
Order for Enforcement of the Act for Securing the Proper Operation of Worker Dispatching Undertakings and Improved Working Conditions for Dispatched Workers	S61 政令第 95 号	H19 政令第 376 号	2.0	H21.4.1	219
Order for Enforcement of the Act on Book-Entry of Company Bonds, Shares, etc.	H14 政令第 362 号	H22 政令第 4 号	5.0	H22.11.26	
Order for Enforcement of the Act on Confirmation, etc. of Release Amounts of Specific Chemical Substances in the Environment and Promotion of Improvements to the Management Thereof	H12 政令第 138 号	H20 政令第 356 号	4.0	H21.12.1	
Order for Enforcement of the Act on Engagement in Trust Business by a Financial Institution	H5 政令第 31 号	H21 政令第 303 号	5.0	H22.11.26	
Order for Enforcement of the Act on Investment Trusts and Investment Corporations	H12 政令第 480 号	H21 政令第 303 号	4.0	H22.6.3	
Order for Enforcement of the Act on Promotion of Use of Alternative Dispute Resolution	H18 政令第 186 号	H23 政令第 403 号	1.0	H24.2.22	73
Order for Enforcement of the Act on Special Measures Concerning Taxation (Limited to the provisions related to nonresidents and foreign corporations)	S32 政令第 43 号	H20 政令第 161 号	4.0	H22.7.9	125

ABC 順目次

A 《ABC順法令一覧》25年7月19日現在

ABC順目次

法外訳 SYS	法令名	所管庁	PDFデータ頁数	○:済 △:未完 →備考
148	新エネルギー利用等の促進に関する特別措置法施行令	経済産業省	8	○
231	特定商取引に関する法律施行令	消費者庁	59	○
21	化学物質の審査及び製造等の規制に関する法律施行令	経済産業省	17	○
194	大規模小売店舗立地法施行令	経済産業省	3	○
53	金融商品の販売等に関する法律施行令	金融庁	11	○
80	公認会計士法施行令	金融庁	26	○
288	民事執行法施行令	法務省	2	○
285	民事保全法施行令	法務省	1	○
133	商品取引所法施行令	経済産業省	60	○
1-2 17	**会社法施行令**	**法務省**	4	○
280	法人税法施行令（外国法人関連部分）	財務省	50	○
212	電子記録債権法施行令	金融庁	17	○
176	食品衛生法施行令	厚生労働省	21	○
143	所得税法施行令（非居住者、外国法人関連部分）	財務省	61	○
19	割賦販売法施行令	経済産業省	39	○
1-7 276	**保険業法施行令**	**金融庁**	252	○
41	貸金業法施行令	金融庁	143	○
67	原子力損害賠償支援機構法施行令	内閣府	17	○

JSB英文六法　　　1st ed.2014.10

A 《ABC 順法令一覧》25 年 7 月 19 日現在

翻訳（英訳）	法令番号	改正	辞書 ver	翻訳日	法なび
Order for Enforcement of the Act on Special Measures for the Promotion of New Energy Use, etc.	H9 政令第 208 号	H20 政令第 16 号	3.0	H21.4.1	97
Order for Enforcement of the Act on Specified Commercial Transactions	S51 政令第 295 号	H21 政令第 217 号	4.0	H21.12.1	157
Order for Enforcement of the Act on the Evaluation of Chemical Substances and Regulation of Their Manufacture, etc.	S49 政令第 202 号	H21 政令第 257 号	5.0	H23.1.20	15
Order for Enforcement of the Act on the Measures by Large-Scale Retail Stores for Preservation of Living Environment	H10 政令第 327 号		5.0	H23.1.20	
Order for Enforcement of the Act on the Sale, etc. of Financial Instruments	H12 政令第 484 号	H21 政令第 303 号	5.0	H22.11.26	
Order for Enforcement of the Certified Public Accountants Act	S27 政令第 343 号	H19 政令第 235 号	3.0	H22.5.10	
Order for Enforcement of the Civil Execution Act	S55 政令第 230 号	H16 政令第 419 号	5.0	H22.12.17	
Order for Enforcement of the Civil Provisional Remedies Act	H2 政令第 284 号		5.0	H22.12.17	
Order for Enforcement of the Commodity Exchange Act	S25 政令第 280 号	H20 政令第 237 号	3.0	H21.4.22	86
Order for Enforcement of the Companies Act	H17 政令第 364 号	H20 政令第 100 号	4.0	H22.3.24	
Order for Enforcement of the Corporation Tax Act（Limited to the provisions related to foreign corporations）	S40 政令第 97 号	H19 政令第 83 号	3.0	H21.8.18	194
Order for Enforcement of the Electronically Recorded Monetary Claims Act	H20 政令第 325 号		5.0	H22.11.26	
Order for Enforcement of the Food Sanitation Act	S28 政令第 229 号	H18 政令第 189 号	2.0	H21.4.1	116
Order for Enforcement of the Income Tax Act（Limited to the provisions related to nonresidents and foreign corporations）	S40 政令第 96 号	H19 政令第 82 号	3.0	H21.8.18	93
Order for Enforcement of the Installment Sales Act	S36 政令第 341 号	H21 政令第 217 号	4.0	H21.12.1	
Order for Enforcement of the Insurance Business Act	H7 政令第 425 号	H21 政令第 201 号	4.0	H22.6.3	
Order for Enforcement of the Money Lending Act	S58 政令第 181 号	H21 政令第 303 号	4.0	H22.6.3	
Order for Enforcement of the Nuclear Damage Compensation Facilitation Corporation Act	H23 政令第 257 号		6.0	H24.5.7	

A《ABC 順法令一覧》25 年 7 月 19 日現在

法外訳 SYS	法令名	所管庁	PDFデータ頁数	○:済 △:未完 →備考
196	対内直接投資等に関する命令	経済産業省	38	○
60	銀行法第 26 条第 2 項に規定する区分等を定める命令	金融庁	20	○
316	労働者派遣事業の適正な運営の確保及び派遣労働者の就業条件の整備等に関する法律施行規則	厚生労働省	71	○
229	特定化学物質の環境への排出量の把握等及び管理の改善の促進に関する法律施行規則	経済産業省	26	○
57	金融機関の信託業務の兼営等に関する法律施行規則	金融庁	130	○
201	短時間労働者の雇用管理の改善等に関する法律施行規則	厚生労働省	30	○
115	裁判外紛争解決手続の利用の促進に関する法律施行規則	法務省	19	○
109	債権管理回収業に関する特別措置法施行規則	法務省	15	○

A 《**ABC 順法令一覧**》25 年 7 月 19 日現在

翻訳（英訳）	法令番号	改正	辞書 ver	翻訳日	法なび
	日本法令外国語訳データベースシステム　最終1覧データ収集日：H25.7.19			
Order on Inward Direct Investment, etc.	S55 総理府・大蔵省・文部省・厚生省・農林水産省・通商産業省・運輸省・郵政省・労働省・建設省令第1号	H22 内閣府・総務省・財務省・文部科学省・厚生労働省・農林水産省・経済産業省・国土交通省・環境省令第2号	5.0	H23.2.19	132
Order Providing for the Categories, etc. Prescribed in Article 26, Paragraph (2) of the Banking Act	H12 総理府・大蔵省令第39号	H18 内閣府・財務省令第6号	3.0	H22.5.10	
Ordinance for Enforcement of the Act for Securing the Proper Operation of Worker Dispatching Undertakings and Improved Working Conditions for Dispatched Workers	S61 労働省令第20号	H19 厚生労働省令第149号	2.0	H21.4.1	220
Ordinance for Enforcement of the Act on Confirmation, etc. of Release Amounts of Specific Chemical Substances in the Environment and Promotion of Improvements to the Management Thereof	H13 内閣府・財務省・文部科学省・厚生労働省・農林水産省・経済産業省・国土交通省・環境省令第1号	H22 内閣府・財務省・文部科学省・厚生労働省・農林水産省・経済産業省・国土交通省・環境省・防衛省令第1号	6.0	H24.4.10	
Ordinance for Enforcement of the Act on Engagement in Trust Business by a Financial Institution	S57 大蔵省令第16号	H21 内閣府令第78号	5.0	H22.11.26	
Ordinance for Enforcement of the Act on Improvement, etc. of Employment Management for Part-Time Workers	H5 労働省令第34号	H23 厚生労働省令第48号	6.0	H23.8.12	
Ordinance for Enforcement of the Act on Promotion of Use of Alternative Dispute Resolution	H18 法務省令第52号	H23 法務省令第39号	1.0	H24.2.22	74
Ordinance for Enforcement of the Act on Special Measures Concerning Claim Management and Collection Businesses	H11 法務省令第4号	H20 法務省令第59号	4.0	H22.3.19	

ABC順目次

A《ABC順法令一覧》25年7月19日現在

法外訳 SYS	法令名	所管庁	PDFデータ頁数	○:済 △:未完 →備考
111	産業活力の再生及び産業活動の革新に関する特別措置法施行規則	経済産業省	79	○
27	外国弁護士による法律事務の取扱いに関する特別措置法施行規則	法務省	10	○
71	経済産業省関係化学物質の審査及び製造等の規制に関する法律施行規則	経済産業省	22	○
81	公認会計士法施行規則	金融庁	77	○
101	航空法施行規則	国土交通省	621	△
131	商品先物取引法施行規則	経済産業省	491	○
156	消費者契約法施行規則	消費者庁	34	○
281	法人税法施行規則（外国法人関連部分）	財務省	11	○
305	預金保険法施行規則	金融庁	39	○
213	電子記録債権法施行規則	金融庁	53	○
165	職業安定法施行規則	厚生労働省	79	○

A 《ABC順法令一覧》25 年 7 月 19 日現在

翻訳（英訳）	日本法令外国語訳データベースシステム 最終1覧データ収集日：H25.7.19				法なび
	法令番号	改正	辞書 ver	翻訳日	
Ordinance for Enforcement of the Act on Special Measures Concerning Revitalization of Industry and Innovation in Industrial Activities	H21 内閣府、総務省、財務省、厚生労働省、農林水産省、経済産業省、国土交通省、環境省令第1号	H23 内閣府・総務省・財務省・厚生労働省・農林水産省・経済産業省・国土交通省・環境省令第1号	6.0	H24.4.19	
Ordinance for Enforcement of the Act on Special Measures concerning the Handling of Legal Services by Foreign Lawyers	S62 法務省令第7号	H23 法務省令第43号	2.0	H21.4.1	20
Ordinance for Enforcement of the Act on the Evaluation of Chemical Substances and Regulation of Their Manufacture, etc. as the Act Relates to the Ministry of Economy, Trade and Industry.	S49 通商産業省令第40号	H22 経済産業省令第7号	5.0	H23.1.20	
Ordinance for Enforcement of the Certified Public Accountants Act	H19 内閣府令第81号		3.0	H22.5.10	
Ordinance for Enforcement of the Civil Aeronautics Act	S27 運輸省令第56号	H20 国土交通省令第73号	3.0	H21.8.18	
Ordinance for Enforcement of the Commodity Derivatives Act	H17 農林水産省・経済産業省令第3号	H22 農林水産省・経済産業省令第5号	5.0	H24.6.18	
Ordinance for Enforcement of the Consumer Contract Act	H19 内閣府令第17号	H21 内閣府令第70号	3.0	H23.1.4	
Ordinance for Enforcement of the Corporation Tax Act (Limited to the provisions related to foreign corporations)	S40 大蔵省令第12号	H20 財務省令第205号	4.0	H21.10.26	
Ordinance for Enforcement of the Deposit Insurance Act	S46 大蔵省令第28号	H22 内閣府・財務省令第1号	5.0	H22.11.26	
Ordinance for Enforcement of the Electronically Recorded Monetary Claims Act	H20 内閣府・法務省令第4号		5.0	H22.11.26	
Ordinance for Enforcement of the Employment Security Act	S22 労働省令第12号	H17 厚生労働省令第154号	2.0	H21.4.1	108

A 《ABC順法令一覧》25年7月19日現在

法外訳SYS	法令名	所管庁	PDFデータ頁数	○:済 △:未完 →備考
177	食品衛生法施行規則	厚生労働省	125	○
128	出入国管理及び難民認定法施行規則	法務省	143	○
144	所得税法施行規則（非居住者，外国法人関連部分）	財務省	9	○
309	労働基準法施行規則	厚生労働省	64	○
11	恩赦法施行規則	法務省	9	○
301	輸出貿易管理令別表第1及び外国為替令別表の規定に基づき貨物又は技術を定める省令	経済産業省	311	○
312	労働安全衛生規則（別表第2、別表第5及び別表第9：H21.厚生労働省令第23号までの改正）	厚生労働省	629	△
264	不動産登記規則	法務省	236	○
1-11 306	連結財務諸表の用語、様式及び作成方法に関する規則	金融庁	94	○
1-10 136	四半期財務諸表等の用語、様式及び作成方法に関する規則	金融庁	58	○
150	新規化学物質の製造又は輸入に係る届出等に関する省令	経済産業省	15	○
10	恩赦法	法務省	4	○
238	特許法	経済産業省	163	○
271	弁理士法	経済産業省	62	○
65	刑法	法務省	87	○

ABC順目次

Ａ 《ABC 順法令一覧》25 年 7 月 19 日現在

翻訳（英訳）	法令番号	改正	辞書 ver	翻訳日	法なび
Ordinance for Enforcement of the Food Sanitation Act	S32 厚生省令第 23 号	H19 厚生労働省令第 156 号	2.0	H21.4.1	117
Ordinance for Enforcement of the Immigration Control and Refugee Recognition Act	S56 法務省令第 54 号	H21 法務省令第 29 号	2.0	H21.6.5	82
Ordinance for Enforcement of the Income Tax Act (Limited to the provisions related to nonresidents and foreign corporations)	S40 大蔵省令第 11 号	H20 財務省令第 24 号	4.0	H22.7.9	
Ordinance for Enforcement of the Labor Standards Act	S22 厚生省令第 23 号		2.0	H21.4.1	215
Ordinance for Enforcement of the Pardon Act	S22 司法省令第 78 号	H18 法務省令第 59 号	1.0	H21.4.1	9
Ordinance of the Ministry Specifying Goods and Technologies Pursuant to Provisions of the Appended Table 1 of the Export Control Order and the Appended Table of the Foreign Exchange Order	H3 通商産業省令第 49 号	H23 経済産業省令第 26 号	7.0		210
Ordinance on Industrial Safety and Health (Appended Tables 2, 5 and 9: up to the revision of Ordinance of the Ministry of Health, Labour and Welfare No. 23 of 2009)	S47 労働省令第 32 号	H18 厚生労働省令第 185 号	3.0	H23.6.27	
Ordinance on Real Property Registration	H17 法務省令第 18 号	H23 法務省令第 5 号	6.0	H24.3.23	
Ordinance on Terminology, Forms, and Preparation Methods of Consolidated Financial Statements	S51 大蔵省令第 28 号	H21 内閣府令第 73 号	5.0	H23.4.22	
Ordinance on Terminology, Forms, and Preparation Methods of Quarterly Financial Statements, etc.	H19 内閣府令第 63 号	H21 内閣府令第 73 号	5.0	H23.5.9	
Ordinance Related to Notification, etc. Concerning the Manufacture or Import of New Chemical Substances	S49 厚生省・通商産業省令第 1 号	H22 厚生労働省・経済産業省・環境省令第 1 号	5.0	H23.1.20	
Pardon Act	S22 法律第 20 号	H11 法律第 160 号	1.0	H21.4.1	8
Patent Act	S34 法律第 121 号	H18 法律第 109 号	2.0	H21.4.1	163
Patent Attorney Act	H12 法律第 49 号	H19 法律第 91 号	3.0	H22.6.2	190
Penal Code	明治 40 法律第 45 号	H19 法律第 54 号	1.0	H21.4.1	40

ＡＢＣ順目次

A《ABC順法令一覧》25年7月19日現在

法外訳 SYS	法令名	所管庁	PDFデータ頁数	○:済 △:未完 →備考
119	人事訴訟法	法務省	26	○
152	植物防疫法	農林水産省	48	○
163	種苗法	農林水産省	59	○
99	港湾法	国土交通省	108	○
185	製造物責任法	内閣府	4	○
43	技術士法	文部科学省	31	○
18	会計法（第4章）	財務省	7	○
298	輸入割当てを受けるべき貨物の品目、輸入の承認を受けるべき貨物の原産地又は船積地域その他貨物の輸入について必要な事項の公表	経済産業省		△
181	生活保護法	厚生労働省	68	○
70	検疫法	厚生労働省	50	○
207	鉄道事業法	国土交通省	51	○
263	不動産登記法	法務省	119	○
262	不動産登記令	法務省	197	○
232	特定商取引に関する法律施行規則	消費者庁	119	○
320	宗教法人法	文部科学省	76	○
290	民事訴訟規則	最高裁判所	119	○
64	刑事訴訟規則	最高裁判所	188	○

ABC順目次

A 《ABC 順法令一覧》25 年 7 月 19 日現在

翻訳（英訳）	法令番号	改正	辞書 ver	翻訳日	法なび
Personal Status Litigation Act	H15 法律第 109 号	H23 法律第 53 号	5.0	H25.1.16	
Plant Protection Act ¥	S25 法律第 151 号	H17 法律第 102 号	2.0	H21.4.1	100
Plant Variety Protection and Seed Act	H10 法律第 83 号	H19 法律第 49 号	2.0	H21.4.1	106
Port and Harbor Act	S25 法律第 218 号	H20 法律第 66 号	3.0	H22.6.18	
Product Liability Act	H6 法律第 85 号		1.0	H21.4.1	124
Professional Engineer Act	S58 法律第 25 号	H18 法律第 50 号	2.0	H21.4.1	30
Public Accounting Act (Chapter IV)	S22 法律第 35 号	H18 法律第 53 号	6.0	H24.3.30	
Public Announcement on the Items of Goods Subject to Import Quotas, the Places of Origin or Places of Shipment of Goods Requiring Approval for Import, and Other Necessary Matters Concerning Import of Goods	S41 通商産業省告示第 170 号	H20 経済産業省告示第 129 号	3.0	H21.5.27	
Public Assistance Act	S25 法律第 144 号	H18 法律第 53 号	2.0	H21.4.1	121
Quarantine Act	S26 法律第 201 号	H18 法律第 106 号	2.0	H21.4.1	43
Railway Business Act	S61 法律第 92 号	H18 法律第 19 号	2.0	H21.4.1	140
Real Property Registration Act	H16 法律第 123 号	H19 法律第 132 号	3.0	H21.10.14	184
Real Property Registration Order	H16 政令第 379 号	H22 政令第 4 号	6.0	H24.3.23	
Regulations for Enforcement of the Act on Specified Commercial Transactions	S51 通商産業省令第 89 号	H16 経済産業省令第 87 号	1.0	H21.4.1	158
Religious Corporations Act	S26 法律第 126 号	H18 法律第 50 号	5.0	H23.1.4	
Rules of Civil Procedure	H8 最高裁判所規則第 5 号	H20 最高裁判所規則第 10 号	3.0	H21.4.1	201
Rules of Criminal Procedure	S23 最高裁判所規則第 32 号	H20 最高裁判所規則第 17 号	4.0	H23.7.28	

ABC 順目次

A 《ABC順法令一覧》25年7月19日現在

法外訳 SYS	法令名	所管庁	PDFデータ頁数	○:済 △:未完 →備考
162	私的独占の禁止及び公正取引の確保に関する法律第9条から第16条までの規定による認可の申請、報告及び届出等に関する規則	公正取引委員会	31	○
321	公正取引委員会の審判に関する規則	公正取引委員会	38	○
76	公正取引委員会の審査に関する規則	公正取引委員会	22	○
322	課徴金の減免に係る報告及び資料の提出に関する規則	公正取引委員会	8	○
167	自衛隊員倫理法	防衛省	15	○
172	障害者自立支援法	厚生労働省	103	○
202	中小企業等協同組合法	経済産業省	288	○
159	社会福祉法	厚生労働省	85	○
221	土壌汚染対策法	環境省	51	○
149	新聞業における特定の不公正な取引方法	公正取引委員会		△
192	大学設置基準	文部科学省	53	○
87	国家賠償法	法務省	2	○
241	統計法	総務省	42	○
257	破壊活動防止法	法務省	23	○
186	測量法	国土交通省		△
145	持続的養殖生産確保法	農林水産省	24	○
249	日本国憲法	その他	27	○

Ⓐ《**ABC 順法令一覧**》25 年 7 月 19 日現在

翻訳（英訳）	法令番号	改正	辞書 ver	翻訳日	法なび
Rules on Applications for Approval, Reporting, Notification, etc. Pursuant to the Provisions of Articles 9 to 16 of the Act on Prohibition of Private Monopolization and Maintenance of Fair Trade	S28 公正取引委員会規則第 1 号	H21 公正取引委員会規則第 13 号	4.0	H22.10.19	105
Rules on Hearings by the Fair Trade Commission	H17 公正取引委員会規則第 8 号	H21 公正取引委員会規則第 6 号	5.0	H22.9.3	
Rules on Investigations by the Fair Trade Commission	H17 公正取引委員会規則第 5 号	H21 公正取引委員会規則第 11 号	5.0	H22.12.2	
Rules on Reporting and the Submission of Supporting Materials in Relation to Immunity from or Reduction of Surcharges	H17 公正取引委員会規則第 7 号	H21 公正取引委員会規則第 12 号	5.0	H23.1.14	
Self-Defense Forces Personnel Ethics Act	H11 法律第 130 号	H19 法律第 80 号	2.0	H21.4.1	110
Services and Supports for Persons with Disabilities Act	H17 法律第 123 号	H18 法律第 94 号	2.0	H21.4.1	112
Small and Medium-Sized Enterprise Cooperatives Act	S24 法律第 181 号	H18 法律第 109 号	2.0	H21.4.1	135
Social Welfare Act	S26 法律第 45 号	H20 法律第 85 号	6.0	H24.1.23	
Soil Contamination Countermeasures Act	H14 法律第 53 号	H21 法律第 23 号	3.0		151
Specific Unfair Trade Practices in the Newspaper Business	H11 公正取引委員会告示第 9 号		3.0	H21.4.1	98
Standards for Establishment of Universities	S31 文部省令第 28 号	H19 文部科学省令第 40 号	3.0	H21.5.28	23
State Redress Act	S22 法律第 125 号		4.0	H22.3.23	
Statistics Act	H19 法律第 53 号		2.0	H21.4.1	165
Subversive Activities Prevention Act	S27 法律第 240 号	H7 法律第 91 号	5.0	H23.9.8	
Survey Act	S24 法律第 188 号	H19 法律第 55 号	3.0	H21.6.23	
Sustainable Aquaculture Production Assurance Act	H11 法律第 51 号	H17 法律第 36 号	4.0	H21.4.1	95
The Constitution of Japan	S21 憲法			H21.4.1	173

A 《ABC 順法令一覧》25 年 7 月 19 日現在

法外訳 SYS	法令名	所管庁	PDFデータ頁数	○:済 △:未完 →備考
197	対内直接投資等に関する命令第3条第3項の規定に基づき財務大臣及び事業所管大臣が定める業種を定める件	経済産業省		△
282	貿易保険法	経済産業省	83	○
135	商標法	経済産業省	123	○
1-3 123	**信託法**	**法務省**	217	○
122	信託業法	金融庁	119	○
266	不正競争防止法（暫定版）	経済産業省	40	○
139	実用新案法	経済産業省	80	○
274	保護司法	法務省	8	○
78	公益通報者保護法	内閣府	10	○
217	電気用品安全法　削除	経済産業省		

A 《ABC 順法令一覧》25 年 7 月 19 日現在

翻訳（英訳）	日本法令外国語訳データベースシステム 最終1覧データ収集日：H25.7.19				法なび
	法令番号	改正	辞書ver	翻訳日	
the public notice on specifying business types to be specified by the Minister of Finance and the minister having jurisdiction over the business pursuant to the provision of Article 3, paragraph (3) of the Order on Inward Direct Investment, etc.	H20 内閣府、総務省、財務省、文部科学省、厚生労働省、農林水産省、経済産業省、国土交通省、環境省告示第1号		3.0	H21.6.16	
Trade Insurance and Investment Act	S25 法律第 67 号	H20 法律第 57 号	5.0	H23.1.20	
Trademark Act	S34 法律第 127 号	H18 法律第 55 号	2.0	H21.4.1	89
Trust Act	H18 法律第 108 号		3.0	H21.11.2	
Trust Business Act	H16 法律第 154 号	H20 法律第 65 号	3.0	H21.9.30	
Unfair Competition Prevention Act (Tentative translation)	H5 法律第 47 号	H23 法律第 62 号	5.0	H23.6.30	186
Utility Model Act	S34 法律第 123 号	H18 法律第 55 号	1.0	H21.4.1	91
Volunteer Probation Officers Act	S25 法律第 204 号	H19 法律第 88 号	4.0	H21.11.13	192
Whistleblower Protection Act	H16 法律第 122 号		1.0	H21.4.1	49
					147

ABC 順目次

B《五十音順法令一覧》25 年 7 月 19 日現在

法外訳 SYS	法令名	所管庁	PDFデータ頁数	○:済 △:未完 →備考
1	アイヌ文化の振興並びにアイヌの伝統等に関する知識の普及及び啓発に関する法律	国土交通省		△
2	医師法	厚生労働省	23	○
3	意匠法	経済産業省	57	○
4	石綿による健康被害の救済に関する法律	環境省	66	○
5	育児休業、介護休業等育児又は家族介護を行う労働者の福祉に関する法律	厚生労働省	62	○
6	遺伝子組換え生物等の使用等の規制による生物の多様性の確保に関する法律	環境省	37	○
7	運輸安全委員会設置法	国土交通省	24	○
8	エネルギーの使用の合理化に関する法律	経済産業省	111	○
9	エネルギー政策基本法	経済産業省	7	○
10	恩赦法	法務省	4	○
11	恩赦法施行規則	法務省	9	○
12	ガス事業法	経済産業省	160	○
13	介護保険法	厚生労働省	377	○
14	会社分割に伴う労働契約の承継等に関する法律	厚生労働省	7	○
1-① 15	**会社法**（第1編第2編第3編第4編）	**法務省**	539	○
1-① 16	**会社法**（第5編第6編第7編第8編）	**法務省**	269	○
1-② 17	**会社法施行令**	**法務省**	4	○
18	会計法（第4章）	財務省	7	○

B 《五十音順法令一覧》25 年 7 月 19 日現在

＊S＝昭和、H＝平成

翻訳（英訳）	日本法令外国語訳データベースシステム 最終1覧データ収集日：H25.7.19				法なび
	法令番号	改正	辞書ver	翻訳日	
Act on the Promotion of Ainu Culture, and Dissemination and Enlightenment of Knowledge about Ainu Tradition, etc.	H9 法律第 52 号	H18 法律第 50 号	2.0	H21.4.1	1
Medical Practitioners' Act	S23 法律第 201 号	H19 法律第 96 号	4.0	H23.1.24	
Design Act	S34 法律第 125 号	H18 法律第 55 号	1.0	H21.4.1	2
Act on Asbestos Health Damage Relief	H18 法律第 4 号		2.0	H21.4.1	3
Act on the Welfare of Workers Who Take Care of Children or Other Family Members Including Child Care and Family Care Leave	H3 法律第 76 号	H16 法律第 160 号	1.0	H21.4.1	4
Act on the Conservation and Sustainable Use of Biological Diversity through Regulations on the Use of Living Modified Organisms	H15 法律第 97 号	H19 法律第 8 号	2.0	H21.4.1	5
Act for Establishment of the Japan Transport Safety Board	S48 法律第 113 号	H20 法律第 26 号	3.0	H22.5.27	
Act on the Rational Use of Energy	S54 法律第 49 号	H20 法律第 47 号	3.0	H21.4.24	6
Basic Act on Energy Policy	H14 法律第 71 号		1.0	H21.4.1	7
Pardon Act	S22 法律第 20 号	H11 法律第 160 号	1.0	H21.4.1	8
Ordinance for Enforcement of the Pardon Act	S22 司法省令第 78 号	H18 法務省令第 59 号	1.0	H21.4.1	9
Gas Business Act	S29 法律第 51 号	H17 法律第 87 号	1.0	H21.4.1	10
Long-Term Care Insurance Act	H9 法律第 123 号	H19 法律第 110 号	2.0	H21.4.1	11
Act on the Succession to Labor Contracts upon Company Split	H12 法律第 103 号	H17 法律第 87 号	2.0	H21.4.1	12
Companies Act (Part I, Part II, Part III and Part IV)	H17 法律第 86 号	H18 法律第 109 号	2.0	H21.4.1	13
Companies Act (Part V, Part VI, Part VII and Part VIII)	H17 法律第 86 号	H18 法律第 109 号	3.0	H21.4.1	13
Order for Enforcement of the Companies Act	H17 政令第 364 号	H20 政令第 100 号	4.0	H22.3.24	
Public Accounting Act (Chapter IV)	S22 法律第 35 号	H18 法律第 53 号	6.0	H24.3.30	

五十音順目次

1st ed.2014.10　　　　　　61　　　　　　JSB英文六法

B《五十音順法令一覧》25年7月19日現在

法外訳 SYS	法令名	所管庁	PDFデータ頁数	○:済 △:未完 →備考
19	割賦販売法施行令	経済産業省	39	○
20	化学物質の審査及び製造等の規制に関する法律（附則第4条未施行 等）	経済産業省	77	○
21	化学物質の審査及び製造等の規制に関する法律施行令	経済産業省	17	○
22	外国人漁業の規制に関する法律	農林水産省	8	○
23	外国人登録法	法務省	30	○
24	外国倒産処理手続の承認援助に関する法律	法務省	54	○
25	外国医師等が行う臨床修練に係る医師法第17条等の特例等に関する法律	厚生労働省	24	○
26	外国弁護士による法律事務の取扱いに関する特別措置法	法務省	44	○
27	外国弁護士による法律事務の取扱いに関する特別措置法施行規則	法務省	10	○
28	外国為替令	経済産業省	114	○
29	外国為替及び外国貿易法（第515条の1未施行 等）	経済産業省	119	○
30	外国等に対する我が国の民事裁判権に関する法律	法務省	15	○
31	家庭用品品質表示法	消費者庁	17	○
32	家畜伝染病予防法	農林水産省	69	○
33	核原料物質、核燃料物質及び原子炉の規制に関する法律	経済産業省	233	○
34	海洋基本法	内閣官房	16	○
35	海洋生物資源の保存及び管理に関する法律	農林水産省	34	○
36	海難審判法	国土交通省	18	○

五十音順目次

JSB英文六法　　　　　1st ed. 2014.10

Ⓑ《五十音順法令一覧》25 年 7 月 19 日現在

翻訳（英訳）	法令番号	改正	辞書 ver	翻訳日	法なび
Order for Enforcement of the Installment Sales Act	S36 政令第 341 号	H21 政令第 217 号	4.0	H21.12.1	
Act on the Evaluation of Chemical Substances and Regulation of Their Manufacture, etc. (Article 4 of the Supplementary Provisions unenforced, etc.)	S48 法律第 117 号	H21 法律第 39 号	4.0	H21.12.1	14
Order for Enforcement of the Act on the Evaluation of Chemical Substances and Regulation of Their Manufacture, etc.	S49 政令第 202 号	H21 政令第 257 号	5.0	H23.1.20	15
Act on Regulation of Fishing Operation by Foreign Nationals	S42 法律第 60 号	H13 法律第 92 号	1.0	H21.4.1	16
Alien Registration Act	S27 法律第 125 号	H16 法律第 152 号	2.0	H21.4.1	17
Act on Recognition of and Assistance for Foreign Insolvency Proceedings	H12 法律第 129 号	H18 法律第 50 号	3.0	H22.11.18	
Law concerning the Exceptional Cases of the Medical Practitioners' Act, Article 17, on the Advanced Clinical Training of Foreign Medical Practitioners, etc.	S62 法律第 29 号	H18 法律第 84 号	2.0	H21.4.1	18
Act on Special Measures concerning the Handling of Legal Services by Foreign Lawyers	S61 法律第 66 号	H15 法律第 128 号	1.0	H21.4.1	19
Ordinance for Enforcement of the Act on Special Measures concerning the Handling of Legal Services by Foreign Lawyers	S62 法務省令第 7 号	H23 法務省令第 43 号	2.0	H21.4.1	20
Foreign Exchange Order	S55 政令第 260 号	H20 政令第 237 号	3.0	H21.5.22	21
Foreign Exchange and Foreign Trade Act	S24 法律第 228 号	H21 法律第 59 号	4.0	H21.12.1	22
Act on the Civil Jurisdiction of Japan with respect to a Foreign State, etc.	H21 法律第 24 号		4.0	H22.3.23	
Household Goods Quality Labeling Act	S37 法律第 104 号	H11 法律第 204 号	2.0	H21.4.1	24
Act on Domestic Animal Infectious Diseases Control	S26 法律第 166 号	H16 法律第 68 号	1.0	H21.4.1	25
Act on the Regulation of Nuclear Source Material, Nuclear Fuel Material and Reactors	S32 法律第 166 号	H19 法律第 84 号	3.0	H21.4.9	42
Basic Act on Ocean Policy	H19 法律第 33 号		2.0	H21.4.1	26
Act on Preservation and Control of Living Marine Resources	H8 法律第 77 号	H19 法律第 77 号	4.0	H21.4.1	27
Act on Marine Accident Inquiry	S22 法律第 135 号	H20 法律第 26 号	3.0	H21.6.16	28

五十音順目次

B《五十音順法令一覧》25年7月19日現在

法外訳 SYS	法令名	所管庁	PDFデータ頁数	○:済 △:未完 →備考
37	肝炎対策基本法	厚生労働省	12	○
38	貨物利用運送事業法	国土交通省	41	○
39	貨物自動車運送事業法	国土交通省	53	○
40	貸金業法	金融庁	157	○
41	貸金業法施行令	金融庁	143	○
42	企業立地の促進等による地域における産業集積の形成及び活性化に関する法律	経済産業省	48	○
43	技術士法	文部科学省	31	○
44	気象業務法	国土交通省	59	○
45	漁業法	農林水産省	133	○
46	行政事件訴訟法	法務省	39	○
47	行政手続法	総務省	39	○
48	行政機関が行う政策の評価に関する法律	総務省	17	○
49	行政機関の保有する個人情報の保護に関する法律	総務省	45	○
50	行政機関の保有する情報の公開に関する法律	総務省	22	○
51	行政相談委員法	総務省	4	○
52	金融商品の販売等に関する法律	金融庁	14	○
53	金融商品の販売等に関する法律施行令	金融庁	11	○
54	金融商品取引法	金融庁	834	○
55	金融商品取引法第2条に規定する定義に関する内閣府令	金融庁	114	○
56	金融機関の信託業務の兼営等に関する法律施行令	金融庁	31	○

B《五十音順法令一覧》25 年 7 月 19 日現在

翻訳（英訳）	法令番号	改正	辞書 ver	翻訳日	法なび
Basic Act on Hepatitis Measures	H21 法律第 97 号		5.0	H22.10.15	
Consigned Freight Forwarding Business Act	H 元法律第 82 号	H14 法律第 77 号	2.0	H22.8.10	
Motor Truck Transportation Business Act	H 元法律第 83 号	H18 法律第 50 号	2.0	H22.8.10	
Money Lending Business Act	S58 法律第 32 号	H20 法律第 74 号	3.0	H21.11.11	
Order for Enforcement of the Money Lending Act	S58 政令第 181 号	H21 政令第 303 号	4.0	H22.6.3	
Act on Formation and Development of Regional Industrial Clusters through Promotion of Establishment of New Business Facilities, etc.	H19 法律第 40 号	H20 法律第 37 号	3.0	H21.4.1	29
Professional Engineer Act	S58 法律第 25 号	H18 法律第 50 号	2.0	H21.4.1	30
Meteorological Service Act	S27 法律第 165 号	H19 法律第 115 号	3.0	H21.4.15	
Fishery Act	S24 法律第 267 号	H19 法律第 77 号	3.0	H21.6.16	31
Administrative Case Litigation Act	S37 法律第 139 号	H19 法律第 109 号	4.0	H22.9.14	
Administrative Procedure Act	H5 法律第 88 号	H17 法律第 73 号	1.0	H21.4.1	32
Government Policy Evaluations Act	H13 法律第 86 号	H15 法律第 23 号	1.0	H21.4.1	33
Act on the Protection of Personal Information Held by Administrative Organs	H15 法律第 58 号	H17 法律第 102 号	2.0	H21.4.1	34
Act on Access to Information Held by Administrative Organs	H11 法律第 42 号	H16 法律第 84 号	1.0	H21.4.1	35
Administrative Counselors Act	S41 法律第 99 号	H11 法律第 160 号	1.0	H21.4.1	36
Act on Sales, etc. of Financial Instruments	H12 法律第 101 号	H18 法律第 66 号	3.0	H22.6.25	
Order for Enforcement of the Act on the Sale, etc. of Financial Instruments	H12 政令第 484 号	H21 政令第 303 号	5.0	H22.11.26	
Financial Instruments and Exchange Act	S23 法律第 25 号	H18 法律第 109 号	3.0	H21.6.16	
Cabinet Office Ordinance on Definitions under Article 2 of the Financial Instruments and Exchange Act	H5 大蔵省令第 14 号	H21 内閣府令第 78 号	3.0	H22.6.25	
Order for Enforcement of the Act on Engagement in Trust Business by a Financial Institution	H5 政令第 31 号	H21 政令第 303 号	5.0	H22.11.26	

五十音順目次

B《五十音順法令一覧》25 年 7 月 19 日現在

法外訳 SYS	法令名	所管庁	PDF データ 頁数	○:済 △:未完 →備考
57	金融機関の信託業務の兼営等に関する法律施行規則	金融庁	130	○
58	銀行法	金融庁	298	○
59	銀行法	金融庁	239	○
60	銀行法第26条第2項に規定する区分等を定める命令	金融庁	20	○
61	刑事収容施設及び被収容者等の処遇に関する法律	法務省	204	○
62	刑事訴訟法(第1編第2編)	法務省	143	○
63	刑事訴訟法(第3編以降)	法務省	42	○
64	刑事訴訟規則	最高裁判所	188	○
65	刑　法	法務省	87	○
66	原子力損害賠償支援機構法	内閣府	42	○
67	原子力損害賠償支援機構法施行令	内閣府	17	○
68	原子力災害対策特別措置法	経済産業省	58	○
69	携帯音声通信事業者による契約者等の本人確認等及び携帯音声通信役務の不正な利用の防止に関する法律	総務省	21	○
70	検疫法	厚生労働省	50	○
71	経済産業省関係化学物質の審査及び製造等の規制に関する法律施行規則	経済産業省	22	○
72	計量法	経済産業省	176	○
73	個人情報の保護に関する法律	内閣府	35	○

JSB英文六法　　　　　　　　　　1st ed.2014.10

B 《五十音順法令一覧》25 年 7 月 19 日現在

翻訳（英訳）	法令番号	改正	辞書ver	翻訳日	法なび
Ordinance for Enforcement of the Act on Engagement in Trust Business by a Financial Institution	S57 大蔵省令第 16 号	H21 内閣府令第 78 号	5.0	H22.11.26	
Banking Act	S56 法律第 59 号	H21 法律第 59 号	4.0	H22.6.2	37
Banking Act	S56 法律第 59 号	H18 法律第 109 号	3.0	H21.6.16	37
Order Providing for the Categories, etc. Prescribed in Article 26, Paragraph (2) of the Banking Act	H12 総理府・大蔵省令第 39 号	H18 内閣府・財務省令第 6 号	3.0	H22.5.10	
Act on Penal Detention Facilities and Treatment of Inmates and Detainees	H17 法律第 50 号	H19 法律第 37 号	2.0	H21.4.1	38
Code of Criminal Procedure (Part I and Part II)	S23 法律第 131 号	H18 法律第 36 号	2.0	H21.4.1	39
Code of Criminal Procedure (Part III ～)	S23 法律第 131 号	H19 法律第 95 号	3.0	H21.4.1	
Rules of Criminal Procedure	S23 最高裁判所規則第 32 号	H20 最高裁判所規則第 17 号	4.0	H23.7.28	
Penal Code	明治 40 法律第 45 号	H19 法律第 54 号	1.0	H21.4.1	40
Nuclear Damage Compensation Facilitation Corporation Act	H23 法律第 94 号		6.0	H24.5.7	
Order for Enforcement of the Nuclear Damage Compensation Facilitation Corporation Act	H23 政令第 257 号		6.0	H24.5.7	
Act on Special Measures Concerning Nuclear Emergency Preparedness	H11 法律第 156 号	H18 法律第 118 号	2.0	H21.4.1	45
Act on Identification, etc. by Mobile Voice Communications Carriers of their Subscribers, etc. and for Prevention of Improper Use of Mobile Voice Communications Services	H17 法律第 31 号		2.0	H21.4.1	41
Quarantine Act	S26 法律第 201 号	H18 法律第 106 号	2.0	H21.4.1	43
Ordinance for Enforcement of the Act on the Evaluation of Chemical Substances and Regulation of Their Manufacture, etc. as the Act Relates to the Ministry of Economy, Trade and Industry.	S49 通商産業省令第 40 号	H22 経済産業省令第 7 号	5.0	H23.1.20	
Measurement Act	H4 法律第 51 号	H18 法律第 10 号	2.0	H21.4.1	44
Act on the Protection of Personal Information	H15 法律第 57 号	H15 法律第 119 号	1.0	H21.4.1	46

日本法令外国語訳データベースシステム 最終1覧データ収集日：H25.7.19

五十音順目次

1st ed.2014.10　　　　　　　　JSB英文六法

B《五十音順法令一覧》25年7月19日現在

法外訳 SYS	法令名	所管庁	PDFデータ頁数	○:済 △:未完 →備考
74	個別労働関係紛争の解決の促進に関する法律	厚生労働省	10	○
75	公正取引委員会の審判費用等に関する政令	公正取引委員会	4	○
76	公正取引委員会の審査に関する規則	公正取引委員会	22	○
77	公益社団法人及び公益財団法人の認定等に関する法律	内閣府	55	○
78	公益通報者保護法	内閣府	10	○
79	公認会計士法	金融庁	137	○
80	公認会計士法施行令	金融庁	26	○
81	公認会計士法施行規則	金融庁	77	○
82	国土利用計画法	国土交通省		△
83	国土形成計画法	国土交通省	16	○
84	国家公務員倫理法	総務省	30	○
85	国家公務員法	人事院	71	○
86	国家行政組織法	総務省	15	○
87	国家賠償法	法務省	2	○
88	国税徴収法(抄)	財務省	3	○
89	国税通則法(抄)	財務省	26	○
90	国籍法	法務省	19	○
91	国際受刑者移送法	法務省	32	○
92	国際捜査共助等に関する法律	法務省	17	○

B《五十音順法令一覧》25年7月19日現在

翻訳（英訳）	法令番号	改正	辞書ver	翻訳日	法なび
Act on Promoting the Resolution of Individual Labor-Related Disputes	H13法律第112号	H16法律第140号	1.0	H21.4.1	47
Cabinet Order on Expenses, etc. for Hearings by the Japan Fair Trade Commission	S23政令第332号	H16政令第201号	4.0	H22.10.28	
Rules on Investigations by the Fair Trade Commission	H17公正取引委員会規則第5号	H21公正取引委員会規則第11号	5.0	H22.12.2	
Act on Authorization of Public Interest Incorporated Associations and Public Interest Incorporated Foundation	H18法律第49号		2.0	H21.4.1	48
Whistleblower Protection Act	H16法律第122号		1.0	H21.4.1	49
Certified Public Accountants Act	S23法律第103号	H19法律第99号	3.0	H22.4.28	50
Order for Enforcement of the Certified Public Accountants Act	S27政令第343号	H19政令第235号	3.0	H22.5.10	
Ordinance for Enforcement of the Certified Public Accountants Act	H19内閣府令第81号		3.0	H22.5.10	
National Land Use Planning Act	S49法律第92号		3.0	H23.2.25	
National Spatial Planning Act	S25法律第205号	H17法律第89号	1.0	H21.4.1	51
National Public Service Ethics Act	H11法律第129号	H17法律第102号	2.0	H21.4.1	52
National Public Service Act	S22法律第120号	H17法律第50号	1.0	H21.4.1	53
National Government Organization Act	S23法律第120号	H18法律第118号	2.0	H21.4.1	54
State Redress Act	S22法律第125号		4.0	H22.3.23	
National Tax Collection Act (Extract)	S34法律第147号	H19法律第102号	4.0	H21.10.26	55
Act on General Rules for National Taxes (Extract)	S37法律第66号	H19法律第6号	4.0	H21.10.26	
Nationality Act	S25法律第147号	H20法律第88号	3.0	H21.5.21	56
Act on the Transnational Transfer of Sentenced Persons	H14法律第66号	H22法律第29号	1.0	H23.12.15	57
Act on International Assistance in Investigation and Other Related Matters	S55法律第69号	H18法律第58号	2.0	H21.4.1	58

五十音順目次

B《五十音順法令一覧》25年7月19日現在

法外訳 SYS	法令名	所管庁	PDFデータ頁数	○:済 △:未完 →備考
93	国際連合安全保障理事会決議第1874号等を踏まえ我が国が実施する貨物検査等に関する特別措置法	外務省	13	○
94	工業標準化法	経済産業省	43	○
95	更生保護事業法	法務省	39	○
96	更生保護法	法務省	63	○
97	港則法	国土交通省	20	○
98	港湾の施設の技術上の基準を定める省令	国土交通省	31	○
99	港湾法	国土交通省	108	○
100	航空法	国土交通省	146	○
101	航空法施行規則	国土交通省	621	△
102	鉱業法	経済産業省	103	○
103	雇用の分野における男女の均等な機会及び待遇の確保等に関する法律	厚生労働省	21	○
104	雇用保険法	厚生労働省	116	○
105	高圧ガス保安法	経済産業省	171	○
106	高度情報通信ネットワーク社会形成基本法	内閣官房	15	○
107	高齢者虐待の防止、高齢者の養護者に対する支援等に関する法律	厚生労働省	18	○
108	債権管理回収業に関する特別措置法（H18.法律第115号による改正のうち，H22.6月18日施行分（第18条第5項）については未反映）	法務省	29	○
109	債権管理回収業に関する特別措置法施行規則	法務省	15	○

B《五十音順法令一覧》25年7月19日現在

翻訳（英訳）	法令番号	改正	辞書ver	翻訳日	法なび
Act on Special Measures concerning Cargo Inspections etc. Conducted by the Government Taking into Consideration United Nations Security Council Resolution 1874, etc.	H22法律第43号		5.0	H24.6.29	
Industrial Standardization Act	S24法律第185号	H17法律第87号	2.0	H21.4.1	59
Offenders Rehabilitation Services Act	H7法律第86号	H17法律第87号	2.0	H21.4.1	60
Offenders Rehabilitation Act	H19法律第88号		3.0	H21.4.1	61
Act on Port Regulations	S23法律第174号	H18法律第68号	2.0	H21.4.1	62
Ministerial Ordinance for the Technical Standards for Port and Harbor Facilities	H19国土交通省令第15号		3.0	H22.6.18	
Port and Harbor Act	S25法律第218号	H20法律第66号	3.0	H22.6.18	
Civil Aeronautics Act	S27法律第231号	H18法律第118号	2.0	H21.4.1	64
Ordinance for Enforcement of the Civil Aeronautics Act	S27運輸省令第56号	H20国土交通省令第73号	3.0	H21.8.18	
Mining Act	S25法律第289号	H16法律第94号	3.0	H21.4.1	65
Act on Securing, Etc. of Equal Opportunity and Treatment between Men and Women in Employment	S47法律第113号	H18法律第82号	1.0	H21.4.1	66
Employment Insurance Act	S49法律第116号	H19法律第30号	2.0	H22.6.1	67
High Pressure Gas Safety Act	S26法律第204号	H17法律第73号	3.0	H21.4.1	68
Basic Act on the Formation of an Advanced Information and Telecommunications Network Society	H12法律第144号		2.0	H21.4.1	69
Act on the Prevention of Elder Abuse, Support for Caregivers of Elderly Persons and Other Related Matters	H17法律第124号	H20法律第42号	4.0	H22.10.6	
Act on Special Measures Concerning Claim Management and Collection Businesses	H10法律第126号	H20法律第74号	3.0	H21.12.25	
Ordinance for Enforcement of the Act on Special Measures Concerning Claim Management and Collection Businesses	H11法務省令第4号	H20法務省令第59号	4.0	H22.3.19	

五十音順目次

B《五十音順法令一覧》25 年 7 月 19 日現在

法外訳 SYS	法令名	所管庁	PDFデータ頁数	○:済 △:未完 →備考
110	産業技術力強化法	経済産業省	23	○
111	産業活力の再生及び産業活動の革新に関する特別措置法施行規則	経済産業省	79	○
112	裁判の迅速化に関する法律	法務省	4	○
113	裁判外紛争解決手続の利用の促進に関する法律	法務省	28	○
114	裁判外紛争解決手続の利用の促進に関する法律施行令	法務省	2	○
115	裁判外紛争解決手続の利用の促進に関する法律施行規則	法務省	19	○
116	裁判所法	法務省	53	○
1-⑨ 117	**財務諸表等の監査証明に関する内閣府令**	**金融庁**	32	○
118	下請代金支払遅延等防止法	公正取引委員会	14	○
119	人事訴訟法	法務省	26	○
120	住生活基本法	国土交通省		△
121	使用済自動車の再資源化等に関する法律	経済産業省	136	○
122	信託業法	金融庁	119	○
1-③ 123	**信託法**	**法務省**	217	○
124	借地借家法	法務省	30	○
125	児童福祉法	厚生労働省	136	○

JSB英文六法　　　　　　　　　　72　　　　　　　　　　1st ed.2014.10

B《五十音順法令一覧》25 年 7 月 19 日現在

翻訳（英訳）	法令番号	改正	辞書 ver	翻訳日	法なび
Industrial Technology Enhancement Act	H12 法律第 44 号	H19 法律第 36 号	2.0	H21.4.1	70
Ordinance for Enforcement of the Act on Special Measures Concerning Revitalization of Industry and Innovation in Industrial Activities	H21 内閣府、総務省、財務省、厚生労働省、農林水産省、経済産業省、国土交通省、環境省令第 1 号	H23 内閣府・総務省・財務省・厚生労働省・農林水産省・経済産業省・国土交通省・環境省令第 1 号	6.0	H24.4.19	
Act on the Expediting of Trials	H15 法律第 107 号		2.0	H21.4.1	71
Act on Promotion of Use of Alternative Dispute Resolution	H16 法律第 151 号	H18 法律第 50 号	1.0	H21.4.1	72
Order for Enforcement of the Act on Promotion of Use of Alternative Dispute Resolution	H18 政令第 186 号	H23 政令第 403 号	1.0	H24.2.22	73
Ordinance for Enforcement of the Act on Promotion of Use of Alternative Dispute Resolution	H18 法務省令第 52 号	H23 法務省令第 39 号	1.0	H24.2.22	74
Court Act	S22 法律第 59 号	H18 法律第 36 号	2.0	H21.4.1	75
Cabinet Office Ordinance on Audit Certification of Financial Statements, etc.	S32 大蔵省令第 12 号	H21 内閣府令第 73 号	5.0	H23.5.10	
Act against Delay in Payment of Subcontract Proceeds, Etc. to Subcontractors	S31 法律第 120 号	H17 法律第 87 号	1.0	H21.4.1	76
Personal Status Litigation Act	H15 法律第 109 号	H23 法律第 53 号	5.0	H25.1.16	
Basic Act for Housing	H18 法律第 61 号		2.0	H21.4.1	77
Act on Recycling, etc. of End-of-Life Vehicles	H14 法律第 87 号	H18 法律第 50 号	2.0	H21.4.1	78
Trust Business Act	H16 法律第 154 号	H20 法律第 65 号	3.0	H21.9.30	
Trust Act	H18 法律第 108 号		3.0	H21.11.2	
Act on Land and Building Leases	H3 法律第 90 号	H19 法律第 132 号	4.0	H22.7.23	
Child Welfare Act	S22 法律第 164 号	H19 法律第 73 号	2.0	H21.4.1	79

1st ed.2014.10　　　　　　　　　　　　　　JSB 英文六法

B《五十音順法令一覧》25 年 7 月 19 日現在

法外訳 SYS	法令名	所管庁	PDF データ頁数	○:済 △:未完 →備考
126	児童買春、児童ポルノに係る行為等の処罰及び児童の保護等に関する法律	法務省	11	○
127	出入国管理及び難民認定法	法務省	130	○
128	出入国管理及び難民認定法施行規則	法務省	143	○
129	出入国管理及び難民認定法第 7 条第 1 項第 2 号の基準を定める省令	法務省	34	○
130	出資の受入れ、預り金及び金利等の取締りに関する法律	法務省	12	○
131	商品先物取引法施行規則	経済産業省	491	○
132	商品取引所法	経済産業省	380	○
133	商品取引所法施行令	経済産業省	60	○
1-⑧ 134	**商業登記法**	**法務省**	92	○
135	商標法	経済産業省	123	○
1-⑩ 136	**四半期財務諸表等の用語、様式及び作成方法に関する規則**	金融庁	58	○
137	地震保険に関する法律	財務省	24	○
138	執行官法	法務省	12	○
139	実用新案法	経済産業省	80	○
140	少年法	法務省	48	○
141	循環型社会形成推進基本法	環境省	20	○
142	所得税法（非居住者、外国法人関連部分）	財務省	35	○

B《五十音順法令一覧》25 年 7 月 19 日現在

翻訳（英訳）	法令番号	改正	辞書 ver	翻訳日	法なび
Act on Punishment of Activities Relating to Child Prostitution and Child Pornography, and the Protection of Children	H11 法律第 52 号	H16 法律第 106 号	1.0	H21.4.1	80
Immigration Control and Refugee Recognition Act	S26 政令第 319 号	H21 法律第 79 号	1.0	H21.12.21	81
Ordinance for Enforcement of the Immigration Control and Refugee Recognition Act	S56 法務省令第 54 号	H21 法務省令第 29 号	2.0	H21.6.5	82
Ministerial Ordinance to Provide for Criteria Pursuant to Article 7, paragraph (1), item (ii) of the Immigration Control and Refugee Recognition Act	H2 法務省令第 16 号	H21 法務省令第 18 号	2.0	H21.10.7	83
Act Regulating the Receipt of Contributions, the Receipt of Deposits, and Interest Rates	S29 法律第 195 号	H19 法律第 85 号	6.0	H23.11.11	84
Ordinance for Enforcement of the Commodity Derivatives Act	H17 農林水産省・経済産業省令第 3 号	H22 農林水産省・経済産業省令第 5 号	5.0	H24.6.18	
Commodity Exchange Act	S25 法律第 239 号	H18 法律第 65 号	3.0	H21.8.18	85
Order for Enforcement of the Commodity Exchange Act	S25 政令第 280 号	H20 政令第 237 号	3.0	H21.4.22	86
Commercial Registration Act	S38 法律第 125 号	H17 法律第 87 号	3.0	H21.6.11	88
Trademark Act	S34 法律第 127 号	H18 法律第 55 号	2.0	H21.4.1	89
Ordinance on Terminology, Forms, and Preparation Methods of Quarterly Financial Statements, etc.	H19 内閣府令第 63 号	H21 内閣府令第 73 号	5.0	H23.5.9	
Act on Earthquake Insurance	S41 法律第 73 号	H11 法律第 160 号	3.0	H22.3.9	90
Court Enforcement Officer Act	S41 法律第 111 号	H19 法律第 18 号	5.0	H22.7.6	
Utility Model Act	S34 法律第 123 号	H18 法律第 55 号	1.0	H21.4.1	91
Juvenile Act	S23 法律第 168 号	H20 法律第 71 号	4.0	H22.3.31	
Basic Act on Establishing a Sound Material-Cycle Society	H12 法律第 110 号		3.0	H21.4.1	92
Income Tax Act (Limited to the provisions related to nonresidents and foreign corporations)	S40 法律第 33 号	H19 法律第 6 号	2.0	H21.4.1	94

1st ed.2014.10　　　　　　　75　　　　　　　JSB 英文六法

B《五十音順法令一覧》25年7月19日現在

法外訳 SYS	法令名	所管庁	PDFデータ頁数	○:済 △:未完 →備考
143	所得税法施行令（非居住者、外国法人関連部分）	財務省	61	○
144	所得税法施行規則（非居住者，外国法人関連部分）	財務省	9	○
145	持続的養殖生産確保法	農林水産省	24	○
146	指定化学物質等の性状及び取扱いに関する情報の提供の方法等を定める省令	経済産業省	6	○
147	新エネルギー利用等の促進に関する特別措置法	経済産業省	15	○
148	新エネルギー利用等の促進に関する特別措置法施行令	経済産業省	8	○
149	新聞業における特定の不公正な取引方法	公正取引委員会		△
150	新規化学物質の製造又は輸入に係る届出等に関する省令	経済産業省	15	○
151	森林・林業基本法	農林水産省	14	○
152	植物防疫法	農林水産省	48	○
153	消費生活用製品安全法	経済産業省	92	○
154	消費者基本法	消費者庁	17	○
155	消費者契約法	消費者庁	60	○
156	消費者契約法施行規則	消費者庁	34	○
157	消費者安全法	消費者庁	25	○
158	消防法	総務省	189	○
159	社会福祉法	厚生労働省	85	○

五十音順目次

B 《五十音順法令一覧》25 年 7 月 19 日現在

翻訳（英訳）	法令番号	改正	辞書 ver	翻訳日	法なび
Order for Enforcement of the Income Tax Act (Limited to the provisions related to nonresidents and foreign corporations)	S40 政令第 96 号	H19 政令第 82 号	3.0	H21.8.18	93
Ordinance for Enforcement of the Income Tax Act (Limited to the provisions related to nonresidents and foreign corporations)	S40 大蔵省令第 11 号	H20 財務省令第 24 号	4.0	H22.7.9	
Sustainable Aquaculture Production Assurance Act	H11 法律第 51 号	H17 法律第 36 号	4.0	H21.4.1	95
Ministerial Ordinance Specifying the Method of Provision of Information on the Properties and Handling of Designated Chemical Substances, etc.	H12 通商産業省令第 401 号	H21 経済産業省令第 27 号	6.0	H24.4.10	
Act on the Promotion of New Energy Usage	H9 法律第 37 号	H17 法律第 87 号	2.0	H21.11.2	96
Order for Enforcement of the Act on Special Measures for the Promotion of New Energy Use, etc.	H9 政令第 208 号	H20 政令第 16 号	3.0	H21.4.1	97
Specific Unfair Trade Practices in the Newspaper Business	H11 公正取引委員会告示第 9 号		3.0	H21.4.1	98
Ordinance Related to Notification, etc. Concerning the Manufacture or Import of New Chemical Substances	S49 厚生省・通商産業省令第 1 号	H22 厚生労働省・経済産業省・環境省令第 1 号	5.0	H23.1.20	
Forest and Forestry Basic Act	S39 法律第 161 号	H15 法律第 119 号	1.0	H21.4.1	99
Plant Protection Act ¥	S25 法律第 151 号	H17 法律第 102 号	2.0	H21.4.1	100
Consumer Product Safety Act	S48 法律第 31 号	H19 法律第 117 号	3.0	H21.4.1	101
Basic Consumer Act	S43 法律第 78 号	H21 法律第 49 号	3.0	H23.1.4	
Consumer Contract Act	H12 法律第 61 号	H21 法律第 49 号	3.0	H23.1.4	102
Ordinance for Enforcement of the Consumer Contract Act	H19 内閣府令第 17 号	H21 内閣府令第 70 号	3.0	H23.1.4	
Consumer Safety Act	H21 法律第 50 号		6.0	H23.4.22	
Fire Service Act	S23 法律第 186 号	H20 法律第 41 号	3.0	H21.3.30	103
Social Welfare Act	S26 法律第 45 号	H20 法律第 85 号	6.0	H24.1.23	

五十音順目次

1st ed.2014.10　　　　　77　　　　　JSB英文六法

B《五十音順法令一覧》25 年 7 月 19 日現在

法外訳 SYS	法令名	所管庁	PDFデータ頁数	○:済 △:未完 →備考
1-⑫ 160	**社債、株式等の振替に関する法律施行令**	**金融庁**	107	○
161	私的独占の禁止及び公正取引の確保に関する法律	公正取引委員会	133	○
162	私的独占の禁止及び公正取引の確保に関する法律第9条から第16条までの規定による認可の申請、報告及び届出等に関する規則	公正取引委員会	31	○
163	種苗法	農林水産省	59	○
164	職業安定法	厚生労働省	58	○
165	職業安定法施行規則	厚生労働省	79	○
166	職業能力開発促進法	厚生労働省	90	○
167	自衛隊員倫理法	防衛省	15	○
1-⑬ 168	**証券情報等の提供又は公表に関する内閣府令**	**金融庁**	39	○
169	資源の有効な利用の促進に関する法律	経済産業省	40	○
170	資産の流動化に関する法律	金融庁	313	○
1-⑭ 171	**資金移動業者に関する内閣府令**	**金融庁**	47	○
172	障害者自立支援法	厚生労働省	103	○
173	食品安全基本法	内閣府	22	○
174	食品安全委員会令	内閣府	2	○
175	食品衛生法	厚生労働省	60	○
176	食品衛生法施行令	厚生労働省	21	○
177	食品衛生法施行規則	厚生労働省	125	○

B 《五十音順法令一覧》25年7月19日現在

翻訳（英訳）	法令番号	改正	辞書ver	翻訳日	法なび
Order for Enforcement of the Act on Book-Entry of Company Bonds, Shares, etc.	H14政令第362号	H22政令第4号	5.0	H22.11.26	
Act on Prohibition of Private Monopolization and Maintenance of Fair Trade	S22法律第54号	H21法律第51号	4.0	H22.10.15	104
Rules on Applications for Approval, Reporting, Notification, etc. Pursuant to the Provisions of Articles 9 to 16 of the Act on Prohibition of Private Monopolization and Maintenance of Fair Trade	S28公正取引委員会規則第1号	H21公正取引委員会規則第13号	4.0	H22.10.19	105
Plant Variety Protection and Seed Act	H10法律第83号	H19法律第49号	2.0	H21.4.1	106
Employment Security Act	S22法律第141号	H19法律第79号	2.0	H21.4.1	107
Ordinance for Enforcement of the Employment Security Act	S22労働省令第12号	H17厚生労働省令第154号	2.0	H21.4.1	108
Human Resources Development Promotion Act	S44法律第64号	H18法律第81号	3.0	H21.5.19	109
Self-Defense Forces Personnel Ethics Act	H11法律第130号	H19法律第80号	2.0	H21.4.1	110
Cabinet Office Ordinance on the Provision and Publication of Information on Securities	H20内閣府令第78号	H21内閣府令第78号	4.0	H22.6.2	
Act on the Promotion of Effective Utilization of Resources	H3法律第48号	H14法律第1号	1.0	H21.4.1	111
Act on Securitization of Assets	H10法律第105号	H20法律第65号	3.0	H21.11.11	
Cabinet Office Ordinance on Funds Transfer Service Providers	H22内閣府令第4号		5.0	H22.11.26	
Services and Supports for Persons with Disabilities Act	H17法律第123号	H18法律第94号	2.0	H21.4.1	112
Food Safety Basic Act	H15法律第48号	H19法律第8号	3.0	H21.4.1	113
Food Safety Commission Order	H15政令第273号	H15政令第505号	3.0	H21.4.1	114
Food Sanitation Act	S22法律第233号	H18法律第53号	2.0	H21.4.1	115
Order for Enforcement of the Food Sanitation Act	S28政令第229号	H18政令第189号	2.0	H21.4.1	116
Ordinance for Enforcement of the Food Sanitation Act	S32厚生省令第23号	H19厚生労働省令第156号	2.0	H21.4.1	117

五十音順目次

B 《五十音順法令一覧》25 年 7 月 19 日現在

法外訳 SYS	法令名	所管庁	PDFデータ頁数	○:済 △:未完 →備考
178	食料・農業・農村基本法	農林水産省	21	○
179	水産基本法	農林水産省	19	○
180	水産資源保護法	農林水産省	46	○
181	生活保護法	厚生労働省	68	○
182	生物多様性基本法	環境省	17	○
183	石油の備蓄の確保等に関する法律	経済産業省	28	○
184	船舶油濁損害賠償保障法	国土交通省	43	○
185	製造物責任法	内閣府	4	○
186	測量法	国土交通省		△
187	租税特別措置法（非居住者、外国法人関連部分）	財務省	226	○
188	租税特別措置法施行令（非居住者,外国法人関連部分）	財務省	379	○
189	総合法律支援法	法務省	52	○
190	総合科学技術会議令	内閣府	2	○
191	大学等における技術に関する研究成果の民間事業者への移転の促進に関する法律	経済産業省	32	○
192	大学設置基準	文部科学省	53	○
193	大規模小売店舗立地法	経済産業省	20	○
194	大規模小売店舗立地法施行令	経済産業省	3	○

五十音順目次

B《五十音順法令一覧》25年7月19日現在

翻訳（英訳）	法令番号	改正	辞書 ver	翻訳日	法なび
Food, Agriculture and Rural Areas Basic Act	H11法律第106号	H17法律第819号	1.0	H21.4.1	118
Fisheries Basic Act	H13法律第819号	H17法律第819号	1.0	H21.4.1	119
Act on the Protection of Fishery Resources	S26法律第313号	H19法律第77号	2.0	H21.4.1	120
Public Assistance Act	S25法律第144号	H18法律第53号	2.0	H21.4.1	121
Basic Act on Biodiversity	H20法律第58号		3.0	H22.5.27	
Oil Stockpiling Act	S50法律第96号		2.0	H21.4.1	122
Act on Liability for Oil Pollution Damage	S50法律第95号	H16法律第37号	2.0	H21.4.1	123
Product Liability Act	H6法律第85号		1.0	H21.4.1	124
Survey Act	S24法律第188号	H19法律第55号	3.0	H21.6.23	
Act on Special Measures Concerning Taxation (Limited to the provisions related to nonresidents and foreign corporations)	S32法律第26号	H19法律第6号	2.0	H21.4.1	126
Order for Enforcement of the Act on Special Measures Concerning Taxation (Limited to the provisions related to nonresidents and foreign corporations)	S32政令第43号	H20政令第161号	4.0	H22.7.9	125
Comprehensive Legal Support Act	H16法律第74号	H20法律第19号	3.0	H21.4.1	127
Cabinet Order for the Council for Science and Technology Policy	H12政令第258号		3.0	H21.5.27	128
Act on the Promotion of Technology Transfer from Universities to Private Business Operators	H10法律第52号	H17法律第87号	2.0	H21.4.1	129
Standards for Establishment of Universities	S31文部省令第28号	H19文部科学省令第40号	3.0	H21.5.28	23
Act on the Measures by Large-Scale Retail Stores for Preservation of Living Environment	H10法律第91号	H12法律第91号	3.0	H21.4.24	130
Order for Enforcement of the Act on the Measures by Large-Scale Retail Stores for Preservation of Living Environment	H10政令第327号		5.0	H23.1.20	

五十音順目次

B《五十音順法令一覧》25 年 7 月 19 日現在

法外訳 SYS	法令名	所管庁	PDFデータ頁数	○:済 △:未完 →備考
195	大規模小売業者による納入業者との取引における特定の不公正な取引方法	公正取引委員会		△
196	対内直接投資等に関する命令	経済産業省	38	○
197	対内直接投資等に関する命令第 3 条第 3 項の規定に基づき財務大臣及び事業所管大臣が定める業種を定める件	経済産業省		△
198	対内直接投資等に関する政令	経済産業省	42	○
199	建物の区分所有等に関する法律	法務省	57	○
200	短時間労働者の雇用管理の改善等に関する法律	厚生労働省	25	○
201	短時間労働者の雇用管理の改善等に関する法律施行規則	厚生労働省	30	○
202	中小企業等協同組合法	経済産業省	288	○
203	地球温暖化対策の推進に関する法律	環境省	39	○
204	知的財産基本法	内閣官房	16	○
205	知的財産高等裁判所設置法	法務省	3	○

五十音順目次

Ⓑ《五十音順法令一覧》25 年 7 月 19 日現在

翻訳（英訳）	日本法令外国語訳データベースシステム　最終1覧データ収集日：H25.7.19				法なび
	法令番号	改正	辞書ver	翻訳日	
Designation of Specific Unfair Trade Practices by Large-Scale Retailers Relating to Trade with Suppliers	H17 公正取引委員会告示第11号		2.0	H21.4.1	131
Order on Inward Direct Investment, etc.	S55 総理府・大蔵省・文部省・厚生省・農林水産省・通商産業省・運輸省・郵政省・労働省・建設省令第1号	H22 内閣府・総務省・財務省・文部科学省・厚生労働省・農林水産省・経済産業省・国土交通省・環境省令第2号	5.0	H23.2.19	132
the public notice on specifying business types to be specified by the Minister of Finance and the minister having jurisdiction over the business pursuant to the provision of Article 3, paragraph (3) of the Order on Inward Direct Investment, etc.	H20 内閣府、総務省、財務省、文部科学省、厚生労働省、農林水産省、経済産業省、国土交通省、環境省告示第1号		3.0	H21.6.16	
Cabinet Order on Inward Direct Investment, etc.	S55 政令第261号	H22 政令第19号	5.0	H23.2.19	133
Act on Building Unit Ownership, etc.	S37 法律第69号	H20 法律第203号	5.0	H23.3.2	
Act on Improvement, etc. of Employment Management for Part-Time Workers	H5 法律第76号	H19 法律第72号	2.0	H21.4.1	134
Ordinance for Enforcement of the Act on Improvement, etc. of Employment Management for Part-Time Workers	H5 労働省令第34号	H23 厚生労働省令第48号	6.0	H23.8.12	
Small and Medium-Sized Enterprise Cooperatives Act	S24 法律第181号	H18 法律第109号	2.0	H21.4.1	135
Act on Promotion of Global Warming Countermeasures	H10 法律第117号	H18 法律第57号	1.0	H21.4.1	136
Intellectual Property Basic Act	H14 法律第122号		1.0	H21.4.1	137
Act for Establishment of the Intellectual Property High Court	H16 法律第119号		2.0	H21.4.1	138

五十音順目次

1st ed.2014.10　　　　　　　JSB英文六法

B《五十音順法令一覧》25 年 7 月 19 日現在

法外訳 SYS	法令名	所管庁	PDFデータ頁数	○:済 △:未完 →備考
206	著作権法	文部科学省	127	○
207	鉄道事業法	国土交通省	51	○
208	電子公告規則	法務省	21	○
209	電子消費者契約及び電子承諾通知に関する民法の特例に関する法律	経済産業省	4	○
210	電子署名及び認証業務に関する法律	経済産業省	30	○
211	電子記録債権法	金融庁	76	○
212	電子記録債権法施行令	金融庁	17	○
213	電子記録債権法施行規則	金融庁	53	○
214	電気事業法	経済産業省	191	○
215	電気事業者による新エネルギー等の利用に関する特別措置法（第 2 条第 2 項第 6 号改正未施行）	経済産業省	11	○
216	電気用品安全法	経済産業省	63	○
217	電気用品安全法　削除	経済産業省		
218	動物の愛護及び管理に関する法律	環境省	29	○
219	動産及び債権の譲渡の対抗要件に関する民法の特例等に関する法律	法務省	20	○
220	土地基本法	国土交通省	8	○
221	土壌汚染対策法	環境省	51	○
222	投資事業有限責任組合契約に関する法律	経済産業省	21	○

五十音順目次

B 《五十音順法令一覧》25 年 7 月 19 日現在

翻訳（英訳）	日本法令外国語訳データベースシステム　最終１覧データ収集日：H25.7.19					法なび
	法令番号	改正	辞書 ver	翻訳日	
Copyright Act	S45 法律第 48 号	H18 法律第 121 号	2.0	H21.4.1	139
Railway Business Act	S61 法律第 92 号	H18 法律第 19 号	2.0	H21.4.1	140
Electronic Public Notice Rules	H18 法務省令第 14 号	H21 法務省令第 5 号	4.0	H22.3.26	
Act on Special Provisions to the Civil Code Concerning Electronic Consumer Contracts and Electronic Acceptance Notice	H13 法律第 95 号		1.0	H21.4.1	141
Act on Electronic Signatures and Certification Business	H12 法律第 102 号	H18 法律第 10 号	1.0	H21.4.1	142
Electronically Recorded Monetary Claims Act	H19 法律第 102 号		3.0	H21.4.1	143
Order for Enforcement of the Electronically Recorded Monetary Claims Act	H20 政令第 325 号		5.0	H22.11.26	
Ordinance for Enforcement of the Electronically Recorded Monetary Claims Act	H20 内閣府・法務省令第 4 号		5.0	H22.11.26	
Electricity Business Act	S39 法律第 170 号	H17 法律第 87 号	1.0	H21.4.1	144
Act on Special Measures Concerning New Energy Use by operators of electric utilities（The revision of Article 2, paragraph (2), item (vi) has not come into force.）	H14 法律第 62 号	H21 法律第 70 号	4.0	H21.12.15	145
Electrical Appliances and Materials Safety Act	S36 法律第 234 号	H19 法律第 116 号	3.0	H21.10.14	146
					147
Act on Welfare and Management of Animals	S48 法律第 105 号	H17 法律第 68 号	2.0	H21.4.1	148
Act on Special Provisions, etc. of the Civil Code Concerning the Perfection Requirements for the Assignment of Movables and Claims	H1 法律第 104 号	H19 法律第 23 号	3.0	H21.5.21	149
Basic Act for Land	H 元法律第 84 号	H11 法律第 160 号	1.0	H21.4.1	150
Soil Contamination Countermeasures Act	H14 法律第 53 号	H21 法律第 23 号	3.0		151
Limited Partnership Act for Investment	H10 法律第 90 号	H16 法律第 34 号	1.0	H21.4.1	152

五十音順目次

1st ed.2014.10　　　　　85　　　　　JSB 英文六法

B《五十音順法令一覧》25年7月19日現在

法外訳 SYS	法令名	所管庁	PDFデータ頁数	○:済 △:未完 →備考
223	投資事業有限責任組合契約に関する法律施行令	経済産業省	13	○
224	投資信託及び投資法人に関する法律	金融庁	268	○
225	投資信託及び投資法人に関する法律施行令	金融庁	158	○
226	特定先端大型研究施設の共用の促進に関する法律	文部科学省	24	○
227	特定化学物質の環境への排出量の把握等及び管理の改善の促進に関する法律	経済産業省	25	○
228	特定化学物質の環境への排出量の把握等及び管理の改善の促進に関する法律施行令	経済産業省	45	○
229	特定化学物質の環境への排出量の把握等及び管理の改善の促進に関する法律施行規則	経済産業省	26	○
230	特定商取引に関する法律	消費者庁	160	○
231	特定商取引に関する法律施行令	消費者庁	59	○
232	特定商取引に関する法律施行規則	消費者庁	119	○
233	特定商品等の預託等取引契約に関する法律	消費者庁	12	○

B 《五十音順法令一覧》25 年 7 月 19 日現在

翻訳（英訳）	法令番号	改正	辞書 ver	翻訳日	法なび
Enforcement Order of the Limited Partnership Act for Investment	H10 政令第 235 号	H16 政令第 173 号	1.0	H21.4.1	153
Act on Investment Trusts and Investment Corporations	S26 法律第 198 号	H20 法律第 65 号	3.0	H21.10.12	154
Order for Enforcement of the Act on Investment Trusts and Investment Corporations	H12 政令第 480 号	H21 政令第 303 号	4.0	H22.6.3	
Act on the Promotion of Public Utilization of the Specific Advanced Large Research Facilities	H6 法律第 78 号	H18 法律第 37 号	3.0	H22.5.27	
Act on Confirmation, etc. of Release Amounts of Specific Chemical Substances in the Environment and Promotion of Improvements to the Management Thereof	H11 法律第 86 号	H14 法律第 152 号	1.0	H21.4.1	155
Order for Enforcement of the Act on Confirmation, etc. of Release Amounts of Specific Chemical Substances in the Environment and Promotion of Improvements to the Management Thereof	H12 政令第 138 号	H20 政令第 356 号	4.0	H21.12.1	
Ordinance for Enforcement of the Act on Confirmation, etc. of Release Amounts of Specific Chemical Substances in the Environment and Promotion of Improvements to the Management Thereof	H13 日内閣府・財務省・文部科学省・厚生労働省・農林水産省・経済産業省・国土交通省・環境省令第 1 号	H22 内閣府・財務省・文部科学省・厚生労働省・農林水産省・経済産業省・国土交通省・環境省・防衛省令第 1 号	6.0	H24.4.10	
Act on Specified Commercial Transactions	S51 法律第 57 号	H21 法律第 49 号	4.0	H21.12.1	156
Order for Enforcement of the Act on Specified Commercial Transactions	S51 政令第 295 号	H21 政令第 217 号	4.0	H21.12.1	157
Regulations for Enforcement of the Act on Specified Commercial Transactions	S51 通商産業省令第 89 号	H16 経済産業省令第 87 号	1.0	H21.4.1	158
Act on the Deposit, etc. Transaction Agreements of Specified Commodities, etc.	S61 法律第 62 号	H21 法律第 49 号	4.0	H21.12.1	

五十音順目次

B《五十音順法令一覧》25 年 7 月 19 日現在

法外訳 SYS	法令名	所管庁	PDFデータ頁数	○:済 △:未完 →備考
234	特定機器に係る適合性評価手続の結果の外国との相互承認の実施に関する法律	総務省	43	○
235	特定特殊自動車排出ガスの規制等に関する法律	環境省	32	○
236	特定電子メールの送信の適正化等に関する法律	総務省	21	○
237	特定電気通信役務提供者の損害賠償責任の制限及び発信者情報の開示に関する法律	総務省	6	○
238	特許法	経済産業省	163	○
239	独立行政法人新エネルギー・産業技術総合開発機構法（第 2 条未施行　等）	経済産業省	50	○
240	独立行政法人産業技術総合研究所法	経済産業省	17	○
241	統計法	総務省	42	○
242	統計調査に用いる産業分類並びに疾病、傷害及び死因分類を定める政令の規定に基づき、産業に関する分類の名称及び分類表を定める等の件	総務省		△
243	逃亡犯罪人引渡法	法務省	22	○
244	都市計画法	国土交通省	149	○
245	入札談合等関与行為の排除及び防止並びに職員による入札等の公正を害すべき行為の処罰に関する法律	公正取引委員会	10	○
246	日本国とアメリカ合衆国との間の相互協力及び安全保障条約第 6 条に基づく施設及び区域並びに日本国における合衆国軍隊の地位に関する協定の実施に伴う郵便法の特例に関する法律	総務省	4	○

五十音順目次

JSB英文六法　　　　　1st ed.2014.10

B《五十音順法令一覧》25年7月19日現在

翻訳（英訳）	法令番号	改正	辞書ver	翻訳日	法なび
Act for Implementation of the Mutual Recognition between Japan and Foreign States in Relation to Results of Conformity Assessment Procedures of Specified Equipment	H13法律第111号	H19法律第92号	3.0	H21.4.1	159
Act on Regulation, Etc. of Emissions from Non-road Special Motor Vehicles	H17法律第51号		1.0	H21.4.1	160
Act on Regulation of Transmission of Specified Electronic Mail	H14法律第26号	H17法律第87号	1.0	H21.4.1	161
Act on the Limitation of Liability for Damages of Specified Telecommunications Service Providers and the Right to Demand Disclosure of Identification Information of the Senders	H13法律第137号		2.0	H21.4.1	162
Patent Act	S34法律第121号	H18法律第109号	2.0	H21.4.1	163
Act on the New Energy and Industrial Technology Development Organization (Article 2 unenforced, etc.)	H14法律第145号	H21法律第70号	4.0	H21.12.1	164
Act on the National Institute of Advanced Industrial Science and Technology	H11法律第203号	H19法律第36号	3.0	H21.12.10	
Statistics Act	H19法律第53号		2.0	H21.4.1	165
Establishment of the nomenclature and classification table concerning industries pursuant to the provision of the Cabinet Order Providing for Industrial Classification and Classification of Diseases, Injuries and Death to be used for Statistical Surveys	H14総務省告示第139号	改正：	1.0	H21.4.1	166
Act of Extradition	S28法律第68号	H19法律第37号	3.0	H22.2.19	167
City Planning Act	S43法律第100号	H20法律第40号	3.0	H21.6.11	168
Act on Elimination and Prevention of Involvement in Bid Rigging, etc. and Punishments for Acts by Employees that Harm Fairness of Bidding, etc.	H14法律第101号	H18法律第110号	2.0	H21.4.1	169
Act on Special Provisions of the Postal Act attendant upon the Enforcement of the "Agreement under Article VI of the Treaty of Mutual Cooperation and Security between Japan and the United States of America regarding Facilities and Areas and the Status of United States Armed Forces in Japan"	S27法律第122号	H17法律第102号	1.0	H21.4.1	170

五十音順目次

B《五十音順法令一覧》25 年 7 月 19 日現在

法外訳 SYS	法令名	所管庁	PDFデータ頁数	○:済 △:未完 →備考
247	日本国とアメリカ合衆国との間の相互協力及び安全保障条約第 6 条に基づく施設及び区域並びに日本国における合衆国軍隊の地位に関する協定の実施に伴う電波法の特例に関する法律	総務省	2	○
248	日本国とアメリカ合衆国との間の相互協力及び安全保障条約第 6 条に基づく施設及び区域並びに日本国における合衆国軍隊の地位に関する協定等の実施に伴う電気通信事業法等の特例に関する法律	総務省	4	○
249	日本国憲法	その他	27	○
250	日本銀行法	財務省	62	○
251	日本電信電話株式会社等に関する法律	総務省	52	○
252	熱供給事業法	経済産業省	22	○
253	農林物資の規格化及び品質表示の適正化に関する法律	農林水産省	49	○
254	半導体集積回路の回路配置に関する法律	経済産業省	48	○
255	排他的経済水域における漁業等に関する主権的権利の行使等に関する法律	農林水産省	19	○
256	犯罪被害者等基本法	内閣府	12	○
257	破壊活動防止法	法務省	23	○
258	破産法	法務省	218	○
259	配偶者からの暴力の防止及び被害者の保護に関する法律	内閣府	29	○
260	ヒトに関するクローン技術等の規制に関する法律	文部科学省	19	○
261	不公正な取引方法	公正取引委員会		△

Ⓑ《五十音順法令一覧》25 年 7 月 19 日現在

翻訳（英訳）	法令番号	改正	辞書 ver	翻訳日	法なび
Act on Special Provisions of the Radio Law Attendant upon the Enforcement of the "Agreement under Article VI of the Treaty of Mutual Cooperation and Security between Japan and the United States of America regarding Facilities and Areas and the Status of United States Armed Forces in Japan"	S27 法律第 108 号	S35 法律第 102 号	2.0	H21.4.1	171
Act on Special Provisions of the Telecommunications Business Law, etc. Attendant upon the Enforcement of the "Agreement under ARTICLE VI of the Treaty of Mutual Cooperation and Security between Japan and the United States of America regarding Facilities and Areas and the Status of United States Armed Forces in Japan"	S27 法律第 107 号	S59 法律第 87 号	2.0	H21.4.1	172
The Constitution of Japan	S21 憲法			H21.4.1	173
Bank of Japan Act	H9 法律第 89 号	H19 法律第 102 号	2.0	H21.4.1	174
Act on Nippon Telegraph and Telephone Corporation, etc.	S59 法律第 85 号	H17 法律第 87 号	1.0	H21.4.1	175
Heat Supply Business Act	S47 法律第 88 号	H16 法律第 94 号	2.0	H21.4.1	176
Act on Standardization and Proper Quality Labeling of Agricultural and Forestry Products	S25 法律第 175 号	H21 法律第 49 号	4.0	H21.4.1	
Act on the Circuit Layout of a Semiconductor Integrated Circuits	S60 法律第 43 号	H18 法律第 50 号	3.0	H21.4.1	177
Act on the Exercise of the Sovereign Right for Fishery, etc. in the Exclusive Economic Zone	H8 法律第 76 号	H13 法律第 91 号	2.0	H21.4.1	178
Basic Act on Crime Victims	H16 法律第 161 号		2.0	H21.4.1	182
Subversive Activities Prevention Act	S27 法律第 240 号	H7 法律第 91 号	5.0	H23.9.8	
Bankruptcy Act	H16 法律第 75 号	H18 法律第 109 号	3.0	H21.10.20	179
Act on the Prevention of Spousal Violence and the Protection of Victims	H13 法律第 31 号	H19 法律第 113 号	2.0	H21.4.1	180
Act on Regulation of Human Cloning Techniques	H12 法律第 146 号		1.0	H21.4.1	181
Designation of Unfair Trade Practices	S57 公正取引委員会告示第 15 号		1.0	H21.4.1	183

五十音順目次

B 《五十音順法令一覧》25 年 7 月 19 日現在

法外訳 SYS	法令名	所管庁	PDFデータ頁数	○:済 △:未完 →備考
262	不動産登記令	法務省	197	○
263	不動産登記法	法務省	119	○
264	不動産登記規則	法務省	236	○
265	不当景品類及び不当表示防止法	消費者庁	13	○
266	不正競争防止法（暫定版）	経済産業省	40	○
267	扶養義務の準拠法に関する法律	法務省	3	○
268	文化財の不法な輸出入等の規制等に関する法律	文部科学省	4	○
269	武力攻撃事態における外国軍用品等の海上輸送の規制に関する法律	防衛省	33	○
270	武力攻撃事態における捕虜等の取扱いに関する法律	防衛省	105	○
271	弁理士法	経済産業省	62	○
272	弁護士法	法務省	107	○
273	保健師助産師看護師法	厚生労働省	55	○
274	保護司法	法務省	8	○
1-⑥ 275	**保険業法**	金融庁	##	△
1-⑦ 276	**保険業法施行令**	金融庁	252	○
277	北海道開発法	国土交通省	2	○
278	法の適用に関する通則法	法務省	22	○
279	法人税法（外国法人関連部分）	財務省	27	○
280	法人税法施行令（外国法人関連部分）	財務省	50	○

B 《五十音順法令一覧》25 年 7 月 19 日現在

翻訳（英訳）	法令番号	改正	辞書ver	翻訳日	法なび
Real Property Registration Order	H16 政令第 379 号	H22 政令第 4 号	6.0	H24.3.23	
Real Property Registration Act	H16 法律第 123 号	H19 法律第 132 号	3.0	H21.10.14	184
Ordinance on Real Property Registration	H17 法務省令第 18 号	H23 法務省令第 5 号	6.0	H24.3.23	
Act against Unjustifiable Premiums and Misleading Representations	S37 法律第 134 号	H17 法律第 35 号	1.0	H21.4.1	185
Unfair Competition Prevention Act (Tentative translation)	H5 法律第 47 号	H23 法律第 62 号	5.0	H23.6.30	186
Act on the Law Applicable to the Obligation of Support	S61 法律第 84 号	H18 法律第 78 号	5.0	H22.12.21	
Act on Controls on the Illicit Export and Import and other matters of Cultural Property	H14 法律第 81 号		1.0	H21.4.1	189
Act on the Restriction of Maritime Transportation of Foreign Military Supplies, etc. in Armed Attack Situations	H16 法律第 116 号	H18 法律第 118 号	4.0	H21.9.1	187
Act on the Treatment of Prisoners of War and Other Detainees in Armed Attack Situations	H16 法律第 117 号	H20 法律第 5 号	3.0	H21.7.16	188
Patent Attorney Act	H12 法律第 49 号	H19 法律第 91 号	3.0	H22.6.2	190
Attorney Act	S24 法律第 205 号	H17 法律第 87 号	3.0	H22.3.12	191
Act on Public Health Nurses, Midwives, and Nurses	S23 法律第 203 号	H21 法律第 78 号	6.0	H24.10.31	
Volunteer Probation Officers Act	S25 法律第 204 号	H19 法律第 88 号	4.0	H21.11.13	192
Insurance Business Act	H7 法律第 105 号	H21 法律第 59 号	3.0	H22.6.2	
Order for Enforcement of the Insurance Business Act	H7 政令第 425 号	H21 政令第 201 号	4.0	H22.6.3	
Hokkaido Development Act	S25 法律第 126 号	H11 法律第 117 号	1.0	H21.4.1	193
Act on General Rules for Application of Laws	H18 法律第 78 号		5.0	H23.4.27	
Corporation Tax Act（Limited to the provisions related to foreign corporations）	S40 法律第 34 号	H19 法律第 6 号	2.0	H21.4.1	195
Order for Enforcement of the Corporation Tax Act（Limited to the provisions related to foreign corporations）	S40 政令第 97 号	H19 政令第 83 号	3.0	H21.8.18	194

五十音順目次

B《五十音順法令一覧》25年7月19日現在

法外訳 SYS	法令名	所管庁	PDFデータ頁数	○:済 △:未完 →備考
281	法人税法施行規則（外国法人関連部分）	財務省	11	○
282	貿易保険法	経済産業省	83	○
283	貿易関係貿易外取引等に関する省令	経済産業省	28	○
284	民事保全法	法務省	36	○
285	民事保全法施行令	法務省	1	○
286	民事再生法	法務省	253	○
287	民事執行法	法務省	154	○
288	民事執行法施行令	法務省	2	○
289	民事訴訟法（暫定版）	法務省	195	○
290	民事訴訟規則	最高裁判所	119	○
291	民事訴訟費用等に関する法律	法務省	50	○
292	民法（第1編第2編第3編）	法務省	232	○
293	民法（第4編第5編）	法務省	106	○
294	民間資金等の活用による公共施設等の整備等の促進に関する法律	内閣府	23	○
295	ものづくり基盤技術振興基本法	経済産業省	10	○
296	有害物質を含有する家庭用品の規制に関する法律	厚生労働省	6	○
297	有限責任事業組合契約に関する法律	経済産業省	35	○
298	輸入割当てを受けるべき貨物の品目、輸入の承認を受けるべき貨物の原産地又は船積地域その他貨物の輸入について必要な事項の公表	経済産業省		△
299	輸入貿易管理令	経済産業省	26	○

B《五十音順法令一覧》25年7月19日現在

翻訳（英訳）	日本法令外国語訳データベースシステム　最終1覧データ収集日：H25.7.19				法なび
	法令番号	改正	辞書ver	翻訳日	
Ordinance for Enforcement of the Corporation Tax Act (Limited to the provisions related to foreign corporations)	S40 大蔵省令第12号	H20 財務省令第205号	4.0	H21.10.26	
Trade Insurance and Investment Act	S25 法律第67号	H20 法律第57号	5.0	H23.1.20	
Ministerial Ordinance on Trade Relation Invisible Trade, etc.	H10 通商産業省令第8号	H19 経済産業省令第67号	3.0	H21.5.22	196
Civil Provisional Remedies Act	H元法律第91号	H23 法律第36号	6.0	H24.3.22	197
Order for Enforcement of the Civil Provisional Remedies Act	H2 政令第284号		5.0	H22.12.17	
Civil Rehabilitation Act	H11 法律第225号	H17 法律第87号	3.0	H21.4.1	198
Civil Execution Act	S54 法律第4号	H19 法律第95号	3.0	H21.4.1	199
Order for Enforcement of the Civil Execution Act	S55 政令第230号	H16 政令第419号	5.0	H22.12.17	
Code of Civil Procedure (Tentative translation)	H8 法律第109号	H23 法律第36号	6.0	H24.3.22	200
Rules of Civil Procedure	H8 最高裁判所規則第5号	H20 最高裁判所規則第10号	3.0	H21.4.1	201
Act on Costs of Civil Procedure	S46 法律第40号	H19 法律第113号	4.0	H21.11.18	
Civil Code (Part I, Part II, and Part III)	明治29法律第89号	H18 法律第78号	2.0	H21.4.1	202
Civil Code (Part IV and Part V)	明治29法律第89号	H18 法律第78号	2.0	H21.4.1	203
Act on Promotion of Private Finance Initiative	H11 法律第117号	H18 法律第53号	3.0	H21.4.1	204
Basic Act on the Promotion of Core Manufacturing Technology	H11 法律第2号		2.0	H21.4.1	205
Act on Control of Household Products Containing Harmful Substances	S48 法律第112号	H21 法律第49号	4.0	H22.2.17	
Limited Liability Partnership Act	H17 法律第40号	H17 法律第87号	1.0	H21.4.1	206
Public Announcement on the Items of Goods Subject to Import Quotas, the Places of Origin or Places of Shipment of Goods Requiring Approval for Import, and Other Necessary Matters Concerning Import of Goods	S41 通商産業省告示第170号	H20 経済産業省告示第129号	3.0	H21.5.27	
Import Trade Control Order	S24 政令第414号	H15 政令第248号	1.0	H21.4.1	208

五十音順目次

1st ed.2014.10　　　95　　　JSB英文六法

B 《五十音順法令一覧》25 年 7 月 19 日現在

法外訳 SYS	法令名	所管庁	PDF データ頁数	○:済 △:未完 →備考
300	輸出貿易管理令（暫定版）	経済産業省	114	○
301	輸出貿易管理令別表第 1 及び外国為替令別表の規定に基づき貨物又は技術を定める省令	経済産業省	311	○
302	輸出貿易管理規則（暫定版）	経済産業省	24	○
303	遺言の方式の準拠法に関する法律	法務省	3	○
304	容器包装に係る分別収集及び再商品化の促進等に関する法律	経済産業省	49	○
305	預金保険法施行規則	金融庁	39	○
1-⑪ 306	連結財務諸表の用語、様式及び作成方法に関する規則	金融庁	94	○
307	労働保険の保険料の徴収等に関する法律	厚生労働省	123	○
308	労働基準法	厚生労働省	66	○
309	労働基準法施行規則	厚生労働省	64	○
310	労働契約法	厚生労働省	7	○
311	労働安全衛生法	厚生労働省	242	○
312	労働安全衛生規則（別表第 2、別表第 5 及び別表第 9：H21.厚生労働省令第 23 号までの改正）	厚生労働省	629	△
313	労働組合法	厚生労働省	46	○
314	労働者派遣事業の適正な運営の確保及び派遣労働者の就業条件の整備等に関する法律	厚生労働省	77	○
315	労働者派遣事業の適正な運営の確保及び派遣労働者の就業条件の整備等に関する法律施行令	厚生労働省	34	○

五十音順目次

B 《五十音順法令一覧》25 年 7 月 19 日現在

翻訳（英訳）	法令番号	改正	辞書ver	翻訳日	法なび
Export Trade Control Order (Tentative translation)	S24 政令第 378 号	H23 政令第 141 号	6.0	H24.4.19	209
Ordinance of the Ministry Specifying Goods and Technologies Pursuant to Provisions of the Appended Table 1 of the Export Control Order and the Appended Table of the Foreign Exchange Order	H3 通商産業省令第 49 号	H23 経済産業省令第 26 号	7.0		210
Export Trade Control Ordinance (Tentative translation)	S24 通商産業省令第 64 号	H22 経済産業省令第 6 号	6.0	H24.4.19	211
Act on the Law Applicable to the Form of Wills	S39 法律第 100 号	H18 法律第 78 号	5.0	H22.12.21	
Act on the Promotion of Sorted Collection and Recycling of Containers and Packaging	H7 法律第 112 号	H18 法律第 76 号	1.0	H21.4.1	212
Ordinance for Enforcement of the Deposit Insurance Act	S46 大蔵省令第 28 号	H22 内閣府・財務省令第 1 号	5.0	H22.11.26	
Ordinance on Terminology, Forms, and Preparation Methods of Consolidated Financial Statements	S51 大蔵省令第 28 号	H21 内閣府令第 73 号	5.0	H23.4.22	
Act on the Collection, etc. of Insurance Premiums of Labor Insurance	S44 法律第 84 号	H19 法律第 110 号	3.0	H21.4.1	213
Labor Standards Act	S22 法律第 49 号	H16 法律第 147 号	1.0	H21.4.1	214
Ordinance for Enforcement of the Labor Standards Act	S22 厚生省令第 23 号		2.0	H21.4.1	215
Labor Contract Act	H19 法律第 128 号		5.0	H22.11.5	
Industrial Safety and Health Act	S47 法律第 57 号	H18 法律第 25 号	1.0	H21.4.1	216
Ordinance on Industrial Safety and Health (Appended Tables 2, 5 and 9: up to the revision of Ordinance of the Ministry of Health, Labour and Welfare No. 23 of 2009)	S47 労働省令第 32 号	H18 厚生労働省令第 185 号	3.0	H23.6.27	
Labor Union Act	S24 法律第 174 号	H17 法律第 87 号	1.0	H21.4.1	217
Act for Securing the Proper Operation of Worker Dispatching Undertakings and Improved Working Conditions for Dispatched Workers	S60 法律第 88 号	H18 法律第 82 号	2.0	H21.4.1	218
Order for Enforcement of the Act for Securing the Proper Operation of Worker Dispatching Undertakings and Improved Working Conditions for Dispatched Workers	S61 政令第 95 号	H19 政令第 376 号	2.0	H21.4.1	219

五十音順目次

B《五十音順法令一覧》25 年 7 月 19 日現在

法外訳 SYS	法令名	所管庁	PDFデータ頁数	○:済 △:未完 →備考
316	労働者派遣事業の適正な運営の確保及び派遣労働者の就業条件の整備等に関する法律施行規則	厚生労働省	71	○
317	労働者災害補償保険法	厚生労働省	86	○
318	労働関係調整法	厚生労働省	17	○
319	老人福祉法	厚生労働省	52	○
320	宗教法人法	文部科学省	76	○
321	公正取引委員会の審判に関する規則	公正取引委員会	38	○
322	課徴金の減免に係る報告及び資料の提出に関する規則	公正取引委員会	8	○
323	預金保険法（暫定版）	金融庁	177	○

五十音順目次

B 《五十音順法令一覧》25年7月19日現在

翻訳（英訳）	日本法令外国語訳データベースシステム　最終1覧データ収集日：H25.7.19					法なび
	法令番号	改正	辞書ver	翻訳日	
Ordinance for Enforcement of the Act for Securing the Proper Operation of Worker Dispatching Undertakings and Improved Working Conditions for Dispatched Workers	S61労働省令第20号	H19厚生労働省令第149号	2.0	H21.4.1	220
Industrial Accident Compensation Insurance Act	S22法律第50号	H19法律第111号	3.0	H21.9.11	
Labor Relations Adjustment Act	S21法律第25号	H16法律第140号	3.0	H21.6.16	221
Act on Social Welfare for the Elderly	S38法律第133号	H20法律第42号	4.0	H22.10.6	
Religious Corporations Act	S26法律第126号	H18法律第50号	5.0	H23.1.4	
Rules on Hearings by the Fair Trade Commission	H17公正取引委員会規則第8号	H21公正取引委員会規則第6号	5.0	H22.9.3	
Rules on Reporting and the Submission of Supporting Materials in Relation to Immunity from or Reduction of Surcharges	H17公正取引委員会規則第7号	H21公正取引委員会規則第12号	5.0	H23.1.14	
Deposit Insurance Act (Tentative translation)	S46法律第34号	H20法律第65号	5.0	H22.11.26	

五十音順目次

C《所管庁別五十音順英文法令一覧》25 年 7 月 19 日現在

法外訳 SYS	法令名	所管庁	PDF データ頁数	○:済 △:未完 →備考
93	国際連合安全保障理事会決議第 1874 号等を踏まえ我が国が実施する貨物検査等に関する特別措置法	外務省	13	○
4	石綿による健康被害の救済に関する法律	環境省	66	○
6	遺伝子組換え生物等の使用等の規制による生物の多様性の確保に関する法律	環境省	37	○
141	循環型社会形成推進基本法	環境省	20	○
182	生物多様性基本法	環境省	17	○
203	地球温暖化対策の推進に関する法律	環境省	39	○
218	動物の愛護及び管理に関する法律	環境省	29	○
221	土壌汚染対策法	環境省	51	○
235	特定特殊自動車排出ガスの規制等に関する法律	環境省	32	○
40	貸金業法	金融庁	157	○
41	貸金業法施行令	金融庁	143	○
52	金融商品の販売等に関する法律	金融庁	14	○
53	金融商品の販売等に関する法律施行令	金融庁	11	○
54	金融商品取引法	金融庁	834	○
55	金融商品取引法第 2 条に規定する定義に関する内閣府令	金融庁	114	○
56	金融機関の信託業務の兼営等に関する法律施行令	金融庁	31	○
57	金融機関の信託業務の兼営等に関する法律施行規則	金融庁	130	○

C 《所管庁別五十音順英文法令一覧》25 年 7 月 19 日現在

＊S＝昭和、H＝平成

翻訳（英訳）	日本法令外国語訳データベースシステム　最終1覧データ収集日：H25.7.19				法なび
	法令番号	改正	辞書ver	翻訳日	
Act on Special Measures concerning Cargo Inspections etc. Conducted by the Government Taking into Consideration United Nations Security Council Resolution 1874, etc.	H22 法律第 43 号		5.0	H24.6.29	
Act on Asbestos Health Damage Relief	H18 法律第 4 号		2.0	H21.4.1	3
Act on the Conservation and Sustainable Use of Biological Diversity through Regulations on the Use of Living Modified Organisms	H15 法律第 97 号	H19 法律第 8 号	2.0	H21.4.1	5
Basic Act on Establishing a Sound Material-Cycle Society	H12 法律第 110 号		3.0	H21.4.1	92
Basic Act on Biodiversity	H20 法律第 58 号		3.0	H22.5.27	
Act on Promotion of Global Warming Countermeasures	H10 法律第 117 号	H18 法律第 57 号	1.0	H21.4.1	136
Act on Welfare and Management of Animals	S48 法律第 105 号	H17 法律第 68 号	2.0	H21.4.1	148
Soil Contamination Countermeasures Act	H14 法律第 53 号	H21 法律第 23 号	3.0		151
Act on Regulation, Etc. of Emissions from Non-road Special Motor Vehicles	H17 法律第 51 号		1.0	H21.4.1	160
Money Lending Business Act	S58 法律第 32 号	H20 法律第 74 号	3.0	H21.11.11	
Order for Enforcement of the Money Lending Act	S58 政令第 181 号	H21 政令第 303 号	4.0	H22.6.3	
Act on Sales, etc. of Financial Instruments	H12 法律第 101 号	H18 法律第 66 号	3.0	H22.6.25	
Order for Enforcement of the Act on the Sale, etc. of Financial Instruments	H12 政令第 484 号	H21 政令第 303 号	5.0	H22.11.26	
Financial Instruments and Exchange Act	S23 法律第 25 号	H18 法律第 109 号	3.0	H21.6.16	
Cabinet Office Ordinance on Definitions under Article 2 of the Financial Instruments and Exchange Act	H5 大蔵省令第 14 号	H21 内閣府令第 78 号	3.0	H22.6.25	
Order for Enforcement of the Act on Engagement in Trust Business by a Financial Institution	H5 政令第 31 号	H21 政令第 303 号	5.0	H22.11.26	
Ordinance for Enforcement of the Act on Engagement in Trust Business by a Financial Institution	S57 大蔵省令第 16 号	H21 内閣府令第 78 号	5.0	H22.11.26	

所管庁別目次

1st ed.2014.10　　　101　　　JSB英文六法

C 《所管庁別五十音順英文法令一覧》25 年 7 月 19 日現在

法外訳 SYS	法令名	所管庁	PDF データ 頁数	○:済 △:未完 →備考
58	銀行法	金融庁	298	○
59	銀行法	金融庁	239	○
60	銀行法第 26 条第 2 項に規定する区分等を定める命令	金融庁	20	○
79	公認会計士法	金融庁	137	○
80	公認会計士法施行令	金融庁	26	○
81	公認会計士法施行規則	金融庁	77	○
1-⑨ 117	財務諸表等の監査証明に関する内閣府令	金融庁	32	○
122	信託業法	金融庁	119	○
1-⑩ 136	四半期財務諸表等の用語、様式及び作成方法に関する規則	金融庁	58	○
1-⑫ 160	社債、株式等の振替に関する法律施行令	金融庁	107	○
1-⑬ 168	証券情報等の提供又は公表に関する内閣府令	金融庁	39	○
170	資産の流動化に関する法律	金融庁	313	○
1-⑭ 171	資金移動業者に関する内閣府令	金融庁	47	○
211	電子記録債権法	金融庁	76	○
212	電子記録債権法施行令	金融庁	17	○
213	電子記録債権法施行規則	金融庁	53	○
224	投資信託及び投資法人に関する法律	金融庁	268	○

所管庁別目次

[C] 《所管庁別五十音順英文法令一覧》25 年 7 月 19 日現在

翻訳（英訳）	法令番号	改正	辞書 ver	翻訳日	法なび
Banking Act	S56 法律第 59 号	H21 法律第 59 号	4.0	H22.6.2	37
Banking Act	S56 法律第 59 号	H18 法律第 109 号	3.0	H21.6.16	37
Order Providing for the Categories, etc. Prescribed in Article 26, Paragraph (2) of the Banking Act	H12 総理府・大蔵省令第 39 号	H18 内閣府・財務省令第 6 号	3.0	H22.5.10	
Certified Public Accountants Act	S23 法律第 103 号	H19 法律第 99 号	3.0	H22.4.28	50
Order for Enforcement of the Certified Public Accountants Act	S27 政令第 343 号	H19 政令第 235 号	3.0	H22.5.10	
Ordinance for Enforcement of the Certified Public Accountants Act	H19 内閣府令第 81 号		3.0	H22.5.10	
Cabinet Office Ordinance on Audit Certification of Financial Statements, etc.	S32 大蔵省令第 12 号	H21 内閣府令第 73 号	5.0	H23.5.10	
Trust Business Act	H16 法律第 154 号	H20 法律第 65 号	3.0	H21.9.30	
Ordinance on Terminology, Forms, and Preparation Methods of Quarterly Financial Statements, etc.	H19 内閣府令第 63 号	H21 内閣府令第 73 号	5.0	H23.5.9	
Order for Enforcement of the Act on Book-Entry of Company Bonds, Shares, etc.	H14 政令第 362 号	H22 政令第 4 号	5.0	H22.11.26	
Cabinet Office Ordinance on the Provision and Publication of Information on Securities	H20 内閣府令第 78 号	H21 内閣府令第 78 号	4.0	H22.6.2	
Act on Securitization of Assets	H10 法律第 105 号	H20 法律第 65 号	3.0	H21.11.11	
Cabinet Office Ordinance on Funds Transfer Service Providers	H22 内閣府令第 4 号		5.0	H22.11.26	
Electronically Recorded Monetary Claims Act	H19 法律第 102 号		3.0	H21.4.1	143
Order for Enforcement of the Electronically Recorded Monetary Claims Act	H20 政令第 325 号		5.0	H22.11.26	
Ordinance for Enforcement of the Electronically Recorded Monetary Claims Act	H20 内閣府・法務省令第 4 号		5.0	H22.11.26	
Act on Investment Trusts and Investment Corporations	S26 法律第 198 号	H20 法律第 65 号	3.0	H21.10.12	154

所管庁別目次

1st ed.2014.10　　　　JSB英文六法

Ⓒ《所管庁別五十音順英文法令一覧》25 年 7 月 19 日現在

法外訳 SYS	法令名	所管庁	PDFデータ頁数	○:済 △:未完 →備考
225	投資信託及び投資法人に関する法律施行令	金融庁	158	○
1-⑥ 275	保険業法	金融庁	1019	△
1-⑦ 276	保険業法施行令	金融庁	252	○
305	預金保険法施行規則	金融庁	39	○
1-⑪ 306	連結財務諸表の用語、様式及び作成方法に関する規則	金融庁	94	○
323	預金保険法（暫定版）	金融庁	177	○
3	意匠法	経済産業省	57	○
8	エネルギーの使用の合理化に関する法律	経済産業省	111	○
9	エネルギー政策基本法	経済産業省	7	○
12	ガス事業法	経済産業省	160	○
19	割賦販売法施行令	経済産業省	39	○
20	化学物質の審査及び製造等の規制に関する法律（附則第 4 条未施行 等）	経済産業省	77	○
21	化学物質の審査及び製造等の規制に関する法律施行令	経済産業省	17	○
28	外国為替令	経済産業省	114	○
29	外国為替及び外国貿易法（第 515 条の 1 未施行 等）	経済産業省	119	○
33	核原料物質、核燃料物質及び原子炉の規制に関する法律	経済産業省	233	○
42	企業立地の促進等による地域における産業集積の形成及び活性化に関する法律	経済産業省	48	○

所管庁別目次

© 《所管庁別五十音順英文法令一覧》25 年 7 月 19 日現在

翻訳（英訳）	日本法令外国語訳データベースシステム 最終１覧データ収集日：H25.7.19				法なび
	法令番号	改正	辞書ver	翻訳日	
Order for Enforcement of the Act on Investment Trusts and Investment Corporations	H12 政令第 480 号	H21 政令第 303 号	4.0	H22.6.3	
Insurance Business Act	H7 法律第 105 号	H21 法律第 59 号	3.0	H22.6.2	
Order for Enforcement of the Insurance Business Act	H7 政令第 425 号	H21 政令第 201 号	4.0	H22.6.3	
Ordinance for Enforcement of the Deposit Insurance Act	S46 大蔵省令第 28 号	H22 内閣府・財務省令第 1 号	5.0	H22.11.26	
Ordinance on Terminology, Forms, and Preparation Methods of Consolidated Financial Statements	S51 大蔵省令第 28 号	H21 内閣府令第 73 号	5.0	H23.4.22	
Deposit Insurance Act (Tentative translation)	S46 法律第 34 号	H20 法律第 65 号	5.0	H22.11.26	
Design Act	S34 法律第 125 号	H18 法律第 55 号	1.0	H21.4.1	2
Act on the Rational Use of Energy	S54 法律第 49 号	H20 法律第 47 号	3.0	H21.4.24	6
Basic Act on Energy Policy	H14 法律第 71 号		1.0	H21.4.1	7
Gas Business Act	S29 法律第 51 号	H17 法律第 87 号	1.0	H21.4.1	10
Order for Enforcement of the Installment Sales Act	S36 政令第 341 号	H21 政令第 217 号	4.0	H21.12.1	
Act on the Evaluation of Chemical Substances and Regulation of Their Manufacture, etc. (Article 4 of the Supplementary Provisions unenforced, etc.)	S48 法律第 117 号	H21 法律第 39 号	4.0	H21.12.1	14
Order for Enforcement of the Act on the Evaluation of Chemical Substances and Regulation of Their Manufacture, etc.	S49 政令第 202 号	H21 政令第 257 号	5.0	H23.1.20	15
Foreign Exchange Order	S55 政令第 260 号	H20 政令第 237 号	3.0	H21.5.22	21
Foreign Exchange and Foreign Trade Act	S24 法律第 228 号	H21 法律第 59 号	4.0	H21.12.1	22
Act on the Regulation of Nuclear Source Material, Nuclear Fuel Material and Reactors	S32 法律第 166 号	H19 法律第 84 号	3.0	H21.4.9	42
Act on Formation and Development of Regional Industrial Clusters through Promotion of Establishment of New Business Facilities, etc.	H19 法律第 40 号	H20 法律第 37 号	3.0	H21.4.1	29

所管庁別目次

© 《所管庁別五十音順英文法令一覧》25 年 7 月 19 日現在

法外訳 SYS	法令名	所管庁	PDF データ 頁数	○：済 △：未完 →備考
68	原子力災害対策特別措置法	経済産業省	58	○
71	経済産業省関係化学物質の審査及び製造等の規制に関する法律施行規則	経済産業省	22	○
72	計量法	経済産業省	176	○
94	工業標準化法	経済産業省	43	○
102	鉱業法	経済産業省	103	○
105	高圧ガス保安法	経済産業省	171	○
110	産業技術力強化法	経済産業省	23	○
111	産業活力の再生及び産業活動の革新に関する特別措置法施行規則	経済産業省	79	○
121	使用済自動車の再資源化等に関する法律	経済産業省	136	○
131	商品先物取引法施行規則	経済産業省	491	○
132	商品取引所法	経済産業省	380	○
133	商品取引所法施行令	経済産業省	60	○
135	商標法	経済産業省	123	○
139	実用新案法	経済産業省	80	○

[C] 《所管庁別五十音順英文法令一覧》25 年 7 月 19 日現在

翻訳（英訳）	法令番号	改正	辞書 ver	翻訳日	法なび
Act on Special Measures Concerning Nuclear Emergency Preparedness	H11 法律第 156 号	H18 法律第 118 号	2.0	H21.4.1	45
Ordinance for Enforcement of the Act on the Evaluation of Chemical Substances and Regulation of Their Manufacture, etc. as the Act Relates to the Ministry of Economy, Trade and Industry.	S49 通商産業省令第 40 号	H22 経済産業省令第 7 号	5.0	H23.1.20	
Measurement Act	H4 法律第 51 号	H18 法律第 10 号	2.0	H21.4.1	44
Industrial Standardization Act	S24 法律第 185 号	H17 法律第 87 号	2.0	H21.4.1	59
Mining Act	S25 法律第 289 号	H16 法律第 94 号	3.0	H21.4.1	65
High Pressure Gas Safety Act	S26 法律第 204 号	H17 法律第 73 号	3.0	H21.4.1	68
Industrial Technology Enhancement Act	H12 法律第 44 号	H19 法律第 36 号	2.0	H21.4.1	70
Ordinance for Enforcement of the Act on Special Measures Concerning Revitalization of Industry and Innovation in Industrial Activities	H21 内閣府、総務省、財務省、厚生労働省、農林水産省、経済産業省、国土交通省、環境省令第 1 号	H23 内閣府・総務省・財務省・厚生労働省・農林水産省・経済産業省・国土交通省・環境省令第 1 号	6.0	H24.4.19	
Act on Recycling, etc. of End-of-Life Vehicles	H14 法律第 87 号	H18 法律第 50 号	2.0	H21.4.1	78
Ordinance for Enforcement of the Commodity Derivatives Act	H17 農林水産省・経済産業省令第 3 号	H22 農林水産省・経済産業省令第 5 号	5.0	H24.6.18	
Commodity Exchange Act	S25 法律第 239 号	H18 法律第 65 号	3.0	H21.8.18	85
Order for Enforcement of the Commodity Exchange Act	S25 政令第 280 号	H20 政令第 237 号	3.0	H21.4.22	86
Trademark Act	S34 法律第 127 号	H18 法律第 55 号	2.0	H21.4.1	89
Utility Model Act	S34 法律第 123 号	H18 法律第 55 号	1.0	H21.4.1	91

所管庁別目次

C 《所管庁別五十音順英文法令一覧》25年7月19日現在

法外訳 SYS	法令名	所管庁	PDFデータ頁数	○:済 △:未完 →備考
146	指定化学物質等の性状及び取扱いに関する情報の提供の方法等を定める省令	経済産業省	6	○
147	新エネルギー利用等の促進に関する特別措置法	経済産業省	15	○
148	新エネルギー利用等の促進に関する特別措置法施行令	経済産業省	8	○
150	新規化学物質の製造又は輸入に係る届出等に関する省令	経済産業省	15	○
153	消費生活用製品安全法	経済産業省	92	○
169	資源の有効な利用の促進に関する法律	経済産業省	40	○
183	石油の備蓄の確保等に関する法律	経済産業省	28	○
191	大学等における技術に関する研究成果の民間事業者への移転の促進に関する法律	経済産業省	32	○
193	大規模小売店舗立地法	経済産業省	20	○
194	大規模小売店舗立地法施行令	経済産業省	3	○
196	対内直接投資等に関する命令	経済産業省	38	○

所管庁別目次

[C] 《所管庁別五十音順英文法令一覧》25 年 7 月 19 日現在

翻訳（英訳）	法令番号	改正	辞書 ver	翻訳日	法なび
Ministerial Ordinance Specifying the Method of Provision of Information on the Properties and Handling of Designated Chemical Substances, etc.	H12 通商産業省令第 401 号	H21 経済産業省令第 27 号	6.0	H24.4.10	
Act on the Promotion of New Energy Usage	H9 法律第 37 号	H17 法律第 87 号	2.0	H21.11.2	96
Order for Enforcement of the Act on Special Measures for the Promotion of New Energy Use, etc.	H9 政令第 208 号	H20 政令第 16 号	3.0	H21.4.1	97
Ordinance Related to Notification, etc. Concerning the Manufacture or Import of New Chemical Substances	S49 厚生省・通商産業省令第 1 号	H22 厚生労働省・経済産業省・環境省令第 1 号	5.0	H23.1.20	
Consumer Product Safety Act	S48 法律第 31 号	H19 法律第 117 号	3.0	H21.4.1	101
Act on the Promotion of Effective Utilization of Resources	H3 法律第 48 号	H14 法律第 1 号	1.0	H21.4.1	111
Oil Stockpiling Act	S50 法律第 96 号		2.0	H21.4.1	122
Act on the Promotion of Technology Transfer from Universities to Private Business Operators	H10 法律第 52 号	H17 法律第 87 号	2.0	H21.4.1	129
Act on the Measures by Large-Scale Retail Stores for Preservation of Living Environment	H10 法律第 91 号	H12 法律第 91 号	3.0	H21.4.24	130
Order for Enforcement of the Act on the Measures by Large-Scale Retail Stores for Preservation of Living Environment	H10 政令第 327 号		5.0	H23.1.20	
Order on Inward Direct Investment, etc.	S55 総理府・大蔵省・文部省・厚生省・農林水産省・通商産業省・運輸省・郵政省・労働省・建設省令第 1 号	H22 内閣府・総務省・財務省・文部科学省・厚生労働省・農林水産省・経済産業省・国土交通省・環境省令第 2 号	5.0	H23.2.19	132

1st ed.2014.10　　　109　　　JSB 英文六法

C 《所管庁別五十音順英文法令一覧》 25 年 7 月 19 日現在

法外訳 SYS	法令名	所管庁	PDF データ 頁数	○：済 △：未完 →備考
197	対内直接投資等に関する命令第 3 条第 3 項の規定に基づき財務大臣及び事業所管大臣が定める業種を定める件	経済産業省		△
198	対内直接投資等に関する政令	経済産業省	42	○
202	中小企業等協同組合法	経済産業省	288	○
209	電子消費者契約及び電子承諾通知に関する民法の特例に関する法律	経済産業省	4	○
210	電子署名及び認証業務に関する法律	経済産業省	30	○
214	電気事業法	経済産業省	191	○
215	電気事業者による新エネルギー等の利用に関する特別措置法（第 2 条第 2 項第 6 号改正未施行）	経済産業省	11	○
216	電気用品安全法	経済産業省	63	○
217	電気用品安全法　削除	経済産業省		
222	投資事業有限責任組合契約に関する法律	経済産業省	21	○
223	投資事業有限責任組合契約に関する法律施行令	経済産業省	13	○
227	特定化学物質の環境への排出量の把握等及び管理の改善の促進に関する法律	経済産業省	25	○

所管庁別目次

JSB英文六法　　　1st ed.2014.10

[C] 《所管庁別五十音順英文法令一覧》25年7月19日現在

翻訳（英訳）	日本法令外国語訳データベースシステム　最終1覧データ収集日：H25.7.19					法なび
	法令番号	改正	辞書ver	翻訳日	
the public notice on specifying business types to be specified by the Minister of Finance and the minister having jurisdiction over the business pursuant to the provision of Article 3, paragraph (3) of the Order on Inward Direct Investment, etc.	H20内閣府、総務省、財務省、文部科学省、厚生労働省、農林水産省、経済産業省、国土交通省、環境省告示第1号		3.0	H21.6.16	
Cabinet Order on Inward Direct Investment, etc.	S55政令第261号	H22政令第19号	5.0	H23.2.19	133
Small and Medium-Sized Enterprise Cooperatives Act	S24法律第181号	H18法律第109号	2.0	H21.4.1	135
Act on Special Provisions to the Civil Code Concerning Electronic Consumer Contracts and Electronic Acceptance Notice	H13法律第95号		1.0	H21.4.1	141
Act on Electronic Signatures and Certification Business	H12法律第102号	H18法律第10号	1.0	H21.4.1	142
Electricity Business Act	S39法律第170号	H17法律第87号	1.0	H21.4.1	144
Act on Special Measures Concerning New Energy Use by operators of electric utilities (The revision of Article 2, paragraph (2), item (vi) has not come into force.)	H14法律第62号	H21法律第70号	4.0	H21.12.15	145
Electrical Appliances and Materials Safety Act	S36法律第234号	H19法律第116号	3.0	H21.10.14	146
					147
Limited Partnership Act for Investment	H10法律第90号	H16法律第34号	1.0	H21.4.1	152
Enforcement Order of the Limited Partnership Act for Investment	H10政令第235号	H16政令第173号	1.0	H21.4.1	153
Act on Confirmation, etc. of Release Amounts of Specific Chemical Substances in the Environment and Promotion of Improvements to the Management Thereof	H11法律第86号	H14法律第152号	1.0	H21.4.1	155

所管庁別目次

C《所管庁別五十音順英文法令一覧》25 年 7 月 19 日現在

法外訳 SYS	法令名	所管庁	PDFデータ頁数	○:済 △:未完 →備考
228	特定化学物質の環境への排出量の把握等及び管理の改善の促進に関する法律施行令	経済産業省	45	○
229	特定化学物質の環境への排出量の把握等及び管理の改善の促進に関する法律施行規則	経済産業省	26	○
238	特許法	経済産業省	163	○
239	独立行政法人新エネルギー・産業技術総合開発機構法（第2条未施行　等）	経済産業省	50	○
240	独立行政法人産業技術総合研究所法	経済産業省	17	○
252	熱供給事業法	経済産業省	22	○
254	半導体集積回路の回路配置に関する法律	経済産業省	48	○
266	不正競争防止法（暫定版）	経済産業省	40	○
271	弁理士法	経済産業省	62	○
282	貿易保険法	経済産業省	83	○
283	貿易関係貿易外取引等に関する省令	経済産業省	28	○
295	ものづくり基盤技術振興基本法	経済産業省	10	○
297	有限責任事業組合契約に関する法律	経済産業省	35	○

© 《所管庁別五十音順英文法令一覧》25年7月19日現在

翻訳（英訳）	法令番号	改正	辞書ver	翻訳日	法なび
Order for Enforcement of the Act on Confirmation, etc. of Release Amounts of Specific Chemical Substances in the Environment and Promotion of Improvements to the Management Thereof	H12政令第138号	H20政令第356号	4.0	H21.12.1	
Ordinance for Enforcement of the Act on Confirmation, etc. of Release Amounts of Specific Chemical Substances in the Environment and Promotion of Improvements to the Management Thereof	H13日内閣府・財務省・文部科学省・厚生労働省・農林水産省・経済産業省・国土交通省・環境省令第1号	H22内閣府・財務省・文部科学省・厚生労働省・農林水産省・経済産業省・国土交通省・環境省・防衛省令第1号	6.0	H24.4.10	
Patent Act	S34法律第121号	H18法律第109号	2.0	H21.4.1	163
Act on the New Energy and Industrial Technology Development Organization (Article 2 unenforced, etc.)	H14法律第145号	H21法律第70号	4.0	H21.12.1	164
Act on the National Institute of Advanced Industrial Science and Technology	H11法律第203号	H19法律第36号	3.0	H21.12.10	
Heat Supply Business Act	S47法律第88号	H16法律第94号	2.0	H21.4.1	176
Act on the Circuit Layout of a Semiconductor Integrated Circuits	S60法律第43号	H18法律第50号	3.0	H21.4.1	177
Unfair Competition Prevention Act (Tentative translation)	H5法律第47号	H23法律第62号	5.0	H23.6.30	186
Patent Attorney Act	H12法律第49号	H19法律第91号	3.0	H22.6.2	190
Trade Insurance and Investment Act	S25法律第67号	H20法律第57号	5.0	H23.1.20	
Ministerial Ordinance on Trade Relation Invisible Trade, etc.	H10通商産業省令第8号	H19経済産業省令第67号	3.0	H21.5.22	196
Basic Act on the Promotion of Core Manufacturing Technology	H11法律第2号		2.0	H21.4.1	205
Limited Liability Partnership Act	H17法律第40号	H17法律第87号	1.0	H21.4.1	206

所管庁別目次

Ⓒ《所管庁別五十音順英文法令一覧》25 年 7 月 19 日現在

法外訳 SYS	法令名	所管庁	PDF データ 頁数	○:済 △:未完 →備考
298	輸入割当てを受けるべき貨物の品目、輸入の承認を受けるべき貨物の原産地又は船積地域その他貨物の輸入について必要な事項の公表	経済産業省		△
299	輸入貿易管理令	経済産業省	26	○
300	輸出貿易管理令（暫定版）	経済産業省	114	○
301	輸出貿易管理令別表第1及び外国為替令別表の規定に基づき貨物又は技術を定める省令	経済産業省	311	○
302	輸出貿易管理規則（暫定版）	経済産業省	24	○
304	容器包装に係る分別収集及び再商品化の促進等に関する法律	経済産業省	49	○
75	公正取引委員会の審判費用等に関する政令	公正取引委員会	4	○
76	公正取引委員会の審査に関する規則	公正取引委員会	22	○
118	下請代金支払遅延等防止法	公正取引委員会	14	○
149	新聞業における特定の不公正な取引方法	公正取引委員会		△
161	私的独占の禁止及び公正取引の確保に関する法律	公正取引委員会	133	○
162	私的独占の禁止及び公正取引の確保に関する法律第9条から第16条までの規定による認可の申請、報告及び届出等に関する規則	公正取引委員会	31	○
195	大規模小売業者による納入業者との取引における特定の不公正な取引方法	公正取引委員会		△

© 《所管庁別五十音順英文法令一覧》25 年 7 月 19 日現在

翻訳（英訳）	日本法令外国語訳データベースシステム 最終 1 覧データ収集日：H25.7.19					法なび
	法令番号	改正	辞書ver	翻訳日	
Public Announcement on the Items of Goods Subject to Import Quotas, the Places of Origin or Places of Shipment of Goods Requiring Approval for Import, and Other Necessary Matters Concerning Import of Goods	S41 通商産業省告示第 170 号	H20 経済産業省告示第 129 号	3.0	H21.5.27	
Import Trade Control Order	S24 政令第 414 号	H15 政令第 248 号	1.0	H21.4.1	208
Export Trade Control Order (Tentative translation)	S24 政令第 378 号	H23 政令第 141 号	6.0	H24.4.19	209
Ordinance of the Ministry Specifying Goods and Technologies Pursuant to Provisions of the Appended Table 1 of the Export Control Order and the Appended Table of the Foreign Exchange Order	H3 通商産業省令第 49 号	H23 経済産業省第 26 号	7.0		210
Export Trade Control Ordinance (Tentative translation)	S24 通商産業省令第 64 号	H22 経済産業省令第 6 号	6.0	H24.4.19	211
Act on the Promotion of Sorted Collection and Recycling of Containers and Packaging	H7 法律第 112 号	H18 法律第 76 号	1.0	H21.4.1	212
Cabinet Order on Expenses, etc. for Hearings by the Japan Fair Trade Commission	S23 政令第 332 号	H16 政令第 201 号	4.0	H22.10.28	
Rules on Investigations by the Fair Trade Commission	H17 公正取引委員会規則第 5 号	H21 公正取引委員会規則第 11 号	5.0	H22.12.2	
Act against Delay in Payment of Subcontract Proceeds, Etc. to Subcontractors	S31 法律第 120 号	H17 法律第 87 号	1.0	H21.4.1	76
Specific Unfair Trade Practices in the Newspaper Business	H11 公正取引委員会告示第 9 号		3.0	H21.4.1	98
Act on Prohibition of Private Monopolization and Maintenance of Fair Trade	S22 法律第 54 号	H21 法律第 51 号	4.0	H22.10.15	104
Rules on Applications for Approval, Reporting, Notification, etc. Pursuant to the Provisions of Articles 9 to 16 of the Act on Prohibition of Private Monopolization and Maintenance of Fair Trade	S28 公正取引委員会規則第 1 号	H21 公正取引委員会規則第 13 号	4.0	H22.10.19	105
Designation of Specific Unfair Trade Practices by Large-Scale Retailers Relating to Trade with Suppliers	H17 公正取引委員会告示第 11 号		2.0	H21.4.1	131

所管庁別目次

ⓒ《所管庁別五十音順英文法令一覧》25 年 7 月 19 日現在

法外訳 SYS	法令名	所管庁	PDF データ 頁数	○:済 △:未完 →備考
245	入札談合等関与行為の排除及び防止並びに職員による入札等の公正を害すべき行為の処罰に関する法律	公正取引委員会	10	○
261	不公正な取引方法	公正取引委員会		△
321	公正取引委員会の審判に関する規則	公正取引委員会	38	○
322	課徴金の減免に係る報告及び資料の提出に関する規則	公正取引委員会	8	○
2	医師法	厚生労働省	23	○
5	育児休業、介護休業等育児又は家族介護を行う労働者の福祉に関する法律	厚生労働省	62	○
13	介護保険法	厚生労働省	377	○
14	会社分割に伴う労働契約の承継等に関する法律	厚生労働省	7	○
25	外国医師等が行う臨床修練に係る医師法第 17 条等の特例等に関する法律	厚生労働省	24	○
37	肝炎対策基本法	厚生労働省	12	○
70	検疫法	厚生労働省	50	○
74	個別労働関係紛争の解決の促進に関する法律	厚生労働省	10	○
103	雇用の分野における男女の均等な機会及び待遇の確保等に関する法律	厚生労働省	21	○
104	雇用保険法	厚生労働省	116	○
107	高齢者虐待の防止、高齢者の養護者に対する支援等に関する法律	厚生労働省	18	○
125	児童福祉法	厚生労働省	136	○

所管庁別目次

JSB英文六法　　　　　　　　　　　　　　　　　1st ed.2014.10

C 《所管庁別五十音順英文法令一覧》25 年 7 月 19 日現在

日本法令外国語訳データベースシステム 最終1覧データ収集日：H25.7.19

翻訳（英訳）	法令番号	改正	辞書 ver	翻訳日	法なび
Act on Elimination and Prevention of Involvement in Bid Rigging, etc. and Punishments for Acts by Employees that Harm Fairness of Bidding, etc.	H14 法律第 101 号	H18 法律第 110 号	2.0	H21.4.1	169
Designation of Unfair Trade Practices	S57 公正取引委員会告示第 15 号		1.0	H21.4.1	183
Rules on Hearings by the Fair Trade Commission	H17 公正取引委員会規則第 8 号	H21 公正取引委員会規則第 6 号	5.0	H22.9.3	
Rules on Reporting and the Submission of Supporting Materials in Relation to Immunity from or Reduction of Surcharges	H17 公正取引委員会規則第 7 号	H21 公正取引委員会規則第 12 号	5.0	H23.1.14	
Medical Practitioners' Act	S23 法律第 201 号	H19 法律第 96 号	4.0	H23.1.24	
Act on the Welfare of Workers Who Take Care of Children or Other Family Members Including Child Care and Family Care Leave	H3 法律第 76 号	H16 法律第 160 号	1.0	H21.4.1	4
Long-Term Care Insurance Act	H9 法律第 123 号	H19 法律第 110 号	2.0	H21.4.1	11
Act on the Succession to Labor Contracts upon Company Split	H12 法律第 103 号	H17 法律第 87 号	2.0	H21.4.1	12
Law concerning the Exceptional Cases of the Medical Practitioners' Act, Article 17, on the Advanced Clinical Training of Foreign Medical Practitioners, etc.	S62 法律第 29 号	H18 法律第 84 号	2.0	H21.4.1	18
Basic Act on Hepatitis Measures	H21 法律第 97 号		5.0	H22.10.15	
Quarantine Act	S26 法律第 201 号	H18 法律第 106 号	2.0	H21.4.1	43
Act on Promoting the Resolution of Individual Labor-Related Disputes	H13 法律第 112 号	H16 法律第 140 号	1.0	H21.4.1	47
Act on Securing, Etc. of Equal Opportunity and Treatment between Men and Women in Employment	S47 法律第 113 号	H18 法律第 82 号	1.0	H21.4.1	66
Employment Insurance Act	S49 法律第 116 号	H19 法律第 30 号	2.0	H22.6.1	67
Act on the Prevention of Elder Abuse, Support for Caregivers of Elderly Persons and Other Related Matters	H17 法律第 124 号	H20 法律第 42 号	4.0	H22.10.6	
Child Welfare Act	S22 法律第 164 号	H19 法律第 73 号	2.0	H21.4.1	79

所管庁別目次

C《所管庁別五十音順英文法令一覧》25 年 7 月 19 日現在

法外訳 SYS	法令名	所管庁	PDF データ頁数	○:済 △:未完 →備考
159	社会福祉法	厚生労働省	85	○
164	職業安定法	厚生労働省	58	○
165	職業安定法施行規則	厚生労働省	79	○
166	職業能力開発促進法	厚生労働省	90	○
172	障害者自立支援法	厚生労働省	103	○
175	食品衛生法	厚生労働省	60	○
176	食品衛生法施行令	厚生労働省	21	○
177	食品衛生法施行規則	厚生労働省	125	○
181	生活保護法	厚生労働省	68	○
200	短時間労働者の雇用管理の改善等に関する法律	厚生労働省	25	○
201	短時間労働者の雇用管理の改善等に関する法律施行規則	厚生労働省	30	○
273	保健師助産師看護師法	厚生労働省	55	○
296	有害物質を含有する家庭用品の規制に関する法律	厚生労働省	6	○
307	労働保険の保険料の徴収等に関する法律	厚生労働省	123	○
308	労働基準法	厚生労働省	66	○
309	労働基準法施行規則	厚生労働省	64	○
310	労働契約法	厚生労働省	7	○
311	労働安全衛生法	厚生労働省	242	○
312	労働安全衛生規則（別表第 2、別表第 5 及び別表第 9：H21.厚生労働省令第 23 号までの改正）	厚生労働省	629	△

C 《所管庁別五十音順英文法令一覧》25年7月19日現在

翻訳（英訳）	法令番号	改正	辞書ver	翻訳日	法なび
Social Welfare Act	S26法律第45号	H20法律第85号	6.0	H24.1.23	
Employment Security Act	S22法律第141号	H19法律第79号	2.0	H21.4.1	107
Ordinance for Enforcement of the Employment Security Act	S22労働省令第12号	H17厚生労働省令第154号	2.0	H21.4.1	108
Human Resources Development Promotion Act	S44法律第64号	H18法律第81号	3.0	H21.5.19	109
Services and Supports for Persons with Disabilities Act	H17法律第123号	H18法律第94号	2.0	H21.4.1	112
Food Sanitation Act	S22法律第233号	H18法律第53号	2.0	H21.4.1	115
Order for Enforcement of the Food Sanitation Act	S28政令第229号	H18政令第189号	2.0	H21.4.1	116
Ordinance for Enforcement of the Food Sanitation Act	S32厚生省令第23号	H19厚生労働省令第156号	2.0	H21.4.1	117
Public Assistance Act	S25法律第144号	H18法律第53号	2.0	H21.4.1	121
Act on Improvement, etc. of Employment Management for Part-Time Workers	H5法律第76号	H19法律第72号	2.0	H21.4.1	134
Ordinance for Enforcement of the Act on Improvement, etc. of Employment Management for Part-Time Workers	H5労働省令第34号	H23厚生労働省令第48号	6.0	H23.8.12	
Act on Public Health Nurses, Midwives, and Nurses	S23法律第203号	H21法律第78号	6.0	H24.10.31	
Act on Control of Household Products Containing Harmful Substances	S48法律第112号	H21法律第49号	4.0	H22.2.17	
Act on the Collection, etc. of Insurance Premiums of Labor Insurance	S44法律第84号	H19法律第110号	3.0	H21.4.1	213
Labor Standards Act	S22法律第49号	H16法律第147号	1.0	H21.4.1	214
Ordinance for Enforcement of the Labor Standards Act	S22厚生省令第23号		2.0	H21.4.1	215
Labor Contract Act	H19法律第128号		5.0	H22.11.5	
Industrial Safety and Health Act	S47法律第57号	H18法律第25号	1.0	H21.4.1	216
Ordinance on Industrial Safety and Health (Appended Tables 2, 5 and 9: up to the revision of Ordinance of the Ministry of Health, Labour and Welfare No. 23 of 2009)	S47労働省令第32号	H18厚生労働省令第185号	3.0	H23.6.27	

所管庁別目次

C 《所管庁別五十音順英文法令一覧》25 年 7 月 19 日現在

法外訳 SYS	法令名	所管庁	PDFデータ頁数	○:済 △:未完 →備考
313	労働組合法	厚生労働省	46	○
314	労働者派遣事業の適正な運営の確保及び派遣労働者の就業条件の整備等に関する法律	厚生労働省	77	○
315	労働者派遣事業の適正な運営の確保及び派遣労働者の就業条件の整備等に関する法律施行令	厚生労働省	34	○
316	労働者派遣事業の適正な運営の確保及び派遣労働者の就業条件の整備等に関する法律施行規則	厚生労働省	71	○
317	労働者災害補償保険法	厚生労働省	86	○
318	労働関係調整法	厚生労働省	17	○
319	老人福祉法	厚生労働省	52	○
1	アイヌ文化の振興並びにアイヌの伝統等に関する知識の普及及び啓発に関する法律	国土交通省		△
7	運輸安全委員会設置法	国土交通省	24	○
36	海難審判法	国土交通省	18	○
38	貨物利用運送事業法	国土交通省	41	○
39	貨物自動車運送事業法	国土交通省	53	○
44	気象業務法	国土交通省	59	○
82	国土利用計画法	国土交通省		△
83	国土形成計画法	国土交通省	16	○
97	港則法	国土交通省	20	○
98	港湾の施設の技術上の基準を定める省令	国土交通省	31	○

Ⓒ《所管庁別五十音順英文法令一覧》25 年 7 月 19 日現在

翻訳（英訳）	法令番号	改正	辞書ver	翻訳日	法なび
Labor Union Act	S24 法律第174 号	H17 法律第87 号	1.0	H21.4.1	217
Act for Securing the Proper Operation of Worker Dispatching Undertakings and Improved Working Conditions for Dispatched Workers	S60 法律第88 号	H18 法律第82 号	2.0	H21.4.1	218
Order for Enforcement of the Act for Securing the Proper Operation of Worker Dispatching Undertakings and Improved Working Conditions for Dispatched Workers	S61 政令第95 号	H19 政令第376 号	2.0	H21.4.1	219
Ordinance for Enforcement of the Act for Securing the Proper Operation of Worker Dispatching Undertakings and Improved Working Conditions for Dispatched Workers	S61 労働省令第20 号	H19 厚生労働省令第149 号	2.0	H21.4.1	220
Industrial Accident Compensation Insurance Act	S22 法律第50 号	H19 法律第111 号	3.0	H21.9.11	
Labor Relations Adjustment Act	S21 法律第25 号	H16 法律第140 号	3.0	H21.6.16	221
Act on Social Welfare for the Elderly	S38 法律第133 号	H20 法律第42 号	4.0	H22.10.6	
Act on the Promotion of Ainu Culture, and Dissemination and Enlightenment of Knowledge about Ainu Tradition, etc.	H9 法律第52 号	H18 法律第50 号	2.0	H21.4.1	1
Act for Establishment of the Japan Transport Safety Board	S48 法律第113 号	H20 法律第26 号	3.0	H22.5.27	
Act on Marine Accident Inquiry	S22 法律第135 号	H20 法律第26 号	3.0	H21.6.16	28
Consigned Freight Forwarding Business Act	H 元法律第82 号	H14 法律第77 号	2.0	H22.8.10	
Motor Truck Transportation Business Act	H 元法律第83 号	H18 法律第50 号	2.0	H22.8.10	
Meteorological Service Act	S27 法律第165 号	H19 法律第115 号	3.0	H21.4.15	
National Land Use Planning Act	S49 法律第92 号		3.0	H23.2.25	
National Spatial Planning Act	S25 法律第205 号	H17 法律第89 号	1.0	H21.4.1	51
Act on Port Regulations	S23 法律第174 号	H18 法律第68 号	2.0	H21.4.1	62
Ministerial Ordinance for the Technical Standards for Port and Harbor Facilities	H19 国土交通省令第15 号		3.0	H22.6.18	

所管庁別目次

1st ed.2014.10　　　121　　　JSB英文六法

C《所管庁別五十音順英文法令一覧》25 年 7 月 19 日現在

法外訳 SYS	法令名	所管庁	PDFデータ頁数	○:済 △:未完 →備考
99	港湾法	国土交通省	108	○
100	航空法	国土交通省	146	○
101	航空法施行規則	国土交通省	621	△
120	住生活基本法	国土交通省		△
184	船舶油濁損害賠償保障法	国土交通省	43	○
186	測量法	国土交通省		△
207	鉄道事業法	国土交通省	51	○
220	土地基本法	国土交通省	8	○
244	都市計画法	国土交通省	149	○
277	北海道開発法	国土交通省	2	○
64	刑事訴訟規則	最高裁判所	188	○
290	民事訴訟規則	最高裁判所	119	○
18	会計法(第 4 章)	財務省	7	○
88	国税徴収法(抄)	財務省	3	○
89	国税通則法(抄)	財務省	26	○
137	地震保険に関する法律	財務省	24	○
142	所得税法(非居住者、外国法人関連部分)	財務省	35	○
143	所得税法施行令(非居住者、外国法人関連部分)	財務省	61	○
144	所得税法施行規則(非居住者,外国法人関連部分)	財務省	9	○

所管庁別目次

© 《所管庁別五十音順英文法令一覧》25 年 7 月 19 日現在

翻訳（英訳）	日本法令外国語訳データベースシステム 最終1覧データ収集日：H25.7.19				法なび
	法令番号	改正	辞書ver	翻訳日	
Port and Harbor Act	S25 法律第218号	H20 法律第66号	3.0	H22.6.18	
Civil Aeronautics Act	S27 法律第231号	H18 法律第118号	2.0	H21.4.1	64
Ordinance for Enforcement of the Civil Aeronautics Act	S27 運輸省令第56号	H20 国土交通省令第73号	3.0	H21.8.18	
Basic Act for Housing	H18 法律第61号		2.0	H21.4.1	77
Act on Liability for Oil Pollution Damage	S50 法律第95号	H16 法律第37号	2.0	H21.4.1	123
Survey Act	S24 法律第188号	H19 法律第55号	3.0	H21.6.23	
Railway Business Act	S61 法律第92号	H18 法律第19号	2.0	H21.4.1	140
Basic Act for Land	H元法律第84号	H11 法律第160号	1.0	H21.4.1	150
City Planning Act	S43 法律第100号	H20 法律第40号	3.0	H21.6.11	168
Hokkaido Development Act	S25 法律第126号	H11 法律第117号	1.0	H21.4.1	193
Rules of Criminal Procedure	S23 最高裁判所規則第32号	H20 最高裁判所規則第17号	4.0	H23.7.28	
Rules of Civil Procedure	H8 最高裁判所規則第5号	H20 最高裁判所規則第10号	3.0	H21.4.1	201
Public Accounting Act (Chapter IV)	S22 法律第35号	H18 法律第53号	6.0	H24.3.30	
National Tax Collection Act（Extract）	S34 法律第147号	H19 法律第102号	4.0	H21.10.26	55
Act on General Rules for National Taxes (Extract)	S37 法律第66号	H19 法律第6号	4.0	H21.10.26	
Act on Earthquake Insurance	S41 法律第73号	H11 法律第160号	3.0	H22.3.9	90
Income Tax Act（Limited to the provisions related to nonresidents and foreign corporations）	S40 法律第33号	H19 法律第6号	2.0	H21.4.1	94
Order for Enforcement of the Income Tax Act（Limited to the provisions related to nonresidents and foreign corporations）	S40 政令第96号	H19 政令第82号	3.0	H21.8.18	93
Ordinance for Enforcement of the Income Tax Act (Limited to the provisions related to nonresidents and foreign corporations)	S40 大蔵省令第11号	H20 財務省令第24号	4.0	H22.7.9	

所管庁別目次

1st ed.2014.10　　　　　　　　JSB英文六法

C《所管庁別五十音順英文法令一覧》25年7月19日現在

法外訳 SYS	法令名	所管庁	PDF データ 頁数	○:済 △:未完 →備考
187	租税特別措置法（非居住者、外国法人関連部分）	財務省	226	○
188	租税特別措置法施行令（非居住者,外国法人関連部分）	財務省	379	○
250	日本銀行法	財務省	62	○
279	法人税法（外国法人関連部分）	財務省	27	○
280	法人税法施行令（外国法人関連部分）	財務省	50	○
281	法人税法施行規則（外国法人関連部分）	財務省	11	○
31	家庭用品品質表示法	消費者庁	17	○
154	消費者基本法	消費者庁	17	○
155	消費者契約法	消費者庁	60	○
156	消費者契約法施行規則	消費者庁	34	○
157	消費者安全法	消費者庁	25	○
230	特定商取引に関する法律	消費者庁	160	○
231	特定商取引に関する法律施行令	消費者庁	59	○
232	特定商取引に関する法律施行規則	消費者庁	119	○
233	特定商品等の預託等取引契約に関する法律	消費者庁	12	○
265	不当景品類及び不当表示防止法	消費者庁	13	○
85	国家公務員法	人事院	71	○
47	行政手続法	総務省	39	○

C 《所管庁別五十音順英文法令一覧》25 年 7 月 19 日現在

翻訳（英訳）	法令番号	改正	辞書 ver	翻訳日	法なび
Act on Special Measures Concerning Taxation (Limited to the provisions related to nonresidents and foreign corporations)	S32 法律第 26 号	H19 法律第 6 号	2.0	H21.4.1	126
Order for Enforcement of the Act on Special Measures Concerning Taxation (Limited to the provisions related to nonresidents and foreign corporations)	S32 政令第 43 号	H20 政令第 161 号	4.0	H22.7.9	125
Bank of Japan Act	H9 法律第 89 号	H19 法律第 102 号	2.0	H21.4.1	174
Corporation Tax Act (Limited to the provisions related to foreign corporations)	S40 法律第 34 号	H19 法律第 6 号	2.0	H21.4.1	195
Order for Enforcement of the Corporation Tax Act (Limited to the provisions related to foreign corporations)	S40 政令第 97 号	H19 政令第 83 号	3.0	H21.8.18	194
Ordinance for Enforcement of the Corporation Tax Act (Limited to the provisions related to foreign corporations)	S40 大蔵省令第 12 号	H20 財務省令第 205 号	4.0	H21.10.26	
Household Goods Quality Labeling Act	S37 法律第 104 号	H11 法律第 204 号	2.0	H21.4.1	24
Basic Consumer Act	S43 法律第 78 号	H21 法律第 49 号	3.0	H23.1.4	
Consumer Contract Act	H12 法律第 61 号	H21 法律第 49 号	3.0	H23.1.4	102
Ordinance for Enforcement of the Consumer Contract Act	H19 内閣府令第 17 号	H21 内閣府令第 70 号	3.0	H23.1.4	
Consumer Safety Act	H21 法律第 50 号		6.0	H23.4.22	
Act on Specified Commercial Transactions	S51 法律第 57 号	H21 法律第 49 号	4.0	H21.12.1	156
Order for Enforcement of the Act on Specified Commercial Transactions	S51 政令第 295 号	H21 政令第 217 号	4.0	H21.12.1	157
Regulations for Enforcement of the Act on Specified Commercial Transactions	S51 通商産業省令第 89 号	H16 経済産業省令第 87 号	1.0	H21.4.1	158
Act on the Deposit, etc. Transaction Agreements of Specified Commodities, etc.	S61 法律第 62 号	H21 法律第 49 号	4.0	H21.12.1	
Act against Unjustifiable Premiums and Misleading Representations	S37 法律第 134 号	H17 法律第 35 号	1.0	H21.4.1	185
National Public Service Act	S22 法律第 120 号	H17 法律第 50 号	1.0	H21.4.1	53
Administrative Procedure Act	H5 法律第 88 号	H17 法律第 73 号	1.0	H21.4.1	32

所管庁別目次

C 《所管庁別五十音順英文法令一覧》25 年 7 月 19 日現在

法外訳 SYS	法令名	所管庁	PDF データ 頁数	○:済 △:未完 →備考
48	行政機関が行う政策の評価に関する法律	総務省	17	○
49	行政機関の保有する個人情報の保護に関する法律	総務省	45	○
50	行政機関の保有する情報の公開に関する法律	総務省	22	○
51	行政相談委員法	総務省	4	○
69	携帯音声通信事業者による契約者等の本人確認等及び携帯音声通信役務の不正な利用の防止に関する法律	総務省	21	○
84	国家公務員倫理法	総務省	30	○
86	国家行政組織法	総務省	15	○
158	消防法	総務省	189	○
234	特定機器に係る適合性評価手続の結果の外国との相互承認の実施に関する法律	総務省	43	○
236	特定電子メールの送信の適正化等に関する法律	総務省	21	○
237	特定電気通信役務提供者の損害賠償責任の制限及び発信者情報の開示に関する法律	総務省	6	○
241	統計法	総務省	42	○
242	統計調査に用いる産業分類並びに疾病、傷害及び死因分類を定める政令の規定に基づき、産業に関する分類の名称及び分類表を定める等の件	総務省		△

所管庁別目次

JSB英文六法　　　　　　　　　　　　1st ed.2014.10

C 《所管庁別五十音順英文法令一覧》25年7月19日現在

翻訳（英訳）	日本法令外国語訳データベースシステム 最終1覧データ収集日：H25.7.19				法なび
	法令番号	改正	辞書ver	翻訳日	
Government Policy Evaluations Act	H13法律第86号	H15法律第23号	1.0	H21.4.1	33
Act on the Protection of Personal Information Held by Administrative Organs	H15法律第58号	H17法律第102号	2.0	H21.4.1	34
Act on Access to Information Held by Administrative Organs	H11法律第42号	H16法律第84号	1.0	H21.4.1	35
Administrative Counselors Act	S41法律第99号	H11法律第160号	1.0	H21.4.1	36
Act on Identification, etc. by Mobile Voice Communications Carriers of their Subscribers, etc. and for Prevention of Improper Use of Mobile Voice Communications Services	H17法律第31号		2.0	H21.4.1	41
National Public Service Ethics Act	H11法律第129号	H17法律第102号	2.0	H21.4.1	52
National Government Organization Act	S23法律第120号	H18法律第118号	2.0	H21.4.1	54
Fire Service Act	S23法律第186号	H20法律第41号	3.0	H21.3.30	103
Act for Implementation of the Mutual Recognition between Japan and Foreign States in Relation to Results of Conformity Assessment Procedures of Specified Equipment	H13法律第111号	H19法律第92号	3.0	H21.4.1	159
Act on Regulation of Transmission of Specified Electronic Mail	H14法律第26号	H17法律第87号	1.0	H21.4.1	161
Act on the Limitation of Liability for Damages of Specified Telecommunications Service Providers and the Right to Demand Disclosure of Identification Information of the Senders	H13法律第137号		2.0	H21.4.1	162
Statistics Act	H19法律第53号		2.0	H21.4.1	165
Establishment of the nomenclature and classification table concerning industries pursuant to the provision of the Cabinet Order Providing for Industrial Classification and Classification of Diseases, Injuries and Death to be used for Statistical Surveys	H14総務省告示第139号	改正：	1.0	H21.4.1	166

所管庁別目次

1st ed.2014.10　　127　　JSB英文六法

C 《所管庁別五十音順英文法令一覧》25 年 7 月 19 日現在

法外訳 SYS	法令名	所管庁	PDF データ 頁数	○:済 △:未完 →備考
246	日本国とアメリカ合衆国との間の相互協力及び安全保障条約第 6 条に基づく施設及び区域並びに日本国における合衆国軍隊の地位に関する協定の実施に伴う郵便法の特例に関する法律	総務省	4	○
247	日本国とアメリカ合衆国との間の相互協力及び安全保障条約第 6 条に基づく施設及び区域並びに日本国における合衆国軍隊の地位に関する協定の実施に伴う電波法の特例に関する法律	総務省	2	○
248	日本国とアメリカ合衆国との間の相互協力及び安全保障条約第 6 条に基づく施設及び区域並びに日本国における合衆国軍隊の地位に関する協定等の実施に伴う電気通信事業法等の特例に関する法律	総務省	4	○
251	日本電信電話株式会社等に関する法律	総務省	52	○
34	海洋基本法	内閣官房	16	○
106	高度情報通信ネットワーク社会形成基本法	内閣官房	15	○
204	知的財産基本法	内閣官房	16	○
73	個人情報の保護に関する法律	内閣府	35	○
77	公益社団法人及び公益財団法人の認定等に関する法律	内閣府	55	○
78	公益通報者保護法	内閣府	10	○
173	食品安全基本法	内閣府	22	○
174	食品安全委員会令	内閣府	2	○
185	製造物責任法	内閣府	4	○

© 《所管庁別五十音順英文法令一覧》25年7月19日現在

翻訳（英訳）	法令番号	改正	辞書ver	翻訳日	法なび
Act on Special Provisions of the Postal Act attendant upon the Enforcement of the "Agreement under Article VI of the Treaty of Mutual Cooperation and Security between Japan and the United States of America regarding Facilities and Areas and the Status of United States Armed Forces in Japan"	S27法律第122号	H17法律第102号	1.0	H21.4.1	170
Act on Special Provisions of the Radio Law Attendant upon the Enforcement of the "Agreement under Article VI of the Treaty of Mutual Cooperation and Security between Japan and the United States of America regarding Facilities and Areas and the Status of United States Armed Forces in Japan"	S27法律第108号	S35法律第102号	2.0	H21.4.1	171
Act on Special Provisions of the Telecommunications Business Law, etc. Attendant upon the Enforcement of the "Agreement under ARTICLE VI of the Treaty of Mutual Cooperation and Security between Japan and the United States of America regarding Facilities and Areas and the Status of United States Armed Forces in Japan"	S27法律第107号	S59法律第87号	2.0	H21.4.1	172
Act on Nippon Telegraph and Telephone Corporation, etc.	S59法律第85号	H17法律第87号	1.0	H21.4.1	175
Basic Act on Ocean Policy	H19法律第33号		2.0	H21.4.1	26
Basic Act on the Formation of an Advanced Information and Telecommunications Network Society	H12法律第144号		2.0	H21.4.1	69
Intellectual Property Basic Act	H14法律第122号		1.0	H21.4.1	137
Act on the Protection of Personal Information	H15法律第57号	H15法律第119号	1.0	H21.4.1	46
Act on Authorization of Public Interest Incorporated Associations and Public Interest Incorporated Foundation	H18法律第49号		2.0	H21.4.1	48
Whistleblower Protection Act	H16法律第122号		1.0	H21.4.1	49
Food Safety Basic Act	H15法律第48号	H19法律第8号	3.0	H21.4.1	113
Food Safety Commission Order	H15政令第273号	H15政令第505号	3.0	H21.4.1	114
Product Liability Act	H6法律第85号		1.0	H21.4.1	124

所管庁別目次

Ⓒ《所管庁別五十音順英文法令一覧》25 年 7 月 19 日現在

法外訳 SYS	法令名	所管庁	PDFデータ頁数	○:済 △:未完 →備考
190	総合科学技術会議令	内閣府	2	○
256	犯罪被害者等基本法	内閣府	12	○
259	配偶者からの暴力の防止及び被害者の保護に関する法律	内閣府	29	○
294	民間資金等の活用による公共施設等の整備等の促進に関する法律	内閣府	23	○
66	原子力損害賠償支援機構法	内閣府	42	○
67	原子力損害賠償支援機構法施行令	内閣府	17	○
22	外国人漁業の規制に関する法律	農林水産省	8	○
32	家畜伝染病予防法	農林水産省	69	○
35	海洋生物資源の保存及び管理に関する法律	農林水産省	34	○
45	漁業法	農林水産省	133	○
145	持続的養殖生産確保法	農林水産省	24	○
151	森林・林業基本法	農林水産省	14	○
152	植物防疫法	農林水産省	48	○
163	種苗法	農林水産省	59	○
178	食料・農業・農村基本法	農林水産省	21	○
179	水産基本法	農林水産省	19	○
180	水産資源保護法	農林水産省	46	○
253	農林物資の規格化及び品質表示の適正化に関する法律	農林水産省	49	○
255	排他的経済水域における漁業等に関する主権的権利の行使等に関する法律	農林水産省	19	○
43	技術士法	文部科学省	31	○

Ⓒ《所管庁別五十音順英文法令一覧》25年7月19日現在

翻訳（英訳）	法令番号	改正	辞書 ver	翻訳日	法なび
Cabinet Order for the Council for Science and Technology Policy	H12政令第258号		3.0	H21.5.27	128
Basic Act on Crime Victims	H16法律第161号		2.0	H21.4.1	182
Act on the Prevention of Spousal Violence and the Protection of Victims	H13法律第31号	H19法律第113号	2.0	H21.4.1	180
Act on Promotion of Private Finance Initiative	H11法律第117号	H18法律第53号	3.0	H21.4.1	204
Nuclear Damage Compensation Facilitation Corporation Act	H23法律第94号		6.0	H24.5.7	
Order for Enforcement of the Nuclear Damage Compensation Facilitation Corporation Act	H23政令第257号		6.0	H24.5.7	
Act on Regulation of Fishing Operation by Foreign Nationals	S42法律第60号	H13法律第92号	1.0	H21.4.1	16
Act on Domestic Animal Infectious Diseases Control	S26法律第166号	H16法律第68号	1.0	H21.4.1	25
Act on Preservation and Control of Living Marine Resources	H8法律第77号	H19法律第77号	4.0	H21.4.1	27
Fishery Act	S24法律第267号	H19法律第77号	3.0	H21.6.16	31
Sustainable Aquaculture Production Assurance Act	H11法律第51号	H17法律第36号	4.0	H21.4.1	95
Forest and Forestry Basic Act	S39法律第161号	H15法律第119号	1.0	H21.4.1	99
Plant Protection Act ¥	S25法律第151号	H17法律第102号	2.0	H21.4.1	100
Plant Variety Protection and Seed Act	H10法律第83号	H19法律第49号	2.0	H21.4.1	106
Food, Agriculture and Rural Areas Basic Act	H11法律第106号	H17法律第819号	1.0	H21.4.1	118
Fisheries Basic Act	H13法律第819号	H17法律第819号	1.0	H21.4.1	119
Act on the Protection of Fishery Resources	S26法律第313号	H19法律第77号	2.0	H21.4.1	120
Act on Standardization and Proper Quality Labeling of Agricultural and Forestry Products	S25法律第175号	H21法律第49号	4.0	H21.4.1	
Act on the Exercise of the Sovereign Right for Fishery, etc. in the Exclusive Economic Zone	H8法律第76号	H13法律第91号	2.0	H21.4.1	178
Professional Engineer Act	S58法律第25号	H18法律第50号	2.0	H21.4.1	30

所管庁別目次

Ⓒ《所管庁別五十音順英文法令一覧》25 年 7 月 19 日現在

法外訳 SYS	法令名	所管庁	PDFデータ頁数	○:済 △:未完 →備考
192	大学設置基準	文部科学省	53	○
206	著作権法	文部科学省	127	○
226	特定先端大型研究施設の共用の促進に関する法律	文部科学省	24	○
260	ヒトに関するクローン技術等の規制に関する法律	文部科学省	19	○
268	文化財の不法な輸出入等の規制等に関する法律	文部科学省	4	○
320	宗教法人法	文部科学省	76	○
10	恩赦法	法務省	4	○
11	恩赦法施行規則	法務省	9	○
1-①15	**会社法**（第1編第2編第3編第4編）	**法務省**	539	○
1-①16	**会社法**（第5編第6編第7編第8編）	**法務省**	269	○
1-②17	**会社法施行令**	**法務省**	4	○
23	外国人登録法	法務省	30	○
24	外国倒産処理手続の承認援助に関する法律	法務省	54	○
26	外国弁護士による法律事務の取扱いに関する特別措置法	法務省	44	○
27	外国弁護士による法律事務の取扱いに関する特別措置法施行規則	法務省	10	○
30	外国等に対する我が国の民事裁判権に関する法律	法務省	15	○
46	行政事件訴訟法	法務省	39	○
61	刑事収容施設及び被収容者等の処遇に関する法律	法務省	204	○
62	刑事訴訟法（第1編第2編）	法務省	143	○

C 《所管庁別五十音順英文法令一覧》25年7月19日現在

翻訳（英訳）	法令番号	改正	辞書 ver	翻訳日	法なび
Standards for Establishment of Universities	S31 文部省令第28号	H19 文部科学省令第40号	3.0	H21.5.28	23
Copyright Act	S45 法律第48号	H18 法律第121号	2.0	H21.4.1	139
Act on the Promotion of Public Utilization of the Specific Advanced Large Research Facilities	H6 法律第78号	H18 法律第37号	3.0	H22.5.27	
Act on Regulation of Human Cloning Techniques	H12 法律第146号		1.0	H21.4.1	181
Act on Controls on the Illicit Export and Import and other matters of Cultural Property	H14 法律第81号		1.0	H21.4.1	189
Religious Corporations Act	S26 法律第126号	H18 法律第50号	5.0	H23.1.4	
Pardon Act	S22 法律第20号	H11 法律第160号	1.0	H21.4.1	8
Ordinance for Enforcement of the Pardon Act	S22 司法省令第78号	H18 法務省令第59号	1.0	H21.4.1	9
Companies Act (Part I, Part II, Part III and Part IV)	H17 法律第86号	H18 法律第109号	2.0	H21.4.1	13
Companies Act (Part V, Part VI, Part VII and Part VIII)	H17 法律第86号	H18 法律第109号	3.0	H21.4.1	13
Order for Enforcement of the Companies Act	H17 政令第364号	H20 政令第100号	4.0	H22.3.24	
Alien Registration Act	S27 法律第125号	H16 法律第152号	2.0	H21.4.1	17
Act on Recognition of and Assistance for Foreign Insolvency Proceedings	H12 法律第129号	H18 法律第50号	3.0	H22.11.18	
Act on Special Measures concerning the Handling of Legal Services by Foreign Lawyers	S61 法律第66号	H15 法律第128号	1.0	H21.4.1	19
Ordinance for Enforcement of the Act on Special Measures concerning the Handling of Legal Services by Foreign Lawyers	S62 法務省令第7号	H23 法務省令第43号	2.0	H21.4.1	20
Act on the Civil Jurisdiction of Japan with respect to a Foreign State, etc.	H21 法律第24号		4.0	H22.3.23	
Administrative Case Litigation Act	S37 法律第139号	H19 法律第109号	4.0	H22.9.14	
Act on Penal Detention Facilities and Treatment of Inmates and Detainees	H17 法律第50号	H19 法律第37号	2.0	H21.4.1	38
Code of Criminal Procedure (Part I and Part II)	S23 法律第131号	H18 法律第36号	2.0	H21.4.1	39

所管庁別目次

C 《所管庁別五十音順英文法令一覧》 25 年 7 月 19 日現在

法外訳 SYS	法令名	所管庁	PDFデータ頁数	○:済 △:未完 備考
63	刑事訴訟法（第3編以降）	法務省	42	○
65	刑　法	法務省	87	○
87	国家賠償法	法務省	2	○
90	国籍法	法務省	19	○
91	国際受刑者移送法	法務省	32	○
92	国際捜査共助等に関する法律	法務省	17	○
95	更生保護事業法	法務省	39	○
96	更生保護法	法務省	63	○
108	債権管理回収業に関する特別措置法（H18.法律第115号による改正のうち，H22.6月18日施行分（第18条第5項）については未反映）	法務省	29	○
109	債権管理回収業に関する特別措置法施行規則	法務省	15	○
112	裁判の迅速化に関する法律	法務省	4	○
113	裁判外紛争解決手続の利用の促進に関する法律	法務省	28	○
114	裁判外紛争解決手続の利用の促進に関する法律施行令	法務省	2	○
115	裁判外紛争解決手続の利用の促進に関する法律施行規則	法務省	19	○
116	裁判所法	法務省	53	○
119	人事訴訟法	法務省	26	○
1-③ 123	**信託法**	**法務省**	217	○
124	借地借家法	法務省	30	○
126	児童買春、児童ポルノに係る行為等の処罰及び児童の保護等に関する法律	法務省	11	○

所管庁別目次

JSB英文六法　　　134　　　1st ed.2014.10

C 《所管庁別五十音順英文法令一覧》25年7月19日現在

翻訳（英訳）	法令番号	改正	辞書ver	翻訳日	法なび
Code of Criminal Procedure (Part III〜)	S23法律第131号	H19法律第95号	3.0	H21.4.1	
Penal Code	明治40法律第45号	H19法律第54号	1.0	H21.4.1	40
State Redress Act	S22法律第125号		4.0	H22.3.23	
Nationality Act	S25法律第147号	H20法律第88号	3.0	H21.5.21	56
Act on the Transnational Transfer of Sentenced Persons	H14法律第66号	H22法律第29号	1.0	H23.12.15	57
Act on International Assistance in Investigation and Other Related Matters	S55法律第69号	H18法律第58号	2.0	H21.4.1	58
Offenders Rehabilitation Services Act	H7法律第86号	H17法律第87号	2.0	H21.4.1	60
Offenders Rehabilitation Act	H19法律第88号		3.0	H21.4.1	61
Act on Special Measures Concerning Claim Management and Collection Businesses	H10法律第126号	H20法律第74号	3.0	H21.12.25	
Ordinance for Enforcement of the Act on Special Measures Concerning Claim Management and Collection Businesses	H11法務省令第4号	H20法務省令第59号	4.0	H22.3.19	
Act on the Expediting of Trials	H15法律第107号		2.0	H21.4.1	71
Act on Promotion of Use of Alternative Dispute Resolution	H16法律第151号	H18法律第50号	1.0	H21.4.1	72
Order for Enforcement of the Act on Promotion of Use of Alternative Dispute Resolution	H18政令第186号	H23政令第403号	1.0	H24.2.22	73
Ordinance for Enforcement of the Act on Promotion of Use of Alternative Dispute Resolution	H18法務省令第52号	H23法務省令第39号	1.0	H24.2.22	74
Court Act	S22法律第59号	H18法律第36号	2.0	H21.4.1	75
Personal Status Litigation Act	H15法律第109号	H23法律第53号	5.0	H25.1.16	
Trust Act	H18法律第108号		3.0	H21.11.2	
Act on Land and Building Leases	H3法律第90号	H19法律第132号	4.0	H22.7.23	
Act on Punishment of Activities Relating to Child Prostitution and Child Pornography, and the Protection of Children	H11法律第52号	H16法律第106号	1.0	H21.4.1	80

所管庁別目次

C 《所管庁別五十音順英文法令一覧》25 年 7 月 19 日現在

法外訳 SYS	法令名	所管庁	PDF データ 頁数	○:済 △:未完 →備考
127	出入国管理及び難民認定法	法務省	130	○
128	出入国管理及び難民認定法施行規則	法務省	143	○
129	出入国管理及び難民認定法第 7 条第 1 項第 2 号の基準を定める省令	法務省	34	○
130	出資の受入れ、預り金及び金利等の取締りに関する法律	法務省	12	○
1-⑧ 134	**商業登記法**	**法務省**	92	○
138	執行官法	法務省	12	○
140	少年法	法務省	48	○
189	総合法律支援法	法務省	52	○
199	建物の区分所有等に関する法律	法務省	57	○
205	知的財産高等裁判所設置法	法務省	3	○
208	電子公告規則	法務省	21	○
219	動産及び債権の譲渡の対抗要件に関する民法の特例等に関する法律	法務省	20	○
243	逃亡犯罪人引渡法	法務省	22	○
257	破壊活動防止法	法務省	23	○
258	破産法	法務省	218	○
262	不動産登記令	法務省	197	○
263	不動産登記法	法務省	119	○
264	不動産登記規則	法務省	236	○

所管庁別目次

[C] 《所管庁別五十音順英文法令一覧》25年7月19日現在

翻訳（英訳）	法令番号	改正	辞書ver	翻訳日	法なび
Immigration Control and Refugee Recognition Act	S26政令第319号	H21法律第79号	1.0	H21.12.21	81
Ordinance for Enforcement of the Immigration Control and Refugee Recognition Act	S56法務省令第54号	H21法務省令第29号	2.0	H21.6.5	82
Ministerial Ordinance to Provide for Criteria Pursuant to Article 7, paragraph (1), item (ii) of the Immigration Control and Refugee Recognition Act	H2法務省令第16号	H21法務省令第18号	2.0	H21.10.7	83
Act Regulating the Receipt of Contributions, the Receipt of Deposits, and Interest Rates	S29法律第195号	H19法律第85号	6.0	H23.11.11	84
Commercial Registration Act	S38法律第125号	H17法律第87号	3.0	H21.6.11	88
Court Enforcement Officer Act	S41法律第111号	H19法律第18号	5.0	H22.7.6	
Juvenile Act	S23法律第168号	H20法律第71号	4.0	H22.3.31	
Comprehensive Legal Support Act	H16法律第74号	H20法律第19号	3.0	H21.4.1	127
Act on Building Unit Ownership, etc.	S37法律第69号	H20法律第203号	5.0	H23.3.2	
Act for Establishment of the Intellectual Property High Court	H16法律第119号		2.0	H21.4.1	138
Electronic Public Notice Rules	H18法務省令第14号	H21法務省令第5号	4.0	H22.3.26	
Act on Special Provisions, etc. of the Civil Code Concerning the Perfection Requirements for the Assignment of Movables and Claims	H1法律第104号	H19法律第23号	3.0	H21.5.21	149
Act of Extradition	S28法律第68号	H19法律第37号	3.0	H22.2.19	167
Subversive Activities Prevention Act	S27法律第240号	H7法律第91号	5.0	H23.9.8	
Bankruptcy Act	H16法律第75号	H18法律第109号	3.0	H21.10.20	179
Real Property Registration Order	H16政令第379号	H22政令第4号	6.0	H24.3.23	
Real Property Registration Act	H16法律第123号	H19法律第132号	3.0	H21.10.14	184
Ordinance on Real Property Registration	H17法務省令第18号	H23法務省令第5号	6.0	H24.3.23	

所管庁別目次

1st ed.2014.10　　　　137　　　　JSB英文六法

©《所管庁別五十音順英文法令一覧》25年7月19日現在

法外訳 SYS	法令名	所管庁	PDFデータ頁数	○:済 △:未完 →備考
267	扶養義務の準拠法に関する法律	法務省	3	○
272	弁護士法	法務省	107	○
274	保護司法	法務省	8	○
278	法の適用に関する通則法	法務省	22	○
284	民事保全法	法務省	36	○
285	民事保全法施行令	法務省	1	○
286	民事再生法	法務省	253	○
287	民事執行法	法務省	154	○
288	民事執行法施行令	法務省	2	○
289	民事訴訟法（暫定版）	法務省	195	○
291	民事訴訟費用等に関する法律	法務省	50	○
292	民法（第1編第2編第3編）	法務省	232	○
293	民法（第4編第5編）	法務省	106	○
303	遺言の方式の準拠法に関する法律	法務省	3	○
167	自衛隊員倫理法	防衛省	15	○
269	武力攻撃事態における外国軍用品等の海上輸送の規制に関する法律	防衛省	33	○
270	武力攻撃事態における捕虜等の取扱いに関する法律	防衛省	105	○
249	日本国憲法	その他	27	○

所管庁別目次

C 《所管庁別五十音順英文法令一覧》25 年 7 月 19 日現在

翻訳（英訳）	日本法令外国語訳データベースシステム　最終1覧データ収集日：H25.7.19				法なび
	法令番号	改正	辞書 ver	翻訳日	
Act on the Law Applicable to the Obligation of Support	S61 法律第 84 号	H18 法律第 78 号	5.0	H22.12.21	
Attorney Act	S24 法律第 205 号	H17 法律第 87 号	3.0	H22.3.12	191
Volunteer Probation Officers Act	S25 法律第 204 号	H19 法律第 88 号	4.0	H21.11.13	192
Act on General Rules for Application of Laws	H18 法律第 78 号		5.0	H23.4.27	
Civil Provisional Remedies Act	H 元法律第 91 号	H23 法律第 36 号	6.0	H24.3.22	197
Order for Enforcement of the Civil Provisional Remedies Act	H2 政令第 284 号		5.0	H22.12.17	
Civil Rehabilitation Act	H11 法律第 225 号	H17 法律第 87 号	3.0	H21.4.1	198
Civil Execution Act	S54 法律第 4 号	H19 法律第 95 号	3.0	H21.4.1	199
Order for Enforcement of the Civil Execution Act	S55 政令第 230 号	H16 政令第 419 号	5.0	H22.12.17	
Code of Civil Procedure (Tentative translation)	H8 法律第 109 号	H23 法律第 36 号	6.0	H24.3.22	200
Act on Costs of Civil Procedure	S46 法律第 40 号	H19 法律第 113 号	4.0	H21.11.18	
Civil Code (Part I, Part II, and Part III)	明治 29 法律第 89 号	H18 法律第 78 号	2.0	H21.4.1	202
Civil Code (Part IV and Part V)	明治 29 法律第 89 号	H18 法律第 78 号	2.0	H21.4.1	203
Act on the Law Applicable to the Form of Wills	S39 法律第 100 号	H18 法律第 78 号	5.0	H22.12.21	
Self-Defense Forces Personnel Ethics Act	H11 法律第 130 号	H19 法律第 80 号	2.0	H21.4.1	110
Act on the Restriction of Maritime Transportation of Foreign Military Supplies, etc. in Armed Attack Situations	H16 法律第 116 号	H18 法律第 118 号	4.0	H21.9.1	187
Act on the Treatment of Prisoners of War and Other Detainees in Armed Attack Situations	H16 法律第 117 号	H20 法律第 5 号	3.0	H21.7.16	188
The Constitution of Japan	S21 憲法			H21.4.1	173

所管庁別目次

1st ed.2014.10　　　　139　　　　JSB英文六法

法令用語日英標準対訳辞書〔前付から〕
（平成 26 年 3 月改訂版）

Standard Legal Terms Dictionary
(March 2014 Edition)

平成 26 年 3 月
March 2014

平成 25 年改訂版はしがき
Preface

　今回の改訂は，平成 25 年度に開催された日本法令外国語訳推進会議における検討結果を踏まえ，収録用語の追加や，訳語の変更等を行うものであり，平成 26 年 3 月 26 日の関係省庁連絡会議で承認されたものである。今回の改訂により，新たに 55 語の収録用語が追加されたほか，収録用語の整理，訳語の変更等が行われ，本書の収録用語数は，3641 語となっている。

　This revision, which includes additional terms and revised translations based on the results of study by the FY2013 Japanese Law Translation Council, was approved at the March 26, 2014, meeting of the Liaison Conference of the Relevant Ministries and Agencies. Through this revision, 55 terms have been added, others have been streamlined, and translations have been revised, bringing the total number of terms in this dictionary to 3641.

　今後も，関係府省のみならず民間団体等が法令の英語訳を行う際に本書が利用され，統一的で信頼できる法令の英語訳が迅速かつ継続的に行われることを期待する。

　It is hoped that not only the relevant ministries, but organizations from the private sector, as well, will continue to use this dictionary in translating the law into English, and that uniform, reliable English translations of laws will continue to be undertaken promptly and continuously.

平成 26 年 3 月　March 2014

日本法令外国語訳推進会議
座　長　柏　木　　昇
Japanese Law Translation Council
Chairperson, Noboru Kashiwagi

＊『法令用語日英標準対訳辞書』は，本シリーズ第 5 巻として刊行する。ここでは，前付のみを便宜のため掲載する（信山社）。

〈参考付録〉　　　　　〔法令用語日英標準対訳辞書（平成26年3月改訂版）〕凡例他前付

日本法令外国語訳推進会議構成員（平成25年度）

柏木　昇	東京大学名誉教授
阿部　博友	一橋大学大学院法学研究科教授
久保田　隆	早稲田大学大学院法務研究科教授
田澤　元章	明治学院大学法学部教授
福田　守利	神田外語大学教授
岩城　肇	弁護士（ディーエルエイ・パイパー東京パートナーシップ 外国法共同事業法律事務所）
児島　幸良	弁護士（森・濱田松本法律事務所）
佐藤　理恵子	弁護士（西村あさひ法律事務所）
キャロル・クリスチャン・ジェイコブソン	外国法事務弁護士
高田　昭英	弁護士（ベーカー＆マッケンジー法律事務所（外国法共同事業））
高橋　聖	弁護士（ＴＭＩ総合法律事務所）
原　悦子	弁護士（アンダーソン・毛利・友常法律事務所）
クリストファー・マーク・ホジェンズ	外国法事務弁護士
若林　剛	弁護士（長島・大野・常松法律事務所）
岩田　太	上智大学法学部教授
星　周一郎	首都大学東京都市教養学部法学系教授

日本法令外国語訳推進会議構成員（平成24年度）

柏木　昇	東京大学名誉教授
岩田　太	上智大学法学部教授
久保田　隆	早稲田大学大学院法務研究科教授
田澤　元章	明治学院大学法学部教授
福田　守利	神田外語大学教授
松下　祐記	千葉大学大学院専門法務研究科准教授
岩城　肇	弁護士（ディーエルエイ・パイパー東京パートナーシップ 外国法共同事業法律事務所）
児島　幸良	弁護士（森・濱田松本法律事務所）
佐藤　理恵子	弁護士（西村あさひ法律事務所）
高田　昭英	弁護士（ベーカー＆マッケンジー法律事務所（外国法共同事業））
高橋　聖	弁護士（TMI総合法律事務所）
原　悦子	弁護士（アンダーソン・毛利・友常法律事務所）
若林　剛	弁護士（長島・大野・常松法律事務所）
鈴鹿　キース　清	外国法事務弁護士
クリストファー・マーク・ホジェンズ	外国法事務弁護士

〔法令用語日英標準対訳辞書（平成 26 年 3 月改訂版）〕凡例他前付　　〈参考付録〉

日本法令外国語訳推進会議構成員（平成 23 年度）

柏木　昇	中央大学法科大学院教授
岩田　太	上智大学法学部教授
久保田　隆	早稲田大学大学院法務研究科教授
田澤　元章	明治学院大学法学部教授
福田　守利	神田外語大学教授
松下　祐記	千葉大学大学院専門法務研究科准教授
井口　直樹	弁護士（アンダーソン・毛利・友常法律事務所）
伊藤　理	弁護士（アレン・アンド・オーヴェリー外国法共同事業法律事務所）
児島　幸良	弁護士（森・濱田松本法律事務所）
佐藤　理恵子	弁護士（西村あさひ法律事務所）
高田　昭英	弁護士（東京青山・青木・狛法律事務所ベーカー＆マッケンジー外国法事務弁護士事務所（外国法共同事業））
山口　芳泰	弁護士（TMI 総合法律事務所）
若林　剛	弁護士（長島・大野・常松法律事務所）
垣貫　ジョン	外国法事務弁護士
鈴鹿　キース　清	外国法事務弁護士
クリストファー・マーク・ホジェンズ	外国法事務弁護士

日本法令外国語訳推進会議構成員（平成 22 年度）

柏木　昇	中央大学法科大学院教授
久保田　隆	早稲田大学大学院法務研究科教授
酒巻　匡	京都大学大学院法学研究科教授
田澤　元章	明治学院大学法学部教授
福田　守利	神田外語大学教授
松下　祐記	千葉大学大学院専門法務研究科准教授
井口　直樹	弁護士（アンダーソン・毛利・友常法律事務所）
伊藤　理	弁護士（アレン・アンド・オーヴェリー外国法共同事業法律事務所）
児島　幸良	弁護士（森・濱田松本法律事務所）
酒井　竜児	弁護士（長島・大野・常松法律事務所）
佐藤　理恵子	弁護士（西村あさひ法律事務所）
達野　大輔	弁護士（東京青山・青木・狛法律事務所ベーカー＆マッケンジー外国法事務弁護士事務所（外国法共同事業））
山口　芳泰	弁護士（TMI 総合法律事務所）
垣貫　ジョン	外国法事務弁護士
鈴鹿　キース　清	外国法事務弁護士

平成 22 年版はしがき
Preface

本書は，統一的で信頼できる法令の英語訳が迅速かつ継続的に行われるようにする目的で作成されたものであり，「翻訳の基本スタンス」及び「法令用語日英対訳辞書」で構成されている。

This dictionary was created with the purpose of enabling the prompt and continuous English translation of laws uniformly and authoritatively, and consists of "Basic Stance for Translation" and "Legal Terms Dictionary".

グローバル化する世界で，我が国の法令が容易かつ正確に理解されることは極めて重要である。とりわけ，国際取引の円滑化（国際競争力の強化），対日投資の促進，法整備支援の推進のほか，我が国に対する国際理解の増進，在日外国人の生活上の利便向上等の観点から，政府による法令外国語訳整備の早急な取組の必要性が指摘された。

In the globalizing world, it is crucially important that the laws of our country are correctly and easily understood. In particular, it has been noted that there is a demand for an immediate effort by the Government to develop foreign language translations of laws in consideration of the facilitation of international transactions (enhancement of international competitiveness), encouragement of investments in Japan, promotion of legislation support, furtherance of global understanding about our country, enhancement of convenience in the lives of foreign residents in Japan, as well as other reasons.

このような状況において，政府は，平成 17 年，「法令外国語訳推進のための基盤整備に関する関係省庁連絡会議」を内閣に設置し，その下に置かれた「実施推進検討会議」において，法令外国語訳推進のための基盤整備に関する事項につき総合的かつ多角的な検討を行い，その下に学者及び弁護士からなる「作業部会」を設け，名古屋大学大学院情報科学研究科等の研究グループ，関係府省等の協力を得ながら，本書の初版を作成した。

In this context, in 2005 the Government established the "Liaison Conference of the Relevant Ministries and Agencies for Developing a Foundation for Promoting Translation of Japanese Laws and Regulations into Foreign Languages" in the Cabinet, comprehensively and multilaterally investigating matters related to infrastructure development for the promotion of the translation of laws into foreign languages with the "Study Council for Promoting Translation of Japanese Laws and Regulations into Foreign Languages" created beneath it, and establishing below that a "working group" composed of scholars and lawyers, and created the first edition of this dictionary with the cooperation of research staff from The University of Nagoya Graduate School of Information Science and other institutions along with the cooperation of relevant ministries.

本書は，平成18年3月23日，実施推進検討会議から関係省庁連絡会議に報告され，同連絡会議において，関係府省が法令の英語訳を行う場合には，本書に準拠するものとされた。したがって，本書は，今後，関係府省が法令の英語訳を行う場合に，その統一性，信頼性を確保するための基本的なルールとなるものであり，民間団体等において法令の翻訳を行う際にも，本書に準拠して行われることを強く期待する。もとより，関係府省等がこれに準拠して翻訳を行った場合でも，いわゆる公定訳とはならないことはいうまでもない。すなわち，法的効力を有するのはあくまでも法令自体であって，翻訳はその理解のための参考資料と位置付けられるものである。

On March 23, 2006, this dictionary was submitted by the Study Council to the Liaison Conference of the Relevant Ministries and Agencies, and when relevant ministries and agencies in the Liaison Conference translate laws into English, they are requested to conform to this dictionary. Accordingly, I strongly anticipate that from hereafter, when relevant governmental departments translate laws into English, this dictionary will provide the basic rules to ensure uniformity and reliabilities, and even when private entities translate laws, they will be translated in compliance with this dictionary. However, even when relevant governmental departments translate in accordance with this dictionary, it goes without saying that such translation is not an official translation. That is to say, only the laws themselves have legal effect, and the translations are posited as reference materials to understand the laws.

本書は，厳しい時間的な制約等の中で，作業部会構成員等の多大な努力によって作成されたものであり，座長の立場から，関係各位の献身的貢献に改めて謝意を表したい。

This dictionary was created through tremendous efforts, under strict time restrictions, by the members of the working group. As chairman, I would like to once again express my gratitude for each of their dedicated contribution.

〈参考付録〉　　　　　〔法令用語日英標準対訳辞書（平成26年3月改訂版）〕凡例他前付

　本書については，上記連絡会議においても，今後の関係府省における翻訳成果や有識者・利用者の意見等を踏まえて必要な改訂を行うこととされており，平成 18 年度から平成 20 年度にかけては法令外国語訳専門家会議，平成 21 年度からは日本法令外国語訳推進会議で改訂作業を行い，平成 19 年度，平成 20 年度及び 21 年度の改訂に続き，平成 22 年 3 月 26 日の関係省庁連絡会議で今回の改訂版が承認された。今後も，本書の内容が更に充実したものになることを期待している。

　The revisions regarded as being necessary for this dictionary based on the subsequent translation outcomes of the relevant ministries and the opinions of experts and users were made by the aforementioned Liaison Conference; and, revision work was conducted from 2006 to 2008 by the Law Translation Expert Council, and thereafter in 2009 by the Japanese Law Translation Council. Following the revisions of 2007, 2008 and 2009, the Liaison Conference of the Relevant Ministries and Agencies confirmed this revised version in March 26, 2010.

　I hope the contents of this dictionary will continue to be further enriched.

平成 22 年 3 月
March 2010

　　　　　　　　　　　　　　　　　　　　　日本法令外国語訳推進会議
　　　　　　　　　　　　　　　　　　　　　座　長　柏　木　　昇
　　　　　　　　　　　　　　　　　　　　　Japanese Law Translation Council
　　　　　　　　　　　　　　　　　　　　　Chairperson, Noboru Kashiwagi

〔法令用語日英標準対訳辞書（平成26年3月改訂版）〕凡例他前付　　〈参考付録〉

作業部会構成員 （平成17年度）

柏木　昇	中央大学法科大学院教授
久保田　隆	早稲田大学大学院法務研究科教授
小島　立	九州大学大学院法学研究院助教授
島並　良	神戸大学大学院法学研究科助教授
田澤　元章	名城大学法学部教授
ダニエル・ローゼン	中央大学法科大学院教授
福田　守利	神田外語大学教授
マルコム・スミス	中央大学法科大学院教授
伊藤　理	弁護士（あさひ・狛法律事務所）
児島　幸良	弁護士（森・濱田松本法律事務所）
小舘　浩樹	弁護士（アンダーソン・毛利・友常法律事務所）
酒井　竜児	弁護士（長島・大野・常松法律事務所）
佐藤　理恵子	弁護士（西村ときわ法律事務所）
達野　大輔	弁護士（東京青山・青木法律事務所）
矢吹　公敏	弁護士（矢吹法律事務所）
山口　芳泰	弁護士（TMI総合法律事務所）

専門家会議構成員 （平成18年度）

柏木　昇	中央大学法科大学院教授
久保田　隆	早稲田大学大学院法務研究科教授
酒巻　匡	京都大学大学院法学研究科教授
田澤　元章	名城大学法学部教授
福田　守利	神田外語大学教授
松下　祐記	名城大学法学部助教授
伊藤　理	弁護士（あさひ・狛法律事務所）
児島　幸良	弁護士（森・濱田松本法律事務所）
酒井　竜児	弁護士（長島・大野・常松法律事務所）
佐藤　理恵子	弁護士（西村ときわ法律事務所）
達野　大輔	弁護士（東京青山・青木法律事務所）
中野　雄介	弁護士（アンダーソン・毛利・友常法律事務所）
山口　芳泰	弁護士（TMI総合法律事務所）
垣貫　ジョン	外国法事務弁護士

専門家会議構成員 （平成19年度）

柏木　昇	中央大学法科大学院教授
久保田　隆	早稲田大学大学院法務研究科教授
酒巻　匡	京都大学大学院法学研究科教授

JSB英文六法　　　146　　　1st ed. 2014.10

〈参考付録〉　　　〔法令用語日英標準対訳辞書（平成26年3月改訂版）〕凡例他前付

田澤　元章	名城大学法学部教授
福田　守利	神田外語大学教授
松下　祐記	名城大学法学部准教授
伊藤　理	弁護士（アレン・アンド・オーヴェリー外国法共同事業法律事務所）
児島　幸良	弁護士（森・濱田松本法律事務所）
酒井　竜児	弁護士（長島・大野・常松法律事務所）
佐藤　理恵子	弁護士（西村あさひ法律事務所）
達野　大輔	弁護士（東京青山・青木・狛法律事務所ベーカー＆マッケンジー外国法事務弁護士事務所（外国法共同事業）
中野　雄介	弁護士（アンダーソン・毛利・友常法律事務所）
山口　芳泰	弁護士（TMI総合法律事務所）
垣貫　ジョン	外国法事務弁護士
鈴鹿　キース　清	外国法事務弁護士

専門家会議構成員（平成20年度）

柏木　昇	中央大学法科大学院教授
久保田　隆	早稲田大学大学院法務研究科教授
酒巻　匡	京都大学大学院法学研究科教授
田澤　元章	明治学院大学法学部教授
福田　守利	神田外語大学教授
松下　祐記	名城大学法学部准教授
伊藤　理	弁護士（アレン・アンド・オーヴェリー外国法共同事業法律事務所）
児島　幸良	弁護士（森・濱田松本法律事務所）
酒井　竜児	弁護士（長島・大野・常松法律事務所）
佐藤　理恵子	弁護士（西村あさひ法律事務所）
達野　大輔	弁護士（東京青山・青木・狛法律事務所ベーカー＆マッケンジー外国法事務弁護士事務所（外国法共同事業）
中野　雄介	弁護士（アンダーソン・毛利・友常法律事務所）
山口　芳泰	弁護士（TMI総合法律事務所）
垣貫　ジョン	外国法事務弁護士
鈴鹿　キース　清	外国法事務弁護士

推進会議構成員（平成21年度）

柏木　昇	中央大学法科大学院教授
久保田　隆	早稲田大学大学院法務研究科教授
酒巻　匡	京都大学大学院法学研究科教授
田澤　元章	明治学院大学法学部教授
福田　守利	神田外語大学教授

〔法令用語日英標準対訳辞書（平成26年3月改訂版）〕凡例他前付 〈参考付録〉

松下　祐記	千葉大学大学院専門法務研究科准教授
井口　直樹	弁護士（アンダーソン・毛利・友常法律事務所）
伊藤　理	弁護士（アレン・アンド・オーヴェリー外国法共同事業法律事務所）
児島　幸良	弁護士（森・濱田松本法律事務所）
酒井　竜児	弁護士（長島・大野・常松法律事務所）
佐藤　理恵子	弁護士（西村あさひ法律事務所）
達野　大輔	弁護士（東京青山・青木・狛法律事務所ベーカー＆マッケンジー外国法事務弁護士事務所（外国法共同事業）
山口　芳泰	弁護士（TMI総合法律事務所）
垣貫　ジョン	外国法事務弁護士
鈴鹿　キース　清	外国法事務弁護士

作業協力

松浦　好治	名古屋大学大学院法学研究科教授
外山　勝彦	名古屋大学大学院情報科学研究科准教授
小川　泰弘	名古屋大学大学院情報科学研究科助教

目　次
Table of Contents

I 翻訳の基本スタンス ································ 29
　Basic Stance on Translation
　1 翻訳の基本方針 ································ 29
　　Basic Guidelines for Translation
　2 翻訳に付記すべき情報等 ························ 31
　　Information to be Appended to Translations

II 法令用語日英対訳辞書 ····························· 33
　Legal Terms Dictionary
　1 凡　例 ·· 33
　　Explanatory Note
　2 特別編 ·· 39
　　Special Volume
　　　法令の形式 ································ 39
　　　Law Format
　　　法令の構成等 ······························ 39
　　　Law Organization
　　　法令の題名等 ······························ 40
　　　Law Titles
　　　法令番号 ·································· 42
　　　Law Numbering
　　　法令の慣用的表現 ·························· 43
　　　Conventionally Used Phrases in Law
　3 全 体 編 ··································· (本書第5巻)
　　Complete Volume

[法令用語日英標準対訳辞書(平成26年3月改訂版)] 凡例他前付　　　〈参考付録〉

I　翻訳の基本スタンス
Basic Stance for Translation

1　翻訳の基本方針

Basic Guidelines for Translation

(1)　基本的な考え方

Fundamental Vision

我が国の法令の英語訳にあたっては,正確で分かりやすく,全体として統一性が確保された翻訳が継続的に行われることを目指すことを基本とする。

The foundations of the English translations of our laws are based on the aspiration for continuous practice of accurate, easy-to-understand, and wholly uniform translations.

(2)　利用者

Intended Users

英米法に関する一定の知識はあるが,日本法及び日本語に関する知識はない者(例えば,法律実務家や企業関係者等)を翻訳の主な利用者として想定し,そのような利用者が法令の原文の趣旨を理解できるよう,正確でわかりやすい翻訳を目指す。

It is assumed that this translation will mostly be used by those who have a certain level of knowledge about Anglo-American law, but do not have knowledge of the Japanese language or Japanese law (for example, law practitioners and business persons), and accurate and easy-to-understand translations that will allow these users to understand the general meaning of the original text is what is intended.

(3)　正確性と分かりやすさ

Accuracy and Understandability

① 翻訳の正確性と分かりやすさの関係については,翻訳の正確性を確保しつつ分かりやすさを重視し,英語を母国語とする者にとって分かりやすい訳(英語として自然で読みやすい訳)を目指す。

The relationship between the accuracy and understandability of translations is such that importance is placed on the understandability of transla-

〈参考付録〉　　〔法令用語日英標準対訳辞書（平成26年3月改訂版）〕凡例他前付

tions while ensuring the accuracy of them, thereby striving for translations that native speakers of English would understand easily (translations read naturally and easily in English).

② 具体的には，個々の用語・言い回し等については，原則として，本書Ⅱの法令用語日英対訳辞書に従って精密に翻訳を行いつつ，例えば，原文では省略されている主語，目的語等を補うなどすることにより，文章全体が英語として自然で読みやすいものとなるよう努める。

Specifically, while accurately translating each term and expression in principle in example, by filling in the subject or object omitted from the original text.

③ また，翻訳自体のみでは原文の正確な意味が伝わらないと考えられる場合や，その他翻訳の理解に資する参考情報がある場合には，脚注等に補足的な説明を記載し，翻訳を補完する。

Furthermore, if the accurate meaning of the original text cannot be conveyed by the translation alone, or if there is other reference information conducive to understanding the translation, supplemental information will be noted in a footnote to complement the translation.

(4) 統一性

Uniformity

翻訳は，原則として，本書Ⅱの法令用語日英対訳辞書に従って行うことにより，全体としての統一性を確保することとする。ただし，①法令用語日英対訳辞書が想定していないが，使い分けを認めるべき事由がある場合，②個々の単語について，法令用語日英対訳辞書に厳密に従うと，節や文のレベルで見た場合に英語として誤解を招く又は不自然なものとなる場合，③その他，これらに準ずる事由がある場合には，適宜，これと異なる訳語を選択することも差し支えない。

In principle, the uniformity of translations made in accordance with part II of this dictionary, the "Legal Terms Dictionary" is to be ensured. However, (1) if there is reason to recognize proper usage not conceived in the Legal Terms Dictionary, (2) if by looking at the clause or sentence, it would cause confusion or sound unnatural in English if the vocabulary of the Legal Terms Dictionary is strictly adhered to, or (3) if there are other similar circumstances, choosing language differing from the Legal Terms Dictionary, as one sees fit is not precluded.

1st ed.2014.10　　　　　　　　　　JSB英文六法

2　翻訳に付記すべき情報等

Information to be Appended to Translations

(1)　翻訳の位置づけ等に関する情報（注）

Information About the Status of the Translations (Note)

本書に準拠した翻訳を公表する場合には，本書に準拠していることや公定訳でないことなどを含め，翻訳の位置づけを明示するとともに，当該翻訳の法改正への対応状況や，準拠している辞書のバージョンについても明確にするため，下記の定型文言を翻訳に付す。

When translations compliant with this dictionary are made public, the standard clause below should be added to it in order to clearly specify the status of the translation, state that compliance with:

（定型文言）

(standard clause)

英文 (English text)：This English translation of this law or regulation has been prepared (up to the revisions of Act No. ○ of ○) in compliance with the Standard Legal Terms Dictionary (March 2008 edition).

　　This is an unofficial translation. Only the original Japanese texts of laws and regulations have legal effect, and translations are to be used solely as reference material to aid in the understanding of Japanese laws and regulations.

The Government of Japan will not be responsible for the accuracy, reliability or currency of the legislative material provided on this Website, or for any consequence resulting from use of the information on this Website. For all purposes of interpreting and applying the law to any legal issue or dispute, users should consult the original Japanese texts published in the Official Gazette.

　(Note) The Japan Law Translation database system website was launched in April 2009 (http://www.japaneselawtranslation.go.jp/). Accordingly, with regards to the status of legal revisions and version of the dictionary the translation is in compliance with, the above standard clause has been modified and the relevant information, such as the status of legal revisions of each translation, is indicated on the upper hand of the screen displaying the respective

〈参考付録〉　　　〔法令用語日英標準対訳辞書（平成26年3月改訂版）〕凡例他前付

translated law. The actual above standard clause is displayed in places such as the search screen.

和文 (Japanese text)：この法令の翻訳は，平成〇年法律第〇号までの改正について，「法令用語日英標準対訳辞書」（平成20年3月版）に準拠して作成したものです。なお，この法令の翻訳は公定訳ではありません。法的効力を有するのは日本語の法令自体であり，翻訳はあくまでその理解を助けるための参考資料です。この翻訳の利用に伴って発生した問題について，一切の責任を負いかねますので，法律上の問題に関しては，官報に掲載された日本語の法令を参照してください。

（注）当該翻訳の法改正への対応状況や，準拠している辞書のバージョンについては，平成21年4月から，日本法令外国語訳データベース・システムのウェブサイト (http://www.japanese-lawtranslation.go.jp/) が開設されたことに伴い，法令ごとに，上記定型文言を改め，法令表示画面上部に当該翻訳の法改正への対応状況等の情報を表示し，上記なお書きについては，検索画面等に表示することとなった。

(2)　辞書への準拠性に関する情報

Information About Compliance with the Standard Legal Terms Dictionary

本書Ⅱの法令用語日英対訳辞書と異なる翻訳を行った場合には，原則として，その旨及びその具体的理由を脚注等に記載する。

In principle, when translations differ from part II "Legal Terms Dictionary" of this dictionary, a note to this effect and the specific reasoning (behind it) will be noted in a footnote:

（記載例）

(Example)

英文：The translation of the Japanese legal term "〇〇" is "xxxx" in the Standard Legal Terms Dictionary (March 2009 edition). However, since the United Nations Convention that formed the basis for this Act uses the English term "xxxxxx" as the term corresponding to said "〇〇," for the purpose of the translation of this Act, "〇〇" will be translated as "xxxxxx."

和文：〇〇は，標準対訳辞書（平成21年3月版）においては，「xxxx」とされているが，本法の基礎となった国連条約は，……の場合について，「xxxxxx」を使用していることから，関連する本法においても，

これに従うこととした。

II　法令用語日英対訳辞書
Legal Terms Dictionary

1　凡　例　Explanatory Note

⑴　構　成　Composition

本辞書は，特別編（法令の形式，法令の構成等，法令の題名等，法令番号，法令の慣用的表現といった特別の項目を整理したもの）と全体編（特別編を含め，収録用語のすべてを50音順に配列したもの）から構成されている。

This Legal Terms Dictionary is composed of the Special Volume (a collection of special sections entitled Law Format, Law Organization, Law Titles, Law Numbering, and Conventionally Used Phrases in Law) and the Complete Volume (including the Special Volume, all of the terms of which are arranged according to the Japanese syllabary.)

⑵　収録用語の選定方針，表記　Term Selection Policy and Expression

①　収録用語には，個別的な法令用語の他，法令の形式に関する事項及び一般的な言い回し等を含む。選定に当たっては，民事・刑事・行政の各分野における典型的な実体法・手続法で共通して多数用いられる基本的用語を始め，主要かつ基本的な法令用語，言い回し等が広く収録されるよう配慮した。

The terms used herein include legal terms, and matters regarding the format of laws and the expressions generally used in statutes. Consideration has been given to including a wide range of fundamental and important legal terms and expressions, starting with the numerous fundamental terms commonly used in quintessential substantive and procedural law from the civil, criminal and administrative fields.

②　収録用語は，法令において現に使用されるものに限られ，講学上の概念等については，主要かつ基本的なものであっても収録していない。

The terms are limited to those used currently in statutes; concepts used only in scholarly works, even if fundamental and important, are not included.

〈参考付録〉　　　　　〔法令用語日英標準対訳辞書（平成26年3月改訂版）〕凡例他前付

③　見出し語は，名詞で示すのを基本とし，他品詞については【動詞】・【形容詞】・【副詞】として項目中に付記する場合がある。

　As a general rule, keywords appear as nouns. For other parts of speech, they may appear as a note within the entry as a [verb]/[adjective]/[adverb].

④　見出し語の直後に，読み方を（　）に入れて示す。

　Immediately after the keyword, the pronunciation will appear in parentheses.

(3)　訳語の選定方針，表記　Translation Word Choice Selection Policy and Expression

①　各収録用語の訳語については，以下の方針によって選定した。

　Each term's translation word choice is selected based on the policies below:

・　英語を母国語とする者が日本法の概念に最も近似のイメージを抱くことができる訳語（概念的に近いだけでなく，認知度が高いなど分かりやすいもの）を選定する。原文の意味から離れ，又は英語として不自然となるような直訳語，新奇な中立的用語・造語等は，可能な限り避ける。

　The words that bear the closest resemblance for native English speakers are selected (not just close conceptually, but highly recognizable, so that the translated word is easy to understand), avoiding as much as possible, words that depart from the meaning of the original text, literal translations that would sound unnatural in English, unprecedented neutral terms, or coined terms.

・　従前の使用例やその傾向については十分に考慮するが，全体としての統一性の確保や分かりやすさの観点から，必要な場合には見直しを行う。

　Previous usage examples and their patterns are considered to the fullest extent, but revisions will be made when necessary for the maintenance of uniformity or from a ease-of-understanding point of view.

・　用語の用いられる分野等によっては，国際法上の用法にも留意する。

　Depending on the field using a term, terms used in international law will also be heeded.

・　当該用語の属する分野全体又は分野相互間の統一性の確保に，可能な限り，努める。

Uniformity of terms within a field or used between several fields will be maintained much as possible.

- 訳語としてローマ字のみを表記することは，特段の必要がない限り，行わない。ただし，注書や括弧書きで，日本語のローマ字表記を参考に示すことができる。

  Unless there is a particular need, translations will not be in Romanized Japanese. However, Romanized Japanese may be written as a reference in explanatory notes or within brackets.

- アメリカ語とイギリス語で訳語が異なる場合，原則として，アメリカ語を優先する。

  As a principle, American English will be preferred when there are differences between American and British English.

- 異なる日本語の用語・表現等は，可能な限り，訳し分ける。訳語が同一になる場合には，誤解・混同を招くおそれがないか留意する。

  Wherever possible, different Japanese terms and expressions will be made distinct when translated. If the translated language is the same, attention will be paid as to whether it has the risk of inviting misunderstanding or confusion.

- 本辞書を利用する場合には，コモン・ロー上の訳語の意味と原語の意味は必ずしも全面的に一致しないことに注意が必要である。本辞書では，日本法上使われている用語に最も近いと思われる英語を訳語としている。しかし，日本法上の原語が翻訳された英語がコモン・ロー上持つ意味と完全に一致することはない。

  ※たとえば，抵当権は mortgage と訳されているが，これは不動産上の約定担保権であるという点では共通であるが，mortgage では歴史的には title が mortgagee（抵当権者）に移転したのに対して日本では抵当不動産の所有権は抵当債権者には移転しない。したがって，抵当権の実行方法は強制競売によるのに対して mortgage の実行方法である foreclosure は原則として title の受戻権（redemption right）の喪失という構成をとった。「抵当権」の訳語に mortgage の言葉を当てたのは，「不動産に対する約定担保権」という本質が共通することから，日本法を知らない英語圏の利用者に「抵当権」に最も近いイメージを伝達できるだろうという期待からである。

  Users of this dictionary should note that the common-law meanings of the translated terms and the meanings of the original Japanese terms are not necessarily identical in every respect. The English words felt

〈参考付録〉　　　　　〔法令用語日英標準対訳辞書（平成26年3月改訂版）〕凡例他前付

to be closest in meaning to the Japanese legal terms are selected as the translations for inclusion in the dictionary. This said, the original Japanese legal terms do not have a perfect semantic correspondence with the translated terms as used at common law.

> ※ For example, the term "抵当権 (teitoken)" is translated as "mortgage", the commonality being that both of these constitute contractual security interests in real property; however, whereas a common-law mortgage was originally a conveyance of title to the mortgagee, in Japan, ownership of mortgaged real property is not transferred to the mortgage holder. Accordingly, whereas a 抵当権 (teitoken) is enforced through a compulsory judicial sale, foreclosure on common-law mortgages principally took the form of forfeiture of the right of redemption. In this particular case, the reason the word "mortgage" was chosen as the translation of "抵当権 (teitoken)" is because it has in common the concept of a contractual security in real property, and can be expected to most closely convey the sense of a "抵当権 (teitoken)" to English speakers with no knowledge of Japanese.

② 名詞については，複数で用いるのが通例である場合を除き，単数形で示す。

Nouns will be presented in singular form, unless customarily used in plural form.

③ 訳語のうち，文脈などから省略してよい場合があり得る部分は，（　）で囲んで示す。

When a portion may be omitted from the translation in context, it will be indicated in parentheses.

④ 訳語のうち，文脈などからいずれを使用してもよい部分は，／を使って併記する。

When several words may be used in context, / will be used.

⑤ 見出し語以外の品詞が【動詞】・【形容詞】・【副詞】として項目中に示されている場合，それぞれ直後に対応する訳語を示す。

When within an item a part of speech other than the keyword appears, [verb]/[adjective]/[adverb] will be indicated immediately after each corresponding translation.

(4)　複数の訳語の使い分け　Multiple Translations

① 本辞書においては，最も適切な訳語を一つ示すことを原則とする。

In principle, in this Legal Terms Dictionary only the most appropriate

translation will be indicated.
② ただし，次の各場合のように，一定の基準の下，複数の訳語の使い分けを認めるのが適切な場合には，(1)(2) という番号を付して複数の訳語を示し，[ ] 内に使い分け基準を示す。この場合，翻訳者は，使い分け基準に従って訳語を選択する必要がある。

However, for each instance below, when it is appropriate to recognize multiple proper translations depending on certain standards, the multiple translations will be affixed with numbers such as (1) (2), and within [ ] the standards for proper use will be indicated. For this, the translator must follow the standards for proper use in selecting the proper translation.

i. 慣例上，特定分野において使用される表現がある場合
When there is precedent for using an expression in a specific field.

ii. 単一の用語ではあるが複数の意味を持つため，使用される場面によって訳語を使い分ける必要がある場合
When there is a need to differentiate the translation word usage based on how a single term is used because it has several meanings.

iii. その他，上記 i.ii. に準ずる事由がある場合
When there are other circumstances equivalent to i or ii above.

③ また，多義的で，訳語との一対一対応や使い分け基準を明確にすることが困難であり，かつ，訳語の統一を図ることに特段の意味がないと考えられる収録用語については，(1)(2)として複数の訳語を示し，使い分け基準は示さない。この場合，翻訳者は，示された複数の訳語の中から，文脈に応じて適宜のものを選択し得る。

Also, when a word has multiple meanings and is difficult to clarify a one-to-one correspondence with the translation and the proper usage standards and there is no particular meaning to attempt uniform translations, multiple translations will be indicated with (1) (2) and the proper usage standards need not be indicated. For this, the translator may select from the indicated multiple translations the one most appropriate based on the context.

(5) 用 例 Examples
① 複数の訳語の使い分けを認める場合や，訳語の正確な理解のために必要な場合には，可能な限り，訳語ごとに用例・使用条文例を示す。

When multiple proper translations are recognized or when necessary for accurate comprehension, examples/textual usage examples will be in-

〈参考付録〉　　　　　〔法令用語日英標準対訳辞書（平成26年3月改訂版）〕凡例他前付

dicated, wherever possible.
②　用例では，どのような文脈において当該訳語が用いられるかが，日本法を理解しない者にも明確となるような典型的な例（条文の該当部分等）を示す。

In examples, what context the translation will be used in and an archetypical example will be indicated in order to clarify matters for even individuals who do not understand Japanese laws.
③　用例は，【用例】として日本語及び英語を付記し，出典条文は（　）内に示す。

Examples will have [Example] affixed to it in English or in Japanese, and reference text will be indicated in parentheses.
④　なお，用例として，英語としての実際上の用法等にかんがみ，訳語とは語順・語形等が異なるものを挙げている場合がある。

In addition, in consideration of actual English usage, examples with a word order and word form different from the translation may be given.

例：してはならない（してはならない）　　must not
　【例】…その権限は，…と解釈してはならない　　the authority must not be construed as …

(6)　注　書　Comments
①　日本法の概念に対応する訳語が存在しない場合や，日本法の概念に類似の訳語は存在するが，内容が完全には一致しない場合等には，【注】として，日本法の概念の説明を付記するよう心がけた。

When there is no translation corresponding to concepts in Japanese law, or when there is a translation akin to a concept in Japanese law but its contents are not completely consistent, an explanation of the concept in Japanese law will be attached as a [comment].
②　その他，日本語のローマ字表記や反対概念，類似概念，出典条文など，訳語の理解に有用な情報についても，【注】として付記する場合がある。

There are instances where Romanized Japanese words, contrasting or similar concepts, text from source material, and other information helpful for the understanding of the translation will be added as a [comment].

(7)　その他　Miscellaneous
本辞書は，原則として，法令中の法律専門用語について英訳を示したものであるが，収録した見出し語の中には，必ずしも法律用語ではないもの，

あるいは法律用語であっても，法文の中で場合によっては一般用語として使われているものもある。例として「充てる」，「主張」などがあるが，これらの用語は，法令翻訳の場合の適切な訳語選択に困難を伴うことが想定される用語として参考掲載したものであり，使用される場面によって多様な意味で用いられ得るものであるから，必ずしも本辞書に示した訳語にとらわれずに条文の意味に即して適切な訳語を使用することが求められる。

In principle, this Legal Terms Dictionary has English translations of specialized legal terminology found in laws, but among the terms entered are those that are not necessarily legal terms or those that are legal terms, but depending on the circumstances, may be used

in laws as a general term. Terms such as "充てる" (allocate, appoint, etc.) and "主張" (claim, assertion, etc.) are examples of this; they are included for reference, as terms that it is expected will be difficult to select the appropriate translation for in a legal translation, Since such terms can be used to convey a variety of meanings depending on the context, it is best not to adhere so strictly to the translations given for them in the dictionary, but to use the appropriate translation in light of the meaning of the text.

2　特別編

〈法令の形式〉

憲　法	Constitution
法　律	Act［原則］
	Code［いわゆる法典］
政　令	Cabinet Order
内閣府令	Cabinet Office Ordinance
省　令	Ordinance of the Ministry［原則］
	Ministerial Ordinance［後に続く語が長い場合］
規　則	Rule
条　例	Prefectural Ordinance［都道府県条例］
	Municipal Ordinance［市町村条例］

〈法令の構成等〉

目　次	Table of Contents
編	Part

〈参考付録〉　　　　　　　　〔法令用語日英標準対訳辞書（平成26年3月改訂版）〕凡例他前付

章	Chapter
節	Section
款	Subsection
目	Division
条	Article (Art.)
項	paragraph (para.)
	(1)(2)(3)　［見出しとして用いる場合］
号	item
	(i)(ii)(iii)　［見出しとして用いる場合］
イ ロ ハ	(a)(b)(c)
(1)(2)(3)	1. 2. 3.
(i)(ii)(iii)	i. ii. iii.
枝 番 号	-1, -2, -3
本　文	main clause
ただし書	proviso
前　段	first sentence
後　段 *	second sentence
附　則	supplementary provisions
別表第…（第…条関係）	appended table … (Re: Art. …)
項 **	row
欄 **	column
別記様式	appended form

＊3文に区切られている場合には，中段が second sentence で，後段は third sentence（4文以上の場合もこれに準じる）。

＊＊表・別表中において，「項」とは縦の線で区画されている区切りをいい，「欄」とは横の線で区画されている区切りをいう。原文（縦書）の表・別表を英語（横書）に翻訳する場合には，「項」が横の線で区画され，「欄」が縦の線で区画されるようにする。

対訳辞書〔前付〕

〈法令の題名等〉

…関係　**Re:**
　【例】輸出貿易管理令別表第一関係 Re: Appended Table 1 of the Export Control Oder

規則
　(1)　**Ordinance**　［法形式が省令の場合］
　　【例】商法施行規則 Ordinance for Enforcement of the Commercial Code
　(2)　**Rule**　［法形式が規則の場合］

1st ed.2014.10　　　　　　　　　　　　　　　　　　　　　　　　　　　　　　　JSB英文六法

【例】民事訴訟規則 Rules of Civil Procedure
(3) **regulation**［就業規則などの場合］

基本法　**Basic Act**
　　【例】原子力基本法 Atomic Energy Basic Act
　　【例】環境基本法 Environment Basic Act
　　【例】男女共同参画社会基本法 Basic Act for Gender-Equal Society
暫定措置法　**Act on Temporary Measures**
施行規則　**Ordinance for Enforcement**
施行法　**Act for Enforcement**
　　【例】刑法施行法 Act for Enforcement of the Penal Code
省令
　(1)　**Ordinance of the Ministry**
　　【例】法務省令 Ordinance of the Ministry of Justice
　　【例】経済産業省令 Ordinance of METI
　　【注】題名にかかわらず法形式が省令の場合は Ordinance を用いる。
　(2)　**Ministerial Ordinance**［後に続く語が長い場合など］
　　【例】出入国管理及び難民認定法第七条第一項第二号の基準を定める省令 Ministerial Ordinance to Provide for Criteria Pursuant to Article 7, paragraph (1), item (ii) of the Immigration Control and Refugee Recognition Act
政令　**Cabinet Order**
　　【注】題名にかかわらず法形式が政令の場合は Cabinet Order を用いる。
設置法　**Act for Establishment**
　　【例】総務省設置法 Act for Establishment of the Ministry of Internal Affairs and Communications
通則法　**Act on General Rules**
　　【例】独立行政法人通則法 Act on General Rules for Incorporated Administrative Agency
特別措置法　**Act on Special Measures**
　　【例】租税特別措置法 Act on Special Measures concerning Taxation
特例に関する法律　**Act on Special Measures**
内閣府令　**Cabinet Office Ordinance**
に関する法律
　(1)　**Act on**［原則］
　　【例】臓器の移植に関する法律 Act on Organ Transplantation

〈参考付録〉　　　　〔法令用語日英標準対訳辞書（平成26年3月改訂版）〕凡例他前付

(2) **…Act**［「に関する法律」を「…Act」とする翻訳がすでに海外において定着している場合］
　【例】行政機関が行う政策の評価に関する法律 Government Policy Evaluations Act

法
(1) **Act**［法律名に使う場合の原則］
　【例】商標法 Trademark Act
(2) **Code**［いわゆる法典］
　【例】民法 Civil Code
　【例】刑法 Penal Code
　【例】商法 Commercial Code
　【例】民事訴訟法 Code of Civil Procedure
　【例】刑事訴訟法 Code of Criminal Procedure
(3) **law**［いわゆる一般名称や科目名としての法律］

法律
(1) **law**［法律一般としての意味の場合］
(2) **Act**［法律名に用いる場合］
(3) **Code**［いわゆる法典］
　【例】民法 Civil Code
　【例】刑法 Penal Code
　【例】商法 Commercial Code
　【例】民事訴訟法 Code of Civil Procedure
　【例】刑事訴訟法 Code of Criminal Procedure

臨時措置法　**Act on Temporary Measures**
　【例】罰金等臨時措置法 Act on Temporary Measures concerning Fines

令　**Cabinet Order**
　【注】法形式が政令の場合。

〈法令番号〉

年法律第…号
　Act No. … of
　【例】平成 11 年法律第 103 号 Act No. 103 of 1999
　【注】政省令等についてもこれに準ずる。

〈法令の慣用的表現〉

…以下
  (1) **... or less** ［原則］
  (2) **not more than ...** ［上限を示すことに重点がある場合］
    【例】3年以下の for not more than 3 years
以下「…」という　**hereinafter referred to as "..."**
以下同じ　**the same applies hereinafter**
以下この…において同じ　**hereinafter the same applies in this ...**
…以上
  (1) **... or more** ［原則］
    【例】20歳以上 20 years of age or more
  (2) **not less than ...** ［下限を示すことに重点がある場合］
    【例】1年以上の for not less than 1 year
  (3) **... or heavier** ［刑の場合］
    【例】罰金以上の刑 fine or heavier punishment
偽りその他不正の手段　**deception or other wrongful means**
及び　**and**
かつ　**and**
…から…以内に　**within ... from ...**
  【例】告示の日の翌日から起算して6か月以内に within 6 months from the day following the date of public notice
…から…までの規定　**provisions ... to ... inclusive**
禁錮以上の刑に処せられた者

a person who has been sentenced to imprisonment or heavier punishment

公布の日　**the date of promulgation**
公布の日から起算して…を経過した日

the day on which ... have elapsed from the date of promulgation

公布の日から起算して…を超えない範囲内において政令で定める日

the day specified by Cabinet Order within a period not exceeding ... from the date of promulgation

この場合において，…中「…」とあるのは，「…」と読み替えるものとする

in this case, the term "..." in ... is deemed to be replaced with "..."

〈参考付録〉　　　　〔法令用語日英標準対訳辞書（平成26年3月改訂版）〕凡例他前付

この法律において，次の各号に掲げる用語の意義は，当該各号に定めるところによる

  in this Act, the meanings of the terms set forth in the following items are as prescribed respectively in those items

この法律において「…」とは，…をいう

  the term "..." as used in this Act means ...

この法律に規定するもののほか，…は，…で定める

  in addition to what is provided for in this Act, ... are prescribed by ...

この法律による改正後の　**revised by this Act**

  【例】この法律による改正後の関連法律の規定 the provisions of concerned Acts revised by this Act

この法律による改正前の　**prior to revision by this Act**

  【例】この法律による改正前の特許法の規定 the provisions of the Patent Act prior to revision by this Act

この法律は，…限り，その効力を失う

  this Act ceases to be effective at the end of ...

この法律は，…から施行する　**this Act comes into effect as of ...**

この法律は，…に関し必要な事項を定めるものとする

  this Act provides for necessary matters concerning ...

この法律は，…を目的とする　**the purpose of this Act is ...**

事項

  (1)　**matter**

  (2)　**information**

  (3)　**particular**

  【注】辞書中，（事項）と表示してある場合は，前後の文脈の応じて適切な訳語を用いる。

してはならない

  (1)　**must not**

    【例】その権限は，…と解釈してはならない the authority must not be construed as …

  (2)　**is prohibited**

    【例】何人も…してはならない it is prohibited for any person to...

しなければならない

  (1)　**must**

  (2)　**shall**

〔法令用語日英標準対訳辞書（平成26年3月改訂版）〕凡例他前付　　　〈参考付録〉

心身の故障のため　**due to mental or physical disorder**
推定する　**is presumed**
速やかに　**promptly**
することができない
(1) **may not**［禁止］
【例】その権利を行使することができない the right may not be exercised
【例】その処分に対しては，不服申立てをすることができない no appeal may be entered against the disposition
(2) **be unable to**［不可能］
【例】罰金を完納することができない者 a person unable to pay the fine in full
することができる　**may**
することを妨げない　**does not preclude**
【例】相手方が申立てをすることを妨げない this does not preclude the adverse party from filing a motion
【例】当事者本人を尋問することを妨げない this does not preclude the examination of the party
することを要しない　**is not required to**
するため…する必要がある　**be necessary that … in order to**
するものとする　**is to**
するよう努めなければならない　**must endeavor to**
前項に規定する…　**… prescribed in the preceding paragraph**
前項に規定する場合において
　in the case prescribed in the preceding paragraph
前項に規定するもののほか，…は，…で定める
　in addition to what is provided for in the preceding paragraph, … is prescribed by …
前項の…　**… set forth in the preceding paragraph**
前項の規定により
　pursuant to the provision of the preceding paragraph
前項の場合において　**in the case referred to in the preceding paragraph**
その法人又は人の業務に関して…をしたときは，行為者を罰するほか，その法人又は人に対して各本条の罰金刑を科する
　When an individual has done … with regard to the business of said

〈参考付録〉　　　　　　　〔法令用語日英標準対訳辞書（平成26年3月改訂版）〕凡例他前付

corporation or individual, not only is the offender punished but also said corporation or individual is punished by the fine prescribed in the respective Articles

ただし… ; provided, however, that ...

ただし，第三者の権利を害することはできない

　; provided, however, that this may not prejudice the rights of a third party

ただし，…は，この限りでない

　; provided, however, that this does not apply to ...

直ちに　immediately

遅滞なく　without delay

次の各号の一に該当する者

　any person who falls under any of the following items

…等

　⑴　**...etc.**〔見出し中に用いられる場合や，定義がなされている場合など，「等」の内容が別の場所に明示されている場合〕

　　【例】（定義等）（Definitions, etc.）

　　【例】船舶又は航空機（以下「船舶等」という。）vessel or aircraft (hereinafter referred to as "vessel, etc.")

　⑵　**such as...**〔例示列挙など「等」の内容が明示されていない場合〕

　　【例】機構の名称，目的，業務の範囲等に関する事項 such matters as the Agency's name, purpose and scope of business

　⑶　**and other (things) with/of similar nature**

　⑷　**or the like**

　　【例】この法律において「薬物犯罪収益等」とは，薬物犯罪収益，薬物犯罪収益に由来する財産又はこれらの財産とこれらの財産以外の財産とが混和した財産をいう In this Act, "drug offense proceeds or the like" means drug offense proceeds, property derived from drug offense proceeds or any other property in which any drug offense proceeds or property derived from drug offense proceeds is mingled with other property（麻薬特例法2条5項）

当分の間　**until otherwise provided for by law**

同様とする　**the same applies to**

とする　**is**

なおその効力を有する　**remain in force**

〔法令用語日英標準対訳辞書（平成26年3月改訂版）〕凡例他前付　　　　　　　〈参考付録〉

並びに　and
　　【例】A及びB，C並びにD　A and B, C, and D
…において準用する…の規定
　　the provision of …, as applied mutatis mutandis pursuant to …
…において準用する場合を含む
　　including the cases where applied mutatis mutandis pursuant to
…において読み替えて準用する…の規定
　　the provision of …, as applied mutatis mutandis pursuant to … after deemed replacement,
に掲げる（事項）　**(matters) set forth in**
　　【例】第2号から第4号までに掲げる（事項）(matters) set forth in items 2 to 4 inclusive
　　【例】次に掲げる（事項）following (matters)
　　※15ページ，121ページ，「事項」参照
に掲げるもののほか　**in addition to what is set forth in**
に限る　**limited to**
　　【例】第1項の資格（政令で定めるものに限る。）qualifications provided by para.1 (limited to those specified by Cabinet Order)
　　【例】ただし，第5条に規定する場合に限る provided, however, that this is limited to the cases prescribed by Art. 5
に代わる　**in lieu of**
に関連する（事項）　**(matters) relevant to**
　　※15ページ，121ページ，「事項」参照
に定めるところにより
　⑴　**pursuant to the provision of**
　⑵　**as provided for by**
に従わないで　**not complying with**
に準ずる
　⑴　**equivalent**［形容詞（同等の，類似の）］
　　【例】これに準ずる方法 equivalent method
　⑵　**is dealt with in the same manner as**［動詞（同様に扱う）］
　　【例】正犯に準ずる is dealt with in the same manner as a principal
に処する　**is punished by**
については，…の例による　**is governed by …**
　　【例】その時効については，国税の例による the prescription is gov-

JSB英文六法　　　　　　　　　168　　　　　　　　　1st ed. 2014.10

〈参考付録〉　　　　　〔法令用語日英標準対訳辞書（平成26年3月改訂版）〕凡例他前付

erned by the same rules as national tax
　【例】前項の場合には，次の例による the cases referred to in the preceding paragraph are governed by the following rules

については，なお従前の例による
the provisions then in force remain applicable
　【例】この法律の施行前にした行為に対する罰則の適用については，なお従前の例による with regard to the application of penal provisions to acts committed prior to the enforcement of this Act, the provisions then in force remain applicable

に照らし　**in light of**

に満たない
　(1)　**less than**〔原則〕
　　【例】一株に満たない端数 a fraction less than one share
　(2)　**under**〔年齢の場合〕
　　【例】14歳に満たない者 a person under 14 years of age

に基づく
　(1)　**based on**〔原則〕
　　【例】専門的知見に基づく意見 opinion based on expert knowledge
　(2)　**pursuant to**〔法令の規定等〕
　　【例】第60条の規定に基づく措置 measures pursuant to Art. 60

のいずれかに該当する　**fall under any of**

…の規定に違反して…した者
any person who, in violation of …, has done …
　【例】第20条の規定に違反して故意に報告しなかった者 any person who has intentionally failed to report in violation of Article 20

…の規定にかかわらず　**notwithstanding the provision of**

…の規定により　**pursuant to the provision of**

…の規定は，…について準用する
the provisions of … apply mutatis mutandis to …

…の規定は，…についても適用する　**the provisions of … also apply to …**

…の日の…日前までに　**… days prior to the date of**

…の日の翌日から起算して
　(1)　**from the day following the date of**〔原則〕
　(2)　**since the day following the date of**〔期間の経過の場合〕
　　【例】告示の日の翌日から起算して1年が経過したときは when one

year has passed since the day following the date of public notice
  (3) **commencing from the day following the date of**
…は，…と解釈してはならない **must not be construed as …**
…は，…と認めるときは **when … find …**
　　【例】裁判所は，適当と認めるときは，…することができる the court may, when it finds appropriate, …
　　【例】主務大臣は，…のおそれがあると認めるときは，…しなければならない the competent minister must, when the minister finds a risk of …, …
…は，他の法律に特別の定めのある場合を除くほか，この法律の定めるところによる

is governed by the provisions of this Act, except as otherwise provided by other acts

不服を申し立てることができない **no appeal may be entered**
別段の定めがある場合を除き **unless otherwise provided for**
別に法律で定める日 **the date specified separately by an act**
又は **or**
みだりに
  (1) **without (good) reason**
　　【注】法律上の「みだりに」は，正当性がないという意味。
  (2) **without (due) cause**
みなす **is deemed**
未満
  (1) **less than**［原則］
　　【例】1万円未満の端数 a fraction less than ten thousand yen
  (2) **under**［年齢の場合］
　　【例】18歳未満の者 a person under 18 years of age
若しくは **or**
　　【例】A，B又はC，D若しくはE A, B, or C, D or E
を超えない **not exceeding**
を超える **exceeding**
を除くほか
  (1) **in addition to**［付加を示す場合］
　　【例】前項の場合を除くほか in addition to the cases referred to in the preceding paragraph

(2) **except**［例外を示す場合］
　【例】特別の措置を講じている場合を除くほか except when special measures are taken

① Companies Act

(Act No. 86 of July 26, 2005)

PART I General Provisions

Chapter I Common Provisions

(Purpose)
Article 1 The formation, organization, operation and management of companies shall be governed by the provisions of this Act, except as otherwise provided by other acts.

(Definitions)
Article 2 In this Act, the meanings of the terms listed in the following items shall be as prescribed respectively in those items:
  (i) "Company" means any Stock Company, General Partnership Company, Limited Partnership Company or Limited Liability Company;
  (ii) "Foreign Company" means such any juridical person incorporated under the law of a foreign country or such other foreign organization that is of the same kind as the Company or is similar to a Company;
  (iii) "Subsidiary" means any entity which is prescribed by the applicable Ordinance of the Ministry of Justice as the juridical person the management of which is controlled by a Company, including, but not limited to, a Stock Company a majority of all votes in which are owned by the Company;
  (iv) "Parent Company" means any entity which is prescribed by the applicable Ordinance of the Ministry of Justice as a juridical person who controls the management of a Stock Company, including, but not limited to, a Company which has a Stock Company as its Subsidiary;
  (v) "Public Company" means any Stock Company the articles of incorporation of which do not require, as a feature of all or part of its shares, the approval of the Stock Company for the acquisition of such shares by transfer;
  (vi) "Large Company" means any Stock Company which satisfies any of the following requirements:
    (a) that the amount of the stated capital in the balance sheet as of the end of its Most Recent Business Year (hereinafter in this (a) and (b) below referring to the balance sheet reported to the annual shareholders' meeting under the provision of Article 439 in cases provided for in the first sentence of such Article, and referring to the balance sheet under Article 435(1) in cases where the first annual shareholders' meeting after the incorporation of the Stock Company has not yet been held) is 500,000,000 yen or more; or
    (b) that the total sum of the amounts in the liabilities section of the balance sheet as of the end of its Most Recent Business Year is 20,000,000,000 yen or more;
  (vii) "Company with Board of Directors" means any Stock Company which has a board of directors, or any Stock Company which is required to have a board of directors under the provisions of this Act;
  (viii) "Company with Accounting Advisors" means any Stock Company which has Accounting Advisor(s);
  (ix) "Company with Auditors" means any Stock Company which has auditor(s) (excluding any Stock Company the articles of incorporation of which provide that the

scope of the audit by its auditor(s) shall be limited to an audit related to accounting), or any Stock Company which is required to have auditor(s) under the provisions of this Act;

(x) "Company with Board of Auditors" means any Stock Company which has a board of auditors, or any Stock Company which is required to have a board of auditors under the provisions of this Act;

(xi) "Company with Accounting Auditors" means any Stock Company which has accounting auditor(s), or any Stock Company which is required to have accounting auditor(s) under the provisions of this Act;

(xii) "Company with Committees" means any Stock Company which has a nominating committee, an audit committee and a compensation committee (hereinafter referred to as "Committees");

(xiii) "Corporation with Class Shares" means any Business Corporation which issues two or more classes of shares with different features as to the matters listed in the items of Article 108(1), including, but not limited to, the Dividend of Surplus;

(xiv) "Class Meeting" means a meeting of Class Shareholders (hereinafter referring to the shareholders of any class of shares of a Company with Class Shares);

(xv) "Outside Director" means a director of any Stock Company who is neither an Executive Director (hereinafter referring to a director of a Stock Company listed in any item of Article 363(1), and any other director who has executed operation of such Stock Company) nor an executive officer, nor an employee, including a manager, of such Stock Company or any of its Subsidiaries, and who has neither ever served in the past as an executive director nor executive officer, nor as an employee, including a manager, of such Stock Company or any of its Subsidiaries;

(xvi) "Outside Company Auditor" means an auditor of any Stock Company who has neither ever served in the past as a director, Accounting Advisor (or, in cases where the accounting advisor is a juridical person, any member thereof who was in charge of its advisory affairs) or executive officer, nor as an employee, including a manager, of such Stock Company or any of its Subsidiaries;

(xvii) "Shares with Restriction on Transfer" means the shares in cases where a Stock Company provides, as a feature of all or part of its shares, that the approval of the Stock Company is required for the acquisition of such shares by transfer;

(xviii) "Shares with Put Option" means the shares in cases where a Stock Company provides, as a feature of all or part of its shares, that a shareholder may demand the Stock Company to redeem such shares;

(xix) "Shares Subject to Call" means the shares in cases where a Stock Company provides, as a feature of all or part of its shares, that such Stock Company may redeem such shares upon the occurrence of specified event;

(xx) "Share Unit" means such certain number in cases where a Stock Company provides in its articles of incorporation that certain number of shares it issues constitute one unit of shares which entitles a shareholder to cast one vote in a shareholders' meeting or Class Meeting;

(xxi) "Share Option" means any right which entitles the holder to acquire shares in a Stock Company by exercising the right against such Stock Company;

(xxii) "Bond with Share Options" means any Bond with attached Share Options;

(xxiii) "Bond" means any monetary claim owed by a Company by allotment under the provisions of this Act and which will be redeemed in accordance with the provisions on the matters listed in the items of Article 676;

(xxiv) "Most Recent Business Year" means the latest of business years for which approval under Article 438(2) (or any approval under Article 436(3) in cases provided for in Article 439(1)) is obtained with respect to the financial statements provided

in Article 435(2) relating to each business year;
(xxv) "Dividend Property" means the property to be distributed in cases where a Stock Company pays the Dividend of Surplus;
(xxvi) "Entity Conversion" means any change, through conversion, from a Company listed in (a) or (b) below, respectively, to another form of Company prescribed immediately thereafter in the said (a) or (b):
  (a) from a Stock Company to a General Partnership Company, Limited Partnership Company or Limited Liability Company;
  (b) from a General Partnership Company, Limited Partnership Company or Limited Liability Company to a Stock Company.
(xxvii) "Absorption-type Merger" means any merger Company(s) effects with another Company(s) whereby the surviving Company succeeds to any and all rights and obligations of the absorbed Company(s);
(xxviii) "Consolidation-type Merger" means any merger effected by two or more Companies whereby the new Company incorporated by the merger succeeds to any and all rights and obligations of the companies consolidated by the merger;
(xxix) "Absorption-type Company Split" means any Company split whereby succeeding Company(s) succeeds after the Company Split, in whole or in part, to any rights and obligations, in whole or in part, in connection with the business of the Stock Company(s) or the Limited Liability Company(s) which is split;
(xxx) "Incorporation-type Company Split" means any Company split whereby new Company(s) incorporated by the Company Split succeeds to any rights and obligations, in whole or in part, in connection with business of the Stock Company(s) or the Limited Liability Company(s) which is split;
(xxxi) "Share Exchange" means any exchange of shares whereby Stock Company(s) cause all of its issued shares (hereinafter referring to the shares issued by a Stock Company) to be acquired by another Stock Company or Limited Liability Company;
(xxxii) "Share Transfer" means any transfer whereby Stock Company(s) cause all of its issued shares to be acquired by a newly incorporated Stock Company;
(xxxiii) "Method of Public Notice" means the method which a Company (including a Foreign Company) adopts to give public notice (excluding those which are required to be effected by publishing the notice in the Official Gazette pursuant to the provisions of this Act or any other acts);
(xxxiv) "Electronic Public Notice" means a Method of Public Notice prescribed by the applicable ordinance of the Ministry of Justice which, through use of an electronic method (hereinafter referring to the method prescribed by the applicable ordinance of the Ministry of Justice which uses information communication technology including, but not limited to, the method which uses electronic data processing system), enables the general public to access such public notice.

(Juridical Personality)
Article 3 A Company shall be a juridical person.

(Domicile)
Article 4 The domicile of a Company shall be the location of its head office.

(Commercial Transaction)
Article 5 Any act which a Company (hereinafter in this Article, in paragraph (1) of the following Article, in Article 8 and in Article 9, including a Foreign Company) carries out as its business and any act which it carries out for its business shall constitute a commercial transaction.

Chapter II Trade Name of Company

(Trade Name)
Article 6 (1) The name of a Company shall be its trade name.
(2) A Company shall use in its trade name the words "Kabushiki-Kaisha," "Gomei-Kaisha," "Goushi-Kaisha" or "Goudou-Kaisha" respectively for Stock Company, General Partnership Company, Limited Partnership Company or Limited Liability Company.
(3) A Company may not use in its trade name any word which makes it likely that the Company may be mistaken for a different form of Company.

(No Use of Name, etc. which is Likely to be Mistaken for a Company)
Article 7 No person who is not a Company may use in its name or trade name any word which makes it likely that the person may be mistaken as a Company.

Article 8 (1) No person may use, with a wrongful purpose, any name or trade name which makes it likely that the person may be mistaken for the other Company.
(2) Any Company the enterprise interests of which have been, or are likely to be, infringed by the use of any name or trade name in violation of the provisions of the preceding paragraph may seek an injunction suspending or preventing the infringement against the person who infringes, or is likely to infringe, those enterprise interests.

(Liability of Company Permitting Others to Use Its Trade Name)
Article 9 Any Company who has permitted others to carry out a business or engage in any enterprise by using the Company's own trade name shall be jointly and severally liable together with such others, vis-a-vis any person who has transacted with such others based on misunderstanding that such Company carries out such business, for the performance of any obligations which may arise from such transaction.

Chapter III Employees of a Company

Section 1 Employees of a Company

(Manager)
Article 10 A Company (hereinafter in this Part including a Foreign Company) may appoint manager(s) and have him/her carry out its business at its head office or branch office.

(Manager's Authority of Representation)
Article 11 (1) A manager shall have authority to do any and all judicial and non-judicial acts on behalf of a Company in connection with its business.
(2) A manager may elect or dismiss other employee(s).
(3) No limitation on a manager's authority of representation may be asserted against a third party without knowledge of such limitation.

(Non-Competition by Manager)
Article 12 (1) A manager may not commit any of the following acts without the permission of the Company:
   (i) engage in his/her own enterprise;
   (ii) carry out, for himself/herself or for a third party, any transaction which is in the

line of business of the Company;
(iii) become an employee of any other Company or merchant (excluding any Company; the same shall apply in Article 24);
(iv) become a director, executive officer or any member who executes the operation of any other Company.
(2) If a manager commits any act listed in item (ii) of the preceding paragraph in violation of the provisions of that paragraph, the amount of the profit obtained by the manager or any third party as a result of such act shall be presumed to be amount of the damage suffered by the Company.

(Apparent Manager)
Article 13 Any employee with a title which holds him/her out as the chief of the business of the head office or any branch office of a Company shall be deemed to have the authority to do any and all non-judicial acts in connection with the business of such head office or branch office, provided, however, that this shall not apply to the cases where his/her counterparty acts with knowledge of his/her actual authority.

(Employees to Whom the Authority of a Certain Kind of Matter or A Specific Matter is Delegated)
Article 14 (1) Any employee to whom the authority of a certain kind of matter or a specific matter in connection with the business is delegated shall have the authority to do any and all non-judicial acts in connection with such matter.
(2) No limitation on the authority of representation of the employee provided in the preceding paragraph may be asserted against a third party without knowledge of such limitation.

(Employees of Stores for the Purpose of Selling Goods)
Article 15 Any employee of a store the purpose of which is the sale, etc. (hereinafter in this Article referring to sale, lease or any other act similar to the foregoing) of goods shall be deemed to have authority to conduct the sale, etc. of the goods located in such store, provided, however, that this shall not apply to the cases where his/her counterparty acts with knowledge of his/her actual authority.

Section 2 Commercial Agents of the Companies

(Duty to Give Notice)
Article 16 When any Commercial Agent (hereinafter in this Section referring to a person who acts on behalf of a Company as an agent or intermediary in any transaction in the ordinary line of business of the Company, and is not an employee of the Company) undertakes any transaction as an agent or intermediary, the Commercial Agent shall give notice of that fact to the Company without delay.

(Non-Competition by Commercial Agent)
Article 17 (1) A Commercial Agent may not carry out any of the following acts without the permission of the Company:
(i) carry out, for himself/herself or for a third party, any transaction which is in the line of business of the Company;
(ii) become a director, executive officer or any member who executes operation of any other Company which carries out the same kind of business as the Company.
(2) If a Commercial Agent commits any act listed in item (i) of the preceding paragraph in violation of provisions of that paragraph, the amount of the profit obtained by the Com-

mercial Agent or any third party as a result of such act shall be presumed to be amount of the damage suffered by the Company.

(Authority to Receive Notice)
Article 18 A Commercial Agent to whom the authority of the sale of goods or the role of intermediary in the same is delegated shall have authority to receive the notice regarding the sale and purchase including, but not limited to, the notice under Article 526(2) of the Commercial Code (Act No. 48 of 1899).

(Cancellation of Commercial Agency Contract)
Article 19 (1) A Company or the Commercial Agent may, when they did not define the period of the commercial agency contract, cancel the contract by giving an advance notice more than two months in advance.
(2) Notwithstanding the provisions of the preceding paragraph, if there is any compelling reason, the Company or its Commercial Agent may cancel the commercial agency contract at any time.

(Right of Retention of Commercial Agent)
Article 20 If any claim arising from acting as an agent or intermediary in any transaction is due, the Commercial Agent can retain any property or negotiable instruments of value which it possesses on behalf of the Company until the satisfaction of such claim, provided, however, that this shall not apply to the cases where the parties otherwise manifest their intention.

Chapter IV Non-Competition after Assignment of Business

(Non-competition by Assignor Company)
Article 21 (1) Unless the parties otherwise manifest their intention, a Company which assigned its business (hereinafter in this Chapter referred to as "Assignor Company") may not carry out the same line of business within the area of the same city, town or village (hereinafter in this Section referring to "ward" for the area in which special wards of Tokyo are located and for the cities designated under Article 252-19(1) of the Local Autonomy Act (Act No. 67 of 1947)), or within the area of any of its neighboring cities, towns or villages for twenty years from the day of the assignment of the business.
(2) In cases where the Assignor Company agreed to a special provision to the effect that it will not carry out the same line of the business, the effectiveness of the special provision shall be limited to the period of thirty years from the day of the assignment of the business.
(3) Notwithstanding the provisions of the preceding two paragraphs, the Assignor Company may not carry out the same line of business with the purpose of unfair competition.

(Liabilities of Assignee Company using the Trade Name of the Assignor Company)
Article 22 (1) In cases where any Company to which any business is assigned (hereinafter in this Chapter referred to as "Assignee Company") continues to use the trade name of the Assignor Company, the Assignee Company shall also be liable for the performance of any obligations having arisen from the business of the Assignor Company.
(2) The provisions of the preceding paragraph shall not apply in cases where the Assignee Company registers, at the location of its head office, without delay after it has accepted

the assignment of the business, a statement to the effect that it will not be liable for the performance of the obligations of the Assignor Company. In cases where the Assignee Company and Assignor Company give notice to the above effect to any third party without delay after the assignment of the business, the provisions of the immediately preceding sentence shall apply to the third party who receives such notice.

(3) In cases where the Assignee Company is liable for the performance of the obligations of the Assignor Company pursuant to the provisions of paragraph (1), the liability of the Assignee Company shall be extinguished upon lapse of two years after the day of the assignment of the business vis-a-vis any obligee who does not demand the performance, or does not give an advance notice of his/her demand, within that period.

(4) In cases provided for in paragraph (1), any performance made vis-a-vis the Assignee Company with respect to any claim arising from the business of the Assignor Company shall remain effective if the performing party is without knowledge and is not grossly negligent.

(Assumption of Obligations by Assignee Company)

Article 23 (1) Even in cases where an Assignee Company does not continue to use the trade name of the Assignor Company, if it advertises to the effect that it will assume the obligations that has arisen from the business of the Assignor Company, the obligees of the Assignor Company may demand the performance against the Assignee Company.

(2) In cases where the Assignee Company is liable for the performance of the obligations of the Assignor Company pursuant to the provisions of the preceding paragraph, the liability of the Assignor Company shall be extinguished upon lapse of two years after the day of the advertisement under that paragraph vis-a-vis any obligee who does not demand the performance, or does not give an advance notice of his/her demand, within that period.

(Assignment of Business to or from a Merchant)

Article 24 (1) In cases where a Company assigns its business to a merchant, such Company shall be deemed to be the assignee provided for in paragraph (1) of Article 16 of the Commercial Code, and the provisions of Article 17 and Article 18 of the Code shall apply.

(2) In cases where a Company accepts assignment of the enterprise of any merchant, such merchant shall be deemed to be the Assignor Company, and the provisions of the preceding two articles shall apply.

PART II Stock Company

Chapter I Incorporation

Section 1 General Provisions

Article 25 (1) A Stock Company may be incorporated by either of the following methods:
  (i) The method by which incorporator(s) subscribe(s) for all Shares Issued at Incorporation (meaning the shares which are issued at incorporation of a Stock Company. The same shall apply hereinafter) pursuant to the provisions of the next Section to Section 8 inclusive; or
  (ii) The method by which, in addition to the subscription by incorporator(s) for the Shares Issued at Incorporation, person(s) who will subscribe for the Shares Issued at Incorporation is/are solicited pursuant to the provisions of the next Section, Sec-

tion 3, Article 39 and Section 6 to Section 9 inclusive.
(2) Each incorporator shall subscribe for one or more Shares Issued at Incorporation in the incorporation of a Stock Company.

Section 2 Preparation of Articles of Incorporation

(Preparation of Articles of Incorporation)
Article 26 (1) In order to incorporate a Stock Company, incorporator(s) shall prepare articles of incorporation, and all incorporators shall sign or affix the name(s) and seal(s) to it.
(2) Articles of incorporation set forth in the preceding paragraph may be prepared by Electromagnetic Records (meaning records produced by electronic forms, magnetic forms, or any other forms unrecognizable by human senses, which are for computer data-processing use as prescribed by the applicable Ordinance of the Ministry of Justice. The same shall apply hereinafter.). In such cases, actions prescribed by the applicable Ordinance of the Ministry of Justice shall be taken in lieu of the signing or the affixing of the names and seals, with respect to the data recorded in such Electromagnetic Records.

(Matters to be Specified or Recorded in the articles of incorporation)
Article 27 Articles of incorporation of a Stock Company shall specify or record the following matters:
(i) Purpose(s);
(ii) Trade name;
(iii) Location of the head office;
(iv) Value of property to be contributed at the incorporation or the lower limit thereof;
(v) Name(s) and address(es) of the incorporator(s).

Article 28 In cases where a Stock Company is to be incorporated, the following matters shall not become effective unless they are specified or recorded in the articles of incorporation referred to in Article 26(1):
(i) Name(s) of person(s) who contribute(s) by any property other than money, the description of such property and the value thereof, and the number of the Shares Issued at Incorporation that are to be allotted to such person(s) (in cases where the Stock Company to be incorporated is a Company with Class Shares, referring to the class(es) and the number of each class of the Shares Issued at Incorporation; the same shall apply in item (i) of Article 32(1));
(ii) Property that is agreed to be assigned to the Stock Company after the formation thereof, the value thereof, and the name of the assignor;
(iii) Compensation or other special benefit which the incorporator(s) is to obtain by the formation of the Stock Company, and the name(s) of such incorporator(s); and
(iv) Expenses regarding the incorporation that are borne by the Stock Company (excluding the fees for the certification of the articles of incorporation, and other expenses which are prescribed by the applicable Ordinance of the Ministry of Justice as expenses that are unlikely to cause harm to the Stock Company)

Article 29 In addition to the matters listed in each item of Article 27 and each item of the preceding article, articles of incorporation of a Stock Company may specify or record the matters which, pursuant to the provisions of this Act, may not become effective unless provided for in the articles of incorporation, or other matters which do not violate any provision of this Act.

(Certification of Articles of Incorporation)

Article 30 (1) Articles of incorporation set forth in Article 26(1) shall not become effective unless they are certified by a notary public.

(2) Articles of incorporation that are certified by a notary public pursuant to the preceding paragraph may not be amended before the formation of the Stock Company except when they are amended under the provisions of Article 33(7) or (9), or Article 37(1) or (2).

(Keeping and Inspection of Articles of Incorporation)

Article 31 (1) The incorporator(s) (or the Stock Company after the formation of such Stock Company) shall keep articles of incorporation at the place designated by the incorporator(s) (or at the head office or branch office of the Stock Company after the formation of such Stock Company).

(2) The incorporator(s) (or, after the formation of such Stock Company, the shareholder(s) and creditor(s) of such Stock Company) may submit the following request at any time during the hours designated by the incorporator(s) (or, after the formation of such Stock Company, during the business hours of such Stock Company); provided, however, that the fees designated by the incorporator(s) (or, after the formation of such Stock Company, such Stock Company) are required to be paid in order to submit the requests listed in item (ii) or item (iv):

(i) If articles of incorporation are prepared in writing, a request to inspect it;

(ii) A request for a transcript or extract of the articles of incorporation referred to in the preceding item;

(iii) If articles of incorporation are prepared by Electromagnetic Records, a request to inspect anything that displays the data recorded in such Electromagnetic Records in a manner prescribed by the applicable Ordinance of the Ministry of Justice; or

(iv) A request that the matters recorded in the Electromagnetic Records set forth in the preceding item be provided by an Electromagnetic Method designated by the incorporator(s) (or, after the formation of such Stock Company, such Stock Company), or a request for any document that contains such data

(3) If, after the formation of a Stock Company, it is necessary for the purpose of exercising the rights of a Member of the Parent Company (meaning the shareholders and other members of the Parent Companies. The same shall apply hereinafter.) of such Stock Company, such Member of the Parent Company may, with the permission of the court, make the requests listed in each item of the preceding paragraph with respect to the articles of incorporation of such Stock Company; provided, however, that, in order to make the requests listed in item (ii) or item (iv) of that paragraph, the fees designated by such Stock Company is required to be paid.

(4) In cases where articles of incorporation are prepared by Electromagnetic Records, for the purpose of the application of the provisions of paragraph (1) with respect to a Stock Company which adopts the measures prescribed by the applicable Ordinance of the Ministry of Justice as the measures that enable its branch offices to respond to the request listed in item (iii) and item (iv) of paragraph (2), "head office and branch office" in that paragraph shall be deemed to be replaced with "head office."

Section 3 Contributions

(Determination of Matters regarding Shares Issued at Incorporation)

Article 32 (1) When incorporator(s) determine the following matters at the incorporation of the Stock Company (excluding matters provided for in the articles of incorpora-

tion), he/she shall obtain the consent of all incorporators:
(i) The number of the Shares Issued at Incorporation that is to be allotted to each incorporator;
(ii) The amount of money to be paid in exchange for the Shares Issued at Incorporation set forth in the preceding item; and
(iii) Matters regarding the amount of the stated capital and capital reserves of the Stock Company after the formation.
(2) In cases where the Stock Company to be incorporated is a Company with Class Shares, if the Shares Issued at Incorporation set forth in item (i) of the preceding paragraph are those which are provided for in the articles of incorporation under the provisions of the first sentence of Article 108(3), the incorporator(s) shall, with the consent of all incorporators, determine the features of such Shares Issued at Incorporation.

(Election of Inspector of Matters Specified or Recorded in the Articles of Incorporation)
Article 33 (1) If articles of incorporation specify or record the matters listed in each item of Article 28, the incorporator(s) shall, without delay after the certification by the notary public under Article 30(1), file a petition for the election of an inspector with the court in order to have the inspector investigate such matters.
(2) In cases where the petition set forth in the preceding paragraph has been filed, the court shall elect the inspector except in case it dismisses such petition as non-conforming.
(3) In cases where the court has elected the inspector set forth in the preceding paragraph, it may fix the amount of the remuneration that the Stock Company after the formation pays to such inspector.
(4) The inspector set forth in paragraph (2) shall conduct necessary investigation and shall report the court by submitting documents or Electromagnetic Records (limited to those prescribed by the applicable Ordinance of the Ministry of Justice) which specifies or records the result of such investigation.
(5) If the court finds it necessary for the purpose of clarification of the contents of the report set forth in the preceding paragraph or of confirmation of the grounds supporting such report, it may request the inspector set forth in paragraph (2) a further report set forth in the preceding paragraph.
(6) When the inspector set forth in paragraph (2) reports pursuant to paragraph (4), he/she shall give the incorporator(s) a copy of the documents set forth in that paragraph, or provide the matters recorded in the Electromagnetic Records set forth in that paragraph by the method prescribed by the applicable Ordinance of the Ministry of Justice.
(7) In cases where the court receives a report under paragraph (4), if it finds the provisions in articles of incorporation relating to matters listed in each item of Article 28 (excluding any matters not subjected to the investigation by the inspector under paragraph (2)) to be improper, it shall make a ruling amending the same.
(8) In cases where some or all of the provisions in articles of incorporation relating to matters listed in each item of Article 28 are amended by a ruling set forth in the preceding paragraph, the incorporator(s) may rescind his/her manifestation of intention relating to subscription for the relevant Shares Issued at Incorporation within one week from the finalization of such ruling.
(9) In the cases prescribed in the preceding paragraph, the incorporator(s) may, with the consent of all incorporators, amend articles of incorporation repealing the provisions which have been amended by such ruling, within one week from the finalization of the ruling set forth in paragraph (7).
(10) The provisions of the preceding nine paragraphs shall not apply to the matters pre-

scribed in following items:
(i) In cases where the total value specified or recorded in the articles of incorporation with respect to the property under item (i) and item (ii) of Article 28 (hereinafter in this Chapter referred to as "Properties Contributed in Kind") does not exceed 5,000,000 yen: Matters listed in item (i) and item (ii) of such Article;
(ii) In cases where the value specified or recorded in the articles of incorporation with respect to the Properties Contributed in Kind that are Securities (meaning the securities provided for in paragraph (1) of Article 2 of the Financial Instruments and Exchange Act (Act No. 25 of 1948), including rights deemed to be securities pursuant to the provisions of paragraph (2) of such Article. The same shall apply hereinafter.) with a market price does not exceed the value calculated by the method prescribed by the applicable Ordinance of the Ministry of Justice as the market price of such Securities: Matters listed in item (i) and item (ii) of Article 28 with respect to such Securities;
(iii) In cases where the verification of an attorney, a legal professional Company, a Certified Public Accountant (including a foreign certified public accountant as defined in Article 16-2(5) of the Certified Public Accountant Act (Act No. 103 of 1948). The same shall apply hereinafter.), an auditing firm, a tax accountant or a tax accountant corporation (in cases where the Properties Contributed in Kind consist of any real estate, referring to such verification and appraisal by a real property appraiser; hereinafter the same shall apply in this item) is obtained with respect to the reasonableness of the value specified or recorded in the articles of incorporation with respect to the Properties Contributed in Kind: Matters listed in item (i) and item (ii) of Article 28 (limited to those relating to the Properties Contributed in Kind so verified).
(11) None of the following persons may provide the verification prescribed in item (iii) of the preceding paragraph:
(i) An incorporator;
(ii) An assignor of property under item (ii) of Article 28;
(iii) A Director at Incorporation (referring to a Director at Incorporation prescribed in paragraph (1) of Article 38) or an Auditor at Incorporation (referring to an Auditor at Incorporation prescribed for in item (ii), paragraph (2) of such Article);
(iv) A person who is subject to the disciplinary action ordering a suspension of operations and for whom the period of such suspension has not yet elapsed; or
(v) A legal professional Company, an auditing Company or a tax accountant Company more than half of whose members are persons who fall under any of the item (i) to (iii) above inclusive.

(Performance of Contributions)
Article 34 (1) Incorporator(s) shall, without delay after subscription for Shares Issued at Incorporation, contribute fully in money or in kind, with respect to the Shares Issued at Incorporation for which he/she has subscribed; provided, however, that, if the consent of all incorporator(s) is obtained, the foregoing provisions do not preclude him/her from performing registration, recording or other acts necessary to assert the creation or transfer of rights against third parties after the formation of the Stock Company.
(2) The contribution in money pursuant to the provisions of the preceding paragraph shall be paid at the Bank, Etc. (meaning a Bank (meaning a bank as defined in Article 2(1) of the Bank Act (Act No. 59 of 1981). The same shall apply in Article 703(1)), a Trust Company (meaning a trust company as defined in Article 2(2) of the Trust Business Act (Act No. 154 of 2004). The same shall apply hereinafter) and other entities pre-

scribed by the applicable Ordinance of the Ministry of Justice as entities equivalent to the same. The same shall apply hereinafter.) designated for payment by the incorporator.

(Assignment of Right to Become a Shareholder of Shares Issued at Incorporation)
Article 35 The assignment of the right to become a shareholder of the Shares Issued at Incorporation by contribution pursuant to the provisions of paragraph (1) of the preceding article (hereinafter in this Chapter referred to as "Performance of Contributions") may not be asserted against the Stock Company after the formation.

(Forfeiture of Right to Become a Shareholder of Shares Issued at Incorporation)
Article 36 (1) In cases where not all of the incorporators fulfill the Performance of Contributions, the incorporators shall set a date and notify any incorporator who does not fulfill the Performance of Contributions that such incorporator shall fulfill the Performance of Contributions by such date.
(2) The notice set forth in the provisions of the preceding paragraph shall be given no later than two weeks prior to the date provided for in such paragraph.
(3) Incorporator(s) who is notified pursuant to the provisions of paragraph (1) shall forfeit the right to become the shareholder of Shares Issued at Incorporation by fulfilling the Performance of Contributions if the same fail to fulfill the Performance of Contributions by the date provided for in such paragraph.

(Provisions on Total Number of Authorized Shares)
Article 37 (1) In cases where the total number of shares that may be issued by a Stock Company (hereinafter referred to as "Total Number of Authorized Shares") is not provided for in the articles of incorporation, the incorporators shall, with the consent of all incorporators, amend the articles of incorporation and create a provision on the Total Number of Authorized Shares prior to the formation of the Stock Company.
(2) In cases where the Total Number of Authorized Shares is provided for in the articles of incorporation, the incorporators may, with the consent of all incorporators, amend the articles of incorporation with respect to the Total Number of Authorized Shares at any time prior to the formation of the Stock Company.
(3) The total number of Shares Issued at Incorporation may not be less than one quarter of the Total Number of Authorized Shares; provided, however, that this shall not apply in cases where the Stock Company to be incorporated is not a Public Company.

Section 4 Election and Dismissal of Officers at Incorporation

(Election of Officers at Incorporation)
Article 38 (1) The incorporator(s) shall elect the Director(s) at Incorporation (meaning person(s) who becomes director(s) at the incorporation. The same shall apply hereinafter) without delay after the fulfillment of the Performance of Contributions.
(2) In the cases listed in the following items, the incorporator(s) shall elect the persons provided for respectively in those items without delay after the fulfillment of the Performance of Contributions:
  (i) In cases where the Stock Company to be incorporated is a Company with Accounting Advisors: Accounting Advisor(s) at Incorporation (meaning a person who becomes an accounting advisor at the incorporation. The same shall apply hereinafter.)

(ii) In cases where the Stock Company to be incorporated is a Company with Auditors (including any Stock Company the articles of incorporation of which provide that the scope of the audit by its auditor(s) is limited to an audit related to accounting): Auditor(s) at Incorporation (meaning a person who becomes an auditor at the incorporation. The same shall apply hereinafter.)
(iii) In cases where the Stock Company to be incorporated is a Company with Accounting Auditors: Accounting Auditor(s) at Incorporation (meaning a person who becomes an accounting auditor at the incorporation. The same shall apply hereinafter.)
(3) Persons who are prescribed in articles of incorporation as Directors at Incorporation, Accounting Advisors at Incorporation, Auditors at Incorporation, and Accounting Auditors at Incorporation shall be deemed to be elected as Directors at Incorporation, Accounting Advisors at Incorporation, Auditors at Incorporation, and Accounting Auditors at Incorporation, respectively, upon the fulfillment of the Performance of Contributions.

Article 39 (1) In cases where a Stock Company to be incorporated is a Company with Board of Directors, there shall be three or more Directors at Incorporation.
(2) In cases where a Stock Company to be incorporated is a Company with Board of Auditors, there shall be three or more Auditors at Incorporation.
(3) A person who may not be a director, accounting advisor, auditor or accounting auditor of a Stock Company after formation pursuant to the provisions of paragraph (1) of Article 331 (including the case where it is applied mutatis mutandis pursuant to Article 335(1)), Article 333(1) or (3), or Article 337(1) or (3) may not become a Director at Incorporation, an Accounting Advisor at Incorporation, an Auditor at Incorporation, or an Accounting Auditor at Incorporation (hereinafter referred to as "Officers at Incorporation"), respectively.

(Method of Election of Officers at Incorporation)
Article 40 (1) The election of the Officers at Incorporation shall be determined by a majority of the votes of the incorporators.
(2) In the cases provided for in the preceding paragraph, an incorporator shall be entitled to one vote for each one Share Issued at Incorporation for which the Performance of Contributions has been fulfilled; provided, however, that, in cases where the Share Unit is provided for in the articles of incorporation, he/she shall be entitled to one vote for each one unit of the Shares Issued at Incorporation.
(3) Notwithstanding the provisions of the preceding paragraph, in cases where the Stock Company to be incorporated is a Company with Class Shares, if it issues Shares Issued at Incorporation of a class for which it is provided that the voting rights may not be exercised in connection with the election of some or all of the directors, with respect to such class of the Shares Issued at Incorporation, the incorporators may not exercise voting rights in connection with the election of the Directors at Incorporation who are to become such directors.
(4) The provisions of the preceding paragraph shall apply mutatis mutandis to the election of Accounting Advisors at Incorporation, Auditors at Incorporation and Accounting Auditors at Incorporation.

(Special Provisions on the Method of Election of Officers at Incorporation)
Article 41 (1) Notwithstanding the provisions of paragraph (1) of the preceding article, in cases where, at the incorporation of a Stock Company, it issues shares of a class for which the matters listed in item (ix) of Article 108(1) (limited to those relating to di-

rectors) are provided, the election of the Directors at Incorporation shall be determined by a majority of the votes (limited to the votes with respect to such class of the Shares Issued at Incorporation) of the incorporators who subscribed for such class of the Shares Issued at Incorporation, consistently with the provisions of articles of incorporation with respect to the matters provided for in item (ix), paragraph (2) of such Article.
(2) In the cases provided for in the preceding paragraph, an incorporator shall be entitled to one vote for each one Share Issued at Incorporation of such class for which the Performance of Contributions is fulfilled; provided, however, that, in cases where the Share Unit is provided for in the articles of incorporation, he/she shall be entitled to one vote for each one unit of the Shares Issued at Incorporation of such class.
(3) The provisions of the preceding two paragraphs shall apply mutatis mutandis to the cases where the shares of a class for which matters listed in item (ix), paragraph (1) of Article 108 (limited to those relating to auditors) are provided are issued at incorporation of the Stock Company.

(Dismissal of Officers at Incorporation)
Article 42 The incorporators may dismiss Officer(s) at Incorporation elected by the incorporators (including those deemed to be elected as Officer(s) at Incorporation pursuant to the provisions of Article 38(3)) at any time prior to the formation of the Stock Company.

(Method of Dismissal of Officers at Incorporation)
Article 43 (1) Dismissal of Officer(s) at Incorporation shall be determined by a majority of the votes of the incorporators (or by a majority of two thirds or more in case of dismissal of Auditor(s) at Incorporation).
(2) In the cases provided for in the preceding paragraph, an incorporator shall be entitled to one vote for each one Share Issued at Incorporation for which the Performance of Contributions has been fulfilled; provided, however, that, in cases where the Share Unit is provided for in the articles of incorporation, he/she shall be entitled to one vote for each one unit of the Shares Issued at Incorporation.
(3) Notwithstanding the provisions of the preceding paragraph, in cases where the Stock Company to be incorporated is a Company with Class Shares, if it issues Shares Issued at Incorporation of a class for which it is provided that the voting rights may not be exercised in connection with the dismissal of some or all of the directors, with respect to such class of the Shares Issued at Incorporation, the incorporators may not exercise voting rights in connection with the dismissal of the Directors at Incorporation who are to become such directors.
(4) The provisions of the preceding paragraph shall apply mutatis mutandis to the dismissal of Accounting Advisors at Incorporation, Auditors at Incorporation and Accounting Auditors at Incorporation.

(Special Provisions on Method of Dismissal of Directors at Incorporation)
Article 44 (1) Notwithstanding the provisions of paragraph (1) of the preceding article, the dismissal of Director(s) at Incorporation who is elected pursuant to the provisions of paragraph (1) of Article 41 shall be determined by a majority of the votes of the incorporators relating to such election.
(2) Notwithstanding the provisions of the preceding paragraph, in cases where there is a provision in the articles of incorporation to the effect that a director who is elected pursuant to the provisions of paragraph (1) of Article 41, or is elected at a Class Organizational Meeting (referring to Class Organizational Meeting provided for in Article

84) or at a Class Meeting may be dismissed by a resolution of the shareholders' meeting, the dismissal of the Director at Incorporation who is elected pursuant to such provisions shall be determined by a majority of the votes of the incorporators.
(3) In the cases provided for in the preceding paragraph, an incorporator shall be entitled to one vote for each one Share Issued at Incorporation of such class for which the Performance of Contributions is fulfilled; provided, however, that, in cases where the Share Unit is provided for in the articles of incorporation, he/she shall be entitled to one vote for each one unit of the Shares Issued at Incorporation of such class.
(4) Notwithstanding the provisions of the preceding paragraph, in cases where a Director at Incorporation is to be dismissed pursuant to the provisions of paragraph (2) above, if Shares Issued at Incorporation of a class for which it is provided that the voting rights may not be exercised in connection with the dismissal of some or all of the directors are to be issued, with respect to such class of the Shares Issued at Incorporation, the incorporators may not exercise voting rights in connection with the dismissal of the Directors at Incorporation who are to become such directors.
(5) The provisions of the preceding four paragraphs shall apply mutatis mutandis to the dismissal of Auditors at Incorporation who are elected pursuant to the provisions of Article 41(1) which shall be applied mutatis mutandis under paragraph (3) of such Article. In such case, the term "majority" in paragraph (1) and paragraph (2) shall be deemed to be replaced with "majority of two thirds or more."

(Special Provisions on Effect of Election or Dismissal of Officers as at Incorporation)

Article 45 (1) In cases where, at the incorporation of a Stock Company, it issues shares of a class for which the matters listed in item (viii) of Article 108(1) are provided, if there are provisions in the articles of incorporation to the effect that a resolution of the Class Meeting is required with respect to the matters listed in the following items as the features of the shares of such class, the matters provided for in each of such items shall not become effective unless, in addition to the determination pursuant to the provisions of Article 40(1) or Article 43(1), there is a determination by a majority of the votes (limited to the votes with respect to the Shares Issued at Incorporation of such class) of the incorporators who subscribe for the Shares Issued at Incorporation of such class in accordance with the applicable provisions of the articles of incorporation:
(i) Election or dismissal of some or all of the directors: Election or dismissal of Directors at Incorporation who are to become such directors;
(ii) Election or dismissal of some or all of the accounting advisors: Election or dismissal of Accounting Advisors at Incorporation who are to become such accounting advisors;
(iii) Election or dismissal of some or all of the auditors: Election or dismissal of Auditors at Incorporation who are to become such auditors;
(iv) Election or dismissal of some or all of the accounting auditors: Election or dismissal of Accounting Auditors at Incorporation who are to become such accounting auditors.
(2) In the cases provided for in the preceding paragraph, an incorporator shall be entitled to one vote for each one Share Issued at Incorporation of such class for which the Performance of Contributions is fulfilled; provided, however, that, in cases where the Share Unit is provided for in the articles of incorporation, he/she shall be entitled to one vote for each one unit of the Shares Issued at Incorporation of such class.

Section 5 Investigation by Directors at Incorporation

Article 46 (1) The Directors at Incorporation (referring to the Directors at Incorporation and Auditor at Incorporation in cases where the Stock Company to be incorporated is a Company with Auditors. The same shall apply hereinafter in this Article.) shall investigate the following matters without delay after their election:
(i) That, with respect to the Properties Contributed in Kind in the cases listed in item (i) or item (ii) of Article 33(10) (if listed in such item, limited to the securities under such item), the value specified or recorded in the articles of incorporation is reasonable;
(ii) That the verification provided for in item (iii) of Article 33(10) is appropriate;
(iii) That the Performance of Contributions has been fulfilled; and
(iv) That, in addition to the matters listed in the preceding three items, the procedures for the incorporation of the Stock Company do not violate the applicable laws and regulations or articles of incorporation.
(2) If, as a result of the investigation pursuant to the preceding paragraph, the Directors at Incorporation find that there is any violation of the applicable laws and regulations or articles of incorporation or there is any inappropriate matter in a matter listed in any item of such paragraph, directors shall give notice to such effect to the incorporator;
(3) In cases where the Stock Company to be incorporated is a Company with Committees, the Director at Incorporation shall give the Representative Executive Officer at Incorporation (referring to the Representative Executive Officer at Incorporation provided for in item (iii) of Article 48(1)) notice to the effect that the investigation under paragraph (1) has been completed, or, if the notice under the preceding paragraph has been given, notice that such notice was given and a description of the contents thereof.

Section 6 Appointment etc. of Representative Directors at Incorporation etc.

(Appointment etc. of Representative Directors at Incorporation)
Article 47 (1) In cases where the Stock Company to be incorporated is a Company with Board of Directors (excluding a Company with Committees), the Directors at Incorporation shall appoint among the Directors at Incorporation a person who shall be the Representative Director (meaning the director who represents the Stock Company. The same shall apply hereinafter.) as at incorporation of the Stock Company (hereinafter referred to as "Representative Director at Incorporation").
(2) The Directors at Incorporation may remove the Representative Director at Incorporation at any time prior to the formation of the Stock Company.
(3) The appointment and removal of the Representative Director at Incorporation pursuant to the provisions of the preceding two paragraphs shall be determined by a majority of the Directors at Incorporation.

(Appointment of Committee Members at Incorporation)
Article 48 (1) In cases where the Stock Company to be incorporated is a Company with Committees, the Director at Incorporation shall:
(i) appoint the following persons (in the next paragraph referred to as "Committee Members at Incorporation") among the Directors at Incorporation:
　(a) Persons who shall be members of the nominating committee at incorporation of the Stock Company:
　(b) Persons who shall be committee members of the audit committee at incorporation of the Stock Company:
　(c) Persons who shall be committee members of the compensation committee at

incorporation of the Stock Company:
(ii) elect persons who shall be the executive officers at incorporation of the Stock Company (hereinafter referred to as "Executive Officers at Incorporation"); and
(iii) appoint among the Executive Officers at Incorporation the persons who shall be the representative executive officers at incorporation of the Stock Company (hereinafter referred to as "Representative Executive Officers at Incorporation"); provided, however, that, if there is only one Executive Officer at Incorporation, such person shall be deemed to have been appointed as the Representative Executive Officer at Incorporation.
(2) At any time prior to the formation of the Stock Company, the Directors at Incorporation may remove the Committee Members at Incorporation or the Representative Executive Officers at Incorporation, or dismiss the Executive Officers at Incorporation.
(3) The decision pursuant to the provisions of the preceding two paragraphs shall be made by a majority of the Directors at Incorporation.

Section 7 Formation of Stock Companies

(Formation of Stock Companies)
Article 49 A Stock Company shall be formed by the registration of the incorporation at the location of its head office.

(Right of Subscribers of Shares)
Article 50 (1) As at formation of a Stock Company, the incorporator shall be a shareholder for the Shares Issued at Incorporation for which the Performance of Contributions has been fulfilled.
(2) The assignment of the right to become a shareholder pursuant to the provisions of the preceding paragraph may not be asserted against the Stock Company after the formation.

(Restrictions on Invalidation or Rescission of Subscription)
Article 51 (1) The proviso to Article 93 and the provisions of Article 94(1) of the Civil Code (Act No. 89 of 1896) shall not apply to the manifestation of intention relating to the subscription for Shares Issued at Incorporation.
(2) After the formation of the Stock Company, the incorporator(s) may not assert the invalidity of his/her subscription for Shares Issued at Incorporation on the grounds of mistake, nor rescind his/her subscription for Shares Issued at Incorporation on the grounds of fraud or duress.

Section 8 Liability of Incorporators

(Liability for Insufficiency of Value of Properties Contributed)
Article 52 (1) If the value of the Properties Contributed in Kind at formation of a Stock Company is substantially short of the value specified or recorded in the articles of incorporation with respect to such Properties Contributed in Kind (or if there is any amendment of the articles of incorporation, the value so amended), the incorporators and Directors at Incorporation shall be jointly and severally liable to such Stock Company for the payment of the amount of such shortfall.
(2) Notwithstanding the provisions of the preceding paragraph, the incorporators (in this paragraph and in item (ii) excluding those who contributed in kind under item (i) of Article 28 or the assignor of the property under item (ii) of the same Article) and Directors at Incorporation shall not be held liable in accordance with such paragraph with

respect to the Properties Contributed in Kind in the following cases:
(i) Where the investigation by the inspector under Article 33(2) has been carried out with respect to the matters listed in item (i) or item (ii) of Article 28; or
(ii) Where such incorporators or Directors at Incorporation prove that they did not fail to exercise due care with respect to the performance of their duties.
(3) In the cases set forth in paragraph (1), the person who carried out the verification provided for in item (iii) of Article 33(10) (hereinafter in this paragraph referred to as "Verifier") shall be jointly and severally liable with the person who assumes the liability under paragraph (1) for the payment of the amount of the shortfall under such paragraph; provided, however, that this shall not apply in cases where such Verifier prove that he/she did not fail to exercise due care with respect to the carrying out such verification.

(Liability for Damages of Incorporators)
Article 53 (1) If an incorporator, Director at Incorporation or Auditor at Incorporation neglects his/her duties with respect to the incorporation of a Stock Company, he/she shall be liable to such Stock Company for damages arising as a result thereof.
(2) If an incorporator, Director at Incorporation or Auditor at Incorporation are with knowledge or grossly negligent in performing his/her duties, such incorporator, Director at Incorporation or Auditor at Incorporation shall be liable to a third party for damages arising as a result thereof.

(Joint and Several Liabilities of Incorporators)
Article 54 In cases where an incorporator, a Director at Incorporation or an Auditor at Incorporation is liable for damages arising in the Stock Company or a third party, if other incorporators, Directors at Incorporation or Auditors at Incorporation are also liable, such persons shall be joint and several obligors.

(Exemption from Liability)
Article 55 An exemption from the obligations assumed by an incorporator or Director at Incorporation pursuant to the provisions of Article 52(1) and the liability assumed by an incorporator, Director at Incorporation or Auditor at Incorporation pursuant to the provisions of Article 53(1) may not be given without the consent of all shareholders.

(Liability in cases of Failure to Form a Stock Company)
Article 56 If the formation of a Stock Company fails, the incorporator(s) shall be jointly and severally liable for any act committed in connection with the incorporation of the Stock Company, and shall bear the costs expended in connection with the incorporation of the Stock Company.

Section 9 Incorporation by Solicitation

Subsection 1 Solicitation of Persons who Subscribe for Shares Issued at Incorporation

(Solicitation of Persons who Subscribe for Shares Issued at Incorporation)
Article 57 (1) Pursuant to the provisions of this Subsection, the incorporators may provide to the effect that subscribers be solicited for the Shares Issued at Incorporation.
(2) Incorporators intending to provide to the effect that the solicitation under the preceding paragraph be carried out shall obtain the consent of all incorporators.

(Provision for Matters regarding Shares Solicited at Incorporation)
Article 58 (1) Whenever the incorporator intends to carry out the solicitation under paragraph (1) of the preceding article, he/she shall decide the following matters with respect to the Shares Solicited at Incorporation (meaning the Shares Issued at Incorporation that are allotted to the persons who accept the solicitation under such paragraph and apply to subscribe for the Shares Issued at Incorporation. The same shall apply hereinafter in this Section.):
  (i) The number of the Shares Solicited at Incorporation (in cases where the Stock Company to be incorporated is a Company with Class Shares, referring to the class(es) and the number of each class of Shares Solicited at Incorporation. The same shall apply hereinafter in this Subsection.);
  (ii) The Amount to be Paid In for Shares Issued at Incorporation (meaning the amount of money which is to be paid in in exchange for one Share Solicited at Incorporation. The same shall apply hereinafter in this Subsection.);
  (iii) The date by or period during which payment is to be made of the money to be paid in in exchange for the Shares Solicited at Incorporation;
  (iv) If there is any arrangement that subscriptions for Shares Solicited at Incorporation may be rescinded in cases where the registration of incorporation is not effected by a certain date, a statement of such arrangement and such date.
(2) If the incorporator intends to determine the matters listed in any item of the preceding paragraph, he/she shall obtain the consent of all incorporators.
(3) The conditions for the solicitation under paragraph (1) of the preceding article, such as the Amount to be Paid In for Shares Solicited at Incorporation, shall be decided uniformly for each such solicitation (or, in cases where the Stock Company to be incorporated is a Company with Class Shares, for each such class and solicitation).

(Subscription for Shares Solicited at Incorporation)
Article 59 (1) The incorporator shall notify the person who, in response to the solicitation under paragraph (1) of Article 57, intends to apply to subscribe for the Shares Solicited at Incorporation of the following matters:
  (i) The date of the certification of the articles of incorporation and the name of the notary public who effected such certification;
  (ii) The matters listed in each item of Article 27, each item of Article 28, each item of Article 32(1) and each item of paragraph (1) of the preceding article;
  (iii) The value of the property contributed by the incorporator(s);
  (iv) The place designated for payment pursuant to the provisions of Article 63(1);
  (v) In addition to the foregoing, any other matters provided by applicable Ordinance of the Ministry of Justice.
(2) In cases where not all of the incorporators fulfill the Performance of Contributions, the incorporators may not give the notice pursuant to the provisions of the preceding paragraph until after the date provided for in Article 36(1).
(3) A person who intends to apply to subscribe for Shares Solicited at Incorporation in response to a solicitation under Article 57(1) shall give the incorporators a document that states the following matters:
  (i) The name and address of the person who intends to apply; and
  (ii) The number of Shares Solicited at Incorporation that he/she intends to subscribe for.
(4) A person who submits the application referred to in the preceding paragraph may, in lieu of the giving of the document under such paragraph, provide the matters to be stated in the document under such paragraph by an Electromagnetic Method, with the approval of the incorporators, subject to the provisions of the applicable Cabinet Order.

In such cases, the person who submitted the application shall be deemed to have given a document under such paragraph.

(5) If there are changes in the matters listed in any item of paragraph (1), the incorporators shall immediately notify persons who submitted applications under paragraph (3) (hereinafter in this Subsection referred to as "Applicants") thereof and of the matters so changed.

(6) It would be sufficient for a notice or demand to an Applicant by the incorporators to be sent to the address under item (i) of paragraph (3) (or, in cases where such Applicant notifies the incorporators of a different place or contact address for the receipt of notices or demand, to such place or contact address).

(7) The notice or demand referred to in the preceding paragraph shall be deemed to have arrived at the time when such notice or demand should normally have arrived.

(Allotment of Shares Solicited at Incorporation)
Article 60 (1) The incorporators shall specify from among the Applicants the persons to whom the Shares Solicited at Incorporation are allotted, and specify the number of the Shares Solicited at Incorporation that are allotted to such persons. In such cases, the incorporators may reduce the number of the Shares Solicited at Incorporation to be allotted to such Applicants to less than the number referred to in item (ii), paragraph (3) of the preceding article.

(2) The incorporator shall notify the Applicant, no later than the day immediately preceding the date referred to in item (iii) of Article 58(1) (or, in case a period is specified under that item, no later than the day immediately preceding the first day of that period), of the number of the Shares Solicited at Incorporation that are allotted to such Applicant.

(Special Provisions on the Subscription for and Allotment of Shares Solicited at Incorporation)
Article 61 The provisions of the preceding two Articles shall not apply in cases where persons who intend to subscribe for Shares Solicited at Incorporation execute contracts for subscriptions for the total number of those shares.

(Subscriptions for Shares Solicited at Incorporation)
Article 62 The persons listed in the following items shall be the subscribers for the number of the Shares Solicited at Incorporation provided for in each such item with respect to the Shares Solicited at Incorporation:
  (i) Applicants: The number of the Shares Solicited at Incorporation as allotted by the incorporators; or
  (ii) Persons who subscribed for the total number of the Shares Solicited at Incorporation under the contracts referred to in the preceding article: The number of the Shares Solicited at Incorporation for which such persons have subscribed.

(Payment of Amount to be Paid In for Shares Solicited at Incorporation)
Article 63 (1) The subscribers for the Shares Solicited at Incorporation shall pay fully the Amount to be Paid In for Shares Solicited at Incorporation for which the subscribers subscribed, at the Bank Etc. designated for payment by the incorporator(s), no later than the date set forth in item (iii) of Article 58(1) or within the period under that item.

(2) Assignment of the right to become a shareholder of the Shares Issued at Incorporation by effecting payment pursuant to the preceding paragraph may not be asserted against the Stock Company after formation.

(3) If a subscriber for the Shares Solicited at Incorporation fails to make payment pursuant to the provisions of paragraph (1), the subscriber shall forfeit the right to become the shareholder of the Shares Solicited at Incorporation by making such payment.

(Certificate of Deposit of Paid Money)
Article 64 (1) In cases where solicitation under Article 57(1) has been carried out, the incorporators may request the Bank, Etc. that handled the payment pursuant to the provisions of Article 34(1) and paragraph (1) of the preceding article to issue a certificate of deposit of a money amount paid in pursuant to such provisions.
(2) The Bank, Etc. that issued the certificate referred to in the preceding paragraph may not assert against the Stock Company after formation any misstatement in such certificate or the existence of restrictions regarding the return of money paid in pursuant to the provisions of Article 34(1) or paragraph (1) of the preceding article.

Subsection 2 Organizational Meeting

(Calling of Organizational Meetings)
Article 65 (1) In cases where solicitation under Article 57(1) is to be carried out, the incorporator shall call a meeting of the Shareholders at Incorporation (meaning shareholders who shall be the shareholders of the Stock Company pursuant to the provisions of Article 50(1) or Article 102(2). The same shall apply hereinafter.) without delay on and after either the date under item (iii), of Article 58(1) or the last day of the period under such item, whichever comes later. (Such meeting is referred to as "Organizational Meeting" hereinafter.)
(2) In the cases referred to in the preceding paragraph, the incorporators may call an Organizational Meeting at any time when the incorporators find it necessary.

(Authority of Organizational Meetings)
Article 66 An Organizational Meeting may resolve only the matters provided for in this Section, the discontinuation of the incorporation of a Stock Company, the conclusion of an Organizational Meeting and other matters regarding the incorporation of a Stock Company.

(Determinations to Call Organizational Meetings)
Article 67 (1) The incorporators shall decide the following matters in cases where the incorporators call an Organizational Meeting:
(i) The date, time and place of the Organizational Meeting;
(ii) The purpose(s) of the Organizational Meeting;
(iii) That Shareholders at Incorporation who do not attend the Organizational Meeting may exercise their votes in writing, if so arranged;
(iv) That Shareholders at Incorporation who do not attend the Organizational Meeting may exercise their votes by an Electromagnetic Method, if so arranged;
(v) In addition to the matters listed in the preceding items, any matters prescribed by the applicable Ordinance of the Ministry of Justice.
(2) In cases where the number of the Shareholders at Incorporation (excluding Shareholders at Incorporation who may not exercise votes on all matters which may be resolved at Organizational Meetings. The same shall apply in the next Article through Article 71.) is one thousand or more, the incorporators shall decide the matters listed in item (iii) of the preceding paragraph.

(Notices of Calling of Organizational Meetings)

Article 68 (1) In order to call an Organizational Meeting, incorporators shall dispatch notice thereof to the Shareholders at Incorporation no later than two weeks (or one week if the Stock Company to be incorporated is not a Public Company, except in cases where the matters listed in item (iii) or item (iv) of paragraph (1) of the preceding article are decided, (or if a shorter period of time is provided for in the articles of incorporation in cases where the Stock Company to be incorporated is a Stock Company other than a Company with Board of Directors, such shorter period of time)) prior to the day of the Organizational Meeting.

(2) The notice referred to in the preceding paragraph shall be in writing in the following cases:
 (i) Where the matters listed in item (iii) or item (iv) of paragraph (1) of the preceding article are decided; or
 (ii) Where the Stock Company to be incorporated is a Company with Board of Directors.

(3) In lieu of the dispatch of the written notice referred to in the preceding paragraph, the incorporators may dispatch the notice by an Electromagnetic Method, with the consent of the Shareholders at Incorporation, in accordance with the provisions of the applicable Cabinet Order. In such cases, such incorporators shall be deemed to have dispatched the written notice under such paragraph.

(4) The notice under the preceding two paragraphs shall specify or record the matters listed in each item of paragraph (1) of the preceding article.

(5) It would be sufficient for a notice or demand to a Shareholder at Incorporation by the incorporators to be sent to the address under item (v) of Article 27, or item (i) of Article 59(3) (or, in cases where such Shareholder at Incorporation notifies the incorporator of a different place or contact address for the receipt of notices or letters of demand, to such place or contact address).

(6) The notice or demand referred to in the preceding paragraph shall be deemed to have arrived at the time when such notice or demand should normally have arrived.

(7) The provisions of the preceding two paragraphs shall apply mutatis mutandis to cases where a writing is given to the Shareholders at Incorporation when giving the notice referred to in paragraph (1), or to cases where the matters to be stated in such writing are provided by an Electromagnetic Method. In such case, the term "to have arrived" in the preceding paragraph shall be deemed to be replaced with "to have been given in such writing or to have been provided by an Electromagnetic Method with such matters."

(Omission of Calling Procedures)
Article 69 Notwithstanding the provisions of the preceding article, Organizational Meetings may be held without the procedures of calling if the consent of all Shareholders at Incorporation is obtained; provided, however, that this shall not apply in cases where the matters listed in item (iii) or item (iv) of Article 67(1) are decided.

(Giving of Organizational Meeting Reference Documents and Voting Forms)
Article 70 (1) In cases where the matters listed in item (iii) of Article 67(1) are decided, the incorporators shall, when dispatching a notice under Article 68(1), give the Shareholders at Incorporation documents stating matters of reference for the exercise of votes (hereinafter in this Subsection referred to as "Organizational Meeting Reference Documents") and documents to be used by the Shareholders at Incorporation to exercise votes (hereinafter in this Subsection referred to as "Voting Forms"), as prescribed by the applicable Ordinance of the Ministry of Justice.

(2) If the incorporators dispatch notices by an Electromagnetic Method referred to in Ar-

ticle 68(3) to Shareholders at Incorporation who have given consent under the same paragraph, the incorporators may provide, in lieu of the giving of Organizational Meeting Reference Documents and Voting Forms pursuant to the provisions of the preceding paragraph, the matters to be specified in such documents by an Electromagnetic Method; provided, however, that, if requested by any Shareholder at Incorporation, the incorporators shall give these documents to such Shareholder at Incorporation.

Article 71 (1) In cases where the matters listed in item (iv) of Article 67(1) are decided, the incorporators shall, when dispatching notice under Article 68(1), give the Shareholders at Incorporation the Organizational Meeting Reference Documents as prescribed by the applicable Ordinance of the Ministry of Justice.
(2) If the incorporators dispatch notices by an Electromagnetic Method referred to in Article 68(3) to Shareholders at Incorporation who have given consent under the same paragraph, the incorporators may provide, in lieu of the giving of Organizational Meeting Reference Documents pursuant to the provisions of the preceding paragraph, the matters to be specified in such documents by an Electromagnetic Method; provided, however, that, if requested by any Shareholder at Incorporation, the incorporators shall give the Organizational Meeting Reference Documents to such Shareholders at Incorporation.
(3) In the cases provided for in paragraph (1), when sending notice to Shareholders at Incorporation who have given consent under Article 68(3) by an Electromagnetic Method referred to in that paragraph, the incorporators shall provide to the Shareholders at Incorporation the matters to be specified in the Voting Forms by such Electromagnetic Method, as prescribed by the applicable Ordinance of the Ministry of Justice.
(4) In the cases provided for in paragraph (1), if any Shareholder at Incorporation who has not given consent under Article 68(3) requests, no later than one week prior to the day of the Organizational Meeting, for the provision of the matters to be specified in the Voting Form by an Electromagnetic Method, the incorporators shall provide such matters to such Shareholder at Incorporation by an Electromagnetic Method, as prescribed by the applicable Ordinance of the Ministry of Justice.

(Number of Votes)
Article 72 (1) Shareholders at Incorporation (excluding Shareholders at Incorporation prescribed by the applicable Ordinance of the Ministry of Justice as entities in a relationship that may allow the Stock Company after the formation to have substantial control of such entity through the holding of one quarter or more of the votes of all shareholders of such entity or other reasons) shall be entitled to one vote for each one Share Issued at Incorporation for which they subscribed at Organizational Meetings; provided, however, that, in cases where a Share Unit is provided for in the articles of incorporation, he/she shall be entitled to one vote for each one unit of the Shares Issued at Incorporation.
(2) In cases where the Stock Company to be incorporated is a Company with Class Shares, if it issues Shares Issued at Incorporation of a class that has restrictions on matters for which votes may be exercised at the shareholders' meeting, the Shareholders at Incorporation may exercise, at the Organizational Meeting, votes with respect to such Shares Issued at Incorporation only in relation to matters that are equivalent to the matters for which they may exercise the votes at the shareholders' meeting.
(3) Notwithstanding the provisions of the preceding paragraph, Shareholders at Incorporation may exercise votes with respect to the Shares Issued at Incorporation for which they subscribed in relation to the discontinuation of the incorporation of the Stock

Company.

(Resolutions of Organizational Meetings)
Article 73 (1) Resolutions of an Organizational Meeting shall be made by a majority of the votes of the Shareholders at Incorporation entitled to exercise their votes at such Organizational Meeting, being a majority of two thirds or more of the votes of such Shareholders at Incorporation who are present at the meeting.
(2) Notwithstanding the provisions of the preceding paragraph, in cases where the articles of incorporation are amended creating a provision to the effect that, as a feature of all shares issued by a Stock Company, the approval of such Stock Company is required for the acquisition of such shares by transfer (excluding cases where the Stock Company to be incorporated is a Company with Class Shares), the resolution of the Organizational Meeting with respect to such amendment in the articles of incorporation shall be made by a majority of the Shareholders at Incorporation entitled to exercise their votes at such Organizational Meeting, being a majority of two thirds or more of the votes of such Shareholders at Incorporation.
(3) In cases where it is intended to create, as a feature of all shares issued by a Stock Company, any provision in articles of incorporation with respect to the matters listed in item (iii) Article 107(1) by amending the articles of incorporation, or to effect any amendment (excluding that which repeals provisions of the articles of incorporation with respect to such matters) in the articles of incorporation with respect to such matters (excluding cases where the Stock Company to be incorporated is a Company with Class Shares), the consent of all Shareholders at Incorporation shall be obtained.
(4) An Organizational Meeting may not resolve matters other than the matters listed in item (ii) of Article 67(1); provided, however, that this shall not apply to amendment in the articles of incorporation or discontinuation of the incorporation of a Stock Company.

(Proxy Voting)
Article 74 (1) Shareholders at Incorporation may exercise their votes by proxy. In such cases, such Shareholders at Incorporation or proxies shall submit to the incorporators a document evidencing the authority of proxy.
(2) The grant of the authority of proxy under the preceding paragraph shall be made for each Organizational Meeting.
(3) The Shareholders at Incorporation or proxies referred to in paragraph (1) may, in lieu of the submission of a document evidencing the authority of proxy, provide the matters to be stated in such document by an Electromagnetic Method with the approval of the incorporators in accordance with the provisions of the applicable Cabinet Order. In such cases, such Shareholders at Incorporation or proxies shall be deemed to have submitted such document.
(4) In cases where the Shareholders at Incorporation are persons who gave consent under Article 68(3), the incorporators may not refuse to grant the approval under the preceding paragraph without justifiable reasons.
(5) The incorporators may restrict the number of proxies who may attend the Organizational Meeting.
(6) The incorporators (or the Stock Company after the formation of such Stock Company. The same shall apply hereinafter in paragraph (3) of the following Article and Article 76(4).) shall keep the documents evidencing the authority of proxy and the Electromagnetic Records which record the matters provided by an Electromagnetic Method under paragraph (3) at a place designated by the incorporators (or at the head office of the Stock Company after the formation. of such Stock Company. The same shall apply

hereinafter in paragraph (3) of the following Article and Article 76(4)) for the period of three months from the day of the Organizational Meeting.
(7) The Shareholders at Incorporation (or the shareholders of the Stock Company after the formation of such Stock Company. The same shall apply hereinafter in paragraph (4) of the following Article and Article 76(5).) may submit the following request at any time during the hours designated by the incorporators (or during the business hours of the Stock Company after the formation of such Stock Company. The same shall apply hereinafter in paragraph (4) of the following Article and Article 76(5).):
  (i) Requests for the inspection or copying of the documents evidencing the authority of proxy; and
  (ii) Requests for the inspection or copying of anything that displays the data recorded in the Electromagnetic Records under the preceding paragraph in a manner prescribed by the applicable Ordinance of the Ministry of Justice.

(Voting in Writing)
Article 75 (1) If the votes are exercised in writing, it shall be exercised by entering the Voting Form with the necessary matters and submitting it to the incorporators no later than the time prescribed by the applicable Ordinance of the Ministry of Justice.
(2) The number of the votes exercised in writing pursuant to the provisions of the preceding paragraph shall be included in the number of the votes of the Shareholders at Incorporation who are present at the meeting.
(3) The incorporators shall keep the Voting Forms submitted pursuant to the provisions of paragraph (1) at a place designated by the incorporators for the period of three months from the day of the Organizational Meeting.
(4) The Shareholders at Incorporation may make requests for the inspection or copying of the Voting Forms submitted pursuant to the provisions of paragraph (1) at any time during the hours designated by the incorporators.

(Voting by Electromagnetic Method)
Article 76 (1) If the vote are exercised by an Electromagnetic Method, it shall be exercised by providing the matters to be entered on the Voting Form to the incorporators by an Electromagnetic Method, with the approval of such incorporators, no later than the time prescribed by the applicable Ordinance of the Ministry of Justice in accordance with the provisions of the applicable Cabinet Order.
(2) In cases where the Shareholders at Incorporation are persons who have given consent under Article 68(3), the incorporators may not refuse to give the approval under the preceding paragraph without justifiable reasons.
(3) The number of the votes exercised by an Electromagnetic Method pursuant to the provisions of paragraph (1) shall be included in the number of the votes of the Shareholders at Incorporation who are present at the meeting.
(4) The incorporators shall keep the Electromagnetic Records which record the matters provided pursuant to the provisions of paragraph (1) at a place designated by the incorporators for the period of three months from the day of the Organizational Meeting.
(5) The Shareholders at Incorporation may, at any time during the hours designated by the incorporators, make a request for the inspection or copying of anything that displays the data recorded in the Electromagnetic Record under the preceding paragraph in a manner prescribed by the applicable Ordinance of the Ministry of Justice.

(Diverse Exercise of Votes)
Article 77 (1) Shareholders at Incorporation may diversely exercise the votes they hold. In such cases, the shareholders shall notify the incorporators to such effect and of the

reasons for the same no later than three days prior to the day of the Organizational Meeting.
(2) If the Shareholders at Incorporation referred to in the preceding paragraph are not persons who subscribed for the Shares Issued at Incorporation on behalf of others, the incorporators may refuse the diverse exercise of the votes held by such Shareholders at Incorporation pursuant to the provisions of the preceding paragraph.

(Accountability of Incorporators)
Article 78 In cases where incorporators are requested by the Shareholders at Incorporation to provide explanations on certain matters at an Organizational Meeting, the incorporators shall provide necessary explanations with respect to such matters; provided, however, that this shall not apply in cases where such matters are not relevant to the matters that are the purpose of the Organizational Meeting, or in cases where such explanations are to the serious detriment of the common interest of the Shareholders at Incorporation, or in other cases prescribed by the applicable Ordinance of the Ministry of Justice as cases where there are justifiable grounds.

(Authority of Chairperson)
Article 79 (1) The chairperson of an Organizational Meeting shall maintain the order of such Organizational Meeting and organize the business of the meeting.
(2) The chairperson of an Organizational Meeting may require any one who does not comply with his/her orders or who otherwise disturbs the order of such Organizational Meeting to leave the room.

(Resolution for Postponement or Adjournment)
Article 80 In cases where there is a resolution for the postponement or adjournment of an Organizational Meeting, the provisions of Article 67 and Article 68 shall not apply.

(Minutes)
Article 81 (1) Minutes shall be prepared with respect to the business of Organizational Meetings pursuant to the provisions of the applicable Ordinance of the Ministry of Justice.
(2) The incorporators (or the Stock Company after the formation of such Stock Company. The same shall apply hereinafter in paragraph (2) of the following Article.) shall keep the minutes referred to in the preceding paragraph at a place designated by the incorporators (or at the head office of the Stock Company if after the incorporation of such Stock Company. The same shall apply hereinafter in paragraph (2) of the following Article.) for the period of ten years from the day of the Organizational Meeting.
(3) The Shareholders at Incorporation (or the shareholders and creditors of the Stock Company after the formation of such Stock Company. The same shall apply hereinafter in paragraph (3) of the following Article.) may submit the following requests at any time during the hours designated by the incorporators (or during the business hours of such Stock Company if after the incorporation of such Stock Company. The same shall apply hereinafter in such paragraph.):
　(i) If the minutes under paragraph (1) are prepared in writing, requests for inspection or copying of such documents; and
　(ii) If the minutes under paragraph (1) are prepared by means of Electromagnetic Records, requests for inspection or copying of anything that displays the data recorded in such Electromagnetic Records in a manner prescribed by the applicable Ordinance of the Ministry of Justice.
(4) If, after the formation of a Stock Company, it is necessary for the purpose of exercising

the rights of a Member of the Parent Company of such Stock Company, he/she may, with the permission of the court, make the requests listed in each item of the preceding paragraph with respect to the minutes referred to in paragraph (1).

(Omission of Resolutions of Organizational Meetings)
Article 82 (1) In cases where incorporators submit a proposal with respect to any matter that is the purpose of an Organizational Meeting, if all Shareholders at Incorporation (limited to those who may exercise their votes with respect to such matter) manifest their intention to agree to such proposal in writing or by means of Electromagnetic Records, it shall be deemed that a resolution to approve such proposal at an Organizational Meeting has been made.
(2) The incorporators shall keep the documents or Electromagnetic Records under the provisions of the preceding paragraph at a place designated by the incorporators for the period of ten years from the day when the resolution of the Organizational Meeting is deemed to have been made pursuant to the provisions of the preceding paragraph.
(3) The Shareholders at Incorporation may submit the following requests at any time during the hours designated by the incorporators:
 (i) Requests for inspection or copying of the documents under the preceding paragraph; and
 (ii) Requests for inspection or copying of anything that displays the data recorded in the Electromagnetic Records under the preceding paragraph in a manner prescribed by the applicable Ordinance of the Ministry of Justice.
(4) If, after the formation of a Stock Company, it is necessary for the purpose of exercising the rights of a Member of the Parent Company of such Stock Company, he/she may, with the permission of the court, make the requests listed in each item of the preceding paragraph with respect to the documents or Electromagnetic Records under paragraph (2).

(Omission of Reports to Organizational Meetings)
Article 83 In cases where the incorporators notify all Shareholders at Incorporation of any matter that is to be reported to an Organizational Meeting, if all Shareholders at Incorporation manifest in writing or by means of Electromagnetic Records their intention to agree that it is not necessary to report such matter to the Organizational Meeting, it shall be deemed that such matter has been reported to the Organizational Meeting.

(Cases of Provision Requiring Resolution of Class Meeting)
Article 84 In cases where the Stock Company to be incorporated is a Company with Class Shares, if there is a provision, as a feature of a certain class of shares to be issued as at the incorporation, to the effect that, with respect to the matter that is subject to the resolution of a shareholders' meeting, in addition to such resolution, the resolution of a Class Meeting constituted by the Class Shareholders of such class of shares is required, such matter shall not become effective unless the resolution is made at a Class Organizational Meeting (meaning a meeting of Class Shareholders at Incorporation (as defined below) of a certain class of the Shares Issued at Incorporation. The same shall apply hereinafter.) constituted by the Class Shareholders at Incorporation (meaning the Shareholders at Incorporation of a certain class of Shares Issued at Incorporation. The same shall apply hereinafter in this Section.) of the Shares Issued at Incorporation of such class in addition to the resolution of the Organizational Meeting, consistently with the provisions of articles of incorporation; provided, how-

ever, that this shall not apply to the case where there exists no Class Shareholder at Incorporation who may exercise the votes at such Class Organizational Meeting.

(Calling and Resolutions of Class Organizational Meetings)
Article 85 (1) In cases where a resolution of a Class Organizational Meeting is to be made pursuant to the provisions of the preceding article, Article 90(1) (including the case where it is applied mutatis mutandis under paragraph (2) of the same Article), Article 92(1) (including the case where it is applied mutatis mutandis under paragraph (3) of the same Article), Article 100(1) or Article 101(1), the incorporators shall call a Class Organizational Meeting.
(2) Resolutions of a Class Organizational Meeting shall be made by a majority of the votes of the Class Shareholders at Incorporation who are entitled to exercise their votes at such Class Organizational Meeting, being a majority of two thirds or more of the votes of such Class Shareholders at Incorporation who are present at the meeting.
(3) Notwithstanding the provisions of the preceding paragraph, resolutions under Article 100(1) shall be made by a majority of the Class Shareholders at Incorporation who are entitled to exercise their votes at such Class Organizational Meeting, being a majority of two thirds or more of the votes of such Class Shareholders at Incorporation.

(Mutatis Mutandis Application of Provisions regarding Organizational Meetings)
Article 86 The provisions of Article 67 through Article 71, Article 72(1), and Article 74 through Article 82 shall apply mutatis mutandis to Class Organizational Meetings. In such cases, the term "Shareholders at Incorporation" in item (iii) and item (iv) of paragraph (1) and paragraph (2) of Article 67, paragraph (1) and paragraph (3) of Article 68, Article 69 through Article 71, paragraph (1) of Article 72, paragraph (1), paragraph (3) and paragraph (4) of Article 74, paragraph (2) of Article 75, paragraph (2) and paragraph (3) of Article 76, Article 77, the main clause of Article 78 and paragraph (1) of Article 82 shall be deemed to be replaced with as "Class Shareholders at Incorporation (meaning Shareholders at Incorporation for a certain class of Shares Issued at Incorporation)."

Subsection 3 Reporting of Matters regarding Incorporation

Article 87 (1) The incorporators shall report matters regarding the incorporation of a Stock Company to an Organizational Meeting.
(2) In the cases listed in the following items, the incorporators shall submit or provide to an Organizational Meeting the documents or Electromagnetic Records that state or record the matters provided for in such items:
  (i) In cases where articles of incorporation provide for the matters listed in each item of Article 28 (excluding the matters provided for in each item of Article 33(10) in cases listed in such items): The content of the report referred to of Article 33(4) of the inspector under paragraph (2) thereof; and
  (ii) In the case listed in item (iii) of Article 33(10): The content of the verification provided in such item.

Subsection 4 Election and Dismissal of Director at Incorporation

(Election of Directors at Incorporation)
Article 88 In cases where the solicitation under Article 57(1) is carried out, the election of the Directors at Incorporation, Accounting Advisors at Incorporation, Auditors at Incorporation and Accounting Auditors at Incorporation shall be made by the resolution of an Organizational Meeting.

(Election of Directors at Incorporation by Cumulative Vote)
Article 89 (1) In cases where the purpose of an Organizational Meeting is the election of two or more Directors at Incorporation, the Shareholders at Incorporation (limited to the Shareholders at Incorporation entitled to exercise their votes with respect to the election of the Directors at Incorporation. The same shall apply hereinafter in this Article) may request the incorporators that the Directors at Incorporation be elected pursuant to the provisions of paragraph (3) through paragraph (5), except as otherwise provided in the articles of incorporation.
(2) The request under the provisions of the preceding paragraph shall be made no later than five days prior to the day of the Organizational Meeting referred to in the same paragraph.
(3) Notwithstanding the provisions of Article 72(1), in cases where a request is made pursuant to the provisions of paragraph (1), a Shareholder at Incorporation shall be entitled to such number of votes as is equal to the number of the Directors at Incorporation to be elected in such Organizational Meeting, for each one Share Issued at Incorporation for which he/she subscribed (or, in cases where the Share Unit is provided for in the articles of incorporation, for each one unit of the Shares Issued at Incorporation for which he/she subscribed) with respect to the resolution of the election of the Directors at Incorporation. In such cases, the Shareholder at Incorporation may exercise his/her votes by casting votes for only one candidate or for two or more candidates.
(4) In the cases set forth in the preceding paragraph, the Directors at Incorporation shall be elected in the order of the votes obtained by respective candidates.
(5) In addition to the matters provided for in the preceding two paragraphs, necessary matters regarding the election of Directors at Incorporation in cases where a request has been made pursuant to the provisions of paragraph (1) shall be prescribed by the applicable Ordinance of the Ministry of Justice.

(Election of Directors at Incorporation by Resolutions of Class Organizational Meetings)
Article 90 (1) Notwithstanding the provisions of Article 88, in cases where, at incorporation of the Stock Company, it issues shares of a class for which the matters listed in item (ix) of Article 108(1) (limited to those relating to directors) are provided, the Directors at Incorporation shall be elected by a resolution of a Class Organizational Meeting constituted by the Class Shareholders at Incorporation of such class of Shares Issued at Incorporation, consistently with the provisions of articles of incorporation with respect to the matters provided for in item (ix), paragraph (2) of such Article.
(2) The provisions of the preceding paragraph shall apply mutatis mutandis to the cases where the shares of a class for which matters listed in item (ix), Article 108(1) (limited to those relating to auditors) are provided are issued at incorporation of the Stock Company.

(Dismissal of Directors at Incorporation)
Article 91 Directors at Incorporation, Accounting Advisors at Incorporation, Auditors at Incorporation or Accounting Auditors at Incorporation who are elected pursuant to the

provisions of Article 88 may be dismissed by resolution of an Organizational Meeting at any time prior to the formation of the Stock Company.

Article 92 (1) Directors at Incorporation who are elected pursuant to the provisions of Article 90(1) may be dismissed by a resolution of a Class Meeting constituted by the Class Shareholders at Incorporation of such class of Shares Issued at Incorporation relating to such election at any time prior to the formation of the Stock Company.
(2) Notwithstanding the provisions of the preceding paragraph, in cases where there is a provision in articles of incorporation to the effect that a director who is elected pursuant to the provisions of Article 41(1), or at a Class Organizational Meeting or at a Class Meeting may be dismissed by a resolution of the shareholders' meeting, a Director at Incorporation who is elected pursuant to the provisions of Article 90(1) may be dismissed by a resolution of an Organizational Meeting at any time prior to the formation of the Stock Company.
(3) The provisions of the preceding two paragraphs shall apply mutatis mutandis to the dismissal of an Auditor at Incorporation who is elected pursuant to the provisions of Article 90(1) applied mutatis mutandis under paragraph (2) of such Article.

Subsection 5 Investigation by Directors at Incorporation

(Investigation by Directors at Incorporation)
Article 93 (1) The Directors at Incorporation (referring to the Directors at Incorporation and Auditors at Incorporation in cases where the Stock Company to be incorporated is a Company with Auditors. The same shall apply hereinafter in this Article.) shall investigate the following matters without delay after their election:
(i) That, with respect to the Properties Contributed in Kind in the cases listed in item (i) or item (ii) of Article 33(10) (if listed in such item, limited to the securities under such item), the value specified or recorded in the articles of incorporation is reasonable;
(ii) That the verification provided for in item (iii) of Article 33(10) is appropriate;
(iii) That the Performance of Contributions by the incorporators and the payments pursuant to the provisions of Article 63(1) have been fulfilled; and
(iv) That, in addition to the matters listed in the preceding three items, the procedures for the incorporation of the Stock Company do not violate applicable laws and regulations or the articles of incorporation.
(2) The Directors at Incorporation shall report the outcome of the investigations pursuant to the provisions of the preceding paragraph to an Organizational Meeting.
(3) In cases where incorporators are asked by the Shareholders at Incorporation to provide explanations on the matters regarding the investigation pursuant to the provisions of the paragraph (1) at an Organizational Meeting, the incorporators shall provide necessary explanations with respect to such matters.

(Special Provisions in Case Directors at Incorporation are Incorporators)
Article 94 (1) In cases where some or all of the Directors at Incorporation (or the Directors at Incorporation and Auditors at Incorporation in cases where the Stock Company to be incorporated is a Company with Auditors) are incorporators, an Organizational Meeting may make a resolution to elect a person to investigate the matters listed in each item of paragraph (1) of the preceding article.
(2) A person who is elected pursuant to the provisions of the preceding paragraph shall conduct the necessary investigation and report the outcome of such investigation to an Organizational Meeting.

Subsection 6　Amendment in Articles of Incorporation

(No Amendment in Articles of Incorporation by Incorporators)
Article 95　In cases where the solicitation under Article 57(1) is carried out, the incorporators may not effect any amendment in the articles of incorporation on and after either the date referred to in item (iii) of Article 58(1) or the first day of the period referred to in the same item, whichever comes earlier, the provisions of Article 33(9) and Article 37(1) and (2) notwithstanding.

(Amendment in Articles of Incorporation at Organizational Meetings)
Article 96　Notwithstanding the provisions of Article 30(2), articles of incorporation may be amended by resolution of an Organizational Meeting.

(Rescission of Subscription for Shares Issued at Incorporation)
Article 97　In cases where it is resolved at the Organizational Meeting to effect an amendment in the articles of incorporation to change the matters listed in each item of Article 28, the Shareholders at Incorporation who dissented from such amendment at such Organizational Meeting may rescind the manifestation of their intention relating to the subscription for such Shares Issued at Incorporation only within two weeks after such resolution.

(Provision for Total Number of Authorized Shares by Resolutions of Organizational Meetings)
Article 98　If, in cases where the solicitation under Article 57(1) is carried out, the Total Number of Authorized Shares is not provided for in the articles of incorporation, the provision on the Total Number of Authorized Shares shall be created by amending the articles of incorporation prior to the formation of the Stock Company by resolution of an Organizational Meeting.

(Special Provisions on Procedures for Amendment in Articles of Incorporation)
Article 99　In cases where the Stock Company to be incorporated is a Company with Classes Shares, if the cases listed in any of the following items apply, the consent of all Class Shareholders at Incorporation of such classes of the Shares Issued at Incorporation in each of such items shall be obtained:
(i) If it is intended to create, as a feature of a certain class of shares, any provision in the articles of incorporation with respect to the matters listed in item (vi) of Article 108(1), or to effect any amendment in the articles of incorporation with respect to such matters (excluding any amendment which repeals the provisions of the articles of incorporation with respect to such matters);
(ii) If it is intended to create any provision in the articles of incorporation pursuant to the provisions of Article 322(2) with respect to a certain class of shares.

Article 100　(1) In cases where the Stock Company to be incorporated is a Company with Class Shares, if it is intended to create, as a feature of a certain class of shares, any provision in the articles of incorporation with respect to the matters listed in item (iv) or item (vii) of Article 108(1) by amending the articles of incorporation, such amendment in the articles of incorporation shall not become effective unless a resolution is made at a Class Organizational Meeting constituted by the following Class Shareholders at Incorporation (in cases where there are two or more classes of Shares Issued at

Incorporation relating to such Class Shareholders at Incorporation, referring to the respective Class Organizational Meetings constituted by Class Shareholders at Incorporation categorized by the class of such two or more classes of Shares Issued at Incorporation. The same shall apply hereinafter in this Article.); provided, however, that this shall not apply to cases where there is no Class Shareholder at Incorporation who may exercise his/her votes at such Class Organizational Meeting:

(i) The Class Shareholders at Incorporation of such class of Shares Issued at Incorporation;

(ii) The Class Shareholders at Incorporation of Shares with Put Option for which there is a provision that the "other share" referred to in item (v)(b) of Article 108(2) shall be such class of share; or

(iii) The Class Shareholders at Incorporation of Shares Subject to Call Option for which there is a provision that the "other shares" referred to in item (vi)(b) of Article 108(2) shall be such class of shares;

(2) The Class Shareholders at Incorporation who, at the Class Organizational Meeting referred to in the preceding paragraph, dissented from such amendment in the articles of incorporation may rescind the manifestation of their intention relating to the subscription for such Shares Issued at Incorporation only within two weeks after the resolution made by such Class Organizational Meeting.

Article 101 (1) In cases where the Stock Company to be incorporated is a Company with Class Shares, if effecting any amendment in articles of incorporation with respect to any of the following matters is likely to cause detriment to the Class Shareholders at Incorporation of any class of Shares Issued at Incorporation, such amendment in the articles of incorporation shall not become effective unless a resolution is made at an Class Organizational Meeting constituted by the Class Shareholders at Incorporation of the Shares Issued at Incorporation of such class (in cases where there are two or more classes of Shares Issued at Incorporation relating to such Class Shareholders at Incorporation, referring to the respective Class Organizational Meetings constituted by the Class Shareholders at Incorporation categorized by the class of such two or more classes of Shares Issued at Incorporation); provided, however, that this shall not apply to cases where there is no Class Shareholder at Incorporation who may exercise his/her votes at such Class Organizational Meeting:

(i) Creation of a new class of shares;

(ii) Changes in the features of shares;

(iii) Increase of the Total Number of Authorized Shares, or the Total Number of Authorized Shares in a Class (meaning the total number of shares in one class that the Stock Company is authorized to issue. The same shall apply hereinafter.).

(2) In cases where any amendment in the articles of incorporation with respect to the Share Unit is to be effected and there is a provision in the articles of incorporation pursuant to the provisions of Article 322(2) with respect to such amendment in the articles of incorporation, the provisions of the preceding paragraph shall not apply to the Class Organizational Meeting constituted by the Class Shareholders at Incorporation of such class of the Shares Issued at Incorporation.

Subsection 7 Special Provisions on Incorporation Procedures

(Special Provisions on Incorporation Procedures)

Article 102 (1) A subscriber for the Shares Solicited at Incorporation may submit the requests listed in each item of Article 31(2) at any time during the hours designated by

the incorporators; provided, however, that, the fees designated by the incorporators are required to be paid in order to submit the requests listed in item (ii) or item (iv) of such paragraph.
(2) As at formation of a Stock Company, the subscriber for the Shares Solicited at Incorporation shall become a shareholder of the Shares Issued at Incorporation for which he/she have made payment pursuant to the provisions of Article 63(1).
(3) The proviso to Article 93 and the provisions of Article 94(1) of the Civil Code shall apply to neither offer of subscription for nor allotment of the Shares Solicited at Incorporation, nor to manifestation of intention relating to contracts under Article 61.
(4) The subscriber for the Shares Solicited at Incorporation may neither assert the invalidity of the his/her subscription for Shares Issued at Incorporation on the ground of mistake, nor rescind his/her subscription for Shares Issued at Incorporation on the ground of fraud or duress after the formation of a Stock Company, or after exercising his/her votes at an Organizational Meeting or Class Organizational Meeting.

(Liabilities of Incorporators)
Article 103 (1) In cases where the solicitation under of Article 57(1) is carried out, for the purpose of the application of the provisions of Article 52(2), "in the following cases" in such paragraph shall be read as "in the cases of item (i)."
(2) In cases where the solicitation under Article 57(1) is carried out, any person (excluding the incorporators) who consents to specifying or recording his/her name and a statement to the effect that he/she supports the incorporation of the Stock Company in any document or Electromagnetic Record regarding such solicitation, including an advertisement for such solicitation, shall be deemed to be an incorporator and the provisions of the preceding Section and the preceding paragraph shall apply.

Chapter II Share

Section 1 General Provisions

(Shareholders' Liabilities)
Article 104 A shareholder's liability shall be limited to the amount of the subscription price of the shares he/she holds.

(Rights of Shareholders)
Article 105 (1) A shareholder shall have the following rights and other rights recognized pursuant to the provisions of this Act with respect to the shares he/she holds:
(i) The right to receive dividends of surplus;
(ii) The right to receive distribution of residual assets;
(iii) The right to cast a vote at shareholders meeting.
(2) Provisions of articles of incorporation that do not give the entirety of the rights listed in item (i) and item (ii) of the preceding paragraph to shareholders shall not be effective.

(Exercise of Rights by Co-owners)
Article 106 If any share is co-owned by two or more persons, the co-owners may not exercise their rights in relation to such share unless they specify one person who exercises the rights in relation to such share, and notify the Stock Company of the name of that person; provided, however, that this shall not apply in cases where the Stock Company agrees to the exercise of such rights.

Art.107　　　　Ⅰ Companies Act, PART II, Chap.II, Sec.1

(Special Provision on Features of Shares)
Article 107 (1) A Stock Company may determine the matters listed in the following items as the features of all shares it issues:
(i) That the approval of such Stock Company shall be required for the acquisition of such shares by assignment;
(ii) That shareholders may demand, that such Stock Company acquire such shares held by such shareholders;
(iii) That such Stock Company may acquire such shares on condition of certain grounds arising.
(2) If a Stock Company determines the matters listed in the following items as the features of all shares it issues, it shall provide for the matters prescribed in each such item in the articles of incorporation:
(i) Regarding the fact that the approval of such Stock Company shall be required for the acquisition of such shares by assignment: The matters listed below:
(a) A statement to the effect that the acquisition of such shares by assignment shall require the approval of such Stock Company;
(b) If the Stock Company is deemed to have effected the approval under Article 136 or Article 137 (1) under certain circumstances, a statement to such effect and a description of such circumstances.
(ii) Regarding the fact that shareholders may demand that such Stock Company acquire shares held by such shareholders: The matters listed below:
(a) A statement to the effect that shareholders may demand that such Stock Company acquire the shares held by such shareholders;
(b) If Bonds of such Stock Company (other than those in relation to Bonds with Share Option) are delivered to such shareholders in exchange for the acquisition of one of the shares referred to in (a), the description of the classes of such Bonds (referring to the classes defined in Article 681 (i). The same shall apply hereinafter in this Part.) and the total amount for each class of Bonds, or the method for calculating such total amount;
(c) If Share Options of such Stock Company (other than those attached to Bonds with Share Option) are delivered to such shareholders in exchange for the acquisition of one of the shares referred to in (a), the features and number of such Share Options, or the method for calculating such number;
(d) If Bonds with Share Option of such Stock Company are delivered to such shareholders in exchange for the acquisition of one of the shares referred to in (a), the matters prescribed in (b) with respect to such Bonds with Share Option, and the matters prescribed in (c) with respect to the Share Options attached to such Bonds with Share Option;
(e) If any property other than shares, etc. (referring to shares, Bonds and Share Options. This shall apply hereinafter.) of such Stock Company is delivered to such shareholders in exchange for the acquisition of one of the shares referred to in (a), the description of the features and number or amount of such property, or the method for calculating such number or amount;
(f) The period during which the shareholders may demand that such Stock Company acquire such shares held by such shareholders.
(iii) Regarding the fact that such Stock Company may acquire such shares on condition of certain grounds arising: The matters listed below:
(a) A statement to the effect that such Stock Company will acquire its shares on the day when certain grounds arise, and of such grounds;
(b) If the grounds referred to in (a) will arise with the arrival of a day to be separately specified by such Stock Company, a statement to that effect;

(c) If a portion of the shares referred to in (a) will be acquired on the day the grounds referred to in (a) arise, a statement to that effect and of the method for determining the portion of shares to be acquired;
(d) If Bonds of such Stock Company (other than those of Bonds with Share Option) are delivered to such shareholders in exchange for the acquisition of one of the shares referred to in (a), the classes of such Bonds and the total amount for each class of Bonds, or the method for calculating such total amounts;
(e) If Share Options of such Stock Company (other than those attached to Bonds with Share Option) are delivered to such shareholders in exchange for the acquisition of one of the shares referred to in (a), the features and number of such Share Options, or the method for calculating such number;
(f) If Bonds with Share Option of such Stock Company are delivered to such shareholders in exchange for the acquisition of one share of the shares referred to in (a), the matters prescribed in (d) with respect to such Bonds with Share Option, and the matters prescribed in (e) with respect to the Share Options attached to such Bonds with Share Option;
(g) If any property other than shares, etc. of such Stock Company is delivered to such shareholders in exchange for the acquisition of one of the shares referred to in (a), the features and number or amount of such property, or the method for calculating such number or amount.

(Shares of Different Classes)
Article 108 (1) A Stock Company may issue two or more classes of shares with different features which have different provisions on the following matters; provided, however, that a Company with Committees and a Public Company may not issue shares of a class that has provisions in relation to the matters listed in item (ix):
(i) Dividends of surplus;
(ii) Distribution of residual assets;
(iii) Capacity to exercise the right to vote at a shareholders meeting;
(iv) That the approval of such Stock Company shall be required for the acquisition of such class shares by assignment;
(v) That shareholders may demand that such Stock Company acquire such class shares held by such shareholders;
(vi) That such Stock Company may acquire such class shares on condition of certain grounds arising;
(vii) That such Stock Company shall acquire all of such class shares by resolution of the shareholders meeting;
(viii) Such of the matters to be resolved at a shareholders meeting (or at a shareholders meeting or board of directors meeting for a Company with Board of Directors, or at a shareholders meeting or board of liquidators meeting for a Company with Board of Liquidators (referring to the Company with Board of Liquidators as provided for Article 478(6). The same shall apply hereinafter in this Article.)), that require, in addition to such resolution, a resolution of a Class Meeting constituted by the Class Shareholders of such class shares.
(ix) That directors or company auditors shall be elected at a Class Meeting constituted by the Class Shareholders of such class shares.
(2) In cases where a Stock Company issues two or more classes of shares with different features that have different provisions on the following matters, it shall provide for the matters prescribed in each of such items and the Total Number of Authorized Shares in a Class in the articles of incorporation:
(i) Regarding dividends of surplus: The method for determining the Dividend Property

Art.108   ① Companies Act, PART II, Chap.II, Sec.1

to be delivered to the shareholders of such classes, the conditions for dividends of surplus, and other features relating to dividends of surplus;
(ii) Regarding the distribution of residual assets: The method for determining the value of the residual assets to be delivered to the shareholders of such classes, the kinds of such residual assets, and other features of treatment relating to the distribution of residual assets;
(iii) Regarding the matter of capacity to exercise the right to vote at shareholders meetings: The following matters:
   (a) The matters in relation to which the voting right may be exercised at a shareholders meeting; and
   (b) If any condition on the exercise of the voting right is to be prescribed for such class shares, such condition.
(iv) Regarding the fact that the approval of such Stock Company shall be required for the acquisition of such class shares by assignment: The matters prescribed in item (i), paragraph (2) of the preceding article with respect to such class shares;
(v) Regarding the fact that shareholders may demand that such Stock Company acquire such class shares held by such shareholders: The following matters:
   (a) The matters prescribed in item (ii), paragraph (2) of the preceding article with respect to such class shares;
   (b) If, in exchange for the acquisition of one share of such class shares, other shares of such Stock Company are delivered to such shareholders, the class of such other shares and the total number of each class, or the method for calculating such number;
(vi) Regarding the fact that such Stock Company may acquire such class shares on condition of certain grounds arising: The following matters:
   (a) The matters prescribed in item (iii), paragraph (2) of the preceding article with respect to such class shares;
   (b) If, in exchange for the acquisition of one share of such class shares, other shares of such Stock Company are delivered to such shareholders, the class of such other shares and the total number of each class, or the method for calculating such number;
(vii) Regarding the fact that such Stock Company shall acquire all of such class of shares by resolution of a shareholders meeting; The following matters:
   (a) The method for determining the value of the acquisition price prescribed in Article 171(1)(i);
   (b) If any condition is to be prescribed on whether or not the resolution of such shareholders meeting may be effected, such condition.
(viii) Regarding such of the matters to be resolved at a shareholders meeting (or at a shareholders meeting or board of directors meeting for a Company with Board of Directors, or at a shareholders meeting or board of liquidators meeting for a Company with Board of Liquidators), that require, in addition to such resolution, a resolution of a Class Meeting constituted by the Class Shareholders of such class shares. The following matters:
   (a) The matters for which the resolution of such Class Meeting is required; and
   (b) If any condition for which the resolution of such Class Meeting is required is to be prescribed, such condition.
(ix) Regarding the fact that directors or company auditors shall be elected at a Class Meeting constituted by the Class Shareholders of such class shares. The following matters:
   (a) The election of directors or company auditors at a Class Meeting constituted by such Class Shareholders and the number of directors or company auditors to be

elected;
(b) If some or all of the directors or company auditors who may be elected pursuant to the provisions of (a) shall be elected jointly with other Class Shareholders, the class of the shares held by such other Class Shareholders, and the number of directors or company auditors to be elected jointly;
(c) If there is any condition that alters the matters listed in (a) or (b), such condition, and the matters listed in (a) or (b) after such alternation in cases where such condition is fulfilled; and
(d) In addition to the matters listed in (a) to (c) inclusive, any matter prescribed by the applicable Ordinance of the Ministry of Justice.
(3) Notwithstanding the provisions of the preceding paragraph, with respect to some or all of the matters prescribed in each item of the same paragraph (limited to the amount of dividends which may be received by Class Shareholders of classes with different features with respect to dividends of surplus, and other matters prescribed by the applicable Ordinance of the Ministry of Justice), it may be provided in the articles of incorporation to the effect that such matters shall be determined by resolution of a shareholders meeting (or at a shareholders meeting or board of directors meeting for a Company with Board of Directors, or at a shareholders meeting or board of liquidators meeting for a Company with Board of Liquidators) by the time of the first issue of such class shares. In such cases, an outline of the features thereof shall be provided for in the articles of incorporation.

(Equality of Shareholders)
Article 109 (1) A Stock Company shall treat its shareholders equally in accordance with the features and number of the shares they hold.
(2) Notwithstanding the provisions of the preceding paragraph, a Stock Company that is not a Public Company may provide in its articles of incorporation to the effect that each shareholder shall be treated differently with respect to the matters regarding the rights listed in each item of Article 105 (1).
(3) In cases where there is a provision in the articles of incorporation that is provided for in the preceding paragraph, the shares held by the shareholders under that paragraph shall be deemed to be class shares with different features with respect to the matters regarding the rights under that paragraph, and the provisions of this Part and Part V shall apply.

(Special Provisions on Procedures for Amendments in Articles of Incorporation)
Article 110 In cases where it is intended to create, as a feature of all shares to be issued by a Stock Company, a provision in the articles of incorporation with respect to the matters listed in Article 107(1)(iii) by amending the articles of incorporation, or to effect any amendment (excluding that which abolishes the provisions of the articles of incorporation with respect to such matters) in the articles of incorporation with respect to such matters (excluding the case where the Stock Company is a Company with Class Shares), the consent of all shareholders shall be obtained.

Article 111 (1) If a Company with Class Shares intends, after it has issued a certain class of shares, to create, as a feature of such class shares, a provision in the articles of incorporation with respect to the matters listed in Article 108(1)(vi) by amending the articles of incorporation, or to effect any amendment to the articles of incorporation with respect to such matters (excluding any amendment which abolishes the provisions of the articles of incorporation with respect to such matters), the consent of all Class

Shareholders who hold such class shares shall be obtained.
(2) In cases where a Company with Class Shares intends to create, as a feature of a certain class of shares, a provision in the articles of incorporation with respect to the matters listed in Article 108(1)(iv) or (vii), such amendment to the articles of incorporation shall not become effective unless a resolution is passed at a Class Meeting constituted by the following Class Shareholders (in cases where there are two or more classes of shares relating to such Class Shareholders, referring to the respective Class Meetings constituted by Class Shareholders categorized by the class of such two or more classes of shares. This shall apply hereinafter in this Article.); provided, however, that this shall not apply to cases where there is no Class Shareholder who can exercise his/her voting right at such Class Meeting:
(i) The Class Shareholders of shares of such class;
(ii) The Class Shareholders of Shares with Put Option for which there is a provision that the "other shares" referred to in Article 108(2)(v)(b) shall be the shares of such class; or
(iii) The Class Shareholders of Shares subject to Call for which there is a provision that the "other shares" referred to in Article 108(2)(vi)(b) shall be the shares of such class.

(Special Provisions on Abolition of Provisions in Articles of Incorporation on Class Shares in relation to Election of Directors)
Article 112 (1) The provisions in the articles of incorporation on the matters listed in Article 108(2)(ix) (limited to those on directors) shall be deemed to have been abolished if, in cases where the number of directors is less than the number prescribed in this Act or the articles of incorporation, hence it is not possible to elect directors in a number sufficient to satisfy such requirement.
(2) The provisions of the preceding paragraph shall apply mutatis mutandis to the provisions of the articles of incorporation on the matters listed in Article 108(2)(ix) (limited to those on company auditors).

(Total Number of Authorized Shares)
Article 113 (1) A Stock Company may not abolish the provisions on the Total Number of Authorized Shares by amending its articles of incorporation.
(2) If it is intended to reduce the Total Number of Authorized Shares by amending the articles of incorporation, the Total Number of Authorized Shares after the amendment may not be less than the total number of the Issued Shares at the time when such amendment to the articles of incorporation becomes effective.
(3) In cases where it is intended to increase the Total Number of Authorized Shares by amending the articles of incorporation, the Total Number of Authorized Shares after the amendment may not exceed the number four times the total number of the Issued Shares at the time when such amendment to the articles of incorporation becomes effective; provided, however, that this shall not apply in cases where the Stock Company is not a Public Company.
(4) The number of the shares which holders of Share Options (excluding Share Options for which the first day of the period prescribed in Article 236(1)(iv) has not yet arrived) acquire pursuant to the provisions of Article 282 may not exceed the number obtained by subtracting the total number of the Issued Shares (excluding Treasury Shares (meaning shares in a Stock Company owned by that Stock Company itself. The same shall apply hereinafter.)) from the Total Number of Authorized Shares.

(Total Number of Authorized Share in a Class)

Article 114 (1) If it is intended to reduce the Total Number of Authorized Shares in a Class of a certain class of shares by amending the articles of incorporation, the Total Number of Authorized Shares in a Class of such class of shares after the amendment may not be less than the total number of the Issued Shares of such class at the time when such amendment to the articles of incorporation becomes effective.
(2) The total sum of the numbers set forth below for a certain class of shares may not exceed the number obtained by subtracting the total number of the Issued Shares of such class (excluding Treasury Shares) from the Total Number of Authorized Shares in a Class of such class of shares.
  (i) The number of "other shares" prescribed in Article 167(2)(iv) which is to be acquired pursuant to the provisions of Article 167(2) by the shareholders (excluding the relevant Stock Company) of Shares with Put Option (excluding those for which the first day of the period prescribed in Article 107(2)(ii)(f) has not yet arrived);
  (ii) The number of "other shares" prescribed in Article 170(2)(iv) which is to be acquired pursuant to the provisions of Article 170(2) by the shareholders (excluding the relevant Stock Company) of Shares subject to Call; and
  (iii) The number of the shares which holders of Share Options (excluding those for which the first day of the period prescribed in Article 236(1)(iv) has not yet arrived) acquire pursuant to the provisions of Article 282.

(Number of Issued Shares with Restricted Voting Right)
Article 115 In cases where a Company with Class Shares is a Public Company, if the number of the shares of a certain class with restriction in relation to matters on which voting right can be exercised at a shareholders meeting (hereinafter in this article referred to as "Shares with Restricted Voting Right") has exceeded one half of the total number of the Issued Shares, the Stock Company shall immediately take measures necessary to reduce the number of the Shares with Restricted Voting Right below one half of the total number of the Issued Shares.

(Dissenting Shareholders' Share Purchase Demand)
Article 116 (1) In the cases listed in the following items, dissenting shareholders may demand that the Stock Company purchase, at a fair price, the shares prescribed in such items held by such shareholders:
  (i) In cases where it is intended to effect a amendment to the articles of incorporation to create a provision on matters listed in Article 107(1)(i) as a feature of all shares issued by a Stock Company: All shares;
  (ii) In cases where it is intended to effect a amendment to the articles of incorporation to create a provision on matters listed in Article 108(1)(iv) or (vii) as the feature of a certain class of shares: The shares prescribed in each item of Article 111(2);
  (iii) In cases where any act listed below is to be performed, if any detriment is likely to be suffered by Class Shareholders who hold a certain class of shares (limited to those provided for in the articles of incorporation under the provisions of Article 322(2)): The shares of such class
    (a) Consolidation of shares or splitting of shares;
    (b) Allotment of Shares without Contribution provided for in Article 185;
    (c) Amendment to the articles of incorporation on the Share Unit;
    (d) Solicitation of persons to subscribe for the shares of such Stock Company (limited to solicitation for which the Stock Company provides for the matters listed in each item of Article 202(1));
    (e) Solicitation of persons to subscribe for the Share Options of such Stock Company (limited to solicitation for which the Stock Company provides for the matters

listed in each item of Article 241(1));
  (f) Allotment of Share Options without Contribution provided for in Article 277.
(2) The "dissenting shareholders" provided for in the preceding paragraph shall mean the shareholders provided for in the following items in the cases listed in the same items:
  (i) In cases where a resolution of a shareholders meeting (including a Class Meeting) is required to perform an act in any item of the preceding paragraph: The following shareholders:
    (a) Shareholders who gave notice to such Stock Company to the effect that they dissented from such act prior to such shareholders meeting and who dissented from such act at such shareholders meeting (limited to those who can exercise voting right at such shareholders meetings);
    (b) Shareholders who cannot exercise voting right at such shareholders meetings.
  (ii) In cases other than those prescribed in the preceding item: All shareholders.
(3) A Stock Company that intends to perform an act in any item of paragraph (1) shall give notice to the shareholders of the shares provided for in each item of that paragraph to the effect that it intends to perform such act, no later than twenty days prior to the day when such act becomes effective (hereinafter in this article and in the next article referred to as "Effective Day").
(4) A public notice may be substituted for the notice pursuant to the provisions of the preceding paragraph.
(5) Demands under the provisions of paragraph (1) (hereinafter in this Section referred to as "Share Purchase Demand") shall be made, within the period from the day twenty days prior to the Effective Day to the day immediately preceding the Effective Day, by disclosing the number of shares relating to such Share Purchase Demand (or, for a Company with Class Shares, the classes of the shares and the number of shares for each class).
(6) Shareholders who have made the Share Purchase Demand may withdraw their Share Purchase Demand only in cases where they obtain the approval of the Stock Company.
(7) If a Stock Company suspends the act in any item of paragraph (1), the Share Purchase Demand shall become ineffective.

(Determination of Price of Shares)
Article 117 (1) In cases where a Share Purchase Demand is made, if an agreement is reached between the shareholder and the Stock Company on the determination of the price of the shares, the Stock Company shall make the payment within sixty days from the Effective Day.
(2) If no agreement is reached within thirty days from the Effective Day on the determination of the price of the shares, the shareholders or the Stock Company may file a petition to the court for a determination of the price within thirty days after the expiration of that period.
(3) Notwithstanding the provisions of paragraph (6) of the preceding article, in the cases provided for in the preceding paragraph, if the petition under that paragraph is not made within sixty days after the Effective Day, the shareholders may withdraw their Share Purchase Demand at any time after the expiration of such period.
(4) The Stock Company shall also pay interest on the price determined by the court which shall be calculated at the rate of 6% per annum from and including the day of the expiration of the period referred to in paragraph (1).
(5) The purchase relating to the Share Purchase Demand shall become effective at the time of payment of the price for such shares.
(6) If a Company Issuing Share Certificate (meaning a Stock Company the articles of incorporation of which have provisions to the effect that share certificate representing

its shares (or, in case of a Company with Class Shares, shares of all classes) shall be issued), has received a Share Purchase Demand with respect to shares for which share certificates are issued, the Stock Company shall pay the price of the shares relating to such Share Purchase Demand in exchange for the share certificate.

(Demand for Purchase of Share Options)

Article 118 (1) In cases where it is intended to effect any amendment to articles of incorporation listed in the following items, the holders of Share Options provided for in any such item may demand that the Stock Company purchase, at a fair price, the Share Options held by the same:

(i) In cases where it is intended to effect a amendment to the articles of incorporation to create a provision on matters listed in Article 107(1)(i) as a feature of all shares issued by a Stock Company: All Share Options;

(ii) In cases where it is intended to effect a amendment to the articles of incorporation to create a provision on matters listed in Article 108(1)(iv) or (vii) as a feature of a certain class of shares: The Share Options for which shares of such class are the underlying shares;

(2) If holders of the Share Options attached to Bonds with Share Option intend to make the demand under the preceding paragraph (hereinafter in this Section referred to as "Share Option Purchase Demand"), they shall also make the demand for the purchase of Bonds with respect to Bonds with Share Option; provided, however, that this shall not apply in cases where it is otherwise provided for with respect to the Share Options attached to Bonds with Share Option.

(3) A Stock Company which intends to effect a amendment to the articles of incorporation listed in each item of paragraph (1) shall give notice to the holders of Share Options provided for in each item of that paragraph, no later than twenty days prior to the day when such amendment to the articles of incorporation becomes effective (hereinafter in this article and in the following article referred to as "Day of Amendment to Articles of Incorporation"), to the effect that such amendment to the articles of incorporation is to be effected.

(4) A public notice may be substituted for the notice pursuant to the provisions of the preceding paragraph.

(5) The Share Option Purchase Demand shall be made, within the period form the day twenty days prior to the Day of Amendment to Articles of Incorporation to the day immediately preceding the Day of Amendment to Articles of Incorporation, by disclosing the features and number of Share Options relating to such Share Option Purchase Demand.

(6) Holders of Share Options who have made the Share Option Purchase Demand may withdraw their Share Option Purchase Demand only in cases where they obtain the approval of the Stock Company.

(7) If a Stock Company suspends the amendment to articles of incorporation provided for in any item of paragraph (1), the Share Option Purchase Demand shall become ineffective.

(Determination of Price of Share Options)

Article 119 (1) In cases where a Share Option Purchase Demand is made, if an agreement on the determination of the price of the Share Options is reached between the holder of Share Options (in cases where such Share Options are attached to Bonds with Share Option, if there is a demand for the purchase of Bonds with respect to such Bonds with Share Option, including such Bonds. The same shall apply in this article.) and the Stock Company, the Stock Company shall make payment within sixty days

Art.120　　　　　Ⅰ Companies Act, PART II, Chap.II, Sec.1

from the Day of the Amendment to the Articles of Incorporation.
(2) If no agreement on the determination of the price of the Share Options is reached within thirty days from the Day of Amendment to Articles of Incorporation, the holders of Share Options or the Stock Company may file a petition to the court for a determination of the price within thirty days after the expiration of that period.
(3) Notwithstanding the provisions of paragraph (6) of the preceding article, in the cases provided for in the preceding paragraph, if the petition under that paragraph is not filed within sixty days after the Day of Amendment to Articles of Incorporation, the holders of Share Options may withdraw their Share Option Purchase Demand at any time after the expiration of such period.
(4) The Stock Company shall also pay interest on the price determined by the court which is calculated at the rate of 6% per annum from and including the day of the expiration of the period referred to in paragraph (1).
(5) The purchase relating to the Share Option Purchase Demand shall become effective at the time of payment of the price for such Share Options.
(6) If a Stock Company has received a Share Option Purchase Demand with respect to any Share Option for which a Share Option certificate is issued, it shall pay the price of the Share Option relating to such Share Option Purchase Demand in exchange for such Share Option certificate.
(7) If a Stock Company has received a Share Option Purchase Demand with respect to a Share Option attached to a Bond with Share Option for which a certificate for Bond with Share Option provided for in Article 249 (ii) is issued, it shall pay the price of the Share Option relating to such Share Option Purchase Demand in exchange for such certificate for Bond with Share Option.

(Giving Benefits on Exercise of Shareholder's Right)
Article 120 (1) A Stock Company may not give property benefits to any person regarding the exercise of shareholders' rights (limited to benefits given for the accounts of such Stock Company or its Subsidiary. The same shall apply hereinafter in this article.).
(2) If a Stock Company gives property benefits to a specific shareholder without charge, it shall be presumed that such Stock Company has given property benefits regarding the exercise of shareholders' rights. The same shall apply in cases where a Stock Company gives property benefits to a specific shareholder for value if the benefit received by such Stock Company or its Subsidiary is insignificant in comparison to such property benefits.
(3) If a Stock Company gives property benefits in violation of the provisions of paragraph (1), the recipient of such benefit shall return the same to such Stock Company or its Subsidiary. In such cases, if the recipient has tendered anything to such Stock Company or its Subsidiary in exchange for such benefit, that person may receive the return of the same.
(4) If a Stock Company gives property benefits in violation of the provisions of paragraph (1), persons prescribed by the applicable Ordinance of the Ministry of Justice as directors (including executive officers for Companies with Committees. The same shall apply hereinafter in this paragraph.) who are involved in giving such benefits shall be jointly and severally liable to such Stock Company for payment of an amount equivalent to the value of the benefit so given; provided, however, that this shall not apply if such persons (excluding the directors who gave such benefit) have proven that they did not fail to exercise due care in discharging their duties.
(5) Exemptions from the obligations set forth in the preceding paragraph may not be given without the consent of all shareholders.

Section 2 Shareholder Registry

(Shareholder Registry)
Article 121 A Stock Company shall prepare a shareholder registry and state or record the following matters (hereinafter referred to as "Matters to be Stated in the Shareholder Registry") in the same:
(i) The names and addresses of shareholders;
(ii) The number of shares held by the shareholders referred to in the preceding item (or the classes of shares and number for each class for a Company with Class Shares);
(iii) The days when the shareholders referred to in item (i) acquired the shares; and
(iv) In cases where the Stock Company is a Company Issuing Share Certificate, the serial numbers of share certificates representing the shares (limited to those for which share certificates are issued) under item (ii).

(Delivery of Documents Stating Matters to be Stated in the Shareholder Registry)
Article 122 (1) The shareholders referred to in item (i) of the preceding article may request that the Stock Company deliver documents stating the matters to be specified in the shareholder registry that are stated or recorded in the shareholder registry with respect to such shareholders, or provide the Electromagnetic Records that record such Matters to be Stated in the Shareholder Registry.
(2) The documents referred to in the preceding paragraph shall be affixed with the signature, or name and seal, of the Representative Director of the Stock Company (referring to the representative executive officer for a Company with Committees. The same shall apply hereinafter in this paragraph and in the following paragraph.).
(3) With respect to the Electromagnetic Records referred to in paragraph (1), the Representative Director of the Stock Company shall implement measures in lieu of the affixing of the signature, or name and seal that is prescribed by the applicable Ordinance of the Ministry of Justice.
(4) The provisions of the preceding three paragraphs shall not apply to a Company Issuing Share Certificate.

(Administrator of Shareholder Registry)
Article 123 A Stock Company may provide in its articles of incorporation to the effect that an Administrator of Shareholder Registry (meaning a person who is responsible on behalf of the Stock Company for the administration of the shareholder registry including preparing and keeping the shareholder registry. The same shall apply hereinafter.) shall be installed, and may entrust such administration to the same.

(Record Date)
Article 124 (1) A Stock Company may, by prescribing a certain date (hereinafter in this Chapter referred to as a "Record Date"), prescribe the shareholders who are stated or recorded in the shareholder registry on the Record Date (hereinafter in this article referred to as "Shareholders as of the Record Date") as the persons who may exercise their rights.
(2) In cases where a Record Date is to be established, the Stock Company shall prescribe the content of the rights which the Shareholders on the Record Date may exercise (limited to those which are exercised within three months from the Record Date).
(3) If a Stock Company has prescribed a Record Date, it shall give public notice of such

Art.125　　　Ⅰ Companies Act, PART II, Chap.II, Sec.2

Record Date and the matters prescribed pursuant to the provisions of the preceding paragraph no later than two weeks prior to such Record Date; provided, however, that this shall not apply if the articles of incorporation provide for such Record Date and such matters.
(4) In cases where the rights that the Shareholders on the Record Date may exercise are voting right at a shareholders meeting or Class Meeting, the Stock Company may prescribe some or all persons who acquire shares on or after such Record Date as persons who may exercise such right; provided, however, that this provision may not prejudice the rights of the Shareholders on the Record Date of such shares.
(5) The provisions of paragraph (1) to paragraph (3) inclusive shall apply mutatis mutandis to the Registered Pledgees of Shares provided for in Article 149 (1).

(Keeping and Making Available for Inspection of Shareholder Registry)
Article 125　(1) A Stock Company shall keep the shareholder registry at its head office (or, in cases where there is an Administrator of Shareholder Registry, at its business office).
(2) Shareholders and creditors may make the following requests at any time during the business hours of the Stock Company. In such cases, the reasons for such requests shall be disclosed.
　(i) If the shareholder registry is prepared in writing, a request for the inspection or copying of such document;
　(ii) If the shareholder registry is prepared by using Electromagnetic Records, a request for the inspection or copying of anything that indicates the matters recorded in such Electromagnetic Records in a manner prescribed by the applicable Ordinance of the Ministry of Justice.
(3) If a request in the preceding paragraph is made, a Stock Company may not refuse such request, except cases it falls under any of the following:
　(i) The shareholder or creditor who made such request (hereinafter in this paragraph referred to as the "Requestor") made the request for a purpose other than for research on securing or exercising his/her rights;
　(ii) The Requestor made the request with the purpose of interfering with the execution of the operations of such Stock Company or prejudicing the common benefit of the shareholders;
　(iii) The Requestor operates or engages in any business which is, in substance, in competition with the operations of such Stock Company;
　(iv) The Requestor made the request in order to report facts to third parties for profit, knowledge of which may be acquired by inspecting or copying the shareholder registry; or
　(v) The Requestor is a person who has reported facts, knowledge of which was acquired by inspecting or copying the shareholder registry, to third parties for profit in the immediately preceding two years.
(4) If it is necessary for a member of the Parent Company of a Stock Company to exercise his/her rights, such member of the Parent Company may, with the permission of the court, make the requests in each item of paragraph (2) with respect to the shareholder registry of such Stock Company. In such cases, the reasons for such requests shall be disclosed.
(5) The court may not grant the permission in the preceding paragraph if grounds provided for in any item of paragraph (3) apply to the member of the Parent Company in the preceding paragraph.

(Notice to Shareholders)

Article 126 (1) It shall be sufficient for a notice or demand to shareholders to be sent by a Stock Company to the addresses of such shareholders stated or recorded in the shareholder registry (or, in cases where such shareholders notify such Stock Company of a different place or contact address for the receipt of notices or demands, to such place or contact address).
(2) The notices or demand in the preceding paragraph shall be deemed to have arrived at the time when such notice or demand should normally have arrived.
(3) If a share is co-owned by two or more persons, the co-owners shall specify one person to receive the notices or demand sent by the Stock Company to shareholders and notify such Stock Company of the name of that person. In such cases, that person shall be deemed to be the shareholder and the provisions of the preceding two paragraphs shall apply.
(4) In cases where there is no notice by co-owners under the provisions of the preceding paragraph, it shall be sufficient for a notice or demand sent by a Stock Company to the co-owners of the shareholders if it is sent to one of them.
(5) The provisions of each of the preceding two paragraphs shall apply mutatis mutandis to cases where, when the notice referred to in Article 299 (1) (including the case where it is applied mutatis mutandis in Article 325) is given, a document is delivered to shareholders or matters to be stated in such document are provided to shareholders by Electromagnetic Means. In such cases, the words "to have arrived" in paragraph (2) shall be read as "to have been effected by delivery of such documents or provision of such matters by Electromagnetic Means."

Section 3 Transfer of Share

Subsection 1 Transfer of Share

(Transfer of Share)
Article 127 Shareholders may transfer the shares held by the same.

(Transfer of Shares in Company Issuing Share Certificate)
Article 128 (1) Transfer of shares in a Company Issuing Share Certificate shall not become effective unless the share certificates representing such shares are delivered; provided, however, that this shall not apply to transfer of shares that arise out of the disposition of Treasury Shares.
(2) Transfer effected prior to the issuance of the share certificate shall not be effective vis-a-vis the Company Issuing Share Certificate.

(Special Provisions on Disposition of Treasury Shares)
Article 129 (1) A Company Issuing Share Certificate shall deliver the share certificates to persons who acquire Treasury Shares without delay after the day of the disposition of such Treasury Shares.
(2) Notwithstanding the provisions of the preceding paragraph, a Company Issuing Share Certificate that is not a Public Company may choose to not deliver the share certificates under that paragraph until the persons under that paragraph so request.

(Perfection of Transfer of Shares)
Article 130 (1) Transfer of shares shall not be perfected against the Stock Company and other third parties unless the name and address of the person who acquires those shares is stated or recorded in the shareholder registry.
(2) For the purpose of the application of the provisions of the preceding paragraph with

respect to a Company Issuing Share Certificate, "the Stock Company and other third parties" in that paragraph shall be read as "the Stock Company."

(Presumption of Rights)
Article 131 (1) A possessor of share certificates shall be presumed to be the lawful owner of the rights in relation to the shares representing such share certificates.
(2) A person who receives delivery of the share certificates shall acquire the rights in relation to the shares represented by such share certificates; provided, however, that this shall not apply if that person has knowledge or is grossly negligent as to the fact of defective title of the transferor.

(Stating or Recording of Matters to be Stated in Shareholder registry Not Requested by Shareholders)
Article 132 In the cases provided for in the following items, a Stock Company shall state or record the Matters to be Stated in the Shareholder Registry relating to the shareholders of the shares referred to in such items:
(i) In cases where it has Issued Shares;
(ii) In cases where it has acquired shares in such Stock Company;
(iii) In cases where it has disposed of Treasury Shares.

(Stating or Recording of Matters to be Stated in Shareholder Registry at Request of Shareholders)
Article 133 (1) A person who has acquired shares from any person other than the Stock Company that issued such shares (excluding such Stock Company, hereinafter in this Section referred to as "Acquirer of Shares") may request that such Stock Company states or records the Matters to be Stated in the Shareholder Registry relating to such shares in the shareholder registry.
(2) Except for the cases prescribed by the applicable Ordinance of the Ministry of Justice as cases of no likelihood of detriment to interested parties, requests pursuant to the provisions of the preceding paragraph shall be made jointly with the person stated or recorded in the shareholder registry as the shareholder of the shares so acquired, or his/her general successors including his/her heirs.

Article 134 The provisions of the preceding paragraph shall not apply in cases where the shares acquired by the Acquirer of Shares are Shares with Restriction on Transfer; provided, however, that this shall not apply in cases where it falls under any of the following:
(i) Such Acquirer of Shares has obtained approval under Article 136 as to an intended acquisition of such Shares with Restriction on Transfer;
(ii) Such Acquirer of Shares has obtained approval under Article 137 (1) as to a completed acquisition of such Shares with Restriction on Transfer;
(iii) Such Acquirer of Shares is a Designated Purchaser provided for in Article 140 (4);
(iv) Such Acquirer of Shares is a person who has acquired the Shares with Restriction on Transfer by general succession including inheritance.

(Acquisition of Shares of Parent Companies Prohibited)
Article 135 (1) A Subsidiary may not acquire the shares of a Stock Company that is its Parent Company (hereinafter in this article referred to as "Parent Company's Shares").
(2) The provisions of the preceding paragraph shall not apply to the following cases:
(i) Cases where the Subsidiary accepts the transfer of the Parent Company's Shares held by another Company in cases where the Subsidiary accepts the assignment of

the entire business of such other Company (including Foreign Companies);
(ii) Cases where the Subsidiary succeeds to the Parent Company's Shares from a Company that is extinguished after a merger;
(iii) Cases where the Subsidiary succeeds to the Parent Company's Shares from another Company by Absorption-type Company Split;
(iv) Cases where the Subsidiary succeeds to the Parent Company's Shares from another Company by Incorporation-type Company Split; or
(v) In addition to the cases provided for in the preceding items, cases prescribed by the applicable Ordinance of the Ministry of Justice.
(3) The Subsidiary shall dispose of the Parent Company's Shares held by the same at an appropriate time.

Subsection 2 Approval Procedures relating to Transfer of Shares

(Requests for Approval by Shareholders)
Article 136 If shareholders of Shares with Restriction on Transfer intend to transfer the Shares with Restriction on Transfer held by the same to others (excluding the Stock Company which issued such Shares with Restriction on Transfer), they may request that such Stock Company make a determination as to whether or not to approve the acquisition by such others of such Shares with Restriction on Transfer.

(Request for Approval by Acquirers of Shares)
Article 137 (1) Acquirers of Shares who have acquired Shares with Restriction on Transfer may request that the Stock Company make a determination as to whether or not to approve the acquisition of such Shares with Restriction on Transfer.
(2) Except for the cases prescribed by the applicable Ordinance of the Ministry of Justice as cases of no likelihood of detriment to interested parties, requests pursuant to the provisions of the preceding paragraph shall be made jointly with the person stated or recorded in the shareholder registry as the shareholder of the shares so acquired, or his/her general successors including his/her heirs.

(Method for Requests for Approval of Transfer)
Article 138 The requests listed in the following items (hereinafter in this Subsection referred to as "Requests for Approval of Transfer") shall be made by disclosing the matters provided for in such items:
(i) Requests pursuant to the provisions of Article 136: The following matters:
  (a) The number of Shares with Restriction on Transfer that the shareholders making such request intend to transfer to others (or, for a Company with Class Shares, the classes of the shares and the number of shares for each class);
  (b) The name of the person accepting the transfer of the Shares with Restriction on Transfer referred to in (a);
  (c) In cases where a Stock Company determines not to give approval under Article 136, if it is requested that such Stock Company or Designated Purchaser provided for in Article 140 (4) purchase the Shares with Restriction on Transfer referred to in (a), the statement to such effect.
(ii) The request pursuant to the provisions of paragraph (1) of the preceding article: The following matters:
  (a) The number of Shares with Restriction on Transfer which the Acquirer of Shares making such request has acquired (or, for a Company with Class Shares, the classes of the shares and the number of shares for each class);

(b) The name of the Acquirer of Shares referred to in (a);
(c) In cases where a Stock Company determines not to effect the approval under paragraph (1) of the preceding article, if it is requested that such Stock Company or the Designated Purchaser provided for in Article 140 (4) purchase the Shares with Restriction on Transfer referred to in (a), a statement to such effect.

(Determination of Approval of transfer)
Article 139 (1) The determination by a Stock Company as to whether or not to grant approval under Article 136 or Article 137 (1) shall be made by resolution of a shareholders meeting (or of a board of directors meeting for a Company with Board of Directors); provided, however, that this shall not apply in cases where it is otherwise provided for in the articles of incorporation.
(2) If a Stock Company has made a determination under the preceding paragraph, it shall notify the person who made the Requests for Approval of Transfer (hereinafter in this Subsection referred to as "Requester for Approval of Transfer") of the content of such determination.

(Purchase by Stock Company or Designated Purchaser)
Article 140 (1) In cases where a Stock Company receives a request under Article 138 (i) (c) or (ii)(c), if it makes a determination to not give approval under Article 136 or Article 137 (1), it shall purchase the Shares with Restriction on Transfer relating to such Requests for Approval of Transfer (hereinafter in this Subsection referred to as "Subject Shares"). In such cases, the following matters shall be prescribed:
(i) A statement to the effect that the Stock Company will purchase the Subject Shares;
(ii) The number of the Subject Shares that will be purchased by the Stock Company (or, for a Company with Class Shares, the classes of the Subject Shares and the number of shares for each class).
(2) The determination of the matters listed in the items of the preceding paragraph shall be made by resolution of a shareholders meeting.
(3) Requesters for Approval of Transfer may not exercise voting right at the shareholders meeting referred to in the preceding paragraph; provided, however, that this shall not apply in cases where all shareholders other than such Requesters for Approval of Transfer may not exercise voting right at the shareholders meeting referred to in that paragraph.
(4) Notwithstanding the provisions of paragraph (1), in the cases provided for in that paragraph, a Stock Company may designate a person to purchase some or all of the Subject Shares (hereinafter in this Subsection referred to as "Designated Purchaser").
(5) The designation pursuant to the provisions of the preceding paragraph shall be made by resolution of the shareholders meeting (or of a board of directors meeting for a Company with Board of Directors); provided, however, that this shall not apply in cases where it is otherwise provided for in the articles of incorporation.

(Notice of Purchases by Stock Company)
Article 141 (1) If a Stock Company has determined the matters listed in any item of paragraph (1) of the preceding article, it shall notify the Requester for Approval of Transfer of such matters.
(2) If a Stock Company intends to give notice pursuant to the provisions of the preceding paragraph, it shall deposit the amount obtained by multiplying the amount of the net assets per share (referring to the amount prescribed by the applicable Ordinance of the Ministry of Justice as the amount of net assets per share. The same shall apply

hereinafter.) by the number of the Subject Shares under item (ii), paragraph (1) of the preceding article, with a depository located in the area where its head office is located, and deliver a document certifying such deposit to the Requester for Approval of Transfer.
(3) In cases where the Subject Shares are the shares of a Company Issuing Share Certificate, the Requester for Approval of Transfer who received delivery of the document referred to in the preceding paragraph shall deposit the share certificates representing the Subject Shares referred to in item (ii), paragraph (1) of the preceding article with a depository located in the area where the head office of such Company Issuing Share Certificate is located within one week from the day of receipt of such delivery. In such cases, such Requester for Approval of Transfer shall give notice of such deposit to such Company Issuing Share Certificate without delay.
(4) If the Requester for Approval of Transfer under the preceding paragraph does not effect the deposit pursuant to the provisions of that paragraph within the period under that paragraph, the Company Issuing Share Certificate may cancel the contract for the sale and purchase of the Subject Shares provided for in item (ii), paragraph (1) of the preceding article.

(Designated Purchaser's Notice to Purchase)
Article 142 (1) If a Designated Purchaser is designated pursuant to the provisions of Article 140(4), he/she shall notify the Requester for Approval of Transfer of the following matters:
(i) A statement to the effect that he/she has been designated as a Designated Purchaser; and
(ii) The number of the Subject Shares that the Designated Purchaser will purchase (or, for a Company with Class Shares, the classes of the Subject Shares and the number of shares for each class).
(2) If a Designated Purchaser intends to give notice pursuant to the provisions of the preceding paragraph, the Designated Purchaser shall deposit the amount obtained by multiplying the amount of the net assets per share by the number of the Subject Shares under item (ii) of that paragraph with a depository located in the area where the head office of the Stock Company is located, and deliver a document certifying such deposit to the Requester for Approval of Transfer.
(3) In cases where the Subject Shares are the shares of a Company Issuing Share Certificate, the Requester for Approval of Transfers who received delivery of the document referred to in the preceding paragraph shall deposit the share certificates representing the Subject Shares referred to in item (ii) of paragraph (1) with a depository located in the area where the head office of such Company Issuing Share Certificate is located within one week from the day of receipt of such delivery. In such cases, such Requester for Approval of Transfer shall give notice of such deposit to the Designated Purchaser without delay.
(4) If the Requester for Approval of Transfer under the preceding paragraph does not effect the deposit pursuant to the provisions of that paragraph within the period under that paragraph, the Designated Purchaser may cancel the contract for the sale and purchase of the Subject Shares provided for in item (ii) of paragraph (1).

(Withdrawal of Requests for Approval of Transfer)
Article 143 (1) A Requester for Approval of Transfer who made a request under Article 138(i)(c) or (ii)(c) may, after he/she has received notice pursuant to the provisions of Article 141(1), withdraw his/her request only in cases where he/she obtains the approval of the Stock Company.

(2) A Requester of Approval of Transfer who made a request under Article 138(i)(c) or (ii)(c) may, after he/she has received notice pursuant to the provisions of paragraph (1) of the preceding article, withdraw his/her request only in cases where he/she obtains the approval of the Designated Purchaser.

(Determination of Sale Price)
Article 144 (1) In cases where notice is given pursuant to the provisions of Article 141(1), the sale price of the Subject Shares under Article 140(1)(ii) shall be prescribed through discussion between the Stock Company and the Requester for Approval of Transfer.
(2) The Stock Company or Requester for Approval of Transfers may file a petition to the court for a determination of the sale price within twenty days from the day when notice is given pursuant to the provisions of Article 141(1).
(3) In order to make the determination under the preceding paragraph, the court shall consider the financial conditions of the Stock Company at the time of the Requests for Approval of Transfer and all other circumstances.
(4) Notwithstanding the provisions of paragraph (1), if a petition under paragraph (2) is made within the period provided for in that paragraph, the amount determined by the court in response to such petition shall be the sale price of the Subject Shares under Article 140(1)(ii).
(5) Notwithstanding the provisions of paragraph (1), if no petition under paragraph (2) is made within the period provided for in that paragraph (except in cases where the discussions under paragraph (1) are successfully concluded within such period), the amount obtained by multiplying the amount of the net assets per share by the number of the Subject Shares under Article 140(1)(ii) shall be the sale price of the Subject Shares.
(6) In cases where a deposit is effected pursuant to the provisions of Article 141(2), if the sale price of the Subject Shares under Article 140(1)(ii) has been finalized, the Stock Company shall be deemed to have paid the sale price, in whole or in part, up to an amount equivalent to the value of the money so deposited.
(7) The provisions of the preceding paragraphs shall apply mutatis mutandis in cases where notice is given pursuant to the provisions of Article 142(1). In such cases, in paragraph (1), the term "Article 140(1)(ii)" shall be read as "Article 142(1)(ii)" and the term "Stock Company" shall be read as "Designated Purchaser"; in paragraph (2), the term "Stock Company" shall be read as "Designated Purchaser"; in paragraph (4) and paragraph (5), the term "Article 140(1)(ii)" shall be read as "Article 142(1)(ii)"; and in the preceding paragraph, the term "Article 141(2)" shall be read as "Article 142(2)," the term "Article 140(1)(ii)" shall be read as "item (ii), paragraph (1) of that article," and the term "Stock Company" shall be read as "Designated Purchaser."

(Cases where Stock Company is Deemed to have Approved)
Article 145 In the cases listed below, the Stock Company shall be deemed to have given the approval under Article 136 or Article 137(1); provided, however, that this shall not apply if otherwise provided for by the agreement between the Stock Company and the Requester for Approval of Transfer:
(i) In cases where the Stock Company has failed to give notice pursuant to the provisions of Article 139(2) within two weeks (or if any shorter period of time is provided for in the articles of incorporation, such shorter period of time) from the day of the request pursuant to the provisions of Article 136 or Article 137(1);
(ii) In cases where the Stock Company has failed to give notice pursuant to the provisions of Article 141(1) within forty days (or if any shorter period of time is provided

for in the articles of incorporation, such shorter period of time) from the day of the notice pursuant to the provisions of Article 139(2) (except the cases where the Designated Purchaser gives notice pursuant to the provisions of Article 142(1) within ten days (or if any shorter period of time is provided in the articles of incorporation, such shorter period of time) from the day of the notice pursuant to the provisions of Article 139(2)).

(iii) In addition to the cases provided for in the preceding two items, the cases prescribed by the applicable Ordinance of the Ministry of Justice.

Subsection 3 Pledging Shares

(Pledge of Shares)
Article 146 (1) Shareholders may pledge the shares held by the same.
(2) Pledge of shares of a Company Issuing Share Certificate shall not become effective unless the share certificates for such shares are delivered.

(Perfection of Pledges of Shares)
Article 147 (1) Pledges of shares shall not be perfected against the Stock Company and other third parties unless the names and addresses of the pledgees are stated or recorded in the shareholder registry.
(2) Notwithstanding the provisions of the preceding paragraph, a pledgee of shares of a Company Issuing Share Certificate may not assert his/her pledge against the Stock Company and other third parties unless he/she is in continuous possession of the share certificates for such shares.
(3) The provisions of Article 364 of the Civil Code shall not apply to shares.

(Entries in Shareholder Registry)
Article 148 A person who pledges shares may request that the Stock Company state or record the following matters in the shareholder registry:
(i) The name and address of the pledgee;
(ii) The shares underlying the pledge.

(Delivery of Documents Stating Matters to be Stated in Shareholder Registry)
Article 149 (1) The pledgees for whom the matters listed in the items of the preceding article are stated or recorded in the shareholder registry (hereinafter referred to as "Registered Pledgees of Shares") may request that the Stock Company deliver documents stating the matters listed in the items of that article with respect to such Registered Pledgees of Shares that are stated or recorded in the shareholder registry, or provide the Electromagnetic Records that record such matters.
(2) The documents in the preceding paragraph shall be affixed with the signature, or name and seal, of the Representative Director of the Stock Company (the representative executive officer for a Company with Committees. The same shall apply hereinafter in this paragraph and in the following paragraph.).
(3) With respect to the Electromagnetic Records referred to in paragraph (1), the Representative Director of the Stock Company shall implement measures in lieu of the affixation of signature, or name and seal prescribed by the applicable Ordinance of the Ministry of Justice.
(4) The provisions of the preceding three paragraphs shall not apply to a Company Issuing Share Certificate.

(Notices to Registered Pledgees of Shares)

Art.150～152   [I] Companies Act, PART II, Chap.II, Sec.3

Article 150 (1) It shall be sufficient for a notice or demand to a Registered Pledgee of Shares to be sent by a Stock Company to the addresses of such Registered Pledgee of Shares stated or recorded in the shareholder registry (or, in cases where such Registered Pledgee of Shares notifies the Stock Company of any different place or contact address for the receipt of notices or demands, to such place or contact address).
(2) The notices or demands referred to in the preceding paragraph shall be deemed to have arrived at the time when such notice or demand should normally have arrived.

(Effect of Pledge of Shares)
Article 151 In cases where a Stock Company carries out any of the acts listed below, the pledge for shares shall be effective with respect to the Monies, etc. (meaning monies and other properties. The same shall apply hereinafter.) which the shareholders of such shares are entitled to receive as a result of such act:
(i) The acquisition of Shares with Put Option pursuant to the provisions Article 167(1);
(ii) The acquisition of Shares subject to Call pursuant to the provisions of paragraph (1) of Article 170(1);
(iii) The acquisition of Class Shares subject to Wholly Call provided for in Article 171(1) pursuant to the provisions of Article 173(1);
(iv) Consolidation of shares;
(v) Share Split;
(vi) Allotment of Shares without Contribution provided for in Article 185;
(vii) Allotment of Share Options without Contribution provided for in Article 277;
(viii) Dividends of surplus;
(ix) Distribution of residual assets;
(x) Entity Conversion;
(xi) Mergers (limited to cases where such Stock Company is to be extinguished as a result of the merger);
(xii) Share Exchange;
(xiii) Share Transfer; or
(xiv) Acquisition of shares (excluding the acts listed in item (i) to item (iii) inclusive).

Article 152 (1) In cases where a Stock Company (excluding a Company Issuing Share Certificate. The same shall apply hereinafter in this article.) carries out the acts listed in item (i) to item (iii) inclusive of the preceding article (limited to the cases where such Stock Company delivers the shares when carrying out such acts), or carries out the act listed in item (vi) of that article, if the pledgees of the pledges under that article are Registered Pledgees of Shares (excluding those for whom the matters listed in each item of Article 148 are stated or recorded in the shareholder registry because of a request pursuant to the provisions of Article 218(5). The same shall apply hereinafter in this Subsection.), the names and addresses of such pledgees shall be stated or recorded in the shareholder registry with respect to the shares under the preceding article that the shareholders are entitled to receive.
(2) In cases where the consolidation of shares has been effected, if the pledgees of the pledge under the preceding article are Registered Pledgees of Shares, the Stock Company shall state or record the names and addresses of such pledgees with respect to the shares that have been consolidated.
(3) In cases where the Share Split has been effected, if the pledgees of the pledge under the preceding article are Registered Pledgees of Shares, the Stock Company shall state or record the names and addresses of such pledgees with respect to the shares that have been split.

Article 153 (1) In the cases provided for in paragraph (1) of the preceding article, the Company Issuing Share Certificate shall deliver the share certificates representing the shares that the shareholders under Article 151 receive to the Registered Pledgees of Shares.
(2) In the cases provided for in paragraph (2) of the preceding article, the Company Issuing Share Certificate shall deliver the share certificates representing the shares that have been consolidated to the Registered Pledgees of Shares.
(3) In the cases provided for in paragraph (3) of the preceding article, the Company Issuing Share Certificate shall deliver the share certificates that will be newly issued with respect to the shares that have been split to the Registered Pledgees of Shares.

Article 154 (1) Registered Pledgees of Shares may receive Monies, etc. (limited to monies) under Article 151, and appropriate them as payment to satisfy their own claims in priority to other creditors.
(2) If the claims under the preceding paragraph have not yet become due and payable, the Registered Pledgees of Shares may have the Stock Company deposit an amount equivalent to the value of the Monies, etc. provided for in that paragraph. In such cases, the pledge shall be effective with respect to the monies so deposited.

Section 4 Acquisition of Own Shares by Stock Company

Subsection 1 General Provisions

Article 155 A Stock Company may acquire shares issued by such Stock Company only in the following cases:
(i) Where the grounds under Article 107(2)(iii)(a) have arisen;
(ii) Where a request has been made under Article 138(i)(c) or (ii)(c);
(iii) Where a resolution has been made under paragraph (1) of the following article;
(iv) Where a request has been made pursuant to the provisions of Article 166(1);
(v) Where a resolution has been made under Article 176(1);
(vi) Where the Stock Company has made a request under the provisions of Article 176(1);
(vii) Where a request has been made pursuant to the provisions of Article 192(1);
(viii) Where the Stock Company has prescribed the matters listed in each item of Article 197(3);
(ix) Where the Stock Company has prescribed the matters listed in each item of Article 234(4);
(x) Where the Stock Company accepts the assignment of the entire business of another Company (including Foreign Companies) in cases where such Stock Company accepts the assignment of own shares held by such other Company;
(xi) Where the Stock Company succeeds to own shares held by a Company that is to be extinguished after merger;
(xii) Where the Stock Company succeeds to own shares held by a Company that is effecting an Absorption-type Company Split; or
(xiii) In addition to the cases listed in the preceding items, in any case prescribed by the applicable Ordinance of the Ministry of Justice.

Art.156~159　　Ⅰ Companies Act, PART II, Chap.II, Sec.4

Subsection 2　Acquisition by Agreement with Shareholders

Division 1　General Provisions

(Determination of Matters regarding Acquisition of Shares)
Article 156　(1) A Stock Company shall prescribe the following matters by resolution of a shareholders meeting in advance in order to acquire for value own shares by agreement with its shareholders; provided, however, that the period under item (iii) cannot exceed one year:
(i) The number of shares to be acquired (or, for a Company with Class Shares, the classes of the shares and the number of shares for each class); and
(ii) The description and total amount of the Monies, etc. (excluding the shares, etc. of such Stock Company. The same shall apply hereinafter in this Subsection.) that will be delivered in exchange for the acquisition of the shares; and
(iii) The period during which the shares can be acquired.
(2) The provisions of the preceding paragraph shall not apply to the cases listed in item (i) and item (ii), and in item (iv) to item (xiii) inclusive of the preceding article.

(Determination of Acquisition Price)
Article 157　(1) Whenever a Stock Company intends to acquire its shares in accordance with a determination pursuant to the provisions of paragraph (1) of the preceding article, it shall prescribe the following matters:
(i) The number of shares to be acquired (or, for a Company with Class Shares, the class of the shares and the number of the shares);
(ii) The description, and the number or amount, or the method for the calculation thereof, of the Monies, etc. that will be delivered in exchange for the acquisition of one share;
(iii) The total amount of Monies, etc. that will be delivered in exchange for the acquisition of the shares; and
(iv) The date on which the offer to transfer the shares will be made.
(2) A Company with Board of Directors shall determine the matters listed in each item of the preceding paragraph by resolution of the board of directors.
(3) The conditions prescribed for the acquisition of shares under paragraph (1) shall be uniform for each determination made under the provisions of that paragraph.

(Notice to Shareholders)
Article 158　(1) A Stock Company shall notify its shareholders (or, for a Company with Class Shares, the Class Shareholders of the classes of the shares it intends to acquire) of the matters listed in each item of paragraph (1) of the preceding article.
(2) A Public Company may substitute a public notice for the notice under the provisions of the preceding paragraph.

(Offers to transfer)
Article 159　(1) If a shareholder who receives a notice pursuant to the provisions of paragraph (1) of the preceding article intends to make an offer to transfer the shares he/she holds, he/she shall disclose to the Stock Company the number of shares (or, for a Company with Class Shares, the classes of the shares and the number of the shares for each class) relating to such offer.
(2) A Stock Company shall be deemed to have accepted, on the date provided for in Article 157(1)(iv), the transfer of shares that the shareholders under the preceding para-

graph offered; provided, however, that if the total number of shares that the shareholders under that paragraph offered (hereinafter in this paragraph referred to as "Total Number of Shares Offered") exceed the number provided for in item (i), paragraph (1) of that article (hereinafter in this paragraph referred to as "Total Number of Shares to be Acquired"), it shall be deemed that the Stock Company has accepted the transfer of the shares in the number obtained by first dividing the Total Number of Shares to be Acquired by the Total Number of Shares Offered, and then multiplying such product by the number of the shares offered by the shareholders under the preceding paragraph (in cases where the number so obtained includes a fraction of less than one, such fraction shall be rounded off).

Division 2 Acquisition from Specific Shareholders

(Acquisition from Specific Shareholders)
Article 160 (1) In conjunction with the determination of the matters listed in each item of Article 156(1), a Stock Company may, by resolution of a shareholders meeting under that paragraph, make a determination to the effect that notice under the provisions of Article 158(1) shall be given to specific shareholders.
(2) If a Stock Company intends to make a determination under the provisions of the preceding paragraph, it shall give notice to the shareholders (or, for a Company with Class Shares, the Class Shareholders of the classes of the shares to be acquired), by the time prescribed by the applicable Ordinance of the Ministry of Justice, to the effect that the shareholders may make the requests under the provisions of the following paragraph.
(3) The shareholders under the preceding paragraph may, by the time prescribed by the applicable Ordinance of the Ministry of Justice, request that they be added to the specific shareholders provided for in paragraph (1) for the proposal for the shareholders meeting under that paragraph.
(4) The specific shareholders under paragraph (1) may not exercise voting right at the shareholders meeting provided for in Article 156(1); provided, however, that this shall not apply in cases where all shareholders other than the specific shareholders under paragraph (1) may not exercise the voting right at such shareholders meeting.
(5) In cases where specific shareholders are prescribed under paragraph (1), for the purpose of the application of the provisions of Article 158(1), "shareholders (or, for a Company with Class Shares, the Class Shareholder of the classes of the shares it intends to acquire)" in such paragraph shall be read as "specific shareholders under Article 160(1)."

(Special Provision on Acquisition of Shares with Market Price)
Article 161 The provisions of paragraph (2) and paragraph (3) of the preceding article shall not apply if, in cases where the shares to be acquired are shares with a market price, the amount of the Monies, etc. to be delivered in exchange for the acquisition of one such share does not exceed the amount of the market price of one such share calculated by the method prescribed by the applicable Ordinance of the Ministry of Justice.

(Special Provision on Acquisition from Heirs)
Article 162 The provisions of Article 160(2) and (3) shall not apply in cases where a Stock Company acquires, from general successors of the shareholders, including their heirs, the shares of such Stock Company that the same acquired by general succession including inheritance; provided, however, that this shall not apply if it falls under any

of the following:
(i) The Stock Company is a Public Company; or
(ii) Such general successors, including heirs exercised the voting right on such shares at a shareholders meeting or Class Meeting.

(Acquisition of Shares from Subsidiaries)
Article 163 In cases where a Stock Company acquires shares in such Stock Company that are held by its Subsidiary, for the purpose of the application of the provisions of Article 156(1), "shareholders meeting" in such paragraph shall be read as "shareholders meeting (or board of directors meeting for a Company with Board of Directors)." In such cases, the provisions of Article 157 to Article 160 inclusive shall not apply.

(Provisions of Articles of Incorporation regarding Acquisition from Specific Shareholders)
Article 164 (1) If a Stock Company intends to make a determination under the provisions of Article 160(1) with respect to the acquisition of shares (or, for a Company with Class Shares, shares of a certain class. The same shall apply in the following paragraph.), it may provide in the articles of incorporation to the effect that the provisions of paragraph (2) and paragraph (3) of that article shall not apply.
(2) If, after the shares are issued, it is intended to create a provision in the articles of incorporation under the provisions of the preceding paragraph with respect to such shares by amending the articles of incorporation, or to effect any amendment (excluding that which abolishes the provisions of the articles of incorporation under that paragraph) in the articles of incorporation with respect to such provisions, the consent of all shareholders who hold such shares shall be obtained.

Division 3 Acquisition of Shares by Market Transactions

Article 165 (1) The provisions of Article 157 to Article 160 inclusive shall not apply in cases where a Stock Company acquires shares in such Stock Company through transactions undertaken by that Stock Company in the market or through a takeover bid provided for in Article 27-2(6) of the Financial Instruments and Exchange Act (hereinafter in this article referred to as "Market Transactions").
(2) A Company with Board of Directors may provide in its articles of incorporation to the effect that the acquisition of own shares by Market Transactions may be prescribed by resolution of a board of directors meeting.
(3) In cases where the provision of the articles of incorporation under the provisions of the preceding paragraph is created, for the purpose of the application of the provisions of Article 156(1), "shareholders meeting" in such paragraph shall be read as "shareholders meeting (or shareholders meeting or board of director's meeting in the cases provided for in Article 165(1))."

Subsection 3 Acquisition of Shares with Put Option and Shares subject to Call

Division 1 Demand for Acquisition of Shares with Put Option

(Demand for Acquisition)
Article 166 (1) Shareholders of Shares with Put Option may demand that the Stock

Company acquire the Shares with Put Option held by such shareholders; provided, however, that this shall not apply if, in cases where the properties provided for in item (ii)(b) to item (ii)(e) inclusive of Article 107(2) is delivered in exchange for the acquisition of such Shares with Put Option, the book value of such properties exceeds the Distributable Amount under Article 461(2) on the day when such demand is made.
(2) The demand pursuant to the provisions of the preceding paragraph shall be submitted by disclosing the number of Shares with Put Option relating to such demand (or, for a Company with Class Shares, the classes of the Shares with Put Option and the number of shares for each class).
(3) If shareholders of a Company Issuing Share Certificate intend to submit demand pursuant to the provisions of paragraph (1) with respect to the Shares with Put Option held by the same, they shall submit the share certificates representing such Shares with Put Option to the Company Issuing Share Certificate; provided, however, that this shall not apply in cases where no share certificate representing such Shares with Put Option is issued.

(Effectuation)
Article 167 (1) A Stock Company shall acquire the Shares with Put Option relating to a demand pursuant to the provisions of paragraph (1) of the preceding article on the day of such demand.
(2) In the cases listed in the following items, a shareholders who submits a demand pursuant to the provisions of paragraph (1) of the preceding article shall become a shareholder provided for in each of such items in accordance with the provisions with respect to the matters provided for in Article 107(2)(ii) (or, for a Company with Class Shares, Article 108(2)(v)) on the day of the demand:
(i) In cases where there is a provision on the matters listed in Article 107(2)(ii)(b): Bondholders of the Bonds under that item (ii)(b);
(ii) In cases where there is a provision on the matters listed in Article 107(2)(ii)(c): Holders of Share Options under that item (ii)(c);
(iii) In cases where there is a provision on the matters listed in Article 107(2)(ii)(d): Bondholders of the Bonds with respect to Bonds with Share Option under that item (ii)(d), and holders of Share Options attached to such Bonds with Share Option;
(iv) In cases where there is a provision on the matters listed in Article 108(2)(v)(b): Shareholders of "other shares" under that item (v)(b);
(3) In the cases provided for in item (iv) of the preceding paragraph, if the number of the "other shares" provided for in such item includes a fraction of less than one share, it shall be rounded off. In such cases, unless otherwise provided in the articles of incorporation, the Stock Company shall, in accordance with the categories of the cases listed in the following items, deliver to the shareholders who submitted demands pursuant to the provisions of paragraph (1) of the preceding article the monies in the amount equivalent to the amount obtained by multiplying the amount provided for in each of such items by such fraction:
(i) In cases where such shares are shares with a market price: The amount calculated by the method prescribed by the applicable Ordinance of the Ministry of Justice as the amount of the market price of one such share;
(ii) In cases other than the cases listed in the preceding item: The amount of net assets per share.
(4) The provisions of the preceding paragraph shall apply mutatis mutandis to cases where there is a fraction with respect to the Bonds and Share Options of such Stock Company. In such cases, the term "amount of net assets per share" in item (ii) of that

paragraph shall be read as "the amount prescribed by the applicable Ordinance of the Ministry of Justice."

Division 2 Acquisitions of Shares subject to Call

(Determination of Day of Acquisition)
Article 168 (1) In cases where there is a provision with respect to the matters listed in Article 107(2)(iii)(b), the Stock Company shall prescribe the day under that item (iii)(b) by resolution of a shareholders meeting (or of a board of director's meeting for a Company with Board of Directors); provided, however, that this shall not apply in cases where it is otherwise provided for in the articles of incorporation.
(2) If a Stock Company prescribes the day under Article 107(2)(iii)(b), the Stock Company shall notify the shareholders of the Shares subject to Call (or, in cases where there is a provision with respect to the matters listed in item (iii)(c) of that paragraph, the shareholders of Shares subject to Call who are determined under the provisions of paragraph (1) of the following article) and the Registered Pledgees of Shares thereof of such date no later than two weeks prior to such day.
(3) A public notice may be substituted for the notice under the provisions of the preceding paragraph.

(Determination of Shares to be Acquired)
Article 169 (1) In cases where there is a provision with respect to the matters listed in Article 107(2)(iii)(c), if a Stock Company intends to acquire Shares subject to Call, it shall determine the Shares subject to Call that it intends to acquire.
(2) The Shares subject to Call under the preceding paragraph shall be determined by resolution of a shareholders meeting (or of a board of directors meeting for a Company with Board of Directors); provided, however, that this shall not apply in cases where it is otherwise provided for in the articles of incorporation.
(3) If a Stock Company makes the determination pursuant to the provisions of paragraph (1), the Stock Company shall immediately notify the shareholders of the Shares subject to Call who are identified pursuant to the provisions of that paragraph and the Registered Pledgees of Shares thereof to the effect that the Stock Company will acquire such Shares subject to Call.
(4) A public notice may be substituted for the notice pursuant to the provisions of the preceding paragraph.

(Effectuation)
Article 170 (1) A Stock Company shall acquire, on the day when the grounds under Article 107(2)(iii)(a) have arisen (or, in cases where there is a provision with respect to the matters listed in item (iii)(c) thereof, on the day listed in item (i) or the day listed in item (ii) below, whichever comes later. The same shall apply in the following paragraph and paragraph (5).), the Shares subject to Call (or, in cases where there is a provision with respect to the matters listed in item (iii)(c), paragraph (2) of that article, those determined pursuant to the provisions of paragraph (1) of the preceding article. The same shall apply in the following paragraph.):
(i) The day when grounds under Article 107(2)(iii)(a) have arisen; or
(ii) The day of notice pursuant to the provisions of paragraph (3) of the preceding article, or the day when two weeks have lapsed from the day of the public notice under paragraph (4) of that article.
(2) In the cases listed in the following items, the shareholders of the Shares subject to Call (excluding the relevant Stock Company) shall become the status provided for in

each of such items in accordance with the provisions with respect to the matters provided for in such item (or, for a Company with Class Shares, Article 108(2)(vi)) on the day when the grounds under Article 107(2)(iii)(a) have arisen:
  (i) In cases where there is a provision on the matters listed in Article 107(2)(iii)(d): Bondholders of the Bonds under that item (iii)(d);
  (ii) In cases where there is a provision on the matters listed in Article 107(2)(iii)(e): Holders of Share Options under that item (iii)(e);
  (iii) In cases where there is a provision on the matters listed in Article 107(2)(iii)(f): Bondholders of the Bonds with respect to Bonds with Share Option under that item (ii)(d), and holders of Share Options attached to such Bonds with Share Option;
  (iv) In cases where there is a provision on the matters listed in Article 108(2)(vi)(b): Shareholders of "other shares" under that item (vi)(b);
(3) A Stock Company shall notify the shareholders of Shares subject to Call and Registered Pledgees of Shares thereof without delay after grounds have arisen under Article 107(2)(iii)(a) (in cases where there is a provision with respect to the matters listed in that item (iii)(c), the shareholders of Shares subject to Call determined pursuant to the provisions of paragraph (1) of the preceding article, and Registered Pledgees of Shares thereof) to the effect that such grounds have arisen; provided, however, that this shall not apply if the Stock Company has given notice under the provisions of Article 168(2) or has given public notice under the provisions of paragraph (3) of that article.
(4) A public notice may be substituted for the notice under the provisions of the preceding paragraph.
(5) The provisions of the preceding paragraphs shall not apply if, in cases where the properties provided for in item (iii)(d) to item (iii)(g) inclusive of Article 107(2) is delivered in exchange for the acquisition of the Shares subject to Call, the book value of such properties exceeds the Distributable Amount under Article 461(2) on the day when the grounds under Article 107(2)(iii)(a) arose.

Subsection 4　Acquisition of Class Shares subject to Wholly Call

(Determinations regarding Acquisition of Class Shares subject to Wholly Call)
Article 171 (1) A Company with Class Shares which has issued Class Shares subject to Wholly Call (meaning the Class Shares that have provisions with respect to the matters listed in Article 108(1)(vii) hereof. The same shall apply in this Subsection.) may acquire all of the Class Shares subject to Wholly Call by resolution of a shareholders meeting. In such cases, the following matters shall be prescribed by resolution of such shareholders meeting:
  (i) If Monies, etc. will be delivered in exchange for the acquisition of the Class Shares subject to Wholly Call, the following matters with respect to such Monies, etc. (hereinafter in this article referred to as "Consideration for Acquisition"):
    (a) If such Consideration for Acquisition consists of the shares in the Stock Company, the classes of such shares and the number of shares for each class, or the method for calculating such numbers;
    (b) If such Consideration for Acquisition consists of the Bonds of the Stock Company (excluding those with respect to the Bonds with Share Option), the classes of such Bonds and the total amount of Bonds for each class, or the method for calculating such total amounts;
    (c) If such Consideration for Acquisition consists of the Share Options of the Stock

Company (excluding those attached to Bonds with Share Option), the features and number of such Share Options, or the method for calculating such number;
  (d) If such Consideration for Acquisition consists of the Bonds with Share Option of the Stock Company, the matters prescribed in (b) above with respect to such Bonds with Share Option, and the matters prescribed in (c) above with respect to the Share Options attached to such Bonds with Share Option; and
  (e) If such Consideration for Acquisition consists of properties other than the shares, etc. of the Stock Company, the description and number or value of such properties, or the method for calculating such number or value.
 (ii) In the cases provided for in the preceding item, the matters regarding the allotment of the Consideration for Acquisition to the shareholders of the Class Shares subject to Wholly Call.
 (iii) The day on which the Stock Company will acquire the Class Shares subject to Wholly Call (hereinafter in this Subsection referred to as "Acquisition Day").
(2) The provisions regarding the matters listed in item (ii) of the preceding paragraph shall stipulate that the Consideration for Acquisition will be allotted in proportion to the number of the Class Shares subject to Wholly Call held by the shareholders (excluding the relevant Stock Company).
(3) The directors, at the shareholders meeting under paragraph (1) above, shall explain the reasons for the need to acquire all of the Class Shares subject to Wholly Call.

(Petition to Court for Determination of Price)
Article 172 (1) In cases where the matters listed in each item of paragraph (1) of the preceding article are prescribed, the following shareholders may file a petition to the court, within twenty days from the day of the shareholders meeting under that paragraph, for a determination of the price of the Class Shares subject to Wholly Call for the acquisition by the Stock Company.
  (i) Shareholders who give notice to such Stock Company to the effect that they dissent from the acquisition by the Stock Company of the Class Shares subject to Wholly Call act prior to such shareholders meeting and do dissent from such acquisition at such shareholders meeting (limited to those who can exercise voting right at such shareholders meeting);
  (ii) Shareholders who cannot exercise voting right at such shareholders meeting.
(2) The Stock Company shall also pay the interest on the price determined by the court which shall be calculated at the rate of 6% per annum from and including the Acquisition Day.

(Effectuation)
Article 173 (1) A Stock Company shall acquire Class Shares subject to Wholly Call on the Acquisition Day.
(2) In the cases listed in the following items, shareholders of the Class Shares subject to Wholly Call other than the Stock Company shall become the person provided for in each of such items in accordance with provisions made by resolution of the shareholders meeting under Article 171(1) on the Acquisition Day:
  (i) In cases where there is a provision on the matters listed in Article 171(1)(i)(a): Shareholders of shares under that item (i)(a);
  (ii) In cases where there is a provision on the matters listed in Article 171(1)(i)(b): Bondholders of Bonds under that item (i)(b);
  (iii) In cases where there is a provision on the matters listed in Article 171(1)(i)(c): Holders of Share Options under that item (i)(c);
  (iv) In cases where there is a provision on the matters listed in Article 171(1)(i)(d):

Bondholders of the Bonds with respect to Bonds with Share Option under that item (i)(d), and holders of Share Options attached to such Bonds with Share Option;

Subsection 5 Demand for Sale to Heirs

(Provisions of Articles of Incorporation regarding Demand for Sale to Heirs)
Article 174 A Stock Company may provide in the articles of incorporation to the effect that it may demand that a person who has acquired shares (limited to Shares with Restriction on Transfer) in such Stock Company by general succession, including inheritance, sell such shares to such Stock Company.

(Determinations regarding Demand for Sale)
Article 175 (1) In cases where there is a provision of the articles of incorporation under the provisions of the preceding article, whenever a Stock Company intends to effect a demand pursuant to the provisions of paragraph (1) of the following article, it shall prescribe the following matters by resolution of a shareholders meeting:
  (i) The number of shares for which the Stock Company intends to effect the demand pursuant to the provisions of paragraph (1) of the following article (or, for a Company with Class Shares, the classes of the shares and the number of shares for each class); and
  (ii) The names of the persons who hold the shares under the preceding item.
(2) The persons under item (ii) of the preceding paragraph may not exercise voting right at the shareholders meeting under that paragraph; provided, however, that this shall not apply in cases where all shareholders other than the persons under that paragraph may not exercise the voting right at such shareholders meeting.

(Demand for Sale)
Article 176 (1) If a Stock Company determines the matters listed in each item of paragraph (1) of the preceding article, it may demand that the persons under item (ii) of that paragraph sell the shares under item (i) of that paragraph to such Stock Company; provided, however, that this shall not apply when one year has lapsed from the day when such Stock Company acquires knowledge of the general succession, including inheritances.
(2) Demands pursuant to the provisions of paragraph (1) shall be made by disclosing the number of shares relating to such demand (or, for a Company with Class Shares, the classes of the shares and the number of shares for each class).
(3) A Stock Company may withdraw a demand under the provisions of paragraph (1) at any time.

(Determination of Sale Price)
Article 177 (1) In cases where notice is given under the provisions of paragraph (1) of the preceding article, the sale price of the shares under Article 175(1)(i) shall be prescribed through discussion between the Stock Company and the persons under item (ii) of that paragraph.
(2) The Stock Company or persons under Article 175(1)(ii) may file a petition to the court for a determination of the sale price within twenty days from the day when a demand is made under the provisions of paragraph (1) of the preceding article.
(3) In order to make the determination under the preceding paragraph, the court shall consider the financial conditions of the Stock Company at the time of the demand pursuant to the provisions of paragraph (1) of the preceding article and all other circum-

Art.178〜182　　Ⅰ Companies Act, PART II, Chap.II, Sec.5

stances.
(4) Notwithstanding the provisions of paragraph (1), if a petition is made under paragraph (2) within the period provided for in that paragraph, the amount determined by the court in response to such petition shall be the sale price of the shares under Article 175(1)(i).
(5) If no petition is made under paragraph (2) within the period provided for in that paragraph (except in cases where the discussions under paragraph (1) are successfully concluded within such period), a demand under the provisions of paragraph (1) of the preceding article shall become ineffective.

Subsection 6 Cancellation of Shares

Article 178 (1) A Stock Company may cancel its Treasury Shares. In such cases, the Stock Company shall determine the number of the Treasury Shares it intends to cancel (or, for a Company with Class Shares, the classes of the shares and the number of Treasury Shares for each class).
(2) For a Company with Board of Directors, the determination under the provisions of the second sentence of the preceding paragraph shall be made by resolution of a board of directors meeting.

Article 179 Deleted

Section 5 Consolidation of Shares

Subsection 1 Consolidation of Shares

(Consolidation of Shares)
Article 180 (1) A Stock Company may consolidate its shares.
(2) Whenever a Stock Company intends to consolidate its shares, it shall determine the following matters by resolution of a shareholders meeting:
　(i) The ratio of the consolidation;
　(ii) The day when the consolidation of shares will become effective;
　(iii) In cases where the Stock Company is a Company with Class Shares, the classes of the shares it will consolidate.
(3) The directors shall, at the shareholders meeting under the preceding paragraph, explain the reasons for the need to consolidate the shares.

(Notices to Shareholders)
Article 181 (1) No later than two weeks prior to the day under item (ii), paragraph (2) of the preceding article, the Stock Company shall notify the shareholders (or, for a Company with Class Shares, referring to the Class Shareholders of the classes of shares under item (iii) of that paragraph. The same shall apply in the following article.) and the Registered Pledgees of the Shares thereof of the matters listed in each item of that paragraph.
(2) A public notice may be substituted for the notice under the provisions of the preceding paragraph.

(Effectuation)
Article 182 On the day provided for in Article 180(2)(ii), the shareholders shall become shareholders of shares in the number obtained by multiplying the number of shares (or, for a Company with Class Shares, shares of the classes provided for in item (iii) of that

paragraph. The same shall apply hereinafter in this Article.) they held on the day immediately preceding that day, by the ratio provided for in item (i) of that paragraph.

Subsection 2 Share Split

(Share Split)
Article 183 (1) A Stock Company may split its shares.
(2) Whenever a Stock Company intends to split its shares, it shall prescribe the following matters by resolution of a shareholders meeting (or of a board of directors meeting for a Company with Board of Directors):
  (i) The ratio of the total number of shares after the increase as a result of the Share Split to the total number of Issued Shares (or, for a Company with Class Shares, Issued Shares of the classes under item (iii)) immediately before the Share Split, and the Record Date relating to such Share Split;
  (ii) The day when the Share Split will become effective;
  (iii) In cases where the Stock Company is a Company with Class Shares, the classes of the shares it splits.

(Effectuation)
Article 184 (1) Shareholders stated or recorded in the shareholder registry on the Record Date (or, for a Company with Class Shares, Class Shareholders of the classes provided for in item (iii), paragraph (2) of the preceding article who are stated or recorded in the shareholder registry on the Record Date) shall acquire, on the day provided for in item (ii) of that paragraph, shares in the number obtained by multiplying the number of shares (or, for a Company with Class Shares, shares of the classes provided for in item (iii) of that paragraph. The same shall apply hereinafter in this paragraph.) they hold on the Record Date, by the ratio provided for in item (i), paragraph (2) of that article.
(2) Notwithstanding the provisions of Article 466, a Stock Company (excluding a Stock Company that in fact issues two or more classes of shares) may, without a resolution of a shareholders meeting, effect a amendment to the articles of incorporation that is intended to increase the Total Number of Authorized Shares on the day provided for in item (ii), paragraph (2) of the preceding article to the extent of the number obtained by multiplying the Total Number of Authorized Shares as of the day immediately preceding such day, by the ratio provided for in item (i) of that paragraph.

Subsection 3 Allotment of Shares without Contribution

(Allotment of Shares without Contribution)
Article 185 A Stock Company may allot the shares of such Stock Company to shareholders (or, for a Company with Class Shares, shareholders of certain classes) without requiring them to make additional contribution (hereinafter in this Subsection referred to as "Allotment of Shares without Contribution").

(Determination of Matters concerning Allotment of Shares without Contribution)
Article 186 (1) Whenever a Stock Company intends to effect the Allotment of Shares without Contribution, it shall prescribe the following matters:
  (i) The number of shares the Stock Company will allot to shareholders (or, for a Company with Class Shares, the classes of shares and the number of shares for each

class), or the method for calculating such number;
(ii) The day when such Allotment of Shares without Contribution becomes effective; and
(iii) In cases where the Stock Company is a Company with Class Shares, the classes of shares held by the shareholders entitled to such Allotment of Shares without Contribution.
(2) The provisions regarding the matters listed in item (i) of the preceding paragraph shall stipulate that the shares under item (i) of that paragraph will be allotted in proportion to the number of shares (or, for a Company with Class Shares, shares of the classes under item (iii) of that paragraph) held by shareholders (or, for a Company with Class Shares, Class Shareholders of shares of the classes under item (iii) of that paragraph) other than such Stock Company.
(3) The determination of the matters listed in each item of paragraph (1) shall be made by resolution of a shareholders meeting (or of a board of directors meeting for a Company with Board of Directors); provided, however, that this shall not apply in cases where it is otherwise provided in the articles of incorporation.

(Effectuation of Allotment of Shares without Contribution)
Article 187 (1) Shareholders to whom the shares under item (i), paragraph (1) of the preceding article have been allotted shall become shareholders of the shares provided for in item (i) of that paragraph on the day provided for in item (ii) of that paragraph.
(2) Without delay after the day provided for in item (ii) of that paragraph, a Stock Company shall notify shareholders (or, for a Company with Class Shares, Class Shareholders of the classes under item (iii) of that paragraph) and the Registered Pledgees of the Shares thereof of the number of the shares (or, for a Company with Class Shares, the classes of the shares and the number of shares for each class) that have been allotted to such shareholders.

Section 6 Share Units

Subsection 1 General Provisions

(Share Unit)
Article 188 (1) A Stock Company may provide in the articles of incorporation, with respect to the shares it issues, to the effect that a fixed number of shares shall constitute one unit of shares, which entitles a shareholder to cast one vote at a shareholders meeting or Class Meeting.
(2) The fixed number in the preceding paragraph may not exceed the number prescribed by the applicable Ordinance of the Ministry of Justice.
(3) A Company with Class Shares shall provide for the Share Unit for each class of its shares.

(Restriction on Rights in relation to Shareholdings less than One Unit)
Article 189 (1) Shareholders who hold shares in a number less than one Share Unit (hereinafter referred to respectively as "Holder of Shares Less than One Unit" and "Shares Less than One Unit") may not exercise voting right at a shareholders meeting or Class Meeting with respect to their Shares Less than One Unit.
(2) A Stock Company may provide in the articles of incorporation to the effect that Holders of Shares Less than One Unit may not exercise some or all rights, other than the following rights, with respect to the relevant Shares Less than One Unit:
(i) The right to take delivery of the Consideration for Acquisition provided for in Arti-

cle 171(1)(i);
(ii) The right to take delivery of Monies, etc. in exchange for the acquisition by the Stock Company of Shares subject to Call;
(iii) The right to receive the Allotment of Shares without Contribution provided for in Article 185;
(iv) The right to demand the purchase of the Shares Less than One Unit pursuant to the provisions of Article 192(1);
(v) The right to receive the distribution of residual assets;
(vi) In addition to the matters listed in the preceding items, any matters prescribed by the applicable Ordinance of the Ministry of Justice.
(3) A Company Issuing Share Certificate may provide in the articles of incorporation to the effect that it may elect to not issue share certificates representing Shares Less than One Unit.

(Disclosure of Reasons)
Article 190 In cases where the Share Unit is to be prescribed, the directors shall explain the reasons for the need to prescribe such Share Unit at the shareholders meeting at which it is intended to amend the articles of incorporation to prescribe such Share Unit.

(Special Provisions on Procedures)
Article 191 Notwithstanding the provisions of Article 466, a Stock Company may effect a amendment to the articles of incorporation that will increase the size of the Share Unit (or, for a Company with Class Shares, the size of the Share Unit for the shares of each class. The same shall apply hereinafter in this article.) or create a provision in the articles of incorporation with respect to the Share Unit without a resolution of a shareholders meeting, in cases that fall under both of the following items:
(i) That the amendment will increase the size of the Share Unit simultaneously with a Share Split, or create a provision in the articles of incorporation with respect to the Share Unit; and
(ii) That the number provided for in (a) below is not less than the number provided for in (b) below:
  (a) The number obtained by dividing the number of the shares held by each shareholder after such amendment to the articles of incorporation by the Share Unit;
  (b) The number of the shares held by each shareholder before such amendment to the articles of incorporation (or, in cases where the Share Unit is prescribed, the number obtained by dividing the number of such shares by the Share Unit).

Subsection 2 Demand for Purchase from Holder of Shares Less than One Unit

(Demand for Purchase of Holder of Shares Less than One Unit)
Article 192 (1) Holders of Shares Less than One Unit may demand that the Stock Company purchase their Shares Less than One Unit.
(2) A demand under the provisions of the preceding paragraph shall be made by disclosing the number of the Shares Less than One Unit relating to that demand (or, for a Company with Class Shares, the classes of the Shares Less than One Unit and the number of shares for each class).
(3) A Holder of Shares Less than One Unit who makes a demand pursuant to the provisions of paragraph (1) may withdraw such demand only if the approval of the Stock Company is obtained.

(Determination of Price of Shares Less than One Unit)

Article 193 (1) In cases where the demand pursuant to the provisions of paragraph (1) of the preceding article is made, the amount provided for in each of the following items in accordance with the categories of the cases listed in such items, shall be the price of the Shares Less than One Unit relating to such demand:

(i) In cases where the Shares Less than One Unit are shares with a market price, the amount calculated by the method prescribed by the applicable Ordinance of the Ministry of Justice as the market price of such Shares Less than One Unit;

(ii) In cases other than the cases listed in the preceding item, the amount prescribed through discussions between the Stock Company and the Holder of Shares Less than One Unit who made the demand under the provisions of paragraph (1) of the preceding article.

(2) In the cases listed in item (ii) of the preceding paragraph, the Holder of Shares Less than One Unit who made the demand pursuant to the provisions of paragraph (1) of the preceding article, or the Stock Company, may file a petition to the court for a determination of the sale price within twenty days from the day when such demand is made.

(3) In order to make the determination under the preceding paragraph, the court shall consider the financial condition of the Stock Company at the time of the demand pursuant to the provisions of paragraph (1) of the preceding article and all other circumstances.

(4) Notwithstanding the provisions of paragraph (1), if petition is filed under paragraph (2) within the period provided for in that paragraph, the amount determined by the court in response to such petition shall be the price of such Shares Less than One Unit.

(5) Notwithstanding the provisions of paragraph (1), in the cases listed in item (ii) of that paragraph, if no petition is filed under paragraph (2) within the period provided for in that paragraph (except in cases where the discussions under item (ii) of paragraph (1) are successfully concluded within such period), the sale price of the Shares Less than One Unit shall be the amount obtained by multiplying the amount of the net assets per share by the number of the Shares Less than One Unit related to the demand pursuant to the provisions of paragraph (1) of the preceding article.

(6) The purchase of the shares related to the demand pursuant to the provisions of paragraph (1) of the preceding article shall become effective as at payment for such shares.

(7) If a Company Issuing Share Certificate is subject to a demand pursuant to the provisions of paragraph (1) of the preceding article with respect to shares for which share certificates have been issued, it shall pay the price of the shares related to such demand in exchange for the share certificates.

Subsection 3 Demand for Sale to Holder of Shares Less than One Unit

Article 194 (1) A Stock Company may provide in the articles of incorporation to the effect that a Holder of Shares Less than One Unit may submit to such Stock Company a Demand for the Sale of Shares Less than One Unit (referring to a demand that the Stock Company sell to a Holder of Shares Less than One Unit such number of shares which, together with the number of Shares Less than One Unit held by such Holder of Shares Less than One Unit, will constitute one Share Unit. The same shall apply hereinafter in this article.).

(2) Demand for the Sale of Shares Less than One Unit shall be made by disclosing the number of the Shares Less than One Unit to be sold to such Holder of Shares Less

than One Unit (or, for a Company with Class Shares, the classes of the Shares Less than One Unit and the number of shares for each class).
(3) A Stock Company that is subject to a Demand for the Sale of Shares Less than One Unit shall sell its Treasury Shares to such Holders of Shares Less than One Unit, unless the Stock Company does not hold, at the time of reception of such Demand for the Sale of Shares Less than One Unit, Treasury Shares in a number corresponding to the number of the Shares Less than One Unit provided for in the preceding paragraph.
(4) The provisions of Article 192(3), and paragraph (1) to paragraph (6) inclusive of the preceding article shall apply mutatis mutandis to Demand for the Sale of Shares Less than One Unit.

Subsection 4 Changes in Share Unit

Article 195 (1) Notwithstanding the provisions of Article 466, a Stock Company may decrease the size of the Share Unit or abolish the provision of the articles of incorporation with respect to the Share Unit by effecting a amendment to the articles of incorporation by decision of the directors (or resolution of a board of directors meeting for a Company with Board of Directors).
(2) In cases where a amendment is made in the articles of incorporation pursuant to the provisions of the preceding paragraph, the Stock Company shall, without delay after the day of the effectuation of such amendment to the articles of incorporation, notify its shareholders (or, for a Company with Class Shares, its Class Shareholders of the classes for which the Share Unit has been changed pursuant to the provisions of that paragraph) to the effect that such amendment to the articles of incorporation has been made.
(3) A public notice may be substituted for the notice under the provisions of the preceding paragraph.

Section 7 Omission to Notices to Shareholders

(Omission of Notices to Shareholders)
Article 196 (1) In cases where notices or demands from a Stock Company do not reach a shareholder for five consecutive years or more, the Stock Company shall no longer be required to give notices or issue demands to such shareholder.
(2) In the cases provided for in the preceding paragraph, the domicile of the Stock Company shall be the place where the obligation of the Stock Company with regard to the shareholder under that paragraph is performed.
(3) The provisions of the preceding two paragraphs shall apply mutatis mutandis to Registered Pledgees of Shares.

(Auction of Shares)
Article 197 (1) A Stock Company may sell shares that fall under both of the following items by auction and tender the proceeds thereof to the shareholders of such shares:
  (i) That there is no requirement to give notice or issue a demand to the shareholder of such shares pursuant to the provisions of paragraph (1) of the preceding article, or Article 294(2); and
  (ii) That the shareholders of such shares have not received dividends of surplus for consecutive five years.
(2) In lieu of sale by auction under the provisions of the preceding paragraph, a Stock Company may sell shares under that paragraph with a market price in an amount calculated by the method prescribed by the applicable Ordinance of the Ministry of Jus-

tice as the market price thereof, and shares under that paragraph without a market price using a method other than auction with the permission of the court. In such cases, if there are two or more directors, the petition for such permission shall be filed with the consent of all directors.
(3) The Stock Company may purchase some or all of the shares sold under the provisions of the preceding paragraph. In such cases, the Stock Company shall prescribe the following matters:
   (i) The number of shares to be purchased (or, for a Company with Class Shares, the classes of shares and the number of shares for each class);
   (ii) The total amount of the monies to be delivered in exchange for the purchase of the shares in the preceding item.
(4) A Company with Board of Directors shall determine the matters listed in each item of the preceding paragraph by resolution of a board of directors meeting.
(5) Notwithstanding the provisions of paragraph (1) and paragraph (2), in cases where there are Registered Pledgees of Shares, the Stock Company may effect the auction under the provisions of paragraph (1), or the sale pursuant to the provisions of paragraph (2), only if such Registered Pledgees of Shares are the persons who fall under both of the following items:
   (i) That there is no requirement to give notice or issue a demand to such persons under the provisions of Article 196(1) applied mutatis mutandis under paragraph (3) of that paragraph; and
   (ii) That the persons have not received the dividends of surplus to which they are entitled under the provisions of Article 154(1) for consecutive five years.

(Objections of Interested Parties)
Article 198 (1) In cases where a Stock Company effects an auction under the provisions of paragraph (1) of the preceding article, or a sale under the provisions of paragraph (2) of that article, the Stock Company shall give public notice to the effect that interested parties, including the shareholders of the shares provided for in paragraph (1) of that article, may state their objections during a certain period of time, and other matters prescribed by the applicable Ordinance of the Ministry of Justice, and shall issue separate demands seeking such objections, if any, to each shareholder of such shares and each Registered Pledgee of Shares thereof; provided, however, that such period cannot be less than three months.
(2) Notwithstanding the provisions of Article 126(1) and Article 150(1), the demands under the provisions of the preceding paragraph shall be sent to the addresses of such shareholders and Registered Pledgees of Shares stated or recorded in the shareholder registry (or, in cases where such shareholders or Registered Pledgees of Shares notify such Stock Company of a different place or contact address for the receipt of notices or demands, to such place or contact address).
(3) Notwithstanding the provisions of Article 126(3) and (4), if a share is co-owned by two or more persons, the demand pursuant to the provisions of paragraph (1) shall be sent to the address of the co-owners specified or recorded in the shareholder registry (or, in cases where such co-owners notify such Stock Company of a different place or contact address for the receipt of notices or demands, to such place or contact address).
(4) The provisions of Article 196(1) (including cases where it is applied mutatis mutandis under paragraph (3) of that paragraph) shall not apply to demands under the provisions of paragraph (1).
(5) In cases where public notice is given under the provisions of paragraph (1) (limited to cases where share certificates representing the shares under paragraph (1) of the preceding article have been issued), if no interested party raises any objection within the

period under paragraph (1), the share certificates representing such shares shall become invalid on the last day of such period.

Section 8 Issue of Shares for Subscription

Subsection 1 Determination of Subscription Requirements

(Determination of Subscription Requirements)

Article 199 (1) Whenever a Stock Company intends to solicit persons to subscribe for shares it issues or for Treasury Shares it disposes of, the Stock Company shall prescribe the following matters with respect to the Shares for Subscription (meaning shares the Stock Company allots to persons who subscribed for those shares in response to such solicitation. The same shall apply hereinafter in this Section.):

(i) The number of Shares for Subscription (or, for a Company with Class Shares, the classes and the number of the Shares for Subscription. The same shall apply hereinafter in this Section.);

(ii) The Amount To Be Paid In (meaning the amount of the monies to be paid in in exchange for one of the Shares for Subscription, or the amount of any property other than monies to be contributed. The same shall apply hereinafter in this Section.) for the Shares for Subscription or the method for calculating such amount;

(iii) If property other than monies will be the subject of the contribution, a statement to such effect and the description and value of such property;

(iv) The day or period for the payment of the monies in exchange for the Shares for Subscription, or the contribution of the property under the preceding item;

(v) If shares are issued, matters regarding the capital and capital reserves that is to be increased.

(2) The determination of the matters listed in each item of the preceding paragraph (hereinafter in this Section referred to as "Subscription Requirements") shall be made by resolution of a shareholders meeting.

(3) In cases where the Amount To Be Paid In under item (ii) of paragraph (1) is particularly favorable to subscribers for the Shares for Subscription, the directors shall, at the shareholders meeting under the preceding paragraph, explain the reasons for the need to solicit such persons with such an offer of the Amount To Be Paid In.

(4) For a Company with Class Shares, if the class of the Shares for Subscription under item (i) of paragraph (1) is that of Shares with Restriction on Transfer, the determination of the Subscription Requirements regarding such class of shares shall not become effective without a resolution of the relevant Class Meeting, except in cases where there is a provision in the articles of incorporation to the effect that, with respect to the solicitation of subscribers for such class shares, a resolution of the Class Meeting constituted by the Class Shareholders of such class shares is not required; provided, however, that this shall not apply to cases where there is no Class Shareholder who can exercise his/her voting right at such Class Meeting.

(5) The Subscription Requirements shall be uniform for each solicitation under paragraph (1).

(Delegation of Determination of Subscription Requirements)

Article 200 (1) Notwithstanding the provisions of paragraphs (2) and (4) of the preceding article, a shareholders meeting may, by means of a resolution, delegate the determination of the Subscription Requirements to the directors (or, for a Company with Board of Directors, the board of directors). In such cases, the shareholders meeting shall

Art.201   Ⅰ Companies Act, PART II, Chap.II, Sec.8

prescribe the maximum number of the Shares for Subscription for which the Subscription Requirements may be determined under such delegation, and the minimum Amount To Be Paid In.
(2) In cases where the minimum Amount To Be Paid In in the preceding paragraph is particularly favorable to subscribers for the Shares for Subscription, the directors shall, at the shareholders meeting under that paragraph, explain the reason for the need to solicit such persons with such an offer of the Amount To Be Paid In.
(3) The resolution under paragraph (1) shall be effective with respect only to solicitations under paragraph (1) of the preceding article under which the date in item (iv) of that paragraph (in cases where a period is determined under that item, the last day of such period) falls within one year from the day of such resolution.
(4) For a Company with Class Shares, if the class of the Shares for Subscription under paragraph (1) is that of Shares with Restriction on Transfer, the delegation of the determination of the Subscription Requirements regarding such class shares shall not become effective without a resolution of the Class Meeting constituted by the Class Shareholders of such class shares, except in cases where there is a provision in the articles of incorporation under paragraph (4) of the preceding article with respect to such class shares; provided, however, that this shall not apply to cases where there is no Class Shareholder who can exercise his/her voting right at such Class Meeting.

(Special Provisions on Determination of Subscription Requirements for Public Company)
Article 201 (1) Except for cases provided for in Article 199(3), for the purpose of the application of the provisions of paragraph (2) of that article to a Public Company, "shareholders meeting" in that paragraph shall be read as "board of directors meeting." In such cases, the provision of the preceding article shall not apply.
(2) In cases where Subscription Requirements are determined by a resolution of the board of directors meeting provided for in Article 199(2) applied by the reading of terms pursuant to the provisions of the preceding paragraph, if a Public Company solicits subscribers for shares with a market price, it may prescribe, in lieu of the matters listed in item (ii), paragraph (1) of that article, the method for determining the Amount To Be Paid In that is appropriate to realize payment in at a fair value.
(3) If a Public Company has determined Subscription Requirements by a resolution of the board of directors meeting provided for in Article 199(2) applied by the reading of terms pursuant to the provisions of the preceding paragraph, that Public Company shall notify the shareholders of such Subscription Requirements (in cases where the method for determining the Amount To Be Paid In has been prescribed, including that method. The same shall apply hereinafter in this Section.) no later than two weeks prior to the day referred to in item (iv), paragraph (1) of that article (or, in cases where a period has been prescribed under that item, no later than two weeks prior to the first day of that period).
(4) A public notice may be substituted for the notice under the provisions of the preceding paragraph.
(5) The provisions of paragraph (3) shall not apply in cases prescribed by the applicable Ordinance of the Ministry of Justice as cases where it is unlikely that the protection of shareholders is compromised, including cases where, with respect to Subscription Requirements, the Stock Company has submitted, no later than two weeks prior to the date provided for in that paragraph, a notice under Article 4(1) or (2) of the Financial Instruments and Exchange Act.

(Cases where Entitlement to Allotment of Shares is Granted to Shareholders)

Article 202 (1) In carrying out solicitation under Article 199(1), the Stock Company may grant entitlement to the allotment of shares to its shareholders. In such cases, the Stock Company shall prescribe the following matters in addition to the Subscription Requirements:
  (i) A statement to the effect that the Stock Company will grant entitlement to the allotment of the Shares for Subscription of that Stock Company (or, for a Company with Class Shares, class shares identical to the class shares held by such shareholders) to shareholders, subject to the application provided for in paragraph (2) of the following article;
  (ii) The day for the application for subscription for the Shares for Subscription referred to in the preceding item.
(2) In the cases provided for in the preceding paragraph, the shareholders under item (i) of that paragraph (excluding the Stock Company) shall be entitled to the allotment of the Shares for Subscription in accordance with the number of shares they hold; provided, however, that if the number of the Shares for Subscription to be allotted to such shareholders includes a fraction of less than one share, it shall be rounded off.
(3) In cases where the Stock Company prescribes the matters listed in each item of paragraph (1), the Subscription Requirements and the matters listed in each item of that paragraph shall be prescribed in accordance with the categories of the cases listed in the following items, by the methods provided for in each of such items:
  (i) In cases where there is a provision in the articles of incorporation to the effect that such Subscription Requirements and the matters listed in each item of paragraph (1) may be prescribed by decision of the directors (excluding the cases where the Stock Company is a Company with Board of Directors): A decision of the directors;
  (ii) In cases where there is a provision in the articles of incorporation to the effect that such Subscription Requirements and the matters listed in each item of paragraph (1) may be prescribed by resolution of the board of directors (excluding the cases listed in the following item): A resolution of the board of directors;
  (iii) In cases where the Stock Company is a Public Company: A resolution of the board of directors;
  (iv) In cases other than those listed in the preceding three items: A resolution of a shareholders meeting;
(4) In cases where a Stock Company prescribes the matters listed in each item of paragraph (1), the Stock Company shall notify the shareholders under item (i) of that paragraph (excluding such Stock Company) of the following matters no later than two weeks prior to the date provided for in item (ii) of that paragraph:
  (i) The Subscription Requirements;
  (ii) The number of Shares for Subscription to be allotted to such shareholders; and
  (iii) The date provided for in item (ii) of paragraph (1).
(5) The provisions of paragraphs (2) to (4) inclusive of Article 199 and the preceding two articles shall not apply in cases where entitlement to the allotment of shares is granted to shareholders under the provisions of paragraphs (1) to (3) inclusive hereof.

Subsection 2 Allotment of Shares for Subscription

(Applications for Shares for Subscription)
Article 203 (1) A Stock Company shall notify persons who intend to subscribe for Shares for Subscription in response to solicitation in Article 199(1) of the matters listed in the following items:
  (i) The trade name of the Stock Company;

(ii) The Subscription Requirements;
(iii) If any money payment is to be made, the place where payments are handled;
(iv) In addition to the matters listed in the preceding three paragraphs, matters prescribed by the applicable Ordinance of the Ministry of Justice.
(2) A person who submits an application to subscribe for Shares for Subscription in response to solicitation in Article 199(1) shall deliver a document that specifies the following matters:
(i) The name and address of the person applying;
(ii) The number of Shares for Subscription for which he/she intends to subscribe.
(3) A person who submits an application under the preceding paragraph may, in lieu of the delivery of the document under that paragraph, provide the matters to be stated in the document under that paragraph by Electromagnetic Means, with the approval of the Stock Company, pursuant to the provisions of the applicable Cabinet Order. In such cases, the person who submitted the application shall be deemed to have delivered the document under that paragraph.
(4) The provisions of paragraph (3) shall not apply in cases where the Stock Company has issued a prospectus provided for in Article 2(10) of the Securities and Exchange Act that states the matters listed in each item of that paragraph to a person who intends to submit the application in paragraph (1), and in other cases prescribed by the applicable Ordinance of the Ministry of Justice as cases where it is unlikely that the protection of persons who intend to submit applications for subscription for Shares for Subscription is compromised.
(5) If there are changes in the matters listed in each item of paragraph (1), the Stock Company shall immediately notify persons who have submitted applications in paragraph (2) (hereinafter in this Subsection referred to as "Applicants") thereof and of the matters so changed.
(6) It shall be sufficient for a notice or demand to an Applicant to be sent by the Stock Company to the address under item (i) of paragraph (2) (or, in cases where such Applicant notifies the Stock Company of a different place or contact address for the receipt of notices or demands, to such place or contact address).
(7) The notices or demands referred to in the preceding paragraph shall be deemed to have arrived at the time when such notice or demand should normally have arrived.

(Allotment of Shares for Subscription)
Article 204 (1) A Stock Company shall specify the persons to whom Shares for Subscription will be allotted from among the Applicants and the number of Shares for Subscription to be allotted to those persons. In such cases, the Stock Company may reduce the number of Shares for Subscription the Stock Company allots to such Applicants below the number under item (ii), paragraph (2) of the preceding article.
(2) In cases where Shares for Subscription are Shares with Restriction on Transfer, the determination under the provisions of the preceding paragraph shall be made by resolution of a shareholders meeting (or of a board of directors meeting for a Company with Board of Directors); provided, however, that this shall not apply in cases where it is otherwise prescribed in the articles of incorporation.
(3) The Stock Company shall notify the Applicants, no later than the day immediately preceding the date referred to in item (iv), paragraph (1) of Article 199 (or, in cases where a period is prescribed under that item, no later than the day immediately preceding the first day of that period), of the number of Shares for Subscription that will be allotted to such Applicants.
(4) In cases where the Stock Company has granted entitlement to the allotment of shares to its shareholders pursuant to the provisions of Article 202, if the shareholders do not

submit, no later than the date under item (ii), paragraph (1) of that article, applications under paragraph (2) of the preceding article, such shareholders shall lose the entitlement to the allotment of Shares for Subscription.

(Special Provision on Subscription and Allotment of Shares for Subscription)
Article 205 The provisions of the preceding two Articles shall not apply in cases where a person who intends to subscribe for Shares for Subscription executes a contract for subscription for the total number of those shares.

(Subscription for Shares for Subscription)
Article 206 The persons listed in the following items shall be the subscribers for Shares for Subscription with respect to the number of Shares for Subscription prescribed in each of such items:
  (i) Applicants: The number of the Shares for Subscription allotted by the Stock Company; or
  (ii) A person who subscribed for all of the Shares for Subscription under a contract in the preceding article: The number of Shares for Subscription for which that person has subscribed.

Subsection 3 Contribution of Property other than Monies

Article 207 (1) If a Stock Company has prescribed the matters listed in Article 199(1)(iii), the Stock Company shall file a petition to the court, without delay after the determination of the Subscription Requirements, for the appointment of an inspector in order to have the inspector investigate the value of the property provided for in that item (hereinafter in this Section referred to as "Properties Contributed in Kind").
(2) In cases where the petition referred to in the preceding paragraph has been filed, the court shall appoint an inspector, except in cases where it dismisses such petition as unlawful.
(3) In cases where the court has appointed the inspector under the preceding paragraph, it may fix the amount of the remuneration that the Stock Company shall pay to such inspector.
(4) The inspector referred to in paragraph (2) shall conduct the necessary investigations and submit a report, either by recording the outcome of such investigations or by providing documents or Electromagnetic Records (limited to those prescribed by the applicable Ordinance of the Ministry of Justice) to the court.
(5) If the court finds it necessary to clarify the contents of the report under the preceding paragraph or to confirm the grounds supporting such report, it may request that the inspector under paragraph (2) submit a further report under the preceding paragraph.
(6) If the inspector under paragraph (2) has submitted the report referred to in paragraph (4), he/she shall deliver to the Stock Company a copy of the documents under such paragraph, or provide the matters recorded in the Electromagnetic Records under such paragraph by the methods prescribed by the applicable Ordinance of the Ministry of Justice.
(7) In cases where the court receives a report under paragraph (4), if it finds the value provided for in Article 199(1)(iii) with respect to Properties Contributed in Kind (excluding a value not subjected to investigation by the inspector under paragraph (2)) to be improper, it shall issue a ruling changing such value.
(8) In cases where the value of Properties Contributed in Kind has been changed, in whole or in part, because of a ruling under the preceding paragraph, the subscriber for Shares for Subscription (limited to a person who tenders Properties Contributed in

Kind. The same shall apply hereinafter in this article.) may rescind his/her applications for subscription for Shares for Subscription, or his/her manifestation of intention relating to the contract provided for in Article 205, limited to within one week from the finalization of such ruling.
(9) The provisions of the preceding paragraphs shall not apply in the cases in each of the following items with respect to the matters prescribed respectively in those items:
   (i) In cases where the total number of the shares to be allotted to the subscribers for the Shares for Subscription does not exceed one tenth (1/10) of the total number of Issued Shares: The value of the Properties Contributed in Kind that are tendered by the subscribers for such Shares for Subscription;
   (ii) In cases where the total sum of the value provided for under Article 199(1)(iii) with respect to the Properties Contributed in Kind does not exceed 5,000,000 yen: The value of such Properties Contributed in Kind;
   (iii) In cases where the value of the securities with market price provided for under Article 199(1)(iii) with respect to Properties Contributed in Kind does not exceed the value calculated by the method prescribed by the applicable Ordinance of the Ministry of Justice as the market price of such securities: The value of the Properties Contributed in Kind with respect to such securities;
   (iv) In cases where the verification of an attorney, a legal professional corporation, a certified public accountant, an auditing firm, a tax accountant or a tax accountant corporation (or in cases where the Properties Contributed in Kind consist of real estate, such verification and an appraisal by a real property appraiser. The same shall apply hereinafter in this item.) is obtained with respect to the reasonableness of the value provided for under Article 199(1)(iii) with respect to Properties Contributed in Kind: The value of the Properties Contributed in Kind so verified;
   (v) In cases where the Properties Contributed in Kind consist of a money claim (limited to claims that have already fallen due) to the Stock Company, and the value provided for under Article 199(1)(iii) with respect to such money claim does not exceed the book value of the debt representing such monetary claim: The value of the Properties Contributed in Kind with respect to such monetary claim
(10) None of the following persons can provide the verification provided in item (iv) of the preceding paragraph:
   (i) A director, an accounting advisor, a company auditor or executive officer, or an employee including a manager;
   (ii) A subscriber for Shares for Subscription;
   (iii) A person who is subject to a suspension of operations for whom the period of such suspension has not elapsed yet; or
   (iv) A legal profession corporation, an auditing firm or a tax accountant corporation with respect to which more than half of its members are persons who fall under either item (i) or item (ii) above.

Subsection 4 Performance of Contributions

(Performance of Contributions)
Article 208 (1) Subscribers for Shares for Subscription (excluding persons who tender Properties Contributed in Kind) shall, on the date or within the period provided for in Article 199(1)(iv), pay in the entire Amount To Be Paid In for the Shares for Subscription for which the subscribers respectively subscribed, at the bank etc. designated by the Stock Company as the place for the handling of payments.
(2) Subscribers for Shares for Subscription (limited to persons who tender Properties Contributed in Kind) shall, on the date or within the period provided for in Article

199(1)(iv), deliver the Properties Contributed in Kind equivalent in value to the entire Amount To Be Paid In of the Shares for Subscription for which the subscribers respectively subscribed.
(3) Subscribers for Shares for Subscription may not set off their obligations to effect payment under the provisions of paragraph (1) or delivery under the provisions of the preceding paragraph (hereinafter in this Subsection referred to as "Performance of Contribution") against claims they have against the Stock Company.
(4) Assignment of the right to become a shareholder of Shares for Subscription by effecting the Performance of Contribution cannot be asserted against the Stock Company.
(5) A subscriber for Shares for Subscription shall lose his/her right to become the shareholder of Shares for Subscription by effecting the Performance of Contribution if he/she fails to effect the Performance of Contribution.

(Timing of Shareholder Status)
Article 209 In the cases listed in the following items, a subscriber for Shares for Subscription shall become the shareholder of the Shares for Subscription for which he/she has effected the Performance of Contribution on the day prescribed in each of such items:
(i) In cases where a date under Article 199(1)(iv) is prescribed: Such date; and
(ii) In cases where a period under Article 199(1)(iv) is prescribed: The day on which the Performance of Contribution is effected.

Subsection 5 Demanding Cessation of Issue of Shares for Subscription

Article 210 In the following cases, if shareholders are likely to suffer disadvantage, shareholders may demand that the Stock Company cease a share issue or disposition of Treasury Shares relating to solicitations under Article 199(1):
(i) In cases where such share issue or disposition of Treasury Shares violates the applicable laws and regulations or articles of incorporation; or
(ii) In cases where such share issue or disposition of Treasury Shares is effected by using a method which is extremely unfair.

Subsection 6 Liabilities relating to Solicitation

(Restrictions on Invalidation or Rescission of Subscription)
Article 211 (1) The proviso to Article 93 and the provisions of Article 94(1) of the Civil Code shall not apply to manifestation of intention relating to applications for subscription for, or the allotment of, Shares for Subscription, or the contract under Article 205.
(2) If one year has elapsed from the day on which a subscriber for Shares for Subscription became a shareholder pursuant to the provisions of Article 209, or if he/she has exercised his/her rights in relation to such shares, he/she may not thereafter assert the invalidity of the subscription for the Shares for Subscription on the grounds of mistake, or rescind the subscription for the Shares for Subscription on the grounds of fraud or duress.

(Liabilities of Persons who Subscribed for Shares with Unfair Amount To Be Paid In)
Article 212 (1) In the cases listed in the following items, subscribers for Shares for Subscription shall be liable to a Stock Company for payment of the amount provided for in such items:

(i) In cases where the subscriber subscribed for the Shares for Subscription at an Amount To Be Paid In that is extremely unfair, in collusion with directors (or directors or executive officers for a Company with Committees): The amount equivalent to the difference between such Amount To Be Paid In and the fair value of such Shares for Subscription;
(ii) In cases where the value of the Properties Contributed in Kind that the subscriber tendered when he/she became a shareholder of the Shares for Subscription pursuant to the provisions of Article 209 is extremely short of the value provided for under Article 199(1)(iii) with respect to the Properties Contributed in Kind: The amount of such shortfall.
(2) In the cases provided for in item (ii) of the preceding paragraph, if the subscriber for Shares for Subscription who tendered the Properties Contributed in Kind is without knowledge and is not grossly negligent as to the fact that the value of such Properties Contributed in Kind is extremely short of the value prescribed under Article 199(1)(iii) with respect to the Properties Contributed in Kind, that subscriber may rescind his/her application for subscription for Shares for Subscription or his/her manifestation of intention relating to the contract provided for in Article 205.

(Liabilities of Directors in case of Shortfall in Value of Property Contributed)
Article 213 (1) In the cases listed in item (ii), paragraph (1) of the preceding article, the following persons (hereinafter in this article referred to as "Directors, etc.") shall be liable to the Stock Company for payment of the amounts listed in such items:
(i) Executive directors who carried out duties regarding the solicitation of subscribers for such Shares for Subscription (or, for a Company with Committees, executive officers. The same shall apply hereinafter in this item.) and other persons prescribed by the applicable Ordinance of the Ministry of Justice as persons who were involved, in the performance of their duties, in the execution of the business of such executive directors;
(ii) If a shareholders meeting has passed a resolution regarding the determination of the value of Properties Contributed in Kind, the persons prescribed by the applicable Ordinance of the Ministry of Justice as the directors who submitted proposals to such shareholders meeting;
(iii) If a board of directors meeting has passed a resolution regarding the determination of the value of Properties Contributed in Kind, the persons prescribed by the applicable Ordinance of the Ministry of Justice as the directors (or, for a Company with Committees, directors or executive officers) who submitted proposals to such board of directors meeting;
(2) Notwithstanding the provisions of the preceding paragraph, the Directors, etc. shall not be liable for Properties Contributed in Kind under that paragraph in the cases listed below:
(i) An investigation has been carried out by an inspector under Article 207(2) with respect to the value of the Properties Contributed in Kind; or
(ii) Such Directors, etc. have proven that they did not fail to exercise care with respect to the performance of their duties.
(3) In the cases provided for in paragraph (1), the person who submitted the verification provided for in Article 207(9)(iv) (hereinafter in this article referred to as "Verifying Person") shall be liable for payment of the amount provided for in item (ii), paragraph (1) of the preceding article to the Stock Company; provided, however, that this shall not apply in cases where such Verifying Person has proven that he/she did not fail to exercise care with respect to the submission of such verification.
(4) In cases where a subscriber for Shares for Subscription bears an obligation to pay an

amount provided for in item (ii), paragraph (1) of the preceding article with respect to Properties Contributed in Kind tendered by the subscriber, if the persons listed as follows bear obligations provided for in such items with respect to such Properties Contributed in Kind, such persons shall be joint and several obligors:
(i) Directors, etc. : The obligations under paragraph (1); and
(ii) Verifying persons: The obligations under the main clause of the preceding paragraph.

Section 9 Share Certificate

Subsection 1 General Provisions

(Provisions of Articles of Incorporation to the effect that Share Certificates be Issued)
Article 214 A Stock Company may provide in the articles of incorporation to the effect that it issues share certificates relating to its shares (or, for a Company with Class Shares, the shares of all classes).

(Issuing of Share Certificate)
Article 215 (1) A Company Issuing Share Certificate shall, without delay after the day of a share issue, issue share certificates for such shares.
(2) If a Company Issuing Share Certificate consolidates shares, it shall issue share certificates for the consolidated shares without delay after the day provided for in Article 180(2)(ii).
(3) If a Company Issuing Share Certificate splits shares, it shall issue share certificates for the split shares (excluding those which have been already issued) without delay after the day provided for in Article 183(2)(ii).
(4) Notwithstanding the provisions of the preceding three paragraphs, a Company Issuing Share Certificate that is not a Public Company may elect to not deliver share certificates under those paragraphs until shareholders so request.

(Matters to be Specified on Share Certificates)
Article 216 A Stock Company shall state the following matters and the serial number on a share certificate, and the Representative Director of the Company Issuing Share Certificate (or the representative executive officer for a Company with Committees) shall affix his/her signature, or name and seal:
(i) The trade name of the Company Issuing Share Certificate;
(ii) The number of shares represented by such share certificates;
(iii) If it is provided that the approval of the Stock Company is required for the acquisition of shares which are represented by such share certificates by assignment, a statement to such effect; and
(iv) For a Company with Class Shares, the class and features of the shares represented by such share certificates.

(Offer Not to Possess Share Certificates)
Article 217 (1) Shareholders of a Company Issuing Share Certificate may make an offer to such Company Issuing Share Certificate to the effect that they do not wish to hold share certificates representing shares held by the same.
(2) The offer pursuant to the provisions of the preceding paragraph shall be made by disclosing the number of shares relating to the offer (or, for a Company with Class Shares, the classes of shares and the number of shares for each class). In such cases, if share

Art.218   Ⅰ Companies Act, PART II, Chap.II, Sec.9

certificates representing such shares have been issued, such shareholders shall submit such share certificates to the Company Issuing Share Certificate.
(3) A Company Issuing Share Certificate that has received an offer under the provisions of paragraph (1) shall state or record in the shareholder registry, without delay, a statement that it will not issue share certificates for the shares referred to in the first sentence of the preceding paragraph.
(4) If a Company Issuing Share Certificate has stated or recorded the statement pursuant to the provisions of the preceding paragraph, it may not issue share certificates for the shares referred to in the first sentence of paragraph (2).
(5) Share certificates submitted pursuant to the provisions of the second sentence of paragraph (2) shall become ineffective when a statement is stated or recorded pursuant to the provisions of paragraph (3).
(6) A shareholder who has made an offer pursuant to the provisions of paragraph (1) may at any time demand that the Company Issuing Share Certificate issue share certificates for the shares referred to in the first sentence of paragraph (2). In such cases, if there are any share certificates that have been submitted pursuant to the provisions of the second sentence of paragraph (2), the cost for the issuing of the share certificates shall be borne by such shareholder.

(Abolition of Provisions of Articles of Incorporation that Share Certificates be Issued)
Article 218 (1) If a Company Issuing Share Certificate intends to effect a amendment to the articles of incorporation to abolish provisions of the articles of incorporation to the effect that it issues share certificates for its shares (or, for a Company with Class Shares, shares of all classes), it shall give public notice of the following matters, and give separate notice thereof to each shareholder and each Registered Pledgee of Shares no later than two weeks prior to the day on which such amendment to the articles of incorporation takes effect:
(i) A statement to the effect that the Stock Company abolishes the provisions of the articles of incorporation to the effect that it issues share certificates for its shares (or, for a Company with Class Shares, shares of all classes);
(ii) The day on which the amendment to the articles of incorporation will take effect; and
(iii) A statement to the effect that the share certificates of such Stock Company shall become invalid on the day provided for in the preceding item.
(2) he share certificates for the shares of a Company Issuing Share Certificate shall become invalid on the day provided for in item (ii) of the preceding paragraph.
(3) Notwithstanding the provisions of paragraph (1), in cases where a Company Issuing Share Certificate that does not issue share certificates for any of its shares intends to effect a amendment to the articles of incorporation to abolish provisions of the articles of incorporation to the effect that it issues share certificates for its shares (or, for a Company with Class Shares, shares of all classes), it shall be sufficient to notify the shareholders and Registered Pledgees of Shares of the matters listed in item (i) and item (ii) of that paragraph no later than two weeks prior to the day provided for in item (ii) of that paragraph.
(4) A public notice may be substituted for the notice under the provisions of the preceding paragraph.
(5) In the cases provided for in paragraph (1), pledgees of shares (excluding Registered Pledgees of Shares) may, no later than the day immediately preceding the day provided for in item (ii) of that paragraph, demand that the Company Issuing Share Certificate state or record the matters listed in each item of Article 148 in the shareholder regis-

try.

Subsection 2　Submission of Share Certificate

(Public Notice in relation to Submission of Share Certificate)
Article 219　(1) In cases where a Company Issuing Share Certificate carries out an act listed in the following items, it shall, more than one month prior to the day when such act takes effect, give public notice to the effect that share certificates for the shares provided for in each of such items be submitted to such Company Issuing Share Certificate before such day, and a separate notice to such effect to each shareholder and each Registered Pledgee of Shares thereof; provided, however, that this shall not apply in cases where the Company Issuing Share Certificate does not issue share certificates for any of its shares:
  (i) Amendments to the articles of incorporation to create provisions of the articles of incorporation with respect to the matters listed in Article 107(1)(i): All shares (or, for a Company with Class Shares, the class shares that have provisions with respect to such matters);
  (ii) Consolidation of shares: All shares (or, for a Company with Class Shares, the class shares under Article 180(2)(iii));
  (iii) Acquisitions of Class Shares subject to Wholly Call provided for in Article 171(1): Such Class Shares subject to Wholly Call;
  (iv) Acquisitions of Shares subject to Call: Such Shares subject to Call;
  (v) Entity Conversion: All shares;
  (vi) Mergers (limited to cases where such Stock Company is to be extinguished as a result of the merger): All shares;
  (vii) Share Exchanges: All shares;
  (viii) Share Transfers: All shares;
(2) If a person fails to submit the share certificates to a Stock Company no later than the day on which an act listed in any item of the preceding paragraph takes effect, the Stock Company may, until such share certificates are submitted, refuse to deliver Monies, etc. to which the shareholders of the shares represented by such share certificates are entitled as a result of such act.
(3) The share certificates representing the shares provided for in each item of paragraph (1) shall become invalid on the day when the act listed in each such item takes effect.

(Cases where Share Certificates cannot be Submitted)
Article 220　(1) In cases where the acts listed in each item of paragraph (1) of the preceding article are carried out, if a person cannot submit share certificates, the Company Issuing Share Certificate may, at the request of that person, give public notice to interested parties to the effect that they can state their objections, if any, during a certain period of time; provided, however, that such period cannot be less than three months.
(2) In cases where public notice is given under the provisions of the preceding paragraph, if no interested party states an objection during the period of time under that paragraph, the Company Issuing Share Certificate may deliver Monies, etc. under paragraph (2) of the preceding article to the person who made the request under the preceding paragraph.
(3) The costs of the public notice under the provisions of paragraph (1) shall be borne by the person who makes the request under that paragraph.

Subsection 3　Registration of Lost Share Certificate

Art.221～224　　1 Companies Act, PART II, Chap.II, Sec.9

(Registry of Lost Share Certificates)
Article 221　A Company Issuing Share Certificate (including a Company Issuing Share Certificate in cases where one year has not elapsed from the day immediately following the day on which such Company Issuing Share Certificate effected a amendment to the articles of incorporation to abolish provisions of the articles of incorporation to the effect that it issues share certificates for its shares (or, for a Company with Class Shares, shares of all classes). The same shall apply hereinafter in this Subsection (excluding Article 223, Article 227 and Article 228(2)).) shall prepare a registry of lost share certificates and state or record the following matters (hereinafter in this Subsection referred to as "Matters to be Stated in the Registry of Lost Share Certificates") in the same:
(i) The serial numbers of the share certificates relating to the request under the provisions of Article 223 (including share certificates that have become invalid under the provisions of Article 218(2) or Article 219(3), and share certificates representing shares in cases where a judgment upholding a claim seeking invalidation of the share issue or the disposition of such shares has become final and binding. The same shall apply hereinafter in this Subsection (excluding Article 228).);
(ii) The names and addresses of persons who have lost share certificates under the preceding item;
(iii) The names and addresses of persons who are stated or recorded in the shareholder registry as the shareholders or Registered Pledgees of Shares of the shares represented by the share certificates (hereinafter in this Subsection, referring to as "Registered Holder.") under paragraph (1); and
(iv) The day on which the matters listed in the preceding three paragraphs are stated or recorded for the share certificates provided for in paragraph (1) (hereinafter in this Subsection referred to as "Day of Registration of Loss of Share Certificate").

(Delegation of Administration of Registry of Lost Share Certificates)
Article 222　For the purpose of the application of the provisions of Article 123 to a Company Issuing Share Certificate, in that Article, "of the shareholder registry" shall be read as "of the shareholder registry and the registry of lost share certificates," and "keeping the shareholder registry" shall be read as "keeping the shareholder registry and the registry of lost share certificates."

(Requests for Registration of Lost Share Certificate)
Article 223　A person who has lost share certificates may make a request for the Company Issuing Share Certificate to state or record the Matters to be Stated in the Registry of Lost Share Certificates for such share certificates (hereinafter referred to as "Registration of Lost Share Certificate").

(Notices to Registered Holders)
Article 224　(1) In cases where a Company Issuing Share Certificate has effected the Registration of Lost Share Certificate in response to a request under the provisions of the preceding article, if the person stated or recorded in the registry of lost share certificates as the person who lost the share certificates relating to such request (hereinafter in this Subsection referred to as "Registrant of Lost Share Certificate") is not the Registered Holder of the shares represented by such share certificates, the Company Issuing Share Certificate shall, without delay, notify such Registered Holder to the effect that the Company Issuing Share Certificate has effected the Registration of Lost Share Certificates for such share certificates, and of the matters listed in items (i), (ii) and (iv) of Article 221.

(2) In cases where share certificates have been submitted to the Company Issuing Share Certificate in order to exercise rights with respect to the shares, if the Registration of Lost Share Certificate has been effected for such share certificates, the Company Issuing Share Certificate shall, without delay, notify the person who submitted such share certificates to the effect that the Registration of Lost Share Certificate has been effected for such share certificates.

(Filing of Application to Cancel by Holders of Share Certificate)

Article 225 (1) A person who holds share certificates subject to the Registration of Lost Share Certificate (excluding the Registrant of Lost Share Certificate for such share certificates) may file an application with the Company Issuing Share Certificate for the cancellation of such Registration of Lost Share Certificate, as prescribed by the applicable Ordinance of the Ministry of Justice; provided, however, that this shall not apply if one year has elapsed from the day immediately following the Day of Registration of the Loss of Share Certificate.
(2) A person who intends to make an application under the provisions of the preceding paragraph shall submit the share certificates referred to in that paragraph to the Company Issuing Share Certificate.
(3) A Company Issuing Share Certificate that has received an application under the provisions of paragraph (1) shall, without delay, notify the Registrant of Lost Share Certificate referred to in that paragraph of the name and address of the person who made the application under the provisions of that paragraph, and of the serial numbers of the share certificates referred to in that paragraph.
(4) On the day on which two weeks have elapsed from the day of the notice under the provisions of the preceding paragraph, the Company Issuing Share Certificate shall cancel the Registration of Lost Share Certificate relating to share certificates submitted pursuant to the provisions of paragraph (2). In such cases, the Company Issuing Share Certificate shall return such share certificates to the person who filed the application under the provisions of paragraph (1).

(Filing of Application to Cancel by Registrant of Lost Share Certificates)

Article 226 (1) A Registrant of Lost Share Certificate may file an application with the Company Issuing Share Certificate, as prescribed by the applicable Ordinance of the Ministry of Justice, to cancel the Registration of Lost Share Certificate (excluding the Registration of Lost Share Certificate for share certificates submitted under the provisions of paragraph (2) of the preceding article in cases where a amendment is effected to the articles of incorporation to abolish provisions of the articles of incorporation to the effect that the Company Issuing Share Certificate issues share certificates for its shares (or, for a Company with Class Shares, shares of all classes)).
(2) A Company Issuing Share Certificate that has received an application under the provisions of the preceding paragraph shall cancel the Registration of Lost Share Certificate relating to such application on the day of the receipt of such application.

(Cancellation of Registration of Lost Share Certificate where Provisions of Articles of Incorporation to Issue Share Certificates are Abolished)

Article 227 In cases where a Company Issuing Share Certificate amends the articles of incorporation to abolish provisions of the articles of incorporation to the effect that the Company Issuing Share Certificate issues share certificates for its shares (or, for a Company with Class Shares, shares of all classes), the Company Issuing Share Certificate shall cancel the Registration of Lost Share Certificate (excluding registrations for share certificates submitted under the provisions of Article 225(2) only if the Registrant of Lost Share Certificate is the Registered Holder of the shares relating to the share certificates subject to such Registration of Lost Share Certificate) on the day of the effectuation of such amendment to the articles of incorporation.

(Invalidation of Share Certificate)
Article 228 (1) Share certificates subject to the Registration of Lost Share Certificate (excluding registrations that have been cancelled) shall become invalid on the day on which one year has elapsed from the day immediately following the Day of Registration of Lost Share Certificate.
(2) In cases where share certificates become invalid under the provisions of the preceding paragraph, the Company Issuing Share Certificate shall reissue share certificates to the Registrant of Lost Share Certificate for such share certificates.

(Relationship with Procedures for Notices seeking Objections)
Article 229 (1) In cases where a Registrant of Lost Share Certificate submits a request under Article 220(1), the Company Issuing Share Certificate may give public notice pursuant to the provisions of that paragraph only if the last day of the period under that paragraph arrives before the day on which one year has elapsed from the day immediately following the Day of Registration of Lost Share Certificate.
(2) If a Company Issuing Share Certificate gives public notice under the provisions of Article 220(1), such Company Issuing Share Certificate shall cancel the Registration of Lost Share Certificate for the share certificates relating to such public notice on the day of such public notice.

(Effect of Registration of Lost Share Certificate)
Article 230 (1) A Company Issuing Share Certificate may not state or record the names and addresses of the persons who acquired shares represented by share certificates subject to the Registration of Lost Share Certificate until the earliest of the following days (hereinafter in this article referred to as the "Day of Cancellation of Registration"):
(i) The day on which such Registration of Lost Share Certificate is cancelled; or
(ii) The day on which one year has elapsed from the day immediately following the Day of Registration of Lost Share Certificate.
(2) A Company Issuing Share Certificate may reissue share certificates subject to the Registration of Lost Share Certificate only after the Day of Cancellation of Registration.
(3) If a Registrant of Lost Share Certificate is not the Registered Holder of the shares represented by the share certificates subject to the Registration of Lost Share Certificate, the shareholders of such shares may not exercise voting right at a shareholders meeting or Class Meeting until the Day of Cancellation of Registration.
(4) An auction pursuant to the provisions of Article 197(1) or a sale pursuant to the provisions of paragraph (2) of that article may not be effected with respect to shares represented by share certificates subject to the Registration of Lost Share Certificate.

(Keeping and Making Available for Inspection of Registry of Lost Share Certificates)
Article 231 (1) A Company Issuing Share Certificate shall keep the registry of lost share certificates at its head office (or, in cases where there is a Administrator of Shareholder Registry, at its sales office).
(2) Any person may submit the following requests at any time during the business hours of a Company Issuing Share Certificate with respect to the registry of lost share cer-

tificates (limited to the portion in which such person has an interest). In such cases, the reasons for such request shall be disclosed.
(i) If the registry of lost share certificates is prepared in writing, a request for the review or copying of such document;
(ii) If the registry of lost share certificates is prepared by Electromagnetic Means, a request for the inspection or copying of anything that indicates the matters recorded in such Electromagnetic Records in a manner prescribed by the applicable Ordinance of the Ministry of Justice.

(Notices to Registrants of Lost Share Certificate)
Article 232 (1) It shall be sufficient for a notice or demand to a Registrant of Lost Share Certificate to be sent by a Company Issuing Share Certificate to the address of such Registrant of Lost Share Certificate stated or recorded in the registry of lost share certificates (or, in cases where such Registrant of Lost Share Certificate notifies the Company Issuing Share Certificate of a different place or contact address for the receipt of notices or demands, to such place or contact address).
(2) The notices or demands referred to in the preceding paragraph shall be deemed to have arrived at the time when such notice or demand should normally have arrived.

(Exception to Application)
Article 233 The provisions of Part III of the Non-Contentious Cases Procedures Act (Act No. 14 of 1898) shall not apply to share certificates.

Section 10 Miscellaneous Provisions

(Treatment of Fractions)
Article 234 (1) In cases where a Stock Company delivers shares in such Stock Company to the persons listed in the following items when any act listed in such items is carried out, if the number of the shares of such Stock Company that shall be delivered to such persons includes a fraction of less than one share, the Stock Company shall sell the number of shares equivalent to the total sum of the fractions by auction (in cases where the total sum includes a fraction of less than one, such fraction shall be rounded off) and shall deliver the proceeds of that auction to such persons in proportion to the fractions attributed to them:
(i) The acquisition of shares under the provisions of Article 170(1): The shareholders of such Stock Company;
(ii) The acquisition of shares under the provisions of Article 173(1): The shareholders of such Stock Company;
(iii) The Allotment of Shares without Contribution provided for in the provisions of Article 185: The shareholders of such Stock Company;
(iv) The acquisition of Share Options pursuant to the provisions of Article 275(1): The holders of the Share Options provided for in of 236(1)(vii)(a);
(v) Mergers (limited to cases where such Stock Company survives the merger): The shareholders or members of the Company which is to be extinguished after the merger;
(vi) The issuing of shares to be issued at the time of incorporation under merger contracts: The shareholders or members of the Company which is to be extinguished after the merger;
(vii) The acquisition of all Issued Shares of another Stock Company by Share Exchange: The shareholders of the Stock Company that effects the Share Exchange;
(viii) The issuing of shares to be issued at the time of incorporation under Share

Transfer plan: The shareholders of the Stock Company that effects the Share Transfer plan;
(2) In lieu of sale by auction under the provisions of the preceding paragraph, a Stock Company may sell shares under that paragraph with a market price in an amount calculated by the method prescribed by the applicable Ordinance of the Ministry of Justice as the market price thereof, and shares under that paragraph without a market price using a method other than auction with the permission of the court. In such cases, if there are two or more directors, the petition for such permission shall be filed with the consent of all directors.
(3) For the purpose of the application of the provisions of the preceding paragraph in cases where the shares under paragraph (1) are sold, "of that auction" in paragraph (1) shall be read as "of that sale."
(4) A Stock Company may purchase some or all of the shares sold pursuant to the provisions of paragraph (2). In such cases, the following matters shall be prescribed:
　(i) The number of shares to be purchased (or, for a Company with Class Shares, the classes of the shares and the number of shares for each class); and
　(ii) The total amount of the monies to be delivered in exchange for the purchase of the shares under the preceding item.
(5) A Company with Board of Directors shall determine the matters listed in each item of the preceding paragraph by resolution of the board of directors.
(6) The provisions of paragraphs (1) to (4) inclusive shall apply mutatis mutandis to cases where Bonds or Share Options of such Stock Company are delivered to the persons provided for in each item of paragraph (1) when any act listed in such items is carried out.

Article 235 (1) If a Share Split or consolidation of shares effected by a Stock Company produces any fraction less than one share in the number of the shares, the Stock Company shall sell the number of shares equivalent to the total sum of the fractions by auction (in cases where the total sum includes a fraction of less than one, such fraction shall be rounded off) and shall deliver the proceeds of that auction to the shareholders in proportion to the fractions attributed to them:
(2) The provisions of paragraphs (2) to (5) inclusive of the preceding article shall apply mutatis mutandis to the cases provided for in the preceding paragraph.

Chapter III　Share Option

Section 1　General Provisions

(Features of Share Option)
Article 236 (1) If a Stock Company issues Share Options, the features of the Share Options shall consist of the following matters:
　(i) The number of the shares underlying the Share Options (or, for a Company with Class Shares, the classes of the shares and the number of shares for each class), or the method for calculating that number;
　(ii) The value of the property to be contributed when such Share Options are exercised or the method for calculating that value;
　(iii) If property other than monies will be the subject of the contribution when Share Options are exercised, a statement to such effect and the description and value of that property;
　(iv) The period during which such Share Options can be exercised;
　(v) Matters regarding the capital and capital reserves that will be increased in cases

where shares will be issued as a result of the exercise of such Share Options;
(vi) If it is arranged that the approval of such Stock Company will be required for the acquisition of such Share Options by assignment, a statement to such effect;
(vii) If it is arranged that such Stock Company may acquire such Share Options on condition of certain grounds arising, the following matters:
   (a) A statement that such Stock Company may acquire its Share Options on the day when certain grounds arise, and of those grounds;
   (b) If it is arranged that the grounds referred to in (a) will arise as at the arrival of a day to be separately prescribed by such Stock Company, a statement of such arrangement;
   (c) If it is arranged that a portion of the Share Options referred to in (a) may be acquired on the day the grounds referred to in (a) arise, a statement of such arrangement and of the method for determining the portion of the Share Options to be acquired;
   (d) If shares in such Stock Company are delivered to the holders of such Share Options in exchange for the acquisition of the Share Options referred to in (a), the number of such shares (or, for a Company with Class Shares, the classes of the shares and the number of shares for each class), or the method for calculating that number;
   (e) If Bonds of such Stock Company (other than those on Bonds with Share Option) are delivered to the holders of such Share Options in exchange for the acquisition of the Share Options referred to in (a), the description of the classes of such Bonds and the total amount for each class of Bonds, or the method for calculating that total amount;
   (f) If other Share Options of such Stock Company (other than those attached to Bonds with Share Option) are delivered to the holders of such Share Options in exchange for the acquisition of the Share Options referred to in (a), the feature and number of such other Share Options, or the method for calculating that number;
   (g) If Bonds with Share Option of such Stock Company are delivered to the holders of such Share Options in exchange for the acquisition of the Share Options referred to in (a), the matters prescribed in (e) for such Bonds with Share Option, and the matters prescribed in (f) for the Share Options attached to such Bonds with Share Option;
   (h) If property other than Share Options, etc. of such Stock Company is delivered to the holders of such Share Options in exchange for the acquisition of the Share Options referred to in (a), a description of the features and number or amount of such property, or the method for calculating that number or amount.
(viii) If it is arranged that in cases where such Stock Company carries out acts listed in sub-items (a) to (e) inclusive below, the Share Options of the Stock Company provided for in sub-items (a) to (e) inclusive is to be delivered to the holders of such Share Options, a statement to that effect and of the conditions of the same:
   (a) Mergers (limited to cases where such Stock Company is to be extinguished as a result of the merger): The Stock Company that survives the merger or the Stock Company incorporated as a result of the merger;
   (b) Absorption-type Company Split: The Stock Company which succeeds, in whole or in part, to any rights and obligations that a Stock Company effecting an Absorption-type Company Split holds in connection with its business;
   (c) Incorporation-type Company Split: The Stock Company incorporated as a result of the Incorporation-type Company Split;
   (d) Share Exchange: The Stock Company that acquires all of the Issued Shares of

the Stock Company effecting the Share Exchange;
  (e) Share Transfer: The Stock Company incorporated as a result of the Share Transfer;
(ix) If, in cases where the number of the shares to be issued to the holder of Share Options who has exercised his/her Share Options includes a fraction of less than one share, such fraction shall be rounded off, a statement to that effect.
(x) If it is arranged to issue Share Option certificates representing such Share Options (excluding those attached to Bonds with Share Option), a statement to that effect.
(xi) In the cases provided for in the preceding item, if the holders of Share Options cannot make, in whole or in part, the demand under the provisions of Article 290, a statement to that effect.
(2) The number of the Share Options attached to Bonds with Share Option shall be uniform for each monetary amount for the Bonds with respect to such Bonds with Share Option.

(Exercise of Rights by Co-owners)
Article 237 If any Share Option is co-owned by two or more persons, the co-owners may not exercise their rights in relation to such Share Option unless they specify one person to exercise the rights in relation to such Share Option, and notify the Stock Company of the name of that person; provided, however, that this shall not apply in cases where the Stock Company has agreed to the exercise of such rights.

Section 2 Share Option Issue

Subsection 1 Determination of Subscription Requirements

(Determination of Subscription Requirements)
Article 238 (1) Whenever a Stock Company intends to solicit subscribers for a Share Option issue, the Stock Company shall prescribe the following matters (hereinafter in this Section referred to as "Subscription Requirements") with respect to the Share Options for Subscription (meaning the Share Options that is to be allotted to persons who subscribed for such Share Options in response to such solicitation. The same shall apply hereinafter in this Chapter.):
(i) The features and number of the Share Options for Subscription;
(ii) In cases where it is arranged that there is no requirement for monies to be paid in in exchange for the Share Options for Subscription, a statement to that effect;
(iii) In cases other than the cases provided for in the preceding item, the Amount To Be Paid In for the Share Options for Subscription (meaning the amount of money to be paid in in exchange for one Share Option for Subscription. The same shall apply hereinafter in this Chapter.) or the method for calculating that amount;
(iv) The day on which the Share Options for Subscription is allotted (hereinafter in this Section referred to as the "Day of Allotment");
(v) If the Stock Company prescribes the date for the payment of monies in exchange for the Share Options for Subscription, that date;
(vi) In cases where Share Options for Subscription are attached to Bonds with Share Option, the matters listed in each item of Article 676;
(vii) In the cases provided for in the preceding item, if the Stock Company otherwise provides for the method for submission of a demand under the provisions of Article 118(1), Article 777(1), Article 787(1), or Article 808(1) with respect to the Share Options for Subscription attached to the Bonds with Share Option under that item,

that provision.
(2) The determination of the Subscription Requirements shall be made by resolution of shareholders meeting.
(3) In the following cases, the directors shall explain at the shareholders meeting referred to in the preceding paragraph the reasons for the need to solicit subscribers for Share Options for Subscription with the offer of the conditions under item (i) or in the amount under item (ii):
  (i) If, in the cases provided for in item (ii) of paragraph (1), the absence of a requirement for the payment in of monies is particularly favorable to relevant persons; or
  (ii) If, in the cases provided for in item (iii) of paragraph (1), the Amount To Be Paid In under that paragraph is particularly favorable to relevant persons.
(4) For a Company with Class Shares, if some or all classes of the shares underlying the Share Options for Subscription are Shares with Restriction on Transfer, the determination of the Subscription Requirements regarding such Share Options for Subscription shall not become effective without a resolution of the relevant Class Meeting, except in cases where there is a provision in the articles of incorporation to the effect that, with respect to the solicitation of subscribers for Share Options for Subscription for which the underlying shares are such class shares, a resolution of the Class Meeting constituted by the Class Shareholders of such class is not required; provided, however, that this shall not apply to cases where there is no Class Shareholder who can exercise his/her voting right at such Class Meeting.
(5) The Subscription Requirements shall be uniform for each solicitation under paragraph (1).

(Delegation of Determination of Subscription Requirements)
Article 239 (1) Notwithstanding the provisions of paragraphs (2) and (4) of the preceding article, a shareholders meeting may delegate the determination of the Subscription Requirements to the directors (or, for a Company with Board of Directors, the board of directors) by resolution. In such cases, the shareholders meeting shall prescribe the following matters:
  (i) The features and maximum number of Share Options for Subscription for which the Subscription Requirements may be determined under such delegation; and
  (ii) In cases where it is arranged that there will be no requirement to pay monies in with respect to the Share Options for Subscription under the preceding item, a statement to that effect;
  (iii) In cases other than those prescribed in the preceding item, the minimum Amount To Be Paid In for Share Options for Subscription.
(2) In the following cases, the directors shall explain at the shareholders meeting referred to in the preceding paragraph the reasons for the need to solicit subscribers for Share Options for Subscription with the offer of the conditions under item (i) or in the amount under item (ii):
  (i) If, in the cases provided for in item (ii) of the preceding paragraph, the absence of a requirement for the payment in of monies is particularly favorable to relevant persons; or
  (ii) If, in the cases provided for in item (iii) of the preceding paragraph, the minimum Amount To Be Paid In under that paragraph is particularly favorable to relevant persons.
(3) Resolutions under paragraph (1) shall be effective with respect only to solicitation under that paragraph under which the date under item (iv), paragraph (1) of the preceding article falls within one year from the day of such resolution.
(4) For a Company with Class Shares, if some or all of the classes of the shares underlying

Art.240〜241   Ⅰ Companies Act, PART II, Chap.III, Sec.2

the Share Options for Subscription are Shares with Restriction on Transfer, the determination of the Subscription Requirements regarding such Share Options for Subscription shall not become effective without a resolution of the relevant Class Meeting, except in cases where there is a provision in the articles of incorporation referred to in paragraph (3) of the preceding article; provided, however, that this shall not apply to the case where there is no Class Shareholder who can exercise his/her voting right at such Class Meeting.

(Special Provisions on Determination of Subscription Requirements for Public Company)
Article 240 (1) Except for the cases listed in each item of Article 238(3), for the purpose of the application of the provisions of paragraph (2) of that article to a Public Company, "shareholders meeting" in that paragraph shall be read as "board of directors meeting." In such cases, the provision of the preceding article shall not apply.
(2) In cases where a Public Company has determined Subscription Requirements by a resolution of a board of directors meeting provided for in Article 238(2) applied by the reading of terms pursuant to the provisions of the preceding paragraph, the Public Company shall notify the shareholders of such Subscription Requirements no later than two weeks prior to the Day of Allotment.
(3) A public notice may be substituted for the notice under the provisions of the preceding paragraph.
(4) The provisions of paragraph (2) shall not apply in cases prescribed by the applicable Ordinance of the Ministry of Justice as cases where it is unlikely that the protection of shareholders is compromised, including cases where, with respect to Subscription Requirements, the Stock Company has submitted, no later than two weeks prior to the Day of Allotment, a notice under Article 4(1) or (2) of the Securities and Exchange Act.

(Cases where Entitlement to Allotment of Share Options is Granted to Shareholders)
Article 241 (1) In carrying out solicitation under Article 238(1), the Stock Company may grant entitlement to the allotment of Share Options to its shareholders. In such cases, in addition to the Subscription Requirements, the Stock Company shall prescribe the following matters:
(i) A statement to the effect that the Stock Company will grant entitlement to the allotment of the Share Options for Subscription of that Stock Company (or, for a Company with Class Shares, the Share Options the shares underlying which have the class identical to the class of the shares held by such shareholders) to shareholders subject to the application provided for in paragraph (2) of the following article;
(ii) The day for the application for subscription for the Share Options for Subscription referred to in the preceding item.
(2) In the cases provided for in the preceding paragraph, the shareholders under item (i) of that paragraph (excluding the Stock Company) shall be entitled to the allotment of the Share Options for Subscription in accordance with the number of shares they hold; provided, however, that if the number of the Share Options for Subscription to be allotted to such shareholders includes a fraction of less than one unit, it shall be rounded off.
(3) In cases where the Stock Company prescribes the matters listed in each item of paragraph (1), the Subscription Requirements and the matters listed in each item of that paragraph shall be prescribed in accordance with the categories of the cases listed in

the following items, by the methods provided for in each of such items:
(i) In cases where there is a provision in the articles of incorporation to the effect that such Subscription Requirements and the matters listed in each item of paragraph (1) may be prescribed by decision of the directors (excluding the cases where the Stock Company is a Company with Board of Directors): A decision of the directors;
(ii) In cases where there is a provision in the articles of incorporation to the effect that such Subscription Requirements and the matters listed in each item of paragraph (1) may be prescribed by resolution of the board of directors (excluding the cases listed in the following item): A resolution of the board of directors;
(iii) In cases where the Stock Company is a Public Company: A resolution of the board of directors;
(iv) In cases other than those listed in the preceding three items: A resolution of a shareholders meeting;
(4) In cases where a Stock Company determines the matters listed in each item of paragraph (1), the Stock Company shall notify the shareholders under item (i) of that paragraph (excluding such Stock Company) of the following matters no later than two weeks prior to the date provided for in item (ii) of that paragraph:
(i) The Subscription Requirements;
(ii) The features and number of Share Options for Subscription to be allotted to such shareholders; and
(iii) The date provided for in item (ii) of paragraph (1).
(5) The provisions of Article 238(2) to (4) inclusive and the preceding two articles shall not apply in cases where entitlement to the allotment of Share Options is granted to the shareholders under the provisions of paragraph (1) to paragraph (3) inclusive hereof.

Subsection 2 Allotment of Share Options for Subscription

(Application for Share Options for Subscription)

Article 242 (1) A Stock Company shall notify persons who intend to subscribe for Share Options for Subscription in response to solicitation in Article 238(1) of the matters listed in the following items:
(i) The trade name of the Stock Company;
(ii) The Subscription Requirements;
(iii) If any payment is to be made when the Share Options are exercised, the place where payments are handled;
(iv) In addition to the matters listed in the preceding three paragraphs, any matter prescribed by the applicable Ordinance of the Ministry of Justice.
(2) A person who applies to subscribe for the Share Options for Subscription in response to solicitation in paragraph (1) of Article 238 shall deliver a document which specifies the following matters:
(i) The name and address of the person applying;
(ii) The number of Share Options for Subscription for which he/she intends to subscribe.
(3) A person who applies referred to in the preceding paragraph may, in lieu of the delivery of the document under such paragraph, provide the matters to be specified in the document under such paragraph by Electromagnetic Means, with the approval of the Stock Company, subject to the provisions of the applicable Cabinet Order. In such cases, the person applying shall be deemed to have delivered the document under such paragraph.
(4) The provisions of paragraph (3) shall not apply in cases where the Stock Company has

Art.243   ① Companies Act, PART II, Chap.III, Sec.2

issued a prospectus provided for in Article 2(10) of the Financial Instruments and Exchange Act that specifies the matters listed in each item of that paragraph to the person who intends to submit the application under paragraph (1), and in other cases prescribed by the applicable Ordinance of the Ministry of Justice as cases where it is unlikely that the protection of persons who intend to submit applications for subscription for Share Options for Subscription are compromised.
(5) If there are changes in the matters listed in each item of paragraph (1), the Stock Company shall immediately notify persons who have submitted applications under paragraph (2) (hereinafter in this Subsection referred to as "Applicants") thereof and of the matter so changed.
(6) In cases where Share Options for Subscription are attached to Bonds with Share Option, Applicants (limited to those who submitted applications solely for Share Options for Subscription) shall be deemed to have applied for subscription for the Bonds with Share Option to which the Share Options for Subscription relating to such applications are attached.
(7) It shall be sufficient for a notice or demand to an applicant to be sent by the Stock Company to the address under item (i) of paragraph (2) (or, in cases where such applicant notifies the Stock Company of a different place or contact address for the receipt of notices or demands, to such place or contact address).
(8) The notices or demands referred to in the preceding paragraph shall be deemed to have arrived at the time when such notice or demand should normally have arrived.

(Allotment of Share Options for Subscription)
Article 243 (1) A Stock Company shall specify the persons from among the Applicants the persons to whom Share Options for Subscription will be allotted, and determine the number of Share Options for Subscription to be allotted to those persons. In such cases, the Stock Company may reduce the number of Share Options for Subscription the Stock Company allots to such Applicants below the number under item (ii), paragraph (2) of the preceding article.
(2) In the following cases, the determination under the provisions of the preceding paragraph shall be made by resolution of a shareholders meeting (or of a board of directors meeting for a Company with Board of Directors); provided, however, that this shall not apply in cases where it is otherwise provided for in the articles of incorporation.
   (i) In cases where some or all of the shares underlying the Share Options for Subscription are Shares with Restriction on Transfer; or
   (ii) In cases where the Share Options for Subscription are Share Options with Restriction on Transfer (meaning Share Options for which it is provided that the acquisition of such Share Options by assignment shall require the approval of the Stock Company. The same shall apply hereinafter in this Chapter.).
(3) The Stock Company shall notify the Applicants, no later than the day immediately preceding the Day of Allotment, of the number of the Share Options for Subscription that will be allotted to such Applicants (in cases where such Share Options for Subscription are attached to Bonds with Share Option, including a description of the classes of Bonds with respect to such Bonds with Share Option and the total amount of money for each class of Bonds).
(4) In cases where the Stock Company has granted entitlement to the allotment of Share Options pursuant to the provisions of Article 241 to its shareholders, if the shareholders do not submit, no later than the date under item (ii), paragraph (1) of that article, applications under paragraph (2) of the preceding article, such shareholders shall lose the entitlement to the allotment of Share Options for Subscription.

(Special Provisions on the Subscription for and Allotment of Share Options for Subscription)

Article 244 (1) The provisions of the preceding two Articles shall not apply in cases where a person who intends to subscribe for Share Options for Subscription executes a contract for subscription for the total number of those Share Options.

(2) For the purpose of the application of the preceding paragraph in cases where the Share Options for Subscription are those attached to Bonds with Share Option, "for subscription for the total number of those Share Options" in that paragraph shall be read as "for subscription for the total number of those Share Options and the total amount of the Bonds to which such Share Options for Subscription are attached."

(Status as Holders of Share Options)

Article 245 (1) The persons listed in the following items shall become the holders of the Share Options for Subscription provided for in such items on the Day of Allotment:
  (i) Applicants: The Share Options for Subscription allotted by the Stock Company; and
  (ii) Persons who subscribed for the total number of the Share Options for Subscription under the provisions of paragraph (1) of the preceding article: The Share Options for Subscription for which those persons have subscribed.

(2) In cases where Share Options for Subscription are attached to Bonds with Share Option, the persons who become holders of the Share Options under the provisions of the preceding paragraph shall become bondholders of the Bonds with respect to the Bonds with Share Option to which such Share Options for Subscription are attached.

Subsection 3 Payments for Share Options for Subscription

Article 246 (1) In the cases provided for under Article 238(1)(iii), holders of Share Options shall pay the entire Amount To Be Paid In for the Share Options for Subscription for which the holders respectively subscribed, at the place for the handling of bank, etc. payments designated by the Stock Company, no later than the day immediately preceding the first day of the period provided for under Article 236(1)(iv) for Share Options for Subscription (or, in the cases provided for under Article 238(1)(v), no later than the date under that item; in paragraph (3) referred to as the "Payment Date")

(2) Notwithstanding the provisions of the preceding paragraph, holders of Share Options may, with the approval of the Stock Company, tender property other than monies equivalent to the Amount To Be Paid In or set off their claims against such Stock Company, in lieu of payment under the provisions of that paragraph.

(3) In the cases provided for under Article 238(1)(iii), holders of Share Options may not exercise the Share Options for Subscription unless they pay in the entire Amount To Be Paid In for their respective Share Options for Subscription (including tendering property other than monies or setting off claims against such Stock Company in lieu of such payment) no later than the Payment Date with respect to such Share Options for Subscription.

Subsection 4 Demand for Discontinuation of Issue of Share Options for Subscription

Article 247 In the following cases, if shareholders are likely to suffer any disadvantage, shareholders may demand that the Stock Company discontinue an issue of the Share Options relating to solicitation under Article 238(1):
  (i) In cases where such Share Option issue violates the applicable laws and regulations

or articles of incorporation; or
(ii) In cases where such Share Option issue is effected by using a method that is extremely unfair.

Subsection 5 Miscellaneous Provisions

Article 248 The provisions of Article 676 through Article 680 shall not apply to the solicitation of subscribers for the Bonds with respect to the Bonds with Share Option.

Section 3 Share Option Registry

(Share Option Registry)
Article 249 A Stock Company shall, without delay after the day Share Options are issued, prepare a Share Option registry and state or record, in accordance with the categories of Share Options listed in the following items, the matters listed in such items (hereinafter referred to as "Matters to be Specified in the Share Option Registry"):
(i) Share Options for which bearer form Share Option certificates are issued (hereinafter in this Chapter referred to as "Bearer Share Options"): The serial numbers of such Share Option certificates and the features and number of such Bearer Share Options; and
(ii) Share Options attached to Bonds with Share Option for which bearer form certificates for Bonds with Share Option (referring to Bond certificates for Bond with Share Option with Issued Certificates (meaning a Bond with Share Option for which it is provided that a Bond certificate shall be issued for the Bond for such Bond with Share Option. The same shall apply hereinafter in this Chapter.). The same shall apply hereinafter.) are issued (hereinafter in this Chapter referred to as "Bearer Bonds with Share Option"): The serial numbers of such certificates for Bonds with Share Option and the features and number of such Share Options; and
(iii) Share Options other than the Share Options listed in the preceding two items: The following matters:
(a) The names and addresses of the holders of Share Options;
(b) The features and number of the Share Options held by the holders of Share Options referred to in (a);
(c) The days when the holders of Share Options referred to in (a) acquired the Share Options; and
(d) If the Share Options referred to in (b) are Share Options with Issued Certificates (meaning Share Options (excluding those attached to Bonds with Share Option) for which it is provided that Share Option certificates are issued for such Share Options. The same shall apply hereinafter in this Chapter.), the serial numbers of the Share Option certificates representing such Share Options (limited to those for which Share Option certificates are issued).
(e) If the Share Options referred to in (b) are attached to Bonds with Share Option with Issued Certificates, the serial numbers of the certificates of Bonds with Share Option for the Bonds with Share Option (limited to those for which certificates of Bonds with Share Option are issued) to which such Share Options are attached.

(Delivery of Documents Stating Matters to be Specified in the Share Option Registry)
Article 250 (1) The holders of Share Options referred to in item (iii)(a) of the preceding article may request that the Stock Company deliver documents stating the Matters to

be Specified in the Share Option Registry that are stated or recorded in the Share Option registry with respect to such holders of Share Options, or provide the Electromagnetic Records that record such Matters to be Specified in the Share Option Registry.
(2) The documents referred to in the preceding paragraph shall be affixed with the signature, or name and seal, of the Representative Director of the Stock Company (referring to the representative executive officer for a Company with Committees. The same shall apply in the following paragraph.).
(3) With respect to the Electromagnetic Records referred to in paragraph (1), the Representative Director of the Stock Company shall implement measures in lieu of the affixation of signature, or name and seal, prescribed by the applicable Ordinance of the Ministry of Justice.
(4) The provisions of the preceding three paragraphs shall not apply to Share Options with Issued Certificates or Share Options attached to Bonds with Share Option with Issued Certificates.

(Administration of Share Option Registry)
Article 251 For the purpose of the application of Article 123 in cases where a Stock Company issues Share Options, in that article, "Administrator of Shareholder Registry" shall be read as "Administrator of Shareholder Registry and Share Option Registry" and "keeping the shareholder registry" shall be read as "keeping the shareholder registry and Share Option registry."

(Keeping and Making Available for Inspection of Share Option Registry)
Article 252 (1) A Stock Company shall keep the Share Option registry at its head office (or, in cases where there is an Administrator of Shareholder Registry, at its business office).
(2) Shareholders and creditors may submit the following requests at any time during the business hours of the Stock Company. In such cases, the reasons for such requests shall be disclosed.
  (i) If the Share Option registry is prepared in writing, a request for the inspection or copying of such document;
  (ii) If the Share Option registry is prepared by Electromagnetic Means, a request for the inspection or copying of anything that indicates the matters recorded in such Electromagnetic Records in a manner prescribed by the applicable Ordinance of the Ministry of Justice.
(3) If a request referred to in the preceding paragraph is made, a Stock Company may not refuse such request unless it falls under any of the following:
  (i) The shareholder or creditor who made such request (hereinafter in this paragraph referred to as the "Requestor") submitted the request for a purpose other than for research on securing or exercising his/her rights;
  (ii) The Requestor made the request with the purpose of interfering with the execution of the operations of such Stock Company or prejudicing the common benefit of the shareholders;
  (iii) The Requestor operates or engages in any business which is, in substance, in competition with the operations of such Stock Company;
  (iv) The Requestor made the request in order to report facts to third parties for profit, knowledge of which may be acquired by inspecting or copying the Share Option registry; or
  (v) The Requestor is a person who has reported facts. Knowledge of which was acquired by reviewing or copying the Share Option registry, to third parties for profit

Art.253〜255   ① Companies Act, PART II, Chap.III, Sec.4

in the immediately preceding two years.
(4) If it is necessary for a member of the Parent Company of a Stock Company to exercise his/her rights, such member of the Parent Company may, with the permission of the court, make the requests set forth in each item of paragraph (2) with respect to the Share Option registry of such Stock Company. In such cases, the reasons for such requests shall be disclosed.
(5) The court may not grant the permission referred to in the preceding paragraph if any circumstance provided for in any item of paragraph (3) applies to the member of the Parent Company referred to in the preceding paragraph.

(Notices to Holders of Share Options)
Article 253 (1) It shall be sufficient for a notice or demand to holders of Share Options to be sent by a Stock Company to the addresses of such holders of Share Options stated or recorded in the Share Options registry (or, in cases where such holders of Share Options notify such Stock Company of a different place or contact address for the receipt of notices or demands, to such place or contact address).
(2) The notices or demands referred to in the preceding paragraph shall be deemed to have arrived at the time when such notice or demand should normally have arrived.
(3) If a Share Option is co-owned by two or more persons, the co-owners shall specify one person who receives the notice or demand sent by the Stock Company to the holders of Share Options and notify such Stock Company of the name of that person. In such case, that person shall be deemed to be the holder of Share Option and the provisions of the preceding two paragraphs shall apply.
(4) In cases where there is no notice by co-owners pursuant to the provisions of the preceding paragraph, it shall be sufficient for a notice or demand sent by a Stock Company to the co-owners of the Share Options if it is sent to one of them.

Section 4　Transfer of Share Option

Subsection 1　Transfer of Share Option

(Transfer of Share Option)
Article 254 (1) Holders of Share Options may transfer the Share Options held by the same.
(2) Notwithstanding the provisions of the preceding paragraph, Share Options attached to Bonds with Share Option may not be transferred on a stand-alone basis; provided, however, that this shall not apply if the Bonds with respect to such Bonds with Share Option are extinguished.
(3) Bonds with respect to Bonds with Share Option may not be transferred on a stand-alone basis; provided, however, that this shall not apply if the Share Options attached to such Bonds with Share Option are extinguished.

(Transfer of Share Options with Issued Certificate)
Article 255 (1) Transfer of Share Options with issued certificates shall not become effective unless the Share Option certificates representing such Share Options with Issued Certificate are delivered; provided, however, that this shall not apply to transfer of Share Options with issued certificates that arise out of the disposition of Own Share Options (meaning Own Share Options that the Stock Company holds. The same shall apply hereinafter in this Chapter.).
(2) Transfer of Share Options attached to Bonds with Share Option with Issued Certificate shall not become effective unless the certificates of Bonds with Share Option for such

Bonds with Share Option with Issued Certificate are delivered; provided, however, that this shall not apply to transfer of Share Options attached to Own Bonds with Share Option (meaning Own Bonds with Share Option that the Stock Company holds. The same shall apply hereinafter in this article and in the following article.) that arise out of the disposition of such Own Bonds with Share Option.

(Special Provisions on Disposition of Own Share Option)
Article 256 (1) A Stock Company shall, without delay after the day of the disposition of its Own Share Options (limited to Share Options with Issued Certificate), deliver the Share Option certificates to the persons who acquired such Own Share Options.
(2) Notwithstanding the provisions of the preceding paragraph, a Stock Company may elect to not deliver Share Option certificates under that paragraph until the persons under that paragraph so request.
(3) A Stock Company shall, without delay after the day of the disposition of its Own Bonds with Share Option (limited to Bond with Share Option with Issued Certificate), deliver the certificates of Bonds with Share Option to the persons who acquire such Own Bonds with Share Option.
(4) The provisions of Article 687 shall not apply to the transfer of Bonds with respect to the Own Bonds with Share Option arising from the disposition of such Own Bonds with Share Option.

(Perfection of Transfer of Share Option)
Article 257 (1) Transfer of Share Options shall not be perfected against the Stock Company and other third parties unless the names and addresses of the person who acquire those Share Options is stated or recorded in the Share Options registry.
(2) For the purpose of the application of the provisions of the preceding paragraph with respect to Share Options with Issued Certificates for which registered Share Option certificates are issued, and Share Options attached to the Bond with Share Option with Issued Certificate for which registered certificates of Bonds with Share Option are issued, "the Stock Company and other third parties" in that paragraph shall be read as "the Stock Company."
(3) The provisions of paragraph (1) shall not apply to any Bearer Share Options or Share Options attached to Bearer Bonds with Share Option.

(Presumption of Rights)
Article 258 (1) A possessor of Share Option certificates shall be presumed to be the lawful owner of the rights in relation to the Share Options with Issued Certificate for such Share Option certificates.
(2) A person who receives delivery of Share Option certificates shall acquire the rights in relation to the Share Options with Issued Certificate for such Share Option certificates; provided, however, that this shall not apply if that person has knowledge or is grossly negligent as to the fact of defective title of the transferor.
(3) A possessor of certificates of Bonds with Share Option shall be presumed to be the lawful owner of the rights in relation to the Share Options attached to Bonds with Share Option with Issued Certificates for such certificates of Bonds with Share Option.
(4) A person who receives delivery of certificates of Bonds with Share Option shall acquire the rights in relation to the Share Options attached to the Bond with Share Option with Issued Certificates for such certificates of Bonds with Share Option; provided, however, that this shall not apply if that person has knowledge or is grossly negligent as to the fact of defective title of the transferor.

Art.259～263   [I] Companies Act, PART II, Chap.III, Sec.4

(Stating or Recording of Matters to be Specified in the Share Option Registry Not Requested by Holders of Share Options)
Article 259 (1) In the cases provided for in the following items, a Stock Company shall state or record the Matters to be Specified in the Share Option Registry relating to the holders of Share Options referred to in such items:
(i) In cases where it has acquired the Share Options of such Stock Company;
(ii) In cases where it has disposed of Own Share Options.
(2) The provisions of the preceding paragraph shall not apply to Bearer Share Options or Share Options attached to Bearer Bonds with Share Option.

(Stating or Recording of Matters to be Specified in the Share Option Registry at Request of Holders of Share Options)
Article 260 (1) A person who has acquired Share Options from a person other than the Stock Company that issued such Share Options (excluding such Stock Company, hereinafter in this Section referred to as "Acquirer of Share Options") may request that such Stock Company state or record, in the Share Option registry, the Matters to be Specified in the Share Option Registry relating to such Share Options.
(2) Except for cases prescribed by the applicable Ordinance of the Ministry of Justice as cases of no likelihood of detriment to interested parties, requests under the provisions of the preceding paragraph shall be made jointly with the person stated or recorded in the Share Option registry as the holder of the Share Options so acquired, or his/her general successors including his/her heirs.
(3) The provisions of the preceding two paragraphs shall not apply to Bearer Share Options or Share Options attached to Bearer Bonds with Share Option.

Article 261 The provisions of the preceding paragraph shall not apply in cases where the Share Options acquired by the Acquirer of Share Options are Share Options with Restriction on Transfer; provided, however, that this shall not apply in cases where it falls under any of the following:
(i) Such Acquirer of Share Options has obtained approval under the following article as to an intended acquisition of such Share Options with Restriction of Transfer;
(ii) Such Acquirer of Share Options has obtained approval under Article 263(1) as to a completed acquisition of such Share Options with Restriction of Transfer;
(iii) Such Acquirer of Share Options is a person who acquired the Share Options with Restriction of Transfer by general succession including inheritance.

Subsection 2 Restriction on Transfer of Shares

(Requests for Approval by Holders of Share Option)
Article 262 If holders of Share Options with Restriction on Transfer intend to transfer Share Options with Restriction on Transfer held by the same to others (excluding the Stock Company which issued such Share Options with Restriction on Transfer), they may request that such Stock Company make a determination as to whether or not to approve the acquisition by such others of such Share Options with Restriction on Transfer.

(Request for Approval by Acquirers of Share Options)
Article 263 (1) Acquirers of Share Options who have acquired Share Options with Restriction on Transfer may request that the Stock Company make a determination as to whether or not to approve the acquisition of such Share Options with Restriction on

Transfer.
(2) Except for cases prescribed by the applicable Ordinance of the Ministry of Justice as cases of no likelihood of detriment to interested parties, requests pursuant to the provisions of the preceding paragraph shall be submitted jointly with the person stated or recorded in the Share Option registry as the holder of the Share Options so acquired, or his/her general successors including his/her heirs.

(Method for Requests for Approval of Transfer)
Article 264 The requests listed in the following items (hereinafter in this Subsection referred to as "Requests for Approval of Transfer") shall be made by disclosing the matters provided for in such items:
(i) Requests under the provisions of Article 262: The following matters:
   (a) The features and number of Share Options with Restriction on Transfer that the holders of Share Options making such request intend to transfer to others;
   (b) The names of the person accepting the transfer of the Share Options with Restriction on Transfer referred to in (a);
(ii) Requests under the provisions of paragraph (1) of the preceding article: The following matters:
   (a) The features and number of Share Options with Restriction on Transfer that the Acquirer of Share Options making such request has acquired;
   (b) The name of the Acquirer of Share Options referred to in (a);

(Determination of Approval of Transfer)
Article 265 (1) The determination by a Stock Company as to whether or not to grant approval under Article 262 or Article 263(1) shall be made by resolution of a shareholders meeting (or of a board of directors meeting for a Company with Board of Directors); provided, however, that this shall not apply in cases where it is otherwise provided for as a feature of the Share Options.
(2) If a Stock Company has made a determination under the preceding paragraph, it shall notify the person who made the Requests for Approval of Transfer of the content of such determination.

(Cases where Stock Company is Deemed to have Approved)
Article 266 In cases where a Stock Company has failed to give notice pursuant to the provisions of paragraph (2) of the preceding article within two weeks (or if any shorter period of time is provided for in the articles of incorporation, such shorter period of time) from the day of the Requests for Approval of Transfer, the Stock Company shall be deemed to have given the approval under Article 262 or Article 263(1); provided, however, that this shall not apply if otherwise provided for by agreement between the Stock Company and the person who made the Requests for Approval of Transfer:

Subsection 3 Pledge of Share Options

(Pledge of Share Options)
Article 267 (1) Holders of Share Options may pledge the Share Options held by the same.
(2) Notwithstanding the provisions of the preceding paragraph, Share Options attached to Bonds with Share Option may not be pledged on a stand-alone basis; provided, however, that this shall not apply if the Bonds with respect to such Bonds with Share Option are extinguished.
(3) Bonds with respect to Bonds with Share Option may not be pledged on a stand-alone

basis; provided, however, that this shall not apply if the Share Options attached to such Bonds with Share Option are extinguished.
(4) Pledges of Share Options with Issued Certificate shall not become effective unless the Share Option certificates for such Share Options with Issued Certificates are delivered.
(5) Pledges of Share Options attached to Bonds with Share Option with Issued Certificate shall not become effective unless the certificates of Bonds with Share Option for such Bonds with Share Option with Issued Certificate are delivered.

(Perfection of Pledges of Share Options)
Article 268 (1) Pledges of Share Options shall not be perfected against the Stock Company and other third parties unless the names and addresses of pledgees are stated or recorded in the Share Option registry.
(2) Notwithstanding the provisions of the preceding paragraph, a pledgee of Share Options with Issued Certificate may not assert his/her pledge against the Stock Company and other third parties unless he/she is in continuous possession of the Share Option certificates for such Share Options with Issued Certificate.
(3) Notwithstanding the provisions of paragraph (1), a pledgee of Share Options attached to Bonds with Share Option with Issued Certificates may not assert his/her pledge against the Stock Company and other third parties unless he/she is in continuous possession of the certificates of Bonds with Share Option for such Bonds with Share Option with Issued Certificate.

(Entries in Share Option Registry)
Article 269 (1) A person who pledges Share Options may request that the Stock Company state or record the following matters in the Share Option registry:
(i) The name and address of the pledgee;
(ii) The Share Options underlying the pledge.
(2) The provisions of the preceding paragraph shall not apply to Bearer Share Options or Share Options attached to Bearer Bonds with Share Option.

(Delivery of Documents Stating Matters to be Specified in the Share Option Registry)
Article 270 (1) The pledgees for whom the matters listed in the items of the preceding article are stated or recorded in the Share Option registry (hereinafter referred to as "Registered Pledgees of Share Options") may request that the Stock Company deliver documents stating the matters listed in the items of that paragraph with respect to such Registered Pledgees of Share Options that are stated or recorded in the Share Option registry, or provide the Electromagnetic Records that record such matters.
(2) The documents referred to in the preceding paragraph shall be affixed with the signature, or name and seal, of the Representative Director of the Stock Company (the representative executive officer for a Company with Committees. The same shall apply in the following paragraph.).
(3) With respect to the Electromagnetic Records referred to in paragraph (1), the Representative Director of the Stock Company shall implement measures in lieu of the affixation of signature, or name and seal prescribed by the applicable Ordinance of the Ministry of Justice.
(4) The provisions of the preceding three paragraphs shall not apply to Share Options with Issued Certificate or Share Options attached to Bonds with Share Option with Issued Certificate.

(Notices to Registered Pledgees of Share Options)

Article 271 (1) It shall be sufficient for a notice or demand to a Registered Pledgees of Share Options to be sent by a Stock Company to the addresses of such Registered Pledgees of Share Options stated or recorded in the Share Option registry (or, in cases where such Registered Pledgees of Share Options notify the Stock Company of any different place or contact address for the receipt of notices or demands, to such place or contact address).

(2) The notices or demands referred to in the preceding paragraph shall be deemed to have arrived at the time when such notice or demand should normally have arrived.

(Effect of Pledge of Share Options)

Article 272 (1) In cases where a Stock Company carries out any of the acts listed below, pledge for Share Options shall be effective with respect to the Monies, etc. which the holders of such Share Options are entitled to receive as a result of such act:
(i) The acquisition of Share Options;
(ii) Entity Conversion;
(iii) Mergers (limited to cases where such Stock Company is to be extinguished as a result of the merger);
(iv) Absorption-type Company Split;
(v) Incorporation-type Company Split;
(vi) Share Exchange; or
(vii) Share Transfer.

(2) Registered Pledgees of Share Options may receive Monies, etc. (limited to monies) under the preceding paragraph, and appropriate them as payment to satisfy their own claims in priority to other creditors.

(3) If the claims under the preceding paragraph have not yet become due and payable, the Registered Pledgees of Share Options may have the Stock Company deposit an amount equivalent to the value of the Monies, etc. provided for in that paragraph. In such cases, the pledge shall be effective with respect to the monies so deposited.

(4) Pledges for Share Options attached to Bonds with Share Option (limited to cases where the property provided for in Article 236(1)(iii) consists of the Bonds with respect to such Bonds with Share Option, and the redemption amount for such Bonds is equal to or more than the value provided for in item (ii) of that paragraph with respect to such Share Options) shall be effective with respect to the shares that holders of such Share Options receive by exercising such Share Options.

Section 5 Acquisition of Own Share Option by Stock Companies

Subsection 1 Acquisition of Share Option pursuant to Subscription Requirements

(Determination of Day of Acquisition)

Article 273 (1) In cases where there are provision with respect to the matters listed in Article 236(1)(vii)(b) as a feature of Share Options subject to Call (meaning Share Options for which there are provisions with respect to the matters listed in item (vii)(a) of that paragraph. The same shall apply hereinafter in this Chapter.), the Stock Company shall determine the day under the same item (vii)(b) by resolution of a shareholders meeting (or of a board of directors meeting for a Company with Board of Directors); provided, however, that this shall not apply in cases where it is otherwise provided as a feature of such Share Options subject to Call.

(2) If a Stock Company determines the day under Article 236(1)(vii)(b), the Stock Compa-

ny shall notify the holders of Share Options subject to Call (or, in cases where there are provisions with respect to the matters listed in item (vii)(c) of that paragraph, the holders of Share Options subject to Call determined under the provisions of paragraph (1) of the following article) and the Registered Pledgees of Share Options thereof of such date, no later than two weeks prior to such day.
(3) A public notice may be substituted for the notice under the provisions of the preceding paragraph.

(Determination of Share Options to be Acquired)
Article 274 (1) In cases where there are provisions with respect to the matters listed in Article 236(1)(vii)(c), if a Stock Company intends to acquire Share Options subject to Call, it shall determine the Share Options subject to Call that it intends to acquire.
(2) The Share Options subject to Call under the preceding paragraph shall be determined by resolution of a shareholders meeting (or of a board of directors meeting for a Company with Board of Directors); provided, however, that this shall not apply in cases where it is otherwise provided as a feature of such Share Options subject to Call.
(3) If a Stock Company makes the determination pursuant to the provisions of paragraph (1), the Stock Company shall immediately notify the holders of Share Options subject to Call who are determined under the provisions of that paragraph and the Registered Pledgees of Share Options thereof to the effect that the Stock Company will acquire such Share Options subject to Call.
(4) A public notice may be substituted for the notice under the provisions of the preceding paragraph.

(Effectuation)
Article 275 (1) A Stock Company shall acquire, on the day when the grounds under item (vii)(a), paragraph (1) of Article 236 have arisen (or, in cases where there is a provision with respect to the matters listed in item (vii)(c) thereof, the day listed in item (i) or the day listed in item (ii) below, whichever comes later. The same shall apply in the following paragraph and paragraph (3)), Share Options subject to Call (or, in cases where there are provisions with respect to the matters listed in item (vii)(c), paragraph (1) of that article, the Share Options subject to Call determined pursuant to the provisions of paragraph (1) of the preceding article. The same shall apply in the following paragraph and paragraph (3)):
(i) The day when the grounds under Article 236(1)(vii)(a) have arisen; or
(ii) The day of notice under the provisions of paragraph (3) of the preceding article, or the day when two weeks have lapsed from the day of the public notice under paragraph (4) of that article.
(2) In cases where the Share Options subject to Call that a Stock Company acquires under the provisions of the preceding paragraph are attached to Bonds with Share Option, the Stock Company shall acquire the Bonds with respect to such Bonds with Share Option on the day when the grounds under Article 236(1)(vii)(a) have arisen.
(3) In the cases listed in the following items, the holders of Share Options subject to Call (excluding the relevant Stock Company) shall acquire the status provided for in each of such items in accordance with the provisions with respect to the matters provided for in such item, on the day when the grounds under Article 236(1)(vii)(a) have arisen:
(i) In cases where there are provisions on the matters listed in Article 236(1)(vii)(d): Shareholders of shares under the same item (vii)(d);
(ii) In cases where there are provision on the matters listed in Article 236(1)(vii)(e): Bondholders of Bonds under the same item (vii)(e);
(iii) In cases where there are provisions on the matters listed in Article 236(1)(vii)(f):

Holders of "other Share Options" under that item (vii)(f);
(iv) In cases where there are provisions on the matters listed in Article 236(1)(vii)(g): Bondholders of the Bonds with respect to Bonds with Share Option under that item (vii)(g), and holders of Share Options attached to such Bonds with Share Option;
(4) Without delay after the grounds under Article 236(1)(vii)(a) have arisen, a Stock Company shall notify the holders of Share Options subject to Call and Registered Pledgees of Share Options thereof (in cases where there are provisions with respect to the matters listed in the same item (vii)(c) thereof, the holders of Share Options subject to Call determined pursuant to the provisions of paragraph (1) of the preceding article, and Registered Pledgees of Share Options thereof) to the effect that such grounds has occurred; provided, however, that this shall not apply if the Stock Company has given notice under the provisions of Article 273(2) or has given public notice under the provisions of paragraph (3) of the same article.
(5) A public notice may be substituted for the notice under the provisions of the preceding paragraph.

Subsection 2 Cancellation of Share Options

Article 276 (1) A Stock Company may cancel its Own Share Options. In such cases, the Stock Company shall determine the features and number of the Own Share Options it intends to cancel.
(2) For a Company with Board of Directors, the determination under the provisions of the second sentence of the preceding paragraph shall be made by resolution of a board of directors meeting.

Section 6 Allotment of Share Options without Contribution

(Allotment of Share Options without Contribution)
Article 277 A Stock Company may allot the Share Options of such Stock Company to shareholders (or, for a Company with Class Shares, shareholders of a certain class) without requiring them to make additional contribution (hereinafter in this Section referred to as "Allotment of Share Options without Contribution").

(Determination of Matters in relation to Allotment of Share Options without Contribution)
Article 278 (1) Whenever a Stock Company intends to effect the Allotment of Share Options without Contribution, it shall prescribe the following matters:
(i) The features and number of the Share Options the Stock Company will allot to shareholders or the method for calculating such number;
(ii) In cases where the Share Options provided for in the preceding item are attached to Bonds with Share Option, the classes of Bonds with respect to such Bonds with Share Option, and the total of the amounts for each Bond or the method for calculating such amount;
(iii) The day when such Allotment of Share Options without Contribution becomes effective; and
(iv) In cases where the Stock Company is a Company with Class Shares, the classes of shares held by shareholders who are entitled to such Allotment of Share Options without Contribution.
(2) The provisions regarding the matters listed in item (i) and item (ii) of the preceding paragraph shall be that the Share Options under item (i) of that paragraph and the

Bonds under item (ii) of that paragraph will be allotted in proportion to the number of shares (or, for a Company with Class Shares, the shares of the classes under item (iv) of that paragraph) held by shareholders (or, for a Company with Class Shares, Class Shareholders of the classes under item (iv) of that paragraph) other than such Stock Company.
(3) The determination of the matters listed in each item of paragraph (1) shall be made by resolution of a shareholders meeting (or of a board of directors meeting for a Company with Board of Directors); provided, however, that this shall not apply in cases where it is otherwise provided for in the articles of incorporation.

(Effectuation of Allotment of Share Options without Contribution)
Article 279 (1) Shareholders to whom the Share Options under item (i), paragraph (1) of the preceding article have been allotted shall become the holders of the Share Options provided for in item (i) of that paragraph on the day provided for in item (iii) of that paragraph (or, in the case provided for in item (ii) of that paragraph, the holders of the Share Options provided for in item (i) of that paragraph and the Bondholders of the Bonds provided for in item (ii) of that paragraph).
(2) No later than the first day of the period provided for in Article 236(1)(iv) with respect to the Share Options provided for in item (i), paragraph (1) of the preceding article, a Stock Company shall notify shareholders (or, for a Company with Class Shares, Class Shareholders of the classes under item (iv), paragraph (1) of the preceding article) and the Registered Pledgees of Shares thereof, of the features and number of the Share Options (in the cases provided for in item (ii), paragraph (1) of the preceding article, including the classes of Bonds that have been allotted to such shareholders and the total of the amounts for each Bond) that have been allotted to such shareholders.

Section 7 Exercising Share Option

Subsection 1 General Provisions

(Exercising Share Option)
Article 280 (1) Share Options shall be exercised by disclosing the following matters:
(i) The features and number of the Share Options to be exercised; and
(ii) The day on which the Share Options will be exercised.
(2) If it is intended to exercise Share Options with Issued Certificate, the holders of such Share Options with Issued Certificate shall submit the Share Option certificates for such Share Options with Issued Certificate to the Stock Company; provided, however, that this shall not apply if no such Share Option certificates have been issued.
(3) If it is intended to exercise Share Options attached to Bonds with Share Option with Issued Certificate, the holders of such Share Options with Issued Certificate shall submit to the Stock Company the certificates of Bonds with Share Option for Bonds with Share Option to which such Share Options are attached. In such case, such Stock Company shall specify in such certificates of Bonds with Share Option to the effect that those Share Options attached to such Bonds with Share Option with Issued Certificate have been extinguished.
(4) Notwithstanding the provisions of the preceding paragraph, in cases where it is intended to exercise Share Options attached to Bonds with Share Option with Issued Certificate, if the Bonds with respect to such Bonds with Share Option with Issued Certificate are extinguished by the exercise of such Share Options, the holders of such Share Options shall submit the certificates of Bonds with Share Option for the Bonds with Share Option to which such Share Options are attached to the Stock Company.

(5) Notwithstanding the provisions of paragraph (3), in cases where it is intended to exercise the Share Options attached to Bonds with Share Option with Issued Certificate after the redemption of the Bonds with respect to such Bonds with Share Option with Issued Certificate, the holders of such Share Options shall submit the certificates of Bonds with Share Option for the Bonds with Share Option to which such Share Options are attached to the Stock Company.
(6) A Stock Company cannot exercise Own Share Options.

(Payment of Amount to be Paid in on Exercise of Share Option)
Article 281 (1) If monies are the subject of the contribution to be made on the exercise of Share Options, the holders of Share Options shall pay in the entire amount of the value provided for in Article 236(1)(ii) with respect to the Share Options relating to such exercise at the place for the handling of bank etc. payments designated by the Stock Company on the day provided for in item (ii), paragraph (1) of the preceding article.
(2) If any property other than monies is the subject of the contribution to be made on the exercise of Share Options, the holders of Share Options shall deliver the property provided for in Article 236(1)(iii) with respect to the Share Options relating to such exercise on the day provided for in item (ii), paragraph (1) of the preceding article. In such cases, if the value of such property falls short of the value provided for in Article 236(1)(ii), the holders of the Share Options shall pay in monies equivalent to the balance thereof at the place for the handling of payments referred to in the preceding paragraph.
(3) Holders of Share Options may not set off their obligations to effect payment under the provisions of paragraph (1) or delivery under the provisions of the preceding paragraph against claims the Holders of Share Options have against the Stock Company.

(Timing of Shareholder Status)
Article 282 Holders of Share Options who have exercised Share Options shall become shareholders of the shares underlying such Share Options on the day when such Share Options are exercised.

(Treatment of Fraction)
Article 283 In cases where Share Options are exercised, if the number of the shares to be issued to the holders of such Share Options includes a fraction of less than one share, the Stock Company shall, in accordance with the categories of the cases listed in the following items, deliver to the holders of such Share Options monies equivalent to the amount obtained by multiplying the amount provided for in each such item by such fraction; provided, however, that this shall not apply in cases where there are provisions with respect to the matters listed in Article 236(1)(ix):
(i) In cases where such shares are shares with a market price: The amount calculated by the method prescribed by the applicable Ordinance of the Ministry of Justice as the market price of one such share; and
(ii) In cases other than the cases listed in the preceding item: The amount of net assets per share.

Subsection 2 Contribution of Property Other than Monies

Article 284 (1) In cases where Share Options for which there are provisions with respect to the matters listed in Article 236(1)(iii) are exercised, a Stock Company shall petition the court, without delay after a delivery of property under the provisions of Arti-

Art.284　　　Ⅰ Companies Act, PART II, Chap.III, Sec.7

cle 281(2), for the appointment of an inspector, in order to have the inspector investigate the value of the property provided for in that item (hereinafter in this Section referred to as "Properties Contributed in Kind").

(2) In cases where the petition referred to in the preceding paragraph has been filed, the court shall appoint an inspector, except in cases where it dismisses such petition as unlawful.

(3) In cases where the court has appointed the inspector under the preceding paragraph, it may fix the amount of the remuneration that the Stock Company shall pay to such inspector.

(4) The inspector referred to in paragraph (2) shall conduct the necessary investigations, and submit a report, either by recording the outcome of such investigations or by providing the documents or Electromagnetic Records (limited to those prescribed by the applicable Ordinance of the Ministry of Justice) to the court.

(5) If the court finds it necessary to clarify the contents of the report under the preceding paragraph or to confirm the grounds supporting such report, it may request that the inspector under paragraph (2) submit a further report under the preceding paragraph.

(6) If the inspector under paragraph (2) has submitted the report referred to in paragraph (4), he/she shall deliver to the Stock Company a copy of the documents under such paragraph, or provide the matters recorded in the Electromagnetic Records under such paragraph by the methods prescribed by the applicable Ordinance of the Ministry of Justice.

(7) In cases where the court receives a report under paragraph (4), if it finds the value provided for in item (iii), paragraph (1) of Article 236 with respect to the Properties Contributed in Kind (excluding a value not subjected to the investigation by the inspector under paragraph (2)) to be improper, it shall issue a ruling changing such value.

(8) In cases where the value of the Properties Contributed in Kind has been changed, in whole or in part, because of a ruling under the preceding paragraph, the holders of the Share Options referred to in paragraph (1) may rescind their manifestation of intention relating to the exercise of their Share Options, limited to within one week from the finalization of such ruling.

(9) The provisions of the preceding paragraphs shall not apply in the cases in each of the following items with respect to the matters prescribed respectively in those items:

(i) In cases where the total number of the shares to be delivered to the holders of Share Options that have been exercised does not exceed one tenth (1/10) of the total number of Issued Shares: The value of the Properties Contributed in Kind that are tendered by the holders of such Share Options;

(ii) In cases where the total sum of the values provided for under Article 236(1)(iii) with respect to the Properties Contributed in Kind does not exceed 5,000,000 yen: The value of such Properties Contributed in Kind;

(iii) In cases where the value provided for under Article 236(1)(iii) with respect to the Properties Contributed in Kind does not exceed the value calculated by the method prescribed by the applicable Ordinance of the Ministry of Justice as the market price of such securities: The value of the Properties Contributed in Kind with respect to such securities;

(iv) In cases where, the verification of an attorney, a legal professional corporation, a certified public accountant, an auditing firm, a tax accountant or a tax accountant corporation (or in cases where the Properties Contributed in Kind consist of real estate, hereinafter in this item referring to such verification and an appraisal by a real property appraiser) is obtained with respect to the reasonableness of the value provided for under Article 236(1)(iii) with respect to Properties Contributed in

Kind: The value of the Properties Contributed in Kind so verified;
(v) In cases where the Properties Contributed in Kind consist of a money claim (limited to claims that have already fallen due), and the value provided for under Article 236(1)(iii) with respect to such money claim does not exceed the book value of the debt representing such money claim: The value of the Properties Contributed in Kind with respect to such monetary claim

(10) None of the following persons can provide the verification provided in item (iv) of the preceding paragraph:
   (i) A director, an accounting advisor, a company auditor or executive officer, or an employee including a manager;
   (ii) A holder of Share Options;
   (iii) A person who has become subject to a suspension of operations for whom the period of such suspension has not elapsed yet; or
   (iv) A legal profession corporation, an auditing firm or a tax accountant corporation with respect to which more than half of its members are the persons who fall under either item (i) or item (ii) above.

Subsection 3 Liabilities

(Liabilities of Persons who Subscribed for Share Options with Unfair Amount To Be Paid In)

Article 285 (1) In the cases listed in the following items, a holder of Share Options who has exercised Share Options shall be liable to the Stock Company for payment of the amount provided for in such items:
   (i) In the cases provided for in Article 238(1)(ii), if the arrangement that there is no requirement for monies to be paid in for Share Options for Subscription is a condition that is extremely unfair (limited to the cases where the holder of the Share Options subscribed for the Share Options in collusion with directors (or, directors or executive officers for a Company with Committees. The same shall apply in the following item.)): The fair value of such Share Options;
   (ii) In the cases provided for in Article 238(1)(iii), if the holder of the Share Options subscribed for the Share Options at an Amount To Be Paid In that is extremely unfair, in collusion with directors: The amount equivalent to the difference between such Amount To Be Paid In and the fair value of such Share Options;
   (iii) In cases where the value of the Properties Contributed in Kind that the holder of the Share Options tendered when he/she became a shareholder pursuant to the provisions of Article 282 is extremely short of the value provided for under Article 236(1)(iii) with respect to the Properties Contributed in Kind: The amount of such shortfall

(2) In the cases provided for in item (iii) of the preceding paragraph, if the holder of the Share Options who tendered the Properties Contributed in Kind is without knowledge and is not grossly negligent as to the fact that the value of such Properties Contributed in Kind is extremely short of the value provided for under item (iii), paragraph (1) of Article 236 with respect to the Properties Contributed in Kind, the holder of the Share Options may rescind his/her manifestation of intention relating to the exercise of the Share Options.

(Liabilities of Directors in case of Shortfall in Value of Property Contributed)

Article 286 (1) In the cases listed in item (iii), paragraph (1) of the preceding article, the following persons (hereinafter in this article referred to as "Directors, etc.") shall be liable to the Stock Company for payment of the amounts listed in such items:

(i) Executive directors who carried out duties regarding the solicitation of such holders of Share Options (or, for a Company with Committees, executive officers. The same shall apply in this item.) and other persons prescribed by the applicable Ordinance of the Ministry of Justice as persons who were involved, in the performance of their duties, in the execution of the business of such executive directors;
(ii) If a shareholders meeting has passed a resolution regarding the determination of the value of the Properties Contributed in Kind, the persons prescribed by the applicable Ordinance of the Ministry of Justice as the directors who submitted proposals to such shareholders meeting;
(iii) If a board of directors meeting has passed a resolution regarding the determination of the value of Properties Contributed in Kind, the persons prescribed by the applicable Ordinance of the Ministry of Justice as the directors (or, for a Company with Committees, directors or executive officers) who submitted proposals to such board of directors meeting;
(2) Notwithstanding the provisions of the preceding paragraph, the Directors, etc. shall not be liable for Properties Contributed in Kind under that paragraph in the cases listed below:
(i) An investigation has been carried out by an inspector under Article 284(2) with respect to the value of the Properties Contributed in Kind; or
(ii) Such Directors, etc. have proven that they did not fail to exercise care with respect to the performance of their duties.
(3) In the cases provided for in paragraph (1), the person who submitted the verification provided for in Article 284(9)(iv) (hereinafter in this article referred to as "Verifying Person") shall be liable for the payment of the amount provided for in item (iii), paragraph (1) of the preceding article to the Stock Company; provided, however, that this shall not apply in cases where such Verifying Person has proven that he/she did not fail to exercise care with respect to the submission of such verification.
(4) In cases where a holder of Share Options bears an obligation to pay an amount provided for in item (iii), paragraph (1) of the preceding article with respect to Properties Contributed in Kind tendered by the holder of Share Options, if the persons listed as follows bear obligations provided for in such items with respect to such Properties Contributed in Kind, such persons shall be joint and several obligors:
(i) Directors, etc. : The obligations under paragraph (1); and
(ii) Verifying Person: The obligations under the main clause of the preceding paragraph.

Subsection 4 Miscellaneous Provisions

Article 287 In addition to the cases provided for in Article 276(1), if a holder of Share Options can no longer exercise the Share Options held by the same, such Share Options shall be extinguished.

Section 8 Certificates for Share Options

Subsection 1 Share Option Certificates

(Issuing of Share Option Certificates)
Article 288 (1) A Stock Company shall, without delay after the day of issue of Share Options with Issued Certificate, issue Share Option certificates for such Share Options with Issued Certificate.
(2) Notwithstanding the provisions of the preceding paragraph, a Stock Company may

elect to not deliver the Share Option certificates under that paragraph until the holders of Share Options so request.

(Matters to be Stated on Share Option Certificate)
Article 289 A Stock Company shall state the following matters and the serial number on a Share Option certificate and the Representative Director of the Stock Company (or the representative executive officer for a Company with Committees) shall affix his/her signature, or name and seal:
(i) The trade name of the Stock Company; and
(ii) The features and number of Share Options with Issued Certificate relating to such Share Option certificates;

(Conversion between Registered Share Option and Bearer Share Option)
Article 290 Holders of Share Options with Issued Certificate may demand at any time that the Stock Company convert their registered Share Option certificates into bearer Share Option certificates, or convert their bearer Share Option certificates into registered Share Option certificates, except in cases where there is an arrangement that such conversion is not possible under the provisions with respect to the matters listed in Article 236(1)(xi).

(Loss of Share Option Certificates)
Article 291 (1) Share Option certificates may be invalidated pursuant to the public notification procedures under Article 142 of the Non-Contentious Cases Procedures Act.
(2) A person who has lost Share Option certificates may not request the re-issuing of their Share Option certificates until after they obtain the decision for invalidation provided for in Article 148(1) of the Non-Contentious Cases Procedures Act.

Subsection 2 Certificates of Bonds with Share Option

Article 292 (1) The certificates of Bonds with Share Option representing Bonds with Share Option with Issued Certificate shall state the features and number of the Share Options attached to such Bonds with Share Option with Issued Certificate, in addition to the matters to be stated under the provisions of Article 697(1).
(2) In cases where it is intended to redeem Bonds with respect to Bonds with Share Option with Issued Certificate, if the Share Options attached to such Bonds with Share Option with Issued Certificate have not been extinguished, the Stock Company may not demand the redemption of the Bonds in exchange for the certificates of Bonds with Share Option representing such Bonds with Share Option with Issued Certificate. In such cases, the Stock Company may, in exchange for the redemption of the Bonds, seek the presentation of such certificates of Bonds with Share Option and may enter a statement on such certificates of Bonds with Share Option to the effect that the Bonds have been redeemed.

Subsection 3 Submission of Share Option Certificate

(Public Notice in relation to Submission of Share Option Certificate)
Article 293 (1) In cases where a Stock Company carries out an act listed in the following items, if it has issued Share Option certificates representing the Share Options provided for in such items (if such Share Options are attached to Bonds with Share Option, hereinafter in this Subsection referring to the certificates of Bonds with Share Option representing such Bonds with Share Option), such Stock Company shall, more than

Art.294　　1 Companies Act, PART II, Chap.III, Sec.8

one month prior to the day when such act takes effect, give public notice to the effect that such Share Option certificates shall be submitted to such Stock Company before such day, and a separate notice to such effect to each holder of such Share Options and each registered pledgee of such Share Options:

(i) Acquisitions of Share Options subject to Call: Such Share Options subject to Call;
(ii) Organizational Changes: All Share Options;
(iii) Mergers (limited to cases where such Stock Company is to be extinguished as a result of the merger): All Share Options;
(iv) Absorption-type Company Split: Share Options under Absorption-type split agreement provided for in Article 758(v)(a);
(v) Incorporation-type Company Split: Share Options under Incorporation-type company split plan provided for in Article 763(x)(a);
(vi) Share Exchange: Share Options under Share Exchange agreement provided for in Article 768(1)(iv)(a); or
(vii) Share Transfer: Share Options under Share Transfer plan provided for in Article 773(1)(ix)(a);

(2) If a person fails to submit Share Option certificates to a Stock Company no later than the day on which the act listed in each item of the preceding paragraph takes effect, the Stock Company may, until such Share Option certificates are submitted, refuse to deliver the Monies, etc. to which the holders of the Share Options representing such Share Option certificates are entitled as a result of such act.

(3) The Share Option certificates representing the Share Options provided for in each item of paragraph (1) shall become invalid on the day when the act listed in each such item takes effect.

(4) The provisions of Article 220 shall apply mutatis mutandis if, in cases where an act listed in any item of paragraph (1) is carried out, a person cannot submit the Share Option certificates.

(Cases Where Bearer Share Option Certificates are not Submitted)
Article 294 (1) Notwithstanding the provisions of Article 132, in cases where the act listed in item (i), paragraph (1) of the preceding article is carried out (limited to cases where, in exchange for the acquisition of Share Options by a Stock Company, shares in such Stock Company are delivered to the holders of such Share Options), if Share Option certificates (hereinafter in this article limited to those in bearer form) are not submitted pursuant to the provisions of that paragraph, the Stock Company is not required to state or record in the shareholder registry the matters listed in Article 121(i) relating to shares that persons who hold such Share Option certificates are entitled to have delivered.

(2) In the cases provided for in the preceding paragraph, a Stock Company is not required to send notices or demands to shareholders of shares that persons who hold Share Option certificates that shall be submitted pursuant to the provisions of paragraph (1) of the preceding article are entitled to have delivered.

(3) Notwithstanding the provisions of Article 249 and Article 259(1), in cases where the act listed in item (i), paragraph (1) of the preceding article is carried out (limited to cases where, in exchange for the acquisition of Share Options by a Stock Company, other Share Options of such Stock Company (excluding those attached to Bonds with Share Option) are delivered to the holders of such Share Options), if no Share Option certificates are submitted pursuant to the provisions of that paragraph, the Stock Company is not required to state or record in the Share Option registry the matters listed in Article 249(iii)(a) relating to such other Share Options (excluding Bearer Share Options) that persons who hold such Share Option certificates are entitled to have deliv-

ered.
(4) In the cases provided for in the preceding paragraph, a Stock Company is not required to send notices or demands to holders of Share Options that persons who hold Share Option certificates that shall be submitted pursuant to the provisions of paragraph (1) of the preceding article are entitled to have delivered.
(5) Notwithstanding the provisions of Article 249 and Article 259(1), in cases where the act listed in item (i), paragraph (1) of the preceding article is carried out (limited to cases where, in exchange for the acquisition of Share Options by a Stock Company, Bonds with Share Option of such Stock Company are delivered to the holders of such Share Options), if no Share Option certificates are submitted pursuant to the provisions of that paragraph, the Stock Company is not required to state or record in the Share Option registry the matters listed in Article 249(iii)(a) relating to Share Options attached to the Bonds with Share Option (excluding Bearer Bonds with Share Option) that persons who hold such Share Option certificates are entitled to have delivered.
(6) In the cases provided for in the preceding paragraph, a Stock Company is not required to send notices or demands to holders of Share Options attached to the Bonds with Share Option that persons who hold Share Option certificates that shall be submitted pursuant to the provisions of paragraph (1) of the preceding article are entitled to have delivered.

Chapter IV Organ

Section 1 Shareholders Meeting and Class Meeting

Subsection 1 Shareholders Meeting

(Authority of Shareholders Meeting)
Article 295 (1) Shareholders' meetings may resolve the matters provided for in this Act, the organization, operations and administration of the Stock Company, and any and all other matters regarding the Stock Company.
(2) Notwithstanding the provisions of the preceding paragraph, for a Company with Board of Directors, a shareholders meeting may resolve only the matters provided for in this Act and the matters provided for in the articles of incorporation.
(3) Provisions of the articles of incorporation which provide to the effect that any organization other than the shareholders meeting, such as directors, executive officers and board of directors, may determine any matter which, pursuant to the provisions of this Act, requires the resolution of the shareholders meeting shall not be effective.

(Calling of Shareholders Meeting)
Article 296 (1) Annual shareholders meeting shall be called within a defined period of time after the end of each business year.
(2) A shareholders meeting may be called whenever necessary.
(3) A shareholders meeting shall be called by directors, except in cases where it is called pursuant to the provisions of paragraph (4) of the following Article.

(Demand for Calling of Meeting by Shareholders)
Article 297 (1) Shareholders having consecutively for the preceding six months or more (or, in cases where shorter period is prescribed in the articles of incorporation, such period or more) not less than three hundredths (3/100) (or, in cases where lesser proportion is prescribed in the articles of incorporation, such proportion) of the votes of all shareholders may demand the directors, by showing the matters which shall be the

Art.298   Ⅰ Companies Act, PART II, Chap.IV, Sec.1

purpose of the shareholders meeting (limited to the matters on which such shareholders may exercise their votes) and the reason of the calling, that they call the shareholders meeting.
(2) For the purpose of the application of the preceding paragraph to a Stock Company which is not a Public Company, "having consecutively for the preceding six months or more (or, in cases where shorter period is prescribed in the articles of incorporation, such period or more)" in that paragraph shall be read as "having."
(3) The number of the votes of the shareholders who may not exercise their votes on the matters that are the purpose of the shareholders meeting referred to in paragraph (1) shall not be included in the number of the votes of all shareholders under that paragraph.
(4) In the following cases, the shareholders who made the demand pursuant to the provisions of paragraph (1) may call the shareholders meeting with the permission of the court.
　(i) In cases where the calling procedure is not effected without delay after the demand pursuant to the provisions of paragraph (1); or
　(ii) In cases where a notice for the calling of the shareholders meeting which designates, as the day of the shareholders meeting, a day falling within the period of eight weeks (or, in cases where any period less than that is provided for in the articles of incorporation, such period) from the day of the demand pursuant to the provisions of paragraph (1) is not dispatched.

(Determination to Call Shareholders Meeting)
Article 298 (1) Directors (in cases where shareholders call a shareholders meeting pursuant to the provisions of paragraph (4) of the preceding Article, such shareholders. The same shall apply in the main clause of the next paragraph and in the following Article to Article 302 inclusive) shall decide the following matters in cases where they call a shareholders meeting:
(i) The date, time and place of the shareholders meeting;
(ii) If there is any matter which is the purpose of the shareholders meeting, such matter;
(iii) That shareholders who do not attend the shareholders meeting may exercise their votes in writing, if so arranged;
(iv) That shareholders may exercise their votes by an Electromagnetic Method, if so arranged;
(v) In addition to the matters listed in the preceding items, any matters prescribed by the applicable Ordinance of the Ministry of Justice.
(2) In cases where the number of the shareholders (excluding shareholders who may not exercise their votes on all matters which may be resolved at a shareholders meetings. The same shall apply in the next Article to Article 302 inclusive) is one thousand or more, the directors shall decide the matters listed in item (iii) of the preceding paragraph; provided, however, that this shall not apply to the cases where such Stock Company is a Stock Company which issues the shares provided for in Article 2(16) of the Financial Instruments and Exchange Act and is an entity prescribed by the applicable Ordinance of the Ministry of Justice.
(3) For the purpose of the application of the provisions of the preceding paragraph to a Company with Board of Directors, "matters which may be resolved at the shareholders meetings" in that that paragraph shall be read as "matters listed in paragraph (2) of the preceding paragraph."
(4) At a Company with Board of Directors, the decision of the maters listed in each item of paragraph (1) shall be made by the resolution of the board of directors, except for

the cases where the shareholders call the Company pursuant to the provisions of paragraph (4) of the preceding Article.

(Notice of Calling of Shareholders' meetings)
Article 299 (1) In order to call the shareholders meeting, the directors shall dispatch the notice thereof to the shareholders no later than two weeks (or one week if the Stock Company is not a Public Company, except in cases where the matters listed in item (iii) or (iv) of paragraph (1) of the preceding Article are decided, (or if a shorter period of time is provided for in the articles of incorporation in cases where the Stock Company is a Stock Company other than the Company with Board of Directors, such shorter period of time)) prior to the day of the shareholders meeting.
(2) The notice referred to in the preceding paragraph shall be in writing in the following cases:
  (i) Where the matters listed in item (iii) or (iv) of paragraph (1) of the preceding Article are decided; or
  (ii) Where the Stock Company is a Company with Board of Directors.
(3) In lieu of the dispatch of the written notice referred to in the preceding paragraph, the directors may dispatch the notice by an Electromagnetic Method, with the consent of the shareholders, in accordance with the provisions of the applicable Cabinet Order. In such cases, such directors shall be deemed to have dispatched the written notice under such paragraph.
(4) The notice under the preceding two paragraphs shall specify or record the matters listed in each item of paragraph (1) of the preceding article.

(Omission of Calling Procedures)
Article 300 Notwithstanding the provisions of the preceding Article, the shareholders meeting may be held without the procedures of calling if the consent of all shareholders is obtained; provided, however, that this shall not apply in cases where the matters listed in item (iii) or item (iv) of Article 298(1) are decided.

(Giving of Reference Documents for Shareholders Meeting and Voting Forms)
Article 301 (1) In cases where the matters listed in item (iii) of Article 298(1) are decided, the directors shall, when dispatching a notice under Article 299(1), give the shareholder the document stating matters of reference for the exercise of votes (hereinafter in this Subsection referred to as "Reference Document for Shareholders Meeting") and the document to be used by the shareholder to exercise the votes (hereinafter in this Subsection referred to as "Voting Form") pursuant to the provisions of the applicable Ordinance of the Ministry of Justice.
(2) If the directors dispatch notices by an Electromagnetic Method referred to in Article 299(3) to the shareholders who have given consent under the same paragraph, the directors may provide, in lieu of the giving of the Reference Documents for Shareholders Meeting and Voting Forms pursuant to the provisions of the preceding paragraph, the matters to be specified in such document by an Electromagnetic Method; provided, however, that, if requested by any shareholder, they shall give these documents to such shareholder.

Article 302 (1) In cases where the matters listed in item (iv) of Article 298(1) are decided, the directors shall, when dispatching a notice under Article 299(1), give the shareholders the Reference Documents for Shareholders Meeting pursuant to the provisions of the applicable Ordinance of the Ministry of Justice.
(2) If the directors dispatch the notice by an Electromagnetic Method referred to in Arti-

Art.303〜304　　Ⅰ Companies Act, PART II, Chap.IV, Sec.1

cle 299(3) to the shareholders who have given consent under the same paragraph, the directors may provide, in lieu of the giving of the Reference Documents for Shareholders Meeting pursuant to the provisions of the preceding paragraph, the matters to be specified in such documents by an Electromagnetic Method; provided, however, that, if requested by any shareholder, the directors shall give the Reference Documents for Shareholders Meeting to such shareholder.
(3) In the case provided for in paragraph (1), when sending notice to the shareholders who have given consent under Article 299(3) by an Electromagnetic Method referred to in the same paragraph, the directors shall provide to the shareholders the matters to be specified in the Voting Forms by such Electromagnetic Method pursuant to the provisions of the applicable Ordinance of the Ministry of Justice.
(4) In the case provided for in paragraph (1), if any shareholder who has not given consent under Article 299(3) requests, no later than one week prior to the day of the shareholders meeting, for the provision of the matters to be specified in the Voting Form by an Electromagnetic Method, the directors shall provide such matters to such shareholder by an Electromagnetic Method pursuant to the provisions of the applicable Ordinance of the Ministry of Justice.

(Shareholders' Right to Propose)
Article 303 (1) Shareholders may demand that the directors include certain matters (limited to the matters on which such shareholders may exercise their votes. The same shall apply in the following paragraph) in the purpose of the shareholders meeting.
(2) Notwithstanding the provisions of the preceding paragraph, at a Company with Board of Directors, only shareholders having consecutively for the preceding six months or more (or, in cases where shorter period is prescribed in the articles of incorporation, such period or more) not less than one hundredth (1/100) (or, in cases where lesser proportion is prescribed in the articles of incorporation, such proportion) of the votes of all shareholders or not less than three hundred (or, in cases where lesser number is prescribed in the articles of incorporation, such number of) votes of all shareholders may demand the directors that the directors include certain matters in the purpose of the shareholders meeting. In such cases, that demand shall be submitted no later than eight weeks (or, in cases where shorter period is prescribed in the articles of incorporation, such period or more) prior to the day of the shareholders meeting.
(3) For the purpose of the application of the preceding paragraph to a Company with Board of Directors which is not a Public Company, "having consecutively for the preceding six months or more (or, in cases where shorter period is prescribed in the articles of incorporation, such period or more)" in that paragraph shall be read as "having."
(4) The number of the votes to which the shareholders who may not exercise their votes on the certain matters referred to in paragraph (2) are entitled shall not be included in the number of the votes of all shareholders under that paragraph.

Article 304 Shareholders may submit proposals at the shareholders meeting with respect to the matters that are the purpose of the shareholders meeting (limited to the matters on which such shareholders may exercise their votes. The same shall apply in paragraph (1) of the following article); provided, however, that this shall not apply in cases where such proposals are in violation of the laws or the articles of incorporation, or in cases where three years have not elapsed from the day on which, with respect to the proposal which is essentially identical to such proposal, affirmative votes not less than one tenths (1/10) (or, in cases where any proportion less than that is provided for in the articles of incorporation, such proportion) of the votes of all shareholders (excluding the shareholders who may not exercise their voting rights on such proposal) were not obtained.

Article 305 (1) Shareholders may demand the directors that, no later than eight weeks (or, in cases where any period less than that is provided for in the articles of incorporation, such period) prior to the day of the shareholders meeting, shareholders be notified of the summary of the proposals which such demanding shareholders intend to submit with respect to the matters that are the purpose of the shareholders meeting (or, in cases where a notice pursuant to paragraph (2) or paragraph (3) of Article 299 is to be given, such summary be specified or recorded in that notice); provided, however, that, for a Company with Board of Directors, only shareholders having consecutively for the preceding six months or more (or, in cases where shorter period is prescribed in the articles of incorporation, such period or more) not less than one hundredth (1/100) (or, in cases where lesser proportion is prescribed in the articles of incorporation, such proportion) of the votes of all shareholders or not less than three hundred (or, in cases where lesser number is prescribed in the articles of incorporation, such number of) votes of all shareholders may make such demand.
(2) For the purpose of the application of the proviso to the preceding paragraph to a Company with Board of Directors which is not a Public Company, "having consecutively for the preceding six months or more (or, in cases where shorter period is prescribed in the articles of incorporation, such period or more)" in that paragraph shall be read as "having."
(3) The number of the votes to which the shareholders who may not exercise their votes on the matters that are the purpose of the shareholders meeting referred to in paragraph (1) are entitled shall not be included in the number of the votes of all shareholders under the proviso to that paragraph.
(4) The provisions of the preceding three paragraphs shall not apply in cases where the proposals under paragraph (1) are in violation of the laws or the articles of incorporation, or in cases where three years have not elapsed from the day on which, with respect to the proposal which is essentially identical to such proposal, affirmative votes not less than one tenths (1/10) (or, in cases where any proportion less than that is provided for in the articles of incorporation, such proportion) of the votes of all shareholders (excluding the shareholders who may not exercise their voting rights on such proposal) were not obtained.

(Election of Inspector on Calling Procedures of Shareholders Meeting)
Article 306 (1) A Stock Company or shareholders who hold not less than one hundredth (1/100) (or, in cases where any proportion less than that is provided for in the articles of incorporation, such proportion) of the votes of all shareholders (excluding the shareholders who may not exercise their votes on all matters which may be resolved at the shareholders meeting) may file a petition with the court, before a shareholders meeting, for the election of an inspector who shall be retained to investigate the calling procedures and method of resolution relating to such shareholders meeting.
(2) For the purpose of the provisions of the preceding paragraph to a Company with Board of Directors which is a Public Company, in that paragraph, "matters which may be resolved at the shareholders meeting" shall be read as "matters listed in item (ii) of Article 298(1)" and "hold" shall be read as "have held, for the consecutive period of six months or more (or, in cases where any period less than that is provided for in the articles of incorporation, such period)"; and for the purpose of the provisions of the preceding paragraph to a Company with Board of Directors which is not a Public Company, "matters which may be resolved at the shareholders meeting" in that paragraph

shall be read as "matters listed in item (ii) of Article 298(1)."
(3) In cases where the petition for the election of an inspector pursuant to the provisions of the preceding two paragraphs has been filed, the court shall elect the inspector except in case it dismisses such petition as non-conforming.
(4) In cases where the court has elected the inspector set forth in the preceding paragraph, it may fix the amount of the compensation which the Stock Company shall pay to such inspector.
(5) The inspector set forth in paragraph (3) shall conduct necessary investigation and shall report the court by submitting the document or Electromagnetic Records (limited to those prescribed by the applicable Ordinance of the Ministry of Justice) which specifies or records the result of such investigation.
(6) If the court finds it necessary to for the purpose of clarification of the contents of the report set forth in the preceding paragraph or of confirmation of the grounds supporting such report, it may request the inspector set forth in paragraph (3) a further report set forth in the preceding paragraph.
(7) When the inspector set forth in paragraph (3) reports pursuant to paragraph (5), he/she shall give the Stock Company (in cases where the person who filed a petition for the election of an inspector was not such Stock Company, such Stock Company and that person) a copy of the document set forth in that paragraph, or provide the matters recorded in the Electromagnetic Records set forth in that paragraph by the method prescribed by the applicable Ordinance of the Ministry of Justice.

(Determination by the Court of the Calling of Shareholders Meeting)
Article 307 (1) In cases where the report under paragraph (5) of the preceding Article is submitted, if the court finds it necessary, it shall order the directors to take some or all of the measures listed below:
(i) To call a shareholders meeting within a defined period of time; and
(ii) To notify the shareholders of the result of the investigation under paragraph (5) of the preceding Article.
(2) In cases where the court orders the measures listed in item (i), paragraph (1) of the preceding Article, the directors shall disclose the content of the report under paragraph (5) of the preceding Article at the shareholders meeting under that paragraph.
(3) In the cases provided for in the preceding paragraph, the directors (or the directors and company auditors for a Company with Auditors) shall investigate the content of the report under paragraph (5) of the preceding Article and report the result thereof to the shareholders meeting under item (i) of paragraph (1).

(Number of Votes)
Article 308 (1) Shareholders (excluding the shareholder prescribed by the applicable Ordinance of the Ministry of Justice as the entity in a relationship that may allow the Stock Company to have substantial control of such entity through the holding of one quarter or more of the votes of all shareholders of such entity or other reasons) shall be entitled to one vote for each one share they hold at the shareholders meeting; provided, however, that, in cases where a Share Unit is provided for in the articles of incorporation, they shall be entitled to one vote for each one unit of the shares.
(2) Notwithstanding the provisions of the preceding paragraph, a Stock Company shall not have any votes with respect to its Treasury Shares.

(Resolution of Shareholders Meetings)
Article 309 (1) Unless otherwise provided for in the articles of incorporation, the resolution of a shareholders meeting shall be made by a majority of the votes of the share-

holders present at the meeting where the shareholders holding a majority of the votes of the shareholders who are entitled to exercise their votes are present.
(2) Notwithstanding the provisions of the preceding paragraph, the resolutions of the following shareholders meetings shall be made by a majority of two thirds (in cases where a higher proportion is provided for in the articles of incorporation, such proportion) or more of the votes of the shareholders present at the meeting where the shareholders holding a majority (in cases where a proportion of one third or more is provided for in the articles of incorporation, such proportion or more) of the votes of the shareholders entitled to exercise their votes at such shareholders meeting are present. In such cases, it is not precluded from providing in the articles of incorporation, in addition to such requirements for resolution, additional requirements including those providing to the effect that the approval of a certain number or more of the shareholders are required:
(i) Shareholders meeting under Article 140(2) and (5);
(ii) Shareholders meeting under Article 156(1) (limited to the case where the specific shareholders under Article 160(1) are to be identified);
(iii) Shareholders meeting under Article 171(1) and Article 175(1);
(iv) Shareholders meeting under Article 180(2);
(v) Shareholders meeting under Article 199(2), Article 200(1), item (iv) of Article 202(3) and Article 204(2);
(vi) Shareholders meeting under Article 238(2), Article 239(1), item (iv) of Article 241(3) and Article 243(2);
(vii) Shareholders meeting under Article 339(1) (limited to the case where directors elected pursuant to the provisions of item (iii) through (v) of Article 342 are to be dismissed or company auditors are to be dismissed);
(viii) Shareholders meeting under Article 425(1);
(ix) Shareholders meeting under Article 447(1) (excluding the cases which fall under both of the following conditions):
(a) That the matters listed in each item of Article 447(1) shall be determined at the annual shareholders meeting; and
(b) That the amount referred to in item (i) of Article 447(1) shall not exceed the amount which is calculated in a manner prescribed by the applicable Ordinance of the Ministry of Justice as the amount of deficit at the day of the annual shareholders meeting referred to in Sub-item (a) (or, in the case provided for in the first sentence of Article 439, the day when the approval under Article 436(3) is effected).
(x) Shareholders' meeting under Article 454(4) (limited to the cases where it is to be arranged that the Dividend Property shall consist of any property other than cash, and that no Right to Demand Distribution of Monies provided for in item (i) of that paragraph shall be granted to the shareholders);
(xi) Shareholders' meeting in cases where the resolution by such shareholders meeting is required pursuant to the provisions of Chapter VI through Chapter VIII;
(xii) Shareholders' meeting in cases where no resolution by such shareholders meeting is required pursuant to the provisions of Part V.
(3) Notwithstanding the provisions of the preceding two paragraphs, the resolutions of the following shareholders meetings (excluding the shareholders meetings of a Company with Class Shares) shall be made by at least half (in cases where a higher proportion is provided for in the articles of incorporation, such proportion or more) of the shareholders entitled to exercise their votes at such shareholders meeting, being a majority of two thirds (in cases where a higher proportion is provided for in the articles of incorporation, such proportion) or more of the votes of such shareholders:

Art.310   ① Companies Act, PART II, Chap.IV, Sec.1

  (i) Shareholders' meetings where the articles of incorporation are amended creating a provision to the effect that, as the features of all shares issued by a Stock Company, the approval of such Stock Company is required for the acquisition of such shares by transfer;
  (ii) Shareholders' meetings under Article 783(1) (limited to such shareholders meeting where the Stock Company which will be absorbed by merger or Stock Company which effects Share Exchange is a Public Company, and some or all of the Cash Etc. to be delivered to the shareholders of such Stock Company consist of Shares with Restriction on Transfer, Etc. (meaning the Shares with Restriction on Transfer, Etc. provided for in paragraph (3) of that paragraph. The same shall apply hereinafter in the following item.)); or
  (iii) Shareholders' meetings under Article 804(1) (limited to such shareholders meeting where the Stock Company which effects merger or Share Transfer is a Public Company, and some or all of the Monies, Etc. to be distributed to the shareholders of such Stock Company consist of Shares with Restriction on Transfer, Etc.).
(4) Notwithstanding the provisions of the preceding three paragraphs, resolutions of the shareholders meetings which effect any amendment in the articles of incorporation (excluding those which repeal such provisions of the articles of incorporation) with respect to the amendment in the articles of incorporation pursuant to the provisions of Article 109(2) shall be made by the majority (in cases where a higher proportion is provided for in the articles of incorporation, such proportion or more) of all shareholders, being a majority equating three quarters (in cases where a higher proportion is provided for in the articles of incorporation, such proportion) or more of the votes of all shareholders.
(5) At a Company with Board of Directors, the shareholders meeting may not resolve matters other than the matters listed in item (ii) of Article 298(1); provided, however, that this shall not apply to the election of the persons provided for in paragraph (1) or paragraph (2) of Article 316, nor to requests for the presence of an accounting auditor under Article 398(2).

(Proxy Voting)
Article 310 (1) Shareholders may exercise their votes by proxy. In such cases, such shareholders or proxies shall submit to the Stock Company a document evidencing the authority of proxy.
(2) The grant of the authority of proxy under the preceding paragraph shall be made for each shareholders meeting.
(3) Shareholders or proxies referred to in paragraph (1) may, in lieu of the submission of the document evidencing the authority of proxy, provide the matters to be stated in such document by an Electromagnetic Method with the approval of the Stock Company in accordance with the provisions of the applicable Cabinet Order. In such cases, such shareholders or proxies shall be deemed to have submitted such document.
(4) In cases where the shareholders are the persons who gave consent under Article 299(3), the Stock Company may not refuse to grant the approval under the preceding paragraph without justifiable reasons.
(5) The Stock Company may restrict the number of proxies who may attend the shareholders meeting.
(6) The Stock Company shall keep the documents evidencing the authority of proxy and the Electromagnetic Records which records the matters provided by the Electromagnetic Method under paragraph (3) at its head office for the period of three months from the day of the shareholders meeting.
(7) The shareholders (excluding the shareholders who may not exercise their votes on all

matters which may be resolved at the shareholders meeting under the preceding paragraph. The same shall apply hereinafter in paragraph (4) of the following Article and in Article 312(5)) may submit the following request at any time during the business hours of the Stock Company:
(i) Request for the inspection or copying of the documents evidencing the authority of proxy; and
(ii) Request for inspection or copying of anything that displays the data recorded in the Electromagnetic Records under the preceding paragraph in a manner prescribed the applicable Ordinance of the Ministry of Justice.

(Voting in Writing)
Article 311 (1) If the votes are exercised in writing, it shall be exercised by entering the Voting Form with necessary matters and submitting it to the Stock Company no later than the time prescribed by the applicable Ordinance of the Ministry of Justice.
(2) The number of the votes exercised in writing pursuant to the provisions of the preceding paragraph shall be included in the number of the votes of the shareholders who are present at the meeting.
(3) The Stock Company shall keep the Voting Forms submitted pursuant to the provisions of paragraph (1) at its head office for the period of three months from the day of the shareholders meeting.
(4) The shareholders may make requests for the inspection or copying of the Voting Forms submitted pursuant to the provisions of paragraph (1) at any time during the business hours of the Stock Company.

(Voting by Electromagnetic Method)
Article 312 (1) If the votes are exercised by an Electromagnetic Method, it shall be exercised by providing the matters to be entered on the Voting Form to the Stock Company by an Electromagnetic Method, with the approval of such Stock Company, no later than the time prescribed by the applicable Ordinance of the Ministry of Justice in accordance with the provisions of the applicable Cabinet Order.
(2) In cases where the shareholders are the persons who have given consent under Article 299(3), the Stock Company may not refuse to give the approval under the preceding paragraph without justifiable reasons.
(3) The number of the votes exercised by an Electromagnetic Method pursuant to the provisions of paragraph (1) shall be included in the number of the votes of the shareholders who are present at the meeting.
(4) The Stock Company shall keep the Electromagnetic Records which record the matters provided pursuant to the provisions of paragraph (1) at its office for the period of three months from the day of the shareholders meeting.
(5) The shareholders may, at any time during the business hours of the Stock Company, make requests for the inspection or copying of anything that displays the data recorded in the Electromagnetic Records under the preceding paragraph in a manner prescribed by the applicable Ordinance of the Ministry of Justice.

(Diverse Exercise of Votes)
Article 313 (1) Shareholders may diversely exercise the votes they hold.
(2) For a Company with Board of Directors, the shareholders under the preceding paragraph shall notify the Stock Company that they will diversely exercise their votes and of the reason thereof no later than three days prior to the day of the shareholders meeting.
(3) If the shareholders referred to in the paragraph (1) are not persons who hold the

shares on behalf of others, the Stock Company may refuse the diverse exercise of the votes held by such shareholders pursuant to the provisions of that paragraph.

(Accountability of Directors, etc.)
Article 314 In cases where a director, an accounting advisor, a company auditor or an executive officer is requested by the shareholders to provide explanations on certain matters at the shareholders meeting, they shall provide necessary explanations with respect to such matters; provided, however, that this shall not apply in cases where such matters are not relevant to the matters that are the purpose of the shareholders meeting, or in cases where such explanations are to the serious detriment of the common interest of the shareholders, or in other cases prescribed by the applicable Ordinance of the Ministry of Justice as the cases where there are justifiable grounds.

(Authority of Chairperson)
Article 315 (1) The chairperson of the shareholders meeting shall maintain the order of such shareholders meeting and organize the business of the meeting.
(2) The chairperson of the shareholders meeting may require any one who does not comply with his/her order or who otherwise disturbs the order of such shareholders meeting to leave the room.

(Investigation of Materials Submitted to the Shareholders Meeting)
Article 316 (1) The shareholders meeting may, by its resolution, elect a person to investigate the materials submitted or provided to such shareholders meeting by the directors, accounting advisors, company auditors, board of company auditors and accounting auditors.
(2) The shareholders meeting which is called pursuant to the provisions of Article 297 may, by its resolution, elect a person who will be charged to investigate the status of the operations and property of the Stock Company.

(Resolution for Postponement or Adjournment)
Article 317 In cases where there is a resolution for the postponement or adjournment of the shareholders meeting, the provisions of Article 298 and Article 299 shall not apply.

(Minutes)
Article 318 (1) Minutes shall be prepared with respect to the business of the shareholders meetings pursuant to the provisions of the applicable Ordinance of the Ministry of Justice.
(2) The Stock Company shall keep the minutes referred to in the preceding paragraph at its head office for the period of ten years from the day of the shareholders meeting.
(3) The Stock Company shall keep copies of the minutes referred to in paragraph (1) at its branch offices for the period of five years from the day of the shareholders meeting; provided, however, that this shall not apply to the cases where such minutes are prepared by Electromagnetic Records and the Stock Company adopts the measures prescribed by the applicable Ordinance of the Ministry of Justice as measures enabling its branch offices to respond to the request listed in item (ii) of the following paragraph.
(4) The shareholders and creditors may submit the following requests at any time during the business hours of the Stock Company:
　(i) If the minutes under paragraph (1) are prepared in writing, requests for inspection or copying of such documents or copies of such documents; and
　(ii) If the minutes under paragraph (1) are prepared by Electromagnetic Records, requests for inspection or copying of anything that displays the data recorded in such

Electromagnetic Records in a manner prescribed by the applicable Ordinance of the Ministry of Justice.
(5) If it is necessary for the purpose of exercising the rights of a Member of the Parent Company of a Stock Company, he/she may, with the permission of the court, make the requests listed in each item of the preceding paragraph with respect to the minutes referred to in paragraph (1).

(Omission of Resolution of Shareholders Meetings)
Article 319 (1) In cases where directors or shareholders submit a proposal with respect to a matter which is the purpose of the shareholders meeting, if all shareholders (limited to those who may exercise their votes with respect to such matter) manifest their intention to agree to such proposal in writing or by means of Electromagnetic Records, it shall be deemed that the resolution to approve such proposal at the shareholders meeting has been made.
(2) The Stock Company shall keep the documents or Electromagnetic Records under the provisions of the preceding paragraph at its head office for a period of ten years from the day when the resolution of the shareholders meeting is deemed to have been made pursuant to the provisions of the preceding paragraph.
(3) The shareholders may submit the following requests at any time during the business hours of the Stock Company:
 (i) Request for inspection or copying of the documents under the preceding paragraph; and
 (ii) Request for inspection or copying of anything that displays the data recorded in the Electromagnetic Records under the preceding paragraph in a manner prescribed by the applicable Ordinance of the Ministry of Justice.
(4) If it is necessary for the purpose of exercising the rights of a Member of the Parent Company of such Stock Company, he/she may, with the permission of the court, make the requests listed in each item of the preceding paragraph with respect to the documents or Electromagnetic Records under paragraph (2).
(5) In cases where it is deemed that the resolutions to approve proposals on all matters that are the purpose of the annual shareholders meeting have been made at the shareholders meeting pursuant to the provisions of paragraph (1), such annual shareholders meeting shall be deemed concluded at that time.

(Omission of Reports to Shareholders Meetings)
Article 320 In cases where the directors notify all shareholders of any matter that is to be reported to the shareholders meeting, if all shareholders manifest in writing or by means of Electromagnetic Records their intention to agree that it is not necessary to report such matter to the shareholders meeting, it shall be deemed that such matter has been reported to the shareholders meeting.

Subsection 2 Class Meeting

(Authority of Class Meeting)
Article 321 Class Meeting may resolve only the matters provided for in this Act and the matters provided for in the articles of incorporation.

(Class Meeting where Detriment to Class Shareholders of Certain Class Likely)
Article 322 (1) In cases where a Company with Class Shares carries out an act listed in the following items, if it is likely to cause detriment to the Class Shareholders of any

class of shares, such act shall not become effective unless a resolution is made at a Class Meeting constituted by the Class Shareholders of the shares of such class (in cases where there are two or more classes of shares relating to such Class Shareholders, referring to the respective Class Meetings constituted by the Class Shareholders categorized by the class of such two or more classes of shares. The same shall apply hereinafter in this Article); provided, however, that this shall not apply to the case where there exists no Class Shareholder who may exercise his/her votes at such Class Meeting:
(i) Amendment of the articles of incorporation with respect to the following matters (excluding those provided for in paragraph (1) or paragraph (2) of Article 111);
   (a) Creation of a new class of the shares;
   (b) Change in the features of the shares;
   (c) Increase of the Total Number of Authorized Shares, or Total Number of Authorized Shares in a Class.
(ii) Consolidation of shares or share split;
(iii) Allotment of share without contribution provided for in Article 185;
(iv) Solicitation of persons who subscribe for the shares of such Stock Company (limited to that which prescribes the matters listed in each item of Article 202(1));
(v) Solicitation of persons who subscribe for the Share Options of such Stock Company (limited to that which prescribes the matters listed in each item of Article 241(1));
(vi) Allotment of Share Option without contribution provided for in Article 277;
(vii) Merger;
(viii) Absorption-type Company Split;
(ix) Succession by Absorption-type Company Split to some or all of the rights and obligations held by another Company with respect to such Company's business;
(x) Incorporation-type Company Split;
(xi) Share Exchange;
(xii) Acquisition of all Issued Shares of another Stock Company by Share Exchange; or
(xiii) Share Transfer.
(2) A Company with Class Shares may provide in the articles of incorporation that, as a feature of a certain class of shares, a resolution of the Class Meeting pursuant to the provisions of the preceding paragraph shall not be required.
(3) The provisions of the paragraph (1) shall not apply to Class Meeting constituted by the Class Shareholders of the class which is subject to the provisions of the articles of incorporation pursuant to the provisions of the preceding paragraph; provided, however, that this shall not apply to the cases where the amendment in the articles of incorporation (excluding the amendment relating to Share Unit) set forth in item (i) of paragraph (1) is carried out.
(4) If, after shares of a certain class are issued, it is intended to create provisions pursuant to the provisions of paragraph (2) with respect to the shares of such class by effecting an amendment in the articles of incorporation, the consent of all Class Shareholders of such class shall be obtained.

(Cases of Provision Requiring Resolution of Class Meeting)
Article 323 If, at a Company with Class Shares, there is a provision, as a feature of a certain class of shares, to the effect that, with respect to the matter that is subject to the resolution of the shareholders meeting (for a Company with Board of Directors, shareholders meeting or board of directors; and for a Company with Board of Liquidators provided for in Article 478(6), shareholders meeting or board of liquidators), in addition to such resolution, the resolution of a Class Meeting constituted by the Class Shareholders of such class of shares is required, such matter shall not become effec-

tive unless the resolution is made at a Class Meeting constituted by the Class Shareholders of the shares of such class in addition to the resolution of the shareholders meeting, board of directors or board of liquidators, consistently with the provisions of articles of incorporation; provided, however, that this shall not apply to the case where there exists no Class Shareholder who may exercise the votes at such Class Meeting.

(Resolution of Class Meetings)
Article 324 (1) Unless otherwise provided for in the articles of incorporation, resolutions of a Class Meeting shall be made by a majority of the votes of the shareholders of that class present at the meeting where the shareholders who hold a majority of the votes of all shareholders of the shares of such class are present.
(2) Notwithstanding the provisions of the preceding paragraph, the resolutions of the following Class Meetings shall be made by a majority of two thirds (in cases where any higher proportion is provided for in the articles of incorporation, such proportion) or more of the votes of the shareholders present at the meeting where the shareholders who hold a majority of the votes (in cases where any proportion of one third or more is provided for in the articles of incorporation, such proportion or more) of the shareholders who are entitled to exercise their votes at such Class Meeting are present. In such cases, it is not precluded from providing in the articles of incorporation, in addition to such requirements for resolution, additional requirements including those providing to the effect that the approval of a certain number or more of the shareholders are required:
  (i) Class Meeting under Article 111(2) (limited to the cases where, as a feature of a certain class of shares, a provision of the articles of incorporation is to be created with respect to the matters listed in item (vii) of Article 108(1));
  (ii) Class Meeting under of Article 199(4) and Article 200(4);
  (iii) Class Meeting under Article 238(4) and Article 239(4);
  (iv) Class Meeting under Article 322(1);
  (v) Class Meeting under Article 339(1) which is applied by the deemed replacement of terms pursuant to the provisions of Article 347(2);
  (vi) Class Meeting under Article 795(4);
(3) Notwithstanding the provisions of the preceding two paragraphs, the resolutions of the following Class Meetings shall be made by a majority (in cases where a higher proportion is provided for in the articles of incorporation, such proportion or more) of the shareholders entitled to exercise their votes at such Class Meeting, being a majority of two thirds (in cases where a higher proportion is provided for in the articles of incorporation, such proportion) or more of the votes of such shareholders:
  (i) Class Meetings under Article 111(2) (limited to the cases where, as a feature of a certain class of shares, a provision of the articles of incorporation is to be created with respect to the matters listed in item (vii) of Article 108(1));
  (ii) Class Meetings under Article 783(3) and Article 804(3).

(Mutatis mutandis Application of Provisions regarding Shareholders Meetings)
Article 325 The provisions of the preceding Subsection (excluding paragraph (1) and paragraph (2) of Article 295, paragraph (1) and paragraph (2) of Article 296, and Article 309) shall apply mutatis mutandis to the Class Meeting. In such cases, in Article 297(1), "all shareholders" shall be deemed to be replaced with "all shareholders (limited to the shareholders of a certain class of shares. The same shall apply hereinafter in this Subsection (excluding Article 308(1))." and "Shareholders" shall be deemed to be replaced with "Shareholders (limited to the shareholders of a certain class of shares.

The same shall apply hereinafter in this Subsection (excluding Article 318(4) and Article 319(3))."

Section 2 Establishment of Organs Other Than Shareholders Meeting

(Establishment of Organs Other Than Shareholders Meeting)
Article 326 (1) A Stock Company shall have one or more directors.
(2) A Stock Company may have a board of directors, an accounting advisor, a company auditor, a board of company auditors, an accounting auditor or Committees as prescribed by the articles of incorporation.

(Obligations to Establish Board of Directors and Other Organizations)
Article 327 (1) The following Stock Company shall have a board of directors.
(i) A Public Company;
(ii) A Company with Board of Company Auditors;
(iii) A Company with Committees.
(2) A Company with Board of Directors (excluding Company with Committees) shall have a company auditor; provided, however, that this shall not apply to a Company with Accounting Advisors that is not a Public Company.
(3) A Company with Accounting Auditors (excluding a Company with Committees) shall have a company auditor.
(4) A Company with Committees may not have a company auditor.
(5) A Company with Committees shall have an accounting auditor.

(Obligations of Large Companies to Establish Board of Company Auditors, etc.)
Article 328 (1) A Large Company (excluding a Company which is not a Public Company and a Company with Committees) shall have a board of company auditors and an accounting auditor.
(2) A Large Company which is not a Public Company shall have an accounting auditor.

Section 3 Election and Dismissal of Officers and Accounting Auditors

Subsection 1 Election

(Election)
Article 329 (1) Officers (meaning directors, accounting advisors and company auditors. The same shall apply hereinafter in this Section and in Article 371(4) and Article 394(3)) and accounting auditors shall be elected by resolution of a shareholders meeting.
(2) In case of the resolution under the preceding paragraph, substitute Officers may be elected as prescribed by the applicable Ordinance of the Ministry of Justice by way of precaution against the cases where there are no Officers in office or the cases where there is a vacancy which results in a shortfall in the number of Officers prescribed in this Act or articles of incorporation.

(Relationship between Stock Company and Officers)
Article 330 The relationship between a Stock Company and its Officers or accounting auditors shall be governed by the provisions on mandate.

(Qualifications of Directors)

Article 331 (1) The following persons may not act as directors:
  (i) A juridical person;
  (ii) An adult ward, a person under curatorship, or a person who is similarly treated under foreign laws and regulations;
  (iii) A person who has been sentenced to a penalty for having violated the provisions of this Act or the Act on General Incorporated Association and General Incorporated Foundation (Act No. 48 of 2006), or for having committed: a crime under Article 197, Article 197-2(1)(i) through (x) or (xiii), Article 198(viii), Article 199, Article 200(i) through (xii), (xx) or (xxi), Article 203(3) or Article 205 (i) through (vi), (xix) or (xx) of the Financial Instruments and Exchange Act; a crime under Articles 255, 256, 258 through 260 or 262 of the Civil Rehabilitation Act (Act No. 225 of 1999); a crime under Articles 65, 66, 68 or 69 of the Act on Recognition and Assistance for Foreign Insolvency Procedures (Act No. 129 of 2000); a crime under Articles 266, 267, 269 through Article 271 or 273 of the Corporate Reorganization Act (Act No. 154 of 2002); or a crime under Articles 265, 266, 268 through 272 or 274 of the Bankruptcy Act, for whom two years have not elapsed since the day on which the execution of the sentence was completed or the sentence no longer applied.
  (iv) A person who violated the provisions of laws and regulations other than those provided for in the preceding item, was sentenced to imprisonment or severer penalty and who has not completed the execution of the sentence or to whom the sentence still applies (excluding persons for whom the execution of the sentence is suspended).
(2) A Stock Company may not provide in the articles of incorporation that directors shall be shareholders; provided, however, that this shall not apply to a Stock Company that is not a Public Company.
(3) A director of a Company with Committees may not concurrently act as an employee including a manager of such Company with Committees.
(4) A Company with Board of Directors shall have three or more directors.

(Directors' Terms of Office)
Article 332 (1) Directors' terms of office shall continue until the conclusion of the annual shareholders meeting for the last business year which ends within two years from the time of their election; provided, however, that this shall not preclude the shortening the term of the directors by the articles of incorporation or by the resolution of the shareholders meeting.
(2) The provisions of the preceding paragraph shall not preclude a Stock Company which is not a Public Company (excluding a Company with Committees) from extending, by the articles of incorporation, the term of office under that paragraph until the conclusion of the annual shareholders meeting for the last business year which ends within ten years from the time of the election.
(3) For the purpose of the application of the provisions under paragraph (1) to the directors of a Company with Committees, "two years" in that paragraph shall be read as "one year."
(4) Notwithstanding the provisions of the preceding three paragraphs, in cases where any of the following amendments in the articles of incorporation is made, the directors' term of office shall expire when such amendment in the articles of incorporation takes effect:
  (i) An amendment in the articles of incorporation to the effect that Committees shall be established;
  (ii) An amendment in the articles of incorporation to repeal the provisions of the articles of incorporation to the effect that Committees shall be established; or

(iii) An amendment in the articles of incorporation to repeal the provisions of the articles of incorporation to the effect that, as a feature of all shares the Stock Company issues, the approval of the Stock Company is required for the acquisition of such shares by transfer (excluding an amendment made by a Company with Committees).

(Qualifications of Accounting Advisors)
Article 333 (1) An accounting advisor shall be a Certified Public Accountant or audit firm, or a certified public tax accountant or tax accountant corporation.
(2) An audit firm or tax accountant corporation which has been elected as the accounting advisor shall appoint, from among its members, a person who is in charge of the affairs of an accounting advisor, and notify the Stock Company to that effect. In such cases, the persons listed in each item of following paragraph may not be appointed.
(3) The following persons may not act as accounting advisors:
　(i) A director, company auditor or executive officer, or an employee, including a manager, of a Stock Company or its Subsidiary;
　(ii) A person who is subject to the disciplinary action ordering a suspension of operations and for whom the period of such suspension has not yet elapsed; or
　(iii) A person who, pursuant to the provisions of Article 43 of the Certified Public Tax Accountant Act (Act No. 237 of 1951), may not engage in the business of the certified public tax accountant prescribed in Article 2(2) of that act.

(Accounting Advisors' Terms of Office)
Article 334 (1) The provisions of Article 332 shall apply mutatis mutandis to the accounting advisors' terms of office.
(2) Notwithstanding the provisions of Article 332 applied mutatis mutandis under the preceding paragraph, in cases where a Company with Accounting Advisors effects an amendment in the articles of incorporation to repeal the provisions of the articles of incorporation to the effect that it shall have an accounting advisor, the accounting advisor's term of office shall expire when such amendment in the articles of incorporation takes effect.

(Qualifications of Company auditors)
Article 335 (1) The provisions of paragraph (1) and paragraph (2) of Article 331 shall apply mutatis mutandis to company auditors.
(2) A company auditor of a Stock Company may not concurrently act as a director, employee, including manager, of that Stock Company or its Subsidiary, and may not act as an accounting advisor (if the accounting advisor is a juridical person, the member who is in charge of its affairs) or an executive officer of such Subsidiary.
(3) A Company with Board of Company auditors shall have three or more company auditors, and the half or more of them shall be Outside Company Auditors.

(Company Auditors' Terms of Office)
Article 336 (1) Company auditors' terms of office shall continue until the conclusion of the annual shareholders meeting for the last business year which ends within four years from the time of their election.
(2) The provisions of the preceding paragraph shall not preclude a Stock Company which is not a Public Company from extending, by the articles of incorporation, the terms of office under that paragraph until the conclusion of the annual shareholders meeting for the last business year which ends within ten years from the time of the election.
(3) The provisions of paragraph (1) shall not preclude providing, by the articles of incorpo-

ration, that the term of office of a company auditor, who is elected as the substitute for a company auditor who retired from office before the expiration of the term of office, shall continue until the time the term of office of the company auditor who retired from office expires.
(4) Notwithstanding the provisions of the preceding three paragraphs, in cases where any of the following amendments in the articles of incorporation is made, the company auditors' terms of office shall expire when such amendment in the articles of incorporation takes effect:
  (i) An amendment in the articles of incorporation to repeal the provisions of the articles of incorporation to the effect that company auditors shall be established;
  (ii) An amendment in the articles of incorporation to the effect that Committees shall be established;
  (iii) An amendment in the articles of incorporation to repeal the provisions of the articles of incorporation to the effect that the scope of the audit by the company auditors shall be limited to an audit related to accounting;
  (iv) An amendment in the articles of incorporation to repeal the provisions of the articles of incorporation to the effect that, as a feature of all shares the Stock Company issues, the approval of the Stock Company is required for the acquisition of such shares by transfer.

(Qualifications of Accounting Auditors)
Article 337 (1) An accounting auditor shall be a Certified Public Accountant or an audit firm.
(2) An audit firm which has been elected as an accounting auditor shall appoint, from among its members, a person who is in charge of the affairs of an accounting auditor, and notify the Stock Company to that effect. In such cases, the person listed in item (ii) of the following paragraph may not be appointed.
(3) The following persons may not act as accounting auditors:
  (i) A person who, pursuant to the provisions of the Certified Public Accountant Act, may not audit the financial statement provided for in Article 435(2);
  (ii) A person who is in continuous receipt of remuneration from a Subsidiary of the Stock Company, or from a director, accounting advisor, company auditor or executive officer of that Subsidiary, for operations other than the operations of the Certified Public Accountant or audit firm, or the spouse of that person; or
  (iii) An audit firm half or more of its members of which are persons listed in the above items.

(Accounting Auditors' Terms of Office)
Article 338 (1) An accounting auditor's term of office shall continue until the conclusion of the annual shareholders meeting for the last business year which ends within one year from the time of their election.
(2) Unless otherwise resolved at the annual shareholders meeting under the preceding paragraph, accounting auditors shall be deemed to have been re-elected at such annual shareholders meeting.
(3) Notwithstanding the provisions of the preceding two paragraphs, in cases where a Company with Accounting Auditors makes any amendment in the articles of incorporation to repeal the provisions of the articles of incorporation to the effect that it shall have an accounting auditor, the accounting auditor's term of office shall expire when such amendment in the articles of incorporation takes effect.

Art.339〜341　　[I] Companies Act, PART II, Chap.IV, Sec.3

Subsection 2 Dismissal

(Dismissal)
Article 339 (1) Officers and accounting auditors may be dismissed at any time by resolution of a shareholders meeting.
(2) A person dismissed pursuant to the provisions of the preceding paragraph shall be entitled to demand damages arising from the dismissal from the Stock Company, except in cases where there are justifiable grounds for such dismissal.

(Dismissal of Accounting Auditors by Company Auditors)
Article 340 (1) The company auditor may dismiss an accounting auditor if that accounting auditor:
　(i) has breached his or her duty in the course of his/her duties, or neglected his/her duties;
　(ii) has engaged in misconduct inappropriate for an accounting auditor; or
　(iii) has difficulty in, or is unable to cope with the execution of his/her duties due to mental or physical disability.
(2) Dismissals pursuant to the provisions of the preceding paragraph shall be effected by the unanimous consent of all company auditors in cases where there are two or more company auditors.
(3) If an accounting auditor is dismissed pursuant to the provisions of paragraph (1), the company auditor (or, in cases where there are two or more company auditors, the company auditor appointed by the company auditors from among themselves) shall report such fact and the reason for dismissal to the first shareholders meeting called after the dismissal.
(4) For the purpose of the application of the provisions of the preceding three paragraphs to a Company with Board of Company Auditors, "company auditor" in paragraph (1) shall be read as "board of company auditors," "company auditors in cases where there are two or more company auditors" in paragraph (2) shall be read as "company auditors," and "company auditor (or, in cases where there are two or more company auditors, the company auditor appointed by the company auditors from among themselves)" in the preceding paragraph shall be read as "the company auditor appointed by the board of company auditors."
(5) For the purpose of the application of the provisions of paragraph (1) through paragraph (3) to a Company with Committees, "a company auditor" in paragraph (1) shall be read as "[an] audit committee," "company auditors in cases where there are two or more company auditors" in paragraph (2) shall be read as "committee members of the audit committee," and "company auditor (or, in cases where there are two or more company auditors, the company auditor appointed by the company auditors from among themselves)" in paragraph (3) shall be read as "committee member appointed by the audit committee."

Subsection 3 Special Provisions on the Procedures for Election and Dismissal

(Resolution at Shareholders Meeting for Election and Dismissal of Officers)
Article 341 Notwithstanding the provisions of Article 309(1), resolutions for the election or dismissal of officers shall be made by the majority (in cases where a higher proportion is provided for in the articles of incorporation, such proportion or more) of the votes of the shareholders present at the meeting where the shareholders holding the majority of the votes (in cases where a proportion of one third or more is provided for

in the articles of incorporation, such proportion or more) of the shareholders entitled to exercise their votes are present.

(Election of Directors by Cumulative Vote)
Article 342 (1) In cases where the purpose of the shareholders meeting is the election of two or more directors, the shareholders (limited to the shareholders entitled to exercise their votes with respect to the election of the directors. The same shall apply hereinafter in this article) may request the Stock Company that the directors be elected pursuant to the provisions of paragraph (3) through paragraph (5), except as otherwise provided in the articles of incorporation.
(2) The request under the provisions of the preceding paragraph shall be made no later than five days prior to the day of the shareholders meeting referred to in that paragraph.
(3) Notwithstanding the provisions of Article 308(1), in cases where a request is made pursuant to the provisions of paragraph (1), a shareholder shall be entitled to such number of votes as is equal to the number of the directors to be elected in such shareholders meeting for each one share the shareholder holds (or, in cases where the Share Unit is provided for in the articles of incorporation, for each one unit of the shares the shareholder holds) with respect to the resolution of the election of the directors. In such cases, the shareholder may exercise his/her votes by casting votes for only one candidate or for two or more candidates.
(4) In the case provided for in the preceding paragraph, the directors shall be elected in the order of the votes obtained by respective candidates.
(5) In addition to the matters provided in the preceding two paragraphs, necessary matters regarding the election of directors in cases where a request has been made pursuant to the provisions of paragraph (1) shall be prescribed by the applicable Ordinance of the Ministry of Justice.
(6) The provisions of the preceding article shall not apply to resolutions for the dismissal of the directors elected pursuant to the provisions of the preceding three paragraphs.

(Consent of Company Auditors to Election of Company Auditors)
Article 343 (1) In cases where a company auditor is in office, directors shall obtain the consent of the company auditor (or, in cases where there are two or more company auditors, the majority of the company auditors) in order to submit a proposal for the election of a company auditor to the shareholders meeting.
(2) The company auditor may request the directors that they include the election of the company auditor in the purpose of the shareholders meeting, or they submit a proposal regarding the election of company auditor to the shareholders meeting.
(3) For the purpose of the application of the preceding two paragraphs to a Company with Board of Company Auditors, "company auditor (or, in cases where there are two or more company auditors, the majority of the company auditors)" in paragraph (1) shall be read as "board of company auditors," and "company auditor may" in the preceding paragraph shall be read as "board of company auditors may."
(4) The provisions of Article 341 shall not apply to resolutions for the dismissal of company auditors.

(Consent of Company Auditors to the Election of Accounting Auditors)
Article 344 (1) At a Company with Auditors, they shall obtain the consent of the company auditor (or, in cases where there are two or more company auditors, the majority of the company auditors) in order to carry out the following acts:
(i) Submitting a proposal for the election of an accounting auditor to a shareholders

meeting;
(ii) Including the dismissal of an accounting auditor in the purpose of the shareholders meeting; or
(iii) Including the refusal to reelect an accounting auditor in the purpose of the shareholders meeting.
(2) A company auditor may request that the directors carry out the following acts:
(i) Submitting a proposal for the election of an accounting auditor to the shareholders meeting;
(ii) Including the election or dismissal of an accounting auditor in the purpose of the shareholders meeting; or
(iii) Including the refusal to reelect an accounting auditor in the purpose of the shareholders meeting.
(3) For the purpose of the application of the preceding two paragraphs to a Company with Board of Company Auditors, "company auditor (or, in cases where there are two or more company auditors, the majority of the company auditors)" in paragraph (1) and "company auditor" in the preceding paragraph shall be read as "board of company auditors."

(Statement of Opinions on Election of Accounting Advisors, etc.)
Article 345 (1) Accounting advisors may state their opinions on the election or dismissal, or resignation of accounting advisors at the shareholders meeting.
(2) A person who has resigned as an accounting advisor may attend the first shareholders meeting called after the resignation and state the fact of the resignation and the reason thereof.
(3) Directors shall notify the person under the preceding paragraph of the fact that the shareholders meeting under that paragraph is to be called, and of the matters listed in item (i) of Article 298(1).
(4) The provisions of paragraph (1) shall apply mutatis mutandis to a company auditor, and the provisions of the preceding two paragraphs shall apply mutatis mutandis to a person who resigned as the company auditor, respectively. In such cases, "accounting advisors" in paragraph (1) shall be read as "company auditors."
(5) The provisions of paragraph (1) shall apply mutatis mutandis to an accounting auditor, and the provisions of paragraph (2) and paragraph (3) shall apply mutatis mutandis to a person who resigned as the accounting auditor and a person dismissed as the accounting auditor pursuant to the provisions of Article 340(1), respectively. In such cases, "on the election or dismissal, or resignation of accounting advisors at the shareholders meeting" in paragraph (1) shall be read as "on the election, dismissal or refusal of reelection, or resignation of accounting auditors, by attending the shareholders meeting," and in paragraph (2), "after the resignation" shall be read with "after the dismissal or resignation," and "the fact of the resignation and the reason thereof" shall be read with "the fact of the resignation and the reason thereof, or opinions on the dismissal."

(Measures when Vacancies arise among Officers)
Article 346 (1) Where there are no Officers in office, or where there is a vacancy which results in a shortfall in the number of Officers prescribed in this Act or articles of incorporation, an Officer who retired from office due to expiration of his/her term of office or resignation shall continue to have the rights and obligations of an Officer until a newly elected officer (including a person who is to temporarily perform the duties of an Officer under the following paragraph) assumes his/her office.
(2) In the case provided for in the preceding paragraph, if the court finds it necessary, it may, in response to a petition by interested persons, elect a person who is to tempo-

rarily perform the duties of an Officer.
(3) In cases where the court has elected a person who is to temporarily perform the duties of an Officer under the preceding paragraph, the court may prescribe the amount of the remuneration that the Stock Company shall pay to that person.
(4) Where there are no accounting auditors in office, or where there is a vacancy which results in a shortfall in the number of accounting auditors prescribed in the articles of incorporation, if an accounting auditor is not elected without delay, the company auditor shall elect a person who is to temporarily perform the duties of an accounting auditor.
(5) The provisions of Article 337 and Article 340 shall apply mutatis mutandis the person who is to temporarily perform the duties of an accounting auditor under the preceding paragraph.
(6) For the purpose of the application of the provisions of paragraph (4) to a Company with Board of Company Auditors, "company auditor" in that paragraph shall be read as "board of company auditors."
(7) For the purpose of the application of the provisions of paragraph (4) to a Company with Committees, "company auditor" in that paragraph shall be read as "audit committee."

(Election of Directors or Company Auditors at Class Meetings)
Article 347 (1) For the purpose of the application of the provisions of Article 329(1), Article 332(1), Article 339(1) and Article 341 to the cases where it issues shares in a class for which there is the provision with respect to the matters listed in item (ix) of Article 108(1) (limited to those relating to directors), "shareholders meeting" in Article 329(1) shall be read as "shareholders meeting (or, for directors, Class Meeting constituted by the Class Shareholders of each class of shares in accordance with the applicable provisions of the articles of incorporation on the matters prescribed in item (ix) Article 108(2))"; "by resolution of a shareholders meeting" in Article 332(1) and Article 339(1) shall be read as "by resolution of a shareholders meeting (or, for directors elected pursuant to the provisions of Article 41(1), or at a Class Meeting under Article 90(1) or a Class Meeting under Article 329(1) applied by reading of terms pursuant to the provisions of Article 347(1), Class Meeting constituted by the Class Shareholders of shares of the class relating to the election of such director (or shareholders meeting in cases where it is otherwise provided in the articles of incorporation, or in cases where, before the expiration of the term of office of such director, there are no longer any shareholders entitled to exercise his/her votes at such Class Meeting))"; "Article 309(1)" in Article 341 shall be read as "Article 309(1) and Article 324"; and "shareholders meeting" in Article 341 shall be read as "shareholders meeting (including the Class Meeting under Article 329(1) and Article 339(1) applied by the reading of terms pursuant to the provisions of Article 347(1))."
(2) For the purpose of the application of the provisions of Article 329(1), Article 339(1) and Article 341 to the cases where it issues shares in a class for which there is the provision with respect to the matters listed in item (ix) of Article 108(1) (limited to those relating to company auditors), "shareholders meeting" in Article 329(1) shall be read as "shareholders meeting (or, for company auditors, Class Meeting constituted by the Class Shareholders of each class of shares in accordance with the applicable provisions of the articles of incorporation on the matters prescribed in item (ix) Article 108(2))"; "the shareholders meeting" in Article 339(1) shall be read as "shareholders meeting (or, for company auditors elected pursuant to the provisions of Article 41(1) applied mutatis mutandis under paragraph (3) of that article, or at a Class Meeting under Article 90(1) applied mutatis mutandis under paragraph (2) of that article or at a Class Meeting under 329(1) applied by the reading of terms pursuant to the provisions

of Article 347(2), Class Meeting constituted by the Class Shareholders of shares of the class relating to the election of such company auditor (or shareholders meeting in cases where it is otherwise provided in the articles of incorporation, or in cases where, before the expiration of the term of office of such company auditor, there are no longer any shareholders entitled to exercise his/her votes at such Class Meeting))"; "Article 309(1)" in Article 341 shall be read as "Article 309(1) and Article 324"; and "shareholders meeting" in Article 341 shall be read as "shareholders meeting (including the Class Meeting under Article 329(1) applied by the reading of terms pursuant to the provisions of Article 347(2))."

Section 4 Directors

(Execution of Operations)
Article 348 (1) The directors shall execute the operations of the Stock Company (excluding a Company with Board of Directors. The same shall apply hereinafter in this article), unless otherwise provided in the articles of incorporation.
(2) In cases where there are two or more directors, the operations of the Stock Company shall be decided by a majority of the directors, unless otherwise provided in the articles of incorporation.
(3) In the case provided for in the preceding paragraph, the directors may not delegate the decisions on the following matters to individual directors:
(i) The election or dismissal of managers;
(ii) The establishment, relocation and abolition of branch offices;
(iii) The matters listed in each item of Article 298(1) (including the cases where such items are applied mutatis mutandis under Article 325);
(iv) The development of systems necessary to ensure that the execution of the duties by the directors complies with the laws and regulations and the articles of incorporation, and other systems prescribed by the applicable Ordinance of the Ministry of Justice as systems necessary to ensure the properness of operations of a Stock Company; or
(v) Exemption from the liability under Article 423(1) pursuant to the provisions of the articles of incorporation under the provisions of Article 426(1).
(4) At a Large Company, the directors shall decide the matters listed in item (iv) of the preceding paragraph.

(Representatives of Companies)
Article 349 (1) The directors shall represent the Stock Company; provided, however, that this shall not apply in cases where Representative Directors or other persons who represent the Company are otherwise designated.
(2) In cases where there are two or more directors referred to in the main clause of the preceding paragraph, each director shall represent the Stock Company individually.
(3) A Stock Company (excluding a Company with Board of Directors) may appoint Representative Directors from among the directors pursuant to the articles of incorporation, or through the appointment by the directors from among themselves pursuant to the provisions of the articles of incorporation, or by resolution of a shareholders meeting.
(4) Representative Directors shall have authority to do any and all judicial and non-judicial acts in connection with the operations of the Stock Company.
(5) No limitation on the authority under the preceding paragraph may be asserted against a third party without knowledge of such limitation.

(Liability for Damages Caused by Acts of Directors)

Article 350 A Stock Company shall be liable for damage caused to third parties by its Representative Directors or other representatives during the course of the performance of their duties.

(Measures when Vacancy arises in Office of Representative Director)
Article 351 (1) Where there are no Representative Directors in office, or where there is a vacancy which results in a shortfall in the number of Representative Directors prescribed in the articles of incorporation, a Representative Director who retired from office due to expiration of his/her term of office or resignation shall continue to have the rights and obligations of a Representative Director until a newly appointed Representative Director (including the person who is to temporarily perform the duties of a Representative Director under the following paragraph) assumes his/her office.
(2) In the case provided for in the preceding paragraph, if the court finds it necessary, it may, in response to the petition by the interested persons, elect a person who is to temporarily perform the duties of a Representative Director.
(3) In cases where the court has elected the person who is to temporarily perform the duties of a Representative Director under the preceding paragraph, the court may prescribe the amount of the remuneration that the Stock Company shall pay to that person.

(Authority of Persons who Perform Duties on Behalf of Directors)
Article 352 (1) A person who is elected by a provisional disposition order provided for in Article 56 of the Civil Provisional Remedies Act (Act No. 91 of 1989) to perform the duties of directors or Representative Directors on behalf of them shall obtain the permission of the court in order to engage in acts that do not belong to the ordinary operations of the Stock Company, unless otherwise provided for in the provisional disposition order.
(2) Any act of the person who performs the duties of directors or Representative Directors on behalf of them that is performed in violation of the provisions of the preceding paragraph shall be void; provided, however, that the Stock Company may not assert that voidness against a third party without knowledge.

(Representation of Companies in Actions between Stock Company and Directors)
Article 353 Notwithstanding the provisions of Article 349(4), in cases where a Stock Company files an action against its directors (including persons who were directors. The same shall apply hereinafter in this article), or the directors of a Stock Company files an action against that Stock Company, a shareholders meeting may designate a person to represent the Stock Company in such action.

(Apparent Representative Directors)
Article 354 In cases where a Stock Company gives the title of president, vice president or other title regarded as having authority to represent the Stock Company to a director who is not a Representative Director, the Stock Company shall be liable to third parties without knowledge for the acts of such director.

(Duty of Loyalty)
Article 355 Directors shall perform their duties for the Stock Company in a loyal manner in compliance with laws and regulations, the articles of incorporation, and resolutions of shareholders meetings.

Art.356～358　　　Ⅰ Companies Act, PART II, Chap.Ⅳ, Sec.4

(Restrictions on Competition and Conflicting Interest Transactions)
Article 356 (1) In the following cases, a director shall disclose the material facts on the relevant transactions at a shareholders meeting and obtain approval of the shareholders meeting:
  (i) If a directors intends to carry out, for himself/herself or for a third party, any transactions in the line of business of the Stock Company;
  (ii) If the director intends to carry out any transactions with the Stock Company for himself/herself or for a third party; or
  (iii) If a Stock Company intends to guarantee debts of a director or otherwise to carry out any transactions with a person other than the director that results in a conflict of interests between the Stock Company and such director.
(2) The provisions of Article 108 of the Civil Code shall not apply to the transactions under item (ii) of the preceding paragraph that are approved under that paragraph.

(Director's Duty to Report)
Article 357 (1) If directors detect any fact likely to cause substantial detriment to the Stock Company, they shall immediately report such fact to the shareholders (or, for a Company with Auditors, the company auditors).
(2) For the purpose of the application of the provisions of the preceding paragraph to a Company with Board of Company Auditors, "shareholders (or, for a Company with Auditors, the company auditors)" in that paragraph shall be read as "board of company auditors."

(Election of Inspector of Execution of Operation)
Article 358 (1) If there are sufficient grounds to suspect misconduct or material facts in violation of laws and regulations or the articles of incorporation in connection with the execution of the operations of a Stock Company, the following shareholders may file a petition for the election of an inspector with the court in order to have the inspector investigate the status of the operations and the financial status of such Stock Company:
  (i) Shareholders who hold not less than three hundredths (3/100) of the votes (or, in cases where a lesser proportion is prescribed in the articles of incorporation, such proportion) of all shareholders (excluding shareholders who may not exercise their votes on all matters which may be resolved at shareholders meetings); or
  (ii) Shareholders who hold not less than three hundredths (3/100) (or, in cases where a lesser proportion prescribed in the articles of incorporation, such proportion) of the Issued Shares (excluding Treasury Shares).
(2) In cases where the petition under the preceding paragraph has been filed, the court shall elect the inspector except in case it dismisses such petition as non-conforming.
(3) In cases where the court has elected the inspector under the preceding paragraph, it may fix the amount of the remuneration that the Stock Company shall pay to such inspector.
(4) The inspector referred to in paragraph (2) may investigate the status of the operations and the financial status of Subsidiaries of the Stock Company if it is necessary in order to perform his/her duties.
(5) The inspector referred to in paragraph (2) shall conduct necessary investigation and shall report the court by submitting the documents or Electromagnetic Records (limited to those prescribed by the applicable Ordinance of the Ministry of Justice) which specifies or records the result of such investigation.
(6) If the court finds it necessary for the purpose of clarification of the contents of the report under the preceding paragraph or of confirmation of the grounds supporting such

report, it may request the inspector under paragraph (2) a further report under the preceding paragraph.
(7) When the inspector under paragraph (2) reports pursuant to paragraph (5), he/she shall give the Stock Company and the shareholders who filed the petition for the election of an inspector a copy of the documents under that paragraph, or provide the matters recorded in the Electromagnetic Records under that paragraph by the method prescribed by the applicable Ordinance of the Ministry of Justice.

(Decision by Court to Call Shareholders Meeting)
Article 359 (1) In cases where the report under paragraph (5) of the preceding Article is submitted, if the court finds it necessary, it shall order the directors to take some or all of the measures listed below:
(i) To call a shareholders meeting within a defined period of time; and
(ii) To notify shareholders of the result of the investigation under paragraph (5) of the preceding Article.
(2) In cases where the court orders the measures listed in item (i), paragraph (1) of the preceding Article, the directors shall disclose the content of the report under paragraph (5) of the preceding Article at the shareholders meeting under that paragraph.
(3) In the cases provided for in the preceding paragraph, the directors (or the directors and company auditors for a Company with Auditors) shall investigate the content of the report under paragraph (5) of the preceding Article and report the result thereof to the shareholders meeting under item (i) of paragraph (1).

(Enjoinment of Acts of Directors by Shareholders)
Article 360 (1) In cases where a director engages, or is likely to engage, in an act outside the scope of the purpose of a Stock Company, or other acts in violation of laws and regulations or the articles of incorporation, if such act is likely to cause substantial detriment to such Stock Company, shareholders having the shares consecutively for the preceding six months or more (or, in cases where a shorter period is prescribed in the articles of incorporation, such period or more) may demand that such director cease such act.
(2) For the purpose of the application of the provisions of the preceding paragraph to a Stock Company which is not a Public Company, "shareholders having the shares consecutively for the preceding six months or more (or, in cases where shorter period is prescribed in the articles of incorporation, such period or more)" in that paragraph shall be read as "shareholders."
(3) For the purpose of the application of the provisions of paragraph (1) to a Company with Auditors or a Company with Committees, "substantial detriment" in that paragraph shall be read as "irreparable detriment."

(Remuneration for Directors)
Article 361 (1) The following matters with respect to the financial benefits received from a Stock Company as a consideration for the execution of the duties, such as remunerations and bonuses, (hereinafter in this Chapter referred to as "Remunerations") of directors shall be fixed by resolution of a shareholders meeting if such matters are not prescribed in the articles of incorporation:
(i) For Remunerations in a fixed amount, that amount;
(ii) For Remunerations the amount of which is not fixed, the specific method for calculating that amount;
(iii) For Remunerations that are not monetary, the specific contents thereof.
(2) Directors who prescribed the matters listed in item (ii) or item (iii) of the preceding

Section 5 Board of Directors
Subsection 1 Authority

(Authority of Board of Directors)
Article 362 (1) Board of directors shall be composed of all directors.
(2) Board of directors shall perform the following duties:
(i) Deciding the execution of the operations of the Company with Board of Directors;
(ii) Supervising the execution of the duties by directors; and
(iii) Appointing and removing Representative Directors.
(3) Board of directors shall appoint Representative Directors from among the directors.
(4) Board of directors may not delegate the decision on the execution of important operations such as the following matters to directors:
(i) The disposal of and acceptance of assignment of important assets;
(ii) Borrowing in a significant amount;
(iii) The election and dismissal of a important employee including managers;
(iv) The establishment, changes or abolition of important structures including branch offices;
(v) Matters prescribed by the applicable Ordinance of the Ministry of Justice as important matters regarding the solicitation of persons who subscribe for Bonds such as the matters listed in item (i) of Article 676;
(vi) The development of systems necessary to ensure that the execution of duties by directors complies with laws and regulations and the articles of incorporation, and other systems prescribed by the applicable Ordinance of the Ministry of Justice as systems necessary to ensure the properness of operations of a Stock Company; or
(vii) Exemption from liability under Article 423(1) pursuant to provisions of the articles of incorporation under the provisions of Article 426(1).
(5) A Company with Board of Directors that is a Large Company shall decide the matters listed in item (vi) of the preceding paragraph.

(Authority of Directors of Companies with Board of Directors)
Article 363 (1) The following directors shall execute the operations of a Company with Board of Directors:
(i) A Representative Director; or
(ii) A director other than a Representative Director, who is appointed by resolution of the board of directors as the director who is to execute the operations of a Company with Board of Directors.
(2) The directors listed in each item of the preceding paragraph shall report the status of the execution of his/her duties to the board of directors at least once every three months.

(Representation of Company in Actions between Companies with Board of Directors and Directors)
Article 364 In the case provided for in Article 353, except when there is designation by a shareholders meeting pursuant to the provisions of that article, the board of directors may designate a person to represent the Company with Board of Directors with respect to the actions under that article.

(Restrictions on Competition and Transactions with Companies with Board of Directors)

Article 365 (1) For the purpose of the application of the provisions of Article 356 to a Company with Board of Directors, "shareholders meeting" in paragraph (1) of that article shall be read as "board of directors."

(2) At a Company with Board of Directors, a director who has engaged in transactions under each item of Article 356(1) shall report the material facts with respect to such transaction to the board of directors without delay after such transaction.

Subsection 2 Operations

(Convenor)

Article 366 (1) A board of directors meetings shall be called by any director; provided, however, that, if the director to call the board of directors meetings is designated by the articles of incorporation or the board of directors, such director shall call the meetings.

(2) In the case provided for in the proviso to the preceding paragraph, directors other than the director designated pursuant to the provision of the proviso to that paragraph (referred to as "Convenor." The same shall apply hereinafter in this Chapter) may demand that the Convenor call the board of directors meeting by indicating to the Convenor the matters that are the purpose of the board of directors meeting.

(3) In cases where, within five days from the day of the demand made pursuant to the provisions of preceding paragraph, a notice of calling of the board of directors meeting which designates as the day of the board of directors meeting a day falling within two weeks from the day of the demand is not dispatched, the directors who made the demand may call the board of directors meeting.

(Demand for Calling of Meeting by Shareholders)

Article 367 (1) If shareholders of a Company with Board of Directors (excluding a Company with Auditors and Company with Committees) recognize that a director engages, or is likely to engage, in an act outside the scope of the purpose of the Company with Board of Directors, or other acts in violation of laws and regulations or the articles of incorporation, they may demand the calling of a board of directors meeting.

(2) The demand pursuant to the provisions of the preceding paragraph shall be made to the directors (or to the Convenor in the case provided for in the proviso to paragraph (1) of the preceding article) by indicating the matters that are the purpose of the board of directors meeting.

(3) The provisions of paragraph (3) of the preceding article shall apply mutatis mutandis to the cases where a demand is made pursuant to the provisions of paragraph (1).

(4) Shareholders who made the demand pursuant to the provisions of paragraph (1) may attend the board of directors meeting which is called pursuant to such demand or which they call pursuant to the provisions of paragraph (3) of the preceding article applied mutatis mutandis under the preceding paragraph and state their opinions.

(Calling Procedures)

Article 368 (1) A person who calls a board of directors meeting shall dispatch the notice thereof to each director (or, for a Company with Auditors, to each director and each company auditor) no later than one week (or if a shorter period of time is prescribed in the articles of incorporation, such period of time) prior to the day of the board of directors meeting.

(2) Notwithstanding the provisions of the preceding paragraph, the board of directors meeting may be held without the procedures of calling if the consent of all directors (or, for a Company with Auditors, directors and company auditors) is obtained.

(Resolution of Board of Directors Meetings)
Article 369 (1) The resolution of a board of directors meeting shall be made by a majority (in cases where a higher proportion is provided for in the articles of incorporation, such proportion or more) of the directors present at the meeting where the majority (in cases where a higher proportion is provided for in the articles of incorporation, such proportion or more) of the directors entitled to participate in the vote are present.
(2) Directors who have a special interest in the resolution under the preceding paragraph may not participate in the vote.
(3) With respect to the business of the board of directors meeting, minutes shall be prepared pursuant to the provisions of the applicable Ordinance of the Ministry of Justice, and if the minutes are prepared in writing, the directors and company auditors present at the meeting shall sign or affix the names and seals to it.
(4) With respect to the matters recorded in Electromagnetic Records in cases where the minutes under the preceding paragraph are prepared by such Electromagnetic Records, an action in lieu of the signing or the affixing of names and seals prescribed by the applicable Ordinance of the Ministry of Justice shall be taken.
(5) Directors who participate in resolutions of the board of directors meeting and do not have their objections recorded in the minutes under paragraph (3) shall be presumed to have agreed to such resolutions.

(Omission of Resolution of Board of Directors Meeting)
Article 370 A Company with Board of Directors may provide in the articles of incorporation to the effect that, in cases where directors submit a proposal with respect to a matter which is the purpose of the resolution of board of directors meeting, if all directors (limited to those who are entitled to participate in votes with respect to such matter) manifest their intention to agree to such proposal in writing or by means of Electromagnetic Records (except for the case, at a Company with Auditors, where a company auditor states his/her objections to such proposal), it shall be deemed that the resolution to approve such proposal at the board of directors meeting has been made.

(Minutes)
Article 371 (1) A Company with Board of Directors shall keep the minutes referred to in Article 369(3) or the documents or Electromagnetic Records which specify or record the manifestation of intention under the preceding article (hereinafter in this article referred to as "Minutes") at its head office for the period of ten years from the day of the board of directors meeting (including the day when a resolution of a board of directors meeting is deemed to have been made pursuant to the provisions of the preceding article).
(2) If it is necessary for the purpose of exercising the rights of a shareholder, he/she may make the following requests at any time during the business hours of a Stock Company:
　(i) If the Minutes under the preceding paragraph are prepared in writing, requests for inspection or copying of such documents; and
　(ii) If the Minutes under the preceding paragraph are prepared in Electromagnetic Records, requests for inspection or copying of anything that displays the data record-

ed in such Electromagnetic Records in a manner prescribed by the applicable Ordinance of the Ministry of Justice.
(3) For the purpose of the application of the provisions of the preceding paragraph to a Company with Auditors or Company with Committees, "at any time during the business hours of a Stock Company" in that paragraph shall be read as "with the permission of the court."
(4) If it is necessary for the purpose of pursuing the liability of Officers or executive officers by a creditor of a Company with Board of Directors, such creditor may, with the permission of the court, make the request set forth in each item of paragraph (2) with respect to the Minutes of such Company with Board of Directors.
(5) The provision of the preceding paragraph shall apply mutatis mutandis to the cases where it is necessary for the purpose of exercising the rights of a Member of the Parent Company of a Company with Board of Directors.
(6) If the court finds that the inspection or copying relating to the requests listed in each item of paragraph (2) applied by the reading of terms under paragraph (3), or a request under paragraph (4) (including the case of the mutatis mutandis application under the preceding paragraph. The same shall apply hereinafter in this paragraph) is likely to cause substantial detriment to such Company with Board of Directors or its Parent Company or Subsidiary, the court may not grant the permission under paragraph (2) applied by the reading of terms under paragraph (3) or the permission under paragraph (4).

(Omission of Report to Board of Directors)
Article 372 (1) In cases where the directors, accounting advisors, company auditors or accounting auditors have notified all directors (or, for a Company with Auditors, directors and company auditors) of matters that are to be reported to a board of directors meeting, it shall be unnecessary to report such matters to a board of directors meeting.
(2) The provisions of the preceding paragraph shall not apply to reports under the provisions of Article 363(2).
(3) For the purpose of the application of the provisions of the preceding two paragraphs to a Company with Committees, "company auditors or accounting auditors" in paragraph (1) shall be read as "accounting auditors or executive officers"; "directors (or, for a Company with Auditors, directors and company auditors)" in paragraph (1) shall be read as "directors"; and "Article 363(2)" in the preceding paragraph shall be read as "Article 417(4)."

(Resolution of Board of Directors by Special Directors)
Article 373 (1) Notwithstanding the provisions of Article 369(1), in cases where a Company with Board of Directors (excluding a Company with Committees) falls under all of the following requirements, the board of directors may provide to the effect that the resolution of the board of directors on the matters listed in item (i) and item (ii) of Article 362(4) may be made, where the majority (in cases where a higher proportion is determined by the board of directors, such proportion or more) of three or more directors appointed in advance (hereinafter in this Chapter referred to as "Special Directors") who are entitled to participate in the vote are present, by the majority (in cases where a higher proportion is determined by the board of directors, such proportion or more) of such directors present:
(i) That there are six or more directors; and
(ii) That one or more of the directors are Outside Directors.
(2) In cases where there is a provision on the vote by Special Directors pursuant to the

Art.374　　　Ⅰ Companies Act, PART II, Chap.IV, Sec.6

provisions of the preceding paragraph, directors other than the Special Directors shall not be required to attend the board of directors meeting that decides the matters listed in item (i) and item (ii) of Article 362(4). For the purpose of the application of the provisions of the main clause of Article 366(1) and Article 368 to such cases, "any director" in the main clause of 366(1) shall be read as "any Special Director (referring to the Special Director provided for in Article 373(1). The same shall apply in Article 368)," "in the articles of incorporation" in Article 368(1) shall be read as "by the board of directors," "each director" in the same paragraph shall be read as "each Special Director," "directors (" in paragraph (2) of that article shall be read as "Special Directors (," and "directors and" in the same paragraph shall be read as "Special Directors and."
(3) The person who is appointed by Special Directors from among themselves shall report without delay after the resolution of the board of directors under the preceding paragraph the content of such resolution to the directors other than the Special Directors.
(4) The provisions of Article 366 (excluding the main clause of paragraph (1)), Article 367, Article 369(1) and Article 370 shall not apply to the board of directors under paragraph (2).

Section 6　Accounting Advisors

(Authority of Accounting Advisors)
Article 374　(1) Accounting advisors shall prepare, jointly with the directors, the Financial Statements (referring to the Financial Statements provided for in Article 435(2). The same shall apply hereinafter in this Chapter) and the supplementary schedules thereof, the Temporary Financial Statements (referring to the Temporary Financial Statements provided for in Article 441(1). The same shall apply hereinafter in this Chapter) as well as the Consolidated Financial Statements (referring to the Consolidated Financial Statements provided for in Article 444(1). The same shall apply in Article 396(1)). In such cases, the accounting advisors shall prepare accounting advisor's report pursuant to the provisions of the applicable Ordinance of the Ministry of Justice.
(2) Accounting advisors may at any time inspect or copy the following things or request reports on accounting from directors and managers or other employees:
　(i) If the account books or the materials relating thereto are prepared in writing, such documents; and
　(ii) If the account books or the materials relating thereto are prepared by Electromagnetic Records, anything that displays the data recorded in such Electromagnetic Records in a manner prescribed by the applicable Ordinance of the Ministry of Justice;
(3) If it is necessary for the purpose of performing duties of an accounting advisor, an accounting advisor may request reports on accounting from a Subsidiary of the Company with Accounting Advisors, or investigate the status of the operations and financial status of the Company with Accounting Advisors or of its Subsidiary.
(4) The Subsidiary under the preceding paragraph may refuse the report or investigation under that paragraph if there are justifiable grounds.
(5) Accounting advisors may not employ a person listed in item (ii) or item (iii) of Article 333(3) in performing their duties.
(6) For the purpose of the application of the provisions of paragraph (1) and paragraph (2) to a Company with Committees, "directors" in paragraph (1) shall be read as "executive officers," and "directors and" in paragraph (2) shall be read as "executive officers and directors, and."

(Accounting Advisor's Duty to Report)

Article 375 (1) If an accounting advisor detect, during the performance of their duties, misconduct or material facts in violation of laws and regulations or the articles of incorporation in connection with the execution of the duties of the directors, they shall report the same to the shareholders (or, for a Company with Auditors, to the company auditors) without delay.

(2) For the purpose of the application of the provisions of the preceding paragraph to a Company with Board of Company Auditors, "shareholders (or, for a Company with Auditors, to the company auditors)" in that paragraph shall be read as "board of company auditors."

(3) For the purpose of the application of the provisions of paragraph (1) to a Company with Committees, "directors" in that paragraph shall be read as "executive officers or directors" and "shareholders (or, for a Company with Auditors, to the company auditors)" in the same paragraph shall be read as "audit committee."

(Attendance at Board of Directors Meetings)

Article 376 (1) Accounting advisors (in cases where accounting advisors are audit firms or tax accountant corporation, referring to the members who are to perform the duties of the accounting advisors. The same shall apply hereinafter in this Article) of a Company with Board of Directors shall attend the board of directors meetings that effect the approval under Article 436(3), Article 441(3) or Article 444(5). In such cases, accounting advisors shall state their opinions if they regard it necessary.

(2) At a Company with Accounting Advisors, a person who is to call the board of directors meetings under the preceding paragraph shall dispatch the notice thereof to each accounting advisor no later than one week (or if a shorter period of time is provided for in the articles of incorporation, such shorter period of time) prior to the day of such board of directors meeting.

(3) In order to hold a board of directors meeting under paragraph (1) without the calling procedures pursuant to the provisions of Article 368(2) at a Company with Accounting Advisors, the consent of all accounting advisors shall be obtained.

(Statement of Opinions at Shareholders Meetings)

Article 377 (1) If an accounting advisor's opinion on matters regarding the preparation of the statements provided for in Article 374(1) differs from those of the directors, the accounting advisor (in cases where the accounting advisors are audit firms or tax accountant corporations, referring to the members who are to perform the duties of the accounting advisors) may state his/her opinion at the shareholders meeting.

(2) For the purpose of the application of the provisions of the preceding paragraph to a Company with Committees, "directors" in that paragraph shall be read as "executive officers."

(Keeping and Inspection of Financial Statements by Accounting Advisors)

Article 378 (1) Accounting advisors shall keep the things listed in the following items at the place designated by the accounting advisors for the period provided for in each such item, pursuant to the applicable Ordinance of the Ministry of Justice:

(i) The Financial Statements and the supplementary schedules thereof, and the accounting advisor's report for each business year: Five years from the day one week (or, for a Company with Board of Directors, two weeks) prior to the day of the annual shareholders meeting (or, in the case provided for in Article 319(1), from the day when the proposal under that paragraph was submitted); and

(ii) The Temporary Financial Statements and the accounting advisor's report: Five

years from the day when the Temporary Financial Statement was prepared.
(2) The shareholders and creditors of a Company with Accounting Advisors may submit the following request to the accounting advisors at any time during the business hours of the Company with Accounting Advisors (except for cases prescribed by the applicable Ordinance of the Ministry of Justice as cases where it is difficult for the accounting advisor to response to the request); provided, however, that the fees designated by such accounting advisors are required to be paid in order to submit the requests listed in item (ii) or item (iv):
(i) If the statements listed in each item of the preceding paragraph are prepared in writing, a request to inspect the statements;
(ii) A request for a transcript or extract of the statements referred to in the preceding item;
(iii) If the statements listed in each item of the preceding paragraph are prepared by Electromagnetic Records, a request to inspect anything that displays the data recorded in such Electromagnetic Records in a manner prescribed by the applicable Ordinance of the Ministry of Justice; or
(iv) A request that the matters recorded in the Electromagnetic Records referred to in the preceding item be provided by an Electromagnetic Method designated by the accounting advisor, or a request for any document which contains such data.
(3) If it is necessary for the purpose of exercising the rights of a Member of the Parent Company of a Company with Accounting Advisors, he/she may, with the permission of the court, make the requests listed in each item of the preceding paragraph with respect to the things of such Company with Accounting Auditors listed in each item of paragraph (1); provided, however, that, in order to make the requests listed in item (ii) or item (iv) of the preceding paragraph, the fees designated by such accounting advisor are required to be paid.

(Remunerations for Accounting Advisors)
Article 379 (1) The Remunerations for accounting advisors shall be fixed by resolution of a shareholders meeting if the amount thereof is not prescribed in the articles of incorporation.
(2) In cases where there are two or more accounting advisors, if there is no provision in the articles of incorporation and no resolution by a shareholders meeting with respect to the Remunerations for each accounting advisor, such Remunerations shall be fixed by discussion by the accounting advisors within the extent of the Remunerations referred to in the preceding paragraph.
(3) Accounting advisors (or, in cases where accounting advisors are audit firms or tax accountant corporation, the members who are to perform the duties of accounting advisors) may state their opinions on Remunerations for the accounting advisors at a shareholders meeting.

(Requests for Indemnification of Expenses)
Article 380 If accounting advisors make the following requests to a Company with Accounting Advisors with respect to the execution of their duties, such Company with Accounting Advisors may not refuse such request except in cases where it proves that the expense or debt relating to such request is not necessary for the execution of the duties of such accounting advisors:
(i) Requests for advancement of expenses;
(ii) Requests for indemnification of the expenses paid and interests thereon from and including the day of the payment; or
(iii) Requests for payment (or, in cases where such debt is not yet due, provision of

reasonable security) to the creditor of a debt incurred.

Section 7 Company Auditors

(Authority of Company Auditors)
Article 381 (1) Company auditors shall audit the execution of duties by directors (or directors and accounting advisors for a Company with Accounting Advisors). In such cases, company auditors shall prepare audit reports pursuant to the provisions of the applicable Ordinance of the Ministry of Justice.
(2) Company auditors may at any time request reports on the business from the directors and accounting advisors and managers and other employees, or investigate the status of the operations and financial status of the Company with Auditors.
(3) Company auditors may, if it is necessary for the purpose of performing duties of the company auditors, request reports on the business from a Subsidiary of the Company with Auditors, or investigate the status of the operations and financial status of its Subsidiary.
(4) The Subsidiary under the preceding paragraph may refuse the report or investigation under that paragraph if there are justifiable grounds.

(Duty to Report to Directors)
Article 382 If company auditors find that directors engage in misconduct, or are likely to engage in such conduct, or that there are facts in violation of laws and regulations or the articles of incorporation or grossly improper facts, they shall report the same to the directors (or, for a Company with Board of Directors, to the board of directors) without delay.

(Duty to Attend Board of Directors Meetings)
Article 383 (1) Company auditors shall attend the board of directors meeting, and shall state their opinions if they find it necessary; provided, however, that, in cases where there are two or more company auditors, if there is a provision on the vote by Special Directors pursuant to the provisions of Article 373(1), the specific company auditor who shall attend the board of directors meeting under paragraph (2) of that article shall be appointed by the company auditors from among the company auditors.
(2) In the case provided for in the preceding article, if company auditors find it necessary, they may demand that the directors (or a Convenor in case provided for in the proviso to Article 366(1)) call the board of directors meeting.
(3) In cases where, within five days from the day of the demand made pursuant to the provisions of preceding paragraph, a notice of calling of the board of directors meeting which designates as the day of the board of directors meeting a day falling within the period of two weeks from the day of the demand are not dispatched, the company auditors who made that demand may call the board of directors meeting.
(4) The provisions of the preceding two paragraphs shall not apply to the board of directors meeting under Article 373(2).

(Duty to Report to Shareholders Meeting)
Article 384 Company auditors shall investigate proposals, documents and other items prescribed by the applicable Ordinance of the Ministry of Justice that directors intend to submit to the shareholders meeting. In such cases, if company auditors find that there is a violation of laws and regulations or the articles of incorporation or a grossly improper fact, they shall report the results of the investigation to a shareholders meeting.

(Enjoinment of Acts of Directors by Company Auditors)
Article 385 (1) In cases where a director engages, or is likely to engage, in an act outside the scope of the purpose of a Stock Company, or other acts in violation of laws and regulations or the articles of incorporation, if such act is likely to cause substantial detriment to such Company with Auditors, company auditors may demand that such director cease such act.
(2) In the cases provided for in the preceding paragraph, if the court orders a director under the preceding paragraph to cease such act by a provisional disposition, the court shall not require the provision of security.

(Representation of Company in Actions between Company with Auditors and Directors)
Article 386 (1) Notwithstanding the provisions of Article 349(4), Article 353 and Article 364, in cases where a Company with Auditors files an action against its directors (including persons who were directors. The same shall apply hereinafter in this article), or the directors file an action against that Company with Auditors, the company auditors shall represent the Company with Auditors in such action.
(2) Notwithstanding the provisions of Article 349(4), in the following cases, the company auditors shall represent the Company with Auditors:
(i) In cases where a Company with Auditors is requested to file an action under Article 847(1) (limited to requests for the filing of actions that pursue the liability of directors); or
(ii) In cases where a Company with Auditors receives notice of suit under Article 849(3) (limited to those related to actions that pursue the liability of directors) and a notice or demand pursuant to the provisions of Article 850(2) (limited to those related to the settlement of a suit relating to an action that pursues the liability of directors).

(Remunerations for Company Auditors)
Article 387 (1) The Remunerations for company auditors shall be fixed by resolution of a shareholders meeting if the amount thereof is not prescribed in the articles of incorporation.
(2) In cases where there are two or more company auditors, if there is no provision in the articles of incorporation and no resolution by a shareholders meeting with respect to the Remunerations for each company auditor, such Remunerations shall be fixed by discussion by the company auditors within the extent of the Remunerations referred to in the preceding paragraph.
(3) Company auditors may state their opinions on Remunerations for the company auditors at a shareholders meeting.

(Requests for Indemnification of Expenses)
Article 388 If company auditors make the following requests to a Company with Auditors (including a Stock Company the articles of incorporation of which provide that the scope of the audit by its company auditors shall be limited to an audit related to accounting) with respect to the execution of their duties, such Company with Auditors may not refuse such request except in cases where it proves that the expense or debt relating to such request is not necessary for the execution of the duties of such company auditors:
(i) Requests for advancement of expenses;
(ii) Requests for indemnification of the expenses paid and the interests thereon from

and including the day of the payment; or
(iii) Requests for the payment (or, in cases where such debt is not yet due, provision of reasonable security) to the creditor of a debt incurred.

(Limitation of Scope of Audit by Provisions of Articles of Incorporation)
Article 389 (1) A Stock Company which is not a Public Company (excluding a Company with Board of Company Auditors and Company with Accounting Auditors) may provide in the articles of incorporation that the scope of the audit by its company auditors shall be limited to an audit related to accounting, notwithstanding the provisions of Article 381(1).
(2) Company auditors of a Stock Company that has the provisions of the articles of incorporation under the provisions of the preceding paragraph shall prepare audit reports pursuant to the applicable Ordinance of the Ministry of Justice.
(3) The company auditors under the preceding paragraph shall investigate the proposals, documents and other items prescribed by the applicable Ordinance of the Ministry of Justice that are related to accounting which the directors intend to submit to a shareholders meeting, and report the results of that investigation to a shareholders meeting.
(4) The company auditors under paragraph (2) may at any time inspect or copy the following things, or request reports on accounting from directors and accounting advisors as well as managers or other employees:
   (i) If the account books or the materials relating thereto are prepared in writing, such documents;
   (ii) If the account books or the materials relating thereto are prepared by Electromagnetic Records, anything that displays the data recorded in such Electromagnetic Records in a manner prescribed by the applicable Ordinance of the Ministry of Justice; or
(5) If it is necessary for the purpose of performing duties of a company auditor under paragraph (2), a company auditor may request reports on accounting from a Subsidiary of the Stock Company, or investigate the status of the operations and financial status of the Stock Company or of its Subsidiary.
(6) The Subsidiary under the preceding paragraph may refuse the report or investigation under that paragraph if there are justifiable grounds.
(7) The provisions from Article 382 through Article 386 shall not apply to a Stock Company which has provisions of the articles of incorporation pursuant to the provisions of paragraph (1).

Section 8 Board of Company Auditors

Subsection 1 Authority

Article 390 (1) Board of company auditors shall be composed of all company auditors.
(2) Board of company auditors shall perform the following duties; provided, however, that the decision in item (iii) may not preclude company auditors from exercising their authority:
   (i) Preparing audit reports;
   (ii) Appointing and removing full-time company auditors; and
   (iii) Deciding audit policy, methods for investigating the status of the operations and financial status of a Company with Board of Company Auditors and other matters regarding the execution of the duties of company auditors.
(3) Board of company auditors shall appoint full-time company auditors from among the

Art.391～394　　　Ⅰ Companies Act, PART II, Chap.IV, Sec.8

company auditors.
(4) If a board of company auditors requests, company auditors shall report the status of the execution of their duties to the board of company auditors at any time.

Subsection 2 Operations

(Convenor)
Article 391 A board of company auditors meeting shall be called by any company auditor.

(Calling Procedures)
Article 392 (1) To call a board of company auditors meeting, a company auditor shall dispatch the notice thereof to each company auditor no later than one week (or if a shorter period of time is prescribed in the articles of incorporation, such shorter period of time) prior to the day of the board of company auditors meeting.
(2) Notwithstanding the provisions of the preceding paragraph, the board of company auditors meeting may be held without the procedures of calling if the consent of all company auditors is obtained.

(Resolution of Board of Company Auditors Meetings)
Article 393 (1) The resolution of a board of company auditors meeting shall be made by a majority of the company auditors.
(2) With respect to the business of the board of company auditors meeting, minutes shall be prepared pursuant to the provisions of the applicable Ordinance of the Ministry of Justice, and if the minutes are prepared in writing, the company auditors present at the meeting shall sign or affix the names and seals to it.
(3) With respect to the matters recorded in Electromagnetic Records in cases where the minutes under the preceding paragraph are prepared in such Electromagnetic Records, an action in lieu of the signing or the affixing of names and seals prescribed by the applicable Ordinance of the Ministry of Justice shall be taken.
(4) Company auditors who participate in resolutions of the board of company auditors meeting and do not have their objections recorded in the minutes under paragraph (2) shall be presumed to have agreed to such resolutions.

(Minutes)
Article 394 (1) A Company with Board of Company Auditors shall keep the minutes referred to in paragraph (2) of the preceding article at its head office for the period of ten years from the day of the board of company auditors meeting.
(2) If it is necessary for the purpose of exercising the rights of a shareholder of a Company with Board of Company Auditors, he/she may, with the permission of the court, make the following requests:
    (i) If the minutes under the preceding paragraph are prepared in writing, requests for inspection or copying of such documents; and
    (ii) If the minutes under the preceding paragraph are prepared by Electromagnetic Records, requests for inspection or copying of anything that displays the data recorded in such Electromagnetic Records in a manner prescribed by the applicable Ordinance of the Ministry of Justice.
(3) The provisions of the preceding paragraph shall apply mutatis mutandis to the cases where it is necessary for the purpose of pursuing the liability of Officers by a creditor of a Company with Auditors and to the cases where it is necessary for the purpose of exercising the rights of a Member of the Parent Company.
(4) If the court finds that the inspection or copying relating to the requests under para-

graph (2) (including the case of the mutatis mutandis application under the preceding paragraph. The same shall apply hereinafter in this paragraph) is likely to cause substantial detriment to such Company with Board of Company Auditors or its Parent Company or Subsidiary, the court may not grant the permission under paragraph (2).

(Omission of Report to Board of Company auditors)
Article 395 In cases where the directors, accounting advisors, company auditors or accounting auditors have notified all company auditors of matters that are to be reported to a board of company auditors meeting, it shall be unnecessary to report such matters to a board of company auditors meeting.

Section 9 Accounting Auditors

(Authority of Accounting Auditors)
Article 396 (1) Accounting auditors shall audit the Financial Statements and the supplementary schedules thereof, the Temporary Financial Statements as well as the Consolidated Financial Statements of a Stock Company pursuant to the provisions of the next Chapter. In such cases, accounting auditors shall prepare accounting audit reports pursuant to the provisions of the applicable Ordinance of the Ministry of Justice.
(2) Accounting auditors may at any time inspect and copy the following things or request reports on accounting from directors and accounting advisors as well as managers or other employees:
  (i) If account books or materials relating thereto are prepared in writing, such documents; and
  (ii) If account books or materials relating thereto are prepared by Electromagnetic Records, anything that displays the data recorded in such Electromagnetic Records in a manner prescribed by the applicable Ordinance of the Ministry of Justice;
(3) Accounting auditors may, if it is necessary for the purpose of performing duties of the accounting auditors, request reports on accounting from a Subsidiary of the Company with Accounting Auditors, or investigate the status of the operations and financial status of the Company with Accounting Auditors or of its Subsidiary.
(4) The Subsidiary under the preceding paragraph may refuse the report or investigation under that paragraph if there are justifiable grounds.
(5) Accounting auditors may not employ a person listed in any of the following items in performing their duties:
  (i) A person listed in item (i) or item (ii) of Article 337(3);
  (ii) A person who is a director, accounting advisor, company auditor, executive officer or employee, including a manager, of a Company with Accounting Auditors; or
  (iii) A person who is in continuous receipt of remuneration from a Company with Accounting Auditors or its Subsidiary for operations other than the operations of the Certified Public Accountant or audit firm.
(6) For the purpose of the application of the provisions of paragraph (2) to a Company with Committees, "directors" in that paragraph shall be read as "executive officers, directors."

(Report to Company Auditors)
Article 397 (1) If accounting auditors detect, during the performance of their duties, misconduct or material facts in violation of laws and regulations or the articles of incorporation in connection with the execution of the duties of the directors, they shall report the same to the company auditors without delay.
(2) If it is necessary for the purpose of performing their duties, company auditors may re-

Art.398～400　　[I] Companies Act, PART II, Chap.IV, Sec.10

quest reports on the accounting auditors' audits from the accounting auditors.
(3) For the purpose of the application of the provisions of paragraph (1) to a Company with Board of Company Auditors, "company auditors" in that paragraph shall be read as "board of company auditors."
(4) For the purpose of the application of the provisions of paragraph (1) and paragraph (2) to a Company with Committees, "directors" in paragraph (1) shall be read as "executive officers or directors," "company auditors" in the same paragraph shall be read as "audit committee," and "company auditors" in paragraph (2) shall be read as "committee members of the audit committee who are appointed by the audit committee."

(Statement of Opinions at Annual Shareholders Meeting)
Article 398 (1) If an accounting auditor's opinion on whether or not the statements provided for in Article 396(1) comply with laws and regulations or the articles of incorporation differs from those of the company auditors, the accounting auditor (in cases where accounting auditors are audit firms or tax accountant corporations, referring to the members who are to perform their duties. The same shall apply in the following paragraph) may attend the annual shareholders meeting and state their opinion.
(2) If there is a resolution of an annual shareholders meeting that requires the attendance of accounting auditors, the accounting auditors shall attend the shareholders meeting and state their opinions.
(3) For the purpose of the application of the provisions of paragraph (1) to a Company with Board of Company Auditors, "company auditors" in that paragraph shall be read as "board of company auditors or company auditors."
(4) For the purpose of the application of the provisions of paragraph (1) to a Company with Committees, "company auditors" in that paragraph shall be read as "audit committee or its committee members."

(Involvement of Company Auditors in Decision on Remunerations for Accounting Auditors)
Article 399 (1) Directors shall obtain the consent of the company auditor (if there are two or more company auditors, the majority of the company auditors) in cases where the directors fix the Remunerations for accounting auditors or persons who are to temporarily perform the duties of accounting auditors.
(2) For the purpose of the application of the preceding paragraph to a Company with Board of Company Auditors, "company auditor (if there are two or more company auditors, the majority of the company auditors)" in that paragraph shall be read as "board of company auditors."
(3) For the purpose of the application of the provisions of paragraph (1) to a Company with Committees, "company auditor (if there are two or more company auditors, the majority of the company auditors)" in that paragraph shall be read as "audit committee."

Section 10　Committees and Executive Officers

Subsection 1 Appointment of Committee Members and Election of Executive Officers

(Appointment of Committee Members)
Article 400 (1) Each Committee shall be composed of three or more committee members.
(2) The committee members of each Committee shall be appointed from among the directors by resolution of the board of directors.

(3) The majority of the committee members of each Committee shall be Outside Directors.
(4) A committee member of the audit committee (hereinafter referred to as "Audit Committee Member") may not concurrently act as an executive officer or Executive Director of a Company with Committees or its Subsidiary, or as an accounting advisor (if the accounting advisor is a juridical person, the member who is to perform the duties of the accounting advisor) or employee, including manager, of a Subsidiary of a Company with Committees.

(Removal of Committee Members)
Article 401 (1) The committee members of each Committee may be removed at any time by resolution of the board of directors.
(2) Where there is a vacancy which results in a shortfall in the number of committee members of each Committee provided for in paragraph (1) of the preceding article (or, if the number of committee members provided for in the articles of incorporation is four or more, that number), a committee member who retired from office due to expiration of his/her term of office or resignation shall continue to have the rights and obligations of a committee member until a newly appointed committee member (including a person who is to temporarily perform the duties of a committee member under the following paragraph) assumes his/her office.
(3) In the case provided for in the preceding paragraph, if the court finds it necessary, it may, in response to a petition by interested persons, elect a person who is to temporarily perform the duties of a committee member.
(4) In cases where the court has elected the person who is to temporarily perform the duties of a committee member under the preceding paragraph, the court may prescribe the amount of the remuneration that the Company with Committees shall pay to that person.

(Election of Executive Officers)
Article 402 (1) A Company with Committees shall have one or more executive officers.
(2) Executive officer shall be elected by resolution of the board of directors.
(3) The relationship between a Company with Committees and its executive officers shall be governed by the provisions on mandate.
(4) The provisions of Article 331(1) shall apply mutatis mutandis to executive officers.
(5) A Stock Company may not provide in the articles of incorporation that the executive officers shall be shareholders; provided, however, that this shall not apply to a Company with Committees that is not a Public Company.
(6) An executive officer may act concurrently as a director.
(7) An executive officer's term of office shall continue until the conclusion of the first board of directors meeting called after the conclusion of the annual shareholders meeting for the last business year ending within one year from the time of their election; provided, however, that this does not preclude the shortening the executive officer's term of office by the articles of incorporation.
(8) Notwithstanding the provisions of the preceding paragraph, in cases where a Company with Committees makes any amendment in the articles of incorporation to repeal the provisions of the articles of incorporation to the effect that Committees shall be established, the executive officer's term of office shall expire when such amendment in the articles of incorporation takes effect.

(Dismissal of Executive Officers)
Article 403 (1) Executive officers may be dismissed at any time by resolution of the

board of directors.
(2) An executive officer dismissed pursuant to the provisions of the preceding paragraph shall be entitled to demand damages arising from the dismissal from the Company with Committees, except in cases where there are justifiable grounds for such dismissal.
(3) The provisions from paragraph (2) through paragraph (4) of Article 402 shall apply mutatis mutandis to the cases where there are no executive officers in office, or where there is a vacancy which results in a shortfall in the number of executive officers prescribed in the articles of incorporation.

Subsection 2 Authority of Committees

(Authority of Committees)
Article 404 (1) A nominating committee shall determine the contents of proposals regarding the election and dismissal of directors (or directors and accounting advisors for a Company with Accounting Advisors) to be submitted to a shareholders meeting.
(2) An audit committee shall perform the following duties:
   (i) Auditing the execution of duties by Executive Officers, Etc. (meaning executive officers and directors, or, for a Company with Accounting Advisors, meaning executive officers, directors and accounting advisors. The same shall apply hereinafter in this Section) and preparing audit reports; and
   (ii) Determining the contents of proposals regarding the election and dismissal of accounting auditors and the refusal to reelect accounting auditors to be submitted to a shareholders meeting.
(3) Notwithstanding the provisions of Article 361(1) and Article 379(1) and (2), a compensation committee shall determine the contents of the Remunerations for individual Executive Officers, Etc. If an executive officer acts concurrently as an employee, including manager, of a Company with Committees, the same shall apply to the contents of the Remunerations for such employee, including manager.
(4) If committee members make the following requests to a Company with Committees with respect to the execution of their duties (limited to that regarding the execution of the duties of the Committee to which such committee members belong. The same shall apply hereinafter in this paragraph), such Company with Committees may not refuse such request except in cases where it proves that the expense or debt relating to such request is not necessary for the execution of the duties of such committee members:
   (i) Requests for advancement of the expenses;
   (ii) Request for the indemnification of the expenses paid and interests thereon from and including the day of the payment; or
   (iii) Requests for the payment (or, in cases where such debt is not yet, provision of reasonable security) to the creditor of a debt incurred.

(Investigations by Audit Committees)
Article 405 (1) Audit Committee Members appointed by the audit committee may at any time request reports on the execution of their duties from Executive Officers, Etc. and employees including managers, or investigate the status of the operations and financial status of the Company with Committees.
(2) Audit Committee Members appointed by the audit committee may, if it is necessary for the purpose of performing duties of the audit committee, request reports on the business from a Subsidiary of the Company with, or investigate the status of the operations and financial status of its Subsidiary.

(3) The Subsidiary under the preceding paragraph may refuse the report or investigation under that paragraph if there are justifiable grounds.
(4) Audit Committee Members under paragraph (1) and paragraph (2) shall comply with resolutions of the audit committee, if any, on matters regarding the collection of the report or investigation under such respective paragraphs.

(Duty to Report to Board of Directors)
Article 406 If Audit Committee Members find that executive officers or directors engage in misconduct, or are likely to engage in such conduct, or that there are facts in violation of laws and regulations or the articles of incorporation or grossly improper facts, they shall report the same to the board of directors without delay.

(Enjoinment of Acts of Executive Officers, Etc. by Audit Committee Members)
Article 407 (1) In cases where an executive officer or director engages, or is likely to engage, in any act outside the scope of the purpose of a Company with Committees, or other acts in violation of laws and regulations or the articles of incorporation, if such act is likely to cause substantial detriment to such Company with Committees, the Audit Committee Members may demand that such executive officer or director cease such act.
(2) In the cases provided for in the preceding paragraph, if the court orders a executive officer or director under the preceding paragraph to cease such act by a provisional disposition, the court shall not require the provision of security.

(Representation of Company in Actions between Company with Committees and Executive Officers or Directors)
Article 408 (1) Notwithstanding the provisions of Article 349(4) applied mutatis mutandis under Article 420(3), and the provisions of Article 353 and Article 364, in cases where a Company with Committees files an action against its executive officers (including persons who were executive officers. The same shall apply hereinafter in this article) or directors (including persons who were directors. The same shall apply hereinafter in this article), or the executive officers or directors of a Company with Committees files an action against that Company with Committees, the persons provided for in each of the following items for the case categories listed in such items shall represent the Company with Committees in such actions:
  (i) In cases where Audit Committee Members are the party to the suit relating to such action: The person designated by the board of directors (or, in cases where the shareholders meeting designates a person to represent the Company with Committees with respect to such action, that person); and
  (ii) In cases other than the case listed in the preceding item: The Audit Committee Member appointed by the audit committee.
(2) Notwithstanding the provisions of the preceding paragraph, in cases where executive officers or directors file an action against the Company with Committees, the service of complaint on the Audit Committee Members (excluding those filing such action) shall be effective service on such Company with Committees.
(3) Notwithstanding the provisions of Article 349(4) applied mutatis mutandis under Article 420(3), in the following cases, the Audit Committee Members shall represent the Company with Committees:
  (i) In cases where a Company with Committees receives a request (limited to requests for the filing of actions that pursue the liability of executive officers or directors) pursuant to the provisions of Article 847(1) (excluding cases where such Audit

Committee Members are the party to the suit relating to such claim); or
(ii) In cases where a Company with Committees receives notice of suit under Article 849(3) (limited to those related to actions that pursue the liability of executive officers or directors) and a notice or demand (limited to those related to the settlement of a suit relating to an action that pursues the liability of executive officers or directors) pursuant to the provisions of Article 850(2) (excluding cases where such Audit Committee Members are the party to the suit relating to these claims).

(Methods for Decisions on Remuneration by Compensation Committee)
Article 409 (1) The compensation committee shall prescribe the policy on decisions on the content of the Remunerations for individual Executive Officers, Etc.
(2) The compensation committee shall comply with the policy under the preceding paragraph in order to make decisions under the provisions of Article 404(3).
(3) In cases where the compensation committee uses what is listed in the following items as the individual Remunerations of Executive Officers, Etc. , it shall decide the matters provided for in each of such item as the contents thereof; provided, however, that the Remunerations for individual accounting advisors shall be that listed in item (i):
(i) Remunerations in a fixed amount: The amount for each individual person;
(ii) Remunerations the amount of which is not fixed: The specific method for calculating that amount for each individual person;
(iii) Remunerations that are not monetary: The specific contents thereof for each individual person.

Subsection 3 Operation of Committees

(Convenors)
Article 410 A Committee shall be called by any committee member of such Committee.

(Calling Procedures)
Article 411 (1) To call a Committee meeting, a committee member of that Committee shall dispatch the notice thereof to each committee member of such Committee no later than one week (or if a shorter period of time is prescribed by the board of directors, such shorter period of time) prior to the day of the Committee meeting.
(2) Notwithstanding the provisions of the preceding paragraph, the Committee meeting may be held without the procedures of calling if the consent of all committee members of such Committee is obtained.
(3) If requested by the Committee, Executive Officers, Etc. shall attend such Committee meeting and provide explanations on the matters requested by such Committee.

(Resolution of Committee Meetings)
Article 412 (1) The resolution of a Committee meeting shall be made by a majority (in cases where a higher proportion is prescribed by the board of directors, such proportion or more) of the committee members present at the meeting where the majority (in cases where a higher proportion is prescribed by the board of directors, such proportion or more) of the committee members entitled to participate in the vote are present.
(2) Committee members who have a special interest in the resolution under the preceding paragraph may not participate in the vote.
(3) With respect to the business of the Committee meeting, minutes shall be prepared pursuant to the provisions of the applicable Ordinance of the Ministry of Justice, and if the minutes are prepared in writing, the committee members present at the meeting

shall sign or affix the names and seals to it.
(4) With respect to the matters recorded in Electromagnetic Records in cases where the minutes under the preceding paragraph are prepared in such Electromagnetic Records, an action in lieu of the signing or the affixing of names and seals prescribed by the applicable Ordinance of the Ministry of Justice shall be taken.
(5) Committee members who participate in resolutions of the Committee meeting and do not have their objections recorded in the minutes under paragraph (3) shall be presumed to have agreed to such resolutions.

(Minutes)
Article 413 (1) A Company with Committees shall keep the minutes referred to in paragraph (3) of the preceding article at its head office for the period of ten years from the day of the Committee meeting.
(2) The directors of a Company with Committees may inspect or copy anything listed in the following items:
  (i) If the minutes under the preceding paragraph are prepared in writing, such documents; and
  (ii) If the minutes under the preceding paragraph are prepared in Electromagnetic Records, anything which indicates the matters recorded in such Electromagnetic Records in a manner prescribed by the applicable Ordinance of the Ministry of Justice.
(3) If it is necessary for the purpose of exercising the rights of a shareholder of a Company with Committees, he/she may, with the permission of the court, make requests for inspection or copying of the things set forth in each item of the preceding paragraph with respect to the minutes under paragraph (1).
(4) The provision of the preceding paragraph shall apply mutatis mutandis to the cases where it is necessary for the purpose of pursuing the liability of committee members by a creditor of a Company with Committees and where it is necessary for the purpose of exercising the rights of a Member of the Parent Company.
(5) If the court finds that the inspection or copying relating to the requests under paragraph (3) (including cases of the mutatis mutandis application under the preceding paragraph. The same shall apply hereinafter in this paragraph) is likely to cause substantial detriment to such Company with Committees or its Parent Company or Subsidiary, the court may not grant the permission under paragraph (3).

(Omission of Report to Committees)
Article 414 In cases where the executive officers, directors, accounting advisors or accounting auditors have notified all committee members of matters that are to be reported to a Committee meeting, it shall be unnecessary to report such matters to a Committee meeting.

Subsection 4 Authority of Directors of Companies with Committees

(Authority of Directors of Companies with Committees)
Article 415 Directors of a Company with Committees may not execute the operations of the Company with Committees unless otherwise provided in this act or any order under this Act.

(Authority of Board of Directors of Company with Committees)
Article 416 (1) The board of directors of a Company with Committees shall perform the following duties notwithstanding the provisions of Article 362:
  (i) Deciding on the following matters and on the execution of other operations of the

Art.416 　 ① Companies Act, PART II, Chap.IV, Sec.10

Company with Committees:
(a) Basic management policy;
(b) The matters prescribed by the applicable Ordinance of the Ministry of Justice as those necessary for the execution of the duties of the audit committee;
(c) In cases where there are two or more executive officers, matters regarding the interrelationship between executive officers including the division of duties between executive officers and hierarchy of commands of executive officers;
(d) The directors to receive requests for the calling of board of directors meeting pursuant to the provisions of paragraph (2) of the following article; or
(e) The development of systems necessary to ensure that the execution of duties by executive officers complies with laws and regulations and the articles of incorporation, and other systems prescribed by the applicable Ordinance of the Ministry of Justice as systems necessary to ensure the properness of operations of a Stock Company.
 (ii) The supervision of the execution of duties by Executive Officers, Etc.
(2) The board of directors of a Company with Committees shall decide the matters listed in item (i)(a) through item (i)(e) of the preceding paragraph.
(3) The board of directors of a Company with Committees may not delegate the execution of the duties listed in each item of paragraph (1) to directors.
(4) The board of directors of a Company with Committees may, by resolution of the same, delegate decisions on the execution of the operations of the Company with Committees to executive officers; provided, however, that this shall not apply to the following matters:
 (i) Decisions under Article 136 or Article 137(1), and the designation under Article 140(4);
 (ii) Decisions on the matters listed in each item of Article 156(1) applied by the reading of terms under Article 165(3);
 (iii) Decisions under Article 262 or Article 263(1);
 (iv) Decisions on the matters listed in each item of Article 298(1);
 (v) Decisions on the contents of proposals to be submitted to a shareholders meeting (excluding those regarding the election and dismissal of directors, accounting advisors and accounting auditors and the refusal to reelect accounting auditors);
 (vi) Approval under Article 356(1) applied by the reading of terms under Article 365(1) (including cases of mutatis mutandis application by the reading of terms under Article 419(2));
 (vii) Designation of the directors to call the board of directors meeting pursuant to the provisions of the proviso to Article 366(1);
 (viii) Appointment of the committee members pursuant to the provisions of Article 400(2) and removal of committee members pursuant to the provisions of Article 401(1);
 (ix) Election of executive officers pursuant to the provisions of Article 402(2) and dismissal of executive officers pursuant to the provisions of Article 403(1);
 (x) Designation of persons to represent Companies with Committees pursuant to the provisions of item (i) of Article 408(1);
 (xi) Appointment of representative executive officers pursuant to the provisions of the first sentence of Article 420(1) and removal of representative executive officers pursuant to the provisions of paragraph (2) of the same article;
 (xii) Exemption from liability under Article 423(1) pursuant to the provisions of the articles of incorporation under the provisions of Article 426(1);
 (xiii) Approvals under Article 436(3), Article 441(3) and Article 444(5);
 (xiv) Decisions on the matters to be decided pursuant to the provisions of Article

454(1) applied by the reading of terms under paragraph (5) of the same article;
(xv) Decisions on the contents of contracts relating to the acts listed in each item of Article 467(1) (excluding those which do not require approval by resolution of shareholders meeting of such Company with Committees);
(xvi) Decisions on the contents of merger agreements (excluding those which do not require approval by resolution of shareholders meeting of such Company with Committees);
(xvii) Decisions on the contents of Absorption-type Company Split agreements (excluding those which do not require approval by resolution of shareholders meeting of such Company with Committees);
(xviii) Decisions on the contents of Incorporation-type Company Split plans (excluding those which do not require approval by resolution of shareholders meeting of such Company with Committees);
(xix) Decisions on the contents of Share Exchange agreements (excluding those which do not require approval by resolution of shareholders meeting of such Company with Committees);
(xx) Decisions on the contents of Share Transfer plans;

(Operations of Board of Directors of Company with Committees)
Article 417 (1) At a Company with Committees, even in cases where there is provision for a Convenor, persons appointed by the Committees from among their committee members may call the board of directors meeting.
(2) Executive officers may demand that the directors under item (i)(d), paragraph (1) of the preceding article call the board of directors meeting by indicating to those directors the matters that are the purpose of the board of directors meeting. In such cases, if a notice of calling of the board of directors meeting which designates as the day of the board of directors meeting a day falling within two weeks from the day of the demand is not dispatched within five days from the day of such demand, such executive officers may call the board of directors meeting.
(3) The persons appointed by the Committees from among the committee members shall report the status of the execution of the duties of such Committees to the board of directors without delay.
(4) The executive officers shall report the status of the execution of their duties to the board of directors at least once every three months. In such cases, executive officers may submit such reports through their agents (limited to other executive officers).
(5) If requested by the board of directors, executive officers shall attend the board of directors meeting and provide explanations on the matters requested by the board of directors.

Subsection 5 Authority of Executive Officers

(Authority of Executive Officers)
Article 418 Executive officers shall perform the following duties:
(i) Deciding on the execution of the operations of the Company with Committees that were delegated to the executive officers by resolution of the board of directors pursuant to the provisions of Article 416(4); and
(ii) The execution of the operations of the Company with Committees.

(Executive officer's Duty to Report to Audit Committee Members)
Article 419 (1) If executive officers detect any fact likely to cause substantial detriment to the Company with Committees, they shall immediately report such fact to the Audit

Committee Members.

(2) The provisions of Article 355, Article 356 and Article 365(2) shall apply mutatis mutandis to executive officers. In such cases, "shareholders meeting" in Article 356(1) shall be read as "board of directors meeting" and "At a Company with Board of Directors, a director who has engaged in transactions under each item of Article 356(1)" in Article 365(2) shall be read as "An executive officer who has engaged in transactions under each item of Article 356(1)."

(3) The provisions of Article 357 shall not apply to Companies with Committees.

(Representative Executive Officers)
Article 420 (1) Board of directors shall appoint representative executive officers from among the executive officers. In such cases, if there is only one executive officer, that person shall be regarded as having been appointed as the representative executive officer.

(2) A representative executive officer may be removed at any time by resolution of the board of directors.

(3) The provisions of Article 349(4) and (5) shall apply mutatis mutandis to representative executive officers, the provisions of Article 352 shall apply mutatis mutandis to a person elected by a provisional disposition order provided for in Article 56 of the Civil Provisional Remedies Act to perform the duties of executive officers or representative executive officers on behalf of the same, and the provisions of Article 401(2) through (4) shall apply mutatis mutandis to the cases where there are no representative executive officers in office, or where there is a vacancy which results in a shortfall in the number of executive officers prescribed in the articles of incorporation, respectively.

(Apparent Representative Executive Officers)
Article 421 In cases where a Company with Committees gives the title of president, vice president or other title regarded as having authority to represent the Company with Committees to an executive officer who is not a representative executive, the Company with Committees shall be liable to third parties without knowledge for the acts of such executive officer.

(Enjoinment of Acts of Executive Officers by Shareholders)
Article 422 (1) In cases where an executive officer engages, or is likely to engage, in an act outside the scope of the purpose of a Company with Committees, or other acts in violation of laws and regulations or the articles of incorporation, if such act is likely to cause irreparable detriment to such Company with Committees, shareholders having the shares consecutively for the preceding six months or more (or, in cases where a shorter period is prescribed in the articles of incorporation, such period or more) may demand that such executive officer cease such act.

(2) For the purpose of the application of the provisions of the preceding paragraph to a Company with Committees which is not a Public Company, "shareholders having the shares consecutively for the preceding six months or more (or, in cases where a shorter period is prescribed in the articles of incorporation, such period or more)" in that paragraph shall be read as "shareholders."

Section 11 Liability for Damages of Officers, Etc.

(Liability for Damages of Officers, Etc. to Stock Company for Damages)
Article 423 (1) If a director, accounting advisor, company auditor, executive officer or accounting auditor (hereinafter in this Section referred to as "Officers, Etc.") neglects

his/her duties, he/she shall be liable to such Stock Company for damages arising as a result thereof.
(2) If a director or executive officer engages in a transaction listed in item (i) of Article 356(1) in violation of the provisions of Article 356(1) (including cases where applied mutatis mutandis under Article 419(2). The same shall apply hereinafter in this paragraph), the amount of the profits obtained by the director, executive officer or a third party as a result of such transaction shall be presumed to be the amount of the damages under the preceding paragraph.
(3) If a Stock Company incurs damages as a result of the transaction provided for in item (ii) or item (iii) of Article 356(1) (including cases where these provisions are applied mutatis mutandis under Article 419(2)), the following directors or executive officers shall be presumed to have neglected their duties:
  (i) Directors and executive officers provided for in Article 356(1) (including cases where applied mutatis mutandis under Article 419(2));
  (ii) Directors and executive officers who decided that the Stock Company would undertake such transaction; or
  (iii) Directors who agreed to the board of directors' resolution approving such transaction (for a Company with Committees, limited to cases where such transaction is a transaction between the Company with Committees and the directors or is a transaction that gives rise to a conflict of interest between the Company with Committees and the directors).

(Exemption from Liability for Damages to Stock Company)
Article 424 An exemption from liability under paragraph (1) of the preceding article may not be given without the consent of all shareholders.

(Partial Exemption from Liability)
Article 425 (1) Notwithstanding the provisions of the preceding paragraph, if the relevant Officers, Etc. are without knowledge and are not grossly negligent in performing their duties, exemption from liability under Article 423(1) may be given by resolution of a shareholders meeting, to the extent of the amount obtained by subtracting the sum of the following amounts (in Article 427(1) referred to as "Minimum Liability Amount") from the amount for which they are liable:
  (i) The amount obtained by multiplying the amount calculated by the method prescribed by the applicable Ordinance of the Ministry of Justice as the amount equivalent to the annual amount of property benefits which such Officers, Etc. have received, or are to receive, from the Stock Company as consideration for the execution of their duties while they are in the office by the numbers provided for in Sub-item (a) through (c) for the categories of Officers, Etc. listed in such Sub-item (a) through (c):
    (a) Representative Directors or representative executive officers: 6;
    (b) directors (excluding Outside Directors) other than Representative Directors or executive officers other than representative executive officers: 4;
    (c) Outside Directors, accounting advisors, company auditors or accounting auditors: 2.
  (ii) In cases where such Officers, Etc. have subscribed for Share Options of such Stock Company (limited to cases listed in each item of Article 238(3)), the amount calculated by the method prescribed by the applicable Ordinance of the Ministry of Justice as the amount equivalent to the amount of the property benefits regarding such Share Options.
(2) In cases under the preceding paragraph, the directors shall disclose the following mat-

ters to the shareholders meeting under that paragraph:
(i) The facts that cause the liability and the amount of the liability for damages;
(ii) The maximum amount for which exemption may be given pursuant to the provisions of the preceding paragraph and the grounds supporting such calculation; and
(iii) The reasons for which exemption from the liability is to be given and the amount for which exemption is to be given.
(3) At a Company with Auditors or Company with Committees, in order to submit proposals regarding the exemption from liability under Article 423(1) (limited to the exemption from liability of directors (excluding those who are Audit Committee Members) and executive officers) to a shareholders meeting, directors shall obtain the consent of the persons provided for in the following items for the Stock Company categories listed in each such item:
(i) Company with Auditors: The company auditor (all company auditors if there are two or more company auditors); and
(ii) Company with Committees: All Audit Committee Members.
(4) In cases where a resolution under paragraph (1) is made, if the Stock Company gives any property benefits prescribed by the applicable Ordinance of the Ministry of Justice including, but not limited to, retirement allowance to the Officers, Etc. in that paragraph after such resolution, the Stock Company shall obtain the approval of a shareholders meeting. The same shall apply if such Officers, Etc. exercise or transfer the Share Options under item (ii) of the same paragraph after such resolution.
(5) In cases where a resolution under paragraph (1) is made, if such Officers, Etc. possess share option certificates that certify the Share Options under the preceding paragraph, such Officers, Etc. shall deposit such share option certificates with the Stock Company without delay. In such cases, such Officers, Etc. may not demand the return of such share option certificates until after the approval under that paragraph is obtained with respect to the transfer under that paragraph.

(Provisions of Articles of Incorporation on Exemption by Directors)
Article 426 (1) Notwithstanding the provisions of Article 424, Companies with Auditors (limited to cases where there are two or more directors) or Companies with Committees may provide in the articles of incorporation that, in cases where the relevant Officers, Etc. are without knowledge and are not grossly negligent in performing their duties, if it is found particularly necessary taking into account the relevant circumstances including, but not limited to, the details of the facts that caused the liability and the status of execution of duties by such Officers, Etc. , exemption may be given with respect to the liability under Article 423(1) by the consent of a majority of the directors (excluding the directors subject to such liability) (or, for Companies with Board of Directors, by resolution of the board of directors) to the extent of the amount which exemption may be given pursuant to the provisions of paragraph (1) of the preceding article.
(2) The provisions of paragraph (3) of the preceding article shall apply mutatis mutandis to cases where a proposal to amend the articles of incorporation to create provisions of the articles of incorporation pursuant to the provisions of the preceding paragraph (limited to provisions of the articles of incorporation to the effect that directors (excluding those who are Audit Committee Members) and executive officers may be exempted from the liability) is submitted to a shareholders meeting, to cases where the consent of directors with respect to exemption from liability under the provisions of the articles of incorporation pursuant to the provisions of that paragraph (limited to exemption from liability of directors (excluding those who are Audit Committee Members) and executive officers) is to be obtained, and to the cases where a proposal re-

garding such exemption from liability is submitted to the board of directors.
(3) If consent (or, for a Company with Board of Directors, a resolution of the board of directors) to the effect that Officers, Etc. shall be exempted from the liability under the provisions of the articles of incorporation pursuant to the provisions of paragraph (1) has been given, the directors shall, without delay, give public notice, or give notice to shareholders, to the effect that any objections to the matters listed in each item of paragraph (2) of the preceding article or to the exemption from liability ought to be stated within a specified period of time; provided, however, that such period may not be shorter than one month.
(4) For the purpose of the application of the provisions of the preceding paragraph to a Stock Company that is not a Public Company, "give public notice, or give notice to shareholders" in that paragraph shall be read as "give notice to shareholders."
(5) If shareholders having not less than three hundredths (3/100) (or, in cases where lesser proportion is prescribed in the articles of incorporation, such proportion) of the votes of all shareholders (excluding Officers, Etc. subject to the liability referred to in paragraph (3)) state objections during the period provided for in that paragraph, the Stock Company may not effect the exemption pursuant to the provisions of the articles of incorporation under the provisions of paragraph (1).
(6) The provisions of paragraph (4) and paragraph (5) of the preceding article shall apply mutatis mutandis to cases where exemption from liability is given pursuant to the provisions of the articles of incorporation under the provisions of paragraph (1).

(Contracts for Limitation of Liability)
Article 427 (1) Notwithstanding the provisions of Article 424, a Stock Company may provide in the articles of incorporation that the Stock Company may enter into contracts with Outside Directors, accounting advisors, Outside Company Auditors or accounting auditors (hereinafter in this article referred to as "Outside Directors, Etc.") to the effect that, if such Outside Directors, Etc. are without knowledge and are not grossly negligent in performing their duties, the liability of the Outside Directors, Etc. under Article 423(1) shall be limited to either an amount specified by the Stock Company in advance within the limit of the amount provided for in the articles of incorporation, or the Minimum Liability Amount, whichever is higher.
(2) If Outside Directors, Etc. who have entered into contracts under the preceding paragraph assume the office of Executive Director, executive officer, or employee, including manager, of such Stock Company or its Subsidiaries, such contracts shall become ineffective from then on.
(3) The provisions of Article 425(3) shall apply mutatis mutandis to cases where a proposal to amend the articles of incorporation to create provisions of the articles of incorporation under the provisions of paragraph (1) (limited to the provisions of the articles of incorporation to the effect that contracts may be entered into with Outside Directors (excluding those who are Audit Committee Members)) is submitted to a shareholders meeting.
(4) If a Stock Company that entered into contracts under paragraph (1) has come to know that it has suffered damages as a result of Outside Directors, Etc. who were the counterparties to such contracts neglecting their duties, the Stock Company shall disclose the following matters at the first shareholders meeting called thereafter:
(i) Matters listed in item (i) and (ii) of Article 425(2);
(ii) The contents of such contracts and reasons for entering into such contracts; and
(iii) The amount for which it was arranged that such Outside Directors, Etc. would be exempted from liability for damages in Article 423(1).
(5) The provisions of Article 425(4) and (5) shall apply mutatis mutandis to cases where it

has been arranged pursuant to contracts under paragraph (1) that Outside Directors, Etc. shall not be liable for damages in excess of the limit provided for in that paragraph.

(Special Provision on Transactions carried out by Director for Himself/Herself)
Article 428 (1) A director or executive officer who has carried out transactions under item (ii) of Article 356(1) (including cases of mutatis mutandis application under Article 419(2)) (limited to transactions carried out for himself/herself) may not be exempted from the liability under Article 423(1) for the reason that the neglect of his/her duties was due to grounds not attributable to such directors or executive officers.
(2) The provisions of the preceding three articles shall not apply to the liability in the preceding paragraph.

(Liability for Damages of Officers, Etc. to Third Parties)
Article 429 (1) If Officers, Etc. are with knowledge or grossly negligent in performing their duties, such Officers, Etc. shall be liable to a third party for damages arising as a result thereof.
(2) The provisions of the preceding paragraph shall also apply if the persons listed in the following items carry out the acts provided for in each such item; provided, however, that this shall not apply if such persons prove that they did not fail to exercise due care with respect to the performance of their duties:
(i) Directors and executive officers: The following acts:
　(a) The giving of false notice with respect to important matters, notice of which shall be given when soliciting persons to subscribe for shares, Share Options, Bonds or Bonds with Share Option, or the making of false statements or records with respect to materials used for explanations regarding the business of the relevant Stock Company and other matters for the purpose of such solicitation;
　(b) The making of false statements or records with respect to important matters to be specified or recorded in Financial Statements and business reports as well as the supplementary schedules thereof and Temporary Financial Statements;
　(c) The false registration; and
　(d) The false public notice (including the measures provided for in Article 440(3));
(ii) Accounting advisors: The making of false statements or records with respect to important matters to be specified or recorded in Financial Statements as well as supplementary schedules thereof, Temporary Financial Statements and accounting advisors' reports;
(iii) Auditors and Audit Committee Members: The making of false statements or records with respect to important matters to be specified or recorded in audit reports;
(iv) Accounting Auditor: The making of false statements or records with respect to important matters to be specified or recorded in accounting audit reports;

(Joint and Several Liabilities of Officers, Etc.)
Article 430 In cases where Officers, Etc. are liable for damages arising in the Stock Company or a third party, if other Officers, Etc. are also liable, such persons shall be joint and several obligors.

Chapter V Accounting

Section 1 Accounting Principle

Article 431 The accounting for a Stock Company shall be subject to the business accounting practices generally accepted as fair and appropriate.

Section 2 Account Books

Subsection 1 Account Books

(Preparation and Retention of Account Books)
Article 432 (1) A Stock Company shall prepare accurate account books in a timely manner pursuant to the applicable Ordinance of the Ministry of Justice.
(2) A Stock Company shall retain its account books and important materials regarding its business for ten years from the time of the closing of the account books.

(Request to Inspect Account Books)
Article 433 (1) Shareholders having not less than three hundredths (3/100) (or, in cases where lesser proportion is prescribed in the articles of incorporation, such proportion) of the votes of all shareholders (excluding shareholders who may not exercise their votes on all matters which may be resolved at a shareholders meeting) or shareholders having not less than three hundredths (3/100) (or, in cases where lesser proportion is prescribed in the articles of incorporation, such proportion) of the Issued Shares (excluding Treasury Shares) may make the following requests at any time during the business hours of the Stock Company. In such cases, the reasons for such requests shall be disclosed.
  (i) If the account books or materials relating thereto are prepared in writing, the requests for inspection or copying of such documents;
  (ii) If the account books or materials relating thereto are prepared by Electromagnetic Records, the requests for inspection or copying of anything that displays the data recorded in such Electromagnetic Records in a manner prescribed by the applicable Ordinance of the Ministry of Justice.
(2) If a request referred to in the preceding paragraph is made, the Stock Company may not refuse the request unless it is found that any of the following apply:
  (i) The shareholder who makes such request (hereinafter in this paragraph referred to as "Requestor") makes the request for a purpose other than for investigation related to the securing or exercising of his/her right;
  (ii) The Requestor makes the request for the purpose of interfering with the execution of the operations of such Stock Company and prejudicing the common benefit of the shareholders;
  (iii) The Requestor operates or engages in business which is, in substance, in competition with the operations of such Stock Company;
  (iv) The Requestor makes the request in order to report facts which he/she may learn by inspecting or copying the account books or materials relating thereto to third parties for profit; or
  (v) The Requestor is a person who has reported facts which he/she learned by inspecting or copying the account books or materials relating thereto to third parties for profit during the last two years.
(3) If it is necessary for the purpose of exercising the rights of a Member of the Parent Company of a Stock Company, he/she may, with the permission of the court, make the

request listed in each item of paragraph (1) with respect to the account books or materials relating thereto. In such cases, the reasons for such request shall be disclosed.
(4) The court may not grant the permission referred to in the preceding paragraph if there are any of the facts provided for in each item of paragraph (2) with respect to the Member of the Parent Company referred to in the preceding paragraph.

(Order to Submit Account Books)
Article 434 The court may, in response to a petition or ex officio, order the parties to a suit to submit account books, in whole or in part.

Subsection 2 Financial Statements, etc.

(Preparation and Retention of Financial Statements, etc.)
Article 435 (1) A Stock Company shall prepare a balance sheet as at the day of its formation pursuant to the applicable Ordinance of the Ministry of Justice.
(2) A Stock Company shall prepare Financial Statements (meaning balance sheets, profit and loss statements and other statements prescribed by the applicable Ordinance of the Ministry of Justice as necessary and appropriate in order to indicate the status of the assets and profits and losses of a Stock Company) and business reports for each business year and supplementary schedules thereof pursuant to the applicable Ordinance of the Ministry of Justice.
(3) Financial Statements and business reports and supplementary schedules thereof may be prepared by Electromagnetic Records.
(4) A Stock Company shall retain its Financial Statements and supplementary schedules thereof for ten years from the time of preparation of the Financial Statements.

(Audit of Financial Statements, etc.)
Article 436 (1) At Companies with Auditors (including Stock Companies the articles of incorporation of which provide that the scope of the audit shall be limited to an audit related to accounting, and excluding the Companies with Accounting Auditors), the Financial Statements and business reports and supplementary schedules thereof under paragraph (2) of the preceding article shall be audited by company auditors pursuant to the applicable Ordinance of the Ministry of Justice.
(2) At Companies with Accounting Auditors, the documents listed in the following items shall be audited by the persons listed in each such item pursuant to the applicable Ordinance of the Ministry of Justice:
　(i) The Financial Statements and supplementary schedules thereof under paragraph (2) of the preceding article: Auditors (or audit committees for Companies with Committees) and accounting auditors;
　(ii) The business reports and supplementary schedules thereof under paragraph (2) of the preceding article: Auditors (or audit committees for Companies with Committees);
(3) At Companies with Board of Directors, the Financial Statements and business report and supplementary schedules thereof under paragraph (2) of the preceding article (or, in cases where the provisions of paragraph (1) or the preceding paragraph apply, those which have been audited as provided for in paragraph (1) and the preceding paragraph) shall be approved by the board of directors.

(Provision of Financial Statements, etc. to Shareholders)
Article 437 At Companies with Board of Directors, directors shall, when giving notice to call annual shareholders meetings, provide to shareholders pursuant to the applicable

Ordinance of the Ministry of Justice the Financial Statements and business reports that have been approved as provided for in paragraph (3) of the preceding paragraph (in cases where the provisions of paragraph (1) or paragraph (2) of the same article apply, including audit reports and accounting audit reports).

(Provision of Financial Statements, etc. to Annual Shareholders Meetings)

Article 438 (1) At Stock Companies listed in the following items, directors shall submit or provide the Financial Statements and business reports provided for in each such item to annual shareholders meetings:
 (i) Companies with Auditors provided for in Article 436(1) (excluding Companies with Board of Directors): Financial Statements and business reports that have been audited pursuant to Article 436(1);
 (ii) Companies with Accounting Auditors (excluding Companies with Board of Directors): Financial Statements and business reports that have been audited pursuant to Article 436(2);
 (iii) Companies with Board of Directors: Financial Statements and business reports that have been approved pursuant to Article 436(3); and
 (iv) Stock Companies other than those listed in the preceding three items: Financial Statements and business reports under Article 435(2).
(2) Financial Statements that have been submitted or provided pursuant to the provisions of the preceding paragraph shall be approved by the annual shareholders meeting.
(3) Directors shall report the contents of the business reports submitted or provided pursuant to the provisions of paragraph (1) to the annual shareholders meeting.

(Special Provision on Companies with Accounting Auditors)

Article 439 With respect to Companies with Accounting Auditors, in cases where the Financial Statements that have been approved pursuant to Article 436(3) satisfy the requirements prescribed by the applicable Ordinance of the Ministry of Justice as statements that accurately indicate the status of the assets and profits and losses of a Stock Company in compliance with applicable laws and regulations and the articles of incorporation, the provisions of paragraph (2) of the preceding article shall not apply. In such cases, directors shall report the contents of such Financial Statements to the annual shareholders meeting.

(Public Notice of Financial Statements)

Article 440 (1) A Stock Company shall give public notice of its balance sheet (or, for a Large Company, its balance sheet and profit and loss statement) without delay after the conclusion of the annual shareholders meeting pursuant to the provisions of the applicable Ordinance of the Ministry of Justice.
(2) Notwithstanding the provisions of the preceding paragraph, with respect to a Stock Company for which the Method of Public Notice is a method listed in item (i) or (ii) of Article 939(1), it shall be sufficient to give public notice of a summary of the balance sheet provided for in the preceding paragraph.
(3) A Stock Company referred to in the preceding paragraph may, without delay after the conclusion of the annual shareholders meeting, pursuant to the provisions of the applicable Ordinance of the Ministry of Justice, take measures to make the information contained in the balance sheet provided for in paragraph (1) available to the general public continually by the Electromagnetic Method until the day on which five years have elapsed from the day of the conclusion of the annual shareholders meeting. In such cases, the provisions of the preceding two paragraphs shall not apply.
(4) The provisions of the preceding three paragraphs shall not apply to Stock Companies

Art.441～442　　　Ⅰ Companies Act, PART Ⅱ, Chap.Ⅴ, Sec.2

that shall submit their securities reports to the Prime Minister pursuant to the provisions of Article 24(1) of the Financial Instruments and Exchange Act.

(Temporary Financial Statements)
Article 441 (1) Stock Companies may prepare the following documents (hereinafter referred to as "Temporary Financial Statements") pursuant to the provisions of the applicable Ordinance of the Ministry of Justice in order to grasp the financial status of such Stock Company as at a certain day (hereinafter in this paragraph referred to as "Temporary Account Closing Day") included in the business year immediately following the Most Recent Business Year:
(i) A balance sheet as at the Temporary Closing Date; and
(ii) A profit and loss statement for the period from the first day of the business year that includes the Temporary Account Closing Day to the Temporary Account Closing Day.
(2) At Companies with Auditors or Companies with Accounting Auditors provided for in Article 436(1), Temporary Financial Statements shall be audited by company auditors or accounting auditors (or, for Companies with Committees, by the audit committee and accounting auditors) pursuant to the provisions of the applicable Ordinance of the Ministry of Justice.
(3) At Companies with Board of Directors, Temporary Financial Statements (or, in cases where the provisions of the preceding paragraph apply, the statements audited under that paragraph) shall be approved by the board of directors.
(4) At Stock Companies listed in the following items, the Temporary Financial Statements provided for in each such item shall be approved by a shareholders meeting; provided, however, that this shall not apply in cases where the Temporary Financial Statements satisfy the requirements prescribed by the applicable Ordinance of the Ministry of Justice as statements that accurately indicate the status of the assets and profits and losses of a Stock Company in compliance with applicable laws and regulations and the articles of incorporation:
(i) Companies with Auditors or Companies with Accounting Auditors provided for in Article 436(1) (in each case excluding Company with Board of Directors): Temporary Financial Statements that have been audited pursuant to paragraph (2);
(ii) Companies with Board of Directors: Temporary Financial Statements that have been approved pursuant to the preceding paragraph; and
(iii) Stock Companies other than those listed in the preceding two items: Temporary Financial Statements under paragraph (1).

(Keeping and Inspection of Financial Statements, Etc.)
Article 442 (1) Stock Companies shall keep the things listed in the each of the following items (hereinafter in this article referred to as "Financial Statements, Etc.") at its head office for the period provided for in each such item:
(i) Financial Statements and business reports for each business year and supplementary schedules thereof (in cases where the provisions of Article 436(1) or (2) apply, including audit reports or accounting audit reports): Five years from the day one week (or, for Companies with Board of Directors, two weeks) prior to the day of the annual shareholders meeting (or, in cases provided for in Article 319(1), from the day when the proposal under that paragraph is made); and
(ii) Temporary Financial Statements (in cases where the provisions of paragraph (2) of the preceding article apply, including audit reports and accounting audit reports): Five years from the day when the Temporary Financial Statements are prepared.
(2) A Stock Company shall keep copies of the Financial Statements, Etc. listed in the fol-

lowing items at its branch offices for the period provided for in each such item; provided, however, that this shall not apply to the cases where the Financial Statements, Etc. are prepared by Electromagnetic Records and the Stock Company adopts the measures prescribed by the applicable Ordinance of the Ministry of Justice as measures enabling its branch offices to respond to the request listed in item (iii) and item (iv) of the following paragraph:
  (i) Financial Statements, Etc. listed in item (i) of the preceding paragraph: Three years from the day one week (or, for a Company with Board of Directors, two weeks) prior to the day of the annual shareholders meeting (or, in cases provided for in Article 319(1), from the day when the proposal under that paragraph is made); and
  (ii) Financial Statements, Etc. listed in item (ii) of the preceding paragraph: Three years from the day when the Temporary Financial Statements under that item are prepared.
(3) The shareholders and creditors may submit the following requests at any time during the business hours of the Stock Company; provided, however, that the fees designated by such Stock Company are required to be paid in order to submit the requests listed in item (ii) or (iv):
  (i) If the Financial Statements, Etc. are prepared in writing, requests for inspection of such documents or copies of such documents;
  (ii) Requests for a transcript or extract of the document referred to in the preceding item;
  (iii) If the Financial Statements, Etc. are prepared by Electromagnetic Records, requests for inspection of anything that displays the data recorded in such Electromagnetic Records in a manner prescribed by the applicable Ordinance of the Ministry of Justice; or
  (iv) Request that the matters recorded in the Electromagnetic Records referred to in the preceding item be provided by Electromagnetic Methods prescribed by the Stock Company, or requests for documents that state such matters.
(4) If it is necessary for the purpose of exercising the rights of a Member of the Parent Company of a Stock Company, he/she may, with the permission of the court, make the requests listed in each item of the preceding paragraph with respect to the Financial Statements, Etc. of such Stock Company; provided, however, that, in order to make the requests listed in item (ii) or (iv) of that paragraph, the fees designated by such Stock Company are required to be paid.

(Order to Submit Financial Statements, etc.)
Article 443 The court may, in response to a petition or ex officio, order the parties to a suit to submit Financial Statements and supplementary schedules thereof, in whole or in part.

Subsection 3 Consolidated Financial Statements

Article 444 (1) A Company with Accounting Auditors may, pursuant to the provisions of the applicable Ordinance of the Ministry of Justice, prepare Consolidated Financial Statements (meaning statements prescribed by the applicable Ordinance of the Ministry of Justice as necessary and appropriate in order to indicate the status of the assets and profits and losses of a business group comprised of such Company with Accounting Auditors and its Subsidiaries. The same shall apply hereinafter) for each business year.
(2) Consolidated Financial Statements may be prepared by Electromagnetic Records.
(3) An entity that is a Large Company as at the last day of a business year and shall sub-

mit a securities report to the Prime Minister pursuant to the provisions of Article 24(1) of the Securities and Exchange Act shall prepare Consolidated Financial Statements for such business year.
(4) Consolidated Financial Statements shall be audited by the company auditors (or, for a Company with Committees, by the audit committee) and accounting auditors pursuant to the provisions of the applicable Ordinance of the Ministry of Justice.
(5) In cases where a Company with Accounting Auditors is a Company with Board of Directors, the consolidated financial statements audited as provided for in the preceding paragraph shall be approved by the board of directors.
(6) In cases where a Company with Accounting Auditors is a Company with Board of Directors, directors shall, when giving notice to call annual shareholders meetings, provide to shareholders, pursuant to the provisions of the applicable Ordinance of the Ministry of Justice, Consolidated Financial Statements that have been approved as provided for in the preceding paragraph.
(7) At Companies with Accounting Auditors listed in the following items, directors shall submit or provide the Consolidated Financial Statements provided for in each such item to the annual shareholders meetings. In such cases, the contents of the Consolidated Financial Statements provided for in each such item and the results of the audit under paragraph (4) shall be reported to the annual shareholders meeting:
  (i) A Company with Accounting Auditors which is a Company with Board of Directors: Consolidated Financial Statements approved as provided for in paragraph (5);
  (ii) A Company with Accounting Auditors other that that listed in the preceding item: Consolidated Financial Statements audited as provided for in paragraph (4).

Section 3 Amounts of Stated Capital, etc.

Subsection 1 General Provisions

(Amounts of Stated Capital and Amounts of Reserves)
Article 445 (1) Unless it is otherwise provided for in this Act, the amount of stated capital of a Stock Company shall be the amount of properties contributed by persons who become shareholders at the incorporation or share issue.
(2) The amount not exceeding half of the amount of the contribution under the preceding paragraph may not be recorded as stated capital.
(3) The amount not recorded as stated capital pursuant to the provisions of the preceding paragraph shall be recorded as capital reserves.
(4) If a Stock Company pays dividends of surplus, it shall record an amount equivalent to one tenth of the amount of the deduction from surplus as a result of the payment of such dividends of surplus as capital reserves or retained earnings reserves (hereinafter referred to as "Reserves"), pursuant to the provisions of the applicable Ordinance of the Ministry of Justice.
(5) The amount to be recorded as stated capital or Reserves at mergers, Absorption-type Company Splits, Incorporation-type Company Splits, Share Exchanges or Share Transfers shall be prescribed by the applicable Ordinance of the Ministry of Justice.

(Amounts of Surplus)
Article 446 The amount of the surplus of a Stock Company shall be the amount obtained by subtracting the sum of the amounts listed in item (v) through (vii) from the sum of the amounts listed in item (i) through (iv):
  (i) The amount obtained by subtracting the sum of the amounts listed in Sub-item (c) through (e) from the sum of the amounts listed in Sub-item (a) through (b) as at the

last day of the Most Recent Business Year:
(a) The amount of assets;
(b) The sum of the book value of Treasury Shares;
(c) The amount of debt;
(d) The sum of the amount of stated capital and Reserves;
(e) The sum of the amounts, other than those listed in Sub-item (c) and (d), recorded in each account title prescribed by the applicable Ordinance of the Ministry of Justice.
(ii) In cases where Treasury Shares are disposed of after the last day of the Most Recent Business Year, the amount obtained by subtracting the book value of such Treasury Shares from the amount of the value received in exchange for such Treasury Shares;
(iii) In cases where the amount of stated capital is reduced after the last day of the Most Recent Business Year, the amount of such reduction (excluding the amount under item (ii), paragraph (1) of the following article);
(iv) In cases where the Reserves are reduced after the last day of the Most Recent Business Year, the amount of such reduction (excluding the amount under item (ii) of Article 448(1));
(v) In cases where Treasury Shares are canceled pursuant to the provisions of Article 178(1) after the last day of the Most Recent Business Year, the amount of the book value of such Treasury Shares;
(vi) The sum of the following amounts in cases where dividend of surplus is paid after the last day of the Most Recent Business Year:
(a) The total book value of the Dividend Property referred to in item (i) of Article 454(1) (excluding the book value of such Dividend Property assigned to shareholders who exercised the Rights to Demand Distribution of Monies provided for in item (i), paragraph (4) of that paragraph);
(b) The sum of the amounts of the money delivered to shareholders who exercised the Rights to Demand Distribution of Monies provided for in item (i) of Article 454(4); and
(c) The sum of the amounts of money paid to shareholders of Disqualified Shares provided for in Article 456.
(vii) The sum of the amounts, other than those listed in the preceding two items, recorded in each account title prescribed by the applicable Ordinance of the Ministry of Justice.

Subsection 2 Reductions, etc. in Amount of Stated Capital

Division 1 Reductions, etc. in Amount of Stated Capital

(Reductions in Amount of Stated Capital)
Article 447 (1) A Stock Company may reduce the amount of its stated capital. In such cases, the following matters shall be decided by resolution of a shareholders meeting:
(i) The amount by which the stated capital is reduced;
(ii) If all or part of the amount by which the stated capital is reduced is to be appropriated to Reserves, a statement to such effect and the amount to be appropriated to Reserves;
(iii) The day on which the reduction in the amount of stated capital takes effect.
(2) The amount under item (i) of the preceding paragraph may not exceed the amount of stated capital as at the day under item (iii) of that paragraph.

Art.448〜449　　　Ⅰ Companies Act, PART II, Chap.V, Sec.3

(3) In cases where a Stock Company reduces the amount of stated capital concurrently with a share issue, if the amount of stated capital after the day on which such reduction in the amount of stated capital takes effect is not less than the amount of stated capital before such day, for the purpose of the application of the provisions of paragraph (1), "resolution of a shareholders meeting" in that paragraph shall be read as "decision of the directors (or, for a Company with Board of Directors, resolution of the board of directors)."

(Reductions in Amount of Reserves)
Article 448 (1) A Stock Company may reduce the amount of its Reserves. In such cases, the following matters shall be decided by resolution of a shareholders meeting:
(i) The amount by which the Reserves are reduced;
(ii) If all or part of the amount by which the Reserves are reduced is to be appropriated to the stated capital, a statement to such effect and the amount to be appropriated to the stated capital;
(iii) The day on which the reduction in the amount of the Reserves takes effect.
(2) The amount under item (i) of the preceding paragraph may not exceed the amount of the Reserves as at the day under item (iii) of that paragraph.
(3) In cases where a Stock Company reduces the amount of the Reserves concurrently with a share issue, if the amount of the Reserves after the day on which such reduction in the amount of the Reserves takes effect is not less than the amount of the Reserves before such day, for the purpose of the application of the provisions of paragraph (1), "resolution of a shareholders meeting" in that paragraph shall be read as "decision of the directors (or, for a Company with Board of Directors, resolution of the board of directors)."

(Objection of Creditors)
Article 449 (1) In cases where a Stock Company reduces the amount of its stated capital or Reserves (hereinafter in this article referred to as "Stated Capitals, Etc.") (excluding cases where the whole of the amount by which the Reserves are reduced is appropriated to the stated capital), creditors of such Stock Company may state their objections to the reduction in the amount of the Capitals, Etc. ; provided, however, that this shall not apply to cases where only the amount of the Reserves is reduced and all of the following apply:
(i) That matters listed in each item of paragraph (1) of the preceding article are decided at the annual shareholders meeting; and
(ii) That the amount referred to in item (i), paragraph (1) of the preceding article does not exceed the amount calculated in the manner prescribed by the applicable Ordinance of the Ministry of Justice as the amount of the deficit as at the day of the annual shareholders meeting referred to in the preceding item (or, in cases provided for in the first sentence of Article 439, the day when the approval under Article 436(3) is given).
(2) In cases where creditors of a Stock Company may state their objections pursuant to the provisions of the preceding paragraph, such Stock Company shall give public notice of the matters listed below in the official gazette and shall give notices inviting objections separately to each known creditor, if any; provided, however, that the period under item (iii) may not be less than one month:
(i) The details of such reduction in the amount of Capitals, Etc. ;
(ii) The matters prescribed by the applicable Ordinance of the Ministry of Justice as the matters regarding the Financial Statements of such Stock Company; and
(iii) A statement to the effect that creditors may state their objections within a certain

period of time.
(3) Notwithstanding the provisions of the preceding paragraph, if a Stock Company gives public notice under that paragraph by Method of Public Notice listed in item (ii) or (iii) of Article 939(1) in accordance with the provisions of the articles of incorporation pursuant to the provisions of that paragraph in addition to the official gazette, the Stock Company is not required to give separate notices under the provisions of the preceding paragraph.
(4) In cases where creditors do not raise any objections within the period under item (iii) of paragraph (2), such creditors shall be deemed to have approved such reduction in the amount of the Capitals, Etc.
(5) In cases where creditors raise objections within the period under item (iii) of paragraph (2), the Stock Company shall make payment or provide equivalent security to such creditors, or entrust equivalent property to a Trust Company, Etc. (meaning Trust Companies and financial institutions that engage in trust business (referring to financial institutions approved under Article 1(1) of the Act on the Concurrent Undertaking of Trust Business by Financial Institutions (Act No. 43 of 1943)). The same shall apply hereinafter) for the purpose of making such creditors receive the payment; provided, however, that this shall not apply if there is no risk of harm to such creditors by such reduction in the amount of Capitals, Etc.
(6) The actions listed in the following items shall take effect on the day provided for in each such item; provided, however, that this shall not apply if the procedures pursuant to the provisions of paragraph (2) through the preceding paragraph have not been completed:
  (i) Reduction in the amount of stated capital: The day under item (iii) of Article 447(1); and
  (ii) Reduction in the amount of the Reserves: The day under item (iii), paragraph (1) of the preceding article.
(7) A Stock Company may change the day provided for in each item of the preceding paragraph at any time before such day.

Division 2 Increases in Amount of Stated Capital, etc.

(Increases in Amount of Stated Capital)
Article 450 (1) A Stock Company may increase the amount of its stated capital by reducing the amount of its surplus. In such cases, the following matters shall be decided:
  (i) The amount by which the surplus is reduced;
  (ii) The day on which the increase in the amount of stated capital takes effect;
(2) Decisions on the matters listed in each of the items of the preceding paragraph shall be made by resolution of a shareholders meeting.
(3) The amount under item (i) of paragraph (1) may not exceed the amount of surplus as at the day under item (ii) of that paragraph.

(Increase in Amount of Reserves)
Article 451 (1) A Stock Company may increase the amount of its Reserves by reducing the amount of its surplus. In such cases, the following matters shall be decided:
  (i) The amount by which the surplus is reduced;
  (ii) The day on which the increase in the amount of the Reserves takes effect;
(2) Decisions on the matters listed in the items of the preceding paragraph shall be made by resolution of a shareholders meeting.
(3) The amount under item (i) of paragraph (1) may not exceed the amount of surplus as at the day under item (ii) of that paragraph.

Division 3 Other Appropriation of Surplus

Article 452 A Stock Company may, by resolution of a shareholders meeting, make the appropriation of its surplus, including, but not limited to, the disposition of loss and funding of voluntary reserves (excluding those provided for in the preceding Division and those which dispose of the property of the Stock Company, including, but not limited to, dividends of surplus). In such cases, the Stock Company shall decide on the amount of such appropriation of surplus and other matters prescribed by the applicable Ordinance of the Ministry of Justice.

Section 4 Dividends of Surplus

(Dividends of Surplus to Shareholders)
Article 453 A Stock Company may distribute dividends of surplus to its shareholders (excluding such Stock Company).

(Decisions on Matters regarding Dividends of Surplus)
Article 454 (1) Whenever a Stock Company intends to distribute dividends of surplus pursuant to the provisions of the preceding article, it shall decide the following matters by resolution of a shareholders meeting:
(i) The kind and total book value of the Dividend Property (excluding the Shares, Etc. of such Stock Company);
(ii) The matters regarding the assignment of the Dividend Property to shareholders;
(iii) The day on which such distribution of dividend of surplus takes effect.
(2) In the cases provided for in the preceding paragraph, if a Stock Company issues two or more classes of shares with different features as to dividends of surplus, the Stock Company may decide the following matters as the matters listed in item (ii) of that paragraph in accordance with the features of such classes of shares:
(i) If there is any arrangement that no Dividend Property is assigned to the shareholders of a certain class of shares, a statement to such effect and such class of shares;
(ii) In addition to the matters listed in the preceding item, if there is any arrangement that each class of shares shall be treated differently with respect to assignment of Dividend Property, a statement to such effect and the details of such different treatment.
(3) The decisions on the matters listed in item (ii) of paragraph (1) shall provide that the Dividend Property is assigned in proportion to the number of the shares (or, in cases where there are decisions on the matters listed in item (ii) of the preceding paragraph, the number of the shares of each class) held by the shareholders (excluding the relevant Stock Company and shareholders of the class of shares referred to in item (i) of the preceding paragraph).
(4) If the Dividend Property consists of property other than monies, the Stock Company may decide the following matters by resolution of a shareholders meeting; provided, however, that the last day of the period referred to in item (i) shall be the day that is or precedes the day referred to in item (iii) of paragraph (1):
(i) If Right to Demand Distribution of Monies (meaning the right to demand that the Stock Company deliver monies in lieu of such Dividend Property. The same shall apply hereinafter in this Chapter) is granted to shareholders, a statement to such effect and the period during which the Right to Demand Distribution of Monies may be exercised; and
(ii) If there is any arrangement that no Dividend Property shall be assigned to share-

holders who hold less than a certain number of shares, a statement to such effect and that number.
(5) A Company with Board of Directors may provided in the articles of incorporation that it may distribute a dividend of surplus only once during a business year by resolution of the board of directors (limited to that where the Dividend Property consists of monies. It is referred to as "Interim Dividend" hereinafter in this Chapter). For the purpose of the application of the provisions of paragraph (1) to the Interim Dividend in such cases, "shareholders meeting" in that paragraph shall be read as "board of directors."

(Exercise of Rights to Demand Distribution of Monies)
Article 455 (1) In the cases provided for in item (i) of paragraph (4) of the preceding article, the Stock Company shall notify shareholders of the matters listed in that item no later than 20 days prior to the last day of the period referred to in that item.
(2) A Stock Company shall pay to shareholders who have exercised the Right to Demand Distribution of Monies, in lieu of the Dividend Property assigned to such shareholders, the monies equivalent to the value of such Dividend Property. In such cases, the amounts provided for in each of the following items for the case categories listed in each such item shall be the value of such Dividend Property:
 (i) In cases where such Dividend Property consists of property with a market price: The amount calculated in the manner prescribed by the applicable Ordinance of the Ministry of Justice as the market price of such Dividend Property;
 (ii) In cases other than those listed in the preceding item: The amount determined by the court in response to a petition by the Stock Company.

(Treatment where Minimum Number of Shares is Prescribed)
Article 456 In cases where the number referred to in item (ii) of Article 454(4) (hereinafter in this article referred to as "Minimum Number of Shares") is prescribed, a Stock Company shall pay to shareholders having shares in a number less than the Minimum Number of Shares (hereinafter in this article referred to as "Disqualified Shares") monies equivalent to the amount obtained by multiplying the amount prescribed as the value of the Dividend Property assigned to shareholders having shares in the Minimum Number of Shares in accordance with the applicable provisions of the second sentence of paragraph (2) of the preceding article by the ratio of the number of such Disqualified Shares to the Minimum Number of Shares.

(Methods of Delivery of Dividend Property)
Article 457 (1) The Dividend Property (including monies paid pursuant to the provisions of Article 455(2) and monies paid pursuant to the provisions of the preceding article. The same shall apply hereinafter in this article) shall be delivered at the address of the shareholders (including Registered Pledgees of Shares. The same shall apply hereinafter in this article) specified or recorded in the shareholder registry, or at other place of which the shareholders have notified the Stock Company (in paragraph (3) referred to as "Address, Etc.").
(2) The cost of the delivery of Dividend Property pursuant to the provisions of the preceding paragraph shall be borne by the Stock Company; provided, however, that, if such cost increases due to reasons attributable to shareholders, such increased amount shall be borne by the shareholders.
(3) The provisions of the preceding two paragraphs shall not apply to the delivery of Dividend Property to shareholders who do not have Address, Etc. in Japan.

(Exclusion from Application)
Article 458 The provisions of Article 453 through the preceding article shall not apply in cases where the amount of the net assets of the Stock Company is less than 3,000,000 yen.

Section 5 Special Provision on Organs that Decide Dividends of Surplus

(Provisions of Articles of Incorporation that Board of Directors Determines Dividends of Surplus)
Article 459 (1) A Company with Accounting Auditors (excluding Companies for which the last day of the term of office of directors falls on a day after the day of the conclusion of the annual shareholders meeting for the last business year ending within one year from the time of their election, and Companies with Auditors that are not Companies with Board of Company Auditors) may provide in the articles of incorporation that the board of directors (for matters listed in item (ii), limited to the board of directors under Article 436(3)) may decide the following matters:
 (i) The matters listed in each item of Article 156(1) in cases other than cases where a decision pursuant to the provisions of Article 160(1) is made;
 (ii) The matters listed in item (i) and (iii) of Article 448(1) in cases that fall under item (ii) of Article 449(1);
 (iii) The matters listed in the second sentence of Article 452; and
 (iv) The maters listed in each item of Article 454(1) and each item of paragraph (4) of that article; provided, however, that the cases where the Dividend Property consists of property other than monies and no Right to Demand Distribution of Monies are granted to shareholders are excluded.
(2) The provisions of the articles of incorporation pursuant to the provisions of the preceding paragraph shall be effective only in cases where the Financial Statements for the Most Recent Business Year satisfy the requirements prescribed by the applicable Ordinance of the Ministry of Justice as accurately indicating the status of the assets and profits and losses of a Stock Company in compliance with applicable laws and regulations and the articles of incorporation.
(3) For the purpose of the application of the provisions of item (i) of Article 449(1) in cases where there is a provision in the articles of incorporation pursuant to the provisions of paragraph (1), "annual shareholders meeting" in that item shall be read as "annual shareholders meeting or board of directors under Article 436(3)."

(Restriction on Rights of Shareholders)
Article 460 (1) In cases where there is a provision in the articles of incorporation pursuant to the provisions of paragraph (1) of the preceding article, a Stock Company may provide in the articles of incorporation that the matters listed in each item of that paragraph shall not be decided by resolution of a shareholders meeting.
(2) The provisions of the articles of incorporation pursuant to the provisions of the preceding paragraph shall be effective only in cases where the Financial Statements for the Most Recent Business Year satisfy the requirements prescribed by the applicable Ordinance of the Ministry of Justice as accurately indicating the status of the assets and profits and losses of a Stock Company in compliance with applicable laws and regulations and the articles of incorporation.

Section 6 Liability related to Dividends of Surplus

(Restriction on Dividends)

Article 461 (1) The total book value of the Monies, Etc. (excluding shares of the relevant Stock Company. The same shall apply hereinafter in this Section) delivered to shareholders as a result of the following acts may not exceed the Distributable Amount as at the day on which such act takes effect:
  (i) The purchase of shares of such Stock Company in response to a demand under item (i)(c) or (2)(c) of Article 138;
  (ii) The acquisition of shares of such Stock Company based on a decision pursuant to the provisions of Article 156(1) (limited to acquisitions of shares by such Stock Company in the cases provided for in Article 163 or Article 165(1));
  (iii) The acquisition of shares of such Stock Company based on a decision pursuant to the provisions of Article 157(1);
  (iv) The acquisition of shares of such Stock Company pursuant to the provisions of Article 173(1);
  (v) The purchase of shares of such Stock Company based on a request pursuant to the provisions of Article 176(1);
  (vi) The purchase of shares of such Stock Company pursuant to the provisions of Article 197(3);
  (vii) The purchase of shares of such Stock Company pursuant to the provisions of Article 234(4); or
  (viii) Dividend of surplus.
(2) The "Distributable Amount" provided for in the preceding paragraph shall mean the amount obtained by subtracting the sum of the amounts listed in item (iii) through (vi) from the sum listed in item (i) and item (ii) (the same shall apply hereinafter in this Section):
  (i) The amount of surplus;
  (ii) The amounts listed below in cases where the approval under Article 441(4) (or the approval under paragraph (3) of that article in the cases provided for in the proviso to that paragraph) is obtained for the Temporary Financial Statements:
    (a) The sum of the amounts recorded in each account title prescribed by the applicable Ordinance of the Ministry of Justice as the amount of profits during the period under item (ii) of Article 441(1); and
    (b) In cases where Treasury Shares are disposed of during the during the period under item (ii) of Article 441(1), the amount of the value received in exchange for such Treasury Shares.
  (iii) The book value of Treasury Shares;
  (iv) In cases where Treasury Shares are disposed of after the last day of the Most Recent Business Year, the amount of the value received in exchange for such Treasury Shares;
  (v) In the cases provided for in item (ii), the sum of the amounts recorded in each account title prescribed by the applicable Ordinance of the Ministry of Justice as the amount of losses during the period under item (ii) of Article 441(1); and
  (vi) Other than those listed in the preceding three items, the sum of the amounts recorded in each account title prescribed by the applicable Ordinance of the Ministry of Justice.

(Liability related to Dividends of Surplus)

Article 462 (1) In cases where a Stock Company carries out an act listed in any item of paragraph (1) of the preceding article in violation of the provisions of that paragraph, persons who received Monies, Etc. as a result of such act, as well as Executing Persons (meaning Executive Directors (or, for a Company with Committees, executive of-

Art.462　　1 Companies Act, PART II, Chap.V, Sec.6

ficers. The same shall apply hereinafter in this paragraph) and other persons prescribed by the applicable Ordinance of the Ministry of Justice as persons involved, in performing their duties, in the execution of the operations by such Executive Directors. The same shall apply hereinafter in this Section) who performed duties regarding such act and, in cases where such act is any of the acts listed below, the persons provided for in each such item shall be jointly and severally liable to such Stock Company for payment of monies in an amount equivalent to the book value of the Monies, Etc. received by the persons who received such Monies, Etc. :

(i) The acts listed in item (ii), paragraph (1) of the preceding article: The following persons:

　(a) In cases where a resolution relating to a decision pursuant to the provisions of Article 156(1) is passed by a shareholders meeting (limited to cases where the total amount of the Monies, Etc. under item (ii) of that paragraph decided by such resolution exceeds the Distributable Amount as at the day of such resolution), the Proposing Directors at Shareholders Meeting (meaning persons prescribed by the applicable Ordinance of the Ministry of Justice as directors who submitted proposals to such shareholders meeting. The same shall apply hereinafter in this paragraph) relating to such shareholders meeting;

　(b) In cases where a resolution relating to a decision pursuant to the provisions of Article 156(1) is passed by a board of directors meeting (limited to cases where the total amount of the Monies, Etc. under item (ii) of that paragraph decided by such resolution exceeds the Distributable Amount as at the day of such resolution), the Proposing Directors at Board of Directors Meeting (meaning persons prescribed by the applicable Ordinance of the Ministry of Justice as directors who submitted proposals to such board of directors meeting (or, for a Company with Committees, directors or executive officers). The same shall apply hereinafter in this paragraph) relating to such board of directors meeting;

(ii) The acts listed in item (iii), paragraph (1) of the preceding article: The following persons:

　(a) In cases where a resolution relating to a decision pursuant to the provisions of Article 157(1) is passed by a shareholders meeting (limited to cases where the total amount under item (iii) of that paragraph decided by such resolution exceeds the Distributable Amount as at the day of such resolution), the Proposing Directors at Shareholders Meeting relating to such shareholders meeting;

　(b) In cases where a resolution relating to a decision pursuant to the provisions of Article 157(1) is passed by a board of directors meeting (limited to cases where the total amount under item (iii) of that paragraph decided by such resolution exceeds the Distributable Amount as at the day of such resolution), the Proposing Directors at Board of Directors Meeting relating to such board of directors meeting;

(iii) The acts listed in item (iv), paragraph (1) of the preceding article: the Proposing Directors at Shareholders Meeting relating to the shareholders meeting under Article 171(1) (limited to such shareholders meeting in cases where the total amount of Consideration for Acquisition under item (i) of that paragraph decided by such resolution exceeds the Distributable Amount as at the day of such resolution);

(iv) The acts listed in item (vi), paragraph (1) of the preceding article: The following persons:

　(a) In cases where a resolution relating to a decision pursuant to the provisions of the second sentence of Article 197(3) is passed by a shareholders meeting (limited to cases where the total amount under item (ii) of that paragraph decided by such resolution exceeds the Distributable Amount as at the day of such reso-

lution), the Proposing Directors at Shareholders Meeting relating to such shareholders meeting;
   (b) In cases where a resolution relating to a decision pursuant to the provisions of the second sentence of Article 197(3) is passed by a board of directors meeting (limited to cases where the total amount under item (ii) of that paragraph decided by such resolution exceeds the Distributable Amount as at the day of such resolution), the Proposing Directors at Board of Directors Meeting relating to such board of directors meeting;
(v) The acts listed in item (vii), paragraph (1) of the preceding article: The following persons:
   (a) In cases where a resolution relating to a decision pursuant to the provisions of the second sentence of Article 234(4) is passed by a shareholders meeting (limited to cases where the total amount under item (ii) of that paragraph decided by such resolution exceeds the Distributable Amount as at the day of such resolution), the Proposing Directors at Shareholders Meeting relating to such shareholders meeting;
   (b) In cases where a resolution relating to a decision pursuant to the provisions of the second sentence of Article 234(4) is passed by a board of directors meeting (limited to cases where the total amount under item (ii) of that paragraph decided by such resolution exceeds the Distributable Amount as at the day of such resolution), the Proposing Directors at Board of Directors Meeting relating to such board of directors meeting;
(vi) The acts listed in item (viii), paragraph (1) of the preceding article: The following persons:
   (a) In cases where a resolution relating to a decision pursuant to the provisions of Article 454(1) is passed by a shareholders meeting (limited to cases where the book value of the Dividend Property decided by such resolution exceeds the Distributable Amount as at the day of such resolution), the Proposing Directors at Shareholders Meeting relating to such shareholders meeting;
   (b) In cases where a resolution relating to a decision pursuant to the provisions of Article 454(1) is passed by a board of directors meeting (limited to cases where the book value of the Dividend Property decided by such resolution exceeds the Distributable Amount as at the day of such resolution), the Proposing Directors at Board of Directors Meeting relating to such board of directors meeting.
(2) Notwithstanding the provisions of the preceding paragraph, Executing Persons and the persons provided for in each item of that paragraph shall not be liable under such paragraph in cases where such persons prove that they did not fail to exercise due care with respect to the performance of their duties.
(3) An exemption from the obligations assumed by Executing Persons and the persons provided for in each item of paragraph (1) pursuant to the provisions of that paragraph may not be given; provided, however, that this shall not apply in cases where all shareholders consent to the exemption from such obligations to the extent of the Distributable Amount as at the time of the act listed in each item of paragraph (1) of the preceding article.

(Restrictions on Remedy Over against Shareholders)
Article 463 (1) In the cases provided for in paragraph (1) of the preceding article, shareholders without knowledge with respect to the fact that the total book value of the Monies, Etc. delivered to shareholders as a result of the acts listed in each item of Article 461(1) exceeds the Distributable Amount as at the day when such act takes effect

shall not be obligated to respond to the remedy over that the Executing Persons who made the payment of monies under paragraph (1) of the preceding article or the persons provided for in each item of that paragraph have against such shareholders, with respect to the Monies, Etc. which such shareholders received.

(2) In the cases provided for in paragraph (1) of the preceding article, creditors of a Stock Company may have the shareholders who are liable pursuant to the provisions of that paragraph pay monies equivalent to the book value of the Monies, Etc. they have received (or, in cases where such value exceeds the amount that the Stock Company owes to such creditors, such amount).

(Liability where Shares are Acquired in Response to Demand for Purchase)
Article 464 (1) In cases where a Stock Company acquires shares in response to the demands pursuant to the provisions of Article 116(1), if the amount of the monies paid to the shareholders who made such demands exceeds the Distributable Amount as at the day when such payment is made, the Executing Persons who performed duties in relation to the acquisition of such shares shall be jointly and severally liable to the Stock Company for payment of such excess amount; provided, however, that this shall not apply in cases where such persons prove that they did not fail to exercise due care with respect to the performance of their duties.

(2) Exemption from the obligations under the preceding paragraph may not be given without the consent of all shareholders.

(Liability in Cases of Deficit)
Article 465 (1) In cases where a Stock Company carries out the acts listed in any of the following items, if the sum of the amounts listed in item (iii), (iv) and (vi) of Article 461(2) when approval under Article 438(2) (or, in cases provided for in the first sentence of Article 439, approval under Article 436(3)) is obtained with respect to the Financial Statements for the business year that contains the day on which such act is carried out (or, if the business year immediately preceding such business year is not the Most Recent Business Year, the business year immediately preceding such business year) exceeds the amount listed in item (i) of that paragraph, the Executing Persons who performed duties in relation to the acts listed in each such item shall be jointly and severally liable to such Stock Company for payment of such excess amount (or, in cases where such excess amount exceeds the amount listed in each such item, the amount listed in each such item). ; provided, however, that this shall not apply in cases where such Executing Persons prove that they did not fail to exercise due care with respect to the performance of their duties:

(i) The purchase of shares of such Stock Company in response to a demand under item (i)(c) or (ii)(c) of Article 138: The total book value of the Monies, Etc. delivered to shareholders as a result of the purchase of such shares;

(ii) The acquisition of shares of such Stock Company based on a decision pursuant to the provisions of Article 156(1) (limited to acquisitions of shares by such Stock Company in cases provided for in Article 163 or Article 165(1)): The total book value of the Monies, Etc. delivered to shareholders as a result of the acquisition of such shares;

(iii) The acquisition of shares of such Stock Company based on a decision pursuant to the provisions of Article 157(1): The total book value of the Monies, Etc. delivered to shareholders as a result of the acquisition of such shares;

(iv) The acquisition of shares of such Stock Company pursuant to the provisions of Article 167(1): The total book value of the Monies, Etc. delivered to shareholders as a result of the acquisition of such shares;

(v) The acquisition of shares of such Stock Company pursuant to the provisions of Article 170(1): The total book value of the Monies, Etc. delivered to shareholders as a result of the acquisition of such shares;
(vi) The acquisition of shares of such Stock Company pursuant to the provisions of Article 173(1): The total book value of the Monies, Etc. delivered to shareholders as a result of the acquisition of such shares;
(vii) The purchase of shares of such Stock Company based on a demand pursuant to the provisions of Article 176(1): The total book value of the Monies, Etc. delivered to shareholders as a result of the purchase of such shares;
(viii) The purchase of shares of such Stock Company pursuant to the provisions of Article 197(3): The total book value of the Monies, Etc. delivered to shareholders as a result of the purchase of such shares;
(ix) The purchase of shares of such Stock Company pursuant to the provisions of Article 234(4): The total book value of the Monies, Etc. delivered to the persons provided for in each item of paragraph (1) of that article as a result of the purchase of such shares;
  (a) Article 234(4): The persons listed in each item of Article 234(1)
  (b) Article 234(4) applied mutatis mutandis pursuant to Article 235(2): The shareholders
(x) Distribution of dividends of surplus (excluding those listed in Sub-item (a) through (c) below): The sum of the amounts listed in Sub-item (a) through (c) in item (vi) of Article 446 with respect to such distribution of dividend of surplus;
  (a) Distribution of dividends of surplus in cases where the matters listed in each item of Article 454(1) are decided at an annual shareholders meeting (or, in cases provided for in the first sentence of Article 439, an annual shareholders meeting or a board of directors meeting under Article 436(3));
  (b) Distribution of dividends of surplus in cases where the matters listed in each item of Article 454(1) are decided at a shareholders meeting for the purpose of deciding the matters listed in each item of Article 447(1) (limited to the cases where the amount under item (i) of that paragraph (or, if there are monies to be paid to shareholders of Disqualified Shares pursuant to the provisions of Article 456, the aggregate amount thereof) does not exceed the amount under item (i) of Article 447(1) and there is no provision with respect to the matters listed in item (ii) of that paragraph);
  (c) Distribution of dividends of surplus in cases where the matters listed in each item of Article 454(1) are decided at a shareholders meeting for the purpose of deciding the matters listed in each item of Article 448(1) (limited to the cases where the amount under item (i) of that paragraph (or, if there are monies to be paid to shareholders of Disqualified Shares pursuant to the provisions of Article 456, the aggregate amount thereof) does not exceed the amount under item (i) of Article 448(1) and there is no provision with respect to the matters listed in item (ii) of that paragraph);
(2) Exemption from the obligations under the preceding paragraph may not be given without the consent of all shareholders.

Chapter VI Changes in Articles of Incorporation

Article 466 A Stock Company may change the articles of incorporation by the resolution of a shareholders meeting after its incorporation.

Chapter VII Assignment of Business

(Approvals of Assignment of Business)
Article 467 (1) In cases where a Stock Company intends to commit any of the following acts, it must obtain the approval of the contracts relating to such acts by the resolution of the shareholders meeting no later than the day immediately preceding the day when such act takes effect (hereinafter in this Chapter referred to as "Effective Day"):
(i) The assignment of the entire business;
(ii) The assignment of significant part of the business (excluding the assignment in which the book value of the assets to be assigned to others by such assignment does not exceed one fifth (1/5) (or, in cases where any proportion less than that is provided for in the articles of incorporation, such proportion) of the amount calculated by the method prescribed by the applicable Ordinance of the Ministry of Justice as the total assets of such Stock Company);
(iii) The acceptance of assignment of entire business of another Company (hereinafter in this article and the next article including juridical persons including Foreign Corporations and other juridical persons);
(iv) The entering into, changing or termination of contracts for the lease of the entire business, contracts for the entrustment of the management of the entire business, contracts for sharing with others the entirety of profit and loss of business and other contracts equivalent to the above;
(v) The acquisition at any time within two years after the incorporation of such Stock Company (hereinafter in this item limited to the Stock Company that was incorporated by the method listed in each item of paragraph (1) of Article 25) of assets of such Stock Company that existed prior to such incorporation and continues to be used for its business; provided, however, that the cases where the proportion of the amount listed in Sub-item (a) to the amount listed in Sub-item (b) does not exceed one fifth (1/5) (or, in cases where any lower proportion is provided for in the articles of incorporation, such proportion) shall be excluded:
(a) The total book value of the assets that are issued as the consideration for such assets;
(b) The amount calculated by the method prescribed by the applicable Ordinance of the Ministry of Justice as the net assets of such Stock Company.
(2) In cases where the act listed in item (iii) of the preceding paragraph is committed, if the assets assigned to the Stock Company which commits such act include shares of such Stock Company, directors must explain the matters regarding such shares at a shareholders meeting under that paragraph.

(Cases where Approval of Assignment of Business is not Required)
Article 468 (1) The provisions of the preceding article shall not apply in cases where other party to the contracts relating to the acts listed in items (i) through (iv) of paragraph (1) of that article (hereinafter in this Chapter referred to as "Assignment of Business") is the Special Controlling Company (hereinafter, in cases where nine tenths (9/10) (or, in cases where any proportion higher than that is provided for in the articles of incorporation, such proportion) or more of the voting rights of all shareholders of a Stock Company are held by other Company, and by Stock Companies all of the issued shares in which are held by such other Company and other juridical persons prescribed by the applicable Ordinance of the Ministry of Justice as entities equivalent to the above, referring to such other Company) of the Stock Company that effects such Assignment of Business.
(2) The provisions of the preceding article shall not apply if, in cases where the act listed

in item (iii) of paragraph (1) of that article is carried out, the proportion of the amount listed in item (i) to the amount listed in item (ii) does not exceed one fifth (1/5) (or, in cases where any lower proportion is provided for in the articles of incorporation, such proportion):
  (i) The total book value of the assets that are issued as the consideration for all business of such other Company;
  (ii) The amount calculated by the method prescribed by the applicable Ordinance of the Ministry of Justice as the amount of the net assets of such Stock Company.
(3) In the cases provided for in the preceding paragraph, if shareholders that hold the shares (limited to those that entitle the shareholders to exercise voting rights at a shareholders meeting under paragraph (1) of the preceding article) in the number prescribed by the applicable Ordinance of the Ministry of Justice notify the Stock Company that carries out the act listed in item (iii), paragraph (1) of the preceding article to the effect that such shareholders dissent from such act, within two weeks from the day of the notice under the provisions of paragraph (3) of the following article or the public notice under paragraph (4) of that article, such Stock Company must obtain the approval of the contract relating to such act by resolution of a shareholders meeting no later than the day immediately preceding the Effective Day.

(Dissenting Shareholders Demand for Purchase of Shares)
Article 469 (1) In cases where Assignment of Business is to be effected, dissenting shareholders may demand that the Stock Company effecting the Assignment of Business purchase the shares held by such shareholders at a fair price; provided, however, that this shall not apply if, in cases where the act listed in item (i), paragraph (1) of Article 467 is carried out, the resolution of a shareholders' meeting under item (iii) of Article 471 is passed simultaneously with the resolution of a shareholders' meeting under that paragraph.
(2) The dissenting shareholders provided for in the preceding paragraph means the shareholders provided for in each of the following items in the cases listed in the same items:
  (i) In cases where a resolution of a shareholders meeting (including a Class Meeting) is required to effect the Assignment of Business: The following shareholders:
    (a) Shareholders who gave notice to such Stock Company to the effect that they dissented from such Assignment of Business prior to such shareholders meeting and who dissented from such Assignment of Business at such shareholders meeting (limited to those who can exercise voting rights at such shareholders meetings);
    (b) Shareholders who cannot exercise voting rights at such shareholders meetings.
  (ii) In cases other than those prescribed in the preceding item: All shareholders.
(3) A Stock Company that intends to effect the Assignment of Business must give notice to its shareholders to the effect that it intends to effect the Assignment of Business (or, in the cases provided for in paragraph (2) of Article 467, to the effect that the Stock Company will carry out the act listed in item (iii), paragraph (1) of that article and of the matters regarding shares under paragraph (2) of that article), no later than twenty days prior to the Effective Day.
(4) A public notice may be substituted for the notice pursuant to the provisions of the preceding paragraph in the following cases:
  (i) In cases where the Stock Company which effects the Assignment of Business is a Public Company;
  (ii) In cases where the Stock Company which effects the Assignment of Business receives the approval of the contract relating to the Assignment of Business by the

resolution of a shareholders meeting under paragraph (1) of Article 467.
(5) Demands under the provisions of paragraph (1) (hereinafter in this Chapter referred to as "Share Purchase Demand") must be made after the day twenty days prior to the effective day but no later than the day immediately preceding the Effective Day, by disclosing the number of shares relating to such Share Purchase Demand (or, for a Company with Classes of Shares, the classes of the shares and the number of shares for each class).
(6) Shareholders who made the Share Purchase Demand may withdraw their Share Purchase Demand only in cases where such shareholders obtain the approval of the Stock Company that effects the Assignment of Business.
(7) If the Assignment of Business is suspended, the Share Purchase Demand shall become ineffective.

(Decision on Share Price)
Article 470 (1) In cases where a Share Purchase Demand is made, if an agreement deciding the price of shares is reached between the shareholder and the Stock Company that effects the Assignment of Business, such Stock Company must make the payment within sixty days from the Effective Day.
(2) If no agreement deciding the price of shares is reached within thirty days from the Effective Day, the shareholders or the Stock Company under the preceding paragraph may petition the court for a determination of the price within thirty days after the expiration of that period.
(3) Notwithstanding the provisions of paragraph (6) of the preceding article, in the cases provided for in the preceding paragraph, if the petition under that paragraph is not made within sixty days after the Effective Day, the shareholders may withdraw their Share Purchase Demand at any time after the expiration of such period.
(4) Stock Companies under paragraph (1) must also pay interest on the price determined by the court which shall be calculated at the rate of 6% per annum from and including the day of the expiration of the period referred to in that paragraph.
(5) The purchase relating to the Share Purchase Demand shall become effective as at payment of the price for such shares.
(6) If a Company issuing share certificates has received a Share Purchase Demand with respect to shares for which share certificates are issued, the Company must pay the price of the shares relating to such Share Purchase Demand in exchange for the share certificates.

Chapter VIII Dissolution

(Grounds for Dissolution)
Article 471 A Stock Company shall dissolve on the grounds listed below:
(i) The expiration of the duration provided for in the articles of incorporation;
(ii) The grounds for dissolution provided for in the articles of incorporation;
(iii) A resolution of a shareholders meeting;
(iv) A merger (limited to cases where such Stock Company is liquidated as a result of the merger);
(v) A ruling to commence bankruptcy procedures; or
(vi) Judgment that orders the dissolution pursuant to the provisions of paragraph (1) of Article 824 or paragraph (1) of Article 833.

(Deemed Dissolution of Dormant Companies)
Article 472 (1) In cases where the Minister of Justice gives a public notice to a dormant

Company (hereinafter in this article referring to a Stock Company for which twelve years have elapsed from the day when a registration regarding such Stock Company was last effected) in Official Gazette to the effect that the dormant Company should submit a notice to the effect that it has not abolished its business pursuant to the applicable Ordinance of the Ministry of Justice to the registry that has jurisdiction over the area where dormant Company's head office is located within two months, if that dormant Company fails to submit that notice, the dormant Company shall be deemed to have dissolved upon expiration of that two month period; provided, however, that this shall not apply if any registration regarding such dormant Company is effected during such period.

(2) If the public notice has been given under the provisions of the preceding paragraph, the registry must issue a notice to such effect to dormant Companies.

(Continuation of Companies)

Article 473 In cases where a Stock Company dissolves on the grounds listed in item (i) through item (iii) of Article 471 (including the cases where Stock Companies are deemed to have dissolved under the provisions of paragraph (1) of the preceding article), the Stock Company may continue in existence by resolution of a shareholders meeting until the completion of the liquidation under the provisions of the following Chapter (in cases where the Stock Company is deemed to have dissolved pursuant to the provisions of that paragraph, limited to the completion within three years from the time of the deemed dissolution).

(Restrictions on Mergers and Other Transactions of Dissolved Stock Companies)

Article 474 In cases where a Stock Company has dissolved, such Stock Company may not carry out the following acts:

(i) Mergers (limited to the cases where such Stock Company survives the merger);

(ii) Succession by Absorption-type Company Split to some or all of the rights and obligations held by another Company with respect to such Company's business.

Chapter IX Liquidation

Section 1 General Provisions

Subsection 1 Commencement of Liquidation

(Causes of Commencement of Liquidation)

Article 475 A Stock Company must go into liquidation in the cases listed below, subject to the provisions of this Chapter:

(i) In cases where the Stock Company has dissolved (excluding the cases where Stock Companies have dissolved on the grounds listed in item (iv) of Article 471 and cases where it dissolved as a result of the ruling to commence bankruptcy procedures and such bankruptcy procedures have not ended);

(ii) In cases where a judgment allowing a claim seeking invalidation of the incorporation of a Stock Company has become final and binding; or

(iii) In cases where a judgment allowing a claim seeking invalidation of the Share Transfer has become final and binding.

(Capacity of Liquidating Stock Companies)

Article 476 Stock Companies that go into liquidation under the provisions of the preceding article (hereinafter referred to as "Liquidating Stock Companies") shall be deemed to remain in existence until the liquidation is completed, to the extent of the purpose of the liquidation.

Subsection 2 Structures for Liquidating Stock Companies

Division 1 Establishment of Structures Other Than Shareholders Meetings

Article 477 (1) A Liquidating Stock Company must have one or more liquidators.
(2) A Liquidating Stock Company may have a board of liquidators, a Company Auditor, a board of Company Auditors or a board of Company Auditors as prescribed by the articles of incorporation.
(3) A Liquidating Stock Company the articles of incorporation of which provide that a board of Company Auditors shall be established must establish a board of liquidators.
(4) A Liquidating Stock Company that was a Public Company or a Large Company when it fell under a case listed in each item of Article 475 must establish a board of Company Auditors.
(5) At a Liquidating Stock Company that was a Company with Committees when it fell under a case listed in each item of Article 475 and to which the provisions of the preceding paragraph apply, an Audit Committee Member shall be the Company Auditor.
(6) The provisions of Section 2 of Chapter IV shall not apply to Liquidating Stock Companies.

Division 2 Assumption of Office and Dismissal of Liquidators and Resignation of Company Auditors

(Assumption of Office of Liquidators)
Article 478 (1) The following persons shall become liquidators of a Liquidating Stock Company:
  (i) A director (excluding cases where persons listed in the following item or in item (iii) exist);
  (ii) A person prescribed by the articles of incorporation;
  (iii) A person who is appointed by resolution of a shareholders meeting.
(2) In the absence of a liquidator under the provisions of the preceding paragraph, the court shall appoint the liquidator in response to the petition by the interested parties.
(3) Notwithstanding the provisions of the preceding two paragraphs, with respect to a Liquidating Stock Company that has dissolved on the grounds listed in item (vi) of Article 471, the court shall appoint the liquidator in response to a petition by the interested parties or the Minister of Justice or ex officio.
(4) Notwithstanding the provisions of paragraphs (1) and (2), with respect to a Liquidating Stock Company that has fallen under the cases listed in item (ii) or item (iii) of Article 475, the court shall appoint the liquidator in response to a petition by the interested parties.
(5) For the purpose of the application of the provisions of item (i) of paragraph (1) and paragraph (3) of Article 335 to a Liquidating Stock Company that was a Company with Committees when it fell under a case listed in each item of Article 475, the word "director" in paragraph (1) shall be read as "director who is not an Audit Committee Member" and the words "Outside Company Auditors" in paragraph (3) of Article 335 shall be read as "who have at no time in the past served as executive directors (excluding Outside Company Auditors), Accounting Advisors (or, in cases where the Ac-

counting Advisors are juridical persons, partners in the same who are in charge of its advisory affairs) or executive officers or managers or other employees of such Company with Board of Company Auditors or any of its Subsidiaries."
(6) The provisions of Article 330 and paragraph (1) of Article 331 shall apply mutatis mutandis to liquidators, and the provisions of paragraph (4) of that article shall apply mutatis mutandis to Companies with Board of Liquidators (hereinafter referring to Liquidating Stock Companies that establish a board of liquidators or Liquidating Stock Companies that must establish a board of liquidators under the provisions of this Act), respectively. In such cases, the word "directors" shall be as "liquidators."

(Dismissal of Liquidators)
Article 479 (1) Liquidators (excluding those appointed by the court pursuant to the provisions of paragraphs (2) through (4) of the preceding article) may be dismissed at any time by resolution of a shareholders meeting.
(2) If there are substantial grounds, the court may dismiss a liquidator in response to the petition by the following shareholders:
(i) Shareholders (excluding the following shareholders) who have held, for the consecutive period of past six months or more (or, in cases where a shorter period is provided for in the articles of incorporation, such period), not less than three hundredths (3/100) of the voting rights of all shareholders (excluding the following shareholders) (or, in cases where a lower proportion is provided for in the articles of incorporation, such proportion):
(a) Shareholders who cannot exercise voting rights on proposals to the effect that liquidators be dismissed; or
(b) Shareholders that are the liquidators related to such petition.
(ii) Shareholders (excluding the following shareholders) who have held, for the consecutive period of six months or more (or, in cases where a shorter period is provided for in the articles of incorporation, such period), not less than three hundredths (3/100) of the issued shares (excluding the shares held by the following shareholders) (or, in cases where a lower proportion is provided for in the articles of incorporation, such proportion):
(a) A shareholder who is the relevant Liquidating Stock Company; or
(b) Shareholders that are the liquidators relating to such petition.
(3) For the purpose of the application of the provisions of the items of the preceding paragraph to Liquidating Stock Companies that are not Public Companies, the words "have held, for the consecutive period of past six months or more (or, in cases where a shorter period is provided for in the articles of incorporation, such period)," in those provisions shall be read as "hold."
(4) The provisions of paragraphs (1) through (3) of Article 346 shall apply mutatis mutandis to liquidators.

(Resignation of Company Auditors)
Article 480 (1) In cases where Liquidating Stock Companies effect any of the following changes in the articles of incorporation, Company Auditors of such Liquidating Stock Companies shall resign when such change in the articles of incorporation takes effect:
(i) Any change in the articles of incorporation to abolish the provisions of the articles of incorporation to the effect that Company Auditors shall be established; or
(ii) Any change in the articles of incorporation to abolish the provisions of the articles of incorporation to the effect that the scope of the audit by the Company Auditors shall be limited to accounting audit.
(2) The provisions of 336 shall not apply to Company Auditors of Liquidating Stock Com-

panies.

Division 3 Liquidators' Duties

(Liquidators' Duties)
Article 481 Liquidators shall perform the following duties:
(i) The conclusion of current business;
(ii) The collection of debts and the performance obligations; and
(iii) The delivery of the residual assets.

(Execution of Business)
Article 482 (1) A liquidator shall execute the business of the Liquidating Stock Companies (hereinafter in this article excluding Companies with Board of Liquidators).
(2) In cases where there are two or more liquidators, the business of the Liquidating Stock Company shall be determined by a majority of the liquidators, unless otherwise provided for in the articles of incorporation.
(3) In the cases provided for in the preceding paragraph, the liquidators cannot delegate the determination on the following matters to individual liquidators:
(i) The appointment or dismissal of a manager;
(ii) The establishment, relocation and abolition of branch offices;
(iii) The matters listed in each item of paragraph (1) of Article 298 (including the case where such items are applied mutatis mutandis under Article 325);
(iv) The development of the system necessary to ensure that the execution of the duties by the liquidators comply with the laws and regulations and the articles of incorporation, and other systems prescribed by the applicable Ordinance of the Ministry of Justice as the systems that are necessary to ensure the proper operations of a Liquidating Stock Company; or
(4) The provisions of Articles 353 through 357, Article 360 and Article 361 shall apply mutatis mutandis to liquidators (as to the provisions of these articles, excluding liquidators appointed by the court under the provisions of paragraphs (2) through (4) of Article 478). In such cases, the words "paragraph (4) of Article 349" in Article 353 shall be read as "paragraph (4) of Article 349 applied mutatis mutandis under paragraph (6) of Article 483," the words "representative director" in Article 354 shall be read as "representative liquidator (referring to the representative liquidator provided for in paragraph (1) of Article 483)," and the words "a Company with Company Auditors or a Companies with Committees" in paragraph (3) of Article 360 shall be read as "a Company with Company Auditors."

(Representatives of Liquidating Stock Companies)
Article 483 (1) A liquidator or liquidators shall represent the Liquidating Stock Company; provided, however, that this shall not apply in cases where representative liquidators (hereinafter referring to liquidators who represent the Liquidating Stock Company) or other persons who represent the Liquidating Stock Company are otherwise prescribed.
(2) In cases where there are two or more liquidators referred to in the main clause of the preceding paragraph, each liquidator shall represent the Liquidating Stock Company individually.
(3) A Liquidating Stock Company (excluding a Company with Board of Liquidators) may appoint representative liquidators from among the liquidators under the articles of incorporation, or through the appointment by the liquidators (hereinafter in this paragraph excluding those that are appointed by the court pursuant to the provisions of

paragraphs (2) through (4) of Article 478) from among themselves pursuant to the applicable provisions of the articles of incorporation, or by the resolution of the shareholders meeting.
(4) In cases where directors become liquidators pursuant to the provisions of item (i), paragraph (1) of Article 478, if representative directors are already specified, such representative directors shall act as the representative liquidators.
(5) In cases where the court appoints liquidators pursuant to the provisions of paragraphs (2) through (4) of Article 478, it may prescribe representative liquidators from among those liquidators.
(6) The provisions of paragraphs (4) and (5) of Article 349 and Article 351 shall apply mutatis mutandis to representative liquidators, and the provisions of Article 352 shall apply mutatis mutandis to persons who are appointed by the provisional disposition order provided for in Article 56 of the Civil Provisional Remedies Act to perform the duties of liquidators or representative liquidators on behalf of them, respectively.

(Commencement of Bankruptcy Procedures for Liquidating Stock Companies)
Article 484 (1) In cases where it has become clear that the assets of a Liquidating Stock Company are not sufficient to fully discharge its debts, liquidators must immediately file a petition for the commencement of bankruptcy procedures.
(2) In cases where a Liquidating Stock Company has become subject to the ruling for the commencement of bankruptcy procedures, if liquidators have transferred their administration to the trustee in bankruptcy, they shall have completed their duties.
(3) In the cases provided for in the preceding paragraph, if the Liquidating Stock Company has already made payments to creditors or distributions to shareholders, the trustee in bankruptcy may retrieve the same.

(Remuneration for Liquidators Appointed by the Court)
Article 485 In cases where the court has appointed the liquidator under the provisions of paragraphs (2) through (4) of Article 478, the court may prescribe the amount of the remuneration that the Liquidating Stock Companies shall pay to such liquidator.

(Liquidators' Liability to Liquidating Stock Companies for Damages)
Article 486 (1) If a liquidator fails to discharge his/her duties, he/she shall be liable to compensate such Liquidating Stock Companies for any losses arising as a result.
(2) If a liquidator engages in any transaction listed in item (i), paragraph (1) of Article 356 applied mutatis mutandis under paragraph (4) of Article 482 in violation of the provisions of the paragraph (1) of Article 356, the amount of the profit obtained by the liquidator or a third party as a result of such transaction shall be presumed to be amount of the losses under the preceding paragraph.
(3) If a Liquidating Stock Company suffers loss as a result of the transaction provided for in item (ii) or (iii) of paragraph (1) of Article 356 applied mutatis mutandis under paragraph (4) of Article 482, the following liquidators shall be presumed to have failed to discharge their duties:
  (i) Liquidators provided for in paragraph (1) of Article 356 applied mutatis mutandis under paragraph (4) of Article 482;
  (ii) Liquidators who decided that the Liquidating Stock Companies would undertake such transaction; or
  (iii) Liquidators who agreed to the board of liquidators' resolution to approve such transaction.
(4) The provisions of Article 424 and paragraph (1) of Article 428 shall apply mutatis mutandis to liquidators' liability under paragraph (1). In such cases, the words "item (ii),

paragraph (1) of Article 356 (including the cases where such item is applied mutatis mutandis under paragraph (2) of Article 419)" in paragraph (1) of Article 428 shall be read as "item (ii), paragraph (1) of Article 356 applied mutatis mutandis under paragraph (4) of Article 482."

(Liquidators' Liability to Third Parties)
Article 487 (1) If liquidators had knowledge or were grossly negligent in discharging their duties, such liquidators shall be liable to compensate losses arising in a third party as a result thereof.
(2) The provisions of the preceding paragraph shall also apply if the liquidators commit the acts provided for in the following items; provided, however, that this shall not apply if such liquidators have proven that they did not fail to exercise due care with respect to the performance of their duties:
(i) The giving of false notice with respect to important matters, the notice of which must be given when soliciting persons to subscribe for shares, Share Options, Bonds or Bonds with Share Options or making of false statement or records with respect to materials used for the explanation regarding the business of such Liquidating Stock Company and other matters for the purpose of such solicitation;
(ii) The making of false statements or records with respect to important matters to be stated or recorded in the property inventory of provided for in paragraph (1) of Article 492 as well as the balance sheet and administrative report in paragraph (1) of Article 494 and annexed detailed statements thereof.
(iii) Registering a false registration; or
(iv) Giving false public notice.

(Joint and Several Liabilities of and Company Auditors)
Article 488 (1) In cases where liquidators or Company Auditors are liable to compensate losses arising in the Liquidating Stock Companies or a third party, if other liquidators or Company Auditors are also liable, such persons shall be joint and several obligors.
(2) In the cases provided for in the preceding paragraph, the provisions of Article 430 shall not apply.

Division 4 Board of Liquidators

(Authority of Board of Liquidators)
Article 489 (1) Board of liquidators shall be organized by all liquidators.
(2) Board of liquidators shall perform the following duties:
(i) Deciding the execution of the business of the Company with Board of Liquidators;
(ii) Supervising the execution of the duties by liquidators; and
(iii) Appointing and removing representative liquidators.
(3) Board of liquidators must appoint representative liquidators from among the liquidators; provided, however, that this shall not apply if there are other representative liquidators.
(4) Board of liquidators may remove representative liquidators it appointed and persons who became representative liquidators pursuant to the provisions of paragraph (4) of Article 483.
(5) If the court has prescribed representative liquidators under the provisions of paragraph (5) of Article 483, the board of liquidators cannot select or remove the representative liquidators.
(6) Board of liquidators cannot delegate the decisions on the execution of important business such as the following matters to the liquidators:

(i) The disposal and acceptance of assignment of important assets;
(ii) The taking out of substantial loans;
(iii) The appointment and dismissal of managers or other important employees;
(iv) The establishment, change or closure of branch offices and other important structures;
(v) The matters listed in item (i) of Article 676 and other matters prescribed by the applicable Ordinance of the Ministry of Justice as important matters regarding the solicitation of persons to subscribe for Bonds;
(vi) The development of systems necessary to ensure that the execution of the duties by the liquidators comply with the laws and regulations and the articles of incorporation, and other systems prescribed by the applicable Ordinance of the Ministry of Justice as the systems necessary to ensure the proper business of a Liquidating Stock Company; or
(7) The following liquidators shall execute the business of the Company with Board of Liquidators:
(i) A representative liquidator; and
(ii) A liquidator other than a representative liquidator who is appointed by the resolution of the board of liquidators as the liquidator who is to execute the business of a Company with Board of Liquidators.
(8) The provisions of paragraph (2) of Article 363, Article 364 and Article 365 shall apply mutatis mutandis to a Company with Board of Liquidators. In such cases, in paragraph (2) of Article 363, the words "each item of the preceding paragraph" shall be read as "each item of paragraph (7) of Article 489," the words "director" shall be read as "liquidator," and the words "board of directors" shall be read as "board of liquidators"; in Article 364, the words "Article 353" shall be read as "Article 353 applied mutatis mutandis under paragraph (4) of Article 482," and the words "board of directors" shall be read as "board of liquidators"; in paragraph (1) of Article 365, words "Article 356" shall be read as "Article 356 applied mutatis mutandis under paragraph (4) of Article 482," and the words "board of directors" shall be read as "board of liquidators"; and in paragraph (2) of Article 365, the words "each item of paragraph (1) of Article 365" shall be read as "each item of paragraph (1) of Article 365 applied mutatis mutandis under paragraph (4) of Article 482," the word "director" shall be read as "liquidator," and the words "to the board of directors" shall be read as "to the board of liquidators."

(Operations of Board of Liquidators)
Article 490 (1) A board of liquidators meeting shall be convened by each liquidator; provided, however, that, if the liquidator who convenes the board of liquidators meeting is prescribed by the articles of incorporation or the board of liquidators, such liquidator shall convene the meeting.
(2) In the case provided for in the proviso to the preceding paragraph, liquidators other than the liquidator prescribed under the provision of the proviso to that paragraph (hereinafter in this paragraph referred to as "Convener") may request the Convener that the Convener convene the board of liquidators meeting by indicating to the Convener the matters that are the purpose of the board of liquidators meeting.
(3) In cases where the Convener fails to send, within five days from the day of the request under the provisions of preceding paragraph, any notice of convocation of a board of liquidators meeting that specifies a day falling within two weeks from the day of that request as the day of the board of liquidators meeting, the liquidators who made that request may convene the board of liquidators meeting.
(4) The provisions of Article 367 and Article 368 shall apply mutatis mutandis to the convocation of the board of liquidators meeting at a Company with Board of Liquidators.

In such cases, in paragraph (1) of Article 367, the words "a Company with Company Auditors and Companies with Committees" shall be read as "a Companies with Committees," and the words "any director" shall be read as "any liquidator"; in paragraph (2) of Article 367, the words "to the directors (or to the Convener in the case provided for in the proviso to paragraph (1) of the preceding article)" shall be read as "to the liquidators (or to the Convener provided for in paragraph (2) of Article 490 in the case provided for in the proviso to paragraph (1) of that article)"; in paragraph (3) and paragraph (4) of Article 367, the words "paragraph (3) of the preceding article" shall be read as "paragraph (3) of Article 490"; in paragraph (1) of Article 368, the words "each director" shall be read as "each liquidator"; and in paragraph (2) of Article 368, the words "directors (or" shall be read as "liquidators (or," and "directors and" shall be read as "liquidators and."

(5) The provisions of Article 369 through Article 371 shall apply mutatis mutandis to Companies with Board of Liquidators. In such cases, in paragraph (1) of Article 369, the words "of the directors" shall be read as "of the liquidators"; in paragraph (2) of Article 369, the words "Directors" shall be read as "Liquidators"; in paragraph (3) of Article 369, the words "directors and" shall be read as "liquidators and"; in paragraph (5) of Article 369, the words "Directors who" shall be read as "Liquidators who"; in Article 370, the words "directors submit" shall be read as "liquidators submit" and the words "directors (" shall be read as "liquidators ("; in paragraph (3) of Article 371, the words "a Company with Company Auditors or Companies with Committees" shall be read as "a Company with Company Auditors"; and in paragraph (4) of Article 371, the words "officers or executive officers" shall be read as "liquidators and Company Auditors."

(6) The provisions of paragraph (1) and paragraph (2) of Article 372 shall apply mutatis mutandis to the report to board of liquidators at a Company with Board of Liquidators. In such cases, in paragraph (1) of Article 372, the words "the directors, Accounting Advisors, Company Auditors or Accounting Auditor(s)" shall be read as "liquidators or Company Auditors," "directors (" shall be read as "liquidators (" and "directors and" shall be read as "liquidators and"; and in paragraph (2) of Article 372, the words "paragraph (2) of Article 363" shall be read as "paragraph (2) of Article 363 applied mutatis mutandis under paragraph (8) of Article 489";

Division 5 Application of Provisions regarding Directors and Others

Article 491 With respect to Liquidating Stock Companies, out of the provisions in Chapter II (excluding Article 155), Chapter III, Section 1 of Chapter IV, paragraph (2) of Article 335, paragraph (1) and paragraph (2) of Article 343, paragraph (3) of Article 345 applied mutatis mutandis under paragraph (4) of that article, Article 359, Section 7 and Section 8 of Chapter IV and Chapter VII, provisions regarding directors, representative directors, board of directors or Company with Board of Directors shall apply to liquidators, representative liquidators, board of liquidators or Company with Board of Liquidators as provisions regarding liquidators, representative liquidators, board of liquidators or Company with Board of Liquidators, respectively.

Subsection 3 Property Inventories

(Preparation of Inventory of Property)
Article 492 (1) Liquidators (or, for Companies with Board of Liquidators, liquidators listed in each item of paragraph (7) of Article 489) must investigate the current status of

the assets of the Liquidating Stock Companies and prepare, pursuant to the provisions of the applicable Ordinance of the Ministry of Justice, the inventory of property and the balance sheet as of the day when the Liquidating Stock Companies has fallen under any of the cases listed in each item of Article 475 (hereinafter in this article and following article referred to as "Inventory of Property"), without delay after assuming the office.
(2) At a Company with Board of Liquidators, the Inventory of Property must be approved by the board of liquidators.
(3) Liquidators must submit or provide the Inventory of Property (or, in cases where the provisions of the preceding paragraph apply, the Inventory of Property approved under that paragraph) to the shareholders meeting and obtain the approval of the same.
(4) A Liquidating Stock Company must retain its Inventory of Property from the time of the preparation of such Inventory of Property until the registration completion of the liquidation at the location of its head office.

(Order to Submit Inventory of Property)
Article 493 The court may, in response to a petition or ex officio, order the parties to a lawsuit to submit the Inventory of Property, in whole or in part.

(Preparation and Retention of Balance Sheet)
Article 494 (1) A Liquidating Stock Company must prepare balance sheet and administrative report regarding each liquidation year (referring to each one year period starting on the day immediately following the day when the Liquidating Stock Companies has fallen under any of the cases listed in each item of Article 475 or the anniversary of that day of the subsequent years (or, in cases where such anniversary does not exist, the immediately preceding day)) as well as annexed detailed statements thereof as prescribed by the applicable Ordinance of the Ministry of Justice.
(2) Balance sheet and administration reports as well as annexed detailed statements thereof under the preceding paragraph may be prepared by using electromagnetic records.
(3) A Liquidating Stock Company must retain its balance sheet under paragraph (1) and annexed detailed statements thereof from the time of the preparation of such balance sheet until the registration of the completion of the liquidation at the location of its head office.

(Audit of Balance Sheet)
Article 495 (1) Companies with Company Auditors (including Liquidating Stock Companies which have the provisions of the articles of incorporation to the effect that the scope of the audit shall be limited to accounting audit) must have the balance sheet and administration reports as well as annexed detailed statements thereof under paragraph (1) of the preceding article audited by Company Auditors pursuant to the applicable Ordinance of the Ministry of Justice.
(2) Companies with Board of Liquidators must have the balance sheet and administration report as well as annexed detailed statements thereof under paragraph (1) of the preceding article (or, in cases where the provisions of the preceding paragraph apply, those which have been audited as provided for in the preceding paragraph) approved by the board of liquidators.

(Keeping and Inspection of Balance Sheet)
Article 496 (1) Liquidating Stock Companies must keep the balance sheet and administration report regarding each liquidating administrative year provided for in paragraph

(1) of Article 494 as well as annexed detailed statements thereof (including, in cases where the provisions of paragraph (1) of the preceding article apply, audit reports, hereinafter in this article referred to as "Balance Sheet") at its head office from the day preceding the day of the annual shareholders meeting (or, in the cases provided for in paragraph (1) of Article 319, from the day when the proposal under that paragraph is submitted) until the registration of the completion of the liquidation at the location of its head office.

(2) Shareholders and creditors may make the following request at any time during the business hours of the Liquidating Stock Company; provided, however, that the expense prescribed by such Liquidating Stock Company must be paid in order to make the request listed in item (ii) or item (iv):
 (i) If the Balance Sheet is prepared in writing, request to inspect such documents;
 (ii) A request for the issuance of a transcript or extract of the documents referred to in the preceding item;
 (iii) If the Balance Sheet are prepared by using electromagnetic records, requests to inspect anything that indicates the matters recorded in such electromagnetic records in a manner prescribed by the applicable Ordinance of the Ministry of Justice; or
 (iv) Requests that the matters recorded in the electromagnetic records referred to in the preceding item be provided by an electromagnetic method prescribed by the Liquidating Stock Company, or requests for the issuance of any document that states such matters.

(3) If it is necessary for a partner of the Parent Company of a Liquidating Stock Company to exercise such partner's rights, such partner may, with the permission of the court, make the requests listed in each item of the preceding paragraph with respect to the Balance Sheet of such Liquidating Stock Company; provided, however, that the expenses prescribed by such Liquidating Stock Company must be paid in order to make the requests listed in item (ii) or item (iv) of that paragraph.

(Provision of Balance Sheet to Annual Shareholders Meeting)
Article 497 (1) At Liquidating Stock Company listed in the following items, liquidators must submit or provide the Balance Sheet and administrative reports provided for in each such item to the annual shareholders meeting:
 (i) Companies with Company Auditors (excluding Companies with Board of Liquidators) provided for in paragraph (1) of Article 495: The Balance Sheets and administrative reports that have been audited under that paragraph;
 (ii) Companies with Board of Liquidators: The Balance Sheets and administration reports that have been approved pursuant to paragraph (2) of Article 495; and
 (iii) Liquidating Stock Companies other than those listed in the preceding two items: The Balance Sheets and administration reports under paragraph (1) of Article 494.
(2) Balance Sheets that have been submitted or provided pursuant to the provisions of the preceding paragraph must be approved by the annual shareholders meeting.
(3) Directors must report the contents of the administrative reports submitted or provided pursuant to the provisions of paragraph (1) to the annual shareholders meeting.

(Order to Submit Balance Sheet)
Article 498 The court may, in response to a petition or ex officio, order the parties to a lawsuit to submit Balance Sheets under paragraph (1) of Article 194 and annexed detailed statements thereof, in whole or in part.

Subsection 4 Performance of Obligations

(Public Notices to Creditors)
Article 499 (1) A Liquidating Stock Company must, without delay after having fallen under each item of Article 475, give public notice in the Official Gazette to the creditors of such Liquidating Stock Companies to the effect that creditors should state their claims during a certain period of time and must give such notices separately to each known creditor, if any; provided, however, that such period cannot be less than two months.
(2) The pubic notice pursuant to the provisions of the preceding paragraph must contain a notation to the effect that such creditors shall be excluded from the liquidation unless they state their claims during such period of time.

(Restrictions on Performance of Obligations)
Article 500 (1) A Liquidating Stock Company cannot perform its obligations during the period of time under paragraph (1) of the preceding article. In such cases, a Liquidating Stock Company cannot be exempted from the liability arising from its failure to perform.
(2) Notwithstanding the provisions of the preceding paragraph, even during the period of time under paragraph (1) of the preceding article, a Liquidating Stock Company may, with the permission of the court, perform its obligations relating to claims of minor claims, claims secured by security interests over the assets of the Liquidating Stock Company, or other claims unlikely to be detrimental to other creditors even if performed. In such cases, if there are two or more liquidators, the petition for such permission must be made with the consent of all of the liquidators.

(Performance of Obligations relating to Conditional Claims)
Article 501 (1) A Liquidating Stock Company may perform its obligations relating to conditional claims, claims of indeterminate duration or other claims of indeterminable amount. In such cases, a petition for the appointment of an appraiser must be filed to the court in order to have such claims evaluated.
(2) In the cases provided for in the preceding paragraph, a Liquidating Stock Company must perform its obligations relating to the claims under that paragraph in accordance with the evaluations by the appraiser under that paragraph.
(3) Any expense for the procedures for the appointment of the appraiser under paragraph (1) shall be borne by the Liquidating Stock Company. The same shall apply to the expense for the summonses and questions for the purpose of the appraiser's appraisal.

(Restrictions on Distribution of Residual Assets before Performance of Obligations)
Article 502 A Liquidating Stock Company cannot distribute its property to its shareholders until after performance of the obligations of such Liquidating Stock Company; provided, however, that this shall not apply in cases where assets regarded as necessary for the performance of obligations relating to a claim that is the subject of dispute as to its existence or otherwise or as to its amount have been withheld.

(Exclusion from Liquidation)
Article 503 (1) Creditors of a Liquidating Stock Company (excluding known creditors) who fail to state their claims during the period under paragraph (1) of Article 499 shall be excluded from the liquidation.
(2) Creditors who are excluded from the liquidation pursuant to the provisions of the pre-

ceding paragraph may demand the performance with respect to the residual assets that are not distributed.
(3) In cases where residual assets of a Liquidating Stock Company have been distributed to some shareholders, the assets necessary for the distribution to shareholders other than such shareholders in the same proportion as that applied for the distribution received by such shareholders shall be deducted from the residual assets under the preceding paragraph.

Subsection 5 Distribution of Residual Assets

(Determination of Matters regarding Distribution of Residual Assets)
Article 504 (1) If a Liquidating Stock Company intends to distribute its residual assets, it must prescribe the following matters by decision of liquidators (or, for a Company with Board of Liquidators, by resolution of the board of liquidators):
(i) Kind of residual assets; and
(ii) Matters regarding the allotment of residual assets to shareholders.
(2) In the cases provided for in the preceding paragraph, if two or more classes of shares with different features as to the distribution of residual assets are issued, the Liquidating Stock Company may prescribe the following matters as the matters listed in item (ii) of that paragraph in accordance with the features of such classes of shares:
(i) If there is any arrangement that no residual assets will be allotted to the shareholders of a certain class of shares, a statement to that effect and such class of shares;
(ii) In addition to the matter listed in the preceding item, if there is an arrangement that each class of shares shall be treated differently with respect to allotment of residual assets, a statement to that effect and the details of such different treatment.
(3) The provisions regarding the matters listed in item (ii) of paragraph (1) must stipulate that the residual assets will be allotted in proportion to the number of the shares (or, in cases where there is a provision with respect to the matters listed in item (ii) of the preceding paragraph, the number of the shares of each class) held by the shareholders (excluding the relevant Liquidating Stock Company and shareholders of the class of shares referred to in item (i) of the preceding paragraph).

(Cases where Residual Assets Consist of Property Other Than Monies)
Article 505 (1) If residual assets consist of property other than monies, shareholders shall have the right to demand distribution of monies (hereinafter in this article referring to the rights to demand that the Liquidating Stock Company deliver monies in lieu of such residual assets). In such cases, the Liquidating Stock Company must prescribe the following matters by resolution of liquidators (or, for a Company with Board of Liquidators, by resolution of board of liquidators):
(i) The period during which rights to demand distribution of monies can be exercised; and
(ii) If there is any arrangement that no residual assets shall be allotted to shareholders who hold less than certain number of shares, a statement to that effect and that number.
(2) In the cases provided for in the preceding paragraph, the Liquidating Stock Company must notify the shareholders of the matters listed in item (i) of that paragraph no later than 20 days prior to the last day of the period referred to such item.
(3) A Liquidating Stock Company must pay to shareholders who exercised rights to demand distribution of monies, in lieu of the residual assets allotted to such shareholders, monies equivalent to the value of such residual assets. In such cases, the amount provided for in each of the following items for the case categories listed in each such

item shall be the value of such residual assets:
(i) In cases where such residual assets consist of property with a market price: The amount calculated in a manner prescribed by the applicable Ordinance of the Ministry of Justice as the market price of such residual assets;
(ii) In cases other than those listed in the preceding item: The amount determined by the court in response to the petition by the Liquidating Stock Company.

(Treatment in case Base Number of Shares is Provided)
Article 506 In cases where the number in item (ii), paragraph (1) of the preceding article (hereinafter in this article referred to as "Minimum Number of Shares") is prescribed, a Liquidating Stock Company must pay to the shareholders who hold shares in a number less than the Minimum Number of Shares (hereinafter in this article referred to as "Below Minimum Shareholding") the monies equivalent to the amount which is obtained by multiplying the amount prescribed as the value of the residual assets allotted to the shareholders who hold shares in the Minimum Number of Shares in accordance with the applicable provisions of the second sentence of paragraph (3) of the preceding article by the ratio of the number shares in such Bellow Minimum Shareholding to the Minimum Number of Shares.

Subsection 6 Conclusion of Liquidation

Article 507 (1) If the administration of a liquidation has concluded, the Liquidating Stock Company must prepare the settlement of accounts pursuant to the provisions of the applicable Ordinance of the Ministry of Justice without delay.
(2) At a Company with Board of Liquidators, the settlement of accounts must be approved by the board of liquidators.
(3) Liquidators must submit or provide the settlement of accounts (or, in cases where the provisions of the preceding paragraph apply, the settlement of accounts approved under that paragraph) to the shareholders meeting and obtain the approval of the same.
(4) If the approval is given under the preceding paragraph, an exemption shall be deemed to have been given for the liquidators' liability for failure to perform their duties; provided, however, that this shall not apply if there has been misconduct regarding the execution of the liquidators' duties.

Subsection 7 Retention of Accounting Materials

Article 508 (1) A Liquidator (or, for a Company with Board of Liquidators, the liquidators listed in each item of paragraph (7) of Article 489) must retain the books of the Liquidating Stock Company as well as any material data regarding the business and liquidation of the same (hereinafter in this article referred to as "Accounting Materials") for a period of ten years from the time of the registration of the completion of the liquidation at the location of head office of the Liquidating Stock Company.
(2) The court may, in response to the petition by the interested parties, appoint a person to act on behalf of the liquidator in the preceding paragraph in retaining the Accounting Materials. In such cases, the provisions of that paragraph shall not apply.
(3) The person appointed pursuant to the provisions of the preceding paragraph must retain the Accounting Materials for a period of ten years from the time of the registration of the completion of the liquidation at the location of head office of the Liquidating Stock Company.
(4) Expenses regarding the procedures for the appointment under the provisions of paragraph (2) shall be borne by the Liquidating Stock Company.

Subsection 8 Exceptions to Application

Article 509 (1) The provisions listed below shall not apply to Liquidating Stock Companies:
  (i) Article 155;
  (ii) In Chapter V, Subsection 2 (excluding paragraph (4) of Article 435, paragraph (3) of Article 440, Article 442 and Article 443) and Subsection 3 of Section 2 as well as Section 3 through Section 5; and
  (iii) In Chapter IV and Chapter V of Part V, portions relating to the procedures of Share Exchange and Share Transfer.
(2) A Liquidating Stock Company may acquire the shares of such Liquidating Stock Company, limited to cases where acquisition is effected without consideration or in other cases prescribed by the applicable Ordinance of the Ministry of Justice.

Section 2 Special Liquidations

Subsection 1 Commencement of Special Liquidations

(Cause of Commencement of Special Liquidation)
Article 510 If the court finds that the grounds listed below exist with respect to a Liquidating Stock Company, it shall order such Liquidating Stock Company to commence special liquidation in response to the filing under the provisions of Article 514:
  (i) The existence of circumstances prejudicial to the implementation of the liquidation; or
  (ii) The suspicion that the Liquidating Stock Company is insolvent (hereinafter in this article and in paragraph (2) of the following article referring to the status where the assets of the Liquidating Stock Company is not sufficient to fully discharge its debts).

(Petition for Commencement of Special Liquidation)
Article 511 (1) Creditors, liquidators, Company Auditors or shareholders may file a petition for the commencement of special liquidation.
(2) If it is suspected that a Liquidating Stock Company is insolvent, liquidators must file a petition for the commencement of the special liquidation.

(Order to Suspend Other Procedures)
Article 512 (1) In cases where a petition is filed for the commencement of the special liquidation, if the court finds it necessary, it may, in response to the petition by the creditors, liquidators, Company Auditors or shareholders or ex officio, order that the following procedures be suspended until a decision is made on the filing of a petition for the commencement of the special liquidation; provided, however, that, with respect to the bankruptcy procedures listed in item (i), this shall be limited to cases where the ruling to commence bankruptcy procedures is not yet been handed down, and with respect to the procedures listed in item (ii), this shall be limited to cases where the creditors that petitioned for such procedures are not likely to suffer undue loss:
  (i) Bankruptcy procedures for the Liquidating Stock Company; or
  (ii) Procedures of compulsory execution, provisional attachment or provisional disposition (excluding those based on general liens and other claims that have general priority) that are already enforced to the assets of the Liquidating Stock Company.
(2) The provisions of the preceding paragraph shall also apply if immediate appeal under

paragraph (5) of Article 890 is filed against a ruling to dismiss the petition for the commencement of special liquidation.

(Restrictions on Withdrawal of Petition for Commencement of Special Liquidation)
Article 513 A person who filed a petition for the commencement of special liquidation may withdraw such petition limited to if it is before the order to commence special liquidation. In such cases, the permission of the court must be obtained if it is after an order to suspend has been issued pursuant to the provisions of the preceding paragraph, a protective disposition has been effected pursuant to the provisions of paragraph (2) of Article 540 or a disposition has been effected pursuant to the provisions of paragraph (2) of Article 541.

(Order to Commence Special Liquidation)
Article 514 In cases where a petition for the commencement of special liquidation has been filed, if the court finds that there are grounds that warrant the commencement of special liquidation, the court shall order the commencement of special liquidation, except in cases falling under any of the following:
(i) If no advance has been made for the expense for the special liquidation procedures;
(ii) If it is clear that there is no expectation of the completion of the liquidation, even by special liquidation;
(iii) If it is clear that invoking the special liquidation is contrary to the general interest of creditors; or
(iv) If the petition for the commencement of special liquidation has been filed with improper purpose, or the petition was otherwise not filed in good faith.

(Suspension of Other Procedures)
Article 515 (1) If an order to commence special liquidation is issued, petition cannot be filed for commencement of bankruptcy procedures, or for compulsory execution, provisional attachment or provisional disposition against the assets of a Liquidating Stock Company, or for property disclosure procedures (hereinafter in this paragraph limited to those in response to a petition under paragraph (1) of Article 197 of the Civil Execution Act (Act No. 4 of 1979)), and the bankruptcy procedures (limited to those for which a ruling to commence bankruptcy procedures has not yet been handed down), the compulsory execution, provisional attachment or provisional disposition procedures already effected against the assets of the Liquidating Stock Company and property disclosure procedures shall be suspended; provided, however, that this shall not apply with respect to the compulsory execution, provisional attachment or provisional disposition or property disclosure procedures pursuant to general liens and other claims that have general priority.
(2) If an order to commence special liquidation has become final and binding, the procedures suspended pursuant to the provisions of the preceding paragraph shall become ineffective in relation to the procedures for the special liquidation.
(3) If an order to commence special liquidation is issued, prescription shall not be completed with respect to the claims of creditors of the Liquidating Stock Company (excluding general liens and other claims that have general priority, claims that have accrued in relation to the Liquidating Stock Company for the procedures for special liquidation and rights to seek reimbursement of expense for the procedures for special liquidation from the Liquidating Stock Company, hereinafter in this Section referred to as "Agreement Claims") until the day on which two months have elapsed from the day of the registration of the rescission of the commencement of special liquidation or reg-

istration of conclusion of special liquidation provided for in item (ii) or item (iii) of paragraph (1) of Article 938.

(Order to Suspend Procedures to Enforce Security Interests)
Article 516 In cases where the court issues an order to commence special liquidation, the court may, in response to a petition by the liquidators, Company Auditors, creditors or shareholders or ex officio, prescribing a reasonable period of time, order the suspension of procedures to enforce a security interest if the court finds that it suits the general interests of the creditors and those who petitioned for the procedures to enforce the security interest (hereinafter in this article referring to procedures to enforce the security interest the assets of the Liquidating Stock Company, procedures to enforce charge on whole company assets or compulsory execution procedures based on the general liens and other claims that have general priority that have already been enforced against the assets of the Liquidating Stock Company) are not likely to suffer undue loss.

(Prohibition of Set-offs)
Article 517 (1) Creditors who hold Agreement Claims (hereinafter in this Section referred to as "Agreement Claim Creditors") may not effect set-offs in the cases listed below:
(i) If such creditors assumed debts owed to the Liquidating Stock Company after the commencement of special liquidation;
(ii) If such creditor assumed debts owed to the Liquidating Stock Company after the Liquidating Stock Company became unable to pay its debts (hereinafter in this Subsection referring to the status under which, due to its lack of capacity to pay, the Liquidating Stock Company is generally and continuously unable to pay debts that are due) by entering into contracts with the Liquidating Stock Company under which assets of the Liquidating Stock Company are to be disposed of for the purpose of offsetting obligations the creditors assume under the contract exclusively against the Agreement Claims or by entering into contracts under which the creditors assume obligations of a person who owes the obligations to the Liquidating Stock Company, and creditors had the knowledge at the time of executing such contracts that the Liquidating Stock Company was unable to pay debts;
(iii) If, in cases where they assumed debts after suspension of payment, they had the knowledge at the time of such assumption of debt that payments had been suspended; provided, however, that this shall not apply if the Liquidating Stock Company was not insolvent at the time of such suspension of payments; or
(iv) If, in cases where such creditors assumed debts after the commencement of special liquidation, they had the knowledge at the time of such assumption that the petition for commencement of special liquidation had been filed.
(2) The provisions of item (ii) through item (iv) of the preceding paragraph shall not apply in cases where the assumption of debt pursuant to the provisions of those provisions is based on any of the causes listed below:
(i) Statutory causes;
(ii) Causes in existence before the Agreement Claim Creditors acquired the knowledge that the Liquidating Stock Company was unable to pay debts, or the petition for suspension of payments or commencement of special liquidation had been filed; or
(iii) Causes that accrued one year or more before the petition for the commencement of special liquidation was filed.

Article 518 (1) Creditors who owe debts to a Liquidating Stock Company cannot effect the set-off in the cases listed below:
  (i) If such creditors acquired Agreement Claims of others after the commencement of special liquidation;
  (ii) If, in cases where such creditors acquired Agreement Claims after Liquidating Stock Company became unable to pay debts, they had the knowledge that the Liquidating Stock Company was unable to pay debts at the time of the acquisition of the Agreement Claims;
  (iii) If, in cases where such creditors acquired Agreement Claims after the suspension of payment, they had the knowledge that the there was suspension of payment at the time of the acquisition of the same; provided, however, that this shall not apply if the Liquidating Stock Company was not unable to pay debts at the time of such suspension of payment;
  (iv) If, in cases where such creditors acquired Agreement Claims after the petition for commencement of special liquidation, they had the knowledge that the commencement of special liquidation had been filed at the time of the acquisition of the Agreement Claims.
(2) The provisions under items (ii) through (iv) of the preceding paragraph shall not apply in cases where the acquisition of the Agreement Claims provided for in those provisions is based on any of the causes listed below:
  (i) Statutory causes;
  (ii) Causes in existence before the persons who assumed debts owed to the Liquidating Stock Company acquired the knowledge that the Liquidating Stock Company was unable to pay debts, or that a petition for suspension of payments or commencement of special liquidation was filed; or
  (iii) Causes that accrued one year or more before the petition for the commencement of special liquidation was filed; or
  (iv) Contracts between the persons who assume debts owed to the Liquidating Stock Company and the Liquidating Stock Company.

Subsection 2 Supervision and Investigations by the Court

(Supervision by the Court)
Article 519 (1) If an order to commence special liquidation is issued, the liquidation of the Liquidating Stock Company shall be subject to supervisions by the court.
(2) If the court finds it necessary, it may seek a statement of opinion with respect to procedures for the special liquidation of such Liquidating Stock Company from the government agency that supervises the business of the Liquidating Stock Company, or entrust the investigations to the same.
(3) The government agency under the preceding paragraph may state its opinion with respect to the procedures for special liquidation of such Liquidating Stock Company to the court.

(Investigations by the Court)
Article 520 The Court may at any time order a Liquidating Stock Company to report the status of its administration of the liquidation and assets, or otherwise conduct investigations that are necessary for the supervision of the liquidation.

(Submission of Inventory of Property to the Court)
Article 521 In cases where an order to commence special liquidation is issued, the Liquidating Stock Company must, without delay after the approval under paragraph (3) of

Article 492 is given, submit the Inventory of Property (hereinafter referring to the Inventory of Property provided for in that paragraph); provided, however, that, if the Inventory of Property is prepared by using electromagnetic records, a document that specifies the matters recorded in such electromagnetic records must be submitted to the court.

(Order to Investigate)
Article 522 (1) If the court finds it necessary after the commencement of special liquidation considering the status of the assets of a Liquidating Stock Company, it may effect the disposition ordering that the matters listed below be investigated by investigators (hereinafter in Article 533 referred to as "Investigation Order") in response to a petition by liquidators, Company Auditors, creditors who have claims equivalent to one tenth or more of the total amount of the claims of creditors that have stated their claims and other creditors known to the Liquidating Stock Company, or shareholders who have held, for the consecutive period of past six months or more (or, in cases where a shorter period is provided for in the articles of incorporation, such period), not less than three hundredths (3/100) of the voting rights of all shareholders (excluding the shareholders that cannot exercise voting rights on all matters on which resolutions can be passed at the shareholders meeting; or, in cases where any proportion less than that is provided for in the articles of incorporation, such proportion) or shareholders who have held, for the consecutive period of past six months or more (or, in cases where a shorter period is provided for in the articles of incorporation, such period), not less than three hundredths (3/100) of the issued shares (excluding treasury shares; or, in cases where a lower proportion is provided for in the articles of incorporation, such proportion) or ex officio:
(i) Circumstances that resulted in the commencement of special liquidation;
(ii) Status of the business and assets of the Liquidating Stock Company;
(iii) Whether or not it is necessary to issue the temporary restraining order pursuant to the provisions of paragraph (1) of Article 540; or
(iv) Whether or not it is necessary to issue the temporary restraining order pursuant to the provisions of paragraph (1) of Article 542;
(v) Whether or not it is necessary to make the Ruling Evaluating Subject Officers' Liability provided for in paragraph (1) of Article 545; or
(vi) Other matters necessary for special liquidation specified by the court.
(2) The amounts of the claims in relation to which creditors who hold security interest (limited to special liens, pledges, mortgages or rights of retention provided for in the provisions of this Act or Commercial Code) with respect to the assets of a Liquidating Stock Company are entitled to payment by exercising those security interests shall not be included in the amount of the claims under the preceding paragraph.
(3) For the purpose of the application of the provisions of paragraph (1) to Liquidating Stock Companies that are not Public Companies, the words "have held, for the consecutive period of six months or more (or, in cases where a shorter period is provided for in the articles of incorporation, such period)," in that paragraph shall be read as "hold."

Subsection 3　Liquidators

(Liquidators' Duty of Fairness and Good Faith)
Article 523 In cases where special liquidation is commenced, liquidators shall assume the duty to perform the liquidation administration in fairness and good faith in relation to creditors, the Liquidating Stock Company and shareholders.

(Dismissal of Liquidators)
Article 524 (1) The court may dismiss liquidators in response to the petition by creditors or shareholders or ex officio if the liquidators do not perform the liquidation administration properly or there otherwise are significant grounds to do so.

(2) The court shall appoint liquidators if there is any vacancy in the office of liquidator.

(3) Even in cases where there are liquidators in office, the court may appoint additional liquidators if the court finds it necessary.

(Liquidators' Agents)
Article 525 (1) If necessary, liquidators may appoint one or more liquidators' agents at their own responsibility to cause them perform the duties of the liquidators.

(2) Permission of the court must be obtained with respect to the appointment of agents of liquidators under the preceding paragraph.

(Remuneration of Liquidators)
Article 526 (1) Liquidators may receive advance payment of the expense, and remuneration determined by the court.

(2) The provisions of the preceding paragraph shall apply mutatis mutandis to liquidators' agents.

Subsection 4 Supervisor

(Appointment of Supervisors)
Article 527 (1) The court may appoint one or more supervisors and grant to such Supervisors the authority to give consent in lieu of the permission under paragraph (1) of Article 535.

(2) Juridical persons may act as supervisors.

(Supervision over Supervisors)
Article 528 (1) The court shall supervise supervisors.

(2) The court may dismiss supervisors in response to the petition by interested parties or ex officio if the supervisors fail to supervise the management of the business and assets of the Liquidating Stock Company properly or there otherwise are significant grounds to do so.

(Performance of Duties by Two or more Supervisors)
Article 529 If there are two or more supervisors, they shall perform their duties jointly; provided, however, that they may perform their duties individually or divide their duties, with the permission of the court.

(Investigations by Supervisors)
Article 530 (1) Supervisors may at any time ask liquidators and Company Auditors of a Liquidating Stock Company and employees, including managers, to provide a report on the business, or investigate the status of the business and property of the Liquidating Stock Company.

(2) Supervisors may, when it is necessary to perform their duties, ask Subsidiaries of a Liquidating Stock Company to provide reports on the business, or investigate the status of the business and assets of Subsidiaries of the Liquidating Stock Company.

(Supervisors' Duty of Care)

Article 531 (1) Supervisors must perform their duties with due care of a prudent manager.

(2) If supervisors fail to exercise the due care under the preceding paragraph, those supervisors shall be jointly and severally liable to compensate losses arising in interested parties.

(Remunerations of Supervisors)

Article 532 (1) Supervisors may receive advance payment of the expense, and remunerations determined by the court.

(2) Supervisors must obtain the permission of the court if, after their appointment, they assign, or assigned claims owed by the Liquidating Stock Company or shares in the Liquidating Stock Company.

(3) Supervisors cannot receive payment of expense or remuneration if they engage in the acts provided for in the preceding paragraph without the permission under the preceding paragraph.

Subsection 5 Investigators

(Appointment of Investigators)

Article 533 In cases where the court issues an Investigation Order, it must appoint one or more investigating members in such Investigation Order, and prescribe the matters that the investigators ought to investigate and the period in which the investigators are to report the outcome of the investigation to the court.

(Mutatis mutandis Application of Provisions on Supervisors)

Article 534 The provisions of the preceding Subsection (excluding paragraph (1) of Article 527 and proviso to Article 529) shall apply mutatis mutandis to supervisors.

Subsection 6 Restrictions on Acts of Liquidating Stock Companies

(Restrictions on Acts of Liquidating Stock Companies)

Article 535 (1) In cases where an order is issued for the commencement of special liquidation, a Liquidating Stock Company must obtain the permission of the court in order to carry out the acts listed below; provided, however, that, if supervisors are appointed under the provisions of paragraph (1) of Article 527, consent of the supervisors must be obtained in lieu of that permission:

(i) The disposal of an asset (excluding the act listed in each item of paragraph (1) of the following article);
(ii) The taking out of a loan;
(iii) The filing of an action;
(iv) A settlement or the entering in an arbitration agreement (referring to the arbitration agreement provided for in paragraph (1) of Article 2 of the Arbitration Act (Act No. 138 of 2003));
(v) A waiver of rights; or
(vi) Other acts designated by the court.

(2) Notwithstanding the provisions of the preceding paragraph, the permission under that paragraph is not required with respect to the act listed in items (i) through (v) of that paragraph in the cases listed below:

(i) If the act is related to an act that involves the amount equivalent to or less than the amount provided for in the Supreme Court Rules; or
(ii) If, in addition to the act listed in the preceding item, the act relates to an act for which the court has held that the permission under the preceding paragraph is not required.
(3) Any act committed without the permission under paragraph (1) or consent of supervisors in lieu thereof shall be ineffective; provided, however, that the above provision may not be asserted against a third party without knowledge.

(Restrictions on Assignment of Business)
Article 536 (1) In cases where an order for commencement of special liquidation is issued, if a Liquidating Stock Company intends to carry out any act listed below, it must obtain the permission of the court:
(i) Assignment of the entire business; or
(ii) Assignment of significant part of the business (excluding the assignment in which the book value of the assets to be assigned by such assignment does not exceed one fifth (1/5) (or, in cases where any lower proportion is provided for in the articles of incorporation, such proportion) of the amount calculated by the method prescribed by the applicable Ordinance of the Ministry of Justice as the total amount of the assets of such Stock Company);
(2) The provisions of paragraph (3) of the preceding article shall apply mutatis mutandis to the acts committed without the permission under the preceding paragraph.
(3) The provisions of Chapter VII (excluding item (v), paragraph (1) of Article 467) shall not apply to the cases of special liquidation.

(Restrictions on Performance of Obligations)
Article 537 (1) In cases where an order is issued for commencement of special liquidation, a Liquidating Stock Company must perform obligations to Agreement Claim Creditors in proportion to the amount of their claims.
(2) Notwithstanding the provisions of the preceding paragraph, a Liquidating Stock Company may, with the permission of the court, perform its obligations relating to minor claims, claims secured by security interests, or other claims that are unlikely to be detrimental to other creditors even if performed in excess of the proportion of the amount of the claims.

(Method of Conversion into Cash)
Article 538 (1) A Liquidating Stock Company may convert its assets into cash pursuant to the provisions of the Civil Execution Act and other laws and regulations on compulsory execution procedures. In such cases, the provisions of item (i), paragraph (1) of Article 535 shall not apply.
(2) A Liquidating Stock Company may convert the assets that underlie the security interest provided for in paragraph (2) of Article 522 (hereinafter in this article and in the following article simply referred to as "Security Interest") into cash pursuant to the provisions of the Civil Execution Act and other laws and regulations on compulsory execution procedures. In such cases, a person who holds such Security Interest (hereinafter in this article and in the following article simply referred to as "Security Interest Holder") may not refuse the conversion into cash.
(3) In the cases of the preceding two paragraphs, the provisions of Article 63 and Article 129 of the Civil Execution Act (including the cases where those provisions are applied mutatis mutandis under that act and other laws and regulations on compulsory execution procedures) shall not apply.

(4) If, in the case of paragraph (2), the amount that the Security Interest Holder is to receive is not fixed yet, the Liquidating Stock Company must deposit the proceeds separately. In such cases, the security interest shall exist with respect to the proceeds so deposited.

(Designating Periods for Disposition by Security Interest Holders)
Article 539 (1) If Security Interest Holders have the right to dispose of the assets that underlie the security interest without relying on the method prescribed by the Act, the court may, in response to the petition by the Liquidating Stock Company, specify the period during which the Security Interest Holders ought to effect the disposition.
(2) Security Interest Holders shall lose their right under the preceding paragraph if they do not effect disposition during the period under the preceding paragraph.

Subsection 7 Dispositions Necessary to Supervise Liquidation

(Temporary Restraining Order regarding Assets of Liquidating Stock Company)
Article 540 (1) In cases where an order is issued for commencement of special liquidation, if the court finds it necessary to supervise the liquidation, the court may, in response to a petition by the creditors, liquidators, Company Auditors or shareholders or ex officio, order the provisional disposition that prohibits the disposition of the property of the Liquidating Stock Company or other necessary temporary restraining orders.
(2) Even during the period from the time when a petition for commencement of special liquidation is filed to the time when a ruling is handed down on such petition, if the court finds it necessary, the court may, in response to the petitions by the creditors, liquidators, Company Auditors or shareholders or ex officio, effect the temporary restraining orders under the provisions of the preceding paragraph. The same shall apply if an immediate appeal in paragraph (5) of Article 890 is filed against the ruling to dismiss the petition for the commencement of special liquidation.
(3) In cases where the court orders the temporary restraining orders under the provisions of the preceding two paragraphs to the effect that the Liquidating Stock Company is prohibited from carrying out the performance of its obligations and other acts that extinguishes its obligation to its creditors, the creditors may not, in relation to the special liquidation, assert the effectiveness of the performance of the obligations and other acts that extinguish its obligations, that were effected in contravention of such temporary restraining orders; provided, however, that this shall be limited to the cases where the creditors had the knowledge that such temporary restraining orders were effected at the time of the creditors' act.

(No Entry in Shareholder registry)
Article 541 (1) In cases where an order is issued for commencement of special liquidation, if the court finds it necessary to supervise the liquidation, the court may, in the shareholder registry in response to the petitions by the creditors, liquidators, Company Auditors or shareholders or ex officio, prohibit a Liquidating Stock Company from stating or recording Matters to be Stated in the Shareholder registry.
(2) Even during the period from the time when a petition for commencement of special liquidation is filed to the time when a ruling is handed down on such petition, if the court finds it necessary, the court may, in response to the petitions by the creditors, liquidators, Company Auditors or shareholders or ex officio, effect the disposition under the provisions of the preceding paragraph. The same shall apply if immediate ap-

peal under paragraph (5) of Article 890 is filed against the ruling to dismiss the petition for the commencement of special liquidation.

(Temporary Restraining Orders on Property of Officers)
Article 542 (1) In cases where an order for commencement of special liquidation is issued, if the court finds it necessary to supervise the liquidation, the court may, with respect to rights to seek damages pursuant to the liability of the incorporators, directors upon incorporation, Company Auditors upon incorporation, Qualified Officers provided for in paragraph (1) of Article 423 or liquidators (hereinafter in this Subsection referred to as "Subject Officers"), in response to the petition by the Liquidating Stock Company or ex officio, effect temporary restraining orders against the assets of such Subject Officers.
(2) Even during the period from the time when a petition for commencement of special liquidation is filed to the time when a ruling is made with respect to such petition, if the court finds it urgently necessary, the court may, in response to the petitions by the Liquidating Stock Company or ex officio, effect a disposition under the provisions of the preceding paragraph. The same shall apply if immediate appeal in paragraph (5) of Article 890 is filed against the ruling to dismiss a petition for the commencement of special liquidation.

(Prohibition of Exemptions from Liability of Officers)
Article 543 In cases where an order is issued for commencement of special liquidation, if the court finds it necessary to supervise the liquidation, the court may, in response to the petitions by the creditors, liquidators, Company Auditors or shareholders or ex officio, effect the disposition that prohibits the exemption of liability of the Subject Officers.

(Rescission of Exemption from Liability of Officers)
Article 544 (1) If an order is issued for commencement of special liquidation, a Liquidating Stock Company may rescind the exemption of liability of Subject Officers effected within one year prior to or after the time when the petition for commencement of special liquidation was filed. The same shall apply with respect to the exemption from the liability of Subject Officers that effected for improper purpose.
(2) The rights of rescission under the provisions of the preceding paragraph shall be exercised by filing an action or defense.
(3) The rights of rescission under the provisions of paragraph (1) cannot be exercised when two years have lapsed from the day when the order was issued for the commencement of special liquidation. The same shall apply if twenty years have elapsed from the day when Subject Officers was exempted from liability.

(Ruling Evaluating Subject Officers' Liability)
Article 545 (1) In cases where an order is issued for commencement of special liquidation, if the court finds it necessary, the court may, in response to the petition by the Liquidating Stock Company or ex officio, pass judgment evaluating the rights to seek damages pursuant to the liability of the Subject Officers (hereinafter in this article referred to as "Ruling Evaluating Subject Officers' Liability")
(2) In cases where the court commences procedures of the Ruling Evaluating Subject Officers' Liability ex officio, it must make the determination to that effect.
(3) If the petition under paragraph (1) is filed or the ruling in the preceding paragraph is made, for the purpose of the nullification of the prescription, it shall be deemed that a judicial claim has been made.

(4) The procedures for the Ruling Evaluating Subject Officers' Liability (excluding those after the Ruling Evaluating Subject Officers' Liability) shall end if the special liquidation is ended.

Subsection 8 Creditors' Meetings

(Convocation of Creditors' meetings)
Article 546 (1) Creditors' meetings may be convened whenever it is required to implement special liquidation.
(2) A Creditors' meeting shall be convened by the Liquidating Stock Company, except in cases where convened pursuant to the provisions of paragraph (3) of the following Article.

(Demand for Convocation of Meeting by Creditors)
Article 547 (1) Agreement Claim Creditors who have Agreement Claims equivalent to one tenth or more of the total amount of the Agreement Claims of Agreement Claim Creditors that have stated their claims and other Agreement Claim Creditors known to the Liquidating Stock Company may demand, by disclosing the matters that are the purpose of the creditors' meeting and the reasons of the convocation, that the Liquidating Stock Company convene a creditors' meeting.
(2) The amount of the Agreement Claims in relation to which Agreement Claim Creditors who hold security interest provided for in paragraph (2) of Article 522 with respect to the assets of a Liquidating Stock Company are entitled by exercising their security interest shall not be included in the amount of the Agreement Claims under the preceding paragraph.
(3) In the following cases, Agreement Claim Creditors who made the demand pursuant under the provisions of paragraph (1) may convene the creditors' meeting with the permission of the court:
  (i) In cases where the convocation procedure is not effected without delay after the demand pursuant to the provisions of paragraph (1); or
  (ii) In cases where a notice for the convocation of the creditors' meeting that specifies a day falling within six weeks from the day of the demand under the provisions of paragraph (1) as the day of the creditors' meeting, is not sent.

(Determination of Convocation of Creditors' Meeting)
Article 548 (1) A person who convenes a creditors' meeting (hereinafter in this Subsection referred to as "Convener") must prescribe the following matters in cases where he/she convenes a creditors' meeting:
  (i) The date, time and place of the creditors' meeting;
  (ii) The matters that are the purpose of the creditors' meeting;
  (iii) If it is to be arranged that Agreement Claim Creditors who do not attend the creditors' meeting may exercise their voting rights by electromagnetic means, a statement to that effect;
  (iv) In addition to the matters listed in the preceding three items, any matters prescribed by the applicable Ordinance of the Ministry of Justice.
(2) In cases where a Liquidating Stock Company convenes a creditors' meeting, such Liquidating Stock Company must prescribe with respect to each Agreement Claim whether or not voting rights can be exercised at the creditors' meeting and the amount of the same.
(3) In cases where a person other than the Liquidating Stock Company convenes a creditors' meeting, such Convener must demand that the Liquidating Stock Company pre-

scribe the matters provided for in the preceding paragraph. In such cases, if that demand is made, the Liquidating Stock Company must prescribe the matters provided for in that paragraph.
(4) Agreement Claim Creditors who hold security interest provided for in paragraph (2) of Article 522 with respect to the property of a Liquidating Stock Companies shall have no voting rights with respect to the amount of the Agreement Claims to the payment of which they are entitled by exercising their security interest.

(Notice of Convocation of Creditors' Meetings)
Article 549 (1) In order to convene a creditors' meeting, the Convener must give the written notice thereof to Agreement Claim Creditors who stated their claims and other Agreement Claim Creditors known to the Liquidating Stock Company and the Liquidating Stock Company, no later than two weeks prior to the day of the creditors' meeting.
(2) In lieu of the sending of the written notice referred to in the preceding paragraph, the Convener may send the notice by an electromagnetic means with the approval of the Agreement Claim Creditors in accordance with the provisions of the applicable Cabinet Order. In such cases, such Convener shall be deemed to have sent the written notice under such paragraph.
(3) The notice under the preceding two paragraphs must state or record the matters listed in each item of paragraph (1) of the preceding article.
(4) The provisions of the preceding three paragraphs shall apply mutatis mutandis to Agreement Claim Creditors that stated their claims and other Agreement Claim Creditors known to the Liquidating Stock Company that hold general liens and other claims that have general priority, claims that have arisen in relation to the Liquidating Stock Company for procedures for special liquidation or rights to seek reimbursement of expenses of procedures for special liquidation from the Liquidating Stock Company.

(Issuance of Reference documents for Creditors' Meetings and Proxy Cards)
Article 550 (1) The Convener must, when giving a notice under paragraph (1) of the preceding article, issue to the Agreement Claim Creditors that stated their claims and other Agreement Claim Creditors known to the Liquidating Stock Company, documents which contain stating the matters provided for under the provisions of paragraph (2) or paragraph (3) of Article 548 with respect to the Agreement Claims held by such Agreement Claim Creditors and maters of reference for the exercising the voting rights (in the following paragraph referred to as "Reference documents for Creditors' Meeting") as well as the document to be used by the Agreement Claim Creditors to exercise the voting rights (hereinafter in this Subsection referred to as "Proxy Card") as prescribed by the applicable Ordinance of the Ministry of Justice.
(2) If the Convener intends to send notices by an electromagnetic means r in paragraph (2) of the preceding article to the Agreement Claim Creditors that have given consent under the same paragraph, the Convener must provide the matters to be specified in such document by an electromagnetic means in lieu of the issuance of the Creditors' Meeting reference documents and Proxy Card under the provisions of the preceding paragraph; provided, however, that, if requested by an Agreement Claim Creditor, the Convener must issue such documents to such Agreement Claim Creditor.

Article 551 (1) In cases where the matters listed in item (iii), paragraph (1) of Article 548 are prescribed, the Convener must, when giving a notice by an electromagnetic means to the Agreement Claim Creditors who have given the consent under paragraph (2) of Article 549, provide to the Agreement Claim Creditors the matters to be

specified in the Proxy Card by such electromagnetic means.
(2) In cases where the matters listed in item (iii), paragraph (1) of Article 548 are prescribed, if an Agreement Claim Creditor who has not given the consent under paragraph (2) of Article 549 makes a request, no later than one week prior to the day of the creditors' meeting, for the provision of the matters to be stated in the Proxy Card by an electromagnetic means, the Convener must provide such matters to such Agreement Claim Creditor by an electromagnetic means, pursuant to the applicable Ordinance of the Ministry of Justice.

(Direction of Creditors' Meeting)
Article 552 (1) Creditors' meeting shall be directed by the court.
(2) If a Convener intends to call a creditors' meeting, the Convener must notify the court in advance of the matters listed in each item of paragraph (1) of Article 548 and the matters provided for under the provisions of paragraph (2) of paragraph (3) of that article.

(Treatment of Voting Rights under Objections)
Article 553 If, with respect to matters prescribed for each Agreement Claim pursuant to the provisions of paragraph (2) or paragraph (3) of Article 548, persons who hold such Agreement Claims or other Agreement Claim Creditors state their objections at a creditors' meeting, the court shall prescribe the same.

(Resolutions of Creditors' Meetings)
Article 554 (1) In order to adopt a matter to be resolved at a resolution at a creditors' meeting, all of the following consents must be obtained:
  (i) The consent of a majority of the voting rights holders present at the meeting (hereinafter in this Subsection and following Subsection referring to the Agreement Claim Creditors that can exercise voting rights); and
  (ii) The consent of persons who hold the voting rights in excess of half of the total voting rights of the voting rights holders present at the meeting.
(2) For the purpose of the application of the provisions of item (i), paragraph (1) of Article 558, if any voting rights holder exercised only some of the voting rights he/she holds as a consent to the matters under the preceding paragraph under the provisions of paragraph (1) of that article (excluding the cases where his/her remaining voting rights were not exercised), for each such voting rights holder, "one" shall be added to the number of the voting rights holders who attended the meeting, and "one" shall be added to the number of the voting rights holders who gave their consent, respectively.
(3) Creditors' meeting cannot pass resolutions with respect to matters other than the matters listed in item (ii), paragraph (1) of Article 548.

(Proxy Voting)
Article 555 (1) Agreement Claim Creditors may exercise voting rights by proxy. In such cases, such Agreement Claim Creditors or proxy must submit to the Convener a document which certifies the power of representation.
(2) The grant of the power of representation under the preceding paragraph must be made for each creditors' meeting.
(3) Agreement Claim Creditors or proxy referred to in paragraph (1) may, in lieu of the submission of the document which certifies the power of representation, provide the matters to be specified in such document by electromagnetic means with the approval of the Convener pursuant to the provisions of the applicable Cabinet Order. In such cases, such Agreement Claim Creditors or proxies shall be deemed to have submitted

such document.

(4) In cases where the Agreement Claim Creditors are the persons who gave consent under paragraph (2) of Article 549, the Convener may not refuse providing the approval under the preceding paragraph without a justifiable ground.

(Voting in Writing)
Article 556 (1) Agreement Claim Creditors who do not attend the creditors' meeting may exercise their voting rights in writing.

(2) The exercise of voting rights in writing shall be effected by entering necessary matters on the Proxy Card and submitting the Proxy Card to the Convener by the time prescribed by the applicable Ordinance of the Ministry of Justice.

(3) Voting rights holders who exercised the voting rights in writing pursuant to the provisions of the preceding paragraph shall be deemed to have been present at the creditors' meeting for the purpose of the provisions of paragraph (1) of Article 554 and paragraph (1) of Article 567.

(Voting through Use of Electromagnetic Means)
Article 557 (1) The exercise of a voting rights by an electromagnetic means shall be effected by providing the matters to be entered in the proxy card to the Convener by an electromagnetic means, with the approval of such Convener, no later than the time prescribed by the applicable Ordinance of the Ministry of Justice in accordance with the provisions of the applicable Cabinet Order.

(2) In cases where the Agreement Claim Creditors are the persons who gave consent under paragraph (2) of Article 549, the Convener may not refuse providing the approval under the preceding paragraph without justifiable grounds.

(3) Voting rights holders who exercised the voting rights by an electromagnetic means under the provisions of paragraph (1) shall be deemed to have been present at the creditors' meeting for the purpose of the application of the provisions of paragraph (1) of Article 554 and paragraph (1) of Article 567.

(Inconsistent Voting)
Article 558 (1) Agreement Claim Creditors may exercise the voting rights they hold without maintaining consistency. In such cases, the Agreement Claim Creditors must notify the Convener to such effect and of the reason thereof no later than three days prior to the day of the creditors' meeting.

(2) If an Agreement Claim Creditor referred to in the preceding paragraph is not a person who holds the Agreement Claims on behalf of others, the Convener may reject the inconsistent exercise of the voting rights held by such Agreement Claim Creditor under the provisions of that paragraph.

(Attendance of Creditors who Hold Security Interest)
Article 559 Creditors' meetings or Conveners may demand that the following creditors are present at the meeting and hear their opinions. In such cases, a resolution must be passed to that effect at a creditors' meeting:

(i) Creditors that hold security interest provided for in paragraph (2) of Article 522; and

(ii) Creditors who hold general liens and other claims that have general priority, claims that have arisen in relation to the Liquidating Stock Company for the procedures for special liquidation or rights to seek from the Liquidating Stock Company reimbursement of expense for the procedures for special liquidation.

(Resolution for Postponement or Continuation)
Article 560 In cases where there is a resolution for the postponement or continuation of the creditors' meeting, the provisions of Article 548 (excluding paragraph (4)) and Article 549 shall not apply.

(Minutes)
Article 561 The Convener must prepare minutes with respect to the business of the creditors' meeting, pursuant to the provisions of the applicable Ordinance of the Ministry of Justice.

(Report to Creditors' Meeting of Outcome of Investigations Liquidators)
Article 562 In cases where an order is issued for the commencement of special liquidation, if the liquidators provided for in paragraph (1) of Article 492 have completed the investigations of the current status of the property of the Liquidating Stock Companies and have prepared the Inventory of Property (hereinafter in this article referring to the Inventory of Property provided for in that paragraph), the Liquidating Stock Company must, without delay, convene the creditors' meeting and report to such creditors' meeting the outcome of the investigations of the status of the operations and assets of the Liquidating Stock Companies as well as the summary of the Inventory of Property, and state its opinions regarding the policy and prospect of the implementation of the liquidation; provided, however, that this shall not apply if the Liquidating Stock Company regards it as appropriate to make the creditors aware of the content of the matters to be reported and such opinions by means other than the statement of the report and opinions to the creditors' meeting.

Subsection 9 Agreements

(Offer of Agreements)
Article 563 A Liquidating Stock Company may offer an agreement to the creditors' meeting.

(Terms and Conditions of Agreements)
Article 564 (1) Terms and conditions regarding the change of some or all of the rights of Agreement Claim Creditors (excluding the security interest provided for in paragraph (2) of Article 522) must be provided for in the Agreements.
(2) The terms and conditions that change some or all of the rights of Agreement Claim Creditors must prescribe reductions of debts and extensions of terms and other general standards for the change in rights.

(Change in Rights under Agreements)
Article 565 Any changes of rights under an agreement must be equal as between Agreement Claim Creditors; provided, however, that this shall not apply in cases where Agreement Claim Creditors that will suffer detriment have given consent, in cases where the equality will not be compromised even if it is otherwise provided with respect to minor Agreement Claims, or in other cases where the equality will not be compromised even if there are differences as between Agreement Claim Creditors.

(Participation of Creditors Holding Security Interest)
Article 566 If a Liquidating Stock Company regards it as necessary in preparing a draft agreement, it may seek the participation of the following creditors:

(i) Creditors that hold security interest provided for in paragraph (2) of Article 522; and
(ii) Creditors that hold general liens and other claims that have general priority.

(Requirements for Adoption of Agreements)
Article 567 (1) Notwithstanding the provisions of paragraph (1) of Article 554, in order to adopt an agreement at a creditors' meeting, all of the following consents must be obtained:
(i) The consent of a majority of the voting rights holders present at the meeting; and
(ii) The consent of persons who hold the voting rights in excess of two thirds (2/3) of the total voting rights of the voting rights holders.
(2) The provisions of paragraph (2) of Article 554 shall apply mutatis mutandis to the application of the provisions of item (i) of the preceding paragraph.

(Petition Seeking Approval of Agreements)
Article 568 If an agreement is adopted, the Liquidating Stock Company must petition the court for approval of the agreement without delay.

(Ruling Approving or Rejecting Agreements)
Article 569 (1) In cases where a petition under the preceding article is filed, the court shall hand down the ruling approving the agreement except for the cases under the following paragraph.
(2) The court shall hand down a ruling rejecting the agreement in cases falling under any of the following:
(i) If the procedures for special liquidation or the agreement violates any provisions of the act, and such deficiency cannot be remedied; provided, however, that this shall not apply if, in cases where the procedures for special liquidation violates provisions of the acts, the degree of such violation is minor;
(ii) If there is no prospect that the agreement will be fulfilled;
(iii) If the agreement was established by unlawful means; or
(iv) If the agreement is contrary to the general interest of the creditors.

(Time of Effectuation of Agreements)
Article 570 Agreements shall take effect upon finalization of the rulings to approve.

(Scope of Effectiveness of Agreements)
Article 571 (1) An agreement shall be effective on behalf of, and shall bind, the Liquidating Stock Company and all Agreement Claim Creditors.
(2) An agreement shall not affect security interest provided for in paragraph (2) of Article 522 held by creditors provided for in that paragraph, rights that Agreement Claim Creditors hold, jointly with guarantors of the Liquidating Stock Company or otherwise with the Liquidating Stock Company, against persons who owe obligations, or collateral provided by persons other than the Liquidating Stock Company for the benefit of the Agreement Claim Creditors.

(Change of Details of Agreements)
Article 572 The details of an agreement may be changed if it is necessary for the implantation of the agreement. In such cases, the provisions of Article 563 through the preceding article shall apply mutatis mutandis.

Subsection 10　Completion of Special Liquidation

(Rulings on Conclusion of Special Liquidation)
Article 573　After the commencement of special liquidation, the court shall hand down a ruling on the conclusion of the special liquidation in response to petitions by liquidators, Company Auditors, creditors, shareholders, or investigators in the cases listed below:
(i) If the special liquidation has been completed; or
(ii) If the special liquidation is no longer necessary.

(Ruling for Commencement of Bankruptcy Procedures)
Article 574　(1) After the commencement of special liquidation, if the court finds, in the cases listed below, facts on the part of the Liquidating Stock Company that constitute cause for the commencement of bankruptcy procedures, the court must make ex officio the ruling for commencement of bankruptcy procedures in accordance with the Bankruptcy Act:
(i) If there is no prospect of an agreement;
(ii) If there is no prospect that the agreement will be implemented; or
(iii) If reliance on the special liquidation is contrary to the general interest of the creditors.
(2) After the commencement of special liquidation, if the court finds, in the cases listed below, facts on the part of the Liquidating Stock Company that constitute cause for the commencement of bankruptcy procedures, the court may make an ex officio ruling for commencement of bankruptcy procedures in accordance with the Bankruptcy Act:
(i) If an agreement is not adopted; or
(ii) If a ruling to reject an agreement has become final and binding;
(3) For the purpose of the application of the provisions of item (iv), paragraph (1) and items (ii) and (iii) of paragraph (2) of Article 71, item (iv), paragraph (1) and items (ii) and (iii) of paragraph (2) of Article 72, Article 160 (excluding item (i) of paragraph (1)), Article 162 (excluding item (ii) of paragraph (1)), paragraph (2) of Article 163, paragraph (1) of Article 164 (including the cases where that paragraph is applied mutatis mutandis under paragraph (1) of that article), Article 166, and paragraph (2) of Article 167 (including the cases where that paragraph is applied mutatis mutandis under paragraph (2) of Article 170) of the Bankruptcy Act in cases where a ruling to commence bankruptcy procedures has been made under the provisions of the preceding two paragraphs, the petition for the commencement of bankruptcy procedures shall be deemed to have been filed at the time when the petition in each of the following items for the case categories listed in each such items were filed:
(i) In cases where there was a petition for the commencement of bankruptcy procedures before the petition for the commencement of special liquidation in bankruptcy procedures that became ineffective because the order to commence special liquidation becoming final and binding: Such petition for the commencement of bankruptcy procedures;
(ii) In cases other than the cases listed in the preceding item: The petition for the commencement of special liquidation
(4) If a ruling to commence bankruptcy procedures is handed down under the provisions of paragraph (1) or paragraph (2), claims that have arisen in relation to the Liquidating Stock Company for the procedures for special liquidation and rights to seek reimbursement of expense regarding the procedures for special liquidation from the Liquidating Stock Company shall constitute preferred claims against the bankrupt's estate.

PART III Companies without Share
Chapter I Incorporation

(Preparation of Articles of Incorporation)
Article 575 (1) In order to incorporate an General Partnership Company, Limited Partnership Company or Limited Liability Company (hereinafter collectively referred to as "Membership Company"), persons who intend to be its partners must prepare articles of incorporation which must be signed by or record the names of and be affixed with the seals, of all partners.
(2) The articles of incorporation in the preceding paragraph may be prepared using electromagnetic records. In such cases, measures prescribed by the applicable Ordinance of the Ministry of Justice must be taken in lieu of signing, or the recording of names and affixing of seals, with respect to the information recorded in such electromagnetic records.

(Matters to be Specified or Recorded in the Articles of Incorporation)
Article 576 (1) Articles of incorporation of Membership Companies must specify or record the following matters:
(i) Purposes;
(ii) Trade name;
(iii) Location of the head office;
(iv) Names and addresses of the partners
(v) Whether the partners are unlimited partners or limited partners; and
(vi) Subject matter invested by the partners (limited to monies, etc. if they are limited partners) and the value and standard of evaluation of the same.
(2) If the Membership Company to be incorporated is a General Partnership Company, a statement that all of the partners are unlimited partners must be specified or recorded as the matter listed in item (v) of the preceding paragraph.
(3) If the Membership Company to be incorporated is a Limited Partnership Company, a statement that some of the partners are unlimited partners and other partners are limited partners must be stated or recorded as the matter listed in item (v) of paragraph (1).
(4) If the Membership Company to be incorporated is a Limited Liability Company, a statement that all of the partners are limited partners must be stated or recorded as the matter listed in item (v) of paragraph (1).

Article 577 In addition to those provided for in the preceding paragraph, articles of incorporation of a Membership Company may state or record matters which, under the provisions of this Act, will not become effective unless provided for in the articles of incorporation, or other matters which do not violate any provision of this Act.

(Performance of Contributions as at Incorporation of Limited Liability Companies)
Article 578 In cases where a Membership Company to be incorporated is a Limited Liability Company, persons who intend to be partners of such Limited Liability Company must pay in the entire sum of monies relating to their partnership contribution or deliver the entire property, other than monies, relating to their contribution after the preparation of the articles of incorporation but before the registration of the incorporation of the Limited Liability Company; provided, however, that, if the consent of all

persons who intend to be partners of the Limited Liability Company is obtained, this shall not preclude them from carrying out registration, recording or other acts necessary to assert the creation or transfer of rights against third parties after the incorporation of the Limited Liability Company.

(Incorporation of Membership Companies)
Article 579 A Membership Company shall be incorporated by the registration of the incorporation at the location of its head office.

Chapter II Partners

Section 1 Responsibility of Partners

(Responsibility of Partners)
Article 580 (1) Partners shall be jointly and severally liable for the performance of obligations of the Membership Company in the cases listed below:
  (i) In cases where the obligations of such Membership Company cannot be fully performed with the assets of the same; or
  (ii) In cases where compulsory execution against the assets of such Membership Company has not been successful (except for the cases where the partners have proven that such Membership Company has financial resources to pay and that the compulsory execution can be effected at ease).
(2) Limited liability partners shall be liable for the performance of the obligations of the Membership Company to the extent of the value of their investment (excluding the value of the contributions already performed to the Membership Company).

(Partners' Defenses)
Article 581 (1) In cases where partners are liable for the performance of the obligations of a Membership Company, the partners may assert defenses against the creditors of such Membership Company that the Membership Company may raise against such creditors.
(2) In the cases provided for in the preceding paragraph, if a Membership Company has a right to set-off, right to rescind or right to terminate against its creditors, the partners may refuse the performance of obligations to such creditors.

(Partners' Liability in relation to Contributions)
Article 582 (1) In cases where a partner provides monies as the subject matter of a partnership contribution, if he/she fails to effect such contribution, such partner must compensate the loss in addition to the payment of interest on such contribution.
(2) In cases where a partner provides claims as the subject matter of a contribution, if the obligor of such claims fails to perform the obligations when they become due, such partner shall be liable for the performance of the same. In such cases, such partner must compensate the loss in addition to the payment of interest on such obligations.

(Special Provision in case of Partners' Liability Change)
Article 583 (1) In cases where a limited partner has become an unlimited partner, the person who has become such unlimited partner shall also be liable as an unlimited partner for the performance of the obligations of the Membership Company that arose before such person became an unlimited partner.
(2) Even in cases where a limited partner (excluding partners of Limited Liability Company) reduce the value of the contributions, such limited partners shall be liable to the

extent of his/her pre-existing liability for the obligations of the Membership Company that arose before the registration to that effect.
(3) Even in cases where an unlimited partner has become a limited partner, the person who has become such a limited partner shall be liable as an unlimited partner for the performance of the obligations of the Membership Company that arose before the registration to such effect.
(4) The liability under the preceding two paragraphs to the creditors of the Membership Company who do not make their claims, or do not give an advance notice of their claims, within two years from the day of such registration shall be extinguished when two years have elapsed from the day of the registration in the preceding two paragraphs.

(Capacity to Act of Minors Permitted to Become Unlimited Partners)
Article 584 A minor who is permitted to become an unlimited partner of a Membership Company shall be deemed to be a person with capacity to act regarding any act committed in his/her capacity as a partner.

Section 2 Assignments of Equity Interests

(Assignment of Equity Interest)
Article 585 (1) A partner cannot assign all or part of his/her equity interests to others without the approval of all other partners.
(2) Notwithstanding the provisions of the preceding paragraph, a limited partner who does not execute business may assign some or all of his/her equity interests to others if the approval of all other partners who execute the business is obtained.
(3) Notwithstanding the provisions of Article 637, if a change in the articles of incorporation arises in conjunction with the assignment of equity interests of any limited partner who does not execute the business, the change in the articles of incorporation due to the assignment of that equity interest may be effected with the consent of all partners who execute the business.
(4) The provisions of the preceding three paragraphs shall not preclude the provisions to the contrary in the articles of incorporation.

(Liability of Partners who Assign Entire Equity Interests)
Article 586 (1) A partner who assigned all of his/her equity interests to others shall be liable to the extent of his/her pre-existing liability for the obligations of the Membership Company that arose before the registration to that effect.
(2) Liability in the preceding paragraph to the creditors of the Membership Company who do not state their claims or do not give an advance notice of their claims, within two years from the day of such registration shall be extinguished when two years have elapsed from the day of the registration in that paragraph.

Article 587 (1) Membership Companies may not accept the assignment of some or all of their own equity interests.
(2) In cases where a Membership Company has acquired any equity interest in such Membership Company, such equity interest shall be extinguished when such Membership Company acquires the same.

Section 3 Liability for Mistaken Acts

(Liability of Limited Partners for Acts Mistaken as Acts of Unlimited Part-

ners)
Article 588 (1) If a limited partner of a Limited Partnership Company engages in an act that causes such limited partner to be mistaken as an unlimited partner, such limited partner shall assume the same liability as that assumed by an unlimited partner in relation to persons who transact with the Limited Partnership Company based on such mistaken belief.
(2) If a limited partner of a Limited Partnership Company or Limited Liability Company engages in an act that causes mistake as to the extent of the limited partner's liability (excluding that in the preceding paragraph), such limited partner shall assume the liability to perform the obligations of such Limited Partnership Company or Limited Liability Company in relation to persons who transact with the Limited Partnership Company or Limited Liability Company on the bases of such mistaken belief, to the extent of the liability so mistaken.

(Responsibility for Acts Mistaken as Acts of Partners)
Article 589 (1) If a person who is neither a partner of a General Partnership Company nor Limited Partnership Company engages in an act that causes such person to be mistaken as an unlimited partner, such person shall assume the same liability as that assumed by an unlimited partner in relation to persons who transact with the General Partnership Company or Limited Partnership Company on the bases of such mistaken belief.
(2) If a person who is a partner in neither a Limited Partnership Company nor Limited Liability Company engages in an act that causes such person to be mistaken as a limited partner, such person shall assume liability to perform the obligations of such Limited Partnership Company or Limited Liability Company in relation to persons who transact with the Limited Partnership Company or Limited Liability Company on the bases of such mistaken belief the to the extent of the liability so mistaken.

Chapter III Administration
Section 1 General Provisions

(Execution of Business)
Article 590 (1) A partner shall execute the business of the Membership Company, unless otherwise provided for in the articles of incorporation.
(2) In cases where there are two or more partners, the business of the Membership Company shall be determined by a majority of the partners, unless otherwise provided for in the articles of incorporation.
(3) Notwithstanding the provisions of the preceding paragraph, each partner may perform the ordinary business of the Membership Company individually; provided, however, that this shall not apply in cases where other partners raise objections before the completion of the same.

(Where Articles of Incorporation Provide for Partners who Execute Business)
Article 591 (1) In cases where partners who execute the business are provided for in the articles of incorporation, if there are two or more partners who execute the business, the business of the Membership Company shall be determined by a majority of the partners who execute the operations, unless otherwise provided for in the articles of incorporation. For the purpose of the application of the provisions of paragraph (3) of the preceding article to such cases, "partner(s)" in that paragraph shall be read as "partner(s) who execute(s) the business."

(2) Notwithstanding the provisions of the preceding paragraph, in the cases provided for in that paragraph, the appointment and dismissal of managers shall be determined by a majority of the partners; provided, however, that this shall not preclude the provision to the contrary in the articles of incorporation.
(3) In cases where partners who execute the business are provided for in the articles of incorporation, if all partners who execute the operations leave the Company, such provisions of the articles of incorporation shall become ineffective.
(4) In cases where partners who execute the business are provided for in the articles of incorporation, partners who execute the business may not resign without justifiable grounds.
(5) Partners who execute the business under the preceding paragraph may be dismissed with the unanimous consent of other partners, limited to cases where there are justifiable grounds.
(6) The provisions of the preceding two paragraphs shall not preclude the provision to the contrary in the articles of incorporation.

(Partners' Investigations regarding Status of Business and Assets of Membership Company)
Article 592 (1) In cases where partners who execute the business are provided for in the articles of incorporation, each partner may investigate the status of the business and assets of the Membership Company even if he/she does not have the rights to execute the business of the same.
(2) The provisions of the preceding paragraph shall not preclude provision to the contrary in the articles of incorporation; provided, however, that even the articles of incorporation may not provide to the effect of restricting the carrying out of investigations by partners provided for in that paragraph at the end of the business year or if there are significant grounds to do so.

Section 2 Partners who Execute Business

(Relationship between Partners Executing Business and Membership Company)
Article 593 (1) Partners who execute the business shall have the duty to perform their duties with due care of a prudent manager.
(2) Partners who execute the business must perform their duties for the Membership Company in a loyal manner in compliance with the laws and regulations and articles of incorporation.
(3) Partners who execute the business must report the status of the execution of their duties whenever there are requests by the Membership Company or other partners, and must report the progress and outcome of their duties without delay after those duties end.
(4) The provisions of Article 646 through 650 of the Civil Code shall apply mutatis mutandis to the relationship between partners who execute the business and the Membership Company. In such cases, "mandated business" in paragraph (1) of Article 646, paragraph (2) of Article 648, Article 649 and Article 650 shall be deemed to be replaced with "their duties," and "mandate" in paragraph (3) of Article 648 of the same Code shall be deemed to be replaced with "duties in the preceding paragraph."
(5) The provisions of the preceding two paragraphs shall not preclude provision to the contrary in the articles of incorporation.

(Non-Competition)

Article 594 (1) Partners who execute the business may not carry out the following acts without the approval of all partners other than such partners; provided, however, that this shall not apply in cases where the articles of incorporation provide otherwise:
  (i) Carrying out, for themselves or for a third party, any transaction which is in the line of business of the Membership Company; or
  (ii) Becoming directors, executive officers or partners who execute the business of a Company the purpose of which is a business that is similar to the business of the Membership Company.
(2) If partners who execute the business carry out any act listed in item (i) of the preceding paragraph in violation of the provisions of that paragraph, the amount of the profit obtained by such partners who execute such business or any third party as a result of such act shall be presumed to be amount of the loss suffered by the Membership Company.

(Restrictions on Transactions involving Conflict of Interest)
Article 595 (1) In the following cases, partners who execute the business must obtain the approval of a majority of the partners other than such partners with respect to such transactions; provided, however, that this shall not apply in cases where the articles of incorporation provide otherwise:
  (i) If partners who execute the business intend to engage in a transaction with the Membership Company for themselves or on behalf of a third party; or
  (ii) If a Membership Company intends to guarantee the debt of partners who execute the business or otherwise to engage in a transaction with any person other than partners that will results in the conflict of interest between the Membership Company and such partners.
(2) The provisions of Article 108 of the Civil Code shall not apply to transactions under item (i) of the preceding paragraph that have received the approval under that paragraph.

(Liability of Partners who Execute Operations to Membership Company for Damages)
Article 596 If partners who execute the business fail to perform their duties, they shall be jointly and severally liable to the Membership Company for losses arising as a result.

(Liability of Limited Partners who Execute Business to Membership Company for Damages)
Article 597 If limited partners who execute the business had knowledge, or was grossly negligent in discharging their duties, such limited partners shall be jointly and severally liable to compensate losses arising in a third party as a result.

(Special Provisions where Juridical Persons are Partners Executing Business)
Article 598 (1) In cases where juridical persons act as partners who execute the business, such juridical persons must appoint persons who are to perform the duties of partners who execute such business and notify other partners of the names and addresses of such persons.
(2) The provisions from Article 593 through the preceding article shall apply mutatis mutandis to the persons who are to perform the duties of partners appointed under the provisions of the preceding paragraph.

(Representatives of Membership Companies)

Article 599 (1) A partner or partners who execute the business shall represent the Membership Company; provided, however, that this shall not apply in cases where partners or other persons who represent the Membership Companies are otherwise designated.
(2) In cases where there are two or more partners who execute the business referred to in the main clause of the preceding paragraph, each partner who executes the business shall represent the Membership Company individually.
(3) A Membership Company may appoint partners who represent the Membership Company from among the partners who execute the business pursuant to the articles of incorporation, or through the appointment by the partners themselves pursuant to the provisions of the articles of incorporation.
(4) Partners who represent the Membership Company shall have authority to do all judicial and non-judicial acts in connection with the operations of the Membership Company.
(5) No limitation on the authority under the preceding paragraph may be asserted against a third party without knowledge.

(Liability for Damages Caused by Acts of Partners who Represent Membership Companies)
Article 600 A Membership Company shall be liable to compensate losses that partners who represent the Membership Company or other representatives caused to third parties in the performance of their duties.

(Representation of Company in Claims between Membership Companies without Share and Partners)
Article 601 Notwithstanding the provisions of paragraph (4) of Article 599, in cases where a Membership Company files an action against any of its partners, or any of the partners files an action against that Membership Company, if there is no representative of the Membership Company with respect to such action (excluding the relevant partner), the representative of the Membership Company in such action may be determined by a majority of the partners other than such partner.

Article 602 Notwithstanding the provisions of paragraph (1) of Article 599, in cases where a partner requests that the Membership Company file an action to pursue the liability of a partner, if the Membership Company fails to file such action within 60 days after the day of such request, such partner making the request may represent the Membership Company with respect to such action; provided, however, that this shall not apply in cases where the purpose of such action is to seek unlawful gains of such partner or a third party or to inflict losses on such Membership Company.

Section 3 Persons who Perform Duties on behalf of Partners Executing Business

Article 603 (1) A person who is appointed by a provisional disposition order provided for in Article 56 of the Civil Provisional Remedies Act to act on behalf of partners who execute the business or partners who represent the Membership Company, in carrying out of the duties of the same, must obtain the permission of the court in order to engage in any act which does not belong to the ordinary business of the Membership Company, unless otherwise provided for in the provisional disposition order.
(2) An act of a person who acts on behalf of partners who execute the business or part-

ners who represent the Membership Company in carrying out duties of the same that is performed in violation of the provisions of the preceding paragraph shall be ineffective; provided, however, that the Membership Company may not assert that ineffectiveness against a third party without knowledge.

Chapter IV Admission and Withdrawal of Partners

Section 1 Admission of Partners

(Admission of Partners)
Article 604 (1) A Membership Company may admit a new partner.
(2) Admission of partners of a Membership Company shall take effect when a change relating to such partner is effected in the articles of incorporation.
(3) Notwithstanding the provisions of the preceding paragraph, in cases where a Limited Liability Company admits a new partner, if the person who intends to become the new partner has not performed all or a part of the payment or delivery relating to the contribution at the time of the change in the articles of incorporation in that paragraph, such person shall become a partner of the Limited Liability Company when such payment or delivery has been completed.

(Responsibility of Admitted Partners)
Article 605 A partner that is admitted after the incorporation of a Membership Company shall also be liable for the performance of obligations of the Membership Company that arose before such admission.

Section 2 Withdrawal of Partners

(Voluntary Withdrawal)
Article 606 (1) In cases where the duration of a Membership Company is not provided by the articles of incorporation, or in cases where the articles of incorporation provide that the Membership Company shall continue to exist for the life of a particular partner, each partner may withdraw at the end of the business year. In such cases, each partner must give advance notice of withdrawal to the Membership Company more than six months in advance.
(2) The provisions of the preceding paragraph do not preclude the Membership Company from provision to the contrary in the articles of incorporation.
(3) Notwithstanding the provisions of the preceding two paragraphs, if there are any unavoidable grounds, any partner may withdraw at any time.

(Statutory Withdrawal)
Article 607 (1) Other than as provided for in the preceding article, paragraph (1) of Article 609, Article 642 and Article 845, partners shall withdraw on the grounds listed below:
(i) Grounds provided for in the articles of incorporation having arisen;
(ii) The consent of all partners;
(iii) Death;
(iv) Mergers (limited to cases where the relevant partner that is a juridical person is liquidated as a result of the merger);
(v) A ruling to commence bankruptcy procedures;
(vi) Dissolution (excluding that resulting from the grounds listed in the preceding two items);

(vii) Being subject to a decision for commencement of guardianship; or
(viii) Removal.
(2) A Membership Company can provide to the effect that no partner shall withdraw due to some or all of the grounds listed in items (v) through (vii) of the preceding paragraph.

(Special Provision in case of Inheritances and Mergers)
Article 608 (1) A Membership Company may provide in its articles of incorporation that, in cases where a partner in the same dies or is liquidated as a result of the merger, the heirs or other general successors of such partner may succeed to the equity interest of such partner.
(2) Notwithstanding the provisions of paragraph (2) of Article 604, in cases where the provisions in the preceding paragraph are prescribed in the articles of incorporation, a general successor in that paragraph (limited to general successors that are not a partner) shall become a partner holding equity interest in that paragraph at the time when the general successor succeeds to such equity interest.
(3) In cases where there is a provision in paragraph (1) in the articles of incorporation, the Membership Company shall be deemed to have effected the change in the articles of incorporation relating to the general successor in that paragraph when such general successor has succeeded to the equity interest under that paragraph.
(4) In cases where there are two or more general successors (limited to general successors that have succeeded to a partnership interest by inheritance and have not performed all or part of the payment in or delivery relating to the partnership contribution) in paragraph (1), each general successor shall be jointly and severally liable for the performance of such payment in or delivery relating to the contribution.
(5) In cases where there are two or more general successors (limited to those who have succeeded to equity interest by inheritance) under paragraph (1), each general successor may not exercise his/her rights with respect to the interest which he/she has succeeded to unless he/she designates one person who exercises the rights with respect to such equity interest; provided, however, that this shall not apply in cases where the Membership Company gives its consent to the exercise of such rights.

(Forcing of Partners to Withdraw by Creditors that have attached Equity Interest)
Article 609 (1) A creditor that has attached the equity interest of a partner may force such partner to withdraw at the end of the business year. In such cases, such creditor must give advance notice thereof to the Membership Company and such partner more than 6 months in advance.
(2) The advance notice under the second sentence of the preceding paragraph shall become ineffective if the partner in that paragraph performs such partner's obligations to the creditor in that paragraph or has provided appropriate security.
(3) A creditor who gives the advance notice under the second sentence of paragraph (1) may petition the court for the disposition necessary to preserve the rights to claim the refund of the equity interest.

(Deemed Changes of Articles of Incorporation upon Withdrawal of Partners)
Article 610 In cases where a partner withdraws pursuant to the provisions of Article 606, paragraph (1) of Article 607, paragraph (1) of the preceding article or paragraph (2) of Article 642 (including the cases where a partner is deemed to have withdrawn under the provisions of Article 845), a Membership Company shall be deemed to have effected a change in the articles of incorporation to abolish the provisions of the arti-

cles of incorporation relating to such partner.

(Refund of Equity Interest in Conjunction with Withdrawal)
Article 611 (1) A partner that has withdrawn may receive the refund of his/her equity interest; provided, however, that this shall not apply in cases where a general successor of such partner becomes a partner under the provisions of paragraph (1) and paragraph (2) of Article 608.
(2) Accounting as between a partner that has withdrawn and the Membership Company must be effected in accordance with the status of the assets of the Membership Company as at the time of the withdrawal.
(3) The equity interest of a withdrawn partner may be refunded in monies regardless of the kind of his/her contribution.
(4) With respect to matters not completed yet as at the time of the withdrawal, accounting may be effected after the completion of the same.
(5) For the purpose of the application of the provisions of paragraph (2) and the preceding paragraph in cases where a partner withdraws due to removal, the words "the time of the withdrawal" in those provisions shall be read as "the time of the filing of an action seeking removal."
(6) In the cases provided for in the preceding paragraph, the Membership Company must also pay interest calculated at the rate of 6% per annum from and including the day of the time of the filing of an action seeking removal.
(7) Attachment on the equity interest of a partner shall be also effective to the rights seeking the refund of the equity interest.

(Liability of Withdrawn Partners)
Article 612 (1) A partner that has withdrawn shall be liable for the obligations of the Membership Company that arose before the registration of the withdrawal to the extent of the partner's pre-existing liability.
(2) The liability under the preceding paragraph shall be extinguished when two years have elapsed from the day of the registration under the preceding paragraph in relation to the creditors of the Membership Company who do not state their claims, or do not give an advance notice of their claims within two years from the day of such registration.

(Demand for Change of Trade Names)
Article 613 In cases where a Membership Company uses the family name or first and family names, or the corporate name, of a partner in its trade name, such partner that has withdrawn may demand that such Membership Company discontinue the use of such family name or first name and family names, or corporate name.

Chapter V Accounting

Section 1 Accounting Principles

Article 614 Accounting of a Membership Company shall be shall be subject to the corporate accounting practices that are generally accepted as fair and appropriate.

Section 2 Accounting Books

(Preparation and Retention of Accounting Books)
Article 615 (1) A Membership Company must prepare accurate accounting books in a

timely manner as prescribed by the applicable Ordinance of the Ministry of Justice.
(2) A Membership Company must retain its accounting books and important materials regarding its business for ten years from the time of the closing of the accounting books.

(Order to Submit Accounting Books)
Article 616 The court may, in response to a petition or ex officio, order the parties to a lawsuit to submit the accounting books, in whole or in part.

Section 3 Financial Statements

(Preparation and Retention of Financial Statements)
Article 617 (1) A Membership Company must prepare a balance sheet as of the day of its incorporation pursuant to the provisions of the applicable Ordinance of the Ministry of Justice.
(2) A Membership Company must prepare financial statements (hereinafter in this Chapter referring to balance sheet and other statements that are prescribed by the applicable Ordinance of the Ministry of Justice to be necessary and appropriate in order to indicate the status of the property of a Membership Company) for each business year pursuant to the provisions of the applicable Ordinance of the Ministry of Justice.
(3) Financial statements may be prepared by using electromagnetic records.
(4) A Membership Company must retain its financial statements for ten years from the time of the preparation of the same.

(Inspection of Financial Statements)
Article 618 (1) Partners of a Membership Company may submit the following requests at any time during the business hours of such Membership Company:
  (i) If the financial statements are prepared in writing, request for inspection or copying of such documents; or
  (ii) If the financial statements are prepared using electromagnetic records, requests for inspection or copying of anything that indicates the matters recorded in such electromagnetic records in a manner prescribed by the applicable Ordinance of the Ministry of Justice.
(2) The provisions of the preceding paragraph shall not preclude provision to the contrary in the articles of incorporation; provided, however, that even the articles of incorporation may not provide to the effect of restricting the submission of requests listed in each item of that paragraph at the end of the business year by partners.

(Order to Submit Financial Statements)
Article 619 The court may, in response to a petition or ex officio, order the parties to a lawsuit to submit financial statements, in whole or in part.

Section 4 Reductions in Stated Capital

Article 620 (1) A Membership Company may reduce the amount of its stated capital to compensate for losses.
(2) The amount by which the stated capital will be reduced under the provisions of the preceding paragraph cannot exceed the amount calculated in the manner prescribed by the applicable Ordinance of the Ministry of Justice as the amount of the losses.

Section 5 Distribution of Profit

(Distribution of Profits)
Article 621 (1) Partners may demand that the Membership Company distribute its profit.
(2) A Membership Company may prescribe matters regarding the method for demanding the distribution of the profit and other matters on the distribution of profit in the articles of incorporation.
(3) Attachment on the equity interest of a partner shall be also effective against the right to demand the distribution of the profits.

(Proportion of Distribution of Profits and Losses among Partners)
Article 622 (1) If there is no provision in the articles of incorporation with respect to the proportion of the distribution of profits and losses, those proportions shall be determined in accordance with the value of each partner's contribution.
(2) If provisions with respect to the proportions of the distribution of either profit or loss alone are provided in the articles of incorporation, it shall be presumed that such proportion is common to distributions of profits and distributions of losses.

(Limited Partners' Responsibility regarding Distribution of Profit)
Article 623 (1) In cases where the book value of the monies, etc. delivered by a Membership Company to a limited partner by the distribution of profit (hereinafter in this paragraph referred to as "Distributed Amount") exceeds the amount of the profit as at the day when such distribution of profit takes place (hereinafter in this Chapter referring to the amount calculated in the manner prescribed by the applicable Ordinance of the Ministry of Justice as the profit of a Membership Company), limited partners who received such distribution of profit shall be jointly and severally liable to such Membership Company for the payment of monies equivalent to such Distributed Amount.
(2) For the purpose of the application of the provisions of paragraph (2) of Article 580 to the partners that received the distribution of profit under the preceding paragraph in the cases provided for in that paragraph, words "to the extent of the value of their investment (excluding the value of the contributions to the Membership Company already performed)" in that paragraph (2) of Article 580 shall be read as "to the extent of the sum of the value of their investment (excluding the value of the contributions to the Membership Company already performed) and the amount by which the Distributed Amount under paragraph (1) of Article 623 exceeds the amount of the profit under that paragraph."

Section 6 Contribution Refunds

Article 624 (1) Partners may demand that the Membership Company refund the monies, etc. that partners have already paid in or delivered as contributions (hereinafter in this Part referred to as "Contribution Refunds"). In such cases, if such monies, etc. consist of any property other than monies, they shall not be precluded from demanding the refund of monies in an amount equivalent to the value of such property.
(2) M Membership Company may prescribe matters regarding the method for demanding the Contribution Refunds and other matters on Contribution Refunds in its articles of incorporation.
(3) Attachment of the equity interest of a partner shall be also effective against the rights to demand a Contribution Refunds.

Section 7 Special Provisions on Accounting of Limited Liability Companies

Subsection 1 Special Provision on Inspection of Financial Statements

Article 625 Creditors of a Limited Liability Company may make the requests listed in each item of paragraph (1) of Article 618 with respect to its financial statements (limited to those prepared within the preceding five years) at any time during the business hours of the Limited Liability Company.

Subsection 2 Special Provisions on Reduction in Stated Capital

(Reductions in Stated Capital where Contribution Refund is Effected)
Article 626 (1) In addition to the cases under paragraph (1) of Article 620, a Limited Liability Company may reduce the amount of its stated capital to effect a Contribution Refund.
(2) The amount of the stated capital to be reduced pursuant to the provisions of the preceding paragraph may not exceed the amount obtained by subtracting the surplus amount as of the day when the Refund of Contributions is effected from Contribution Refund Amount provided for in paragraph (2) of Article 632.
(3) The amount of the stated capital to be reduced by Partnership Interest Refund Amount pursuant to the provisions of the paragraph (1) may not exceed the amount obtained by subtracting the surplus amount as of the day when the Refund of Equity Interests is effected from Equity Interest Refund Amount provided for in paragraph (1) of Article 635.
(4) The term "surplus amount" provided for in the preceding two paragraphs shall mean the amount obtained by subtracting the total sum of the amounts listed in item (ii) through item (iv) from the amount listed in item (i) (the same shall apply to Subsection 4 and Subsection 5):
(i) Amount of assets;
(ii) Amount of debt;
(iii) Amount of stated capital; and
(iv) Other than those listed in the preceding two items, the total sum of the amounts accounted for in each line item prescribed by the applicable Ordinance of the Ministry of Justice.

(Objection of Creditors)
Article 627 (1) In cases where a Limited Liability Company reduces the amount of stated capital, creditors of such Limited Liability Company may state their objections to the reduction in the stated capital to such Limited Liability Company.
(2) In cases provided for in the preceding paragraph, the Limited Liability Company must give public notice of the matters listed below in the Official Gazette and must give notice of the same separately to each known creditor; provided, however, that the period under item (ii) cannot be less than one month:
(i) The details of such reduction in stated capital; and
(ii) A statement to the effect that creditors may state their objections within a certain period of time.
(3) Notwithstanding the provisions of the preceding paragraph, if, in addition to a notice in the Official Gazette, a Limited Liability Company effects the public notice under that

paragraph in a manner listed in item (ii) or item (iii) of paragraph (1) of Article 939 in accordance with the provisions of the articles of incorporation under the provisions of that paragraph, the Limited Liability Company shall no longer be required to give separate notices under the provisions of the preceding paragraph.
(4) In cases where the creditors do not raise any objection within the period under item (ii) of paragraph (2), such creditors shall be deemed to have approved such reduction of in the stated capital.
(5) In cases where the creditors raise any objection within the period under item (ii) of paragraph (2), the Limited Liability Company must make the payment or provide appropriate security to such creditors, or entrust equivalent assets to a qualified trust company for the purpose of assuring the payment to such creditors; provided, however, that this shall not apply if such reduction in the stated capital is unlikely to be detrimental to such creditors.
(6) The reduction in stated capital shall take effect on the day when the procedures in each of the preceding paragraphs has ended.

Subsection 3 Special Provisions concerning Distribution of Profits

(Restriction on Distribution of Profits)
Article 628 In cases where the book value of the monies, etc. delivered to partners of a Limited Liability Company through the distribution of profits (hereinafter in this Subsection referred to as "Distributed Amount") exceeds the amount of the profit as at the day when such distribution of profit takes place, such distribution of profit cannot be effected. In such cases, the Limited Liability Company may reject demands under the provisions of paragraph (1) of Article 621.

(Liability for Distribution of Profits)
Article 629 (1) In cases where a Limited Liability Company effects the distribution of profit in violation of the provisions of the preceding paragraph, the partners that executed the operations in connection with such distribution of profits shall be jointly and severally liable to such Limited Liability Company, together with the partners that received such distribution of profits, for payment of the monies in an amount equivalent to such Distributed Amount; provided, however, that this shall not apply in cases where such partners who executed such operations have proven that they did not fail to exercise due care with respect to the performance of their duties;
(2) Exemption from the obligations in the preceding paragraph cannot be given; provided, however, that this shall not apply in cases where consent of all partners is obtained with respect to the exemption of such obligations, to the extent of the amount of profits as at the day when the distribution of profits takes place.

(Restrictions on Right to Obtain Reimbursement from Partners)
Article 630 (1) In the cases provided for in paragraph (1) of the preceding article, if partners that received the distribution of profits are without knowledge with respect to the fact that the Distributed Amount exceeds the amount of the profit as at the day when such distribution of profit takes place, such partners shall not be obliged to respond to a demand for reimbursement by the partners who executed the operations in connection with such distribution of profit with respect to such Distributed Amount.
(2) In the cases provided for in paragraph (1) of the preceding article, creditors of a Limited Liability Company may have the partners that received the distribution of profits pay monies equivalent to the Distributed Amount (or, in cases where such Distributed

Amount exceeds the amount which the Limited Liability Company owes to such creditors, such amount owed).
(3) The provisions of paragraph (2) of Article 623 shall not apply to partners in a Limited Liability Company.

(Liability in Cases of Deficit)
Article 631 (1) In cases where a Limited Liability Company effects the distribution of profits, if a deficit (hereinafter in this paragraph referring to the amount calculated by the method prescribed by the applicable Ordinance of the Ministry of Justice as the amount of the deficit of the Limited Liability Company) occurs at the end of the business year that contains the day on which such distribution of profit takes place, partners that executed the operations in connection with such distribution of profit with respect to such Distributed Amount shall be jointly and severally liable to such Limited Liability Company, together with the partners who received such distribution of profit, for payment of the amount of that deficit (or, if the amount of such deficit exceeds the Distributed Amount, such Distributed Amount); provided, however, that this shall not apply in cases where such partners who executed such operations have proven that they did not fail to exercise due care with respect to the performance of their duties:
(2) Exemption from the obligations in the preceding paragraph cannot be given without the consent of all partners.

Subsection 4 Special Provisions on Contribution Refunds

(Restrictions on Contribution Refunds)
Article 632 (1) Notwithstanding the provisions of paragraph (1) of Article 624, partners in a Limited Liability Company may not make the demand under the provisions of the first sentence of that paragraph except in cases where the value of partner's contributions will be reduced by changes in the articles of incorporation.
(2) In cases where the book value of the monies, etc. delivered by a Limited Liability Company to a partner by Contribution Refunds (hereinafter in this Subsection referred to as "Amount of Contribution Refunds") exceeds the amount of surplus as of the day when a demand is made under the provisions of the first sentence of paragraph (1) of Article 624 (in cases where the reduction in the stated capital under paragraph (1) of Article 626 is effected, hereinafter in this Subsection referring to the amount of surplus after such reduction), or the reduction in the value of partner's contributions in the preceding paragraph, whichever is lower, such Contribution Refunds cannot be effected. In such cases, the Limited Liability Company may reject the demand under the provisions of the first sentence of paragraph (1) of Article 624.

(Partner's Liability for Contribution Refunds)
Article 633 (1) In cases where a Limited Liability Company effects the Contribution Refunds in violation of the provisions of the preceding paragraph, the partners who executed the operations in connection with such Contribution Refunds shall be jointly and severally liable to such Limited Liability Company, together with the partners who received such Contribution Refunds, for payment of the monies in an amount equivalent to such Amount of Contribution Refunds; provided, however, that this shall not apply in cases where such partners who executed such operations have proven that they did not fail to exercise due care in the performance of their duties:
(2) Exemption from the obligations under the preceding paragraph may not be given; provided, however, that this shall not apply in cases where consent of all partners is ob-

tained with respect to the exemption of such obligations to the extent of the surplus as at the day when the Contribution Refunds takes place.

(Restrictions on Rights to Obtain Reimbursement from Partners)
Article 634 (1) In the cases provided for in paragraph (1) of the preceding article, if partners who received the Contribution Refund are without knowledge with respect to the fact that the Amount of Contribution Refunds exceeds the amount of surplus as at the day when such Contribution Refunds takes place, such partners shall not have the obligation to respond to the demand for reimbursement by the partners that executed the operations in connection with such Contribution Refunds with respect to such Amount of Contribution Refunds.
(2) In the cases provided for in paragraph (1) of the preceding article, creditors of a Limited Liability Company may have the partners that received the Contribution Refunds pay the monies equivalent to the Amount of Contribution Refunds (or, in cases where such Amount of Contribution Refunds exceeds the amount that the Limited Liability Company owes to such creditors, such amount owed).

Subsection 5 Special Provisions on Refund of Equity Interest in Conjunction with Withdrawals

(Objection of Creditors)
Article 635 (1) In cases where the book value of the monies, etc. delivered by a Limited Liability Company to partners through equity interest refund (hereinafter in this Subsection referred to as "Partnership Interest Refund Amount") exceeds the surplus as of the day when such equity interest refund takes place, creditors of such Limited Liability Company may state their objections as to the equity interest refund to such Limited Liability Company.
(2) In cases provided for in the preceding paragraph, the Limited Liability Company must make the public notice of the matters listed below in the Official Gazette and must give notice of the same separately to each known creditor, if any; provided, however, that the period in item (ii) cannot be less than one month (or, in cases where the Partnership Interest Refund Amount exceeds the amount calculated by the method prescribed by the applicable Ordinance of the Ministry of Justice as the amount of the net assets of such Limited Liability Company, two months):
(i) The details of the equity interest refund that exceeds such surplus; and
(ii) A statement to the effect that creditors may state their objections within a certain period of time.
(3) Notwithstanding the provisions of the preceding paragraph, if, in addition to using the Official Gazette, a Limited Liability Company effects the public notice in that paragraph in a manner listed in item (ii) or (iii) of paragraph (1) of Article 939 in accordance with the provisions of the articles of incorporation under the provisions of that paragraph, the Limited Liability Company shall no longer be required to give separate notices under the provisions of the preceding paragraph; provided, however, that this shall not apply in cases where the Partnership Interest Refund Amount exceeds the amount calculated by the method prescribed by the applicable Ordinance of the Ministry of Justice as the amount of the net assets of such Limited Liability Company.
(4) In cases where the creditors do not raise any objection within the period in item (ii) of paragraph (2), such creditors shall be deemed to have approved such equity interest refund.
(5) In cases where the creditors raise objections within the period in item (ii) of paragraph (2), the Limited Liability Company must make the payment or provide appropriate se-

curity to such creditors, or entrust appropriate assets to a qualified trust company with the purpose of assuring the payment to such creditors; provided, however, that this shall not apply if, in cases where the Partnership Interest Refund Amount does not exceed the amount calculated by the method prescribed by the applicable Ordinance of the Ministry of Justice as the net assets of such Limited Liability Company, such equity interest refund is unlikely to be detrimental to such creditors.

(Responsibility of Partners who Execute Operations)
Article 636 (1) In cases where a Limited Liability Company effects an equity interest refund in violation of the provisions of the preceding paragraph, the partners who executed the operations in connection with such equity interest refund shall be jointly and severally liable to such Limited Liability Company, together with the partners who received such equity interest refund, for payment of the monies in the amount equivalent to such Partnership Interest Refund Amount; provided, however, that this shall not apply in cases where such partners who executed the operations regarding the refund of equity interest have proven that they did not fail to exercise due care in the performance of their duties:
(2) Exemptions from the obligations under the preceding paragraph cannot be given; provided, however, that this shall not apply in cases where consent of all partners is obtained with respect to the exemption of such obligations to the extent of the surplus as at the day when the equity interest refund takes place.

Chapter VI Change in Articles of Incorporation

(Change in Articles of Incorporation)
Article 637 A Membership Company may change its articles of incorporation with the consent of all partners, unless otherwise provided for in the articles of incorporation.

(Change in Kind of Membership Company by Change in Articles of Incorporation)
Article 638 (1) A General Partnership Company shall, by effecting the change in the articles of incorporation listed in each of the following items, become a Membership Company of the kind listed in each such item:
(i) Changes in the articles of incorporation that admits limited partners: Limited Partnership Company;
(ii) Changes of the articles of incorporation to convert some of its partners into limited partners: Limited Partnership Company;
(iii) Changes of the articles of incorporation to convert all of its partners into limited partners: Limited Liability Company.
(2) A Limited Partnership Company shall, by effecting the change in the articles of incorporation listed in each of the following items, become a Membership Company of the kind listed in each such item:
(i) Changes in the articles of incorporation to convert all of its partners into unlimited partners: General Partnership Company; and
(ii) Changes in the articles of incorporation to convert all of its partners into limited partners: Limited Liability Company.
(3) A Limited Liability Company shall, by effecting the change in the articles of incorporation listed in each of the following items, become a Membership Company of the kind listed in each such item:
(i) Changes in the articles of incorporation to convert all of its partners into unlimited partners: General Partnership Company;

(ii) Changes in the articles of incorporation to admit unlimited partners: Limited Partnership Company; and
(iii) Changes in the articles of incorporation to convert some of its partners into unlimited partners: Limited Partnership Company.

(Deemed Changes in Articles of Incorporation on Withdrawal of Partners of a Limited Partnership Company)
Article 639 (1) In cases where, due to withdrawal of limited partners, partners of a Limited Partnership Company consist only of unlimited partners, such Limited Partnership Company shall be deemed to have effected a change in the articles of incorporation to become an General Partnership Company.
(2) In cases where, due to withdrawal of unlimited partners, partners of a Limited Partnership Company consist only of limited partners, such Limited Partnership Company shall be deemed to have effected changes in the articles of incorporation to become a Limited Liability Company.

(Performance of Contributions in Changing Articles of Incorporation)
Article 640 (1) In cases where changes in the articles of incorporation listed in item (iii) of paragraph (1) or item (ii) of paragraph (2) of Article 638 is to be effected, if partners of the Membership Company that effects such changes in the articles of incorporation have not performed all or part of the payment in or delivery relating to the contributions to the Limited Liability Company after such changes in the articles of incorporation, such changes in the articles of incorporation shall take effect on the day when such payment in and delivery have been completed.
(2) In cases where changes in the articles of incorporation to become a Limited Liability Company are deemed to have been effected pursuant to the provisions of paragraph (2) of the preceding article, if the partners have not performed all or part of the payment in or delivery relating to the partners' contributions, such payment in or delivery must be completed within one month of the day when such changes in the articles of incorporation are deemed to have been effected; provided, however, that this shall not apply in cases where changes in the articles of incorporation to become a General Partnership Company or Limited Partnership Company are effected within such period.

Chapter VII Dissolution

(Grounds for Dissolution)
Article 641 A Membership Company shall dissolve on the grounds listed below:
(i) The expiration of the duration provided for in the articles of incorporation;
(ii) The grounds for dissolution provided for in the articles of incorporation having arisen
(iii) The consent of all partners;
(iv) The absence of all partners;
(v) A merger (limited to cases where such Membership Company is liquidated as a result of the merger);
(vi) A ruling for commencement of bankruptcy procedures; or
(vii) A judgment ordering the dissolution under the provisions of paragraph (1) of Article 824 or paragraph (1) of Article 833.

(Continuation of Membership Companies)
Article 642 (1) In cases where a Membership Company dissolves on the grounds listed in items (i) through (iii) of the preceding article, the Membership Company may con-

tinue in existence by the consent of some or all partners until the completion of the liquidation under the provisions of the following Chapter.
(2) In the case provided for in the preceding paragraph, partners who have not given consent to the continuation of the Membership Company shall withdraw on the day when it is determined that the Membership Company will continue in existence.

(Restrictions on Mergers of Dissolved Membership Company)
Article 643 In cases where a Membership Company has dissolved, such Membership Company cannot engage in the following acts:
 (i) Mergers (limited to the cases where such Membership Company survives the merger);
 (ii) Succession by Absorption-type Company Split to some or all of the rights and obligations held by another Company with respect to such Company's business.

Chapter VIII Liquidation

Section 1 Commencement of Liquidation

(Causes of Commencement of Liquidation)
Article 644 A Membership Company must go into liquidation in the cases listed below subject to the provisions of this Chapter:
 (i) In cases where the Membership Company has dissolved (excluding the cases where Membership Companies have dissolved on the grounds listed in item (v) of Article 641 and cases where Membership Companies have dissolved as a result of a ruling for commencement of bankruptcy procedures and such bankruptcy procedures have not ended);
 (ii) In cases where a judgment allowing a claim seeking invalidation of the incorporation has become final and binding; or
 (iii) In cases where a judgment which permits a claim seeking rescission of the incorporation has become final and binding.

(Capacity of Liquidating Membership Companies)
Article 645 Membership Companies that go into liquidation themselves under the provisions of the preceding article (hereinafter referred to as "Liquidating Membership Companies") shall be deemed to remain in existence until the completion of liquidation to the extent of the purpose of the liquidation.

Section 2 Liquidators

(Establishment of Liquidators)
Article 646 A Liquidating Membership Company must have one or more liquidators.

(Assumption of Office of Liquidators)
Article 647 (1) The following persons shall become liquidators of a Liquidating Membership Company:
 (i) A partner who executes the operations (excluding the cases where persons listed in the following item or in item (iii) exist);
 (ii) A person prescribed by the articles of incorporation; or
 (iii) A person prescribed by the consent of a majority of partners (or, if partners who execute the operations are provided for in the articles of incorporation, those part-

Art.648～652　　　Ⅰ Companies Act, PART III, Chap.VIII, Sec.2

ners).
(2) In the absence of a liquidator under the provisions of the preceding paragraph, the court shall appoint a liquidator in response to the petition by the interested parties.
(3) Notwithstanding the provisions of the preceding two paragraphs, with respect to a Liquidating Membership Company that has dissolved on the grounds listed in item (iv) of item (vii) of Article 641, the court shall appoint a liquidator in response to a petition by interested parties or the Minister of Justice or ex officio.
(4) Notwithstanding the provisions of paragraphs (1) and (2), with respect to a Liquidating Membership Company that has fallen under the cases listed in item (ii) or (iii) of Article 644, the court shall appoint a liquidator in response to a petition by the interested parties.

(Dismissal of Liquidators)
Article 648 (1) Liquidators (excluding those appointed by the court under the provisions of paragraphs (2) through (4) of the preceding article) may be dismissed at any time.
(2) Dismissals under the provisions of the preceding paragraph shall be determined by a majority of the partners unless otherwise provided for in the articles of incorporation.
(3) If there are significant grounds, the court may dismiss a liquidator in response to a petition by the partners or other interested parties.

(Liquidators' Duties)
Article 649 Liquidators shall perform the following duties:
(i) The conclusion of current business;
(ii) The collection of debts and the performance of obligations; and
(iii) To deliver the residual assets.

(Execution of Business)
Article 650 (1) A liquidator shall execute the operations of the Liquidating Membership Company.
(2) In cases where there are two or more liquidators, the operations of the Liquidating Membership Company shall be decided by a majority of the liquidators, unless otherwise provided for in the articles of incorporation.
(3) Notwithstanding the provisions of the preceding paragraph, in cases where there are two or more partners, assignment of some or all of the business of a Liquidating Membership Company shall be decided by a majority of the partners.

(Relationship between Liquidators and Liquidating Membership Company)
Article 651 (1) The relationship between a Liquidating Membership Company and its liquidators shall be governed by the applicable provisions on mandate.
(2) The provisions of paragraph (2) of Article 593, Article 594 and Article 595 shall apply mutatis mutandis to liquidators. In such cases, "partners other than such partners" in paragraph (1) of Article 594 and paragraph (1) of Article 595 shall be deemed to be read as "partners (or, in cases where such liquidators are partners, partners other than such liquidators)."

(Liquidators' Liability for Damages to Liquidating Membership Company)
Article 652 If liquidators fail to discharge their duties, the liquidators shall be jointly and severally liable to compensate such Liquidating Membership Company for losses arising as a result.

(Liquidators' Liability for Damages to Third Parties)

Article 653 If liquidators had knowledge or was grossly negligent in discharging the duties of the same, such liquidators shall be jointly and severally liable to compensate losses arising in a third party as a result.

(Special Provisions where Juridical Persons are Liquidators)
Article 654 (1) In case where juridical persons act as liquidators, such juridical persons must appoint persons who are to perform the duties of such liquidators and notify the partners of the names and addresses of such persons.

(2) The provisions of the preceding three articles shall apply mutatis mutandis to the persons who are to perform the duties of liquidators appointed under the provisions of the preceding paragraph.

(Representatives of Liquidating Membership Company)
Article 655 (1) A liquidator or liquidators shall represent the Liquidating Membership Company; provided, however, that this shall not apply in cases where liquidators or other persons who represent the Liquidating Membership Company are otherwise prescribed.

(2) In cases where there are two or more liquidators referred to in the main clause of the preceding paragraph, each liquidator shall represent the Liquidating Membership Company individually.

(3) A Liquidating Membership Company may appoint liquidators who represent the Liquidating Membership Company from among the liquidators pursuant to the articles of incorporation, or through the appointment by the liquidators (hereinafter in this paragraph excluding those appointed by the court under the provisions of paragraph (2) through paragraph (4) of Article 647) from among themselves pursuant to the provisions of the articles of incorporation.

(4) In cases where partners who execute the operations become liquidators pursuant to the provisions of item (i), paragraph (1) of Article 647, if the partners that represent the Membership Company are already prescribed, such partners that represent the Membership Company shall become the liquidators that represent the Liquidating Membership Company.

(5) In cases where the court appoints liquidators under the provisions of paragraph (2) through paragraph (4) of Article 647, the court may prescribe liquidators that represent the Liquidating Membership Company from among those liquidators.

(6) The provisions of paragraph (4) and paragraph (5) of Article 599 shall apply mutatis mutandis to liquidators that represent the Liquidating Membership Company, and the provisions of Article 603 shall apply mutatis mutandis to persons that are appointed by a provisional disposition order provided for in Article 56 of the Civil Provisional Remedies Act to perform the duties of liquidators or liquidators who represent the Liquidating Membership Company on behalf of them, respectively.

(Commencement of Bankruptcy Procedures with respect to Liquidating Membership Company)
Article 656 (1) In cases where it has become clear that the assets of a Liquidating Membership Company are not sufficient to fully discharge its debts, liquidators must immediately file a petition for the commencement of bankruptcy procedures.

(2) In cases where a Liquidating Membership Company is subject to a ruling for the commencement of bankruptcy procedures, if liquidators have transferred the administration of the same to the trustee in bankruptcy, liquidators shall be have completed their duties.

(3) In the cases provided for in the preceding paragraph, if the Liquidating Membership

Company has already made payments to creditors or distributions to partners, the trustee in bankruptcy may retrieve the same.

(Remuneration for Liquidators Appointed by the Court)
Article 657 In cases where the court has appointed a liquidator under the provisions of paragraphs (2) through (4) of Article 647, the court may prescribe the amount of the remuneration that the Liquidating Membership Company shall pay to such liquidator.

Section 3 Inventory of Property

(Preparation of Inventory of Property)
Article 658 (1) Liquidators must investigate the current status of the property of the Liquidating Membership Companies and prepare, pursuant to the provisions of the applicable Ordinance of the Ministry of Justice, an inventory of property and the balance sheet as of the day when the Liquidating Membership Companies fell under cases listed in any of the item of Article 644 (hereinafter in this Section referred to as "Inventory of Property") and notify each partner of the details of the same, without delay after assuming office.
(2) Liquidating Membership Companies must retain its Inventory of Property from the time of the preparation of such Inventory of Property until the registration completion of the liquidation at the location of its head office.
(3) Liquidating Membership Companies must report every month the current status of the liquidation at the request of the partners.

(Orders to Submit Inventory of Property)
Article 659 The court may, in response to a petition or ex officio, order parties to a lawsuit to submit the Inventory of Property, in whole or in part.

Section 4 Performance of Obligations

(Public Notices to Creditors)
Article 660 (1) A Liquidating Membership Company (hereinafter in this paragraph and in the following article limited to Limited Liability Companies) must, without delay after having fallen under a case listed in any item of Article 644, give public notice in the Official Gazette to the creditors of such Liquidating Membership Companies to the effect that creditors should state their claims during a certain period of time and must give notice of the same separately to each known creditor, if any; provided, however, that such period cannot be less than two months.
(2) The pubic notice pursuant to the provisions of the preceding paragraph must contain a notation to the effect that such creditors will be excluded from the liquidation unless they state their claims during such period of time.

(Restrictions on Performance of Obligations)
Article 661 (1) A Liquidating Membership Company cannot perform its obligations during the period of time under paragraph (1) of the preceding article. In such cases, a Liquidating Membership Company cannot be exempted from the liability arising from its failure to perform.
(2) Notwithstanding the provisions of the preceding paragraph, even during the period of time under paragraph (1) of the preceding article, a Liquidating Membership Company may, with the permission of the court, perform its obligations relating to minor claims,

claims secured by security interests over the assets of the Liquidating Membership Company, or other claims unlikely to be detrimental to other creditors even if performed. In such cases, if there are two or more liquidators, the petition for such permission must be made with the consent of all of them.

(Performance of Obligations relating to Conditional Claims)
Article 662 (1) A Liquidating Membership Company may perform obligations relating to conditional claims, claims the duration of indeterminate duration or other claims of indeterminate amount. In such cases, a petition for the appointment of an appraiser must be filed with the court in order to have such claims evaluated.
(2) In the cases provided for in the preceding paragraph, a Liquidating Membership Company must perform its obligations relating to the claims under that paragraph in accordance with the evaluation by the appraiser under that paragraph.
(3) The expenses of the procedures for the appointment of the appraiser under paragraph (1) shall be borne by the Liquidating Membership Company. The same shall apply to the expense of summonses and questions for the purpose of appraiser's evaluation.

(Demand for Performance of Contributions)
Article 663 In cases where the current assets of a Liquidating Membership Company are not sufficient to fully discharge its debts, if there are partners who have not performed all or part of their contributions, such Liquidating Membership Company may have such partners make their contributions, notwithstanding the provisions of the articles of incorporation relating to such contributions.

(Restrictions on Distribution of Residual Assets before Performance of Obligations)
Article 664 A Liquidating Membership Company cannot distribute its assets to its partners until after performance of the obligations of such Liquidating Membership Company; provided, however, that this shall not apply in cases where assets regarded as necessary for the performance of obligations relating to a claim that is the subject of dispute as to its existence or otherwise or as to its amount have been withheld.

(Exclusion from Liquidation)
Article 665 (1) Creditors of a Liquidating Membership Company (excluding known creditors; hereinafter in this article limited to Limited Liability Companies) who fail to state their claims during the period under paragraph (1) of Article 660 shall be excluded from the liquidation.
(2) Creditors who are excluded from the liquidation pursuant to the provisions of the preceding paragraph may demand the performance solely with respect to the residual assets that are not distributed.
(3) In cases where residual assets of a Liquidating Membership Company have been distributed to some partners, the assets necessary for the distribution to partners other than such partners in the same proportion as that applied for the distribution received by such partners shall be deducted from the residual assets under the preceding paragraph.

Section 5 Distribution of Residual Assets

(Proportion of Distribution of Residual Assets)
Article 666 If there is no provision in the articles of incorporation with respect to the proportions of the distribution of residual assets, that proportions shall be prescribed

in accordance with the value of each partner's contribution.

Section 6 End of Liquidation Administrations

Article 667 (1) If the administration of a liquidation has ended, the Liquidating Membership Company must carry out the accounting relating to the liquidation and obtain the approval of the partners without delay.

(2) If partners do not raise objections to the accounting under the preceding paragraph within one month, the partners shall be deemed to have approved such accounting; provided, however, that this shall not apply if there is any misconduct regarding the execution of the liquidators' duties.

Section 7 Voluntary Liquidation

(Method to Dispose of Assets)

Article 668 (1) A Membership Company (hereinafter in this Section limited to a General Partnership Company and a Limited Partnership Company) may prescribe, by the articles of incorporation or by the consent of all partners, the method of the disposition of the assets of such Membership Company in cases where such Membership Company is dissolved on the grounds listed in items (i) through (iii) of Article 641.

(2) The provisions of Section 2 through the immediately preceding Section shall not apply to Membership Companies that have prescribed the method of the disposition of assets under the preceding paragraph.

(Preparation of Inventory of Property)

Article 669 (1) In cases where a Membership Company that determines the method of the disposition of assets under paragraph (1) of the preceding article is dissolved on the grounds listed in items (i) through (iii) of Article 641, the Liquidating Membership Company (hereinafter in this Section limited to a General Partnership Company and a Limited Partnership Company) must prepare, pursuant to the provisions of the applicable Ordinance of the Ministry of Justice, the inventory of property and the balance sheet as of the day of the dissolution within two weeks after the day of the dissolution.

(2) In cases where a Membership Company that has not prescribed the method of the disposition of assets under paragraph (1) of the preceding article is dissolved on the grounds listed in items (i) through (iii) of Article 641, if it prescribes the method of the disposition of assets in that paragraph after the dissolution, the Liquidating Membership Company must prepare, pursuant to the provisions of the applicable Ordinance of the Ministry of Justice, an inventory of property and the balance sheet as of the day of the dissolution within two weeks of the day of such prescribing of the method of the disposition of assets.

(Objection of Creditors)

Article 670 (1) In cases where a Membership Company has prescribed the method of the disposition of assets under paragraph (1) of Article 668, creditors of the Liquidating Membership Company after the dissolution thereof may state their objections to such method of the disposition of assets to such Liquidating Membership Company.

(2) In cases provided for in the preceding paragraph, the Liquidating Membership Company must, within two weeks from the day of the dissolution (or, in the cases provided for in paragraph (2) of the preceding article, of the day when such method of disposition of the assets is prescribed), give public notice of the matters listed below in the

Official Gazette and must give notice of the same separately to each known creditor, if any; provided, however, that the period under item (ii) cannot be less than one month:
(i) A statement that liquidation will be effected in accordance with the method of the disposition of assets under paragraph (1) of Article 668; and
(ii) A statement to the effect that creditors may state their objections within a certain period of time.
(3) Notwithstanding the provisions of the preceding paragraph, if, in addition to using the Official Gazette, a Liquidating Membership Company effects public notice under that paragraph in a manner listed in item (ii) or (iii) of paragraph (1) of Article 939 in accordance with the provisions of the articles of incorporation under the provisions of that paragraph, the Liquidating Membership Company shall no longer be required to give separate notices under the provisions of the preceding paragraph.
(4) In cases where the creditors do not raise objections within the period under item (ii) of paragraph (2), such creditors shall be deemed to have approved such disposition of assets.
(5) In cases where the creditors raise objections within the period under item (ii) of paragraph (2), the Liquidating Membership Company must make payment to or provide appropriate security to such creditors, or entrust appropriate assets to a qualified trust company for the purpose of assuring the payment to such creditors.

(Consents of Creditors that have attached Equity Interest)
Article 671 (1) In cases where a Membership Company prescribes the method of the disposition of assets under paragraph (1) of Article 668, if there are creditors that have attached the equity interest of partners, consent of those creditors must be obtained if the Liquidating Membership Company after the dissolution intends to dispose of its assets.
(2) If the Liquidating Membership Company under the preceding paragraph disposes of its assets in violation of the provisions of that paragraph, creditors that attached the equity interests of partners may demand that such Liquidating Membership Company pay an amount equivalent to those equity interests.

Section 8 Retention of Accounting Materials

Article 672 (1) A Liquidator (or, in cases where the method of the disposition of assets in paragraph (1) of Article 668 is prescribed, a partner that represents the Liquidating Membership Company) must retain the books of the Liquidating Membership Company as well as any material data regarding the business and liquidation of the same (hereinafter in this article referred to as "Accounting Materials") for a period of ten years from the time of the registration of completion of the liquidation at the location of head office of the Liquidating Membership Company.
(2) Notwithstanding the provisions of the preceding paragraph, in cases where a person who retains the Accounting Materials has been prescribed by the articles of incorporation or by a majority of the partners, that person must retain the Accounting Materials for a period of ten years from the time of registration of the completion of the liquidation at the location of head office of the Liquidating Membership Company.
(3) The court may, in response to a petition by interested parties, appoint a person to act on behalf of the liquidator in paragraph (1) or the person who retains the Accounting Materials under the provisions of the preceding paragraph in the retaining the Accounting Materials. In such cases, the provisions of the preceding two paragraphs shall not apply.
(4) The person appointed pursuant to the provisions of the preceding paragraph must re-

tain the Accounting Materials for a period of ten years from the time of the registration of the completion of the liquidation at the location of head office of the Liquidating Membership Company.
(5) The expenses regarding the procedures for the appointment under the provisions of paragraph (3) shall be borne by the Liquidating Membership Company.

Section 9 Extinctive Prescription of Partner's Liability

Article 673 (1) The liability of the partner in Article 580 shall be extinguished in relation to the creditors of the Liquidating Membership Company who do not state their claims, or do not give advance notice of their claims within five years from the day of the registration of the dissolution at the location of head office of the Liquidating Membership Company, when five years have elapsed from the day of such registration.
(2) Creditors of the Liquidating Membership Company may demand that the Liquidating Membership Company make the payment, even after the lapse of the period under the preceding paragraph, if there are residual assets not distributed to partners.

Section 10 Exceptions to Application

(Exceptions to Application)
Article 674 The provisions listed below shall not apply to Liquidating Membership Company:
(i) Section 1 of Chapter IV;
(ii) Article 606, paragraph (1) of Article 607 (excluding items (iii) and (iv)) and Article 609;
(iii) In Chapter V, Section 3 (excluding paragraph (4) of Article 617, Article 618 and Article 619) through Section 6 and Subsection 2 of Section 7; and
(iv) item (iii) of paragraph (1) and item (ii) of paragraph (2) of Article 638.

(Special Provisions on Withdrawal of Partners due to Inheritances and Mergers)
Article 675 In cases where a partner in a Liquidating Membership Company dies or is liquidated as a result of the merger, the heirs or other general successors of such partner, may succeed to the equity interest of such partner even in the absence of the provisions of the articles of incorporation under paragraph (1) of Article 608. In such cases, the provisions of paragraphs (4) and (5) of that article shall apply mutatis mutandis.

PART IV Bonds

Chapter I General Provisions

(Determination of Matters on Bonds for Subscription)
Article 676 Whenever a Company intends to solicit persons who subscribe for the Bonds it issues, the Company must determine the following matters with respect to the Bonds for subscription (hereinafter in this Part referring to the Bonds that will be allotted to the persons who subscribed for those Bonds in response to such solicitation):
(i) The total amount of Bonds for subscription;
(ii) The amount of each Bond for subscription;
(iii) The interest rate for the Bonds for subscription;

(iv) The method and due date for the redemption of the Bonds for subscription;
(v) The method and due date for payment of the interest;
(vi) If Bond certificates are to be issued, the statement to that effect;
(vii) If it is to be arranged that bondholders may not make the demand under the provisions of Article 698, in whole or in part, the statement to that effect;
(viii) If it is to be arranged that bond manager may perform the act listed in item (ii), paragraph (1) of Article 706 in the absence of the resolution of the bondholders' meeting, the statement to that effect;
(ix) The amount to be paid in for each Bond for subscription (hereinafter in this Chapter referring to the amount of monies to be paid in in exchange for each Bond for subscription) or the minimum amount thereof, or the method for calculating those amounts;
(x) The due date for payment in of the monies in exchange for the Bond for subscription;
(xi) If it is to be arranged that the issue of the Bonds for subscription will not be carried out in their entirety in cases where the persons to whom the Bonds for subscription will be allotted are not prescribed for the total amount of the bonds by a certain day, the statement to that effect and that certain day; and
(xii) In addition to the matters listed in each of the above items, matters prescribed by applicable Ordinance of the Ministry of Justice.

(Applications for Bonds for Subscription)
Article 677 (1) A Company must notify persons who intend to subscribe for Bonds for subscription in response to the solicitation under the preceding paragraph of the matters listed in the following items:
(i) The trade name of the Company;
(ii) The matters listed in each item of the preceding Article relating to such solicitation;
(iii) In addition to the matters listed in the preceding two items, matters prescribed by the applicable Ordinance of the Ministry of Justice.
(2) A person who intends to apply the subscription for the Bonds for subscription in response to the solicitation in the preceding paragraph must deliver a document that specifies the following matters:
(i) The name and address of the person applying;
(ii) The amount of the Bonds for subscription for which he/she intends to subscribe and the number of Bonds for each amount; and
(iii) If the Company has prescribed the minimum amount under item (ix) of the preceding article, the preferred amount for payment.
(3) A person who submits an application in paragraph (1) may, in lieu of the delivery of the document in that paragraph, provide the matters to be stated in the document in that paragraph by an electromagnetic means with the approval of the Company pursuant to the provisions of the applicable Cabinet Order. In such cases, the person who submitted the application shall be deemed to have delivered the document in that paragraph.
(4) The provisions of paragraph (1) shall not apply in cases where the Company has issued the prospectus prescribed in paragraph (10) of Article 2 of the Financial Instruments and Exchange Act that states the matters listed in each item of that paragraph to a person who intends to submit the application under paragraph (1), and in other cases that are prescribed by the applicable Ordinance of the Ministry of Justice as the cases where it is unlikely that the protection of persons who intend to submit the application for the subscription for Bonds for subscription will be compromised.
(5) If there are changes in the matters listed in any item of paragraph (1), the Company

must immediately notify persons who have submitted applications in paragraph (2) (hereinafter in this Subsection referred to as "Applicants") thereof and of the matters so changed.
(6) It shall be sufficient for a notice or letters of demand to an Applicant to be sent by the Company to the address under item (i) of paragraph (2) (or, in cases where such Applicant notifies the Company of a different place or contact address for the receipt of notices or letters of demand, to such place or contact address).
(7) The notice or letters of demand referred to in the preceding paragraph shall be deemed to have arrived at the time when such notice or letter of demand should normally have arrived.

(Allotment of Bonds for Subscription)
Article 678 (1) A Company must specify the persons to whom Bonds for subscription will be allotted from among the Applicants, and the amount, and the number for each amount, of the Bonds for subscription to be allotted to those persons. In such cases, the Company may reduce the number for each amount of Bonds for subscription that are to be allotted to such Applicants below the number under item (ii), paragraph (2) of the preceding article.
(2) The Company must notify the Applicants, no later than the day immediately preceding the date referred to in item (x) of Article 676 of the amount, and the number for each amount, of the Bonds for subscription that will be allotted to such Applicant.

(Special Provision on Subscription and Allotment of Bonds for Subscription)
Article 679 The provisions of the preceding two Articles shall not apply in cases where a person who intends to subscribe for the Bonds for subscription executes a contract for the subscription for the total amount of those Bonds.

(Bondholders of Bonds for Subscription)
Article 680 The person listed in the following items shall be the Bondholders of the Bonds for subscription provided for in each of such items:
(i) Applicants: The Bonds for subscription allotted by the Company; or
(ii) A person who subscribed for all amount of the Bonds for subscription under the contract referred to in the preceding article: The Bonds for subscription which such person has subscribed.

(Bond Registry)
Article 681 A Company must, without delay after the day when Bonds are issued, prepare a bond registry and state or record the following matters (hereinafter referred to as "Matters to be Specified in Bond Registry") in that registry:
(i) The matters listed in items (iii) through (xiii) of Article 676 and other matters prescribed by the applicable Ordinance of the Ministry of Justice as the matters that specify the features of the Bonds (hereinafter in this Part referred to as "Class");
(ii) For each Class, the total amount of the Bonds and the amount of each Bond;
(iii) The amount of the monies paid in in exchange for each Bond, and the day of the payment in;
(iv) The name and address of the Bondholders (excluding the Bondholders of bearer Bonds (hereinafter in this Part referring to Bonds for which bearer form Bond certificates are issued));
(v) The days when the Bondholders in the preceding item acquired each Bond;
(vi) If bond certificates are issued, the serial number of the Bond certificates, the days of issue, whether the bond certificates are registered certificates or bearer certifi-

cates, and the number of the bearer bond certificates;
(vii) In addition to the foregoing, matters prescribed by applicable Ordinance of the Ministry of Justice.

(Delivery of Document Stating Matters to be Stated in Bond Registry)
Article 682 (1) Bondholders (excluding the bondholders of bearer bonds) may request the Company that issued the Bonds (hereinafter in this Part referred to as "Bond-issuing Company") to deliver the documents stating the Matters to be Stated in Bond Registry that are stated or recorded in the bond registry with respect to such bondholders, or provide the electromagnetic records that records such Matters to be Stated in Bond Registry.
(2) The document referred to in the preceding paragraph must be affixed with the signature, or name and seal, of the representative of the Bond-issuing Company.
(3) With respect to the electromagnetic records referred to in paragraph (1), the representative of the Bond-issuing Company must implement measures in lieu of the affixation of signature, or name and seal prescribed by the applicable Ordinance of the Ministry of Justice.
(4) The provisions of the preceding three paragraphs shall not apply in cases where there is provision to the effect that bond certificates shall be issued for such bonds.

(Management of Bond Registry)
Article 683 A Company may appoint a manager of the Bond Registry (hereinafter referring to a person who shall be responsible on behalf of the Company for the administration regarding the bond registry such as preparing and keeping the bond registry) and may entrust such administration of the registry to the same.

(Keeping and Making Available for Inspection of Bond Registry)
Article 684 (1) A Bond-issuing Company must keep the Bond Registry at its head office (or, in case a manager of Bond Registry is appointed, at its business office).
(2) The Bondholders and other persons prescribed by the applicable Ordinance of the Ministry of Justice may make the following requests at any time during the business hours of the bond-issuing Company. In such cases, the reasons for such request must be disclosed.
(i) If the Bond Registry is prepared in writing, the request for the inspection or copying of such document;
(ii) If the Bond Registry is prepared by using electromagnetic records, the request for the inspection or copying of the thing that indicates the matters recorded in such electromagnetic records in a manner prescribed by the applicable Ordinance of the Ministry of Justice.
(3) If the request referred to in the preceding paragraph is made, the bond-issuing Company may not refuse such request unless:
(i) The person who made such request, made the request for a purpose other than for the research on securing or exercising his/her rights;
(ii) The person who made such request, made the request in order to report the fact which he/she may learn by reviewing or copying the bond registry to third parties for profit; or
(iii) The person who makes the request is a person who has reported the facts, knowledge of which was acquired by inspecting or copying the bond registry, to third parties for profit in the immediately preceding two years.
(4) In cases where a bond-issuing Company is a Stock Company, if it is necessary for a partner in the Parent Company of such bond-issuing Company to exercise his/her

right, such partner in the Parent Company may, with the permission of the court, make the request in each item of paragraph (2) with respect to the bond registry of such bond-issuing Company. In such cases, the reasons of such request must be disclosed.
(5) The court may not grant the permission in the preceding paragraph if grounds provided for in any item of paragraph (3) apply to the partner of the parent Company in the preceding paragraph.

(Notices to Bondholders)
Article 685 (1) It shall be sufficient for a notice or demand letter to bondholders to be sent by a bond-issuing Company to the address of such bondholders stated or recorded in the bond registry (or, in cases where such bondholders notify such bond-issuing Company of a different place or contact address for receipt of notices or demand letters, to such place or contact address).
(2) The notices or demand letters referred to in the preceding paragraph shall be deemed to have arrived at the time when such notice or demand letter should normally have arrived.
(3) If a bond is co-owned by two or more persons, the co-owners must specify one person to receive the notices or demand letters sent by the bond-issuing Company to bondholders and notify such bond-issuing Company of the name of that person. In such cases, that person shall be deemed to be the bondholder and the provisions of the preceding two paragraphs shall apply mutatis mutandis.
(4) In cases where there is no notice by co-owners under the provisions of the preceding paragraph, it shall be sufficient for a notice or demand letter sent by a bond-issuing Company to the co-owners of the bondholders if it is sent to one of them.
(5) The provisions of the preceding paragraphs shall apply mutatis mutandis to the cases where, when the notice in paragraph (1) of Article 720 is given, a document is delivered or matters to be stated in such document are provided to the bondholders by an electromagnetic means. In such cases, the words "to have arrived" in paragraph (2) shall be read as "to have been effected by delivery of such documents or provision of such matters by electromagnetic means."

(Exercise of Rights by Co-owners)
Article 686 If a bond is co-owned by two or more persons, the co-owners may not exercise their rights in relation to such bond unless they specify one person to exercise the rights in relation to such bond, and notify the Company of the name of that person; provided, however, that this shall not apply in cases where the Company has agreed to the exercise of such rights.

(Assignment of Bonds with Issued Certificates)
Article 687 Assignment Bonds for which there is provision to the effect that bond certificates shall be issued shall not become effective unless bond certificates relating to such bonds are delivered.

(Perfection of Assignment of Bonds)
Article 688 (1) Assignment of bonds cannot be asserted against the bond-issuing Company and other third parties unless the name and addresses of the persons who acquire those bonds is stated or recorded in the Bond Registry.
(2) For the purpose of the application of the provisions of the preceding paragraph in cases where there is provision to the effect that bond certificates shall be issued with respect to such bonds, the words "the bond-issuing Company and other third parties" in that paragraph shall be read as "the bond-issuing Company."

(3) The provisions of the preceding two paragraphs shall not apply to bearer bonds.

(Presumption of Rights)
Article 689 (1) A possessor of bond certificates shall be presumed to be the lawful owner of the right in relation to the Bonds for such bond certificates.
(2) A person who takes the delivery of bond certificates shall acquire the rights in relation to the bonds for such bond certificates; provided, however, that this shall not apply if that person has knowledge or is grossly negligent.

(Stating or Recording Matters to be Stated in Bond Registry without Request from Bondholders)
Article 690 (1) In the cases provided for in the following items, the bond-issuing Company must state or record the Matters to be Stated in Bond Registry relating to the bondholders referred to in such items:
(i) In cases where the bondholders have acquired the bonds of such bond-issuing Company;
(ii) In cases where the bondholders have disposed of own bonds.
(2) The provisions of the preceding paragraph shall not apply to any bearer bond.

(Stating or Recording Matters to be Stated in Bond Registry as Requested by Bondholders)
Article 691 (1) A person who has acquired bonds from any person other than the bond-issuing Company (excluding such bond-issuing Company) may request that such bond-issuing Company state or record the Matters to be Stated in Bond Registry relating to such bonds in the Bond Registry.
(2) Except for the cases prescribed by the applicable Ordinance of the Ministry of Justice as the case of no likelihood of harm to interested parties, requests under the provisions of the preceding paragraph must be made jointly with the person stated or recorded in the Bond Registry as the bondholder of the bonds so acquired, or his/her general successor(s) including his/her heir(s).
(3) The provisions of the preceding two paragraphs shall not apply to any bearer bond.

(Pledges of Bonds with Issued Certificates)
Article 692 Pledges of bonds for which there is provision to the effect that bond certificates shall be issued, shall not become effective, unless Bond certificates relating to such bonds are delivered.

(Perfection of Pledge of Bonds)
Article 693 (1) Pledge of bonds cannot be asserted against the Bond-issuing Company and other third parties unless the names and addresses of the pledgees are stated or recorded in the Bond Registry.
(2) Notwithstanding the provisions of the preceding paragraph, a pledgee of bonds for which there is provision to the effect that bond certificates shall be issued may not assert his/her pledge against the Bond-issuing Company and other third parties unless he/she is in continuous possession of the bond certificates relating to such bonds.

(Entries in Bond Registry regarding Pledges)
Article 694 (1) A person who pledges bonds may request the bond-issuing Company to state or record the following matters in the Bond Registry:
(i) The name and address of the pledgee;
(ii) The bond underlying the pledge.

(2) The provisions of the preceding paragraph shall not apply in cases where there is provision to the effect that bond certificates will be issued.

(Delivery of Documents Stating Matters to be Stated in Bond Registry regarding Pledges)
Article 695 (1) The pledgees for whom the matters listed in each of the items of paragraph (1) of the preceding article are stated or recorded in the Bond Registry may request that bond-issuing Company deliver documents stating the matters listed in each of the items of that paragraph with respect to such pledgees that are stated or recorded in the Bond Registry, or provide the Electromagnetic Records that record such matters.
(2) The documents in the preceding paragraph must be affixed with the signature, or name and seal, of a representative of the bond-issuing Company.
(3) With respect to the Electromagnetic Records in paragraph (1), the representative of the bond-issuing Company must implement measures in lieu of the affixation of signature, or name and seal prescribed by the applicable Ordinance of the Ministry of Justice.

(Issuing of Bond Certificates)
Article 696 A bond-issuing Company must, without delay after the day of a bond issue for which there is provision to the effect that bond certificates shall be issued, issue bond certificates for such bonds.

(Matters to be Stated on Bond Certificates)
Article 697 (1) A bond-issuing Company must state the following matters and the serial number on a bond certificate, and the representative of the bond-issuing Company must affix his/her signature, or name and seal:
(i) The trade name of the bond-issuing Company;
(ii) The amount of bonds relating to such bond certificates;
(iii) The Class of bonds relating to such bond certificates;
(2) Coupons may be attached to bond certificates.

(Conversions between Registered Bonds and Bearer Bonds)
Article 698 Bondholders of bonds for which bond certificates are issued may demand at any time that the bond-issuing Company convert their registered bond certificates into bearer bond certificates, or convert their bearer bond certificates into registered bond certificates, except in cases where there is an arrangement under provisions with respect to the matters listed in item (vii) of Article 676 that such conversion is not possible.

(Loss of Bond Certificates)
Article 699 (1) Bond certificates may be invalidated pursuant to the public notification procedures under Article 142 of the Non-Contentious Cases Procedures Act.
(2) Persons who have lost bond certificates may not request the reissuing of their bond certificates until after they obtain the invalidation provided for in paragraph (1) of Article 148 of the Non-Contentious Cases Procedures Act.

(Redemption of Bonds where Coupons Missing)
Article 700 (1) In cases where a bond-issuing Company redeems a bond for which a bond certificates is issued before it matures, if a coupon attached to the bond is missing, the bond-issuing Company must deduct the amount of the claim for interest on

the bond indicated on such coupon from the redemption amount; provided, however, that this shall not apply if such claim has fallen due.
(2) The possessor of the coupon in the preceding paragraph may demand at any time that the bond-issuing Company pay the amount that must be deducted under the provisions of that paragraph in exchange for the coupon.

(Extinctive Prescription of Right to Claim Redemption of Bonds)
Article 701 (1) The right to claim the redemption of bonds shall be extinguished by prescription if not exercised for ten years.
(2) The right to claim interest on bonds and the right to claim under the provisions of paragraph (2) of the preceding Article shall be extinguished by prescription if not exercised for five years.

Chapter II Bond Managers

(Establishment of Bond Managers)
Article 702 In cases where a Company will issue bonds, the Company must specify a bond manager and entrust the receipt of payments, the preservation of rights of claim on behalf of the bondholders and other administration of the bonds to that manager; provided, however, that this shall not apply in cases where the amount of each bond is 100,000,000 yen or more, and other cases prescribed by the applicable Ordinance of the Ministry of Justice as cases where it is unlikely that the protection of bondholders will be compromised.

(Qualifications of Bond Managers)
Article 703 A bond manager must be a person listed as follows:
  (i) A bank;
  (ii) A trust company; and
  (iii) In addition to the above, a person prescribed by the applicable Ordinance of the Ministry of Justice as a person equivalent to the above.

(Obligations of Bond Managers)
Article 704 (1) Bond managers must perform the administration of bonds in a fair and sincere manner on behalf of the bondholders.
(2) Bond managers must manage the bonds with due care of a prudent manager to the bondholders.

(Bond Manager's Power of Representation)
Article 705 (1) A manager shall have authority to do all judicial and non-judicial acts on behalf of bondholders that are necessary to receive payment of claims relating to the bonds or to preserve the realization of claims relating to the bonds.
(2) In cases where a bond manager has received payment under the preceding paragraph, the bondholders may claim payment of the redeemed amount of bonds and interest from the bond manager. In such cases, if there is provision to the effect that bond certificates shall be issued, the bondholders must claim the payment of such redeemed amount in exchange for the bond certificates, and the payment of such interest in exchange for the coupons.
(3) The right to claim under the provisions of the first sentence of the preceding paragraph shall be extinguished by prescription if not exercised for ten years.
(4) If it is necessary for a bond manager to carry out the acts under paragraph (1) with re-

spect to bonds that the bond manager has been entrusted to administer, the bond manager may, with the permission of the court, investigate the status of the business and assets of the bond-issuing Company.

Article 706 (1) A bond manager may not carry out the following acts without a resolution of a bondholders' meeting; provided, however, that this shall not apply with respect to the act listed in item (ii) if there is provision with respect to the matters listed in item (viii) of Article 676:
  (i) With respect to all of the bonds, granting extension for the payment of those bonds, or releasing, or settling liability arising from the failure to perform the obligations of those bonds (excluding the acts listed in the following item);
  (ii) With respect to all of the bonds, prosecuting lawsuits, or proceeding with bankruptcy procedures, rehabilitation procedures, reorganization procedures or procedures regarding special liquidation (excluding the act under paragraph (1) of the preceding article).
(2) If a bond manager carries out the acts listed in item (ii) of the preceding paragraph without a resolution of a bondholders' meeting under the provisions of the proviso to that paragraph, the bond manager must, without delay, give public notice to such effect and separate notice thereof to each known bondholder.
(3) The public notice under the provisions of the preceding paragraph must be made in accordance with the method of public notice used by the bond-issuing Company; provided, however, that, if that method is electromagnetic public notice, such public notice must be effected by publication in the Official Gazette.
(4) If it is necessary for a bond manager to carry out the acts listed in each item of paragraph (1) with respect to bonds that the bond manager has been entrusted to administer, the bond manager may, with the permission of the court, investigate the status of the business and assets of the bond-issuing Company.

(Appointment of Special Agent)
Article 707 In cases where there is conflict between the interests of the bondholders and those of the bond manager, if it is necessary to carry out judicial and non-judicial acts on behalf of bondholders, the court must, in response to a petition by the bondholders' meeting, appoint a special agent.

(Method of Acts of Bond Managers)
Article 708 If a bond manager or a special agent under the preceding article performs judicial or non-judicial acts on behalf of bondholders, he/she need not identify individual bondholders.

(Special Provisions for Multiple Bond Managers)
Article 709 (1) If there are two or more bond managers, these persons must perform the acts within their authority jointly.
(2) In the cases provided for in the preceding paragraph, if bond managers have accepted payments under paragraph (1) of Article 705, the bond managers shall be jointly and severally liable for payment of the amount so tendered.

(Liability of Bond Manager)
Article 710 (1) If bond managers commit acts in violation of this Act or resolutions of the bondholders' meeting, they shall be jointly and severally liable to compensate bondholders for losses arising as a result.
(2) A bond manager shall be liable to compensate bondholders for losses if the bond man-

ager commits any of the following acts after, or within three months prior to, the bond-issuing Company having failed to redeem bonds or pay interest on the same, or having suspended payments; provided, however, that this shall not apply if such bond manager has proven that he/she did not fail to manage the Bonds with due diligence, or that such losses were not caused by such acts:
(i) Accepting, with respect to an obligation relating to a claim of such bond manager, the tender of a security or an act regarding the extinguishment of the obligation from the bond-issuing Company;
(ii) Assigning a claim of such bond manager to a person who has a special relationship prescribed by the applicable Ordinance of the Ministry of Justice with such bond manager (limited to cases where the person who has such special relationship has accepted with respect to an obligation relating to such claim, the tender of a security or an act regarding the extinguishment of the obligation, from the bond-issuing Company); or
(iii) In cases where such bond manager has a claim against the bond-issuing Company, entering into a contract with the bond-issuing Company for disposal of assets of the bond-issuing Company, or entering into a contract under which the bond manager assumes the obligations that a person owes to the bond-issuing Company, in each case for the sole purpose of setting off obligations to the bond-issuing Company that the bond manager assumes under the contract against the bond manager's claim against the bond-issuing Company.
(iv) In cases where such bond manager has an obligation to the bond-issuing Company, accepting the assignment of a claim against the bond-issuing Company and setting off such obligation against such claim.

(Resignation of Bond Managers)
Article 711 (1) A bond manager may resign with the consent of the bond-issuing Company and the bondholders' meeting. In such cases, if there is no other bond manager, such bond manager must specify a bond manager to succeed to the administration of the bonds, in advance.
(2) Notwithstanding the provisions of the preceding paragraph, a bond manager may resign on any ground provided for in the entrustment contract under the provisions of Article 702; provided, however, that this shall not apply if such contract does not have provisions regarding bond managers to succeed to the administration of the bonds.
(3) Notwithstanding the provisions of paragraph (1), a bond manager may resign with the permission of the court if there are unavoidable reasons.

(Liability of Bond Managers after Resignation)
Article 712 The provisions of paragraph (2) of Article 710 shall apply mutatis mutandis to a person who resigned as bond manager under the provisions of paragraph (2) of the preceding article after, or within three months prior to, the bond-issuing Company having failed to redeem bonds or pay interest, or having suspended payments.

(Dismissal of Bond Managers)
Article 713 The court may dismiss a bond manager in response to a petition by a bond-issuing Company or a bondholders' meeting if such bond manager has violated the bond manager's obligations, if the bond manager is not fit to handle the administration for which the bond manager is responsible, or if there are other justifiable grounds.

(Succession to Bond Manager's Administration of Bonds)
Article 714 (1) In cases where a bond manager has fallen under any of the following cir-

cumstances, if there is no other bond manager, the bond-issuing Company must specify a bond manager to succeed to the administration of the bonds, and entrust the administration of the bonds to such person on behalf of the bondholders. In such cases, the bond-issuing Company must convene a bondholders' meeting without delay in order to obtain the consent of the same, and if such consent cannot be obtained, must file a petition for the permission of the court in lieu of such consent:
(i) If the bond manager is no longer a person listed in any item of Article 703;
(ii) If the bond manager has resigned under the provisions of paragraph (3) of Article 711;
(iii) If the bond manager has been dismissed under the provisions of the preceding paragraph; or
(iv) If the bond manager has been dissolved.
(2) In the cases provided for in the first sentence of the preceding paragraph, if a bond-issuing Company does not convene a meeting under the provisions of the second sentence of that paragraph or file a petition under the second sentence of that paragraph within two months of the day on which the bond-issuing Company fell under any of the circumstances in each item of that paragraph, the bond-issuing Company shall forfeit the benefit of time in relation to the total amount of such bonds.
(3) In the cases provided for in the first sentence of paragraph (1), if there are unavoidable reasons, interested parties may petition the court for the appointment of a bond manager to succeed to the administration of the bonds.
(4) In cases where a bond-issuing Company has specified the bond manager to succeed to the administration of the bonds under the provisions of the first sentence of paragraph (1) (excluding cases where the consent of a bondholders' meeting has been obtained), or in cases where a bond manager has been appointed to succeed to the administration of the bonds under the provisions of the preceding paragraph, the bond-issuing Company must, without delay, give public notice to such effect and separate notice thereof to each known bondholder.

Chapter III Bondholders' Meeting

(Constitution of Bondholders' Meetings)
Article 715 Bondholders' meetings for each Class of bonds shall be constituted by bondholders.

(Authority of Bondholders' Meetings)
Article 716 Bondholders' meetings may make resolutions on matters provided for in this Act, and matters in relation to the interests of the bondholders.

(Convocation of Bondholders' Meetings)
Article 717 (1) Bondholders' meetings may, where necessary, be convened at any time.
(2) Bondholders' meetings shall be convened by the bond-issuing Company or bond manager, except in cases where a bondholders' meeting is convened under the provisions of paragraph (3) of the following article.

(Demand for Convocation of Meeting by Bondholders)
Article 718 (1) Bondholders who hold not less than one tenth (1/10) of the total amount of bonds of a certain Class (excluding bonds that have been redeemed) may demand that the bond-issuing Company or bond manager convene a bondholders' meeting, by disclosing the matters that form the purpose of the bondholders' meeting and the rea-

sons for the convocation.
(2) The sum of the amount of bonds of such Class held by the bond-issuing Company itself shall not be included in the calculation of the total amount of the bonds under the preceding paragraph.
(3) In the following cases, the bondholders who made the demand under the provisions of paragraph (1) may convene a bondholders' meeting with the permission of the court.
  (i) In cases where the convocation procedure is not effected without delay after the demand pursuant to the provisions of paragraph (1); or
  (ii) In cases where notice of the convocation of a bondholders' meeting stating a day falling within an eight-week period after the day of the demand under the provisions of paragraph (1) as the day of the bondholders' meeting, is not sent.
(4) Bondholders of bearer bonds who intend to make a demand pursuant to the provisions of paragraph (1) or to effect the convocation pursuant to the provisions of the preceding paragraph must present their bond certificates to the bond-issuing Company or bond manager.

(Determination of Convocation of Bondholders' Meeting)
Article 719 A person who convenes a bondholders' meeting (hereinafter in this Chapter referred to as "Convener") must specify the following matters in cases where he/she convenes a bondholders' meeting:
(i) The date, time and place of the bondholders' meeting;
(ii) The matters that form the purpose of the bondholders' meeting;
(iii) If it is to be arranged that bondholders who do not attend the bondholders' meeting may exercise voting rights by electromagnetic means, a statement to such effect;
(iv) In addition to the matters listed in the preceding three items, matters prescribed by the applicable Ordinance of the Ministry of Justice.

(Notice of Convocation of Bondholders' Meetings)
Article 720 (1) In order to convene a bondholders' meeting, the Convener must give written notice thereof to known bondholders and the bond-issuing Company, as well as to the bond manager if appointed, no later than two weeks prior to the day of the bondholders' meeting.
(2) In lieu of sending the written notice referred to in the preceding paragraph, the Convener may send a notice by electromagnetic means with the consent of bondholders, pursuant to the provisions of the applicable Cabinet Order. In such cases, such Convener shall be deemed to have sent the written notice under that paragraph.
(3) The notice under the preceding two paragraphs must state or record the matters listed in each item of the preceding article.
(4) In cases where a bond-issuing Company issues bearer bond certificates, in order to convene a bondholders' meeting, the Convener must give public notice to the effect that a bondholders' meeting will be convened and of the matters listed in each item of the preceding article no later than three weeks prior to the day of the bondholders' meeting.
(5) The public notice pursuant to the provisions of the preceding paragraph must be given in accordance with the method of public notice used by the bond-issuing Company; provided, however, that, in cases where the Convener is a person other than the bond-issuing Company, if such method is electromagnetic public notice, such public notice must be effected by publication in the Official Gazette.

(Delivery of Bondholders' Meeting Reference Documents and Proxy Cards)

Art.721〜724　　　Ⅰ Companies Act, PART IV, Chap.III

Article 721 (1) The Convener must, when giving notice under paragraph (1) of the preceding article, deliver documents containing reference materials for exercising voting rights (hereinafter in this article referred to as "Bondholders' Meeting Reference Documents") and the documents to be used by bondholders to exercise voting rights (hereinafter in this Chapter referred to as "Proxy Cards") to known bondholders, pursuant to the provisions of the applicable Ordinance of the Ministry of Justice.
(2) If the Convener intends to send notice by the electromagnetic means in paragraph (2) of the preceding article to bondholders who have given consent under the same paragraph, they may provide, by electromagnetic means in lieu of the delivery of the Bondholders' Meeting Reference Documents and Proxy cards under the provisions of the preceding paragraph, the matters to be stated in such documents; provided, however, that, if there is a request from a bondholder, the Convener must deliver such documents to such bondholder.
(3) In cases where public notice is given pursuant to the provisions of paragraph (4) of the preceding article, if there is a request by a bondholder of bearer bonds no later than one week prior to the day of the bondholders' meeting, the Convener must immediately deliver the Bondholders' Meeting Reference Documents and Proxy Cards to such bondholder.
(4) In lieu of the delivery of the Bondholders' Meeting Reference Documents and Proxy Cards under the provisions of the preceding paragraph, the Convener may provide the matters to be stated in such documents by electromagnetic means with the consent of bondholders, pursuant to the provisions of the applicable Cabinet Order. In such cases, such Convener shall be deemed to have delivered those documents under the provisions of that paragraph.

Article 722 (1) In cases where the matters listed in item (iii) of Article 719 are specified, the Convener must, when giving notice by electromagnetic means to bondholders who have given consent under paragraph (2) of Article 720, provide to the bondholders, by such electromagnetic means, the matters to be specified in the Proxy Card, pursuant to the provisions of the applicable Ordinance of the Ministry of Justice.
(2) In cases where the matters listed in item (iii) of Article 719 are specified, if there is a request from a bondholder who did not give consent under paragraph (2) of Article 720 no later than one week prior to the day of the bondholders' meeting, for the provision of the matters to be stated on the proxy card by electromagnetic means, the Convener must immediately provide such matters to such bondholder by electromagnetic means, pursuant to the provisions of the applicable Ordinance of the Ministry of Justice.

(Amount of Voting Rights)
Article 723 (1) Bondholders shall have voting rights at bondholders' meetings in proportion to the total amounts of bonds of the relevant Classes they hold (excluding amounts already redeemed).
(2) Notwithstanding the provisions of the preceding paragraph, a bond-issuing Company shall not have voting rights with respect to its own bonds that it holds.
(3) Bondholders of bearer bonds who intend to exercise voting rights must present their bond certificates to the Convener no later than one week prior to the day of a bondholders' meeting.

(Resolutions of Bondholders' Meetings)
Article 724 (1) In order to pass a matter to be resolved at a bondholders' meeting, the consent of persons who hold more than half of the total amount of voting rights of vot-

ing rights holders (hereinafter in this Chapter referring to the bondholders who can exercise voting rights) present at the meeting must be obtained.
(2) Notwithstanding the provisions of the preceding paragraph, in order to pass the following matters at a bondholders' meeting, the consent of persons who hold not less than one fifth (1/5) of the total amount of voting rights of voting rights holders, being not less than two thirds (2/3) of the total amount of voting rights of voting rights holders present at the meeting, must be obtained.
  (i) Matters regarding the acts listed in each item of Article 706; and
  (ii) Matters for which a resolution of a bondholders' meeting is required under the provisions of paragraph (1) of Article 706, paragraph (1) of Article 736, the proviso to paragraph (1) of Article 737 and Article 738.
(3) Bondholders' meetings may not pass resolutions on matters other than those listed in item (ii) of Article 719.

(Proxy Voting)
Article 725 (1) Bondholders may exercise voting rights by proxy. In such cases, such bondholders or proxies must submit to the Convener a document certifying such power of representation.
(2) The grant of the power of representation under the preceding paragraph must be made for each bondholders' meeting.
(3) Bondholders or proxies referred to in paragraph (1) may, in lieu of the submission of the document certifying the power of representation, provide the matters to be stated in such document by electromagnetic means with the approval of the Convener pursuant to the provisions of the applicable Cabinet Order. In such cases, such bondholders or proxies shall be deemed to have submitted such document.
(4) In cases where the bondholders are persons who gave consent under paragraph (2) of Article 720, the Convener may not refuse to grant approval under the preceding paragraph without reasonable grounds.

(Voting in Writing)
Article 726 (1) Bondholders who do not attend a bondholders' meeting may exercise voting rights in writing.
(2) The exercise of voting rights in writing shall be effected by entering the necessary matters on the Proxy Card and submitting the Proxy Card to the Convener by the time prescribed by the applicable Ordinance of the Ministry of Justice.
(3) The number of voting rights exercised in writing under the provisions of the preceding paragraph shall be included in the number of the voting rights of the bondholders present at the meeting.

(Voting by Electromagnetic Means)
Article 727 (1) The exercise of voting rights by electromagnetic means shall be effected by providing the matters to be entered on the proxy card to the Convener by electromagnetic means, with the approval of such Convener, no later than the time prescribed by the applicable Ordinance of the Ministry of Justice, pursuant to the provisions of the applicable Cabinet Order.
(2) In cases where the bondholders are persons who have given consent under paragraph (2) of Article 720, the Convener may not refuse to grant approval under the preceding paragraph without justifiable grounds.
(3) The amount of the voting rights exercised by electromagnetic means under the provisions of paragraph (1) shall be included in the amount of the voting rights of the bondholders present at the meeting.

(Inconsistent Voting)
Article 728 (1) Bondholders may exercise the voting rights they hold without maintaining consistency. In such cases, the bondholders must notify the Convener to such effect and of the reasons for the same no later than three days prior to the day of the bondholders' meeting.
(2) If a bondholder in the preceding paragraph is not a person who holds bonds on behalf of others, the Convener may reject the inconsistent exercise of the voting rights held by such bondholder under the provisions of that paragraph.

(Attendance of Representative of Bond-issuing Company)
Article 729 (1) Bond-issuing Company or bond managers may state their opinions by having a representative or agent attend the bondholders' meeting, or in writing; provided, however, that, for bond managers, this shall not apply if that bondholders' meeting is convened for the appointment of a special agent under Article 707.
(2) Bondholders or Conveners may, when they regard it as necessary, demand the attendance of a Bond-issuing Company's representative or agent attend a meeting. In such cases, for attendance at a bondholders' meeting, a resolution must be passed to the effect that such demand will be made.

(Resolution for Postponement or Continuation)
Article 730 In cases where a resolution has been passed for the postponement or continuation of the bondholders' meeting, the provisions of Articles 719 and 720 shall not apply.

(Minutes)
Article 731 (1) Minutes must be prepared with respect to the business of the bondholders' meeting, pursuant to the provisions of the applicable Ordinance of the Ministry of Justice.
(2) The bond-issuing Company must keep the minutes in the preceding paragraph at its head office for a period of ten years from the day of a bondholders' meeting.
(3) The bond manager and bondholders may make the following requests at any time during the business hours of the Bond-issuing Company:
  (i) If the minutes in paragraph (1) are prepared in writing, requests for the inspection or copying of such documents; and
  (ii) If the minutes in paragraph (1) are prepared using electromagnetic records, requests for the inspection or copying of anything that indicates the matters recorded in such electromagnetic records in a manner prescribed by the applicable Ordinance of the Ministry of Justice.

(Petitions for Approval of Resolutions of Bondholders' Meetings)
Article 732 When a resolution is made at a bondholders' meeting, the Convener must file a petition with the court for the approval of such resolution within one week of the day of such resolution.

(Rejection of Resolutions of Bondholders' Meetings)
Article 733 The court cannot approve a resolution of a bondholders' meeting in cases falling under any of the following:
  (i) If the procedures for the convocation of the bondholders' meeting or the method of the resolution of the bondholders' meeting violates laws and regulations or the matters stated or recorded in materials used for explaining the business of such

bond-issuing Company or other matters regarding the solicitation in Article 676;
(ii) If the resolution was adopted by an unlawful method;
(iii) If the resolution is extremely unfair; or
(iv) If the resolution is contrary to the general interests of bondholders.

(Effectiveness of Resolutions of Bondholders' Meetings)
Article 734 (1) A resolution of a bondholders' meeting shall not be become effective unless the approval of the court is obtained.
(2) A resolution of a bondholders' meeting shall be effective against all bondholders who hold bonds of the relevant Class.

(Public Notice of Rulings Approving or Rejecting Resolutions of Bondholders' Meetings)
Article 735 If a ruling has been given approving or rejecting a resolution of a bondholders' meeting, the bond-issuing Company must give public notice to that effect without delay.

(Appointment of Representative Bondholders)
Article 736 (1) A bondholders' meeting may appoint, by resolution of the same, one or more representative bondholders from among bondholders who hold bonds representing not less than one thousandth (1/1000) of the total amount of bonds of the relevant Class (excluding amounts already redeemed), and entrust decisions on the matters on which resolutions are to be passed at bondholders' meetings to such representative bondholders.
(2) The provisions of paragraph (2) of Article 718 shall apply mutatis mutandis to the total amount of the Bonds provided for in the preceding paragraph.
(3) In cases where there are two or more representative bondholders, unless otherwise provided for at a bondholders' meeting, the decisions on the matters provided for in paragraph (1) shall be made by a majority of those representative bondholders.

(Execution of Resolutions of Bondholders' Meetings)
Article 737 (1) Resolutions of bondholders' meetings shall be executed by the bond manager or representative bondholders (except where there is a bond manager); provided, however, that this shall not apply if the person who executes resolutions of bondholders' meetings is separately prescribed by a resolution of a bondholders' meeting.
(2) The provisions under paragraphs (1) through (3) of Article 705, and under Articles 708 and 709 shall apply mutatis mutandis to cases where a representative bondholder or person responsible for the execution of resolutions of bondholders' meetings prescribed under the provisions of the proviso to the preceding paragraph (hereinafter in this Chapter referred to as "Resolution Administrator") executes the resolutions of bondholders' meetings.

(Dismissal of Representative Bondholders)
Article 738 A bondholders' meeting may, at any time by resolution of the same, dismiss or change the matters entrusted to the representative bondholders or Resolution Administrator.

(Forfeiture of the Benefit of Time for Failure to Pay Interest on Bonds)
Article 739 (1) If a bond-issuing Company fails to pay interest on bonds, or fails to periodically partially redeem bonds in cases where it must carry out that redemption, pur-

suant to a resolution of a bondholders' meeting, the person who executes such resolution may give written notice to the bond-issuing Company to the effect that that bond-issuing Company must make payment within a defined period of time, and to the effect that, if payment is not made within such period of time, the bond-issuing Company shall forfeit the benefit of time as to the total amount of such bonds, provided, however, that such period may not be less than two months.
(2) A person who executes a resolution under the preceding paragraph may, in lieu of the written notice under the provisions of that paragraph, provide the matters to be notified under the provisions of that paragraph by electromagnetic means, with the approval of the bond-issuing Company, pursuant to the provisions of the applicable Cabinet Order. In such cases, the person who executes such resolution shall be deemed to have given such written notice.
(3) If a Bond-issuing Company fails to make the payment in paragraph (1) within the period in that paragraph, it shall forfeit the benefit of time with respect to the total amount of such bonds.

(Special Provisions on Objection Procedures for Creditors)
Article 740 (1) In order for a bondholder to raise an objection under the provisions of Article 449, Article 627, Article 635, Article 670, Article 779 (including cases where applied mutatis mutandis under paragraph (2) of Article 781), Article 789 (including cases where applied mutatis mutandis under paragraph (2) of Article 793), Article 799 (including cases where applied mutatis mutandis under paragraph (2) of Article 802) or Article 810 (including cases where applied mutatis mutandis in paragraph (2) of Article 813), the objection must be raised by resolution of a bondholders' meeting. In such cases, the court may, in response to a petition by interested parties, extend the period during which objections can be raised on behalf of bondholders.
(2) Notwithstanding the provisions of the preceding paragraph, a bond manager may raise objections on behalf of bondholders; provided, however, that this shall not apply in cases where there is provision to the contrary in a contract relating to entrustment under the provisions of Article 702.
(3) For the purpose of the application of the provisions of paragraph (2) of Article 449, paragraph (2) of Article 627, (hereinafter in this paragraph including cases where applied mutatis mutandis under paragraph (2) of Article 781), paragraph (2) of Article 789 (hereinafter in this paragraph including cases where applied mutatis mutandis under paragraph (2) of Article 793), paragraph (2) of Article 799 (hereinafter in this paragraph including cases where applied mutatis mutandis under paragraph (2) of Article 802) or paragraph (2) of Article 810 (hereinafter in this paragraph including cases where applied mutatis mutandis under paragraph (2) of Article 813) to a bond-issuing Company, the words "known creditors" in paragraph (2) of Article 449, paragraph (2) of Article 627, paragraph (2) of Article 635, paragraph (2) of Article 670, paragraph (2) of Article 779 and paragraph (2) of Article 799 shall be read as "known creditors (if there is a bond manager, including such bond manager)" and the words "known creditors (limited to those who can raise objections under the provisions of that paragraph)" in paragraph (2) of Article 789 and paragraph (2) of Article 810 shall be read as "known creditors (limited to those who can raise objections under the provisions of that paragraph, and, if there is a bond manager, including such bond manager)."

(Remuneration for Bond Managers)
Article 741 (1) With the permission of the court, a bond-issuing Company may bear the cost of the remuneration to be paid to the bond manager, representative bondholders or Resolution Administrator, the costs necessary for handling the administration of the

bond-issuing Company, and the interest that accrues from and including the day of disbursement of the remuneration and costs, as well as amounts of compensation for losses suffered by those persons for handling the administration of the bond-issuing Company in the absence of negligence, unless there is provisions in the contracts with the bond-issuing Company.
(2) The petition for permission under the preceding paragraph shall be made by the bond managers, representative bondholders or Resolution Administrator.
(3) With respect to the remuneration, costs and interest as well as amounts of compensation in paragraph (1), the bond managers, representative bondholders or Resolution Administrator shall have the right to obtain reimbursement, before the bondholders, from the proceeds of payments received under paragraph (1) of Article 705 (including cases where that paragraph is applied mutatis mutandis under paragraph (2) of Article 737).

(Burden of Costs of Bondholders' Meetings)
Article 742 (1) The costs of bondholders' meetings shall be borne by the bond-issuing Company.
(2) The costs of the petition in Article 732 shall be borne by the bond-issuing Company; provided, however, that the court may, in response to the petition by the bond-issuing Company or other interested parties or ex officio, separately prescribe a persons from among the Convener and other interested parties to bear some or all of the costs.

Part V Entity Conversion, Merger, Company Split, Share Exchange, and Share Transfer

Chapter I Entity Conversion

Section 1 Common Provisions

(Preparation of Entity Conversion Plan)
Article 743 A Company may effect Entity Conversion. In such cases, the Company shall prepare an Entity Conversion plan.

Section 2 Entity Conversion of a Stock Company

(Entity Conversion Plan of a Stock Company)
Article 744 (1) In cases where a Stock Company effects Entity Conversion, the Stock Company shall prescribe the following matters in the Entity Conversion plan:
(i) whether a Membership Company after the Entity Conversion (hereinafter referred to as the "Membership Company after Entity Conversion") is a General Partnership Company, Limited Partnership Company, or Limited Liability Company;
(ii) the purpose, trade name, and location of the head office of the Membership Company after Entity Conversion;
(iii) the following matters concerning the partners of the Membership Company after Entity Conversion:
(a) the names and domiciles of the partners;
(b) whether the partners are unlimited partners or limited partners; and
(c) the value of contributions by the partners;
(iv) in addition to what is listed in the preceding two items, the matters provided for in the articles of incorporation of the Membership Company after Entity Conversion;

Art.745　　　　　　Ⅰ Companies Act, Part V, Chap.I, Sec.2

(v) if the Membership Company after Entity Conversion is to deliver to shareholders of the Stock Company effecting the Entity Conversion Monies, etc. (excluding the equity interests of the Membership Company after Entity Conversion; hereinafter the same shall apply in this item and the following item) in lieu of the shares thereof when effecting the Entity Conversion, the following matters concerning such Monies, etc.:
   (a) if such Monies, etc. are Bonds of the Membership Company after Entity Conversion, the description of the classes of such Bonds (meaning the classes of Bonds prescribed in Article 107(2)(ii)(b); hereinafter the same shall apply in this Part) and the total amount for each class of Bonds, or the method for calculating that total amount;
   (b) if such Monies, etc. are property other than Bonds of the Membership Company after Entity Conversion, the description of the features and number or amount of such property, or the method for calculating such number or amount;
(vi) in the case prescribed in the preceding item, matters concerning the allotment of Monies, etc. set forth in that item to shareholders of the Stock Company effecting the Entity Conversion (excluding the Stock Company effecting the Entity Conversion);
(vii) if the Stock Company effecting Entity Conversion has issued Share Options, the description of the amount of Monies, etc. that the Membership Company after Entity Conversion will deliver in lieu of such Share Options to holders of such Share Options at the time of the Entity Conversion, or the method for calculating such amount;
(viii) in the case prescribed in the preceding item, matters concerning the allotment of Monies, etc. set forth in that item to holders of Share Options of the Stock Company effecting the Entity Conversion; and
(ix) the day on which the Entity Conversion becomes effective (hereinafter referred to as the "Effective Day" in this Chapter)
(2) If the Membership Company after Entity Conversion is a General Partnership Company, it shall provide that all of the partners are unlimited partners in prescribing the matter set forth in item (iii)(b) of the preceding paragraph.
(3) If the Membership Company after Entity Conversion is a Limited Partnership Company, it shall provide that some of the partners are unlimited partners and other partners are limited partners in prescribing the matter set forth in paragraph (1)(iii)(b).
(4) If the Membership Company after Entity Conversion is a Limited Liability Company, it shall provide that all of the partners are limited partners in prescribing the matter set forth in paragraph (1)(iii)(b).

(Effectuation, etc. of Entity Conversion of a Stock Company)
Article 745 (1) A Stock Company effecting Entity Conversion shall become a Membership Company on the Effective Day.
(2) A Stock Company effecting Entity Conversion shall, in accordance with the provisions on the matters listed in paragraph (1)(ii) to (iv) of the preceding Article, be deemed to have effected changes to the articles of incorporation relating to such matters on the Effective Day.
(3) Shareholders of a Stock Company effecting Entity Conversion shall, in accordance with the provisions on the matters set forth in paragraph (1)(iii) of the preceding Article, become partners of the Membership Company after Entity Conversion on the Effective Day.
(4) In cases where there are provisions on the matter set forth in item (v)(a) of paragraph (1) of the preceding Article, shareholders of the Stock Company effecting Entity Con-

version shall, in accordance with the provisions on the matter set forth in item (vi) of that paragraph, become bondholders of the Bonds set forth in item (v)(a) of that paragraph on the Effective Day.
(5) The Share Options of a Stock Company effecting Entity Conversion shall be extinguished on the Effective Day.
(6) The provisions of the preceding paragraphs shall not apply in cases where procedures under the provisions of Article 779 are not completed yet or where the Entity Conversion is cancelled.

Section 3 Entity Conversion of a Membership Company

(Entity Conversion Plan of a Membership Company)
Article 746 In cases where a Membership Company effects Entity Conversion, the Membership Company shall prescribe the following matters in the Entity Conversion plan:
(i) the purpose, trade name, location of the head office, and Total Number of Authorized Shares of the Stock Company after the Entity Conversion (hereinafter referred to as the "Stock Company after Entity Conversion" in this Article);
(ii) in addition to what is provided for in the preceding item, the matters provided for in the articles of incorporation of the Stock Company after Entity Conversion;
(iii) the names of the directors of the Stock Company after Entity Conversion;
(iv) the matters provided for in (a) to (c) below for the categories of cases listed respectively therein:
  (a) in cases where the Stock Company after Entity Conversion is a Company with Accounting Advisors: the name(s) of the Accounting Advisor(s) of the Stock Company after Entity Conversion;
  (b) in cases where the Stock Company after Entity Conversion is a Company with Company Auditors (including any Stock Company the articles of incorporation of which provide that the scope of the audit by its company auditor(s) is limited to an audit related to accounting): the name(s) of the company auditor(s) of the Stock Company after Entity Conversion; and
  (c) in cases where the Stock Company after Entity Conversion is a Company with Accounting Auditors: the name(s) of the accounting auditor(s) of the Stock Company after Entity Conversion;
(v) the number of shares (or, for a Company with Class Shares, the classes of the shares and the number of the shares for each class) of the Stock Company after Entity Conversion to be acquired by partners of the Membership Company effecting Entity Conversion, when effecting the Entity Conversion, or the method for calculating such numbers;
(vi) matters concerning the allotment of the shares set forth in the preceding item to partners of the Membership Company effecting Entity Conversion;
(vii) if the Stock Company after Entity Conversion is to deliver to partners of the Membership Company effecting the Entity Conversion Monies, etc. (excluding the shares of the Stock Company after Entity Conversion; hereinafter the same shall apply in this item and the following item) in lieu of the equity interests thereof when effecting the Entity Conversion, the following matters concerning such Monies, etc.:
  (a) if such Monies, etc. are Bonds of the Stock Company after Entity Conversion (excluding those pertaining to Bonds with Share Options), the description of the classes of such Bonds and the total amount for each class of Bonds, or the method for calculating that total amount;

(b) if such Monies, etc. are Share Options of the Stock Company after Entity Conversion (excluding those attached to Bonds with Share Options), the description of the features and number of such Share Options, or the method for calculating such number;
(c) if such Monies, etc. are Bonds with Share Options of the Stock Company after Entity Conversion, the matters prescribed in (a) concerning such Bonds with Share Options and the matters prescribed in (b) concerning the Share Options attached to such Bonds with Share Options; and
(d) if such Monies, etc. are property other than Bonds, etc. (meaning Bonds and Share Options; hereinafter the same shall apply in this Part) of the Stock Company after Entity Conversion, the description of the features and number or amount of such property, or the method for calculating such number or amount;
(viii) in the case prescribed in the preceding item, matters concerning the allotment of Monies, etc. set forth in that item to partners of the Membership Company effecting the Entity Conversion; and
(ix) the Effective Day.

(Effectuation, etc. of Entity Conversion of a Membership Company)
Article 747 (1) A Membership Company effecting Entity Conversion shall become a Stock Company on the Effective Day.
(2) A Membership Company effecting Entity Conversion shall, in accordance with the provisions on the matters listed in item (i) and item (ii) of the preceding Article, be deemed to have effected changes to the articles of incorporation relating to such matters on the Effective Day.
(3) Partners of a Membership Company effecting Entity Conversion shall, in accordance with the provisions on the matters set forth in item (vi) of the preceding Article, become shareholders of the shares set forth in item (v) of that Article on the Effective Day.
(4) In the cases listed in the following items, partners of a Membership Company effecting Entity Conversion shall become the persons specified respectively in those items, in accordance with the provisions on the matters set forth in item (viii) of the preceding Article, on the Effective Day:
(i) in cases where there is a provision on the matters set forth in (a) of item (vii) of the preceding Article: bondholders of the Bonds set forth in (a) of that item;
(ii) in cases where there is a provision on the matters set forth in (b) of item (vii) of the preceding Article: holders of the Share Options set forth in (b) of that item; and
(iii) in cases where there is a provision on the matters set forth in (c) of item (vii) of the preceding Article: bondholders of the Bonds pertaining to Bonds with Share Options set forth in (c) of that item, and holders of the Share Options attached to such Bonds with Share Options.
(5) The provisions of the preceding paragraphs shall not apply in cases where procedures under the provisions of Article 779 (excluding paragraph (2) (ii)) as applied mutatis mutandis pursuant to Article 781(2) are not completed yet or where the Entity Conversion is cancelled.

Chapter II Merger

Section 1 Common Provisions

(Conclusion of a Merger Agreement)
Article 748 A Company may effect a merger with another Company. In such cases, the

merging Companies shall conclude a merger agreement.

Section 2 Absorption-type Merger

Subsection 1 Absorption-type Merger in Which a Stock Company Survives

(Absorption-type Merger Agreement in Which a Stock Company Survives)
Article 749 (1) In the case where a Company effects an Absorption-type Merger, if the Company surviving the Absorption-type Merger (hereinafter referred to as the "Company Surviving Absorption-type Merger") is a Stock Company, it shall prescribe the following matters in the Absorption-type Merger agreement:
(i) the trade names and domiciles of the Company Surviving Absorption-type Merger that is a Stock Company (hereinafter referred to as the "Stock Company Surviving Absorption-type Merger" in this Part) and the Company absorbed in the Absorption-type Merger (hereinafter referred to as the "Company Absorbed in Absorption-type Merger" in this Part);
(ii) if the Stock Company Surviving Absorption-type Merger is to deliver to shareholders of the Company Absorbed in Absorption-type Merger that is a Stock Company (hereinafter referred to as the "Stock Company Absorbed in Absorption-type Merger" in this Part) or to partners of the Company Absorbed in Absorption-type Merger that is a Membership Company (hereinafter referred to as the "Membership Company Absorbed in Absorption-type Merger" in this Part) Monies, etc. in lieu of the shares or equity interests thereof when effecting the Absorption-type Merger, the following matters concerning such Monies, etc.:
  (a) if such Monies, etc. are shares of the Stock Company Surviving Absorption-type Merger, the description of the number of such shares (or, for a Company with Class Shares, the classes of the shares and the number of the shares for each class) or the method for calculating such numbers, and matters concerning the amount of the stated capital and capital reserves of the Stock Company Surviving Absorption-type Merger;
  (b) if such Monies, etc. are Bonds of the Stock Company Surviving Absorption-type Merger (excluding those pertaining to Bonds with Share Options), the description of the classes of such Bonds and the total amount for each class of Bonds, or the method for calculating that total amount;
  (c) if such Monies, etc. are Stock Options of the Stock Company Surviving Absorption-type Merger (excluding those attached to Bonds with Share Options), the description of the features and number of such Share Options, or the method for calculating such number;
  (d) if such Monies, etc. are Bonds with Share Options of the Stock Company Surviving Absorption-type Merger, the matters prescribed in (b) concerning such Bonds with Share Options and the matters prescribed in (c) concerning the Share Options attached to such Bonds with Share Options; or
  (e) if such Monies, etc. are property other than shares, etc. of the Stock Company Surviving Absorption-type Merger, the description of the features and number or amount of such property, or the method for calculating such number or amount;
(iii) in the case prescribed in the preceding item, matters concerning the allotment of Monies, etc. set forth in that item to shareholders of the Stock Company Absorbed in Absorption-type Merger (excluding the Stock Company Absorbed in Absorption-type Merger and the Stock Company Surviving Absorption-type Merger) or to

partners of the Membership Company Absorbed in Absorption-type Merger (excluding the Stock Company Surviving Absorption-type Merger);
(iv) if the Stock Company Absorbed in Absorption-type Merger has issued Share Options, the following matters concerning the Share Options of the Stock Company Surviving Absorption-type Merger or monies that the Stock Company Surviving Absorption-type Merger will deliver in lieu of such Share Options to holders of such Share Options at the time of the Absorption-type Merger:
(a) when delivering Share Options of the Stock Company Surviving Absorption-type Merger to holders of Share Options of the Stock Company Absorbed in Absorption-type Merger, the description of the features and number of such Share Options, or the method for calculating such number;
(b) in the case prescribed in (a), if the Share Options of the Stock Company Absorbed in Absorption-type Merger set forth in (a) are Share Options attached to Bonds with Share Options, a statement to the effect that the Stock Company Surviving Absorption-type Merger will succeed to the obligations relating to the Bonds pertaining to such Bonds with Share Options and the description of the classes of the Bonds subject to such succession and the total amount for each class of Bonds, or the method for calculating that total amount; and
(c) when delivering monies to holders of Share Options of the Stock Company Absorbed in Absorption-type Merger, the description of the amount of such monies or the method for calculating such amount;
(v) in the case prescribed in the preceding item, matters concerning allotment of the Share Options of the Stock Company Surviving Absorption-type Merger or monies set forth in that item to holders of Share Options of the Stock Company Absorbed in Absorption-type Merger; and
(vi) the day on which the Absorption-type Merger becomes effective (hereinafter referred to as the "Effective Day" in this Section).
(2) In the case prescribed in the preceding paragraph, if the Stock Company Absorbed in Absorption-type Merger is a Company with Class Shares, the Stock Company Surviving Absorption-type Merger and the Stock Company Absorbed in Absorption-type Merger may provide for the following matters in prescribing the matters set forth in item (iii) of that paragraph in accordance with the features of the classes of shares issued by the Stock Company Absorbed in Absorption-type Merger:
(i) if there is any arrangement that no Monies, etc. are allotted to shareholders of a certain class of shares, a statement to such effect and such class of shares; and
(ii) in addition to the matters listed in the preceding item, if there is any arrangement that each class of shares shall be treated differently with respect to allotment of Monies, etc., a statement to such effect and the details of such different treatment.
(3) In the case prescribed in paragraph (1), the provisions on the matters listed in item (iii) of that paragraph shall be such that the Monies, etc. are delivered in proportion to the number of the shares (or, in cases where there are provisions on the matters listed in item (ii) of the preceding paragraph, the number of the shares of each class) held by the shareholders of the Stock Company Absorbed in Absorption-type Merger (excluding the Stock Company Absorbed in Absorption-type Merger and the Stock Company Surviving Absorption-type Merger and shareholders of the class of shares referred to in item (i) of the preceding paragraph).

(Effectuation, etc. of an Absorption-type Merger in Which a Stock Company Survives)
Article 750 (1) A Stock Company Surviving Absorption-type Merger shall succeed to the rights and obligations of a Company Absorbed in Absorption-type Merger on the

Effective Day.
(2) Dissolution of a Company Absorbed in Absorption-type Merger resulting from the Absorption-type Merger may not be duly asserted against a third party until the registration of the Absorption-type Merger has been completed.
(3) In the cases listed in the following items, the shareholders of a Stock Company Absorbed in Absorption-type Merger or partners of a Membership Company Absorbed in Absorption-type Merger shall become the persons specified respectively in those items, in accordance with the provisions on the matters set forth in paragraph (1) (iii) of the preceding Article, on the Effective Day:
  (i) in cases where there is a provision on the matters set forth in (a) of item (ii) of paragraph (1) of the preceding Article: shareholders of shares set forth in (a) of that item;
  (ii) in cases where there is a provision on the matters set forth in (b) of item (ii) of paragraph (1) of the preceding Article: bondholders of Bonds set forth in (b) of that item;
  (iii) in cases where there is a provision on the matters set forth in (c) of item (ii) of paragraph (1) of the preceding Article: holders of Share Options set forth in (c) of that item; or
  (iv) in cases where there is a provision on the matters set forth in (d) of item (ii) of paragraph (1) of the preceding Article: bondholders of the Bonds pertaining to Bonds with Share Options set forth in (d) of that item, and holders of the Share Options attached to such Bonds with Share Options.
(4) The Share Options of a Stock Company Absorbed in Absorption-type Merger shall be extinguished on the Effective Day.
(5) In the case prescribed in item (iv)(a) of paragraph (1) of the preceding Article, the holders of Share Options of a Stock Company Absorbed in Absorption-type Merger shall, in accordance with the provisions on the matters set forth in item (v) of that paragraph, become holders of Share Options of a Stock Company Surviving Absorption-type Merger set forth in item (iv)(a) of that paragraph on the Effective Day.
(6) The provisions of the preceding paragraphs shall not apply in cases where procedures under the provisions of Article 789 (excluding paragraph (1)(iii) and paragraph (2)(iii), and including the case where it is applied mutatis pursuant to Article 793(2)) or Article 799 are not completed yet or where the Absorption-type Merger is cancelled.

Subsection 2 Absorption-type Merger in Which a Membership Company Survives

(Absorption-type Merger Agreement in Which a Membership Company Survives)

Article 751 (1) In the case where a Company effects an Absorption-type Merger, if the Company Surviving Absorption-type Merger is a Membership Company, it shall prescribe the following matters in the Absorption-type Merger agreement:
  (i) the trade names and domiciles of the Company Surviving Absorption-type Merger that is a Membership Company (hereinafter referred to as the "Membership Company Surviving Absorption-type Merger" in this Section) and the Company Absorbed in Absorption-type Merger;
  (ii) if shareholders of the Stock Company Absorbed in Absorption-type Merger or partners of the Membership Company Absorbed in Absorption-type Merger are to become partners of the Membership Company Surviving Absorption-type Merger when effecting the Absorption-type Merger, the matters provided for in (a) to (c) below for the categories of Membership Company Surviving Absorption-type

Art.751 ① Companies Act, Part V, Chap.II, Sec.2

Merger listed respectively therein:
   (a) General Partnership Company: the names and domiciles of the partners and the value of contributions by the partners;
   (b) Limited Partnership Company: the names and domiciles of the partners, whether the partners are unlimited partners or limited partners, and the value of contributions by the partners; or
   (c) Limited Liability Company: the names and domiciles of the partners and the value of contributions by the partners;
(iii) if the Membership Company Surviving Absorption-type Merger is to deliver to shareholders of the Stock Company Absorbed in Absorption-type Merger or partners of the Membership Company Absorbed in Absorption-type Merger Monies, etc. (excluding the equity interests of the Membership Company Surviving Absorption-type Merger) in lieu of the shares or equity interests thereof when effecting the Absorption-type Merger, the following matters concerning such Monies, etc.:
   (a) if such Monies, etc. are Bonds of the Membership Company Surviving Absorption-type Merger, the description of the classes of such Bonds and the total amount for each class of Bonds, or the method for calculating that total amount; or
   (b) if such Monies, etc. are property other than Bonds of the Membership Company Surviving Absorption-type Merger, the description of the features and number or amount of such property, or the method for calculating such number or amount;
(iv) in the case prescribed in the preceding item, matters concerning allotment of Monies, etc. set forth in that item to shareholders of the Stock Company Absorbed in Absorption-type Merger (excluding the Stock Company Absorbed in Absorption-type Merger and the Membership Company Surviving Absorption-type Merger) or partners of the Membership Company Absorbed in Absorption-type Merger (excluding the Membership Company Surviving Absorption-type Merger);
(v) if the Stock Company Absorbed in Absorption-type Merger has issued Share Options, the description of the amount of Monies, etc. that the Membership Company Surviving Absorption-type Merger will deliver in lieu of such Share Options to holders of such Share Options at the time of the Absorption-type Merger, or the method for calculating such amount;
(vi) in the case prescribed in the preceding item, matters concerning the allotment of Monies, etc. set forth in that item to holders of Share Options of the Stock Company Absorbed in Absorption-type Merger; and
(vii) the Effective Day.
(2) In the case prescribed in the preceding paragraph, if the Stock Company Absorbed in Absorption-type Merger is a Company with Class Shares, the Membership Company Surviving Absorption-type Merger and the Stock Company Absorbed in Absorption-type Merger may provide for the following matters in prescribing the matters set forth in item (iv) of that paragraph in accordance with the features of the classes of shares issued by the Stock Company Absorbed in Absorption-type Merger:
   (i) if there is any arrangement that no Monies, etc. are allotted to shareholders of a certain class of shares, a statement to such effect and such class of shares; and
   (ii) in addition to the matters listed in the preceding item, if there is any arrangement that each class of shares shall be treated differently with respect to allotment of Monies, etc., a statement to such effect and the details of such different treatment.
(3) In the case prescribed in paragraph (1), the provisions on the matters listed in item (iv) of that paragraph shall be such that the Monies, etc. are delivered in proportion to the

number of the shares (or, in cases where there are provisions on the matters listed in item (ii) of the preceding paragraph, the number of the shares of each class) held by shareholders of the Stock Company Absorbed in Absorption-type Merger (excluding the Stock Company Absorbed in Absorption-type Merger and the Membership Company Surviving Absorption-type Merger and shareholders of the class of shares referred to in item (i) of the preceding paragraph).

(Effectuation, etc. of an Absorption-type Merger in Which a Membership Company Survives)

Article 752 (1) A Membership Company Surviving Absorption-type Merger shall succeed to the rights and obligations of the Company Absorbed in Absorption-type Merger on the Effective Day.

(2) Dissolution of the Company Absorbed in Absorption-type Merger resulting from the Absorption-type Merger may not be duly asserted against a third party until the registration of the Absorption-type Merger has been completed.

(3) In the case prescribed in item (ii) of paragraph (1) of the preceding Article, the shareholders of the Stock Company Absorbed in Absorption-type Merger or partners of the Membership Company Absorbed in Absorption-type Merger shall, in accordance with the provisions on the matters set forth in that item, become partners of the Membership Company Surviving Absorption-type Merger on the Effective Day. In such cases, the Membership Company Surviving Absorption-type Merger shall be deemed to have effected changes to the articles of incorporation relating to the partners set forth in that item on the Effective Day.

(4) In cases where there are provisions on the matter set forth in item (iii)(a) of paragraph (1) of the preceding Article, the shareholders of the Stock Company Absorbed in Absorption-type Merger or partners of the Membership Company Absorbed in Absorption-type Merger shall, in accordance with the provisions on the matter set forth in item (iv) of that paragraph, become bondholders of Bonds set forth in item (iii)(a) of that paragraph on the Effective Day.

(5) The Share Options of the Stock Company Absorbed in Absorption-type Merger shall be extinguished on the Effective Day.

(6) The provisions of the preceding paragraphs shall not apply in cases where procedures under the provisions of Article 789 (excluding paragraph (1)(iii) and paragraph (2)(iii), and including the case where it is applied mutatis pursuant to Article 793(2)) or Article 799 (excluding paragraph (2)(iii)) as applied mutatis mutandis pursuant to Article 802(2) are not completed yet or where the Absorption-type Merger is cancelled.

Section 3 Consolidation-type Merger

Subsection 1 Consolidation-type Merger by Which a Stock Company is Incorporated

(Consolidation-type Merger Agreement by Which a Stock Company is Incorporated)

Article 753 (1) In the case where two or more Companies effect a Consolidation-type Merger, if the Company incorporated through the Consolidation-type Merger (hereinafter referred to as the "Company Incorporated through Consolidation-type Merger" in this Part) is a Stock Company, it shall prescribe the following matters in the Consolidation-type Merger agreement:

(i) the trade names and domiciles of the companies consolidated by the Consolidation-type Merger (hereinafter referred to as the "Companies Consolidated through

Art.753　　　① Companies Act, Part V, Chap.II, Sec.3

Consolidation-type Merger" in this Part);
(ii) the purpose, trade name, location of the head office, and Total Number of Authorized Shares of the Company Incorporated through Consolidation-type Merger that is a Stock Company (hereinafter referred to as the "Stock Company Incorporated through Consolidation-type Merger" in this Part);
(iii) in addition to what is provided for in the preceding item, the matters provided for in the articles of incorporation of the Stock Company Incorporated through Consolidation-type Merger;
(iv) the names of the Directors at Incorporation of the Stock Company Incorporated through Consolidation-type Merger;
(v) the matters provided for in (a) to (c) below for the categories of cases listed respectively therein:
  (a) in cases where the Stock Company Incorporated through Consolidation-type Merger is a Company with Accounting Advisors: the name(s) of the Accounting Advisor(s) at Incorporation of the Stock Company Incorporated through Consolidation-type Merger;
  (b) in cases where the Stock Company Incorporated through Consolidation-type Merger is a Company with Company Auditors (including any Stock Company the articles of incorporation of which provide that the scope of the audit by its company auditor(s) is limited to an audit related to accounting): the name(s) of the Company Auditor(s) at Incorporation of the Stock Company Incorporated through Consolidation-type Merger; or
  (c) in cases where the Stock Company Incorporated through Consolidation-type Merger is a Company with Accounting Auditors: the name(s) of the Accounting Auditor(s) at Incorporation of the Stock Company Incorporated through Consolidation-type Merger;
(vi) the number of shares (or, for a Company with Class Shares, the classes of the shares and the number of the shares for each class) of the Stock Company Incorporated through Consolidation-type Merger to be delivered by the Stock Company Incorporated through Consolidation-type Merger to shareholders of the Company(ies) Consolidated through Consolidation-type Merger that is a Stock Company (hereinafter referred to as the "Stock Company(ies) Consolidated through Consolidation-type Merger" in this Part) or to partners of the Company(ies) Consolidated through Consolidation-type Merger that is a Membership Company (hereinafter referred to as the "Membership Company(ies) Consolidated through Consolidation-type Merger" in this Part), when effecting the Consolidation-type Merger, or the method for calculating such numbers, and matters concerning the amount of the stated capital and capital reserves of the Stock Company Incorporated through Consolidation-type Merger;
(vii) matters concerning allotment of the shares set forth in the preceding item to shareholders of the Stock Company(ies) Consolidated through Consolidation-type Merger (excluding the Stock Company(ies) Consolidated through Consolidation-type Merger) or to partners of the Membership Company(ies) Consolidated through Consolidation-type Merger;
(viii) if the Stock Company Incorporated through Consolidation-type Merger is to deliver to shareholders of the Stock Company(ies) Consolidated through Consolidation-type Merger or to partners of the Membership Company(ies) Consolidated through Consolidation-type Merger Bonds, etc. of the Stock Company Incorporated through Consolidation-type Merger in lieu of the shares or equity interests thereof when effecting the Consolidation-type Merger, the following matters concerning such Bonds, etc.:

(a) if such Bonds, etc. are Bonds of the Stock Company Incorporated through Consolidation-type Merger (excluding those pertaining to Bonds with Share Options), the description of the classes of such Bonds and the total amount for each class of Bonds, or the method for calculating that total amount;
(b) if such Bonds, etc. are Share Options of the Stock Company Incorporated through Consolidation-type Merger (excluding those attached to Bonds with Share Options), the description of the features and number of such Share Options, or the method for calculating such number; or
(c) if such Bonds, etc. are Bonds with Share Options of the Stock Company Incorporated through Consolidation-type Merger, the matters prescribed in (a) concerning such Bonds with Share Options and the matters prescribed in (b) concerning the Share Options attached to such Bonds with Share Options;
(ix) in the case prescribed in the preceding item, matters concerning the allotment of Bonds, etc. set forth in that item to shareholders of the Stock Company(ies) Consolidated through Consolidation-type Merger (excluding the Stock Company(ies) Consolidated through Consolidation-type Merger) or partners of the Membership Company(ies) Consolidated through Consolidation-type Merger;
(x) if the Stock Company(ies) Consolidated through Consolidation-type Merger has issued Share Options, the following matters concerning the Share Options of the Stock Company Incorporated through Consolidation-type Merger or monies that the Stock Company Incorporated through Consolidation-type Merger will deliver in lieu of such Share Options to holders of such Share Options at the time of the Consolidation-type Merger:
(a) when delivering Share Options of the Stock Company Surviving Absorption-type Merger to holders of Share Options of the Stock Company Absorbed in Absorption-type Merger, the description of the features and number of such Share Options, or the method for calculating such number;
(b) in the case prescribed in (a), if the Share Options of the Stock Company(ies) Consolidated through Consolidation-type Merger set forth in (a) are Share Options attached to Bonds with Share Options, a statement to the effect that the Stock Company Incorporated through Consolidation-type Merger will succeed to the obligations relating to the Bonds pertaining to such Bonds with Share Options and the description of the classes of the Bonds subject to such succession and the total amount for each class of Bonds, or the method for calculating that total amount; and
(c) when delivering monies to holders of Share Options of the Stock Company(ies) Consolidated through Consolidation-type Merger, the description of the amount of such monies or the method for calculating such amount; and
(xi) in the case prescribed in the preceding item, matters concerning the allotment of the Share Options of the Stock Company Incorporated through Consolidation-type Merger or monies set forth in that item to holders of Share Options of the Stock Company(ies) Consolidated through Consolidation-type Merger.
(2) In the case prescribed in the preceding paragraph, if all or part of the Stock Company(ies) Consolidated through Consolidation-type Merger are Companies with Class Shares, the Companies Consolidated through Consolidation-type Merger may provide for the following matters in prescribing the matters set forth in item (vii) of that paragraph (limited to matters pertaining to shareholders of the Stock Company(ies) Consolidated through Consolidation-type Merger; the same shall apply in the following paragraph) in accordance with the features of the classes of shares issued by the Stock Company(ies) Consolidated through Consolidation-type Merger:
(i) if there is any arrangement that no shares of the Stock Company Incorporated

Art.754　　　　Ⅰ **Companies Act, Part V, Chap.II, Sec.3**

through Consolidation-type Merger are allotted to shareholders of a certain class of shares, a statement to such effect and such class of shares; and

(ii) in addition to the matters listed in the preceding item, if there is any arrangement that each class of shares shall be treated differently with respect to allotment of shares of the Stock Company Incorporated through Consolidation-type Merger, a statement to such effect and the details of such different treatment.

(3) In the case prescribed in paragraph (1), the provisions on the matters listed in item (vii) of that paragraph shall be such that shares of the Stock Company Incorporated through Consolidation-type Merger shall be delivered in proportion to the number of the shares (or, in cases where there are provisions on the matters listed in item (ii) of the preceding paragraph, the number of the shares of each class) held by shareholders of the Stock Company(ies) Consolidated through Consolidation-type Merger (excluding the Companies Consolidated through Consolidation-type Merger and shareholders of the class of shares referred to in item (i) of the preceding paragraph).

(4) The provisions of the preceding two paragraphs shall apply mutatis mutandis to paragraph (1)(ix). In such cases, the term "shares of the Stock Company Incorporated through Consolidation-type Merger" in the preceding two paragraphs shall be deemed to be replaced with "Bonds, etc. of the Stock Company Incorporated through Consolidation-type Merger."

(Effectuation, etc. of Consolidation-type Merger by Which a Stock Company is Incorporated)

Article 754　(1) A Stock Company Incorporated through Consolidation-type Merger shall succeed to the rights and obligations of the Companies Consolidated through Consolidation-type Merger on the day of its formation.

(2) In the case prescribed in paragraph (1) of the preceding Article, the shareholders of the Stock Company(ies) Consolidated through Consolidation-type Merger or partners of the Membership Company(ies) Consolidated through Consolidation-type Merger shall become shareholders of the shares set forth in item (vi) of that paragraph, in accordance with the provisions on the matters set forth in item (vii) of that paragraph, on the day of formation of the Stock Company Incorporated through Consolidation-type Merger.

(3) In the cases listed in the following items, shareholders of a Stock Company(ies) Consolidated through Consolidation-type Merger or partners of a Membership Company(ies) Consolidated through Consolidation-type Merger shall become the persons specified respectively in those items, in accordance with the provisions on the matters set forth in paragraph (1)(ix) of the preceding Article, on the day of formation of the Stock Company Incorporated through Consolidation-type Merger:

(i) in cases where there is a provision on the matters set forth in (a) of item (viii) of paragraph (1) of the preceding Article: bondholders of Bonds set forth in (a) of that item;

(ii) in cases where there is a provision on the matters set forth in (b) of item (viii) of paragraph (1) of the preceding Article: holders of Share Options set forth in (b) of that item; or

(iii) in cases where there is a provision on the matters set forth in (c) of item (viii) paragraph (1) of the preceding Article: bondholders of the Bonds pertaining to Bonds with Share Options set forth in (c) of that item, and holders of the Share Options attached to such Bonds with Share Options.

(4) The Share Options of a Stock Company(ies) Consolidated through Consolidation-type Merger shall be extinguished on the day of formation of the Stock Company Incorporated through Consolidation-type Merger.

(5) In the case prescribed in item (x)(a) of paragraph (1) of the preceding Article, the holders of Share Options of a Stock Company(ies) Consolidated through Consolidation-type Merger shall, in accordance with the provisions on the matters set forth in item (xi) of that paragraph, become holders of Share Options of the Stock Company Incorporated through Consolidation-type Merger set forth in item (x)(a) of that paragraph on the day of formation of the Stock Company Incorporated through Consolidation-type Merger.

Subsection 2 Consolidation-type Merger by Which a Membership Company is Incorporated

(Consolidation-type Merger Agreement by Which a Membership Company is Incorporated)
Article 755 (1) In the case where two or more Companies effect a Consolidation-type Merger, if the Company Incorporated through Consolidation-type Merger is a Membership Company, it shall prescribe the following matters in the Consolidation-type Merger agreement:
(i) the trade names and domiciles of the Companies Consolidated through Consolidation-type Merger;
(ii) whether the Company Incorporated through Consolidation-type Merger that is a Membership Company (hereinafter referred to as the "Membership Company Incorporated through Consolidation-type Merger" in this Part) is a General Partnership Company, a Limited Partnership Company, or a Limited Liability Company;
(iii) the purpose, trade name, location of the head office of the Membership Company Incorporated through Consolidation-type Merger;
(iv) the following matters concerning the partners of the Membership Company Incorporated through Consolidation-type Merger:
  (a) the names and domiciles of the partners;
  (b) whether the partners are unlimited partners or limited partners; and
  (c) the value of contributions by the partners;
(v) in addition to what is listed in the preceding two items, the matters provided for in the articles of incorporation of the Membership Company Incorporated through Consolidation-type Merger;
(vi) if the Membership Company Incorporated through Consolidation-type Merger is to deliver to shareholders of the Stock Company(ies) Consolidated through Consolidation-type Merger or to partners of the Membership Company(ies) Consolidated through Consolidation-type Merger Bonds of the Membership Company Incorporated through Consolidation-type Merger in lieu of the shares or equity interests thereof when effecting the Consolidation-type Merger, the description of the classes of such Bonds and the total amount for each class of Bonds, or the method for calculating that total amount
(vii) in the case prescribed in the preceding item, matters concerning allotment of Bonds set forth in that item to shareholders of the Stock Company(ies) Consolidated through Consolidation-type Merger (excluding the Stock Company(ies) Consolidated through Consolidation-type Merger) or to partners of the Membership Company(ies) Consolidated through Consolidation-type Merger;
(viii) if the Stock Company(ies) Consolidated through Consolidation-type Merger has issued Share Options, the description of the amount of monies that the Membership Company Incorporated through Consolidation-type Merger shall deliver in lieu of such Share Options to holders of such Share Options at the time of the Consolidation-type Merger, or the method for calculating such amount

(ix) n the case prescribed in the preceding item, matters concerning allotment of monies set forth in that item to holders of Share Options of the Stock Company(ies) Consolidated through Consolidation-type Merger.
(2) If the Membership Company Incorporated through Consolidation-type Merger is a General Partnership Company, it shall provide that all of the partners are unlimited partners in prescribing the matter set forth in item (iv)(b) of the preceding paragraph.
(3) If the Membership Company Incorporated through Consolidation-type Merger is a Limited Partnership Company, it shall provide that some of the partners are unlimited partners and other partners are limited partners in prescribing the matter set forth in paragraph (1)(iv)(b).
(4) If the Membership Company Incorporated through Consolidation-type Merger is a Limited Liability Company, it shall provide that all of the partners are limited partners in prescribing the matter set forth in paragraph (1)(iv)(b).

(Effectuation, etc. of Consolidation-type Merger by Which a Membership Company is Incorporated)
Article 756 (1) A Membership Company Incorporated through Consolidation-type Merger shall succeed to the rights and obligations of the Companies Consolidated through Consolidation-type Merger on the day of its formation.
(2) In the case prescribed in paragraph (1) of the preceding Article, the shareholders of the Stock Company(ies) Consolidated through Consolidation-type Merger or partners of the Membership Company(ies) Consolidated through Consolidation-type Merger shall become partners of the Membership Company Incorporated through Consolidation-type Merger, in accordance with the provisions on the matters set forth in item (iv) of that paragraph, on the day of formation of the Membership Company Incorporated through Consolidation-type Merger.
(3) In cases where there are provisions on the matter set forth in item (vi) of paragraph (1) of the preceding Article, the shareholders of a Stock Company(ies) Consolidated through Consolidation-type Merger or partners of a Membership Company(ies) Consolidated through Consolidation-type Merger shall, in accordance with the provisions on the matter set forth in item (vii) of that paragraph, become bondholders of Bonds set forth in item (vi) of that paragraph on the day of formation of the Membership Company Incorporated through Consolidation-type Merger.
(4) The Share Options of a Stock Company(ies) Consolidated through Consolidation-type Merger shall be extinguished on the day of formation of the Membership Company Incorporated through Consolidation-type Merger.

Chapter III Company Split

Section 1 Absorption-type Company Split

Subsection 1 Common Provisions

(Conclusion of an Absorption-type Company Split Agreement)
Article 757 A Company (limited to a Stock Company or a Limited Liability Company) may effect an Absorption-type Company Split. In such cases, such Company shall conclude an Absorption-type Company Split agreement with the Company which succeeds to all or part of the rights and obligations held by such Company in connection with its business by transfer from such Company (hereinafter referred to as the "Succeeding Company in Absorption-type Company Split" in this Part).

Subsection 2 Absorption-type Company Split Which Causes a Stock Company to Succeed to Rights and Obligations

(Absorption-type Company Split Agreement Which Causes a Stock Company to Succeed to Rights and Obligations)

Article 758 In the case where a Company effects an Absorption-type Company Split, if the Succeeding Company in Absorption-type Company Split is a Stock Company, it shall prescribe the following matters in the Absorption-type Company Split agreement:

(i) the trade names and domiciles of the Company effecting the Absorption-type Company Split (hereinafter referred to as the "Splitting Company in Absorption-type Company Split" in this Part) and the Succeeding Company in Absorption-type Company Split that is a Stock Company (hereinafter referred to as the "Succeeding Stock Company in Absorption-type Company Split" in this Part);

(ii) matters concerning the assets, obligations, employment agreements, and any other rights and obligations that the Succeeding Stock Company in Absorption-type Company Split succeeds to by transfer from the Splitting Company in Absorption-type Company Split through the Absorption-type Company Split (excluding obligations pertaining to shares of the Splitting Company in Absorption-type Company Split that is a Stock Company (hereinafter referred to as the "Splitting Stock Company in Absorption-type Company Split" in this Part) and of the Succeeding Stock Company in Absorption-type Company Split and to Share Options of the Splitting Stock Company in Absorption-type Company Split);

(iii) when the Succeeding Stock Company in Absorption-type Company Split succeeds to shares of the Splitting Stock Company in Absorption-type Company Split or of the Succeeding Stock Company in Absorption-type Company Split through the Absorption-type Company Split, matters concerning such shares;

(iv) if the Succeeding Stock Company in Absorption-type Company Split is to deliver to the Splitting Company in Absorption-type Company Split Monies, etc. in lieu of all or part of the rights and obligations in connection with the business thereof when effecting the Absorption-type Company Split, the following matters concerning such Monies, etc.:

(a) if such Monies, etc. are shares of the Succeeding Stock Company in Absorption-type Company Split, the description of the number of such shares (or, for a Company with Class Shares, the classes of the shares and the number of the shares for each class) or the method for calculating such numbers, and matters concerning the amount of the stated capital and capital reserves of the Succeeding Stock Company in Absorption-type Company Split;

(b) if such Monies, etc. are Bonds of the Succeeding Stock Company in Absorption-type Company Split (excluding those pertaining to Bonds with Share Options), the description of the classes of such Bonds and the total amount for each class of Bonds, or the method for calculating that total amount;

(c) if such Monies, etc. are Stock Options of the Succeeding Stock Company in Absorption-type Company Split (excluding those attached to Bonds with Share Options), the description of the features and number of such Share Options, or the method for calculating such number;

(d) if such Monies, etc. are Bonds with Share Options of the Succeeding Stock Company in Absorption-type Company Split, the matters prescribed in (b) concerning such Bonds with Share Options and the matters prescribed in (c) concerning the Share Options attached to such Bonds with Share Options; and

Art.759　　Ⅰ Companies Act, Part V, Chap.III, Sec.1

  (e) if such Monies, etc. are property other than shares, etc. of the Succeeding Stock Company in Absorption-type Company Split, the description of the features and number or amount of such property, or the method for calculating such number or amount;
(v) if the Succeeding Stock Company in Absorption-type Company Split is to deliver to holders of Share Options of the Splitting Stock Company in Absorption-type Company Split Share Options of the Succeeding Stock Company in Absorption-type Company Split in lieu of such Share Options at the time of the Absorption-type Company Split, the following matters concerning such Share Options:
  (a) the description of the features of the Share Options (hereinafter referred to as "Share Options under Absorption-type Company Split Agreement" in this Part) held by holders of Share Options of the Splitting Stock Company in Absorption-type Company Split who shall receive delivery of Share Options of the Succeeding Stock Company in Absorption-type Company Split;
  (b) the description of the features and number of Share Options of the Succeeding Stock Company in Absorption-type Company Split to be delivered to holders of Share Options under Absorption-type Company Split Agreement, or the method for calculating such number; and
  (c) if Share Options under Absorption-type Company Split Agreement are Share Options attached to Bonds with Share Options, a statement to the effect that the Succeeding Stock Company in Absorption-type Company Split will succeed to the obligations relating to the Bonds pertaining to such Bonds with Share Options and the description of the classes of the Bonds subject to such succession and the total amount for each class of Bonds, or the method for calculating that total amount;
(vi) in the case prescribed in the preceding item, matters concerning allotment of the Share Options of the Succeeding Stock Company in Absorption-type Company Split set forth in that item to holders of Share Options under Absorption-type Company Split Agreement;
(vii) the day on which the Absorption-type Company Split becomes effective (hereinafter referred to as the "Effective Day" in this Section);
(viii) if the Splitting Stock Company in Absorption-type Company Split conducts any one of the following acts on the Effective Day, a statement to that effect:
  (a) acquisition of shares under the provisions of paragraph (1) of Article 171 (limited to the case where the Consideration for Acquisition prescribed in item (i) of that paragraph is only the shares of the Succeeding Stock Company in Absorption-type Company Split (excluding shares that had been held by the Splitting Stock Company in Absorption-type Company Split prior to effecting the Absorption-type Company Split, and including shares prescribed by the applicable Ordinance of the Ministry of Justice as those equivalent to shares of the Succeeding Stock Company in Absorption-type Company Split; the same shall apply in (b))); or
  (b) payment of dividends of surplus (limited to the case where the Dividend Property is only the shares of the Succeeding Stock Company in Absorption-type Company Split).

(Effectuation, etc. of an Absorption-type Company Split Which Causes a Stock Company to Succeed to Rights and Obligations)
Article 759 (1) A Succeeding Stock Company in Absorption-type Company Split shall succeed to the rights and obligations of the Splitting Company in Absorption-type Company Split, in accordance with the provisions of the Absorption-type Company

Split agreement, on the Effective Day.
(2) Notwithstanding the provisions of the preceding paragraph, if a creditor of the Splitting Company in Absorption-type Company Split who is able to state an objection (limited to a creditor to whom the separate notice set forth in Article 789(2) (excluding item (iii) and including the case where it is applied mutatis mutandis pursuant to Article 793(2); hereinafter the same shall apply in this paragraph and the following paragraph) shall be given; the same shall apply in the following paragraph) pursuant to the provisions of Article 789(1)(ii) (including the case where it is applied mutatis mutandis pursuant to Article 793(2); the same shall apply in the following paragraph) has not received the separate notice set forth in Article 789(2), such creditor may request the Splitting Company in Absorption-type Company Split to perform the obligations to the extent of the value of property held by the Splitting Company in Absorption-type Company Split on the Effective Day, even in the case where such creditor is not allowed, under the Absorption-type Company Split agreement, to request the Splitting Company in Absorption-type Company Split to perform the obligations after the Absorption-type Company Split.
(3) Notwithstanding the provisions of paragraph (1), if a creditor of the Splitting Company in Absorption-type Company Split who is able to state an objection pursuant to the provisions of paragraph (1)(ii) of Article 789 has not received the separate notice set forth in paragraph (2) of that Article, such creditor may request the Succeeding Stock Company in Absorption-type Company Split to perform the obligations to the extent of the value of property to which it has succeeded, even in the case where such creditor is not allowed, under the Absorption-type Company Split agreement, to request the Succeeding Stock Company in Absorption-type Company Split to perform the obligations after the Absorption-type Company Split.
(4) In the cases listed in the following items, the Splitting Company in Absorption-type Company Split shall become the persons specified respectively in those items, in accordance with the provisions of the Absorption-type Company Split agreement, on the Effective Day:
  (i) in cases where there is a provision on the matters set forth in (a) of item (iv) of the preceding Article: shareholders of shares set forth in (a) of that item;
  (ii) in cases where there is a provision on the matters set forth in (b) of item (iv) of the preceding Article: bondholders of Bonds set forth in (b) of that item;
  (iii) in cases where there is a provision on the matters set forth in (c) of item (iv) of the preceding Article: holders of Share Options set forth in (c) of that item; or
  (iv) in cases where there is a provision on the matters set forth in (d) of item (iv) of the preceding Article: bondholders of the Bonds pertaining to Bonds with Share Options set forth in (d) of that item, and holders of the Share Options attached to such Bonds with Share Options.
(5) In the case prescribed in item (v) of the preceding Article, the Share Options under Absorption-type Company Split Agreement shall be extinguished and holders of the Share Options under Absorption-type Company Split Agreement shall become holders of the Share Options of the Succeeding Stock Company in Absorption-type Company Split set forth in item (v)(b) of that Article, in accordance with the provisions on the matters set forth in item (vi) of that Article, on the Effective Day.
(6) The provisions of the preceding paragraphs shall not apply in cases where procedures under the provisions of Article 789 (excluding paragraph (1)(iii) and paragraph (2)(iii), and including the case where it is applied mutatis pursuant to Article 793(2)) or Article 799 are not completed yet or where the Absorption-type Company Split is cancelled.

Art.760　　　① Companies Act, Part V, Chap.III, Sec.1

Subsection 3 Absorption-type Company Split Which Causes a Membership Company to Succeed to Rights and Obligations

(Absorption-type Company Split Agreement Which Causes a Membership Company to Succeed to Rights and Obligations)
Article 760 In the case where a Company effects an Absorption-type Company Split, if the Succeeding Company in Absorption-type Company Split is a Membership Company, it shall prescribe the following matters in the Absorption-type Company Split agreement:
  (i) the trade names and domiciles of the Splitting Company in Absorption-type Company Split and the Succeeding Company in Absorption-type Company Split that is a Membership Company (hereinafter referred to as the "Succeeding Membership Company in Absorption-type Company Split" in this Part);
  (ii) matters concerning the assets, obligations, employment agreements, and any other rights and obligations that the Succeeding Membership Company in Absorption-type Company Split succeeds to by transfer from the Splitting Company in Absorption-type Company Split through the Absorption-type Company Split (excluding obligations pertaining to shares of the Splitting Stock Company in Absorption-type Company Split);
  (iii) when the Succeeding Membership Company in Absorption-type Company Split succeeds to shares of the Splitting Stock Company in Absorption-type Company Split through the Absorption-type Company Split, matters concerning such shares;
  (iv) if the Splitting Company in Absorption-type Company Split is to become a partner of the Succeeding Membership Company in Absorption-type Company Split when effecting the Absorption-type Company Split, the matters provided for in (a) to (c) below for the categories of Succeeding Membership Company in Absorption-type Company Split listed respectively therein:
    (a) General Partnership Company: the name and domicile of the partner and the value of the contribution by the partner;
    (b) Limited Partnership Company: the name and domicile of the partner, whether the partner is an unlimited partner or a limited partner, and the value of the contribution by the partner; or
    (c) Limited Liability Company: the name and domicile of the partner and the value of the contribution by the partner;
  (v) if the Succeeding Membership Company in Absorption-type Company Split is to deliver to the Splitting Company in Absorption-type Company Split Monies, etc. (excluding the equity interests of the Succeeding Membership Company in Absorption-type Company Split) in lieu of all or part of the rights and obligations in connection with the business thereof when effecting the Absorption-type Company Split, the following matters concerning such Monies, etc.:
    (a) if such Monies, etc. are Bonds of the Succeeding Membership Company in Absorption-type Company Split, the description of the classes of such Bonds and the total amount for each class of Bonds, or the method for calculating that total amount; or
    (b) if such Monies, etc. are property other than Bonds of the Succeeding Membership Company in Absorption-type Company Split, the description of the features and number or amount of such property, or the method for calculating such number or amount;
  (vi) the Effective Day;
  (vii) if the Splitting Stock Company in Absorption-type Company Split conducts any

one of the following acts on the Effective Day, a statement to that effect:
(a) acquisition of shares under the provisions of paragraph (1) of Article 171 (limited to the case where the Consideration for Acquisition prescribed in item (i) of that paragraph is only equity interests of the Succeeding Membership Company in Absorption-type Company Split (excluding equity interests that had been held by the Splitting Stock Company in Absorption-type Company Split prior to effecting the Absorption-type Company Split, and including shares prescribed by the applicable Ordinance of the Ministry of Justice as those equivalent to equity interests of the Succeeding Membership Company in Absorption-type Company Split; the same shall apply in (b)); or
(b) payment of dividends of surplus (limited to the case where the Dividend Property is only equity interests of the Succeeding Membership Company in Absorption-type Company Split).

(Effectuation, etc. of an Absorption-type Company Split Which Causes a Membership Company to Succeed to Rights and Obligations)

Article 761 (1) A Succeeding Membership Company in Absorption-type Company Split shall succeed to the rights and obligations of the Splitting Company in Absorption-type Company Split, in accordance with the provisions of the Absorption-type Company Split agreement, on the Effective Day.
(2) Notwithstanding the provisions of the preceding paragraph, if a creditor of the Splitting Company in Absorption-type Company Split who is able to state an objection (limited to a creditor to whom the separate notice set forth in Article 789(2) (excluding item (iii) and including the case where it is applied mutatis mutandis pursuant to Article 793(2); hereinafter the same shall apply in this paragraph and the following paragraph) shall be given; the same shall apply in the following paragraph) pursuant to the provisions of Article 789(1)(ii) (including the case where it is applied mutatis mutandis pursuant to Article 793(2); the same shall apply in the following paragraph) has not received the separate notice set forth in Article 789(2), such creditor may request the Splitting Company in Absorption-type Company Split to perform the obligations to the extent of the value of property held by the Splitting Company in Absorption-type Company Split on the Effective Day, even in the case where such creditor is not allowed, under the Absorption-type Company Split agreement, to request the Splitting Company in Absorption-type Company Split to perform the obligations after the Absorption-type Company Split.
(3) Notwithstanding the provisions of paragraph (1), if a creditor of the Splitting Company in Absorption-type Company Split who is able to state an objection pursuant to the provisions of paragraph (1)(ii) of Article 789 has not received the separate notice set forth in paragraph (2) of that Article, such creditor may request the Succeeding Membership Company in Absorption-type Company Split to perform the obligations to the extent of the value of property to which it has succeeded, even in the case where such creditor is not allowed, under the Absorption-type Company Split agreement, to request the Succeeding Membership Company in Absorption-type Company Split to perform the obligations after the Absorption-type Company Split.
(4) In the case prescribed in item (iv) of the preceding Article, the Splitting Company in Absorption-type Company Split shall, in accordance with the provisions on the matters set forth in that item, become a partner of the Succeeding Membership Company in Absorption-type Company Split on the Effective Day. In such cases, the Succeeding Membership Company in Absorption-type Company Split shall be deemed to have effected changes to the articles of incorporation relating to the partner set forth in that item on the Effective Day.

(5) In cases where there are provisions on the matter set forth in (a) of item (v) of the preceding Article, the Splitting Company in Absorption-type Company Split shall, in accordance with the provisions of the Absorption-type Company Split agreement, become bondholders of Bonds set forth in (a) of that item on the Effective Day.
(6) The provisions of the preceding paragraphs shall not apply in cases where procedures under the provisions of Article 789 (excluding paragraph (1)(iii) and paragraph (2)(iii), and including the case where it is applied mutatis pursuant to Article 793(2)) or Article 799 (excluding paragraph (2)(iii)) as applied mutatis mutandis pursuant to Article 802(2) are not completed yet or where the Absorption-type Merger is cancelled.

Section 2 Incorporation-type Company Split

Subsection 1 Common Provisions

(Preparation of an Incorporation-type Company Split Plan)
Article 762 (1) A Stock Company(ies) and/or a Limited Liability Company(ies) may effect an Incorporation-type Company Split. In such cases, such Company(ies) shall prepare an Incorporation-type Company Split plan.
(2) In the case where two or more Stock Companies and/or Limited Liability Companies jointly effect an Incorporation-type Company Split, said two or more Stock Companies and/or Limited Liability Companies shall prepare an Incorporation-type Company Split plan jointly.

Subsection 2 Incorporation-type Company Split by Which a Stock Company is Incorporated

(Incorporation-type Company Split Plan by Which a Stock Company is Incorporated)
Article 763 In the case where a Stock Company(ies) and/or a Limited Liability Company(ies) effect an Incorporation-type Company Split, if the Company incorporated through the Incorporation-type Company Split (hereinafter referred to as the "Company Incorporated through Incorporation-type Company Split" in this Part) is a Stock Company, said company(ies) shall prescribe the following matters in the Incorporation-type Company Split plan:
(i) the purpose, trade name, location of the head office, and the Total Number of Authorized Shares of the Company Incorporated through Incorporation-type Company Split that is a Stock Company (hereinafter referred to as the "Stock Company Incorporated through Incorporation-type Company Split" in this Part);
(ii) in addition to what is provided for in the preceding item, the matters provided for in the articles of incorporation of the Stock Company Incorporated through Incorporation-type Company Split;
(iii) the names of the Directors at Incorporation of the Stock Company Incorporated through Incorporation-type Company Split;
(iv) the matters provided for in (a) to (c) below for the categories of cases listed respectively therein:
  (a) in cases where the Stock Company Incorporated through Incorporation-type Company Split is a Company with Accounting Advisors: the name(s) of the Accounting Advisor(s) at Incorporation of the Stock Company Incorporated through Incorporation-type Company Split;
  (b) in cases where the Stock Company Incorporated through Incorporation-type Company Split is a Company with Auditors (including any Stock Company the

articles of incorporation of which provide that the scope of the audit by its company auditor(s) is limited to an audit related to accounting): the name(s) of the Company Auditor(s) at Incorporation of the Stock Company Incorporated through Incorporation-type Company Split; and

(c) in cases where the Stock Company Incorporated through Incorporation-type Company Split is a Company with Accounting Auditors: the name(s) of the Accounting Auditor(s) at Incorporation of the Stock Company Incorporated through Incorporation-type Company Split;

(v) matters concerning the assets, obligations, employment agreements, and any other rights and obligations that the Stock Company Incorporated through Incorporation-type Company Split succeeds to by transfer from the Company(ies) effecting the Incorporation-type Company Split (hereinafter referred to as the "Splitting Company(ies) in Incorporation-type Company Split" in this Part) through the Incorporation-type Company Split (excluding obligations pertaining to shares and Share Options of the Splitting Company(ies) in Incorporation-type Company Split that is a Stock Company(ies) (hereinafter referred to as the "Splitting Stock Company(ies) in Incorporation-type Company Split" in this Part));

(vi) the number of shares (or, for a Company with Class Shares, the classes of the shares and the number of the shares for each class) of the Stock Company Incorporated through Incorporation-type Company Split to be delivered by the Stock Company Incorporated through Incorporation-type Company Split to the Splitting Company(ies) in Incorporation-type Company Split in lieu of all or part of the rights and obligations in connection with the business thereof when effecting the Incorporation-type Company Split, or the method for calculating such numbers, and matters concerning the amount of the stated capital and capital reserves of the Stock Company Incorporated through Incorporation-type Company Split;

(vii) if two or more Stock Companies and/or Limited Liability Companies are to jointly effect the Incorporation-type Company Split, matters concerning allotment of the shares set forth in the preceding item to the Splitting Company(ies) in Incorporation-type Company Split;

(viii) if the Stock Company Incorporated through Incorporation-type Company Split is to deliver to shareholders of the Splitting Company(ies) in Incorporation-type Company Split Bonds, etc. of the Stock Company Incorporated through Incorporation-type Company Split in lieu of all or part of the rights and obligations in connection with the business thereof when effecting the Incorporation-type Company Split, the following matters concerning such Bonds, etc.:

(a) if such Bonds, etc. are Bonds of the Stock Company Incorporated through Incorporation-type Company Split (excluding those pertaining to Bonds with Share Options), the description of the classes of such Bonds and the total amount for each class of Bonds, or the method for calculating that total amount;

(b) if such Bonds, etc. are Share Options of the Stock Company Incorporated through Incorporation-type Company Split (excluding those attached to Bonds with Share Options), the description of the features and number of such Share Options, or the method for calculating such number; or

(c) if such Bonds, etc. are Bonds with Share Options of the Stock Company Incorporated through Incorporation-type Company Split, the matters prescribed in (a) concerning such Bonds with Share Options and the matters prescribed in (b) concerning the Share Options attached to such Bonds with Share Options;

(ix) in the case prescribed in the preceding item, if two or more Stock Companies and/or Limited Liability Companies are to jointly effect the Incorporation-type Company Split, matters concerning allotment of Bonds, etc. set forth in that item to the

Art.764   [I] Companies Act, Part V, Chap.III, Sec.2

Splitting Company(ies) in Incorporation-type Company Split;
(x) if the Stock Company Incorporated through Incorporation-type Company Split is to deliver to holders of Share Options of the Splitting Stock Company(ies) in Incorporation-type Company Split Share Options of the Stock Company Incorporated through Incorporation-type Company Split in lieu of such Share Options at the time of the Incorporation-type Company Split, the following matters concerning such Share Options:
   (a) the description of the features of the Share Options (hereinafter referred to as the "Share Options under Incorporation-type Company Split Plan" in this Part) held by holders of Share Options of the Splitting Stock Company(ies) in Incorporation-type Company Split who will receive delivery of Share Options of the Stock Company Incorporated through Incorporation-type Company Split;
   (b) the description of the features and number of the Share Options of the Stock Company Incorporated through Incorporation-type Company Split to be delivered to holders of Share Options under Incorporation-type Company Split Plan, or the method for calculating such number; and
   (c) if the Share Options under Incorporation-type Company Split Plan are Share Options attached to Bonds with Share Options, a statement to the effect that the Stock Company Incorporated through Incorporation-type Company Split will succeed to the obligations relating to the Bonds pertaining to such Bonds with Share Options and the description of the classes of the Bonds subject to such succession and the total amount for each class of Bonds, or the method for calculating that total amount;
(xi) in the case prescribed in the preceding item, matters concerning allotment of the Share Options of the Stock Company Incorporated through Incorporation-type Company Split set forth in that item to holders of Share Options under Incorporation-type Company Split Plan; and
(xii) if the Splitting Stock Company(ies) in Incorporation-type Company Split conducts any one of the following acts on the day of formation of the Stock Company Incorporated through Incorporation-type Company Split, a statement to that effect:
   (a) acquisition of shares under the provisions of paragraph (1) of Article 171 (limited to the case where the Consideration for Acquisition prescribed in item (i) of that paragraph is only shares of the Stock Company Incorporated through Incorporation-type Company Split (including shares prescribed by the applicable Ordinance of the Ministry of Justice as those equivalent thereto; the same shall apply in (b)); or
   (b) payment of dividends of surplus (limited to the case where the Dividend Property is only shares of the Stock Company Incorporated through Incorporation-type Company Split).

(Effectuation, etc. of an Incorporation-type Company Split by Which a Stock Company is Incorporated)
Article 764 (1) A Stock Company Incorporated through Incorporation-type Company Split shall succeed to the rights and obligations of the Splitting Company(ies) in Incorporation-type Company Split, in accordance with the provisions of the Incorporation-type Company Split plan, on the day of its formation.
(2) Notwithstanding the provisions of the preceding paragraph, if a creditor of the Splitting Company(ies) in Incorporation-type Company Split who is able to state an objection (limited to a creditor to whom the separate notice set forth in Article 810(2) (excluding item (iii) and including the case where it is applied mutatis mutandis pursuant to Article 813(2); hereinafter the same shall apply in this paragraph and the following

paragraph) shall be given; the same shall apply in the following paragraph) pursuant to the provisions of Article 810(1)(ii) (including the case where it is applied mutatis mutandis pursuant to Article 813(2); the same shall apply in the following paragraph) has not received the separate notice set forth in Article 810(2), such creditor may request the Splitting Company(ies) in Incorporation-type Company Split to perform the obligations to the extent of the value of property held by the Splitting Company(ies) in Incorporation-type Company Split on the day of formation of the Stock Company Incorporated through Incorporation-type Company Split, even in the case where such creditor is not allowed, under the Incorporation-type Company Split plan, to request the Splitting Company(ies) in Incorporation-type Company Split plan to perform the obligations after the Incorporation-type Company Split.

(3) Notwithstanding the provisions of paragraph (1), if a creditor of the Splitting Company(ies) in Incorporation-type Company Split who is able to state an objection pursuant to the provisions of paragraph (1)(ii) of Article 810 has not received the separate notice set forth in paragraph (2) of that Article, such creditor may request the Stock Company Incorporated through Incorporation-type Company Split to perform the obligations to the extent of the value of property to which it has succeeded, even in the case where such creditor is not allowed, under the Incorporation-type Company Split plan, to request the Stock Company Incorporated through Incorporation-type Company Split to perform the obligations after the Incorporation-type Company Split.

(4) In the case prescribed in the preceding Article, the Splitting Company(ies) in Incorporation-type Company Split shall become a shareholder(s) of shares set forth in item (vi) of that Article, in accordance with the provisions of the Incorporation-type Company Split plan, on the day of formation of the Stock Company Incorporated through Incorporation-type Company Split.

(5) In the cases listed in the following items, the Splitting Company(ies) in Incorporation-type Company Split shall become the person(s) specified respectively in those items, in accordance with the provisions on the Incorporation-type Company Split plan, on the day of formation of the Stock Company Incorporated through Incorporation-type Company Split:

(i) in cases where there is a provision on the matters set forth in (a) of item (viii) of the preceding Article: Bondholders of Bonds set forth in (a) of that item;

(ii) in cases where there is a provision on the matters set forth in (b) of item (viii) of the preceding Article: holders of Share Options set forth in (b) of that item; or

(iii) in cases where there is a provision on the matters set forth in (c) of item (viii) of the preceding Article: bondholders of the Bonds pertaining to Bonds with Share Options set forth in (c) of that item, and holders of the Share Options attached to such Bonds with Share Options.

(6) With regard to the application of the provisions of the preceding two paragraphs in the case where two or more Stock Companies and/or Limited Liability Companies are to jointly effect an Incorporation-type Company Split, the phrase "provisions of the Incorporation-type Company Split plan" in paragraph (4) shall be deemed to be replaced with "provisions on the matters set forth in item (vii) of that Article," and the phrase "provisions of the Incorporation-type Company Split plan" in the preceding paragraph shall be deemed to be replaced with "provisions on the matters set forth in item (ix) of the preceding Article."

(7) In the case prescribed in item (x) of the preceding Article, the Share Options under Incorporation-type Company Split Plan shall be extinguished and holders of the Share Options under Incorporation-type Company Split Plan shall become holders of the Share Options of the Stock Company Incorporated through Incorporation-type Company Split set forth in item (x)(b) of that Article, in accordance with the provisions on the

matters set forth in item (xi) of that Article, on the day of formation of the Stock Company Incorporated through Incorporation-type Company Split.

Subsection 3 Incorporation-type Company Split by Which a Membership Company is Incorporated

(Incorporation-type Company Split Plan by Which a Membership Company is Incorporated)
Article 765 (1) In the case where a Stock Company(ies) and/or a Limited Liability Company(ies) effect an Incorporation-type Company Split, if the Company Incorporated through Incorporation-type Company Split is a Membership Company, said company(ies) shall prescribe the following matters in the Incorporation-type Company Split plan:
(i) whether the Company Incorporated through Incorporation-type Company Split which is a Membership Company (hereinafter referred to as the "Membership Company Incorporated through Incorporation-type Company Split" in this Part) is a General Partnership Company, Limited Partnership Company, or Limited Liability Company;
(ii) the purpose, trade name, and location of the head office of the Membership Company Incorporated through Incorporation-type Company Split;
(iii) the following matters concerning the partners of the Membership Company Incorporated through Incorporation-type Company Split:
(a) the names and domiciles of the partners;
(b) whether the partners are unlimited partners or limited partners; and
(c) the value of contributions by the partners;
(iv) in addition to what is listed in the preceding two items, the matters provided for in the articles of incorporation of the Membership Company Incorporated through Incorporation-type Company Split;
(v) matters concerning the assets, obligations, employment agreements, and any other rights and obligations that the Membership Company Incorporated through Incorporation-type Company Split succeeds to by transfer from the Splitting Company(ies) in Incorporation-type Company Split through the Incorporation-type Company Split (excluding obligations pertaining to shares and Share Options of the Splitting Stock Company(ies) in Incorporation-type Company Split);
(vi) if the Membership Company Incorporated through Incorporation-type Company Split is to deliver to the Splitting Company(ies) in Incorporation-type Company Split Bonds of the Membership Company Incorporated through Incorporation-type Company Split in lieu of all or part of the rights and obligations in connection with the business thereof when effecting the Incorporation-type Company Split, the description of the classes of such Bonds and the total amount for each class of Bonds, or the method for calculating that total amount;
(vii) in the case prescribed in the preceding item, if two or more Stock Companies and/or Limited Liability Companies are to jointly effect the Incorporation-type Company Split, matters concerning allotment of Bonds set forth in that item to the Splitting Company(ies) in Incorporation-type Company Split; and
(viii) if the Splitting Stock Company(ies) in Incorporation-type Company Split conducts any one of the following acts on the day of formation of the Membership Company Incorporated through Incorporation-type Company Split, a statement to that effect:
(a) acquisition of shares under the provisions of paragraph (1) of Article 171 (limited to the case where the Consideration for Acquisition prescribed in item (i) of

that paragraph is only shares of the Membership Company Incorporated through Incorporation-type Company Split (including shares prescribed by the applicable Ordinance of the Ministry of Justice as those equivalent thereto; the same shall apply in (b)); or
  (b) payment of dividends of surplus (limited to the case where the Dividend Property is only shares of the Membership Company Incorporated through Incorporation-type Company Split).
(2) If the Membership Company Incorporated through Incorporation-type Company Split is a General Partnership Company, it shall provide that all of the partners are unlimited partners in prescribing the matter set forth in item (iii)(b) of the preceding paragraph.
(3) If the Membership Company Incorporated through Incorporation-type Company Split is a Limited Partnership Company, it shall provide that some of the partners are unlimited partners and other partners are limited partners in prescribing the matter set forth in paragraph (1)(iii)(b).
(4) If the Membership Company Incorporated through Incorporation-type Company Split is a Limited Liability Company, it shall provide that all of the partners are limited partners in prescribing the matter set forth in paragraph (1)(iii)(b).

(Effectuation, etc. of an Incorporation-type Company Split by Which a Membership Company is Incorporated)

Article 766 (1) A Membership Company Incorporated through Incorporation-type Company Split shall succeed to the rights and obligations of the Splitting Company(ies) in Incorporation-type Company Split, in accordance with the provisions of the Incorporation-type Company Split plan, on the day of its formation.
(2) Notwithstanding the provisions of the preceding paragraph, if a creditor of the Splitting Company(ies) in Incorporation-type Company Split who is able to state an objection (limited to a creditor to whom the separate notice set forth in Article 810(2) (excluding item (iii) and including the case where it is applied mutatis mutandis pursuant to Article 813(2); hereinafter the same shall apply in this paragraph and the following paragraph) shall be given; the same shall apply in the following paragraph) pursuant to the provisions of Article 810(1)(ii) (including the case where it is applied mutatis mutandis pursuant to Article 813(2); the same shall apply in the following paragraph) has not received the separate notice set forth in Article 810(2), such creditor may request the Splitting Company(ies) in Incorporation-type Company Split to perform the obligations to the extent of the value of property held by the Splitting Company(ies) in Incorporation-type Company Split on the day of formation of the Membership Company Incorporated through Incorporation-type Company Split, even in the case where such creditor is not allowed, under the Incorporation-type Company Split plan, to request the Splitting Company(ies) in Incorporation-type Company Split to perform the obligations after the Incorporation-type Company Split.
(3) Notwithstanding the provisions of paragraph (1), if a creditor of the Splitting Company(ies) in Incorporation-type Company Split who is able to state an objection pursuant to the provisions of paragraph (1)(ii) of Article 810 has not received the separate notice set forth in paragraph (2) of that Article, such creditor may request the Membership Company Incorporated through Incorporation-type Company Split to perform the obligations to the extent of the value of property to which it has succeeded, even in the case where such creditor is not allowed, under the Incorporation-type Company Split plan, to request the Membership Company Incorporated through Incorporation-type Company Split to perform the obligations after the Incorporation-type Company Split.
(4) In the case prescribed in paragraph (1) of the preceding Article, the Splitting

Company(ies) in Incorporation-type Company Split shall become a partner(s) of the Membership Company Incorporated through Incorporation-type Company Split, in accordance with the provisions on the matter set forth in item (iii) of that paragraph, on the day of formation of the Membership Company Incorporated through Incorporation-type Company Split.
(5) In cases where there are provisions on the matter set forth in item (vi) of paragraph (1) of the preceding Article, a Splitting Company(ies) in Incorporation-type Company Split shall, in accordance with the provisions of the Incorporation-type Company Split plan, become a bondholder(s) of Bonds set forth in that item on the day of formation of the Membership Company Incorporated through Incorporation-type Company Split.
(6) With regard to the application of the provisions of the preceding paragraph in the case where two or more Stock Companies and/or Limited Liability Companies are to jointly effect an Incorporation-type Company Split, the phrase "in accordance with the provisions of the Incorporation-type Company Split plan, become a bondholder(s) of Bonds set forth in that item" in that paragraph shall be deemed to be replaced with "in accordance with the provisions on the matter set forth in item (vii) of that paragraph, become bondholders of Bonds set forth in item (vi) of that paragraph."

Chapter IV Share Exchange and Share Transfer

Section 1 Share Exchange

Subsection 1 Common Provisions

(Conclusion of a Share Exchange Agreement)
Article 767 A Stock Company may effect Share Exchange. In such cases, the Stock Company shall conclude a Stock Exchange agreement with the company acquiring all of its Issued Shares (limited to a Stock Company or a Limited Liability Company; hereinafter referred to as the "Wholly Owning Parent Company in Share Exchange" in this Part).

Subsection 2 Share Exchange Which Causes a Stock Company to Acquire the Issued Shares

(Share Exchange Agreement Which Causes a Stock Company to Acquire the Issued Shares)
Article 768 (1) In the case where a Stock Company effects a Share Exchange, if the Wholly Owning Parent Company in Share Exchange is a Stock Company, it shall prescribe the following matters in the Share Exchange agreement:
(i) the trade names and domiciles of the Stock Company effecting the Share Exchange (hereinafter referred to as the "Wholly Owned Subsidiary Company in Share Exchange" in this Part) and the Wholly Owning Parent Company in Share Exchange which is a Stock Company (hereinafter referred to as the "Wholly Owning Parent Stock Company in Share Exchange" in this Part);
(ii) if the Wholly Owning Parent Stock Company in Share Exchange is to deliver to shareholders of the Wholly Owned Subsidiary Company in Share Exchange Monies, etc. in lieu of the shares thereof when effecting the Share Exchange, the following matters concerning such Monies, etc.:
(a) if such Monies, etc. are shares of the Wholly Owning Parent Stock Company in Share Exchange, the description of the number of such shares (or, for a Company with Class Shares, the classes of the shares and the number of the shares for

each class) or the method for calculating such numbers, and matters concerning the amount of the stated capital and capital reserves of the Wholly Owning Parent Stock Company in Share Exchange;
  (b) if such Monies, etc. are Bonds of the Wholly Owning Parent Stock Company in Share Exchange (excluding those pertaining to Bonds with Share Options), the description of the classes of such Bonds and the total amount for each class of Bonds, or the method for calculating that total amount;
  (c) if such Monies, etc. are Stock Options of the Wholly Owning Parent Stock Company in Share Exchange (excluding those attached to Bonds with Share Options), the description of the features and number of such Share Options, or the method for calculating such number;
  (d) if such Monies, etc. are Bonds with Share Options of the Wholly Owning Parent Stock Company in Share Exchange, the matters prescribed in (b) concerning such Bonds with Share Options and the matters prescribed in (c) concerning the Share Options attached to such Bonds with Share Options; or
  (e) if such Monies, etc. are property other than shares, etc. of the Wholly Owning Parent Stock Company in Share Exchange, the description of the features and number or amount of such property, or the method for calculating such number or amount;
 (iii) in the case prescribed in the preceding item, matters concerning the allotment of Monies, etc. set forth in that item to shareholders of the Wholly Owned Subsidiary Company in Share Exchange (excluding the Wholly Owning Parent Stock Company in Share Exchange);
 (iv) if the Wholly Owning Parent Stock Company in Share Exchange is to deliver to holders of Share Options of the Wholly Owned Subsidiary Company in Share Exchange Share Options of the Wholly Owning Parent Stock Company in Share Exchange in lieu of such Share Options at the time of the Share Exchange, the following matters concerning such Share Options:
  (a) the description of the features of the Share Options (hereinafter referred to as "Share Options under Share Exchange Agreement" in this Part) held by holders of Share Options of the Wholly Owned Subsidiary Company in Share Exchange who will receive delivery of Share Options of the Wholly Owning Parent Stock Company in Share Exchange;
  (b) the description of the features and number of Share Options of the Wholly Owning Parent Stock Company in Share Exchange to be delivered to holders of Share Options under Share Exchange Agreement, or the method for calculating such number; and
  (c) if Share Options under Share Exchange Agreement are Share Options attached to Bonds with Share Options, a statement to the effect that the Wholly Owning Parent Stock Company in Share Exchange will succeed to the obligations relating to the Bonds pertaining to such Bonds with Share Options and the description of the classes of the Bonds subject to such succession and the total amount for each class of Bonds, or the method for calculating that total amount;
 (v) in the case prescribed in the preceding item, matters concerning the allotment of the Share Options of the Wholly Owning Parent Stock Company in Share Exchange set forth in that item to holders of Share Options under Share Exchange Agreement; and
 (vi) the day on which the Share Exchange becomes effective (hereinafter referred to as the "Effective Day" in this Section).
(2) In the case prescribed in the preceding paragraph, if the Wholly Owned Subsidiary Company in Share Exchange is a Company with Class Shares, the Wholly Owned Sub-

sidiary Company in Share Exchange and the Wholly Owning Parent Stock Company in Share Exchange may provide for the following matters in prescribing the matters set forth in item (iii) of that paragraph in accordance with the features of the classes of shares issued by the Wholly Owned Subsidiary Company in Share Exchange:
(i) if there is any arrangement that no Monies, etc. are allotted to shareholders of a certain class of shares, a statement to such effect and such class of shares; and
(ii) in addition to the matters listed in the preceding item, if there is any arrangement that each class of shares shall be treated differently with respect to allotment of Monies, etc., a statement to such effect and the details of such different treatment.
(3) In the case prescribed in paragraph (1), the provisions on the matters listed in item (iii) of that paragraph shall be such that the Monies, etc. are delivered in proportion to the number of the shares (or, in cases where there are provisions on the matters listed in item (ii) of the preceding paragraph, the number of the shares of each class) held by shareholders of the Wholly Owned Subsidiary Company in Share Exchange (excluding the Wholly Owning Parent Stock Company in Share Exchange and shareholders of the class of shares referred to in item (i) of the preceding paragraph).

(Effectuation, etc. of a Share Exchange Which Causes a Stock Company to Acquire the Issued Shares)
Article 769 (1) The Wholly Owning Parent Stock Company in Share Exchange shall acquire all of the Issued Shares of the Wholly Owned Subsidiary Company in Share Exchange (excluding shares of the Wholly Owned Subsidiary Company in Share Exchange already held by the Wholly Owning Parent Stock Company in Share Exchange) on the Effective Day.
(2) In the case set forth in the preceding paragraph, the Wholly Owned Subsidiary Company in Share Exchange shall be deemed to have given the approval set forth in Article 137(1) with regard to the acquisition of shares of the Wholly Owned Subsidiary Company in Share Exchange (limited to Shares with a Restriction on Transfer, and excluding those already held by the Wholly Owning Parent Stock Company in Share Exchange prior to the Effective Day) by the Wholly Owning Parent Stock Company in Share Exchange.
(3) In the cases listed in the following items, shareholders of the Wholly Owned Subsidiary Company in Share Exchange shall become the persons specified respectively in those items, in accordance with the provisions on the matters set forth in paragraph (1)(iii) of the preceding Article, on the Effective Day:
(i) in cases where there is a provision on the matters set forth in (a) of item (ii) of paragraph (1) of the preceding Article: shareholders of shares set forth in (a) of that item;
(ii) in cases where there is a provision on the matters set forth in (b) of item (ii) of paragraph (1) of the preceding Article: bondholders of Bonds set forth in (b) of that item;
(iii) in cases where there is a provision on the matters set forth in (c) of item (ii) of paragraph (1) of the preceding Article: holders of Share Options set forth in (c) of that item; or
(iv) in cases where there is a provision on the matters set forth in (d) of item (ii) of paragraph (1) of the preceding Article: bondholders of the Bonds pertaining to Bonds with Share Options set forth in (d) of that item, and holders of the Share Options attached to such Bonds with Share Options.
(4) In the case prescribed in paragraph (1)(iv) of the preceding Article, the Share Options under Share Exchange Agreement shall be extinguished and holders of the Share Options under Share Exchange Agreement shall become holders of the Share Options of

the Wholly Owning Parent Stock Company in Share Exchange set forth in item (iv)(b) of that Article, in accordance with the provisions on the matters set forth in item (v) of that Article, on the Effective Day.
(5) In the case prescribed in (c) of item (iv) of paragraph (1) of the preceding Article, the Wholly Owning Parent Stock Company in Share Exchange shall succeed to the obligations relating to the Bonds pertaining to Bonds with Share Options set forth in (c) of that item on the Effective Day.
(6) The provisions of the preceding paragraphs shall not apply in cases where procedures under the provisions of Article 789 or Article 799 are not completed yet or where the Share Exchange is cancelled.

Subsection 3 Share Exchange Which Causes a Limited Liability Company to Acquire the Issued Shares

(Share Exchange Which Causes a Limited Liability Company to Acquire the Issued Shares)
Article 770 (1) In the case where a Stock Company effects a Share Exchange, if the Wholly Owning Parent Company in Share Exchange is a Limited Liability Company, it shall prescribe the following matters in the Share Exchange agreement:
  (i) the trade names and domiciles of the Wholly Owned Subsidiary Company in Share Exchange and the Wholly Owning Parent Company in Share Exchange which is a Limited Liability Company (hereinafter referred to as the "Wholly Owning Parent Limited Liability Company in Share Exchange" in this Part);
  (ii) if shareholders of the Wholly Owned Subsidiary Company in Share Exchange are to become partners of the Wholly Owning Parent Limited Liability Company in Share Exchange when effecting the Share Exchange, the names and domiciles of the partners and the value of contributions by the partners;
  (iii) if the Wholly Owning Parent Limited Liability Company in Share Exchange is to deliver to shareholders of the Wholly Owned Subsidiary Company in Share Exchange Monies, etc. (excluding the equity interests of the Wholly Owning Parent Limited Liability Company in Share Exchange) in lieu of the shares thereof when effecting the Share Exchange, the following matters concerning such Monies, etc.:
    (a) if such Monies, etc. are Bonds of the Wholly Owning Parent Limited Liability Company in Share Exchange, the description of the classes of such Bonds and the total amount for each class of Bonds, or the method for calculating that total amount; or
    (b) if such Monies, etc. are property other than Bonds of the Wholly Owning Parent Limited Liability Company in Share Exchange, the description of the features and number or amount of such property, or the method for calculating such number or amount;
  (iv) in the case prescribed in the preceding item, matters concerning the allotment of Monies, etc. set forth in that item to shareholders of the Wholly Owned Subsidiary Company in Share Exchange (excluding the Wholly Owning Parent Limited Liability Company in Share Exchange); and
  (v) the Effective Day.
(2) In the case prescribed in the preceding paragraph, if the Wholly Owned Subsidiary Company in Share Exchange is a Company with Class Shares, the Wholly Owned Subsidiary Company in Share Exchange and the Wholly Owning Parent Limited Liability Company in Share Exchange may provide for the following matters in prescribing the matters set forth in item (iv) of that paragraph in accordance with the features of the classes of shares issued by the Wholly Owned Subsidiary Company in Share Ex-

Art.771〜772　　　Ⅰ Companies Act, Part V, Chap.IV, Sec.2

change:
(i) if there is any arrangement that no Monies, etc. are allotted to shareholders of a certain class of shares, a statement to such effect and such class of shares; and
(ii) in addition to the matters listed in the preceding item, if there is any arrangement that each class of shares shall be treated differently with respect to allotment of Monies, etc., a statement to such effect and the details of such different treatment.
(3) In the case prescribed in paragraph (1), the provisions on the matters listed in item (iv) of that paragraph shall be such that the Monies, etc. are delivered in proportion to the number of the shares (or, in cases where there are provisions on the matters listed in item (ii) of the preceding paragraph, the number of the shares of each class) held by shareholders of the Wholly Owned Subsidiary Company in Share Exchange (excluding the Wholly Owning Parent Limited Liability Company in Share Exchange and shareholders of the class of shares referred to in item (i) of the preceding paragraph).

(Effectuation, etc. of a Share Exchange Which Causes a Limited Liability Company to Acquire the Issued Shares)
Article 771　(1) The Wholly Owning Parent Limited Liability Company in Share Exchange shall acquire all of the Issued Shares of the Wholly Owned Subsidiary Company in Share Exchange (excluding shares of the Wholly Owned Subsidiary Company in Share Exchange already held by the Wholly Owning Parent Limited Liability Company in Share Exchange) on the Effective Day.
(2) In the case set forth in the preceding paragraph, the Wholly Owned Subsidiary Company in Share Exchange shall be deemed to have given the approval set forth in Article 137(1) with regard to the acquisition of shares of the Wholly Owned Subsidiary Company in Share Exchange (limited to Shares with a Restriction on Transfer, and excluding those already held by the Wholly Owning Parent Limited Liability Company in Share Exchange prior to the Effective Day) by the Wholly Owning Parent Limited Liability Company in Share Exchange.
(3) In the case prescribed in item (ii) of paragraph (1) of the preceding Article, the shareholders of the Wholly Owned Subsidiary Company in Share Exchange shall, in accordance with the provisions on the matters set forth in that item, become partners of the Wholly Owning Parent Limited Liability Company in Share Exchange on the Effective Day. In such cases, the Wholly Owning Parent Limited Liability Company in Share Exchange shall be deemed to have effected changes to the articles of incorporation relating to the partners set forth in that item on the Effective Day.
(4) In cases where there are provisions on the matter set forth in item (iii)(a) of paragraph (1) of the preceding Article, the shareholders of the Wholly Owned Subsidiary Company in Share Exchange shall, in accordance with the provisions on the matter set forth in item (iv) of that paragraph, become bondholders of Bonds set forth in item (iii)(a) of that paragraph on the Effective Day.
(5) The provisions of the preceding paragraphs shall not apply in cases where procedures under the provisions of Article 799 (excluding paragraph (2)(iii)) as applied mutatis mutandis pursuant to Article 802(2) are not completed yet or where the Share Exchange is cancelled.

Section 2　Share Transfer

(Preparation of a Share Transfer Plan)
Article 772　(1) A Stock Company(ies) may effect a Share Transfer. In such cases, such company(ies) shall prepare a Share Transfer plan.
(2) In the case where two or more Stock Companies jointly effect a Share Transfer, said

two or more Stock Companies shall prepare the Share Transfer plan jointly.

(Share Transfer Plan)
Article 773 (1) In the case where a Stock Company(ies) effects a Share Transfer, said company(ies) shall prescribe the following matters in the Share Transfer plan:
 (i) the purpose, trade name, location of the head office, and the Total Number of Authorized Shares of the Stock Company Incorporated through Share Transfer (hereinafter referred to as the "Wholly Owning Parent Company Incorporated through Share Transfer" in this Part);
 (ii) in addition to what is provided for in the preceding item, the matters provided for in the articles of incorporation of the Wholly Owning Parent Company Incorporated through Share Transfer;
 (iii) the names of the Directors at Incorporation of the Wholly Owning Parent Company Incorporated through Share Transfer;
 (iv) the matters provided for in (a) to (c) below for the categories of cases listed respectively therein:
  (a) in cases where the Wholly Owning Parent Company Incorporated through Share Transfer is a Company with Accounting Advisors: the name(s) of the Accounting Advisor(s) at Incorporation of the Wholly Owning Parent Company Incorporated through Share Transfer;
  (b) in cases where the Wholly Owning Parent Company Incorporated through Share Transfer is a Company with Company Auditors (including a Stock Company the articles of incorporation of which provide that the scope of the audit by its company auditor(s) is limited to an audit related to accounting): the name(s) of the Company Auditor(s) at Incorporation of the Wholly Owning Parent Company Incorporated through Share Transfer; or
  (c) in cases where the Wholly Owning Parent Company Incorporated through Share Transfer is a Company with Accounting Auditors: the name(s) of the Accounting Auditor(s) at Incorporation of the Wholly Owning Parent Company Incorporated through Share Transfer;
 (v) the number of shares (or, for a Company with Class Shares, the classes of the shares and the number of the shares for each class) of the Wholly Owning Parent Company Incorporated through Share Transfer to be delivered by the Wholly Owning Parent Company Incorporated through Share Transfer to shareholders of the Stock Company effecting the Share Transfer (hereinafter referred to as the "Wholly Owned Subsidiary Company in Share Transfer" in this Part) in lieu of the shares thereof, when effecting the Share Transfer, or the method for calculating such numbers, and matters concerning the amount of the stated capital and capital reserves of the Wholly Owning Parent Company Incorporated through Share Transfer;
 (vi) matters concerning allotment of the shares set forth in the preceding item to shareholders of the Wholly Owned Subsidiary Company in Share Transfer;
 (vii) if the Wholly Owning Parent Company Incorporated through Share Transfer is to deliver to shareholders of the Wholly Owned Subsidiary Company in Share Transfer Bonds, etc. of the Wholly Owning Parent Company Incorporated through Share Transfer in lieu of the shares thereof when effecting the Share Transfer, the following matters concerning such Bonds, etc.:
  (a) if such Bonds, etc. are Bonds of the Wholly Owning Parent Company Incorporated through Share Transfer (excluding those pertaining to Bonds with Share Options), the description of the classes of such Bonds and the total amount for each class of Bonds, or the method for calculating that total amount;
  (b) if such Bonds, etc. are Share Options of the Wholly Owning Parent Company

Incorporated through Share Transfer (excluding those attached to Bonds with Share Options), the description of the features and number of such Share Options, or the method for calculating such number; or
  (c) if such Bonds, etc. are Bonds with Share Options of the Wholly Owning Parent Company Incorporated through Share Transfer, the matters prescribed in (a) concerning such Bonds with Share Options and the matters prescribed in (b) concerning the Share Options attached to such Bonds with Share Options;
(viii) in the case prescribed in the preceding item, matters concerning allotment of Bonds, etc. set forth in that item to shareholders of the Wholly Owned Subsidiary Company in Share Transfer;
(ix) if the Wholly Owning Parent Company Incorporated through Share Transfer is to deliver to holders of Share Options of the Wholly Owned Subsidiary Company in Share Transfer Share Options of the Wholly Owning Parent Company Incorporated through Share Transfer in lieu of such Share Options at the time of the Share Transfer, the following matters concerning such Share Options:
  (a) the description of the features of the Share Options (hereinafter referred to as "Share Options under Share Transfer Plan" in this Part) held by holders of Share Options of the Wholly Owned Subsidiary Company in Share Transfer who will receive delivery of Share Options of the Wholly Owning Parent Company Incorporated through Share Transfer;
  (b) the description of the features and number of Share Options of the Wholly Owning Parent Company Incorporated through Share Transfer to be delivered to holders of Share Options under Share Transfer Plan, or the method for calculating such number; and
  (c) if Share Options under Share Transfer Plan are Share Options attached to Bonds with Share Options, a statement to the effect that the Wholly Owning Parent Company Incorporated through Share Transfer will succeed to the obligations relating to the Bonds pertaining to such Bonds with Share Options and the description of the classes of the Bonds subject to such succession and the total amount for each class of Bonds, or the method for calculating that total amount; and
(x) in the case prescribed in the preceding item, matters concerning allotment of the Share Options of the Wholly Owning Parent Company Incorporated through Share Transfer set forth in that item to holders of Share Options under Share Transfer Plan.
(2) In the case prescribed in the preceding paragraph, if the Wholly Owned Subsidiary Company in Share Transfer is a Company with Class Shares, the Wholly Owned Subsidiary Company in Share Transfer may provide for the following matters in prescribing the matters set forth in item (vi) of that paragraph in accordance with the features of the classes of shares issued by the Stock Company Absorbed in Absorption-type Merger:
  (i) if there is any arrangement that no shares of the Wholly Owning Parent Company Incorporated through Share Transfer are allotted to shareholders of a certain class of shares, a statement to such effect and such class of shares; and
  (ii) in addition to the matters listed in the preceding item, if there is any arrangement that each class of shares shall be treated differently with respect to allotment of shares of the Wholly Owning Parent Company Incorporated through Share Transfer, a statement to such effect and the details of such different treatment.
(3) In the case prescribed in paragraph (1), the provisions on the matters listed in item (vi) of that paragraph shall be such that shares of the Wholly Owning Parent Company Incorporated through Share Transfer are delivered in proportion to the number of the

shares (or, in cases where there are provisions on the matters listed in item (ii) of the preceding paragraph, the number of the shares of each class) held by the shareholders of the Wholly Owned Subsidiary Company in Share Transfer (excluding the shareholders of the class of shares referred to in item (i) of the preceding paragraph).
(4) The provisions of the preceding two paragraphs shall apply mutatis mutandis to the matters mentioned in paragraph (1)(viii). In such cases, the term "shares of the Wholly Owning Parent Company Incorporated through Share Transfer" in the preceding two paragraphs shall be deemed to be replaced with "Bonds, etc. of the Wholly Owning Parent Company Incorporated through Share Transfer."

(Effectuation, etc. of a Share Transfer)
Article 774 (1) The Wholly Owning Parent Company Incorporated through Share Transfer shall acquire all of the Issued Shares of the Wholly Owned Subsidiary Company in Share Transfer on the day of its formation.
(2) The shareholders of the Wholly Owned Subsidiary Company in Share Transfer shall, in accordance with the provisions on the matters set forth in item (vi) of the preceding Article, become shareholders of the shares set forth in item (v) of that paragraph on the day of formation of the Wholly Owning Parent Company Incorporated through Share Transfer.
(3) In the cases listed in the following items, the shareholders of the Wholly Owned Subsidiary Company in Share Transfer shall become the persons specified respectively in those items, in accordance with the provisions on the matters set forth in paragraph (1)(viii) of the preceding Article, on the day of formation of the Wholly Owning Parent Company Incorporated through Share Transfer:
  (i) in cases where there is a provision on the matters set forth in (a) of item (vii) of paragraph (1) of the preceding Article: bondholders of Bonds set forth in (a) of that item;
  (ii) in cases where there is a provision on the matters set forth in (b) of item (vii) of paragraph (1) of the preceding Article: holders of Share Options set forth in (b) of that item; or
  (iii) in cases where there is a provision on the matters set forth in (c) of item (vii) of paragraph (1) of the preceding Article: bondholders of the Bonds pertaining to Bonds with Share Options set forth in (c) of that item, and holders of the Share Options attached to such Bonds with Share Options.
(4) In the case prescribed in item (ix) of paragraph (1) of the preceding Article, the Share Options under Share Transfer Plan shall be extinguished and the holders of the Share Options under Share Transfer Plan shall become holders of the Share Options of the Wholly Owning Parent Company Incorporated through Share Transfer set forth in item (ix)(b) of that paragraph, in accordance with the provisions on the matters set forth in item (x) of that paragraph, on the day of formation of the Wholly Owning Parent Company Incorporated through Share Transfer.
(5) In the case prescribed in (c) of item (ix) of paragraph (1) of the preceding Article, the Wholly Owning Parent Company Incorporated through Share Transfer shall succeed to the obligations relating to the Bonds pertaining to Bonds with Share Options set forth in (c) of that item on the day of its formation.

Chapter V Procedures of Entity Conversion, Merger, Company Split, Share Exchange, and Share Transfer

Section 1 Procedures of Entity Conversion

Subsection 1 Procedures for a Stock Company

(Keeping and Inspection, etc. of Documents, etc. Concerning an Entity Conversion Plan)

Article 775 (1) A Stock Company effecting Entity Conversion shall, from the day on which the Entity Conversion plan began to be kept until the day on which the Entity Conversion becomes effective (hereinafter referred to as the "Effective Day" in this Section), keep documents or Electromagnetic Records that state or record the contents of the Entity Conversion plan and other matters prescribed by the applicable Ordinance of the Ministry of Justice at its head office.

(2) The "day on which the Entity Conversion plan began to be kept" prescribed in the preceding paragraph means the earliest of the following days:
 (i) the day on which the consent of all shareholders of the Stock Company effecting the Entity Conversion has been gained with regard to the Entity Conversion plan;
 (ii) if the Stock Company effecting the Entity Conversion has issued Share Options, the day of the notice under the provisions of paragraph (3) of Article 777 or the day of the public notice set forth in paragraph (4) of that Article, whichever is earlier; or
 (iii) the day of the public notice under the provisions of paragraph (2) of Article 779 or the day of the demand under the provisions of that paragraph, whichever is earlier.

(3) Shareholders and creditors of a Stock Company effecting Entity Conversion may make the following requests to said Stock Company at any time during its business hours; provided, however, that the fees designated by said Stock Company are required to be paid in order to make the requests set forth in item (ii) or item (iv):
 (i) requests for inspection of the documents set forth in paragraph (1);
 (ii) requests for delivery of a transcript or extract of the documents set forth in paragraph (1);
 (iii) requests for inspection of anything that indicates the matters recorded in the Electromagnetic Records set forth in paragraph (1) in a manner prescribed by the applicable Ordinance of the Ministry of Justice; and
 (iv) requests that the matters recorded in the Electromagnetic Records set forth in paragraph (1) be provided by the Electromagnetic Method designated by the Stock Company, or requests for the delivery of any document that states such matters.

(Approval, etc. of the Entity Conversion Plan of a Stock Company)

Article 776 (1) A Stock Company effecting Entity Conversion shall obtain the consent of all shareholders of said Stock Company with regard to the Entity Conversion plan by the day immediately preceding the Effective Day.

(2) A Stock Company effecting Entity Conversion shall notify its Registered Pledgees of Shares and Registered Pledgees of Share Options thereof that it will effect Entity Conversion, by twenty days prior to the Effective Day.

(3) A public notice may be substituted for the notice under the provisions of the preceding paragraph.

(Demand for Purchase of Share Options)

Article 777 (1) In cases where a Stock Company effects Entity Conversion, holders of

Share Options of the Stock Company effecting Entity Conversion may demand that the Stock Company purchase, at a fair price, the Share Options held by the same.
(2) If holders of the Share Options attached to Bonds with Share Options intend to make the demand under the preceding paragraph (hereinafter referred to as a "Share Option Purchase Demand" in this Section), they shall also make the demand for the purchase of the Bonds pertaining to Bonds with Share Options; provided, however, that this shall not apply in cases where it is otherwise provided for with respect to the Share Options attached to such Bonds with Share Options.
(3) A Stock Company which intends to effect Entity Conversion shall notify the holders of Share Options thereof that it will effect Entity Conversion, by twenty days prior to the Effective Day.
(4) A public notice may be substituted for the notice under the provisions of the preceding paragraph.
(5) A Share Option Purchase Demand shall be made, within the period from the day twenty days prior to the Effective Day to the day immediately preceding the Effective Day, by disclosing the features and number of Share Options relating to such Share Option Purchase Demand.
(6) Holders of Share Options who have made a Share Option Purchase Demand may withdraw their Share Option Purchase Demands only in cases where they obtain the approval of the Stock Company effecting Entity Conversion.
(7) If the Entity Conversion is cancelled, the Share Option Purchase Demands shall become ineffective.

(Determination, etc. of Price of Share Options)
Article 778 (1) In cases where a Share Option Purchase Demand is made, if an agreement on the determination of the price of the Share Options (in cases where such Share Options are those attached to Bonds with Share Options, if there is a demand for the purchase of Bonds pertaining to such Bonds with Share Options, they shall include such Bonds; hereinafter the same shall apply in this Article) is reached between the holder of Share Options and the Stock Company effecting Entity Conversion (after the Effective Day, the Membership Company after Entity Conversion; hereinafter the same shall apply in this Article), the Stock Company shall make payment within sixty days from the Effective Day.
(2) If no agreement on the determination of the price of the Share Options is reached within thirty days from the Effective Day, holders of Share Options or the Membership Company after Entity Conversion may file a petition to the court for a determination of the price within thirty days after the expiration of that period.
(3) Notwithstanding the provisions of paragraph (6) of the preceding Article, in the cases prescribed in the preceding paragraph, if the petition under that paragraph is not filed within sixty days from the Effective Day, holders of Share Options may withdraw their Share Option Purchase Demands at any time after the expiration of such period.
(4) The Membership Company after Entity Conversion shall also pay interest on the price determined by the court which shall be calculated at the rate of six percent per annum from and including the day of the expiration of the period referred to in paragraph (1).
(5) The purchase of Share Options relating to a Share Option Purchase Demand shall become effective on the Effective Day.
(6) If a Stock Company effecting Entity Conversion receives a Share Option Purchase Demand with respect to a Share Option for which a Share Option certificate is issued, it shall pay the price of the Share Option relating to such Share Option Purchase Demand in exchange for the Share Option certificate.
(7) If a Stock Company effecting Entity Conversion receives a Share Option Purchase De-

mand with respect to a Share Option attached to a Bond with a Share Option for which a certificate for a Bond with a Share Option is issued, it shall pay the price of the Share Option relating to such Share Option Purchase Demand in exchange for such certificate for a Bond with a Share Option.

(Objections of Creditors)
Article 779 (1) Creditors of a Stock Company effecting Entity Conversion may state their objections to the Entity Conversion to such Stock Company.
(2) A Stock Company effecting Entity Conversion shall give public notice of the matters listed below in the official gazette and shall give notices separately to each known creditor, if any; provided, however, that the period under item (iii) may not be less than one month:
(i) a statement that Entity Conversion will be effected;
(ii) the matters prescribed by the applicable Ordinance of the Ministry of Justice as the matters regarding the Financial Statements (meaning the Financial Statements prescribed in Article 435(2); hereinafter the same shall apply in this Chapter) of the Stock Company effecting Entity Conversion; and
(iii) a statement to the effect that creditors may state their objections within a certain period of time.
(3) Notwithstanding the provisions of the preceding paragraph, if a Stock Company effecting Entity Conversion gives public notice under that paragraph by the Method of Public Notice listed in item (ii) or item (iii) of paragraph (1) of Article 939 in accordance with the provisions of the articles of incorporation under the provisions of that paragraph in addition to the official gazette, the Stock Company is not required to give separate notices under the provisions of the preceding paragraph.
(4) In cases where creditors do not raise any objections within the period under paragraph (2)(iii), such creditors shall be deemed to have approved the Entity Conversion.
(5) In cases where creditors raise objections within the period under paragraph (2)(iii), the Stock Company effecting Entity Conversion shall make payment or provide reasonable security to such creditors, or entrust equivalent property to a Trust Company, etc. for the purpose of having such creditors receive the payment; provided, however, that this shall not apply if there is no risk of harm to such creditors by such Entity Conversion.

(Change of the Effective Day of Entity Conversion)
Article 780 (1) A Stock Company effecting Entity Conversion may change the Effective Day.
(2) In the cases prescribed in the preceding paragraph, the Stock Company effecting Entity Conversion shall give public notice of the changed Effective Day by the day immediately preceding the original Effective Day (or, immediately preceding the changed Effective Day, in the case where the changed Effective Day comes before the original Effective Day).
(3) When the Effective Day is changed pursuant to the provisions of paragraph (1), the provisions of this Subsection and Article 745 shall apply by deeming the changed Effective Day to be the Effective Day.

Subsection 2 Procedures for a Membership Company

Article 781 (1) A Membership Company effecting Entity Conversion shall obtain the consent of all partners of the Membership Company with regard to the Entity Conversion plan by the day immediately preceding the Effective Day; provided, however, that

this shall not apply in cases where it is otherwise provided for in the articles of incorporation.
(2) The provisions of Article 779 (excluding paragraph (2)(ii)) and the preceding Article shall apply mutatis mutandis to a Membership Company effecting Entity Conversion. In such cases, the term "Stock Company effecting Entity Conversion" in Article 779(3) shall be deemed to be replaced with "Membership Company (limited to a Limited Liability Company) effecting Entity Conversion," and the term "and Article 745" in paragraph (3) of the preceding Article shall be deemed to be replaced with "and Article 747 and paragraph (1) of the following Article."

Section 2 Procedures of an Absorption-type Merger, etc.

Subsection 1 Procedures for a Company Absorbed in Absorption-type Merger, a Splitting Company in Absorption-type Company Split, and a Wholly Owned Subsidiary Company in Share Exchange

Division 1 Procedures for a Stock Company

(Keeping and Inspection, etc. of Documents, etc. Concerning an Absorption-type Merger Agreement, etc.)

Article 782 (1) Each of the Stock Companies listed in the following items (hereinafter referred to as an "Absorbed Stock Company, etc." in this Division) shall, from the day on which the Absorption-type Merger Agreement, etc. began to be kept until the day on which six months have elapsed from the day on which the Absorption-type Merger, Absorption-type Company Split or Share Exchange (hereinafter referred to as an "Absorption-type Merger, etc." in this Section) becomes effective (hereinafter referred to as the "Effective Day" in this Section) (or, in the case of a Stock Company Absorbed in Absorption-type Merger, until the Effective Day), keep documents or Electromagnetic Records that state or record the contents of the matters specified respectively in those items (hereinafter referred to as the "Absorption-type Merger Agreement, etc." in this Section) and other matters prescribed by the applicable Ordinance of the Ministry of Justice at its head office:
(i) Stock Company Absorbed in Absorption-type Merger: the Absorption-type Merger agreement;
(ii) Splitting Stock Company in Absorption-type Company Split: the Absorption-type Company Split agreement; and
(iii) Wholly Owned Subsidiary Company in Share Exchange: the Share Exchange agreement.
(2) The "day on which the Absorption-type Merger Agreement, etc. began to be kept" prescribed in the preceding paragraph means the earliest of the following days:
(i) if the Absorption-type Merger Agreement, etc. is required to be approved by a resolution of a shareholders meeting (including a Class Meeting), the day two weeks prior to the day of the shareholders meeting (or, in the cases prescribed in paragraph (1) of Article 319, the day when the proposal under that paragraph is submitted);
(ii) if there are shareholders who are to receive the notice under the provisions of paragraph (3) of Article 785, the day of the notice under the provisions of that paragraph or the day of the public notice under paragraph (4) of that Article, whichever is earlier;
(iii) if there are holders of Share Options who are to receive the notice under the pro-

visions of paragraph (3) of Article 787, the day of the notice under the provisions of that paragraph or the day of the public notice under paragraph (4) of that Article, whichever is earlier
(iv) if the procedures under the provisions of Article 789 are required to be carried out, the day of the public notice under the provisions of paragraph (2) of that Article or the day of the notice under the provisions of that paragraph, whichever is earlier; or
(v) in cases other than those prescribed in the preceding items, the day on which two weeks have elapsed from the day of conclusion of the Absorption-type Company Split agreement or the Share Exchange agreement.
(3) Shareholders and creditors of an Absorbed Stock Company, etc. (or, in the case of a Wholly Owned Subsidiary Company in Share Exchange, shareholders and holders of Share Options) may make the following requests to said Absorbed Stock Company, etc. at any time during its business hours; provided, however, that the fees designated by said Absorbed Stock Company, etc. are required to be paid in order to make the requests set forth in item (ii) or item (iv):
(i) requests for inspection of the documents set forth in paragraph (1);
(ii) requests for delivery of a transcript or extract of the documents set forth in paragraph (1);
(iii) requests for inspection of anything that indicates the matters recorded in the Electromagnetic Records set forth in paragraph (1) in a manner prescribed by the applicable Ordinance of the Ministry of Justice; and
(iv) requests that the matters recorded in the Electromagnetic Records set forth in paragraph (1) be provided by the Electromagnetic Method designated by the Absorbed Stock Company, etc., or requests for the delivery of any document that states such matters.

(Approval, etc. of the Absorption-type Merger Agreement, etc.)
Article 783 (1) An Absorbed Stock Company, etc. shall obtain the approval of the Absorption-type Merger Agreement, etc. by a resolution of a shareholders meeting by the day immediately preceding the Effective Day.
(2) Notwithstanding the provisions of the preceding paragraph, in the cases where the Stock Company Absorbed in Absorption-type Merger or the Wholly Owned Subsidiary Company in Share Exchange is not a Company with Classes of Shares, if all or part of the Monies, etc. to be delivered to shareholders of the Stock Company Absorbed in Absorption-type Merger or the Wholly Owned Subsidiary Company in Share Exchange (hereinafter referred to as the "Consideration for the Merger, etc." in this Article) are Equity Interests, etc. (meaning equity interests of a Membership Company or those prescribed by the applicable Ordinance of the Ministry of Justice as being equivalent thereto; hereinafter the same shall apply in this Article), the consent of all shareholders of the Stock Company Absorbed in Absorption-type Merger or the Wholly Owned Subsidiary Company in Share Exchange shall be obtained with regard to the Absorption-type Merger agreement or the Share Exchange agreement.
(3) In the cases where the Stock Company Absorbed in Absorption-type Merger or the Wholly Owned Subsidiary Company in Share Exchange is a Company with Classes of Shares, if all or part of the Consideration for the Merger, etc. are Shares with a Restriction on Transfer, etc. (meaning Shares with a Restriction on Transfer and those prescribed by the applicable Ordinance of the Ministry of Justice as being equivalent thereto; hereinafter the same shall apply in this Chapter), the Absorption-type Merger or the Share Exchange shall not become effective without a resolution of a Class Meeting constituted by the Class Shareholders of the class of shares subject to the al-

lotment of the Shares with a Restriction on Transfer, etc. (excluding Shares with a Restriction on Transfer) (in cases where there are two or more classes of shares relating to such Class Shareholders, the respective Class Meetings constituted by Class Shareholders categorized by the class of such two or more classes of shares); provided, however, that this shall not apply to cases where there is no Class Shareholder who is able to exercise a voting right at such Class Meeting.
(4) In the cases where the Stock Company Absorbed in Absorption-type Merger or the Wholly Owned Subsidiary Company in Share Exchange is a Company with Classes of Shares, if all or part of the Consideration for the Merger, etc. are Equity Interests, etc., the Absorption-type Merger or the Share Exchange shall not become effective without the consent of all shareholders of the class subject to the allotment of the Equity Interests, etc.
(5) An Absorbed Stock Company, etc. shall notify its Registered Pledgees of Shares (excluding the Registered Pledgees of Shares in the cases prescribed in paragraph (3) of the following Article) and Registered Pledgees of Share Options concerning the Share Options specified in the items of Article 787(3) that it will effect the Absorption-type Merger, etc. by twenty days prior to the Effective Day.
(6) A public notice may be substituted for the notice under the provisions of the preceding paragraph.

(Cases Where Approval of the Absorption-type Merger Agreement, etc. Is Not Required)
Article 784 (1) The provisions of paragraph (1) of the preceding Article shall not apply in the cases where the Company Surviving Absorption-type Merger, the Succeeding Company in Absorption-type Company Split or the Wholly Owning Parent Company in Share Exchange (hereinafter referred to as the "Surviving Company, etc." in this Division) is the Special Controlling Company of the Absorbed Stock Company, etc.; provided, however, that this shall not apply in the cases where all or part of the value of the merger, etc. in the Absorption-type Merger or Share Exchange is Shares with a Restriction on Transfer, etc., and the Absorbed Stock Company, etc. is a Public Company and not a Company with Class Shares.
(2) In the cases prescribed in the main clause of the preceding paragraph, in any one of the following cases where shareholders of the Absorbed Stock Company, etc. are likely to suffer disadvantage, shareholders of the Absorbed Stock Company, etc. may demand that the Absorbed Stock Company, etc. refrain from effecting the Absorption-type Merger, etc.:
  (i) in cases where the Absorption-type Merger, etc. violates the applicable laws and regulations or articles of incorporation; or
  (ii) in cases where the matters set forth in Article 749(1)(ii) or (iii), Article 751(1)(iii) or (iv), Article 758(iv), Article 760(iv) or (v), Article 768(1)(ii) or (iii), or Article 770(1)(iii) or (iv) are grossly improper in light of the financial status of the Absorbed Stock Company, etc. or the Surviving Company, etc.
(3) The provisions of the preceding Article and the preceding paragraph shall not apply in cases where the sum of the book value of the assets that the Succeeding Company in Absorption-type Company Split succeeds to through the Absorption-type Company Split does not exceed one-fifth (or, in cases where a lesser proportion is prescribed in the articles of incorporation of the Splitting Stock Company in Absorption-type Company Split, such proportion) of the amount calculated by the method specified by the applicable Ordinance of the Ministry of Justice as the total assets of the Splitting Stock Company in Absorption-type Company Split.

Art.785〜786　　　　　Ⅰ Companies Act, Part V, Chap.V, Sec.2

(Dissenting Shareholders' Share Purchase Demand)
Article 785 (1) In cases of effecting an Absorption-type Merger, etc. (excluding the following cases), dissenting shareholders may demand that the Absorbed Stock Company, etc. purchase, at a fair price, the shares held by such shareholders:
(i) in cases prescribed in Article 783(2); or
(ii) in cases prescribed in paragraph (3) of the preceding Article.
(2) The "dissenting shareholders" provided for in the preceding paragraph shall mean the shareholders provided for in the following items in the cases listed in the same items (excluding shareholders entitled to allotment of Equity Interests, etc. prescribed in Article 783(4) in the cases prescribed in that paragraph):
(i) in cases where a resolution of a shareholders meeting (including a Class Meeting) is required to effect the Absorption-type Merger, etc.: the following shareholders:
(a) shareholders who gave notice to such Absorbed Stock Company, etc. to the effect that they dissented from such Absorption-type Merger, etc. prior to such shareholders meeting and who dissented from such Absorption-type Merger, etc. at such shareholders meeting (limited to those who can exercise voting rights at such shareholders meeting);
(b) shareholders who are unable to exercise voting rights at such shareholders meeting; and
(ii) in cases other than those prescribed in the preceding item: all shareholders.
(3) An Absorbed Stock Company, etc. shall notify its shareholders (excluding shareholders entitled to allotment of Equity Interests, etc. prescribed in Article 783(4) in the cases prescribed in that paragraph) that it will effect an Absorption-type Merger, etc. and the trade name and domicile of the Surviving Company, etc., by twenty days prior to the Effective Day; provided, however, that this shall not apply in the cases listed in the items of paragraph (1).
(4) In the following cases, a public notice may be substituted for the notice under the provisions of the preceding paragraph:
(i) in cases where the Absorbed Stock Company, etc. is a Public Company; or
(ii) in cases where the Absorbed Stock Company, etc. obtains the approval of the Absorption-type Merger Agreement, etc. by the resolution of a shareholders meeting set forth in Article 783(1).
(5) Demands under the provisions of paragraph (1) (hereinafter referred to as a "Share Purchase Demand" in this Division) shall be made, within the period from the day twenty days prior to the Effective Day to the day immediately preceding the Effective Day, by disclosing the number of shares relating to such Share Purchase Demand (or, for a Company with Classes of Shares, the classes of the shares and the number of shares for each class).
(6) Shareholders who made Share Purchase Demands may withdraw their Share Purchase Demands only in cases where such shareholders obtain the approval of the Absorbed Stock Company, etc.
(7) If the Absorption-type Merger, etc. is cancelled, the Share Purchase Demands shall become ineffective.

(Determination, etc. of Price of Shares)
Article 786 (1) In cases where a Share Purchase Demand is made, if an agreement on the determination of the price of the shares is reached between the shareholder and the Absorbed Stock Company, etc. (or, after the Effective Day in cases of effecting an Absorption-type Merger, the Company Surviving Absorption-type Merger; hereinafter the same shall apply in this Article), the Absorbed Stock Company, etc. shall make payment within sixty days from the Effective Day.

(2) If no agreement on the determination of the price of the shares is reached within thirty days from the Effective Day, shareholders or the Absorbed Stock Company, etc. may file a petition to the court for a determination of the price within thirty days after the expiration of that period.
(3) Notwithstanding the provisions of paragraph (6) of the preceding Article, in the cases prescribed in the preceding paragraph, if the petition under that paragraph is not filed within sixty days from the Effective Day, shareholders may withdraw their Share Purchase Demands at any time after the expiration of such period.
(4) The Absorbed Stock Company, etc. shall also pay interest on the price determined by the court which shall be calculated at the rate of six percent per annum from and including the day of the expiration of the period referred to in paragraph (1).
(5) The purchase of shares relating to a Share Purchase Demand shall become effective on the Effective Day (or, in the case of effecting an Absorption-type Company Split, at the time of payment of the price of such shares).
(6) If a Company Issuing Share Certificates receives a Share Purchase Demand with respect to shares for which share certificates are issued, the Company must pay the price of the shares relating to such Share Purchase Demand in exchange for the share certificates.

(Demand for Purchase of Share Options)
Article 787 (1) In cases of carrying out any one of the acts listed in the following items, holders of Share Options of the Absorbed Stock Company, etc. provided for in those items may demand that the Absorbed Stock Company, etc. purchase, at a fair price, the Share Options held by the same:
  (i) Absorption-type Merger: Share Options other than those for which provisions on the matters set forth in Article 749(1)(iv) or (v) meet the conditions set forth in item (iii) of Article 236(1) (limited to those related to (a) of that item);
  (ii) Absorption-type Company Split (limited to cases where the Succeeding Company in Absorption-type Company Split is a Stock Company): among the following Share Options, Share Options other than those for which provisions on the matters set forth in Article 758(v) or (vi) meet the conditions set forth in item (viii) of Article 236(1) (limited to those related to (b) of that item):
    (a) Share Options under Absorption-type Company Split Agreement; and
    (b) Share Options other than Share Options under Absorption-type Company Split Agreement and for which there are provisions to the effect that, in the case of effecting an Absorption-type Company Split, Share Options of the Succeeding Stock Company in Absorption-type Company Split shall be delivered to holders of such Share Options; or
  (iii) Share Exchange (limited to cases where the Wholly Owning Parent Company in Share Exchange is a Stock Company): Among the following Share Options, Share Options other than those for which provisions on the matters set forth in item (iv) or item (v) of Article 768(1) meet the conditions set forth in item (viii) of Article 236(1) (limited to those related to (d) of that item):
    (a) Share Options under Share Exchange Agreement; and
    (b) Share Options other than Share Options under Share Exchange Agreement and for which there are provisions to the effect that, in the case of effecting a Share Exchange, Share Options of the Wholly Owning Parent Stock Company in Share Exchange shall be delivered to holders of such Share Options.
(2) If holders of the Share Options attached to Bonds with Share Options intend to make the demand under the preceding paragraph (hereinafter referred to as a "Share Option Purchase Demand" in this Division), they shall also make a demand for the purchase

Art.788 **① Companies Act, Part V, Chap.V, Sec.2**

of the Bonds pertaining to Bonds with Share Options; provided, however, that this shall not apply in cases where it is otherwise provided for with respect to the Share Options attached to such Bonds with Share Options.
(3) The Absorbed Stock Companies, etc. listed in the following items shall notify holders of Share Options provided for in those items that they will effect an Absorption-type Merger, etc. and the trade name and domicile of the Surviving Company, etc., by twenty days prior to the Effective Day:
 (i) Stock Company Absorbed in Absorption-type Merger: all Share Options;
 (ii) Splitting Stock Company in Absorption-type Company Split in cases where the Succeeding Company in Absorption-type Company Split is a Stock Company: the following Share Options:
  (a) Share Options under Absorption-type Company Split Agreement; and
  (b) Share Options other than Share Options under Absorption-type Company Split Agreement and for which there are provisions to the effect that, in the case of effecting an Absorption-type Company Split, Share Options of the Succeeding Stock Company in Absorption-type Company Split shall be delivered to holders of such Share Options;
 (iii) Wholly Owned Subsidiary Company in Share Exchange in cases where the Wholly Owning Parent Company in Share Exchange is a Stock Company: the following Share Options:
  (a) Share Options under Share Exchange Agreement; and
  (b) Share Options other than Share Options under Share Exchange Agreement and for which there are provisions to the effect that, in the case of effecting a Share Exchange, Share Options of the Wholly Owning Parent Stock Company in Share Exchange shall be delivered to holders of such Share Options.
(4) A public notice may be substituted for the notice under the provisions of the preceding paragraph.
(5) A Share Option Purchase Demand shall be made, within the period from the day twenty days prior to the Effective Day to the day immediately preceding the Effective Day, by disclosing the features and number of Share Options relating to such Share Option Purchase Demand.
(6) Holders of Share Options who have made Share Option Purchase Demands may withdraw their Share Option Purchase Demands only in cases where they obtain the approval of the Absorbed Stock Company, etc.
(7) If the Absorption-type Merger, etc. is cancelled, the Share Option Purchase Demands shall become ineffective.

(Determination, etc. of Price of Share Options)
Article 788 (1) In cases where a Share Option Purchase Demand is made, if an agreement on the determination of the price of the Share Options (in cases where such Share Options are those attached to Bonds with Share Options, if there is a demand for the purchase of Bonds pertaining to such Bonds with Share Options, they shall include such Bonds; hereinafter the same shall apply in this Article) is reached between the holder of Share Options and the Absorbed Stock Company, etc. (or, after the Effective Day in cases of effecting an Absorption-type Merger, the Company Surviving Absorption-type Merger; hereinafter the same shall apply in this Article), the Absorbed Stock Company, etc. shall make payment within sixty days from the Effective Day.
(2) If no agreement on the determination of the price of the Share Options is reached within thirty days from the Effective Day, holders of Share Options or the Absorbed Stock Company, etc. may file a petition to the court for a determination of the price within thirty days after the expiration of that period.

(3) Notwithstanding the provisions of paragraph (6) of the preceding Article, in the cases prescribed in the preceding paragraph, if the petition under that paragraph is not filed within sixty days from the Effective Day, holders of Share Options may withdraw their Share Option Purchase Demands at any time after the expiration of such period.
(4) The Absorbed Stock Company, etc. shall also pay interest on the price determined by the court which shall be calculated at the rate of six percent per annum from and including the day of the expiration of the period referred to in paragraph (1).
(5) The purchase of Share Options relating to a Share Option Purchase Demand shall become effective at the times provided for in the following items for the categories of Share Options set forth respectively in those items:
  (i) Share Options provided for in paragraph (1)(i) of the preceding Article: the Effective Day;
  (ii) Share Options set forth in paragraph (1)(ii)(a) of the preceding Article: the Effective Day.
  (iii) Share Options set forth in paragraph (1)(ii)(b) of the preceding Article: the time of payment of the price of such Share Options;
  (iv) Share Options set forth in paragraph (1)(iii)(a) of the preceding Article: the Effective Day.
  (v) Share Options set forth in paragraph (1)(iii)(b) of the preceding Article: the time of payment of the price of such Share Options.
(6) If an Absorbed Stock Company, etc. receives a Share Option Purchase Demand with respect to a Share Option for which a Share Option certificate is issued, it shall pay the price of the Share Option relating to such Share Option Purchase Demand in exchange for the Share Option certificate.
(7) If an Absorbed Stock Company, etc. receives a Share Option Purchase Demand with respect to a Share Option attached to a Bond with a Share Option for which a certificate for a Bond with a Share Option is issued, it shall pay the price of the Share Option relating to such Share Option Purchase Demand in exchange for such certificate for a Bond with a Share Option.

(Objections of Creditors)
Article 789 (1) In the cases listed in the following items, the creditors provided for in those items may state their objections to the Absorption-type Merger, etc. to the Absorbed Stock Company, etc.:
  (i) in cases of effecting an Absorption-type Merger: creditors of the Stock Company Absorbed in Absorption-type Merger;
  (ii) in cases of effecting an Absorption-type Company Split: creditors of the Splitting Stock Company in Absorption-type Company Split who are unable to request the Splitting Stock Company in Absorption-type Company Split to perform the obligations (including performance of the guarantee obligations that the Splitting Stock Company in Absorption-type Company Split jointly and severally assumes with the Succeeding Company in Absorption-type Company Split as a guarantor) (or, in the case where there are provisions on the matter set forth in Article 758(viii) or Article 760(vii), creditors of the Splitting Stock Company in Absorption-type Company Split); and
  (iii) in cases where the Share Options under Share Exchange Agreement are Share Options attached to Bonds with Share Options: bondholders pertaining to such Bonds with Share Options.
(2) In cases where all or part of the creditors of the Absorbed Stock Company, etc. are able to state their objection pursuant to the provisions of the preceding paragraph, the Absorbed Stock Company, etc. shall give public notice of the matters listed below in

the official gazette and shall give notices separately to each known creditor (limited to one who is able to state an objection pursuant to the provisions of such paragraph), if any; provided, however, that the period under item (iv) may not be less than one month:
(i) a statement that an Absorption-type Merger, etc. will be effected;
(ii) the trade name and domicile of the Surviving Company, etc.;
(iii) the matters prescribed by the applicable Ordinance of the Ministry of Justice as the matters regarding the Financial Statements of the Absorbed Stock Company, etc. and the Surviving Company, etc. (limited to a Stock Company); and
(iv) a statement to the effect that creditors may state their objections within a certain period of time.
(3) Notwithstanding the provisions of the preceding paragraph, if the Absorbed Stock Company, etc. gives public notice under that paragraph by the Method of Public Notice listed in item (ii) or item (iii) of paragraph (1) of Article 939 in accordance with the provisions of the articles of incorporation under the provisions of that paragraph in addition to the official gazette, the Absorbed Stock Company, etc. is not required to give separate notices under the provisions of the preceding paragraph (excluding such notices to creditors of the obligations of the Splitting Stock Company in Absorption-type Company Split that have arisen due to a tort in the case of effecting an Absorption-type Company Split).
(4) In cases where creditors do not raise any objections within the period under paragraph (2)(iv), such creditors shall be deemed to have approved the Absorption-type Merger, etc.
(5) In cases where creditors raise objections within the period under paragraph (2)(iv), the Absorbed Stock Company, etc. shall make payment or provide reasonable security to such creditors, or entrust equivalent property to a Trust Company, etc. for the purpose of having such creditors receive the payment; provided, however, that this shall not apply if there is no risk of harm to such creditors by such Absorption-type Merger, etc.

(Change in the Effective Day of an Absorption-type Merger, etc.)
Article 790 (1) An Absorbed Stock Company, etc. may change the Effective Day by agreement with the Surviving Company, etc.
(2) In the cases prescribed in the preceding paragraph, the Absorbed Stock Company, etc. shall give public notice of the changed Effective Day by the day immediately preceding the original Effective Day (or, immediately preceding the changed Effective Day, in the case where the changed Effective Day comes before the original Effective Day).
(3) When the Effective Day is changed pursuant to the provisions of paragraph (1), the provisions of this Section and Article 750, Article 752, Article 759, Article 761, Article 769, and Article 771 shall apply by deeming the changed Effective Day to be the Effective Day.

(Keeping and Inspection, etc. of Documents, etc. Concerning an Absorption-type Company Split or Share Exchange)
Article 791 (1) The Splitting Stock Company in Absorption-type Company Split or the Wholly Owned Subsidiary Company in Share Exchange shall, without delay after the Effective Day, prepare what are provided for in the following items for the categories set forth respectively in those items, jointly with the Succeeding Company in Absorption-type Company Split or the Wholly Owning Parent Company in Share Exchange:
(i) Splitting Stock Company in Absorption-type Company Split: documents or Electromagnetic Records that state or record the rights and obligations that the Succeed-

ing Company in Absorption-type Company Split succeeded to by transfer from the Splitting Stock Company in Absorption-type Company Split through the Absorption-type Company Split and any other matters prescribed by the applicable Ordinance of the Ministry of Justice as those concerning an Absorption-type Company Split; and
  (ii) Wholly Owned Subsidiary Company in Share Exchange: documents or Electromagnetic Records that state or record the number of shares of the Wholly Owned Subsidiary Company in Share Exchange acquired by the Wholly Owning Parent Company through the Share Exchange and any other matters prescribed by the applicable Ordinance of the Ministry of Justice as those concerning a Share Exchange.
(2) A Splitting Stock Company in Absorption-type Company Split or a Wholly Owned Subsidiary Company in Share Exchange shall, for a period of six months from the Effective Day, keep the documents or Electromagnetic Records set forth in the items of the preceding paragraph at its head office.
(3) Shareholders, creditors and any other interested parties of a Splitting Stock Company in Absorption-type Company Split may make the following requests to the Splitting Stock Company in Absorption-type Company Split at any time during its business hours; provided, however, that the fees designated by said Splitting Stock Company in Absorption-type Company Split are required to be paid in order to make the requests set forth in item (ii) or item (iv):
  (i) requests for inspection of the documents set forth in the preceding paragraph;
  (ii) requests for delivery of a transcript or extract of the documents set forth in the preceding paragraph;
  (iii) requests for inspection of anything that indicates the matters recorded in the Electromagnetic Records set forth in the preceding paragraph in a manner prescribed by the applicable Ordinance of the Ministry of Justice; and
  (iv) requests that the matters recorded in the Electromagnetic Records set forth in the preceding paragraph be provided by the Electromagnetic Method designated by the Splitting Stock Company in Absorption-type Company Split, or requests for the delivery of any document that states such matters.
(4) The provisions of the preceding paragraph shall apply mutatis mutandis to a Wholly Owned Subsidiary Company in Share Exchange. In such cases, the phrase "shareholders, creditors and any other interested parties of a Splitting Stock Company in Absorption-type Company Split" shall be deemed to be replaced with "persons who were shareholders or holders of Share Options of the Wholly Owned Subsidiary Company in Share Exchange as of the Effective Day."

(Special Provisions on Dividends of Surplus, etc.)
Article 792 The provisions of Article 458 and Part II, Chapter V, Section 6 shall not apply to the acts listed below:
  (i) acquisition of shares set forth in Article 758(viii)(a) or Article 760(vii)(a); and
  (ii) distribution of dividends of surplus set forth in Article 758(viii)(b) or Article 760(vii)(b).

Division 1 Procedures for a Membership Company

Article 793 (1) A Membership Company conducting any one of the acts below shall obtain the consent of all partners of the Membership Company with regard to the Absorption-type Merger Agreement, etc. by the day immediately preceding the Effective Day; provided, however, that this shall not apply in cases where it is otherwise provid-

Art.794 　　　 ① Companies Act, Part V, Chap.V, Sec.2

ed for in the articles of incorporation:
(i) Absorption-type Merger (limited to cases where the Membership Company shall be extinguished through the Absorption-type Merger); or
(ii) Absorption-type Company Split (limited to cases where another Company succeeds to all of the rights and obligations held by such Membership Company (limited to a Limited Liability Company) in connection with its business).
(2) The provisions of Article 789 (excluding paragraph (1)(iii) and paragraph (2)(iii)) and Article 790 shall apply mutatis mutandis to a Membership Company Absorbed in Absorption-type Merger or a Splitting Company in Absorption-type Company Split, which is a Limited Liability Company (hereinafter referred to as the "Splitting Limited Liability Company in Absorption-type Company Split" in this Section). In such cases, the phrase "Creditors of the Splitting Stock Company in Absorption-type Company Split who are unable to request the Splitting Stock Company in Absorption-type Company Split to perform the obligations (including performance of the guarantee obligations that the Splitting Stock Company in Absorption-type Company Split jointly and severally assumes with the Succeeding Company in Absorption-type Company Split as a guarantor) (or, in the case where there are provisions on the matter set forth in Article 758(viii) or Article 760(vii), creditors of the Splitting Stock Company in Absorption-type Company Split)" in Article 789(1)(ii) shall be deemed to be replaced with "Creditors of the Splitting Stock Company in Absorption-type Company Split who are unable to request the Splitting Stock Company in Absorption-type Company Split to perform the obligations (including performance of the guarantee obligations that the Splitting Stock Company in Absorption-type Company Split jointly and severally assumes with the Succeeding Company in Absorption-type Company Split as a guarantor)" and the term "Absorbed Stock Company, etc." in paragraph (3) of that Article shall be deemed to be replaced with "Membership Company Absorbed in Absorption-type Merger (limited to a Limited Liability Company in the case where the Company Surviving Absorption-type Merger is a Stock Company or a Limited Liability Company) or the Splitting Limited Liability Company in Absorption-type Company Split."

Subsection 2　Procedures for the Company Surviving Absorption-type Merger, the Succeeding Company in Absorption-type Company Split and the Wholly Owning Parent Company in Share Exchange

Division 1　Procedures for a Stock Company

(Keeping and Inspection, etc. of Documents, etc. Concerning an Absorption-type Merger Agreement, etc.)
Article 794　(1) The Stock Company Surviving Absorption-type Merger, the Succeeding Stock Company in Absorption-type Company Split or the Wholly Owning Parent Stock Company in Share Exchange (hereinafter referred to as the "Surviving Stock Company, etc." in this Division) shall, from the day on which the Absorption-type Merger Agreement, etc. began to be kept until the day on which six months have elapsed from the Effective Day, keep documents or Electromagnetic Records that state or record the contents of the Absorption-type Merger Agreement, etc. and other matters prescribed by the applicable Ordinance of the Ministry of Justice at its head office.
(2) The "day on which the Absorption-type Merger Agreement, etc. began to be kept" prescribed in the preceding paragraph means the earliest of the following days:
(i) if the Absorption-type Merger Agreement, etc. is required to be approved by a resolution of a shareholders meeting (including a Class Meeting), the day two weeks prior to the day of the shareholders meeting (or, in the cases prescribed in para-

graph (1) of Article 319, the day when the proposal under that paragraph is submitted);
(ii) the day of the notice under the provisions of paragraph 3 of Article 797 or the day of the public notice under paragraph (4) of that Article, whichever is earlier; or
(iii) if the procedures under the provisions of Article 799 are required to be carried out, the day of the public notice under the provisions of paragraph (2) of that Article or the day of the notice under the provisions of that paragraph, whichever is earlier.
(3) Shareholders and creditors of a Surviving Stock Company, etc. (or, in the case where the Monies, etc. to be delivered to shareholders of the Wholly Owned Subsidiary Company in Share Exchange are limited to shares of the Wholly Owning Parent Stock Company in Share Exchange or those prescribed by the applicable Ordinance of the Ministry of Justice as being equivalent thereto (excluding the case prescribed in Article 768(1)(iv)(c)), shareholders) may make the following requests to said Surviving Stock Company, etc. at any time during its business hours; provided, however, that the fees designated by said Surviving Stock Company, etc. are required to be paid in order to make the requests set forth in item (ii) or item (iv):
(i) requests for inspection of the documents set forth in paragraph (1);
(ii) requests for delivery of a transcript or extract of the documents set forth in paragraph (1);
(iii) requests for inspection of anything that indicates the matters recorded in the Electromagnetic Records set forth in paragraph (1) in a manner prescribed by the applicable Ordinance of the Ministry of Justice; and
(iv) requests that the matters recorded in the Electromagnetic Records set forth in paragraph (1) be provided by the Electromagnetic Method designated by the Surviving Stock Company, etc., or requests for the delivery of any document that states such matters.

(Approval, etc. of the Absorption-type Merger Agreement, etc.)
Article 795 (1) A Surviving Stock Company, etc. shall obtain the approval of the Absorption-type Merger Agreement, etc. by a resolution of a shareholders meeting by the day immediately preceding the Effective Day.
(2) In the cases listed below, a director shall explain to that effect at the shareholders meeting set forth in the preceding paragraph:
(i) in cases where the amount prescribed by the applicable Ordinance of the Ministry of Justice as the amount of obligations that the Stock Company Surviving Absorption-type Merger or the Succeeding Stock Company in Absorption-type Company Split succeeds to by transfer from the Company Absorbed in Absorption-type Merger or the Splitting Company in Absorption-type Company Split (referred to as the "Amount of Succeeded Obligations" in the following item) exceeds the amount prescribed by the applicable Ordinance of the Ministry of Justice as the amount of assets that the Stock Company Surviving Absorption-type Merger or the Succeeding Stock Company in Absorption-type Company Split succeeds to by transfer from the Company Absorbed in Absorption-type Merger or the Splitting Company in Absorption-type Company Split (referred to as the "Amount of Succeeded Assets" in the following item);
(ii) in cases where the book value of the Monies, etc. (excluding shares, etc. of the Stock Company Surviving Absorption-type Merger or the Succeeding Stock Company in Absorption-type Company Split) delivered by the Stock Company Surviving Absorption-type Merger or the Succeeding Stock Company in Absorption-type Company Split to shareholders of the Stock Company Absorbed in Absorption-type

Art.796　① Companies Act, Part V, Chap.V, Sec.2

Merger, to partners of the Membership Company Absorbed in Absorption-type Merger or to the Splitting Company in Absorption-type Company Split exceeds the amount obtained by deducting the Amount of Succeeded Obligations from the Amount of Succeeded Assets; or
  (iii) in cases where the book value of the Monies, etc. (excluding shares, etc. of the Wholly Owning Parent Stock Company in Share Exchange) delivered by the Wholly Owning Parent Stock Company in Share Exchange to shareholders of the Wholly Owned Subsidiary Company in Share Exchange exceeds the amount prescribed by the applicable Ordinance of the Ministry of Justice as the amount of shares of the Wholly Owned Subsidiary Company in Share Exchange to be acquired by the Wholly Owning Parent Stock Company in Share Exchange.
(3) In cases where the assets of the Company Absorbed in Absorption-type Merger or the Splitting Company in Absorption-type Company Split include shares of the Stock Company Surviving Absorption-type Merger or the Succeeding Stock Company in Absorption-type Company Split, a director shall explain the matters concerning such shares at the shareholders meeting set forth in paragraph (1).
(4) Where the Surviving Stock Company, etc. is a Company with Class Shares, in the cases listed in the following items, an Absorption-type Merger, etc. shall not become effective without a resolution of a Class Meeting constituted by Class Shareholders of the class of shares provided for respectively in those items (limited to Shares with a Restriction on Transfer and for which the provisions of the articles of incorporation set forth in Article 199(4) do not exist) (in cases where there are two or more classes of shares relating to such Class Shareholders, the respective Class Meetings constituted by Class Shareholders categorized by the class of such two or more classes of shares); provided, however, that this shall not apply to cases where there is no Class Shareholder who is able to exercise a voting right at such Class Meeting:
  (i) in cases where the Monies, etc. delivered to shareholders of the Stock Company Absorbed in Absorption-type Merger or to partners of the Membership Company Absorbed in Absorption-type Merger are shares of the Stock Company Surviving Absorption-type Merger: the class of shares set forth in Article 749(1)(ii)(a);
  (ii) in cases where the Monies, etc. delivered to the Splitting Company in Absorption-type Company Split are shares of the Succeeding Stock Company in Absorption-type Company Split: the class of shares set forth in Article 758(iv)(a); or
  (iii) in cases where the Monies, etc. delivered to shareholders of the Wholly Owned Subsidiary Company in Share Exchange are shares of the Wholly Owning Parent Stock Company in Share Exchange: the class of shares set forth in Article 768(1)(ii)(a).

(Cases Where Approval of the Absorption-type Merger Agreement, etc. Is Not Required, etc.)
Article 796　(1) The provisions of paragraphs (1) to (3) of the preceding Article shall not apply in the cases where the Company Absorbed in Absorption-type Merger, the Splitting Company in Absorption-type Company Split or the Wholly Owned Subsidiary Company in Share Exchange (hereinafter referred to as the "Absorbed Company, etc." in this Division) is the Special Controlling Company of the Surviving Stock Company, etc.; provided, however, that this shall not apply in the cases where all or part of the Monies, etc. to be delivered to shareholders of the Stock Company Absorbed in Absorption-type Merger or the Wholly Owned Subsidiary Company in Share Exchange, to partners of the Membership Company Absorbed in Absorption-type Merger or to the Splitting Company in Absorption-type Company Split are Shares with a Restriction on Transfer, etc. of the Surviving Stock Company, etc., and the Surviving Stock Com-

pany, etc. is not a Public Company.
(2) In the cases prescribed in the main clause of the preceding paragraph, in any one of the following cases where shareholders of the Surviving Stock Company, etc. are likely to suffer disadvantage, shareholders of the Surviving Stock Company, etc. may demand that the Surviving Stock Company, etc. refrain from effecting the Absorption-type Merger, etc.:
  (i) in cases where the Absorption-type Merger, etc. violates the applicable laws and regulations or articles of incorporation; or
  (ii) in cases where the matters set forth in Article 749(1)(ii) or (iii), Article 758(iv) or Article 768(1)(ii) or (iii) are grossly improper in light of the financial status of the Surviving Stock Company, etc. or the Absorbed Company, etc.
(3) The provisions of paragraphs (1) to (3) of the preceding Article shall not apply in cases where the amount set forth in item (i) does not exceed one-fifth (or, in cases where a lesser proportion is prescribed in the articles of incorporation of the Surviving Stock Company, etc., such proportion) of the amount set forth in item (ii); provided, however, that this shall not apply in the cases listed in the items of paragraph (2) of the preceding Article or the cases prescribed in the proviso to paragraph (1):
(i) the total amount of the amounts listed below:
    (a) the amount obtained by multiplying the number of shares of the Surviving Stock Company, etc. to be delivered to shareholders of the Stock Company Absorbed in Absorption-type Merger or the Wholly Owned Subsidiary Company in Share Exchange, to partners of the Membership Company Absorbed in Absorption-type Merger or to the Splitting Company in Absorption-type Company Split (hereinafter referred to as "Shareholders, etc. of the Absorbed Company, etc." in this item) by the amount of net assets per share;
    (b) the total amount of the book value of Bonds, Share Options or Bonds with Share Options of the Surviving Stock Company, etc. to be delivered to Shareholders, etc. of the Absorbed Company, etc.; and
    (c) the total amount of the book value of property other than shares, etc. of the Surviving Stock Company, etc. to be delivered to Shareholders, etc. of the Absorbed Company, etc.; and
  (ii) the amount calculated by the method specified by the applicable Ordinance of the Ministry of Justice as the total assets of the Surviving Stock Company, etc.
(4) In the cases prescribed in the main clause of the preceding paragraph, if shareholders that hold the shares (limited to those that entitle the shareholders to exercise voting rights at a shareholders meeting under paragraph (1) of the preceding article) in the number prescribed by the applicable Ordinance of the Ministry of Justice notify the Surviving Stock Company, etc. to the effect that such shareholders dissent from the Absorption-type Merger, etc., within two weeks from the day of the notice under the provisions of paragraph (3) of the following Article or the public notice under paragraph (4) of that Article, such Surviving Stock Company, etc. must obtain the approval of the Absorption-type Merger Agreement, etc. by a resolution of a shareholders meeting no later than the day immediately preceding the Effective Day.

(Dissenting Shareholders' Share Purchase Demand)
Article 797 (1) In cases of effecting an Absorption-type Merger, etc., dissenting shareholders may demand that the Surviving Stock Company, etc. purchase, at a fair price, the shares held by such shareholders.
(2) The "dissenting shareholders" provided for in the preceding paragraph shall mean the shareholders provided for in the following items in the cases listed in the same items:
  (i) in cases where a resolution of a shareholders meeting (including a Class Meeting)

is required to effect the Absorption-type Merger, etc.: the following shareholders:
  (a) shareholders who gave notice to such Surviving Stock Company, etc. to the effect that they dissented from such Absorption-type Merger, etc. prior to such shareholders meeting and who dissented from such Absorption-type Merger, etc. at such shareholders meeting (limited to those who can exercise voting rights at such shareholders meeting);
  (b) shareholders who are unable to exercise voting rights at such shareholders meeting; and
 (ii) in cases other than those prescribed in the preceding item: all shareholders;
(3) A Surviving Stock Company, etc. shall notify its shareholders that it will effect an Absorption-type Merger, etc. and the trade name and domicile of the Absorbed Company, etc. (or, in the cases prescribed in Article 795(3), the fact that it will effect an Absorption-type Merger, etc., the trade name and domicile of the Absorbed Company, etc. and the matters concerning shares set forth in that paragraph), by twenty days prior to the Effective Day.
(4) In the following cases, a public notice may be substituted for the notice under the provisions of the preceding paragraph:
 (i) in cases where the Surviving Stock Company, etc. is a Public Company; or
 (ii) in cases where the Surviving Stock Company, etc. obtains the approval of the Absorption-type Merger Agreement, etc. by the resolution of a shareholders meeting set forth in Article 795(1).
(5) Demands under the provisions of paragraph (1) (hereinafter referred to as the "Share Purchase Demand" in this Division) shall be made, within the period from the day twenty days prior to the Effective Day to the day immediately preceding the Effective Day, by disclosing the number of shares relating to such Share Purchase Demand (or, for a Company with Classes of Shares, the classes of the shares and the number of shares for each class).
(6) Shareholders who made Share Purchase Demands may withdraw their Share Purchase Demands only in cases where such shareholders obtain the approval of the Surviving Stock Company, etc.
(7) If the Absorption-type Merger, etc. is cancelled, the Share Purchase Demands shall become ineffective.

(Determination, etc. of Price of Shares)
Article 798 (1) In cases where a Share Purchase Demand is made, if an agreement on the determination of the price of the shares is reached between the shareholder and the Surviving Stock Company, etc., the Surviving Stock Company, etc. shall make payment within sixty days from the Effective Day.
(2) If no agreement on the determination of the price of the shares is reached within thirty days from the Effective Day, shareholders or the Surviving Stock Company, etc. may file a petition to the court for a determination of the price within thirty days after the expiration of that period.
(3) Notwithstanding the provisions of paragraph (6) of the preceding Article, in the cases prescribed in the preceding paragraph, if the petition under that paragraph is not filed within sixty days from the Effective Day, shareholders may withdraw their Share Purchase Demands at any time after the expiration of such period.
(4) The Surviving Stock Company, etc. shall also pay interest on the price determined by the court which shall be calculated at the rate of six percent per annum from and including the day of the expiration of the period referred to in paragraph (1).
(5) The purchase of shares relating to a Share Purchase Demand shall become effective at the time of payment of the price of such shares.

(6) If a Company Issuing Share Certificates receives a Share Purchase Demand with respect to shares for which share certificates are issued, the Company must pay the price of the shares relating to such Share Purchase Demand in exchange for the share certificates.

(Objections of Creditors)
Article 799 (1) In the cases listed in the following items, the creditors provided for in those items may state their objections to the Absorption-type Merger, etc. to the Surviving Stock Company, etc.:
  (i) in cases of effecting an Absorption-type Merger: creditors of the Stock Company Surviving Absorption-type Merger;
  (ii) in cases of effecting an Absorption-type Company Split: creditors of the Succeeding Stock Company in Absorption-type Company Split; or
  (iii) in cases of effecting a Share Exchange other than where the Monies, etc. to be delivered to shareholders of the Wholly Owned Subsidiary Company in Share Exchange are only shares of the Wholly Owning Parent Stock Company in Share Exchange or those prescribed by the applicable Ordinance of the Ministry of Justice as being equivalent thereto, or in the cases prescribed in Article 768(1)(iv): creditors of the Wholly Owning Parent Stock Company in Share Exchange.
(2) In cases where the creditors of the Surviving Stock Company, etc. are able to state their objection pursuant to the provisions of the preceding paragraph, the Surviving Stock Company, etc. shall give public notice of the matters listed below in the official gazette and shall give notices separately to each known creditor, if any; provided, however, that the period under item (iv) may not be less than one month:
  (i) a statement that an Absorption-type Merger, etc. will be effected;
  (ii) the trade name and domicile of the Absorbed Company, etc.;
  (iii) the matters prescribed by the applicable Ordinance of the Ministry of Justice as the matters regarding the Financial Statements of the Surviving Stock Company, etc. and the Absorbed Company, etc. (limited to a Stock Company); and
  (iv) a statement to the effect that creditors may state their objections within a certain period of time.
(3) Notwithstanding the provisions of the preceding paragraph, if the Surviving Stock Company, etc. gives public notice under that paragraph by Method of Public Notice listed in item (ii) or item (iii) of paragraph (1) of Article 939 in accordance with the provisions of the articles of incorporation under the provisions of that paragraph in addition to the official gazette, the Surviving Stock Company, etc. is not required to give separate notices under the provisions of the preceding paragraph.
(4) In cases where creditors do not raise any objections within the period under paragraph (2)(iv), such creditors shall be deemed to have approved the Absorption-type Merger, etc.
(5) In cases where creditors raise objections within the period under paragraph (2)(iv), the Surviving Stock Company, etc. shall make payment or provide reasonable security to such creditors, or entrust equivalent property to a Trust Company, etc. for the purpose of having such creditors receive the payment; provided, however, that this shall not apply if there is no risk of harm to such creditors by such Absorption-type Merger, etc.

(Special Provisions on Cases Where the Monies, etc. to Be Delivered to Shareholders, etc. of the Absorbed Company, etc. Are the Parent Company's Shares of the Surviving Stock Company, etc.)
Article 800 (1) Notwithstanding the provisions of Article 135(1), in cases where all or

Art.801　　　Ⅰ Companies Act, Part V, Chap.V, Sec.2

part of the Monies, etc. to be delivered to shareholders of the Stock Company Absorbed in Absorption-type Merger or the Wholly Owned Subsidiary Company in Share Exchange, to partners of the Membership Company Absorbed in Absorption-type Merger or to the Splitting Company in Absorption-type Company Split (hereinafter referred to as "Shareholders, etc. of the Absorbed Company, etc." in this paragraph) are the Parent Company's Shares (meaning the Parent Company's Shares prescribed in paragraph (1) of that Article; hereinafter the same shall apply in this Article) of the Surviving Stock Company, etc., the Surviving Stock Company, etc. may acquire such Parent Company's Shares in a number not exceeding the total number of such Parent Company's Shares to be delivered to the Shareholders, etc. of the Absorbed Company, etc. at the time of the Absorption-type Merger, etc.
(2) Notwithstanding the provisions of Article 135(3), the Surviving Stock Company, etc. set forth in the preceding paragraph may hold the Parent Company's Shares of the Surviving Stock Company, etc. until the Effective Day; provided, however, that this shall not apply when the Absorption-type Merger, etc. is cancelled.

(Keeping and Inspection, etc. of Documents, etc. Concerning an Absorption-type Merger, etc.)
Article 801　(1) The Stock Company Surviving Absorption-type Merger shall, without delay after the Effective Day, prepare documents or Electromagnetic Records that state or record the rights and obligations that the Stock Company Surviving Absorption-type Merger succeeded to by transfer from the Company Absorbed in Absorption-type Merger through the Absorption-type Merger and any other matters prescribed by the applicable Ordinance of the Ministry of Justice as those concerning an Absorption-type Merger.
(2) The Succeeding Stock Company in Absorption-type Company Split (limited to the Succeeding Stock Company in Absorption-type Company Split where the Limited Liability Company effects the Absorption-type Company Split) shall, without delay after the Effective Day, prepare, jointly with the Splitting Limited Liability Company in Absorption-type Company Split, documents or Electromagnetic Records that state or record the rights and obligations that the Succeeding Stock Company in Absorption-type Company Split succeeded to by transfer from the Splitting Limited Liability Company in Absorption-type Company Split through the Absorption-type Company Split and any other matters prescribed by the applicable Ordinance of the Ministry of Justice as those concerning an Absorption-type Company Split.
(3) Each of the Surviving Stock Companies, etc. listed in the following items shall, for a period of six months from the Effective Day, keep what are specified respectively in those items at its head office:
　(i) Stock Company Surviving Absorption-type Merger: documents or Electromagnetic Records set forth in paragraph (1);
　(ii) Succeeding Stock Company in Absorption-type Company Split: documents or Electromagnetic Records set forth in the preceding paragraph or Article 791(1)(i); and
　(iii) Wholly Owning Parent Stock Company in Share Exchange: documents or Electromagnetic Records set forth in Article 791(1)(ii).
(4) Shareholders and creditors of the Stock Company Surviving Absorption-type Merger may make the following requests to said Stock Company Surviving Absorption-type Merger at any time during its business hours; provided, however, that the fees designated by said Stock Company Surviving Absorption-type Merger are required to be paid in order to make the requests set forth in item (ii) or item (iv):
　(i) requests for inspection of the documents set forth in item (i) of the preceding paragraph;

(ii) requests for delivery of a transcript or extract of the documents set forth in item (i) of the preceding paragraph;
(iii) requests for inspection of anything that indicates the matters recorded in the Electromagnetic Records set forth in item (i) of the preceding paragraph in a manner prescribed by the applicable Ordinance of the Ministry of Justice; and
(iv) requests that the matters recorded in the Electromagnetic Records set forth in item (i) of the preceding paragraph be provided by the Electromagnetic Method designated by the Stock Company Surviving Absorption-type Merger, or requests for the delivery of any document that states such matters.
(5) The provisions of the preceding paragraph shall apply mutatis mutandis to the Succeeding Stock Company in Absorption-type Company Split. In such cases, the phrase "shareholders and creditors" in that paragraph shall be deemed to be replaced with "shareholders, creditors and any other interested parties," and the term "item (i) of the preceding paragraph" in the items of that paragraph shall be deemed to be replaced with "item (ii) of the preceding paragraph."
(6) The provisions of paragraph (4) shall apply mutatis mutandis to the Wholly Owning Parent Stock Company in Share Exchange. In such cases, the phrase "shareholders and creditors" in that paragraph shall be deemed to be replaced with "shareholders and creditors (or, in cases where Monies, etc. to be delivered to shareholders of the Wholly Owned Subsidiary Company in Share Exchange are limited to shares of the Wholly Owning Parent Stock Company in Share Exchange or those prescribed by the applicable Ordinance of the Ministry of Justice as being equivalent thereto (excluding the case prescribed in Article 768(1)(iv)(c)), shareholders of the Wholly Owning Parent Stock Company in Share Exchange)," and the term "item (i) of the preceding paragraph" in the items of that paragraph shall be deemed to be replaced with "item (iii) of the preceding paragraph."

Division 2 Procedures for a Membership Company

Article 802 (1) A Membership Company conducting any one of the acts listed in the following items (hereinafter referred to as the "Surviving Membership Company, etc." in this Article) shall, in the cases specified respectively in those items, obtain the consent of all partners of the Surviving Membership Company, etc. with regard to the Absorption-type Merger Agreement, etc. by the day immediately preceding the Effective Day; provided, however, that this shall not apply in cases where it is otherwise provided for in the articles of incorporation:
(i) Absorption-type Merger (limited to cases where the Membership Company shall survive in the Absorption-type Merger): the cases prescribed in Article 751(1)(ii);
(ii) succession of all or part of the rights and obligations held by another Company in connection with its business through an Absorption-type Company Split: the cases prescribed in Article 760(iv); or
(iii) acquisition of all of the Issued Shares of a Stock Company through a Share Exchange: the cases prescribed in Article 770(1)(ii).
(2) The provisions of Article 799 (excluding paragraph (2)(iii)) and Article 800 shall apply mutatis mutandis to a Surviving Membership Company, etc. In such cases, the term "shares of the Wholly Owning Parent Stock Company in Share Exchange" in Article 799(1)(iii) shall be deemed to be replaced with "equity interests of the Wholly Owning Parent Limited Liability Company in Share Exchange," and the phrase "thereto, or in the cases prescribed in Article 768(1)(iv)" in that item shall be deemed to be replaced with "thereto."

Art.803　　　Ⅰ Companies Act, Part Ⅴ, Chap.Ⅴ, Sec.3

Section 3　Procedures of a Consolidation-type Merger, etc.

Subsection 1　Procedures for Companies Consolidated through Consolidation-type Merger, Splitting Company(ies) in Incorporation-type Company Split or the Wholly Owned Subsidiary Company in Share Transfer

Division 1　Procedures for a Stock Company

(Keeping and Inspection, etc. of Documents, etc. Concerning a Consolidation-type Merger Agreement, etc.)

Article 803　(1) Each of the Stock Companies listed in the following items (hereinafter referred to as a "Consolidated Stock Company, etc." in this Division) shall, from the day on which the Consolidation-type Merger Agreement, etc. began to be kept until the day on which six months have elapsed from the day of formation of the Company Incorporated through Consolidation-type Merger, the Company Incorporated through Incorporation-type Company Split, or the Wholly Owning Parent Company Incorporated through Share Transfer (hereinafter referred to as an "Incorporated Company" in this Division) (or, for a Stock Company(ies) Consolidated through Consolidation-type Merger, the day of formation of the Company Incorporated through Consolidation-type Merger), keep documents or Electromagnetic Records that state or record the contents of what are specified respectively in those items (hereinafter referred to as the "Consolidation-type Merger Agreement, etc." in this Section) and other matters prescribed by the applicable Ordinance of the Ministry of Justice at its head office:

(i) Stock Company(ies) Consolidated through Consolidation-type Merger: the Consolidation-type Merger agreement;

(ii) Splitting Stock Company(ies) in Incorporation-type Company Split: the Incorporation-type Company Split plan; and

(iii) Wholly Owned Subsidiary Company in Share Transfer: the Share Transfer plan.

(2) The "day on which the Consolidation-type Merger Agreement, etc. began to be kept" prescribed in the preceding paragraph means the earliest of the following days:

(i) if the Consolidation-type Merger Agreement, etc. is required to be approved by a resolution of a shareholders meeting (including a Class Meeting), the day two weeks prior to the day of the shareholders meeting (or, in the cases prescribed in paragraph (1) of Article 319, the day when the proposal under that paragraph is submitted);

(ii) if there are shareholders who are to receive the notice under the provisions of paragraph (3) of Article 806, the day of the notice under the provisions of that paragraph or the day of the public notice under paragraph (4) of that Article, whichever is earlier;

(iii) if there are holders of Share Options who are to receive the notice under the provisions of paragraph (3) of Article 808, the day of the notice under the provisions of that paragraph or the day of the public notice under paragraph (4) of that Article, whichever is earlier;

(iv) if the procedures under the provisions of Article 810 are required to be carried out, the day of the public notice under the provisions of paragraph (2) of that Article or the day of the notice under the provisions of that paragraph, whichever is earlier; or

(v) in cases other than those prescribed in the preceding items, the day on which two weeks have elapsed from the day of preparation of the Incorporation-type Company Split plan.

(3) Shareholders and creditors of a Consolidated Stock Company, etc. (or, in the case of a Wholly Owned Subsidiary Company in Share Transfer, shareholders and holders of Share Options) may make the following requests to said Consolidated Stock Company, etc. at any time during its business hours provided, however, that the fees designated by said Consolidated Stock Company, etc. are required to be paid in order to make the requests set forth in item (ii) or item (iv):
(i) requests for inspection of the documents set forth in paragraph (1);
(ii) requests for delivery of a transcript or extract of the documents set forth in paragraph (1);
(iii) requests for inspection of anything that indicates the matters recorded in the Electromagnetic Records set forth in paragraph (1) in a manner prescribed by the applicable Ordinance of the Ministry of Justice; and
(iv) requests that the matters recorded in the Electromagnetic Records set forth in paragraph (1) be provided by the Electromagnetic Method designated by the Consolidated Stock Company, etc., or requests for the delivery of any document that states such matters.

(Approval, etc. of the Consolidation-type Merger Agreement, etc.)
Article 804 (1) A Consolidated Stock Company, etc. shall obtain the approval of the Consolidation-type Merger Agreement, etc. by a resolution of a shareholders meeting.
(2) Notwithstanding the provisions of the preceding paragraph, in the cases where the Company Incorporated through Consolidation-type Merger is a Membership Company, consent of all shareholders of the Stock Company(ies) Consolidated through Consolidation-type Merger shall be obtained with regard to the Consolidation-type Merger agreement.
(3) In the cases where the Stock Company(ies) Consolidated through Consolidation-type Merger or the Wholly Owned Subsidiary Company in Share Transfer is a Company with Classes of Shares, if all or part of the shares, etc. of the Stock Company Incorporated through Consolidation-type Merger or the Wholly Owning Parent Stock Company Incorporated through Share Transfer to be delivered to shareholders of the Stock Company(ies) Consolidated through Consolidation-type Merger or the Wholly Owned Subsidiary Company in Share Transfer are Shares with a Restriction on Transfer, etc., the Consolidation-type Merger or the Share Transfer shall not become effective without a resolution of a Class Meeting constituted by Class Shareholders of the class of shares subject to the allotment of the Shares with a Restriction on Transfer, etc. (excluding Shares with a Restriction on Transfer) (in cases where there are two or more classes of shares relating to such Class Shareholders, the respective Class Meetings constituted by Class Shareholders categorized by the class of such two or more classes of shares); provided, however, that this shall not apply to cases where there is no Class Shareholder able to exercise a voting right at such Class Meeting.
(4) A Consolidated Stock Company, etc. shall notify its Registered Pledgees of Shares (excluding the Registered Pledgees of Shares in the cases prescribed in the following Article) and Registered Pledgees of Share Options concerning the Share Options specified in the items of Article 808(3) that it will effect the Consolidation-type Merger, the Incorporation-type Company Split or the Share Transfer (hereinafter referred to as a "Consolidation-type Merger, etc." in this Section) within two weeks from the day of resolution of the shareholders meeting set forth in paragraph (1) (or, in the cases prescribed in paragraph (2), the day of obtainment of the consent of all shareholders set forth in that paragraph).
(5) A public notice may be substituted for the notice under the provisions of the preceding paragraph.

(Cases Where Approval of the Incorporation-type Company Split Plan Is Not Required)
Article 805 The provisions of paragraph (1) of the preceding Article shall not apply in cases where the sum of the book value of the assets that the Company Incorporated through Incorporation-type Company Split succeeds to through the Incorporation-type Company Split does not exceed one-fifth (or, in cases where a lesser proportion is prescribed in the articles of incorporation of the Splitting Stock Company(ies) in Incorporation-type Company Split, such proportion) of the amount calculated by the method specified by the applicable Ordinance of the Ministry of Justice as the total assets of the Splitting Stock Company(ies) in Incorporation-type Company Split.

(Dissenting Shareholders' Share Purchase Demand)
Article 806 (1) In cases of effecting a Consolidation-type Merger, etc. (excluding the following cases), dissenting shareholders may demand that the Consolidated Stock Company, etc. purchase, at a fair price, the shares held by such shareholders:
(i) in cases prescribed in Article 804(2); and
(ii) in cases prescribed in the preceding Article.
(2) The "dissenting shareholders" provided for in the preceding paragraph shall mean the shareholders provided for in the following items:
(i) shareholders who gave notice to such Consolidated Stock Company, etc. to the effect that they dissented from such Consolidation-type Merger, etc. prior to the shareholders meeting set forth in Article 804(1) (in cases where a resolution of a Class Meeting is required to effect the Consolidation-type Merger, etc., including such Class Meeting) and who dissented from such Consolidation-type Merger, etc. at such shareholders meeting (limited to those who can exercise voting rights at such shareholders meeting); and
(ii) shareholders who are unable to exercise voting rights at such shareholders meeting.
(3) A Consolidated Stock Company, etc. shall notify its shareholders that it will effect a Consolidation-type Merger, etc. and the trade names and domiciles of the Companies Consolidated through Consolidation-type Merger, the Splitting Company(ies) in Incorporation-type Company Split or the Wholly Owned Subsidiary Company in Share Transfer (hereinafter referred to as the "Consolidated Company, etc." in this Section) and the Incorporated Company, within two weeks from the day of resolution of the shareholders meeting set forth in Article 804(1); provided, however, that this shall not apply in the cases listed in the items of paragraph (1).
(4) A public notice may be substituted for the notice under the provisions of the preceding paragraph.
(5) Demands under the provisions of paragraph (1) (hereinafter referred to as a "Share Purchase Demand" in this Division) shall be made, within twenty days from the day of the notice under the provisions of paragraph (3) or the public notice under the preceding paragraph, by disclosing the number of shares relating to such Share Purchase Demand (or, for a Company with Classes of Shares, the classes of the shares and the number of shares for each class).
(6) Shareholders who made Share Purchase Demands may withdraw their Share Purchase Demands only in cases where such shareholders obtain the approval of the Consolidated Stock Company, etc.
(7) If the Consolidation-type Merger, etc. is cancelled, the Share Purchase Demand shall become ineffective.

(Determination, etc. of Price of Shares)

Article 807 (1) In cases where a Share Purchase Demand is made, if an agreement on the determination of the price of the shares is reached between the shareholder and the Consolidated Stock Company, etc. (or, after the day of formation of the Company Incorporated through Consolidation-type Merger in cases of effecting a Consolidation-type Merger, the Company Incorporated through Consolidation-type Merger; hereinafter the same shall apply in this Article), the Consolidated Stock Company, etc. shall make payment within sixty days from the day of formation of the Incorporated Company.

(2) If no agreement on the determination of the price of the shares is reached within thirty days from the day of formation of the Incorporated Company, shareholders or the Consolidated Stock Company, etc. may file a petition to the court for a determination of the price within thirty days after the expiration of that period.

(3) Notwithstanding the provisions of paragraph (6) of the preceding Article, in the cases prescribed in the preceding paragraph, if the petition under that paragraph is not filed within sixty days from the day of formation of the Incorporated Company, shareholders may withdraw their Share Purchase Demands at any time after the expiration of such period.

(4) The Consolidated Stock Company, etc. shall also pay interest on the price determined by the court which shall be calculated at the rate of six percent per annum from and including the day of the expiration of the period referred to in paragraph (1).

(5) The purchase of shares relating to a Share Purchase Demand shall become effective on the day of formation of the Incorporated Company (or, in the case of effecting an Incorporation-type Company Split, at the time of payment of the price of such shares).

(6) If a Company Issuing a Share Certificate receives a Share Purchase Demand with respect to shares for which share certificates are issued, the Company must pay the price of the shares relating to such Share Purchase Demand in exchange for the share certificates.

(Demand for Purchase of Share Options)

Article 808 (1) In cases of carrying out any one of the acts listed in the following items, holders of Share Options of the Consolidated Stock Company, etc. provided for in those items may demand that the Consolidated Stock Company, etc. purchase, at a fair price, the Share Options held by the same:

(i) Consolidation-type Merger: Share Options other than those for which provisions on the matters set forth in Article 753(1)(x) or (xi) meet the conditions set forth in item (viii) of Article 236(1) (limited to those related to (a) of that item);

(ii) Incorporation-type Company Split (limited to cases where the Company Incorporated through Incorporation-type Company Split is a Stock Company): among the following Share Options, Share Options other than those for which provisions on the matters set forth in Article 763(x) or (xi) meet the conditions set forth in item (viii) of Article 236(1) (limited to those related to (c) of that item):

(a) Share Options under Incorporation-type Company Split Plan; and

(b) Share Options other than Share Options under Incorporation-type Company Split Plan and for which there are provisions to the effect that, in the case of effecting an Incorporation-type Company Split, Share Options of the Stock Company Incorporated through Incorporation-type Company Split shall be delivered to holders of such Share Options; or

(iii) Share Exchange: among the following Share Options, Share Options other than those for which provisions on the matters set forth in Article 773(1)(ix) or (x) meet the conditions set forth in item (viii) of Article 236(1) (limited to those related to

Art.808　　　　　　　1 Companies Act, Part V, Chap.V, Sec.3

(e) of that item):
(a) Share Options under Share Transfer Plan; and
(b) Share Options other than Share Options under Share Transfer Plan and for which there are provisions to the effect that, in the case of effecting a Share Transfer, Share Options of the Wholly Owning Parent Company Incorporated through Share Transfer shall be delivered to holders of such Share Options.
(2) If holders of the Share Options attached to Bonds with Share Options intend to make the demand under the preceding paragraph (hereinafter referred to as a "Share Option Purchase Demand" in this Division), they shall also make the demand for the purchase of the Bonds pertaining to Bonds with Share Options; provided, however, that this shall not apply in cases where it is otherwise provided for with respect to the Share Options attached to such Bonds with Share Options.
(3) The Consolidated Stock Company, etc. listed in the following items shall notify holders of Share Options provided for in those items that they will effect a Consolidation-type Merger, etc. and the trade names and domiciles of the Consolidated Company, etc. and the Incorporated Company, within two weeks from the day of resolution of the shareholders meeting set forth in Article 804(1) (or, in the cases prescribed in paragraph (2) of that Article, the day of obtainment of the consent of all shareholders set forth in that paragraph, and in the cases prescribed in Article 805, the day of preparation of the Incorporation-type Company Split plan):
(i) Stock Company(ies) Consolidated through Consolidation-type Merger: all Share Options;
(ii) Splitting Stock Company(ies) in Incorporation-type Company Split in cases where the Company Incorporated through Incorporation-type Company Split is a Stock Company: the following Share Options:
(a) Share Options under Incorporation-type Company Split Plan; and
(b) Share Options other than Share Options under Incorporation-type Company Split Plan and for which there are provisions to the effect that, in the case of effecting an Incorporation-type Company Split, Share Options of the Stock Company Incorporated through Incorporation-type Company Split shall be delivered to holders of such Share Options; and
(iii) Wholly Owned Subsidiary Company in Share Transfer: the following Share Options:
(a) Share Options under Share Transfer Plan; and
(b) Share Options other than Share Options under Share Transfer Plan and for which there are provisions to the effect that, in the case of effecting a Share Transfer, Share Options of the Wholly Owning Parent Company Incorporated through Share Transfer shall be delivered to holders of such Share Options.
(4) A public notice may be substituted for the notice under the provisions of the preceding paragraph.
(5) A Share Option Purchase Demand shall be made, within twenty days from the day of the notice under the provisions of paragraph (3) or the public notice under the preceding paragraph, by disclosing the number of shares relating to such Share Option Purchase Demand.
(6) Holders of Share Options who have made Share Option Purchase Demands may withdraw their Share Option Purchase Demands only in cases where they obtain the approval of the Consolidated Stock Company, etc.
(7) If the Consolidation-type Merger, etc. is cancelled, the Share Option Purchase Demands shall become ineffective.

(Determination, etc. of Price of Share Options)

Article 809 (1) In cases where a Share Option Purchase Demand is made, if an agreement on the determination of the price of the Share Options (in cases where such Share Options are those attached to Bonds with Share Options, if there is a demand for the purchase of Bonds pertaining to such Bonds with Share Options, they shall include such Bonds; hereinafter the same shall apply in this Article) is reached between the holder of Share Options and the Consolidated Stock Company, etc. (after the day of formation of the Company Incorporated through Consolidation-type Merger in cases of effecting a Consolidation-type Merger, the Company Incorporated through Consolidation-type Merger; hereinafter the same shall apply in this Article), the Consolidated Stock Company, etc. shall make payment within sixty days from the day of formation of the Incorporated Company.
(2) If no agreement on the determination of the price of the Share Options is reached within thirty days from the day of formation of the Incorporated Company, holders of Share Options or the Consolidated Stock Company, etc. may file a petition to the court for a determination of the price within thirty days after the expiration of that period.
(3) Notwithstanding the provisions of paragraph (6) of the preceding Article, in the cases prescribed in the preceding paragraph, if the petition under that paragraph is not filed within sixty days from the day of formation of the Incorporated Company, holders of Share Options may withdraw their Share Option Purchase Demands at any time after the expiration of such period.
(4) The Consolidated Stock Company, etc. shall also pay interest on the price determined by the court which shall be calculated at the rate of six percent per annum from and including the day of the expiration of the period referred to in paragraph (1).
(5) The purchase of Share Options relating to the Share Option Purchase Demands shall become effective at the times provided for in the following items for the categories of Share Options set forth respectively in those items:
  (i) Share Options provided for in paragraph (1)(i) of the preceding Article: the day of formation of the Company Incorporated through Consolidation-type Merger;
  (ii) Share Options set forth in paragraph (1)(ii)(a) of the preceding Article: the day of formation of the Company Incorporated through Incorporation-type Company Split;
  (iii) Share Options set forth in paragraph (1)(ii)(b) of the preceding Article: the time of payment of the price of such Share Options;
  (iv) Share Options set forth in paragraph (1)(iii)(a) of the preceding Article: the day of formation of the Wholly Owning Parent Company Incorporated through Share Transfer; and
  (v) Share Options set forth in paragraph (1)(iii)(b) of the preceding Article: the time of payment of the price of such Share Options.
(6) If a Consolidated Stock Company, etc. receives a Share Option Purchase Demand with respect to a Share Option for which a Share Option certificate is issued, it shall pay the price of the Share Option relating to such Share Option Purchase Demand in exchange for the Share Option certificate.
(7) If a Consolidated Stock Company, etc. receives a Share Option Purchase Demand with respect to a Share Option attached to a Bond with a Share Option for which a certificate for a Bond with a Share Option is issued, it shall pay the price of the Share Option relating to such Share Option Purchase Demand in exchange for such certificate for Bond with Share Option.

(Objections of Creditors)
Article 810 (1) In the cases listed in the following items, the creditors provided for in those items may state their objections to the Consolidation-type Merger, etc. to the Consolidated Stock Company, etc.:

(i) in cases of effecting a Consolidation-type Merger: creditors of the Stock Company(ies) Consolidated through Consolidation-type Merger;
(ii) in cases of effecting an Incorporation-type Company Split: creditors of the Splitting Stock Company(ies) in Incorporation-type Company Split who are unable to request the Splitting Stock Company(ies) in Incorporation-type Company Split to perform the obligations (including performance of the guarantee obligations that the Splitting Stock Company(ies) in Incorporation-type Company Split jointly and severally assumes with the Company Incorporated through Incorporation-type Company Split as a guarantor) (or, in the case where there are provisions on the matter set forth in Article 763(xii) or Article 765(1)(viii), creditors of the Splitting Stock Company(ies) in Incorporation-type Company Split); or
(iii) in cases where the Share Options under Share Transfer Plan are Share Options attached to Bonds with Share Options: bondholders pertaining to such Bonds with Share Options.
(2) In cases where all or part of the creditors of the Consolidated Stock Company, etc. are able to state their objection pursuant to the provisions of the preceding paragraph, the Consolidated Stock Company, etc. shall give public notice of the matters listed below in the official gazette and shall give notices separately to each known creditor (limited to one who is able to state an objection pursuant to the provisions of such paragraph), if any; provided, however, that the period under item (iv) may not be less than one month:
(i) a statement that a Consolidation-type Merger, etc. will be effected;
(ii) the trade name and domicile of the other Consolidated Company(ies), etc. and the Incorporated Company;
(iii) the matters prescribed by the applicable Ordinance of the Ministry of Justice as the matters regarding the Financial Statements of the Consolidated Stock Company, etc.; and
(iv) a statement to the effect that creditors may state their objections within a certain period of time.
(3) Notwithstanding the provisions of the preceding paragraph, if the Consolidated Stock Company, etc. gives public notice under that paragraph by the Method of Public Notice listed in item (ii) or item (iii) of paragraph (1) of Article 939 in accordance with the provisions of the articles of incorporation under the provisions of that paragraph in addition to the official gazette, the Consolidated Stock Company, etc. is not required to give separate notices under the provisions of the preceding paragraph (excluding such notices to creditors of the obligations of the Splitting Stock Company(ies) in Incorporation-type Company Split that have arisen due to a tort in the case of effecting an Incorporation-type Company Split).
(4) In cases where creditors do not raise any objections within the period under paragraph (2)(iv), such creditors shall be deemed to have approved the Consolidation-type Merger, etc.
(5) In cases where creditors raise objections within the period under paragraph (2)(iv), the Consolidated Stock Company, etc. shall make payment or provide reasonable security to such creditors, or entrust equivalent property to a Trust Company, etc. for the purpose of having such creditors receive the payment; provided, however, that this shall not apply if there is no risk of harm to such creditors by such Consolidation-type Merger, etc.

(Keeping and Inspection, etc. of Documents, etc. Concerning an Incorporation-type Company Split or Share Transfer)
Article 811 (1) The Splitting Stock Company(ies) in Incorporation-type Company Split

or the Wholly Owned Subsidiary Company in Share Transfer shall, without delay after the day of formation of the Company Incorporated through Incorporation-type Company Split or the Wholly Owning Parent Company Incorporated through Share Transfer, prepare what are provided for in the following items for the categories set forth respectively in those items, jointly with the Company Incorporated through Incorporation-type Company Split or the Wholly Owning Parent Company Incorporated through Share Transfer:

(i) Splitting Stock Company(ies) in Incorporation-type Company Split: documents or Electromagnetic Records that state or record the rights and obligations that the Company Incorporated through Incorporation-type Company Split succeeded to by transfer from the Splitting Stock Company(ies) in Incorporation-type Company Split through the Incorporation-type Company Split and any other matters prescribed by the applicable Ordinance of the Ministry of Justice as those concerning an Incorporation-type Company Split; and

(ii) Wholly Owned Subsidiary Company in Share Transfer: documents or Electromagnetic Records that state or record the number of shares of the Wholly Owned Subsidiary Company in Share Transfer acquired by the Wholly Owning Parent Company Incorporated through Share Transfer and any other matters prescribed by the applicable Ordinance of the Ministry of Justice as those concerning a Share Transfer.

(2) The Splitting Stock Company(ies) in Incorporation-type Company Split or the Wholly Owned Subsidiary Company in Share Transfer shall, for a period of six months from the day of formation of the Company Incorporated through Incorporation-type Company Split or the Wholly Owning Parent Company Incorporated through Share Transfer, keep the documents or Electromagnetic Records set forth in the items of the preceding paragraph at its head office.

(3) Shareholders, creditors and any other interested parties of a Splitting Stock Company(ies) in Incorporation-type Company Split may make the following requests to the Splitting Stock Company(ies) in Incorporation-type Company Split at any time during its business hours; provided, however, that the fees designated by said Splitting Stock Company(ies) in Incorporation-type Company Split are required to be paid in order to make the requests set forth in item (ii) or item (iv):

(i) requests for inspection of the documents set forth in the preceding paragraph

(ii) requests for delivery of a transcript or extract of the documents set forth in the preceding paragraph;

(iii) requests for inspection of anything that indicates the matters recorded in the Electromagnetic Records set forth in the preceding paragraph in a manner prescribed by the applicable Ordinance of the Ministry of Justice; and

(iv) requests that the matters recorded in the Electromagnetic Records set forth in the preceding paragraph be provided by the Electromagnetic Method designated by the Splitting Stock Company(ies) in Incorporation-type Company Split, or requests for the delivery of any document that states such matters.

(4) The provisions of the preceding paragraph shall apply mutatis mutandis to a Wholly Owned Subsidiary Company in Share Transfer. In such cases, the phrase "shareholders, creditors and any other interested parties of a Splitting Stock Company(ies) in Incorporation-type Company Split" shall be deemed to be replaced with "persons who were shareholders or holders of Share Options of the Wholly Owned Subsidiary Company in Share Transfer as of the day of formation of the Wholly Owning Parent Company Incorporated through Share Transfer."

(Special Provisions on Dividends of Surplus, etc.)

Art.812〜814　　　① Companies Act, Part V, Chap.V, Sec.3

Article 812 The provisions of Article 458 and Part II, Chapter V, Section 6 shall not apply to the acts listed below:
(i) acquisition of shares set forth in Article 763(xii)(a) or Article 765(1)(viii)(a); and
(ii) Distribution of dividends of surplus set forth in Article 763(xii)(b) or Article 765(1)(viii)(b).

Division 2 Procedure for a Membership Company

Article 813 (1) A Membership Company conducting any one of the acts below shall obtain the consent of all partners of the Membership Company with regard to the Consolidation-type Merger Agreement, etc.; provided, however, that this shall not apply in cases where it is otherwise provided for in the articles of incorporation:
(i) Consolidation-type Merger; or
(ii) Incorporation-type Company Split (limited to cases where another Company succeeds to all of the rights and obligations held by such Membership Company (limited to a Limited Liability Company) in connection with its business).
(2) The provisions of Article 810 (excluding paragraph (1)(iii) and paragraph (2)(iii)) shall apply mutatis mutandis to a Membership Company(ies) Consolidated through Consolidation-type Merger or a Splitting Company(ies) in Incorporation-type Company Split, which is a Limited Liability Company (hereinafter referred to as the "Splitting Limited Liability Company in Incorporation-type Company Split" in this Section). In such cases, the phrase "Creditors of the Splitting Stock Company(ies) in Incorporation-type Company Split who are unable to request the Splitting Stock Company(ies) in Incorporation-type Company Split to perform the obligations (including performance of the guarantee obligations that the Splitting Stock Company(ies) in Incorporation-type Company Split jointly and severally assumes with the Company Incorporated through Incorporation-type Company Split as a guarantor) (or, in the case where there are provisions on the matter set forth in Article 763(xii) or Article 765(1)(viii), creditors of the Splitting Stock Company(ies) in Incorporation-type Company Split)" in paragraph (1)(ii) of Article 810 shall be deemed to be replaced with "Creditors of the Splitting Stock Company(ies) in Incorporation-type Company Split who are unable to request the Splitting Stock Company(ies) in Incorporation-type Company Split to perform the obligations (including performance of the guarantee obligations that the Splitting Stock Company(ies) in Incorporation-type Company Split jointly and severally assumes with the Company Incorporated through Incorporation-type Company Split as a guarantor)" and the term "Consolidated Stock Company, etc." in paragraph (3) of that Article shall be deemed to be replaced with "Membership Company(ies) Consolidated through Consolidation-type Merger (limited to a Limited Liability Company in the case where the Company Incorporated through Consolidation-type Merger is a Stock Company or a Limited Liability Company) or the Splitting Limited Liability Company in Incorporation-type Company Split."

Subsection 2 Procedures for the Company Incorporated through Consolidation-type Merger, the Company Incorporated through Incorporation-type Company Split and the Wholly Owning Parent Company Incorporated through Share Transfer

Division 1 Procedures for a Stock Company

(Special Provisions on Incorporation of a Stock Company)
Article 814 (1) The provisions of Part II, Chapter I (excluding Article 27 (excluding

items (iv) and (v)), Article 29, Article 31, Article 39, Section 6 and Article 49) shall not apply to incorporation of a Stock Company Incorporated through Consolidation-type Merger, a Stock Company Incorporated through Incorporation-type Company Split or a Wholly Owning Parent Company Incorporated through Share Transfer (hereinafter referred to as an "Incorporated Stock Company" in this Division).

(2) The articles of incorporation of an Incorporated Stock Company shall be prepared by the Consolidated Company, etc.

(Keeping and Inspection, etc. of Documents, etc. Concerning a Consolidation-type Merger Agreement, etc.)

Article 815 (1) The Stock Company Incorporated through Consolidation-type Merger shall, without delay after the day of its formation, prepare documents or Electromagnetic Records that state or record the rights and obligations that the Stock Company Incorporated through Consolidation-type Merger succeeded to by transfer from the Companies Consolidated through Consolidation-type Merger and any other matters prescribed by the applicable Ordinance of the Ministry of Justice as those concerning a Consolidation-type Merger.

(2) The Stock Company Incorporated through Incorporation-type Company Split (limited to the Stock Company Incorporated through Incorporation-type Company Split where only a Limited Liability Company(ies) effects the Incorporation-type Company Split) shall, without delay after the day of its formation, prepare, jointly with the Splitting Limited Liability Company in Incorporation-type Company Split, documents or Electromagnetic Records that state or record the rights and obligations that the Stock Company Incorporated through Incorporation-type Company Split succeeded to by transfer from the Splitting Limited Liability Company in Incorporation-type Company Split through the Incorporation-type Company Split and any other matters prescribed by the applicable Ordinance of the Ministry of Justice as those concerning an Incorporation-type Company Split.

(3) Each of the Incorporated Stock Companies, etc. listed in the following items shall, for a period of six months from the day of its formation, keep what are specified respectively in those items at its head office:
  (i) Stock Company Incorporated through Consolidation-type Merger: the documents or Electromagnetic Records set forth in paragraph (1) and documents or Electromagnetic Records that state or record the contents of the Consolidation-type Merger agreement and other matters prescribed by the applicable Ordinance of the Ministry of Justice;
  (ii) Stock Company Incorporated through Incorporation-type Company Split: the documents or Electromagnetic Records set forth in the preceding paragraph or Article 811(1)(i); and
  (iii) Wholly Owning Parent Company Incorporated through Share Transfer: the documents or Electromagnetic Records set forth in Article 811(1)(ii).

(4) Shareholders and creditors of the Stock Company Incorporated through Consolidation-type Merger may make the following requests to said Stock Company Incorporated through Consolidation-type Merger at any time during its business hours; provided, however, that the fees designated by said Stock Company Incorporated through Consolidation-type Merger are required to be paid in order to make the requests set forth in item (ii) or item (iv):
  (i) requests for inspection of the documents set forth in item (i) of the preceding paragraph;
  (ii) requests for delivery of a transcript or extract of the documents set forth in item (i) of the preceding paragraph;

(iii) requests for inspection of anything that indicates the matters recorded in the Electromagnetic Records set forth in item (i) of the preceding paragraph in a manner prescribed by the applicable Ordinance of the Ministry of Justice; and
(iv) requests that the matters recorded in the Electromagnetic Records set forth in item (i) of the preceding paragraph be provided by the Electromagnetic Method designated by the Stock Company Incorporated through Consolidation-type Merger, or requests for the delivery of any document that states such matters.
(5) The provisions of the preceding paragraph shall apply mutatis mutandis to the Stock Company Incorporated through Incorporation-type Company Split. In such cases, the phrase "shareholders and creditors" in that paragraph shall be deemed to be replaced with "shareholders, creditors and any other interested parties," and the term "item (i) of the preceding paragraph" in the items of the items of that paragraph shall be deemed to be replaced with "item (ii) of the preceding paragraph."
(6) The provisions of paragraph (4) shall apply mutatis mutandis to the Wholly Owning Parent Company Incorporated through Share Transfer. In such cases, the phrase "shareholders and creditors" in that paragraph shall be deemed to be replaced with "shareholders and holders of Share Options," and the term "item (i) of the preceding paragraph" in the items of that paragraph shall be deemed to be replaced with "item (iii) of the preceding paragraph."

Division 2 Procedures for a Membership Company

(Special Provisions on Incorporation of a Membership Company)
Article 816 (1) The provisions of Article 575 and Article 578 shall not apply to incorporation of a Membership Company Incorporated through Consolidation-type Merger or a Membership Company Incorporated through Incorporation-type Company Split (referred to as an "Incorporated Membership Company" in the following paragraph).
(2) The articles of incorporation of an Incorporated Membership Company shall be prepared by the Consolidated Company, etc.

Part VI Foreign Company

(Foreign Company's Representatives in Japan)
Article 817 (1) When a Foreign Company intends to carry out transactions continuously in Japan, it shall specify its representatives in Japan. In such cases, one or more of such representatives in Japan shall be those whose domiciles are in Japan.
(2) A Foreign Company's representatives in Japan shall have the authority to do any and all judicial and extra-judicial acts on behalf of such foreign company in connection with its business.
(3) No limitation on the authority under the preceding paragraph may be asserted against a third party without knowledge of such limitation.
(4) A Foreign Company shall be liable for damage caused to third parties by its representatives in Japan during the course of the performance of their duties.

(Prohibition, etc. of Continuous Transactions Prior to Registration)
Article 818 (1) A Foreign Company may not carry out transactions continuously in Japan before completing registration of a Foreign Company.
(2) A person who has carried out transactions in violation of the provisions of the preceding paragraph shall be liable, jointly and severally with the Foreign Company, to perform any obligations that have arisen from such transactions to the counterparty.

(Public Notice of What is Equivalent to a Balance Sheet)
Article 819 (1) A Foreign Company (limited to one for which the same kind of Company or the most similar Company in Japan is a Stock Company) that has completed registration of a Foreign Company shall, pursuant to the provisions of the applicable Ordinance of the Ministry of Justice, give public notice in Japan of what is equivalent to a balance sheet without delay after the conclusion of the same kind of procedure as the approval set forth in Article 438(2) or a procedure similar thereto.
(2) Notwithstanding the provisions of the preceding paragraph, with respect to a Foreign Company for which the Method of Public Notice is a method listed in Article 939(1)(i) or (ii), it shall be sufficient to give public notice of a summary of what is equivalent to a balance sheet provided for in the preceding paragraph.
(3) A Foreign Company referred to in the preceding paragraph may, without delay after the conclusion of the procedure set forth in paragraph (1), pursuant to the provisions of the applicable Ordinance of the Ministry of Justice, take measures to make the information contained in what is equivalent to the balance sheet provided for in that paragraph available to the general public continually by the Electromagnetic Method until the day on which five years have elapsed from the day of the conclusion of such procedure. In such cases, the provisions of the preceding two paragraphs shall not apply.
(4) The provisions of the preceding three paragraphs shall not apply to Foreign Companies that shall submit their securities reports to the Prime Minister pursuant to the provisions of Article 24(1) of the Securities and Exchange Act.

(Resignation of Representatives in Japan Whose Domiciles Are in Japan)
Article 820 (1) A Foreign Company that has completed registration of a Foreign Company may, when all of its representatives in Japan (limited to those whose domiciles are in Japan) intend to resign, give public notice to creditors of the Foreign Company to the effect that they are able to state their objections, if any, during a certain period of time and shall give notice separately to each known creditor, if any; provided, however, that such period may not be less than one month.
(2) In cases where creditors raise objections within the period under the preceding paragraph, the Foreign Company set forth in that paragraph shall make payment or provide reasonable security to such creditors, or entrust equivalent property to a Trust Company, etc. for the purpose of having such creditors receive the payment; provided, however, that this shall not apply if there is no risk of harm to such creditors by the resignation set forth in that paragraph.
(3) The resignation set forth in paragraph (1) shall become effective by completing the registration thereof after the completion of the procedures set forth in the preceding two paragraphs.

(Pseudo-Foreign Company)
Article 821 (1) A Foreign Company that has its head office in Japan or whose main purpose is to conduct business in Japan may not carry out transactions continuously in Japan.
(2) A person who has carried out transactions in violation of the provisions of the preceding paragraph shall be liable, jointly and severally with the Foreign Company, to perform obligations that have arisen from such transactions to the counterparty.

(Liquidation of a Foreign Company's Property in Japan)
Article 822 (1) The court may, in response to a petition by interested persons or ex offi-

cio, order commencement of the liquidation of all of a Foreign Company's property in Japan in the cases listed below:
(i) in cases where the Foreign Company receives the order under the provisions of Article 827(1); or
(ii) in cases where the Foreign Company stops carrying out transactions continuously in Japan.
(2) In the cases set forth in the preceding paragraph, the court shall appoint the liquidator.
(3) The provisions of Article 476, the provisions of Part II, Chapter IX, Section 1, Subsection 2, the provisions of Article 492, the provisions of Subsection 4 of that Section, the provisions of Article 508, and the provisions of Section 2 of that Chapter (excluding Article 510, Article 511 and Article 514) shall apply mutatis mutandis to the liquidation of a Foreign Company's property in Japan under the provisions of paragraph (1), excluding those that are not applicable by their nature.
(4) The provisions of Article 820 shall not apply in cases where a Foreign Company is ordered to commence the liquidation set forth in paragraph (1) and where all of the Foreign Company's representatives in Japan (limited to those whose domiciles are in Japan) intend to resign.

(Application of Other Acts)
Article 823 With regard to application of other Acts, a Foreign Company shall be deemed to be the same kind of Company or the most similar kind of Company in Japan; provided, however, that this shall not apply when it is otherwise provided by other Acts.

Part VII Miscellaneous Provisions

Chapter I Dissolution Order, etc. for a Company

Section 1 Dissolution Order for a Company

(Dissolution Order for a Company)
Article 824 (1) In the cases listed below, if the court finds that the existence of a Company is unallowable for securing public interests, it may, in response to a petition by the Minister of Justice, shareholders, partners, creditors or any other interested parties, order the dissolution of the Company:
(i) when the Company is incorporated for an illegal purpose;
(ii) when the Company fails to commence its business within one year from the day of its formation or suspends its business continuously for one year or more, without justifiable grounds; or
(iii) in cases where an executive director, an executive officer or a partner who executes the business has committed an act that goes beyond or abuses the authority of the Company prescribed by laws and regulations or the articles of incorporation or that violates criminal laws and regulations, if such person commits such act continuously or repeatedly despite receiving a written warning from the Minister of Justice.
(2) When a shareholder, a partner, a creditor or any other interested party files the petition set forth in the preceding paragraph, the court may, in response to a petition by the Company, order the person who filed the petition set forth in that paragraph to provide reasonable security.
(3) When a Company intends to file the petition under the provisions of the preceding paragraph, it shall make a prima facie showing that the petition set forth in paragraph (1) has been filed in bad faith.

(4) The provisions of Article 75(5) and (7) and Articles 76 to 80 of the Code of Civil Procedure (Act No. 109 of 1996) shall apply mutatis mutandis to the security to be provided with respect to the petition set forth in paragraph (1) pursuant to the provisions of paragraph (2).

(Temporary Restraining Order Concerning Property of a Company)
Article 825 (1) In cases where the petition set forth in paragraph (1) of the preceding Article is filed, the court may, in response to a petition by the Minister of Justice or shareholders, partners, creditors or any other interested parties or ex officio, issue a disposition ordering administration by an administrator (referred to as an "Administration Order" in the following paragraph) or any other necessary temporary restraining order with respect to the property of the Company until a ruling is handed down on the petition set forth in that paragraph.
(2) When the court issues an Administration Order, it shall appoint an administrator in such Administration Order.
(3) The court may, in response to a petition by the Minister of Justice or shareholders, partners, creditors or any other interested parties or ex officio, dismiss the administrator set forth in the preceding paragraph.
(4) When the court appoints the administrator set forth in paragraph (2), it may specify the amount of remuneration to be paid by the Company to such administrator.
(5) The administrator set forth in paragraph (2) shall be supervised by the court.
(6) The court may order the administrator set forth in paragraph (2) to report the status of the property of the Company and to account for the administration thereof.
(7) The provisions of Article 644, Article 646, Article 647 and Article 650 of the Civil Code shall apply mutatis mutandis to the administrator set forth in paragraph (2). In such cases, the term "mandator" in Article 646, Article 647 and Article 650 of that Act shall be deemed to be replaced with "Company."

(Duty of a Government Agency, etc. to Give Notice to the Minister of Justice)
Article 826 If a court or any other government agency, a public prosecutor or an official comes to know in the course of their duties that there are grounds for filing the petition set forth in paragraph (1) of Article 824 or giving the warning set forth in item (iii) of that paragraph, such entity or person shall give notice to that effect to the Minister of Justice.

Section 2 Order of Prohibition of Continuous Transactions or Closure of a Business Office of a Foreign Company

Article 827 (1) In the cases listed below, the court may, in response to a petition by the Minister of Justice, shareholders, partners, creditors or any other interested parties, order the prohibition of a Foreign Company to carry out transactions continuously in Japan or the closure of its business office established in Japan:
(i) when the Foreign Company conducts business for an illegal purpose;
(ii) when the Foreign Company fails to commence its business within one year from the day of registration of the Foreign Company or suspends its business continuously for one year or more, without justifiable grounds;
(iii) when the Foreign Company stops payment without justifiable grounds; or
(iv) in cases where the Foreign Company's representative in Japan or any other person who executes its business has committed an act that goes beyond or abuses the authority of the Foreign Company prescribed by laws and regulations or that violates criminal laws and regulations, if such person continuously or repeatedly com-

Art.828　　　Ⅰ Companies Act, Part VII, Chap.II, Sec.1

mits such act despite receiving a written warning from the Minister of Justice.
(2) The provisions of Article 824, paragraphs (2) to (4), and the preceding two Articles shall apply mutatis mutandis to the cases set forth in the preceding paragraph. In such cases, the term "preceding paragraph" in Article 824(2), the term "paragraph (1)" in paragraph (3) and paragraph (4) of that Article, and the term "paragraph (1) of the preceding Article" in Article 825(1) shall be deemed to be replaced with "Article 827(1)," the term "Article 824(1)" in the preceding Article shall be deemed to be replaced with "paragraph (1) of the following Article" and the term "item (iii) of that paragraph" in that Article shall be deemed to be replaced with "item (iv) of that paragraph."

Chapter II Suits

Section 1 Actions Concerning the Organization of a Company

(Actions Seeking Invalidation of Acts Concerning the Organization of a Company)
Article 828 (1) Invalidation of the acts listed in the following items may only be asserted by filing an action during the periods specified respectively in those items:
(i) incorporation of a Company: within two years from the day of formation of the Company;
(ii) share issue after the formation of a Stock Company: within six months from the day on which the share issue became effective (or, for a Stock Company which is not a Public Company, within one year from the day on which the share issue became effective);
(iii) disposition of Treasury Shares: within six months from the day on which the disposition of Treasury Shares became effective (or, for a Stock Company which is not a Public Company, within one year from the day on which the disposition of Treasury Shares became effective);
(iv) Share Option (in cases where the Share Options are those attached to Bonds with Share Options, it shall include the Bonds pertaining to Bonds with Share Options; hereinafter the same shall apply in this Chapter) issue: within six months from the day on which the Share Option issue became effective (or, for a Stock Company which is not a Public Company, within one year from the day on which the Share Option issue became effective);
(v) reduction in the amount of stated capital of a Stock Company: within six months from the day on which the reduction in the amount of stated capital became effective;
(vi) Entity Conversion of a Company: within six months from the day on which the Entity Conversion became effective;
(vii) Absorption-type Merger of a Company: within six months from the day on which the Absorption-type Merger became effective;
(viii) Consolidation-type Merger of a Company: within six months from the day on which the Consolidation-type Merger became effective;
(ix) Absorption-type Company Split of a Company: within six months from the day on which the Absorption-type Company Split became effective;
(x) Incorporation-type Company Split: within six months from the day on which the Incorporation-type Company Split became effective;
(xi) Share Exchange of a Stock Company: within six months from the day on which the Share Exchange became effective; and
(xii) Share Transfer of a Stock Company: within six months from the day on which the Share Transfer became effective.

[2009年4月1日訳]　　1 Companies Act, Part VII, Chap.II, Sec.1　　Art.828

(2) An action seeking invalidation of the acts listed in the following items may be filed only by the persons specified respectively in those items:
(i) the act set forth in item (i) of the preceding paragraph: a Shareholder, etc. (meaning a shareholder, director or liquidator (or, for a Company with Company Auditors, it means a shareholder, director, company auditor or liquidator, and for a Company with Committees, it means a shareholder, director, executive officer or liquidator); hereinafter the same shall apply in this Section) of the incorporated Stock Company or a Partner, etc. (meaning a partner or liquidator; hereinafter the same shall apply in this paragraph) of the incorporated Membership Company;
(ii) the act set forth in item (ii) of the preceding paragraph: a Shareholder, etc. of the relevant Stock Company;
(iii) the act set forth in item (iii) of the preceding paragraph: a Shareholder, etc. of the relevant Stock Company;
(iv) the act set forth in item (iv) of the preceding paragraph: a Shareholder, etc. or a holder of Share Options of the relevant Stock Company;
(v) the act set forth in item (v) of the preceding paragraph: a Shareholder, etc., the trustee in bankruptcy or a creditor, who did not give approval to the reduction in the amount of stated capital, of the relevant Stock Company;
(vi) the act set forth in item (vi) of the preceding paragraph: a person who was a Shareholder, etc. or a Partner, etc. of the Company effecting the Entity Conversion as of the day on which such act became effective or a Shareholder, etc., a Partner, etc., the trustee in bankruptcy or a creditor, who did not give approval to the Entity Conversion, of the Company after the Entity Conversion;
(vii) the act set forth in item (vii) of the preceding paragraph: a person who was a Shareholder, etc. or a Partner, etc. of the Company effecting the Absorption-type Merger as of the day on which such act became effective or a Shareholder, etc., a Partner, etc., the trustee in bankruptcy or a creditor, who did not give approval to the Absorption-type Merger, of the Company Surviving Absorption-type Merger;
(viii) the act set forth in item (viii) of the preceding paragraph: a person who was a Shareholder, etc. or a Partner, etc. of the Company effecting the Consolidation-type Merger as of the day on which such act became effective or a Shareholder, etc., a Partner, etc., the trustee in bankruptcy or a creditor, who did not give approval to the Consolidation-type Merger, of the Company incorporated through the Consolidation-type Merger;
(ix) the act set forth in item (ix) of the preceding paragraph: a person who was a Shareholder, etc. or a Partner, etc. of the Company that has concluded the Absorption-type Company Split agreement as of the day on which such act became effective or a Shareholder, etc., a Partner, etc., the trustee in bankruptcy or a creditor, who did not give approval to the Absorption-type Company Split, of the Company that has concluded the Absorption-type Company Split agreement;
(x) the act set forth in item (x) of the preceding paragraph: a person who was a Shareholder, etc. or a Partner, etc. of the Company effecting the Incorporation-type Company Split as of the day on which such act became effective or a Shareholder, etc., a Partner, etc., the trustee in bankruptcy or a creditor, who did not give approval to the Incorporation-type Company Split, of the Company effecting the Incorporation-type Company Split or the Company incorporated through the Incorporation-type Company Split;
(xi) the act set forth in item (xi) of the preceding paragraph: a person who was a Shareholder, etc. or a Partner, etc. of the Company that has concluded the Share Exchange agreement as of the day on which such act became effective or a Shareholder, etc., a Partner, etc., the trustee in bankruptcy or a creditor, who did not give

approval to the Share Exchange, of the Company that has concluded the Share Exchange agreement; and
(xii) the act set forth in item (xii) of the preceding paragraph: a person who was a Shareholder, etc. or a Partner, etc. of the Company that has concluded the Share Exchange agreement as of the day on which such act became effective or a Shareholder, etc., a Partner, etc., the trustee in bankruptcy or a creditor, who did not give approval to the Share Exchange, of the Company that has concluded the Share Exchange agreement.

(Action for Declaratory Judgment of Absence of a New Share Issue, etc.)
Article 829 With regard to the acts below, confirmation of the absence of the acts may be claimed by filing an action:
(i) share issue after the formation of a Stock Company;
(ii) disposition of Treasury Shares; and
(iii) Share Option issue.

(Action for Declaratory Judgment of Absence or Invalidation of a Resolution of a Shareholders Meeting, etc.)
Article 830 (1) With regard to a resolution of a shareholders meeting, Class Meeting, Organizational Meeting or Class Organizational Meeting (hereinafter referred to as a "Shareholders Meeting, etc." in this Section and Article 937(1)(i)(g)), confirmation of the absence of the resolution may be claimed by filing an action.
(2) With regard to a resolution of a Shareholders Meeting, etc., confirmation of invalidation of the resolution may be claimed by filing an action based on the reason that the contents of the resolution violate laws and regulations.

(Action Seeking Revocation of a Resolution of a Shareholders Meeting, etc.)
Article 831 (1) In the cases listed in the following items, a Shareholder, etc. (or, in cases where the Shareholders Meeting, etc. set forth respectively in each such item is an Organizational Meeting or a Class Organizational Meetings, a Shareholder, etc., a Shareholder at Incorporation, a Director at Incorporation or a Company Auditor at Incorporation) may, within three months from the day of resolution of the Shareholders Meeting, etc., claim revocation of the resolution by filing an action. The same shall apply to a person who becomes a director, company auditor or liquidator (or, in cases where such resolution is a resolution of a shareholders meeting or Class Meeting, it shall include a person who has the rights and obligations of a director, company auditor or liquidator pursuant to the provisions of Article 346(1) (including cases where it is applied mutatis mutandis pursuant to Article 479(4)), and in cases where such resolution is a resolution of an Organizational Meeting or Class Organizational Meeting, it shall include a Director at Incorporation or a Company Auditor at Incorporation) by rescission of such resolution:
(i) when the calling procedures or the method of resolution of the Shareholders Meeting, etc. violate laws and regulations or the articles of incorporation or are grossly improper;
(ii) when the contents of the resolution of the Shareholders Meeting, etc. violate the articles of incorporation; or
(iii) when a grossly improper resolution is made as a result of a person having a special interest in the resolution of the Shareholders Meeting, etc. exercising a voting right.
(2) In cases where an action set forth in the preceding paragraph is filed, even if the calling procedures or the method of resolution of the Shareholders Meeting, etc. are in vi-

olation of laws and regulations or the articles of incorporation, the court may dismiss the claim prescribed in that paragraph if it finds that the facts in violation are not serious and will not affect the resolution.

(Action Seeking Rescission of the Incorporation of a Membership Company)
Article 832 In the cases listed in the following items, the persons specified respectively in those items may claim rescission of the incorporation of the Membership Company within two years from the day of formation of the Membership Company:
(i) when a partner is able to rescind such partner's manifestation of intention relating to the incorporation pursuant to the provisions of the Civil Code or any other acts: such partner; or
(ii) when a partner incorporates a Membership Company having the knowledge that it will be detrimental to its creditor: such creditor.

(Action Seeking Dissolution of a Company)
Article 833 (1) In the cases listed below, if there are unavoidable circumstances, a shareholder having not less than one-tenths (or, in cases where a lesser proportion is prescribed in the articles of incorporation, such proportion) of the voting rights of all shareholders (excluding shareholders who are unable to exercise voting rights on all matters which may be resolved at the shareholders meeting) or a shareholder having not less than one-tenth (or, in cases where a lesser proportion is prescribed in the articles of incorporation, such proportion) of the Issued Shares (excluding Treasury Shares) may claim dissolution of the Stock Company by filing an action:
(i) when a Stock Company faces an extreme difficulty in executing business and the Stock Company suffers or is likely to suffer irrepara.le harm; or
(ii) when the management or disposition of property of a Stock Company is extremely unreasonable and puts the existence of the Stock Company at risk.
(2) In cases where there are unavoidable circumstances, partners of a Membership Company may claim dissolution of the Membership Company by filing an action.

(Defendant)
Article 834 With regard to the actions listed in the following items (hereinafter collectively referred to as an "Action Concerning Organization of Company" in this Section), the persons specified respectively in those items shall be the defendant:
(i) an action seeking invalidation of the incorporation of a Company: the incorporated Company;
(ii) an action seeking invalidation of a share issue after the formation of a Stock Company (referred to as an "Action Seeking Invalidation of New Share Issue" in Article 840(1)): The Stock Company that has issued the shares;
(iii) an action seeking invalidation of a disposition of Treasury Shares: the Stock Company that has disposed of the Treasury Shares;
(iv) an action seeking invalidation of a Share Option issue: the Stock Company that has issued the Share Options;
(v) an action seeking invalidation of a reduction in the amount of stated capital of a Stock Company: the relevant Stock Company;
(vi) an action seeking invalidation of an Entity Conversion of a Company: the Company after the Entity Conversion;
(vii) an action seeking invalidation of an Absorption-type Merger of a Company: the Company surviving the Absorption-type Merger;
(viii) an action seeking invalidation of a Consolidation-type Merger of a Company: the Company incorporated through the Consolidation-type Merger;

Art.835〜836　　Ⅰ Companies Act, Part VII, Chap.II, Sec.1

(ix) an action seeking invalidation of an Absorption-type Company Split of a Company: the Company that has concluded the Absorption-type Company Split agreement;
(x) an action seeking invalidation of an Incorporation-type Company Split: the Company(ies) effecting the Incorporation-type Company Split and the Company incorporated through the Incorporation-type Company Split;
(xi) an action seeking invalidation of a Share Exchange of a Stock Company: the Company that has concluded the Share Exchange agreement;
(xii) an action seeking invalidation of a Share Transfer of a Stock Company: the Stock Company(ies) effecting the Share Transfer and the Stock Company incorporated through the Share Transfer;
(xiii) an action for declaratory judgment of absence of a share issue after the formation of a Stock Company: the Stock Company that has issued the shares;
(xiv) an action for declaratory judgment of absence of a disposition of Treasury Shares: the Stock Company that has disposed of the Treasury Shares;
(xv) an action for declaratory judgment of absence of a Share Option issue: the Stock Company that has issued the Share Options;
(xvi) an action for declaratory judgment of absence of a resolution of a Shareholders Meeting, etc. or invalidation of a resolution of a Shareholders Meeting, etc. based on a reason that the contents of such resolution violate laws and regulations: the relevant Stock Company;
(xvii) an action seeking revocation of a resolution of a Shareholders Meeting, etc.: the relevant Stock Company;
(xviii) an action seeking rescission of the incorporation of a Membership Company under the provisions of Article 832(i): such Membership Company;
(xix) an action seeking rescission of the incorporation of a Membership Company under the provisions of Article 832(ii): such Membership Company and the partner set forth in that item;
(xx) an action seeking dissolution of a Stock Company: the relevant Stock Company; and
(xxi) an action seeking dissolution of a Membership Company: such Membership Company.

(Jurisdiction over and Transfer of an Action)
Article 835　(1) An Action Concerning Organization of Company shall be under the exclusive jurisdiction of the district court having jurisdiction over the location of the head office of the Company which is the defendant.
(2) When two or more district courts have jurisdiction pursuant to the provisions of items (ix) to (xii) of the preceding Article, the actions listed in those items shall be under the jurisdiction of the district court with which an action was filed first.
(3) In cases set forth in the preceding paragraph, a court may, even when the suit pertaining to such action is under its jurisdiction, transfer the suit to another court with jurisdiction, in response to a petition or ex officio, if it finds it necessary for avoiding substantial detriment or delay.

(Order to Provide Security)
Article 836　(1) With regard to an Action Concerning Organization of Company which may be filed by a shareholder or a Shareholder at Incorporation, the court may, in response to a petition by the defendant, order the shareholder or the Shareholder at Incorporation who has filed such Action Concerning Organization of Company to provide reasonable security; provided, however, that this shall not apply when such shareholder is a director, company auditor, executive officer or liquidator or when such Share-

holder at Incorporation is a Director at Incorporation or a Company Auditor at Incorporation.
(2) The provisions of the preceding paragraph shall apply mutatis mutandis to Actions Concerning the Organization of a Company which may be filed by creditors.
(3) In order for a defendant to file the petition set forth in paragraph (1) (including the cases where it is applied mutatis mutandis pursuant to the preceding paragraph), the defendant shall make a prima facie showing that the action filed by the plaintiff is in bad faith

(Mandatory Consolidation of Oral Arguments, etc.)
Article 837 When several suits relating to an Action Concerning Organization of Company for the same claim are pending simultaneously, the oral arguments and judicial decisions thereof shall be made in consolidation.

(Persons Affected by an Upholding Judgment)
Article 838 A final and binding judgment upholding a claim relating to an Action Concerning Organization of Company shall also be effective against third parties.

(Effects of a Judgment of Invalidation, Revocation or Rescission)
Article 839 When a judgment upholding a claim relating to an Action Concerning Organization of Company (limited to any one of the actions listed in Article 834(i) to (xii), (xviii) and (xix)) becomes final and binding, the act that is held to be invalid or revoked or rescinded by such judgment (in cases where a Company was incorporated by such act, it shall include such incorporation, and in cases where shares or Share Options were delivered at the time of such act, it shall include such shares or Share Options) shall become ineffective from then on.

(Effects of a Judgment of Invalidation of New Share Issue)
Article 840 (1) When a judgment upholding a claim relating to an Action Seeking Invalidation of a New Share Issue becomes final and binding, the relevant Stock Company shall pay, to the shareholders of such shares as of the time such judgment became final and binding, monies equivalent to the amount of payment received from them or the value of the property delivered by them as of the time of the delivery. In such cases, when such Stock Company is a Company Issuing Share Certificates, the Stock Company may request such shareholders to return the old share certificates representing such shares (meaning the share certificates representing the shares that became ineffective pursuant to the provisions of the preceding Article; hereinafter the same shall apply in this Section) in exchange for the payment of such monies.
(2) When the amount of the monies set forth in the preceding paragraph is extremely unreasonable in light of the status of the Company property as of the time the judgment set forth in that paragraph became final and conclusive, the court may, in response to a petition by the Stock Company or shareholders set forth in the first sentence of that paragraph, order an increase or decrease of such amount.
(3) The petition set forth in the preceding paragraph shall be filed within six months from the day the judgment set forth in that paragraph became final and conclusive.
(4) In the cases prescribed in the first sentence of paragraph (1), the pledges on the shares set forth in the first sentence of that paragraph shall be effective with respect to the monies set forth in that paragraph.
(5) In the cases prescribed in the first sentence of paragraph (1), Registered Pledgees of Shares with respect to the pledges set forth in the preceding paragraph may receive the monies set forth in paragraph (1) from the Stock Company set forth in the first

sentence of that paragraph, and appropriate them as payment to satisfy their own claims in priority to other creditors.

(6) If the claims under the preceding paragraph are not yet due and payable, the Registered Pledgees of Share Options may have the Stock Company set forth in the first sentence of paragraph (1) deposit an amount equivalent to the value of the monies provided for in that paragraph. In such cases, the pledges shall be effective with respect to the monies so deposited.

(Effects of a Judgment of Invalidation of Disposition of Treasury Shares)
Article 841 (1) When a judgment upholding a claim relating to an action seeking invalidation of a disposition of Treasury Shares becomes final and binding, the relevant Stock Company shall pay, to shareholders of such Treasury Shares as of the time such judgment became final and binding, monies equivalent to the amount of payment received from them or the value of the property delivered by them as of the time of the delivery. In such cases, when such Stock Company is a Company Issuing Share Certificates, the Stock Company may request such shareholders to return the old share certificates representing such Treasury Shares in exchange for the payment of such monies.

(2) The provisions of paragraphs (2) to (6) of the preceding Article shall apply mutatis mutandis to the cases set forth in the preceding paragraph. In such cases, the term "shares" in paragraph (4) of that Article shall be deemed to be replaced with "Treasury Shares."

(Effects of a Judgment of Invalidation of Share Option Issue)
Article 842 (1) When a judgment upholding a claim relating to an action seeking invalidation of a Share Option issue becomes final and binding, the relevant Stock Company shall pay, to the holders of such Share Options as of the time such judgment became final and binding, monies equivalent to the amount of payment received from them or the value of the property delivered by them as of the time of the delivery. In such cases, when such Stock Company has issued Share Option certificates pertaining to such Share Options (or, in cases where such Share Options are those attached to Bonds with Share Options, certificates of Bonds with Share Options pertaining to such Bonds with Share Options; hereinafter the same shall apply in this paragraph), the Stock Company may request holders of the Share Options to return the Share Option certificates pertaining to the Share Options that became ineffective pursuant to the provisions of Article 839 in exchange for the payment of such monies.

(2) The provisions of paragraphs (2) to (6) of Article 840 shall apply mutatis mutandis to the cases set forth in the preceding paragraph. In such cases, the term "shareholders" in paragraph (2) of that Article shall be deemed to be replaced with "holders of Share Options," the term "shares" in paragraph (4) of that Article shall be deemed to be replaced with "Share Options," and the term "Registered Pledgees of Shares" set forth in paragraphs (5) and (6) of that Article shall be deemed to be replaced with "Registered Pledgees of Share Options."

(Effects of a Judgment of Invalidation of a Merger or Company Split)
Article 843 (1) When a judgment upholding a claim relating to an action seeking invalidation of any one of the acts listed in the following items becomes final and binding, the Company that carried out such act shall be liable jointly and severally to perform the obligations assumed by the Companies specified respectively in those items after the day on which such act became effective:

(i) Absorption-type Merger: the Company surviving the Absorption-type Merger;

(ii) Consolidation-type Merger: the Company incorporated through the Consolidation-type Merger;
(iii) Absorption-type Company Split: the Company succeeding to all or part of the rights and obligations held by the Company effecting the Absorption-type Company Split in connection with its business by transfer from such Company; or
(iv) Incorporation-type Company Split: the Company incorporated through the Incorporation-type Company Split.
(2) In the cases prescribed in the preceding paragraph, the property acquired, after the day on which the acts listed in the items of that paragraph became effective, by the Companies specified respectively in those items shall be co-owned by the Companies that carried out such acts; provided, however, that in cases where the act set forth in item (iv) of that paragraph has been carried out by a single Company, the property acquired by the Company specified in that item shall be owned by the single Company that carried out such act.
(3) In the cases prescribed in paragraph (1) and the main clause of the preceding paragraph, each Company's portion of the obligations to be assumed set forth in paragraph (1) and share of co-ownership of property set forth in the main clause of the preceding paragraph shall be decided through discussion among the Companies.
(4) If no agreement is reached in the discussion set forth in the preceding paragraph with regard to each Company's portion of the obligations to be assumed set forth in paragraph (1) and share of co-ownership of property set forth in the main clause of the preceding paragraph, the court shall come to a decision, in response to a petition by the Companies, by taking into account the amount of property of each Company as of the time the act set forth in any one of the items of paragraph (1) became effective and all other circumstances.

(Effects of a Judgment of Invalidation of a Share Exchange or Share Transfer)
Article 844 (1) In cases where a judgment upholding a claim relating to an action seeking invalidation of a Share Exchange or Share Transfer of a Stock Company has become final and binding, if the Stock Company acquiring all of the Issued Shares (hereinafter referred to as the "Former Wholly Owning Parent Company" in this Article) of the Stock Company effecting the Share Exchange or Share Transfer (hereinafter referred to as the "Former Wholly Owned Subsidiary Company" in this Article) has delivered the shares of the Former Wholly Owning Parent Company (hereinafter referred to as the "Shares of the Former Wholly Owning Parent Company" in this Article) at the time of the Share Exchange or Share Transfer, the Former Wholly Owning Parent Company shall deliver to shareholders pertaining to the Shares of the Former Wholly Owning Parent Company as of the time such judgment became final and conclusive the shares of the Former Wholly Owned Subsidiary Company (hereinafter referred to as the "Shares of the Former Wholly Owned Subsidiary Company" in this Article) that had been held, at the time of the Share Exchange or Share Transfer, by the persons who received delivery of the Shares of the Former Wholly Owning Parent Company. In such cases, when such Former Wholly Owning Parent Company is a Company Issuing Share Certificates, the Former Wholly Owning Parent Company may request such shareholders to return the old share certificates representing such Shares of the Former Wholly Owning Parent Company in exchange for the delivery of such Shares of the Former Wholly Owned Subsidiary Company.
(2) In the cases prescribed in the first sentence of the preceding paragraph, pledges on the Shares of the Former Wholly Owning Parent Company shall be effective with respect to the Shares of the Former Wholly Owned Subsidiary Company.
(3) When the pledgees with respect to the pledges set forth in the preceding paragraph

Art.845〜847　　　Ⅰ Companies Act, Part VII, Chap.II, Sec.2

are Registered Pledgees of Shares, the Former Wholly Owning Parent Company shall, without delay after the judgment set forth in paragraph (1) became final and conclusive, notify the Former Wholly Owned Subsidiary Company of the matters listed in the items of Article 148 regarding such Registered Pledgees of Shares.
(4) The Former Wholly Owned Subsidiary Company that has received the notice under the provisions of the preceding paragraph shall, when it states or records in the shareholder registry the Matters to Be Stated in the Shareholder Registry relating to the shares underlying the pledges of the Registered Pledgees of Shares set forth in that paragraph, immediately state or record in such shareholder registry the matters listed in the items of Article 148 regarding such Registered Pledgees of Shares.
(5) In the cases prescribed in paragraph (3), when the Former Wholly Owned Subsidiary Company set forth in that paragraph is a Company Issuing Share Certificates, the Former Wholly Owning Parent Company shall deliver the share certificates representing the Shares of the Former Wholly Owned Subsidiary Company set forth in paragraph (2) Crestec

(Effects of a Judgment of Invalidation or Rescission of the Incorporation of a Membership Company)
Article 845 In cases where a judgment upholding a claim relating to an action seeking invalidation or rescission of the incorporation of a Membership Company becomes final and binding, if the cause of the invalidation or rescission is attributable only to part of the partners, the Membership Company may continue in existence with the consent of all of the other partners. In such cases, the partners attributable to the cause shall be deemed to have withdrawn.

(Liability for Damages in Cases Where the Plaintiff Is Defeated)
Article 846 In cases where the plaintiffs who filed Actions Concerning the Organization of a Company are defeated, if the plaintiffs were in bad faith or grossly negligent, they shall be jointly and severally liable to compensate the defendant for damages.

Section 2　Action for Pursing the Liability, etc. of a Stock Company

(Action for Pursuing Liability, etc.)
Article 847 (1) A shareholder (excluding a Holder of Shares Less than One Unit who is unable to exercise rights pursuant to the provisions of the articles of incorporation) having the shares consecutively for the preceding six months or more (or, in cases where a shorter period is prescribed in the articles of incorporation, such period or more) may demand the Stock Company, in writing or by any other method prescribed by the applicable Ordinance of the Ministry of Justice, to file an action for pursuing the liability of an incorporator, Director at Incorporation, Company Auditor at Incorporation, Officer, etc. (meaning the Officer, etc. prescribed in Article 423(1); hereinafter the same shall apply in this Article) or liquidator, an action seeking the return of the benefits set forth in Article 120(3) or an action seeking payment under the provisions of Article 212(1) or Article 285(1) (hereinafter referred to as an "Action for Pursuing Liability, etc." in this Section); provided, however, that this shall not apply in cases where the purpose of the Action for Pursuing Liability, etc. is to seek unlawful gains of such shareholder or a third party or to inflict damages on such Stock Company.
(2) With regard to application of the provisions of the preceding paragraph to a Stock Company that is not a Public Company, the phrase "A shareholder (excluding a Holder of Shares Less than One Unit who is unable to exercise rights pursuant to the provisions of the articles of incorporation)" in that paragraph shall be deemed to be replaced

with "A shareholder."
(3) When the Stock Company does not file an Action for Pursuing Liability, etc. within sixty days from the day of the demand under the provisions of paragraph (1), the shareholder who has made such demand may file an Action for Pursuing Liability, etc. on behalf of the Stock Company.
(4) In cases where the Stock Company does not file an Action for Pursuing Liability, etc. within sixty days from the day of the demand under the provisions of paragraph (1), if there is a request by the shareholder who made such demand or the incorporator, Director at Incorporation, Company Auditor at Incorporation, Officer, etc. or liquidator set forth in that paragraph, it shall, without delay, notify the person who made such a request of the reason for not filing an Action for Pursuing Liability, etc. in writing or by any other method prescribed by the applicable Ordinance of the Ministry of Justice.
(5) Notwithstanding the provisions of paragraphs (1) and (3), in cases where the Stock Company is likely to suffer irrepara.le harm through the elapse of the period set forth in those paragraphs, the shareholder set forth in paragraph (1) may immediately file an Action for Pursuing Liability, etc. on behalf of the Stock Company; provided, however, that this shall not apply in the cases prescribed in the proviso to that paragraph.
(6) The Action for Pursuing Liability, etc. set forth in paragraph (3) or the preceding paragraph shall be deemed to be an action relating to a claim which is not a claim based on a property right in calculating the value of the subject-matter of the suit.
(7) When a shareholder files an Action for Pursuing Liability, etc., the court may, in response to a petition by the defendant, order such shareholder to provide reasonable security.
(8) When the defendant intends to file the petition set forth in the preceding paragraph, the defendant shall make a prima facie showing that the Action for Pursuing Liability, etc. has been filed in bad faith.

(Jurisdiction of an Action)
Article 848 An Action for Pursuing Liability, etc. shall be under the exclusive jurisdiction of the district court having jurisdiction over the location of the head office of the Stock Company.

(Intervention)
Article 849 (1) A shareholder or a Stock Company may intervene in a suit relating to an Action for Pursuing Liability, etc. either as a coparty or for assisting either of the parties; provided, however, that this shall not apply when it will unduly delay the court proceedings or impose an excessive administrative burden on the court.
(2) In order for a Stock Company to intervene in a suit relating to an Action for Pursuing Liability, etc. to assist a director (excluding an Audit Committee Member), executive officer, liquidator or a person who was formerly in such a position, it shall obtain the consent of the persons specified in the following items for the categories listed respectively in those items:
　(i) Company with Company Auditors: the company auditor (in cases where there are two or more company auditors, each of such company auditors); or
　(ii) Company with Committees: each Audit Committee Member.
(3) When a shareholder files an Action for Pursuing Liability, etc., the shareholder shall give notice of suit to the Stock Company without delay.
(4) When a Stock Company files an Action for Pursuing Liability, etc. or receives the notice of suit set forth in the preceding paragraph, it shall give public notice to that effect or give notice thereof to its shareholders without delay.
(5) With regard to application of the provisions of the preceding paragraph to a Stock

Company that is not a Public Company, the phrase "give public notice to that effect or give notice thereof to its shareholders" in that paragraph shall be deemed to be replaced with "give notice to that effect to its shareholders."

(Settlement)
Article 850 (1) The provisions of Article 267 of the Code of Civil Procedure shall not apply to the subject-matter of a suit relating to an Action for Pursuing Liability, etc. in cases where a Stock Company is not a party to settlement in such suit; provided, however, that this shall not apply when such Stock Company has given approval.
(2) In the case prescribed in the preceding paragraph, the court shall notify the Stock Company of the contents of the settlement and give the Stock Company notice to the effect that it should state its objection to such settlement, if any, within two weeks.
(3) In cases where the Stock Company does not raise any objections in writing within the period set forth in the preceding paragraph, it shall be deemed to have given the approval for shareholders to effect a settlement with the contents of the notice under the provisions of that paragraph.
(4) The provisions of Article 55, Article 120(5), Article 424 (including the cases where it is applied mutatis mutandis pursuant to Article 486(4)), Article 462(3) (limited to the portion pertaining to the obligations assumed for the portion not exceeding the Distributable Amount prescribed in the proviso to that paragraph), Article 464(2) and Article 465(2) shall not apply in cases of effecting a settlement in a suit relating to an Action for Pursuing Liability, etc.

(Conduct of a Suit of a Person Who is No Longer a Shareholder)
Article 851 (1) Even where a shareholder who has filed an Action for Pursuing Liability, etc. or a shareholder who has intervened in a suit relating to the Action for Pursuing Liability, etc. as a coparty ceases to be a shareholder during the pendency of such suit, such person may conduct the suit in the following cases:
(i) when such person acquires shares of the Wholly Owning Parent Company (meaning a Stock Company holding all of the Issued Shares of a certain Stock Company or a Stock Company prescribed by the applicable Ordinance of the Ministry of Justice as being equivalent thereto; hereinafter the same shall apply in this Article) of the relevant Stock Company through a Share Exchange or Share Transfer of such Stock Company; or
(ii) when such person acquires shares of the Stock Company incorporated through the merger or the Stock Company surviving a merger, or the Wholly Owning Parent Company thereof, through a merger in which the relevant Stock Company is a Company extinguished by the Merger
(2) The provisions of the preceding paragraph shall apply mutatis mutandis when, in the case set forth in item (i) of that paragraph (including the cases where it is applied mutatis mutandis pursuant to this paragraph or the following paragraph), the shareholder set forth in the preceding paragraph ceases to be a shareholder of shares of the Wholly Owning Parent Company of the relevant Stock Company during the pendency of the suit set forth in that paragraph. In such cases, the term "the relevant Stock Company" in that paragraph (including the cases where it is applied mutatis mutandis pursuant to this paragraph or the following paragraph) shall be deemed to be replaced with "the relevant Wholly Owning Parent Company."
(3) The provisions of paragraph (1) shall apply mutatis mutandis when, in the case set forth in item (ii) of that paragraph (including the cases where it is applied mutatis mutandis pursuant to the preceding paragraph or this paragraph), the shareholder set forth in paragraph (1) ceases to be a shareholder of shares of the Stock Company in-

corporated through the merger or the Stock Company surviving a merger, or the Wholly Owning Parent Company thereof, during the pendency of the suit set forth in that paragraph. In such cases, the term "the relevant Stock Company" in that paragraph (including the cases where it is applied mutatis mutandis pursuant to the preceding paragraph and this paragraph) shall be deemed to be replaced with "the Stock Company incorporated through the merger or the Stock Company surviving a merger, or the Wholly Owning Parent Company thereof."

(Demand for Costs, etc.)
Article 852 (1) In cases where a shareholder who has filed an Action for Pursuing Liability, etc. wins the suit (including cases of partially winning the suit), if the shareholder has paid the necessary costs (excluding court costs) or is to pay a fee to an attorney or a legal professional corporation with respect to the suit relating to the Action for Pursuing Liability, etc., the shareholder may demand the relevant Stock Company to pay an amount that is found to be reasonable, not exceeding the amount of such costs or the amount of such fee.
(2) Even in cases where a shareholder who has filed an Action for Pursuing Liability, etc. loses the case, the shareholder shall not be obligated to compensate the relevant Stock Company for the damages arising as a result thereof, except when the shareholder was in bad faith.
(3) The provisions of the preceding two paragraphs shall apply mutatis mutandis to any shareholder who intervened in the suit set forth in paragraph (1) of Article 849 pursuant to the provisions of that paragraph.

(Action for a Retrial)
Article 853 (1) In cases where an Action for Pursuing Liability, etc. has been filed, if the plaintiff and the defendant, in conspiracy, caused the court to render a judgment for the purpose of prejudicing the rights of the Stock Company, which are the subject-matter of the suit relating to the Action for Pursuing Liability, etc., the Stock Company or shareholders may enter an appeal against the final judgment that became final and conclusive, by filing an action for a retrial.
(2) The provisions of the preceding Article shall apply mutatis mutandis to the appeal for a retrial set forth in the preceding paragraph.

Section 3 Action Seeking Dismissal of an Officer of a Stock Company

(Action Seeking Dismissal of an Officer of a Stock Company)
Article 854 (1) If, notwithstanding the presence of misconduct or material facts in violation of laws and regulations or the articles of incorporation in connection with the execution of the duties of an officer (meaning the officer prescribed in Article 329(1); hereinafter the same shall apply in this Section), a proposal to dismiss such officer is rejected at the shareholders meeting or a resolution of the shareholders meeting to dismiss such officer fails to become effective pursuant to the provisions of Article 323, the following shareholders may demand dismissal of such officer by filing an action within thirty days from the day of such shareholders meeting:
(i) a shareholder (excluding the following shareholders) holding consecutively for the preceding six months or more (or, in cases where a shorter period is prescribed in the articles of incorporation, such period or more) not less than three-hundredths (or, in cases where a lesser proportion is prescribed in the articles of incorporation, such proportion) of the voting rights of all shareholders (excluding the following shareholders):

(a) a shareholder who is unable to exercise a voting right with respect to the proposal to dismiss such officer; and
(b) a shareholder who is the officer pertaining to such demand; and
(ii) a shareholder (excluding the following shareholders) holding consecutively for the preceding six months or more (or, in cases where a shorter period is prescribed in the articles of incorporation, such period or more) not less than three-hundredths (or, in cases where a lesser proportion is prescribed in the articles of incorporation, such proportion) of the Issued Shares (excluding the shares held by the following shareholders):
(a) a shareholder who is such Stock Company; and
(b) a shareholder who is the officer pertaining to such demand.
(2) With regard to application of the provisions of the items of the preceding paragraph to a Stock Company that is not a Public Company, the phrase "holding consecutively for the preceding six months or more (or, in cases where a shorter period is prescribed in the articles of incorporation, such period or more)" in those provisions shall be deemed to be replaced with "holding."
(3) With regard to application of the provisions of paragraph (1) in cases where the class of shares for which there are provisions on the matters set forth in Article 108(1)(ix) (limited to those relating to directors) have been issued, the term "shareholders meeting" in that paragraph shall be deemed to be replaced with "shareholders meeting (including the Class Meeting set forth in Article 339(1) as applied mutatis mutandis by replacing the terms pursuant to the provisions of Article 347(1))."
(4) With regard to application of the provisions of paragraph (1) in cases where the class of shares for which there are provisions on the matters set forth in Article 108(1)(ix) (limited to those relating to company auditors) have been issued, the term "shareholders meeting" in that paragraph shall be deemed to be replaced with "shareholders meeting (including the Class Meeting set forth in Article 339(1) as applied mutatis mutandis by replacing the terms pursuant to the provisions of Article 347(2))."

(Defendants)
Article 855 With regard to the action set forth in paragraph (1) of the preceding Article (referred to as an "Action Seeking Dismissal of an Officer of a Stock Company" in the following Article and Article 937(1)(i)(j)), the relevant Stock Company and the officer set forth in paragraph (1) of the preceding Article shall be the defendants.

(Jurisdiction over an Action)
Article 856 An Action Seeking Dismissal of an Officer of a Stock Company shall be under the exclusive jurisdiction of the district court having jurisdiction over the location of the head office of the relevant Stock Company.

Section 4 Action Concerning Special Liquidation

(Jurisdiction over an Action Seeking Rescission of Exemption from Liability of an Officer)
Article 857 The action set forth in Article 544(2) shall be under the exclusive jurisdiction of the Special Liquidation Court (meaning the Special Liquidation Court prescribed in Article 880(1); the same shall apply in paragraph (3) of the following Article).

(Action for Objection to a Ruling Evaluating a Subject Officer's Liability)
Article 858 (1) A person who is dissatisfied with a Ruling Evaluating a Subject Officer's

Liability (meaning the Ruling Evaluating a Subject Officer's Liability prescribed in Article 545(1); hereinafter the same shall apply in this Article) may file an action for objection within the unextendable period of one month from the day of receiving the service under the provisions of Article 899(4).
(2) With regard to the action set forth in the preceding paragraph, the Liquidating Stock Company shall be the defendant if the person filing the action is the Subject Officer (meaning the Subject Officer prescribed in Article 542(1); hereinafter the same shall apply in this paragraph), and the Subject Officer shall be the defendant if such person is the Liquidating Stock Company.
(3) The action set forth in paragraph (1) shall be under the exclusive jurisdiction of the Special Liquidation Court.
(4) A judgment for the action set forth in paragraph (1) shall approve, change or revoke the Ruling Evaluating the Subject Officer's Liability, except in cases of dismissing the action as being unlawful.
(5) A judgment that has approved or changed the Ruling Evaluating the Subject Officer's Liability shall have the same effect as a judgment ordering performance, with regard to compulsory execution.
(6) With regard to a judgment that has approved or changed the Ruling Evaluating the Subject Officer's Liability, the court in charge of the case may make a declaration of provisional execution pursuant to the provisions of Article 259(1) of the Code of Civil Procedure.

Section 5 Action Seeking Removal of Partner of Membership Company, etc.

(Action Seeking Removal of Partner of Membership Company)
Article 859 If any one of the following grounds applies to a partner of a Membership Company (hereinafter referred to as the "Subject Partner" in this Article and Article 861(i)), such Membership Company may demand removal of the Subject Partner by filing an action, based on a resolution adopted by a majority of the partners other than the Subject Partner:
(i) a failure to perform the obligation of contribution;
(ii) a violation of the provisions of Article 594(1) (including the cases where it is applied mutatis mutandis pursuant to Article 598(2));
(iii) engagement in misconduct in executing duties or involvement in execution of duties when having no right to execute the duties;
(iv) engagement in misconduct in representing the Membership Company or conducting an act by representing the Membership Company when having no authority of representation; or
(v) in addition to what is provided for in the preceding items, a failure to fulfill an important obligation.

(Action Seeking Extinguishment of Right to Execute Business or Authority of Representation of Partner Executing Business of Membership Company)
Article 860 If any one of the following grounds apply to a partner executing the business of a Membership Company (hereinafter referred to as the "Subject Managing Partner" in this Article and item (ii) of the following Article), such Membership Company may demand extinguishment of the right to execute business or the authority of representation of the Subject Managing Partner by filing an action, based on a resolution adopted by a majority of the partners other than the Subject Managing Partner:
(i) when there are any of the grounds listed in the items of the preceding Article; or

(ii) when the partner is too incompetent to execute the business of the Membership Company or to represent the Membership Company.

(Defendants)
Article 861 With regard to the actions listed in the following items, the persons specified respectively in those items shall be the defendants.
(i) the action set forth in Article 859 (referred to as an "Action Seeking Removal of Partner of Membership Company" in the following Article and Article 937(1)(i)(k)): the Subject Partner; and
(ii) the action set forth in the preceding Article (referred to as an "Action Seeking Extinguishment of Right to Execute Business or Authority of Representation of Partner Executing Business of Membership Company" in the following Article and Article 937(1)(i)(l)): the Subject Managing Partner.

(Jurisdiction over an Action)
Article 862 An Action Seeking Removal of Partner of Membership Company and an Action Seeking Extinguishment of Right to Execute Business or Authority of Representation of Partner Executing Business of Membership Company shall be under the exclusive jurisdiction of the district court having jurisdiction over the location of the head office of the relevant Membership Company.

Section 6 Action Seeking Rescission of Disposition of Property of a Liquidating Membership Company

(Action Seeking Rescission of Disposition of Property of a Liquidating Membership Company)
Article 863 (1) When a Liquidating Membership Company (limited to a General Partnership Company or a Limited Partnership Company; hereinafter the same shall apply in this paragraph) commits any one of the acts listed in the following items, the persons specified respectively in those items may demand rescission of such act by filing an action; provided, however, that this shall not apply if there is no risk of harm to such persons by such acts:
(i) disposition of property of the Liquidating Membership Company in violation of the provisions of Article 670: a creditor of the Liquidating Membership Company; or
(ii) disposition of property of the Liquidating Membership Company in violation of the provisions of Article 671(1): a creditor who has attached the equity interest of a partner of the Liquidating Membership Company.
(2) The provisions of the proviso to Article 424(1), Article 425 and Article 426 of the Civil Code shall apply mutatis mutandis to the cases set forth in the preceding paragraph. In such cases, the phrase "from such act" in the proviso to Article 424(1) of the Civil Code shall be deemed to be replaced with "from any one of the acts listed in the items of Article 863 of the Companies Act (Act No. 86 of 2005)."

(Defendants)
Article 864 With regard to the action set forth in paragraph (1) of the preceding Article, the counterparties to the acts set forth in the items of that paragraph or the subsequent purchasers shall be the defendants.

Section 7 Action Seeking Rescission of Performance, etc. of a Bond-Issuing Company

(Action Seeking Rescission of Performance, etc. of a Bond-Issuing Company)
Article 865 (1) When a bond-issuing Company's payment to a bondholder, settlement effected with a bondholder, or other act conducted against or with a bondholder is grossly improper, the bond manager may demand rescission of such act by filing an action.
(2) The action set forth in the preceding paragraph may not be filed when six months have elapsed from the time when the bond manager learned about the fact that serves as the cause for the rescission of the act set forth in that paragraph. The same shall apply when one year has elapsed from the time of the act set forth in that paragraph.
(3) In the cases prescribed in paragraph (1), if there is a resolution of bondholders meeting, a representative bondholder or a Resolution Administrator (meaning the Resolution Administrator prescribed in Article 737(2)) may also demand rescission of the act set forth in paragraph (1) by filing an action; provided, however, that this shall not apply when one year has elapsed from the time of the act set forth in that paragraph.
(4) The provisions of the proviso to Article 424(1) and Article 425 of the Civil Code shall apply mutatis mutandis to the cases set forth in paragraph (1) and the main clause of the preceding paragraph. In such cases, the phrase "from such act" in the proviso to Article 424(1) of that Act shall be deemed to be replaced with "from the act prescribed in Article 865(1) of the Companies Act," the phrase "the fact that the obligee is to be prejudiced" in that paragraph shall be deemed to be replaced with "that such act is grossly improper," and the term "obligees" in Article 425 shall be deemed to be replaced with "bondholders."

(Defendants)
Article 866 With regard to the action set forth in paragraph (1) or paragraph (3) of the preceding Article, the counterparty to the act set forth in paragraph (1) of that Article or the subsequent purchaser shall be the defendant.

(Jurisdiction over an Action)
Article 867 The action set forth in paragraph (1) or paragraph (3) of Article 865 shall be under the exclusive jurisdiction of the district court having jurisdiction over the location of the head office of the bond-issuing Company.

Chapter III Non-Contentious Cases

Section 1 General Provisions

(Jurisdiction over Non-Contentious Cases)
Article 868 (1) A non-contentious case under the provisions of this Act (excluding the cases prescribed in the following paragraph to paragraph (5)) shall be under the exclusive jurisdiction of the district court having jurisdiction over the location of the head office of the Company.
(2) A case relating to a petition for permission for the following Inspection, etc. (meaning inspection, copying, delivery of a transcript or extract, provision of certain matters or delivery of a document that states such matters; the same shall apply in Article 870(i)) of documents or Electromagnetic Records prepared or kept by a Stock Company pursuant to the provisions of this Act, filed by a Member of the Parent Company (limited to a shareholder or member of the Parent Company, which is a Company), shall be under the exclusive jurisdiction of the district court having jurisdiction over the location

of the head office of such Stock Company:
 (i) inspection, copying or delivery of a transcript or extract of the documents; and
 (ii) inspection or copying of anything that indicates the matters recorded in the Electromagnetic Records, provision of such matters by an Electromagnetic Method or delivery of a document that states such matters.
(3) A case relating to a petition for a judicial decision under the provisions of Article 705(4), Article 706(4), Article 707, Article 711(3), Article 713, Article 714(1) and (3), Article 718(3), Article 732, Article 740(1) and Article 741(1) shall be under the exclusive jurisdiction of the district court having jurisdiction over the location of the head office of the bond-issuing Company.
(4) A case relating to liquidation of a Foreign Company under the provisions of Article 822(1) and a case relating to a judicial decision under the provisions of Article 827(1) or a temporary restraining order under the provisions of Article 825(1) as applied mutatis mutandis pursuant to Article 827(2) shall be under the exclusive jurisdiction of the district court having jurisdiction over the location of such Foreign Company's business office in Japan (or, in cases where no business office is established in Japan, the location of the domicile of the representative in Japan).
(5) A case in relation to the petition set forth in paragraph (4) of Article 843 shall be under the exclusive jurisdiction of the court in charge of the first instance of an action seeking invalidation of any one of the acts listed in the items of paragraph (1) of that Article.

(Prima Facie Showing)
Article 869 In cases of filing a petition for permission under the provisions of this Act, a prima facie showing shall be made with regard to the fact that serves as the cause thereof.

(Hearing of Statements)
Article 870 When the court makes the judicial decisions listed in the following items from among judicial decisions relating to non-contentious cases under the provisions of this Act (excluding Part II, Chapter IX, Section 2), it shall hear statements by the persons specified respectively in those items (excluding the petitioner in cases of items (iv) and (vi)):
 (i) a judicial decision relating to a petition for permission for Inspection, etc. of documents or Electromagnetic Records prepared or kept by a Stock Company pursuant to the provisions of this Act: the relevant Stock Company;
 (ii) a determination of the amount of remuneration for a person who is temporarily to perform the duties of a director, accounting advisor, company auditor, Representative Director, committee member, executive officer or representative executive officer appointed pursuant to the provisions of Article 346(2), Article 351(2) or Article 401(3) (including cases where it is applied mutatis mutandis pursuant to Article 403(3) or Article 420(3)), a liquidator, a person who is temporarily to perform the duties of a liquidator or representative liquidator appointed pursuant to the provisions of Article 346(2) as applied mutatis mutandis pursuant to Article 479(4) or the provisions of Article 351(2) as applied mutatis mutandis pursuant to Article 483(6), an inspector, or the administrator set forth in Article 825(2) (including cases where it is applied mutatis mutandis pursuant to Article 827(2)): the relevant Company and the person receiving the remuneration;
 (iii) a judicial decision on dismissal of a liquidator or a bond manager: such liquidator or bond manager;
 (iv) a determination of the price of the shares or Share Options (in cases where such

Share Options are those attached to Bonds with Share Options, if there is a demand for the purchase of Bonds pertaining to such Bonds with Share Options, they shall include such Bonds) under the provisions of Article 117(2), Article 119(2), Article 172(1), Article 193(2) (including cases where it is applied mutatis mutandis pursuant to Article 194(4)), Article 470(2), Article 778(2), Article 786(2), Article 788(2), Article 798(2), Article 807(2), or Article 809(2): a person who is able to file a petition for a determination of the price;

(v) a judicial decision under the provisions of Article 33(7): a Director at Incorporation, the person who contributes property other than monies set forth in Article 28(i) and the assignor set forth in item (ii) of that Article;

(vi) a determination of the sale price of shares under the provisions of paragraph (2) of Article 144 (including the cases where it is applied mutatis mutandis pursuant to paragraph (7) of that Article) or Article 177(2): a person who is able to file a petition for a determination of the sale price (in cases where there is the Designated Purchaser prescribed in Article 140(4), such person shall include the Designated Purchaser);

(vii) a judicial decision under the provisions of Article 207(7) or Article 284(7): the relevant Stock Company and a person who contributes property other than monies pursuant to the provisions of Article 199(1)(iii) or Article 236(1)(iii);

(viii) a judicial decision under the provisions of Article 455(2)(ii) or Article 505(3)(ii): the relevant shareholder;

(ix) a judicial decision under the provisions of Article 456 or Article 506: the relevant shareholder;

(x) a judicial decision under the provisions of Article 732: an interested party;

(xi) a judicial decision upholding a petition under the provisions of Article 740(1): the bond-issuing Company;

(xii) a judicial decision on the petition for permission set forth in Article 741(1): the bond-issuing Company;

(xiii) a judicial decision under the provisions of Article 824(1): the relevant Company;

(xiv) a judicial decision under the provisions of Article 827(1): the relevant Foreign Company; and

(xv) a judicial decision on the petition set forth in Article 843(4): the Company that carried out the act prescribed in that paragraph.

(Appending of the Reason)

Article 871 A judicial decision for a non-contentious case under the provisions of this Act shall append the reason thereof; provided, however, that this shall not apply to the following judicial decisions:

(i) the judicial decision set forth in item (ii) of the preceding Article; and

(ii) the judicial decisions listed in the items of Article 874.

(Immediate Appeal)

Article 872 An immediate appeal may be entered against the judicial decisions listed in the following items by the persons specified respectively in those items:

(i) a judicial decision on a temporary restraining order under the provisions of Article 609(3) or Article 825(1) (including the cases where it is applied mutatis mutandis pursuant to Article 827(2)): an interested party;

(ii) a judicial decision on a petition under the provisions of Article 840(2) (including the cases where it is applied mutatis mutandis pursuant to Article 841(2)): the petitioner, shareholders and the Stock Company;

(iii) a judicial decision on a petition under the provisions of Article 840(2) as applied

mutatis mutandis pursuant to Article 842(2): the petitioner, holders of Share Options and the Stock Company; and
(iv) the judicial decisions listed in the items of Article 870: The petitioner and the persons specified respectively in those items (or, for the judicial decisions listed in items (ii), (v) and (vii) of that Article, it shall only be the persons specified respectively in those items).

(Stay of Execution of the Judicial Decision of the Prior Instance)
Article 873 The immediate appeal set forth in the preceding Article shall have the effect of staying execution; provided, however, that this shall not apply to an immediate appeal against the following judicial decisions:
(i) the judicial decision set forth in Article 870(ii);
(ii) the judicial decision set forth in Article 870(iii);
(iii) the judicial decisions set forth in Article 870(v) and (vii); and
(iv) the judicial decisions set forth in Article 870(xi).

(Restrictions on Appeal)
Article 874 No appeal may be entered against the following judicial decisions:
(i) a judicial decision on the appointment or selection of a person who is temporarily to perform the duties of a director, accounting advisor, company auditor, Representative Director, committee member, executive officer or representative executive officer prescribed in item (ii) of Article 870, a liquidator, a representative liquidator, a liquidator who represents a Liquidating Membership Company, a person who is temporarily to perform the duties of a liquidator or representative liquidator prescribed in that item, an inspector, the appraiser set forth in Article 501(1) (including the cases where it is applied mutatis mutandis pursuant to Article 822(3)) or Article 662(1), the person who retains Accounting Materials set forth in Article 508(2) (including the cases where it is applied mutatis mutandis pursuant to Article 822(3)) or Article 672(3), a special agent of a bond manager or the bond manager to succeed to the administration of bonds set forth in Article 714(3);
(ii) a judicial decision on appointment or dismissal of the administrator set forth in Article 825(2) (including the cases where it is applied mutatis mutandis pursuant to Article 827(2));
(iii) a judicial decision under the provisions of Article 825(6) (including the cases where it is applied mutatis mutandis pursuant to Article 827(2)); and
(iv) a judicial decision upholding a petition for permission under the provisions of this Act (excluding the judicial decisions listed in Article 870(i) and (xii)).

(Exclusion from Application of the Provisions of the Non-Contentious Cases Procedures Act)
Article 875 The provisions of Article 15 of the Non-Contentious Cases Procedures Act shall not apply to non-contentious cases under the provisions of this Act.

(Supreme Court Rules)
Article 876 In addition to what is provided for in this Act, necessary matters concerning the procedures of non-contentious cases under the provisions of this Act shall be specified by the Supreme Court Rules.

Section 2 Special Provisions on the Procedures of Increasing or Decreasing the Refund after a Judgment of Invalidation of a New Share Issue

(Mandatory Consolidation of Hearings, etc.)
Article 877 When several cases relating to the petition set forth in Article 840(2) (including the cases where it is applied mutatis mutandis pursuant to Article 841(2) and Article 842(2)) are pending simultaneously, the hearings and judicial decisions thereof shall be made in consolidation.

(Effects of a Judicial Decision)
Article 878 (1) A judicial decision on the petition set forth in Article 840(2) (including the cases where it is applied mutatis mutandis pursuant to Article 841(2)) shall be effective against all of the shareholders.
(2) A judicial decision on the petition set forth in Article 840(2) as applied mutatis mutandis pursuant to Article 842(2) shall be effective against all of the holders of Share Options.

Section 3 Special Provisions on the Procedures of Special Liquidation

Subsection 1 Common Provisions

(Jurisdiction over a Special Liquidation Case)
Article 879 (1) Notwithstanding the provisions of Article 868(1), in cases where a juridical person has a majority of the voting rights of all shareholders of a Stock Company (excluding shareholders who are unable to exercise voting rights on all the matters which may be resolved at the shareholders meeting; the same shall apply in the following paragraph), if a special liquidation case, a bankruptcy case, a rehabilitation case or a reorganization case (hereinafter referred to as a "Special Liquidation Case, etc." in this Article) is pending with regard to such juridical person (hereinafter referred to as the "Parent Juridical Person" in this Article), a petition for commencement of special liquidation relating to such Stock Company may be filed alternatively with the district court before which the Special Liquidation Case, etc. of the Parent Juridical Person is pending.
(2) In cases where the Stock Company prescribed in the preceding paragraph, or the Parent Juridical Person and the Stock Company prescribed in that paragraph have a majority of the voting rights of all shareholders of another Stock Company, a petition for commencement of special liquidation relating to such other Stock Company may be filed alternatively with the district court before which the Special Liquidation Case, etc. of the Parent Juridical Person is pending.
(3) With regard to application of the preceding two paragraphs, the shareholder prescribed by the applicable Ordinance of the Ministry of Justice set forth in Article 308(1) shall be deemed to have voting rights with respect to the shares which such shareholder holds.
(4) Notwithstanding the provisions of Article 868(1), in cases where a Stock Company has, pursuant to the provisions of Article 444, prepared Consolidated Financial Statements of that Stock Company or another Stock Company for the Most Recent Business Year and the contents thereof have been reported to the annual shareholders meeting of that Stock Company, if a Special Liquidation Case, etc. is pending with regard to that Stock Company, a petition for commencement of special liquidation relating to such other Stock Company may be filed alternatively with the district court be-

fore which the Special Liquidation Case, etc. of that Stock Company is pending.

(Jurisdiction over and Transfer of an Ordinary Liquidation Case after Commencement of Special Liquidation)
Article 880 (1) Notwithstanding the provisions of Article 868(1), if an order to commence special liquidation is issued with regard to a Liquidating Stock Company, a case relating to a petition under the provisions of Part II, Chapter IX, Section 1 (excluding Article 508) (referred to as an "Ordinary Liquidation Case" in the following paragraph) relating to such Liquidating Stock Company shall be under the jurisdiction of the district court (hereinafter referred to as the "Special Liquidation Court" in this Section) before which the special liquidation case of such Liquidating Stock Company is pending.
(2) In cases where a special liquidation case relating to a Liquidating Stock Company is pending before a district court other than the district court before which an Ordinary Liquidation Case relating to the same Liquidating Stock Company is pending and an order to commence special liquidation has been issued, if it is found reasonable for processing such Ordinary Liquidation Case, the court (meaning a judge or a panel of judges handling the Ordinary Liquidation Case) may transfer such Ordinary Liquidation Case to the special liquidation court ex officio.

(Prima Facie Showing)
Article 881 The provisions of Article 869 shall not apply to a petition for permission under the provisions of Part II, Chapter IX, Section 2 (excluding Article 547(3)).

(Appending of the Reason)
Article 882 (1) A ruling concerning procedures of special liquidation against which an immediate appeal may be entered shall append the reason thereof; provided, however, that this shall not apply to a ruling under the provisions of paragraph (1) of Article 526 (including the cases where it is applied mutatis mutandis pursuant to paragraph (2) of that Article) and Article 532(1) (including the cases where it is applied mutatis mutandis pursuant to Article 534).
(2) The provisions of Article 871 shall not apply to a ruling concerning procedures of special liquidation.

(Service of a Written Judgment)
Article 883 The provisions of Part I, Chapter V, Section 4 of the Code of Civil Procedure (excluding Article 104) shall apply mutatis mutandis to the service of a written judgment under the provisions of this Section.

(Appeal)
Article 884 (1) A person who has an interest in a judicial decision concerning procedures of special liquidation may enter an immediate appeal against such judicial decision only in the case where there are special provisions in this Section.
(2) The immediate appeal set forth in the preceding paragraph shall have the effect of staying execution except as otherwise provided by this Section.
(3) The provisions of Article 20 of the Non-Contentious Cases Procedures Act shall not apply to a ruling concerning procedures of special liquidation.

(Public Notice)
Article 885 (1) A public notice under the provisions of this Section shall be effected by publication in an official gazette.

(2) The public notice set forth in the preceding paragraph shall become effective on the day immediately following the day of publication.

(Inspection, etc. of Documents Concerning a Case)
Article 886 (1) An interested party may make a request to a court clerk for inspection of the documents or any other articles (hereinafter referred to as the "Documents, etc." in this Article and paragraph (1) of the following Article) submitted to the court or prepared by the court based on the provisions of Part II, Chapter IX, Section 2 or this Section or Part I of the Non-Contentious Cases Procedures Act (or, in cases where an order to commence special liquidation has been issued, Part II, Chapter IX, Section 1 or Section 2, or Section 1 of this Chapter (limited to the portions pertaining to a case relating to a petition under the provisions of Part II, Chapter IX, Section 1) or this Section, or Part I of the Non-Contentious Cases Procedures Act) (including the provisions of this Act or any other Acts applied mutatis mutandis under these provisions).
(2) An interested party may make a request to a court clerk for copying of the Documents, etc., delivery of the original, a transcript or an extract thereof, or delivery of a certificate of matters concerning the case.
(3) The provisions of the preceding paragraph shall not apply to sound recording tapes or video tapes (including objects on which certain matters are recorded by a method equivalent thereto) among the Documents, etc. In such cases, a court clerk shall permit reproduction of these objects if there is a request from an interested party for such objects.
(4) Notwithstanding the provisions of the preceding three paragraphs, the persons listed in the following items may not make a request under the provisions of the preceding three paragraphs until any one of the orders, temporary restraining orders, dispositions or judicial decisions specified respectively in those items has been issued; provided, however, that this shall not apply in cases where any such person is a petitioner with respect to commencement of special liquidation:
  (i) an interested party other than the Liquidating Stock Company: an order to suspend under the provisions of Article 512, a temporary restraining order under the provisions of Article 540(2), a disposition under the provisions of Article 541(2), or a judicial decision relating to a petition for commencement of special liquidation; or
  (ii) the Liquidating Stock Company: a judicial decision designating the date of the hearing on which the Liquidating Stock Company is to be summoned concerning a petition for commencement of special liquidation or the order, temporary restraining order, disposition or judicial decision specified in the preceding item.
(5) The provisions of Article 91(5) of the Code of Civil Procedure shall apply mutatis mutandis to the Documents, etc.

(Restrictions on Inspection, etc. of a Detrimental Part)
Article 887 (1) In cases where a prima facie showing is made that any one of the following Documents, etc. include a part (hereinafter referred to as a "Detrimental Part") where inspection or copying thereof, delivery of the original or a transcript or an extract thereof, or reproduction thereof (hereinafter referred to as "Inspection, etc." in this Article) by interested parties is likely to cause considerable detriment to the implementation of liquidation of the Liquidating Stock Company, the court may, in response to a petition from the Liquidating Stock Company that submitted such Documents, etc. or by an investigator, limit the persons who are able to request Inspection, etc. of the Detrimental Part to the person who has filed such petition and the Liquidating Stock Company:
  (i) Documents, etc. relating to a report under the provisions of Article 520 or a report

of the results of the investigation prescribed in Article 522(1); or
   (ii) Documents, etc. submitted to the court for obtaining the permission set forth in Article 535(1) or Article 536(1).
(2) When the petition set forth in the preceding paragraph is filed, interested parties (excluding the person who has filed the petition set forth in that paragraph and the Liquidating Stock Company; the same shall apply in the following paragraph) may not request Inspection, etc. of the Detrimental Part until the judicial decision on such petition becomes final and binding.
(3) An interested party who intends to request Inspection, etc. of the Detrimental Part may file a petition for revocation of the ruling under the provisions of paragraph (1) with the special liquidation court on the basis that the requirements prescribed in that paragraph are not satisfied or are no longer satisfied.
(4) An immediate appeal may be entered against a ruling to dismiss the petition set forth in paragraph (1) or against a judicial decision relating to the petition set forth in the preceding paragraph.
(5) A ruling to revoke the ruling under the provisions of paragraph (1) shall not become effective until it is final and binding.

Subsection 2 Special Provisions on Procedures for Commencement of Special Liquidation

(Petition for Commencement of Special Liquidation)
Article 888 (1) When a creditor or shareholder files a petition for commencement of special liquidation, such creditor or shareholder shall make a prima facie showing of the grounds that serve as the cause for commencement of special liquidation.
(2) When a creditor files a petition for commencement of special liquidation, the creditor shall also make a prima facie showing of the presence of the claims the creditor holds.
(3) When filing a petition for commencement of special liquidation, the petitioner shall prepay the amount specified by the court as expenses for the procedures of special liquidation prescribed in Article 514(i).
(4) An immediate appeal may be entered against a ruling concerning the prepayment of expenses set forth in the preceding paragraph.

(Order to Suspend Other Procedures)
Article 889 (1) The court may change or revoke an order to suspend under the provisions of Article 512.
(2) An immediate appeal may be entered against the order to suspend set forth in the preceding paragraph and a ruling under the provisions of that paragraph.
(3) The immediate appeal set forth in the preceding paragraph shall not have the effect of staying execution.
(4) In cases where the judicial decision prescribed in paragraph (2) or a judicial decision relating to the immediate appeal set forth in that paragraph is made, the written judgment thereof shall be served on the parties.

(Order to Commence Special Liquidation)
Article 890 (1) When the court issues an order to commence special liquidation, it shall immediately give public notice to that effect and serve the written judgment of the order to commence special liquidation on the Liquidating Stock Company.
(2) An order to commence special liquidation shall become effective when the written judgment thereof is served on the Liquidating Stock Company.
(3) When an order to commence special liquidation is issued, the expenses for the proce-

dures of special liquidation shall be borne by the Liquidating Stock Company.
(4) Only the Liquidating Stock Company may enter an immediate appeal against an order to commence special liquidation.
(5) Only the petitioner may enter an immediate appeal against a judicial decision that dismissed a petition for commencement of special liquidation.
(6) The court that has issued an order to commence special liquidation shall, in cases where the immediate appeal set forth in paragraph (4) has been entered, if a ruling to revoke such order becomes final and binding, immediately give public notice to that effect.

(Order to Suspend Procedures to Enforce Security Interests)
Article 891 (1) The court shall, when issuing an order to suspend under the provisions of Article 516, hear statements by the petitioner of the procedures to enforce security interests prescribed in that Article.
(2) The court may change or revoke the order to suspend set forth in the preceding paragraph.
(3) Only the petitioner set forth in paragraph (1) may enter an immediate appeal against the order to suspend set forth in paragraph (1) and a ruling to change under the provisions of the preceding paragraph.
(4) The immediate appeal set forth in the preceding paragraph shall not have the effect of staying execution.
(5) In cases where the judicial decision prescribed in paragraph (3) or a judicial decision on the immediate appeal set forth in that paragraph is made, the written judgment thereof shall be served on the parties.

Subsection 3 Special Provisions on Procedure of Implementation of Special Liquidation

(Investigation Order)
Article 892 (1) The court may change or revoke an Investigation Order (meaning an Investigation Order prescribed in Article 522(1); the same shall apply in the following paragraph).
(2) An immediate appeal may be entered against an order to investigate and a ruling under the provisions of the preceding paragraph.
(3) The immediate appeal set forth in the preceding paragraph shall not have the effect of staying execution.
(4) In cases where the judicial decision prescribed in paragraph (2) or a judicial decision on the immediate appeal set forth in that paragraph is made, the written judgment thereof shall be served on the parties.

(Dismissal and Remuneration, etc. of a Liquidator)
Article 893 (1) The court shall, in cases of dismissing a liquidator pursuant to the provisions of Article 524(1), hear statements from such liquidator.
(2) An immediate appeal may be filed against a judicial decision on dismissal under the provisions of article 524(1).
(3) The immediate appeal set forth in the preceding paragraph shall not have the effect of staying execution.
(4) An immediate appeal may be filed against a ruling under the provisions of paragraph (1) of Article 526 (including the cases where it is applied mutatis mutandis pursuant to paragraph (2) of that Article).

(Dismissal and Remuneration, etc. of a Supervisor)
Article 894 (1) The court shall, in cases of dismissing a supervisor, hear statements from such supervisor.
(2) An immediate appeal may be filed against a ruling under the provisions of Article 532(1).

(Dismissal and Remuneration, etc. of an Investigator)
Article 895 The provisions of the preceding Article shall apply mutatis mutandis pursuant to investigators.

(Petition for Permission of Assignment of Business)
Article 896 (1) A liquidator shall, in cases of filing a petition for the permission set forth in Article 536(1), hear the opinions of the known creditors and report the contents thereof to the court.
(2) The court shall, in cases of issuing the permission set forth in Article 536(1), hear the opinions of the Labor Union, etc. (meaning the labor union if there is a labor union consisting of a majority of the employees and any other workers of the Liquidating Stock Company, and the person representing a majority of the employees and any other workers of the Liquidating Stock Company if there is no labor union consisting of a majority of the employees and any other workers of the Liquidating Stock Company).

(Designating Periods for Disposition by Security Interest Holders)
Article 897 (1) An immediate appeal may be entered against a judicial decision relating to the petition set forth in Article 539(1).
(2) In cases where the judicial decision set forth in the preceding paragraph or a judicial decision relating to the immediate appeal set forth in that paragraph is made, the written judgment thereof shall be served on the parties.

(Temporary Restraining Order, etc. Concerning Property of a Liquidating Stock Company)
Article 898 (1) The court may change or revoke any one of the following judicial decisions:
(i) a temporary restraining order under the provisions of Article 540(1) or (2);
(ii) a disposition under the provisions of Article 541(1) or (2);
(iii) a temporary restraining order under the provisions of Article 542(1) or (2); or
(iv) a disposition under the provisions of Article 543.
(2) An immediate appeal may be entered against the judicial decisions listed in the items of the preceding paragraph and a ruling under the provisions of that paragraph.
(3) The immediate appeal set forth in the preceding paragraph shall not have the effect of staying execution.
(4) In cases where the judicial decision prescribed in paragraph (2) or a judicial decision relating to the immediate appeal set forth in that paragraph is made, the written judgment thereof shall be served on the parties.
(5) When the court makes the judicial decision set forth in paragraph (1)(ii), it shall immediately give public notice to that effect. The same shall apply when it makes a ruling to change or revoke such judicial decision.

(Ruling Evaluating the Subject Officer's Liability)
Article 899 (1) When a Liquidating Stock Company intends to file the petition set forth in Article 545(1), it shall make a prima facie showing with regard to the fact that serves as the cause thereof.

(2) A Ruling Evaluating the Subject Officer's Liability (meaning the Ruling Evaluating the Subject Officer's Liability prescribed in Article 545(1); hereinafter the same shall apply in this Article) and a ruling to dismiss the petition set forth in the preceding paragraph shall append the reason therefor.
(3) The court shall, when making the judicial decision prescribed in the preceding paragraph, hear statements from the Subject Officer (meaning the Subject Officer prescribed in Article 542(1)).
(4) In cases where a Ruling Evaluating the Subject Officer's Liability is made, the written judgment thereof shall be served on the parties.
(5) When the action set forth in Article 858(1) is not filed within the period set forth in that paragraph or is dismissed, the Ruling Evaluating the Subject Officer's Liability shall have the same effect as a final and binding judgment ordering performance.

(Judicial Decision Relating to the Petition for Permission to Call a Bondholders' Meeting)
Article 900 An immediate appeal may be entered against a ruling to dismiss the petition for permission set forth in Article 547(3).

(Ruling Approving or Rejecting an Agreement)
Article 901 (1) An interested party may state an opinion on whether the agreement relating to the petition set forth in Article 568 should be approved.
(2) When the court makes the ruling approving the agreement set forth in Article 569(1), it shall immediately give public notice to that effect.
(3) An immediate appeal may be entered against a judicial decision relating to the petition set forth in Article 568. In such cases, the period for entering an immediate appeal against the ruling approving the agreement set forth in the preceding paragraph shall be two weeks from the day on which the public notice under the provisions of that paragraph has become effective.
(4) The provisions of the preceding three paragraphs shall apply mutatis mutandis to cases of changing the details of an agreement pursuant to the provisions of Article 572.

Subsection 4 Special Provisions on Procedures of Completion of Special Liquidation

(Judicial Decision Relating to a Petition for the Conclusion of Special Liquidation)
Article 902 (1) When the court makes a ruling to conclude special liquidation, it shall immediately give public notice to that effect.
(2) An immediate appeal may be entered against a judicial decision relating to a petition for the conclusion of special liquidation. In such cases, the period for entering an immediate appeal against a ruling to conclude special liquidation shall be two weeks from the day on which the public notice under the provisions of the preceding paragraph has become effective.
(3) A ruling to conclude special liquidation shall not become effective until it is final and binding.
(4) The court that has made a ruling to conclude special liquidation shall, in cases where the immediate appeal set forth in paragraph (2) has been entered, if a ruling to revoke such ruling becomes final and binding, immediately give public notice to that effect.

Section 4 Special Provisions on Procedures of Liquidation of a Foreign Company

(Application Mutatis Mutandis of the Provisions on Procedures of Special Liquidation)
Article 903 The provisions of the preceding Section shall apply mutatis mutandis to liquidation of a Foreign Company's property in Japan under the provisions of Article 822(1), excluding those that are not applicable by their nature.

Section 5 Special Provisions on Procedures of a Dissolution Order, etc. for a Company

(Participation of the Minister of Justice)
Article 904 (1) When the court makes a judicial decision relating to the petition set forth in Article 824(1) or Article 827(1), it shall seek the opinion of the Minister of Justice.
(2) The Minister of Justice may, when the court carries out a hearing concerning the case relating to the petition set forth in the preceding paragraph, attend such hearing.
(3) The court shall notify the Minister of Justice that a case relating to the petition set forth in paragraph (1) became pending and of the date of the hearing set forth in the preceding paragraph.
(4) The Minister of Justice may enter an immediate appeal against a judicial decision to dismiss the petition set forth in paragraph (1).

(Special Provisions on a Temporary Restraining Order Concerning Property of a Company)
Article 905 (1) In cases where the court issues the temporary restraining order set forth in Article 825(1) (including the cases where it is applied mutatis mutandis pursuant to Article 827(2)), the expenses referred to in the main clause of Article 26 of the Non-Contentious Cases Procedures Act shall be borne by the Company or Foreign Company. The same shall apply to the necessary expenses with regard to such temporary restraining order.
(2) In cases where an immediate appeal has been entered against the temporary restraining order set forth in the preceding paragraph or against a judicial decision dismissing a petition under the provisions of Article 825(1) (including the cases where it is applied mutatis mutandis pursuant to Article 827(2)), if the court of the appeal revokes the judicial decision of the prior instance by finding that such immediate appeal has grounds, the court costs required for the procedures in such appeal instance and the court costs required for the procedures in the prior instance, which had been borne by the appellant, shall be borne by the Company or Foreign Company.

Article 906 (1) An interested party may make a request to a court clerk for inspection of documents relating to the report or account set forth in Article 825(6) (including the cases where it is applied mutatis mutandis pursuant to Article 827(2)).
(2) An interested party may make a request to a court clerk for the copying of the documents set forth in the preceding paragraph or delivery of the original, transcript or an extract thereof.
(3) The provisions of the preceding paragraph shall not apply to sound recording tapes or video tapes (including objects on which certain matters are recorded by a method equivalent thereto) among the documents set forth in paragraph (1). In such cases, a court clerk shall permit reproduction of these objects if there is such a request from

an interested party for such objects.
(4) The Minister of Justice may make a request to a court clerk for inspection of the documents set forth in paragraph (1).
(5) The provisions of Article 91(5) of the Code of Civil Procedure shall apply mutatis mutandis to the documents set forth in paragraph (1).

Chapter IV Registration

Section 1 General Provisions

(Common Provisions)
Article 907 The matters to be registered pursuant to the provisions of this Act (excluding the matters pertaining to the registration of the temporary restraining order set forth in Article 938(3)) shall be registered in the commercial registry through application by a party or commission of a court clerk, in accordance with the provisions of the Commercial Registration Act (Act No. 125 of 1963).

(Effects of Registration)
Article 908 (1) The matters to be registered pursuant to the provisions of this Act may not be duly asserted against a third party who has no knowledge of such matters until after the registration. The same shall apply after the registration, if a third party did not know that such matters were registered based on justifiable grounds.
(2) A person who has registered false matters intentionally or by negligence may not duly assert the falsity of such matters against a third party without knowledge of such falsity.

(Registration of a Change and Registration of an Extinction)
Article 909 When there is a change to the matters registered pursuant to the provisions of this Act or when such matters becomes extinct, the party shall have the registration of the change or the registration of the extinction completed without delay.

(Period for Registration)
Article 910 The period for the registration of those matters to be registered pursuant to the provisions of this Act which require the permission of a government agency shall be counted from the day of the arrival of the written permission.

Section 2 Registration of a Company

Subsection 1 Registration at the Location of the Head Office

(Registration of Incorporation of a Stock Company)
Article 911 (1) The registration of incorporation of a Stock Company shall be completed at the location of the head office within two weeks from whichever of the following days that is later:
(i) the day on which the investigation under the provisions of paragraph (1) of Article 46 ended (or, in cases where the Stock Company to be incorporated is a Company with Committees, the day on which the Representative Executive Officer at Incorporation received the notice under the provisions of paragraph (3) of that Article); or
(ii) the day specified by the incorporator.
(2) Notwithstanding the provisions of the preceding paragraph, in cases of making the so-

Art.911　Ⅰ Companies Act, Part VII, Chap.IV, Sec.2

licitation set forth in Article 57(1), the registration set forth in the preceding paragraph shall be completed within two weeks from whichever of the following days that is the latest:
(i) the day of the conclusion of an Organizational Meeting;
(ii) if the resolution of a Class Organizational Meeting set forth in Article 84 is made, the day of such resolution;
(iii) if the resolution of the Organizational Meeting set forth in Article 97 is made, the day on which two weeks have elapsed from the day of such resolution;
(iv) if the resolution of a Class Organizational Meeting set forth in Article 100(1) is made, the day on which two weeks have elapsed from the day of such resolution; or
(v) if the resolution of a Class Organizational Meeting set forth in Article 101(1) is made, the day of such resolution.
(3) The following matters shall be registered upon the registration set forth in paragraph (1):
(i) the purpose;
(ii) the trade name;
(iii) the addresses of the head office and branch offices;
(iv) if there are provisions in the articles of incorporation with regard to the duration or the grounds for dissolution of the Stock Company, such provisions;
(v) the amount of stated capital;
(vi) the Total Number of Authorized Shares;
(vii) the details of the shares it issues (or, for a Company with Class Shares, the Total Number of Authorized Shares in a Class and the details of the shares of each class);
(viii) if there are provisions in the articles of incorporation with regard to the Share Unit, such Share Unit;
(ix) the total number of the Issued Shares and the class(es) and the number of each class of the Issued Shares;
(x) if the Stock Company is a Company Issuing Share Certificates, a statement to that effect;
(xi) if there is an Administrator of the Shareholder Registry, the name, domicile and business office of the Administrator;
(xii) if the Stock Company has issued Share Options, the following matters:
  (a) the number of the Share Options;
  (b) the matters listed in Article 236(1)(i) to (iv);
  (c) in addition to the matters set forth in (b), if conditions on the exercise of the Share Options have been prescribed, such conditions; and
  (d) the matters listed in Article 236(1)(vii) and Article 238(1)(ii) and (iii);
(xiii) the names of the directors;
(xiv) the name and domicile of the Representative Director (excluding the cases prescribed in item (xxii));
(xv) if the Stock Company is a Company with a Board of Directors, a statement to that effect;
(xvi) if the Stock Company is a Company with Accounting Advisors, a statement to that effect, the name(s) of the accounting advisor(s) and the place set forth in Article 378(1);
(xvii) if the Stock Company is a Company with Auditors (including a Stock Company the articles of incorporation of which provide that the scope of the audit by its company auditors shall be limited to an audit related to accounting), a statement to that effect and the name(s) of the company auditor(s);
(xviii) if the Stock Company is a Company with a Board of Company Auditors, a state-

ment to that effect and the fact that those among the company auditors who are Outside Company Auditors are Outside Company Auditors;

(xix) if the Stock Company is a Company with Accounting Auditors, a statement to that effect and the name(s) of the accounting auditor(s);

(xx) if the Stock Company has a person who is temporarily to perform the duties of an accounting auditor who has been appointed pursuant to the provisions of Article 346(4), such person's name;

(xxi) if there are provisions on the vote by Special Directors under the provisions of Article 373(1), the following matters:
  (a) a statement to the effect that there are provisions on the vote by Special Directors under the provisions of Article 373(1);
  (b) the names of the Special Directors; and
  (c) a statement to the effect that those among the directors who are Outside Directors are Outside Directors;

(xxii) if the Stock Company is a Company with Committees, a statement to that effect and the following matters:
  (a) a statement to the effect that those among the directors who are Outside Directors are Outside Directors;
  (b) the names of the committee members and executive officers of each Committee; and
  (c) the name and domicile of the representative executive officer;

(xxiii) if there are provisions in the articles of incorporation with regard to exemption from liability of directors, accounting advisors, company auditors, executive officers or accounting auditors under the provisions of Article 426(1), such provisions of the articles of incorporation;

(xxiv) if there are provisions in the articles of incorporation with regard to the conclusion of contracts for the limitation of liabilities assumed by Outside Directors, accounting advisors, Outside Company Auditors or accounting auditors under the provisions of Article 427(1), such provisions of the articles of incorporation;

(xxv) if the provisions of the articles of incorporation set forth in the preceding item are related to Outside Directors, a statement to the effect that those among the directors who are Outside Directors are Outside Directors;

(xxvi) if the provisions of the articles of incorporation set forth in item (xxiv) are related to Outside Company Auditors, a statement to the effect that those among the company auditors who are Outside Company Auditors are Outside Company Auditors;

(xxvii) when taking measures under the provisions of paragraph (3) of Article 440, the matters prescribed by the applicable ordinance of the Ministry of Justice which are necessary for making the information contained in the balance sheet provided for in paragraph (1) of that Article available to the general public;

(xxviii) if there are provisions in the articles of incorporation with regard to the Method of Public Notice under the provisions of Article 939(1), such provisions of the articles of incorporation;

(xxix) if the provisions of the articles of incorporation set forth in the preceding item provide that electronic public notice shall be the Method of Public Notice, the following matters:
  (a) the matters prescribed by the applicable ordinance of the Ministry of Justice which are necessary for making the information to be publicly notified through electronic public notice available to the general public; and
  (b) if there are provisions of the articles of incorporation under the provisions of the second sentence of Article 939(3), such provisions of the articles of incor-

Art.912〜913   Ⅰ Companies Act, Part VII, Chap.IV, Sec.2

poration; and
(xxx) if there are no provisions of the articles of incorporation set forth in item (xxviii), a statement to the effect that publication in an official gazette shall be the Method of Public Notice pursuant to the provisions of Article 939(4).

(Registration of Incorporation of a General Partnership Company)
Article 912 The registration of incorporation of a General Partnership Company shall be completed by registering the following matters at the location of the head office:
(i) the purpose;
(ii) the trade name;
(iii) the addresses of the head office and branch offices;
(iv) if there are provisions in the articles of incorporation with regard to the duration or the grounds for dissolution of the General Partnership Company, such provisions;
(v) the names and domiciles of the partners;
(vi) the name of the partner representing the General Partnership Company (limited to cases where there is a partner(s) not representing the General Partnership Company);
(vii) if the partner representing the General Partnership Company is a juridical person, the name and domicile of the person who is to perform the duties of such partner;
(viii) if there are provisions in the articles of incorporation with regard to the Method of Public Notice under the provisions of Article 939(1), such provisions of the articles of incorporation;
(ix) if the provisions of the articles of incorporation set forth in the preceding item provide that electronic public notice shall be the Method of Public Notice, the following matters:
  (a) the matters prescribed by the applicable ordinance of the Ministry of Justice which are necessary for making the information to be publicly notified through electronic public notice available to the general public; and
  (b) if there are provisions of the articles of incorporation under the provisions of the second sentence of Article 939(3), such provisions of the articles of incorporation; and
(x) if there are no provisions of the articles of incorporation set forth in item (viii), a statement to the effect that publication in an official gazette shall be the Method of Public Notice pursuant to the provisions of Article 939(4).

(Registration of Incorporation of a Limited Partnership Company)
Article 913 The registration of incorporation of a Limited Partnership Company shall be completed by registering the following matters at the location of the head office:
(i) the purpose;
(ii) the trade name;
(iii) the addresses of the head office and branch offices;
(iv) if there are provisions in the articles of incorporation with regard to the duration or the grounds for dissolution of the Limited Partnership Company, such provisions;
(v) the names and domiciles of the partners;
(vi) a statement as to whether the partners are limited partners or unlimited partners;
(vii) the subjects of the contributions by limited partners, the value thereof and the value of the contributions already performed;
(viii) the name of the partner representing the Limited Partnership Company (limited to cases where there is a partner(s) not representing the Limited Partnership

Company);
(ix) if the partner representing the Limited Partnership Company is a juridical person, the name and domicile of the person who is to perform the duties of such partner;
(x) if there are provisions in the articles of incorporation with regard to the Method of Public Notice under the provisions of Article 939(1), such provisions of the articles of incorporation;
(xi) if the provisions of the articles of incorporation set forth in the preceding item provide that electronic public notice shall be the Method of Public Notice, the following matters:
  (a) the matters prescribed by the applicable ordinance of the Ministry of Justice which are necessary for making the information to be publicly notified through electronic public notice available to the general public; and
  (b) if there are provisions of the articles of incorporation under the provisions of the second sentence of Article 939(3), such provisions of the articles of incorporation; and
(xii) if there are no provisions of the articles of incorporation set forth in item (x), a statement to the effect that publication in an official gazette shall be the Method of Public Notice pursuant to the provisions of Article 939(4).

(Registration of Incorporation of a Limited Liability Company)
Article 914 The registration of incorporation of a Limited Liability Company shall be completed by registering the following matters at the location of the head office:
(i) the purpose;
(ii) the trade name;
(iii) the addresses of the head office and branch offices;
(iv) if there are provisions in the articles of incorporation with regard to the duration or the grounds for dissolution of the Limited Liability Company, such provisions;
(v) the amount of stated capital;
(vi) the names of the partners who execute the business of the Limited Liability; Company
(vii) the name and domicile of the partner representing the Limited Liability Company;
(viii) if the partner representing the Limited Liability Company is a juridical person, the name and domicile of the person who is to perform the duties of such partner;
(ix) if there are provisions in the articles of incorporation with regard to the Method of Public Notice under the provisions of Article 939(1), such provisions of the articles of incorporation;
(x) if the provisions of the articles of incorporation set forth in the preceding item provide that electronic public notice shall be the Method of Public Notice, the following matters:
  (a) the matters prescribed by the applicable ordinance of the Ministry of Justice which are necessary for making the information to be publicly notified through electronic public notice available to the general public; and
  (b) if there are provisions of the articles of incorporation under the provisions of the second sentence of Article 939(3), such provisions of the articles of incorporation; and
(xi) if there are no provisions of the articles of incorporation set forth in item (ix), a statement to the effect that publication in an official gazette shall be the Method of Public Notice pursuant to the provisions of Article 939(4).

(Registration of a Change)
Article 915 (1) When there is a change to the matters listed in the items of Article

911(3) or in the items of the preceding three Articles with regard to a Company, the registration of the change shall be completed at the location of the head office within two weeks.
(2) Notwithstanding the provisions of the preceding paragraph, in cases where the period set forth in Article 199(1)(iv) has been prescribed, it shall be sufficient to complete the registration of a change resulting from a share issue within two weeks from the last day of such period.
(3) Notwithstanding the provisions of paragraph (1), it shall be sufficient to complete the registration of a change based on any one of the following grounds within two weeks from the last day of each month:
(i) exercise of Share Options; or
(ii) the demand under the provisions of Article 166(1) (limited to cases where the matters listed in Article 107(2)(ii)(c) or (d) or Article 108(2)(v)(b) are provided for as the features of shares).

(Registration of Relocation of the Head Office to the Jurisdictional District of Another Registry)
Article 916 When a Company relocates its head office to the jurisdictional district of another registry, the registration of relocation shall be completed at the old location and the matters specified in the following items for the categories of Companies set forth respectively in those items shall be registered at the new location within two weeks:
(i) Stock Company: the matters listed in the items of Article 911(3);
(ii) General Partnership Company: the matters listed in the items of Article 912;
(iii) Limited Partnership Company: the matters listed in the items of Article 913; and
(iv) Limited Liability Company: the matters listed in the items of Article 914.

(Registration of a Provisional Disposition, etc. Suspending Execution of Duties)
Article 917 When a provisional disposition order suspending execution of duties by any one of the persons specified in the following items for the categories of Companies set forth respectively in those items or appointing a person who will perform such duties on behalf of the former person is issued or a ruling changing or revoking such provisional disposition order is made, the registration thereof shall be completed at the location of the head office:
(i) Stock Company: a director, accounting advisor, company auditor, Representative Director, committee member, executive officer or representative executive officer;
(ii) General Partnership Company: a partner;
(iii) Limited Partnership Company: a partner; or
(iv) Limited Liability Company: a partner executing business.

(Registration of a Manager)
Article 918 When a Company appoints a manager or a manager's authority of representation becomes extinct, the registration thereof shall be completed at the location of the head office.

(Registration of a Change of Kind of a Membership Company)
Article 919 When a Membership Company becomes a Membership Company of another kind pursuant to the provisions of Article 638, the registration of dissolution shall be completed with regard to the Membership Company as it was prior to the change of kind and the registration of incorporation shall be completed with regard to the Membership Company as it will be after the change of kind, at the location of the head of-

fice, within two weeks from the day on which the change to the articles of incorporation prescribed in that Article became effective.

(Registration of an Entity Conversion)
Article 920 When a Company effects an Entity Conversion, the registration of dissolution shall be completed with regard to the Company as it was prior to the Entity Conversion and the registration of incorporation shall be completed with regard to the Company as it will be after the Entity Conversion, at the location of the head office, within two weeks from the day on which the Entity Conversion became effective.

(Registration of an Absorption-type Merger)
Article 921 When a Company effects an Absorption-type Merger, the registration of dissolution shall be completed with regard to the Company absorbed through the Absorption-type Merger and the registration of a change shall be completed with regard to the Company surviving the Absorption-type Merger, at the location of the head office, within two weeks from the day on which the Absorption-type Merger became effective.

(Registration of a Consolidation-type Merger)
Article 922 (1) In cases where two or more Companies effect a Consolidation-type Merger, if the Company incorporated through the Consolidation-type Merger is a Stock Company, the registration of dissolution shall be completed with regard to the Companies consolidated through the Consolidation-type Merger and the registration of incorporation shall be completed with regard to the Company incorporated through the Consolidation-type Merger, at the location of the head office, within two weeks from the days specified in the following items for the categories of cases set forth respectively in those items:

(i) in cases where the Companies consolidated through the Consolidation-type Merger are only Stock Companies: whichever of the following days that is the latest:
  (a) the day of the resolution of the shareholders meeting set forth in Article 804(1);
  (b) if a resolution of a Class Meeting is required to effect the Consolidation-type Merger, the day of such resolution;
  (c) the day on which twenty days have elapsed from the day of the notice under the provisions of paragraph (3) of Article 806 or the public notice set forth in paragraph (4) of that Article;
  (d) if the Companies consolidated through the Consolidation-type Merger have issued Share Options, the day on which twenty days have elapsed from the day of the notice under the provisions of paragraph (3) of Article 808 or the public notice set forth in paragraph (4) of that Article;
  (e) the day on which the procedures under the provisions of Article 810 have been completed; or
  (f) the day decided on by an agreement between the Companies consolidated through the Consolidation-type Merger;

(ii) in cases where the Companies consolidated through the Consolidation-type Merger are only Membership Companies: whichever of the following days that is the latest:
  (a) the day on which the consent of all partners set forth in paragraph (1) of Article 813 has been obtained (or, in the cases prescribed in the proviso to that paragraph, the day on which the procedures provided for in the articles of incorporation have been completed);
  (b) the day on which the procedures under the provisions of Article 810 as applied

Art.923〜924　　　Ⅰ Companies Act, Part VII, Chap.IV, Sec.2

mutatis mutandis pursuant to Article 813(2) have been completed; or
(c) the day decided on by an agreement between the Companies consolidated through the Consolidation-type Merger; and
(iii) in cases where the Companies consolidated through the Consolidation-type Merger include both a Stock Company(ies) and a Membership Company(ies): Whichever of the days specified in the preceding two items that is later.
(2) In cases where two or more Companies effect a Consolidation-type Merger, if the Company incorporated through the Consolidation-type Merger is a Membership Company, the registration of dissolution shall be completed with regard to the Companies consolidated through the Consolidation-type Merger and the registration of incorporation shall be completed with regard to the Company incorporated through the Consolidation-type Merger, at the location of the head office, within two weeks from the days specified in the following items for the categories of cases set forth respectively in those items:
(i) in cases where the Companies consolidated through the Consolidation-type Merger are only Stock Companies: whichever of the following days that is the latest:
(a) the day on which the consent of all partners set forth in Article 804(2) has been obtained;
(b) if the Companies consolidated through the Consolidation-type Merger have issued Share Options, the day on which twenty days have elapsed from the day of the notice under the provisions of paragraph (3) of Article 808 or the public notice set forth in paragraph (4) of that Article;
(c) the day on which the procedures under the provisions of Article 810 have been completed; or
(d) the day decided on by an agreement between the Companies consolidated through the Consolidation-type Merger;
(ii) in cases where the Companies consolidated through the Consolidation-type Merger are only Membership Companies: whichever of the following days that is the latest:
(a) the day on which the consent of all partners set forth in paragraph (1) of Article 813 has been obtained (or, in the cases prescribed in the proviso to that paragraph, the day on which the procedures provided for in the articles of incorporation have been completed);
(b) the day on which the procedures under the provisions of Article 810 as applied mutatis mutandis pursuant to Article 813(2) have been completed; or
(c) the day decided on by an agreement between the Companies consolidated through the Consolidation-type Merger; and
(iii) in cases where the Companies consolidated through the Consolidation-type Merger include both a Stock Company(ies) and a Membership Company(ies): Whichever of the days specified in the preceding two items that is later.

(Registration of an Absorption-type Company Split)
Article 923　When a Company effects an Absorption-type Company Split, the registration of a change shall be completed with regard to the Company effecting the Absorption-type Company Split and the Company succeeding to all or part of the rights and obligations held by such Company in connection with its business by transfer from such Company, at the location of the head office, within two weeks from the day on which the Absorption-type Company Split became effective.

(Registration of an Incorporation-type Company Split)
Article 924　(1) In cases where a Stock Company(ies) and/or a Limited Liability

Company(ies) effect an Incorporation-type Company Split, if the Company incorporated through the Incorporation-type Company Split is a Stock Company, the registration of a change shall be completed with regard to the Company(ies) effecting the Incorporation-type Company Split and the registration of incorporation shall be completed with regard to the Company incorporated through the Incorporation-type Company Split, at the location of the head office, within two weeks from the days specified in the following items for the categories of cases set forth respectively in those items:
(i) in cases where the Company(ies) effecting the Incorporation-type Company Split is only a Stock Company(ies), whichever of the following days that is the latest:
  (a) in cases other than those prescribed in Article 805, the day of the resolution of the shareholders meeting set forth in Article 804(1);
  (b) if a resolution of a Class Meeting is required to effect the Incorporation-type Company Split, the day of such resolution;
  (c) in cases other than those prescribed in Article 805, the day on which twenty days have elapsed from the day of the notice under the provisions of paragraph (3) of Article 806 or the public notice set forth in paragraph (4) of that Article;
  (d) if there are holders of Share Options who are to receive the notice under the provisions of paragraph (3) of Article 808, the day on which twenty days have elapsed from the day of the notice under the provisions of that paragraph or the public notice set forth in paragraph (4) of that Article;
  (e) if the procedures under the provisions of Article 810 need to be carried out, the day on which such procedures are completed; or
  (f) the day decided on by the Stock Company effecting the Incorporation-type Company Split (or, in cases where two or more Stock Companies jointly effect the Incorporation-type Company Split, the day decided on by an agreement between such two or more Stock Companies effecting the Incorporation-type Company Split);
(ii) in cases where the Company(ies) effecting the Incorporation-type Company Split is only a Limited Liability Company(ies), whichever of the following days that is the latest:
  (a) the day on which the consent of all partners set forth in paragraph (1) of Article 813 has been obtained (or, in the cases prescribed in the proviso to that paragraph, the day on which the procedures provided for in the articles of incorporation have been completed);
  (b) if the procedures under the provisions of Article 810 as applied mutatis mutandis pursuant to Article 813(2) need to be carried out, the day on which such procedures were completed; or
  (c) the day decided on by the Limited Liability Company effecting the Incorporation-type Company Split (or, in cases where two or more Limited Liability Companies jointly effect the Incorporation-type Company Split, the day decided on by an agreement between such two or more Limited Liability Companies effecting the Incorporation-type Company Split); and
(iii) in cases where the Company(ies) effecting the Incorporation-type Company Split include both a Stock Company(ies) and a Limited Liability Company(ies), Whichever of the days specified in the preceding two items that is later.
(2) In cases where a Stock Company(ies) and/or a Limited Liability Company(ies) effect an Incorporation-type Company Split, if the Company incorporated through the Incorporation-type Company Split is a Membership Company, the registration of a change shall be completed with regard to the Company(ies) effecting the Incorporation-type Company Split and the registration of incorporation shall be completed with regard to the Company incorporated through the Incorporation-type Company Split, at the loca-

Art.925 　　　Ⅰ Companies Act, Part VII, Chap.IV, Sec.2

tion of the head office, within two weeks from the days specified in the following items for the categories of cases set forth respectively in those items:
(i) in cases where the Company(ies) effecting the Incorporation-type Company Split is only a Stock Company(ies), whichever of the following days that is the latest:
  (a) in cases other than those prescribed in Article 805, the day of the resolution of the shareholders meeting set forth in Article 804(1);
  (b) if a resolution of a Class Meeting is required to effect the Incorporation-type Company Split, the day of such resolution;
  (c) in cases other than those prescribed in Article 805, the day on which twenty days have elapsed from the day of the notice under the provisions of paragraph (3) of Article 806 or the public notice set forth in paragraph (4) of that Article;
  (d) if the procedures under the provisions of Article 810 need to be carried out, the day on which such procedures were completed; or
  (e) the day decided on by the Stock Company effecting the Incorporation-type Company Split (or, in cases where two or more Stock Companies jointly effect the Incorporation-type Company Split, the day decided on by an agreement between such two or more Stock Companies effecting the Incorporation-type Company Split);
(ii) in cases where the Company(ies) effecting the Incorporation-type Company Split is only a Limited Liability Company(ies), whichever of the following days that is the latest:
  (a) the day on which the consent of all partners set forth in paragraph (1) of Article 813 has been obtained (or, in the cases prescribed in the proviso to that paragraph, the day on which the procedures provided for in the articles of incorporation have been completed);
  (b) if the procedures under the provisions of Article 810 as applied mutatis mutandis pursuant to Article 813(2) need to be carried out, the day on which such procedures were completed; or
  (c) the day decided on by the Limited Liability Company effecting the Incorporation-type Company Split (or, in cases where two or more Limited Liability Companies jointly effect the Incorporation-type Company Split, the day decided on by an agreement between such two or more Limited Liability Companies effecting the Incorporation-type Company Split); and
(iii) in cases where the Company(ies) effecting the Incorporation-type Company Split include both a Stock Company(ies) and a Limited Liability Company(ies), whichever of the days specified in the preceding two items that is later.

(Registration of a Share Transfer)
Article 925 In cases where a Stock Company(ies) effects a Share Transfer, the registration of incorporation shall be completed with regard to the Stock Company incorporated through the Share Transfer, at the location of the head office, within two weeks from whichever of the following days that is the latest:
(i) the day of the resolution of the shareholders meeting set forth in Article 804(1);
(ii) if a resolution of a Class Meeting is required to effect the Share Transfer, the day of such resolution;
(iii) the day on which twenty days have elapsed from the day of the notice under the provisions of paragraph (3) of Article 806 or the public notice set forth in paragraph (4) of that Article;
(iv) if there are holders of Share Options who are to receive the notice under the provisions of paragraph (3) of Article 808, the day on which twenty days have elapsed from the day of the notice under the provisions of that paragraph or the public no-

tice set forth in paragraph (4) of that Article;
(v) if the procedures under the provisions of Article 810 need to be carried out, the day on which such procedures were completed; or
(vi) the day decided on by the Stock Company effecting the Share Transfer (or, in cases where two or more Stock Companies jointly effect the Share Transfer, the day decided on by an agreement between such two or more Stock Companies effecting the Share Transfer).

(Registration of Dissolution)
Article 926 When a Company is dissolved pursuant to the provisions of Article 471(i) to (iii) or Article 641(i) to (iv), the registration of dissolution shall be completed at the location of the head office within two weeks.

(Registration of Continuation)
Article 927 When a Company continues in existence pursuant to the provisions off Article 473, Article 642(1) or Article 845, the registration of continuation shall be completed at the location of the head office within two weeks.

(Registration of a Liquidator)
Article 928 (1) When the person set forth in Article 478(1)(i) becomes a liquidator of a Liquidating Stock Company, the following matters shall be registered at the location of the head office within two weeks from the day of dissolution:
(i) the name of the liquidator;
(ii) the name and domicile of the representative liquidator; and
(iii) if the Liquidating Stock Company is a Company with a Board of Liquidators, a statement to that effect.
(2) When the person set forth in Article 647(1)(i) becomes a liquidator of a Liquidating Membership Company, the following matters shall be registered at the location of the head office within two weeks from the day of dissolution:
(i) the name of the liquidator;
(ii) the name of the liquidator representing the Liquidating Membership Company (limited to cases where there is a liquidator(s) not representing the Liquidating Membership Company); and
(iii) if the liquidator representing the Liquidating Membership Company is a juridical person, the name and domicile of the person who is to perform the duties of the liquidator.
(3) When a liquidator is appointed, the matters listed in the items of paragraph (1) shall be registered in the case of a Liquidating Stock Company and the matters listed in the items of the preceding paragraph shall be registered in the case of a Liquidating Membership Company, at the location of the head office, within two weeks.
(4) The provisions of Article 915(1) shall apply mutatis mutandis to the registration under the provisions of the preceding three paragraphs, and the provisions of Article 917 shall apply mutatis mutandis to a liquidator, representative liquidator or liquidator representing a Liquidating Membership Company.

(Registration of Completion of Liquidation)
Article 929 When liquidation is completed, the registration of the completion of liquidation shall be completed at the location of the head office within two weeks from the days specified in the following items for the categories of Companies set forth respectively in those items:
(i) Liquidating Stock Company: the day of the approval set forth in Article 507(3);

(ii) Liquidating Membership Company (limited to a General Partnership Company or a Limited Partnership Company): the day of the approval set forth in Article 667(1) (or, in cases where the method of disposition of property set forth in Article 668(1) has been prescribed, the day on which such disposition of property has been completed); and
(iii) Liquidating Membership Company (limited to a Limited Liability Company): the day of the approval set forth in Article 667(1).

Subsection 2 Registration at the Location of a Branch Office

(Registration at the Location of a Branch Office)
Article 930 (1) In the cases listed in the following items (excluding cases where the branch offices prescribed in those items are within the jurisdictional district of the registry having jurisdiction over the location of the head office), the registration at the location of a branch office shall be completed at the location of the relevant branch office within the periods specified respectively in those items:
(i) in cases where a branch office is established at the time of the incorporation of a Company (excluding the cases prescribed in the following item to item (iv)), within two weeks from the day the registration of incorporation was completed at the location of the head office;
(ii) in cases where a branch office is established by the Company Incorporated through Consolidation-type Merger at the time of the Consolidation-type Merger, within three weeks from the days specified in the items of Article 922(1) or in the items of Article 922(2);
(iii) in cases where a branch office is established by the Company Incorporated through Incorporation-type Company Split at the time of the Incorporation-type Company Split, within three weeks from the days specified in the items of Article 924(1) or in the items of Article 924(2);
(iv) in cases where a branch office is established by the Stock Company Incorporated through Share Transfer at the time of the Share Transfer, within three weeks from whichever of the days listed in the items of Article 925 that is the latest; and
(v) in cases where a branch office is established after the formation of a Company, within three weeks from the day of establishment of the branch office.
(2) The following matters shall be registered upon the registration at the location of a branch office; provided, however, that it shall be sufficient to register the matter set forth in item (iii) when a branch office is established within the jurisdictional district of the registry having jurisdiction over the location of an existing branch office:
(i) the trade name;
(ii) the address of the head office; and
(iii) the address(es) of the branch office(s) (limited to those within the jurisdictional district of the registry having jurisdiction over the location of the relevant branch office).
(3) When there is a change to the matters listed in the items of the preceding paragraph, the registration of the change shall be completed at the location of the relevant branch office within three weeks.

(Registration of Relocation of a Branch Office to the Jurisdictional District of Another Registry)
Article 931 When a Company relocates a branch office to the jurisdictional district of another registry, the registration of relocation shall be completed at the old location (ex-

cluding cases where the old location is within the jurisdictional district of the registry having jurisdiction over the location of the head office) within three weeks, and the matters specified in the items of paragraph (2) of the preceding Article shall be registered at the new location (excluding cases where the new location is within the jurisdictional district of the registry having jurisdiction over the location of the head office; hereinafter the same shall apply in this Article) within four weeks; provided, however, that it shall be sufficient to register the matter set forth in item (iii) of that paragraph at the new location when a branch office is relocated to the jurisdictional district of the registry having jurisdiction over the location of an existing branch office.

(Registration of a Change, etc. with Regard to a Branch Office)
Article 932 In the cases prescribed in Articles 919 to 925 and Article 929, the registration prescribed in these provisions shall be completed also at the location(s) of the branch office(s) within three weeks from the days prescribed in these provisions; provided, however, that the registration of a change prescribed in Article 921, Article 923 or Article 924 shall be completed only in cases where there is a change to the matters listed in the items of Article 930(2).

Section 3 Registration of a Foreign Company

(Registration of a Foreign Company)
Article 933 (1) When a Foreign Company specifies its representative(s) in Japan for the first time pursuant to the provisions of Article 817(1), registration of the Foreign Company shall be completed at the locations specified in the following items for the categories of cases set forth respectively in those items, within three weeks:
(i) in cases where no business office is established in Japan, the location(s) of the domicile(s) of its representative(s) in Japan (limited to those whose domicile is in Japan); or
(ii) in cases where a business office is established in Japan, the location of such business office.
(2) Upon the registration of a Foreign Company, the matters listed in the items of Article 911(3) or in the items of Articles 912 to 914 shall be registered and also the following matters shall be registered, in accordance with the same kind of Company or the most similar kind of Company in Japan:
(i) the law governing the incorporation of the Foreign Company;
(ii) the name(s) and domicile(s) of its representative(s) in Japan;
(iii) if the same kind of Company or the most similar Company in Japan is a Stock Company, the method of giving public notice under the provisions of the governing law prescribed in item (i);
(iv) in the cases prescribed in the preceding item, if the Foreign Company intends to take the measure prescribed in Article 819(3), the matters prescribed by the applicable ordinance of the Ministry of Justice which are necessary for making the information contained in what is equivalent to the balance sheet provided for in paragraph (1) of that Article available to the general public;
(v) if there are provisions with regard to the Method of Public Notice under the provisions of Article 939(2), such provisions;
(vi) if the provisions set forth in the preceding item provide that electronic public notice shall be the Method of Public Notice, the following matters:
(a) the matters prescribed by the applicable ordinance of the Ministry of Justice which are necessary for making the information to be publicly notified through electronic public notice available to the general public; and

Art.934〜935　　　Ⅰ Companies Act, Part VII, Chap.IV, Sec.3

(b) if there are provisions under the provisions of the second sentence of Article 939(3), such provisions; and
(vii) if there are no provisions set forth in item (v), a statement to the effect that publication in an official gazette shall be the Method of Public Notice pursuant to the provisions of Article 939(4).
(3) With regard to application of the provisions of the preceding paragraph concerning a business office established in Japan by a Foreign Company, such business office shall be deemed to be the branch office prescribed in Article 911(3)(iii), Article 912(iii), Article 913(iii) or Article 914(iii).
(4) The provisions of Article 915 and Articles 918 to 929 shall apply mutatis mutandis to Foreign Companies. In such cases, the term "two weeks" in these provisions shall be deemed to be replaced with "three weeks" and the term "location of the head office" in those provisions shall be deemed to be replaced with "location(s) of the domicile(s) of its representative(s) in Japan (limited to those whose domicile is in Japan) (or, for a Foreign Company that has established a business office in Japan, the location of such business office)."
(5) When a matter that should be registered pursuant to the provisions of the preceding paragraphs arises in a foreign country, the period for registration shall be counted from the day on which the notice thereof reached a representative in Japan.

(Registration, etc. of Appointment of a Representative in Japan)
Article 934　(1) In cases where a Foreign Company that has not established a business office in Japan specifies a new representative in Japan after registration of the Foreign Company (excluding cases where the location of the domicile of the relevant representative is within the jurisdictional district of the registry having jurisdiction over the location of the domicile of another representative in Japan), the registration of the Foreign Company shall also be completed at the location of the domicile of such newly specified representative in Japan, within three weeks.
(2) In cases where a Foreign Company that has established a business office(s) in Japan establishes a new business office in Japan after registration of the Foreign Company (excluding cases where the location of the relevant business office is within the jurisdictional district of the registry having jurisdiction over the location of another registered business office), the registration of the Foreign Company shall also be completed at the location of such newly established business office in Japan, within three weeks.

(Registration, etc. of the Relocation of the Domicile of a Representative in Japan)
Article 935　(1) When a representative in Japan of a Foreign Company that has not established a business office in Japan relocates such representative's domicile to the jurisdictional district of another registry after registration of the Foreign Company, the registration of relocation shall be completed at the location of the old domicile within three weeks and the registration of the Foreign Company shall be completed at the location of the new domicile within four weeks; provided, however, that it shall be sufficient to have the relocation of the domicile registered at the location of the new domicile when such representative relocates such representative's domicile to the jurisdictional district of the registry having jurisdiction over the location of the domicile of another registered representative in Japan.
(2) When a Foreign Company that has established a business office in Japan relocates its business office to the jurisdictional district of another registry after registration of the Foreign Company, the registration of relocation shall be completed at the old location within three weeks and the registration of the Foreign Company shall be completed at

the new location within four weeks; provided, however, that it shall be sufficient to have the relocation of the business office registered at the new location when it relocates a business office to the jurisdictional district of the registry having jurisdiction over the location of the domicile of another registered business office.

(Registration, etc. of Establishment of a Business Office in Japan)
Article 936 (1) When a Foreign Company that has not established a business office in Japan establishes a business office in Japan after registration of the Foreign Company, the registration of the establishment of the business office shall be completed at the location(s) of the domicile(s) of its representative(s) in Japan within three weeks and the registration of the Foreign Company shall be completed at the location of the business office within four weeks; provided, however, that it shall be sufficient to have the establishment of the business office registered when it establishes a business office to the jurisdictional district of the registry having jurisdiction over the location of the domicile of a registered representative in Japan.
(2) When a Foreign Company that has established a business office in Japan closes all of its business offices in Japan after registration of the Foreign Company, the registration of the closure of the business office shall be complete at the location(s) of its business office(s) within three weeks and the registration of the Foreign Company shall be completed at the location(s) of the domicile(s) of its representative(s) in Japan within four weeks, except in cases where all of its representatives in Japan of such Foreign Company intend to resign; provided, however, that it shall be sufficient to have the closure of all business offices registered when the location(s) of the domicile(s) of its representative(s) in Japan is within the jurisdictional district of the registry having jurisdiction over the location of the registered business office(s).

Section 4 Commissioning of Registration

(Commissioning of Registration by a Judicial Decision)
Article 937 (1) In the following cases, a court clerk shall commission the registration, ex officio, to the registry having jurisdiction over the location of the head office (or, in the cases prescribed in item (i)(g), if the matters listed in the items of Article 930(2) have been registered as a result of such resolution, the head office and the branch office(s) pertaining to such registration) of the Company without delay:
(i) when a judgment upholding a claim relating to any one of the following actions becomes final and binding:
  (a) an action seeking invalidation of the incorporation of a Company;
  (b) an action seeking invalidation of a share issue after the formation of a Stock Company;
  (c) an action seeking invalidation of an issue of Share Options (in cases where such Share Options are those attached to Bonds with Share Options, they shall include the Bonds pertaining to such Bonds with Share Options; hereinafter the same shall apply in this Section);
  (d) an action seeking invalidation of a reduction in the amount of stated capital of a Stock Company;
  (e) an action for a declaratory judgment of absence of a share issue after the formation of a Stock Company;
  (f) an action for a declaratory judgment of absence of a Share Option issue;
  (g) the following actions in cases where matters resolved at a Shareholders Meeting, etc. have been registered:
  1. an action for a declaratory judgment of absence of a resolution of a Shareholders

Art.937　　　Ⅰ Companies Act, Part VII, Chap.IV, Sec.4

　　　　　Meeting, etc. or invalidation of a resolution of a Shareholders Meeting, etc. on the basis that the contents of such resolution violate laws and regulations; or
　　　　2. an action seeking revocation of a resolution of a Shareholders Meeting, etc.;
　　　(h) an action seeking rescission of the incorporation of a Membership Company;
　　　(i) an action seeking dissolution of a Company;
　　　(j) an action Seeking Dismissal of an Officer of a Stock Company;
　　　(k) an Action Seeking Removal of Partner of Membership Company; or
　　　(l) an Action Seeking Extinguishment of Right to Execute Business or Authority of Representation of Partner Executing Business of Membership Company;
　(ii) when any one of the following judicial decisions is made:
　　　(a) a judicial decision on the appointment of a person who is temporarily to perform the duties of a director, accounting advisor, company auditor, Representative Director, committee member, executive officer or representative executive officer under the provisions of Article 346(2), Article 351(2) or Article 401(3) (including the cases where it is applied mutatis mutandis pursuant to Article 403(3) and Article 420(3));
　　　(b) a judicial decision on the appointment of a person who is temporarily to perform the duties of a liquidator or representative liquidator under the provisions of Article 351(2) as applied mutatis mutandis pursuant to Article 346(2) or Article 483(6) as applied mutatis mutandis pursuant to Article 479(4) (excluding the judicial decision prescribed in paragraph (2)(i) of the following Article);
　　　(c) a judicial decision revoking the judicial decision set forth in (a) or (b) (excluding the judicial decision prescribed in paragraph (2)(ii) of the following Article);
　　　(d) a judicial decision revoking a judicial decision on the appointment or selection of a liquidator, a representative liquidator or a liquidator who represents a Liquidating Membership Company (excluding the judicial decision prescribed in paragraph (2)(iii) of the following Article); or
　　　(e) a judicial decision on the dismissal of a liquidator (excluding the judicial decision prescribed in paragraph (2)(iv) of the following Article); and
　(iii) when any one of the following judicial decisions becomes final and binding:
　　　(a) a judicial decision revoking the judicial decision set forth in (e) of the preceding item; or
　　　(b) a judicial decision ordering the dissolution of a Company under the provisions of Article 824(1).
(2) When a judicial decision ordering the prohibition of a Foreign Company's continuous transactions in Japan or closure of its business office in Japan under the provisions of Article 827(1) becomes final and binding, a court clerk shall commission the registration, ex officio, to the registry having jurisdiction over the locations specified in the following items for the categories of Foreign Companies set forth respectively in those items without delay:
　(i) Foreign Company that has not established a business office in Japan: The location(s) of the domicile(s) of its representative(s) in Japan (limited to those whose domicile is in Japan); and
　(ii) Foreign Company that has established a business office(s) in Japan: The location(s) of such business office(s).
(3) In cases where a judgment upholding a claim relating to the actions listed in the following items becomes final and binding, a court clerk shall commission the registrations specified respectively in those items, ex officio, to the registry having jurisdiction over the location of the head office of each Company without delay:
　(i) an action seeking invalidation of an Entity Conversion of a Company: registration of dissolution with regard to the Company after the Entity Conversion and registra-

tion of restoration with regard to the Company effecting the Entity Conversion;
(ii) an action seeking invalidation of an Absorption-type Merger of a Company: registration of a change with regard to the Company Surviving Absorption-type Merger and registration of restoration with regard to the Company absorbed by the Absorption-type Merger;
(iii) an action seeking invalidation of a Consolidation-type Merger of a Company: registration of dissolution with regard to the Company incorporated through the Consolidation-type Merger and registration of restoration with regard to the Companies consolidated through the Consolidation-type Merger;
(iv) an action seeking invalidation of an Absorption-type Company Split of a Company: registration of a change with regard to the Company effecting the Absorption-type Company Split and the Company succeeding to all or part of the rights and obligations held by such Company in connection with its business by transfer from such Company;
(v) an action seeking invalidation of an Incorporation-type Company Split: registration of a change with regard to the Company(ies) effecting the Incorporation-type Company Split and registration of dissolution with regard to the Company incorporated through the Incorporation-type Company Split;
(vi) an action seeking invalidation of a Share Exchange of a Stock Company: registration of a change with regard to the Stock Company effecting the Share Transfer (limited to cases where there are provisions on the matters set forth in Article 768(1)(iv)) and the Company acquiring all of the Issued Shares of the Stock Company effecting the Share Transfer; and
(vii) an action seeking invalidation of a Share Exchange of a Stock Company(ies): registration of a change with regard to the Company(ies) effecting the Share Transfer (limited to cases where there are provisions on the matters set forth in Article 773(1)(ix)) and registration of dissolution with regard to the Stock Company incorporated through the Share Transfer.
(4) In the cases prescribed in the preceding paragraph, if the matters listed in the items of paragraph (2) of Article 930 have been registered as a result of the Entity Conversion, merger or company split that is the subject of the claim relating to any one of the actions listed in the items of that paragraph, the court clerk shall, in addition, commission the registrations specified in the items of the preceding paragraph to the registry(ies) having jurisdiction over the location(s) of the branch office(s) of each Company.

(Commissioning of Registration by a Juridical Decision Concerning Special Liquidation)

Article 938 (1) In the cases listed in the following items, a court clerk shall commission the registrations specified respectively in those items, ex officio, to the registry having jurisdiction over the location of the head office (or, in the cases set forth in item (iii), if a ruling to conclude special liquidation is made due to completion of special liquidation, the head office and branch office(s)) of the Liquidating Stock Company without delay:
(i) when an order to commence special liquidation is issued, registration of commencement of special liquidation;
(ii) when a ruling to revoke an order to commence special liquidation becomes final and binding, registration of revocation of commencement of special liquidation; and
(iii) when a ruling to conclude special liquidation becomes final and binding, registration of conclusion of special liquidation.
(2) In the following cases, a court clerk shall commission the registration, ex officio, to

the registry having jurisdiction over the location of the head office of the Liquidating Stock Company without delay:
(i) when the court makes a judicial decision on the appointment of a person who is temporarily to perform the duties of a liquidator or representative liquidator under the provisions of Article 351(2) as applied mutatis mutandis pursuant to Article 346(2) or Article 483(6) as applied mutatis mutandis pursuant to Article 479(4) after the commencement of special liquidation;
(ii) when the court makes a judicial decision revoking the judicial decision set forth in the preceding item;
(iii) when the court makes a judicial decision revoking a judicial decision on the appointment or selection of a liquidator or representative liquidator after the commencement of special liquidation;
(iv) when the court makes a judicial decision on the dismissal of a liquidator after the commencement of special liquidation; and
(v) when a judicial decision revoking the judicial decision set forth in the preceding item becomes final and binding.
(3) In the following cases, a court clerk shall commission the registration of such temporary restraining order, ex officio, without delay:
(i) when the court issues a temporary restraining order under the provisions of Article 540(1) or (2) concerning a right which is categorized as the property of the Liquidating Stock Company and which is registered; and
(ii) when the court issues a temporary restraining order under the provisions of Article 542(1) or (2) concerning a registered right.
(4) The provisions of the preceding paragraph shall apply mutatis mutandis to cases where the temporary restraining order prescribed in that paragraph is changed or revoked or in cases where such temporary restraining order becomes ineffective.
(5) The provisions of the preceding two paragraphs shall apply mutatis mutandis to registered rights.
(6) The provisions of the preceding paragraphs shall apply mutatis mutandis to the liquidation of a Foreign Company's property in Japan under the provisions of Article 822(1), excluding those that are not applicable by their nature.

Chapter V Public Notice

Section 1 General Provisions

(Method of Public Notice of a Company)
Article 939 (1) A Company may prescribe any one of the following methods as the Method of Public Notice in its articles of incorporation:
(i) publication in an official gazette;
(ii) publication in a daily newspaper that publishes matters on current affairs; or
(iii) electronic public notice.
(2) A Foreign Company may prescribe any one of the methods listed in the items of the preceding paragraph as the Method of Public Notice.
(3) In cases where a Company or a Foreign Company prescribes to the effect that the method set forth in item (iii) of paragraph (1) shall be the Method of Public Notice, it shall be sufficient to prescribe to the effect that electronic public notice shall be the Method of Public Notice. In such cases, the method set forth in item (i) or item (ii) of that paragraph may be prescribed as the Method of Public Notice for cases where it is unable to give public notice by way of electronic public notice due to an accident or other unavoidable circumstances.

(4) The Method of Public Notice of a Company or a Foreign Company that does not have the provisions under the provisions of paragraph (1) or paragraph (2) shall be the method set forth in paragraph (1)(i).

(Public Notice Period, etc. of Electronic Public Notice)

Article 940 (1) In cases where a Stock Company or a Membership Company gives public notice under the provisions of this Act by way of electronic public notice, it shall give public notice by way of electronic public notice continuously until the days specified in the following items for the categories of public notice set forth respectively in those items:
  (i) public notice in cases where the public notice shall be given a certain period prior to a specified date pursuant to the provisions of this Act: such specified date;
  (ii) public notice under the provisions of Article 440(1): the day on which five years have elapsed from the day of the conclusion of the annual shareholders meeting set forth in that paragraph;
  (iii) public notice to the effect that objections may be stated within the period specified in the public notice: the day on which such period has elapsed; and
  (iv) public notice other than that set forth in the preceding three items: the day on which one month has elapsed from the start of such public notice.
(2) In cases where a Foreign Company gives public notice under the provisions of Article 819(1) by way of electronic public notice, it shall give public notice by way of electronic public notice continuously until the day on which five years have elapsed from the day of the conclusion of the procedure set forth in that paragraph.
(3) Notwithstanding the provisions of the preceding two paragraphs, in cases where an Interruption of Public Notice (meaning that the information, which was made available to the general public, is no longer made available or that such information has been altered after being made available to the general public; hereinafter the same shall apply in this paragraph) occurs during the period in which public notice was to be given by way of electronic public notice pursuant to these provisions (hereinafter referred to as the "Public Notice Period" in this Chapter), if all of the following conditions are met, such Interruption of Public Notice shall not affect the effects of such public notice:
  (i) the Company is without knowledge and is not grossly negligent or the Company has justifiable grounds with regard to the occurrence of the Interruption of Public Notice;
  (ii) the total time during which the Interruption of Public Notice has occurred does not exceed one-tenth of the Public Notice Period; and
  (iii) promptly after learning about the occurrence of the Interruption of Public Notice, the Company has given public notice of such fact, the time when the Interruption of Public Notice occurred and the details of the Interruption of Public Notice by appending such information to the relevant public notice.

Section 2 Electronic Public Notice Investigation Body

(Electronic Public Notice Investigation)

Article 941 A Company that intends to give public notice under the provisions of this Act or another Act (excluding the public notice under the provisions of Article 440(1); hereinafter the same shall apply in this Section) by way of electronic public notice shall request a person who has been registered by the Minister of Justice (hereinafter referred to as an "Investigation Body" in this Section) to carry out an investigation as to whether the information contained in such public notice is being made available to the general public during the Public Notice Period, pursuant to the provisions of the applicable Ordinance of the Ministry of Justice.

(Registration)
Article 942 (1) The registration set forth in the preceding Article (hereinafter simply referred to as the "Registration" in this Section) shall be made through an application by a person who intends to conduct the investigation under the provisions of that Article (hereinafter referred to as the "Electronic Public Notice Investigation" in this Section).
(2) A person who intends to obtain the Registration shall pay a fee to the amount specified by the applicable Cabinet Order by giving consideration to the actual cost.

(Grounds for Disqualification)
Article 943 A person who falls under any one of the following categories of persons may not obtain the Registration:
(i) a person who has been sentenced to a fine or a severer punishment for the violation of the provisions of this Section or the provisions of Article 955(1) as applied mutatis mutandis pursuant to Article 92(5) of the Agricultural Cooperatives Act (Act No. 132 of 1947), Article 34-20(6) of the Certified Public Accountants Act, Article 121(5) of the Fisheries Cooperatives Act (Act No. 242 of 1948), Article 33(7) of the Small and Medium-Sized Enterprise Cooperatives Act (Act No. 181 of 1949) (including the cases where it is applied mutatis mutandis pursuant to Article 20 of the Export Fisheries Promotion Act (Act No. 154 of 1954) and Article 5-23(3) and Article 47(2) of the Act on Organizations of Small and Medium Sized Enterprises (Act No. 185 of 1957)), Article30-28(6) of the Attorneys Act (Act No. 205 of 1949) (including the cases where it is applied mutatis mutandis pursuant to Article 43(3) of that Act), Article 55(3) of the Ship Owners' Mutual Insurance Union Act (Act No. 177 of 1950), Article 45-2(6) of the Judicial Scrivener Act (Act No. 197 of 1950), Article 40-2(6) of the Land and House Investigator Act (Act No. 228 of 1950), Article 11(9) of the Commodity Exchange Act (Act No. 239 of 1950), Article 13-20-2(6) of the Administrative Scrivener Act (Act No. 4 of 1951), Article 48-2(3) of the Act on Securities Investment Trust and Securities Investment Corporations (Act No. 198 of 1951) (including the cases where it is applied mutatis mutandis pursuant to Article 49-13(2) and (3) and Article 59 of that Act) and Article 186-2(4) of that Act, Article 48-19-2(6) of the Certified Public Tax Accountant Act (including the cases where it is applied mutatis mutandis pursuant to Article 49-12(3) of that Act), Article 87-4(4) of the Shinkin Bank Act (Act No. 238 of 1951), Article 15(6) of the Export and Import Transaction Act (Act No. 299 of 1952) (including the cases where it is applied mutatis mutandis pursuant to Article 19-6 of that Act), Article 55(5) of the Loan Security Act for Small and Medium Sized Fishery Industry (Act No. 346 of 1952), Article 91-4(4) of the Labor Bank Act (Act No. 227 of 1953), Article 9(7) of the Act on Research and Development Partnership concerning Mining and Manufacturing Technology (Act No. 81 of 1961), Article 48-3(5) of the Agricultural Credit Guarantee Insurance Act (Act No. 204 of 1961) (including the cases where it is applied mutatis mutandis pursuant to Article 48-9(7) of that Act), Article 25-23-2(6) of the Act on Public Consultants on Social and Labor Insurance (Act No. 89 of 1968), Article 23(6) of the Act on Foreign Securities Brokers (Act No. 5 of 1971), Article 8-2(5) of the Forestry Partnership Act (Act No. 36 of 1978), Article 49-2(2) of the Banking Act, Article 84(7) of the Financial Instruments and Exchange Act (Act No. 77 of 1988), Article 67-2 and Article 217(3) of the Insurance Business Act (Act No. 105 of 1995), Article 194(4) and Article 288(3) of the Act on Securitization of Assets (Act No. 105 of 1998), Article 53-2(6) of the Patent Attorney Act (Act No.

49 of 2000), Article 96-2(4) of the Norinchukin Bank Act (Act No. 93 of 2001) and Article 57(6) of the Trust Business Act (hereinafter collectively referred to as the "Electronic Public Notice Related Provisions" in this Section) or the violation of an order based on the provisions this Section and where two years have yet to elapse from the day on which the execution of the sentence has been completed or the sentence has become no longer applicable;
(ii) a person whose Registration has been rescinded pursuant to the provisions of Article 954 and where two years have yet to elapse from the day of such rescission; or
(iii) a juridical person where the Directors, etc. engaged in the business thereof (meaning directors, executive officers, partners executing business, inspectors, company auditors or persons equivalent thereto; the same shall apply in Article 947) include a person who falls under any one of the preceding two items.

(Registration Standards)
Article 944 (1) When a person who has filed an application for a Registration pursuant to the provisions of Article 942(1) satisfies all of the following requirements, the Minister of Justice shall complete the Registration of such person. In such cases, the necessary procedures concerning a Registration shall be prescribed by the applicable Ordinance of the Ministry of Justice:
(i) the person shall carry out the Electronic Public Notice Investigation by using the computers (including input-output devices; hereinafter the same shall apply in this item) and Programs (meaning instructions given to a computer, combined so as to obtain a certain result; hereinafter the same shall apply in this item) necessary for the Electronic Public Notice Investigation, which satisfy all of the following requirements:
   (a) such computers and Programs shall allow users to inspect, through the Internet, the information that is publicly notified by way of electronic public notice;
   (b) necessary measures shall be taken for preventing persons from making such computers fail to operate in accordance with the purpose of use or making them operate against the purpose of use by damaging such computers or Electromagnetic Records to be used by such computers, giving false information or wrongful instructions to such computers or any other method;
   (c) such computers and Programs shall have the function of preserving the information and instructions that have been input into such computers and the information received through the Internet throughout the period of carrying out the Electronic Public Notice Investigation; and
(ii) the necessary implementation method for carrying out the Electronic Public Notice Investigation appropriately shall have been prescribed.
(2) The Registration shall be completed by stating or recording the following matters in the Investigation Body registry:
(i) the date of the Registration and the Registration number;
(ii) the name and domicile of the person who obtained the Registration, and in the case of a juridical person, the name of the representative thereof; and
(iii) the location of the place of business where the person who obtained the Registration will carry out the Electronic Public Notice Investigation.

(Renewal of Registration)
Article 945 (1) Unless a Registration is renewed at an interval of not less than three years as specified by the applicable Cabinet Order, it shall become ineffective by the expiration of such period.
(2) The provisions of the preceding three Articles shall apply mutatis mutandis to the re-

newal of a Registration set forth in the preceding paragraph.

(Obligation, etc. of Investigation)
Article 946 (1) When being requested to carry out an Electronic Public Notice Investigation, an Investigation Body shall carry out the Electronic Public Notice Investigation except in cases where there are justifiable grounds.
(2) An Investigation Body shall carry out an Electronic Public Notice Investigation fairly and by the method prescribed by the applicable Ordinance of the Ministry of Justice.
(3) In cases where an Investigation Body carries out an Electronic Public Notice Investigation, such Investigation Body shall report to the Minister of Justice the trade name of the person who has requested the Electronic Public Notice Investigation (hereinafter referred to as the "Investigation Entruster" in this Section) and any other matters prescribed by the applicable Ordinance of the Ministry of Justice, pursuant to the provisions of the applicable Ordinance of the Ministry of Justice.
(4) An Investigation Body shall, without delay after an Electronic Public Notice Investigation, notify the Investigation Entruster of the results of the Electronic Public Notice Investigation, pursuant to the provisions of the applicable Ordinance of the Ministry of Justice.

(Cases Where an Electronic Public Notice Investigation Is Unable to Be Carried Out)
Article 947 An Investigation Body is unable to carry out an Electronic Public Notice Investigation with regard to public notice given by any one of the following persons by way of electronic public notice or with regard to the public notice in the cases prescribed by the applicable Ordinance of the Ministry of Justice as those where such persons or Directors, etc. thereof were involved in the public notice given by way of electronic public notice:
(i) the relevant Investigation Body;
(ii) the Parent Stock Company (meaning a Stock Company which has the relevant Investigation Body as its Subsidiary Company) in cases where the relevant Investigation Body is a Stock Company;
(iii) a juridical person whose Directors, etc. or employees (including those who have been in either of such positions within the past two years; the same shall apply in the following item) constitute more than half of the Directors, etc. of the relevant Investigation Body; or
(iv) a juridical person whose Directors, etc. or employees include the relevant Investigation Body (excluding one who is a juridical person) or a Director, etc. having the authority of representation of the relevant Investigation Body.

(Notification of a Change in the Place of Business)
Article 948 When an Investigation Body intends to change the location of the place of business where Electronic Public Notice Investigations will be carried out, such Investigation Body shall give notification to the Minister of Justice by two weeks prior to the day of such change.

(Business Rules)
Article 949 (1) An Investigation Body shall prescribe rules concerning the business of Electronic Public Notice Investigations (referred to as the "Business Rules" in the following paragraph) and notify the Minister of Justice thereof prior to the commencement of the business of Electronic Public Notice Investigations. The same shall apply when the Investigation Body intends to change the Business Rules.

(2) The Business Rules shall provide for the implementation method of Electronic Public Notice Investigations, fees concerning Electronic Public Notice Investigations and any other matters prescribed by the applicable Ordinance of the Ministry of Justice.

(Suspension or Discontinuance of Business)
Article 950 When an Investigation Body intends to suspend or discontinue all or part of the business of Electronic Public Notice Investigations, such Investigation Body shall notify the Minister of Justice to that effect in advance, pursuant to the provisions of the applicable Ordinance of the Ministry of Justice.

(Keeping and Inspection, etc. of Financial Statements, etc.)
Article 951 (1) An Investigation Body shall, within three months from the end of each business year, prepare an inventory of property, a balance sheet, profit and loss statement or settlement of accounts, and business report (including Electromagnetic Records in cases where Electromagnetic Records are prepared in lieu of preparation of these documents; referred to as the "Financial Statements, etc." in the following paragraph) for such business year, and keep them at such Investigation Body's place of business for five years.

(2) An Investigation Entruster or any other interested party may make the following requests to an Investigation Body at any time during the business hours of the Investigation Body; provided, however, that such person shall pay the fee designated by the Investigation Body when making the request set forth in item (ii) or item (iv):
(i) when the Financial Statements, etc. are prepared in the form of documents, requests for the inspection or copying of such documents;
(ii) requests for the delivery of a transcript or extract of the documents set forth in the preceding item;
(iii) when the Financial Statements, etc. are prepared in the form of Electromagnetic Records, requests for inspection or copying of anything that indicates the matters recorded in such Electromagnetic Records in a manner prescribed by the applicable Ordinance of the Ministry of Justice; and
(iv) requests that the matters recorded in the Electromagnetic Records set forth in the preceding item be provided by the Electromagnetic Method designated by the Investigation Body, or requests for the delivery of any document that states such matters.

(Compliance Order)
Article 952 When the Minister of Justice finds that an Investigation Body no longer complies with any one of the items of Article 944(1), the minister may order the Investigation Body to take necessary measures for complying with these provisions.

(Order for Improvement)
Article 953 When the Minister of Justice finds that an Investigation Body violates the provisions of Article 946, the minister may order the Investigation Body to carry out Electronic Public Notice Investigations or to take necessary measures to improve the method of Electronic Public Notice Investigation or the method of any other business.

(Rescission, etc. of Registration)
Article 954 When an Investigation Body falls under any one of the following items, the Minister of Justice may rescind the Registration of the Investigation Body or order the suspension of all or part of the business of Electronic Public Notice Investigations for a set period:

(i) when the Investigation Body falls under Article 943(i) or (iii);
(ii) when the Investigation Body violates the provisions of Article 947 (including the cases where it is applied mutatis mutandis pursuant to the Electronic Public Notice Related Provisions) to Article 950, Article 951(1) or paragraph (1) of the following Article (including the cases where it is applied mutatis mutandis pursuant to the Electronic Public Notice Related Provisions);
(iii) when the Investigation Body rejects a request under the provisions of the items of Article 951(2) or the items of paragraph (2) of the following Article (including the cases where it is applied mutatis mutandis pursuant to the Electronic Public Notice Related Provisions) without justifiable grounds;
(iv) when the Investigation Body violates the order set forth in Article 952 or in the preceding Article (including the cases where it is applied mutatis mutandis pursuant to the Electronic Public Notice Related Provisions); or
(v) when the Investigation Body obtains the Registration set forth in Article 941 by wrongful means.

(Statements, etc. in an Investigation Record Book, etc.)
Article 955 (1) An Investigation Body shall, pursuant to the provisions of the applicable Ordinance of the Ministry of Justice, keep investigation records or what is prescribed by the applicable Ordinance of the Ministry of Justice as being equivalent thereto (hereinafter referred to as the "Investigation Record Book, etc." in this Article), state or record the matters prescribed by the applicable Ordinance of the Ministry of Justice concerning Electronic Public Notice Investigations, and preserve such Investigation Record Book, etc.
(2) An Investigation Entruster or any other interested party may make the following requests to an Investigation Body with regard to the Investigation Record Book, etc. preserved by such Investigation Body pursuant to the provisions of the preceding paragraph or paragraph (2) of the following Article (limited to the portions in which such person has an interest) at any time during the business hours of the Investigation Body; provided, however, that such person shall pay the fee designated by the Investigation Body when making such requests:
(i) when the Investigation Record Book, etc. is prepared in the form of documents, requests for the delivery of a copy of such documents; and
(ii) when the Investigation Record Book, etc. is prepared in the form of Electromagnetic Records, requests that the matters recorded in such Electromagnetic Records be provided by the Electromagnetic Method designated by the Investigation Body, or requests for the delivery of any document that states such matters.

(Succession of an Investigation Record Book, etc.)
Article 956 (1) When an Investigation Body intends to discontinue all of its business of Electronic Public Notice Investigation or when its Registration is rescinded pursuant to the provisions of Article 954, the Investigation Body shall have another Investigation Body succeed to the Investigation Record Book, etc. set forth in paragraph (1) of the preceding Article (including the cases where it is applied mutatis mutandis pursuant to the Electronic Public Notice Related Provisions), which the former Investigation Body has preserved.
(2) An Investigation Body that has succeeded to the Investigation Record Book, etc. set forth in the preceding paragraph pursuant to the provisions of that paragraph shall preserve such Investigation Record Book, etc. pursuant to the provisions of the applicable Ordinance of the Ministry of Justice.

(Implementation of the Business of Electronic Public Notice Investigation by the Minister of Justice)

Article 957 (1) When no person obtains a Registration, when a notification to suspend or discontinue all or part of the business of Electronic Public Notice Investigation under the provisions of Article 950 is given, when rescinding a Registration or ordering an Investigation Body to suspend all or part of the business of Electronic Public Notice Investigation pursuant to the provisions of Article 954, when it becomes difficult for an Investigation Body to implement all or part of the business of Electronic Public Notice Investigation due to a natural disaster or on any other grounds, or in any other cases where it is found necessary, the Minister of Justice may himself/herself carry out all or part of the business of Electronic Public Notice Investigation.

(2) The succession of the business of Electronic Public Notice Investigation and any other necessary matters in cases where the Minister of Justice himself/herself carries out all or part of the business of Electronic Public Notice Investigation pursuant to the provisions of the preceding paragraph shall be prescribed by the applicable Ordinance of the Ministry of Justice.

(3) A person who seeks the Electronic Public Notice Investigation carried out by the Minister of Justice pursuant to the provisions of paragraph (1) shall pay a fee to the amount specified by the applicable Cabinet Order by giving consideration to the actual cost.

(Reports and Inspections)

Article 958 (1) The Minister of Justice may, to the extent necessary for the enforcement of this Act, have an Investigation Body report on the status of such Investigation Body's business or accounting, or have officials of the Minister of Justice enter the office or place of business of an Investigation Body and inspect the status of the business or the books, documents or any other articles.

(2) An official shall, when conducting an on-site inspection pursuant to the provisions of the preceding paragraph, carry an identification card and present it to the person(s) concerned.

(3) The authority to conduct on-site inspections under paragraph (1) shall not be construed as being vested for criminal investigation.

(Public Notice)

Article 959 In the following cases, the Minister of Justice shall give public notice to that effect in an official gazette:

(i) when the minister completes a Registration;

(ii) when the minister confirms that a Registration became ineffective pursuant to the provisions of Article 945(1);

(iii) when the notification set forth in Article 948 or Article 950 is given;

(iv) when the minister rescinds a Registration or orders the suspension of all or part of the business of Electronic Public Notice Investigation pursuant to the provisions of Article 954; or

(v) when the Minister of Justice himself/herself carries out all or part of the business of Electronic Public Notice Investigation pursuant to the provisions of Article 957(1) or when the minister ceases to carry out all or part of the business of Electronic Public Notice Investigation that the minister had carried out himself/herself

Part VIII Penal Provisions

(Crime of an Aggravated Breach of Trust by a Director, etc.)

Art.960～962　　① Companies Act, Part VIII, Chap.V, Sec.2

Article 960　(1) When any one of the following persons, for the purpose of promoting such person's own interest or the interest of a third party or inflicting damage on a Stock Company, commits an act in breach of such person's duties and causes financial damages to such Stock Company, such person shall be punished by imprisonment with work for not more than ten years or a fine of not more than ten million yen, or both:
(i) an incorporator;
(ii) a Director at Incorporation or Company Auditor at Incorporation;
(iii) a director, accounting advisor, company auditor or executive officer;
(iv) a person to perform duties on behalf of a director, company auditor or executive officer who has been appointed based on a provisional disposition order under the provisions of Article 56 of the Civil Provisional Remedies Act;
(v) a person who is temporarily to perform the duties of a director, accounting advisor, company auditor, Representative Director, committee member, executive officer or representative executive officer appointed pursuant to the provisions of Article 346(2), Article 351(2) or Article 401(3) (including the cases where it is applied mutatis mutandis pursuant to Article 403(3) and Article 420(3));
(vi) a manager;
(vii) an employee to whom the authority of a certain kind of matter or a specific matter concerning business has been delegated; or
(viii) an inspector.
(2) The provisions of the preceding paragraph shall also apply when any one of the following persons, for the purpose of promoting such person's own interest or the interest of a third party or inflicting damage on a Liquidating Stock Company, commits an act in breach of such person's duties and causes financial damages to such Liquidating Stock Company:
(i) a liquidator of the Liquidating Stock Company;
(ii) a person to perform duties on behalf of a liquidator of the Liquidating Stock Company who has been appointed based on a provisional disposition order under the provisions of Article 56 of the Civil Provisional Remedies Act;
(iii) a person who is temporarily to perform the duties of a liquidator or representative liquidator appointed pursuant to the provisions of Article 346(2) as applied mutatis mutandis pursuant to Article 479(4) or Article 351(2) as applied mutatis mutandis pursuant to Article 483(6);
(iv) a liquidator's agent;
(v) a supervisor; or
(vi) an investigator.

(Crime of an Aggravated Breach of Trust by a Representative Bondholder, etc.)
Article 961　When a representative bondholder or a Resolution Administrator (meaning the Resolution Administrator prescribed in Article 737(2); the same shall apply hereinafter), for the purpose of promoting such person's own interest or the interest of a third party or inflicting damage on a bondholder, commits an act in breach of such person's duties and causes financial damages to the bondholder, such person shall be punished by imprisonment with work for not more than five years or a fine of not more than five million yen, or both.

(Attempted Crime)
Article 962　Attempts of the crimes set forth in the preceding two Articles shall be punished.

(Crimes That Put Company Property at Risk)

Article 963 (1) When the person set forth in Article 960(1)(i) or (ii) makes a false statement to or conceals facts from a court, an Organizational Meeting or a Class Organizational Meeting with regard to payment or delivery under the provisions of Article 34(1) or Article 63(1) or the matters listed in the items of Article 28, such person shall be punished by imprisonment with work for not more than five years or a fine of not more than five million yen, or both.

(2) The provisions of the preceding paragraph shall also apply when any one of the persons listed in Article 960(1)(iii) to (v) makes a false statement to or conceals facts from a court, a shareholders meeting or a Class Meeting with regard to the matters set forth in Article 199(1)(iii) or Article 236(1)(iii).

(3) The provisions of paragraph (1) shall also apply when an inspector makes a false statement to or conceals facts from a court with regard to the matters set forth in the items of Article 28, Article 199(1)(iii) or Article 236(1)(iii).

(4) The provisions of paragraph (1) shall also apply when a person appointed pursuant to the provisions of Article 94(1) makes a false statement to or conceals facts from an Organizational Meeting with regard to payment or delivery under the provisions of Article 34(1) or Article 63(1) or the matters set forth in the items of Article 28.

(5) The provisions of paragraph (1) shall also apply when any one of the persons listed in Article 960(1)(iii) to (vii) falls under any one of the following items:

(i) when the person, under any name, unlawfully acquires shares of a Stock Company on the account of such Stock Company;

(ii) when the person pays dividends of surplus in violation of the provisions of laws and regulations or the articles of incorporation; or

(iii) when the person disposes of a Stock Company's property for the purpose of speculative trading outside the scope of the purpose of the Stock Company.

(Crime of Use of False Documents, etc.)

Article 964 (1) When any one of the following persons, in soliciting subscribers for shares, Share Options, Bonds or Bonds with Share Options, uses materials providing explanations about the business of the Company or any other matters, advertisements for such solicitation or any other documents concerning such solicitation that contain false statements with regard to important matters or, in cases where Electromagnetic Records have been prepared in lieu of preparation of such documents, uses such Electromagnetic Records that contain false records with regard to important matters for the administration of such solicitation, such person shall be punished by imprisonment with work for not more than five years or a fine of not more than five million yen, or both:

(i) any one of the persons listed in Article 960(1)(i) to (vii);

(ii) a partner who executes the business of a Membership Company;

(iii) a person to perform duties on behalf of a partner who executes the business of a Membership Company, who has been appointed based on a provisional disposition order under the provisions of Article 56 of the Civil Provisional Remedies Act; or

(iv) a person to whom solicitation of subscribers for shares, Share Options, Bonds or Bonds with Share Options has been entrusted.

(2) The provisions of the preceding paragraph shall also apply when a person who carries out the secondary distribution of shares, Share Options, Bonds or Bonds with Share Options uses documents concerning such secondary distribution that contain false statements with regard to important matters or, in cases where Electromagnetic Records have been prepared in lieu of preparation of such documents, uses such Electromagnetic Records that contain false records with regard to important matters for the

Art.965～968　　　Ⅰ Companies Act, Part VIII, Chap.V, Sec.2

administration of such secondary distribution.

(Crime of Borrowing and Depositing of Money)
Article 965　When any one of the persons listed in Article 960(1)(i) to (vii) borrows and deposits money for disguising the payment relating to a share issue, such person shall be punished by imprisonment with work for not more than five years or a fine of not more than five million yen, or both. The same shall apply to any person who accepts such borrowing and depositing of money.

(Crime of Excessive Issue of Shares)
Article 966　When any one of the following persons issues shares exceeding the total number of shares that may be issued by a Stock Company, such person shall be punished by imprisonment with work for not more than five years or a fine of not more than five million yen:
(i) An incorporator
(ii) A Director at Incorporation or Executive Officer at Incorporation
(iii) A director or executive officer or a liquidator of a Liquidating Stock Company
(iv) a person to perform duties on behalf of a director or executive officer or a liquidator of a Liquidating Stock Company who has been appointed based on a provisional disposition order under the provisions of Article 56 of the Civil Provisional Remedies Act; or
(v) a person who is temporarily to perform the duties of a director or executive officer or a liquidator of a Liquidating Stock Company appointed pursuant to the provisions of Article 346(2) (including the cases where it is applied mutatis mutandis pursuant to Article 479(4)) or Article 401(3) as applied mutatis mutandis pursuant to Article 403(3).

(Crime of the Giving or Acceptance of a Bribe by a Director, etc.)
Article 967　(1) When any one of the following persons accepts, solicits or promises to accept property benefits in connection with such person's duties, in response to a wrongful request, such person shall be punished by imprisonment with work for not more than five years or a fine of not more than five million yen:
(i) any one of the persons listed in the items of Article 960(1) or the items of Article 960(2);
(ii) the person prescribed in Article 961; or
(iii) an accounting auditor or a person who is temporarily to perform the duties of an accounting auditor appointed pursuant to the provisions of Article 346(4).
(2) A person who has given, offered or promised to give the benefits set forth in the preceding paragraph shall be punished by imprisonment with work for not more than three years or a fine of not more than three million yen.

(Crime of the Giving or Acceptance of a Bribe in Relation to Exercise of a Right of a Shareholder, etc.)
Article 968　(1) A person who has accepted, solicited or promised to accept property benefits in relation to any one of the following matters, in response to a wrongful request, shall be punished by imprisonment with work for not more than five years or a fine of not more than five million yen:
(i) statement of opinions or exercise of a voting right at a shareholders meeting, Class Meeting, Organizational Meeting or Class Organizational Meeting, bondholders meeting or creditors meeting;
(ii) exercise of the right of a shareholder prescribed in Article 210 or Article 247, Arti-

cle 297(1) or (4), Article 303(1) or (2), Article 304, Article 305(1) or Article 306(1) or (2) (including the cases where these provisions are applied mutatis mutandis pursuant to Article 325), Article 358(1), Article 360(1) or (2) (including the cases where these provisions are applied mutatis mutandis pursuant to Article 482(4)), Article 422(1) or (2), Article 426(5), Article 433(1) or Article 479(2), exercise of the right of a shareholder or creditor prescribed in Article 511(1) or Article 522(1) or exercise of the right of a creditor prescribed in Article 547(1) or (3);

(iii) exercise of a right of a bondholder holding Bonds of not less than one-tenth of the total amount of Bonds (excluding bonds that have been redeemed);

(iv) filing of the action prescribed in Article 828(1), Articles 829 to 831, Article 833(1), Article 847(3) or (5), Article 853, Article 854 or Article 858 (limited to one filed by a shareholder or creditor of a Stock Company or a person holding Share Options or Bonds with Share Options of a Stock Company); or

(v) a shareholder's intervention in a suit under the provisions of Article 849(1).

(2) The provisions of the preceding paragraph shall also apply to a person who has given, offered or promised to give the benefits set forth in that paragraph.

(Confiscation and Collection of Equivalent Value)
Article 969 In the cases set forth in Article 967(1) or paragraph (1) of the preceding Article, the benefits accepted by the offender shall be confiscated. When it is not possible to confiscate all or part of such benefits, an equivalent value thereof shall be collected.

(Crime of the Giving of Benefits in Relation to Exercise of a Right of a Shareholder)
Article 970 (1) When any one of the persons listed in Article 960(1)(iii) to (vi) or any other employee of a Stock Company gives property benefits on the account of such Stock Company or its Subsidiary Company in relation to the exercise of a right of a shareholder, such person shall be punished by imprisonment with work for not more than three years or a fine of not more than three million yen.

(2) The provisions of the preceding paragraph shall also apply to a person who has, knowingly, received the benefits set forth in that paragraph or caused such benefits to be given to a third party.

(3) The provisions of paragraph (1) shall also apply to a person who has requested the person prescribed in that paragraph to give to him/her or a third party the benefits set forth in that paragraph on the account of a Stock Company or its Subsidiary Company in relation to the exercise of a right of a shareholder.

(4) When a person who has committed either of the crimes set forth in the preceding two paragraphs intimidates the person prescribed in paragraph (1) with regard to committing such crime, the former person shall be punished by imprisonment with work for not more than five years or a fine of not more than five million yen.

(5) A person who has committed any one of the crimes set forth in the preceding three paragraphs may be punished by cumulative imposition of both imprisonment with work and a fine in light of the circumstances.

(6) When a person who has committed the crime set forth in paragraph (1) surrenders, the punishment may be reduced or such person may be exempted from punishment.

(Crime Committed Outside Japan)
Article 971 (1) The crimes set forth in Articles 960 to 963, Article 965, Article 966, Article 967(1), Article 968(1) and paragraph (1) of the preceding Article shall also apply to persons who committed such crimes outside Japan.

(2) The crimes set forth in Article 967(2), Article 968(2) and paragraphs (2) to (4) of the

preceding Article shall be governed by Article 2 of the Penal Code (Act No. 45 of 1907).

(Application of Penal Provisions to Juridical Persons)
Article 972 When the person prescribed in Article 960, Article 961, Articles 963 to 966, Article 967(1) or Article 970(1) is a juridical person, these provisions and the provisions of Article 962 shall apply respectively to the director, executive officer or any other officer executing business, or the manager who has committed such act.

(Crime of Violation of an Order to Suspend Business)
Article 973 A person who has violated an order to suspend all or part of the business of Electronic Public Notice Investigation (meaning the Electronic Public Notice Investigation prescribed in Article 942(1)) under the provisions of Article 954 shall be punished by imprisonment with work for not more than one year or a fine of not more than one million yen, or both.

(Crime of False Notification, etc.)
Article 974 A person who falls under any one of the following items shall be punished by a fine of not more than three hundred thousand yen:
(i) a person who has failed to give notification under the provisions of Article 950 or has given false notification;
(ii) a person who, in violation of the provisions of paragraph (1) of Article 955, has failed to state or record in an Investigation Record Book, etc. (meaning the Investigation Record Book, etc. prescribed in that paragraph; hereinafter the same shall apply in this item) the matters prescribed by the applicable Ordinance of the Ministry of Justice concerning Electronic Public Notice Investigations prescribed in that paragraph, or has stated or recorded false matters, or who, in violation of the provisions of that paragraph or Article 956(2), has failed to preserve an Investigation Record Book, etc.; or
(iii) a person who has failed to make a report under the provisions of paragraph (1) of Article 958 or has made a false report, or who has refused, obstructed or avoided an inspection under the provisions of that paragraph.

(Dual Liability)
Article 975 When the representative of a juridical person, or an agent, employee or other worker of a juridical person or individual commits any one of the violations set forth in the preceding two Articles with regard to the business of such juridical person or individual, not only the offender shall be punished but also such juridical person or individual shall be punished by the fine prescribed in the respective Articles.

(Acts to be Punished by a Non-Penal Fine)
Article 976 When an incorporator, Director at Incorporation, Company Auditor at Incorporation, Executive Officer at Incorporation, director, accounting advisor or member who is to perform the duties thereof, company auditor, executive officer, accounting auditor or member who is to perform the duties thereof, liquidator, liquidator's agent, member who executes the business of a Membership Company, person to perform duties on behalf of a director, company auditor, executive officer, liquidator or partner who executes the business of a Membership Company who has been appointed based on a provisional disposition order under the provisions of Article 56 of the Civil Provisional Remedies Act, person who is temporarily to perform the duties of a director, accounting advisor, company auditor, Representative Director, committee member, exec-

utive officer or representative executive officer prescribed in Article 960(1)(v), person who is temporarily to perform the duties of a liquidator or representative liquidator prescribed in paragraph (2)(iii) of that Article, person who is temporarily to perform the duties of an accounting auditor prescribed in Article 967(1)(iii), inspector, supervisor, investigator, Administrator of the Shareholder Registry, manager of the Bond Registry, bond manager, bond manager to succeed to the administration of the bonds, representative bondholder, Resolution Administrator, Foreign Company's representative in Japan or manager falls under any one of the following items, such person shall be punished by a non-penal fine of not more than one million yen; provided, however, that this shall not apply when such act should be made subject to a criminal punishment:

(i) when the person fails to complete a registration under the provisions of this Act;
(ii) when the person fails to give public notice or notice under the provisions of this Act or has given improper public notice or notice;
(iii) when the person fails to disclose matters under the provisions of this Act;
(iv) when, in violation of the provisions of this Act, the person refuses to allow the inspection or copying of documents or anything that indicates the matters recorded in Electromagnetic Records in a manner prescribed by the applicable Ordinance of the Ministry of Justice, to deliver a transcript or extract of documents, to provide matters recorded in Electromagnetic Records by an Electromagnetic Method or to deliver a document that states such matters, without justifiable grounds;
(v) when the person obstructs an inspection under the provisions of this Act;
(vi) when the person makes a false statement to or conceals facts from a government agency, shareholders meeting, Class Meeting, Organizational Meeting or Class Organizational Meeting, bondholders meeting or creditors meeting;
(vii) when the person fails to state or record matters to be stated or recorded in the articles of incorporation, shareholder registry, registry of lost share certificates, Share Option registry, Bond Registry, minutes, inventory of property, accounting books, balance sheet, profit and loss statement, business report, administrative report, annexed detailed statements set forth in Article 435(2) or Article 494(1), accounting advisor's report, audit report, accounting audit report, settlement of accounts, or the documents or Electromagnetic Records set forth in Article 122(1), Article 149(1), Article 250(1), Article 270(1), Article 682(1), Article 695(1), Article 782(1), Article 791(1), Article 794(1), Article 801(1) or (2), Article 803(1), Article 811(1) or Article 815(1) or (2), or states or records false matters;
(viii) when the person fails to keep books, documents or Electromagnetic Records in violation of the provisions of Article 31(1) or the provisions of Article 74(6), Article 75(3), Article 76(4), Article 81(2) or Article 82(2) (including the cases where these provisions are applied mutatis mutandis pursuant to Article 86), Article 125(1), Article 231(1) or Article 252(1), Article 310(6), Article 311(3), Article 312(4), Article 318(2) or (3) or Article 319(2) (including the cases where these provisions are applied mutatis mutandis pursuant to Article 325), Article 371(1) (including the cases where these provisions are applied mutatis mutandis pursuant to Article 490(5)), Article 378(1), Article 394(1), Article 413(1), Article 442(1) or (2), Article 496(1), Article 684(1), Article 731(2), Article 782(1), Article 791(2), Article 794(1), Article 801(3), Article 803(1), Article 811(2) or Article 815(3);
(ix) when the person fails to provide an explanation about the matters for which an explanation was sought by shareholders or Shareholders at Incorporation at a shareholders meeting, Class Meeting, Organizational Meeting or Class Organizational Meeting, without justifiable grounds;
(x) when the person acquires shares in violation of the provisions of paragraph (1) of Article 135 or fails to dispose of shares in violation of the provisions of paragraph

(3) of that Article;
(xi) when the person cancels shares in violation of the provisions of Article 178(1) or (2);
(xii) when the person sells shares by auction or by any other method in violation of the provisions of Article 197(1) or (2);
(xiii) when the person issues share certificates, Share Option certificates or Bond certificates prior to the day of issue of the shares, Share Options or Bonds;
(xiv) when the person fails to issue share certificates, Share Option certificates or Bond certificates without delay in violation of the provisions of Article 215(1), Article 288(1) or Article 696;
(xv) when the person fails to state matters to be stated in share certificates, Share Option certificates or Bond certificates or states false matters;
(xvi) when the person fails to cancel a Registration of Lost Share Certificate in violation of the provisions of Article 225(4), Article 226(2), Article 227 or Article 229(2);
(xvii) when the person states or records matters in a shareholder registry in violation of the provisions of Article 230(1);
(xviii) when the person fails to call a shareholders meeting in violation of the provisions of Article 296(1) or a court order under the provisions of Article 307(1)(i) (including the cases where it is applied mutatis mutandis pursuant to Article 325) or Article 359(1)(i);
(xix) when, in cases where a demand under the provisions of Article 303(1) or (2) (including the cases where they are applied mutatis mutandis pursuant to Article 325) has been filed, the person fails to include the matter pertaining to such demand in the purpose of the shareholders meeting or Class Meeting;
(xx) when the person fails to appoint enough Outside Company Auditors to constitute half or more of the company auditors in violation of the provisions of Article 335(3);
(xxi) when, in cases where a request under the provisions of Article 343(2) (including the cases where it is applied mutatis mutandis by replacing terms pursuant to the provisions of Article 347(2)) or Article 344(2) has been filed, the person fails to include the matter pertaining to such request in the purpose of a shareholders meeting or Class Meeting or fails to submit the proposal pertaining to such request to a shareholders meeting or Class Meeting;
(xxii) when, in cases where there is a shortfall in the number of directors, accounting advisors, company auditors, executive officers or accounting auditors prescribed in this Act or the articles of incorporation, the person fails to carry out the procedures for appointing a person(s) to assume such position (including the appointment of a person who is temporarily to perform the duties of an accounting auditor);
(xxiii) when the person fails to make a report to a board of directors or board of liquidators or makes a false report in violation of the provisions of Article 365(2) (including the cases where it is applied mutatis mutandis pursuant to Article 419(2) and Article 489(8));
(xxiv) when the person fails to select a full-time company auditor in violation of the provisions of Article 390(3);
(xxv) when the person fails to record capital reserves or Reserves in violation of the provisions of Article 445(3) or (4) or reduces the amount of Reserves in violation of the provisions of Article 448;
(xxvi) when the person reduces the amount of stated capital or Reserves, refunds equity interest, disposes of property of a Membership Company, effects an Entity Conversion, Absorption-type Merger, Consolidation-type Merger, Absorption-type Company Split, Incorporation-type Company Split, Share Exchange or Share Trans-

fer, or effects the resignation of all of a Foreign Company's representatives in Japan in violation of the provisions of Article 449(2) or (5), Article 627(2) or (5), Article 635(2) or (5), Article 670(2) or (5), Article 779(2) or (5) (including the cases where they are applied mutatis mutandis pursuant to Article 781(2)), Article 789(2) or (5) (including the cases where they are applied mutatis mutandis pursuant to Article 793(2)), Article 799(2) or (5) (including the cases where they are applied mutatis mutandis pursuant to Article 802(2)), Article 810(2) or (5) (including the cases where they are applied mutatis mutandis pursuant to Article 813(2)) or Article 820(1) or (2);

(xxvii) when the person fails to file a petition for the commencement of bankruptcy procedures in violation of the provisions of Article 484(1) or Article 656(1) or fails to file a petition for the commencement of special liquidation in violation of the provisions of Article 511(2);

(xxviii) when the person inappropriately prescribes the period set forth in Article 499(1), Article 660(1) or Article 670(2) for the purpose of delaying the completion of liquidation;

(xxix) when the person performs obligations in violation of the provisions of Article 500(1), Article 537(1) or Article 661(1);

(xxx) when the person distributes property of a Liquidating Stock Company or Liquidating Membership Company in violation of the provisions of Article 502 or Article 664;

(xxxi) when the person violates the provisions of Article 535(1) or Article 536(1);

(xxxii) when the person violates a temporary restraining order under the provisions of Article 540(1) or (2) or Article 542(1) or (2);

(xxxiii) when the person issues Bonds in violation of the provisions of Article 702 or fails to specify a bond manager to succeed to the administration of the bonds in violation of the provisions of Article 714(1);

(xxxiv) when the person violates a court order under the provisions of Article 827(1); or

(xxxv) when the person fails to request an Electronic Public Notice Investigation in violation of the provisions of Article 941.

Article 977 A person who falls under any one of the following items shall be punished by a non-penal fine of not more than one million yen:

(i) a person who fails to make a report or makes a false report in violation of the provisions of Article 946(3);

(ii) a person who, in violation of the provisions of Article 951(1), fails to keep Financial Statements, etc. (meaning the Financial Statements, etc. prescribed in that paragraph; the same shall apply hereinafter) or fails to state or record matters to be stated or recorded in Financial Statements, etc. or states or records false matters; or

(iii) a person who refuses any one of the requests listed in the items of Article 951(2) or the items of Article 955(2) without justifiable grounds.

Article 978 A person who falls under any one of the following items shall be punished by a non-penal fine of not more than one million yen:

(i) a Company that uses in its trade name any word which makes it likely that the Company may be mistaken for a different form of Company in violation of the provisions of Article 6(3);

(ii) a person who uses in such person's own name or trade name any word which makes it likely that the person may be mistaken for a Company in violation of the

provisions of Article 7; or
(iii) a person who uses any name or trade name which makes it likely that the person may be mistaken for another Company (including a Foreign Company).

Article 979 (1) A person who engages in business by using the name of a Company prior to the formation of such Company shall be punished by a non-penal fine of an amount equivalent to the registration and license tax for the incorporation of the Company.
(2) The provisions of the preceding paragraph shall also apply to a person who carries out a transaction in violation of the provisions of Article 818(1) or Article 821(1).

② Order for Enforcement of the Companies Act

(Cabinet Order No. 364 of December 14, 2005)

The Cabinet hereby enacts this Cabinet Order pursuant to the provisions of the Companies Act (Act No. 86 of 2005).

(Consent to the Provision of Matters to Be Stated in Writing by Electromagnetic Means)
Article 1 (1) A person (referred to as the "Provider" in the following paragraph) who intends to provide the matters listed in the following provisions by electromagnetic means (meaning the Electromagnetic Means prescribed in Article 2, item (xxxiv) of the Companies Act (hereinafter referred to as the "Act"); the same shall apply hereinafter) shall, as provided by Ordinance of the Ministry of Justice, indicate to the intended recipient of said matters the type and details of Electromagnetic Means used, and shall obtain consent therefrom in writing or by Electromagnetic Means in advance:
(i) Article 59, paragraph (4) of the Act;
(ii) Article 74, paragraph (3) of the Act (including the cases where it is applied mutatis mutandis pursuant to Article 86 of the Act);
(iii) Article 76, paragraph (1) of the Act (including the cases where it is applied mutatis mutandis pursuant to Article 86 of the Act);
(iv) Article 203, paragraph (3) of the Act;
(v) Article 242, paragraph (3) of the Act;
(vi) Article 310, paragraph (3) of the Act (including the cases where it is applied mutatis mutandis pursuant to Article 325 of the Act);
(vii) Article 312, paragraph (1) of the Act (including the cases where it is applied mutatis mutandis pursuant to Article 325 of the Act);
(viii) Article 555, paragraph (3) of the Act (including the cases where it is applied mutatis mutandis pursuant to Article 822, paragraph (3) of the Act);
(ix) Article 557, paragraph (1) of the Act (including the cases where it is applied mutatis mutandis pursuant to Article 822, paragraph (3) of the Act);
(x) Article 677, paragraph (3) of the Act;
(xi) Article 721, paragraph (4) of the Act;
(xii) Article 725, paragraph (3) of the Act;
(xiii) Article 727, paragraph (1) of the Act;
(xiv) Article 739, paragraph (2) of the Act.
(2) The Provider who has obtained consent pursuant to the provisions of the preceding paragraph shall not provide the relevant matters to the recipient set forth in the same paragraph by Electromagnetic Means if said recipient has indicated in writing or by Electromagnetic Means to the effect that he/she is not to be provided with said matters by Electromagnetic Means; provided, however, that this shall not apply in the case where said recipient gives his/her consent again pursuant to the provisions of said paragraph.

(Consent to Notification by Electromagnetic Means)
Article 2 (1) A person who intends to issue a notice by Electromagnetic Means under the provisions listed below (referred to as the "Notice Issuer" in the following paragraph) shall, as provided by Ordinance of the Ministry of Justice, indicate to the intended recipient of said notice the type and details of Electromagnetic Means used, and shall obtain consent therefrom in writing or by Electromagnetic Means in advance:

(i) Article 68, paragraph (3) of the Act (including the cases where it is applied mutatis mutandis pursuant to Article 86 of the Act);
(ii) Article 299, paragraph (3) of the Act (including the cases where it is applied mutatis mutandis pursuant to Article 325 of the Act);
(iii) Article 549, paragraph (2) of the Act (including paragraph (4) of the same Article (including the cases where it is applied mutatis mutandis pursuant to Article 822, paragraph (3) of the Act) and the cases where it is applied mutatis mutandis pursuant to Article 822, paragraph (3) of the Act);
(iv) Article 720, paragraph (2) of the Act.
(2) The Notice Issuer who has obtained consent pursuant to the provisions of the preceding paragraph shall not issue a notice to the recipient set forth in the same paragraph by Electromagnetic Means if said recipient has indicated in writing or by Electromagnetic Means to the effect that he/she is not to receive said notice by Electromagnetic Means; provided however, that this shall not apply in the case where said recipient gives his/her consent again pursuant to the provisions of said paragraph.

(Registration of Investigative Bodies for Electronic Public Notices and the Amount of Fees Pertaining to Applications for Renewal Thereof)
Article 3 The amount of fees specified by Cabinet Order, set forth in Article 942, paragraph (2) of the Act (including the case where it is applied mutatis mutandis pursuant to Article 945, paragraph (2) of the Act), shall be 420,600 yen.

(The Valid Period of Registration for Investigative Bodies for Electronic Public Notices)
Article 4 The period specified by Cabinet Order under Article 945, paragraph (1) of the Act shall be three years.

Trust Act

(Act No. 108 of December 15, 2006)

Chapter I General Provisions (Article 1 to Article 13)
Chapter II Trust Property, etc. (Article 14 to Article 25)
Chapter III Trustees, etc.
　Section 1 Trustees' Powers (Article 26 to Article 28)
　Section 2 Duties, etc. of a Trustee (Article 29 to Article 39)
　Section 3 Trustee Liabilities, etc. (Article 40 to Article 47)
　Section 4 Expenses, etc. and Trust Fees, etc. of the Trustee (Article 48 to Article 55)
　Section 5 Changing, etc. of Trustees
　　Subsection 1 Termination of the Trustee's Duty as Trustee (Article 56 to Article 58)
　　Subsection 2 Duties, etc. of the Former Trustee (Article 59 to Article 61)
　　Subsection 3 Appointment of New Trustees (Article 62)
　　Subsection 4 Trust Property Administrators, etc. (Article 63 to Article 74)
　　Subsection 5 Succession, etc. to Rights and Duties upon a Change in Trustees (Article 75 to Article 78)
　Section 6 Special Rules on Trusts with Two or More Trustees (Article 79 to Article 87)
Chapter IV Beneficiaries, etc.
　Section 1 Acquisition and Exercise of Rights by Beneficiaries (Article 88 to Article 92)
　Section 2 Beneficial Interest, etc.
　　Subsection 1 Assignment, etc. of Beneficial Interest (Article 93 to Article 98)
　　Subsection 2 Waiver of Beneficial Interest (Article 99)
　　Subsection 3 Distribution claims as a beneficiary (Article 100 to Article 102)
　　Subsection 4 The Beneficiary's Right to Demand that the Trustee Acquire Beneficiary's Beneficial Interest (Article 103 and Article 104)
　Section 3 Special Rules on Decision-Making Methods Involving Two or More Beneficiaries
　　Subsection 1 General Provisions (Article 105)
　　Subsection 2 Beneficiaries Meetings (Article 106 to Article 122)
　Section 4 Trust Caretakers, etc.
　　Subsection 1 Trust Caretakers (Article 123 to Article 130)
　　Subsection 2 Trust Supervisors (Article 131 to Article 137)
　　Subsection 3 Beneficiaries' Agents (Article 138 to Article 144)
Chapter V Settlors (Article 145 to Article 148)
Chapter VI Modification, Consolidation, and Split of trusts
　Section 1 Modification of Trusts (Article 149 and Article 150)
　Section 2 Consolidation of Trusts (Article 151 to Article 154)
　Section 3 Split of Trusts
　　Subsection 1 Absorption-Type Trust Splits (Article 155 to Article 158)
　　Subsection 2 Creation-Type Trust Splits (Article 159 to Article 162)
Chapter VII Termination and Liquidation of Trusts
　Section 1 Termination of Trusts (Article 163 to Article 174)
　Section 2 Liquidation of Trusts (Article 175 to Article 184)
Chapter VIII Special Rules on Trusts With Certificates of Beneficial Interests
　Section 1 General Provisions (Article 185 to Article 193)

Section 2　Special Rules on the Assignment of Beneficial Interest, etc. (Article 194 to Article 206)
　　　Section 3　Certificates of Beneficial Interest (Article 207 to Article 211)
　　　Section 4　Special Rules on the Rights and Duties, etc. of the Relevant Parties (Article 212 to Article 215)
　　Chapter IX　Special Rules on Limited Liability Trusts
　　　Section 1　General Provisions (Article 216 to Article 221)
　　　Section 2　Special Rules on Accounting, etc. (Article 222 to Article 231)
　　　Section 3　Registration of Limited Liability Trusts (Article 232 to Article 247)
　　Chapter X　Special Rules on Limited Liability Trusts With Certificates of Beneficial Interest (Article 248 to Article 257)
　　Chapter XI　Special Rules on Trusts with No Provisions on the Beneficiary (Article 258 to Article 261)
　　Chapter XII　Miscellaneous Provision
　　　Section 1　Non-Contentious Case (Article 262 to Article 264)
　　　Section 2　Public Notice, etc. (Article 265 and Article 266)
　　Chapter XIII　Penal Provisions (Article 267 to Article 271)
　　　Supplementary Provisions

Chapter I　General Provisions

(Purpose)
Article 1　The requirements, effect, etc. of a trust shall be governed by the provisions of this Act in addition to the provisions of other laws and regulations.

(Definitions)
Article 2　(1) The term "trust" as used in this Act means an arrangement in which a specific person, by employing any of the methods listed in the items of the following Article, administers or disposes of property in accordance with a certain purpose (excluding the purpose of exclusively promoting the person's own interests; the same shall apply in said Article) and conducts any other acts that are necessary to achieve such purpose.
(2) The term "act of trust" as used in this Act means a juridical act specified in each of the following items for the categories of trusts listed in the respective items:
　(i) a trust created by the method set forth in item (i) of the following Article: a trust agreement as set forth in said item;
　(ii) a trust created by the method set forth in item (ii) of the following Article: a will as set forth in said item; and
　(iii) a trust created by the method set forth in item (iii) of the following Article: a manifestation of such intention in a document or electromagnetic record (meaning an electromagnetic record as prescribed in said item) as set forth in said item.
(3) The term "trust property" as used in this Act means any and all property which belongs to a trustee and which should be administered or disposed of through a trust.
(4) The term "settlor" as used in this Act means a person who creates a trust by any of the methods listed in the items of the following Article.
(5) The term "trustee" as used in this Act means a person who is under an obligation to administer or dispose of property that belongs to the trust property and to conduct any other acts that are necessary to achieve the purpose of a trust as provided for by the terms of trust.
(6) The term "beneficiary" as used in this Act means a person who holds a beneficial interest in a trust.

(7) The term "beneficial interest" as used in this Act means a claim based on the terms of trust pertaining to the obligation of a trustee to distribute property that is among trust property to a beneficiary or to make any other distribution involving the trust property (hereinafter referred to as a "distribution claim as a beneficiary"), and the right to request a trustee or any other person to carry out certain acts under the provisions of this Act in order to secure such a claim.
(8) The term the "trustee's own property" as used in this Act means any and all property which belongs to a trustee and which is not among the trust property.
(9) The term "obligations covered by the trust property" as used in this Act means obligations on which the trustee is liable to perform through the use of property that belongs to the trust property.
(10) The term "consolidation of trusts" as used in this Act means the consolidation of the whole of the trust properties of two or more trusts that have the same trustee into the trust property of a single new trust.
(11) As used in this Act: the term "absorption-type trust split" means the transfer of a part of a trust's trust property into the trust property of another trust that has the same trustee; the term "creation-type trust split" means the transfer of a part of a trust's trust property into the trust property of a new trust that has the same trustee; and the term "split of trust" means an absorption-type trust split or creation-type trust split.
(12) The term "limited liability trust" as used in this Act means a trust in which a trustee is only liable to perform all of the obligations covered by the trust property only by using property that belongs to the trust property.

(Method of Creating a Trust)
Article 3 A trust shall be created by any of the following methods:
(i) by concluding an agreement with a specific person to the effect that the person will be assigned property, that the person will be granted a security interest in property, or that property will otherwise be disposed of to the person, and that said specific person should administer or dispose of such property in accordance with a certain purpose and carry out any other acts that are necessary for achieving such purpose (hereinafter referred to as a "trust agreement");
(ii) by making a will to the effect that property will be assigned to a specific person, that a specific person will granted a security interest in property, or that property will otherwise be disposed of to a specific person, and that the specific person should administer or dispose of such property in accordance with a certain purpose and carry out any other acts that are necessary for achieving such purpose; or
(iii) by manifestation of an intention for a specific person to administer or dispose of a certain portion of the property that the person holds in accordance with a certain purpose and for the person to conduct any other acts that are necessary for achieving such purpose by the person, with the manifestation of such intention being evidenced by a notarial deed or any other document or electromagnetic record (meaning a record made in an electronic form, a magnetic form, or any other form not recognizable to human perception and which is used in information processing by computers as specified by Ordinance of the Ministry of Justice; the same shall apply hereinafter) in which said purpose, the matters necessary for specifying said property, and other matters specified by Ordinance of the Ministry of Justice have been stated or recorded.

(The Coming into Effect of a Trust)
Article 4 (1) A trust created by the method set forth in item (i) of the preceding Article

shall become effective when a trust agreement is concluded between the person who is to be the settlor and another person who is to be the trustee.

(2) A trust created by the method set forth in item (ii) of the preceding Article shall become effective when the will takes effect.

(3) A trust created by the method set forth in item (iii) of the preceding Article shall become effective when the events specified in the following items take place for the cases listed in the respective items:

(i) where the trust is created by means of a notarial deed or any other document or electromagnetic record authenticated by a notary (hereinafter referred to as a "notarial deed, etc." in this item and the following item): when the notarial deed, etc. is executed; or

(ii) where the trust is created by means of a document or electromagnetic record other than a notarial deed, etc.: when notice is given by means of an instrument bearing a fixed date to the third party designated as the person who is to be the beneficiary (if there are two or more such third parties, to one of them), with regard to the fact that the trust has been created and the contents thereof.

(4) Notwithstanding the provisions of the preceding three paragraphs, when a trust is subject to a condition precedent or a designated time of commencement by the terms of trust, said trust shall become effective when the condition precedent is fulfilled or when the time of commencement arrives.

(Call to Undertake the Trust by Will)

Article 5 (1) Where a trust is created by the method set forth in Article 3, item (ii), if the will contains a provision designating a particular person to be the trustee, any interested party may specify a reasonable period of time and call on the person designated as the one who is to be the trustee to give a definite answer within that period of time with regard to whether the specific person will undertake the trust; provided, however, that if the will designates a condition precedent or a time of commencement for the provision, this may only be done after the condition precedent is fulfilled or after the time of commencement arrives.

(2) Where a call for an answer is made under the provisions of the preceding paragraph, if the person designated as the one who is to be the trustee fails to give a definite answer to the settlor's heir within the period set forth in said paragraph, it shall be deemed that such person does not undertake the trust.

(3) For the purpose of the application of the provisions of the preceding paragraph in cases where the settlor has no heir at the time in question, the phrase "the settlor's heir" in said paragraph shall be deemed to be replaced with "the beneficiary (if there are two or more beneficiaries at that time, to one of them, and if there is a trust caretaker at that time, to the trust caretaker)."

(Appointment of a Trustee by the Court in the Case of a Testamentary Trust)

Article 6 (1) Where a trust is created by the method set forth in Article 3, item (ii), if the will contains no provision concerning the designation of a trustee or if the person designated as the one who is to be the trustee does not undertake or is unable to undertake the trust, the court may appoint a trustee on the petition of an interested party.

(2) The judicial decision on the petition set forth in the preceding paragraph shall include the reasons for said decision.

(3) A beneficiary or the current trustee may file an immediate appeal against a judicial decision on the appointment of a trustee under the provisions of paragraph (1).

(4) The immediate appeal set forth in the preceding paragraph shall have the effect of a stay of execution.

(Qualification of a Trustee)
Article 7 No trust may be created with a minor, adult ward, or person under curatorship serving as a trustee.

(Prohibition on the Trustee's Enjoyment of Benefit)
Article 8 No trustee may benefit from the trust under any name, except where the trustee benefits from the trust as its beneficiary.

(Prohibition of Trusts for Evasion of the Law)
Article 9 A person who may not enjoy a certain property right under laws and regulations may not enjoy, as a beneficiary, the same benefit as that derived from holding such right.

(Prohibition on Trusts for Suits)
Article 10 No trust may be created for the primary purpose of having another person conduct any procedural act.

(Cancellation of Fraudulent Trusts, etc.)
Article 11 (1) Where a settlor has created a trust with the knowledge that it would harm the settlor's creditor, the creditor may, irrespective of whether or not the trustee had knowledge of the fact that the creditor would be harmed, request the court for a rescission under the provisions of Article 424, paragraph (1) of the Civil Code (Act No. 89 of 1896), with the trustee as the defendant; provided, however, that this shall not apply where there are any beneficiaries at the time, all or some of who had no knowledge of the fact that the creditor would be harmed at the time when they became aware that they had been designated as beneficiaries (meaning being designated as an initial beneficiary or new beneficiary after a change in the provisions of the terms of trust or as a result of the exercise of the right to designate or change a beneficiary prescribed in Article 89, paragraph (1); the same shall apply hereinafter) or when they acquired beneficial interests.
(2) Where a judgment upholding a request under the provisions of the preceding paragraph has become final and binding, if a creditor (excluding one who is the settlor) who has a claim pertaining to an obligation covered by the trust property had no knowledge at the time when the creditor acquired the claim of the fact that would harm the creditor, the settlor shall be liable to perform the obligation covered by the trust property to the creditor who holds such a claim; provided, however, that such performance shall be limited to the value of the property to be transferred from the trustee to the settlor by reason of the rescission under the provisions of said paragraph.
(3) For the purpose of the application of the provisions of the preceding paragraph, the right that the trustee has pursuant to the provisions of Article 49, paragraph (1) (including cases where applied mutatis mutandis pursuant to Article 53, paragraph (2) and Article 54, paragraph (4)) shall be deemed to be a monetary claim.
(4) Where a settlor has created a trust with the knowledge that it would harm the settlor's creditor, if a beneficiary has been distributed property by the trustee from among the trust property, the creditor may request the court for a rescission under the provisions of Article 424, paragraph (1) of the Civil Code, with the beneficiary as the defendant; provided, however, that this shall not apply where said beneficiary had no knowledge of the fact that the creditor would be harmed at the time when the said beneficiary became aware to have been designated as a beneficiary or when the said beneficiary acquired a beneficial interest.

(5) Where a settlor has created a trust with the knowledge that it would harm the settlor's creditor, the creditor may demand, by a suit designating a beneficiary as a defendant, that the beneficiary assign the beneficiary's beneficial interest to the settlor. In this case, the provisions of the proviso to the preceding paragraph shall apply mutatis mutandis.
(6) The provisions of Article 426 of the Civil Code shall apply mutatis mutandis to the right to make a demand under the provisions of the preceding paragraph.
(7) When designating a beneficiary or assigning a beneficial interest, it shall not be permitted to, for the purpose of unjustly circumventing the application of the provisions of the main clause of paragraph (1), the main clause of paragraph (4) or the first sentence of paragraph (5), designate a person who has no knowledge of the fact that any creditor could be harmed (hereinafter referred to as a "person without knowledge" in this paragraph) as a beneficiary without value (including cases where such designation is made with value that should be deemed to be equal to a designation being made without value; hereinafter the same shall apply in this paragraph), or assign a beneficial interest to a person without knowledge without value.
(8) With regard to a person who has become a beneficiary as a result of the designation of a beneficiary or the acquisition of a beneficial interest in violation of the provisions of the preceding paragraph, the provisions of the proviso to paragraph (1) and the proviso to paragraph (4) (including cases where applied mutatis mutandis pursuant to the second sentence of paragraph (5)) shall not apply.

(Avoidance of Fraudulent Trusts, etc.)
Article 12 (1) For the purpose of the application of the provisions of Article 160, paragraph (1) of the Bankruptcy Act (Act No. 75 of 2004) to a trust created with a bankrupt person as the settlor, the phrase "the person who has benefited from" in the items of said paragraph shall be deemed to be replaced with "all or part of the beneficiaries who have benefited from."
(2) Where a bankrupt has created a trust as the settlor with the knowledge that it would harm the bankruptcy creditors, the bankruptcy trustee may demand, by filing an action against the beneficiary, that the beneficiary return the beneficial interest to the bankruptcy estate. In this case, the provisions of the proviso to paragraph (4) of the preceding Article shall apply mutatis mutandis.
(3) For the purpose of the application of the provisions of Article 127, paragraph (1) of the Civil Rehabilitation Act (Act No. 225 of 1999) to a trust created with a debtor under rehabilitation procedure as the settlor, the phrase "the person who has benefited from" in the items of said paragraph shall be deemed to be replaced with "all or part of the beneficiaries who have benefited from."
(4) Where a rehabilitation debtor has created a trust as the settlor with the knowledge that it would harm the rehabilitation creditors, a supervisor with avoiding powers or a trustee in charge of rehabilitation proceedings may demand, by filing an action against a beneficiary, that the beneficiary return the beneficial interest to the assets of rehabilitation debtor (meaning the assets of rehabilitation debtor as prescribed in Article 12, paragraph (1), item (i) of the Civil Rehabilitation Act; the same shall apply in Article 25, paragraph (4)). In this case, the provisions of the proviso to paragraph (4) of the preceding Article shall apply mutatis mutandis.
(5) The provisions of the preceding two paragraphs shall apply mutatis mutandis to a company under reorganization (meaning a company under reorganization as prescribed in Article 2, paragraph (7) of the Corporate Reorganization Act (Act No. 154 of 2002) or a company under reorganization as prescribed in Article 169, paragraph (7) of the Act on Special Rules, etc. for Reorganization Proceedings for Financial Institutions, etc. (Act

No. 95 of 1996)) or a cooperative financial institution under reorganization (meaning a cooperative financial institution under reorganization as prescribed in Article 4, paragraph (7) of the Act on Special Rules, etc. for Reorganization Proceedings for Financial Institutions, etc). In this case, in paragraph (3), the phrase "the provisions of Article 127, paragraph (1) of the Civil Rehabilitation Act (Act No. 225 of 1999)" shall be deemed to be replaced with "the provisions of Article 86, paragraph (1) of the Corporate Reorganization Act (Act No. 154 of 2002) and Article 57, paragraph (1) and Article 223, paragraph (1) of the Act on Special Rules, etc. for Reorganization Proceedings for Financial Institutions, etc. (Act No. 95 of 1996)," and the phrase "the items of said paragraph" shall be deemed to be replaced with "these provisions," and in the preceding paragraph, the term "rehabilitation creditors" shall be deemed to be replaced with "reorganization creditors or secured reorganization creditors," and the phrase "supervisor with avoidance powers or a trustee in charge of rehabilitation proceedings" shall be deemed to be replaced with "trustee in charge of reorganization proceedings," and the phrase "the assets of rehabilitation debtor (meaning the assets of rehabilitation debtor prescribed in Article 12, paragraph (1), item (i) of the Civil Rehabilitation Act; the same shall apply in Article 25, paragraph (4))" shall be deemed to be replaced with "the assets of the company under reorganization (meaning assets of a company under reorganization as prescribed in Article 2, paragraph (14) of the Corporate Reorganization Act or assets of a company under reorganization as prescribed in Article 169, paragraph (14) of the Act on Special Rules, etc. for Reorganization Proceedings for Financial Institutions, etc.) or assets of a cooperative financial institution under reorganization (meaning assets of a cooperative financial institution under reorganization as prescribed in Article 4, paragraph (14) of the Act on Special Rules, etc. for Reorganization Proceedings for Financial Institutions, etc.)"

(Accounting Principles)
Article 13 The accounting for a trust shall be subject to accounting practices that are generally accepted as fair and appropriate.

Chapter II Trust Property, etc.

(Requirements for Perfection Concerning Property that Belongs to Trust Property)
Article 14 With regard to any property for which the acquisition, loss, and modification of any right may not be duly asserted against a third party unless it is registered, the fact that such property belongs to the trust property may not be duly asserted against a third party unless the fact that the property is under the trust is registered.

(Succession of a Defect in the Possession of Property That Belongs to Trust Property)
Article 15 A trustee shall succeed to a settlor's defect in possession of property that belongs to the trust property.

(Scope of Trust Property)
Article 16 In addition to property specified by the terms of trust as being among trust property, the following property shall be among the trust property:
(i) any property obtained by the trustee as a result of the administration, disposition, loss or damage of, or any other events occurring to property that belongs to the trust property; and

(ii) any property that has come to be among the trust property pursuant to the provisions of the following Article, Article 18, Article 19 (including cases where applied mutatis mutandis by replacing the relevant terms and phrases pursuant to the provisions of Article 84; hereinafter the same shall apply in this item), Article 226, paragraph (3), Article 228, paragraph (3), and Article 254, paragraph (2) (including any co-ownership interest that is deemed to be among the trust property pursuant to the provisions of Article 18, paragraph (1) (including cases where applied mutatis mutandis pursuant to paragraph (3) of said Article) and any property that is made to be among the trust property as a result of the division under the provisions of Article 19).

(Accession, etc. of Property that belongs to Trust Property)
Article 17 Where property that belongs to trust property is joined by accession to or mixture with the trustee's own property or any property that belongs to the trust property of another trust, or where processing is conducted using these properties as materials, those properties that are among the trust properties of the respective trusts and the property that belongs to the trustee's own property shall be deemed to belong to their respective owners, and the provisions of Article 242 to Article 248 of the Civil Code shall apply.

Article 18 (1) Where property that belongs to the trust property becomes indistinguishable from property that belongs to the trustee's own property (excluding the case prescribed in the preceding Article), it shall be deemed that a co-ownership interest in either of these properties is an interest in both the trust property and the trustee's own property. In this case, the shares of such co-ownership interests shall be in proportion to the prices of the respective properties as of the time when they became indistinguishable from each other.
(2) The co-ownership interests set forth in the preceding paragraph shall be presumed to be equal.
(3) The provisions of the preceding two paragraphs shall apply mutatis mutandis where a trustee of a trust also serves as a trustee of another trust, and where properties that are among the trust properties of these trusts have become indistinguishable from each other (excluding the case prescribed in the preceding Article). In this case, the phrase "the trust property and the trustee's own property" in paragraph (1) shall be deemed to be replaced with "the trust properties of these trusts."

(Division of Properties in Co-ownership that Are Among Both the Trust Property and the Trustee's Own Property, etc.)
Article 19 (1) Where a co-ownership interest in a specific property that belongs to a trustee is an interest in both the trust property and the trustee's own property, such property may be divided by the following methods:
(i) by the method specified by the terms of trust;
(ii) based on an agreement between the trustee and the beneficiary (if there is a trust caretaker at the time in question, the trust caretaker); and
(iii) based on a decision by the trustee in cases where the division of the property in question is considered to be necessary to a reasonable extent in order to achieve the purpose of the trust and where it is clear that the division will not harm the interests of the beneficiary, or where there are justifiable grounds for the division in light of the impact of the division on the trust property, the purpose and manner of the division, the substantial status of the relationship between the trustee and the beneficiary as interested parties and other relevant circumstances.

(2) In the case prescribed in the preceding paragraph, if the agreement set forth in item (ii) of said paragraph is not reached or if it is impossible to effect the division by any of the methods listed in the items of said paragraph for other reasons, the trustee or the beneficiary (if there is a trust caretaker at the time in question, the trust caretaker) may submit a demand to the court for the division of the property in co-ownership set forth in said paragraph.

(3) Where a co-ownership interest in a specific property that belongs to a trustee is an interest in both the trust property and the trust property of another trust, such property may be divided by the following methods:
  (i) by the method specified by the terms of trust of both trusts;
  (ii) based on an agreement between the beneficiaries of both trusts (if there is a trust caretaker for each trust at the time in question, the trust caretakers); and
  (iii) based on a decision by the trustees of both trusts in cases where the partition of the property in question is considered to be necessary to a reasonable extent in order to achieve the purpose of each trust and where it is clear that the division will not harm the interest of the beneficiaries, or where there are justifiable grounds for the division in light of the impact of the division on the trust properties, the purpose and manner of the division, the status of the substantial relationship of interests between the trustees and the beneficiaries, and other relevant circumstances.

(4) In the case prescribed in the preceding paragraph, if the agreement set forth in item (ii) of said paragraph is not reached or if it is impossible to make the division by any of the methods listed in the items of said paragraph for other reasons, the beneficiary of each trust (if there is a trust caretaker at the time in question, the trust caretaker) may submit a demand to the court for the division of the property in co-ownership set forth in said paragraph.

(Special Rules for the Confusion of Property That Belongs to Trust Property)

Article 20 (1) Where ownership and any other real right existing on a single property have each come to be among either the trust property and the trustee's own property or among the trust property of another trust, such other real right shall not be extinguished, notwithstanding the provisions of the main clause of Article 179, paragraph (1) of the Civil Code.

(2) Where any real right other than ownership and any other right for which the said real right is the object have come to exist with respect to the trust property and the trustee's own property or among the trust property of another trust, such other right shall not be extinguished, notwithstanding the provisions of the first sentence of Article 179, paragraph (2) of the Civil Code.

(3) In the following cases, the claim set forth therein shall not be extinguished, notwithstanding the provisions of the main clause of Article 520 of the Civil Code:
  (i) where an obligation pertaining to a claim belonging to the trust property has vested in the trustee (excluding the case where such obligation has become an obligation covered by the trust property);
  (ii) where a claim pertaining to an obligation covered by the trust property has vested in the trustee (excluding the case where such claim has come to belong to the trust property);
  (iii) where an obligation pertaining to a claim belonging to the trustee's own property or the trust property of another trust has vested in the trustee (limited to the case where such obligation has become an obligation covered by the trust property); and
  (iv) where a claim pertaining to a trustee's obligation (excluding an obligation covered by the trust property) has vested in the trustee (limited to the case where such claim has come to belong to the trust property).

(Scope of Obligations Covered by the Trust Property)
Article 21 (1) Obligations pertaining to the following claims shall be obligations covered by the trust property:
(i) a distribution claim as a beneficiary;
(ii) a right arising with respect to property that belongs to the trust property from a cause that occurred prior to the creation of the trust;
(iii) a claim arising against the settlor prior to the creation of the trust, for which it is provided by the terms of trust that the obligation pertaining to said claim is an obligation covered by the trust property;
(iv) a beneficiary's right to demand that the trustee acquire the distribution claim as a beneficiary interest under the provisions of Article 103, paragraph (1) or paragraph (2);
(v) a right arising from an act which is conducted in the interest of the trust property and which falls within the scope of the trustee's powers;
(vi) a right arising from any of the following acts which is conducted in the interest of the trust property and which does not fall within the scope of the trustee's powers;
    (a) an act that may not be rescinded pursuant to the provisions of Article 27, paragraph (1) or paragraph (2) (including cases where these provisions are applied mutatis mutandis pursuant to Article 75, paragraph (4); the same shall apply in (b)) (excluding cases where the other party to the act did not know, at the time of the act, that the act was being conducted in the interest of the trust property (excluding the act of establishing or transferring a right with respect to property that belongs to the trust property));
    (b) an act that may be rescinded pursuant to the provisions of Article 27, paragraph (1) or paragraph (2) but has not yet been rescinded;
(vii) a right arising from a disposition or any other act prescribed in Article 31, paragraph (6) or from an act prescribed in paragraph (7) of said Article, which may not be rescinded pursuant to these provisions or which may be rescinded pursuant to these provisions but has not yet been rescinded;
(viii) a right arising from a tort committed by the trustee in the course of the trust administration; and
(ix) in addition to what is listed in item (v) to the preceding item, a right arising in the course of the trust administration.
(2) With regard to obligations pertaining to the following rights which fall within the scope of obligation covered by the trust property, a trustee shall be liable to perform such obligations only by using property that belongs to the trust property:
(i) a distribution claim as a beneficiary;
(ii) a trust claim (meaning a claim pertaining to an obligation covered by the trust property, other than a distribution claim as a beneficiary; the same shall apply hereinafter) in cases where the terms of trust contains the provision set forth in Article 216, paragraph (1) and a registration has been made as provided for in Article 232;
(iii) in addition to those listed in the preceding two items, a trust claim in cases where the trustee is deemed to only be liable for using property that belongs to the trust property to satisfy said claim, pursuant to the provisions of this Act; and
(iv) a trust claim in cases where there is an agreement between the trustee and the holder of the trust claim (hereinafter referred to as a "trust creditor") to the effect that the trustee is to be liable to satisfy said claim only by using property that belongs to the trust property.

(Restriction on the Set-Off of Claims, etc. that Are Among the Trust Property)

Article 22 (1) A person who holds a claim pertaining to an obligation which the trustee is liable to perform only by using property that belongs to trustee's own property or the trust property of another trust (referred to as the "trustee's own property, etc." in item (i)) (such obligations shall be referred to as "obligations covered by trustee's own property only, etc." in item (i) and item (ii)) may not use said claim to set off the obligation pertaining to a claim belonging to the trust property; provided, however, that this shall not apply in the following cases:
  (i) where, either at the time when a person acquired the claim or at the time when a person assumed the obligation pertaining to a claim belonging to the trust property, whichever occurred later, the said person who holds the claim pertaining to the obligation covered by the trustee's own property only, etc. did not know and was not negligent in failing to know that the claim belonging to the trust property did not belong to the trustee's own property, etc.; or
  (ii) where, either at the time when a person acquired a claim or at the time when a person assumed the obligation pertaining to a claim belonging to the trust property, whichever occurred later, the person who holds the claim pertaining to the obligation covered by the trustee's own property only, etc. did not know and was not negligent in failing to know that the obligation covered by the trustee's own property only, etc. is liable was not an obligation covered by the trust property.
(2) The provisions of the main clause of the preceding paragraph shall not apply in the cases listed in the items of Article 31, paragraph (2) in which the trustee has approved the set-off set forth in said paragraph.
(3) A person who holds a claim pertaining to an obligation covered by the trust property (limited to an obligation that the trustee is liable to perform only by using property that belongs to the trust property) may not use said claim to set off against the person's obligation pertaining to a claim belonging to the trustee's own property; provided, however, that this shall not apply where, at the time when said person acquired the claim or when the person assumed the obligation pertaining to the claim belonging to the trustee's own property, whichever occurred later, the person who holds the claim pertaining to the obligation covered by the trust property did not know and was not negligent in failing to know that the claim belonging to the trustee's own property did not belong to the trust property.
(4) The provisions of the main clause of the preceding paragraph shall not apply where the trustee has approved the set-off set forth in said paragraph.

(Restriction, etc. on Execution, etc. Against Property that Belongs to Trust Property)
Article 23 (1) Except where based on a claim pertaining to an obligation covered by the trust property (including a right arising with respect to property that belongs to the trust property; the same shall apply in the following paragraph), no execution, provisional seizure, provisional disposition, or exercise of a security interest or an auction (excluding an auction for the exercise of a security interest; the same shall apply hereinafter) nor collection proceedings for delinquent national tax (including a procedure to be enforced pursuant to the provisions on collection proceedings for delinquent national tax; the same shall apply hereinafter) may be enforced against property that belongs to the trust property.
(2) In addition to a creditor who holds a claim pertaining to an obligation covered by the trust property, where a trust has been created by the method set forth in Article 3, item (iii), if the settlor has created the trust with the knowledge that it would harm settlor's creditor(s), notwithstanding the provisions of the preceding paragraph, a person who holds a claim against the settlor (limited to cases where the settlor is a trust-

ee) which has arisen prior to the creation of the trust may commence a execution, provisional seizure, provisional disposition or exercise of a security interest, or an auction, or may commence collection proceedings for delinquent national tax against property that belongs to the trust property; provided, however, that this shall not apply where there are beneficiaries at the time in question, and when all or some of those beneficiaries did not know, at the time when they became aware that they had been designated as beneficiaries or when they acquired beneficial interests, of the fact that the creditor would be harmed.

(3) The provisions of Article 11, paragraph (7) and paragraph (8) shall apply mutatis mutandis to the application of the provisions of the preceding paragraph.

(4) The provisions of the preceding two paragraphs shall not apply when two years have elapsed since the trust set forth in paragraph (2) was created.

(5) A trustee or beneficiary may assert an objection to the execution, provisional seizure, provisional disposition or exercise of a security interest, or auction that is being commenced in violation of the provisions of paragraph (1) or paragraph (2). In this case, the provisions of Article 38 of the Civil Execution Act (Act No. 4 of 1979) and the provisions of Article 45 of the Civil Preservation Act (Act No. 91 of 1989) shall apply mutatis mutandis.

(6) A trustee or beneficiary may assert an objection to the collection proceeding for delinquent national tax that are being enforced in violation of the provisions of paragraph (1) or paragraph (2). In this case, the assertion of the objection shall be made by entering an appeal against the collection proceedings of delinquent national tax.

(Payment, etc. of Expenses, Costs, or Remuneration)
Article 24 (1) Where a beneficiary who has filed an action to assert an objection under the provisions of paragraph (5) or paragraph (6) of the preceding Article has won the beneficiary's case (completely or partially), if the beneficiary has paid any expenses or costs (excluding court costs) that were necessary in relation to the action or if the beneficiary is liable for paying remuneration to an attorney-at-law, legal professional corporation, judicial scrivener, or judicial scrivener corporation, such expenses, costs, or remuneration shall be paid from the trust property, up to the amount considered reasonable, not exceeding the actual amount thereof.

(2) Even where the beneficiary who filed the action set forth in the preceding paragraph has lost the beneficiary's case, the beneficiary shall not be liable to compensate the trustee for any damage arising from the action, except where the beneficiary was in bad faith.

(Relationship between Trust Property and Bankruptcy Proceedings, etc. Against a Trustee)
Article 25 (1) Even where an order for the commencement of bankruptcy is entered against a trustee, no property that belongs to the trust property shall be included in the bankruptcy estate.

(2) In the case referred to in the preceding paragraph, no distribution claim as a beneficiary shall be the bankruptcy claims. The same shall apply to a trust claim that the trustee is liable to satisfy only by using property that belongs to the trust property.

(3) In the case referred to in paragraph (1), discharge of an obligation pertaining to a trust claim (excluding a trust claim prescribed in the preceding paragraph) based on a discharge order as set forth in Article 252, paragraph (1) of the Bankruptcy Act may not be asserted to the trust property.

(4) Even where an order for the commencement of rehabilitation proceedings is entered against a trustee, no trust property shall be included in the rehabilitation debtor's as-

sets.
(5) In the case referred to in the preceding paragraph, no distribution claim as a beneficiary shall be included in the rehabilitation claims. The same shall apply to a trust claim that the trustee is liable to satisfy only by using property that belongs to the trust property.
(6) In the case referred to in paragraph (4), a discharge of or modification to an obligation pertaining to a trust claim (excluding a trust claim as prescribed in the preceding paragraph) by a rehabilitation plan, an order for the confirmation of the rehabilitation plan, or discharge order set forth in Article 235, paragraph (1) of the Civil Rehabilitation Act may not be asserted to the trust property.
(7) The provisions of the preceding three paragraphs shall apply mutatis mutandis where an order for the commencement of reorganization is entered against a trustee. In this case, the term " rehabilitation debtor's assets" in paragraph (4) shall be deemed to be replaced with " of reorganization company's assets (meaning the assets of a company under reorganization as prescribed in Article 2, paragraph (14) of the Corporate Reorganization Act or the assets of a company in reorganization as prescribed in Article 169, paragraph (14) of the Act on Special Rules, etc. for Reorganization Proceedings for Financial Institutions, etc.) or the assets of a cooperative financial institution under reorganization (meaning the assets of a cooperative financial institution under reorganization as prescribed in Article 4, paragraph (14) of the Act on Special Rules, etc. for Reorganization Proceedings for Financial Institutions, etc)," the term "rehabilitation claims" in paragraph (5) shall be deemed to be replaced with "reorganization claims or secured reorganization claims," and the phrase "rehabilitation plan, an order for the confirmation of the rehabilitation plan, or an order of discharge set forth in Article 235, paragraph (1) of the Civil Rehabilitation Act" in the preceding paragraph shall be deemed to be replaced with "reorganization plan or an order for the confirmation of the reorganization plan."

Chapter III Trustees, etc.
Section 1 Trustees' Powers

(Scope of the Trustee's Powers)
Article 26 A trustee shall have the power to administer or dispose of property that belongs to the trust property and to conduct any other acts that are necessary to achieve the purpose of the trust; provided, however, that this shall not preclude such power from being restricted by the terms of trust.

(Rescission of Acts Conducted by Trustee Beyond the Powers)
Article 27 (1) Where an act conducted by a trustee for the trust property does not fall within the scope of the trustee's powers, a beneficiary may rescind such act, if all of the following conditions are met:
(i) that the other party to the act knew, at the time of the act, that the act was conducted for the trust property; and
(ii) that the other party to the act knew or was grossly negligent in failing to know, at the time of the act, that the act did not fall within the scope of the trustee's powers.
(2) Notwithstanding the provisions of the preceding paragraph, where an act conducted by a trustee to establish or transfer a right for property that belongs to the trust property (limited to such property for which a trust registration as set forth in Article 14 may be made) does not fall within the scope of trustee's powers, a beneficiary may rescind such act, if all of the following conditions are met:

(i) that at the time of the act, the trust registration as set forth in Article 14 existed with regard to the property that belongs to the trust property; and
(ii) that the other party to the act knew or was grossly negligent in failing to know, at the time of the act, that the act did not fall within the scope of the trustee's powers.
(3) When any one of the two or more beneficiaries has exercised the right to rescind under the provisions of the preceding two paragraphs, the rescission shall also be effective for other beneficiaries.
(4) The right to rescind under the provisions of paragraph (1) or paragraph (2) shall be extinguished by prescription if it is not exercised within three months from the time when the beneficiary (if there is a trust caretaker at the time in question, the trust caretaker) became aware of the existence of the grounds for rescission. The same shall apply when one year has elapsed from the time of the act.

(Delegation of Trust administration to a Third Party)
Article 28 In the following cases, a trustee may delegate the trust administration to a third party:
(i) where it is provided by the terms of trust that the trust administration is to be or may be delegated to a third party;
(ii) where the terms of trust does not contain any provisions concerning the delegation of the trust administration to a third party, but delegating the trust administration to a third party is considered to be appropriate in light of the purpose of the trust; and
(iii) where it is provided by the terms of trust that the trust administration shall not be delegated to a third party, but delegating the trust administration to a third party is considered to be unavoidable in light of the purpose of the trust.

Section 2 Duties, etc. of a Trustee

(The Trustee's Duty of Care)
Article 29 (1) A trustee shall administer trust affairs in line with the purpose of the trust.
(2) A trustee shall administer trust affairs with the due care of a prudent manager; provided, however, that if terms of trust otherwise provide, the trustee shall administer trust affairs with such care as provided for by the terms of trust.

(Duty of Loyalty)
Article 30 A trustee shall administer trust affairs and conduct any other acts faithfully on behalf of the beneficiary.

(Restriction on Acts that Create Conflicts of Interest)
Article 31 (1) A trustee shall not carry out the following acts:
(i) causing property that belongs to the trust property (including any right for such property) to be included in the trustee's own property, or causing property that belongs to the trustee's own property (including any right for such property) to be included in the trust property;
(ii) causing property that belongs to the trust property (including any right for such property) to be included in the trust property of another trust;
(iii) carrying out an act for the trust property with a third party while serving as the third party's agent; and
(iv) establishing a security interest on property that belongs to the trust property in

order to secure a claim pertaining to an obligation that the trustee is liable to perform only by using property that belongs to the trustee's own property, or carrying out any other act with a third party for the trust property which would create a conflict of interest between the trustee or an interested party thereof and the beneficiary.
(2) Notwithstanding the provisions of the preceding paragraph, in any of the following cases, a trustee may carry out the acts listed in the items of said paragraph; provided, however, that this shall not apply in the case set forth in item (ii) if it is provided for by the terms of trust that the trustee may not carry out said acts even in the case set forth in said item:
(i) where it is provided by the terms of trust that the trustee is allowed to carry out said acts;
(ii) where the trustee has disclosed the material facts and obtained approval from the beneficiary for carrying out said acts;
(iii) where any right to property that belongs to the trust property has been included in the trustee's own property by reason of inheritance or any other universal succession; or
(iv) where, in order to achieve the purpose of the trust, it is considered reasonably necessary for the trustee to carry out said acts, and it is clear that said acts conducted by the trustee will not harm the interests of the beneficiary, or where there are justifiable grounds for the trustee to carry out said acts in light of the impact of said acts on the trust property, the purpose and manner of the acts, the status of a substantial relationship between the trustee and the beneficiary which makes the trustee an interested party, and other relevant circumstances.
(3) A trustee shall, when the trustee has carried out any of the acts listed in the items of paragraph (1), give notice of the material facts concerning said act to a beneficiary; provided, however, that if the terms of trust otherwise provides for, such provisions shall prevail.
(4) Where the act set forth in paragraph (1), item (i) or item (ii) is carried out in violation of the provisions of paragraph (1) or paragraph (2), such act shall be void.
(5) The act set forth in the preceding paragraph shall become effective retroactively as of the time of the act, if it is ratified by the beneficiary.
(6) In the case prescribed in paragraph (4), when a trustee has disposed of or carried out any other act regarding the property set forth in paragraph (1), item (i) or item (ii) with a third party, a beneficiary may rescind the disposition or other act only if the third party knew or was grossly negligent in failing to know that the act set forth in paragraph (1), item (i) or item (ii) was carried out in violation of the provisions of paragraph (1) or paragraph (2). In this case, the provisions of Article 27, paragraph (3) and paragraph (4) shall apply mutatis mutandis.
(7) Where an act set forth in paragraph (1), item (iii) or item (iv) has been carried out in violation of the provisions of paragraph (1) and paragraph (2), a beneficiary may rescind the act only if the third party knew or was grossly negligent in failing to know that such act was conducted in violation of these provisions. In this case, the provisions of Article 27, paragraph (3) and paragraph (4) shall apply mutatis mutandis.

Article 32 (1) With regard to an act that a trustee may carry out in the course of administering trust affairs based on the trustee's powers as a trustee, if the trustee's failure to carry out such an act would be contrary to the interests of a beneficiary, the trustee may not conduct such act on the account of the trustee's own property or on the account of an interested party thereof.
(2) Notwithstanding the provisions of the preceding paragraph, in any of the following

cases, a trustee may carry out the act prescribed in said paragraph on the account of the trustee's own property or on the account of the interested party thereof; provided, however, that this shall not apply in the case set forth in item (ii) if it is provided by the terms of trust that the trustee may not carry out said act on the account of the trustee's own property or on the account of an interested party thereof even in the case set forth in said item:
  (i) where it is provided by the terms of trust that the trustee is allowed to carry out said act on the account of the trustee's own property or on the account of an interested party thereof; or
  (ii) where the trustee has disclosed the material facts and obtained approval from the beneficiary for carrying out said act on the account of the trustee's own property or on the account of an interested party thereof.
(3) A trustee shall, when the trustee has carried out the act prescribed in paragraph (1) on the account of the trustee's own property or on the account of an interested party thereof, give notice to the beneficiary of the material facts concerning the act; provided, however, that if the terms of trust otherwise provides for, such provisions shall prevail.
(4) Where a trustee has carried out an act prescribed in paragraph (1) in violation of the provisions of paragraph (1) and paragraph (2), the beneficiary may deem that said act has been conducted in the interests of the trust property; provided, however, that this may not harm rights of any third party.
(5) The rights under the provisions of the preceding paragraph shall be extinguished when one year has elapsed from the time of the act.

(Duty of Equity)
Article 33 In the case of a trust with two or more beneficiaries, the trustee shall perform duties of the trustee equitably on behalf of these beneficiaries.

(Duty to Segregate Property)
Article 34 (1) A trustee shall segregate property that belongs to the trust property from property that belongs to the trustee's own property and that which belongs to the trust property of other trusts by the method specified in each of the following items for the categories of property listed in the respective items; provided, however, that if the terms of trust otherwise provides for the method of segregation, such provisions shall prevail:
  (i) property for which a trust registration set forth in Article 14 may be made (excluding the property set forth in item (iii)): by said trust registration;
  (ii) property for which a trust registration set forth in Article 14 may not be made (excluding the property set forth in the following item): either of the methods specified in (a) or (b) below for the categories of property listed in (a) or (b), respectively:
    (a) movables (excluding monies): by retaining property that belongs to the trust property separately from property that belongs to the trustee's own property and the trust property of other trusts in the manner whereby they can be distinguished from each other on sight; or
    (b) monies and any property other than those set forth in (a): by clarifying the accounting thereof; or
  (iii) property specified by Ordinance of the Ministry of Justice: by a method specified by Ordinance of the Ministry of Justice for the appropriate segregation of the property.
(2) Notwithstanding the provisions of the proviso to the preceding paragraph, a trustee

shall not be exempted from the duty for trust registration set forth in Article 14 for the property set forth in item (i) of said paragraph.

(Duty to Appoint and Supervise a Third Party when Delegating the Trust administration)
Article 35 (1) When delegating the trust administration to a third party pursuant to the provisions of Article 28, the trustee shall delegate said administration to a suitable person in light of the purpose of the trust.
(2) A trustee, when the trustee has delegated the trust administration to a third party pursuant to the provisions of Article 28, shall conduct the necessary and appropriate supervision of the third party in order to achieve the purpose of the trust.
(3) When a trustee has delegated the trust administration to any of the following third parties, the provisions of the preceding two paragraphs shall not apply; provided, however, that when the trustee becomes aware that the third party is unsuitable or unfaithful or that the administration of affairs by the third party is inappropriate, the trustee shall give notice to the beneficiary to that effect, cancel the delegation to the third party, or take other necessary measures:
(i) a third party designated by the terms of trust; or
(ii) in cases where it is provided by the terms of trust that the trust administration shall be delegated to a third party designated by the settlor or the beneficiary, the third party designated pursuant to such provisions.
(4) Notwithstanding the provisions of the proviso to the preceding paragraph, if the terms of trust otherwise provides for, such provisions shall prevail.

(Duty to Report on the Processing Status Trust administration)
Article 36 A settlor or beneficiary may request that a trustee to report on the processing status of trust administration as well as the status of property that belongs to the trust property and the obligation covered by the trust property.

(Duty to Prepare, Report On, and Preserve Books, etc.)
Article 37 (1) A trustee shall prepare books and other documents or electromagnetic records relating to the trust property, as provided for by Ordinance of the Ministry of Justice, in order to clarify the accounts on trust affairs as well as the status of property that belongs to the trust property and the obligation covered by the trust property.
(2) A trustee shall prepare a balance sheet, profit and loss statement, and any other documents or electromagnetic records specified by Ordinance of the Ministry of Justice, once each year, at a certain time, as provided for by Ordinance of the Ministry of Justice.
(3) When a trustee has prepared the documents or electromagnetic records set forth in the preceding paragraph, the trustee shall report to a beneficiary (if there is a trust caretaker at the time in question, to the trust caretaker) on the content thereof; provided, however, that if the terms of trust otherwise provides for, such provisions shall prevail.
(4) Where a trustee has prepared the documents or electromagnetic records set forth in paragraph (1), the trustee shall preserve said documents (if electromagnetic records are prepared in lieu of said documents by the method specified by Ordinance of the Ministry of Justice, such electromagnetic records) or said electromagnetic records (if documents are prepared in lieu of said electromagnetic records, such documents) for ten years from the date of their preparation (or until the date of the completion of the liquidation of the trust if this occurs within said ten-year period; the same shall apply in the following paragraph); provided, however, that this shall not apply where the

trustee has delivered said documents or copies thereof to the beneficiary (if there are two or more beneficiaries at the time in question, to all beneficiaries; if there is a trust caretaker at the time in question, to the trust caretaker; the same shall apply in the proviso to paragraph (6)), or has provided the beneficiary with information on the matters recorded in said electromagnetic records by the method specified by Ordinance of the Ministry of Justice.

(5) Where a trustee has prepared or acquired a written contract relating to the disposition of property that belongs to the trust property or any other documents or electromagnetic records concerning the trust administration, the trustee shall preserve said documents (if electromagnetic records are prepared in lieu of said documents by the method specified by Ordinance of the Ministry of Justice, such electromagnetic records) or said electromagnetic records (if documents are prepared in lieu of said electromagnetic records, such documents) for ten years from the date of the preparation or acquisition. In this case, the provisions of the proviso to the preceding paragraph shall apply mutatis mutandis.

(6) Where a trustee has prepared the documents or electromagnetic records set forth in paragraph (2), the trustee shall preserve said documents (if electromagnetic records are prepared in lieu of said documents by the method specified by Ordinance of the Ministry of Justice, such electromagnetic records) or said electromagnetic records (if documents are prepared in lieu of said electromagnetic records, such documents) until the date of the completion of the liquidation of the trust; provided, however that this shall not apply where the trustee has, after ten years have elapsed from the date of their preparation, delivered said documents or copies thereof to the beneficiary, or has provided the beneficiary with information on the matters recorded in said electromagnetic records by the method specified by Ordinance of the Ministry of Justice.

(Request to Inspect, etc. of the Books, etc.)

Article 38 (1) A beneficiary may make the following requests to a trustee. In this case, in making such a request, the reasons therefor shall be specified:
  (i) a request to inspect or copy the documents set forth in paragraph (1) or paragraph (5) of the preceding Article; and
  (ii) a request to inspect or copy any object which shows the matters recorded in the electromagnetic records set forth in paragraph (1) or paragraph (5) of the preceding Article by a method specified by Ordinance of the Ministry of Justice.

(2) The trustee may not refuse a request set forth in the preceding paragraph when such a request has been received, except where it is found to fall under any of the following cases:
  (i) where the person making such request (hereinafter referred to as the "requester" in this paragraph) has made the request for purposes other than an investigation related to the securement or exercise of the requester's rights;
  (ii) where the requester has made the request at an inappropriate time;
  (iii) where the requester has made the request for the purpose of disturbing the trust administration or harming the common interests of the beneficiaries;
  (iv) where the requester operates or engages in a business which is effectively in competition with business pertaining to the trust;
  (v) where the requester has made the request in order to inform a third party, for profit, of any fact that the requester may learn by way of inspecting or copying documents or any other object under the provisions of the preceding paragraph; or
  (vi) where the requester has informed a third party, for profit, of any fact that the requester has learned by way of inspecting or copying documents or any other object under the provisions of the preceding paragraph within the past two years.

(3) The provisions of the preceding paragraph (excluding item (i) and item (ii)) shall not apply when there are two or more beneficiaries of a trust and the request set forth in paragraph (1) is made by all beneficiaries, or when there is only one beneficiary of the trust and the request set forth in said paragraph is made by such beneficiary.
(4) Where it is provided by the terms of trust that a request to inspect or copy documents or any other object under the provisions of paragraph (1) is to be restricted with regard to any information other than the those listed below if a beneficiary gives consent for such restriction, the beneficiary who has given such consent (including the beneficiary's successor; hereinafter the same shall apply in this Article) may not revoke the consent:
  (i) information that is indispensable for preparing the documents or electromagnetic records set forth in paragraph (2) of the preceding Article or any other material information concerning the trust; and
  (ii) information that is unlikely to harm the interests of any person other than said beneficiary.
(5) Upon receiving a request to inspect or copy documents or any other object under the provisions of paragraph (1) from a beneficiary who has given the consent as set forth in the preceding paragraph, a trustee may refuse such a request, except for the part that falls under the information listed in the items of the preceding paragraph.
(6) An interested party may make the following requests to a trustee:
  (i) a request to inspect or copy the documents set forth in paragraph (2) of the preceding Article; and
  (ii) a request to inspect or copy any object which shows the matters recorded in the electromagnetic records set forth in paragraph (2) of the preceding Article by a method specified by Ordinance of the Ministry of Justice.

(Request for the Disclosure of Names, etc. of Other Beneficiaries)
Article 39 (1) In the case of a trust with two or more beneficiaries, each beneficiary may request that trustee disclose the following matters by an appropriate method. In this case, in making such a request, the reasons therefor shall be specified:
  (i) the names and addresses of the other beneficiaries; and
  (ii) the content of the beneficial interest held by other beneficiaries.
(2) A trustee may not refuse a request set forth in the preceding paragraph when such a request has been received, except where it is found to fall under any of the following cases:
  (i) where the person making such request (hereinafter referred to as the "requester" in this paragraph) has made the request for purposes other than an investigation related to the securement or exercise of the requester's rights;
  (ii) where the requester has made the request at an inappropriate time;
  (iii) where the requester has made the request for the purpose of disturbing the trust administration or harming the common interests of the beneficiaries;
  (iv) where the requester operates or engages in business which is effectively in competition with business pertaining to the trust;
  (v) where the requester has made the request in order to inform a third party, for profit, of any fact that the requester may learn by way of the disclosure under the provisions of the preceding paragraph; or
  (vi) where the requester has informed a third party, for profit, of any fact that the requester learned by way of the disclosure under the provisions of the preceding paragraph within the past two years.
(3) Notwithstanding the provisions of the preceding two paragraphs, if the terms of trust otherwise provides, such provisions shall prevail.

Section 3 Trustee Liabilities, etc.

(Trustee Liability to Compensate for Losses, etc.)
Article 40 (1) When any of the cases listed in the following items has occurred due to the trustee's breach of the duties, the beneficiary may demand that the trustee take the measures specified in the respective items; provided, however, that this shall not apply to the measures specified in item (ii), if it is extremely difficult to restore the trust property, if the restoration would require excessive expenses, or if there are other special circumstances where it is inappropriate to have the trustee restore the trust property:
(i) where any loss to the trust property has occurred: compensation for such loss; and
(ii) where any change to the trust property has occurred: restoration of the trust property.
(2) Where a trustee has delegated the trust administration to a third party in violation of the provisions of Article 28, if any loss or change to the trust property has occurred, the trustee may not be released from liability as set forth in the preceding paragraph unless the trustee proves that such loss or change would have occurred even if the trustee had not delegated the trust administration to the third party.
(3) Where a trustee has carried out any act in violation of the provisions of Article 30, Article 31, paragraph (1) and paragraph (2) or Article 32, paragraph (1) and paragraph (2), the trustee shall be presumed to have caused a loss to the trust property in the same amount as the amount of the profit obtained by the trustee or an interested party thereof as a result of such act.
(4) Where a trustee has administered property that belongs to the trust property in violation of the provisions of Article 34, if any loss or change to the trust property has occurred, the trustee may not be released from the liability set forth in paragraph (1) unless the trustee proves that such loss or change would have occurred even if the trustee had segregated the relevant property in accordance with the provisions of said Article.

(Joint and Several Liability of the Officers of a Trustee Who Is a Juridical Person)
Article 41 Where a trustee that is a juridical person has incurred liability under the provisions of the preceding Article, the trustee's director, executive officer, or any other person equivalent thereto shall be jointly and severally liable together with the juridical person to compensate the beneficiary for any loss or to restore the trust property if the trustee's director, executive officer, or any other person equivalent thereto was willful or grossly negligent for an act that the juridical person carried out in violation of laws and regulations or the provisions of the terms of trust.

(Release from Liability to Compensate for Losses, etc.)
Article 42 Beneficiaries may grant a release from the following liabilities:
(i) liability under the provisions of Article 40; and
(ii) liability under the provisions of the preceding Article.

(Limitation to the Term for Claims Pertaining to Liability to Compensate for Losses, etc.)
Article 43 (1) The extinctive prescription for a claim pertaining to liability under the provisions of Article 40 shall be governed by the provisions on extinctive prescription for claims pertaining to liability arising from the failure to perform an obligation.

(2) The claim pertaining to liability under the provisions of Article 41 shall be extinguished by prescription if it is not exercised within ten years.
(3) The period of the extinctive prescription for a beneficiary's claim pertaining to liability under the provisions of Article 40 or Article 41 shall not begin to run until the beneficiary becomes aware that the beneficiary has been designated as a beneficiary (if there is no beneficiary at the time in question, until a trust caretaker is appointed).
(4) The claim prescribed in the preceding paragraph shall be extinguished when 20 years have elapsed from the time when any loss or change occurred to the trust property due to the trustee's breach of the duties.

(Cessation of a Trustee's Acts At the Demand of the Beneficiary)
Article 44 (1) Where a trustee has acted or is likely to act in violation of laws and regulations or the provisions of the terms of trust, if said action is likely to cause substantial harm to the trust property, the beneficiary may demand that the trustee cease said action.
(2) Where a trustee has acted or is likely to act in violation of the provisions of Article 33, if said action is likely to cause substantial harm to some of the beneficiaries, those beneficiaries may demand that the trustee cease said action.

(Payment of Expenses, Costs, or Remuneration, etc.)
Article 45 (1) Where a beneficiary who has filed a suit pertaining to the demand under the provisions of Article 40, Article 41, or the preceding Article has won the case (completely or partially), if the beneficiary has paid any expenses or costs (excluding court costs) that were necessary in relation to the suit or if the beneficiary is liable for paying remunerations to an attorney-at-law, legal professional corporation, judicial scrivener, or judicial scrivener corporation, such expenses, costs, or remuneration shall be paid from the trust property, up to the amount considered reasonable, not exceeding the actual amount thereof.
(2) Even where the beneficiary who filed the action set forth in the preceding paragraph has lost the case, the beneficiary shall not be liable to compensate the trustee for any damage arising from the action, except where the beneficiary was in bad faith.

(Appointment of an Inspector)
Article 46 (1) When there are sufficient grounds to suspect misconduct or material facts in violation of laws and regulations or the provisions of the terms of trust in connection with the trust administration by a trustee, the beneficiary may file a petition with the court for the appointment of an inspector in order to have the inspector investigate the status of the trust administration as well as the status of property that belongs to the trust property and the obligation covered by the trust property.
(2) When a petition set forth in the preceding paragraph is filed, the court shall appoint an inspector, except where it dismisses the petition as unlawful.
(3) A judicial decision dismissing the petition set forth in paragraph (1) shall include the reasons therefor.
(4) No appeal may be entered against a judicial decision on the appointment of an inspector under the provisions of paragraph (1).
(5) The inspector set forth in paragraph (2) may receive remuneration as determined by the court from the trust property.
(6) The court, before making a judicial decision determining the remuneration for an inspector under the provisions of the preceding paragraph, shall hear statements from the trustee and the inspector set forth in paragraph (2).
(7) A trustee or an inspector set forth in paragraph (2) may file an immediate appeal

Art.47~48　　　　　　　③ Trust Act, Chap.III, Sec.4

against a judicial decision determining the remuneration for the inspector made under the provisions of paragraph (5).

Article 47 (1) An inspector set forth in paragraph (2) of the preceding Article may, when it is necessary in order for the inspector to perform the duties, request that a trustee report on the status of the trust administration as well as the status of the trust property that belongs to the trust property and the obligation covered by the trust property, and may investigate the books, documents, and any other objects pertaining to the trust.
(2) An inspector set forth in paragraph (2) of the preceding Article shall conduct the necessary investigation, and shall report to the court through the submission of documents or electromagnetic records (limited to such record specified by Ordinance of the Ministry of Justice) in which the results of the investigation are stated or recorded.
(3) When the court finds it necessary for clarifying the contents of or confirming the basis of the report set forth in the preceding paragraph, it may request that the inspector set forth in paragraph (2) of the preceding Article make a further report set forth in the preceding paragraph.
(4) An inspector set forth in paragraph (2) of the preceding Article shall, when the inspector has made a report set forth in paragraph (2), deliver to the trustee and the person who filed the petition set forth in paragraph (1) of said Article a copy of the documents set forth in paragraph (2), or shall provide them with information on the matters recorded in the electromagnetic records set forth in said paragraph by the method specified by Ordinance of the Ministry of Justice.
(5) When a trustee has received a copy of the documents or information on the matters recorded in the electromagnetic records by the method specified by Ordinance of the Ministry of Justice under the provisions of the preceding paragraph, the trustee shall immediately give notice to the beneficiaries (excluding the beneficiary who filed the petition set forth in paragraph (1) of the preceding Article; the same shall apply in the following paragraph) to that effect; provided, however, that if the terms of trust otherwise provides for, such provisions shall prevail.
(6) Where a report set forth in paragraph (2) has been made, the court, when it finds it necessary, shall order the trustee to give notice of the results of the investigation set forth in said paragraph to the beneficiary or to take any other appropriate measures to make public the content of the report.

Section 4　Expenses, etc. and Trust Fees, etc. for the Trustee

(Reimbursement of Expenses, etc. from the Trust Property)
Article 48 (1) Where a trustee has paid, from the trustee's own property, expenses that are considered to be necessary for the trust administration, the trustee may receive reimbursement for such expenses and interest thereon accruing from the date of payment (hereinafter referred to as "expenses, etc.") from the trust property; provided, however, that if the terms of trust otherwise provides for, such provisions shall prevail.
(2) When a trustee needs expenses for the trust administration, the trustee may receive advance payment thereof from the trust property; provided, however, that if the terms of trust otherwise provides for, such provisions shall prevail.
(3) In order to receive advance payment of expenses from the trust property pursuant to the provisions of the main clause of the preceding paragraph, a trustee shall give notice to a beneficiary of the amount of advance payment to be received and the basis for the calculation of such amount; provided, however, that if the terms of trust otherwise provides for, such provisions shall prevail.

(4) Notwithstanding the provisions of paragraph (1) or paragraph (2), where a trustee has incurred liability under the provisions of Article 40, the trustee may not receive reimbursement for expenses, etc. or advance payment of expenses until after the trustee performs such liability; provided, however, that if the terms of trust otherwise provides for, such provisions shall prevail.
(5) In the case referred to in paragraph (1) or paragraph (2), a trustee shall not be precluded from receiving reimbursement for expenses, etc. or advance payment of expenses from a beneficiary based on an agreement between the trustee and the beneficiary.

(Method of Reimbursement, etc. for Expenses, etc.)
Article 49 (1) Where a trustee may receive reimbursement for expenses, etc. or advance payment of expenses from the trust property pursuant to the provisions of paragraph (1) or paragraph (2) of the preceding Article, said trustee may transfer monies that belong to the trust property to the coffers of trustee's own property, up to the amount receivable.
(2) In the case prescribed in the preceding paragraph, when necessary, a trustee may dispose of property that belongs to the trust property (excluding such property whose disposal would make it impossible to achieve the purpose of the trust); provided, however, that if the terms of trust otherwise provides for, such provisions shall prevail.
(3) In the case prescribed in paragraph (1), if any of the items of Article 31, paragraph (2) apply, a trustee may transfer property that belongs to the trust property other than monies, to the coffers of trustee's own property, instead of exercising the right under the provisions of paragraph (1); provided, however, that if the terms of trust otherwise provides for, such provisions shall prevail.
(4) When proceedings are commenced for execution against or for the exercise of a security interest in property that belongs to the trust property, the right that a trustee has pursuant to the provisions of paragraph (1) shall be deemed to be a monetary claim in relation to such proceedings.
(5) In the case referred to in the preceding paragraph, a trustee who has proved that the trustee has the right prescribed in said paragraph by means of a document certifying the existence of said right may also demand a distribution under the proceedings for execution or for the exercise of a security interest set forth in said paragraph.
(6) The right that a trustee has pursuant to the provisions of paragraph (1) with regard to expenses, etc. for the preservation, liquidation, or distribution of property that belongs to the trust property, which has been conducted in the common interest of creditors (limited to creditors who hold claims pertaining to the obligation covered by the trust property; hereinafter the same shall apply in this paragraph and the following paragraph) shall, in the proceedings for execution or for the exercise of a security interest set forth in paragraph (4), prevail over the rights of other creditors (in cases where such expenses, etc. were not beneficial to all creditors, those who did not benefit from such expenses, etc. shall be excluded). In this case, said right has the same rank in the order of priority as a statutory lien prescribed in Article 307, paragraph (1) of the Civil Code.
(7) The right that a trustee has pursuant to the provisions of paragraph (1) with regard to the expenses, etc. which fall under the following items shall, in the proceedings for execution against or for the exercise of a security interest in the property set forth in the respective items, as set forth in paragraph (4), prevail over the rights of other creditors for the amount specified in the respective items:
(i) the amount of expenses paid for the preservation of property that belongs to the trust property or any other amount that is considered to be necessary for maintaining the value of such property: such amount; and

(ii) the amount of expenses paid for the improvement of property that belongs to the trust property or any other amount that is considered to be conducive to increasing the value of such property: such amount or the amount of the increase in value at the time in question, whichever is smaller.

(Subrogation of a Trustee through Performance of Obligations Covered by the Trust Property)
Article 50 (1) Where a trustee has performed an obligation covered by the trust property by using trustee's own property, when the trustee acquires the right under the provisions of paragraph (1) of the preceding Article through such performance, the trustee shall be subrogated to the creditor who holds the claim pertaining to said obligation covered by the trust property. In this case, the right that the trustee has pursuant to the provisions of said paragraph shall be deemed to be a monetary claim in relation to such subrogation.
(2) When a trustee is subrogated to the creditor set forth in the preceding paragraph pursuant to the provisions of said paragraph, the trustee shall give notice to the creditor, without delay, to the effect that the claim held by the creditor is a claim pertaining to an obligation covered by the trust property and that the trustee has performed said obligation by using the trustee's own property.

(Reimbursement of Expenses, etc. and Simultaneous Performance)
Article 51 A trustee may, before the right that the trustee has pursuant to the provisions of Article 49, paragraph (1) is extinguished, refuse to perform the obligation of distribution involving the trust property to a beneficiary or a holder of a vested right prescribed in Article 182, paragraph (1), item (ii); provided, however, that if the terms of trust otherwise provides, such provisions shall prevail.

(Measures for Trust Property that Is Insufficient for the Reimbursement of Expenses, etc.)
Article 52 (1) Where a trustee wishes to receive reimbursement for expenses, etc. or advance payment of expenses from the trust property pursuant to the provisions of Article 48, paragraph (1) or paragraph (2) but the trust property (excluding any property that may not be disposed of pursuant to the provisions of Article 49, paragraph (2); the same shall apply in item (i) and paragraph (4)) is insufficient to provide such reimbursement or advance payment, the trustee may terminate the trust if the trustee has given notice of the following matters to the settlor and the beneficiary but has not received reimbursement of expenses, etc. or advance payment of expenses from the settlor or the beneficiary even when a reasonable period of time set forth in item (ii) has elapsed:
(i) a statement to the effect that the trustee is unable to receive reimbursement of expenses, etc. or advance payment of expenses due to the insufficient trust property; and
(ii) a statement to the effect that the trustee will terminate the trust if the trustee is unable to receive reimbursement of expenses, etc. or advance payment of expenses from the settlor or the beneficiary within a reasonable period of time specified by the trustee.
(2) For the purpose of the application of the provisions of the preceding paragraph in cases where there is no settlor at the time in question, the phrase "the settlor and the beneficiary" and "the settlor or the beneficiary" in said paragraph shall be deemed to be replaced with "the beneficiary."
(3) For the purpose of the application of the provisions of paragraph (1) in cases where

there is no beneficiary at the time in question, the phrase "the settlor and the beneficiary" and "the settlor or the beneficiary" in said paragraph shall be deemed to be replaced with "the settlor."
(4) Where the trust property is insufficient to provide for reimbursement of expenses, etc. or advance payment of expenses pursuant to the provisions of Article 48, paragraph (1) or paragraph (2), or if there is neither a settlor nor a beneficiary at the time in question, the trustee may terminate the trust.

(Compensation for Damages Out of the Trust Property)
Article 53 (1) In the cases listed in the following items, a trustee may receive compensation from the trust property for the amount of damages specified in the respective items; provided, however, that if the terms of trust otherwise provides for, such provisions shall prevail:
 (i) where the trustee has suffered any damages in the course of administering trust affairs, in the absence of trustee's own negligence: the amount of such damages; and
 (ii) where the trustee has suffered any damages in the course of administering trust affairs due to an international or negligent act of a third party (excluding the case set forth in the preceding item): the amount of compensation that may be demanded from such third party.
(2) The provisions of Article 48, paragraph (4) and paragraph (5), Article 49 (excluding paragraph (6) and paragraph (7)), and the preceding two Articles shall apply mutatis mutandis to the compensation for damages from the trust property under the provisions of the preceding paragraph.

(Trust Fees for the Trustee)
Article 54 (1) In addition to the case where the provisions of Article 512 of the Commercial Code (Act No. 48 of 1899) shall apply to the undertaking of acceptance of a trust, a trustee may receive trust fees (meaning a property benefit to be received by a trustee as the consideration for the trust administration; the same shall apply hereinafter) from the trust property only where it is provided by the terms of trust that the trustee shall receive trust fees from the trust property.
(2) In the case referred to in the preceding paragraph, the amount of trust fees shall be, if the terms of trust contains provisions concerning the amount of trust fees or the calculation method thereof, determined pursuant to such provisions, and if there are no such provisions, a reasonable amount.
(3) In the absence of provisions of the terms of trust as set forth in the preceding paragraph, a trustee shall, in order to receive trust fees from the trust property, give notice to a beneficiary of the amount of trust fees and the basis for the calculation of such amount.
(4) The provisions of Article 48, paragraph (4) and paragraph (5), Article 49 (excluding paragraph (6) and paragraph (7)), Article 51, and Article 52, as well as the provisions of Article 648, paragraph (2) and paragraph (3) of the Civil Code, shall apply mutatis mutandis to the trustee's trust fees.

(Exercise of a Security Interest by the Trustee)
Article 55 In the case of a trust created with a security interest as the trust property, if it is provided by the terms of trust that the beneficiary shall be the creditor of the claim to be secured by said security interest, the trustee may, as the holder of the security interest, file a petition for the enforcement of the security interest and be distributed the proceeds of the sale or be delivered payment monies, within the scope of trust affairs.

Section 5 Changing, etc. of Trustees
Subsection 1 Termination of a Trustee's Duty as Trustee

(Grounds for Termination of a Trustee's Duty as Trustee)
Article 56 (1) A trustee's duty as trustee shall terminate on the following grounds, in addition to the completion of the liquidation of the trust; provided, however, that in the case of the termination on the grounds set forth in item (iii), if the terms of trust otherwise provides, such provisions shall prevail:
(i) the death of the individual who is the trustee:
(ii) a ruling for commencement of guardianship or commencement of curatorship against the individual who is the trustee:
(iii) an order for the commencement of bankruptcy proceedings against the trustee (excluding cases of dissolution by an order for the commencement of bankruptcy proceedings);
(iv) the dissolution of the juridical person who is the trustee for reasons other than a merger;
(v) the resignation of the trustee under the provisions of the following Article;
(vi) the dismissal of the trustee under the provisions of Article 58; or
(vii) any grounds specified by the terms of trust.
(2) Where the juridical person who is the trustee has effected a merger, the judicial person that survives the merger or judicial person that is incorporated through the merger shall take over the trustee's duty. Where the judicial person who is the trustee has effected a company split, the same shall apply to the juridical person that succeeds to the rights and duties of the trustee as a result of the company split.
(3) Notwithstanding the provisions of the preceding paragraph, if the terms of trust otherwise provides for, such provisions shall prevail.
(4) Where the grounds set forth in paragraph (1), item (iii) occur, if the trustee's duty as trustee does not terminate pursuant to the provisions of the proviso to said paragraph, the bankrupt shall perform the duties of the trustee.
(5) A trustee's duty as trustee shall not terminate on the grounds that the trustee has been handed an order for the commencement of rehabilitation proceedings; provided, however, that if the terms of trust otherwise provides for, such provisions shall prevail.
(6) In the case prescribed in the main clause of the preceding paragraph, when there is a rehabilitation trustee, the right of the trustee to perform the trustee's duties and administer and dispose of property that belongs to the trust property shall be vested exclusively in the rehabilitation trustee. The same shall apply where there is a provisional administrator in charge of rehabilitation proceedings.
(7) The provisions of the preceding two paragraphs shall apply mutatis mutandis where the trustee is given an order for the commencement of reorganization proceedings. In this case, the phrase "there is a rehabilitation trustee" in the preceding paragraph shall be deemed to be replaced with "there is a reorganization trustee (excluding the period set forth in Article 74, paragraph (2) of the Corporate Reorganization Act (including cases where applied mutatis mutandis pursuant to Article 47 and Article 213 of the Act on Special Rules, etc. for Reorganization Proceedings for Financial Institutions, etc.))."

(Resignation of the Trustee)
Article 57 (1) The trustee may resign from the office as trustee with the permission of

the settlor and the beneficiary; provided, however, that if the terms of trust otherwise provides for, such provisions shall prevail.
(2) The trustee may resign from the office as trustee with the permission of the court when there is a compelling reason.
(3) When filing a petition for the permission set forth in the preceding paragraph, the trustee shall make a prima facie showing of the facts constituting the grounds for the petition.
(4) A judicial decision dismissing the petition for permission set forth in paragraph (2) shall include the reasons therefor.
(5) No appeal may be entered against a judicial decision on permission for resignation under the provisions of paragraph (2).
(6) The provisions of the main clause of paragraph (1) shall not apply where there is no settlor at the time in question.

(Dismissal of the Trustee)
Article 58 (1) The settlor and the beneficiary may, based on an agreement between them, dismiss the trustee at any time.
(2) When the settlor and the beneficiary have dismissed a trustee at a time that is detrimental to the trustee, the settlor and the beneficiary shall compensate the trustee for any damages; provided, however, that this shall not apply if there was a compelling reason for such dismissal.
(3) Notwithstanding the provisions of the preceding two paragraphs, if the terms of trust otherwise provides, such provisions shall prevail.
(4) When the trustee has caused a substantial detriment to the trust property through a breach of the duties or where there are other material grounds, the court may, upon the petition of a settlor or a beneficiary, dismiss the trustee.
(5) Before dismissing the trustee pursuant to the provisions of the preceding paragraph, the court shall hear a statement from the trustee.
(6) The judicial decision on the petition for permission set forth in paragraph (4) shall include the reasons for said decision.
(7) A settlor, trustee or beneficiary may file an immediate appeal against a judicial decision of dismissal under the provisions of paragraph (4).
(8) The provisions of paragraph (1) and paragraph (2) shall not apply where there is no settlor at the time in question.

Subsection 2 Duties, etc. of the Former Trustee

(Former Trustee's Duty to Give Notice and Retain Property, etc.)
Article 59 (1) Where a trustee's duty as trustee has been terminated on any of the grounds listed in Article 56, paragraph (1), item (iii) to item (vii), the person who was the trustee (hereinafter referred to as the "former trustee") shall give notice of the termination to a beneficiary; provided, however, that if the terms of trust otherwise provides for, such provisions shall prevail.
(2) Where a trustee's duty as trustee has been terminated on the grounds listed in Article 56, paragraph (1), item (iii), the former trustee shall give notice to the bankruptcy trustee of the content and location of property that belongs to the trust property, the content of the obligation covered by the trust property, and other matters specified by Ordinance of the Ministry of Justice.
(3) Where a trustee's duty as trustee has been terminated on any of the grounds listed in Article 56, paragraph (1), item (iv) to item (vii), the former trustee shall continue to retain property that belongs to the trust property until a new trustee (if a trust prop-

Art.60　　　　　　　　3 Trust Act, Chap.III, Sec.5

erty administrator is appointed pursuant to the provisions of Article 64, paragraph (1), the trust property administrator; hereinafter referred to as a "new trustee, etc." in this Section) becomes able to administer trust affairs, and shall carry out the necessary actions for the transfer of trust affairs; provided, however, that if the terms of trust otherwise provides, the new trustee's duties may be expanded.
(4) Notwithstanding the provisions of the preceding paragraph, where a trustee's duty as trustee has been terminated on the grounds listed in Article 56, paragraph (1), item (v) (limited to the case under the provisions of Article 57, paragraph (1)), the former trustee shall continue to have the rights and duties of a trustee until a new trustee, etc. becomes able to administer trust affairs; provided, however, that if the terms of trust otherwise provides, such provisions shall prevail.
(5) In the cases referred to in paragraph (3) (excluding the case prescribed in the main clause of the preceding paragraph), if the former trustee attempts to dispose of property that belongs to the trust property, a beneficiary may demand that the former trustee cease to dispose of the property; provided, however, that this shall not apply after a new trustee, etc. becomes able to administer trust affairs.

(Duty of the Former Trustee's Heir to Give Notice and Retain Property, etc.)
Article 60 (1) Where a trustee's duty as trustee has been terminated on any of the grounds listed in Article 56, paragraph (1), item (i) or item (ii), if the former trustee's heir (if there is a statutory agent at the time in question, the statutory agent) or guardian or curator of an adult trustee (hereinafter collectively referred to as the "former trustee's heir, etc." in this Section) knows such a fact, the former trustee's heir, etc. shall give notice of the fact to a known beneficiary; provided, however, that if the terms of trust otherwise provides for, such provisions shall prevail.
(2) Where a trustee's duty as trustee has been terminated on any of the grounds listed in Article 56, paragraph (1), item (i) or item (ii), the former trustee's heir, etc. shall continue to retain property that belongs to the trust property until a new trustee, etc. or an incorporated trust property administrator becomes able to administer trust affairs, and shall carry out the necessary actions for the transfer of trust affairs.
(3) In the case referred to in the preceding paragraph, if the former trustee's heir, etc. attempts to dispose of property that belongs to the trust property, a beneficiary may demand that the former trustee's heir, etc. cease to dispose of the property; provided, however, that this shall not apply after a new trustee, etc. or an incorporated trust property administrator becomes able to administer trust affairs.
(4) Where a trustee's duty as trustee has been terminated on the grounds listed in Article 56, paragraph (1), item (iii), the bankruptcy trustee shall continue to retain property that belongs to the trust property until a new trustee, etc. becomes able to administer trust affairs, and shall carry out the necessary actions for the transfer of trust affairs.
(5) In the case referred to in the preceding paragraph, if the bankruptcy trustee attempts to dispose of property that belongs to the trust property, a beneficiary may demand that the bankruptcy trustee cease to dispose of the property; provided, however, that this shall not apply after a new trustee, etc. becomes able to administer trust affairs.
(6) The former trustee's heir, etc. or the bankruptcy trustee may demand reimbursement, from the new trustee, etc. or from the incorporated trust property administrator, of expenses paid for carrying out the actions under the provisions of paragraph (1), paragraph (2) or paragraph (4), and for interest thereon accruing from the date of payment.
(7) The provisions of Article 49, paragraph (6) and paragraph (7) shall apply mutatis mutandis to the right that the former trustee's heir, etc. or the bankruptcy trustee has pursuant to the provisions of the preceding paragraph.

(Payment of Expenses, Costs, or Remuneration, etc.)

Article 61 (1) Where a beneficiary who has filed an action pertaining to the demand under the provisions of Article 59, paragraph (5), or paragraph (3) or paragraph (5) of the preceding Article has won the case (completely or partially), if the beneficiary has paid any expenses or costs (excluding court costs) that were necessary in relation to the action or if the beneficiary is liable to pay remuneration to an attorney-at-law, legal professional corporation, judicial scrivener, or judicial scrivener corporation, such expenses, costs, or remunerations shall be paid from the trust property, up to the amount considered reasonable, not exceeding the actual amount thereof.
(2) Even where the beneficiary who filed the action set forth in the preceding paragraph has lost the case, the beneficiary shall not be liable to compensate the trustee for any damage arising from the action, except where the beneficiary was in bad faith.

Subsection 3 Appointment of a New Trustee

Article 62 (1) Where a trustee's duty as trustee has been terminated on any of the grounds listed in the items of Article 56, paragraph (1), if the terms of trust contains no provisions concerning a new trustee, or where the person designated by the provisions of the terms of trust as a person who is to be the new trustee does not undertake or is unable to undertake the trust, the settlor and the beneficiary may, based on an agreement between them, appoint a new trustee.
(2) Where a trustee's duty as trustee has been terminated on any of the grounds listed in the items of Article 56, paragraph (1), if the terms of trust contains provisions designating a particular person to be the new trustee, any interested party may specify a reasonable period of time and call on the person designated as the one to be the new trustee to give a definite answer within that period of time with regard to whether the person will accept the duty; provided, however, that if the terms of trust designates a condition precedent or a time of commencement for the provisions, this may only be done after the condition precedent is fulfilled or after the time of commencement arrives.
(3) Where a call for an answer is made under the provisions of the preceding paragraph, if the person designated as the one who is to be the new trustee fails to give a definite answer to the settlor and the beneficiary (if there are two or more beneficiaries at the time in question, to one of them; if there is a trust caretaker at the time in question, to the trust caretaker) within the period set forth in said paragraph, it shall be deemed that the person does not accept the duty.
(4) In the case referred to in paragraph (1), the court may, at the petition of an interested party, appoint a new trustee when it finds it necessary in light of the status of discussions pertaining to the agreement set forth in said paragraph and any other circumstances.
(5) The judicial decision on the petition set forth in the preceding paragraph shall include the reasons for said decision.
(6) The settlor, beneficiary, or the current trustee may file an immediate appeal against a judicial decision on the appointment of a new trustee under the provisions of paragraph (4).
(7) The immediate appeal set forth in the preceding paragraph shall have the effect of a stay of execution.
(8) For the purpose of the application of the provisions of the preceding paragraphs in cases where there is no settlor at the time in question, the phrase "the settlor and the beneficiary may, based on an agreement between them" in paragraph (1) shall be deemed to be replaced with "the beneficiary may," the phrase "the settlor and the ben-

eficiary" in paragraph (3) shall be deemed to be replaced with "the beneficiary," and the phrase "status of discussions pertaining to the agreement set forth in said paragraph" in paragraph (4) shall be deemed to be replaced with "status of the beneficiary."

Subsection 4 Trust Property Administrators, etc.

(Trust Property Administration Orders)
Article 63 (1) Where a trustee's duty as trustee has been terminated on any of the grounds listed in the items of Article 56, paragraph (1), at the petition of an interested party, the court may, when a new trustee has not yet been appointed and when it finds it to be necessary, make a disposition ordering administration by a trust property administrator (hereinafter referred to as a "trust property administration order" in this Subsection) until a new trustee is appointed.
(2) A judicial decision dismissing the petition set forth in the preceding paragraph shall include the reasons therefor.
(3) The court may change or revoke a trust property administration order.
(4) An interested party may file an immediate appeal against a trust property administration order and an order made under the provisions of the preceding paragraph.

(Appointment of Trust Property Administrators, etc.)
Article 64 (1) When the court issues a trust property administration order, it shall appoint a trust property administrator therein.
(2) No appeal may be entered against a judicial decision on the appointment of a trust property administrator made under the provisions of the preceding paragraph.
(3) When the court has made a judicial decision on the appointment of a trust property administrator under the provisions of paragraph (1), it shall immediately give public notice of the following matters:
  (i) a statement to the effect that a trust property administrator has been appointed; and
  (ii) the name of the trust property administrator.
(4) The provisions of item (ii) of the preceding paragraph shall apply mutatis mutandis where there is a change to the matters set forth in said item.
(5) Where a trust property administration order is issued, when a court clerk becomes aware of the existence of any registered right that belongs to the trust property, the court clerk shall, on the own authority of the court clerk and without delay, commission a registration of the trust property administration order.
(6) When a judicial decision is made to revoke a trust property administration order or when a new trustee who has been appointed after a trust property administration order was issued has filed a petition to commission the cancellation of the registration of the trust property administration order, a court clerk shall, on the own authority of the court clerk and without delay, commission the cancellation of the registration of the trust property administration order.

(Effect of Juridical Acts by a Former Trustee)
Article 65 (1) After a judicial decision on the appointment of a trust property administrator has been made under the provisions of paragraph (1) of the preceding Article, no juridical act conducted by the former trustee with respect to property that belongs to the trust property may be asserted as effective in relation to the trust property.
(2) Any juridical act conducted by the former trustee on the day on which the judicial decision on the appointment of a trust property administrator is made under the provision of paragraph (1) of the preceding Article shall be presumed to have been conduct-

ed after said judicial decision was made.

(Trust Property Administrator's Powers)

Article 66 (1) Where a trust property administrator is appointed pursuant to the provisions of Article 64, paragraph (1), a trustee's right to perform the duties and administer and dispose of property that belongs to the trust property shall be vested exclusively in the trust property administrator.
(2) When there are two or more trust property administrators, they shall act within the scope of their power jointly; provided, however, that with the permission of the court, they may perform their duties severally or divide their duties among themselves.
(3) When there are two or more trust property administrators, it shall be sufficient if a third party make manifestation of intention to any one of them.
(4) A trust property administrator shall obtain the court's permission in order to carry out any actions beyond the scope of the following acts:
  (i) an act of preservation; and
  (ii) an act with the intent to use or improve property that belongs to the trust property, to the extent that such act does not change the nature of such property.
(5) Any act conducted by a trust property administrator in violation of the provisions of the preceding paragraph shall be void; provided, however, that the trust property administrator may not duly assert this against a third party who has no knowledge of such violation.
(6) When filing a petition for the permission set forth in the proviso to paragraph (2) or paragraph (4), a trust property administrator shall make a prima facie showing of the facts constituting the grounds for the petition.
(7) A judicial decision dismissing the petition for permission set forth in the proviso to paragraph (2) or paragraph (4) shall include the reasons therefor.
(8) No appeal may be entered against a judicial decision on the permission under the provisions of the proviso to paragraph (2) or paragraph (4).

(Administration of Property that Belongs to Trust Property)

Article 67 A trust property administrator shall commence the administration of property that belongs to the trust property immediately after assuming the office.

(Standing to Sue or to Be Sued)

Article 68 In an action relating to the trust property, a trust property administrator shall be either a plaintiff or defendant.

(Trust Property Administrator's Duties, etc.)

Article 69 A trust property administrator, when performing the duties, shall assume the same duties and liabilities as a trustee.

(Resignation and Dismissal of Trust Property Administrators)

Article 70 The provisions of Article 57, paragraph (2) to paragraph (5) shall apply mutatis mutandis to the resignation of a trust property administrator, and the provisions of Article 58, paragraph (4) to paragraph (7) shall apply mutatis mutandis to the dismissal of a trust property administrator. In this case, the phrase "there is a compelling reason" in Article 57, paragraph (2) shall be deemed to be replaced with "there are justifiable grounds."

(Remuneration, etc. for Trust Property Administrators)

Article 71 (1) A trust property administrator may receive such amounts for advance pay-

ment of expenses and remuneration as determined by the court from the trust property.
(2) The court, before it makes a judicial decision determining the amount of expenses or remuneration under the provisions of the preceding paragraph, shall hear the statement of the trust property administrator.
(3) A trust property administrator may file an immediate appeal against a judicial decision determining the amount of expenses or remuneration under the provisions of paragraph (1).

(Transfer, etc. of Trust Affairs from Trust Property Administrator to New Trustee)
Article 72 The provisions of Article 77 shall apply mutatis mutandis where a new trustee assumes the office as trustee after the appointment of a trust property administrator. In this case, the phrase "the beneficiary (if there are two or more beneficiaries at the time in question, from all of them, and if there is a trust caretaker at the time in question, from the trust caretaker)" in paragraph (1) of said Article and the phrase "beneficiary (if there is a trust caretaker at the time in question, the trust caretaker; the same shall apply in the following paragraph)" in paragraph (2) of said Article, and the term "the beneficiary" in paragraph (3) of said Article shall be deemed to be replaced with "the new trustee," and the term "the beneficiary" in paragraph (2) of said Article shall be deemed to be replaced with "the new trustee."

(Powers of the Person Performing a Trustee's Duties on Behalf of the Trustee)
Article 73 The provisions of Article 66 shall apply mutatis mutandis to a person performing the trustee's duties on behalf of the trustee who has been appointed by an order of provisional disposition to appoint a person to perform the duties of a trustee on behalf of the trustee.

(Ownership, etc. of Trust Property Upon Termination of Trustee's Duty as Trustee Due to Death of the Trustee)
Article 74 (1) When a trustee' duty as trustee has been terminated on the grounds set forth in Article 56, paragraph (1), item (i), the trust property shall be incorporated as a juridical person.
(2) In the case prescribed in the preceding paragraph, at the petition of an interested party, the court may, when it finds it to be necessary, make a disposition ordering administration of the trust by an incorporated trust property administrator (hereinafter referred to as an "incorporated trust property administration order" in paragraph (6)).
(3) The provisions of Article 63, paragraph (2) to paragraph (4) shall apply mutatis mutandis to a case pertaining to the petition set forth in the preceding paragraph.
(4) When the new trustee assumes the office of trustee, it shall be deemed that the juridical person set forth in paragraph (1) was never incorporated; provided, however, that this shall not preclude the effect of any acts conducted by the incorporated trust property administrator within the scope of the powers of the said administrator.
(5) The incorporated trust property administrator's authority of representation shall be extinguished when a new trustee becomes able to administer trust affairs.
(6) The provisions of Article 64 shall apply mutatis mutandis where an incorporated trust property administration order is issued, and the provisions of Article 66 to Article 72 shall apply to an incorporated trust property administrator.

Subsection 5 Succession, etc. to Rights and Duties upon a Change of Trustees

(Succession, etc. to Rights and Duties Concerning the Trust)
Article 75 (1) Where a trustee's duty as trustee has been terminated on any of the grounds listed in the items of Article 56, paragraph (1), when a new trustee has assumed the duty, it shall be deemed that the new trustee has succeeded to, at the time of the termination of the former trustee's duty, the former trustee's rights and duties concerning the trust existing as of that time.
(2) Notwithstanding the provisions of the preceding paragraph, where a trustee's duty as trustee has been terminated on the grounds listed in the items of Article 56, paragraph (1), item (v) (limited to the case under the provision of Article 57, paragraph (1); excluding the case referred to in the proviso to Article 59, paragraph (4)), it shall be deemed that the new trustee has succeeded to, at the time of assumption of the office by a new trustee, etc., the former trustee's rights and duties concerning the trust existing as of that time.
(3) The provisions of the preceding two paragraphs shall not preclude the effect of any act carried out by the former trustee, a trust property administrator, or an incorporated trust property administrator within the scope of their powers before the new trustee assumes the office as the new trustee.
(4) The provisions of Article 27 shall apply mutatis mutandis where the former trustee has carried out any act that does not fall within the scope of the powers of the former trustee before the new trustee, etc. assumes the office as a trustee.
(5) Where the former trustee (including the trustee's heir; hereinafter the same shall apply in this Article) has incurred liability under the provision of Article 40, or where a director, executive officer, or any other person equivalent thereto (hereinafter referred to as a "director, etc." in this paragraph) of the former trustee who is a juridical person has incurred liability under the provision of Article 41, the new trustee, etc. or incorporated trust property administrator may make a claim against the former trustee or its director, etc. under the provisions of Article 40 or Article 41.
(6) Where the former trustee may receive reimbursement of expenses, etc. or compensation for damages, or where the former trustee may receive trust fees from the trust property, the former trustee may make a demand of the new trustee, etc. or incorporated trust property administrator for reimbursement of expenses, etc., compensation for damages, or payment of trust fees; provided, however, that the new trustee, etc. or incorporated trust property administrator shall only be liable for using property that belongs to the trust property to perform this obligation.
(7) The provisions of Article 48, paragraph (4) and Article 49, paragraph (6) and paragraph (7) shall apply mutatis mutandis to the right that the former trustee has under the provisions of the preceding paragraph.
(8) Execution, execution of a provisional seizure or provisional disposition, procedures for the exercise of a security interest, or an auction which has already been commenced against property that belongs to the trust property before a new trustee assumes the office of trustee, may be continued against the new trustee.
(9) The former trustee may retain property that belongs to the trust property until the former trustee receives satisfaction of the claim pertaining to the demand under the provisions of paragraph (6).

(Liabilities of the Former Trustee and the New Trustee for Obligations Succeeded To)
Article 76 (1) Even where obligations pertaining to trust claims are succeeded to by the

new trustee pursuant to the provisions of paragraph (1) or paragraph (2) of the preceding Article, the former trustee shall be liable to perform the obligations thus succeeded to using the former trustee's own property; provided, however, that this shall not apply if the former trustee is only liable for using property that belongs to the trust property to perform such obligations.
(2) Where the new trustee has succeeded to the obligations prescribed in the main clause of the preceding paragraph, the new trustee shall only be liable for using property that belongs to the trust property to perform those obligations.

(Transfer, etc. of Trust Affairs from the Former Trustee to the New Trustee, etc.)
Article 77 (1) Where the new trustee, etc. assumes the office of trustee, the former trustee shall, without delay, settle the accounts on trust affairs and request approval for the settlement of accounts from a beneficiary (if there are two or more beneficiaries at the time in question, from all of them; if there is a trust caretaker at the time in question, from the trust caretaker), and shall transfer trust affairs as required in order for the new trustee, etc. to administer them.
(2) Where a beneficiary (if there is a trust caretaker at the time in question, the trust caretaker; the same shall apply in the following paragraph) has approved the settlement of accounts set forth in the preceding paragraph, the former trustee shall be deemed to have been released from the liability to the beneficiary to transfer trust affairs under the provisions of said paragraph; provided, however, that this shall not apply if the former trustee has committed misconduct in the course of the duties.
(3) Where a beneficiary has not made any objection within one month from the time when the beneficiary was requested by the former trustee to give an approval for the settlement of accounts set forth in paragraph (1), the beneficiary shall be deemed to have approved the settlement of accounts set forth in said paragraph.

(Transfer, etc. of Trust Affairs from the Former Trustee's Heir, etc. or the Bankruptcy Trustee to the New Trustee, etc.)
Article 78 The provisions of the preceding Article shall apply to the former trustee's heir, etc. in cases where the trustee's duty as trustee has been terminated on the grounds set forth in Article 56, paragraph (1), item (i) or item (ii), and to the bankruptcy trustee in cases where the trustee's duty as trustee has been terminated on the grounds set forth in Article 56, paragraph (1), item (iii).

Section 6 Special Rules for Trusts with Two or More Trustees

(Trust Property in Co-ownership Without Share Subject to Certain Restrictions on the Disposition of Shares)
Article 79 In the case of a trust with two or more trustees, the trust property shall be deemed to be held under co-ownership without share, subject to certain restrictions on the disposition of their shares.

(Method of Trust administration)
Article 80 (1) In the case of a trust with two or more trustees, decisions on the trust administration shall be made by the majority of the trustees.
(2) Notwithstanding the provisions of the preceding paragraph, decisions on an act of preservation may be made by each trustee independently.
(3) Where a decision is made on the trust administration pursuant to the provisions of the preceding two paragraphs, each trustee may execute trust affairs based on such deci-

sion.
(4) Notwithstanding the provisions of the preceding three paragraphs, where terms of trust contains provisions concerning the division of duties among the trustees, each trustee shall make decisions on the trust administration and execute those affairs pursuant to such provisions.
(5) With regard to an act to be conducted in the interests of the trust property based on a decision on the trust administration made under the provisions of the preceding two paragraphs, each trustee shall have the authority to represent the other trustee(s).
(6) Notwithstanding the provisions of the preceding paragraphs, if the terms of trust otherwise provides for, such provisions shall prevail.
(7) In the case of a trust with two or more trustees, it shall be sufficient for a third party to make a manifestation of intention to any one of them; provided, however, that if the terms of trust otherwise provides for manifestation of intention by a beneficiary, such provisions shall prevail.

(Standing to Sue or to Be Sued of Trustees with Segregated Duties)
Article 81 In the case prescribed in paragraph (4) of the preceding Article, each trustee shall stand as a plaintiff or defendant with respect to duties of the said trustee in any action against the trust property on behalf of the other trustee(s).

(Delegation to Other Trustees to Make Decisions on the Trust administration)
Article 82 In the case of a trust with two or more trustees, no trustee may delegate the other trustee(s) to make decisions on the trust administration (excluding those falling within the scope of the ordinary business), except where terms of trust otherwise provides for or there is a compelling reason to do so.

(Assumption of Obligations in Administering Trust Affairs)
Article 83 (1) In the case of a trust with two or more trustees, where each trustee has assumed an obligation to a third party in the course of administering trust affairs, these trustees shall be joint and several obligors.
(2) Notwithstanding the provisions of the preceding paragraph, where terms of trust contain a provision concerning the division of duties among the trustees, when either of these trustees has assumed an obligation to a third party in the course of administering trust affairs pursuant to such provisions, the other trustees shall be liable only by using property that belongs to the trust property to perform the obligation; provided, however, that where the third party knew, at the time of the act causing the assumption of the obligation, that said act was conducted in the course of administering trust affairs and that there were two or more trustees for the trust, and did not know and was not negligent in failing to know that the terms of trust contained provisions concerning the division of duties among the trustees, the other trustee(s) may not duly assert such provisions on the division of duties against the third party.

(Special Rules for Division of Property in Co-ownership which Is Both Trust Property and the Trustee's Own Property, etc.)
Article 84 For the purpose of the application of the provisions of Article 19 in the case of a trust with two or more trustees, the phrase "Where a co-ownership interest in a specific property that belongs to a trustee is an interest in both the trust property and the trustee's own property" in paragraph (1) of said Article shall be deemed to be replaced with "Where a co-ownership interest in a specific property that belongs to a trustee is an interest in both the trust property and the trustee's own property, when there are two or more trustees for the trust pertaining to said trust property"; the

term "trustee" in paragraph (1), item (ii) of said Article shall be deemed to be replaced with "trustee whose own property includes the co-ownership interests"; the term "trustee" in paragraph (1), item (iii) of said Article shall be deemed to be replaced with "trustee whose own property includes the co-ownership interests"; the term "trustee" in paragraph (2) of said Article shall be deemed to be replaced with "trustee whose own property includes the co-ownership interests"; the phrase "Where a co-ownership interest in a specific property that belongs to a trustee is an interest in both the trust property and the trust property of another trust" in paragraph (3) of said Article shall be deemed to be replaced with "Where a co-ownership interest in a specific property that belongs to a trustee is an interest in both the trust property and the trust property of another trust, when there are two or more trustees for the trust pertaining to said trust property or such other trust"; in paragraph (3), item (iii) of the said Article, the term "trustee" shall be deemed to be replaced with "trustee to whom the co-ownership interests for each trust property belong" and the phrase "based on a decision by the trustee" shall be deemed to be replaced with "based on an agreement between the trustees"; and in paragraph (4) of said Article, the term "item (ii)" shall be deemed to be replaced with "item (ii) and item (iii)."

(Special Rules for Trustee Liability, etc.)
Article 85 (1) In the case of a trust with two or more trustees, where two or more trustees have incurred liability under the provisions of Article 40 for an act that they have committed in breach of their duties, these trustees who have committed such an act shall be joint and several obligors.
(2) For the purpose of the application of the provisions of Article 40, paragraph (1) and Article 41 in the case of a trust with two or more trustees, the term "beneficiary" in these provisions shall be deemed to be replaced with "beneficiary or the other trustee(s)."
(3) In the case of a trust with two or more trustees, if any of these trustees is released from liability under the provisions of Article 40 or Article 41 pursuant to the provisions of Article 42, no other trustee may file a claim to hold the person who would have incurred liability under the provisions of Article 40 or Article 41 liable; provided, however, that if the terms of trust otherwise provides, such provisions shall prevail.
(4) For the purpose of the application of the provisions of Article 44 in the case of a trust with two or more trustees, the term "beneficiary" in paragraph (1) of said Article shall be deemed to be replaced with "beneficiary or the other trustee(s)" and the term "those beneficiaries" shall be deemed to be replaced with "those beneficiaries or the other trustee(s)."

(Special Rules for a Change of Trustees, etc.)
Article 86 (1) For the purpose of the application of the provisions of Article 59 in the case of a trust with two or more trustees, the term "beneficiary" in paragraph (1) of said Article shall be deemed to be replaced with "beneficiary and the other trustee(s)," and the phrase "a trustee's duty as trustee" in paragraph (3) and paragraph (4) of said Article shall be deemed to be replaced with "all trustees' duties as trustees."
(2) For the purpose of the application of the provisions of Article 60 in the case of a trust with two or more trustees, the term "beneficiary" in paragraph (1) of said Article shall be deemed to be replaced with "beneficiary and the other trustee(s)," and the phrase "a trustee's duty as trustee" in paragraph (2) and paragraph (4) of said Article shall be deemed to be replaced with "all trustees' duties as trustees."
(3) For the purpose of the application of the provisions of Article 74, paragraph (1) in the case of a trust with two or more trustees, the phrase "a trustee's duty as trustee" in

said paragraph shall be deemed to be replaced with "all trustees' duties as trustees."
(4) In the case of a trust with two or more trustees, when one of these trustees' duty as a trustee has been terminated on any of the grounds listed in the items of Article 56 paragraph (1), notwithstanding the provisions of Article 75, paragraph (1) and paragraph (2), the other trustee(s) shall succeed to the rights and duties concerning the trust existing as of the time of termination of said duty, by operation of law, and shall perform the terminated duties of such trustee; provided, however, that if the terms of trust otherwise provides for, such provisions shall prevail.

(Special Rules for the Termination of a Trust)
Article 87 (1) For the purpose of the application of the provisions of Article 163, item (iii) in the case of a trust with two or more trustees, the phrase "where the trust lacks a trustee" in said item shall be deemed to be replaced with "where of the trust lacks all of its trustees."
(2) In the case of a trust with two or more trustees, the trust shall also be terminated in cases where the trust lacks any of the trustees and the duties of such trustee are not performed by any other trustee pursuant to the provisions of the proviso to paragraph (4), and the trustee's office has not been filled by a new trustee within one year.

Chapter IV Beneficiary, etc.

Section 1 Acquisition and Exercise of Rights by a Beneficiary

(Acquisition of Beneficial Interest)
Article 88 (1) A person designated by the provisions of terms of trust as one who is to be a beneficiary (including a person designated as an initial beneficiary or as a new beneficiary after a change as a result of the exercise of the right to designate or change beneficiaries as prescribed in paragraph (1) of the following Article) shall acquire a beneficial interest by operation of law; provided, however, that if the terms of trust otherwise provides, such provisions shall prevail.
(2) If a person designated as one who is to be a beneficiary as prescribed in the preceding paragraph does not know that the person has acquired a beneficial interest pursuant to the provisions of said paragraph, the trustee shall notify such person to that effect without delay; provided, however, that if the terms of trust otherwise provides for, such provisions shall prevail.

(Right to Designate or Change Beneficiaries)
Article 89 (1) In the case of a trust with provisions on the persons who have the right to designate or change beneficiaries, the right to designate or change a beneficiary shall be exercised by manifestation of intention to do so to the trustee.
(2) Notwithstanding the provisions of the preceding paragraph, the right to designate or change a beneficiary may be exercised through a will.
(3) Where the right to designate or change beneficiaries is exercised through a will pursuant to the provisions of the preceding paragraph, if the trustee does not know of such exercise, the acquisition of the status of a beneficiary through the exercise of said right may not be duly asserted against such trustee.
(4) When the person who was a beneficiary has lost beneficial interest as a result of the exercise of the right to change beneficiaries, the trustee shall notify such person to that effect without delay; provided, however, that if the terms of trust otherwise provides for, such provisions shall prevail.
(5) The right to designate or change beneficiaries shall not be succeeded to through in-

heritance; provided, however, that if the terms of trust otherwise provides for, such provisions shall prevail.
(6) For the purpose of the application of the provisions of paragraph (1) in cases where the person who has the right to designate or change beneficiaries is a trustee, the term "trustee" in said paragraph shall be deemed to be replaced with "person who is to be a beneficiary."

(Special Rules for a Trust with Provisions on the Acquisition of Beneficial Interest Upon the Settlor's Death, etc.)
Article 90 (1) In the case of the trusts set forth in each of the following items, the settlor under those items shall have the right to change the beneficiaries; provided, however, that if the terms of trust otherwise provides for, such provisions shall prevail:
  (i) a trust with provisions that a person designated as one who is to be a beneficiary is to acquire a beneficial interest at the time of the settlor's death; and
  (ii) a trust with provisions that a beneficiary is to receive distribution involving the trust property at the time of the settlor's death or thereafter.
(2) The beneficiary set forth in item (ii) of the preceding paragraph shall not have rights as a beneficiary until the settlor under said item dies; provided, however, that if the terms of trust otherwise provides for, such provisions shall prevail.

(Special Rules for Trusts with Provisions on the Acquisition of New Beneficial Interest by Another Party Upon the Beneficiary's Death)
Article 91 A trust with provisions that upon the beneficiary's death, the beneficial interest held by said beneficiary shall be extinguished and another person shall acquire a new beneficial interest (including provisions that upon the death of the predecessor beneficiary, another person shall acquire a beneficial interest as the successor beneficiary) shall be effective, in cases where any beneficiary who is alive when 30 years have elapsed since the creation of the trust acquires a beneficial interest pursuant to said provisions, until such beneficiary dies or until the beneficial interest of such beneficiary is extinguished.

(Prohibition by Provisions in the Terms of Trust of a Beneficiary's Exercise of Rights)
Article 92 No restrictions may be imposed by the provisions of the terms of trust on the beneficiary's exercise of the following rights:
(i) the right to file a petition with the court under the provisions of this Act;
(ii) the right to call for a definite answer under the provisions of Article 5, paragraph (1);
(iii) the right to assert an objection under the provisions of Article 23, paragraph (5) or paragraph (6);
(iv) the right to demand payment under the provisions of Article 24, paragraph (1);
(v) the right to rescind under the provisions of Article 27, paragraph (1) or paragraph (2) (including cases where these provisions are applied mutatis mutandis pursuant to Article 75, paragraph (4));
(vi) the right to rescind under the provisions of Article 31, paragraph (6) or paragraph (7);
(vii) the right to request a report under the provisions of Article 36;
(viii) the right to request to inspect or copy materials under the provisions of Article 38, paragraph (1) or paragraph (6);
(ix) the right to demand compensation for a loss or restoration of the trust property under the provisions of Article 40;

(x) the right to demand compensation for a loss or restoration of the trust property under the provisions of Article 41;
(xi) the right to demand a cessation under the provisions of Article 44;
(xii) the right to demand payment under the provisions of Article 45, paragraph (1);
(xiii) the right to demand a cessation under the provisions of Article 59, paragraph (5);
(xiv) the right to demand a cessation under the provisions of Article 60, paragraph (3) or paragraph (5);
(xv) the right to demand payment under the provisions of Article 61, paragraph (1);
(xvi) the right to call for a definite answer under the provisions of Article 62, paragraph (2);
(xvii) the right to waive a beneficial interest under the provisions of Article 99, paragraph (1);
(xviii) the beneficiary's right to demand that the trustee acquire the beneficial interest under the provisions of Article 103, paragraph (1) or paragraph (2);
(xix) the right to call for a definite answer under the provisions of Article 131, paragraph (2);
(xx) the right to call for a definite answer under the provisions of Article 138, paragraph (2);
(xxi) the right to request the delivery of documents or provision of records under the provisions of Article 187, paragraph (1);
(xxii) the right to request to inspect or copy materials under the provision of Article 190, paragraph (2);
(xxiii) the right to request that a matter be stated or recorded in the registry under the provisions of Article 198, paragraph (1)
(xxiv) the right to demand compensation or payment of monies under the provisions of Article 226, paragraph (1);
(xxv) the right to demand compensation or payment of monies under the provisions of Article 228, paragraph (1); and
(xxvi) the right to demand compensation for a loss under the provisions of Article 254, paragraph (1).

Section 2 Beneficial Interest, etc.

Subsection 1 Assignment, etc. of Beneficial Interest

(Assignability of Beneficial Interest)
Article 93 (1) A beneficiary may assign a beneficial interest to another; provided, however, that this shall not apply if the nature thereof does not permit assignment.
(2) The provisions of the preceding paragraph shall not apply if the terms of trust otherwise provide; provided, however, that such provisions of the terms of trust may not be duly asserted against a third party who has no knowledge of such provisions.

(Requirements for Perfection of the Assignment of Beneficial Interest)
Article 94 (1) The assignment of a beneficial interest may not be duly asserted against a trustee or any other third party unless the assignor gives notice of the assignment to the trustee or the trustee acknowledges the same.
(2) The notice and acknowledgement set forth in the preceding paragraph may not be duly asserted against a third party other than a trustee unless they are made by means of an instrument bearing a certified date.

(Trustee's Defense Upon the Assignment of a Beneficial Interest)

Article 95 A trustee may duly assert as a defense against the assignor any grounds that have arisen in relation to the assignor before the notice or acknowledgment set forth in paragraph (1) of the preceding Article is made.

(Pledges of Beneficial Interest)
Article 96 (1) A beneficiary may create a pledge on a beneficial interest; provided, however, that this shall not apply if the nature thereof does not permit such a pledge.

(2) The provisions of the preceding paragraph shall not apply if the terms of trust otherwise provides for; provided, however, that such provisions of the terms of trust may not be duly asserted against a third party who has no knowledge of such provisions.

(Effect of Pledges of Beneficial Interest)
Article 97 A pledge on a beneficial interest shall exist against the following monies, etc. (meaning monies or other property; hereinafter the same shall apply in this Article and the following Article):

(i) monies, etc. that the beneficiary who holds the pledged beneficial interest has received from the trustee as distribution involving the trust property;

(ii) monies, etc. that the beneficiary who holds the pledged beneficial interest receives by demanding that the trustee acquire the beneficial interest as prescribed in Article 103, paragraph (6);

(iii) monies, etc. that the beneficiary who holds the pledged beneficial interest receives through the consolidation of beneficial interests or splitting of a beneficial interest as a result of a modification of the trust;

(iv) monies, etc. that the beneficiary who holds the pledged beneficial interest receives through the consolidation or split of trust(s) (meaning consolidation of a trust or split of a trust, the same applies hereinafter); and

(v) in addition to what is listed in the preceding items, monies, etc. that the beneficiary who holds the pledged beneficial interest receives in lieu of such beneficial interest.

Article 98 (1) A person who has created a pledge on a beneficial interest may receive monies, etc. set forth in the preceding Article (limited to monies) and appropriate them for payment of a claim of the person prior to other creditors.

(2) Before the claim set forth in the preceding paragraph becomes due, the person who has created the pledge on a beneficial interest may have the trustee deposit an amount equivalent to the monies, etc. prescribed in said paragraph. In this case, a pledge shall exist on such deposited monies.

Subsection 2 Waiver of Beneficial Interest

Article 99 (1) A beneficiary may make a manifestation of intention to waive a beneficial interest to the trustee; provided, however, that this shall not apply where the beneficiary is a party to the terms of trust.

(2) When a beneficiary has made a manifestation of intention as under the provisions of the preceding paragraph, the beneficiary shall be deemed to have never held the beneficial interest; provided, however, that this may not prejudice a third party's rights.

Subsection 3 Distribution claims as a beneficiary

(Trustee Liability for Distribution claims as a beneficiary)

Article 100 The trustee shall only be liable for using property that belongs to the trust property to perform obligations pertaining to distribution claims as a beneficiary.

(Relationship between Distribution claim as a beneficiary and Trust Claims)
Article 101 Distribution claim as a beneficiary shall be subordinated to trust claims.

(Limitation to the Term of a Distribution claim as a beneficiary)
Article 102 (1) Except for the matters specified in the following paragraph and paragraph (3), the extinctive prescription for distribution claim as a beneficiary shall be governed by the provisions on the extinctive prescription for claims.
(2) The extinctive prescription for a distribution claim as a beneficiary shall not begin to run until the beneficiary becomes aware that the beneficiary has been designated as a beneficiary (if there is no beneficiary at the time in question, until the trust caretaker is appointed).
(3) The extinctive prescription for a distribution claim as a beneficiary may be invoked only in the following cases:
(i) where the trustee, without delay after the expiration of the period of extinctive prescription, specified a reasonable period of time and notified the beneficiary of the existence and content of the distribution claim as a beneficiary, but did not receive the beneficiary's request for performance within such period; or
(ii) where, after the expiration of the period of extinctive prescription, the beneficiary's whereabouts are unknown, or there are justifiable grounds for not notifying the beneficiary under the provisions of the preceding item, in light of the provisions of the terms of trust, the status of the beneficiary, the loss of the relevant materials, and other relevant circumstances.
(4) A distribution claim as a beneficiary shall be extinguished when 20 years have elapsed since it became possible to exercise it.

Subsection 4 The Beneficiary's Right to Demand that the Trustee Acquire the Beneficial Interest of the Beneficiary

(Beneficiary's Demand that the Trustee Acquire the Beneficial Interest of the Beneficiary)
Article 103 (1) Where a modification is to be made to a trust regarding the following matters (referred to as a "material modification of a trust" in paragraph (3)), a beneficiary who is likely to suffer damages from the modification may demand that the trustee acquire the beneficial interest of the beneficiary at a fair price; provided, however, that where a modification of a trust is to be made regarding the matters listed in item (i) or item (ii), there need not be any likelihood of suffering any damage from the modification:
(i) a change in the purpose of the trust;
(ii) restrictions on the assignment of a beneficial interest;
(iii) a reduction of trustee liability or release therefrom in whole or in part (excluding the case where the terms of trust contains provisions on the scope of such a reduction or release and the method of making decisions thereon);
(iv) a change in the content of a distribution claim as a beneficiary (excluding the case where the terms of trust contains provisions on the scope of such a change to the content and the method of making decisions thereon); and
(v) any matter provided for by the terms of trust.
(2) Where a trust is to be consolidated or split, a beneficiary who is likely to suffer any damage from the consolidation or split may demand that the trustee acquire the bene-

Art.104   ③ Trust Act, Chap.IV, Sec.2

ficial interest of the beneficiary at a fair price; provided, however, that where the consolidation or split of the trust is to involve a modification of the trust regarding the matters listed in item (i) or item (ii) of the preceding paragraph, there need not be any likelihood of suffering any damages from the consolidation or split.
(3) When the beneficiary set forth in the preceding two paragraphs has participated in the decision to make a material modification to the trust or to consolidate or split the trust (hereinafter referred to as a "material modification to the trust, etc." in this Chapter), and has made manifestation of intention in the decision-making process to approve such material modification of the trust, etc., the provisions of the preceding two paragraphs shall not apply to such beneficiary.
(4) The trustee shall notify the beneficiary of the following matters within 20 days from the date of the decision to make a material modification to the trust, etc.:
   (i) a statement to the effect that a material modification is to be made to the trust, etc.;
   (ii) the day on which the material modification to the trust, etc. becomes effective (referred to as the "effective day" in paragraph (1) of the following Article); and
   (iii) conditions for cancellation of the material modification to the trust, etc., if any such conditions are specified.
(5) Public notice in an official gazette may be substituted for the notification under the provisions of the preceding paragraph.
(6) A demand under the provisions of paragraph (1) or paragraph (2) (hereinafter referred to as the "(beneficiary's) demand that the trustee acquire the beneficial interest" in this Subsection) shall be made within 20 days from the date of the notice under the provisions of paragraph (4) or the date of the public notice under the provisions of the preceding paragraph, and the contents of the beneficial interest for which the beneficiary is making the demand that the trustee acquire the beneficial interest shall be specified.
(7) The beneficiary who has made the demand that the trustee acquire the beneficial interest of the beneficiary may revoke the demand that the trustee acquire the beneficial interest only where the beneficiary has obtained approval from the trustee.
(8) When a material modification of the trust, etc. is cancelled, the beneficiary's demand that the trustee acquire the beneficial interest shall cease to be effective.

(Determination of the Price of a Beneficial Interest, etc.)
Article 104 (1) Where a beneficiary's demand that the trustee acquire the beneficial interest has been made, if an agreement is reached between the trustee and the beneficiary on the determination of the price of the beneficial interest, the trustee shall pay the price before 60 days have elapsed from the date of the beneficiary's demand that the trustee acquire the beneficial interest (or the effective day if it has not arrived by said date).
(2) If no agreement is reached on the determination of the price of the beneficial interest within 30 days from the date of the beneficiary's demand that the trustee acquire the beneficial interest, the trustee or the beneficiary may file a petition with the court for the determination of the price within 30 days after said 30-day period has elapsed.
(3) The court, in making a judicial decision to determine the price under the provision of the preceding paragraph, shall hear statements from the persons who may file the petition set forth in said paragraph.
(4) The judicial decision on the petition set forth in paragraph (2) shall include the reasons for said decision.
(5) The petitioner and any person who may file a petition set forth in said paragraph may file an immediate appeal against a judicial decision on the determination of the price under the provisions of paragraph (2).

(6) The immediate appeal set forth in the preceding paragraph shall have the effect of a stay of execution.
(7) Notwithstanding the provisions of paragraph (7) of the preceding Article, in the case prescribed in paragraph (2), if no petition set forth in said paragraph has been made within 60 days from the date of the beneficiary's demand that the trustee acquire the beneficial interest of the beneficiary, the beneficiary may revoke the demand that the trustee acquire the beneficial interest at any time after the expiration of such period.
(8) The trustee set forth in paragraph (1) shall also pay interest on the price determined by the court for the period from the date on which the period set forth in said paragraph elapsed.
(9) The acquisition of a beneficial interest by the trustee in response to a beneficiary's demand that the trustee acquire the beneficial interest of the beneficiary shall become effective at the time of payment of the monies equivalent to the price of the beneficial interest.
(10) When a beneficiary's demand that the trustee acquire the beneficial interest of the beneficiary is made with regard to a beneficial interest for which a certificate of beneficial interest (meaning a certificate of beneficial interest prescribed in Article 185, paragraph (1); hereinafter the same shall apply in this Chapter) is issued, monies equivalent to the price of the beneficial interest to be acquired in response to the beneficiary's demand that the trustee acquire the beneficial interest shall be paid in exchange for the certificate of beneficial interest.
(11) The trustee shall only be liable for using property that belongs to the trust property to perform obligations pertaining to a beneficiary's demand that the trustee acquire the beneficial interest of the beneficiary; provided, however, that if an terms of trust or the decision to make a material modification to the trust, etc. has otherwise provided for, such provisions shall prevail.
(12) When the trustee has acquired a beneficial interest pursuant to the provisions of paragraph (1) or paragraph (2) of the preceding Article, the beneficial interest shall be extinguished; provided, however, that if terms of trust or the decision to make such material modification of the trust, etc. has otherwise provided for, such provisions shall prevail.

Section 3 Special Rules on Decision-Making Methods Involving Two or More Beneficiaries

Subsection 1 General Provisions

Article 105 (1) In the case of a trust with two or more beneficiaries, the beneficiaries' decisions (excluding decisions on the exercise of the rights listed in the items of Article 92) shall be made with the unanimous consent of all beneficiaries; provided, however, that if the terms of trust otherwise provides, such provisions shall prevail.
(2) In the case referred to in the proviso to the preceding paragraph, if it is provided in the terms of trust that beneficiaries' decisions shall be made by majority vote at a beneficiaries meeting, the provisions of the following Subsection shall apply; provided, however, that if the terms of trust otherwise provides, such provisions shall prevail.
(3) Notwithstanding the provisions of the proviso to paragraph (1) or the preceding paragraph, provisions of the terms of trust on the method of making decisions on release from liability under the provisions of Article 42 shall be effective only if they are provisions to the effect that such decisions are to be made by majority vote at a beneficiaries meeting as provided for in the following Subsection.
(4) The provisions of the proviso to paragraph (1) and the preceding two paragraphs shall

not apply to exemptions from liability listed as follows:
(i) a total exemption from liability under the provisions of Article 42;
(ii) a partial exemption from liability under the provisions of Article 42, item (i) (limited to liability arising in cases where the trustee was willful or grossly negligent in the performance of the duties); and
(iii) a partial exemption from liability under the provisions of Article 42, item (ii).

Subsection 2 Beneficiaries Meetings

(Convocation of Beneficiaries Meetings)
Article 106 (1) A beneficiaries meeting may be convened at any time when necessary.
(2) A beneficiaries meeting shall be convened by a trustee (if there is a trust supervisor at the time in question, a trustee or trust supervisor).

(Beneficiary's Request for Convocation)
Article 107 (1) A beneficiary may request that a trustee (if there is a trust supervisor at the time in question, a trustee or trust supervisor) convene a beneficiaries meeting by pointing out a matter which is a subject for a beneficiaries meeting and showing the reasons for convocation.
(2) In the following cases, when significant harm to the trust property is likely to occur, the beneficiary who has made the request under the provisions of the preceding paragraph may convene a beneficiaries meeting:
(i) where convocation procedures are not conducted without delay after the request was made under the provisions of the preceding paragraph; or
(ii) where a notice of convocation of a beneficiaries meeting which designates, as the date of the beneficiaries meeting, any day falling within a period of eight weeks from the date of the request under the provisions of the preceding paragraph, is not issued.

(Decision to Convene a Beneficiaries Meeting)
Article 108 A person who convenes a beneficiaries meeting (hereinafter referred to as a "convener" in this Subsection) shall specify the following matters when convening the beneficiaries meeting:
(i) the date and place of the beneficiaries meeting;
(ii) if there is any matter that is the subject of a beneficiaries meeting, such matter;
(iii) if there is an arrangement in which beneficiaries who do not attend the beneficiaries meeting are entitled to exercise their votes by electromagnetic means (meaning the means of using an electronic data processing system or any other means of using information and communications technology which is specified by Ordinance of the Ministry of Justice; hereinafter the same shall apply in this Subsection), a statement to that effect; and
(iv) in addition to what is listed in the preceding items, any matters specified by Ordinance of the Ministry of Justice.

(Notice of Convocation of a Beneficiaries Meeting)
Article 109 (1) In order to convene a beneficiaries meeting, the convener shall issue a written notice to the known beneficiaries and the trustee (if there is a trust supervisor at the time in question, to known beneficiaries, a trustee and the trust supervisor), no later than two weeks prior to the date of the beneficiaries meeting.
(2) In lieu of issuing the written notice set forth in the preceding paragraph, the convener may issue a notice by electromagnetic means with the consent of those persons who

are to receive the notice set forth in said paragraph, as provided for by Cabinet Order. In this case, the convener shall be deemed to have issued the written notice set forth in said paragraph.

(3) The matters listed in the paragraphs of the preceding Article shall be stated or recorded in the notice set forth in the preceding two paragraphs.

(4) In order to convene a beneficiaries meeting in cases where bearer certificates of beneficial interest are issued, the convener shall give public notice in an official gazette to the effect that a beneficiaries meeting is being convened and with regard to the matters listed in the items of the preceding Article, no later than three weeks prior to the date of the beneficiaries meeting.

(Delivery of Reference Documents for a Beneficiaries Meeting and Voting Cards, etc.)

Article 110 (1) Upon issuing a notice set forth in paragraph (1) of the preceding Article, the convener shall deliver to known beneficiaries, as provided for by Ordinance of the Ministry of Justice, documents stating matters which may be of reference for the exercise of voting rights (hereinafter referred to as "reference documents for the beneficiaries meeting" in this Article) and documents by which the beneficiaries are to exercise their voting rights (hereinafter referred to as "voting cards" in this Subsection).

(2) When the convener issues a notice by an electromagnetic means set forth in paragraph (2) of the preceding Article to the beneficiaries who have given their consent as set forth in said paragraph, the convener may, in lieu of delivering reference documents for the beneficiaries meeting and voting cards under the provisions of the preceding paragraph, provide information on the matters that should be stated in these documents by electromagnetic means; provided, however, that when requested by a beneficiary, the convener shall deliver these documents to said beneficiary.

(3) Where the convener has given public notice under the provisions of paragraph (4) of the preceding Article, when the convener is requested by a beneficiary holding a bearer beneficial interest (meaning a beneficial interest for which a bearer certificate of beneficial interest is issued; the same shall apply in Chapter VIII) by one week prior to the date of the beneficiaries meeting, the convener shall immediately deliver reference documents for the beneficiaries meeting and a voting card to such beneficiary.

(4) In lieu of delivering reference documents for the beneficiaries meeting and the voting cards under the provisions of the preceding paragraph, the convener may, with the consent of the beneficiary, as provided for by Cabinet Order, provide information on the matters that should be stated in these documents by electromagnetic means. In this case, the convener shall be deemed to have delivered these documents under the provisions of said paragraph.

Article 111 (1) Where the convener has specified the matters set forth in Article 108, item (iii), the convener shall, when giving notice by electromagnetic means to the beneficiaries who have given their consent as set forth in Article 109, paragraph (2), provide these beneficiaries, with the information on the matters that should be stated in the voting cards by said electromagnetic means, as provided by Ordinance of the Ministry of Justice.

(2) Where the convener has specified the matters set forth in Article 108, item (iii), when the convener is requested by any beneficiary who has not given the consent as set forth in Article 109, paragraph (2), by no later than one week prior to the date of the beneficiaries meeting, to provide such beneficiary with the information on the matters that should be stated in the voting card by electromagnetic means, the convener shall immediately provide such beneficiary with the information on such matters by electro-

magnetic means.

(Beneficiary's Voting Rights)
Article 112 (1) At a beneficiaries meeting, a beneficiary shall have voting rights based on the matters specified in the following items for the cases listed in the respective items:
(i) where the content of the beneficial interests is equal: the number of beneficial interests: or
(ii) in cases other than the case set forth in the preceding item: the value of each beneficial interest as of the time of the decision to convene the beneficiaries meeting.
(2) Notwithstanding the provisions of the preceding paragraph, if a beneficial interest belongs to the trust property of the trust to which the beneficial interest pertains, the trustee shall have no voting rights with regard to such beneficial interest.

(Resolutions at Beneficiaries Meetings)
Article 113 (1) A resolution at a beneficiaries meeting shall be adopted by a majority of the votes of the beneficiaries present, when the beneficiaries who are present at the meeting hold a majority of the voting rights of all the beneficiaries who are entitled to exercise their voting rights.
(2) Notwithstanding the provisions of the preceding paragraph, resolutions at beneficiaries meetings regarding each of the following matters shall be adopted by at least a two-thirds majority of the votes of the beneficiaries present, when the beneficiaries who are present hold a majority of the voting rights of all the beneficiaries who are entitled to exercise their voting rights at said beneficiaries meeting:
(i) a release from liability under the provisions of Article 42 (excluding a release set forth in the items of Article 105, paragraph (4));
(ii) an agreement prescribed in Article 136, paragraph (1), item (i);
(iii) an agreement prescribed in Article 143, paragraph (1), item (i);
(iv) an agreement prescribed in Article 149, paragraph (1) or paragraph (2), item (i), or the manifestation of an intent as prescribed in paragraph (3) of said Article;
(v) an agreement prescribed in Article 151, paragraph (1) or paragraph (2), item (i);
(vi) an agreement prescribed in Article 155, paragraph (1) or paragraph (2), item (i);
(vii) an agreement prescribed in Article 159, paragraph (1) or paragraph (2), item (i); and
(viii) an agreement prescribed in Article 164, paragraph (1).
(3) Notwithstanding the provisions of the preceding two paragraphs, with regard to the material modification of a trust, etc. pertaining to the matters listed in Article 103, paragraph (1), item (ii) to item (iv) (in the case of the matter set forth in item (iv), excluding such a matter that would change the balance among beneficiaries), the resolution at the beneficiaries meeting shall be adopted by at least half of the beneficiaries who are entitled to exercise their voting rights at said beneficiaries meeting, and by at least a two-thirds majority of the votes of such beneficiaries.
(4) Notwithstanding the provisions of the preceding three paragraphs, with regard to the material modification of a trust, etc. pertaining to the matters listed in Article 103, paragraph (1), item (i) or item (iv) (in the case of the matters set forth in item (iv), limited to such a matter that would change the balance among beneficiaries), the resolution at the beneficiaries meeting shall be adopted by at least half of all of the beneficiaries, and by at least a three-fourths majority of the votes of all beneficiaries.
(5) A beneficiaries meeting may adopt no resolution on any matters other than the matters set forth in Article 108, item (ii).

(Proxy Voting)
Article 114 (1) A beneficiary may exercise the voting rights by proxy. In this case, such beneficiary or the proxy shall submit a document to the convener certifying the authority of representation.
(2) The authority of representation set forth in the preceding paragraph shall be granted for each beneficiaries meeting.
(3) In lieu of submitting a document certifying the authority of representation, beneficiary or the proxy as set forth in paragraph (1) may, with the approval of the convener, provide the information on the matters that should be stated in said document by electromagnetic means, as provided for by Cabinet Order. In this case, the beneficiary or the proxy shall be deemed to have submitted said document.
(4) The convener may not refuse to give approval as set forth in the preceding paragraph to a beneficiary who has given the consent as set forth in Article 109, paragraph (2), without justifiable grounds.

(Voting in Writing)
Article 115 (1) A beneficiary who does not attend a beneficiaries meeting may exercise the voting rights in writing.
(2) The exercise of voting rights in writing shall be performed by stating the necessary matters in a voting card and submitting the voting card containing those matters to the convener by the time specified by Ordinance of the Ministry of Justice.
(3) Voting rights exercised in writing pursuant to the provisions of the preceding paragraph shall be deemed to be voting rights exercised by voting right holders present at the meeting.

(Voting by Electromagnetic Means)
Article 116 (1) The exercise of a voting right by electromagnetic means shall be performed, with the consent of the convener, by providing the convener with the information on the matters that should be stated in a voting card by electromagnetic means, by the time specified by Ordinance of the Ministry of Justice, as provided for by Cabinet Order.
(2) The convener may not refuse to give the consent as set forth in the preceding paragraph to a beneficiary who has given the consent as set forth in Article 109, paragraph (2), without justifiable grounds.
(3) Voting rights exercised by electromagnetic means pursuant to the provisions of paragraph (1) shall be deemed to be voting rights exercised by voting right holders present at the meeting.

(Diverse Voting)
Article 117 (1) A beneficiary may exercise the voting rights differently. In this case, such beneficiary shall give notice to the convener to that effect and of the reasons therefor no later than three days prior to the date of the beneficiaries meeting.
(2) If the beneficiary set forth in the preceding paragraph is not a person who holds a beneficial interest on behalf of others, the convener may refuse to allow such a beneficiary to exercise the voting rights differently pursuant to the provisions of said paragraph.

(Attendance of the Trustee, etc.)
Article 118 (1) The trustee (in the case of a trustee who is a juridical person, its representative or agent; the same shall apply in the following paragraph) may attend a beneficiaries meeting or state opinions in writing.
(2) A beneficiaries meeting or its convener may, when it or the convener finds it neces-

sary, demand that the trustee attend the meeting. In this case, a resolution shall be passed at a beneficiaries' meeting demanding such attendance.

(Resolution for Postponement or Continuation)
Article 119 Where a resolution is adopted at a beneficiaries meeting for the postponement or continuation thereof, the provisions of Articles 108 and 109 shall not apply.

(Minutes of Meetings)
Article 120 The convener shall prepare the minutes with regard to the business of a beneficiaries meeting as provided for by Ordinance of the Ministry of Justice.

(Effect of Resolutions at Beneficiaries Meetings)
Article 121 A resolution made at a beneficiaries meeting shall be effective against all beneficiaries of the trust.

(Burden of Expenses for Beneficiaries Meetings)
Article 122 (1) A person who has paid the expenses necessary for a beneficiaries meeting may demand reimbursement thereof from a trustee.
(2) The trustee shall only be liable for using property that belongs to the trust property to perform the obligation pertaining to the demand under the provisions of the preceding paragraph.

Section 4　Trust Caretakers, etc.

Subsection 1　Trust Caretakers

(Appointment of a Trust Caretaker)
Article 123 (1) Provisions may be established in terms of trust to designate a person who is to be the trust caretaker in cases where there is no beneficiary at the time in question.
(2) If the terms of trust contains provisions designating a particular person to be the trust caretaker, any interested party may specify a reasonable period of time and call on the person designated as the one who is to be the trust caretaker to give a definite answer within that period of time with regard to whether the person will accept the office; provided, however, that if the terms of trust designates a condition precedent or a time of commencement to said provisions, this may only be done after the condition precedent is fulfilled or after the time of commencement arrives.
(3) Where a call for an answer is made under the provisions of the preceding paragraph, if the person designated as the one who is to be the trust caretaker fails to give a definite answer to the settlor (if there is no settlor at the time in question, to the trustee) within the period set forth in said paragraph, it shall be deemed that the person does not accept the office.
(4) Where there is no beneficiary at the time in question, if the terms of trust contains no provisions concerning a trust caretaker or if the person designated by the provisions of the terms of trust as the one who is to be the trust caretaker does not accept or is unable to accept the office, the court may appoint a trust caretaker at the petition of an interested party.
(5) When a judicial decision on the appointment of a trust caretaker has been made under the provisions of the preceding paragraph, it shall be deemed that the provisions set forth in paragraph (1) were established in the terms of trust with regard to the appointed trust caretaker.

(6) The judicial decision on the petition set forth in paragraph (4) shall include the reasons for said decision.
(7) The settlor or the trustee, or the trust caretaker at the time in question, may file an immediate appeal against a judicial decision on the appointment of a trust caretaker under the provisions of paragraph (4).
(8) The immediate appeal set forth in the preceding paragraph shall have the effect of a stay of execution.

(Qualifications of Trust Caretakers)
Article 124 None of the following persons may serve as a trust caretaker:
  (i) a minor or an adult ward or person under curatorship; and
  (ii) the person who is the trustee of the trust in question.

(Trust Caretakers' Powers)
Article 125 (1) A trust caretaker shall have the power to conduct any and all acts in or out of court in the trust caretaker's own name on behalf of a beneficiary in connection with the beneficiary's rights; provided, however, that if the terms of trust otherwise provides for, such provisions shall prevail.
(2) When there are two or more trust caretakers, they shall carry out acts within the scope of their powers jointly; provided, however, that if the terms of trust otherwise provides for, such provisions shall prevail.
(3) When there is a trust caretaker, any notice to be given to a beneficiary pursuant to the provisions of this Act shall be given to the trust caretaker.

(Duties of the Trust Caretaker)
Article 126 (1) The trust caretaker shall exercise the powers set forth in paragraph (1) of the preceding Article with the due care of a prudent manager.
(2) The trust caretaker shall exercise the powers set forth in paragraph (1) of the preceding Article sincerely and equitably on behalf of the beneficiary.

(Expenses, etc. and Remuneration of the Trust Caretaker)
Article 127 (1) A trust caretaker may demand from the trustee the expenses that are considered to be necessary for the administration of the affairs concerned and interest thereon accruing from the date of payment.
(2) In the following cases, a trust caretaker may demand compensation from a trustee for the amount of damages specified in the respective items:
  (i) where the trust caretaker has suffered any damages in the course of administering the relevant affairs, absent the trust caretaker's own negligence: the amount of such damages; or
  (ii) where the trust caretaker has suffered any damages in the course of administering the relevant affairs through the intentional or negligent act of a third party (excluding the case set forth in the preceding item): the amount of compensation that may be demanded from the third party.
(3) In addition to the case where the provisions of Article 512 of the Commercial Code shall apply, the trust caretaker may demand remuneration from the trustee only where it is provided by an terms of trust that the trust caretaker shall receive remuneration.
(4) The trustee shall only be liable for using property that belongs to the trust property to perform an obligation pertaining to the demand under the provisions of the preceding three paragraphs.
(5) In the case referred to in paragraph (3), if the terms of trust contains provisions concerning the amount of remuneration or the calculation method thereof, the amount of

remuneration shall be determined pursuant to such provisions, and if there are no such provisions, the amount of remuneration shall be a reasonable amount.
(6) Where the court has appointed a trust caretaker pursuant to the provisions of Article 123, paragraph (4), it may determine the remuneration for the trust caretaker.
(7) When a judicial decision concerning the remuneration for a trust caretaker is made under the provisions of the preceding paragraph, it shall be deemed that the provisions set forth in paragraph (3) and the provisions on the amount of remuneration set forth in paragraph (5) were included in the terms of trust with regard to the trust caretaker.
(8) Before the court makes a judicial decision on the remuneration for a trust caretaker under the provisions of paragraph (6), it shall hear the statements of the trustee and the trust caretaker.
(9) The trustee and the trust caretaker may file an immediate appeal against a judicial decision on the remuneration for a trust caretaker under the provisions of paragraph (6).

(Termination of Trust Caretaker's Duty as Trust Caretaker)
Article 128 (1) The provisions of Article 56 shall apply mutatis mutandis to the termination of a trust caretaker's duty as trust caretaker. In this case, the term "following Article" in paragraph (1), item (v) of said Article shall be deemed to be replaced with "following Article as applied mutatis mutandis pursuant Article 128, paragraph (2)," and the term "Article 58" in item (vi) of said paragraph shall be deemed to be replaced with "Article 58 as applied mutatis mutandis pursuant to Article 128, paragraph (2)."
(2) The provisions of Article 57 shall apply mutatis mutandis to the resignation of a trust caretaker, and the provisions of Article 58 shall apply mutatis mutandis to the dismissal of a trust caretaker.

(Appointment, etc. of a New Trust Caretaker)
Article 129 (1) The provisions of Article 62 shall apply mutatis mutandis to the appointment of a new trust caretaker in cases where a trust caretaker's duty as trust caretaker has been terminated pursuant to the provisions of the items of Article 56, paragraph (1) as applied mutatis mutandis pursuant to paragraph (1) of the preceding Article (referred to as the "new trust caretaker" in the following paragraph).
(2) Where the new trust caretaker assumes the office, the person who has been the trust caretaker shall, without delay, transfer affairs to the new trust caretaker as required in order for the new trust caretaker to administer the relevant affairs.
(3) When a beneficiary comes into existence and the person who has been the trust caretaker as set forth in the preceding paragraph then learns of said person who has become the beneficiary, the person who has been the trust caretaker shall report to said person who has become the beneficiary on the process and results of the relevant affairs without delay.

(Termination of the Administration of Affairs by a Trust Caretaker)
Article 130 (1) The administration of affairs by a trust caretaker shall terminate on the following grounds; provided, however, that in the case of termination on the grounds set forth in item (ii), if the terms of trust otherwise provides, such provisions shall prevail:
(i) a beneficiary has come into existence;
(ii) the settlor has manifested trust caretaker an intent to terminate the administration of affairs by the trust caretaker to the trust caretaker; or
(iii) any grounds specified by the terms of trust.
(2) Where the administration of affairs by a trust caretaker has terminated pursuant to the provisions of the preceding paragraph, the person who has been the trust caretaker

shall, without delay, report to the beneficiary on the process and results of the relevant affairs; provided, however, that this shall apply only where a beneficiary comes into existence and the person who has been the trust caretaker then learns of said person who has become the beneficiary.

Subsection 2 Trust Supervisors

(Appointment of a Trust Supervisor)
Article 131 (1) Provisions may be established in the terms of trust to designate a person who is to be the trust supervisor in cases where there is a beneficiary at the time in question.
(2) If an terms of trust contains provisions designating a particular person to be the trust supervisor, any interested party may specify a reasonable period of time and call on the person designated as the one who is to be the trust supervisor to give a definite answer within that period of time with regard to whether the person will accept the office; provided, however, that if the terms of trust designates a condition precedent or a time of commencement to the provisions, this may only be done after the condition precedent is fulfilled or after the time of commencement arrives.
(3) Where a call for an answer is made under the provisions of the preceding paragraph, if the person designated as the one who is to be the trust supervisor fails to give a definite answer to the settlor (if there is no settlor at the time in question, to the trustee) within the period set forth in said paragraph, it shall be deemed that the person not accept the office.
(4) When there are special circumstances wherein a beneficiary is unable to supervise a trustee appropriately, if the terms of trust contains no provisions concerning a trust supervisor or if the person designated by provisions of the terms of trust as the one who is to be the trust supervisor does not accept or is unable to accept the office, the court may appoint a trust supervisor at the petition of an interested party.
(5) When a judicial decision on the appointment of a trust supervisor has been made under the provisions of the preceding paragraph, it shall be deemed that the provisions set forth in paragraph (1) were established in the terms of trust with regard to the appointed trust supervisor.
(6) The judicial decision on the petition set forth in paragraph (4) shall include the reasons for said decision.
(7) A settler, trustee, or beneficiary, or the trust supervisor at the time in question may file an immediate appeal against a judicial decision on the appointment of a trust supervisor under the provisions of paragraph (4).
(8) The immediate appeal set forth in the preceding paragraph shall have the effect of a stay of execution.

(Trust Supervisors' Powers)
Article 132 (1) A trust supervisor shall have the power to carry out any and all acts in or out of court in the trust supervisor's own name on behalf of a beneficiary in connection with the rights listed in the items of Article 92 (excluding item (xvii), item (xviii), item (xxi) and item (xxiii)); provided, however, that if the terms of trust otherwise provides for, such provisions shall prevail.
(2) When there are two or more trust supervisors, they shall carry out acts within the scope of their power jointly; provided, however, that if the terms of trust otherwise provides for, such provisions shall prevail.

(Duties of a Trust Supervisor)

Article 133 (1) A trust supervisor shall exercise the powers set forth in paragraph (1) of the preceding Article with the due care of a prudent manager.
(2) A trust supervisor shall exercise the powers set forth in paragraph (1) of the preceding Article sincerely and equitably on behalf of the beneficiary.

(Termination of a Trust Supervisor's Duty as Trust Supervisor)
Article 134 (1) The provisions of Article 56 shall apply mutatis mutandis to the termination of a trust supervisor's duty as trust supervisor. In this case, the term "following Article" in paragraph (1), item (v) of said Article shall be deemed to be replaced with "following Article as applied mutatis mutandis pursuant Article 134, paragraph (2)," and the term "Article 58" in item (vi) of said paragraph shall be deemed to be replaced with "Article 58 as applied mutatis mutandis pursuant to Article 134, paragraph (2)."
(2) The provisions of Article 57 shall apply mutatis mutandis to the resignation of a trust supervisor, and the provisions of Article 58 shall apply mutatis mutandis to the dismissal of a trust supervisor.

(Appointment, etc. of a New Trust Supervisor)
Article 135 (1) The provisions of Article 62 shall apply mutatis mutandis to the appointment of a new trust supervisor in cases where a trust supervisor's duty as trust supervisor has been terminated pursuant to the provisions of the items of Article 56, paragraph (1) as applied mutatis mutandis pursuant to paragraph (1) of the preceding Article (referred to as a "new trust supervisor" in the following paragraph).
(2) Where a new trust supervisor assumes the office, the person who has been a trust supervisor shall, without delay, report to the beneficiary on the process and results of the affairs concerned, and transfer affairs as required in order for the new trust supervisor to administer the relevant affairs.

(Termination of the Administration of Affairs by a Trust Supervisor)
Article 136 (1) The administration of affairs by a trust supervisor shall terminate on the following grounds, in addition to the completion of the liquidation of the trust; provided, however, that in the case of the termination on the grounds set forth in item (i), if the terms of trust otherwise provides for, such provisions shall prevail:
(i) the settlor and the beneficiary have agreed to terminate the administration of affairs by a trust supervisor; or
(ii) any grounds specified by the terms of trust.
(2) Where the administration of affairs by a trust supervisor has been terminated pursuant to the provisions of the preceding paragraph, the person who has been the trust supervisor shall, without delay, report to the beneficiary on the process and results of the affairs concerned.
(3) The provisions of paragraph (1), item (i) shall not apply where there is no settlor at the time in question.

(Application Mutatis Mutandis of Provisions on Trust Caretakers)
Article 137 The provisions of Article 124 and Article 127 shall apply mutatis mutandis to a trust supervisor. In this case, the phrase "Article 123, paragraph (4)" in paragraph (6) of said Article shall be deemed to be replaced with "Article 131, paragraph (4)."

Subsection 3 Beneficiaries' Agents

(Appointment of a Beneficiary's Agent)
Article 138 (1) Provisions may be established in the terms of trust to designate a person

who is to be the beneficiary's agent, while specifying the beneficiary or beneficiaries whom the person is to represent.
(2) If an terms of trust contains provisions designating a particular person to be the beneficiary's agent, any interested party may specify a reasonable period of time and call on the person designated as the one who is to be the beneficiary's agent to give a definite answer within that period of time with regard to whether the person will accept the office; provided, however, that if the terms of trust designates a condition precedent or a time of commencement to the provisions, this may only be done after the condition precedent is fulfilled or after the time of commencement arrives.
(3) Where a call for an answer is made under the provisions of the preceding paragraph, if the person designated as the one who is to be the beneficiary's agent fails to give a definite answer to the settlor (if there is no settlor at the time in question, to the trustee) within the period set forth in said paragraph, it shall be deemed that the person does not accept the office.

(Powers of the Beneficiary's Agent)
Article 139 (1) The beneficiary's agent shall have the power to conduct any and all acts in or out of court on behalf of the beneficiary or beneficiaries whom the agent represents in connection with their rights (excluding the rights pertaining to a release from the liability under the provisions of Article 42); provided, however, that if the terms of trust otherwise provides, such provisions shall prevail.
(2) When a beneficiary's agent conducts any act in or out of court on behalf of the beneficiary or beneficiaries whom the agent represents, it shall be sufficient for the agent to indicate the scope of the beneficiaries whom the agent represents.
(3) When there are two or more beneficiary's agents for a single beneficiary, they shall conduct acts within the scope of their power jointly; provided, however, that if the terms of trust otherwise provides for, such provisions shall prevail.
(4) When there is a beneficiary's agent, the beneficiary or beneficiaries represented by the beneficiary's agent may not exercise their rights, except for the rights listed in the items of Article 92 and the rights specified by the terms of trust.

(Duties of a Beneficiary's Agent)
Article 140 (1) A beneficiary's agent shall exercise the power set forth in paragraph (1) of the preceding Article with the due care of a prudent manager.
(2) A beneficiary's agent shall exercise the power set forth in paragraph (1) of the preceding Article sincerely and equitably on behalf of the beneficiary or beneficiaries whom the agent represents.

(Termination of the Beneficiary's Agent's Duty as the Beneficiary's Agent)
Article 141 (1) The provisions of Article 56 shall apply mutatis mutandis to the termination of a beneficiary's agent's duty as the beneficiary's agent. In this case, the term the "following Article" in paragraph (1), item (v) of said Article shall be deemed to be replaced with "following Article as applied mutatis mutandis pursuant Article 141, paragraph (2)," and the term "Article 58" in item (vi) of said paragraph shall be deemed to be replaced with "Article 58 as applied mutatis mutandis pursuant to Article 141, paragraph (2)."
(2) The provisions of Article 57 shall apply mutatis mutandis to the resignation of a beneficiary's agent, and the provisions of Article 58 shall apply mutatis mutandis to the dismissal of a beneficiary's agent.

(Appointment of a New Beneficiary's Agent)

Article 142 (1) The provisions of Article 62 shall apply mutatis mutandis to a new beneficiary's agent in cases where a beneficiary's agent's duty as the beneficiary's agent has been terminated pursuant to the provisions of the items of Article 56, paragraph (1) as applied mutatis mutandis pursuant to paragraph (1) of the preceding Article. In this case, the term "an interested party" in Article 62, paragraph (2) and paragraph (4) shall be deemed to be replaced with "the settlor or any beneficiary represented by the beneficiary's agent."

(2) Where a new beneficiary's agent assumes the office, the person who has been the beneficiary's agent shall, without delay, make a report to the beneficiary or beneficiaries whom the person who has been the beneficiary's agent represents on the process and results of the relevant affairs, and shall transfer affairs as required in order for the new beneficiary's agent to administer the relevant affairs.

(Termination of the Administration of Affairs by a Beneficiary's Agent)
Article 143 (1) The administration of affairs by a beneficiary's agent shall terminate on the following grounds, in addition to the completion of the liquidation of the trust; provided, however, that in case of termination on the grounds set forth in item (i), if the terms of trust otherwise provides, such provisions shall prevail:
 (i) the settlor and the beneficiary or beneficiaries represented by the beneficiary's agent have agreed to terminate the administration of affairs by a beneficiary's agent; or
 (ii) any grounds specified by the terms of trust.
(2) Where the administration of affairs by a beneficiary's agent has terminated pursuant to the provisions of the preceding paragraph, the person who has been the beneficiary's agent shall, without delay, make a report to the beneficiary or beneficiaries whom the agent has represented on the process and results of the relevant affairs.
(3) The provisions of paragraph (1), item (i) shall not apply where there is no settlor at the time in question.

(Application Mutatis Mutandis of Provisions on Trust Caretakers)
Article 144 The provisions of Article 124 and Article 127, paragraph (1) to paragraph (5) shall apply mutatis mutandis to a beneficiary's agent.

Chapter V Settlors

(Settlors' Rights, etc.)
Article 145 (1) Terms of trust may provide for a settlor not to have all or part of the rights under the provisions of this Act.
(2) Terms of trust may provide for the settlor also to have all or part of the following rights:
 (i) the right to assert an objection under the provisions of Article 23, paragraph (5) or paragraph (6);
 (ii) the right to rescind under the provisions of Article 27, paragraph (1) or paragraph (2) (including cases where these provisions are applied mutatis mutandis pursuant to Article 75, paragraph (4));
 (iii) the right to rescind under the provisions of Article 31, paragraph (6) or paragraph (7);
 (iv) the right under the provisions of Article 32, paragraph (4);
 (v) the right to request to inspect or copy materials under the provisions of Article 38, paragraph (1);

(vi) the right to request the disclosure under the provisions of Article 39, paragraph (1);
(vii) the right to demand compensation for a loss or restoration of the trust property under the provisions of Article 40;
(viii) the right to demand compensation for a loss or restoration of the trust property under the provisions of Article 41;
(ix) the right to demand a cessation under the provisions of Article 44;
(x) the right to file a petition for the appointment of an inspector under the provisions of Article 46, paragraph (1);
(xi) the right to demand a cessation under the provisions of Article 59, paragraph (5);
(xii) the right to demand a cessation under the provisions of Article 60, paragraph (3) or paragraph (5);
(xiii) the right to demand compensation or payment of monies under the provisions of Article 226, paragraph (1);
(xiv) the right to demand compensation or payment of monies under the provisions of Article 228, paragraph (1); and
(xv) the right to demand compensation for a loss under the provisions of Article 254, paragraph (1).

(3) For the purpose of the application of the provisions of Article 24, Article 45 (including cases where applied mutatis mutandis pursuant to Article 226, paragraph (6), Article 228, paragraph (6), and Article 254, paragraph (3)), or Article 61 in cases where the provisions of an terms of trust are established as set forth in the preceding paragraph with regard to the rights listed in item (i), item (vii) to item (ix), or item (xi) to item (xv) of said paragraph, the term "beneficiary" shall be deemed to be replaced with "settlor or beneficiary."

(4) Terms of trust may provide for a trustee to have the following duties:
(i) the duty to notify the settlor of the matters of which the trustee should notify the beneficiary (if there is a trust caretaker at the time in question, the matters of which the trustee should notify the trust caretaker; the same shall apply in the following item) pursuant to the provisions of this Act;
(ii) the duty to report to the settlor the matters which the trustee should report to the beneficiary pursuant to the provisions of this Act; and
(iii) the duty to request that the settlor give an approval for the settlement of accounts for which the trustee is to give approval pursuant to the provisions of Article 77, paragraph (1) or Article 184, paragraph (1).

(5) For the purpose of the application of the provisions of paragraph (1), paragraph (2) and the preceding paragraph in the case of a trust with two or more settlors, the term "settlor" in these provisions shall be deemed to be replaced with "all or some of the settlors."

(Transfer of Status as the Settlor)
Article 146 (1) The status of a settlor may be transferred to a third party with the consent of the trustee and the beneficiary or by the method specified by the terms of trust.
(2) For the purpose of the application of the provisions of the preceding paragraph in the case of a trust with two or more settlors, the phrase "the trustee and the beneficiary" shall be deemed to be replaced with "other settlor(s), the trustee and the beneficiary."

(Settlor's Heir in a Testamentary Trust)
Article 147 Where a trust is created by the method set forth in Article 3, item (ii), the settlor's heir shall not succeed to the status of settlor by inheritance; provided, how-

ever, that if the terms of trust otherwise provides for, such provisions shall prevail.

(Special Rules for Trusts, etc. with Provisions on the Acquisition of Beneficial Interest Upon the Death of the Settlor)
Article 148 In the case of a trust set forth in each of the items of Article 90, paragraph (1), when there is no beneficiary for the trust or no beneficiary has any right as a beneficiary at the time in question pursuant to the provisions of Article 90, paragraph (2), the settlor shall have the rights listed in the items of Article 145, paragraph (2), and the trustee shall have the duties listed in the items of Article 145, paragraph (4); provided, however, that if the terms of trust otherwise provides, such provisions shall prevail.

Chapter VI Modification, Consolidation, and Split of trusts
Section 1 Modification of Trusts

(Agreement, etc. among the Relevant Parties)
Article 149 (1) A trust may be modified at the agreement of the settlor, the trustee, and the beneficiary. In this case, in making such a modification, the contents of the terms of trust after modification shall be specified:
(2) Notwithstanding the provisions of the preceding paragraph, in the cases listed in the following items, a trust may be modified by the methods specified in the respective items. In this case, the trustee shall, without delay, give notice of the contents of the terms of trust after modification, to the settlor in the case set forth in item (i), or to the settlor and the beneficiary in the case set forth in item (ii):
(i) where it is clear that the modification is not contrary to the purpose of the trust: an agreement between the trustee and the beneficiary; or
(ii) where it is clear that the modification is not contrary to the purpose of the trust and that it conforms to the interests of the beneficiary: the trustee's manifestation of such intent in a document or electromagnetic record.
(3) Notwithstanding the provisions of the preceding two paragraphs, in the cases listed in the following items, a trust may be modified by the persons specified in the respective items manifesting their intent to do so to the trustee. In this case, in the case set forth in item (ii), the trustee shall, without delay, notify the settlor of the contents of the terms of trust after modification:
(i) where it is clear that the modification will not harm the interests of the trustee: the settlor and the beneficiary; or
(ii) where it is clear that the modification is not contrary to the purpose of the trust and that it will not harm the interests of the trustee: the beneficiary.
(4) Notwithstanding the provisions of the preceding three paragraphs, if the terms of trust otherwise provides for, such provisions shall prevail.
(5) Where there is no settlor at the time in question, the provisions of paragraph (1) and paragraph (3), item (i) shall not apply, and the phrase "to the settlor in the case set forth in item (i), or to the settlor and the beneficiary in the case set forth in item (ii)" in paragraph (2) shall be deemed to be replaced with "to the beneficiary in the case set forth in item (ii)."

(Judicial Decision Ordering the Modification of a Trust Due to Special Circumstances)
Article 150 (1) When, due to the special circumstances that were unforeseeable at the time of an act of trust, the provisions of the terms of trust concerning the method of

trust administration no longer conforms to the interests of the beneficiary in light of the purpose of the trust, the status of the trust property, and any other relevant circumstances, the court may order a modification of the trust at the petition of the settlor, the trustee or the beneficiary.

(2) In filing the petition set forth in the preceding paragraph, the provisions of the terms of trust after modification to which the petition pertains shall be specified.

(3) Before the court makes a judicial decision on the petition set forth in paragraph (1), it shall hear the statement of the trustee.

(4) A judicial decision on the petition set forth in paragraph (1) shall include a summary of the reasons for said decision.

(5) The settlor, the trustee, or the beneficiary may file an immediate appeal against the judicial decision on the petition set forth in paragraph (1).

(6) The immediate appeal set forth in the preceding paragraph shall have the effect of a stay of execution.

Section 2 Consolidation of Trusts

(Agreement, etc. among the Relevant Parties)

Article 151 (1) Trusts may be consolidated by the agreement of the settlors, trustees, and beneficiaries of the former trusts. In this case, in effecting such a consolidation, the following matters shall be specified:

(i) the contents of the terms of trust after consolidation of the trusts;

(ii) if there is any change in the contents of the beneficial interest provided for by the terms of trust, such contents and the reasons for the change;

(iii) if monies or any other property is delivered to a beneficiary upon the consolidation of the trusts, the content and value of such property;

(iv) the day on which the consolidation of the trusts becomes effective; and

(v) other matters specified by Ordinance of the Ministry of Justice.

(2) Notwithstanding the provisions of the preceding paragraph, in the cases listed in the following items, trusts may be consolidated by the methods specified in the respective items. In this case, the trustee shall, without delay, give notice of the matters listed in the items of said paragraph, to the settlor in the case set forth in item (i), or to the settlor and the beneficiary in the case set forth in item (ii):

(i) where it is clear that the consolidation is not contrary to the purpose of the trust: an agreement between the trustee and the beneficiary; or

(ii) where it is clear that the consolidation is not contrary to the purpose of the trust and that it conforms to the interests of the beneficiary: the trustee's manifestation of such intent in a document or electromagnetic record.

(3) Notwithstanding the provisions of the preceding two paragraphs, if each terms of trust otherwise provides for, such provisions shall prevail.

(4) Where there is no settlor at the time in question, the provisions of paragraph (1) shall not apply, and the phrase "to the settlor in the case set forth in item (i), or to the settlor and the beneficiary in the case set forth in item (ii)" in paragraph (2) shall be deemed to be replaced with "to the beneficiary in the case set forth in item (ii)."

(Objections by the Creditors)

Article 152 (1) Where trusts are to be consolidated, creditors who hold claims pertaining to obligations covered by the trust properties of the former trusts may state their objections to the trustees with regard to the consolidation of the trusts; provided, however, that this shall not apply if there is no risk of such creditors being harmed by the consolidation of the trusts.

(2) Where all or some of the creditors set forth in the preceding paragraph may state their objections pursuant to the provisions of said paragraph, the trustee shall give public notice of the following matters in the official gazette, and shall give notice of the same separately to each of the known creditors as set forth in said paragraph; provided, however, that the period set forth in item (ii) may not be less than one month:
(i) a statement to the effect that the trusts are to be consolidated;
(ii) a statement to the effect that the creditors set forth in the preceding paragraph may state their objections within a certain period of time; and
(iii) other matters specified by Ordinance of the Ministry of Justice.
(3) Notwithstanding the provisions of the preceding paragraph, a trustee who is a juridical person may substitute public notice (limited to public notice given by the following methods) for the separate notice to each creditor under the provisions of said paragraph:
(i) publication in a major daily newspaper which publishes matters on current events; or
(ii) electronic public notice (meaning, among methods of public notice, a method wherein measures are taken to make the information that should be given in a public notice available to many and unspecified persons by electromagnetic means (meaning an electromagnetic means prescribed in Article 2, item (xxxiv) of the Companies Act (Act No. 86 of 2005), which is prescribed in said item; the same shall apply in the following Section)).
(4) If any creditors set forth in paragraph (1) do not state any objections within the period set forth in paragraph (2), item (ii), such creditors shall be deemed to have accepted the consolidation of the trusts.
(5) When any creditors set forth in paragraph (1) state their objections within the period set forth in paragraph (2), item (ii), the trustee shall make payment or provide reasonable security to such creditors, or shall entrust adequate property to a trust company, etc. (meaning a trust company or a financial institution engaging in the trust business (meaning a financial institution authorized under Article 1, paragraph (1) of the Act on the Concurrent Undertaking of Trust Business by Financial Institutions (Act No. 43 of 1943)); the same shall apply in the following Section) for the purpose of having such creditors receive payment; provided, however, that this shall not apply if there is no risk of such creditors being harmed by the consolidation of the trusts.

(Scope of Obligations Covered by Trust Property After Consolidation of Trusts)
Article 153 Where trusts are consolidated, the obligations covered by the trust properties of the former trusts shall become obligations covered by trust property after the consolidation.

Article 154 Where trusts are consolidated, the obligations covered only by the trust property (meaning obligation covered by the trust property which may be paid only out of property belonging to the trust property, hereinafter the same shall apply in this Chapter) among obligations covered by the trust property with regard to the previous trusts referred to in the preceding Article, shall be obligations covered only by the trust property after consolidation of trusts.

Section 3 Split of trusts

Subsection 1 Absorption-Type Trust Splits

(Agreement, etc. among the Relevant Parties)

Article 155 (1) An absorption-type trust split may be effected at the agreement of the settlor, the trustee, and the beneficiary of a trust. In this case, in effecting such a split, the following matters shall be specified:
(i) the contents of the terms of trust after the absorption-type trust split;
(ii) if there is a change in the contents of the beneficial interest provided for by the terms of trust, such contents and the reasons for the change;
(iii) if monies or any other property is delivered to a beneficiary in the absorption-type trust split, the contents and value of such property;
(iv) the day on which the absorption-type trust split becomes effective;
(v) the contents of any property to be transferred;
(vi) if there is any obligation which will, as a result of the absorption-type trust split, cease to be an obligation covered by the trust property of a trust that transfers a part of its trust property to another trust (hereinafter referred to as the "split trust" in this Subsection), and will become an obligation covered by the trust property of the other trust to which said part of the trust property is transferred (hereinafter referred to as the "succeeding trust"), the matters concerning such obligation; and
(vii) other matters specified by Ordinance of the Ministry of Justice.
(2) Notwithstanding the provisions of the preceding paragraph, in the cases listed in the following items, an absorption-type trust split may be effected by the methods specified in the respective items. In this case, the trustee shall, without delay, give notice of the matters listed in the items of said paragraph, to the settlor in the case set forth in item (i), or to the settlor and the beneficiary in the case set forth in item (ii):
(i) where it is clear that the split is not contrary to the purpose of the trust: an agreement between the trustee and the beneficiary; or
(ii) where it is clear that the split is not contrary to the purpose of the trust and that it conforms to the interests of the beneficiary: the trustee's manifestation of such intent in a document or electromagnetic record.
(3) Notwithstanding the provisions of the preceding two paragraphs, if each terms of trust otherwise provides for, such provisions shall prevail.
(4) Where there is no settlor at the time in question, the provisions of paragraph (1) shall not apply, and the phrase "to the settlor in the case set forth in item (i), or to the settlor and the beneficiary in the case set forth in item (ii)" in paragraph (2) shall be deemed to be replaced with "to the beneficiary in the case set forth in item (ii)."

(Objections by the Creditors)

Article 156 (1) Where an absorption-type trust split is effected, creditors who hold claims pertaining to obligations covered by the trust property of the split trust or the succeeding trust may state their objections to the trustee with regard to the absorption-type trust split; provided, however, that this shall not apply if there is no risk of such creditors being harmed by the absorption-type trust split.
(2) Where all or some of the creditors set forth in the preceding paragraph may state their objections pursuant to the provisions of said paragraph, the trustee shall give public notice of the following matters in the official gazette, and shall give notice of the same separately to each of the known creditors set forth in said paragraph; provided, however, that the period set forth in item (ii) may not be less than one month:
(i) a statement to the effect that the absorption-type trust split is to be effected;
(ii) a statement to the effect that the creditors set forth in the preceding paragraph may state their objections within a certain period of time; and
(iii) other matters specified by Ordinance of the Ministry of Justice.

(3) Notwithstanding the provisions of the preceding paragraph, a trustee who is a juridical person may substitute public notice (limited to public notice given by the following methods) for the separate notice to each creditor under the provisions of said paragraph:
(i) publication in a major daily newspaper which publishes matters on current events; or
(ii) electronic public notice.
(4) If no creditors set forth in paragraph (1) state any objections within the period set forth in paragraph (2), item (ii), such creditors shall be deemed to have accepted the absorption-type trust split.
(5) When any creditors set forth in paragraph (1) state their objections within the period set forth in paragraph (2), item (ii), the trustee shall make payment or provide reasonable security to such creditors, or shall entrust adequate property to a trust company, etc. for the purpose of having such creditors receive payment; provided, however, that this shall not apply if there is no risk of such creditors being harmed by the absorption-type trust split.

(Scope of Obligations Covered by the Trust Property of a Split Trust and That of a Succeeding Trust After an Absorption-Type Trust Split)
Article 157 Where an absorption-type trust split is effected, the obligation set forth in Article 155, paragraph (1), item (vi) shall cease to be an obligation covered by the trust property of the split trust after the absorption-type trust split, and shall become an obligation covered by the trust property of the succeeding trust after the absorption-type trust split. In this case, any obligation which was an obligation covered only by the trust property of the split trust shall become an obligation covered only by the trust property of the succeeding trust.

Article 158 Where a creditor who may state objections pursuant to the provisions of Article 156, paragraph (1) (limited to creditors to whom separate notice should be given pursuant to the provisions of paragraph (2) of said Article) has not been given notice as set forth in paragraph (2) of said Article, the creditor may also demand, based on the claim which the creditor has held since prior to the absorption-type trust split and which falls under any of the following items, that the trustee perform the obligation pertaining to said claim by using the property specified in the respective items; provided, however, that such performance shall be limited, in the case of the property set forth in item (i), to the value of the property to be transferred to the succeeding trust as of the day on which the absorption-type trust split becomes effective, and in the case of the property set forth in item (ii), to the value of the trust property of the split trust as of said day:

(i) a claim pertaining to an obligation covered by the trust property of the split trust (excluding claims pertaining to the obligation set forth in Article 155, paragraph (1), item (vi)): property that belongs to the trust property of the succeeding trust after the absorption-type trust split; or
(ii) a claim pertaining to an obligation covered by the trust property of the succeeding trust (limited to claims pertaining to the obligation set forth in Article 155, paragraph (1), item (vi)): property that belongs to the trust property of the split trust after the absorption-type trust split.

Subsection 2 Creation-Type Trust Splits

(Agreement, etc. among the Relevant Parties)

Article 159 (1) A creation-type trust split may be effected at the agreement of the settlor, the trustee, and the beneficiary of a trust. In this case, in effecting such a split, the following matters shall be specified:
(i) the contents of the terms of trust after the creation-type trust split;
(ii) if there is a change in the contents of the beneficial interest provided for by the terms of trust, such contents and the reasons for the change;
(iii) if monies or any other property is delivered to the beneficiary in the creation-type trust split, the contents and value of such property;
(iv) the day on which the creation-type trust split becomes effective;
(v) the contents of any property to be transferred;
(vi) if there is any obligation which will, as a result of the creation-type trust split, cease to be an obligation covered by the trust property of the former trust and become an obligation covered by the trust property of the new trust, matters concerning such obligation; and
(vii) other matters specified by Ordinance of the Ministry of Justice.
(2) Notwithstanding the provisions of the preceding paragraph, in the cases listed in the following items, a creation-type trust split may be effected by the methods specified in the respective items. In this case, the trustee shall, without delay, give notice of the matters listed in the items of said paragraph, to the settlor in the case set forth in item (i), or to the settlor and the beneficiary in the case set forth in item (ii):
(i) where it is clear that the split is not contrary to the purpose of the trust: an agreement between the trustee and the beneficiary; or
(ii) where it is clear that the split is not contrary to the purpose of the trust and that it conforms to the interests of the beneficiary: the trustee's manifestation of intention in a document or electromagnetic record.
(3) Notwithstanding the provisions of the preceding two paragraphs, if each terms of trust otherwise provides for, such provisions shall prevail.
(4) Where there is no settlor at the time in question, the provision of paragraph (1) shall not apply, and the phrase "to the settlor in the case set forth in item (i), or to the settlor and the beneficiary in the case set forth in item (ii)" in paragraph (2) shall be deemed to be replaced with "to the beneficiary in the case set forth in item (ii)."

(Objections by the Creditors)
Article 160 (1) Where a creation-type trust split is to be effected, creditors who hold claims pertaining to obligations covered by the trust property of the former trust may state their objections to the creation-type trust split to the trustee; provided, however, that this shall not apply if there is no risk of such creditors being harmed by the creation-type trust split.
(2) Where all or some of the creditors set forth in the preceding paragraph may state their objections pursuant to the provisions of said paragraph, the trustee shall give public notice of the following matters in an official gazette, and shall give notice of the same separately to each of the known creditors set forth in said paragraph; provided, however, that the period set forth in item (ii) may not be less than one month:
(i) a statement to the effect that the creation-type trust split is to be effected;
(ii) a statement to the effect that the creditors set forth in the preceding paragraph may state their objections within a certain period of time; and
(iii) other matters specified by Ordinance of the Ministry of Justice.
(3) Notwithstanding the provisions of the preceding paragraph, a trustee who is a juridical person may substitute public notice (limited to public notice given by the following methods) for the separate notice to each creditor under the provisions of said paragraph:

Art.161～163　　　　　　3 Trust Act, Chap.VII, Sec.1

(i) publication in a major daily newspaper which publishes matters on current events; or
(ii) electronic public notice.
(4) If creditors set forth in paragraph (1) do not state any objections within the period set forth in paragraph (2), item (ii), such creditors shall be deemed to have accepted the creation-type trust split.
(5) When creditors set forth in paragraph (1) state their objections within the period set forth in paragraph (2), item (ii), the trustee shall make payment or provide reasonable security to such creditors, or shall entrust adequate property to a trust company, etc. for the purpose of having such creditors receive payment; provided, however, that this shall not apply if there is no risk of such creditors being harmed by the creation-type trust split.

(Scope of Obligations Covered by the Trust Property of the Former Trust and That of the New Trust After a Creation-Type Trust Split)
Article 161 Where a creation-type trust split is effected, the obligation set forth in Article 159, paragraph (1), item (vi) shall cease to be an obligation covered by the trust property of the former trust after the creation-type trust split, and shall become an obligation covered by the trust property of the new trust after the creation-type trust split. In this case, any obligation which was an obligation covered only by the trust property of the former trust shall be an obligation covered only by the trust property of the new trusty.

Article 162 Where a creditor who may state an objection pursuant to the provisions of Article 160, paragraph (1) (limited to such a creditor to whom a separate notice should be given pursuant to the provisions of paragraph (2) of said Article) has not been given notice as set forth in paragraph (2) of said Article, the creditor may also demand, based on a claim which the creditor has held since before the creation-type trust split which falls under any of the following items, that the trustee perform the obligation pertaining to said claim by using the property specified in the respective items; provided, however, that such performance shall be limited, in the case of the property set forth in item (i), to the value of the trust property of the new trust as of the day on which the creation-type trust split becomes effective, and in the case of the property set forth in item (ii), to the value of the trust property of the former trust as of said day:
(i) a claim pertaining to an obligation covered by the trust property of the former trust (excluding a claim pertaining to the obligation set forth in Article 159, paragraph (1), item (vi)): property that belongs to the trust property of the new trust after the creation-type trust split; or
(ii) a claim which has become a claim pertaining to an obligation covered by the trust property of the new trust (limited to a claim pertaining to the obligation set forth in Article 159, paragraph (1), item (vi)): property that belongs to the trust property of the former trust after the creation-type trust split.

Chapter VII　Termination and Liquidation of Trusts

Section 1　Termination of a Trust

(Grounds for Termination of a Trust)
Article 163 In addition to cases under the provisions of the following Article, a trust shall terminate in the following cases:
(i) where the purpose of the trust has been achieved or where it has become impossi-

ble to achieve the purpose of the trust;
(ii) where the trustee has continuously held all beneficial interests in the form of the trustee's own property for one year;
(iii) where the trust lacks a trustee and the office has not been filled with a new trustee for one year;
(iv) where the trustee has terminated the trust pursuant to the provisions of Article 52 (including cases where applied mutatis mutandis pursuant to Article 53, paragraph (2) and Article 54, paragraph (4));
(v) where the trust is consolidated with another trust;
(vi) where a judicial decision ordering the termination of the trust has been rendered pursuant to the provisions of Article 165 or Article 166;
(vii) where an order for the commencement of bankruptcy proceedings has been entered against the trust property;
(viii) where the settlor is given an order for the commencement of bankruptcy proceedings, an order for the commencement of rehabilitation proceedings, or an order for the commencement of reorganization proceedings, and the trust agreement is cancelled under the provisions of Article 53, paragraph (1) of the Bankruptcy Act, Article 49, paragraph (1) of the Civil Rehabilitation Act or Article 61, paragraph (1) of the Corporate Reorganization Act (including cases where applied mutatis mutandis pursuant to Article 41, paragraph (1) and Article 206, paragraph (1) of the Act on Special Rules, etc. for Reorganization Proceedings for Financial Institutions, etc.); or
(ix) where any grounds specified by the terms of trust occur.

(Termination of a Trust by Agreement Between the Settlor and the Beneficiary)

Article 164 (1) A settlor and a beneficiary may terminate a trust at any time by an agreement between them.
(2) When a settlor and a beneficiary have terminated a trust at a time that is detrimental to the trustee, the settlor and the beneficiary shall compensate the trustee for any damages; provided, however, that this shall not apply if there was a compelling reason for the trust to be terminated at that time.
(3) Notwithstanding the provisions of the preceding two paragraphs, if the terms of trust otherwise provides for, such provisions shall prevail.
(4) The provisions of paragraph (1) and paragraph (2) shall not apply where there is no settlor at the time in question.

(Judicial Decisions Ordering the Termination of a Trust Due to Special Circumstances)

Article 165 (1) When it has become clear that, due to the special circumstances that were unforeseeable at the time of the terms of trust, the termination of a trust has come to be in the best interest of the beneficiary in light of the purpose of the trust, the status of the trust property, and any other relevant circumstances, the court may, at the petition of the settlor, the trustee, or the beneficiary, order the termination of the trust.
(2) Before the court makes a judicial decision on the petition set forth in the preceding paragraph, it shall hear the statement of the trustee.
(3) The judicial decision on the petition set forth in paragraph (1) shall include the reasons for said decision.
(4) The settlor, the trustee, or the beneficiary may file an immediate appeal against a judicial decision on the petition set forth in paragraph (1).

(5) The immediate appeal set forth in the preceding paragraph shall have the effect of a stay of execution.

(Judicial Decisions Ordering the Termination of a Trust to Ensure the Public Interest)
Article 166 (1) In the following cases, when the court finds the existence of a trust to be unallowable from the perspective of ensuring the public interest, it may, at the petition of the Minister of Justice, the settlor, the beneficiary, a trust creditor, or any other interested party, order the termination of the trust:
  (i) where the trust was created for an unlawful purpose; or
  (ii) where the trustee has committed an act that goes beyond or abuses the trustee's power as prescribed by laws and regulations or the terms of trust or has committed an act in violation of criminal laws and regulations, and where the trustee continuously or repeatedly commits said act despite having received a written warning from the Minister of Justice.
(2) Before the court makes a judicial decision on the petition set forth in the preceding paragraph, it shall hear the statement of the trustee.
(3) The judicial decision on the petition set forth in paragraph (1) shall include the reasons for said decision.
(4) The person who has filed the petition set forth in paragraph (1) or the settlor, the trustee, or the beneficiary may file an immediate appeal against the judicial decision on the petition set forth in said paragraph.
(5) The immediate appeal set forth in the preceding paragraph shall have the effect of a stay of execution.
(6) When the settlor, the beneficiary, a trust creditor, or any other interested party has filed a petition set forth in paragraph (1), the court may, at the petition of the trustee, order the person who has filed the petition set forth in said paragraph to provide reasonable security.
(7) When filing a petition under the provisions of the preceding paragraph, the trustee shall make a prima facie showing of the fact that the petition set forth in paragraph (1) was filed in bad faith.
(8) The provisions of Article 75, paragraph (5) and paragraph (7) and Article 76 to Article 80 of the Code of Civil Procedure (Act No. 109 of 1996) shall apply mutatis mutandis to the security to be provided upon the filing of a petition set forth in paragraph (1) pursuant to the provisions of paragraph (6).

(Duty of Government Agencies, etc. to Notify the Minister of Justice)
Article 167 If a court or any other government agency, a public prosecutor, or an official comes to know in the course of performing their duties that there are grounds for filing the petition set forth in paragraph (1) of the preceding Article or for giving the warning set forth in item (ii) of said paragraph, such entity or person shall notify the Minister of Justice to that effect.

(Participation by the Minister of Justice)
Article 168 (1) Before the court makes a judicial decision on a petition set forth in Article 166, paragraph (1), it shall seek the opinion of the Minister of Justice.
(2) When the court conducts a hearing on a case based on the petition set forth in the preceding paragraph, the Minister of Justice may attend said hearing.
(3) The court shall notify the Minister of Justice of the fact that a case based on the petition set forth in paragraph (1) is pending and of the date of the hearing set forth in the preceding paragraph.

(4) The Minister of Justice may file an immediate appeal against a judicial decision to dismiss the petition set forth in paragraph (1).

(Temporary Restraining Order on Trust Property)
Article 169 (1) Where a petition set forth in Article 166, paragraph (1) has been filed, the court may, at the petition of the Minister of Justice, the settlor, the beneficiary, a trust creditor, or any other interested party or on its own authority, render a disposition ordering administration by an administrator (referred to as an "administration order" in the following Article) or may issue any other temporary restraining order that is necessary with regard to the trust property.
(2) The court may change or revoke a temporary restraining order issued under the provisions of the preceding paragraph.
(3) An interested party may file an immediate appeal against a temporary restraining order under the provisions of paragraph (1) and against an order under the provisions of the preceding paragraph.

Article 170 (1) When the court issues an administration order, it shall appoint an administrator therein.
(2) The administrator set forth in the preceding paragraph shall be supervised by the court.
(3) The court may order the administrator set forth in paragraph (1) to make a report on the status of property that belongs to the trust property and the obligation covered by the trust property, and to settle the administrative accounting thereof.
(4) The provisions of Article 64 to Article 72 shall apply mutatis mutandis to the administrator set forth in paragraph (1). In this case, the term "former trustee" in Article 65 shall be deemed to be replaced with "trustee."
(5) When a temporary restraining order under the provisions of paragraph (1) of the preceding Article (excluding an administration order) is issued against any registered right that belongs to the trust property, the court clerk shall, on the clerk's own authority and without delay, commission a registration of said temporary restraining order.
(6) The provisions of the preceding paragraph shall apply mutatis mutandis where a temporary restraining order prescribed in said paragraph is changed or revoked or where such temporary restraining order has ceased to be effective.

(Burden of Expenses or Costs for Temporary Restraining Orders)
Article 171 (1) Where the court has issued a temporary restraining order under the provisions of Article 169, paragraph (1), the expenses set forth in the main clause of Article 26 of the Non-Contentious Cases Procedures Act (Act No. 14 of 1898) shall be borne by the trustee. The same shall apply to any expenses necessary for such temporary restraining order.
(2) Where an immediate appeal is filed against the temporary restraining order set forth in the preceding paragraph or a judicial decision to dismiss the petition set forth in Article 169, paragraph (1), when the court in charge of the appeal finds for said immediate appeal and revokes the judicial decision of prior instance, the court costs required for the proceedings in said instance of appeal, as well as the court costs required for the proceedings in the prior instance that had been borne by the appellant, shall be borne by the trustee.

(Inspection of Materials Related to a Temporary Restraining Order)
Article 172 (1) An interested party may make a request to the court clerk to inspect ma-

terials relating to the report or settlement of accounts set forth in Article 170, paragraph (3).
(2) An interested party may make a request to the court clerk to copy the materials set forth in the preceding paragraph or for the issuance of an authenticated copy, transcript, or extract thereof.
(3) The provisions of the preceding paragraph shall not apply with respect to materials set forth in paragraph (1) which have been prepared in the form of audiotapes or videotapes (including objects on which certain matters are recorded by any means equivalent thereto). In this case, the court clerk shall permit the reproduction of these objects at the request of an interested party.
(4) The Minister of Justice may make a request to the court clerk to inspect the materials set forth in paragraph (1).
(5) The provisions of Article 91, paragraph (5) of the Code of Civil Procedure shall apply mutatis mutandis to the materials set forth in paragraph (1).

(Appointment of a New Trustee)
Article 173 (1) Where the court has ordered the termination of a trust pursuant to the provisions of Article 166, paragraph (1), it may, at the petition of the Minister of Justice, the settlor, the beneficiary, a trust creditor, or any other interested party or on its own authority, appoint a new trustee for the liquidation of the trust.
(2) No appeal may be entered against a judicial decision on the appointment of a new trustee under the provisions of the preceding paragraph.
(3) When a new trustee is appointed pursuant to the provisions of paragraph (1), the former trustee's duty as trustee shall terminate.
(4) The new trustee set forth in paragraph (1) may receive amounts of advance payment for expenses and remuneration determined by the court from the trust property.
(5) Before the court makes a judicial decision determining the amount of advance payment for expenses or remuneration under the provisions of the preceding paragraph, it shall hear the statement of the new trustee set forth in paragraph (1).
(6) The new trustee set forth in paragraph (1) may file an immediate appeal against a judicial decision determining the amount of advance payment for expenses or remuneration under the provisions of paragraph (4).

(Restriction on Absorption-Type Trust Splitting of a Terminated Trust)
Article 174 Where a trust has terminated, it cannot effect an absorption-type trust split in which said trust will be the succeeding trust.

Section 2 Liquidation of a Trust

(Grounds for Commencement of Liquidation)
Article 175 A trust shall go into liquidation as provided for in this Section in cases where the trust has terminated (excluding cases where the trust has terminated on the grounds set forth in Article 163, item (v) and cases where the trust has terminated due to an order for the commencement of bankruptcy proceedings against the trust property and bankruptcy proceedings have not yet been closed).

(Constructive Existence of a Trust)
Article 176 Even where a trust has terminated, such trust shall be deemed to continue to exist until the liquidation is completed.

(Duties of the Liquidation Trustee)

Article 177 The trustee after the termination of a trust (hereinafter referred to as a "liquidation trustee") shall perform the following duties:
  (i) conclusion of pending duties;
  (ii) collection of claims which are among the trust property and performance of obligations pertaining to trust claims;
  (iii) performance of obligations pertaining to distribution claims as a beneficiary (excluding those for the distribution of residual assets); and
  (iv) distribution of residual assets.

(Powers of the Liquidation Trustee)
Article 178 (1) A liquidation trustee shall have the power to conduct any and all acts necessary for the liquidation of a trust; provided, however, that if the terms of trust otherwise provides, such provisions shall prevail.
(2) In the following cases, a liquidation trustee may put property that belongs to the trust property up for auction:
  (i) where the beneficiary or the holder of a vested right as prescribed in Article 182, paragraph (1), item (ii) (hereinafter collectively referred to as a "beneficiary, etc." in this Article) has refused or is unable to receive property that belongs to the trust property, and the liquidation trustee has made a demand that such a person receive said property and has specified a reasonable period of time therefor; or
  (ii) where the whereabouts of a beneficiary, etc. are unknown.
(3) When the liquidation trustee has put property that belongs to the trust property up for auction pursuant to the provisions of item (i) of the preceding paragraph, the liquidation trustee shall, without delay, give notice to that effect to the beneficiary, etc.
(4) Where the value of any property is likely to decline due to damage or any other reason, the liquidation trustee may put such property up for auction without making the demand set forth in paragraph (2), item (i).

(Commencement of Bankruptcy Proceedings Against Trust Property in Liquidation)
Article 179 (1) When it becomes clear, with regard to a trust in liquidation, that property that belongs to the trust property is insufficient for the payment of its obligations in full, the liquidation trustee shall immediately file a petition for the commencement of bankruptcy proceedings against the trust property.
(2) Where an order for the commencement of bankruptcy proceedings has been entered against the trust property, if the liquidation trustee has already made any payments to a creditor who holds a claim pertaining to an obligation covered by the trust property, the bankruptcy trustee may reclaim such payment.

(Performance of Obligations Pertaining to Conditional Claims, etc.)
Article 180 (1) The liquidation trustee may perform obligations pertaining to conditional claims, claims with indefinite durations, or any other unliquidated claims. In this case, the liquidation trustee shall file a petition with the court for the appointment of an appraiser in order to have these claims appraised.
(2) In the case referred to in the preceding paragraph, the liquidation trustee shall perform obligations pertaining to any of the claims set forth in said paragraph according to the appraisal by the appraiser set forth in said paragraph.
(3) Expenses for the procedures for the appointment of an appraiser as set forth in paragraph (1) shall be borne by the liquidation trustee. The same shall apply to expenses for inquiries made and questions asked by such appraiser for the sake of the appraisal.
(4) A judicial decision dismissing the petition set forth in paragraph (1) shall include the

reasons therefor.
(5) No appeal may be entered against a judicial decision on the appointment of an appraiser under the provisions of paragraph (1).
(6) The provisions of the preceding paragraphs shall not apply where the liquidation trustee, the beneficiary, the trust creditors, and the holders of vested rights as prescribed in Article 182, paragraph (1), item (ii) have otherwise agreed.

(Restriction on the Distribution of Residual Assets Prior to Performance of Obligations)
Article 181 The liquidation trustee may not distribute property that belongs to the trust property to the beneficiary for residual assets, etc. prescribed in paragraph (2) of the following Article until after the liquidation trustee has performed the obligations set forth in Article 177, item (ii) and item (iii); provided, however, that this shall not apply where the liquidation trustee has reserved assets that are considered to be necessary for performing said obligations.

(Vesting of Residual Assets)
Article 182 (1) Residual assets shall vest in the following persons:
(i) the person designated by the terms of trust as the person who is to be the beneficiary in relation to distribution claim as a beneficiary involving the distribution of residual assets (referred to as the "beneficiary for residual assets" in the following paragraph); and
(ii) the person designated by the terms of trust as a person in whom residual assets should be vested (hereinafter referred to as the "holder of a vested right" in this Section).
(2) Where the terms of trust contains no provisions concerning the designation of a beneficiary for residual assets or holder of a vested right (hereinafter collectively referred to as a "beneficiary etc. for residual assets." in this paragraph) or where all persons designated by the provisions of the terms of trust as beneficiaries for residual assets, etc. have waived their rights, it shall be deemed as having been provided by the terms of trust that the settlor or settlor's heir or other universal successor is to be designated as the holder of a vested right.
(3) When the vesting of residual assets is not determined pursuant to the provisions of the preceding two paragraphs, residual assets shall vest in a liquidation trustee.

(Holder of a Vested Right)
Article 183 (1) A person designated by the provisions of the terms of trust as one who is to be a holder of a vested right shall acquire a claim pertaining to the obligation to distribute residual assets by operation of law; provided, however, that if the terms of trust otherwise provides for, such provisions shall prevail.
(2) The provisions of Article 88, paragraph (2) shall apply mutatis mutandis to a person designated as one who is to be a holder of a vested right as prescribed in the preceding paragraph.
(3) A person who has become a holder of a vested right by the provisions of the terms of trust may make a manifestation of intention to the trustee to waive the said right; provided, however, that this shall not apply where the person who has become a holder of a vested right is a party to the act of trust.
(4) When a person who has become a holder of a vested right as prescribed in the main clause of the preceding paragraph has made a manifestation of intention under the provisions of said paragraph, the person shall be deemed to have never held rights as a holder of a vested right; provided, however, that this may not harm the rights of a third

party.
(5) The provisions of Article 100 and Article 102 shall apply mutatis mutandis to the claim held by a holder of a vested right which pertains to an obligation to distribute residual assets.
(6) A holder of a vested right shall be deemed to be a beneficiary during the liquidation of the trust.

(Completion of the Duties of the Liquidation Trustee, etc.)
Article 184 (1) When a liquidation trustee has completed the duties, the liquidation trustee shall, without delay, settle the final accounts related to trust affairs and request approval for the settlement of accounts from all of the beneficiaries (if there is a trust caretaker at the time in question, from the trust caretaker) and vested right holders as of the time of the termination of the trust (hereinafter collectively referred to as the "beneficiaries, etc." in this Article).
(2) Where a beneficiary, etc. has approved the settlement of accounts set forth in the preceding paragraph, the liquidation trustee shall be deemed to have been released from liability in relation to such beneficiary, etc.; provided, however, that this shall not apply if there has been any misconduct in the liquidation trustee's performance of the duties.
(3) Where a beneficiary, etc. has stated no objections within one month from the time when the beneficiary was requested by the liquidation trustee to give approval for the settlement of accounts set forth in paragraph (1), the beneficiary, etc. shall be deemed to have approved of the settlement of accounts set forth in said paragraph.

Chapter VIII Special Rules for Trusts With Certificate of Beneficial Interest

Section 1 General Provisions

(Provisions of The Terms of trust on the Issuance of Certificate of Beneficial Interest)
Article 185 (1) The terms of trust may provide for a certificate(s) indicating one, two, or more beneficial interests (hereinafter referred to as a "certificate of beneficial interest") to be issued as provided for in this Chapter.
(2) The provisions of the preceding paragraph shall not preclude the terms of trust from providing that no certificate of beneficial interest shall be issued for a beneficial interest of specific content.
(3) In the case of a trust with provisions as set forth in paragraph (1) (hereinafter referred to as a "trust with certificate of beneficial interest"), the provisions set forth in the preceding two paragraphs may not be changed by making modifications to the trust.
(4) In the case of a trust with no provisions as set forth in paragraph (1), the provisions set forth in said paragraph or paragraph (2) may not be established by making modifications to the trust.

(Beneficial Interest Registry)
Article 186 A trustee of a trust with certificate of beneficial interest shall, without delay, prepare a beneficial interest registry, and state or record therein the following matters (hereinafter referred to as the "matters to be stated in the beneficial interest registry" in this Chapter):
(i) the content of the distribution claim as a beneficiary pertaining to each beneficial interest and other matters specified by Ordinance of the Ministry of Justice as mat-

ters that specify the content of the beneficial interest;
(ii) the serial number of the certificate of beneficial interest pertaining to each beneficial interest, the date of issue, whether each certificate of beneficial interest is a registered certificate or bearer certificate, and the number of bearer beneficial interests;
(iii) the name and address of the beneficiary pertaining to each beneficial interest (excluding beneficiaries of bearer beneficial interests);
(iv) the day on which the beneficiary set forth in the preceding item acquired each beneficial interest; and
(v) in addition to what is listed in the preceding items, the matters specified by Ordinance of the Ministry of Justice.

(Delivery of Documents Stating the Matters to Be Stated in the Beneficial Interest Registry)
Article 187 (1) A beneficiary of a beneficial interest for which there are provisions as set forth in Article 185, paragraph (2) may request that the trustee of a trust with certificate of beneficial interest deliver to the beneficiary a document stating the matters to be stated in the beneficial interest registry, which are stated or recorded in the beneficial interest registry about said beneficiary, or that said trustee provide the beneficiary with an electromagnetic record containing such matters to be stated in the beneficial interest registry.
(2) The trustee of a trust with certificate of beneficial interest (in the case of a trustee who is a juridical person, its representative; the same shall apply in the following paragraph) shall sign or affix the trustee's name and seal to the document set forth in the preceding paragraph.
(3) With respect to the electromagnetic record set forth in paragraph (1), the trustee of a trust with certificate of beneficial interest shall take the measures specified by Ordinance of the Ministry of Justice as an alternative to signing or affixing trustee's name and seal.
(4) For the purpose of the application of the provisions of the preceding two paragraphs in cases where there are two or more trustees for a trust with certificate of beneficial interest, the phrase "trustee of a trust with certificate of beneficial interest" in these provisions shall be deemed to be replaced with "all trustees of a trust with certificates of beneficial interest."

(Beneficial Interest Registry Administrator)
Article 188 The trustee of a trust with certificate of beneficial interest may appoint a beneficial interest registry administrator (meaning a person who prepares and keeps a beneficial interest registry and executes other affairs concerning the beneficial interest registry on behalf of the trustee of a trust with certificate of beneficial interest; the same shall apply hereinafter), and may delegate the administration of such affairs to the same.

(Record Date)
Article 189 (1) The trustee of trust with certificate of beneficial interest may specify a certain date (hereinafter referred to as the "record date" in this Article), and designate the beneficiaries who have been stated or recorded in the beneficial interest registry as of the record date (hereinafter referred to as the "beneficiaries as of the record date" in this Article) as the persons who are entitled to exercise their rights.
(2) The provisions of the preceding paragraph shall not apply to any beneficiaries of bearer beneficial interests.

(3) When designating the record date, the trustee of a trust with certificate of beneficial interest shall specify the content of the rights that the beneficiaries as of the record date are entitled to exercise (limited to such rights to be exercised within three months from the record date).
(4) When the trustee of a trust with certificate of beneficial interest has designated the record date, the trustee shall give public notice in an official gazette, no later than two weeks prior to the record date, with regard to the record date and the matters specified pursuant to the provisions of the preceding paragraph; provided, however, that this shall not apply if the terms of trust contains provisions on the record date and the content of the rights that the beneficiaries as of the record date are entitled to exercise.
(5) Notwithstanding the provisions of paragraph (1), paragraph (3), and the main clause of the preceding paragraph, if the terms of trust otherwise provides, such provisions shall prevail.

(Keeping and Inspection, etc. of the Beneficial Interest Registry)
Article 190 (1) The trustee of trust with certificate of beneficial interest shall keep a beneficial interest registry at the trustee's address (in cases where the trustee is a juridical person (excluding cases where there is a beneficial interest registry administrator at the time in question), its principal office; in cases where there is a beneficial interest registry administrator at the time in question, the administrator's business office).
(2) The settlor, beneficiary, and any other interested party may make the following requests of the trustee of a trust with certificate of beneficial interest. In this case, in making such a request, the reasons therefor shall be specified:
  (i) if the beneficial interest registry has been prepared in the form of a document, a request to inspect or copy such document; and
  (ii) if the beneficial interest registry has been prepared in the form of an electromagnetic record, a request to inspect or copy any object which shows the matters recorded in the electromagnetic record by a method specified by Ordinance of the Ministry of Justice.
(3) The trustee of a trust with certificate of beneficial interest may not refuse a request set forth in the preceding paragraph when such a request has been received, except where it is found to fall under any of the following cases:
  (i) where the person making such request (hereinafter referred to as the "requester" in this paragraph) has made the request for purposes other than an investigation related to the securement or exercise of requester's rights;
  (ii) where the requester has made the request at an inappropriate time;
  (iii) where the requester has made the request for the purpose of disturbing the trust administration or harming the common interests of the beneficiaries;
  (iv) where the requester operates or engages in business which is effectively in competition with business pertaining to the trust;
  (v) where the requester has made the request in order to inform a third party, for profit, of any fact that the requester may learn by way of inspecting or copying documents or any other object under the provisions of the preceding paragraph; or
  (vi) where the requester has informed a third party, for profit, of any fact that the requester has learned by way of inspecting or copying documents or any other object under the provisions of the preceding paragraph within the past two years.
(4) Where any of the requests set forth in paragraph (2) is made with regard to the matters listed in Article 186, item (iii) or item (iv) (limited to the matters concerning a beneficial interest not subject to the provisions set forth in Article 185, paragraph (2)),

if the terms of trust otherwise provides for, such provisions shall prevail.

(Notices, etc. Given to Beneficiaries)
Article 191 (1) It shall be sufficient for the trustee of a trust with certificate of beneficial interest to send any notice that the trustee gives to a beneficiary or demand that the trustee makes, to the beneficiary's address as stated or recorded in the beneficial interest registry (if a beneficiary has notified the trustee of a different place or contact address for receiving notices or demands, to such place or contact address).
(2) The notice or demand set forth in the preceding paragraph shall be deemed to have reached the addressee at the time when the notice or demand should have normally reached.
(3) If a beneficial interest in a trust with certificate of beneficial interest is co-owned by two or more persons, the co-owners shall designate one person who is to receive any notice or demand sent by the trustee of the trust with beneficiary certificate to the beneficiaries, and shall notify the trustee of that person's name. In this case, said person shall be deemed to be a beneficiary and the provisions of the preceding two paragraphs shall apply thereto.
(4) Where there has been no notification from the co-owners under the provisions of the preceding paragraph, it shall be sufficient for the trustee of the trust with certificate of beneficial interest to send any notice that the trustee is to give to the co-owners of the beneficial interest or any demand that the trustee is to make, to any one of them.
(5) When the trustee of a trust with certificate of beneficial interest should give notice to the beneficiaries of bearer beneficial interest, it shall be sufficient for the trustee to send notices only to such beneficiaries whose names and addresses are known to the trustee. In this case, the trustee shall give public notice in an official gazette of the matters of which to notify them.

(Exercise of Rights by Beneficiaries with Bearer Beneficial Interests)
Article 192 (1) When a beneficiary with a bearer beneficial interest wishes to exercise the right against the trustee of a trust with certificate of beneficial interest or any other person, the beneficiary shall present the certificate of beneficial interest to the trustee or such other person.
(2) When a beneficiary with a bearer beneficial interest wishes to exercise the voting right at a beneficiaries meeting, the beneficiary shall present the certificate of beneficial interest to the convener prescribed in Article 108 no later than one week prior to the date of the beneficiaries meeting.

(Exercise of Rights by Co-owners)
Article 193 If a beneficial interest in a trust with certificate of beneficial interest is co-owned by two or more persons, the co-owners may not exercise the rights of their beneficial interest unless they designate one person who is to exercise the rights of said beneficial interest and notify the trustee of the trust with certificate of beneficial interest of that person's name; provided, however, that this shall not apply where the trustee has consented to the exercise of said rights.

Section 2 Special Rules for Assignment of a Beneficial Interest, etc.

(Assignment of a Beneficial Interest for Which a Certificate of Beneficial Interest Has Been Issued)
Article 194 The assignment of a beneficial interest in a trust with certificate of beneficial interest (excluding a beneficial interest subject to the provisions set forth in Arti-

cle 185, paragraph (2)) shall not be effective unless the certificate of beneficial interest pertaining to such assigned beneficial interest is delivered.

(Requirements for the Perfection of an Assignment of a Beneficial Interest in a Trust With Certificate of Beneficial Interest)
Article 195 (1) The assignment of a beneficial interest in a trust with certificate of beneficial interest may not be duly asserted against the trustee of the trust with certificate of beneficial interest unless the name and address of the person who has acquired the beneficial interest has been stated or recorded in the beneficial interest registry.
(2) For the purpose of the application of the provisions of the preceding paragraph with regard to a beneficial interest subject to the provisions set forth in Article 185, paragraph (2), the phrase "trustee" of the same paragraph shall be deemed to be replaced with "trustee or any third party."
(3) The provisions of paragraph (1) shall not apply to bearer beneficial interests.

(Presumption of Rights, etc.)
Article 196 (1) The possessor of a certificate of beneficial interest shall be presumed to be the lawful owner of the beneficial interest pertaining to said certificate of beneficial interest.
(2) A person who has received the delivery of a certificate of beneficial interest shall acquire the rights of the beneficial interest pertaining to said certificate of beneficial interest; provided, however, that this shall not apply if the person was in bad faith or with gross negligence.

(Stating or Recording Matters to Be Stated in the Beneficial Interest Registry without the Request of the Beneficiary)
Article 197 (1) In the cases listed in the following items, the trustee of a trust with certificate of beneficial shall, as provided for by Ordinance of the Ministry of Justice, state or record in the beneficial interest registry the matters to be stated in the beneficial interest registry which pertain to the beneficiary of the beneficial interest specified in the respective items:
 (i) where the trustee has acquired a beneficial interest in the trust with certificate of beneficial interest and said beneficial interest has not been extinguished; or
 (ii) where the trustee has disposed of the beneficial interest in the trust with certificates of beneficial interest set forth in the preceding item.
(2) The trustee of a trust with certificate of beneficial interest shall, where the consolidation of beneficial interests is effected by making a modification to the trust, state or record in the beneficial interest registry the matters to be stated in the beneficial interest registry which pertain to such consolidated beneficial interests.
(3) The trustee of a trust with certificate of beneficial interest shall, where the splitting of a beneficial interest is effected by making a modification to the trust, state or record in the beneficial interest registry the matters to be stated in the beneficial interest registry which pertain to such split beneficial interest.
(4) The provisions of the preceding three paragraphs shall not apply to bearer beneficial interests.

(Stating or Recording Matters to Be Stated in the Beneficial Interest Registry at the Beneficiary's Request)
Article 198 (1) A person (excluding the trustee) who has acquired a beneficial interest in a trust with certificates of beneficial interest from a person other than the trustee of the trust with certificate of beneficial interest may request that the trustee of the trust

with certificate of beneficial interest, state or record in the beneficial interest registry the matters to be stated in the beneficial interest registry which pertain to said beneficial interest.
(2) The request under the provisions of the preceding paragraph shall be made jointly with the person who is stated or recorded in the beneficial interest registry as the beneficiary of the beneficial interest thus acquired or the person's heir or any other general successor, except in cases specified by Ordinance of the Ministry of Justice where there is no risk of harm to the interest of any interested party.
(3) The provisions of the preceding two paragraphs shall not apply to bearer beneficial interests.

(Pledges of Beneficial Interests for Which Certificate of Beneficial Interest Have Been Issued)
Article 199 A pledge of a beneficial interest for a trust with certificate of beneficial interest (excluding a beneficial interest subject to the provisions set forth in Article 185, paragraph (2)) shall not be effective unless the certificate of beneficial interest pertaining to such pledged beneficial interest is delivered.

(Requirements for the Perfection of a Pledge of a Beneficial Interest in a Trust With Certificate of Beneficial Interest)
Article 200 (1) The pledgee of a beneficial interest in a trust with certificate of beneficial interest (excluding a beneficial interest subject to the provisions set forth in Article 185, paragraph (2)) may not duly assert the right of pledge against the trustee of the trust with certificate of beneficial interest or against any other third party unless the pledge continues to possess the certificate of beneficial interest pertaining to such pledged beneficial interest.
(2) A pledge of a beneficial interest subject to the provisions set forth in Article 185, paragraph (2) may not be duly asserted against the trustee of a trust with certificate of beneficial interest or against any other third party unless the name and address of the pledgee has been stated or recorded in the beneficial interest registry.

(Stating, etc. Matters Related to a Pledge in the Beneficial Interest Registry)
Article 201 (1) A person who has created a pledge on a beneficial interest for a trust with certificates of beneficial interest may request the trustee of a trust with certificate of beneficial interest to state or record the following matters in the beneficial interest registry:
(i) the name and address of the pledgee; and
(ii) the beneficial interest that is the subject matter of the pledge.
(2) The provisions of the preceding paragraph shall not apply to bearer beneficial interests.

(Delivery of Documents Stating the Matters Stated in the Beneficial Interest Registry Which Relate to a Pledge)
Article 202 (1) A pledgee for whom the matters listed in the items of paragraph (1) of the preceding Article have been stated or recorded in the beneficial interest registry (hereinafter referred to as a "registered pledgee of a beneficial interest" in this Section) may request that the trustee of a trust with certificate of beneficial interest deliver a document to the registered pledge of a beneficial interest, stating the matters listed in the respective items of said paragraph, which are stated or recorded in the beneficial interest registry of said registered pledgee of a beneficial interest, or may request that said trustee provide the registered pledgee of a beneficial interest with an

electromagnetic record containing such matters.
(2) The trustee (in the case of a trustee who is a juridical person, its representative; the same shall apply in the following paragraph) of a trust with certificates of beneficial interest shall sign or affix trustee's (or the representative's) name and seal to the document set forth in the preceding paragraph.
(3) With respect to the electromagnetic record set forth in paragraph (1), the trustee of a trust with certificates of beneficial interest shall take the measures specified by Ordinance of the Ministry of Justice as an alternative to signing or affixing trustee's name and seal.
(4) For the purpose of the application of the provisions of the preceding two paragraphs in cases where there are two or more trustees for the trust with certificate of beneficial interest, the phrase "trustee of a trust with certificate of beneficial interest" in these provisions shall be deemed to be replaced with "all trustees of the trust with certificate of beneficial interest."

(Notices, etc. Given to the Registered Pledgee of a Beneficial Interest)
Article 203 (1) It shall be sufficient for the trustee of a trust with certificate of beneficial interest to send any notice that the trustee gives to a registered pledgee of a beneficial interest or demand that the trustee makes, to the address of the registered pledgee of the beneficial interest that is stated or recorded in the beneficial interest registry (if the registered pledgee of a beneficial interest has notified the trustee of a different place or contact address for receiving notices or demands, to such place or contact address).
(2) The notice or demand set forth in the preceding paragraph shall be deemed to have reached the addressee at the time when the notice or demand should have normally reached.

(Stating, etc. Matters in the Beneficial Interest Registry Concerning the Consolidation or Split of Beneficial Interest)
Article 204 (1) The trustee of a trust with certificate of beneficial interest shall, where the consolidation of beneficial interests is effected by making a modification to the trust and the pledgee of the pledge on any of said beneficial interests is a registered pledgee of the beneficial interest, state or record in the beneficial interest registry the name and address of such pledgee with regard to such consolidated beneficial interest.
(2) The trustee of a trust with certificates of beneficial interest shall, where the splitting of a beneficial interest is effected by making a modification to the trust and the pledgee of the pledge on said beneficial interest is a registered pledgee of the beneficial interest, state or record in the beneficial interest registry the name and address of such pledgee with regard to such split beneficial interest.

Article 205 (1) In the case prescribed in paragraph (1) of the preceding Article, the trustee of the trust with certificates of beneficial interest shall deliver the certificate of beneficial interest for the consolidated beneficial interest to the registered pledgee of the beneficial interest.
(2) In the case prescribed in paragraph (2) of the preceding Article, the trustee of the trust with certificates of beneficial interest shall deliver the certificates of beneficial interest for the split beneficial interests to the registered pledgee of the beneficial interest.

(Requirements for Perfection Regarding a Beneficial Interest for Which No Certificate of Beneficial Interest Have Been Issued)

Art.206〜208　　　③ Trust Act, Chap.VIII, Sec.3

Article 206 (1) With regard to a beneficial interest that is subject to the provisions set forth in Article 185, paragraph (2) which belongs to the trust property of another trust, the fact that said beneficial interest belongs to trust property of said other trust may not be duly asserted against the trustee of a trust with certificate of beneficial interest or against any other third party unless such fact that said beneficial interest belongs to the trust property of the other trust is stated or recorded in the beneficial interest registry.

(2) The trustee of the other trust to which the beneficial interest set forth in the preceding paragraph belongs may request that the trustee of the trust with certificate of beneficial interest state or record in the beneficial interest registry the fact that said beneficial interest belongs to the trust property of the other trust.

(3) For the purpose of the application of the provisions of Article 187 in cases where the relevant facts have been stated or recorded in the beneficial interest registry under the provisions of the preceding paragraph, in paragraph (1) of said Article, the phrase "a beneficiary of a beneficial interest for which there are provisions as set forth in Article 185, paragraph (2)" shall be deemed to be replaced with "the trustee of another trust to which a beneficial interest set forth in Article 206, paragraph (1) belongs," the term "said beneficiary" shall be deemed to be replaced with "said beneficial interest," and the phrase "the matters to be stated in the beneficial interest registry, which are stated or recorded in the beneficial interest registry about said beneficiary" shall be deemed to be replaced with "the matters to be stated in the beneficial interest registry, which are stated or recorded in the beneficial interest registry about said beneficiary (including the fact that said beneficial interest belongs to the trust property of the other trust)."

Section 3 Certificates of Beneficial Interest

(Issuance of Certificate of Beneficial Interest)
Article 207 The trustee of a trust with certificate of beneficial interest shall, as provided for by the terms of trust, issue certificates of beneficial interest pertaining to the beneficial interests concerned without delay.

(Notification of Desire Not to Possess Certificate of Beneficial Interest)
Article 208 (1) A beneficiary of a trust with certificates of beneficial interest may notify the trustee of the trust with certificate of beneficial interest to the effect that the beneficiary of a trust with certificates of beneficial interest does not desire to possess a certificate of beneficial interest pertaining to the beneficial interest that such beneficiary holds; provided, however, that if the terms of trust otherwise provides, such provisions shall prevail.

(2) In a notifying the trustee under the provisions of the preceding paragraph, the beneficiary shall specify the content of the beneficial interest to which the notification pertains. In this case, if a certificate of beneficial interest pertaining to said beneficial interest has already been issued, the beneficiary shall return said certificate of beneficial interest to the trustee of the trust with the certificate of beneficial interest.

(3) The trustee of a trust with s certificates of beneficial interest who has received a notification under the provisions of paragraph (1) shall, without delay, state or record in the beneficial interest registry a statement to the effect that the trustee will not issue a certificate of beneficial interest pertaining to the beneficial interest set forth in the first sentence of the preceding paragraph.

(4) When the trustee of a trust with certificate of beneficial interest has stated or recorded the relevant statements under the provisions of the preceding paragraph, the trustee

may not issue a certificate of beneficial interest pertaining to the beneficial interest set forth in the first sentence of paragraph (2).
(5) A certificate of beneficial interest submitted under the provisions of the second sentence of paragraph (2) shall be become invalid at the time when the relevant statement is stated or recorded under the provisions of paragraph (3).
(6) A beneficiary who has notified the trustee under the provisions of paragraph (1) may at any time demand that the trustee of the trust with certificate of beneficial interest issue a certificate of beneficial interest pertaining to the beneficial interest set forth in the first sentence of paragraph (2). In this case, if there any certificate of beneficial interest was returned under the provisions of the second sentence of said paragraph, the expenses for issuing a certificate of beneficial interest shall be borne by said beneficiary.
(7) The provisions of the preceding paragraphs shall not apply to bearer certificate of beneficial interest.

(Matters to Be Stated on a Certificate of Beneficial Interest)
Article 209 (1) On a certificate of beneficial interest, the serial number and the following matters shall be stated, and the trustee of the trust with the certificate of beneficial interest (in the case of a trustee who is a juridical person, its representative) shall sign or affix the trustee's (or the representative's) name and seal to it:
(i) a statement to the effect that the certificate of beneficial interest is a certificate of beneficial interest of the trust with the certificate of beneficial interest;
(ii) the names and addresses of the initial settlor and trustee of the trust with the certificate of beneficial interest;
(iii) if the certificate of beneficial interest is a registered certificate, the name of the beneficiary;
(iv) the content of the distribution claim as a beneficiary pertaining to each beneficial interest, and other matters specified by Ordinance of the Ministry of Justice as matters that specify the content of the beneficial interest;
(v) any provisions of the terms of trust concerning reimbursement of expenses, etc. and compensation for damages to the trustee of the trust with the certificate of beneficial interest;
(vi) the method of calculation for trust fees, and the method and time of payment of such fees;
(vii) if there are restrictions on the assignment of the beneficial interest indicated by the registered certificate of beneficial interest, a statement to that effect and the content of such restrictions;
(viii) any provisions of the terms of trust concerning the exercise of rights by the beneficiary (including matters concerning trust supervisors and beneficiaries' agents); and
(ix) other matters specified by Ordinance of the Ministry of Justice.
(2) For the purpose of the application of the provisions of the preceding paragraph in cases where there are two or more trustees for the trust with the certificate of beneficial interest, the phrase "trustee of the trust that issued the certificate of beneficial interest" in these provisions shall be deemed to be replaced with "all trustees of the trust that issued the certificate of beneficial interest."

(Conversion of Registered Certificate and Bearer Certificate)
Article 210 The beneficiary of a beneficial interest for which a certificate of beneficial interest has been issued, may at any time demand that the said beneficiary's registered certificate of beneficial interest be converted into a bearer certificate, or that the

said beneficiary's bearer certificate of beneficial interest be converted into a registered certificate; provided, however, that if the terms of trust otherwise provides for, such provisions shall prevail.

(Loss of a Certificate of Beneficial Interest)
Article 211 (1) A certificate of beneficial interest may be invalidated through the public notification procedure prescribed in Article 142 of the Non-Contentious Cases Procedures Act.
(2) A person who has lost the certificate of beneficial interest may not request the re-issuance thereof until after the person obtains an order of nullification as prescribed in Article 148, paragraph (1) of the Non-Contentious Cases Procedures Act.
(3) When a person who has lost the certificate of beneficial interest has filed a petition for public notification as prescribed in Article 156 of the Non-Contentious Cases Procedures Act, said person who has lost the certificate of beneficial interest may provide reasonable deposit and have the trustee of the certificate of beneficial interest perform the obligations pertaining to the certificate of beneficial interest.

Section 4 Special Rules on the Rights and Duties, etc. of the Relevant Parties

(Special Rules on the Duties of the Trustee of a Trust With Certificates of Beneficial Interests)
Article 212 (1) In the case of a trust with certificates of beneficial interest, notwithstanding the provisions of the proviso to Article 29, paragraph (2), no provision of the terms of trust may mitigate the duty set forth in the main clause of said paragraph.
(2) The provisions of Article 35, paragraph (4) shall not apply to a trust with certificate of beneficial interests.

(Special Rules on The Terms of trust Providing for Restrictions on the Exercise of Rights by a Beneficiary)
Article 213 (1) In the case of a trust with beneficiary certificates, notwithstanding the provisions of Article 92, item (i), item (v), item (vi), and item (viii), provisions may be established in the terms of trust to the effect that, with regard to all or part of the following rights, such rights may be exercised only by a beneficiary who holds a beneficial interest which represents not less than three-hundredths of the voting rights of all beneficiaries (or any smaller proportion provided for by the terms of trust; hereinafter the same shall apply in this paragraph) or a beneficiary who holds beneficial interest which represents not less than three-hundredths of the total number of existing beneficial interests:
(i) the right to rescind under the provisions of Article 27, paragraph (1) or paragraph (2) (including cases where these provisions are applied mutatis mutandis pursuant to Article 75, paragraph (4));
(ii) the right to rescind under the provisions of Article 31, paragraph (6) or paragraph (7);
(iii) the right to request to inspect or copy materials under the provisions of Article 38, paragraph (1); and
(iv) the right to file a petition for the appointment of an inspector under the provisions of Article 46, paragraph (1).
(2) In the case of a trust with certificate of beneficial interests, notwithstanding the provisions of Article 92, item (i), provisions may be established in the terms of trust to the effect that, with regard to all or part of the following rights, such rights may be exer-

cised only by a beneficiary who holds a beneficial interest which represents not less than one-tenth of the voting rights of all beneficiaries (or any smaller proportion provided for by the terms of trust; hereinafter the same shall apply in this paragraph) or a beneficiary who holds a beneficial interest which represents not less than one-tenth of the total number of existing beneficial interests:
  (i) the right to file a petition for a judicial decision to order the modification of the trust under the provisions of Article 150, paragraph (1); and
  (ii) the right to file a petition for a judicial decision to order the termination of the trust under the provisions of Article 165, paragraph (1).
(3) The provisions of the preceding two paragraphs shall not apply to a trust with certificate of beneficial interests if disclosure under the provisions of Article 39, paragraph (1) is restricted by the provisions of the terms of trust as set forth in paragraph (3) of said Article.
(4) In the case of a trust with beneficiary certificates, notwithstanding the provisions of Article 92, item (xi), provisions may be established in the terms of trust to the effect that the right to demand a cessation under the provisions of Article 44, paragraph (1) may be exercised only by a beneficiary who has continually held a beneficial interest during the preceding six months (or any shorter period provided for by the terms of trust).

(Special Rules on Decision-Making Methods Involving Two or More Beneficiaries)
Article 214 In the case of a trust with certificates of beneficial interest that has two or more beneficiaries, unless otherwise provided for by the terms of trust, it shall be deemed as having been provided for by the terms of trust that a beneficiaries' decision (excluding a decision on the exercise of the rights listed in the items of Article 92) shall be made by a majority vote at a beneficiaries meeting pursuant to the provisions of Chapter IV, Section 3, Subsection 2.

(Special Rules on the Settlor's Rights)
Article 215 In the case of a trust with certificates of beneficial interest among the rights granted to a settlor under the provisions of this Act, the following rights shall be exercised by a beneficiary:
  (i) the right to request a report under the provisions of Article 36;
  (ii) the right to file a petition under the provisions of Article 58, paragraph (4) (including cases where applied mutatis mutandis pursuant to Article 134, paragraph (2), and Article 141, paragraph (2)), Article 62, paragraph (4) (including cases where applied mutatis mutandis pursuant to Article 135, paragraph (1) and Article 142, paragraph (1)), Article 63, paragraph (1), Article 74, paragraph (2), Article 131, paragraph (4), Article 150, paragraph (1), Article 165, paragraph (1), Article 166, paragraph (1), Article 169, paragraph (1), or Article 173, paragraph (1);
  (iii) the right to call for a definite answer under the provisions of Article 62, paragraph (2), Article 131, paragraph (2), or Article 138, paragraph (2);
  (iv) the right to request to inspect, copy, be delivered, or have reproduced materials under the provisions of Article 172, paragraph (1) or paragraph (2) or the second sentence of paragraph (3) of said Article; and
  (v) the right to request to inspect or copy materials under the provisions of Article 190, paragraph (2).

Chapter IX Special Rules for Limited Liability Trusts

Section 1 General Provisions

(Requirements for a Limited Liability Trust)
Article 216 (1) A limited liability trust shall become effective as a limited liability trust when it is provided by the terms of trust that the trustee is liable to perform all obligation covered by the trust property only by using property that belongs to the trust property, and when a registration of such provisions is made as provided for in Article 232.
(2) The terms of trust set forth in the preceding paragraph shall provide for the following matters:
(i) the purpose of the limited liability trust;
(ii) the name of the limited liability trust;
(iii) the names and addresses of the settlor(s) and the trustee(s);
(iv) the place where the principal trust affairs for the limited liability trust are to be administered (referred to as the "place for the administration of affairs" in Section 3);
(v) the method of administration or disposition of property that belongs to the trust property; and
(vi) other matters specified by Ordinance of the Ministry of Justice.

(Restrictions on Execution, etc. Against Property That Belongs to Trustee's Own Property)
Article 217 (1) In the case of a limited liability trust, no performance may be compelled nor may provisional seizure, provisional disposition, exercise of a security interest, auction, or proceedings for collection of delinquent national taxes be carried out against property that belongs to the trustee's own property, based on a claim pertaining to any obligations covered by trust property (excluding obligations pertaining to the right set forth in Article 21, paragraph (1), item (viii)).
(2) The trustee may assert an objection to performance that was compelled or to, provisional seizure, provisional disposition, exercise of a security interest, or an auction that was carried out in violation of the provisions of the preceding paragraph. In this case, the provisions of Article 38 of the Civil Execution Act and the provisions of Article 45 of the Civil Preservation Act shall apply mutatis mutandis.
(3) The trustee may assert an objection to proceedings for collection of delinquent national taxes that were carried out in violation of the provision of paragraph (1). In this case, the assertion of the objection shall be made by entering an appeal against the proceedings for collection of delinquent national taxes.

(Name, etc. of a Limited Liability Trust)
Article 218 (1) In the name of a limited liability trust, the characters representing the term "limited liability trust" shall be used.
(2) No person may use, in its name or trade name, any characters which make it likely that a trust that is not a limited liability trust, will be mistaken for a limited liability trust.
(3) No person may use, with a wrongful purpose, any name or trade name which makes it likely that a limited liability trust, will be mistaken for another limited liability trust.
(4) Any trustee of a limited liability trust whose business interests have been, or are likely to be, infringed by the use of any name or trade name in violation of the provisions of the preceding paragraph may seek an injunction suspending or preventing the infringement against the person who has or is likely to infringe those business interests.

(Duty of Clear Indication to the Counterparty)
Article 219 A trustee may not, in conducting a transaction as the trustee of a limited liability trust, duly assert against the other party to the transaction as such unless the trustee has clearly indicated to that effect to the other party.

(Effect of Registration)
Article 220 (1) The matters to be registered pursuant to the provisions of this Chapter may not be duly asserted against a third party who has no knowledge of such matters until after the registration. The same shall apply after the registration if a third party did not know that such matters were registered, based on justifiable grounds.
(2) A person who has registered false matters willfully or negligently with regard to the matters to be registered pursuant to the provisions of this Chapter may not duly assert the falsity of such matters against a third party who has no knowledge of such falsity.

(Modification of a Trust to Abolish Provisions on Limited Liability Trust Status)
Article 221 When a modification is made to a trust to abolish the provision set forth in Article 216, paragraph (1) and a registration of termination set forth in Article 235 is made, the provisions of this Chapter shall not apply to the trust after the modification.

Section 2 Special Rules on Accounting, etc.

(Special Rules on the Duty to Prepare, Report on, and Preserve Books, etc.)
Article 222 (1) Notwithstanding the provisions of Article 37 and Article 38, the preparation of books and other documents or electromagnetic records pertaining to a limited liability trust, reporting on their content, and preservation of these materials, as well as the inspection and copying of the same shall be governed by the provisions of the following paragraph to paragraph (9).
(2) The trustee shall prepare the accounting books for a limited liability trust as provided for by Ordinance of the Ministry of Justice.
(3) The trustee shall, promptly after a limited liability trust has become effective, prepare a balance sheet as of the day on which it became effective, as provided for by Ordinance of the Ministry of Justice.
(4) A trustee shall, once each year at a certain time as provided for by Ordinance of the Ministry of Justice, prepare a balance sheet and profit and loss statement for the limited liability trust, as well as annexed detailed statements of these and other documents or electromagnetic records specified by Ordinance of the Ministry of Justice.
(5) When the trustee has prepared the documents or electromagnetic records set forth in the preceding paragraph, the trustee shall report to the beneficiary (if there is a trust caretaker at the time in question, to the trust caretaker) on the content thereof; provided, however, that if the terms of trust otherwise provides for, such provisions shall prevail.
(6) Where a trustee has prepared the accounting books set forth in paragraph (2), the trustee shall preserve said books (if electromagnetic records have been prepared in lieu of documents by the method specified by Ordinance of the Ministry of Justice, such electromagnetic records; if documents have been prepared in lieu of electromagnetic records, such documents) for ten years from the date of their preparation (or until the date of the completion of the liquidation of the trust if this occurs within said ten-year period; the same shall apply in the following paragraph); provided, however,

that this shall not apply where the trustee has delivered said documents or copies thereof to the beneficiary (if there are two or more beneficiaries at the time in question, to all beneficiaries; if there is a trust caretaker at the time in question, to the trust caretaker; the same shall apply in paragraph (8)), or has provided the beneficiary with information on the matters recorded in said electromagnetic records by the method specified by Ordinance of the Ministry of Justice.

(7) Where the trustee has prepared or acquired a written contract pertaining to the disposition of property that belongs to the trust property or any other documents or electromagnetic records concerning the trust administration, the trustee shall preserve said documents or electromagnetic records (if electromagnetic records have been prepared in lieu of said documents by the method specified by Ordinance of the Ministry of Justice, such electromagnetic records; if documents have been prepared in lieu of said electromagnetic records, such documents) for ten years from the date of their preparation or acquisition. In this case, the provisions of the proviso to the preceding paragraph shall apply mutatis mutandis.

(8) Where a trustee has prepared the balance sheet set forth in paragraph (3) and the documents or electromagnetic records set forth in paragraph (4) (hereinafter referred to as the "balance sheet, etc." in this paragraph and Article 224, paragraph (2), item (i)), the trustee shall preserve said balance sheet, etc. (if electromagnetic records have been prepared in lieu of documents by the method specified by Ordinance of the Ministry of Justice, such electromagnetic records; if documents have been prepared in lieu of electromagnetic records, such documents) until the date of the completion of the liquidation of the trust; provided, however that this shall not apply where the trustee has, after ten years have elapsed from the date of their preparation, delivered said documents or copies thereof to the beneficiary, or has provided the beneficiary with information on the matters recorded in said electromagnetic records by the method specified by Ordinance of the Ministry of Justice.

(9) For the purpose of the application of the provisions of Article 38 to a limited liability trust, the phrase "paragraph (1) or paragraph (5) of the preceding Article" in the items of paragraph (1) of said Article shall be deemed to be replaced with "Article 222, paragraph (2) or paragraph (7)," and the phrase "paragraph (2) of the preceding Article" in paragraph (4), item (i) of said Article and the items of paragraph (6) of said Article shall be deemed to be replaced with "Article 222, paragraph (3) or paragraph (4)."

(Court's Order to Submit Documents)
Article 223 The court may, upon petition or on its own authority, order the parties to a lawsuit to submit all or part of the documents set forth in paragraph (2) to paragraph (4) of the preceding Article.

(Trustee Liability to Third Parties)
Article 224 (1) In the case of a limited liability trust, if the trustee was willful or grossly negligent in the course of administering trust affairs, the trustee shall be liable to compensate for any damages suffered by a third party arising therefrom.

(2) The provisions of the preceding paragraph shall also apply when a trustee of a limited liability trust has committed the following acts; provided, however, that this shall not apply if the trustee proves that the trustee did not fail to exercise due care in committing said act:
(i) making false statements or records on the matters that should be stated or recorded in the balance sheet, etc.;
(ii) making a false registration; or
(iii) giving false public notice.

(3) In the cases referred to in the preceding two paragraphs, when there is another trustee who is also liable to compensate for damages in addition to the trustee set forth in those paragraphs, these trustees shall be joint and several obligors.

(Restriction on Distribution of Trust Property to the Beneficiary)
Article 225 In the case of a limited liability trust, no distribution of trust property may be made to the beneficiary beyond the maximum distributable amount (meaning the maximum amount that may be distributed to the beneficiary, as calculated by the method specified by Ordinance of the Ministry of Justice within the amount of net assets; hereinafter the same shall apply in this Section).

(Liability Relating to the Distribution of Trust Property to the Beneficiary)
Article 226 (1) Where a trustee has distributed trust property to the beneficiary in violation of the provisions of the preceding Article, the persons listed in the following items shall have the joint and several liability specified in the respective items (in the case of the beneficiary set forth in item (ii), joint and several liability up to the amount of each distribution actually received); provided, however, that this shall not apply where the trustee proves that the trustee did not fail to exercise due care in performing the duties:

(i) the trustee: the liability to compensate the trust property with monies equivalent to the book value of the distribution (hereinafter referred to as the "distributed amount" in this Section); and

(ii) the beneficiary to whom the distribution was made: the liability to pay to the trustee monies equivalent to each distributed amount actually received.

(2) Where the trustee has satisfied the whole or part of the liability specified in item (i) of the preceding paragraph, the beneficiary set forth in item (ii) of said paragraph shall be released from the liability specified in item (ii) of said paragraph up to the amount obtained by multiplying the amount of liability satisfied by the ratio of the distributed amount as set forth in item (ii) of said paragraph to the distributed amount set forth in item (i) of said paragraph, and where the beneficiary has satisfied the liability specified in item (ii) of said paragraph in whole or in part, the trustee shall be released from the liability specified in item (i) of said paragraph up to the amount of liability satisfied.

(3) Monies paid by the beneficiary to the trustee pursuant to the provisions of paragraph (1) (limited to the part pertaining to item (ii)) shall belong to the trust property.

(4) No release may be granted for the liability prescribed in paragraph (1); provided, however, that this shall not apply where all beneficiaries consent to grant a release from said liability up to the maximum distributable amount as of the day on which the distribution was made.

(5) In the case prescribed in the main clause of paragraph (1), when there is another trustee who also has the liability set forth in item (i) of said paragraph in addition to the trustee set forth therein, these trustees shall be joint and several obligors.

(6) The provisions of Article 45 shall apply mutatis mutandis to any action pertaining to the claim under the provisions of paragraph (1).

(Restriction on Demands for Reimbursement from the Beneficiary)
Article 227 (1) In the case prescribed in the main clause of paragraph (1) of the preceding Article, if the beneficiary to whom the distribution was made had no knowledge of the fact that the amount of said distribution exceeded the maximum distributable amount as of the day on which said distribution was made, the beneficiary shall not be liable to satisfy the demand by the trustee for reimbursement with regard to the distributed amount.

(2) In the case prescribed in the main clause of paragraph (1) of the preceding Article, a trust creditor may have the beneficiary to whom the distribution was made, pay monies equivalent to the amount delivered (or the amount of the claim held by said trust creditor if the amount delivered exceeds the amount of the claim).

(Liability in Case of Deficit)
Article 228 (1) Where a trustee has distributed trust property to a beneficiary, if any deficit (meaning the amount obtained by deducting the amount of assets on the balance sheet from the amount of liabilities on the same in cases where the amount of liabilities exceeds the amount of assets; hereinafter the same shall apply in this paragraph) occurs as of the time set forth in Article 222, paragraph (4), when it first comes after the day on which said delivery was made, the persons listed in the following items shall have the joint and several liability specified in the respective items (in the case of the beneficiary set forth in item (ii), the joint and several liability up to the amount of each delivery actually received); provided, however, that this shall not apply where the trustee has proved that the trustee did not fail to exercise due care in performing trustee's duties:
  (i) the trustee: the liability to compensate the trust property with monies equivalent to the deficit (or the amount delivered if the deficit exceeds the distributed amount); and
  (ii) the beneficiary to whom the distribution was made: the liability to pay to the trustee monies equivalent to the deficit (or the amount of each delivery actually received if the deficit exceeds the amount delivered).
(2) Where the trustee has satisfied the liability specified in item (i) of the preceding paragraph in whole or in part, the beneficiary set forth in item (ii) of said paragraph shall be released from the liability specified in item (ii) of said paragraph up to the amount obtained by multiplying the amount of liability satisfied by the ratio of the distributed amount as set forth in item (ii) of said paragraph to the amount delivered as set forth in item (i) of said paragraph, and where the beneficiary has satisfied the liability specified in item (ii) of said paragraph in whole or in part, the trustee shall be released from the liability specified in item (i) of said paragraph up to the amount of liability satisfied.
(3) Monies paid by the beneficiary to the trustee pursuant to the provisions of paragraph (1) (limited to the part pertaining to item (ii)) shall fall under the trust property.
(4) No release may be granted for the liability prescribed in paragraph (1) without the consent of all beneficiaries.
(5) In the case prescribed in the main clause of paragraph (1), when there is another trustee who also has the liability set forth in item (i) of said paragraph in addition to the trustee set forth therein, these trustees shall be joint and several obligors.
(6) The provisions of Article 45 shall apply mutatis mutandis to any action pertaining to the demand under the provisions of paragraph (1).

(Public Notice to Creditors)
Article 229 (1) Without delay after assuming the office, the liquidation trustee of a limited liability trust shall give public notice in an official gazette to the effect that trust creditors should file their claims during a certain period of time, and shall give notice of the same separately to each known creditor; provided, however that said period may not be less than two months.
(2) The public notice under the provisions of the preceding paragraph shall be accompanied by a supplementary note that those trust creditors shall be excluded from the liquidation if they fail to file during said period.

(Restriction on Performance of Obligations)
Article 230 (1) A liquidation trustee of a limited liability trust may not perform any obligations of the limited liability trust in liquidation during the period set forth in paragraph (1) of the preceding Article. In this case, the liquidation trustee may not be released from the liability arising from the failure to perform such obligations.
(2) Notwithstanding the provisions of the preceding paragraph, even during the period set forth in paragraph (1) of the preceding Article, a liquidation trustee may, with the permission of the court, perform obligations pertaining to small claims, claims secured by security interests existing on property that belongs to the trust property of the limited liability trust in liquidation, and any other claims that are unlikely to harm other creditors even if they are performed. In this case, when there are two or more liquidation trustees, a petition for such permission shall be filed with the consent of all of them.
(3) When filing a petition for the permission set forth in the preceding paragraph, the liquidation trustee shall make a prima facie showing of the facts constituting the grounds for the petition.
(4) A judicial decision dismissing the petition set forth in paragraph (2) shall include the reasons therefor.
(5) No appeal may be entered against a judicial decision on the permission for performance under the provisions of paragraph (2).

(Exclusion from Liquidation)
Article 231 (1) Trust creditors of a limited liability trust in liquidation (excluding known creditors) who have not filed their claims during the period set forth in Article 229, paragraph (1) shall be excluded from the liquidation.
(2) Trust creditors excluded from the liquidation under the provisions of the preceding paragraph may demand satisfaction of their claims only with respect to undistributed residual assets.
(3) Where there are two or more beneficiaries, when residual assets of the limited liability trust in liquidation have been distributed to some of those beneficiaries, the assets necessary for delivery to beneficiaries other than said beneficiaries at the same proportion as that applied to the delivery received by those who have received it, shall be deducted from the residual assets set forth in the preceding paragraph.

Section 3 Registration of a Limited Liability Trust

(Registration of the Provisions on Limited Liability Trust Status)
Article 232 When the terms of trust has provided as set forth in Article 216, paragraph (1) the terms of trust, a registration of its provisions on the limited liability trust status shall be made within two weeks, by registering the following matters:
(i) the purpose of the limited liability trust;
(ii) the name of the limited liability trust;
(iii) the name and address of the trustee;
(iv) the place of administration of affairs of the limited liability trust;
(v) if a trust property administrator or incorporated trust property administrator has been appointed under the provisions of Article 64, paragraph (1) (including cases where applied mutatis mutandis pursuant to Article 74, paragraph (6)), the name and address thereof;
(vi) if the terms of trust contains provisions on the termination of the trust under the provisions of Article 163, item (ix), such provisions; and
(vii) if the trust is a trust with accounting auditors (meaning a trust with accounting auditors as prescribed in Article 248, paragraph (3); the same shall apply in Article

240, item (iii)), a statement to that effect and the names of the accounting auditors.

(Registration of Changes)
Article 233 (1) When there is a change to the place of administration of affairs of a limited liability trust, a registration of such change shall be made within two weeks at the former place of administration of affairs, and the matters listed in the items of the preceding Article shall be registered at the new place of administration of affairs.
(2) When there is a change to the place of administration of affairs of a limited liability trust within the jurisdictional district of the same registry office, it shall be sufficient to make a registration of such change.
(3) When there is a change to any of the matters listed in the items of the preceding Article (excluding item (iv)), a registration of such change shall be made within two weeks.

(Registration of Provisional Disposition Orders to Suspend the Execution of Duties, etc.)
Article 234 When an provisional disposition order is given to suspend the execution of duties by a trustee of a limited liability trust or to appoint a person who will execute such duties on behalf of the trustee, or when an order is given to change or revoke such provisional disposition order, a registration of such order shall be made at the place of administration of affairs of the trust.

(Registration of Termination)
Article 235 When a limited liability trust has terminated pursuant to the provisions of Article 163 (excluding the part pertaining to item (vi) and item (vii)) or Article 164, paragraph (1) or paragraph (3), or when a modification has been made to a trust to abolish the provisions set forth in Article 216, paragraph (1), a registration of the termination shall be made within two weeks.

(Registration of Liquidation Trustee)
Article 236 (1) When a limited liability trust has terminated, if the trustee at the time of the termination of the limited liability trust will be the liquidation trustee, the name and address of the liquidation trustee shall be registered within two weeks from the date of the termination.
(2) The provisions of the preceding paragraph shall also apply when a liquidation trustee is appointed pursuant to the provisions of the terms of trust or the provisions of Article 62, paragraph (1) or paragraph (4) or Article 173, paragraph (1).
(3) The provisions of Article 233, paragraph (3) shall apply mutatis mutandis to the registration under the provisions of the preceding two paragraphs.

(Registration of the Completion of Liquidation)
Article 237 When the liquidation of a limited liability trust has been completed, a registration of the completion of the liquidation shall be made within two weeks from the date of approval of the settlement of accounts set forth in Article 184, paragraph (1).

(Registry Office with Jurisdiction and the Registry)
Article 238 (1) Affairs for registration of a limited liability trust shall be administered by the Legal Affairs Bureau or District Legal Affairs Bureau, the branch bureau thereof, or the branch office of any of those bureaus, which has jurisdiction over the place of administration of affairs of the limited liability trust.
(2) A registry office shall keep a limited liability trust registry.

(Application for Registration)

Article 239 (1) Registrations under the provisions of Article 232 and Article 233 shall be made upon application by the trustee, and registrations under the provisions of Article 235 to Article 237 shall be made upon application by the liquidation trustee.

(2) Notwithstanding the provisions of the preceding paragraph, where a trust property administrator or incorporated trust property administrator has been appointed, registrations under the provisions of Article 232 and Article 233 (excluding a registration under the provisions of Article 246) shall be made upon application by such trust property administrator or incorporated trust property administrator.

(Attachments to a Registration of the Provisions on Limited Liability Trust Status)

Article 240 The following documents shall be attached to a written application for the registration of the provisions on limited liability trust status:

(i) a document certifying the terms of trust setting forth the limited liability trust;

(ii) if the trustee is a juridical person, a certificate of registered matters for the juridical person; provided, however, that this shall not apply where the head office or principal office of the juridical person is located within the jurisdictional district of the registry office;

(iii) in the case of a trust with an accounting auditor(s), the following documents:

  (a) a document certifying acceptance of the office(s);

  (b) if the accounting auditor is a juridical person, a certificate of registered matters for the juridical person; provided, however, that this shall not apply where the head office or principal office of the juridical person is located within the jurisdictional district of the registry office; and

  (c) if the accounting auditor is not a juridical person, a document certifying that the accounting auditor is a person prescribed in Article 249, paragraph (1).

(Attachments to a Registration of Changes)

Article 241 (1) When filing a written application for the registration of a change in the place of administration of affairs or a registration of a change in any of the matters listed in the items of Article 232 (excluding item (iv)), a document certifying the change in the place of administration of affairs or the change in the relevant registered matter shall be attached.

(2) When filing a written application for a registration of a change due to a new trustee who is a juridical person having assumed the office of trustee, the document set forth in item (ii) of the preceding Article shall be attached thereto.

(3) When filing a written application for a registration of a change due to an accounting auditor's assumption of the office, the document set forth in item (iii)(b) or (c) of the preceding Article shall be attached.

(Attachments to a Registration of Termination)

Article 242 When filing a written application for the registration of the termination of a limited liability trust, a document certifying the grounds for the termination shall be attached.

(Attachments to a Registration of Liquidation Trustee)

Article 243 (1) When filing a written application for the registration of a liquidation trustee in cases where any of the persons listed in the following items has become the liquidation trustee, the documents set forth in the respective items shall be attached:

(i) a person appointed by the provisions of the terms of trust: the following documents:
   (a) a document certifying that said provisions of the terms of trust exist; and
   (b) a document certifying that the appointed person has accepted the office;
(ii) a person appointed pursuant to the provisions of Article 62, paragraph (1): the following documents:
   (a) a document certifying that the agreement set forth in Article 62, paragraph (1) has been reached; and
   (b) a document set forth in (b) of the preceding item; or
(iii) a person appointed by the court pursuant to the provisions of Article 62, paragraph (4) or Article 173, paragraph (1): a document certifying the appointment.
(2) The provisions of Article 240 (limited to the part pertaining to item (ii)) shall apply mutatis mutandis to the registration of a liquidation trustee who is a juridical person.

(Attachments to the Registration of a Change Concerning the Liquidation Trustee)
Article 244 (1) When filing a written application for the registration of a change due to a liquidation trustee leaving the office, a document certifying that the office has been left shall be attached.
(2) When filing a written application for the registration of a change to any of the matters prescribed in Article 236, paragraph (1), a document certifying the change to the relevant registered matter shall be attached.
(3) The provisions of Article 241, paragraph (2) shall apply mutatis mutandis to the registration of a change due to a liquidation trustee who is a juridical person having assumed the office of liquidation trustee.

(Attachments to the Registration of the Completion of Liquidation)
Article 245 When filing a written application for the registration of the completion of liquidation, a document certifying that the settlement of accounts set forth in Article 184, paragraph (1) has been approved shall be attached.

(Commission of a Registration by Juridical Decision)
Article 246 In the following cases, a court clerk shall, on the clerk's own authority, and without delay, commission the registry office that has jurisdiction over the place of administration of affairs of a limited liability trust to make a registration of the respective matters:
(i) where any of the following judicial decisions has been made:
   (a) a judicial decision dismissing the trustee, trust property administrator, or incorporated trust property administrator under the provisions of Article 58, paragraph (4) (including cases where applied mutatis mutandis pursuant to Article 70 (including cases where applied mutatis mutandis pursuant to Article 74, paragraph (6))); or
   (b) a judicial decision appointing a trust property administrator or incorporated trust property administrator pursuant to the provisions of Article 64, paragraph (1) (including cases where applied mutatis mutandis pursuant to Article 74, paragraph (6)); or
(ii) where any of the following judicial decisions has become final and binding:
   (a) a judicial decision revoking the judicial decision set forth in (a) of the preceding item; or
   (b) a judicial decision ordering the termination of a trust under the provisions of Article 165 or Article 166.

(Application Mutatis Mutandis of the Commercial Registration Act and the Civil Preservation Act)

Article 247 With regard to the registration of a limited liability trust, the provisions of Article 2 to Article 5, Article 7 to Article 15, Article 17 (excluding paragraph (3)), Article 18 to Article 19-2, Article 20, paragraph (1) and paragraph (2), Article 21 to Article 24, Article 26, Article 27, Article 51 to Article 53, Article 71, paragraph (1), Article 132 to Article 137, and Article 139 to Article 148 of the Commercial Registration Act (Act No. 125 of 1963), and the provisions of Article 56 of the Civil Preservation Act shall apply mutatis mutandis. In this case, in Article 51, paragraph (1) of the Commercial Registration Act, the phrase "head office" shall be deemed to be replaced with "place of administration of affairs (meaning the place of administration of affairs as prescribed in Article 216, paragraph (2), item (iv) of the Trust Act (Act No. 108 of 2006); the same shall apply hereinafter)," and the term "relocation" shall be deemed to be replaced with "change"; in Article 51, paragraph (1) and Article 52, paragraph (2), paragraph (3), and paragraph (5) of said Act, the phrase "new location" shall be deemed to be replaced with "new place of administration of affairs"; in Article 51, paragraph (1) and paragraph (2) and Article 52 of said Act, the phrase "former location" shall be deemed to be replaced with "former place of administration of affairs"; in Article 71, paragraph (1), the term "dissolution" shall be deemed to be replaced with "termination of a limited liability trust"; and in Article 56 of the Civil Preservation Act, the phrase "representative or any other officer of a juridical person" shall be deemed to be replaced with "trustee or liquidation trustee of a limited liability trust," and the phrase "location of the head office and principal office or secondary office of the juridical person" shall be deemed to be replaced with "place of administration of affairs (meaning the place of administration of affairs as prescribed in Article 216, paragraph (2), item (iv) of the Trust Act (Act No. 108 of 2006) of the limited liability trust)."

Chapter X Special Rules on Limited Liability Trusts With Certificate of Beneficial Interest

(Appointment of an Accounting Auditor, etc.)

Article 248 (1) A limited liability trust which is a trust with certificates of beneficial interest (hereinafter referred to as a "limited liability trust with certificate of beneficial interest") may appoint an accounting auditor by the provisions of the terms of trust.

(2) A limited liability trust with certificate of beneficial interest which has reported a total of 20 billion yen or more in the liabilities section of its most recent balance sheet (meaning a balance sheet prepared at the most recent time set forth in Article 222, paragraph (4)) shall appoint an accounting auditor.

(3) In the case of a trust whose terms of trust has the provisions set forth in paragraph (1) and a trust prescribed in the preceding paragraph (hereinafter collectively referred to as a "trust with accounting auditors"), provisions designating an accounting auditor shall be established in the terms of trust.

(Qualifications of an Accounting Auditor, etc.)

Article 249 (1) An accounting auditor shall be a certified public accountant (including a foreign certified public accountant (meaning a foreign certified public accountant as prescribed in Article 16-2, paragraph (5) of the Certified Public Accountant Act (Act No. 103 of 1948)); the same shall apply in paragraph (3), item (ii)) or an auditing firm.

(2) An auditing firm which has been appointed as an accounting auditor shall select, from among its members, a person who is to perform the duties of an accounting auditor,

and notify the trustee thereof. In this case, the person set forth in item (ii) of the following paragraph may not be selected.
(3) None of the following persons may serve as an accounting auditor:
   (i) a person who, pursuant to the provisions of the Certified Public Accountant Act, may not audit the documents or electromagnetic records prescribed in Article 222, paragraph (4);
   (ii) a person who continuously receives remuneration from the trustee or an interested party thereof for business other than that of a certified public accountant or auditing firm, or the spouse of such person; and
   (iii) an auditing firm wherein half or more of the members fall under the preceding item.

(Measures to Be Taken in the Event of a Vacancy in the Position of Accounting Auditor)
Article 250 (1) In the case of a trust with accounting auditors, when there is a vacancy in the position of accounting auditor, the settlor and the beneficiary shall appoint, based on an agreement between them, a new accounting auditor within two months from the time when such vacancy of accounting auditor occurred.
(2) In the case prescribed in the preceding paragraph, if there is no settlor at the time in question or no agreement has been reached as set forth in said paragraph after the expiration of two months from the time when a vacancy of accounting auditor occurred, a new accounting auditor may be appointed independently by the beneficiary.
(3) In the cases prescribed in the preceding two paragraphs, when there are two or more beneficiaries, the trustee (if there is a trust supervisor at the time in question, the trustee or trust supervisor) shall convene a beneficiaries meeting without delay in order to appoint a new accounting auditor pursuant to the provisions of the preceding two paragraphs.
(4) When a new accounting auditor has been appointed pursuant to the provisions of paragraph (1) or paragraph (2), it shall be deemed that the provisions set forth in Article 248, paragraph (3) were established in the terms of trust with regard to the appointed new accounting auditor.
(5) Where there is a vacancy in the position of accounting auditor, an accounting auditor who has left office due to resignation shall continue to hold the rights and duties of an accounting auditor until a new accounting auditor is appointed.

(Resignation and Dismissal of Accounting Auditors)
Article 251 The provisions of the main clause of Article 57, paragraph (1) shall apply mutatis mutandis to the resignation of an accounting auditor, and the provisions of Article 58, paragraph (1) and paragraph (2) shall apply mutatis mutandis to the dismissal of an accounting auditor.

(Powers of the Accounting Auditor)
Article 252 (1) An accounting auditor shall audit the documents or electromagnetic records set forth in Article 222, paragraph (4). In this case, an accounting auditor shall prepare an accounting audit report as provided for by Ordinance of the Ministry of Justice.
(2) An accounting auditor may, at any time, inspect and copy the following objects or request a trustee to make a report on accounting:
   (i) if the accounting books or materials relating thereto are prepared in the form of documents, such documents; and
   (ii) if accounting books or materials relating thereto are prepared in the form of elec-

tromagnetic records, any object which indicates the matters recorded in the electromagnetic records by a method specified by Ordinance of the Ministry of Justice.
(3) An accounting auditor, in the course of performing the duties, may not employ a person who falls under any of the following:
 (i) the person set forth in Article 249, paragraph (3) item (i) or item (ii);
 (ii) the trustee or an interested party thereof; or
 (iii) a person who continuously receives remuneration from the trustee or an interested party thereof for business other than that of a certified public accountant or auditing firm.
(4) For the purpose of the application of the provisions of Article 222, paragraph (4), paragraph (5) and paragraph (8) in the case of a trust with accounting auditors, the term "prepare" in paragraph (4) of said Article shall be deemed to be replaced with "prepare and receive an accounting audit set forth in Article 252, paragraph (1) of," the phrase "the content thereof" in paragraph (5) of said Article shall be deemed to be replaced with "the content thereof and an accounting audit report," the phrase "prepared" in paragraph (8) of said Article shall be deemed to be replaced with "prepared and received an accounting audit set forth in Article 252, paragraph (1) of," and the phrase "such documents)" in paragraph (8) of said Article shall be deemed to be replaced with "such documents) and the accounting audit report."

(Accounting Auditor's Duty of Care)
Article 253 An accounting auditor shall perform the duties with the due care of a prudent manager.

(Accounting Auditor's Liability to Compensate for Losses, etc.)
Article 254 (1) When any loss has occurred to the trust property due to an accounting auditor's negligence in the performance of the duties, the beneficiary may demand that the accounting auditor compensate for such loss.
(2) Monies or other property delivered by the accounting auditor to the trustee as compensation for the loss under the provisions of the preceding paragraph shall belong to the trust property.
(3) The provisions of Article 42 (limited to the part pertaining to item (i)) and Article 105, paragraph (3) and paragraph (4) (excluding item (iii)) shall apply mutatis mutandis to a release from liability under the provisions of paragraph (1), the provisions of Article 43 shall apply mutatis mutandis to the claim pertaining to liability under the provisions of paragraph (1), and the provisions of Article 45 shall apply mutatis mutandis to an action pertaining to the demand under the provisions of paragraph (1). In this case, the phrase "the trustee has shown bad faith or gross negligence in the performance of the duties" in Article 105, paragraph (4), item (ii) shall be deemed to be replaced with "the accounting auditor has shown bad faith or gross negligence in the performance of the duties."

(Accounting Auditor's Liability to Third Parties)
Article 255 (1) In the case of a trust with accounting auditors, if an accounting auditor was willful or grossly negligent in the performance of the duties, the accounting auditor shall be liable to compensate for any damage suffered by a third party arising therefrom.
(2) The provisions of the preceding paragraph shall also apply when the accounting auditor of a trust with accounting auditors has made a false statement or record on the matters that should be stated or recorded in the accounting audit report set forth in Article 252, paragraph (1); provided, however, that this shall not apply if the account-

ing auditor proves that the accounting auditor did not fail to exercise due care in carrying out said act.
(3) In the cases referred to in the preceding two paragraphs, when there is another accounting auditor who is also liable to compensate for the damages in addition to the accounting auditor set forth therein, these accounting auditors shall be joint and several obligors.

(Expenses, etc. and Remuneration of Accounting Auditor)
Article 256 The provisions of Article 127, paragraph (1) to paragraph (5) shall apply mutatis mutandis to expenses and interest thereon accruing from the date of payment, compensation for damages, and remuneration payable to an accounting auditor.

(Special Rules for Beneficiaries Meetings)
Article 257 For the purpose of the application of the provisions of Article 118 in cases where the terms of trust for a trust with accounting auditors does not otherwise provide as set forth in Article 214, the phrase "the same shall apply in the following paragraph)" in Article 118, paragraph (1) shall be deemed to be replaced with "the same shall apply in the following paragraph) and an accounting auditor," and the term "trustee" in Article 118, paragraph (2) shall be deemed to be replaced with "trustee or accounting auditor."

Chapter XI Special Rules for a Trust with No Provisions on Beneficiaries

(Requirements for a Trust With No Provisions on the Beneficiary)
Article 258 (1) A trust with no provisions on the beneficiary (including provisions on the method for specifying a beneficiary; the same shall apply hereinafter) may be created by the method set forth in Article 3, item (i) or item (ii).
(2) In the case of a trust with no provisions on the beneficiary, provisions on the beneficiary may be established by making a modification to the trust.
(3) In the case of a trust with provisions on the beneficiary, such provisions on the beneficiary may not be abolished by making a modification to the trust.
(4) When a trust with no provisions on the beneficiary is to be created by the method set forth in Article 3, item (ii), provisions to designate a trust caretaker shall be established. In this case, no provisions may be established to restrict the trust caretaker's power to exercise the rights listed in the items of Article 145, paragraph (2) (excluding item (vi)).
(5) In the case of a trust with no provisions on the beneficiary which was created by the method set forth in Article 3, item (ii) and for which there are no provisions for designating a trust caretaker, if there are provisions on the executor, the executor shall appoint a trust caretaker. In this case, when the executor has appointed a trust caretaker, it shall be deemed that the provisions set forth in the first sentence of the preceding paragraph were established in the terms of trust with regard to the appointed trust caretaker.
(6) In the case of a trust with no provisions on the beneficiary which was created by the method set forth in Article 3, item (ii) and for which there are no provisions designating a trust caretaker, if there are no provisions on the executor or if the person designated as the one who is to be the executor does not appoint or is unable to appoint a trust caretaker, the court may appoint a trust caretaker at the petition of an interested party. In this case, when a judicial decision on the appointment of a trust caretaker has

been made, it shall be deemed that the provisions set forth in the first sentence of paragraph (4) were established in the terms of trust with regard to the appointed trust caretaker.
(7) The provisions of Article 123, paragraph (6) to paragraph (8) shall apply mutatis mutandis to a judicial decision on the petition set forth in the preceding paragraph.
(8) In the case of a trust with no provisions on the beneficiary which was created by the method set forth in Article 3, item (ii), the trust shall terminate where there is a vacancy in the position of trust caretaker and the position has not been filled with a new trust caretaker for one year.

(Duration of a Trust with No Provisions on the Beneficiary)
Article 259 The duration of a trust with no provisions on the beneficiary may not exceed 20 years.

(Settlor's Rights in a Trust with No Provisions on the Beneficiary)
Article 260 (1) In the case of a trust with no provisions on the beneficiary which was created by the method set forth in Article 3, item (i), it shall be deemed as having been provided that the settlor (if there are two or more settlors, all settlors) shall have the rights listed in the items of Article 145, paragraph (2) (excluding item (vi)) and that the trustee shall have the duties listed in the items of paragraph (4) of said Article. In this case, such provisions may not be changed by making a modification to the trust.
(2) In the case of a trust with no provisions on the beneficiary which was created by the method set forth in Article 3, item (ii), if it is deemed, pursuant to the provisions of the second sentence of Article 258, paragraph (5) or the second sentence of paragraph (6) of said Article, that the provisions set forth in the first sentence of paragraph (4) of said Article have been established, it is not allowable to restrict the trust caretaker's power to exercise the rights listed in the items of Article 145, paragraph (2) (excluding item (vi)) by making a modification to the trust.

(Application of This Act)
Article 261 (1) For the purpose of the application of the provisions of this Act listed in the left-hand column of the following table with regard to a trust with no provisions on the beneficiary, the terms and phrases listed in the middle column of said table shall be deemed to be replaced with the terms and phrases listed in the right-hand column of said table, respectively:

Article 19, paragraph (1), item (iii) and paragraph (3), item (iii)	will not harm the interests of the beneficiary	will not hinder the achievement of the purpose of the trust
	between the trustee and the beneficiary	that the trustee has with regard to the purpose of the trust
Article 19, paragraph (3), item (ii)	agreement between the beneficiaries of both trusts (if there is a trust administrator for each trust at the time in question, the trust administrators)	agreement between the trust administrator of the trust with no provisions on the beneficiary and the beneficiary of the other trust (if there is a trust administrator at the time in question, the trust administrator), or on an agreement between the trust administrators of both trusts with no provisions on

		the beneficiary
Article 30	on behalf of the beneficiary	for the achievement of the purpose of the trust
Article 31, paragraph (1), item (iv)	would cause a conflict of interest between the trustee or an interested party thereof and the beneficiary	would be in the interest of the trustee or an interested party thereof and impede the achievement of the purpose of the trust
Article 31, paragraph (2), item (iv)	will not harm the interests of the beneficiary	will not hinder the achievement of the purpose of the trust
	between the trustee and the beneficiary	that the trustee has with regard to the purpose of the trust
Article 32, paragraph (1)	be contrary to the interest of a beneficiary	hinder the achievement of the purpose of the trust
Proviso to Article 37, paragraph (4)	beneficiary (beneficiaries)	settlor(s)
	to the trust administrator	to the trust administrator or settlor
Proviso to Article 37, paragraph (6)	beneficiary	settlor
Article 38, paragraph (2), item (iii)	harming the common interests of the beneficiaries	hindering the achievement of the purpose of the trust
Article 57, paragraph (1)	the settlor and the beneficiary	the settlor (if there is a trust administrator at the time in question, the settlor and the trust administrator)
Article 58, paragraph (1)	The settlor and the beneficiary may, at any time based on an agreement between them	The settlor may, at any time (if there is a trust administrator at the time in question, the settlor and the trust administrator may, at any time based on an agreement between them)
Article 58, paragraph (2)	the settlor and the beneficiary have	the settlor has (if there is a trust administrator at the time in question, the settlor and the trust administrator have)
	the settlor and the beneficiary	the settlor
Article 62, paragraph (1)	the settlor and the beneficiary may, based on an agreement between them	the settlor may (if there is a trust administrator at the time in question, the settlor and the trust administrator may, based on an agreement between them,)
Article 62, paragraph (3)	the settlor and the beneficiary (if there are two or more beneficiaries at the time in question, to one of them; if there is a trust administrator at the time in question, to the trust administrator)	the settlor (if there is a trust administrator at the time in question, to the settlor and the trust administrator)

Article 62, paragraph (4)	status of discussions pertaining to the agreement set forth in said paragraph	status of the settlor (if there is a trust administrator at the time in question, the status of discussions pertaining to the agreement set forth in said paragraph)
Article 62, paragraph (8)	"the beneficiary may"	"the trust administrator may"
	"the beneficiary"	"the trust administrator"
	"status of the beneficiary"	"status of the trust administrator"
Article 125, paragraph (1)	on behalf of a beneficiary	for the achievement of the purpose of the trust
Article 126, paragraph (2)	on behalf of the beneficiary	for the achievement of the purpose of the trust
Article 146, paragraph (1)	the trustee and the beneficiary	the trustee
Article 146, paragraph (2)	other settlor(s), the trustee, and the beneficiary.	other settlor(s) and the trustee
Article 149, paragraph (1)	the settlor, the trustee, and the beneficiary	the settlor and the trustee (if there is a trust administrator at the time in question, the settlor, the trustee, and the trust administrator)
Article 149, paragraph (2) (excluding item (i))	to the settlor and the beneficiary	to the settlor (if there is a trust administrator at the time in question, to the settlor and the trust administrator)
	is not contrary to the purpose of the trust and that it conforms to the interests of the beneficiary	is necessary for the achievement of the purpose of the trust
Article 149, paragraph (3), item (i)	the settlor and the beneficiary	the settlor (if there is a trust administrator at the time in question, to the settlor and the trust administrator)
Article 149, paragraph (5)	to the beneficiary	to the trust administrator
Article 150, paragraph (1)	no longer conforms to the interest of the beneficiary	comes to hinder the achievement of the purpose of the trust
Article 151, paragraph (1)	the settlors, trustees, and beneficiaries of the former trusts	the settlors and trustees of the former trusts (if there are trust administrators at the time in question, the settlors, the trustees, and the trust administrators)
Article 151, paragraph (2) (excluding item (i))	to the settlor and the beneficiary	to the settlor (if there is a trust administrator at the time in question, to the settlor and the trust administrator)

	is not contrary to the purpose of the trust and that it conforms to the interests of the beneficiary	is necessary for the achievement of the purpose of the trust
Article 151, paragraph (4)	to the beneficiary	to the trust administrator
Article 155, paragraph (1)	the settlor, the trustee, and the beneficiary	the settlor and the trustee (if there is a trust administrator at the time in question, the settlor, the trustee, and the trust administrator)
Article 155, paragraph (2) (excluding item (i))	to the settlor and the beneficiary	to the settlor (if there is a trust administrator at the time in question, to the settlor and the trust administrator)
	is not contrary to the purpose of the trust and that it conforms to the interests of the beneficiary	is necessary for the achievement of the purpose of the trust
Article 155, paragraph (4)	to the beneficiary	to the trust administrator
Article 159, paragraph (1)	the settlor, the trustee, and the beneficiary	the settlor and the trustee (if there is a trust administrator at the time in question, the settlor, the trustee, and the trust administrator)
Article 159, paragraph (2) (excluding item (i))	to the settlor and the beneficiary	to the settlor (if there is a trust administrator at the time in question, to the settlor and the trust administrator)
	is not contrary to the purpose of the trust: an agreement between the trustee and the beneficiary	is necessary for the achievement of the purpose of the trust
Article 159, paragraph (4)	to the beneficiary	to the trust administrator
Article 164, paragraph (1)	The settlor and the beneficiary may, at any time based on an agreement between them	The settlor may, at any time (if there is a trust administrator at the time in question, the settlor and the trust administrator may, at any time based on an agreement between them)
Article 164, paragraph (2)	the settlor and the beneficiary have	the settlor has (if there is a trust administrator at the time in question, the settlor and the trust administrator have)
	the settlor and the beneficiary	the settlor
Article 165, paragraph (1)	has come to be in the best interest of the beneficiary	has come to be reasonable

Proviso to Article 222, paragraph (6)	Beneficiary (beneficiaries)	settlor(s)
	to the trust administrator	to the trust administrator or the settlor
Proviso to Article 222, paragraph (8)	beneficiary	settlor
Article 243, paragraph (1), item (ii)(a)	the agreement	the settlor's manifest intent (if there is a trust administrator at the time in question, the agreement between the settlor and the trust administrator) as

(2) With regard to expenses, etc., compensation for loss, and trust fees for a trustee in the case of a trust with no provisions on the beneficiary, the provisions of Article 48, paragraph (5) (including cases where applied mutatis mutandis pursuant to Article 53, paragraph (2) and Article 54, paragraph (4)) shall not apply.
(3) With regard to a modification of a trust in the case of a trust with no provisions on the beneficiary, the provisions of Article 149, paragraph (2), item (i) and paragraph (3), item (ii) shall not apply.
(4) With regard to the consolidation of trusts in the case of trusts with no provisions on the beneficiary, the provisions of Article 151, paragraph (2), item (i) shall not apply.
(5) With regard to the split of a trust in the case of a trust with no provisions on the beneficiary, the provisions of Article 155, paragraph (2), item (i) and Article 159, paragraph (2), item (i) shall not apply.

Chapter XII Miscellaneous Provisions

Section 1 Non-Contentious Cases

(Jurisdiction over Non-Contentious Cases Relating to Trusts)

Article 262 (1) Unless otherwise provided for in this Article, a non-contentious case under the provisions of this Act shall be subject to the jurisdiction of the district court having jurisdiction over the location of the address of the trustee.
(2) For the purpose of the application of the provisions of the preceding paragraph in cases where there are two or more trustees, the phrase "address of the trustee" in said paragraph shall be deemed to be replaced with "address of any of the trustees."
(3) A case pertaining to a petition to the court filed under the provisions of this Act after the termination of a trustee's duty as trustee and prior to the assumption of the office by a new trustee shall be subject to the jurisdiction of the district court having jurisdiction over the address of the former trustee.
(4) For the purpose of the application of the provisions of the preceding paragraph in cases where there are two or more trustees, the phrase "termination of a trustee's duty as trustee" in said paragraph shall be deemed to be replaced with "termination of all trustees' duties as trustees," and for the purpose of the application of the provisions of said paragraph in cases where there are two or more former trustees, the phrase "address of the former trustee" in said paragraph shall be deemed to be replaced with "address of any of the former trustees."
(5) A case pertaining to a petition set forth in Article 6, paragraph (1) or Article 258, paragraph (6) shall be subject to the jurisdiction of the district court having jurisdiction over the testator's last address.

(Special Rules for Procedures for Non-Contentious Cases Relating to Trusts)
Article 263 With regard to non-contentious cases under the provisions of this Act, the provisions of Article 15 of the Non-Contentious Cases Procedures Act shall not apply.

(Supreme Court Rules)
Article 264 In addition to what is provided for in this Act, the necessary matters concerning procedures for non-contentious cases under the provisions of this Act shall be prescribed by the Rules of the Supreme Court.

Section 2 Public Notice, etc.

(Method of Public Notice in the Case of a Trustee Who Is a Juridical Person)
Article 265 In cases where a trustee (after the termination of a trustee's duty as trustee and prior to the assumption of the duty by a new trustee, the former trustee) is a juridical person, public notice under the provisions of this Act (excluding Article 152, paragraph (2), Article 156, paragraph (2), Article 160, paragraph (2) and Article 229, paragraph (1)) shall be given in accordance with the method of public notice (including the period of public notice) which is used by said juridical person.

(Special Rules for Public Notice Procedures, etc. in the Case of the Merger, etc. of a Trustee Who Is a Juridical Person)
Article 266 (1) Where it is provided that creditors of a juridical person may state their objections through a public notice, separate notice, or other procedures with regard to an entity conversion, merger, or any other act to be conducted by the juridical person pursuant to the provisions of the Companies Act and other laws, when a trustee is such a juridical person intends to conduct such an act, creditors who hold claims pertaining to obligation covered by the trust property that the trustee is only liable for using property that belongs to the trust property to perform shall not be included in the scope of such creditors who may state their objections through such procedures with regard to said act.
(2) For the purpose of the application of the provisions on the transfer of a business of a juridical person under the provisions of the Companies Act and other Acts, a trust created by the method set forth in Article 3, item (iii) shall be included in the scope of acts subject to these provisions; provided, however, that this shall not apply if such Acts otherwise provide.

Chapter XIII Penal Provisions

(Crime of Bribery by or of the Trustee, etc. of a Limited Liability Trust With Certificate of Beneficial Interest)
Article 267 (1) When any of the following persons, in connection with such person's duties, has accepted, solicited, or promised to accept a bribe, the person shall be punished by imprisonment with work for not more than three years or a fine of not more than three million yen. When such person has committed misconduct or failed to conduct an appropriate act due to such a bribe, the person shall be punished by imprisonment with work for not more than five years or a fine of not more than five million yen:
  (i) a trustee (including a former trustee or liquidation trustee; the same shall apply hereinafter) of a limited liability trust with certificate of beneficial interest;

(ii) a trust property administrator of a limited liability trust with certificate of beneficial interest;
(iii) a person who acts for the trustee of a limited liability trust with certificate of beneficial interest, who was appointed by an order of provisional disposition prescribed in Article 56 of the Civil Preservation Act;
(iv) an incorporated trust property administrator of a limited liability trust with certificate of beneficial interest;
(v) a trust caretaker of a limited liability trust with certificate of beneficial interest;
(vi) a trust supervisor of a limited liability trust with certificate of beneficial interest;
(vii) a beneficiary's agent in a limited liability trust with certificate of beneficial interest;
(viii) an inspector of a limited liability trust with certificate of beneficial interest; and
(ix) an accounting auditor.
(2) A person who has given, offered, or promised to offer a bribe prescribed in the preceding paragraph shall be punished by imprisonment with work for not more than three years or a fine of not more than three million yen.
(3) In the case referred to in paragraph (1), any bribe accepted by the offender shall be confiscated. If the whole or part of the bribe cannot be confiscated, the equivalent value thereof shall be collected.

(Crimes Committed Outside Japan)
Article 268 (1) The crime set forth in paragraph (1) of the preceding Article shall also apply to a person who has committed the crime set forth in said paragraph outside Japan.
(2) The crime set forth in paragraph (2) of the preceding Article shall be governed by the provisions of Article 2 of the Penal Code (Act No. 45 of 1907).

(Application of Penal Provisions to Juridical Persons)
Article 269 If the person prescribed in Article 267, paragraph (1) is a juridical person, the provisions of said paragraph shall apply to the director, executive officer, or any other officer executing business or manager who has committed such act.

(Acts to Be Punished by Non-Criminal Fine)
Article 270 (1) Where the trustee, the former trustee's heir, etc. as prescribed in Article 60, paragraph (1), the trust property administrator, a person who acts for the trustee who was appointed by an order of provisional disposition prescribed in Article 56 of the Civil Preservation Act, or the incorporated trust property administrator, trust caretaker, trust supervisor, beneficiary's agent, or inspector falls under any of the following, such person shall be punished by a non-penal fine of not more than one million yen; provided, however, that this shall not apply if the act in question should be subject to a criminal punishment:
(i) when the person has failed to give public notice or other notice under the provisions of this Act or has given improper public notice or other notice;
(ii) when the person has failed to disclose matters under the provisions of this Act;
(iii) when the person has, in violation of the provisions of this Act, refused to allow the inspection or copying of documents or any object which indicates the matters recorded in electromagnetic records by a method specified by Ordinance of the Ministry of Justice, without justifiable grounds;
(iv) when the person has failed to give a report under the provisions of this Act or when the person has given a false report;
(v) when the person has obstructed an investigation under the provisions of this Act;

Art.270　　　　　　③ Trust Act, Chap.XIII

 (vi) when the person has failed to prepare or preserve the documents or electromagnetic records set forth in Article 37, paragraph (1), paragraph (2) or paragraph (5) or the minutes set forth in Article 120 (limited to cases where it is provided by the terms of trust that the beneficiaries' decision shall be made by a majority vote at a beneficiaries meeting as provided for in Chapter IV, Section 3, Subsection 2), when the person has failed to state or record matters that should be stated or recorded in such documents or records, or when the person has made false statements or records;

 (vii) when the person has effected a consolidation of trusts or split of a trust in violation of the provisions of Article 152, paragraph (2) or paragraph (5), Article 156, paragraph (2) or paragraph (5) or Article 160, paragraph (2) or paragraph (5);

 (viii) when the person has, in violation of the provision of Article 179, paragraph (1), failed to file a petition for the commencement of bankruptcy proceedings; or

 (ix) when the person has, in violation of the provision of Article 181, distributed property that belongs to the trust property in liquidation.

(2) Where the trustee, the trust property administrator, a person who acts for the trustee who was appointed by an order of provisional disposition prescribed in Article 56 of the Civil Preservation Act, or the incorporated trust property administrator, trust supervisor, or beneficial interest registry administrator of a trust with certificates of beneficial interest falls under any of the following, such person shall be punished by a non-criminal fine of not more than one million yen; provided, however, that this shall not apply if the act in question should be subject to criminal punishment:

 (i) when the person has failed to prepare or preserve the minutes set forth in Article 120 (limited to cases where the terms of trust does not otherwise provide as set forth in Article 214) or the beneficial interest registry set forth in Article 186, when the person has failed to state or record matters that should be stated or recorded in these documents or records, or when the person has made false statements or records;

 (ii) when the person has, in violation of the provisions of Article 187, paragraph (1) or Article 202, paragraph (1), refused to deliver documents or provide electromagnetic records;

 (iii) when the person has, in violation of the provisions of Article 190, paragraph (1), failed to keep the beneficial interest registry set forth in Article 186;

 (iv) when the person has, in violation of the provisions of Article 207, failed to issue a certificate of beneficial interest without delay; or

 (v) when the person has, in violation of the provisions of Article 209, failed to state matters on a certificate of beneficial interest or has made false statements.

(3) Where the trustee, the trust property administrator, a person who acts for the trustee who was appointed by an order of provisional disposition prescribed in Article 56 of the Civil Preservation Act, or the incorporated trust property administrator of a limited liability trust falls under any of the following, such person shall be punished by a non-criminal fine of not more than one million yen; provided, however, that this shall not apply if the act in question should be subject to criminal punishment:

 (i) when the person has failed to make a registration under the provisions of Chapter IX, Section 3;

 (ii) when the person has failed to prepare or preserve the accounting books set forth in Article 222, paragraph (2), the balance sheet set forth in paragraph (3) of said Article or the documents or electromagnetic records set forth in paragraph (4) or paragraph (7) of said Article, when the person has failed to state or record matters that should be stated or recorded in these documents or records, or when the person has made false statements or records;

(iii) when the person has, with the intention of delaying the completion of the liquidation, inappropriately specified the period set forth in Article 229, paragraph (1); or
(iv) when the person has performed any obligation in violation of the provisions of Article 230, paragraph (1).
(4) When the trustee, the trust property administrator, a person who acts for the trustee who was appointed by an order of provisional disposition prescribed in Article 56 of the Civil Preservation Act, or the incorporated trust property administrator or trust supervisor of a trust with accounting auditors has, in violation of the provisions of Article 250, paragraph (3), failed to carry out the procedures for appointing an accounting auditor, such person shall be punished by a non-criminal fine of not more than one million yen; provided, however, that this shall not apply if the act in question should be subject to criminal punishment.

Article 271 A person who falls under any of the following shall be punished by a non-criminal fine of not more than one million yen:
(i) a person who has, in violation of the provisions of Article 218, paragraph (1), failed to use the characters representing the term "limited liability trust" in the name of a limited liability trust;
(ii) a person who has, in violation of the provisions of Article 218, paragraph (2), used, in its name or trade name, any characters which make it likely that a trust will be mistaken for a limited liability trust; or
(iii) a person who has, in violation of the provisions of Article 218, paragraph (3), used any name or trade name which makes it likely that a limited liability trust will be mistaken for another limited liability trust.

Supplementary Provisions

(Effective Date)
(1) This Act shall come into effect as of the day specified by Cabinet Order within a period not exceeding one year and six months from the date of its promulgation.

(Transitional Measures Concerning a Declaration of Trust)
(2) The provisions of Article 3, item (iii) shall not apply until the day on which one year has elapsed from the date of enforcement of this Act.

(Transitional Measures Concerning Trusts with No Provisions on the Beneficiary)
(3) Until a date specified separately by law, a trust with no provisions on the beneficiary (excluding trusts to be created for academic activities, art, charity, worship, religion, or any other public interest) may not be created by designating, as the trustee, a person other than a juridical person specified by Cabinet Order as having sufficient financial basis and personnel structure to appropriately administer trust affairs concerning said trust.
(4) The date specified separately by law set forth in the preceding paragraph shall be considered in light of the status of the review of trusts with no provisions on their beneficiaries which are created for academic activities, art, charity, worship, religion, or other public interest, as well as other circumstances concerned, and shall be determined based on such consideration.

④ Trust Business Act

(Act No. 154 of December 3, 2004)

The Trust Business Act (Act No. 65 of 1922) shall be fully revised.

Chapter I General Provisions (Articles 1 and 2)
Chapter II Trust Companies
  Section 1 General Provisions (Articles 3 to 16)
  Section 2 Major Shareholders (Articles 17 to 20)
  Section 3 Business (Articles 21 to 31)
  Section 4 Accounting (Articles 32 to 35)
  Section 5 Supervision (Articles 36 to 50)
  Section 6 Special Provisions Concerning Specific Trusts (Articles 50-2 to 52)
Chapter III Foreign Trust Business Operators (Articles 53 to 64)
Chapter IV Persons Authorized to Give Directions (Articles 65 and 66)
Chapter V Agents for Trust Agreement
  Section 1 General Provisions (Articles 67 to 73)
  Section 2 Business (Articles 74 to 76)
  Section 3 Accounting (Articles 77 and 78)
  Section 4 Supervision (Articles 79 to 84)
  Section 5 Miscellaneous Provisions (Article 85)
Chapter VI Miscellaneous Provisions (Articles 86 to 90)
Chapter VII Penal Provisions (Articles 91 to 100)
  Supplementary Provisions

Chapter I General Provisions

(Purpose)
Article 1 The purpose of this Act is to ensure the protection of the settlors and beneficiaries of trusts by securing fairness in the acceptance of trusts and other transactions related thereto through the provision of the necessary matters for such persons as those carrying out Trust Business, and thereby to contribute to the sound development of the national economy.

(Definitions)
Article 2 (1) The term "Trust Business" as used in this Act shall mean business that is carried out for accepting trusts (excluding business involving the receipt of deposits of money to be allocated for costs pertaining to other transactions and excluding such business incidental to other transactions which are specified by a Cabinet Order as being found not to interfere with the protection of settlors and beneficiaries thereof after taking into consideration of the content and other matters of such transactions,; the same shall apply hereinafter).
(2) The term "Trust Company" as used in this Act shall mean a person who has been licensed by the Prime Minister under Article 3 or registered by the Prime Minister under Article 7(1).
(3) The term "Custodian Type Custodian Trust Business" as used in this Act shall mean business that is carried out for accepting only those trusts that fall under any of the following items:

(i) trusts wherein trust property is managed or disposed of (including performance of any act as may be necessary for achieving the purpose of said trust; the same shall apply hereinafter) only under instructions from the settlor or any person delegated by the settlor to give instructions (limited to the cases where the settlor or the person delegated by the settlor to give instructions is a person other than those specified by a Cabinet Order as having a close share-capital or personal relationship with the trustee); or

(ii) trusts wherein trust property is only preserved, or only utilized or improved to the extent that it does not change the nature of the property.

(4) The term "Custodian Type Trust Company" as used in this Act shall mean a company which has been registered by the Prime Minister under Article 7(1).

(5) The term "Foreign Trust Business Operator" as used in this Act shall mean a person who carries out Trust Business in a foreign country according to that country's laws and regulations (excluding a Trust Company).

(6) The term "Foreign Trust Company" as used in this Act shall mean a company which has been licensed by the Prime Minister under Article 53(1) or registered by the Prime Minister under Article 54(1).

(7) The term "Custodian Type Foreign Trust Company" as used in this Act shall mean a company which has been registered by the Prime Minister under Article 54(1).

(8) The term "Agency for Trust Agreements" as used in this Act shall mean business that is carried out for acting as an agent (limited to the case of acting as an agent for a Trust Company or a Foreign Trust Company) or an intermediary in concluding a trust agreement (excluding the case where the trustee of a trust based on said trust agreement is to be a person who has issued beneficial interest in said trust (including securities or a deed indicating said beneficial interest) (meaning an issuer as prescribed in Article 2(5) of the Financial Instruments and Exchange Act (Act No. 25 of 1948))).

(9) The term "Agent for Trust Agreement" as used in this Act shall mean an agency which has been registered by the Prime Minister under Article 67(1).

Chapter II Trust Companies

Section 1 General Provisions

(License)

Article 3 No person may carry out Trust Business without obtaining a license from the Prime Minister.

(Application for License)

Article 4 (1) A person who wishes to obtain the license set forth in the preceding Article shall submit to the Prime Minister a written application therefor stating the following matters:

(i) the trade name;

(ii) the amount of stated capital;

(iii) the names of directors and company auditors (in the case of a company with committees, directors and executive officers; the same shall apply in Article 8(1));

(iv) in the case of a company with accounting advisors, the names of the accounting advisors;

(v) where the person carries out business other than trust business, the type of business; and

(vi) the names and locations of the head office and other business offices.

(2) The following documents shall be attached to the written application set forth in the

preceding paragraph:
(i) the articles of incorporation;
(ii) a certificate of the registered matters of the company;
(iii) a statement of operational procedures;
(iv) a balance sheet;
(v) a document stating expected income and expenditures; and
(vi) other documents specified by a Cabinet Office Ordinance.
(3) The statement of operational procedures set forth in item (iii) of the preceding paragraph shall state the following matters:
(i) the type of trust property accepted;
(ii) the method of management or disposition of trust property:
(iii) the method of management of segregated trust property;
(iv) the system for carrying out trust business;
(v) in cases where part of trust business is delegated to a third party, the content of trust business delegated as well as standards and procedures pertaining to selection of the person delegated with said part of trust business (excluding the case where business listed in the items of Article 22(3) is delegated);
(vi) where the person carries out Business for the Sale and Purchase, etc. of Beneficial Interest in Trust (which means business related to conducting the sale and purchase of beneficial interest in trust as prescribed in Article 65-5(1) of the Financial Instruments and Exchange Act; the same shall apply hereinafter), the system for carrying out said business; and
(vii) other matters specified by a Cabinet Office Ordinance.

(Licensing Standards)
Article 5 (1) Where an application for a license under Article 3 has been filed, the Prime Minister shall examine whether the person filing said application (referred to as the "Applicant" in the following paragraph) conforms to the following standards:
(i) that the provisions of the articles of incorporation and the statement of operational procedures conform to laws and regulations and are also sufficient for the proper execution of trust business;
(ii) that the applicant has a sufficient financial basis to allow for the sound execution of trust business; and
(iii) in light of personnel composition, the applicant has knowledge and experience that allow for the right execution of trust business and also has sufficient social credibility.
(2) When the Applicant falls under any of the following items, or when the written application set forth in paragraph (1) of the preceding Article or any of the attached documents listed in the items of paragraph (2) of that Article include any false statements or fail to state any material facts, the Prime Minister shall not grant said Applicant a license.
(i) a person who is not a stock company (limited to stock companies in which the following entities are present):
(a) a board of directors; and
(b) company auditors or committees (meaning committees as prescribed in Article 2(xii) of the Companies Act (Act No. 86 of 2005));
(ii) a stock company whose amount of stated capital is less than the amount specified by a Cabinet Order as necessary and appropriate for the protection of settlors or beneficiaries;
(iii) a stock company whose amount of net assets is less than the amount prescribed in the preceding item;

(iv) a stock company which intends to use a trade name that is identical to a trade name already in use by another Trust Company or a trade name that is likely to cause misidentification with another Trust Company;
(v) a stock company for which the renewal of a registration under Article 7(3) has been refused pursuant to the provisions of Article 10(1), whose license under Article 3 has been rescinded pursuant to the provisions of Article 44(1), whose registration under Article 7(1), Article 50-2(1), or Article 52(1) has been rescinded pursuant to the provisions of Article 45(1), for which the renewal of a registration under Article 7(3), as applied mutatis mutandis pursuant to Article 50-2(2), has been refused pursuant to the provisions of paragraph (6) of that Article, whose registration under Article 67(1) has been rescinded pursuant to the provisions of Article 82(1), whose license under Article 3 of the Secured Bonds Trust Act (Act No. 52 of 1905) has been rescinded pursuant to the provisions of Article 12 of that Act, whose authorization under Article 1(1) of the Act on Provision, etc. of Trust Business by Financial Institutions (Act No. 43 of 1943) has been rescinded pursuant to the provisions of Article 10 of that Act, or a stock company whose license, registration, or authorization of the same kind (including permission or any other administrative disposition similar to said license, registration, or authorization; hereinafter the same shall apply in this item, item (viii)(d), and item (x)(a)) which was obtained in a foreign state has been rescinded or one for which the renewal of said license, registration, or authorization has been refused pursuant to the provisions of laws and regulations of the foreign state that are equivalent to this Act, the Secured Bonds Trust Act, or the Act on Provision, etc. of Trust Business by Financial Institutions, and where five years have yet to elapse since the date of rescission (in the case that a renewal is refused, the day on which a disposition for said refusal to renew was made; the same shall apply in item (viii)(d), (e), and (f) and item (x)(a));
(vi) a stock company which has been sentenced to a fine (including punishment equivalent thereto pursuant to the laws and regulations of a foreign state) for violating the provisions of this Act, the Trust Act (Act No. 108 of 2006), the Secured Bonds Trust Act, the Act on Provision, etc. of Trust Business by Financial Institutions, the Financial Instruments and Exchange Act, the Act on Investment Trusts and Investment Corporations (Act No. 198 of 1951), the Act on Regulation of Business Pertaining to Commodity Investment (Act No. 66 of 1991), the Act on Liquidation of Assets (Act No. 105 of 1998), the Copyright Management Business Act (Act No. 131 of 2000), or any other law specified by a Cabinet Order, or pursuant to the provisions of laws and regulations of a foreign state that are equivalent thereto, and where five years have yet to elapse since the day on which execution of the sentence was completed or since the day on which the stock company has ceased to be subject to execution of the sentence;
(vii) a stock company whose business other than trust business is not related to trust business, or a stock company for which carrying out said other business is found to be likely to interfere with the proper and reliable operations of its trust business;
(viii) a stock company whose directors or executive officers (including consultants, advisers, or any other persons who, irrespective of title, are found to have power that is equivalent to or greater than directors or executive officers over said company; hereinafter the same shall apply in this item, Article 44(2), Article 45(2) and Article 50-2(6)(viii)), accounting advisors, or company auditors include a person who falls under any of the following:
  (a) an adult ward or a person under curatorship, or any person who is treated similarly thereto under the laws and regulations of a foreign state;
  (b) a bankrupt who has not obtained restoration of rights, or any person who is

treated similarly thereto under the laws and regulations of a foreign state;
(c) a person who has been sentenced to imprisonment without work or a severer punishment (including punishment equivalent thereto pursuant to the laws and regulations of a foreign state) and for whom five years have yet to elapse since the day on which execution of the sentence was completed or since the day on which the person ceased to be subject to execution of the sentence;
(d) in regard to a juridical person for which the renewal of a registration under Article 7(3) has been refused pursuant to the provisions of Article 10(1), whose license under Article 3 has been rescinded pursuant to the provisions of Article 44(1), whose registration under Article 7(1), Article 50-2(1), or Article 52(1) has been rescinded pursuant to the provisions of Article 45(1), for which the renewal of a registration under Article 7(3) as applied mutatis mutandis pursuant to Article 50-2(2) has been refused pursuant to the provisions of paragraph (6) of that Article, for which the renewal of a registration under Article 7(3) as applied mutatis mutandis pursuant to Article 54(2) has been refused pursuant to the provisions of paragraph (6) of that Article, whose license under Article 53(1) has been rescinded pursuant to the provisions of Article 59(1), whose registration under Article 54(1) has been rescinded pursuant to the provisions of Article 60(1), or whose registration under Article 67(1) has been rescinded pursuant to the provisions of Article 82(1), or in regard to a juridical person whose license under Article 3 of the Secured Bonds Trust Act has been rescinded pursuant to the provisions of Article 12 of that Act, whose authorization under Article 1(1) of the Act on Provision, etc. of Trust Business by Financial Institutions has been rescinded pursuant to the provisions of Article 10 of that Act, or whose license, registration, or authorization of the same kind which was obtained in a foreign state has been rescinded or for whom the renewal of said license, registration, or authorization has been refused pursuant to the provisions of laws and regulations of the foreign state that are equivalent to this Act, the Secured Bonds Trust Act, or the Act on Provision, etc. of Trust Business by Financial Institutions, a person who, within thirty days prior to the rescission, was a director or executive officer, accounting advisor, or a person equivalent thereto, or who was a representative of the relevant juridical person in Japan (which means a Representative in Japan as prescribed in Article 53(2)) and for whom five years have yet to elapse since the date of rescission;
(e) a person whose registration under Article 67(1) has been rescinded pursuant to the provisions of Article 82(1), and for whom five years have yet to elapse since the date of rescission;
(f) a person whose registration of the same kind as registration under Article 67(1) but which is obtained in a foreign state pursuant to the provisions of laws and regulations of the foreign state that are equivalent to this Act has been rescinded, or for whom the renewal of said registration has been refused and for whom five years have yet to elapse since the date of rescission;
(g) a director, executive officer, accounting advisor, or company auditor who has received a dismissal order pursuant to the provisions of Article 44(2) or Article 45(2), a Representative in Japan or a resident officer of a branch office who has received a dismissal order pursuant to the provisions of Article 59(2) or Article 60(2), an officer who has received a dismissal order pursuant to the provisions of Article 82(2), or a director, executive officer, accounting advisor, company auditor, or a person equivalent thereto who has received a dismissal order pursuant to the provisions of laws and regulations of a foreign state that are equivalent to this Act, where five years have yet to elapse since the date of receipt of

said disposition; or
- (h) a person who has been sentenced to a fine (including punishment equivalent thereto pursuant to the laws and regulations of a foreign state) for violating the provisions of any of the Acts prescribed in item (vi), the Companies Act, or any laws and regulations of a foreign state that are equivalent thereto, or for committing an offense set forth in Article 204, Article 206, Article 208, Article 208-3, Article 222, or Article 247 of the Penal Code (Act No. 45 of 1907), an offense set forth in the Act on Punishment of Physical Violence and Other Related Matters (Act No. 60 of 1926), or an offense set forth in Article 46, Article 47, Article 49, or Article 50 of the Act to Prevent Unjust Acts by Organized Crime Group Members (Act No. 77 of 1991), and for whom five years have yet to elapse since the day on which execution of the sentence was completed or since the day on which the person has ceased to be subject to execution of the sentence;

(ix) a stock company whose Major Shareholders who are individuals (when the applicant is the Subsidiary Company of a Holding Company (meaning a Holding Company as prescribed in Article 9(5)(i) of the Act on Prohibition of Private Monopolization and Maintenance of Fair Trade (Act No. 54 of 1947); the same shall apply hereinafter), including Major Shareholders of said Holding Company; the same shall apply in the following item) include a person who falls under any of the following:
- (a) an adult ward or a person under curatorship, or a person who is treated similarly thereto under the laws and regulations of a foreign state, whose statutory agent falls under any of (a) to (h) inclusive of the preceding item; or
- (b) a person who falls under any of (b) to (h) inclusive of the preceding item;

(x) a stock company whose Major Shareholders who are juridical persons include a person who falls under any of the following:
- (a) a person for whom the renewal of a registration under Article 7(3) has been refused pursuant to the provisions of Article 10(1), whose license under Article 3 has been rescinded pursuant to the provisions of Article 44(1), whose registration under Article 7(1), Article 50-2(1), or Article 52(1) has been rescinded pursuant to the provisions of Article 45(1), for whom the renewal of a registration under Article 7(3) as applied mutatis mutandis pursuant to Article 50-2(2), has been refused pursuant to the provisions of paragraph (6) of that Article, for whom the renewal of a registration under Article 7(3) as applied mutatis mutandis pursuant to Article 54(2), has been refused pursuant to the provisions of paragraph (6) of that Article, whose license under Article 53(1) has been rescinded pursuant to the provisions of Article 59(1), whose registration under Article 54(1) has been rescinded pursuant to the provisions of Article 60(1), whose registration under Article 67(1) has been rescinded pursuant to the provisions of Article 82(1), whose license under Article 3 of the Secured Bonds Trust Act has been rescinded pursuant to the provisions of Article 12 of that Act, or whose authorization under Article 1(1) of the Act on Provision, etc. of Trust Business by Financial Institutions has been rescinded pursuant to the provisions of Article 10 of that Act, or whose license, registration, or authorization of the same kind which has been obtained in a foreign state has been rescinded pursuant to provisions of laws and regulations of the foreign state that are equivalent to this Act, the Secured Bonds Trust Act, or the Act on Provision, etc. of Trust Business by Financial Institutions, and for whom five years have yet to elapse since the date of rescission;
- (b) a person who has been sentenced to a fine (including punishment equivalent

thereto pursuant to laws and regulations of a foreign state) for violating the provisions of any of the laws prescribed in item (vi) or the provisions of any laws and regulations of a foreign state that are equivalent thereto, and for whom five years have yet to elapse since the day on which execution of the sentence was completed or since the day on which the person has ceased to be subject to execution of the sentence; or

(c) a person whose directors or executive officers who represent a juridical person, accounting advisors, company auditors, or persons equivalent thereto include a person who falls under any of item (viii)(a) to (h) inclusive.

(3) The amount specified by a Cabinet Order set forth in item (ii) of the preceding paragraph shall not be less than one hundred million yen.

(4) The amount of net assets set forth in paragraph (2)(iii) shall be calculated pursuant to the provisions of a Cabinet Office Ordinance.

(5) The term "Major Shareholder" set forth in paragraph (2)(ix) and (x) shall mean a person who holds not less than twenty-hundredths (in cases where there is any fact specified by a Cabinet Office Ordinance as a one that is presumed to have a material influence on decisions about the company's finances and business policies, fifteen-hundredths) of the voting rights (including those pertaining to shares which cannot be asserted against an issuer pursuant to the provisions of Article 147(1) or Article 148(1) of the Act on Transfer of Bonds, Shares, etc. (Act No. 75 of 2001), and excluding those specified by a Cabinet Office Ordinance which have been specified in consideration of the condition of holding or other circumstances; hereinafter referred to as "Subject Voting Rights" in this Article and Article 17(1)) of all shareholders or investors of the company (for a stock company, excluding voting rights for shares which can be exercised only for part of the matters that can be resolved at a shareholder's meeting, but including voting rights for shares which are deemed to be held pursuant to the provisions of Article 879(3) of the Companies Act,; the same shall apply hereinafter).

(6) The term "Subsidiary Company" set forth in paragraph (2)(ix) shall mean a company for which the majority of the voting rights of all shareholders are held by another company. In this case, where a company and one or more of its subsidiaries hold the majority of the voting rights of all shareholders of another company, or one or more of the subsidiary companies of the first company hold the majority of the voting rights of all shareholders of another company, said another company shall be deemed to be the Subsidiary Company of the first company.

(7) With regard to the application of the provisions of paragraph (5) in the cases listed in the following items, the Subject Voting Rights prescribed in those items shall be deemed to be held:

(i) in cases where the person has the authority to exercise Subject Voting Rights of the company or the authority to give instructions for the exercise of said Subject Voting Rights pursuant to a trust agreement or any other agreement or the provisions of law: said Subject Voting Rights;

(ii) in cases where a person who has a relationship of stock-ownership, relationship of relatives, or any other special relationship specified by a Cabinet Order with a company, holds voting rights in that company: said Subject Voting Rights held by the person who has said special relationship with the company.

(8) When the Prime Minister finds it necessary in light of the standards for examination under the provisions of paragraph (1), the Prime Minister may, to the extent deemed necessary, impose conditions on the license under Article 3 or make changes thereto.

(Reduction of Stated Capital)
Article 6 When a Trust Company (excluding a Custodian Type Trust Company) intends

to reduce the amount of its stated capital, it shall obtain authorization therefor from the Prime Minister.

(Registration)
Article 7 (1) A person who has been registered by the Prime Minister may, notwithstanding the provisions of Article 3, carry out Custodian Type Trust Business.
(2) The validity of registration set forth in the preceding paragraph shall be three years from the date of registration.
(3) A person who intends to continue to carry out Custodian Type Trust Business after the expiration of the validity shall apply for renewal of its registration within the period specified by a Cabinet Order.
(4) When a registration has been renewed as set forth in the preceding paragraph, the validity of the registration shall be three years from the day following the date of expiration of the validity of the previous registration.
(5) A person who wishes to have the registration renewed as under paragraph (3) shall pay fees therefor pursuant to the provisions of a Cabinet Order.
(6) Where an application has been filed for the renewal of a registration under paragraph (3), when no disposition pertaining to the application has been made prior to the expiration of the validity of the registration, the previous registration shall remain in force until a disposition is made even after the expiration of the validity thereof.

(Application for Registration)
Article 8 (1) A person applying for registration under paragraph (1) of the preceding Article (including the renewal of a registration under paragraph (3) of that Article; the same shall apply in Article 10(1), Article 45(1)(iii), and Article 91(iii)) (referred to as "Applicant" in Article 10(1)) shall submit a written application to the Prime Minister stating the following matters:
(i) the trade name;
(ii) the amount of stated capital;
(iii) the names of directors and company auditors;
(iv) in the case of a company with accounting advisors, the names of the accounting advisors;
(v) where the person carries out business other than trust business, the type of business; and
(vi) the names and locations of the head office and other business offices.
(2) The following documents shall be attached to the written application set forth in the preceding paragraph:
(i) the articles of incorporation;
(ii) the company's certificate of registered matters;
(iii) a statement of operational procedures;
(iv) a balance sheet; and
(v) other documents specified by a Cabinet Office Ordinance.
(3) The statement of operational procedures set forth in item (iii) of the preceding paragraph shall state the following matters:
(i) the type of trust property accepted;
(ii) the method of management or disposition of trust property:
(iii) the method of segregated management of trust property;
(iv) the system for carrying out trust business;
(v) in cases where part of trust business is delegated to a third party, the content of trust business delegated as well as standards and procedures pertaining to selection of a person delegated with said part of trust business (excluding the case

where business listed in the items of Article 22(3) is delegated); and
(vi) other matters specified by a Cabinet Office Ordinance.

(Registration in the Registry)
Article 9 (1) Where an application for registration under Article 7(1) has been filed, the Prime Minister shall register the following matters in the Custodian Type Trust Companies' registry except when the Prime Minister refuses to register the Applicant pursuant to the provisions of paragraph (1) of the following Article:
(i) the matters listed in the items of paragraph (1) of the preceding Article; and
(ii) the date of registration and the registration number.
(2) The Prime Minister shall make the Custodian Type Trust Companies' registry available for public inspection.

(Refusal of Registration)
Article 10 (1) When the Applicant falls under any of the following items or when the written application set forth in Article 8(1) or any of the attached documents listed in the items of paragraph (2) of that Article include any false statements or fail to state any material facts, the Prime Minister shall refuse to register the Applicant:
(i) a person who falls under any of the items of Article 5(2) (excluding items (ii) and (iii));
(ii) a stock company whose amount of stated capital is less than the amount specified by a Cabinet Order as necessary and appropriate for the protection of settlors or beneficiaries;
(iii) a stock company whose amount of net assets is less than the amount prescribed in the preceding item;
(iv) a stock company for whom provisions of the articles of incorporation or the statement of operational procedures do not conform to laws and regulations or are not sufficient for it to properly execute Custodian Type Trust Business; or
(v) a stock company which, in light of its personnel composition, is found not to have the knowledge and experience that would allow for the right execution of Custodian Type Trust Business.
(2) The amount of net assets set forth in item (iii) of the preceding paragraph shall be calculated pursuant to the provisions of a Cabinet Office Ordinance.

(Security Deposit)
Article 11 (1) A Trust Company shall deposit a security deposit with the closest official depository to its head office.
(2) The amount of the security deposit set forth in the preceding paragraph shall be the amount specified by a Cabinet Order in consideration of the contents of trust business and the necessity of protecting the beneficiaries.
(3) When a Trust Company concludes a contract under which the other party promises to deposit the required security deposit on behalf of said Trust Company in accordance with an order of the Prime Minister, and has notified the Prime Minister to that effect pursuant to the provisions of a Cabinet Order, said Trust Company may elect not to deposit all or part of the security deposit set forth in paragraph (1) with regard to the money to be deposited under said contract (hereinafter referred to as the "Contract Amount" in this Article) during the period in which said contract remains in force.
(4) When the Prime Minister finds it necessary for the protection of the beneficiaries, he/she may order the party who has concluded the contract set forth in the preceding paragraph with a Trust Company or said Trust Company to deposit all or part of the Contract Amount.

(5) No Trust Company shall begin trust business until it has deposited the security deposit set forth in paragraph (1) (including conclusion of a contract set forth in paragraph (3)) and has notified the Prime Minister to that effect.
(6) The beneficiary of a trust shall have the right to receive, in preference over other creditors, payment of claims arising with regard to the trust from the security deposit made by the Trust Company that is the trustee of the trust.
(7) The matters necessary for execution of the right set forth in the preceding paragraph shall be specified by a Cabinet Order.
(8) When the amount of the security deposit (including the Contract Amount; the same shall apply in paragraph (10)) falls short of the amount specified by a Cabinet Order set forth in paragraph (2), the Trust Company shall, within three weeks from the day specified by a Cabinet Office Ordinance, deposit (including conclusion of a contract set forth in paragraph (3)) the amount of such shortfall, and notify the Prime Minister to that effect without delay.
(9) A security deposit to be deposited pursuant to the provisions of paragraph (1) or the preceding paragraph may be substituted by national government bond certificates, municipal bond certificates, or other securities specified by a Cabinet Office Ordinance (including book-entry transferred bonds prescribed in Article 278(1) of the Act on Transfer of Bonds, Shares, etc.)
(10) When a transfer of trust property to a new trustee or assignment of trust property to a person entitled thereto has been completed in a case where the renewal of a registration under Article 7(3) has not been effected, when a license under Article 3 has been rescinded pursuant to the provisions of Article 44(1), when a registration under Article 7(1) has been rescinded pursuant to the provisions of Article 45(1), when a license under Article 3 or a registration under Article 7(1) ceases to be effective pursuant to the provision Article 46(1), or when the amount of the security deposit exceeds the amount specified by a Cabinet Order as prescribed in paragraph (2), all or part of the security deposit deposited pursuant to the provisions of paragraph (1), (4), or (8) may be refunded pursuant to the provisions of a Cabinet Order.
(11) In addition to what is prescribed in each of the preceding paragraphs, necessary matters regarding security deposits shall be specified by a Cabinet Office Ordinance and an Ordinance of the Ministry of Justice.

(Notification of Changes)
Article 12 (1) When there is a change in any of the matters listed in the items of Article 4(1), a Trust Company (excluding Custodian Type Trust Company) shall notify the Prime Minister to that effect within two weeks from the date of said change.
(2) When there is a change in any of the matters listed in the items of Article 8(1), a Custodian Type Trust Company shall notify the Prime Minister to that effect within two weeks from the date of said change.
(3) When the Prime Minister has received a notification set forth in the preceding paragraph, the Minister shall register to that effect in the Custodian Type Trust Companies' registry.

(Changes to the Statement of Operational Procedures)
Article 13 (1) When a Trust Company (excluding a Custodian Type Trust Company) intends to change its statement of operational procedures, it shall obtain approval therefor from the Prime Minister.
(2) When a Custodian Type Trust Company intends to change its statement of operational procedures, it shall notify the Prime Minister to that effect in advance.

(Trade Name)
Article 14 (1) A Trust Company shall use the word "trust" in its trade name.

(2) A person who is not a Trust Company shall not use, in its name or trade name, any word that is likely to cause the misunderstanding that the person is a Trust Company; provided, however, that this shall not apply to a person who has obtained a license under Article 3 of the Secured Bonds Trust Act or authorization under Article 1(1) of the Act on Provision, etc. of Trust Business by Financial Institutions.

(Prohibition on Name Lending)
Article 15 No Trust Company shall have another person carry out Trust Business in its own name.

(Restriction, etc. on Concurrent Positions Being Held by Directors)
Article 16 (1) Where a director (in the case of a company with committees, an executive officer) who engages in the full time business, of a Trust Company, engages in the full time business of another company or carries out business, the director shall obtain the approval of the Prime Minister.

(2) The provisions of the proviso to Article 331(2) (including the case where it is applied mutatis mutandis pursuant to Article 335(1) of the Companies Act), Article 332(2) (including the case where it is applied mutatis mutandis pursuant to Article 334(1) of that Act), Article 336(2), and the proviso to Article 402(5) of that Act shall not apply to Trust Companies.

Section 2 Major Shareholders

(Notification by Major Shareholders)
Article 17 (1) A person who has become a Major Shareholder of a Trust Company (meaning a Major Shareholder as prescribed in Article 5(5); the same shall apply hereinafter) shall submit a notification of Subject Voting Rights Held to the Prime Minister, stating the Ratio of the Subject Voting Rights Held (meaning the rate calculated by dividing the number of Subject Voting Rights held by a person holding said Subject Voting Rights by the number of voting rights of all shareholders of said Trust Company), the purpose of such holding, and other matters specified by a Cabinet Office Ordinance without delay.

(2) A document in which the Major Shareholder swears that the shareholder does not fall under Article 5(2)(ix) and (x) and other documents specified by a Cabinet Office Ordinance shall be attached to the notification of Subject Voting Rights Held set forth in the preceding paragraph.

(Order on Measures)
Article 18 Where a Major Shareholder of a Trust Company falls under any of Article 5(2), item (ix), sub-item (a) or (b) or item (x), sub-item (a), (b), or (c), the Prime Minister may order said Major Shareholder to take measures so that the aid Major Shareholder will cease to be a Major Shareholder of said Trust Company or other necessary measures, and may specify a period not exceeding three months therefor.

(Notification by Persons Who Have Ceased to Be Major Shareholders)
Article 19 When a Major Shareholder of a Trust Company has ceased to be a Major Shareholder of said Trust Company, the Major Shareholder shall notify the Prime Minister to that effect without delay.

(Application to Holding Companies Which Have a Trust Company as Their Subsidiary Company)
Article 20 The provisions of the preceding three Articles shall apply mutatis mutandis to the shareholders or investors of a Holding Company which has a Trust Company as its Subsidiary Company (meaning a Subsidiary Company as prescribed in Article 5(6); the same shall apply hereinafter except in Article 51).

Section 3 Business

(Scope of Business)
Article 21 (1) In addition to Trust Business, a Trust Company may carry out Agency for Trust Agreements, Business for the Sale and Purchase, etc. of Beneficial Interest in Trust, and property management business (limited to business for managing property of the same kind as the trust property stated in the statement of operational procedures (meaning a statement of operational procedures as set forth in Article 4(2)(iii) or Article 8(2)(iii)) of said Trust Company by the same method as the method of managing said trust property).
(2) In addition to business carried out pursuant to the provisions of the preceding paragraph, a Trust Company may, with the approval of the Prime Minister, carry out business that is not likely to interfere with the proper and reliable operation of its trust business and which is related thereto.
(3) When a Trust Company wishes to obtain the approval set forth in the preceding paragraph, it shall submit a written application to the Prime Minister with a document stating the content and method of business to be carried out as well as reasons for carrying out said business attached thereto.
(4) When a Trust Company intends to change the content or method of business carried out pursuant to the provisions of paragraph (2), it shall obtain approval therefor from the Prime Minister.
(5) A Trust Company may not carry out business other than business carried out pursuant to the provisions of paragraphs (1) and (2).
(6) Where a written application for a license under Article 3 or for registration under Article 7(1) includes a statement to the effect that the applicant carries out business other than business carried out pursuant to paragraph (1), when said applicant has obtained said license or registration, the applicant shall be deemed to have obtained approval set forth in paragraph (2) with regard to carrying out said business.

(Delegation of Trust Business)
Article 22 (1) A Trust Company may delegate to a third party part of its trust business with regard to the delegated trust property only when all of the following requirements are fulfilled:
(i) that the delegation of a part of trust business and the person who is delegated with the trust business (where the delegated party has not been settled, standards and procedures pertaining to selection thereof) have been made clear in the terms of trust; and
(ii) that the person who is delegated with the trust business is a person who is able to rightly execute the delegated trust business.
(2) With regard to the application of the provisions of Article 28 and Article 29 (excluding paragraph (3)) and the provisions of Chapter VII pertaining to these provisions in cases where a Trust Company has delegated its trust business, the term "Trust Company" in these provisions shall be deemed to be replaced with "Trust Company (includ-

ing a person who has been delegated by said Trust Company)."
(3) The provisions of the preceding two paragraphs (excluding paragraph (1), item (ii)) shall not apply to the case where the following business is delegated:
(i) business pertaining to the act of preserving trust property;
(ii) business for the purpose of utilizing or improving trust property within an extent that does not change the nature of the trust property; or
(iii) business not falling under either of the preceding two items which is specified by a Cabinet Office Ordinance as being found not to interfere with the protection of the beneficiaries.

(Trust Company Liability Pertaining to delegation of Trust Business)
Article 23 (1) A Trust Company shall be liable for compensating for damages caused to a beneficiary with regard to business conducted by a person delegated with trust business by said Trust Company; provided, however, that this shall not apply to the case where a Trust Company has taken appropriate care in selecting an delegated person and made efforts to prevent the damages caused to a beneficiary with regard to the business conducted by the delegated person under the delegation.
(2) The preceding paragraph shall not apply to cases where the Trust Company has delegated trust business to any of the third parties listed in the following items (in the case of the third party listed in item (i) or (ii), limited to a party having a close shareholding or personnel relationship with the settlor as specified by a Cabinet Order and not having a close shareholding or personnel relationship with the trustee as specified by a Cabinet Order); provided, however, that this shall not apply to cases where the Trust Company knows that the delegated party is unsuitable or untrustworthy or that the delegated party is not carrying out the delegated trust business appropriately, and fails to notify the beneficiaries (in cases where a beneficiary has a trust manager or agent at that time, including said trust manager or agent; the same shall apply in item (iii) of this paragraph, Article 29-3 and Article 51(1)(v)) thereof, fails to cancel the delegation to the delegated party, or fails to take any other necessary measures:
(i) a third party designated in the terms of trust;
(ii) in cases where the terms of trust specifies to the effect that the Trust Company will delegate the trust business to a third party designated by the settlor, the third party designated in accordance therewith; or
(iii) in cases where the terms of trust specifies to the effect that the Trust Company will delegate the trust business to a third party designated by the beneficiary, the third party designated in accordance therewith.

(Rules for Acts Pertaining to Acceptance of a Trust)
Article 24 (1) No Trust Company shall commit the following acts (in the case of accepting a trust under a Specific Trust Agreement prescribed in the following Article, excluding acts listed in item (v)) with regard to acceptance of trusts:
(i) the act of informing a settlor of a false fact;
(ii) the act of providing a settlor with a assertive conclusion on an uncertain matter or informing a settlor of something that is likely to cause the settlor to misunderstand that an uncertain matter is certain;
(iii) the act of promising to provide a settlor, beneficiary, or third party with special profits, or providing special profits (including the act of having a third party promise to provide special profits or having a third party provide special profits thereto);
(iv) the act of promising to compensate a settlor, beneficiary, or third party in cases where any loss has occurred with regard to beneficial interest in trust, the act of promising to supplement any shortfall in the case that a pre-determined amount of

Art.24-2　　　　　④ Trust Business Act, Chap.II, Sec.3

profits is not obtained, the act of compensating for losses in cases where any loss has occurred with regard to beneficial interest in trust or the act of supplementing any shortfall in the case that a pre-determined amount of profits is not obtained (including the act of having a third party promise to conduct or conduct said acts, but excluding the case of compensating for losses caused by an accident imputable to the Trust Company's own liability); and

(v) other acts specified by a Cabinet Office Ordinance as lacking in protection for the settlors.

(2) A Trust Company shall accept a trust appropriate in light of the status of the settlors' knowledge, experience, and property and the purpose of concluding the trust agreement, and carry out its business so as not to lack protection for the settlors.

(Application Mutatis Mutandis of the Financial Instruments and Exchange Act)

Article 24-2　The provisions of Chapter III, Section 1, Subsection 5 of the Financial Instruments and Exchange Act (Professional Investors) (excluding Article 34-2(6) to (8) inclusive (Cases Where Professional Investors Are Deemed to Be Customers Other Than Professional Investors) and Article 34-3(5) and (6) (Cases Where Juridical Persons Who Are Customers Other than Professional Investors Are Deemed to Be Professional Investors)), the provisions of Chapter III, Section 2, Subsection 1 of that Act (General Rules) (excluding Article 35 to Article 36-4 inclusive (Scope of Business of Persons Who Engage in Type I Financial Instruments Business or Investment Management Business; Scope of Additional Business of Persons Who Only Engage in Type II Financial Instruments Business or Investment Advisory and Agency Business; Duty of Good Faith to Customers; Posting of Signs; Prohibition on Name Lending; Prohibition on Administration of Bonds, etc.), Article 37(1)(ii) (Regulations on Advertising, etc.), Article 37-2 (Obligation to Clarify in Advance), Article 37-3(1)(ii) to (iv) inclusive and (vi) and 37-3(3) (Delivery of Documents Prior to the Conclusion of a Contract), Article 37-4 (Delivery of Documents upon Conclusion of a Contract, etc.), Article 37-5 (Delivery of Documents Pertaining to Receipt of Security Deposits), Article 38(i) and (ii) and Article 38-2 (Prohibited Acts), Article 39(1), Article 39(2)(ii), Article 39(3) and (5) (Prohibition of Compensation of Loss, etc.), Article 40(i) (Rule of Suitability), and Article 40-2 to Article 40-5 inclusive (Best Execution Policy; Prohibition of Sales and Purchases, etc. where Separate Management Is Not Maintained; Restriction on Sales, etc. of Securities to Professional Investors; Obligation to Provide Professional Investors with Information Regarding Securities)), and the provisions of Article 45 (Miscellaneous Provisions) of that Act (excluding items (iii) and (iv)) shall apply mutatis mutandis to acceptance by a Trust Company of a trust under a trust agreement (meaning those that are specified by a Cabinet Office Ordinance as trust agreements with the risk of a trust principal loss caused by fluctuation in the interest rate, currency value, quotations on a Financial Instruments Market (meaning a Financial Instruments Market as prescribed in Article 2(14) of that Act), or any other index; hereinafter referred to as a "Specific Trust Agreement"). In this case, the term "Contract for a Financial Instruments Transaction" and "Financial Instruments Business" in these provisions shall respectively be deemed to be replaced with "Specific Trust Agreement" and "business for the conclusion of Specific Trust Agreements"; the term "Financial Instruments Transaction" in these provisions (excluding Article 34 of that Act) shall be deemed to be replaced with "conclusion of Specific Trust Agreements"; the term "contract to carry out Acts for a Financial Instruments Transaction (meaning acts listed in the items of Article 2(8); the same shall apply hereinafter) with a customer as the other party or on behalf of a customer" in Article 34 of that Act shall be deemed to be replaced with "Specific Trust Agreements prescribed in Article 24-2 of the Trust Business Act"; the term "the trade name or name and address" in Article 37-3(1)(i) of the Financial Instruments and Exchange Act shall be deemed to be replaced with "the address"; the term "Article 37-4(1)" in Article 37-6(1) of that Act shall be deemed to be replaced with "Article 26(1) of the Trust Business Act"; the terms "Sales and Purchases or Other Transactions of Securities, etc." and "item (i) of the preceding paragraph" in Article 39(2)(i) of the Financial Instruments and Exchange Act shall respectively be deemed to be replaced with "conclusion of Specific Trust Agreements" and "Compensation of Losses, etc. (meaning compensation for losses or supplementation of profit as prescribed in Article 24(1)(iv) of the Trust Business Act; the same shall apply in item (iii))"; the term "Sales and Purchases or Other Transactions of Securities, etc." and "provided under item (iii) of the preceding paragraph" in Article 39(2)(iii) of the Financial Instruments and Exchange Act shall respectively be deemed to be replaced with "conclusion of Specific Trust Agreements" and "pertaining to compensation of losses, etc."; and the term "Problematic Conduct" in Article 39(4) of that Act shall be deemed to be replaced with "an accident imputable to a Trust Company." In addition, the necessary technical replacement of terms shall be specified by a Cabinet Order.

(Explanation of the Content of a Trust Agreement)
Article 25 When a Trust Company accepts a trust under a trust agreement, it shall in advance provide the settlor with the trade name of said Trust Company as well as an explanation on the matters listed in items (iii) to (xvi) inclusive of paragraph (1) of the following Article (when the trust company accepts a trust under a Specific Trust Agreement, the matters listed in that items shall be excluded); provided, however, that this shall not apply to the cases specified by a Cabinet Office Ordinance as cases where omission of such explanation will not interfere with the protection of the settlor.

(Delivery of Documents on Concluding a Trust Agreement)
Article 26 (1) When a Trust Company has accepted a trust under a trust agreement, it shall deliver a document specifying the following matters to the settlor without delay; provided, however, that this shall not apply to the cases specified by a Cabinet Office Ordinance as cases where not delivering said documents will not interfere with the protection of the settlor.
(i) the year, month, and day of conclusion of the trust agreement;
(ii) the name of the settlor, and the trade name of the trustee;
(iii) the purposes of the trust;
(iv) matters concerning the trust property;
(v) matters concerning the period of the trust agreement;
(vi) matters concerning the method of management or disposition of trust property (with regard to a trust not falling under any of the items of Article 2(3), including the policy for management or disposition of trust property);
(vii) in cases where trust business is to be delegated (excluding the cases where business listed in the items of Article 22(3) is to be delegated), the contents of trust business to be delegated as well as the name and address or location of the person to be delegated with said business (where the delegated party has not been settled, the standards and procedures pertaining to selection thereof);
(viii) in cases where any transaction listed in the items of Article 29(2) is to be conducted, the fact that said transaction will take place and an outline of said transaction;
(ix) matters concerning the beneficiaries;

(x) matters concerning delivery of the trust property;
(xi) matters concerning the trust fees;
(xii) matters concerning taxes and other costs related to the trust property;
(xiii) matters concerning the accounting period for the trust property;
(xiv) matters concerning reports on the status of management or disposition of the trust property;
(xv) matters concerning termination of the trust agreement by agreement; and
(xvi) any other matters specified by a Cabinet Office Ordinance.
(2) A Trust Company may, in lieu of delivering the document set forth in the preceding paragraph, provide the information that is to be contained in the document under that paragraph by Electromagnetic Means (meaning a method using an electronic data processing system or other methods using information and communications technology which are specified by a Cabinet Office Ordinance; the same shall apply hereinafter), with the approval of the settlor, pursuant to the provisions of a Cabinet Order. In this case, the Trust Company shall be deemed to have delivered said document.
(3) The accounting period for the trust property prescribed in paragraph (1)(xiii) shall not exceed one year, unless otherwise provided for in a Cabinet Office Ordinance.

(Delivery of Reports on the Status of Trust Property)
Article 27 (1) A Trust Company shall prepare a report on the status of trust property delegated thereto for each accounting period therefor, and deliver it to the beneficiaries of said trust property; provided, however, that this shall not apply to the cases specified by a Cabinet Office Ordinance as the cases where not delivering said report will not interfere with the protection of the beneficiaries.
(2) The provisions of paragraph (2) of the preceding Article shall apply mutatis mutandis to the delivery of a report on the status of trust property set forth in the preceding paragraph to the beneficiaries.

(Trust Companies' Duty of Loyalty, etc.)
Article 28 (1) Trust Companies shall loyally carry out trust business or other business for beneficiaries in accordance with the main purpose of trust.
(2) Trust Companies shall carry out trust business with due care of a prudent manager in accordance with the main purpose of trust.
(3) Trust Companies shall, pursuant to the provisions of a Cabinet Office Ordinance, develop a system for managing property entrusted thereto as trust property, its own property, and property entrusted thereto as the trust property of other trusts in a segregated manner, and shall develop other systems to avoid damage being done to trust property and to prevent Trust Business from losing credibility pursuant to the provisions of Article 34 of the Trust Act.

(Rules of Conducts Pertaining to Trust Property)
Article 29 (1) No Trust Company shall commit the following acts with regard to entrusted trust property:
(i) an act of conducting a transaction under conditions which are different from those for ordinary transactions and because of which the transaction will cause damage to the trust property;
(ii) an act of conducting a transaction which is unnecessary in light of the purpose of the trust, the status of the trust property, or the policy for the management or disposition of the trust property;
(iii) an act of conducting a transaction (excluding one specified by a Cabinet Office Ordinance) in pursuit of the Trust Company's own interests or the interests of a per-

son other than the beneficiary of the trust property by using information on said trust property; and

(iv) other acts specified by a Cabinet Office Ordinance as those which are likely to cause damages to trust property or to cause Trust Business to lose credibility.

(2) No Trust Company shall conduct the following transactions, except in cases where there are provisions to the effect that any of the following transactions are to be conducted and provisions on the outline of said transaction, in the terms of trust, or the case where the approval of the beneficiaries (in cases where a beneficiary has a trust manager or an agent at that time, including said trust manager or agent) has been obtained in advance, in writing or by Electromagnetic Means, by disclosing material facts relating to said transaction (excluding the case where there are provisions in the act of trust to the effect that said Trust Company may not conduct said transaction), which is specified by a Cabinet Office Ordinance as a case where conducting said transaction will not interfere with the protection of the beneficiaries:

(i) a transaction between the Trust Company itself or its Interested Person (meaning a person specified by a Cabinet Order as having a share-capital relationship or a close personal relationship) and the trust property;

(ii) a transaction between the trust property of one trust and the trust property of another trust;

(iii) a transaction conducted with a third party for the trust property ih which the Trust Company acts as an agent of the third party.

(3) Where a Trust Company has conducted any of the transactions set forth in the items of the preceding paragraph, it shall prepare, with respect to each accounting period for the trust property, a document stating the status of said transaction during said period, and shall deliver said document to the beneficiary of said trust property; provided, however, that this shall not apply to the cases specified by a Cabinet Office Ordinance as cases where not delivering said document will not interfere with the protection of the beneficiaries.

(4) The provisions of Article 26(2) shall apply mutatis mutandis to the delivery of a document set forth in the preceding paragraph to the beneficiary.

(Major Change, etc. to Trust)

Article 29-2 (1) When a Trust Company intends to make any material modification to a trust (meaning a modification to a trust pertaining to the matters listed in the items of Article 103(1) of the Trust Act) or to consolidate or split a trust (hereinafter referred to as "Material Modification, etc. to the Trust" in this Article), it shall give public notice of the following matters pursuant to the provisions of a Cabinet Office Ordinance or send a notice to the respective beneficiaries (in cases where a beneficiary has a trust manager or an agent at that time, including said trust manager or agent; hereinafter the same shall apply in this Article), excluding the cases where such changes, etc. are not in conflict with the purpose of the trust and such changes, etc. are clearly in line with the beneficiaries' interests or any other cases specified by a Cabinet Office Ordinance.

(i) that it intends to make Major Changes, etc. to the Trust;

(ii) that a beneficiary who have any objection to the Major Changes, etc. to the Trust should raise their objections within a certain period of time; and

(iii) any other matters specified by a Cabinet Office Ordinance.

(2) The period set forth in item (ii) of the preceding paragraph shall not be less than one month.

(3) No Material Modification, etc. to the Trust prescribed in paragraph (1) shall be effected in cases where the number of beneficial interests in the trust held by beneficiaries

who raised objections within the period prescribed in paragraph (1)(ii) exceeds half of the total number of beneficial interests in said trust (or, if the conditions of each beneficial interest are not the same, cases where the price of beneficial interest in the trust held by such beneficiaries exceeded half of the total price of the beneficial interests in the trust as of the time of the public notice or notice pursuant to the provision of that paragraph, or any other cases specified by a Cabinet Office Ordinance).

(4) The provisions of the preceding three paragraphs shall not apply to a case to which any of the following items applies:
   (i) when the act of trust provides that Material Modification, etc. to the Trust are subject to majority vote at a beneficiaries meeting;
   (ii) when the approval of beneficiaries holding beneficial interests exceeding half of the total number of the beneficial interests in the trust (or, if the conditions of each beneficial interest are not the same, the total price of said beneficial interests in the trust or any others specified by a Cabinet Office Ordinance) has been obtained by a method other than that specified in the preceding item; or
   (iii) in addition to the cases listed in the preceding two items, those specified by a Cabinet Office Ordinance as cases equivalent thereto.

(5) With regard to a trust agreement to be concluded between a Trust Company and a large number of settlors pursuant to same general conditions of trust, the trust pertaining to said general conditions of trust shall be deemed to be a single trust pursuant to the provisions of said trust agreement and the provisions of each of the preceding paragraphs shall apply.

(Explanation of the Scope, etc. of Reimbursement or Advance Payment of Expenses, etc.)
Article 29-3 When a Trust Company is trying to reach an agreement prescribed in Article 48(5) of the Trust Act (including the cases where it is applied mutatis mutandis pursuant to Article 54(4) of that Act) with a beneficiary, it shall provide an explanation on the scope of reimbursement of Expenses, etc. (meaning Expenses, etc. prescribed in Article 48(1) of that Act) or trust fees to be paid pursuant to said agreement, or on the scope of advance payment of expenses or trust fees to be paid pursuant to said agreement, as well as other matters specified by a Cabinet Office Ordinance.

(Exceptions to Public Notice of a Trust)
Article 30 Where a Trust Company registers a transfer under Article 3 of the Act on National Government Bonds (Act No. 34 of 1906) or where there is any other registration specified by a Cabinet Office Ordinance or an Ordinance of the Ministry of Finance with regard to Registered National Government Bonds (meaning national government bonds registered pursuant to the provisions of Article 2(2) of that Act) which the Trust Company holds as trust property pursuant to the provisions of a Cabinet Office Ordinance or an Ordinance of the Ministry of Finance and which are registered by clearly indicating that said registered national government bonds are trust property, with regard to the application of the provisions of Article 14 of the Trust Act, such registration shall be deemed to be registration of a trust.

(Offsetting of Obligations Pertaining to Trust Property)
Article 31 (1) A Trust Company may offset the claim on a trust property whose obligor is a Clearing Organization (meaning a Financial Instruments Clearing Organization as prescribed in Article 2(29) of the Financial Instruments and Exchange Act; hereinafter the same shall apply in this paragraph) (limited to cases where the Clearing Organization has become the obligor due to the assumption of obligations (limited to assump-

tion of obligations undertaken on Assumption of Financial Instruments Obligations as prescribed in Article 156-3(1)(vi) of that Act; hereinafter the same shall apply in this paragraph)) against another trust property's obligations (limited to those assumed as consideration for assumption of obligations by the Clearing Organization); provided, however, that this shall not apply to cases where otherwise provided for in the act of trust.

(2) When a Trust Company which has offset claims pursuant to the provisions of the preceding paragraph causes any damage to the trust property arising from said set-off, it shall be liable for compensating for the damages.

Section 4 Accounting

(Business Year)
Article 32 The business year of a Trust Company shall be from April 1 of a given year to March 31 of the next year.

(Business Report)
Article 33 A Trust Company shall prepare a business report with respect to each business year and submit it to the Prime Minister within three months from the end of each business year.

(Public Inspection of Explanatory Documents Concerning the Status of Business and Property)
Article 34 (1) A Trust Company shall prepare an explanatory document stating matters specified by a Cabinet Office Ordinance as those concerning the status of business and property with respect to each business year, and shall keep copies thereof at all of its business offices and thereby make it available for public inspection for one year from the day on which the period specified by a Cabinet Office Ordinance has elapsed after the end of each business year.

(2) The explanatory document prescribed in the preceding paragraph may be prepared in the form of an Electromagnetic Record (meaning a record in electronic form, magnetic form, or any other form not recognizable to human perception, which is used in information processing by computers and which is specified by a Cabinet Office Ordinance; the same shall apply hereinafter).

(3) When the explanatory document prescribed in paragraph (1) has been prepared in the form of an Electromagnetic Record, a Trust Company may take measures specified by a Cabinet Office Ordinance as those for making information contained in said explanatory document available to unspecified many persons by Electromagnetic Means at its business offices. In this case, the explanatory document prescribed in that paragraph shall be deemed to have been made available for public inspection.

(Denial of a Shareholder's Right to Inspect the Books)
Article 35 The provisions of Article 433 of the Companies Act shall not apply to accounting books of a Trust Company (excluding Custodian Type Trust Companies; hereinafter the same shall apply in this Article to Article 39 inclusive) and materials relevant thereto (limited to those pertaining to trust property).

Section 5 Supervision

(Authorization for Mergers)

Article 36 (1) A merger wherein all or part of the parties thereto are Trust Companies shall not be effected without the authorization of the Prime Minister.
(2) A Trust Company that wishes to obtain authorization under the preceding paragraph shall submit a written application to the Prime Minister stating the matters listed in the items of Article 4(1) with regard to the stock company surviving the merger or the stock company to be incorporated upon merger (referred to as a "Post-Merger Trust Company" in paragraph (4)).
(3) A merger agreement and any other document specified by a Cabinet Office Ordinance shall be attached to the written application set forth in the preceding paragraph.
(4) When an application for authorization set forth in paragraph (1) has been filed, the Prime Minister shall examine whether the Post-Merger Trust Company conforms to the standards listed in the items of Article 5(1). In this case, when the Post-Merger Trust Company falls under any of the requirements listed in the items of Article 5(2), or when the written application set forth in paragraph (2) or the attached documents set forth in the preceding paragraph include any false statements or fail to state any material facts, the Prime Minister shall not grant the authorization.
(5) A stock company to be incorporated upon merger under authorization set forth in paragraph (1) shall be deemed to have obtained a license from the Prime Minister under Article 3 at the time of incorporation thereof.

(Authorization for an Incorporation-Type Company Split)
Article 37 (1) An incorporation-type company split implemented by a Trust Company for the purpose of having a newly incorporated stock company succeed to the whole of its Trust Business (referred to as "Incorporation-Type Company Split" in the following paragraph and paragraph (5)) shall not be effected without the authorization of the Prime Minister.
(2) A Trust Company that wishes to obtain the authorization set forth in the preceding paragraph shall submit a written application to the Prime Minister stating the matters listed in the items of Article 4(1) with regard to the stock company to be incorporated by the Incorporation-Type Company Split (referred to as the "Incorporated Company" in paragraph (4)).
(3) A company split plan and any other document specified by a Cabinet Office Ordinance shall be attached to the written application set forth in the preceding paragraph.
(4) When an application has been filed for the authorization set forth in paragraph (1), the Prime Minister shall examine whether the Incorporated Company conforms to the standards listed in the items of Article 5(1). In this case, when the Incorporated Company falls under any of the conditions listed in the items of Article 5(2), or when the written application set forth in paragraph (2) or the attached documents set forth in the preceding paragraph include any false statement or fail to state any material fact, the Prime Minister shall not grant the authorization.
(5) A stock company to be incorporated in an Incorporation-Type Company Split with authorization under paragraph (1) shall be deemed to have obtained a license from the Prime Minister under Article 3 at the time of incorporation.

(Authorization for an Absorption-Type Split)
Article 38 (1) An absorption-type split implemented by a Trust Company for the purpose of having another stock company succeed to the whole or a part of its Trust Business (referred to as "Absorption-Type Split" in the following paragraph and paragraph (5)) shall not be effected without the authorization of the Prime Minister; provided, however, that this shall not apply to Absorption-Type Split in which only Custodian Type Trust Business is succeeded to.

(2) A Trust Company that wishes to obtain the authorization set forth in the preceding paragraph shall submit a written application to the Prime Minister stating the following matters with regard to the stock company which will succeed to all or a part of Trust Business upon the Absorption-Type Split (hereinafter referred to as "Succeeding Company" in this Article):
(i) the matters listed in the items of Article 4(1); and
(ii) the contents of Trust Business to be succeeded to by the Succeeding Company.
(3) A company split plan and any other document specified by a Cabinet Office Ordinance shall be attached to the written application set forth in the preceding paragraph.
(4) When an application has been filed for the authorization set forth in paragraph (1), the Prime Minister shall examine whether the Succeeding Company conforms to the standards listed in the items of Article 5(1). In this case, when the Succeeding Company falls under any of the conditions listed in the items of Article 5(2), or when the written application set forth in paragraph (2) or the attached documents set forth in the preceding paragraph include any false statement or fail to state any material fact, the Prime Minister shall not grant the authorization.
(5) A stock company which succeeds to the entirety of Trust Business through an Absorption-Type Split with the authorization under paragraph (1) shall be deemed to have obtained a license from the Prime Minister under Article 3 at the time of succession.

(Authorization for a Business Transfer)
Article 39 (1) A transfer by a Trust Company to another Trust Company of all or part of its Trust Business (referred to as a "Business Transfer" in the following paragraph) shall not be effected without the authorization of the Prime Minister; provided, however, that this shall not apply to a Business Transfer in which only Custodian Type Trust Business is transferred.
(2) A Trust Company that wishes to obtain the authorization set forth in the preceding paragraph shall submit a written application to the Prime Minister stating the following matters with regard to a Trust Company which will acquire all or part of Trust Business under said Business Transfer (hereinafter referred to as the "Assignee Company"):
(i) the matters listed in the items of Article 4(1); and
(ii) the contents of Trust Business to be succeeded to by the Assignee Company.
(3) A business transfer agreement and any other document specified by a Cabinet Office Ordinance shall be attached to the written application set forth in the preceding paragraph.
(4) When an application has been filed for the authorization set forth in paragraph (1), the Prime Minister shall examine whether the Assignee Company conforms to the standard listed in the items of Article 5(1). In this case, when the Assignee Company falls under any of the conditions listed in the items of Article 5(2), or when the written application set forth in paragraph (2) or the attached documents set forth in the preceding paragraph include any false statement or fail to state any material fact, the Prime Minister may not grant an authorization.
(5) The provisions of each of the preceding paragraphs shall apply mutatis mutandis to the transfer of Trust Business in whole or in part by a Trust Company to a Foreign Trust Company. In this case, the term and phrases listed in the middle column of the following table in the provisions listed in the left-hand column of the same table shall be deemed to be replaced with the terms and phrases listed in the right-hand column of said table.

| paragraph (2), item (i) | the items of Article 4(1) | the items of Article 53(2) |

| paragraph (4) | the items of Article 5(1) | the items of Article 53(5) |
| | the items of Article 5(2) | the items of Article 53(6) |

(Succession to Rights and Obligations)
Article 40 (1) A Trust Company surviving a merger or a Trust Company incorporated in a merger shall succeed to the rights and obligations which the Trust Company extinguished in the merger had held in regard to business, based on authorization from or any other disposition made by the Prime Minister.
(2) The provisions of the preceding paragraph shall apply mutatis mutandis to a Trust Company which succeeds to the whole of Trust Business through a company split.

(Notifications, etc.)
Article 41 (1) When a Trust Company has come to fall under any of the following items, it shall notify the Prime Minister to that effect without delay:
  (i) when the Trust Company has filed a petition for commencement of bankruptcy proceedings, commencement of rehabilitation proceedings, or commencement of reorganization proceedings;
  (ii) when the Trust Company has effected a merger (excluding the case where said Trust Company has been extinguished in a merger), when it has had a part of its Trust Business succeeded to due to a company split, or when it has had transferred a part of its Trust Business; or
  (iii) when the Trust Company falls under any other cases prescribed by a Cabinet Office Ordinance.
(2) When a Trust Company has come to fall under any of the following items, the person specified in each of the relevant items shall notify the Prime Minister to that effect without delay:
  (i) when the Trust Company has closed its Trust Business (including the cases where the Trust Company has had all of its Trust Business succeeded to due to a company split, and the cases where the Trust Company has had all of its Trust Business transferred): said Trust Company;
  (ii) when the Trust Company has been extinguished due to a merger: the person who was a director or executive officer representing the company or a company auditor;
  (iii) when the Trust Company has been dissolved due to an order for the commencement of bankruptcy proceedings: the bankruptcy trustee; and
  (iv) when the Trust Company has been dissolved for a reason other than a merger or the commencement of bankruptcy proceedings: the liquidator.
(3) When a Trust Company intends to close its Trust Business, effect a merger (limited to a merger in which said Trust Company will be extinguished), dissolve due to any reason other than a merger or the commencement of bankruptcy proceedings, have its Trust Business succeeded to in whole or in part due to a company split, or transfer its Trust Business in whole or in part, it shall, by thirty days prior to the date when any of these events takes place, give public notice to that effect and post a notice to that effect in a place easily seen by the public at all of its business offices, pursuant to the provisions of a Cabinet Office Ordinance.
(4) When a Trust Company has given the public notice set forth in the preceding paragraph, it shall immediately notify the Prime Minister to that effect.
(5) When a Trust Company (excluding a Custodian Type Trust Company; hereinafter the same shall apply in this paragraph) has been registered pursuant to Article 7(1) or Article 52(1), or when a Custodian Type Trust Company has been registered pursuant to Article 52(1), the Trust Company or the Custodian Type Trust Company shall, without

delay, give public notice to that effect and post a notice to that effect in a place easily seen by the public at all of its business offices, pursuant to the provisions of a Cabinet Office Ordinance.
(6) The provisions of Article 940(1) (excluding item (ii)) and 940(3) (Public Notice Period, etc. of Electronic Public Notice) of the Companies Act shall apply mutatis mutandis to the cases where a Trust Company gives a public notice pursuant to the provisions of this Act or any other Act (excluding the public notice to be made pursuant to the provisions of the Companies Act) by means of electronic public notice. In this case, any necessary technical replacement of terms shall be specified by a Cabinet Order.

(Inspections, etc.)
Article 42 (1) When the Prime Minister finds it necessary for securing the sound and appropriate operations of a Trust Company's trust business, the Prime Minister may order said Trust Company, a person who conducts transactions with said Trust Company with regard to said business, or a Holding Company which has said Trust Company as a subsidiary company to submit reports or materials that should be used as a reference concerning the business or property of said Trust Company, and may have the officials enter a business office or any other facility of said Trust Company or a business office or office of the Holding Company which has said Trust Company as a Subsidiary Company, and have them ask questions about the status of its business or property and inspect its books, documents, and other relevant items.
(2) When the Prime Minister finds it especially necessary for securing the sound and appropriate operations of a Trust Company's trust business, the Prime Minister may, to the extent of that necessity, order the Major Shareholders of said Trust Company or the Major Shareholders of a Holding Company which has said Trust Company as a subsidiary company to submit notifications under Article 17 to Articles 19 inclusive or to take measures under those Articles, or to submit reports or materials that should be used as a reference concerning the business or property of said Trust Company, and may have the officials enter the business offices or offices of such Major Shareholders, and have them ask questions about notifications or measures under Article 17 to Article 19 inclusive or the status of business or property of said Trust Company, and may have them inspect the documents or other relevant items of said Major Shareholders.
(3) When the Prime Minister finds it especially necessary for securing the sound and appropriate operations of a Trust Company's trust business, the Prime Minister may, to the extent of that necessity, order a person who has been delegated with business by said Trust Company to submit reports or materials that should be used as a reference concerning the business or property of said Trust Company, and may have the officials enter a facility of a person who has been delegated with business by said Trust Company, and have them ask questions about the status of the business or property of said Trust Company and inspect the books, documents, and other relevant items.
(4) A person who has been delegated with business by a Trust Company as set forth in the preceding paragraph may refuse to submit a report or materials, may refuse questioning, and may refuse to undergo inspection under the provisions of that paragraph when there are justifiable grounds.
(5) An official who carries out an inspection pursuant to the provisions of paragraphs (1) to (3) inclusive shall carry a certificate for identification and present it to the persons concerned.
(6) The authority for inspection under the provisions of paragraphs (1) to (3) inclusive shall not be construed as being for criminal investigation.

(Order to Improve Business Operations)

Article 43 When the Prime Minister finds it necessary for securing the sound and appropriate operations of a Trust Company's trust business in light of the status of business or property of said Trust Company, the Prime Minister may, within the limits of that necessity, order said Trust Company to change the contents of its statement of operational procedures, deposit its property, or take other measures necessary to improve the operation of business or the status of property.

(Supervisory Dispositions against an Investment-Based Trust Company)
Article 44 (1) Where a Trust Company (excluding an Custodian Type Trust Company; hereinafter the same shall apply in this Article) falls under any of the following items, the Prime Minister may rescind the Trust Company's license under Article 3, or may order said Trust Company to suspend its business operations in whole or in part and specify a period not exceeding six months therefor.
  (i) when the Trust Company has come to fall under any of Article 5(2)(i) to (vi) inclusive;
  (ii) when the Trust Company is found to have fallen under any of the items of Article 5(2) at the time when it obtained a license under Article 3;
  (iii) when the Trust Company has ceased to have a sufficient personnel composition to allow for the right execution of trust business;
  (iv) when the Trust Company is found to have obtained a license under Article 3 by wrongful means;
  (v) when the Trust Company has violated any condition attached to a license under Article 3;
  (vi) when the Trust Company has violated laws and regulations or a disposition made by the Prime Minister pursuant to laws and regulations; or
  (vii) when the Trust Company has committed an act that is harmful to the public interest.
(2) When a director or executive officer, an accounting advisor, or a company auditor of a Trust Company has come to fall under any of Article 5(2)(viii)(a) to (h) inclusive, or has committed any act that falls under item (v) or (vi) of the preceding paragraph, the Prime Minister may order said Trust Company to dismiss said director, executive officer, accounting advisor, or company auditor.

(Supervisory Dispositions against a Custodian Type Trust Company)
Article 45 (1) Where an Custodian Type Trust Company falls under any of the following items, the Prime Minister may rescind said Custodian Type Trust Company's registration under Article 7(1), or may order said Custodian Type Trust Company to suspend its business operations in whole or in part and specify a period not exceeding six months therefor:
  (i) when said Custodian Type Trust Company has come to fall under any of Article 5(2)(i) or items (iv) to (vi) inclusive of that paragraph;
  (ii) when said Custodian Type Trust Company has come to fall under any of Article 10(1)(ii) to (v) inclusive;
  (iii) when said Custodian Type Trust Company is found to have been registered under Article 7(1) by wrongful means;
  (iv) when said Custodian Type Trust Company has violated laws and regulations or a disposition made by the Prime Minister pursuant to laws and regulations; or
  (v) when said Custodian Type Trust Company has committed an act that is harmful to the public interest.
(2) When a director or executive officer, an accounting advisor, or a company auditor of a Custodian Type Trust Company has come to fall under any of Article 5(2)(viii)(a) to (h)

inclusive, or has committed any act that falls under item (iv) of the preceding paragraph, the Prime Minister may order said Custodian Type Trust Company to dismiss said director, executive officer, accounting advisor, or company auditor.

(Loss of Effect of a License or Registration)
Article 46 (1) When a Trust Company has come to fall under any of the items of Article 41(2), said Trust Company's license under Article 3 or its registration under Article 7(1) shall cease to be effective.
(2) When a Trust Company (excluding a Custodian Type Trust Company) has obtained a registration under Article 7(1) or Article 52(1), said Trust Company's license under Article 3 shall cease to be effective.
(3) When a Custodian Type Trust Company has obtained a license under Article 3 or a registration under Article 52(1), said Custodian Type Trust Company's registration under Article 7(1) shall cease to be effective.

(Cancellation of Registration)
Article 47 When the Prime Minister has not renewed a registration under Article 7(3) or has rescinded a registration under Article 7(1) pursuant to the provisions of Article 45(1), or when a registration under Article 7(1) has ceased to be effective pursuant to the provisions of paragraph (1) or (3) of the preceding Article, the Prime Minister shall cancel said registration.

(Public Notice of Overseeing Dispositions)
Article 48 When the Prime Minister has rescinded a license under Article 3 pursuant to the provisions of Article 44(1), has rescinded a registration under Article 7(1) pursuant to the provisions of Article 45(1), or has ordered suspension of business in whole or in part pursuant to the provisions of Article 44(1) or Article 45(1), the Prime Minister shall give a public notice to that effect.

(Procedures for Dismissal in the Case of Rescission, etc. of a License, etc.)
Article 49 (1) In the cases where the Prime Minister has not renewed a registration under Article 7(3), has rescinded a license under Article 3 pursuant to the provisions of Article 44(1), or has rescinded a registration under Article 7(1) pursuant to the provisions of Article 45(1), with regard to an application under Article 58(4) of the Trust Act, the term "settlor or beneficiary" in that paragraph shall be deemed to be replaced with "settlor, beneficiary, or the Prime Minister."
(2) With regard to the application of Article 62(2) of the Trust Act in the cases set forth in the preceding paragraph, the term "interested party" in that paragraph shall be deemed to be replaced with "interested party or the Prime Minister."
(3) In the cases referred to in paragraph (1), a trustee which was formerly a Trust Company shall be deemed to be a Trust Company for the period until the court dismisses the trustee which was formerly the Trust Company.

(Opinion, etc. of the Prime Minister in Liquidation Proceedings, etc.)
Article 50 (1) In liquidation proceedings, bankruptcy proceedings, rehabilitation proceedings, reorganization proceedings, or recognition assistance proceedings for a Trust Company, the court may request the opinion of the Prime Minister, or may request that an inspection or investigation be carried out thereby.
(2) When the Prime Minister finds it necessary, the Prime Minister may state an opinion to the court pertaining to the proceedings prescribed in the preceding paragraph.
(3) The provisions of Article 42(1), (5) and (6) shall apply mutatis mutandis to cases

where the Prime Minister receives a request for inspection or investigation from the court pursuant to the provision of paragraph (1).

Section 6 Special Provisions Concerning Specific Trusts

(Special Provisions Concerning Trusts Created by Any of the Methods Listed in Article 3(iii) of the Trust Act)

Article 50-2 (1) A person who intends to create a trust by any of the methods listed in Article 3(iii) of the Trust Act shall be registered by the Prime Minister in the cases specified by a Cabinet Order as the cases where many persons (meaning persons of a number specified by a Cabinet Order or more; the same shall apply in paragraph (10)) may acquire beneficial interest in said trust; provided, however, that this shall not apply to the cases specified by a Cabinet Order as the cases where the creation of such a trust will not interfere with the protection of the beneficiaries of said trust.

(2) The provisions of Article 7(2) to (6) inclusive shall apply mutatis mutandis to the registration set forth in the preceding paragraph.

(3) A person who wishes to be registered under paragraph (1) (including renewal of a registration under Article 7(3), as applied mutatis mutandis pursuant to the preceding paragraph; the same shall apply in paragraph (6), as well as in Article 45(1)(iii) and Article 91 as applied pursuant to the replacement of terms under the provisions of paragraph (12)) (referred to as the "Applicant" in paragraph (6)) shall submit a written application to the Prime Minister stating the following matters:

(i) the trade name;

(ii) the amount of stated capital;

(iii) the names of the directors and company auditors (in the case of a company with committees, the directors and executive officers; and in the case of a Holding Company, the managing members);

(iv) in the case of a company with accounting advisors, the names of the accounting advisors;

(v) the type of business relating to affairs pertaining to trusts created by any of the methods listed in Article 3(iii) of the Trust Act;

(vi) where the person carries out business other than the business set forth in the preceding item, the type of business; and

(vii) the names and locations of business offices which carry out affairs pertaining to trusts created by any of the methods listed in Article 3(iii) of the Trust Act.

(4) The following documents shall be attached to the written application set forth in the preceding paragraph:

(i) the articles of incorporation;

(ii) a certificate of the registered matters of the company (meaning a company prescribed in Article 2(i) of the Companies Act; the same shall apply in paragraph (6));

(iii) a document stating the content and method of affairs pertaining to trusts created by any of the methods listed in Article 3(iii) of the Trust Act;

(iv) a balance sheet; and

(v) other documents specified by a Cabinet Office Ordinance.

(5) The document set forth in item (iii) of the preceding paragraph shall state the following matters:

(i) the type of trust property of trusts created by any of the methods listed in Article 3(iii) of the Trust Act;

(ii) the method of management or disposition of the trust property;

(iii) the method of segregated management of the trust property;

(iv) the system for carrying out affairs pertaining to trusts created by any of the meth-

ods listed in Article 3(iii) of the Trust Act;
(v) in cases where part of affairs pertaining to trusts created by any of the methods listed in Article 3(iii) of the Trust Act is delegated to a third party, the content of the affairs delegated thereto as well as the standards and procedures pertaining to the selection of the person delegated with said part of the affairs (excluding the case where affairs that fall under any of the items of Article 22(3) are delegated);
(vi) where the person carries out Business for the Sale and Purchase, etc. of Beneficial Interest in Trust, the system for carrying out said business; and
(vii) other matters specified by a Cabinet Office Ordinance.
(6) When the Applicant falls under any of the following items, or when the written application set forth in paragraph (3) or any of the attached documents listed in the items of paragraph (4) include any false statements or fail to state any material facts, the Prime Minister shall refuse to register the Applicant:
(i) a person who is not a company;
(ii) a company whose amount of stated capital is less than the amount specified by a Cabinet Order as necessary and appropriate for the protection of the beneficiaries;
(iii) a company whose amount of net assets is less than the amount prescribed in the preceding item;
(iv) a company for whom provisions of the articles of incorporation or provisions of the document set forth in paragraph (4)(iii) do not conform to laws and regulations or are not sufficient for it to properly execute affairs pertaining to trusts created by any of the methods listed in Article 3(iii) of the Trust Act;
(v) a company which, in light of its personnel composition, is found not to have the knowledge and experience that would allow for the right execution of affairs pertaining to trusts created by any of the methods listed in Article 3(iii) of the Trust Act;
(vi) a company which falls under Article 5(2)(v) or (vi);
(vii) a company whose other business is found to be contrary to the public interest, or a company for which carrying out said other business is likely to interfere with the proper and reliable execution of its affairs pertaining to trusts; or
(viii) a company whose directors or executive officers, accounting advisors, or company auditors include a person who falls under any of Article 5(2)(viii)(a) to (h) inclusive.
(7) The amount of net assets set forth in item (iii) of the preceding paragraph shall be calculated pursuant to the provisions of a Cabinet Office Ordinance.
(8) Where an application has been filed for registration under paragraph (1), the Prime Minister shall register the following matters in the registry of self-declared trusts except when the Prime Minister refuses to register said trust pursuant to the provisions of paragraph (6):
(i) the matters listed in the items of paragraph (3); and
(ii) the date of registration and the registration number.
(9) The Prime Minister shall make the registry of self-settled trusts available for public inspection.
(10) When a person who has been registered under paragraph (1) has created a trust by any of the methods listed in Article 3(iii) of the Trust Act (limited to the cases specified by a Cabinet Order as the cases where many persons may acquire beneficial interest in said trust), the person shall, pursuant to the provisions of a Cabinet Office Ordinance, have a person other than said registered person who is specified by a Cabinet Order inspect the status of the property belonging to the relevant trust property or other matters relating to said property.
(11) A person who has been registered under paragraph (1) shall, pursuant to the provi-

Art.50-2   ④ Trust Business Act, Chap.II, Sec.6

sions of a Cabinet Office Ordinance, ensure that carrying out other business will not interfere with the proper and reliable execution of affairs pertaining to trusts set forth in that paragraph.

(12) Where a trust under paragraph (1) is created based on the registration under that paragraph, the provisions of Article 11 (excluding the part pertaining to rescission and loss of effect of a license under paragraph (10)), Article 12(2) and (3), Article 13(2), Article 15, Article 22, Article 23, Article 24(1) (limited to the part pertaining to items (iii) and (iv) (excluding the part pertaining to settlor in these provisions)), Article 27 to Article 29 inclusive, Article 29-2 (excluding paragraph (5)), Article 29-3 to Article 31 inclusive, Article 33, Article 34, Article 40, Article 41 (excluding paragraph (5)), Article 42, Article 43, Article 45 (excluding paragraph (1)(ii)), Article 46(1) (excluding the part pertaining to loss of effect of a license), Article 47, Article 48 (excluding the part pertaining to rescission of license), Article 49 (excluding the part pertaining to rescission of license), and the preceding Article, and the provisions of Chapter VII pertaining to these provisions shall apply by deeming a person who has been registered under paragraph (1) to be a Trust Company (in Article 12(2) and (3), Article 13(2), Article 45, and Article 47, a Custodian Type Trust Company). In this case, the term "trust business" and "Trust Business" in these provisions shall be deemed to be replaced with "affairs pertaining to trusts created by any of the methods listed in Article 3(iii) of the Trust Act" and the phrase "registration under Article 7(1)" in said provisions shall be deemed to be replaced with the phrase "registration under Article 50-2(1)." The terms and phrases listed in the middle column of the following table in the provisions listed in the left-hand column of the same table shall be deemed to be replaced with the terms and phrases listed in the right-hand column of said table.

Article 11(10)	the renewal of a registration under Article 7(3)	the renewal of a registration under Article 7(3) as applied mutatis mutandis pursuant to Article 50-2(2)
Article 12(2)	the items of Article 8(1)	the items of Article 50-2(3)
Article 12(3)	the Administration-Focused Trust Companies' registry	the registry of self-settled trusts
Article 13(2)	its statement of operational procedures	any document stating the content and method of affairs pertaining to a trust created by any of the methods listed in Article 3(iii) of the Trust Act
Article 22(3)	business	affairs pertaining to trusts created by any of the methods listed in Article 3(iii) of the Trust Act
Article 28(1)	other business	other affairs
Article 33	business report	self-settled trust report
Article 34(1)	business	affairs pertaining to trusts created by any of the methods listed in Article 3(iii) of the Trust Act
	all its business offices	all its business offices which handle affairs pertaining to trusts created by any of the methods listed in that item
Article 40(1)	business	affairs pertaining to trusts created by any of the methods listed in Article 3(iii) of the Trust Act

④ Trust Business Act, Chap.II, Sec.6 — Art.50-2

Article 41(2)(ii)	or a company auditor	a company auditor, or a member who executed business of the company
Article 41(3)	all of its business offices	all of its business offices which handle affairs pertaining to trusts created by any of the methods listed in that item
Article 42(1)	said business	said affairs
	the business or property of said Trust Company	the affairs or property
	status of business	status of affairs
Article 42(2)	notifications or measures under Article 17 to Article 19 inclusive or the status of business or property of said Trust Company	the affairs or property
Article 42(3)	business by	affairs by
	concerning the business	concerning the affairs
Article 42(4)	business	affairs
Article 43	status of business	status of affairs pertaining to trusts created by any of the methods listed in Article 3(iii) of the Trust Act
	its statement of operational procedures	any documents stating the content and method of affairs pertaining to a trust created by any of the methods listed in that item
	other measures necessary to improve the operation of business	other measures necessary to improve the operation of the affairs
Article 45(1)	business operations	affairs pertaining to trusts created by any of the methods listed in Article 3(iii) of the Trust Act
Article 45(1)(i)	Article 5(2)(i) or items (iv) to (vi) inclusive of that paragraph	Article 50-2(6)(i) to (vii) inclusive
Article 45(2)	or company auditor	or company auditor, or a member who executes business of the company
Article 47	renewed a registration under Article 7(3)	renewed a registration under Article 7(3) as applied mutatis mutandis pursuant to Article 50-2(2)
	paragraph (1) or (3) of the preceding Article	paragraph (1) of the preceding Article
Article 48	Article 44(1) or Article 45(1)	Article 45(1)
	business	affairs pertaining to trusts created by any of the methods listed in Article 3(iii) of the Trust Act
Article 49(1)	renewed a registration under Article 7(3)	renewed a registration under Article 7(3) as applied mutatis mutandis pursuant to Article 50-2(2)

4 信託業法

Art.51 ④ Trust Business Act, Chap.II, Sec.6

(Special Provisions Concerning Trusts Created between Persons Who Belong to Same Group of Companies)
Article 51 (1) The provisions of Article 3 and the preceding Article shall not apply to the acceptance of a trust which falls under all of the following requirements:
  (i) that the settlor, trustee, and beneficiary are companies which belong to the same group of companies (meaning a company (including a foreign company; hereinafter the same shall apply in this item and paragraph (10)) and a group of Subsidiary Companies of said company; hereinafter referred to as "Company Group" in this Article);
  (ii) that, in cases where a Special Purpose Company (meaning a Special Purpose Company as prescribed in Article 2(3) of the Act on Liquidation of Assets) is a beneficiary, no person who does not belong to the same Company Group as the trustee has acquired Asset Backed Securities (which mean Asset Backed Securities as prescribed in paragraph (11) of that Article; the same shall apply in paragraph (8)(ii)) issued by said Special Purpose Company;
  (iii) that no Silent Partnership Agreement pertaining to business of investment in beneficial interest in trust (meaning a silent partnership agreement prescribed in Article 535 of the Commercial Code (Act No. 48 of 1899); the same shall apply in paragraph (8)(iii)) has been concluded with a person who does not belong to the same Company Group as the trustee;
  (iv) any requirements specified by a Cabinet Office Ordinance as equivalent to the preceding two items; and
  (v) that the trust agreement includes a condition to the effect that the trustee may give up duties without the consent of the settlor or beneficiary in cases where trust has ceased to fulfill any of the requirements listed in the preceding items.
(2) A person who will accept a trust as set forth in the preceding paragraph shall notify the Prime Minister to that effect in advance.
(3) In addition to the trust agreement pertaining to the relevant trust, documents specified by a Cabinet Office Ordinance as those proving that said trust falls under all of the requirements listed in the items of paragraph (1) shall be attached to the notification set forth in the preceding paragraph.
(4) When trust under paragraph (1) has ceased to fall under any of the requirements listed in the items of that paragraph, the Prime Minister may order the trustee of the trust under that paragraph to take measures so that the trustee will cease to be a trustee or to take other necessary measures, and may specify a period not exceeding three months therefor.
(5) When a trustee of a trust under paragraph (1) has ceased to be a trustee of the trust under that paragraph, or has learned that the trust under that paragraph has ceased to fall under any of the requirements listed in the items of that paragraph, the trustee e shall notify the Prime Minister to that effect without delay.
(6) When the Prime Minister finds it especially necessary for confirming the status pertaining to a trust under paragraph (1), the Prime Minister may, to the extent of that necessity, order the settlor, trustee, or beneficiary of the trust under that paragraph to submit a notification under paragraph (2) or the preceding paragraph or reports or materials that should be used as a reference concerning measures under paragraph (4), or may have the officials enter a business office, office, or other facility of the trustee, and have them ask questions about the notification under paragraph (2) or the preceding paragraph or measures under paragraph (4), or inspect the documents or other relevant items of the trustee (limited to those necessary for a notification under paragraph (2) or the preceding paragraph or measures under paragraph (4)).

(7) The provisions of Article 42(5) and (6) shall apply mutatis mutandis to an inspection under the provisions of the preceding paragraph.
(8) No beneficiary of a trust under paragraph (1) shall commit the following acts:
   (i) the act of allowing a person who does not belong to the same Company Group as the trustee acquire beneficial interest in said trust;
   (ii) the act of allowing a person who does not belong to the same Company Group as the trustee acquire Asset Backed Securities pertaining to beneficial interest in said trust;
   (iii) the act of concluding a Silent Partnership Agreement pertaining to business related to investment in a beneficial interest in said trust with a person who does not belong to the same Company Group as the trustee; or
   (iv) other acts specified by a Cabinet Office Ordinance as equivalent to the preceding two items.
(9) No Financial Instruments Business Operator (meaning a Financial Instruments Business Operator as prescribed in Article 2(9) of the Financial Instruments and Exchange Act, and including a person who is deemed to be a Financial Instruments Business Operator pursuant to the provisions of Article 65-5(2) of that Act) or a Registered Financial Institution (meaning a Registered Financial Institution as prescribed in Article 2(11) of that Act, and including a person who is deemed to be a Registered Financial Institution pursuant to the provisions of Article 2(4) of the Act on Provision, etc. of Trust Business by Financial Institutions) shall sell a beneficial interest in a trust under paragraph (1) to a person who does not belong to the same Company Group as the trustee, nor shall act as an agent or an intermediary in such selling.
(10) The term "Subsidiary Company" as set forth in paragraph (1)(i) shall mean a company for which the majority of the voting rights of all shareholders or all persons who made capital contributions are held by another company. In this case, a company for which the majority of the voting rights of all shareholders or persons who made capital contribution are held by another company and one or more of its subsidiary companies or by one or more subsidiary companies of said other company shall be deemed to be the Subsidiary Company of said other company.

(Special Provisions Concerning Trusts Pertaining to Specified University Technology Transfer Project)
Article 52 (1) The provisions of Article 3 shall not apply to the acceptance of a trust by a person who has obtained the approval of the Minister of Education, Culture, Sports, Science and Technology and the Minister of Economy, Trade and Industry with regard to a plan for the implementation of a Specified University Technology Transfer Project (meaning a Specified University Technology Transfer Project as prescribed in Article 2(1) of the Act on the Promotion of Technology Transfer from Universities to Private Business Operators (Act No. 52 of 1998); hereinafter the same shall apply in this Article) pursuant to the provisions of Article 4(1) of that Act (referred to as an "Approved Business Operator" in paragraph (3)) as a Specified University Technology Transfer Project based on registration by the Prime Minister (hereinafter referred to as "Acceptance of a Trust that Falls under the Category of a Specified University Technology Transfer Project" in this Article).
(2) The provisions of Article 8 (excluding paragraph (1), item (iv)), Article 9, and Article 10 (excluding paragraph (1), item (ii)) shall apply mutatis mutandis to the registration set forth in the preceding paragraph. In this case, the terms and phrases listed in the middle column of the following table in the provisions listed in the left-hand column of the same table shall be deemed to be replaced with the terms and phrases listed in the right-hand column of the same table.

Art.52　　　　　　　④ Trust Business Act, Chap.II, Sec.6

Article 8(1)(i)	the trade name	the trade name or name
Article 8(1)(ii)	of stated capital	of stated capital or contribution
Article 8(1)(iii)	directors and company auditors	officers
Article 8(1)(v)	trust business	trust business (limited to business which falls under the category of a Specified University Technology Transfer Project)
Article 8(1)(vi)	the head office and other business offices	the main business offices or offices or other business offices or offices
Article 8(2)(i)	the articles of incorporation	the articles of incorporation or the articles of endowment
Article 8(2)(ii)	a certificate of the registered matters of the company	a certificate of the registered matters
Article 9(1) and (2)	the Administration-Focused Trust Companies' registry	the registry of approved business operators for a specified university technology transfer project
Article 10(1)(i)	items (ii) and (iii)	items (i) to (iv) inclusive
Article 10(1)(iii)	a stock company whose amount of net assets is less than the amount prescribed in the preceding item	a juridical person whose amount of net assets is less than the amount of stated capital or contribution
Article 10(1)(iv)	the articles of incorporation	the articles of incorporation or the articles of endowment
	Administration-Focused Trust Business	Acceptance of a Trust that Falls under the category of a Specified University Technology Transfer Project
	stock company	juridical person
Article 10(1)(v)	Administration-Focused Trust Business	Acceptance of a Trust that Falls under the category of a Specified University Technology Transfer Project
	stock company	juridical person

(3) When an Approved Business Operator accepts a trust with a registration set forth in paragraph (1), the provisions of Article 11 (excluding the parts pertaining to the non-renewal of a registration as well as rescission and loss of effect of license, which are set forth in paragraph (10)), Article 12(2) and (3), Article 13(2), Article 21 to Article 24 inclusive, Article 25 to Article 29-3 inclusive, Article 33, Article 34, Article 41 (excluding paragraph (5)), Article 42 (excluding paragraph (2)), Article 43, Article 45, Article 46 (excluding the part pertaining to loss of effect of license), Article 47 (excluding the parts pertaining to the non-renewal of a registration), Article 48 (excluding the parts pertaining to rescission of license), Article 49 (excluding the parts pertaining to the non-renewal of a registration and rescission of a license), and Article 50, as well as the provisions of Chapter VII that are relevant to these provisions shall apply, by deeming such Approved Business Operator to be a Trust Company (in Article 12(2) and (3), Article 13(2), Article 45, Article 46(3), and Article 47, an Custodian Type Trust Company). In this case, the terms and phrases listed in the middle column of the following table in the provisions listed in the left-hand column of the same table shall be deemed to be replaced with the terms and phrases listed in the right-hand column of the same table.

4 Trust Business Act, Chap.II, Sec.6 — Art.52

Article 11(1)	head office	main business office or office
Article 11(10)	registration under Article 7(1)	registration under Article 52(1)
Article 12(3)	Administration-Focused Trust Companies' registry	the registry of approved business operators for specified university technology transfer projects
Article 21(1)	In addition to Trust Business, a Trust Company may carry out Trust Agreement Agency Business, Business for the Sale and Purchase, etc. of Beneficial Interest in Trust, and property management business	In addition to Trust Business (limited to that which falls under the category of a Specified University Technology Transfer Project; the same shall apply hereinafter) and Specified University Technology Transfer Projects (excluding those which fall under the category of Trust Business), a Trust Company may, in relation to a Specified University Technology Transfer Project, carry out Trust Agreement Agency Business, Business for the Sale and Purchase, etc. of Beneficial Interest in Trust, and property management business
	Article 4(2)(iii) or Article 8(2)(iii)	Article 8(2)(iii) as applied mutatis mutandis pursuant to Article 52(2)
Article 21(6)	for a license under Article 3 or for registration under Article 7(1)	for registration under Article 52(1)
	license or registration	registration
Article 24(1)	the following acts (in the case of accepting a trust under a Specific Trust Agreement as prescribed in the following Article, excluding acts listed in item (v))	the following acts
Article 25	the trade name	the trade name or name
	the matters listed in items (iii) to (xvi) inclusive of paragraph (1) of the following Article (when the trust company accepts a trust under a Specific Trust Agreement, the matters listed in that items shall be excluded)	the matters listed in items (iii) to (xvi) inclusive of paragraph (1) of the following Article
Article 26(1)(ii)	the trade name	the trade name or name
Article 34(1) and (3)	business offices	business offices or offices
Article 41(2)(i)	when the Trust Company has abolished its Trust Business (including the cases where the Trust Company has had all of its Trust Business succeeded to due to a company split, and the cases	when the Trust Company has abolished its Trust Business (including the cases where the Trust Company has had all of its Trust Business succeeded to due to a company split, and the cases where the Trust Company

	where the Trust Company has had transferred all of its Trust Business):	has had transferred all of its Trust Business), or when approval under Article 4(1) of the Act on the Promotion of Technology Transfer from Universities to Private Business Operators has been rescinded pursuant to the provisions of Article 5(2) of that Act:
	Trust Company	business operator
Article 41(2)(ii)	the company	the business operator
	a director or executive officer representing the company or a company auditor	an officer representing the company
Article 41(3)	business offices	business offices or offices
Article 42(1)	a business office or any other facility of said Trust Company	a business office, office, or any other facility of said Approved Business Operator
Article 45(1)	registration under Article 7(1)	registration under Article 52(1)
Article 45(1)(i)	Article 5(2)(i) or items (iv) to (vi) inclusive of that paragraph	Article 5(2)(v) or (vi)
Article 45(1)(ii)	has come to fall under any of Article 10(1)(ii) to (v) inclusive	has come to fall under any of Article 10(1)(iii) to (v) inclusive as applied mutatis mutandis pursuant to Article 52(2)
Article 45(1)(iii)	registered under Article 7(1)	registered under Article 52(1)
Article 45(2)	a director or executive officer, an accounting advisor, or a company auditor	an officer
Article 46(1)	registration under Article 7(1)	registration under Article 52(1)
Article 46(3)	a license under Article 3 or a registration under Article 52(1)	a license under Article 3 or Article 53(1), or a registration under Article 7(1) or Article 54(1)
	registration under Article 7(1)	registration under Article 52(1)
Article 47	registration under Article 7(1)	registration under Article 52(1)
Article 48	registration under Article 7(1)	registration under Article 52(1)
	Article 44(1) or Article 45(1)	Article 45(1)
Article 49(1)	registration under Article 7(1)	registration under Article 52(1)

Chapter III Foreign Trust Business Operators

(Licenses)
Article 53 (1) A Foreign Trust Business Operator may carry out Trust Business at a branch office which said Foreign Trust Business Operator has established as a base of its trust business in Japan (hereinafter referred to as the "Main Branch Office") and other branch offices which said Foreign Trust Business Operator has established in Ja-

pan only when said Foreign Trust Business Operator has obtained a license for said Main Branch Office from the Prime Minister, notwithstanding the provisions of Article 3.

(2) A person who wishes to obtain a license set forth in the preceding paragraph (referred to as "Applicant" in paragraphs (5) and (6)) shall specify a representative who will be in charge of the business of all branch offices carrying out trust business (hereinafter referred to as "Representative in Japan") and submit a written application to the Prime Minister stating the following matters:
(i) the trade name and the location of the head office;
(ii) the amount of stated capital;
(iii) the names of the officers (meaning directors and executive officers, accounting advisors, and company auditors, or persons equivalent thereto; the same shall apply hereinafter);
(iv) where the person carries out business other than trust business at any branch office, the type of business;
(v) the names and locations of the Main Branch Office and other branch offices; and
(vi) the name of the Representative in Japan and the address of the Representative in Japan.

(3) The following documents shall be attached to the written application set forth in the preceding paragraph;
(i) the articles of incorporation and a certificate of the registered matters of the company (including documents equivalent thereto);
(ii) a statement of operational procedures;
(iii) a balance sheet;
(iv) a document stating expected income and expenditures; and
(v) other documents specified by a Cabinet Office Ordinance.

(4) The provisions of Article 4(3) shall apply mutatis mutandis to the statement of operational procedures set forth in item (ii) of the preceding paragraph.

(5) Where an application has been filed under paragraph (1), the Prime Minister shall examine whether the applicant conforms to the following standards:
(i) that the provisions of the articles of incorporation (including documents equivalent thereto) and the statement of operational procedures conform to laws and regulations and are also sufficient for the proper execution of trust business;
(ii) that the applicant has a sufficient financial basis to allow for the sound execution of trust business; and
(iii) in light of the personnel composition of each branch office, the applicant has the knowledge and experience that will allow for the right execution of trust business, and also has sufficient social credibility.

(6) When the applicant falls under any of the following items, or when the written application set forth in paragraph (2) or any of the attached documents listed in the items of paragraph (3) include any false statements or fail to state any material facts, the Prime Minister shall not give a license.
(i) a person who is not a juridical person of the same kind as a stock company;
(ii) a juridical person whose amount of stated capital under paragraph (2)(ii) is less than the amount specified by a Cabinet Order as necessary and appropriate for the protection of settlors or beneficiaries;
(iii) a juridical person whose amount of net assets is less than the amount prescribed in the preceding item;
(iv) a juridical person that intends to use a name that is identical to a trade name or name that is being used by another Trust Company or Foreign Trust Company, or a name that is likely to cause misidentification with another Trust Company or For-

Art.53　　　　4 Trust Business Act, Chap.III

eign Trust Company, at any of its branch offices;
(v) a juridical person for which the renewal of a registration under Article 7(3), as applied mutatis mutandis pursuant to paragraph (2) of the following Article, has been refused pursuant to the provisions of paragraph (6) of that Article, whose license under paragraph (1) has been rescinded pursuant to the provisions of Article 59(1), whose registration under paragraph (1) of the following Article has been rescinded pursuant to the provisions of Article 60(1), whose registration under Article 67(1) has been rescinded pursuant to the provisions of Article 82(1), whose license under Article 3 of the Secured Bonds Trust Act has been rescinded pursuant to the provisions of Article 12 of that Act, or whose authorization under Article 1(1) of the Act on Provision, etc. of Trust Business by Financial Institutions has been rescinded pursuant to the provisions of Article 10 of that Act, or whose license, registration, or authorization of the same kind (including permission or any other administrative disposition similar to said license, registration, or authorization) which has been obtained in the state in which its head office is located has been rescinded or to whom renewal of said license, registration, or authorization has been refused pursuant to the provisions of laws and regulations of that state that are equivalent to this Act, the Secured Bonds Trust Act, or the Act on Provision, etc. of Trust Business by Financial Institutions, and for whom five years have yet to elapse since the date of rescission (where a renewal has been refused, the day on which the disposition of refusal to renew was made);
(vi) a juridical person who has been sentenced to a fine (including punishment equivalent thereto pursuant to laws and regulations of a foreign state) for violating the provisions of any of the laws prescribed in Article 5(2)(vi) or the provisions of laws and regulations of a foreign state that are equivalent thereto, and for whom five years have yet to elapse since the day on which execution of the sentence was completed or since the day on which the person has ceased to be subject to execution of the sentence;
(vii) a juridical person whose other business carried out at any of its branch offices is business that is not related to its trust business, or a juridical person for which carrying out said other business is found to be likely to interfere with the proper and reliable operation of its trust business;
(viii) a juridical person whose officers (including persons who are found to have power equivalent to or greater than that of an officer of said juridical person, irrespective of title; the same shall apply in Article 59(2) and Article 60(2)) and Representatives in Japan include a person who falls under any of Article 5(2)(viii)(a) to (h) inclusive; or
(ix) a juridical person for which the regulatory authorities pertaining to Trust Business in a foreign state have yet to confirm that its Major Shareholders (including persons equivalent thereto) are persons who are not likely to interfere with the sound and appropriate operations of trust business.
(7) The amount of stated capital set forth in paragraph (2)(ii) shall be calculated pursuant to the provisions of a Cabinet Office Ordinance.
(8) The amount of net assets set forth in paragraph (6)(iii) shall be calculated pursuant to the provisions of a Cabinet Office Ordinance.
(9) When the Prime Minister finds it necessary in light of the standards for examination under the provisions of paragraph (5), the Prime Ministermay, to the extent of that necessity, impose conditions on the license under paragraph (1) or change such conditions.

(Registration)

④ Trust Business Act, Chap.III　　　　　　　　　　　　　　　　　　　　Art.54

Article 54 (1) Where the Main Branch Office of a Foreign Trust Business Operator has been registered by the Prime Minister, said Foreign Trust Business Operator may carry out Custodian Type Trust Business at said Main Branch Office and other branch offices that it has established in Japan, notwithstanding the provisions of Article 3, Article 7(1), and paragraph (1) of the preceding Article.
(2) The provisions of Article 7(2) to (6) inclusive shall apply mutatis mutandis to the registration set forth in the preceding paragraph.
(3) A person who wishes to be registered under paragraph (1) (including the renewal of a registration under Article 7(3) as applied mutatis mutandis pursuant to the preceding paragraph; the same shall apply in paragraph (6), Article 60(1)(iii) and Article 91(iii)) (referred to as the "Applicant" in paragraph (6)) shall specify a Representative in Japan and submit a written application to the Prime Minister stating the following matters:
(i) the trade name and the location of the head office;
(ii) the amount of stated capital;
(iii) the names of the officers;
(iv) where the representative carries out business other than trust business at any of the branch offices, the type of business;
(v) the names and locations of the Main Branch Office and other branch offices; and
(vi) the name of the Representative in Japan and the address in Japan.
(4) The following documents shall be attached to the written application set forth in the preceding paragraph:
(i) the articles of incorporation and a certificate of the registered matters of the company (including documents equivalent thereto);
(ii) a statement of operational procedures;
(iii) a balance sheet; and
(iv) other documents specified by a Cabinet Office Ordinance.
(5) The provisions of Article 8(3) shall apply mutatis mutandis to the statement of operational procedures set forth in item (ii) of the preceding paragraph.
(6) When the Applicant falls under any of the following items, or when the written application set forth in paragraph (3) or any of the attached documents listed in the items of paragraph (4) include any false statements or fail to state any material facts, the Prime Minister shall refuse to register the Applicant:
(i) a person who falls under any of the items of paragraph (6) of the preceding Article (excluding items (ii) and (iii));
(ii) a juridical person whose amount of stated capital under paragraph (3)(ii) is less than the amount specified by a Cabinet Order as necessary and appropriate for the protection of settlors or beneficiaries;
(iii) a juridical person whose amount of net assets is less than the amount prescribed in the preceding item;
(iv) a juridical person whose provisions in its articles of incorporation (including documents equivalent thereto) or statement of operational procedures does not conform to laws and regulations or are not sufficient to allow it to properly execute Custodian Type Trust Business; or
(v) a juridical person for which any of the branch offices is found, in light of its personnel composition, to not have the knowledge and experience that would allow for the right execution of Custodian Type Trust Business.
(7) The amount of stated capital set forth in paragraph (3)(ii) shall be calculated pursuant to the provisions of a Cabinet Office Ordinance.
(8) The amount of net assets set forth in paragraph (6)(iii) shall be calculated pursuant to the provisions of a Cabinet Office Ordinance.
(9) Where an application has been filed for registration under paragraph (1), the Prime

Art.55〜57　　　　　　4 Trust Business Act, Chap.III

Minister shall register the following matters in the Custodian Type Foreign Trust Companies' registry, except when the Prime Minister refuses to register the Applicant pursuant to the provisions of paragraph (6):
(i) the matters listed in the items of paragraph (3); and
(ii) the date of registration and the registration number.
(10) The Prime Minister shall make the Custodian Type Foreign Trust Companies' registry available for public inspection.

(Loss Reserves, etc.)
Article 55 (1) A Foreign Trust Company (excluding Custodian Type Foreign Trust Companies) shall, for each accounting period, set aside loss reserves at its Main Branch Office in an amount not less than the amount obtained by multiplying the amount of profits pertaining to the business carried out at all branch offices by a ratio which does not exceed one tenth and which is specified by a Cabinet Office Ordinance, until the amount of loss reserves reaches the amount specified by a Cabinet Order under Article 53(6)(ii).
(2) The provisions of the preceding paragraph shall apply mutatis mutandis to Custodian Type Foreign Trust Companies. In this case, the term "Article 53(6)(ii)" in that paragraph shall be deemed to be replaced with "Article 54(6)(ii)".
(3) The loss reserves set aside pursuant to the provisions of the preceding two paragraphs shall not otherwise be used except when appropriated to compensation of a net loss pertaining to the business of all branch offices for each accounting period, with approval thereof from the Prime Minister.
(4) A Foreign Trust Company shall, pursuant to the provisions of a Cabinet Office Ordinance, retain assets in Japan equivalent to the total sum of the loss reserves set aside pursuant to the provisions of paragraph (1) or (2), the amount of security deposits specified by a Cabinet Office Ordinance, and the amount of liability belonging to the account of all branch offices as specified by a Cabinet Office Ordinance.

(Notification of Changes to Any of the Matters Stated in a Written Application)
Article 56 (1) When there is a change in any of the matters listed in the items of Article 53(2), a Foreign Trust Company (excluding Custodian Type Foreign Trust Companies) shall notify the Prime Minister to that effect within two weeks from the date of said change.
(2) When there is a change in any of the matters listed in the items of Article 54(3), a Custodian Type Foreign Trust Company shall notify the Prime Minister to that effect within two weeks from the date of said change.
(3) When the Prime Minister has received a notification set forth in the preceding paragraph, the Prime Minister shall register to that effect in the Custodian Type Foreign Trust Companies' registry.

(Notifications, etc.)
Article 57 (1) When a Foreign Trust Company has come to fall under any of the following items, it shall notify the Prime Minister to that effect without delay:
(i) when the Foreign Trust Company has filed for the commencement of bankruptcy proceedings, commencement of rehabilitation proceedings, or commencement of reorganization proceedings in Japan, or when it has filed for any proceedings of the same kind in the state where its head office is located, pursuant to the laws and regulations of said state;
(ii) when the Foreign Trust Company has effected a merger (excluding the case where

said Foreign Trust Company is extinguished due to a merger), when it has had a part of its Trust Business succeeded to, when it has succeeded to Trust Business in whole or in part, when it has transferred a part of its Trust Business, or when it has acquired Trust Business in whole or in part; or
(iii) when the Foreign Trust Company falls under any other cases prescribed by a Cabinet Office Ordinance.
(2) When a Foreign Trust Company has come to fall under any of the following items, the person specified in each of the relevant items shall notify the Prime Minister to that effect without delay:
(i) when the Foreign Trust Company has closed trust business at all of its branch offices (including the cases where the Foreign Trust Company has closed all of its Trust Business in foreign countries, where it has had all of its Trust Business conducted in foreign countries succeeded to, where it has had transferred all of its Trust Business conducted in foreign countries, where it has had all of its Trust Business conducted at the branch offices succeeded to, and where it has had transferred all of its Trust Business conducted at its branch offices): said Foreign Trust Business Operator or the person who formerly was said Foreign Trust Business Operator;
(ii) when the Foreign Trust Company has been extinguished due to a merger: a person who was the officer of said Foreign Trust Business Operator;
(iii) when an order for the commencement of bankruptcy proceedings has been issued to the Foreign Trust Company, or when any proceedings of the same kind as bankruptcy proceedings have been commenced in the state where its head office is located pursuant to the laws and regulations of said state: the bankruptcy trustee or the person who holds a position equivalent to bankruptcy trustee in said state; and
(iv) when the Trust Company has been dissolved due to any reason other than a merger or the commencement of bankruptcy proceedings (including the case where liquidation of a branch has been commenced): the liquidator or a person who holds a position equivalent to liquidator in the state where its head office is located.
(3) When a Foreign Trust Company intends to close Trust Business carried out at all of its branch offices (including closure of all Trust Business carried out in foreign countries), to effect a merger (limited to a merger upon which said Foreign Trust Company extinguishes), to dissolve due to any reason other than a merger or the commencement of bankruptcy proceedings, to have all of its Trust Business conducted at branch offices succeeded to (including succession to all of its Trust Business in foreign countries), to have a part of its Trust Business conducted at branch offices succeeded to, to transfer all Trust Business at its branch offices (including transfer of all Trust Business in foreign countries) or transfer a part of Trust Business carried out at its branch offices, it shall, by thirty days prior to the date when any of these events is to take place, give public notice to that effect and post a notice to that effect in a place easily seen by the public at all of its business offices, pursuant to the provisions of a Cabinet Office Ordinance.
(4) When a Foreign Trust Company has given public notice as set forth in the preceding paragraph, it shall immediately notify the Prime Minister to that effect.
(5) When a Foreign Trust Company (excluding an Custodian Type Foreign Trust Company; hereinafter the same shall apply in this paragraph) has been registered pursuant to Article 52(1) or Article 54(1), or when an Custodian Type Foreign Trust Company has been registered pursuant to Article 52(1), the Foreign Trust Company or the Custodian Type Foreign Trust Company shall, without delay, give public notice to that effect and post a notice to that effect in a place easily seen by the public at all of its business offices, pursuant to the provisions of a Cabinet Office Ordinance.
(6) The provisions of Article 940(1) (excluding item (ii)) and 940(3) (Public Notice Period,

etc. of Electronic Public Notice), Article 941 (Electronic Public Notice Investigation), Article 946 (Obligation, etc. of Investigation), Article 947 (Cases Where an Electronic Public Notice Investigation Is Unable to Be Carried Out), Article 951(2) (Keeping and Inspection, etc. of Financial Statements, etc.), Article 953 (Order for Improvement), and Article 955 (Statements, etc. in an Investigation Record Book, etc.) of the Companies Act shall apply mutatis mutandis to the cases where a Foreign Trust Company gives public notice pursuant to the provisions of this Act or any other Act (excluding public notice to be given pursuant to the provisions of the Companies Act) by means of Electronic Public Notice (meaning Electronic Public Notice as prescribed in Article 2(xxxiv) (Definitions) of that Act). In this case, the term "the preceding two paragraphs" in Article 940(3) of that Act shall be deemed to be replaced with "paragraph (1)," and any necessary technical replacement of terms shall be specified by a Cabinet Order.

(Inspections, etc.)
Article 58 (1) When the Prime Minister finds it necessary for securing the sound and appropriate operations of a Foreign Trust Company's trust business, he/she may order said Foreign Trust Company or a person who conducts transactions with a branch office of said Foreign Trust Company with regard to said business to submit reports or materials that should be used as a reference concerning the business or property of said branch office, or have the officials enter said branch office or any other facility, and have them ask questions about the status of business or property, or inspect the books and documents or other relevant items.
(2) When the Prime Minister finds it especially necessary for securing the sound and appropriate operations of trust business of a Foreign Trust Company, the Prime Minister may, to the extent of that necessity, order a person who has been delegated with business by said Foreign Trust Company to submit reports or materials that should be used as a reference concerning the business or property of said Foreign Trust Company, or may have officials enter the facilities of a person who has been delegated with business by said Foreign Trust Company, and have them ask questions about the status of business or property of said Foreign Trust Company, or inspect the books, documents, or other relevant items.
(3) A person who has been delegated with business by a Foreign Trust Company as set forth in the preceding paragraph may refuse to submit a report or materials, may refuse questioning, and may refuse to undergo an inspection under the provisions of that paragraph when there are justifiable grounds.
(4) An official who carries out an inspection pursuant to the provisions of paragraph (1) or (2) shall carry a certificate for identification and present it to the persons concerned.
(5) The authority for inspection under the provisions of paragraphs (1) and (2) shall not be construed as being for criminal investigation.

(Supervisory Dispositions against an Investment-Based Foreign Trust Company)
Article 59 (1) Where a Foreign Trust Company (excluding an Custodian Type Foreign Trust Company; hereinafter the same shall apply in this Article) falls under any of the following items, the Prime Minister may rescind its license under Article 53, paragraph (1), or may order said Foreign Trust Company to suspend business operations at its branch offices in whole or in part specifying a period not exceeding six months therefor:
(i) when the Foreign Trust Company has come to fall under any of Article 53(6)(i) to (vi) inclusive;

(ii) when the Foreign Trust Company is found to have fallen under any of the items of Article 53(6) at the time when it obtained a license under paragraph (1) of that Article;
(iii) when any of the branch offices of the Foreign Trust Company has ceased to have a sufficient personnel composition to allow for the right execution of trust business;
(iv) when the Foreign Trust Company is found to have obtained a license under Article 53(1) by wrongful means;
(v) when the Foreign Trust Company has violated any condition attached to a license under Article 53(1);
(vi) when the Foreign Trust Company has violated laws and regulations or any disposition made by the Prime Minister pursuant to laws and regulations; or
(vii) when the Foreign Trust Company has committed an act that is harmful to the public interest.
(2) When a Foreign Trust Company's Representative in Japan or a resident officer in a branch office thereof has come to fall under any of Article 5(2)(viii)(a) to (h) inclusive, or has committed an act that falls under item (v) or (vi) of the preceding paragraph, the Prime Minister may order said Foreign Trust Company to dismiss said representative or said officer.

(Supervisory Disposition against a Custodian Type Foreign Trust Company)
Article 60 (1) Where a Custodian Type Foreign Trust Company falls under any of the following items, the Prime Minister may rescind its registration under Article 54(1) or may order said Custodian Type Foreign Trust Company to suspend business operations at its branch offices in whole or in part and specify a period not exceeding six months therefor:
(i) when the Custodian Type Foreign Trust Company has come to fall under Article 53(6)(i) or any of items (iv) to (vi) inclusive of that paragraph;
(ii) when the Custodian Type Foreign Trust Company has come to fall under any of Article 54(6)(ii) to (v) inclusive;
(iii) when the Custodian Type Foreign Trust Company is found to have been registered under Article 54(1) by wrongful means;
(iv) when the Custodian Type Foreign Trust Company has violated laws and regulations or a disposition made by the Prime Minister pursuant to laws and regulations; or
(v) when the Custodian Type Foreign Trust Company has committed an act that is harmful to the public interest.
(2) When an Custodian Type Foreign Trust Company's Representative in Japan or a resident officer in a branch office thereof has come to fall under any of Article 5(2)(viii)(a) to (h) inclusive, or has committed an act that falls under item (iv) of the preceding paragraph, the Prime Minister may order said Custodian Type Foreign Trust Company to dismiss said representative or said officer.

(Application Mutatis Mutandis of Provisions on Dismissal Procedures in the Case of Rescission, etc. of a License, etc.)
Article 61 The provisions of Article 49 shall apply mutatis mutandis to the a case where the Prime Minister has not renewed a registration under Article 7(3) as applied mutatis mutandis pursuant to Article 54(2), the case where the Prime Minister has rescinded a license under Article 53(1) pursuant to the provisions of Article 59(1), or the case when the Prime Minister has rescinded a registration under Article 54(1) pursuant to the provisions of paragraph (1) of the preceding Article.

(Opinion, etc. of the Prime Minister in Liquidation Proceedings, etc.)
Article 62 (1) In liquidation proceedings, bankruptcy proceedings, rehabilitation proceedings, reorganization proceedings, or recognition and assistance proceedings conducted in Japan in relation to a Foreign Trust Company, the court may request the opinion of the Prime Minister, and may request that an inspection or investigation be carried out thereby.
(2) The provisions of Article 50(2) and (3) shall apply mutatis mutandis to the case prescribed in the preceding paragraph.

(Application of This Act)
Article 63 (1) The provisions of Chapter II (excluding the provisions of Article 3 to Article 10 inclusive, Article 12, Article 14(2), Article 17 to Article 21 inclusive, Article 32, Article 35 to Article 42 inclusive, Article 44, Article 45, and Article 49 to Article 52 inclusive) and the provisions of Chapter VII pertaining to these provisions shall apply by deeming a Foreign Trust Company to be a Trust Company, an Custodian Type Foreign Trust Company to be an Custodian Type Trust Company, and a Foreign Trust Company's Representative in Japan and the resident officer of a branch office thereof (excluding a company auditor or a person equivalent thereto) to be a director of a Trust Company. In this case, the terms and phrases listed in the middle column of the following table in the provisions listed in the left-hand column of the same table shall be deemed to be replaced with the terms and phrases listed in the right-hand column of said table.

Article 11(1)	head office	main branch office
Article 11(10)	renewal of a registration under Article 7(3)	renewal of a registration under Article 7(3) as applied mutatis mutandis pursuant to Article 54(2)
	Article 44(1)	Article 59(1)
	license under Article 3	license under Article 53(1)
	Article 45(1)	Article 60(1)
	registration under Article 7(1)	registration under Article 54(1)
Article 14(1), Article 25 and Article 26(1)(ii)	trade name	name of branch offices
Article 24-2	"the address	"the address of the branch offices
	"Article 26(1) of the Trust Business Act";	"Article 26(1) of the Trust Business Act"; the term "officer" in Article 38 of the Financial Instruments and Exchange Act shall be deemed to be replaced with "officers (including Representative Persons in Japan)";
Article 33	with respect to each business year	with respect to each period from April of every year to March of the next year
	of each business year	of said period
Article 34	with respect to each business year	with respect to each period from April of every year to March of the next year
	of each business year	of said period

	business offices	branch offices
Article 46(1)	Article 41(2)	Article 57(2)
	license under Article 3	license under Article 53(1)
	registration under Article 7(1)	registration under Article 54(1)
Article 46(2)	registration under Article 7(1) or Article 52(1)	registration under Article 52(1) or Article 54(1)
	license under Article 3	license under Article 53(1)
Article 46(3)	license under Article 3 or a registration under Article 52(1)	registration under Article 52(1) or license under Article 53(1)
	registration under Article 7(1)	registration under Article 54(1)
Article 47	renewal of a registration under Article 7(3)	renewal of a registration under Article 7(3) as applied mutatis mutandis pursuant to Article 54(2)
	Article 45(1)	Article 60(1)
	registration under Article 7(1)	registration under Article 54(1)
Article 48	Article 44(1)	Article 59(1)
	license under Article 3	license under Article 53(1)
	Article 45(1)	Article 60(1)
	registration under Article 7(1)	registration under Article 54(1)

(2) The provisions of Article 21 shall apply mutatis mutandis to the business conducted by a Foreign Trust Company at its branch offices, and the provisions of Article 39 shall apply mutatis mutandis to the cases where a Foreign Trust Company transfers Trust Business conducted at its branches. In this case, the terms and phrases listed in the middle column of the following table in the provisions listed in the left-hand column of the same table shall be deemed to be replaced with the terms and phrases listed in the right-hand column of said table.

Article 21(1)	Article 4(2)(iii)	Article 53(3)(ii)
	Article 8(2)(iii)	Article 54(4)(ii)
Article 21(6)	license under Article 3	license under Article 53(1)
	registration under Article 7(1)	registration under Article 54(1)

(Notification of Establishment of an Office for Resident Officers of a Foreign Trust Business Operator, etc.)

Article 64 (1) Where a Foreign Trust Business Operator intends to establish an office for its resident officers or any other facility in Japan for the purpose of conducting the following business (including the case where a Foreign Trust Business Operator intends to conduct said business at a facility that has been established for other purposes), it shall notify the Prime Minister of the content of said business, the location of said facility, and other matters specified by a Cabinet Office Ordinance in advance:
(i) the collection or provision of information concerning Trust Business; and
(ii) other business related to Trust Business.
(2) When the Prime Minister finds it necessary, the Prime Minister may request a Foreign Trust Business Operator to submit a report or materials concerning the business listed in the items of the preceding paragraph which is conducted at the facility set forth in that paragraph.

(3) When a Foreign Trust Business Operator has closed a facility set forth in paragraph (1), has closed any business listed in the items of that paragraph which is conducted at said facility, or has changed any of the matters notified pursuant to the provisions of that paragraph, it shall notify the Prime Minister to that effect without delay.

Chapter IV Persons Authorized to Give Directions

(Duty of Loyalty of Persons Authorized to Give Directions)
Article 65 A person who carries out business related to providing instructions on methods of management or disposition of trust property (hereinafter referred to as a "Person Authorized to Give Directions" in the following Article) shall, in accordance with the main purpose of trust, loyally provide instructions on the management or disposition of trust property for the benefit of the beneficiaries.

(Rules of Conduct for Persons Authorized to Give Directions)
Article 66 No Person Authorized to Give Directions shall commit any of the following acts with regard to the trust property regarding which the person gives instructions:
(i) the act of instructing the trustee to conduct a transaction under conditions which are different from those for ordinary transactions, and under which a transaction will cause damage to the trust property;
(ii) the act of instructing the trustee to conduct a transaction which is unnecessary in light of the purpose of the trust, the status of the trust property, or the policy for the management or disposition of trust property;
(iii) the act of instructing the trustee to conduct a transaction (excluding that specified by a Cabinet Office Ordinance) in pursuit of one's own interests or in the interests of a person other than the beneficiary pertaining to the trust property, by using information on said trust property; and
(iv) other acts specified by a Cabinet Office Ordinance as those which are likely to cause damage to the trust property.

Chapter V Agent for Trust Agreement

Section 1 General Provisions

(Registration)
Article 67 (1) No person may carry out Agency for Trust Agreements without being registered by the Prime Minister.
(2) A person who carries out Agency for Trust Agreements shall carry out Agency for Trust Agreements for a Trust Company or a Foreign Trust Company (hereinafter referred to as "Principal Trust Company") under authorization by said Trust Company or Foreign Trust Company.

(Application for Registration)
Article 68 (1) A person who wishes to be registered under paragraph (1) of the preceding Article (referred to as "Applicant" in Article 70) shall submit a written application to the Prime Minister stating the following matters:
(i) the trade name or name;
(ii) in the case of a juridical person, the names of the officers;
(iii) the names and locations of the business offices or offices where the person carries out Agency for Trust Agreements;

(iv) the trade name of the Principal Trust Company;
(v) where the person carries out other business, the type of business; and
(vi) other matters specified by a Cabinet Office Ordinance.
(2) The following documents shall be attached to the written application set forth in the preceding paragraph:
(i) a document pledging that the person falls under neither Article 70(i) nor (ii);
(ii) a statement of operational procedures;
(iii) in the case of a juridical person, the articles of incorporation and a certificate of the registered matters of the company (including documents equivalent thereto); and
(iv) other documents specified by a Cabinet Office Ordinance.
(3) The matters that should be stated in a statement of operational procedures set forth in item (ii) of the preceding paragraph shall be specified by a Cabinet Office Ordinance.

(Registration in Registry)

Article 69 (1) Where an application has been filed for registration under Article 67(1), the Prime Minister shall register the following matters in the registry for Agents for Trust Agreement except when the Prime Minister refuses to register the Applicant pursuant to the provisions of the following Article:
(i) the matters listed in the items of paragraph (1) of the preceding Article; and
(ii) the date of registration and the registration number.
(2) The Prime Minister shall make the registry for Trust Agreement available for public inspection.

(Refusal of Registration)

Article 70 When an Applicant falls under any of the following items, or when the written application set forth in Article 68(1) or any of the attached documents listed in the items of paragraph (2) of that Article include any false statements or fail to state any material facts, the Prime Minister shall refuse to register the Applicant:
(i) in cases where the Applicant is an individual, a person who falls under any of Article 5(2)(viii)(a) to (h) inclusive;
(ii) in cases where the Applicant is a juridical person, a person who falls under any of the following:
  (a) a person who falls under Article 5(2)(x)(a) or (b); or
  (b) a person whose officers include a person who falls under any of Article 5(2)(viii)(a) to (h) inclusive;
(iii) a person who is found not to have established the system necessary for the right execution of Agency for Trust Agreements; or
(iv) a person whose other business is found to be contrary to the public interest.

(Notification of Changes)

Article 71 (1) When there is a change in any of the matters listed in the items of Article 68(1), the Agent for Trust Agreement shall notify the Prime Minister to that effect within two weeks from the date of said change.
(2) When the Prime Minister has received a notification set forth in the preceding paragraph, the Prime Minister shall register to that effect in the registry for Agent for Trust Agreement.
(3) When an Agent for Trust Agreement has changed its statement of operational procedures under Article 68(2)(ii), it shall notify the Prime Minister to that effect without delay.

(Posting of Signs)

Article 72 (1) An Agent for Trust Agreement shall post a sign in the format specified by a Cabinet Office Ordinance in a place easily viewable by the public at each business office or office where it carries out Agency for Trust Agreements.

(2) No person other than an Agent for Trust Agreement shall post a sign as set forth in the preceding paragraph or any sign similar thereto.

(Prohibition on Name Lending)
Article 73 No Agent for Trust Agreement shall have another person carry out Agency for Trust Agreements in its own name.

Section 2 Business

(Explanations to Clients)
Article 74 When an Agent for Trust Agreement acts as an agent (limited to the cases where it acts as an agent for a Trust Company or a Foreign Trust Company; hereinafter the same shall apply in this Chapter) or an intermediary in concluding a trust agreement, it shall clearly explain to the client the following matters in advance:
(i) the trade name of the Principal Trust Company;
(ii) the role that the Trust Agreement Agent plays in concluding a trust agreement, either as an agent or as an intermediary; and
(iii) other matters specified by a Cabinet Office Ordinance.

(Segregated Management)
Article 75 Where an Agent for Trust Agreement has received a deposit of property from a client with regard to business in which it acts as an agent or intermediary in concluding a trust agreement, it shall manage said property separately from its own property and any property deposited in relation to conclusion of other trust agreements.

(Application Mutatis Mutandis)
Article 76 The provisions of Article 24 and Article 25 shall apply mutatis mutandis to business carried out by an Agent for Trust Agreement that is related to acting as an agent or an intermediary in concluding a trust agreement. In this case, the phrase "the following acts (in the case of accepting a trust under a Specific Trust Agreement prescribed in the following Article, excluding acts listed in item (v))" in Article 24(1) shall be deemed to be replaced with "the following acts," the term "matters (in the case of accepting a trust under a Specific Trust Agreement, excluding the matters listed in that item)" in Article 25 shall be deemed to be replaced with "matters," and the term "said Trust Company" in the same provisions shall be deemed to be replaced with "trustee."

Section 3 Accounting

(Reports on Agency for Trust Agreements)
Article 77 (1) An Agent for Trust Agreement shall prepare a report on its Agency for Trust Agreements with respect to each business year and submit it to the Prime Minister within three months from the end of each business year.

(2) The Prime Minister shall make reports on Agency for Trust Agreements as set forth in the preceding paragraph available for public inspection, with the exception of matters that are likely to do harm to a secret of the settlor or beneficiary and matters that are likely to cause an unreasonable disadvantage in the business performance of said

Agent for Trust Agreement.

(Public Inspection of Explanatory Documents of Principal Trust Companies)
Article 78 (1) An Agent for Trust Agreement shall keep copies of explanatory documents prepared by the Principal Trust Company pursuant to the provisions of Article 34(1) with respect to each business year of said Principal Trust Company at all of its business offices or offices where it carries out Agency for Trust Agreements, and shall thereby make it available for public inspection.
(2) When an explanatory document prescribed in the preceding paragraph has been prepared in the form of an Electromagnetic Record, all business offices or offices carrying out Agency for Trust Agreements may take measures specified by a Cabinet Office Ordinance as those for making information contained in said explanatory document available to unspecified many persons by Electromagnetic Means. In this case, the explanatory documents prescribed in that paragraph shall be deemed to have been made available for public inspection.

Section 4 Supervision

(Notification of Cessation of Business, etc.)
Article 79 When an Agent for Trust Agreement has come to fall under any of the following items, the persons prescribed in those items shall notify the Prime Minister to that effect within thirty days from that date:
(i) when a Trust Agreement Agent has closed Agency for Trust Agreements (including when it has had the whole Agency for Trust Agreements succeeded to due to company split or has transferred the whole Agency for Trust Agreements): the individual or juridical person;
(ii) when an individual who is an Agent for Trust Agreement has died: the individual's heir;
(iii) when a juridical person who is an Agent for Trust Agreement has been extinguished due to merger: the person who was an officer representing the juridical person;
(iv) when a juridical person who is an Agent for Trust Agreement has been dissolved due to an order for the commencement of bankruptcy proceedings: the bankruptcy trustee;
(v) when a juridical person who is an Agent for Trust Agreement has been dissolved for a reason other than a merger or an order for the commencement of bankruptcy proceedings: the liquidator.

(Site Inspections, etc.)
Article 80 (1) When the Prime Minister finds it necessary for securing the sound and appropriate operations of the agency business for trust agreements by an Agent for Trust Agreement, the Prime Minister may order said Agent for Trust Agreement or a person who conducts transactions with said Agent for Trust Agreement with regard to said business to submit reports or materials that should be used as a reference concerning the business of said Agent for Trust Agreement, or may have officials enter a business office or office of said Agent for Trust Agreement, ask questions about the status of business, and inspect the books, documents, and other relevant items.
(2) An official who carries out inspections pursuant to the provisions of the preceding paragraph shall carry a certificate for identification and present it to the persons concerned.
(3) The authority for inspection under the provisions of paragraph (1) shall not be con-

strued as being for criminal investigation.

(Order to Improve Business Operations)
Article 81 When the Prime Minister finds it necessary for securing the sound and appropriate operations of the business of an Agent for Trust Agreement in light of the status of business of said Agent for Trust Agreement, the Prime Minister may, to the extent of that necessity, order said Agent for Trust Agreement to change its statement of operational procedures or take any other measures necessary to improve the operations of the business.

(Supervisory Dispositions)
Article 82 (1) Where an Agent for Trust Agreement falls under any of the following items, the Prime Minister may rescind the registration of said Agent for Trust Agreement under Article 67(1), or may order said Agent for Trust Agreement to suspend its business operations in whole or in part and specifying a period not exceeding six months therefor:
(i) when the Trust Agreement Agent has come to fall under any of the items of Article 70 (excluding item (ii)(b));
(ii) when the Trust Agreement Agent is found to have been registered under Article 67(1) by wrongful means;
(iii) when the Trust Agreement Agent has violated laws or regulations or a disposition made by the Prime Minister pursuant to laws and regulations; or
(iv) when the Trust Agreement Agent has committed an act that is harmful to the public interest.
(2) When an officer of an Agent for Trust Agreement has come to fall under any of (a) to (h) inclusive of Article 5(2)(viii), or has committed an act that falls under item (iii) of the preceding paragraph, the Prime Minister may order said Agent for Trust Agreement to dismiss said officer.

(Loss of Effect of Registration)
Article 83 When an Agent for Trust Agreement Agent has come to fall under any of the items of Article 79, or when all entrustment agreements it has concluded with entrusting trust companies have terminated, the registration under Article 67(1) of said Trust Agreement Agent shall cease to be effective.

(Cancellation of Registration)
Article 84 When the Prime Minister has rescinded a registration under Article 67(1) pursuant to the provisions of Article 82(1), or when a registration under Article 67(1) has ceased to be effective pursuant to the provisions of the preceding Article, the Prime Minister shall cancel said registration.

Section 5 Miscellaneous Provisions

(Entrusting Trust Company Liability for Damages)
Article 85 A Principal Trust Company of an Agent for Trust Agreement shall be liable for compensation for damages caused to a client with regard to business carried out by an Agent for Trust Agreement that is related to acting as an agency or an intermediary in concluding a trust agreement; provided, however, that this shall not apply to the case where an Principal Trust Company has paid reasonable attention in entrusting said Agent for Trust Agreement and has made efforts to prevent damages which have been caused to a client with regard to business carried out by the Agent for Trust

Agreement that is related to acting as an agent or an intermediary in concluding a trust agreement.

Chapter VI Miscellaneous Provisions

(Submission of Materials to the Minister of Finance, etc.)
Article 86 (1) When the Minister of Finance finds it necessary for planning or designing systems for Trust Business, in relation to a system for disposal of failed financial institutions and financial risk management under the Minister's jurisdiction, the Minister may request that the Prime Minister provide the necessary materials and explanations therefor.
(2) When the Minister of Finance finds it particularly necessary for planning or designing systems for Trust Business, in relation to a system for disposal of failed financial institutions and financial crisis management under the Minister's jurisdiction, the Minister may, to the extent of that necessity, request Trust Companies, Foreign Trust Companies, or Agents for Trust Agreement to provide materials or explanation or any other cooperation.

(Delegation of Authority)
Article 87 (1) The Prime Minister shall delegate the authority under this Act (excluding that specified by a Cabinet Order) to the Commissioner of the Financial Services Agency.
(2) The Commissioner of the Financial Services Agency may, pursuant to the provisions of a Cabinet Order, delegate part of the authority delegated pursuant to the provisions of the preceding paragraph to the Directors-General of the Local Finance Bureaus or the Directors-General of the Local Finance Branch Bureaus.

(Application)
Article 88 The term "trust company" as used in laws and regulations other than this Act and orders issued based thereon shall include Foreign Trust Companies, except as otherwise provided.

(Delegation to Cabinet Office Ordinance)
Article 89 In addition to what is provided in this Act, application procedures, procedures for submission of documents, matters to be stated, and the preservation period with regard to a license, registration, authorization, or approval under the provisions of this Act and other matters necessary to enforce this Act shall be prescribed by a Cabinet Office Ordinance.

(Transitional Measures)
Article 90 Where an order is established or revised pursuant to the provisions of this Act, the necessary transitional measures (including those concerning penal provisions) may be prescribed by said order to the extent reasonably required along with said establishment or revision.

Chapter VII Penal Provisions

Article 91 A person who falls under any of the following items shall be punished by imprisonment with work for not more than three years, a fine of not more than three million yen, or both:

(i) a person who, in violation of the provisions of Article 3, has carried out Trust Business without obtaining a license;
(ii) a person who has obtained a license under Article 3 or Article 53(1) by wrongful means;
(iii) a person who has been registered under Article 7(1), Article 50-2(1), Article 52(1) or Article 54(1) by wrongful means;
(iv) a person who, in violation of the provisions of Article 15, has had another person carry out Trust Business;
(v) a person who, in violation of the provisions of Article 50-2(1), has created any trust by means specified in Article 3(iii) of the Trust Act without being registered;
(vi) a person who, in violation of the provisions of Article 67(1), has carried out Agency for Trust Agreements without being registered;
(vii) a person who has been registered under Article 67(1) by wrongful means; or
(viii) a person who, in violation of the provisions of Article 73, has had another person carry out Agency for Trust Agreements.

Article 92 A person who falls under any of the following items shall be punished by imprisonment with work for not more than two years, a fine of not more than three million yen, or both:
(i) a person who has violated any of the conditions attached pursuant to the provisions of Article 5(8) or Article 53(9);
(ii) a person who has violated an order to suspend business operations under the provisions of Article 44(1) or Article 45(1);
(iii) a person who has violated an order to suspend business operations under the provisions of Article 59(1) or Article 60(1); or
(iv) a person who has violated an order to suspend business operations under the provisions of Article 82(1).

Article 93 A person who falls under any of the following items shall be punished by imprisonment with work for not more than one year, a fine of not more than three million yen, or both:
(i) a person who has made a false statement in a written application under the provisions of Article 4(1) or any of the documents to be attached thereto pursuant to the provisions of paragraph (2) of that Article, and submitted it;
(ii) a person who has made a false statement in a written application under the provisions of Article 8(1) (including the cases where it is applied mutatis mutandis pursuant to Article 52(2)) or Article 50-2(3) or any of the documents to be attached thereto pursuant to the provisions of Article 8(2) (including the cases where it is applied mutatis mutandis pursuant to Article 52(2)) or Article 50-2(4), and submitted it;
(iii) a person who, in violation of the provisions of Article 21(2) (including the cases where it is applied mutatis mutandis pursuant to Article 63(2)), has carried out business other than Trust Business, Agency for Trust Agreements, Business for the Sale and Purchase, etc. of Beneficial Interest in Trust and property management business without obtaining approval;
(iv) a person who, in violation of the provisions of Article 24(1)(i), (iii), or (iv) (including the cases where these provisions are applied mutatis mutandis pursuant to Article 76), has committed any of the acts listed in these provisions;
(v) a person who has violated the provisions of Article 29(2);
(vi) a person who has failed to submit a report under the provisions of Article 33, or has submitted a false report;

(vii) a person who has failed to make an explanatory document under the provisions of Article 34(1) available for public inspection or who has failed to take any measures specified by a Cabinet Office Ordinance as those for making information recorded in an Electromagnetic Record under the provisions of paragraph (3) of that Article available to unspecified many persons by Electromagnetic Means, or a person who has made an explanatory document including a false statement available for public inspection or who has taken measures for making information recorded in an Electromagnetic Record including a false record available to unspecified many persons by Electromagnetic Means;

(viii) a person who has made a false statement in a written application under the provisions of Article 36(2) or in any of the documents to be attached thereto pursuant to the provisions of paragraph (3) of that Article, and submitted it;

(ix) a person who has made a false statement in a written application under the provisions of Article 37(2) or in any of the documents to be attached thereto pursuant to the provisions of paragraph (3) of that Article, and submitted it;

(x) a person who has made a false statement in a written application under the provisions of Article 38(2) or in any of the documents to be attached thereto pursuant to the provisions of paragraph (3) of that Article, and submitted it;

(xi) a person who has made a false statement in a written application under the provisions of Article 39(2) (including the cases where it is applied mutatis mutandis pursuant to paragraph (5) of that Article (including the cases where it is applied mutatis mutandis pursuant to Article 63(2)) and Article 63(2)) or in any of the documents to be attached thereto pursuant to the provisions of Article 39(3) (including the cases where it is applied mutatis mutandis pursuant to paragraph (5) of that Article (including the cases where it is applied mutatis mutandis pursuant to Article 63(2)) and Article 63(2)), and submitted it;

(xii) a person who has failed to give a public notice under the provisions of Article 41(3) or (5), or who has given a false public notice;

(xiii) a person who has failed to submit a report or material under the provisions of Article 42(1) (including the cases where it is applied mutatis mutandis pursuant to Article 50(3) (including the cases where it is applied mutatis mutandis pursuant to Article 62(2))) or Article 42(2) or (3), or who has submitted a false report or material;

(xiv) a person who has failed to respond to questioning by officials under the provisions of Article 42(1) (including the cases where it is applied mutatis mutandis pursuant to Article 50(3) (including the cases where it is applied mutatis mutandis pursuant to Article 62(2))) or Article 42(2) or (3), who has given a false answer thereto, or who has refused, obstructed, or avoided an inspection under these provisions;

(xv) a person who has failed to make a notification under the provisions of Article 51(2) or who has made a false statement in a written notice set forth in that paragraph or in any of the documents to be attached thereto pursuant to the provisions of paragraph (3) of that Article and submitted it;

(xvi) a person who has violated an order under the provisions of Article 51(4);

(xvii) a person who has failed to make a notification under the provisions of Article 51(5) or has made a false notification;

(xviii) a person who has failed to submit a report or material under the provisions of Article 51(6), or has submitted a false report or material;

(xix) a person who has failed to respond to questioning by the officials under the provisions of Article 51(6), who has given a false answer thereto, or who has refused, obstructed, or avoided an inspection under these provisions;

Art.94　　　④ Trust Business Act, Chap.VII, Sec.5

(xx) a person who has violated the provisions of Article 51(8) or (9);
(xxi) a person who has made a false statement in a written application under the provisions of Article 53(2) or in any of the documents to be attached thereto pursuant to the provisions of paragraph (3) of that Article, and submitted it;
(xxii) a person who has made a false statement in a written application under the provisions of Article 54(3) or in any of the documents to be attached thereto pursuant to the provisions of paragraph (4) of that Article, and submitted it;
(xxiii) a person who has failed to give public notice under the provisions of Article 57(3) or (5) or has given a false public notice;
(xxiv) a person who has failed to submit a report or material under the provisions of Article 58(1) or (2), or has submitted a false report or material;
(xxv) a person who has failed to respond to questioning by officials under the provisions of Article 58(1) or (2), who has given a false answer thereto, or who has refused, obstructed, or avoided an inspection under these provisions;
(xxvi) a person who has made a false statement in a written application under the provisions of Article 68(1) or in any of the documents to be attached thereto pursuant to the provisions of paragraph (2) of that Article, and submitted it;
(xxvii) a person who has failed to submit a report under the provisions of Article 77(1), or who has submitted a false report;
(xxviii) a person who has failed to make an explanatory document under the provisions of Article 78(1) available for public inspection, who has failed to take any measures specified by a Cabinet Office Ordinance as those for making information recorded in an Electromagnetic Record under the provisions of paragraph (2) of that Article available to unspecified many persons by Electromagnetic Means, who has made an explanatory document including a false statement available for public inspection, or who has taken measures for making information recorded in an Electromagnetic Record including a false record available to unspecified many persons by Electromagnetic Means;
(xxix) a person who has failed to submit a report or material under the provisions of Article 80(1), or who has submitted a false report or material; or
(xxx) a person who has failed to respond to questioning by officials under the provisions of Article 80(1), who has given a false answer, or who has refused, obstructed, or avoided an inspection under these provisions;

Article 94 A person who falls under any of the following items shall be punished by imprisonment with work for not more than one year, a fine of not more than one million yen, or both:
(i) a person who, in violation of the provisions of Article 6, has reduced the amount of stated capital without obtaining authorization;
(ii) a person who, in violation of the provisions of Article 11(5), has begun trust business;
(iii) a person who, in violation of the provisions of Article 13(1), has changed the statement of operational procedures without obtaining authorization;
(iv) a person who, in violation of the provisions of Article 16(1), has been engaged in routine business at another company or who has carried out business without obtaining approval;
(v) a person who has violated an order under the provisions of Article 18 (including the cases where it is applied mutatis mutandis pursuant to Article 20);
(vi) a person who, in violation of the provisions of Article 21(4) (including the cases where it is applied mutatis mutandis pursuant to Article 63(2)), has changed the content or method of business without obtaining approval; or

(vii) a person who has violated the provisions of Article 39(2) (excluding item (ii)) of the Financial Instruments and Exchange Act, as applied mutatis mutandis pursuant to Article 24-2 (hereinafter referred to as the "Financial Instruments and Exchange Act as Applied Mutatis Mutandis").

Article 95 In the case of item (vii) of the preceding Article, property benefits obtained by an offender or a knowing third party shall be confiscated. When such property benefits cannot be confiscated in whole or in part, a value equivalent thereto shall be collected.

Article 96 A person who falls under any of the following items shall be punished by imprisonment with work for not more than six months, a fine of not more than five hundred thousand yen, or both:
(i) a person who, in violation of the provisions of Article 11(8), has failed to make a deposit;
(ii) a person who has failed to submit a written notice under the provisions of Article 17(1) (including the cases where it is applied mutatis mutandis pursuant to Article 20) or any of the documents to be attached thereto pursuant to the provisions of Article 17(2) (including the cases where it is applied mutatis mutandis pursuant to Article 20), or who has submitted a written notice or a document to be attached thereto which is false;
(iii) a person who has made a false statement in a written application under the provisions of Article 21(3) (including the cases where it is applied mutatis mutandis pursuant to Article 63(2)) or in any of the documents to be attached thereto and submitted it;
(iv) a person who has failed to indicate any of the matters prescribed in Article 37(1) (excluding item (ii)) of the Financial Instruments and Exchange Act as Applied Mutatis Mutandis, or has made a false indication thereof;
(v) a person who has violated the provisions of Article 37(2) of the Financial Instruments and Exchange Act as Applied Mutatis Mutandis;
(vi) a person who, in violation of the provisions of Article 37-3(1) (excluding items (ii) to (iv) inclusive and item (vi)) of the Financial Instruments and Exchange Act as Applied Mutatis Mutandis, has failed to deliver a document, who has delivered a document that lacks a statement on any of the matters prescribed in that paragraph or a document that includes a false statement, who has provided information that is lacking in any of the matters prescribed in that paragraph, or who has provided false information by the method prescribed in Article 34-2(4) of the Financial Instruments and Exchange Act as applied mutatis mutandis pursuant to Article 37-3(2);
(vii) in the case where a document set forth in Article 26(1) is delivered or where an Electromagnetic Means set forth in paragraph (2) of that Article is adopted, a person who has failed to deliver or provide the Electromagnetic Record made by said means or who has delivered or provided a false document or Electromagnetic Record;
(viii) a person who has failed to deliver a report under the provisions of Article 27(1) or who has delivered a report that includes a false statement; or
(ix) a person who has failed to deliver a document under the provisions of Article 29(3) or who has delivered a false document.

Article 97 A person who falls under any of the following items shall be punished by a fine of not more than three hundred thousand yen:

Art.98　　　　4 Trust Business Act, Chap.VII, Sec.5

(i) a person who has failed to make a notification under the provisions of Article 12(1) or (2) or who has made a false notification;
(ii) a person who has failed to make a notification under the provisions of Article 13(2) or who has made a false notification;
(iii) a person who has violated the provisions of Article 14(2);
(iv) a person who has failed to make a notification under the provisions of Article 19 (including the cases where it is applied mutatis mutandis pursuant to Article 20) or who has made a false notification;
(v) a person who has failed to make a notification under the provisions of Article 41(1), (2) or (4) or who has made a false notification;
(vi) a person who has failed to make a notification under the provisions of Article 56(1) or (2) or who has made a false notification;
(vii) a person who has failed to make a notification under the provisions of Article 57(1), (2) or (4) or who has made a false notification;
(viii) a person who, in violation of the provisions of Article 955(1) (Statement, etc. in Investigation Record Registry, etc.) of the Companies Act, as applied mutatis mutandis pursuant to Article 57(6), has failed to state or record the matters specified by an Ordinance of the Ministry of Justice concerning an investigation of the electronic public notice prescribed in Article 955(1) of that Act in an Investigation Record Registry, etc. (meaning an investigation record registry, etc. as prescribed in that paragraph; hereinafter the same shall apply in this item) or who has made a false statement or record, or a person who, in violation of the provisions of that paragraph, has failed to preserve an Investigation Record Registry, etc.;
(ix) a person who has failed to make a notification under the provisions of Article 71(1) or (3) or who has made a false notification;
(x) a person who has violated the provisions of Article 72(1);
(xi) a person who, in violation of the provisions of Article 72(2), has posted a sign set forth in paragraph (1) of that Article or a sign similar thereto; or
(xii) a person who has failed to make a notification under the provisions of Article 79 or who has made a false notification.

Article 98　(1) When a representative of a juridical person (including an entity that is not a juridical person for which a representative or an administrator has been designated; hereinafter the same shall apply in this paragraph), an agent, employee, or other worker of a juridical person, or an individual has committed an act in violation of any of the provisions listed in the following items with regard to the business or property of said juridical person or individual, not only shall the offender be punished, but said juridical person shall be punished as well by the fine prescribed in those items, and said individual shall be punished by the fine prescribed in the Articles referred to in the respective items:
(i) Article 92: a fine of not more than three hundred million yen;
(ii) Article 93 (excluding items (iii), (xii), and (xxiii)): a fine of not more than two hundred million yen;
(iii) Article 94(v) or (vii): a fine of not more than one hundred million yen; and
(iv) Article 91, Article 93(iii), (xii), or (xxiii), Article 94 (excluding items (v) and (vii)), or the preceding two Articles: the fine prescribed in the respective Articles.
(2) Where an entity that is not a juridical person is punished pursuant to the provisions of the preceding paragraph, its representative or administrator shall represent the entity in its procedural acts, and the provisions of the Acts concerning criminal actions in which a juridical person is the accused or the suspect shall apply mutatis mutandis.

Article 99 In the cases that fall under any of the following items, the officer or liquidator of a Trust Company, the Representative in Japan or liquidator of a Foreign Trust Company, or the Agent for Trust Agreement (when said Agent for Trust Agreement Agent is a juridical person, the officer or liquidator thereof) shall be punished by a non-criminal fine of not more than one million yen:

(i) when having violated an order under the provisions of Article 43;
(ii) when having failed to appropriate reserves or having used them in violation of the provisions of Article 55(1) (including the cases where it is applied mutatis mutandis pursuant to paragraph (2)) or Article 55(3);
(iii) when not retaining any assets in Japan, in violation of the provisions of Article 55(4);
(iv) when having failed to request an investigation under Article 941 (Investigation of the Electronic Public Notice) of the Companies Act, in violation of the provisions of that Article, as applied mutatis mutandis pursuant to Article 57(6);
(v) when not carrying out the management of property that should be carried out pursuant to the provisions of Article 75;
(vi) when having violated an order under the provisions of Article 81; or
(vii) when not carrying out the management of trust property that should be carried out pursuant to the provisions of Article 34 of the Trust Act.

Article 100 A person who falls under any of the following items shall be punished by a non-criminal fine of not more than one million yen:

(i) a person who, in violation of an order under the provisions of Article 11(4), has failed to make a deposit;
(ii) a person who, in violation of the provisions of Article 29-2, has effected Major Changes, etc. to a Trust, who has consolidated trusts, or who has split a trust;
(iii) a person who, in violation of the provisions of Article 50-2(10), has refused an inspection;
(iv) a person who, in violation of the provisions of Article 946(3) (Obligation of Inspection, etc.) of the Companies Act as applied mutatis mutandis pursuant to Article 57(6), has failed to make a report or has made a false report;
(v) a person who has refused any of the requests listed in the items of Article 951(2) (Keeping and Inspection, etc. of Financial Statements, etc.) or the items of Article 955(2) (Statement, etc. in Investigation Record Registry, etc.) of the Companies Act, as applied mutatis mutandis pursuant to Article 57(6), without justifiable grounds;
(vi) a person who has failed to make a notification under the provisions of Article 64(1) or (3), or who has made a false notification;
(vii) a person who has failed to submit a report or material under the provisions of Article 64(2), or who has submitted a false report or material; or
(viii) a person who has violated the provisions of Article 66.

[2010年6月2日訳]

⑥ Insurance Business Act

(Act No. 105 of June 7, 1995)

Part I: General Provisions (Article 1 - Article 2-2)
Part II: Insurance Companies, etc.
  Chapter I: General Rules (Article 3 - Article 8-2)
  Chapter II: Stock Companies That Conduct Insurance Business and Mutual Companies
    Section 1: Special Provisions on Stock Companies That Conduct Insurance Business (Article 9 - Article 17-7)
    Section 2: Mutual Companies
      Subsection 1: General Rules (Article 18 - Article 21)
      Subsection 2: Incorporation (Article 22 - Article 30-15)
      Subsection 3: Rights and Obligations of Members (Article 31 - Article 36)
      Subsection 4: Administrative Organs
        Division 1: General Members' Councils (Article 37 - Article 41)
        Division 2: General Representative Members' Councils (Article 42 - Article 50)
        Division 3: Establishment, etc. of Administrative Organs Other than General Members' Councils and General Representative Members' Councils (Article 51 - Article 53-12)
        Division 4: Directors and Boards of Directors (Article 53-13 - Article 53-16)
        Division 5: Accounting Advisors (Article 53-17)
        Division 6: Company Auditors and Boards of Company Auditors (Article 53-18 - Article 53-21)
        Division 7: Accounting Auditors (Article 53-22 and Article 53-23)
        Division 8: Committees and Executive Officers (Article 53-24 - Article 53-32)
        Division 9: Officer, etc. Liability for Damages (Article 53-33 - Article 53-37)
      Subsection 5: Accounting, etc. in Mutual Companies
        Division 1: Accounting Principles (Article 54)
        Division 2: Financial Statements, etc. (Article 54-2 - Article 54-10)
        Division 3: Payments of Interest on Funds, Redemption of Funds, and Distributions of Surplus (Article 55 - Article 55-4)
        Division 4: Reserves for Redemption of Funds and Deficiency Reserves (Article 56 - Article 59)
      Subsection 6: Solicitation of Additional Funds (Article 60 and Article 60-2)
      Subsection 7: Solicitation of Subscribers for Bonds Issued by a Mutual Company (Article 61 - Article 61-10)
      Subsection 8: Amendment of the Articles of Incorporation (Article 62)
      Subsection 9: Transfer, etc. of Business. (Article 62-2)
      Subsection 10: Miscellaneous Provisions (Article 63 - Article 67-2)
    Section 3: Entity Conversion
      Subsection 1: Entity Conversion from a Stock Company to a Mutual Company (Article 68 - Article 84-2)
      Subsection 2: Entity Conversion from a Mutual Company to a Stock Company (Article 85 - Article 96-16)
  Chapter III: Business (Article 97 - Article 105-3)
  Chapter IV: Subsidiary Companies, etc. (Article 106 - Article 108)
  Chapter V: Accounting (Article 109 - Article 122-2)
  Chapter VI: Supervision (Article 123 - Article 134)
  Chapter VII: Portfolio Transfers of Insurance Contracts, Transfer or Acquisition of

6 Insurance Business Act,

　　　Business, and Entrustment of Business and Property
　Section 1: Portfolio Transfers of Insurance Contracts (Article 135 - Article 141)
　Section 2: Transfer or Acquisition of Business (Article 142 and Article 143)
　Section 3: Entrustment of Business and Property Management (Article 144 - Article 151)
Chapter VIII: Dissolution, Mergers, Company Splits, and Liquidation
　Section 1: Dissolution (Article 152 - Article 158)
　Section 2: Mergers
　　Subsection 1: General Rules (Article 159)
　　Subsection 2: Merger Agreements (Article 160 - Article 165)
　　Subsection 3: Merger Procedures
　　　Division 1: Procedures for an Extinguished Stock Company (Article 165-2 - Article 165-8)
　　　Division 2: Procedures for a Stock Company Surviving an Absorption-Type Merger (Article 165-9 - Article 165-13)
　　　Division 3: Procedures for a Stock Company Established by Consolidation-Type Merger (Article 165-14)
　　　Division 4: Procedures for an Extinguished Mutual Company (Article 165-15 - Article 165-18)
　　　Division 5: Procedures for a Mutual Company Surviving an Absorption-Type Merger (Article 165-19 - Article 165-21)
　　　Division 6: Procedures for a Mutual Company Established by a Consolidation-Type Merger (Article 165-22)
　　　Division 7: Special Provisions on the Merger of Stock Companies (Article 165-23 and Article 165-24)
　　　Division 8: Public Notice, etc. after a Merger (Article 166)
　　Subsection 4: Effectuation, etc. of a Merger (Article 167 - Article 173)
　Section 3: Company Splits (Article 173-2 - Article 173-8)
　Section 4: Liquidation (Article 174 - Article 184)
Chapter IX: Foreign Insurers
　Section 1: General Rules (Article 185 - Article 193)
　Section 2: Business, Accounting, etc. (Article 193-2 - Article 199)
　Section 3: Supervision (Article 200 - Article 207)
　Section 4: Abolition, etc. of Insurance Business (Article 208 - Article 213)
　Section 5: Miscellaneous Provisions (Article 214 - Article 218)
　Section 6: Special Provisions on Specified Juridical Persons (Article 219 - Article 240)
Chapter X: Special Measures, etc. for the Protection of Policyholders, etc.
　Section 1: Modification of Contract Conditions (Article 240-2 - Article 240-13)
　Section 2: Dispositions, etc. by the Prime Minister Related to Business and Property Management, etc.
　　Subsection 1: Suspension of Business, Order for Consultation on a Merger, etc., and Business and Property Management (Article 241)
　　Subsection 2: Business and Property Management (Article 242 - Article 249-3)
　　Subsection 3: Modification of the Contract Conditions in a Merger, etc. (Article 250 - Article 255-5)
　Section 3: Order, etc. to Implement Procedures for a Merger, etc. (Article 256 - Article 258)
　Section 4: Financial Assistance, etc. Provided by Policyholders Protection Corporations
　　Subsection 1: Policyholders Protection Corporations
　　　Division 1: General Rules (Article 259 - Article 265)

Division 2: Members (Article 265-2 - Article 265-5)
Division 3: Establishment (Article 265-6 - Article 265-11)
Division 4: Management (Article 265-12 - Article 265-22)
Division 5: General Councils (Article 265-23 - Article 265-27-5)
Division 6: Business (Article 265-28 - Article 265-31)
Division 7: Obligatory Contributions (Article 265-32 - Article 265-35)
Division 8: Finances and Accounting (Article 265-36 - Article 265-44)
Division 9: Supervision (Article 265-45 - Article 265-47)
Division 10: Miscellaneous Provisions (Article 265-48)
Subsection 2: Financial Assistance, etc.
Division 1: Petitions, etc. for Financial Assistance (Article 266 - Article 270-3)
Division 2: Succession of Insurance Contracts (Article 270-3-2 - Article 270-3-14)
Division 3: Assumption of Insurance Contracts (Article 270-4 - Article 270-6-5)
Division 4: Financial Assistance for Covered Insurance Proceeds (Article 270-6-6 and Article 270-6-7)
Subsection 3: Purchase of Insurance Claims, etc. (Article 270-6-8 - Article 270-6-10)
Subsection 4: Miscellaneous Provisions (Article 270-7 - Article 270-9)
Section 5: Miscellaneous Provisions (Article 271 - Article 271-2-3)
Chapter XI: Shareholders
Section 1: General Rules (Article 271-3 - Article 271-9)
Section 2: Special Measures Pertaining to Insurance Companies' Major Shareholders
Subsection 1: General Rules (Article 271-10 and Article 271-11)
Subsection 2: Supervision (Article 271-12 - Article 271-16)
Subsection 3: Miscellaneous Provisions (Article 271-17)
Section 3: Special Provisions on Insurance Holding Companies
Subsection 1: General Rules (Article 271-18 - Article 271-20)
Subsection 2: Business and Subsidiary Companies (Article 271-21 - Article 271-22)
Subsection 3: Accounting (Article 271-23 - Article 271-26)
Subsection 4: Supervision (Article 271-27 - Article 271-30)
Subsection 5: Miscellaneous Provisions (Article 271-31)
Section 4: Miscellaneous Provisions (Article 271-32 and Article 271-33)
Chapter XII: Special Provisions on Low-Cost, Short-Term Insurers
Section 1: General Rules (Article 272 - Article 272-10)
Section 2: Business, etc. (Article 272-11 - Article 272-14)
Section 3: Accounting (Article 272-15 - Article 272-18)
Section 4: Supervision (Article 272-19 - Article 272-28)
Section 5: Portfolio Transfers, etc. of Insurance Contracts (Article 272-29 and Article 272-30)
Section 6: Shareholders
Subsection 1: Low-Cost, Short-Term Insurers' Major Shareholders (Article 272-31 - Article 272-34)
Subsection 2: Low-Cost, Short-Term Insurance Holding Companies (Article 272-35 - Article 272-40)
Subsection 3: Miscellaneous Provisions (Article 272-41 - Article 272-43)
Chapter XIII: Miscellaneous Provisions (Article 273 - Article 274-2)
Part III: The Offering of Insurance
Chapter I: General Rules (Article 275)
Chapter II: Insurance Agents and Affiliated Insurance Companies, etc.
Section 1: Insurance Agents (Article 276 - Article 282)

Section 2: Affiliated Insurance Companies, etc. (Article 283 - Article 285)
Chapter III: Insurance Brokers (Article 286 - Article 293)
Chapter IV: Business (Article 294 - Article 301-2)
Chapter V: Supervision (Article 302 - Article 308)
Part IV: Designated Dispute Resolution Organizations
Chapter I: General Rules (Article 308-2 - Article 308-4)
Chapter II: Business (Article 308-5 - Article 308-17)
Chapter III: Supervision (Article 308-18 - Article 308-24)
Part V: Miscellaneous Provisions (Article 309 - Article 314)
Part VI: Penal Provisions (Article 315 - Article 339)
Supplementary Provisions

Part I General Provisions

(Purpose)
Article 1 The purpose of this Act is, in view of the public nature of the Insurance Business, to protect Policyholders, etc. by ensuring the sound and appropriate business operation of persons conducting Insurance Business and by ensuring fairness in Insurance Solicitation, and thereby to contribute to the stability of the lives of the citizens and to the sound development of the national economy.

(Definitions)
Article 2 (1) The term "Insurance Business" as used in this Act means the business (except business listed in the following items) of underwriting the risks listed in the items of Article 3, paragraph (4) or the items of Article 3, paragraph (5) with insurance for which premiums are received under a contract for the payment of a fixed amount of insurance proceeds in connection with the life or death of an individual, with insurance for which premiums are received under a contract for compensation of damages caused by specific and accidental events, or with any other class of insurance.
(i) Those provided in other Acts.
(ii) The following business:
  (a) That which a local government enters into with its residents as the other parties;
  (b) That which a company, etc. (meaning a company (including a foreign company; hereinafter the same shall apply in this item) or any other enterprise (excluding any enterprise specified by Cabinet Order)) or an organization comprised of officers or employees (including former officers or employees; hereinafter the same shall apply in this item) enters into with its officers or employees, or their relatives (limited to those specified by Cabinet Order; hereinafter the same shall apply in this item) as the other parties;
  (c) That which a labor union enters into with its union members (including former union members) or their relatives as the other parties;
  (d) That which one company enters into with another company that belongs to the same group (meaning the group of a company and its Subsidiary Companies) as the other party;
  (e) That which a school (meaning a school as prescribed in Article 1 of the School Education Act (Act No. 26 of 1947)) or an organization comprised of its students enters into with its students as the other parties;
  (f) That which a regional organization (meaning a regional organization as prescribed in Article 260-2, paragraph (1) of the Local Autonomy Act (Act No. 67 of

1947) that falls under the requirements listed in the items of paragraph (2) of that Article) enters into with its members as the other party; and
      (g) Business specified by Cabinet Order as being equivalent to those listed from (a) to (f) inclusive.
    (iii) That for which the other parties are persons whose number does not exceed the number specified by Cabinet Order (except those specified by Cabinet Order).
(2) The term "Insurance Company" as used in this Act means a person who conducts Insurance Business under the license from the Prime Minister prescribed in Article 3, paragraph (1).
(3) The term "Life Insurance Company" as used in this Act means an Insurance Company which has obtained the life insurance business license set forth in Article 3, paragraph (4).
(4) The term "Non-Life Insurance Company" as used in this Act means an Insurance Company which has obtained the non-life insurance business license set forth in Article 3, paragraph (5).
(5) The term "Mutual Company" as used in this Act means an association established pursuant to this Act for the purpose of conducting Insurance Business, whose policyholders are the members thereof.
(6) The term "Foreign Insurer" as used in this Act means a person conducting Insurance Business in a foreign state in accordance with the laws and regulations of the foreign state (excluding Insurance Companies).
(7) The term "Foreign Insurance Company, etc." as used in this Act means a Foreign Insurer which has obtained the license from the Prime Minister set forth in Article 185, paragraph (1).
(8) The term "Foreign Life Insurance Company, etc." as used in this Act means a Foreign Insurance Company, etc. which has obtained the foreign life insurance business license set forth in Article 185, paragraph (4).
(9) The term "Foreign Non-Life Insurance Company, etc." as used in this Act means a Foreign Insurance Company, etc. which has obtained the foreign non-life insurance business license set forth in Article 185, paragraph (5).
(10) The term "Foreign Mutual Company" as used in this Act means a foreign juridical person akin to a Mutual Company, or a similar foreign juridical person, which was established in accordance with the laws and regulations of a foreign state.
(11) The term "All Shareholders' Voting Rights, etc." as used in this Act means voting rights of all shareholders or investors (in the case of a Stock Company, excluding voting rights related to shares which do not allow exercising voting rights for any of the matters which may be resolved at a shareholders' meeting, but including voting rights related to shares for which holders are deemed to have voting rights pursuant to the provisions of Article 879, paragraph (3) (Jurisdiction Over a Special Liquidation Case) of the Companies Act (Act No. 86 of 2005); the same shall apply hereinafter in this Article, the following Article, Article 100-2-2, Article 106, Article 107, Article 127, Article 260, Part II, Chapters XI and XII and Article 333).
(12) The terms "Subsidiary Company" and "Subsidiary" as used in this Act mean a company in which another company holds voting rights exceeding 50 percent of All Shareholders' Voting Rights, etc. In such a case, if a first company and one or more of its Subsidiary Companies, or if one or more of the Subsidiary Companies of such first company, own voting rights exceeding 50 percent of All Shareholders' Voting Rights, etc. in a second company, said second company shall be deemed to be the Subsidiary Company of the first company.
(13) The term "Major Shareholder Threshold" as used in this Act means 20 percent (15 percent in the case where a person who satisfies the requirements specified by Cabi-

net Office Ordinance as one with regard to which a fact exists that is expected to have a material effect on the decisions on the financial and business policies of the company, holds voting rights in the company) of all shareholders' voting rights.
(14) The term "Insurance Company's Major Shareholder" as used in this Act means a person that holds a number of voting rights in an Insurance Company equal to or exceeding the Major Shareholder Threshold (including a person who holds such number of voting rights in the name of another person (or under a fictitious name); the same shall apply hereinafter), and is established under the authorization set forth in Article 271-10, paragraph (1) or has obtained the authorization prescribed in Article 271-10, paragraph (1) or the proviso to Article 271-10, paragraph (2).
(15) In the case prescribed in paragraph (12) and the preceding paragraph, the voting rights held by a company or a person who holds voting rights shall not include any voting rights from shares or equity interests held in the form of trust property pertaining to a monetary or securities trust (limited to cases where the settlor or the beneficiary may exercise the voting rights or may give instructions to the company or the holder of the voting rights on the exercise of such voting rights) or any of the voting rights specified by Cabinet Office Ordinance, but shall include voting rights from the Shares or equity interests which are held as trust property and whose voting rights the other company or the person holding voting rights in the Insurance Company may, as a settlor or beneficiary, exercise or give instructions on the exercise (excluding those specified by Cabinet Office Ordinance) and any voting rights from the shares which cannot be asserted against the issuer pursuant to the provisions of Article 147, paragraph (1) or Article 148, paragraph (1) of the Act on Transfer of Bonds, Shares, etc. (Act No. 75 of 2001).
(16) The term "Insurance Holding Company" as used in this Act means a Holding Company (meaning a Holding Company as prescribed in Article 9, paragraph (4), item (i) (Holding Company) of the Act on Prohibiting Private Monopolies and Ensuring Fair Trade (Act No. 54 of 1947); the same shall apply hereinafter) whose Subsidiary Companies are Insurance Companies, which has been established under the authorization set forth in Article 271-18, paragraph (1) or which obtains authorization prescribed in Article 271-18, paragraph (1) or the proviso to paragraph (3).
(17) The term "Low-Cost, Short-Term Insurance Business" as used in this Act means, within the Insurance Business, the business of underwriting only insurance that has a term of coverage of within the period of two years or less specified by Cabinet Order, and for which the insurance proceeds do not exceed the amount of ten million yen or less specified by Cabinet Order (except those specified by Cabinet Order).
(18) The term "Low-Cost, Short-Term Insurer" as used in this Act means a person who has obtained the registration set forth in Article 272, paragraph (1) and who conducts Low-Cost, Short-Term Insurance Business.
(19) The term "Life Insurance Agent" as used in this Act means an officer (excluding officers with the authority of representation and company auditors and members of audit committees (hereinafter referred to as "Audit Committee Members"); hereinafter the same shall apply in this Article) or employee of a Life Insurance Company (including Foreign Life Insurance Companies, etc.; hereinafter the same shall apply in this paragraph) or the employee of such a person, and any person delegated by a Life Insurance Company (including an association or foundation that is not a juridical person and has provisions on representative persons or administrators) or the officer or employee of such a person, who acts as an agent or intermediary for the conclusion of an insurance contract on behalf of the Life Insurance Company.
(20) The term "Non-Life Insurance Agent" as used in this Act means an officer or employee of a Non-Life Insurance Company (including Foreign Companies, etc.; the same

shall apply in the following paragraph), Non-Life Insurance Representative, or the officer or employee of such a person.

(21) The term "Non-Life Insurance Representative" as used in this Act means a person delegated by a Non-Life Insurance Company, who acts as an agent or intermediary for the conclusion of insurance contracts on its behalf (including an association or foundation that is not a juridical person and has provisions on representative persons or administrators), and who is not an officer or employee of the Non-Life Insurance Company.

(22) The term "Low-Cost, Short-Term Insurance Agent" as used in this Act means an officer or employee of a Low-Cost, Short-Term Insurer, or a person delegated by a Low-Cost, Short-Term Insurer (including an association or foundation that is not a juridical person and has provisions on representative persons or administrators) or an officer or employee of such a person, who acts as an agent or intermediary for the conclusion of insurance contracts on behalf of the Low-Cost, Short-Term Insurer.

(23) The term "Insurance Agent" as used in this Act means a Life Insurance Agent, a Non-Life Insurance Agent, or a Low-Cost, Short-Term Insurance Agent.

(24) The term "Affiliated Insurance Company, etc." as used in this Act means the Insurance Company (including foreign insurance companies, etc.) or the Low-Cost, Short-Term Insurer, which is to be the insurer in the insurance contracts offered by Life Insurance Agents, Non-Life Insurance Agents, or Low-Cost, Short-Term Insurance Agents.

(25) The term "Insurance Broker" as used in this Act means a person who acts as an intermediary for the conclusion of an insurance contract other than the intermediation that Life Insurance Agents, Non-Life Insurance Representatives, and Low-Cost, Short-Term Insurance Agents (including an association or foundation that is not a juridical person and has provisions on representative persons or administrators) carry out on behalf of their Affiliated Insurance Companies, etc.

(26) The term "Insurance Solicitation" as used in this Act means acting as an agent or intermediary for conclusion of an insurance contract.

(27) The term "Method of Public Notice" as used in this Act means the Method of Public Notice prescribed in Article 2, item (xxxiii) (Definitions) of the Companies Act with regard to stock companies and foreign companies that are foreign insurance companies, etc. and the method by which mutual companies and foreign insurance companies, etc. (excluding foreign companies; hereinafter the same shall apply in this paragraph) give public notice with regard to mutual companies and foreign insurance companies, etc. (except cases where provisions of this Act or other Acts prescribe that a method of publication in the official gazette is to be used).

(28) The term "Designated Dispute Resolution Organization" as used in this Act means a person who has obtained the designation under Article 308-2, paragraph (1).

(29) The term "Life Insurance Services" as used in this Act means business conducted by a Life Insurance Company pursuant to the provisions of Article 97, Article 98 and Article 99; business conducted by a Life Insurance Company pursuant to the provisions of any other laws; and Insurance Solicitation in which a Life Insurance Agent engages for said Life Insurance Company.

(30) The term "Non-Life Insurance Services" as used in this Act means business conducted by a Non-Life Insurance Company pursuant to the provisions of Article 97, Article 98 and Article 99 (excluding business for paying Insurance Proceeds, etc. (meaning the Insurance Proceeds, etc. set forth in Article 16-2 (Limitations on Insurance Proceeds, etc. for Damages, etc. Caused by an Absence from Work) of the Automobile Liability Insurance Act (Act No. 97 of 1955)) from liability insurance as set forth in Article 5 (Compulsory Execution of Contracts for Liability Insurance or Mutual Aid Lia-

Art.2 ⑥ Insurance Business Act, Part I

bility Insurance) of that Act (referred to as the "Automobile Damage Liability Insurance Business" in paragraphs (32) and (34))); business conducted by a Non-Life Insurance Company pursuant to the provisions of any other laws; and Insurance Solicitation in which a Non-Life Insurance Agent engages for said Non-Life Insurance Company.

(31) The term "Foreign Life Insurance Services" as used in this Act means business conducted by a Foreign Life Insurance Company, etc. pursuant to the provisions of Article 97, Article 98, Article 99 and Article 100 as applied mutatis mutandis pursuant to Article 199; and Insurance Solicitation in which a Life Insurance Agent engages for said Foreign Life Insurance Company, etc.

(32) The term "Foreign Non-Life Insurance Services" as used in this Act means business conducted by a Foreign Non-Life Insurance Company, etc. pursuant to the provisions of Article 97, Article 98, Article 99 and Article 100 as applied mutatis mutandis pursuant to Article 199 (excluding the Automobile Damage Liability Insurance Business); and Insurance Solicitation in which a Non-Life Insurance Agent engages for said Foreign Non-Life Insurance Company, etc.

(33) The term "Specified Life Insurance Services" as used in this Act means business that the Underwriting Member referred to in Article 219, paragraph (1), of a Specified Juridical Person referred to in said paragraph, which has obtained a specified life insurance business license under paragraph (4) of that Article, conducts pursuant to the provisions of Article 97, Article 98, Article 99 and Article 100 as applied mutatis mutandis pursuant to Article 199; and Insurance Solicitation in which a Life Insurance Agent engages for said Underwriting Member.

(34) The term "Specified Non-Life Insurance Services" as used in this Act means business that the Underwriting Member referred to in Article 219, paragraph (1), of a Specified Juridical Person as set forth in said paragraph, which has obtained a specified non-life insurance business license under paragraph (5) of that Article, conducts pursuant to the provisions of Article 97, Article 98, Article 99 and Article 100 as applied mutatis mutandis pursuant to Article 199 (excluding the Automobile Damage Liability Insurance Business); and Insurance Solicitation in which a Non-Life Insurance Agent engages for said Underwriting Member.

(35) The term "Low-Cost, Short-Term Insurance Services" as used in this Act means business that a Low-Cost, Short-Term Insurer conducts pursuant to the provisions of Article 272-11, paragraph (1); and Insurance Solicitation in which a Low-Cost, Short-Term Insurance Agent engages for said Low-Cost, Short-Term Insurer.

(36) The term "Insurance Solicitation by Insurance Brokers" as used in this Act means the intermediation that Insurance Brokers performs for the conclusion of insurance contracts.

(37) The term "Insurance Services, etc." as used in this Act means Life Insurance Services, Non-Life Insurance Services, Foreign Life Insurance Services, Foreign Non-Life Insurance Services, Specified Life Insurance Services, Specified Non-Life Insurance Services, Low-Cost, Short-Term Insurance Services, and Insurance Solicitation by Insurance Brokers.

(38) The term "Complaint Processing Procedures" as used in this Act means procedures for processing the Complaints Related to Insurance Services, etc. (meaning complaints related to Insurance Services, etc; the same shall apply in Article 308-7, Article 308-8 and Article 308-12).

(39) The term "Dispute Resolution Procedures" as used in this Act means procedures to resolve Disputes Related to Insurance Services, etc. (meaning disputes related to Insurance Services, etc. that can be settled between the parties; the same shall apply in Article 308-7, Article 308-8 and Articles 308-13 to 308-15 inclusive) without using

court proceedings.
(40) The term "Dispute Resolution Services, etc." as used in this Act means business for Complaint Processing Procedures and Dispute Resolution Procedures as well as business incidental thereto.
(41) The term "Category of Dispute Resolution Services, etc." as used in this Act means categorization of Dispute Resolution Services, etc. as being for Life Insurance Services, Non-Life Insurance Services, Foreign Life Insurance Services, Foreign Non-Life Insurance Services, Specified Life Insurance Services, Specified Non-Life Insurance Services, Low-Cost, Short-Term Insurance Services, or for Insurance Solicitation by Insurance Brokers.
(42) The term "Basic Contract for the Implementation of Dispute Resolution Procedures" as used in this Act means a contract concluded between a Designated Dispute Resolution Organization and an Insurance Service Provider (meaning an Insurance Company, Foreign Life Insurance Company, etc., Licensed Specified Juridical Person as defined in Article 223, paragraph (1), Low-Cost, Short-Term Insurer, or Insurance Broker; the same shall apply hereinafter) with regard to the implementation of Dispute Resolution Services, etc.

Article 2-2 (1) Any person listed in the following items shall be deemed to be a holder of voting rights in an Insurance Company, etc. (meaning Insurance Companies or Low-Cost, Short-Term Insurers; the same shall apply hereinafter) amounting to the number specified in those items, and the provisions of Part II, Chapter XI, Sections 1 and 2, Chapters XII and XIII, and Parts V and VI shall apply to such person:
  (i) An organization that is not a juridical person (limited to an organization specified by Cabinet Office Ordinance as those equivalent to a juridical person): the number of voting rights in the Insurance Company, etc. that the organization holds in its own name;
  (ii) A company required to prepare its financial statements and other documents on a consolidated basis pursuant to the provisions of Cabinet Office Ordinance (referred to as "Company Subject to Standards for Consolidation" in the following item), for which the companies and other juridical persons to be consolidated (including organizations that are not juridical persons as listed in the preceding item; and hereinafter referred to as "Companies, etc." in this paragraph) include an Insurance Company, etc., and that is not consolidated in any other company's financial statements or other documents: the number calculated pursuant to the provisions of Cabinet Office Ordinance as representing the company's substantial influence on the Insurance Company, etc.;
  (iii) Where a Company, etc. (excluding one that is consolidated in the financial statements and other documents of a company that falls under the type of company listed in the preceding item, limited to one that holds voting rights in an Insurance Company, etc.) that is not a Company Subject to Standards for Consolidation belongs to a Group of Companies, etc. (meaning the group of the relevant Company, etc., the group of another Company, etc. in which the relevant Company, etc. holds majority voting rights, or the group of a Company, etc. specified by Cabinet Office Ordinance as a Company, etc. to which the relevant Company, etc. is otherwise closely related; hereinafter the same shall apply in this paragraph), and where the total number of voting rights held in an Insurance Company, etc. by all of the Companies etc. belonging to the Group of Companies, etc (hereinafter referred to as the "Number of Voting Rights Held by the Group of Companies, etc." in this item and the next item) is equal to or exceeds the Major Shareholder Threshold (such Group of Companies, etc. are hereinafter referred to as "Specified Group of Com-

panies, etc." in this item and the next item), a Company, etc. in the Specified Group of Companies, etc. , in which no other Company, etc. holds majority voting rights: the Number of Voting Rights Held by the Group of Companies, etc. in the Specified Group of Companies, etc. ;
(iv) Where no Company, etc. in a Specified Group of Companies, etc. falls under the type of Company, etc. listed in the preceding item, a Company, etc. whose assets in the balance sheet are the largest among the Companies, etc. belonging to the Specified Group of Companies, etc. : the Number of Voting Rights Held by the Group of Companies, etc. in the Specified Group of Companies, etc.
(v) An individual who, by virtue of holding majority voting rights in Companies, etc. that hold voting rights in an Insurance Company, etc. (including any of the persons listed from item (ii) to the preceding item inclusive; hereinafter the same shall apply in this item), is deemed to hold at least 20 percent of all shareholders' voting rights in the Insurance Company, etc. , in terms of the number of voting rights held in the Insurance Company, etc. by such Companies, etc. (for those falling under any of the categories listed in the preceding items, the number specified in the relevant item), taken together (counting in any voting rights held by said individual in the Insurance Company, etc.; the number thus calculated is hereinafter referred to as the "Grand Total Number of Voting Rights" in this item): the Grand Total Number of Voting Rights for the individual.
(vi) A person who holds voting rights in an Insurance Company, etc. (including a person falling under any of the categories listed in the preceding items; hereinafter the same shall apply in this item) who is deemed to hold at least 20 percent of all shareholders' voting rights in the Insurance Company, etc. , in terms of the number of voting rights held by said person in the Insurance Company, etc. (for a person falling under any of the categories listed in the preceding items, the number specified in the relevant item) and the number of voting rights held in the same Insurance Company, etc. by his/her Joint Holder(s) (meaning any other holder(s) of voting rights in the Insurance Company, etc. (including those falling under any of the categories listed in the preceding times) who has (have) agreed with said person on concerted action in acquiring or transferring the shares pertaining to the voting rights, or in exercising the voting and other rights as shareholders of that Insurance Company, etc. (excluding, where the person who holds the voting rights is a company falling under the category listed in item (ii), any Company, etc. to be consolidated in the financial statements and other documents of said company; excluding, where the person who holds the voting rights is a Company, etc. falling under the category prescribed in item (iii) or (iv), any other Company, etc. in the Group of Companies, etc. to which said Company, etc. belongs; and excluding, where the person who holds the voting rights is an individual falling under the category listed in the preceding item, any Company, etc. in which the individual holds majority voting rights; but including any person who has a special relationship as specified by Cabinet Order with the person who holds the voting rights)) (for a Joint Holder falling under any of the categories listed in the preceding items, the number prescribed in the relevant item), taken together (the total number thus calculated is hereinafter referred to as the "Number of Voting Rights Jointly Held" in this item): the Number of Voting Rights Jointly Held.
(vii) A person specified by Cabinet Office Ordinance as being equivalent to a person listed in any of the preceding items: the number calculated pursuant to the provisions of Cabinet Office Ordinance as representing the person's substantive influence on the Insurance Companies, etc.
(2) In the case referred to in the items of the preceding paragraph, the provisions of para-

graph (15) of the preceding Article, shall apply mutatis mutandis to voting rights deemed to be held by a person listed in any of items of that paragraph and voting rights held by the holder of the voting rights.

Part II Insurance Company, etc.

Chapter I General Rules

(Licenses)
Article 3 (1) No person may conduct Insurance Business without having first obtained a license from the Prime Minister.
(2) The license set forth in the preceding paragraph consists of two types: a life insurance business license and the non-life insurance business license.
(3) The same person may not obtain both a life insurance business license and the non-life insurance business license.
(4) A life insurance business license shall be a license for business undertakings for underwriting classes of insurance as listed in item (i) or for underwriting classes of insurance as listed in item (ii) or (iii) in addition to the classes listed in item (i).
  (i) Insurance for which premiums are received under a contract to pay fixed insurance proceeds in connection with the survival or death of individuals (including the physical state of an individual whom a doctor has diagnosed as having no longer than a certain period of time left to live; hereinafter the same shall apply in this paragraph and the following paragraph) (excluding that pertaining only to death, as under the following sub-item (c)).
  (ii) Insurance for which insurance premiums are received under a contract to pay fixed insurance proceeds in connection with the following events or to compensate for damages to the individual caused by such events:
    (a) That an individual has contracted a disease;
    (b) An individual's condition that was caused by an injury or disease;
    (c) An individual's death that was directly caused by an injury;
    (d) Cases specified by Cabinet Office Ordinance as those similar to what is listed in (a) or (b) (excluding the death of an individual); and
    (e) Treatment (including those specified by Cabinet Office Ordinance as procedures similar to treatment) concerning those listed in (a), (b), or (d).
  (iii) Under the classes of insurance listed in item (i) of the following paragraph, reinsurance pertaining to the classes of insurance listed in the preceding two items.
(5) A non-life insurance business license shall be a license for business undertakings for underwriting the classes of insurance as listed in item (i) or for underwriting the classes of insurance as listed in item (ii) or (iii) in addition to the classes listed in item (i).
  (i) Insurance for which premiums are received under a contract to compensate for damages caused by specific accidental events (excluding the classes of insurance listed in the following item).
  (ii) Classes of insurance listed in item (ii) of the preceding paragraph.
  (iii) Among the classes of insurance listed in item (i) of the preceding paragraph, insurance related to the death of an individual between the time he/she leaves his/her residence for overseas travel and the time he/she returns to his/her residence (hereinafter referred to in this item as "Overseas Travel Period") or the death of an individual directly caused by a disease contracted during the Overseas Travel Period.
(6) Sureties from surety bond services (meaning business for guaranteeing the perfor-

mance of contractual obligations or legal and regulatory obligations and receiving consideration therefor, which is conducted out by setting the amount of consideration, establishing a reserve, and distributing the risks through reinsurance, based on actuarial science, or by using any other methods inherent to insurance) shall be deemed to be the underwriting of the classes of insurance listed in item (i) of the preceding paragraph, and the consideration pertaining to the surety shall be deemed to be the insurance premium pertaining to the classes of insurance set forth in that item.

(License Application Procedures)
Article 4 (1) A person who seeks to obtain a license set forth in paragraph (1) of the preceding Article shall submit to the Prime Minister a written application for the license detailing the following particulars:
(i) Trade name or company name;
(ii) Amount of capital or total amount of funds;
(iii) Name of the director and company auditor (director and executive officer in the case of a company with committees (meaning a Stock Company or Mutual Company with a nominating committee, audit committee, and compensation committee (hereinafter referred to as "Committees" except for Chapter X); the same shall apply hereinafter)).
(iv) Type of license desired; and
(v) Location of the head office or principal office.
(2) The following documents and other documents specified by Cabinet Office Ordinance shall be attached to the written application for a license set forth in the preceding paragraph:
(i) Articles of incorporation;
(ii) Statement of business procedures;
(iii) General policy conditions; and
(iv) Statement of calculation procedures for insurance premiums and policy reserves.
(3) In the case referred to in the preceding paragraph, if the articles of incorporation under item (i) of that paragraph have been created as electromagnetic records (meaning a record that is created by an electronic method, magnetic method or any other method which does not allow recognition by human sensory perception and is specified by Cabinet Office Ordinance as suitable for use in information processing by a computer; the same shall apply hereinafter), the electromagnetic records may be attached in place of the documents.
(4) The documents listed in paragraph (2), items (ii) to (iv) inclusive must detail the particulars specified by Cabinet Office Ordinance.

(Licensing Examination Standards)
Article 5 (1) Whenever an application has been filed for a license set forth in Article 3, paragraph (1), the Prime Minister shall examine whether it conforms to the following standards:
(i) the person who filed the application (hereinafter referred to as the "Applicant" in this paragraph) has a sufficient financial basis to perform the business of an Insurance Company soundly and efficiently, and that said Applicant has favorable prospects for income and expenditures pertaining to said business;
(ii) in light of such particulars as personnel structure, etc. , the Applicant has the knowledge and experience necessary to perform the business of an Insurance Company appropriately, fairly, and efficiently, and that said Applicant sufficient social credibility; and
(iii) the particulars detailed in the documents listed in paragraph (2), items (ii) and (iii)

of the preceding Article conform to the following standards:
- (a) the contents of the insurance contracts have no risk of lacking in protection for the policyholders, the persons to be insured, beneficiaries of insurance proceeds, and other relevant persons (hereinafter referred to as "Policyholders, etc.");
- (b) no specific persons are subject to unfair or discriminatory treatment under the contents of the insurance contracts;
- (c) the contents of the insurance contracts pose no risk of encouraging or inducing conduct that is harmful to public policy and good morals;
- (d) the rights and obligations of the Policyholders, etc. and other contents of the insurance contracts are specified clearly and simply for the Policyholders, etc. ; and
- (e) any other standards specified by Cabinet Office Ordinance.

(iv) the particulars detailed in the documents listed in paragraph (2), item (iv) of the preceding Article conform to the following standards:
- (a) the calculation procedures for insurance premiums and policy reserves are reasonable and proper, based on actuarial science;
- (b) no specific persons are subject to unfair or discriminatory treatment with regard to insurance premiums; and
- (c) any other standards specified by Cabinet Office Ordinance.

(2) If and to the extent that the Prime Minister finds it necessary for the public interest in light of examination standards prescribed in the preceding paragraph, he/she may impose conditions on the license referred to in Article 3, paragraph (1) or change such conditions.

(Administrative Organs)
Article 5-2 An Insurance Company shall be a Stock Company or a Mutual Company and shall have in place the following administrative organs:
(i) Board of directors;
(ii) Board of company auditors or committees; and
(iii) Accounting auditor.

(Amount of Capital or Total Amount of Funds)
Article 6 (1) The amount of capital or total amount of funds (including the reserves for redemption of funds set forth in Article 56) of an Insurance Company shall be equal to or greater than the amount specified by Cabinet Order.

(2) The amount specified by Cabinet Order under the preceding paragraph shall not be less than one billion yen.

(Trade Names and Names)
Article 7 (1) An Insurance Company shall, in its trade name or name, use terms specified by Cabinet Office Ordinance for indicating that it is a Life Insurance Company or a Non-Life Insurance Company.

(2) No person other than an Insurance Company shall use, in its trade name or name, any term which would indicate that the person is an Insurance Company.

(Prohibition on Name Lending)
Article 7-2 An Insurance Company shall not cause another person to conduct Insurance Business in the name of the Insurance Company.

(Prohibition on the Concurrent Holding of Positions by Directors, etc.)

Article 8 (1) Directors engaging in the day-to-day business of an Insurance Company (in the case of a company with committees, executive officer) shall not conduct the day-to-day business of any other company, except for the cases authorized by the Prime Minister.
(2) Whenever an application has been filed for the authorization referred to in the preceding paragraph, the Prime Minister may only grant the authorization if he/she finds that the particulars given in the application are unlikely to interfere with the sound and appropriate business operation of the Insurance Company.

(Eligibility of Directors, etc.)
Article 8-2 (1) Directors engaging in the day-to-day business of an Insurance Company (in the case of a company with committees, executive officer) shall have the knowledge and experience to carry out business management of an Insurance Company appropriately, fairly and efficiently, and shall have sufficient social credibility.
(2) No person who has become subject to the ruling for the commencement of bankruptcy proceedings and who has not been restored his/her rights, or a person who is treated the same as such a person under the laws and regulations of a foreign state, shall be appointed as a director, executive officer or auditor of an Insurance Company.

Chapter II Stock Companies That Conduct Insurance Business and Mutual Companies
Section 1 Special Provisions on Stock Companies That Conduct Insurance Business

(Methods of Public Notice)
Article 9 (1) A Stock Company that conducts Insurance Business (hereinafter referred to as a "Stock Company" in this Section) shall specify any of the following methods as the Method of Public Notice in its articles of incorporation:
(i) Publication in a daily newspaper that publishes the particulars of current events; or
(ii) Electronic Public Notice (for Stock Companies and Foreign Insurance Companies, etc. that are foreign companies, meaning the Electronic Public Notice provided for in Article 2, item (xxxiv) (Definitions) of the Companies Act, and for Mutual Companies and a Foreign Insurance Companies, etc. (that are other than foreign companies), any of those Method of Public Notice meeting the definition provided in that item which allow many and unspecified persons to access the information that is published by electromagnetic means (meaning the electromagnetic means defined in that item); the same shall apply hereinafter).
(2) The provisions of Article 940, paragraph (1) (excluding item (ii)) and paragraph (3) (Period of Public Notice, etc. by Electronic Public Notice) of the Companies Act shall apply mutatis mutandis to the cases where a Stock Company gives public notice under this Act in the form of an electronic public notice. In this case, any other necessary technical changes in interpretation shall be specified by Cabinet Order.

(Offer for Offered Shares, etc.)
Article 10 A Stock Company shall, whenever it gives notice pursuant to the provisions of Article 59, paragraph (1) (Subscription for Shares Solicited at Incorporation), Article 203, paragraph (1) (Applications for Offered Shares) or Article 242, paragraph (1) (Subscription for Offered Share Options) of the Companies Act, give notice of the particulars listed in the items of Article 59, paragraph (1), the items of Article 203, paragraph (1) or the items of Article 242, paragraph (1), respectively, as well as any provisions in

its articles of incorporation as set forth in the second sentence of Article 113 (including the cases where it is applied mutatis mutandis pursuant to Article 272-18).

(Reference Date)
Article 11 For the purpose of applying to a Stock Company the provisions of Article 124, paragraph (2) (Record Date) of the Companies Act, the term "three months" in that paragraph shall be deemed to be replaced with "three months (or four months for the right to exercise a voting right at an annual shareholders' meeting and any other right specified by Cabinet Office Ordinance."

(Qualifications, etc. of Directors, etc.)
Article 12 (1) For the purpose of applying the provisions of Article 331, paragraph (1), item (iii) (Qualifications of Directors) of the Companies Act (including the cases where it is applied mutatis mutandis pursuant to Article 335, paragraph (1) (Qualifications of Company Auditors) and Article 402, paragraph (4) (Election of Executive Officers) of that Act) to a Stock Company, the term "this Act" in that item shall be deemed to be replaced with "the Insurance Business Act, this Act."
(2) The provisions of the proviso to Article 331, paragraph (2) (including the cases where it is applied mutatis mutandis pursuant to Article 335, paragraph (1) of the Companies Act), Article 332, paragraph (2) (Directors' Terms of Office) (including the cases where it is applied mutatis mutandis pursuant to Article 334, paragraph (1) (Accounting advisors' terms of office), Article 336, paragraph (2) (Company Auditors' Terms of Office), Article 389, paragraph (1) (Limitation of Scope of Audit by Provisions of Articles of Incorporation), and the proviso to Article 402, paragraph (5) of the Companies Act shall not apply to a Stock Company.

(Voting Forms, etc. and Reference Documents for Shareholders' Meetings)
Article 13 For the purpose of applying the provisions of Article 301, paragraph (1) (Delivery of Voting Forms and Reference Documents for a Shareholders' Meeting), Article 432, paragraph (1) (Preparation and Retention of Account Books), Article 435, paragraphs (1) and (2) (Preparation and Retention of Financial Statements, etc.), Article 436, paragraphs (1) and (2) (Audit of Financial Statements, etc.), Article 439 (Special Provisions on Companies with Accounting Auditors), and Article 440, paragraph (1) (Public Notice of Financial Statements) of the Companies Act to a Stock Company, the term "Ordinance of the Ministry of Justice" in said provisions shall be deemed to be replaced with "Cabinet Office Ordinance."

(Exclusion from Application, etc. of Provisions Regarding Requests to Inspect, etc. Account Books)
Article 14 (1) The provisions of Article 433 (Request to Inspect Account Books) of the Companies Act shall not apply to account books of a Stock Company and materials relating thereto.
(2) For the purpose of applying the provisions of Article 442, paragraph (3) (Retention and Inspection of Financial Statements, etc.) of the Companies Act to a Stock Company, the term "and creditors" in that paragraph shall be deemed to be replaced with ", Policyholders, beneficiaries of insurance proceeds, and other creditors and insurers."

(Reserves)
Article 15 Notwithstanding the provisions of Article 445, paragraph (4) (Amounts of Capital and Amounts of Reserves) of the Companies Act, in the case where a Stock Company pays dividends of surplus, it shall record the amount equivalent to one-fifth

Art.16 ⑥ Insurance Business Act, Part II, Chap.II, Sec.1

of the amount of the deduction from surplus as a result of the payments of such dividends of surplus as capital reserves or retained earnings reserves (hereinafter referred to as "Reserves"), pursuant to the provisions of Cabinet Office Ordinance.

(Retention and Inspection, etc. of Documents, etc. Related to a Reduction of Capital, etc.)
Article 16 (1) A Stock Company shall keep at each of its business offices the documents or electromagnetic records in which any proposal for a reduction (excluding the cases where the whole of the amount by which the Reserves are reduced is appropriated to the capital) of the capital or Reserves (hereinafter referred to as "capital, etc." in this Section) and any other particulars specified by Cabinet Office Ordinance are detailed or recorded, for a period ranging from two weeks before the date of the shareholders' meeting related to the resolution on the reduction (or, the date of the board of directors meeting where Article 447, paragraph (3) (Reductions in Amount of Capital) or Article 448, paragraph (3) (Reductions in Amount of Reserves) of the Companies Act Applies) to six months from the Effective Date of the reduction of the capital, etc.; provided, however, that this shall not apply to the cases where only the amount of the Reserves is reduced and all of the following are met:
(i) An annual shareholders' meeting has decided on the particulars listed in the items of Article 448, paragraph (1) inclusive of the Companies Act; and
(ii) The amount set forth in Article 448, paragraph (1), item (i) of the Companies Act does not exceed the amount calculated in the manner specified by Cabinet Office Ordinance as the amount of the deficit as of the date of the annual shareholders' meeting referred to in the preceding item (or, in the cases provided for in the first sentence of Article 439 (Special Provisions on Companies with Accounting Auditors) of that Act, the date of authorization under Article 436, paragraph (3) (Audit of Financial Statements, etc.).
(2) Shareholders, Policyholders and other creditors of a Stock Company may make the following requests at any time during the operating hours of the company; provided, however, that they pay the fees determined by the Stock Company if making a request falling under item (ii) or (iv):
(i) A request to inspect the documents set forth in the preceding paragraph;
(ii) A request for a certified copy or extract of the documents set forth in the preceding paragraph;
(iii) A request to inspect anything that shows the particulars recorded in the electromagnetic records set forth in the preceding paragraph in a manner specified by Cabinet Office Ordinance; or
(iv) A request to be provided with the particulars recorded in the electromagnetic records set forth in the preceding paragraph by the electromagnetic means (meaning any of the methods using an electronic data processing system or any other information and communication technology and specified by Cabinet Office Ordinance; the same shall apply hereinafter) designated by the Stock Company, or to be issued a document detailing such particulars.
(3) For the purpose of applying the provisions of paragraph (1), item (i) to the cases where the articles of incorporation include provisions as set forth in Article 459, paragraph (1) (Provisions in the Articles of Incorporation for the Board of Directors to Determine Dividends of Surplus) of the Companies Act, the term "annual shareholders' meeting" in that item shall be deemed to be replaced with "annual shareholders' meeting or the board of directors under Article 436, paragraph (3) of the Companies Act."

(Objections by the Creditors)

Article 17 (1) Where a Stock Company reduces the amount of its capital, etc. (excluding the cases where the whole of the amount by which the Reserves are reduced is appropriated to the capital), Policyholders or other creditors of such Stock Company may raise their objections to the reduction in the amount of the capital, etc. to the Stock Company; provided, however, that this shall not apply to the cases where only the amount of the Reserves is reduced and all items of paragraph (1) of the preceding Article are met.

(2) Where Policyholders or other creditors of a Stock Company may raise their objections pursuant to the provisions of the preceding paragraph, said Stock Company shall give public notice of the following particulars below in the official gazette and by the Method of Public Notice stipulated in the company's articles of incorporation; provided, however, that the period under item (iii) may not be less than one month:

(i) The details of such reduction in the amount of the capital, etc. ;

(ii) The particulars specified by Cabinet Office Ordinance regarding the financial statements of such Stock Company;

(iii) That Policyholders or other creditors may raise their objections within a certain period of time; and

(iv) In addition to what is listed in the preceding three items, any particulars specified by Cabinet Office Ordinance.

(3) Where Policyholders or other creditors do not raise any objections within the period under item (iii) of the preceding paragraph, such Policyholders or other creditors shall be deemed to have approved such reduction in the amount of the capital, etc.

(4) Where Policyholders or other creditors raise objections within the period under paragraph (2), item (iii), the Stock Company in paragraph (1) shall make payment or provide equivalent security to such policyholders or other creditors, or entrust equivalent property to a trust company, etc. (meaning a trust company as defined in Article 2, paragraph (2) (Definitions) of the Trust Business Act (Act No. 154 of 2004); the same shall apply hereinafter) or financial institution conducting Trust Business (meaning a financial institution approved under Article 1, paragraph (1) (Authorization for Trust Business) of the Act on Provision, etc. of Trust Business by Financial Institutions (Act No. 43 of 1943)); the same shall apply hereinafter) for the purpose of ensuring that such Policyholders or other creditors receive the payment; provided, however, that this shall not apply to the cases where the reduction of the capital, etc. poses no risk of harming the interest of such Policyholders or other creditors.

(5) The provisions of the preceding paragraph shall not apply to the Policyholders or to any rights held by other persons pertaining to insurance contracts (excluding insurance claims that have already arisen at the time of public notice under paragraph (2) due to the occurrence of insured events or for other reasons, and any other right specified by Cabinet Order (referred to as "Insurance Claims, etc." hereinafter in this Section, as well as in Section 3 and Chapter VIII, Sections 2 and 3)).

(6) Any resolution pertaining to the reduction of the capital, etc. under Article 447, paragraph (1) (Reductions in Amount of Capital) or Article 448, paragraph (1) (Reductions in Amount of Reserves) of the Companies Act shall be invalid if the number of Policyholders who have raised their objections within the period set forth in paragraph (2), item (iii) (excluding the holders of policies under which Insurance Claims, etc. had already arisen at the time of public notice under that paragraph (but limited to those policies that would be terminated with the payment of the Insurance Claims, etc.); hereinafter the same shall apply in this paragraph, as well as in paragraph (4) of the following Article) exceeds one fifth of the total number of Policyholders, and the amount specified by Cabinet Office Ordinance as the credits (excluding Insurance Claims, etc.) belonging to the insurance contracts of the Policyholders who have stat-

ed such objections exceeds one fifth of the total amount of credits belonging to the Policyholders.
(7) In addition to what is provided for in the preceding paragraphs, any necessary particulars for the application of those provisions shall be specified by Cabinet Order.

(Effectuation)
Article 17-2 (1) The reduction of the amounts listed in the following items takes effect on the dates specified by the items, respectively; provided, however, that this shall not apply to the cases where the procedure under the preceding Article has not been completed, or if a resolution pertaining to the reduction of the capital, etc. under Article 447, paragraph (1) (Reductions in Amount of Capital) or Article 448, paragraph (1) (Reductions in Amount of Reserves) of the Companies Act becomes null or void pursuant to the provisions of Article 17, paragraph (6):
(i) Reduction of the capital: the date specified in Article 447, paragraph (1), item (iii) of the Companies Act; and
(ii) Reduction of Reserves: the date specified in Article 448, paragraph (1), item (iii) of the Companies Act.
(2) A Stock Company may change the dates specified in items (i) and (ii) of the preceding paragraph at any time before the relevant dates.
(3) Notwithstanding the provisions of paragraph (1), any reduction of the capital of a Stock Company shall not be effective unless it is approved by the Prime Minister.
(4) Any reduction of the capital, etc. pursuant to the provisions of the preceding Article (or, pursuant to the provisions of that Article and the preceding paragraph for any reduction of the capital) shall also be effective against the Policyholders who have stated their objections under that Article, paragraph (6) and other persons who hold any right (other than Insurance Claims, etc.) pertaining to insurance contracts involving the Policyholders.

(Special Provisions on Registration)
Article 17-3 (1) The following documents shall be attached to a written application for a registration of change due to a reduction of the capital of a Stock Company, in addition to the documents specified in Articles 18, Article 19 (Documents Attached to Written Applications) and Article 46 (General Rules on Attached Documents) of the Commercial Registration Act (Act No. 125 of 1963):
(i) A document certifying that the public notice under Article 17, paragraph (2) has been given;
(ii) Where any Policyholder or other creditor has stated objection under Article 17, paragraph (4), a document certifying that the company has made payment or provided equivalent security to such Policyholder or other creditor, or has entrusted equivalent property to a trust company, etc. for the purpose of ensuring that such Policyholder or other creditor receive the payment, or that the reduction of the capital poses no risk of harming the interest of such Policyholder or other creditor; and
(iii) A document certifying that the number of Policyholders who stated their objections under Article 17, paragraph (6) has not exceeded one fifth of the total number of Policyholders as indicated in that paragraph, or a document certifying that the amount specified by Cabinet Office Ordinance as belonging to such Policyholders as indicated in that paragraph has not exceeded one fifth of the total amount as indicated in that paragraph.
(2) The provisions of Article 70 (Registration of Changes Due to a Reduction of Capital) of the Commercial Registration Act shall not apply to a registration of change due to a

reduction of the capital of a Stock Company.

(Retention and Inspection, etc. of Documents, etc. Related to a Reduction of Capital, etc.)

Article 17-4 (1) A Stock Company shall keep at each of its business offices the documents or electromagnetic records in which the progress of the procedures provided for in Article 17 and any other particulars specified by Cabinet Office Ordinance as related to the reduction of the capital, etc. are detailed or recorded, for six months from the Effective Date of the reduction of the capital, etc.

(2) Shareholders, Policyholders and other creditors of a Stock Company may make the following requests at any time during the operating hours of the company; provided, however, that they pay the fees determined by the Stock Company if making a request falling under item (ii) or (iv):

(i) A request to inspect the documents set forth in the preceding paragraph;

(ii) A request for a certified copy or extract of the documents set forth in the preceding paragraph;

(iii) A request to inspect anything that shows the particulars recorded in the electromagnetic records set forth in the preceding paragraph in a manner specified by Cabinet Office Ordinance; or

(iv) A request to be provided with the particulars recorded in the electromagnetic records set forth in the preceding paragraph by the electromagnetic means designated by the Stock Company, or to be issued a document detailing such particulars.

(Exclusions from Application, etc.)

Article 17-5 (1) The provisions of Article 449 (Objections by the Creditors) of the Companies Act shall not apply to the reduction of the capital, etc. of a stock company.

(2) For the purpose of applying to a Stock Company the provisions of Article 740, paragraph (1) (Special Provisions on Objection Procedures for Creditors) of the Companies Act, the following text shall be inserted after the term "Article 810" in that paragraph: ", or Article 17, Article 70, Article 165-7 (including the cases where it is applied mutatis mutandis pursuant to Article 165-12 of the Insurance Business Act), Article 165-24 or Article 173-4 of the Insurance Business Act."

(Restrictions, etc. on Dividends of Surplus to Shareholders, etc.)

Article 17-6 (1) Where any amount is credited to assets in the balance sheet pursuant to the provisions of the first sentence of Article 113 (including the cases where it is applied mutatis mutandis pursuant to Article 272-18), a Stock Company shall not take any of the following actions unless such amount has been fully amortized.

(i) Purchase of any share of the Stock Company at a request made under sub-item (c) of item (i) or sub-item (c) of item (ii) of Article 138 (Method for Requests for Authorization of Transfer) of the Companies Act;

(ii) Acquisition of any share of the Stock Company based on a decision under Article 156, paragraph (1) (Determination of Matters Regarding Acquisition of Shares) of the Companies Act (but limited to acquisition of any share of the Stock Company where Article 163 (Acquisition of Shares from Subsidiaries) or Article 165, paragraph (1) (Acquisition of Shares by Market Transactions) of that Act applies);

(iii) Acquisition of any share of the Stock Company based on a decision under Article 157, paragraph (1) (Determination of Acquisition Price) of the Companies Act;

(iv) Acquisition of any share of the Stock Company under Article 173, paragraph (1) (Effectuation) of the Companies Act (excluding the cases where no money or other property is delivered);

(v) Purchase of any share of the Stock Company at a request made under Article 176, paragraph (1) (Demand for Sale) of the Companies Act;
(vi) Purchase of any share of the Stock Company under Article 197, paragraph (3) (Auction of Shares) of the Companies Act;
(vii) Purchase of any share of the Stock Company under Article 234, paragraph (4) (Treatment of Fractions) of the Companies Act (including the cases where it is applied mutatis mutandis pursuant to Article 235, paragraph (2) (Treatment of Fractions) of that Act); and
(viii) Dividend of surplus.
(2) The provisions of Article 463, paragraph (2) (Restrictions on Remedy Over Against Shareholders) of the Companies Act shall apply mutatis mutandis to the cases where a Stock Company, in violation of the provisions of the preceding paragraph, has taken any of the actions listed in the items of that Article. In this case, any other necessary technical change in interpretation shall be specified by Cabinet Order.
(3) For the purpose of applying to a Stock Company the provisions of Article 446, item (vii) (Amounts of Surplus), Article 461, paragraph (2), item (ii), sub-item (a) and item (vi) of that paragraph (Restriction on Dividends) of the Companies Act, the term "Ordinance of the Ministry of Justice" in these items shall be deemed to be replaced with "Cabinet Office Ordinance."

(Particulars Registered in Registering Incorporation)
Article 17-7 (1) In registering the incorporation of a Stock Company, the particulars listed in the items of Article 911, paragraph (3) (Registration of a Stock Company's Incorporation) of the Companies Act shall be registered, along with any provisions in its articles of incorporation in the second sentence of Article 113 (including the cases where it is applied mutatis mutandis pursuant to Article 272-18).
(2) Where any change has occurred in the particulars prescribed in the preceding paragraph, the Stock Company shall complete the registration of such a change within two weeks at the location of its head office.

Section 2 Mutual Companies

Subsection 1 General Rules

(Juridical Personality)
Article 18 A Mutual Company shall be a juridical person.

(Address)
Article 19 The address of a Mutual Company shall be at the location of its principal office.

(Name)
Article 20 A Mutual Company shall use the term "Sogo-Kaisha" (which means "Mutual Company") in its name.

(Mutatis Mutandis Application of the Companies Act)
Article 21 (1) The provisions of Article 8 (Prohibition on the Use of a Name, etc. That is Likely to Be Mistaken for That of a Company) of the Companies Act shall apply mutatis mutandis to the use of a misleading trade name or any other name that might evoke a Mutual Company; the provisions of Article 9 (Liability of a Company That Permits Others to Use Its Trade Name) of that Act shall apply mutatis mutandis to a Mutual

Company; the provisions of Part I, Chapter III, Section 1 (Employees of a Company) of that Act shall apply mutatis mutandis to the employees of a Mutual Company; the provisions of Section 2 of said Chapter (excluding Article 18) (Commercial Agents of a Company) shall apply mutatis mutandis to a person acting as an agent or intermediary in transactions for a Mutual Company; and the provisions of Chapter IV of said Part (excluding Article 24) (Non Competition after Assignment of Business) shall apply mutatis mutandis to the cases where a Mutual Company either assigns its business, or takes over any business or operations, respectively. In this case, the term "Company (including a Foreign Company, hereinafter the same shall apply in this Part)" in Article 10 (Managers) of that Act shall be deemed to be replaced with "Mutual Company"; any other necessary technical changes in interpretation shall be specified by Cabinet Order.

(2) The provisions of Part II, Chapter I (excluding Article 501 to 503 inclusive and Article 523) (General Provisions) of the Commercial Code (Act No. 48 of 1899) shall apply mutatis mutandis to the actions taken by a Mutual Company; the provisions of Chapter II of said Part (Buying and Selling) shall apply mutatis mutandis to the buying and selling carried out by a Mutual Company with a merchant or another Mutual Company (including any Foreign Mutual Company); the provisions of Chapter III of said Part (Current Account) shall apply mutatis mutandis to the contracts pertaining to set-offs carried out by a Mutual Company with its usual counter Parties; the provisions of Chapter V of said Part (excluding Article 545) (Brokerage Services) shall apply mutatis mutandis a Mutual Company's actions as an intermediary with regard to commercial transactions between third Parties; and the provisions of Chapter VI of said Part (excluding Article 558) (Commission Agent Services) and Article 593 (Deposits)) of said Code shall apply mutatis mutandis to a Mutual Company, respectively. In this case, any other necessary technical changes in interpretation shall be specified by Cabinet Order.

(3) For the purpose of applying mutatis mutandis the provisions of the Companies Act to the provisions of this Part (excluding the preceding Section, paragraph (1), Article 67-2 and Article 217, paragraph (3)) and Part VI (excluding Article 332-2), the term "electromagnetic record" in the provisions of that Act (including other provisions of that Act as applied mutatis mutandis pursuant to the relevant provisions) shall be deemed to be replaced with "electromagnetic record (meaning the electromagnetic record prescribed in Article 4, paragraph (3) of the Insurance Business Act)"; the term "electromagnetic means" in that Act shall be deemed to be replaced with "electromagnetic means (meaning the electromagnetic means defined in Article 16, paragraph (2), item (iv) of the Insurance Business Act)"; and the term "Ordinance of the Ministry of Justice" in that Act shall be deemed to be replaced with "Cabinet Office Ordinance," respectively.

(4) For the purpose of applying mutatis mutandis the provisions of the Companies Act to the provisions of this Section (excluding paragraph (1), Divisions 1 and 2 of Subsection 4, and Article 67-2) and Chapter VIII, Section 4, the terms "Stock Company" and "Company with a Board of Directors" in the provisions of that Act (including other provisions of that Act as applied mutatis mutandis pursuant to the relevant provisions) shall be deemed to be replaced with "Mutual Company"; the term "shareholder" in that Act shall be deemed to be replaced with "member"; the term "Subsidiary Company" in that Act shall be deemed to be replaced with "de facto Subsidiary Company (meaning a de facto Subsidiary Company as defined in Article 33-2, paragraph (1) of the Insurance Business Act)"; the term "head office" in that Act shall be deemed to be replaced with "principal office"; the term "branch office" in that Act shall be deemed to be replaced with "secondary office"; the term "operating hours" in that Act shall be

deemed to be replaced with "business hours"; the term "shareholders' meeting" in that Act shall be deemed to be replaced with "general members' council meeting (or, General Representative Members' Council Meeting, where the company has such a council)"; and the term "annual shareholders' meeting" in that Act shall be deemed to be replaced with "annual general members' council meeting (or the annual General Representative Members' Council Meeting, where the company has such a council)," respectively, unless provided otherwise.

Subsection 2 Incorporation

(Articles of Incorporation)
Article 22 (1) In order to incorporate a Mutual Company, the incorporators shall prepare its articles of incorporation, and all incorporators shall sign or affix the names and seals to it.
(2) The articles of incorporation set forth in the preceding paragraph may be prepared in the form of electromagnetic record. In this case, actions specified by Cabinet Office Ordinance shall be taken in lieu of the signing or the affixing of the names and seals, with respect to the data recorded on such electromagnetic record.

(Particulars Detailed or Recorded in the Articles of Incorporation)
Article 23 (1) The following particulars must be detailed or recorded in the articles of incorporation of a Mutual Company:
(i) Purpose(s);
(ii) Name;
(iii) Location of the principal office;
(iv) Total amount of funds (including the reserves for redemption of funds under Article 56);
(v) Provisions on the rights of fund contributors;
(vi) Method of redemption of funds;
(vii) Method of distributing dividends of surplus;
(viii) Method of Public Notice; and
(ix) Name and address of the incorporator.
(2) The Method of the Public Notice listed in item (viii) of the preceding paragraph shall be either:
(i) Publication in a daily newspaper that publishes the particulars of current events; or
(ii) Electronic public notice.
(3) Provisions in the articles of incorporation to the effect that electronic public notice is to be the Method of Public Notice shall suffice for a Mutual Company to designate the method listed in item (ii) of the preceding paragraph as its Method of Public Notice in its articles of incorporation. In this case, the company may designate the method listed in item (i) of the preceding paragraph as the Method of Public Notice in case the electronic means is not available for public notice due to an accident or for any other compelling reason.
(4) The provisions of Article 30 (Certification of the Articles of Incorporation) of the Companies Act shall apply mutatis mutandis to certification of the articles of incorporation set forth in paragraph (1) of the preceding Article. In this case, the term "Article 33, paragraph (7) or (9), or Article 37, paragraph (1) or (2)" in Article 30, paragraph (2) of that Act shall be deemed to be replaced with "Article 33, paragraph (7) or (9) as applied mutatis mutandis pursuant to Article 24, paragraph (2) of the Insurance Business Act"; any other necessary technical change in interpretation shall be specified by Cabinet Order.

Article 24 (1) Where a Mutual Company is to be incorporated, the following particulars shall not become effective unless they are detailed or recorded in the articles of incorporation referred to in Article 22, paragraph (1):
  (i) Property that it is agreed will be assigned to the Mutual Company after the establishment thereof, the value thereof, and the name of the assignor;
  (ii) Compensation or any other special benefit which the incorporators are to obtain by establishing the Mutual Company, and the names of such incorporators; and
  (iii) Expenses for the incorporation that are borne by the Mutual Company (excluding the fees for the certification of the articles of incorporation and the other expenses specified by Cabinet Office Ordinance as posing no risk of harming the interest of the Mutual Company).
(2) The provisions of Article 33 (Election of an Inspector of Matters Specified or Recorded in the Articles of Incorporation), Article 868, paragraph (1) (Jurisdiction over Non-Contentious Cases), Article 870 (limited to the segment pertaining to items (ii) and (v)) (Hearing of Statements), Article 871 (Appending of Reasons), Article 872 (limited to the segment pertaining to item (iv)) (Immediate Appeals), Article 874 (limited to the segment pertaining to item (i)) (Restrictions on Appeal), Article 875 (Exclusion from Application of the Provisions of the Non-Contentious Cases Procedures Act) and Article 876 (Supreme Court Rules) of the Companies Act shall apply mutatis mutandis to investigations by an inspector of any of the particulars listed in the items of the preceding paragraph where the Article of incorporation of a Mutual Company include any entry or record of that particular. In this case, the term "rescind the manifestation of his/her intention to subscribe for the relevant Shares Issued at Incorporation" in Article 33, paragraph (8) of that Act shall be deemed to be replaced with "resign from his/her office"; the term "Article 28, items (i) and (ii)" in paragraph (10), item (i) and the term "Article 28, item (i) or (ii)" in items (ii) and (iii) of that Article shall be deemed to be replaced with "Article 24, paragraph (1), item (i) of the Insurance Business Act," the term "items (i) and (ii) of that Article" in Article 33, paragraph (10), item (i) of that Act shall be deemed to be replaced with "that item," and the terms "Article 38, paragraph (1)" and "item (ii) of paragraph (2) of the same Article" in Article 33, paragraph (11), item (iii) of that Act shall be deemed to be replaced with "Article 30-10, paragraph (1) of the Insurance Business Act" and "that paragraph," respectively; any other necessary technical changes in interpretation shall be specified by Cabinet Order.

Article 25 In addition to the particulars listed in the items of Article 23, paragraph (1) and the items of paragraph (1) of the preceding Article, any other particulars may be detailed or recorded in the articles of incorporation of a Mutual Company, including those which, pursuant to the provisions of this Act, do not take effect unless prescribed in the articles of incorporation, so long as they do not violate the provisions of this Act.

(Retention and Inspection, etc. of the Articles of Incorporation)
Article 26 (1) The incorporators (or the Mutual Company after the establishment of such Mutual Company) shall keep the articles of incorporation at the place designated by the incorporators (or each office of the Mutual Company after the establishment of such Mutual Company).
(2) The incorporators (after the establishment of the Mutual Company, the members and creditors of such Mutual Company) may make the following requests at any time during the hours designated by the incorporators (after the establishment of such Mutual Company, during its business hours); provided, however, that they pay the fees deter-

mined by the incorporators (after the establishment of the Mutual Company, such Mutual Company) if making a request falling under item (ii) or (iv):
  (i) Where the articles of incorporation have been prepared in writing, a request to inspect them;
  (ii) A request for a certified copy or extract of the articles of incorporation referred to in the preceding item;
  (iii) Where the articles of incorporation are prepared in the form of electromagnetic record, a request to inspect anything that shows the particulars recorded in such electromagnetic records in a manner specified by Cabinet Office Ordinance; or
  (iv) A request to be provided with the particulars recorded in the electromagnetic records set forth in the preceding item by the electromagnetic means designated by the incorporators (after the establishment of the Mutual Company, such Mutual Company), or to be issued a document detailing such particulars.
(3) Where the articles of incorporation are prepared in the form of electromagnetic record, for the purpose of applying the provisions of paragraph (1) to a Mutual Company that adopts the measures specified by Cabinet Office Ordinance as the measures that enable its secondary offices to respond to the requests listed in items (iii) and (iv) of the preceding paragraph, the term "each office" shall be deemed to be replaced with "principal office."

(Solicitation of Funds at Incorporation by a Mutual Company)
Article 27 The incorporators shall solicit contributions to the total amount of funds in incorporating a Mutual Company pursuant to the provisions of this Subsection.

(Offers to Contribute Funds)
Article 28 (1) The incorporators shall notify those who seek to offer contributions of funds in response to the solicitation under the preceding Article of the following particulars:
  (i) Date of the articles of incorporation and the name of the notary who certified them;
  (ii) Particulars listed in the items of Article 23, paragraph (1) and the items of Article 24, paragraph (1);
  (iii) Location of the bank(s), etc. (meaning any bank (meaning a bank as set forth in Article 2, paragraph (1) (Definitions, etc) of the Banking Act (Act No. 59 of 1981), trust company, or any other institution specified by Cabinet Office Ordinance as equivalent to a bank or trust company; hereinafter the same shall apply in this Part) where the payment of contribution of funds is handled; and
  (iv) In addition to what is listed in the preceding three items, any other particulars specified by Cabinet Office Ordinance.
(2) A person who offers to contribute funds in response to the solicitation under the preceding Article shall submit to the incorporators a document detailing the following particulars:
  (i) Name and address of the person making the offer; and
  (ii) Planned amount of funds to contribute.
(3) A person who makes an offer under the preceding paragraph may, in lieu of submitting the document prescribed in that paragraph, and pursuant to the provisions of Cabinet Order, provide the particulars that are required to be included in such document by electromagnetic means, with the consent of the incorporators. In this case, the person who has made the offer shall be deemed to have submitted the document prescribed in that paragraph.
(4) The incorporators shall immediately notify a person who has made an offer under paragraph (2) (hereinafter referred to as "Offeror" in this Subsection) of any changes

in the particulars listed in the items of paragraph (1) and of the particulars affected by the changes.
(5) It shall be sufficient for a notice or demand to be sent by the incorporators to an Offeror at the address specified under paragraph (2), item (i) (where the Offeror has notified the incorporators of a different place or contact address for the receipt of notices or demands, to such place or contact address).
(6) The notice or demand under the preceding paragraph shall be deemed to have arrived at the time such notice or demand would normally have arrived.

(Allocation of Funds)
Article 29 (1) The incorporators shall select among the Offerors the persons who must contribute funds, and shall determine the amount of contribution to be allocated to each of them. In this case, the incorporators may reduce the amounts of the contributions of funds to be made by such Offerors from the amount prescribed in paragraph (2), item (ii) of the preceding Article.
(2) The incorporators shall, without delay following any decision under the preceding paragraph, notify the Offerors of the amount of contributions of funds to be made by each of them.

(Special Provisions on Offers to Contribute Funds as Solicited at Incorporation and the Allocation Thereof)
Article 30 The provisions of the preceding two Articles shall not apply to the cases where a person who seeks to contribute funds as solicited at incorporation concludes a contract stipulating the contribution of the total amount of such funds.

(Fund Subscription)
Article 30-2 The persons listed in the following items shall be fund subscribers solicited at incorporation in the amounts specified in the items:
(i) Offerors: the amount of their contributions of funds as allocated thereto by the incorporators; and
(ii) A person who, under a contract as set forth in the previous Article, has subscribed for the total amount of funds solicited at incorporation: the amount of funds subscribed for.

(Payment of Funds)
Article 30-3 (1) Each fund subscriber solicited at incorporation shall, without delay following the receipt of the notice under Article 29, paragraph (2), pay the full amount of money pertaining to his/her contribution of funds solicited at incorporation, at the place of payment listed in Article 28, paragraph (1), item (iii).
(2) The incorporators shall notify any fund subscriber solicited at incorporation who has not made the payment set forth in the preceding paragraph to the effect that such payment is to be made by a date designated thereby.
(3) The notice under the preceding paragraph shall be given no later than two weeks before the date prescribed in that paragraph.
(4) No assignment of the right to become a fund subscriber of a Mutual Company at its incorporation by making a payment pursuant to the provisions of paragraph (1) may be duly asserted against the Mutual Company thus established.
(5) A fund subscriber solicited at incorporation who has received the notice under paragraph (2) shall, if he/she fails to make the payment by the date prescribed in that paragraph, lose his/her right to become a fund contributor of a Mutual Company at incorporation by making such payment.

(Certificate of Deposit for Monies Paid)
Article 30-4 (1) The incorporators may request the bank, etc. that handled the payment pursuant to the provisions of paragraph (1) of the preceding Article to issue a certificate of deposit for monies equivalent to the amount paid in pursuant to the provisions of that paragraph.
(2) The bank, etc. that issued the certificate referred to in the preceding paragraph may not assert against the Mutual Company after its establishment anything detailed on such certificate which differs from the truth or the existence of restrictions regarding the return of money paid in pursuant to the provisions of paragraph (1) of the preceding Article.

(Restrictions, etc. on the Invalidation or Recession of Subscription)
Article 30-5 (1) Fund subscribers solicited at incorporation may make the requests listed in the items of Article 26, paragraph (2) at any time during the hours designated by the incorporators; provided, however, that they shall pay the fees determined by the incorporators if making a request that falls under item (ii) or (iv) of that paragraph.
(2) The proviso to Article 93 (Concealment of True Intent) and the provisions of Article 94, paragraph (1) (Fictitious Manifestation of Intention) of the Civil Code (Act No. 89 of 1896) shall not apply to the manifestation of an intention to offer or allocate contributions of funds solicited at incorporation, and a contract under Article 30.
(3) After the establishment of the Mutual Company, a fund subscriber solicited at incorporation may neither assert the invalidity of his/her contribution of funds solicited at incorporation on the grounds of a mistake, nor may he/she cancel his/her contribution of funds solicited at incorporation on the grounds of fraud or duress.

(Solicitation of Members)
Article 30-6 (1) The incorporators shall, pursuant to the provisions of this Subsection, solicit members in incorporating a Mutual Company.
(2) One hundred or more members shall be required for incorporating a Mutual Company.

(Application for Membership)
Article 30-7 (1) The incorporators shall notify those who are willing to apply for membership in response to the solicitation under paragraph (1) of the preceding Article of the following particulars:
(i) Date of the articles of incorporation and the name(s) of the notary (or notaries) who certified them;
(ii) Particulars listed in the items of Article 23, paragraph (1) and the items of Article 24, paragraph (1);
(iii) Names and addresses of the fund contributors (including the fund subscribers), and the amount of contribution (including the amount to be contributed) by each of the contributors;
(iv) Number of the members to be solicited at incorporation;
(v) Any provisions in the articles of incorporation under the second sentence of Article 113 (including the cases where it is applied mutatis mutandis pursuant to Article 272-18); and
(vi) In addition to what is listed in the preceding five items, any other particular specified by Cabinet Office Ordinance.
(2) A person who applies for membership in response to the solicitation under paragraph (1) of the preceding Article shall prepare and submit to the incorporators two copies of a signed document detailing the following particulars:

(i) Name and address of the person applying for membership; and
(ii) Kind of insurance to which belongs the insurance contract that the person is willing to conclude with the Mutual Company.
(3) A person who files an application under the preceding paragraph may, in lieu of submitting the document prescribed in that paragraph, and pursuant to the provisions of Cabinet Order, provide the particulars that are required to be included in such document by electromagnetic means, with the consent of the incorporators. In this case, the person who has filed the application shall be deemed to have submitted the document prescribed in that paragraph.
(4) The provisions of Article 30-5, paragraph (2) shall apply mutatis mutandis to the manifestation of an intention to apply for membership prior to the establishment of a Mutual Company. In this case, any other necessary technical change in interpretation shall be specified by Cabinet Order.

(Organizational Meetings)
Article 30-8 (1) If all payments have been completed for contributions comprising the total amount of funds, and the number of persons who have submitted to the incorporators the documents set forth in paragraph (2) of the preceding Article has reached the number set forth in paragraph (1), item (iv) of the same Article (referred to as "Completion of Payments, etc." in the following paragraph), the incorporators shall, without delay, convene a meeting of prospective members of the Mutual Company (hereinafter referred to as an "Organizational Meeting" in this Section).
(2) After the Completion of Payments, etc. , the incorporators may convene an Organizational Meeting whenever they find it necessary.
(3) An Organizational Meeting may adopt resolutions only on the particulars provided for in this Section, the discontinuation of the incorporation of the Mutual Company, the conclusion of Organizational Meetings, and other particulars regarding the incorporation of the Mutual Company.
(4) Each prospective member shall be entitled to one vote at an Organizational Meeting.
(5) Resolutions at an Organizational Meeting are adopted by a three-quarters majority of the votes, provided that at least half of the prospective members are present.
(6) The provisions of Article 67 (Determination to Convene an Organizational Meeting), Article 68 (excluding items in paragraph (2)) (Notices of Convocation for Organizational Meetings), Articles 70 and Article 71 (Delivery of Voting Forms and Reference Documents for an Organizational Meeting), Article 73, paragraph (4) (Resolutions at Organizational Meetings), Article 74 to 76 inclusive (Proxy Voting, Voting in Writing, and Voting by Electromagnetic Means), Article 78 to 80 inclusive (Accountability of Incorporators, Authority of the Chairperson, and Resolutions for Postponement or Adjournment), and Article 81 (excluding paragraph (4)) (Minutes) of the Companies Act shall apply mutatis mutandis to Organizational Meetings of a Mutual Company; and the provisions of Article 830 (Action for a Declaratory Judgment as to the Absence or Invalidity of a Resolution of a Shareholders' Meeting, etc.), Article 831 (Action to Revoke a Resolution of a Shareholders' Meeting, etc.), Article 834 (limited to the segment pertaining to items (xvi) and (xvii)) (Defendant), Article 835, paragraph (1) (Jurisdiction over Actions), Article 836, paragraphs (1) and (3) (Order to Provide Security), Article 837 (Mandatory Consolidation of Oral Arguments, etc.), Article 838 (Persons Affected by a Judgment Being Upheld), Article 846 (Liability for Damages Where a Judgment Is Entered Against the Plaintiff), and Article 937, paragraph (1) (limited to the segment pertaining to item (i), sub-item (g)) (Commissioning of Registration by Judicial Decision) of that Act shall apply mutatis mutandis to an action for a declaratory judgment as to the absence or invalidity of a resolution of a Mutual Com-

pany's Organizational Meeting and to an action to rescind a resolution of a Mutual Company's Organizational Meeting, respectively. In this case, the terms "Shareholders at Incorporation" in those provisions (excluding Article 67, paragraph (2) and Article 831, paragraph (1) of that Act), and "Shareholders at Incorporation (excluding Shareholders at Incorporation who may not exercise their voting rights on all matters which may be resolved at Organizational Meetings. The same shall apply in the following Article to Article 71 inclusive)" in Article 67, paragraph (2) of that Act shall be deemed to be replaced with "prospective members"; the term "two weeks (or one week if the Stock Company to be incorporated is not a Public Company, except in cases where the particulars listed in item (iii) or item (iv) of paragraph (1) of the preceding Article are decided, (or if a shorter period of time is provided for in the articles of incorporation in cases where the Stock Company to be incorporated is a Stock Company other than a Company with Board of Directors, such shorter period of time))" in Article 68, paragraph (1) of that Act shall be deemed to be replaced with "two weeks"; the term "shall be in writing in the following cases" in Article 68, paragraph (2) shall be deemed to be replaced with "shall be in writing"; the term "Article 27, item (v), or Article 59, paragraph (3), item (i)" in Article 68, paragraph (5) shall be deemed to be replaced with "Article 30-7, paragraph (2), item (i) of the Insurance Business Act"; the term "a Shareholder, etc. (or, in cases where the Shareholders' Meeting, etc. set forth in each such item is an Organizational Meeting or a Class Organizational Meeting, a Shareholder, etc., a Shareholder at Incorporation, a Director at Incorporation, or a Company Auditor at Incorporation" in Article 831, paragraph (1) shall be deemed to be replaced with "members, directors, auditors, or liquidators (or, members, directors, executive officers, or liquidators in a company with Committees), or prospective members, directors at incorporation (meaning directors at incorporation as set forth in Article 30-10, paragraph (1) of the Insurance Business Act; hereinafter the same shall apply in this paragraph) or company auditors at incorporation (meaning the company auditors at incorporation set forth in paragraph (1) of that Article; hereinafter the same shall apply in this paragraph) of a Mutual Company"; and the term "a director, company auditor or liquidator pursuant to the provisions of Article 346(1) (including cases where it is applied mutatis mutandis pursuant to Article 479(4)), and in cases where such resolution is a resolution at an Organizational Meeting or Class Organizational Meeting, this shall include a Director at Incorporation or a Company Auditor at Incorporation" in the same paragraph of the Companies Act shall be deemed to be replaced with "directors, company auditors, liquidators, directors at incorporation or company auditors at incorporation"; and any other necessary technical changes in interpretation shall be specified by Cabinet Order.

(Reporting of the Particulars of Incorporation)
Article 30-9 (1) The incorporators shall report the particulars of the incorporation of a Mutual Company at the Organizational Meeting.
(2) In the cases listed in the following items, the incorporators shall submit or provide at the Organizational Meeting the documents or electromagnetic record in which the particulars specified in the relevant item are detailed or recorded:
(i) Where the articles of incorporation provide for the particulars listed in the items of Article 24, paragraph (1) (excluding the particulars specified in the items of Article 33, paragraph (10) of the Companies Act in the cases listed in such items as applied mutatis mutandis pursuant to Article 24, paragraph (2)): the content of the report set forth in Article 33, paragraph (4) as applied mutatis mutandis pursuant to Article 24, paragraph (2) that is to be submitted by the inspector under Article 33, paragraph (2) as applied mutatis mutandis pursuant to Article 24, paragraph (2);

and
(ii) In the case listed in Article 33, paragraph (10), item (iii) of the Companies Act as applied mutatis mutandis pursuant to Article 24, paragraph (2): the content of the verification provided in Article 33, paragraph (10), item (iii) of that Act as applied mutatis mutandis pursuant to Article 24, paragraph (2).

(Election, etc. of Directors at Incorporation, etc.)
Article 30-10 (1) The election of the directors at incorporation (meaning the persons who become directors at the incorporation of a Mutual Company; the same shall apply hereinafter), accounting advisors at incorporation (meaning the persons who become accounting advisors at the incorporation of a Mutual Company; the same shall apply hereinafter), auditors at incorporation (meaning the persons who become company auditors at the incorporation of a Mutual Company; the same shall apply hereinafter) and accounting auditors at incorporation (meaning the persons who become accounting auditors at the incorporation of a Mutual Company; the same shall apply hereinafter) shall be made by a resolution of the Organizational Meeting.
(2) Three or more persons shall be elected as directors at incorporation.
(3) Three or more persons shall be elected as auditors at incorporation where the Mutual Company to be incorporated is a company with a board of company auditors (meaning a Stock Company or Mutual Company which has a board of company auditors; the same shall apply hereinafter).
(4) A person who is precluded from being a director, accounting advisor, company auditor or accounting auditor of the Mutual Company after its establishment, pursuant to the provisions of Article 8-2, paragraph (2), Article 53-2, paragraph (1) (including the cases where it is applied mutatis mutandis pursuant to Article 53-5, paragraph (1)), Article 333, paragraph (1) or (3) of the Companies Act as applied mutatis mutandis pursuant to Article 53-4, or Article 337, paragraph (1) or (3) of that Act as applied mutatis mutandis pursuant to Article 53-7 may not be elected as director at incorporation, accounting advisor at incorporation, auditor at incorporation or accounting auditor at incorporation, respectively.
(5) Directors at incorporation, accounting advisors at incorporation, auditors at incorporation or accounting auditors at incorporation who are elected pursuant to the provisions of paragraph (1) may be dismissed by a resolution of the Organizational Meeting at any time prior to the establishment of the Mutual Company.
(6) The provisions of Article 47 (Appointment, etc. of Representative Directors at Incorporation) of the Companies Act shall apply mutatis mutandis to the appointment and removal of the representative director at incorporation (meaning the person who becomes representative director at the incorporation of a Mutual Company; the same shall apply hereinafter) of a Mutual Company (other than a company with Committees); and the provisions of Article 48 (Appointment of Committee Members at Incorporation) of that Act shall apply mutatis mutandis to the appointment of committee members at incorporation (meaning the persons who become committee members at the incorporation of a Mutual Company; the same shall apply hereinafter) of a Mutual Company (limited to a company with Committees), the election of its executive officers at incorporation (meaning the persons who become executive officers at the incorporation of a Mutual Company; the same shall apply hereinafter) and the appointment of its representative executive officer at incorporation (meaning the person who becomes representative executive officer at the incorporation of a Mutual Company; the same shall apply hereinafter), and the removal and dismissal of those persons, respectively. In this case, any other necessary technical change in interpretation shall be specified by Cabinet Order.

(Investigations by Directors at Incorporation, etc.)
Article 30-11 (1) The directors at incorporation (meaning the directors at incorporation and auditors at incorporation where the Mutual Company to be incorporated is a company with auditors (meaning a Stock Company or Mutual Company that has company auditors; the same shall apply hereinafter)) shall investigate the following particulars without delay after their election:
(i) That, with respect to the properties contributed in kind, etc. in the cases listed in Article 33, paragraph (10), item (i) or (ii) of the Companies Act as applied mutatis mutandis pursuant to Article 24, paragraph (2) (if listed in Article 33, paragraph (10), item (ii) as applied mutatis mutandis pursuant to Article 24, paragraph (2), limited to the securities under such item), the value indicated or recorded in the articles of incorporation is reasonable;
(ii) That the verification provided for in Article 33, paragraph (10), item (iii) of the Companies Act as applied mutatis mutandis pursuant to Article 24, paragraph (2) is appropriate;
(iii) That the funds solicited at the incorporation of the Mutual Company have been fully subscribed for;
(iv) That the payments pursuant to the provisions of Article 30-3, paragraph (1) have been completed;
(v) That the number of prospective members is no less than one hundred (100); and
(vi) That, in addition to the particulars listed in the preceding five items, the procedures for the incorporation of the Mutual Company do not violate applicable laws and regulations or the articles of incorporation.
(2) The provisions of Article 93, paragraphs (2) and (3) (Investigation by Directors at Incorporation), and Article 94 (Special Provisions in Case Directors at Incorporation are Incorporators) of the Companies Act shall apply mutatis mutandis to the investigation under the preceding paragraph. In this case, any other necessary technical change in interpretation shall be specified by Cabinet Order.

(Amendments, etc. to the Articles of Incorporation at Incorporation)
Article 30-12 (1) The incorporators may not effect any amendment to the articles of incorporation once the notice under Article 29, paragraph (2) has been given, notwithstanding the provisions of Article 33, paragraph (9) of the Companies Act as applied mutatis mutandis pursuant to Article 24, paragraph (2).
(2) Notwithstanding the provisions of Article 30, paragraph (2) of the Companies Act as applied mutatis mutandis pursuant to Article 23, paragraph (4), the articles of incorporation may be amended by a resolution at an Organizational Meeting.
(3) Where an Organizational Meeting has adopted a resolution to amend the articles of incorporation in a manner that modifies any of the particulars listed in the items of Article 24, paragraph (1), the incorporators may resign from their offices, provided that they do so within two weeks of the adoption of the resolution.

(Timing of Establishment)
Article 30-13 (1) A Mutual Company shall be established by registering its incorporation at the location of its principal office.
(2) A person who has submitted the document set forth in Article 30-7, paragraph (2) shall, without delay following the establishment of the Mutual Company and after the Mutual Company has received the license prescribed in Article 3, paragraph (1) or made a registration under Article 272, paragraph (1), apply for an insurance contract with the Mutual Company.

(Mutatis Mutandis Application of the Companies Act)

Article 30-14 The provisions of Part II, Chapter I, Section 8 (excluding Article 52, paragraph (2), item (ii)) (Liability of the Incorporators) and Article 103, paragraph (2) (Liability of the Incorporators) of the Companies Act shall apply mutatis mutandis to the liabilities of incorporators, directors at incorporation or auditors at incorporation of a Mutual Company. In this case, the term "(in this paragraph and in item (ii) excluding those who contributed in kind under Article 28, item (i) or the assignor of the properties under item (ii) of the same Article)" in Article 52, paragraph (2) (Liability for Insufficiency of Value of Properties Contributed) of that Act shall be deemed to be replaced with "(excluding the assignor of the properties under Article 24, paragraph (1), item (i) of the Insurance Business Act)"; the term "Article 28, item (i) or (ii)" in Article 52, paragraph (2), item (i) shall be deemed to be replaced with "Article 24, paragraph (1), item (i) of the Insurance Business Act"; the term "Article 33, paragraph (10), item (iii)" in Article 52, paragraph (3) shall be deemed to be replaced with "Article 33, paragraph (10), item (iii) as applied mutatis mutandis pursuant to Article 24, paragraph (2) of the Insurance Business Act"; and in Article 103, paragraph (2) of that Act, the term "In cases where the solicitation under Article 57, paragraph (1) is carried out," shall be deemed to be deleted, and the terms "such solicitation" and "the preceding paragraph" shall be deemed to be replaced with "solicitation under Article 27 or Article 30-6, paragraph (1) of the Insurance Business Act" and "Article 52, paragraph (2) (excluding item (ii))," respectively; any technical change in interpretation shall be specified by Cabinet Order.

(Actions to Invalidate Incorporation)

Article 30-15 The provisions of Article 828, paragraph (1) (limited to the segment pertaining to item (i)) and paragraph (2) (limited to the segment pertaining to item (i) (Actions to Invalidate Acts Concerning the Organization of a Company), Article 834 (limited to the segment pertaining to item (i)) (Defendant), Article 835, paragraph (1) (Jurisdiction over Actions), Article 836, paragraphs (1) and (3) (Order to Provide Security), Articles 837 to 839 inclusive (Mandatory Consolidation of Oral Arguments, etc., Persons Affected by a Judgment Being Upheld, Effects of a Judgment of Invalidity, Revocation or Rescission), Article 846 (Liability for Damages Where a Judgment Is Entered Against the Plaintiff), and Article 937, paragraph (1) (limited to the segment pertaining to item (i), sub-item (a)) (Commissioning of Registration by a Judicial Decision) of the Companies Act shall apply mutatis mutandis to an action to invalidate the incorporation of a Mutual Company. In this case, the term "a Shareholder, etc. (meaning a shareholder, director or liquidator (or, for a Company with Company Auditors, it means a shareholder, director, company auditor or liquidator, and for a Company with Committees, it means a shareholder, director, executive officer or liquidator); hereinafter the same shall apply in this Section)" in Article 828, paragraph (2), item (i) of that Act shall be deemed to be replaced with "members, directors, company auditors or liquidators (or members, directors, executive officers, or liquidators in a company with Committees)"; any other necessary technical change in interpretation shall be specified by Cabinet Order.

Subsection 3 Rights and Obligations of Members

(Obligations of Members)

Article 31 The obligations of a member shall be limited to the amount of his/her insurance premium payments.

(Notices and Demands)
Article 32 (1) **It shall be sufficient for any notice or demand to an Applicant for member**ship, or member of a Mutual Company to be sent to the place or contact address of which the Applicant or member has notified the incorporators or Mutual Company; provided, however, that this shall not apply to a notice or demand on any particular pertaining to the insurance relationship.

(2) The notice or demand in the main clause of the preceding paragraph shall be deemed to have arrived at the time when such notice or demand would normally have arrived.

(3) The provisions of the main clause of paragraph (1) and the preceding paragraph shall apply mutatis mutandis to the cases where a document is delivered to the members in giving a notice under Article 299, paragraph (1) of the Companies Act as applied mutatis mutandis pursuant to Article 41, paragraph (1) or where the particulars that are required to be included in such document are provided by electromagnetic means. In this case, the term "to have arrived" in the preceding paragraph shall be deemed to be replaced with "to have been effected by delivery of such document or provision of such particulars by electromagnetic means"; and any other necessary technical change in interpretation shall be specified by Cabinet Order.

(Members List)
Article 32-2 (1) A Mutual Company shall, pursuant to the provisions of Cabinet Office Ordinance, prepare a members list in which it details or records the particulars specified by Cabinet Office Ordinance as particulars required for such members list.

(2) A Mutual Company shall keep its members list at its principal office.

(3) A member or creditor may make the following requests at any time during the business hours of the Mutual Company. In this case, however, the member or creditor shall disclose the reason for his/her request:
 (i) Where the members list has been prepared in writing, a request to investigate or copy the written document; or
 (ii) Where the members list has been prepared in the form of electromagnetic record, a request to investigate or copy anything that shows the particulars recorded on such electromagnetic record in a manner specified by Cabinet Office Ordinance.

(4) A Mutual Company may not reject any request made under the preceding paragraph unless:
 (i) The member or creditor making such request (hereinafter referred to as "Requestor" in this paragraph) does so with any other intent than to investigate in connection with the protection or exercise his/her rights;
 (ii) The Requestor makes a request with the intent to preclude the Mutual Company from performing its business or to harm the common interest of the members;
 (iii) The Requestor operates, or engages in, any business that is substantially in a competitive relationship with the business of the Mutual Company;
 (iv) The Requestor makes a request with the intent to inform a third party of any fact obtained by investigating or copying the members list for material gain; or
 (v) The Requestor has, within the past two years, informed a third party of any fact learned by investigating or copying the members list for material gain.

(Reference Date)
Article 33 (1) For the purpose of identifying the persons who shall exercise their rights as members, a Mutual Company may deem the persons who enjoy its membership on a certain date within four months prior to the date of exercising such rights as the members who shall exercise said rights.

(2) A Mutual Company that has fixed the "certain date" set forth in the preceding paragraph shall give public notice of such date no later than two weeks before the date; provided, however, that this shall not apply to the cases where said date is fixed by the articles of incorporation.
(3) The rights set forth in paragraph (1) shall not include any right provided for otherwise in this Act or the rights specified by Cabinet Order such as the right to distribution of surplus.

(Benefits Provided for the Exercise of the Rights of a Member or Representative Member)
Article 33-2 (1) A Mutual Company shall not provide a person with economic benefits for the exercise of his/her member's rights or representative member's rights (limited to benefits given on the account of the Mutual Company or its de facto Subsidiary Company (meaning a juridical person whose management is deemed to be controlled by the Mutual Company pursuant to the provisions of Cabinet Office Ordinance, such as a Stock Company in which the Mutual Company holds the majority of all shareholders' voting rights; the same shall apply hereinafter).
(2) The provisions of Article 120, paragraphs (2) to (5) inclusive (Benefits Provided for the Exercise of a Shareholder's Right) of the Companies Act shall apply mutatis mutandis to the case set forth in the preceding paragraph; and the provisions of Part VII, Chapter II, Section 2 (excluding Article 847, paragraph (2), Article 849, paragraph (5), and Article 851, paragraph (1), item (i) and paragraph (2)) (Liability Actions, etc. Against a Stock Company) of that Act shall apply mutatis mutandis to an action for the return of benefits under Article 120, paragraph (3) of that Act as applied mutatis mutandis pursuant to this paragraph, respectively. In this case, the term "paragraph (1)" in Article 120, paragraphs (3) and (4) of that Act shall be deemed to be replaced with "Article 33-2, paragraph (1) of the Insurance Business Act"; the term "all shareholders" in Article 120, paragraph (5) shall be deemed to be replaced with "all members"; the term "A shareholder (excluding a Holder of Shares Less than One Unit who is unable to exercise rights pursuant to the provisions of the articles of incorporation) having the shares" in Article 847, paragraph (1) (Liability Actions, etc.) of that Act shall be deemed to be replaced with "person who has been a member"; and the term "shareholder" in Article 847, paragraph (3) to (5) inclusive and (7) shall be deemed to be replaced with "member"; and any other necessary technical change in interpretation shall be specified by Cabinet Order.

(Grounds for Withdrawal)
Article 34 (1) A member shall withdraw his/her membership on any of the following grounds:
(i) Termination of the insurance relationship; or
(ii) Occurrence of an event specified in the articles of incorporation.
(2) In the event of a member's death (excluding where the death falls under the items of the preceding paragraph) or a member being extinguished in a merger, the heir or any other general successor to the member shall assume the rights and obligations of the member.
(3) Where the deceased or extinguished member set forth in the previous paragraph has two or more general successors (meaning general successors by inheritance and limited to those who have not effected the payment of insurance premiums in whole or in part; hereinafter the same shall apply in this paragraph), the general successors shall assume the obligation of effecting the insurance premium payments jointly and severally.

(4) If a deceased or extinguished member has two or more general successors (limited to general successors by inheritance; hereinafter the same shall apply in this paragraph), the general successors may not exercise the member's rights that they have assumed, unless they appoint one person to exercise such rights.

(Claims for a Refund)
Article 35 A withdrawn member may, pursuant to the terms of the articles of incorporation or insurance contract, claim refund of the money associated with his/her rights; provided, however, that this shall not apply to the cases where the withdrawn member is replaced by another person.

(Prescription)
Article 36 The claim for refund set forth in the preceding Article shall lapse by prescription, unless exercised within three years.

Subsection 4 Administrative Organs
Division 1 General Members' Councils

(Voting Rights)
Article 37 Each member shall be entitled to one vote at a general members' council meeting.

(Authority of General Members' Councils)
Article 37-2 The general members' council may resolve only the matters provided for in this Act and the matters provided for in the articles of incorporation.

(Resolutions of a General Members' Council)
Article 37-3 (1) Unless otherwise provided for in this Act or the articles of incorporation, a resolution of the general members' council is adopted by the majority vote of the attending members at a session where at least half of the members are present.
(2) A general members' council may not adopt a resolution on any other matter than matters listed in Article 298, paragraph (1), item (ii) of the Companies Act as applied mutatis mutandis pursuant to Article 41, paragraph (1); provided, however, that this shall not apply to a request for the appointment of a person set forth in Article 316, paragraph (1) or (2) of that Act as applied mutatis mutandis pursuant to Article 41, paragraph (1), or for the attendance of the accounting auditors set forth in Article 398, paragraph (2) of that Act as applied mutatis mutandis pursuant to Article 53-23.

(Right to Demand the Convocation of the General Members' Council)
Article 38 (1) Members having consecutively for the preceding six months or more (or, in cases where shorter period is prescribed in the articles of incorporation, such period) not less than three thousandths (or in cases where lesser proportion is prescribed in the articles of incorporation, such proportion) of the total membership, or three thousand (or in cases where smaller number is prescribed in the articles of incorporation) or more members of a Mutual Company (or, in mutual Low-Cost, Short-Term Insurers specified by Cabinet Order (hereinafter referred to as a "Specified Mutual Company"), members equal to or exceeding the number specified by Cabinet Order), who have been members of the Mutual Company may,,by showing matters which are a purpose for a general members' council meeting (limited to matters on which the general members' council may adopt a resolution; hereinafter the same shall apply in this

Division) and the reason for convocation, demand that the directors call a general members' council meeting.
(2) In the following cases, members who have made a demand pursuant to the provisions of the preceding paragraph may call a general members' council with the permission of the court.
   (i) In cases where the convocation procedures are not effected without delay after the demand pursuant to the provisions of the preceding paragraph; or
   (ii) In cases where the notice for the convocation of the general members' council which designates, as the date of the general members' council meeting, a date falling within the period of eight weeks (or in cases where any period less than that is provided for in the articles of incorporation, such period) from the day of a demand pursuant to the provisions of the preceding paragraph, is not given.
(3) The provisions of Article 868, paragraph (1) (Jurisdiction over Non-Contentious Cases), Article 869 (Prima Facie Showing), Article 871 (Appending of Reasons), Article 874 (limited to the segment pertaining to item (iv)) (Restrictions on Appeal), Article 875 (Exclusion from Application of the Provisions of the Non-Contentious Cases Procedures Act) and Article 876 (Supreme Court Rules) of the Companies Act shall apply mutatis mutandis to the previous paragraph. In this case, any other necessary technical change in interpretation shall be specified by Cabinet Order.

(Right to Submit Proposals)
Article 39 (1) Members having consecutively for the preceding six months or more (or, in cases where shorter period is prescribed in the articles of incorporation, such period) no less than one thousandth (or in cases where lesser proportion is prescribed in the articles of incorporation, such proportion) of the total membership, or one thousand (or in case where smaller number is prescribed by the articles of incorporation) or more members of a Mutual Company (or, in a Specified Mutual Company, members equal to or exceeding the number prescribed by Cabinet Order, who have been members of the Mutual Company, may demand that the directors include certain items (limited to matters on which the general members' council may adopt a resolution) in the agenda for a general members' council meeting. In this case, the demand shall be submitted no later than eight weeks (or any shorter period prescribed by the articles of incorporation) prior to the date of the general members' council meeting.
(2) A member may submit a proposal at a general members' council meeting with respect to any agenda item for the meeting; provided, however, that this shall not apply to the cases where the proposal is in violation of any applicable law or regulation or the articles of incorporation, or where three years have not elapsed since the day on which an essentially identical proposal was not approved by at least one tenth (1/10) of the votes of the members (or any smaller proportion prescribed by the articles of incorporation) of the general members' council.
(3) Members representing at least one thousandth (or any smaller proportion prescribed by the articles of incorporation) of the total membership, or one thousand (or any smaller number prescribed by the articles of incorporation) or more members of a Mutual Company (or, in a Specified Mutual Company, members equal to or exceeding the number specified by Cabinet Order set forth in paragraph (1)), who have been members of the Mutual Company without interruption for the preceding six months (or any shorter period prescribed by the articles of incorporation), may demand the directors that, no later than eight weeks (or any shorter period prescribed by the articles of incorporation) prior to the date of the general members' council, members be notified of the outline of any proposal to be submitted by said member with respect to an agenda item of the meeting (or, where a notice is to be given under Article 299, paragraph (2)

Art.40〜41　6 Insurance Business Act, Part II, Chap.II, Sec.2

(excluding the items (i) and (ii)) or (3) of the Companies Act as applied mutatis mutandis pursuant to Article 41, paragraph (1), such outline be described in, or recorded on, that notice); provided, however, that this shall not apply to the cases where the proposal is in violation of any applicable law or regulation or the articles of incorporation, or where three years have not elapsed since the day on which an essentially identical proposal was not approved by at least one tenth of the membership (or any smaller proportion prescribed by the articles of incorporation) in the general members' council.

(Right to Demand the Election of Inspector for a General Members' Council)
Article 40　(1) A Mutual Company or members representing at least one thousandth (or any smaller proportion prescribed by the articles of incorporation) of the total membership, or one thousand (or any smaller number prescribed by the articles of incorporation) or more members of a Mutual Company (or, in a Specified Mutual Company, members equal to or exceeding the number specified by Cabinet Order set forth in paragraph (1) of the preceding Article), who have been members of the Mutual Company without interruption for the preceding six months (or any shorter period prescribed by the articles of incorporation), may file a petition with the court, prior to a session of the general members' council, for the election of an inspector to be retained to investigate the convocation procedures and method of resolution of such a council.
(2) The provisions of Article 306, paragraphs (3) to (7) inclusive (Election of Inspector on Calling Procedures of Shareholders' Meeting) and Article 307 (Determination by The Court of the Calling of Shareholders' Meeting) of the Companies Act shall apply mutatis mutandis to the preceding paragraph. In this case, the term "preceding two paragraphs" in Article 306, paragraph (3) of that Act shall be deemed to be replaced with "Article 40, paragraph (1) of the Insurance Business Act"; the term "Stock Company" in Article 306, paragraphs (4) and (7) shall be deemed to be replaced with "Mutual Company"; the term "shareholders' meeting" in Article 307 of that Act shall be deemed to be replaced with "general members' council meeting"; and the term "shareholders" in Article 307, paragraph (1), item (ii) of that Act shall be deemed to be replaced with "members"; any other necessary technical change in interpretation shall be specified by Cabinet Order.
(3) The provisions of Article 868, paragraph (1) (Jurisdiction over Non-Contentious Cases), Article 870 (limited to the segment pertaining to item (ii)) (Hearing of Statements), Article 871 (Appending of Reasons), Article 872 (limited to the segment pertaining to item (iv)) (Immediate Appeal), Article 874 (limited to the segment pertaining to item (i)) (Restrictions on Appeal), Article 875 (Exclusion from Application of the Provisions of the Non-Contentious Cases Procedures Act) and Article 876 (Supreme Court Rules) of the Companies Act shall apply mutatis mutandis to the preceding two paragraphs. In this case, any other necessary technical change in interpretation shall be specified by Cabinet Order.

(Mutatis Mutandis Application of the Companies Act)
Article 41　(1) The provisions of Article 296 (Convocation of Shareholders' Meetings), Article 298 (excluding the proviso to paragraphs (2) and (3)) (Determination to Convoke a Shareholders' Meeting), Article 299 (excluding items of paragraph (2)) (Notice of Convocation for a Shareholders' Meeting), Article 300 to 302 inclusive (Omission of Convocation Procedures, Delivery of Voting Forms and Reference Documents for a Shareholders' Meeting), Article 310 to 312 inclusive (Proxy Voting, Voting in Writing, Voting by Electromagnetic Means), Article 314 to 317 inclusive (Accountability of Directors, etc., Authority of Chairperson, Investigation of Materials Submitted to the

Shareholders' Meeting, Resolution for Postponement or Adjournment), Article 318 (excluding paragraph (5)) (Minutes), Article 319 (excluding paragraph (4)) (Omission of Resolution of Shareholders' Meetings) and Article 320 (Omission of Reports to Shareholders' Meetings) of the Companies Act shall apply mutatis mutandis to the general members' council of a Mutual Company. In this case, the terms "Stock Company" and "company with board of directors" in those provisions shall be deemed to be replaced with "Mutual Company"; the term "head office" in those provisions shall be deemed to be replaced with "principal office"; the term "operating hours" in those provisions shall be deemed to be replaced with "business hours"; the term "Annual shareholders' meeting" in Article 296, paragraph (1) of that Act shall be deemed to be replaced with "Annual general members' council meeting"; the term "paragraph (4) of the following Article" in Article 296, paragraph (3), and the term "paragraph (4) of the preceding Article" in Article 298, paragraphs (1) and (4) of that Act shall be deemed to be replaced with "Article 38, paragraph (2) and Article 50, paragraph (2) of the Insurance Business Act"; the term "(excluding shareholders who may not exercise their voting rights on all matters which may be resolved at a shareholders' meetings. The same shall apply in the following Article to Article 302 inclusive)" in Article 298, paragraph (2) shall be deemed to be deleted; the term "two weeks (or one week if the Stock Company is not a Public Company, except in cases where the particulars listed in paragraph (1), item (iii) or (iv) of the preceding Article are decided, (or if a shorter period of time is provided for in the articles of incorporation in cases where the Stock Company is a Stock Company other than the Company with Board of Directors, such shorter period of time))" in Article 299, paragraph (1) of that Act shall be deemed to be replaced with "two weeks"; the term "in the following cases" in Article 299, paragraph (2) shall be deemed to be deleted; the term "Reference Documents for a Shareholders' Meeting" in Articles 301 and 302 of that Act shall be deemed to be replaced with "reference documents for a general members' council meeting"; the term "shareholders (excluding the shareholders who may not exercise their voting rights on all matters which may be resolved at the shareholders' meeting under the preceding paragraph. The same shall apply hereinafter in paragraph (4) of the following Article and in Article 312, paragraph (5))" in Article 310, paragraph (7) of that Act shall be deemed to be replaced with "members"; the term "Article 297" in Article 316, paragraph (2) of that Act shall be deemed to be replaced with "Article 38 of the Insurance Business Act"; the term "branch offices" in Article 318, paragraph (3) of that Act shall be deemed to be replaced with "secondary offices"; and the term "all shareholders (limited to those who may exercise their voting rights with respect to such matter)" in Article 319, paragraph (1) of that Act shall be deemed to be replaced with "all members"; any other necessary technical change in interpretation shall be specified by Cabinet Order.

(2) The provisions of Article 830 (Action for a Declaratory Judgment as to the Absence or Invalidity of a Resolution of a Shareholders' Meeting, etc.), Article 831 (Action to Revoke a Resolution of a Shareholders' Meeting, etc.), Article 834 (limited to the segment pertaining to items (xvi) and (xvii)) (Defendant), Article 835, paragraph (1) (Jurisdiction over Actions), Article 836, paragraphs (1) and (3) (Order to Provide Security), Article 837 (Mandatory Consolidation of Oral Arguments, etc.), Article 838 (Persons Affected by a Judgment Being Upheld), Article 846 (Liability for Damages Where a Judgment Is Entered Against the Plaintiff), and Article 937, paragraph (1) (limited to the segment pertaining to item (i), sub-item (g)) (Commissioning of Registration by a Judicial Decision) of the Companies Act shall apply mutatis mutandis to an action for a declaratory judgment as to the absence or invalidity of a resolution of the general members' council of a Mutual Company and to an action to rescind a resolu-

tion of the general members' council of a Mutual Company. In this case, the term "a Shareholder, etc. (or, in cases where the Shareholders' Meeting, etc. set forth in each such item is an Organizational Meeting or a Class Organizational Meeting, a Shareholder, etc., a Shareholder at Incorporation, a Director at Incorporation or a Company Auditor at Incorporation)" in Article 831, paragraph (1) of that Act shall be deemed to be replaced with "members, directors, company auditors or liquidators of a Mutual Company (or, in a company with Committees, members, directors, executive officers or liquidators)"; and the term "a director, company auditor or liquidator pursuant to the provisions of Article 346(1) (including cases where it is applied mutatis mutandis pursuant to Article 479(4)), and in cases where such resolution is the resolution of an Organizational Meeting or Class Organizational Meeting, it shall include a Director at Incorporation or a Company Auditor at Incorporation)" in Article 831, paragraph (1) of that Act shall be deemed to be replaced with "directors, company auditors or liquidators (including a person who assumes the rights and obligations of a director, company auditor or liquidator pursuant to the provisions of Article 53-12, paragraph (1) of the Insurance Business Act (including the cases where it is applied mutatis mutandis pursuant to Article 180-5, paragraph (4) of that Act)"; any other necessary technical replacement of terms shall be specified by Cabinet Order.

Division 2 General Representative Members' Councils

(Establishment of a General Representative Members' Council and Representative Members' Terms of Office, etc.)
Article 42 (1) A Mutual Company may, pursuant to the provisions of its articles of incorporation, establish an administrative organ composed of the representative members elected from among its members (hereinafter referred to as "General Representative Members' Council"), in lieu of a general members' council.
(2) The articles of incorporation set forth in the preceding paragraph shall specify the particulars prescribed by Cabinet Office Ordinance, such as the number, term of office, and method of election of representative members.
(3) The term of office of a representative member shall not exceed four years.

(Voting Rights of Representative Members)
Article 43 Each representative member shall be entitled to one vote at General Representative Members' Council Meetings.

(Authority of the General Representative Members' Council)
Article 43-2 (1) The General Representative Members' Council may resolve only the matters provided for in this Act and the matters provided for in the articles of incorporation.
(2) Any provisions in the articles of incorporation to the effect that the directors, executive officers, board of directors or any other organ than the general members' council or General Representative Members' Council may decide on a matter which requires a resolution of the general members' council (or General Representative Members' Council, where the company has such a council) pursuant to the provisions of this Act shall be null and void.

(Method of Adopting, etc. Resolutions of the General Representative Members' Council)
Article 44 (1) Unless otherwise provided for in this Act or the articles of incorporation, a resolution at a General Representative Members' Council Meeting is adopted by the

majority vote of the attending representative members at a session where at least half of the representative members are present; provided, however, the number of the general representatives required to attend the General Representative Members' Council Meeting shall not be less than one-third of the total number of general representatives, notwithstanding the provisions of the articles of incorporation.

(2) The General Representative Members' Council may not adopt a resolution on any other matter than matters listed in Article 298, paragraph (1), item (ii) of the Companies Act as applied mutatis mutandis pursuant to Article 49, paragraph (1); provided, however, that this shall not apply to electing the person set forth in Article 316, paragraph (1) or (2) of that Act as applied mutatis mutandis pursuant to Article 49, paragraph (1), or to requiring the attendance of accounting auditors under Article 398, paragraph (2) of that Act as applied mutatis mutandis pursuant to Article 53-23.

(Proxy Voting)
Article 44-2 (1) A representative member may exercise his/her voting right by proxy, where the articles of incorporation include any provisions to that effect. In this case, such representative member shall designate only one proxy, and the representative member or proxy shall submit to the Mutual Company a document certifying the authority of proxy.
(2) Any proxy under the preceding paragraph shall be a representative member.
(3) The provisions of Article 310 (excluding paragraphs (1) and (5)) (Proxy Voting) of the Companies Act shall apply mutatis mutandis to paragraph (1). In this case, the term "preceding paragraph" in paragraph (2) of that Article and the term "paragraph (1)" in paragraph (3) of that Article shall be deemed to be replaced with "Article 44-2, paragraph (1) of the Insurance Business Act"; the term "Stock Company" in Article 310, paragraphs (3), (4), (6) and (7) shall be deemed to be replaced with "Mutual Company"; the term "Article 299, paragraph (3)" in Article 310, paragraph (4) shall be deemed to be replaced with "Article 299, paragraph (3) as applied mutatis mutandis pursuant to Article 49, paragraph (1) of the Insurance Business Act"; and the term "shareholders (excluding the shareholders who may not exercise their voting rights on all matters which may be resolved at the shareholders' meeting under the preceding paragraph. The same shall apply in paragraph (4) of the following Article and in Article 312, paragraph (5))" in Article 310, paragraph (7) shall be deemed to be replaced with "members"; any other necessary technical change in interpretation shall be specified by Cabinet Order.

(Right to Demand Convocation of a General Representative Members' Council Meeting)
Article 45 (1) Members representing at least three thousandths (or any smaller proportion prescribed by the articles of incorporation) of the total membership, or three thousand (or any smaller number prescribed by the articles of incorporation) or more members of a Mutual Company (or, in a Specified Mutual Company, members equal to or exceeding the number specified by Cabinet Order set forth in Article 38, paragraph (1)), who have been members of the Mutual Company without interruption for the preceding six months (or any shorter period prescribed by the articles of incorporation), or nine (or any smaller number prescribed by the articles of incorporation) or more representative members may demand the directors to convene a General Representative Members' Council Meeting by indicating the proposed agenda for the meeting (limited to matters on which the General Representative Members' Council may adopt a resolution; hereinafter the same shall apply in this Division) and the reason for the convocation.

Art.46　⑥ Insurance Business Act, Part II, Chap.II, Sec.2

(2) In the following cases, a member or a representative member who made a demand pursuant to the provisions of the preceding paragraph may convene the General Representative Members' Council Meeting with the permission of the court.
  (i) Where the convening procedure is not effected without delay after a demand pursuant to the provisions of the preceding paragraph; or
  (ii) Where a notice for the convocation of a General Representative Members' Council Meeting which designates, as the date of the General Representative Members' Council Meeting, a date falling within the period of eight weeks (or any shorter period prescribed by the articles of incorporation) from the day of a demand pursuant to the provisions of the preceding paragraph, is not given.
(3) The provisions of Article 868, paragraph (1) (Jurisdiction over Non-Contentious Cases), Article 869 (Prima Facie Showing), Article 871 (Appending of the Reason), Article 874 (limited to the segment pertaining to item (iv)) (Restrictions on Appeal), Article 875 (Exclusion from Application of the Provisions of the Non-Contentious Cases Procedures Act) and Article 876 (Supreme Court Rules) of the Companies Act shall apply mutatis mutandis to the preceding paragraph. In this case, any other necessary technical change in interpretation shall be specified by Cabinet Order.

(Right to Submit Proposals)
Article 46　(1) Members representing at least one thousandth (or any smaller proportion prescribed by the articles of incorporation) of the total membership, or one thousand (or any smaller number prescribed by the articles of incorporation) or more members of a Mutual Company (or, in a Specified Mutual Company, members equal to or exceeding the number specified by Cabinet Order set forth in Article 39, paragraph (1)), who have been members of the Mutual Company without interruption for the preceding six months (or any shorter period prescribed by the articles of incorporation), or three (or any smaller number prescribed by the articles of incorporation) or more representative members may demand the directors to include certain items (limited to matters on which the General Representative Members' Council may adopt a resolution) in the agenda for the General Representative Members' Council Meeting. In this case, the demand shall be submitted no later than eight weeks (or any shorter period prescribed by the articles of incorporation) prior to the date of the General Representative Members' Council Meeting.
(2) Representative members may submit a proposal at a General Representative Members' Council Meeting with respect to any agenda item for the meeting; provided, however, that this shall not apply to the cases where the proposal is in violation of any applicable law or regulation or the articles of incorporation, or where three years have not elapsed since the day on which an essentially identical proposal was not approved at a General Representative Members' Council Meeting by at least one tenth of the representative members (or any smaller proportion prescribed by the articles of incorporation).
(3) Members representing at least one thousandth (or any smaller proportion prescribed by the articles of incorporation) of the total membership, or one thousand (or any smaller number prescribed by the articles of incorporation) or more members of a Mutual Company (or, in a Specified Mutual Company, members equal to or exceeding the number specified by Cabinet Order set forth in Article 39, paragraph (1)), who have been members of the Mutual Company without interruption for the preceding six months (or any shorter period prescribed by the articles of incorporation), or three (any smaller number prescribed by the articles of incorporation) or more representative members may demand the directors that, no later than eight weeks (or any shorter period prescribed by the articles of incorporation) prior to the date of the General

Representative Members' Council Meeting, members be notified of the outline of any proposal to be submitted with respect to an agenda item of the meeting (or, where a notice is to be given under Article 299, paragraph (2) (excluding the items) or (3) of the Companies Act as applied mutatis mutandis pursuant to Article 49, paragraph (1), such outline be described in, or recorded on, that notice); provided, however, that this shall not apply to the cases where the proposal is in violation of any applicable law or regulation or the articles of incorporation, or where three years have not elapsed since the day on which an essentially identical proposal was not approved at a General Representative Members' Council Meeting by at least one tenth of the representative members (or any smaller proportion prescribed by the articles of incorporation).

(Right to Demand the Election of an Inspector for a General Representative Members' Council Meeting)

Article 47 (1) A Mutual Company, members representing at least one thousandth (or any smaller proportion prescribed by the articles of incorporation) of the total membership, or one thousand (or any smaller number prescribed by the articles of incorporation) or more members of a Mutual Company (or, in a Specified Mutual Company, members equal to or exceeding the number specified by Cabinet Order set forth in Article 39, paragraph (1)), who have been members of the Mutual Company without interruption for the preceding six months (or any shorter period prescribed by the articles of incorporation), or three (or any smaller number prescribed by the articles of incorporation) or more representative members may file a petition with the court, prior to the session of the General Representative Members' Council, for the election of an inspector who shall be retained to investigate the convocation procedures and method of resolution related to such a council.

(2) The provisions of Article 306, paragraphs (3) to (7) inclusive (Election of an Inspector for the Convocation Procedures of a Shareholders' Meeting) and Article 307 (Determination by the Court of the Calling of Shareholders' Meeting) of the Companies Act shall apply mutatis mutandis to the preceding paragraph. In this case, the term "preceding two paragraphs" in Article 306, paragraph (3) of that Act shall be deemed to be replaced with "Article 40, paragraph (1) of the Insurance Business Act"; the term "Stock Company" in Article 306, paragraphs (4) and (7) shall be deemed to be replaced with "Mutual Company"; the term "shareholders' meeting" in Article 307 of that Act shall be deemed to be replaced with "General Representative Members' Council Meeting"; and the term "shareholders" in paragraph (1), item (ii) of that Article shall be deemed to be replaced with "representative members"; any other necessary technical change in interpretation shall be specified by Cabinet Order.

(3) The provisions of Article 868, paragraph (1) (Jurisdiction over Non-Contentious Cases), Article 870 (limited to the segment pertaining to item (ii)) (Hearing of Statements), Article 871 (Appending of the Reason), Article 872 (limited to the segment pertaining to item (iv)) (Immediate Appeal), Article 874 (limited to the segment pertaining to item (i)) (Restrictions on Appeal), Article 875 (Exclusion from Application of the Provisions of the Non-Contentious Cases Procedures Act) and Article 876 (Supreme Court Rules) of the Companies Act shall apply mutatis mutandis to the preceding two paragraphs. In this case, any other necessary technical change in interpretation shall be specified by Cabinet Order.

(Delivery, etc. of Reference Documents and Voting Forms for a General Representative Members' Council Meeting)

Article 48 (1) The directors (or, where members or representative members convene the General Representative Members' Council pursuant to the provisions of Article

Art.49   6 Insurance Business Act, Part II, Chap.II, Sec.2

45, paragraph (2), such members or representative members; hereinafter the same shall apply in this Article) shall, when dispatching a notice under Article 299, paragraph (1) of the Companies Act as applied mutatis mutandis pursuant to paragraph (1) of the following Article with relevant changes in interpretation, give the representative members documents detailing particulars of reference with regard to the exercise of voting rights pursuant to the provisions of Cabinet Office Ordinance.

(2) If the directors dispatch notices by electromagnetic means referred to in Article 299, paragraph (3) of the Companies Act as applied mutatis mutandis pursuant to paragraph (1) of the following Article with relevant changes in interpretation to the representative members who have given consent under the same paragraph, the directors may, in lieu of giving the documents pursuant to the provisions of the preceding paragraph, provide the particulars that are required to be included in such documents by electromagnetic means; provided, however, that, if requested by any representative member, they shall give these documents to such representative member.

(3) Where the matters listed in Article 298, paragraph (1), item (iii) of the Companies Act as applied mutatis mutandis pursuant to paragraph (1) of the following Article with relevant changes in interpretation are decided, the directors shall, when giving a notice under Article 299, paragraph (1) of that Act as applied mutatis mutandis pursuant to paragraph (1) of the following Article, provide the representative members with documents to be used by the representative members to exercise their voting rights (hereinafter referred to as "Voting Forms" in this Article) pursuant to the provisions of Cabinet Office Ordinance.

(4) If the directors give a notice by electromagnetic means referred to in Article 299, paragraph (3) of the Companies Act as applied mutatis mutandis pursuant to paragraph (1) of the following Article with relevant changes in interpretation to the representative members who have given consent under the same paragraph, the directors may, in lieu of giving out Voting Forms pursuant to the provisions of the preceding paragraph, provide the particulars that are required to be included in such documents by electromagnetic means; provided, however, that, if requested by any representative member, the directors shall give their voting form to such representative member.

(5) Where the matters listed in Article 298, paragraph (1), item (iv) of the Companies Act as applied mutatis mutandis pursuant to paragraph (1) of the following Article with relevant changes in interpretation are decided, the directors shall, when giving a notice to the representative members who have given consent under Article 299, paragraph (3) of the Companies Act by electromagnetic means referred to in the same paragraph, provide the representative members with the particulars that are required to be included in the Voting Forms by such electromagnetic means pursuant to the provisions of Cabinet Office Ordinance.

(6) In the cases prescribed in the preceding paragraph, if any representative member who has not given consent under Article 299, paragraph (3) of the Companies Act as applied mutatis mutandis pursuant to paragraph (1) of the following Article requests, no later than one week prior to the date of the General Representative Members' Council Meeting, to be provided the particulars that are required to be included in the Voting Forms by electromagnetic means, the directors shall, immediately, provide such particulars to such representative member by electromagnetic means pursuant to the provisions of Cabinet Office Ordinance.

(Mutatis Mutandis Application of the Companies Act)
Article 49 (1) The provisions of Article 296 (Convocation of Shareholders' Meetings), Article 298 (excluding paragraphs (2) and (3)) (Determination to Convoke a Shareholders' Meeting), Article 299 (excluding paragraph (2), items (i) and (ii)) (Notice of

Calling of Shareholders' Meetings), Article 300 (Omission of Calling Procedures), Article 311 (Voting in Writing), Article 312 (Voting by Electromagnetic Method), Article 314 to 317 inclusive (Accountability of Directors, etc., Authority of Chairperson, Investigation of Materials Submitted to a Shareholders' Meeting, Resolution for Postponement or Adjournment) and Article 318 (excluding paragraph (5)) (Minutes) of the Companies Act shall apply mutatis mutandis to the General Representative Members' Council of a Mutual Company. In this case, the terms "Stock Company" and "company with board of directors" in those provisions shall be deemed to be replaced with "Mutual Company"; the term "head office" in those provisions shall be deemed to be replaced with "principal office"; the term "operating hours" in those provisions shall be deemed to be replaced with "business hours"; the term "shareholder" in those provisions (excluding Article 298, paragraph (1) (excluding items), Article 298, paragraph (4), Article 311, paragraph (4), Article 312, paragraph (5), Article 314 and Article 318, paragraph (4)) shall be deemed to be replaced with "representative member"; the term "Annual shareholders' meeting" in Article 296, paragraph (1) of that Act shall be deemed to be replaced with "Annual General Representative Members' Council Meeting"; the term "paragraph (4) of the following Article" in Article 296, paragraph (3) shall be deemed to be replaced with "Article 45, paragraph (2) of the Insurance Business Act"; the terms "paragraph (4) of the preceding Article" and "shareholder" in Article 298, paragraph (1) (excluding the items) and Article 298, paragraph (4) of that Act shall be deemed to be replaced with "Article 45, paragraph (2) of the Insurance Business Act" and "member or representative member," respectively; the term "two weeks (or one week if the Stock Company is not a Public Company, except in cases where the particulars listed in items (iii) and (iv), paragraph (1) of the preceding Article are decided, (or if a shorter period of time is provided for in the articles of incorporation in cases where the Stock Company is a Stock Company other than the Company with Board of Directors, such shorter period of time))" in Article 299, paragraph (1) of that Act shall be deemed to be replaced with "two weeks"; the term "in the following cases" in Article 299, paragraph (2) shall be deemed to be deleted; the term "shareholders" in Article 311, paragraph (4) and Article 312, paragraph (5) of that Act shall be deemed to be replaced with "members"; the terms "by the shareholders" and "common interest of the shareholders" in Article 314 of that Act shall be deemed to be replaced with "by the representative members" and "common interest of the representative members," respectively; the term "Article 297" in Article 316, paragraph (2) of that Act shall be deemed to be replaced with "Article 45 of the Insurance Business Act"; the term "branch offices" in Article 318, paragraph (3) of that Act shall be deemed to be replaced with "secondary offices"; and the term "shareholders" in Article 318, paragraph (4) of that Act shall be deemed to be replaced with "members"; any other necessary technical change in interpretation shall be specified by Cabinet Order.

(2) The provisions of Article 830 (Action for a Declaratory Judgment as to the Absence or Invalidity of a Resolution of a Shareholders' Meeting, etc.), Article 831 (Action to Revoke a Resolution of a Shareholders' Meeting, etc.), Article 834 (limited to the segment pertaining to items (xvi) and (xvii)) (Defendant), Article 835, paragraph (1) (Jurisdiction over Actions), Article 836, paragraphs (1) and (3) (Order to Provide Security), Article 837 (Mandatory Consolidation of Oral Arguments, etc.), Article 838 (Persons Affected by a Judgment Being Upheld), Article 846 (Liability for Damages Where a Judgment Is Entered Against the Plaintiff), and Article 937, paragraph (1) (limited to the segment pertaining to item (i), sub-item (g)) (Commissioning of Registration by Judicial Decision) of the Companies Act shall apply mutatis mutandis to an action for a declaratory judgment as to the absence or invalidity of a resolution of the General Representative Members' Council of a Mutual Company and to an action to

revoke a resolution of the General Representative Members' Council of a Mutual Company. In this case, the term "a Shareholder, etc. (or, in cases where the Shareholders' Meeting, etc. set forth respectively in each such item is an Organizational Meeting or a Class Organizational Meetings, a Shareholder, etc., a Shareholder at Incorporation, a Director at Incorporation or a Company Auditor at Incorporation)" in Article 831, paragraph (1) of that Act shall be deemed to be replaced with "members, directors, company auditors or liquidators of a Mutual Company (or, in a company with Committees, members, directors, executive officers or liquidators)"; and the term "a director, company auditor or liquidator pursuant to the provisions of Article 346(1) (including cases where it is applied mutatis mutandis pursuant to Article 479(4)), and in cases where such resolution is a resolution of an Organizational Meeting or Class Organizational Meeting, it shall include a Director at Incorporation or a Company Auditor at Incorporation)" in the same Article shall be deemed to be replaced with "directors, company auditors or liquidators (including a person who assumes the rights and obligations of a director, executive officer or liquidator pursuant to the provisions of Article 53-12, paragraph (1) of the Insurance Business Act (including the cases where it is applied mutatis mutandis pursuant to Article 180-5, paragraph (4) of that Act)"; any other necessary technical change in interpretation shall be specified by Cabinet Order.

(Right to Demand the Convocation of a General Members' Council)
Article 50 (1) Even where a Mutual Company has established a General Representative Members' Council pursuant to the provisions of Article 42, paragraph (1), members representing at least five thousandths (or any smaller proportion prescribed by the articles of incorporation) of the total membership (or, in a Specified Mutual Company, members equal to or exceeding the number specified by Cabinet Order), who have been members of the Mutual Company without interruption for the preceding six months (or any shorter period prescribed by the articles of incorporation), may demand the directors to convene the general members' council with the purpose of abolishing the General Representative Members' Council or modifying any particular prescribed by the articles of incorporation pursuant to the provisions of paragraph (2) in that Article, by indicating the proposed agenda for the meeting and the reason for the convocation.

(2) In the following cases, the members who made a demand pursuant to the provisions of the preceding paragraph may convene a general members' council meeting with the permission of the court.
  (i) Where the convening procedure is not effected without delay after a demand pursuant to the provisions of the preceding paragraph; or
  (ii) Where a notice for the convocation of the general members' council which designates, as the date of the general members' council meeting, a date falling within the period of eight weeks (or any shorter period provided for in the articles of incorporation) from the day of a demand pursuant to the provisions of the preceding paragraph, is not given.

(3) The provisions of Article 868, paragraph (1) (Jurisdiction over Non-Contentious Cases), Article 869 (Prima Facie Showing), Article 871 (Appending of the Reason), Article 874 (limited to the segment pertaining to item (iv)) (Restrictions on Appeal), Article 875 (Exclusion from Application of the Provisions of the Non-Contentious Cases Procedures Act) and Article 876 (Supreme Court Rules) of the Companies Act shall apply mutatis mutandis to the preceding paragraph. In this case, any other necessary technical change in interpretation shall be specified by Cabinet Order.

(4) Where a resolution modifying any particular prescribed by the articles of incorporation pursuant to the provisions of Article 42, paragraph (2) is adopted by the general mem-

bers' council convened pursuant to the provisions of the preceding three paragraphs, the General Representative Members' Council may not adopt a resolution amending the articles of incorporation regarding the particular thus modified, unless three years have elapsed since the day on which the amendment of the articles of incorporation came into effect regarding such particular.

Division 3 Establishment of Administrative Organs Other than General Members' Councils and General Representative Members' Councils, etc.

(Administrative Organs)
Article 51 (1) A Mutual Company shall have in place the following administrative organs:
(i) Board of directors; and
(ii) Company auditors or Committees.
(2) A Mutual Company may have accounting advisors, a board of company auditors or accounting auditors pursuant to the provisions of the articles of incorporation.
(3) A Mutual Company that is an Insurance Company and a Mutual Company listed in Article 272-4, paragraph (1), item (i), sub-item (b) (other than a company with Committees) shall have in place a board of company auditors and an accounting auditor.
(4) A company with Committees shall not have any company auditors.
(5) A company with Committees shall have accounting auditors.

(Election)
Article 52 (1) Officers (meaning directors, accounting advisors and company auditors; hereinafter the same shall apply in this Division) and accounting auditors shall be elected by a resolution of the general members' council (or General Representative Members' Council, where the company has such a council; hereinafter the same shall apply in this Subsection).
(2) In adopting a resolution under the preceding paragraph, substitute officers may be elected as prescribed by Cabinet Office Ordinance as a precaution against cases in which there are no officers in office or where there is a vacancy which results in a shortfall in the number of officers prescribed by this Act or the articles of incorporation.

(Relationship between a Mutual Company and Its Officers, etc.)
Article 53 The relationship held by a Mutual Company with its officers and accounting auditors shall be governed by the provisions on mandate.

(Qualifications, etc. of Directors)
Article 53-2 (1) None of the following persons may act as a director:
(i) A juridical person;
(ii) An adult ward, a person under curatorship, or a person who is similarly treated under foreign laws and regulations;
(iii) A person who has been sentenced to a penalty for having violated the provisions of this Act, the Companies Act or the Act on General Incorporated Associations and General Incorporated Foundations (Act No. 48 of 2006), or for having committed: a crime under Article 197 (Crime of False Statements in a Securities Registration Report, etc.), Article 197-2, items (i) to (x)-3 inclusive or (xiii) (Crime of Solicitation of Securities by Unregistered Agents. etc.), Article 198, item (viii) (Crime of

Violating a Court's Restrictive Injunction or Order for Suspension), Article 199 (Crime of Refusal to Report, etc.), Article 200, items (i) to (xii)-2 inclusive or item (xxi) (Crime of Non-Submission of a Correction Report, etc.), Article 203, paragraph (3) (Bribery of an Officer or Staff Member of a Financial Instruments Transaction Business Operators, etc.) or Article 205, items (i) to (vi) inclusive, item (xvi) or (xx) (Crime of Non-Submission of Written Notice, etc. on Specified Solicitation, etc.) of the Financial Instruments and Exchange Act (Act No. 25 of 1948); a crime under Article 549 (Crime of Fraudulent Reorganization), Article 550 (Crime of Providing a Specific Creditor, etc. with Collateral, etc.), Article 552 to 555 inclusive (Crime of Refusal to Report or Undergo Investigation, etc., Crime of Destruction of Materials on the Status of Business and Property, etc., Crime of Obstruction of the Duties of a Bankruptcy Trustee, etc.) or Article 557 (Bribery) of the Act on Special Measures, etc. concerning Reorganization Proceedings for Financial Institutions, etc. (Act No. 95 of 1996); a crime under Article 255 (Crime of Fraudulent Rehabilitation), Article 256 (Crime of Providing a Specific Creditor, etc. with Collateral), Article 258 to 260 inclusive (Crime of Refusal to Report or Undergo Investigation, etc., Crime of Destruction of Materials on the Status of Business and Property, etc., Crime of Obstruction of the Duties of a Supervising Commissioner, etc.) or Article 262 (Bribery) of the Civil Rehabilitation Act (Act No. 225 of 1999); a crime under Article 65 (Crime of Refusal to Report or Be Investigated, etc.), Article 66 (Crime of Obstruction of the Duties of a Recognition Trustee, etc.), Article 68 (Bribery) or Article 69 (Crime of Disposal or Export of Property without Permission) of the Act on Recognition of and Assistance for Foreign Insolvency Proceedings (Act No. 129 of 2000); a crime under Article 265 (Crime of Fraudulent Bankruptcy), Article 266 (Crime of Providing a Specific Creditor, etc. with Collateral), Article 268 to 272 inclusive (Crime of Refusal to Explain or Be Investigated, etc., Crime of Refusing to Disclose Important Property, etc., Crime of Destruction of Materials on the Status of Business and Property, etc., Crime of Refusal to Explain at a Hearing, etc., Crime of Obstruction of the Duties of a Bankruptcy Trustee, etc.), or Article 274 (Bribery) of the Bankruptcy Act (Act No. 75 of 2004), for whom two years have not elapsed since the day on which the execution of the sentence was completed or the sentence ceased to apply; or

(iv) A person who was sentenced to imprisonment or severer punishment for violating the provisions of laws and regulations other than those provided for in the preceding item, and who has not completed the execution of the sentence or to whom the sentence still applies (excluding persons for whom the execution of the sentence is suspended).

(2) A director of a company with Committees may not concurrently serve as a manager or any other employee of such company with Committees.

(3) A Mutual Company shall have three or more directors.

(Directors' Terms of Office)

Article 53-3 (1) Directors' terms of office shall continue until the conclusion of the annual general members' council meeting (or annual General Representative Members' Council Meeting, where the company has such meeting; hereinafter the same shall apply in this Subsection) for the last business year which ends within two years from the time of their election; provided, however, that this shall not preclude the shortening of the their terms of office by the articles of incorporation or by a resolution of the general members' council.

(2) For the purpose of applying the provisions of the preceding paragraph to the directors of a company with Committees, the term "two years" in that paragraph shall be

deemed to be replaced with "one year."
(3) The provisions of Article 332, paragraph (4) (excluding item (iii)) (Directors' terms of office) of the Companies Act shall apply mutatis mutandis to the terms of office of the directors of a Mutual Company. In this case, the term "preceding three paragraphs" in that paragraph shall be deemed to be replaced with "Article 53-3, paragraphs (1) and (2) of the Insurance Business Act"; any other necessary technical change in interpretation shall be specified by Cabinet Order.

(Qualifications, etc. of Accounting Advisors)
Article 53-4 The provisions of Article 333 (Qualifications of Accounting Advisors) and Article 334 (excluding Article 332, paragraph (2) and Article 332, paragraph (4), item (iii) of the Companies Act as applied mutatis mutandis pursuant to Article 334, paragraph (1)) (Accounting Advisors' Terms of Office) of the Companies Act shall apply mutatis mutandis to the accounting advisors of a Mutual Company. In this case, any other necessary technical change in interpretation shall be specified by Cabinet Order.

(Qualifications, etc. of Company Auditors)
Article 53-5 (1) The provisions of Article 53-2, paragraph (1) shall apply mutatis mutandis to the company auditors of a Mutual Company. In this case, any other necessary technical change in interpretation shall be specified by Cabinet Order.
(2) A company auditor of a Mutual Company may concurrently serve neither as a director, or manager or any other employee of that Mutual Company or its de facto Subsidiary Company, nor as an executive officer or accounting advisor (or, where the accounting advisor is a juridical person, any member of that juridical person who is supposed to carry out relevant duties) of such de facto Subsidiary Company.
(3) A company with a board of company auditors shall have three or more company auditors, of whom half or more shall be outside company auditors (meaning those company auditors of a Mutual Company who have never been a director, executive officer or accounting advisor (or, if the accounting advisor is a juridical person, any member of that juridical person who is supposed to carry out relevant duties), or manager or any other employee of the Mutual Company or its de facto Subsidiary Company; the same shall apply hereinafter).

(Company Auditors' Terms of Office)
Article 53-6 (1) Company auditors' terms of office shall continue until the conclusion of the annual general members' council meeting for the last business year which ends within four years from the time of their election.
(2) The provisions of Article 336, paragraphs (3) and (4) (limited to the segment pertaining to item (ii) (Company Auditors' Terms of Office) of the Companies Act shall apply mutatis mutandis to the company auditors of a Mutual Company. In this case, the term "paragraph (1)" in paragraph (3) of that Article shall be deemed to be replaced with "Article 53-6, paragraph (1) of the Insurance Business Act"; any other necessary technical change in interpretation shall be specified by Cabinet Order.

(Qualifications, etc. of Accounting Auditors)
Article 53-7 The provisions of Article 337 (Qualifications of Accounting Auditors) and Article 338, paragraphs (1) and (2) (Accounting Auditors' Terms of Office) of the Companies Act shall apply mutatis mutandis to the accounting auditors of a Mutual Company; and the provisions of Article 338, paragraph (3) of that Act shall apply mutatis mutandis to the accounting auditors of a Mutual Company other than that set forth in Article 53-14, paragraph (5), respectively. In this case, the term "Article 435, para-

graph (2)" in Article 337, paragraph (3), item (i) of that Act shall be deemed to be replaced with "Article 54-3, paragraph (2) of the Insurance Business Act"; any other necessary technical change in interpretation shall be specified by Cabinet Order.

(Dismissal)
Article 53-8 (1) Officers and accounting auditors of a Mutual Company may be dismissed at any time by a resolution of the general members' council.
(2) A person dismissed pursuant to the provisions of the preceding paragraph shall be entitled to demand from the Mutual Company compensation for damages arising from the dismissal, except in cases where there are justifiable reasons for such dismissal.

(Dismissal of Accounting Auditors by Company Auditors, etc.)
Article 53-9 (1) The company auditor may dismiss an accounting auditor if that accounting auditor:
(i) has breached his/her professional obligations or neglected his/her duties.
(ii) has engaged in conduct unbecoming of an accounting auditor; or
(iii) has difficulty in, or is unable to cope with the execution of his/her duties due to a mental or physical disorder.
(2) Any dismissal pursuant to the provisions of the preceding paragraph shall be effected by the unanimous consent of all company auditors, where the company has two or more company auditors.
(3) If an accounting auditor is dismissed pursuant to the provisions of paragraph (1), the company auditor (or, where the company has two or more company auditors, a company auditor appointed from among themselves) shall report such fact and the reason for dismissal to the first general members' council meeting convened after the dismissal.
(4) For the purpose of applying the provisions of the preceding three paragraphs to a company with a board of company auditors, the term "company auditor" in paragraph (1) shall be deemed to be replaced with "board of company auditors"; the term "company auditors, where the company has two or more company auditors" in paragraph (2) shall be deemed to be replaced with "company auditors"; and the term "company auditor (or, where the company has two or more company auditors, a company auditor appointed from among themselves)" in the preceding paragraph shall be deemed to be replaced with "company auditor appointed by the board of company auditors."
(5) For the purpose of applying the provisions of paragraphs (1) to (3) inclusive to a company with Committees, the term "company auditor" in paragraph (1) shall be deemed to be replaced with "audit committee"; the term "company auditors, where the company has two or more company auditors" in paragraph (2) shall be deemed to be replaced with "Audit Committee Members"; and the term "company auditor (or, where the company has two or more company auditors, a company auditor appointed from among themselves)" in paragraph (3) shall be deemed to be replaced with "audit committee member appointed by the committee."

(Method of Adopting Resolution for Election, etc. of Officers)
Article 53-10 (1) Notwithstanding the provisions of Article 37, paragraph (1) and Article 44, paragraph (1), resolutions of the general members' council for the election or dismissal of officers are adopted by the majority vote (or any larger proportion prescribed by the articles of incorporation) of the attending members (or, where the company has a General Representative Members' Council, representative members) at a session where at least half (or any other proportion larger than one third prescribed by the articles of incorporation) of the members (or representative members) are present.
(2) Notwithstanding the provisions of the preceding paragraph, in case where dismissal of

a company auditor is to be resolved, it shall be adopted by a resolution set forth in Article 62, paragraph (2).

(Mutatis Mutandis Application of the Companies Act)
Article 53-11 The provisions of Article 343 (Consent of Company Auditors to Election of Company Auditors) (excluding paragraph (4)) of the Companies Act shall apply mutatis mutandis to the election of the company auditors of a Mutual Company; the provisions of Article 344 (Consent of Company Auditors to the Election of Accounting Auditors) of that Act shall apply mutatis mutandis to the election of the accounting auditors of a Mutual Company; and the provisions of Article 345 (Statement of Opinions on Election of Accounting Advisors, etc.) of that Act shall apply mutatis mutandis to the statement of opinions regarding the election or dismissal, or resignation of the accounting advisors, company auditors or accounting auditors of a Mutual Company. In this case, the term "Article 298, paragraph (1), item (i)" in paragraph (3) of that Article shall be deemed to be replaced with "Article 298, paragraph (1), item (i) as applied mutatis mutandis pursuant to Article 41, paragraph (1) or Article 49, paragraph (1) of the Insurance Business Act"; any other necessary technical change in interpretation shall be specified by Cabinet Order.

(Measures for Vacancies Arising among the Officers, etc.)
Article 53-12 (1) Where a Mutual Company has no officers or where any vacancy arises which results in a shortfall in the number of officers prescribed by this Act or the articles of incorporation, an officer who retired from office due to the expiration of his/her term of office or resignation shall retain the rights and obligations of an officer until a newly elected officer (including a person who is to temporarily carry out the duties of an officer under the following paragraph) assumes his/her office.
(2) In the case prescribed in the preceding paragraph, the court may, if it finds necessary, appoint a person to temporarily carry out the duties of an officer, in response to a petition filed by any interested party.
(3) The court may, if it has appointed a person to temporarily carry out the duties of an officer under the preceding paragraph, specify the amount of the remuneration to be paid thereto by the Mutual Company.
(4) Where a Mutual Company has no accounting auditors or where any vacancy arises which results in a shortfall in the number of accounting auditors prescribed by the articles of incorporation, and an accounting auditor is not elected without delay, the company auditor shall appoint a person to temporarily carry out the duties of an accounting auditor.
(5) The provisions of Article 337 of the Companies Act as applied mutatis mutandis pursuant to Article 53-7 and the provisions of Article 53-9 shall apply mutatis mutandis to the person who is to temporarily carry out the duties of an accounting auditor under the preceding paragraph. In this case, any other necessary technical change in interpretation shall be specified by Cabinet Order.
(6) For the purpose of applying the provisions of paragraph (4) to a company with a board of company auditors, the term "company auditor" in that paragraph shall be deemed to be replaced with "board of company auditors."
(7) For the purpose of applying the provisions of paragraph (4) to a company with Committees, the term "company auditor" in that paragraph shall be deemed to be replaced with "audit committee."
(8) The provisions of Article 868, paragraph (1) (Jurisdiction over Non-Contentious Cases), Article 870 (limited to the segment pertaining to item (ii)) (Hearing of Statements), Article 871 (Appending of the Reason), Article 872 (limited to the segment

pertaining to item (iv)) (Immediate Appeal), Article 874 (limited to the segment pertaining to item (i)) (Restrictions on Appeal), Article 875 (Exclusion from Application of the Provisions of the Non-Contentious Cases Procedures Act), Article 876 (Supreme Court Rules) and Article 937, paragraph (1) (limited to the segment pertaining to item (ii), sub-items (a) and (c)) (Commissioning of Registration by a Judicial Decision) of the Companies Act shall apply mutatis mutandis to paragraphs (2) and (3). In this case, any other necessary technical change in interpretation shall be specified by Cabinet Order.

Division 4 Directors and Boards of Directors

(Authority of the Directors)
Article 53-13 (1) The following directors execute the business of the Mutual Company:
(i) A representative director; and
(ii) A director other than a representative director, who is appointed by resolution of the board of directors as the director who is to execute the business of the Mutual Company.
(2) The directors listed in the items of the preceding paragraph shall report the status of the execution of his/her duties to the board of directors at least once in every three months.

(Authority, etc. of the Board of Directors)
Article 53-14 (1) A board of directors shall be composed of all of the directors.
(2) The board of directors shall carry out the following duties:
(i) Deciding the execution of the Mutual Company's business;
(ii) Supervising the execution of duties by directors; and
(iii) Appointing and removing representative directors.
(3) The board of directors shall appoint the representative director from among the directors.
(4) The board of directors may not delegate decisions on the execution of important business, such as the following particulars, to directors. :
(i) The appropriation of and acceptance of assignment of important assets;
(ii) Borrowing in a significant large amounts;
(iii) The election and dismissal of an important employee including a manager;
(iv) The establishment, modification or abolition of secondary offices and other important structures;
(v) The particulars specified by Cabinet Office Ordinance as important particulars of the solicitation of persons who subscribe for bonds (meaning the bonds as defined in that Article), such as the particular listed in Article 61, item (i);
(vi) Revision of a system necessary for ensuring that the execution of duties by directors complies with laws and regulations and the articles of incorporation, and of any other system specified by Cabinet Office Ordinance as a system necessary for ensuring propriety in the business of a Mutual Company; or
(vii) Exemption from liability under Article 53-33, paragraph (1) pursuant to the provisions of the articles of incorporation under Article 426, paragraph (1) of the Companies Act as applied mutatis mutandis pursuant to Article 53-36 with relevant changes in interpretation.
(5) In a Mutual Company that is an Insurance Company and a Mutual Company listed in Article 272-4, paragraph (1), item (i), sub-item (b), the board of directors shall decide on the particulars listed in item (vi) of the preceding paragraph.

(Mutatis Mutandis Application of the Companies Act)
Article 53-15 The provisions of Article 350 (Liability for Damages Caused by Directors' Actions), Article 352 (Authority of Persons Who Perform Duties on Behalf of Directors), Article 354 to 357 inclusive (Apparent Representative Directors, Duty of Loyalty, Restrictions on Competition and Conflict of Interest Transactions, Director's Duty to Report), Article 358 (excluding paragraph (1), item (ii)) (Election of Inspector of Execution of Operation), Article 359 (Decision by the Court to Call a Shareholders' Meeting), Article 360, paragraph (1) (Prohibition of Directors' Actions by the Shareholders), Article 361 (Remuneration for Directors) and Article 365, paragraph (2) (Restrictions on Competition and Transactions with Companies with a Board of Directors) of the Companies Act shall apply mutatis mutandis to the directors of a Mutual Company; the provisions of Article 349, paragraphs (4) and (5) (Representatives of Companies), and Article 351 (Measures When Vacancy Arises in the Office of a Representative Director) of that Act shall apply mutatis mutandis to the representative director of a Mutual Company; the provisions of Article 868, paragraph (1) (Jurisdiction over Non-Contentious Cases), Article 869 (Prima Facie Showing), Article 870 (limited to the segment pertaining to item (ii)) (Hearing of Statements), Article 871 (Appending of Reasons), Article 872 (limited to the segment pertaining to item (iv)) (Immediate Appeal), Article 874 (limited to the segment pertaining to items (i) and (iv)) (Restrictions on Appeal), Article 875 (Exclusion from Application of the Provisions of the Non-Contentious Cases Procedures Act) and Article 876 (Supreme Court Rules) of that Act shall apply mutatis mutandis to the directors or representative director of a Mutual Company; and the provisions of Article 937, paragraph (1) (limited to the segment pertaining to item (ii), sub-items (a) and (c)) (Commissioning of Registration by Judicial Decision) of that Act shall apply mutatis mutandis to the representative director of a Mutual Company. In this case, the term "shareholders' meeting" in Article 356, paragraph (1) of that Act shall be deemed to be replaced with "board of directors"; the term "shareholders" in Article 358, paragraph (1) of that Act shall be deemed to be replaced with "members or representative members"; the term "Shareholders who hold not less than 3 percent of the voting rights (or, in cases where a lesser proportion is prescribed in the articles of incorporation, such proportion) of all shareholders (excluding shareholders who may not exercise their voting rights on all matters which may be resolved at shareholders' meetings)" in Article 358, paragraph (1), item (i) of that Act shall be deemed to be replaced with "Members representing at least three thousandths (or any smaller proportion prescribed by the articles of incorporation) of the total membership, or three thousand (or any smaller number prescribed by the articles of incorporation) or more members of a Mutual Company (or, in a Specified Mutual Company, members equal to or exceeding the number specified by Cabinet Order set forth in Article 38, paragraph (1) of the Insurance Business Act), who have been members of the Mutual Company without interruption for the preceding six months (or any shorter period prescribed by the articles of incorporation) (or, where the company has a General Representative Members' Council, those persons, or nine (or any other smaller number prescribed by the articles of incorporation) or more representative members)"; the term "shareholders" in Article 358, paragraph (7) shall be deemed to be replaced with "members or representative members"; the term "shareholders" in Article 359, paragraph (1), item (ii) of that Act shall be deemed to be replaced with "members (or, where the company has a General Representative Members' Council, representative members)"; and the terms "shareholders having the shares" and "substantial detriment" in Article 360, paragraph (1) of that Act shall be deemed to be replaced with "persons who have been members" and "irreparable damages," respectively; any other necessary technical change in interpretation shall be prescribed by

(Management of Boards of Directors)
Article 53-16 The provisions of Part II, Chapter IV, Section 5, Subsection 2 (excluding Article 367, and Article 371, paragraphs (3) and (5)) (Operations) of the Companies Act shall apply mutatis mutandis to the management of the board of directors of a Mutual Company; and the provisions of Article 868, paragraph (1) (Jurisdiction over Non-Contentious Cases), Article 869 (Prima Facie Showing), Article 870 (limited to the segment pertaining to item (i)) (Hearing of Statements), the main clause of Article 871 (Appending of the Reason), Article 872 (limited to the segment pertaining to item (iv)) (Immediate Appeal), the main clause of Article 873 (Stay of Execution of the Judicial Decision of the Prior Instance), Article 875 (Exclusion from Application of the Provisions of the Non-Contentious Cases Procedures Act) and Article 876 (Supreme Court Rules) of that Act shall apply mutatis mutandis to an application for permission under Article 371, paragraph (2) or (4) of that Act as applied mutatis mutandis pursuant to this Article with relevant changes in interpretation. In this case, the terms "shareholder" and "at any time during the business hours of a Stock Company" in Article 371, paragraph (2) (Minutes) of that Act shall be deemed to be replaced with "member (or, where the company has a General Representative Members' Council, such representative members)" and "with the permission of the court," respectively; the term "Parent Company or Subsidiary" in Article 371, paragraph (6) shall be deemed to be replaced with "de facto Subsidiary Company as defined in Article 33-2, paragraph (1) of the Insurance Business Act"; the term "Article 363, paragraph (2)" in Article 372, paragraphs (2) and (3) (Omission of Report to Board of Directors) of that Act shall be deemed to be replaced with "Article 53-13, paragraph (2) of the Insurance Business Act"; the term "Article 417, paragraph (4)" in Article 372, paragraph (3) shall be deemed to be replaced with "Article 417, paragraph (4) as applied mutatis mutandis pursuant to Article 53-30, paragraph (5) of the Insurance Business Act"; and the term "Article 362, paragraph (4), items (i) and (ii)" in Article 373, paragraphs (1) and (2) (Resolution of board of directors by special directors) of that Act shall be deemed to be replaced with "Article 53-14, paragraph (4), items (i) and (ii) of the Insurance Business Act"; any other necessary technical change in interpretation shall be specified by Cabinet Order.

Division 5　Accounting Advisors

(Authority, etc. of Accounting Advisors)
Article 53-17 The provisions of Part II, Chapter IV, Section 6 (excluding Article 378, paragraph (1), item (ii) and Article 378, paragraph (3)) (Accounting Advisors) of the Companies Act shall apply mutatis mutandis to the accounting advisors of a Mutual Company. In this case, the terms "Article 435, paragraph (2)," "supplementary schedules thereof, the Temporary Financial Statements (referring to the Temporary Financial Statements provided for in Article 441, paragraph (1), hereinafter the same shall apply in this Chapter)" and "Article 444, paragraph (1)" in Article 374, paragraph (1) (Authority of Accounting Advisors) of that Act shall be deemed to be replaced with "Article 54-3, paragraph (2) of the Insurance Business Act," "annex detailed statement thereto" and "Article 54-10, paragraph (1) of the Insurance Business Act," respectively; the term "Article 333, paragraph (3), item (ii) or (iii)" in Article 374, paragraph (5) shall be deemed to be replaced with "Article 333, paragraph (3), item (ii) or (iii) as applied mutatis mutandis pursuant to Article 53-4 of the Insurance Business Act"; the term "Article 436, paragraph (3), Article 441, paragraph (3) or Article 444, paragraph

(5)" in Article 376, paragraph (1) (Attendance at board of directors meetings) of that Act shall be deemed to be replaced with "Article 54-4, paragraph (3) or Article 54-10, paragraph (5) of the Insurance Business Act"; the term "Article 368, paragraph (2)" in Article 376, paragraph (3) of that Act shall be deemed to be replaced with "Article 368, paragraph (2) as applied mutatis mutandis pursuant to Article 53-16 of the Insurance Business Act"; and the term "Article 319, paragraph (1)" in Article 378, paragraph (1), item (i) (Retention and Inspection of Financial Statements by Accounting Advisors) of that Act shall be deemed to be replaced with "Article 319, paragraph (1) as applied mutatis mutandis pursuant to Article 41, paragraph (1) of the Insurance Business Act"; any other necessary technical change in interpretation shall be specified by Cabinet Order.

Division 6 Company Auditors and Board of Company Auditors

(Authority of Company Auditors)
Article 53-18 (1) The company auditors shall audit the execution of duties by directors (or, in a company with accounting advisors (meaning a Stock Company or Mutual Company which has accounting advisors; the same shall apply hereinafter), directors and accounting advisors). In this case, the company auditors shall prepare audit reports pursuant to the provisions of Cabinet Office Ordinance.
(2) The company auditors may at any time request a business report from the directors and accounting advisors, and managers and other employees, or investigate the status of the business and property of the Mutual Company.
(3) The company auditors may, if it is necessary for the purpose of carrying out their duties, request a business report from a de facto Subsidiary Company of the Mutual Company, or investigate the status of the business and property of such de facto Subsidiary Company.
(4) The de facto Subsidiary Company set forth in the preceding paragraph may refuse to submit reports or undergo investigation as set forth in that paragraph if there are justifiable grounds for it to do so.

(Authority of Board of Company Auditors)
Article 53-19 (1) The board of company auditors shall be composed of all company auditors.
(2) The board of company auditors shall carry out the following duties; provided, however, that a decision under item (iii) may not preclude company auditors from exercising their authority:
 (i) Preparing audit reports;
 (ii) Appointing and removing full-time company auditors; and
 (iii) Deciding on the particulars of the execution of the duties of company auditors, such as audit policy and method of investigating the status of the business and property of the company with board of company auditors.
(3) The board of company auditors shall appoint full-time company auditors from among the company auditors.
(4) The company auditors shall report the status of the execution of their duties to the board of company auditors whenever the latter so requests.

(Mutatis Mutandis Application of the Companies Act)
Article 53-20 The provisions of Article 382 to 388 inclusive (Duty to Report to Directors, Duty to Attend Board of Directors Meetings, Duty to Report to Shareholders'

Meetings, Prohibition of Directors' Actions by the Company Auditors, Representation of Company in Actions between Company with Auditors and Directors, Remunerations for Company Auditors, Requests for Indemnification of Expenses) of the Companies Act shall apply mutatis mutandis to the company auditors of a Mutual Company. In this case, the term "Article 373, paragraph (1)" in Article 383, paragraph (1) of that Act shall be deemed to be replaced with "Article 373, paragraph (1) as applied mutatis mutandis pursuant to Article 53-16 of the Insurance Business Act"; the term "proviso to Article 366, paragraph (1)" in Article 383, paragraph (2) shall be deemed to be replaced with "proviso to Article 366, paragraph (1) as applied mutatis mutandis pursuant to Article 53-16 of the Insurance Business Act"; the term "Article 373, paragraph (2)" in Article 383, paragraph (4) shall be deemed to be replaced with "Article 373, paragraph (2) as applied mutatis mutandis pursuant to Article 53-16 of the Insurance Business Act"; the term "Article 349, paragraph (4), Article 353 and Article 364" in Article 386, paragraph (1) of that Act and the term "Article 349, paragraph (4)" in Article 386, paragraph (2) shall be deemed to be replaced with "Article 349, paragraph (4) as applied mutatis mutandis pursuant to Article 53-15 of the Insurance Business Act"; the term "Article 847, paragraph (1)" in Article 386, paragraph (2), item (i) of that Act shall be deemed to be replaced with "Article 847, paragraph (1) as applied mutatis mutandis pursuant to Article 53-37 of the Insurance Business Act"; and the terms "Article 849, paragraph (3)" and "Article 850, paragraph (2)" in Article 386, paragraph (2), item (ii) of that Act shall be deemed to be replaced with "Article 849, paragraph (3) as applied mutatis mutandis pursuant to Article 53-37 of the Insurance Business Act" and "Article 850, paragraph (2) as applied mutatis mutandis pursuant to Article 53-37 of the Insurance Business Act," respectively; any other necessary technical change in interpretation shall be specified by Cabinet Order.

(Management of Boards of Company Auditors)
Article 53-21 The provisions of Part II, Chapter IV, Section 8, Subsection 2 (Operations) of the Companies Act shall apply mutatis mutandis to the management of the board of company auditors of a Mutual Company; and the provisions of Article 868, paragraph (1) (Jurisdiction over Non-Contentious Cases), Article 869 (Prima Facie Showing), Article 870 (limited to the segment pertaining to item (i)) (Hearing of Statements), the main clause of Article 871 (Appending of the Reason), Article 872 (limited to the segment pertaining to item (iv)) (Immediate Appeal), the main clause of Article 873 (Stay of Execution of the Judicial Decision of the Prior Instance), Article 875 (Exclusion from Application of the Provisions of the Non-Contentious Cases Procedures Act) and Article 876 (Supreme Court Rules) of that Act shall apply mutatis mutandis to the application for permission under Article 394, paragraph (2) of that Act (including the cases where it is applied mutatis mutandis pursuant to Article 394, paragraph (3); hereinafter the same shall apply in this Article) as applied mutatis mutandis pursuant to this Article. In this case, the term "shareholder" in Article 394, paragraph (2) (Minutes) of that Act shall be deemed to be replaced with "member (or, where the company has a General Representative Members' Council, representative member)"; the term "and to the cases where it is necessary for the purpose of exercising the rights of a Member of the Parent Company" in Article 394, paragraph (3) shall be deemed to be deleted; and the term "Parent Company or Subsidiary" in Article 394, paragraph (4) shall be deemed to be replaced with "de facto Subsidiary Company as defined in Article 33-2, paragraph (1) of the Insurance Business Act"; any other necessary technical change in interpretation shall be specified by Cabinet Order.

Division 7 Accounting Auditors

(Authority, etc. of Accounting Auditors)
Article 53-22 (1) The accounting auditors shall audit the financial statements (meaning the financial statements as defined in Article 54-3, paragraph (2); hereinafter the same shall apply in this Subsection), annexed detailed statements thereto and consolidated financial statements (meaning the consolidated financial statements as defined in Article 54-10, paragraph (1)) of the Mutual Company pursuant to the provisions of the following Subsection. In this case, the accounting auditors shall prepare accounting audit reports pursuant to the provisions of Cabinet Office Ordinance.
(2) The accounting auditors may at any time inspect and copy the following materials or request reports on accounting from the directors and accounting advisors and managers or other employees:
   (i) Any account book (meaning the accounting book as defined in Article 54-2, paragraph (1); hereinafter the same shall apply in this Subsection) or related material prepared in writing; and
   (ii) Where account books or related materials are prepared in the form of electromagnetic record, anything that displays the data recorded on such electromagnetic record in a manner specified by Cabinet Office Ordinance.
(3) The accounting auditors may, if it is necessary for the purpose of carrying out their duties, request a report on accounting from a de facto Subsidiary Company of the company with accounting auditors, or investigate the status of the business and property of the company with accounting auditors or such de facto Subsidiary Company.
(4) The de facto Subsidiary Company set forth in the preceding paragraph may refuse to submit a report or undergo investigation as set forth in that paragraph if there are justifiable grounds for it to do so.
(5) The accounting auditors shall not employ a person falling under any of the following items in carrying out their duties:
   (i) A person listed in Article 337, paragraph (3), item (i) or (ii) of the Companies Act as applied mutatis mutandis pursuant to Article 53-7;
   (ii) A person who is a director, executive officer, accounting advisor or company auditor, or manager or any other employee of the company with accounting auditors or its de facto Subsidiary Company; or
   (iii) A person who is in continuous receipt of remuneration from the company with accounting auditors or its de facto Subsidiary Company for any business other than those carried out as a certified public accountant or audit firm.
(6) For the purpose of applying the provisions of paragraph (2) to a Mutual Company that is a company with Committees, the term "directors" in that paragraph shall be deemed to be replaced with "directors, executive officers."

(Mutatis Mutandis Application of the Companies Act)
Article 53-23 The provisions of Article 397 to 399 inclusive (Report to Company Auditors, Statement of Opinions at the Annual Shareholders' Meeting, Involvement of Company Auditors in Decision on Remunerations for Accounting Auditors) of the Companies Act shall apply mutatis mutandis to the accounting auditors of a Mutual Company. In this case, the term "Article 396, paragraph (1)" in Article 398, paragraph (1) of that Act shall be deemed to be replaced with "Article 53-22, paragraph (1) of the Insurance Business Act"; any other necessary technical change in interpretation shall be specified by Cabinet Order.

Art.53-24〜53-26　⑥ Insurance Business Act, Part II, Chap.II, Sec.2

Division 8 Committees and Executive Officers

(Appointment, etc. of Committee Members)
Article 53-24 (1) Each Committee shall be composed of three or more committee members.
(2) The members of each Committee shall be appointed from among the directors by a resolution of the board of directors.
(3) The majority of the members of each Committee must be outside directors (meaning those directors of a Mutual Company who are neither executive directors (meaning a director of a Mutual Company listed in Article 53-13, paragraph (1), item (i) or (ii) or any other director who has executed the business of the Mutual Company; the same shall apply hereinafter) or executive officers, nor a manager or any other employee of the Mutual Company or its de facto Subsidiary Company, and have never served as an executive director or executive officer, or as a manager or any other employee of the Mutual Company or its de facto Subsidiary Company; the same shall apply hereinafter).
(4) An audit committee member may not concurrently serve as an executive officer or executive director of a company with Committees or its de facto Subsidiary Company, or as an accounting advisor (or, where the accounting advisor is a juridical person, any staff member of the juridical person, who is to carry out the relevant duties) or manager or any other employee of a de facto Subsidiary Company of the company with Committees.

(Removal, etc. of Committee Members)
Article 53-25 (1) A committee member may be removed at any time by a resolution of the board of directors.
(2) The provisions of Article 401, paragraphs (2) to (4) inclusive (Removal of Committee Members), Article 868, paragraph (1) (Jurisdiction over Non-Contentious Cases), Article 870 (limited to the segment pertaining to item (ii)) (Hearing of Statements), Article 871 (Appending of Reasons), Article 872 (limited to the segment pertaining to item (iv)) (Immediate Appeals), Article 874 (limited to the segment pertaining to item (i)) (Restrictions on Appeal), Article 875 (Exclusion from Application of the Provisions of the Non-Contentious Cases Procedures Act), Article 876 (Supreme Court Rules) and Article 937, paragraph (1) (limited to the segment pertaining to item (ii), sub-items (a) and (c)) (Commissioning of Registration by Judicial Decision) of the Companies Act shall apply mutatis mutandis to the committee members of a company with Committees. In this case, the term "paragraph (1) of the preceding Article" in Article 401, paragraph (2) of that Act shall be deemed to be replaced with "Article 53-24, paragraph (1) of the Insurance Business Act"; any other necessary technical change in interpretation shall be specified by Cabinet Order.

(Election, etc. of Executive Officers)
Article 53-26 (1) A company with Committees shall have one or more executive officers.
(2) An executive officer shall be elected by a resolution of the board of directors.
(3) The relationship between a company with Committees and its executive officers shall be governed by the provisions on mandate.
(4) The provisions of Article 53-2, paragraph (1) shall apply mutatis mutandis to an executive officer.
(5) An executive officer may serve concurrently as a director.
(6) An executive officer's term of office shall continue until the conclusion of the first

board of directors meeting convened after the conclusion of the annual general members' council meeting for the last business year ending within one year from the time of their election; provided, however, that this shall not preclude the shortening of his/her term of office by the articles of incorporation.

(7) The provisions of Article 402, paragraph (8) (Election of Executive Officers) of the Companies Act shall apply mutatis mutandis to the terms of office of the executive officers of a Mutual Company. In this case, the term "the preceding paragraph" in that paragraph shall be deemed to be replaced with "Article 53-26, paragraph (6) of the Insurance Business Act"; any other necessary technical change in interpretation shall be specified by Cabinet Order.

(Dismissal, etc. of Executive Officers)
Article 53-27 (1) An executive officer may be dismissed at any time by a resolution of the board of directors.

(2) An executive officer dismissed pursuant to the provisions of the preceding paragraph may demand from the company with Committees compensation for damages arising from the dismissal, unless the company has justifiable grounds for his/her dismissal.

(3) The provisions of Article 401, paragraphs (2) to (4) inclusive of the Companies Act as applied mutatis mutandis pursuant to Article 53-25, paragraph (2), and the provisions of Article 868, paragraph (1) (Jurisdiction over Non-Contentious Cases), Article 870 (limited to the segment pertaining to item (ii)) (Hearing of Statements), Article 871 (Appending of the Reason), Article 872 (limited to the segment pertaining to item (iv)) (Immediate Appeal), Article 874 (limited to the segment pertaining to item (i)) (Restrictions on Appeal), Article 875 (Exclusion from Application of the Provisions of the Non-Contentious Cases Procedures Act), Article 876 (Supreme Court Rules) and Article 937, paragraph (1) (limited to the segment pertaining to item (ii), sub-items (a) and (c)) (Commissioning of Registration by a Judicial Decision) of that Act shall apply mutatis mutandis to the cases where a Mutual Company has no executive officer or any vacancy in the number of executive officers prescribed by the articles of incorporation. In this case, any other necessary technical change in interpretation shall be specified by Cabinet Order.

(Authority, etc. of Committees)
Article 53-28 (1) The nominating Committee shall determine the contents of proposals to be submitted to the general members' council regarding the election and dismissal of directors (or, in a company with accounting advisors, directors and accounting advisors).

(2) The audit Committee shall carry out the following duties:
 (i) Auditing the execution of duties by executive officers, etc. (meaning executive officers and directors, or, in a company with accounting advisors, executive officers, directors and accounting advisors; hereinafter the same shall apply in this Division) and preparing audit reports; and
 (ii) Determining the contents of proposals to be submitted to the general members' council regarding the election and dismissal of accounting auditors, and the non-reappointment of accounting auditors.

(3) Notwithstanding the provisions of Article 361, paragraph (1) of the Companies Act as applied mutatis mutandis pursuant to Article 53-15, and the provisions of Article 379, paragraphs (1) and (2) of that Act as applied mutatis mutandis pursuant to Article 53-17, the compensation committee shall determine the contents of remunerations, etc. (meaning the property considerations received from the Mutual Company in exchange for execution of duties, such as remunerations and bonuses; hereinafter the same shall

Art.53-28   6 Insurance Business Act, Part II, Chap.II, Sec.2

apply in this paragraph) for individual executive officers, etc. Where an executive officer serves concurrently as a manager or any other employee of the company with Committees, the same shall apply to the contents of remunerations, etc. for such manager or other employee.
(4) A company with Committees may not refuse any of the following requests made to it by a committee member with respect to the execution of his/her duties (limited to a request regarding the execution of the duties of the committee to which he/she belongs; hereinafter the same shall apply in this paragraph), unless the company proves that the expenses or obligations pertaining to the request are not necessary for the execution of the duties of such committee member:
  (i) A request for advance payment of expenses;
  (ii) A request for reimbursement of paid expenses and any interest incurred thereon from the date of payment; or
  (iii) A request for payment of any obligation incurred (or, where the obligation is not yet due, furnishing of reasonable security) to the creditor.
(5) The provisions of Article 405 to 409 inclusive (Investigations by Audit Committees, Duty to Report to the Board of Directors, Prohibition of Executive Officers' Actions, etc. by Audit Committee Members, Representation of a Company with Committees in Actions between the Company and Its Executive Officers or Directors, Methods for Decisions on Remuneration by the Compensation Committee) of the Companies Act shall apply mutatis mutandis to the Committees or committee members of a company with Committees. In this case, the term "provisions of Article 349, paragraph (4) applied mutatis mutandis under Article 420, paragraph (3), and the provisions of Article 353 and Article 364" in Article 408, paragraph (1) of that Act shall be deemed to be replaced with "provisions of Article 349, paragraph (4) as applied mutatis mutandis pursuant to Article 420, paragraph (3) as applied mutatis mutandis pursuant to Article 53-32 of the Insurance Business Act"; the term "Article 349, paragraph (4) applied mutatis mutandis under Article 420, paragraph (3)" in Article 408, paragraph (3) shall be deemed to be replaced with "Article 349, paragraph (4) as applied mutatis mutandis pursuant to Article 420, paragraph (3) as applied mutatis mutandis pursuant to Article 53-32 of the Insurance Business Act"; the term "Article 847, paragraph (1)" in Article 408, paragraph (3), item (i) of that Act shall be deemed to be replaced with "Article 847, paragraph (1) as applied mutatis mutandis pursuant to Article 53-37 of the Insurance Business Act"; the terms "Article 849, paragraph (3)" and "Article 850, paragraph (2)" in Article 408, paragraph (3), item (ii) of that Act shall be deemed to be replaced with "Article 849, paragraph (3) as applied mutatis mutandis pursuant to Article 53-37 of the Insurance Business Act" and "Article 850, paragraph (2) as applied mutatis mutandis pursuant to Article 53-37 of the Insurance Business Act," respectively; and the term "Article 404, paragraph (3)" in Article 409, paragraph (2) of that Act shall be deemed to be replaced with "Article 53-28, paragraph (3) of the Insurance Business Act"; any other necessary technical change in interpretation shall be specified by Cabinet Order.
(6) The provisions of Part II, Chapter IV, Section 10, Subsection 3 (Operation of Committees) of the Companies Act shall apply mutatis mutandis to the management of the Committees of a company with Committees; and the provisions of Article 868, paragraph (1) (Jurisdiction over Non-Contentious Cases), Article 869 (Prima Facie Showing), Article 870 (limited to the segment pertaining to item (i)) (Hearing of Statements), the main clause of Article 871 (Appending of the Reason), Article 872 (limited to the segment pertaining to item (iv)) (Immediate Appeal), the main clause of Article 873 (Stay of Execution of the Judicial Decision of the Prior Instance), Article 875 (Exclusion from Application of the Provisions of the Non-Contentious Cases Procedures

Act) and Article 876 (Supreme Court Rules) of that Act shall apply mutatis mutandis to the application for permission under Article 413, paragraph (3) of that Act (including the cases where it is applied mutatis mutandis pursuant to Article 413, paragraph (4); hereinafter the same shall apply in this paragraph) as applied mutatis mutandis pursuant to this Article. In this case, the term "shareholder" in Article 413, paragraph (3) (Minutes) shall be deemed to be replaced with "member (or, where the company has a General Representative Members' Council, representative member"; the term "and where it is necessary for the purpose of exercising the rights of a Member of the Parent Company" in Article 413, paragraph (4) shall be deemed to be deleted"; and the term "or its Parent Company or Subsidiary" in Article 413, paragraph (5) of that Act shall be deemed to be replaced with "or its de facto Subsidiary Company as defined in Article 33-2, paragraph (1) of the Insurance Business Act; any other necessary technical change in interpretation shall be specified by Cabinet Order.

(Authority of the Directors of a Company with Committees)
Article 53-29 The directors of a company with Committees may not execute the business of the company with Committees unless otherwise provided for in this Act or any order pursuant to this Act.

(Authority of the Board of Directors of a Company with Committees)
Article 53-30 (1) Notwithstanding the provisions of Article 53-14, the board of directors of a company with Committees shall carry out the following duties:
(i) Making decisions on the following particulars and any other decision on the execution of the company with Committees' business:
  (a) Basic management policy;
  (b) Particulars specified by Cabinet Office Ordinance as necessary for the execution of the duties of the audit committee;
  (c) In a Mutual Company with two or more executive officers, the particulars of the interrelationship between executive officers, such as allocation of duties and line of control among executive officers;
  (d) The directors to receive requests for the convocation of a board of directors meeting under Article 417, paragraph (2) of the Companies Act as applied mutatis mutandis pursuant to paragraph (5); and
  (e) Establishment of a system to ensure that the execution of duties by executive officers conforms to the applicable laws and regulations and the articles of incorporation, as well as any other system required by Cabinet Office Ordinance to ensure the properness of the Mutual Company's business: and
(ii) Supervising the execution of duties by executive officers, etc.
(2) The board of directors of a company with Committees shall decide on the particulars listed in item (i), sub-items (a) to (e) inclusive of the preceding paragraph.
(3) The board of directors of a company with Committees may not delegate to a director the execution of duties listed in paragraph (1), item (i) or (ii).
(4) The board of directors of a company with Committees may, by adopting a resolution, delegate to an executive officer decisions on the execution of the company's business; provided, however, that this shall not apply to the following particulars:
(i) Decisions on the particulars listed in the items of Article 298, paragraph (1) of the Companies Act as applied mutatis mutandis to Article 41, paragraph (1) or Article 49, paragraph (1);
(ii) Decisions on the contents of proposals to be submitted to the general members' council (excluding those regarding the election and dismissal of directors, accounting advisors and accounting auditors, and the non-reappointment of accounting au-

ditors);
(iii) Authorization under Article 356, paragraph (1) of the Companies Act as applied mutatis mutandis pursuant to Article 53-15 (including the cases where it is applied mutatis mutandis pursuant to the first sentence of Article 419, paragraph (2) of that Act as applied mutatis mutandis pursuant to Article 53-32);
(iv) Designation of the directors to convene a board of directors meetings under the proviso to Article 366, paragraph (1) of the Companies Act as applied mutatis mutandis pursuant to Article 53-16;
(v) Appointment of committee members under Article 53-24, paragraph (2) and removal of committee members under Article 53-25, paragraph (1);
(vi) Election of executive officers under Article 53-26, paragraph (2) and dismissal of executive officers under Article 53-27, paragraph (1);
(vii) Designation of persons to represent the company with Committees under Article 408, paragraph (1), item (i) of the Companies Act as applied mutatis mutandis pursuant to Article 53-28, paragraph (5);
(viii) Appointment of the representative executive officer under the first sentence of Article 420, paragraph (1) of the Companies Act as applied mutatis mutandis pursuant to Article 53-32 and removal of the representative executive officer under Article 420, paragraph (2) of that Act as applied mutatis mutandis pursuant to Article 53-32;
(ix) Exemption from liability under Article 53-33, paragraph (1) pursuant to the provisions of the articles of incorporation under Article 426, paragraph (1) of the Companies Act as applied mutatis mutandis pursuant to Article 53-36 with relevant changes in interpretation;
(x) Authorization under Article 54-4, paragraph (3) and Article 54-10, paragraph (5);
(xi) Decisions on the contents of any contract involving the actions listed in the items of Article 62-2, paragraph (1);
(xii) Decisions on the contents of any entity conversion plan; and
(xiii) Decisions on the contents of any merger agreement.
(5) The provisions of Article 417 (Operations of Board of Directors of Company With Committees) of the Companies Act shall apply mutatis mutandis to the operation of the board of directors of a company with Committees. In this case, the term "paragraph (1), item (i)-2 of the preceding Article" in paragraph (2) of that Article shall be deemed to be replaced with "Article 53-30, paragraph (1), item (i), sub-item (d) of the Insurance Business Act"; any other necessary technical change in interpretation shall be specified by Cabinet Order.

(Authority of Executive Officers)
Article 53-31 The executive officers shall carry out the following duties:
(i) Making decisions on the execution of the company with Committees' business as delegated by a resolution of the board of directors under paragraph (4) of the preceding Article; and
(ii) Executing the company with Committees' business.

(Mutatis Mutandis Application of the Companies Act)
Article 53-32 The provisions of Article 419 (excluding the second sentence of paragraph (2)) (Executive Officer's Duty to Report to Audit Committee Members), Article 421 (Apparent Representative Executive Officers) and Article 422, paragraph (1) (Prohibition of Executive Officers' Actions by Shareholders) of the Companies Act shall apply mutatis mutandis to the executive officers of a company with Committees; the provisions of Article 420 (Representative Executive Officers) shall apply mutatis mutandis

to the representative executive officer of a company with Committees; the provisions of Article 868, paragraph (1) (Jurisdiction over Non-Contentious Cases), Article 869 (Prima Facie Showing), Article 870 (limited to the segment pertaining to item (ii)) (Hearing of Statements), Article 871 (Appending of the Reason), Article 872 (limited to the segment pertaining to item (iv)) (Immediate Appeal), Article 874 (limited to the segment pertaining to items (i) and (iv)) (Restrictions on Appeal), Article 875 (Exclusion from Application of the Provisions of the Non-Contentious Cases Procedures Act) and Article 876 (Supreme Court Rules) of that Act shall apply mutatis mutandis to the executive officers or representative executive officer of a company with Committees; and the provisions of Article 937, paragraph (1) (limited to the segment pertaining to item (ii), sub-items (a) and (c)) (Commissioning of Registration by a Judicial Decision) of that Act shall apply mutatis mutandis to the representative executive officer of a company with Committees. In this case, the term "Article 355, Article 356 and Article 365, paragraph (2)" in the first sentence of Article 419, paragraph (2) of that Act shall be deemed to be replaced with "Article 355, Article 356 and Article 365, paragraph (2) as applied mutatis mutandis pursuant to Article 53-15 of the Insurance Business Act"; the term "Article 357" in Article 419, paragraph (3) shall be deemed to be replaced with "Article 357 as applied mutatis mutandis pursuant to Article 53-15 of the Insurance Business Act"; the terms "Article 349, paragraphs (4) and (5)," "Article 352" and "Article 401, paragraphs (2) to (4) inclusive" in Article 420, paragraph (3) of that Act shall be deemed to be replaced with "Article 349, paragraphs (4) and (5) as applied mutatis mutandis pursuant to Article 53-15 of the Insurance Business Act," "Article 352 as applied mutatis mutandis pursuant to Article 53-15 of that Act" and "Article 401, paragraphs (2) to (4) inclusive as applied mutatis mutandis pursuant to Article 53-25 of the Insurance Business Act," respectively; and the term "shareholders having the shares" in Article 422, paragraph (1) of that Act shall be deemed to be replaced with "persons who have been members"; any other necessary technical change in interpretation shall be specified by Cabinet Order.

Division 9 Officer, etc. Liability

(Officer, etc. Liability to a Mutual Company)
Article 53-33 (1) Directors, executive officers, accounting advisors, company auditors or accounting auditors (hereinafter referred to as "Officers, etc." in this Division) who have been negligent in their duties shall be liable to the Mutual Company for any damage resulting from such negligence.
(2) Where a director or executive officer has conducted a transaction set forth in Article 356, paragraph (1), item (i) (Restrictions on Competition and Transactions Involving a Conflict of Interest) of the Companies Act in violation of the provisions of Article 356, paragraph (1) of that Act as applied mutatis mutandis pursuant to Article 53-15 (including the cases where it is applied mutatis mutandis pursuant to the first sentence of Article 419, paragraph (2) of that Act as applied mutatis mutandis pursuant to the preceding Article; hereinafter the same shall apply in this paragraph), the amount of the profits obtained by the director, executive officer or a third party as a result of such transaction shall be presumed to be the amount of the damages set forth in the preceding paragraph.
(3) Where a Mutual Company incurs any damages as a result of a transaction set forth in Article 356, paragraph (1), item (ii) or (iii) of the Companies Act as applied mutatis mutandis pursuant to Article 53-15 (including the cases where it is applied mutatis mutandis pursuant to the first sentence of Article 419, paragraph (2) of that Act as applied mutatis mutandis pursuant to the preceding Article), the following directors or

executive officers shall be presumed to have been negligent in their duties:
(i) The directors or executive officers set forth in Article 356, paragraph (1) of the Companies Act as applied mutatis mutandis pursuant to Article 53-15 (including the cases where it is applied mutatis mutandis pursuant to the first sentence of Article 419, paragraph (2) of that Act as applied mutatis mutandis pursuant to the preceding Article);
(ii) The directors or executive officers who decided that the Mutual Company would carry out such transaction; or
(iii) The directors who agreed to the board of directors' resolution approving such a transaction (in a company with Committees, limited to the cases where such transaction is carried out between the company with Committees and the directors or gives rise to a conflict of interest between the company with Committees and the directors).

(Exemption from Liability for Damages to a Mutual Company)
Article 53-34 Officers, etc. may not be exempted from the liability under paragraph (1) of the preceding Article without the consent of all members.

(Officer Liability, etc. for Damages to Third Parties)
Article 53-35 (1) Officers, etc. shall be liable for any damages incurred by a third party as a result of their bad faith or gross negligence in carrying out their duties.
(2) The provisions of the preceding paragraph shall also apply where the persons listed in the following items have acted as provided for in the relevant items; provided, however, that this shall not apply to the cases where such persons prove that they did not fail to exercise due care in carrying out their duties:
(i) Directors and executive officers: the following actions:
  (a) Giving false notice with respect to an important particular of which notice is required to by given in soliciting funds or subscribers for company bonds (meaning the company bonds as defined in Article 61), or including a false detail or record in a material used in explaining the business or any other particular of the Mutual Company for the purpose of such solicitation;
  (b) Including a false detail or record of an important particular that must be entered or recorded in financial statements and business reports, and annexed detailed statements thereto;
  (c) Making a false registration; and
  (d) Giving a false public notice (including the measures provided for in Article 54-7, paragraph (3));
(ii) Accounting advisors: including a false detail or record with regard to an important particular that must be detailed or recorded in financial statements and annexed detailed statements thereto, and accounting advisors' reports:
(iii) Auditors and Audit Committee Members: including a false detail or record with regard to an important particular that must be detailed or recorded in an audit report: and
(iv) Accounting auditors: including a false detail or record with regard to an important particular that must be detailed or recorded in an accounting audit report.

(Mutatis Mutandis Application of the Companies Act)
Article 53-36 The provisions of Article 425 (excluding paragraph (1), item (ii), the second sentence of paragraphs (4) and (5)) (Partial Exemption from Liability), Article 426 (excluding paragraph (4)) (Provisions of the Articles of Incorporation on Exemption by Directors), Article 427 (Limited Liability Contracts), Article 428 (Special Provisions

on Transactions Carried Out by a Director for Himself/Herself) and Article 430 (Officers' Joint and Several Liability, etc.) of the Companies Act shall apply mutatis mutandis to the liability for damages of the Officers, etc. of a Mutual Company. In this case, the terms "Article 423, paragraph (1)" and "Article 424" in those provisions shall be deemed to be replaced with "Article 53-33, paragraph (1) of the Insurance Business Act" and "Article 53-34 of the Insurance Business Act," respectively; the term "resolution" in Article 425, paragraph (1) of that Act shall be deemed to be replaced with "the resolution set forth in Article 62, paragraph (2) of the Insurance Business Act"; the term "the consent of directors with respect to an exemption from liability under the provisions of the articles of incorporation pursuant to the provisions of that paragraph (limited to exemptions from liability for directors (excluding those who are Audit Committee Members) and executive officers) is to be obtained, and to the cases where a proposal regarding such exemption from liability" in Article 426, paragraph (2) of that Act shall be deemed to be replaced with "a proposal regarding an exemption from liability pursuant to the provisions of the articles of incorporation under that paragraph (limited to exemptions from liability for directors (excluding those who are Audit Committee Members) and executive officers)"; the term "shareholders having not less than 3 percent (or, in cases where lesser proportion is prescribed in the articles of incorporation, such proportion) of the voting rights of all shareholders (excluding Officers, etc. subject to the liability referred to in paragraph (3))" in Article 426, paragraph (5) shall be deemed to be replaced with "members representing at least three thousandths (or any smaller proportion prescribed by the articles of incorporation) of the total membership (excluding the number of members who are Officers, etc. subject to the liability referred to in paragraph (3)) of a Mutual Company (or, in a Specified Mutual Company, members equal to or exceeding the number specified by Cabinet Order set forth in Article 38, paragraph (1) of the Insurance Business Act)"; and the term "Article 425, paragraphs (4) and (5)" in Article 427, paragraph (5) of that Act shall be deemed to be replaced with "the first sentence of Article 425, paragraph (4)"; any other necessary technical change in interpretation shall be prescribed by Cabinet Order.

(Liability Actions, etc. Against a Mutual Company)
Article 53-37 The provisions of Part VII, Chapter II, Section 2 (excluding Article 847, paragraph (2), Article 849, paragraph (5), Article 851, paragraph (1), item (i) and Article 851, paragraph (2)) (Liability Actions, etc. Against a Stock Company) of the Companies Act shall apply mutatis mutandis to an action for accountability in a Mutual Company; and the provisions of Section 3 of said Chapter (excluding Article 854, paragraph (1), item (i), sub-item (a) and Article 854, paragraphs (2) to (4) inclusive) (Action to Dismiss the Officer of a Stock Company) and Article 937, paragraph (1) (limited to the segment pertaining to item (i), sub-item (j)) (Commissioning of Registration by a Judicial Decision) of that Act shall apply mutatis mutandis to an action to dismiss the officer of a Mutual Company. In this case, the terms "A shareholder (excluding a Holder of Shares Less than One Unit who is unable to exercise rights pursuant to the provisions of the articles of incorporation) having the shares" and "Article 423, paragraph (1)" in Article 847, paragraph (1) (Action to Dismiss the Officer of a Stock Company) of that Act shall be deemed to be replaced with "persons who have been members" and "Article 53-33, paragraph (1) of Insurance Business Act," respectively; the term "shareholder" in Article 847, paragraphs (3) to (5) inclusive and (7) shall be deemed to be replaced with "member"; and the provisions of Article 854, paragraph (1), item (i) of that Act shall be deemed to be replaced with "members representing at least three thousandths (or any smaller proportion prescribed by the articles of incorporation) of

the total membership, or three thousand (or any smaller number prescribed by the articles of incorporation) or more members of a Mutual Company (or, in a Specified Mutual Company, members equal to or exceeding the number specified by Cabinet Order set forth in Article 38, paragraph (1) of the Insurance Business Act), who have been members of the Mutual Company without interruption for the preceding six months (or any shorter period prescribed by the articles of incorporation) (or, where the company has a General Representative Members' Council, those members or nine (or any smaller number prescribed by the articles of incorporation) or more representative members"; any other necessary technical change in interpretation shall be prescribed by Cabinet Order.

Subsection 5 Mutual Companies' Accounting, etc.

Division 1 Accounting Principles

Article 54 A Mutual Company's accounting shall be subject to such business accounting practices that are generally accepted as fair and adequate.

Division 2 Financial Statements, etc.

(Preparation and Retention, etc. of Accounting Books)
Article 54-2 (1) A Mutual Company shall prepare accurate account books in a timely manner pursuant to the provisions of Cabinet Office Ordinance.
(2) A Mutual Company shall retain its account books and important materials regarding its business for ten years from the time of the closing of the account books.
(3) The court may, upon petition or by its own authority, order a party to litigation to submit its accounting books in whole or in part.

(Preparation and Retention of Financial Statements, etc.)
Article 54-3 (1) A Mutual Company shall prepare a balance sheet as of the date of its establishment pursuant to the provisions of Cabinet Office Ordinance.
(2) A Mutual Company shall, pursuant to the provisions of Cabinet Office Ordinance, prepare financial statements (meaning the balance sheet, profit and loss statement, proposal on appropriation of surplus or disposal of losses and any other statement specified by Cabinet Office Ordinance as necessary and appropriate in order to indicate the status of the Mutual Company's property and profits or losses; hereinafter the same shall apply in this Division) and a business report for each business year and their annexed detailed statements.
(3) The financial statements, business report, and annexed detailed statements may be prepared in the form of electromagnetic record.
(4) A Mutual Company shall retain its financial statements and annexed detailed statements thereto for ten years from the time of preparation of the financial statements.

(Auditing, etc. of Financial Statements, etc.)
Article 54-4 (1) In a Mutual Company (other than a company with accounting auditors), the financial statements and business report and their annexed detailed statements under paragraph (2) of the preceding Article, shall be audited by the company auditors pursuant to the provisions of Cabinet Office Ordinance.
(2) In a company with accounting auditors, the documents listed in the following items shall be audited by the persons listed in the relevant items pursuant to the provisions of Cabinet Office Ordinance:

(i) The financial statements and annexed detailed statements thereto set forth in paragraph (2) of the preceding Article: the company auditors (or, in a company with Committees, the audit committee) and accounting auditors; and
(ii) The business report and annexed detailed statements thereto set forth in paragraph (2) of the preceding Article: the company auditors (or, in a company with Committees, the audit committee).
(3) The financial statements and business report, and annexed detailed statements thereto audited under the preceding two paragraphs shall be approved by the board of directors.

(Provision of Financial Statements, etc. to Members)
Article 54-5 In giving a notice of convocation of the annual general members' council meeting (or, where the company has a General Representative Members' Council Meeting, such a council meeting; hereinafter the same shall apply in this Subsection), the directors shall, pursuant to the provisions of Cabinet Office Ordinance, provide the members (or, in a Mutual Company with a General Representative Members' Council, representative members; hereinafter the same shall apply in this Subsection) with the financial statements and business report (including any audit report or accounting audit report) that have been approved under paragraph (3) of the preceding Article.

(Submission, etc. of Financial Statements, etc. at the Annual General Members' Council Meeting)
Article 54-6 (1) The directors shall submit or provide the financial statements and business report approved under Article 54-4, paragraph (3) at the annual general members' council meeting.
(2) The financial statements submitted or provided pursuant to the provisions of the preceding paragraph shall be approved at the annual general members' council meeting.
(3) The directors shall report the contents of the business report submitted or provided pursuant to the provisions of paragraph (1) at the annual general members' council meeting.
(4) In a company with accounting auditors, for the purpose of applying the provisions of the preceding two paragraphs to the cases where the financial statements approved under Article 54-4, paragraph (3) satisfy the requirements specified by Cabinet Office Ordinance for accurate indication of the status of a Mutual Company's property and profits or losses in compliance with the applicable laws and regulations and the articles of incorporation, the term "financial statements" in paragraph (2) shall be deemed to be replaced with "proposal on appropriation of surplus or disposal of losses"; and the term "business report" in the preceding paragraph shall be deemed to be replaced with "financial statements (excluding the proposal on appropriation of surplus or disposal of losses) and business report."

(Public Notice of Financial Statements)
Article 54-7 (1) A Mutual Company shall, pursuant to the provisions of Cabinet Office Ordinance, give public notice of its balance sheet (or, in a Mutual Company set forth in Article 53-14, paragraph (5), its balance sheet and profit and loss statement) without delay after the conclusion of the annual general members' council meeting.
(2) Notwithstanding the provisions of the preceding paragraph, it shall be sufficient for a Mutual Company which adopts, as its Method of Public Notice, publication in a daily newspaper that publishes the particulars of current events, to give public notice of the gist of the balance sheet set forth in that paragraph.
(3) Pursuant to the provisions of Cabinet Office Ordinance, the Mutual Company set forth

in the preceding paragraph may, without delay after the conclusion of the annual general members' council meeting, take measures to make the information contained in the balance sheet provided for in paragraph (1) constantly available to many and unspecified persons by electromagnetic means for a period of five years from the date on which the annual general members' council meeting was concluded. The provisions of the preceding two paragraphs shall not apply in this case.
(4) The provisions of the preceding three paragraphs shall not apply to a Mutual Company which is to submit its securities report to the Prime Minister pursuant to the provisions of Article 24, paragraph (1) (Submission of Securities Report) of the Financial Instruments and Exchange Act.

(Retention and Inspection, etc. of Financial Statements, etc.)
Article 54-8 (1) A Mutual Company shall retain its financial statements and business report for each business year, and their annexed detailed statements (including the audit report or accounting audit report; hereinafter referred to as "Financial Statements, etc." in this Article) at its principal office for a period of five years from the day that is two weeks before the date of the annual general members' council meeting (or, in the case of Article 319, paragraph (1) of the Companies Act as applied mutatis mutandis pursuant to Article 41, paragraph (1), the date of the proposal set forth in that paragraph).
(2) A Mutual Company shall keep the copies of its Financial Statements, etc. for each business year at its secondary offices for a period of three years from the day that is two weeks before the date of its annual general members' council meeting (or, in the case of Article 319, paragraph (1) of the Companies Act as applied mutatis mutandis pursuant to Article 41, paragraph (1), the date of the proposal set forth in that paragraph); provided, however, that this shall not apply to the cases where the Financial Statements, etc. have been prepared in the form of electromagnetic records, if the Mutual Company adopts the measures specified by Cabinet Office Ordinance in order to enable its secondary offices to meet the requests listed in items (iii) and (iv) of the following paragraph.
(3) The creditors and insured persons of a Mutual Company, such as Policyholders and beneficiaries of insurance proceeds, may make the following requests at any time during the business hours of the Mutual Company; provided, however, that they pay the fees determined by the Mutual Company in making a request falling under item (ii) or (iv):
(i) Where the Financial Statements, etc. have been prepared in writing, a request to inspect or copy such documents;
(ii) A request for a certified copy or extract of the documents referred to in the preceding item;
(iii) Where the Financial Statements, etc. are prepared in the form of electromagnetic records, a request to inspect anything that shows the particulars recorded in the electromagnetic records in a manner specified by Cabinet Office Ordinance; or
(iv) A request to be provided with the particulars recorded in the electromagnetic records set forth in the preceding item by the electromagnetic means determined by the Mutual Company, or to be issued a document detailing such particulars.

(Order to Submit Financial Statements, etc.)
Article 54-9 The court may, upon petition or by its own authority, order a party to litigation to submit in whole or in Part the financial statements and annexed detailed statements thereto.

(Consolidated Financial Statements)

Article 54-10 (1) A company with accounting auditors may, pursuant to the provisions of Cabinet Office Ordinance, prepare consolidated financial statements (meaning those statements specified by Cabinet Office Ordinance as necessary and appropriate in order to indicate the status of the property and profits or losses of a corporate group comprised of the company with accounting auditors and its de facto Subsidiary Companies; hereinafter the same shall apply in this Article) for each business year.

(2) Consolidated financial statements may be prepared in the form of electromagnetic records.

(3) An entity that is a Mutual Company set forth in Article 53-14, paragraph (5) as of the last day of a business year shall submit a securities report to the Prime Minister pursuant to the provisions of Article 24, paragraph (1) of the Financial Instruments and Exchange Act and shall prepare consolidated financial statements for the business year.

(4) Consolidated financial statements shall be audited by the company auditors (or, in a company with Committees, the audit committee) and accounting auditors, pursuant to the provisions of Cabinet Office Ordinance.

(5) The consolidated financial statements audited under the preceding paragraph shall be approved by the board of directors.

(6) The provisions of Article 54-5 and Article 54-6, paragraphs (1) and (3) shall apply mutatis mutandis to consolidated financial statements. In this case, the term "contents of the business report" in Article 54-6, paragraph (3) shall be deemed to be replaced with "contents of the consolidated financial statements and the result of audit under Article 54-10, paragraph (4)"; any technical change in interpretation shall be specified by Cabinet Order.

Division 3 Payment of Interest on Funds, Redemption of Funds and Distributions of Surplus

(Restrictions on Payment of Interest on Funds, etc.)

Article 55 (1) Payment of interest on funds may be made in an amount not exceeding the amount of net assets on the balance sheet after the sum total of the following amounts (referred to as "maximum limit of interest payment" in Article 55-3, paragraph (3), item (i)) has been deducted therefrom:

(i) The total amount of funds;

(ii) The deficiency reserves and the reserves for redemption of funds set forth in Article 56 (including the total amount of any reduction of the reserves for redemption of funds pursuant to the provisions of Article 59, paragraph (2); the same shall apply in the following paragraph); and

(iii) Other amounts specified by Cabinet Office Ordinance.

(2) Redemption of funds or distribution of surplus may be made in an amount not exceeding the amount of net assets on the balance sheet after deducting the sum total of the following amounts (referred to as "maximum limit of redemption, etc." in Article 55-3, paragraph (3), item (ii)); provided, however, that such redemption or distribution may only be effected after the amount credited to assets in the balance sheet pursuant to the provisions of the first sentence of Article 113 (including the cases where it is applied mutatis mutandis pursuant to Article 272-18) has been amortized in full:

(i) The total amount of funds;

(ii) The deficiency reserves and the reserves for redemption of funds set forth in Article 56;

(iii) The amount of interest on funds paid under the preceding paragraph;

(iv) The deficiency reserves to be set aside for the accounting period; and
(v) Other amounts specified by Cabinet Office Ordinance.
(3) Where a Mutual Company has made any payment of interest on funds, or redemption of funds or distribution of surplus in violation of the provisions of the preceding two paragraphs, a creditor of the Mutual Company may cause it to refund the money thus expended.

(Distributions of Surplus)
Article 55-2 (1) Any distribution of surplus shall be made in conformity with the standards specified by Cabinet Office Ordinance for fair and equitable distribution.
(2) A Mutual Company shall, as the particulars listed in Article 23, paragraph (1), item (vii), prescribe in its articles of incorporation that, where the company makes an appropriation of surplus for each accounting period, it shall set aside at least the amount calculated by multiplying the appropriable amount specified by Cabinet Office Ordinance by a certain proportion as the reserves for distributing surplus to members pursuant to the provisions of Cabinet Office Ordinance.
(3) The certain proportion set forth in the preceding paragraph shall not be less than the proportion specified by Cabinet Office Ordinance.
(4) Notwithstanding the provisions of the preceding two paragraphs, a Mutual Company may, where it faces unavoidable circumstances in light of the status of its settlement of account, prescribe in its articles of incorporation that, so far as the appropriation of surplus for the accounting period is concerned, the company shall set aside as the Reserves specified by Cabinet Office Ordinance under paragraph (2) the amount calculated by multiplying the amount prescribed by Cabinet Office Ordinance under paragraph (2) by a ratio that is smaller than that prescribed by Cabinet Office Ordinance under the preceding paragraph.
(5) Any provisions in the articles of incorporation under the preceding paragraph shall not take effect unless it is approved by the Prime Minister.

(Liability for Payment of Interest on Funds, etc.)
Article 55-3 (1) Where a Mutual Company has paid any interest on funds in violation of the provisions of Article 55, paragraph (1), or made any redemption of funds or distribution of surplus in violation of the provisions of paragraph (2) of the same Article, the persons who were granted any money due to such action (referred to as "payment of interest on funds, etc." hereinafter in this Article as well as in the following Article) and the persons listed in the following items shall jointly and severally assume the obligation to pay to the Mutual Company the exact amount of money that those recipients have been granted:
(i) The executing person who has carried out any duty related to the payment of interest on funds, etc. (meaning the executive director (or, in a company with Committees, executive officer) or any other person specified by Cabinet Office Ordinance as having participated, in the course of functions, in the execution of duties to be carried out by the executive director); and
(ii) Where the annual general members' council meeting has adopted a resolution pertaining to a proposal related to the appropriation of surplus or disposal of losses (limited to the cases where the contents of the proposal approved by the resolution are in violation of the provisions of Article 55, paragraph (1) or (2)), the person specified by Cabinet Office Ordinance as the director who has presented the proposal to the annual general members' council meeting.
(2) Notwithstanding the provisions of the preceding paragraph, a person listed in item (i) or (ii) of that paragraph shall not assume the obligation under that paragraph, if the

person proves that he/she did not fail to exercise due care in carrying out his/her duties.
(3) A person listed in the items of paragraph (1) may not be exempted from the obligation under that paragraph; provided, however, that this shall not apply if all of the members agree to exempt the person from the obligation to the amount prescribed in the relevant items in the cases listed in the following items:
  (i) In the case of a payment of interest on funds: maximum limit of interest payment; or
  (ii) In the case of a redemption of funds or distribution of surplus (excluding the cases set forth in the proviso to Article 55, paragraph (2)): maximum limit of redemption, etc.

(Restrictions, etc. on Right to Obtain Reimbursement from Members)
Article 55-4 Where a Mutual Company has made any payment of interest on funds, etc. in violation of the provisions of Article 55, paragraph (1) or (2), a member without knowledge of such violation shall not be obliged to meet any request for reimbursement made by a person listed in the items of paragraph (1) of the preceding Article who has paid the money prescribed in that paragraph.

Division 4 Reserve for Redemption of Funds and Deficiency Reserve

(Establishment of Reserve for Redemption of Funds)
Article 56 (1) A Mutual Company shall, in redeeming its funds, set aside the amount of money to be redeemed as the reserves for redemption of funds.
(2) A Mutual Company shall, if it has been released from any debt pertaining to its funds, deduct the amount of debt thus relieved from the total amount of its funds and set it aside as the reserves for redemption of funds.

(Reduction of Reserve for Redemption of Funds)
Article 57 (1) A Mutual Company may reduce the amount of the reserves for redemption of funds by a resolution of the general members' council (or General Representative Members' Council, where the company has such a council).
(2) The resolution set forth in the preceding paragraph shall be a resolution under Article 62, paragraph (2).
(3) The documents prescribed in Articles 18, 19 and 46 of the Commercial Registration Act as well as the following documents shall be attached to a written application for registration of change due to any reduction of the reserves for redemption of funds pursuant to the provisions of paragraph (1):
  (i) A written statement certifying that the company has given a public notice under Article 17, paragraph (2) as applied mutatis mutandis pursuant to the following paragraph with relevant changes in interpretation;
  (ii) Where any Policyholder or other creditor has stated his/her objection under Article 17, paragraph (4) as applied mutatis mutandis pursuant to the following paragraph with relevant changes in interpretation, a written statement certifying that the company has made payment or provided equivalent security to such Policyholder or other creditor or entrusted equivalent property to a trust company, etc. for the purpose of ensuring that such Policyholder or other creditor receive the payment, or that the reduction of the reserves for redemption of funds poses no risk of harming the interest of such Policyholder or other creditor; and
  (iii) A written statement certifying that the number of the Policyholders who have

Art.58 ⑥ Insurance Business Act, Part II, Chap.II, Sec.2

stated their objections under Article 17, paragraph (6) as applied mutatis mutandis pursuant to the following paragraph with relevant changes in interpretation has not exceeded one fifth of the total number of Policyholders set forth in that paragraph, or a written statement certifying that the amount specified by Cabinet Office Ordinance as belonging to such Policyholders has not exceeded one fifth of the total amount set forth in that paragraph.

(4) The provisions of Article 16, paragraph (1) (excluding the proviso thereto) and (2), Article 17 (excluding the proviso to paragraph (1)), Article 17-2, paragraph (4), and Article 17-4 shall apply mutatis mutandis to a reduction of the reserves for redemption of funds under paragraph (1). In this case, the term "reduction of the capital, etc." in those provisions shall be deemed to be replaced with "reduction of the reserves for redemption of funds"; the terms "A Stock Company" and "ranging from two weeks before the date of the shareholders' meeting pertaining to the resolution on the reduction of the capital, etc. (or, the date of the board of directors meeting where Article 447, paragraph (3) (Reductions in Amount of Capital) or Article 448, paragraph (3) (Reductions in Amount of Reserves) of the Companies Act Applies) to six months from the Effective Date of the reduction of the capital, etc." in Article 16, paragraph (1) shall be deemed to be replaced with "In the case of Article 57, paragraph (1), a Mutual Company" and "ranging from two weeks before the date of the general members' council (or General Representative Members' Council, where the company has such a council) pertaining to the resolution under that paragraph to six months from the date of the reduction of the reserves for redemption of funds" respectively; the term "Where a Stock Company reduces the amount of its capital, etc. (excluding the cases where the whole of the amount by which the Reserves are reduced is appropriated to the capital)" in Article 17, paragraph (1) shall be deemed to be replaced with "In the case of Article 57, paragraph (1)"; and the term "Article 447, paragraph (1) (Reductions in amount of the Capital) or Article 448, paragraph (1) (Reductions in amount of Reserves) of the Companies Act" in Article 17, paragraph (6) shall be deemed to be replaced with "Article 57, paragraph (1)"; any other necessary technical change in interpretation shall be specified by Cabinet Order.

(5) Any reduction of the reserves for redemption of funds under paragraph (1) shall not take effect unless it is approved by the Prime Minister.

(6) The provisions of Article 828, paragraph (1) (limited to the segment pertaining to item (v)) and (2) (limited to the segment pertaining to item (v)) (Actions to Invalidate Acts Concerning the Organization of a Company), Article 834 (limited to the segment pertaining to item (v)) (Defendant), Article 835, paragraph (1) (Jurisdiction over Actions), Article 836 to 839 inclusive (Order to Provide Security, Mandatory Consolidation of Oral Arguments, etc., Persons Affected by Where a Judgment Being Upheld, Effects of a Judgment of Invalidity, Revocation or Rescission), Article 846 (Liability for Damages Where a Judgment Is Entered Against the Plaintiff), and Article 937, paragraph (1) (limited to the segment pertaining to item (i), sub-item (d)) (Commissioning of Registration by a Judicial Decision) of the Companies Act shall apply mutatis mutandis to an action to invalidate a reduction of the reserves for redemption of funds. In this case, the term "shareholders, etc." in Article 828, paragraph (2), item (v) of that Act shall be deemed to be replaced with "members, directors, company auditors or liquidators (or, in a company with Committees, members, directors, executive officers or liquidators) of a Mutual Company"; any other necessary technical change in interpretation shall be specified by Cabinet Order.

(Deficiency Reserve)
Article 58 A Mutual Company shall set aside at least three thousandths of the amount

expended in each accounting period for appropriation of surplus (including that Part of the reserves set forth in Article 55-2, paragraph (2) that is to be set aside pursuant to the provisions of Cabinet Office Ordinance) as the deficiency reserve, until such time as its funds (including the reserves for redemption of funds set forth in Article 56) reach their full amount (or any larger amount prescribed by the articles of incorporation).

(Reduction of Deficiency Reserve, etc. to Compensate Losses)
Article 59 (1) The loss compensation reserves may not be reduced, except in the case of allocating it to loss compensation.
(2) By derogation from Article 57, the reserves for redemption of funds may be reduced to compensate for the losses, where the deficiency reserves is not sufficient to cover the whole losses.

Subsection 6 Solicitation of Additional Funds

(Solicitation of Additional Funds)
Article 60 (1) A Mutual Company may, even after its establishment, solicit additional funds by a resolution of the general members' council (or General Representative Members' Council, where the company has such a council; hereinafter the same shall apply in this paragraph). In this case, the Mutual Company shall determine the amount of such additional funds by a resolution of the general members' council.
(2) The resolution specified in the preceding paragraph shall be a resolution under Article 62, paragraph (2).

(Offer of Contributions of Funds)
Article 60-2 (1) A Mutual Company shall notify the persons who seek to make an offer to contribute funds in response to solicitation under paragraph (1) of the preceding Article of the following particulars:
　(i) Particulars listed in Article 23, paragraph (1), item (ii) and items (iv) to (vi) inclusive;
　(ii) The amount of the additional funds to be solicited, the rights enjoyed by the contributors to the funds and the method of redemption of the funds;
　(iii) Payment date; and
　(iv) The banks, etc. and other places where the payment of contribution of funds is to be handled.
(2) A person who offers to contribute to funds in response to the solicitation under paragraph (1) of the preceding Article shall submit to the Mutual Company a document detailing the following particulars:
　(i) Name and address of the person who makes the offer; and
　(ii) Planned amount of contribution of funds.
(3) In addition to the documents specified in Articles 18 and 46 of the Commercial Registration Act as applied mutatis mutandis pursuant to Article 67, the following documents shall be attached to the written application for registration of change due to any solicitation of additional funds under paragraph (1) of the preceding Article:
　(i) A document certifying the offer of a contribution of funds or a contract under Article 30 as applied mutatis mutandis pursuant to the following paragraph; and
　(ii) A document certifying that payment has been made to the funds under Article 30-3, paragraph (1) as applied mutatis mutandis pursuant to the following paragraph.
(4) The provisions of Article 28, paragraphs (3) to (6) inclusive, Article 29 to 30-2 inclusive, Article 30-3 (excluding paragraphs (2) and (3)), Article 30-5, paragraphs (2) and

(3) of this Act and Article 209 (Timing of Shareholders Status) (excluding item (ii)) of the Companies Act shall apply mutatis mutandis to the solicitation of additional funds under paragraph (1) of the preceding Article. In this case, the term "incorporators" in those provisions shall be deemed to be replaced with "Mutual Company"; the term "preceding paragraph" in Article 28, paragraph (3) shall be deemed to be replaced with "Article 60-2, paragraph (2)"; the terms "the items of paragraph (1)" and "paragraph (2)" in Article 28, paragraph (4) shall be deemed to be replaced with "Article 60-2 the items of paragraph (1)" and "paragraph (2) of the same Article," respectively; the term "paragraph (2), item (i)" in Article 28, paragraph (5) shall be deemed to be replaced with "Article 60-2, paragraph (2), item (i)"; the term "paragraph (2), item (ii) of the preceding Article" in Article 29, paragraph (1) shall be deemed to be replaced with "Article 60-2, paragraph (2), item (ii)"; the term "the preceding two Articles" in Article 30 shall be deemed to be replaced with "Article 60-2, paragraph (1) (excluding item (iii)), and Article 28, paragraphs (3) to (6) inclusive and the preceding Article as applied mutatis mutandis pursuant to paragraph (4) of the same Article"; the terms "without delay" and "Article 28, paragraph (1), item (iii)" in Article 30-3, paragraph (1) shall be deemed to be replaced with "on the date set forth in Article 60-2, paragraph (1), item (iii)" and "Article 60-2, paragraph (1), item (iv)," respectively; the term "solicited at incorporation who has received the notice under paragraph (2) shall, unless he/she makes the payment by the date set forth in that paragraph" in Article 28, paragraph (5) be deemed to be replaced with", unless he/she makes the payment by the date set forth in paragraph (1)"; and the term "After the establishment of the Mutual Company" in Article 30-5, paragraph (3) shall be deemed to be replaced with "After a year has elapsed since the date of registration of change due to a solicitation of additional funds under Article 60, paragraph (1)"; any other necessary technical change in interpretation shall be specified by Cabinet Order.

(5) The provisions of Article 828, paragraph (1) (limited to the segment pertaining to item (ii)) and (2) (limited to the segment pertaining to item (ii)) (Actions to Invalidate Acts Concerning the Organization of a Company), Article 834 (limited to the segment pertaining to item (ii)) (Defendant), Article 835, paragraph (1) (Jurisdiction over Actions), Article 836, paragraphs (1) and (3) (Order to Provide Security), Article 837 to 840 inclusive (Mandatory Consolidation of Oral Arguments, etc., Persons Affected by a Judgment Being Upheld, Effects of a Judgment of Invalidity, Revocation or Rescission, Effects of a Judgment Invalidating New Share Issue), Article 846 (Liability for Damages Where a Judgment Is Entered Against the Plaintiff), and Article 937, paragraph (1) (limited to the segment pertaining to item (i), sub-item (b)) (Commissioning of Registration by a Judicial Decision) of the Companies Act shall apply mutatis mutandis to an action to invalidate a solicitation of additional funds under paragraph (1) of the preceding Article; and the provisions of Article 868, paragraph (1) (Jurisdiction over Non-Contentious Cases), the main clause of Article 871 (Appending of the Reason), Article 872 (limited to the segment pertaining to item (ii)) (Immediate Appeal), the main clause of Article 873 (Stay of Execution of the Judicial Decision of the Prior Instance), Article 875 to 877 inclusive (Exclusion from Application of the Provisions of the Non-Contentious Cases Procedures Act, Supreme Court Rules, Mandatory Consolidation of Hearings, etc.) and Article 878, paragraph (1) (Effect of Judicial Decision) of that Act shall apply mutatis mutandis to an application under Article 840, paragraph (2) of that Act as applied mutatis mutandis pursuant to this paragraph. In this case, the term "shareholders, etc." in Article 828, paragraph (2), item (ii) of that Act shall be deemed to be replaced with "members, directors, company auditors or liquidators (or, in a company with Committees, members, directors, executive officers or liquidators) of a Mutual Company"; any other necessary technical change in interpretation shall be speci-

Subsection 7 Solicitation of Subscribers for Bonds Issued by Mutual Company

(Determination of the Particulars of Bonds for Subscription)
Article 61 Before a Mutual Company seeks to solicit persons to subscribe for the bonds (meaning the monetary claims against the Mutual Company which accrue as a result of any allocation made by the Mutual Company pursuant to the provisions of this Act and which are to be redeemed under the conditions that have been fixed with regard to the following particulars; hereinafter the same shall apply in this Subsection) that it issues, the company shall establish the following particulars with regard to the bonds for subscription (meaning the bonds that will be allocated to the persons who have subscribed for such bonds in response to the solicitation; hereinafter the same shall apply in this Subsection):
(i) The total monetary amount of the bonds for subscription;
(ii) The monetary amount of each bond for subscription;
(iii) The interest rate on the bonds for subscription;
(iv) The method and due date of redemption of the bonds for subscription;
(v) The method and due date of interest payment;
(vi) If bond certificates will be issued, that fact;
(vii) If it will be arranged that bondholders may not make, in whole or in part, a demand under Article 698 of the Companies Act as applied mutatis mutandis pursuant to Article 61-5, that fact;
(viii) If it will be arranged that the bond administrator may take the action listed in Article 61-7, paragraph (4), item (ii) in the absence of a resolution of the bondholders meeting, that fact;
(ix) The amount to be paid in for each bond for subscription (meaning the amount of money to be paid in exchange for each bond for subscription: hereinafter the same shall apply in this Subsection) or the minimum amount thereof, or the method of calculating such amount;
(x) Due date for payment of the money in exchange for the bonds for subscription;
(xi) If it will be arranged that the bonds for subscription will not be issued in their entirety if the persons to whom the bonds for subscription will be allocated have not been established by a certain date for the total monetary amount of the bonds, that fact and that certain date; and
(xii) In addition to what is listed in the preceding items, particulars specified by Cabinet Office Ordinance.

(Offer to Subscribe for Bonds)
Article 61-2 (1) A Mutual Company shall notify the persons who seek to make an offer to subscribe for bonds in response to a solicitation under the preceding Article of the following particulars:
(i) Name of the Mutual Company;
(ii) Particulars listed in the items of the preceding Article pertaining to such solicitation; and
(iii) In addition to what is listed in the preceding two items, particulars specified by Cabinet Office Ordinance.
(2) A person who offers to subscribe for bonds in response to the solicitation under the preceding Article shall submit to the Mutual Company a document detailing the following particulars:

Art.61-3～61-5   ⑥ Insurance Business Act, Part II, Chap.II, Sec.2

(i) Name and address of the person who makes the offer;
(ii) The total par value of the bonds for which he/she seeks to subscribe and the number of bonds by par value; and
(iii) Where the Mutual Company has prescribed the minimum amount under item (ix) of the preceding Article, the preferred amount to be paid in.
(3) A person who makes an offer under the preceding paragraph may, in lieu of submitting the document prescribed in that paragraph, and pursuant to the provisions of Cabinet Order, provide the particulars that are required to be included in such document by electromagnetic means, with the consent of the Mutual Company. In this case, the person who has made the offer shall be deemed to have submitted the document prescribed in that paragraph.
(4) The provisions of paragraph (1) shall not apply to the cases where the Mutual Company has issued to the person who seeks to make an offer under paragraph (1) the prospectus prescribed in Article 2, paragraph (10) (Definitions) of the Financial Instruments and Exchange Act that details the particulars listed in the items of paragraph (1), or to any other case specified by Cabinet Office Ordinance as posing no risk to the protection of persons who seek to offer to subscribe for bonds.
(5) The Mutual Company shall immediately notify a person who has made an offer under paragraph (2) (hereinafter referred to as "Offeror" in this Subsection) of any change in the particulars listed in the items of paragraph (1) and the particular affected by the change.
(6) It shall be sufficient for a notice or demand to an Offeror to be sent by the Mutual Company to the address specified under paragraph (2), item (i) (or to any other place or contact address of which the Offeror has notified the Mutual Company for the receipt of notices or demands).
(7) The notice or demand in the preceding paragraph shall be deemed to have arrived at the time when such notice or demand would normally have arrived.

(Allocation of Bonds for Subscription)
Article 61-3 (1) The Mutual Company shall select from among the Offerors the persons to receive allocation of the bonds for subscription, and determine the par value, and the number by name, of the bonds for subscription to be allocated to each of such persons. In this case, the Mutual Company may reduce the number of the bonds for subscription to be allocated to each Offeror for each name from the number prescribed in paragraph (2), item (ii) of the preceding Article.
(2) The Mutual Company shall notify the Offerors, no later than the day immediately preceding the date referred to in Article 61, item (x) of the par value, and the number by name, of the bonds for subscription that will be allocated to each Offeror.

(Special Provisions on Offers for Bonds for Subscription and the Allocation Thereof)
Article 61-4 The provisions of the preceding two Articles shall not apply to the cases where a person who seeks to subscribe for bonds concludes a contract for the subscription for the total amount of those bonds.

(Mutatis Mutandis Application of the Companies Act)
Article 61-5 The provisions of Article 680 to 683 inclusive (Bondholders of Bonds for Subscription, Bond Registry, Delivery of Document Stating Matters to Be Stated in Bond Registry, Management of Bond Registry), Article 684 (excluding paragraphs (4) and (5)) (Retention of the Bond Registry and Making It Available for Inspection) and Article 685 to 701 inclusive (Notices to Bondholders, Exercise of Rights by Co-own-

ers, Assignment of Bonds with Issued Certificates, Perfection of Assignment of Bonds, Presumption of Rights, Stating or Recording Matters to Be Stated in Bond Registry Without Request from Bondholders, Stating or Recording Matters to Be Stated in Bond Registry as Requested by Bondholders, Pledges of Bonds with Issued Certificates, Perfection of Pledge of Bonds, Entries in Bond Registry Regarding Pledges, Delivery of Documents Stating Matters to Be Stated in Bond Registry Regarding Pledges, Perfection Requirements for Bonds Belonging to Trust Property, etc., Issuing of Bond Certificates, Matters to Be Stated on Bond Certificates, Conversions between Registered Bonds and Bearer Bonds, Loss of Bond Certificates, Redemption of Bonds where Coupons Missing, Extinctive Prescription of Right to Claim Redemption of Bonds) of the Companies Act shall apply mutatis mutandis to the cases where a Mutual Company issues bonds. In this case, the term "bond-issuing Company" in those provisions shall be deemed to be replaced with "bond-issuing mutual company"; the term "the preceding Article" in Article 680, item (ii) of that Act shall be deemed to be replaced with "Article 61-4 of the Insurance Business Act"; the term "Article 676, items (iii) though (viii)" in Article 681, item (i) of that Act shall be deemed to be replaced with "Article 61, items (iii) to (viii) inclusive of the Insurance Business Act"; the term "Article 720, paragraph (1)" in Article 685, paragraph (5) of that Act shall be deemed to be replaced with "Article 720, paragraph (1) as applied mutatis mutandis pursuant to Article 61-8, paragraph (2) of the Insurance Business Act"; and the term "Article 676, item (vii)" in Article 698 of that Act shall be deemed to be replaced with "Article 61, item (vii) of the Insurance Business Act"; any technical change in interpretation shall be specified by Cabinet Order.

(Designation of Bond Administrator)
Article 61-6 In issuing bonds, a Mutual Company shall designate a bond administrator to be entrusted with the receipt of payments, preservation of claims and other bond administration on behalf of the bondholders; provided, however, that this shall not apply to the cases where the par value of each bond is one hundred million yen or more, or any other case specified by Cabinet Office Ordinance as posing no risk to the protection of bondholders.

(Authority, etc. of Bond Administrator)
Article 61-7 (1) The bond administrator shall have the authority to carry out any action in or out of court to receive payments of claims pertaining to the bonds on behalf of the bondholders, or to secure the realization of claims pertaining to the bonds.
(2) Where the bond administrator has received any payment under the preceding paragraph, the bondholders may demand the payment of the redeemed amount of bonds and interest thereon from the bond administrator. In this case, the bondholders shall demand the payment of such redeemed amount in exchange for bond certificates, and the payment of such interest in exchange for coupons, if the issuance of bond certificates is stipulated.
(3) Any claim under the first sentence of the preceding paragraph shall lapse by prescription if not exercised within ten years.
(4) The bond administrator shall not take the following actions without a resolution of the bondholders meeting; provided, however, that this shall not apply to the actions listed in item (ii), if there is a stipulation with respect to the particulars listed in Article 61, item (viii):
(i) suspension of his/her payment for the entirety of the bonds, exemption from any liability resulting from a default on his/her debt, or settlement (excluding the actions listed in the following item);

Art.61-8 ⑥ Insurance Business Act, Part II, Chap.II, Sec.2

(ii) Procedural actions with respect to the entirety of the bonds, or any action involved in bankruptcy procedures, rehabilitation procedures, corporate reorganization procedures or procedures for special liquidation (excluding the action set forth in paragraph (1)).

(5) The bond administrator shall, if he/she has taken the action listed in item (ii) of the preceding paragraph without a resolution of the bondholders meeting pursuant to the proviso to that paragraph, give public notice of this without delay, and notify each of the known bondholders thereof.

(6) A public notice under the preceding paragraph shall be made in accordance with the Method of Public Notice adopted by the bond-issuing mutual company; provided, however, that such public notice shall be given by way of publication in the Official Gazette, where that method is electronic public notice.

(7) The bond administrator may, if it is necessary for taking the action listed in paragraph (1) or the items of paragraph (4) with respect to the bonds with whose administration he/she has been entrusted, investigate with the permission of the court the status of the business and property of the bond-issuing mutual company.

(8) The provisions of Article 703 (Qualifications of Bond Managers), Article 704 (Obligations of Bond Managers), Article 707 to 714 inclusive (Appointment of Special Agent, Method of Acts of Bond Managers, Special Provisions on Multiple Bond Managers, Liability of Bond Manager, Resignation of Bond Managers, Liability of Bond Managers after Resignation, Dismissal of Bond Managers, Succession to Bond Manager's Administration of Bonds), Article 868, paragraph (3) (Jurisdiction over Non-Contentious Cases), Article 869 (Prima Facie Showing), Article 870 (limited to the segment pertaining to item (iii)) (Hearing of Statements), Article 871 (Appending of the Reason), Article 872 (limited to the segment pertaining to item (iv)) (Immediate Appeal), Article 874 (limited to the segment pertaining to items (i) and (iv)) (Restrictions on Appeal), Article 875 (Mandatory Consolidation of Hearings, etc.) and Article 876 (Supreme Court Rules) of the Companies Act shall apply mutatis mutandis to a bond administrator. In this case, the term "bond-issuing company" in those provisions shall be deemed to be replaced with "bond-issuing mutual company"; the term "this Act" in Article 710, paragraph (1) of that Act shall be deemed to be replaced with "the Insurance Business Act"; and the term "Article 702" in Article 711, paragraph (2) of that Act shall be deemed to be replaced with "Article 61-6 of the Insurance Business Act"; any other necessary technical change in interpretation shall be specified by Cabinet Order.

(Bondholders Meeting)
Article 61-8 (1) The bondholders shall form a bondholders meeting for each class of bond (meaning the class of bond set forth in Article 681, item (i) of the Companies Act as applied mutatis mutandis pursuant to Article 61-5).

(2) The provisions of Part IV, Chapter III (excluding Article 715 and Article 740, paragraph (3)) (Bondholders' Meeting), Part VII, Chapter II, Section 7 (Action to Rescind Performance, etc. by a Company That Issues Bonds), Article 868, paragraph (3) (Jurisdiction over Non-Contentious Cases), Article 869 (Prima Facie Showing), Article 870 (limited to the segment pertaining to item (x) to (xii) inclusive) (Hearing of Statements), Article 871 (Appending of the Reason), Article 872 (limited to the segment pertaining to item (iv)) (Immediate Appeal), Article 873 (Stay of Execution of the Judicial Decision of the Prior Instance), Article 874 (limited to the segment pertaining to item (iv)) (Restrictions on Appeal), Article 875 (Mandatory Consolidation of Hearings, etc.) and Article 876 (Supreme Court Rules) of the Companies Act shall apply mutatis mutandis to the cases where a Mutual Company issues bonds. In this case, the term "bond-issuing

company" in those provisions shall be deemed to be replaced with "bond-issuing mutual company"; the term "under Article 705, paragraphs (1) to (3) inclusive, and under Articles 708 and 709" in Article 737, paragraph (2) (Execution of Resolutions of Bondholders' Meetings) of that Act shall be deemed to be replaced with "of Article 61-7, paragraphs (1) to (3) inclusive of the Insurance Business Act, and the provisions of Articles 708 and 709 as applied mutatis mutandis pursuant to Article 61-7, paragraph (8) of that Act"; and the term "the provisions of Article 449, Article 627, Article 635, Article 670, Article 779 (including the cases where applied mutatis mutandis pursuant to paragraph (2) of Article 781), Article 789 (including the cases where applied mutatis mutandis pursuant to paragraph (2) of Article 793), Article 799 (including the cases where applied mutatis mutandis pursuant to paragraph (2) of Article 802) or Article 810 (including the cases where applied mutatis mutandis pursuant to paragraph (2) of Article 813)" in Article 740, paragraph (1) (Special provisions on objection procedures for creditors) of that Act shall be deemed to be replaced with "Article 17 (excluding the proviso to paragraph (1)) of the Insurance Business Act as applied mutatis mutandis pursuant to Article 57, paragraph (4) of that Act, and Articles 88 and 165-17 (including the cases where it is applied mutatis mutandis pursuant to Article 165-20 of that Act) of that Act"; any other necessary technical change in interpretation shall be specified by Cabinet Order.

(Application of Secured Bond Trust Act, etc.)
Article 61-9 For the purpose of applying the Secured Bond Trust Act (Act No. 52 of 1905) and other laws and regulations specified by Cabinet Order, the bonds shall, pursuant to the provisions of Cabinet Order, be deemed to be bonds as defined in Article 2, item (xxiii) (Definitions) of the Companies Act.

(Special Provision on Short-Term Bonds)
Article 61-10 (1) A bond registry shall not be required for the bonds which meet all of the following requirements (referred to as "Short-Term Bonds" in the following paragraph):
(i) The par value of each bond is not less than one hundred million yen;
(ii) The due date for redemption of the principal is fixed on a day within one year from the payment date of the total amount of the bonds, and no judgment has been made authorizing installment payments;
(iii) The due date for interest payment is fixed on the same day as the due date for redemption under the preceding item; and
(iv) No security is furnished pursuant to the provisions of the Secured Bond Trust Act.
(2) The provisions of Article 61-6 to 61-8 inclusive shall not apply to Short-Term Bonds.

Subsection 8 Amendment in the Articles of Incorporation

Article 62 (1) Any amendment to the articles of incorporation shall require a resolution of the general members' council (or General Representative Members' Council, where the company has such a council).
(2) Notwithstanding the provisions of Article 37-3, paragraph (1) and Article 44, paragraph (1), the resolution set forth in the preceding paragraph is adopted by a three-quarter majority vote of the attending members at a session where at least half of the members are present (or by a three-quarter majority vote of the attending representative members at a session at which at least half of the representative members are present).

Subsection 9 Assignment, etc. of Business

Article 62-2 (1) A Mutual Company shall, before it takes any of the following actions, have the contract for the relevant action authorized by a resolution of the general members' council no later than the day immediately preceding the Effective Date of the action:
(i) Assignment of the whole of business;
(ii) Assignment of any important Part of the business (excluding the cases where the book value of the assets to be transferred by such assignment does not exceed one fifth (or any smaller proportion prescribed by the articles of incorporation) of the amount of the total assets of the Mutual Company as calculated by the method specified by Cabinet Office Ordinance);
(iii) Acquisition of the whole of business of another company (including a Mutual Company, foreign company or any other juridical person); or
(iv) Acquisition at any time within two years after the establishment of the Mutual Company (limited to the cases where it was incorporated pursuant to the provisions of Subsection 2; hereinafter the same shall apply in this item) of any asset that has existed since before its establishment and is to be used constantly for conducting its business; provided, however, that this shall not apply to the cases where the ratio of the amount listed in (a) to that listed in (b) does not exceed one fifth (or any smaller proportion prescribed by the articles of incorporation):
(a) The total book value of the property to be delivered in exchange for the asset;
(b) The amount of the net assets of the Mutual Company as calculated by the method specified by Cabinet Office Ordinance.
(2) The resolution set forth in the preceding paragraph shall be a resolution under paragraph (2) of the preceding Article.

Subsection 10 Miscellaneous Provisions

(Non-Member Contract)
Article 63 (1) A Mutual Company may, by provisions in its articles of incorporation, exclude from its membership the holders of non-participating policies or any other class of insurance policy specified by Cabinet Office Ordinance.
(2) The articles of incorporation set forth in the preceding paragraph shall specify the class of insurance policy to which that paragraph applies, as well as other particulars specified by Cabinet Office Ordinance.
(3) A Mutual Company shall not underwrite the insurance policies set forth in paragraph (1) over the limit specified by Cabinet Office Ordinance.
(4) Pursuant to the provisions of Cabinet Office Ordinance, a Mutual Company shall, if it underwrites any of the insurance policies set forth in paragraph (1), separate the accounting for such insurance policies from that for the insurance policies held by the members.
(5) The provisions of Part III, Chapter VI (Marine Insurance) of the Commercial Code shall apply mutatis mutandis to the insurance policies set forth in paragraph (1) (limited to those which fall under the category of a marine insurance contract). In this case, any other necessary technical change in interpretation shall be specified by Cabinet Order.
(6) In addition to what is prescribed in the preceding paragraphs, necessary particulars of the insurance policies set forth in paragraph (1) shall be specified by Cabinet Office Ordinance.

(Mutatis Mutandis Application of the Companies Act)

Article 63-2 Article 824 (Dissolution Order for a Company), Article 826 (Duty of a Government Agency, etc. to Give Notice to the Minister of Justice), Article 868, paragraph (1) (Jurisdiction over Non-Contentious Cases), Article 870 (Hearing of Statements) (limited to the portion pertaining to item (xiii)), the main text of Article 871 (Appending of the Reason), Article 872 (Immediate Appeal) (limited to the portion pertaining to item (iv)), the main text of Article 873 (Stay of Execution of the Judicial Decision of the Prior Instance), Article 875 (Exclusion from Application of the Provisions of the Non-Contentious Cases Procedures Act), Article 876 (Supreme Court Rules), Article 904 (Participation of the Minister of Justice) and Article 937, paragraph (1) (Commissioning of Registration by a Judicial Decision) (limited to the portion pertaining to sub-item (b) of item (iii)) of the Companies Act shall apply mutatis mutandis to an order for dissolution of a Mutual Company; Article 825 (Special Provisions on a Temporary Restraining Order Concerning Property of a Company), Article 868, paragraph (1), Article 870 (limited to the portion pertaining to item (ii)), Article 871, Article 872 (limited to the portions pertaining to items (i) and (iv)), Article 873, Article 874 (Restrictions on Appeal) (limited to the portions pertaining to items (ii) and (iii)), Article 875, Article 876, Article 905 and Article 906 (Special Provisions on a Temporary Restraining Order Concerning Property of a Company) of said Act shall apply mutatis mutandis to preservation of properties of a Mutual Company in case where a petition under Article 824, paragraph (1) of that Act as applied mutatis mutandis pursuant to this Article has been filed. In this case, technical replacement of terms as may be necessary shall be specified by Cabinet Order.

(Registration of Incorporation)

Article 64 (1) A Mutual Company shall complete its registration of incorporation at the location of its principal office within two weeks from the date of conclusion of the Organizational Meeting (or from the date of resignation of the incorporators pursuant to the provisions of Article 30-12, paragraph (3)).

(2) The following particulars shall be registered in the registration under the preceding paragraph:

(i) Particulars listed in Article 23, paragraph (1), items (i), (ii) and (iv) to (vii) inclusive;
(ii) The location of the offices;
(iii) The names of the directors;
(iv) The name and address of the representative director (excluding the cases set forth in item (xi));
(v) If the company is a company with accounting advisors, that fact, and the names of the accounting advisors and the place set forth in Article 378, paragraph (1) of the Companies Act as applied mutatis mutandis pursuant to Article 53-17;
(vi) If the company is a company with auditors, that fact and the names of the company auditors;
(vii) If the company is a company with a board of company auditors, that fact, and if there are outside auditors among its auditors, that fact;
(viii) If the company is a company with accounting auditors, that fact and the names of the accounting auditors;
(ix) The name of a person appointed pursuant to the provisions of Article 53-12, paragraph (4) temporarily to carry out the duties of an accounting auditor;
(x) If it is stipulated that the special directors (meaning the special directors as defined in Article 373, paragraph (1) of the Companies Act; the same shall apply hereinafter) may adopt a resolution under that paragraph as applied mutatis mutandis pursuant to Article 53-16, the following particulars:

Art.64   6 Insurance Business Act, Part II, Chap.II, Sec.2

    (a) That it is stipulated that the special directors may adopt a resolution under Article 373, paragraph (1) of the Companies Act as applied mutatis mutandis pursuant to Article 53-16,
    (b) The names of the special directors, and
    (c) The fact that any outside directors among the directors, are outside directors;
 (xi) If the company is a company with Committees, that fact and the following particulars:
    (a) The fact that any outside directors among the directors, are outside directors,
    (b) The names of the members of each committee and its executive officers, and
    (c) The name and address of its representative executive officer;
 (xii) Any provisions in the articles of incorporation for the exemption from liabilities of directors, executive officers, accounting advisors, company auditors or accounting auditors under Article 426, paragraph (1) of the Companies Act as applied mutatis mutandis pursuant to Article 53-36;
 (xiii) Any provisions in the articles of incorporation for the conclusion of contracts regarding the limit of the liabilities to be assumed by outside directors, accounting advisors, outside company auditors or accounting auditors under Article 427, paragraph (1) of the Companies Act as applied mutatis mutandis pursuant to Article 53-36;
 (xiv) If the provisions of the articles of incorporation set forth in the preceding item concern outside directors, the fact that any outside directors among the directors, are outside directors;
 (xv) If the provisions in the articles of incorporation set forth in item (xiii) concern outside auditors, the fact that any outside auditors among the auditors, are outside auditors;
 (xvi) If the relevant company seeks to take measures referred to in Article 54-7, paragraph (3), among the particulars necessary for allowing many and unspecified persons to receive the information contained in the balance sheet set forth in paragraph (1) of that Article, those specified by Cabinet Office Ordinance;
 (xvii) Provisions in the articles of incorporation for the Method of Public Notice under Article 23, paragraph (1), item (viii);
 (xviii) If the provisions in the articles of incorporation set forth in the preceding item specify electronic public notice as the Method of Public Notice, the following particulars:
    (a) Particulars prescribed in Article 911, paragraph (3), item (xxix), sub-item (a) (Registration of Incorporation of a Stock Company) of the Companies Act which are necessary for ensuring that the information made public by electronic public notice is available to many and unspecified persons; and
    (b) Any provisions in the articles of incorporation under the second sentence of Article 23, paragraph (3); and
 (xix) Any provisions in the articles of incorporation under the second sentence of Article 113 (including the cases where it is applied mutatis mutandis pursuant to Article 272-18).
(3) The provisions of Article 915, paragraph (1) (Registration of a Change), Article 916 (limited to the segment pertaining to item (i)) (Registration of Relocation of Head Office to a District under the Jurisdiction of Another Registry), Article 918 (Registration of a Manager) and Part VII, Chapter IV, Section 2, Subsection 2 (excluding Article 932) (Registration at the Location of a Branch Office) of the Companies Act shall apply mutatis mutandis to a Mutual Company; and the provisions of Article 917 (limited to the segment pertaining to item (i)) (Registration of a Provisional Disposition, etc. Suspending Execution of Duties) of that Act shall apply mutatis mutandis to the directors,

executive officers, accounting advisors, company auditors, representative director, committee members or representative executive officer of a Mutual Company. In this case, the term "the items of Article 911, paragraph (3) and the items of the three preceding Articles" in Article 915, paragraph (1) of that Act shall be deemed to be replaced with "the items of Article 64, paragraph (2) of the Insurance Business Act"; any other necessary technical change in interpretation shall be specified by Cabinet Order.

(Application for Registration of Incorporation)
Article 65 The following documents shall be attached to a written application under paragraph (1) of the preceding Article, in addition to the documents set forth in Article 18, Article 46 and Article 47, paragraph (3) of the Commercial Registration Act as applied mutatis mutandis pursuant to Article 67:
(i) Articles of incorporation;
(ii) A document certifying the offer to contribute funds or the contract set forth in Article 30;
(iii) List of prospective members;
(iv) In the case of a solicitation of members, a document certifying each prospective member's application for membership;
(v) Where the articles of incorporation include any detail or record of the particulars listed in the items of Article 24, paragraph (1), the following documents:
  (a) A document containing the investigative report of the inspector or the directors at incorporation (or the directors at incorporation and company auditors at incorporation, where the Mutual Company to be incorporated is a company with auditors) and annexed documents thereto;
  (b) In the case listed in Article 33, paragraph (10), item (ii) of the Companies Act as applied mutatis mutandis pursuant to Article 24, paragraph (2), a document certifying the market value of the securities set forth in that item; and
  (c) In the case listed in Article 33, paragraph (10), item (iii) of the Companies Act as applied mutatis mutandis pursuant to Article 24, paragraph (2), a document containing the verification set forth in that item and attached documents thereto;
(vi) A certified copy of any juridical decision on the report of the inspector;
(vii) A certificate of deposit of money under Article 30-4, paragraph (1);
(viii) A document regarding the appointment of the representative director at incorporation by the directors at incorporation;
(ix) Where the Mutual Company to be incorporated is a company with Committees, a document regarding the election of the executive officers at incorporation, and the appointment of the committee members at incorporation and representative executive officer at incorporation;
(x) Minutes of the Organizational Meeting;
(xi) A document certifying that the directors at incorporation, company auditors at incorporation and representative director at incorporation (or the directors at incorporation, committee members at incorporation, executive officers at incorporation and representative executive officer at incorporation, where the Mutual Company to be incorporated is a company with Committees) elected or appointed pursuant to the provisions of this Act have accepted the assumption of office;
(xii) Where accounting advisors at incorporation or accounting auditors at incorporation have been elected, the following documents:
  (a) A document certifying that they have accepted the assumption of office;
  (b) Where they are juridical persons, Certificates of Registered Particulars for such juridical persons, provided, however, that this shall not apply to the cases where

the principal offices of such juridical persons are located within the district under the jurisdiction of the relevant registry office; and
  (c) Where they are not juridical persons, a document certifying that the accounting advisors at incorporation meet the requirement of Article 333, paragraph (1) of the Companies Act as applied mutatis mutandis pursuant to Article 53-4, or that the accounting auditors at incorporation meet the requirement of Article 337, paragraph (1) of that Act as applied mutatis mutandis pursuant to Article 53-7; and
 (xiii) Where it is stipulated that the special directors may adopt a resolution under Article 373, paragraph (1) of the Companies Act as applied mutatis mutandis pursuant to Article 53-16, a document certifying the appointment of the special directors and their acceptance of the assumption of office.

(Registries)
Article 66 A registry office shall keep a registry of mutual companies.

(Mutatis Mutandis Application of the Companies Act and the Commercial Registration Act to the Registration of Mutual Companies)
Article 67 The provisions of Part VII, Chapter IV, Section 1 (excluding Article 907) (General Provisions) of the Companies Act, and the provisions of Article 1-3 to 5 inclusive (Registry Office, Delegation of Affairs, Suspension of Affairs, Registrar, Disqualification of Registrar), Article 7 to 15 inclusive (Prohibition on Carrying Out of Registries and Other Documents, Loss and Restoration of Registries, Prevention of Loss of Registry, etc., Issuance of Certificate of Registered Matters, Issuance of Documents Specifying Extract of Matters Registered, Inspection of Annexed Documents, Certificate of Seal Impression, Certification of Matters Required for Verification of Measures to Identify the Creator of Electromagnetic Records and Other Matters, Fees, Registration Upon Application by a Relevant Party, Registration upon Commission), Article 17 to 27 inclusive (Method of Application for Registration, Documents to Be Attached to Written Application, Electromagnetic Record to be Attached to Written Application, Submission of Seal Impression, Acceptance of Applications, Receipt, Order of Registration, Identity Confirmation by Registrar, Dismissal of Application, Registration to be Made After Lapse of Period for Filing Action, Change in Administrative Zone, etc., Prohibition of Registration of Identical Trade Name at Same Location), Article 31 (Registration of Exemption of Liabilities Upon Transfer of Enterprise or Business), Article 33 (Cancellation of Registration of Trade Name), Article 44 to 46 inclusive (Registration of Company's Manager, General Rules on Documents to be Attached), Article 47, paragraphs (1) and (3) (Registration of Incorporation), Article 48 to 55 inclusive (Registration to be Made at Location of Branch Offices, Registration of Relocation of Head Office, Registration of Change of Directors and Other Officers, Registration of Change of Person Who is to Temporarily Perform Duties of Accounting Auditor), and Article 132 to 148 inclusive (Correction, Application for Cancellation, Ex Officio Cancellation, Exclusion from Application of the Administrative Procedure Act, Exclusion from Application of the Act on Access to Information Held by Administrative Organs, Exclusion from Application of the Act on Protection of Personal Information Held by Administrative Organs, Request for Review, Handling of Request for Review Case, Exclusion from Application of the Administrative Appeal Act, Delegation to Ordinance of the Ministry) of the Commercial Registration Act shall apply mutatis mutandis to a registration regarding a Mutual Company. In this case, the terms "trade name," "business office (or, in a company, head office; hereinafter the same shall apply in this Article" and "business office pertaining to" in Article 27 of the latter Act shall

be deemed to be replaced with "trade name or name," "principal office" and "principal office pertaining to," respectively; the term "shareholders' meeting or class shareholders' meeting" in Article 46, paragraph (2) of that Act shall be deemed to be replaced with "general members' council (or General Representative Members' Council, where the company has such a council)"; the terms "Article 319, paragraph (1) (including the cases where it is applied mutatis mutandis pursuant to Article 325 of the Companies Act) or Article 370 (including the cases where it is applied mutatis mutandis pursuant to Article 490, paragraph (5) of that Act) of the Companies Act" and "shareholders' meeting or class shareholder meeting" in Article 46, paragraph (3) of that Act shall be deemed to be replaced with "Article 319, paragraph (1) of the Companies Act as applied mutatis mutandis pursuant to Article 41, paragraph (1) of the Insurance Business Act, or Article 370 of the Companies Act as applied mutatis mutandis pursuant to Article 53-16 or 180-15 of the Insurance Business Act" and "general members' council", respectively; the term "Article 416, paragraph (4) of the Companies Act" in Article 46, paragraph (4) shall be deemed to be replaced with "Article 53-30, paragraph (4) of the Insurance Business Act"; and the terms "head office" and "branch offices" in the provisions of Article 48 to 53 inclusive of that Act shall be deemed to be replaced with "principal office" and "secondary offices," respectively; any other necessary technical change in interpretation shall be specified by Cabinet Order.

(Mutatis Mutandis Application of the Companies Act on Electronic Public Notice)

Article 67-2 The provisions of Article 940, paragraphs (1) and (3) (Public Notice Period, etc. of Electronic Public Notice), Article 941 (Electronic Public Notice Investigation), Article 946 (Obligation, etc. of Investigation), Article 947 (Cases Where an Electronic Public Notice Investigation Is Unable to Be Carried Out), Article 951, paragraph (2) (Retention and Inspection, etc. of Financial Statements, etc.), Article 953 (Order for Improvement), and Article 955 (Statements, etc. in an Investigation Record Book, etc.) of the Companies Act shall apply mutatis mutandis to the cases where a Mutual Company gives public notice under this Act or any other Act in the form of electronic public notice. In this case, the terms "Article 440, paragraph (1)" and "annual shareholders' meeting" in Article 940, paragraph (1), item (ii) of that Act shall be deemed to be replaced with "Article 54-7, paragraph (1) of the Insurance Business Act" and "annual general members' council meeting (or annual General Representative Members' Council Meeting, where the company has such a council)," respectively; the term "the preceding two paragraphs" in Article 940, paragraph (3) of that Act shall be deemed to be replaced with "paragraph (1)"; and the term "public notice under this Act or any other Act (excluding the public notice under Article 440, paragraph (1)" in Article 941 of that Act shall be deemed to be replaced with "public notice under the Insurance Business Act (excluding the public notice under Article 54-7, paragraph (1) of that Act"; any other necessary technical change in interpretation shall be specified by Cabinet Order.

Section 3 Entity Conversion
Subsection 1 Entity Conversion from Stock Company to Mutual Company

(Entity Conversion)
Article 68 (1) A stock Insurance Company may convert to a mutual Insurance Company.
(2) A Stock Company that is a Low-Cost, Short-Term Insurer may convert to a Mutual Company that is a Low-Cost, Short-Term Insurer.

Art.69　　⑥ Insurance Business Act, Part II, Chap.II, Sec.3

(3) Any entity conversion under the preceding two paragraphs (hereinafter referred to as "Entity Conversion" in this Subsection) shall require a solicitation of funds in order to raise the total amount of the funds of the Mutual Company after the Entity Conversion to or over the amount specified in one of the following items depending on the case:
  (i) Entity Conversion under paragraph (1): the amount specified by Cabinet Order set forth in Article 6, paragraph (1); or
  (ii) Entity Conversion under the preceding paragraph: the amount specified by Cabinet Order set forth in Article 272-4, paragraph (1), item (ii).
(4) The total amount of the funds set forth in the preceding paragraph may be comprised in whole or in Part of a Reserves set aside at the time of Entity Conversion. In this case, the converting company shall not be required to solicit funds under that paragraph to the extent covered by the reserve.
(5) The Reserves set forth in the preceding paragraph shall be deemed to be the reserves for redemption of funds, to which the provisions of this Act (excluding Article 56) shall apply.
(6) In the case of an Entity Conversion, the converting company may set aside a deficiency reserves in addition to the reserves set forth in paragraph (4).

(Authorization of Entity Conversion Plan)
Article 69 (1) A Stock Company shall, if it seeks to convert to a Mutual Company, prepare an Entity Conversion plan to be approved by a resolution at a shareholders' meeting.
(2) The resolution set forth in the preceding paragraph shall be a resolution under Article 309, paragraph (2) (Resolution of shareholders' meetings) of the Companies Act.
(3) A Stock Company, if it seeks to adopt a resolution under paragraph (1), shall provide an outline of the Entity Conversion plan in the notice to be given pursuant to Article 299, paragraph (1) (Notices of Convocation for Shareholders' Meetings) of the Companies Act.
(4) A Stock Company shall detail the following particulars in its Entity Conversion plan:
  (i) The total amount of funds of the Mutual Company to be established by the Entity Conversion (hereinafter referred to as "Converted Mutual Company" in this Subsection);
  (ii) The amounts of the reserves set forth in paragraph (4) of the preceding Article and of the deficiency reserves set forth in paragraph (6) of that Article;
  (iii) The particulars of compensation to shareholders and holders of share options;
  (iv) The particulars of the rights of Policyholders after the Entity Conversion; and
  (v) The day on which the Entity Conversion takes effect (hereinafter referred to as "Effective Date" in this Subsection) and other particulars specified by Cabinet Office Ordinance.
(5) A Stock Company which has adopted a resolution under paragraph (1) shall, within two weeks from the date of the resolution, notify each of the registered pledgees of shares and registered pledgees of share options of the planned Entity Conversion.
(6) A notice under the preceding paragraph may be replaced by a public notice.
(7) The provisions of Article 219, paragraph (1) (limited to the segment pertaining to item (v)), (2) and (3) (Public Notice in Relation to Submission of Share Certificate), Article 220 (Cases where Share Certificates cannot be Submitted), and Article 293, paragraph (1) (limited to the segment pertaining to item (ii)) (Public Notice in relation to Submission of Share Option Certificate) of the Companies Act shall apply mutatis mutandis to a converting Stock Company. In this case, any other necessary technical change in interpretation shall be specified by Cabinet Order.

(Retention and Inspection, etc. of Documents Related to Entity Conversion Plans, etc.)

Article 69-2 (1) A converting Stock Company shall, for the period from the Day on Which the Entity Conversion plan Began to Be Kept to the Effective Date, keep at each of its business offices the documents or electromagnetic records in which the details of the Entity Conversion plan and any other particulars specified by Cabinet Office Ordinance are detailed or recorded.

(2) The term "the Day on Which the Entity Conversion plan Began to Be Kept" in the preceding paragraph refers to the earliest of the date listed in the following items:

(i) The day two weeks before the date of the shareholders' meeting set forth in paragraph (1) of the preceding Article (or, in the case of Article 319, paragraph (1) (Omission of Resolution of Shareholders' Meetings) of the Companies Act, the date of proposal under that paragraph);

(ii) Where the converting Stock Company has issued share options, the date of notice under Article 777, paragraph (3) of the Companies Act as applied mutatis mutandis pursuant to Article 71 or the date of public notice set forth in Article 777, paragraph (4) of that Act as applied mutatis mutandis pursuant to Article 71, whichever is earlier; or

(iii) The date of public notice under paragraph (2) of the following Article.

(3) The creditors of a converting Stock Company, such as shareholders and Policyholders, may make the following requests to the company at any time during its operating hours; provided, however, that they pay the fees determined by the Stock Company in making a request falling under item (ii) or (iv):

(i) A request to inspect the documents set forth in paragraph (1);

(ii) A request to be issued a certified copy or extract of the documents set forth in paragraph (1);

(iii) A request to inspect anything that shows the particulars recorded in the electromagnetic records set forth in paragraph (1) in a manner specified by Cabinet Office Ordinance; or

(iv) A request to be provided with the particulars recorded in the electromagnetic records set forth in paragraph (1) by the electromagnetic means determined by the converting Stock Company, or to be issued a document detailing such particulars.

(4) The Converted Mutual Company shall, for six months from the Effective Date, keep at each of its offices the documents or electromagnetic records in which the details of the Entity Conversion plan and any other particulars specified by Cabinet Office Ordinance are detailed or recorded.

(5) Policyholders or other creditors of a Converted Mutual Company may make the following requests to the company at any time during its business hours; provided, however, that they pay the fees determined by the Converted Mutual Company in making a request falling under item (ii) or (iv):

(i) A request to inspect the documents set forth in the preceding paragraph;

(ii) A request for a certified copy or extract of the documents set forth in the preceding paragraph;

(iii) A request to inspect anything that shows the particulars recorded in the electromagnetic records set forth in the preceding paragraph in a manner specified by Cabinet Office Ordinance; or

(iv) A request to be provided with the particulars recorded in the electromagnetic records set forth in the preceding paragraph by the electromagnetic means determined by the Converted Mutual Company, or to be issued a document detailing such particulars.

Art.70～71　⑥ Insurance Business Act, Part II, Chap.II, Sec.3

(Objections of Creditors)

Article 70 (1) Policyholders or other creditors of a converting Stock Company may state to the company their objections to the Entity Conversion.

(2) A converting Stock Company shall publish the following particulars in the Official Gazette and by the Method of Public Notice prescribed by its articles of incorporation; provided, however, that the period for item (iv) may not be shorter than one month:
(i) The fact that an Entity Conversion will be carried out;
(ii) The name and address of the Converted Mutual Company;
(iii) Particulars specified by Cabinet Office Ordinance as pertaining to the financial statements of the converting Stock Company;
(iv) The fact that Policyholders or other creditors of the converting Stock Company may state their objections within a certain period of time; and
(v) In addition to what is listed in the preceding items, particulars specified by Cabinet Office Ordinance.

(3) Where no Policyholders or other creditors have stated their objections within the period set forth in item (iv) of the preceding paragraph, such Policyholders or creditors shall be deemed to have approved the Entity Conversion.

(4) Where any Policyholder or other creditor has stated his/her objection under paragraph (2), item (iv), the converting Stock Company shall make payment or provide equivalent security to such Policyholder or other creditor, or entrust equivalent property to a trust company, etc. for the purpose of ensuring that such Policyholder or other creditor receive the payment; provided, however, that this shall not apply to the cases where the Entity Conversion poses no risk of harming the interest of such Policyholder or other creditor;

(5) The provisions of the preceding paragraph shall not apply to the Policyholders or any rights held by other persons pertaining to insurance contracts (other than Insurance Claims, etc.).

(6) Any resolution of authorization under Article 69, paragraph (1) shall be null and void if the number of the Policyholders who have stated their objections within the period set forth in paragraph (2), item (iv) (excluding the holders of policies under which Insurance Claims, etc. had already arisen at the time of public notice under the paragraph (2) (but limited to those policies that would be terminated with the payment of the Insurance Claims, etc.); hereinafter the same shall apply in this paragraph and the following paragraph) exceeds one fifth of the total number of Policyholders, and the amount specified by Cabinet Office Ordinance as the credits (other than Insurance Claims, etc.) belonging to the insurance contracts of the Policyholders who have stated such objections exceeds one fifth of the total amount of credits belonging to the Policyholders.

(7) An Entity Conversion carried out pursuant to the provisions of the preceding paragraphs shall also be effective against the Policyholders who have stated their objections under the preceding paragraph and other persons who hold any right (other than Insurance Claims, etc.) pertaining to the insurance contracts involving the Policyholders.

(8) In addition to what is provided for in the preceding paragraphs, necessary particulars for the application of those provisions shall be specified by Cabinet Order.

(Demand for Purchase of Share Options, etc.)

Article 71 The provisions of Article 777 (Demand for Purchase of Share Options), Article 778 (Determination on Value of Share Options, etc.), Article 868, paragraph (1) (Jurisdiction over Non-Contentious Cases), Article 870 (limited to the segment pertaining to item (iv)) (Hearing of Statements), the main clause of Article 871 (Appending of the Reason), Article 872 (limited to the segment pertaining to item (iv)) (Immediate Appeal), the main clause of Article 873 (Stay of Execution of the Judicial Decision of the Prior Instance), Article 875 (Mandatory Consolidation of Hearings, etc.) and Article 876 (Supreme Court Rules) of the Companies Act shall apply mutatis mutandis to the cases where the converting Stock Company has issued share options. In this case, the term "converted membership company" in Article 778, paragraph (1), Article 778, paragraph (2), and Article 778, paragraph (4) of that Act shall be deemed to be replaced with "Converted Mutual Company (meaning a Converted Mutual Company as defined in Article 69, paragraph (4), item (i) of the Insurance Business Act"; any other necessary technical change in interpretation shall be specified by Cabinet Order.

(Contract during Procedure of Entity Conversion)
Article 72 (1) A converting Stock Company shall, if it seeks to conclude an insurance contract on or after the day following the date of public notice under Article 70, paragraph (2), notify the prospective Policyholder to the effect that the company is going through the procedure of Entity Conversion to obtain his/her consent.
(2) A Policyholder who has given his/her consent under the preceding paragraph shall not be deemed to be a Policyholder for the purpose of applying the following Article to Article 77 inclusive.

(Policyholders Meeting)
Article 73 Where the number of the Policyholders who have stated their objections within the period set forth in Article 70, paragraph (2), item (iv) or the amount of their credits as specified by Cabinet Office Ordinance set forth in paragraph (6) of the same Article has not exceeded the proportion specified in that paragraph, the directors of the converting Stock Company shall convene a policyholders meeting without delay following the completion of the procedure prescribed in the same Article.

(Method of Adopting Resolution, etc.)
Article 74 (1) Each Policyholder shall be entitled to one vote at the policyholders meeting.
(2) A resolution of the policyholders meeting is adopted by a three-quarter majority vote of the attending Policyholders at a session where at least half of the Policyholders are present.
(3) The provisions of Article 67, paragraph (1) (Determination to Call Organizational Meetings), Article 68 (excluding the items in paragraph (2) and paragraphs (5) to (7) inclusive) (Notices of Calling of Organizational Meetings), Articles 70 and 71 (Giving of Organizational Meeting Reference Documents and Voting Forms), Article 74 to 76 inclusive (Proxy Voting, Voting in Writing, Voting by Electromagnetic Method), Article 78 to 80 inclusive (Accountability of Incorporators, Authority of Chairperson, Resolution for Postponement or Adjournment), Article 81, paragraphs (1) to (3) inclusive (Minutes) and Article 316, paragraph (1) (Investigation of Materials Submitted to the Shareholders' Meeting) of the Companies Act shall apply mutatis mutandis to the policyholders meeting; and the provisions of Article 830 (Action for a Declaratory Judgment as to the Absence or Invalidity of a Resolution of a Shareholders' Meeting, etc.), Article 831 (Action to Revoke a Resolution of a Shareholders' Meeting, etc.), Article 834 (limited to the segment pertaining to items (xvi) and (xvii)) (Defendant), Article 835, paragraph (1) (Jurisdiction over Actions), Article 836, paragraphs (1) and (3) (Order to Provide Security), Article 837 (Mandatory Consolidation of Oral Arguments, etc.), Article 838 (Persons Affected by a Judgment Being Upheld), Article 846 (Liability for Damages Where a Judgment Is Entered Against the Plaintiff), and Article 937,

paragraph (1) (limited to the segment pertaining to item (i), sub-item (g)) (Commissioning of Registration by a Judicial Decision) of that Act shall apply mutatis mutandis to an action for a declaratory judgment as to the absence or invalidity of a resolution of the policyholders meeting and to an action to rescind a resolution of the policyholders meeting. In this case, the terms "incorporators," "shareholders at incorporation" and "Stock Company" in those provisions shall be deemed to be replaced with "converting Stock Company," "policyholders" and "Mutual Company," respectively; the term "in the following cases" in Article 68, paragraph (2) of that Act shall be deemed to be deleted; the term "head office" in Article 74, paragraph (6) of that Act shall be deemed to be replaced with "principal office"; the term "shareholders" in Article 74, paragraph (7) of that Act shall be deemed to be replaced with "members"; and the terms "a Shareholder, etc. (or, in cases where the Shareholders' Meeting, etc. set forth respectively in each such item is an Organizational Meeting or a Class Organizational Meetings, a Shareholder, etc., a Shareholder at Incorporation, a Director at Incorporation or a Company Auditor at Incorporation)" and "a director, company auditor or liquidator pursuant to the provisions of Article 346(1) (including cases where it is applied mutatis mutandis pursuant to Article 479(4)), and in cases where such resolution is a resolution of an Organizational Meeting or Class Organizational Meeting, it shall include a Director at Incorporation or a Company Auditor at Incorporation)" in Article 831, paragraph (1) of that Act shall be deemed to be replaced with "policyholders, directors, company auditors or liquidators (or, in a company with Committees, Policyholders, directors, executive officers or liquidators" and "directors, company auditors or liquidators," respectively; any other necessary technical change in interpretation shall be specified by Cabinet Order.

(4) It shall be sufficient for a notice or demand to a Policyholder to be sent by the converting Stock Company to the place or address which the Policyholder has notified to the Stock Company for the receipt of notices or demands.

(5) The notice or demand set forth in the preceding paragraph shall be deemed to have arrived at the time when such notice or demand would normally have arrived.

(6) The provisions of the preceding two paragraphs shall apply mutatis mutandis to the delivery of documents to Policyholders in giving a notice under Article 68, paragraph (1) of the Companies Act as applied mutatis mutandis pursuant to paragraph (3) and provision by electromagnetic means of the particulars that are required to be included in such documents. In this case, the term "to have arrived" in the preceding paragraph shall be deemed to be replaced with "to have been effected by delivery of such document or provision of such particulars by electromagnetic means"; and any other necessary technical change in interpretation shall be specified by Cabinet Order.

(Report of Directors)
Article 75 The directors shall report to the policyholders meeting the particulars related to an Entity Conversion.

(Resolution of Policyholders Meeting)
Article 76 (1) The policyholders meeting shall, in its resolutions, adopt the articles of incorporation of the Converted Mutual Company and other particulars required for the organization of the Converted Mutual Company, and elect the persons to serve as directors of the Converted Mutual Company.

(2) In the following cases, the policyholders meeting shall elect the persons set forth in the relevant items:
  (i) Where the Converted Mutual Company is a company with accounting advisors, the persons to serve as accounting advisors of the Converted Mutual Company;

(ii) Where the Converted Mutual Company is a company with auditors, the persons to serve as company auditors of the Converted Mutual Company; and
   (iii) Where the Converted Mutual Company is a company with accounting auditors, the persons to serve as accounting auditors of the Converted Mutual Company.
(3) The resolution set forth in Article 69, paragraph (1) may be amended by a resolution under paragraph (1); provided, however, that such amendment may not harm the interest of the creditors of the converting Stock Company.
(4) Any amendment under the preceding paragraph that poses the risk of causing any damage to the interest of shareholders shall be subject to the authorization of the shareholders' meeting. In this case, the provisions of Article 69, paragraph (2) shall apply mutatis mutandis.
(5) The resolution of authorization set forth in Article 69, paragraph (1) shall lose its effect without the authorization of the shareholders' meeting set forth in the preceding paragraph.
(6) The policyholders meeting may not adopt a resolution on any other matter than that listed in Article 67, paragraph (1), item (ii) of the Companies Act as applied mutatis mutandis pursuant to Article 74, paragraph (3); provided, however, that this shall not apply to a decision on the articles of incorporation of the Converted Mutual Company or on any other particular that is necessary for the organization of the Converted Mutual Company, and the election of the persons specified in paragraphs (1) and (2).

(General Council of Representative Policyholders)
Article 77 (1) The converting Stock Company may, by a resolution under Article 69, paragraph (1), establish an administrative organ composed of representative members elected from among the Policyholders (hereinafter referred to as "General Council of Representative Policyholders") in lieu of the policyholders meeting.
(2) The resolution set forth in the preceding paragraph shall specify the particulars specified by Cabinet Office Ordinance, such as the number and election method of representative members.
(3) Policyholders of a converting Stock Company (excluding the holders of the policies for which Insurance Claims, etc. had already arisen at the time of public notice under the following paragraph (but limited to those policies that would be terminated with the payment of the Insurance Claims, etc.); the same shall apply in that paragraph and paragraph (5)) may state to the converting Stock Company their objections to the resolution set forth in paragraph (1).
(4) A converting Stock Company shall give public notice of the following particulars within two weeks from the date of the resolution set forth in paragraph (1); provided, however, that such period for item (ii) may not be shorter than one month:
   (i) Contents of the resolution set forth in paragraph (1);
   (ii) The fact that Policyholders of the converting Stock Company may state their objections within a certain period of time; and
   (iii) In addition to what is listed in the preceding two items, particulars specified by Cabinet Office Ordinance.
(5) Any resolution under paragraph (1) shall be null and void if the number of Policyholders who have stated their objections within the period set forth in item (ii) of the preceding paragraph exceeds one fifth of the total number of Policyholders, and the amount specified by Cabinet Office Ordinance as the credits (other than Insurance Claims, etc.) belonging to the insurance contracts of the Policyholders who have stated such objections exceeds one fifth of the total amount of credits belonging to the Policyholders.
(6) The provisions of Article 44-2 (excluding the second sentence of paragraph (3)) and

Article 73 to the preceding Article inclusive shall apply mutatis mutandis to the General Council of Representative Policyholders. In this case, the term "the preceding paragraph" in Article 310, paragraph (2) of the Companies Act as applied mutatis mutandis pursuant to the first sentence of Article 44-2, paragraph (3) and the term "paragraph (1)" in Article 310, paragraph (3) shall be deemed to be replaced with "Article 44-2, paragraph (1) of the Insurance Business Act"; the term "Article 299, paragraph (3)" in Article 310, paragraph (4) shall be deemed to be replaced with "Article 68, paragraph (3) as applied mutatis mutandis pursuant to Article 74, paragraph (3) of the Insurance Business Act"; the term "shareholders (excluding the shareholders who may not exercise their voting rights on all matters which may be resolved at the shareholders' meeting under the preceding paragraph. The same shall apply hereinafter in paragraph (4) of the following Article and in Article 312, paragraph (5))" in Article 310, paragraph (7) shall be deemed to be replaced with "Policyholders or members"; the term "Article 74 to 76 inclusive" in Article 74, paragraph (3) shall be deemed to be replaced with "Articles 75 and 76"; and the term "Policyholder" in Article 74, paragraph (4) shall be deemed to be replaced with "representative member"; any other necessary technical change in interpretation shall be specified by Cabinet Order.

(Solicitation of Funds in Entity Conversion)
Article 78 (1) A converting Stock Company shall, if it seeks to solicit additional funds for the Converted Mutual Company, solicit the required amount of such funds without delay following the conclusion of the policyholders meeting or General Council of Representative Policyholders (or, in the case of Article 76, paragraph (4), following the authorization of the shareholders' meeting set forth in that paragraph).
(2) A converting Stock Company shall notify the persons who seek to offer contributions to its funds in response to a solicitation under the preceding paragraph of the following particulars:
(i) Particulars listed in Article 23, paragraph (1), item (ii) and items (iv) to (vi) inclusive;
(ii) Amount of the additional funds to be solicited, the rights enjoyed by the contributors to the funds and the method of redemption of the funds;
(iii) Payment date; and
(iv) Location of the banks, etc. where the payment of contribution of funds is handled.
(3) The provisions of Article 28, paragraphs (2) to (6) inclusive, Article 29 to 30-2 inclusive, Article 30-3 (excluding paragraphs (2) and (3)), and Article 30-5, paragraphs (2) and (3) shall apply mutatis mutandis to a solicitation under (1). In this case, the term "incorporators" in those provisions shall be deemed to be replaced with "converting Stock Company"; the terms "funds solicited at incorporation" and "funds of a Mutual Company at incorporation" in those provisions shall be deemed to be replaced with "funds solicited under Article 78, paragraph (1)"; the term "the items in paragraph (1)" in Article 28, paragraph (4) shall be deemed to be replaced with "the items of Article 78, paragraph (2)"; the term "the preceding two Articles" in Article 30 shall be deemed to be replaced with "Article 78, paragraph (2) (excluding item (iii)) and Article 28, paragraphs (2) to (6) inclusive as applied mutatis mutandis pursuant to Article 30, paragraph (3)"; the term "Mutual Company thus established" in Article 30-4, paragraph (4) shall be deemed to be replaced with "Converted Mutual Company"; and the term "After the establishment of the Mutual Company" in Article 30-5, paragraph (3) shall be deemed to be replaced with "After the Entity Conversion"; any other necessary technical change in interpretation shall be specified by Cabinet Order.

(Policyholders Meeting after Solicitation of Funds)

Article 79 (1) In the case of paragraph (1) of the preceding Article, the directors of the converting Stock Company shall, without delay after the total amount of the funds solicited under that paragraph has been paid in, convene a second policyholders meeting or General Council of Representative Policyholders.

(2) The persons to serve as directors (or directors and company auditors, where the Converted Mutual Company is a company with auditors) of the Converted Mutual Company shall investigate whether the total amount of the funds solicited under paragraph (1) of the preceding Article has been subscribed for and paid in, and report the result to the policyholders meeting or General Council of Representative Policyholders set forth in the preceding paragraph.

(3) The provisions of Article 94 (Special Provisions in case Directors at Incorporation are Incorporators) of the Companies Act shall apply mutatis mutandis to the policyholders meeting or General Council of Representative Policyholders set forth in paragraph (1), where all or some of the persons to serve as directors of the Converted Mutual Company are directors or executive officers of the converting Stock Company. In this case, the term "the particulars listed in the items of paragraph (1) of the preceding Article" in paragraph (1) of the same Article shall be deemed to be replaced with "whether the total amount of the funds solicited under Article 78, paragraph (1) of the Insurance Business Act has been subscribed for and paid in"; any other necessary technical change in interpretation shall be specified by Cabinet Order.

(Authorization of Entity Conversion)

Article 80 (1) An Entity Conversion shall not take effect without the authorization of the Prime Minister.

(2) Whenever an application has been filed for the authorization referred to in the preceding paragraph, the Prime Minister shall examine whether it conforms to the following standards:
  (i) The Converted Mutual Company would have a sufficient financial basis to execute the business of an Insurance Company, etc. in a sound and efficient manner;
  (ii) The Entity Conversion poses no risk of harming the rights of Policyholders; and
  (iii) In addition to what is listed in the preceding two items, the Entity Conversion poses no risk of precluding the sound business operation of an Insurance Company, etc.

(Effectuation, etc. of Entity Conversion)

Article 81 (1) A converting Stock Company shall become a Mutual Company on the Effective Date.

(2) The shares and share options of a converting Stock Company shall become null and void on the Effective Date.

(3) The Policyholders of a converting Stock Company shall become members of the Converted Mutual Company on the Effective Date.

(4) The provisions of the preceding three paragraphs shall not apply to the cases where a procedure under Article 70 has not been completed or where the Entity Conversion has been voluntarily abandoned.

(Public Notice, etc. of Entity Conversion)

Article 82 (1) A Converted Mutual Company shall, without delay following the Entity Conversion, give public notice of the effect that an Entity Conversion has been carried out and publish the particulars specified by Cabinet Office Ordinance. The same shall apply to the cases where a converting Stock Company has voluntarily abandoned the

planned Entity Conversion after giving a public notice under Article 70, paragraph (2).
(2) A Converted Mutual Company shall, for six months following the Effective Date, keep at each of its offices the documents or electromagnetic records in which the progress of the procedures under Article 70 and any other particulars specified by Cabinet Office Ordinance as being involved in an Entity Conversion are detailed or recorded.
(3) Policyholders or other creditors of a Converted Mutual Company may make the following requests to the company at any time during its business hours; provided, however, that they pay the fees determined by the Mutual Company in making a request falling under item (ii) or (iv):
(i) A request to inspect the documents set forth in the preceding paragraph;
(ii) A request for a certified copy or extract of the documents set forth in the preceding paragraph;
(iii) A request to inspect anything that shows the particulars recorded in the electromagnetic records set forth in the preceding paragraph in a manner specified by Cabinet Office Ordinance; or
(iv) A request to be provided with the particulars recorded in the electromagnetic records set forth in the preceding paragraph by the electromagnetic means determined by the Converted Mutual Company, or to be issued a document detailing such particulars.

(Pledge on Former Shares)
Article 83 The provisions of Article 151 (excluding the items) and Article 154 (Effect of pledge of shares) of the Companies Act shall apply mutatis mutandis to the monies which the shareholders are entitled to receive as a result of any Entity Conversion of a Stock Company. In this case, any other necessary technical change in interpretation shall be specified by Cabinet Order.

(Registration)
Article 84 (1) Where a Stock Company has carried out an Entity Conversion, the converting Stock Company shall make a registration of dissolution within two weeks from the date of Entity Conversion at the location of its head office and within three weeks from said date at the location of its branch offices; and the Converted Mutual Company shall complete registration of incorporation within two weeks from the date of Entity Conversion at the location of its principal office and within three weeks from said date at the location of its secondary offices.
(2) The following documents shall be attached to a written application for the registration of incorporation of a Mutual Company under the preceding paragraph, in addition to those specified in Articles 18, 19 and 46 of the Commercial Registration Act as applied mutatis mutandis pursuant to Article 67:
(i) Entity Conversion plan;
(ii) Articles of incorporation;
(iii) A document certifying that a public notice under Article 70, paragraph (2) has been given;
(iv) The minutes of the shareholders' meeting and policyholders meeting (or General Council of Representative Policyholders, where the company has such a council);
(v) Where any Policyholder or other creditor has stated his/her objection under Article 70, paragraph (4), a document certifying that the company has made payment or provided equivalent security to such Policyholder or other creditor, or entrusted equivalent property to a trust company, etc. for the purpose of ensuring that such Policyholder or other creditor receive the payment, or a document certifying that the Entity Conversion poses no risk of harming the interest of such Policyholder

or other creditor;
(vi) A document certifying that the number of Policyholders who have stated their objections under Article 70, paragraph (6) has not exceeded one fifth of the total number of Policyholders, or a document certifying that the amount specified by Cabinet Office Ordinance set forth in that paragraph as the credits belonging to such Policyholders has not exceeded one fifth of the total amount set forth in that paragraph;
(vii) Where the converting Stock Company is a company issuing share certificates, a document certifying that a public notice has been given under the main clause of Article 219, paragraph (1) of the Companies Act as applied mutatis mutandis pursuant to Article 69, paragraph (7), or a document certifying that the company has not issued share certificates for all of the shares.
(viii) Where the converting Stock Company has issued share options, a document certifying that a public notice has been given under Article 293, paragraph (1) of the Companies Act as applied mutatis mutandis pursuant to Article 69, paragraph (7), or a document certifying that the company has not issued any stock option certificate under that paragraph.
(ix) A document certifying that the directors (or directors and company auditors, where the Converted Mutual Company is a company with auditors) of the Converted Mutual Company have accepted the assumption of office;
(x) Where accounting advisors or accounting auditors have been elected for the Converted Mutual Company, the following documents;
 (a) A document certifying that they have accepted the assumption of office,
 (b) Where they are juridical persons, Certificates of Registered Particulars for such juridical persons, provided, however, that this shall not apply to the cases where the principal offices of such juridical persons are located within the district under the jurisdiction of the relevant registry office, and
 (c) Where they are not juridical persons, a document certifying that the accounting advisors meet the requirement of Article 333, paragraph (1) of the Companies Act as applied mutatis mutandis pursuant to Article 53-4, or that the accounting auditors meet the requirement of Article 337, paragraph (1) of that Act as applied mutatis mutandis pursuant to Article 53-7;
(xi) Where funds have been solicited, a document certifying the offer to contribute funds or a contract under Article 30 as applied mutatis mutandis pursuant to Article 78, paragraph (3); and
(xii) Where funds have been solicited, a document certifying that payment has been made to the funds under Article 30-3, paragraph (1) as applied mutatis mutandis pursuant to Article 78, paragraph (3).
(3) Articles 76 and 78 (Registration of Entity Conversion) of the Commercial Registration Act shall apply mutatis mutandis to the case of paragraph (1). In this case, any other necessary technical change in interpretation shall be specified by Cabinet Order.

(Action to Invalidate an Entity Conversion)
Article 84-2 (1) The invalidity of an Entity Conversion may only be asserted in an action filed within six months from the Effective Date.
(2) An action to invalidate an Entity Conversion may only be filed by a person who was a shareholder, etc. (meaning a person who was a shareholder, director, company auditor or liquidator (or, in a company with Committees, a shareholder, director, executive officer or liquidator); hereinafter the same shall apply in this Section) of the converting Stock Company on the Effective Date, or a member, etc. (meaning a member, director, company auditor or liquidator (or, in a company with Committees, a member, director,

Art.85〜86　⑥ Insurance Business Act, Part II, Chap.II, Sec.3

executive officer or liquidator); hereinafter the same shall apply in this Section) or bankruptcy trustee of the Converted Mutual Company or a creditor of the Converted Mutual Company who has not approved of the Entity Conversion.
(3) An action to nullify an Entity Conversion is filed against the Converted Mutual Company.
(4) The provisions of Article 835, paragraph (1) (Jurisdiction over Actions), Article 836 to 839 inclusive (Order to Provide Security, Mandatory Consolidation of Oral Arguments, etc., Persons Affected by a Judgment Being Upheld), Article 846 (Liability for Damages Where a Judgment Is Entered Against the Plaintiff) and Article 937, paragraph (3) (limited to the segment pertaining to item (i)) (Commissioning of Registration by a Judicial Decision) of the Companies Act shall apply mutatis mutandis to an action to invalidate an Entity Conversion; the provisions of Article 840 (Effects of a Judgment of Invalidity of New Share Issue) of that Act shall apply mutatis mutandis to a judgment of invalidity of an Entity Conversion accompanied by the solicitation of funds set forth in Article 78, paragraph (1); and the provisions of Article 868, paragraph (1) (Jurisdiction over Non-Contentious Cases), the main clause of Article 871 (Appending of the Reason), Article 872 (limited to the segment pertaining to item (ii)) (Immediate Appeal), the main clause of Article 873 (Stay of Execution of the Judicial Decision of the Prior Instance), Article 875 to 877 inclusive (Mandatory Consolidation of Hearings, etc., Supreme Court Rules, Mandatory Consolidation of Hearings, etc.) and Article 878, paragraph (1) (Effects of a Judicial Decision) of that Act shall apply mutatis mutandis to an application under Article 840, paragraph (2) of that Act as applied mutatis mutandis pursuant to this paragraph. In this case, the term "shareholder" in Article 878, paragraph (1) shall be deemed to be replaced with "shareholder or member"; any other necessary technical change in interpretation shall be specified by Cabinet Order.

Subsection 2　Entity Conversion from Mutual Company to Stock Company

(Entity Conversion)
Article 85　(1) A mutual Insurance Company may convert to a stock Insurance Company.
(2) A Mutual Company that is a Low-Cost, Short-Term Insurer may convert to a Stock Company that is a Low-Cost, Short-Term Insurer.

(Authorization of Entity Conversion Plan)
Article 86　(1) A Mutual Company shall, if it seeks to carry out an Entity Conversion under the preceding Article (hereinafter referred to as "Entity Conversion" in this Subsection), prepare an Entity Conversion plan to be approved by a resolution of the general members' council (or General Representative Members' Council, where the company has such a council; hereinafter the same shall apply in this Subsection).
(2) The resolution set forth in the preceding paragraph shall be a resolution under Article 62, paragraph (2).
(3) A Mutual Company, if it seeks to adopt a resolution under paragraph (1), shall provide an outline of the Entity Conversion plan in the notice to be given pursuant to Article 299, paragraph (1) of the Companies Act as applied mutatis mutandis pursuant to Article 41, paragraph (1) or Article 49, paragraph (1).
(4) A Mutual Company shall prescribe the following particulars in its Entity Conversion plan:
 (i) The purpose, trade name, location of the head office and total number of authorized shares of the Stock Company to be established by the Entity Conversion (hereinafter referred to as "Converted Stock Company" in this Subsection);

(ii) In addition to what is listed in the preceding item, particulars specified by the articles of incorporation of the Converted Stock Company;
(iii) Names of the directors of the Converted Stock Company;
(iv) For each category set forth in the following, the corresponding particulars specified therein:
(a) Where the Converted Stock Company is a company with accounting advisors: the names of the persons to serve as accounting advisors of the Converted Stock Company,
(b) Where the Converted Stock Company is a company with auditors: the names of the company auditors of the Converted Stock Company, or
(c) Where the Converted Stock Company is a company with accounting auditors: the names of the accounting auditors of the Converted Stock Company;
(v) The number of shares (or the classes of share and the number of shares by class, where the Converted Stock Company is a company with class shares) to be acquired by the members of the converting Mutual Company or the method of calculating such number, and particulars of the capital and Reserves of the Converted Stock Company;
(vi) Particulars related to the allocation of the shares set forth in the preceding item to the members of the converting Mutual Company;
(vii) The amount of, and calculation method for, any money granted to the members of the converting Mutual Company;
(viii) Particulars related to the allocation of the money set forth in the preceding item to the members of the converting Mutual Company;
(ix) The method of selling any additional fraction of shares to be issued as a result of the allocation of shares to the members of the converting Mutual Company and any other particular specified by Cabinet Office Ordinance regarding such sale.
(x) The method of purchasing any fraction of shares arising under the preceding item and any other particular specified by Cabinet Office Ordinance regarding such purchase;
(xi) Particulars related to the rights of Policyholders after the Entity Conversion; and
(xii) The day on which the Entity Conversion takes effect (hereinafter referred to as "Effective Date" in this Subsection) and any other particular specified by Cabinet Office Ordinance.
(5) A Mutual Company shall, as a particular to be prescribed by the articles of incorporation pursuant to the provisions of item (ii) of the preceding paragraph, include in the Converted Stock Company's articles of incorporation a principle pertaining to the policy dividends set forth in Article 114, paragraph (1) (including the cases where it is applied mutatis mutandis pursuant to Article 272-18).

(Retention and Inspection, etc. of Documents Related to Entity Conversion Plans, etc.)

Article 87 (1) A converting Mutual Company shall, for the period ranging from the commencement date for the keeping of an Entity Conversion plan to the Effective Date, keep at each of its offices the documents or electromagnetic records in which the Entity Conversion plan and any other particulars specified by Cabinet Office Ordinance are detailed or recorded.
(2) The term "the commencement date for the keeping of an Entity Conversion plan" in the preceding paragraph refers to the date listed in any of the following items, whichever is earlier:
(i) The day that is two weeks before the date of the general members' council meeting set forth in paragraph (1) of the preceding Article (or, in the case of Article 319,

paragraph (1) of the Companies Act as applied mutatis mutandis pursuant to Article 41, paragraph (1), the date of proposal under that paragraph); or

(ii) The date of public notice under paragraph (2) of the following Article.

(3) Policyholders or other creditors of a converting Mutual Company may make the following requests to the company at any time during its business hours; provided, however, that they pay the fees determined by the Mutual Company in making a request falling under item (ii) or (iv):

(i) A request to inspect the documents set forth in paragraph (1);

(ii) A request for a certified copy or extract of the documents set forth in paragraph (1);

(iii) A request to inspect anything that shows the particulars recorded in the electromagnetic records set forth in paragraph (1) in a manner specified by Cabinet Office Ordinance; or

(iv) A request to be provided with the particulars recorded in the electromagnetic records set forth in paragraph (1) by the electromagnetic means determined by the converting Mutual Company, or to be issued a document detailing such particulars.

(4) The Converted Stock Company shall, for six months from the Effective Date, keep at each of its business offices the documents or electromagnetic records in which the details of the Entity Conversion plan and any other particulars specified by Cabinet Office Ordinance are detailed or recorded.

(5) The creditors of a Converted Stock Company, such as Shareholders and Policyholders, may make the following requests to the company at any time during its operating hours; provided, however, that they pay the fees determined by the Converted Stock Company in making a request falling under item (ii) or (iv):

(i) A request to inspect the documents set forth in the preceding paragraph;

(ii) A request for a certified copy or extract of the documents set forth in the preceding paragraph;

(iii) A request to inspect anything that shows the particulars recorded in the electromagnetic records set forth in the preceding paragraph in a manner specified by Cabinet Office Ordinance; or

(iv) A request to be provided with the particulars recorded in the electromagnetic records set forth in the preceding paragraph by the electromagnetic means determined by the Converted Stock Company, or to be issued a document detailing such particulars.

(Objections of Creditors)

Article 88 (1) Policyholders or other creditors of a converting Mutual Company may state to the company their objections to the Entity Conversion.

(2) A converting Mutual Company shall give public notice of the following particulars in the Official Gazette and by the Method of Public Notice prescribed by its articles of incorporation; provided, however, that the period for item (iii) may not be shorter than one month:

(i) The fact that an Entity Conversion will be carried out;

(ii) The trade name and address of the Converted Stock Company;

(iii) The fact that Policyholders or other creditors of the converting Mutual Company may state their objections within a certain period of time; and

(iv) In addition to what is listed in the preceding three items, particulars specified by Cabinet Office Ordinance.

(3) Where no Policyholders or other creditors have stated their objections within the period set forth in item (iii) of the preceding paragraph, such Policyholders or creditors shall be deemed to have approved the Entity Conversion.

(4) Where any Policyholder or other creditor has stated his/her objection under paragraph

(2), item (iii), the converting Mutual Company shall make payment or provide equivalent security to such Policyholder or other creditor, or entrust equivalent property to a trust company, etc. for the purpose of ensuring that such Policyholder or other creditor receive the payment; provided, however, that this shall not apply to the cases where the Entity Conversion poses no risk of harming the interest of such Policyholder or other creditor;

(5) The provisions of the preceding paragraph shall not apply to the Policyholders or any rights held by other persons pertaining to insurance contracts (other than Insurance Claims, etc.).

(6) Any resolution of authorization under Article 86, paragraph (1) shall be null and void if the number of the Policyholders who have stated their objections within the period set forth in paragraph (2), item (iii) (excluding the holders of policies under which Insurance Claims, etc. had already arisen at the time of public notice under the paragraph (2) (but limited to those policies that would be terminated with the payment of the Insurance Claims, etc.); the same shall apply hereinafter in this paragraph and in the following paragraph) exceeds one fifth of the total number of Policyholders, and the amount specified by Cabinet Office Ordinance as the credits (other than Insurance Claims, etc.) belonging to the insurance contracts of the Policyholders who have stated such objections exceeds one fifth of the total amount of credits belonging to the Policyholders.

(7) An Entity Conversion carried out pursuant to the provisions of the preceding paragraphs shall also be effective against the Policyholders who have stated their objections under the preceding paragraph and other persons who hold any right (other than Insurance Claims, etc.) pertaining to the insurance contracts involving the Policyholders.

(8) A converting Mutual Company shall, if it seeks to conclude an insurance contract on or after the day following the date of public notice under paragraph (2), notify the prospective Policyholder to the effect that the company is going through Entity Conversion procedures.

(9) In addition to what is provided for in the preceding paragraphs, necessary particulars for the application of those provisions shall be specified by Cabinet Order.

(Redemption of Funds, etc.)

Article 89 (1) A converting Mutual Company shall, where it has any amount of unredeemed funds, redeem the full amount of its funds as stipulated in the Entity Conversion plan; provided, however, that this shall not apply to any amount of credits pertaining to the funds delivered for the purpose of contribution in kind in issuing shares under Article 92.

(2) The provisions of Article 55, paragraph (2) and Article 56 shall not apply to an Entity Conversion from a Mutual Company to a Stock Company.

(Allocation of Shares or Monies to Members)

Article 90 (1) The members of a converting Mutual Company shall receive allocation of the Converted Stock Company's shares or monies as stipulated in the Entity Conversion plan.

(2) The allocation of shares or monies set forth in the preceding paragraph shall be made in accordance with the amount of contribution of each member (meaning the amount calculated pursuant to the provisions of Cabinet Office Ordinance as equivalent to the balance of the amount paid by a member as the insurance premiums and the profits obtained by investing the money received as such insurance premiums which have neither been allocated to the payment of benefits such as insurance proceeds or re-

funds, nor to business or other expenditures, after deducting the amount of assets to be retained for the performance of obligations under the insurance contract with the member).
(3) The provisions of Article 234, paragraph (1) (excluding all items) and (2) to (5) inclusive (Treatment of Fractions), Article 868, paragraph (1) (Jurisdiction over Non-Contentious Cases), Article 869 (Prima Facie Showing), Article 871 (Appending of the Reason), Article 874 (limited to the segment pertaining to item (iv)) (Restrictions on Appeal), Article 875 (Exclusion from Application of the Provisions of the Non-Contentious Cases Procedures Act) and Article 876 (Supreme Court Rules) of the Companies Act shall apply mutatis mutandis to the allocation of shares to the members of a converting Mutual Company pursuant to the provisions of the preceding two paragraphs. In this case, any other necessary technical change in interpretation shall be specified by Cabinet Order.
(4) In addition to what is provided for in the preceding three paragraphs, particulars required for the allocation of shares or monies in the case of an Entity Conversion shall be specified by Cabinet Order.

(Amount of Surplus in Entity Conversion, etc.)
Article 91 (1) A converting Mutual Company shall, as a particular to be prescribed by the articles of incorporation pursuant to the provisions of Article 86, paragraph (4), item (ii), determine the amount of surplus in Entity Conversion.
(2) A Converted Stock Company may not distribute the surplus in excess of the amount of the net assets on the balance sheet after deduction of the amount of surplus in Entity Conversion.
(3) The amount of surplus in Entity Conversion shall be the total amount calculated for all withdrawn members as specified by Cabinet Office Ordinance in accordance with Cabinet Office Ordinance set forth in paragraph (2) of the preceding Article.
(4) In addition to what is provided for in paragraph (1) and the preceding paragraph, the amount to be set aside as capital reserves on Entity Conversion, the reduction of surplus in Entity Conversion and other particulars required for calculations on Entity Conversion shall be specified by Cabinet Office Ordinance.

(Issuance of Shares on Entity Conversion)
Article 92 A converting Mutual Company may, in carrying out the Entity Conversion, issue shares of the Converted Stock Company, in addition to the allocation of shares under Article 90, paragraph (1). In this case, the Entity Conversion plan shall stipulate the following particulars:
(i) The number of the shares to be issued pursuant to the provisions of this Article (hereinafter referred to as "Shares Issued on Entity Conversion" in this Subsection) (or, in a company with class shares, the classes and number of the Shares Issued on Entity Conversion; hereinafter the same shall apply in this Subsection);
(ii) The amount to be paid in for the Shares Issued on Entity Conversion (meaning the amount of money to be paid, or of non-monetary properties to be delivered, in exchange for a share issued on Entity Conversion; hereinafter the same shall apply in this Subsection);
(iii) Where contribution is to be made in the form of non-monetary property, that fact and the description and value of such property;
(iv) The date of the payment of money in exchange for the Shares Issued on Entity Conversion or the delivery of the property set forth in the preceding item;
(v) Particulars of the capital and capital reserves to be increased.

(Offer to Subscribe, etc. for Shares Issued on Entity Conversion)
Article 93 (1) A converting Mutual Company shall notify the persons who seek to make an offer to subscribe for Shares Issued on Entity Conversion of the following particulars:
  (i) The trade name of the Converted Stock Company;
  (ii) Particulars listed in the items of the preceding Article;
  (iii) Places where any payment of money is to be handled; and
  (iv) In addition to what is listed in the preceding three items, particulars specified by Cabinet Office Ordinance.
(2) A person who offers to subscribe for Shares Issued on Entity Conversion shall submit to the converting Mutual Company a document detailing the following particulars:
  (i) The name and address of the person who makes the offer; and
  (ii) The number of Shares Issued on Entity Conversion for which the person seeks to subscribe.
(3) A person who makes an offer under the preceding paragraph may, in lieu of submitting the document prescribed in that paragraph, and pursuant to the provisions of Cabinet Order, provide the particulars that are required to be included in such document by electromagnetic means, with the consent of the converting Mutual Company. In this case, the person who has made the offer shall be deemed to have submitted the document prescribed in that paragraph.
(4) The converting Mutual Company shall immediately notify a person who has made an offer under paragraph (2) (hereinafter referred to as "Offeror" in this Subsection) of any change in the particulars listed in the items of paragraph (1) and the particular affected by the change.
(5) It shall be sufficient for a notice or demand to an Offeror to be sent by the converting Mutual Company to the address specified under paragraph (2), item (i) (or to any other place or contact address of which the Offeror has notified the Mutual Company for the receipt of notices or demands).
(6) The notice or demand set forth in the preceding paragraph shall be deemed to have arrived at the time when such notice or demand would normally have arrived.
(7) The provisions of Article 10 shall apply mutatis mutandis to a notice given by the converting Mutual Company under paragraph (1). In this case, any other necessary technical change in interpretation shall be specified by Cabinet Order.

(Allocation of Shares Issued on Entity Conversion)
Article 94 (1) The converting Mutual Company shall select from among the Offerors the persons to receive allocation of the Shares Issued on Entity Conversion, and determine the number of the Shares Issued on Entity Conversion to be allocated to each of such persons. In this case, the Mutual Company may reduce the number of the Shares Issued on Entity Conversion to be allocated to each Offeror from the number prescribed in paragraph (2), item (ii) of the preceding Article.
(2) The converting Mutual Company shall notify the Offerors, no later than the day immediately preceding the date referred to in Article 92, item (iv) of the number of the Shares Issued on Entity Conversion that will be allocated to each Offeror.

(Subscription for Shares Issued on Entity Conversion)
Article 95 An Offeror shall be a subscriber for Shares Issued on Entity Conversion for the number of such shares allocated by the converting Mutual Company.

(Performance of Contribution)
Article 96 (1) Subscribers for Shares Issued on Entity Conversion (other than those who

deliver properties under Article 92, item (iii) (hereinafter referred to as "Properties Contributed in Kind" in this Subsection)) shall, by the date set forth in item (iv) of the same Article, pay the full amount to be paid in for the Shares Issued on Entity Conversion allocated to each of them at any of the places where such payment is to be handled under Article 93, paragraph (1), item (iii).
(2) Subscribers for Shares Issued on Entity Conversion (limited to those who deliver Properties Contributed in Kind) shall, by the date set forth in Article 92, item (iv), deliver the Properties Contributed in Kind equivalent to the full amount to be paid in for the Shares Issued on Entity Conversion allocated to each of them.
(3) A subscriber for Shares Issued on Entity Conversion may not set off his/her obligation of payment under paragraph (1) or delivery under the preceding paragraph (hereinafter referred to as "Performance of Contribution" in this Subsection) against any claim against the converting Mutual Company.
(4) Any assignment of the right to become a holder of Shares Issued on Entity Conversion by Performance of Contribution may not be duly asserted against the Converted Stock Company.
(5) A subscriber for Shares Issued on Entity Conversion who fails to perform contribution shall lose his/her right to become a holder of Shares Issued on Entity Conversion by the Performance of Contribution.

(Timing of Obtaining Shareholder Status)
Article 96-2 A subscriber for Shares Issued on Entity Conversion shall, on the Effective Date, become the holder of the Shares Issued on Entity Conversion for which he/she has performed contribution.

(Restrictions on the Invalidation or Recession of Subscription)
Article 96-3 (1) The proviso to Article 93 (Concealment of True Intention) and the provisions of Article 94, paragraph (1) (Fictitious Manifestation of Intention) of the Civil Code shall not apply to the manifestation of an intention to offer to subscribe for Shares Issued on Entity Conversion or to the manifestation of an intention to allocate them.
(2) A subscriber for Shares Issued on Entity Conversion may neither assert the invalidity of his/her subscription for Shares Issued on Entity Conversion on the grounds of a mistake, nor rescind his/her subscription for Shares Issued on Entity Conversion on the grounds of fraud or duress, after one year has lapsed since the Effective Date or he/she has exercised any right regarding his/her shares.

(Contribution of Non-Monetary Property)
Article 96-4 The provisions of Article 207 (Contribution of Property Other than Monies), Article 212 (excluding paragraph (1), item (i)) (Liabilities of Persons Who Subscribed for Shares with Unfair Amount to Be Paid in), Article 213 (excluding paragraph (1), items (i) and (iii)) (Liabilities of Directors in Case of Shortfall in Value of Property contributed), Article 868, paragraph (1) (Jurisdiction over Non-Contentious Cases), Article 870 (limited to the segment pertaining to items (ii) and (vii)) (Hearing of Statements), Article 871 (Appending of the Reason), Article 872 (limited to the segment pertaining to item (iv)) (Immediate Appeal), Article 874 (limited to the segment pertaining to item (i)) (Restrictions on Appeal), Article 875 (Exclusion from Application of the Provisions of the Non-Contentious Cases Procedures Act) and Article 876 (Supreme Court Rules) of the Companies Act shall apply mutatis mutandis to any stipulation for the particulars listed in Article 92, item (iii); and the provisions of Part VII, Chapter II, Section 2 (Liability Actions, etc. Against a Stock Company) of that Act shall

apply mutatis mutandis to an action for payment under Article 212 (excluding paragraph (1), item (i)) of that Act as applied mutatis mutandis pursuant to this Article. In this case, the term "director" in Article 207, paragraph (10), item (i) of that Act shall be deemed to be replaced with "director of the converting Mutual Company set forth in Article 86, paragraph (1) of the Insurance Business Act"; the terms "Article 209" and "Article 199, paragraph (1), item (iii)" in Article 207, paragraph (2) shall be deemed to be replaced with "Article 96-2 of the Insurance Business Act" and "Article 92, item (iii) of that Act," respectively; the terms "Article 199, paragraph (1), item (iii)" and "application for subscription for shares for subscription or his/her manifestation of intention related to the contract provided for in Article 205" in Article 212, paragraph (2) of that Act shall be deemed to be replaced with "Article 92, item (iii) of the Insurance Business Act" and "application," respectively; and the term "shareholders having the shares" in Article 847, paragraph (1) of that Act shall be deemed to be replaced with "shareholders having the shares (or, where six months (or any shorter period prescribed by the articles of incorporation; hereinafter the same shall apply in this paragraph) have not lapsed since the Effective Date of an Entity Conversion, persons who had been members from six months prior until the Effective Date of the Entity Conversion and have been holding the shares without interruption since the Effective Date of the Entity Conversion)"; any other necessary technical change in interpretation shall be specified by Cabinet Order.

(Share Exchange on Entity Conversion)
Article 96-5 (1) A converting Mutual Company may, at the time of Entity Conversion, carry out a share exchange on Entity Conversion (meaning an exchange of shares whereby a converting Mutual Company causes all of the shares of the Converted Stock Company to be acquired by another Stock Company (hereinafter referred to as "Wholly Owning Parent Company for Share Exchange on Entity Conversion" in this Subsection) at the time of the Entity Conversion; hereinafter the same shall apply in this Subsection).
(2) A converting Mutual Company shall, in carrying out a share exchange on Entity Conversion, conclude a contract for share exchange on Entity Conversion with the Wholly Owning Parent Company for Share Exchange on Entity Conversion.
(3) The provisions of Article 791 (excluding paragraph (1), item (i) and paragraph (3)) (Retention and Inspection, etc. of Documents, etc. Related to an Absorption-Type Split or Share Exchange) of the Companies Act shall apply mutatis mutandis to a converting Mutual Company carrying out a share exchange on Entity Conversion; the provisions of Article 309, paragraph (2) (excluding all items) (Resolution of Shareholders' Meetings), Article 324, paragraph (2) (excluding all items (Resolution of Class Meetings) and Part V, Chapter V, Section 2, Subsection 2, Division 1 (excluding Article 795, paragraph (4), items (i) and (ii), Article 796, paragraph (3), item (i), sub-item (b), Article 799, paragraph (1), items (i) and (ii), Article 800, Article 801, paragraphs (1) and (2), Article 801, paragraph (3), items (i) and (ii), and Article 801, paragraph (5)) (Procedures for Stock Company) of that Act shall apply mutatis mutandis to a Wholly Owning Parent Company for Share Exchange on Entity Conversion; and the provisions of Article 868, paragraph (1) (Jurisdiction over Non-Contentious Cases), Article 870 (limited to the segment pertaining to item (iv)) (Hearing of Statements), the main clause of Article 871 (Appending of the Reason), Article 872 (limited to the segment pertaining to item (iv)) (Immediate Appeal), the main clause of Article 873 (Stay of Execution of the Judicial Decision of the Prior Instance), Article 875 (Exclusion from Application of the Provisions of the Non-Contentious Cases Procedures Act) and Article 876 (Supreme Court Rules) of that Act shall apply mutatis mutandis to an application under

Article 798, paragraph (2) of that Act as applied mutatis mutandis pursuant to this paragraph. In this case, any other necessary technical change in interpretation shall be specified by Cabinet Order.

(Allocation, etc. of Shares of Wholly Owning Parent Company for Share Exchange to Members)
Article 96-6 (1) Notwithstanding the provisions of Article 90, paragraph (1), the members of a converting Mutual Company carrying out a share exchange on Entity Conversion shall, pursuant to the provisions of the Entity Conversion plan, receive allocation of shares issued, or monies granted, at the time of the share exchange by the Wholly Owning Parent Company for Share Exchange on Entity Conversion.
(2) The provisions of Article 90, paragraphs (2) to (4) inclusive shall apply mutatis mutandis to the case set forth in the preceding paragraph. In this case, the term "the preceding paragraph" in paragraph (2) of the same Article shall be deemed to be replaced with "Article 96-6, paragraph (1)"; the term "the preceding two paragraphs" in Article 90, paragraph (3) shall be deemed to be replaced with "Article 96-6, paragraph (1) and the preceding paragraph"; and the term "the preceding three paragraphs" in Article 90, paragraph (4) shall be deemed to be replaced with "Article 96-6, paragraph (1) and the preceding two paragraphs"; any other necessary technical change in interpretation shall be specified by Cabinet Order.
(3) Where a converting Mutual Company issuing shares pursuant to the provisions of Article 92 carries out a share exchange on Entity Conversion, the subscribers for shares who have made payments or delivered contributions in kind for their shares shall, pursuant to the provisions of the Entity Conversion plan, receive allocation of shares issued, or monies delivered, at the time of the share exchange by the Wholly Owning Parent Company for Share Exchange on Entity Conversion.

(Particulars of Share Exchange on Entity Conversion to be Prescribed by Entity Conversion Plan, etc.)
Article 96-7 In the case of a share exchange on Entity Conversion, the Entity Conversion plan and the contract for share exchange on Entity Conversion shall prescribe the following particulars:
(i) The names, trade names and addresses of the converting Mutual Company and the Wholly Owning Parent Company for Share Exchange on Entity Conversion;
(ii) The following particulars regarding any Shares, etc. (meaning shares or monies; hereinafter the same shall apply in this Section) issued or granted by the Wholly Owning Parent Company for Share Exchange on Entity Conversion to the members of the converting Mutual Company (including the subscribers for the shares issued pursuant to the provisions of Article 92; hereinafter the same shall apply in this Article) in carrying out the share exchange on Entity Conversion;
  (a) Where the Shares, etc. are the shares of the Wholly Owning Parent Company for Share Exchange on Entity Conversion, the number of such shares (or, in a company with class shares, the classes of share and the numbers of shares by class) or the method of its calculation, and the particulars of the amounts of capital and Reserves of the Wholly Owning Parent Company for Share Exchange on Entity Conversion, or
  (b) Where the Shares, etc. are monies, the amount of such monies or the method of its calculation;
(iii) In the case of the preceding item, the particulars of the allocation of the Shares, etc. set forth in that item to the members of the converting Mutual Company (excluding the Wholly Owning Parent Company for Share Exchange on Entity Conver-

sion);
(iv) The method of selling any additional fraction of shares to be issued as a result of the allocation of shares to the members of the converting Mutual Company and any other particular specified by Cabinet Office Ordinance regarding such sale.
(v) The method of purchasing any additional fraction of shares arising under the preceding item and any other particular specified by Cabinet Office Ordinance regarding such purchase; and
(vi) The day on which the Entity Conversion and share exchange on Entity Conversion take effect.

(Share Transfer on Entity Conversion)
Article 96-8 (1) A converting Mutual Company may, at the time of Entity Conversion, carry out a share transfer on Entity Conversion (meaning a transfer whereby a converting Mutual Company or two or more converting mutual companies cause(s) all of the shares of the Converted Stock Company (including, in the case set forth in paragraph (1), item (ix) of the following Article, the Stock Company set forth in that item) to be acquired by a new Stock Company to be incorporated (hereinafter referred to as "Wholly Owning parent Company Formed by Share Transfer on Entity Conversion" in this Subsection) at the time of the Entity Conversion).
(2) The provisions of Article 96-6 shall apply mutatis mutandis to a share transfer on Entity Conversion. In this case, the term "Wholly Owning Parent Company for Share Exchange on Entity Conversion" in paragraph (1) of the same Article shall be deemed to be replaced with "Wholly Owning Parent Company Formed by Share Transfer on Entity Conversion"; the term "Article 96-6, paragraph (1)" in Article 96-6, paragraph (2) shall be deemed to be replaced with "Article 96-6, paragraph (1) as applied mutatis mutandis pursuant to Article 96-8, paragraph (2)"; and the term "Wholly Owning Parent Company for Share Exchange on Entity Conversion" in Article 96-6, paragraph (3) shall be deemed to be replaced with "Wholly Owning Parent Company Formed by Share Transfer on Entity Conversion"; any other necessary technical change in interpretation shall be specified by Cabinet Order.

(Particulars of Share Transfer on Entity Conversion to be Prescribed by Entity Conversion Plan, etc.)
Article 96-9 (1) In the case of a share transfer on Entity Conversion, the Entity Conversion plan shall prescribe the following particulars:
(i) The purpose of the Wholly Owning Parent Company Formed by Share Transfer on Entity Conversion, the trade name, the location of its head office, and the total number of authorized shares;
(ii) In addition to what is listed in the preceding item, particulars specified by the articles of incorporation of the Wholly Owning Parent Company Formed by Share Transfer on Entity Conversion;
(iii) The names of the persons to serve as directors at the incorporation of the Wholly Owning Parent Company Formed by Share Transfer on Entity Conversion;
(iv) For each of the following categories, the particulars set forth therein:
(a) Where the Wholly Owning Parent Company Formed by Share Transfer on Entity Conversion is a company with accounting advisors: the names of the persons to serve as accounting advisors at the incorporation of the Wholly Owning Parent Company Formed by Share Transfer on Entity Conversion,
(b) Where the Wholly Owning Parent Company Formed by Share Transfer on Entity Conversion is a company with auditors: the names of the persons to serve as company auditors at the incorporation of the Wholly Owning Parent Company

Art.96-9　⑥ Insurance Business Act, Part II, Chap.II, Sec.3

　　　　Formed by Share Transfer on Entity Conversion, or
　　(c) Where the Wholly Owning Parent Company Formed by Share Transfer on Entity Conversion is a company with accounting auditors: the names of the persons to serve as accounting auditors at the incorporation of the Wholly Owning Parent Company Formed by Share Transfer on Entity Conversion;
　(v) The number of the shares (or, in a company with class shares, the classes of share and the numbers of shares by class) to be issued by the Wholly Owning Parent Company Formed by Share Transfer on Entity Conversion to the members of the converting Mutual Company (including the subscribers for shares issued pursuant to the provisions of Article 92; hereinafter the same shall apply in this Article) in carrying out the share transfer on Entity Conversion or the method of calculating such number, and the particulars of the amounts of the capital and Reserves of the Wholly Owning Parent Company Formed by Share Transfer on Entity Conversion;
　(vi) Particulars of the allocation of the shares set forth in the preceding item to the members of the converting Mutual Company;
　(vii) The amount of any money to be granted by the Wholly Owning Parent Company Formed by Share Transfer on Entity Conversion to the members of the converting Mutual Company in carrying out the share transfer on Entity Conversion or the method of calculating such amount;
　(viii) In the case of the preceding item, the particulars of the allocation of the money set forth in that item to the members of the converting Mutual Company; and
　(ix) In jointly incorporating a Wholly Owning Parent Company Formed by Share Transfer on Entity Conversion with another converting Mutual Company or a Stock Company, that fact, and the particulars listed in Article 773, paragraph (1), items (ix) and (x) (Share Transfer Plan) of the Companies Act regarding the share options of the Stock Company.
(2) The provisions of Part II, Chapter I (excluding Article 27 (excluding items (iv) and (v)), Article 29, Article 31, Article 39, Section 6 and Article 49) (Incorporation) of the Companies Act shall not apply to the incorporation of a Wholly Owning Parent Company Formed by Share Transfer on Entity Conversion.
(3) The articles of incorporation of a Wholly Owning Parent Company Formed by Share Transfer on Entity Conversion shall be drafted by the converting Mutual Company carrying out the share transfer on Entity Conversion (or, in the case of paragraph (1), item (ix), the converting Mutual Company carrying out the share transfer on Entity Conversion and the Stock Company set forth in that item).
(4) The provisions of Article 811 (excluding paragraph (1), item (i)) (Retention and Inspection , etc. of Documents, etc. Related to an Incorporation-type Company Split or Share Transfer) of the Companies Act shall apply mutatis mutandis to a converting Mutual Company carrying out a share transfer on Entity Conversion; the provisions of Article 219, paragraph (1) (limited to the segment pertaining to item (viii)), (2) and (3) (Public Notice in Relation to Submission of Share Certificate), Article 220 (Cases Where Share Certificates Cannot be Submitted), Article 293, paragraph (1) (limited to the segment pertaining to item (vii)) and (2) to (4) inclusive (Public Notice in Relation to Submission of Share Option Certificate), Article 309, paragraph (2) (excluding the items) and (3) (limited to the segment pertaining to item (iii)) (Resolution of Shareholders' Meetings), Article 324, paragraph (2) (excluding the items) and (3) (limited to the segment pertaining to item (ii)) (Resolution of Class Meetings), and Part V, Chapter V, Section 3, Subsection 1, Division 1 (excluding Article 803, paragraph (1), items (i) and (ii), Article 805, Article 808, paragraph (1), items (i) and (ii), Article 808, paragraph (3), items (i) and (ii), Article 810, paragraph (1), items (i) and (ii), Article 811, paragraph (1), item (i), Article 811, paragraph (3), and Article 812) (Procedures for

Stock Company) of that Act shall apply mutatis mutandis to a Stock Company set forth in paragraph (1), item (ix); and the provisions of Article 815, paragraph (3) (limited to the segment pertaining to item (iii)), (4) and (6) (Retention and Inspection, etc. of Documents, etc. Related to a Consolidation-type Merger Agreement, etc.) of that Act shall apply mutatis mutandis to a Wholly Owning Parent Company Formed by Share Transfer on Entity Conversion. In this case, any other necessary technical change in interpretation shall be specified by Cabinet Order.

(Authorization of Entity Conversion)
Article 96-10 (1) An Entity Conversion shall not take effect without the authorization of the Prime Minister.
(2) Whenever an application has been filed for the authorization set forth in the preceding paragraph, the Prime Minister shall examine whether it conforms to the following standards:
  (i) The Converted Stock Company has a sufficient financial basis to execute its business in a sound and efficient manner;
  (ii) The Entity Conversion poses no risk of harming the rights of Policyholders;
  (iii) The allocation of shares or money under Article 90 or 96-6 (including the cases where it is applied mutatis mutandis pursuant to Article 96-8, paragraph (2)) has been carried out appropriately; and
  (iv) In addition to what is listed in the preceding three items, the Entity Conversion poses no risk of precluding sound business operation.

(Effectuation, etc. of Entity Conversion)
Article 96-11 (1) A converting Mutual Company shall become a Stock Company on the Effective Date (or, in the case of a share transfer on Entity Conversion, the date of the establishment of the Wholly Owning Parent Company Formed by Share Transfer on Entity Conversion).
(2) The members of a converting Mutual Company shall, on the Effective Date, become holders of the shares set forth in Article 86, paragraph (4), item (v) pursuant to the provisions on the particulars listed in Article 86, paragraph (4), item (vi).
(3) The provisions of the preceding two paragraphs shall not apply to the cases where a procedure under Article 88 has not been completed or where the Entity Conversion has been voluntarily abandoned.

Article 96-12 (1) Notwithstanding the provisions of paragraph (2) of the preceding Article and Article 96-2, the Wholly Owning Parent Company for Share Exchange on Entity Conversion shall acquire all of the issued shares of a Converted Stock Company (excluding the shares of the Converted Stock Company held by the Wholly Owning Parent Company for Share Exchange on Entity Conversion) on the Effective Date, where the converting Mutual Company carries out a share exchange on Entity Conversion.
(2) Notwithstanding the provisions of paragraph (2) of the preceding Article and Article 96-2, the members of a converting Mutual Company (including the subscribers for the shares issued pursuant to the provisions of Article 92) shall become holders of the shares set forth in Article 96-7, item (ii), sub-item (a) on the Effective Date pursuant to the provisions on the particulars listed in item (iii) of the same Article, where the converting Mutual Company carries out a share exchange on Entity Conversion.
(3) The provisions of the preceding two paragraphs shall not apply to the cases where a procedure under Article 88 has not been completed or where the Entity Conversion has been voluntarily abandoned.

Article 96-13 (1) Notwithstanding the provisions of Article 96-11, paragraph (2) and Article 96-2, the Wholly Owning Parent Company Formed by Share Transfer on Entity Conversion shall, on the date of its establishment, acquire all of the shares to be allocated to members pursuant to the provisions of Article 90, paragraph (1) (including the shares issued pursuant to the provisions of Article 92 and the shares issued by the Stock Company set forth in Article 96-9, paragraph (1), item (ix)), where the converting Mutual Company carries out a share transfer on Entity Conversion.
(2) Notwithstanding the provisions of Article 96-11, paragraph (2) and Article 96-2, the members of a converting Mutual Company (including the subscribers for the shares issued pursuant to the provisions of Article 92 and the shareholders of the Stock Company set forth in Article 96-9, paragraph (1), item (ix)) shall, on the date of the establishment of the Wholly Owning Parent Company Formed by Share Transfer on Entity Conversion, become holders of the shares set forth in Article 96-9, paragraph (1), item (v) pursuant to the provisions on the particulars listed in Article 96-9, paragraph (1), item (vi), where the converting Mutual Company carries out a share exchange on Entity Conversion.
(3) The provisions of Article 774, paragraphs (4) and (5) (Effectuation, etc. of Share Transfer) of the Companies Act shall apply mutatis mutandis to the case of Article 96-9, paragraph (1), item (ix). In this case, any other necessary technical change in interpretation shall be specified by Cabinet Order.

(Registration)
Article 96-14 (1) Where a Mutual Company has carried out an Entity Conversion, the converting Mutual Company shall complete registration of dissolution within two weeks from the date of Entity Conversion at the location of its principal office and within three weeks from said date at the location of its secondary offices; and the Converted Stock Company shall make a registration of incorporation within two weeks from the date of Entity Conversion at the location of its head office and within three weeks from said date at the location of its branch offices.
(2) The provisions of Article 89 (limited to the segment pertaining to item (i) to (iv) inclusive) (Registration of Share Exchange) of the Commercial Registration Act shall apply mutatis mutandis to a share exchange on Entity Conversion carried out by a converting Mutual Company; and the provisions of Article 925 (excluding items (ii) and (iv)) (Registration of Share Transfer) and Article 930, paragraph (1) (limited to the segment pertaining to item (iv)) (Registration at Location of Branch Offices) of the Companies Act, and the provisions of Article 90 (Registration of Share Transfer) of the Commercial Registration Act shall apply mutatis mutandis to a share transfer on Entity Conversion carried out by a converting Mutual Company. In this case, any other necessary technical change in interpretation shall be specified by Cabinet Order.
(3) The following documents shall be attached to a written application for registration of incorporation under paragraph (1), in addition to those specified in Articles 18, 19 and 46 of the Commercial Registration Act as applied mutatis mutandis pursuant to Article 67:
(i) Entity Conversion plan;
(ii) articles of incorporation;
(iii) The minutes of the Mutual Company's general members' council;
(iv) A document certifying that the directors (or directors and company auditors, where the Converted Stock Company is a company with auditors) of the Converted Stock Company have accepted the assumption of office;
(v) Where accounting advisors or accounting auditors have been appointed for the

Converted Stock Company, the following documents;
(a) A document certifying that they have accepted the assumption of office,
(b) Where they are juridical persons, Certificates of Registered Particulars for such juridical persons, provided, however, that this shall not apply to the cases where the principal offices of such juridical persons are located within the district under the jurisdiction of the relevant registry office, and
(c) Where they are not juridical persons, a document certifying that the accounting advisors meet the requirement of Article 333, paragraph (1) of the Companies Act as applied mutatis mutandis pursuant to Article 53-4, or that the accounting auditors meet the requirement of Article 337, paragraph (1) of that Act as applied mutatis mutandis pursuant to Article 53-7;
(vi) A document certifying a contract with any administrator of the shareholder registry;
(vii) A document certifying that a public notice under Article 88, paragraph (2) has been given;
(viii) Where any Policyholder or other creditor has stated his/her objection under Article 88, paragraph (4), a document certifying that the company has made payment or provided equivalent security to such Policyholder or other creditor, or entrusted equivalent property to a trust company, etc. for the purpose of ensuring that such Policyholder or other creditor receive the payment, or a document certifying that the Entity Conversion poses no risk of harming the interest of such Policyholder or other creditor;
(ix) A document certifying that the number of Policyholders who have stated their objections under Article 88, paragraph (6) has not exceeded one fifth of the total number of Policyholders, or a document certifying that the amount specified by Cabinet Office Ordinance set forth in that paragraph as the credits belonging to such Policyholders has not exceeded one fifth of the total amount set forth in that paragraph; and
(x) Where shares have been issued on the Entity Conversion pursuant to the provisions of Article 92, the following documents:
(a) A document certifying the offers to subscribe for the shares;
(b) Where contribution is to be made in the form of money, a document certifying that payments have been made under Article 96, paragraph (1);
(c) Where contribution is to be made in the form of non-monetary property, the following documents;
1. Where an inspector has been elected, a document containing the investigative report of the inspector and annexed documents thereto,
2. In the cases listed in Article 207, paragraph (9), item (iii) of the Companies Act as applied mutatis mutandis pursuant to Article 96-4, a document certifying the market value of the securities,
3. In the cases listed in Article 207, paragraph (9), item (iv) of the Companies Act as applied mutatis mutandis pursuant to Article 96-4, a document containing the verification set forth in that item and annexed documents thereto, and
4. In the cases listed in Article 207, paragraph (9), item (v) of the Companies Act as applied mutatis mutandis pursuant to Article 96-4, the accounting books carrying the monetary claim set forth in that item; and
(d) Certified copy of any judicial decision on the report of the inspector.
(4) In addition to the documents set forth in Articles 18, 19 (Documents to be Attached to Written Application) and 46 (General Rules for Attached Documents) of the Commercial Registration Act, and Article 89 (limited to the segment pertaining to item (i) to (iv) inclusive) of that Act as applied mutatis mutandis pursuant to paragraph (2), and

Art.96-15～96-16　⑥ Insurance Business Act, Part II, Chap.II, Sec.3

the documents listed in the items of the preceding paragraph, a Certificate of Registered Particulars for the Mutual Company (unless the principal office of the Mutual Company is located within the district under the jurisdiction of the relevant registry office) shall be attached to a written application for registration of change due to any share exchange on Entity Conversion carried out by a Wholly Owning Parent Company for Share Exchange on Entity Conversion.

(5) In addition to the documents set forth in Articles 18, 19 and 46 of the Commercial Registration Act, and Article 90 of that Act as applied mutatis mutandis pursuant to paragraph (2), and the documents listed in the items of paragraph (3), a Certificate Registered Particulars for the Mutual Company (unless the principal office of the Mutual Company is located within the district under the jurisdiction of the relevant registry office) shall be attached to a written application for incorporation due to any share transfer on Entity Conversion.

(6) The provisions of Articles 76 and 78 (Registration of Entity Conversion) of the Commercial Registration Act shall apply mutatis mutandis to the cases of paragraph (1); and the provisions of Article 46, paragraph (3) of that Act as applied mutatis mutandis pursuant to Article 67 shall apply mutatis mutandis to the cases of Article 3, item (iii), paragraph (4) and the preceding paragraph (limited to the segment pertaining to the documents listed in Article 3, item (iii)). In this case, any other necessary technical change in interpretation shall be specified by Cabinet Order.

(Mutatis Mutandis Application of Provisions on Entity Conversion from Stock Company to Mutual Company)
Article 96-15 The provisions of Article 82 shall apply mutatis mutandis to an Entity Conversion from a Mutual Company to a Stock Company. In this case, the term "Article 70, paragraph (2)" in paragraph (1) of the same Article shall be deemed to be replaced with "Article 88, paragraph (2)"; and the term "Article 70" in Article 82, paragraph (2) shall be deemed to be replaced with "Article 88"; any other necessary technical change in interpretation shall be specified by Cabinet Order.

(Actions to Invalidate Entity Conversion)
Article 96-16 (1) The invalidity of an Entity Conversion may only be asserted in an action filed within six months from the Effective Date (or, in the case of a share transfer on Entity Conversion, the date of the establishment of the Wholly Owning Parent Company Formed by Share Transfer on Entity Conversion; the same shall apply in the following paragraph).

(2) An action to invalidate an Entity Conversion may only be filed by the person listed in the relevant of the following items for the category of cases set forth in that item:
  (i) In the case of an Entity Conversion accompanied by a share exchange on Entity Conversion, a person who was a member, etc. of the converting Mutual Company or a shareholder, etc. of the Wholly Owning Parent Company for Share Exchange on Entity Conversion as of the Effective Date, or a shareholder, etc. or bankruptcy trustee of the Converted Stock Company or a creditor of the Converted Stock Company who has not approved of the Entity Conversion or a shareholder, etc. or bankruptcy trustee of the Wholly Owning Parent Company for Share Exchange on Entity Conversion;
  (ii) In the case of an Entity Conversion accompanied by a share transfer on Entity Conversion, a person who was a member, etc. of the converting Mutual Company as of the Effective Date, or a shareholder, etc. or bankruptcy trustee of the Converted Stock Company or the Stock Company set forth in Article 96-9, paragraph (1), item (ix) or a creditor of such Stock Company who has not approved of the En-

tity Conversion or a shareholder, etc. or bankruptcy trustee of the Wholly Owning Parent Company Formed by Share Transfer on Entity Conversion; or
   (iii) In any other case than those listed in the preceding two paragraphs, a person who was a member, etc. of the converting Mutual Company as of the Effective Date, or a shareholder, etc. or bankruptcy trustee of the Converted Stock Company or a creditor of the Converted Stock Company who has not approved of the Entity Conversion.
(3) An action to invalidate an Entity Conversion is filed against the person listed in the relevant of the following items for the category of cases set forth in that item:
   (i) In the case of item (i) of the preceding paragraph, the Converted Stock Company and the Wholly Owning Parent Company for Share Exchange on Entity Conversion;
   (ii) In the case of item (ii) of the preceding paragraph, the Converted Stock Company and the Wholly Owning Parent Company Formed by Share Transfer on Entity Conversion; or
   (iii) In the case of item (iii) of the preceding paragraph, the Converted Stock Company.
(4) The provisions of Article 835, paragraph (1) (Jurisdiction over Actions), Article 836 to 839 inclusive (Order to Provide Security, Mandatory Consolidation of Oral Arguments, etc., Persons Affected by a Judgment Being Upheld, Effects of a Judgment of Invalidity, Revocation or Rescission), Article 846 (Liability for Damages Where a Judgment Is Entered Against the Plaintiff), and Article 937, paragraph (3) (limited to the segment pertaining to item (i)) and (4) (Commissioning of Registration by a Judicial Decision) of the Companies Act shall apply mutatis mutandis to an action to invalidate an Entity Conversion; the provisions of Article 840 (Effects of a Judgment of Invalidity of New Share Issue) of that Act shall apply mutatis mutandis to a judgment of invalidity of an Entity Conversion accompanied by the issuance of shares on Entity Conversion under Article 92; the provisions of Article 844 (Effects of a Judgment of Invalidity of a Share Exchange or Share Transfer) of that Act shall apply mutatis mutandis to a judgment of invalidity of an Entity Conversion accompanied by a share exchange on Entity Conversion or share transfer on Entity Conversion; and the provisions of Article 868, paragraph (1) (Jurisdiction over Non-Contentious Cases), the main clause of Article 871 (Appending of the Reason), Article 872 (limited to the segment pertaining to item (ii)) (Immediate Appeal), the main clause of Article 873 (Stay of Execution of the Judicial Decision of the Prior Instance), Article 875 to 877 inclusive (Exclusion from Application of the Provisions of the Non-Contentious Cases Procedures Act, Supreme Court Rules, Mandatory Consolidation of Hearings, etc.) and Article 878, paragraph (1) (Effect of Judicial Decision) of that Act shall apply mutatis mutandis to an application under Article 840, paragraph (2) of that Act as applied mutatis mutandis pursuant to this paragraph. In this case, the term "shareholder" in Article 878, paragraph (1) shall be deemed to be replaced with "shareholder or member"; any other necessary technical change in interpretation shall be specified by Cabinet Order.
(5) For the purpose of applying the provisions of Article 475 (Causes of Commencement of Liquidation) of the Companies Act to a Wholly Owning Parent Company Formed by Share Transfer on Entity Conversion, the term "in the cases listed below" in that Article shall be deemed to be replaced with "in the cases listed below or the cases where a judgment in favor of any claim in an action to invalidate an Entity Conversion accompanied by a share transfer on Entity Conversion under Article 96-8, paragraph (1) of the Insurance Business Act has become final and binding."

Chapter III Business

(Scope of Business, etc.)
Article 97 (1) An Insurance Company may, in accordance with the types of licenses provided by Article 3, paragraph (2), underwrite insurance.
(2) An Insurance Company shall invest assets such as money received as insurance premiums by any of the methods specified by Cabinet Office Ordinance, such as acquisition of securities.

Article 97-2 (1) An Insurance Company shall not invest assets specified by Cabinet Office Ordinance, in excess of the amount calculated pursuant to the provisions of Cabinet Office Ordinance.
(2) In addition to the provisions under the preceding paragraph, the amount of assets as specified by Cabinet Office Ordinance to be invested by an Insurance Company regarding one person (including any party specially related to that one person as specified by Cabinet Office Ordinance, with said person; the same shall apply in the following paragraph) shall not exceed the amount calculated pursuant to the provisions of Cabinet Office Ordinance.
(3) If an Insurance Company has a Subsidiary or a party to which it is specially related as specified by Cabinet Office Ordinances (hereinafter referred to in this Article as "Subsidiary Companies, etc."), the total amount of assets as specified by Cabinet Office Ordinance to be invested in any one person by the Insurance Company and its Subsidiary Companies, etc. , or by such Subsidiary Companies, etc. shall not exceed the amount calculated pursuant to the provisions of Cabinet Office Ordinance.

Article 98 (1) An Insurance Company may, in addition to the business it carries out pursuant to the provisions of Article 97, carry out the following and other business incidental thereto:
(i) Business agency or standing in for the administrative services (limited to those specified by Cabinet Office Ordinance) of other insurance companies (including Foreign Insurers) for Low-Cost, Short-Term Insurers, shipowners' mutual insurance associations (meaning shipowners' mutual insurance associations prescribed in Article 2, paragraph (1) (Definition) of the Act on Shipowners' Mutual Insurance Associations (Act No. 177 of 1950)), and other persons conducting financial business;
(ii) Guarantee of obligation;
(iii) Underwriting (excluding that carried out for the purpose of secondary distribution) of National Government Bonds, local government bonds or Government-Guaranteed Bonds (hereinafter referred to as "National Government Bonds, etc." in this Article) or handling of public offerings of the National Government Bonds, etc. pertaining to that underwriting;
(iv) Acquisition or transfer (not for the purpose of asset investment) of monetary claims (including those indicated in any of the certificates specified by Cabinet Office Ordinance, such as certificates of negotiable deposits);
(iv)-2 Underwriting (excluding that carried out for the purpose of secondary distribution) of Specified Company Bonds issued by Special Purpose Companies (excluding Specified Short-Term Company Bonds and limited to those where only nominative monetary claims or rights of beneficiary of trust into which nominative monetary claims are placed are acquired using the money gained through the issuance of that Specified Company Bonds under Asset Securitization Plans) and any other securities specified by Cabinet Office Ordinance as those equivalent thereto (hereinafter referred to as "Specified Company Bonds, etc." in this item) or handling of public offering of the Specified Company Bonds, etc. pertaining to that underwriting;

(iv)-3 Acquisition or transfer of short-term Company bonds, etc. (except those for the investment of assets);

(v) Handling of a private placement of securities (except those that fall under monetary claims indicated on the certificates prescribed in item (iv) and Short-Term Bonds, etc.);

(vi) Derivative Transactions (excluding those which are carried out for the investment of assets and those which fall under the category of Transactions of Securities-Related Derivatives; the same shall apply in the following item) that are specified by Cabinet Office Ordinance (excluding those that fall under the category of business listed in item (iv));

(vii) Intermediation, brokerage or agency for Derivative Transactions (limited to those specified by Cabinet Office Ordinance);

(viii) Transactions where the relevant parties promise to give and receive money calculated based on the difference between the reference value that they have determined in advance, in terms of an indicator such as interest rate, currency value, commodity price or price of Carbon Dioxide Equivalent Quotas (meaning carbon dioxide equivalent quotas defined in Article 2, paragraph (6) (Definitions) of the Act on Promotion of Global Warming Countermeasures (Act No. 117 of 1998) or any other quotas similar thereto; the same shall apply in item (iv), paragraph (2) of the following Article) on the one hand, and the actual numerical value of that indicator at a fixed point of time in the future, on the other, or any equivalent transactions thereto, that are specified by Cabinet Office Ordinance (referred to as "Financial Derivative Transactions" in the next item) which are transactions found unlikely to damage the soundness of management of an Insurance Company as specified by Cabinet Office Ordinance (excluding those which are carried out for the purpose of asset investment and those falling under the categories of business listed in items (iv) and (vi));

(ix) Intermediation, brokerage or agency for Financial Derivative Transactions (excluding business that falls under the category of business specified in item (vii) and those specified by Cabinet Office Ordinance);

(x) Over-the-Counter Transactions of Securities-Related Derivatives (limited to those that are settled through giving and receiving the difference in the case where the securities pertaining to that Over-the-Counter Transactions of Securities-Related Derivatives fall under the category of monetary claims that are indicated in the form of certificates as prescribed in item (iv) and are not Short-Term Company Bonds, etc.; the same shall apply in the following item) (except those which are carried out for the investment of assets); and

(xi) Intermediation, brokerage or agency for Over-the-Counter Transactions of Securities-Related Derivatives.

(2) An Insurance Company shall, if it seeks to conduct the business listed in the preceding paragraph, item (i), specify its content and obtain authorization from the Prime Minister.

(3) The term "Government-Guaranteed Bonds" in paragraph (1), item (iii) means bonds, such as company bonds, for which redemption of the principal and payment of interest are guaranteed by the government.

(4) Business provided for in paragraph (1), item (iv) concerning the monetary claims indicated on the certificates prescribed in the same item which fall under securities and business provided for in the same paragraph, item (iv)-3 concerning Short-Term Bonds, etc. include business through which the actions listed in Article 2, paragraph (8), items (i) to (vi) inclusive and items (viii) to (x) inclusive (Definitions) of the Financial Instruments and Exchange Act are taken.

Art.99 ６ Insurance Business Act, Part II, Chap.III, Sec.3

(5) The terms "special purpose company," "asset securitization program" or "specified company bond" in paragraph (1), item (iv)-2 mean the special purpose company, asset securitization program, or specified company bond prescribed in Article 2, paragraph (3), (4), or (7) (Definitions) of the Act on the Liquidation of Assets (Act No. 105 of 1998), respectively, and the term "specified short-term bond" means the specified short-term bond prescribed in Article 2, paragraph (8) of the same Act.

(6) The term "Short-Term Bonds, etc." set forth in paragraph (1), items (iv)-3, (v), and (x), and paragraph (4) means the following bonds:

(i) Short-Term Bonds prescribed in Article 66, item (i) (Ownership of Rights) of the Act on Transfer of Bonds, Shares, etc. ;

(ii) Deleted

(iii) Short-term investment corporation bonds prescribed in Article 139-12, paragraph (1) (Special Provisions Pertaining to Short-term Investment Corporation Bonds) of the Act on Investment Trust and Investment Corporation (Act No. 198 of 1951);

(iv) Short-Term Bonds prescribed in Article 54-4, paragraph (1) (Issuance of Short-Term Bonds) of the Shinkin Bank Act (Act No. 238 of 1951);

(v) Short-Term Bonds prescribed in Article 61-10, paragraph (1);

(vi) Specified Short-Term Bonds prescribed in the preceding paragraph;

(vii) Short-term Norinchukin Bank debentures prescribed in Article 62-2, paragraph (1) (Issuance of Short-Term Norinchukin Bank Debentures) of the Norinchukin Bank Act (Act No. 93 of 2001); and

(viii) Of the rights to be indicated in bonds issued by foreign juridical persons for which ownership of the rights is to be decided based on the entry or record in the transfer account registry pursuant to the provisions of the Act on Transfer of Bonds, Shares, etc. (excluding bonds having a nature of company bonds with share warrant), those that satisfy all of the following requirements:

(a) The amount of each right is not below hundred million yen;

(b) There are provisions on a fixed due date for redemption of the principal that is within one year from the day on which the total amount of the rights has been paid, and there are no provisions on an installment plan; and

(c) There are provisions to make the due date for the payment of interest the same date as the due date for the redemption of the principal set forth in (b).

(7) The "Handling of Private Placement of Securities" set forth in paragraph (1), item (v) means to handle the Private Placement of Securities (meaning the private placement of securities prescribed in Article 2, paragraph (3) (Definitions) of the Financial Instruments and Exchange Act).

(8) The term "Derivative Transactions" or "Transactions of Securities-Related Derivatives" set forth in paragraph (1), item (vi) or (vii) respectively means the Derivative Transactions prescribed in Article 2, paragraph (20) (Definitions) of the Financial Instruments and Exchange Act or the Transactions of Securities-Related Derivatives prescribed in Article 28, paragraph (8), item (vi) (Definitions) of that Act.

(9) The term "Over-the-Counter Transactions of Securities-Related Derivatives" in paragraph (1), item (x) or (xi) means the actions listed in Article 28, paragraph (8), item (iv) (Definitions) of the Financial Instruments and Exchange Act

Article 99 (1) An Insurance Company may, in addition to the business it carries out pursuant to the provisions of Article 97 and the preceding Article, carry out, with regard to the securities or transactions listed in the items of Article 33, paragraph (2) of the Financial Instruments and Exchange Act (Prohibition, etc. of Securities Services by Financial Institutions), business through which the actions listed in the items of the same paragraph (excluding business carried out pursuant to the provisions of the preceding Article, paragraph (1)) and business specified by Cabinet Office Ordinance as incidental thereto, within a limit so as not to preclude the performance of business under Article 97.

(2) In addition to the business it carries out pursuant to the provisions of Article 97 and the preceding Article, an Insurance Company may conduct the following businesses, within a limit so as not to preclude the performance of business under Article 97:
  (i) Subscription or commissioning the administration of bonds such as local government bonds or company bonds; and
  (ii) Trust business concerning secured bonds that is carried out pursuant to the Secured Bond Trust Act.
  (iii) Investment Advisory Business as defined in Article 28, paragraph (6) (General Rules) of the Financial Instruments and Exchange Act;
  (iv) Conclusion of a contract on obtaining or transferring Carbon Dioxide Equivalent Quotas or business for providing intermediation, brokerage, or agency therefor (excluding business conducted pursuant to paragraph (1) of the preceding Article) that is specified by Cabinet Office Ordinance; and
  (v) Fund transfer business defined in Article 2, paragraph (2) (Definitions) of the Act on Financial Settlements (Act No. 59 of 2009).

(3) A Life Insurance Company may, in addition to the business it carries out pursuant to the provisions of Article 97 and the preceding Article, carry out business through which it underwrites trusts for insurance proceeds paid (hereinafter referred to as "Insurance-Proceed Trust Services"), within a limit so as not to preclude the performance of business under Article 97, notwithstanding the provisions of the Trust Business Act.

(4) An Insurance Company shall, if it seeks to conduct business prescribed in paragraph (1) pursuant to the provisions of the same paragraph, set forth the contents and method of any such business in connection with which the other parties are many and unspecified, and obtain authorization from the Prime Minister. The same shall apply if an Insurance Company seeks to modify the contents and method of business for which it obtained said authorization.

(5) An Insurance Company shall obtain authorization from the Prime Minister if it seeks to conduct business listed in the items of paragraph (2) pursuant to the provisions of the same paragraph.

(6) An Insurance Company shall, with regard to business listed in items (i), (ii) and (v) of paragraph (2), be deemed to be a bank (a company including a stock company or bank prescribed by laws and regulations in the case of a Mutual Company) pursuant to the provisions of Cabinet Order, for the purpose of the application of the laws and regulations specified by Cabinet Order, such as the Secured Bond Trust Act. In this case, the provisions of the proviso (Trade Name) of Article 14, paragraph (2) of the Trust Business Act shall not apply.

(7) A Life Insurance Company shall, if it seeks to engage in Insurance-Proceed Trust Services, set forth the method and obtain authorization from the Prime Minister. The same shall apply if a Life Insurance Company seeks to modify the method of business for which it obtained said authorization.

(8) The provisions of Article 11 (Business Deposits), Article 22 (Entrustment of Trust Business), Article 23 (Liability of Trust Company Pertaining to Entrustment of Trust Business), and Articles 24 to 31 inclusive (Conduct Rules Pertaining to Underwriting of Trust, Application mutatis mutandis of the Financial Instruments and Exchange Act, Explanation of Contents of Trust Contract, Written Issuance at Conclusion of Trust Contract, Issuance of Report on Trust Property Situation, Duty of Loyalty of Trust Company, etc., Conduct Rules Pertaining to Trust Property, Change of Important

Art.99　　⑥ **Insurance Business Act, Part II, Chap.III, Sec.3**

Trust, etc., Explanation of Reimbursement of Costs, etc. or Scope of Advance Payment, etc., Special Measures for Public Notice of Trusts, and Debt Set-off Pertaining to Trust Property), Article 42 (Inspection, etc.), and Article 49 (Dismissal Procedure in the Case of Rescission, etc. of License, etc.) of the Trust Business Act and Article 6 (Conclusion of Trust Contract on Loss Compensation, etc.) of the Act on Provision, etc. of Trust Business by Financial Institutions shall apply mutatis mutandis to cases where a Life Insurance Company engage in Insurance-Proceed Trust Services pursuant to the provisions of paragraph (3). In this case, the phrases listed in the middle column of the following table in the provisions of the Trust Business Act listed in the left column of the table shall be deemed to be replaced with the phrases listed in the right column of the table.

Article 11, paragraph (10)	In the case where the registration under Article 7, paragraph (3) is not renewed, in the case where the license under Article 3 is rescinded pursuant to the provisions of Article 44, paragraph (1), in the case where the registration under Article 7, paragraph (1) is rescinded pursuant to the provisions of Article 45, paragraph (1), or the license under Article 3 or registration under Article 7, paragraph (1) pursuant to the provisions of Article 46, paragraph (1)	In the case where the license under Article 3, paragraph (1) of the Insurance Business Act is rescinded pursuant to the provisions of Articles 133 or 134 of the same Act, or the license under Article 3, paragraph (1) of the same Act pursuant to the provisions of Article 273 of the same Act
Article 42, paragraph (2)	Notification or measures under Article 17 to 19 inclusive or said	Said
Article 49, paragraph (1)	In the case where the registration under Article 7, paragraph (3) is not renewed, in the case where the license under Article 3 is rescinded pursuant to the provisions of Article 44, paragraph (1), or the registration under Article 7, paragraph (1) pursuant to the provisions of Article 45, paragraph (1)	License under Article 3, paragraph (1) of the Insurance Business Act pursuant to the provisions of Article 133 or 134 of the same Act

(9) In the case where a Life Insurance Company entrusts a third party to act as an agent or intermediary for the conclusion of a trust contract underwritten pursuant to the provisions of paragraph (3), the Life Insurance Company shall be deemed to be a trust company and the provisions of Article 2, paragraph (8) (Definitions) and Chapter V (including penal provisions pertaining to these provisions) of the Trust Business Act shall apply. In this case, the term "affiliated trust company" in the same Chapter means "affiliated Life Insurance Company" and "Article 34, paragraph (1)" in Article 78, paragraph (1) of the same Act means "Article 111, paragraphs (1) and (2) of the Insurance Business Act."

(10) A Life Insurance Company that engages in Insurance-Proceed Trust Services pursuant to the provisions of paragraph (3) shall be deemed to be a trust company pursuant to the provisions of Cabinet Order, with regard to the application of what is specified by Cabinet Order in the laws and regulations on taxation with regard to said Insurance-

Proceed Trust Services.

(Restriction on Other Business)
Article 100 An Insurance Company may not conduct business other than business it conducts pursuant to the provisions of Article 97 and the preceding two Articles and business conducted pursuant to other Acts.

(Measures Concerning Business Operations)
Article 100-2 Unless provided otherwise in this Act or any other Act, an Insurance Company shall, pursuant to the provisions of Cabinet Office Ordinance, take measures to ensure sound and appropriate management, such as explanation of important particulars of its business to its customers, appropriate handling of customer information acquired in relation to its business, and proper execution of any business entrusted to a third party.

(Establishment of a System for the Protection of Customers' Interests)
Article 100-2-2 (1) Whenever an Insurance Company, its Parent Financial Institution, etc. or Subsidiary Financial Institution, etc. conducts any transaction, such Insurance Company shall, pursuant to the provisions of Cabinet Office Ordinance, properly manage information connected with the business conducted by itself or its Subsidiary Financial Institution, etc. (limited to Insurance Business and any other business specified by Cabinet Office Ordinance), and establish a system for properly supervising the status of implementation of said business or taking any other measures necessary so that the interests of the customer of said business will not be unjustly impaired.
(2) The term "Parent Financial Institution, etc." as used in the preceding paragraph means a person that holds the majority of all shareholders' voting rights in an Insurance Company, and any other person that is specified by Cabinet Order as being closely related to said Insurance Company and which is an Insurance Company, Bank, Financial Instruments Transaction Business Operator (meaning a Financial Instruments Transaction Business Operator as defined in Article 2, paragraph (9) (Definitions) of the Financial Instruments and Exchange Act; the same shall apply hereinafter), or any other person conducting financial business that is specified by Cabinet Order.
(3) The term "Subsidiary Financial Institution, etc." as used in paragraph (1) means a person in which an Insurance Company holds the majority of All Shareholders' Voting Rights, etc. , and any other person that is specified by Cabinet Order as being closely related to said Insurance Company and which is an Insurance Company, Bank, Financial Instruments Transaction Business Operator, or any other person conducting financial business that is specified by Cabinet Order.

(Transactions, etc. with Specified Related Parties)
Article 100-3 An Insurance Company shall not make the following transactions or take the following actions with any Specified Related Party (meaning its Subsidiary Company, its Major Shareholder, the Insurance Holding Company of which it is a Subsidiary, or a Subsidiary of such Insurance Holding Company (other than the relevant Insurance Company itself); hereinafter the same shall apply in this Article), or any other parties to which an Insurance Company is specially related as specified by Cabinet Order, or with a customer of a Specified Related Party; provided, however, that this shall not apply to the cases where the authorization to make such transactions or take such actions is obtained from the Prime Minister for any of the compelling reasons specified by Cabinet Office Ordinance:
(i) Any transaction with the Specified Related Party, such as the purchase and sale of

assets, carried out on significantly different terms and conditions from those applied to normal transactions of said Insurance Company; and
(ii) Any transaction made or action taken with the Specified Related Party or the customer of the Specified Related Party which is equivalent to the transaction listed in the preceding item and which is specified by a Cabinet Office Ordinance as posing a risk to the sound and appropriate business operation of said Insurance Company.

(Restriction on Becoming an Unlimited Partner, etc.)
Article 100-4 An Insurance Company may not become an unlimited partner or a partner who executes the business of a membership company.

(Exclusion from Application of the Act on Prohibition of Private Monopolization and Maintenance of Fair Trade)
Article 101 (1) The provisions set forth in the Act on Prohibition of Private Monopolization and Maintenance of Fair Trade shall not apply to the following actions, which are taken with the authorization set forth in the following Article, paragraph (1); provided, however, that this shall not apply to the cases where any unfair trade practices are used, where the substantial restraint of competition in certain fields of trade unjustly harms the interests of Policyholders or the persons insured, or where one month has passed from the day of the public notice that was given under the provisions of Article 105, paragraph (4) (unless the Prime Minister has rendered a disposition under the provisions of Article 103 in response to the request in Article 105, paragraph (3)):
(i) Concerted actions carried out by a Non-Life Insurance Company with another Non-Life Insurance Company (including foreign non-life insurance companies, etc.) with regard to business specific to the aviation Insurance Business (meaning the business of underwriting insurance whose purpose is to insure aircraft (including rockets; hereinafter the same shall apply in this item) or cargo transported by aircraft, or insurance concerning liability for the compensation of damage caused by an aircraft accident; including business connected with underwriting injury insurance for persons on board the aircraft), the nuclear Insurance Business (meaning the business of underwriting insurance whose purpose is to insure a nuclear facility, or liability insurance for damages caused by an accident at a nuclear facility), the Automobile Liability Insurance Business based on the provisions of the Automobile Liability Insurance Act, or the business under an earthquake insurance contract prescribed in the Act on Earthquake Insurance (Act No. 73 of 1966); and
(ii) Concerted actions taken by a Non-Life Insurance Company with another Non-Life Insurance Company (including foreign non-life insurance companies, etc.) involving all or part of the following actions in connection with a reinsurance contract or insurance contract for reinsurance, if it is found that there is a risk of extreme disadvantage to a Policyholder or those insured unless a Non-Life Insurance Company and another Non-Life Insurance Company (including foreign non-life insurance companies, etc.) jointly provide for reinsurance in advance to carry out risk distribution or equalization with regard to business connected with the underwriting of insurance not listed in the preceding item:
(a) Ruling on contents of insurance contracts (except those pertaining to the insurance rate);
(b) Ruling on the method of damage obligatory contribution;
(c) Ruling on another party or amount concerning reinsurance transactions; and
(d) Ruling on the reinsurance rate and reinsurance fee.
(2) If a request under the provisions of Article 105, paragraph (3) is made concerning a Section of the contents of concerted actions, the provisions of the main clause of the

preceding paragraph shall be deemed applicable notwithstanding the provisions of the proviso of the preceding paragraph (limited to the Parts pertaining to the public notice that was given under the provisions of paragraph (4) of the same Article) for Sections of the contents of the concerted actions which do not pertain to the request.

(Authorization of Concerted Actions)
Article 102 (1) If a Non-Life Insurance Company seeks to carry out concerted actions under the provisions of the items of paragraph (1) of the preceding Article or modify its contents, it shall obtain authorization from the Prime Minister.
(2) The Prime Minister shall not grant the authorization of the preceding paragraph unless he/she finds that the contents of the concerted actions pertaining to the application for authorization of the same paragraph conform to the following items:
(i) There is no unjust harm to the interest of Policyholders or those insured;
(ii) The business is not unfairly discriminatory;
(iii) There is no unreasonable restraint of enrollment and withdrawal; and
(iv) It stays within the minimum necessary level in light of risk distribution or equalization, or any other purpose of the concerted actions.

(Order to Change of Concerted Actions and Rescission of Authorization)
Article 103 The Prime Minister shall, if he/she finds that the contents of the concerted actions pertaining to the authorization of the preceding Article, paragraph (1) no longer conform to the items of the same Article, paragraph (2), order the Non-Life Insurance Company to modify the contents of the concerted actions or rescind the authorization.

(Notification of Abolition of Concerted Actions)
Article 104 A Non-Life Insurance Company shall, upon abolishing concerted actions notify the Prime Minister of this without delay.

(Relationship with the Fair Trade Commission)
Article 105 (1) If the Prime Minister seeks to grant the authorization set forth in Article 102, paragraph (1), he/she shall, in advance, obtain the consent of the Fair Trade Commission.
(2) The Prime Minister shall, upon rendering a disposition under the provisions of Article 103 or accepting a notification under the provisions of the preceding Article, notify the Fair Trade Commission of this without delay.
(3) The Fair Trade Commission may, if it finds that the contents of the concerted actions which obtained the authorization set forth in Article 102, paragraph (1) no longer conform to the items of the same Article, paragraph (2), request the Prime Minister to render a disposition under the provisions of Article 103.
(4) The Fair Trade Commission shall, upon making a request under the provisions of the preceding paragraph, give public notice of this in the official gazette.

(Obligation to Conclude a Contract ,etc. with a Designated Dispute Resolution Organization for Life Insurance Services)
Article 105-2 (1) A Life Insurance Company shall take the measures specified in the following items according to the category of cases set forth in the respective items:
(i) in cases where there is a Designated Dispute Resolution Organization for Life Insurance Services (meaning a Designated Dispute Resolution Organization for which the Category of Dispute Resolution Services, etc. is Life Insurance Services; hereinafter the same shall apply in this Article): measures to conclude a Basic

Contract for the Implementation of Dispute Resolution Procedures for Life Insurance Services with a single Designated Dispute Resolution Organization for Life Insurance Services;
(ii) in cases where there is no Designated Life Insurance Dispute Resolution Organization: Complaint Processing Measures (meaning measures to have the person set forth in Article 308-13, paragraph (3), item (iii) provide advice or guidance to the employee or any other workers working to process complaints from the customers (including Policyholders, etc. other than customers; the same shall apply in this item) or any other measures specified by Cabinet Office Ordinance as being equivalent thereto; the same shall apply in the following Article, Article 272-13-2 and Article 299-2)) and Dispute Resolution Measures (meaning measures seeking to resolve disputes with customers through Certified Dispute Resolution Procedures (meaning Certified Dispute Resolution Procedures as defined in Article 2, item (iii) (Definition) of the Act on Promotion of Use of Alternative Dispute Resolution (Act No. 151 of 2004)) or any other measures specified by Cabinet Office Ordinance as being equivalent thereto; the same shall apply in the following Article, Article 272-13-2 and Article 299-2) concerning Life Insurance Services.
(2) A Life Insurance Company shall, if it has taken measures to conclude a Basic Contract for the Implementation of Dispute Resolution Procedures pursuant to the provisions of the preceding paragraph, publicize the trade name or name of the Designated Dispute Resolution Organization for Life Insurance Services that is the counterparty to said Basic Contract for the Implementation of Dispute Resolution Procedures.
(3) The provisions of paragraph (1) shall not apply for the periods specified in the following items according to the category of cases set forth in the respective items:
(i) if the relevant case which had fallen under the cases set forth in paragraph (1), item (i), has come to fall under the cases set forth in item (ii) of that paragraph: the period specified by the Prime Minister as the period necessary to take the measures specified in that item at the time of granting authorization for abolition of Dispute Resolution Services, etc. under Article 308-23, paragraph (1) or rescinding the designation under Article 308-24, paragraph (1);
(ii) if the relevant case had fallen under the cases set forth in paragraph (1), item (i), and the abolition of Dispute Resolution Services, etc. of a single Designated Dispute Resolution Organization for the Life Insurance Services under that item has been authorized under Article 308-23, paragraph (1) or the designation under Article 308-2, paragraph (1) of a single Designated Dispute Resolution Organization for Life Insurance Services under that item has been rescinded pursuant to Article 308-24, paragraph (1) (excluding the case set forth in the preceding item): the period specified by the Prime Minister at the time of granting such authorization or making such rescission, as the period necessary for taking the measures specified in paragraph (1), item (i); and
(iii) if the relevant case which had fallen under the cases set forth in paragraph (1), item (ii) has come to fall under the cases set forth in item (i) of that paragraph: the period specified by the Prime Minister at the time of designation under Article 308-2, paragraph (1), as the period necessary to take the measures specified in that item.

(Obligation to Conclude a Contract, etc. with a Designated Dispute Resolution Organization for Non-Life Insurance Services)
Article 105-3 (1) A Non-Life Insurance Company shall take the measures specified in the following items according to the category of cases set forth in the respective items:

(i) in cases where there is a Designated Dispute Resolution Organization for Non-Life Insurance Services (meaning a Designated Dispute Resolution Organization for which the Category of Dispute Resolution Services, etc. is Non-Life Insurance Services; hereinafter the same shall apply in this Article): measures to conclude a Basic Contract for the Implementation of Dispute Resolution Procedures for Non-Life Insurance Services with a single Designated Dispute Resolution Organization for Non-Life Insurance Services; or

(ii) in cases where there is no Designated Dispute Resolution Organization for Non-Life Insurance Services: Complaint Processing Measures and Dispute Resolution Measures concerning Non-Life Insurance Services.

(2) A Non-Life Insurance Company shall, if it has taken measures to conclude a Basic Contract for the Implementation of Dispute Resolution Procedures pursuant to the provisions of the preceding paragraph, publicize the trade name or name of the Designated Dispute Resolution Organization for Non-Life Insurance Services that is the counterparty to said Basic Contract for the Implementation of Dispute Resolution Procedures.

(3) The provisions of paragraph (1) shall not apply for the periods specified in the following items according to the category of cases set forth in the respective items:

(i) if the relevant case which had fallen under the cases set forth in paragraph (1), item (i), has come to fall under the cases set forth in item (ii) of that paragraph: the period specified by the Prime Minister at the time of granting authorization for abolition of Dispute Resolution Services, etc. under Article 308-23, paragraph (1) or rescinding the designation under Article 308-24, paragraph (1), as the period necessary to take the measures specified in that item;

(ii) if the relevant case had fallen under the cases set forth in paragraph (1), item (i), and the abolition of Dispute Resolution Services, etc. of a single Designated Dispute Resolution Organization for Non-Life Insurance Services under that item has been authorized under Article 308-23, paragraph (1) or the designation under Article 308-2, paragraph (1) of a single Designated Dispute Resolution Organization for Non-Life Insurance Services under that item has been rescinded pursuant to Article 308-24, paragraph (1) (excluding the case set forth in the preceding item): the period specified by the Prime Minister at the time of granting such authorization or making such rescission, as the period necessary for taking the measures specified in paragraph (1), item (i); and

(iii) if the relevant case which had fallen under the cases set forth in paragraph (1), item (ii) has come to fall under the cases set forth in item (i) of that paragraph: the period specified by the Prime Minister at the time of designation under Article 308-2, paragraph (1), as the period necessary to take the measures specified in that item.

Chapter IV Subsidiary, etc.

(Scope of an Insurance Company's Subsidiaries, etc.)

Article 106 (1) An Insurance Company shall not have as its Subsidiary any company other than a company that falls under any of the categories specified in the following items (hereinafter such companies shall be referred to as "Companies Eligible to Be Subsidiaries" in this Article):

(i) A Life Insurance Company;
(ii) A Non-Life Insurance Company;
(ii)-2 A Low-Cost, Short-Term Insurer;
(iii) A Bank;

Art.106　⑥ Insurance Business Act, Part II, Chap.IV, Sec.3

(iv) A long term credit bank as defined in Article 2 (Definitions) of the Long Term Credit Bank Act (Act No. 187 of 1952) (hereinafter referred to as "Long Term Credit Bank");

(iv)-2 Fund transfer specialists defined in Article 2, paragraph (3) (Definitions) of the Act on Financial Settlements (excluding those falling under the company set forth in item (ix)) which exclusively conduct Fund Transfer Business (meaning the fund transfer business defined in paragraph (2) of that Article) or any other business specified by Cabinet Office Ordinance (referred to as "Companies Specialized in Fund Transfer" in Article 271-22, paragraph (1), item (iv)-2);

(v) A Financial Instruments Transaction Business Operator that, apart from the Securities Services (meaning Securities Services as defined in Article 28, paragraph (8) (General Rules) of the Financial Instruments and Exchange Act; the same shall apply hereinafter), exclusively conducts any of the business specified by Cabinet Office Ordinance, such as business in which any of the actions listed in Article 35, paragraph (1), items (i) to (viii) inclusive (Scope of Business of Persons Who Engage in Type 1 Financial Instruments Transaction Business or Investment Management) of that Act (hereinafter referred to as "Company Specializing in Securities") are taken;

(vi) A Financial Instruments Intermediary as defined in Article 2, paragraph (12) (Definitions) of the Financial Instruments and Exchange Act that, apart from the Financial Instruments Intermediation Services (meaning the Financial Instruments Intermediation Services defined in Article 2, paragraph (11) (Definitions) of that Act and limited to those in which the following actions are taken in the course of trade; hereinafter the same shall apply in this item), exclusively conducts any of the business specified by Cabinet Office Ordinance, such as business incidental to Financial Instruments Intermediation Services (hereinafter referred to as "Company Specialized in Securities Intermediation");

(a) Acts listed in Article 2, paragraph (11), item (i) (Definitions) of the Financial Instruments and Exchange Act;

(b) Intermediation for the entrustment of the purchase and sale of securities on Financial Instruments Exchange Markets prescribed in Article 2, paragraph (17) (Definitions) of the Financial Instruments and Exchange Act or Foreign Financial Instruments Markets prescribed in Article 2, paragraph (8), item (iii), sub-item (b) (Definitions) of that Act (excluding actions listed in (c));

(c) Intermediation for the entrustment of actions listed in item (iii) or (v) of Article 28, paragraph (8) (General Rules) of the Financial Instruments and Exchange Act; and

(d) Actions listed in Article 2, paragraph (11), item (iii) of the Financial Instruments and Exchange Act.

(vii) A trust company specialized in the Trust Business (meaning the Trust Business defined in Article 1, paragraph (1) of the Act on Provision of Trust Business by Financial Institutions; the same shall apply in item (viii), sub-item (a) of the following paragraph) (hereinafter referred to as "Companies Specialized in Trust Business");

(viii) Foreign companies that conduct Insurance Business;

(ix) Foreign companies that engage in Banking (meaning Banking prescribed in Article 2, paragraph (2) (Definitions, etc.) of the Banking Act; the same shall apply hereinafter) (excluding those that fall under the category of companies specified in preceding item);

(x) Foreign companies that engage in Securities Services (excluding those that fall under the category of companies specified in item (viii));

(xi) Foreign Companies that conduct Trust Business (means Trust Business pre-

scribed in Article 2, paragraph (1) (Definitions) of the Trust Business Act; the same shall apply hereinafter) (excluding those that fall under the category of companies specified in item (viii));
(xii) Companies that exclusively operate Dependent Services or Finance-Related Services (limited, in case of those which operate Dependent Services, to companies that operate Dependent Services mainly for business operated by the Insurance Company, its Subsidiary Companies (limited to those that fall under any of the categories in item (i), (ii) or (viii); the same shall apply in paragraph (7)) or other entities specified by Cabinet Office Ordinance as being similar to the Insurance Company and its Subsidiary Companies, and in case of those which operate Finance-Related Services and fall under any of the following business categories, to the cases specified in for the respective categories):
(a) Companies which operate Specialized Banking-Related Services, Specialized Securities-Related Services and a Specialized Trust-Related Services: limited to the case where, among all voting rights in the company, the total voting rights held by the Insurance Company's Banking Subsidiaries, etc. exceed the total voting rights held by the Insurance Company and its Subsidiaries (other than its Banking Subsidiaries, etc. Securities Subsidiaries, etc. and Trust Subsidiaries, etc.), and the total voting rights held by the Insurance Company's Securities Subsidiaries, etc. exceed the total voting rights held by the Insurance Company and its Subsidiaries (other than its Banking Subsidiaries, etc., Securities Subsidiaries, etc. and Trust Subsidiaries, etc.), and the total voting rights held by the Insurance Company's Trust Subsidiaries, etc. exceed the total voting rights held by the Insurance Company and its Subsidiaries (other than its Banking Subsidiaries, etc., Securities Subsidiaries, etc. and Trust Subsidiaries, etc.);
(b) Companies which operate Specialized Banking-Related Services and Specialized Securities-Related Services (excluding those falling under the category listed in (a)): limited to the case where, among all voting rights in the company, the total voting rights held by the Insurance Company's Banking Subsidiaries, etc. exceed the total voting rights held by the Insurance Company and its Subsidiaries (other than its Banking Subsidiaries, etc. and Securities Subsidiaries, etc.), and the total voting rights held by the Insurance Company's Securities Subsidiaries, etc. exceed the total voting rights held by the Insurance Company and its Subsidiaries (other than its Banking Subsidiaries, etc. and Securities Subsidiaries, etc.);
(c) Companies which operate Specialized Banking-Related Services and Specialized Trust-Related Services (excluding those falling under the category listed in (a)): limited to the case where, among all voting rights in the company, the total voting rights held by the Insurance Company's Banking Subsidiaries, etc. exceed the total voting rights held by the Insurance Company and its Subsidiaries (other than its Banking Subsidiaries, etc. and Trust Subsidiaries, etc.), and the total voting rights held by the Insurance Company's Trust Subsidiaries, etc. exceed the total voting rights held by the Insurance Company and its Subsidiaries (other than its Banking Subsidiaries, etc. and Trust Subsidiaries, etc.);
(d) Companies which operate Specialized Securities-Related Services and a Specialized Trust-Related Services (excluding those falling under the category listed in (a)): limited to the case where, among all voting rights in the company, the total voting rights held by the Insurance Company's Securities Subsidiaries, etc. exceed the total voting rights held by the Insurance Company and its Subsidiaries (other than its Securities Subsidiaries, etc. and Trust Subsidiaries,

Art.106   ⑥ Insurance Business Act, Part II, Chap.IV, Sec.3

etc.), and the total voting rights held by the Insurance Company's Trust Subsidiaries, etc. exceeds the total voting rights held by the Insurance Company and its Subsidiaries (other than its Securities Subsidiaries, etc. and Trust Subsidiaries, etc.);
  (e) Companies which operate Specialized Banking-Related Services (excluding those falling under the category listed in (a), (b) or (c)): limited to the case where, among all voting rights in the company, the total voting rights held by the Insurance Company's Banking Subsidiaries, etc. exceed the total voting rights held by the Insurance Company and its Subsidiaries (other than its Banking Subsidiaries, etc.);
  (f) Companies which operate Specialized Securities-Related Services (other than a company falling under (a), (b) or (d)): limited to the case where among all voting rights in the company, the total voting rights held by the Insurance Company's Securities Subsidiaries, etc. exceed the total voting rights held by the Insurance Company and its Subsidiaries (other than its Securities Subsidiaries, etc.); and
  (g) Companies which operate Specialized Trust-Related Services (excluding those falling under the category listed in (a), (c) or (d)); limited to the case where, among all voting rights in the company, the total voting rights held by the Insurance Company's Trust Subsidiaries, etc. exceed the total voting rights held by the Insurance Company and its Subsidiaries (other than its Trust Subsidiaries, etc.);
 (xiii) Companies specified by Cabinet Office Ordinance as those exploring new business fields or conducting new business activities found to contribute considerably to the improvement of management (limited to the case where, among all voting rights in the company, the total voting rights held by the Insurance Company and its Subsidiaries other than those falling under the categories listed in the preceding item and specified by Cabinet Office Ordinance (such excluded companies shall be referred to as "Specified Subsidiary" in paragraph (7) of the following Article) does not exceed the Voting Right Holding Threshold prescribed in paragraph (1) of the same Article); and
 (xiv) Among Holding Companies whose Subsidiaries consist exclusively of companies falling under any of the categories specified in the preceding items, those specified by Cabinet Office Ordinance (including those which are scheduled to become such Holding Companies).
(2) In the preceding paragraph, the meanings of the terms listed in the following items shall be prescribed respectively in those items:
  (i) Dependent Services: Business specified by Cabinet Office Ordinance as being dependent on the business of an Insurance Company or a company falling under any of item (ii)-2 to (xi) inclusive of the preceding paragraph;
  (ii) Finance-Related Services: Business specified by Cabinet Office Ordinance as being incidental or related to the Insurance Business, Banking, Securities Services or Trust Business;
  (iii) Specialized Banking-Related Services: Business specified by Cabinet Office Ordinance as incidental or related exclusively to Banking;
  (iv) Specialized Securities-Related Services: Business specified by Cabinet Office Ordinance as being incidental or related exclusively to the Securities Services;
  (v) Specialized Trust-Related Services: Business specified by Cabinet Office Ordinance as being incidental or related exclusively to the Trust Business.
  (vi) Banking Subsidiary, etc. : An Insurance Company's Subsidiary that falls under any of the following categories:
    (a) A Bank (including a Long Term Credit Bank; hereinafter the same shall apply in

this item) or a foreign company that operates in banking;
  (b) A Holding Company falling under item (xiv) of the preceding paragraph which has a company falling under (a) as its Subsidiary; or
  (c) Any other company that is the Subsidiary of a Bank that is itself a Subsidiary of an Insurance Company and specified by Cabinet Office Ordinance;
(vii) Securities Subsidiary, etc. : An Insurance Company's Subsidiary that falls under any of the following categories:
  (a) A Company Specializing in Securities, Company Specializing in Securities Intermediation, or foreign company engaged in Securities Services;
  (b) A Holding Company that falls under the category listed in item (xiv) of the preceding paragraph and which has a company that falls under the category listed in (a) above as its Subsidiary; and
  (c) Any other company that is a Subsidiary of that Insurance Company and that is a Subsidiary of a Company Specializing in Securities or a Subsidiary of a Company Specializing in Securities Intermediation and is specified by Cabinet Office Ordinance; and
(viii) Trust Subsidiary, etc. : An Insurance Company's Subsidiary that falls under any of the following categories:
  (a) A Bank that operates in the Trust Business under the authorization set forth in Article 1, paragraph (1) (Authorization for Trust Business) of the Act on the Provision, etc. of Trust Business by Financial Institutions (hereinafter referred to as "Trust Bank" in this item);
  (b) A Company Specialized in Trust Business or a foreign company that operates in the Trust Business;
  (c) A Holding Company that falls under the category listed in item (xiv) of the preceding paragraph and which has a company that falls under the category listed in (a) or (b) above as its Subsidiary; and
  (d) Any other company that is a Subsidiary of that Insurance Company and that is a Subsidiary of a Trust Bank or a Subsidiary of a Company Specialized in Trust Services and is specified by Cabinet Office Ordinance.
(3) The provisions of paragraph (1) shall not apply where a company other than a Company Eligible to Be a Subsidiary became the Subsidiary of that Insurance Company following any of the events specified by Cabinet Office Ordinance, such as the acquisition of shares or equity interests as a result of the exercise of security rights by the Insurance Company or its Subsidiaries; provided, however, that the Insurance Company shall take necessary measures for making the company, which became to its Subsidiary in a manner as described as above, cease to be its Subsidiary by the day on which one year has elapsed from the date on which that event arose.
(4) An Insurance Company shall, if it seeks to have as its Subsidiary any of the Companies Eligible to Be a Subsidiary listed in paragraph (1), items (i) to (xii) inclusive or (xiv) (other than a company specialized in Dependent Services (meaning Dependent Services falling under paragraph (2), item (i); hereinafter the same shall apply in this paragraph and paragraph (7)) or in any business specified by Cabinet Office Ordinance as ancillary or related to the Insurance Business (for a company operates Dependent Services, limited to one that operates them mainly for business operated by the Insurance Company); referred to as "Insurance Company, etc. Eligible to Be a Subsidiary" hereinafter in this Article as well as in paragraph (4), item (i) of the following Article), obtain in advance the authorization from the Prime Minister, unless it receives an authorization for business acquisition, merger or company split under Article 142, Article 167, paragraph (1) or Article 173-6, paragraph (1).
(5) The provisions of the preceding paragraph shall not apply where an Insurance Compa-

ny, etc. Eligible to Be a Subsidiary became the Subsidiary of an Insurance Company due to the acquisition of its shares or equity interests as a result of the exercise of security rights by the Insurance Company or its Subsidiary, or any other justifiable event specified by Cabinet Office Ordinance; provided, however, that the Insurance Company shall take necessary measures for the Insurance Company, etc. Eligible to Be a Subsidiary to stop being its Subsidiary by the day on which one year has elapsed from the date on which the cause arose, unless the Insurance Company has obtained an authorization from the Prime Minister to allow the Insurance Company etc. Eligible to Be a Subsidiary that became its Subsidiary, continue to be its Subsidiary.
(6) The provisions of paragraph (4) shall apply mutatis mutandis to the cases where an Insurance Company seeks make a company it has as its Subsidiary which falls under any of the categories prescribed in the items of paragraph (1) into a Subsidiary that falls under any of the categories prescribed in the items of that paragraph (limited to an Insurance Company, etc. Eligible to Be a Subsidiary).
(7) In a case falling under item (xii) of paragraph (1), or paragraph (4), the Prime Minister shall establish standards for whether a company is operating Dependent Services mainly for an Insurance Company, its Subsidiaries, any other similar company specified by Cabinet Office Ordinance, or for the business conducted by an Insurance Company.

(Restrictions on the Acquisition of Voting Rights, etc. by an Insurance Company, etc.)
Article 107 (1) An Insurance Company and its Subsidiaries may not acquire or hold voting rights in a Domestic Company (excluding companies falling under the category listed in paragraph (1), items (i) to (vii) inclusive of the preceding Article, (xii) or (xiv) ; hereinafter the same shall apply in this Article) in a total number that exceeds the Voting Right Holding Threshold (meaning the number equal to 5 percent of All Shareholders' Voting Rights, etc. in the Domestic Company; the same shall apply in this Article).
(2) The provisions of the preceding paragraph shall not apply to the cases where an Insurance Company and its Subsidiaries, following any of the events specified by Cabinet Office Ordinance such as the acquisition of shares or equity interests through exercise of security rights, comes to acquire or hold voting rights in a Domestic Company if the total number of the voting right held by the Insurance Company and its Subsidiaries exceeds the Voting Right Holding Threshold; provided, however, that the Insurance Company and/or the Subsidiaries shall not continue to hold the part of the voting rights which it came to acquire or hold in excess of the Voting Right Holding Threshold after one year from the day on which it came to acquire or hold the voting rights, unless the Insurance Company has in advance obtained approval for holding such portion of the voting rights from the Prime Minister.
(3) In the case referred to in the proviso in the preceding paragraph, if the total number of voting rights acquired or held by the Insurance Company and its Subsidiaries exceeds 50 percent of All Shareholders' Voting Rights, etc. in a Domestic Company, the Prime Minister's approval given under that paragraph shall not cover the part of the voting rights which the Insurance Company and its Subsidiaries came to acquire or hold in excess of 50 percent; and the approval of the Prime Minister shall be given on the condition that the Insurance Company and its Subsidiaries promptly dispose of voting rights they came to acquire or hold in excess of the Voting Right Holding Threshold.
(4) Notwithstanding the provisions of paragraph (1), in the case listed in any of the following items, even if the total number of voting rights which an Insurance Company and its Subsidiaries will hold in a Domestic Company on the day prescribed in the respec-

tive items exceeds the Voting Right Holding Threshold, the Insurance Company and its Subsidiaries may hold them after that day; provided, however, that the Prime Minister shall not grant the authorization (or the license in the case of item (vi); the same shall apply in the next paragraph) referred to in the following items, if the total number voting rights that the relevant Insurance Company and its Subsidiaries will hold in the Domestic Company in the case referred to in the respective items exceeds 50 percent of All Shareholders' Voting Rights, etc. in that Domestic Company:
- (i) If the Insurance Company has received the authorization set forth in paragraph (4) of the preceding Article and made a Subsidiary Insurance Company, etc. that is Eligible to Be a Subsidiary its Subsidiary (limited to the cases specified by Cabinet Office Ordinance): the day on which that company becomes its Subsidiary
- (ii) If the Insurance Company has received the authorization set forth in Article 142 and been transferred any other party's business under (limited to the cases specified by Cabinet Office Ordinance): the day on which the transfer is carried out;
- (iii) If a company that has been established by Joint Incorporation-Type Split following authorization under Article 173-6, paragraph (1) has obtained a license under Article 3, paragraph (1) and become an Insurance Company: the day companion which it obtains the license;
- (iv) If the Insurance Company has succeeded any other party's business through an absorption-type split following authorization set forth in Article 173-6, paragraph (1) (limited to the cases specified by Cabinet Office Ordinance): the day on which the absorption-type split is carried out;
- (v) If the Insurance Company is established by Merger under the authorization set forth in Article 167, paragraph (1): the day on which the Insurance Company is established; and
- (vi) If the Insurance Company carries out a Merger under the authorization set forth in Article 167, paragraph (1) (limited to the cases where the Insurance Company survives the merger): the day on which the Merger is carried out.
(5) The Prime Minister's authorization set forth in the items of the preceding paragraph shall be given on the condition that, the portion of the voting rights in the Domestic Company that an Insurance Company and its Subsidiaries hold in excess of the Voting Right Holding Threshold as of the day specified in the respective items will be disposed of in accordance with standards set by the Prime Minister by the day on which five years has elapsed from the day.
(6) If an Insurance Company and its Subsidiaries come to hold a total number of voting rights in a Domestic Company which is in excess of the Voting Right Holding Threshold, the portion in excess of the Voting Right Holding Threshold shall be deemed to be acquired or held by that Insurance Company.
(7) In the cases of the referred to in the preceding paragraphs, with respect to acquisition or holding of voting rights in a company specified by Cabinet Office Ordinance as that exploring new business fields or as those engaged in new business activities which are found to significantly contribute to improvement of business management, a Specified Subsidiary shall be deemed not to be a Subsidiary of the Insurance Company.
(8) The provisions of Article 2, paragraph (15) shall apply mutatis mutandis to the voting rights acquired or held by an Insurance Company or its Subsidiaries under any of the preceding paragraphs.

Article 108 Deleted

Chapter V Accounting

(Business Year)
Article 109 The Business Year of an Insurance Company shall run from 1 April to 31 March of the next year.

(Business Report, etc.)
Article 110 (1) An Insurance Company shall, for each business year, prepare an interim business report and business report describing the status of its business and property for submission to the Prime Minister.
(2) Where an Insurance Company has a Subsidiary or any other company to which it is specially related as specified by Cabinet Office Ordinance (referred to as "Subsidiary Company, etc." hereinafter in this Chapter as well as in the following Chapter), the Insurance Company shall, for each business year, prepare in addition to the report set forth in the preceding paragraph an interim business report and business report describing the status of the business and property of the Insurance Company and its Subsidiary, etc. in a consolidated manner for submission to the Prime Minister.
(3) The particulars for inclusion in the reports set forth in the preceding two paragraphs, their submission dates and other necessary particulars regarding those reports shall be specified by Cabinet Office Ordinance.

(Public Inspection, etc. of Explanatory Documents on Business and Property Status)
Article 111 (1) An Insurance Company shall, for each business year, prepare explanatory documents detailing the particulars specified by Cabinet Office Ordinance as pertaining to the status of its business and property, and keep them for public inspection at its head office or principal office and branch offices or secondary offices, or any other equivalent place specified by Cabinet Office Ordinance.
(2) If an Insurance Company has a Subsidiary, etc. , the Insurance Company shall, for each business year, prepare in addition to the explanatory documents set forth in the preceding paragraph explanatory documents detailing, with regard to the Insurance Company and its Subsidiary, etc. , the particulars specified by Cabinet Office Ordinance as pertaining to the status of the business and property of the Insurance Company and its Subsidiary, etc. in a consolidated manner, and keep them for public inspection at the Insurance Company's head office or principal office and its branch offices or secondary offices, or any other equivalent place specified by Cabinet Office Ordinance.
(3) The explanatory documents set forth in the preceding two paragraphs may be prepared in the form of electromagnetic record.
(4) Where the explanatory documents set forth in paragraph (1) or (2) are prepared in the form of electromagnetic record, the Insurance Company may take the measures specified by Cabinet Office Ordinance as measures to ensure that the information recorded in the electromagnetic records is available to many and unspecified persons at its head office or principal office and its branch offices or secondary offices, or any other equivalent place specified by Cabinet Office Ordinance. In this case, the explanatory documents set forth in paragraph (1) or (2) shall be deemed to be kept for public inspection pursuant to the provisions of paragraph (1) or (2).
(5) In addition to what is provided for in the preceding paragraphs, the period for making the documents set forth in paragraph (1) or (2) available for public inspection and any other particular that is necessary in order to apply the provisions of the preceding paragraphs shall be specified by Cabinet Office Ordinance.
(6) An Insurance Company shall endeavor to disclose, in addition to the particulars set forth in paragraph (1) or (2), any particular that should serve as reference for Policyholders and other customers in knowing the status of the business and property of the

Insurance Company and its Subsidiary, etc.

(Special Provisions on Valuation of Shares)
Article 112 (1) An Insurance Company may, if the current value of the quoted shares that it owns (excluding those shares which are accounted for under the Special Account set forth in Article 118, paragraph (1); hereinafter the same shall apply in this paragraph) exceeds the acquisition value of such shares, attach to the shares any value that exceeds their acquisition value but does not exceed their current value with the authorization of the Prime Minister, pursuant to the provisions of Cabinet Office Ordinance.
(2) Any profit recorded as a result of revaluation under the preceding paragraph shall be set aside as a Reserve specified by Cabinet Office Ordinance.

(Amortization of Business Expenditures, etc.)
Article 113 An Insurance Company may credit to the assets on the balance sheet an amount pertaining to its business expenditures for the first five years following the establishment of the Insurance Company as well as any other amount specified by Cabinet Office Ordinance. In this case, the Insurance Company shall, pursuant to the provisions of its articles of incorporation, amortize the amount thus credited within ten years from the establishment of the Insurance Company.

(Policy Dividend)
Article 114 (1) Any policy dividend (meaning the distribution to Policyholders, in whole or in Part, of those profits obtained by investing insurance premiums and the money received as insurance premiums which have neither been allocated to any payments such as insurance proceeds or refunds, nor to any business or other expenditures, where such distribution is stipulated in the insurance contracts, the same shall apply hereinafter) distributed by a stock Insurance Company shall meet the standards specified by Cabinet Office Ordinance as standards for fair and equitable distribution.
(2) A Cabinet Office Ordinance shall specified how to fund the reserves for policy dividends as well as any other necessary particular pertaining to Policyholder dividends.

(Price Fluctuation Reserve)
Article 115 (1) An Insurance Company shall, with regard to the assets specified by Cabinet Office Ordinance as susceptible to losses due to price fluctuation, such as shares (referred to as "Shares, etc." in the following paragraph), within its portfolio, set aside as a price fluctuation reserves the amount calculated pursuant to the provisions of Cabinet Office Ordinance; provided, however, that this shall not apply to any amount exempted from these funding standards by virtue of an authorization granted by the Prime Minister to relieve the Insurance Company of these standards in whole or in part.
(2) The Reserves set forth in the preceding paragraph shall not be reduced unless it is allocated to compensation for any excess amount of the losses due to buying and selling, etc. of Shares, etc. (meaning losses due to buying and selling, revaluation and fluctuation in foreign exchange rates, and losses on redemption) over the profits due to buying and selling, etc. of Shares, etc. (meaning profits due to buying and selling, revaluation and fluctuation in foreign exchange rates (excluding any profit credited as a result of revaluation under Article 112, paragraph (1)), and gains on redemption); provided, however, that this shall not apply to the cases where the Prime Minister has approved such reduction.

(Policy Reserve)

Article 116 (1) An Insurance Company shall, for each accounting period, set aside a certain amount of money as a policy reserves to prepare for future performance of obligations under its insurance contracts.

(2) The Prime Minister may set necessary standards for the method of funding the policy reserves pertaining to the long-term insurance contracts specified by Cabinet Office Ordinance, as well as for the levels of the coefficients that should constitute the basis for calculating the amount of the policy reserve, such as expected mortality.

(3) In addition to what is provided for in the preceding two paragraphs, the method of funding the policy reserves pertaining to any reinsured insurance contract and any other particular necessary to the funding of the policy reserves shall be specified by Cabinet Office Ordinance.

(Reserve for Outstanding Claims)

Article 117 (1) For each business year, an Insurance Company shall set aside a certain amount of money as reserves for outstanding claims, where it has any payments due, such as insurance proceeds or refunds (hereinafter referred to as "Insurance Proceeds, etc." in this paragraph), under its insurance contracts, or any other equivalent payment specified by Cabinet Office Ordinance that has not been recorded as an expenditure for Insurance Proceeds, etc.

(2) A Cabinet Office Ordinance shall specify the necessary particulars of the funding of the reserves for outstanding claims set forth in the preceding paragraph.

(Statutory Lien for Policyholders, etc. in Life Insurance Company)

Article 117-2 (1) In a Life Insurance Company, the Policyholders (excluding the holders of reinsurance policies) and the persons who have any of the following rights (excluding the rights pertaining to reinsurance) shall enjoy a statutory lien against the whole assets of the Life Insurance Company for the total amount of money paid for the insurers and for the amount of the relevant right, respectively:

(i) Insurance Claims;

(ii) The right to demand compensation for losses (other than the right listed in the preceding item); or

(iii) The right to demand a payment, such as refund, dividend of surplus or policy dividend (other than insurance proceeds).

(2) The statutory lien set forth in the preceding paragraph shall be ranked next in priority to the statutory lien set forth in Article 306, item (i) of the Civil Code (Statutory lien for expenses for common interest).

(Special Accounts)

Article 118 (1) An Insurance Company shall, as regards performance-linked insurance contracts (meaning the insurance contracts stipulating that insurance proceeds, refunds or other benefits shall be paid to the Policyholders in accordance with the performance of investment of the money received as insurance premiums) and any other class of insurance contract specified by Cabinet Office Ordinance, create a Special Account to separate the property managed under such insurance contracts from other properties (hereinafter referred to as "Special Account" in this Article).

(2) Unless provided otherwise in Cabinet Office Ordinance, an Insurance Company shall not take any of the following actions:

(i) Transferring any property to be accounted for under a Special Account to a Non-Special Account or to another Special Account; or

(ii) Transferring to a Special Account any property other than a property to be ac-

counted for under the Special Account.
(3) A Cabinet Office Ordinance shall specify how to manage the property belonging to a Special Account and any other necessary particulars for Special Accounts.

Article 119 Deleted

(Appointment of Actuary, etc.)
Article 120 (1) The board of directors of an Insurance Company (limited to a Life Insurance Company or a Non-Life Insurance Company meeting the requirements specified by Cabinet Office Ordinance. The same shall apply in the paragraph (3) and in Article 122) shall appoint an actuary to Participate with regard to the particulars specified by Cabinet Office Ordinance as actuarial particulars involving, among others, the method of calculating insurance premiums.
(2) The actuary shall be a person with necessary knowledge and experience with regard to actuarial science who meets the requirements specified by Cabinet Office Ordinance.
(3) An Insurance Company shall, if it has appointed an actuary or if its actuary has left office, notify the Prime Minister of this without delay, pursuant to the provisions of Cabinet Office Ordinance.

(Actuary's Duties)
Article 121 (1) The actuary shall, for each accounting period, check the following particulars pursuant to the provisions of Cabinet Office Ordinance and submit to the board of directors a written opinion describing his/her findings:
  (i) Whether the policy reserves pertaining to the insurance contracts specified by Cabinet Office Ordinance has been funded according to sound actuarial practice;
  (ii) Whether policy dividends or dividends of surplus to members have been distributed in a fair and equitable manner; and
  (iii) Any other particular specified by Cabinet Office Ordinance.
(2) The actuary shall, without delay following the submission to the board of directors of the written opinion set forth in the preceding paragraph, submit a copy of the written opinion to the Prime Minister.
(3) The Prime Minister may request the actuary to provide explanations about the copy of his/her written opinion set forth in the preceding paragraph and to present an opinion on any other particular within the scope of his/her duties.
(4) In addition to what is provided for in the preceding three paragraphs, any necessary particulars of a written opinion as set forth in paragraph (1) shall be specified by Cabinet Office Ordinance.

(Dismissal of Actuary)
Article 122 The Prime Minister may order an Insurance Company to dismiss its actuary, if the latter has violated any provisions of this Act or any dispositions of the Prime Minister under this Act.

(Designation, etc.)
Article 122-2 (1) The Prime Minister may, on application, designate a general incorporated association that he/she considers to conform to the following standards regarding the business set forth in the following paragraph as a person to conduct such business:
  (i) The incorporated association is found to have sufficient accounting and technical expertise to ensure proper performance of its business; and

(ii) In addition to the standard set forth in the preceding item, the incorporated association has the ability to implement its business in a fair and appropriate manner.
(2) An incorporated association designated pursuant to the provisions of the preceding paragraph (hereinafter referred to as "Designated Association" in this Article) shall conduct any of the following business:
(i) Developing and training persons with expert knowledge and skills on actuarial science;
(ii) Conducting necessary research and study, preparing statistics, collecting data, or providing information regarding actuarial science;
(iii) Any business involving the levels of coefficients that should constitute the basis for calculating the amount of the policy reserves set forth in Article 116, paragraph (2) or pertaining to any other actuarial particular, with which the Prime Minister has entrusted it; or
(iv) Business incidental to any of the business listed in the preceding three items.
(3) The Prime Minister may, if he/she finds that an improvement is required in the operation of business set forth in the preceding paragraph, order the Designated Association to take necessary measures for such improvement.
(4) The Prime Minister may, if he/she finds it necessary for ensuring proper operation of business specified in paragraph (2), request the Designated Association to submit as necessary a report on the services under that paragraph or its property, or cause his/her officials to enter the Designated Association's offices, ask questions about the business provided for in that paragraph or its property or inspect its books and documents and other related materials.
(5) The Prime Minister may rescind a designation under paragraph (1) (referred to as "Designation" in item (ii) and the following paragraph), if the Designated Association:
(i) is found to be unable to implement its business under paragraph (2) in a fair and appropriate manner;
(ii) has committed any wrongful conduct in relation to the Designation; or
(iii) has violated an order under paragraph (3).
(6) In addition to what is provided for in the preceding paragraphs, the procedure of Designation and any other necessary particulars involving Designated Associations shall be specified by Cabinet Office Ordinance.

Chapter VI Supervision

(Change of Particulars Prescribed in Statement of Business Procedures, etc.)
Article 123 (1) An Insurance Company must obtain authorization from the Prime Minister if it seeks to modify the particulars prescribed in the documents listed in Article 4, paragraph (2), items (ii) to (iv) inclusive (except the particulars specified by Cabinet Office Ordinance as being not very likely to impair the protection of Policyholders, etc.).
(2) An Insurance Company shall, if it seeks to modify the particulars specified by Cabinet Office Ordinance set forth in the preceding paragraph in the case where it seeks to modify the particulars prescribed in the documents prescribed in the same paragraph, notify the Prime Minister thereof in advance.

(Authorization of Change of Particulars Prescribed in Statement of Business Procedures, etc.)
Article 124 Whenever an application has been filed for the authorization referred to in the preceding Article, paragraph (1), the Prime Minister shall examine whether the particulars set forth in each of the following items conform to the standards prescribed

in the relevant item:
(i) particulars given in the documents listed in Article 4, paragraph (2), items (ii) and (iii): the standards set forth in Article 5, paragraph (1), item (iii), sub-items (a) to (e) inclusive; and
(ii) particulars given in the documents listed in Article 4, paragraph (2), item (iv): the standards set forth in Article 5, paragraph (1), item (iv), sub-item (a) to (c) inclusive.

(Notification, etc. of Change of Particulars Prescribed in Statement of Business Procedures, etc.)
Article 125 (1) In the case where a notification under the provisions of Article 123, paragraph (2) is made, it shall be deemed that the change pertaining to said notification was made on the day on which ninety days have passed since the day immediately following the date on which the Prime Minister received said notification.
(2) The Prime Minister may, if he/she finds that the particulars of a notification under the provisions of Article 123, paragraph (2) conform to the standards listed in Article 5, paragraph (1), item (iii), sub-item (a) to (e) inclusive of or item (iv), sub-item (a) to (c) inclusive, shorten the period of time prescribed in the preceding paragraph to a period of time found to be reasonable. In this case, the Prime Minister shall, without delay, give notice of the shortened period of time to the person that made said notification.
(3) The Prime Minister may, if there are reasonable grounds requiring a reasonable period of time for examining whether the particulars of a notification under the provisions of Article 123, paragraph (2) conform to the standards listed in Article 5, paragraph (1), item (iii), sub-items (a) to (e) inclusive or item (iv), sub-items (a) to (c) inclusive and if the Prime Minister finds that said examination will not terminate within the period of time prescribed in paragraph (1), extend the period of time to a period found to be reasonable. In this case, the Prime Minister shall, without delay, give notice of the extended period of time and the reasons for the extension to the person that made said notification.
(4) The Prime Minister may, if he/she finds that the particulars of the notification under the provisions of Article 123, paragraph (2) do not conform to the standards listed in Article 5, paragraph (1), item (iii), sub-items (a) to (e) inclusive or item (iv), sub-items (a) to (c) inclusive, order the person that made said notification to modify the particulars of said notification for a limited period or revoke said notification, limited to within a period of time until the day on which ninety days have passed since the day following the date on which said notification was received (the extended period of time in the case where the period of time is extended pursuant to the provisions of the preceding paragraph).

(Authorization of an amendment in the articles of incorporation)
Article 126 Any resolutions of the shareholders' meeting or the general members' council or the General Representative Members' Council concerning any amendment in the articles of incorporation involving the following particulars of an Insurance Company shall not come into effect without obtaining the authorization of the Prime Minister:
(i) Trade name or name;
(ii) The particulars of the redemption of funds;
(iii) Reasons for the withdrawal of members;
(iv) The set number of representative members and the particulars of how they are selected;
(v) The particulars of the contract set forth in Article 63, paragraph (1);

(vi) The particulars of the policy on Policyholders' dividends in a Converted Stock Company set forth in Article 86, paragraph (5);
(vii) The particulars of the appropriation of residual assets set forth in Article 182;
(viii) The particulars of the policy set forth in Article 240-5, paragraph (5).

(Particulars Requiring Notice)
Article 127 (1) An Insurance Company shall, if it falls under any of the following items, notify the Prime Minister of this pursuant to the provisions of Cabinet Office Ordinance:
(i) If it has commenced Insurance Business;
(ii) If it seeks to have a company falling under the category specified in Article 106, paragraph (1), item (xii) or (xiii) (excluding one for which paragraph (4) provides that in order to have such a company as its Subsidiary, an Insurance Company is to obtain authorization) become its Subsidiary (excluding the case where it seeks to accept a transfer of business or to effect a merger or company split upon obtaining authorization pursuant to the provisions of Article 142, Article 167, paragraph (1) or Article 173-6, paragraph (1));
(iii) If its Subsidiary ceases to be its Subsidiary (excluding the case where it accepted a business or demerged upon obtaining authorization under the provisions of Article 142 or Article 173-6, paragraph (1)), or if a Subsidiary that falls under the category of an Insurance Company, etc. That Is Eligible to Be a Subsidiary prescribed in Article 106, paragraph (4) becomes a Subsidiary that does not fall under the category of an Insurance Company, etc. That Is Eligible to Be a Subsidiary;
(iv) If it seeks to increase the amount of capital or the total amount of funds;
(v) If it modifies the articles of incorporation with regard to particulars other than those provided for otherwise;
(vi) If it seeks to establish an branch office or secondary office or representative office in a foreign state;
(vii) If its voting rights are acquired or come to be held by a single shareholder, in excess of 5 percent of all shareholders' voting rights; or;
(viii) If it falls under any of the other cases specified by a Cabinet Office Ordinance (Cabinet Office Ordinance or Ordinance of the Ministry of Finance for those pertaining to the financial bankruptcy processing system and financial crisis management).
(2) The provisions of Article 2, paragraph (15) shall apply mutatis mutandis to the voting rights in an Insurance Company to be acquired or held by one shareholder prescribed in the preceding paragraph, item (vii).

(Submission of Reports or Materials)
Article 128 (1) The Prime Minister may, if he/she finds it necessary for protecting the Policyholders, etc. and for ensuring the sound and appropriate business operation of an Insurance Company, require the Insurance Company to submit reports or materials concerning the status of its business or property.
(2) If and to the extent that the Prime Minister finds it particularly necessary for protecting the Policyholders, etc. and for ensuring the sound and appropriate business operation of an Insurance Company, he/she may require said Insurance Company's Subsidiary, etc. (meaning a Subsidiary Company or any other juridical person specified by Cabinet Office Ordinance as one whose operations are controlled by the Insurance Company; the same shall apply in the following paragraph and the following Article, paragraphs (2) and (3)) or a person the Insurance Company has entrusted with its business, to submit reports or materials that would helpful to understand the status of

the business or property of the Insurance Company.
(3) An Insurance Company's Subsidiary, etc. or a person that an Insurance Company has entrusted with its business may refuse to submit reports or materials required under the provisions of the preceding paragraph if there are justifiable grounds for it to do so.

(Inspection)
Article 129 (1) The Prime Minister may, if he/she finds it necessary for protecting the Policyholders, etc. and for ensuring the sound and appropriate business operation of an Insurance Company, have his/her officials enter a facility of the Insurance Company, such as a business or other office, ask questions about the status of its business or property, or inspect relevant objects such as books and documents.
(2) If and to the extent that the Prime Minister finds it particularly necessary in entering a site, asking questions, or conducting an inspection under the preceding paragraph, he/she may have his/her officials enter a facility of the Insurance Company's Subsidiary, etc. or of a person the Insurance Company has entrusted with its business, have such officials question the Insurance Company or ask questions about any particulars that are necessary for their inspection, or have such officials inspect relevant objects such as books and documents.
(3) An Insurance Company's Subsidiary, etc. or a person that an Insurance Company has entrusted with its business may refuse the questioning and inspection under the provisions of the preceding paragraph if there are justifiable grounds for it to do so.

(Standard of Soundness)
Article 130 The Prime Minister may use the following amounts with respect to an Insurance Company and establish whether or not the Insurance Company has an appropriate level of solvency in terms of its ability to pay for Insurance Proceeds, etc. as the standard by which the soundness of its business management is determined:
  (i) Total amount of the items specified by Cabinet Office Ordinance such as capital, funds and reserves; and
  (ii) Amount calculated pursuant to the provisions of Cabinet Office Ordinance as the amount for coping with possible risks exceeding standard predictions that may occur due to any events pertaining to the insurance being underwritten, such as insured events.

(Order for Modification of the Particulars Prescribed in Statement of Business Procedures, etc.)
Article 131 If and to the extent that the Prime Minister finds it necessary for protecting the Policyholders, etc. and for ensuring the sound and appropriate business operation of an Insurance Company in light of the status of the business or property of the Insurance Company or a change in the circumstances, he/she may order the Insurance Company to modify the particulars prescribed in the documents listed in Article 4, paragraph (2), items (ii) to (iv) inclusive.

(Suspension of Business, etc.)
Article 132 (1) If the Prime Minister finds it necessary for protecting the Policyholders, etc. and for ensuring the sound and appropriate business operation of an Insurance Company in light of the status of the business or property of the Insurance Company or the status of the assets of the Insurance Company and its Subsidiary, etc. , he/she may request the Insurance Company to submit an improvement program for ensuring soundness in its management by identifying particulars with regard to which measures are to be taken as well as due dates or order changes to the submitted improvement

program, or, to the extent that the Prime Minister finds necessary, he/she may order the full or partial suspension of business of the Insurance Company with due dates, or order the deposit of property of the Insurance Company or other necessary measures for supervision.
(2) An order under the provisions of the preceding paragraph (including the request for submission of an improvement program) that it is found to be necessary to issue due to an Insurance Company's level of solvency in terms of its ability to pay for Insurance Proceeds, etc. , must be an order specified by Cabinet Office Ordinance or Ordinance of the Ministry of Finance that corresponds to the Insurance Company's level of solvency in terms of its ability to pay for Insurance Proceeds, etc.

(Rescission of License, etc.)
Article 133　The Prime Minister may, if an Insurance Company has come to fall under any of the following items, order the full or partial suspension of the business of the Insurance Company or the dismissal of the director, executive officer, accounting advisor, or company auditor, or rescind the license set forth in Article 3, paragraph (1):
(i) If it is in violation of laws and regulations, disposition of the Prime Minister pursuant to laws and regulations, or particularly important particulars among those prescribed in the documents listed in the items of Article 4, paragraph (2);
(ii) If it is in violation of the conditions attached to said license; and
(iii) If it engages in conduct prejudicial to the public interest.

Article 134　The Prime Minister may, if he/she finds that the property status of an Insurance Company is significantly worsening and that it is not appropriate for it to continue in the Insurance Business from the viewpoint of protecting Policyholders, etc. , rescind the license of the Insurance Company set forth in Article 3, paragraph (1).

Chapter VII　Portfolio Transfers of Insurance Contracts, Assignment or Acquisition of Business, and Entrustment of Business and Property Administration

Section 1　Portfolio Transfers of Insurance Contracts

(Portfolio Transfers of Insurance Contracts)
Article 135　(1) An Insurance Company may, pursuant to the provisions of this Act, transfer insurance contracts to another Insurance Company (including a Foreign Insurance Company, etc.; hereinafter the same shall apply in this paragraph) under an Agreement with such other Insurance Company (hereinafter referred to as "Transferee Company" in this Section).
(2) A transfer of insurance contracts shall cover the whole insurance contracts for which the policy reserves is calculated on the same basis (excluding the insurance contracts specified by Cabinet Office Ordinance, such as those for which an insured event had occurred by the time of public notice under Article 137, paragraph (1) (limited to those contracts which would be terminated with the payment of the insurance proceeds pertaining to the insured event)).
(3) An Agreement under paragraph (1) shall provide for the particulars of the transfer of the Insurance Company's property which accompanies the transfer of insurance contracts. In this case, the Insurance Company which seeks to transfer insurance contracts (hereinafter referred to as "Transferor Company" in this Section) shall retain the property deemed necessary to protect the interest of the Transferor Company's

creditors other than the Policyholders to which pertains the insurance contracts to be transferred under the Agreement (hereinafter referred to as "Affected Policyholders" in this Section).

(4) In an Agreement under paragraph (1), the Transferor Company may stipulate minor changes to the clauses of the insurance contracts to be transferred under the Agreement, so long as such changes are not disadvantageous to the Policyholders.

(Resolution on Transfer of Insurance Contracts)

Article 136 (1) Any transfer of insurance contracts under paragraph (1) of the preceding Article shall require a resolution at a shareholders' meeting or a general members' council meeting (or a General Representative Members' Council Meeting, where the company has such a council) (referred to as "Shareholders' Meeting, etc." hereinafter in this Chapter, as well as in Chapters VIII and X) in both the Transferor Company and the Transferee Company (other than a Foreign Insurance Company, etc.).

(2) The resolution set forth in the preceding paragraph shall be a resolution under Article 309, paragraph (2) (Resolution of shareholders' meetings) of the Companies Act or under Article 62, paragraph (2) above.

(3) In adopting a resolution under paragraph (1), the Transferor Company and the Transferee Company shall describe the gist of the Agreement set forth in paragraph (1) of the preceding Article in the notice to be given under Article 299, paragraph (1) (Notice of Calling of Shareholders' Meetings) of the Companies Act (including the cases where it is applied mutatis mutandis pursuant to Article 41, paragraph (1) and Article 49, paragraph (1)).

(Retention, etc. of Documents Pertaining to the Transfer of Insurance Contracts)

Article 136-2 (1) The directors (or, in a company with Committees, executive officers) of the Transferor Company shall keep at each of its business offices or offices the documents specified by Cabinet Office Ordinance, such as the written Agreement concluded under paragraph (1) of the preceding Article, for a period ranging from two weeks before the date of the Shareholders' Meeting, etc. set forth in Article 136, paragraph (1) to the end of the period specified pursuant to the provisions of paragraph (2) of the following Article in a supplementary note to the public notice set forth in paragraph (1) of the following Article.

(2) A shareholder or a Policyholder of the Transferor Company may, within the company's operating hours or business hours, make a request to inspect the documents set forth in the preceding paragraph, or may request a certified copy or extract of such documents in exchange for the fees determined by the Transferor Company.

(Public Notice of, and Filing of Objection to, Transfer of Insurance Contracts)

Article 137 (1) The Transferor Company shall, within two weeks from the date of the resolution set forth in Article 136, paragraph (1), give public notice of the gist of the Agreement concluded under Article 135, paragraph (1), and the balance sheets of the Transferor Company and the Transferee Company (for a Foreign Insurance Company, etc., the balance sheet for its Insurance Business in Japan), as well as other particulars specified by Cabinet Office Ordinance.

(2) The public notice set forth in the preceding paragraph shall include a supplementary note to the effect that any affected Policyholder who is opposed to the transfer must state his/her objection within a certain period of time.

(3) The period under the preceding paragraph cannot be less than one month.

(4) A transfer of insurance contracts shall not be carried out where the number of the Af-

fected Policyholders who have stated their objections within the period set forth in paragraph (2) exceeds one fifth of all Affected Policyholders, and the amount specified by Cabinet Office Ordinance as the credits belonging to the insurance contracts of the Affected Policyholders who have thus stated their objections (excluding any insurance claim, etc. (meaning the Insurance Claims, etc. set forth in Article 17, paragraph (5)) that had arisen with regard to such insurance contracts by the time of public notice under paragraph (1)) exceeds one fifth of the amount prescribed as the credits belonging to all Affected Policyholders.

(5) Where the number of the Affected Policyholders who have stated their objections within the period set forth in paragraph (2) or the amount of credits specified by Cabinet Office Ordinance set forth in the preceding paragraph for such Policyholders does not exceed the proportion specified in that paragraph, all of the Affected Policyholders shall be deemed to have approved the transfer of insurance contracts.

(Suspension of Conclusion of Insurance Contracts)
Article 138 The Transferor Company shall not conclude any insurance contract that belongs to the same class as the insurance contracts to be transferred, for the period ranging from the time of the adoption of the resolution under Article 136, paragraph (1) to the time of execution or renunciation of the transfer of insurance contracts.

(Authorization of Transfer of Insurance Contracts)
Article 139 (1) Any transfer of insurance contracts shall be not become effective without the authorization of the Prime Minister.
(2) Whenever an application has been filed for the authorization set forth in the preceding paragraph, the Prime Minister shall examine whether it conforms to the following standards:
(i) the transfer of insurance contracts is appropriate in light of the protection of Policyholders, etc. ;
(ii) it is certain that the Transferee Company will perform its business in an appropriate, fair and efficient manner following the transfer of insurance contracts; and
(iii) the transfer poses no risk of unduly harming the interest of the creditors of the Transferor Company other than the Affected Policyholders.

(Public Notice, etc. of Transfer of Insurance Contracts)
Article 140 (1) The Transferor Company shall, following the transfer of insurance contracts, give public notice of without delay the fact that a transfer of insurance contracts has been carried out and other particulars specified by Cabinet Office Ordinance. The same shall apply where the company has renounced the transfer of insurance contracts.
(2) The Transferee Company shall, if it has received any transfer of insurance contracts, notify the Policyholders affected by the transfer of insurance contracts thereof (or, where any minor change to the transferred insurance contracts under Article 135, paragraph (4) is stipulated in the Agreement set forth in paragraph (1) of the same Article, of the fact that it has received a transfer of insurance contracts and the contents of such minor change) within three months from such transfer.
(3) Where the Transferor Company has outstanding loans or other claims against Policyholders, and such claims are to be assigned to the Transferee Company under the Agreement on the transfer of insurance contracts set forth in Article 135, paragraph (1), a notice in the form of an instrument carrying a fixed date under Article 467 (Requirement for Assertion of Assignment of Nominative Claims Against Third Parties) of the Civil Code shall be deemed to have been given to the Policyholders if a public

notice under the first sentence of paragraph (1) has been given, in accordance with the Method of Public Notice specified by the company, by way of publication in a daily newspaper that publishes the particulars of current events. In this case, the date of the public notice shall be deemed to be the fixed date.

(Membership through Transfer of Insurance Contracts)
Article 141 Where insurance contracts are transferred to a Mutual Company, the Policyholders affected by the transfer become members of the Mutual Company; provided, however, that this shall not apply to the cases where the articles of incorporation of the Transferee Company do not grant membership to the Policyholders with the same class of insurance contracts as those covered by the transfer agreement.

Section 2 Assignment or Acquisition of Business

(Authorization of Assignment or Acquisition of Business)
Article 142 Unless otherwise specified by Cabinet Office Ordinance, any assignment or acquisition of business involving Insurance Company or insurance companies shall be not become effective without the authorization of the Prime Minister.

(Special Provisions on Insurance Companies Engaged in Insurance-Proceed Trust Services)
Article 143 (1) Where a Mutual Company engaged in Insurance-Proceed Trust Services has adopted a resolution on the transfer of all insurance contracts, and the general members' council (or the General Representative Members' Council, where the company has such a council) or the board of directors has adopted a resolution on the assignment of business including Insurance-Proceed Trust Services, the Mutual Company shall, within two weeks from the date of the latter resolution, give public notice of the effect that any beneficiary of a monetary trust (hereinafter referred to as "Beneficiary" in this Article) who is opposed to the gist of the resolution and the assignment of business must state their objections within a certain period of time.
(2) The period under the preceding paragraph cannot be less than one month.
(3) Where no beneficiaries have stated their objections during the period set forth in paragraph (1), the beneficiaries shall be deemed to have approved the assignment of business.

Section 3 Entrustment of Business and Property Administration

(Entrustment of Business and Property Administration)
Article 144 (1) An Insurance Company may, pursuant to the provisions of this Act, entrust another Insurance Company (including a Foreign Insurance Company, etc. (unless otherwise p specified by Cabinet Office Ordinance); hereinafter the same shall apply in this paragraph) with the administration of its business and property under an Agreement with such other Insurance Company (hereinafter referred to as "Entrusted Company" in this Section).
(2) Any entrustment of the administration business set forth in the preceding paragraph shall require a resolution of the Shareholders' Meeting, etc. in both the Insurance Company entrusting the administration business (hereinafter referred to as "Entrusting Company" in this Section) and the Entrusted Company (other than a Foreign Insurance Company, etc.).
(3) The resolution set forth in the preceding paragraph shall be a resolution under Article 309, paragraph (2) (Resolution of shareholders' meetings) of the Companies Act or un-

der Article 62, paragraph (2) above.
(4) The provisions of Article 136, paragraph (3) shall apply mutatis mutandis to the adoption of a resolution under paragraph (2).

(Authorization of Entrustment of Business and Property Administration)
Article 145 (1) Any entrustment of business and property administration under paragraph (1) of the preceding Article shall be not become effective without the authorization of the Prime Minister.
(2) Whenever an application has been filed for the authorization set forth in the preceding paragraph, the Prime Minister shall examine whether it conforms to the following standards:
(i) the entrustment of administration is necessary and appropriate in light of the protection of Policyholders, etc. ; and
(ii) it is certain that the Entrusted Company will perform business to which the entrustment of administration pertains in an appropriate, fair and efficient manner.

(Public Notice and Registration)
Article 146 (1) The Entrusting Company shall, without delay following the authorization set forth in paragraph (1) of the preceding Article, give public notice of the gist of the Agreement set forth in Article 144, paragraph (1) (hereinafter referred to as "Administration Entrustment Agreement" in this Section) and register the entrustment of the administration business, and the Entrusted Company's trade name, name and its head office or principal office, or its principal branch in Japan (meaning the principal branch in Japan set forth in Article 187, paragraph (1), item (iv)).
(2) The registration set forth in the preceding paragraph shall be made at the location of the Entrusted Company's head office or principal office.
(3) The following documents shall be attached to a written application for the registration set forth in paragraph (1), in addition to the documents set forth in Articles 18 and 19 (Documents to be Attached to Written Application) and Article 46 (General Rules on Attached Documents) of the Commercial Registration Act (including the cases where it is applied mutatis mutandis pursuant to Article 67):
(i) A copy of the Administration Entrustment Agreement; and
(ii) The minutes of the Shareholders' Meeting, etc. of the Entrusted Company (other than a Foreign Insurance Company, etc.).

(Internal Relationship)
Article 147 Unless provided otherwise in this Act, the relationship between the Entrusting Company and the Entrusted Company shall be governed by the provisions on mandate.

(External Relationship)
Article 148 (1) The Entrusted Company shall, in taking any action on behalf of the Entrusting Company, such as the conclusion of an insurance contract, indicate that it does so on behalf of the Entrusting Company.
(2) Any action taken without the indication set forth in the preceding paragraph shall be deemed to have been taken on the Entrusted Company's own account.
(3) The provisions of Article 11, paragraphs (1) and (3) (Manager's Authority of Representation) of the Companies Act shall apply mutatis mutandis to an Entrusted Company. In this case, the terms "a Company" and" business" in paragraph (1) of the same Article shall be deemed to be replaced with "the Entrusting Company set forth in Article 144, paragraph (2) of the Insurance Business Act" and "business and properties," re-

spectively; any other necessary technical change in interpretation shall be specified by Cabinet Order.
(4) The provisions of Article 78 (Liability for Damages Pertaining to the Actions of the Representative) of the Act on General Incorporated Associations and General Incorporated Foundations shall apply mutatis mutandis to an Entrusting Company. In this case, the term "representative director or any other representative" in that Article shall be deemed to be replaced with "Entrusted Company set forth in Article 144, paragraph (1) of the Insurance Business Act."

(Amendment or Cancellation of Administration Entrustment Agreement)
Article 149 (1) Any amendment to an Administration Entrustment Agreement or cancellation of an Administration Entrustment Agreement shall require a resolution of the Shareholders' Meeting, etc. in both the Entrusting Company and the Entrusted Company (other than a Foreign Insurance Company, etc.).
(2) The amendment or cancellation set forth in the preceding paragraph shall be not become effective without the authorization of the Prime Minister.
(3) The provisions of Article 144, paragraphs (3) and (4) shall apply mutatis mutandis to the adoption of a resolution under paragraph (1).

(Public Notice, etc. of Amendment or Termination of Administration Entrustment Agreement)
Article 150 (1) If an Entrusting Company has obtained authorization under paragraph (2) of the preceding Article, it shall give public notice of this without delay. The same shall apply if an Administration Entrustment Agreement has been terminated due to any cause other than the cancellation set forth in paragraph (1) of the same Article.
(2) The provisions of Article 146, paragraph (3) shall apply mutatis mutandis to the registration of any amendment to an Administration Entrustment Agreement or cancellation of an Administration Entrustment Agreement. In this case, the term "following documents" in that paragraph shall be deemed to be replaced with "following documents (or, in the case of termination due to any other cause than cancellation, the document listed in item (i) and a document certifying the occurrence of the cause of termination)"; and the term "Administration Entrustment Agreement" in Article 146, paragraph (3), item (i) shall be deemed to be replaced with "Administration Entrustment Agreement (or, in the case of any amendment, Administration Entrustment Agreement thus amended)."

Article 151 Deleted

Chapter VIII Dissolution, Merger, Company Split and Liquidation

Section 1 Dissolution

(Causes of Dissolution)
Article 152 (1) For the purpose of applying the provisions of Article 471 (Grounds for Dissolution) of the Companies Act to Stock Companies that conduct Insurance Business, the term "below" in that Article shall be deemed to be replaced with "in item (iii) to (vi) inclusive."
(2) The provisions of Article 471 of the Companies Act as applied with the change in interpretation set forth in the preceding paragraph shall apply mutatis mutandis to a

Mutual Company. In this case, the term "a shareholders' meeting" in item (iii) of that Article shall be deemed to be replaced with "a general members' council meeting (or a General Representative Members' Council Meeting, where the company has such a council)"; any other necessary technical change in interpretation shall be specified by Cabinet Order.
(3) An Insurance Company, etc. shall dissolve due to the following causes (or, for a Stock Company that conducts Insurance Business, the cause listed in item (ii)), in addition to the causes listed in Article 471, items (iii) to (vi) inclusive of the Companies Act as applied with the change in interpretation set forth in paragraph (1) (including the cases where it is applied mutatis mutandis pursuant to the preceding paragraph):
(i) Transfer of all insurance contracts; or
(ii) Cancellation of a license under Article 3, paragraph (1) or a registration under Article 272, paragraph (1).

(Authorization of Dissolution, etc.)
Article 153 (1) None of the following shall be effective without authorization of the Prime Minister:
(i) A resolution of the Shareholders' Meeting, etc. that approves dissolution of the Insurance Company, etc. ;
(ii) A resolution of the shareholders' meeting that approves abolition of the Insurance Business; and
(iii) A merger in which the parties solely consist of stock companies or include a Stock Company or stock companies conducting Insurance Business (excluding a merger under Article 167, paragraph (1); the same shall apply in the following paragraph).
(2) Whenever an application has been filed for the authorization set forth in the preceding Article, the Prime Minister shall examine whether it conforms to the following standards:
(i) If the application for authorization is from an Insurance Company, that the dissolution or abolition of Insurance Business by resolution, or that the merger, is inevitable in light of the status of business and property of the Insurance Company; or
(ii) That the dissolution or abolition of Insurance Business envisaged by the resolution, or that the planned merger, poses no risk to the protection of Policyholders, etc.
(3) The Prime Minister is not to grant the authorization referred to in paragraph (1), if the Insurance Company, etc. that has submitted the application under paragraph (1) (limited to a Stock Company or a Mutual Company whose articles of incorporation include the provisions set forth in Article 63, paragraph (1)) is the insurer under any existing insurance contracts (excluding the insurance contracts specified by Cabinet Order, such as those for which an insured event had occurred by the date of the application (limited to those contracts which would be terminated with the payment of the insurance proceeds pertaining to the insured event)).

(Public Notice of Dissolution, etc.)
Article 154 Upon obtaining the authorization set forth in paragraph (1) the Insurance Company, etc. , of the preceding Article shall, without delay, give public notice of that effect and details of the particulars for which the authorization is granted pursuant to the provisions of Cabinet Office Ordinance.

(Registration of Dissolution due to Transfer of Insurance Contracts)
Article 155 The following documents shall be attached to a written application for registration of dissolution due to the cause listed in Article 152, paragraph (3), item (i), in

addition to the documents set forth in Articles 18, 19 and 46 of the Commercial Registration Act as applied mutatis mutandis pursuant to Article 67, and in Article 71, paragraph (3) of that Act as applied mutatis mutandis pursuant to Article 158:
(i) The minutes of the Shareholders' Meeting, etc. of the Transferee Company (other than a Foreign Insurance Company, etc.) set forth in Article 135, paragraph (1) (including the cases where it is applied mutatis mutandis pursuant to Article 272-29);
(ii) A document certifying that a public notice has been given under Article 137, paragraph (1) (including the cases where it is applied mutatis mutandis pursuant to Article 272-29);
(iii) A document certifying that the number of those Affected Policyholders set forth in Article 137, paragraph (2) (including the cases where it is applied mutatis mutandis pursuant to Article 272-29) who have stated their objections within the period set forth in that paragraph, or the amount of credits specified by Cabinet Office Ordinance set forth in Article 137, paragraph (4) (including the cases where it is applied with relevant changes in interpretation pursuant to the provisions of Article 251, paragraph (2) and where it is applied mutatis mutandis pursuant to Article 272-29; hereinafter the same shall apply in this item) as belonging to such Affected Policyholders has not exceeded the proportion set forth in Article 137, paragraph (4); and
(iv) A document certifying any public notice given under Article 250, paragraph (4).

(Procedure, etc. of Dissolution for Mutual Company)
Article 156 Any resolution on the dissolution of a Mutual Company shall be a resolution under Article 62, paragraph (2).

(Retention, etc. of Documents Pertaining to a Dissolution)
Article 156-2 (1) A Mutual Company shall, for the period ranging from two weeks before the date of the general members' council meeting (or General Representative Members' Council Meeting, where the company has such a council) pertaining to the resolution on its dissolution to the date of such resolution (or, where the resolution is adopted by the General Representative Members' Council, the day that is one month after the date of public notice under paragraph (1) of the following Article), keep at each of its offices the documents or electromagnetic records in which the dissolution proposal and any other particulars specified by Cabinet Office Ordinance are detailed or recorded.
(2) Members of a Mutual Company may make the following requests to the company at any time during its business hours; provided, however, that they pay the fees determined by the Mutual Company in making a request falling under item (ii) or (iv):
(i) A request to inspect the documents set forth in the preceding paragraph;
(ii) A request for a certified copy or extract of the documents set forth in the preceding paragraph;
(iii) A request to inspect anything that shows the particulars recorded in the electromagnetic records set forth in the preceding paragraph in a manner specified by Cabinet Office Ordinance; or
(iv) A request to be provided with the particulars recorded in the electromagnetic records set forth in the preceding paragraph by the electromagnetic means determined by the Mutual Company, or to be issued a document detailing such particulars.

Article 157 (1) Where the General Representative Members' Council has adopted a resolution on dissolution, the Mutual Company shall, within two weeks from the date of such resolution, give public notice of the gist of the resolution and its balance sheet, as

well as any other particular specified by Cabinet Office Ordinance.
(2) In the case set forth in the preceding paragraph, members representing at least five thousandths (or, in a Specified Mutual Company, members equal to or exceeding the number specified by Cabinet Order set forth in Article 50, paragraph (1)), who have been members of the Mutual Company without interruption for the preceding six months may demand the directors to convene the general members' council with the purpose of discussing the particulars of the resolution, by indicating the proposed agenda for the meeting and the reason for the convocation. In this case, the demand shall be made within one month from the date of public notice under that paragraph.
(3) In the case referred to in the preceding paragraph, the resolution of the General Representative Members' Council shall lose its effect, unless the general members' council adopts a resolution approving the resolution of the General Representative Members' Council on dissolution within six weeks from the date of demand under that paragraph.
(4) The provisions of Article 156 shall apply mutatis mutandis to the resolution of the general members' council set forth in the preceding paragraph. In this case, any other necessary technical change in interpretation shall be specified by Cabinet Order.

Article 158 The provisions of Article 926 (Registration of Dissolution) of the Companies Act, and Article 71, paragraphs (1) and (3) (Registration of Dissolution) of the Commercial Registration Act shall apply mutatis mutandis to a Mutual Company. In this case, the term "Article 478, paragraph (1), item (i) of the Companies Act" in Article 71, paragraph (3) of the Commercial Registration Act shall be deemed to be replaced with "Article 180-4, paragraph (1), item (i) of the Insurance Business Act"; any other necessary technical change in interpretation shall be specified by Cabinet Order.

Section 2 Merger

Subsection 1 General Rules

Article 159 (1) A Mutual Company may merge with another Mutual Company or a Stock Company that conducts Insurance Business. In this case, a merger agreement shall be concluded between the mutual companies or between the Mutual Company and the Stock Company.
(2) In the case referred to in the preceding paragraph, the company surviving the merger or the company incorporated by the merger shall be the company that falls under one of the following items in the case set forth in each of those items:
 (i) Where a Mutual Company merges with another Mutual Company: a Mutual Company; or
 (ii) Where a Mutual Company merges with a Stock Company that conducts Insurance Business: a Mutual Company or a Stock Company that conducts Insurance Business.

Subsection 2 Merger Agreement

(Absorption-Type Merger Agreement between Mutual Companies)
Article 160 Where mutual companies carry out an absorption-type merger (meaning any merger that a Mutual Company effects with another Mutual Company or a Stock Company, whereby the surviving mutual or Stock Company succeeds to any and all rights and obligations of the absorbed mutual or Stock Company; the same shall apply hereinafter), the absorption-type merger agreement shall provide for the following particu-

lars:
(i) The names and addresses of the Mutual Company surviving the absorption-type merger (hereinafter referred to as the "Mutual Company Surviving the Absorption-Type Merger" in this Section) and the Mutual Company extinguished in the merger (hereinafter referred to as "Absorbed Mutual Company" in this Section);
(ii) The amount of any money to be granted to the members of the Absorbed Mutual Company;
(iii) The particulars of the rights of the Policyholders of the Absorbed Mutual Company following the merger;
(iv) The date on which the Merger takes effect; and
(v) Any other particular specified by Cabinet Office Ordinance.

(Consolidation-Type Merger Agreement between Mutual Companies)
Article 161 Where mutual companies carry out a consolidation-type merger (meaning any merger effected by two or more mutual companies or by two or more mutual and stock companies, whereby the new mutual or Stock Company established in the merger succeeds to any and all rights and obligations of the mutual or stock companies consolidated by the merger; the same shall apply hereinafter), the consolidation-type merger agreement shall provide for the following particulars:
(i) The names and addresses of the Mutual Companies that will be extinguished in the merger (hereinafter referred to as "Consolidated Mutual Companies" in this Section);
(ii) The purpose and name of the Mutual Company to be established in the merger (hereinafter referred to as the "Mutual Company Established by the Consolidation-Type Merger" in this Section) and the address of its principal office;
(iii) In addition to what is listed in the preceding item, particulars specified by the articles of incorporation of the Mutual Company Established by the Consolidation-Type Merger;
(iv) The names of the directors at incorporation of the Mutual Company Established by the Consolidation-Type Merger;
(v) The particulars set forth in the following items in accordance with the categories provided therein:
 (a) Where the Mutual Company Established by the Consolidation-Type Merger is a company with accounting advisors: the names of the accounting advisors at incorporation of the Mutual Company Established by the Consolidation-Type Merger;
 (b) Where the Mutual Company Established by the Consolidation-Type Merger is a company with auditors: the names of the company auditors at incorporation of the Mutual Company Established by the Consolidation-Type Merger; or
 (c) Where the Mutual Company Established by the Consolidation-Type Merger is a company with accounting auditors: the names of the accounting auditors at incorporation of the Mutual Company Established by the Consolidation-Type Merger;
(vi) The amount of any money to be granted to the members of the Consolidated Mutual Companies;
(vii) The particulars of the rights of Policyholders following the merger; and
(viii) Any other particular specified by Cabinet Office Ordinance.

(Absorption-Type Merger Agreement between Stock and Mutual Companies Survived by Mutual Company)
Article 162 (1) In an absorption-type merger between a Stock Company and a Mutual

Art.163 ⑥ Insurance Business Act, Part II, Chap.VIII, Sec.2

Company where the surviving Insurance Company, etc. is the Mutual Company, the merger agreement shall provide for the following particulars:
(i) The trade names, names and addresses of the Stock Company extinguished in the merger (hereinafter referred to as "Absorbed Stock Company" in this Section) and the Mutual Company Surviving the Absorption-Type Merger;
(ii) The method of compensation for the shareholders and holders of share options of the Absorbed Stock Company;
(iii) The particulars of the Reserves of the Mutual Company Surviving the Absorption-Type Merger;
(iv) The particulars of the rights of the Policyholders of the Absorbed Stock Company following the merger;
(v) The date on which the merger takes effect; and
(vi) Any other particular specified by Cabinet Office Ordinance.
(2) The provisions of Article 68, paragraph (6) shall apply mutatis mutandis to the absorption-type merger set forth in the preceding paragraph. In this case, the term "deficiency reserves in addition to the reserves set forth in paragraph (4)" in that paragraph shall be deemed to be replaced with "deficiency reserve"; any other necessary technical change in interpretation shall be specified by Cabinet Order.
(3) The provisions of Article 72, paragraph (1) shall apply mutatis mutandis to the Absorbed Stock Company set forth in paragraph (1), item (i). In this case, the terms "Article 70, paragraph (2)" and "Entity Conversion" in that paragraph shall be deemed to be replaced with "Article 165-7, paragraph (2)" and "absorption-type merger," respectively; and the term "to obtain his/her consent" shall be deemed to be deleted; any other necessary technical change in interpretation shall be specified by Cabinet Order.
(4) The provisions of Article 83 shall apply mutatis mutandis to the absorption-type merger set forth in paragraph (1). In this case, any other necessary technical change in interpretation shall be specified by Cabinet Order.

(Consolidation-Type Merger between Stock and Mutual Companies Incorporating Mutual Company)
Article 163 (1) In a consolidation-type merger between a Stock Company (or stock companies) and a Mutual Company where the Insurance Company, etc. to be incorporated is a Mutual Company, the merger agreement shall provide for the following particulars:
(i) The trade names, names and addresses of the Stock Company (or stock companies) extinguished in the merger (hereinafter referred to as "Consolidated Stock Company" in this Section) and the consolidated mutual company;
(ii) The purpose and name of the Mutual Company Established by the Consolidation-Type Merger and the address of its principal office;
(iii) In addition to what is listed in the preceding item, particulars specified by the articles of incorporation of the Mutual Company Established by the Consolidation-Type Merger;
(iv) The names of the directors at incorporation of the Mutual Company Established by the Consolidation-Type Merger;
(v) The particulars set forth in the following items in accordance with the categories provided therein:
 (a) Where the Mutual Company Established by the Consolidation-Type Merger is a company with accounting advisors: the names of the accounting advisors at incorporation of the Mutual Company Established by the Consolidation-Type Merger;
 (b) Where the Mutual Company Established by the Consolidation-Type Merger is a

company with auditors: the names of the company auditors at incorporation of the Mutual Company Established by the Consolidation-Type Merger; or
     (c) Where the Mutual Company Established by the Consolidation-Type Merger is a company with accounting auditors: the names of the accounting auditors at incorporation of the Mutual Company Established by the Consolidation-Type Merger;
   (vi) The method of compensation for the shareholders and holders of share options of the Consolidated Stock Company;
   (vii) The amount of any money to be granted to the members of the consolidated mutual company;
   (viii) The particulars of the Reserves of the Mutual Company Established by the Consolidation-Type Merger;
   (ix) The particulars of the rights of Policyholders following the merger; and
   (x) Any other particular specified by Cabinet Office Ordinance.
(2) The provisions of paragraph (2) of the preceding Article shall apply mutatis mutandis to the consolidation-type merger set forth in the preceding paragraph; and the provisions of paragraph (3) of that Article shall apply mutatis mutandis to a Consolidated Stock Company. In this case, the term "absorption-type merger" in Article 162, paragraph (3) shall be deemed to be replaced with "consolidation-type merger"; any other necessary technical change in interpretation shall be specified by Cabinet Order.
(3) The provisions of Article 83 shall apply mutatis mutandis to the consolidation-type merger set forth in paragraph (1). In this case, any other necessary technical change in interpretation shall be specified by Cabinet Order.

(Absorption-Type Merger Agreement between Stock and Mutual Companies Survived by Stock Company)
Article 164 (1) In an absorption between a Stock Company and a Mutual Company where the surviving Insurance Company, etc. is the Stock Company, the merger agreement shall provide for the following particulars:
   (i) The trade names, names and addresses of the Stock Company surviving the merger (hereinafter referred to as "Stock Company Surviving the Absorption-Type Merger" in this Section) and the Absorbed Mutual Company;
   (ii) The following particulars of any share, etc. (meaning any share or money; hereinafter the same shall apply in this Section) to be granted to the members of the Absorbed Mutual Company by the Stock Company Surviving the Absorption-Type Merger in carrying out the merger:
     (a) Where the share, etc. is the shares of the Stock Company Surviving the Absorption-Type Merger, the number of such shares (or, in a company with class shares, the classes of such shares and the number of shares by class) or the method of calculating such number, and the particulars of the amounts of capital and Reserves of the Stock Company Surviving the Absorption-Type Merger; or
     (b) Where the share, etc. is money, the amount of such money or the method of calculating the amount;
   (iii) Where the preceding item applies, the particulars of the allocation of Shares, etc. to the members of the Absorbed Mutual Company (excluding the Stock Company Surviving the Absorption-Type Merger) under that item;
   (iv) The method of sale for the new shares to be issued for fractional lots generated by the allocation of shares to the members of the Absorbed Mutual Company, and any other particular specified by Cabinet Office Ordinance regarding such sale;
   (v) Where the shares set forth in the preceding item are purchased, the method of the purchase and any other particular specified by Cabinet Office Ordinance regarding

Art.165　　6 Insurance Business Act, Part II, Chap.VIII, Sec.2

such purchase;
(vi) The amount of any money to be granted to the contributors to the funds of the Absorbed Mutual Company;
(vii) The particulars of the rights of the Policyholders of the Absorbed Mutual Company following the merger;
(viii) The particulars of the amount of surplus from consolidation;
(ix) The date on which the merger takes effect; and
(x) Any other particular specified by Cabinet Office Ordinance.
(2) The provisions of the main clause of Article 89, paragraph (1) and Article 89, paragraph (2) shall apply mutatis mutandis to the absorption-type merger set forth in the preceding paragraph. In this case, the terms "converting Mutual Company," "Effective Date" and "entity conversion plan" in paragraph (1) of the same Article shall be deemed to be replaced with "Absorbed Mutual Company," "date set forth in Article 164, paragraph (1), item (ix)" and "absorption-type merger agreement set forth in Article 164, paragraph (1)," respectively; any other necessary technical change in interpretation shall be specified by Cabinet Order.
(3) The provisions of Article 90 shall apply mutatis mutandis to the absorption-type merger set forth in paragraph (1); and the provisions of Article 162, paragraph (3) shall apply mutatis mutandis to an Absorbed Mutual Company. In this case, the terms "members of a converting mutual company," "Converted Stock Company" and "entity conversion plan" in Article 90, paragraph (1) shall be deemed to be replaced with "members of an Absorbed Mutual Company," "Stock Company Surviving the Absorption-Type Merger" and "absorption-type merger agreement set forth in Article 164, paragraph (1)" respectively; and the term "Article 165-7, paragraph (2)" in Article 162, paragraph (3) shall be deemed to be replaced with "Article 165-17, paragraph (2)"; any other necessary technical change in interpretation shall be specified by Cabinet Order.
(4) The provisions of Article 91 shall apply mutatis mutandis to a Stock Company Surviving an Absorption-Type Merger. In this case, the term "amount of surplus in Entity Conversion" in that Article shall be deemed to be replaced with "amount of merger surplus"; the term "as a particular to be specified by the articles of incorporation pursuant to the provisions of Article 86, paragraph (4), item (ii)" in Article 91, paragraph (1) shall be deemed to be replaced with "in its articles of incorporation"; the term "paragraph (3) of the preceding Article" in Article 91, paragraph (2) shall be deemed to be replaced with "paragraph (2) of the preceding Article as applied mutatis mutandis pursuant to Article 164, paragraph (3)"; and the terms "capital Reserve on Entity Conversion" and "calculations on Entity Conversion" in Article 91, paragraph (4) shall be deemed to be replaced with "capital Reserve on an absorption-type merger under Article 164, paragraph (1)" and "calculations on such absorption-type merger," respectively; any other necessary technical change in interpretation shall be specified by Cabinet Order.

(Consolidation-Type Merger Agreement between Stock and Mutual Companies Incorporating Stock Company)
Article 165 (1) In a consolidation-type merger between a Stock Company (or stock companies) and a Mutual Company where the Insurance Company, etc. to be incorporated is a Stock Company, the merger agreement shall provide for the following particulars:
(i) The trade names, names and addresses of the consolidated companies (meaning the Consolidated Stock Company and the consolidated mutual company; hereinafter the same shall apply in this Section);
(ii) The purpose, trade name, address of the head office, and total number of authorized shares of the Stock Company to be established in the merger (hereinafter re-

ferred to as "Stock Company Established by Consolidation-Type Merger" in this Section);
(iii) In addition to what is listed in the preceding item, particulars specified by the articles of incorporation of the Stock Company Established by the Consolidation-Type Merger;
(iv) The names of the persons to serve as directors at the incorporation of the Stock-Company Established by the Consolidation-Type Merger;
(v) The particulars set forth in the following items in accordance with the categories provided therein:
  (a) Where the Stock-Company Established by the Consolidation-Type Merger is a company with accounting advisors: the names of the persons to serve as accounting advisors at the incorporation of the Stock Company Established by the Consolidation-Type Merger;
  (b) Where the Stock Company Established by the Consolidation-Type Merger is a company with auditors: the names of the persons to serve as company auditors at the incorporation of the Stock Company Established by the Consolidation-Type Merger; or
  (c) Where the Stock Company Established by the Consolidation-Type Merger is a company with accounting auditors: the names of the persons to serve as accounting auditors at the incorporation of the Stock Company Established by the Consolidation-Type Merger;
(vi) The number of the Stock Company Established by the Consolidation-Type Merger's shares (or, in a company with class shares, the classes of share and the number of shares by class) to be granted by the company in carrying out the merger to the shareholders of the Consolidated Stock Company in lieu of the latter company's shares, or the method of calculating such number;
(vii) The number of the Stock Company Established by the Consolidation-Type Merger's shares (or, in a company with class shares, the classes of shares and the number of shares by class) to be granted by the company in carrying out the merger to the members of the consolidated mutual company;
(viii) The particulars of the amounts of the capital and reserves of the Stock Company Established by the Consolidation-Type Merger;
(ix) The particulars of the allocation of shares under item (vi) or (vii) to the shareholders of the Consolidated Stock Company (excluding any Consolidated Stock Company or consolidated mutual company) or the members of the consolidated mutual company (excluding any Consolidated Stock Company or consolidated mutual company);
(x) The method of sale for the new shares to be issued for fractional lots generated by the allocation of shares to the members of the consolidated mutual company, and any other particular specified by Cabinet Office Ordinance regarding such sale;
(xi) Where the shares set forth in the preceding item are purchased, the method of the purchase and any other particular specified by Cabinet Office Ordinance regarding such purchase;
(xii) Where a Consolidated Stock Company has issued share options, the following particulars of the Stock Company Established by the Consolidation-Type Merger's share options or money to be granted by the latter company in carrying out the merger to the holders of share options of the Consolidated Stock Company in lieu of such share options:
  (a) Where share options of the Stock Company Established by the Consolidation-Type Merger are granted to the holders of stock options of the Consolidated Stock Company, the contents and number of the share options thus granted and

Art.165　　⑥ Insurance Business Act, Part II, Chap.VIII, Sec.2

the method of calculating such number;
(b) In the case prescribed in (a), if the share options of the Consolidated Stock Company set forth in (a) are share options attached to bonds, the fact that the Stock Company Established by the Consolidation-Type Merger will assume the obligations pertaining to the bonds (meaning bonds as defined in Article 2, item (xxiii) of the Companies Act; the same shall apply in this sub-item) with stock options, and the classes of bonds covered by such assumption and the total value of the bonds by class or the method of calculating such amount; or
(c) Where any money is granted to the holders of stock options of a Consolidated Stock Company other than that set forth in (a), the amount of such money or the method of calculating such amount;
(xiii) Where the preceding item applies, the particulars of the allocation of Stock Company Established by the Consolidation-Type Merger's share options or money to the holders of share options of the Consolidated Stock Company set forth in that item;
(xiv) The amount of any money to be granted to the shareholders of the Consolidated Stock Company, or the contributors to the funds and the members of the consolidated mutual company;
(xv) The particulars of the rights of Policyholders following the merger;
(xvi) The particulars of the amount of surplus from consolidation; and
(xvii) Any other particular specified by Cabinet Office Ordinance.
(2) In the case prescribed in the preceding paragraph, the consolidated companies may, where all or any of the consolidated stock company is a company with class shares, prescribe the following particulars as particulars listed in item (vi) of that paragraph, depending on the class structure of the shares issued by the Consolidated Stock Company:
(i) If they do not allocate shares of the Stock Company Established by the Consolidation-Type Merger to any specific class of shareholder, that fact and the relevant class of share; and
(ii) In addition to what is listed in the preceding item, if they treat each class of share in a different manner in allocating shares of the Stock Company Established by the Consolidation-Type Merger, that fact and a description of such different treatment.
(3) Where paragraph (1) applies, the provisions for the particulars listed in item (vi) of that paragraph shall include a clause that the shares of the Stock Company Established by the Consolidation-Type Merger shall be allocated in accordance with the number of shares (or, where the articles of incorporation include provisions for the particulars listed in item (ii) of the preceding paragraph, the number of shares by class) held by each shareholder of the Consolidated Stock Company (excluding any Consolidated Stock Company, consolidated mutual company or holder of the class of share set forth in item (i) of the preceding paragraph).
(4) The provisions of the main clause of Article 89, paragraph (1) and Article 89, paragraph (2) shall apply mutatis mutandis to the consolidation-type merger set forth in paragraph (1). In this case, the terms "converting Mutual Company," "Effective Date" and "entity conversion plan" in paragraph (1) of the same Article shall be deemed to be replaced with "consolidated mutual company," "date of the establishment of the Stock Company Established by the Consolidation-Type Merger" and "consolidation-type merger agreement set forth in Article 165, paragraph (1)," respectively; any other necessary technical change in interpretation shall be specified by Cabinet Order.
(5) The provisions of Article 90 shall apply mutatis mutandis to the consolidation-type merger set forth in paragraph (1); and the provisions of Article 162, paragraph (3) shall apply mutatis mutandis to a consolidated mutual company. In this case, the terms

"members of a converting Mutual Company," "Converted Stock Company" and "entity conversion plan" in Article 90, paragraph (1) shall be deemed to be replaced with "members of a consolidated mutual company," "Stock Company Established by the Consolidation-Type Merger" and "consolidation-type merger agreement set forth in Article 165, paragraph (1)" respectively; and the term "Article 165-7, paragraph (2)" in Article 162, paragraph (3) shall be deemed to be replaced with "Article 165-17, paragraph (2)"; any other necessary technical change in interpretation shall be specified by Cabinet Order.

(6) The provisions of Article 91 shall apply mutatis mutandis to a Stock Company Established by the Consolidation-Type Merger. In this case, the term "amount of surplus in Entity Conversion" in that Article shall be deemed to be replaced with "amount of surplus from consolidation"; the term "Article 86, paragraph (4), item (ii)" in Article 91, paragraph (1) shall be deemed to be replaced with "Article 165, paragraph (1), item (iii)"; the term "paragraph (2) of the preceding Article" in Article 91, paragraph (3) shall be deemed to be replaced with "paragraph (2) of the preceding Article as applied mutatis mutandis pursuant to Article 165, paragraph (5)"; and the terms "capital Reserve on Entity Conversion" and "calculations on Entity Conversion" in Article 91, paragraph (4) shall be deemed to be replaced with "capital reserves on a consolidation-type merger under Article 165, paragraph (1)" and "calculations on such consolidation-type merger," respectively; any other necessary technical change in interpretation shall be specified by Cabinet Order.

Subsection 3 Procedure of Merger

Division 1 Procedures for Extinguished Stock Companies

(Retention and Inspection, etc. of Documents Related to a Merger Agreement, etc.)

Article 165-2 (1) An Extinguished Stock Company (meaning an Absorbed Stock Company or a Consolidated Stock Company; hereinafter the same shall apply in this Section) shall, for the period ranging from any of the following dates, whichever is the earliest, to the date on which the merger takes effect (hereinafter referred to as "Effective Date" in this Section), keep at each of its business offices the documents or electromagnetic records in which the details of the merger agreement and any other particulars specified by Cabinet Office Ordinance are detailed or recorded.

(i) The day that is two weeks before the date of the shareholders' meeting set forth in paragraph (1) of the following Article or the class meeting set forth in paragraph (5) of the same Article;

(ii) The date of notice under Article 165-4, paragraph (1) or the date of public notice under paragraph (2) of the same Article, whichever is earlier; or

(iii) The date of public notice under Article 165-7, paragraph (2).

(2) The creditors of an Extinguished Stock Company, such as shareholders and Policyholders, may make the following requests to the company at any time during its operating hours; provided, however, that they pay the fees determined by the Extinguished Stock Company in making a request falling under item (ii) or (iv):

(i) A request to inspect the documents set forth in the preceding paragraph;

(ii) A request for a certified copy or extract of the documents set forth in the preceding paragraph;

(iii) A request to inspect anything that shows the particulars recorded in the electromagnetic records set forth in the preceding paragraph in a manner specified by Cabinet Office Ordinance; or

Art.165-3~165-4　[6] Insurance Business Act, Part II, Chap.VIII, Sec.2

(iv) A request to be provided with the particulars recorded in the electromagnetic records set forth in the preceding paragraph by the electromagnetic means determined by the Extinguished Stock Company, or to be issued a document detailing such particulars.

(Authorization of Merger Agreement)
Article 165-3 (1) An extinguished stock company shall have its merger agreement approved by a resolution of the shareholders' meeting by the day before the Effective Date.
(2) The resolution set forth in the preceding paragraph to be adopted by an extinguished stock company shall be a resolution under Article 309, paragraph (2) (Resolution of shareholders' meetings) of the Companies Act.
(3) An extinguished stock company shall, if it seeks to adopt a resolution under paragraph (1), provide an outline of the merger agreement in the notice to be given pursuant to Article 299, paragraph (1) (Notice of Calling of Shareholders' Meetings) of the Companies Act.
(4) Notwithstanding the provisions of paragraph (2), where the merger involves an extinguished stock company that is a public company (meaning a public company as defined in Article 2, item (v) (Definitions) of the Companies Act; hereinafter the same shall apply in this Section), and all or Part of the Shares, etc. to be distributed to the shareholders of the extinguished stock company are shares with restriction on transfer, the resolution set forth in paragraph (1) shall be a resolution under Article 309, paragraph (3) of that Act; provided, however, that this shall not apply to the cases where the extinguished stock company is a company with class shares.
(5) In a consolidation-type merger involving a Consolidated Stock Company that is a company with class shares, where all or Part of the shares of the Stock Company Established by the Consolidation-Type Merger to be distributed to the shareholders of the Consolidated Stock Company are shares with restriction on transfer, the merger shall be null and void unless approved by a resolution of the class meeting composed of the holders of the class of share (excluding shares with restriction on transfer) for which the shares with restriction on transfer are to be distributed (or, where the shares with restriction on transfer are to be distributed to the holders of two or more classes of share, the class meetings each composed of the holders of one of such classes of share); provided, however, that this shall not apply to the cases where no shareholders can exercise their voting rights in the relevant class meeting.
(6) Any resolution by a Consolidated Stock Company under the preceding paragraph shall be a resolution under Article 324, paragraph (3) (Resolution of Class Meetings) of the Companies Act.

(Notice, etc. to Shareholders, etc.)
Article 165-4 (1) An extinguished stock company shall, no later than twenty days before the Effective Date, notify its shareholders and the registered pledgees of its shares, and the holders of its share options and the registered pledgees of its share options of the planned merger, and of the trade name or name and address of the Mutual Company Surviving the Absorption-Type Merger, or the Stock Company conducting Insurance Business or Mutual Company to be incorporated by the merger (hereinafter referred to as "Formed Company" in this Section).
(2) A notice under the preceding paragraph may be replaced with a public notice.
(3) The provisions of Article 219, paragraph (1) (limited to the segment pertaining to item (vi)), (2) and (3) (Public Notice in Relation to Submission of Share Certificate), Article 220 (Cases Where Share Certificates Cannot be Submitted), and Article 293, para-

graph (1) (limited to the segment pertaining to item (iii) (Public Notice in Relation to Submission of Share Option Certificate) of the Companies Act shall apply mutatis mutandis to an extinguished stock company. In this case, any other necessary technical change in interpretation shall be specified by Cabinet Order.

(Right to Request Purchase of Shares)
Article 165-5 (1) The following shareholders may request the extinguished stock company to purchase the shares that they hold at a fair price:
(i) A shareholder who, prior to the shareholders' meeting to approve the merger agreement (including the class meeting; hereinafter the same shall apply in this item), has given notice to the extinguished stock company of his/her intent to oppose the merger, and has actually opposed the merger at the shareholders' meeting (limited to a shareholder who can exercise his/her voting rights at the shareholders' meeting); and
(ii) A shareholder who cannot exercise his/her voting rights at the shareholders' meeting.
(2) The provisions of Article 785, paragraphs (5) to (7) inclusive (Dissenting Shareholders' Share Purchase Demand), Article 786 (Determination, etc. of Price of Shares), Article 868, paragraph (1) (Jurisdiction over Non-Contentious Cases), Article 870 (limited to the segment pertaining to item (iv)) (Hearing of Statements), the main clause of Article 871 (Appending of the Reason), Article 872 (limited to the segment pertaining to item (iv)) (Immediate Appeal), the main clause of Article 873 (Stay of Execution of the Judicial Decision of the Prior Instance), Article 875 (Exclusion from Application of the Provisions of the Non-Contentious Cases Procedures Act) and Article 876 (Supreme Court Rules) of the Companies Act shall apply mutatis mutandis to a request made under the preceding paragraph. In this case, any other necessary technical change in interpretation shall be specified by Cabinet Order.

(Right to Request Purchase of Share Options)
Article 165-6 (1) A holder of share options of an extinguished stock company may request the company to purchase the share options that he/she holds at a fair price:
(2) The provisions of Article 787, paragraphs (5) to (7) inclusive (Demand for Purchase of Share Options), Article 788 (Determination, etc. of Price of Share Options), Article 868, paragraph (1) (Jurisdiction over Non-Contentious Cases), Article 870 (limited to the segment pertaining to item (iv)) (Hearing of Statements), the main clause of Article 871 (Appending of the Reason), Article 872 (limited to the segment pertaining to item (iv)) (Immediate Appeal), the main clause of Article 873 (Stay of Execution of the Judicial Decision of the Prior Instance), Article 875 (Exclusion from Application of the Provisions of the Non-Contentious Cases Procedures Act) and Article 876 (Supreme Court Rules) of the Companies Act shall apply mutatis mutandis to a request made under the preceding paragraph. In this case, any other necessary technical change in interpretation shall be specified by Cabinet Order.

(Objections of Creditors)
Article 165-7 (1) Policyholders or other creditors of an extinguished stock company may state to the company their objections to the merger.
(2) An extinguished stock company shall give public notice of the following particulars in the Official Gazette and by the Method of Public Notice prescribed by its articles of incorporation; provided, however, that the period for item (iv) may not be shorter than one month:
(i) The fact that a merger will be carried out;

(ii) The trade names or names and addresses of the Mutual Company Surviving the Absorption-Type Merger or other consolidated companies (meaning consolidated stock companies and Consolidated Mutual Companies; the same shall apply in Article 165-17, paragraph (2)) and the Formed Company;
(iii) The particulars specified by Cabinet Office Ordinance as pertaining to the financial statements of an extinguished stock company;
(iv) The fact that Policyholders or other creditors of the extinguished stock company may state their objections within a certain period of time; and
(v) In addition to what is listed in the preceding items, particulars specified by Cabinet Office Ordinance.
(3) Where no Policyholders or other creditors have stated their objections within the period set forth in item (iv) of the preceding paragraph, such Policyholders or other creditors shall be deemed to have approved the merger.
(4) The provisions of Article 70, paragraphs (4) to (8) inclusive shall apply mutatis mutandis to objections of creditors under paragraph (1). In this case, the term "paragraph (2), item (iv)" in paragraphs (5) and (6) of the same Article shall be deemed to be replaced with "Article 165-7, paragraph (2), item (iv)"; any other necessary technical change in interpretation shall be specified by Cabinet Order.

(Change in Effective Date of Absorption-Type Merger)
Article 165-8 (1) An Absorbed Stock Company may change the Effective Date in an agreement with the Mutual Company Surviving the Absorption-Type Merger.
(2) In the case set forth in the preceding paragraph, the Absorbed Stock Company shall give public notice of the Effective Date thus changed by the day before the original Effective Date (or, where the changed Effective Date falls before the original Effective Date, the changed Effective Date).
(3) Where the Effective Date has been changed pursuant to the provisions of paragraph (1), the changed Effective Date shall be deemed to be the Effective Date for the purpose of applying the provisions of this Section.

Division 2 Procedures for a Stock Company Surviving an Absorption-Type Merger

(Retention and Inspection, etc. of Documents Related to an Absorption-Type Merger Agreement, etc.)
Article 165-9 (1) A Stock Company Surviving an Absorption-Type Merger shall, for the period ranging from any of the following dates, whichever is the earliest, to the day that is six months after the Effective Date, keep at each of its business offices the documents or electromagnetic records in which the details of the absorption-type merger agreement and any other particulars specified by Cabinet Office Ordinance are detailed or recorded.
(i) Where the merger agreement needs to be approved by a resolution of the shareholders' meeting (including the class meeting), the day that is two weeks before the date of the shareholders' meeting;
(ii) The date of notice under Article 165-4, paragraph (1) as applied mutatis mutandis pursuant to Article 165-12 or the date of public notice under Article 165-4, paragraph (2) as applied mutatis mutandis pursuant to Article 165-12, whichever is earlier; or
(iii) The date of public notice under Article 165-7, paragraph (2) as applied mutatis mutandis pursuant to Article 165-12.
(2) The creditors of a Stock Company Surviving an Absorption-Type Merger, such as

Shareholders and Policyholders, may make the following requests to the company at any time during its operating hours; provided, however, that they pay the fees determined by the Stock Company Surviving the Absorption-Type Merger in making a request falling under item (ii) or (iv):
(i) A request to inspect the documents set forth in the preceding paragraph;
(ii) A request for a certified copy or extract of the documents set forth in the preceding paragraph;
(iii) A request to inspect anything that shows the particulars recorded in the electromagnetic records set forth in the preceding paragraph in a manner specified by Cabinet Office Ordinance; or
(iv) A request to be provided with the particulars recorded in the electromagnetic records set forth in the preceding paragraph by the electromagnetic means determined by the Stock Company Surviving the Absorption-Type Merger, or to be issued a document detailing such particulars.

(Authorization of Absorption-Type Merger Agreement, etc.)
Article 165-10 (1) A Stock Company Surviving an Absorption-Type Merger shall have its merger agreement approved by a resolution of the shareholders' meeting by the day before the Effective Date.
(2) The resolution set forth in the preceding paragraph to be adopted by the Stock Company Surviving the Absorption-Type Merger shall be a resolution under Article 309, paragraph (2) (Resolution of Shareholders' Meetings) of the Companies Act.
(3) A Stock Company Surviving an Absorption-Type Merger, if it seeks to adopt a resolution under paragraph (1), shall provide an outline of the absorption-type merger agreement in the notice to be given pursuant to Article 299, paragraph (1) (Notice of Calling of Shareholders' Meetings) of the Companies Act.
(4) Where a Stock Company Surviving an Absorption-Type Merger succeeds to the assets of the Absorbed Mutual Company including its own shares, its directors shall explain the particulars of such shares in the shareholders' meeting set forth in paragraph (1).
(5) In an absorption-type merger wherein the company surviving the merger is a company with class shares, and in which the Shares, etc. to be granted to the members of the Absorbed Mutual Company are shares of the Stock Company Surviving the Absorption-Type Merger, the merger shall be null and void unless approved by a resolution of the class meeting composed of the holders of the class of share set forth in Article 164, paragraph (1), item (ii), sub-item (a) (limited to the shares with restriction on transfer which are not covered by the provisions in the articles of incorporation set forth in Article 199, paragraph (4) (Determination of Subscription Requirements) of the Companies Act) (or, where the shares are to be granted to the holders of two or more classes of share, the class meetings each composed of the holders of one of such classes of share); provided, however, that this shall not apply to the cases where no shareholders can exercise their voting rights in the relevant class meeting.
(6) Any resolution by a Stock Company Surviving an Absorption-Type Merger under the preceding paragraph shall be a resolution under Article 324, paragraph (3) (Resolution of Class Meetings) of the Companies Act.

(Cases where Authorization of an Absorption-Type Merger Agreement is not Required, etc.)
Article 165-11 (1) The provisions of the preceding Article paragraphs (1) to (4) inclusive shall not apply where the amount set forth in item (i) does not exceed one fifth (or any smaller proportion prescribed by the articles of incorporation of the Stock Company Surviving the Absorption-Type Merger) of the amount set forth in item (ii); provided,

however, that this shall not apply to cases where all or part of the Shares, etc. delivered to members of an Absorbed Mutual Company are shares with restriction on transfer of the Stock Company Surviving the Absorption-Type Merger and where the Stock Company Surviving the Absorption-Type Merger is not a Public Company:
(i) The total of the following amounts:
  (a) The amount calculated by multiplying the number of Stock Company Surviving the Absorption-Type Merger's shares to be distributed to the members of the Absorbed Mutual Company by the amount of net assets per share (meaning the amount of net assets per share set forth in Article 141, paragraph (2) (Notice of purchases by Stock Company) of the Companies Act); and
  (b) The amount of money to be granted to the members of the Absorbed Mutual Company;
(ii) The amount of net assets of the Stock Company Surviving the Absorption-Type Merger as calculated by the method specified by Cabinet Office Ordinance.
(2) In the case prescribed in the main clause of the preceding paragraph, an absorption-type merger agreement shall be approved by a resolution of the shareholders' meeting by the day before the Effective Date, where the holders of the number of shares specified by Cabinet Office Ordinance (limited to those who can exercise their voting rights at the shareholders' meeting set forth in paragraph (1) of the preceding Article) have notified to the Stock Company Surviving the Absorption-Type Merger of their intention to oppose to the merger within two weeks from the date of notice under Article 165-4, paragraph (1) as applied mutatis mutandis pursuant to the following Article or the date of public notice under Article 165-4, paragraph (2) as applied mutatis mutandis pursuant to the following Article.

(Provision on Mutatis Mutandis Application)
Article 165-12　The provisions of Article 165-4, Article 165-5, paragraph (2) and Article 165-7 of this Act of this Act and Article 797, paragraphs (1) and (2) (Dissenting Shareholders' Share Purchase Demand) of the Companies Act shall apply mutatis mutandis to a Stock Company Surviving an Absorption-Type Merger. In this case, the term "and address" in Article 165-4, paragraph (1) shall be deemed to be replaced with ", address and, where Article 165-10, paragraph (4) applies, the particulars of the shares set forth in that paragraph"; any other necessary technical change in interpretation shall be specified by Cabinet Order.

(Retention and Inspection, etc. of Documents Related to Absorption-Type Merger, etc.)
Article 165-13　(1) A Stock Company Surviving an Absorption-Type Merger shall, without delay following the Effective Date, prepare documents or electromagnetic records in which the rights and obligations of the Absorbed Mutual Company assumed by the Stock Company Surviving the Absorption-Type Merger as a result of the absorption-type merger and any other particulars specified by Cabinet Office Ordinance as being involved in an absorption-type merger are detailed or recorded.
(2) A Stock Company Surviving an Absorption-Type Merger shall, for six months from the Effective Date, keep at each of its business offices documents or electromagnetic records set forth in the preceding paragraph.
(3) The creditors of a Stock Company Surviving an Absorption-Type Merger, such as Shareholders and Policyholders, may make the following requests to the company at any time during its operating hours; provided, however, that they pay the fees determined by the Stock Company Surviving the Absorption-Type Merger in making a request falling under item (ii) or (iv):

(i) A request to inspect the documents set forth in the preceding paragraph;
(ii) A request for a certified copy or extract of the documents set forth in the preceding paragraph;
(iii) A request to inspect anything that shows the particulars recorded in the electromagnetic records set forth in the preceding paragraph in a manner specified by Cabinet Office Ordinance; or
(iv) A request to be provided with the particulars recorded in the electromagnetic records set forth in the preceding paragraph by the electromagnetic means determined by the Stock Company Surviving the Absorption-Type Merger, or to be issued a document detailing such particulars.

Division 3 Procedures for a Stock Company Established by Consolidation-Type Merger

Article 165-14 (1) The provisions of Part II, Chapter I (excluding Article 27 (excluding items (iv) and (v)), Article 29, Article 31, Article 39, Section 6 and Article 49) (Incorporation) of the Companies Act shall not apply to the incorporation of a Stock Company Established by a Consolidation-Type Merger.
(2) The articles of incorporation of a Stock Company Established by a Consolidation-Type Merger shall be drafted by the consolidated companies.
(3) The provisions of the preceding Article shall apply mutatis mutandis to a Stock Company Established by a Consolidation-Type Merger. In this case, any other necessary technical change in interpretation shall be specified by Cabinet Order.

Division 4 Procedures for Extinguished Mutual Companies

(Retention and Inspection, etc. of Documents Related to a Merger Agreement, etc.)
Article 165-15 (1) An extinguished mutual company (meaning an Absorbed Mutual Company or a consolidated mutual company; hereinafter the same shall apply in this Section) shall, for the period ranging from any of the following dates, whichever is earlier, to the Effective Date, keep at each of its offices the documents or electromagnetic records in which the details of the merger agreement and any other particulars specified by Cabinet Office Ordinance are detailed or recorded.
(i) The day that is two weeks before the date of the general members' council meeting (or General Representative Members' Council Meeting, where the company has such a council; hereinafter the same shall apply in this Subsection) set forth in paragraph (1) of the following Article; or
(ii) The date of public notice under Article 165-17, paragraph (2).
(2) Policyholders or other creditors of an extinguished mutual company may make the following requests to the company at any time during its business hours; provided, however, that they pay the fees determined by the extinguished mutual company in making a request falling under item (ii) or (iv):
(i) A request to inspect the documents set forth in the preceding paragraph;
(ii) A request for a certified copy or extract of the documents set forth in the preceding paragraph;
(iii) A request to inspect anything that shows the particulars recorded in the electromagnetic records set forth in the preceding paragraph in a manner specified by Cabinet Office Ordinance; or
(iv) A request to be provided with the particulars recorded in the electromagnetic re-

cords set forth in the preceding paragraph by the electromagnetic means determined by the extinguished mutual company, or to be issued a document detailing such particulars.

(Authorization of Merger Agreement)
Article 165-16 (1) An extinguished mutual company shall have its merger agreement approved by a resolution of the general members' council by the day before the Effective Date.
(2) The resolution set forth in the preceding paragraph to be adopted by an extinguished mutual company shall be a resolution under Article 62, paragraph (2).

(Objections of Creditors)
Article 165-17 (1) Policyholders or other creditors of an extinguished mutual company may state to the company their objections to the merger.
(2) An extinguished mutual company shall give public notice of the following particulars in the Official Gazette and by the Method of Public Notice prescribed by its articles of incorporation; provided, however, that the period for item (iii) may not be shorter than one month:
(i) The fact that a merger will be carried out;
(ii) The trade names or names and addresses of the Company Surviving the Absorption-Type Merger (meaning the Mutual Company Surviving the Absorption-Type Merger or Stock Company Surviving the Absorption-Type Merger; hereinafter the same shall apply in this Section) or other consolidated companies and the Formed Company;
(iii) The fact that Policyholders or other creditors of the extinguished mutual company may state their objections within a certain period of time; and
(iv) In addition to what is listed in the preceding items, any particular specified by Cabinet Office Ordinance.
(3) Where no Policyholders or other creditors have stated their objections within the period set forth in item (iii) of the preceding paragraph, such Policyholders or other creditors shall be deemed to have approved the merger.
(4) The provisions of Article 88, paragraphs (4) to (6) inclusive shall apply mutatis mutandis to objections of creditors under paragraph (1). In this case, the term "paragraph (2), item (iii)" in paragraphs (4) and (6) of the same Article shall be deemed to be replaced with "Article 165-17, paragraph (2), item (iii)"; any other necessary technical change in interpretation shall be specified by Cabinet Order.

(Change in Effective Date of an Absorption-Type Merger)
Article 165-18 (1) An Absorbed Mutual Company may change the Effective Date in an agreement with the Company Surviving the Absorption-Type Merger.
(2) In the case set forth in the preceding paragraph, the Absorbed Mutual Company shall give public notice of the Effective Date thus changed by the day before the original Effective Date (or, where the changed Effective Date falls before the original Effective Date, the changed Effective Date).
(3) Where the Effective Date has been changed pursuant to the provisions of paragraph (1), the changed Effective Date shall be deemed to be the Effective Date for the purpose of applying the provisions of this Section.

Division 5 Procedures for a Mutual Company Surviving an Absorption-Type Merger

(Retention and Inspection, etc. of Documents Related to an Absorption-Type Merger Agreement, etc.)

Article 165-19 (1) A Mutual Company Surviving an Absorption-Type Merger shall, for the period ranging from any of the following dates, whichever is earlier, to the day that is six months after the Effective Date, keep at each of its offices the documents or electromagnetic records in which the details of the absorption-type merger agreement and any other particulars specified by Cabinet Office Ordinance are detailed or recorded.

(i) The day that is two weeks before the date of the general members' council meeting set forth in Article 165-16, paragraph (1) as applied mutatis mutandis pursuant to the following Article; or

(ii) The date of public notice under Article 165-17, paragraph (2) as applied mutatis mutandis pursuant to the following Article.

(2) Policyholders or other creditors of a Mutual Company Surviving an Absorption-Type Merger may make the following requests to the company at any time during its business hours; provided, however, that they pay the fees determined by the Mutual Company Surviving the Absorption-Type Merger in making a request falling under item (ii) or (iv):

(i) A request to inspect the documents set forth in the preceding paragraph;

(ii) A request for a certified copy or extract of the documents set forth in the preceding paragraph;

(iii) A request to inspect anything that shows the particulars recorded in the electromagnetic records set forth in the preceding paragraph in a manner specified by Cabinet Office Ordinance; or

(iv) A request to be provided with the particulars recorded in the electromagnetic records set forth in the preceding paragraph by the electromagnetic means determined by the Mutual Company Surviving the Absorption-Type Merger, or to be issued a document detailing such particulars.

(Mutatis Mutandis Application of Provisions)

Article 165-20 The provisions of Articles 165-16 and 165-17 shall apply mutatis mutandis to a Mutual Company Surviving an Absorption-Type Merger. In this case, any other necessary technical change in interpretation shall be specified by Cabinet Order.

(Retention and Inspection, etc. of Documents Related to an Absorption-Type Merger, etc.)

Article 165-21 (1) A Mutual Company Surviving an Absorption-Type Merger shall, without delay following the Effective Date, prepare documents or electromagnetic records in which the rights and obligations of the Absorbed Mutual Company or Absorbed Stock Company which are assumed by the Mutual Company Surviving the Absorption-Type Merger as a result of the absorption-type merger and any other particulars specified by Cabinet Office Ordinance as being involved in an absorption-type merger are detailed or recorded.

(2) A Mutual Company Surviving an Absorption-Type Merger shall, for six months from the Effective Date, keep at each of its offices documents or electromagnetic records set forth in the preceding paragraph.

(3) Policyholders or other creditors of a Mutual Company Surviving an Absorption-Type Merger may make the following requests to the company at any time during its business hours; provided, however, that they pay the fees determined by the Stock Company Surviving the Absorption-Type Merger in making a request falling under item (ii) or (iv):

(i) A request to inspect the documents set forth in the preceding paragraph;
(ii) A request for a certified copy or extract of the documents set forth in the preceding paragraph;
(iii) A request to inspect anything that shows the particulars recorded in the electromagnetic records set forth in the preceding paragraph in a manner specified by Cabinet Office Ordinance; or
(iv) A request to be provided with the particulars recorded in the electromagnetic records set forth in the preceding paragraph by the electromagnetic means determined by the Mutual Company Surviving the Absorption-Type Merger, or to be issued a document detailing such particulars.

Division 6 Procedures for a Mutual Company Established by Consolidation-Type Merger

Article 165-22 (1) The provisions of Chapter II, Section 2, Subsection 2 (excluding Article 23 (excluding paragraph (1), item (ix) and paragraph (4)), Article 25, Article 26, Article 30-10, paragraphs (2) to (4) inclusive and (6), and Article 30-13, paragraph (1)) shall not apply to the incorporation of a Mutual Company Established by a Consolidation-Type Merger.
(2) The articles of incorporation of a Mutual Company Established by a Consolidation-Type Merger shall be drafted by the consolidated companies.
(3) The provisions of the preceding Article shall apply mutatis mutandis to a Mutual Company Established by a Consolidation-Type Merger. In this case, any other necessary technical change in interpretation shall be specified by Cabinet Order.

Division 7 Special Provisions on the Merger of Stock Companies

(Special Provisions on the Retention and Inspection, etc. of Documents Related to Merger Agreements, etc.)
Article 165-23 For the purpose of applying the provisions of Article 782, paragraph (1), Article 794, paragraph (1) (Retention and Inspection, etc. of Documents, etc. Related to an Absorption-type Merger Agreement, etc.) and Article 803, paragraph (1) (Retention and Inspection, etc. of Documents, etc. Related to a Consolidation-type Merger Agreement, etc.) of the Companies Act to a merger of stock companies that conducts Insurance Business pursuant to Article 748 (Conclusion of a Merger Agreement) of that Act, the terms "Ordinance of the Ministry of Justice" and "its head office" in those provisions shall be deemed to be replaced with "Ordinance of the Ministry of Justice or Cabinet Office Ordinance" and "each of its business offices," respectively.

(Special Provisions on Objections of the Creditors)
Article 165-24 (1) Policyholders or other creditors of a stock company conducting Insurance Business that seeks to carry out a merger under Article 748 (Conclusion of a Merger Agreement) of the Companies Act (limited to the cases where the company to survive the merger or to be incorporated by the merger is a stock company conducting Insurance Business) (hereinafter referred to as "Merging Company under the Companies Act" in this Section) may state to the company their objections to the merger.
(2) In the case set forth in the preceding paragraph, a Merging Company under the Companies Act shall give public notice of the following particulars in the Official Gazette and by the Method of Public Notice prescribed by its articles of incorporation; provid-

ed, however, that the period for item (iv) may not be shorter than one month:
(i) The fact that a merger will be carried out;
(ii) The trade names and addresses of the merging companies and the company to survive the merger or the company to be incorporated by the merger;
(iii) The particulars specified by Cabinet Office Ordinance as pertaining to the financial statements of the companies set forth in the preceding item;
(iv) The fact that Policyholders or other creditors of the Merging Company under the Companies Act may state their objections within a certain period of time; and
(v) In addition to what is listed in the preceding items, any particular specified by Cabinet Office Ordinance.
(3) Where no Policyholders or other creditors have stated their objections within the period set forth in item (iv) of the preceding paragraph, such Policyholders or other creditors shall be deemed to have approved the merger.
(4) Where any Policyholder or other creditor has stated his/her objection under paragraph (2), item (iv), the merging company under the Company Act shall make payment or provide equivalent security to such Policyholder or other creditor, or entrust equivalent property to a trust company, etc. for the purpose of ensuring that such Policyholder or other creditor receive the payment; provided, however, that this shall not apply to the cases where the merger poses no risk of harming the interest of such Policyholder or other creditor;
(5) The provisions of the preceding paragraph shall not apply to the Policyholders or any rights held by other persons pertaining to insurance contracts (other than Insurance Claims, etc.).
(6) Any resolution approving the merger under shall be null and void if the number of the Policyholders who have stated their objections within the period set forth in paragraph (2), item (iv) (excluding the holders of policies under which Insurance Claims, etc. had arisen by the time of public notice under paragraph (2) (but limited to those policies that would be terminated with the payment of the Insurance Claims, etc.); hereinafter the same shall apply in this paragraph and the following paragraph) exceeds one fifth of the total number of Policyholders, and the amount specified by Cabinet Office Ordinance as the credits (other than Insurance Claims, etc.) belonging to the insurance contracts of the Policyholders who have stated such objections exceeds one fifth of the total amount of credits belonging to the Policyholders.
(7) A merger carried out pursuant to the provisions of the preceding paragraphs shall also be effective against the Policyholders who have stated their objections under the preceding paragraph and other persons who hold any right (other than Insurance Claims, etc.) pertaining to the insurance contracts involving the Policyholders.
(8) In addition to what is provided for in the preceding paragraphs, necessary particulars for the application of those provisions shall be specified by Cabinet Order.
(9) The provisions of Articles 789, 799 and 810 (Objections of Creditors) of the Companies Act shall not apply to a Merging Company under the Companies Act.

Division 8 Public Notice, etc. after Merger

Article 166 (1) An Insurance Company, etc. surviving a merger or an Insurance Company, etc. incorporated by a merger shall, without delay following the merger, give public notice of the fact that the merger has been carried out and the particulars specified by Cabinet Office Ordinance. The same shall apply where an Insurance Company, etc. that has given public notice under paragraph (2) of the preceding Article (including the cases where it is applied mutatis mutandis pursuant to Article 165-12), Article 165-17, paragraph (2) (including the cases where it is applied mutatis mutandis pursuant to

Article 165-20) or paragraph (2) of the preceding Article has renounced the planned merger.
(2) An Insurance Company, etc. surviving a merger or an Insurance Company, etc. incorporated by a merger shall, for six months from the date of the merger, keep at each of its business offices or offices the documents or electromagnetic records in which the progress of the procedures provided for in Article 165-7 (including the cases where it is applied mutatis mutandis pursuant to Article 165-20), Article 165-17 (including the cases where it is applied mutatis mutandis pursuant to Article 165-20) and any other particulars specified by Cabinet Office Ordinance as being involved in a merger are detailed or recorded.
(3) The creditors, such as Shareholders and Policyholders, of an Insurance Company, etc. surviving a merger or an Insurance Company, etc. incorporated by a merger may make the following requests at any time during its operating hours or business hours; provided, however, that they pay the fees determined by the Insurance Company, etc. in making a request falling under item (ii) or (iv):
(i) A request to inspect the documents set forth in the preceding paragraph;
(ii) A request for a certified copy or extract of the documents set forth in the preceding paragraph;
(iii) A request to inspect anything that shows the particulars recorded in the electromagnetic records set forth in the preceding paragraph in a manner specified by Cabinet Office Ordinance; or
(iv) A request to be provided with the particulars recorded in the electromagnetic records set forth in the preceding paragraph by the electromagnetic means determined by the Insurance Company, etc. surviving a merger or the Insurance Company, etc. incorporated by a merger, or to be issued a document detailing such particulars.

Subsection 4 Effectuation, etc. of Merger

(Authorization of Merger)
Article 167 (1) Any merger involving an Insurance Company, etc. (limited to the cases where the Insurance Company, etc. survives the merger or where an Insurance Company, etc. is established by the merger) shall be null and void without the authorization of the Prime Minister.
(2) Whenever an application has been filed for the authorization set forth in the preceding paragraph, the Prime Minister shall examine whether it conforms to the following standards:
(i) The merger is appropriate in light of the protection of Policyholders, etc. ;
(ii) If the application for authorization is from an Insurance Company, that the merger poses no risk of impeding the appropriate competitive relationships among insurance companies; and
(iii) It is certain that the Insurance Company, etc. surviving the merger or the Insurance Company, etc. established by the merger will perform its business in an appropriate, fair and efficient manner following the merger.
(3) The Prime Minister must not give the authorization set forth in paragraph (1) for any application made under that paragraph for a merger between an Insurance Company and a Low-Cost, Short-Term Insurer, unless the company surviving the merger or the company established by the merger is an Insurance Company.

(Deemed License, etc.)
Article 168 (1) A Stock Company or Mutual Company established by a merger with the

authorization set forth in paragraph (1) of the preceding Article shall, at the time of its establishment, be deemed to obtain the license from the Prime Minister set forth in Article 3, paragraph (1) where the merger involves an Insurance Company, or the registration set forth in Article 272, paragraph (1) where the merger does not involve any Insurance Company.
(2) The license set forth in the preceding paragraph shall be either of the two types of license listed in Article 3, paragraph (2), whichever was obtained under paragraph (1) of the same Article by the Insurance Company that is extinguished in the merger.

(Effectuation, etc. of Merger)
Article 169 (1) A Mutual Company Surviving an Absorption-Type Merger shall, on the Effective Date, succeed to the rights and obligations of the absorbed company (meaning the Absorbed Mutual Company or Absorbed Stock Company; hereinafter the same shall apply in this Section).
(2) The dissolution of an absorbed company following a merger may not be duly asserted against a third party prior to the registration of the merger.
(3) The shares and share options of an Absorbed Stock Company shall expire on the Effective Date.
(4) The Policyholders of an absorbed company shall gain membership in the Mutual Company Surviving the Absorption-Type Merger on the Effective Date; provided, however, that this shall not apply to the cases where the Mutual Company Surviving the Absorption-Type Merger's articles of incorporation do not grant membership to the Policyholders with the same class of insurance contracts as those covered by the merger agreement.
(5) The provisions of the preceding paragraphs shall not apply where the procedure set forth in Article 165-7 or 165-17 (including the cases where it is applied mutatis mutandis pursuant to Article 165-20) has not been completed, or where the absorption-type merger has been voluntarily abandoned.

Article 169-2 (1) A Mutual Company Established by a Consolidation-Type Merger shall, on the date of its establishment, succeed to the rights and obligations of the consolidated companies.
(2) The Policyholders of a consolidated company shall gain membership in the Mutual Company Established by a Consolidation-Type Merger on the date of the latter's establishment; provided, however, that this shall not apply to the cases where the Mutual Company Established by the Consolidation-Type Merger's articles of incorporation do not grant membership to the Policyholders with the same class of insurance contracts as those covered by the merger agreement.
(3) The shares and share options of a Consolidated Stock Company shall expire on the date of the establishment of the Mutual Company Established by the Consolidation-Type Merger.

Article 169-3 (1) A Stock Company Surviving an Absorption-Type Merger shall succeed to the rights and obligations of the absorbed company on the Effective Date.
(2) The dissolution of an absorbed company following a merger may not be duly asserted against a third party prior to the registration of the merger.
(3) Where the merger agreement provides for the particulars listed in Article 164, paragraph (1), item (ii), sub-item (a), the members of an Absorbed Mutual Company shall, on the Effective Date, become holders of the shares set forth in said sub-item pursuant to the provisions of the merger agreement on the particulars listed in Article 164, paragraph (1), item (iii).

(4) The provisions of the preceding three paragraphs shall not apply where the procedure set forth in Article 165-7 as applied mutatis mutandis pursuant to Article 165-12 or in Article 165-17 has not been completed, or where the absorption-type merger has been voluntarily abandoned.

Article 169-4 (1) A Stock Company Established by a Consolidation-Type Merger shall, on the date of its establishment, succeed to the rights and obligations of the consolidated companies.
(2) The shareholders or members of a consolidated company shall, on the date of the establishment of the Stock Company Established by the Consolidation-Type Merger, become the holders of the shares set forth in Article 165, paragraph (1), item (vi) or (vii) pursuant to the provisions of the merger agreement on the particulars listed in Article 165, paragraph (1), item (ix).
(3) The share options of a Consolidated Stock Company shall expire on the date of the establishment of the Stock Company Established by the Consolidation-Type Merger.
(4) In the case prescribed in Article 165, paragraph (1), item (xii), sub-item (a), the holders of share options of a Consolidated Stock Company shall, on the date of the establishment of the Stock Company Established by the Consolidation-Type Merger, become holders of the latter company's share options as set forth in said sub-item, pursuant to the provisions of the merger agreement on the particulars listed in Article 165, paragraph (1), item (xiii).

(Registration of Merger)
Article 169-5 (1) Where a Mutual Company or stock company has undergone an absorption-type merger, it shall make, at the location of its principal office or head office, a registration of dissolution for the absorbed company and a registration of change for the Company Surviving the Absorption-Type Merger, within two weeks from the date on which the merger took effect.
(2) Where two or more Mutual Companies or Stock Companies are involved in a consolidation-type merger, they shall complete, at the location of their principal offices or head offices, registrations of dissolution for the consolidated companies and a registration of incorporation for the Formed Company, within two weeks from the dates specified in each of the following items in accordance with the categories provided therein:
 (i) Where the consolidated companies only include stock companies, any of the following dates, whichever is the latest:
  (a) The date of the resolution at the shareholders' meeting set forth in Article 165-3, paragraph (1);
  (b) Where a resolution of the class meeting is required for the merger, the date of such resolution;
  (c) The day on which twenty days have elapsed since a notice under Article 165-4, paragraph (1) or a public notice under paragraph (2) of the same Article was given;
  (d) The date of completion of the procedure set forth in Article 165-7; or
  (e) Any date fixed by the consolidated companies in an agreement;
 (ii) Where the consolidated companies only include Mutual Companies, any of the following dates, whichever is the latest:
  (a) The date of the resolution of the general members' council set forth in Article 165-16, paragraph (1);
  (b) The date of completion of the procedure set forth in Article 165-17; or
  (c) Any date fixed by the consolidated companies in an agreement; or
 (iii) Where the consolidated companies include a Stock Company (or stock companies)

and a Mutual Company, any of the dates specified in the preceding two items, whichever is the latest.
(3) In the cases prescribed in the preceding two paragraphs, the Mutual Company or Stock Company shall also complete the registration(s) set forth in the applicable provisions at the location of its (their) branch offices or secondary offices, within three weeks from the date specified in the applicable provision; provided, however, that a registration of change under paragraph (1) shall only be made where the change affects any of the particulars listed in the items of Article 930, paragraph (2) (Registration at Location of Branch Offices) of the Companies Act (including the cases where it is applied mutatis mutandis pursuant to Article 64, paragraph (3)).

(Application for Registration of Merger, etc.)
Article 170 (1) The following documents shall be attached to a written application for registration of change due to a merger under Article 159, paragraph (1) and Article 165-23, in addition to the documents set forth in Articles 18 and 19 (Documents to be Attached to Written Application) and Article 46 (General Rules on Attached Documents) of the Commercial Registration Act (including the cases where they are applied mutatis mutandis pursuant to Article 67), and Article 80 (Registration of Absorption-Type Merger) of that Act (including the cases where it is applied mutatis mutandis pursuant to paragraph (3)):
(i) A document certifying that a public notice has been given under Article 165-7, paragraph (2) (including the cases where it is applied mutatis mutandis pursuant to Article 165-12), Article 165-17, paragraph (2) (including the cases where it is applied mutatis mutandis pursuant to Article 165-20) or Article 165-24, paragraph (2);
(ii) For an extinguished stock company or Stock Company Surviving an Absorption-Type Merger, a document certifying that the number of the Policyholders who raised their objections within the period set forth in Article 165-7, paragraph (2), item (iv) (including the cases where it is applied mutatis mutandis pursuant to Article 165-12) has not exceeded one fifth of the total number of Policyholders set forth in Article 70, paragraph (6) (including the cases where it is applied with relevant changes in interpretation pursuant to the provisions of Article 255, paragraph (2) (hereinafter referred to as "The Cases of Application with Relevant Changes in Interpretation Pursuant to the Provision of Article 255, paragraph (2)"in this item); hereinafter the same shall apply in this item) as applied mutatis mutandis pursuant to Article 165-7, paragraph (4) (including the cases where it is applied mutatis mutandis pursuant to Article 165-12; hereinafter the same shall apply in this item) (or, in The Cases of Application with Relevant Changes in Interpretation Pursuant to the Provision of Article 255, paragraph (2), one tenth of such total number), or a document certifying that the amount of credits specified by Cabinet Office Ordinance set forth in Article 70, paragraph (6) as applied mutatis mutandis pursuant to Article 165-7, paragraph (4) as belonging to such Policyholders has not exceeded one fifth (or, in The Cases of Application with Relevant Changes in Interpretation Pursuant to the Provision of Article 255, paragraph (2), one tenth) of the total amount set forth in Article 70, paragraph (6) as applied mutatis mutandis pursuant to Article 165-7, paragraph (4);
(iii) For an extinguished Mutual Company or a Mutual Company Surviving an Absorption-Type Merger, a document certifying that the number of the Policyholders who raised their objections within the period set forth in Article 165-17, paragraph (2), item (iii) (including the cases where it is applied mutatis mutandis pursuant to Article 165-20) has not exceeded one fifth of the total number of Policyholders set forth in Article 88, paragraph (6) (including the cases where it is applied with rele-

Art.171   6 Insurance Business Act, Part II, Chap.VIII, Sec.2

vant changes in interpretation pursuant to the provisions of Article 255, paragraph (2) (hereinafter referred to as "The Cases of Application with Relevant Changes in Interpretation Pursuant to the Provision of Article 255, paragraph (2)"in this item); hereinafter the same shall apply in this item) as applied mutatis mutandis pursuant to Article 165-17, paragraph (4) (including the cases where it is applied mutatis mutandis pursuant to Article 165-20; hereinafter the same shall apply in this item) (or, in The Cases of Application with Relevant Changes in Interpretation Pursuant to the Provision of Article 255, paragraph (2), one tenth of such total number), or a document certifying that the amount of credits specified by Cabinet Office Ordinance set forth in Article 88, paragraph (6) as applied mutatis mutandis pursuant to Article 165-17, paragraph (4) as belonging to such Policyholders has not exceeded one fifth (or, in The Cases of Application with Relevant Changes in Interpretation Pursuant to the Provision of Article 255, paragraph (2), one tenth) of the total amount set forth in Article 88, paragraph (6) as applied mutatis mutandis pursuant to Article 165-17, paragraph (4);

(iv) For a Merging Company under the Companies Act, a document certifying that the number of the Policyholders who raised their objections within the period set forth in Article 165-24, paragraph (2), item (iv) has not exceeded one fifth of the total number of Policyholders set forth in paragraph (6) of the same Article (including the cases where it is applied with relevant changes in interpretation pursuant to the provisions of Article 255, paragraph (2) (hereinafter referred to as "The Cases of Application with Relevant Changes in Interpretation Pursuant to the Provision of Article 255, paragraph (2)"in this item); hereinafter the same shall apply in this item) (or, in The Cases of Application with Relevant Changes in Interpretation Pursuant to the Provision of Article 255, paragraph (2), one tenth of such total number), or a document certifying that the amount of credits specified by Cabinet Office Ordinance set forth in Article 165-24, paragraph (6) as belonging to such Policyholders has not exceeded one fifth (or, in The Cases of Application with Relevant Changes in Interpretation Pursuant to the Provision of Article 255, paragraph (2), one tenth) of the total amount set forth in that paragraph; and

(v) A document certifying any public notice made under Article 254, paragraph (3).

(2) The documents listed in the items of the preceding paragraph shall be attached to a written application for registration of incorporation due to a merger under Article 159, paragraph (1) and Article 165-23, in addition to the documents set forth in Articles 18, 19 and 46 of the Commercial Registration Act (including the cases where they are applied mutatis mutandis pursuant to Article 67), and Article 81 (Registration of Consolidation-Type Merger) of that Act (including the cases where it is applied mutatis mutandis pursuant to the following paragraph).

(3) The provisions of Article 79 to 83 inclusive (Registration of Merger) of the Commercial Registration Act shall apply mutatis mutandis to a registration pertaining to a Mutual Company. In this case, any other necessary technical change in interpretation shall be specified by Cabinet Order.

(Actions to Invalidate a Merger)

Article 171 The provisions of Article 828, paragraph (1) (limited to the segment pertaining to items (vii) and (viii)) and (2) (limited to the segment pertaining to items (vii) and (viii)) (Actions to Invalidate Acts Concerning the Organization of a Company), Article 834 (limited to the segment pertaining to items (vii) and (viii)) (Defendant), Article 835, paragraph (1) (Jurisdiction over Actions), Article 836 to 839 inclusive (Order to Provide Security, Mandatory Consolidation of Oral Arguments, etc., Persons Affected by a Judgment Being Upheld, Effects of a Judgment of Invalidity, Revocation or Rescission), Article 843 (excluding paragraph (1), items (iii) and (iv), and the proviso to paragraph (2)) (Effects of a Judgment of Invalidity of a Merger), Article 846 (Liability for Damages Where a Judgment Is Entered Against the Plaintiff), and Article 937, paragraph (3) (limited to the segment pertaining to items (ii) and (iii)) and (4) (Commissioning of Registration by a Judicial Decision) of the Companies Act shall apply mutatis mutandis to an action to invalidate a merger under Article 159, paragraph (1); and the provisions of Article 868, paragraph (5) (Jurisdiction over Non-Contentious Cases), Article 870 (limited to the segment pertaining to item (xv)) (Hearing of Statements), the main clause of Article 871 (Appending of the Reason), Article 872 (limited to the segment pertaining to item (iv)) (Immediate Appeal), the main clause of Article 873 (Stay of Execution of the Judicial Decision of the Prior Instance), Article 875 (Exclusion from Application of the Provisions of the Non-Contentious Cases Procedures Act) and Article 876 (Supreme Court Rules) of that Act shall apply mutatis mutandis to an application under Article 843, paragraph (4) of that Act as applied mutatis mutandis pursuant to this Article. In this case, the term "members, etc." in Article 828, paragraph (2), items (vii) and (viii) of that Act shall be deemed to be replaced with "members, directors, company auditors or liquidator(s) (or, in a company with Committees, members, directors, executive officers or liquidator(s)) of a Mutual Company"; any other necessary technical change in interpretation shall be specified by Cabinet Order.

Article 172 Deleted

Article 173 Deleted

Section 3 Company Split

(Split of Stock Company Conducting Insurance Business)
Article 173-2 (1) Where a Stock Company that conducts Insurance Business (hereinafter referred to as "Stock Insurance Company" in this Section) transfers its insurance contracts in a company split (hereinafter referred to as "Split" in this Section), the transfer shall cover the whole insurance contracts for which the policy reserves is calculated on the same basis (excluding the insurance contracts specified by Cabinet Order, such as those for which an insured event had occurred by the time of public notice under Article 173-4, paragraph (2) (limited to those contracts which would be terminated with the payment of the insurance proceeds pertaining to the insured event)).
(2) A Stock Insurance Company that transfers its insurance contracts in a Split may, in the relevant incorporation-type company split plan or absorption-type split agreement (hereinafter referred to as "Split Plan, etc."), stipulate minor changes to the clauses of the insurance contracts to be transferred in the Split, so long as such changes are not disadvantageous to the Policyholders.

(Retention and Inspection, etc. of Documents Pertaining to a Split, etc.)
Article 173-3 For the purpose of applying the provisions of Article 782, paragraph (1) (Retention and Inspection. etc. of Documents, etc. Related to an Absorption-type Merger Agreement, etc.), Article 794, paragraph (1) (Retention and Inspection, etc. of Documents, etc. Related to an Absorption-type Merger Agreement, etc.) and Article 803, paragraph (1) (Retention and Inspection, etc. of Documents, etc. Related to a Consolidation-type Merger Agreement, etc.) of the Companies Act to a Stock Insurance Company involved in a Split, the terms "particulars prescribed by the Ordinance of the Ministry of Justice" and "head office" in those provisions shall be deemed to be

Art.173-4   ⑥ Insurance Business Act, Part II, Chap.VIII, Sec.3

replaced with "particulars prescribed by a Ordinance of the Ministry of Justice and particulars specified by Cabinet Office Ordinance" and "business offices," respectively.

(Objections of Creditors)

Article 173-4 (1) Where a Stock Insurance Company is involved in a Split, the persons listed in the following items may state their objections thereto to the Stock Insurance Company set forth in each of those items:

(i) Policyholders or other creditors (limited to the creditors set forth in Article 789, paragraph (1), item (ii) (Objections of Creditors) of the Companies Act) of a splitting company in an absorption-type split (meaning a Stock Company or limited liability company carrying out an absorption-type split; hereinafter the same shall apply in this Article) that is a Stock Insurance Company: the splitting company in an absorption-type split;

(ii) Policyholders or other creditors of a succeeding company in an absorption-type split (meaning a Stock Company, general Partnership company, limited Partnership company or limited liability company assuming, in whole or in Part, the rights and obligations of the splitting company in an absorption-type split with regard to its business; the same shall apply hereinafter) that is a Stock Insurance Company: the succeeding company in an absorption-type split; and

(iii) Policyholders or other creditors (limited to the creditors set forth in Article 810, paragraph (1), item (ii) (Objections of Creditors) of the Companies Act) of a splitting company in an incorporation-type company split (meaning a Stock Company or limited liability company carrying out an incorporation-type company split; hereinafter the same shall apply in this Article) that is a Stock Insurance Company: the splitting company in an incorporation-type company split.

(2) In the case set forth in the preceding paragraph, a Stock Insurance Company falling under any of the items of that paragraph (hereinafter referred to as "Split-Involved Company" in this Article) shall give public notice of the following particulars in the Official Gazette and by the Method of Public Notice prescribed by the Split-Involved Company in its articles of incorporation, and notify each of the known creditors of said particulars (limited to the creditors set forth in Article 789, paragraph (3) or Article 810, paragraph (3) of the Companies Act); provided, however, that the period set forth in item (iv) may not be shorter than one month:

(i) The fact that a Split will be carried out;

(ii) The trade name and address of the companies listed in (a) or (b) in accordance with the categories of Split set forth in (a) and (b):

  (a) In the case of an absorption-type split: the splitting company in an absorption-type split and the succeeding company in an absorption-type split; or

  (b) In the case of an incorporation-type split: the splitting company in an incorporation-type company split and the Stock Company, general Partnership company, limited Partnership company or limited liability company to be incorporated by the Split.

(iii) The particulars specified by Cabinet Office Ordinance as pertaining to the financial statements of a Stock Company falling under (a) or (b) of the preceding item;

(iv) The fact that Policyholders or other creditors of the Split-Involved Company may raise their objections within a certain period of time; and

(v) In addition to what is listed in the preceding items, particulars specified by Cabinet Office Ordinance.

(3) Where no Policyholders or other creditors have raised their objections within the period set forth in item (iv) of the preceding paragraph, such Policyholders or other creditors shall be deemed to have approved the merger.

(4) Where any Policyholder or other creditor has raised his/her objection under paragraph (2), item (iv), the Split-Involved Company shall make payment or provide equivalent security to such Policyholder or other creditor, or entrust equivalent property to a trust company, etc. for the purpose of ensuring that such Policyholder or other creditor receive the payment; provided, however, that this shall not apply to the cases where the Split poses no risk of harming the interest of such Policyholder or other creditor.
(5) The provisions of the preceding paragraph shall not apply to the Policyholders or any rights held by other persons pertaining to insurance contracts (other than Insurance Claims, etc.).
(6) Any Split shall be invalid if the number of the Policyholders who have raised their objections within the period set forth in paragraph (2), item (iv) (excluding the holders of policies under which Insurance Claims, etc. had already arisen at the time of public notice under the paragraph (2) (but limited to those policies that would be terminated with the payment of the Insurance Claims, etc.); hereinafter the same shall apply in this paragraph and the following paragraph) exceeds one fifth of the total number of Policyholders (limited to those who may raise their objections pursuant to the provisions of paragraph (1)), and the amount specified by Cabinet Office Ordinance as the credits (other than Insurance Claims, etc.) belonging to the insurance contracts of the Policyholders who have raised such objections exceeds one fifth of the total amount of credits belonging to the Policyholders (limited to those who may raise their objections pursuant to the provisions of paragraph (1)).
(7) A Split carried out pursuant to the provisions of the preceding paragraphs shall also be effective against the Policyholders who have raised their objections under the preceding paragraph and other persons who hold any right (other than Insurance Claims, etc.) pertaining to the insurance contracts involving the Policyholders.
(8) In addition to what is provided for in the preceding paragraphs, the necessary particulars for applying those provisions shall be specified by Cabinet Order.
(9) The provisions of Articles 789 and 799 (Objections of Creditors) and Article 810 of the Companies Act shall not apply to a Stock Insurance Company falling under paragraph (1), item (i) or (ii).
(10) For the purpose of applying to the cases set forth in paragraph (1) the provisions of Article 759, paragraphs (2) and (3) (Effectuation, etc. of an Absorption-type Company Split Which Causes a Stock Company to Succeed to Rights and Obligations), Article 761, paragraphs (2) and (3) (Effectuation, etc. of an Absorption-type Company Split Which Causes a Membership Company to Succeed to Rights and Obligations), Article 764, paragraphs (2) and (3) (Effectuation, etc. of an Incorporation-type Company Split by Which a Stock Company is Incorporated), and Article 766, paragraphs (2) and (3) (Effectuation, etc. of an Incorporation-type Company Split by Which a Membership Company is Incorporated), Article 791, paragraph (1), item (i) (Retention and Inspection, etc. of Documents, etc. Related to an Absorption-type Company Split or Share Exchange), Article 801, paragraph (2) (Retention and Inspection, etc. of Documents, etc. Related to an Absorption-type Merger, etc.) and Article 811, paragraph (1), item (i) (Retention and Inspection, etc. of Documents, etc. Related to an Incorporation-type Company Split or Share Transfer) of the Companies Act, the term "objections pursuant to the provisions of Article 789, paragraph (1), item (ii) (including the cases where it is applied mutatis mutandis pursuant to Article 793, paragraph (2); the same shall apply in the following paragraph)" in Article 759, paragraph (2) and Article 761, paragraph (2) of that Act shall be deemed to be replaced with "objections pursuant to the provisions of Article 789, paragraph (1), item (ii) (including the cases where it is applied mutatis mutandis pursuant to Article 793, paragraph (2); the same shall apply in

Art.173-4   ⑥ Insurance Business Act, Part II, Chap.VIII, Sec.3

the following paragraph) or the provisions of Article 173-4, paragraph (1) of the Insurance Business Act"; the term "individual notification under Article 789, paragraph (2) (excluding item (iii) and including the cases where it is applied mutatis mutandis pursuant to Article 793, paragraph (2); the same shall apply hereinafter in this paragraph as well as in the following paragraph)" in Article 759, paragraph (2) and Article 761, paragraph (2) of that Act shall be deemed to be replaced with "individual notification under Article 789, paragraph (2) (excluding item (iii) and including the cases where it is applied mutatis mutandis pursuant to Article 793, paragraph (2); the same shall apply hereinafter in this paragraph as well as in the following paragraph) or under Article 173-4, paragraph (2) of the Insurance Business Act"; the term "objections pursuant to the provisions of Article 810, paragraph (1), item (ii) (including the cases where it is applied mutatis mutandis pursuant to Article 813, paragraph (2); the same shall apply in the following paragraph)" in Article 764, paragraph (2) and Article 766, paragraph (2) of that Act shall be deemed to be replaced with "objections pursuant to the provisions of Article 810, paragraph (1), item (ii) (including the cases where it is applied mutatis mutandis pursuant to Article 813, paragraph (2); the same shall apply in the following paragraph) or the provisions of Article 173-4, paragraph (1) of the Insurance Business Act"; the term "individual notification under Article 810, paragraph (2) (excluding item (iii) and including the cases where it is applied mutatis mutandis pursuant to Article 813, paragraph (2); the same shall apply hereinafter in this paragraph as well as in the following paragraph)" in Article 764, paragraph (2) and Article 766, paragraph (2) of that Act shall be deemed to be replaced with "individual notification under Article 810, paragraph (2) (excluding item (iii) and including the cases where it is applied mutatis mutandis pursuant to Article 813, paragraph (2); the same shall apply hereinafter in this paragraph as well as in the following paragraph) or under Article 173-4, paragraph (2) of the Insurance Business Act"; the term "individual notification under Article 789, paragraph (2)" in Article 759, paragraph (2) and Article 761, paragraph (2) of that Act shall be deemed to be replaced with "individual notification under Article 789, paragraph (2) or under Article 173-4, paragraph (2) of the Insurance Business Act"; the term "individual notification under Article 810, paragraph (2)" in Article 764, paragraph (2) and Article 766, paragraph (2) of that Act shall be deemed to be replaced with "individual notification under Article 810, paragraph (2) or under Article 173-4, paragraph (2) of the Insurance Business Act"; the terms "Article 789, paragraph (1), item (ii)" and "paragraph (2) of the same Article" in Article 759, paragraph (3) and Article 761, paragraph (3) of that Act shall be deemed to be replaced with "Article 789, paragraph (1), item (ii) or Article 173-4, paragraph (1) of the Insurance Business Act" and "Article 789, paragraph (2) or Article 173-4, paragraph (2) of that Act," respectively; and the terms "Article 810, paragraph (1), item (ii)" and "Article 810, paragraph (2)" in Article 764, paragraph (3) and Article 766, paragraph (3) of that Act shall be deemed to be replaced with "Article 810, paragraph (1), item (ii) or Article 173-4, paragraph (1) of the Insurance Business Act" and "Article 810, paragraph (2) or Article 173-4, paragraph (2) of that Act," respectively; and the term "Ordinance of the Ministry of Justice" in Article 791, paragraph (1), item (i), Article 801, paragraph (2) and Article 811, paragraph (1), item (i) of that Act shall be deemed to be replaced with "Cabinet Office Ordinance," respectively.

(11) The provisions of Article 759, paragraphs (2) and (3), Article 761, paragraphs (2) and (3), Article 764, paragraphs (2) and (3), and Article 766, paragraphs (2) and (3) of the Companies Act shall not apply to the creditor specified by Cabinet Order, such as a person holding any right pertaining to an insurance contract, a Beneficiary of money trust pertaining to the Insurance-Proceed Trust Services set forth in Article 99, paragraph (3).

(Suspension of Conclusion of Insurance Contracts)
Article 173-5 A Stock Insurance Company that transfers its insurance contracts in a Split shall not conclude any insurance contract that belongs to the same type as the insurance contracts to be transferred, for the period ranging from the time of adoption of the resolution on the Split to the time of execution or renunciation of the Split.

(Authorization of Split of Stock Insurance Company)
Article 173-6 (1) Any Split of a Stock Insurance Company shall be null and void without the authorization of the Prime Minister.
(2) Whenever an application has been filed for the authorization set forth in the preceding paragraph, the Prime Minister shall examine whether it conforms to the following standards:
  (i) The Split is appropriate in light of the protection of Policyholders, etc. ;
  (ii) If the application for authorization is from an Insurance Company, that the Split poses no risk of impeding the appropriate competitive relationships among Insurance Companies; and
  (iii) It is certain that the Stock Insurance Company applying for the authorization will perform its business in an appropriate, fair and efficient manner following the Split.
(3) The Prime Minister may not approve any application made under paragraph (1) pertaining to a Split that involves the transfer of insurance contracts of an Insurance Company, unless the company that acquires the insurance contracts is an Insurance Company.

(Public Notice, etc. of Split)
Article 173-7 (1) A Stock Insurance Company that transfers its insurance contracts in a Split shall, following the Split, give public notice of without delay the fact that its insurance contracts have been transferred in the Split and other particulars specified by Cabinet Office Ordinance. The same shall apply where the company has renounced the Split.
(2) A Stock Insurance Company that has acquired insurance contracts in a Split shall, within three months from the date of the Split, notify the Policyholders affected by the transfer of insurance contracts in the Split thereof (or, where any minor change under Article 173-2, paragraph (2) is stipulated in the Split Plan, etc. with regard to the insurance contracts transferred in the Split, of the fact that it has acquired the insurance contracts in the Split and the contents of such minor change).
(3) Where a Stock Insurance Company that transfers its insurance contracts in a Split has outstanding loans or other claims against Policyholders, and such claims are to be assigned to the Stock Insurance Company that acquires the insurance contracts under the Split Plan, etc. , a notice in the form of an instrument carrying a fixed date under Article 467 (Requirement for Assertion of Assignment of Nominative Claims Against Third Parties) of the Civil Code shall be deemed to have been given to the Policyholders if a public notice under the first sentence of paragraph (1) has been given by way of publication in a daily newspaper that publishes the particulars of current events. In this case, the date of the public notice shall be deemed to be the fixed date.

(Registration of Split)
Article 173-8 (1) The following documents shall be attached to a written application for registration of incorporation due to an incorporation-type split, in addition to the documents specified in Articles 18 and 19 (Documents to be Attached to Written Application), Article 46 (General Rules on Attached Documents), Article 86 (excluding item

(viii)) (Registration of Company Split) and Article 109, paragraph (2) (excluding that segment in item (iii) pertaining to the documents listed in Article 86, item (viii) of that Act and including the cases where it is applied mutatis mutandis pursuant to Article 116, paragraph (1) and Article 125 of that Act) (Registration of Company Split) of the Commercial Registration Act:

(i) A document certifying that a public notice under Article 173-4, paragraph (2) has been given;

(ii) Where any Policyholder or other creditor has raised his/her objection under Article 173-4, paragraph (4), a document certifying that the company has made payment or provided equivalent security to such Policyholder or other creditor, or entrusted equivalent property to a trust company, etc. for the purpose of ensuring that such Policyholder or other creditor receive the payment, or a document certifying that the Split poses no risk of harming the interest of such Policyholder or other creditor;

(iii) A document certifying that the number of Policyholders who raised their objections under Article 173-4, paragraph (6) has not exceeded one fifth of the total number of Policyholders, or a document certifying that the amount specified by Cabinet Office Ordinance set forth in that paragraph as the credits belonging to such Policyholders has not exceeded one fifth of the total amount set forth in that paragraph;

(2) The documents listed in the items of the preceding paragraph shall be attached to a written application for registration of change due to an absorption-type split carried out by a Stock Company, general Partnership company, limited Partnership company or limited liability company that is the succeeding company in an absorption-type split, in addition to the documents set forth in the following provisions of the Commercial Registration Act: Article 18, Article 19, Article 46, Article 85 (excluding the segment pertaining to the documents listed in item (iii) or (viii) of the same Article with regard to a Stock Insurance Company) (Registration of Company Split), Article 93 (General Rules on Attached Documents) (including the cases where it is applied mutatis mutandis pursuant to Articles 111 and 118 of that Act) and Article 109, paragraph (1) (excluding that segment in item (ii) pertaining to the documents listed in Article 85, item (viii) of that Act and including the cases where it is applied mutatis mutandis pursuant to Article 106, paragraph (1) and Article 125 of that Act).

Section 4 Liquidation

(Appointment and Dismissal of Liquidators by Prime Minister)
Article 174 (1) The Prime Minister shall appoint liquidators, at the request of interested persons or the Minister of Justice, or without any party's request, where an Insurance Company, etc. has dissolved on the grounds listed in Article 471, item (vi) (Grounds for Dissolution) of the Companies Act as applied with relevant changes in interpretation pursuant to the provisions of Article 152, paragraph (1) (including the cases where it is applied mutatis mutandis pursuant to Article 152, paragraph (2)), or at the request of interested persons or without any party's request where no one is entitled to become a liquidator pursuant to the provisions of Article 180-4, paragraph (1) or under Article 478, paragraph (1) (Assumption of Office of Liquidators) of that Act or where an Insurance Company, etc. falls under Article 180, item (ii) or under Article 475, item (ii) (Causes of Commencement of Liquidation) of that Act.

(2) For the purpose of applying the provisions of Article 477, paragraph (4) (Establishment of Structures Other than Shareholders' Meetings) of the Companies Act to a Stock Company that conducts Insurance Business, the term "Large Company" in that para-

graph shall be deemed to be replaced with "Insurance Company or a Stock Company listed in Article 272-4, paragraph (1), item (i), sub-item (b) of the Insurance Business Act."

(3) The provisions of Article 478, paragraphs (2) to (4) inclusive of the Companies Act shall not apply to a Stock Company that conducts Insurance Business.

(4) Notwithstanding the provisions of Article 180-4, paragraph (1) or Article 478, paragraph (1) of the Companies Act, the Prime Minister shall appoint liquidators where an Insurance Company, etc. has dissolved due to the cancellation of a license under Article 3, paragraph (1) or a registration under Article 272, paragraph (1).

(5) The provisions of Article 8-2, paragraph (2) shall apply mutatis mutandis to the liquidator(s) of a Stock Company that conducts Insurance Business.

(6) For the purpose of applying to a Stock Company that conducts Insurance Business, the provisions of Article 331, paragraph (1), item (iii) (Qualifications of Directors) of the Companies Act as applied mutatis mutandis pursuant to Article 478, paragraph (6) of that Act, the term "this Act" in that item shall be deemed to be replaced with "the Insurance Business Act, this Act."

(7) The Prime Minister may, if he/she appoints liquidators pursuant to the provisions of paragraph (1), (4) or (9), designate from among them a liquidator (hereinafter referred to as "Representative Liquidator" in this Section) who represents the Stock Company or Mutual Company to be liquidated (hereinafter referred to as "Insurance Company in Liquidation, etc." in this Section).

(8) The liquidator(s) (excluding the persons appointed by the Prime Minister and the liquidator(s) in the case of special liquidation) shall, within two weeks from the date of their assumption of office, notify the Prime Minister of the following particulars; provided, however, that this shall not apply to the cases where special liquidation has commenced in the meantime.
  (i) Grounds for the dissolution (or, for an Insurance Company in Liquidation, etc. falling under Article 180, item (ii) or under Article 475, item (ii) of the Companies Act, that fact) and the date of dissolution; and
  (ii) The name(s) and address(es) of the liquidator(s).

(9) In the case of the liquidation of an Insurance Company, etc. (other than a special liquidation), the Prime Minister may dismiss a liquidator, if he/she finds material grounds for such dismissal. In this case, the Prime Minister may appoint another liquidator.

(10) For the purpose of applying the provisions of Article 479 (Dismissal of Liquidators) of the Companies Act to the liquidation of a Stock Company that conducts Insurance Business, the term "court pursuant to the provisions of paragraphs (2) to (4) inclusive of the preceding Article" in paragraph (1) of that Article shall be deemed to be replaced with "Prime Minister"; and the term "liquidator" in paragraph (2) of that Article shall be deemed to be replaced with "liquidator (other than a person appointed by the Prime Minister)."

(11) The provisions of Article 73, paragraphs (1) and (3) (Registration of Liquidators), and Article 74, paragraph (1) (Registration of Change with Regard to Liquidators) of the Commercial Registration Act (including the cases where it is applied mutatis mutandis pursuant to Article 183, paragraph (2)) shall apply mutatis mutandis to a liquidator appointed by the Prime Minister. In this case, any other necessary technical change in interpretation shall be specified by Cabinet Order.

(12) The Prime Minister shall, where he/she dismisses a liquidator pursuant to the provisions of paragraph (9), commission a registration to that effect to the registry office with jurisdiction over the head office or principal office of the Insurance Company in Liquidation, etc.

(Remuneration for Liquidators Appointed by Prime Minister)
Article 175 (1) A liquidator appointed pursuant to the provisions of paragraphs (1), (4) or (9) of the preceding Article may receive remuneration from the Insurance Company in Liquidation, etc.
(2) The amount of the remuneration set forth in the preceding paragraph shall be determined by the Prime Minister.

(Submission of Closing Financial Statements, etc.)
Article 176 The liquidator(s) of an Insurance Company in Liquidation, etc. (other than the liquidator(s) in the case of a special liquidation) shall, if the Shareholders' Meeting, etc. has approved the material set forth in Article 492, paragraph (3) (Preparation of Inventory of Property) or Article 497, paragraph (2) (Provision of Balance Sheet to Annual Shareholders' Meeting) (including the cases where they are applied mutatis mutandis pursuant to Article 180-17), or Article 507, paragraph (3) (Conclusion of Liquidation) (including the cases where it is applied mutatis mutandis pursuant to Article 183, paragraph (1)) of the Companies Act, submit such material (or, where such material has been prepared in the form of electromagnetic record or where an electromagnetic record has been prepared in lieu of such material, the electromagnetic record specified by Cabinet Office Ordinance or a document describing the information contained in the electromagnetic record) to the Prime Minister without delay.

(Cancellation of Insurance Contracts after Dissolution)
Article 177 (1) Where an Insurance Company, etc. has dissolved on the grounds listed in Article 471, item (iii) or (vi) (Grounds for Dissolution) of the Companies Act as applied with relevant changes in interpretation pursuant to the provisions of Article 152, paragraph (1) (including the cases where it is applied mutatis mutandis pursuant to Article 152, paragraph (2)) or in Article 152, paragraph (3), item (ii), a Policyholder may cancel his/her insurance contract prospectively.
(2) In the case referred to in the preceding paragraph, any insurance contract that is not cancelled by the Policyholder pursuant to the provisions of that paragraph shall lose its effect on the day that is three months after the date of dissolution.
(3) In the cases set forth in the preceding two paragraphs, the Insurance Company in Liquidation, etc. shall refund to the Policyholder the amount of money reserved for the insured, any unearned premium (meaning the insurance premium paid for that Part of the period of insurance stipulated in an insurance contract which had not lapsed by the time at which the insurance contract was cancelled or lost its effect) and any other amount of money specified by Cabinet Office Ordinance.

(Permission of Performance during Period for Stating Claims)
Article 178 For the purpose of applying the provisions of Article 500 (Restrictions on Performance of Obligations) of the Companies Act to the liquidation of a Stock Company that conducts Insurance Business, the term "court" in paragraph (2) of that Article shall be deemed to be replaced with "Prime Minister."

(Order for Supervision of Liquidation)
Article 179 (1) In the case of the liquidation of an Insurance Company, etc. (other than a special liquidation), the Prime Minister may, if he/she finds it necessary, order the Insurance Company in Liquidation, etc. to deposit its properties or to take any other necessary measure for supervising the liquidation.
(2) The provisions of Article 128, paragraph (1), Article 129, paragraph (1), Article 272-22, paragraph (1) and Article 272-23, paragraph (1) shall apply mutatis mutandis to the

case referred to in the preceding paragraph, if the Prime Minister finds it necessary for supervising the liquidation of an Insurance Company in Liquidation, etc.

(Causes of Commencement of Mutual Company's Liquidation)
Article 180 A Mutual Company shall go into liquidation in the following cases, pursuant to the provisions of this Section:
(i) Where the company has dissolved (excluding the cases where it has dissolved on the grounds listed in Article 471, item (iv) of the Companies Act as applied mutatis mutandis pursuant to Article 152, paragraph (2) and where it has dissolved as a result of a ruling for the commencement of bankruptcy proceedings and such bankruptcy proceedings have not ended); or
(ii) Where a judgment allowing an action to invalidate the company's incorporation has become final and binding.

(Capacity of Mutual Companies in Liquidation)
Article 180-2 A Mutual Company that goes into liquidation pursuant to the provisions of the preceding Article (hereinafter referred to as a "Mutual Company in Liquidation" in this Section) shall be deemed to remain in existence until the liquidation is completed, to the extent of the purpose of the liquidation.

(Administrative Organs of Mutual Companies in Liquidation Other than General Members' Councils and General Representative Members' Councils)
Article 180-3 (1) A Mutual Company in Liquidation shall have one or more liquidator(s) and company auditor(s).
(2) A Mutual Company in Liquidation may have a board of liquidators or a board of company auditors as prescribed by its articles of incorporation.
(3) A Mutual Company in Liquidation whose articles of incorporation provide for the establishment of a board of company auditors shall also have a board of liquidators.
(4) In a Mutual Company in Liquidation that was a company with Committees when it fell under Article 180, item (i) or (ii), the Audit Committee Members shall become the company auditors.
(5) The provisions of Article 51 shall not apply to a Mutual Company in Liquidation.

(Assumption of Office of Liquidators)
Article 180-4 (1) The following persons shall become the liquidators of a Mutual Company in Liquidation:
(i) Directors (unless the company has a person falling under the following item or item (iii));
(ii) Person(s) prescribed by the articles of incorporation; and
(iii) Person(s) elected by a resolution of the general members' council (or General Representative Members' Council, where the company has such a council).
(2) For the purpose of applying the provisions of item (i) of the preceding paragraph and Article 53-5, paragraph (3) to a Mutual Company in Liquidation that was a company with Committees when it fell under Article 180, item (i) or (ii), the term "Directors" in item (i) of the preceding paragraph shall be deemed to be replaced with "Directors other than Audit Committee Members"; and the term "outside company auditors (meaning those company auditors of a Mutual Company who have never been a director, executive officer or accounting advisor (or, if the accounting advisor is a juridical person, any member of that juridical person who is supposed to carry out relevant duties), or manager or any other employee of the Mutual Company or any of its de facto Subsidiaries; the same shall apply hereinafter)" in Article 180, paragraph (3) shall be

Art.180-5 6 Insurance Business Act, Part II, Chap.VIII, Sec.4

deemed to be replaced with "persons who have never been a director, executive officer or accounting advisor (or, if the accounting advisor is a juridical person, any member of that juridical person who is supposed to carry out relevant duties), or manager or any other employee of the company with a board of auditors or any of its de facto Subsidiaries."
(3) The provisions of Article 8-2, paragraph (2), Article 53 and Article 53-2, paragraph (1) shall apply mutatis mutandis to the liquidator(s) of a Mutual Company in Liquidation; and the provisions of Article 53-2, paragraph (3) shall apply mutatis mutandis to the liquidators of a Mutual Company with a board of liquidators (meaning a mutual liquidating company that has a board of liquidators; hereinafter the same shall apply in this Section). In this case, any other necessary technical change in interpretation shall be specified by Cabinet Order.

(Dismissal of Liquidators)
Article 180-5 (1) A liquidator (other than a person appointed by the Prime Minister pursuant to the provisions of Article 174, paragraph (1), (4) or (9)) may be dismissed at any time by a resolution of the general members' council (or General Representative Members' Council, where the company has such a council).
(2) The court may, if it finds any material grounds, dismiss a liquidator under the preceding paragraph in response to a petition filed by members representing at least three thousandths (or any smaller proportion prescribed by the articles of incorporation) of the total membership, or three thousand (or any smaller number prescribed by the articles of incorporation) or more members of the Mutual Company (or, in a Specified Mutual Company, members equal to or exceeding the number specified by Cabinet Order set forth in Article 38, paragraph (1)), who have been members of the Mutual Company without interruption for the preceding six months (or any shorter period prescribed by the articles of incorporation) (or, in a company with a General Representative Members' Council, those members or nine (or any smaller number prescribed by the articles of incorporation) or more representative members).
(3) The provisions of Article 868, paragraph (1) (Jurisdiction over Non-Contentious Cases), Article 870 (limited to the segment pertaining to item (iii)) (Hearing of Statements), the main clause of Article 871 (Appending of the Reason), Article 872 (limited to the segment pertaining to item (iv)) (Immediate Appeal), Article 875 (Exclusion from Application of the Provisions of the Non-Contentious Cases Procedures Act) and Article 876 (Supreme Court Rules) of the Companies Act shall apply mutatis mutandis to a petition under the preceding paragraph; and the provisions of Article 937, paragraph (1) (limited to the segment pertaining to item (ii), sub-item (e) and item (iii), sub-item (a)) (Commissioning of Registration by a Judicial Decision) of that Act shall apply mutatis mutandis to a judicial decision on the dismissal of a liquidator under paragraph (1). In this case, any other necessary technical change in interpretation shall be specified by Cabinet Order.
(4) The provisions of Article 53-12, paragraphs (1) to (3) inclusive, and the provisions of Article 868, paragraph (1), Article 870 (limited to the segment pertaining to item (ii)), Article 871, Article 872 (limited to the segment pertaining to item (iv)), Article 874 (limited to the segment pertaining to item (i)) (Restrictions on Appeal), Article 875, Article 876 and Article 937, paragraph (1) (limited to the segment pertaining to item (ii), sub-items (b) and (c)) of the Companies Act shall apply mutatis mutandis to the liquidator set forth in paragraph (1). In this case, any other necessary technical change in interpretation shall be specified by Cabinet Order.

(Company Auditor's Term of Office)

Article 180-6 The provisions of Article 53-6 shall not apply to the company auditors of a Mutual Company in Liquidation.

(Liquidator's Duties)
Article 180-7 The liquidator(s) of a Mutual Company in Liquidation shall carry out the following duties:
(i) Completion of pending transactions;
(ii) Collection of debts and performance of obligations; and
(iii) Distribution of residual assets.

(Execution of Business)
Article 180-8 (1) The liquidator(s) shall execute the business of the Mutual Company in Liquidation (other than a Mutual Company with a board of liquidators; hereinafter the same shall apply in this Article).
(2) If a Mutual Company in Liquidation has two or more liquidators, the business of the company is decided by the majority of the liquidators, unless otherwise provided for in the articles of incorporation.
(3) In the case set forth in the preceding paragraph, the liquidators may not delegate to any liquidator a decision regarding any of the following particulars:
(i) Appointment or dismissal of a manager;
(ii) Establishment, relocation or abolition of a secondary office;
(iii) Particulars listed in the items of Article 298, paragraph (1) of the Companies Act as applied mutatis mutandis pursuant to Article 41, paragraph (1) or Article 49, paragraph (1); or
(iv) Revision of a system to ensure that the liquidators carry out their duties in compliance with applicable laws and regulations and the articles of incorporation, and any other system required by Cabinet Office Ordinance for ensuring that the business of a Mutual Company in Liquidation is executed in an appropriate manner.
(4) The provisions of Article 353 to 357 inclusive (Representation of Companies in Actions Between Stock Company and Directors, Apparent Representative Directors, Duty of Loyalty, Restrictions on Competition and Conflicting Interest Transactions, Director's Duty to Report), Article 360, paragraph (1) (Prohibition of Directors' Actions by the Shareholders) and Article 361 (Remuneration for Directors) of the Companies Act shall apply mutatis mutandis to a liquidator (with regard to the provisions of Article 361 of that Act, other than a liquidator appointed by the Prime Minister pursuant to the provisions of Article 174, paragraph (1), (4) or (9)). In this case, the term "Article 349, paragraph (4)" in Article 353 of that Act shall be deemed to be replaced with "Article 349, paragraph (4) as applied mutatis mutandis pursuant to Article 180-9, paragraph (5) of the Insurance Business Act"; the term "a Representative Director" in Article 354 of that Act shall be deemed to be replaced with "the Representative Liquidator"; and the terms "shareholders having the shares" and "substantial detriment" in Article 360, paragraph (1) of that Act shall be deemed to be replaced with "persons who have been members of the company" and "irreparable damage," respectively; any other necessary technical change in interpretation shall be specified by Cabinet Order.

(Representative of Mutual Company in Liquidation)
Article 180-9 (1) The liquidator(s) shall represent the Mutual Company in Liquidation; provided, however, that this shall not apply to the cases where the liquidating Insurance Company appoints a Representative Liquidator or any other person to act as its representative.
(2) Where a Mutual Company in Liquidation has two or more liquidators, each of the liqui-

Art.180-11   ⑥ Insurance Business Act, Part II, Chap.VIII, Sec.4

dators shall represent the company for the purpose of the main clause of the preceding paragraph.
(3) A Mutual Company in Liquidation (other than a Mutual Company with a board of liquidators) may appoint a Representative Liquidator from among its liquidators (excluding a person appointed by the Prime Minister pursuant to the provisions of Article 174, paragraph (1), (4) or (9); hereinafter the same shall apply in this paragraph) in accordance with its articles of incorporation, by mutual vote of the liquidators pursuant to the provisions of its articles of incorporation, or by a resolution of the general members' council (or General Representative Members' Council, where the company has such a council).
(4) Where a representative director has been appointed, the representative director shall act as the Representative Liquidator if the directors become the liquidators pursuant to the provisions of Article 180-4, paragraph (1), item (i).
(5) The provisions of Article 349, paragraphs (4) and (5) (Representatives of Companies) and Article 351 (Measures when Vacancy Arises in Office of Representative Director) of the Companies Act shall apply mutatis mutandis to the Representative Liquidator of a Mutual Company in Liquidation; the provisions of Article 352 (Authority of Persons Who Perform Duties on Behalf of Directors) of that Act shall apply mutatis mutandis to a person appointed by a provisional disposition order under Article 56 (Commission of Registration of Provisional Disposition for Stay of Execution of Duties by Representative of Juridical Person, etc.) of the Civil Provisional Relief Act to act for a liquidator or the Representative Liquidator of a Mutual Company in Liquidation; the provisions of Article 868, paragraph (1) (Jurisdiction over Non-Contentious Cases), Article 869 (Prima Facie Showing), Article 870 (limited to the segment pertaining to item (ii)) (Hearing of Statements), Article 871 (Appending of the Reason), Article 872 (limited to the segment pertaining to item (iv)) (Immediate Appeal), Article 874 (limited to the segment pertaining to items (i) and (iv)) (Restrictions on Appeal), Article 875 (Exclusion from Application of the Provisions of the Non-Contentious Cases Procedures Act) and Article 876 (Supreme Court Rules) of the Companies Act shall apply mutatis mutandis to the liquidator(s) or Representative Liquidator of a Mutual Company in Liquidation; and the provisions of Article 937, paragraph (1) (limited to the segment pertaining to item (ii), sub-items (b) and (c)) (Commissioning of Registration by a Judicial Decision) of that Act shall apply mutatis mutandis to a person who must carry out the duties of the temporary Representative Liquidator of a Mutual Company in Liquidation. In this case, any other necessary technical change in interpretation shall be specified by Cabinet Order.

(Commencement of Bankruptcy Proceedings for Mutual Company in Liquidation)
Article 180-10 (1) The liquidators shall, if it has become clear that the assets of the Mutual Company in Liquidation are not sufficient to fully discharge its debts, immediately file a petition for commencement of bankruptcy proceedings.
(2) If a Mutual Company in Liquidation has become subject to a ruling for the commencement of bankruptcy proceedings, the liquidator(s) shall be deemed to have accomplished their duties when they have transferred their tasks to the bankruptcy trustee.
(3) In the case prescribed in the preceding paragraph, the bankruptcy trustee may recover any payment made to creditors by the Mutual Company in Liquidation.

(Liquidator's Liability for Damages to Mutual Company in Liquidation)
Article 180-11 (1) A liquidator shall be liable to the Mutual Company in Liquidation for any damage caused by the failure to carry out his/her (their) duties.

(2) Where a liquidator has carried out the transaction listed in Article 356, paragraph (1), item (i) of the Companies Act in violation of Article 356, paragraph (1) of that Act as applied mutatis mutandis pursuant to Article 180-8, paragraph (4), the amount of the profit gained by the liquidator or any third party from such transaction shall be presumed to be the amount of the damage set forth in the preceding paragraph.
(3) Any of the following liquidators shall be presumed to have failed to carry out his/her duties if the Mutual Company in Liquidation has suffered any damage from the transaction set forth in Article 356, paragraph (1), item (ii) or (iii) of the Companies Act as applied mutatis mutandis pursuant to Article 180-8, paragraph (4):
  (i) A liquidator falling under Article 356, paragraph (1) of the Companies Act as applied mutatis mutandis pursuant to Article 180-8, paragraph (4);
  (ii) A liquidator who decided that the Mutual Company in Liquidation carry out such transaction; or
  (iii) A liquidator who agreed to the board of liquidators' resolution to approve such transaction.
(4) The provisions of Article 53-34 and the provisions of Article 428, paragraph (1) (Special Provision on Transactions Carried out by Director for Himself/Herself) of the Companies Act shall apply mutatis mutandis to the liability of a liquidator under paragraph (1). In this case, the term "Article 356, paragraph (1), item (ii) (including the cases where it is applied mutatis mutandis pursuant to Article 419, paragraph (2))" in Article 428, paragraph (1) of that Act shall be deemed to be replaced with "Article 356, paragraph (1), item (ii) as applied mutatis mutandis pursuant to Article 180-8, paragraph (4) of the Insurance Business Act"; any other necessary technical change in interpretation shall be specified by Cabinet Order.

(Liquidator's Liability for Damages to a Third Party)
Article 180-12 (1) A liquidator of a Mutual Company in Liquidation shall be liable to a third party for any damage caused by his/her bad faith or gross negligence in carrying out his/her duties.
(2) The provisions of the preceding paragraph shall also apply where the liquidator set forth in that paragraph has acted as follows; provided, however, that this shall not apply to the cases where the liquidator has proven that he/she did not fail to exercise due care in so acting:
  (i) Giving false notice with respect to any important particular of which notice must be given in soliciting subscribers for bonds (meaning the bonds set forth in Article 61), or including a false detail or record in any material used to explain the Mutual Company in Liquidation's business or other particulars for the purpose of such solicitation;
  (ii) Including a false detail or record with regard to any important particular that must be detailed or recorded in the inventory of property, etc. set forth in Article 492, paragraph (1) of the Companies Act as applied mutatis mutandis pursuant to Article 180-17 or the balance sheet and administrative report set forth in Article 494, paragraph (1) of that Act as applied mutatis mutandis pursuant to Article 180-17, or in the annexed detailed statements thereto;
  (iii) Making a false registration; or
  (iv) Giving false public notice.

(Joint and Several Liability of Liquidators and Company Auditors)
Article 180-13 (1) If a liquidator or company auditor is liable for any damage caused to the Mutual Company in Liquidation or a third party, and the other liquidator(s) or company auditor(s) are also liable for such damages, the other liquidator(s) or company

auditor(s) shall be his/her joint and several obligors.
(2) The provisions of Article 430 of the Companies Act as applied mutatis mutandis pursuant to Article 53-36 shall not apply to the case set forth in the preceding paragraph.

(Authority, etc. of Board of Liquidators)
Article 180-14 (1) The board of liquidators of a Mutual Company in Liquidation shall be composed of all of its liquidators.
(2) The board of liquidators shall carry out the following duties:
  (i) Decisions on the execution of business of the Mutual Company with a board of liquidators;
  (ii) Supervision of the execution of duties by the liquidators; and
  (iii) Appointment and removal of the Representative Liquidator.
(3) The board of liquidators shall appoint the Representative Liquidator from among the liquidators; provided, however, that this shall not apply to the cases where the Representative Liquidator has been appointed otherwise.
(4) The board of liquidators may remove the Representative Liquidator that it has appointed or the person who has become the Representative Liquidator pursuant to the provisions of Article 180-9, paragraph (4).
(5) Where the Prime Minister has appointed the Representative Liquidator of a Mutual Company in Liquidation pursuant to the provisions of Article 174, paragraph (7), the board of liquidators may not appoint or remove the Representative Liquidator.
(6) The board of liquidators may not delegate to any liquidator an important decision on the execution of business, including on any of the following particulars:
  (i) The appropriation of and acceptance of assignment of important assets ;
  (ii) Contracting of a large amount of debt;
  (iii) Appointment or removal of a manager or any other important employee;
  (iv) Establishment, change or abolition of a secondary office or any other important structure;
  (v) The particulars specified by Cabinet Office Ordinance as important particulars of the solicitation of subscribers for bonds (meaning the bonds set forth in Article 61), such as the particulars listed in Article 61, item (i); or
  (vi) Revision of a system to ensure that the liquidators carry out their duties in compliance with applicable laws and regulations and the articles of incorporation, and any other system required by Cabinet Office Ordinance for ensuring that the business of a Mutual Company in Liquidation is executed in an appropriate manner.
(7) The business of a Mutual Company with a board of liquidators shall be executed by:
  (i) The Representative Liquidator in a Mutual Company in Liquidation; or
  (ii) A liquidator other than the Representative Liquidator appointed by a resolution of the board of liquidators to execute the business of the Mutual Company with a board of directors.
(8) A liquidator listed in the items of the preceding paragraph shall report, at least once in every three months, the status of execution of his/her duties to the board of liquidators.
(9) The provisions of Article 364 (Representation of Company in Actions between Companies with Board of Directors and Directors) and Article 365 (Restrictions on Competition and Transactions with Companies with Board of Directors) of the Companies Act shall apply mutatis mutandis to a Mutual Company with a board of liquidators. In this case, the term "Article 353" in Article 364 of that Act shall be deemed to be replaced with "Article 353 as applied mutatis mutandis pursuant to Article 180-8, paragraph (4) of the Insurance Business Act"; the term "Article 356" in Article 365, paragraph (1) of that Act shall be deemed to be replaced with "Article 356 as applied mutatis mutandis

pursuant to Article 180-8, paragraph (4) of the Insurance Business Act"; and the term "the items of Article 356, paragraph (1)" in Article 365, paragraph (2) of that Act shall be deemed to be replaced with "the items of Article 356, paragraph (1) as applied mutatis mutandis pursuant to Article 180-8, paragraph (4) of the Insurance Business Act"; any other necessary technical change in interpretation shall be specified by Cabinet Order.

(Operations of Board of Liquidators)
Article 180-15 The provisions of Part II, Chapter IV, Section 5, Subsection 2 (excluding Article 367, Article 371, paragraphs (3) and (5), Article 372, paragraph (3), and Article 373) (Operations) of the Companies Act shall apply mutatis mutandis to the operations of the board of liquidators of a Mutual Company with a board of liquidators; and the provisions of Article 868, paragraph (1) (Jurisdiction over Non-Contentious Cases), Article 869 (Prima Facie Showing), Article 870 (limited to the segment pertaining to item (i)) (Hearing of Statements), the main clause of Article 871 (Appending of the Reason), Article 872 (limited to the segment pertaining to item (iv)) (Immediate Appeal) the main clause of Article 873 (Stay of Execution of the Judicial Decision of the Prior Instance), Article 875 (Exclusion from Application of the Provisions of the Non-Contentious Cases Procedures Act) and Article 876 (Supreme Court Rules) of that Act shall apply mutatis mutandis to an application for permission under Article 371, paragraph (2) or (4) of that Act as applied mutatis mutandis pursuant to this Article. In this case, the terms "shareholder" and "at any time during the business hours of a Stock Company" in Article 371, paragraph (2) (Minutes) of that Act shall be deemed to be replaced with "member (or representative member, where the company has a General Representative Members' Council)" and "with the permission of the court," respectively; the term "Parent Company or Subsidiary" in Article 371, paragraph (6) of that Act shall be deemed to be replaced with "de facto Subsidiaries as set forth in Article 33-2, paragraph (1) of the Insurance Business Act"; and the term "Article 363, paragraph (2)" in Article 372, paragraph (2) (Omission of report to board of directors) of that Act shall be deemed to be replaced with "Article 180-14, paragraph (8) of the Insurance Business Act"; any other necessary technical change in interpretation shall be specified by Cabinet Order.

(Application of Provisions on Directors, etc.)
Article 180-16 For the purpose of applying to a Mutual Company in Liquidation the provisions of Chapter II, Section 2, Subsection 3; Chapter II, Section 2, Subsection 4, Divisions 1 and 2; Article 53-5, paragraph (2); Article 343, paragraphs (1) and (2) of the Companies Act as applied mutatis mutandis pursuant to Article 53-11; Article 345, paragraph (3) of that Act as applied mutatis mutandis pursuant to Article 345, paragraph (4) of that Act as applied mutatis mutandis pursuant to Article 53-11; Article 359 of that Act as applied mutatis mutandis pursuant to Article 53-15; Chapter II, Section 2, Subsection 4, Division 6; and Article 62-2, the provisions pertaining to a director, representative director, board of directors or Mutual Company shall be deemed applicable to a liquidator, Representative Liquidator, board of liquidators or Mutual Company with board of liquidators, respectively.

(Inventory of Property, etc.)
Article 180-17 The provisions of Part II, Chapter IX, Section 1, Subsection 3 (excluding Article 496, paragraph (3) and Article 497, paragraph (1), item (iii)) (Property Inventories) of the Companies Act shall apply mutatis mutandis to a Mutual Company in Liquidation. In this case, the terms "the items of Article 489, paragraph (7)" and "the

items of Article 475" in Article 492, paragraph (1) (Preparation of Inventory of Property) of that Act shall be deemed to be replaced with "Article 180-14, paragraph (7), item (i) or (ii) of the Insurance Business Act" and "Article 180, item (i) or (ii) of that Act," respectively; and the term "the items of Article 475" in Article 494, paragraph (1) (Preparation and Retention of Balance Sheet) of that Act shall be deemed to be replaced with "Article 180, item (i) or (ii) of the Insurance Business Act"; any other necessary technical change in interpretation shall be specified by Cabinet Order.

(Order of Appropriation of Property)
Article 181 (1) The liquidator(s) of a Mutual Company in Liquidation shall perform the obligations, and redeem the funds of the Mutual Company.
(2) In the case referred to in the preceding paragraph, the funds shall not be redeemed prior to the performance of the Mutual Company's obligations.

(Performance of Obligations, etc.)
Article 181-2 The provisions of Part II, Chapter IX, Section 1, Subsection 4 (Performance of Obligations), Article 868, paragraph (1) (Jurisdiction over Non-Contentious Cases), Article 871 (Appending of the Reason), Article 874 (limited to the segment pertaining to item (i)) (Restrictions on Appeal), Article 875 (Exclusion from Application of the Provisions of the Non-Contentious Cases Procedures Act) and Article 876 (Supreme Court Rules) of the Companies Act shall apply mutatis mutandis to a Mutual Company in Liquidation. In this case, the term "the items of Article 475" in Article 499, paragraph (1) (Public Notices to Creditors) of that Act shall be deemed to be replaced with "Article 180, item (i) or (ii) of the Insurance Business Act"; and the term "court" in Article 500, paragraph (2) of that Act shall be deemed to be replaced with "Prime Minister"; any other necessary technical change in interpretation shall be specified by Cabinet Order.

(Distribution of Residual Assets)
Article 182 (1) Unless otherwise provided in the articles of incorporation, any appropriation of the residual assets of a Mutual Company in Liquidation shall be made by a resolution of the general members' council (or General Representative Members' Council, where the company has such a council).
(2) The residual assets of a Mutual Company in Liquidation shall be distributed to its members or disposed of in a manner that contributes to the protection of Policyholders, etc.
(3) Any distribution of the residual assets of a Mutual Company in Liquidation to its members shall be made in accordance with the members' amount of contribution (meaning the amount calculated pursuant to the provisions of Cabinet Office Ordinance as that part of the profits obtained by investing the insurance premiums paid by the members and the amount of money received as such insurance premiums which have neither been allocated to any payments such as insurance proceeds or refunds, nor to any business or other expenditures (including any refund under Article 177, paragraph (3)).
(4) Any measures of the residual assets of a Mutual Company in Liquidation in a manner that contributes to the protection of Policyholders, etc. under paragraph (2) shall be made in an amount not exceeding the total amount calculated in accordance with Cabinet Office Ordinance set forth in the preceding paragraph for all withdrawing members, pursuant to the provisions of Cabinet Office Ordinance.
(5) The resolution set forth in paragraph (1) shall be a resolution under Article 62, paragraph (2).
(6) Any resolution under paragraph (1) shall be null and void without the authorization of

the Prime Minister.

(Completion of Liquidation Process, etc.)
Article 183 (1) The provisions of Article 507 (Conclusion of Liquidation), Article 508 (Retention of Accounting Materials), Article 868, paragraph (1) (Jurisdiction over Non-Contentious Cases), Article 871 (Appending of the Reason), Article 874 (limited to the segment pertaining to item (i)) (Restrictions on Appeal), Article 875 (Exclusion from Application of the Provisions of the Non-Contentious Cases Procedures Act) and Article 876 (Supreme Court Rules) of the Companies Act shall apply mutatis mutandis to a Mutual Company in Liquidation. In this case, the term "the items of Article 489, paragraph (7)" in Article 508, paragraph (1) of that Act shall be deemed to be replaced with "Article 180-14, paragraph (7), item (i) or (ii) of the Insurance Business Act"; any other necessary technical change in interpretation shall be specified by Cabinet Order.
(2) The provisions of Article 928 (excluding paragraph (2)) (Registration of a Liquidator), Article 929 (limited to the segment pertaining to item (i)) (Registration of Completion of Liquidation) and the main clause of Article 932 (Registration of a Change, etc. with Regard to a Branch Office) of the Companies Act, and Article 73 to 75 inclusive (Registration of Liquidators, Registration of Change Related to Liquidator, Registration of Completion of Liquidation) of the Commercial Registration Act shall apply mutatis mutandis to a registration regarding the liquidation of a Mutual Company. In this case, any other necessary technical change in interpretation shall be specified by Cabinet Order.

(Mutatis Mutandis Application of the Companies Act to the Special Liquidation of a Mutual Company)
Article 184 The provisions of Part II, Chapter IX, Section 2 (excluding Article 522, paragraph (3) and Article 541) (Special Liquidations), Part VII, Chapter II, Section 4 (Action Concerning Special Liquidation), Part VII, Chapter III, Sections 1 (excluding Article 868, paragraphs (2) to (5) inclusive and Article 870 to 874 inclusive) (General Provisions) and 3 (excluding Article 879, Article 880, and Article 898, paragraphs (1), (2) and (5)) (Special Provisions on Procedures of Special Liquidation), and Article 938, paragraphs (1) to (5) inclusive (Commissioning of Registration by a Juridical Decision Concerning Special Liquidation) of the Companies Act shall apply mutatis mutandis to a Mutual Company in Liquidation. In this case, the term "shareholders who have held, for the consecutive period of the past six months or more (or, in cases where a shorter period is provided for in the articles of incorporation, such period), not less than 3 percent of the voting rights held by all of the shareholders (excluding the shareholders that cannot exercise voting rights on all matters on which resolutions can be passed at the shareholders' meeting; or, in cases where any proportion less than that is provided for in the articles of incorporation, such proportion) or shareholders who have held, for the consecutive period of the past six months or more (or, in cases where a shorter period is provided for in the articles of incorporation, such period), not less than 3 percent of the issued shares (excluding treasury shares; or, in cases where a lower proportion is provided for in the articles of incorporation, such proportion)" in Article 522, paragraph (1) (Order to investigate) of that Act shall be deemed to be replaced with "members representing at least three thousandths (or any smaller proportion prescribed by the articles of incorporation) of the total membership, or three thousand (or any smaller number prescribed by the articles of incorporation) or more members of the Mutual Company (or, in a Specified Mutual Company, members equal to or exceeding the number specified by Cabinet Order set forth in Article 38, paragraph (1) of the Insurance Business Act), who have been members of the Mutual Company with-

out interruption for the preceding six months (or any shorter period prescribed by the articles of incorporation)"; the term "assigned claims owed by the Liquidating Stock Company or shares in" in Article 532, paragraph (2) (Remunerations of Supervisors) of that Act shall be deemed to be replaced with "acquire any claim against"; the term "Chapter VII (excluding Article 467, paragraph (1), item (v))" in Article 536, paragraph (3) (Restrictions on Assignment of Business) of that Act shall be deemed to be replaced with "Article 62-2 of the Insurance Business Act"; and the term "Article 492, paragraph (1)" in Article 562 (Report to Creditors' Meeting of Outcome of Investigations by Liquidators) of that Act shall be deemed to be replaced with "Article 492, paragraph (1) as applied mutatis mutandis pursuant to Article 180-17 of the Insurance Business Act"; any other necessary technical change in interpretation shall be specified by Cabinet Order.

Chapter IX Foreign Insurers

Section 1 General Rules

(License)
Article 185 (1) A Foreign Insurer may, only in cases where it established a branch office, etc. in Japan (meaning an office in Japan, such as a branch office or secondary office, of the Foreign Insurer, or the office of a person delegated by the Foreign Insurer to act as an agent for the underwriting of insurance for the Foreign Insurer's Insurance Business in Japan; the same shall apply hereinafter in this Section to Section 5 inclusive) and obtained a license of the Prime Minister, transact Insurance Business under that license at said branch office, etc. , notwithstanding the provisions of Article 3, paragraph (1).
(2) The license set forth in the preceding paragraph refers to two types of licenses: the foreign life insurance business license and the foreign non-life insurance business license.
(3) The same person cannot obtain both the foreign life insurance business license and the foreign non-life insurance business license.
(4) The foreign life insurance business license shall be a license pertaining to the business of underwriting the classes of insurance listed in Article 3, paragraph (4), item (i) or, in addition, underwriting the classes of insurance listed in the same paragraph, items (ii) or (iii).
(5) The foreign non-life insurance business license shall be a license pertaining to the business of underwriting the classes of insurance listed in Article 3, paragraph (5), item (i) or, in addition, underwriting the classes of insurance listed in the same paragraph, item (ii) or (iii).
(6) A Foreign Insurance Company, etc. shall, except as otherwise specified by Cabinet Office Ordinance, conclude, in Japan, an insurance contract pertaining to any persons with an address or residence in Japan or property located in Japan, or vessels or aircraft with Japanese nationality.

(Foreign Insurers, etc. Without Branch Offices, etc. in Japan)
Article 186 (1) A Foreign Insurer without a branch office, etc. in Japan shall not conclude an insurance contract pertaining to any persons with an address or residence in Japan or property located in Japan, or vessels or aircrafts with Japanese nationality (except for insurance contracts specified by Cabinet Order; the same shall apply in the following paragraph); provided, however, that this shall not apply to insurance contracts pertaining to the permission set forth in the same paragraph.

(2) A person that seeks to apply to a Foreign Insurer without a branch office, etc. in Japan for an insurance contract pertaining to any persons with an address or residence in Japan or property located in Japan, or vessels or aircrafts with Japanese nationality, shall obtain the permission of the Prime Minister pursuant to the provisions of Cabinet Office Ordinance before the application is made.

(3) The Prime Minister shall not grant the permission set forth in the preceding paragraph in the case where the insurance contract is found to fall under any of the following items:
   (i) The contents of that insurance contract are in violation of laws and regulations or are unfair;
   (ii) In place of concluding that insurance contract, it is easy to conclude an insurance contract between insurance companies or foreign insurance companies, etc. which have equivalent or favorable conditions relative to that insurance contract;
   (iii) The conditions of that insurance contract are significantly less balanced compared to the conditions that shall normally be attached in the case of concluding an insurance contract similar to that contract between insurance companies or foreign insurance companies, etc. ;
   (iv) There is a risk of unjustifiable infringement to the interests of the insured and other relevant persons due to the conclusion of that insurance contract; and
   (v) There is a risk of adverse effect to the sound development of the Insurance Business in Japan or harm to the public interest due to the conclusion of that insurance contract.

(Application Procedures for a License, etc.)

Article 187 (1) A Foreign Insurer that seeks to obtain the license set forth in Article 185, paragraph (1) shall submit a written application for a license to the Prime Minister, detailing the following particulars:
   (i) The name of the home country of that Foreign Insurer (meaning the country where that Foreign Insurer started Insurance Business or the country that enacted laws and regulations in relation to the establishment of a juridical person pertaining to that Foreign Insurer; hereinafter the same shall apply in this Section to Section 4 inclusive) and the name or trade name or denomination of that Foreign Insurer, address or location of the head office or principal office, and date of commencement or establishment of Insurance Business;
   (ii) Name and address of the representative person in Japan;
   (iii) Types of license desired; and
   (iv) Principal branch in Japan (meaning the branch office, etc. which the Foreign Insurer has prescribed as the headquarters of Insurance Business in Japan; hereinafter the same shall apply in this Section to Section 4 inclusive).

(2) A certificate proving the following particulars which was issued by the competent organization in the home country shall be attached to the written application for a license set forth in the preceding paragraph:
   (i) That the commencement of Insurance Business of that Foreign Insurer or the establishment of a juridical person pertaining to that Foreign Insurer was done lawfully; and
   (ii) That the Foreign Insurer is lawfully conducting Insurance Business in its home country that are similar to the Insurance Business it seeks to conduct in Japan after obtaining that license.

(3) In addition to what is prescribed in the preceding paragraph, the following documents and other documents specified by Cabinet Office Ordinance shall be attached to the written application for a license set forth in paragraph (1):

Art.188〜190　⑥ Insurance Business Act, Part II, Chap.IX, Sec.1

(i) Articles of incorporation or equivalent documents;
(ii) Statement of business procedures in Japan;
(iii) General policy conditions of the insurance contract concluded in Japan; and
(iv) Statement of calculation procedures for insurance premiums and policy reserves pertaining to the insurance contract concluded in Japan.

(4) The documents listed in item (ii) to (iv) inclusive of the preceding paragraph must detail the particulars specified by Cabinet Office Ordinance.

(5) The provisions of Article 5 shall apply mutatis mutandis to cases where an application has been filed for the license set forth in Article 185, paragraph (1). In this case, the term "business of an Insurance Company" in Article 5, paragraph (1), items (i) and (ii) shall be deemed to be replaced with "business in Japan of a Foreign Insurance Company, etc.", the term "the preceding Article, paragraph (2), items (ii) and (iii)" in the same paragraph, item (iii) shall be deemed to be replaced with "Article 187, paragraph (3), items (ii) and (iii)", and the term "the preceding Article, paragraph (2), item (iv)" in the same paragraph, item (iv) shall be deemed to be replaced with "Article 187, paragraph (3), item (iv)".

(Conditions for a License)
Article 188　(1) The Prime Minister may, in the case where the Insurance Business that a Foreign Insurer which applied for a foreign life insurance business license seeks to conduct in Japan only involves the underwriting of insurance contracts in which the insurance proceeds are indicated in a foreign currency and for which the counter parties are the persons specified by Cabinet Order, grant a license set forth in Article 185, paragraph (1) with conditions attached to the effect that the Foreign Insurer may only conduct business that is related to that insurance contract.

(2) The provisions specified by a Cabinet Order, such as Article 196, shall not apply to Foreign Life Insurance Companies, etc. , which obtained the license set forth in Article 185, paragraph (1) attached with conditions set forth in the preceding paragraph; any necessary special measures concerning the application of this Act may be specified by Cabinet Order.

(3) Special measures regarding the application procedures for a license set forth in Article 185, paragraph (1) of a Foreign Insurer in the case prescribed in paragraph (1) and other necessary particulars involving the application of the provisions of paragraph (1) shall be specified by Cabinet Order.

(Public Notice of Prime Minister)
Article 189　The Prime Minister shall, whenever he/she grants the license set forth in Article 185, paragraph (1), give public notice thereof and the particulars listed in the items of Article 187, paragraph (1) in the official gazette without delay. The same shall apply if a notification is made under the provisions of Article 209 on the change of particulars listed in the same paragraph, items (i), (ii) or (iv).

(Deposit)
Article 190　(1) A Foreign Insurance Company, etc. shall deposit money to the deposit office closest to the principal branch in Japan in the amount specified by Cabinet Order deemed to be necessary and appropriate to protect Policyholders, etc. in Japan.

(2) The Prime Minister may, if he/she finds it necessary to protect Policyholders, etc. in Japan, order a Foreign Insurance Company, etc. to deposit money in the amount found to be reasonable, in addition to the amount specified by Cabinet Order of the preceding paragraph, prior to commencing Insurance Business in Japan.

(3) If Foreign Insurance Company, etc. , pursuant to the provisions of Cabinet Order, con-

cludes a contract pursuant to the provisions of Cabinet Order under which the required deposit will be deposited for that Foreign Insurance Company, etc. at the order of the Prime Minister, and notifies the Prime Minister of this, said Foreign Insurance Company, etc. may choose not to deposit all or part of the amount set forth in the preceding two paragraphs in the amount that it has been decided will be deposited under that contract while the contract is in effect (hereinafter referred to in this Article as "Contract Amount").

(4) The Prime Minister may, if he/she finds it necessary to protect Policyholders, etc. in Japan, order any persons who have concluded the contract set forth in the preceding paragraph with a Foreign Insurance Company, etc. or that Foreign Insurance Company, etc. to deposit all or part of the amount corresponding to the Contract Amount.

(5) A Foreign Insurance Company, etc. shall not commence Insurance Business pertaining to its license unless it has deposited (including the conclusion of the contract set forth in paragraph (3); the same shall apply in paragraph (8)) the deposit set forth in paragraph (1) (including the following deposit in the case where a company is ordered to deposit the money set forth in paragraph (2) pursuant to the provisions of the same paragraph) and notified the Prime Minister of this.

(6) Policyholders under insurance contracts in Japan, the insured, or any persons who shall receive insurance proceeds have the right to receive payment ahead of other obligees with regard to the deposit pertaining to that Foreign Insurance Company, etc. concerning claims resulting from an insurance contract.

(7) The necessary particulars related to the execution of the rights set forth in the preceding paragraph shall be specified by Cabinet Order.

(8) If a deposit amount (including Contract Amount) has come short of the amount specified by Cabinet Order which is referred to in paragraph (1) for any reason such as the execution of the rights set forth in paragraph (6), the Foreign Insurance Company, etc. shall deposit the deficit within two weeks from the date specified by Cabinet Office Ordinance and notify the Prime Minister of this without delay.

(9) A Foreign Insurance Company, etc. may replace the deposit set forth in paragraph (1), paragraph (2), or the preceding paragraph with national government bond certificates, local government bond certificates, or other securities specified by Cabinet Office Ordinance (including transfer bonds specified by Article 278, paragraph (1) (Deposit of Transfer Bonds) of the Act on Transfer of Corporate Bonds, Shares, etc.; the same shall apply in Article 223, paragraph (10), Article 272-5, paragraph (9) and Article 291, paragraph (9)).

(10) A deposit which was deposited pursuant to the provisions of paragraph (1), (2), (4), or (8) may be reclaimed pursuant to the provisions of Cabinet Order in a case under any of the following items:

(i) If the license set forth in Article 185, paragraph (1) pertaining to that Foreign Insurance Company, etc. is revoked pursuant to the provisions of Articles 205 or 206; and

(ii) If the license set forth in Article 185, paragraph (1) pertaining to that Foreign Insurance Company, etc. loses its validity pursuant to the provisions of Article 273.

(11) In addition to what is specified in the preceding paragraphs, the necessary particulars of deposits shall be specified by Cabinet Office Ordinance and Ordinance of the Ministry of Justice.

(Trade Name or Denomination of a Foreign Insurance Company, etc.)

Article 191 The provisions of Article 7, paragraph (2) shall not apply to a Foreign Insurance Company, etc.

(Representative Person in Japan)

Article 192 (1) Representative persons in Japan of a Foreign Insurance Company, etc. (except for foreign companies prescribed in Article 2, item (ii) (Definitions) of the Companies Act; hereinafter the same shall apply in this paragraph to paragraph (3) inclusive) shall have the authority to take any action in or out of court in connection with the business in Japan of that Foreign Insurance Company, etc.

(2) Restrictions on the right set forth in the preceding paragraph may not be asserted against a third party without knowledge of such restrictions.

(3) A Foreign Insurance Company, etc. shall bear responsibility for the compensation of damage caused to a third party in connection with representative persons in Japan carrying out their duties.

(4) Representative persons in Japan of a Foreign Insurance Company, etc. shall, even after retiring from their posts, have rights and duties as representative persons in Japan until the registration of Article 22 (Registration of Manager) of the Commercial Code or Article 933, paragraph (2) (Registration of Foreign Company) of the Companies Act (including the cases where it is applied mutatis mutandis pursuant to Article 215) regarding the name and address and other locations of representative persons who shall act in their place or public notice under the provisions of the second sentence of Article 189 is made.

(5) Representative persons in Japan of a Foreign Insurance Company, etc. shall not engage in the day-to-day business of other company, except if authorized by the Prime Minister.

(6) Whenever an application has been filed for the authorization referred to in the preceding paragraph, the Prime Minister may only grant the authorization if he/she finds that the particulars given in the application are unlikely to interfere with the sound and appropriate business operation of the Foreign Insurance Company, etc. in Japan.

(Foreign Mutual Company)

Article 193 (1) A Foreign Mutual Company shall prescribe representative persons in Japan if it seeks to continue conducting in Japan. In this case, at least one of the representative persons in Japan shall be a person with an address in Japan.

(2) The provisions of Article 818 (Prohibition, etc. of Continuous Transactions Prior to Registration) and Article 819 (Public Notice of What is Equivalent to a Balance Sheet) of the Companies Act shall apply mutatis mutandis to a Foreign Mutual Company. In this case, the term "foreign company registered as a foreign company (limited to those where similar companies or their closest equivalents in Japan are stock companies)" in the same Article, paragraph (1) shall be deemed to be replaced with "Foreign Mutual Company registered as a Foreign Mutual Company", the term "Article 438, paragraph (2)" in the same Article, paragraph (1) shall be deemed to be replaced with "Article 54-6, paragraph (2) of the Insurance Business Act," and the term "Article 939, paragraph (1), item (i) or (ii)" in the same Article, paragraph (2) shall be deemed to be replaced with "Article 217, paragraph (1), item (i) of the Insurance Business Act." In addition, the necessary technical change in interpretation shall be specified by Cabinet Order.

Section 2 Business, Accounting, etc.

(Establishment of System for Protection of Customers' Interests)

Article 193-2 (1) Whenever a Foreign Insurance Company, etc. , or its Parent Financial Institution, etc. or Subsidiary Financial Institution, etc. conducts any transaction, such Foreign Insurance Company, etc. shall, pursuant to the provisions of Cabinet Office

Ordinance, properly manage the information on business conducted by itself or its Subsidiary Financial Institution, etc. (limited to Insurance Business and any other business specified by Cabinet Office Ordinance) and establish a system for properly supervising the status of implementation of said business or taking any other measures necessary so that the interests of the customer of said business will not be unjustly impaired.

(2) The term "Parent Financial Institution, etc." as used in the preceding paragraph means a person who holds the majority of All Shareholders' Voting Rights, etc. in a Foreign Insurance Company, etc. and any other person that is specified by Cabinet Order as being closely related to said Foreign Insurance Company, etc. and which is an Insurance Company, Bank, Financial Instruments Transaction Business Operator, or any other person conducting financial business that is specified by Cabinet Order.

(3) The term "Subsidiary Financial Institution, etc." as used in paragraph (1) means a person in which a Foreign Insurance Company, etc. holds the majority of All Shareholders' Voting Rights, etc. , and any other person that is specified by Cabinet Order as being closely related to said Foreign Insurance Company, etc. and which is an Insurance Company, Bank, Financial Instruments Transaction Business Operator, or any other person conducting financial business that is specified by Cabinet Order.

(Transactions, etc. with Specially Related Parties)

Article 194 A Foreign Insurance Company, etc. shall not make any of the following transactions or actions with parties to which it is specially related as specified by a Cabinet Order (hereinafter referred to as a "Specially Related Party" in this Article) or a customer of any Specially Related Party; provided, however, that this shall not apply where the Prime Minister has approved such transaction or action for any of the compelling reasons specified by a Cabinet Office Ordinance:

(i) Any transaction, such as the purchase and sale of assets, conducted with a Specially Related Party in a branch office, etc. of the Foreign Insurance Company, etc. on significantly different terms and conditions from those applied to normal transactions of the Foreign Insurance Company, etc. ; or

(ii) Any transaction or action taken with a Specially Related Party or a customer related to a Specially Related Party in a branch office, etc. of the Foreign Insurance Company, etc. that is equivalent to the transaction listed in the preceding item and specified by a Cabinet Office Ordinance as posing a risk to the sound and appropriate management of the Insurance Business conducted by the Foreign Insurance Company, etc. in Japan.

(Submission of Closing Financial Statements of Head Office or Principal Office)

Article 195 A Foreign Insurance Company, etc. shall, for each business year, submit to the Prime Minister an inventory of property, balance sheet, profit and loss statement and business report prepared in its head office or principal office, pursuant to the provisions of a Cabinet Office Ordinance, within a reasonable period of time following the end of the business year.

(Retention and Inspection, etc. of the Articles of Incorporation, etc.)

Article 196 (1) The representative person of a Foreign Insurance Company, etc. in Japan shall keep in its principal branch in Japan its articles of incorporation or any other equivalent document (or, for a Foreign Mutual Company, such document and its members list in Japan), or a electromagnetic record thereof.

(2) The representative person of a Foreign Insurance Company, etc. in Japan shall, pursu-

ant to the provisions of a Cabinet Office Ordinance, keep in its principal branch in Japan the document or electromagnetic record set forth in the preceding Article for five years from the day following the date of its submission pursuant to the provisions of that Article.
(3) The representative person of a Foreign Insurance Company, etc. in Japan shall, pursuant to the provisions of a Cabinet Office Ordinance, prepare the following documents and annex detailed statements thereto for each accounting period of the business year in Japan and keep them in its principal branch in Japan for five years from the day following the date of the end of the business year in Japan covered by such accounting.
(i) Balance sheet for Insurance Business conducted in Japan;
(ii) Profit and loss statement for Insurance Business conducted in Japan; and
(iii) Business report for Insurance Business conducted in Japan.
(4) The documents set forth in the preceding paragraph may be prepared in the form of electromagnetic record.
(5) The creditors and insured of a Foreign Insurance Company, etc. , such as Policyholders and beneficiaries of insurance proceeds, may make the following requests at any time during the hours in which the Foreign Insurance Company, etc. should be doing business; provided, however, that they pay the fees determined by the Foreign Insurance Company, etc. in making a request falling under item (ii) or (iv):
(i) Where the documents set forth in paragraphs (1) to (3) inclusive are prepared in writing, a request to inspect such documents;
(ii) A request for a certified copy or extract of the documents referred to in the preceding item;
(iii) Where the documents set forth in paragraphs (1) to (3) inclusive are prepared in the form of electromagnetic record, a request to inspect anything that shows the particulars recorded in the electromagnetic records in a manner specified by a Cabinet Office Ordinance; or
(iv) A request to be provided with the particulars recorded in the electromagnetic records set forth in the preceding item by the electromagnetic means determined by the Foreign Insurance Company, etc. , or to be issued a document detailing such particulars.

(Obligation to Hold Assets in Japan)
Article 197 A Foreign Insurance Company, etc. shall, pursuant to the provisions of a Cabinet Office Ordinance, hold in Japan the assets equivalent to the sum total of the amount calculated pursuant to the provisions of a Cabinet Office Ordinance on the basis of the policy reserves and reserves for outstanding claims set aside in Japan pursuant to the provisions of Article 116, paragraph (1) and 117, paragraph (1) as applied mutatis mutandis pursuant to Article 199, and the amount specified by a Cabinet Office Ordinance as equivalent to equity capital, such as the deposit set forth in Article 190.

(Mutatis Mutandis Application of the Companies Act, etc.)
Article 198 (1) The provisions of Article 8 (No Use of Name, etc. that is likely to be mistaken for a company) of the Companies Act shall apply mutatis mutandis to the use of a trade name or name that is likely to be mistaken for a Foreign Mutual Company; the provisions of Article 9 (Liability of Company Permitting Others to Use Its Trade Name) of that Act shall apply mutatis mutandis to the name of a Foreign Mutual Company; the provisions of Part I, Chapter III, Section 1 (Employees of a Company) of that Act shall apply mutatis mutandis to the employees of a Foreign Mutual Company; the provisions of Part I, Chapter III, Section 2 (excluding Article 18) (Commercial Agents of the Companies) of that Act shall apply mutatis mutandis to a person acting as an

agent or intermediary in a transaction for a Foreign Mutual Company; the provisions of Part I, Chapter IV (excluding Article 24) (Non Competition after Assignment of Business) of that Act shall apply mutatis mutandis to the cases where a Foreign Mutual Company has assigned its business or acquired any business or operation; and the provisions of Article 54, Article 54-2 and Article 54-3, paragraphs (1) and (4) shall apply mutatis mutandis to the books and other materials of a Foreign Mutual Company. In this case, any technical change in interpretation required shall be specified by Cabinet Order.

(2) The provisions of Part II, Chapter I (excluding Article 501 to 503 inclusive and Article 523) (General Provisions) of the Commercial Code shall apply mutatis mutandis to the actions taken by a Foreign Mutual Company; the provisions of Part II, Chapter II (Buying or Selling) of said Code shall apply mutatis mutandis to buying or selling between a Foreign Mutual Company and a merchant or Mutual Company (including a Foreign Mutual Company); the provisions of Part II, Chapter III (Current Account) of said Code shall apply mutatis mutandis to a contract pertaining to set-offs between a Foreign Mutual Company and a person with which it has normal transactions; the provisions of Part II, Chapter V (excluding Article 545) (Brokerage Business) of said Code shall apply mutatis mutandis to the acting as an intermediary by a Foreign Mutual Company in a commercial transaction between third parties; and the provisions of Part II, Chapter VI (excluding Article 558) (Commission Agent Business) and Article 593 (Deposit) of said Code shall apply mutatis mutandis to a Foreign Mutual Company.

(Mutatis Mutandis Application of Provisions on Business, etc.)
Article 199 The provisions of Article 97, Article 97-2, paragraphs (1) and (2), Article 98, Article 99, paragraphs (1), (2) and (4) to (6) inclusive, Article 100 and Article 100-2 shall apply mutatis mutandis to the business of the branch offices, etc. of a Foreign Insurance Company, etc. ; the provisions of Article 99, paragraphs (3) and (7) to (10) inclusive shall apply mutatis mutandis to the business of the branch offices, etc. of a Foreign Life Insurance Company, etc. ; the provisions of Article 101 to 105 inclusive shall apply mutatis mutandis to concerted actions taken by a Foreign Non-Life Insurance Company, etc. with another Non-Life Insurance Company (including a Foreign Non-Life Insurance Company, etc.); the provisions of Article 7-2, Article 109, Article 110, paragraphs (1) and (3), Article 111, paragraph (1) and paragraphs (3) to (6) inclusive, Article 112, Article 114 to 118 inclusive, and Article 120 to 122 inclusive shall apply mutatis mutandis to a Foreign Insurance Company, etc. ; the provisions of Article 105-2 shall apply mutatis mutandis to a Foreign Life Insurance Company, etc. ; and the provisions of Article 105-3 shall apply mutatis mutandis to a Foreign Non-Life Insurance Company, etc. In this case, the term "Article 3, paragraph (2)" in Article 97, paragraph (1) shall be deemed to be replaced with "Article 185, paragraph (2)"; the term "Mutual Company" in Article 99, paragraph (6) shall be deemed to be replaced with "Foreign Mutual Company"; the term "In the case where the license of Article 3, paragraph (1) of the Insurance Business Act is cancelled pursuant to the provisions of Article 133 or 134 of that Act, or in the case where the license of Article 3, paragraph (1) of that Act loses its effect pursuant to the provisions of Article 273 of that Act" in Article 99, paragraph (8) shall be deemed to be replaced with "In the case where the license of Article 185, paragraph (1) of the Insurance Business Act is cancelled pursuant to the provisions of Article 205 or 206 of that Act, or in the case where the license of Article 185, paragraph (1) of that Act loses its effect pursuant to the provisions of Article 273 of that Act"; the term "Article 3, paragraph (1) of the Insurance Business Act pursuant to the provisions of Article 133 or 134 of that Act" in Article 99, paragraph (8) shall be deemed to be replaced with "Article 185, paragraph (1) of the Insurance Business Act

Art.199 ⑥ Insurance Business Act, Part II, Chap.IX, Sec.2

pursuant to the provisions of Article 205 or 206 of that Act"; the term "Article 111, paragraphs (1) and (2)" in Article 99, paragraph (9) shall be deemed to be replaced with "Article 111, paragraph (1) as applied mutatis mutandis pursuant to Article 199"; the term "Designated Dispute Resolution Organization for Life Insurance Services" in the items of paragraph (1) of Article 105-2, paragraph (2) of that Article and item (ii) of paragraph (3) of that Article shall be deemed to be replaced with "Designated Dispute Resolution Organization for Foreign Life Insurance Services"; the term "Life Insurance Services" in the items of paragraph (1) of that Article shall be deemed to be replaced with "Foreign Life Insurance Services"; the term "Designated Dispute Resolution Organization for Non-Life Insurance Services" in the items of paragraph (1) of Article 105-3, paragraph (2) of that Article and item (ii) of paragraph (3) of that Article shall be deemed to be replaced with "Designated Dispute Resolution Organization for Foreign Non-Life Insurance Services"; the term "Non-Life Insurance Services" in the items of paragraph (1) of that Article shall be deemed to be replaced with "Foreign Non-Life Insurance Services"; the term "business year" in Article 109 shall be deemed to be replaced with "business year in Japan"; the term "for each business year, prepare an interim business report and business report describing the status of its business and property" in Article 110, paragraph (1) shall be deemed to be replaced with "for each business year in Japan, prepare an interim business report and business report describing the status of its business and property in Japan"; the term "for each business year, prepare explanatory documents detailing the particulars specified by Cabinet Office Ordinance as pertaining to the status of its business and property" in Article 111, paragraph (1) shall be deemed to be replaced with "for each business year in Japan, prepare explanatory documents detailing the particulars specified by Cabinet Office Ordinance as pertaining to the status of its business and property in Japan"; the term "its head office or principal office and its branch offices or secondary offices, or any other equivalent place specified by a Cabinet Office Ordinance" in Article 111, paragraphs (1) and (4) shall be deemed to be replaced with "the branch office of the Foreign Insurance Company, etc. in Japan or any other equivalent place specified by a Cabinet Office Ordinance"; the term "business and property of the Insurance Company and its Subsidiary, etc." in Article 111, paragraph (6) shall be deemed to be replaced with "business and property of the Foreign Insurance Company, etc. in Japan"; the term "owns" in Article 112, paragraph (1) shall be deemed to be replaced with "owns in Japan"; the term ", pursuant to the provisions of a Cabinet Office Ordinance" in Article 112, paragraph (1) shall be deemed to be deleted; the term "set aside as a reserve" in Article 112, paragraph (2) shall be deemed to be replaced with "set aside in Japan as a reserve"; the term "Policyholders" in Article 114, paragraph (1) shall be deemed to be replaced with "Policyholders in Japan"; the terms "within its portfolio" and "set aside as price fluctuation reserve" in Article 115, paragraph (1) shall be deemed to be replaced with "within its portfolio in Japan" and "set aside in Japan as price fluctuation reserve," respectively; the term "Shares, etc." in Article 115, paragraph (2) shall be deemed to be replaced with "Shares, etc. in Japan"; the terms "each accounting period," "insurance contracts" and "set aside a certain amount of money" in Article 116, paragraph (1) shall be deemed to be replaced with "each accounting period of the business year in Japan," "insurance contracts in Japan" and "set aside in Japan a certain amount of money," respectively; the term "funding the policy reserve" in Article 116, paragraph (2) shall be deemed to be replaced with "funding in Japan the policy reserve"; the term "insurance contract" in Article 116, paragraph (3) shall be deemed to be replaced with "insurance contract in Japan"; the terms "each accounting period," "insurance contracts," "as expenditure" and "reserves for outstanding claims" in Article 117, paragraph (1) shall be deemed to be replaced with "each accounting period of the business year in Japan," "insurance contracts in Japan," "in Japan as expenditure" and "reserves for outstanding claims in Japan," respectively; the terms "insurance contract specified by a Cabinet Office Ordinance" and "create" in Article 118, paragraph (1) shall be deemed to be replaced with "insurance contract in Japan specified by a Cabinet Office Ordinance" and "create in Japan," respectively; the terms "board of directors," "Life Insurance Company or a Non-Life Insurance Company meeting the requirements specified by a Cabinet Office Ordinance," "actuary" and "method of calculating insurance premiums" in Article 120, paragraph (1) shall be deemed to be replaced with "representative person," "Foreign Life Insurance Company, etc. or a Foreign Non-Life Insurance Company, etc. meeting the requirements specified by a Cabinet Office Ordinance," "actuary of the Foreign Insurance Company, etc. in Japan" and "method of calculating the insurance premiums applicable to the insurance contracts concluded in Japan," respectively; the term "actuary" in Article 120, paragraph (2) shall be deemed to be replaced with "actuary of a Foreign Insurance Company, etc. in Japan"; the terms "Insurance Company" and "actuary" in Article 120, paragraph (3) shall be deemed to be replaced with "Foreign Insurance Company, etc." and "actuary in Japan" respectively; the terms "actuary," "each accounting period," and "board of directors" in Article 121 shall be deemed to be replaced with "actuary of a Foreign Insurance Company, etc. in Japan," "each accounting period of the business year in Japan" and "representative person of the Foreign Insurance Company, etc. in Japan," respectively; and the terms "Insurance Company" and "actuary" in Article 122 shall be deemed to be replaced with "Foreign Insurance Company, etc." and "actuary in Japan", respectively.

Section 3 Supervision

(Submission of Reports or Materials)
Article 200 (1) The Prime Minister may, if he/she finds it necessary to protect Policyholders, etc. in Japan by ensuring the sound and appropriate business operation of a Foreign Insurance Company, etc. in Japan, request the Foreign Insurance Company, etc. or a person acting as an agent for the underwriting of insurance prescribed in Article 185, paragraph (1) to submit reports or materials concerning the status of its business in Japan or property of the Foreign Insurance Company, etc.

(2) If and to the extent that the Prime Minister finds it particularly necessary to protect Policyholders, etc. in Japan by ensuring the sound and appropriate business operation of a Foreign Insurance Company, etc. in Japan, he/she may request any Specially Related Party of the Foreign Insurance Company, etc. (meaning a Specially Related Party as prescribed in Article 194; the same shall apply in the following paragraph and the following Article) or person the Foreign Insurance Company, etc. has entrusted with its business in Japan (except for the person acting as an agent for the underwriting of insurance set forth in the preceding paragraph; the same shall apply in the next paragraph), to submit reports or materials that would be helpful to understand the status of the business in Japan or property of the Foreign Insurance Company, etc. .

(3) A Specially Related Party of a Foreign Insurance Company, etc. or person that a Foreign Insurance Company, etc. has entrusted with its business in Japan may refuse to submit reports or materials required under the preceding paragraph if there are justifiable grounds for it to do so.

(On-Site Inspection)
Article 201 (1) The Prime Minister may, if he/she finds it necessary to protect Policyholders, etc. in Japan by ensuring the sound and appropriate business operation of a

Foreign Insurance Company, etc. in Japan, have his/her officials enter a branch office, etc. of the Foreign Insurance Company, etc. , ask questions on the status of its business in Japan or property of the Foreign Insurance Company, etc. , or inspect relevant items such as books and documents.
(2) If and to the extent that the Prime Minister finds it particularly necessary in entering a site, asking questions, or conducting an inspection under the preceding paragraph, he/she may have his/her officials enter a facility of any Specially Related Party of the Foreign Insurance Company, etc. or person the Foreign Insurance Company, etc. has entrusted with its business in Japan, have such officials question the Foreign Insurance Company, etc. or ask questions about particulars that are necessary for the inspection, or have such officials inspect relevant items such as books and documents.
(3) A Specially Related Party of a Foreign Insurance Company, etc. or a person that a Foreign Insurance Company, etc. has entrusted with its business in Japan may refuse the questioning and inspection under the provisions of the preceding paragraph if there are justifiable grounds for it to do so.

(Standard of Soundness)
Article 202 The Prime Minister may use the following amounts with respect to a Foreign Insurance Company, etc. and establish whether or not the Foreign Insurance Company, etc. has an appropriate level of solvency in terms of its ability to pay Insurance Proceeds, etc. as the standard by which the soundness of its business management in Japan is determined:
(i) Total amount of the items specified by Cabinet Office Ordinance, such as the deposit set forth in Article 190; and
(ii) Amount calculated pursuant to the provisions of Cabinet Office Ordinance as the amount for coping with possible risks exceeding standard predictions that may occur due to any events pertaining to the insurance being underwritten in Japan, such as insured events.

(Order to Change Regarding Particulars Prescribed in Statement of Business Procedures, etc.)
Article 203 If and to the extent that the Prime Minister finds it necessary to protect Policyholders, etc. in Japan by ensuring the sound and appropriate business operation of a Foreign Insurance Company, etc. in Japan in light of the situation of the business or property of the Foreign Insurance Company, etc. or a change in the circumstances, he/she may order the Foreign Insurance Company, etc. to modify the particulars prescribed in the documents listed in Article 187, paragraph (3), items (ii) to (iv) inclusive.

(Suspension of Business, etc.)
Article 204 (1) If the Prime Minister finds it necessary to protect Policyholders, etc. in Japan by ensuring the sound and appropriate business operation of a Foreign Insurance Company, etc. in Japan in light of the status of the business or property of the Foreign Insurance Company, etc. , he/she may request that Foreign Insurance Company, etc. to submit an improvement plan for ensuring soundness in the business operation of that Foreign Insurance Company, etc. in Japan or order a change to the submitted improvement plan by designating the particulars and the time limit for which measures must be taken, or, to the extent the Prime Minister finds necessary, he/she may order suspension of the whole or part of business of that Foreign Insurance Company by setting a limit or order deposit of property of that Foreign Insurance Company or other measures necessary for the purpose of supervision.

(2) An order under the preceding paragraph(including the request of submission of an improvement plan) that it is found to be necessary to issue due to the level of solvency of the Foreign Insurance Company, etc. in terms of its ability to pay Insurance Proceeds, etc., must be an order specified by Cabinet Office Ordinance or Ordinance of the Ministry of Finance for the category that corresponds to the level of solvency of the Foreign Insurance Company, etc. in terms of its ability to pay Insurance Proceeds, etc.

(Rescission of License, etc.)
Article 205 The Prime Minister may, if a Foreign Insurance Company, etc. has come to fall under any of the following items, order the full or partial suspension of the business in Japan of the Foreign Insurance Company, etc. or the dismissal of the representative person in Japan, or rescind the license set forth in Article 185, paragraph (1):
  (i) If it is in violation of laws and regulations (including foreign laws and regulations), the measures of the Prime Minister pursuant to laws and regulations, or particularly vital particulars among those prescribed in the documents listed in the items of Article 187, paragraph (3)
  (ii) If it is in violation of the conditions attached to the license set forth in Article 185, paragraph (1) or the license obtained in its country for Insurance Business (including any administrative measures similar to said license, such as permission or registration; the same shall apply in Article 209, item (vii)); and
  (iii) If it engages in conduct that is prejudicial to the public interest.

Article 206 The Prime Minister may, if he/she finds that the situation of the property of a Foreign Insurance Company, etc. is significantly worsening and that it is not appropriate for it to continue in the Insurance Business in Japan from the viewpoint of protecting Policyholders, etc. in Japan, rescind the license of the Foreign Insurance Company, etc. set forth in Article 185, paragraph (1).

(Mutatis Mutandis Application of Provisions Concerning Supervision)
Article 207 The provisions in Article 123 to 125 inclusive shall apply mutatis mutandis to a Foreign Insurance Company, etc. In this case, the term "Article 4, paragraph (2), items (ii) to (iv) inclusive" in Article 123, paragraph (1) shall be deemed to be replaced with "Article 187, paragraph (3), items (ii) to (iv) inclusive," the term "Article 4, paragraph (2), items (ii) and (iii)" in Article 124, paragraph (1) shall be deemed to be replaced with "Article 187, paragraph (3), items (ii) and (iii)," the term "Article 5, paragraph (1), item (iii), sub-items (a) to (e) inclusive" in Article 124, paragraph (1) shall be deemed to be replaced with "Article 5, paragraph (1), item (iii), sub-items (a) to (e) inclusive as applied mutatis mutandis pursuant to Article 187, paragraph (5)," the term "Article 4, paragraph (2), item (iv)" in the same Article, item (ii) shall be deemed to be replaced with "Article 187, paragraph (3), item (iv)," the term "Article 5, paragraph (1), item (iv), sub-items (a) to (c) inclusive" in the same Article, item (ii) shall be deemed to be replaced with "Article 5, paragraph (1), item (iv), sub-items (a) to (c) inclusive as applied mutatis mutandis pursuant to Article 187, paragraph (5)," and the term "Article 5, paragraph (1), item (iii), sub-items (a) to (e) inclusive or item (iv), sub-items (a) to (c) inclusive" in Article 125 shall be deemed to be replaced with "Article 5, paragraph (1), item (iii), sub-items (a) to (e) inclusive or item (iv), sub-items (a) to (c) inclusive as applied mutatis mutandis pursuant to Article 187, paragraph (5)."

Section 4 Abolition of Insurance Business, etc.

(Abolition of Insurance Business in Japan)

Article 208 A Foreign Insurance Company, etc. shall, if it seeks to abolish its Insurance Business in Japan (excluding the cases falling under paragraph (6) of the following Article), obtain authorization from the Prime Minister.

(Notification by Foreign Insurance Company, etc.)
Article 209 If a Foreign Insurance Company, etc. falls under any of the following items, it shall notify the Prime Minister of this without delay pursuant to the provisions of Cabinet Office Ordinance:
(i) it has started its Insurance Business in Japan;
(ii) it has modified any of the particulars listed in Article 187, paragraph (1), item (i), (ii) or (iv), or any of the particulars prescribed by the document listed in Article 187, paragraph (3), item (i);
(iii) it has modified the amount of its capital or contribution, or the total amount of its funds;
(iv) it has carried out an Entity Conversion;
(v) it has merged, transferred or succeeded to a business through a company split, or assigned or acquired the whole or an important Part of a business (other than a business that only pertains to branch offices, etc.);
(vi) it has dissolved (for any other reason than a merger) or abolished its Insurance Business;
(vii) it has had its license for Insurance Business canceled in its home country;
(viii) it has become subject to a ruling for the commencement of bankruptcy proceedings; or
(ix) it falls under any of the other cases specified by Cabinet Office Ordinance.

(Mutatis Mutandis Application of Provisions on Portfolio Transfers of Insurance Contracts)
Article 210 (1) The provisions of Chapter VII, Section 1 shall apply mutatis mutandis to the comprehensive transfer of insurance contracts in Japan by a Foreign Insurance Company, etc. In this case, the term "creditors" in Article 135, paragraph (3) shall be deemed to be replaced with "creditors of branch offices, etc. set forth in Article 185, paragraph (1)"; the term "Transferor Company and the Transferee Company" in Article 136, paragraphs (1) and (3) shall be deemed to be replaced with "Transferee Company"; the terms "two weeks before the date of the Shareholders' Meeting, etc. set forth in paragraph (1) of the preceding Article," "written agreement concluded under Article 135, paragraph (1)" and "business offices or offices" in Article 136-2, paragraph (1) shall be deemed to be replaced with "the date of preparation of the written agreement concluded under Article 135, paragraph (1) (hereinafter referred to as "Transfer Agreement" in this Section)," "Transfer Agreement" and "branch offices, etc.," respectively; the term "shareholder or Policyholder of the Transferor Company" in Article 136-2, paragraph (2) shall be deemed to be replaced with "affected Policyholder"; the term "resolution set forth in Article 136, paragraph (1)" in Article 137, paragraph (1) shall be deemed to be replaced with "preparation of the Transfer Agreement"; the terms "the time of the adoption of resolution under Article 136, paragraph (1)" and "shall not conclude" in Article 138 shall be deemed to be replaced with "the time of preparation of the Transfer Agreement" and "shall not conclude in Japan," respectively; and the term "creditors" in Article 139, paragraph (2), item (iii) shall be deemed to be replaced with "creditors of branch offices, etc. set forth in Article 185, paragraph (1)."
(2) Any Foreign Insurance Company, etc. that has transferred all of its insurance contracts in Japan shall be deemed to have abolished its Insurance Business in Japan. The provi-

sions of Article 208 shall not apply in this case.

(Mutatis Mutandis Application of Provisions on the Transfer or Acceptance of Business, and Entrustment of Business and Property Administration)
Article 211 The provisions of Article 142 shall apply mutatis mutandis to a transfer or acceptance of business in Japan involving a Foreign Insurance Company, etc. or foreign insurance companies, etc. ; and the provisions of Chapter VII, Section 3 shall apply mutatis mutandis where a Foreign Insurance Company, etc. has entrusted the administration of its business and property in Japan. In this case, the term "both the Insurance Company entrusting administration of business (hereinafter referred to as "Entrusting Company" in this Section) and the Entrusted Company" in Article 144, paragraph (2) shall be deemed to be replaced with "the Entrusted Company"; the term "head office or principal office" in Article 146, paragraph (2) shall be deemed to be replaced with "principal branch in Japan set forth in that paragraph"; the term ", Article 19" in item (iii) of that paragraph shall be deemed to be replaced with "and Article 19," the term "and Article 46 (General Rules on Attached Documents) of the Commercial Registration Act (including the cases where they are applied mutatis mutandis pursuant to Article 67)" in Article 146, paragraph (3) shall be deemed to be replaced with "(including the cases where they are applied mutatis mutandis pursuant to Article 216, paragraph (1)"; the term "Entrusting Company set forth in Article 144, paragraph (2) of the Insurance Business Act" in Article 148, paragraph (3) shall be deemed to be replaced with "Foreign Insurance Company, etc. as defined in Article 2, paragraph (7) of the Insurance Business Act that has entrusted the administration of its business and property in Japan"; the term "Article 144, paragraph (1) of the Insurance Business Act" in Article 148, paragraph (4) shall be deemed to be replaced with "Article 144, paragraph (1) of the Insurance Business Act as applied mutatis mutandis pursuant to Article 211 of that Act"; and the term "both the Entrusting Company and the Entrusted Company" in Article 149, paragraph (1) shall be deemed to be replaced with "the Entrusted Company"; any other necessary technical changes in interpretation shall be specified by Cabinet Order.

(Liquidation of a Foreign Insurance Company, etc.)
Article 212 (1) A Foreign Insurance Company, etc. shall, if it falls under any of the following items, liquidate the whole of its property in Japan:
  (i) its license under Article 185, paragraph (1) has been cancelled pursuant to the provisions of Article 205 or 206; or
  (ii) its license under Article 185, paragraph (1) has lost its effect pursuant to the provisions of Article 273.
(2) If a Foreign Insurance Company, etc. goes into liquidation pursuant to the provisions of the preceding paragraph, the Prime Minister shall appoint (a) liquidator(s) at the request of any interested person or without any party's request. The same shall apply where he/she dismisses the liquidator(s).
(3) The Prime Minister shall, where he/she dismisses a liquidator pursuant to the provisions of the preceding paragraph, commission the registry office with jurisdiction over the principal branch of the Foreign Insurance Company in Liquidation, etc. in Japan to make a registration to that effect.
(4) The provisions of Article 500 (Restrictions on Performance of Obligations) of the Companies Act as applied with relevant changes in interpretation pursuant to the provisions of Article 178, and the provisions of Article 476 (Capacity of Liquidating Stock Companies), Part II, Chapter IX, Section 1, Subsection 2 (Structures for Liquidating Stock Companies), Article 492 (Preparation of an Inventory of Property), Part II,

Chapter IX, Section 1, Subsection 4 (excluding Article 500) (Performance of Obligations), Article 508 (Retention of Accounting Materials), Part II, Chapter IX, Section 2 (excluding Articles 510, 511 and 514) (Special Liquidations), Part VII, Chapter III, Sections 1 (General Provisions) and 3 (Special Provisions on Procedures of Special Liquidation) and Article 938, paragraphs (1) to (5) inclusive (Commissioning of Registration by a Juridical Decision on Special Liquidation) of that Act shall apply mutatis mutandis to the liquidation of the property of a Foreign Insurance Company, etc. in Japan under paragraph (1), unless their specific characters forbid such application. In this case, any other necessary technical changes in interpretation shall be specified by Cabinet Order.

(5) The provisions of Article 177 shall apply mutatis mutandis to the liquidation of a Foreign Insurance Company, etc. under paragraph (1); the provisions of Article 175 and Article 179, paragraph (1) shall apply mutatis mutandis to the liquidation of a Foreign Insurance Company, etc. under paragraph (1) (excluding the cases to which apply the provisions of Part II, Chapter IX, Section 2 (excluding Articles 510, 511 and 514), Part VII, Chapter III, Sections 1 and 3, and Article 938, paragraphs (1) to (5) inclusive of the Companies Act as applied mutatis mutandis pursuant to the preceding paragraph; hereinafter the same shall apply in this paragraph); and the provisions of Article 200, paragraph (1) and Article 201, paragraph (1) shall apply mutatis mutandis to the liquidation of a Foreign Insurance Company, etc. under paragraph (1) where the Prime Minister finds it necessary for supervising the liquidation of the Foreign Insurance Company in Liquidation, etc. In this case, the term "date of dissolution" in Article 177, paragraph (2) shall be deemed to be replaced with "date of cancellation or expiration of the license issued to the Foreign Insurance Company, etc. under Article 185, paragraph (1)"; the term "Insurance Company in Liquidation, etc." in Article 177, paragraph (3) shall be deemed to be replaced with "Foreign Insurance Company in Liquidation, etc."; the terms "paragraph (1), (4) or (9) of the preceding Article" and "Insurance Company in Liquidation, etc." in Article 175 shall be deemed to be replaced with "Article 212, paragraph (2)" and "Foreign Insurance Company in Liquidation, etc.," respectively; and the term "Insurance Company in Liquidation, etc." in Article 179, paragraph (1) shall be deemed to be replaced with "Foreign Insurance Company in Liquidation, etc."; any other necessary technical change in interpretation shall be specified by Cabinet Order.

(6) The provisions of Article 812 (Resignation of Representatives in Japan Whose Domiciles Are in Japan) of the Companies Act shall not apply to a Foreign Insurance Company, etc. (other than a Foreign Mutual Company) that has obtained a license from the Prime Minister set forth in Article 185, paragraph (1).

(Mutatis Mutandis Application of the Companies Act)

Article 213 The provisions of Article 822, paragraphs (1) to (3) inclusive (Liquidation of a Foreign Company's Property in Japan), Part VII, Chapter I, Section 2 (Order of Prohibition of Continuous Transactions or Closure of a Business Office of a Foreign Company), Part VII, Chapter III, Sections 1 (General Provisions), 4 (Special Provisions on Liquidation Proceedings of a Foreign Company) and 5 (Special Provisions on Procedures of a Dissolution Order, etc. for a Company), Article 937, paragraph (2) (Commissioning of Registration by a Judicial Decision), and Article 938, paragraph (6) (Commissioning of Registration by a Juridical Decision Concerning Special Liquidation) of the Companies Act shall apply mutatis mutandis where a Foreign Mutual Company has established a secondary office or other office in Japan. In this case, any other necessary technical change in interpretation shall be specified by Cabinet Order.

Section 5 Miscellaneous Provisions

(Registry)
Article 214 A registry office shall keep a registry of foreign mutual companies.

(Mutatis Mutandis Application of the Companies Act)
Article 215 The provisions of Part VII, Chapter IV, Section 1 (excluding Article 907) (General Provisions), and Article 933 (excluding paragraph (1), item (i) and paragraph (2), item (vii)) (Registration of Foreign Company), Article 934, paragraph (2) (Registration, etc. of Appointment of a Representative in Japan), Article 935, paragraph (2) (Registration, etc. of the Relocation of the Domicile of a Representative in Japan) and Article 936, paragraph (2) (Registration, etc. of Establishment of a Business Office in Japan) of the Companies Act shall apply mutatis mutandis to the registration of a Foreign Mutual Company. In this case, the term "this Act" in Part VII, Chapter IV, Section 1 (excluding Article 907) of that Act shall be deemed to be replaced with "the Insurance Business Act and this Act"; any other necessary technical change in interpretation shall be specified by Cabinet Order.

(Mutatis Mutandis Application of the Commercial Registration Act)
Article 216 The provisions of Article 1-3 to 5 inclusive (Registry Office, Delegation of Affairs, Suspension of Affairs, Registrar, Disqualification of Registrar), Article 7 to 15 inclusive (Prohibition on Carrying Out of Registries and Other Documents, Loss and Restoration of Registries, Prevention of Loss of Registry, Issuance of Certificate of Registered Matters, Issuance of Documents Specifying Extract of Matters Registered, Inspection of Annexed Documents, Certificate of Seal Impression, Certification of Matters Required for Verification of Measures to Identify the Creator of Electromagnetic Records and Other Matters, Fees, Registration Upon Application by a Relevant Party, Registration upon Commission), Article 17, paragraphs (1), (2) and (4) (Method of Application for Registration), Article 18 to 19-2 inclusive (Documents to be Attached to Written Application, Electromagnetic Record to be Attached to Written Application), Article 20, paragraphs (1) and (2) (Submission of Seal Impression), Article 21 to 23-2 inclusive (Acceptance of Applications, Receipt, Order of Registration, Identify Confirmation by Registrar), Article 24 (excluding items (xi) and (xii)) (Dismissal of Application), Article 25 to 27 inclusive (Registration to be Made after Lapse of Period for Filing Action, Change in Administrative Zone, etc., Prohibition of Registration of Identical Trade Name at Same Location), Article 33 (Cancellation of Registration of Trade Name), Articles 44 and 45 (Registration of Company's Manager), Articles 51 and 52 (Registration of Relocation of Head Office), Article 128 (Applicant), Article 129 (Registration of Foreign Company), Article 130, paragraphs (1) and (3) (Registration of Change), and Article 132 to 148 inclusive (Correction, Application for Cancellation, Ex Officio Cancellation, Exclusion from Application of the Administrative Procedure Act, Exclusion from Application of the Act on Access to Information Held by Administrative Organs, Request for Review, Handling of Request of Review Case, Exclusion from Application of the Administrative Appeal Act, Delegation to Ordinance of the Ministry) of the Commercial Registration Act shall apply mutatis mutandis to a registration regarding a Foreign Mutual Company. In this case, the term "or the particulars that are required to be included in a written application pursuant to the provisions of the preceding paragraph" in Article 17, paragraph (4) of that Act shall be deemed to be deleted; the term "preceding two paragraphs" in Article 17, paragraph (4) of that Act shall be deemed to be replaced with "that paragraph"; the term "head office" in Article 51, paragraph (1) of that Act shall be deemed to be replaced with "office in Japan"; the

term "a foreign company under Article 933, paragraph (1) of the Companies Act" in Article 129, paragraph (1) of that Act shall be deemed to be replaced with "the establishment of an office of a Foreign Mutual Company"; the term "the company has designated its representative person in Japan or established a business office in Japan" in Article 129, paragraph (3) of that Act shall be deemed to be replaced with "the company has established an office in Japan"; and the terms "for registration under the preceding two paragraphs," "registration has been made under the preceding two paragraphs" and "documents set forth in the preceding two paragraphs" in Article 130, paragraph (3) of that Act shall be deemed to be replaced with "for registration under the preceding paragraph," "registration has been made under that paragraph" and "document set forth in that paragraph," respectively; any other necessary technical change in interpretation shall be specified by Cabinet Order.

(Method of Public Notice by a Foreign Insurance Company, etc.)
Article 217 (1) A Foreign Insurance Company, etc. (limited to a foreign company or Foreign Mutual Company; the same shall apply in the following paragraph and paragraph (3)) shall designate as its Method of Public Notice:
(i) Publication in a daily newspaper that publishes the particulars of current events; or
(ii) Electronic public notice.
(2) Where a Foreign Insurance Company, etc. designates the method listed in item (ii) of the preceding paragraph as its Method of Public Notice, it shall be sufficient for the company to prescribe that electronic public notice shall be its Method of Public Notice. In this case, the company may designate the method listed in item (i) of that paragraph as the Method of Public Notice to be adopted where it is unable to give an electronic public notice due to an accident or any other unavoidable circumstances.
(3) The provisions of Article 940, paragraph (1) (excluding item (i)) and (3) (Public Notice Period, etc. of Electronic Public Notice), Article 941 (Electronic Public Notice Investigation), Article 946 (Obligation, etc. of Investigation), Article 947 (Cases Where an Electronic Public Notice Investigation Is Unable to Be Carried Out), Article 951, paragraph (2) (Retention and Inspection, etc. of Financial Statements, etc.), Article 953 (Order for Improvement), and Article 955 (Statements, etc. in an Investigation Record Book, etc.) of the Companies Act shall apply mutatis mutandis where a Foreign Insurance Company, etc. gives public notice under this Act or any other Act in the form of electronic public notice. In this case, the terms "Article 440, paragraph (1)" and "annual shareholders' meeting" in Article 940, paragraph (1), item (ii) of that Act shall be deemed to be replaced with "Article 819, paragraph (1) as applied mutatis mutandis pursuant to Article 193, paragraph (2) of the Insurance Business Act" and "procedure" respectively; the term "the preceding two paragraphs" in Article 940, paragraph (3) of that Act shall be deemed to be replaced with "paragraph (1)"; and the term "public notice under this Act or any other Act (excluding the public notice under Article 440, paragraph (1)" in Article 941 of that Act shall be deemed to be replaced with "public notice under the Insurance Business Act (excluding the public notice under Article 819, paragraph (1) as applied mutatis mutandis pursuant to Article 193, paragraph (2) of that Act"; any other necessary technical change in interpretation shall be specified by Cabinet Order.
(4) The Method of Public Notice by a Foreign Insurance Company, etc. (other than a foreign company or Foreign Mutual Company) shall be publication in a daily newspaper that publishes the particulars of current events.

(Notification of Establishment of a Representative Office in a Foreign State, etc.)

Article 218 (1) If a Foreign Insurer who does not have a license as set forth in Article 185, paragraph (1) falls under any of the following items and if item (i) applies, the insurer shall notify the Prime Minister of this and of the content of the relevant business, the location of the offices conducting such business and any other particular specified by Cabinet Office Ordinance and, if item (ii), (iii) or (iv) applies, shall notify the Prime Minister of this without delay:
  (i) The insurer seeks to establish a resident office in a foreign state or any other office in Japan to conduct any of the following business (including the cases where it seeks to conduct such business in an office that has been established for any other purpose):
    (a) Collection or provision of information regarding the Insurance Business; or
    (b) Any other business related to the Insurance Business;
  (ii) The insurer has abolished the office set forth in the preceding item;
  (iii) The insurer has abolished the business listed in item (i), sub-item (a) or (b) that were provided at the office set forth in that item; or
  (iv) The insurer has modified any of the particulars for which it has provided notification under item (i).
(2) The Prime Minister may, if he/she finds it necessary for the public interest, request the Foreign Insurer set forth in the preceding paragraph to submit a report or materials concerning the business listed in item (i), sub-item (a) or (b) of that paragraph that is conducted at the office set forth in that item.

Section 6 Special Provisions on Specified Juridical Persons

(Licensing)
Article 219 (1) A juridical person falling under both of the following items (hereinafter referred to as "Specified Juridical Person" in this Section) may designate a person (hereinafter referred to as "General Representative" in this Section) to act as an underwriting agent for those members of the Specified Juridical Person who provide insurance underwriting (hereinafter referred to as "Underwriting Members") for the juridical person's Insurance Business in Japan, or as a business agent for the Specified Juridical Person and its Underwriting Members for such Insurance Business in Japan, and obtain a license from the Prime Minister for its Underwriting Members to conduct Insurance Business in Japan:
  (i) It was incorporated under a special foreign law or regulation; and
  (ii) Pursuant to a special provisions of foreign laws or regulations, its members are allowed to conduct Insurance Business in the relevant foreign state without obtaining a license for Insurance Business (including any administrative measure similar to such license, such as permission or registration);
(2) The license set forth in the preceding paragraph shall be in two types: a specified life insurance business license and a specified non-life insurance business license.
(3) The same Specified Juridical Person may not obtain both a specified life insurance business license and a specified non-life insurance business license.
(4) A specified life insurance business license shall be a license for Underwriting Members to underwrite the type of insurance listed in Article 3, paragraph (4), item (i) as a business undertaking in Japan or, in addition, to underwrite the type of insurance listed in Article 3, paragraph (4), item (ii) or (iii).
(5) A specified non-life insurance business license shall be a license for an Underwriting Member to underwrite the type of insurance listed in Article 3, paragraph (5), item (i) as a business undertaking in Japan or, in addition, to underwrite the type of insurance listed in Article 3, paragraph (5), item (ii) or (iii).

Art.220〜221　⑥ Insurance Business Act, Part II, Chap.IX, Sec.6

(6) The Underwriting Members of a Specified Juridical Person that has obtained a license under paragraph (1) may, notwithstanding the provisions of Article 3, paragraph (1) and Article 185, paragraph (1), conduct Insurance Business in Japan in the offices of their general agent in accordance with the type of license issued under paragraph (2).

(Application Procedures for Licensing)
Article 220 (1) Any Specified Juridical Person that seeks to obtain the license set forth in paragraph (1) of the preceding Article shall submit to the Prime Minister a written application for a license detailing the following particulars:
  (i) The trade name or name, address of the head office or principal office, and date of the incorporation of the Specified Juridical Person;
  (ii) The name of the country that enacted the law or regulation under which the Specified Juridical Person was incorporated (hereinafter referred to as "Country with Jurisdiction over Incorporation" in this Section);
  (iii) The name and address of the person who represents the Specified Juridical Person and its Underwriting Members in Japan (hereinafter referred to as the "Representative Person in Japan" in this Section);
  (iv) The type of license desired; and
  (v) The principal branch of the Specified Juridical Person and its Underwriting Members in Japan (meaning the head office of the General Representative; hereinafter the same shall apply in this Section).
(2) A certificate issued by the competent authorities of the Country with Jurisdiction over Incorporation certifying that the Specified Juridical Person was incorporated legally and that its Underwriting Members legally conduct the same type of Insurance Business as that which they seek to conduct in Japan, in the Country with Jurisdiction over Incorporation, shall be attached to the written application for a license set forth in the preceding paragraph.
(3) In addition to what is listed in the preceding paragraph, the following documents and other documents specified by Cabinet Office Ordinance shall be attached to the written application for the license set forth in paragraph (1):
  (i) The articles of incorporation of the Specified Juridical Person or any other equivalent document;
  (ii) A statement of business procedures pertaining to the business of the Underwriting Members in Japan;
  (iii) The general policy conditions pertaining to the insurance contracts to be concluded by the Underwriting Members in Japan;
  (iv) A statement on the calculation methods for the insurance premiums and policy reserves pertaining to the insurance contracts to be concluded by the Underwriting Members in Japan; and
  (v) A document indicating the name or trade name, and address or location of the head office of the person specified by Cabinet Office Ordinance with whom the Underwriting Members may consult for the purpose of confirming the contents of insurance contracts in connection with the insurance underwriting business that they conduct in Japan.
(4) The documents listed in item (ii) to (iv) inclusive of the preceding paragraph must detail the particulars specified by Cabinet Office Ordinance.

(Licensing Examination Standards)
Article 221 (1) Whenever an application has been filed for the license set forth in Article 219, paragraph (1), the Prime Minister shall examine whether it conforms to the following standards:

(i) The person that filed the application (hereinafter referred to as "Applicant" in this paragraph) has, in light of its human resource structure, etc., the necessary knowledge and experience to carry out the business of the Underwriting Members in an appropriate, fair and efficient manner, and must have sufficient social credibility;
(ii) The Applicant has sufficient property to ensure the performance of the insurance contract obligations of the Underwriting Members pursuant to the laws and regulations of the Country with Jurisdiction over Incorporation or the bylaws of the juridical person, and has taken other measures for the protection of Policyholders, etc. in a sufficient manner;
(iii) The prospects of revenues and expenditures for the Insurance Business the Underwriting Members would conduct in Japan are satisfactory
(iv) The particulars detailed in the documents listed in paragraph (3), item (ii) and (iii) of the preceding Article conform to the standards listed in Article 5, paragraph (1), item (iii), sub-item (a) to (e) inclusive; and
(v) The particulars detailed in the documents listed in paragraph (3), item (iv) of the preceding Article conform to the standards listed in Article 5, paragraph (1), item (iv), sub-items (a) to (c) inclusive.
(2) If and to the extent that the Prime Minister finds it necessary for the public interest in light of standards for examination prescribed in the preceding paragraph, he/she may impose conditions on the license referred to in Article 219, paragraph (1) or change them.

(Public Notice by the Prime Minister)
Article 222 If the Prime Minister has granted a license under Article 219, paragraph (1), he/she shall publish that fact and the particulars listed in the items of Article 220, paragraph (1) without delay in the Official Gazette. The same shall apply where the Prime Minister has been notified pursuant to Article 234 of the modification of any particular listed in Article 220, paragraph (1), item (i), (ii), (iii) or (v).

(Deposits)
Article 223 (1) A Specified Juridical Person that has obtained a license under Article 219, paragraph (1) (hereinafter referred to as "Licensed Specified Juridical Person") shall deposit the amount of money specified by Cabinet Order as necessary and appropriate for the protection of Policyholders, etc. in Japan with the deposit office located nearest to its principal branch in Japan.
(2) If the Prime Minister finds it necessary for the protection of Policyholders, etc. in Japan, he/she may order a Licensed Specified Juridical Person to deposit, in addition to the amount of money specified by Cabinet Order set forth in the preceding paragraph, the amount of money that he/she finds appropriate prior to the commencement of Insurance Business in Japan by its Underwriting Members.
(3) If a Licensed Specified Juridical Person has concluded an agreement stipulating that a required amount of deposit be made for the Licensed Specified Juridical Person by order of the Prime Minister pursuant to the provisions of Cabinet Order and has notified the Prime Minister of this, it may withhold in whole or in Part the deposit under the preceding two paragraphs regarding the amount to be deposited under said agreement (hereinafter referred to as the "Contract Amount" in this Article), so long as the agreement remains in effect.
(4) If the Prime Minister finds it necessary for the protection of Policyholders, etc. in Japan, he/she may order a person who has concluded with a Licensed Specified Juridical Person an agreement as set forth in the preceding paragraph or the Licensed Specified Juridical Person concerned to make a deposit in an amount corresponding to the whole

Art.224　⑥ Insurance Business Act, Part II, Chap.IX, Sec.6

or Part of the Contract Amount.
(5) Underwriting Members may not commence Insurance Business under a license referred to in Article 219, paragraph (1), unless the Licensed Specified Juridical Person has made the deposit under paragraph (1) (including any deposit made following an order for the deposit of money under paragraph (2) pursuant to the provisions of that paragraph) (including the conclusion of an agreement under paragraph (3); the same shall apply in paragraph (9)) and has notified the Prime Minister of this.
(6) The Policyholders, insurers or beneficiaries of insurance contracts concluded by Underwriting Members in Japan shall, with regard to any credit arising out of the insurance contracts, have a priority claim over other creditors on the deposit pertaining to the Licensed Specified Juridical Person.
(7) For the purpose of applying the provisions of the preceding paragraph, a Licensed Specified Juridical Person shall be deemed to have jointly and severally guaranteed the obligations of its Underwriting Members under the insurance contracts that they have concluded in Japan.
(8) The necessary particulars for enforcing a claim under paragraph (6) shall be specified by Cabinet Order.
(9) If and when the amount of a deposit (including the Contract Amount) falls below the amount specified by Cabinet Order set forth in paragraph (1) for reasons such as the enforcement of a claim under paragraph (6), the Licensed Specified Juridical Person shall compensate for the shortfall within two weeks from the date specified by Cabinet Office Ordinance, and notify the Prime Minister to that effect without delay.
(10) A Licensed Specified Juridical Person may deposit any of the securities specified by Cabinet Office Ordinance, such as a national government bond or local government bond, in lieu of the deposit set forth in paragraph (1), (2) or the preceding paragraph.
(11) The deposit made pursuant to the provisions of paragraph (1), (2), (4) or (9) may be recovered pursuant to the provisions of Cabinet Order, if and when:
　(i) The license granted to the Licensed Specified Juridical Person under Article 219, paragraph (1) is cancelled pursuant to the provisions of Article 231 or 232; or
　(ii) The license granted to the Licensed Specified Juridical Person under Article 219, paragraph (1) loses its effect pursuant to the provisions of Article 236.
(12) In addition to what is provided for in the preceding paragraphs, necessary particulars of a deposit shall be specified by Cabinet Office Ordinance/Ordinance of the Ministry of Justice.

(Notification on Underwriting Members Conducting Insurance Business in Japan, etc.)
Article 224　(1) A Representative Person in Japan shall notify the Prime Minister in advance of the names and addresses of the Underwriting Members to conduct Insurance Business in Japan, as well as the name or trade name, and address or location of the head office of the person specified by Cabinet Office Ordinance set forth in Article 220, paragraph (3), item (v). The same shall apply to any change in a particular of which notification has been given.
(2) A Representative Person in Japan shall keep at its principal branch in Japan a list of the Underwriting Members conducting Insurance Business in Japan.
(3) Policyholders and beneficiaries of insurance proceeds in connection with the business of the Underwriting Members in Japan, and other creditors and insured parties, may make any of the following requests to the General Representative at any time during the hours in which it should be doing business; provided, however, that they must pay the fees determined by the General Representative in making a request falling under item (ii) or (iv):

(i) Where the list set forth in the preceding paragraph has been prepared in writing, a request to inspect such a document;
(ii) A request for a certified copy or extract of the documents referred to in the preceding item;
(iii) Where the list set forth in the preceding paragraph has been prepared in the form of electromagnetic records, a request to inspect anything that shows the particulars recorded in the electromagnetic records in a manner specified by Cabinet Office Ordinance; or
(iv) A request to be provided with the particulars recorded in the electromagnetic records set forth in the preceding item by the electromagnetic means determined by the General Representative, or to be issued a document detailing such particulars.

(Modification of Particulars Prescribed in a Statement of Business Procedures, etc.)
Article 225 (1) A Licensed Specified Juridical Person shall obtain authorization from the Prime Minister when it seeks to modify any of the particulars prescribed in the documents listed in Article 220, paragraph (3), items (ii) to (iv) inclusive (excluding the particulars specified by Cabinet Office Ordinance as posing little risk to the protection of Policyholders, etc. in Japan).
(2) A Licensed Specified Juridical Person shall, when it seeks to modify any of the particulars that are prescribed in the preceding paragraph and are specified by Cabinet Office Ordinance set forth in that paragraph, notify the Prime Minister to that effect in advance.
(3) The provisions of Articles 124 and 125 shall apply mutatis mutandis to the authorization under paragraph (1) and the notification set forth in the preceding paragraph. In this case, the term "Article 4, paragraph (2), items (ii) and (iii)" in Article 124, item (i) shall be deemed to be replaced with "Article 220, paragraph (3), items (ii) and (iii)"; and the term "Article 4, paragraph (2), item (iv)" in Article 124, item (ii) shall be deemed to be replaced with "Article 220, paragraph (3), item (iv)."

(Submission of Reports and Materials)
Article 226 (1) If the Prime Minister finds it necessary to protect Policyholders, etc. in Japan by ensuring the sound and appropriate business operation of the Underwriting Members in Japan, he/she may request the Licensed Specified Juridical Person, Underwriting Members or General Representative to submit a report or materials concerning the status of the business or property of the Licensed Specified Juridical Person or its Underwriting Members in Japan.
(2) If and to the extent that the Prime Minister finds it particularly necessary for the protection of Policyholders, etc. in Japan and for ensuring the sound and appropriate business operation of the Underwriting Members in Japan, he/she may request the Licensed Specified Juridical Person to which the Underwriting Members belong or a person the Underwriting Members have entrusted with their business in Japan (other than the Underwriting Members or General Representative; referred to as a "Person That a Licensed Specified Juridical Person, etc. Has Entrusted With Its Business" in the following paragraph, and paragraphs (2) and (3) of the following Article) to submit a report or materials that should serve as a reference concerning the status of the business or property of the Licensed Specified Juridical Person or Underwriting Members in Japan.
(3) A Person That a Licensed Specified Juridical Person, etc. Has Entrusted With Its Business may refuse to submit reports or materials required under the preceding paragraph if there are justifiable grounds for it to do so.

(On-Site Inspections)

Article 227 (1) If the Prime Minister finds it necessary for ensuring the sound and appropriate business operation of the Underwriting Members in Japan and for protecting Policyholders, etc. in Japan, he/she may have his/her officials enter the offices of the General Representative, ask questions on the status of the business or property of the Licensed Specified Juridical Person or its Underwriting Members, or inspect relevant items such as books and documents.

(2) If and to the extent that the Prime Minister finds it to be particularly necessary in entering a site, asking questions, or conducting an inspection pursuant to the provisions of the preceding paragraph, he/she may have his/her officials enter the office of a Person That the Licensed Specified Juridical Person, etc. Has Entrusted With Its Business, have such officials question the Licensed Specified Juridical Person or its Underwriting Members or ask questions about any particulars that are necessary for their inspection, or have such officials inspect relevant materials such as books and documents.

(3) A Person That a Licensed Specified Juridical Person, etc. Has Entrusted With Its Business may refuse the questioning and inspection under the preceding paragraph if there are justifiable grounds for it to do so.

(Standard of Soundness)

Article 228 The Prime Minister may use the following amounts with respect to a Licensed Specified Juridical Person and establish whether or not the Underwriting Members have an appropriate level of solvency in terms of their ability to pay Insurance Proceeds, etc. as the standard by which the soundness of the Underwriting Members' business management in Japan is determined:

(i) The sum total of the amounts specified by Cabinet Office Ordinance, such as the deposit under Article 223; and

(ii) An amount calculated pursuant to the provisions of Cabinet Office Ordinance as the amount corresponding to that part of risks which might materialize beyond normal expectations for any reasons pertaining to the insurance underwritten in Japan by the Underwriting members, such as the occurrence of insured events.

(Order to Modify Particulars Prescribed in a Statement of Business Procedures, etc.)

Article 229 If and to the extent that the Prime Minister finds it necessary for protecting Policyholders, etc. in Japan and for ensuring the sound and appropriate business operation of the Underwriting Members in Japan in light of the status of the business or property of the Licensed Specified Juridical Person and Underwriting Members or any changes in the circumstances, he/she may order the Licensed Specified Juridical Person to modify the particulars prescribed in the documents listed in Article 220, paragraph (3), items (ii) to (iv) inclusive.

(Suspension of Business, etc.)

Article 230 (1) If the Prime Minister finds it necessary for protecting the Policyholders, etc. in Japan and for ensuring the sound and appropriate business operation of the Underwriting Members in Japan in light of the status of the business or property of the Licensed Specified Juridical Person or Underwriting Members, he/she may request the Licensed Specified Juridical Person or Underwriting Members to submit an improvement program to ensure the soundness of the business operations of the Underwriting Members in Japan by identifying particulars for which measures must be taken

as well as a time limit or order the modification of the submitted improvement program, or may, to the extent that he/she finds necessary, order the full or partial suspension of the business in Japan with a time limit or order the deposit of property or other measures necessary for supervision.
(2) An order under the preceding paragraph (including the request for submission of an improvement program) that it is found to be necessary to issue due to the Underwriting Members' level of solvency in terms of their ability to pay Insurance Proceeds, etc. , must be an order specified by Cabinet Office Ordinance or Ordinance of the Ministry of Finance for the category that corresponds to the Underwriting Members' level of solvency in terms of their ability to pay Insurance Proceeds, etc.

(Rescission of a License, etc.)
Article 231 The Prime Minister may order the full or partial suspension of business in Japan by the Underwriting Members or the dismissal of the Representative Person in Japan, or rescind the license set forth in Article 219, paragraph (1), if a Licensed Specified Juridical Person or its Underwriting Member:
(i) violates a law or regulation (including foreign law or regulation), any measures of the Prime Minister pursuant to a law or regulation, or any of the particularly important particulars prescribed in the documents listed in Article 220, paragraph (3), items (i) to (iv) inclusive;
(ii) violates any of the conditions attached to the license; or
(iii) engages in any conduct that harms public interest.

Article 232 If the Prime Minister finds that the status of the property of a Licensed Specified Juridical Person or its Underwriting Members has deteriorated so significantly that it is not appropriate for the Underwriting Members to conduct Insurance Business in Japan from the viewpoint of protecting Policyholders, etc. in Japan, he/she may cancel the license issued to the Licensed Specified Juridical Person under Article 219, paragraph (1).

(Authorization of Abolition of a General Representative)
Article 233 A Licensed Specified Juridical Person shall, when it seeks to abolish its General Representative, obtain authorization from the Prime Minister.

(Notification by Licensed Specified Juridical Person)
Article 234 If a Licensed Specified Juridical Person falls under any of the following items, it shall notify the Prime Minister of this without delay:
(i) its Underwriting Members have started their Insurance Business in Japan;
(ii) it has modified any of the particulars listed in Article 220, paragraph (1), item (i), (ii), (iii) or (v), or any of the particulars provided for in the document listed in Article 220, paragraph (3), item (i);
(iii) it has carried out an Entity Conversion;
(iv) it has assigned the whole of its business;
(v) it has dissolved (for any other reason than a merger);
(vi) it has been subject to a ruling for the commencement of bankruptcy proceedings;
(vii) its Underwriting Member conducting Insurance Business in Japan has been subject to a ruling for the commencement of bankruptcy proceedings; or
(viii) When it falls under any other case specified by Cabinet Office Ordinance.

(Liquidation of Licensed Specified Juridical Person and Underwriting Members)

Art.234 ⑥ Insurance Business Act, Part II, Chap.IX, Sec.6

Article 235 (1) A Licensed Specified Juridical Person and its Underwriting Members shall, when it falls under any of the following items, liquidate the whole of their property in Japan when:
  (i) the license issued to the Licensed Specified Juridical Person under Article 219, paragraph (1) has been canceled pursuant to the provisions of Article 231 or 232; or
  (ii) the license issued to the Licensed Specified Juridical Person under Article 219, paragraph (1) has lost its effect pursuant to the provisions of the following Article.
(2) The Prime Minister shall appoint (a) liquidator(s) at the request of interested persons or without any party's request, where a Licensed Specified Juridical Person and its Underwriting Members go into liquidation pursuant to the provisions of the preceding paragraph. The same shall apply to the dismissal of such liquidator(s).
(3) The Prime Minister shall, where he/she dismisses a liquidator pursuant to the provisions of the preceding paragraph, commission a registration to that effect to the registry office with jurisdiction over the principal branch of the liquidating Licensed Specified Juridical Person and its Underwriting Members in Japan.
(4) The provisions of Article 500 (Restrictions on Performance of Obligations) of the Companies Act as applied with relevant changes in interpretation pursuant to the provisions of Article 178, and the provisions of Article 476 (Capacity of Liquidating Stock Companies), Part II, Chapter IX, Section 1, Subsection 2 (Structures for Liquidating Stock Companies), Article 492 (Preparation of Inventory of Property), Part II, Chapter IX, Section 1, Subsection 4 (excluding Article 500) (Performance of Obligations), Article 508 (Retention of Accounting Materials), Part II, Chapter IX, Section 2 (excluding Articles 510, 511 and 514) (Special Liquidations), Part VII, Chapter III, Sections 1 (General Provisions) and 3 (Special Provisions on the Procedures of Special Liquidation) and Article 938, paragraphs (1) to (5) inclusive (Commissioning of Registration by a Juridical Decision Concerning Special Liquidation) of that Act shall apply mutatis mutandis to the liquidation of the property of a Licensed Specified Juridical Person and its Underwriting Members under paragraph (1), unless their specific characters forbid such application. In this case, any other necessary technical change in interpretation shall be specified by Cabinet Order.
(5) The provisions of Article 177 shall apply mutatis mutandis to the liquidation of a Licensed Specified Juridical Person and its Underwriting Members under paragraph (1); the provisions of Article 175 and Article 179, paragraph (1) shall apply mutatis mutandis to the liquidation of a Licensed Specified Juridical Person and its Underwriting Members under paragraph (1) (excluding the cases to which apply the provisions of Part II, Chapter IX, Section 2 (excluding Articles 510, 511 and 514), Part VII, Chapter III, Sections 1 and 3, and Article 938, paragraphs (1) to (5) inclusive of the Companies Act as applied mutatis mutandis pursuant to the preceding paragraph; hereinafter the same shall apply in this paragraph); and the provisions of Article 226, paragraph (1) and Article 227, paragraph (1) shall apply mutatis mutandis to the liquidation of a Licensed Specified Juridical Person and its Underwriting Members under paragraph (1) where the Prime Minister finds it necessary for supervising the liquidation of the liquidating Licensed Specified Juridical Person and its Underwriting Members. In this case, the term "date of dissolution" in Article 177, paragraph (2) shall be deemed to be replaced with "date of cancellation or expiration of the license issued to the Licensed Specified Juridical Person under Article 219, paragraph (1)"; the term "Insurance Company in Liquidation, etc." in Article 177, paragraph (3) shall be deemed to be replaced with "liquidating Underwriting Members"; the terms "paragraph (1), (4) or (9) of the preceding Article" and "Insurance Company in Liquidation, etc." in Article 175 shall be deemed to be replaced with "Article 235, paragraph (2)" and "liquidating Li-

censed Specified Juridical Person and its Underwriting Members," respectively; and the term "Insurance Company in Liquidation, etc." in Article 179, paragraph (1) shall be deemed to be replaced with "liquidating Licensed Specified Juridical Person and its Underwriting Members"; any other necessary technical change in interpretation shall be specified by Cabinet Order.

(Expiration of License)
Article 236 (1) The license from the Prime Minister to a Licensed Specified Juridical Person set forth in Article 219, paragraph (1) shall, when it falls under any of the following items, lose its effect when:
  (i) all of its Underwriting Members have abolished their Insurance Business in Japan; or
  (ii) no Underwriting Members start their Insurance Business in Japan within six months from the date of obtaining such license (excluding the cases where the Licensed Specified Juridical Person has received in advance the authorization of the Prime Minister for any compelling reason).
(2) Where any of Article 234, items (iv) to (vi) inclusive applies and the notification under Article 234 has been made, the license from the Prime Minister to the Licensed Specified Juridical Person that has made such notification shall lose its effect.

(Public Notice by Prime Minister)
Article 237 In the following cases, the Prime Minister shall give public notice to the relevant effect in the Official Gazette:
  (i) When he/she orders suspension of the whole or part of Underwriting Members' business in Japan under Article 230, paragraph (1) or Article 231, or under Article 240, paragraph (1) as applied pursuant to the provisions of Article 240;
  (ii) When he/she rescinds the license set forth in Article 219, paragraph (1) canceled pursuant to the provisions of Article 231 or 232;
  (iii) any measures ordering the administration of business and property by an insurance administrator under Article 241, paragraph (1) as applied pursuant to the provisions of Article 240, or any order under Article 258, paragraph (1) as applied pursuant to the provisions of Article 240; and
  (iv) When the license granted under Article 219, paragraph (1) loses its effect pursuant to the provisions of the preceding Article.

(Public Notice)
Article 238 Any public notice given by a Licensed Specified Juridical Person or its Underwriting Members pursuant to the provisions of this Act shall be published in a daily newspaper that publishes the particulars of current events.

(Notification by General Representative, etc.)
Article 239 A person who seeks to act as General Representative for a Specified Juridical Person that seeks to obtain the license set forth in Article 219, paragraph (1) or the Underwriting Members of the Specified Juridical Person shall, by the time of application for such license, shall notify the Prime Minister of the particulars specified by Cabinet Office Ordinance, such as the relevant fact, the contents of its business and the method of managing the property of the Underwriting Members in Japan. The same shall apply to any change in a particular with regard to which notification has been given.

(Application of this Act, etc.)

Article 240 (1) This Act shall apply as follows where a Specified Juridical Person has obtained the license set forth in Article 219, paragraph (1):
(i) For the purpose of applying the provisions of Article 185, paragraph (6); Article 186, paragraph (3); Article 191; Article 197; Article 97, Article 97-2, paragraphs (1) and (2), Article 98 to 100-2 inclusive, Article 112, and Article 114 to 122 inclusive as applied mutatis mutandis pursuant to Article 199; Article 210; Part II, Chapter X (excluding Articles 262, 265-2, 265-3, 265-6 and 265-42); Part III; and Part V (including the penal provisions pertaining thereto), the Underwriting Members of a Licensed Specified Juridical Person shall be deemed to be a Foreign Insurance Company, etc., or a Foreign Life Insurance Company, etc. or Foreign Non-Life Insurance Company, etc. in accordance with the type of license issued under Article 219, paragraph (2). In this case, the term "Article 190" in Article 197 shall be deemed to be replaced with "Article 223"; the term "Article 185, paragraph (2)" in Article 97, paragraph (1) as applied mutatis mutandis pursuant to Article 199 shall be deemed to be replaced with "Article 219, paragraph (2)"; and the terms "In the case where the license of Article 185, paragraph (1) of the Insurance Business Act is canceled pursuant to the provisions of Article 205 or 206 of that Act, or in the case where the license of Article 185, paragraph (1) of that Act loses its effect pursuant to the provisions of Article 273 of that Act" and "Article 185, paragraph (1) of the Insurance Business Act pursuant to the provisions of Article 205 or 206 of that Act" in Article 99, paragraph (8) as applied mutatis mutandis pursuant to Article 199 shall be deemed to be replaced with "In the case where the license of Article 219, paragraph (1) of the Insurance Business Act is canceled pursuant to the provisions of Article 231 or 232 of that Act, or in the case where the license of Article 219, paragraph (1) of that Act loses its effect pursuant to the provisions of Article 236 of that Act" and "Article 219, paragraph (1) of the Insurance Business Act pursuant to the provisions of Article 231 or 232 of that Act," respectively.
(ii) For the purpose of applying the provisions of Article 101 to 105 inclusive (including the penal provisions pertaining thereto) as applied mutatis mutandis pursuant to Article 199, those Underwriting Members of a Specified Juridical Person with the specified non-life insurance business license who conduct Insurance Business in Japan shall be deemed to be a Foreign Non-Life Insurance Company, etc.
(iii) For the purpose of applying the provisions of Article 195; Article 7-2, Article 110, paragraphs (1) and (3), and Article 111, paragraph (1) and paragraphs (3) to (6) inclusive as applied mutatis mutandis pursuant to Article 199; Article 262; Article 265-2; Article 265-3; Article 265-6; and Article 265-42 (including the penal provisions pertaining thereto), a Licensed Specified Juridical Person shall be deemed to be a Foreign Insurance Company, etc. In this case, the term "inventory of property, balance sheet" in Article 195 shall be deemed to be replaced with "balance sheet of the Licensed Specified Juridical Person and its Underwriting Members"; the term "its business and property in Japan" in Article 110, paragraph (1) as applied mutatis mutandis pursuant to Article 199 shall be deemed to be replaced with "the business and property of the Licensed Specified Juridical Person and its Underwriting Members in Japan"; the term "its business and property in Japan" in Article 111, paragraph (1) as applied mutatis mutandis pursuant to Article 119 shall be deemed to be replaced with "the business and property of the Licensed Specified Juridical Person and its Underwriting Members in Japan"; the term "the branch office of the Foreign Insurance Company, etc. in Japan or any other equivalent place specified by Cabinet Office Ordinance" in Article 111, paragraphs (1) and (4) as applied mutatis mutandis pursuant to Article 119 shall be deemed to be replaced with "the head office and branch offices of the General Representative set forth in Article 219,

paragraph (1) or any other equivalent place specified by Cabinet Office Ordinance"; and the term "business and property of the Foreign Insurance Company, etc. in Japan" in Article 111, paragraph (6) as applied mutatis mutandis pursuant to Article 119 shall be deemed to be replaced with "business and property of the Licensed Specified Juridical Person and its Underwriting Members in Japan."

(iii)-2 For the purpose of applying the provisions of Article 105-2 as applied mutatis mutandis pursuant to Article 199, a Specified Juridical Person which has obtained a specified life insurance business license shall be deemed to be a Foreign Life Insurance Company, etc. In this case, the term "Designated Dispute Resolution Organization for Foreign Life Insurance Services" in the items of paragraph (1) of Article 105-2, paragraph (2) of that Article and item (ii) of paragraph (3) of that Article as applied mutatis mutandis pursuant to Article 199 shall be deemed to be replaced with "Designated Dispute Resolution Organization for Specified Life Insurance Services"; and the term "Foreign Life Insurance Services" in the items of paragraph (1) of that Article shall be deemed to be replaced with "Specified Life Insurance Services."

(iii)-3 For the purpose of applying the provisions of Article 105-3 as applied mutatis mutandis pursuant to Article 199, a Specified Juridical Person which has obtained a specified non-life insurance business license shall be deemed to be a Foreign Non-Life Insurance Company, etc. In this case, the term "Designated Dispute Resolution Organization for Foreign Non-Life Insurance Services" in the items of paragraph (1) of Article 105-3, paragraph (2) of that Article and item (ii) of paragraph (3) of that Article as applied mutatis mutandis pursuant to Article 199 shall be deemed to be replaced with "Designated Dispute Resolution Organization for Specified Non-Life Insurance Services"; and the term "Foreign Non-Life Insurance Services" in the items of paragraph (1) of that Article shall be deemed to be replaced with "Specified Non-Life Insurance Services."

(iv) For the purpose of applying the provisions of Articles 192 and 196 (including the penal provisions pertaining thereto), a Representative Person in Japan shall be deemed to be the representative person of a Foreign Insurance Company, etc. in Japan. In this case, the terms "Policyholders, beneficiaries of insurance benefits, other creditors and insurers of a Foreign Insurance Company, etc.," "Foreign Insurance Company, etc. should be doing business" and "determined by the Foreign Insurance Company, etc." in Article 196, paragraph (5) shall be deemed to be replaced with "Policyholders, beneficiaries of insurance benefits, other creditors and insurers of Underwriting Members," "General Representative should be doing business" and "determined by the General Representative," respectively.

(v) For the purpose of applying the provisions of Article 109 as applied mutatis mutandis pursuant to Article 199, and Article 142 and Chapter VII, Section 3 as applied mutatis mutandis pursuant to Article 211 (including the penal provisions pertaining thereto), a Licensed Specified Juridical Person and its Underwriting Members shall be deemed to be a Foreign Insurance Company, etc.

(vi) The provisions of Article 218 shall not apply to the Underwriting Members of a Licensed Specified Juridical Person.

(2) For the purpose of applying the laws and regulations specified by Cabinet Order, such as the Act on Compensation for Nuclear Damage (Act No. 147 of 1961), the Underwriting Members of a Licensed Specified Juridical Person shall be deemed, pursuant to the provisions of Cabinet Order, as a Foreign Insurance Company, etc. , or a Foreign Life Insurance Company, etc. or Foreign Non-Life Insurance Company, etc. in accordance with the type of license issued under Article 219, paragraph (2).

Chapter X Special Measures, etc. for Protection of Policyholders, etc.

Section 1 Modification of Contract Conditions

(Reporting of Modification of Contract Conditions)
Article 240-2 (1) An Insurance Company (including a Foreign Insurance Company, etc.; hereinafter the same shall apply in this Section, excluding Article 240-5 and Article 240-6) may report to the Prime Minister to the effect that it will modify the clause of its contract (hereinafter referred to as a "Modification of Contract Conditions" in this Section), such as a reduction in the insurance proceeds and other modifications to contract clauses with regard to insurance contracts pertaining to that Insurance Company (excluding Contracts Exempt from Modification) in the case that there is a probability that the continuation of that Insurance Company's Insurance Business (In the case of Foreign Insurance Companies, etc., Insurance Business in Japan. Hereinafter the same shall apply in this Article, Article 240-11, Article 241 and Article 262) will be difficult in the light of the state of its business or property.
(2) In the case that an Insurance Company reports as set forth in the preceding paragraph, that Insurance Company shall show that there is a probability that the continuation of its Insurance Business will be difficult unless it makes a Modification of Contract Conditions, and that a Modification of Contract Conditions is inevitable for the protection of Insurance Policyholders, etc. (in the case of Foreign Insurance Companies, etc., Policyholders, etc. in Japan. Hereinafter the same shall apply in this Chapter), and the reason in writing.
(3) If the Prime Minister finds there to be grounds in the report set forth in paragraph (1), he/she shall approve the report.
(4) The term "Contracts Exempt from Modification," as prescribed in paragraph (1), refers to the insurance contracts specified by Cabinet Order, such as those for which an insured event has already occurred by the date of reference of the Modification of Contract Conditions (limited to those contracts which would be terminated with the payment of the insurance proceeds pertaining to the insured event).

(Suspension of Business, etc.)
Article 240-3 If the Prime Minister finds it necessary for the protection of Insurance Policyholders, etc. , in cases approved in paragraph (3) of the preceding Article, he/she may order that Insurance Company to suspend its business pertaining to the cancellation of said Insurance Company's insurance contracts and other necessary measures with a time limit.

(Limitations on Modification of Contract Conditions)
Article 240-4 (1) A Modification of Contract Conditions shall not affect the rights pertaining to an insurance contract corresponding to the policy reserves that must be accumulated by the date of reference of said Modification of Contract Conditions.
(2) Concerning the assumed interest rate that is to become the basis of calculation for the payments that are modified by the Modification of Contract Conditions, such as insurance proceeds and refunds, from the standpoint of the protection of Insurance Policyholders, etc. , the assumed interest rate shall not be less than the rate specified by Cabinet Order, taking into account the Insurance Company's property operating situation and other circumstances.

(Resolution of Modification of Contract Conditions)

Article 240-5 (1) An Insurance Company, when it seeks to carry out a Modification of Contract Conditions, shall obtain approval as set forth in Article 240-2, paragraph (3), and after that, a resolution mandating the Modification of Contract Conditions shall be passed by the Shareholders' Meeting, etc. of the Insurance Company.
(2) Cases described in the preceding paragraph shall be resolved as set forth in Article 309, paragraph (2) (Resolutions of a Shareholders' Meeting) or under Article 62, paragraph (2) of the Companies Act.
(3) An Insurance Company, in cases where a resolution is carried out as set forth in paragraph (1), shall, in a notice pursuant to the provisions of Article 299, paragraph (1) of the Companies Act (Notices of Convocation for Shareholders' Meetings) (including the cases where it is applied mutatis mutandis pursuant to Article 41, paragraph (1) and Article 49, paragraph (1)), show the particulars specified by Cabinet Office Ordinance, such as the reason why the Modification of Contract Conditions is inevitable, the details of the Modification of Contract Conditions, a forecast of the business and property situation after the Modification of Contract Conditions is effected, the particulars of funding and the handling of debts against creditors apart from Insurance Policyholders, etc. and the particulars of management responsibility.
(4) In cases where a resolution is carried out as set forth in paragraph (1), where there is a policy on monetary payments concerning the insurance contracts pertaining to the Modification of Contract Conditions, such as policy dividend and the distribution of the surplus, the Insurance Company shall show the details in the notice set forth in the preceding paragraph.
(5) Concerning the policy set forth in the preceding paragraph, the Insurance Company shall describe or record the policy in its articles of incorporation.

(Special Provisions concerning Extraordinary Resolutions, etc. of Shareholders' Meeting, etc., pertaining to Modification of Contract Conditions)
Article 240-6 (1) Resolutions set forth in paragraph (1) of the preceding Article of an Insurance Company that is a Stock Company, or resolutions listed in Article 309, paragraph (2), item (iv), (v), (ix), (xi), or (xii) of the Companies Act (Resolution of Shareholders' Meetings), or listed in Article 324, paragraph (2), item (i) or (iv) of that Act (Resolution of Class Meetings), or resolutions pursuant to the provisions of Article 69, paragraph (2), Article 136, paragraph (2), Article 144, paragraph (3), Article 165-3, paragraph (2), or Article 165-10, paragraph (2) of that Act that are to be decided together with said resolutions, may be made provisionally with the two-thirds majority vote of the attending shareholders, notwithstanding these provisions.
(2) Resolutions of a Shareholders' Meeting or a class meeting listed in the items of Article 309, paragraph (3) or in Article 324, paragraph (3), items (i) and (ii) of the Companies Act, or resolutions pursuant to the provisions of Article 323 of that Act (in the case that the provisions require a resolution of a class meeting), or in Article 165-3, paragraph (4) and Article 165-3, paragraph (6), or Article 165-10, paragraph (6) of that Act that are to be decided together with resolutions as set forth in paragraph (1) of the preceding Article of an Insurance Company that is a Stock Company may be made provisionally with the two-thirds majority vote of the attending shareholders at a session where the majority of the shareholders are present, notwithstanding these provisions.
(3) Resolutions as set forth in paragraph (1) of the preceding Article of an Insurance Company that is a Mutual Company, or resolutions pursuant to the provisions of Article 57, paragraph (2), Article 60, paragraph (2), Article 62, paragraph (2), Article 62-2, paragraph (2), Article 86, paragraph (2), Article 136, paragraph (2), Article 144, paragraph (3), Article 156, or Article 165-16, paragraph (2) (including the cases where it is applied mutatis mutandis pursuant to Article 165-20) that are to be decided together

Art.240-7   [6] Insurance Business Act, Part II, Chap.X, Sec.1

with said resolutions may be made provisionally with the three-quarter majority vote of the attending members (or, where the company has a General Representative Members' Council, attending representative members).
(4) In the case that a resolution is made provisionally pursuant to the provisions of paragraph (1) (hereinafter referred to as "Provisional Resolution" in this Article), the Insurance Company shall notify the purpose of said Provisional Resolution to its shareholders and shall call a subsequent Shareholders' Meeting within one month of the date of adoption of the Provisional Resolution.
(5) In the case where a Provisional Resolution is approved by majority as prescribed in paragraph (1) at the Shareholders' Meeting set forth in the preceding paragraph, a resolution on the particulars of said Provisional Resolution shall be deemed to have existed when said approval was given.
(6) The provisions of the preceding two paragraphs shall apply mutatis mutandis to cases where a resolution is made provisionally pursuant to the provisions of paragraph (2). In these cases, the term "paragraph (1)" in the preceding paragraph shall be deemed to be replaced with the term "paragraph (2)."
(7) The provisions of paragraph (4) and paragraph (5) shall apply mutatis mutandis to cases where a resolution is made provisionally pursuant to the provisions of paragraph (3). In these cases, the term "shareholders" in paragraph (4) shall be deemed to be replaced with the term "Members" (in cases where a General Representative Members' Council has been established, "representative members"), the term "Shareholders' Meeting" in that paragraph and in paragraph (5) shall be deemed to be replaced with the term "general members' council meeting" (or "General Representative Members' Council Meeting," where the company has such a council), and the term "paragraph (1)" in that paragraph shall be deemed to be replaced with the term "paragraph (3)."

(Retention, etc. of Documents Related to the Modification of Contract Conditions)
Article 240-7 (1) From two weeks prior to the date the resolution shall be made as set forth in Article 240-5, paragraph (1) (in the case of Foreign Insurance Companies, etc., the date the decision was made concerning the Modification of Contract Conditions) until the date of issuance of the public notice pursuant to the provisions of Article 240-13, paragraph (1), the Insurance Company shall keep a document or electromagnetic records describing or recording the particulars specified by Cabinet Office Ordinance, such as the reason why the Modification of Contract Conditions is inevitable, the details of the Modification of Contract Conditions, a forecast of the business and property situation after the Modification of Contract Conditions is effected, the particulars of the funding and the handling of debts against creditors apart from Insurance Policyholders, etc., and the particulars of management responsibility (in cases where there is a policy pursuant to the provisions of Article 240-5, paragraph (4), including the contents of the policy), at the company's business offices and other offices (in the case of Foreign Insurance Companies, etc., branch offices, etc. pursuant to the provisions of Article 185, paragraph (1)).
(2) Shareholders or Insurance Policyholders of the Insurance Company (in the case of Foreign Insurance Companies, etc., Insurance Policyholders in Japan) may make the following listed requests to that Insurance Company at any time during its operating hours or business hours; however, that they shall pay the fees determined by the Insurance Company in making a request falling under item (ii) or (iv);
(i) A request to inspect the documents set forth in the preceding paragraph;
(ii) A request for a certified copy or extract of the documents set forth in the preceding paragraph;

(iii) A request to inspect anything that shows the particulars recorded in the electromagnetic records set forth in the preceding paragraph in a manner specified by a Cabinet Office Ordinance;
(iv) A request to be provided with the particulars recorded in the electromagnetic records set forth in the preceding paragraph by the electromagnetic means determined by that Insurance Company, or to be issued a document detailing such particulars.

(Insurance Inspectors)
Article 240-8 (1) If the Prime Minister finds it necessary, in cases approved as set forth in Article 240-2, paragraph (3), he/she may appoint an Insurance Inspector and cause that Insurance Inspector to investigate relevant particulars such as the content of the Modification of Contract Conditions.
(2) In the case referred to in the preceding paragraph, the Prime Minister shall specify the particulars that must be investigated by the Insurance Inspector and the deadline by which he/she must report the investigation findings to the Prime Minister.
(3) If the Prime Minister finds that the Insurance Inspector is not carrying out the investigation appropriately, he/she may dismiss the Insurance Inspector.
(4) The provisions of Article 80 and Article 81, paragraph (1) (Duty of Care and Advance Payment of Costs and Compensation of Trustees) of the Corporate Rehabilitation Act (Act No. 154 of 2002) shall apply mutatis mutandis to the Insurance Inspector. In this case, the term "court" in that paragraph shall be deemed to be replaced with "the Prime Minister," and any technical changes in interpretation required shall be specified by a Cabinet Order.
(5) The costs and compensation prescribed in Article 81, paragraph (1) of the Corporate Rehabilitation Act, as applied mutatis mutandis pursuant to the preceding paragraph, shall be borne by an Insurance Company (referred to as the "Company Being Investigated" in the following Article and in Article 318-2) as provided in Article 240-2, paragraph (1).

(Investigations, etc., by Insurance Inspectors)
Article 240-9 (1) The Insurance Inspector may request directors, executive officers, accounting advisors, company auditors, accounting auditors, and managers or any other employee of the Company Being Investigated, and any person who has resigned from these positions, to make a report on the status of the business and property of the Company Being Investigated (with regard to any person who has resigned from these positions, limited to the status of particulars that could have been known by said person during the period when he/she was engaged to work for that Company Being Investigated), or inspect relevant items such as the books and documents of the Company Being Investigated.
(2) The Insurance Inspector may, when it is necessary to carry out his/her duty, inquire with, or request the cooperation of, relevant persons such as government agencies, public entities.

(Confidentiality Obligation of Insurance Inspectors)
Article 240-10 (1) The Insurance Inspector shall not divulge any secret learned in the course of his/her duties. The same shall apply after the Insurance Inspector resigns from office.
(2) When the Insurance Inspector is a juridical person, its officers and employees who are engaged in the duties of the Insurance Inspector shall not divulge any secret learned in the course of his/her duties. The same shall apply after said officers or employees

are no longer engaged in the duties of the Insurance Inspector.

(Approval for the Modification of Contract Conditions)
Article 240-11 (1) In cases where a resolution (in the case of Foreign Insurance Companies, etc., a decision concerning the Modification of Contract Conditions; hereinafter the same shall apply in this Section) pursuant to the provisions of Article 240-5, paragraph (1) (including cases where it is deemed that there was a resolution as set forth in Article 240-5, paragraph (1) pursuant to the provisions of Article 240-6, paragraph (5) (including the cases where it is applied mutatis mutandis to paragraph (6) and paragraph (7) of that Article)), after that resolution, the Insurance Company shall, without delay, seek the approval of the Prime Minister concerning the Modification of Contract Conditions pertaining to that resolution.
(2) The Prime Minister shall not grant approval set forth in the preceding paragraph except in cases where measures necessary for the continuation of Insurance Business have been undertaken by that Insurance Company, and the Modification of Contract Conditions pertaining to the resolution as set forth in Article 240-5, paragraph (1) is found necessary for the continuation of Insurance Business of that Insurance Company, and appropriate from the standpoint of the protection of Insurance Policyholders, etc.

(Notice of the Modification of Contract Conditions and Raising of Objections, etc.)
Article 240-12 (1) In cases where approval is granted as set forth in paragraph (1) of the preceding Article, within two weeks of the date of said approval being granted, the Insurance Company shall make a public notice of the main contents of the Modification of Contract Conditions pertaining to the resolution set forth in Article 240-5, paragraph (1), and shall also notify the Insurance Policyholders who are subject to the Modification of Contract Conditions (hereinafter referred to as "Policyholders Subject to the Modification" in this Article) in writing of the contents of the Modification of Contract Conditions under the resolution set forth in that paragraph.
(2) In the case referred to in the preceding paragraph, the Insurance Company shall attach the documents specified by Cabinet Office Ordinance, such as documents showing the reason why the Modification of Contract Conditions is inevitable, documents showing a forecast of the business and property situation after the Modification of Contract Conditions is effected, documents showing the particulars of funding and the handling of debts against creditors other than Insurance Policyholders, etc. , and documents showing to the particulars of management responsibility (in cases where there is a policy pursuant to the provisions set forth in Article 240-5, paragraph (4), including documents showing the content of the policy). Moreover, the Insurance Company shall attach a supplementary note to the effect that any Policyholder Subject to the Modification who has an objection must raise that objection within a set period of time.
(3) The period under the preceding paragraph cannot be less than a month.
(4) Contract conditions shall not be modified when the number of Policyholders Subject to the Modification who have raised objections within the period of time set forth in paragraph (2) exceeds one tenth of the total number of Policyholders Subject to the Modification and the amount specified by a Cabinet Office Ordinance as an amount equivalent to the sum of the claims pertaining to the insurance contracts of Policyholders Subject to the Modification who have raised such objections exceeds one tenth of the total amount of that amount of Policyholders Subject to the Modification.
(5) When the number of Policyholders Subject to the Modification who have raised their objections within the period of time set forth in paragraph (2) or the amount specified

by a Cabinet Office Ordinance belonging to those Policyholders as set forth in the preceding paragraph does not exceed the percentage specified in that paragraph, all of said Policyholders Subject to the Modification shall be deemed to have approved said Modification of Contract Conditions.

(Public Notice, etc. of the Modification of Contract Conditions)
Article 240-13 (1) An Insurance Company shall, without delay after the Modification of Contract Conditions, make a public notice of the fact a Modification of Contract Conditions has been made and any other particulars specified by Cabinet Office Ordinance. The same shall apply even when a Modification of Contract Conditions is not made.
(2) An Insurance Company shall, within three months after the Modification of Contract Conditions, notify the Insurance Policyholders pertaining to said Modification of Contract Conditions of the content of the rights and duties of Insurance Policyholders after said Modification of Contract Conditions.

Section 2 Dispositions, etc., by the Prime Minister on Business and Property Management, etc.

Subsection 1 Suspension of Business, Orders for Merger Consultations, etc., and Business and Property Management

(Suspension of Business, Orders for Merger Consultations, etc., and Business and Property Management)
Article 241 (1) If the Prime Minister finds that the continuation of Insurance Business will be difficult in light of the status of the business or property of an Insurance Company, etc. , or Foreign Insurance Company, etc. , or if he/she finds that the management of that business (in the case of Foreign Insurance Companies, etc., their business in Japan; hereinafter the same shall apply in this Article to Article 255-2 inclusive) is extremely inappropriate and that there is a risk that the continuation of Insurance Business could bring about a situation lacking in protection for Insurance Policyholders, etc. , the Prime Minister may order the whole or partial suspension of business, a merger, a transfer of insurance contracts (in the case of Foreign Insurance Companies, etc., the transfer of insurance contracts in Japan) or an agreement for the acquisition of the shares of that Insurance Company, etc. , or Foreign Insurance Company, etc. , by another Insurance Company, etc. , Foreign Insurance Company, etc. , or Insurance Holding Company, etc. (referred to as "Merger, etc." in Article 247, paragraph (1); Article 256 to Article 258 inclusive; Article 270-3-2, paragraph (4) and Article 270-3-2, paragraph (5); and Article 270-4, Article 270-4, paragraph (4) and Article 270-4, paragraph (5)) or any other necessary measure against that Insurance Company, etc. , or Foreign Insurance Company, etc. , or make a disposition ordering business and property management (in the case of Foreign Insurance Companies, etc., property located in Japan; the same shall apply in the following Article and Article 246-2 to Article 247-2 inclusive) by an Insurance Administrator.
(2) The term "Insurance Holding Company, etc." as used in this Chapter means the following:
(i) An Insurance Holding Company;
(ii) A Low-Cost, Short-Term Insurance Holding Company prescribed in Article 272-37, paragraph (2);
(iii) A company that has received the approval under Article 271-18, paragraph (1) to become a Holding Company whose Subsidiaries include an Insurance Company, due to an acquisition of shares;

(iv) A company that has received approval, as set forth in Article 272-35, paragraph (1), to become a Holding Company whose Subsidiaries include a Low-Cost, Short-Term Insurer, due to an acquisition of shares;
(v) A company, other than the companies listed in the preceding items (excluding an Insurance Company, etc., and Foreign Insurance Company, etc.), whose Subsidiaries include an Insurance Company, etc., or Foreign Insurance Company, etc., or which is attempting to make such company its Subsidiary.
(3) An Insurance Company, etc., or Foreign Insurance Company, etc., shall, when the continuation of its Insurance Business will be difficult in light of the state of its business or property, notify the Prime Minister to that effect and of the reason in writing.

Subsection 2 Business and Property Management

(Appointment, etc., of an Insurance Administrator)
Article 242 (1) When a disposition ordering business and property management by an Insurance Administrator has been issued under the provisions of paragraph (1) of the preceding Article (hereinafter referred to as "Disposition Ordering Management" in this Subsection and Article 258, paragraph (2)), the right to represent an Insurance Company, etc., or Foreign Insurance Company, etc., that has been rendered that disposition (hereinafter referred to as a "Managed Company"), execute its business, and manage and dispose of its property (in the case of the right to represent a Foreign Insurance Company, etc., limited to the scope of Insurance Business in Japan) shall be vested exclusively in an Insurance Administrator. The same shall apply to the rights of the directors and executive officers under the provisions of Article 828, paragraph (1) and Article 828, paragraph (2) (Actions to Invalidate Acts Concerning the Organization of a Company) (including the cases where it is applied mutatis mutandis pursuant to Article 30-15; Article 57, paragraph (6); Article 60-2, paragraph (5); and Article 171) and Article 831, paragraph (1) (Action to Revoke a Resolution of a Shareholders' Meeting, etc.) (including the cases where it is applied mutatis mutandis pursuant to Article 41, paragraph (2) and Article 49, paragraph (2)) and the provisions of Article 84-2, paragraph (2) and Article 96-16, paragraph (2) of the Companies Act.
(2) The Prime Minister shall, together with the Disposition Ordering Management, appoint one or several Insurance Administrators.
(3) The Prime Minister may order the Insurance Administrators to take necessary measures regarding the business and property management of the Managed Company.
(4) If the Prime Minister finds it necessary, he/she may appoint further Insurance Administrators after appointing Insurance Administrators pursuant to the provisions of paragraph (2), or when he/she finds that the Insurance Administrators are not appropriately managing the business and property of the Managed Company, dismiss the Insurance Administrators.
(5) If the Prime Minister has appointed Insurance Administrators pursuant to the provisions of paragraph (2) or the preceding paragraph or if he/she has dismissed Insurance Administrators pursuant to that paragraph, he/she shall notify the Managed Company of this, as well as giving public notice of that fact in the Official Gazette.
(6) The provisions of Article 69, Article 70, Article 80, and Article 81, paragraph (1) and Article 81, paragraph (5) (Execution of Duty by Several Trustees, Appointment of Trustee Representatives, Duty of Care, and Advance Payment of Costs and Compensation of a Trustee) of the Corporate Rehabilitation Act and the provisions of Article 78 (Liability for Damages with regard to Acts of Representative Persons) of the Act on General Incorporated Associations and General Incorporated Foundations shall apply mutatis mutandis to Insurance Administrators and the Managed Company, respective-

ly. In this case, the term "permission of a court" in Article 69, paragraph (1) of the Corporate Rehabilitation Act shall be deemed to be replaced with "approval of the Prime Minister," the term "trustee representatives" in Article 70 of that Act shall be deemed to be replaced with "Insurance Administrator Representatives," the term "permission of a court" in paragraph (2) in that Article shall be deemed to be replaced with "Approval of the Prime Minister," the term "court" in Article 81, paragraph (1) of that Act shall be deemed to be replaced with "the Prime Minister," the term "trustee representatives" in paragraph (5) in that Article shall be deemed to be replaced with "Insurance Administrator Representatives," and the term "representative directors and other representative persons" in Article 78 of the Act on General Incorporated Associations and General Incorporated Foundations shall be deemed to be replaced with "Insurance Administrators."

Article 243 (1) An Insurance Company, etc. , may become an Insurance Administrator or an Insurance Administrator Representative.
(2) An Insurance Company, etc. , if requested by the Prime Minister to become an Insurance Administrator, shall not refuse in the absence of justifiable grounds.
(3) A Policyholders Protection Corporation may become an Insurance Administrator or an Insurance Administrator Representative and undertake the business of such.

(Notices and Registration)
Article 244 (1) If the Prime Minister shall issues a Disposition Ordering Management, he/she shall immediately notify the district court with jurisdiction over the location of the head office or principal office of the Managed Company of this, and attach a certified copy of the written order to a written commission and commission its registration in the registry of the head office or principal office of the Managed Company (in the case of a Foreign Insurance Company, etc., the location of a branch office, etc. as prescribed in Article 185, paragraph (1)).
(2) The name and address of the Insurance Administrator shall also be registered in the registration of the preceding paragraph.
(3) The provisions of paragraph (1) shall apply mutatis mutandis when modifications occur to particulars listed in the preceding paragraph.

(Suspension of Business)
Article 245 When a Disposition Ordering Management has been issued, the Managed Company shall suspend its business, except for those listed as follows; provided, however, that this shall not apply to a portion business when the Prime Minister finds it necessary that said portion not be suspended pursuant to a report by the Insurance Administrator.
(i) Where a contract has been concluded under the provisions of Article 270-6-7, paragraph (3) with an Affiliated Corporation as prescribed in Article 266, paragraph (1), business for paying insurance proceeds or any other benefit under a Covered Insurance Contract as prescribed in Article 270-3, paragraph (2), item (i) (hereinafter referred to as a "Covered Insurance Contract" in this Article) (limited to the amount calculated by multiplying the amount of the insurance proceeds or any other benefit under the Covered Insurance Contract by the rate specified by Cabinet Office Ordinance or Ordinance of the Ministry of Finance, in consideration of the type of Covered Insurance Contract, the assumed interest rate, any other content, and the timing that the insured event pertaining to said claim occurred, etc.; hereinafter referred to as "Covered Insurance Proceeds"), based on a creditor's right to claim Insurance Proceeds or any other right claimed by the creditor, as specified

Art.246~247-2 ⑥ Insurance Business Act, Part II, Chap.X, Sec.2

Cabinet Order, under said Covered Insurance Contract (hereinafter referred to as "Services for Paying Covered Insurance Proceeds").
(ii) Business involving the cancellation of specified Covered Insurance Contracts (meaning those Covered Insurance Contracts specified by a Cabinet Office Ordinance or Ordinance of the Ministry of Finance as contracts having little necessity to maintain in order to protect Insurance Policyholders, etc.; the same shall apply hereinafter) within the period of time specified by a Cabinet Office Ordinance or Ordinance of the Ministry of Finance (excluding business involving the payment of cancellation refunds or any other similar benefits; hereinafter referred to as "Business for Canceling Specified Covered Insurance Contracts").

(Prohibition on Entry of Name Changes for Shareholders)
Article 246 If a Managed Company (excluding a Foreign Insurance Company, etc.) is a Stock Company and the Prime Minister finds it necessary, the Prime Minister may prohibit the entry of a name change for the shareholders.

(Insurance Administrator's Duty to Report)
Article 246-2 An Insurance Administrator shall, without delay after taking office, investigate and report the following particulars to the Prime Minister:
(i) The course of events that lead to the circumstances under which the Managed Company received a Disposition Ordering Management;
(ii) The situation of the business and property of the Managed Company;
(iii) Any other necessary particular.

(Approval of Plans)
Article 247 (1) If the Prime Minister finds it necessary for the protection of Insurance Policyholders, etc. , that the maintenance of insurance contracts pertaining to the Managed Company (in the case of Foreign Insurance Companies, etc., insurance contracts in Japan; hereinafter the same shall apply in this Chapter, excluding Article 254 and Article 270-7, paragraph (1)) or business involving the cancellation of specified Covered Insurance Contracts or any other business be conducted smoothly, he/she may order the Insurance Administrator to prepare a plan, including the following particulars, related to business and property management:
(i) A policy related to the liquidation and rationalization of the business of the Managed Company; and
(ii) Measures to carry out smoothly a Merger, etc. , pertaining to the Managed Company.
(2) An Insurance Administrator shall obtain the approval of the Prime Minister when he/she has prepared the plan set forth in the preceding paragraph.
(3) An Insurance Administrator shall, without delay, when he/she has the approval set forth in the preceding paragraph, move on to the implementation of the plan set forth in paragraph (1) pertaining to said approval.
(4) An Insurance Administrator may, when unavoidable circumstances arise, receive approval from the Prime Minister and change or abolish the plan set forth in paragraph (1).
(5) If the Prime Minister finds it necessary for the protection of Insurance Policyholders, etc. , he/she may order the Insurance Administrator to change or abolish the plan set forth in paragraph (1).

(Investigations, etc., by Insurance Administrators)
Article 247-2 (1) The Insurance Administrator may request directors, executive officers,

accounting advisors, company auditors, accounting auditors, and managers or any other employee of the Managed Company, and any person who has resigned from these positions, to make a report on the status of the business and property of the Managed Company (with regard to any person who has resigned from these positions, limited to the status of particulars that could have been known by said person during the period when he/she was engaged to work for that Managed Company), or inspect the books, documents, or any other items of the Managed Company.
(2) The Insurance Administrator may, when it is necessary to carry out his/her duty, inquire with, or request the cooperation of, government agencies, public entities, or any other person.

(Confidentiality Obligation of Insurance Administrators, etc.)
Article 247-3 (1) The Insurance Administrator and Insurance Administrator Representative (hereinafter referred to as "Insurance Administrator, etc." in this Article) shall not divulge any secret learned in the course of his/her duties. The same shall apply after the Insurance Administrator, etc. , resigns from office.
(2) When the Insurance Administrator, etc. , is a juridical person, its officers and employees who are engaged in the duties of the Insurance Administrator, etc. , shall not divulge any secret learned in the course of duty. The same shall apply after said officers or employees are no longer engaged in the duties of the Insurance Administrator, etc.

(Measures to Clarify Managers' Responsibility for the Bankruptcy of a Managed Company)
Article 247-4 (1) An Insurance Administrator shall, in order to cause directors, executive officers, accounting advisers, company auditors or accounting auditors of a Managed Company, or any person who has resigned from these positions, to perform his/her civil responsibility based on the breach of professional obligations, file an action with the court or take other necessary measures.
(2) An Insurance Administrator shall, if, in the course of his/her duties, he/she comes to consider that a crime has been committed, take the necessary measures toward prosecution.

(Transactions between an Insurance Administrator and a Managed Company)
Article 247-5 (1) An Insurance Administrator shall obtain the approval of the Prime Minister before carrying out, for himself/herself or for a third party, any transaction with the Managed Company. In this case, the provisions of Article 108 (Self-Contract and Representation of Both Parties) of the Civil Code shall not apply.
(2) An action shall be null and void if the approval set forth in the preceding paragraph has not been obtained; provided, however, that this may not be duly asserted against a third party without knowledge.

(Rescission of Dispositions Ordering Management by Insurance Administrator)
Article 248 (1) If the Prime Minister finds that there is no longer any need for a Disposition Ordering Management, he/she shall rescind that Disposition Ordering Management.
(2) The provisions of Article 244, paragraph (1) shall apply mutatis mutandis to the case set forth in the preceding paragraph.

(Special Provisions on Extraordinary Resolutions, etc., at Shareholders' Meetings, etc.)

Article 249 (1) In a Managed Company that is a Stock Company (excluding a Foreign Insurance Company, etc.; hereinafter the same shall apply in this Article and the following Article), resolutions at a Shareholders' Meeting or class meeting listed in Article 309, paragraph (2), item (iv), (v), (ix), (xi), or (xii) (Resolutions at Shareholders' Meetings) or Article 324, paragraph (2), item (i) or (iv) (Resolutions at Class Meetings) of the Companies Act, or resolutions pursuant to the provisions of Article 69, paragraph (2), Article 136, paragraph (2), Article 144, paragraph (3), Article 165-3, paragraph (2), or Article 165-10, paragraph (2), may be made provisionally with the two-thirds majority vote of the attending shareholders, notwithstanding these provisions.

(2) In a Managed Company that is a Stock Company, resolutions at a Shareholders' Meeting or class meeting listed in the items of Article 309, paragraph (3) or in Article 324, paragraph (3), items (i) and (ii) of the Companies Act or resolutions pursuant to the provisions of Article 323 (Cases of Provisions Requiring Resolution at a Class Meeting) of that Act or Article 165-3, paragraph (4) or Article 165-3, paragraph (6), or Article 165-10, paragraph (6) may be made provisionally with the two-thirds majority vote of the attending shareholders at a session where the majority of the shareholders are present, notwithstanding these provisions.

(3) In a Managed Company that is a Mutual Company, resolutions pursuant to the provisions of Article 57, paragraph (2), Article 60, paragraph (2), Article 62, paragraph (2), Article 62-2, paragraph (2), Article 86, paragraph (2), Article 136, paragraph (2), Article 144, paragraph (3), Article 156 or Article 165-16, paragraph (2) (including the cases where it is applied mutatis mutandis pursuant to Article 165-20) may be made provisionally with a three-quarters majority vote of the members attending the meeting (or attending the General Representative Members' Council meeting, where the company has such a council), notwithstanding these provisions.

(4) In the case where a resolution is made provisionally pursuant to the provisions of paragraph (1) (hereinafter referred to as a "Provisional Resolution" in this Article), the Managed Company shall notify its shareholders of the purpose of said Provisional Resolution and shall call a subsequent Shareholders' Meeting within one month of the date of adoption of said Provisional Resolution.

(5) In the case where a Provisional Resolution is approved by a majority as prescribed in paragraph (1) at the Shareholders' Meeting set forth in the preceding paragraph, a resolution on the particulars of said Provisional Resolution shall be deemed to have existed when said approval was given.

(6) The provisions of the preceding two paragraphs shall apply mutatis mutandis to cases where a resolution is made provisionally pursuant to the provisions of paragraph (2). In this case, the term "paragraph (1)" in the preceding paragraph shall be deemed to be replaced with the term "paragraph (2)."

(7) The provisions of paragraph (4) and paragraph (5) shall apply mutatis mutandis to cases where a resolution is made provisionally pursuant to the provisions of paragraph (3). In this case, the term "shareholders" in paragraph (4) shall be deemed to be replaced with the term "members present at the relevant meeting (or, where the company has a General Representative Members' Council, the representative members present)," the term "Shareholders' Meeting" in that paragraph and in paragraph (5) shall be deemed to be replaced with the term "general members' council meeting" (or "General Representative Members' Council Meeting," where the company has such a council), and the term "paragraph (1)" in that paragraph shall be deemed to be replaced with the term "paragraph (3)."

(Permission in lieu of Extraordinary Resolution of Shareholders' Meeting, etc.)

Article 249-2 (1) In the case where a Managed Company that is a Stock Company is unable to satisfy its obligations with its property, that Managed Company may obtain permission of a court and act with regard to the following particulars, notwithstanding the provisions of Article 447, paragraph (1) (Reductions in Amount of capital), Article 467, paragraph (1), items (i) and (ii) (Approvals of Assignment of Business), and Article 471, item (iii) (Grounds for Dissolution) of the Companies Act and the provisions of Article 136 (including the cases where it is applied mutatis mutandis pursuant to Article 272-29; the same shall apply in the following paragraph):
(i) Assignment of all or a material portion of business;
(ii) Reduction in the amount of capital;
(iii) Dissolution;
(iv) Transfer of insurance contracts.
(2) In the case where a Managed Company that is a Mutual Company is unable to satisfy its obligations with its property, that Managed Company may obtain permission of a court and act with regard to the following particulars, notwithstanding the provisions of Article 62-2, paragraph (1), items (i) and (ii), Article 136, and Article 156:
(i) Assignment of all or a material portion of business;
(ii) Transfer of insurance contracts;
(iii) Dissolution.
(3) The Insurance Administrator may obtain permission of a court and dismiss directors, executive officers, accounting advisers, company auditors, or accounting auditors of the Managed Company, notwithstanding the provisions of Article 339, paragraph (1) (Dismissal), Article 347, paragraph (1) (Election of Directors or Company Auditors at Class Meetings), or Article 403, paragraph (1) (Dismissal of Executive Officers) of the Companies Act or the provisions of Article 53-8, paragraph (1) or Article 53-27, paragraph (1).
(4) In the case where the Insurance Administrator seeks to dismiss directors, executive officers, accounting advisers, company auditors, or accounting auditors of the Managed Company pursuant to the provisions of the preceding paragraph, when the number of directors, executive officers, accounting advisers, company auditors, or accounting auditors will fail to meet the number prescribed by an Act or by the articles of incorporation by carrying out the dismissals, the Insurance Administrator may obtain permission of a court and appoint directors, executive officers, accounting advisers, company auditors, or accounting auditors of the Managed Company, notwithstanding the provisions of Article 329, paragraph (1) (Election), Article 347, paragraph (1) or Article 402, paragraph (2) (Election of Executive Officers) of the Companies Act or the provisions of Article 52, paragraph (1) or Article 53-26, paragraph (2).
(5) The directors, accounting advisers, company auditors, or accounting auditors of the Managed Company who have been elected pursuant to the provisions of the preceding paragraph shall retire from their posts at the conclusion of the first annual Shareholders' Meeting or annual general members' council meeting (in cases where there is a General Representative Members' Council, the Annual General Representative Members' Council Meeting) convened after the end of the business year during which they were appointed, and executive officers shall retire from their posts at the conclusion of the first meeting of the board of directors held after the conclusion of the first Annual Shareholders' Meeting convened after the end of the business year during which they were appointed.
(6) When the permissions prescribed in paragraph (1) to paragraph (4) inclusive (hereinafter referred to as "Replacement Permissions" in this Article and the following Article) have been obtained, it shall be deemed that a resolution of the Shareholders' Meeting, etc. , class meeting, or board of directors has been made concerning the particulars of

said Replacement Permissions. With regard to the application of the provisions in Article 16, paragraph (1), Article 136-2, paragraph (1) (including the cases where it is applied mutatis mutandis pursuant to Article 272-29), and Article 250, paragraphs (3) and (5) in this case, the term "two weeks before the date of the Shareholders' Meeting pertaining to the resolution on the reduction (excluding the cases where the whole of the amount by which the reserves are reduced is appropriated to the capital) of the capital or reserves (hereinafter referred to as "capital, etc." in this Section) (or, the date of the board of directors meeting where Article 447, paragraph (3) (Reductions in Amount of Capital) or Article 448, paragraph (3) (Reductions in Amount of Reserves) of the Companies Act applies)" in Article 60, paragraph (1) shall be deemed to be replaced with "a date within two weeks from the date of receipt of the permission set forth in Article 249-2, paragraph (1) pertaining to the reduction (excluding the cases where the whole of the amount by which the reserves are reduced is appropriated to the capital) of the capital or reserves," the term "two weeks before the date of the Shareholders' Meeting, etc. set forth in Article 136, paragraph (1) in the preceding Article" in Article 136-2 shall be deemed to be replaced with "a date within two weeks from the date of receipt of the permission set forth in Article 249-2, paragraph (1) or (2) pertaining to the transfer of insurance contracts," and the terms "the public notice set forth in the following paragraph" in Article 250, paragraph (3) and "the public notice set forth in the preceding paragraph" in paragraph (5) in that Article shall be deemed to be replaced with "the public notice set forth in Article 249-2, paragraph (8)"; and the provisions of Article 156-2 and Article 250, paragraph (4) shall not apply.

(7) The district court with jurisdiction over the location of the head office or principle office of that Managed Company shall have jurisdiction over the particulars of Replacement Permissions.

(8) The court shall, when it has made a decision on Replacement Permissions, serve that written decision on the Managed Company and make a public notice as to the gist of that decision.

(9) The public notice made pursuant to the provisions of the preceding paragraph shall be published in the Official Gazette.

(10) The decision on Replacement Permissions shall take effect as of the time it has been served on the Managed Company under the provisions of paragraph (8).

(11) Shareholders or members may make an immediate appeal against the decision on Replacement Permissions within an unextendable period of one week from the date of the public notice set forth in paragraph (8). In this case, when the immediate appeal is against a decision on Replacement Permissions pertaining to dissolution, it shall have the effect of a stay of execution.

(12) The provisions of Article 2 to Article 4 inclusive (Court with Jurisdiction, Priority Jurisdiction and Transfer, Designations of Courts with Jurisdiction), Article 15 (Statements and Attendance of a Public Prosecutor), Article 16 (Obligation to Notify a Public Prosecutor), Article 18, paragraphs (1) and (2) (Effect of Decisions), and Article 20 (Appeals) of the Act on Procedures in Non-Contentious Cases (Act No. 14 of 1898) shall not apply concerning the particulars of Replacement Permissions.

(Special Provisions on Registration Pertaining to Replacement Permissions)
Article 249-3 In cases where Replacement Permissions for the particulars listed in item (ii) or (iii) of paragraph (1) of the preceding Article, item (iii) of paragraph (2) of that Article, or in paragraph (3) or (4) of that Article have been granted, a certified copy or extract of the written decision for said Replacement Permissions shall be attached to the written application for registration for said particulars.

Subsection 3 Modification of Contract Conditions in Merger, etc.

(Modification of Contract Conditions in Transfer of Insurance Contracts)
Article 250 (1) In addition to the minor modifications prescribed in Article 135, paragraph (4) (including the cases where it is applied mutatis mutandis pursuant to Article 210, paragraph (1) and Article 272-29) made to the contract set forth in Article 135, paragraph (1) (including the cases where it is applied mutatis mutandis pursuant to Article 210, paragraph (1) and Article 272-29), an Insurance Company, etc. , or Foreign Insurance Company, etc. , may, in the cases that fall under the following listed cases, prescribe a reduction in the insurance proceeds and any other modifications to contract clauses with regard to insurance contracts (excluding specified contracts) that will be transferred pursuant to that contract (excluding said minor modifications, that reduce the policy reserves that must be reserved from Insurance Premiums received after the time of the public notice, etc., prescribed in paragraph (3), item (i) with regard to Covered Insurance Contracts other than specified Covered Insurance Contracts (referred to as Covered Insurance Contracts prescribed in Article 270, paragraph (3), item (i)), and modifications that will establish disadvantageous content related to cancellation refunds or any other similar benefits specified by a Cabinet Office Ordinance or Ordinance of the Ministry of Finance that accrue after the time of the public notice, etc., prescribed in that item with regard to specified Covered Insurance Contracts compared to other insurance proceeds or any other benefits pertaining to said specified Covered Insurance Contracts; hereinafter referred to in this Subsection as "Modifications to Contract Conditions"):
(i) In the case where agreement to a transfer of insurance contracts pertaining to all insurance contracts has been ordered pursuant to the provisions of Article 241, paragraph (1), when said insurance contracts are to be transferred;
(ii) In the case where the company is a Managed Company, when a transfer of insurance contracts pertaining to all or some insurance contracts is to be made in accordance with a plan as set forth in Article 247, paragraph (1) that has received approval as set forth in paragraph (2) in that Article (including the approval of modification as set forth in paragraph (4) in that Article);
(iii) In the case where the company is a Bankrupt Insurance Company as prescribed in Article 260, paragraph (2) that has received the recognition of the Prime Minister as set forth in Article 268, paragraph (1) or Article 270, paragraph (1), when insurance contracts pertaining to all its insurance contracts are to be transferred to a Relief Insurance Company as prescribed in Article 260, paragraph (3) (excluding the case given in the preceding two items).
(2) In the case where insurance contracts are to be transferred as set forth in the item (i) or (iii) in the preceding paragraph, all the insurance contracts pertaining to that Insurance Company, etc. , or Foreign Insurance Company, etc. , (including insurance contracts relevant to Business for Canceling Specified Covered Insurance Contracts), other than specified contracts, shall be transferred collectively.
(3) The term "Specified Contracts" prescribed in the preceding two paragraphs refers to the following:
(i) Insurance contracts for which an insured event (limited to insurance contracts which would be terminated with the payment of the insurance proceeds pertaining to the insured event) has already occurred at the Time of the Public Notice set forth in the following paragraph (when payment pertaining to said insurance contracts has already been suspended at the time of said public notice in the case where a whole or partial suspension of business has been ordered pursuant to the

Art.251　　　⑥ Insurance Business Act, Part II, Chap.X, Sec.2

provisions of Article 241, paragraph (1) and payment pertaining to insurance contracts has been suspended or in the case where business has been suspended pursuant to the provisions of Article 245 (including the cases where it is applied mutatis mutandis pursuant to Article 258, paragraph (2)), paragraph (5) in this Article, Article 254, paragraph (4), or Article 255-2, paragraph (3), and payment pertaining to insurance contracts has been suspended; referred to as "Time of Public Notice, etc." in the following item);
　(ii) Insurance contracts for which the insured period has already terminated at the Time of Public Notice, etc. (including those that, at the Time of Public Notice, etc., were cancelled during the insured period and any others for which a cause of termination of insurance contracts has occurred (excluding those for which payment pertaining to insurance contracts has been suspended pursuant to an order under the provisions of Article 240-3), and excluding those given in the preceding item).
(4) In the case set forth in paragraph (1), an Insurance Company, etc. , shall, on the date of mailing convocation notices for the Shareholders' Meeting, etc. , set forth in Article 136, paragraph (1) (including the cases where it is applied mutatis mutandis pursuant to Article 272-29), make public notice to the effect that said Shareholders' Meeting, etc. , will be held and that a resolution to transfer insurance contracts that include said Modifications of Contract Conditions is the purpose of the meeting; a Foreign Insurance Company, etc. , shall, on the date the contracts set forth in Article 135, paragraph (1) are created, make public notice to the effect that contracts that contain said Modifications of Contract Conditions have been issued.
(5) The Insurance Company, etc. , or Foreign Insurance Company, etc. , set forth in paragraph (1) shall suspend all of its business (excluding Business for Paying Covered Insurance Proceeds and Business for Canceling Specified Covered Insurance Contracts) from the Time of Public Notice as set forth in the preceding paragraph, excluding the case where, already at the Time of Public Notice, the suspension of all of its business has been ordered pursuant to the provisions of Article 241, paragraph (1) or all of its business has been suspended pursuant to the provisions of the main clause of Article 245 (including the cases where it is applied mutatis mutandis pursuant to Article 258, paragraph (2)), the main clause of this paragraph, the main clause of Article 254, paragraph (4), or the main clause of Article 255-2, paragraph (3); provided, however, that this shall not apply to a portion of its business in the case that the Prime Minister has found it necessary that the portion of business not be suspended pursuant to a report from that Insurance Company, etc. , or Foreign Insurance Company, etc.

(Special Provisions on Public Notice of Transfer of Insurance Contracts and Raising of Objections)
Article 251　(1) In the case where insurance contracts are to be transferred as set forth in the paragraph (1) in the preceding Article, the public notice set forth in Article 137, paragraph (1) (including the cases where it is applied mutatis mutandis pursuant to Article 210, paragraph (1)and Article 272-29) shall include a supplementary note on the main content of modifications in the rights and duties of Insurance Policyholders caused by a Modification of Contract Conditions and any other particulars specified by Cabinet Office Ordinance or Ordinance of the Ministry of Finance.
(2) With regard to the application of the provisions of Article 135, paragraph (2) and Article 137, paragraph (4) (including the cases where it is applied mutatis mutandis pursuant to Article 210, paragraph (1) and Article 272-29; hereinafter the same shall apply in this paragraph) in the case where insurance contracts are to be transferred as set forth in the paragraph (1) in the preceding Article, "insurance contracts for which an insured event has already occurred at the Time of Public Notice set forth in Article

137, paragraph (1) (limited to insurance contracts which would be terminated with the payment of the insurance proceeds pertaining to the insured event) and any other insurance contracts specified by a Cabinet Order" in Article 135, paragraph (2) shall be deemed to be replaced with "Specified Contracts prescribed in Article 250, paragraph (3)," and the terms "one fifth" and "at the Time of Public Notice under the provisions of paragraph (1) with regard to said insurance contracts" in Article 137, paragraph (4) shall be deemed to be replaced with "one tenth" and "for said insurance contracts, in the case that said insurance contracts are Specified Contracts as prescribed in Article 250, paragraph (3)," respectively.

(Effect of Transfer of Insurance Contracts Accompanied by Modification in Contract Conditions)
Article 252 When a transfer of insurance contracts has taken place as set forth in Article 250, paragraph (1), the Transferee Company prescribed in Article 135, paragraph (1) shall assume the claims and obligations pertaining to insurance contracts pertaining to the transfer of insurance contracts under the conditions set forth after the Modifications to Contract Conditions specified in the contract set forth in Article 135, paragraph (1) (including the cases where it is applied mutatis mutandis pursuant to Article 210, paragraph (1) and Article 272-29; hereinafter the same shall apply in this Article) have been made with regard to said insurance contracts.

(Notice of Modification of Contract Conditions)
Article 253 With regard to the application of the provisions of Article 140, paragraph (2) (including the cases where it is applied mutatis mutandis pursuant to Article 210, paragraph (1) and Article 272-29; hereinafter the same shall apply in this Article) in the case where a transfer of insurance contracts has taken place as set forth in Article 250, paragraph (1), the term "the fact that a transfer of insurance contracts has been received and the content of said minor modifications when the minor modifications prescribed in the paragraph (4) in that Article have been established" in Article 140, paragraph (2) shall be deemed to be replaced with "the fact that a transfer of insurance contracts has been received and the content of the rights and duties of Insurance Policyholders after said Modification of Contract Conditions when the Modification of Contract Conditions prescribed in Article 250, paragraph (1) (including the minor modifications prescribed in Article 135, paragraph (4), hereinafter the same shall apply in this paragraph) has been established."

(Modification of Contract Conditions in a Merger Agreement)
Article 254 (1) An Insurance Company, etc. , may, in the cases that fall under the following listed cases, specify Modifications of Contract Conditions with regard to insurance contracts (excluding Specified Contracts) pertaining to that Insurance Company, etc. , in merger agreements:
  (i) In the case where agreement to a merger has been ordered pursuant to the provisions of Article 241, paragraph (1), when a merger is sought;
  (ii) In the case where the company is a Managed Company, when a merger is to be made in accordance with a plan as set forth in Article 247, paragraph (1) that has received approval as set forth in paragraph (2) in that Article (including the approval of modifications as set forth in paragraph (4) in that Article);
  (iii) In the case where the company is a Bankrupt Insurance Company as prescribed in Article 260, paragraph (2) that has received the recognition of the Prime Minister as set forth in Article 268, paragraph (1) or Article 270, paragraph (1), when a merger is to be made that will result in the survival of a Relief Insurance Company

as prescribed in Article 260, paragraph (3) (excluding the case given in the preceding two items).
(2) The provisions of Article 250, paragraph (3) shall apply mutatis mutandis to the Specified Contracts prescribed in the preceding paragraph. In this case, the term "the following paragraph" shall be deemed to be replaced with "Article 254, paragraph (3)."
(3) The Insurance Company, etc., shall, on the date of mailing convocation notices for the Shareholders' Meeting, etc., at which a resolution will be made on the approval set forth in Article 783, paragraph (1) (Approval, etc., of the Absorption-type Merger Agreements, etc.), Article 795, paragraph (1) (Approval, etc., of the Absorption-type Merger Agreements, etc.), or Article 804, paragraph (1) (Approval, etc. of the Consolidation-type Merger Agreements, etc.) of the Companies Act, or Article 165-3, paragraph (1), Article 165-10, paragraph (1), or Article 165-16, paragraph (1) (including the cases where it is applied mutatis mutandis pursuant to Article 165-20), make public notice to the effect that said Shareholders' Meeting, etc., will be held and that a resolution on the approval of a merger agreement is the purpose of the meeting.
(4) The Insurance Company, etc., set forth in paragraph (1) shall suspend all of its business (excluding Business for Paying Covered Insurance Proceeds and Business for Canceling Specified Covered Insurance Contracts) from the Time of Public Notice as set forth in the preceding paragraph, excluding the case where, already at the Time of Public Notice, the suspension of all of its business has been ordered pursuant to the provisions of Article 241, paragraph (1) or all of its business has been suspended pursuant to the provisions of the main clause of Article 245 (including the cases where it is applied mutatis mutandis pursuant to Article 258, paragraph (2)), the main clause of Article 250, paragraph (5), the main clause of this paragraph, or the main clause of Article 255-2, paragraph (3); provided, however, that this shall not apply to a portion of its business in the case that the Prime Minister has found it necessary that the portion of business not be suspended pursuant to a report from that Insurance Company, etc.

(Special Provisions on Public Notice of Merger and Raising of Objections)
Article 255 (1) The Insurance Company, etc., set forth in paragraph (1) in the preceding Article, shall attach a supplementary note to the public notice under the provisions of Article 165-7, paragraph (2) (including the cases where it is applied mutatis mutandis pursuant to Article 165-12), Article 165-17, paragraph (2) (including the cases where it is applied mutatis mutandis pursuant to Article 165-20), or Article 165-24, paragraph (2) on the main content of modifications in the rights and duties of Insurance Policyholders caused by a Modification of Contract Conditions and any other particulars specified by Cabinet Office Ordinance or Ordinance of the Ministry of Finance.
(2) With regard to the application of the provisions of Article 70, paragraph (6), as applied mutatis mutandis pursuant to Article 165-7, paragraph (4) (including the cases where it is applied mutatis mutandis pursuant to Article 165-12), Article 88, paragraph (6), as applied mutatis mutandis pursuant to Article 165-17, paragraph (4) (including the cases where it is applied mutatis mutandis pursuant to Article 165-20), or Article 165-24, paragraph (6) in the case where a merger is to be made as set forth in paragraph (1) in the preceding Article, in these provisions, the term "insurance contracts under which the Insurance Claims, etc., had already arisen at the Time of Public Notice under the provisions of that paragraph (limited to those contracts that would be terminated with payment pertaining to said Insurance Claims, etc.)" shall be deemed to be replaced with "insurance contracts prescribed in Article 250, paragraph (3), as applied mutatis mutandis pursuant to Article 254, paragraph (2)," the term "one fifth" shall be deemed to be replaced with "one tenth," the term "Insurance Claims, etc." shall be deemed to

be replaced with "insurance claims pertaining to the Specified Contracts prescribed in Article 250, paragraph (3), as applied mutatis mutandis pursuant to Article 254, paragraph (2), and any other rights specified by a Cabinet Order."
(3) In the case of a merger as set forth in paragraph (1) in the preceding Article, the Insurance Company, etc. , that survives after the merger or the Insurance Company, etc. , that is incorporated by the merger shall, within three months after the merger, notify the Insurance Policyholders of the Insurance Company, etc. , of that paragraph to that effect and of the content of the rights and duties of Insurance Policyholders after the Modification of Contract Conditions.

(Modification of Contract Conditions in an Acquisition of Shares)
Article 255-2 (1) An Insurance Company, etc. , or Foreign Insurance Company, etc. , may, in the following cases (limited to cases in which shares are acquired in order to set in place the particulars specified by the Prime Minister and the Minister of Finance as necessary for ensuring the sound and appropriate business operation of said Insurance Company, etc., or Foreign Insurance Company, etc., and for protecting Insurance Policyholders, etc.), prepare a plan to modify contract conditions and modify the contract conditions of insurance contracts (excluding Specified Contracts) with that Insurance Company, etc. , or Foreign Insurance Company, etc. In this case, the main content of changes in the rights and duties of Insurance Policyholders caused by the Modification of Contract Conditions and any other particulars specified by Cabinet Office Ordinance or Ordinance of the Ministry of Finance shall be specified in the plan to modify contract conditions:
(i) If an agreement has been ordered, pursuant to the provisions of Article 241, paragraph (1) for it to become the Subsidiary of another Insurance Company, etc. or Foreign Insurance Company, etc. or of an Insurance Holding Company, etc. through an acquisition of its shares, and it becomes the Subsidiary of another Insurance Company, etc. or Foreign Insurance Company, etc. or of an Insurance Holding Company, etc. through the acquisition of its shares;
(ii) If it is a Managed Company and has become the Subsidiary of another Insurance Company, etc. or Foreign Insurance Company, etc. or of an Insurance Holding Company, etc. through an acquisition of its shares in accordance with a plan as set forth in Article 247, paragraph (1) for which the approval set forth in the paragraph (2) in that Article has been received (including the approval of the modifications set forth in the paragraph (4) in that Article);
(iii) If it is a Bankrupt Insurance Company as prescribed in Article 260, paragraph (2) that has received the recognition of the Prime Minister as set forth in Article 268, paragraph (1), and become the Subsidiary of a Relief Insurance Company or Relief Insurance Holding Company, etc. , as prescribed in Article 260, paragraph (3) through an acquisition of its shares (excluding the case given in the preceding two items).
(2) The provisions of Article 250, paragraph (3) shall apply mutatis mutandis to the Specified Contracts prescribed in the preceding paragraph. In this case, the term "the following paragraph" in paragraph (3), item (i) in that Article shall be deemed to be replaced with "Article 255-4, paragraph (1)."
(3) An Insurance Company, etc. , or Foreign Insurance Company, etc. , that seeks to make the Modification of Contract Conditions set forth in paragraph (1) (hereinafter referred to as "Modified Company" in this Subsection) shall suspend all of its business (excluding Business for Paying Covered Insurance Proceeds and Business for Canceling Specified Covered Insurance Contracts) from the Time of Public Notice as set forth in Article 255-4, paragraph (1), excluding the case where, already at the time of public

Art.255-3～255-4   ⑥ Insurance Business Act, Part II, Chap.X, Sec.2

notice, the suspension of all of its business has been ordered pursuant to the provisions of Article 241, paragraph (1) or all of its business has been suspended pursuant to the provisions of the main clause of Article 245 (including the cases where it is applied mutatis mutandis pursuant to Article 258, paragraph (2)), the main clause of Article 250, paragraph (5), the main clause of Article 254, paragraph (4), or the main clause of this paragraph; provided, however, that this shall not apply to a portion of its business in the case that the Prime Minister has found it necessary that the portion of business not be suspended pursuant to a report from that Insurance Company, etc. , or Foreign Insurance Company, etc.

(Retention, etc. of Documents Related to the Modification of Contract Conditions,)
Article 255-3 (1) A Modified Company shall, from the date of public notice under the provisions of the paragraph (1) in the following Article until the last day of the period of the supplementary note attached to the public notice of the paragraph (1) in that Article pursuant to the provisions of the paragraph (2) in that Article, keep the documents or electromagnetic records in which the details of the plan to modify contract conditions and any other particulars specified by Cabinet Office Ordinance or Ordinance of the Ministry of Finance are detailed or recorded, at the company's business offices or other offices.
(2) Insurance Policyholders under an insurance contract that is to be modified pursuant to a plan to modify contract conditions (referred to as "Policyholders Subject to the Modification" in the following Article) may make the following requests to the Modified Company during its operating hours or business hours; provided, however, that they pay the expenses determined by that Modified Company in making a request falling under item (ii) or (iv):
(i) A request to inspect the documents set forth in the preceding paragraph;
(ii) A request to be issued a certified copy or extract of the documents set forth in the preceding paragraph;
(iii) A request to inspect anything that shows the particulars recorded in the electromagnetic records set forth in the preceding paragraph by a manner specified by a Cabinet Office Ordinance or Ordinance of the Ministry of Finance;
(iv) A request to be provided with the particulars recorded in the electromagnetic records set forth in the preceding paragraph by electromagnetic means determined by that Modified Company, or to be issued a document detailing such particulars.

(Public Notice of Modification of Contract Conditions and Raising of Objections)
Article 255-4 (1) A Modified Company shall, on the day of preparation of a plan to modify contract conditions, make a public notice on the gist of the plan to modify contract conditions and the balance sheet and any other particulars specified by Cabinet Office Ordinance or Ordinance of the Ministry of Finance.
(2) The public notice set forth in the preceding paragraph shall include a supplementary note to the effect that any Policyholder Subject to the Modification who has an objection must raise that objections within a set period of time.
(3) The period under the preceding paragraph cannot be less than one month.
(4) Contract conditions shall not be modified when the number of Policyholders Subject to the Modification who have raised objections within the period of time set forth in paragraph (2) exceeds one tenth of the total number of Policyholders Subject to the Modification and the amount specified by a Cabinet Office Ordinance or Ordinance of the Ministry of Finance as an amount equivalent to the sum of the claims pertaining to the

insurance contracts of Policyholders Subject to the Modification who have raise d such objections exceeds one tenth of the total amount of that amount of Policyholders Subject to the Modification.
(5) When the number of Policyholders Subject to the Modification who have raised their objections within the period of time set forth in paragraph (2) or the amount specified by a Cabinet Office Ordinance or Ordinance of the Ministry of Finance belonging to those Policyholders as set forth in the preceding paragraph does not exceed the percentage specified in that paragraph, all of said Policyholders Subject to the Modification shall be deemed to have approved said Modification of Contract Conditions.

(Public Notice, etc., of the Modification of Contract Conditions)
Article 255-5 (1) A Modified Company shall, without delay after the Modification of Contract Conditions, make a public notice of the fact a Modification of Contract Conditions has been made and of particulars specified by Cabinet Office Ordinance or Ordinance of the Ministry of Finance. The same shall apply even when a Modification of Contract Conditions is not made.
(2) A Modified Company shall, within three months after the Modification of Contract Conditions, notify the Insurance Policyholders pertaining to said Modification of Contract Conditions of the content of the rights and duties of Insurance Policyholders after said Modification of Contract Conditions.

Section 3 Order, etc. for Implementation of Procedures for a Merger, etc.

(Designation of the Other Party to Consultations for a Merger, etc.)
Article 256 (1) The Prime Minister may, when an Insurance Company (including a Foreign Insurance Company, etc.; hereinafter the same shall apply in this Chapter, except in Article 260, paragraph (1), item (ii), Article 260, paragraph (6), and Article 260, paragraph (8), item (ii), and Article 270-6) falls under the category of a Bankrupt Insurance Company (meaning a Bankrupt Insurance Company as prescribed in Article 260, paragraph (2); hereinafter the same shall apply in this Section) and he/she finds it necessary, designate another Insurance Company or Insurance Holding Company, etc. , as the other party with which that Bankrupt Insurance Company shall hold a consultation pertaining to a Merger, etc. , and recommend that other Insurance Company or Insurance Holding Company, etc. to agree to participate in the consultation.
(2) If and to the extent that the Prime Minister finds it necessary for making the recommendation set forth in the preceding paragraph, he/she may deliver material related to the status of the business or property of a Bankrupt Insurance Company or an Insurance Company recognized as having a high probability of becoming a Bankrupt Insurance Company to another Insurance Company or Insurance Holding Company, etc. , and make any other necessary preparations for said recommendation.
(3) The Prime Minister may, request necessary cooperation, concerning the recommendation set forth in the paragraph (1) or the preparations set forth in the preceding paragraph, from the Policyholders Protection Corporation to which the Bankrupt Insurance Company or the Insurance Company recognized as having a high probability of becoming a Bankrupt Insurance Company has entered as a member.

(Mediation of the Merger Conditions, etc.)
Article 257 (1) The Prime Minister may, when no agreement is reached in the case set forth in paragraph (1) of the preceding Article, hear in advance the opinions of the Bankrupt Insurance Company pertaining to the recommendation set forth in that para-

Art.258〜260   ⑥ Insurance Business Act, Part II, Chap.X, Sec.4

graph and the opinions of the other Insurance Company or Insurance Holding Company, etc. , that received the recommendation set forth in that paragraph, indicate the conditions and conduct necessary mediation.
(2) The provisions of paragraph (2) and paragraph (3) of the preceding Article, shall apply mutatis mutandis to the mediation set forth in the preceding paragraph. In this case, the term "Bankrupt Insurance Company or an Insurance Company recognized as having a high probability of becoming a Bankrupt Insurance Company" in paragraph (2) in that Article shall be deemed to be replaced with "Bankrupt Insurance Company."

(Order to Implement Merger Proceedings etc.)
Article 258 (1) The Prime Minister may, in the case set forth in paragraph (1) of the preceding Article, when the other Insurance Company or Insurance Holding Company, etc. , of that paragraph has consented to the conditions pertaining to the mediation, order the Bankrupt Insurance Company pertaining to the mediation set forth in that paragraph to conduct the proceedings necessary to execute the Merger, etc. , in accordance with said conditions.
(2) The provisions of Article 245 shall apply mutatis mutandis in the case set forth in the preceding paragraph (excluding the case where a Disposition Ordering Management has been received). In this case, the term "Insurance Administrator" in the proviso of that Article shall be deemed to be replaced with "said Bankrupt Insurance Company."

Section 4 Financial Assistance, etc., Provided by Policyholders Protection Corporations

Subsection 1 Policyholders Protection Corporations

Division 1 General Rules

(Purpose)
Article 259 The purpose of a policyholders protection corporation (hereinafter referred to as a "Corporation" in this Section, the following Section, Part V, and Part VI) is to protect Insurance Policyholders, etc. , by providing financial assistance in the transfer, etc. , of insurance contracts pertaining to a Bankrupt Insurance Company, providing executive management for the succeeding Insurance Company, underwriting insurance contracts, providing financial assistance pertaining to the payment of Covered Insurance Proceeds, and purchasing the Insurance Claims, etc. , thereby maintaining credibility in Insurance Business.

(Definitions)
Article 260 (1) The term "Transfer, etc., of Insurance Contracts" as used in this Section refers to the following:
 (i) The transfer, between a Bankrupt Insurance Company and another Insurance Company, of insurance contracts pertaining to all or some of the insurance contracts pertaining to a Bankrupt Insurance Company;
 (ii) The survival, by a merger of a Bankrupt Insurance Company (excluding a Foreign Insurance Company, etc.) and another Insurance Company, of that other Insurance Company;
 (iii) That which is performed in order to set in place the particulars specified by the Prime Minister and the Minister of Finance as necessary for ensuring sound and appropriate operations in the business of a Bankrupt Insurance Company (in the case of Foreign Insurance Companies, etc., business in Japan; hereinafter the same

shall apply in the following paragraph and the following Subsection) and for protecting Insurance Policyholders, etc. , by the acquisition of the shares of that Bankrupt Insurance Company under another Insurance Company or Insurance Holding Company, etc.
(2) The term "Bankrupt Insurance Company" as used in this Section means the following:
   (i) A company that will likely suspend the payment of insurance proceeds or that has suspended the payment of insurance proceeds in the light of the status of its business or property (in the case of Foreign Insurance Companies, etc., property located in Japan; hereinafter the same shall apply in the following item);
   (ii) A company that is unable to satisfy its obligations with its property or a company at which a situation will likely arise in which it is unable to satisfy its obligations with its property.
(3) The term "Relief Insurance Company" as used in this Section means a company that is not a Bankrupt Insurance Company among Insurance Companies that conduct a Transfer, etc. , of Insurance Contracts; the term "Relief Insurance Holding Company, etc." means an Insurance Holding Company, etc. that acquires the shares specified in paragraph (1), item (iii).
(4) The term "Financial Assistance" as used in this Section means the donation of money, the purchase of assets, or the Securing of Damage.
(5) The term "Securing of Damage" as used in this Section means, in the case where a loss is caused by the collection of the assets specified in the following items at amounts that fall below their book value or by any other reason, the making up of all or part of the amount of said loss to the company specified in each of the items based on a contract that was concluded in advance:
   (i) Assets assumed by a Relief Insurance Company, a Secondary Successor Insurance Company (meaning an Insurance Company which is other than a Successor Insurance Company, that succeeds in the Succession to Inherited Insurance Contracts; the same shall apply hereinafter), or a Secondary Transferee Insurance Company (meaning an Insurance Company that receives a Secondary Transfer of Insurance Contracts ; the same shall apply hereinafter) by the transfer of insurance contracts as prescribed in paragraph (1), item (i), paragraph (8), item (i), or paragraph (11) or by a merger as prescribed in paragraph (1), item (ii) or paragraph (8), item (ii): That Relief Insurance Company, Secondary Successor Insurance Company, or Secondary Transferee Insurance Company.
   (ii) The assets of an Insurance Company whose shares were acquired as prescribed in paragraph (1), item (iii) or paragraph (8), item (iii): That Insurance Company.
(6) The term "Successor Insurance Company" as used in this Section refers to an Insurance Company, the main purpose of that is to take over the insurance contracts of a Bankrupt Insurance Company by a transfer of insurance contracts or merger and to manage and dispose of said taken over insurance contracts, that is formed as the Subsidiary of a Corporation (meaning a company in which the Corporation holds voting rights exceeding 50 percent of all shareholders' voting rights; the same shall apply hereinafter).
(7) The term "Succession of Insurance Contracts" as used in this Section means the taking over, by a Successor Insurance Company, of the insurance contracts of a Bankrupt Insurance Company by a transfer of insurance contracts or merger and the management and disposition of said taken over insurance contracts.
(8) The term "Succession to Inherited Insurance Contracts" as used in this Section refers to the following:
   (i) The transfer, between a Successor Insurance Company and another Insurance Company, of insurance contracts that represent all or part of those pertaining to

the Successor Insurance Company;
(ii) The survival, by a merger between a Successor Insurance Company and another Insurance Company, of the other Insurance Company;
(iii) That that is performed in order to set in place the particulars specified by the Prime Minister and the Minister of Finance as necessary for ensuring the sound and appropriate business operation of a Successor Insurance Company and for protecting Insurance Policyholders, etc. , by the acquisition of the shares of that Successor Insurance Company under another Insurance Company or Insurance Holding Company, etc.
(9) The term "Underwriting Insurance Contracts" as used in this Section refers to the receiving of a transfer of insurance contracts pertaining to all or a part of the insurance contracts of a Bankrupt Insurance Company pursuant to a contract between a Corporation and that Bankrupt Insurance Company.
(10) The term "Management and Disposition of Insurance Contracts" as used in this Section refers to the acceptance of Insurance Premiums and the payment of insurance proceeds, refunds, or any other benefit based on insurance contracts, the utilization of money accepted as Insurance Premiums under insurance contracts and any other assets, the conclusion of reinsured insurance contracts pertaining to insurance contracts, the transfer of insurance contracts to Insurance Companies, and any other particulars specified by Cabinet Office Ordinance or Ordinance of the Ministry of Finance as pertaining to insurance contracts.
(11) The term "Secondary Transfer of Insurance Contracts" as used in this Section refers to the transfer, between an Organization that has underwritten insurance contracts and an Insurance Company, of insurance contracts that represent all or part of those that had been taken over by the underwriting thereof.

(Juridical Personality)
Article 261 A protection Corporation shall be a juridical person.

(Kinds of Corporations)
Article 262 (1) A Corporation shall, for each class of license for Insurance Business, accept as its members insurance companies that have received a license that falls under that Class of License.
(2) The Classes of License set forth in the preceding paragraph shall be the following two classes:
(i) Life insurance business licenses, foreign life insurance business licenses, and specified life insurance business licenses;
(ii) Non-life insurance business licenses, foreign non-life insurance business licenses, and specified non-life insurance business licenses.

(Name)
Article 263 (1) A Corporation shall use the term "Hoken Keiyakusha Hogo Kiko" (which means "Policyholders Protection Corporation") in its name.
(2) No person other than a Corporation shall use any term "Policyholders Protection Corporation" in its name.

(Registration)
Article 264 (1) A Corporation must complete its registration pursuant to the provisions of a Cabinet Order.
(2) No particulars that must be registered pursuant to the provisions of the preceding paragraph may be duly asserted against a third party prior to the registration.

(Mutatis Mutandis Application of the Act on General Incorporated Associations and General Incorporated Foundations)
Article 265 The provisions of Article 4 (Address) and Article 78 (Liability for Damages Due to the Actions of the Representative) of the Act on General Incorporated Associations and General Incorporated Foundations shall apply mutatis mutandis to a Corporation.

Division 2 Members

(Member Qualifications, etc.)
Article 265-2 (1) Those holding qualifications to be members of a Corporation shall be limited to Insurance Companies (excluding Insurance Companies specified by a Cabinet Order; hereinafter the same shall apply in the following Article).
(2) A Corporation shall not refuse entry to those who hold the qualifications to be members nor set unreasonable conditions with respect to that entry.

(Obligation to Join, etc.)
Article 265-3 (1) An Insurance Company shall join, as a member, one Corporation that accepts as its members insurance companies that have received a license that belongs to the class of license prescribed in Article 262, paragraph (2) (hereinafter referred to as "Class of License" in the following paragraph) that is the same as its license.
(2) A person who seeks to receive a license set forth in Article 3, paragraph (1), Article 185, paragraph (1), or Article 219, paragraph (1) (excluding persons specified by a Cabinet Order) shall, at the time of application for that license, undertake the procedures for joining one Corporation that accepts as its members insurance companies that are to receive the license falling under the Class of License that is the same as that license, pursuant to the provisions of a Cabinet Office Ordinance or Ordinance of the Ministry of Finance.
(3) A person who has undertaken the procedures to join a Corporation pursuant to the provisions of the preceding paragraph will become a member of said Corporation upon receiving the license set forth in that paragraph.
(4) Whenever an Insurance Company becomes a member of a Corporation pursuant to the provisions of the preceding paragraph, the Corporation shall promptly report this to the Prime Minister and the Minister of Finance.

(Withdrawal, etc.)
Article 265-4 (1) A member shall withdraw for the following reasons:
  (i) Rescission of license;
  (ii) Expiration of license.
(2) A member may not withdraw from a Corporation, except in the cases occurring under the reasons listed in the items of the preceding paragraph or in the case where the member receives approval from the Prime Minister and Minister of Finance and becomes a member of another Corporation.
(3) In the case where a member withdraws from a Corporation, when there are expenses incurred by said Corporation to perform obligations pertaining to the following listed borrowing of funds, the member shall assume the obligation to pay as its obligatory contribution an amount calculated by said Corporation pursuant to the provisions of a Cabinet Office Ordinance or Ordinance of the Ministry of Finance as the expenses that must be borne by the members:
  (i) The borrowing of funds performed pursuant to the provisions of Article 265-42 in

order to implement the business listed in Article 265-28, paragraph (1), items (iii) to (vii) inclusive and Article 265-28, paragraph (2), items (i) to (iii) inclusive that said Corporation has decided to carry out by the day of that withdrawal;
(ii) The borrowing of funds that will be performed pursuant to the provisions of Article 265-42 in order to implement the business listed in Article 265-28, paragraph (1), items (iii) to (vii) inclusive and Article 265-28, paragraph (2), items (i) to (iii) inclusive that said Corporation has decided to carry out by the day of that withdrawal.
(4) Whenever an application has been filed for the approval set forth in paragraph (2), the Prime Minister and Minister of Finance may only give their approval if the member to which the application pertains conforms to the following standards:
(i) Said member has satisfied the obligations it bears as a member of the Corporation it seeks to withdraw from;
(ii) Said member appears certain to perform the obligation to pay as its obligatory contribution the amount calculated as prescribed in the preceding paragraph pursuant to the provisions of that paragraph;
(iii) Said member has undertaken procedures to enter another Corporation as a member.

(Monetary Penalties for Members)
Article 265-5 A Corporation may, pursuant to the provisions specified by the articles of incorporation, impose a monetary penalty on a member that has violated any provision of this Section or the Corporation's articles of incorporation or any other rules.

Division 3 Establishment

(Founders)
Article 265-6 In order to form a Corporation, ten or more insurance companies that seek to become its members must become the founders.

(Organizational Meetings)
Article 265-7 (1) The founders shall, after preparing articles of incorporation and a business plan, invite those who seek to become members, make a public notice of these together with the time and location at least two weeks before the date the meeting shall be held, and hold an Organizational Meeting.
(2) Approval of the articles of incorporation and business plan and the decision on any other particulars necessary for the incorporation of a Corporation shall depend on resolutions at the Organizational Meetings.
(3) The agenda of the Organizational Meeting set forth in the preceding paragraph is decided by a two-thirds majority vote of those in attendance at a meeting where at least one half of the founders and the persons with the qualifications to become members who have notified the founders in writing by the date of the Organizational Meeting that they will become members are present.
(4) The following particulars and any other particulars that are necessary to the operation of business in the business year including the date of incorporation of a Corporation may be decided by the resolution of the Organizational Meeting, notwithstanding the provisions of Article 265-25 and Article 265-34, paragraph (3):
(i) The preparation of business rules;
(ii) The decision of the budget and financial plan for the business year including the date of incorporation of the Corporation;
(iii) The decision of the obligatory contribution rate prescribed in Article 265-34, paragraph (1), items (i) and (ii).

(5) The provisions of Article 265-26, paragraph (2) shall apply mutatis mutandis in the case where the particulars prescribed in the preceding paragraph are made the business of the Organizational Meeting pursuant to the provisions of that paragraph. In this case, the term "items (i), (iii), and (v) of the preceding Article," shall be deemed to be replaced with "Article 265-7, paragraph (4), item (i)."
(6) The provisions of Article 265-27-4 and Article 265-27-5 shall apply mutatis mutandis to the resolutions of the Organizational Meeting.

(Application for Authorization for Establishment)
Article 265-8 (1) The founders shall, without delay after the end of the Organizational Meeting, apply for approval for incorporation by submitting to the Prime Minister and Minister of Finance an application for approval detailing the following particulars:
(i) Name;
(ii) Office address;
(iii) Names of the officers and members.
(2) Documents detailing the articles of incorporation, business plan, and any other particulars specified by Cabinet Office Ordinance or Ordinance of the Ministry of Finance shall be attached to the application for approval set forth in the preceding paragraph.

(Approval for Establishment)
Article 265-9 (1) Whenever an application has been filed for the approval under the provisions in paragraph (1) of the preceding Article, the Prime Minister and Minister of Finance shall examine whether the application conforms to the following standards:
(i) The procedure of incorporation and the content of the articles of incorporation and business plan conform to the provisions of laws and regulations;
(ii) There are no false details in the articles of incorporation and business plan.
(iii) There are no persons among the officers who fall under any of the items listed in Article 265-16;
(iv) It is found to be certain that business operation will be undertaken appropriately;
(v) The organization of the Corporation pertaining to the application conforms to the provisions of this Act.
(2) The Prime Minister and Minister of Finance shall, if they find as a result of the examination pursuant to the provisions of the preceding paragraph that the application conforms to the standards given in that paragraph, authorize the incorporation.

(Succession of Business)
Article 265-10 When an approval for incorporation has been granted, the founders shall, without delay, hand over business to the president of a Corporation.

(Period of Establishment, etc.)
Article 265-11 (1) A Corporation shall be established upon completing the registration of its incorporation at the location of its principal office.
(2) When a Corporation has completed the registration of its incorporation as set forth in the preceding paragraph, it shall notify the Prime Minister and Minister of Finance of this without delay.

Division 4 Management

(Articles of Incorporation)
Article 265-12 (1) A Corporation's articles of incorporation must detail the following particulars:

(i) Purpose;
(ii) Name;
(iii) Office address;
(iv) The particulars of the members;
(v) The particulars of the officers;
(vi) The particulars of the management committee and the evaluation examination board;
(vii) The particulars of the General Representative Members' Council;
(viii) The particulars of its business and the execution thereof;
(ix) The particulars of obligatory contributions;
(x) Particulars related to finances and accounting;
(xi) Particulars related to dissolution;
(xii) Particulars related to the amendment of the articles of incorporation;
(xiii) Method of Public Notices.
(2) Modifications to a Corporation's articles of incorporation shall be null and void without the approval of the Prime Minister and Minister of Finance.

(Decisions on Officers and Business)
Article 265-13 (1) A Corporation shall have one president, two or more directors, and one or more auditors as officers.
(2) The business of a Corporation shall be decided by the majority of the president and directors, unless otherwise provided for in the articles of incorporation.

(Duties and Authority of Officers)
Article 265-14 (1) The president shall represent a Corporation and preside over its business.
(2) The directors shall, as determined by the president, represent a Corporation, assist the president in administering the business of the Corporation, act on behalf of the president when he/she has had an accident, and perform the duties of the president when his/her position is vacant.
(3) The auditors shall audit the state of a Corporation's business and accounting, and report the results of those audits to the General Representative Members' Council.
(4) The auditors may, when it is found necessary based on the results of audits, submit opinions to the president or to the Prime Minister and Minister of Finance.

(Appointment, Dismissal, and Term of Office of Officers)
Article 265-15 (1) Officers shall be appointed or dismissed at General Representative Members' Council Meetings pursuant to the provisions of the articles of incorporation; provided, however, that the officers at the time of incorporation shall be appointed at an Organizational Meeting.
(2) The appointment and dismissal of officers under the provisions of the preceding paragraph shall be null and void without the approval of the Prime Minister and Minister of Finance,
(3) The term of office of officers shall be a period of time within two years as specified by the articles of incorporation; provided, however, that the term of office of officers at the time of incorporation shall be a period of time within two years as specified at the Organizational Meeting.
(4) Officers may be reappointed.

(Grounds for Disqualification of Officers)
Article 265-16 Persons who fall under any of the following items may not become offi-

cers:
(i) In the case where a Corporation had its approval for incorporation rescinded pursuant to the provisions of Article 265-47, a person who was an officer within the 30 days prior to the date of that rescission, where five years have not elapsed from the date of that rescission;
(ii) An adult ward or a person under curatorship or a bankrupt who has not obtained a restoration of rights;
(iii) A person who has been sentenced to imprisonment without work or severer punishment, where five years have not elapsed from the date that execution finished or the date he/she became no longer subject to that execution;
(iv) A person who has been sentenced to punishment by fine pursuant to the provisions of this Act, where five years have not elapsed from the date that execution finished or the date he/she became no longer subject to that execution.

(Prohibition of Concurrent Holding of Posts by Auditors)
Article 265-17 No auditor shall concurrently hold the post of president, director, management committee member, evaluation examination board member, or employee of a Corporation.

(Restrictions on Authority of Representation)
Article 265-18 With regard to particulars with regard to which there exists conflict of interests between a Corporation and the president or directors, these persons shall not have authority of representation. In this case, the auditor shall represent the Corporation, pursuant to the provisions specified by the articles of incorporation.

Article 265-18-2 The president may appoint, from among the employees of a Corporation, an agent who has the authority to undertake all action in and out of court related to a portion of the business of the Corporation.

(Management Committees)
Article 265-19 (1) A Corporation shall have a management committee (hereinafter referred to as the "Committee" in this Chapter).
(2) The Committee shall respond to consultation by the president and deliberate on matters that are important to the management of the Corporation's business (excluding the particulars of the evaluation of the property of a Bankrupt Insurance Company as prescribed in paragraph (2) of the following Article) in addition to dealing with the matters under its authority pursuant to this Act.
(3) The Committee may state its opinion to the president as to the management of the Corporation's business.
(4) Members of the Committee shall be appointed by the president, having received the approval of the Prime Minister and Minister of Finance, from among persons with relevant knowledge and experience needed for appropriate management of the Corporation's business.
(5) In addition to what is provided for in the preceding paragraphs, necessary particulars of the organization and management of the Committee shall be specified by a Cabinet Office Ordinance or Ordinance of the Ministry of Finance.

(Evaluation Examination Boards)
Article 265-20 (1) A Corporation shall have an evaluation examination board (hereinafter referred to as "Examination Board").
(2) The Examination Board shall respond to consultation by the president and deliberate

on matters that are important in the evaluation of the property of a Bankrupt Insurance Company (in the case of Foreign Insurance Companies, etc., property located in Japan) that is a member of the Corporation in addition to dealing with the particulars under its authority pursuant to the provisions of the following Subsection.
(3) Members of the Examination Board shall be appointed by the president, having received the approval of the Prime Minister and Minister of Finance, from among persons with relevant knowledge and experience or expert knowledge regarding insurance or evaluation of property.
(4) In addition to what is provided for in the preceding three paragraphs, necessary particulars of the organization and management of the Examination Board shall be specified by a Cabinet Office Ordinance or Ordinance of the Ministry of Finance.

(Confidentiality Obligation, etc., of Officers, etc.)
Article 265-21 The Corporation's officers (meaning officers as set forth in Article 265-13, paragraph (1); hereinafter the same shall apply) or employees, members of the Committee, members of the Examination Board, or those who held these positions, shall not divulge or misappropriate any secret learned regarding their duties.

(Status of Officers, etc., as Government Employees)
Article 265-21-2 With regard to the application of the Penal Code (Act No. 45 of 1907) and any other penal provisions, a Corporation's officers and employees, members of the Committee, and members of the Examination Board shall be deemed to be employees engaged in public service pursuant to laws and regulations.

(Public Inspection, etc., of the List of Members)
Article 265-22 A Corporation shall, pursuant to the provisions of a Cabinet Office Ordinance or Ordinance of the Ministry of Finance, prepare a list of members, submit this to the Prime Minister and Minister of Finance, and make it available for public inspection.

Division 5 General Councils

(Convocation of the General Council)
Article 265-23 (1) The president shall, pursuant to the provisions of the articles of incorporation, call an ordinary General Council Meeting once every business year.
(2) If the president finds it necessary, he/she may call an extraordinary General Council Meeting.

(Attendance of Designated Employees at Meetings)
Article 265-24 Employees designated by the Prime Minister and Minister of Finance, respectively, may attend a General Council Meeting and state their opinions.

(Matters to Be Decided at General Council Meetings)
Article 265-25 In addition to what is specified elsewhere in this Act, decisions on the following matters must be effected by resolution of the General Council:
(i) The amendment of the articles of incorporation;
(ii) Decisions on or modifications to the budget and financial plan;
(iii) Preparation of or modifications to business rules;
(iv) Settlement of accounts;
(v) Dissolution;

(vi) Any other matters specified by the articles of incorporation.

(Agenda of a General Council Meeting)
Article 265-26 (1) A General Council may not open a meeting or vote on a resolution without the attendance of at least one half of its total members.
(2) Decisions on the agenda of a General Council meeting are effected by the majority vote of those in attendance at the meeting, and the chairperson makes the decisions in the event of a tie; provided, however, that decisions on the matters listed in items (i), (iii), and (v) of the preceding Article, are effected by a two-thirds majority vote of those present.
(3) The chairperson shall be governed by the provisions specified in the articles of incorporation.

(Extraordinary General Council Meetings)
Article 265-27 The president shall call an extraordinary General Council meeting when a one-fifth or more of all of the members indicate a matter that is a subject for a meeting and so request; provided, however, that a percentage that differs with the percentage of one-fifth of all of the members can be specified by the articles of incorporation.

(Convocation of General Council Meetings)
Article 265-27-2 A notice of convocation for a General Council Meeting shall be made in accordance with the method specified by the articles of incorporation at least five days prior to the day of the General Council Meeting, and shall indicate the matter that is the subject of that General Council Meeting.

(Matters to Be Resolved at a General Council Meeting)
Article 265-27-3 Only the matters for which notice was given in advance pursuant to the provisions of the preceding Article may be resolved at a General Council Meeting; provided, however, that this shall not apply when otherwise provided for in the articles of incorporation.

(Voting Rights of the Members)
Article 265-27-4 (1) The voting rights of members shall be equal.
(2) Members who do not attend a General Council Meeting may vote in writing or through a proxy.
(3) The provisions of the preceding two paragraphs shall not apply in the case where they are otherwise provided for in the articles of incorporation.

(Case of No Voting Rights)
Article 265-27-5 When a decision is to be made regarding the relationship between a Corporation and a certain member, that member shall have no voting rights.

Division 6 Business

(Business)
Article 265-28 (1) A Corporation shall undertake the following business in order to accomplish the purpose specified in Article 259:
(i) Business as an Insurance Administrator or Insurance Administrator Representative under the provisions of Article 243, paragraph (3);
(ii) The receipt and management of obligatory contributions under the provisions of

Art.265-29〜265-30　⑥ Insurance Business Act, Part II, Chap.X, Sec.4

the following Division;
(iii) Financial Assistance in the Transfer, etc. , of Insurance Contracts, Succession to Insurance Contracts, Succession to Inherited Insurance Contracts, and Secondary Transfer of Insurance Contracts under the provisions of the following Subsection;
(iv) Business for providing executive management for the Successor Insurance Company and any other Succession of Insurance Contracts under the provisions of the following Subsection;
(v) The Underwriting of Insurance Contracts pertaining to a Bankrupt Insurance Company and the Management and Disposition of Insurance Contracts pertaining to the Underwriting of Insurance Contracts under the provisions of the following Subsection;
(vi) Financial Assistance pertaining to the payment of Covered Insurance Proceeds under the provisions of the following Subsection;
(vii) Purchasing the Insurance Claims, etc. under the provisions of Subsection 3; .
(viii) The submission of a list of Insurance Policyholders under the provisions of Chapter IV, Section 6 (Authority, etc., of Policyholders Protection Corporations) and Chapter VI, Section 4 (Authority of Policyholders Protection Corporations) of the Act on Special Treatment of Corporate Reorganization Proceedings, etc. and Other Insolvency Proceedings by Financial Institutions, etc. , and any other business under these provisions;
(ix) Business incidental to what is listed in the preceding items.
(2) In addition to the business listed in the items of the preceding paragraph, a Corporation may conduct the following business within the limit that this does not interfere with the performance of business listed in item (iii) to (vii) inclusive of that paragraph:
(i) Loans of funds to its members;
(ii) Loans of funds to Insurance Policyholders, etc. , of a Bankrupt Insurance Company;
(iii) Purchase of the property of Insurance Companies in Liquidation (meaning Insurance Companies connected with the liquidation; hereinafter the same shall apply in Article 270-8-2 and Article 270-8-3) under the provisions of Subsection 4;
(iv) Business incidental to that listed in the preceding three items.

(Entrustment of Business)
Article 265-29 (1) A Corporation may not entrust its business to another party, except in the following cases:
(i) The case where the Corporation entrusts the acceptance of Insurance Premiums and any other business specified by a Cabinet Office Ordinance or Ordinance of the Ministry of Finance among business involving the Management and Disposition of Insurance Contracts (hereinafter referred to as the "Insurance Premiums Acceptance Services, etc." in this Article) to an Insurance Company or any other party;
(ii) The case where the Corporation receives the approval of the Prime Minister and Minister of Finance in advance and entrusts business other than Insurance Premiums Acceptance Services, etc. , to an Insurance Company or any other party.
(2) An Insurance Company that a Corporation has entrusted with its Insurance Premiums Acceptance Services, etc. , or business for which it has received the approval set forth in item (ii) of the preceding paragraph, may conduct that business, notwithstanding the provisions of Article 100 (including the cases where it is applied mutatis mutandis pursuant to Article 199).

(Business Rules)
Article 265-30 (1) With regard to the business listed in each of the items of Article 265-28, paragraph (1) and paragraph (2) (hereinafter referred to as "Financial Assistance

Services, etc."), a Corporation shall prepare business rules related to the implementation of Financial Assistance Services, etc., and receive the approval of the Prime Minister and Minister of Finance before beginning Financial Assistance Services, etc. The same shall apply when the organization seeks to modify these rules.
(2) The business rules set forth in the preceding paragraph shall specify the particulars of Financial Assistance, the particulars of the Succession of Insurance Contracts, the particulars of the Underwriting of Insurance Contracts, the particulars of the receipt of obligatory contributions, the particulars of the purchase of Insurance Claims, etc. and any other particulars specified by Cabinet Office Ordinance or Ordinance of the Ministry of Finance.
(3) The Prime Minister and Minister of Finance may, when they find that the business rules approved as set forth in paragraph (1) are inappropriate for the proper and reliable operation of Financial Assistance Services, etc., order their modification.

(Requests for the Submission of Materials, etc.)
Article 265-31 (1) A Corporation may request its members to submit materials when it is necessary for it to conduct its business, except in the cases where the submission of materials is requested pursuant to other provisions of this Section.
(2) Members who have been requested to submit materials pursuant to the provisions of the preceding paragraph shall submit such materials without delay.
(3) If the Prime Minister finds it to be particularly necessary for the implementation of a Corporation's business, in the case where there has been a request from the Corporation, he/she may deliver materials to the Corporation or allow the Corporation inspect such materials.

Division 7 Obligatory Contributions

(Insurance Policyholders Protection Funds)
Article 265-32 (1) A Corporation shall establish Insurance Policyholders Protection Funds as funds to be allocated for covering expenses incurred in implementing Financial Assistance Services, etc.
(2) Insurance Policyholders Protection Funds may not be used except in the case where they are allocated for covering expenses incurred in implementing Financial Assistance Services, etc.

(Payment of Obligatory Contributions)
Article 265-33 (1) A member shall pay its obligatory contribution to a Corporation, pursuant to the provisions of the articles of incorporation, during each of the Corporation's business years, to be allocated for covering expenses incurred in implementing Financial Assistance Services, etc.; provided, however, that this shall not apply with regard to the business year after a business year in which the balance of Insurance Policyholders Protection Funds at the end of that business year of the Corporation reaches an amount calculated pursuant to the provisions of the articles of incorporation as a sufficient amount in light of the estimated amount of expenses the Corporation will incur in implementing Financial Assistance Services, etc.
(2) A Corporation may, in the cases listed in the following items, exempt members corresponding to the Insurance Companies specified in each of the items from obligatory contribution pursuant to the provisions of the articles of incorporation, notwithstanding the provisions of the main clause of the preceding paragraph:
(i) When authorization has been granted by the Prime Minister as set forth in Article 268, paragraph (1): the Bankrupt Insurance Company pertaining to said authoriza-

Art.265-34   ⑥ Insurance Business Act, Part II, Chap.X, Sec.4

tion;
(ii) When a supplementary note has been included by the Prime Minister as set forth in Article 269, paragraph (1): the Bankrupt Insurance Company pertaining to said supplementary note;
(iii) When authorization has been granted by the Prime Minister as set forth in Article 270, paragraph (1): the Bankrupt Insurance Company pertaining to said authorization;
(iv) When a Successor Insurance Company has been formed: that Successor Insurance Company.

(Amount of Obligatory Contributions)
Article 265-34 (1) The amount of obligatory contributions that members must pay during each of a Corporation's business years shall be the total of the following amounts (in the case where a minimum amount of obligatory contribution has been set by the articles of incorporation, an amount equivalent to that minimum amount when that total amount is less than that minimum amount; hereinafter referred to as "Annual Amount of Obligatory Contribution" in this paragraph) for each member; provided, however, that the amount of the obligatory contribution that must be paid by members in the business year including the day of incorporation of the Corporation shall be an amount calculated by dividing the Annual Amount of Obligatory Contribution by 12 and multiplying this by the number of months in the business year including the day of incorporation of the Corporation:
(i) An amount calculated by multiplying the obligatory contribution rate by an amount calculated pursuant to the provisions of a Cabinet Office Ordinance or Ordinance of the Ministry of Finance as the amount of Insurance Premiums received over the year by each member;
(ii) An amount calculated by multiplying the obligatory contribution rate by an amount calculated pursuant to the provisions of a Cabinet Office Ordinance or Ordinance of the Ministry of Finance as the amount of liabilities that must be reserved to be allocated to the payment of policy reserves and any other Insurance Proceeds, etc. , by each member at the end of the business year.
(2) The number of months set forth in the provisions of the proviso to the preceding paragraph shall be one month when a fraction of less than one month results when calculated according to the calendar.
(3) The obligatory contribution rate set forth in the items of paragraph (1) shall be established by a Corporation after resolution by a General Representative Members' Council.
(4) A Corporation shall obtain the approval of the Prime Minister and Minister of Finance when it establishes the obligatory contribution rate set forth in the items of paragraph (1) or when it seeks to modify these rates.
(5) The obligatory contribution rate set forth in the items of paragraph (1) shall be established such that they conform to the following standards:
(i) The percentage is such that a Corporation's long-term finances will be balanced in light of the estimated amount of expenses the Corporation will incur in implementing Financial Assistance Services, etc. ;
(ii) The rate is such that certain members are not subject to discriminatory treatment (excluding what is done according to the soundness of the members' operation).
(6) If the obligatory contribution rate is established in conformity with the standards listed in item (i) of the preceding paragraph and the soundness of a member's operation can no longer be maintained due to the payment of obligatory contribution, the provisions of that paragraph must not be interpreted as preventing the temporary establish-

ment of an obligatory contribution rate that does not conform with said standards.

(Late Payment Charges)
Article 265-35 (1) Members shall pay a late payment charge to the Corporation in the case where they do not pay obligatory contribution by the deadline established in the articles of incorporation.
(2) The amount of the late payment charge shall be an amount calculated by multiplying the unpaid obligatory contribution by 14.5% a year in accordance with the number of days from the day after the deadline to the day of payment inclusive.

Division 8 Finances and Accounting

(Business Year)
Article 265-36 A Corporation's business year shall be from 1 April to 31 March of the following year inclusive; provided, however, that the business year including the day of incorporation of the Corporation shall be from the day of that incorporation to the first March 31 thereafter inclusive.

(Budget, etc.)
Article 265-37 (1) A Corporation that accepts as its members Insurance Companies that have received a license that falls under the Class of License described in Article 262, paragraph (2), item (i) (hereinafter referred to as "Life Insurance Policyholders Protection Corporation" in this paragraph and in Article 265-42-2) shall, every business year, prepare a budget and financial plan and receive the approval of the Prime Minister and Minister of Finance before the start of that business year (in the business year that includes the day of incorporation of the Life Insurance Policyholders Protection Corporation, without delay after incorporation). The same shall apply when the Corporation seeks to modify these.
(2) A Corporation that accepts as its members Insurance Companies that have received a license that falls under the Class of License described in Article 262, paragraph (2), item (ii) (hereinafter referred to as "Non-Life Insurance Policyholders Protection Corporation" in this paragraph) shall, every business year, prepare a budget and financial plan and submit these to the Prime Minister and Minister of Finance before the start of that business year (in the business year that includes the day of incorporation of the Non-Life Insurance Policyholders Protection Corporation, without delay after incorporation). The same shall apply when the Corporation has modified these.

(Approval, etc., of Financial Statements, etc.)
Article 265-38 (1) Every business year, the president shall prepare an inventory of property, balance sheet, and profit and loss statement, and a business report and statement of accounts according to the budget classifications for that business year (referred to as "Financial Statements, etc." in the following paragraph and following Article) and submit these to the auditor at least four weeks prior to the first ordinary General Council Meeting to be called after the end of that business year.
(2) The president shall attach the written opinion of the auditor to the Financial Statements, etc., set forth in the preceding paragraph, submit these to the ordinary General Council Meeting set forth in that paragraph, and request its approval.

Article 265-39 (1) Every business year, a Corporation shall, within three months of the end of that business year, submit the Financial Statements, etc., that received the approval of the ordinary General Council Meeting set forth in paragraph (2) of the pre-

Art.265-40〜265-43 ⑥ Insurance Business Act, Part II, Chap.X, Sec.4

ceding Article, to the Prime Minister and Minister of Finance and receive their approval.
(2) A Corporation shall, when it submits Financial Statements, etc. , to the Prime Minister and Minister of Finance pursuant to the provisions of the preceding paragraph, attach to these the written opinion of the auditor on the Financial Statements, etc.
(3) A Corporation shall without delay, when it has received the approval of the Prime Minister and Minister of Finance under the provisions of paragraph (1), give public notice of the inventory of property, balance sheet, and profit and loss statement in the Official Gazette, and shall keep the Financial Statements, etc. , annexed detailed statement, and the written opinion of the auditor set forth in the preceding paragraph at each office, and provide these for public inspection for a period of time specified by a Cabinet Office Ordinance or Ordinance of the Ministry of Finance.

(Separate Accounting)
Article 265-40 With regard to accounting related to business pertaining to the Management and Disposition of Insurance Contracts pertaining to the Underwriting of Insurance Contracts (including business incidental to this), a Corporation shall arrange Special Accounts, separate from other accounting (hereinafter referred to as "Special Insurance Accounts") for each Bankrupt Insurance Company pertaining to the Underwriting of Insurance Contracts.

(Abolition of Special Insurance Accounts)
Article 265-41 (1) A Corporation shall, in the case where it has underwritten insurance contracts pertaining to a Bankrupt Insurance Company that is its member, abolish the Special Insurance Account established for said Bankrupt Insurance Company when there is no longer a need to manage any of the insurance contracts pertaining to the Underwriting of Insurance Contracts due to termination, transfer, or any other reason.
(2) The Corporation shall, when it has abolished a Special Insurance Account under the provisions of the preceding paragraph, vest the property and debt belonging to said Special Insurance Account to a general account (meaning accounts other than the Corporation's Special Insurance Accounts (including Special Accounts prescribed in Article 118, paragraph (1) as applied by deeming the Corporation as an Insurance Company pursuant to the provisions of Article 270-6, paragraph (2)); the same shall apply in Article 270-5)).

(Borrowings)
Article 265-42 A Corporation may, when it finds it necessary for conducting Financial Assistance Services, etc. , receive the approval of the Prime Minister and Minister of Finance and borrow funds (including refinancing), within the amount specified by a Cabinet Order, from an Insurance Company or financial institution specified by a Cabinet Office Ordinance or Ordinance of the Ministry of Finance.

(Government Guarantee)
Article 265-42-2 The government may guarantee an obligation pertaining to the borrowing set forth in the preceding Article of a Life Insurance Policyholders Protection Corporation within the amount approved by a Diet resolution, notwithstanding the provisions of Article 3 of the Act on Limitations of Government Financial Assistance to Juridical Persons (Act No. 24 of 1946).

(Investment of Surplus Funds)
Article 265-43 Surplus funds occurring in the course of business of a Corporation, ex-

cluding those belonging to Special Insurance Accounts, shall be invested by the following methods:
(i) Retention in national government bonds or any other securities designated by the Prime Minister and Minister of Finance;
(ii) Deposit in financial institutions designated by the Prime Minister and Minister of Finance;
(iii) Any other method specified by a Cabinet Office Ordinance or Ordinance of the Ministry of Finance.

(Delegation to Cabinet Office Ordinance or Ordinance of the Ministry of Finance)
Article 265-44 The particulars that are necessary to a Corporation's finances and accounting, in addition to what is provided for in Article 265-36 to the preceding Article inclusive, shall be specified by a Cabinet Office Ordinance or Ordinance of the Ministry of Finance.

Division 9 Supervision

(Supervision)
Article 265-45 (1) The Corporation shall be supervised by the Prime Minister and Minister of Finance.
(2) The Prime Minister and Minister of Finance may, when they find it necessary for the enforcement of the provisions of this Section, issue orders necessary for supervision to a Corporation.
(3) The Prime Minister and Minister of Finance may, when an officer of a Corporation engages in conduct that violates this Act, orders based on this Act or dispositions based on these, or the articles of incorporation or business rules, order said Corporation to dismiss that officer. In this case, when the Corporation has dismissed said officer after obtaining a resolution of the General Council, that dismissal shall take effect when the General Representative Members' Council has reached a resolution, notwithstanding the provisions of Article 265-15, paragraph (2).

(Report and On-Site Inspections)
Article 265-46 The Prime Minister and Minister of Finance may, within the limit necessary for the enforcement of the provisions of this Section, order a Corporation to submit a report or material related to its business or property, or have their officials enter the Corporation's office and inspect the state of its business or property or its books and documents or any other objects, or have such officials question the relevant persons.

(Rescission of Establishment Approval)
Article 265-47 The Prime Minister and Minister of Finance may, when a Corporation falls under any of the following items, rescind the approval of incorporation set forth in Article 265-9, paragraph (2):
(i) When it has violated this Act, orders based on this Act or the articles of incorporation or business rules of said Corporation;
(ii) When it has violated dispositions under the provisions of Article 265-30, paragraph (3) or Article 265-45, paragraph (2) or the first sentence of paragraph (3);
(iii) When it is found that the continuation of its business would be difficult due to the state of its business or property;
(iv) When it has engaged in conduct that harms the public interest.

Division 10 Miscellaneous Provisions

(Dissolution)
Article 265-48 (1) A Corporation shall dissolve due to the following reasons:
  (i) The resolution of the General Representative Members' Council;
  (ii) Rescission of approval of incorporation under the provisions of the preceding Article.
(2) Dissolution under the reason given in item (i) of the preceding paragraph shall be null and void without the approval of the Prime Minister and Minister of Finance.
(3) A Corporation shall, when there are residual assets after it has performed its obligations in the case of dissolution, vest said residual assets, pursuant to the provisions of a Cabinet Office Ordinance or Ordinance of the Ministry of Finance, in the other Corporations that its members join.
(4) Requisite measures related to the dissolution of a Corporation, in addition to what is provided for in the preceding paragraph, may be specified by a Cabinet Order, within the scope deemed reasonably necessary.

Subsection 2 Financial Assistance, etc.

Division 1 Petitions for Financial Assistance, etc.

(Petitions for Financial Assistance for the Transfer, etc. of Insurance Contracts)
Article 266 (1) The Relief Insurance Company or the Relief Insurance Holding Company, etc. may, in conjunction with a Bankrupt Insurance Company, petition the Corporation with which that Bankrupt Insurance Company is affiliated as a member (hereinafter referred to as "Affiliated Corporation" in this and the following Subsections) to extend Financial Assistance with regard to the transfer, etc. of insurance contracts.
(2) An Affiliated Corporation may, when it finds it necessary in the case referred to in the preceding paragraph, request the Relief Insurance Company or the Relief Insurance Holding Company, etc. that made the petition under that paragraph, and the Bankrupt Insurance Company or other relevant persons, for the submission of materials.
(3) Within the Financial Assistance prescribed in paragraph (1), the purchase of the property shall be conducted pertaining to the property of the Bankrupt Insurance Company pertaining to the transfer, etc. of insurance contracts.

(Petition Related to the Succession, etc. to Insurance Contracts)
Article 267 (1) If the transfer, etc. of insurance contracts is one that has been specified as being difficult by a Cabinet Office Ordinance and Ordinance of the Ministry of Finance on the grounds such as that there is no prospect of finding a Relief Insurance Company or Relief Insurance Holding Company, etc. , a Bankrupt Insurance Company may petition its Affiliated Corporation to succeed in a Succession to Insurance Contracts or Underwriting of Insurance Contracts (hereinafter referred to as "Succession, etc. to Insurance Contracts"), to .
(2) A Bankrupt Insurance Company shall, in the case of making the petition under the preceding paragraph, submit, to its Affiliated Corporation, materials which illustrate the content of the negotiation with other Insurance Companies or Insurance Holding Companies, etc. on the transfer, etc. of insurance contracts, and other materials specified by a Cabinet Office Ordinance and Ordinance of the Ministry of Finance.
(3) A Bankrupt Insurance Company may, when petitioning for the Succession of Insurance

Contracts under the provisions of paragraph (1), also petition the Affiliated Corporation to extend it Financial Assistance with regard to the Succession of Insurance Contracts (limited to donations of money or purchase of property).

(4) The provisions of paragraphs (2) and (3) of the preceding Article shall apply mutatis mutandis to the Financial Assistance of the preceding paragraph. In this case, the term "the Relief Insurance Company or the Relief Insurance Holding Company, etc. that filed the application in that paragraph, and the Bankrupt Insurance Company" in paragraph (2) of that Article shall be deemed to be replaced with "the Bankrupt Insurance Company."

(Authorization of Eligibility for the Transfer, etc. of Insurance Contracts)

Article 268 (1) In the case referred to in Article 266, paragraph (1), the Bankrupt Insurance Company and Relief Insurance Company, or the Bankrupt Insurance Company and Relief Insurance Holding Company, etc. which carry out the transfer, etc. of insurance contracts shall obtain the authorization of the Prime Minister for the transfer, etc. of insurance contracts by the time that the petition under that paragraph is made.

(2) The application for authorization of the preceding paragraph shall be filed jointly by the Bankrupt Insurance Company and Relief Insurance Company or Bankrupt Insurance Company and Relief Insurance Holding Company, etc. set forth in that paragraph.

(3) The Prime Minister may grant the authorization under paragraph (1), only in cases that fall under all of the following requirements:
  (i) The transfer, etc. of insurance contracts contributes to the protection of Policyholders, etc. ;
  (ii) The extension of Financial Assistance by the Affiliated Corporation is indispensable to the smooth implementation of the transfer, etc. of insurance contracts; and
  (iii) There is a risk of loss of credibility in the Insurance Business in the case that all of the business of the Bankrupt Insurance Company pertaining to the transfer, etc. of insurance contracts are abolished or the Bankrupt Insurance Company is dissolved, without a transfer of insurance contracts, etc.

(4) If the Prime Minister has given the authorization under paragraph (1), he/she shall notify the Affiliated Corporation of this.

(5) If an Affiliated Corporation receives a notice under the provisions of the preceding paragraph, it shall promptly report this to the Minister of Finance.

(6) If a company attempting to acquire shares of a Bankrupt Insurance Company has filed an application for approval under Article 271-18, paragraph (1) to acquire shares and become a Holding Company whose Subsidiaries include an Insurance Company (hereinafter referred to as "Holding Company Approval" in this paragraph), the Prime Minister may not give the authorization under the provisions of paragraph (1) until after Holding Company Approval has been given for that company.

(Special Provisions on Authorization of Eligibility for the Transfer, etc. of Insurance Contracts)

Article 269 (1) The Prime Minister may, only in cases that fall under all of the following requirements, make a supplementary note in the recommendation of Article 256, paragraph (1), notwithstanding the provisions of paragraph (1) of the preceding Article, that the petition under Article 266, paragraph (1) may be made:
  (i) The abolition of all business of a Bankrupt Insurance Company or the dissolution of the Bankrupt Insurance Company pertaining to the recommendation of Article 256, paragraph (1) falls under the requirements listed in paragraph (3), item (iii) of the preceding Article; and
  (ii) The extension of Financial Assistance by the Affiliated Corporation is indispens-

able to the transfer, etc. of insurance contracts pertaining to said recommendation.
(2) The provisions of paragraphs (4) and (5) of the preceding Article shall apply mutatis mutandis to cases in which the supplementary note of the preceding paragraph was made.

(Authorization of Eligibility for Succession, etc. to Insurance Contracts)
Article 270 (1) In the case referred to in Article 267, paragraph (1), the Bankrupt Insurance Company shall obtain the authorization of the Prime Minister in regard to the Succession, etc. to Insurance Contracts of that paragraph by the time that the petition under that paragraph is made.
(2) The Prime Minister may give the authorization of the preceding paragraph, only in cases that fall under all of the following requirements:
   (i) The Succession, etc. to Insurance Contracts contributes to the protection of Policyholders, etc. ;
   (ii) There is a risk that without the Succession, etc. to Insurance Contracts, the Insurance Business would lose credibility in the event that all of the business of the Bankrupt Insurance Company that is petitioning the Affiliated Corporation for the Succession, etc. to Insurance Contracts were abolished or if the Bankrupt Insurance Company were dissolved,; and
   (iii) In the case that petition is made for Financial Assistance under the provisions of Article 267, paragraph (3), the extension of said Financial Assistance is indispensable to the smooth implementation of the Succession of Insurance Contracts.
(3) If the Prime Minister has given the authorization under paragraph (1), he/she shall notify the Affiliated Corporation of this.
(4) If an Affiliated Corporation receives a notice under the provisions of the preceding paragraph, it shall promptly report this to the Minister of Finance.

(Evaluation of the Property of a Bankrupt Insurance Company)
Article 270-2 (1) A Bankrupt Insurance Company making the petition under Article 266, paragraph (1) or Article 267, paragraph (1) shall seek the confirmation of the Affiliated Corporation regarding the appropriateness of the evaluation the company made of its property (for a Foreign Insurance Company, etc., property in Japan; hereinafter the same shall apply in this Subsection) without delay at the same time that the petition was made or after the petition was made (referred to as "Property Self-Evaluation" in the next paragraph and paragraph (4)).
(2) If an Affiliated Corporation determines, after discussion by the Examination Board, that the Property Self-Evaluation for which confirmation under the preceding paragraph is being sought is appropriate, it shall notify the Bankrupt Insurance Company which requested this that the Property Self-Evaluation has been confirmed as appropriate.
(3) If an Affiliated Corporation finds it necessary for making a determination under the preceding paragraph, it may conduct an examination to evaluate the property of the Bankrupt Insurance Company that made said request.
(4) If an Affiliated Corporation determines, after discussion by the Examination Board, that the Property Self-Evaluation for which confirmation under paragraph (1) is being sought is not appropriate, it shall notify the Bankrupt Insurance Company which made the relevant request of this, and shall conduct an examination to evaluate the property of that Bankrupt Insurance Company.
(5) After confirming that the evaluation based on the examination under the provisions of the preceding paragraph is appropriate and after discussion by the Examination Board, the Affiliated Corporation shall notify the Bankrupt Insurance Company that made the

relevant request of the content of the evaluation.
(6) If an Affiliated Corporation has made a notification under paragraph (2) or the preceding paragraph, it shall immediately report the particulars of the notification to the Prime Minister and Minister of Finance.

(Financial Assistance for the Transfer, etc. of Insurance Contracts)
Article 270-3 (1) After making a notification under paragraph (2) or paragraph (5) of the preceding Article to the Bankrupt Insurance Company which filed the petition under Article 266, paragraph (1), Affiliated Corporation shall make a decision without delay, after discussion by the Committee, on whether to extend the Financial Assistance pertaining to said petition.
(2) The amount of the Financial Assistance under the provisions of the preceding paragraph (limited to donation of money) shall be an amount equivalent to that calculated by adding the amount listed in item (iii) to the amount remaining after the deduction of the amount listed in item (ii) from the amount listed in item (i) with regard to the Bankrupt Insurance Company to which said Financial Assistance pertains:
  (i) With regard to a Bankrupt Insurance Company's insurance contracts that fall under the category of insurance contract specified by a Cabinet Office Ordinance and Ordinance of the Ministry of Finance (hereinafter referred to as a "Covered Insurance Contract"), the amount specified by a Cabinet Office Ordinance and Ordinance of the Ministry of Finance as the liability that must be saved for allocation to the payment of Insurance Proceeds, etc. and for policy reserves (referred to as "Specified Policy Reserves, etc." in the following item and Article 270-5, paragraph (2)) multiplied by the rate specified by a Cabinet Office Ordinance and Ordinance of the Ministry of Finance by taking into consideration the kind of Covered Insurance Contract, expected interest rate, other content, etc. ;
  (ii) The amount of the asset value of that Bankrupt Insurance Company -- based on the evaluation of property confirmed under the provisions of paragraph (2) or paragraph (5) of the preceding Article (referred to as "Confirmed Evaluation of Property" in Article 270-5, paragraph (2)) -- which has been calculated as per Cabinet Office Ordinance and Ordinance of the Ministry of Finance as being the amount which corresponds to the Specified Policy Reserve, etc. pertaining to the Covered Insurance Contract; and
  (iii) The amount of expense, which has been approved by the Affiliated Corporation as being necessary for the smooth transfer, etc. of the insurance contracts pertaining to said Financial Assistance, among the expenses that fall under those specified by a Cabinet Office Ordinance and Ordinance of the Ministry of Finance as expenses which are deemed necessary for the transfer, etc. of insurance contracts pertaining to that Bankrupt Insurance Company.
(3) The Affiliated Corporation shall, when it has made the decision under paragraph (1), immediately report the particulars specified by Cabinet Office Ordinance and Ordinance of the Ministry of Finance, as those related to the decision, to the Prime Minister and Minister of Finance.
(4) The Affiliated Corporation shall, when it makes a decision to extend Financial Assistance under the provisions of paragraph (1), conclude a contract concerning said Financial Assistance with the Insurance Company or Insurance Holding Company, etc. that petitioned for said Financial Assistance, and that is to be the party to said Financial Assistance.
(5) When damage security is included in the Financial Assistance pertaining to the contract of the preceding paragraph, the Relief Insurance Company or the Relief Insurance Holding Company, etc. pertaining to that contract, under that contract, shall, if

profits are accrued from the assets pertaining to said damage security, commit in that contract that it shall pay all or part of said profits to the Affiliated Corporation pertaining to that contract, or, as one that will have said assets from the transfer, etc. of insurance contracts, to take measures for making payment to the Affiliated Corporation pertaining to that contract.

Division 2 Succession of Insurance Contracts

(Succession of Insurance Contracts)
Article 270-3-2 (1) The Affiliated Corporation may, when it finds it necessary in the case of receiving a petition on the Succession of Insurance Contracts under the provisions of Article 267, paragraph (1), make a request that the Prime Minister take the measures under the provisions of Article 256, paragraph (1) be taken before making the decisions listed in items (i) and (ii) of paragraph (6) pertaining to said petition.
(2) The Prime Minister shall, without delay, notify the Affiliated Corporation, when the measures under the provisions of Article 256, paragraph (1) pursuant to the provisions of the preceding paragraph are requested, of whether said measures may be taken, and, in the case that said measures are to be taken, of the content of those measures.
(3) The Affiliated Corporation shall, when the content of the notification of the Prime Minister under the provisions of the preceding paragraph is to the effect that the measures under the provisions of Article 256, paragraph (1) are to be taken, stay the implementation of the procedure pertaining to the decision listed in paragraph (6), items (i) and (ii); provided, however, that this shall not apply to the confirmation procedures under the provisions of Article 270-2.
(4) In the case that the Prime Minister takes the measures under the provisions of Article 256, paragraph (1) the Bankrupt Insurance Company which petitioned for the Succession of Insurance Contracts under the provisions of Article 267, paragraph (1) shall, when that Bankrupt Insurance Company has reached an agreement pertaining to Merger, etc. , without delay, withdraw said petition.
(5) In the case prescribed in the preceding paragraph, when no agreement pertaining to Merger, etc. is reached, the Bankrupt Insurance Company of that paragraph shall, without delay, notify the Affiliated Corporation of this.
(6) The Affiliated Corporation shall, when it finds it unnecessary to make the request under the provisions of paragraph (1) of the Prime Minister, when the content of the notification of the Prime Minister under the provisions of paragraph (2) is to the effect that the measures under the provisions of Article 256, paragraph (1) cannot be taken, or when the notification under the provisions of the preceding paragraph is made, promptly, after discussion by the Committee, make the decision listed in items (i) and (ii) pertaining to the petition under paragraph (1) or the decision listed in item (ii):
  (i) Ruling to the effect that the Affiliated Corporation will incorporate, as its Subsidiary, the Successor Insurance Company, which will carry out a transfer of insurance contracts from the Bankrupt Insurance Company or merge with that company to take over the insurance contracts from that company; and
  (ii) Ruling to the effect that the Successor Insurance Company shall carry out a transfer of insurance contracts from the Bankrupt Insurance Company or merge with that company to take over the insurance contracts from that company.
(7) The Affiliated Corporation shall, when making a decision under the preceding paragraph on the Succession of Insurance Contracts pertaining to a petition it has received under Article 267, paragraph (3), also make a decision, after discussion by the Committee, on whether to extend the Financial Assistance pertaining to said petition.
(8) The provisions of paragraph (2) of the preceding Article shall apply mutatis mutandis

to the amount of Financial Assistance under the provisions of the preceding paragraph (limited to donation of money), the provisions of paragraph (3) of that Article shall apply mutatis mutandis in the case that the Affiliated Corporation makes a decision under the preceding two paragraphs, and the provisions of paragraph (4) of that Article shall apply mutatis mutandis in the case that the Affiliated Corporation makes a decision to extend Financial Assistance pursuant to the provisions of the preceding paragraph. In this case, the term "transfer, etc. of insurance contracts" in paragraph (2) of that Article shall be deemed to be replaced with "Succession of Insurance Contracts," and the term "Insurance Company or Insurance Holding Company, etc. which filed the application for said Financial Assistance that becomes the party of said Financial Assistance" in paragraph (4) of that Article shall be deemed to be replaced with "Bankrupt Insurance Company which filed the application for said Financial Assistance."
(9) The Bankrupt Insurance Company that has made a petition under paragraph (1) may, when the Affiliated Corporation makes a decision listed in paragraph (6), items (i) or (ii), transfer all or part of the insurance contracts to the Successor Insurance Company pertaining to the decision, or may merge with that company.

(Incorporation of Successor Insurance Company, etc.)
Article 270-3-3 (1) The Affiliated Corporation shall, when it makes a decision listed in paragraph (6), item (i) of the preceding Article, after discussion by the Committee on the content of the contribution pertaining to the decision, become the incorporator for the incorporation of the Stock Company which will be the Successor Insurance Company, and make a contribution for the incorporation of the Stock Company, of which it became the incorporator for said incorporation, as its Subsidiary.
(2) In addition to the case prescribed in the preceding paragraph, the Affiliated Corporation shall, when it seeks to make a contribution to the Successor Insurance Company, go through Committee discussions thereon.
(3) The Affiliated Corporation shall, when it makes the contribution prescribed in the preceding two paragraphs, promptly report the content of the contribution to the Prime Minister and Minister of Finance about the content.

(Managing the Successor Insurance Company)
Article 270-3-4 (1) A Corporation shall manage a Successor Insurance Company (limited to those incorporated by said Corporation; hereinafter the same shall apply in this Article, Article 270-3-6, and Article 270-3-10) to enable its optimal implementation of the following particulars:
  (i) When the decision listed in Article 270-3-2, paragraph (6), item (ii) is made, the transfer of insurance contracts or merger shall be carried out to take over the insurance contracts from the Bankrupt Insurance Company that was the subject of the decision; and
  (ii) In managing and disposing the insurance contracts or in implementing other business, these shall be carried out in accordance with the guidelines specified in the following paragraph.
(2) A Corporation shall create guidelines on the management and disposition of the insurance contracts of a Successor Insurance Company and other business, and, upon obtaining the approval of the Prime Minister, make the guidelines public.
(3) A Corporation may offer any guidance and advice necessary for the management of a Successor Insurance Company.
(4) If a Corporation assigns the shares of a Successor Insurance Company or makes other dispositions, it shall promptly report this to the Prime Minister and Minister of Finance.

(Non-Application of Article 467 of the Companies Act)
Article 270-3-5 The provisions of Article 467, paragraph (1), item (v) of the Companies Act (Approvals of Assignment of Business) shall not apply to the property confirmed under the provisions of Article 270-2, paragraph (2) or Article 270-2, paragraph (5), in the case that the Corporation owns all of the issued shares of the Successor Insurance Company.

(Succession Agreements)
Article 270-3-6 (1) A Corporation shall conclude an agreement with a Successor Insurance Company that includes the following particulars (hereinafter referred to as "Succession Agreement"):
  (i) That the Successor Insurance Company with which the Succession Agreement has been concluded (hereinafter referred to as "Successor Insurance Company Under the Agreement") is to set in place the particulars listed in Article 270-3-4, paragraph (1), items (i) and (ii);
  (ii) The Successor Insurance Company Under the Agreement may petition the Corporation to purchase the assets of that Successor Insurance Company Under the Agreement; and
  (iii) The Successor Insurance Company Under the Agreement shall, when it seeks to conclude a contract concerning the borrowing of the funds that fall under the guaranteed obligation prescribed in Article 270-3-8, paragraph (1), obtain the approval of the Corporation on the content of that contract to be concluded.
(2) A Corporation shall, when it concludes a Succession Agreement, immediately report the content of the agreement to the Prime Minister and Minister of Finance.

(Purchase of Property)
Article 270-3-7 (1) A Corporation shall, when it receives a petition under paragraph (1), item (ii) of the preceding Article, make a decision, after discussion by the Examination Board and the Committee, on whether to purchase the property pertaining to said petition, without delay.
(2) A Corporation shall, when it makes a decision under the provisions of the preceding paragraph, immediately report to the Prime Minister and Minister of Finance the particulars of the decision.
(3) A Corporation shall, when it makes a decision to purchase the property under the provisions of paragraph (1), conclude a contract concerning the purchase of the property with the Successor Insurance Company Under the Agreement that petitioned for the purchase of the property.

(Loans of Funds and Obligation Guarantee)
Article 270-3-8 (1) For loans of funds that the Successor Insurance Company Under the Agreement finds to be necessary for the smooth implementation of business, the Corporation may, upon petition by the Successor Insurance Company Under the Agreement for a loan of such funds or upon petition to guarantee an obligation pertaining to the borrowing of the funds by the Successor Insurance Company Under the Agreement, after discussions by the Committee, extend said loan or guarantee said obligation when it recognizes these as being necessary.
(2) A Corporation shall, when it concludes a contract pertaining to the loan or guarantee of obligation under the preceding paragraph with the Successor Insurance Company Under the Agreement pursuant to the provisions of that paragraph, immediately report to the Prime Minister and Minister of Finance the content of the contract.

(Compensation for Losses)

Article 270-3-9 A Corporation may, when an amount has been accounted for pursuant to what is specified by a Cabinet Order for the amount of loss accrued by the Successor Insurance Company Under the Agreement by the implementation of business under the specifications of the Succession Agreement, give compensation for said losses, after discussions by the Committee, within the scope of that amount.

(Request for Reporting)

Article 270-3-10 A Corporation may, when it is necessary in order for it to conduct the business under the provisions of this Division, request a Successor Insurance Company to report on the status of the implementation of the Succession Agreement or on finances.

(Petitions for Financial Assistance for Succession to Inherited Insurance Contracts)

Article 270-3-11 (1) The Secondary Successor Insurance Company or Secondary Successor Insurance Holding Company, etc. (meaning Insurance Holding Companies, etc. that succeed in the Succession to Inherited Insurance Contracts; the same shall apply hereinafter) may petition the Corporation that incorporated the Successor Insurance Company pertaining to the inherited insurance contracts to be succeeded to (hereinafter referred to as "Incorporating Corporation") to jointly extend Financial Assistance for Succession to Inherited Insurance Contracts (limited to damage security) with the Successor Insurance Company.

(2) The Incorporating Corporation may, when it finds it necessary in the case referred to in the preceding paragraph, request the Secondary Successor Insurance Company or Secondary Successor Insurance Holding Company, etc. , which made the petition under that paragraph, and the Successor Insurance Company and other relevant persons to submit materials.

(Authorization, etc. of Eligibility for Succession to Inherited Insurance Contracts)

Article 270-3-12 (1) In the case referred to in paragraph (1) of the preceding Article, the Successor Insurance Company and Secondary Successor Insurance Company, which implement the Succession to Inherited Insurance Contracts, or the Successor Insurance Company and Secondary Successor Insurance Holding Company, etc. , shall obtain the authorization of the Prime Minister for the Succession to Inherited Insurance Contracts by the time that the petition under that paragraph is made.

(2) The provisions of Article 268, paragraph (2) to Article 268, paragraph (6) inclusive (except for paragraph (3), item (iii)) shall apply mutatis mutandis to the authorization of the preceding paragraph. In this case, the term "Bankrupt Insurance Company and Relief Insurance Company or Bankrupt Insurance Company and Relief Insurance Holding Company, etc." in paragraph (2) of that Article shall be deemed to be replaced with "Successor Insurance Company and Secondary Successor Insurance Company or Successor Insurance Company and Secondary Successor Insurance Holding Company, etc.," the term "transfer, etc. of insurance contract" in paragraph (3) of that Article shall be deemed to be replaced with "Succession to Inherited Insurance Contracts," the term "Affiliated Corporation" shall be deemed to be replaced with "Incorporating Corporation," the term "Affiliated Corporation" in paragraphs (4) and (5) of that Article shall be deemed to be replaced with "Incorporating Corporation," and the term "Bankrupt Insurance Company" in paragraph (6) of that Article shall be deemed to be

Art.270-3-13〜270-3-14　⑥ Insurance Business Act, Part II, Chap.X, Sec.4

replaced with "Successor Insurance Company."
(3) The provisions of Article 270-2 shall apply mutatis mutandis to cases in which a petition under paragraph (1) of the preceding Article is made. In this case, the term "Bankrupt Insurance Company" in Article 270-2 shall be deemed to be replaced with "Successor Insurance Company," the term "Affiliated Corporation" shall be deemed to be replaced with "Incorporating Corporation," and the term "its property (for a Foreign Insurance Company, etc., property in Japan; hereinafter the same shall apply in this Subsection)" in paragraph (1) of that Article shall be deemed to be replaced with "its property."

(Designation of the Other Party to Consultations on Succession to Inherited Insurance Contracts, etc.)
Article 270-3-13 (1) The Prime Minister may designate another Insurance Company or Insurance Holding Company, etc. as the other party with which the Successor Insurance Company shall hold a consultation pertaining to Succession to Inherited Insurance Contracts and recommend that other Insurance Company or Insurance Holding Company, etc. to participate in the consultation.
(2) The provisions of Article 256, paragraphs (2) and (3) and Article 257 shall apply mutatis mutandis to the recommendation of the preceding paragraph. In this case, the term "Bankrupt Insurance Company or an Insurance Company recognized as having a high probability of becoming a Bankrupt Insurance Company" in Article 256, paragraph (2) shall be deemed to be replaced with "Successor Insurance Company of that paragraph," the term "Policyholders Protection Corporation to which a Bankrupt Insurance Company or the Insurance Company that is recognized as having a high probability of becoming a Bankrupt Insurance Company has joined as a member" in Article 256, paragraph (3) shall be deemed to be replaced with "Policyholders Protection Corporation which incorporated the Successor Insurance Company of Article 270-3-13, paragraph (1)," and the term "Bankrupt Insurance Company" in Article 257, paragraph (1) shall be deemed to be replaced with "Successor Insurance Company."
(3) The Prime Minister may, only when he/she finds that the extension of Financial Assistance by the Incorporating Corporation is indispensable for Succession to Inherited Insurance Contracts pertaining to the recommendation of paragraph (1), make a supplementary note in said recommendation, notwithstanding the provisions of paragraph (1) of the preceding Article, that a petition under Article 270-3-11, paragraph (1) may be made.
(4) The provisions of Article 268, paragraph (4) and Article 268, paragraph (5) shall apply mutatis mutandis to the case that the supplementary note of the preceding paragraph is made.

(Financial Assistance in the Succession to Inherited Insurance Contracts)
Article 270-3-14 (1) The Incorporating Corporation shall, without delay after making the notification under Article 270-2, paragraph (2) or (5), as applied mutatis mutandis pursuant to Article 270-3-12, paragraph (3) to the Successor Insurance Company which made the petition under Article 270-3-11, paragraph (1), make a decision, after discussion by the Committee, on whether to extend the Financial Assistance pertaining to said petition.
(2) The provisions of Article 270-3, paragraph (3) shall apply mutatis mutandis in the case that the Incorporating Corporation makes the decision under the preceding paragraph, the provisions of paragraph (4) of that Article shall apply mutatis mutandis in the case that the Incorporating Corporation makes a decision to extend Financial Assistance pursuant to the provisions of the preceding paragraph, and the provisions of paragraph

(5) of that Article shall apply mutatis mutandis to the Secondary Successor Insurance Company or Secondary Successor Insurance Holding Company, etc. which concludes the contract of paragraph (4) of that Article, as applied mutatis mutandis pursuant to this paragraph. In this case, the term "transfer, etc. of insurance contracts" in paragraph (5) of that Article shall be deemed to be replaced with "Succession to Inherited Insurance Contracts," and the term "Affiliated Corporation" shall be deemed to be replaced with "Incorporating Corporation."

Division 3 Underwriting of Insurance Contract

(Underwriting of Insurance Contracts)
Article 270-4 (1) The Affiliated Corporation may, when it finds it necessary in the case of receiving a petition for underwriting for the insurance contracts under the provisions of Article 267, paragraph (1), make request the Prime Minister that the measures under the provisions of Article 256, paragraph (1) be taken before underwriting the insurance contracts pertaining to said petition.
(2) The Prime Minister shall, without delay, notify the Affiliated Corporation, when the measures under the provisions of Article 256, paragraph (1) pursuant to the provisions of the preceding paragraph are requested, of whether said measures may be taken, and, in the case that said measures are to be taken, of the content of those measures.
(3) The Affiliated Corporation shall, when the content of the notification of the Prime Minister under the provisions of the preceding paragraph is to the effect that the measures under the provisions of Article 256, paragraph (1) shall be taken, stay the implementation of the procedure pertaining to the Underwriting of Insurance Contracts; provided, however, that this shall not apply to the confirmation procedure under the provisions of Article 270-2.
(4) In the case that the Prime Minister takes the measures under the provisions of Article 256, paragraph (1) under the provisions of paragraph (1), the Bankrupt Insurance Company which applied for the Underwriting of Insurance Contracts under the provisions of Article 267, paragraph (1) shall, when that Bankrupt Insurance Company has reached an agreement pertaining to a Merger, etc. , withdraw said petition without delay.
(5) In the case prescribed in the preceding paragraph, when no agreement pertaining to Merger, etc. is reached, the Bankrupt Insurance Company under that paragraph shall, without delay, notify the Affiliated Corporation of this.
(6) The Affiliated Corporation shall, when it finds it unnecessary to make the request under the provisions of paragraph (1) to the Prime Minister, when the content of the notification of the Prime Minister under the provisions of paragraph (2) is to the effect that the measures under the provisions of Article 256, paragraph (1) cannot be taken, or when the notification under the provisions of the preceding paragraph is made, promptly, after discussion by the Committee, make a decision listed in items (i) and (ii) pertaining to the petition under paragraph (1) or the decision listed in item (ii).
(7) The provisions of Article 270-3, paragraph (3) shall apply mutatis mutandis to the case that the Affiliated Corporation makes the decision under the preceding paragraph.
(8) The Bankrupt Insurance Company pertaining to the petition under paragraph (1) may, when the Affiliated Corporation makes a decision under the provisions of paragraph (6), transfer all or part of the relevant insurance contracts to said Affiliated Corporation pursuant to the contract with the Affiliated Corporation concerning the Underwriting of Insurance Contracts.
(9) The provisions of Article 135, paragraphs (2) to (4) inclusive, Article 136 to 140 inclusive, Article 155, Article 210, and Article 250 to 253 inclusive shall apply mutatis mu-

Art.270-5〜270-5　⑥ Insurance Business Act, Part II, Chap.X, Sec.4

tandis to the transfer of insurance contracts from the Bankrupt Insurance Company pertaining to the Underwriting of Insurance Contracts to the Affiliated Corporation. In this case, the term "paragraph (1)" in Article 135, paragraphs (3) and (4) shall be deemed to be replaced with "Article 270-4, paragraph (8)," the term "paragraph (1) of the preceding Article" "Transferor Company and the Transferee Company (other than a Foreign Insurance Company, etc.)," and "hereinafter in this Chapter, as well as in Chapter VIII and X" in Article 136, paragraph (1) shall be deemed to be replaced with "Article 270-4, paragraph (8)," "Transferor Company," and "Article 250, paragraph (4)," respectively. The term "Transferor Company and the Transferee Company" and "paragraph (1) of the preceding Article," in Article 136, paragraph (3) shall be deemed to be replaced with "Transferor Company" and "Article 270-4, paragraph (8)," respectively. The term "Article 135, paragraph (1)" and "Transferee Company" in Article 137, paragraph (1) shall be deemed to be replaced with "Article 270-4, paragraph (8)" and "Policyholders Protection Corporation of which that Insurance Company is a member (referred to as "Affiliated Corporation" in Articles 140, 155 and 252)," respectively. The term "the following standards" in Article 139, paragraph (2) shall be deemed to be replaced with "standards listed in items (i) and (iii)." The terms "Transferee Company," "Article 135, paragraph (1)," and "Article 135, paragraph (4)" in Article 140, paragraph (2) shall be deemed to be replaced with "Affiliated Corporation," "Article 270-4, paragraph (8)," and "Article 135, paragraph (4) as applied mutatis mutandis pursuant to paragraph (9) of that Article," respectively. The terms "Article 135, paragraph (1)" and "Transferee Company" in Article 140, paragraph (3) shall be deemed to be replaced with "Article 270-4, paragraph (8)" and "Affiliated Corporation," respectively. The term "minutes of the Shareholders' Meeting, etc. of the Transferee Company (other than a Foreign Insurance Company, etc.) set forth in Article 135, paragraph (1) (including the cases where it is applied mutatis mutandis pursuant to Article 272-29)" in Article 155, item (i) shall be deemed to be replaced with "minutes of the General Council of Affiliated Corporation." The term "written agreement concluded under Article 135, paragraph (1) (hereinafter referred to as "Transfer Agreement" in this Section)" in Article 210, paragraph (1) shall be deemed to be replaced with "contract concluded under Article 270-4, paragraph (8) (hereinafter referred to as "Transfer Contract" in this Section)." The term "Article 135, paragraph (1) (including the cases where it is applied mutatis mutandis pursuant to Article 210, paragraph (1) and Article 272-29)," "Article 268, paragraph (1) or Article 270, paragraph (1)," and "Relief Insurance Company as prescribed in Article 260, paragraph (3)" in Article 250, paragraph (1) shall be deemed to be replaced with "Article 270-4, paragraph (8)," "Article 270, paragraph (1)," and "Policyholders Protection Corporation of which that Bankrupt Insurance Company is a member," respectively. The term "Article 135, paragraph (1)" in Article 250, paragraph (4) shall be deemed to be replaced with "Article 270-4, paragraph (8)." The terms "Article 135, paragraph (1) (including the cases where it is applied mutatis mutandis pursuant to Article 210, paragraph (1) and Article 272-29; hereinafter the same shall apply in this Article)" and "Transferee Company prescribed in Article 135, paragraph (1)" in Article 252 shall be deemed to be replaced with "Article 270-4, paragraph (8)" and "Affiliated Corporation," respectively. Any other technical change in interpretation required shall be specified by a Cabinet Order.

(Transfer to Special Insurance Account pertaining to Underwriting of Insurance Contracts, etc.)

Article 270-5 (1) The Affiliated Corporation shall, when it underwrites the insurance contracts pursuant to the provisions of the preceding Article, incorporate the property of the Bankrupt Insurance Company pertaining to the Underwriting of Insurance Contracts, which it inherited with the transfer of insurance contracts pertaining to the Underwriting of Insurance Contracts, into the Special Insurance Account created for the purpose of that Bankrupt Insurance Company.

(2) The Affiliated Corporation shall, when it underwrites the insurance contracts pursuant to the provisions of the preceding Article, transfer, from the general account to the Special Insurance Account created for the purpose of that Bankrupt Insurance Company, the amount equivalent to the amount remaining after the deduction of the amount listed in item (ii) from the amount listed in item (i) with regard to the Bankrupt Insurance Company pertaining to said assumption of insurance contracts:

(i) The amount of Specified Policy Reserve, etc. pertaining to the Covered Insurance Contract pertaining to that Bankrupt Insurance Company, multiplied by the rate specified by a Cabinet Office Ordinance and Ordinance of the Ministry of Finance by taking into consideration the kind of that Covered Insurance Contract, expected interest rate, other content, etc. ; and

(ii) The amount of the asset value of that Bankrupt Insurance Company, based on the Confirmed Evaluation of Property, which has been calculated as per Cabinet Office Ordinance and Ordinance of the Ministry of Finance as being the amount which corresponds to the Specified Policy Reserve, etc. pertaining to the Covered Insurance Contract.

(3) The Affiliated Corporation shall, when it underwrites the insurance contracts pursuant to the provisions of the preceding Article, take over the documents of the Bankrupt Insurance Company pertaining to said assumption of insurance contracts listed in Article 4, paragraph (2), items (ii) to (iv) inclusive.

(4) The Affiliated Corporation may, when an amount has been accounted pursuant to what is specified by Cabinet Order for the amount of loss accrued by the Special Insurance Account by the implementation of business involving the Management and Disposition of Insurance Contracts pertaining to the assumption of insurance contracts under the provisions of the preceding Article (including incidental business), transfer the amount from the general account to that Special Insurance Account, after discussion by the Committee, within the scope of that amount.

(Application of this Act to Corporations Conducting Insurance Business)

Article 270-6 (1) A Corporation may, notwithstanding the provisions of Article 3, paragraph (1), conduct Insurance Business to the extent necessary for the Management and Disposition of Insurance Contracts which were transferred pursuant to the contract concerning the Underwriting of Insurance Contracts concluded under the provisions of Article 270-4, paragraph (8).

(2) The application of this Act in the case that a Corporation conducts Insurance Business pursuant to the provisions of the preceding paragraph shall be prescribed as follows:

(i) For the purpose of applying the provisions of Article 9, paragraph (1) (limited to the sections pertaining to item (i)), Article 97, Article 97-2, paragraphs (1) and (2), Article 98, Chapter V of Part II (except for Articles 109, 113, and 114), Article 123 to 125 inclusive, Article 131, Sections 1 and 3 of Chapter VII of that Part, and Article 309 (including the penal provisions pertaining to the provisions), a Corporation shall be deemed to be an Insurance Company. In this case, the term "Article 3, paragraph (2)" in Article 97, paragraph (1) shall be deemed to be replaced with "Bankrupt Insurance Company prescribed in Article 260, paragraph (2) pertaining to the assumption of insurance contracts prescribed in paragraph (9) of that Article," the term "the following business and other business" in Article 98, paragraph (1) shall be deemed to be replaced with "business listed in items (i) and (ii)," the term "board of directors" in Article 120, paragraph (1) and Article 121, paragraphs

(1) and (2) shall be deemed to be replaced with "president of the Policyholders Protection Corporation," the term "or general members' council meeting (or General Representative Members' Council Meeting, where the company has such a council) (referred to as 'Shareholders' Meeting, etc.' hereinafter in this Chapter, as well as in Chapter VIII and X)" in Article 136, paragraph (1) shall be deemed to be replaced with ", general members' council meeting (or General Representative Members' Council Meeting, where the company has such a council) or General Representative Members' Council Meeting of the Policyholders Protection Corporation (referred to as 'Shareholders' Meeting, etc.' in Article 144, paragraph (2) and Article 149, paragraph (1)," the terms "director (or, in a company with Committees, executive officers) of the Transferor Company" and "from two weeks before the date of the Shareholders' Meeting, etc. set forth in paragraph (1) of the preceding Article" in Article 136-2, paragraph (1) shall be deemed to be replaced with "director of the Policyholders Protection Corporation," and "from the date of the General Council of the Policyholders Protection Corporation of paragraph (1) of the preceding Article as applied with relevant changes in interpretation pursuant to the provisions of Article 270-6, paragraph (2), item (i)," respectively.

(ii) For the purpose of applying the provisions of Article 101 to 105 inclusive (including the penal provisions pertaining to the provisions), the Corporation shall be deemed to be a Non-Life Insurance Company in the case that the license which had been received by the Bankrupt Insurance Company pertaining to the Underwriting of Insurance Contracts, which was a member of said Corporation, falls under the Classes of License listed in Article 262, paragraph (2), item (ii); and

(iii) For the purpose of applying the provisions of Article 114, the Corporation shall be deemed to be a Stock Company that is an Insurance Company.

(3) In the case that a Corporation conducts Insurance Business pursuant to the provisions of paragraph (1), said Corporation shall, with regard to the application of the Automobile Liability Insurance Act and other laws and regulations specified by a Cabinet Order, be deemed to be an Insurance Company, or, according to the kind of membership license, a Life Insurance Company or Non-Life Insurance Company pursuant to the provisions of a Cabinet Order.

(Request for Financial Assistance in the Secondary Transfer of Insurance Contracts)

Article 270-6-2 (1) The Secondary Transferee Insurance Company may request the Corporation that underwrote the insurance contracts it seeks to have transferred pursuant to the Secondary Transfer of Insurance Contracts (hereinafter referred to as "Underwriting Corporation") to extend Financial Assistance in the Secondary Transfer of Insurance Contracts (limited to security against damages).

(2) The Underwriting Corporation may, when it finds it necessary in the case referred to in the preceding paragraph, ask the Secondary Transferee Insurance Company that made the request under that paragraph and other relevant persons to submit materials.

(Authorization of Eligibility for the Secondary Transfer of Insurance Contracts)

Article 270-6-3 (1) In the case referred to in paragraph (1) of the preceding Article, the Underwriting Corporation and the Secondary Transferee Insurance Company, which implement the Secondary Transfer of Insurance Contracts, shall obtain the authorization of the Prime Minister for the Secondary Transfer of Insurance Contracts by the time that the request under that paragraph is made.

(2) The provisions of Article 268, paragraphs (2) to (5) inclusive (except for paragraph (3), item (iii)) shall apply mutatis mutandis to the authorization of the preceding paragraph. In this case, the term "Bankrupt Insurance Company and Relief Insurance Company or Bankrupt Insurance Company and Relief Insurance Holding Company, etc." in paragraph (2) of that Article shall be deemed to be replaced with "Underwriting Corporation and Secondary Transferee Insurance Company," the term "transfer, etc. of insurance contracts" in paragraph (3) of that Article shall be deemed to be replaced with "Secondary Transfer of Insurance Contracts," the term "Affiliated Corporation" shall be deemed to be replaced with "Underwriting Corporation," and the term "Affiliated Corporation" in paragraphs (4) and (5) of that Article shall be deemed to be replaced with "Underwriting Corporation."

(Designation of Another Party to Consultations on the Secondary Transfer of Insurance Contracts, etc.)

Article 270-6-4 (1) The Prime Minister may designate an Insurance Company as the other party with which the Underwriting Corporation shall hold consultations pertaining to the Secondary Transfer of Insurance Contracts and recommend that that Insurance Company participate in the consultation.

(2) The provisions of Article 256, paragraphs (2) and (3) and Article 257 shall apply mutatis mutandis to the recommendation of the preceding paragraph. In this case, the term "Bankrupt Insurance Company or Insurance Company recognized as having a high probability of becoming a Bankrupt Insurance Company" in Article 256, paragraph (2) shall be deemed to be replaced with "Underwriting Corporation of that paragraph," the term "another Insurance Company or Insurance Holding Company, etc." shall be deemed to be replaced with "Insurance Company," the term "Bankrupt Insurance Company or Policyholders Protection Corporation which an Insurance Company that is recognized as having a high probability of becoming a Bankrupt Insurance Company has joined as a member" in Article 256, paragraph (3) shall be deemed to be replaced with "Underwriting Corporation of Article 270-6-4, paragraph (1)," the term "Bankrupt Insurance Company" in Article 257, paragraph (1) shall be deemed to be replaced with "Underwriting Corporation," and the term "other Insurance Company or Insurance Holding Company, etc." shall be deemed to be replaced with "Insurance Company."

(3) The Prime Minister may, only when he/she finds that the extension of Financial Assistance by the Underwriting Corporation is indispensable for the Secondary Transfer of Insurance Contracts pertaining to the recommendation of paragraph (1), make a supplementary note in said recommendation, notwithstanding the provisions of paragraph (1) of the preceding Article, that the petition under Article 270-6-2, paragraph (1) may be made.

(4) The provisions of Article 268, paragraph (4) and Article 268, paragraph (5) shall apply mutatis mutandis to the case that the supplementary note of the preceding paragraph is made.

(Financial Assistance for the Secondary Transfer of Insurance Contracts)

Article 270-6-5 (1) The Underwriting Corporation shall, when it receives the petition under the provisions of Article 270-6-2, paragraph (1), without delay make a decision, after discussion by the Examination Board and the Committee, on whether to extend the Financial Assistance pertaining to said petition.

(2) The provisions of Article 270-3, paragraph (3) shall apply mutatis mutandis to the case that the Underwriting Corporation makes a decision under the preceding paragraph, and the provisions of paragraph (4) of that Article shall apply mutatis mutandis in the

case that the Underwriting Corporation makes a decision to extend Financial Assistance pursuant to the provisions of the preceding paragraph. In this case, the term "Insurance Company or Insurance Holding Company, etc. which made the request for said Financial Assistance that becomes a party to said Financial Assistance" in paragraph (4) of that Article shall be deemed to be replaced with "Secondary Transferee Insurance Company."

(3) The Secondary Transferee Insurance Company which concludes a contract under Article 270-3, paragraph (4), as applied mutatis mutandis pursuant to the preceding paragraph, shall, if profits are accrued from the assets pertaining to said damage security pertaining to that contract, commit in that contract that it shall pay all or part of said profits to the Underwriting Corporation pertaining to that contract.

Division 4 Financial Assistance for the Payment of Covered Insurance Proceeds

(Petitions for Financial Assistance for the Payment of Covered Insurance Proceeds)

Article 270-6-6 (1) The following Insurance Companies (referred to as "Specified Insurance Company" under Subsection 4) may petition the Affiliated Corporation to extend Financial Assistance in connection with the payment of Covered Insurance Proceeds (limited to donations of monies):

(i) An Insurance Company which has been ordered to suspend all or part of its business pursuant to the provisions of Article 241, paragraph (1), or which has suspended its business and is suspending its payments pertaining to the insurance contract pursuant to the provisions of Article 245 (including the cases where it is applied mutatis mutandis pursuant to Article 258, paragraph (2)), Article 250, paragraph (5) (including the cases where it is applied mutatis mutandis pursuant to Article 270-4, paragraph (9)), Article 254, paragraph (4) or Article 255-2, paragraph (3); and

(ii) An Insurance Company whose bankruptcy proceedings or reorganization proceedings are pending before the court and that is suspending its payments pertaining to the insurance contract.

(2) The Affiliated Corporation may, when it finds it necessary in the case referred to in the preceding paragraph, request the Specified Insurance Company that made the petition under that paragraph and other relevant persons to submit materials.

(Financial Assistance for the Payment of Covered Insurance Proceeds)

Article 270-6-7 (1) An Affiliated Corporation shall, when it receives a petition under paragraph (1) of the preceding Article, make a decision without delay, after discussion by the Committee, on whether to extend the Financial Assistance for the payment of the Covered Insurance Proceeds under said petition.

(2) An Affiliated Corporation shall, when it has made a decision under the preceding paragraph, immediately report on the particulars of the decision to the Prime Minister and the Minister of Finance.

(3) An Affiliated Corporation shall, when it has made the decision to extend Financial Assistance for the payment of Covered Insurance Proceeds pursuant to the provisions of paragraph (1), conclude a contract concerning the Financial Assistance for the payment of the Covered Insurance Proceeds with the Specified Insurance Company which filed the relevant petition.

Subsection 3 Purchase of Insurance Claims, etc.

(Purchase of Insurance Claims, etc.)
Article 270-6-8 (1) An Affiliated Corporation may, in the case that the Specified Insurance Company has suspended all of its payments pertaining to the insurance contract, make a decision, after discussion by the Committee, to purchase Insurance Claims pertaining to the Covered Insurance Contract and other rights specified by a Cabinet Order (limited to those whose purpose is not security interest; hereinafter referred to as "Insurance Claim, etc." in this Subsection).
(2) The purchase under the preceding paragraph shall be made in such a way that the Insurance Claim, etc. under the preceding paragraph is purchased based on the request of the creditor pertaining to the Insurance Claim, etc. , within the period during which all payments pertaining to the insurance contract are suspended, at the amount of the insurance proceeds under the Covered Insurance Contract and of other benefits, multiplied by the rate specified by a Cabinet Office Ordinance and Ordinance of the Ministry of Finance by taking into consideration what is the kind of that Covered Insurance Contract, the expected interest rate, other content, the time when the insured event pertaining to that request took place, etc. (hereinafter referred to as "Purchase Amount"); provided, however, that the Affiliated Corporation shall, in the case that it called for the Insurance Claim, etc. pertaining to the purchase and when the amount which was collected from the calling deducted by the amount specified by a Cabinet Office Ordinance and Ordinance of the Ministry of Finance as the cost of said purchase exceeds the Purchase Amount pertaining to said purchase, pay this excess amount to the creditor pertaining to said Insurance Claim, etc.
(3) The Affiliated Corporation shall, when it has made the decision under paragraph (1), immediately report on the particulars of the decision to the Prime Minister and Minister of Finance.

(Public Notice, etc. of Purchase)
Article 270-6-9 (1) The Affiliated Corporation shall, when it has made the decision under paragraph (1) of the preceding Article, promptly provide for the purchase location pertaining to the purchase of the Insurance Claim, etc. of that paragraph, the payment method for the Purchase Amount, and other particulars specified by Cabinet Office Ordinance and Ordinance of the Ministry of Finance, and give public notice thereof.
(2) The Affiliated Corporation shall, when it makes the payment under the provisions of the proviso of paragraph (2) of the preceding Article, in advance, after discussion by the Committee, provide for the payment amount, payment period, and other particulars specified by Cabinet Office Ordinance and Ordinance of the Ministry of Finance, and give public notice thereof.
(3) The provisions of paragraph (3) of the preceding Article shall apply mutatis mutandis to cases in which the particulars prescribed in the preceding paragraph are provided.

(Concerning Taxation)
Article 270-6-10 (1) In the case that a person entitled to the Insurance Claim, etc. receives payment of the Purchase Amount pertaining to the purchase under the provisions of Article 270-6-8, paragraph (2) with regard to said Insurance Claim, etc. , said payment of Purchase Amount received (in the case that the person who received the payment of that Purchase Amount receives payment for the Insurance Claim, etc. pertaining to that Purchase Amount under the provisions of the proviso of that paragraph, that amount of payment received is included) shall be deemed to be the amount of the insurance proceeds and of other benefits based on the Covered Insurance Contract

pertaining to said Insurance Claim, etc., and the provisions of the Income Tax Act (Act No. 33 of 1965) and other laws and regulations concerning income tax shall apply.
(2) In the case that the provisions of the preceding paragraph shall apply, necessary particulars involving the application of the special provisions of the proviso of Article 4-2 and Article 4-3 of the Act on Special Measures concerning Taxation (Act No. 26 of 1957) and other provisions of that paragraph shall be specified by a Cabinet Order.
(3) For the purpose of applying the provisions of the Inheritance Tax Act (Act No. 73 of 1950) and other laws and regulations concerning inheritance tax or gift tax pertaining to the payment of the Purchase Amount received in the case that payment of the Purchase Amount pertaining to the purchase of the Insurance Claim, etc. under the provisions of Article 270-6-8, paragraph (2) (in the case that the payment of said Insurance Claim, etc. pertaining to the Purchase Amount is received within three years of the occurrence of the insured event pertaining to said Insurance Claim, etc. under the provisions of the proviso of that paragraph, that amount of payment received is included; hereinafter the same shall apply in this paragraph) is received, the term "insurance proceeds (mutual aid money)" in Article 3, paragraph (1), item (i) of that Act shall be deemed to be "insurance proceeds (the Purchase Amount prescribed in Article 270-6-10, paragraph (2) of the Insurance Business Act (Act No. 105 of 1995); referred to as "Purchase Amount" in Article 5, paragraph (2)) and mutual aid money," the term "said recipient of insurance proceeds" shall be deemed to be "said recipient of insurance proceeds (any person who received payment of said Purchase Amount and," and the term "its equivalent" in Article 5, paragraph (2) of that Act shall be deemed to be "its equivalent (including the Purchase Amount; hereinafter the same shall apply)."

Subsection 4 Miscellaneous Provisions

(Loans to Members)
Article 270-7 (1) The lending of funds under Article 265-28, paragraph (2), item (i), within the extent of the amount that is found necessary, may be made in the following cases, based on an application therefor, limited to those in which it is found that the loan is necessary and appropriate for the smooth payment of insurance proceeds and other benefits by the members of the Corporation (for a Foreign Insurance Company, etc., insurance proceeds and other benefits pertaining to the insurance contract in Japan; hereinafter the same shall apply in this paragraph):
(i) In the case that a member of the Corporation is late in the payment of insurance proceeds or other benefits, or there is a risk of a member being late in a payment, due to temporary financial circumstances; and
(ii) In the case that a member of the Corporation that is the Specified Insurance Company concluded a contract under the provisions of Article 270-6-7, paragraph (3) with said Corporation.
(2) The loan of funds of item (i) of the preceding paragraph shall comply with the requirement that the calling of loan claims pertaining to the loan of funds is found to be certain and with other requirements specified by a Cabinet Office Ordinance and Ordinance of the Ministry of Finance.
(3) Whenever an application has been filed for the lending of funds under the provisions of paragraph (1), a Corporation shall make a decision, after discussion by the Committee, on whether to lend the funds.
(4) A Corporation shall, if it has made the decision to lend the funds referred to in paragraph (1) pursuant to the provisions of the preceding paragraph, immediately report on the particulars of the decision to the Prime Minister and Minister of Finance.

(Loans to Policyholders, etc.)

Article 270-8 (1) If the members of a Corporation are Specified Insurance Companies, the lending of funds under Article 265-28, paragraph (2), item (ii) may be made to any person who is a Policyholder, etc. in an insurance contract with said member as specified by a Cabinet Office Ordinance and Ordinance of the Ministry of Finance, and who is a entitled to the Insurance Claims and other rights specified by a Cabinet Office Ordinance and Ordinance of the Ministry of Finance (hereinafter referred to as "Qualified Person" in this Article), within the extent of the amount specified by a Cabinet Office Ordinance and Ordinance of the Ministry of Finance as the amount which they find that said Qualified Person is to receive based on said rights, when said lending is based on the application of said Qualified Person.

(2) The lending of funds under the preceding paragraph must be backed by the finding that the Qualified Person will certainly pay the debt pertaining to the loan of funds through payments of insurance proceeds and other benefits it will receive based on the rights of that paragraph, and in compliance with other requirements specified by a Cabinet Office Ordinance and Ordinance of the Ministry of Finance.

(3) A Corporation shall, if its member has become a Specified Insurance Company, make a decision, after discussion by the committee, on whether to lend funds to the Qualified Person of the member.

(4) A Corporation shall, when it has made the decision to loan the funds of paragraph (1) pursuant to the provisions of the preceding paragraph, immediately report on the particulars of the decision to the Prime Minister and Minister of Finance, and promptly, after discussion by the Committee, provide for the enquiry location pertaining to the loan of said funds, loan method, and other particulars specified by Cabinet Office Ordinance and Ordinance of the Ministry of Finance, and give public notice thereof.

(Petitions to Purchase the Assets of Insurance Companies in Liquidation)

Article 270-8-2 (1) An Insurance Company in Liquidation may petition a Corporation (limited to on of which that Insurance Company in Liquidation was a member) to purchase the assets of that Insurance Company in Liquidation.

(2) A Corporation may, when it finds it necessary in the case referred to in the preceding paragraph, request the Insurance Company in Liquidation that made the petition under that paragraph and other relevant persons to submit materials.

(Purchase of Assets of an Insurance Company in Liquidation)

Article 270-8-3 (1) A Corporation shall, when it receives a petition under paragraph (1) of the preceding Article, make a decision without delay, after discussion by the Examination Board and the committee, on whether to purchase the assets pertaining to said petition.

(2) A Corporation shall, when it has made the decision under the provisions of the preceding paragraph, immediately report on the particulars of the decision to the Prime Minister and Minister of Finance.

(3) A Corporation shall, when it has made the decision to purchase the assets pursuant to the provisions of paragraph (1), conclude a contract concerning the purchase of said assets with the Insurance Company in Liquidation which made to the petition for the purchase of said assets.

(Special Provisions on Taxation)

Article 270-9 (1) The registration and license tax shall not be imposed for the registration under the provisions of Article 244 (including the cases where it is applied mutatis mutandis pursuant to Article 248, paragraph (2)).

(2) Where a Corporation has accepted insurance contracts pertaining to a member Bankrupt Insurance Company pursuant to the provisions of Article 270-4, when it has acquired the right to real estate or movables from the transfer of property of that Bankrupt Insurance Company that accompanies the acceptance of that insurance contract prescribed in the contract concerning the acceptance of insurance contracts concluded pursuant to the provisions of Article 270-4, paragraph (8), the registration and license tax shall not be imposed for the registration of the transfer of said right to real estate or movables, limited to those which will be registered within one year after the acquisition pursuant to the provisions of the Ordinance of the Ministry of Finance.

(3) Where a Successor Insurance Company has acquired the right to real estate pursuant to the transfer of insurance contracts of the Bankrupt Insurance Company or a merger with that Bankrupt Insurance Company (referred to as "Transfer, etc. of Insurance Contracts Based on a Decision" in the following paragraph) that had been recognized as being qualified under the provisions of Article 270, paragraph (1) based on the decision listed in Article 270-3-2, paragraph (6), item (ii) under the provisions of Article 270-3-2, paragraph (6), the registration and license tax shall not be imposed for the registration of the transfer of said right to real estate, limited to that which will be registered within one year after the acquisition pursuant to the provisions of the Ordinance of the Ministry of Finance.

(4) The assignment of land or rights attached to the land, which the Successor Insurance Company acquired by the transfer of insurance contracts based on a decision, etc. (the assignment prescribed in Article 62-3, paragraph (2), item (i), sub-item (a) of the Act on Special Measures concerning Taxation), shall not fall under the assignment of land, etc. prescribed in Article 62-3, paragraph (2), item (i) of that Act, with regard to the application of the provisions of that Article and Articles 63, 68-68, and 68-69 of that Act pertaining to the Successor Insurance Company.

Section 5 Miscellaneous Provisions

(Opinion of the Prime Minister, etc. on Liquidation Proceedings, etc.)
Article 271 (1) The court may seek the Prime Minister's opinion or make him/her a request for an inspection or investigation regarding the liquidation procedures, bankruptcy procedures, rehabilitation procedures, reorganization procedures or approval assistance procedures of an Insurance Company, etc. or Foreign Insurance Company, etc.

(2) If the Prime Minister finds it necessary, he/she may state his/her opinion to the court on the procedures prescribed in the preceding paragraph.

(3) The provisions of Article 129, paragraph (1), Article 201, paragraph (1), Article 227, paragraph (1) and Article 272-23, paragraph (1) shall apply mutatis mutandis to cases where the Prime Minister has received a request for inspection or investigation from court pursuant to the provisions of paragraph (1).

(Special Provisions pertaining to Assignment of Revolving Mortgages)
Article 271-2 (1) When the Managed Company seeks to assign a revolving mortgage together with all of the claims it shall guarantee before the principal is established, through the assigning of property which will be carried out in conjunction with the assignment of insurance contracts to the Successor Insurance Company (meaning the Successor Insurance Company prescribed in Article 260, paragraph (6); the same shall apply in paragraph (5) and Article 271-2-3, paragraph (1), item (iii)), other insurance companies, or the Corporation that will underwrite (meaning the Underwriting of Insurance Contract prescribed in Article 260, paragraph (9); the same shall apply in

paragraph (5)) the insurance contracts of that Managed Company (hereinafter referred to as "Successor Insurance Company, etc." in this Article), that Managed Company and that Successor Insurance Company, etc. may give public notice to the effect that the revolving mortgagor with an objection shall raise its objections to that Managed Company with regard to the following particulars within a certain period, or make the demand thereof:
(i) The fact that the revolving mortgage shall be assigned from that Managed Company to that Successor Insurance Company, etc. and the date thereof; and
(ii) The fact that the revolving mortgage shall guarantee said claim even after the revolving mortgage is assigned.
(2) The period referred to in the preceding paragraph shall not be less than two weeks.
(3) When the revolving mortgagor pertaining to the public notice or demand of paragraph (1) does not raise its objections to the particulars listed in the items of that paragraph within the period referred to in that paragraph, it shall be deemed that the revolving mortgagor consents to the particular listed in item (i) of that paragraph and that the revolving mortgagor and the Successor Insurance Company, etc. pertaining to the public notice or demand of that paragraph agree on the particular listed in item (ii) of that paragraph, respectively.
(4) When the revolving mortgagor raises its objections to part of the particulars listed in the items of paragraph (1), it shall be deemed that it has raised objections to all of the particulars listed in the items of that paragraph.
(5) The provisions of all preceding paragraphs shall apply mutatis mutandis to the case that the Successor Insurance Company or Corporation that underwrote the insurance contracts seeks to assign the revolving mortgage together with all of the claims it shall guarantee before the principal is established, through the assigning of property which will be carried out in conjunction with the assignment of insurance contracts to another Insurance Company.

(Special Provisions on Application Procedures for Registration, etc. of a Revolving Mortgage Transfer)
Article 271-2-2 (1) To apply for the registration of the revolving mortgage transfer in the case referred to in paragraph (3) of the preceding Article (including the cases where it is applied mutatis mutandis pursuant to paragraph (5) of that Article), information proving that public notice or demand was given and that the revolving mortgagor did not raise its objections within the period referred to in paragraph (1) of that Article (including the cases where it is applied mutatis mutandis pursuant to paragraph (5) of that Article) shall be provided with the application information.
(2) The registration of a change in the revolving mortgage to the effect of adding claims pertaining to the assignment to the scope of claims which are to be guaranteed by the revolving mortgage in the case set forth in paragraph (3) of the preceding Article (including the cases where it is applied mutatis mutandis pursuant to paragraph (5) of that Article) may be applied for only by the revolving mortgagor when the information prescribed in the preceding paragraph is provided along with the application information.

(Special Provisions on the Continuation of Business)
Article 271-2-3 (1) Each of the persons listed in the following items may, in the case that he/she has succeeded, through the transfer of an insurance contract or through a merger prescribed in those items, to rights and duties under a contract for business that he/she cannot conduct or a contract restricting his/her engagement in such business pursuant to laws and regulations on said persons' operations, continue to conduct

the business under said contracts until the expiration date, if a duration is prescribed in said contract, or for a limited period of within two years from the date of succession, if no such duration is prescribed:
(i) An Insurance Company which has received the recommendation set forth in Article 256, paragraph (1), Article 270-3-13, paragraph (1), or Article 270-6-4, paragraph (1): transfer of insurance contract pertaining to said recommendation or merger;
(ii) A Relief Insurance Company, Secondary Successor Insurance Company, or Secondary Transferee Insurance Company, which has received the authorization set forth in Article 268, paragraph (1), Article 270-3-12, paragraph (1), or Article 270-6-3, paragraph (1) : transfer of insurance contracts pertaining to said authorization or merger; and
(iii) A Successor Insurance Company or Corporation, which carries out the transfer of insurance contracts pertaining to the authorization set forth in Article 270, paragraph (1) from, or the merge with, the Bankrupt Insurance Company which has received said authorization (meaning the Bankrupt Insurance Company prescribed in Article 260, paragraph (2)): transfer of that insurance contract or merger.
(2) Persons prescribed in the preceding paragraph may, in the case that there is a special circumstance in light of the convenience, etc. of the user of the business under the contracts prescribed in that paragraph, create a plan for managing said business for a specified period, and when said plan is approved by the Prime Minister, continue said business within the extent that the total amount of that contract of the day of the transfer of the insurance contract or merger is not exceeded, and, in accordance with said plan, renew the contract whose period set forth in that paragraph has expired or by exceeding the period set forth in that paragraph.

Chapter XI Shareholders

Section 1 General Rules

(Submission of Written Notices Pertaining to the Holding of Voting Rights in an Insurance Company, etc.)

Article 271-3 (1) A person who holds voting rights exceeding 5 percent of all shareholders' voting rights in a single Insurance Company or voting rights exceeding 5 percent of all shareholders' voting rights in a single Insurance Holding Company (excluding the State, a local public entity, or any juridical person specified by Cabinet Order as one equivalent thereto (referred to as the "State, etc." in Article 271-10); such person is hereinafter referred to as a "Large-Volume Holder of Insurance Company Voting Rights" in this Chapter and in Article 333) shall, pursuant to the provisions of Cabinet Office Ordinance, submit a written notice detailing the following particulars (hereinafter referred to in this Chapter as a "Statement of Insurance Company Voting Right Holdings") to the Prime Minister within five days (Sundays and other holidays specified by Cabinet Order are not included in the number of days; the same shall apply in paragraph (1) of the next Article) from the day on which he/she became a Large-Volume Holder of Insurance Company Voting Rights (within the number of days specified by Cabinet Office Ordinance in the where the number of voting rights held has not increased or in any other case specified by Cabinet Office Ordinance):
(i) The particulars of the Proportion of Voting Rights Held (meaning the proportion calculated by dividing the number of voting rights that a Large-Volume Holder of Insurance Company Voting Rights holds in an Insurance Company or Insurance Holding Company in which that Large-Volume Holder of Insurance Company Voting Rights is the holder of voting rights exceeding 5 percent of all shareholders'

voting rights, by the number of all shareholders' voting rights in that Insurance Company or Insurance Holding Company; hereinafter the same shall apply in this Chapter), the particulars of acquisition funding, the purpose of holding the voting rights, and any other particulars specified by Cabinet Office Ordinance as important particulars of the holding of voting rights in an Insurance Company or Insurance Holding Company:

(ii) The trade name or name and address;

(iii) In the case of a juridical person, the amount of its capital (including the total amount of contribution) and the name of its representative person; and

(iv) In the case where the person conducts business, the name and location of the business office and the type of the business.

(2) The provisions of Article 2, paragraph (15) shall apply mutatis mutandis to the voting rights held by a Large-Volume Holder of Insurance Company Voting Rights in the case referred to in the preceding paragraph.

(Submission of a Statement of Changes to a Statement of Insurance Company Voting Right Holdings)

Article 271-4 (1) A Large-Volume Holder of Insurance Company Voting Rights shall, in the case where any particulars listed in the items of paragraph (1) of the preceding Article have been changed (in the case of a change in the Proportion of Voting Rights Held, it shall be limited to a case where the rate has increased or decreased by 1 percent or more) after the day on which he/she became a holder of voting rights exceeding 5 percent of all shareholders' voting rights in a single Insurance Company or voting rights exceeding 5 percent of all shareholders' voting rights in a single Insurance Holding Company, he/she shall, pursuant to the provisions of Cabinet Office Ordinance, submit a report pertaining to that change (hereinafter referred to as a "Statement of Changes" in this Article and the next Article) to the Prime Minister within five days from that day (within the number of days specified by Cabinet Office Ordinance in the case where the number of voting rights held has not increased or in any other case specified by Cabinet Office Ordinance); provided, however, that this shall not apply to the case where a Statement of Changes has already been submitted based on a 1 percent or greater decrease in the Proportion of Voting Rights Held and the Proportion of Voting Rights Held detailed in that Statement of Changes is 5 percent or less, or to any other case specified by Cabinet Office Ordinance.

(2) A person submitting a Statement of Changes based on a decrease in the Proportion of Voting Rights Held shall, in a case that conforms to the standards specified by Cabinet Order for a case where a large number of voting rights have been transferred within a short period, also detail the particulars of the party to whom the voting rights were transferred and the Consideration received in that Statement of Changes, pursuant to the provisions of Cabinet Office Ordinance.

(3) When circumstances that compel a person to submit another Statement of Changes have arisen by the day preceding the day of submission of a Statement of Insurance Company Voting Right Holdings or a Statement of Changes (hereinafter referred to as "Required Documents" in this Section), that Statement of Changes shall be submitted to the Prime Minister at the same time as the submission of the Required Documents that have yet to be submitted, notwithstanding the provisions of the main clause of paragraph (1).

(4) A person who has submitted Required Documents shall, if he/she finds that the contents detailed in said documents differ from fact or that said documents insufficiently detail or lack a particular that is required to be included or a fact that is necessary for preventing a misinterpretation, submit a correction report to the Prime Minister.

Art.271-5 ⑥ Insurance Business Act, Part II, Chap.XI, Sec.1

(5) The provisions of Article 2, paragraph (15) shall apply mutatis mutandis to the voting rights held by a Large-Volume Holder of Insurance Company Voting Rights in the case referred to in paragraphs (1) and (2).

(Special Provisions on Statements of Holdings in Insurance Company Voting Rights, etc.)

Article 271-5 (1) Notwithstanding the provisions of Article 271-3, paragraph (1), a Statement of Insurance Company Voting Right Holdings pertaining to voting rights held by a Bank, Financial Instruments Transaction Business Operator (limited to one that conducts Securities Services), trust company, or any other person specified by Cabinet Office Ordinance who has notified the Prime Minister of a Reference date, where the purpose of holding such voting rights is not for controlling the business activities of the Insurance Company or Insurance Holding Company that has issued the shares related to those voting rights (excluding the case where the Proportion of Voting Rights Held has exceeded the number specified by Cabinet Office Ordinance and any case specified by Cabinet Office Ordinance by taking into consideration the manner in which they are held and other circumstances; hereinafter referred to as "Voting Rights Subject to Special Provisions" in this Act) shall be submitted to the Prime Minister by detailing the particulars of the status of holding for those voting rights as of the Reference Date on which the Proportion of Voting Rights Held exceeded 5 percent for the first time and that are specified by Cabinet Office Ordinance, by the fifteenth day of the month following the month containing said Reference Date, pursuant to the provisions of Cabinet Office Ordinance.

(2) A Statement of Changes pertaining to Voting Rights Subject to Special Provisions (excluding one pertaining to a change where the voting rights become those that are not Voting Rights Subject to Special Provisions) shall be submitted to the Prime Minister by the days respectively prescribed in the following items for the categories of cases listed in those items, pursuant to the provisions of Cabinet Office Ordinance:

(i) A case where the Proportion of Voting Rights Held on a Reference Date that comes after the Reference Date pertaining to the Statement of Insurance Company Voting Right Holdings set forth in the preceding paragraph increased or decreased by 1 percent or more from the Proportion of Voting Rights Held that was detailed in that Statement of Insurance Company Voting Right Holdings or any other case where there was an important change to particulars specified by Cabinet Office Order prescribed in that paragraph: The fifteenth day of the month following the month containing said later Reference Date;

(ii) A case where the circumstances came to conform to the standards specified by Cabinet Office Ordinance for a case in which the Proportion of Voting Rights Held considerably increased or decreased by the last day of any month after the month containing the Reference Date pertaining to the Statement of Insurance Company Voting Right Holdings: The fifteenth day of the month following the month containing said last day;

(iii) A case where the Proportion of Voting Rights Held on a Reference Date that comes after the Reference Date pertaining to the Statement of Changes increased or decreased by 1 percent or more from the Proportion of Voting Rights Held that was detailed in that Statement of Changes or any other case where there was an important change to particulars specified by Cabinet Office Order prescribed in the preceding paragraph: The fifteenth day of the month following the month containing that later reference date; and

(iv) A case specified by Cabinet Office Ordinance as a case equivalent to any of the preceding three items: The day specified by Cabinet Office Ordinance.

(3) The Reference Date set forth in the preceding two paragraphs means the last day of the month in which a person specified by Cabinet Office Ordinance prescribed in paragraph (1) notified the Prime Minister pursuant to the provisions of Cabinet Office Ordinance and that of every three months thereafter.

(4) The provisions of Article 2, paragraph (15) shall apply mutatis mutandis to the Voting Rights Subject to Special Provisions held by a Large-Volume Holder of Insurance Company Voting Rights in the case referred to in paragraphs (1) and (2).

(Order to Submit Correction Report)

Article 271-6 In the case where Required Documents have been submitted pursuant to the provisions of Article 271-3, paragraph (1), Article 271-4, paragraph (1) or (3), or paragraph (1) or (2) of the preceding Article, the Prime Minister may, if he/she finds that there is a formal deficiency in the Required Documents or that the Required Documents insufficiently detail an important particular that is required to be included, order the person who has submitted the Required Documents to submit a correction report. In this case, a hearing shall be carried out irrespective of the categories of procedures for hearing statements under Article 13, paragraph (1) (Procedures Prerequisite for Adverse Dispositions) of the Administrative Procedure Act (Act No. 88 of 1993).

Article 271-7 The Prime Minister may, if he/she has discovered that Required Documents include a false detail with regard to an important particular, fail to detail an important particular that is required to be included, or fail to detail any fact that is necessary for preventing a misinterpretation, order the person who has submitted the Required Documents, at any time, to submit a correction report. In this case, a hearing shall be carried out irrespective of the categories of procedures for hearing statements under Article 13, paragraph (1) (Procedures Prerequisite for Adverse Dispositions) of the Administrative Procedure Act.

(Submission of Reports or Materials by a Large-Volume Holder of Insurance Company Voting Rights)

Article 271-8 The Prime Minister may, if he/she suspects that Required Documents include a false detail with regard to an important particular, fail to detail an important particular that is required to be included, or fail to detail a fact that is necessary for preventing a misinterpretation, order the Large-Volume Holder of Insurance Company Voting Rights that has submitted the Required Documents to submit reports or materials that should serve as reference in connection with the particulars that are required to be included in the Required Documents or facts that are necessary for preventing a misinterpretation.

(On-site Inspection of a Large-Volume Holder of Insurance Company Voting Rights)

Article 271-9 (1) The Prime Minister may, if he/she suspects that Required Documents include a false detail with regard to an important particular, fail to detail an important particular that is required to be included, or fail to detail any fact that is necessary for preventing a misinterpretation, have his/her officials enter an office or any other facility of the Large-Volume Holder of Insurance Company Voting Rights who has submitted the Required Documents, ask questions concerning the particulars that are required to be included in the Required Documents or facts necessary for avoiding misunderstanding, or inspect books and documents or other objects of that Large-Volume Holder of Insurance Company Voting Rights.

(2) The official that carries out the entry, questioning, or inspection under the provisions of the preceding paragraph shall indicate the reason for the entry, questioning, or inspection to the other party.

Section 2 Special Provisions Pertaining to an Insurance Company's Major Shareholders

Subsection 1 General Rules

(Authorization, etc. to Be Obtained by an Insurance Company's Major Shareholders)

Article 271-10 (1) A person who seeks to become the holder of a number of voting rights in an Insurance Company equal to or exceeding the Major Shareholder Threshold or a person who seeks to establish a company or any other juridical person that is the holder of a number of voting rights in an Insurance Company equal to or exceeding the Major Shareholder Threshold (excluding the State, etc., a company that seeks to become a Holding company as prescribed in Article 271-18, paragraph (1), the person prescribed in that paragraph, and an Insurance Holding Company that seeks to make the Insurance Company its Subsidiary) through any of the following transactions or actions shall obtain authorization from the Prime Minister in advance:
   (i) Acquisition of voting rights in the Insurance Company by the person who seeks to become the holder of such voting rights (excluding acquisition of shares through exercise of security rights or acquisition of voting rights by any other cause specified by Cabinet Office Ordinance);
   (ii) Acquisition of a license set forth in Article 3, paragraph (1), through a company that holds a number of voting rights equal to or exceeding the Major Shareholder Threshold, by the person who seeks to become the holder of said voting rights; or
   (iii) Any other transactions or actions specified by Cabinet Order.
(2) A person who became the holder of a number of voting rights in an Insurance Company equal to or exceeding the Major Shareholder Threshold due to a cause other than the transactions or actions listed in the items of the preceding paragraph (excluding the State, etc., an Insurance Holding Company, and a Specified Holding Company prescribed in Article 271-18, paragraph (2); hereinafter referred to "Specified Major Shareholder" in this Article and Article 333) shall take necessary measures for becoming a person who is no longer the holder of a number of voting rights in the Insurance Company equal to or exceeding the Major Shareholder Threshold by the day on which one year has elapsed from the end of the Business Year of that Insurance Company including the date on which said cause arose (hereinafter referred to as the "Last Day of the Grace Period" in this paragraph and paragraph (4)); provided, however, that this shall not apply to the cases where that Specified Major Shareholder has obtained authorization from the Prime Minister to remain the holder of a number of voting rights in an Insurance Company equal to or exceeding the Major Shareholder Threshold even after the Last Day of the Grace Period.
(3) If a Specified Major Shareholder becomes a person who is no longer the holder of a number of voting rights equal in an Insurance Company equal to or exceeding the Major Shareholder Threshold due to a measure required under the preceding paragraph, he/she shall notify the Prime Minster of this without delay. The same applies if a Specified Major Shareholder becomes a person who is no longer the holder of a number of voting rights in the Insurance Company equal to or exceeding the Major Shareholder Threshold without such measures.
(4) The Prime Minister may order a person who became the holder of a number of voting

rights in an Insurance Company equal to or exceeding the Major Shareholder Threshold or a company or any other juridical person established as the holder of a number of voting rights in an Insurance Company equal to or exceeding the Major Shareholder Threshold through any of the transactions or actions listed in the items of paragraph (1) without obtaining the authorization set forth in that paragraph or a person who remains the holder of a number of voting rights in an Insurance Company equal to or exceeding the Major Shareholder Threshold even after the Last Day of the Grace Period without obtaining the authorization set forth in the proviso to paragraph (2), to take necessary measures to cease being the holder of a number of voting rights in an Insurance Company equal to or exceeding the Major Shareholder Threshold.

Article 271-11 Whenever an application has been filed for the authorization set forth in paragraph (1) of the preceding Article or the proviso to paragraph (2) of the preceding Article, the Prime Minister shall examine whether it conforms to the following standards:

(i) If the person who applied for the authorization (hereinafter referred to in this Article as "Applicant") is a company or any other juridical person, or if a company or any other juridical person is to be established under the authorization, that the following standards are met:

(a) In light of the particulars of the acquisition funding, the purpose of holding the voting rights, or any other particulars involved in the holding of a number of voting rights in an Insurance Company equal to or exceeding the Major Shareholder Threshold by that Applicant or the company or any other juridical person to be established under the authorization (hereinafter referred to as the "Juridical Person Applicant, etc." in this item), there shall be no risk of impairing the sound and appropriate business operation of the Insurance Company in which that Juridical Person Applicant, etc. is or will become the holder of a number of voting rights equal to or exceeding the Major Shareholder Threshold;

(b) In light of the status of property and income and expenditure of the Juridical Person Applicant, etc. and its Subsidiaries (including any company that will become a Subsidiary), there shall be no risk of impairing the sound and appropriate business operation of the Insurance Company in which that Juridical Person Applicant, etc. is or will become the holder of a number of voting rights equal to or exceeding the Major Shareholder Threshold;

(c) In light of such particulars as its personnel structure, etc. , the Juridical Person Applicant, etc. must have sufficient understanding concerning the public nature of the Insurance Business and must have sufficient social credibility; and

(ii) In cases other than the cases listed in the preceding items, that the following standards are met:

(a) In light of the particulars of the acquisition funding, the purpose of holding the voting rights, or any other particulars of the holding of a number of voting rights in an Insurance Company equal to or exceeding the Major Shareholder Threshold by that Applicant, there shall be no risk of impairing the sound and appropriate business operation of the Insurance Company in which that Applicant is or will become the holder of a number of voting rights equal to or exceeding the Major Shareholder Threshold;

(b) In light of the status of the property of the Applicant (including the status of income and expenditure in the case where that Applicant is a person who conducts business), there shall be no risk of impairing the sound and appropriate business operation of the Insurance Company in which that Applicant is or will become the holder of a number of voting rights equal to or exceeding the Major

Art.271-12〜271-15　⑥ Insurance Business Act, Part II, Chap.XI, Sec.2

Shareholder Threshold; and

(c) That Applicant has sufficient understanding of the public nature of the Insurance Business and holds sufficient social credibility.

Subsection 2 Supervision

(Submission of Reports or Materials by an Insurance Company's Major Shareholder)

Article 271-12 If and to the extent that the Prime Minister finds it particularly necessary for protecting Policyholders, etc. and for ensuring the sound and appropriate business operation of an Insurance Company in requesting the Insurance Company to submit reports or materials pursuant to the provisions of Article 128, paragraph (1), he/she may request an Insurance Company's Major Shareholders who are the holders of a number of voting rights in the relevant Insurance Company equal to or exceeding the Major Shareholder Threshold, to submit reports or materials that could be helpful concerning the status of the business or property of that Insurance Company, indicating the reasons therefor.

(On-site Inspection of an Insurance Company's Major Shareholders)

Article 271-13 (1) If and to the extent that the Prime Minister finds it particularly necessary for protecting Policyholders, etc. and for ensuring the sound and appropriate business operation of an Insurance Company in carrying out the entry, questioning, or inspection of the Insurance Company under the provisions of Article 129, paragraph (1), he/she may have an official to enter an office or any other facility of an Insurance Company's Major Shareholder that holds a number of voting rights in the relevant Insurance Company equal to or exceeding the Major Shareholder Threshold, ask questions concerning the status of the business or property of the Insurance Company or the Insurance Company's Major Shareholder, or inspect books and documents and other items of the Insurance Company's Major Shareholder.

(2) The official that carries out the entry, questioning, or inspection pursuant to the provisions of the preceding paragraph shall indicate the reason for the entry, questioning, or inspection to the other party.

(Order for an Insurance Company's Major Shareholder to Take Measures)

Article 271-14 The Prime Minister may, when an Insurance Company's Major Shareholder no longer conforms to the standards listed in the items of Article 271-11 (in the case where conditions are imposed on the authorization set forth in Article 271, paragraph (1) or the proviso to Article 271, paragraph (2) pertaining to that Insurance Company's Major Shareholder, based on the provisions of Article 310, paragraph (1), such standards shall include those conditions), order that Insurance Company's Major Shareholder to take necessary measures for conforming to the standards by designating the time limit for taking the measures.

(Request, etc. for an Insurance Company's Major Shareholder to Submit an Improvement Plan)

Article 271-15 (1) If and to the extent that the Prime Minister finds it particularly necessary for protecting the Policyholders, etc. and for ensuring the sound and appropriate business operation of an Insurance Company in light of the status of business or property (in the case that the Insurance Company's Major Shareholder is a company or any other juridical person, this includes the status of property of Subsidiaries of the Insurance Company's Major Shareholder or any other companies to which it is specially related as specified by Cabinet Office Ordinance to the Insurance Company's Major Shareholder) of the Insurance Company's Major Shareholder (limited to a person who holds voting rights exceeding 50 percent of all shareholders' voting rights in the Insurance Company; hereinafter the same shall apply in this Article), the Prime Minister may request the Insurance Company's Major Shareholder to submit an improvement plan for ensuring soundness in the business operation of the Insurance Company or order amendment of the submitted improvement plan by designating the particulars with regard to which measures must be taken and the time limit therefor, or may, to the extent necessary for achieving this, order measures necessary for supervision.

(2) Where the Prime Minister has issued an Insurance Company's Major Shareholder an order under the preceding paragraph, if he/she finds it necessary in light of the state of implementation of the measures under that order, he/she may order the Insurance Company in which the Insurance Company's Major Shareholder holds voting rights exceeding 50 percent of all shareholders' voting rights to take measures necessary for ensuring the sound and appropriate business operation of the Insurance Company.

(Rescission, etc. of the Authorization Granted to an Insurance Company's Major Shareholder)

Article 271-16 (1) The Prime Minister may, when an Insurance Company's Major Shareholder has violated any laws and regulations or a disposition given by the Prime Minister based on any laws and regulations or has engaged in conduct that harms the public interest, order the Insurance Company's Major Shareholder to take necessary measures for the purpose of supervision, or rescind the authorization set forth in Article 271-10, paragraph (1) or the proviso to Article 271-10, paragraph (2) for the Insurance Company's Major Shareholder. In this case, the authorization set forth in paragraph (1) of that Article that pertains to establishment shall be deemed to be granted to the company or other juridical person that has been established under the authorization which constitutes the relevant Insurance Company's Major Shareholder.

(2) An Insurance Company's Major Shareholder shall, when authorization set forth in Article 271-10, paragraph (1) or the proviso to Article 271-10, paragraph (2) has been rescinded pursuant to the provisions of the preceding paragraph, take necessary measures for ceasing to be the holder of a number of voting rights in an Insurance Company equal to or exceeding the Major Shareholder Threshold within a period designated by the Prime Minister.

Subsection 3 Miscellaneous Provision

(Application of this Act to an Insurance Company's Major Foreign Shareholders)

Article 271-17 Any special provisions and technical replacement of terms for applying this Act to a foreign national or a foreign juridical person that is the holder of a number of voting rights in an Insurance Company equal to or exceeding the Major Shareholder Threshold (hereinafter referred to as an "Insurance Company's Major Foreign Shareholder" in this Article) and any other necessary particulars for the application of the provisions of this Act to an Insurance Company's Major Foreign Shareholders shall be specified by Cabinet Order.

Section 3 Special Provisions Pertaining to Insurance Holding Company

Subsection 1 General Rules

(Authorization to be Obtained by Insurance Holding Company, etc.)
Article 271-18 (1) A company which seeks to become a Holding Company whose Subsidiaries include an Insurance Company, or a person who seeks to establish such a Holding Company through any of the following transactions or actions must obtain authorization from the Prime Minister in advance:
  (i) Acquisition of Voting Rights in the Insurance Company by the company or its Subsidiary (excluding acquisition of shares through exercise of security rights or acquisition of voting rights by any other cause specified by Cabinet Office Ordinance);
  (ii) Acquisition of the license set forth in Article 3, paragraph (1) by its Subsidiary; or
  (iii) Any other transaction or action specified by Cabinet Order.
(2) When a company becomes a Holding Company whose Subsidiaries include an Insurance Company through a cause other than the transactions or actions listed in the items of the preceding paragraph (hereinafter referred to as "Specified Holding Company") it shall notify the Prime Minister of the fact that it has become a Holding Company whose Subsidiaries include an Insurance Company and of other particulars specified by Cabinet Office Ordinance, within three months after the end of the relevant Business Year including the day on which said cause arose.
(3) A Specified Holding Company shall take necessary measures to stop being a Holding Company whose Subsidiaries include an Insurance Company by the day on which one year has elapsed from the end of the Business Year that contains the day on which the cause referred to in the preceding paragraph arose (hereinafter referred to as the "Last Day of the Grace Period" in this paragraph and paragraph (5)); provided, however, that this shall not apply to the cases where said Specified Holding Company has obtained authorization from the Prime Minister to continue being a Holding Company whose Subsidiaries include an Insurance Company even after the Last Day of the Grace Period.
(4) If a Specified Holding Company has ceased to be a Holding Company whose Subsidiaries include an Insurance Company due to the measures required under the preceding paragraph, it shall notify the Prime Minister of this without delay. The same applies if a Specified Holding Company has ceased to be a Holding Company whose Subsidiaries include an Insurance Company without such measures.
(5) The Prime Minister may order a company that has become a Holding Company whose Subsidiaries include an Insurance Company or a person who established such a Holding Company due to any of the transactions or actions listed in the items of paragraph (1) without obtaining the authorization set forth in that paragraph, or a company that continues to be a Holding Company whose Subsidiaries include an Insurance Company even after the Last Day of the Grace Period without obtaining the authorization set forth in the proviso to paragraph (3), to take necessary measures to stop being a Holding Company whose Subsidiaries include an Insurance Company.

Article 271-19 (1) Whenever an application has been filed for the authorization set forth in paragraph (1) or the proviso to paragraph (3) of the preceding Article, the Prime Minister shall examine whether it conforms to the following standards:
  (i) The company that has filed the application for authorization or which is to be established under the authorization (hereinafter referred to as the "Applicant, etc." in this Article) and its Subsidiaries (including companies scheduled to become its

Subsidiaries; hereinafter the same shall apply in the following item) have good prospects for income and expenditure of the business;
(ii) In light of such particulars as its personnel structure, etc. , the Applicant, etc. has the knowledge and experience that will enable the Applicant, etc. to perform the business management of an Insurance Company that is or is scheduled to become its Subsidiary appropriately and fairly and must have sufficient social credibility.
(iii) The business content of the Subsidiary of the Applicant, etc. does not fall under Article 271-22, paragraph (3), item (i) or (ii).
(2) An Insurance Holding Company (excluding one established in accordance with the laws and regulations of the foreign state) shall be a stock company shall have the following organs:
(i) Board of directors;
(ii) Board of company auditors or committees; and
(iii) Accounting auditors.

(Qualification, etc. for Directors, etc. of Insurance Holding Company)
Article 271-19-2 (1) A person who has become subject to the decision under the commencement of bankruptcy proceedings and has not had restored his/her rights, or a person who is treated the same as such a person under the laws and regulations of a foreign state, may not be appointed as a director, executive officer or auditor of an Insurance Holding Company.
(2) The following provisions of the Companies Act shall not apply to an Insurance Holding Company: the proviso to Article 331, paragraph (2) (Qualifications of Directors) (including the cases where it is applied mutatis mutandis pursuant to Article 335, paragraph (1) (Qualifications of Company Auditors) of that Act), Article 332, paragraph (2) (Directors' Terms of Office) (including the cases where it is applied mutatis mutandis pursuant to Article 334, paragraph (1) (Accounting Advisors' Terms of Office) of that Act), Article 336, paragraph (2) (Company Auditors' Terms of Office) and the proviso to Article 402, paragraph (5) (Election of Executive Officers).
(3) An Insurance Holding Company may not become an unlimited partner or a partner who executes the business of a membership company.

(Mutatis Mutandis Application of Provisions on an Insurance Company's Major Shareholders)
Article 271-20 The provisions of Article 271-17 shall apply mutatis mutandis to a Holding Company whose Subsidiaries include an Insurance Company which was established in accordance with the laws and regulations of a foreign state.

Subsection 2 Business and Subsidiary Companies

(Scope of Business of an Insurance Holding Company, etc.)
Article 271-21 (1) An Insurance Holding Company may not conduct business other than managing the operations of its Insurance Company Subsidiaries the operations of the companies listed in Article 271-22, paragraph (1), items (ii)-2 to (xiv) inclusive, and the operations of any other company that has become its Subsidiary with the approval of the Prime Minister under Article 271-22, paragraph (1) or the proviso to Article 271-22, paragraph (4), or any other business incidental thereto.
(2) An Insurance Holding Company shall endeavor to ensure the sound and appropriate business operation of its Insurance Company Subsidiaries.

(Establishment of a System for the Protection of Customers' Interests)

Article 271-21-2 (1) When an Insurance Company that is the Subsidiary of a Insurance Holding Company, or the Parent Financial Institution, etc. or Subsidiary Financial Institution, etc. of a Insurance Holding Company conducts a transaction, such Insurance Holding Company shall, pursuant to the provisions of Cabinet Office Ordinance, properly manage the information on business conducted by its Insurance Company Subsidiaries or by its Subsidiary Financial Institutions, etc. (limited to the Insurance Business and any other business specified by Cabinet Office Ordinance) and establish a system for properly supervising the status of implementation of said business or taking any other measures necessary so that the interests of the customer of said business will not be unjustly impaired.
(2) The term "Parent Financial Institution, etc." as used in the preceding paragraph means the person who holds the majority of all shareholders' voting rights in an Insurance Holding Company, and any other person that is specified by Cabinet Order as being closely related to said Insurance Holding Company and which is an Insurance Company, Bank, Financial Instruments Transaction Business Operator, or any other person conducting financial business that is specified by Cabinet Order.
(3) The term "Subsidiary Financial Institution, etc." as used in paragraph (1) means a person in which an Insurance Holding Company holds the majority of All Shareholders' Voting Rights, etc. , and any other person specified by Cabinet Order as being closely related to said Insurance Holding Company and which is an Insurance Company (excluding said Insurance Holding Company's Insurance Company Subsidiaries), Bank, Financial Instruments Transaction Business Operator, or any other person conducting financial business that is specified by Cabinet Order.

(Scope of Subsidiaries of an Insurance Holding Company, etc.)
Article 271-22 (1) An Insurance Holding Company must receive the advance approval of the Prime Minister if it seeks to make any company other than the following its Subsidiary:
(i) a Life Insurance Company;
(ii) a Non-Life Insurance Company;
(ii)-2 Low-Cost, Short-Term Insurer;
(iii) a bank;
(iv) a Long Term Credit Bank;
(iv)-2 a Company Specialized in Fund Transfers;
(v) a Company Specializing in Securities;
(vi) a Company Specializing in Securities Intermediation;
(vii) a Company Specializing in Trusts;
(viii) a foreign company that conducts Insurance Business;
(ix) Foreign companies which operate in the Banking business (other than a company falling under the preceding item);
(x) a foreign company that conducts any Securities Services (other than a company falling under either of the preceding two items);
(xi) Foreign companies which operate in the Trust Business (other than a company falling under any of the preceding three items);
(xii) Companies which exclusively conduct the following business (limited, in case of those conducting business specified in (a) below, to companies that conduct such business mainly for business being conducted by the relevant Insurance Holding Company, its Subsidiaries (limited to persons that fall under any of the categories in items (i), (ii) and (viii); the same shall apply in paragraph (5)) or other entities specified by Cabinet Office Ordinance as being similar thereto):
(a) Business specified by Cabinet Office Ordinance as being dependent on the busi-

[2010年6月2日訳] ⑥ Insurance Business Act, Part II, Chap.XI, Sec.3   Art.271-22

ness of an Insurance Company or any of the companies listed in item (ii)-2 to the preceding item inclusive (referred to as "Dependent Services" in paragraph (5)); or
(b) Finance-Related Services listed in Article 106, paragraph (2), item (ii);
(xiii) Companies specified by Cabinet Office Ordinance as those exploring new business fields or conducting new business activities found to contribute considerably to the improvement of management (limited to a company in which a person specified by Cabinet Office Ordinance provided for in the preceding item holds voting rights exceeding the number calculated by multiplying All Shareholders' Voting Rights, etc. in the company by the rate specified by Cabinet Office Ordinance); or
(xiv) a Holding Company whose only Subsidiaries are companies listed in the preceding items and to be specified by Cabinet Office Ordinance (including a company that is scheduled to become such Holding Company).
(2) An Insurance Holding Company that seeks to receive the approval set forth in the preceding paragraph shall submit to the Prime Minister a written application detailing the business content, amount of capital and human resource structure of the company covered by the application for approval, as well as other particulars specified by Cabinet Office Ordinance.
(3) Whenever an application has been filed for the approval set forth in paragraph (1), unless the content of the business that the company to which the application pertains conducts or seeks to conduct falls under any of the following cases, the Prime Minister shall give such approval:
(i) it poses the risk of undermining the social credibility of the Insurance Company Subsidiaries of the Insurance Holding Company that filled the application because it falls under either (a) or (b), below:
(a) it may harm the public policy and good morals; or
(b) it may preclude the stable lives of the citizenry or sound development of the national economy; or
(ii) it is likely to damage the soundness of management of the company covered by the application in light of the amount of capital, human resource structure, etc. of the company, and any such damage to its managerial soundness in turn poses the risk of damaging the soundness of management of the Insurance Company Subsidiaries of the Insurance Holding Company that filled the application .
(4) The provisions of paragraph (1) shall not apply where a company other than those listed in the items of the same paragraph becomes a Subsidiary Company of the Insurance Holding Company as a result of the acquisition of shares or equity interests through the exercise of a security rights by the Insurance Holding Company or any of its Subsidiary Companies, or any other justifiable event to be specified by Cabinet Office Ordinance; provided, however, that the Insurance Holding Company shall, unless the Prime Minister approves that such company continue to be its Subsidiary Company, take necessary measures for ensuring that the company will cease to be its Subsidiary Company within one year from the date of such event.
(5) In the case referred to in paragraph (1), item (xii), the Prime Minister shall set the standards for to determining whether a company primarily performs Dependent Services for business conducted by the Insurance Holding Company, its Subsidiaries or any other similar company specified by Cabinet Office Ordinance.
(6) The relevant provisions of the Banking Act or the Long Term Credit Bank Act shall apply in lieu of the provisions of the preceding paragraphs to any Insurance Holding Company that seeks to become a Bank Holding Company (meaning a Bank Holding Company as defined in Article 2, paragraph (13) (Definitions, etc.) of the Banking Act; the same shall apply hereafter in this paragraph as well as in Article 272-39, paragraph

(6)) or a Long Term Credit Bank Holding Company (meaning a Long Term Credit Bank Holding Company as defined in Article 16-4, paragraph (1) (Scope of Subsidiary Companies, etc.) of the Long Term Credit Bank Act; the same shall apply hereafter in this paragraph as well as in Article 272-39, paragraph (6)) by making a bank or Long Term Credit Bank its Subsidiary, or that already is a Bank Holding Company or Long Term Credit Bank Holding Company.

Subsection 3 Accounting

(Business Year of Insurance Holding Companies)
Article 271-23 The business year of an Insurance Holding Company shall run from 1 April to 31 March of the next year.

(Insurance Holding Companies' Business Reports, etc.)
Article 271-24 (1) An Insurance Holding Company shall, for each business year, prepare for submission to the Prime Minister an interim business report and business report describing in a consolidated manner the status of business or property of the Insurance Holding Company, and its Subsidiaries and any other company to which it is specially related as specified by Cabinet Office Ordinance (referred to as "Subsidiary Companies, etc." hereafter in this Subsection as well as in the following Subsection)
(2) The particulars for inclusion in the interim business report and business report, submission dates, and other necessary particulars of those reports shall be specified by Cabinet Office Ordinance.

(Public Inspection, etc. of Explanatory Documents on the Status of Business and Property Pertaining to Insurance Holding Company)
Article 271-25 (1) An Insurance Holding Company shall, for each business year, prepare explanatory documents describing, with regard to the Insurance Holding Company and its Subsidiary Companies, etc. , the particulars specified by Cabinet Office Ordinance as pertaining to the status of the business and property of the Insurance Holding Company and its Subsidiary Companies, etc. in a consolidated manner, and keep them for public inspection in the head office and branch offices of its Insurance Company Subsidiaries or any other equivalent place specified by Cabinet Office Ordinance.
(2) The explanatory documents set forth in the preceding paragraph may be prepared in the form of electromagnetic record.
(3) Where the explanatory documents set forth in paragraph (1) are prepared in the form of electromagnetic record, the Insurance Holding Company may take the measures to be specified by Cabinet Office Ordinance as measures to ensure that the information recorded in the electromagnetic records is available to many and unspecified persons by electromagnetic means at the head office and branch offices of its Insurance Company Subsidiaries or any other equivalent place to be specified by Cabinet Office Ordinance. In this case, the explanatory documents set forth in that paragraph shall be deemed to be kept for public inspection pursuant to the provisions of that paragraph.
(4) In addition to what is provided in the preceding three paragraphs, the period for making the documents set forth in paragraph (1) available for public inspection and any other necessary particulars involved in the application of these provisions of preceding paragraphs shall be specified by Cabinet Office Ordinance.
(5) An Insurance Holding Company shall endeavor to disclose, in addition to what is set forth in paragraph (1), any particular that would be helpful for the Policyholders and other customers of its Insurance Company Subsidiaries to know the status of the business and property of the Insurance Holding Company and its Subsidiary Companies,

etc.

(Particulars for Inclusion in the Business Reports, etc. of an Insurance Holding Company)
Article 271-26 The particulars for inclusion in the business report and supplementary schedules prepared by an Insurance Holding Company pursuant to the provisions of Article 435, paragraph (2) (Preparation and Retention of Financial Statements, etc.) of the Companies Act, are specified by Cabinet Office Ordinance.

Subsection 4 Supervision

(Submission of Reports or Materials by Insurance Holding Company, etc.)
Article 271-27 (1) In requesting an Insurance Company to submit a report or materials pursuant to the provisions of Article 128, paragraph (1), if the Prime Minister finds it particularly necessary for protecting the Policyholders, etc. and for ensuring the sound and appropriate business operation of the Insurance Company, he/she may request the Insurance Holding Company of which the Insurance Company is a Subsidiary, that Insurance Holding Company's Subsidiary, etc. (meaning a Subsidiary of the Insurance Holding Company or any other person to be specified by Cabinet Office Ordinance as a juridical person whose operations are controlled by the Insurance Holding Company; the same shall apply in the following paragraph, and paragraphs (2) and (4) of the following Article), or a person the Insurance Holding Company has entrusted with its business, to submit a report or materials that should serve as reference regarding the status of the business or property of the Insurance Company, indicating the reason therefor.
(2) An Insurance Holding Company's Subsidiary, etc. or a person that an Insurance Holding Company has entrusted with its business may refuse to submit reports or materials under the preceding paragraph if there are justifiable grounds for it to do so.

(On-Site Inspection of Insurance Holding Company, etc.)
Article 271-28 (1) If and to the extent that the Prime Minister finds it particularly necessary for protecting the Policyholders, etc. and for ensuring the sound and appropriate business operation of the Insurance Company in making an entry, asking questions, or conducting inspection in an Insurance Company pursuant to the provisions of Article 129, paragraph (1), he/she may have his/her officials enter an office or any other facility of the Insurance Holding Company of which the Insurance Company is a Subsidiary to ask questions on the status of the business or property of the Insurance Company or Insurance Holding Company, or inspect the books and documents and other materials of the Insurance Holding Company.
(2) If and to the extent that the Prime Minister finds it particularly necessary for protecting the Policyholders, etc. and for ensuring the sound and appropriate business operation of the Insurance Company in making an entry, asking questions, or conducting inspection in an Insurance Company pursuant to the provisions of Article 129, paragraph (1), he/she, may have his/her officials enter the business office or any other facility of an Insurance Holding Company's Subsidiary, etc. of which the Insurance Company is a Subsidiary or the business office or any other facility of a person the Insurance Holding Company has entrusted with its business, have such officials question the Insurance Company or ask questions about any particulars that are necessary for their inspection, or have such officials inspect books and documents and other materials.
(3) The personnel who make an entry, ask questions or conduct inspection under the preceding two paragraphs shall indicate to the other party the reason for such entry, ques-

tioning or inspection.
(4) The provisions of paragraph (2) of the preceding Article shall apply mutatis mutandis to the questioning and inspection of an Insurance Holding Company's Subsidiary, etc. or of a person that an Insurance Holding Company has entrusted with its business under paragraph (2).

(Request for Submission of Improvement Plan, etc. by Insurance Holding Company, etc.)
Article 271-29 (1) If the Prime Minister finds it necessary for protecting the Policyholders, etc. and for ensuring the sound and proper business operation of an Insurance Holding Company's Insurance Company Subsidiaries, in light of the status of the business of said Insurance Holding Company or the property of the Insurance Holding Company and its Subsidiary Companies, etc. , the Prime Minister may request the Insurance Holding Company to submit an improvement plan for ensuring soundness in the management of the relevant Insurance Companies by designating particulars with regard to which measures must be taken and the time limit thereof, or may order, to the extent necessary for achieving this, measures necessary for supervision.
(2) In giving an order to an Insurance Holding Company under the preceding paragraph (including the request for submission of an improvement plan), if the Prime Minister finds it particularly necessary in light of conditions regarding the implementation of the ordered measures, he/she may order its Insurance Company Subsidiaries to take necessary measures for ensuring sound and appropriate business operation.

(Rescission of Authorization Pertaining to Insurance Holding Company, etc.)
Article 271-30 (1) The Prime Minister may, when an Insurance Holding Company has violated a law or regulation, its articles of incorporation or any disposition of the Prime Minister pursuant to a law or regulation, or has engaged in any conduct that harms the public interest, order the Insurance Holding Company to dismiss its directors, executive officers, accounting advisors or company auditors or to take necessary measures for the purpose of supervision, rescind the authorization given to the Insurance Holding Company under Article 271-18, paragraph (1) or the proviso to Article 271-18, paragraph (3), or order its Insurance Company Subsidiaries to suspend its business in whole or in part. In this case, the authorization set forth in paragraph (1) of that Article that was granted for establishment of the Insurance Holding Company shall be deemed to be granted to the Insurance Holding Company established under the authorization.
(2) An Insurance Holding Company shall, when the authorization set forth in Article 271-18, paragraph (1) or the proviso to Article 271-18, paragraph (3) is rescinded pursuant to the provisions of the preceding paragraph, take necessary measures to ensure that it will stop being a Holding Company whose Subsidiaries include an Insurance Company within a period designated by the Prime Minister.
(3) When the measures prescribed in the preceding paragraph have been taken, the day on which such measures were taken shall be deemed to be the date of occurrence of the event set forth in Article 171-10, paragraph (2) for the purpose of applying the provisions of the preceding paragraph where the company that has taken such measures continues to be the holder of a number of voting rights in an Insurance Company equal to or exceeding the Major Shareholder Threshold.
(4) If a Holding Company whose Subsidiaries include an Insurance Company falls under any of the following items and the Prime Minister finds it to be necessary, the Prime Minister may order that Holding Company's Insurance Company Subsidiaries to suspend its business in whole or in part:
(i) it has become a Holding Company whose Subsidiaries include an Insurance Compa-

ny due to any of the transactions or actions listed in the items of that paragraph without the authorization required in Article 271-18, paragraph (1);
(ii) it was established as a Holding Company whose Subsidiaries include an Insurance Company without the authorization required in Article 271-18, paragraph (1);
(iii) it continues to be a Holding Company whose Subsidiaries include an Insurance Company even after the Last Day of the Grace Period set forth in Article 271-18, paragraph (3) without the authorization set forth in the proviso thereto; or
(iv) it has had the authorization under Article 271-18, paragraph (1) or the proviso to Article 271-18, paragraph (3) rescinded pursuant to the provisions of paragraph (1), and continues to be a Holding Company whose Subsidiaries include an Insurance Company after the end of the period designated by the Prime Minister under paragraph (2) without taking the measures set forth in that paragraph.

Subsection 5 Miscellaneous Provisions

(Authorization of Merger, Company Split, or Transfer of Business Involving Insurance Holding Company)
Article 271-31 (1) Any Merger involving an Insurance Holding Company or Insurance Holding Companies (limited to a merger as a result of which a company that was an Insurance Holding Company before the merger survives as an Insurance Holding Company) shall not be effective without authorization of the Prime Minister.
(2) No company split of which an Insurance Holding Company is party (limited to the case where the Insurance Holding Company which had its business succeeded by another party through the company split or the Insurance Holding Company which succeeded to another party's business through the company split continues to exist as a Insurance Holding Company even after the company split) shall be effective without authorization of the Prime Minister, except for the cases specified by Cabinet Order.
(3) No transfer of business where an Insurance Holding Company transfers or receives the whole or part of its or any other party's business (limited to the case where the Insurance Holding Company which transferred or received transfer of its or any other party's business continues to exist as an Insurance Holding Company even after the transfer or the receipt) shall be effective without authorization of the Prime Minister, except for the cases specified by Cabinet Order.
(4) The provisions of Article 271-19, paragraph (1) apply mutatis mutandis whenever an application has been filed for the authorization set forth in the preceding three paragraphs.

Section 4 Miscellaneous Provisions

(Particulars Requiring Notice)
Article 271-32 (1) If an Insurance Company's Major Shareholder (including a person who used to be an Insurance Company's Major Shareholder) falls under any of the following items, it shall notify the Prime Minister of this pursuant to the provisions of Cabinet Office Ordinance:
(i) If it becomes the Insurance Company's Major Shareholder under the authorization set forth in Article 271-10, paragraph (1) or is formed as the Insurance Company's Major Shareholder subject to such authorization;
(ii) If it comes to hold voting rights exceeding 50 percent of all shareholders' voting rights in the Insurance Company;
(iii) If it ceases to be the holder of a number of voting rights in an Insurance Company equal to or exceeding the Major Shareholder Threshold (excluding the case re-

Art.271-33   ⑥ Insurance Business Act, Part II, Chap.XI, Sec.4

ferred to in item (v));
(iv) If it ceases to hold voting rights exceeding 50 percent of all shareholders' voting rights in the Insurance Company (excluding the cases referred to in the preceding and following items);
(v) If it dissolves (including when a judgment invalidating its formation, share transfer, merger (limited to a merger for forming a company or any other juridical person that becomes the holder of a number of voting rights in an Insurance Company equal to or exceeding the Major Shareholder Threshold) or incorporation-type split has become final and binding);
(vi) If its voting rights are acquired or come to be held by a single shareholder, in excess of 50 percent of all shareholders' voting rights; or
(vii) If it falls under any other case specified by Cabinet Office Ordinance.
(2) If an Insurance Holding Company (including a former Insurance Holding Company) falls under any of the following items, it shall notify the Prime Minister of this pursuant to the provisions of Cabinet Office Ordinance:
(i) If it becomes an Insurance Holding Company subject to the authorization set forth in Article 271-18, paragraph (1) or is established as an Insurance Holding Company subject to such authorization;
(ii) If it stops being a Holding Company whose Subsidiaries include an Insurance Company (excluding the case referred to in item (v));
(iii) If it seeks to make any of the companies listed in the items of Article 271-22, paragraph (1) (except when it seeks to merge, Split or acquire a business with the authorization set forth in Article 271-31, paragraph (1), (2) or (3)) its Subsidiary;
(iv) If its Subsidiary ceases to be its Subsidiary (except when it splits or assigns a business with the authorization set forth in Article 271-31, paragraph (2) or (3), and the case referred to in item (ii));
(v) If it dissolves (including when a judgment invalidating its incorporation, share transfer, merger (limited to a merger for incorporating a Holding Company whose Subsidiaries include an Insurance Company) or incorporation-type split has become final and binding);
(vi) If it seeks to modify the amount of capital;
(vii) If its voting rights are acquired or come to be held by a single shareholder, in excess of 5 percent of all shareholders' voting rights; or
(viii) If it falls under any other case specified by Cabinet Office Ordinance.
(3) The provisions of Article 2, paragraph (15) shall apply mutatis mutandis to voting rights in an Insurance Company's Major Shareholder or an Insurance Holding Company which were acquired or have come to be held by the single shareholder set forth in paragraph (1), item (vi) or the preceding paragraph, item (vii).

(Expiration of Authorization)
Article 271-33 (1) The authorization set forth in Article 271-10, paragraph (1) shall lose its effect when it falls under any of the following items; and the authorization set forth in the proviso to Article 271-10, paragraph (2) shall lose its effect when it falls under item (ii) or (iii):
(i) The particulars covered by the authorization were not implemented within six months from the date of such authorization (except when the Prime Minster had given approval thereto for any compelling reason);
(ii) The Insurance Company's Major Shareholder subject to the authorization ceases to be the holder of a number of voting rights in an Insurance Company equal to or exceeding the Major Shareholder Threshold; or
(iii) The Insurance Company's Major Shareholder subject to the authorization has re-

ceived the authorization set forth in Article 271-18, paragraph (1) or the proviso to Article 271-18, paragraph (3) to make the Insurance Company subject to the authorization its Subsidiary.
(2) The authorization set forth in Article 271-18, paragraph (1) shall lose its effect when it falls under any of the following items; and the authorization set forth in the proviso to Article 271-18, paragraph (3) shall lose its effect when it falls under item (ii):
  (i) The particulars covered by the authorization were not implemented within six months from the date of such authorization (except when the Prime Minster had given approval thereto for any compelling reason); or
  (ii) The Insurance Holding Company subject to the authorization is no longer a Holding Company whose Subsidiaries include an Insurance Company.

Chapter XII Special Provisions on Low-Cost, Short-Term Insurers

Section 1 General Rules

(Registration)
Article 272 (1) A person registered with the Prime Minister may, notwithstanding the provisions of Article 3, paragraph (1), provide Low-Cost, Short-Term Insurance Services.
(2) A Low-Cost, Short-Term Insurer shall be a small-scale entrepreneur (meaning an entrepreneur receiving insurance premiums in an amount not exceeding the standard specified by Cabinet Office Ordinance; the same shall apply in Article 272-26, paragraph (1), item (iii)).

(Application Procedure for Registration)
Article 272-2 (1) An Applicant for the registration set forth in paragraph (1) of the preceding Article shall submit to the Prime Minister a written application for registration detailing the following particulars:
  (i) its trade name or name;
  (ii) the amount of capital or the total amount of funds;
  (iii) the names of directors and company auditors (or, in a company with Committees, directors and executive officers);
  (iv) in a company with accounting advisors, the names of accounting advisors;
  (v) when it conducts any other business than Low-Cost, Short-Term Insurance Services, the content of such business; and
  (vi) the addresses of its head office and other offices.
(2) The following documents, as well as other documents to be specified by Cabinet Office Ordinance, shall be attached to the written application set forth in the preceding paragraph:
  (i) Articles of incorporation;
  (ii) Statement of business procedures;
  (iii) General policy conditions; and
  (iv) Statement of calculation procedures for insurance premiums and policy reserve.
(3) The provisions of Article 4, paragraph (3) shall apply mutatis mutandis to the attachment of the articles of incorporation set forth in paragraph (2), item (i) pursuant to the provisions of the preceding paragraph.
(4) The documents listed in paragraph (2), items (ii) to (iv) inclusive must detail the particulars specified by Cabinet Office Ordinance.

(Registration to Registry)
Article 272-3 (1) Whenever an application has been filed for the registration under Article 272, paragraph (1), unless the Prime Minister denies the Applicant registration pursuant to the provisions of paragraph (1) of the following Article, the Prime Minister shall register the following particulars in the registry of Low-Cost, Short-Term Insurers:
(i) The particulars listed in the items of paragraph (1) of the preceding Article; and
(ii) The date and number of registration.
(2) The Prime Minister shall make the registry of Low-Cost, Short-Term Insurers available for public inspection.

(Refusal of Registration)
Article 272-4 (1) The Prime Minister shall deny an Applicant registration if the Applicant falls under any of the following items, or if the written application or a document attached thereto includes any false detail or fails to detail a material fact:
(i) A person that is not a Stock Company or Mutual Company (limited to a company that falls under the following sub-items in accordance with the categories set forth in those items):
(a) A Stock Company or Mutual Company (hereinafter referred to as "Stock Company, etc." in this paragraph) whose capital or total funds (including the reserves for redemption of funds set forth in Article 56; the same shall apply in the following item) is less than the amount specified by Cabinet Order: a company with a board of directors and company auditors or Committees; or
(b) Any other Stock Company, etc. than the Stock Company, etc. listed in (a): a company with a board of directors and board of company auditors or Committees, and accounting auditors;
(ii) A Stock Company, etc. whose capital or total funds is less than the amount specified by Cabinet Order as necessary and appropriate for the protection of Policyholders, etc.;
(iii) A Stock Company, etc. whose net assets are less than the amount specified by Cabinet Order which is provided for in the preceding item;
(iv) A Stock Company, etc. whose articles of incorporation include any provisions that do not conform to laws and regulations.
(v) A Stock Company, etc., whose documents listed in Article 272-2, paragraph (2), items (ii) and (iii) include any particular that does not conform to the following standards:
(a) Its insurance contracts do not include any stipulation that poses a risk to the protection of Policyholders, etc.;
(b) Its insurance contracts do not include any stipulation that constitutes undue discriminatory treatment against specific persons;
(c) Its insurance contracts do not include any stipulation that poses the risk of facilitating or inducing conduct with prejudice to the public policy and good morals;
(d) Its insurance contracts do not include any stipulation that entails acceptance of excessive risk in light of the solvency of the Stock Company, etc.; and
(e) The stipulations of its insurance contracts, including on the rights and obligations of Policyholders, etc., are clear and plain to Policyholders, etc.;
(vi) A Stock Company, etc. whose calculation procedures for insurance premiums and policy reserves as described in the document listed in Article 272-2, paragraph (2), item (iv) have not been confirmed by the actuary as reasonable and appropriate based on actuarial science.

(vii) A Stock Company, etc. whose license under Article 3, paragraph (1) was rescinded pursuant to the provisions of Article 133 or 134, whose registration under Article 272, paragraph (1) was canceled pursuant to the provisions of Article 272-26, paragraph (1) or Article 272-27 or whose registration under Article 276 or 286 was canceled pursuant to the provisions of Article 307, paragraph (1), or against which a similar type of license or registration under the relevant provisions of a foreign law or regulation equivalent to this Act (including any permission or other administrative disposition similar to such license or registration) was canceled in the foreign state concerned, without five years having elapsed since the date of such cancellation;

(viii) A Stock Company, etc. sentenced to a fine (including any equivalent punishment under a foreign law or regulation) for violating the provisions of this Act, the Act concerning Regulation, etc. of Receiving of Capital Subscription, Deposits, Interest on Deposits, etc. (Act No. 195 of 1954) or an equivalent foreign law or regulation, without five years having elapsed since the execution of the sentence was terminated or since it was no longer subject to the execution of the sentence;

(ix) A Stock Company, etc. that conducts any other business than the business set forth in the proviso to Article 272-11, paragraph (2) to be specified by Cabinet Office Ordinance, or is found to pose the risk of obstructing the appropriate and secure performance of its Low-Cost, Short-Term Insurance Services;

(x) A Stock Company, etc. whose directors, executive officers, accounting advisors or company auditors include any person:
  (a) who was subject to a ruling for the commencement of bankruptcy proceedings and whose rights have not been restored, or who is receiving any similar treatment under a foreign law or regulation;
  (b) who was sentenced to imprisonment without work or severer punishment (including any equivalent punishment under a foreign law or regulation), without five years having elapsed since the execution of the sentence was terminated or since he/she was no longer subject to the execution of the sentence;
  (c) whose license under Article 3, paragraph (1) was rescinded pursuant to the provisions of Article 133 or 134, whose license under Article 185, paragraph (1) was canceled pursuant to the provisions of Article 205 or 206, whose license under Article 219, paragraph (1) was canceled pursuant to the provisions of Article 231 or 232, whose registration under Article 272, paragraph (1) was canceled pursuant to the provisions of Article 272-26, paragraph (1) or Article 272-27 or whose registration under Article 276 or 286 was canceled pursuant to the provisions of Article 307, paragraph (1), or against whom a similar type of license or registration under the relevant provisions of a foreign law or regulation equivalent to this Act (including any permission or other administrative disposition similar to such license or registration) was canceled in the foreign state concerned, and who had been a director, executive officer, accounting advisor or company auditor, or the Representative Person in Japan (including any similar post) of the company at any time during the 30 (thirty) days prior to the date of the cancellation, without five years having elapsed since the date of such cancellation;
  (d) whose registration under Article 276 or 286 was rescinded pursuant to the provisions of Article 307, paragraph (1) or against whom a similar type of registration under the relevant provisions of a foreign law or regulation equivalent to this Act (including any permission or other administrative disposition similar to such registration) was canceled, without five years having elapsed since the date of such cancellation;

(e) who was subject to an order for dismissal as director, executive officer, accounting advisor or company auditor pursuant to the provisions of Article 133, an order for dismissal as Representative Person in Japan pursuant to the provisions of Article 205 or 231, an order for dismissal as director, executive officer, accounting advisor or company auditor pursuant to the provisions of Article 272-26, paragraph (2), or order for dismissal as director, executive officer, accounting advisor or company auditor or Representative Person in Japan (including any similar post) under the relevant provisions of a foreign law or regulation equivalent to this Act, without five years having elapsed since the date of such disposition; or

(f) who was sentenced to a fine (including any equivalent punishment under a foreign law or regulation) for violating a provisions of any of the Acts set forth in item (viii) or the Act to Prevent Unjust Acts by Organized Crime Group Members, etc. (Act No. 77 of 1991), or a provisions of any foreign law or regulation equivalent to those Acts, or for committing a crime under the Penal Code or the Act on Punishment of Physical Violence and Other Related Matters (Act No. 60 of 1926), without five years having elapsed since the execution of the sentence was terminated or since he/she was no longer subject to the execution of the sentence;

(xi) A Stock Company, etc. without sufficient human resource structure to provide Low-Cost, Short-Term Insurance Services in an appropriate manner; or

(xii) An Insurance Company.

(2) The amount of net assets set forth in item (iii) of the preceding paragraph shall be calculated pursuant to the provisions of a Cabinet Office Ordinance.

(Deposit)

Article 272-5 (1) A Low-Cost, Short-Term Insurer shall deposit the amount of money to be specified by Cabinet Order as necessary and appropriate for the protection of Policyholders, etc. with the deposit office located nearest to its head office or principal office.

(2) If the Prime Minister finds it necessary for the protection of Policyholders, etc. , he/she may order a Low-Cost, Short-Term Insurer to deposit, in addition to the amount of money set forth in the preceding paragraph to be specified by Cabinet Order, the amount of money that he/she finds appropriate prior to the commencement of its Low-Cost, Short-Term Insurance Services.

(3) If a Low-Cost, Short-Term Insurer has concluded an agreement stipulating that a required amount of deposit be deposited for the Low-Cost, Short-Term Insurer by order of the Prime Minister pursuant to the provisions of a Cabinet Order and has notified the Prime Minister of this, the insurer may withhold in whole or in part the deposit under the preceding two paragraphs regarding the amount to be deposited under said agreement (hereinafter referred to as the "Contract Amount" in this Article), so long as the agreement remains in effect.

(4) If the Prime Minister finds it necessary for the protection of Policyholders, etc. , he/she may order a person who has concluded with a Low-Cost, Short-Term Insurer the agreement set forth in the preceding paragraph or the Low-Cost, Short-Term Insurer concerned to make a deposit in an amount corresponding to the whole or part of the Contract Amount.

(5) A Low-Cost, Short-Term Insurer must not commence Low-Cost, Short-Term Insurance Services, unless it has made the deposit under paragraph (1) (including any deposit made pursuant to the provisions of paragraph (2) following an order for deposit of money under that paragraph) or concluded the agreement set forth in paragraph (3),

and has notified the Prime Minister thereof.
(6) The Policyholders, insured parties or beneficiaries pertaining to insurance contracts have, with regard to any credit arising out of the insurance contracts, a priority claim over other creditors on the deposit pertaining to the Low-Cost, Short-Term Insurer.
(7) Any necessary particular in enforcing a claim under the preceding paragraph shall be specified by Cabinet Order.
(8) If the amount of its deposit (including the Contract Amount) falls below the amount set forth in paragraph (1) to be specified by Cabinet Order for reasons such as the enforcement of a claim under paragraph (6), the Low-Cost, Short-Term Insurer shall compensate for the shortfall or conclude the agreement set forth in paragraph (3) (simply referred to as "Make a Deposit" in Article 319, item (xi)) within two weeks from the date specified by Cabinet Office Ordinance, and notify the Prime Minister thereof without delay.
(9) A national government bond, local government bond or any other securities to be specified by Cabinet Office Ordinance may be deposited in lieu of the deposit set forth in paragraph (1), (2) or the preceding paragraph.
(10) The deposit made pursuant to the provisions of paragraph (1), (2), (4) or (8) may be recovered pursuant to the provisions of a Cabinet Order, if and when:
  (i) the registration made under Article 272, paragraph (1) is canceled pursuant to the provisions of Article 272-26, paragraph (1) or Article 272-27; or
  (ii) the registration made under Article 272, paragraph (1) loses its effect pursuant to the provisions of Article 273, paragraph (1) or (3).
(11) In addition to what is specified for in the preceding paragraphs, any necessary particulars of deposits shall be prescribed by Cabinet Office Ordinance/Ordinance of the Ministry of Justice.

(Low-Cost, Short-Term Insurers' Liability Insurance Contracts)
Article 272-6 (1) A Low-Cost, Short-Term Insurer that has concluded a Low-Cost, Short-Term Insurer's liability insurance contract pursuant to the provisions of a Cabinet Order may, with the Prime Minister's approval, withhold part of the deposit to be made under the preceding Article, paragraph (1), (2) or (8), or choose not to conclude the agreement set forth in paragraph (3) of the same Article, depending on the amount insured by the contract, so long as the contract remains in effect.
(2) If the Prime Minister finds it necessary for the protection of Policyholders, etc. , he/she may order a Low-Cost, Short-Term Insurer that has concluded the Low-Cost, Short-Term Insurer's liability insurance contract set forth in the preceding paragraph to deposit in whole or in part that part of the deposit under the preceding Article, paragraph (1), (2) or (8) which the insurer may withhold or for which it may choose not to conclude the agreement set forth in paragraph (3) of the same Article.
(3) In addition to what is prescribed in the preceding two paragraphs, any necessary particular of Low-Cost, Short-Term Insurers' liability insurance contracts shall be specified by a Cabinet Office Ordinance.

(Notification of Change)
Article 272-7 (1) If there has been a change in any of the particulars listed in the items of Article 272-2, paragraph (1), the Low-Cost, Short-Term Insurer shall notify the Prime Minister of this within two weeks from the day on which the change occurred.
(2) The Prime Minister shall register the effect of any notice received under the preceding paragraph to the registry of Low-Cost, Short-Term Insurers.

(Posting of Sign, etc.)

Article 272-8 (1) A Low-Cost, Short-Term Insurer shall, at a conspicuous location in each of its offices, post a sign in the form to be specified by Cabinet Office Ordinance.
(2) Any person other than a Low-Cost, Short-Term Insurer shall not post the sign set forth in the preceding paragraph or any similar sign thereto.
(3) For the purpose of applying the provisions of Article 7, paragraph (2) to a Low-Cost, Short-Term Insurer, the term "letters that run the risk of mistaking the entity for an Insurance Company" shall be deemed to be replaced with "letters that run the risk of mistaking the entity for an Insurance Company (excluding the letters to be specified by Cabinet Office Ordinance as indicating that the entity is a Low-Cost, Short-Term Insurer)."

(Prohibition of Name Lending)
Article 272-9 A Low-Cost, Short-Term Insurer shall not have another person provide Low-Cost, Short-Term Insurance Services in the name of the Low-Cost, Short-Term Insurer.

(Restriction on Concurrent Holding of Posts by Director, etc.)
Article 272-10 (1) A director (in the case of a company with committees, executive officer) engaging in the day-to-day business of a Low-Cost, Short-Term Insurer shall not engage in the day-to-day business of another company, except when authorized by the Prime Minister.
(2) Whenever an application has been filed for the authorization set forth in the preceding paragraph, unless the Prime Minister finds that the particulars given in the application pose the risk of interfering with the sound and appropriate business operation of the Low-Cost, Short-Term Insurer's business, the Prime Minister shall grant such authorization.

Section 2 Business, etc.

(Scope of Business)
Article 272-11 (1) A Low-Cost, Short-Term Insurer may conduct Low-Cost, Short-Term Insurance Business and any other business incidental thereto.
(2) A Low-Cost, Short-Term Insurer may not conduct any business other than what is provided pursuant to the provisions of the preceding paragraph; provided however, that this shall not apply when the Low-Cost, Short-Term Insurer has received the approval of the Prime Minister pursuant to the provisions of Cabinet Office Ordinance for any business specified by Cabinet Office Ordinance as related to Low-Cost, Short-Term Insurance Services which are found to pose no risk to the insurer in performing Low-Cost, Short-Term Insurance Services in an appropriate and secure manner.
(3) Where a written application for the registration set forth in Article 272, paragraph (1) includes an indication that the Applicant seeks to conduct any other business than what is provided for pursuant to the provisions of paragraph (1), the Applicant shall be deemed to have received the approval set forth in the proviso to the preceding paragraph conduct such business if its application for registration is accepted.

(Method of Investment)
Article 272-12 A Low-Cost, Short-Term Insurer shall invest money received as insurance premiums and other assets by any of the following methods:
   (i) Deposit with any of the banks or financial institutions specified by Cabinet Office Ordinance;
   (ii) Acquisition of national government bonds or any other securities specified by Cabi-

net Office Ordinance as equivalent thereto; or
(iii) Any other method specified by Cabinet Office Ordinance as equivalent to the methods listed in the preceding two items.

(Amount of Insurance Proceeds for One Policyholder, etc.)

Article 272-13 (1) A Low-Cost, Short-Term Insurer shall not, with regard to any one single Policyholder, underwrite policies with a total amount of insurance proceeds exceeding the amount specified by Cabinet Order.

(2) The provisions of Article 100-2, Article 100-3 and Article 100-4 shall apply mutatis mutandis to a Low-Cost, Short-Term Insurer. In this case, the terms "Insurance Company's Major Shareholder" and "Insurance Holding Company" in Article 100-3 shall be deemed to be replaced with "Low-Cost, Short-Term Insurer's Major Shareholder provided for in Article 272-34, paragraph (1)" and "Low-Cost, Short-Term Insurance Holding Company as defined in Article 272-37, paragraph (2)," respectively.

(Obligation to Conclude a Contract, etc. with a Designated Dispute Resolution Organization for Low-Cost, Short-Term Insurance Services)

Article 272-13-2 (1) A Low-Cost, Short-Term Insurer shall take the measures specified in the following items according to the category of cases set forth in the respective items:
(i) in cases where there is a Designated Dispute Resolution Organization for Low-Cost, Short-Term Insurance Services (meaning a Designated Dispute Resolution Organization for which the Category of Dispute Resolution Services, etc. is Low-Cost, Short-Term Insurance Services; hereinafter the same shall apply in this Article): measures to conclude a Basic Contract for the Implementation of Dispute Resolution Procedures for Low-Cost, Short-Term Insurance Services with a single Designated Dispute Resolution Organization for Low-Cost, Short-Term Insurance Services;
(ii) in cases where there is no Designated Dispute Resolution Organization for Low-Cost, Short-Term Insurance Services: Complaint Processing Measures and Dispute Resolution Measures concerning Low-Cost, Short-Term Insurance Services.

(2) A Low-Cost, Short-Term Insurer shall, when it has taken measures to conclude a Basic Contract for the Implementation of Dispute Resolution Procedures pursuant to the provisions of the preceding paragraph, publicize the trade name or name of the Designated Dispute Resolution Organization for Low-Cost, Short-Term Insurance Services that is the counterparty to said Basic Contract for the Implementation of Dispute Resolution Procedures.

(3) The provisions of paragraph (1) shall not apply for the periods specified in the following items according to the category of cases set forth in the respective items:
(i) when the relevant case which had fallen under the cases set forth in paragraph (1), item (i), has come to fall under the cases set forth in item (ii) of that paragraph: the period specified by the Prime Minister at the time of granting authorization for abolition of Dispute Resolution Services, etc. under Article 308-23, paragraph (1) or rescinding the designation under Article 308-24, paragraph (1), as the period necessary to take the measures specified in that item;
(ii) when the relevant case had fallen under the cases set forth in paragraph (1), item (i), and the abolition of Dispute Resolution Services, etc. of a single Designated Dispute Resolution Organization for Low-Cost, Short-Term Insurance Services under that item has been authorized under Article 308-23, paragraph (1) or the designation under Article 308-2, paragraph (1) of a single Designated Dispute Resolution Organization for Low-Cost, Short-Term Insurance Services under that item

has been rescinded pursuant to Article 308-24, paragraph (1) (excluding the case set forth in the preceding item): the period specified by the Prime Minister at the time of granting such authorization or making such rescission, as the period necessary for taking the measures specified in paragraph (1), item (i); and
(iii) when the relevant case which had fallen under the cases set forth in paragraph (1), item (ii) has come to fall under the cases set forth in item (i) of that paragraph: the period specified by the Prime Minister at the time of designation under Article 308-2, paragraph (1), as the period necessary to take the measures specified in that item.

(Scope of a Low-Cost, Short-Term Insurer's Subsidiary Companies, etc.)
Article 272-14 (1) A Low-Cost, Short-Term Insurer shall not have as its Subsidiary any company other than one that conducts business that is dependent on its own business, or any other business specified by Cabinet Office Ordinance as incidental or related thereto.
(2) A Low-Cost, Short-Term Insurer shall, when it seeks to take as its Subsidiary a company specialized in any of the business set forth in the preceding paragraph specified by Cabinet Office Ordinance, receive in advance the approval of the Prime Minister, unless it receives the authorization for business acquisition, merger or company split set forth in Article 142 as applied mutatis mutandis pursuant to Article 272-30, paragraph (1), or in Article 167, paragraph (1) or Article 173-6, paragraph (1).

Section 3 Accounting

(Business Year)
Article 272-15 The business year of a Low-Cost, Short-Term Insurer shall run from 1 April to 31 March of the next year.

(Business Report, etc.)
Article 272-16 (1) A Low-Cost, Short-Term Insurer shall, for each business year, prepare a business report describing the status of its business and property for submission to the Prime Minister.
(2) A Low-Cost, Short-Term Insurer that is also a Stock Company, etc. falling under Article 272-4, paragraph (1), item (i), sub-item (b) (referred to as "Specified Low-Cost, Short-Term Insurer" in the following paragraph and the following Article) shall, in addition to the business report set forth in the preceding paragraph, prepare an interim business report for submission to the Prime Minister.
(3) The provisions of Article 110, paragraph (2) shall apply mutatis mutandis where a Specified Low-Cost, Short-Term Insurer has any Subsidiary or any other person to which it is specially related as specified by Cabinet Office Ordinance (referred to as "Subsidiary Company, etc." in the following Article and Article 272-25, paragraph (1)); and the provisions of Article 110, paragraph (3) shall apply mutatis mutandis to a Low-Cost, Short-Term Insurer. In this case, the term "the preceding two paragraphs" in Article 110, paragraph (3) shall be deemed to be replaced with "Article 272-16, paragraphs (1) and (2), and the preceding paragraph."

(Explanatory Documents on Business and Property Status)
Article 272-17 The provisions of Article 111, paragraph (1) and paragraphs (3) to (6) inclusive shall apply mutatis mutandis to a Low-Cost, Short-Term Insurer; and the provisions of Article 111, paragraph (2) shall apply mutatis mutandis to a Specified Low-Cost, Short-Term Insurer with any Subsidiary Company, etc.

(Mutatis Mutandis Application of Provisions on the Amortization of Business Expenditures, etc.)

Article 272-18 The provisions of Article 113, Article 115, Article 116, paragraphs (1) and (3), Article 117, and Article 120 to 122 inclusive shall apply mutatis mutandis to a Low-Cost, Short-Term Insurer; and the provisions of Article 114 shall apply mutatis mutandis to a Stock Company that is also a Low-Cost, Short-Term Insurer. In this case, the term "the preceding two paragraphs" in Article 116, paragraph (3) shall be deemed to be replaced with "paragraph (1)"; and the term "policy reserves pertaining to the insurance contracts specified by Cabinet Office Ordinance has been funded according to a sound actuarial practice" in Article 121, paragraph (1), item (i) shall be deemed to be replaced with "insurance premiums pertaining to the insurance contracts specified by Cabinet Office Ordinance are calculated using a reasonable and relevant method based on actuarial science, and whether the policy reserves pertaining thereto has been funded using a reasonable and relevant method based on actuarial science."

Section 4 Supervision

(Modification of Particulars Prescribed in Statement of Business Procedures, etc.)

Article 272-19 (1) A Low-Cost, Short-Term Insurer shall, when it seeks to modify any of the particulars prescribed in the documents listed in Article 272-2, paragraph (2), items (ii) to (iv) inclusive, give advance notification thereof to the Prime Minister.

(2) Where the notification prescribed in the preceding paragraph pertains to the modification of any particular prescribed in the document listed in Article 272-2, paragraph (2), item (iv), the Low-Cost, Short-Term Insurer shall submit a written opinion confirming the actuary's finding that the method of calculating the insurance premiums and policy reserves prescribed in the document is reasonable and relevant based on actuarial science.

(3) The necessary the particulars of the written opinion set forth in the preceding paragraph shall be specified by Cabinet Office Ordinance.

(Notification, etc. of the Modification of Particulars Prescribed in Statement of Business Procedures, etc.)

Article 272-20 (1) Where a notification was made under the preceding Article, the modification pertaining to such notification shall be deemed to be made on the day when sixty days have passed since the day following the date of receipt by the Prime Minister of the notification (or, on the day following the date of receipt of such notification, where the notification solely pertains to a modification in any of the particulars prescribed in the document listed in Article 272-2, paragraph (2), item (iv)).

(2) If the Prime Minister finds that the particulars of a notification under the preceding Article (other than a notification solely pertaining to a modification in any of the particulars prescribed in the document listed in Article 272, paragraph (2), item (iv)) conform to the standards listed in Article 272-4, paragraph (1), item (v), he/she may shorten the period prescribed in the preceding paragraph to any period of time that he/she finds reasonable. In this case, the Prime Minister shall, without delay, give notice of the shortened period of time to the person that made the notification.

(3) The Prime Minister may, when there is reasonable ground to believe that a reasonable period of time is required to examine whether the particulars of a notification under the preceding Article conform to the standards listed in Article 272-4, paragraph (1),

item (v), and that such examination will not be completed within the period of time prescribed in paragraph (1), extend the period of time to any period that he/she finds reasonable. In this case, the Prime Minister shall, without delay, give notice of the extended period of time and the reason for the extension to the person that made the notification.

(4) If the Prime Minister finds that the particulars of a notification under the preceding Article do not conform to the standards listed in Article 272-4, paragraph (1), item (v), he/she may order the person that made the notification to modify any of the particulars of the notification within a specified period time, or to revoke the notification, provided that such order be issued within sixty days from the day following the date of receipt of such notification (or within any extended period of time pursuant to the provisions of the preceding paragraph).

(Particulars Requiring Notice)
Article 272-21 (1) If a Low-Cost, Short-Term Insurer falls under any of the following items, it shall notify the Prime Minister of this pursuant to the provisions of a Cabinet Office Ordinance:
(i) If it begins Low-Cost, Short-Term Insurance Business;
(ii) If its Subsidiary ceases to be its Subsidiary (except when it assigns its business or splits with the authorization set forth in Article 142 as applied mutatis mutandis pursuant to Article 272-30, paragraph (1), or Article 173-6, paragraph (1));
(iii) If it seeks to increase the amount of capital or the total amount of funds;
(iv) If it modifies its articles of incorporation;
(v) If its voting rights are acquired or come to be held by a single shareholder, in excess of 5 percent of all shareholders' voting rights; or
(vi) If it falls under any of the other cases specified by Cabinet Office Ordinance (or Cabinet Office Ordinance/Ordinance of the Ministry of Finance in the cases pertaining to the financial bankruptcy processing system and financial crisis management).
(2) The provisions of Article 2, paragraph (15) shall apply mutatis mutandis to the voting rights in a Low-Cost, Short-Term Insurer acquired or held by the single shareholder set forth in item (v) of the preceding paragraph.

(Submission of Reports or Materials)
Article 272-22 (1) If the Prime Minister finds it necessary for protecting the Policyholders, etc. and for ensuring the sound and appropriate business operation of a Low-Cost, Short-Term Insurer, he/she may request the Low-Cost, Short-Term Insurer to submit a reports or materials concerning the status of its business or property.
(2) If and to the extent that the Prime Minister finds it particularly necessary for protecting the Policyholders, etc. and for ensuring the sound and appropriate business operation of a Low-Cost, Short-Term Insurer, he/she may request the Low-Cost, Short-Term Insurer's Subsidiary Company, etc. (meaning its Subsidiary or any other juridical person whose management is specified as being be controlled by the Low-Cost, Short-Term Insurer under a Cabinet Office Ordinance; the same shall apply in the following paragraph and paragraphs (2) and (3) of the following Article) or a person the Low-Cost, Short-Term Insurer has entrusted with its business to submit a report or materials that should serve as reference concerning the condition of the business or property of the Low-Cost, Short-Term Insurer, within the limit necessary.
(3) A Low-Cost, Short-Term Insurer's Subsidiary Company, etc. or a person that a Low-Cost, Short-Term Insurer has entrusted with its business may refuse to submit reports or materials required under the preceding paragraph if there are justifiable

grounds for it to do so.

(On-Site Inspection)
Article 272-23 (1) If the Prime Minister finds it necessary for protecting the Policyholders, etc. and for ensuring the sound and appropriate business operation of a Low-Cost, Short-Term Insurer, he/she may have his/her officials enter a business office, any other office or any other facility of the Low-Cost, Short-Term Insurer to ask questions on the status of its business or property, or inspect books and documents and other materials.
(2) The Prime Minister may, when and to the extent that he/she finds it particularly necessary in making an entry, asking questions, or conducting inspection pursuant to the provisions of the preceding paragraph, have his/her officials enter a facility of a Low-Cost, Short-Term Insurer's Subsidiary Company, etc. or a person the Low-Cost, Short-Term Insurer has entrusted with its business, have such officials question the Low-Cost, Short-Term Insurer or ask questions about any particulars that are necessary for their inspection, or have such officials inspect books and documents and other materials.
(3) A Low-Cost, Short-Term Insurer's Subsidiary Company, etc. or a person that a Low-Cost, Short-Term Insurer has entrusted with its business may refuse the questioning and inspection set forth in the preceding paragraph if there are justifiable grounds for it to do so.

(Order to Modify Regarding Particulars Prescribed in Statement of Business Procedures, etc.)
Article 272-24 (1) If the Prime Minister finds that the particulars prescribed by a Low-Cost, Short-Term Insurer in the document listed in Article 272-2, paragraph (2), item (iv) fall under any of the following items, he/she may order the Low-Cost, Short-Term Insurer to modify any of the particulars prescribed in the document listed in that item within a specified period of time:
(i) The method of calculating insurance premiums is not found to be reasonable and relevant based on actuarial science, in light of the rate of Insurance Proceeds, etc. (meaning the rate found by dividing the amount of the insurance proceeds and other benefits (including any other payment specified by Cabinet Office Ordinance as equivalent thereto) which became payable under insurance contracts within the business year concerned) by the amount of insurance premiums specified by Cabinet Office Ordinance as received under the insurance contracts; or
(ii) The method of calculating the policy reserves is not found to be reasonable and relevant based on actuarial science.
(2) In addition to the cases prescribed in the preceding paragraph, the Prime Minister may, when and to the extent that he/she finds it necessary, in light of the status of the business or property of a Low-Cost, Short-Term Insurer or changing circumstances, for protecting the Policyholders, etc. and for ensuring the sound and appropriate business operation of the Low-Cost, Short-Term Insurer, order the Low-Cost, Short-Term Insurer to modify any of the particulars prescribed in the documents listed in Article 272-2, paragraph (2), items (ii) to (iv) inclusive.

(Business Improvement Order)
Article 272-25 (1) If the Prime Minister finds it necessary, in light of the status of the business or property of a Low-Cost, Short-Term Insurer or the status of the property of its Subsidiary Company, etc. , for protecting the Policyholders, etc. and for ensuring the sound and appropriate business operation of the Low-Cost, Short-Term Insurer,

he/she may request the Low-Cost, Short-Term Insurer to submit an improvement program for ensuring the soundness of its management by specifying particulars with regard to which measures must be taken as well as a time limit or order the modification of the submitted improvement program, or order necessary measures for the purpose of supervision.

(2) An order under the preceding paragraph that it is found to be necessary to issue due to the Low-Cost, Short-Term Insurer's level of solvency in terms of its ability to pay Insurance Proceeds, etc. , must be an order specified by Cabinet Office Ordinance or Ordinance of the Ministry of Finance for the category that corresponds to the Low-Cost, Short-Term Insurer's level of solvency in terms of its ability to pay Insurance Proceeds, etc.

(Cancellation of Registration, etc.)
Article 272-26 (1) The Prime Minister may order the total or partial suspension of the business of a Low-Cost, Short-Term Insurer for a specified period of time, or cancel the registration set forth in Article 272, paragraph (1), if and when the Low-Cost, Short-Term Insurer:
  (i) falls under any of Article 272-4, paragraph (1), items (i) to (iv) inclusive, item (vii), (viii) or (xi);
  (ii) obtains the registration set forth in Article 272, paragraph (1) by wrongful means;
  (iii) ceases to be a small-scale entrepreneur or violates any other provisions of a law or regulation;
  (iv) violates any disposition by the Prime Minister pursuant to a law or regulation or any of the particularly important particulars prescribed in the documents listed in the items of Article 272-2, paragraph (2); or
  (v) engages in any action with prejudice to the public interest.
(2) Where any director, executive officer, accounting advisor or company auditor of a Low-Cost, Short-Term Insurer falls under any of Article 272-4, paragraph (1), item (x), sub-items (a) to (f) inclusive, violates any provisions of a law or regulation, or acts as listed in item (iv) or (v) of the preceding paragraph, the Prime Minister may order the Low-Cost, Short-Term Insurer to dismiss the director, executive officer, accounting advisor or company auditor.

Article 272-27 If the Prime Minister finds that, from the viewpoint of protecting Policyholders, etc. , it is inappropriate for a Low-Cost, Short-Term Insurer to engage in Low-Cost, Short-Term Insurance Services, because of extreme deterioration in the status of its property, the Prime Minister may cancel the registration of such Low-Cost, Short-Term Insurer under Article 272, paragraph (1).

(Mutatis Mutandis Application of Provisions on the Standard of Soundness)
Article 272-28 The provisions of Article 130 shall apply mutatis mutandis to a Low-Cost, Short-Term Insurer.

Section 5 Portfolio Transfers, etc. of Insurance Contracts

(Mutatis Mutandis Application of Provisions on Portfolio Transfers of Insurance Contracts)
Article 272-29 The provisions of Chapter VII, Section 1 shall apply mutatis mutandis to the transfer of insurance contracts of a Low-Cost, Short-Term Insurer. In this case, the term "Foreign Insurance Company, etc." in Article 135, paragraph (1) shall be deemed to be replaced with "Foreign Insurance Company, etc. or Low-Cost, Short-Term Insur-

er."

(Mutatis Mutandis Application of Provisions on the Transfer or Acceptance of Business, and Entrustment of Activity and Property)
Article 272-30 (1) The provisions of Article 142 shall apply mutatis mutandis to the transfer or acceptance of business involving a Low-Cost, Short-Term Insurer or Low-Cost, Short-Term Insurers.
(2) The provisions of Chapter VII, Section 3 shall apply mutatis mutandis to entrustment of the administration of business and property by a Low-Cost, Short-Term Insurer. In this case, the term "Foreign Insurance Company, etc. (unless otherwise specified by a Cabinet Office Ordinance)" in Article 144, paragraph (1) shall be deemed to be replaced with "Foreign Insurance Company, etc. (unless otherwise specified by a Cabinet Office Ordinance) or Low-Cost, Short-Term Insurer."

Section 6 Shareholders

Subsection 1 Low-Cost, Short-Term Insurers' Major Shareholders

(Approval Pertaining to Holders of Voting Rights in a Low-Cost, Short-Term Insurer, etc. Equal to or Exceeding the Major Shareholder Threshold)
Article 272-31 (1) Any person who seeks to become the holder of a number of voting rights in a Low-Cost, Short-Term Insurer equal to or exceeding the Major Shareholder Threshold or to form a company or juridical person that is the holder of a number of voting rights in a Low-Cost, Short-Term Insurer equal to or exceeding the Major Shareholder Threshold through any of the following transactions or actions (other than the State, etc. set forth in Article 271-10, paragraph (1), the company set forth in Article 272-35, paragraph (1) that seeks to become a Holding Company, the person set forth in that paragraph or the Low-Cost, Short-Term Insurance Holding Company set forth in Article 272-37, paragraph (2) that seeks to make a Low-Cost, Short-Term Insurer its Subsidiary Company), shall obtain the approval of the Prime Minister in advance:
(i) Acquisition of voting rights in a Low-Cost, Short-Term Insurer by a person seeking to hold the relevant voting rights (except for those obtained by the acquisition of shares through the exercise of a security interest or due to any other event specified by Cabinet Office Ordinance);
(ii) An action through which the registration set forth in Article 272, paragraph (1), is obtained, through a company that holds a number of voting rights in a Low-Cost, Short-Term Insurer equal to or exceeding the Major Shareholder Threshold, by the person seeking to become the holder of said voting rights); or
(iii) Any other transaction or action specified by Cabinet Order.
(2) Any person that has become the holder of a number of voting rights in a Low-Cost, Short-Term Insurer equal to or exceeding the Major Shareholder Threshold due to any other event than the transactions or actions listed in the items of the preceding paragraph (other than the National Government, etc. set forth in Article 271-10, paragraph (1), the Specified Low-Cost, Short-Term Insurance Holding Company set forth in Article 272-35, paragraph (2) or the Specified Low-Cost, Short-Term Insurance Holding Company set forth in Article 272-37, paragraph (2); referred to as a "Low-Cost, Short-Term Insurer's Specified Major Shareholder" hereafter in this Article as well as in Article 333) shall take necessary measures for ensuring that it will cease to be the holder of a number of voting rights in a Low-Cost, Short-Term Insurer equal to or exceeding the Major Shareholder Threshold by the date one year after the last day of the Low-

Cost, Short-Term Insurer's business year in which the event occurred (referred to as the "Last Day of the Grace Period" hereafter in this paragraph as well as in paragraph (4)); provided, however, that this shall not apply where the Low-Cost, Short-Term Insurer's Specified Major Shareholder has received approval from the Prime Minister for continuing to be the holder of a number of voting rights in the Low-Cost, Short-Term Insurer equal to or exceeding the Major Shareholder Threshold after the Last Day of the Grace Period.

(3) If a Low-Cost, Short-Term Insurer's Specified Major Shareholder has ceased to be the holder of a number of voting rights in the Low-Cost, Short-Term Insurer equal to or exceeding the Major Shareholder Threshold due to the measures set forth in the preceding paragraph, it shall notify the Prime Minister of this without delay. The same applies if it has ceased to be the holder of a number of voting rights in the Low-Cost, Short-Term Insurer equal to or exceeding the Major Shareholder Threshold without such measures.

(4) The Prime Minister may order a person who has become the holder of a number of voting rights in a Low-Cost, Short-Term Insurer equal to or exceeding the Major Shareholder Threshold through any of the transactions or actions listed in the items of paragraph (1) or a company or any other juridical person formed as the holder of a number of voting rights in a Low-Cost, Short-Term Insurer equal to or exceeding the Major Shareholder Threshold, without receiving the approval set forth in paragraph (1), or a person that continues to be the holder of a number of voting rights in a Low-Cost, Short-Term Insurer equal to or exceeding the Major Shareholder Threshold, even after the Last Day of the Grace Period, without receiving the approval set forth in the proviso to paragraph (2), to take necessary measures for ensuring that it will cease to be the holder of a number of voting rights in the Low-Cost, Short-Term Insurer equal to or exceeding the Major Shareholder Threshold.

(5) The provisions of Article 2, paragraph (15) shall apply mutatis mutandis to the voting rights held by the holder of a number of voting rights in a Low-Cost, Short-Term Insurer equal to or exceeding the Major Shareholder Threshold, in the cases referred to in the preceding paragraphs.

(Application Procedure for Approval)

Article 272-32 (1) Any person that seeks to receive the approval set forth in the preceding Article, paragraph (1) or the proviso to paragraph (2) shall submit to the Prime Minister a written application for approval detailing the following particulars:

(i) the particulars of the Proportion of Voting Rights Held (meaning the proportion calculated by dividing the number of voting rights the Applicant for approval holds in the Low-Cost, Short-Term Insurer to which the approval pertains, by all shareholders' voting rights in the Low-Cost, Short-Term Insurer; the same shall apply in Article 272-36, paragraph (1) and Article 272-42, paragraph (1)), the particulars of the acquisition funding, the purpose of holding the voting rights, and other particulars specified by Cabinet Office Ordinance as important particulars of the holding of voting rights in a Low-Cost, Short-Term Insurer;

(ii) its trade name, name, and address;

(iii) for a juridical person, the amount of capital or contribution and the name of its representative person; and

(iv) for a business entity, the names and addresses of its business offices and the type of its business.

(2) The written application for approval set forth in the preceding paragraph shall be attached with a document containing a pledge that the application does not fall under paragraph (1), item (i), sub-item (c) or item (ii), sub-item (c) of the following Article as

well as any other document specified by Cabinet Office Ordinance.
(3) The provisions of Article 2, paragraph (15) shall apply mutatis mutandis to the voting rights held by the person submitting the written application for approval in the case referred to in paragraph (1).

Article 272-33 (1) Whenever an application has been filed for the approval under Article 272-31, paragraph (1) or the proviso to Article 272-31, paragraph (2), with the exception of cases falling under any of the following, the Prime Minister shall give such approval:
(i) The person that filed the application for approval (hereinafter referred to as "Applicant" in this Article) is a company or any other juridical person, or where a company or any other juridical person is to be formed with the approval, any of the following applies:
 (a) In light of the particulars of the acquisition funding, the purpose of holding the voting rights or any other particular involved in the holding of a number of voting rights in a Low-Cost, Short-Term Insurer equal to or exceeding the Major Shareholder Threshold by the company or any other juridical person to be formed with the approval (hereinafter referred to as "Juridical Person Applicant, etc." in this item), the application poses a risk to the sound and appropriate business operation of the Low-Cost, Short-Term Insurer in which the Juridical Person Applicant, etc. holds, or will hold, a number of voting rights equal to or exceeding the Major Shareholder Threshold;
 (b) In light of the condition of the property and balance of payment of the Juridical Person Applicant, etc. and its Subsidiary Companies (including any prospective Subsidiary Company), the application poses a risk to the sound and appropriate business operation of the Low-Cost, Short-Term Insurer in which the Juridical Person-Applicant, etc. holds, or will hold, a number of voting rights equal to or exceeding the Major Shareholder Threshold; or
 (c) The Juridical Person Applicant, etc. falls under any of the following:
1. A person whose license under Article 3, paragraph (1) was canceled pursuant to the provisions of Article 133 or 134, whose license under Article 185, paragraph (1) was canceled pursuant to the provisions of Article 205 or 206, whose license under Article 219, paragraph (1) was canceled pursuant to the provisions of Article 231 or 232, whose registration under Article 272, paragraph (1) was canceled pursuant to the provisions of Article 272-26, paragraph (1) or Article 272-27 or whose registration under Article 276 or 286 was canceled pursuant to the provisions of Article 307, paragraph (1), or whose license or registration of a similar type obtained under a foreign law or regulation equivalent to this Act (including any permission or other administrative disposition similar to such license or registration) was canceled in the foreign state concerned, without five years having elapsed since the date of such cancellation.
2. A person sentenced to a fine (including any equivalent punishment under a foreign law or regulation) for violating a provisions of any of the actions set forth in Article 272-4, paragraph (1), item (viii) or any foreign law or regulation equivalent thereto, without five years having elapsed since the execution of the sentence was terminated or since it was no longer subject to the execution of the sentence;
3. A person whose officers include the person listed in Article 331, paragraph (1), item (ii) of the Companies Act (Qualifications of Directors) or Article 331, paragraph (1), item (iii) of that Act as applied with relevant changes in interpretation pursuant to the provisions of Article 12, paragraph (1), or a person falling under

Art.272-34   6 Insurance Business Act, Part II, Chap.XII, Sec.6

any of Article 272-4, paragraph (1), item (x), sub-items (a) to (f) inclusive; or
(ii) In any other case than that listed in the preceding item, any of the following applies:
 (a) In light of the particulars of the acquisition funding, the purpose of holding the voting rights or any other particular involved in the holding of a number of voting rights in the Low-Cost, Short-Term Insurer equal to or exceeding the Major Shareholder Threshold by the Applicant, the application poses a risk to the sound and appropriate business operation of the Low-Cost, Short-Term Insurer in which the Applicant holds, or will hold, a number of voting rights equal to or exceeding the Major Shareholder Threshold;
 (b) In light of the status of the property of the Applicant (including the condition of balance of payment, where the Applicant is a business entity), the application poses a risk to the sound and appropriate business operation of the Low-Cost, Short-Term Insurer in which the Applicant holds, or will hold, a number of voting rights equal to or exceeding the Major Shareholder Threshold; or
 (c) The Applicant falls under any of the following points:
 1. An adult ward or person under curatorship, or any other person receiving a similar treatment under a foreign law or regulation, whose statutory representative falls under Article 331, paragraph (1), item (ii) of the Companies Act or Article 331, paragraph (1), item (iii) of that Act as applied with relevant changes in interpretation pursuant to the provisions of Article 12, paragraph (1), or any of Article 272-4, paragraph (1), item (x), sub-items (a) to (f) inclusive; or
 2. A person falling under Article 331, paragraph (1), item (ii) of the Companies Act or Article 331, paragraph (1), item (iii) of that Act as applied with relevant changes in interpretation pursuant to the provisions of Article 12, paragraph (1), or any of Article 272-4, paragraph (1), item (x), sub-items (a) to (f) inclusive.
(2) The provisions of Article 2, paragraph (15) shall apply mutatis mutandis to the voting rights held by the Applicant in the case referred to in the preceding paragraph.

(Mutatis Mutandis Application of Provisions on Supervision)
Article 272-34 (1) The provisions of Article 271-12 to 271-14 inclusive and 271-16 shall apply mutatis mutandis to a Low-Cost, Short-Term Insurer's Major Shareholder that holds a number of voting rights in a Low-Cost, Short-Term Insurer equal to or exceeding the Major Shareholder Threshold (meaning a person that has received the approval to hold such voting rights following any of the transactions or actions listed in items of Article 272-31, paragraph (1), was formed with the approval set forth in the same paragraph, or has received the approval set forth in the proviso to paragraph (2) of the same Article; the same shall apply hereinafter). In this case, the term "Article 128, paragraph (1)" in Article 271-12 shall be deemed to be replaced with "Article 272-22, paragraph (1)"; the term "Article 129, paragraph (1)" in Article 271-13 shall be deemed to be replaced with "Article 272-23, paragraph (1)"; the terms "the items of Article 271-11" and "authorization set forth in the proviso of Article 271, paragraph (1) or (2)" in Article 271-14 shall be deemed to be replaced with "Article 272-33, paragraph (1), items (i) and (ii)" and "approval set forth in Article 272-31, paragraph (1) or the proviso to Article 272-31, paragraph (2)," respectively; the terms "authorization of the Insurance Company's Major Shareholder set forth in the proviso of Article 271-10, paragraph (1) or (2)," "authorizations set forth in Article 271-10, paragraph (1)" and "said authorization" in Article 271-16, paragraph (1) shall be deemed to be replaced with "approval of the Insurance Company's Major Shareholder set forth in Article 272-31, paragraph (1) or the proviso to Article 272-31, paragraph (2)," "approvals set forth in Article 272-31, paragraph (1)," and "said approval," respectively; and the term "autho-

rization set forth in the proviso of Article 271-10, paragraph (1) or (2)" in Article 271-16, paragraph (2) shall be deemed to be replaced with "approval set forth in Article 272-31, paragraph (1) or the proviso to Article 272-31, paragraph (2)."p
(2) The provisions of Article 2, paragraph (15) shall apply mutatis mutandis to the voting rights held by the holder of a number of voting rights in a Low-Cost, Short-Term Insurer equal to or exceeding the Major Shareholder Threshold in the case referred to in the preceding paragraph.

Subsection 2 Low-Cost, Short-Term Insurance Holding Company

(Approval Pertaining to Low-Cost, Short-Term Insurance Holding Company, etc.)
Article 272-35 (1) Any company that seeks to become a Holding Company whose Subsidiaries include a Low-Cost, Short-Term Insurer through any of the following transactions or actions, or any person that seeks to incorporate a Holding Company whose Subsidiaries include a Low-Cost, Short-Term Insurer must receive in advance the approval of the Prime Minister:
  (i) Acquisition of voting rights in the Low-Cost, Short-Term Insurer by the company or any of its Subsidiaries (excluding through the acquisition of shares by the exercise of a security interest or any other event specified by Cabinet Office Ordinance);
  (ii) Any action by a Subsidiary of the company to obtain the registration set forth in Article 272, paragraph (1); or
  (iii) Any other transaction or action specified by Cabinet Order.
(2) Any company that has become a Holding Company whose Subsidiaries include a Low-Cost, Short-Term Insurer following any other event than the transactions or actions listed in items of the preceding paragraph (hereinafter referred to as "Specified Low-Cost, Short-Term Insurance Holding Company") shall, within three months from the end of the business year in which the event occurred, notify the Prime Minister of the fact that the company has become a Holding Company whose Subsidiaries include a Low-Cost, Short-Term Insurer, as well as other particulars specified by Cabinet Office Ordinance.
(3) A Specified Low-Cost, Short-Term Insurance Holding Company shall take necessary measures to ensure that it will cease to be a Holding Company whose Subsidiaries include a Low-Cost, Short-Term Insurer by the date that is one year after the last day of the business year in which the event set forth in the preceding paragraph occurred (referred to as "Last Day of the Grace Period" hereafter in this paragraph as well as in paragraph (5)); provided, however, that this shall not apply where the Prime Minister approves that the Specified Low-Cost, Short-Term Insurance Holding Company continue as a Holding Company whose Subsidiaries include a Low-Cost, Short-Term Insurer after the Last Day of the Grace Period.
(4) If a Specified Low-Cost, Short-Term Insurance Holding Company has ceased to be a Holding Company whose Subsidiaries include a Low-Cost, Short-Term Insurer due to the measures taken under the preceding paragraph, it shall notify the Prime Minister of this without delay. The same applies if it has ceased to be a Holding Company whose Subsidiaries include a Low-Cost, Short-Term Insurer without such measures.
(5) The Prime Minister may order any company that has become a Holding Company whose Subsidiaries include a Low-Cost, Short-Term Insurer due to any of the transactions or actions listed in the items of paragraph (1) or was incorporated as a Holding Company whose Subsidiaries include a Low-Cost, Short-Term Insurer, without the approval set forth in paragraph (1), or any company that continues as a Holding Company whose Subsidiaries include a Low-Cost, Short-Term Insurer after the Last Day of the

Grace Period without the approval set forth in the proviso to paragraph (3), to take necessary measures to ensure that it will cease to be a Holding Company whose Subsidiaries include a Low-Cost, Short-Term Insurer.

Article 272-36 (1) A person seeking to receive the approval set forth in the preceding Article, paragraph (1) or the proviso to paragraph (3) must submit a written application for approval to the Prime Minister detailing the following particulars:
(i) the particulars of the Proportion of Voting Rights Held, the particulars of the acquisition funding, the purpose of holding the voting rights, and other particulars specified by Cabinet Office Ordinance as important particulars of the holding of voting rights in a Low-Cost, Short-Term Insurer;
(ii) its trade name;
(iii) the amount of capital;
(iv) the names of its directors and company auditors (or, in a company with Committees, directors and executive officers); and
(v) the names and addresses of its head office and other offices.
(2) The written application for approval set forth in the preceding paragraph shall be attached with the articles of incorporation, the balance sheet, the profit and loss statement, a document containing a pledge that the application does not fall under paragraph (1), item (iii) of the following Article, and other documents specified by Cabinet Office Ordinance.

Article 272-37 (1) Whenever an application has been filed for the approval referred to in Article 272-35, paragraph (1) or the proviso to Article 272-35, paragraph (3), with the exception of cases falling under any of the following, the Prime Minister shall give such approval:
(i) in light of the status of the property and balance of payment of the company that filed the application for approval or the company to be incorporated with the approval (hereinafter referred to as "Applicant, etc." in this Article) and its Subsidiaries (including any prospective Subsidiaries), the Applicant, etc. poses a risk to the sound and appropriate business operation of the Low-Cost, Short-Term Insurer that is, or will be its Subsidiary;
(ii) in light of its human resource structure, etc. , the Applicant, etc. does not have the necessary knowledge and experience for ensuring the appropriate and fair management of the Low-Cost, Short-Term Insurer that is, or will be, its Subsidiary;
(iii) the Applicant, etc. falls under Article 272-33, paragraph (1), item (i), sub-item (c); or
(iv) the business content of any Subsidiary of the Applicant, etc. falls under item of Article 272-39, paragraph (3).
(2) A Low-Cost, Short-Term Insurance Holding Company (meaning a Holding Company whose Subsidiaries include a Low-Cost, Short-Term Insurer that has received the approval to hold the relevant voting rights following any of the transactions or actions listed in items of Article 272-35, paragraph (1), was incorporated with the approval set forth in Article 272-35, paragraph (1), or has received the approval set forth in the proviso to Article 272-35, paragraph (3); the same shall apply hereinafter) shall be a Stock Company that has the following organs, unless it was incorporated in accordance with the laws and regulations of the foreign state:
(i) Board of directors;
(ii) Board of company auditors or Committees; and
(iii) Accounting auditors.

[2010年6月2日訳] ⑥ Insurance Business Act, Part II, Chap.XII, Sec.6 Art.272-37-2〜272-39

(Qualification, etc. for Directors, etc. of Low-Cost, Short-Term Insurance Holding Company)
Article 272-37-2 (1) The following provisions in the Companies Act shall not apply to a Low-Cost, Short-Term Insurance Holding Company: the proviso to Article 331, paragraph (2) (Qualifications of Directors) (including the cases where it is applied mutatis mutandis pursuant to Article 335, paragraph (1) (Qualifications of Company Auditors) of that Act), Article 332, paragraph (2) (Directors' Terms of Office) (including the cases where it is applied mutatis mutandis pursuant to Article 334, paragraph (1) (Accounting Advisors' Terms of Office) of that Act), Article 336, paragraph (2) (Company Auditors' Terms of Office) and the proviso to Article 402, paragraph (5) (Election of Executive Officers).
(2) A Low-Cost, Short-Term Insurance Holding Company may not become an unlimited partner or a partner who executes the business of a membership company.

(Scope of Business of Low-Cost, Short-Term Insurance Holding Company, etc.)
Article 272-38 (1) A Low-Cost, Short-Term Insurance Holding Company may not conduct business other than managing the operation of any company falling under items of paragraph (1) of the following Article and any other company that has become its Subsidiary with the approval of the Prime Minister set forth in Article 272-39, paragraph (1) or the proviso to Article 272-39, paragraph (4), or any other business incidental thereto.
(2) A Low-Cost, Short-Term Insurance Holding Company shall, in conducting its business, endeavor to ensure the sound and appropriate business operation of its Low-Cost, Short-Term Insurer Subsidiaries.

(Scope of Subsidiaries of a Low-Cost, Short-Term Insurance Holding Company, etc.)
Article 272-39 (1) A Low-Cost, Short-Term Insurance Holding Company must receive advance approval from the Prime Minister, when it seeks to make any company other than the companies that fall under any of the categories specified in the following items its Subsidiary:
(i) A Low-Cost, Short-Term Insurer; or
(ii) A company specialized in business that is dependent on the business conducted by a Low-Cost, Short-Term Insurer, or any business specified by Cabinet Office Ordinance as incidental or related thereto.
(2) A Low-Cost, Short-Term Insurance Holding Company that seeks to receive the approval set forth in the preceding paragraph shall submit to the Prime Minister a written application detailing the business content, amount of capital and human resource structure of the company covered by the application for approval, as well as other particulars specified by Cabinet Office Ordinance.
(3) Whenever an application has been filed for the approval referred to in paragraph (1), with the exception of cases in which the content of the business that the company to which the application pertains conducts or seeks to conducts falls under one of the following items, the Prime Minister shall give such approval:
(i) it may harm the public policy and good morals; or
(ii) it is likely to damage the soundness in management of the company covered by the application in light of the amount of capital, human resource structure, etc. of the company, and any such damage to its managerial soundness in turn poses the risk of damaging the soundness in the management of the Low-Cost, Short-Term Insurer Subsidiaries of the Low-Cost, Short-Term Insurance Holding Company that

Art.272-40　⑥ Insurance Business Act, Part II, Chap.XII, Sec.6

has filed the application.
(4) The provisions of paragraph (1) shall not apply where a company not falling under paragraph (1), item (i) or (ii) becomes a Subsidiary of the Low-Cost, Short-Term Insurance Holding Company following the acquisition of shares or equity interests through the exercise of security interest by the Low-Cost, Short-Term Insurance Holding Company or any of its Subsidiaries, or any other justifiable event specified by Cabinet Office Ordinance; provided, however, that the Low-Cost, Short-Term Insurance Holding Company shall, unless the Prime Minister approves that such company continue to be its Subsidiary, take necessary measures to ensure that the company will cease to be its Subsidiary within one year from the date of such event.
(5) The provisions of Article 271-22 shall apply in lieu of the provisions of paragraph (1) of the preceding Article and the preceding paragraphs to any Low-Cost, Short-Term Insurance Holding Company that seeks to become an Insurance Holding Company by making an Insurance Company its Subsidiary, or any Low-Cost, Short-Term Insurance Holding Company that already is an Insurance Holding Company.
(6) The relevant provisions of the Banking Act or the Long Term Credit Bank Act shall apply in lieu of the provisions of paragraph (1) of the preceding Article and paragraphs (1) to (4) inclusive to any Low-Cost, Short-Term Insurance Holding Company that seeks to become a Bank Holding Company or Long Term Credit Bank Holding Company by making a Bank or Long Term Credit Bank its Subsidiary, or any Low-Cost, Short-Term Insurance Holding Company that already is a Bank Holding Company or Long Term Credit Bank Holding Company.

⑥ **(Mutatis Mutandis Application of Provisions on Accounting, Supervision, etc.)**
Article 272-40 (1) The provisions of Article 271-23 shall apply mutatis mutandis to the business year of a Low-Cost, Short-Term Insurance Holding Company; the provisions of Article 271-24 shall apply mutatis mutandis to an interim business report or business report describing in a consolidated manner the status of the business and property of a Low-Cost, Short-Term Insurance Holding Company, its Subsidiaries and any other company to which it is specially related as specified by Cabinet Office Ordinance (hereinafter referred to as "Subsidiary Companies, etc." in this Article); the provisions of Article 271-25, paragraphs (1) to (4) inclusive shall apply mutatis mutandis to explanatory documents describing the particulars specified by Cabinet Office Ordinance as pertaining to the status of the business and property of a Low-Cost, Short-Term Insurance Holding Company and its Subsidiary Companies, etc. in a consolidated manner with regard to the Low-Cost, Short-Term Insurance Holding Company and its Subsidiary Companies, etc.; the provisions of Article 271-25, paragraph (5) shall apply mutatis mutandis to a Low-Cost, Short-Term Insurance Holding Company; and the provisions of Article 271-26 shall apply mutatis mutandis to the particulars for inclusion in the business report and annexed detailed statements of a Low-Cost, Short-Term Insurance Holding Company.
(2) The provisions of Article 271-27 shall apply mutatis mutandis to a Low-Cost, Short-Term Insurance Holding Company whose Subsidiaries include a Low-Cost, Short-Term Insurer, a Low-Cost, Short-Term Insurance Holding Company's Subsidiary, etc. (meaning a Subsidiary or any other person to be prescribed by Cabinet Office Ordinance as a juridical person whose management is controlled by the Low-Cost, Short-Term Insurance Holding Company; hereinafter the same shall apply in this Article) or a person the Low-Cost, Short-Term Insurance Holding Company has entrusted with its business; the provisions of Article 271-28, paragraph (1) shall apply mutatis mutandis to a Low-Cost, Short-Term Insurance Holding Company whose Subsidiaries include a Low-Cost, Short-Term Insurer; the provisions of Article 271-28, paragraphs (2)

and (4) shall apply mutatis mutandis to a Low-Cost, Short-Term Insurance Holding Company's Subsidiary, etc. and a person that a Low-Cost, Short-Term Insurance Holding Company has entrusted with its business; the provisions of Article 271-28, paragraph (3) shall apply mutatis mutandis to the personnel who make an entry, ask questions or conduct inspection under those provisions; the provisions of Article 271-29, paragraph (1) shall apply mutatis mutandis to a Low-Cost, Short-Term Insurance Holding Company; the provisions of Article 271-29, paragraph (2) shall apply mutatis mutandis to a Low-Cost, Short-Term Insurer that is the Subsidiary of a Low-Cost, Short-Term Insurance Holding Company; and the provisions of Article 271-30 shall apply mutatis mutandis to a Low-Cost, Short-Term Insurance Holding Company or a Low-Cost, Short-Term Insurer that is the Subsidiary of a Low-Cost, Short-Term Insurance Holding Company. In this case, the term "Article 128, paragraph (1)" in Article 271-27, paragraph (1) shall be deemed to be replaced with "Article 272-22, paragraph (1)"; the term "Article 129, paragraph (1)" in Article 271-28, paragraphs (1) and (2) shall be deemed to be replaced with "Article 272-23, paragraph (1)"; the terms "authorization given to the Insurance Holding Company under Article 271-18, paragraph (1) or the proviso to Article 271-18, paragraph (3)," "authorization set forth in Article 271-18, paragraph (1)" and "said authorization" in Article 271-30, paragraph (1) shall be deemed to be replaced with "approval given to the Insurance Holding Company under Article 272-35, paragraph (1) or the proviso to Article 272-35, paragraph (3)," "approval set forth in Article 272-35, paragraph (1)" and "said approval," respectively; the term "authorization set forth in Article 271-18, paragraph (1) or the proviso to Article 271-18, paragraph (3)" in Article 271-30, paragraph (2) shall be deemed to be replaced with "approval set forth in Article 272-35, paragraph (1) or the proviso to Article 272-35, paragraph (3)"; the term "Article 271-10, paragraph (2)" in Article 271-30, paragraph (3) shall be deemed to be replaced with "Article 272-31, paragraph (2)"; the term "authorization set forth in Article 271-18, paragraph (1)" in Article 271-30, paragraph (4), items (i) and (ii) shall be deemed to be replaced with "approval set forth in Article 272-35, paragraph (1)"; the term "Article 271-18, paragraph (3) without the authorization set forth in the proviso thereto" in Article 271-30, paragraph (4), item (iii) shall be deemed to be replaced with "Article 272-35, paragraph (3) without the approval set forth in the proviso thereto"; and the term "authorization under Article 271-18, paragraph (1) or the proviso to Article 271-18, paragraph (3)" in Article 271-30, paragraph (4), item (iv) shall be deemed to be replaced with "approval under Article 272-35, paragraph (1) or the proviso to Article 272-35, paragraph (3)."

Subsection 3 Miscellaneous Provisions

(Application of this Act to Low-Cost, Short-Term Insurers' Major Foreign Shareholders and to Foreign Low-Cost, Short-Term Insurance Holding Companies)
Article 272-41 A Cabinet Order shall prescribe special provisions and technical changes in interpretation in applying this Act to a foreign national or foreign juridical person that is the holder of a number of voting rights in a Low-Cost, Short-Term Insurer equal to or exceeding the Major Shareholder Threshold and to a person incorporated in accordance with the laws and regulations of a foreign state whose Subsidiaries include a Low-Cost, Short-Term Insurer (hereinafter referred to as a "Low-Cost, Short-Term Insurer's Major Foreign Shareholder, etc." in this Article), as well as any other particular necessary for applying the provisions of this Act to a Low-Cost, Short-Term Insurer's Major Foreign Shareholder, etc.

Art.272-42 ⑥ Insurance Business Act, Part II, Chap.XII, Sec.6

(Particulars Requiring Notice)

Article 272-42 (1) If a Low-Cost, Short-Term Insurer's Major Shareholder (including a person that used to be a Low-Cost, Short-Term Insurer's Major Shareholder) falls under any of the following items, it shall notify the Prime Minister of this pursuant to the provisions of a Cabinet Office Ordinance:

(i) If it becomes the Low-Cost, Short-Term Insurer's Major Shareholder subject to the approval set forth in Article 272-31, paragraph (1) or is formed as the Low-Cost, Short-Term Insurer's Major Shareholder subject to such approval;

(ii) If any of the particulars listed in the items of Article 272-32, paragraph (1) are modified (excluding any modification in the Proportion of Voting Rights Held;

(iii) If it comes to hold voting rights exceeding 50 percent of all shareholders' voting rights in the Low-Cost, Short-Term Insurer;

(iv) If it ceases to be the holder of a number of voting rights in the Low-Cost, Short-Term Insurer equal to or exceeding the Major Shareholder Threshold (excluding the case referred to in item (vi));

(v) If it ceases to hold voting rights exceeding 50 percent of all shareholders' voting rights in the Low-Cost, Short-Term Insurer (excluding the cases referred to in the preceding and following items);

(vi) If it dissolves (including the case where a court judgment invalidating the establishment, share transfer, Merger (limited to a Merger having resulted in establishment of a company or any other juridical person that becomes the holder of a number of voting rights in a Low-Cost, Short-Term Insurer equal to or exceeding the Major Shareholder Threshold) or an Incorporation-Type Split pertaining to the holder has become final and binding);

(vii) If its voting rights are acquired or come to be held by a single shareholder, in excess of 50 percent of all shareholders' voting rights; or

(viii) If it falls under any other case specified by Cabinet Office Ordinance.

(2) If a Low-Cost, Short-Term Insurance Holding Company (including a former Low-Cost, Short-Term Insurance Holding Company) falls under any of the following items, it shall notify the Prime Minister of this pursuant to the provisions of Cabinet Office Ordinance:

(i) it becomes a Low-Cost, Short-Term Insurance Holding Company subject to the approval set forth in Article 272-35, paragraph (1) or is incorporated as a Low-Cost, Short-Term Insurance Holding Company subject to such approval;

(ii) it ceases to be a Holding Company whose Subsidiaries include a Low-Cost, Short-Term Insurer (excluding the case referred to in item (v));

(iii) it seeks to make any of the companies listed in items of Article 272-39, paragraph (1) its Subsidiary;

(iv) such Subsidiary ceases to be its Subsidiary (excluding the case referred to in item (ii));

(v) the holder dissolves (including the case where a court judgment invalidating the establishment, share transfer, Merger (limited to a Merger for incorporating a Holding Company to make a Low-Cost, Short-Term Insurer its Subsidiary) or Incorporation-Type Split has become final and binding);

(vi) it seeks to modify the amount of capital;

(vii) its voting rights constituting over 5 percent of all shareholders' voting rights, are acquired or come to be held by a single shareholder; or

(viii) the holder falls under any other case specified by Cabinet Office Ordinance.

(3) The provisions of Article 2, paragraph (15) shall apply mutatis mutandis to voting rights in a Low-Cost, Short-Term Insurer's Major Shareholder or in a Low-Cost, Short-Term Insurance Holding Company which were acquired or have come to be held

by the single shareholder set forth in paragraph (1), item (vii) or the preceding paragraph, item (vii).

(Expiration of Approval)
Article 272-43 The provisions of Article 271-33, paragraph (1) shall apply mutatis mutandis to the approval given to a Low-Cost, Short-Term Insurer's Major Shareholder under Article 272-31, paragraph (1) or the proviso to Article 272-31, paragraph (2); and the provisions of Article 271-33, paragraph (2) shall apply mutatis mutandis to the approval given to a Low-Cost, Short-Term Insurance Holding Company under Article 272-35, paragraph (1) or the proviso to Article 272-35, paragraph (3).

Chapter XIII Miscellaneous Provisions

(Expiration of License or Registration)
Article 273 (1) The license set forth Article 3, paragraph (1) or Article 185, paragraph (1), or the registration set forth in Article 272, paragraph (1) shall lose its effect for an Insurance Company (including a Foreign Insurance Company, etc.) or a Low-Cost, Short-Term Insurer falling under any of the following items (item (i) or (v) for a Foreign Insurance Company, etc.):
  (i) It has abolished its Insurance Business (for a Foreign Insurance Company, etc., its Insurance Business in Japan; the same shall apply in item (v));
  (ii) It has dissolved (including when a judgment invalidating its incorporation, share transfer, merger (limited to a merger for incorporating an Insurance Company) or an incorporation-type split has become final and binding);
  (iii) A Stock Company operating in the Insurance Business has transferred all of its insurance contracts;
  (iv) A Stock Company operating in the Insurance Business has carried out a company split, effectively transferring all of its insurance contracts; or
  (v) It does not start its Insurance Business within six months from the date of obtaining such license or registration (except when it received in advance the approval of the Prime Minister for any compelling reason).
(2) When a notification was made under Article 209 following any of the events listed in Article 209, items (v) to (viii) inclusive (for a notification under Article 209, item (v), limited to the notification of a merger through which the Foreign Insurance Company, etc. will be extinguished, a company split resulting in the transfer in whole of the business of the Foreign Insurance Company, etc. or an assignment of the whole business), the license granted by the Prime Minister to the notifying Foreign Insurance Company, etc. under Article 185, paragraph (1) shall lose its effect.
(3) The registration set forth in Article 272, paragraph (1) shall lose its effect when the Low-Cost, Short-Term Insurer obtains the license set forth in Article 3, paragraph (1).

(Public Notice by Prime Minister)
Article 274 In the following cases, the Prime Minister shall give public notice of the relevant fact in the Official Gazette:
  (i) When he/she orders suspension of the whole or part of the business (for a Foreign Insurance Company, etc., its business in Japan) pursuant to the provisions of Article 132, paragraph (1), Article 133, Article 204, paragraph (1), Article 205, Article 241, paragraph (1) or Article 272-26, paragraph (1);
  (ii) he/she has canceled the license set forth in Article 3, paragraph (1) or Article 185, paragraph (1), or the registration set forth in Article 272, paragraph (1), pursuant to the provisions of Article 133, Article 134, Article 205, Article 206, Article 272-26,

Art.275　⑥ Insurance Business Act, Part III, Chap.I

paragraph (1) or Article 272-27;
(iii) he/she has made a disposition ordering the administration of business and property by the Insurance Administrator pursuant to the provisions of Article 241, paragraph (1) or issued an order pursuant to the provisions of Article 258, paragraph (1);
(iv) When the license granted under Article 3, paragraph (1) or Article 185, paragraph (1) has loses effect pursuant to the provisions of the preceding Article;
(v) When he/she rescinds the authorization set forth in Article 271-10, paragraph (1) or the proviso to Article 271-10, paragraph (2) pursuant to the provisions of Article 271-16, paragraph (1);
(vi) When he/she rescinds the authorization set forth in Article 271-18, paragraph (1) or the proviso to Article 271-18, paragraph (3) pursuant to the provisions of Article 271-30, paragraph (1);
(vii) When he/she orders suspension of the whole or part of the business of an Insurance Holding Company's Insurance Company Subsidiaries, pursuant to the provisions of Article 271-30, paragraph (1);
(viii) When he/she orders suspension of the whole or part of the business of an Insurance Company pursuant to the provisions of Article 271-30, paragraph (4); or
(ix) the authorization set forth in Article 271-10, paragraph (1) or the proviso to Article 271-10, paragraph (2) or in Article 271-18, paragraph (1) or the proviso to Article 271-18, paragraph (3) has lost its effect pursuant to the provisions of Article 271-33.

Part III Insurance Solicitation

Chapter I General Rules

(Restrictions on Insurance Solicitation)
Article 275 (1) Insurance Solicitation may not take place other than as provided for in each of the following items with the person set forth in the relevant item engaging in the stipulated Insurance Solicitation:
(i) A Life Insurance Agent registered under the following Article: agency or intermediation for its Affiliated Insurance Company, etc. in concluding insurance contracts (for a bank serving as a Life Insurance Agent or any other person specified by Cabinet Order (hereinafter referred to as "Bank, etc." in this Article), or an director or employee thereof, this shall be limited to the cases specified by Cabinet Office Ordinance as posing little risk to the protection of Policyholders, etc.)
(ii) An officer (other than an officer with authority of representation, or an auditor or audit committee member; the same shall apply hereinafter in this Article, as well as in Articles 283 and 302.) or an employee of a Non-Life Insurance Company (including a Foreign Non-Life Insurance Company, etc.; hereinafter the same shall apply in this Part), or a Non-Life Insurance Representative registered under the following Article or an officer or employee thereof: agency or intermediation for its Affiliated Insurance Company, etc. in concluding insurance contracts (for a Bank, etc. serving as a Non-Life Insurance Representative, or an officer or employee thereof, this shall be limited to the cases specified by Cabinet Office Ordinance as posing little risk to the protection of Policyholders, etc.)
(iii) A Specified Low-Cost, Short-Term Insurance Agent (meaning a Low-Cost, Short-Term Insurance Agent that engages in Insurance Solicitation only for the class of insurance defined in Article 3, paragraph (5), item (i) or any other class of insurance specified by Cabinet Office Ordinance, and who has not been delegated by the

Low-Cost, Short-Term Insurer; the same shall apply hereinafter) or a Low-Cost, Short-Term Insurance Agent registered under the following Article: agency or intermediation for its Affiliated Insurance Company, etc. in concluding insurance contracts (for a Bank, etc. serving as a Low-Cost, Short-Term Insurance Agent, or an officer or employee thereof, this shall be limited to the cases specified by Cabinet Office Ordinance as posing little risk to the protection of Policyholders, etc.)

(iv) An Insurance Broker registered under Article 286, or an officer or employee thereof: intermediation in concluding insurance contracts (where the insurer is a Foreign Insurer that is not a Foreign Insurance Company, etc., this shall be limited to the cases specified by Cabinet Order; for a Bank, etc. serving as an Insurance Broker, or an officer or employee thereof, this shall be limited to the cases specified by Cabinet Office Ordinance as posing little risk to the protection of Policyholders, etc.), excluding intermediation for the conclusion of insurance contracts that a Life Insurance Agent, Non-Life Insurance Agent, or Low-Cost, Short-Term Insurance Agent does for its Affiliated Insurance Company, etc.

(2) Notwithstanding the provisions of any other Act, a Bank, etc. may engage in Insurance Solicitation by way of registration under the following Article or Article 286.

Chapter II Insurance Agents and Affiliated Insurance Companies, etc.

Section 1 Insurance Agents

(Registration)

Article 276 A Specified Insurance Agent (meaning a Life Insurance Agent, Non-Life Insurance Representative, or Low-Cost, Short-Term Insurance Agent (other than a Specified Low-Cost, Short-Term Insurance Agent); the same shall apply hereinafter) shall be registered with the Prime Minister pursuant to the provisions of this Act.

(Application for registration)

Article 277 (1) A person applying for a registration under the preceding Article shall submit to the Prime Minister a written application detailing the following particulars:

(i) Trade name or name and birth date;
(ii) Name and location of the office;
(iii) Trade name, name of the Affiliated Insurance Company, etc. ;
(iv) Any other type of business conducted by the Applicant; and
(v) Any other particular specified by Cabinet Office Ordinance.

(2) The following documents shall be attached to the written application set forth in the preceding paragraph:

(i) A written statement pledging that the Applicant does not fall under any of Article 279, paragraph (1), items (i) to (v) inclusive, item (vii) or (viii) (excluding the reference to Article 279, paragraph (1), item (vi)), item (ix) (excluding the reference to Article 279, paragraph (1), item (vi)), item (x) or (xi);

(ii) Where the Applicant is a juridical person (including an association or foundation that is not a juridical person and has a designated representative person or manager; hereinafter the same shall apply in this Part), a written statement indicating the names and addresses of its officers (including the representative person or manager of an association or foundation that is not a juridical person; hereinafter the same shall apply in this Part except for Articles 283 and 302); and

(iii) In addition to what is listed in the preceding two items, any other document specified by Cabinet Office Ordinance.

(Registration process)
Article 278 (1) Whenever an application has been filed for the registration under Article 276, unless the Prime Minister denies the Applicant registration pursuant to the provisions of paragraphs (1) to (3) inclusive of the following Article, the Prime Minister shall immediately register the following particulars in the registry of Life Insurance Agents, the registry of Non-Life Insurance Representatives, or the registry of Low-Cost, Short-Term Insurance Agents maintained at the location specified by Cabinet Office Ordinance:
(i) Particulars listed in items of paragraph (1) of the preceding Article; and
(ii) Date and number of registration.
(2) Whenever the Prime Minister has made a registration under the provisions of the preceding paragraph, he/she shall notify the Applicant and the Affiliated Insurance Company, etc. of this without delay.

(Denial of Registration)
Article 279 (1) The Prime Minister shall deny an Applicant registration if the Applicant falls under any of the following items, or if the written application or a document attached thereto includes a false detail with regard to an important particular or fails to detail a material fact:
(i) A bankrupt whose rights have not been restored or a person receiving any similar treatment under a foreign law or regulation;
(ii) A person sentenced to imprisonment or severer punishment (including any equivalent punishment under a foreign law or regulation), without three years having elapsed since the execution of the sentence was terminated or since he/she was no longer subject to the execution of the sentence;
(iii) A person sentenced to fine (including any equivalent punishment under a foreign law or regulation) for violating the provisions of this Act or of an equivalent foreign law or regulation, without three years having elapsed since the execution of the sentence was terminated or since he/she was no longer subject to the execution of the sentence;
(iv) A person whose registration under Article 276 above was cancelled pursuant to the provisions of Article 307, paragraph (1), without three years having elapsed since the date of the cancellation (including, where the cancellation of registration was made against a juridical person, a person who had been an officer of the juridical person at any time during the thirty days prior to the date of the cancellation, without three years having elapsed since that date); or a person against whom a similar registration under any provisions of a foreign law or regulation equivalent to this Act was cancelled in the foreign state concerned (including any permission or other administrative measures similar to the registration; hereinafter referred to as "Registration, etc." in this item), without three years having elapsed since the date of the cancellation (including, where the cancellation of Registration, etc. was made against a juridical person, a person who had been an officer of the juridical person at any time during the thirty days prior to the date of the cancellation, without three years having elapsed since that date);
(v) An adult ward or person under curatorship, or any other person receiving a similar treatment under a foreign law or regulation;
(vi) A person who had engaged in any extremely inappropriate conduct in connection with Insurance Solicitation during the three years prior to the date of application;
(vii) An Insurance Broker, or any of its officers or any of its employees engaged in Insurance Solicitation;

[2010年6月2日訳]　**6 Insurance Business Act, Part III, Chap.II, Sec.1**　　Art.280

(viii) A minor who does not have the business capacity of an adult regarding sales and whose statutory representative falls under any of the preceding items;
(ix) A juridical person whose officers include at least one person falling under any of item (i) to (vi) inclusive;
(x) An individual whose employees engaged in Insurance Solicitation include at least one person falling under item (vii); or
(xi) A juridical person whose officers or employees engaged in Insurance Solicitation include at least one person falling under item (vii).

(2) If the Prime Minister seeks to deny an Applicant registration pursuant to the provisions of the preceding paragraph, he/she shall notify the Applicant of this in advance and require the appearance of the Applicant or his/her representative at an opinion hearing to be held by an official designated by the Prime Minister in order to provide an opportunity to submit any further evidence in support of the application.
(3) In the case referred to in the preceding paragraph, the Prime Minister may deny an Applicant registration without hearing any opinion, if the person summoned for the hearing fails to appear without justifiable grounds.
(4) If the Prime Minister has denied an Applicant registration pursuant to the provisions of the preceding three paragraphs, he/she shall notify the Applicant of this in writing without delay.

(Notice, etc. of a Change, etc.)
Article 280　(1) If a Specified Insurance Agent has come to fall under any of the following items, the person specified in the relevant item shall notify the Prime Minister of this without delay:
(i) Any of the particulars listed in the items of Article 277, paragraph (1) have changed: the Specified Insurance Agent affected by the change;
(ii) It has abolished its Insurance Solicitation business: the individual who served as the Specified Insurance Agent or the officer representing the juridical person that served as the Specified Insurance Agent;
(iii) The individual serving as the Specified Insurance Agent has died: his/her heir;
(iv) The juridical person serving as the Specified Insurance Agent has become the subject of a ruling for the commencement of bankruptcy proceedings: the bankruptcy trustee;
(v) The juridical person serving as the Specified Insurance Agent has extinguished due to merger (for an association or foundation that is not a juridical person, any action equivalent to merger; the same shall apply in the following item): the person who served as the officer representing the juridical person; or
(vi) The juridical person serving as the Specified Insurance Agent has dissolved (for an association or foundation that is not a juridical person, any action equivalent to dissolution) for a reason other than a merger or a ruling for the commencement of bankruptcy proceedings: its liquidator (for an association or foundation that is not a juridical person, its representative person or the person who served as its manager).
(2) Whenever the Prime Minister receives notice under the preceding paragraph for the reason specified in item (i), he/she shall register the particulars of the notice in the registry of Life Insurance Agents, the registry of Non-Life Insurance Representatives, or the registry of Low-Cost, Short-Term Insurance Agents, and notify the Affiliated Insurance Company, etc. of this.
(3) Registration of a Specified Insurance Agent shall lose its effect if and when said Agent falls under any of paragraph (1), items (ii) to (vi) inclusive.

(Registration and license tax and fees)
Article 281 An Applicant for registration under Article 276 (including a person who files a report under paragraph (1), item (i) of the preceding Article when such report is deemed to be a new registration pursuant to the provisions of item (xxxvii) of Appended Table 1 of the Registration and License Tax Act (Act No. 35 of 1967)) shall pay the registration and license tax pursuant to the provisions of that Act in the case of item (i), or a fee in an amount specified by Cabinet Order taking the actual cost into consideration in the case of item (ii)
(i) Any application for registration under Article 277, paragraph (1) (including a report filed under paragraph (1), item (i) of the preceding Article above when such report is deemed to be a new registration pursuant to the provisions of Article 34 of the Registration and License Tax Act) submitted upon entrustment by the Affiliated Insurance Company, etc. (excluding any entrustment for a limited time based on temporary needs and specified as such by Cabinet Office Ordinance); or
(ii) Any application which does not fall under the preceding item.

(Restriction on Life Insurance Agents)
Article 282 (1) A Life Insurance Company (including a Foreign Life Insurance Company, etc.; hereinafter the same shall apply in this Part) shall not entrust a Life Insurance Agent of another Life Insurance Company with any Insurance Solicitation on its own behalf.
(2) A Life Insurance Agent may neither serve as an officer or employee of another Life Insurance Company, or as an employee of any such person, nor may an agent engage in Insurance Solicitation under delegation from another Life Insurance Company or serve as an officer or employee of a person that engages in Insurance Solicitation under delegation from another Life Insurance Company.
(3) The provisions of the preceding two paragraphs shall not apply to a Life Insurance Agent that has two or more Affiliated Insurance Companies, etc. if specified by Cabinet Order as posing little risk to the protection of Policyholders, etc. in light of the person's capacity to perform in business involving Insurance Solicitation and other conditions.

Section 2 Affiliated Insurance Companies, etc.

(Liability of Affiliated Insurance Companies, etc.)
Article 283 (1) An Affiliated Insurance Company, etc. shall be liable for any damage caused by an Insurance Agent to a Policyholder involving Insurance Solicitation.
(2) The provisions of the preceding paragraph shall not apply when
(i) With regard to Insurance Solicitation by an Insurance Agent who is an officer of the Affiliated Insurance Company, etc. (for a Life Insurance Company, including a Life Insurance Agent who is an employee of such officer), the Affiliated Insurance Company, etc. used due care in appointing the officer and has made reasonable efforts in relation to Insurance Solicitation by such person to prevent the damage caused to the Policyholder;
(ii) With regard to Insurance Solicitation by an Insurance Agent who is an employee of the Affiliated Insurance Company, etc. (for a Life Insurance Company, including a Life Insurance Agent who is an employee of such employee), the Affiliated Insurance Company, etc. used due care in recruiting the employee (other than an employee of a Life Insurance Company's employee) and has made reasonable efforts in relation to Insurance Solicitation by such person to prevent the damage caused to the Policyholder; or

(iii) With regard to Insurance Solicitation by a Specified Insurance Agent upon entrustment by the Affiliated Insurance Company, etc., or an officer or employee thereof, the Affiliated Insurance Company, etc. used due care in entrusting the Specified Insurance Agent with such solicitation and has made reasonable efforts in relation to Insurance Solicitation by such person to prevent the damage caused to the Policyholder.

(3) The provisions of paragraph (1) shall not prevent the Affiliated Insurance Company, etc. to exercise its right to obtain reimbursement from the Insurance Agent concerned.

(4) The provisions of Article 724 of the Civil Code (Time limit for seeking compensation for damage caused by tort) shall apply mutatis mutandis to any claim under paragraph (1).

(Application for Registration, etc. through Affiliated Insurance Company, etc. as Agent)

Article 284 A Specified Insurance Agent or a person falling under any of Article 280, paragraph (1), items (ii) to (vi) inclusive may appoint the Affiliated Insurance Company, etc. as his/her agent in applying for a registration under Article 277, paragraph (1), or in filing a report under Article 280, paragraph (1) or Article 302.

(Registry of Specified Insurance Agents)

Article 285 (1) An Affiliated Insurance Company, etc. shall, pursuant to the provisions of Cabinet Office Ordinance, maintain a registry of Specified Insurance Agents acting on its behalf at its head office or principal office, or at one of its branch offices or secondary offices (for a Foreign Insurance Company, etc., at its branch office, etc. set forth in Article 185, paragraph (1)).

(2) Any interested person may require the Affiliated Insurance Company, etc. as necessary to provide access to the registry set forth in the preceding paragraph for inspection.

Chapter III Insurance Broker

(Registration)

Article 286 An Insurance Broker shall be registered with the Prime Minister pursuant to the provisions of this Act.

(Application for Registration)

Article 287 (1) A person applying for a registration under the preceding Article shall submit to the Prime Minister a written application detailing the following particulars:

(i) Trade name, name and address;
(ii) Name and location of the office;
(iii) Class(es) of insurance contract to be dealt in;
(iv) Any other type of business conducted by the Applicant; and
(v) Any other particular specified by Cabinet Office Ordinance.

(2) The following documents shall be attached to the written application set forth in the preceding paragraph:

(i) A written statement pledging that the Applicant does not fall under any of Article 289, paragraph (1), items (i) to (v) inclusive, item (vii) or (viii) (excluding the reference to Article 289, paragraph (1), item (vi)), item (ix) (excluding the reference to Article 289, paragraph (1), item (vi)) or item (x);

(ii) In the case where the person is juridical person, a written statement indicating the names and addresses of its officers; and
(iii) In addition to what is listed in the preceding two items, any other document specified by Cabinet Office Ordinance.

(Registration Process)
Article 288 (1) Whenever an application has been filed for the registration under Article 286, unless the Prime Minister denies the Applicant registration pursuant to the provisions of paragraphs (1) to (3) inclusive of the following Article, the Prime Minister shall immediately register the following particulars in the registry of Insurance Brokers maintained at the location specified by Cabinet Office Ordinance:
(i) The particulars listed in items of paragraph (1) of the preceding Article; and
(ii) The date and number of registration.
(2) Whenever the Prime Minister has made a registration under the provisions of the preceding paragraph, he/she shall notify the Applicant of this without delay.
(3) The Prime Minister shall make the registry of Insurance Brokers available for public inspection.

(Denial of Registration)
Article 289 (1) The Prime Minister shall deny an Applicant registration if the Applicant falls under any of the following items, or if the written application or a document attached thereto includes a false detail with regard to an important particular or fails to detail a material fact:
(i) A bankrupt whose rights have not been restored or a person receiving any similar treatment under a foreign law or regulation;
(ii) A person sentenced to imprisonment or severer punishment (including any equivalent punishment under a foreign law or regulation), without three years having elapsed since the execution of the sentence was terminated or since he/she was no longer subject to the execution of the sentence;
(iii) A person sentenced to fine (including any equivalent punishment under a foreign law or regulation) for violating the provisions of this Act or of an equivalent foreign law or regulation, without three years having elapsed since the execution of the sentence was terminated or since he/she was no longer subject to the execution of the sentence;
(iv) A person whose registration under Article 286 was cancelled pursuant to the provisions of Article 307, paragraph (1), without three years having elapsed since the date of the cancellation (including, where the cancellation of registration was made against a juridical person, a person who had been an officer of the juridical person at any time during the thirty days prior to the date of the cancellation, without three years having elapsed since that date), or a person against whom a similar registration under the provisions of a foreign law or regulation equivalent to this Act was canceled in the foreign state concerned (including any permission or other administrative measures similar to the registration; hereinafter referred to as "Registration, etc." in this item), without three years having elapsed since the date of the cancellation (including, where the cancellation of Registration, etc. was made against a juridical person, a person who had been an officer of the juridical person at any time during the thirty days prior to the date of the cancellation, without three years having elapsed since that date);
(v) An adult ward or person under curatorship, or any other person receiving a similar treatment under a foreign law or regulation;
(vi) A person who had engaged in any extremely inappropriate conduct in connection

with Insurance Solicitation during the three years prior to the date of application;
(vii) An Insurance Company, etc. or Foreign Insurance Company, etc., any of its officers (other than an officer who is also an Insurance Agent), or an Insurance Agent (for an employee of a Non-Life Insurance Representative, limited to those engaged in Insurance Solicitation);
(viii) An individual whose employees engaged in Insurance Solicitation include at least one person falling under any of the preceding items;
(ix) A juridical person whose officers or employees engaged in Insurance Solicitation include at least one person falling under any of item (i) to (vii) inclusive; or
(x) A person who does not have sufficient capacity to appropriately perform in business involving Insurance Solicitation.
(2) If the Prime Minister seeks to deny an Applicant registration pursuant to the provisions of the preceding paragraph, he/she shall notify the Applicant of this in advance and require the appearance of the Applicant or his/her representative at an opinion hearing to be held by an official designated by the Prime Minister in order to provide an opportunity to produce any further evidence in support of the application.
(3) In the case referred to in the preceding paragraph, the Prime Minister may deny an Applicant registration without hearing any opinion, if the person summoned for the hearing fails to appear without justifiable grounds.
(4) If the Prime Minister has denied an Applicant registration pursuant to the provisions of the preceding three paragraphs, he/she shall notify the Applicant of this in writing without delay..

(Notice, etc. of a Change, etc.)
Article 290 (1) If an Insurance Broker has come to fall under any of the following items, the person specified in the relevant item shall notify the Prime Minister of this without delay:
(i) Any of the particulars listed in the items of Article 287, paragraph (1) have changed: the Insurance Broker affected by the change;
(ii) It has abolished its Insurance Solicitation business: the individual who served as the Insurance Broker or the officer representing the juridical person that served as the Insurance Broker;
(iii) The individual serving as the Insurance Broker has died: his/her heir;
(iv) The juridical person serving as an Insurance Broker has become the subject of a ruling for the commencement of bankruptcy proceedings: its bankruptcy trustee;
(v) The juridical person serving as an Insurance Broker has extinguished due to merger (for an association or foundation that is not a juridical person, any action equivalent to merger; the same shall apply in the following item): the person who served as the officer representing the juridical person; or
(vi) The juridical person serving as an Insurance Broker has dissolved (for an association or foundation that is not a juridical person, any action equivalent to dissolution) for a reason other than a merger or ruling for the commencement of bankruptcy proceedings: its liquidator (for an association or foundation that is not a juridical person, its representative person or the person who served as its manager).
(2) Whenever the Prime Minister receives notice under the preceding paragraph for the reason provided in item (i), he/she shall register the particulars of the notice on the registry of Insurance Brokers.
(3) An Insurance Broker's registration becomes invalid if the broker comes to fall under any of paragraph (1), items (ii) to (vi) inclusive.

(Security Deposit)

Article 291 (1) An Insurance Broker shall make a security deposit with the deposit office located nearest to its principal office.

(2) The security deposit as set forth in the preceding paragraph shall be in an amount specified by Cabinet Order, taking into consideration the business characteristics of the Insurance Broker and the necessity of protecting Policyholders, etc.

(3) If an Insurance Broker has concluded a contract stipulating that a required amount of security deposit will be made for the Insurance Broker by order of the Prime Minister pursuant to the provisions of Cabinet Order and has notified the Prime Minister of this, the broker may withhold in whole or in Part the security deposit under paragraph (1) regarding the amount to be deposited under said contract (hereinafter referred to as the "Contract Amount" in this Article), so long as the contract remains in effect.

(4) If the Prime Minister finds it necessary for the protection of Policyholders, etc., he/she may order a person who has concluded with an Insurance Broker a contract as set forth in the preceding paragraph or the Insurance Broker concerned to make a deposit in an amount corresponding to the whole or Part of the Contract Amount.

(5) An Insurance Broker may not act as an intermediary in concluding an insurance contract, unless he/she has made the security deposit under paragraph (1) (including the conclusion of a contract under paragraph (3)) and has notified the Prime Minister of this.

(6) A Policyholder who entrusted an Insurance Broker with acting as an intermediary in concluding an insurance contract, the insured covered by the insurance contract or the Beneficiary of the insurance contract shall, with regard to any credit arising out of any such action as an intermediary in concluding the insurance contract, have a priority claim over other creditors on the security deposit made by the Insurance Broker.

(7) Any other necessary particular for enforcing a claim as set forth in the preceding paragraph shall be specified by Cabinet Order.

(8) If the amount of a security deposit (including the Contract Amount; the same shall apply in paragraph (10)) falls below the amount specified by Cabinet Order under paragraph (2) for reasons such as the enforcement of a claim under paragraph (6), the Insurance Broker shall compensate for the shortfall within two weeks from the date specified by Cabinet Office Ordinance (including the conclusion of a contract under paragraph (3); the same shall apply in Article 319, item (xii)), and notify the Prime Minister of this without delay.

(9) The security deposit to be made pursuant to the provisions of paragraph (1) or the preceding paragraph may be in the form of a national government bond, local government bond or any other securities specified by Cabinet Office Ordinance.

(10) The security deposit made pursuant to the provisions of paragraph (1), (4) or (8) may be fully or Partly recovered with the Prime Minister's authorization, if and when:

(i) Any of the item (ii) to (vi) inclusive of paragraph (1) of the preceding Article applies;

(ii) The relevant registration is canceled pursuant to the provisions of Article 307, paragraph (1) or (2) ; or

(iii) The security deposit exceeds the amount specified by Cabinet Order under paragraph (2) for reasons such as changing business characteristics.

(11) The Prime Minister may, in giving an authorization as set forth in the preceding paragraph, designate a period for the recovery and the recoverable amount of the security deposit, within the limit that he/she finds necessary for ensuring the payment of any claim that has arisen out of action as an intermediary in concluding an insurance contract.

(12) In addition to what is provided for in the preceding paragraphs, any necessary particular of security deposits shall be specified by Cabinet Office Ordinance/Ordinance of

(Insurance Brokers Liability Insurance Contract)

Article 292 (1) An Insurance Broker who has concluded an Insurance Broker's liability insurance contract pursuant to the provisions of Cabinet Order may, with the Prime Minister's authorization, withhold in whole or in part the security deposit to be made under paragraph (1) of the preceding Article (including the conclusion of a contract under paragraph (3) of that Article; the same shall apply in the following paragraph) in accordance with the amount of insurance proceeds under the contract, so long as the contract remains in effect.

(2) If the Prime Minister finds it necessary for the protection of Policyholders, etc., he/she may order an Insurance Broker who has concluded an Insurance Broker's liability insurance contract as set forth in the preceding paragraph to make in whole or in Part that Part of the security deposit under paragraph (1) of the preceding Article which may be withheld.

(3) In addition to what is provided for in the preceding two paragraphs, any necessary particular for Insurance Brokers liability insurance contracts shall be specified by Cabinet Office Ordinance.

(Mutatis Mutandis Application of the Commercial Code)

Article 293 The provisions of Articles 543, 544 and 546 to 550 inclusive (Brokerage Business) of the Commercial Code shall apply mutatis mutandis to action as an intermediary by an Insurance Broker in concluding an insurance contract in which the insurer is supposed to be a Mutual Company (including a Foreign Mutual Company).

Chapter IV Business

(Explanation to Customer)

Article 294 An Insurance Agent shall, when seeking to engage in Insurance Solicitation, clearly communicate in advance the following particulars to customers:
(i) Trade name or name of the Affiliated Insurance Company, etc. ;
(ii) Whether he/she will act as an agent of the Affiliated Insurance Company, etc. or as an intermediary in concluding an insurance contract; and
(iii) Any other particular specified by Cabinet Office Ordinance.

(Prohibition of Self-Contract)

Article 295 (1) A Non-Life Insurance Representative or Insurance Broker shall not make it his/her primary business purpose to engage in Insurance Solicitation for insurance contracts in which he/she or his/her employer is the Policyholder or the insured (for an Insurance Broker, limited to those contracts specified by Cabinet Office Ordinance; referred to as "Self-Contracts" in the following paragraph).

(2) For the purpose of applying the provisions of the preceding paragraph, a Non-Life Insurance Representative or Insurance Broker shall be deemed to have made it his/her primary business purpose to engage in Insurance Solicitation for Self-Contracts, when the total amount of insurance premiums for the Self-Contracts solicited by the Non-Life Insurance Representative or Insurance Broker, as calculated pursuant to the provisions of Cabinet Office Ordinance, exceeds 50 percent of the total amount of insurance premiums for all contracts solicited by the Non-Life Insurance Representative or Insurance Broker, as calculated pursuant to the provisions of Cabinet Office Ordinance.

(Clear Indication of Name, etc. of Insurance Broker)
Article 296 (1) If an Insurance Broker seeks to act as an intermediary in concluding an insurance contract, he/she shall deliver to the customer a document detailing the following particulars pursuant to the provisions of Cabinet Office Ordinance:
(i) Trade name, name and address of the Insurance Broker;
(ii) The particulars of the Insurance Broker' authority
(iii) The particulars of the Insurance Broker' liability; and
(iv) In addition to what is listed in the preceding three items, any particular specified by Cabinet Office Ordinance.
(2) In lieu of the delivery of a written statement under the preceding paragraph, an Insurance Broker may, with the authorization of the customer pursuant to the provisions of Cabinet Order, communicate the particulars that are required to be included in the written statement by a method using an electronic data processing system or any other method using information and communications technology pursuant to the provisions of Cabinet Office Ordinance. In this case, the Insurance Broker shall be deemed to have delivered the written statement.

(Information to be Disclosed by Insurance Brokers)
Article 297 An Insurance Broker shall, upon request of a customer, disclose the amount of commission, reward or any other consideration that he/she receives for acting as an intermediary in concluding the insurance contract, or any other particular specified by Cabinet Office Ordinance.

(Particulars for Inclusion in a Closing Document)
Article 298 For the purpose of applying the provisions of Article 546, paragraph (1) of the Commercial Code (Obligation to Prepare and Deliver Closing Document) (including the cases where it is applied mutatis mutandis pursuant to Article 293) to an Insurance Broker, the term "its outline" in the paragraph shall be deemed to be replaced with "the particulars specified by Cabinet Office Ordinance."

(Insurance Broker's Obligation of Good Faith)
Article 299 An Insurance Broker shall act in good faith for the benefit of the customer in acting as an intermediary for the conclusion of an insurance contract.

(Obligation to Conclude a Contract, etc. with a Designated Dispute Resolution Organization for Insurance Solicitation by Insurance Brokers)
Article 299-2 (1) An Insurance Broker shall take the measures specified in the following items according to the category of cases set forth in the respective items:
(i) in cases where there is a Designated Dispute Resolution Organization for Insurance Solicitation by Insurance Brokers (meaning a Designated Dispute Resolution Organization for which the Category of Dispute Resolution Services, etc. is Insurance Solicitation by Insurance Brokers; hereinafter the same shall apply in this Article): measures to conclude a Basic Contract for the Implementation of Dispute Resolution Procedures for Insurance Solicitation by Insurance Brokers with a single Designated Dispute Resolution Organization for Insurance Solicitation by Insurance Brokers;
(ii) in cases where there is no Designated Dispute Resolution Organization for Insurance Solicitation by Insurance Brokers: Complaint Processing Measures and Dispute Resolution Measures concerning Insurance Solicitation by Insurance Brokers.
(2) An Insurance Broker shall, when it has taken measures to conclude a Basic Contract for the Implementation of Dispute Resolution Procedures pursuant to the provisions

of the preceding paragraph, publicize the trade name or name of the Designated Dispute Resolution Organization for Insurance Solicitation by Insurance Brokers that is the counterparty to said Basic Contract for the Implementation of Dispute Resolution Procedures.
(3) The provisions of paragraph (1) shall not apply for the periods specified in the following items according to the category of cases set forth in the respective items:
  (i) when the relevant case which had fallen under the cases set forth in paragraph (1), item (i), has come to fall under the cases set forth in item (ii) of that paragraph: the period specified by the Prime Minister at the time of granting authorization for abolition of Dispute Resolution Services, etc. under Article 308-23, paragraph (1) or rescinding the designation under Article 308-24, paragraph (1), as the period necessary to take the measures specified in that item;
  (ii) when the relevant case had fallen under the cases set forth in paragraph (1), item (i), and the abolition of Dispute Resolution Services, etc. of a single Designated Dispute Resolution Organization for Insurance Solicitation by Insurance Brokers under that item has been authorized under Article 308-23, paragraph (1) or the designation under Article 308-2, paragraph (1) of a single Designated Dispute Resolution Organization for Insurance Solicitation by Insurance Brokers under that item has been rescinded pursuant to Article 308-24, paragraph (1) (excluding the case set forth in the preceding item): the period specified by the Prime Minister at the time of granting such authorization or making such rescission, as the period necessary for taking the measures specified in paragraph (1), item (i); and
  (iii) when the relevant case which had fallen under the cases set forth in paragraph (1), item (ii) has come to fall under the cases set forth in item (i) of that paragraph: the period specified by the Prime Minister at the time of designation under Article 308-2, paragraph (1), as the period necessary to take the measures specified in that item.

(Prohibited Acts Pertaining to Conclusion of Insurance Contract or Insurance Solicitation)

Article 300 (1) An Insurance Company, etc. or Foreign Insurance Company, etc. , any officer thereof (other than an officer who is an Insurance Agent), an Insurance Agent, or an Insurance Broker or any officer or employee thereof shall not take any of the following actions in relation to the conclusion of an insurance contract or Insurance Solicitation (for the conclusion of a specified insurance contract provided in the following Article and related act as an agent or intermediary, excluding the non-disclosure of any important particular stipulated in the insurance contract contained in the provisions of item (i) and the act specified in item (ix):
  (i) Falsely informing the Policyholder or the insured, or failing to disclose thereto any important particular stipulated in the insurance contract;
  (ii) Encouraging the Policyholder or the insured to give false information about any important particular to an Insurance Company, etc. or Foreign Insurance Company, etc. ;
  (iii) Preventing or discouraging the Policyholder or the insured from informing an Insurance Company, etc. or Foreign Insurance Company, etc. of a material fact;
  (iv) Inducing the Policyholder or the insured to apply for a new insurance contract without informing him/her of any fact that would work to his/her disadvantage in the termination of an already effected insurance contract, or terminating an already effected insurance contract by inducing the Policyholder or the insured to apply for a new contract;
  (v) Promising to offer, or actually offering, to the Policyholder or the insured a discount

Art.300-2　⁶ Insurance Business Act, Part III, Chap.IV

or rebate on insurance premiums, or any other special advantage;
(vi) Telling or indicating to the Policyholder or the insured, or any other unspecified person a misleading message regarding the features of an insurance contract in comparison with other contracts;
(vii) Making a conclusive statement, or telling or indicating a misleading message to the Policyholder, the insured, or an unspecified person so that he/she may believe that a certain amount of money will be obtained in the future as a dividend to Policyholders, dividend of surplus to members or any other benefit whose amount is specified as uncertain by Cabinet Office Ordinance.
(viii) Inducing the Policyholder or the insured to offer an insurance contract, knowing that the Specified Related Party of the Insurance Company, etc. or Foreign Insurance Company, etc. (meaning a Specified Related Party as set forth in Article 100-3 (including the cases where it is applied mutatis mutandis pursuant to Article 272-13, paragraph (2); the same shall apply in Article 301) or a Specially Related Party as set forth in Article 194, other than an Insurance Holding Company or Low-Cost, Short-Term Insurance Holding Company whose Subsidiaries include the Insurance Company, etc. or Foreign Insurance Company, etc. (referred to as "Insurance Holding Company, etc." hereinafter in this Article as well as in Article 301-2), a Subsidiary of the Insurance Holding Company, etc. (other than an Insurance Company, etc. or Foreign Insurance Company, etc.), or a person conducting Insurance Business) has promised to offer, or actually offered, a special advantage to the Policyholder or the insured.
(ix) In addition to what is listed in the preceding items, any other action specified by Cabinet Office Ordinance as posing risk to the protection of Policyholders, etc.
(2) The provisions of the preceding paragraph, item (v) shall not apply where an Insurance Company, etc. or Foreign Insurance Company, etc. makes such offer based on a document listed in any of the items of Article 4, paragraph (2), the items of Article 187, paragraph (3) or the items of Article 272-2, paragraph (2).

(Mutatis Mutandis Application of the Financial Instruments and Exchange Act)
Article 300-2　The provisions of Chapter III, Section 1, Subsection 5 (excluding Article 34-2, paragraphs (6) to (8) inclusive (Cases Where a Professional Investor Is Deemed to Be a Customer Other than a Professional Investor) and Article 34-3, paragraphs (5) and (6) (Cases Where a Juridical Person Who Is a Customer Other than a Professional Investor Is Deemed to Be a Professional Investor)) (Professional Investors) and Article 45 (excluding items (iii) and (iv)) (Miscellaneous Provisions) of the Financial Instruments and Exchange Act shall apply mutatis mutandis to the conclusion of a specified insurance contract (meaning an insurance contract specified by Cabinet Office Ordinance as entailing the risk of loss due to any changes in interest rates, currency values, financial instruments market prices as set forth in Article 2, paragraph (14) of that Act or any other indicator (meaning the risk that the total amount of insurance premiums to be paid by the customer following the conclusion of the insurance contract may exceed the total insurance proceeds, reimbursements and other benefits to be paid out to the customer following the conclusion of the contract); hereinafter the same shall apply in this Article) effected by an Insurance Company, etc. or Foreign Insurance Company, etc. , or a contract stipulating any specific action as an intermediary for the benefit of a customer in concluding a specified insurance contract; the provisions of Section 2, Subsection 1 of the same Chapter (excluding Article 35 to 36-4 inclusive (Scope of Business for Persons Who Engage in Type 1 Financial Instruments Transaction Business or Investment Management Business, Scope of Subsidiary Busi-

nesses of Persons Who Only Engage in Type II Financial Instruments Business or Investment Advisory and Agency Business, Duty of Good Faith to Customers, Posting of Signs, Prohibition of Name-Lending and Prohibition of Administration of Company Bonds, etc.), Article 37, paragraph (1), item (ii) (Regulation of Advertising, etc.), Article 37-2 (Obligation to Clarify Conditions of Transactions in Advance), Article 37-3, paragraph (1), items (ii) and (vi) and Article 37-3, paragraph (3) (Delivery of Document Prior to Conclusion of Contract), Article 37-5 to Article 37-7 inclusive (Delivery of Document Pertaining to Receipt of Security Deposit; Cancellation by a Written Statement; and Obligation to Execute Contract with Designated Dispute Resolution Organization), Article 38, items (i) and (ii) and Article 38-2 (Prohibited Acts), the proviso of Article 39, paragraph (3) and Article 39, paragraph (5) (Prohibition of Loss Compensation, etc.), Article 40-2 to Article 40-5 inclusive (Best Execution Policy, etc.; Prohibition of Purchase and Sale, etc. Where Separate Management Is Not Ensured; (General Rules)) shall apply mutatis mutandis to the conclusion of a specified insurance contract by an Insurance Company, etc., Foreign Insurance Company, etc., Insurance Agent or Insurance Broker and related actions as an agent or intermediary. In this case, the terms "financial instruments transaction contract" and "financial instruments transaction business" in those provisions shall be deemed to be replaced with "specified insurance contract, etc.," and "the conclusion of a specified insurance contract, or any related action as an agent or intermediary," respectively; in Article 34 of that Act, the term "the Act of Executing a Financial Instruments Transaction (meaning actions listed in the items of Article 2, paragraph (8); the same shall apply hereinafter) with a customer as the other party or on behalf of a customer" shall be deemed to be replaced with "effecting a specified insurance contract (meaning a specified insurance contract provided in Article 300-2 of the Insurance Business Act; the same shall apply hereinafter) or acting as an intermediary for the benefit of a customer in concluding a specified insurance contract"; in Article 37, paragraph (2) of that Act, the term "the Act of Executing a Financial Instruments Transaction" shall be deemed to be replaced with "the conclusion of specified insurance contracts"; in Article 37-3, paragraph (1) of that Act, the term "when it seeks to conclude a Contract for a Financial Instruments Transaction" shall be deemed to be replaced with "when it seeks to conclude a Contract for a Financial Instruments Transaction or actions as an agent or intermediary in concluding a specified insurance contract" and the term "the following particulars" with "the following particulars and any other important particular stipulated by an insurance contract as provided in Article 300, paragraph (1), item (i) of the Insurance Business Act"; in Article 37-3, paragraph (1), item (i) of that Act, the term "Financial Instruments Transaction Business Operators, etc." shall be deemed to be replaced with "Insurance Company, etc. (meaning an Insurance Company, etc. as defined in Article 2-2, paragraph (1) of the Insurance Business Act), Foreign Insurance Company, etc. (meaning a Foreign Insurance Company, etc. as defined in Article 2, paragraph (7) of that Act) or Insurance Broker (meaning an Insurance Broker as defined in paragraph (25) of the same Article) concluding a specified insurance contract, etc."; in Article 37-3, paragraph (1), item (v) of that Act, the term "financial instruments transaction business conducted" shall be deemed to be replaced with "specified insurance contract concluded"; in Article 38, paragraph (1) of that Act, the term "employee" shall be deemed to be replaced with "employee (excluding an Insurance Agent as defined in Article 2, paragraph (23) of the Insurance Business Act; the same shall apply in Article 39, paragraph (3))"; in Article 39, paragraph (1), item (i) of that Act, the term "purchase and sale or any other transaction of Securities (excluding a purchase and sale on condition of repurchase for which the repurchase price is set in advance and other transactions specified by Cabinet Order) or of Derivative Transactions (hereinafter re-

Art.301　⑥ Insurance Business Act, Part III, Chap.IV

ferred to as a 'Purchase and Sale or Other Transaction of Securities, etc.' in this Article)" shall be deemed to be replaced with "the conclusion of a specified insurance contract"; the term "securities or derivative transactions (hereinafter referred to as 'securities, etc.' in this Article)" with "specified insurance contract," the term "customer (in the case where a Trust Company, etc. (meaning a trust company or financial institution that has obtained authorization under Article 1, paragraph (1) of the Act on the Provision of Trust Business by Financial Institutions; the same shall apply hereinafter) conducts the purchase and sale of Securities or Derivative Transactions on the account of the person who has established a trust under a trust contract, including said person who established the trust; hereinafter the same shall apply in this Article)" with "the customer," the term "loss" with "loss (meaning, where the total amount of insurance premiums to be paid by the customer following the conclusion of the specified insurance contract exceeds the total insurance proceeds, reimbursements and other benefits to be paid out to the customer following the conclusion of the contract, the total amount of premium payment less the total insurance proceeds, reimbursements and other benefits; hereinafter the same shall apply in this Article)," and the term "to supplement" with "to supplement, outside the stipulations of the specified insurance contract"; in Article 39, paragraph (1), items (ii) and (iii) of that Act, the term "the Purchase and Sale or Other Transaction of Securities, etc." shall be deemed to be replaced with "the conclusion of a specified insurance contract," the term "securities, etc." with "specified insurance contract," and the term "to add to" with "to add to, outside the stipulations of the specified insurance contract"; in Article 39, paragraph (2) of that Act, the term "the Purchase and Sale or Other Transaction of Securities, etc." shall be deemed to be replaced with "the conclusion of a specified insurance contract"; in Article 39, paragraph (3) of that Act, the term "determined by Cabinet Office Ordinance as a potential cause" shall be deemed to be replaced with "a potential cause"; in Article 40, item (i) of that Act, the term "financial instruments transaction business" with "the conclusion of a specified insurance contract, etc."; in Article 45, item (ii) of that Act, the term "Article 37-2 to 37-6 inclusive, Article 40-2, paragraph (4) and Article 43-4" shall be deemed to be replaced with "Articles 37-3 (as far as any of the particulars listed in the items of Article 37-3, paragraph (1) is concerned, excluding Article 37-3, paragraph (1), items (ii) and (vi) and Article 37-3, paragraph (3)) and 37-4"; and any other necessary technical replacement of terms shall be specified by Cabinet Order.

Article 301 An Insurance Company, etc. or Foreign Insurance Company, etc. shall not act in any of the following ways or make any of the following transactions in relation to the conclusion of an insurance contract by a Specified Related Party (meaning a Specified Related Party as defined in Article 100-3 (limited to a person conducting Insurance Business) or, in the case of a Foreign Insurance Company, etc., a Specially Related Party as defined in Article 194 (limited to a person conducting Insurance Business); hereinafter the same shall apply in this Article) or any Insurance Solicitation involving the Specified Related Party:
(i) Promising to offer, or actually offering, any special advantage to the Policyholder or the insured in an insurance contract where the Specified Related Party is the insurer; or
(ii) Acting or making a transaction with the Specified Related Party, or with the Policyholder or the insured in an insurance contract where the Specified Related Party is the insurer, provided that the action or transaction is equivalent to that listed in the preceding item and is specified by Cabinet Office Ordinance as posing a risk of harming the fairness of Insurance Solicitation

Article 301-2 An Insurance Holding Company, etc. and any Subsidiary thereof (other than an Insurance Company, etc. or Foreign Insurance Company, etc.) may not act any of the following ways or make any of the following transactions in connection with the conclusion of an insurance contract by any Insurance Company, etc. or Foreign Insurance Company, etc. that is a Subsidiary of the Insurance Holding Company, etc. , or in connection with Insurance Solicitation for the Insurance Company, etc. or Foreign Insurance Company, etc. :
(i) Promising to offer, or actually offering, any special advantage to the Policyholder or the insured in an insurance contract where the Insurance Company, etc. or Foreign Insurance Company, etc. is the insurer; or
(ii) Acting or making a transaction with the Policyholder or the insured in an insurance contract where the Insurance Company, etc. or Foreign Insurance Company, etc. is the insurer, provided that the action or transaction is equivalent to that listed in the preceding item and is specified by Cabinet Office Ordinance as posing a risk of harming the fairness of Insurance Solicitation.

Chapter V Supervision

(Notification Pertaining to Directors and Employees)
Article 302 A Non-Life Insurance Representative, Small-Claims and Short-Term Insurance Agent or Insurance Broker shall, when it seeks to appoint any of its officers or employees to act as Insurance Agents (limited to a specified Low-Cost, Short-Term Insurance Agent for an officer or employee of a Low-Cost, Short-Term Insurance Agent), notify the Prime Minister of the person's name and birth date. The same shall apply to any change in a particular with regard to which notification has been given, the cessation of Insurance Solicitation by any of the officers or employees covered by the notification, and the death of any such person.

(Keeping of Books and Documents)
Article 303 An Insurance Broker shall, pursuant to the provisions of Cabinet Office Ordinance, prepare and keep at each of its offices books and documents on its business, and enter therein the dates of insurance contracts and any other particulars specified by Cabinet Office Ordinance for each Policyholder.

(Submission of Business Reports)
Article 304 An Insurance Broker shall, pursuant to the provisions of Cabinet Office Ordinance, prepare a business report for each business year and submit it to the Prime Minister within three months from the end of the previous business year.

(On-Site Inspection, etc.)
Article 305 The Prime Minister may, within the limit necessary for the enforcement of this Act, order a Specified Insurance Agent or Insurance Broker to submit any report or data that should serve as a reference on its business or property, or have his/her officials enter an office of the Specified Insurance Agent or Insurance Broker to inspect the condition of its business or property or books and documents and other materials, or to ask questions of relevant persons.

(Business Improvement Order)
Article 306 When the Prime Minister finds, with regard to the business of a Specified

Insurance Agent or Insurance Broker, any fact that might harm the interest of Policyholders, etc. , he/she may order, within the limit necessary for the protection of Policyholders, etc. , the Specified Insurance Agent or Insurance Broker to take necessary measures to improve its business operations.

(Cancellation of Registration, etc.)

Article 307 (1) The Prime Minister may cancel the registration of a Specified Insurance Agent or Insurance Broker under Article 276 or 286 above, or order total or partial suspension of its business for a period not exceeding six months when:
 (i) The Specified Insurance Agent falls under any of Article 279, paragraph (1), items (i) to (iii) inclusive, (iv) (limited to the segment meaning any provisions of a foreign law or regulation equivalent to this Act), (v), (vii), (viii) (excluding the reference to Article 279, paragraph (1), item (vi)), item (ix) (excluding the reference to Article 279, paragraph (1), item (vi)), item (x) or (xi), or the Insurance Broker falls under any of Article 289, paragraph (1), items (i) to (iii) inclusive, (iv) (limited to the segment meaning "any provisions of a foreign law or regulation equivalent to this Act"), (v), (vii), (viii) (excluding the reference to Article 279, paragraph (1), item (vi)), item (ix) (excluding the reference to Article 279, paragraph (1), item (vi)) or item (x);
 (ii) The registration under Article 276 or 286 was obtained by wrongful means; or
 (iii) The Specified Insurance Agent or Insurance Broker violates any provisions of this Act or any measures by the Prime Minister based on this Act, or is found to have engaged in any other extremely inappropriate conduct in connection with Insurance Solicitation.
(2) If the Prime Minister cannot ascertain the location of the office of a Specified Insurance Agent or Insurance Broker, or the whereabouts of a Specified Insurance Agent or Insurance Broker (in the case of a juridical person, the whereabouts of the director who represents the juridical person), he/she may issue public notice of that fact and cancel the registration of the Specified Insurance Agent or Insurance Broker if the person does not report within thirty days from the date of the public notice, pursuant to the provisions of Cabinet Office Ordinance.
(3) The provisions of Chapter III of the Administrative Procedure Act (Adverse Dispositions) shall not apply to any measures under the preceding paragraph.

(Deregistration, etc.)

Article 308 (1) The Prime Minister shall deregister a Specific Insurance Agent or Insurance Broker when
 (i) He/she has canceled, pursuant to the provisions of paragraph (1) or (2) of the preceding Article above, any registration under Article 276 or 286 above; or
 (ii) Any registration under Article 276 has lost its effect pursuant to the provisions of Article 280, paragraph (3), or any registration under Article 286 has lost its effect pursuant to the provisions of Article 290, paragraph (3).
(2) If the Prime Minister has deregistered a Specified Insurance Agent pursuant to the provisions of the preceding paragraph, he/she shall notify the Specified Insurance Agent's Affiliated Insurance Company, etc. of this. In this case, the Affiliated Insurance Company, etc. shall delete the entries pertaining to the Specified Insurance Agent from the registry stipulated in Article 285, paragraph (1).

Part IV Designated Dispute Resolution Organizations

Chapter I General Rules

(Designation of Person to Conduct Dispute Resolution Services, etc.)
Article 308-2 (1) The Prime Minister may designate a person satisfying the following requirements as the person to conduct Dispute Resolution Services, etc. , upon that person's application:
(i) that the relevant person is a juridical person (including an association or foundation without judicial personality for which a representative person or administrator has been designated, and excluding a juridical person established under laws and regulations of a foreign state and any other foreign organizations; the same shall apply in item (iv), sub-item (d));
(ii) that the relevant person is not a person who has had the designation under this paragraph rescinded pursuant to Article 308-24, paragraph (1) and for whom five years have not passed since the date of rescission, nor is the relevant person a person who has had the designation under the provisions of other Acts specified by Cabinet Order as pertaining to business equivalent to Dispute Resolution Services, etc. rescinded and for whom five years have not passed since the date of rescission;
(iii) that the relevant person is not a person who has been sentenced to a fine (including a punishment under laws and regulations of a foreign state equivalent to this) for violating the provisions of this Act or the Attorney Act (Act No. 205 of 1949) or laws and regulations of a foreign state equivalent thereto and for whom five years have not passed since the day when the execution of the punishment terminated or he/she became free from the execution of the punishment;
(iv) that the relevant person has no Officers falling under any of the following categories of persons:
  (a) an adult ward or a person under curatorship, or a person who is treated in the same manner under laws and regulations of a foreign state;
  (b) a bankrupt who has not obtained restoration of rights, or a person who is treated in the same manner under laws and regulations of a foreign state;
  (c) a person who has been sentenced to or a severer punishment (including punishment under laws and regulations of a foreign state equivalent to this) and for whom five years have not passed since the day when the execution of the punishment terminated or he/she became free from the execution of the punishment;
  (d) in cases where the designation under this paragraph has been rescinded under the provisions of Article 308-24, paragraph (1) or an administrative disposition similar to said designation in a foreign state pursuant to the provisions of laws and regulations of the foreign state which are equivalent to this Act has been rescinded, a person who was an Officer (including persons treated in the same manner under laws and regulations of a foreign state; the same shall apply in this sub-item (d)) of the juridical person within one month prior to the date of rescission and for whom five years have not passed since the date of rescission, or in cases where the designation under the provisions of other Acts specified by Cabinet Order as pertaining to business equivalent to Dispute Resolution Services, etc. or an administrative disposition similar to said designation in a foreign state as specified by Cabinet Order under the provisions of laws and regulations of the foreign state which are equivalent to said other Acts has been rescinded, a person who was an Officer of the juridical person within one month

prior to the date of rescission and for whom five years have not passed from the date of rescission; or
(e) a person who has been sentenced to a fine (including punishment under laws and regulations of a foreign state equivalent to this) for violating the provisions of this Act, the Attorney Act, or laws and regulations of a foreign state equivalent thereto and for whom five years have not passed since the day when the execution of the punishment terminated or he/she became free from the execution of the punishment;
(v) that the relevant person has a sufficient financial and technical basis to properly implement Dispute Resolution Services, etc. ;
(vi) that the composition of the Officers or employees has no risk of causing hindrance to the fair implementation of Dispute Resolution Services, etc. ;
(vii) that the rules concerning the implementation of Dispute Resolution Services, etc. (hereinafter referred to as the "Operational Rules") conform to laws and regulations and are found sufficient for the fair and appropriate implementation of Dispute Resolution Services, etc. pursuant to the provisions of this Act; and
(viii) that, as a result of hearing the opinions pursuant to the following paragraph, the proportion of the number of Insurance Service Providers who have stated their objections to the particulars of the cancellation of the Basic Contract for the Implementation of Dispute Resolution Procedures, other contents of the Basic Contract for the Implementation of Dispute Resolution Procedures (excluding the particulars listed in the items of paragraph (2) of Article 308-7), and other contents of the Operational Rules (excluding the particulars which are to be the content thereof as provided by paragraph (3) of that Article and the particulars that are necessary to conforming to the standards listed in the items of paragraph (4) of that Article and item (i) of paragraph (5) of that Article) (limited to objections with reasonable grounds attached thereto) to the total number of Insurance Service Providers has become less than the proportion specified by Cabinet Order.
(2) Any person who seeks to file the application under the preceding paragraph shall, in advance and pursuant to the provisions of Cabinet Office Ordinance, explain the contents of the Operational Rules to the Insurance Service Provider and hear opinions therefrom as to whether they have any objections thereto (in cases where there are objections, reasons therefor shall be included) and prepare a document detailing the results thereof.
(3) When the Prime Minister seeks to make the designation under paragraph (1), he/she shall consult the Minister of Justice in advance with regard to the fact that the relevant person satisfies the requirements listed in items (v) to (vii) inclusive of that paragraph (limited to the part related to the operation of Dispute Resolution Procedures, and with regard to the requirements set forth in item (vii), limited to the requirement pertaining to the standards listed in the items of paragraph (4) of Article 308-7 and the items of paragraph (5) of that Article).
(4) The designation under paragraph (1) shall be made for each Category of Dispute Resolution Services, etc. and the proportion under item (viii) of that item shall be calculated for each Category of Dispute Resolution Services, etc.
(5) When the Prime Minister has made the designation under paragraph (1), he/she shall give public notice of the trade name or name and the location of the principal business office or office of the Designated Dispute Resolution Organization, the Category of Dispute Resolution Services, etc. related to said designation, as well as the day on which he/she made the designation in the official gazette.

(Application for Designation)

Article 308-3 (1) A person who seeks to obtain the designation set forth in paragraph (1) of the preceding Article shall submit a written application for designation detailing the following particulars to the Prime Minister:
  (i) the Category of Dispute Resolution Services, etc. for which the relevant person seeks to obtain designation;
  (ii) the trade name or name;
  (iii) the name and location of the principal business office or office or any other business offices or offices for Dispute Resolution Services, etc. ; and
  (iv) the name(s) or trade name(s) of the Officer(s).
(2) The following documents shall be attached to the written application for designation under the preceding paragraph:
  (i) a document to pledge that the person satisfies the requirements set forth in items (iii) and (iv) of paragraph (1) of the preceding Article;
  (ii) the articles of incorporation and the juridical person's certificate of registered particulars (including those equivalent thereto);
  (iii) the Operational Rules;
  (iv) documents detailing the particulars of the organization;
  (v) an inventory of assets, a balance sheet, and any other documents that certify that the relevant person has the necessary financial basis for conducting Dispute Resolution Services, etc. which are specified by Cabinet Office Ordinance;
  (vi) the documents prescribed in paragraph (2) of the preceding Article and any other documents specified by Cabinet Office Ordinance as those that prove that the relevant person satisfies the requirements set forth in item (viii) of paragraph (1) of that Article; and
  (vii) in addition to what is provided for in the preceding items, documents specified by Cabinet Office Ordinance.
(3) In the case referred to in the preceding paragraph, when the articles of incorporation, inventory of assets, or balance sheet has been prepared in the form of an Electromagnetic Record, such Electromagnetic Record may be attached in lieu of the written documents.

(Obligation of Confidentiality, etc.)
Article 308-4 (1) A Dispute Resolution Mediator (meaning the Dispute Resolution Mediator appointed under Article 308-13, paragraph (2); the same shall apply in the following paragraph, paragraph (2) of the following Article and Article 308-7, paragraphs (2) and (4)) or an Officer or employee of the Designated Dispute Resolution Organization, or a person who was formerly in such position shall not divulge to another person or use for his/her own interest any confidential information learned during the course of Dispute Resolution Services, etc.
(2) With regard to the application of the Penal Code and other penal provisions, a Dispute Resolution Mediator or an Officer or employee of the Designated Dispute Resolution Organization who is engaged in Dispute Resolution Services, etc. shall be deemed to be officials engaged in public service under laws and regulations.

Chapter II Business

(Business of a Designated Dispute Resolution Organization)
Article 308-5 (1) A Designated Dispute Resolution Organization shall perform Dispute Resolution Services, etc. pursuant to the provisions of this Act and Operational Rules.
(2) A Designated Dispute Resolution Organization (including the Dispute Resolution Mediators) may receive obligatory contributions, fees, or any other remuneration for per-

Art.308-6〜308-7　⑥ Insurance Business Act, Part IV, Chap.II

forming the Dispute Resolution Services, etc. pursuant to the Basic Contract for the Implementation of Dispute Resolution Procedures or any other contracts concluded with the Member Insurance Service Provider (meaning the Insurance Service Provider with whom a Basic Contract for the Implementation of Dispute Resolution Procedures have been concluded; hereinafter the same shall apply in this Part) who is the party or with the customer thereof (including the Policyholder, etc. other than a customer; hereinafter the same shall apply in this Part) or with persons other than these persons.

(Entrustment of Operation of Complaint Processing Procedures or Dispute Resolution Procedures)
Article 308-6 A Designated Dispute Resolution Organization shall not entrust the operation of Complaint Processing Procedures or Dispute Resolution Procedures to persons other than other Designated Dispute Resolution Organizations or a person who has obtained the designation under the provisions of other Acts specified by Cabinet Order as related to business equivalent to the Dispute Resolution Services, etc. (referred to as the "Entrusted Dispute Resolution Organization" in Article 308-13, paragraph (4) and (5)).

(Operational Rules)
Article 308-7 (1) A Designated Dispute Resolution Organization shall set forth Operational Rules for the following particulars:
(i) the particulars of the contents of the Basic Contract for the Implementation of Dispute Resolution Procedures;
(ii) the particulars of the conclusion of a Basic Contract for the Implementation of Dispute Resolution Procedures;
(iii) the particulars of the implementation of Dispute Resolution Services, etc. ;
(iv) the particulars of the obligatory contribution to be borne by the Member Insurance Service Providers with regard to the cost required for the Dispute Resolution Services, etc. ;
(v) when collecting fees for the implementation of Dispute Resolution Services, etc. from the Member Insurance Service Provider who is the relevant party or from the customer thereof (hereinafter simply referred to as the "Party" in this Part), the particulars of such fees;
(vi) the particulars of coordination with other Designated Dispute Resolution Organizations, national organs, local governments, private enterprises, or any other persons processing complaints or implementing dispute resolution;
(vii) the particulars of complaint processing regarding Dispute Resolution Services, etc. ; and
(viii) in addition to what is listed in the preceding items, particulars specified by Cabinet Office Ordinance as those necessary for the implementation of Dispute Resolution Services, etc.
(2) The Basic Contract for the Implementation of Dispute Resolution Procedures as referred to in item (i) of the preceding paragraph shall provide the following particulars:
(i) that the Designated Dispute Resolution Organization is to commence Complaint Processing Procedures or Dispute Resolution Procedures based on the application for the resolution of Complaints Related to Insurance Services, etc. from the customer of the Member Insurance Service Provider or on application for Dispute Resolution Procedures by the Party;
(ii) that the Designated Dispute Resolution Organization or a Dispute Resolution Mediator may, when Complaint Processing Procedures has been commenced, or when

Dispute Resolution Procedures based on an application by the customer of the Member Insurance Service Provider has been commenced, request that the Member Insurance Service Provider respond to these procedures, and in cases of such request, said Member Insurance Service Provider shall not refuse such request without justifiable grounds;

(iii) that a Designated Dispute Resolution Organization or Dispute Resolution Mediator may request the Member Insurance Service Provider to make reports or submit books and documents or any other articles in the course of Complaint Processing Procedures or Dispute Resolution Procedures, and that said Member Insurance Service Provider shall not refuse such request without justifiable grounds;

(iv) that a Dispute Resolution Mediator may prepare a settlement proposal necessary for the resolution of Disputes Related to Insurance Services, etc. in the course of Dispute Resolution Procedures and recommend that the Party accept such proposal;

(v) that, in cases where, in connection with the Dispute Resolution Procedures, there is no prospect of reaching a settlement between the Parties to the dispute through the recommendation to accept the settlement proposal under the preceding item, if the Dispute Resolution Mediator find it reasonable in light of the nature of the case, intention of the Parties, the status of implementation of procedures by the Parties, or any other circumstances, he/she may prepare a Special Conciliation Proposal necessary for the resolution of a Dispute Related to Insurance Services, etc. and present it to the Parties with reasons attached thereto;

(vi) that, if Dispute Resolution Procedures are commenced for claims with litigation pending, a Member Insurance Service Provider must report that said litigation is pending, the grounds for the claims in said litigation, and the progress of said litigation to the Designated Dispute Resolution Organization;

(vii) that, if litigation involving the claims subject to the Dispute Resolution Procedures is filed, a Member Insurance Service Provider must report that said litigation has been filed and the grounds for the claims in said litigation to the Designated Dispute Resolution Organization;

(viii) in addition to what is provided for in the preceding two items, that if a Member Insurance Service Provider has been demanded to make reports on the progress of litigation involving the claims subject to Dispute Resolution Procedures or any other particulars, he/she must report such particulars to the Designated Dispute Resolution Organization;

(ix) that if the litigation referred to in item (vi) or (vii) comes to no longer be pending in court, or if the court decision in the litigation has become final and binding, the Member Insurance Service Provider must report this to the Designated Dispute Resolution Organization and give the details thereof;

(x) that a Member Insurance Service Provider must provide necessary information or take other measures necessary for informing the implementation of Dispute Resolution Services, etc. by a Designated Dispute Resolution Organization to its customer; and

(xi) in addition to what is provided for in the preceding items, particulars specified by Cabinet Office Ordinance as those necessary for the promotion of the processing of Complaints Related to Insurance Services, etc. or the resolution of Disputes Related to Insurance Services, etc.

(3) The Operational Rules concerning particulars involved in the conclusion of a Basic Contract for the Implementation of Dispute Resolution Procedures under paragraph (1), item (ii) shall provide that, in cases where a Designated Dispute Resolution Organization has received an application for the conclusion of a Basic Contract for the Im-

Art.308-7   [6] Insurance Business Act, Part IV, Chap.II

plementation of Dispute Resolution Procedures from a Member Insurance Service Provider, except in cases where it is expected to be uncertain whether said Member Insurance Service Provider will perform the obligations under the Basic Contract for the Implementation of Dispute Resolution Procedures or any other obligations regarding the implementation of Dispute Resolution Services, etc. , said Designated Dispute Resolution Organization shall not refuse such application.

(4) The Operational Rules concerning the particulars listed in paragraph (1), item (iii), must conform to the following standards:

(i) measures have been taken to ensure coordination between Complaint Processing Procedures and Dispute Resolution Procedures;

(ii) a method has been established for appointing the Dispute Resolution Mediator and, in cases where the Dispute Resolution Mediator has an interest with the Party to the Dispute Related to Insurance Services, etc. or where there are any other causes that are likely to hinder the fair implementation of Dispute Resolution Procedures, the method has been established for excluding such Dispute Resolution Mediator;

(iii) with regard to a Designated Dispute Resolution Organization that is to carry out the operations of Dispute Resolution Procedures with regard to Disputes Related to Insurance Services, etc. of which a Party is the Substantial Controller, etc. (meaning a person specified by Cabinet Office Ordinance as one who substantially controls business of the Designated Dispute Resolution Organization or who has a material influence on business thereof through the holding of the shares of the Designated Dispute Resolution Organization, financing to the Designated Dispute Resolution Organization or any other causes) of the Designated Dispute Resolution Organization or the Subsidiary Company, etc. (meaning a person specified by Cabinet Office Ordinance as one whose business is substantially controlled by the Designated Dispute Resolution Organization through the holding of shares and any other causes) of the Designated Dispute Resolution Organization, measures have been taken for preventing said Substantial Controller, etc. , Subsidiary Company, etc. , or Designated Dispute Resolution Organization to exercise undue influence on the Dispute Resolution Mediator;

(iv) if the Dispute Resolution Mediator is not an attorney-at-law (excluding cases where, with regard to the Dispute Resolution Procedures carried out for a dispute set forth in Article 3, paragraph (1), item (vii) (Business) of the Judicial Scrivener Act (Act No. 197 of 1950), the Dispute Resolution Mediator is a judicial scrivener as set forth in paragraph (2) of that Article) and expert knowledge on the interpretation and application of laws and regulations is required for the implementation of Dispute Resolution Procedures, measures have been taken to receive the advice of an attorney-at-law;

(v) an appropriate method has been established for the notice to be given in implementing the Dispute Resolution Procedures;

(vi) a standard operation process has been established from the commencement to the termination of Dispute Resolution Procedures;

(vii) the requirements and methods have been established for filing an application with the Designated Dispute Resolution Organization for the resolution of a Complaint Related to Insurance Services, etc. by the customer of a Member Insurance Service Provider or for filing an application for Dispute Resolution Procedures with the Designated Dispute Resolution Organization by a Party to the Dispute Related to Insurance Services, etc. ;

(viii) the Designated Dispute Resolution Organization has established procedures for promptly notifying any customer of the Member Insurance Service Provider that

would be the other Party to a Dispute Related to Insurance Services, etc. , of any application that the organization has received for Dispute Resolution Procedures from the Member Insurance Service Provider, and to confirm with such customer whether it will request the implementation of Dispute Resolution Procedures in response to this;
(ix) the Designated Dispute Resolution Organization has established procedures for promptly notifying any Member Insurance Service Provider that would be the other Party to the Dispute Related to Insurance Services, etc. , of any application that the organization has received for Dispute Resolution Procedures under item (vii) from the customer of the Member Insurance Service Provider;
(x) a method has been established for retaining, returning, and other handling of books and documents and any other articles which have been submitted in the course of Dispute Resolution Procedures;
(xi) a method has been established for handling the confidential information of the Parties to the Dispute Related to Insurance Services, etc. or of a third party, which is to be included in opinions to be entered or the books and documents or any other articles to be submitted or presented in the course of Dispute Resolution Procedures, in accordance with the nature of such confidential information; the same applies to the confidential information contained in the dispute resolution procedures record referred to in Article 308-13, paragraph (9);
(xii) that the requirements and methods have been established for the Parties to a Dispute Related to Insurance Services, etc. to terminate the Dispute Resolution Procedures;
(xiii) it is stipulated that the Dispute Resolution Mediator will promptly terminate Dispute Resolution Procedures and notify the Parties to the Dispute Related to Insurance Services, etc. if the Dispute Resolution Mediator judges there to be no prospect of reaching a settlement between the Parties to a Dispute Related to Insurance Services, etc. ; and
(xiv) measures have been established to have the Dispute Resolution Mediator or an Officer or employee of the Designated Dispute Resolution Organization securely retain the confidential information learned in the course of Dispute Resolution Services, etc.
(5) The Operational Rules concerning the particulars listed in paragraph (1), items (iv) and (v) must conform to the following standards:
(i) provisions have been made for the amount of the obligatory contribution set forth in paragraph (1), item (iv), the fees referred to in item (v) of that paragraph, or the calculation and payment methods for them (collectively referred to as the "Amount of Obligatory Contribution, etc." in the following item); and
(ii) the Amount of Obligatory Contribution, etc. is not grossly inappropriate.
(6) The term "Special Conciliation Proposal" as used in paragraph (2), item (v) means, except for the following cases, a settlement proposal for the Member Insurance Service Provider to accept:
(i) if the customer of the Member Insurance Service Provider who is the relevant party (hereinafter simply referred to as the "Customer" in this paragraph) does not accept the relevant settlement proposal;
(ii) if, at the time of the relevant settlement proposal, litigation had not been filed involving a claim which had become the subject matter of the Dispute Resolution Procedures, but is filed in connection with that claim by the day on which one month has elapsed from the day when the Member Insurance Service Provider came to know that the Customer had accepted the settlement proposal and is not withdrawn by that day;

Art.308-8～308-10   6 Insurance Business Act, Part IV, Chap.II

(iii) if, at the time of the relevant settlement proposal, litigation had been filed involving a claim which had become the subject matter of the relevant Dispute Resolution Procedures, and said litigation has not been withdrawn by the day on which one month has elapsed from the day when the Member Insurance Service Provider came to know that the Customer had accepted the settlement proposal; or
(iv) with regard to a Dispute Related to Insurance Services, etc. for which Dispute Resolution Procedures have been implemented, if an arbitration agreement defined in Article 2, paragraph (1) (Definitions) of the Arbitration Act (Act No. 138 of 2003) has been entered into or a settlement or conciliation not through said settlement proposal has been reached between the Parties by the day on which one month has elapsed from the day when the Member Insurance Service Provider came to know that the Customer had accepted the settlement proposal.
(7) Changes to the Operational Rules shall not come into effect without the authorization of the Prime Minister.
(8) When the Prime Minister seeks to grant the authorization under the preceding paragraph, he/she shall consult the Minister of Justice in advance as to whether the Operational Rules subject to said authorization conform to the standards set forth in the items of paragraph (4) and the items of paragraph (5) (limited to the part related to the operation of Dispute Resolution Procedures).

(Publication, etc. of the Fact of Non-Performance of the Basic Contract for the Implementation of Dispute Resolution Procedures)
Article 308-8 (1) In cases where non-performance of the obligations to be incurred by a Member Insurance Service Provider under a Basic Contract for the Implementation of Dispute Resolution Procedures arises, when a Designated Dispute Resolution Organization has heard opinions from said Member Insurance Service Provider and finds there are no justifiable grounds for such non-performance, said Designated Dispute Resolution Organization shall publicize and report to the Prime Minister the trade name or name of said Member Insurance Service Provider and the fact of such non-performance, without delay.
(2) A Designated Dispute Resolution Organization shall endeavor to provide information, consultation or any other support to a Member Insurance Service Provider or any other person to preemptively prevent Complaints Related to Insurance Services, etc. and Disputes Related to Insurance Services, etc. , or to promote the processing of Complaints Related to Insurance Services, etc. and the resolution of Disputes Related to Insurance Services, etc.

(Prohibition of Use of Organized Crime Group Member, etc.)
Article 308-9 A Designated Dispute Resolution Organization shall not have an Organized Crime Group Member, etc. (meaning the Organized Crime Group Member, etc. as defined in Article 2, item (vi) (Definitions) of the Act on Prevention of Unjust Acts by Organized Crime Group Member (hereinafter referred to as the "Organized Crime Group Member" in this Article) or a person for whom five years have not passed from the day on which such person ceased to be an Organized Crime Group Member) engaged in Dispute Resolution Services, etc. or use him/her as an assistant in Dispute Resolution Services.

(Prohibition of Discriminatory Treatment)
Article 308-10 A Designated Dispute Resolution Organization shall not treat any particular Member Insurance Service Provider in an unjust, discriminatory manner.

(Preservation of Records)

Article 308-11 A Designated Dispute Resolution Organization shall, except for those under the provisions of Article 308-13, paragraph (9) and pursuant to the provisions of Cabinet Office Ordinance, prepare and preserve records concerning Dispute Resolution Services, etc.

(Complaint Processing Procedures by a Designated Dispute Resolution Organization)

Article 308-12 When a customer of a Member Insurance Service Provider files an application for resolution of a Complaint Related to Insurance Services, etc. , a Designated Dispute Resolution Organization shall respond to requests for consultation, provide necessary advice to the customer, investigate the circumstances pertaining to such Complaint Related to Insurance Services, etc. , notify said Member Insurance Service Provider of the substance and content of such Complaint Related to Insurance Services, etc. , and demand that said Member Insurance Service Provider process the complaint expeditiously.

(Dispute Resolution Procedures by a Designated Dispute Resolution Organization)

Article 308-13 (1) The Parties to the Dispute Related to Insurance Services, etc. may file an application for Dispute Resolution Procedures with the Designated Dispute Resolution Organization with whom the Member Insurance Service Provider has concluded a Basic Contract for the Implementation of Dispute Resolution Procedures for the purpose of resolving Disputes Related to Insurance Services, etc. related to the Member Insurance Service Provider.

(2) When a Designated Dispute Resolution Organization has received the application under the preceding paragraph, it shall appoint Dispute Resolution Mediators.

(3) Dispute Resolution Mediators shall be appointed from among persons who are of the highest moral character and fall under any of the following items (excluding persons who have an interest with the Parties pertaining to the application under paragraph (1)). In this case, at least one of the Dispute Resolution Mediators shall be a person who falls under item (i) or (iii) (in cases where said application is that related to a dispute provided in Article 3, paragraph (1), item (vii) (Business) of the Judicial Scrivener Act, item (i), (iii) or (iv)):

(i) an attorney-at-law who has been engaged in his/her profession for five years or more in total;

(ii) a person who has been engaged in Insurance Services, etc. for ten years or more in total;

(iii) a person who has specialized knowledge and experience on consultation for the complaints which have arisen between the consumer and the enterprise with regard to consumer affairs or on any other particular of consumer affairs as provided by Cabinet Office Ordinance;

(iv) in cases where the application is that related to the dispute prescribed in Article 3, paragraph (1), item (vii) of the Judicial Scrivener Act, a judicial scrivener as prescribed in paragraph (2) of that Article who has been engaged in business involving legal representation in summary court, etc. defined in that paragraph for five years or more in total; or

(v) persons specified by Cabinet Office Ordinance as those equivalent to the persons listed in the preceding items.

(4) A Designated Dispute Resolution Organization shall have the application under paragraph (1) proceed into Dispute Resolution Procedures through the Dispute Resolution

Art.308-13   ⑥ Insurance Business Act, Part IV, Chap.II

Mediator appointed under paragraph (2) (hereinafter simply referred to as the "Dispute Resolution Mediator" in this Article and paragraph (1) of the following Article); provided, however, that in cases where the Dispute Resolution Mediator finds that it is not appropriate to carry out Dispute Resolution Procedures on the grounds that it is acceptable to recognize the customer of the Member Insurance Service Provider who is a Party to said application as a person who has sufficient ability to properly resolve the Dispute Related to Insurance Services, etc. or on any other grounds, or where he/she finds that the Parties have filed the application under paragraph (1) for improper purposes and without reason, he/she shall not implement Dispute Resolution Procedures, and when the Dispute Resolution Mediator finds it appropriate to have the application proceed into procedures equivalent to Dispute Resolution Procedures to be conducted by an Entrusted Dispute Resolution Organization, the Designated Dispute Resolution Organization shall entrust the operations of Dispute Resolution Procedures to an Entrusted Dispute Resolution Organization.

(5) If a Dispute Resolution Mediator has decided not to implement Dispute Resolution Procedures pursuant to the proviso to the preceding paragraph, or has decided to entrust the operations to an Entrusted Dispute Resolution Organization, the Designated Dispute Resolution Organization shall notify the person who filed the application under paragraph (1) of this, appending the reasons therefor.

(6) A Dispute Resolution Mediator may hear opinions of the Parties or witnesses, request said persons to submit written reports, or request the Parties to submit books and documents and other articles that will be helpful, and may prepare a settlement plan necessary for the resolution of the case and recommend the Parties to accept said plan, or provide a Special Conciliation (meaning to present the Special Conciliation Proposal prescribed in Article 308-7, paragraph (6)); .

(7) Dispute Resolution Procedures shall not be open to the public; provided, however, that a Dispute Resolution Mediator may allow the attendance of a person who is considered appropriate with the consent of the Parties.

(8) A Designated Dispute Resolution Organization shall, prior to the commencement of Dispute Resolution Procedures and pursuant to the provisions of Cabinet Office Ordinance, deliver a document containing the following particulars or provide the Electromagnetic Record in which such particulars are recorded and make an explanation thereof to the customer of the Member Insurance Service Provider who is a party to the dispute:

(i) the particulars of the fees to be paid by the customer;

(ii) the standard operation process from the commencement to the termination of Dispute Resolution Procedures as provided in Article 308-7, paragraph (4), item (vi); and

(iii) in addition to what is listed in the preceding two items, particulars specified by Cabinet Office Ordinance.

(9) A Designated Dispute Resolution Organization shall, pursuant to the provisions of Cabinet Office Ordinance, prepare and preserve a dispute resolution procedures record detailing the following particulars, for Dispute Resolution Procedures it has implemented:

(i) the date on which the Parties to the Dispute Related to Insurance Services, etc. filed the application for Dispute Resolution Procedures;

(ii) the name or trade name of the Parties to the Dispute Related to Insurance Services, etc. and the agents thereof;

(iii) the names of the Dispute Resolution Mediators;

(iv) the particulars of the Dispute Resolution Procedures;

(v) the results of the Dispute Resolution Procedures (including the reasons for the

termination of the Dispute Resolution Procedures and the date thereof); and
(vi) in addition to what is listed in the preceding items, particulars necessary for clarifying the contents of the implemented Dispute Resolution Procedures which are specified by Cabinet Office Ordinance.

(Interruption of Prescription)
Article 308-14 (1) In cases where the Dispute Resolution Mediators terminate the Dispute Resolution Procedures on the grounds that there is no prospect of reaching a settlement between the Parties to the relevant Dispute Related to Insurance Services, etc. through the Dispute Resolution Procedures, when the Party to said Dispute Related to Insurance Services, etc. that filed the application for said Dispute Resolution Procedure files an action for the claims which were the subject matter of said Dispute Resolution Procedures within one month from the day on which he/she received the notice of the termination, with regard to the interruption of prescription, it shall be deemed that the action was filed at the time when the claim was made through Dispute Resolution Procedures.
(2) The provisions of the preceding paragraph shall also apply in cases where the abolition of Dispute Resolution Services, etc. by a Designated Dispute Resolution Organization has been authorized under Article 308-23, paragraph (1) or the designation under Article 308-2, paragraph (1) has been rescinded under Article 308-24, paragraph (1) and there is a Dispute Related to Insurance Services, etc. for which Dispute Resolution Procedures have been implemented as of the day of authorization or rescission, when the Party to the Dispute Related to Insurance Services, etc. that filed the application for Dispute Resolution Procedures files an action for the claims which were the subject matter of the Dispute Resolution Procedures within one month from the day on which said Party received the notice under Article 308-23, paragraph (3) or Article 308-24, paragraph (3) or the day on which the Party came to know of the authorization or rescission whichever comes earlier.

(Suspension of Court Proceeding(s))
Article 308-15 (1) In cases where litigation is pending between the Parties to a Dispute Related to Insurance Services, etc. , with regard to said Dispute Related to Insurance Services, etc. , when there are any of the following grounds and the Parties to said Dispute Related to Insurance Services, etc. have filed a joint petition, the court in charge of the case may decide to suspend court proceedings for a fixed period of not longer than four months:
(i) that, with regard to the relevant Dispute Related to Insurance Services, etc. , Dispute Resolution Procedures have been implemented between the Parties to the Dispute Related to Insurance Services, etc. ; and
(ii) in addition to the case referred to in the preceding item, that an agreement to achieve a resolution of the relevant Dispute Related to Insurance Services, etc. through Dispute Resolution Procedures has been reached between the Parties to the Dispute Related to Insurance Services, etc.
(2) The court in charge of the case may rescind the decision under the preceding paragraph at any time.
(3) No appeal may be entered against a decision dismissing the application under paragraph (1) or a decision rescinding the decision under paragraph (1).

(Public Inspection of the Registry of Member Insurance Service Providers)
Article 308-16 A Designated Dispute Resolution Organization shall make the registry of the Member Insurance Service Providers available for public inspection.

(Restriction on Use of Name)
Article 308-17 A person who is not a Designated Dispute Resolution Organization (excluding persons who have been designated under Article 156-39, paragraph (1) (Designation of Person to Conduct Dispute Resolution Services, etc.) of the Financial Instruments and Exchange Act and any other persons specified by Cabinet Order as those similar thereto) shall not use any term in its name or trade name that is likely to mislead people to understand that said person is a Designated Dispute Resolution Organization.

Chapter III Supervision

(Notification of Changes)
Article 308-18 (1) If there has been any change in the particulars listed in Article 308-3, paragraph (1), item (ii) to (iv) inclusive, a Designated Dispute Resolution Organization shall notify the Prime Minister of this.
(2) If the Prime Minister has received notice of a change to the trade name or name of a Designated Dispute Resolution Organization or to the location of the principal business office or office thereof, the Prime Minister shall give public notice of this in the official gazette.

(Notification of the Conclusion, etc. of a Basic Contract for the Implementation of Dispute Resolution Procedures)
Article 308-19 If a Designated Dispute Resolution Organization falls under any of the following items, it shall notify the Prime Minister of this pursuant to the provisions of Cabinet Office Ordinance:
(i) it has concluded a Basic Contract for the Implementation of Dispute Resolution Procedures with an Insurance Service Provider or has terminated said Basic Contract for the Implementation of Dispute Resolution Procedures; and
(ii) in addition to what is listed in the preceding item, cases specified by Cabinet Office Ordinance.

(Submission of Report on Business)
Article 308-20 (1) A Designated Dispute Resolution Organization shall, for each business year, prepare a report on Dispute Resolution Services, etc. pertaining to the relevant business year and submit it to the Prime Minister.
(2) The particulars for inclusion, the submission date, and any other particulars necessary for the report under the preceding paragraph shall be specified by Cabinet Office Ordinance.

(Order for Production of Reports and On-Site Inspection)
Article 308-21 (1) When the Prime Minister finds it necessary for the fair and appropriate execution of Dispute Resolution Services, etc. , he/she may order a Designated Dispute Resolution Organization to make reports or submit materials concerning the business thereof, or have his/her officials enter the business office or office or any other facilities of a Designated Dispute Resolution Organization to inquire about the status of business of said Designated Dispute Resolution Organization or inspect the books and documents or other articles.
(2) If and to the extent that the Prime Minister finds it especially necessary for the fair and appropriate execution of Dispute Resolution Services, etc. , he/she may order a

Member Insurance Service Provider of the Designated Dispute Resolution Organization or a person the Designated Dispute Resolution Organization has entrusted with its business, to make reports or submit materials, or may have his/her officials enter the business office or office or any other facilities of these persons, inquire about the status of business of said Designated Dispute Resolution Organization, or inspect books and documents or other articles of these persons.

(Business Improvement Order)
Article 308-22 (1) If and to the extent that the Prime Minister finds it necessary for ensuring the fair and appropriate execution of Dispute Resolution Services, etc. with regard to the Designated Dispute Resolution Organization's management of the Dispute Resolution Services, etc. , he/she may order necessary measures for improving the business operation of the relevant Designated Dispute Resolution Organization.
(2) In cases where a Designated Dispute Resolution Organization falls under any of the following items, when the Prime Minister seeks to give the order under the preceding paragraph, he/she shall consult with the Minister of Justice in advance:
  (i) cases where the Designated Dispute Resolution Organization has come to no longer satisfy the requirements set forth in Article 308-2, paragraph (1), items (v) to (vii) inclusive (limited to the part pertaining to the operations of Dispute Resolution Procedures, the requirement set forth in item (vii) of that paragraph shall be one pertaining to the standards listed in the items of paragraph (4) of Article 308-7 or the items of paragraph (5) of that Article; hereinafter the same shall apply in this item) or where the Designated Dispute Resolution Organization is found likely to come to no longer satisfy the requirements set forth in Article 308-2, paragraph (1), items (v) to (vii) inclusive; or
  (ii) cases where the Designated Dispute Resolution Organization has violated the provisions of Article 308-5, Article 308-6, Article 308-9, or Article 308-13 (limited to cases where such violation is one that is related to the operations of Dispute Resolution Procedures).

(Suspension or Abolition of Dispute Resolution Services, etc.)
Article 308-23 (1) When a Designated Dispute Resolution Organization seeks to suspend (excluding the suspension on the grounds prescribed in the following paragraph) or abolish all or part of the Dispute Resolution Services, etc. , it shall obtain authorization from the Prime Minister.
(2) If a Designated Dispute Resolution Organization has suspended all or part of its Dispute Resolution Services, etc. due to a natural disaster or any other inevitable grounds, it shall immediately notify the Prime Minister of this, appending the reasons therefor. The same applies if the Designated Dispute Resolution Organization recommences all or part of its suspended Dispute Resolution Services, etc.
(3) A Designated Dispute Resolution Organization that has obtained the authorization for suspension or abolition under paragraph (1) or that has implemented the suspension under the preceding paragraph shall notify the Parties for which Complaint Processing Procedures or Dispute Resolution Procedures have been implemented (if another Designated Dispute Resolution Organization or a person with the legally provided for designation specified by Cabinet Order as involving business equivalent to Dispute Resolution Services, etc. (hereinafter collectively referred to as the "Entrusting Dispute Resolution Organization" in this paragraph), has entrusted the relevant Designated Dispute Resolution Organization with its business, this includes procedures for processing complaints of the Entrusting Dispute Resolution Organization in connection with the entrustment or procedures for dispute resolution; the same shall apply in

paragraph (4) of the following Article), the Member Insurance Service Providers other than said Parties, and other Designated Dispute Resolution Organization(s), of the fact of the suspension or abolition within two weeks from the day of said suspension or abolition or on the day of said suspension or abolition. The same shall apply when the Designated Dispute Resolution Organization recommences all or part of the suspended Dispute Resolution Services, etc.

(Rescission of Designation, etc.)
Article 308-24 (1) When a Designated Dispute Resolution Organization falls under any of the following items, the Prime Minister may rescind the designation under Article 308-2, paragraph (1) or order the suspension of all or part of its business by specifying a period not exceeding six months:
(i) when the Designated Dispute Resolution Organization has come to no longer satisfy the requirements listed in Article 308-2, paragraph (1), items (ii) to (vii) inclusive, or the Designated Dispute Resolution Organization is found to have not fallen under any of the items of that paragraph at the time when receiving the designation;
(ii) when the Designated Dispute Resolution Organization has received the designation under Article 308-2, paragraph (1) by wrongful means; or
(iii) when the Designated Dispute Resolution Organization has violated laws and regulations or a disposition under laws and regulations.
(2) In cases where a Designated Dispute Resolution Organization falls under any of the following items, when the Prime Minister seeks to make a disposition or order under the preceding paragraph, he/she shall consult with the Minister of Justice in advance:
(i) cases where the Designated Dispute Resolution Organization has come to no longer satisfy the requirements listed in Article 308-2, paragraph (1), items (v) to (vii) inclusive (limited to the part pertaining to the operations of Dispute Resolution Procedures, the requirement set forth in item (vii) of that paragraph shall be limited to one related to the standards listed in the items of Article 308-7, paragraph (4) or the items of paragraph (5) of that Article; hereinafter the same shall apply in this item), or the Designated Dispute Resolution Organization is found not to have satisfied the requirements set forth in Article 308-2, paragraph (1), items (v) to (vii) inclusive at the time it received the designation under Article 308-2, paragraph (1); or
(ii) cases where the Designated Dispute Resolution Organization has violated the provisions of Article 308-5, Article 308-6, Article 308-9, or Article 308-13 (limited to cases where such violation is one that is related to the operation of Dispute Resolution Procedure).
(3) If the Prime Minister has rescinded a designation under Article 308-2, paragraph (1) pursuant to the provisions of paragraph (1), he/she shall give public notice of this in the official gazette.
(4) Any person who has received a disposition of rescission of the designation under Article 308-2, paragraph (1) or an order for suspension of all or part of its business pursuant to the provisions of paragraph (1) shall, within two weeks from the day of said disposition or order, notify the Parties for which Complaint Processing Procedures or Dispute Resolution Procedures had been implemented, a Member Insurance Service Provider other than the Parties, and other Designated Dispute Resolution Organization(s) to the effect that he/she has received the disposition or order.

Part V Miscellaneous Provisions

(Revocation of an Offer for an Insurance Contract, etc.)
Article 309 (1) Any person that has made an offer for an insurance contract to an Insurance Company, etc. or a Foreign Insurance Company, etc. , or any of the Policyholders of such company (hereinafter referred to as "Offeror, etc." in this Article) may revoke or cancel the offer in writing (hereinafter referred to as "Revocation of an Offer, etc." in this Article), unless:
  (i) A document detailing the particulars for the Revocation of an Offer, etc. for an insurance contract has been issued to the Offeror, etc. pursuant to the provisions of a Cabinet Office Ordinance, and eight days have elapsed counting from the issue date of such document or the date of the offer, whichever is later;
  (ii) The Offeror, etc. made the offer to conclude the insurance contract for the purpose of, or on behalf of, its operation or business;
  (iii) The offer was made by a general incorporated association or general incorporated foundation, a juridical person formed under a special Act, a non-incorporated association or foundation with a designated representative or administrator, or the national government or a local government;
  (iv) The insurance contract has a term of coverage of one year or less;
  (v) The Offeror, etc. is required by law to take out the insurance contract; or
  (vi) The Offeror, etc. has offered the insurance contract at a business office or any other office or facility of an Insurance Company, etc. , Foreign Insurance Company, etc. , Specified Insurance Agent, Insurance Broker, or otherwise, and the situation falls under any of the cases specified by Cabinet Order as posing no risk to the protection of the Offeror, etc.
(2) In the case referred to in item (i) of the preceding paragraph, an Insurance Company, etc. or Foreign Insurance Company, etc. may, in lieu of issuing of the document set forth in that item, provide the relevant person with the particulars that are required to be included in the document by a method using an electronic data processing system or any other method using information and communication technology to be specified by Cabinet Office Ordinance, pursuant to the provisions of a Cabinet Order and with the approval of the Applicant, etc. In this case, the Insurance Company, etc. or Foreign Insurance Company, etc. shall be deemed to have issued that document.
(3) Where the method set forth in the first sentence of the preceding paragraph (other than the method to be specified by Cabinet Office Ordinance) is used in lieu of issuing the document set forth in paragraph (1), item (i), the particulars that are required to be included in that document shall be deemed to have arrived with the Offeror, etc. when they have been recorded on a file stored in the computer used by the Offeror, etc.
(4) The Revocation of an Offer, etc. for an insurance contract shall take effect when the document on the Revocation of the Offer, etc. is issued.
(5) If a Revocation of an Offer, etc. for an insurance contract has been effected, the Insurance Company, etc. or Foreign Insurance Company, etc. may not demand from the Offeror, etc. payment for any damages, penalties or other money for the Revocation of the Offer, etc.; provided, however, that this shall not apply, in the case of revocation of an insurance contract under paragraph (1), to the amount of money specified by Cabinet Office Ordinance as equivalent to the insurance premium for the period leading to the date of such revocation.
(6) If a Revocation of an Offer, etc. for an insurance contract has been effected, the Insurance Company, etc. or Foreign Insurance Company, etc. shall promptly refund to the Offeror, etc. any money received in connection with the insurance contract; provided, however, that this shall not apply, in the case of revocation of an insurance contract

under paragraph (1), to that part of the money received as prepayment of the insurance premium pertaining to the insurance contract which corresponds to the amount set forth in the preceding paragraph specified by Cabinet Office Ordinance.
(7) If a Revocation of an Offer, etc. for an insurance contract has been effected, the Specified Insurance Agent or any other person engaged in Insurance Solicitation shall promptly refund to the Offeror, etc. any money received in connection with the insurance contract.
(8) An Insurance Broker or any other person engaged in Insurance Solicitation that has paid to an Insurance Company, etc. or Foreign Insurance Company, etc. any damages or other money for the Revocation of an Offer, etc. for an insurance contract may not, in connection with such payment, demand from the person who effected the Revocation of the Offer, etc. payment of any damages or other money.
(9) The Revocation of an Offer, etc. for an insurance contract shall not take effect if any event that gives rise to payment of an insurance proceeds has occurred by the time of such Revocation of the Offer, etc.; provided, however, that this shall not apply where the person who effected the Revocation of the Offer, etc. knew that an event giving rise to payment of insurance proceeds had occurred by the time of such Revocation of the Offer, etc.
(10) Any special provisions in an insurance contract that violate any of the provisions of paragraphs (1) and (4) to (9) inclusive shall be null and void if it is disadvantageous to the Offeror, etc.

(Condition for Authorization, etc.)
Article 310 (1) The Prime Minister, or the Prime Minister and the Minister of Finance, may impose conditions on any authorization, permission or approval (referred to as "Authorization, etc." in the following paragraph and Article 312) prescribed in this Act or change them.
(2) The conditions set forth in the preceding paragraph shall, in light of the purpose of the Authorization, etc. , be the minimum necessary for ensuring assured implementation of the particulars of the Authorization, etc. .

(Carrying and Showing of Identification card by Inspecting Personnel, etc.)
Article 311 (1) The personnel who make an entry, ask questions or conduct inspection under Article 122-2, paragraph (4), Article 129 (including the cases where it is applied mutatis mutandis pursuant to Article 179, paragraph (2) and Article 271, paragraph (3)), Article 201 (including the cases where it is applied mutatis mutandis pursuant to Article 212, paragraph (6) and Article 271, paragraph (3)), Article 227 (including the cases where it is applied mutatis mutandis pursuant to Article 235, paragraph (5) and Article 271, paragraph (3)), Article 265-46, Article 271-9, Article 271-13 (including the cases where it is applied mutatis mutandis pursuant to Article 272-34, paragraph (1)), Article 271-28 (including the cases where it is applied mutatis mutandis pursuant to Article 272-40, paragraph (2)), Article 272-23 (including the cases where it is applied mutatis mutandis pursuant to Article 179, paragraph (2) and Article 271, paragraph (3)), Article 305 or Article 308-21 shall carry their identification cards with them and show it on the request of a relevant person.
(2) The authority to make an entry, ask questions or conduct inspection prescribed in the preceding paragraph shall not be construed as given for any criminal investigation.

(Consultation with Minister of Finance)
Article 311-2 (1) Before the Prime Minister finds that reaching any of the following dispositions with regard to an Insurance Company, etc. , a Foreign Insurance Company,

etc. or a licensed specified juridical person could have a serious impact on the maintenance of the credibility of Insurance Services, he/she shall consult in advance with the Minister of Finance on the necessary measures for maintaining the credibility of Insurance Services:
  (i) An order for total or partial suspension of business under Article 132, paragraph (1), Article 133, Article 204, paragraph (1), Article 205, Article 230, paragraph (1), Article 231, Article 241, paragraph (1), Article 271-30, paragraph (1) or (4) (including the cases where it is applied mutatis mutandis pursuant to Article 272-40, paragraph (2)), or Article 272-26, paragraph (1);
  (ii) An order for suspension of business under Article 240-3;
  (iii) Cancellation of the license set forth in Article 3, paragraph (1), Article 185, paragraph (1) or Article 219, paragraph (1), or the registration set forth in Article 272, paragraph (1) under Article 133, Article 134, Article 205, Article 206, Article 231, Article 232, Article 272-26, paragraph (1) or Article 272-27; or
  (iv) A disposition ordering the administration of business and property by an Insurance Administrator under Article 241, paragraph (1).
(2) Before the Prime Minister finds that if a Corporation were to conduct any of the business listed in the following items pursuant to his/her disposition listed in the relevant item, the condition of the funds available to the Corporation would deteriorate extremely, thus posing the risk of a serious impact on the maintenance of the credibility of the Insurance Business, he/she shall consult in advance with the Minister of Finance on the necessary measures for maintaining the credibility of the Insurance Business:
  (i) The authorization set forth in Article 268, paragraph (1), Article 270, paragraph (1), Article 270-3-12, paragraph (1) or Article 270-6-3, paragraph (1), or the supplementary note set forth in Article 269, paragraph (1), Article 270-3-13, paragraph (3) or Article 270-6-4, paragraph (3): the Financial Assistance set forth in Article 265-28, paragraph (1), item (iii) for transfer, etc. of insurance contracts (meaning the transfer, etc. of insurance contracts set forth in Article 260, paragraph (1)), succession of insurance contracts (meaning the succession of insurance contracts set forth in Article 260, paragraph (7)), Succession to Inherited Insurance Contracts (meaning the Succession to Inherited Insurance Contracts set forth in Article 260, paragraph (8)) or retransfer of insurance contracts (meaning the retransfer of insurance contracts set forth in Article 260, paragraph (11)); or
  (ii) The authorization set forth in Article 270, paragraph (1): the Underwriting of Insurance Contracts set forth in Article 265-28, paragraph (1), item (v).

(Notice to Minister of Finance)
Article 311-3 (1) If the Prime Minister has reached any of the following dispositions, he/she shall promptly notify the Minister of Finance of this:
  (i) The license set forth in Article 3, paragraph (1), Article 185, paragraph (1) or Article 219, paragraph (1), or the registration set forth in Article 272, paragraph (1);
  (ii) The authorization or approval set forth in Article 106, paragraph (4) (limited to the cases where the applicant seeks to make a Subsidiary out of an Insurance Company that falls under the category of Bankrupt Insurance Company as defined in Article 260, paragraph (2) or any other Insurance Company specified by Cabinet Office Ordinance/Ordinance of the Ministry of Finance), Article 139, paragraph (1) (including the cases where it is applied mutatis mutandis pursuant to Article 272-29), Article 142 (including the cases where it is applied mutatis mutandis pursuant to Article 272-30, paragraph (1)), Article 153, paragraph (1), Article 167, paragraph (1), Article 208, Article 233, Article 271-10, paragraph (1), the proviso to Article 271-10,

Art.311-4   6 Insurance Business Act, Part V

paragraph (2), Article 271-18, paragraph (1), the proviso to Article 271-18, paragraph (3), Article 271-31, paragraphs (1) to (3) inclusive, Article 272-31, paragraph (1), the proviso to Article 272-31, paragraph (2), Article 272-35, paragraph (1) or the proviso to Article 272-35, paragraph (3);

(iii) Giving of an order (including any request for the submission of an improvement program) set forth in Article 132, paragraph (1), Article 133, Article 204, paragraph (1), Article 205, Article 230, paragraph (1), Article 231, Article 240-3, Article 241, paragraph (1), Article 247, paragraph (5), Article 258, paragraph (1), Article 271-6, Article 271-7, Article 271-10, paragraph (4), Article 271-14 (including the cases where it is applied mutatis mutandis pursuant to Article 272-34, paragraph (1)), Article 271-15, Article 271-16, paragraph (1) (including the cases where it is applied mutatis mutandis pursuant to Article 272-34, paragraph (1), Article 271-18, paragraph (5), Article 271-29 or Article 271-30, paragraph (1) or (4) (including the cases where any of those provisions is applied mutatis mutandis pursuant to Article 272-40, paragraph (2)), Article 272-25, paragraph (1), Article 272-26, paragraph (1) or (2), Article 272-31, paragraph (4), or Article 272-35, paragraph (5);

(iv) Rescission of the license set forth in Article 3, paragraph (1), Article 185, paragraph (1) or Article 219, paragraph (1) pursuant to the provisions of Article 133, 134, 205, 206, 231 or 232, or cancellation of the registration set forth in Article 272, paragraph (1) pursuant to the provisions of Article 272-26, paragraph (1) or Article 272-27;

(v) Rescission of the authorization set forth in Article 271-10, paragraph (1) or the proviso to Article 271-10, paragraph (2) pursuant to the provisions of Article 271-16, paragraph (1), rescission of the authorization set forth in Article 271-18, paragraph (1) or the proviso to Article 271-18, paragraph (3) pursuant to the provisions of Article 271-30, paragraph (1), rescission of the approval set forth in Article 272-31, paragraph (1) or the proviso to Article 272-31, paragraph (2) pursuant to the provisions of Article 271-16, paragraph (1) as applied mutatis mutandis pursuant to Article 272-34, paragraph (1), or rescission of the approval set forth in Article 272-35, paragraph (1) or the proviso to Article 272-35, paragraph (3) pursuant to the provisions of Article 271-30, paragraph (1) as applied mutatis mutandis pursuant to Article 272-40, paragraph (2);

(vi) Any disposition ordering the administration of business and property by an Insurance Administrator under Article 241, paragraph (1); or

(vii) The approval set forth in Article 247, paragraph (2) or (4).

(2) If the Prime Minister has received notice under any of the following provisions (for notice under the provisions listed in item (i) or (iv), limited to one involving the cases specified by Cabinet Office Ordinance/Ordinance of the Ministry of Finance), promptly notify the Minister of Finance of this:

(i) Article 127, paragraph (1) (limited to the segment pertaining to item (viii) of that paragraph);

(ii) Article 209 (limited to the segment pertaining to item (v) to (viii) inclusive of that Article);

(iii) Article 234 (limited to the segment pertaining to item (iv) to (vii) inclusive of that Article); or

(iv) Article 272-21, paragraph (1) (limited to the segment pertaining to item (vi)).

(Submission of Materials to the Minster of Finance, etc.)

Article 311-4 (1) If the Minister of Finance finds it necessary for planning or drafting a system for Insurance Services in connection with the financial bankruptcy processing system and financial crisis management under his/her jurisdiction, he/she shall re-

quest the Prime Minister to submit materials and provide explanations as necessary.
(2) If and to the extent that the Minister of Finance finds it particularly necessary for designing or planning a system pertaining to the Insurance Business in connection with the financial bankruptcy processing system and financial crisis management under his/her jurisdiction, he/she may request an Insurance Company, etc. , a Foreign Insurance Company, etc. , the General Representative of a licensed specified juridical person (meaning the General Representative set forth in Article 219, paragraph (1)), an Insurance Company's Major Shareholder, an Insurance Holding Company, a Low-Cost, Short-Term Insurer's Major Shareholder, a Low-Cost, Short-Term Insurance Holding Company or any other relevant person to submit materials or to provide explanations or other cooperation.

(Delegation to Cabinet Office Ordinance, etc.)
Article 312 In addition to what is prescribed in this Act, the procedures for application and submission of documents for Authorization, etc. under this Act and any other particular necessary for the implementation of this Act shall be specified by Cabinet Office Ordinance (or Cabinet Office Ordinance/Ordinance of the Ministry of Finance for any particular of a Corporation and its business).

(Delegation of Authority)
Article 313 (1) The Prime Minister shall delegate his/her authority under this Act (excluding those specified by Cabinet Order) to the Commissioner of the Financial Services Agency
(2) The Commissioner of the Financial Services Agency may, pursuant to the provisions of a Cabinet Order, delegate part of the authority that has been delegated pursuant to the provisions of the preceding paragraph to the Director-Generals of Local Finance Bureaus or Local Finance Branch Offices.

(Transitional Measures)
Article 314 Whenever an order is enacted, revised or abolished pursuant to this Act, necessary transitional measures (including transitional measures concerning penal provisions) may be provided for by that order, to the extent considered reasonably necessary for its enactment, revision or abolition.

Part VI Penal Provisions

Article 315 Any person who falls under any of the following items shall be punished by imprisonment with work for not more than three years or a fine of not more than three million yen, or both:
(i) A person who has conducted Insurance Services without obtaining the license of the Prime Minister, in violation of the provisions of Article 3, paragraph (1);
(ii) A person who had another person conduct Insurance Services in violation of Article 7-2 (including the cases where it is applied mutatis mutandis pursuant to Article 199);
(iii) A person who has obtained the registration set forth in Article 272, paragraph (1) by wrongful means;
(iv) A person who had another person to conduct Low-Cost, Short-Term Insurance Services in violation of Article 272-9; and
(v) Any person who has violated the provisions of Article 39, paragraph (1) of the Financial Instruments and Exchange Act, as applied mutatis mutandis pursuant to

Article 300-2.

Article 315-2 In any of the following cases of violation, a person who has committed the violation shall be punished by imprisonment with work for not more than two years or a fine of amount more than three million yen, or both:
(i) When a person has, without obtaining the authorization of the Prime Minister under the provisions of Article 271-18, paragraph (1), by any of the transactions or actions listed in the items of the same paragraph, become a Holding Company whose Subsidiaries include an Insurance Company, or incorporated a Holding Company whose Subsidiaries include an Insurance Company;
(ii) When the person had been, in violation of Article 271-18, paragraph (3), a Holding Company whose Subsidiaries included an Insurance Company beyond the Last Day of the Grace Period prescribed in the same paragraph;
(iii) When the person had been a Holding Company whose Subsidiaries included an Insurance Company in violation of the order under the provisions of Article 271-18, paragraph (5), or when the person had been, in violation of Article 271-30, paragraph (2), a Holding Company whose Subsidiaries included an Insurance Company beyond the period of time designated by the Prime Minister prescribed in the same paragraph;
(iv) When the person has, without obtaining the approval of the Prime Minister under the provisions of Article 272-35, paragraph (1), through any of the transactions or actions listed in the items of the same paragraph, become a Holding Company whose Subsidiaries include a Low-Cost, Short-Term Insurer, or incorporated a Holding Company whose Subsidiaries include a Low-Cost, Short-Term Insurer;
(v) When the person had been, in violation of Article 272-35, paragraph (3), a Holding Company whose Subsidiaries included a Low-Cost, Short-Term Insurer beyond the Last Day of the Grace Period prescribed in the same paragraph; and
(vi) When the person had been a Holding Company whose Subsidiaries included a Low-Cost, Short-Term Insurer in violation of the order under the provisions of Article 272-35, paragraph (5), or when the person had been, in violation of the provisions of Article 271-30, paragraph (2), as applied mutatis mutandis pursuant to Article 272-40, paragraph (2), a Holding Company whose Subsidiaries included a Low-Cost, Short-Term Insurer beyond the period of time designated by the Prime Minister prescribed in the same paragraph.

Article 316 Any person who falls under any of the following items shall be punished by imprisonment with work for not more than two years or a fine of not more than three million yen, or both:
(i) Any person who has violated the conditions imposed pursuant to the provisions of Article 5, paragraph (2) (including the cases where it is applied mutatis mutandis pursuant to Article 187, paragraph (5)) or Article 221, paragraph (2);
(ii) Any person who has violated the order for the whole or partial suspension of the business under the provisions of Article 132, paragraph (1), Article 133, Article 204, paragraph (1), Article 205, Article 230, paragraph (1), Article 231, Article 241, paragraph (1), Article 271-30, paragraph (1) or (4) (including the cases where it is applied mutatis mutandis pursuant to Article 272-40, paragraph (2)), or Article 272-26, paragraph (1);
(iii) Any person who has violated the order for suspension of the business under the provisions of Article 240-3;
(iv) Any person who has violated the provisions of Article 186, paragraph (1);
(v) Any person who has violated the conditions imposed pursuant to the provisions of

Article 188, paragraph (1);

(vi) Any person who has violated the provisions of Article 190, paragraph (5), Article 223, paragraph (5), or Article 272-5, paragraph (5); and

(vii) Any person who has conducted business in violation of Article 245 (including the cases where it is applied mutatis mutandis pursuant to Article 258, paragraph (2)), Article 250, paragraph (5) (including the cases where it is applied mutatis mutandis pursuant to Article 270-4, paragraph (9)), Article 254, paragraph (4), or Article 255-2, paragraph (3).

Article 316-2 Any person who falls under any of the following items shall be punished by imprisonment with work for not more than one year or a fine of not more than three million yen, or both:

(i) Any person who, in violation of the provisions of Article 24, paragraph (1), item (i), (iii), or (iv) of the Trust Business Act, as applied mutatis mutandis pursuant to Article 99, paragraph (8) (including the cases where it is applied mutatis mutandis pursuant to Article 199), has acted as listed in those provisions;

(ii) Any person who has violated the provisions of Article 29, paragraph (2) of the Trust Business Act, as applied mutatis mutandis pursuant to Article 99, paragraph (8) (including the cases where it is applied mutatis mutandis pursuant to Article 199);

(iii) Any person who has failed to submit the report or materials under the provisions of Article 42, paragraphs (1) to (3) inclusive of the Trust Business Act, as applied mutatis mutandis pursuant to Article 99, paragraph (8) (including the cases where it is applied mutatis mutandis pursuant to Article 199), or has submitted a false report or materials; and

(iv) Any person who has failed to answer the questions asked by the officials under the provisions of Article 42, paragraphs (1) to (3) inclusive of the Trust Business Act, as applied mutatis mutandis pursuant to Article 99, paragraph (8) (including the cases where it is applied mutatis mutandis pursuant to Article 199) or has made a false answer, or has refused, obstructed, or avoided the inspection under the provisions.

Article 316-3 Any person who falls under any of the following items shall be punished by imprisonment with work for not more than one year or a fine of not more than three million yen, or both:

(i) Any person who has submitted a written application for designation under Article 308-3, paragraph (1) or a document or Electromagnetic Records to be attached thereto pursuant to the provisions of paragraph (2) of that Article, in which he/she has included a false detail or record;

(ii) Any person who has violated the provisions of Article 308-9;

(iii) Any person who has failed to submit a report under Article 308-20, paragraph (1) or has submitted a report that includes any false detail;

(iv) Any person who has failed to submit a report or material pursuant to the provisions of Article 308-21, paragraph (1) or (2) or submitted to a false report or material; any person who has failed to answer the questions asked by the officials under these provisions or has made a false answer, or has refused, obstructed, or avoided the inspection under these provisions; and

(v) Any person who has violated the order under Article 308-22, paragraph (1).

Article 317 A person who falls under any of the following items shall be punished by imprisonment with work for not more than one year or a fine of not more than three mil-

lion yen:
(i) Any person who, in violation of Article 110, paragraph (1) (including the cases where it is applied mutatis mutandis pursuant to Article 199) or paragraph (2) (including the cases where it is applied mutatis mutandis pursuant to Article 272-16, paragraph (3)), Article 195, Article 271-24, paragraph (1) (including the cases where it is applied mutatis mutandis pursuant to Article 272-40, paragraph (1)), or Article 272-16, paragraph (1) or (2), has failed to submit the document or electromagnetic record prescribed in the provisions, or has submitted documents or electromagnetic records in which he/she has failed to detail or record the particulars that must be detailed or recorded or in which he/she has included a false detail or record;
(i)-2 Any person who, in violation of Article 111, paragraph (1) (including the cases where it is applied mutatis mutandis pursuant to Article 199 and Article 272-17) or paragraph (2) (including the cases where it is applied mutatis mutandis pursuant to Article 272-17), or Article 271-25, paragraph (1) (including the cases where it is applied mutatis mutandis pursuant to Article 272-40, paragraph (1)), has failed to make the document prescribed in the provisions available for public inspection, or who, in violation of Article 111, paragraph (4) (including the cases where it is applied mutatis mutandis pursuant to Article 199 and Article 272-17) or Article 271-25, paragraph (3) (including the cases where it is applied mutatis mutandis pursuant to Article 272-40, paragraph (1)), has failed to take the measure specified by Cabinet Office Ordinance which makes the information recorded in the electromagnetic record prescribed in Article 111, paragraph (3) (including the cases where it is applied mutatis mutandis pursuant to Article 199 and Article 272-17) or Article 271-25, paragraph (2) (including the cases where it is applied mutatis mutandis pursuant to Article 272-40, paragraph (1)) available to many and unspecified persons by electromagnetic means, or who, in violation of these provisions, has made documents in which he/she has failed to detail the particulars that are required to be included or in which he/she has included a false detail available for public inspection, or who has taken measures to make the information recorded in electronic records in which he/she has failed to record the particulars that are required to be recorded in the electromagnetic records or in which he/she has included a false record available to many and unspecified persons by electromagnetic means;
(ii) Any person who has failed to submit the reports or materials under the provisions of Article 128, paragraph (1) or (2), Article 200, paragraph (1) or (2), Article 226, paragraph (1) or (2), Article 271-8, Article 271-12 (including the cases where it is applied mutatis mutandis pursuant to Article 272-34, paragraph (1)), Article 271-27, paragraph (1) (including the cases where it is applied mutatis mutandis pursuant to Article 272-40, paragraph (2)), or Article 272-22, paragraph (1) or (2), or has submitted false reports or materials;
(iii) Any person who has failed to answer the questions under the provisions of Article 129, paragraph (1) or (2), Article 201, paragraph (1) or (2), Article 227, paragraph (1) or (2), Article 271-9, paragraph (1), Article 271-13, paragraph (1) (including the cases where it is applied mutatis mutandis pursuant to Article 272-34, paragraph (1)), Article 271-28, paragraph (1) or (2) (including the cases where it is applied mutatis mutandis pursuant to Article 272-40, paragraph (2)), or Article 272-23, paragraph (1) or (2), or has made a false answer, or has refused, obstructed, or avoided the inspection under the provisions;
(iv) Any person who has violated the order under the provisions of Article 179, paragraph (1) (including the cases where it is applied mutatis mutandis pursuant to Article 212, paragraph (5) and Article 235, paragraph (5));

(v) Any person who has failed to submit the reports or materials under the provisions of Article 128, paragraph (1) or Article 272-22, paragraph (1), as applied mutatis mutandis pursuant to Article 179, paragraph (2), the provisions of Article 200, paragraph (1), as applied mutatis mutandis pursuant to Article 212, paragraph (5), or the provisions of Article 226, paragraph (1), as applied mutatis mutandis pursuant to Article 235, paragraph (5), or has submitted false reports or materials;

(vi) Any person who has failed to answer any question under the provisions of Article 129, paragraph (1) or Article 272-23, paragraph (1), as applied mutatis mutandis pursuant to Article 179, paragraph (2), the provisions of Article 201, paragraph (1), as applied mutatis mutandis pursuant to Article 212, paragraph (5), the provisions of Article 227, paragraph (1), as applied mutatis mutandis pursuant to Article 235, paragraph (5), or Article 129, paragraph (1), Article 201, paragraph (1), Article 227, paragraph (1), or Article 272-23, paragraph (1), as applied mutatis mutandis pursuant to Article 271, paragraph (3), or has made a false answer, or has refused, obstructed, or avoided the inspection under the provisions;

(vii) Any person who has violated the order (except for orders for the dismissal of the director, executive officer, accounting advisor, or company auditor, or for the full or partial suspension of business) under the provisions of Article 271-30, paragraph (1) (including the cases where it is applied mutatis mutandis pursuant to Article 272-40, paragraph (2)); and

(viii) Any person who has violated any condition attached pursuant to the provisions of Article 310, paragraph (1) (limited to those pertaining to the authorization under the provisions of the proviso of Article 271-18, paragraph (1) or (3), or the approval under the provisions of the proviso of Article 272-35, paragraph (1) or (3)).

Article 317-2 Any person who falls under any of the following items shall be punished by imprisonment with work for not more than one year or a fine of not more than one million yen, or both:

(i) Any person who, in violation of the provisions of Article 11, paragraph (5) of the Trust Business Act, as applied mutatis mutandis pursuant to Article 99, paragraph (8) (including the cases where it is applied mutatis mutandis pursuant to Article 199), has commenced Insurance-Proceed Trust Services;

(ii) Any person who has violated the provisions of Article 24-2 of the Trust Business Act, as applied mutatis mutandis pursuant to Article 99, paragraph (8) (including the cases where it is applied mutatis mutandis pursuant to Article 199), or the provisions of Article 39, paragraph (2) of the Financial Instruments and Exchange Act, as applied mutatis mutandis pursuant to Article 300-2.

(iii) Any person who has submitted a written application for registration set forth in Article 272-2, paragraph (1) or a document set forth in the same Article, paragraph (2) which includes a false detail;

(iv) Any person who is not any of the persons listed in the items of Article 275, paragraph (1) and has engaged in Insurance Solicitation;

(v) A person who has obtained the registration set forth in Article 276 or Article 286 by wrongful means;

(vi) Any person who has violated the provisions of Article 291, paragraph (5);

(vii) Any person who, in violation of Article 300, paragraph (1), has acted as listed in item (i) to (iii) inclusive of the same paragraph;

(viii) Any person who, in violation of Article 37-3, paragraph (1) (except for items (ii) and (vi)) of the Financial Instruments and Exchange Act, as applied mutatis mutandis pursuant to Article 300-2, has failed to deliver a document or has delivered a document that does not detail the particulars prescribed in the same paragraph or

Art.317-3〜319　　　⑥ Insurance Business Act, Part VI

that includes false details; or any person who has provided information lacking said particulars or has provided false particulars by the method specified in Article 34-2, paragraph (4) of that Act as applied mutatis mutandis pursuant to paragraph (2) of that Article; and
(ix) Any person who has violated the order for the full or partial suspension of business under the provisions of Article 307, paragraph (1).
(x) Any person who, in violation of the provisions of Article 308-4, paragraph (1), has divulged any information learned in the course of his/her duties or has used such information for his/her own interest;

Article 317-3 In the case referred to in item (ii) in the preceding Article, the property interest received by the offender or a third person who knows the circumstances shall be confiscated. Where it is not possible to confiscate the whole or part of it, the value thereof shall be collected.

Article 318 Any person who has violated the provisions of Article 240-10, Article 247-3, or Article 265-21 shall be punished by imprisonment with work for not more than one year or a fine of not more than five hundred thousand yen.

Article 318-2 (1) When the director, executive officer, accounting advisor, company auditor, accounting auditor, or manager or other employee of a Company Being Investigated, or any person who has resigned from these positions has failed to make a report under the provisions of Article 240-9, paragraph (1), or has made a false report, or has refused, obstructed, or evaded the inspection under the provisions of the same paragraph, he/she shall be punished by imprisonment with work for not more than one year or a fine of not more than five hundred thousand yen.
(2) When the director, executive officer, accounting advisor, company auditor, accounting auditor, or manager or other employee of a Managed Company, or any person who has resigned from these positions has failed to make a report under the provisions of Article 247-2, paragraph (1), or has made a false report, or has refused, obstructed, or avoided the inspection under the provisions of the same paragraph, he/she shall be punished by imprisonment with work for not more than one year or a fine of not more than five hundred thousand yen.

Article 319 Any person who falls under any of the following items shall be punished by imprisonment with work for not more than six months or a fine of not more than five hundred thousand yen, or both:
(i) Any person who, in violation of the provisions of Article 11, paragraph (8) of the Trust Business Act, as applied mutatis mutandis pursuant to Article 99, paragraph (8) (including the cases where it is applied mutatis mutandis pursuant to Article 199), has failed to Make a Deposit;
(ii) Any person who has failed to indicate the particulars prescribed in the provisions of Article 24, paragraph (2) of the Trust Business Act, as applied mutatis mutandis pursuant to Article 99, paragraph (8) (including the cases where it is applied mutatis mutandis pursuant to Article 199), or the provisions of paragraph (1) or Article 37, paragraph (1) (except for item (ii)) of the Financial Instruments and Exchange Act, as supplied mutatis mutandis pursuant to Article 300-2, or has indicated false particulars;
(iii) Any person who has violated the provisions of Article 24-2 of the Trust Business Act, as applied mutatis mutandis pursuant to Article 99, paragraph (8) (including the cases where it is applies mutatis mutandis pursuant to Article 199), or the pro-

visions of Article 37, paragraph (2) of the Financial Instruments and Exchange Act, as applied mutatis mutandis pursuant to Article 300-2;
(iv) Any person who, in violation of the provisions of Article 37-3, paragraph (1) (except for item (ii) to (iv) inclusive and item (vi)) of the Financial Instruments and Exchange Act, as applied mutatis mutandis pursuant to Article 24-2 of the Trust Business Act, as applied mutatis mutandis pursuant to Article 99, paragraph (8) (including the cases where it is applied mutatis mutandis pursuant to Article 199), has failed to deliver a document, or has delivered a document that does not detail the particulars prescribed in the same paragraph or a document that includes false details; or any person who has provided information lacking said particulars or has provided false particulars by the method specified in Article 34-2, paragraph (4) of that Act as applied mutatis mutandis pursuant to paragraph (2) of that Article;
(v) Any person who has failed to deliver a document under the provisions of Article 26, paragraph (1) of the Trust Business Act, as applied mutatis mutandis pursuant to Article 99, paragraph (8) (including the cases where it is applied mutatis mutandis pursuant to Article 199), or has delivered a false document;
(vi) Any person who has failed to deliver a report under the provisions of Article 27, paragraph (1) of the Trust Business Act, as applied mutatis mutandis pursuant to Article 99, paragraph (8) (including the cases where it is applied mutatis mutandis pursuant to Article 199), or has delivered a report that includes false details;
(vii) Any person who has failed to deliver a document under the provisions of Article 29, paragraph (3) of the Trust Business Act, as applied mutatis mutandis pursuant to Article 99, paragraph (8) (including the cases where it is applied mutatis mutandis pursuant to Article 199), or has delivered a false document;
(viii) Any person who, in violation of Article 190, paragraph (8), has failed to Make a Deposit for the shortfall set forth in the same paragraph;
(ix) Any person who, in violation of Article 223, paragraph (9), has failed to Make a Deposit for the shortfall set forth in the same paragraph;
(x) Any person who has submitted a written application for approval set forth in Article 272-36, paragraph (1) or a document set forth in paragraph (2) of the same Article in which he/she has included false details;
(xi) Any person who, in violation of Article 272-5, paragraph (8), has failed to Make a Deposit for the shortfall set forth in the same paragraph;
(xii) Any person who, in violation of Article 291, paragraph (8), has failed to deposit the security deposit for the shortfall set forth in the same paragraph; and
(xiii) Any person who has failed to deliver the document under the provisions of Article 37-4, paragraph (1) of the Financial Instruments and Exchange Act, as applied mutatis mutandis pursuant to Article 300-2, or has delivered a document that includes false details; or a person or who has provided false particulars by the method specified in Article 34-2, paragraph (4) of that Act as applied mutatis mutandis pursuant to paragraph (2) of that Article.

Article 319-2 Any person who has failed to prepare or preserve the records under Article 308-11 or Article 308-13, paragraph (9), or has prepared false records shall be punished by a fine of not more than one million yen.

Article 319-3 A person who falls under any of the following items shall be punished by a fine of not more than five hundred thousand yen:
(i) Any person who has failed to submit the report or materials under the provisions of Article 265-46, or has submitted a false report or materials;
(ii) Any person who has failed to answer any question under the provisions of Article

Art.320   6 Insurance Business Act, Part VI

265-46, or has made a false answer, or has refused, obstructed, or avoided the inspection under the provisions of the same Article;
(iii) Any person who has failed to make a report under the provisions of Article 270-3, paragraph (3) (including the cases where it is applied mutatis mutandis pursuant to Article 270-3-2, paragraph (8), Article 270-3-14, paragraph (2), Article 270-4, paragraph (7), and Article 270-6-5, paragraph (2)), Article 270-3-3, paragraph (3), Article 270-3-4, paragraph (4), Article 270-3-6, paragraph (2), Article 270-3-7, paragraph (2), Article 270-3-8, paragraph (2), Article 270-6-7, paragraph (2), Article 270-6-8, paragraph (3) (including the cases where it is applied mutatis mutandis pursuant to Article 270-6-9, paragraph (3)), Article 270-7, paragraph (4), Article 270-8, paragraph (4), or Article 270-8-3, paragraph (2), or has made a false report;
(iv) Any person who has failed to make a report under the provisions of Article 270-3-10, or has made a false report; and
(v) Any person who has suspended or abolished all or part of the Dispute Resolution Services, etc. without obtaining an authorization under Article 308-23, paragraph (1).

Article 320 A person who falls under any of the following items shall be punished by a fine of not more than three hundred thousand yen:
(i) Any person who, without obtaining authorization, has acted with regard to particulars which require authorization under the provisions of Article 102, paragraph (1) (including the cases where it is applied mutatis mutandis pursuant to Article 199);
(i)-2 Any person who has failed to make a report under the provisions of Article 122-2, paragraph (4) or has made a false report, or has refused, obstructed, or avoided the inspection under the provisions of the same paragraph;
(i)-3 Any person who has failed to submit the materials under the provisions of Article 265-31, paragraph (1), Article 266, paragraph (2) (including the cases where it is applied mutatis mutandis pursuant to Article 267, paragraph (4)), Article 267, paragraph (2), Article 270-3-11, paragraph (2), Article 270-6-2, paragraph (2), Article 270-6-6, paragraph (2), and Article 270-8-2, paragraph (2), or has submitted false materials;
(ii) Any person who has submitted a written application for registration set forth in Article 277, paragraph (1), a document set forth in the same Article, paragraph (2), a written application for registration set forth in Article 287, paragraph (1), or a document set forth in the same Article, paragraph (2) in which he/she has included false details;
(iii) Any person who, in violation of Article 303, has failed to keep books and documents, has failed to enter the particulars prescribed in the same Article in the books and documents, has included false entries in the books and documents, or has failed to preserve the books and documents;
(iv) Any person who has, in violation of Article 304, failed to submit the documents prescribed in the same Article, who has submitted documents in which he/she has failed to detail particulars that are required to be included, or who has submitted documents in which he/she has included false details;
(v) Any person who has failed to submit the report or materials under the provisions of Article 305, or has submitted false reports or materials;
(vi) Any person who has failed to answer any question under the provisions of Article 305 or has made a false answer, or has refused, obstructed, or avoided the inspection under the provisions of the same Article; and
(vii) Any person who has violated the order under the provisions of Article 306.
(viii) Any person who has failed to make a report under Article 308-8, paragraph (1),

or has made a false report;
(ix) Any person who has failed to make a notification under Article 308-18, paragraph (1), Article 308-19 or Article 308-23, paragraph (2), or has made a false notification; and
(x) Any person who has failed to make a notification under Article 308-23, paragraph (3) or Article 308-24, paragraph (4), or has made a false notification.

Article 321 (1) When the representative person or agent of a juridical person (including an association or foundation that is not a juridical person and has provisions on representative persons or administrators; hereinafter the same shall apply in this paragraph) or representative, employee or other worker of a juridical person or individual has committed the violation set forth in the provisions listed in the following items with regard to the business or property of said juridical person or individual, not only the offender shall be punished but also said juridical person shall be punished by the fine prescribed respectively in those items, and said individual shall be punished by the fine prescribed in the respective Articles:
(i) Article 315, item (v), or Article 316, items (i) to (iii) inclusive, item (vi) or (vii); a fine of not more than three hundred million yen; any of the dates specified in the preceding two items, whichever is the latest.
(ii) Article 316-2, Article 316-3 (excluding item (ii)) or Article 317, items (i) to (iii) inclusive, items (vii) or (viii); a fine of not more than two hundred million yen;
(iii) Article 317-2, item (ii); a fine of not more than one hundred million yen; and
(iv) Article 315 (except for item (v)), Article 315-2, Article 316, item (iv) or (v), Article 316-3, item (ii), Article 317, items (iv) to (vi) inclusive, Article 317-2 (except for item (ii)), or Article 318-2 to the preceding Article inclusive; a fine prescribed in the respective Articles.
(2) In the case where the provisions of the preceding paragraph apply to an association or foundation that is not a juridical person, its representative person or administrator shall represent said association or foundation in any procedural acts, and the provisions of the Acts concerning criminal procedures in the cases where a juridical person is the accused or a suspect shall apply mutatis mutandis.

(Special Breach of Trust Crime of Director, etc.)
Article 322 (1) When any of the following persons, for the purpose of promoting his/her own interest or the interest of a third party, or inflicting damage on an Insurance Company etc. , engages in conduct in breach of his/her duty and causes financial loss to the Insurance Company, etc. , he/she shall be punished by imprisonment with work for not more than ten years or a fine of not more than ten million yen, or both:
(i) Insurance administrator or actuary of an Insurance Company, etc. ;
(ii) Incorporator of a Mutual Company;
(iii) Director or company auditor of a Mutual Company at the time of its incorporation;
(iv) Director, executive officer, accounting advisor or company auditor of a Mutual Company;
(v) Acting director, executive officer or auditor of a Mutual Company who has been appointed pursuant to the provisional disposition order prescribed in Article 56 of the Civil Provisional Relief Act;
(vi) Any person who shall carry out the duties of a temporary director, accounting advisor, company auditor, representative director, committee member, executive officer or representative executive officer who has been appointed pursuant to the provisions of Article 53-15, paragraph (2) of the Companies Act, as applied mutatis mutandis pursuant to Article 53-15, Article 401, paragraph (3) of that Act, as ap-

plied mutatis mutandis pursuant to Article 53-25, paragraph (2) (including the cases where it is applied mutatis mutandis pursuant to Article 53-27, paragraph (3)) or Article 401, paragraph (3) of that Act, as applied mutatis mutandis pursuant to Article 420, paragraph (3) of that Act, as applied mutatis mutandis pursuant to Article 53-32;
(vii) Manager of a Mutual Company;
(viii) Employee of a Mutual Company to whom a type of particular or a specific particular of its business has been delegated; and
(ix) Inspector (limited to those pertaining to a Mutual Company).
(2) When any of the following persons, for the purpose of promoting his/her own interest or the interest of a third party, or inflicting damage on a liquidating mutual company, engages in conduct in breach of his/her duty and causes financial loss to the liquidating mutual company, the same punishment as in the preceding paragraph shall apply:
(i) Liquidator of a liquidating mutual company;
(ii) Acting liquidator of a liquidating mutual company who has been appointed pursuant to the provisional disposition order prescribed in Article 56 of the Civil Provisional Relief Act;
(iii) Any person who shall carry out the duties of a temporary liquidator or Representative Liquidator of a liquidating mutual company who has been appointed pursuant to the provisions of Article 53-12, paragraph (2), as applied mutatis mutandis pursuant to Article 180-5, paragraph (4), or the provisions of Article 351, paragraph (2) of the Companies Act, as applied mutatis mutandis pursuant to Article 180-9, paragraph (5);
(iv) Representative for a liquidator of a liquidating mutual company;
(v) Supervising committee member of a liquidating mutual company; and
(vi) Examination committee member of a liquidating mutual company.
(3) Any person who has attempted a crime set forth in the preceding two paragraphs shall be punished.

(Special Breach of Trust Crime of Representative Bondholder, etc.)
Article 323 (1) When a representative bondholder or resolution executor (meaning a resolution executor prescribed in Article 737, paragraph (2) of the Companies Act, as applied mutatis mutandis pursuant to Article 61-8, paragraph (2); the same shall apply hereinafter) of a Mutual Company, for the purpose of promoting his/her own interest or the interest of a third party, or inflicting damage on a bondholder, engages in conduct in breach of his/her duty and causes financial loss to the bondholder, he/she shall be punished by imprisonment with work for not more than five years or a fine of not more than five million yen, or both.
(2) Any person who has attempted the crime set forth in the preceding paragraph shall be punished.

(Crime of Endangerment to Corporate Assets)
Article 324 (1) In the case where an insurance administrator of a Stock Company operating in the Insurance Business (hereinafter referred to in this Part as "Stock Company") or actuary falls under any of the following items, he/she shall be punished by imprisonment with work for not more than five years or a fine of not more than five million yen, or both:
(i) When he/she, regarding particulars listed in Article 199, paragraph (1), item (iii) or Article 236, paragraph (1), item (iii) of the Companies Act, has made a false statement or has concealed any fact from the court or shareholders' meeting or class shareholders' meeting;

(ii) When he/she, irrespective of whether on behalf of him/herself or on someone else's behalf, has wrongfully acquired shares or has obtained shares for the purpose of pledging them on the account of a Stock Company;
(iii) When he/she has made a dividend of surplus in violation of laws and regulations or articles of incorporation; and
(iv) When he/she has disposed the property of a Stock Company for the objective of speculative trading outside the scope of the purpose of the Stock Company.
(2) In the case where an insurance administrator of a Mutual Company, actuary, any person listed in Article 322, paragraph (1), items (ii) to (ix) inclusive, or any person appointed pursuant to the provisions of Article 94, paragraph (1) of the Companies Act, as applied mutatis mutandis pursuant to Article 30-11, paragraph (2) or Article 79, paragraph (3), falls under any of the following items, he/she shall be punished by the same punishment as that of the preceding paragraph:
(i) When he/she, regarding the number of members, acceptance of the total amount of funds, or payment pertaining to the contribution of funds, or particulars listed in the items of Article 24, paragraph (1), in the case of the incorporation of a Mutual Company, has made a false statement or has concealed any fact from the court or Organizational Meeting;
(ii) When he/she, in violation of laws and regulations or articles of incorporation, has depreciated the funds, paid interest on the funds, or distributed the surplus; and
(iii) When he/she has disposed the property of a Mutual Company for the objective of speculative trading outside the scope of the purpose of the Mutual Company.
(3) When an insurance administrator of a Mutual Company, any of the persons listed in Article 322, paragraph (1), items (iv) to (vi) inclusive or item (ix), or any person who shall be the director, accounting advisor, company auditor or executive officer of a Stock Company, in the case of an Entity Conversion from a Mutual Company into a Stock Company, regarding the subscription or payment of shares or delivery of non-monetary property or particulars listed in Article 92, item (iii) has made a false statement or has concealed any fact from the Prime Minister or court, or from the general members' council or General Representative Members' Council, he/she shall be punished by imprisonment with work for not more than three years or a fine of not more than three million yen, or both.
(4) When an insurance administrator, director, accounting advisor, company auditor or executive officer of a Stock Company, an acting director, accounting advisor, company auditor or executive officer of a Stock Company who has been appointed pursuant to the provisional disposition order prescribed in Article 56 of the Civil Provisional Relief Act, any person who shall carry out the duties of a temporary director, accounting advisor, company auditor, representative director, committee member, executive officer or representative executive officer who has been appointed pursuant to the provisions of Article 346, paragraph (2), Article 351, paragraph (2), or Article 401, paragraph (3) of the Companies Act (including the cases where it is applied mutatis mutandis pursuant to Article 403, paragraph (3) and Article 420, paragraph (3)) or inspector, or any person who shall be the director, accounting advisor, company auditor or executive officer of a Mutual Company, in the case of an Entity Conversion from a Stock Company into a Mutual Company, regarding the acceptance of the total amount of funds or payment pertaining to the contribution of funds, has made a false statement or has concealed any fact from the policyholders meeting or General Council of Representative Policyholders, the same punishment as in the preceding paragraph shall apply.

(Crime of Using False Documents, etc.)
Article 325 (1) When any of the persons listed in Article 322, paragraph (1), items (i) to

Art.324

(viii) inclusive or any person who has been entrusted with the solicitation of funds or subscribers to the bonds of a Mutual Company (meaning bonds prescribed in Article 61), in soliciting subscribers for the shares, funds, share options, bonds (meaning bonds prescribed in Article 61 and bonds prescribed in Article 2, item (xxiii) of the Companies Act; hereinafter the same shall apply in this paragraph), or bonds with a share option, has used materials explaining the business of an Insurance Company, etc. or other particulars or an advertisement or other documents related to said subscription which include a false detail with regard to an important particular, or has offered electromagnetic records that include a false record with regard to an important particular for carrying out affairs for said solicitation for subscription in the case where electromagnetic records have been created in lieu of said documents, he/she shall be punished by imprisonment with work for not more than five years or a fine of not more than five million yen, or both.

(2) When any person who offers the bonds of a Mutual Company (meaning bonds prescribed in Article 61) has used documents concerning the secondary distribution which include a false detail with regard to an important particular, or has offered electromagnetic records that include a false record with regard to an important particular for carrying out affairs for said secondary distribution in the case where electromagnetic records have been created in lieu of said documents, the same punishment as in the preceding paragraph shall apply.

(3) When an insurance administrator of a Mutual Company or any persons listed in Article 322, paragraph (1), items (iv) to (viii) inclusive, in the case of an Entity Conversion from a Mutual Company into a Stock Company, in soliciting subscribers for the shares prescribed in Article 92, has used materials explaining the business of the Stock Company following the Entity Conversion or other matters or an advertisement or other documents related to said subscription which include a false detail with regard to an important particular, or has offered electromagnetic records that include a false record with regard to an important particular for carrying out affairs for said solicitation for subscription in the case where electromagnetic records have been created in lieu of said documents, the same punishment as in paragraph (1) shall apply.

(4) When an insurance administrator, director, accounting advisor, company auditor or executive officer of a Stock Company, an acting director, company auditor or executive officer of a Stock Company who has been appointed pursuant to the provisional disposition order prescribed in Article 56 of the Civil Provisional Relief Act, any person who shall carry out the duties of a temporary director, accounting advisor, company auditor, representative director, committee member, executive officer or representative executive officer who has been appointed pursuant to the provisions of Article 346, paragraph (2), Article 351, paragraph (2), or Article 401, paragraph (3) of the Companies Act (including the cases where it is applied mutatis mutandis pursuant to Article 403, paragraph (3) and Article 420, paragraph (3) of that Act) or manager or an employee who has been entrusted with a type of particular or a specific particular of its other operations, in soliciting the funds prescribed in Article 78, paragraph (1), in the case of an Entity Conversion from a Stock Company into a Mutual Company, has used an advertisement or other documents related to the subscription of funds which include a false detail with regard to an important particular, or has offered electromagnetic records that include a false detail with regard to an important particular for carrying out affairs for said solicitation for subscription in the case where electromagnetic records have been created in lieu of said documents, the same punishment as in paragraph (1) shall apply.

(Crime of Fake Payment)

Article 326 (1) When any of the persons listed in Article 322, paragraph (1), items (i) to (viii) inclusive has made a fake payment to give the false appearance of a payment to fund contributions or payment for shares, he/she shall be punished by imprisonment with work for not more than five years or a fine of not more than five million yen, or both. The same shall apply to any person who has acted as a party to such fake payment.

(2) When any of the persons prescribed in the preceding Article, paragraph (3), in the case of an Entity Conversion from a Mutual Company into a Stock Company, has made a fake payment to give a false appearance of payment for shares pertaining to subscription under the provisions of Article 92, the same punishment as in the preceding paragraph shall apply. The same shall apply to any person who has acted as a party to such fake payment.

(3) When any of the persons prescribed in the preceding Article, paragraph (4), in the case of an Entity Conversion from a Stock Company into a Mutual Company, has made a fake payment to give a false appearance of payment set forth in Article 30-3, paragraph (1), as applied mutatis mutandis pursuant to Article 78, paragraph (3), the same punishment as in paragraph (1) shall apply. The same shall apply to any person who has acted as a party to such fake payment.

(Crime of Over Issuance of Shares)
Article 327 When an insurance administrator of a Stock Company has issued an aggregate number of shares exceeding the total number of shares that a Stock Company may issue, he/she shall be punished by imprisonment with work for not more than five years or a fine of not more than five million yen.

(Crime of Bribery of Director, etc.)
Article 328 (1) When any of the following persons has accepted, or requested or promised a property benefit based on an unlawful request concerning his/her duties, he/she shall be punished by imprisonment with work for not more than five years or a fine of not more than five million yen:

(i) Any person listed in the items of Article 322, paragraph (1) or the items of paragraph (2);

(ii) Any person prescribed in Article 323;

(iii) Accounting auditor of a Mutual Company or any person who shall carry out the duties of a temporary accounting auditor who has been appointed pursuant to the provisions of Article 53-12, paragraph (4); and

(iv) Insurance inspector of an Insurance Company.

(2) Any person who has given, or offered or promised to give the benefit set forth in the preceding paragraph shall be punished by imprisonment with work for not more than three years or a fine of not more than three million yen.

(Crime of Bribery Concerning Exercise of Rights of Members, etc.)
Article 329 (1) Any person who, concerning the following particulars, has accepted, or requested or promised a property benefit based on an unlawful request shall be punished by imprisonment with work for not more than five years or a fine of not more than five million yen:

(i) The making of remarks or exercise of voting rights at a general members' council meeting, General Representative Members' Council Meeting, Organizational Meeting, bondholders meeting or creditors meeting of a Mutual Company, policyholders meeting or General Council of Representative Policyholders in the case where a Stock Company shall carry out the Entity Conversion set forth in Article

68, paragraph (1), or creditors meeting of a Foreign Mutual Company;
(ii) The exercise of rights of a member or representative member prescribed in Article 38, paragraph (1) or (2), Article 39, Article 40, paragraph (1), Article 45, paragraph (1) or (2), Article 46, Article 47, paragraph (1), Article 50, paragraph (1) or (2), Article 358, paragraph (1) (except for item (ii)) or Article 360, paragraph (1) of the Companies Act, as applied mutatis mutandis pursuant to Article 53-15, Article 422, paragraph (1) of the same Act, as applied mutatis mutandis pursuant to Article 53-32, Article 426, paragraph (5) of the same Act, as applied mutatis mutandis pursuant to Article 53-36, or Article 360, paragraph (1) of the same Act, as applied mutatis mutandis pursuant to Article 180-5, paragraph (2) or Article 180-8, paragraph (4); or the exercise of rights of a member or obligee prescribed in Article 511, paragraph (1) or Article 522, paragraph (1) of the same Act, as applied mutatis mutandis pursuant to Article 184; or the exercise of rights of an obligee prescribed in Article 547, paragraph (1) or (3) of the same Act, as applied mutatis mutandis pursuant to Article 184;
(iii) The exercise of rights of an aggregate number of members that corresponds to five thousandths, three thousandths, one thousandth or more of the total number of members or three thousand or one thousand or more members (in the case of a Specified Mutual Company, the number of members specified by Cabinet Order prescribed in Article 38, paragraph (1), Article 39, paragraph (1) or Article 50, paragraph (1) or more), nine or three or more representative members, or a bondholder who holds bonds equivalent to one-tenth or more of the total amount (excluding the amount of bonds which have been redeemed) of bonds of a Mutual Company (meaning the bonds prescribed in Article 61; hereinafter the same shall apply in this item);
(iv) The filing of litigation prescribed in this Act or the Companies Act, as applied mutatis mutandis pursuant to this Act (limited to those filed by a member or an obligee of a Mutual Company); and
(v) The intervention by a member under the provisions of Article 849, paragraph (1) of the Companies Act, as applied mutatis mutandis pursuant to this Act.
(2) The same punishment as in the preceding paragraph shall apply to any person who has given, or offered or promised to give the benefit set forth in the same paragraph.

(Confiscation and Collection of Equivalent Value)
Article 330 In the case referred to in Article 328, paragraph (1) or the preceding Article, paragraph (1), a benefit accepted by an offender shall be confiscated. When the whole or a part of the benefit cannot be confiscated, an equivalent sum of money shall be collected.

(Crime of Benefit Sharing Concerning Exercise of Rights of Shareholder, etc.)
Article 331 (1) When an insurance administrator of an Insurance Company, etc. , or any of the persons listed in Article 322, paragraph (1), items (iv) to (vii) inclusive or other employee of a Mutual Company, concerning the exercise of rights of a shareholder or member or representative member, has given a property benefit with regards to the account of the Insurance Company, etc. or its Subsidiary Company (meaning the Subsidiary Company prescribed in Article 2, item (iii) of the Companies Act (its de facto Subsidiary Company in the case where the Insurance Company, etc. is a Mutual Company); the same shall apply in paragraph (3)), he/she shall be punished by imprisonment with work for not more than three years or a fine of not more than three million yen.
(2) The same punishment as in the preceding paragraph shall apply to any person who,

with knowledge, has been given the benefit set forth in the same paragraph or has caused a third party to give such benefit.
(3) The same punishment as in paragraph (1) shall apply to any person who, concerning the exercise of rights of a shareholder or member or representative member, has requested the person prescribed in the same paragraph to give the benefit set forth in the same paragraph to him/her or to a third party with regards to the account of the Insurance Company, etc. or its Subsidiary.
(4) When any person who has committed a crime set forth in the preceding two paragraphs has intimidated a person prescribed in paragraph (1) regarding the execution of the crime, he/she shall be punished by imprisonment with work for not more than five years or a fine of not more than five million yen.
(5) Imprisonment with work and fines may be imposed cumulatively, pursuant to the circumstances, on any person who has committed a crime set forth in the preceding three paragraphs.
(6) When any person who has committed a crime set forth in paragraph (1) has surrendered himself/herself to authorities, the punishment thereof may be reduced or remitted.

(Crimes Committed Outside Japan)
Article 331-2 (1) The crimes set forth in Article 322 to 324 inclusive, Article 326, Article 327, Article 328, paragraph (1), Article 329, paragraph (1) and the preceding Article, paragraph (1) shall also apply to any person who has committed these crimes outside Japan.
(2) The crimes set forth in Article 328, paragraph (2), Article 329, paragraph (2), and the preceding Article, paragraph (2) to (4) inclusive shall be governed by Article 2 of the Penal Code.

(Application of Penal Provisions to Juridical Person)
Article 332 When a person prescribed in Article 322 to 327 inclusive, Article 328, paragraph (1), Article 329, paragraph (1), or Article 331, paragraph (1) is a juridical person, said provisions and the provisions of Article 322, paragraph (3) and Article 323, paragraph (2) shall respectively apply to the director, executive officer, other officer who executes business, or manager who has acted in the relevant way.

(Crime of False Notification, etc.)
Article 332-2 Any person who, in violation of Article 955, paragraph (1) of the Companies Act, as applied mutatis mutandis pursuant to Article 67-2 or Article 217, paragraph (3), has failed to detail or record what is specified by Ordinance of the Ministry of Justice concerning the Investigation of Electronic Public Notice prescribed in the same paragraph in the registry of studies, etc. (meaning the registry of studies, etc. prescribed in the same paragraph; hereinafter the same shall apply in this Article), who has included a false detail or record in the registry of studies, etc. , or who has not preserved the registry of studies, etc. , in violation of the same paragraph, shall be punished by a fine of not more than three hundred thousand yen.

(Dual Liability)
Article 332-3 When a representative person of a juridical person, or an agent, employee or other worker of a juridical person or individual, has committed the violation set forth in the preceding Article with regard to the business of said juridical person or individual, not only the offender shall be punished but also said juridical person or individual shall be punished by the punishment prescribed in the same Article.

(Acts Which Shall be Punishable by Non-Criminal Fine)
Article 333 (1) If the incorporator of an Insurance Company, etc. , the director at the time of the incorporation of said Insurance Company, etc. , its executive officer at the time of incorporation, company auditor at the time of incorporation, its director, executive officer, or accounting advisor, or the member who is to act as such; its company auditor or accounting auditor or the member who is to act as such; its liquidator; its Entrusted Company as prescribed in Article 144, paragraph (1) (including the cases where it is applied mutatis mutandis pursuant to Article 272-30, paragraph (2)); its insurance administrator or insurance inspector; its liquidator representative as set forth in Article 525, paragraph (1) of the Companies Act (including the cases where it is applied mutatis mutandis pursuant to Article 184); its supervising committee member as set forth in Article 527, paragraph (1) of the same Act (including the cases where it is applied mutatis mutandis pursuant to Article 184); its examination committee member as set forth in Article 533 of the same Act (including the cases where it is applied mutatis mutandis pursuant to Article 184); the person who is to act as its director, executive officer, company auditor, or liquidator and who has been appointed pursuant to a provisional disposition order prescribed in Article 56 of the Civil Provisional Remedies Act; the person who is to act as its temporary director, accounting advisor, company auditor, representative director, committee member, executive officer, or representative executive officer as prescribed in Article 322, paragraph (1), item (vi) or in Article 960, paragraph (1), item (v) of the Companies Act; the person who is to act as its temporary liquidator or Representative Liquidator as prescribed in Article 322, paragraph (2), item (iii) or in Article 960, paragraph (2), item (iii) of the same Act; the person who is to act as its temporary accounting auditor as prescribed in Article 328, paragraph (1), item (iii) or Article 967, paragraph (1), item (iii) of the same Act; its inspector, the administrator of its shareholder registry, the administrator of its bond registry, its bond administrator, the bond administrator succeeding to its affairs, its representative bondholder, its resolution executor, or its manager; the Representative Person in Japan of a Foreign Insurance Company, etc. , the liquidator of said Foreign Insurance Company, its Entrusted Company as prescribed in Article 144, paragraph (1), as applied mutatis mutandis pursuant to Article 211, or its insurance administrator, insurance inspector, or manager; the person representing a licensed Specified Juridical Person and its subscription members in Japan; a person who has concluded a contract set forth in Article 190, paragraph (3) with a Foreign Insurance Company, etc. , a person who has concluded a contract set forth in Article 223, paragraph (3) with a licensed Specified Juridical Person, or a person who has concluded a contract set forth in Article 272-5, paragraph (3) with a Low-Cost, Short-Term Insurer; the officer of a Corporation; a Large-Volume Holder of Insurance Company Voting Rights (including the person who used to be the relevant Large-Volume Holder of Insurance Company Voting Rights, if said Large-Volume Holder of Insurance Company Voting Rights has ceased to be a Large-Volume Holder of Insurance Company Voting Rights, and if the Large-Volume Holder of Insurance Company Voting Rights is a juridical person (including organizations without juridical personality which are listed in Article 2-2, paragraph (1), item (i); hereinafter the same applies in this paragraph except for items (lxiv) and (lxx)), this means its director, executive officer, or accounting advisor, or the member who is to act as such; its company auditor, representative person, or manager, the member who executes its business, or its liquidator); an Insurance Company's Major Shareholder or a Low-Cost, Short-Term Insurer's Major Shareholder (including the person who used to be the relevant Insurance Company's Major Shareholder or Low-Cost, Short-Term Insurer's Major Shareholder, if said Insurance Company's Ma-

jor Shareholder or Low-Cost, Short-Term Insurer's Major Shareholder has ceased to be the Insurance Company's Major Shareholder or Low-Cost, Short-Term Insurer's Major Shareholder, and if the Insurance Company's Major Shareholder or Low-Cost, Short-Term Insurer's Major Shareholder is a juridical person, this means its director, executive officer, or accounting advisor, or the member who is to act as such, its company auditor, representative person, or manager, the member who executes its business, or its liquidator); a Specified Major Shareholder or Low-Cost, Short-Term Insurer's Specified Major Shareholder (including the person who used to be the relevant Specified Major Shareholder or Low-Cost, Short-Term Insurer's Specified Major Shareholder, if said Specified Major Shareholder or Low-Cost, Short-Term Insurer's Specified Major Shareholder has ceased to be a person that holds a number of voting rights in an Insurance Company equal to or exceeding the Major Shareholder Threshold, etc., and if the Specified Major Shareholder or Low-Cost, Short-Term Insurer's Specified Major Shareholder is a juridical person, this means its director, executive officer, or accounting advisor, or the member who is to act as such, its company auditor, representative person, or manager, the member who executes its business, or its liquidator); the director, executive officer, or accounting advisor of an Insurance Holding Company or Low-Cost, Short-Term Insurance Holding Company (including the company that used to be the relevant Insurance Holding Company or Low-Cost, Short-Term Insurance Holding Company, if said Insurance Holding Company or Low-Cost, Short-Term Insurance Holding Company has ceased to be an Insurance Holding Company or Low-Cost, Short-Term Insurance Holding Company), or the member who is to act as such; or its company auditor, its manager, or its liquidator; or the director, executive officer, or accounting advisor of a Specified Holding Company or Specified Low-Cost, Short-Term Insurance Holding Company (including the company that used to be the relevant Specified Holding Company or Specified Low-Cost, Short-Term Insurance Holding Company, if said Specified Holding Company or Specified Low-Cost, Short-Term Insurance Holding Company has ceased to have an Insurance Company, etc. as its Subsidiary), or the member who is to act as such; or its company auditor, its manager, the member who executes its business, or its liquidator falls under any of the following items, he/she shall be subject to a non-criminal fine of not more than one million yen; provided, however, that this does not apply if a criminal punishment is to be imposed for the relevant action:

(i) (Deleted);
(ii) When he/she has engaged in the day-to-day business of another company, in violation of Article 8, paragraph (1), Article 192, paragraph (5) or Article 272-10, paragraph (1);
(iii) When he/she has failed to complete his/her registration under the provisions of this Act or the Companies Act, as applied mutatis mutandis pursuant to this Act;
(iv) When he/she has failed to give public notice or notice under the provisions of this Act or the Companies Act, as applied mutatis mutandis pursuant to this Act, or has given an unauthorized public notice or notice;
(v) When he/she has failed to make a disclosure under the provisions of this Act or the Companies Act, as applied mutatis mutandis pursuant to this Act;
(vi) When he/she, in violation of this Act or the Companies Act, as applied mutatis mutandis pursuant to this Act after a deemed replacement, has refused, without justifiable grounds, to allow the inspection of documents or of an object that shows, by a method specified by Cabinet Office Ordinance, the particulars recorded in electromagnetic records, or has refused to issue a certified copy or extract of a document, to provide the particulars that are recorded in an electromagnetic record by electromagnetic means, or to issue a document detailing such particulars;

(vii) When he/she has refused, obstructed, or evaded an inspection under the provisions of this Act or the Companies Act, as applied mutatis mutandis pursuant to this Act;
(viii) When he/she, regarding particulars prescribed in this Act or the Companies Act, as applied mutatis mutandis pursuant to this Act, has made a false statement or has concealed any fact from a government agency, general members' council, General Representative Members' Council, Organizational Meeting, policyholders meeting, General Council of Representative Policyholders, bondholders meeting, or creditors meeting;
(ix) When he/she has failed to detail or record the particulars that are required to be detailed or recorded or has included a false detail or record in the articles of incorporation, minutes of general members' council meeting, General Representative Members' Council Meeting, Organizational Meeting, board of directors, committee on important property, Committees, board of company auditors, policyholders meeting, General Council of Representative Policyholders, bondholders meeting or creditors meeting, roster of members, accounting books, balance sheet, profit and loss statement, business report, annexed detailed statement of Article 494, paragraph (1) of the Companies Act, as applied mutatis mutandis pursuant to Article 54-3, paragraph (2) or Article 180-17, accounting advisory report, audit report, accounting auditing report, statement of accounts, bond registry, inventory of property, business report, or document or electromagnetic record set forth in Article 682, paragraph (1) or Article 695, paragraph (1), Article 165-2, paragraph (1), Article 165-9, paragraph (1), Article 165-13, paragraph (1), Article 165-15, paragraph (1), Article 165-19, paragraph (1) or Article 165-21, paragraph (1) of the same Act, as applied mutatis mutandis pursuant to Article 61-5;
(x) When he/she has failed to keep books or documents or a statement or electromagnetic record in violation of this Act or the Companies Act, as applied mutatis mutandis pursuant to this Act;
(xi) When he/she, without justifiable grounds, has failed to explain the particulars with regard to which a person who seeks to be a member or a member, representative member, or Policyholder has requested an explanation at the general members' council meeting, General Representative Members' Council Meeting, Organizational Meeting, policyholders meeting or General Council of Representative Policyholders;
(xii) When he/she, in violation of Article 15, Article 56 to 59 inclusive, Article 91, paragraph (4), Article 112, paragraph (2) (including the cases where it is applied mutatis mutandis pursuant to Article 199) or Article 115 (including the cases where it is applied mutatis mutandis pursuant to Articles 199 and 272-18), has failed to report any Reserves or reserves funds, or has failed to make Reserves, or has withdrawn from such Reserves;
(xiii) When he/she, in violation of Article 17, paragraph (2) or (4) (including the cases where the provisions are applied mutatis mutandis pursuant to Article 57, paragraph (4)), Article 70, paragraph (2) or (4) (including the cases where it is applied mutatis mutandis pursuant to Article 165-7, paragraph (4) (including the cases where it is applied mutatis mutandis pursuant to Article 165-12)), Article 77, paragraph (4), Article 88, paragraph (2)or (4) (including the cases where it is applied mutatis mutandis pursuant to Article 165-17, paragraph (4) (including the cases where it is applied mutatis mutandis pursuant to Article 165-20)), Article 137, paragraphs (1) to (3) inclusive (including the cases where the provisions are applied mutatis mutandis pursuant to Article 210, paragraph (1) (including the cases where it is applied mutatis mutandis pursuant to Article 270-4, paragraph (9)), Article

270-4, paragraph (9) and Article 272-29), Article 165-7, paragraph (2) (including the cases where it is applied mutatis mutandis pursuant to Article 165-12), Article 165-17, paragraph (2) (including the cases where it is applied mutatis mutandis pursuant to Article 165-20), Article 165-24, paragraph (2) or (4), Article 173-4, paragraph (2) or (4) Article 240-12, paragraphs (1) to (3) inclusive, Article 251, paragraph (1) (including the cases where it is applied mutatis mutandis pursuant to Article 270-4, paragraph (9)), Article 255, paragraph (1), or Article 255-4, paragraphs (1) to (3) inclusive, has reduced the amount of capital or reserves or withdrawn from depreciation reserves for redemption of funds, has made an Entity Conversion, established a General Council of Representative Policyholders, transferred an insurance contract, conducted a merger, split a company, amended the contract conditions prescribed in Article 240-2, paragraph (1), or amended the contract conditions prescribed in Article 250, paragraph (1);

(xiv) When he/she has failed to make the particulars of a request under Article 39, paragraph (1) or Article 46, paragraph (1) the purpose of a general members' council meeting or General Representative Members' Council Meeting in the case where such a request has been made;

(xv) When he/she has failed to call a general members' council meeting or General Representative Members' Council Meeting in violation of a court order under the provisions of Article 307, paragraph (1), item (i) of the Companies Act, as applied mutatis mutandis pursuant to Article 40-2, paragraph (2) or Article 47, paragraph (2) or the provisions of Article 359, paragraph (1), item (i) of the same Act, as applied mutatis mutandis pursuant to Article 53-15, or Article 296, paragraph (1) of the same Act, as applied mutatis mutandis pursuant to Article 41, paragraph (1) or Article 49, paragraph (1);

(xvi) When he/she, in violation of the provisions of Articles 301 or 302 of the Companies Act, as applied mutatis mutandis pursuant to Article 41, paragraph (1), or the provisions of Article 48 or the provisions of Article 54-5 (including the cases where it is applied mutatis mutandis pursuant to Article 54-10, paragraph (6)), has failed to issue a document or statement, or has failed to provide information by electromagnetic means in giving a notice of convocation for a general members' council meeting or General Representative Members' Council Meeting;

(xvii) When he/she has failed to carry out the procedure for the appointment of a director, accounting advisor, company auditor, executive officer or accounting auditor (including the appointment of any person who shall carry out the duties of a temporary accounting auditor) in the case where his/her number shall fall short of the number specified by this Act or the articles of incorporation;

(xviii) When he/she has failed to appoint half or more outside company auditors as company auditors in violation of Article 53-5, paragraph (3);

(xix) When he/she has failed to make particulars of a request under Article 343, paragraph (2) or Article 344, paragraph (2) of the Companies Act, as applied mutatis mutandis pursuant to Article 53-11 the purpose of a general members' council meeting or General Representative Members' Council Meeting in the case where such a request has been made, or has failed to submit a proposal pertaining to such a request to the general members' council meeting or General Representative Members' Council Meeting;

(xx) When he/she, in violation of the provisions of Article 365, paragraph (2) of the Companies Act (including the cases where it is applied mutatis mutandis pursuant to Article 419, paragraph (2) of the same Act, as applied mutatis mutandis pursuant to Article 53-32), as applied mutatis mutandis pursuant to Article 53-15, or the provisions of Article 365, paragraph (2) of the same Act, as applied mutatis mutandis

Art.333   ⑥ Insurance Business Act, Part VI

pursuant to Article 180-14, paragraph (9), has failed to make a report to a board of directors or board of liquidators, or has made a false report;

(xxi) When he/she has failed to select full-time company auditors in violation of Article 53-19, paragraph (3);

(xxii) When he/she has issued debenture shares prior to the date of the issuance of bonds (meaning bonds prescribed in Article 61);

(xxiii) When he/she has failed to issue debenture shares without delay in violation of Article 696 of the Companies Act, as applied mutatis mutandis pursuant to Article 61-5;

(xxiv) When he/she has failed to detail the particulars that are required to be included on the debenture shares, or has included a false detail on the debenture shares

(xxv) When he/she, in violation of Article 61-6, has issued bonds (meaning bonds prescribed in Article61), or, in violation of Article 714, paragraph (1) of the Companies Act, as applied mutatis mutandis pursuant to Article 61-7, paragraph (8), has failed to prescribe a bond administrator who shall succeed to the affairs;

(xxvi) When he/she, in violation of Article 941 of the Companies Act, as applied mutatis mutandis pursuant to Article 67-2 or Article 217, paragraph (3), has failed to seek the investigation set forth in the same Article;

(xxvii) When he/she has made an Entity Conversion in violation of Article 69, Article 78 or Article 86;

(xxviii) When he/she, in violation of Article 98, paragraph (2) or Article 99, paragraph (4), first sentence or paragraph (5) (including the cases where the provisions are applied mutatis mutandis pursuant to Article 199), has conducted business prescribed in these provisions without obtaining authorization, or, in violation of the proviso of Article 272-11, paragraph (2), has conducted business prescribed in the proviso of the same paragraph without obtaining approval;

(xxix) When he/she, in violation of Article 99, paragraph (4), second sentence (including the cases where it is applied mutatis mutandis pursuant to Article 199; hereinafter the same shall apply in this item), has changed the content or method of the business prescribed in the second sentence of the same paragraph without obtaining authorization;

(xxx) When he/she has conducted any other business in violation of Article 100 (including the cases where it is applied mutatis mutandis pursuant to Article 199), Article 271-21, paragraph (1), Article 272-11, paragraph (2) or Article 272-38, paragraph (1);

(xxxi) When he/she, in violation of Article 100-4 (including the cases where it is applied mutatis mutandis pursuant to Article 272-13, paragraph (2)), Article 271-19-2, paragraph (3), or Article 272-37-2, paragraph (2), has become an unlimited partner or a partner who executes the business of a membership company;

(xxxii) When he/she, in violation of Article 106, paragraph (1), has made a company other than the a Company Eligible to Be a Subsidiary prescribed in the same paragraph (except for the Japanese company prescribed in Article 107, paragraph (1)) a Subsidiary, or, in violation of Article 272-14, paragraph (1), has made a company other than the company that exclusively operates in the business specified by Cabinet Office Ordinance prescribed in the same paragraph its Subsidiary;

(xxxiii) When he/she has made an Insurance Company, etc. Eligible to Be a Subsidiary prescribed in Article 106, paragraph (4) a Subsidiary without obtaining the authorization of the Prime Minister under the provisions of the same paragraph or has made a company listed in the items of the same Article, paragraph (1) into a Subsidiary that falls under any of the companies listed in another of these items (limited to an Insurance Company, etc. Eligible to Be a Subsidiary prescribed in the same Article, paragraph (4)) without obtaining the authorization of the Prime Minister under the provisions of the same Article, paragraph (4), as applied mutatis mutandis pursuant to the same Article, paragraph (6), or has made a company that exclusively operates in the business specified by Cabinet Office Ordinance prescribed in the same paragraph a Subsidiary without obtaining the approval of the Prime Minister under the provisions of Article 272-14, paragraph (2);

(xxxiv) When he/she has violated Article 107, paragraph (1) or the proviso of paragraph (2);

(xxxv) When he/she has violated the conditions imposed pursuant to the provisions of Article 107, paragraph (3) or (5);

(xxxvi) When he/she, in violation of Articles 116 or 117 (including the cases where the provisions are applied mutatis mutandis pursuant to Articles 199 and 272-18), has failed to reserves policy reserves or reserves for outstanding claims;

(xxxvii) When he/she has acted as listed in the items of Article 118, paragraph (2), in violation of the same paragraph (including the cases where it is applied mutatis mutandis pursuant to Article 199);

(xxxviii) When he/she, in violation of Article 120, paragraph (1) (including the cases where it is applied mutatis mutandis pursuant to Articles 199 and 272-18), has failed to carry out the procedures for the appointment of an actuary or has appointed a person who fails to satisfy the requirements specified by Cabinet Office Ordinance set forth in Article 120, paragraph (2) (including the cases where it is applied mutatis mutandis pursuant to Articles 199 and 272-18) to the position of actuary, or, in violation of Article 120, paragraph (3) (including the cases where it is applied mutatis mutandis pursuant to Articles 199 and 272-18; hereinafter the same shall apply in this item), has failed to give the notification under the provisions of the same paragraph;

(xxxix) When he/she has violated the order under the provisions of Article 122 (including the cases where it is applied mutatis mutandis pursuant to Articles 199 and 272-18, Article 190, paragraph (4), Article 223, paragraph (4), Article 242, paragraph (3), Article 258, paragraph (1) or Article 272-5, paragraph (4), or the order under the provisions of Article 132, paragraph (1), Article 204, paragraph (1), Article 230, paragraph (1), Article 240-3, Article 241, paragraph (1) or Article 272-25, paragraph (1) (including orders for the submission of improvement programs, except orders for the whole or partial suspension of business);

(xl) When he/she has modified the particulars prescribed in the documents prescribed in the provisions under Article 123, paragraph (1) (including the cases where it is applied mutatis mutandis pursuant to Article 207) or Article 225, paragraph (1) without obtaining the authorization under these provisions;

(xli) When he/she has failed to give the notification under the provisions of Article 123, paragraph (2) (including the cases where it is applied mutatis mutandis pursuant to Article 207) or Article 225, paragraph (2), or has modified the particulars specified by Cabinet Office Ordinance set forth in Article 123, paragraph (1) (including the cases where it is applied mutatis mutandis pursuant to Article 207) or Article 225, paragraph (1) within a period of time prescribed in Article 125, paragraph (1) (the shortened or extended period of time in the case where said period of time has been shortened or extended under the provisions of Article 125, paragraph (2) or (3) (including the cases where the provisions are applied mutatis mutandis pursuant to Article 207 and Article 225, paragraph (3))) (including the cases where it is applied mutatis mutandis pursuant to Article 207 and Article 225, paragraph (3));

(xlii) When he/she has violated the order for the revocation of change or notification under the provisions of Article 125, paragraph (4) (including the cases where it is

Art.333　　　　　　　　6 Insurance Business Act, Part VI

applied mutatis mutandis pursuant to Article 207 and Article 225, paragraph (3)) or Article 272-20, paragraph (4);

(xliii) When he/she has failed to give the notification under the provisions of Article 127, paragraph (1), Article 209, Article 218, paragraph (1), Article 234, Article 239, Article 271-32, paragraph (1) or (2), Article 272-21, paragraph (1), or Article 272-42, paragraph (1) or (2), or has given a false notification;

(xliv) When he/she has violated the order under the provisions of Article 131, Article 203, Article 229, or Article 272-24, paragraph (1) or (2);

(xlv) When he/she, in violation of Article 136 (including the cases where it is applied mutatis mutandis pursuant to Article 210, paragraph (1) (including the cases where it is applied mutatis mutandis pursuant to Article 270-4, paragraph (9); the same shall apply in the following item), Article 270-4, paragraph (9) and Article 272-29), has carried out the procedure for the transfer of an insurance contract;

(xlvi) When he/she has concluded an insurance contract in violation of Article 138 (including the cases where it is applied mutatis mutandis pursuant to Article 210, paragraph (1), Article 270-4, paragraph (9) and Article 272-29);

(xlvii) When he/she, in violation of Article 176, has failed to submit a document or statement or electromagnetic record, or has submitted a document or statement or electromagnetic record in which he/she has failed to detail or record the particulars that must be detailed or recorded or in which he/she has included a false detail or record;

(xlviii) When he/she, in violation of Article 180-10, paragraph (1), has failed to file a petition for the commencement of bankruptcy proceedings, or, in violation of Article 511, paragraph (2) of the Companies Act, as applied mutatis mutandis pursuant to Article 184, has failed to file a petition for the commencement of special liquidation;

(xlix) When he/she has disposed of property in violation of Article 181;

(l) When he/she has unjustifiably prescribed the period of time set forth in Article 499, paragraph (1) of the Companies Act, as applied mutatis mutandis pursuant to Article 181-2, for the purpose of delaying the completion of the liquidation;

(li) When he/she has performed obligations in violation of the provisions of Article 500, paragraph (1) of the Companies Act, as applied mutatis mutandis pursuant to Article 181-2, or the provisions of Article 537, paragraph (1) of the same Act, as applied mutatis mutandis pursuant to Article 184;

(lii) When he/she has distributed the property of a liquidating mutual company in violation of Article 502 of the Companies Act, as applied mutatis mutandis pursuant to Article 181-2;

(liii) When he/she has violated Article 535, paragraph (1) of the Companies Act, as applied mutatis mutandis pursuant to Article 184, or Article 536, paragraph (1);

(liv) When he/she has violated the temporary restraining order under the provisions of Article 540, paragraph (1) or (2) of the Companies Act, as applied mutatis mutandis pursuant to Article 184, or Article 542;

(lv) When he/she, in violation of Article 197, has failed to hold assets in Japan of an amount corresponding to the total amount prescribed in the same Article;

(lvi) When he/she has violated a court order under the provisions of Article 827, paragraph (1)of the Companies Act, as applied mutatis mutandis pursuant to Article 213;

(lvii) When he/she has failed to submit reports or materials under the provisions of Article 218, paragraph (2), or has submitted false reports or materials;

(lviii) When he/she has failed to report the findings of the study by the due date set forth in Article 240-8, paragraph (2);

(lix) When he/she, in violation of Article 241, paragraph (3), has failed to make a proposal, or has made a false proposal;
(lx) When he/she has failed to transfer tasks to an insurance administrator who has been appointed by the Prime Minister pursuant to the provisions of Article 242, paragraph (2);
(lxi) When he/she, without justifiable grounds, has refused to be an insurance administrator in violation of Article 243, paragraph (2);
(lxii) When he/she has failed to transfer tasks to a director, executive officer or liquidator of a Managed Company prescribed in Article 242, paragraph (1), notwithstanding the rescission of the disposition that orders the management prescribed in Article 248, paragraph (1) pursuant to the same paragraph;
(lxiii) When he/she has failed to make the submission or give the notification under the provisions of Article 271-3, paragraph (1), Article 271-4, paragraph (1), (3) or (4), Article 271-5, paragraph (1) or (2), Article 271-6, Article 271-7, Article 271-10, paragraph (3), Article 271-18, paragraph (2) or (4), Article 272-31, paragraph (3), or Article 272-35, paragraph (2)or (4), or has made a false submission or gave a false notification;
(lxiv) When he/she, without obtaining authorization from the Prime Minister under Article 271-10, paragraph (1), has become the holder of a number of voting rights in an Insurance Company equal to or exceeding the Major Shareholder Threshold or has established a company or any other juridical person that is the holder of a number of voting rights in an Insurance Company equal to or exceeding the Major Shareholder Threshold through any of the transactions or actions listed in the items of that paragraph;
(lxv) When he/she, in violation of Article 271-10, paragraph (2) was the holder of a number of voting rights in an Insurance Company equal to or exceeding the Major Shareholder Threshold beyond the Last Day of the Grace Period provided for in the same paragraph;
(lxvi) When he/she, in violation of the order under the provisions of Article 271-10, paragraph (4), was the holder of a number of voting rights in an Insurance Company equal to or exceeding the Major Shareholder Threshold, or, in violation of Article 271-16, paragraph (2) was the holder of a number of voting rights in an Insurance Company equal to or exceeding the Major Shareholder Threshold upon exceeding the period designated by the Prime Minister prescribed in the same paragraph;
(lxvii) When he/she has violated the order (including orders for the submission of improvement programs) under the provisions of Article 271-14 (including the cases where it is applied mutatis mutandis pursuant to Article 272-34, paragraph (1)), Article 271-15, Article 271-16, paragraph (1) (including the cases where it is applied mutatis mutandis pursuant to Article 272-34, paragraph (1)), or Article 271-29 (including the cases where it is applied mutatis mutandis pursuant to Article 272-40, paragraph (2));
(lxviii) When he/she, without obtaining the approval of the Minister of Finance prescribed in Article 271-22, paragraph (1), has made a company other than the companies listed in the items of the same paragraph a Subsidiary;
(lxix) When he/she has failed to give the notification or make the submission under the provisions of Article 272-19, paragraph (1) or (2) or has modified the particulars prescribed in the documents prescribed in the provisions under Article 272-19, paragraph (1) within a period of time prescribed in Article 272-20, paragraph (1) (the shortened or extended period of time in the case where said period of time has been shortened or extended under the provisions of the same Article, paragraph (2)

or (3));
(lxx) When he/she, without obtaining authorization from the Prime Minister under Article 272-31, paragraph (1), has, through any of the transactions or actions listed in the items of the same paragraph, become the holder of a number of voting rights in a Low-Cost, Short-Term Insurer equal to or exceeding the Major Shareholder Threshold , or has incorporated a company or formed another juridical person that is the holder of a number of voting rights in a Low-Cost, Short-Term Insurer equal to or exceeding the Major Shareholder Threshold;
(lxxi) When he/she, in violation of Article 272-31, paragraph (2), was the holder of a number of voting rights in a Low-Cost, Short-Term Insurer equal to or exceeding the Major Shareholder Threshold beyond the Last Day of the Grace Period provided for in the same paragraph;
(lxxii) When he/she, in violation of the order under the provisions of Article 272-31, paragraph (4), was the holder of a number of voting rights in a Low-Cost, Short-Term Insurer equal to or exceeding the Major Shareholder Threshold, or, in violation of Article 271-16, paragraph (2) as applied mutatis mutandis pursuant to Article 272-34, paragraph (1), was the holder of a number of voting rights in a Low-Cost, Short-Term Insurer equal to or exceeding the Major Shareholder Threshold upon exceeding the period designated by the Prime Minister prescribed in the same paragraph;
(lxxiii) When he/she, without obtaining the approval of the Prime Minister under the provisions of Article 272-39, paragraph (1), has made a company other than the companies listed in the items of the same paragraph a Subsidiary; and
(lxxiv) When he/she has violated the conditions imposed pursuant to the provisions of Article 310, paragraph (1).
(2) In the case where an insurance administrator of a Stock Company or an insurance administrator of a Foreign Insurance Company, etc. falls under any of the items of Article 976 of the Companies Act, he/she shall be punished by a non-criminal fine of not more than one million yen; provided, however, that this shall not apply when a punishment shall be given for the action.

Article 333-2 Any person who falls under either of the following shall be punished by a non-criminal fine of not more than one million yen:
(i) Any person who has, in violation of Article 946, paragraph (3) of the Companies Act, as applied mutatis mutandis pursuant to Article 67-2 or Article 217, paragraph (3), failed to make a report, or has made a false report; and
(ii) Any person who, without justifiable grounds, has refused any of the requests listed in Article 67-2, or the items of Article 951, paragraph (2) of the Companies Act, as applied mutatis mutandis pursuant to Article 217, paragraph (3), or the items of Article 955, paragraph (2).

Article 334 In the case where a director, executive officer, accounting advisor or a member who shall carry out its duties, company auditor or liquidator of a Life Insurance Company that engages in Insurance-Proceed Trust Services, Entrusted Company prescribed in Article 144, paragraph (1), insurance administrator, supervising committee member of a liquidating Stock Company or liquidating mutual company who has been appointed pursuant to the provisions of Article 527, paragraph (1) of the Companies Act (including the cases where it is applied mutatis mutandis pursuant to Article 184), acting director, accounting advisor, company auditor, representative director, committee member, executive officer or representative executive officer of a Stock Company or Mutual Company who has been appointed pursuant to the provisional disposition order prescribed in Article 56 of the Civil Provisional Relief Act, acting liquidator or Representative Liquidator of a liquidating stock company or liquidating mutual company who has been appointed pursuant to the provisional disposition order prescribed in the same Article, any person who shall carry out the duties of a temporary officer or temporary liquidator who has been appointed pursuant to the provisions of Article 346, paragraph (2) of the Companies Act (including the cases where it is applied mutatis mutandis pursuant to Article 479, paragraph (4) of the same Act), any person who shall carry out the duties of a temporary committee member or temporary executive officer who has been appointed pursuant to the provisions of Article 401, paragraph (3) of the same Act (including the cases where it is applied mutatis mutandis pursuant to Article 403, paragraph (3) of the same Act), any person who shall carry out the duties of a temporary officer or temporary liquidator who has been appointed pursuant to the provisions of Article 53-12, paragraph (2) (including the cases where it is applied mutatis mutandis pursuant to Article 180-5, paragraph (4)), any person who shall carry out the duties of a temporary committee member or any person who shall carry out the duties of a temporary executive officer or manager who has been appointed pursuant to the provisions of Article 401, paragraph (3) of the same Act, as applied mutatis mutandis pursuant to Article 53-25, paragraph (2) (including the cases where it is applied mutatis mutandis pursuant to Article 53-27, paragraph (3)), or a Representative Person in Japan of a Foreign Life Insurance Company, etc. that engages in Insurance-Proceed Trust Services, liquidator, Entrusted Company prescribed in Article 144, paragraph (1), as applied mutatis mutandis pursuant to Article 211, insurance administrator or manager, falls under any of the following items, he/she shall be punished by a non-criminal fine of not more than one million yen:

(i) When he/she, without obtaining authorization, has engaged in Insurance-Proceed Trust Services in violation of Article 99, paragraph (7), first sentence (including the cases where it is applied mutatis mutandis pursuant to Article 199);

(ii) When he/she, without obtaining the authorization under the provisions of Article 99, paragraph (7), second sentence (including the cases where it is applied mutatis mutandis pursuant to Article 199; hereinafter the same shall apply in this item), has changed the method of Insurance-Proceed Trust Services prescribed in the same paragraph, second sentence;

(iii) When he/she, in violation of the order pursuant to Article 6 of the Act on Provision, etc. of Trust Services by Financial Institutions, as applied mutatis mutandis pursuant to Article 99, paragraph (8) (including the cases where it is applied mutatis mutandis pursuant to Article 199), has made a supplementary or auxiliary trust contract; and

(iv) When he/she, in violation of Article 34 of the Trust Act (Act No. 108 of 2006), has failed to carry out the management of trust property that he/she is to carry out pursuant to the provisions of the same Article.

Article 335 Any person who falls under any of the following items shall be punished by a non-criminal fine of not more than one million yen:

(i) Any person who has violated Article 7, paragraph (2)

(ii) Any person who, in violation of the order under the provisions of Article 11, paragraph (4) of the Trust Business Act, as applied mutatis mutandis pursuant to Article 99, paragraph (8) (including the cases where it is applied mutatis mutandis pursuant to Article 199), has failed to Make a Deposit;

(iii) Any person who, in violation of Article 29-2 of the Trust Business Act, as applied mutatis mutandis pursuant to Article 99, paragraph (8) (including the cases where it is applied mutatis mutandis pursuant to Article 199), has made changes regard-

Art.336~337-3 ⑥ Insurance Business Act, Part VI

ing important trusts, or has consolidated or split trusts;
(iv) Any person who has violated Article 272-8, paragraph (1)
(v) Any person who, in violation of Article 272-8, paragraph (2), has posted a sign under the provisions of the same Article, paragraph (1) or a similar sign;
(vi) Any person who has submitted a written application for approval set forth in Article 272-32, paragraph (1) or a document set forth in the same Article, paragraph (2) in which he/she has included a false detail; and
(vii) Any person who has violated the provisions of Article 308-16.

Article 336 In the case where an officer of an agency falls under either of the following items, he/she shall be punished by a non-criminal fine of not more than five hundred thousand yen:
(i) When he/she, in violation of Article 265-22, has failed to make the registry prescribed in the same Article available for public inspection; and
(ii) When he/she has violated the order under the provisions of Article 265-45, paragraph (2) or (3).

Article 337 Any person who falls under any of the following items shall be punished by a non-criminal fine of not more than five hundred thousand yen:
(i) Any person who, in violation of Article 186, paragraph (2) has offered an insurance contract prescribed in the same paragraph without obtaining permission;
(ii) Any person who has failed to give the notification under the provisions of Article 280, paragraph (1), Article 290, paragraph (1), or Article 302, or gave a false notification; and
(iii) Any person who, in violation of the order under the provisions of Article 291, paragraph (4) or Article 292, paragraph (2), has failed to Make a Deposit.

Article 337-2 In the case where an officer of an agency falls under any of the following items, he/she shall be punished by a non-criminal fine of not more than two hundred thousand yen:
(i) When he/she, in the case where the authorization of the Prime Minister and Minister of Finance is required pursuant to the provisions of Part II, Chapter X, Section 4, has not obtained the authorization thereof;
(ii) When he/she has failed to complete his/her registration in violation of Cabinet Order under the provisions of Article 264, paragraph (1);
(iii) When he/she has violated Article 265-2, paragraph (2);
(iv) When he/she has conducted business other than what is prescribed in Article 265-28;
(v) When he/she has failed to submit a document prescribed in Article 265-37 or Article 265-39, paragraph (1) or (2), or has submitted a false document;
(vi) When he/she has invested surplus funds in the course of business in violation of Article 265-43; and
(vii) When he/she has failed to make a report under the provisions of Article 268, paragraph (5) (including the cases where it is applied mutatis mutandis pursuant to Article 269, paragraph (2), Article 270-3-12, paragraph (2), Article 270-3-13, paragraph (4), Article 270-6-3, paragraph (2), and Article 270-6-4, paragraph (4)), Article 270, paragraph (4), or Article 270-2, paragraph (6) (including the cases where it is applied mutatis mutandis pursuant to Article 270-3-12, paragraph (3)), or has made a false report.

Article 337-3 Any person who has violated Article 263, paragraph (2) shall be punished by a non-criminal fine of not more than one million yen.

Article 338 Any person who, in violation of Article 8, paragraph (1) of the Companies Act, as applied mutatis mutandis pursuant to Article 21, has used a denomination or trade name that runs the risk of mistaking the entity for a Mutual Company, shall be punished by a non-criminal fine of not more than one million yen.

Article 339 A person who, in violation of the provisions of Article 308-17, used any character which would indicate that the person is a Designated Dispute Resolution Organization shall be punished by a non-criminal fine of not more than one hundred thousand yen.

Supplementary Provisions

(Effective Date)
Article 1 This Act shall come into effect as of the date specified by Cabinet Order within a period not exceeding one year from the day of promulgation; provided, however, that the provisions of Article 106 of these Supplementary Provisions shall come into effect as of the day of promulgation.

(Special Provisions Pertaining to the Specific Insurance Undertakings of a Specified Insurance Company)
Article 1-2 (1) In case of an application for the license set forth in Article 3, paragraph (1) (limited to the case where the business to be licensed includes insurance underwriting listed in Article 3, paragraph (4), item (ii) or Article 3, paragraph (5), item (ii); the same shall apply in the following paragraph), the Prime Minister may, until otherwise stipulated, attach any necessary condition to such license pursuant to the provisions of Article 5, paragraph (2) for ensuring that the license will neither bring a drastic change in the management environment pertaining to the specific insurance undertakings (meaning undertakings for insurance underwriting listed in Article 3, paragraph (4), item (ii) or Article 3, paragraph (5), item (ii); hereinafter the same shall apply in this Article) of a Specified Insurance Company (meaning an Insurance Company or Foreign Insurance Company, etc. the management of which depends relatively heavily on insurance underwriting listed in Article 3, paragraph (4), item (ii) or Article 3, paragraph (5), item (ii); hereinafter the same shall apply in this Article), nor pose any risk to the soundness in the business of the Specified Insurance Company.
(2) Where an Insurance Company makes another Insurance Company its Subsidiary with the authorization set forth in Article 106, paragraph (4), or Article 142 or Article 167, paragraph (1) (limited to the case where a Life Insurance Company makes a Non-Life Insurance Company its Subsidiary or where a Non-Life Insurance Company makes a Life Insurance Company its Subsidiary), the Prime Minister may, until otherwise stipulated, attach any necessary condition to the license granted to that other Insurance Company under Article 3, paragraph (1) for ensuring that the license will neither bring any drastic change in the management environment pertaining to the specific insurance undertakings of the Specified Insurance Company nor pose any risk to the soundness in the business of the Specified Insurance Company.
(3) In case of an application for authorization or notification, pursuant to the provisions of Article 123, paragraph (1) or (2), of any modification of the particulars prescribed in the document set forth in Article 123, paragraph (1) pertaining to the specific insurance undertakings, the Prime Minister shall, until otherwise stipulated, consider in addition to the standards set forth in the items of Article 124 and in Article 125, para-

graph (4), whether such modification will bring any drastic change in the management environment of the Specified Insurance Company pertaining to the specific insurance undertakings or pose any risk to the soundness in the business of the Specified Insurance Company, in examining the particulars of the application or notification.

(Special Provisions on Business)
Article 1-2-2 A Policyholders Protection Corporation (hereinafter referred to as a "Corporation") may, until otherwise stipulated, conduct the business set forth in the following Article, in addition to business set forth in Article 265-28.

(Special Provisions on the Business of a Partner Bank)
Article 1-2-3 A Corporation may conclude with a bank whose purposes include the management and disposition of assets purchased from a Bankrupt Insurance Company, etc. (meaning a Bankrupt Insurance Company as set forth in Article 260, paragraph (2); the same shall apply in Article 1-3 of the Supplementary Provisions), Successor Insurance Company (meaning a Successor Insurance Company as set forth in Article 260, paragraph (6)) or Insurance Company in Liquidation (meaning an Insurance Company in Liquidation as set forth in Article 265-28, paragraph (2), item (iii); the same shall apply in Article 1-2-5, paragraph (1), item (iii) of the Supplementary Provisions); the same shall apply in Article 1-2-5, paragraph (4) and Article 1-2-7, paragraph (1) of the Supplementary Provisions) (hereinafter referred to as "Asset Management and Collection Services") an agreement regarding Asset Management and Collection Services (hereinafter referred to as "Agreement"), and conduct the following business to implement the Agreement:
(i) Provide, for the banks that have concluded the Agreement (hereinafter referred to as "Partner Banks"), compensation for losses under Article 1-2-6 of the Supplementary Provisions or loans under Article 1-2-7, paragraph (1) of the Supplementary Provisions, or the guarantee of obligations set forth in that paragraph pertaining to any debt contracted by the Partner Banks;
(ii) Receive the money to be paid by the Partner Banks pursuant to the provisions of paragraph (1), item (ii) of the following Article;
(iii) Provide necessary guidance and advice for the Partner Banks to perform Asset Management and Collection Services; and
(iv) Conduct necessary investigations for the purpose of business set forth in item (i) or the preceding item.

(Agreements)
Article 1-2-4 (1) An Agreement shall contain the following provisions:
(i) That the Partner Bank shall, where it concludes a contract of entrustment with a Corporation following an offer from the latter to entrust the former with the purchase of assets under paragraph (1) of the following Article, purchase the assets pertaining to such entrustment on behalf of the Corporation and perform Asset Management and Collection Services pertaining to the assets thus purchased;
(ii) That the Partner Bank shall, when it has any amount calculated pursuant to the provisions of a Cabinet Order as profit from the business conducted under the Agreement, pay the amount corresponding to such profit to the Corporation for each business year;
(iii) That the Partner Bank shall, when it seeks to conclude a contract regarding the purchase of assets under item (i) or a contract regarding the borrowing of funds to be covered by the guarantee of obligations set forth in Article 1-2-7, paragraph (1) of the Supplementary Provisions, receive in advance the approval of the Corpora-

tion with regard to the content of the prospective contract;
  (iv) That the Partner Bank shall promptly prepare, for approval by the Corporation, an implementation plan and a financial plan for Asset Management and Collection Services pertaining to any purchase of assets under item (i);
  (v) That the Partner Bank shall, when it seeks to modify the implementation plan or financial plan set forth in the preceding item, receive in advance the approval of the Corporation; and
  (vi) That the Partner Bank shall submit to the Corporation the interim business report and business report when submitting these reports to the Prime Minister pursuant to the provisions of Article 19, paragraph (1) or (2) (Business Report, etc.) of the Banking Act.
(2) A Corporation shall, if it seeks to conclude an Agreement, determine the content of the Agreement after discussion by the Committee, and must have this authorized by the Prime Minister and the Minister of Finance.
(3) Whenever an application has been filed for the authorization set forth in the preceding paragraph, the Prime Minister and the Minister of Finance may not give the relevant authorization unless they find that the content of the Agreement to which the application pertains conforms to the applicable provisions of laws and regulations and that the bank seeking to conclude the Agreement with the Corporation is capable of performing Asset Management and Collection Services under the Agreement in an appropriate manner.

(Entrustment of Purchase of Assets, etc.)
Article 1-2-5 (1) The Corporation may entrust a Partner Bank with the purchase of assets on its behalf where:
  (i) it decides to provide financial assistance including the purchase of assets pursuant to the provisions of Article 270-3, paragraph (1) or Article 270-3-2, paragraph (7);
  (ii) it decides to purchase the assets of a partner Successor Insurance Company pursuant to the provisions of Article 270-3-7, paragraph (1); or
  (iii) it decides to purchase the assets of an Insurance Company in Liquidation pursuant to the provisions of Article 270-8-3, paragraph (1).
(2) The Corporation shall, when it makes an offer of entrustment under the preceding paragraph, determine after discussion by the Examination Board and the Committee the purchase value of the assets covered by the decision set forth in that paragraph as well as other conditions regarding such entrustment including the compensation for losses set forth in the following Article, for presentation to the Partner Bank concerned.
(3) The Corporation shall, when it has concluded with a Partner Bank any contract for entrusting the purchase of assets under paragraph (1), immediately report to the Prime Minister and the Minister of Finance the content of such contract.
(4) Where a Corporation has concluded any contract with a Partner Bank for the entrustment set forth in the preceding paragraph, the contract for the purchase of assets shall be concluded by the Partner Bank with the Bankrupt Insurance Company, etc. , notwithstanding the provisions of Article 270-3, paragraph (4) (including the cases where it is applied mutatis mutandis pursuant to Article 270-3-2, paragraph (8)), Article 270-3-7, paragraph (3) and Article 270-8-3, paragraph (3).

(Compensation for Losses)
Article 1-2-6 The Corporation may compensate a Partner Bank for any loss within the scope of the amount accounted pursuant to what is specified by a Cabinet Order for the amount of loss accrued by the Partner Bank in the implementation of business un-

der the specifications of the Agreement.

(Loan of Funds and Obligation Guarantee)
Article 1-2-7 (1) The Corporation may, when it finds it necessary in the case of receiving an application from a Partner Bank for the loan of any funds required for the purchase of assets from a Bankrupt Insurance Company, etc. under the Agreement or any other funds required for the smooth implementation of Asset Management and Collection Services under the Agreement, or for an obligation guarantee pursuant to the borrowing of such funds by the Partner Bank, extend, after discussion by the Committee, the loan or obligation guarantee.
(2) The Corporation shall, when it concludes a contract pertaining to the loan or obligation guarantee of the preceding paragraph with a Partner Bank pursuant to the provisions of that paragraph, immediately report to the Prime Minister and the Minister of Finance the content of the contract.

(Financial Arrangements)
Article 1-2-8 The Corporation shall endeavor to secure financial arrangements required by the Partner Banks for the smooth implementation of Asset Management and Collection Services under the Agreement.

(Request for Cooperation)
Article 1-2-9 The Corporation may, when it is necessary for conducting business listed in the items of Article 1-2-3 of the Supplementary Provisions, inquire of or request cooperation from government agencies, public entities or any other relevant persons.

(Request for Reports)
Article 1-2-10 The Corporation may, when it is necessary for conducting business listed in the items of Article 1-2-3 of the Supplementary Provisions, request a Partner Bank to report on the status of the implementation of the Agreement or finances.

(Application of this Act)
Article 1-2-11 For the purpose of applying the provisions of Article 265-30, paragraph (1) to the cases where the business listed in the items of Article 1-2-3 of the Supplementary Provisions are provided, the term "business listed in each of the items of Article 265-28, paragraph (1) and Article 265-28, paragraph (2)" in Article 265-30, paragraph (1) shall be deemed to be replaced with "business listed in each of the items of Article 265-28, paragraph (1) and Article 265-28, paragraph (2) (including business listed in the items of Article 1-2-3 of the Supplementary Provisions)."

(Special Provisions on Taxation)
Article 1-2-12 (1) Where a Partner Bank has acquired any right to real estate following the purchase of assets as delegated by the Corporation set forth in Article 1-2-4, paragraph (1), item (i) of the Supplementary Provisions pursuant to the provisions of the Agreement (referred to as "Purchase of Assets Pursuant to the Agreement" in the following paragraph), the registration of transfer of rights on the real estate shall not be subject to the registration and license tax, as long as such registration is made within three years from the acquisition pursuant to the provisions of the applicable Ordinance of the Ministry of Finance.
(2) For the purpose of applying to a Partner Bank the provisions of Articles 62-3, 63, 68-68 and 68-69 of the Act on Special Measures concerning Taxation, the conveyance of

any land acquired by a Partner Bank following the Purchase of Assets Pursuant to the Agreement or the assignment of any right over the land (meaning the conveyance set forth in Article 62-3, paragraph (2), item (i), sub-item (a) of that Act) shall not constitute the conveyance of land, etc. set forth in Article 62-3, paragraph (2), item (i) of that Act.

(Assistance of Government Pertaining to Financial Assistance to Specified Members or Special Members, etc.)
Article 1-2-13 (1) The Government may, when it finds that if the Life Insurance Policyholders Protection Corporation (meaning the Life Insurance Policyholders Protection Corporation set forth in Article 265-37, paragraph (1); the same shall apply hereafter in this Article, as well as in the following Article and Article 1-2-15 of the Supplementary Provisions) was to cover the costs of Financial Assistance and other business for its members (limited to those subject to the disposition ordering administration under Article 242, paragraph (1) by 31 March 2003 and any other members to be specified by Cabinet Order; referred to as "Specified Members" in Article 1-2-15, paragraph (1) of the Supplementary Provisions) solely with the obligatory contributions paid by the members of the Life Insurance Policyholders Protection Corporation pursuant to the provisions of Article 265-33, paragraph (1), the financial conditions of the members of the Life Insurance Policyholders Protection Corporation would deteriorate significantly, making it difficult to maintain the credibility of the insurance industry and hence posing the risk of causing unexpected disruptions in the lives of the citizenry and the financial market (limited to the cases where the total amount of such costs exceeds the amount to be specified by Cabinet Order), provide assistance to the Life Insurance Policyholders Protection Corporation in an amount corresponding to the whole or part of such costs (limited to those required for the business specified by Cabinet Order (referred to as "Specified Activities" in the following paragraph, the following Article and Article 1-2-15 of the Supplementary Provisions) within the amount prescribed by the budget.
(2) The Government may, when it finds that if the Life Insurance Policyholders Protection Corporation was to cover the costs of Financial Assistance and other business for its members (limited to those subject to the disposition ordering administration under Article 242, paragraph (1) between 1 April 2003 and 31 March 2006 and any other members to be specified by Cabinet Order; referred to as "Special Members" in Article 1-2-15, paragraph (2) of the Supplementary Provisions) solely with the obligatory contributions paid by the members of the Life Insurance Policyholders Protection Corporation pursuant to the provisions of Article 265-33, paragraph (1), the financial conditions of the members of the Life Insurance Policyholders Protection Corporation would deteriorate significantly, making it difficult to maintain the credibility of the insurance industry and hence posing the risk of causing unexpected disruptions in the lives of the citizenry and the financial market (limited to the cases where the total amount of such costs exceeds the amount to be specified by Cabinet Order), provide assistance to the Life Insurance Policyholders Protection Corporation in an amount corresponding to the whole or part of such costs (limited to those required for the Specified Activities) within the amount prescribed by the budget.
(3) The necessary procedure for implementing the provisions of the preceding paragraph shall be specified by Cabinet Order.

(Assistance of Government Pertaining to Financial Assistance to Members under Special Provisions, etc.)
Article 1-2-14 (1) The Government may, when it finds that if the Life Insurance Policy-

holders Protection Corporation were to cover the costs of Financial Assistance and other business for its members (limited to those subject to the disposition ordering administration under Article 242, paragraph (1) between 1 April 2006 and 31 March 2012 and any other members to be specified by Cabinet Order; referred to as "Members under Special Provisions" in paragraph (3) of the following Article) solely with the obligatory contributions paid by the members of the Life Insurance Policyholders Protection Corporation pursuant to the provisions of Article 265-33, paragraph (1), the financial conditions of the members of the Life Insurance Policyholders Protection Corporation would deteriorate significantly, making it difficult to maintain the credibility of the insurance industry and hence posing the risk of causing serious consequences in the lives of the citizenry and the financial market (limited to the cases where the sum total of the amount of outstanding debts of the Life Insurance Policyholders Protection Corporation as of the date specified by Cabinet Order and the amount to be specified by Cabinet Order as the amount of additional debts that would be incurred if the Life Insurance Policyholders Protection Corporation had to finance such costs through borrowings exceeds the amount to be specified by Cabinet Order taking into consideration the long-term balance of payments of the Life Insurance Policyholders Protection Corporation), provide assistance to the Life Insurance Policyholders Protection Corporation in an amount corresponding to the whole or part of such costs (limited to those required for the Specified Activities) within the amount prescribed by the budget.

(2) The necessary procedure for implementing the provisions of the preceding paragraph shall be specified by Cabinet Order.

(Payment to National Treasury)
Article 1-2-15 (1) For each business year, the Life Insurance Policyholders Protection Corporation shall pay to the Treasury any amount calculated pursuant to the provisions of a Cabinet Order as the profit earned by the Specified Activities pertaining to the Specified Members, to the total amount of the assistance of the Government already provided pursuant to the provisions of Article 1-2-13, paragraph (1) of the Supplementary Provisions less any amount already paid to the Treasury pursuant to the provisions of this paragraph.

(2) For each business year, the Life Insurance Policyholders Protection Corporation shall pay to the Treasury any amount calculated pursuant to the provisions of a Cabinet Order as the profit earned by the Specified Activities pertaining to the Special Members, to the total amount of the assistance of the Government already provided pursuant to the provisions of Article 1-2-13, paragraph (2) of the Supplementary Provisions less any amount already paid to the Treasury pursuant to the provisions of this paragraph.

(3) For each business year, the Life Insurance Policyholders Protection Corporation shall pay to the Treasury any amount calculated pursuant to the provisions of a Cabinet Order as the profit earned by the Specified Activities pertaining to the Members under Special Provisions, to the total amount of the assistance of the Government already provided pursuant to the provisions of paragraph (1) of the preceding Article less any amount already paid to the Treasury pursuant to the provisions of this paragraph.

(4) The procedure of payment and other necessary the particulars of payments under the preceding three paragraphs shall be specified by Cabinet Order.

(Special Provisions on Financial Assistance, etc.)
Article 1-3 (1) Notwithstanding the provisions of Article 270-3, paragraph (2) (including the cases where it is applied mutatis mutandis pursuant to Article 270-3-2, paragraph (8)), the amount of the Financial Assistance provided by a Corporation under Article

266, paragraph (1) or Article 267, paragraph (3) for the applications received by 31 March 2001 under Article 266, paragraph (1) or Article 267, paragraph (3) (limited to the donation of money; hereinafter referred to as "Financial Assistance in the Special Provision Period") shall be, for each of the Bankrupt Insurance Companies covered by the Financial Assistance in the Special Provision Period, the amount calculated by adding the amounts listed in items (iii) and (iv) to the difference calculated by subtracting the amount listed in item (ii) from the amount listed in item (i):

(i) The amount calculated by multiplying the sum total of the amount of the policy reserves pertaining to those insurance contracts of the Bankrupt Insurance Company which meet the requirements for insurance contracts to be specified by Cabinet Office Ordinance and Ordinance of the Ministry of Finance (referred to as "Covered Insurance Contracts in the Special Provision Period" in the following item and the following paragraph) and any other amount to be specified by Cabinet Office Ordinance and Ordinance of the Ministry of Finance as the liabilities to be retained for allocation to the payment of Insurance Proceeds, etc. (referred to as "Specified Policy Reserve, etc." in that item and that paragraph) by the ratio to be specified by Cabinet Office Ordinance and Ordinance of the Ministry of Finance;

(ii) The amount of the asset value of that Bankrupt Insurance Company, based on the evaluation of property confirmed under the provisions of Article 270-2, paragraph (2) or (5) (referred to as "Confirmed Evaluation of Property" in the following paragraph), which has been calculated as per Cabinet Office Ordinance and Ordinance of the Ministry of Finance as being the amount which corresponds to the Specified Policy Reserve, etc. pertaining to the Covered Insurance Contracts in the Special Provision Period;

(iii) With regard to those insurance contracts of the Bankrupt Insurance Company which meet the requirements for insurance contracts to be specified by Cabinet Office Ordinance and Ordinance of the Ministry of Finance and have been subject to the Modification of Contract Conditions (meaning the modification of the contract conditions set forth in Article 250, paragraph (1)) under Article 250, 254 or 255-2, or the Modification of Contract Conditions in reorganization proceedings, the amount calculated pursuant to the provisions of a Cabinet Office Ordinance and Ordinance of the Ministry of Finance as the additional amount required due to the difference between the modified conditions of contract and the original conditions of contract where it is stipulated that insurance proceeds or benefits shall be paid in amounts as prescribed under the original conditions of contract for any insured event (other than any of the insured events to be specified by Cabinet Office Ordinance and Ordinance of the Ministry of Finance) that has occurred by 31 March 2001 (excluding the amount of any Financial Assistance pertaining to the payment of Covered Insurance Proceeds); and

(iv) That part of the amount of the costs meeting the requirements for expected costs of the transfer, etc. of insurance contracts (meaning the Transfer, etc., of Insurance Contracts set forth in Article 260, paragraph (1); hereinafter the same shall apply in this item) or succession of insurance contracts (meaning the succession of insurance contracts set forth in Article 260, paragraph (7); hereinafter the same shall apply in this item) pertaining to the Bankrupt Insurance Company to be specified by Cabinet Office Ordinance and Ordinance of the Ministry of Finance which the Corporation finds necessary for the smooth implementation of the Transfer, etc. , of Insurance Contracts or succession of insurance contracts pertaining to the Financial Assistance in the Special Provision Period.

(2) With regard to the underwriting of insurance contracts under Article 267, paragraph (1) for the applications under that paragraph that a Corporation has received by 31

March 2001 (hereinafter referred to as "Underwriting in the Special Provision Period"), the amount to be transferred by the Corporation from the General Account (meaning the General Account set forth in Article 265-41, paragraph (2)) to the Special Insurance Account created for the Bankrupt Insurance Company pertaining to the Underwriting in the Special Provision Period shall be, for the Bankrupt Insurance Company pertaining to the Underwriting in the Special Provision Period, the amount calculated by adding the amount listed in item (iii) to the difference calculated by subtracting the amount listed in item (ii) from the amount listed in item (i), notwithstanding the provisions of Article 270-5, paragraph (2):
(i) The amount calculated by multiplying the amount of the Specified Policy Reserve, etc. for the Covered Insurance Contracts in the Special Provision Period pertaining to the Bankrupt Insurance Company by the ratio to be specified by Cabinet Office Ordinance and Ordinance of the Ministry of Finance;
(ii) The amount of the asset value of that Bankrupt Insurance Company, based on the Confirmed Evaluation of Property, which has been calculated as per Cabinet Office Ordinance and Ordinance of the Ministry of Finance as being the amount which corresponds to the Specified Policy Reserve, etc. pertaining to the Covered Insurance Contracts in the Special Provision Period; and
(iii) With regard to those insurance contracts of the Bankrupt Insurance Company which meet the requirements for insurance contracts to be specified by Cabinet Office Ordinance and Ordinance of the Ministry of Finance and have been subject to the Modification of Contract Conditions (meaning the modification of the contract conditions set forth in Article 250, paragraph (1)) under Article 250 as applied mutatis mutandis pursuant to Article 270-4, paragraph (9) or the Modification of Contract Conditions in reorganization proceedings, the amount calculated pursuant to the provisions of a Cabinet Office Ordinance and Ordinance of the Ministry of Finance as the additional amount required due to the difference between the modified conditions of contract and the original conditions of contract where it is stipulated that insurance proceeds or benefits shall be paid in amounts as prescribed under the original conditions of contract for any insured event (other than any of the insured events to be specified by Cabinet Office Ordinance and Ordinance of the Ministry of Finance) that has occurred by 31 March 2001 (excluding the amount of any Financial Assistance for the payment of Covered Insurance Proceeds).
(3) For the purpose of applying the provisions of Article 245 to the case set forth in item (iii) of paragraph (1) or item (iii) of the preceding paragraph, the term "(hereinafter referred to as 'Business for Paying Covered Insurance Proceeds')" in that Article shall be deemed to be replaced with "(including business for paying insurance proceeds or benefits in the amounts set forth in item (iii) of paragraph (1) or item (iii) of paragraph (2) of Article 1-3 of the Supplementary Provisions)."
(4) Notwithstanding the provisions of Article 112 of the Corporate Reorganization Act (including the cases where it is applied mutatis mutandis pursuant to Article 160-40 of the Act on Special Treatment, etc. of Corporate Reorganization Proceedings and Other Insolvency Proceedings by Financial Institutions, etc.), insurance proceeds or benefits may be paid in the amounts set forth in paragraph (1), item (iii) or paragraph (2), item (iii) in the case set forth in paragraph (1), item (iii) or paragraph (2), item (iii) (excluding the case of Article 177-29, paragraph (1) of the Act on Special Treatment, etc. of Corporate Reorganization Proceedings and Other Insolvency Proceedings by Financial Institutions, etc.).

(Special Provisions on Financial Assistance for the Payment of Covered Insurance Proceeds)

Article 1-3-2 For the purpose of applying the provisions of Article 245 and the provisions of Article 177-29, paragraph (1) (Special Provisions on Payment of Covered Insurance Proceeds) of the Act on Special Treatment. etc. of Corporate Reorganization Proceedings and Other Insolvency Proceedings by Financial Institutions, etc. to the cases where a Corporation has received any application under Article 270-6-6, paragraph (1) by 31 March 2001, the terms "pertaining to a Covered Insurance Contract," and "the insurance proceeds under a Covered Insurance Contract" in Article 245 shall be deemed to be replaced with "pertaining to a Covered Insurance Contract (including the Covered Insurance Contracts in the Special Provision Period prescribed in Article 1-3, paragraph (1), item (i) of the Supplementary Provisions (hereinafter referred to as 'Covered Insurance Contracts in the Special Provision Period'))" and "insurance proceeds under a Covered Insurance Contract (excluding the Covered Insurance Contracts in the Special Provision Period," respectively; the term ") or the insurance proceeds and other benefits under the Covered Insurance Contracts in the Special Provision Period (limited to the amount calculated by multiplying the insurance proceeds and other benefits under the Covered Insurance Contracts in the Special Provision Period by the ratio to be specified by Cabinet Office Ordinance and Ordinance of the Ministry of Finance) (" shall be deemed to be inserted before the term "hereinafter referred to as 'Services for Paying Covered Insurance Proceeds' " in Article 245; and the term "Contracts Qualified for Compensation set forth in Article 270-3, paragraph (2), item (i) of the Insurance Business Act (" in Article 177-29, paragraph (1) of that Act shall be deemed to be replaced with "Contracts Qualified for Compensation set forth in Article 270-3, paragraph (2), item (i) of the Insurance Business Act (including the Covered Insurance Contracts in the Special Provision Period as defined in Article 1-3, paragraph (1), item (i) of the Supplementary Provisions of the Insurance Business Act)."

(Special Provisions on the Purchase of Insurance Claims, etc.)

Article 1-3-3 For the purpose of applying the provisions of Articles 270-6-8 and 270-6-10 to the cases where a Corporation has made any decision under Article 270-6-8, paragraph (1) by 31 March 2001, the term "the Covered Insurance Contract" in that paragraph shall be deemed to be replaced with "the Covered Insurance Contract (including the Covered Insurance Contracts in the Special Provision Period as defined in Article 1-3, paragraph (1), item (i) of the Supplementary Provisions (hereinafter referred to as "Covered Insurance Contracts in the Special Provision Period" in this Article); the same shall apply in Article 270-6-10)"; the term "the Covered Insurance Contract" in Article 270-6-8, paragraph (2) shall be deemed to be replaced with "the Covered Insurance Contract (excluding the Covered Insurance Contracts in the Special Provision Period)"; and the term "or the amount calculated by multiplying the insurance proceeds and other benefits under the Covered Insurance Contracts in the Special Provision Period by the ratio to be specified by Cabinet Office Ordinance/Ordinance of the Ministry of Finance" shall be deemed to be inserted before the term "(hereinafter referred to as" in Article 270-6-8, paragraph (2).

(Special Provisions on Obligatory Contributions)

Article 1-4 For each of the business years from the business year in which a Corporation is established to the business year to which belongs the date prescribed in Article 1-6, paragraph (1) of the Supplementary Provisions to be specified by Cabinet Order, the obligatory contribution rate to be determined by the Corporation pursuant to the provisions of Article 265-34, paragraph (3) shall not, for each type of license prescribed in Article 262, paragraph (2), be less than the rate to be specified by Cabinet Order taking into consideration the expected amount of cost required by the Corporation for Financial Assistance Services, etc. pertaining to the Insurance Companies with the same type of license and the financial conditions of such Insurance Companies.

(Special Provisions on Borrowings, Guarantee by Government, etc.)
Article 1-5 (1) For the purpose of applying the provisions of Article 265-42 to any Financial Assistance in the Special Provision Period or Underwriting in the Special Provision Period by a Corporation, the term "Insurance Company" in that Article shall be deemed to be replaced with "Insurance Company, the Bank of Japan."
(2) Where the provisions of the preceding paragraph applies, the Bank of Japan may provide loans of funds to a Corporation, notwithstanding the provisions of Article 43, paragraph (1) of the Bank of Japan Act (Act No. 89 of 1997).
(3) Where a Corporation borrows any funds pursuant to the provisions of Article 265-42 as applied with relevant replacement of terms under paragraph (1), the Government may, when it finds necessary, provide guarantee for the obligations of the Corporation pertaining to the borrowing within the limit of the amount to be specified by way of a resolution of the Diet, notwithstanding the provisions of Article 3 of the Act on the Limitations of Government Financial Assistance to Juridical Persons.

(Separate Accounting)
Article 1-6 (1) The Non-Life Insurance Policyholders Protection Corporation (meaning the Non-Life Insurance Policyholders Protection Corporation prescribed in Article 265-37, paragraph (2); the same shall apply hereinafter) shall, at the end of the business year to which belongs the day to be specified by Cabinet Order as the date of termination of the business pertaining to the Financial Assistance in the Special Provision Period and the Underwriting in the Special Provision Period, create a Special Account (hereinafter referred to as "Liquidation Account") to arrange for the separate accounting of any outstanding borrowings guaranteed by the Government under paragraph (3) of the preceding Article, with regard to the account related to the performance obligations pertaining to such borrowings.
(2) The Non-Life Insurance Policyholders Protection Corporation shall, at the end of the business year prescribed in the preceding paragraph, impute to the Liquidation Account the obligations pertaining to the borrowings set forth in that paragraph and any claims on obligatory contributions (meaning claims on any unpaid amount of obligatory contribution to be paid under Article 265-33, paragraph (1); hereinafter the same shall apply in this paragraph), and transfer from the Insurance Policyholders Protection Funds prescribed in Article 265-32, paragraph (1) to the Liquidation Account the amount corresponding to the balance of the fund as of the end of that business year, to the limit of the amount of the borrowings less the amount of the claims on obligatory contribution.

(Special Obligatory Contributions)
Article 1-7 (1) The members of the Non-Life Insurance Policyholders Protection Corporation shall, with regard to each of the business years from the business year after the business year prescribed in paragraph (1) of the preceding Article until the business year that includes the day when the Non-Life Insurance Policyholders Protection Corporation abolishes the Liquidation Account pursuant to the provisions of Article 1-9 of the Supplementary Provisions, where the amount of obligations pertaining to borrowings to be imputed to the Liquidation Account pursuant to the provisions of paragraph (2) of the preceding Article exceeds the amount of the assets belonging to the Liquidation Account, pay obligatory contributions to the Non-Life Insurance Policyholders

Protection Corporation pursuant to the provisions of the articles of incorporation as funds to be allocated by the Non-Life Policyholders Protection Corporation to the performance of such obligations, in addition to the obligatory contribution set forth in Article 265-33, paragraph (1).
(2) The provisions of Article 265-33, paragraph (2), the main clause of Article 265-34, paragraphs (1), (3) and (4) and Article 265-35 shall apply mutatis mutandis to the obligatory contribution to be paid under the preceding paragraph.
(3) The obligatory contribution rate to be determined by the Non-Life Insurance Policyholders Protection Corporation under Article 265-34, paragraph (3) as applied mutatis mutandis pursuant to the preceding paragraph shall not be less than the rate to be determined by the Prime Minister and the Minister of Finance taking into consideration the amount required for the performance of obligations pertaining to borrowings imputed to the Liquidation Account pursuant to the provisions of paragraph (2) of the preceding Article and the amount of the assets belonging to the Liquidation Account.

(Special Provisions on Budget Approval, etc.)
Article 1-8 (1) For each of the business years from the business year in which the Non-Life Insurance Policyholders Protection Corporation is established to the business year in which the Liquidation Account is abolished pursuant to the provisions of the following Article, where the Liquidation Account is created, or to the business year to which belongs the date prescribed in Article 1-6, paragraph (1) of the Supplementary Provisions to be specified by Cabinet Order, where the Liquidation Account is not created, the Non-Life Insurance Policyholders Protection Corporation shall, notwithstanding the provisions of Article 265-37, have its budget and financial plan for the business year approved by the Prime Minister and the Minister of Finance, prior to the start of the business year (or, for the business year in which the Non-Life Insurance Policyholders Protection Corporation is established, without delay after its establishment). The same shall apply to any amendment thereto.
(2) The provisions of the preceding paragraph shall not preclude the incorporators of the Non-Life Insurance Policyholders Protection Corporation, acting on its behalf, from applying for, and receiving the approval of the Prime Minister and the Minister of Finance under the preceding paragraph for its budget and financial plan adopted by way of a resolution of the Organizational Meeting pursuant to the provisions of Article 265-7, paragraph (4), prior to the start of the business year in which the Non-Life Insurance Policyholders Protection Corporation is established.

(Abolition of Liquidation Account)
Article 1-9 The Non-Life Insurance Policyholders Protection Corporation shall abolish the Liquidation Account on the day when the performance of the obligations pertaining to the borrowings imputed to the Liquidation Account pursuant to the provisions of Article 1-6, paragraph (2) of the Supplementary Provisions is completed.

(Application of this Act)
Article 1-10 The provisions of this Act shall apply as follows where the Liquidation Account is created in the Non-Life Insurance Policyholders Protection Corporation pursuant to the provisions of Article 1-6, paragraph (1) of the Supplementary Provisions:
(i) For the purpose of applying the provisions of Article 265-28, paragraph (1), item (ii), the term "and the obligatory contribution set forth in Article 1-7, paragraph (1) of the Supplementary Provisions" shall be deemed to be added at the end of that item; and
(ii) For the purpose of applying the provisions of Article 265-41, paragraph (2), the

term "and the Liquidation Account prescribed in Article 1-6, paragraph (1) of the Supplementary Provisions" shall be inserted before the term "; the same shall apply in Article 270-5."

(Penal Provisions)
Article 1-11 (1) Any officer or functionary who has failed to report under Article 1-2-5, paragraph (3) or Article 1-2-7, paragraph (2) of the Supplementary Provisions or made a false report shall be punished by a fine of not more than five hundred thousand yen.
(2) Any person who has failed to make a report under Article 1-2-10 of the Supplementary Provisions or has made a false report shall be punished by a fine of not more than five hundred thousand yen.
(3) When the representative person, or any agent, employee or other worker of a juridical person has committed the violation set forth in the preceding paragraph in connection with the business or property of the juridical person, such juridical person, in addition to the perpetrator, shall be punished under that paragraph.

Article 1-12 Any officer of the Non-Life Insurance Policyholders Protection Corporation who has failed to receive the approval of the Prime Minister and the Minister of Finance pursuant to the provisions of Article 1-8, paragraph (1) of the Supplementary Provisions, where such approval is required, shall be punished by a non-criminal fine of not more than two hundred thousand yen.

(Special Provisions on Partial Payment in Kind of Amount Corresponding to Policy Reserve Pertaining to Dissolved Welfare Pension Fund, etc.)
Article 1-13 (1) Where a dissolved welfare pension fund, etc. as defined in Article 113, paragraph (1) of the Defined-Benefit Corporation Pension Act (Act No. 50 of 2001) (hereinafter referred to as "Dissolved Welfare Pension Fund, etc." in this Article) pays in kind part of the amount corresponding to the policy reserves (meaning the policy reserves prescribed in Article 113, paragraph (1) of that Act) pursuant to the provisions of Article 114, paragraph (1) of that Act (meaning the payment in kind prescribed in Article 114, paragraph (1) of that Act; hereinafter the same shall apply in this Article), the provisions of this Act shall apply to the delivery for allocation to such payment in kind of any assets pertaining to life insurance contracts concluded by the Dissolved Welfare Pension Fund, etc. from a Life Insurance Company (including a Foreign Life Insurance Company, etc.; hereinafter the same shall apply in this Article), by deeming such delivery as the payment of insurance proceeds, refunds or other benefits in an amount corresponding to the value of the assets pursuant to the provisions of a Cabinet Office Ordinance.
(2) When a Life Insurance Company that has concluded a contract with the Government Pension Investment Fund regarding the management and investment of the funds receives from a Dissolved Welfare Pension Fund, etc. the transfer of assets pertaining to the payment in kind pursuant to the provisions of Article 114, paragraph (4) of the Defined-Benefit Corporation Pension Act, the provisions of this Act shall apply to the transfer of assets by deeming such transfer as the receipt of insurance premiums pertaining to life insurance contracts concluded with the Government Pension Investment Fund in an amount corresponding to the value of the assets, pursuant to the provisions of a Cabinet Office Ordinance.

(Repeal of Acts on the Control of Insurance Solicitation, etc.)
Article 2 The following Acts shall be repealed:
(i) The Act on the Control of Insurance Solicitation (Act No. 171 of 1948); and

(ii) The Foreign Insurance Providers Act (Act No. 184 of 1949).

(Transitional Measures for License)
Article 3 (1) The persons that have obtained the license of the competent minister set forth in Article 1, paragraph (1) of the Insurance Business Act before amendment (hereinafter referred to as the "Former Act") by the time when this Act enters into force (including the persons deemed to have obtained the license of the competent minister set forth in Article 1, paragraph (1) of the Former Act pursuant to the provisions of Article 159 of the Former Act, or any Act other than the Former Act or any order pursuant thereto (referred to as the "Provision of Article 159 of the Former Act, etc." in the following paragraph) shall be deemed to obtain the license of the Ministry of Finance set forth in Article 3, paragraph (1) of the Insurance Business Act as amended (hereinafter referred to as the "New Act") when this Act enters into force.
(2) The license of the Financial Minister set forth in Article 3, paragraph (1) of the New Act that the persons prescribed in the preceding paragraph are deemed to have obtained (hereinafter referred to as the "Insurance Companies Licensed under the Former Act") pursuant to the provisions of that paragraph shall be the life insurance business license as defined in Article 3, paragraph (4) of the New Act or the non-life insurance business license as defined in paragraph (5) of that Article, in accordance with the category of business, i. e. the life insurance business or non-life insurance business, in which the person was allowed to operate under the license set forth in Article 1, paragraph (1) of the Former Act (including the license that the person is deemed to have obtained pursuant to the Provision of Article 159 of the Former Act, etc.).

Article 4 Those documents listed in Article 1, paragraph (2), items (i) to (iv) inclusive of the Former Act which have been submitted to the competent minister for the Insurance Companies Licensed under the Former Act by the time when this Act enters into force shall be deemed to be the corresponding documents listed in the items of Article 4, paragraph (2) of the New Act (for the document listed in Article 1, paragraph (2), item (iv) of the Former Act, as the document listed in Article 4, paragraph (2), item (iv) of the New Act).

(Transitional Measures for Amount of Capital or Total Amount of Funds)
Article 5 (1) The provisions of Article 6, paragraph (1) of the New Act shall not apply to those Insurance Companies Licensed under the Former Act for which the amount of capital or the total amount of funds (including the reserves under Article 65 of the Former Act) is less than the amount set forth in that paragraph to be specified by Cabinet Order at the time when this Act enters into force, for a period of five years counting from the Effective Date of this Act (hereinafter referred to as the "Effective Date") (or, for an Insurance Company Licensed under the Former Act which has obtained the authorization of the Prime Minister set forth in Article 79, paragraph (1) or Article 93, paragraph (1) of the New Act within the five-year period, until the date of the Entity Conversion thus authorized).
(2) Where the Insurance Company Licensed under the Former Act to which the provisions of the preceding paragraph is applied is a Mutual Company, for the period of time specified by the preceding paragraph, the company may set aside as a reserves all or part of the amount that may be allocated to the redemption of funds or distribution of surplus specified in Article 55, paragraph (2) of the New Act, until such time as the total amount of funds (including the reserves for redemption of funds set forth in Article 56 of the New Act (including any amount deemed to have been set aside as the re-

serves for redemption of funds pursuant to the provisions of the following paragraph and Article 39 of the Supplementary Provisions)) reaches the amount set forth in Article 6, paragraph (1) of the New Act to be specified by Cabinet Order.
(3) The Reserve set aside pursuant to the provisions of the preceding paragraph shall be deemed to have been set aside as the reserves for redemption of funds set forth in Article 56 of the New Act.

(Transitional Measures for Trade Name or Name)
Article 6 The provisions of Article 7, paragraph (2) of the New Act shall not apply for six months counting from the Effective Date to a person using any term that may be understood as indicating an Insurance Company at the time when this Act enters into force.

(Transitional Measures for Share Application Certificates)
Article 7 (1) The provisions of Article 9, paragraph (1) of the New Act shall apply to the share application certificate set forth in Article 175, paragraph (1) (Method of Share Application) of the Commercial Code where the incorporators start the solicitation of shareholders on or after the Effective Date; with regard to the share application certificates where the incorporators started the solicitation of shareholders before the Effective Date, the provisions then in force shall remain applicable.
(2) The provisions of Article 9, paragraph (1) of the New Act as applied mutatis mutandis pursuant to paragraph (2) of that Article shall apply to the share application certificate set forth in Article 280-6 (Share Application Certificate) of the Commercial Code or the subscription warrant set forth in Article 280-6-2, paragraph (1) (Subscription Warrant) of said Code where the board of directors or shareholders' meeting adopts any resolution on the issuance of new shares under Article 280-2 (Decision on the Particulars of the Issuance of New Shares) of said Code after the Effective Date.

(Transitional Measures for Grounds for Disqualification of Director, etc.)
Article 8 For the purpose of applying the provisions of Article 254-2, item (iii) (Grounds for Disqualification of Director) of the Commercial Code (including the cases where it is applied mutatis mutandis pursuant to Article 280, paragraph (1) (Company Auditor) and Article 430, paragraph (2) (Liquidator) of said Code) as applied with relevant replacements of terms pursuant to Article 12, paragraph (1) of the New Act, a person punished pursuant to the provisions of the Former Act (including the provisions of the Former Act that are to remain applicable pursuant to these Supplementary Provisions) shall be deemed to have been punished pursuant to the provisions of the New Act on the day when the person received the original punishment.

(Transitional Measures for Retained Earnings Reserve)
Article 9 The provisions of Article 14 of the New Act shall apply to the accumulation of the retained earnings Reserve for the business years that start on or after the Effective Date.

(Transitional Measures for Restrictions on Dividend, etc.)
Article 10 The provisions of Article 15 of the New Act shall apply to the dividend of profit or the distribution of money set forth in Article 293-5, paragraph (1) (Interim Dividend) of the Commercial Code pertaining to a resolution adopted by the board of directors or shareholders' meeting in a session held on or after the Effective Date, or to the cancellation of shares set forth in the proviso to Article 212, paragraph (1) or Article 212-2, paragraph (1) (Cancellation of Shares) of said Code; with regard to the

dividend of profit or the distribution of money set forth in Article 293-5, paragraph (1) pertaining to a resolution adopted by the board of directors or shareholders' meeting in a session held before the Effective Date, the provisions then in force shall remain applicable.

(Transitional Measures for Denial of Shareholders' Right to Inspect Books)
Article 11 The provisions of Article 16 of the New Act shall not apply to any request made by shareholders before the Effective Date for the inspection or copying of accounting books and documents set forth in Article 293-6, paragraph (1) (Shareholders' Right to Inspect Books) of the Commercial Code.

(Transitional Measures for Reduction of Capital)
Article 12 The provisions of Article 17 of the New Act shall apply to the reduction of capital pertaining to a resolution of the shareholders' meeting adopted in a session held on or after the Effective Date; with regard to the reduction of capital pertaining to a resolution of the shareholders' meeting adopted in a session before the Effective Date, the provisions then in force shall remain applicable.

(Transitional Measures for Statutory Lien for Policyholders, etc.)
Article 13 With regard to the statutory lien under Article 32 of the Former Act or the right under Article 33 of the Former Act in existence at the time when this Act enters into force, the provisions then in force shall remain applicable.

(Transitional Measures for Mutual Companies)
Article 14 The Mutual Companies under the Former Act in existence at the time when this Act enters into force shall be deemed to be Mutual Companies under the New Act.

(Transitional Measures for Actions by the Directors, etc. of a Mutual Company)
Article 15 The actions prescribed in the Commercial Code or the Act on Special Measures for the Commercial Code as applied mutatis mutandis pursuant to the Former Act which were taken or were required to have been taken before the Effective Date by the incorporators, directors, representative director, company auditors, accounting auditors or liquidators of a Mutual Company under the Former Act in existence at the time when this Act enters into force shall be deemed to be the actions prescribed in the relevant provisions of the Commercial Code or the Act on Special Measures for the Commercial Code as applied mutatis mutandis pursuant to the New Act which were taken or were required to have been taken by the incorporators, directors, representative director, company auditors, accounting auditors or liquidators of a Mutual Company under the New Act on the day when the original actions were taken or were required to have been taken, except when these Supplementary Provisions specify otherwise.

(Transitional Measures for Actions, etc. of the Managers, etc. of Mutual Company)
Article 16 (1) With regard to an action taken before the Effective Date by a manager that a Mutual Company under the provisions of the Former Act which still exists at the time of the enforcement of this Act, has appointed (including an employee prescribed in Article 42 of the Commercial Code (Apparent Manager) or Article 43 of the same Act (Employee Entrusted with Certain Type of Task or Specific Task) as applied muta-

tis mutandis pursuant to Article 42 of the Former Act) pursuant to the provisions of Article 37 of the Commercial Code (Appointment of Manager) as applied mutatis mutandis pursuant to Article 42 of the Former Act), and with regard to any other particulars that were true of such manager before the Effective Date, the day on which said particulars were true is deemed to be the day on which such particulars were true for a manager that a Mutual Company under the New Act has appointed (including an employee prescribed in Article 42 or 43 of said Code as applied mutatis mutandis pursuant to that paragraph) pursuant to the provisions of Article 37 of the Commercial Code as applied mutatis mutandis pursuant to Article 21, paragraph (1) of the New Act, and the provisions of Article 38 to 43 inclusive (Commercial Employee) of the Commercial Code as applied mutatis mutandis pursuant to Article 21, paragraph (1) of the New Act apply.

(2) For the purpose of applying Article 46 to 48 inclusive, Article 50 and Article 51 (Commercial Agent) of the Commercial Code as applied mutatis mutandis pursuant to Article 21, paragraph (1) of the New Act, the day on which the relevant actions took place and the relevant other particulars were present prior to the Effective Date prescribed in Article 46 to 48 inclusive, Article 50 and Article 51 of the Commercial Code as applied mutatis mutandis pursuant to Article 42 of the Former Act regarding a Mutual Company under the Former Act is deemed to be the day on which said actions took place and other particulars were present for the Mutual Company under the New Act.

(3) Any claim filed with the court before the Effective Date pertaining to a Mutual Company under the Former Act in existence at the time when this Act enters into force by the members, creditors or other interested persons of the Mutual Company under the Former Act pursuant to Article 58 (Order for Dissolution) or any other provisions of the Commercial Code as applied mutatis mutandis pursuant to the Former Act, and any order issued by the court pertaining to such claim before the Effective Date shall be deemed to be a claim filed with the court or an order issued by the court on the date of the original claim or order pertaining to a Mutual Company under the New Act pursuant to the corresponding provisions of the Commercial Code as applied mutatis mutandis pursuant to the New Act, except when these Supplementary Provisions specify otherwise.

(Transitional Measures for Commercial Books, etc. of Mutual Company)

Article 17 The commercial books, financial statements or other accounting documents prepared before the Effective Date pursuant to the provisions of the Commercial Code as applied mutatis mutandis pursuant to the Former Act by a Mutual Company under the Former Act in existence at the time when this Act enters into force shall be deemed to have been prepared on the dates of the original preparation by a Mutual Company under the New Act pursuant to the corresponding provisions of the Commercial Code as applied mutatis mutandis pursuant to the New Act.

(Transitional Measures for Incorporation of Mutual Company)

Article 18 The provisions of Part II, Chapter II, Section 2, Subsection 2 of the New Act shall apply to the procedure of incorporation of a Mutual Company whose articles of incorporation are certified on or after the Effective Date under Article 167 (Certification of Articles of Incorporation) of the Commercial Code as applied mutatis mutandis pursuant to Article 22, paragraph (4) of the New Act, and to the registration of incorporation of a Mutual Company and application thereof made on or after the Effective Date; with regard to the procedure of incorporation (excluding the registration of incorporation and application thereof) of a Mutual Company whose articles of incorporation were certified before the Effective Date under Article 167 of the Commercial

Code as applied mutatis mutandis pursuant to Article 42 of the Former Act, the provisions then in force shall remain applicable.

(Transitional Measures for Mutual Company's Articles of Incorporation)
Article 19 Details of the particulars listed in Article 34, items (i) to (ix) inclusive of the Former Act in the articles of incorporation of a Mutual Company under the Former Act in existence at the time when this Act enters into force and of a Mutual Company whose incorporation shall remain governed by the provisions then in force pursuant to the provisions of the preceding Article are deemed to be details of the particulars listed in the corresponding items among of Article 22, paragraph (2), items (i) to (viii) inclusive and Article 22, paragraph (3), item (ii) of the New Act (or, for the particulars listed in Article 34, item (i) of the Former Act, the particulars listed in Article 22, paragraph (2), item (i) of the New Act); any details of the particulars listed in Article 34, item (x) of the Former Act in such articles of incorporation are deemed not to exist.

(Transitional Measures for Application for Registration of Incorporation)
Article 20 The provisions of Article 28, item (ii) of the New Act shall not apply to any application for registration of incorporation made by a Mutual Company whose incorporation shall remain governed by the provisions then in force pursuant to the provisions of Article 18 of the Supplementary Provisions.

(Transitional Measures for Actions to Hold Incorporators of a Mutual Company Accountable)
Article 21 The provisions of Article 267 to 268-3 inclusive (Lawsuit to Hold Directors Accountable) of the Commercial Code as applied mutatis mutandis pursuant to Article 196 (Exemption from Liability of, and Representative Action against Incorporators) of said Code as applied mutatis mutandis pursuant to Article 30 of the New Act shall apply to any action filed by members on or after the Effective Date under Article 267, paragraph (1) of the Commercial Code as applied mutatis mutandis pursuant to Article 196 of said Code as applied mutatis mutandis pursuant to Article 30 of the New Act or under Article 267, paragraph (3) of the Commercial Code as applied mutatis mutandis pursuant to Article 196 of said Code as applied mutatis mutandis pursuant to Article 30 of the New Act; with regard to any action filed by members before the Effective Date under Article 57, paragraph (1) of the Former Act as applied mutatis mutandis pursuant to Article 41 of the Former Act or under Article 267, paragraph (3) of the Commercial Code as applied mutatis mutandis pursuant to Article 57, paragraph (2) of the Former Act as applied mutatis mutandis pursuant to Article 41 of the Former Act, the provisions then in force shall remain applicable.

(Transitional Measures for Set-Offs Pertaining to Payment of Insurance Premiums)
Article 22 With regard to set-offs pertaining to the payment of those insurance premiums under Article 45 of the Former Act which were required to have been paid by members before the Effective Date, the provisions then in force shall remain applicable.

(Transitional Measures for Notices and Demands)
Article 23 The provisions of Article 32 of the New Act shall apply to any notice or demand issued on or after the Effective Date under the main clause of paragraph (1) of that Article; with regard to any notice or demand issued before the Effective Date un-

der the main clause of Article 50 of the Former Act, the provisions then in force shall remain applicable.

(Transitional Measures for Withdrawing Members)
Article 24 The provisions of Articles 35 and 36 of the New Act shall apply to the members who withdraw on or after the Effective Date; with regard to the members who withdrew before the Effective Date, the provisions then in force shall remain applicable.

(Transitional Measures for Voting Rights of Members and Representative Members)
Article 25 If the exceptional specification prescribed in the proviso to Article 52 of the Former Act (including the cases where it is applied mutatis mutandis pursuant to Article 51, paragraph (2) of the Former Act) has been detailed in the articles of incorporation of a Mutual Company under the Former Act which are in existence at the time when this Act enters into force, such details are deemed not to exist.

(Transitional Measures for the Right to Make Proposals at General Members' Councils, etc.)
Article 26 The provisions of Article 38 to 40 inclusive of the New Act shall apply to any request made by members on or after the Effective Date for any of the particulars prescribed in those provisions; with regard to any request made before the Effective Date under Article 52-2, paragraph (1), Article 53, paragraph (1) or Article 53-2, paragraph (1) of the Former Act, the provisions then in force shall remain applicable.

(Transitional Measures for Resolutions of the General Members' Council, etc.)
Article 27 Any resolution adopted before the Effective Date, pursuant to any of the provisions of the Commercial Code or Act on Special Measures for the Commercial Code as applied mutatis mutandis pursuant to the Former Act, on the appointment of directors or company auditors, or any other matter by the general members' council (including the administrative organ established in lieu of such council under Article 51, paragraph (1) of the Former Act) of a Mutual Company under the Former Act in existence at the time when this Act enters into force, except those specified in other Article of these Supplementary Provisions, shall be deemed to be a resolution adopted pursuant to the corresponding provisions of the Commercial Code as applied mutatis mutandis pursuant to the New Act on the date of the original resolution by the general members' council of a Mutual Company under the New Act or the administrative organ established under Article 51, paragraph (1) of the Former Act that is deemed to be the General Representative Members' Council established under Article 42, paragraph (1) of the New Act pursuant to the provisions of Article 29 of the Supplementary Provisions.

(Transitional Measures for the Mutatis Mutandis Application of the Commercial Code, etc. Pertaining to General Members' Councils)
Article 28 (1) The provisions of the Commercial Code and Act on Special Measures for the Commercial Code as applied mutatis mutandis pursuant to Article 41 of the New Act shall apply to the sessions of the general members' council for which the convocation notice set forth in Article 232, paragraph (1) (Convocation Notice) of the Commercial Code as applied mutatis mutandis pursuant to Article 41 of the New Act is issued on or after the Effective Date; with regard to the sessions of general members' council for which the convocation notice set forth in Article 232, paragraph (1) of the

Commercial Code as applied mutatis mutandis pursuant to Article 54 of the Former Act was issued before the Effective Date, the provisions then in force shall remain applicable.

(2) Where the articles of incorporation of a Mutual Company under the Former Act in existence at the time when this Act enters into force specify any exceptional standard pursuant to the proviso to Article 52-2, paragraph (1), the proviso to Article 53, paragraph (1) or the proviso to Article 53-2, paragraph (1) of the Former Act, the details of such standard are deemed not to exist when the proportion of the number of members to the total number of members or the number of members thus detailed exceeds the proportion of the number of members to the total number of members or the number of members prescribed in Article 38, paragraph (1), Article 39, paragraph (1) or Article 40, paragraph (1) of the New Act, respectively.

(Transitional Measures for the Establishment of a General Representative Members' Council, etc.)

Article 29 (1) Where a Mutual Company under the Former Act in existence at the time when this Act enters into force has established the administrative organ prescribed in Article 51, paragraph (1) of the Former Act, such administrative organ shall be deemed to be a General Representative Members' Council as set forth in Article 42, paragraph (1) of the New Act when the specification in the articles of incorporation set forth in Article 51, paragraph (1) of the Former Act conforms to the provisions of Article 42, paragraphs (2) and (3) of the New Act.

(2) Where a Mutual Company under the Former Act in existence at the time when this Act enters into force has established the administrative organ prescribed in Article 51, paragraph (1) of the Former Act, such administrative organ shall be deemed to be a General Representative Members' Council as set forth in Article 42, paragraph (1) of the New Act only for a period of one year counting from the Effective Date when the specification in the articles of incorporation set forth in Article 51, paragraph (1) of the Former Act does not conform to the provisions of Article 42, paragraphs (2) and (3) of the New Act.

(3) In the case prescribed in the preceding paragraph, when the Mutual Company under the Former Act prescribed in that paragraph modifies its articles of incorporation within the period prescribed in that paragraph so that they may conform to the provisions of Article 42, paragraphs (2) and (3)of the New Act, the administrative organ prescribed in Article 51, paragraph (1) of the Former Act of the Mutual Company under the Former Act shall be deemed to be a General Representative Members' Council as set forth in Article 42, paragraph (1) of the New Act even after the expiration of the period.

(4) The members of the administrative organ deemed to be a General Representative Members' Council as set forth in Article 42, paragraph (1) of the New Act pursuant to the provisions of the preceding three paragraphs shall be deemed to be the representative members set forth in that paragraph.

(Transitional Measures for Method of Adopting Resolutions of General Council, of Representative Members etc.)

Article 30 The provisions of Articles 43 and 44 of the New Act shall apply to the sessions of the General Representative Members' Council set forth in Article 42, paragraph (1) of the New Act (including the administrative organ prescribed in Article 51, paragraph (1) of the Former Act which is deemed to be a General Council pursuant to the provisions of the preceding Article) for which the convocation notice set forth in Article 232, paragraph (1) (Convocation Notice) of the Commercial Code as applied

Art.31～32　⑥ Insurance Business Act, Part VI

mutatis mutandis pursuant to Article 49 of the New Act is issued on or after the Effective Date; with regard to the sessions of the administrative organ prescribed in Article 51, paragraph (1) of the Former Act that is deemed to be the General Council set forth in Article 42, paragraph (1) of the New Act pursuant to the provisions of paragraph (1) or (2) of the preceding Article for which the convocation notice set forth in Article 232, paragraph (1) of the Commercial Code as applied mutatis mutandis pursuant to Article 54 of the Former Act as applied mutatis mutandis pursuant to Article 51, paragraph (2) of the Former Act was issued before the Effective Date, the provisions then in force shall remain applicable.

(Transitional Measures for Right to Make Proposals at a General Representative Members' Council Meeting, etc.)
Article 31　(1) The provisions of Article 45 to 47 inclusive of the New Act shall apply to any request made on or after the Effective Date by members or the representative members set forth in Article 42, paragraph (1) of the New Act (including those who shall be deemed to be the representative members set forth in Article 42, paragraph (1) of the New Act pursuant to the provisions of Article 29, paragraph (4) of the Supplementary Provisions) regarding the particulars prescribed in Article 45, paragraph (1), Article 46, paragraph (1) or Article 47, paragraph (1) of the New Act; with regard to any request made before the Effective Date pursuant to the provisions of Article 52-2, paragraph (1), Article 53, paragraph (1) or Article 53-2, paragraph (1) of the Former Act as applied mutatis mutandis pursuant to Article 51, paragraph (2) of the Former Act, the provisions then in force shall remain applicable.
(2) The provisions of Article 28, paragraph (2) of the Supplementary Provisions shall apply mutatis mutandis to any exceptional standard specified in the articles of incorporation of a Mutual Company under the Former Act in existence at the time when this Act enters into force, pursuant to the proviso to Article 52-2, paragraph (1), the proviso to Article 53, paragraph (1) or the proviso to Article 53-2, paragraph (1) of the Former Act as applied mutatis mutandis pursuant to Article 51, paragraph (2) of the Former Act.
(3) Where the articles of incorporation of a Mutual Company under the Former Act in existence at the time when this Act enters into force describe the number of the persons who shall be deemed to be the representative members set forth in Article 42, paragraph (1) of the New Act pursuant to the provisions of Article 29, paragraph (4) of the Supplementary Provisions pursuant to the proviso to Article 52-2, paragraph (1), the proviso to Article 53, paragraph (1) or the proviso to Article 53-2, paragraph (1) of the Former Act as applied mutatis mutandis pursuant to Article 51, paragraph (2) of the Former Act, such details are deemed not to exist when the number thus detailed exceeds the number of representative members prescribed in Article 45, paragraph (1), Article 46, paragraph (1) or Article 47, paragraph (1) of the New Act.

(Transitional Measures for Sending of Reference Documents for General Representative Members' Council)
Article 32　The provisions of Article 48 of the New Act shall apply to that convocation notice set forth in Article 232, paragraph (1) (Convocation Notice) of the Commercial Code as applied mutatis mutandis pursuant to Article 49 of the New Act that is issued on or after the Effective Date; with regard to that convocation notice set forth in Article 232, paragraph (1) of the Commercial Code as applied mutatis mutandis pursuant to Article 54 of the Former Act as applied mutatis mutandis pursuant to Article 51, paragraph (2) of the Former Act which was issued before the Effective Date, the provisions then in force shall remain applicable.

(Transitional Measures for Mutatis Mutandis Application of the Commercial Code Pertaining to General Representative Members' Council)

Article 33 The provisions of the Commercial Code as applied mutatis mutandis pursuant to Article 49 of the New Act shall apply to the sessions of the General Council set forth in Article 42, paragraph (1) of the New Act (including an administrative organ prescribed in Article 51, paragraph (1) of the Former Act which is deemed to be a General Representative Members' Council pursuant to the provisions of Article 29 of the Supplementary Provisions) for which the convocation notice set forth in Article 232, paragraph (1) (Convocation Notice) of the Commercial Code as applied mutatis mutandis pursuant to Article 49 of the New Act is issued on or after the Effective Date; with regard to the sessions of an administrative organ as prescribed in Article 51, paragraph (1) of the Former Act which is deemed to be a General Council as set forth in Article 42, paragraph (1) of the New Act pursuant to the provisions of Article 29, paragraph (1) or (2) of the Supplementary Provisions for which the convocation notice set forth in Article 232, paragraph (1) of the Commercial Code as applied mutatis mutandis pursuant to Article 54 of the Former Act as applied mutatis mutandis pursuant to Article 51, paragraph (2) of the Former Act was issued before the Effective Date, the provisions then in force shall remain applicable.

(Transitional Measures for Resolutions, etc. Adopted by Mutual Company's Board of Directors, etc.)

Article 34 The resolutions adopted, and other powers used before the Effective Date pursuant to the provisions of the Commercial Code or Act on Special Measures for the Commercial Code as applied mutatis mutandis pursuant to the Former Act by the board of directors or board of company auditors of a Mutual Company under the Former Act in existence at the time when this Act enters into force shall be deemed to be the resolutions adopted, and other powers used on the dates of the original resolutions or use of powers by the board of directors or board of company auditors of a Mutual Company under the New Act pursuant to the corresponding provisions of the Commercial Code or Act on Special Measures for the Commercial Code as applied mutatis mutandis pursuant to the New Act.

(Transitional Measures for Mutatis Mutandis Application of Commercial Code Pertaining to Directors of Mutual Company)

Article 35 (1) The provisions of Article 8 of the Supplementary Provisions shall apply mutatis mutandis to any application of the provisions of Article 254-2 (Grounds for Disqualification of Director) of the Commercial Code as applied mutatis mutandis pursuant to Article 51, paragraph (2) of the New Act.

(2) The provisions of Article 267 to 268-3 inclusive (Lawsuit to Hold Directors Accountable) of the Commercial Code as applied mutatis mutandis pursuant to Article 51, paragraph (2) of the New Act shall apply to any request for filing the action set forth in Article 267, paragraph (1) of the Commercial Code as applied mutatis mutandis pursuant to Article 51, paragraph (2) of the New Act or any filing of the action set forth in Article 267, paragraph (3) of the Commercial Code as applied mutatis mutandis pursuant to Article 51, paragraph (2) of the New Act, made by members on or after the Effective Date; with regard to any request for filing the action set forth in Article 57, paragraph (1) of the Former Act, or any filing of the action set forth in Article 267, paragraph (3) of the Commercial Code as applied mutatis mutandis pursuant to Article 57, paragraph (2) of the Former Act, made by members before the Effective Date, the provisions then in force shall remain applicable.

Art.36〜38　　　　6 Insurance Business Act, Part VI

(3) The provisions of Article 264 (Duty not to Compete) of the Commercial Code as applied mutatis mutandis pursuant to Article 51, paragraph (2) of the New Act shall apply to the transactions carried out by directors on or after the Effective Date.

(Transitional Measures for Members List)
Article 36　The members list kept pursuant to the provisions of Article 56 of the Former Act by the directors of a Mutual Company under the Former Act in existence at the time when this Act enters into force shall be deemed to be the members list set forth in Article 52, paragraph (1) of the New Act.

(Transitional Measures for the Mutatis Mutandis Application of the Commercial Code Pertaining to the Company Auditors of a Mutual Company)
Article 37　(1) The provisions of Article 8 of the Supplementary Provisions shall apply mutatis mutandis to any application of the provisions of Article 254-2 (Grounds for Disqualification of Director) of the Commercial Code as applied mutatis mutandis pursuant to Article 53, paragraph (2) of the New Act.
(2) The provisions of Article 267 to 268-3 inclusive (Lawsuit to Hold Directors Accountable) of the Commercial Code as applied mutatis mutandis pursuant to Article 53, paragraph (2) of the New Act shall apply to any request for filing the action set forth in Article 267, paragraph (1) of the Commercial Code as applied mutatis mutandis pursuant to Article 53, paragraph (2) of the New Act or any filing of the action set forth in Article 267, paragraph (3) of the Commercial Code as applied mutatis mutandis pursuant to Article 53, paragraph (2) of the New Act, made by members on or after the Effective Date; with regard to any request for filing the action set forth in Article 57, paragraph (1) of the Former Act as applied mutatis mutandis pursuant to Article 62 of the Former Act or any filing of the action set forth in Article 267, paragraph (3) of the Commercial Code as applied mutatis mutandis pursuant to Article 57, paragraph (2) of the Former Act as applied mutatis mutandis pursuant to Article 62 of the Former Act, made by members before the Effective Date, the provisions then in force shall remain applicable.

(Transitional Measures for Deficiency Reserve)
Article 38　(1) The provisions of Article 54 of the New Act shall apply to the accumulation of the deficiency reserves set forth in that Article pertaining to the business years that start on or after the Effective Date; with regard to the accumulation of the reserves set forth in Article 63, paragraph (1) of the Former Act pertaining to the business years that started before the Effective Date, the provisions then in force shall remain applicable.
(2) The reserves set forth in Article 63, paragraph (1) of the Former Act in existence at the time when this Act enters into force pertaining to a Mutual Company under the Former Act and the reserves set forth in paragraph (1) of that Article to which the provisions then in force are to remain applicable pursuant to the provisions of the preceding paragraph shall be deemed to have been set aside as the deficiency reserves set forth in Article 54 of the New Act.
(3) The accounting practices for settlement purposes where the amount of the reserves set forth in Article 63, paragraph (1) of the Former Act that are deemed to have been set aside as the deficiency reserves set forth in Article 54 of the New Act pursuant to the provisions of the preceding paragraph exceeds the total amount of the funds prescribed in Article 54 of the New Act (including the reserves for redemption of funds set forth in Article 56 of the New Act) or the amount specified in the articles of incorporation shall be specified by Cabinet Office Ordinance.

(Transitional Measures for Funds and Reserve for Redemption of Funds)
Article 39 The funds under the Former Act and the reserves under Article 65 of the Former Act pertaining to a Mutual Company under the Former Act in existence at the time when this Act enters into force shall be deemed to be the funds under the New Act and the reserves for redemption of funds set aside pursuant to the provisions of Article 56 of the New Act, respectively.

(Transitional Measures for Distribution of Surplus)
Article 40 The provisions of Article 58 of the New Act shall apply to the distribution of surplus pertaining to the business years that start on or after the Effective Date; with regard to the distribution of surplus set forth in Article 66 of the Former Act pertaining to the business years that started before the Effective Date, the provisions then in force shall remain applicable.

(Transitional Measures for Research and Development Expenditure, etc.)
Article 41 (1) That amount of money prescribed in Article 286-2 (Deferral of Test and Research Expenditure and Development Expenditure) of the Commercial Code as applied mutatis mutandis pursuant to Article 67 of the Former Act which was expended before the Effective Date by a Mutual Company under the Former Act in existence at the time when this Act enters into force shall be deemed to be that amount of money prescribed in Article 286-3 of the Commercial Code as applied mutatis mutandis pursuant to Article 59, paragraph (1) of the New Act which was expended on the date of the original expenditure by a Mutual Company under the New Act.
(2) The provisions of Article 286-4 (Deferral of New Share Issue Cost) of the Commercial Code as applied mutatis mutandis pursuant to Article 59, paragraph (1) of the New Act shall apply to that amount of cost required for the public offering of funds prescribed in that Article that is expended in the business years that start on or after the Effective Date.
(3) That amount of cost required for the public offering of funds prescribed in Article 286-4 of the Commercial Code as applied mutatis mutandis pursuant to Article 59, paragraph (1) of the New Act which was expended in the business years that started before the Effective Date by a Mutual Company under the Former Act in existence at the time when this Act enters into force may be credited to assets on the balance sheet for the accounting period of the first business year that starts on or after the Effective Date, after deducting the minimum amount that would have been amortized if the provisions of Article 286-4 of the Commercial Code had applied to the accounting periods before the accounting period of the first business year that starts on or after the Effective Date. In this case, not less than the straight-line amount shall be amortized in each of the accounting periods that fall within the amortization period under that Article after deducting the period that has already elapsed.
(4) The provisions of Article 294 (Inspection of Business and Property Condition of Company) of the Commercial Code as applied mutatis mutandis pursuant to Article 59, paragraph (1) of the New Act shall apply where the members or representative members prescribed in Article 294, paragraph (1) of the Commercial Code make the request set forth in that paragraph on or after the Effective Date. In this case, the business executed before the Effective Date by a Mutual Company under the Former Act in existence at the time when this Act enters into force shall be deemed to have been executed on the date of the original business execution by a Mutual Company under the New Act.

(Transitional Measures for Public Offering of Funds)
Article 42 The provisions of Article 60 of the New Act shall apply to any public offering of funds started by a Mutual Company on or after the Effective Date.

(Transitional Measures for Registry)
Article 43 The Registry of Mutual Insurance Companies kept in a registry office at the time when this Act enters into force shall be deemed to be the Registry of Mutual Insurance Companies set forth in Article 64 of the New Act.

(Transitional Measures for Mutatis Mutandis Application of Commercial Registration Act)
Article 44 The dispositions, procedures and other actions prior to the Effective Date under the Commercial Registration Act as applied mutatis mutandis pursuant to the Imperial Ordinance set forth in Article 79 of the Former Act shall be deemed to be the corresponding actions under the Commercial Registration Act as applied mutatis mutandis pursuant to Article 65 of the New Act.

(Transitional Measures for Mutatis Mutandis Application of Act on Procedures for Non-Contentious Cases)
Article 45 The procedures started before the Effective Date under the Act on Procedures for Non-Contentious Cases as applied mutatis mutandis pursuant to the Imperial Ordinance set forth in Article 79 of the Former Act shall be deemed to be the procedures under the Act on Procedures for Non-Contentious Cases as applied mutatis mutandis pursuant to Article 66 of the New Act.

(Transitional Measures for Entity Conversion from Stock Company to Mutual Company)
Article 46 The provisions of Part II, Chapter II, Section 3, Subsection 1 of the New Act shall apply to the Entity Conversion set forth in Article 68, paragraph (1) of the New Act pertaining to the resolution of the shareholders' meeting set forth in Article 69, paragraph (1) of the New Act where it is carried out on or after the Effective Date; with regard to the Entity Conversion set forth in Article 19, paragraph (1) of the Former Act pertaining to the resolution of the shareholders' meeting set forth in Article 20, paragraph (1) of the Former Act, the provisions then in force shall remain applicable where it was carried out before the Effective Date.

(Transitional Measures for Scope of Business)
Article 47 (1) Those Insurance Companies Licensed under the Former Act which, at the time when this Act enters into force and with the authorization of the competent minister pursuant to the proviso to Article 5, paragraph (1) of the Former Act, conduct business for acting as an agent or intermediary, on behalf of any of the other companies conducting non-life insurance business as prescribed in the proviso to that paragraph, in transactions within the scope of the latter's non-life insurance business, shall be deemed to obtain the authorization set forth in Article 98, paragraph (2) of the New Act at the time when this Act enters into force.
(2) Those Insurance Companies Licensed under the Former Act which, at the time when this Act enters into force, conduct business set forth in Article 98, paragraph (1), item (i) of the New Act (excluding the business prescribed in the preceding paragraph) shall notify the Minister of Finance of the content of such business within six months from the Effective Date.
(3) Those Insurance Companies Licensed under the Former Act which have made the no-

tification set forth in the preceding paragraph shall be deemed to obtain the authorization set forth in Article 98, paragraph (2) of the New Act for conducting business to which the notification pertains on the Effective Date.

Article 48 (1) Those Insurance Companies Licensed under the Former Act which, at the time when this Act enters into force, conduct business set forth in Article 99, paragraph (1) of the New Act, shall notify the Minister of Finance of the content of such business within six months from the Effective Date.
(2) Those Insurance Companies Licensed under the Former Act which have made the notification set forth in the preceding paragraph shall be deemed to obtain the authorization set forth in Article 99, paragraph (4) of the New Act for conducing business to which the notification pertains on the Effective Date.
(3) Those Insurance Companies Licensed under the Former Act which, at the time when this Act enters into force and with the authorization of the competent minister pursuant to the proviso to Article 5, paragraph (1) of the Former Act, conduct business for accepting trusts prescribed in the proviso to that paragraph, shall be deemed to obtain the authorization set forth in Article 99, paragraph (7) of the New Act at the time when this Act enters into force.

(Transitional Measures for Exclusion from Application of Anti-Monopoly Act)
Article 49 (1) With regard to those Agreements, contracts and other concerted actions (hereinafter referred to as "Concerted Actions" in this Article) listed in the items of Article 12-3 of the Former Act (including the cases where it is applied mutatis mutandis pursuant to Article 19 of the Foreign Insurance Providers Act to be repealed under Article 2 of the Supplementary Provisions (hereinafter referred to as the "Former Foreign Insurance Providers Act")) which have been entered into by the time when this Act enters into force by those Insurance Companies Licensed under the Former Act that are deemed to have obtained the non-life insurance business license set forth in Article 3, paragraph (5) of the New Act pursuant to the provisions of Article 3 of the Supplementary Provisions and those foreign insurance providers prescribed in Article 2, paragraph (1) of the Former Foreign Insurance Operators Act (hereinafter referred to as "Non-Life Insurance Companies, etc. Licensed under the Former Act" in this Article) that are deemed to have obtained the foreign non-life insurance business license set forth in Article 185, paragraph (5) of the New Act pursuant to the provisions of Article 72 of the Supplementary Provisions, with other Non-Life Insurance Companies, etc. Licensed under the Former Act, the provisions of Article 12-3 to 12-7 inclusive of the Former Act (including the cases where they are applied mutatis mutandis pursuant to Article 19 of the Former Foreign Insurance Providers Act) (including the penal provisions pertaining thereto) shall remain in force for a period of two years counting from the Effective Date, provided that all of the Non-Life Insurance Companies, etc. Licensed under the Former Act involved in the Concerted Actions have notified the Minister of Finance pursuant to the provisions of the applicable Ordinance of the Ministry of Finance within three months from the Effective Date.
(2) For the purpose of applying the provisions of Article 12-5, paragraph (3) of the Former Act (including the cases where it is applied mutatis mutandis pursuant to Article 19 of the Former Foreign Insurance Operators Act) to any application of the provisions of the preceding paragraph, the provisions of Article 12, paragraphs (3) and (4) of the Former Act shall remain in force.
(3) With regard to those Concerted Actions prescribed in paragraph (1) that constitute the Concerted Actions listed in Article 101, paragraph (1), items (i) and (ii) of the New Act, the Non-Life Insurance Companies, etc. Licensed under the Former Act set forth in

Art.50～51　　　　　[6] Insurance Business Act, Part VI

paragraph (1) may, even in the period prescribed in that paragraph, apply for the authorization set forth in Article 102, paragraph (1) of the New Act. In this case, where any disposition has been adopted to the effect that the authorization shall be given within such period, the provisions of paragraph (1) shall cease to apply on the day when the authorization takes effect.

(Transitional Measures for Shareholding in Overseas Affiliated Company, etc.)
Article 50 (1) An Insurance Company Licensed under the Former Act as of the time this Act enters into force, which holds shares (limited to those with voting rights) or equity interests (hereinafter referred to as "Shares, etc." in this Article) exceeding 50 percent of the total number of issued shares (limited to those with voting rights) or total amount of contribution (hereinafter referred to as "Issued Shares, etc." in this Article) in a company listed in the items of Article 108, paragraph (1) of the New Act shall notify the Minister of Finance of this within three months from the Effective Date.
(2) If an Insurance Company Licensed under the Former Act as of the time this Act enters into force has received the permission listed in item (i) or if the acquisition of Shares, etc. (limited an acquisition that has not been executed by the Effective Date) in the notice under item (ii) is an acquisition of Shares, etc. that constitute over 50 percent of the Issued Shares, etc. in a company listed in the items of Article 108, paragraph (1) of the New Act, the Insurance Company Licensed under the Former Act shall notify the Minister of Finance of this within three months from the Effective Date:
　(i) Permission under Article 21, paragraph (2) (Capital Transactions that Require Permission of Minister of Finance) of the Foreign Exchange and Foreign Trade Act (Act No. 228 of 1949); or
　(ii) Notification under Article 22, paragraph (1), item (iv) (Notification Pertaining to External Direct Investment by Resident) of the Foreign Exchange and Foreign Trade Act (limited to the cases where, for the relevant notification, the period during which the acquisition of the Shares, etc. pertaining to the notification is prohibited pursuant to the provisions of Article 23, paragraph (1) of that Act without the recommendation of the Minister of Finance under Article 23, paragraph (2) (Examination of Content and Recommendation of Modification Pertaining to Capital Transaction, etc.) of that Act has lapsed, or the notification of the acceptance of the recommendation has been made pursuant to the provisions of Article 23, paragraph (4) of that Act).
(3) The provisions of Article 106, paragraph (2) of the New Act as applied mutatis mutandis pursuant to Article 108, paragraph (2) of the New Act shall apply mutatis mutandis to the Shares, etc. acquired or owned by the Insurance Company Licensed under the Former Act in the cases set forth in the preceding two paragraphs.
(4) An Insurance Company Licensed under the Former Act that has notified pursuant to the provisions of paragraph (1) or (2) shall be deemed to have received the authorization set forth in Article 108, paragraph (1) of the New Act as of the Effective Date.

(Transitional Measures concerning Required Documents for the Minister of Finance)
Article 51　The provisions of Article 110 of the New Act shall apply to the business report prescribed in paragraph (1) of that Article pertaining to the business years that start on or after the Effective Date; with regard to the documents set forth in Article 82, paragraph (1) of the Former Act pertaining to the business years that started before the Effective Date, the provisions then in force shall remain applicable.

(Transitional Measures for Public Inspection of Explanatory Documents on

Business and Property Status)
Article 52 The provisions of Article 111 of the New Act shall apply to the explanatory documents prescribed in that Article pertaining to the business years that start on or after the Effective Date.

(Transitional Measures for Special Provisions on Valuation of Shares)
Article 53 (1) The provisions of Article 112 of the New Act shall apply to the valuation of shares pertaining to the business years that start on or after the Effective Date; with regard to the valuation of shares pertaining to the business years that started before the Effective Date, the provisions then in force shall remain applicable.
(2) The reserves set forth in Article 84, paragraph (2) of the Former Act in existence at the time when this Act enters into force pertaining to an Insurance Company Licensed under the Former Act or the reserves set forth in paragraph (2) of that Article to which the provisions then in force are to remain applicable pursuant to the provisions of the preceding paragraph shall be deemed to have been set aside as the reserves set forth in Article 112, paragraph (2) of the New Act to be prescribed by an Ordinance of the Ministry of Finance.

(Transitional Measures for Amortization of Incorporation Expenditures and Business Expenditures)
Article 54 For the purpose of applying the provisions of Article 113, paragraph (1) of the New Act to any amount of the incorporation expenditures prescribed in Article 85, paragraph (1) of the Former Act or the business expenditures for the initial five years pertaining to an Insurance Company Licensed under the Former Act that has not been amortized by the time when this Act enters into force, such amount shall be deemed to have been credited to assets on the balance sheet pursuant to the provisions of Article 113, paragraph (1) of the New Act.

(Transitional Measures for Policy Dividend)
Article 55 The provisions of Article 114 of the New Act shall apply to any distribution of the policy dividend prescribed in paragraph (1) of that Article pertaining to the business years that start on or after the Effective Date.

(Transitional Measures for Price Fluctuation Reserve)
Article 56 (1) The provisions of Article 115 of the New Act shall apply to the accumulation of the price fluctuation reserves set forth in paragraph (1) of that Article pertaining to the business years that start on or after the Effective Date; with regard to the accumulation of the reserves set forth in Article 86 of the Former Act pertaining to the business years that started before the Effective Date, the provisions then in force shall remain applicable.
(2) The reserves set forth in Article 86 of the Former Act in existence at the time when this Act enters into force pertaining to an Insurance Company Licensed under the Former Act and the reserves set forth in that Article to which the provisions then in force are to remain applicable pursuant to the provisions of the preceding paragraph shall be deemed to have been set aside as the price fluctuation reserves set forth in Article 115, paragraph (1) of the New Act.
(3) Where the amount of reserves as set forth in Article 86 of the Former Act that are deemed to have been set aside as the price fluctuation reserves set forth in Article 115, paragraph (1) of the New Act pursuant to the provisions of the preceding paragraph exceeds the amount set forth in Article 115, paragraph (1) of the New Act to be calculated pursuant to the provisions of the applicable Ordinance of the Ministry of Fi-

nance, necessary particulars in accounting for such excess amount for settlement purposes shall be prescribed by the Ordinance of the Ministry of Finance.

(Transitional Measures for Policy Reserve)
Article 57 (1) The provisions of Article 116 of the New Act shall apply to the accumulation of the policy reserves set forth in paragraph (1) of that Article pertaining to the business years that start on or after the Effective Date; with regard to the accumulation of the policy reserves set forth in Article 88, paragraph (1) of the Former Act pertaining to the business years that started before the Effective Date, the provisions then in force shall remain applicable.
(2) The policy reserves set forth in Article 88, paragraph (1) in existence at the time when this Act enters into force pertaining to an Insurance Company Licensed under the Former Act and the reserves set forth in that paragraph to which the provisions then in force are to remain applicable pursuant to the provisions of the preceding paragraph shall be deemed to have been set aside as the policy reserves set forth in Article 116, paragraph (1) of the New Act.

(Transitional Measures for Reserve for Outstanding Claims)
Article 58 The provisions of Article 117 of the New Act shall apply to the accumulation of the reserves for outstanding claims set forth in paragraph (1) of that Article pertaining to the business years that start on or after the Effective Date.

(Transitional Measures for Special Accounts)
Article 59 Where an Insurance Company Licensed under the Former Act has created, by the time when this Act enters into force, a Special Account for the assets corresponding to the amount of the policy reserves set forth in Article 88, paragraph (1) of the Former Act pertaining to the insurance contracts set forth in Article 118, paragraph (1) of the New Act to be specified by an Ordinance of the Ministry of Finance for the purpose of ensuring separate accounting from other assets, such separate account shall be deemed to be the separate account created pursuant to the provisions of Article 118, paragraph (1) of the New Act.

(Transitional Measures for Appointment of Actuary, etc.)
Article 60 (1) The provisions of Article 120 of the New Act shall not apply to an Insurance Company Licensed under the Former Act that is deemed to have obtained the non-life insurance business license set forth in Article 3, paragraph (5) of the New Act pursuant to the provisions of Article 3 of the Supplementary Provisions, for a period of three months counting from the Effective Date.
(2) An actuary that has been appointed by the time when this Act enters into force pursuant to the provisions of Article 89, paragraph (1) of the Former Act shall be deemed to be the actuary appointed on the Effective Date pursuant to the provisions of Article 120, paragraph (1) of the New Act.
(3) The provisions of Article 120, paragraph (2) of the New Act shall not apply to an actuary who is deemed to be appointed pursuant to the provisions of paragraph (1) of that Article pursuant to the provisions of the preceding paragraph, for a period of two years counting from the Effective Date.

(Transitional Measures for Actuary's Duties)
Article 61 The provisions of Article 121 of the New Act shall apply to the duties of an actuary concerning the particulars for business years that start on or after the Effective Date; with regard to the duties of an actuary concerning the particulars for busi-

ness years that started before the Effective Date of an Insurance Company Licensed under the Former Act that is deemed to have obtained the life insurance business license set forth in Article 3, paragraph (4) of the New Act pursuant to the provisions of Article 3 of the Supplementary Provisions, the provisions then in force shall remain applicable. In this case, the competent minister prescribed in Article 90, paragraph (2) of the Former Act to whom the provisions then in force shall remain applicable shall be the Prime Minister.

(Transitional Measures for Dismissal of Actuary)
Article 62 The provisions of Article 122 of the New Act shall apply to the dismissal of an actuary for any of the actions taken on or after the Effective Date; with regard to the dismissal of an actuary for any of the neglect or actions taken before the Effective Date, the provisions then in force shall remain applicable. In this case, the competent minister prescribed in Article 89, paragraph (2) of the Former Act to whom the provisions then in force shall remain applicable shall be the Prime Minister.

(Transitional Measures for Authorization, etc. of Modification Pertaining to Statement of Business Procedures, etc.)
Article 63 (1) Where an Insurance Company Licensed under the Former Act has applied, by the time this Act enters into force, for the authorization of the competent minister pertaining to the modification of particulars prescribed in any of the documents listed in Article 1, paragraph (2), items (ii) to (iv) inclusive of the Former Act pursuant to the provisions of Article 10, paragraph (1) of the Former Act, such application shall be deemed to be the application for the authorization of the Minister of Finance set forth in Article 123, paragraph (1) of the New Act. In this case, the particulars to be modified shall be deemed to be outside the scope of the particulars set forth in that paragraph to be prescribed by an Ordinance of the Ministry of Finance even when such particulars do fall under the particulars prescribed by the Ordinance of the Ministry of Finance set forth in that paragraph.
(2) Where an Insurance Company Licensed under the Former Act has applied, by the time this Act enters into force, for the authorization of the competent minister pertaining to the modification of particulars prescribed in the document listed in Article 1, paragraph (2), item (i) of the Former Act pursuant to the provisions of Article 10, paragraph (1) of the Former Act, such application shall be deemed to be an application subject to the authorization set forth in Article 126 of the New Act when the particulars to be modified fall under any of the particulars listed in the items of that Article.
(3) In the case prescribed in the preceding paragraph, when the particulars to be modified do not fall under any of the particulars listed in the items of Article 126 of the New Act, the modification shall take effect at the time when this Act enters into force, and the application set forth in Article 127 of the New Act shall be deemed to be filed as of the Effective Date pertaining to the particulars listed in item (iii) of that Article.

(Transitional Measures Concerning Suspension of Business, etc.)
Article 64 (1) Any order for the suspension of business under Article 12, paragraph (1) of the Former Act issued prior to the Effective Date shall be deemed to be the disposition ordering total or partial suspension of business prescribed in, and made under, Article 132 of the New Act.
(2) Where any notification and public notice were given under Article 12, paragraph (3) of the Former Act before the Effective Date pertaining to an order for the suspension of business under paragraph (1) of that Article, the disposition for ordering total or partial suspension of business prescribed in Article 132 of the New Act may be made under

that Article by continuing the procedure as prescribed in Article 12, paragraphs (2) and (4) of the Former Act on and after the Effective Date.

(Transitional Measures Concerning Rescission of License, etc.)
Article 65 (1) For the purpose of applying the provisions of item (i) or (iii) of Article 133 of the New Act, any action under Article 12, paragraph (1) of the Former Act committed before the Effective Date by an Insurance Company Licensed under the Former Act shall be deemed to be the action prescribed in item (i) or (iii) of Article 133 of the New Act.
(2) Where any notification and public notice were given under Article 12, paragraph (3) of the Former Act before the Effective Date pertaining to a disposition under paragraph (1) of that Article, a disposition under Article 133 of the New Act that is equivalent to the original disposition may be made by continuing the procedure as prescribed in Article 12, paragraph (4) of the Former Act on and after the Effective Date.

(Transitional Measures for Portfolio Transfers of Insurance Contracts)
Article 66 The provisions of Part II, Chapter VII, Section 1 of the New Act shall apply to the transfer of insurance contracts pertaining to a resolution at a shareholders' meeting, or a general members' council meeting or a General Representative Members' Council Meeting set forth in Article 42, paragraph (1) of the New Act (including an administrative organ prescribed in Article 51, paragraph (1) of the Former Act which is deemed to be a General Representative Members' Council Meeting as set forth in Article 42, paragraph (1) of the New Act pursuant to the provisions of Article 29 of the Supplementary Provisions) (hereinafter referred to as the "Shareholders' Meeting, etc."), adopted in a session for which the convocation notice set forth in Article 232, paragraph (1) (Convocation Notice) of the Commercial Code (including the cases where it is applied mutatis mutandis pursuant to Articles 41 and 49 of the New Act) is given on or after the Effective Date; with regard to the transfer of insurance contracts pertaining to a resolution of the Shareholders' Meeting, etc. adopted in a session for which the convocation notice set forth in Article 232, paragraph (1) of the Commercial Code (including the cases where it is applied mutatis mutandis pursuant to Article 54 of the Former Act (including the cases where it is applied mutatis mutandis pursuant to Article 51, paragraph (2) of the Former Act)) was given before the Effective Date, the provisions then in force shall remain applicable.

(Transitional Measures for Entrustment of Business and Property Administration)
Article 67 For the purpose of applying the provisions of Article 146 to 150 inclusive of the New Act, those contracts set forth in Article 92, paragraph (1) of the Former Act and authorized under Article 93 of the Former Act which are in force at the time when this Act enters into force shall be deemed to be the contracts set forth in Article 144, paragraph (1) of the New Act.

(Transitional Measures for Arrangement Proceedings)
Article 68 The provisions of the Commercial Code on corporate arrangement as applied mutatis mutandis pursuant to Article 151 of the New Act shall apply where the application or notification set forth in Article 381 (Initiation of Arrangement Proceedings) of said Code is made on or after the Effective Date; where the application or notification set forth in Article 381 of the Commercial Code as applied mutatis mutandis pursuant to Article 78 of the Former Act was made before the Effective Date, the provisions then in force shall remain applicable.

(Transitional Measures Concerning Dissolution, etc.)

Article 69 The provisions of Part II, Chapter VIII, Section 2 of the New Act shall apply to the dissolution of an Insurance Company on the grounds prescribed in Article 152 of the New Act that emerge on or after the Effective Date; with regard to the dissolution of an Insurance Company under the Former Act on the grounds prescribed in Article 108, paragraph (1) of the Former Act that emerged before the Effective Date, the provisions then in force shall remain applicable.

(Transitional Measures for Merger)

Article 70 The provisions of Part II, Chapter VIII, Section 3 of the New Act shall apply to any merger pertaining to a resolution of the Shareholders' Meeting, etc. adopted in a session for which the convocation notice set forth in Article 232, paragraph (1) (Convocation Notice) of the Commercial Code (including the cases where it is applied mutatis mutandis pursuant to Articles 41 and 49 of the New Act) is given on or after the Effective Date; with regard to any merger pertaining to a resolution of the Shareholders' Meeting, etc. adopted in a session for which the convocation notice set forth in Article 232, paragraph (1) of the Commercial Code (including the cases where it is applied mutatis mutandis pursuant to Article 54 of the Former Act (including the cases where it is applied mutatis mutandis pursuant to Article 51, paragraph (2) of the Former Act)) was given before the Effective Date, the provisions then in force shall remain applicable.

(Transitional Measures for Liquidation Procedure, etc.)

Article 71 (1) The provisions of Part II, Chapter VIII, Section 4 of the New Act shall apply to any liquidation pertaining to the dissolution of an Insurance Company on the grounds prescribed in Article 152 of the New Act that emerge on or after the Effective Date; with regard to any liquidation pertaining to the dissolution of an Insurance Company under the Former Act on the grounds prescribed in Article 108, paragraph (1) of the Former Act that emerged before the Effective Date, the provisions then in force shall remain applicable.

(2) The provisions of Article 267 to 268-3 inclusive (Lawsuit to Hold Directors Accountable) of the Commercial Code as applied mutatis mutandis pursuant to Article 430, paragraph (2) (Provisions for Mutatis Mutandis Application Concerning Liquidation) of said Code as applied mutatis mutandis pursuant to Article 183, paragraph (1) of the New Act shall apply to any request for filing the action set forth in Article 267, paragraph (1) of the Commercial Code as applied mutatis mutandis pursuant to Article 430, paragraph (2) of said Code as applied mutatis mutandis pursuant to Article 183, paragraph (1) of the New Act or any filing of the action set forth in Article 267, paragraph (3) of the Commercial Code as applied mutatis mutandis pursuant to Article 430, paragraph (2) of said Code as applied mutatis mutandis pursuant to Article 183, paragraph (1) of the New Act, made by members on or after the Effective Date; with regard to any request for filing the action set forth in Article 57, paragraph (1) of the Former Act as applied mutatis mutandis pursuant to Article 77 of the Former Act or any filing of the action set forth in Article 267, paragraph (3) of the Commercial Code as applied mutatis mutandis pursuant to Article 57, paragraph (2) of the Former Act, made by members before the Effective Date, the provisions then in force shall remain applicable.

(Transitional Measures for Business License Pertaining to Foreign Insurance Company, etc.)

Article 72 (1) A person that has obtained by the time when this Act enters into force the license of the Minister of Finance set forth in Article 3, paragraph (1) of the Former Foreign Insurance Providers Act (including a person who is deemed to have obtained the license of the Minister of Finance set forth in that paragraph pursuant to the provisions of paragraph (3) or (5) of the Supplementary Provisions to the Former Foreign Insurance Providers Act) shall be deemed to obtain the license of the Minister of Finance set forth in Article 185, paragraph (1) of the New Act at the time when this Act enters into force.

(2) The license of the Minister of Finance set forth in Article 185, paragraph (1) of the New Act that the person prescribed in the preceding paragraph (hereinafter referred to as "Foreign Insurance Company, etc. Licensed under the Former Foreign Insurance Providers Act") shall be deemed to have received pursuant to the provisions of that paragraph shall be the foreign life insurance business license set forth in Article 185, paragraph (4) of the New Act or the foreign non-life insurance business license set forth in paragraph (5) of that Article, according to whether the person is the foreign life insurance provider or foreign non-life insurance provider set forth in Article 2, paragraph (1) of the Former Foreign Insurance Providers Act.

(Transitional Measures for Written Application for License, etc.)
Article 73 (1) The particulars listed in the items of Article 4, paragraph (1) of the Former Foreign Insurance Providers Act which are described in the written application set forth in that paragraph pertaining to a Foreign Insurance Company, etc. Licensed under the Former Foreign Insurance Providers Act (or, where the notification set forth in Article 7, paragraph (1) of the Former Foreign Insurance Providers Act has been made, such particulars as modified by the notification) shall be deemed to be the particulars listed in the corresponding items of Article 187, paragraph (1) of the New Act which are described in the written application for license set forth in that paragraph.

(2) Those documents listed in Article 4, paragraph (1), items (i) to (v) inclusive of the Former Foreign Insurance Providers Act pertaining to a Foreign Insurance Company, etc. Licensed under the Former Foreign Insurance Providers Act which have been submitted to the Minister of Finance by the time when this Act enters into force shall be deemed to be the documents listed in the corresponding items of Article 187, paragraph (3) of the New Act (or, for the document listed in item (iv) or (v) of Article 4, paragraph (4) of the Former Foreign Insurance Providers Act, the document listed in Article 187, paragraph (3), item (iv) of the New Act).

(Transitional Measures for Condition for License)
Article 74 Where the content of Insurance Business in Japan as prescribed in Article 1 of the Former Foreign Insurance Providers Act, conducted by a Foreign Insurance Company, etc. Licensed under the Former Foreign Insurance Providers Act at the time when this Act enters into force falls under the case prescribed in Article 188, paragraph (1) of the New Act, the condition set forth in Article 188, paragraph (1) of the New Act shall be attached to that license of the Minister of Finance set forth in Article 185, paragraph (1) of the New Act which the person shall be deemed to obtain at the time when this Act enters into force pursuant to the provisions of Article 72 of the Supplementary Provisions.

(Transitional Measures for Deposit by Foreign Insurance Company, etc.)
Article 75 (1) The things deposited by a Foreign Insurance Company, etc. Licensed under the Former Foreign Insurance Providers Act pursuant to the provisions of Article 8 of the Former Foreign Insurance Providers Act by the time this Act enters into force

shall be deemed to have been deposited under Article 190, paragraph (1) of the New Act.

(2) For the purpose of applying the provisions of Article 190, paragraph (8) of the New Act to the Foreign Insurance Company, etc. Licensed under the Former Foreign Insurance Providers Act set forth in the preceding paragraph, the amount to be specified by Cabinet Office Ordinance as the amount of deposits pertaining to those things deposited under the preceding paragraph that are deemed to have been deposited under paragraph (1) of that Article pursuant to the provisions of the preceding paragraph shall be deemed to be the amount set forth in paragraph (1) of that Article to be specified by Cabinet Order under paragraph (8) of that Article, for a period of five years counting from the Effective Date.

(3) In the case set forth in paragraph (1), any right of priority enjoyed by a person prescribed in Article 9, paragraph (1) or (2) of the Former Foreign Insurance Providers Act on the things deposited under Article 8 of the Former Foreign Insurance Providers Act at the time this Act enters into force shall be deemed to be the right prescribed in Article 190, paragraph (6) of the New Act.

(4) In the case referred to in the preceding paragraph, any special provisions for Article 190, paragraph (6) of the New Act and other particulars necessary for applying the provisions of that Article where the Foreign Insurance Company, etc. Licensed under the Former Foreign Insurance Providers Act is a Foreign Mutual Company shall be specified by Cabinet Order.

(Transitional Measures for Representative Person in Japan, etc.)
Article 76 The provisions of Article 192, paragraphs (1) and (2) of the New Act shall also apply to the particulars that arose before the Effective Date. In this case, for the purpose of applying the provisions of Article 192, paragraphs (1) and (2) of the New Act, the notification and public notice set forth in Article 7, paragraph (1) of the Former Foreign Insurance Providers Act shall be deemed to be the public notice set forth in Article 192, paragraph (2) of the New Act, provided that they be given before the Effective Date.

(Transitional Measures for Mutatis Mutandis Application of Provisions of Commercial Code on Business Offices of Foreign Company Pertaining to Foreign Mutual Company)
Article 77 A Foreign Mutual Company that has obtained the license set forth in Article 3, paragraph (1) of the Former Foreign Insurance Providers Act by the time when this Act enters into force shall be deemed to continue its transactions in Japan pursuant to the provisions of Article 479, paragraph (1) (Business Offices of Foreign Company) of the Commercial Code as applied mutatis mutandis pursuant to Article 193 of the New Act; the particulars registered by the Foreign Mutual Company pursuant to the provisions of Article 45, paragraph (3) (Registration of Establishment of Juridical Person) and Article 46 (Matters to be Registered upon Registration of Formation and Registration of Change) of the Civil Code as applied mutatis mutandis pursuant to Article 49, paragraph (1) (Registration of Foreign Juridical Person) of said Code shall be deemed to have been registered pursuant to the provisions of Article 479, paragraphs (3) and (4) of the Commercial Code as applied mutatis mutandis pursuant to Article 193 of the New Act.

(Transitional Measures for Submission of Closing Financial Statements of the Head Office or Principal Office, and Retention and Inspection, etc. of the Articles of Incorporation, etc.)

Article 78 (1) The provisions of Article 195, and Article 196, paragraphs (2) and (4) (limited to the segment pertaining to the documents prescribed in Article 195 of the New Act) of the New Act shall apply to the documents prescribed in Article 195 of the New Act pertaining to the business years of a Foreign Insurance Company, etc. that end on or after the Effective Date; with regard to the documents prescribed in Article 12 of the Former Foreign Insurance Providers Act pertaining to the business years that ended before the Effective Date, the provisions then in force shall remain applicable. In this case, those documents set forth in that Article to be submitted pursuant to the provisions of that Article to which the provisions then in force shall remain applicable shall be submitted to the Prime Minister.

(2) The articles of incorporation or any equivalent document, and the members list in Japan, kept by the Representative Person in Japan of a Foreign Insurance Company, etc. Licensed under the Former Foreign Insurance Providers Act at the time when this Act enters into force, pursuant to the provisions of Article 17, paragraph (1) of the Former Foreign Insurance Providers Act, shall be deemed to be kept pursuant to the provisions of Article 196, paragraph (1) of the New Act.

(3) The provisions of paragraphs (3), (4) (limited to the segment pertaining to paragraph (3) of that Article) and (5) of Article 196 of the New Act shall apply to the documents prescribed in paragraph (3) of that Article pertaining to the business years in Japan that start on or after the Effective Date; with regard to the documents prescribed in Article 17, paragraph (1) of the Former Foreign Insurance Providers Act (other than the documents prescribed in the preceding two paragraphs) pertaining to the business years that started before the Effective Date, the provisions then in force shall remain applicable.

(Transitional Measures for Obligation of Foreign Insurance Company, etc. to Hold Assets in Japan)
Article 79 For the purpose of applying the provisions of Article 197 of the New Act to a Foreign Company, etc. Licensed under the Former Foreign Insurance Providers Act, the term "sum total" in that Article shall be deemed to be replaced with "sum total multiplied by the proportion to be specified by Cabinet Office Ordinance," for a period of five years counting from the Effective Date.

(Transitional Measures for Acts, etc of Manager, etc of Foreign Mutual Company, etc.)
Article 80 (1) For the purpose of applying the provisions of Articles 38 to 43 inclusive (Commercial Employee) of the Commercial Code as applied mutatis mutandis pursuant to Article 198, paragraph (1) of the New Act to actions prior to the Effective Date of the manager appointed by a Foreign Mutual Company that has obtained the license set forth in Article 3, paragraph (1) of the Former Foreign Insurance Providers Act by the time this Act enters into force, pursuant to the provisions of Article 37 (Appointment of Manager) of the Commercial Code as applied mutatis mutandis pursuant to Article 18 of the Former Foreign Insurance Providers Act (including the employee prescribed in Article 42 (Apparent Manager) or Article 43 (Employee with Certain Types of Entrustment or Specific Entrustment) as applied mutatis mutandis pursuant to Article 18 of the Former Foreign Insurance Providers Act), and other particulars involving said manager, such actions and other particulars shall be deemed to be particulars involving the manager appointed by a Foreign Mutual Company under the New Act pursuant to the provisions of Article 37 of the Commercial Code as applied mutatis mutandis pursuant to Article 198, paragraph (1) of the New Act (including the employee prescribed in Article 42 or 43 of said Code as applied mutatis mutandis pursuant to

that paragraph).
(2) For the purpose of applying the provisions of Article 46 to 48 inclusive, 50 and 51 (Commercial Agent) of the Commercial Code as applied mutatis mutandis pursuant to Article 198, paragraph (1) of the New Act, those actions and other particulars prescribed in Articles 46 to 48 inclusive, 50 and 51 of the Commercial Code as applied mutatis mutandis pursuant to Article 18 of the Former Foreign Insurance Providers Act which took place before the Effective Date concerning a Foreign Mutual Company under the Former Foreign Insurance Providers Act shall be deemed to be actions and other particulars of a Foreign Mutual Company under the New Act, which took place as of the original dates.

(Transitional Measures for Commercial Books, etc of Foreign Mutual Company)
Article 81 The books and other documents prepared prior to the Effective Date by a Foreign Mutual Company under the Former Foreign Insurance Providers Act in existence at the time when this Act enters into force, pursuant to the provisions of Part I, Chapter V (Commercial Books) of the Commercial Code as applied mutatis mutandis pursuant to Article 18 of the Former Foreign Insurance Providers Act, shall be deemed to have been prepared by a Foreign Mutual Company under the New Act as of the dates of the original preparation, pursuant to the corresponding provisions of Part I, Chapter V of the Commercial Code as applied mutatis mutandis pursuant to Article 198 of the New Act.

(Transitional Measures for Mutatis Mutandis Application of Provisions on Business and Accounting, etc. Pertaining to Foreign Insurance Companies, etc.)
Article 82 (1) Those Foreign Insurance Companies, etc. Licensed under the Former Foreign Insurance Providers Act, that conduct business set forth in Article 98, paragraph (1), item (i) of the New Act as applied mutatis mutandis pursuant to Article 199 of the New Act at the time when this Act enters into force shall notify the Minister of Finance of the content of such business within six months from the Effective Date.
(2) Those Foreign Insurance Companies, etc. Licensed under the Former Foreign Insurance Providers Act which have made the notification set forth in the preceding paragraph shall be deemed to have received as of the Effective Date the authorization set forth in Article 98, paragraph (2) of the New Act as applied mutatis mutandis pursuant to Article 199 of the New Act.

Article 83 The provisions of Article 110 of the New Act as applied mutatis mutandis pursuant to Article 199 of the New Act shall apply to the business report prescribed in Article 110, paragraph (1) of the New Act pertaining to the business years in Japan that start on or after the Effective Date; with regard to the business report prescribed in Article 11, paragraph (1) of the Former Foreign Insurance Providers Act pertaining to the business years in Japan that started before the Effective Date, the provisions then in force shall remain applicable. In the cases where the provisions then in force shall remain applicable, the business report set forth in that paragraph shall be submitted to the Prime Minister.

Article 84 The provisions of Article 111 of the New Act as applied mutatis mutandis pursuant to Article 199 of the New Act shall apply to the explanatory documents prescribed in Article 111 of the New Act pertaining to the business years in Japan that start on or after the Effective Date.

Article 85 The provisions of Article 112 of the New Act as applied mutatis mutandis pursuant to Article 199 of the New Act shall apply to the valuation of shares pertaining to the business years in Japan that start on or after the Effective Date.

Article 86 The provisions of Article 114 of the New Act as applied mutatis mutandis pursuant to Article 199 of the New Act shall apply to any distribution of the policy dividend prescribed in Article 114, paragraph (1) of the New Act pertaining to the business years in Japan that start on or after the Effective Date.

Article 87 The provisions of Article 115 of the New Act as applied mutatis mutandis pursuant to Article 199 of the New Act shall apply to the accumulation of the price fluctuation reserves set forth in Article 115, paragraph (1) of the New Act pertaining to the business years in Japan that start on or after the Effective Date.

Article 88 (1) The provisions of Article 116 of the New Act as applied mutatis mutandis pursuant to Article 199 of the New Act shall apply to the accumulation of the policy reserves set forth in Article 116, paragraph (1) of the New Act pertaining to the business years in Japan that start on or after the Effective Date; with regard to the accumulation of the policy reserves set forth in Article 13 of the Former Foreign Insurance Providers Act pertaining to the business years in Japan that started before the Effective Date, the provisions then in force shall remain applicable.
(2) The policy reserves set forth in Article 13 of the Former Foreign Insurance Providers Act in existence at the time when this Act enters into force pertaining to a Foreign Insurance Company, etc. Licensed under the Former Foreign Insurance Providers Act and the policy reserves set forth in that Article to which the provisions then in force are to remain applicable pursuant to the provisions of the preceding paragraph shall be deemed to have been set aside in Japan as policy reserves pursuant to the provisions of Article 116 of the New Act as applied mutatis mutandis pursuant to Article 199 of the New Act.

Article 89 (1) The provisions of Article 117 as applied mutatis mutandis pursuant to Article 199 of the New Act shall apply to the accumulation of the reserves for outstanding claims set forth in Article 117, paragraph (1) of the New Act pertaining to the business years in Japan that start on or after the Effective Date; with regard to the accumulation of the reserves for outstanding claims set forth in Article 13 of the Former Foreign Insurance Providers Act pertaining to the business years in Japan that started before the Effective Date, the provisions then in force shall remain applicable.
(2) The reserves for outstanding claims set forth in Article 13 of the Former Foreign Insurance Providers Act in existence at the time when this Act enters into force pertaining to a Foreign Insurance Company, etc. Licensed under the Former Foreign Insurance Providers Act and the reserves for outstanding claims set forth in that Article to which the provisions then in force are to remain applicable pursuant to the provisions of the preceding paragraph shall be deemed to have been set aside in Japan as reserves for outstanding claims pursuant to the provisions of Article 117 of the New Act as applied mutatis mutandis pursuant to Article 199 of the New Act.

Article 90 Where a Foreign Insurance Company, etc Licensed under the Former Foreign Insurance Providers Act in existence at the time when this Act enters into force has created a Special Account to ensure separate accounting from other property for the property corresponding to the amount of the policy reserves set forth in Article 13 of the Former Foreign Insurance Providers Act pertaining to the insurance contracts set forth in Article 118, paragraph (1) of the New Act as applied mutatis mutandis pursuant to Article 199 of the New Act to be specified by an Ordinance of the Ministry of Finance, such Special Account shall be deemed to be the Special Account created pursuant to the provisions of Article 118, paragraph (1) of the New Act as applied mutatis mutandis pursuant to Article 199 of the New Act.

Article 91 The provisions of Article 120 of the New Act as applied mutatis mutandis pursuant to Article 199 of the New Act shall not apply to a Foreign Insurance Company, etc. Licensed under the Former Foreign Insurance Providers Act for a period of three months counting from the Effective Date.

(Transitional Measures for Suspension of Business, etc.)
Article 92 (1) Any order for the suspension of business in Japan issued under Article 22, paragraph (1) of the Former Foreign Insurance Providers Act before the Effective Date shall be deemed to be the disposition ordering total or partial suspension of business prescribed in Article 204 of the New Act taken under that Article.

(2) Where any notification and public notice were given under Article 22, paragraph (3) of the Former Foreign Insurance Providers Act before the Effective Date pertaining to an order for the suspension of business under paragraph (1) of that Article, the disposition for ordering total or partial suspension of business prescribed in Article 204 of the New Act may be taken under that Article by continuing the procedure as prescribed in Article 22, paragraphs (2) and (4) of the Former Foreign Insurance Providers Act on and after the Effective Date.

(Transitional Measures for Rescission of License, etc.)
Article 93 (1) For the purpose of applying the provisions of Article 205 of the New Act, an action prescribed in Article 22, paragraph (1) of the Former Foreign Insurance Providers Act that was taken before the Effective Date by a Foreign Insurance Company, etc. Licensed under the Former Foreign Insurance Providers Act shall be deemed to be the action prescribed in Article 205, item (i) of the New Act.

(2) Where any notification and public notice were given under Article 22, paragraph (3) of the Former Foreign Insurance Providers Act before the Effective Date pertaining to a disposition under paragraph (1) of that Article, a disposition corresponding to such disposition may be taken under Article 205 of the New Act by continuing the procedure as prescribed in Article 22, paragraph (4) of the Former Foreign Insurance Providers Act on and after the Effective Date.

(Transitional Measures Concerning Authorization of Modification Pertaining to Statement of Business Procedures, etc.)
Article 94 Where a Foreign Insurance Company, etc. Licensed under the Former Foreign Insurance Providers Act has applied, by the time when this Act enters into force, for the authorization of the competent minister pertaining to the modification of any of the particulars prescribed in the documents listed in Article 4, paragraph (4), items (ii) to (v) inclusive of the Former Foreign Insurance Providers Act pursuant to the provisions of Article 10, paragraph (1) of the Former Act as applied mutatis mutandis pursuant to Article 19 of the Former Foreign Insurance Providers Act, such application shall be deemed to be an application for the authorization of the Minister of Finance set forth in Article 123, paragraph (1) of the New Act as applied mutatis mutandis pursuant to Article 207 of the New Act. In this case, the particulars to be modified shall be deemed to be outside the scope of the particulars set forth in that paragraph to be prescribed

by an Ordinance of the Ministry of Finance even when such particulars do fall under the particulars prescribed by the Ordinance of the Ministry of Finance set forth in that paragraph.

(Transitional Measures Concerning Portfolio Transfers of Insurance Contracts by Foreign Insurance Company, etc.)
Article 95 The provisions of Part II, Chapter VII, Section 1 of the New Act as applied mutatis mutandis pursuant to Article 210, paragraph (1) of the New Act shall apply to the transfer of insurance contracts pertaining to that written Agreement pertaining to the Agreement set forth in Article 135, paragraph (1) of the New Act as applied mutatis mutandis pursuant to Article 210, paragraph (1) of the New Act that is prepared by a Foreign Insurance Company, etc. on or after the Effective Date; with regard to the transfer of insurance contracts pertaining to that written Agreement pertaining to the Agreement set forth in Article 211, paragraph (1) of the Former Foreign Insurance Providers Act which was prepared before the Effective Date, the provisions then in force shall remain applicable.

(Transitional Measures for Liquidation of Foreign Insurance Company, etc.)
Article 96 The provisions of Article 212 of the New Act shall apply to a Foreign Insurance Company, etc. that falls under any of the items of paragraph (1) of that Article on or after the Effective Date; with regard to the foreign insurance provider set forth in Article 26, paragraph (1) of the Former Foreign Insurance Providers Act that fell under the case prescribed in that paragraph before the Effective Date, the provisions then in force shall remain applicable.

(Transitional Measures for Order to Close Business Office, etc. Issued to Secondary Office, etc. of Foreign Insurance Providers)
Article 97 Where the foreign insurance provider set forth in Article 29 of the Former Foreign Insurance Providers Act has established any secondary offices or other offices in Japan, or where a person specialized in solicitation on behalf of a foreign insurance provider has established any business offices or other offices, the provisions then in force shall remain applicable to any event before the Effective Date that fell under any of the items of Article 484, paragraph (1) (Order to Close Business Offices) of the Commercial Code as applied mutatis mutandis pursuant to Article 29 of the Former Foreign Insurance Providers Act.

(Transitional Measures for Registry of Foreign Mutual Insurance Companies)
Article 98 The registry of foreign mutual insurance companies set forth in Article 31 of the Former Foreign Insurance Providers Act shall be deemed to be the registry of foreign mutual insurance companies prescribed in Article 214 of the New Act.

(Transitional Measures for Mutatis Mutandis Application of Commercial Registration Act Pertaining to Foreign Mutual Company)
Article 99 Any disposition, procedure or other action taken prior to the Effective Date under the provisions of the Commercial Registration Act as applied mutatis mutandis pursuant to Article 33 of the Former Foreign Insurance Providers Act shall be deemed to be the corresponding action under the provisions of the Commercial Registration Act as applied mutatis mutandis pursuant to Article 216, paragraph (1) of the New Act.

(Transitional Measures for Mutatis Mutandis Application of Act on Procedures for Non-Contentious Cases Pertaining to Foreign Mutual Company)

Article 100 Any procedure commenced before the Effective Date under the provisions of the Act on Procedures for Non-Contentious Cases as applied mutatis mutandis pursuant to Article 33 of the Former Foreign Insurance Providers Act shall be deemed to be a procedure under the provisions of the Act on Procedures for Non-Contentious Cases as applied mutatis mutandis pursuant to Article 217 of the New Act.

(Transitional Measures Concerning Notification of Establishment of Foreign Insurer's Representative Office, etc.)

Article 101 That foreign insurer prescribed in Article 2, paragraph (1) of the Former Foreign Insurers Act which has established an office falling under Article 218, paragraph (1), item (i) of the New Act by the time this Act enters into force and that is not a Foreign Insurance Company, etc. Licensed under the Former Foreign Insurers Act shall, within six months from the Effective Date, notify the content of the business listed in (a) or (b) of that item concerning such office, the location of the office to conduct business and other particulars set forth in Article 218, paragraph (1) of the New Act to be prescribed by an Ordinance of the Ministry of Finance, unless it obtains, in the meantime, the license set forth in Article 185, paragraph (1) of the New Act, or has abolished such office or the business listed in (a) or (b) of that item. In this case, such notification shall be deemed to be notification made under Article 218, paragraph (1) of the New Act.

(Transitional Measures for Order for Suspension of Business)

Article 102 (1) Any order for the suspension of business under Article 100, paragraph (1) of the Former Act or order for the suspension of business in Japan under Article 23, paragraph (1) of the Former Foreign Insurance Providers Act, issued before the Effective Date, shall be deemed to be the disposition ordering total or partial suspension of business prescribed in Article 241 of the New Act, issued under that Article.

(2) Where any notification and public notice under Article 12, paragraph (3) of the Former Act as applied mutatis mutandis pursuant to Article 100, paragraph (3) of the Former Act were given before the Effective Date pertaining to an order for the suspension of business issued under paragraph (1) of that Article, or where any notification and public notice under Article 22, paragraph (3) of the Former Insurance Providers Act as applied mutatis mutandis pursuant to Article 23, paragraph (3) of the Former Foreign Insurance Providers Act were given before the Effective Date pertaining to an order for the suspension of business in Japan issued under paragraph (1) of that Article, the disposition ordering total or partial suspension of business prescribed in Article 241 of the New Act may be made under that Article by continuing the procedure as prescribed in Article 12, paragraph (4) of the Former Act as applied mutatis mutandis pursuant to Article 100, paragraphs (2) and (3) of the Former Act, or in Article 22, paragraph (4) of the Former Foreign Insurance Providers Act as applied mutatis mutandis pursuant to Article 23, paragraphs (2) and (3) of the Former Foreign Insurance Providers Act, on and after the Effective Date.

(Transitional Measures for Order for Administration of Business and Property)

Article 103 (1) Any order for the administration of business and property under Article 100, paragraph (1) of the Former Act, and order for the administration of business and property in Japan under Article 23, paragraph (1) of the Former Foreign Insurance Providers Act, issued before the Effective Date, shall be deemed to be the disposition ordering the administration of business and property by an insurance administrator prescribed in Article 241 of the New Act, made under that Article; the insurance ad-

ministrator pertaining to the original order for the administration of business and property or order for the administration of business and property in Japan shall be deemed to be the insurance administrator pertaining to the disposition ordering the administration of business and property.
(2) Where any notification and public notice under Article 12, paragraph (3) of the Former Act as applied mutandis pursuant to Article 100, paragraph (3) of the Former Act were given before the Effective Date pertaining to an order for the administration of business and property issued under paragraph (1) of that Article, or where any notification and public notice under Article 22, paragraph (3) of the Former Foreign Insurance Providers Act as applied mutatis mutandis pursuant to Article 23, paragraph (3) of the Former Foreign Insurance Providers Act were given before the Effective Date pertaining to an order for the administration of business and property in Japan issued under paragraph (1) of that Article, the disposition ordering the administration of business and property by an insurance administrator prescribed in Article 241 of the New Act may be made under that Article by continuing the procedure as prescribed in Article 12, paragraph (4) of the Former Act as applied mutatis mutandis pursuant to Article 100, paragraphs (2) and (3) of the Former Act, or in Article 22, paragraph (4) of the Former Foreign Insurance Providers Act as applied mutatis mutandis pursuant to Article 23, paragraphs (2) and (3) of the Former Foreign Insurance Providers Act, on and after the Effective Date.

(Transitional Measures for Order for Transfer of Insurance Contracts)
Article 104 (1) Where any notification and public notice under Article 12, paragraph (3) of the Former Act as applied mutatis mutandis pursuant to Article 100, paragraph (3) of the Former Act were given before the Effective Date pertaining to an order for the transfer of contracts issued under paragraph (1) of that Article, or where any notification and public notice under Article 22, paragraph (3) of the Former Foreign Insurance Providers Act as applied mutatis mutandis pursuant to Article 23, paragraph (3) of the Former Foreign Insurance Providers Act were given before the Effective Date pertaining to an order for the transfer of insurance contracts in Japan issued under paragraph (1) of that Article, the provisions of Article 100 and Article 121 to 126 of the Former Act, and Article 23 of the Former Foreign Insurance Providers Act shall remain in force with regard to the transfer of contracts or transfer of insurance contracts in Japan pertaining to such orders, until the day before the date of the Designation set forth in Article 259, paragraph (1) of the New Act.
(2) For the purpose of applying the provisions of Article 100, paragraph (3), Article 121, paragraph (5), Article 122, paragraphs (2) and (3) and Article 126 of the Former Act, and Article 23, paragraphs (3) and (4) of the Former Foreign Insurance Providers Act, which are to remain in force pursuant to the provisions of the preceding paragraph, the provisions of Article 12, paragraphs (3) and (4), Article 103, Article 104, Article 109, the proviso to Article 111, paragraph (2), Article 114, Article 115, Article 117, Article 118 and Article 120 of the Former Act, and Article 22, paragraphs (3) and (4) of the Former Foreign Insurance Providers Act shall remain in force. In this case, the term "Article 39, paragraph (2) of this Act" in Article 109 of the Former Act shall be deemed to be replaced with "Article 62, paragraph (2) of the Insurance Business Act (Act No. 105 of 1995)."
(3) For the purpose of applying penal provisions to actions taken before the period prescribed in paragraph (1) lapses, the provisions prescribed in that paragraph, which are to remain in force pursuant to the provisions of that paragraph, shall remain in force even after the period prescribed in that paragraph has lapsed.
(4) Where the provisions of Article 100 and Article 121 to 126 of the Former Act, or Arti-

cle 23 of the Former Foreign Insurance Providers Act, which are to remain in force pursuant to the provisions of paragraph (1), apply, the provisions of Part II, Chapter VII, Section 1 of the New Act (including the cases where they are applied mutatis mutandis pursuant to Article 210, paragraph (1) of the New Act) shall not apply, notwithstanding the provisions of Articles 66 and 95 of the Supplementary Provisions.

(Deleted)
Article 105 Deleted.

(Deleted)
Article 106 Deleted.

(Transitional Measures Concerning Lapse of License)
Article 107 The provisions of Article 272, paragraph (1), item (v) of the New Act shall apply to the license of the Prime Minister set forth in Article 3, paragraph (1) of the New Act, and the license of the Prime Minister set forth in Article 185, paragraph (1) of the New Act, obtained by an Insurance Company or a Foreign Insurance Company, etc. on or after the Effective Date; with regard to the license of the competent minister set forth in Article 1, paragraph (1) of the Former Act, and the license of the Minister of Finance set forth in Article 3, paragraph (1) of the Former Foreign Insurance Providers Act, issued before the Effective Date pertaining to an Insurance Company Licensed under the Former Act or a Foreign Insurance Company, etc. Licensed under the Former Foreign Insurance Providers Act, the provisions then in force shall remain applicable.

(Transitional Measures for Registration of Life Insurance Agents and Non-Life Insurance Representatives)
Article 108 Those Life Insurance Agents (including the persons who are deemed to be registered on the registry of Life Insurance Agents pursuant to the provisions of Article 4, paragraph (2) of the Former Solicitation Control Act pursuant to the provisions of paragraph (2) of the Supplementary Provisions to the Act for Partial Revision of the Act on the Control of Insurance Solicitation (Act No. 152 of 1951)) and Non-Life Insurance Representative that have obtained the registration set forth in Article 3 of the Former Solicitation Control Act by the time this Act enters into force (hereinafter referred to as "Life Insurance Agents, etc. Registered under the Former Act") shall be deemed to have obtained the registration with the Ministry of Finance set forth in Article 276 of the New Act, at the time when this Act enters into force.

(Transitional Measures for Registry of Life Insurance Agents, etc.)
Article 109 (1) The registry of Life Insurance Agents and registry of Non-Life Insurance Representatives under Article 4, paragraph (1) of the Former Solicitation Control Act in existence at the time this Act enters into force shall be deemed to be the registry of Life Insurance Agents and registry of Non-Life Insurance Representatives under Article 278, paragraph (1) of the New Act.
(2) The provisions of Article 278, paragraph (2) of the New Act shall apply to those persons who shall be deemed to have obtained the registration with the Minister of Finance set forth in Article 276 of the New Act at the time when this Act enters into force, pursuant to the provisions of the preceding Article and who have not received the notice under Article 4, paragraph (3) of the Former Solicitation Control Act, and to their Affiliated Insurance Companies.

(Transitional Measures for Refusal of Registration Pertaining to Life Insurance Agents, etc.)
Article 110 (1) For the purpose of applying the provisions of Article 279, paragraph (1), item (iii) of the New Act, a person who was sentenced to a fine pursuant to the provisions of the Former Solicitation Control Act (including the provisions of the Former Solicitation Control Act that are to remain applicable pursuant to these Supplementary Provisions as provisions then in force) shall be deemed to have been sentenced to a fine as of the date of the original punishment for violating a provisions of the New Act.
(2) For the purpose of applying the provisions of Article 279, paragraph (1), item (iv) of the New Act, a person whose registration under Article 3, paragraph (1) of the Former Solicitation Control Act was canceled pursuant to the provisions of Article 7-2 or Article 20, paragraph (1) of the Former Solicitation Control Act shall be deemed to have had his/her registration under Article 276 of the New Act canceled pursuant to the provisions of Article 307, paragraph (1) of the New Act as of the date of the original punishment.

(Transitional Measures for Affiliated Insurance Company's Liability for Damages)
Article 111 The provisions of Article 283 of the New Act shall apply to any liability for the damages inflicted on or after the Effective Date by a Life Insurance Agent or Non-Life Insurance Agent upon Policyholders in connection with Insurance Solicitation; with regard to any liability for the damages inflicted before the Effective Date upon Policyholders by a Life Insurance Agent, an officer or employee of a Non-Life Insurance Company, or a Non-Life Insurance Representative in connection with solicitation, the provisions then in force shall remain applicable.

(Transitional Measures for Registry of Life Insurance Agents and Non-Life Insurance Representatives)
Article 112 Any registry of Life Insurance Agents or Non-Life Insurance Representatives under Article 13, paragraph (1) of the Former Solicitation Control Act in existence at the time when this Act enters into force shall be deemed to be the registry regarding Life Insurance Agents or Non-Life Insurance Representatives set forth in Article 285, paragraph (1) of the New Act.

(Transitional Measures for Refusal of Registration Pertaining to Insurance Broker)
Article 113 For the purpose of applying the provisions of Article 289, paragraph (1), item (iii) of the New Act, a person who was sentenced to a fine pursuant to the provisions of the Former Act, the Former Solicitation Control Act or the Former Foreign Insurance Providers Act (including the provisions of the Former Act, the Former Solicitation Control Act and the Foreign Insurance Providers Act that are to remain applicable pursuant to these Supplementary Provisions as provisions then in force) shall be deemed to have been sentenced to a fine as of the date of the original punishment for violating a provisions of the New Act.

(Transitional Measures for Notification of Officers or Employees of a Non-Life Insurance Representative)
Article 114 Any notification of officers or employees of a Non-Life Insurance Representative under Article 8 of the Former Solicitation Control Act made before the Effective Date shall be deemed to be notification under Article 302 of the New Act.

(Transitional Measures for Notification, etc. of a Change, etc. in a Life Insurance Agent, etc.)

Article 115 (1) The provisions of Articles 7 and 26 of the Former Solicitation Control Act shall remain in force with regard to those Life Insurance Agents, etc. Registered under the Former Act who have not made the notification required under Article 7 of the Former Solicitation Control Act by the time when this Act enters into force. In this case, the term "Minister of Finance" in Article 7 of the Former Solicitation Control Act, which is to remain in force, shall be deemed to be replaced with "Prime Minister."

(2) The provisions of Article 7-3 (limited to the segment pertaining to item (ii)) of the Former Solicitation Control Act shall remain in force with regard to the Life Insurance Agents, etc. Registered under the Former Act who make, on or after the Effective Date, the notification required under Article 7, paragraph (3) of the Former Solicitation Control Act, which is to remain in force pursuant to the provisions of the preceding paragraph. In this case, the term "Minister of Finance" in Article 7-3 (limited to the segment pertaining to item (ii)), which is to remain in force, shall be deemed to be replaced with "Prime Minister."

(Transitional Measures for Cancellation of Registration, etc.)

Article 116 For the purpose of applying the provisions of Article 307, paragraph (1) of the New Act, any action falling under Article 7-2, item (iii) or any of the items of Article 20, paragraph (1) of the Former Solicitation Control Act that was taken before the Effective Date by a Life Insurance Agent, etc. Registered under the Former Act shall be deemed to be the action prescribed in item (ii) or (iii) of Article 307, paragraph (1) of the New Act.

(Transitional Measures for Deletion of Registration, etc.)

Article 117 Any Life Insurance Agents, etc. Registered under the Former Act who fell under any of the items of Article 7-3 of the Former Solicitation Control Act before the Effective Date and have not had its registration deleted under that Article by the time when this Act enters into force shall be deemed to fall under Article 308, paragraph (1), item (ii) of the New Act.

(Transitional Measures for Officers, etc. of Foreign Life Insurance Providers)

Article 118 (1) The officers or employees of a foreign life insurance provider that has obtained the license of the Minister of Finance set forth in Article 3, paragraph (1) of the Former Foreign Insurance Providers Act by the time this Act enters into force may, notwithstanding the provisions of Article 275 of the New Act, carry out Insurance Solicitation for a period of six months counting from the Effective Date (or until the date, within such six months, of any disposition refusing the registration under Article 279, paragraphs (1) to (3) inclusive of the New Act). The same shall apply where said period has elapsed even though such persons have applied for the registration set forth in Article 277 of the New Act within said period, until such time as the registration or the disposition refusing the registration is made, with regard to the application.

(2) The Minister of Finance may, within the period prescribed in the preceding paragraph, order the abolition of business, or total or partial suspension of business when the officers or employees of a foreign life insurance provider prescribed in the preceding paragraph fall under item (i) or (iii) of Article 307, paragraph (1) of the New Act.

(3) For the purpose of applying the provisions of Article 279, paragraph (1) of the New Act, any order for the abolition of Insurance Solicitation business issued under the preceding paragraph to the officers or employees of a foreign life insurance operator prescribed in paragraph (1) shall be deemed to be cancellation of the registration set

forth in Article 276 of the New Act under Article 307, paragraph (1) of the New Act.

(Transitional Measures for Insurance Broker)
Article 119 (1) An Insurance Broker registered under Article 286 of the New Act shall, when it seeks to act or to cause any of its officers or employees to act as intermediary in concluding the long-term insurance contracts to be specified by Cabinet Order, determine the method by which it will do so, and shall, for the interim, obtain authorization from the Prime Minister. The same shall apply where it seeks to modify the method thus authorized.
(2) The Prime Minister may, when an Insurance Broker authorized under the preceding paragraph has violated this Act or any disposition of the Prime Minister pursuant to this Act, or has engaged in conduct that harms the public interest, cancel the authorization set forth in that paragraph.
(3) Necessary particulars for the authorization set forth in paragraph (1) shall be specified by Cabinet Office Ordinance.

(Transitional Measures for Revocation, etc. of Application for Insurance Contract)
Article 120 The provisions of Article 309 of the New Act shall apply to the applications for insurance contracts received by an Insurance Company or Foreign Insurance Company, etc. on or after the Effective Date, or the insurance contracts concluded on or after the Effective Date (excluding those for which applications were made before the Effective Date).

(Deleted)
Article 121 Deleted.

(Transitional Measures for Particulars Requiring Registration)
Article 122 (1) An Insurance Company Licensed under the Former Act shall, within six months from the Effective Date, register the particulars newly requiring registration under the New Act.
(2) No other registration may be filed before the registration set forth in the preceding paragraph; any such registration must be filed at the same time as the registration set forth in that paragraph.
(3) When any change has occurred in the particulars set forth in paragraph (1) before making the registration set forth in that paragraph, the registration set forth in that paragraph shall be made without delay regarding the original particulars.
(4) For any violation of the provisions of the preceding three paragraphs, the representative director of the Insurance Company Licensed under the Former Act shall be punished by a non-criminal fine of not more than one million yen.

(Effect of Dispositions or Procedures Pursuant to Provisions of Former Act, etc.)
Article 123 The authorization, approval and other dispositions, or application and other procedures made before the Effective Date under the provisions of the Former Act, the Former Solicitation Control Act or the Former Foreign Insurance Providers Act, or any of the orders pursuant thereto, which are covered by the Supplementary Provisions of the New Act or any of the orders pursuant thereto, shall be deemed to be authorization, approval and other dispositions, or application and other procedures made under the corresponding provisions of the New Act or the orders pursuant thereto.

(Transitional Measures Concerning Penal Provisions)
Article 124 With regard to the application of penal provisions to actions taken prior to the enforcement of this Act, and to actions taken subsequent to the enforcement of this Act pertaining to any of the particulars to which the provisions then in force are to remain applicable pursuant to these Supplementary Provisions, the provisions then in force shall remain applicable.

(Delegation to Cabinet Order)
Article 125 In addition to what is provided for in Article 3 to the preceding Article inclusive of these Supplementary Provisions, necessary transitional measures for the enforcement of this Act shall be specified by Cabinet Order.

(Review)
Article 126 At an appropriate time after the enforcement of this Act, the Government shall, taking into consideration the status of enforcement of this Act and changing socioeconomic conditions surrounding Insurance Services, among other factors, review the system prescribed in this Act pertaining to Insurance Services, and when it finds it necessary, take required measures based on its findings.

Supplementary Provisions [Act No. 55 of May 21, 1997] [Extract]

(Effective Date)
Article 1 This Act shall come into effect as of 1 June 1997.

Supplementary Provisions [Act No. 72 of June 6, 1997]

(Effective Date)
(1) This Act shall come into effect as of the Effective Date of the Act for Partial Revision of the Commercial Code, etc. (Act No. 71 of 1997).

(Transitional Measures)
(2) With regard to any merger pertaining to a merger agreement concluded prior to the enforcement of this Act, the provisions then in force shall remain applicable subsequent to the enforcement of this Act.

(Transitional Measures for Application of Penal Provisions)
(3) With regard to the application of penal provisions to actions taken prior to the enforcement of this Act, and to actions taken subsequent to the enforcement of this Act where the provisions then in force are to remain applicable pursuant to the provisions of the preceding paragraph, the provisions then in force shall remain applicable.

Supplementary Provisions [Act No. 102 of June 20, 1997] [Extract]

(Effective Date)
Article 1 This Act shall come into effect as of the Effective Date of the Act for Establishment of the Financial Supervisory Agency (Act No. 101 of 1997).

(Transitional Measures for Dispositions, etc. Made by Minister of Finance, etc.)
Article 2 (1) The licensing, permission, authorization, approval, Designation and other dispositions, or notification and other actions taken by the Minister of Finance or other

organs of the State pursuant to the provisions of the Secured Bond Trust Act, Trust Business Act, Norinchukin Bank Act, Mutual Loan Business Act, Act on Simplification of Banking Business Procedures, etc. , Act on Provision, etc. of Trust Business by Financial Institutions, Act on Prohibition of Private Monopolization and Maintenance of Fair Trade, Agricultural Cooperative Association Act, Securities and Exchange Act, Act on Non-Life Insurance Rating Organizations, Fisheries Cooperative Association Act, Act on the Cooperative Associations of Small and Medium Enterprises, etc. , Act on Financial Businesses by Cooperative, Shipowners Mutual Insurance Association Act, Securities Investment Trust Act, Shinkin Bank Act, Long-Term Credit Bank Act, Loan Trust Act, Medium and Small Fishery Loan Guarantee Act, Credit Guarantee Companies Act, Labor Bank Act, Foreign Exchange Bank Act, Automobile Liability Security Act, Agricultural Credit Guarantee Insurance Act, Act on Financial Institutions' Merger and Conversion, Act on Foreign Securities Brokers, Deposit Insurance Act, Act on the Promotion of Introduction of Industry, etc. into Agricultural Regions, Agricultural and Fishery Cooperation Savings Insurance Act, Banking Act, Act on Controls, etc. on Money Lending, Act on Regulation, etc. on Investment Advisory Business Pertaining to Securities, Act on Regulation, etc. for Mortgage Corporations, Financial Futures Trading Act, Act on Regulation, etc. on Advanced Payment Certificate, Act on Regulations of Business Pertaining to Commodities Investment, Act on Special Provisions for the Narcotics and Psychotropics Control Act, etc. and Other Matters for the Prevention of Activities Encouraging Illicit Conduct and Other Activities Involving Controlled Substances through International Cooperation, Act on the Regulation of Business Pertaining to Specified Claims, etc. , Act on Revision, etc. of Related Acts for the Reform of Financial System and Securities Exchange System, Act on Preferred Equity Investment by Cooperative Structured Financial Institution, Real Estate Specified Joint Enterprise Act, Insurance Business Act, Act on Special Treatment, etc. of Corporate Reorganization Proceedings and Other Insolvency Proceedings of Financial Institution, Act on the Merger of the Norinchukin Bank and the Federation of Credit Agricultural Cooperatives, etc. , Bank of Japan Act, or Act on Special Measures, etc. for Merger Procedures Pertaining to Banks, etc. for the Creation of Bank Holding Company (hereinafter referred to as the "Former Secured Bond Trust Act, etc."), prior to revision by this Act, shall be deemed to be licensing, permission, authorization, approval, Designation and other dispositions, or notification and other actions taken by the Prime Minister or other corresponding organs of the State pursuant to the corresponding provisions of the Secured Bond Trust Act, Trust Business Act, Norinchukin Bank Act, Mutual Loan Business Act, Act on Simplification of Banking Business Procedures, etc. , Act on Provision, etc. of Trust Business by Financial Institutions, Act on Prohibition of Private Monopolization and Maintenance of Fair Trade, Agricultural Cooperative Association Act, Securities and Exchange Act, Act on Non-Life Insurance Rating Organizations, Fisheries Cooperative Association Act, Act on the Cooperative Associations of Small and Medium Enterprises, etc. , Act on Financial Businesses by Cooperative, Shipowners Mutual Insurance Association Act, Securities Investment Trust Act, Shinkin Bank Act, Long-Term Credit Bank Act, Loan Trust Act, Medium and Small Fishery Loan Guarantee Act, Credit Guarantee Companies Act, Labor Bank Act, Foreign Exchange Bank Act, Automobile Liability Security Act, Agricultural Credit Guarantee Insurance Act, Act on Financial Institutions' Merger and Conversion, Act on Foreign Securities Brokers, Deposit Insurance Act, Act on the Promotion of Introduction of Industry, etc. into Agricultural Regions, Agricultural and Fishery Cooperation Savings Insurance Act, Banking Act, Act on Controls, etc. on Money Lending, Act on Regulation, etc. on Investment Advisory Business Pertaining to Securities, Act on Regulation, etc. for Mortgage Corporations, Financial Futures

Trading Act, Act on Regulation, etc. on Advanced Payment Certificate, Act on Regulations of Business Pertaining to Commodities Investment, Act on Special Provisions for the Narcotics and Psychotropics Control Act, etc. and Other Matters for the Prevention of Activities Encouraging Illicit Conduct and Other Activities Involving Controlled Substances through International Cooperation, Act on the Regulation of Business Pertaining to Specified Claims, etc. , Act on Revision, etc. of Related Acts for the Reform of Financial System and Securities Exchange System, Act on Preferred Equity Investment by Cooperative Structured Financial Institution, Real Estate Specified Joint Enterprise Act, Insurance Business Act, Act on Special Treatment, etc. of Corporate Reorganization Proceedings and Other Insolvency Proceedings of Financial Institution, Act on the Merger of the Norinchukin Bank and the Federation of Credit Agricultural Cooperatives, etc. , Bank of Japan Act, or Act on Special Measures, etc. for Merger Procedures Pertaining to Banks, etc. for the Creation of Bank Holding Company, revised by this Act (hereinafter referred to as the "New Secured Bond Trust Act, etc.").

(2) The applications, notifications and other actions that have been addressed to the Minister of Finance or other organs of the State pursuant to the provisions of the Former Secured Bond Trust Act, etc. by the time when this Act enters into force shall be deemed to be applications, notifications and other actions addressed to the Prime Minister or other corresponding organs of the State pursuant to the corresponding provisions of the New Secured Bond Trust Act, etc.

(3) For the purpose of applying the provisions of the New Secured Bond Trust Act, etc. to the particulars with regard to which a person is required to make a report to, give notice to, file a submission with, or go through any other procedures with the Minister of Finance or other organs of the State pursuant to the provisions of the Former Secured Bond Trust Act, etc. , any such particulars for which the relevant procedures have not been completed by the Effective Date of this Act shall be deemed to be particulars with regard to which a person is required to make a report to, give notice to, file a submission with, or go through any other procedures with the Prime Minister or other corresponding organs of the State pursuant to the corresponding provisions of the New Secured Bond Trust Act, etc. , but for which the relevant procedure has not been completed.

(Transitional Measures Concerning Penal Provisions)
Article 5 With regard to the application of penal provisions to actions taken prior to the enforcement of this Act, the provisions then in force shall remain applicable.

(Delegation to Cabinet Order)
Article 6 In addition to what is provided for in Article 2 to the preceding Article inclusive of the Supplementary Provisions, necessary transitional measures for the enforcement of this Act shall be specified by Cabinet Order.

Supplementary Provisions [Act No. 117 of December 10, 1997] [Extract]

(Effective Date)
Article 1 This Act shall come into effect as of the day on which twenty days have elapsed from the day of promulgation.

Supplementary Provisions [Act No. 120 of December 12, 1997] [Extract]

(Effective Date)
Article 1 This Act shall come into effect as of the date to be specified by Cabinet Order within a period not exceeding three months from the day of promulgation.

(Review)
Article 10 Where five years have elapsed from the enforcement of this Act, the Government shall, taking into consideration the status of enforcement of the Banking Act revised by the provisions of Article 1 (hereinafter referred to as the "New Banking Act"), the Long-Term Credit Bank Act revised by the provisions of Article 2 (hereinafter referred to as the "New Long-Term Credit Bank Act") and the Insurance Business Act revised by the provisions of Article 4 (hereinafter referred to as the "New Insurance Business Act"), and changing socioeconomic conditions surrounding Banking and the Insurance Business, among other factors, review the systems pertaining to the bank holding companies prescribed in Article 2, paragraph (13) of the New Banking Act, the Long Term Credit Bank holding companies prescribed in Article 16-4, paragraph (1) of the New Long-Term Credit Bank Act and the insurance holding companies prescribed in Article 2, paragraph (16) of the New Insurance Business Act, and when it finds it necessary, take required measures based on its findings.

Supplementary Provisions [Act No. 121 of December 12, 1997] [Extract]

(Effective Date)
Article 1 This Act shall come into effect as of the Effective Date of the Act on the Revision, etc. of Finance-Related Acts Accompanying the Lifting of Prohibition on the Incorporation of Holding Companies, etc. (Act No. 120 of 1997).

Supplementary Provisions [Act No. 106 of June 15, 1998]

This Act shall come into effect as of the Effective Date (1 September 1998) of the Act on the Liquidation of Specified Assets by Special Purpose Companies (Act No. 105 of 1998); provided, however, that the provisions revising Article 5 of the Supplementary Provisions to the Local Tax Act in Article 17 shall come into effect as of 1 April 1999.

Supplementary Provisions [Act No. 107 of June 15, 1998] [Extract]

(Effective Date)
Article 1 This Act shall come into effect as of 1 December 1998; provided, however, that the provisions listed in the following items shall come into effect as of the date specified in the relevant item:
(i) The provisions adding a Chapter after Chapter IV of the Securities and Exchange Act (limited to the segment pertaining to Article 79-29, paragraph (1)) and provisions revising Article 189, paragraphs (2) and (4) of that Act in Article 1, the provisions of Article 21, the provisions revising Part II, Chapter X, Section 2, Subsection 1 of the Insurance Business Act (limited to the segment pertaining to Article 265-6) in Article 22, the provisions of Article 23 and the provisions of Article 25, and the provisions of Article 40, Article 42, Article 58, Article 136, Article 140, Article 143, Article 147, Article 149, Article 158, Article 164, Article 187 (excluding the provisions revising Article 4, item (lxxix) of the Ministry of Finance Establishment Act (Act No. 144 of 1949) and Article 188 to 190 inclusive of the Supplementary

Provisions: 1 July 1998

(Transitional Measures Accompanying Partial Revision to Insurance Business Act)

Article 130 (1) The provisions of Article 97-2, paragraph (2) (including the cases where it is applied mutatis mutandis pursuant to Article 199 of the Insurance Business Act revised by the provisions of Article 22 (hereinafter referred to as "New Insurance Business Act") of the New Insurance Business Act shall not apply, for a period of one year counting from the Effective Date, to the investment of assets on behalf of one single person (meaning the one single person prescribed in Article 97-2, paragraph (2) of the New Insurance Business Act; the same shall apply in the following paragraph) by an Insurance Company (meaning an Insurance Company as defined in Article 2, paragraph (2) of the New Insurance Business Act; the same shall apply hereinafter) (including a Foreign Insurance Company, etc. (meaning a Foreign Insurance Company, etc. as defined in Article 2, paragraph (7) of the New Insurance Business Act; the same shall apply hereinafter) or a Licensed Specified Juridical Person (meaning a Licensed Specified Juridical Person as defined in Article 223, paragraph (1) of the New Insurance Business Act; the same shall apply hereinafter); hereinafter the same shall apply in this paragraph), if the amount of assets prescribed in Article 97-2, paragraph (2) of the New Insurance Business Act which are invested by the Insurance Company on behalf of said single person exceeds, at the time when this Act enters into force, the amount calculated pursuant to the provisions of that paragraph, provided that the Insurance Company notifies the Financial Reconstruction Commission of this within three months from the Effective Date.

(2) The provisions of Article 97-2, paragraph (3) of the New Insurance Business Act shall not apply, for a period of one year counting from the Effective Date, to an Insurance Company and its Subsidiary Companies, etc. (meaning Subsidiary Companies, etc. as defined in that paragraph; hereinafter the same shall apply in this paragraph) that have invested, at the time when this Act enters into force, the assets prescribed in that paragraph on behalf of one single person in a total amount that exceeds the amount calculated pursuant to the provisions of that paragraph, or to the investment of such assets by the Subsidiary Companies, etc. of the Insurance Company on behalf of said single person, provided that the Insurance Company notifies the Financial Reconstruction Commission of this within three months from the Effective Date.

Article 131 The provisions of Articles 100-3 and 194 of the New Insurance Business Act shall apply to transactions made or actions taken on or subsequent to the Effective Date by an Insurance Company or a Foreign Insurance Company, etc. ; with regard to transactions made or actions taken by an Insurance Company or a Foreign Insurance Company, etc. prior to the Effective Date, the provisions then in force shall remain applicable.

Article 132 (1) The provisions of Article 106, paragraph (1) of the New Insurance Business Act shall not apply, for a period of one year counting from the Effective Date, to any Subsidiary (meaning any Subsidiary as defined in Article 2, paragraph (13) of the New Insurance Business Act; hereinafter the same shall apply in this Article) of an Insurance Company that is not a Company Eligible to Be a Subsidiary as defined in Article 106, paragraph (1) of the New Insurance Business Act at the time when this Act enters into force, provided that the Insurance Company notifies the Financial Reconstruction Commission of this within three months from the Effective Date.

(2) If the company under the notice in the preceding paragraph that is not a Company Eli-

gible to Be a Subsidiary has ceased to be the Subsidiary of the Insurance Company set forth in that paragraph, said Insurance Company shall notify the Prime Minister of this without delay.
(3) Until the date to be specified by Cabinet Order, but no later than 31 March 2000, the term "bank as defined in Article 2, paragraph (4) (Definitions, etc.) of the Banking Act" in Article 106, paragraph (1), item (iii) of the New Insurance Business Act shall be deemed to be replaced with "bank as defined in Article 2, paragraph (4) (Definitions, etc.) of the Banking Act that falls under the category of bankrupt financial institutions prescribed in Article 2, paragraph (4) (Definitions) of the Deposit Insurance Act (Act No. 34 of 1971)"; and the term "Long Term Credit Bank as defined in Article 2 (Definitions) of the Long Term Credit Bank Act" in Article 106, paragraph (1), item (iv) of the New Insurance Business Act shall be deemed to be replaced with "Long Term Credit Bank as defined in Article 2 (Definitions) of the Long Term Credit Bank Act that falls under the category of bankrupt financial institutions prescribed in Article 2, paragraph (4) (Definitions) of the Deposit Insurance Act."
(4) Any authorization given by the Prime Minister pursuant to the provisions of Article 106, paragraph (1) or Article 108, paragraph (1) of the Insurance Business Act prior to its revision by the provisions of Article 22 (hereinafter referred to as the "Former Insurance Business Act"), conditions attached to such authorization, or applications made pursuant to those provisions pertaining to such authorization before the Effective Date shall be deemed to be the authorization prescribed in Article 106, paragraph (4) of the New Insurance Business Act given by the Prime Minister pursuant to the provisions of that paragraph, conditions attached to such authorization or applications made pursuant to the provisions of that paragraph pertaining to such authorization.
(5) If an Insurance Company has made any Insurance Company, etc. That Is Eligible to Be a Subsidiary as defined in Article 106, paragraph (4) of the New Insurance Business Act (excluding any company in which the Insurance Company holds shares or equity interests with the authorization set forth in Article 106, paragraph (1) or Article 108, paragraph (1) of the Former Insurance Business Act; the same shall apply in the following paragraph) its Subsidiary by the time when this Act enters into force, the Insurance Company shall notify the Financial Reconstruction Commission of this within three months from the Effective Date.
(6) An Insurance Company that has given notice under the preceding paragraph shall be deemed to have received as of the Effective Date the authorization set forth in Article 106, paragraph (4) of the New Insurance Business Act to make the Insurance Company, etc. Eligible to Be a Subsidiary to which the notice pertains its Subsidiary.
(7) The provisions of Article 107, paragraph (1) of the New Insurance Business Act shall not apply, for a period of one year counting from the Effective Date, to the ownership of Shares, etc. (meaning Shares, etc. as defined in Article 2, paragraph (12) of the New Insurance Business Act; hereinafter the same shall apply in this paragraph) by an Insurance Company or any of its Subsidiaries in a domestic company (meaning a domestic company as defined in Article 107, paragraph (1) of the New Insurance Business Act; hereinafter the same shall apply in this paragraph), where the Insurance Company or the Subsidiary owns, at the time when this Act enters into force, Shares, etc. in the domestic company in a total number that exceeds its shareholding threshold, etc. (meaning the shareholding threshold, etc. prescribed in Article 107, paragraph (1) of the New Insurance Business Act; hereinafter the same shall apply in this paragraph), provided that the Insurance Company notify the Financial Reconstruction Commission of this within three months from the Effective Date. In this case, for the purpose of applying the provisions of that Article to the ownership of Shares, etc. in the domestic company on and subsequent to the date, the Insurance Company and its Subsidiaries

shall be deemed to have acquired as of the date the Shares, etc. of the domestic company in excess of the shareholding threshold, etc. following the events prescribed in the main clause of paragraph (2) of that Article.

Article 133 The provisions of Article 110, paragraphs (2) and (3), Article 111, paragraphs (1) to (3) inclusive (including the cases where the provisions of paragraphs (1) and (3) of that Article are applied mutatis mutandis pursuant to Article 199 of the New Insurance Business Act), Article 271-8, and Article 271-9, paragraphs (1) and (2) of the New Insurance Business Act shall apply to the documents of an Insurance Company (including a Foreign Insurance Company, etc. or a Licensed Specified Juridical Person; hereinafter the same shall apply in this Article) or Insurance Holding Company (meaning an Insurance Holding Company as defined in Article 2, paragraph (16) of the New Insurance Business Act; hereinafter the same shall apply in this Article) prescribed in those provisions pertaining to the business years or fiscal years that start on or subsequent to 1 April 1998; with regard to the business report and other documents of an Insurance Company or Insurance Holding Company pertaining to the business years or fiscal years that started prior to the date, the provisions then in force shall remain applicable.

Article 134 (1) The provisions of Article 132, paragraph (2), Article 204, paragraph (2) and Article 230, paragraph (2) of the New Insurance Business Act shall apply to any order (including any demand for the submission of an improvement program) issued on or subsequent to 1 April 1999 under Article 132, paragraph (1), Article 204, paragraph (1) or Article 230, paragraph (1) of the New Insurance Business Act, respectively.
(2) Any demands for the submission of an improvement program under Article 130, paragraph (1), Article 202, paragraph (1) or Article 228, paragraph (1) of the Former Insurance Business Act, and orders for modification under Article 130, paragraph (2), Article 202, paragraph (2) or Article 228, paragraph (2) of the Former Insurance Business Act issued prior to the Effective Date shall be deemed to be demands for the submission of an improvement program, and orders for modification issued under Article 132, paragraph (1), Article 204, paragraph (1) or Article 230, paragraph (1) of the New Insurance Business Act, respectively.

Article 135 Any authorization given by the Prime Minister pursuant to the provisions of Article 8, paragraph (1) of the Former Insurance Business Act as applied mutatis mutandis pursuant to Article 192, paragraph (3) of the Former Insurance Business Act, conditions attached to such authorization, or applications made pursuant to the provisions of that paragraph pertaining to the authorization set forth in that paragraph prior to the Effective Date shall be deemed to be authorization given by the Prime Minister pursuant to the provisions of Article 192, paragraph (3) of the New Insurance Business Act, conditions attached to such authorization or applications made pursuant to the provisions of that paragraph pertaining to the authorization set forth in that paragraph.

Article 136 (1) An Insurance Company (including a Foreign Insurance Company, etc. or a Licensed Specified Juridical Person) that seeks to become an incorporator or a member of the Policyholders Protection Corporation prescribed in Article 259 of the New Insurance Business Act (hereinafter referred to as the "Corporation") may, prior to the Effective Date, proceed with the preparation of the articles of incorporation, the holding of sessions of the Organizational Meeting and other actions necessary for incorporating the Corporation, necessary actions for participating in the Corporation, and necessary actions for managing business for the business year to which belongs the date of incorporation of the Corporation, as prescribed in Article 261 to 263 inclusive, Article 265 to 265-3 inclusive, Article 265-5, Article 265-7, Article 265-12, Article 265-13, Article 265-15 to 265-17 inclusive, Article 265-30 and Article 265-34 of the New Insurance Business Act, and Article 1-4 of the Supplementary Provisions of the New Insurance Business Act.

(2) The incorporators of a Corporation may, prior to the Effective Date, apply for the authorization of the incorporation of the Corporation and the authorization of the appointment of officers and, on behalf of the Corporation, the authorization of the Corporation's business procedures, the budget and financial plan for the business year to which belongs the date of its incorporation and the obligatory contribution rates, and receive the authorization from the Minister of Finance, as prescribed in Article 265-8, Article 265-9, Article 265-15, Article 265-30 and Article 265-34 of the New Insurance Business Act, and Article 1-8 of the Supplementary Provisions of the New Insurance Business Act. In this case, such authorization shall come into effect as of the Effective Date.

Article 137 (1) The provisions of Article 265-2, paragraph (2) and Article 265-3, paragraph (1) of the New Insurance Business Act shall not apply to any Insurance Company (including any Foreign Insurance Company, etc.; hereinafter the same shall apply in this Article and the following Article), in cases where the Prime Minister, pursuant to the provisions of Article 241 of the Former Insurance Business Act, has issued an order for suspension of all or part of its business (or, for a Foreign Insurance Company, etc., its business in Japan; hereinafter the same shall apply in this Article), the transfer of insurance contracts or consultation on merger (or, for a Foreign Insurance Company, etc., consultation on the transfer of insurance contracts in Japan) or has rendered a disposition ordering the administration of its business and property (or, for a Foreign Insurance Company, etc., its property located in Japan; the same shall apply in the following paragraph) by an insurance administrator, at the time when this Act enters into force.

(2) Where the condition of the business and property of an Insurance Company to which the provisions of the preceding paragraph shall apply is found to have returned to normal after this Act enters into force, as attested by the relevant Designation by the Prime Minister, the provisions of Article 265-2, paragraph (2) and Article 265-3, paragraph (1) of the New Insurance Business Act shall apply as of the date of such Designation.

Article 138 With regard to any Policyholders Protection Fund as defined in Article 259, paragraph (2) of the Former Insurance Business Act in existence at the time when this Act enters into force (including a fund in the course of liquidation; referred to as "Policyholders Protection Fund" in the following Article to Article 141 inclusive of the Supplementary Provisions) that includes among its business participants (meaning the business participants prescribed in Article 260, paragraph (5), item (iv) of the Former Insurance Business Act), at the time when this Act enters into force, any Insurance Company to which the provisions of paragraph (1) of the preceding Article shall apply but for which no decision has been made to provide Financial Assistance (meaning the Financial Assistance prescribed in Article 260, paragraph (5), item (v) of the Former Insurance Business Act), the provisions of Article 259 to 270 inclusive of the Former Insurance Business Act and Article 105 of the Supplementary Provisions to the Former Insurance Business Act shall remain in force even after this Act enters into force, for a period to be specified by Cabinet Order counting from the Effective Date. In this case, the term "Article 241" in Article 268, paragraph (1), item (i) of the Former Insurance Business Act, which is to remain in force, shall be deemed to be replaced with "Article 241 of the Insurance Business Act prior to its revision by the provisions of Article 22 of the Act on Revision, etc. of Related Acts for the Financial System Reform (Act No. 107 of 1998)."

Article 139 With regard to any Policyholders Protection Fund in existence at the time when this Act enters into force that conducts Financial Assistance Business, etc. (meaning Financial Assistance Business, etc. prescribed in Article 259, paragraph (1) of the Former Insurance Business Act; the same shall apply in the following Article) at the time when this Act enters into force, the Former Insurance Business Act shall remain in force even after this Act enters into force until Financial Assistance Business, etc. is completed, within the limit necessary for executing Financial Assistance Business, etc. In this case, the terms "Minister of Finance" and "Ordinance of the Ministry of Finance" in Part II, Chapter X, Section 2 (excluding Article 267, paragraph (5), Article 269, paragraph (2) and Article 270, paragraph (3)) of the Former Insurance Business Act shall be deemed to be replaced with "Prime Minister and the Minister of Finance" and "Cabinet Office Ordinance and Ordinance of the Ministry of Finance," respectively; and the terms "incompetent" and "quasi-incompetent" in Article 259, paragraph (1), item (iii) of the Former Insurance Business Act shall be deemed to be replaced with "adult ward" and "person under curatorship," respectively; any necessary technical change in interpretation shall be specified by Cabinet Order.

Article 140 (1) The Policyholders Protection Fund set forth in the preceding Article may, until a date to be specified by Cabinet Order, propose to the incorporators of a Corporation or the Corporation that the Corporation should succeed to Financial Assistance Business, etc. conducted by the Policyholders Protection Fund, and those assets and liabilities which have come to belong to the Policyholders Protection Fund as a result of executing Financial Assistance Business, etc. (hereinafter referred to as the "Financial Assistance, etc. Business Property" in this Article).

(2) A Corporation or the incorporators of a Corporation shall, when they seek to consent to any proposal made under the preceding paragraph, receive approval at an Organizational Meeting or General Representative Members' Council Meeting of the Corporation.

(3) A decision in favor of approval under the preceding paragraph is effected at the Organizational Meeting by a two-thirds majority vote of those present at a session attended by at least half of the incorporators and the persons qualified to become members that have applied to become members of the Corporation, in writing, to the incorporators by the date of the session of the Organizational Meeting; or at General Representative Members' Council by a two-thirds majority vote of those present at a session attended by at least half of its members.

(4) A Corporation or the incorporators of a Corporation shall, when the resolution for approval under paragraph (2) was adopted at an Organizational Meeting or at a General Representative Members' Council Meeting, apply without delay for the authorization of the Ministry of Finance.

(5) When the authorization set forth in the preceding paragraph was given, the Corporation shall succeed to Financial Assistance Services, etc. provided by the Policyholders Protection Fund and the Financial Assistance, etc. Business Property, set forth in paragraph (1), as of the date of such authorization (or, when the authorization was given to the incorporators of the Corporation prior to the date of establishment of the Corporation, as of the date of establishment of the Corporation).

(6) Where a Corporation has succeeded to Financial Assistance Services, etc. pursuant to the provisions of the preceding paragraph, the Former Insurance Business Act shall remain in force with regard to the Corporation until Financial Assistance Services, etc. is completed, within the limit necessary for executing Financial Assistance Services, etc. In this case, the terms "Minister of Finance" and "Ordinance of the Ministry of Finance" in Part II, Chapter X, Section 2 (excluding Article 267, paragraph (5), Article 269, paragraph (2) and Article 270, paragraph (3)) of the Former Insurance Business Act shall be deemed to be replaced with "Prime Minister and the Minister of Finance" and "Cabinet Office Ordinance and Ordinance of the Ministry of Finance," respectively; and the terms "incompetent" and "quasi-incompetent" in Article 259, paragraph (1), item (iii) of the Former Insurance Business Act shall be deemed to be replaced with "adult ward" and "person under curatorship," respectively; any technical change in interpretation required shall be specified by Cabinet Order.

(7) For the purpose of applying the provisions of the Former Insurance Business Act that shall remain in force pursuant to the provisions of the preceding paragraph, the Corporation that has succeeded to Financial Assistance Business, etc. pursuant to the provisions of paragraph (5) shall be deemed to be a Policyholders Protection Fund and may conduct Financial Assistance Business, etc. thus succeeded to, notwithstanding the provisions of Article 265-28 of the New Insurance Business Act.

(8) The Corporation shall, when it conducts Financial Assistance Business, etc. to which it has succeeded pursuant to the provisions of the preceding paragraph, create a Special Account (hereinafter referred to as "Ongoing Business Account") to arrange for the separate accounting of Financial Assistance Business, etc. In this case, any Financial Assistance, etc. Business Property succeeded to pursuant to the provisions of paragraph (5) shall be credited to the Ongoing Business Account as of the date of such succession.

(9) For the purpose of applying the provisions of Article 265-41, paragraph (2) of the New Insurance Business Act during the period in which the Ongoing Business Account is in place pursuant to the provisions of the preceding paragraph, the term "and the Ongoing Business Account prescribed in Article 138, paragraph (7) of the Supplementary Provisions to the Act on Revision, etc. of Related Acts for the Financial System Reform (Act No. 107 of 1998)" shall be deemed to be inserted before the term "; the same shall apply in Article 270-5" in Article 265-41, paragraph (2) of the New Insurance Business Act.

(10) The Corporation shall, when Financial Assistance Services, etc. succeeded to pursuant to the provisions of paragraph (5) has been completed, abolish the Ongoing Business Account, and impute any residual assets in existence at the time of such abolishment to the General Account set forth in Article 265-41, paragraph (2) of the New Insurance Business Act.

Article 141 With regard to the obligation for a person who has been an officer or functionary of a Policyholders Protection Fund not to reveal any secret that he/she had access to in the course of duties, the provisions then in force shall remain applicable even after this Act enters into force.

Article 142 The provisions of Article 263, paragraph (2) of the New Insurance Business Act shall not apply, for a period of six months counting from the Effective Date, to a person that uses the term "Hoken Keiyakusha Hogo Kiko" (which means "Policyholders Protection Corporation") in its name at the time when this Act enters into force.

(Delegation of Authorities)

Article 147 (1) The Prime Minister shall delegate his/her authorities under these Supplementary Provisions (excluding the authorities to be specified by Cabinet Order) to the Commissioner of the Financial Services Agency.
(2) The authorities delegated to the Commissioner of the Financial Services Agency pursuant to the provisions of the preceding paragraph, and the authorities of the Minister of Agriculture, Forestry and Fisheries and Minister of Health, Labour and Welfare under these Supplementary Provisions may be delegated in part to the heads of the Regional Financial Bureaus or Regional Financial Offices (or, for the authorities of the Minister of Agriculture, Forestry and Fisheries and Minister of Health, Labour and Welfare, the heads of the Regional Financial Branch Offices), pursuant to the provisions of a Cabinet Order.

(Effect of Dispositions, etc.)
Article 188 Those dispositions, procedures or other actions taken before this Act (or, for the provisions listed in the items of Article 1 of the Supplementary Provisions, such provisions) enters into force pursuant to the provisions of the respective Acts prior to its revision (including any orders pursuant thereto; hereinafter the same shall apply in this Article), which are covered by the corresponding provisions of the respective Acts as revised, shall be deemed to have been carried out pursuant to such corresponding provisions of the respective Acts as revised, unless provided otherwise in these Supplementary Provisions.

(Transitional Measures for Application of Penal Provisions)
Article 189 With regard to the application of penal provisions to actions taken prior to the enforcement of this Act (or, for the provisions listed in the items of Article 1 of the Supplementary Provisions, such provisions), and to actions taken subsequent to the enforcement of this Act where the provisions then in force are to remain applicable pursuant to the provisions of these Supplementary Provisions, the provisions then in force shall remain applicable.

(Delegation of Other Transitional Measures to Cabinet Order)
Article 190 In addition to what is provided for in Article 2 to 146 inclusive, Article 153 and Article 169 of the Supplementary Provisions, and the preceding Article, necessary transitional measures for the enforcement of this Act shall be specified by Cabinet Order.

(Review)
Article 191 (1) Subsequent to the enforcement of this Act, the Government shall, when it finds it necessary, take necessary measures to maintain the credibility of the insurance industry, taking into consideration the status of implementation of the system pertaining to special measures, etc. for the protection of Policyholders, etc. under the New Insurance Business Act and the condition of soundness in management of Insurance Companies, among other factors.
(2) In addition to what is provided for in the preceding paragraph, the Government shall, within five years from the enforcement of this Act, review the financial systems revised by this Act, taking into consideration the status of implementation of the provisions revised by this Act and changing socioeconomic conditions surrounding the financial sector, among other factors, and when it finds it necessary, take required measures based on its findings.

Supplementary Provisions [Act No. 131 of October 16, 1998]

(Effective Date)
Article 1 This Act shall come into effect as of the Effective Date of the Act for Establishment of the Financial Reconstruction Commission (Act No. 130 of 1998).

(Transitional Measures)
Article 2 (1) The licensing, permission, authorization, approval, Designation and other dispositions, or notification and other actions taken by the Prime Minister or other organs of the State pursuant to the provisions of the Secured Bond Trust Act, Trust Business Act, Norinchukin Bank Act, Mutual Loan Business Act, Act on Simplification of Banking Business Procedures, etc. , Act on Provision, etc. of Trust Business by Financial Institutions, Act on Prohibition of Private Monopolization and Maintenance of Fair Trade, Agricultural Cooperative Association Act, Securities and Exchange Act, Act on Non-Life Insurance Rating Organizations, Fisheries Cooperative Association Act, Act on the Cooperative Associations of Small and Medium Enterprises, etc. , Act on Financial Businesses by Cooperative, Shipowners Mutual Insurance Association Act, Local Tax Act, Act on Securities Investment Trust and Securities Investment Corporations, Shinkin Bank Act, Long-Term Credit Bank Act, Loan Trust Act, Medium and Small Fishery Loan Guarantee Act, Credit Guarantee Companies Act, Labor Bank Act, Automobile Liability Security Act, Agricultural Credit Guarantee Insurance Act, Act on Earthquake Insurance, Registration and License Tax Act, Act on Financial Institutions' Merger and Conversion, Act on Foreign Securities Brokers, Act on the Promotion of Introduction of Industry, etc. into Agricultural Regions, Agricultural and Fishery Cooperation Savings Insurance Act, Banking Act, Act on Controls, etc. on Money Lending, Act on Regulation, etc. on Investment Advisory Business Pertaining to Securities, Act on Regulation, etc. for Mortgage Corporations, Financial Futures Trading Act, Act on Regulation, etc. on Advanced Payment Certificate, Act on Regulations of Business Pertaining to Commodities Investment, Act on Special Provisions for the Narcotics and Psychotropics Control Act, etc. and Other Matters for the Prevention of Activities Encouraging Illicit Conduct and Other Activities Involving Controlled Substances through International Cooperation, Act on the Regulation of Business Pertaining to Specified Claims, etc. , Act on Revision, etc. of Related Acts for the Reform of Financial System and Securities Exchange System, Act on Preferred Equity Investment by Cooperative Structured Financial Institution, Real Estate Specified Joint Enterprise Act, Insurance Business Act, Act on Special Treatment, etc. of Corporate Reorganization Proceedings and Other Insolvency Proceedings of Financial Institution, Act on the Merger of the Norinchukin Bank and the Federation of Credit Agricultural Cooperatives, etc. , Bank of Japan Act, Act on Special Measures, etc. for Merger Procedures Pertaining to Banks, etc. for the Creation of Bank Holding Company, Act on the Liquidation of Specified Assets by Special Purpose Companies, or Act on Revision, etc. of Related Acts for the Financial System Reform, prior to its revision by this Act (hereinafter referred to as "Former Secured Bond Trust Act, etc."), shall be deemed to be licensing, permission, authorization, approval, Designation and other dispositions, or notification and other actions taken by the Financial Reconstruction Commission or other corresponding organs of the State pursuant to the corresponding provisions of the Secured Bond Trust Act, Trust Business Act, Norinchukin Bank Act, Mutual Loan Business Act, Act on Simplification of Banking Business Procedures, etc. , Act on Provision, etc. of Trust Business by Financial Institutions, Act on Prohibition of Private Monopolization and Maintenance of Fair Trade, Agricultural Cooperative Association Act, Securities and Exchange Act, Act on Non-Life Insurance Rating Organizations, Fisheries Cooperative Association Act, Act on the Cooperative Associa-

tions of Small and Medium Enterprises, etc., Act on Financial Businesses by Cooperative, Shipowners Mutual Insurance Association Act, Local Tax Act, Act on Securities Investment Trust and Securities Investment Corporations, Shinkin Bank Act, Long-Term Credit Bank Act, Loan Trust Act, Medium and Small Fishery Loan Guarantee Act, Credit Guarantee Companies Act, Labor Bank Act, Automobile Liability Security Act, Agricultural Credit Guarantee Insurance Act, Act on Earthquake Insurance, Registration and License Tax Act, Act on Financial Institutions' Merger and Conversion, Act on Foreign Securities Brokers, Act on the Promotion of Introduction of Industry, etc. into Agricultural Regions, Agricultural and Fishery Cooperation Savings Insurance Act, Banking Act, Act on Controls, etc. on Money Lending, Act on Regulation, etc. on Investment Advisory Business Pertaining to Securities, Act on Regulation, etc. for Mortgage Corporations, Financial Futures Trading Act, Act on Regulation, etc. on Advanced Payment Certificate, Act on Regulations of Business Pertaining to Commodities Investment, Act on Special Provisions for the Narcotics and Psychotropics Control Act, etc. and Other Matters for the Prevention of Activities Encouraging Illicit Conduct and Other Activities Involving Controlled Substances through International Cooperation, Act on the Regulation of Business Pertaining to Specified Claims, etc., Act on Revision, etc. of Related Acts for the Reform of Financial System and Securities Exchange System, Act on Preferred Equity Investment by Cooperative Structured Financial Institution, Real Estate Specified Joint Enterprise Act, Insurance Business Act, Act on Special Treatment of Corporate Reorganization Proceedings and Other Insolvency Proceedings of Financial Institution, Act on the Merger of the Norinchukin Bank and the Federation of Credit Agricultural Cooperatives, etc., Bank of Japan Act, Act on Special Measures, etc. for Merger Procedures Pertaining to Banks, etc. for the Creation of Bank Holding Company, Act on the Liquidation of Specified Assets by Special Purpose Companies, or Act on Revision, etc. of Related Acts for the Financial System Reform, revised by this Act (hereinafter referred to as "New Secured Bond Trust Act, etc.").

(2) Applications, notifications and other actions that have been addressed to the Prime Minister or other organs of the State pursuant to the provisions of the Former Secured Bond Trust Act, etc. by the time when this Act enters into force shall be deemed to be applications, notifications and other actions addressed to the Financial Reconstruction Commission or other corresponding organs of the State pursuant to the corresponding provisions of the New Secured Bond Trust Act, etc.

(3) For the purpose of applying the provisions of the New Secured Bond Trust Act, etc. to the particulars with regard to which a person is required to make a report to, give notice to, file a submission with, or go through any other procedures with the Prime Minister or other organs of the State pursuant to the provisions of the Former Secured Bond Trust Act, etc., any such particulars for which the relevant procedures have not been completed by the Effective Date of this Act shall be deemed to be particulars with regard to which a person is required to make a report to, give notice to, file a submission with, or go through any other procedures with the Financial Reconstruction Commission or other corresponding organs of the State pursuant to the corresponding provisions of the New Secured Bond Trust Act, etc., but for which the relevant procedures have not been completed.

Article 3 Any orders pursuant to the provisions of the Former Secured Bond Trust Act, etc. that are effective at the time when this Act enters into force shall be effective as orders issued pursuant to the corresponding provisions of the New Secured Bond Trust Act, etc.

Art.4～1   ⑥ Insurance Business Act, Part VI

Article 4 With regard to the application of penal provisions to actions taken prior to the enforcement of this Act, the provisions then in force shall remain applicable.

(Delegation to Cabinet Order)
Article 5 In addition to what is provided for in the preceding three Articles, necessary transitional measures for the enforcement of this Act shall be specified by Cabinet Order.

Supplementary Provisions [Act No. 125 of August 13, 1999] [Extract]

(Effective Date)
Article 1 This Act shall come into effect as of the date to be specified by Cabinet Order within a period not exceeding six months from the day of promulgation; provided, however, that the provisions revising Article 285-4, Article 285-5, paragraph (2), Article 285-6, paragraphs (2) and (3), Article 290, paragraph (1) and Article 293-5, paragraph (3) of the Commercial Code in Article 1, and the provisions revising Article 23, paragraph (3) and Article 24, paragraph (1) of the Norinchukin Bank Act (Act No. 42 of 1923) in Article 6 of the Supplementary Provisions, the provisions revising Article 39-3, paragraph (3) and Article 40-2, paragraph (1) of the Shoko Chukin Bank Act (Act No. 14 of 1936) in Article 7 of the Supplementary Provisions, the provisions revising Article 52, paragraph (1) of the Agricultural Cooperative Association Act (Act No. 132 of 1947) in Article 9 of the Supplementary Provisions, the provisions revising Article 53, paragraph (3) of the Securities and Exchange Act (Act No. 25 of 1948) and deleting paragraph (4) of that Article in Article 10 of the Supplementary Provisions, the provisions revising Article 56, paragraph (1) of the Fisheries Cooperative Association Act (Act No. 242 of 1948) in Article 11 of the Supplementary Provisions, the provisions adding an Article after Article 5-5 of the Act on Financial Businesses by Cooperative (Act No. 183 of 1949) and revising Article 12, paragraph (1) of that Act in Article 12 of the Supplementary Provisions, the provisions revising Article 42, paragraph (1) of the Shipowners Mutual Insurance Association Act (Act No. 177 of 1950) in Article 13 of the Supplementary Provisions, the provisions revising Article 55-3, paragraph (3) and Article 57, paragraph (1) of the Shinkin Bank Act (Act No. 238 of 1951) in Article 16 of the Supplementary Provisions, the provisions revising Article 61, paragraph (1) of the Labor Bank Act (Act No. 227 of 1953) in Article 18 of the Supplementary Provisions, the provisions revising Article 17-2, paragraph (3) of the Banking Act (Act No. 59 of 1981) and deleting paragraph (4) of that Article in Article 23 of the Supplementary Provisions, the provisions of Article 26 of the Supplementary Provisions, the provisions adding a paragraph to Article 15 of the Insurance Business Act (Act No. 105 of 1995), revising Article 55, paragraphs (1) and (2), Article 102, paragraph (1) and Article 112-2, paragraph (3) of that Act, deleting Article 112-2, paragraph (4) of that Act, revising Article 115, paragraph (2), Article 118, paragraph (1), Article 119 and Article 199 of that Act and deleting Article 59, paragraph (2) and Article 90, paragraph (2) of the Supplementary Provisions to that Act in Article 27 of the Supplementary Provisions, the provisions revising Article 7, paragraph (2) of the Act on Special Measures for the Commercial Code on the Procedure of Cancellation of Shares (Act No. 55 of 1997) in Article 29 of the Supplementary Provisions and the provisions revising Article 101, paragraph (1) and Article 102, paragraph (3) of the Act on the Liquidation of Specified Assets by Special Purpose Companies (Act No. 105 of 1998) in Article 31 of the Supplementary Provisions shall come into effect as of 1 April 2000.

(Transitional Measures for Audit Report)

Article 2 With regard to particulars for inclusion in audit reports to be prepared for the financial years that ended prior to the enforcement of this Act, the provisions then in force shall remain applicable. The same shall apply to particulars for inclusion in audit reports to be prepared for the business years that ended prior to the enforcement of this Act with regard to the Norinchukin Bank, Agricultural Cooperative Associations and Federations of Agricultural Cooperatives, Fisheries Cooperative Associations, Federations of Fisheries Cooperatives, Fish Processors' Cooperative Associations and Federations of Fish Processors' Cooperatives, Credit Cooperatives and Federations of Credit Cooperatives (meaning federations of cooperatives that conduct the business set forth in Article 9-9, paragraph (1), item (i) of the Small and Medium-Sized Enterprise Cooperatives Act (Act No. 181 of 1949); the same shall apply in the following Article), Shinkin Banks and Federations of Shinkin Banks, Labor Banks and Federations of Labor Banks, and Mutual Companies (meaning Mutual Companies as defined in Article 2, paragraph (5) of the Insurance Business Act; the same shall apply in the following Article).

(Transitional Measures for Valuation of Monetary Claims, etc.)
Article 3 With regard to the valuation of monetary claims, company bonds and other bonds, and shares and other equity interests acquired by contribution (hereinafter referred to as "Valuation of Monetary Claims, etc." in this Article) for the accounting periods in the financial years that started prior to the enforcement of the amending provisions listed in the proviso to Article 1 of the Supplementary Provisions, the provisions then in force shall remain applicable. The same shall apply to the Valuation of Monetary Claims, etc. listed in the following items:
(i) Valuation of Monetary Claims, etc. as of the end of the business years that started prior to the enforcement of the amending provisions listed in the proviso to Article 1 of the Supplementary Provisions with regard to the Norinchukin Bank, the Shoko Chukin Bank, Agricultural Cooperative Associations and Federations of Agricultural Cooperatives, Fisheries Cooperative Associations, Federations of Fisheries Cooperatives, Fish Processors' Cooperative Associations and Federations of Fish Processors' Cooperatives, Credit Cooperatives and Federations of Credit Cooperatives, Shipowners Mutual Insurance Cooperatives, Shinkin Banks and Federations of Shinkin Banks, and Labor Banks and Federations of Labor Banks;
(ii) Valuation of Monetary Claims, etc. for the accounting periods in the business periods (meaning the business periods prescribed in Article 133, paragraph (2) of the Act on Securities Investment Trust and Securities Investment Corporations (Act No. 198 of 1951)) that started prior to the enforcement of the amending provisions listed in the proviso to Article 1 of the Supplementary Provisions with regard to securities investment corporations (meaning securities investment corporations as defined in Article 2, paragraph (11) of that Act; and
(iii) Valuation of Monetary Claims, etc. for the accounting periods in the business years that started prior to the enforcement of the amending provisions listed in the proviso to Article 1 of the Supplementary Provisions with regard to Mutual Companies.

Supplementary Provisions [Act No. 151 of December 8, 1999] [Extract]

(Effective Date)
Article 1 This Act shall come into effect as of 1 April 2000.

Article 4 With regard to the application of penal provisions to actions taken prior to the enforcement of this Act, the provisions then in force shall remain applicable.

Supplementary Provisions [Act No. 160 of December 22, 1999] [Extract]

(Effective Date)
Article 1 This Act (excluding Articles 2 and 3) shall come into effect as of 6 January 2001; provided, however, that the provisions listed in the following items shall come into effect as of the date specified in the relevant item:
(ii) The provisions of Chapter III (excluding Article 3) and the following Article: 1 July 2000;

Supplementary Provisions [Act No. 225 of December 22, 1999] [Extract]

(Effective Date)
Article 1 This Act shall come into effect as of the date to be specified by Cabinet Order within a period not exceeding six months from the day of promulgation.

(Transitional Measures Accompanying Partial Revision to Civil Code, etc.)
Article 25 With regard to the treatment of the particulars specified in the legal provisions listed in the following items pertaining to any petition for the commencement of composition filed prior to the enforcement of this Act or any ruling for the commencement of composition made prior or subsequent to the enforcement of this Act based on such petition, the provisions then in force shall remain applicable, notwithstanding those provisions revised by the Supplementary Provisions to this Act:
(i) Article 398-3, paragraph (2) of the Civil Code;
(ii) Article 33-12-3, paragraph (1), item (i), sub-item (c) of the Mariners Insurance Act;
(iii) Article 59, paragraph (3) and Article 68-3, paragraph (2) of the Agricultural and Fishing Cooperatives Savings Insurance Act;
(iv) Article 22-2, paragraph (1), item (i), sub-item (c) of the Employment Insurance Act;
(v) Article 135-36 of the Act on Procedures for Non-Contentious Cases;
(vi) Article 309-2, paragraph (1), item (ii), and Article 383, paragraphs (1) and (2) of the Commercial Code;
(vii) Article 54, paragraph (1), item (vii), Article 64-10, paragraph (1) and Article 79-53, paragraph (1), item (ii) of the Securities and Exchange Act;
(viii) Article 2, paragraph (3), item (i) of the Small and Medium-Sized Enterprise Credit Insurance Act;
(ix) Article 20, paragraph (2), Article 24, Article 37, paragraph (1), Article 38, paragraph (4), Article 67, paragraph (1), Article 78, paragraph (1), Article 79, paragraph (2), items (ii) to (iv) inclusive, Article 80, paragraph (1), and Article 163, items (ii) and (iv) of the Corporate Rehabilitation Act.
(x) Article 30 of the Act on the Management of the State's Credits, etc. ;
(xi) Article 27, paragraph (1), item (v) of the Installment Sales Act;
(xii) Article 22, paragraph (1), item (viii) and Article 33, paragraph (1) of the Act on Foreign Securities Brokers;
(xiii) Row 12 and Row 17 of sub-item (d) of Appended Table 1 to the Act on Civil Court Costs, etc. ;
(xiv) Article 36, paragraph (1), item (v) of the Act on the Sale of Residential Land and Buildings Reserved by Advance Installments;

(xv) Article 2, paragraph (2), item (i) of the Act on Mutual Relief System for the Prevention of Bankruptcies of Small and Medium-sized Enterprises;
(xvi) Article 46, paragraph (1) of the Banking Act;
(xvii) Article 111, paragraph (4), item (ii) of the Act on the Liquidation of Specified Assets by Special Purpose Companies;
(xviii) Article 66, Article 151 and Article 271, paragraph (1) of the Insurance Business Act;
(xix) Article 24, paragraph (1), Article 26, Article 27, Article 31, Article 45, Article 48, paragraph (1), items (ii) to (iv) inclusive and Article 49, paragraph (1) of the Act on Special Treatment of Corporate Reorganization Proceedings and Other Insolvency Proceedings by Financial Institutions, etc. ; and
(xx) Article 40, paragraphs (1) and (3) of the Act on Punishment of Organized Crimes and Control of Crime Proceeds.

(Transitional Measures on Application of Penal Provisions)
Article 26 With regard to the application of penal provisions to actions taken prior to the enforcement of this Act and to actions taken subsequent to the enforcement of this Act where the provisions then in force are to remain applicable pursuant to the Supplementary Provisions to this Act, the provisions then in force shall remain applicable.

Supplementary Provisions [Act No. 14 of March 31, 2000] [Extract]

(Effective Date)
Article 1 This Act shall come into effect as of 1 April 2000.

Supplementary Provisions [Act No. 91 of May 31, 2000]

(Effective Date)
(1) This Act shall come into effect as of the Effective Date of the Act for Partial Revision of the Commercial Code, etc. (Act No. 90 of 2000).

(Transitional Measures)
(2) Where the Effective Date of this Act comes before the Effective Date of the provisions of Article 8 of the Supplementary Provisions to the Act on the Center for Food Quality, Labeling and Consumer Services (Act No. 183 of 1999), the term "Article 27" in the provisions revising Article 19-5-2, Article 19-6, paragraph (1), item (iv) and Article 27 of the Act on Standardization and Proper Quality Labeling of Agricultural and Forestry Products in Article 31 shall be deemed to be replaced with "Article 26."

Supplementary Provisions [Act No. 92 of May 31, 2000] [Extract]

(Effective Date)
Article 1 This Act shall come into effect as of the date to be specified by Cabinet Order within a period not exceeding three months from the day of promulgation; provided, however, that the provisions adding an Article after Article 265-42 of the Insurance Business Act and revising Articles 275 and 317-2 of that Act in Article 1, and the provisions of Article 19 of the Supplementary Provisions shall come into effect as of 1 April 2001.

(Transitional Measures)
Article 3 The provisions of Part II, Chapter II, Section 3 of the New Insurance Business

Act shall apply to any Entity Conversion (meaning Entity Conversion as defined in Article 68, paragraph (2) or Article 86, paragraph (1) of the New Insurance Business Act) pertaining to a resolution of the shareholders' meeting or general members' council meeting (or General Representative Members' Council Meeting, where the company has such a council) (hereinafter referred to as "Shareholders' Meeting, etc.") adopted in a session for which the convocation notice set forth in Article 232, paragraph (1) of the Commercial Code (including the cases where it is applied mutatis mutandis pursuant to Articles 41 and 49 of the New Insurance Business Act) is issued on or subsequent to the Effective Date; with regard to any Entity Conversion (meaning Entity Conversion as defined in Article 68, paragraph (2) or Article 86, paragraph (1) of the Insurance Business Act prior to its revision by the provisions of Article 1 (hereinafter referred to as "Former Insurance Business Act")) pertaining to a resolution of the Shareholders' Meeting, etc. adopted in a session for which the convocation notice set forth in Article 232, paragraph (1) of the Commercial Code (including the cases where it is applied mutatis mutandis pursuant to Articles 41 and 49 of the Former Insurance Business Act) was issued prior to the Effective Date, the provisions then in force shall remain applicable.

Article 4 The provisions of Article 117-2 of the New Insurance Business Act shall also apply to claims pertaining to the insurance contracts concluded prior to the Effective Date.

Article 5 The provisions of Articles 136-2 and 137 of the New Insurance Business Act shall apply to any transfer of insurance contracts pertaining to a resolution of the Shareholders' Meeting, etc. adopted in a session for which the convocation notice set forth in Article 232, paragraph (1) of the Commercial Code (including the cases where it is applied mutatis mutandis pursuant to Articles 41 and 49 of the New Insurance Business Act) is issued on or subsequent to the Effective Date; with regard to any transfer of insurance contracts pertaining to a resolution of the Shareholders' Meeting, etc. adopted in a session for which the convocation notice set forth in Article 232, paragraph (1) of the Commercial Code (including the cases where it is applied mutatis mutandis pursuant to Articles 41 and 49 of the Former Insurance Business Act) was issued prior to the Effective Date, the provisions then in force shall remain applicable.

Article 6 The provisions of Articles 156-2 and 157 of the New Insurance Business Act shall apply to any dissolution pertaining to a resolution of the general members' council (or General Representative Members' Council, where the company has such a council; hereinafter the same shall apply in this Article) adopted in a session for which the convocation notice set forth in Article 232, paragraph (1) of the Commercial Code as applied mutatis mutandis pursuant to Articles 41 and 49 of the New Insurance Business Act is issued on or subsequent to the Effective Date; with regard to any dissolution pertaining to a resolution of the general members' council adopted in a session for which the convocation notice set forth in Article 232, paragraph (1) of the Commercial Code as applied mutatis mutandis pursuant to Articles 41 and 49 of the Former Insurance Business Act was issued prior to the Effective Date, the provisions then in force shall remain applicable.

Article 7 The provisions of Part II, Chapter VIII, Section 3 of the New Insurance Business Act shall apply to any merger pertaining to a resolution of the Shareholders' Meeting, etc. adopted in a session for which the convocation notice set forth in Article 232, paragraph (1) of the Commercial Code (including the cases where it is applied mutatis mutandis pursuant to Articles 41 and 49 of the New Insurance Business Act) is issued on or subsequent to the Effective Date; with regard to any merger pertaining to a resolution of the Shareholders' Meeting, etc. adopted in a session for which the convocation notice set forth in Article 232, paragraph (1) of the Commercial Code (including the cases where it is applied mutatis mutandis pursuant to Articles 41 and 49 of the Former Insurance Business Act) was issued prior to the Effective Date, the provisions then in force shall remain applicable.

Article 8 The provisions of Articles 136-2 and 137 of the New Insurance Business Act as applied mutatis mutandis pursuant to Article 210, paragraph (1) of the New Insurance Business Act shall apply to any transfer of insurance contracts pertaining to that Agreement set forth in Article 135, paragraph (1) of the New Insurance Business Act as applied mutatis mutandis pursuant to Article 210, paragraph (1) of the New Insurance Business Act that is prepared by a Foreign Insurance Company, etc. (meaning a Foreign Insurance Company, etc. as defined in Article 2, paragraph (7) of the New Insurance Business Act) on or subsequent to the Effective Date; with regard to any transfer of insurance contracts pertaining to that Agreement set forth in Article 135 of the Former Insurance Business Act as applied mutatis mutandis pursuant to Article 210, paragraph (1) of the Former Insurance Business Act which was prepared prior to the Effective Date, the provisions then in force shall remain applicable.

Article 9 The provisions of Part II, Chapter X, Section 1, Subsection 2 of the New Insurance Business Act shall apply to any disposition ordering the administration of business and property by an insurance administrator under Article 241, paragraph (1) of the New Insurance Business Act, made on or subsequent to the Effective Date; with regard to any disposition ordering the administration of business and property by an insurance administrator under Article 241 of the Former Insurance Business Act, made prior to the Effective Date, the provisions then in force shall remain applicable.

Article 10 The provisions of Part II, Chapter X, Section 1, Subsection 3 of the New Insurance Business Act shall apply to any modification of the contract conditions where an order for consultation on Merger, etc. is issued under Article 241, paragraph (1) of the New Insurance Business Act, where a disposition ordering the administration of business and property by an insurance administrator is made under that paragraph, or where the certification set forth in Article 268, paragraph (1) of the New Insurance Business Act is given, on or subsequent to the Effective Date; with regard to any modification of the contract conditions where an order for the transfer of insurance contracts or for consultation on merger was issued under Article 241 of the Former Insurance Business Act, where a disposition ordering the administration of business and property by an insurance administrator was made under that Article, or where the certification set forth in Article 268, paragraph (1) of the Former Insurance Business Act was given, prior to the Effective Date, the provisions then in force shall remain applicable.

Article 11 The provisions of Article 257 of the New Insurance Business Act shall apply to any mediation conducted on or subsequent to the Effective Date pertaining to the recommendation set forth in Article 256, paragraph (1) of the New Insurance Business Act; with regard to any mediation conducted prior to the Effective Date pertaining to the recommendation set forth in Article 256, paragraph (1) of the Former Insurance Business Act, the provisions then in force shall remain applicable.

Article 12 The provisions of Article 265-37 of the New Insurance Business Act shall apply to the approval, submission or modification of budgets and financial plans pertaining to the business years that start on or subsequent to the Effective Date; with regard to the approval, submission or modification of budgets and financial plans pertaining to the business years that started prior to the Effective Date, the provisions then in force shall remain applicable.

Article 13 The provisions of Article 265-39, paragraph (3) of the New Insurance Business Act shall apply to the documents set forth in that paragraph for the business years that start on or subsequent to the Effective Date; with regard to the documents set forth in that paragraph for the business years that started prior to the Effective Date, the provisions then in force shall remain applicable.

Article 14 The provisions of Part II, Chapter X, Section 2, Subsection 2, Division 1 of the New Insurance Business Act shall apply to Financial Assistance pertaining to any decision on the Financial Assistance set forth in Article 270-3, paragraph (1) of the New Insurance Business Act made on or subsequent to the Effective Date; with regard to Financial Assistance pertaining to any decision on the Financial Assistance set forth in Article 270-3, paragraph (1) of the Former Insurance Business Act made prior to the Effective Date, the provisions then in force shall remain applicable.

Article 15 The provisions of Part II, Chapter X, Section 2, Subsection 2, Division 3 of the New Insurance Business Act shall apply to the underwriting of insurance contracts pertaining to any decision on the date of concluding an Agreement regarding the underwriting of insurance contracts set forth in Article 270-4, paragraph (6) of the New Insurance Business Act, made on or subsequent to the Effective Date; with regard to the underwriting of insurance contracts pertaining to any decision on the date of concluding an Agreement regarding the underwriting of insurance contracts set forth in Article 270-4, paragraph (6) of the Former Insurance Business Act, made prior to the Effective Date, the provisions then in force shall remain applicable.

(Transitional Measures for Application of Penal Provisions)
Article 29 With regard to the application of penal provisions to actions taken prior to the enforcement of this Act (or, for the provisions set forth in the proviso to Article 1 of the Supplementary Provisions, such provisions), and to actions taken subsequent to the enforcement of this Act where the provisions then in force are to remain applicable pursuant to the provisions of these Supplementary Provisions, the provisions then in force shall remain applicable.

(Delegation of Other Transitional Measures to Cabinet Order)
Article 30 In addition to what is provided for in Article 2 to 17 inclusive of the Supplementary Provisions and the preceding Article, necessary transitional measures for the enforcement of this Act shall be specified by a Cabinet order.

(Review)
Article 31 Within three years from the enforcement of this Act, the Government shall review the system for the protection of Policyholders, etc. revised by this Act, taking into consideration the status of implementation of the system, etc. pertaining to special measures, etc. for the protection of Policyholders, etc. and the condition of soundness in management of Insurance Companies, among other factors, and when it finds it necessary, take necessary measures to maintain the credibility of the insurance in-

dustry, based on its findings.

Supplementary Provisions [Act No. 96 of May 31, 2000] [Extract]

(Effective Date)
Article 1 This Act shall come into effect as of 1 December 2000 (hereinafter referred to as "Effective Date").

(Effect of Dispositions, etc.)
Article 49 Those dispositions, procedures or other actions taken prior to the enforcement of this Act (or, for the provisions listed in the items of Article 1 of the Supplementary Provisions, such provisions) enter into force pursuant to the provisions of the respective Acts prior to its revision which are covered by the corresponding provisions of the respective Acts as revised, shall be deemed to have been carried out pursuant to such corresponding provisions of the respective Acts as revised, unless provided otherwise in these Supplementary Provisions.

(Transitional Measures for Application of Penal Provisions)
Article 50 With regards to the application of penal provisions to actions taken prior to the enforcement of this Act, the provisions then in force shall remain applicable.

(Delegation of Other Transitional Measures to Cabinet Order)
Article 51 In addition to what is provided for in Article 2 to 11 inclusive of the Supplementary Provisions and the preceding Article, necessary transitional measures for the enforcement of this Act shall be specified by Cabinet Order.

(Review)
Article 52 Where five years have elapsed from the enforcement of this Act, the Government shall, taking into consideration the status of enforcement of the New Securities and Exchange Act and the New Financial Futures Trading Act and changing socioeconomic conditions, among other factors, review the systems pertaining to securities exchanges as defined in Article 2, paragraph (16) of the New Securities and Exchange Act and financial futures exchanges as defined in Article 2, paragraph (6) of the New Financial Futures Trading Act, and when it finds it necessary, take required measures based on its findings.

Supplementary Provisions [Act No. 97 of May 31, 2000] [Extract]

(Effective Date)
Article 1 This Act shall come into effect as of the date to be specified by Cabinet Order within a period not exceeding six months from the day of promulgation (hereinafter referred to as "Effective Date").

(Partial Revision of the Insurance Business Act)
Article 56 (1) Omitted.
(2) For the purpose of applying the provisions of Article 98, paragraph (5) of the Insurance Business Act revised by the provisions of the preceding paragraph, a former special purpose company and the asset securitization plan and specified bonds of the special purpose company shall be deemed to be a special purpose company incorporated pursuant to the provisions of the New Asset Liquidation Act and the asset securitization

plan and specified bonds of the special purpose company, respectively.

(Effect of Dispositions, etc.)
Article 64 Those dispositions, procedures or other actions taken before this Act (or, for the provisions set forth in the proviso to Article 1 of the Supplementary Provisions, such provisions) enters into force pursuant to the provisions of the relevant Acts prior to their revision (including any orders pursuant thereto; hereinafter the same shall apply in this Article), which are covered by the corresponding provisions of the relevant Acts as revised, shall be deemed to have been carried out pursuant to such corresponding provisions of the relevant Acts as revised, unless provided otherwise in these Supplementary Provisions.

(Transitional Measures for Application of Penal Provisions)
Article 65 With regard to the application of penal provisions to actions taken prior to the enforcement of this Act (or, for the provisions set forth in the proviso to Article 1 of the Supplementary Provisions, such provisions), and to actions taken subsequent to the enforcement of this Act where the provisions then in force are to remain applicable pursuant to the provisions of these Supplementary Provisions, the provisions then in force shall remain applicable.

Article 66 For the purpose of applying the provisions (excluding the penal provisions that shall apply pursuant to the provisions of the preceding Article) of the Act on Punishment of Organized Crimes and Control, etc. of Crime Proceeds revised by the provisions of Article 62 of the Supplementary Provisions (hereinafter referred to as "New Organized Crimes Punishment Act" in this Article), the crimes set forth in Article 171, Article 172, Article 174, Article 179, paragraph (1), and Article 182, paragraphs (2) and (4) of the Former Asset Liquidation Act, which is to remain in force pursuant to the provisions of the main clause of Article 2, paragraph (1) of the Supplementary Provisions shall be deemed to be the crimes listed in Appended Table 58 to the New Organized Crimes Punishment Act; and the crimes set forth in Article 228, Article 230, Article 235, paragraph (1), and Article 236, paragraphs (2) and (4) of the Former Investment Trust Act, where the provisions then in force are to remain applicable pursuant to the provisions of the preceding Article, shall be deemed to be the crimes listed in Appended Table 23 to the New Organized Crimes Punishment Act.

(Delegation of Other Transitional Measures to Cabinet Order)
Article 67 In addition to what is provided for in these Supplementary Provisions, necessary transitional measures for the enforcement of this Act shall be specified by Cabinet Order.

(Review)
Article 68 Within five years from the enforcement of this Act, the Government shall, taking into consideration the status of enforcement of the New Asset Liquidation Act, the New Investment Trust Act and the Building Lots and Buildings Transaction Business Act revised by Article 8 (hereinafter referred to as "New Building Lots and Buildings Transaction Business Act" in this Article) and changing socioeconomic conditions, among other factors, review the provisions of the New Asset Liquidation Act and New Investment Trust Act, and the system pertaining to the authorized building lots and buildings traders prescribed in Article 50-2, paragraph (2) of the New Building Lots and Buildings Transaction Business Act, and when it finds it necessary, take required measures based on its findings.

Supplementary Provisions [Act No. 126 of November 27, 2000] [Extract]

(Effective Date)
Article 1 This Act shall come into effect as of the date to be specified by Cabinet Order within a period not exceeding five months from the day of promulgation.

(Transitional Measures Concerning Penal Provisions)
Article 2 With regard to the application of penal provisions to actions taken prior to the enforcement of this Act, the provisions then in force shall remain applicable.

Supplementary Provisions [Act No. 129 of November 29, 2000] [Extract]

(Effective Date)
Article 1 This Act shall come into effect as of the date to be specified by Cabinet Order within a period not exceeding six months from the day of promulgation.

Supplementary Provisions [Act No. 7 of March 30, 2001] [Extract]

(Effective Date)
Article 1 This Act shall come into effect as of 1 April 2001.

Supplementary Provisions [Act No. 41 of June 8, 2001] [Extract]

(Effective Date)
Article 1 This Act shall come into effect as of 1 April 2002.

Supplementary Provisions [Act No. 50 of June 15, 2001] [Extract]

(Effective Date)
Article 1 This Act shall come into effect as of 1 April 2002; provided, however, that the provisions listed in the following items shall come into effect as of the date specified in the relevant item:
  (i) The provisions of Article 9 of the Supplementary Provisions: the day of promulgation;
  (ii) The provisions of Article 7 of the Supplementary Provisions: the date to be specified by Cabinet Order within a period not exceeding one year from the day of promulgation; and
  (iii) The provisions of Article 111 to 114 inclusive and Article 115, paragraph (2), and the provisions of Articles 4, 10, 16 and 35 of the Supplementary Provisions: the date to be specified by Cabinet Order within a period not exceeding two years and six months from the day of promulgation

Supplementary Provisions [Act No. 75 of June 27, 2001] [Extract]

(Effective Date, etc.)
Article 1 This Act shall come into effect as of 1 April 2002 (hereinafter referred to as "Effective Date"), and apply to short-term company bonds, etc. issued on or subsequent to the Effective Date.

(Transitional Measures on Application of Penal Provisions)
Article 7 With regard to the application of penal provisions to actions taken prior to the Effective Date and to actions taken on or subsequent to the Effective Date where the provisions then in force are to remain applicable pursuant to these Supplementary Provisions, the provisions then in force shall remain applicable.

(Delegation of Other Transitional Measures to Cabinet Order)
Article 8 In addition to what is provided for in these Supplementary Provisions, necessary transitional measures for the enforcement of this Act shall be specified by Cabinet Order.

(Review)
Article 9 Where five years have elapsed after the enforcement of this Act, the Government shall, taking into consideration the status of enforcement of this Act and changing socioeconomic conditions, among other factors, review the system pertaining to institutions for transfer, and when it finds it necessary, take required measures based on its findings.

Supplementary Provisions [Act No. 80 of June 29, 2001]

This Act shall come into effect as of the Effective Date of the Act for Partial Revision of the Commercial Code, etc.

Supplementary Provisions [Act No. 117 of November 9, 2001] [Extract]

(Effective Date)
Article 1 This Act shall come into effect as of the date to be specified by Cabinet Order within a period not exceeding six months from the day of promulgation; provided, however, that the provisions listed in the following items shall come into effect as of the date specified in the relevant item:
(i) In Article 1, the provisions deleting Article 17-2 of the Banking Act and the provisions revising Article 47, paragraph (2) of that Act (limited to the segment deleting the term "Article 17-2"); in Article 3, the provisions deleting Article 112-2 of the Insurance Business Act and the provisions revising Article 270-6, paragraph (2), item (i) of that Act; in Article 4, the provisions deleting Article 55-3 of that Act; the provisions of Articles 8, 9, 13 and 14; and the provisions of the following Article, Article 9 and Article 13 to 16 inclusive of the Supplementary Provisions: the day on which one month has elapsed from the day of promulgation.

(Transitional Measures for Shareholders of Insurance Company)
Article 5 (1) For the purpose of applying the provisions of Chapter X-2 (excluding the provisions of Section 3) of the Insurance Business Act as revised by the provisions of Article 3 (hereinafter referred to as "New Insurance Business Act"), any owners of shares in an Insurance Company in existence at the time when this Act enters into force shall be deemed to become owners of shares in the Insurance Company as of the Effective Date following an event other than the transactions or actions listed in the items of Article 271-10, paragraph (1) of the New Insurance Business Act.
(2) Any Insurance Company that has made another Insurance Company its Subsidiary by the time when this Act enters into force, with the authorization set forth in Article

106, paragraph (4) or the proviso to Article 106, paragraph (5) of the Insurance Business Act prior to its revision by the provisions of Article 3, shall be deemed to have received as of the Effective Date the authorization set forth in Article 271-10, paragraph (1) of the New Insurance Business Act for the ownership of shares in such another Insurance Company.

(Delegation of Authorities)
Article 13 (1) The Prime Minister shall delegate his/her authority under these Supplementary Provisions (excluding the authorities to be specified by Cabinet Order) to the Commissioner of the Financial Services Agency.
(2) The authorities delegated to the Commissioner of the Financial Services Agency pursuant to the provisions of the preceding paragraph may be delegated in part to the heads of the Regional Financial Bureaus or Regional Financial Offices, pursuant to the provisions of a Cabinet Order.

(Effect of Dispositions, etc.)
Article 14 Those dispositions, procedures or other actions taken before the amending provisions of this Act enter into force pursuant to the provisions of the respective Acts prior to its revision (including any orders pursuant thereto; hereinafter the same shall apply in this Article), which are covered by the corresponding provisions of the respective Acts as revised, shall be deemed to have been carried out pursuant to such corresponding provisions of the respective Acts as revised, unless provided otherwise in these Supplementary Provisions.

(Transitional Measures Concerning Penal Provisions)
Article 15 With regard to the application of penal provisions to actions taken prior to the enforcement of the amending provisions of this Act and to actions taken subsequent to the enforcement of the amending provisions pertaining to the particulars to which the provisions then in force are to remain applicable pursuant to these Supplementary Provisions, the provisions then in force shall remain applicable.

(Delegation of Other Transitional Measures to Cabinet Order)
Article 16 In addition to what is provided for in Article 2 to the preceding Article inclusive of the Supplementary Provisions, necessary transitional measures for the enforcement of this Act (including transitional measures pertaining to penal provisions) shall be specified by Cabinet Order.

(Review)
Article 23 Where five years have elapsed after the enforcement of this Act, the Government shall, taking into consideration the status of enforcement of the New Banking Act, the New Long-Term Credit Bank Act and the New Insurance Business Act, and changing socioeconomic conditions surrounding banking and the insurance business, among other factors, review the systems pertaining to Bank Major Shareholders as defined in Article 2, paragraph (10) of the New Banking Act, Long-Term Credit Bank Major Shareholders as defined in Article 16-2-2, paragraph (5) of the New Long-Term Credit Bank Act and Insurance Companies' Major Shareholders as defined in Article 2, paragraph (14) of the New Insurance Business Act, and when it finds it necessary, take required measures based on its findings.

Supplementary Provisions [Act No. 129 of November 28, 2001] [Extract]

(Effective Date)
(1) This Act shall come into effect as of 1 April 2002.

(Transitional Measures for Application of Penal Provisions)
(2) With regard to the application of penal provisions to actions taken prior to the enforcement of this Act and to actions taken subsequent to the enforcement of this Act where the provisions then in force are to remain applicable pursuant to the provisions of this Act, the provisions then in force shall remain applicable.

Supplementary Provisions [Act No. 150 of December 12, 2001]

This Act shall come into effect as of the Effective Date of the Act for Partial Revision of the Commercial Code and the Act on Special Measures for the Commercial Code on the Audit, etc. of Stock Company; provided, however, that the provisions of Article 21, paragraph (5) shall come into effect as of the Effective Date of the amending provisions listed in the proviso to Article 1 of the Supplementary Provisions to that Act, and the provisions of Article 24 shall come into effect as of the day of promulgation.

Supplementary Provisions [Act No. 45 of May 29, 2002]

(Effective Date)
(1) This Act shall come into effect as of the date to be specified by Cabinet Order within a period not exceeding one year from the day of promulgation.

(Transitional Measures)
(2) Where the Effective Date of this Act comes before the Effective Date of the provisions of Article 2 of the Act for Partial Revision of the Agricultural Cooperative Association Act, etc. (Act No. 94 of 2001), the term "Article 30, paragraph (12)" in the provisions revising Article 30, paragraph (12) of the Agricultural Cooperative Association Act in Article 9 shall be deemed to be replaced with "Article 30, paragraph (11)."

Supplementary Provisions [Act No. 47 of May 29, 2002] [Extract]

(Effective Date)
Article 1 This Act shall come into effect as of the date to be specified by Cabinet Order within a period not exceeding six months from the day of promulgation.

Supplementary Provisions [Act No. 65 of June 12, 2002] [Extract]

(Effective Date)
Article 1 This Act shall come into effect as of 6 January 2003; provided, however, that the provisions listed in the following items shall come into effect as of the date specified in the relevant item:
  (ii) The provisions of Article 3, and of Article 3, Article 58 to 78 inclusive and Article 82 of the Supplementary Provisions: the date to be specified by Cabinet Order within a period not exceeding five years from the Effective Date of this Act (hereinafter referred to as "Effective Date");

(Transitional Measures Accompanying Partial Revision of Insurance Business Act)

Article 72 The provisions of Article 61-9 of the Insurance Business Act prior to its revision by the provisions of the preceding Article shall remain in force with regard to registered company bonds, etc. under the Former Bond, etc. Registry Act, which is to remain in force pursuant to the provisions of Article 3 of the Supplementary Provisions.

(Transitional Measures for Application of Penal Provisions)
Article 84 With regard to the application of penal provisions to actions taken prior to the enforcement of this Act (or, for the provisions listed in the items of Article 1 of the Supplementary Provisions, such provisions; hereinafter the same shall apply in this Article) and to actions taken subsequent to the enforcement of this Act where the provisions then in force are to remain applicable pursuant to these Supplementary Provisions, the provisions then in force shall remain applicable.

(Delegation of Other Transitional Measures to Cabinet Order)
Article 85 In addition to what is provided for in these Supplementary Provisions, necessary transitional measures for the enforcement of this Act shall be specified by Cabinet Order.

(Review)
Article 86 Where five years have elapsed from the enforcement of this Act, the Government shall, taking into consideration the status of enforcement of the New Act on Transfer of Bonds, etc. , the New Securities and Exchange Act and the New Financial Futures Trading Act, and changing socioeconomic conditions, among other factors, review the systems pertaining to Subscriber's Protective Trusts as defined in Article 2, paragraph (11) of the New Act on Transfer of Bonds, etc. , Settlement Institutions of Securities Transactions as defined in Article 2, paragraph (31) of the New Securities and Exchange Act and Settlement Institutions for Financial Futures as defined in Article 2, paragraph (15) of the New Financial Futures Trading Act, and when it finds it necessary, take required measures based on its findings.

Supplementary Provisions [Act No. 79 of July 3, 2002] [Extract]

(Effective Date)
Article 1 This Act shall come into effect as of 1 August 2002.

Supplementary Provisions [Act No. 155 of December 13, 2002] [Extract]

(Effective Date)
Article 1 This Act shall come into effect as of the Effective Date of the Corporate Rehabilitation Act (Act No. 54 of 2002).

(Transitional Measures for Application of Penal Provisions)
Article 3 With regard to the application of penal provisions to actions taken prior to the enforcement of this Act and to actions taken subsequent to the enforcement of this Act where the provisions then in force are to remain applicable pursuant to the provisions of this Act, the provisions then in force shall remain applicable.

Supplementary Provisions [Act No. 39 of May 9, 2003] [Extract]

(Effective Date)
Article 1 This Act shall come into effect as of the date to be specified by Cabinet Order within a period not exceeding one month from the day of promulgation; provided, however, that the provisions revising Articles 277 and 302, and the provisions of Article 5 to 7 inclusive of the Supplementary Provisions shall come into effect as of 1 September 2003.

(Transitional Measures for Consolidated Financial Statements, etc. Pertaining to Mutual Company)
Article 2 The following provisions shall not apply to a Mutual Company (meaning a Mutual Company as defined in Article 2, paragraph (5) of the Insurance Business Act revised by this Act (hereinafter referred to as "New Act"); the same shall apply hereinafter), until the conclusion of the first session of the general members' council (or General Representative Members' Council, where the company has such a council; the same shall apply hereinafter) convened for the business year subsequent to the enforcement of this Act:
(i) Article 21-8, paragraph (7) and Article 21-10, paragraph (2) of the Act on Special Measures for the Commercial Code on the Audit, etc. of Stock Company (Act No. 22 of 1974; hereinafter referred to as "Act on Special Measures for the Commercial Code") as applied mutatis mutandis pursuant to Article 52-3, paragraph (2) of the New Act, and Article 4, paragraph (2), item (ii), Article 7, paragraph (3) and Article 7, paragraph (5) (limited to the segment regarding consolidated Subsidiaries) of the Act on Special Measures for the Commercial Code as applied mutatis mutandis pursuant to Article 59, paragraph (1) of the New Act; and
(ii) Article 21-32, paragraphs (1) to (5) inclusive of the Act on Special Measures for the Commercial Code as applied mutatis mutandis pursuant to Article 52-3, paragraph (2) of the New Act, and Article 18, paragraph (4), Article 19-2 and Article 19-3 of the Act on Special Measures for the Commercial Code as applied mutatis mutandis pursuant to Article 59, paragraph (1) of the New Act.

(Transitional Measures for Consolidated Financial Statements of Mutual Company Not Submitting Securities Report)
Article 3 (1) For the purpose of applying the provisions listed in the items of the preceding Article to a Mutual Company that does not fall under the category of Mutual Companies required to submit to the Prime Minister the securities report prescribed in Article 24, paragraph (1) of the Securities and Exchange Act (Act No. 25 of 1948) within the period specified in the main clause of that paragraph (hereinafter referred to as "Mutual Companies Submitting the Securities Report"), the preceding Article as well as the following paragraph to paragraph (4) inclusive below shall be effective until otherwise stipulated.
(2) The provisions listed in the items of the preceding Article shall not apply to a Mutual Company that does not fall under the category of Mutual Companies Submitting the Securities Report.
(3) Where the Mutual Company set forth in the preceding paragraph falls under the category of Mutual Companies Submitting the Securities Report, the provisions listed in the items of the preceding Article shall not apply to the Mutual Company until the conclusion of the first session of the general members' council convened for the business year subsequent thereto.
(4) Where a Mutual Company that fell under the category of Mutual Companies Submitting the Securities Report at the end of a business year (limited to a company to which the provisions listed in the items of the preceding Article applied) ceases to fall under

the category of Mutual Companies Submitting the Securities Report prior to the conclusion of the first session of the general members' council convened for the business year subsequent to the end of the business year, the provisions listed in the items of the preceding Article shall apply to the Mutual Company even after it ceases to fall under the category until the conclusion of the session of the general members' council, notwithstanding the provisions of paragraph (2).

(Transitional Measures for Interim Business Report)
Article 4 The provisions of Article 110 of the New Act (including the cases where the provisions of paragraphs (1) and (3) of that Article are applied mutatis mutandis pursuant to Article 199 of the New Act) shall apply to the documents prescribed in Article 110 of the New Act pertaining to the business years that start on or subsequent to 1 April 2004; with regard to the documents pertaining to the business years that started prior to the date, the provisions then in force shall remain applicable.

(Transitional Measures Accompanying a Modification of the Registered Particulars of a Life Insurance Agent and Non-Life Insurance Representative)
Article 5 (1) With regard to the modification of any particulars registered for an individual that has obtained the registration set forth in Article 276 of the Insurance Business Act prior to its revision by this Act (hereinafter referred to as "Former Act") by the time when the provisions revising Article 277 enter into force (other than a person whose birth date has been registered on the registry of Life Insurance Agents or the registry of Non-Life Insurance Representatives by the time when the provisions revising Article 277 enter into force; hereinafter referred to as "Person Without a Registered Birth Date"), the provisions then in force shall remain applicable.
(2) If a Person Without a Registered Birth Date (other than a person who has made the notification set forth in the following paragraph) seeks to give notice of any change in address to which the provisions then in force are applicable pursuant to the provisions of the preceding paragraph, he/she shall notify the Prime Minister of his/her birth date in lieu of his/her address. In this case, the provisions of the New Act shall apply to the modification of any particulars registered subsequent to such notification, regarding the person who made the notification, notwithstanding the provisions of the preceding paragraph.
(3) A Person Without a Registered Birth Date who has not given notice of any change in address to which the provisions then in force are to remain applicable pursuant to the provisions of paragraph (1) may notify the Prime Minister of his/her birth date. In this case, the provisions of the New Act shall apply to the modification of any particulars registered subsequent to such notification, regarding the person who made the notification, notwithstanding the provisions of paragraph (1).
(4) A Person Without a Registered Birth Date may make the notification set forth in the preceding paragraph via his/her Affiliated Insurance Company (meaning the Affiliated Insurance Company prescribed in Article 2, paragraph (20) of the New Act; the same shall apply hereinafter) acting as his/her agent.
(5) Whenever the Prime Minister receives notice under paragraph (3), he/she shall register the birth date to which the notice pertains in the registry of Life Insurance Agents or the registry of Non-Life Insurance Representatives, and notify the Affiliated Insurance Company of this.
(6) Any person that has made a false notification regarding the notification set forth in paragraph (3) shall be punished by a non-criminal fine of not more than five hundred thousand yen.

(Transitional Measures Accompanying Modification of Particulars Requiring Reporting for Officers and Employees of Non-Life Insurance Representatives and Insurance Brokers)

Article 6 (1) With regard to the modification of any particulars in a notice that has been filed with regard to a person reported as an officer or employee (excluding a person of whose birth date the Prime Minister will have been notified by the time the provisions revising Article 302 enter into force; hereinafter referred to as a "Person With an Unreported Birth Date") by the time when the provisions revising Article 302 enter into force, the provisions then in force shall remain applicable.

(2) A Non-Life Insurance Representative (meaning a Non-Life Insurance Representative as defined in Article 2, paragraph (19) of the New Act; the same shall apply hereinafter) or an Insurance Broker (meaning an Insurance Broker as defined in Article 2, paragraph (21) of the New Act; the same shall apply hereinafter) shall, in notifying any change in the address of a Person With an Unreported Birth Date (excluding a person for whom the notification set forth in the following paragraph has been made) to which the provisions then in force are to remain applicable pursuant to the provisions of the preceding paragraph, notify the Prime Minister of his/her birth date in lieu of the address. In this case, the provisions of the New Act shall apply to the modification of any particulars under a notification made subsequent to the notification, regarding the person for whom the notification was made, notwithstanding the provisions of the preceding paragraph.

(3) A Non-Life Insurance Representative or an Insurance Broker may notify the Prime Minister of the birth date of a Person With an Unreported Birth Date with regard to whom no notice has been filed for any change in address to which the provisions then in force are to remain applicable. In this case, the provisions of the New Act shall apply to the modification of any particulars of a notification subsequent to said notification, regarding the person for whom the notification was made, notwithstanding the provisions of paragraph (1).

(4) A Non-Life Insurance Representative may make the notification set forth in the preceding paragraph via its Affiliated Insurance Company acting as its agent.

(5) Any person that has made a false notification regarding the notification set forth in paragraph (3) shall be punished by a non-criminal fine of not more than five hundred thousand yen.

(Delegation of Authorities)

Article 7 (1) The Prime Minister shall delegate his/her authority under Article 5, paragraph (3) of the Supplementary Provisions and paragraph (3) of the preceding Article to the Commissioner of the Financial Services Agency.

(2) The Commissioner of the Financial Services Agency may, pursuant to the provisions of a Cabinet Order, delegate part of the authority that has been delegated pursuant to the provisions of the preceding paragraph to the Director-Generals of Local Finance Bureaus or Local Finance Branch Offices.

(Transitional Measures Concerning Penal Provisions)

Article 8 With regard to the application of penal provisions to actions taken prior to the enforcement of this Act (or, for the provisions prescribed in the proviso to Article 1 of the Supplementary Provisions, such provisions; hereinafter the same shall apply in this Article) and to actions taken subsequent to the enforcement of this Act where the provisions then in force are to remain applicable pursuant to these Supplementary Provisions, the provisions then in force shall remain applicable.

(Delegation of Other Transitional Measures to Cabinet Order)
Article 9 In addition to what is provided for in these Supplementary Provisions, necessary transitional measures for the enforcement of this Act shall be specified by Cabinet Order.

(Review)
Article 11 Within three years from the enforcement of this Act, the Government shall review the system for the protection of Policyholders, etc. revised by this Act, taking into consideration the status of implementation of the system, etc. pertaining to special measures, etc. for the protection of Policyholders, etc. and the condition of soundness in management of Insurance Companies, among other factors, and when it finds it necessary, take necessary measures to maintain the credibility of the insurance industry, based on its findings.

Supplementary Provisions [Act No. 54 of May 30, 2003] [Extract]

(Effective Date)
Article 1 This Act shall come into effect as of 1 April 2004.

(Transitional Measures for Application of Penal Provisions)
Article 38 With regard to the application of penal provisions to actions taken prior to the enforcement of this Act, the provisions then in force shall remain applicable.

(Delegation of Other Transitional Measures to Cabinet Order)
Article 39 In addition to what is provided for in this Act, necessary transitional measures to accompany the enforcement of this Act shall be specified by Cabinet Order.

(Review)
Article 40 Where five years have elapsed from the enforcement of this Act, the Government shall review the financial systems revised by this Act, taking into consideration the status of implementation of the provisions revised by this Act and changing socioeconomic conditions, among other factors, and when it finds it necessary, take required measures based on its findings.

Supplementary Provisions [Act No. 129 of July 25, 2003] [Extract]

(Effective Date)
Article 1 This Act shall come into effect as of the date to be specified by Cabinet Order within a period not exceeding one month from the day of promulgation.

(Delegation of Transitional Measures to Cabinet Order)
Article 2 Necessary transitional measures for the enforcement of this Act shall be specified by Cabinet Order.

Supplementary Provisions [Act No. 132 of July 30, 2003] [Extract]

(Effective Date)
Article 1 This Act shall come into effect as of the date to be specified by Cabinet Order within a period not exceeding three months from the day of promulgation; provided, however, that where the Effective Date of the Act for Partial Revision of the Insurance

Business Act (Act No. 39 of 2003) comes after the Effective Date of this Act, the provisions revising Article 52-3, paragraphs (2) and (3) and Article 65 of the Insurance Business Act (Act No. 105 of 1995) in Article 5 of the Supplementary Provisions shall come into effect as of the Effective Date of the Act for Partial Revision of the Insurance Business Act.

Supplementary Provisions [Act No. 134 of August 1, 2003] [Extract]

(Effective Date)
Article 1 This Act shall come into effect as of the date to be specified by Cabinet Order within a period not exceeding one year from the day of promulgation.

(Transitional Measures Accompanying Partial Revision to Insurance Business Act)
Article 35 With regard to a statutory lien pertaining to any claims emerging from that employment relationship set forth in Article 295, paragraph (1) of the Former Commercial Code as applied mutatis mutandis pursuant to Article 59, paragraph (1) of the Insurance Business Act prior to its revision by the provisions of the preceding Article which started prior to the Effective Date, the provisions then in force shall remain applicable.

Supplementary Provisions [Act No. 76 of June 2, 2004] [Extract]

(Effective Date)
Article 1 This Act shall come into effect as of the Effective Date of the Bankruptcy Act (Act No. 75 of 2004; referred to as "New Bankruptcy Act" in paragraph (8) of the following Article, and in Article 3, paragraph (8), Article 5, paragraph (8), (16) and (21), Article 8, paragraph (3) and Article 13 of the Supplementary Provisions).

(Delegation to Cabinet Order)
Article 14 In addition to what is provided for in Article 2 to the preceding Article inclusive of the Supplementary Provisions, necessary transitional measures for the enforcement of this Act shall be specified by Cabinet Order.

Supplementary Provisions [Act No. 87 of June 9, 2004] [Extract]

(Effective Date)
Article 1 This Act shall come into effect as of the date to be specified by Cabinet Order within a period not exceeding one year from the day of promulgation.

(Transitional Measures for Repeal of Public Notice, etc.)
Article 2 (1) The provisions then in force shall remain applicable to public notice in the case of any action filed under Article 104, paragraph (1), Article 136, paragraph (1), Article 140, Article 141, Article 247, paragraph (1), Article 252, Article 280-15, paragraph (1), Article 363, paragraph (1), Article 372, paragraph (1), Article 374-12, paragraph (1), Article 374-28, paragraph (1), Article 380, paragraph (1), Article 415, paragraph (1) or Article 428, paragraph (1) of the Commercial Code prior to its revision by the provisions of Article 1 (hereinafter referred to as "Former Commercial Code" in this Article) (including the cases where those provisions are applied mutatis mutandis pursuant to the Former Commercial Code or any other Act), any action filed under Article 73-14, paragraph (1) of the Agricultural Cooperative Association Act prior to its revi-

sion by the provisions of Article 6, any action filed under Article 101-15, paragraph (1) of the Securities and Exchange Act prior to its revision by the provisions of Article 7, any action filed under Article 94, paragraph (2) of the Act on Securities Investment Trust and Securities Investment Corporations prior to its revision by the provisions of Article 13 (referred to as "Former Investment Trust Act" in the following paragraph), any action filed under Article 100-16, paragraph (1) of the Act on the Organization of Small and Medium-Sized Enterprise Association prior to its revision by the provisions of Article 15, any action filed under Article 34-18, paragraph (1) of the Financial Futures Trading Act prior to its revision by the provisions of Article 18, any action filed under Article 84, paragraph (1) of the Insurance Business Act prior to its revision by the provisions of Article 19, or any action filed under Article 22, paragraph (1), Article 38, paragraph (2) or (3), Article 79, paragraph (1), Article 95, paragraph (1) or Article 125, paragraph (1) of the Intermediate Companies Act prior to its revision by the provisions of Article 23, prior to the enforcement of this Act.

(2) The provisions then in force shall remain applicable to public notice and notification in the case of any payment made under Article 309, paragraph (1) of the Former Commercial Code (including the cases where it is applied mutatis mutandis pursuant to the Former Commercial Code or any other Act), any resolution adopted under Article 64, paragraph (1) or Article 67, paragraph (1) of the Limited Liability Companies Act prior to its revision by the provisions of Article 3, any security interest exercised by an Entrusted Company pursuant to the provisions of Article 82, paragraph (1) of the Secured Bond Trust Act prior to its revision by the provisions of Article 5, any payment made under Article 139-5, paragraph (1) of the Former Investment Trust Act, any payment made under Article 111, paragraph (1) of the Act on the Liquidation of Assets prior to its revision by the provisions of Article 20, any resolution adopted under Article 10-17, paragraph (1) or (7) of the Act to Promote the Creation of New Business Undertakings prior to its revision by the provisions of Article 21, or any payment made under Article 111, paragraph (1) of the Act on the Liquidation of Specified Assets by Special Purpose Companies prior to its revision by the provisions of Article 1 of the Act for Partial Revision of the Act on the Liquidation of Specified Assets by Special Purpose Companies, etc. prior to its revision by the provisions of Article 24, which is to remain in force pursuant to the provisions of Article 2, paragraph (1) of the Supplementary Provisions to that Act, prior to the enforcement of this Act.

(Transitional Measures for the Application of Penal Provisions)
Article 3 With regard to the application of penal provisions to actions taken prior to the enforcement of this Act and to actions taken subsequent to the enforcement of this Act where the provisions then in force shall be applicable under the preceding Article, the provisions then in force shall remain applicable.

Supplementary Provisions [Act No. 88 of June 9, 2004] [Extract]

(Effective Date)
Article 1 This Act shall come into effect as of the date to be specified by Cabinet Order within a period not exceeding five years from the day of promulgation (hereinafter referred to as "Effective Date"); provided, however, that the provisions of Article 34, paragraph (7) to (16) inclusive of the Supplementary Provisions shall come into effect as of the Effective Date of the Companies Act (Act No. 86 of 2005).

(Transitional Measures Accompanying Partial Revision to the Insurance Business Act)

Article 41 (1) Where the period (hereinafter referred to as "Closure Period" in this Article) prescribed in Article 11, paragraph (1) of the Insurance Business Act prior to its revision by the provisions of Article 6 (hereinafter referred to as "Former Insurance Business Act" in this Article) for a Stock Company that conducts Insurance Business (meaning a Stock Company that conducts Insurance Business as defined in Article 9, paragraph (1) of the Former Insurance Business Act; hereinafter referred to as a "Company" in this Article) starts to elapse prior to the Partial Enforcement Date and expires subsequent to the Partial Enforcement Date, the Company set forth in that paragraph may choose not to change any of the details or records in the shareholders list even after the Partial Enforcement Date until the expiration of the Closure Period.

(2) With regard to a Company (including a Company that obtained certification for its articles of incorporation prior to the Partial Enforcement Date but was established subsequent to the Partial Enforcement Date (hereinafter referred to as "Company in the Course of Incorporation" in this paragraph)) whose articles of incorporation include provisions pertaining to the Closure Period as of the Partial Enforcement Date but do not include any provisions pertaining to the certain date set forth in Article 11, paragraph (2) of the Former Insurance Business Act, a resolution for an amendment in the articles of incorporation shall be deemed to be adopted as of the Partial Enforcement Date (or, for a Company in the Course of Incorporation, the date of its establishment) to designate the first day of the Closure Period as the certain date set forth in that paragraph, in order to specify the persons to exercise rights as shareholders or pledgees. In this case, a resolution of the board of directors shall determine the content of such rights.

(Transitional Measures for Application of Penal Provisions)
Article 135 With regards to the application of penal provisions to actions taken prior to the enforcement of this Act and to actions taken subsequent to the enforcement of this Act where the provisions then in force shall remain applicable or remain in force pursuant to these Supplementary Provisions, the provisions then in force shall remain applicable.

(Delegation of Other Transitional Measures to Cabinet Order)
Article 136 In addition to what is provided for in these Supplementary Provisions, necessary transitional measures for the enforcement of this Act shall be specified by Cabinet Order.

(Review)
Article 137 Where five years have elapsed from the enforcement of this Act, the Government shall, taking into consideration the status of implementation of the provisions revised by this Act and changing socioeconomic conditions, among other factors, review the settlement system pertaining to the transactions of Shares, etc. revised by this Act, and when it finds it necessary, take required measures based on its findings.

Supplementary Provisions [Act No. 97 of June 9, 2004] [Extract]

(Effective Date)
Article 1 This Act shall come into effect as of 1 April 2005 (hereinafter referred to as "Effective Date"); provided, however, that the provisions listed in the following items shall come into effect as of the date specified in the relevant item:
(i) In Article 1, the provisions revising Article 33-3, Article 64-2, paragraphs (1) and (2) and Article 64-7, paragraph (5) of the Securities Exchange Act, the provisions re-

vising Article 65-2, paragraph (5) of that Act (limited to the segment replacing the term "and (vii)" with ", (vii) and (xii)") and the provisions revising Article 144, Article 163, paragraph (2) and Article 207, paragraph (1), item (i) and paragraph (2) of that Act; in Article 2, the provisions revising Article 36, paragraph (2) of the Act on Foreign Securities Brokers (hereinafter referred to as "Foreign Securities Brokers Act" in this Article); in Article 4, the provisions revising Article 10-5 of the Act on Securities Investment Trust and Securities Investment Corporations (hereinafter referred to as "Investment Trust Act" in this Article); in Article 6, the provisions revising Article 29-3 of the Act on Regulation, etc. of Securities Investment Advisory Services (hereinafter referred to as "Investment Advisory Business Act" in this Article); the provisions of Articles 11 and 12; in Article 13, the provisions adding terms to Article 9-8, paragraph (6), item (i) of the Small and Medium-Sized Enterprise Cooperatives Act; and the provisions of Article 14 to 19 inclusive: the day of promulgation of this Act;

(Transitional Measures for Application of Penal Provisions)
Article 22 With regard to the application of penal provisions to actions taken prior to the enforcement of this Act (or, for the provisions listed in the items of Article 1 of the Supplementary Provisions, such provisions; hereinafter the same shall apply in this Article) and to actions taken subsequent to the enforcement of this Act where the provisions then in force are to remain applicable pursuant to the provisions of Article 3 of the Supplementary Provisions, the provisions then in force shall remain applicable

(Delegation of Other Transitional Measures to Cabinet Order)
Article 23 In addition to what is provided for in these Supplementary Provisions, necessary transitional measures for the enforcement of this Act shall be specified by Cabinet Order.

(Review)
Article 24 Where five years have elapsed from the enforcement of this Act, the Government shall, taking into consideration the status of implementation of the provisions revised by this Act and changing socioeconomic conditions, among other factors, review the financial systems revised by this Act, and when it finds it necessary, take required measures based on its findings.

Supplementary Provisions [Act No. 105 of June 11, 2004] [Extract]

(Effective Date)
Article 1 This Act shall come into effect as of 1 April 2006; provided, however, that the provisions of Article 17, paragraph (3) (limited to the segment applying mutatis mutandis the provisions of Article 14 of the Act on General Rules), Article 30, and the following Article to Article 5 inclusive of the Supplementary Provisions, Article 7 of the Supplementary Provisions and Article 39 of the Supplementary Provisions shall come into effect as of the day of promulgation.

(Delegation to Cabinet Order)
Article 39 In addition to what is provided for in Article 2 to 13 inclusive of the Supplementary Provisions, Article 15 of the Supplementary Provisions, Article 16 of the Supplementary Provisions and Article 19 of the Supplementary Provisions, necessary transitional measures accompanying the incorporation of the Government Pension Investment Fund and other necessary transitional measures for the enforcement of this

Act shall be specified by Cabinet Order.

Supplementary Provisions [Act No. 124 of June 18, 2004] [Extract]

(Effective Date)
Article 1 This Act shall come into effect as of the Effective Date of the New Act on the Registration of Immovables.

(Transitional Measures)
Article 2 In the case that the Effective Date of this Act falls after the Effective Date of Act on the Protection of Personal Information Held by Administrative Organs, then in Article 52, the provisions revising Article 114-3 and Article 117 to 119 inclusive of the Commercial Registration Act, the term "Article 114-3" shall be deemed to be replaced with "Article 114-4."

Supplementary Provisions [Act No. 147 of December 1, 2004] [Extract]

(Effective Date)
Article 1 This Act shall come into effect as of the date to be specified by Cabinet Order within a period not exceeding six months from the day of promulgation.

Supplementary Provisions [Act No. 154 of December 3, 2004] [Extract]

(Effective Date)
Article 1 This Act shall come into effect as of the date to be specified by Cabinet Order within a period not exceeding six months from the day of promulgation (hereinafter referred to as "Effective Date").

(Effect of Dispositions, etc.)
Article 121 Those dispositions, procedures or other actions taken pursuant to the provisions of the respective Acts prior to the enforcement of this Act (including any orders pursuant thereto; hereinafter the same shall apply in this Article), which are covered by the corresponding provisions of the respective Acts as revised, shall be deemed to have been carried out pursuant to such corresponding provisions of the respective Acts as revised, unless provided otherwise in these Supplementary Provisions.

(Transitional Measures Concerning Penal Provisions)
Article 122 With regard to the application of penal provisions to actions taken prior to the enforcement of this Act and to actions taken subsequent to the enforcement of this Act where the provisions then in force are to remain applicable pursuant to these Supplementary Provisions, the provisions then in force shall remain applicable.

(Delegation of Other Transitional Measures to Cabinet Order)
Article 123 In addition to what is provided for in these Supplementary Provisions, necessary transitional measures accompanying the enforcement of this Act shall be specified by Cabinet Order.

(Review)
Article 124 The Government shall, within three years from the enforcement of this Act, review the status of enforcement of this Act, and when it finds it necessary, take re-

quired measures based on its findings.

Supplementary Provisions [Act No. 159 of December 8, 2004] [Extract]

(Effective Date)
Article 1 This Act shall come into effect as of 1 July 2005.

Supplementary Provisions [Act No. 38 of May 2, 2005] [Extract]

(Effective Date)
Article 1 This Act shall come into effect as of the date to be specified by Cabinet Order within a period not exceeding one year from the day of promulgation (hereinafter referred to as "Effective Date"); provided, however, that the provisions listed in the following items shall come into effect as of the date specified in the relevant item:
  (i) In Article 1, The provisions revising Article 59, paragraph (1) of the Insurance Business Act (limited to the segment replacing the term "the term "Article 130, paragraph (3) of that Act" shall be deemed to be replaced with "Article 48, paragraph (2) of the Insurance Business Act" and the term "Ordinance of the Ministry of Justice" shall be deemed to be replaced with "Cabinet Office Ordinance"" with "the term "by an Ordinance of the Ministry of Justice as electronic public notice (meaning the electronic public notice set forth in Article 66, paragraph (6) of the Insurance Business Act; the same shall apply hereinafter)" shall be deemed to be replaced with "electromagnetic means (meaning the electromagnetic means set forth in Article 48, paragraph (2) of the Insurance Business Act) by Cabinet Office Ordinance""), the provisions revising Article 258, paragraph (2) of that Act, the provisions revising Article 270-4, paragraph (9) of that Act (excluding the segment adding the term "(including the cases where it is applied mutatis mutandis pursuant to Article 272-29)" after the term "Article 135, paragraph (1)" and adding the term "and Article 272-29" after the term "(Article 210, paragraph (1)" in Article 155, item (i)) and the provisions revising Article 271-4, paragraph (1) of that Act, and the provisions revising Article 1-2-13 of the Supplementary Provisions to that Act (limited to the segment adding a paragraph to that Article): the date to be specified by Cabinet Order within a period not exceeding three months from the day of promulgation; and
  (ii) In Article 1, the provisions revising Article 118 of the Insurance Business Act, the provisions revising Article 199 of that Act (limited to the segment replacing the term "establish" with "shall establish"), the provisions revising Article 245 of that Act, the provisions revising Article 247, paragraph (1) of that Act, the provisions revising Article 250 of that Act (limited to the segment replacing the term "Insurance Company" in paragraph (1) of that Article with "Insurance Company, etc. or Foreign Insurance Company, etc.," the segment adding the term "and Article 272-29" after the term "Article 210, paragraph (1)" in that paragraph, the segment replacing the term "Insurance Company" in paragraph (2) of that Article with "Insurance Company, etc. or Foreign Insurance Company, etc.," the segment replacing the term "the Insurance Company set forth in paragraph (1), when it is not a Foreign Insurance Company, etc." in paragraph (4) of that Article with "in the case referred to in paragraph (1), in the Insurance Company, etc.," the segment adding the term "(including the cases where it is applied mutatis mutandis pursuant to Article 272-29)" after the term "Article 136, paragraph (1)" in that paragraph, the segment replacing the term "when it is a Foreign Insurance Company, etc." in that paragraph with "in the Insurance Company, etc." and the segment replacing the term "Insurance Company" in paragraph (5) of that Article with "Insurance Company,

etc. or Foreign Insurance Company, etc."), the provisions revising Article 254 of that Act (limited to the segment adding the term "and Business for Canceling Specified Covered Insurance Contracts" after the term "Business for Paying Covered Insurance Proceeds" in paragraph (4) of that Article), the provisions revising Article 255-2 of that Act (limited to the segment adding the term "and Business for Canceling Specified Covered Insurance Contracts" after the term "Business for Paying Covered Insurance Proceeds" in paragraph (3) of that Article), the provisions revising Article 267 of that Act, the provisions revising Article 270-3 of that Act, the provisions revising Article 270-5, paragraph (2), item (i) of that Act and the provisions revising Article 270-6-8, paragraph (2) of that Act, and the provisions revising Article 1-2-14 of the Supplementary Provisions to that Act and the provisions changing the number of that Article into Article 1-2-15 of the Supplementary Provisions to that Act and adding an Article after Article 1-2-13 of the Supplementary Provisions to that Act; and in Article 3, the provisions revising Article 440 of the Act on Special Treatment of Corporate Reorganization Proceedings and Other Insolvency Proceedings by Financial Institutions, etc. and the provisions revising Article 445 of that Act: 1 April 2006.

(Transitional Measures)
Article 2 (1) In the cases set forth in each of the following items, a person conducting Specified Insurance Business (meaning Insurance Business as defined in Article 2, paragraph (1) of the Insurance Business Act as revised by the provisions of Article 1 (hereinafter referred to as the "New Insurance Business Act") that does not fall under the category of Insurance Business defined in Article 2, paragraph (1) of the Insurance Business Act prior to its revision by the provisions of Article 1 (hereinafter referred to as "Former Insurance Business Act"); the same shall apply hereinafter) at the time when this Act enters into force may, notwithstanding the provisions of Article 3, paragraph (1) of the New Insurance Business Act, conduct Specified Insurance Business until the date specified in each of those items:
(i) In the case that the abolition of the Specified Insurance Business is ordered pursuant to the provisions of Article 272-26, paragraph (1) or of Article 272-27 of the New Insurance Business Act as applied with relevant changes in interpretation pursuant to the provisions of Article 4, paragraph (1) of the Supplementary Provisions: On the date said abolition was ordered
(ii) In the case that an application is made for a license as set forth in Article 3, paragraph (1) of the New Insurance Business Act or an application for registration is made for a license as set forth in Article 272, paragraph (1) of the New Insurance Business Act within two years of the Effective Date (except in cases that fall under the preceding item): On the date of the disposition refusing the license or registration
(iii) In the case that a person who has committed to receive the transfer of insurance contracts from a person conducting Specified Insurance Business or succeed to insurance contracts from a person conducting Specified Insurance Business (limited to persons who have applied for approval of the transfer or succession of said insurance contracts pursuant to the provisions of Article 4, paragraphs (7), (8), (11) and (12) of the Supplementary Provisions within two years of the Effective Date) files an application for a license set forth in Article 3, paragraph (1) of the New Insurance Business Act or registration set forth in Article 272, paragraph (1) of the New Insurance Business Act within two years of the Effective Date (except in cases that fall under the preceding two items): On the date of the disposition refusing the license or registration

(iv) In cases that are not covered by any of the preceding three items: On the date two years after the Effective Date
(2) Among persons who are actually conducing Specified Insurance Business at the time when this Act enters into force, for persons who only manage business and property under insurance contracts that were underwritten before the Effective Date (except for persons subject to a disposition refusing the license set forth in Article 3, paragraph (1) of the of the New Insurance Business Act or the registration set forth in Article 272, paragraph (1) of the New Insurance Business Act), notwithstanding the provisions of the preceding paragraph, the provisions then in force shall remain applicable.
(3) A person who is actually conducting Specified Insurance Business at the time when this Act enters into force (excluding persons who are provided for in the preceding paragraph, persons who are listed in the items of Article 5, paragraph (1) of the Supplementary Provisions, and persons who have licenses as set forth in Article 3, paragraph (1) of the of the New Insurance Business Act or who have registrations as set forth in Article 272, paragraph (1) of the New Insurance Business Act; hereinafter referred to as "Specified Insurers") shall transfer, pursuant to its contract with an Insurance Company (including a Foreign Insurance Company, etc.; hereinafter the same shall apply in this Article) or Low-Cost, Short-Term Insurer, any insurance contract under which it manages the relevant business and property, or shall entrust the management of such business and property under such insurance contracts pursuant to its contract with an Insurance Company or Low-Cost, Short-Term Insurer corresponding with cases listed in the items of paragraph (1), after the date specified by the items and until one year from the date specified by the items.
(4) A Specified Insurer may conduct business and property management pertaining to insurance contracts underwritten before the date specified in the items until one year from the date under the provisions of the preceding paragraph (when the Prime Minister recognizes that there are compelling reasons making it impossible to effect the transfer of the insurance contracts and the entrusting of business and property management pertaining to insurance contracts as set forth in the same paragraph, until a date designated by the Prime Minister) notwithstanding the provisions of Article 3, paragraph (1) of the New Insurance Business Law, corresponding to cases listed in the items of paragraph (1).

(Report by Specified Insurers)
Article 3 (1) A Specified Insurer who continues to conduct Specified Insurance Business pursuant to paragraph (1) or (4) of the preceding Article (including a person who seeks to be a Specified Insurer pursuant to the paragraph (2) of that Article) shall submit a written notice detailing the particulars listed in the following to the Prime Minister by the day when six months have passed since the Effective Date (or, if the underwriting of the insurance is performed for the first time after the Effective Date, the date of such underwriting; hereinafter the same shall apply in this Article); provided, however, that this shall not apply to a person who applies for the license set forth in Article 3, paragraph (1) of the New Insurance Business Act or for the registration set forth in Article 272, paragraph (1) of the New Insurance Business Act by the day on which such six months have passed.
(i) Name or trade name
(ii) When the person is a juridical person, the amount of capital or contribution or total amount of funds
(iii) When the person is a juridical person (including an association or foundation that is not a juridical person and has provisions on representative persons or administrators), the name of the officer (including a representative persons or administra-

tor of an association or foundation that is not a juridical person)
(iv) Location of head office and other offices
(2) The following documents must be attached to the written notice in the preceding paragraph.
 (i) Insurance clause (including those relevant to this)
 (ii) Documents giving the particulars of the Policyholders, particulars of the person acting as an agent or intermediary for the conclusion of an insurance contract on behalf of a Specified Insurer, and other particulars specified by Cabinet Office Ordinance as the content and means of business.
 (iii) Inventory of property, balance sheets, income and expenditure account statement, profit and loss statements and other documents that disclose the situation of the property and business
 (iv) Other documents specified by Cabinet Office Ordinance
(3) If a Specified Insurer who continues to conduct Specified Insurance Business pursuant to paragraph (1) or (4) of the preceding Article comes to fall under any of the following items, the person specified in the relevant item shall notify the Prime Minister of this within thirty days from the date in question:
 (i) it has abolished its Specified Insurance Business: the Specified Insurer
 (ii) it has extinguished due to merger: the person who was the officer representing the Specified Insurer
 (iii) it has dissolved due to a ruling to commence bankruptcy proceedings: the bankruptcy trustee
 (iv) it has dissolved for reasons other than merger or the commencement of bankruptcy proceedings: the liquidator
 (v) it has transferred all insurance contracts, or all of its business has been succeeded to or assigned: the Specified Insurer

(Application of Provisions of the New Insurance Business Act to Specified Insurers)
Article 4 (1) When a Specified Insurer continues to conduct Specified Insurance Business pursuant to the provisions of Article 2, paragraph (1) or (4) of the Supplementary Provisions, such Specified Insurer shall be deemed to be a Low-Cost, Short-Term Insurer, and the provisions of Article 100-2 to 100-4 of the New Insurance Business Act, as applied mutatis mutandis pursuant to Article 272-13, paragraph (2), Article 272-16, paragraph (1) and the provisions of Article 272-16, Article 272-22 to 272-24 of the New Insurance Business Act and the provisions of Article 272-25, paragraph (1), Article 272-26 and 272-27 of the New Insurance Business Act (including the penal provisions pertaining thereto) shall apply. In this case, the term "measures to ensure" in Article 100-2 of the New Insurance Business Act as applied mutatis mutandis pursuant to Article 272-13, paragraph (2) of the New Insurance Business Act shall be deemed to be replaced with "measures (limited to those specified by Cabinet Office Ordinance) to ensure"; the term "the Specified Insurer shall not make any of the following transactions or act in any of the following ways; provided, however, that this shall not apply where the Prime Minister has approved such transaction or action for any of the compelling reasons specified by a Cabinet Office Ordinance" in Article 100-3 of the New Insurance Business Act as applied mutatis mutandis pursuant to Article 272-13, paragraph (2) of the New Insurance Business Act shall be deemed to be replaced with "the Specified Insurer shall not make any of the following transactions or act in any of the following ways (limited to those specified by Cabinet Office Ordinance)," the term "particulars detailed in the documents included in Article 272-2, paragraph (2), item (iv)" in Article 272-24, paragraph (1) of the New Insurance Business Act shall be

deemed to be replaced with "particulars detailed as part of the method of calculating insurance premiums or the method of calculating policy reserve," the term "particulars detailed in the documents included in that item" shall be deemed to be replaced with "such particulars," the term "particulars detailed in the documents included in Article 272-2, paragraph (2), items (ii) to (iv)" in Article 272, paragraph (2) shall be deemed to be replaced with "insurance clause (including those relevant to this) or particulars detailed as the method of calculating insurance premiums or the method of calculating policy reserve," the term "the following items" in Article 272-26, paragraph (1) of the New Insurance Business Act shall be deemed to be replaced with "items (i) and (iii) to (v)," the term "rescind the registration according to Article 272, paragraph (1)"shall be deemed to be replaced with "order for abolishing of the business," the term "from Article 272-4, paragraph (1), items (i) to (iv), (vii)" in item (i) of that paragraph shall be deemed to be replaced with "Article 272-4, paragraph (1), item (vii)," the term "in the event that the Specified Insurer is no longer a small business, other laws and regulations" in item (iii) of that paragraph shall be deemed to be replaced with "laws and regulations," the term "documents included in each of the items in Article 272-2, paragraph (2)" in item (iv) of that paragraph shall be deemed to be replaced with "insurance clause (including those relevant to this)," the term "the director, executive officer, and accounting adviser or company auditor" in paragraph (2) of that Article shall be deemed to be replaced with "the officer (including a representative persons or administrator of an association or foundation that is not a juridical person)," the term "laws and regulations in the event that it falls under any of the provisions in Article 272-4, paragraph (1), item (x), sub-items (a) to (f)" in Article 272, paragraph (2) shall be deemed to be replaced with "laws and regulations," the term "canceling registration set forth in Article 272, paragraph (1)" in Article 272-27 of the New Insurance Business Act shall be deemed to be replaced with "order for abolishing of the business"; and the term "the incorporator, director at the time of incorporation, the executive officer at the time of incorporation, the company auditor at the time of incorporation, the director, executive officer, accounting advisor or any member who is supposed to carry out such duties and the company auditor" in Article 333, paragraph (1) of the New Insurance Business Act shall be deemed to be replaced with "the incorporator, officer (including a representative person or administrator of an association or foundation that is not a juridical person)."

(2) For the purpose of applying the provisions of Article 272-4, paragraph (1), Article 272-33, paragraph (1), and Article 272-37, paragraph (1) of the New Insurance Business Act in the event that the Specified Insurer as a juridical person (including an association or foundation that is not a juridical person and has provisions on representative persons or administrators) is ordered to abolish Specified Insurance Business pursuant to the provisions of Article 272-26, paragraph (1) or Article 272-27 of the New Insurance Business Act applied with relevant changes in interpretation pursuant to the provisions of the preceding paragraph, the Specified Insurer being ordered to execute such abolishment shall be deemed to be a person having cancellation of registration set forth in Article 272, paragraph (1) of the New Insurance Business Act pursuant to the provisions of Article 272-26, paragraph (1) or Article 272-27 of the New Insurance Business Act, and the date on which such abolishment was ordered shall be deemed to be the date of cancellation of registration set forth in Article 272, paragraph (1) of the New Insurance Business Act pursuant to the provisions of Article 272-26, paragraph (1) or Article 272-27 of the New Insurance Business Act.

(3) For the purpose of applying the provisions of Article 272-4, paragraph (1), Article 272-33, paragraph (1), and Article 272-37, paragraph (1) of the New Insurance Business Act in the event that the Specified Insurer as an individual is ordered to abolish Speci-

fied Insurance Business pursuant to the provisions of Article 272-26, paragraph (1) or Article 272-27 of the New Insurance Business Act applied with relevant changes in interpretation pursuant to the provisions of paragraph (1), the individual shall be deemed to be a person who is subject to Article 272-4, paragraph (1), item (x), sub-item (c) of the New Insurance Business Act until five years have passed since the day on which the individual was ordered to execute such abolishment.

(4) The particulars for inclusion in the business reports set forth in Article 272-16, paragraph (1) of the New Insurance Business Act applied in paragraph (1), their submission dates and other necessary particulars of those written reports shall be specified by Cabinet Office Ordinance.

(5) The provisions of Article 272-16, paragraph (1) of the New Insurance Business Act applied in paragraph (1) shall apply from the business year on which ends after the day on which six months have elapsed from the Effective Date.

(6) The Prime Minister shall, pursuant to the provisions of Cabinet Office Ordinance, make portions of a business report that is referred to in Article 272-16, paragraph (1) of the New Insurance Business Act as applied pursuant to paragraph (1), available for public inspection that are recognized as necessary for protection of Policyholders, etc. , with the exception of any particulars that risk causing a breach of confidence and any particulars that risk putting a Specified Insurer that is deemed to be a Low-Cost, Short-Term Insurer pursuant to Article 272-16, paragraph (1) of the New Insurance Business Act applied in paragraph (1) at an unfair disadvantage in the administration of its business.

(7) When a Specified Insurer who continues to conduct Specified Insurance Business executes a transfer of insurance contracts pursuant to the provisions of Article 2, paragraph (1) or (4) of the Supplementary Provisions, such Specified Insurer shall be deemed to be a Low-Cost, Short-Term Insurer, and the provisions of Part II, Chapter VII, Section 1 of the New Insurance Business Act (including the penal provisions pertaining thereto) shall apply mutatis mutandis pursuant to Article 272-29 of the New Insurance Business Act. In this case, the term "Transferor Company and Transferee Company" in Article 136, paragraphs (1) and (3) of the New Insurance Business Act as applied mutatis mutandis in Article 272-29 shall be deemed to be replaced with "Transferee Company," the terms "The directors (or in a company with Committees, executive officers)" and "two weeks before of the date of Shareholders' Meeting, etc. set forth in paragraph (1) of the preceding Article" in Article 136-2, paragraph (1) of the New Insurance Business Act as applied mutatis mutandis in Article 272-29 of the New Insurance Business Act shall be deemed to be replaced with "the officers (including representative persons or administrators of an association or foundation that is not a juridical person)" and "the date of preparation of the Transfer Agreement concluded under Article 135, paragraph (1) (hereinafter referred to as "Transfer Agreement" in this Section)," respectively; the term "the Transfer Agreement concluded under Article 135, paragraph (1) and other" shall be deemed to be replaced with "Transfer Agreement and other," the term "A shareholder or Policyholder of the Transferor Company" in paragraph (2) of the same Article shall be deemed to be replaced with "Affected Policyholders," the term "the time of the adoption of the resolution under Article 136, paragraph (1)" in Article 138 of the New Insurance Business Act as applied mutatis mutandis pursuant to Article 272-29 of the New Insurance Business Act shall be deemed to be replaced with "the time of the creation of Transfer Agreement," the term "the incorporator, the director at the incorporation, the executive officer at the incorporation, the company auditor at the incorporation, the director, the executive officer, the accounting advisor or the member who is supposed to carry out such duties and the company auditor" in Article 333, paragraph (1) in the New Insurance Business

Act shall be deemed to be replaced with "the officer"; any technical change in interpretation required shall be specified by Cabinet Order.
(8) When a Specified Insurer continues to conduct Specified Insurance Business pursuant to the provisions of Article 2, paragraph (1) or (4) of the Supplementary Provisions, such Specified Insurer shall be deemed to be a Low-Cost, Short-Term Insurer, and the provisions of Article 142 of the New Insurance Business Act as applied mutatis mutandis pursuant to Article 272-30, paragraph (1) of the New Insurance Business Act shall apply.
(9) When a Specified Insurer who continues to conduct Specified Insurance Business pursuant to the provisions of Article 2, paragraph (1) or (4) of the Supplementary Provisions entrusts business and property management, such Specified Insurer shall be deemed to be a Low-Cost, Short-Term Insurer, and the provisions of Articles 144, 145, Article 146, paragraph (1) and Articles 147 to 149 of the New Insurance Business Act as applied mutatis mutandis in Article 272-30, paragraph (2) of the New Insurance Business Act, and the provisions of Article 150, paragraph (1) of the New Insurance Business Act (including the penal provisions pertaining thereto) shall apply. In this case, the term "the Insurance Company entrusting the administration (hereinafter referred to as "Entrusting Company" in this Section) and the Entrusted Company" in Article 144, paragraph (2) of the New Insurance Business Act as applied mutatis mutandis pursuant to Article 272-30, paragraph (2) of the New Insurance Business Act shall be deemed to be replaced with "Entrusted Company," the term "publish the gist of the Agreement set forth in Article 146, paragraph (1) (hereinafter referred to as "Administration Entrustment Agreement" in this Section) and register the entrustment of administration, and the Entrusted Company's trade name, name and its head office or principal office, or its principal branch store in Japan (meaning the principal branch store in Japan set forth in Article 187, paragraph (1), item (iv))" in Article 146, paragraph (1) of the New Insurance Business Act as applied mutatis mutandis pursuant to Article 272-30, paragraph (2) of the New Insurance Business Act shall be deemed to be replaced with "publish the gist of the Agreement set forth in Article 146, paragraph (1) (hereinafter referred to as "Administration Entrustment Agreement" in this Section)"; and the term "the Entrusting Company and the Entrusted Company" in Article 149, paragraph (1) of the New Insurance Business Act as applied mutatis mutandis pursuant to Article 272-30, paragraph (2) of the New Insurance Business Act shall be deemed to be replaced with "Entrusted Company."
(10) The provisions of the Part II, Chapter II, Section 1 and Chapter VIII of the New Insurance Business Act shall not be applied to a Specified Insurer who continues to conduct Specified Insurance Business pursuant to the provisions of Article 2, paragraph (1) or (4) of the Supplementary Provisions.
(11) When a Specified Insurer continues to conduct Specified Insurance Business pursuant to the provisions of Article 2, paragraph (1) or (4) of the Supplementary Provisions, such Specified Insurer shall be deemed to be a Low-Cost, Short-Term Insurer, and the provisions of Article 167, paragraphs (1) and (2) of the New Insurance Business Act shall apply.
(12) When a Specified Insurer continues to conduct Specified Insurance Business pursuant to the provisions of Article 2, paragraph (1) or (4) of the Supplementary Provisions, such Specified Insurer shall be deemed to be a Low-Cost, Short-Term Insurer, and the provisions of Article 173-6, paragraphs (1) and (2) of the New Insurance Business Act shall apply.
(13) A Specified Insurer who continues to conduct Specified Insurance Business pursuant to the provisions of Article 2, paragraph (1) or (4) of the Supplementary Provisions shall receive approval from the Prime Minister when he/she seeks to abolish Specified

Insurance Business.

(14) Any public notice given by a Specified Insurer who continues to conduct Specified Insurance Business pursuant to the provisions of Article 2, paragraph (1) or (4) of the Supplementary Provisions, pursuant to the provisions of the New Insurance Business Act applied in paragraph (7) or (9) shall be published in a daily newspaper that publishes the particulars of current events.

(15) When a Specified Insurer continues to conduct Specified Insurance Business pursuant to the provisions of Article 2, paragraph (1) or (4) of the Supplementary Provisions, such Specified Insurer shall be deemed to be an Insurance Company, etc. , or Affiliated Insurance Company, etc. , the person acting as an agent or intermediary for the conclusion of an insurance contract on behalf of such Specified Insurer shall be deemed to be an Insurance Agent or Specified Insurance Agent, and the provisions of Article 283, Article 294, Article 300, paragraph (1) (limited to the segment pertaining to items (i) to (iv), (vi), (vii), and (ix)), Article 305, Article 306, Article 307, paragraph (1) and Article 309 (including the penal provisions pertaining thereto) shall apply. In this case, the term "any of the following items" in Article 307, paragraph (1) of the New Insurance Business Act shall be deemed to be replaced with "the item (i) or (iii)," and "cancel the registration set forth in Article 276 or 286" shall be deemed to be replaced with "order abolition of the business."

(16) For the purpose of applying the provisions of Article 272-4, paragraph (1) and Article 279, paragraph (1) of the New Insurance Business Act in the case where the Specified Insurer is ordered to abolish the business pursuant to the provisions of Article 307, paragraph (1) of the New Insurance Business Act applied with relevant changes in interpretation pursuant to the provisions of the preceding paragraph, the person who is ordered such abolishment shall be deemed to be a person of whom is canceled the registration set forth in Article 276 of the New Insurance Business Act, and the day of which such abolishment is ordered shall be deemed to be the day of cancellation of the registration set forth in Article 276 of the New Insurance Business Act pursuant to the provisions of Article 307, paragraph (1) of the New Insurance Business Act.

(Transitional Measure regarding Public-interest Corporation, etc.)
Article 5 (1) A juridical person (excluding the following) established pursuant to the provisions of Article 34 of the Civil Code (Act No. 89 of 1896), which conducts Specified Insurance Business at the time when this Act enters into force may continue to conduct Specified Insurance Business notwithstanding the provisions of Article 3, paragraph (1) of the New Insurance Business Act until otherwise stipulated.
  (i) A juridical person that has completed the registration set forth in Article 106, paragraph (1) of the Act to Re-Arrange the Related Acts in Line with the Enforcement of the Act on General Incorporated Associations and General Incorporated Foundations and the Act on the Authorization, etc. of Public-Interest Incorporated Associations and Public-Interest Incorporated Foundations (Act No. 50 of 2006. Hereinafter referred to as "Revising Act") (referred to as "Public-Interest Corporation Transfer Registration" in paragraph (5)) with the authorization set forth in Article 44 of the Revising Act
  (ii) A juridical person that has completed the registration set forth in Article 106, paragraph (1) of the Revising Act (referred to as "General Incorporated Association, etc., Transfer Registration" in paragraph (5)) as applied mutatis mutandis pursuant to Article 121, paragraph (1) of the Revising Act, with the approval set forth in Article 45 of the Revising Act
(2) The Japan Chambers of Commerce and Industry, societies of commerce and industry or Central Federations of Societies of Commerce and Industry who conduct Specified

Insurance Business at the time when this Act enters into force can continuously conduct Specified Insurance Business notwithstanding the provisions of Article 3, paragraph (1) of the New Insurance Business Act until otherwise stipulated.
(3) When Specified Insurance Business is continuously conducted pursuant to the provisions of the preceding two paragraphs, the person conducting business shall be deemed to be an Insurance Company, etc. , or Affiliated Insurance Company, etc. the person acting as an agent or intermediary for the conclusion of an insurance contract on behalf of such Specified Insurer shall be deemed to be an Insurance Agent or a Specified Insurance Agent, and the provisions (including the penal provisions pertaining thereto) of Article 283 and Article 300, paragraph (1) (limited to the segment pertaining to items (i) to (iii)) shall apply.
(4) For the purpose of applying the provisions of Article 95 and Article 96 of the Revising Act in the case where the Specified Insurance Business is continuously conducted pursuant to the provisions of paragraph (1), the term "business of a special case juridical person under the Civil Code" in Article 95 of the Revising Act shall be deemed to be replaced with "business of a special case juridical person under the Civil Code (including Specified Insurance Business prescribed in Article 2, paragraph (1) of the Supplementary Provisions of the Act on Partial Revision of the Insurance Business Act, etc. (Act No. 38 of 2005); the same shall apply in the following paragraph)," the term "order" in Article 96, paragraph (1) of the Revising Act shall be deemed to be replaced with "order (including the order of which make it comply with the provisions of Article 300, paragraph (1) (limited to the segment pertaining to items (i) to (iii)) of the Insurance Business Act (Act No. 105 of 1995))," and "order by" in paragraph (2) of the same Article shall be deemed to be replaced with "order by (including the order of which make it comply with the provisions of Article 300, paragraph (1) of the New Insurance Business Act (limited to the segment pertaining to items (i) to (iii))."
(5) A juridical person that was established pursuant to the provisions of Article 34 of the Civil Code, which is actually conducting Specified Insurance Business at the time when this Act enters into force, and which is listed in the items of paragraph (1) (excluding a person with the registration set forth in Article 272, paragraph (1) of the New Insurance Business Act; hereinafter referred to as "Transferred Juridical Person" in this Article) can manage business and the property under an insurance contract that the person underwrote before the day of the Public-Interest Corporation Transfer Registration or General Incorporated Association etc. , Transfer Registration (hereinafter, named generically as "Transfer Registration" in this Article) notwithstanding the provisions of Article 3, paragraph (1) of the New Insurance Business Act for a period of one year counting from the day of the Transfer Registration (or until the day that the Prime Minister designates when he/she recognizes that there are compelling reasons for the following insurance contract and the entrustment pertaining to the management of the business and property not to be transferred).
(6) In the case referred to in the preceding paragraph, such Transferred Juridical Person shall, by the day on which on year has passed described in the same paragraph, and pursuant to its contract with an Insurance Company (including Foreign Insurance Company, etc; hereinafter the same shall apply in this Article) or Low-Cost, Short-Term Insurer, transfer any insurance contract under which the person manages the relevant business and property, or entrust the management of business and property under such insurance contract pursuant to the contract with an Insurance Company or Low-Cost, Short-Term Insurer.
(7) A Transferred Juridical Person that manages the business and property pertaining to an insurance contract underwritten before the day of the Transfer Registration pursuant to the provisions of paragraph (5) shall be deemed to be a Low-Cost, Short-Term

Insurer, and the provisions of Article 272-22, Article 272-23, Article 272-25, paragraph (1), Article 272-26, and Article 272-27 of the New Insurance Business Act (including the penal provisions pertaining thereto) shall apply. In this case, the term "items listed in following" and the term "cancel registration set forth in Article 272, paragraph (1)" in Article 272-26, paragraph (1) of the New Insurance Business Act shall be deemed to be replaced with "items (i) and (iii) to (v)" and "order for abolishing of the business" respectively; the term "Article 272-4, paragraph (1), items (i) to (iv), items (vii) and (viii)" in item (i) of the same paragraph shall be deemed to be replaced with "Article 272-4, paragraph (1), item (viii)," the term "in the case where the Specified Insurer is no longer a small business, other laws and regulations" in item (iii) of the same paragraph shall be "laws and regulations," the term "documents included in each of the items in Article 272-2, paragraph (2)" in item (iv) of the same paragraph shall be deemed to be replaced with "insurance contract (including those relevant thereto)," the term "the director, executive officer, and accounting adviser or company auditor" and "laws and regulations in the case where it falls under any of the provisions in Article 272-4, paragraph (1), item (x), sub-items (a) to (f) inclusive" in paragraph (2) of the same Article shall be deemed to be replaced with "the officer" and "laws and regulations" respectively; the term "cancel registration set forth in Article 272, paragraph (1)" in Article 272-27 of the New Insurance Business Act shall be deemed to be replaced with "order for abolishing of the business," the term "the incorporator, the director at the incorporation, the executive officer at the incorporation, the company auditor at the incorporation, the director, the executive officer, the accounting advisor or the member who is supposed to carry out such duties and the auditor" in Article 333, paragraph (1) in the New Insurance Business Act shall be "the officer," and other necessary technical change in interpretation shall be specified by Cabinet Order.

(8) A Transferred Juridical Person that manages business and property pertaining to an insurance contract underwritten before the day of the Transfer Registration pursuant to the provisions of paragraph (5) shall be deemed to be a Specified Insurer who continues to conduct Specified Insurance Business pursuant to the provisions of Article 2, paragraph (1) or (4) of the Supplementary Provisions, and the provisions of Article 3 of the Supplementary Provisions (excluding paragraph (2)), the preceding Article (limited to paragraph (7) to (12) and (14)), following Article (limited to paragraphs (2) and (5)), and Articles 8 and 16 of the Supplementary Provisions shall apply. In this case, the term "by the day when six months have passed since the Effective Date (or, if the underwriting of the insurance is performed for the first time after the Effective Date, the date of such underwriting; hereinafter the same shall apply in this Article)" in Article 3, paragraph (1) of the Supplementary Provisions shall be deemed to be replaced with "after the day on which the Transfer Registration provided in Article 5, paragraph (1) of the Supplementary Provisions was registered without delay" and the term ": provided, however, that this shall not apply to a person who applies for the license set forth in Article 3, paragraph (1) of the New Insurance Business Act or for the registration set forth in Article 272, paragraph (1) of the New Insurance Business Act by the day on which such six months have passed" in the Article 3, paragraph (1) of the Supplementary Provisions shall be deemed to be deleted; the term "by the day when two years have passed since the Effective Date" in paragraph (2) of the following Article shall be deemed to be replaced with "shall apply pursuant to the provisions of paragraph (8) of the preceding Article by the day when six years have passed since the Effective Date of the Revising Act," the term "five years have passed since the Effective Date" in paragraph (8) of the preceding Article, Article 8, paragraph (2) and Article 16, paragraph (18) of the Supplementary Provisions shall be deemed to be replaced with "eight years have passed since the Effective Date of the Revising Act," the term "by

the day when two years have passed since the Effective Date" in Article 8, paragraph (2) and Article 16, paragraphs (1), (17) and (18) of the Supplementary Provisions shall be deemed to be replaced with "shall apply pursuant to the provisions of Article 5, paragraph (8) of the Supplementary Provisions by the day when six years have passed since the Effective Date of the Revising Act," and the term "seven years have passed since the Effective Date" in Article 16, paragraph (1) shall be deemed to be replaced with "ten years have passed since the Effective Date of the Revising Act"; any technical change in interpretation required shall be specified by Cabinet Order.

(Transitional Measures, etc. Concerning Examination Licensing Standards)
Article 6 (1) The provisions of Article 6, paragraph (1) of the New Insurance Business Act shall not apply to Specified Insurers who have applied for a license as set forth in Article 3, paragraph (1) of the New Insurance Business Act (limited to persons whose capital amount at the time of the application for that license exceeds five hundred million yen and is less than the amount specified by Cabinet Order as set forth in Article 6, paragraph (1) of the New Insurance Business Act) for a period of five years counting from the Effective Date.
(2) The provisions of Article 6, paragraph (1) of the New Insurance Business Act shall not apply to a license applicant as set forth in Article 3, paragraph (1) of the New Insurance Business Act who has committed that he/she will receive the transfer of insurance contracts from a Specified Insurer or succeed to insurance contracts from a Specified Insurer (limited to persons who have filed an application for approval of the transfer or succession of that insurance contract pursuant to the provisions of Article 4, paragraphs (7), (8), (11) and (12) of the Supplementary Provisions until the date two years after the Effective Date, and to persons whose capital amount at the time of the application for that license exceeds five hundred million yen and is less than the amount specified by Cabinet Order as set forth in Article 6, paragraph (1) of the New Insurance Business Act) for a period of five years counting from the Effective Date.
(3) Where the person to whom the provisions of the preceding paragraph is applied is a Mutual Company, for a period of five years set forth in the same paragraph, said person may set aside as a reserves all or part of the amount that may be allocated to the redemption of funds or distribution of surplus specified in Article 55, paragraph (2) of the New Insurance Business Act, until such time as the total amount of funds (including the reserves for redemption of funds set forth in Article 56 of the New Insurance Business Act (including any amount deemed to have been set aside as the reserves for redemption of funds pursuant to the provisions of the following paragraph)) reaches the amount set forth in Article 6, paragraph (1) of the New Insurance Business Act to be specified by Cabinet Order.
(4) The reserves set aside pursuant to the provisions of the preceding paragraph shall be deemed to have been set aside as the reserves for redemption of funds set forth in Article 56 of the New Insurance Business Act.
(5) The Prime Minister may attach necessary conditions pursuant to the provisions of Article 5, paragraph (2) of the New Insurance Business Act concerning Specified Insurers as prescribed in paragraph (1) or concerning the issuance of licenses to license applicants as prescribed in paragraph (2), with regard to underwriting of insurance contracts by the other party, contents of insurance contracts, and other particulars to said licenses.

(Transitional Measures for Registry)
Article 7 (1) The Registry of Mutual Insurance Companies kept in a registry office at the time when this Act enters into force shall be deemed to be the Registry of Mutual In-

surance Companies set forth in Article 64 of the New Insurance Business Act.
(2) The Registry of Foreign Mutual Insurance Companies kept in a registry office at the time when this Act enters into force shall be deemed to be the Registry of Foreign Mutual Insurance Companies set forth in Article 214 of the New Insurance Business Act.

(Transitional Measures for the Insurance Company, etc., which was a Specified Insurer)
Article 8 (1) The provisions of Article 113 of the New Insurance Business Act shall not be applied to the Insurance Company which applied for a license set forth in Article 3, paragraph (1) of the New Insurance Business Act and received the license set forth in the same paragraph following the application of the provisions of Article 6, paragraph (2) of the Supplementary Provisions.
(2) The Insurance Company which was a Specified Insurer or the Insurance Company which received transfer of the insurance contract from a Specified Insurer or succeeded to the insurance contract from a Specified Insurer (limited to the person who applied for the approval of transfer or succession of insurance contract pursuant to the provisions of Article 4, paragraph (7), (8), (11) or (12) of the Supplementary Provisions and applied for the license set forth in Article 3, paragraph (1) in the New Insurance Business Act by the day when two years have passed since the Effective Date) may, with giving a notification to the Prime Minister, be relieved of the requirement of accumulating the policy reserves specified by a Cabinet Office Ordinance set forth in Article 116, paragraph (1) of the New Insurance Business Act for the accounting period that ends by the day when five years have passed since the Effective Date.

(Transitional Measures regarding Suspension of Business and Approval of Plan)
Article 9 The provisions of Article 245 (including the cases where it is applied mutatis mutandis pursuant to Article 258, paragraph (2) of the New Insurance Business Act) and Article 247, paragraph (1) of the New Insurance Business Act shall apply to the disposition ordering the management of the business and property after 1 April 2006 by the Insurance Administrator pursuant to the provisions of Article 241, paragraph (1) of the New Insurance Business Act; with regard to a disposition ordering the management of the business and property before that day by the Insurance Administrator pursuant to the provisions of Article 241, paragraph (1) of the Former Insurance Business Act, the provisions then in force shall remain applicable.

(Transitional Measures regarding Modification of Contract Condition in Transfer, etc., of Insurance Contracts)
Article 10 The provisions of Article 250 (including the cases where it is applied mutatis mutandis pursuant to Article 270-4, paragraph (9) of the New Insurance Business Act), Article 254 or 255-2 of the New Insurance Business Act, shall apply to the Modification of Contract Conditions in the transfer of insurance contracts, merger agreement, or acquisition of shares in the case where the order for consultation on Merger, etc. or disposition ordering the management of the business and property by the Insurance Administrator pursuant to the provisions of Article 241, paragraph (1) of the New Insurance Business Act is issued or in the case where the Insurance Company (including Foreign Insurance Companies, etc.; hereinafter the same shall apply in this Article) falls under the category of the Bankrupt Insurance Company prescribed in Article 260, paragraph (2) of the New Insurance Business Act after 1 April 2006; with regard to the Modification of Contract Conditions in the transfer of insurance contracts,

merger Agreement, or acquisition of shares in the case where the order for consultation on Merger, etc. or disposition ordering the management of the business and property by the Insurance Administrator pursuant to the provisions of Article 241, paragraph (1) of the New Insurance Business Act is issued or in the case where the Insurance Company (including Foreign Insurance Companies, etc.; hereinafter the same shall apply in this Article) falls under the category of the Bankrupt Insurance Company prescribed in Article 260, paragraph (2) of the New Insurance Business Act before 1 April 2006, the provisions then in force shall remain applicable.

(Transitional Measures regarding Financial Assistance, etc.)
Article 11　The provisions of Part II, Chapter X, Section 4, Subsection 2 of the New Insurance Business Act shall apply to Financial Assistance Services, etc. prescribed in Article 265-30 of the New Insurance Business Act executed by the Life Insurance Policyholders Protection Corporation pertaining to the person who falls under the category of the Bankrupt Insurance Company prescribed in Article 260, paragraph (2) of the New Insurance Business Act after 1 April 2006; with regard to Financial Assistance Services, etc. prescribed in Article 265-30 of the Former Insurance Business Act executed by the Life Insurance Policyholders Protection Corporation pertaining to the person who falls under the category of the Bankrupt Insurance Company prescribed in Article 260, paragraph (2) of the Former Insurance Business Act before 1 April 2006, the provisions then in force shall be remain applicable.

(Transitional Measures regarding Purchase of Insurance Claims)
Article 12　The provisions of Article 270-6-8, paragraph (2) of the New Insurance Business Act shall apply to the purchase of Insurance Claims, etc. prescribed in Article 270-6-8, paragraph (1) of the New Insurance Business Act pertaining to the person who falls under the category of the Bankrupt Insurance Company prescribed in Article 260, paragraph (2) of the New Insurance Business Act after 1 April 2006; with regard to the purchase of Insurance Claims prescribed in Article 270-6-8, paragraph (1) of the Former Insurance Business Act pertaining to the person who falls under the category of the Bankrupt Insurance Company prescribed in Article 260, paragraph (2) of the Former Insurance Business Act before 1 April 2006, the provisions then in force shall be remain applicable.

(Transitional Measures regarding Submission of a Statement of Changes for a Statement of Insurance Company Voting Right Holdings)
Article 13　The provisions of Article 271-4, paragraph (1) of the New Insurance Business Act shall apply to the submission of a Statement of Changes prescribed in Article 271-4, paragraph (1) of the New Insurance Business Act in the case where there are modifications to particulars listed in items of Article 271-3, paragraph (1) of the New Insurance Business Act after the day specified in Article 1, paragraph (1) of the Supplementary Provisions; with regard to the submission of a Statement of Changes prescribed in Article 271-4, paragraph (1) of the Former Insurance Business Act in the case where there are modifications to particulars listed in items of Article 271-3, paragraph (1) of the Former Insurance Business Act before that day, the provisions then in force shall be remain applicable.

(Transitional Measures regarding Business Report, etc. pertaining to Insurance Holding Company)
Article 14　The provisions of Article 271-24 of the New Insurance Business Act shall apply to an interim business report and business report prescribed in paragraph (1) of

Art.15　⑥ Insurance Business Act, Part VI

the same Article pertaining to the business year which starts after the Effective Date; with regard to the business report prescribed in Article 271-24, paragraph (1) of the Former Insurance Business Act pertaining to the business year which started before the Effective Date, the provisions then in force shall remain applicable.

(Transitional Measures regarding Juridical Persons That Conduct Specified Insurance Business)

Article 15 (1) In the case where the juridical person (excluding stock companies; hereinafter the same shall apply in this Article) conducting Specified Insurance Business at the time when this Act enters into force applied for the registration set forth in Article 272, paragraph (1) of the New Insurance Business Act, the provisions of Article 272-4, paragraph (1), item (i) of the New Insurance Business Act shall not be applied.

(2) For the purpose of applying the provisions of Article 272-2, paragraph (1) and Article 272-4, paragraph (1) of the New Insurance Business Act to the juridical person in the preceding paragraph, the term "the amount of capital or the total amount of funds" in Article 272-2, paragraph (1), item (ii) of the New Insurance Business Act shall be deemed to be replaced with "the amount of contribution or the total amount of funds," the term "directors and company auditors (or, in a company with Committees, directors and executive officers)" in item (iii) of the same paragraph shall be deemed to be replaced with "officers," the term "whose capital or total funds" in Article 272-4, paragraph (1), item (ii) of the New Insurance Business Act shall be deemed to be replaced with "whose contribution or total funds," the term "Stock Company, etc." shall be deemed to be replaced with "juridical person," the term "Stock Company, etc." in the provisions of item (iii) to (viii) inclusive of the same paragraph shall be deemed to be replaced with "juridical person," the term "any business other than what is set forth in the proviso to Article 272-11, paragraph (2) to be specified by Cabinet Office Ordinance, or." and the term "Stock Company, etc." in item (ix) of the same paragraph shall be deemed to be replaced with "any other business that" and "juridical person," respectively; the term "directors, executive officers, accounting advisers or company auditors" and "Stock Company, etc." in item (x) of the same paragraph shall be deemed to be replaced with "officers" and "juridical person," respectively, and the term "Stock Company, etc." in item (xi) of the same paragraph shall be deemed to be replaced with "juridical person."

(3) Any reduction of the amount of the contribution or total amount of the fund of the Low-Cost, Short-Term Insurer (hereinafter referred to as "Specified Low-Cost, Short-Term Insurer" in this Article) who is the juridical person under paragraph (1) and received the registration set forth in Article 272, paragraph (1) of the New Insurance Business Act shall be null and void without the approval of the Prime Minister.

(4) A person (excluding administrative agencies and other persons specified by a Cabinet Order) who holds the right to request inspection of the accounting books and accounting documents of a Specified Low-Cost, Short-Term Insurer pursuant to the provisions of other Acts may not exercise such right unless receiving the approval of the Prime Minister.

(5) For the purpose of applying the provisions of Article 272-11, paragraph (2) and Article 272-26 of the New Insurance Business Act to a Specified Low-Cost, Short-Term Insurer, the term "to be specified by Cabinet Office Ordinance as related to Low-Cost, Short-Term Insurance Services" in the same paragraph shall be deemed to be deleted, the term "Article 272-4, paragraph (1), items (i) to (iv) inclusive" in Article 272-26, paragraph (1), item (i) of the New Insurance Business Act shall be deemed to be replaced with "Article 272-4, paragraph (1), items (ii) to (iv) inclusive as applied with relevant changes in interpretation pursuant to the provisions of Article 15, paragraph

(2) of the Supplementary Provisions of the Act on Partial Revision of the Insurance Business Act, etc. (Act No. 38 of 2005)" and the term "director, executive officer, accounting advisor or company auditor" in paragraph (2) of the same Article shall be deemed to be replaced with "officer."

(6) A Specified Low-Cost, Short-Term Insurer cannot be a Transferee Company prescribed in Article 135, paragraph (1) of the New Insurance Business Act as applied mutatis mutandis pursuant to Article 272-29 of the New Insurance Business Act, notwithstanding of that Article.

(7) In the case where a Specified Low-Cost, Short-Term Insurer is a Transferor Company prescribed in Article 135, paragraph (3) of the New Insurance Business Act as applied mutatis mutandis pursuant to Article 272-29 of the New Insurance Business Act, the term "the Transferor Company and the Transferee Company" in Article 136, paragraphs (1) and (3) of the New Insurance Business Act as applied mutatis mutandis pursuant to Article 272-29 of the New Insurance Business Act shall be deemed to be replaced with "the Transferee Company," the terms "directors (or, in a company with Committees, executive officers)," "for a period ranging from two weeks before the date of the Shareholders' Meeting, etc. set forth in paragraph (1) of the preceding Article," and "the Transfer Agreement concluded under Article 135, paragraph (1) and other" in Article 136-2, paragraph (1) of the New Insurance Business Act as applied mutatis mutandis pursuant to Article 272-29 of the New Insurance Business Act shall be deemed to be replaced with "officers," "on the creation day of the contract pertaining to the contract set forth in Article 135, paragraph (1) (hereinafter defined as "Transfer Agreement")," and "the Transfer Agreement and other," respectively; the term "A shareholder or Policyholder of the Transferor Company" in paragraph (2) of the same Article shall be deemed to be replaced with "An Affected Policyholder,", and the term "the time of the adoption of the resolution under Article 136, paragraph (1)" in Article 138 of the New Insurance Business Act as applied mutatis mutandis pursuant to Article 272-29 of the New Insurance Business Act shall be deemed to be replaced with "the time of preparation of the Transfer Agreement."

(8) A Specified Low-Cost, Short-Term Insurer cannot be an Entrusted Company prescribed in Article 144, paragraph (1) of the New Insurance Business Act as applied mutatis mutandis pursuant to Article 272-30, paragraph (2) of the New Insurance Business Act notwithstanding the provisions of that paragraph.

(9) In the case where a Specified Low-Cost, Short-Term Insurer is an Entrusting Company prescribed in Article 144, paragraph (2) of the New Insurance Business Act as applied mutatis mutandis pursuant to Article 272-30, paragraph (2) of the New Insurance Business Act, the term "both the Insurance Company entrusting the administration (hereinafter referred to as "Entrusting Company" in this Section) and" in Article 144, paragraph (2) shall be deemed to be deleted; the term ", in addition to the documents set forth in Articles 18 and 19 (Documents to be attached to written application) and Article 46 (General rules on attached documents) of the Commercial Registration Act (including the cases where they are applied mutatis mutandis pursuant to Article 67)" in Article 146, paragraph (3) of the New Insurance Business Act as applied mutatis mutandis pursuant to Article 272-30, paragraph (2) of the New Insurance Business Act shall be deemed to be deleted; and the term "both the Entrusting Company and" in Article 149, paragraph (1) of the New Insurance Business Act as applied mutatis mutandis pursuant to Article 272-30, paragraph (2) of the New Insurance Business Act shall be deemed to be deleted.

(10) A Specified Low-Cost, Short-Term Insurer shall not specify the reason of dissolution in the articles of incorporation notwithstanding the provisions of other Acts.

(11) A Specified Low-Cost, Short-Term Insurer shall obtain authorization from the Prime

Art.15　　　　　　⑥ Insurance Business Act, Part VI

　　　Minister when the Specified Low-Cost, Short-Term Insurer seeks to dissolve or abolish the Specified Insurance Business.
(12) The provisions of Article 153, paragraph (2) of the New Insurance Business Act shall apply mutatis mutandis to the application for approval set forth in the preceding paragraph, the provisions of Article 153, paragraph (3) shall apply mutatis mutandis to the Specified Low-Cost, Short-Term Insurer who applied for the approval set forth in the preceding paragraph, and the provisions of Article 154 of the New Insurance Business Act shall apply mutatis mutandis to the Specified Low-Cost, Short-Term Insurer who received the approval set forth in the same paragraph respectively.
(13) The merger of a Specified Low-Cost, Short-Term Insurer shall be null and void without the approval of the Prime Minister.
(14) The provisions of Article 167, paragraph (2) of the New Insurance Business Act shall apply mutatis mutandis to the application for the approval of the preceding paragraph.
(15) A juridical person that is established by merger upon receiving the approval set forth in paragraph (13) shall be deemed that the juridical person received the registration set forth in Article 272, paragraph (1) of the New Insurance Business Act at such establishment.
(16) A company split by a Specified Low-Cost, Short-Term Insurer shall be null and void without the approval of the Prime Minister.
(17) The provisions of Article 173-6, paragraph (2) of the New Insurance Business Act shall apply mutatis mutandis to the application for the approval set forth in the preceding paragraph.
(18) For the purpose of applying the provisions of Part II, Chapter X, Section 2 of the New Insurance Business Act to a Specified Low-Cost, Short-Term Insurer, the term "In the case set forth in paragraph (1), an Insurance Company, etc." and the term "a Foreign Insurance Company, etc.," in Article 250, paragraph (4) of the New Insurance Business Act shall be deemed to be replaced with "In the case of paragraph (1), an Insurance Company, etc. (excluding the Specified Low-Cost, Short-Term Insurer prescribed in Article 15, paragraph (3) of the Supplementary Provisions of the Act on Partial Revision of the Insurance Business Act, etc. (Act No. 38 of 2005))" and "a Foreign Insurance Company, etc. (including the Specified Low-Cost, Short-Term Insurer prescribed in Article 15, paragraph (3) of the Supplementary Provisions of that Act)," respectively; the term "The Insurance Company, etc., set forth in paragraph (1)" and the term "the purpose of the meeting" in Article 254, paragraph (3) of the New Insurance Business Act shall be deemed to be replaced with "In the case of paragraph (1), the Insurance Company, etc. (excluding the Specified Low-Cost, Short-Term Insurer (meaning the Specified Low-Cost, Short-Term Insurer prescribed in Article 15, paragraph (3) of the Supplementary Provisions of the Act on Partial Revision of the Insurance Business Act, etc.; hereinafter the same shall apply in this paragraph))" and "the purpose of the meeting; the Specified Low-Cost, Short-Term Insurer, etc. shall, on the date the merger agreement was created, make public notice to the effect that contracts that contain said Modifications of Contract Conditions have been issued."
(19) For the purpose of applying the provisions of Article 333 of the New Insurance Business Act to a Specified Low-Cost, Short-Term Insurer, the term "the incorporator, the director at the incorporation, the executive officer at the incorporation, the company auditor at the incorporation, the director, the executive officer, the accounting advisor or the member who is supposed to carry out such duties and the company auditor" in paragraph (1) of the same Article shall be deemed to be replaced with "the incorporator, the officer."
(20) The Method of Public Notice for a Specified Low-Cost, Short-Term Insurer shall be publication in a daily newspaper that publishes the particulars of current events.

(Transitional Measures regarding Low-Cost, Short-Term Insurer, etc., who was a Specified Insurer)

Article 16 (1) A Low-Cost, Short-Term Insurer that was a Specified Insurer or a Low-Cost, Short-Term Insurer that received the transfer of, or succeeded to, the insurance contracts from a Specified Insurer (limited to a person who applied for the approval of transfer or succession of said insurance contracts pursuant to the provisions of Article 4, paragraph (7), (8), (11) or (12) of the Supplemental Provisions by the day when two years have passed since the Effective Date and for the registration set forth in Article 272, paragraph (1) of the New Insurance Business Act) may, notwithstanding the provisions of Article 3, paragraph (1) of the New Insurance Business Act, underwrite insurance with insurance proceeds of more than the amount specified by Cabinet Order set forth in Article 2, paragraph (17) of the New Insurance Business Act and less than the amount specified by Cabinet Order, until the day on which seven years have passed since the Effective Date.

(2) A Low-Cost, Short-Term Insurer shall, when underwriting insurance whose insurance proceeds exceed the amount specified by Cabinet Order set forth in Article 2, paragraph (17) of the New Insurance Business Act pursuant to the provisions of the preceding paragraph, have reinsurance whose insurance proceeds equal or exceed that excess amount with an Insurance Company (including Foreign Insurance Companies, etc.; hereinafter the same shall apply in this Article) pursuant to Cabinet Office Ordinance.

(3) When underwriting insurance whose insurance proceeds exceed the amount specified by Cabinet Order set forth in Article 2, paragraph (17) of the New Insurance Business Act pursuant to the provisions of paragraph (1), a Low-Cost, Short-Term Insurer shall, in advance, submit notice detailing the trade name and name of the Insurance Company with which the reinsurance is effected, and contents of the reinsurance as well as other particulars specified by Cabinet Office Ordinance to the Prime Minister.

(4) When underwriting insurance whose insurance proceeds exceed the amount specified by Cabinet Order set forth in Article 2, paragraph (17) of the New Insurance Business Act pursuant to the provisions of paragraph (1), a Low-Cost, Short-Term Insurer shall, in advance, disclose the particulars listed below to the customers.

  (i) Trade name and name of the Insurance Company with which the reinsurance is effected
  (ii) Amount of reinsurance proceeds to be effected and other contents of the reinsurance.
  (iii) Other particulars specified by Cabinet Office Ordinance.

(5) When the underwriting of the insurance whose insurance proceeds exceed the amount specified by Cabinet Order provided in the Article 2, paragraph (17) of the New Insurance Business Act pursuant to the provisions of paragraph (1) is performed, the provisions of the paragraph (2) shall not apply to a Low-Cost, Short-Term Insurer for whom the effecting reinsurance pertaining to such insurance with a Foreign Insurer was approved by the Prime Minister as falling under any of the following cases. In this case, pursuant to the provisions of a Cabinet Office Ordinance, such Low-Cost, Short-Term Insurer shall have reinsurance whose insurance proceeds equal or exceed that excess amount with said Foreign Insurer.

  (i) The contents of the reinsurance do not violate the laws and regulations, or are not unfair.
  (ii) Instead of said reinsurance, effecting reinsurance with an Insurance Company on the terms equivalent to or more favorable than those of said reinsurance is difficult.
  (iii) Effecting such reinsurance poses no risk of unduly harming the interest of the in-

Art.16

sured and other relevant persons.

(6) In the case the reinsurance contract is entered into with a Foreign Insurer pursuant to the provisions of the preceding paragraph, the term "trade name and name of an Insurance Company" in paragraph (4), item (i) shall be deemed to be replaced with "trade name and name of a Foreign Insurer."

(7) When giving an approval set forth in paragraph (5), the Prime Minister may confirm with the Insurance Company whether it falls under any case of item (ii) of the same paragraph.

(8) When an approval set forth in paragraph (5) was made, the Prime Minister may rescind the approval of the same paragraph when effecting reinsurance with such Foreign Insurer does not fall under the cases listed in the items of the same paragraph. In this case, the Low-Cost, Short-Term Insurer set forth in the same paragraph shall, without delay, have reinsurance whose insurance proceeds equal or exceed the excess amount set forth in the second sentence of the same paragraph with the other Insurance Company or Foreign Insurer.

(9) The Specified Insurer may, if it received the registration set forth in Article 272, paragraph (1) of the New Insurance Business Act, manage business or properties pertaining to the insurance contract which was underwritten prior to such registration and whose insurance proceeds exceed the amount specified by Cabinet Order set forth in Article 2, paragraph (17) of the New Insurance Business Act, notwithstanding the provisions of Article 3, paragraph (1) of the New Insurance Business Act.

(10) Notwithstanding the provisions of Article 3, paragraph (1) of the New Insurance Business Act, a Low-Cost, Short-Term Insurer may manage business or properties pertaining to the insurance contract which was underwritten prior to the Effective Date or during the period when the Specified Insurer conducted Specified Insurance Business pursuant to the provisions of Article 2, paragraph (1) of the Supplementary Provisions and whose insurance proceeds exceed the amount specified by Cabinet Order set forth in Article 2, paragraph (17) of the New Insurance Business Act, after the Specified Insurer received the transfer of, or succeeded to, such insurance contract.

(11) In the case of paragraph (9) or the case in the preceding paragraph, a Low-Cost, Short-Term Insurer shall effect reinsurance with an Insurance Company or a Foreign Insurer whose insurance proceeds equals or exceed the excess amount prescribed in paragraph (9) or the preceding paragraph, pursuant to the provisions of a Cabinet Office Ordinance.

(12) A Low-Cost, Short-Term Insurer shall, if it effected reinsurance with an Insurance Company or a Foreign Insurer pursuant to the provisions in the preceding paragraph, submit notice detailing the trade name and name of such Insurance Company or Foreign Insurer and other particulars specified by Cabinet Office Ordinance to the Prime Minister without delay,.

(13) A Specified Insurer may, if it received the registration set forth in Article 272, paragraph (1) of the New Insurance Business Act, manage business or properties pertaining to the insurance contract which was underwritten prior to such registration and whose term of coverage exceeds the period specified by Cabinet Order set forth in Article 2, paragraph (17) of the New Insurance Business Act, notwithstanding the provisions of Article 3, paragraph (1) of the New Insurance Business Act.

(14) A Low-Cost, Short-Term Insurer who has committed that it will receive the transfer of insurance contracts from a Specified Insurer or succeed to insurance contracts from a Specified Insurer, or a Low-Cost, Short-Term Insurer who received the transfer of insurance contracts from a Specified Insurer or succeeded insurance contracts from a Specified Insurer may, notwithstanding the provisions of Article 3, paragraph (1) of the New Insurance Business Act, receive the transfer of insurance contracts which were

underwritten prior to the Effective Date or during the period when the Specified Insurer conducted Specified Insurance Business pursuant to the provisions of Article 2, paragraph (1) of the Supplementary Provisions and whose term of coverage exceeds the period specified by Cabinet Order set forth in Article 2, paragraph (17) of the New Insurance Business Act or succeed to such insurance contracts, and manage business and properties pertaining to such insurance contracts.

(15) In the cases of paragraphs (1), (5), (9), (10), and (13) or of the preceding paragraph, the term "conducts Low-Cost, Short-Term Insurance Business" in Article 2, paragraph (18) of the New Insurance Business Act shall be deemed to be replaced with "conducts Low-Cost, Short-Term Insurance Business (including Insurance Business conducted pursuant to the provisions of Article 16, paragraph (1), (9), (10), (13) or (14) of the Supplementary Provisions of Act on Partial Revision of Insurance Business Act etc.(Act No. 38 of 2005)," the term "Low-Cost, Short-Term Insurance Business" in Article 272, paragraph (1) of the New Insurance Business Act shall be deemed to be replaced with "Low-Cost, Short-Term Insurance Business (including Insurance Business conducted pursuant to the provisions of Article 16, paragraph (1), (9), (10), (13) or (14) of the Supplementary Provisions of Act on Partial Revision of Insurance Business Act etc.; the same shall apply in paragraph (1), item (v) of the following Article, Article 272-4, paragraph (1), items (ix) and (xi), Article 272-5, paragraphs (2) and (5), Article 272-9, Article 272-11, paragraphs (1) and (2), Article 272-21, paragraph (1), item (i), Article 272-27 and Article 315, item (iv))", and the term "(xi)" in Article 272-26, paragraph (1), item (i) of the New Insurance Business Act shall be deemed to be replaced with "(xi) of Article 272-4, paragraph (1) as applied with the change in interpretation pursuant to Article 16, paragraph (15) of the Supplementary Provisions of Act on Partial Revision of Insurance Business Act etc."

(16) In paragraph (13) or (14), necessary particulars regarding the accumulation of policy reserves performed by a Low-Cost, Short-Term Insurer set forth in Article 116, paragraph (1) of the New Insurance Business Act as applied mutates mutandis pursuant to Article 272-18 of the New Insurance Business Act.

(17) The provisions of Article 113 of the New Insurance Business Act applied mutatis mutandis to Article 272-18 of the New Insurance Business Act shall not apply to a Low-Cost, Short-Term Insurer who received a transfer of insurance contracts from a Specified Insurer or succeeded insurance contracts from a Specified Insurer (limited to a person who applied for the approval of transfer or succession of said insurance contracts pursuant to the provisions of Article 4, paragraph (7), (8), (11) or (12) of the Supplemental Provisions by the day when two years have passed since the Effective Date, or a person who applied for the registration of Article 272, paragraph (1) of the New Insurance Business Act).

(18) The Low-Cost, Short-Term Insurer who was a Specified Insurer, or the Low-Cost, Short-Term Insurer who received the transfer of insurance contracts from a Specified Insurer or succeeded to insurance contracts from a Specified Insurer (limited to a person who applied for the approval of transfer or succession of said insurance contracts pursuant to the provisions of Article 4, paragraph (7), (8), (11) or (12) of the Supplemental Provisions or applied for the registration set forth in Article 272, paragraph (1) of the New Insurance Business Act by the day when two years have passed since the Effective Date) may, by notifying the Prime Minister, be relieved of the requirement of accumulating of the policy reserves specified by a Cabinet Office Ordinance set forth in Article 116, paragraph (1) of the New Insurance Business Act as applied mutatis mutandis pursuant to Article 272, paragraph (18) of the New Insurance Business Act for the accounting period that ends by the day when five years have passed since the Effective Date.

(Transitional Measures regarding Posting of Sign)
Article 17 The provisions of Article 272-8, paragraph (2) of the New Insurance Business Act does not apply to a person who posts a sign set forth in paragraph (1) of the same Article or a sign similar to this at the time when this Act enters into force, until the day on which six months have passed from the Effective Date.

(Penal Provisions)
Article 19 (1) A person who has failed to submit notice pursuant to the provisions of Article 3, paragraph (1) of the Supplementary Provisions and documents that must be attached pursuant to the provisions of paragraph (2) of the same Article, or a person who has submitted such documents but failed to detail the particulars that are required to be detailed therein or included false details shall be punished by imprisonment with work for not more than five years or by a fine of not more than three million yen.
(2) When a representative person or administrator of a juridical person (including an association or foundation that is not a juridical person and has provisions on representative persons or administrators; hereinafter the same shall apply in this paragraph) or any agent, employee or other worker of a juridical person or an individual has done the violation set forth in the preceding paragraph with regard to the business of said juridical person or individual, not only the offender shall be punished but also said juridical person or individual shall be punished by the fine prescribed in the respective paragraph.

(Delegation to Cabinet Office Ordinance)
Article 34 In addition to what is provided for in the Supplementary Provisions, the procedures for application pertaining to the authorization or approval pursuant to the provisions of the Supplementary Provisions, submission of documents, and any other particular that is necessary in order for this Act to be implemented shall be specified by Cabinet Office Ordinance.

(Transitional Measures Concerning Penal Provisions)
Article 35 With regard to the application of penal provisions to actions taken prior to the enforcement of this Act and actions taken after the enforcement of this Act in the cases where the provisions then in force are to remain applicable pursuant to the provisions of the Supplementary Provisions, the provisions then in force shall remain applicable.

(Delegation of Authority)
Article 36 (1) The Prime Minister shall delegate his/her authority under the Supplementary Provisions (except for authority to be specified by Cabinet Order) to the Commissioner of Financial Services Agency.
(2) With regard to the authority delegated to the Commissioner of Financial Services Agency pursuant to the provisions in the preceding paragraph, part of it may be delegated to the Director-Generals of Local Finance Bureaus or Local Finance Branch Bureaus pursuant to the provisions of a Cabinet Order.

(Delegation to Cabinet Order)
Article 37 In addition to what is provided for in the Supplementary Provisions, necessary transitional measures regarding the enforcement of the Act will be specified by Cabinet Order.

(Review)

Article 38 (1) Within three years after the enforcement of this Act, the government shall consider the implementations of systems, etc. , pertaining to special measures, etc. for protection of Policyholders, etc. , including government assistance for Life Insurance Policyholders Protection Corporation and Financial Assistance, etc. , by Life Insurance Policyholders Protection Corporation, the financial conditions of Life Insurance Policyholders Protection Corporation, and the soundness of the management of an Insurance Company, among other factors, examine the bearing of expenses required for the Financial Assistance, etc. , of Life Insurance Policyholders Protection Corporation and necessities, etc. for the continuation of the provisions pertaining to the government assistance, and conduct an appropriate review.

(2) Within five years after the enforcement of the Act, the government shall consider the status of business for which reinsurance is effected with an Insurance Company and other business of a Low-Cost, Short-Term Insurer, the conditions of diversification of insurance that an Insurance Company underwrites, as well as the changes in economic and social conditions, review systems pertaining to the Insurance Business specified in this Act, and take necessary measures based on its results, when necessary.

Supplementary Provisions [Act No. 87 of July 26, 2005] [Extract]

This Act shall come into effect as of the Effective Date of the Companies Act.

Supplementary Provisions [Act No. 102 of October 21, 2005] [Extract]

(Effective Date)
Article 1 This Act shall come into effect as of the Effective Date of Postal Service Privatization Act.

(Transitional Measures Concerning Penal Provisions)
Article 117 With regard to the application of penal provisions to actions taken prior to the enforcement of this Act; actions taken after the enforcement of this Act in the cases where the provisions then in force are to remain applicable pursuant to the provisions of the Supplementary Provisions; actions taken prior to the lapse of the provisions of Article 38-8 of the Former Postal Money Order Act (limited to the segment pertaining to items (ii) and (iii)) that are to remain in force pursuant to the provisions of Article 9, paragraph (1) of the Supplementary Provisions even after the enforcement of this Act; actions taken prior to the lapse of the provisions of Article 70 of the Former Postal Transfer Act (limited to the segment pertaining to items (ii) and (iii)) that are to remain in force pursuant to the provisions of Article 13, paragraph (1) of the Supplementary Provisions after the enforcement of this Act; actions taken prior to the invalidation of the provisions of Article 8 of the Former Act on the Entrustment of Postal Transfer Deposit and Contribution (limited to the segment pertaining to items (ii)) that are to remain in force pursuant to the provisions of Article 27, paragraph (1) of the Supplementary Provisions even after the enforcement of this Act; actions taken before the lapse of the provisions of Article 70 of the Former Public Companies Act (limited to the segment pertaining to items (ii)) that are to remain in force pursuant to the provisions of Article 39, paragraph (2) of the Supplementary Provisions even after the enforcement of this Act; actions taken prior to the lapse of the provisions of Article 71 and 72 of the Former Public Companies Act (limited to the segment pertaining to items (xv)) that are to remain in force pursuant to the provisions of Article 42, paragraph (1) of the Supplementary Provisions even after the enforcement of this Act; and actions taken prior to the specified day pertaining to the post savings bank prescribed

in Article 104 of the Postal Service Privatization Act in the cases where the provisions of Article 2, paragraph (2) of the Supplementary Provisions is applicable, the provisions then in force are to remain applicable.

Supplementary Provisions [Act No. 10 of March 31, 2006] [Extract]

(Effective Date)
Article 1 This Act shall come into effect as of 1 April 2006.

(Transitional Measures Concerning Penal Provisions)
Article 211 With regard to the application of penal provisions to actions taken prior to the enforcement of this Act (with regard to the provisions listed in the items of Article 1 of the Supplementary Provisions, those provisions; hereinafter the same shall apply in this Article) and actions taken after the enforcement of this Act in the cases where the provisions then in force are to remain applicable pursuant to the provisions of the Supplementary Provisions, the provisions then in force shall remain applicable.

(Delegation of Other Transitional Measures to Cabinet Order)
Article 212 In addition to what is provided for in the Supplementary Provisions, necessary transitional measures concerning the enforcement of this Act shall be specified by Cabinet Order.

Supplementary Provisions [Act No. 50 of June 2, 2006] [Extract]

(Effective Date)
(1) This Act shall come into effect as of the Effective Date of Act on General Incorporated Associations and General Incorporated Foundations.

(Adjustment Provisions)
(2) If the Effective Date of the Act for Partial Revision of the Penal Code, etc. to Respond to an Increase in International and Organized Crimes and Advancement of Information Processing (Act No. of 2006) is after the Effective Date, for the purpose of applying the provisions of appended table 62 of the Act for Punishment of Organized Crimes and Control of Crime Proceeds (Act No. 136 of 1999; hereinafter referred to as the "Organized Crime Punishment Act") from the Effective Date to the day before the enforcement of that Act, the term "crime set forth in Article 157 (aggravated breach of trust of director etc.) of the Intermediate Corporation Act (Act No. 49 of 2001)" in the same table shall be deemed to be replaced with "crime of Article 334 (aggravated breach of trust of director etc.) of the Act on General Incorporated Associations and General Incorporated Foundations (Act No.48 of 2006)."
(3) In addition to what is provided for in the provisions in the preceding paragraph, with regard to the application of the provisions of the Organized Crime Punishment Act until the day before the Effective Date of the Act for Partial Revision of the Penal Code, etc. to Respond to an Increase in International and Organized Crimes and Advancement of Information Processing in the case referred to in the preceding paragraph, a crime set forth in Article 157 of the Former Intermediate Corporation Act(aggravated breach of trust of director, etc.) where the provisions then in force remain applicable pursuant to the provisions of Article 457 shall be deemed to be a crime listed in the appended table 62 of the Organized Crime Punishment Act.

Supplementary Provisions [Act No. 65 of June 14, 2006] [Extract]

(Effective Date)

Article 1 This Act shall come into effect as of the date specified by Cabinet Order within a period not exceeding one year and six months from the day of promulgation (hereinafter referred to as the "Effective Date"); provided, however, that the provisions set forth in the following items shall come into effect as of the day prescribed respectively in those items.

(i) Provision of Article 1; revised provisions in Article 30-4, paragraph (2), item (ii) of the Agricultural Cooperative Association Act in Article 8 (limited to the segment which revises "Article 197, paragraph (1), items (i) to (iv) inclusive or item (vii) or paragraph (2), Article 198, items (i) to (x) inclusive, item (xviii) or (xiv)" to "Article 197, Article 197-2, items (i) to (x) or (xiii), Article 198, item (viii)"); revised provisions in Article 34-4, paragraph (2), item (ii) of the Act on Fishing Cooperatives in Article 9 (limited to the segment which revises "Article 197, paragraph (1), items (i) to (iv) inclusive or item (vii) or paragraph (2), Article 198, items (i) to (x) inclusive, item (xviii) or (xix)" to "Article 197, Article 197-2, items (i) to (x) or item (xiii), Article 198, item (viii)"); revised provisions in Article 5-4, paragraph (4), item (iv) of the Act on Financial Services by Cooperative in Article 11 (limited to the segment which revises "Article 197, paragraph (1), items (i) to (iv) inclusive or item (vii) or paragraph (2)" to "Article 197" and "Article 198, items (i) to (x) inclusive, item (xviii) or (xix) (Crime of Solicitation of Securities by Unregistered Agents etc)" to "Article 197-2, items (i) to (x) or item (xiii) (Crime of Solicitation of Securities by Unregistered Agents. etc), Article 198, item (viii) (Crime of Violating Prohibition Order or Order for Suspension by Court)"; revised provisions in Article 34, item (iv) of the Shinkin Bank Act in Article 13 (limited to the segment which revises "Article 197, paragraph (1), items (i) to (iv) inclusive or item (vii) or paragraph (2)" to "Article 197" and "Article 198, items (i) to (x) inclusive, item (xviii) or (xix) (Crime of Solicitation of Securities by Unregistered Agents etc)" to "Article 197-2, items (i) to (x) or item (xiii) (Crime of Solicitation of Securities by Unregistered Agents etc), Article 198, item (viii) (Crime of Violating Prohibition Order or Order for Suspension by Court)"; revised provisions in Article 34, item (iv) of the Labor Bank Act in Article 15 (limited to the segment which revises "Article 197, paragraph (1), items (i) to (iv) inclusive or item (vii) or paragraph (2)" to "Article 197" and "Article 198, items (i) to (x) inclusive, item (xviii) or (xix) (Crime of Solicitation of Securities by Unregistered Agents etc)" to "Article 197-2, items (i) to (x) or item (xiii) (Crime of Solicitation of Securities by Unregistered Agents etc), Article 198, item (viii) (Crime of Violating Prohibition Order or Order for Suspension by Court)"; revised provisions in Article 53-2, paragraph (1), item (iii) of the Insurance Business Act in Article 18 (limited to the segment which revises "Article 197, paragraph (1), items (i) to (iv) inclusive or item (vii) or paragraph (2)" to "Article 197" and "Article 198, items (i) to (x) inclusive, item (xviii) or (xix) (Crime of Solicitation of Securities by Unregistered Agents etc)" to "Article 197-2, items (i) to (x) or item (xiii) (Crime of Solicitation of Securities by Unregistered Agents etc), Article 198, item (viii) (Crime of Violating Prohibition Order or Order for Suspension by Court)"; revised provisions in Article 24-4, item (iv) of the Norinchukin Bank Act in Article 19 (limited to the segment which revises "Article 197, paragraph (1), items (i) to (iv) inclusive or item (vii) or paragraph (2), or Article 198, items (i) to (x) inclusive, item (xviii) or (xix)" to "Article 197, Article 197-2, items (i) to (x) or item (xiii), Article 198, item (viii)"); and Supplementary Provisions, Article 2, Article 4, Article 182, paragraph (1), Article 184, paragraph (1), Article 187, paragraph (1), Article 190, paragraph (1), Article 193, paragraph (1), Article 196,

paragraph (1) and Article 198, paragraph (1): the day on which 20 days have passed from the day of promulgation.
(ii) Provision of Article 3 of the Supplementary Provisions: the Effective Date of the Act for Partial Revision of the Penal Code to Respond to an Increase in International and Organized Crimes and Advancement of Information Processing (Act No. of 2006) or the Effective Date of the provisions listed in the preceding item, whichever comes later.
(iii) Provisions of Article 2 (excluding revised provisions in Article 27-23 of the Securities and Exchange Act (excluding the segment that adds "and Article 27-26" under "Article 27-25, paragraph (1)"); revised provisions in Article 27-24 of the same Act; revised provisions in Article 27-25 of the same Act; revised provisions in Article 27-26 of the same Act (excluding the segment which revises "control business activities of a company, an issuer of share certificates etc." to "act in any way specified by Cabinet Order as making a significant change in and having a significant impact on the business activities of an issuer of share certificates, etc., (referred to as an "Important Proposed Action, etc." in paragraphs (4) and (5))" and the segment which adds paragraph (3) in the same Article); revised provisions in Article 27-27 of the same Act and revised provisions in Article 27-30, item (ii) of that Act (excluding the segment which revises "Article 27-10, paragraph (2)" to "Article 27-10, paragraphs (8) and (12)" and the segment that adds "or (11)" under "Article 27-10, paragraph (1)")); and provisions of Article 7, Article 8 and Article 12 of the Supplementary Provisions: the date specified by Cabinet Order within a period not exceeding six months from the day of promulgation.
(iv) Revised provisions in Article 27-23 of the Securities and Exchange Act in Article 2 (excluding the segment which adds "and Article 27-26" under "Article 27-25, paragraph (1)"); revised provisions in Article 27-24 of the same Act; revised provisions in Article 27-25 of the same Act; revised provisions in Article 27-26 of the same Act (excluding the segment which revises "control business activities of a company, an issuer of share certificate etc." to "act in any way specified by Cabinet Order as making a significant change in and having a significant impact on the business activities of an issuer of share certificates etc. (referred to as an "Important Proposed Action, etc." in paragraphs (4) and (5))" and the segment which adds paragraph (3) in the same Article); revised provisions in Article 27-27 of the same Act and revised provisions in Article 27-30, item (ii) of the same Act (excluding the segment which revises "Article 27-10, paragraph (2)" to "Article 27-10, paragraphs (8) and (12)" and the segment that adds "or (11)" under "Article 27-10, paragraph (1)"); and provisions from Article 9 to Article 11 and 13 of the Supplementary Provisions: the day specified by Cabinet Order within a period not exceeding one year from the day of promulgation.
(v) The provisions of Article 4: the Effective Date of the Act on General Incorporated Associations and General Incorporated Foundations (Act No. 48 of 2006)

(Transitional Measures associated with Partial Revision of Insurance Business Act)
Article 196 (1) With regard to the applications of the provisions of Article 53-2, paragraph (1), item (iii) of the Revised Insurance Business Act (hereinafter referred to as the New Insurance Business Act in this paragraph) (including the cases where it is applied mutatis mutandis pursuant to the provisions of Article 53-5, paragraph (1), Article 53-26, paragraph (4), and Article 180-4, paragraph (3) of the New Insurance Business Act) pursuant to the provisions of Article 18 (limited to the revised provisions in Article 53-2, paragraph (1), item (iii) (limited to the segments that revise "Article 197,

paragraph (1), items (i) to (iv) inclusive or item (vii) or paragraph (2)" to "Article 197", and "Article 198, items (i) to (x) inclusive, item (xviii) or (xix) (Crime of Solicitation of Securities by Unregistered Agents, etc)" to "Article 197-2, items (i) to (x) inclusive or item (xiii) (Crime of Solicitation of Securities by Unregistered Agents. etc), Article 198, item (viii) (Crime of Violating Prohibition Order or Order for Suspension by Court)", any person who has violated Article 197, paragraph (1), items (i) to (iv) inclusive, or item (vii), paragraph (2) or Article 198, items (i) to (x) inclusive, item (xviii) or (xix) of the pre-revision Securities and Exchange Act pursuant to the provisions of Article 1 (including these provisions where the provisions then in force remain applicable pursuant to the provisions of Article 218 of the Supplementary Provisions) and who has been punished shall be deemed to have violated Article 197, Article 197-2, items (i) to (x) inclusive or item (xiii), or Article 198, item (viii) of the revised Securities and Exchange Act pursuant to the provisions of Article 1, and to have been punished.

(2) With regard to the application of the provisions of Article 53-2, paragraph (1), item (iii) of the Revised Insurance Business Act (hereinafter referred to as the "Newly Revised Insurance Business Act" in this paragraph) (including the cases where it is applied mutatis mutandis pursuant to Article 53-5, paragraph (1), Article 53-26, paragraph (4) and Article 180-4, paragraph (3) of the Newly Revised Insurance Business Act), pursuant to the provisions of Article 18 (limited to the revised provisions in Article 53-2, paragraph (1), item (iii) (limited to the segments that revise "Securities and Exchange Act" to "Financial Instruments and Exchange Act", "(xxi) or (xxii)" to "(xx) or (xxi)", "securities company etc." to "Financial Instruments Transaction Business Operators, etc." and "(xv) or (xvi)" to "(xix) or (xx)"), any person who has violated the provisions of Article197 Article 197-2, items (i) to (x) inclusive or item (xiii), Article 198, item (viii), Article 199, Article 200, items (i) to (xii) inclusive, items (xxi) or (xxii), Article 203, paragraph (3) or Article 205, items (i) to (vi) inclusive, item (xv) or (xvi) of the Former Securities and Exchange Act (including these provisions where the provisions then in force remain applicable pursuant to the provisions of Article 218 of the Supplementary Provisions) and has been punished shall be deemed to have violated the provisions of Article 197, Article 197-2, items (i) to (x) inclusive or item (xiii), Article 198, item (viii), Article199, Article 200, items (i) to (xii) inclusive, items (xx) or (xxi), Article 203, paragraph (3) or Article 205, items (i) to (vi) inclusive, item (xix) or (xx) of the New Financial Instruments and Exchange Act and to have been punished.

Article 197 If an Insurance Company, etc. (meaning an Insurance Company, etc. provided in Article 2-2, paragraph (1) of the Revised Insurance Business Act pursuant to the provisions of Article 18 (hereinafter meaning "Revised Insurance Business Act"), a Foreign Insurance Company, etc. (meaning a Foreign Insurance Company, etc. provided in Article 2, paragraph (7) of the Revised Insurance Business Act), or an Insurance Broker (meaning an Insurance Broker provided in Article 2, paragraph (25) of the Revised Insurance Business Act), in the case where an application for a specified insurance contract, etc. (meaning as a specified insurance contract, etc. provided in Article 34 of the New Financial Instruments and Exchange Act as applied mutatis mutandis pursuant to Article 300-2 of the Revised Insurance Business Act with relevant changes in interpretation) from a customer (limited to an individual listed in Article 2, paragraph (31), item (iv) of the New Financial Instruments and Exchange Act) for the first time after the enforcement of this Act is received, and has notified such customer prior to the enforcement of this Act pursuant to an example set forth in Article 34 of the New Financial Instruments and Exchange Act as applied mutatis mutandis pursuant to Article 300-2 of the Revised Insurance Business Act that such customer may file an application pursuant to the provisions of Article 34-2, paragraph (1) of the New Financial Instruments and Exchange Act as applied mutatis mutandis pursuant to Article 300-2 of the Revised Insurance Business Act after the enforcement of this Act, a notification provided in Article 34 of the New Financial Instruments and Exchange Act as applied mutatis mutandis pursuant to Article 300-2 of the Revised Insurance Business Act shall be deemed to have been made to such customer.

(Delegation of Authority)
Article 216 (1) The Prime Minister shall delegate his/her authority under the Supplementary Provisions (except for authority to be specified by Cabinet Order) to the Commissioner of Financial Services Agency.
(2) With regard to the authority delegated to the Commissioner of Financial Services Agency pursuant to the provisions in the preceding paragraph, part of it may, pursuant to the provisions of a Cabinet Order, be delegated to the Director-Generals of Local Finance Bureaus or the Director-General of Local Finance Branch Bureaus.

(Effect of Dispositions, etc.)
Article 217 Dispositions imposed, procedures taken or other actions taken prior to the enforcement of this Act pursuant to the provisions of the Former Securities and Exchange Act, the Former Act on Securities Investment Trust and Securities Investment Corporations, or Former Trust Business Act or orders based on those, for which the corresponding provisions exist in the provisions of the New Financial Instruments and Exchange Act shall be deemed to have been imposed, taken or committed pursuant to the corresponding provisions of the New Financial Instruments and Exchange Act, except as otherwise provided for in this Supplementary Provision.

(Transitional Measures regarding the Application of Penal Provisions)
Article 218 With regard to the application of penal provisions to actions taken prior to the enforcement of this Act (in provisions listed in the items of Article 1 of the Supplementary Provisions, such provision. Hereinafter the same shall apply in this Article) and actions taken after the enforcement of this Act where the provisions previously in force remain applicable pursuant to the provisions of the Supplementary Provisions and remain in force, the provisions then in force shall remain applicable.

(Delegation of Other Transitional Measures to Cabinet Order, etc.)
Article 219 (1) In addition to what is prescribed in the Supplementary Provisions, transitional measures necessary for the enforcement of this Act shall be specified by Cabinet Order.
(2) Transitional measures necessary for a procedure concerning a registration associated with a partial revision of the Securities and Exchange Act pursuant to the provisions of Article 3 shall be specified by an Ordinance of the Ministry of Justice

(Review)
Article 220 Within five years after the enforcement of this Act, the government shall review the conditions of the enforcement of this Act and take necessary measures based on its results, when necessary.

Supplementary Provisions [Act No. 109 of December 15, 2006] [Extract]

This Act shall come into effect as of the Effective Date of New Trust Act; provided, however, the provisions listed in the following items shall come into effect as of the day

prescribed respectively in those items.
(i) Provisions of Article 9 (limited to the revised provisions in Article 7 of the Commercial Code, Article 25 (limited to the revised provisions in Article 251, item (xxiv) of Act on Securities Investment Trust and Securities Investment Corporations), Article 37 (limited to the revised provisions in Article 76, item (vii) of Act on Mergers and Conversions by Financial Institutions), Article 49 (limited to the revised provisions in Article 17-6, paragraph (1), item (vii), Article 53-12, paragraph (8), Article 53-15, Article 53-25, paragraph (2), Article 53-27, paragraph (3), Article 53-32, Article 180-5, paragraphs (3) and (4) as well as Article 180-9, paragraph (5) of the Insurance Business Act), Article 55 (limited to the revised provisions in Article 76, paragraph (6), Article 85, Article 168, paragraph (5), Article 171, paragraph (6) and Article 316, paragraph (1), item (xxiii) of the Act on Liquidation of Assets), Article 59, Article 75 and Article 77 (excluding the provisions which revises the table of contents in the Companies Act, the provisions which adds two items in Article 132 of the same Act, the provisions which adds Subsection 1 after Article 154 in the Part II Chapter II Section 3 in the same Act, the provisions which adds after the Article 272 in Part II Chapter III Section 4 of the same Act, the provisions which adds Article 1 after the Article 695 of the same Act and the revised provisions in Article 943, item (i) of the same Act: the day of promulgation.

Supplementary Provisions [Act No. 74 of June 1, 2007] [Extract]

(Effective Date)
Article 1 This Act shall come into effect as of 1 October 2008, provided, however, that the provisions set forth in following items shall come into effect as of the day prescribed respectively in those items.
(i) The provisions Article 3 to 22, 25 to 30, 101 and 102 of the Supplementary Provisions: the date to be specified by a Cabinet within a period no exceeding six months from the day of promulgation.

(Transitional Measures Accompanying Partial Revision to Insurance Business Act)
Article 77 With respect to application to the provisions of Insurance Business Act about short-term commercial and industrial bonds which a juridical person prior to the conversion has published before the enforcement, the short-term commercial and industrial bonds shall be deemed to be short-term company bonds, etc. prescribed in Article 98, paragraph (6) of that Act.

(Transitional Measures regarding the Disposition, etc.)
Article 100 Those dispositions, procedures or other actions taken before this Act enters into force pursuant to the provisions of the respective Acts prior to its revision (including any orders pursuant thereto; hereinafter the same shall apply in this Article), which are covered by the corresponding provisions of the respective Acts as revised, shall be deemed to have been carried out pursuant to such corresponding provisions of the respective Acts as revised, unless provided otherwise in these Supplementary Provisions.

(Transitional Measures regarding the Application of Penal Provisions)
Article 101 With regard to the application of penal provisions to actions taken prior to the enforcement of this Act (in provisions listed in the items of Article 1 of the Supplementary Provisions, such provision. Hereinafter the same shall apply in this Article)

and actions taken after the enforcement of this Act where the provisions previously in force remain applicable pursuant to the provisions of the Supplementary Provisions and remain in force pursuant to the provisions of the Supplementary Provisions, the provisions then in force shall remain applicable.

(Delegation of Other Transitional Measures to Cabinet Order etc.)
Article 102 In addition to what is provided for in the Supplementary Provisions, necessary transitional measures concerning the enforcement of this Act shall be specified by Cabinet Order.

[7] Order for Enforcement of the Insurance Business Act

(Cabinet Order No. 425 of December 22, 1995)

Pursuant to the provisions of the Insurance Business Act (Act No. 105 of 1995) and for the purpose of enforcement of said Act, the Cabinet hereby enacts this Cabinet Order in replacement of the Order for Enforcement of the Insurance Business Act (Imperial Ordinance No. 904 of 1939) in its entirety.

Table of Contents
Chapter I General Provisions (Article 1 - Article 2)
Chapter II Insurance Companies, Foreign Insurance Companies, etc. and Low-Cost, Short-Term Insurers
　Section 1 Insurance Companies, Foreign Insurance Companies, etc. and Low-Cost, Short-Term Insurers (Article 2-2 - Article 37-9)
　Section 2 Special Provisions on Low-Cost, Short-Term Insurers (Article 38 - Article 38-15)
Chapter III Insurance Solicitation (Article 39 - Article 44-6)
Chapter IV Miscellaneous Provisions (Article 45 - Article 47-3)
　Supplementary Provisions

Chapter I General Provisions

(Definitions)
Article 1 In this Cabinet Order, the terms "Insurance Business," "Insurance Company," "Life Insurance Company," "Non-Life Insurance Company," "Mutual Company," "Foreign Insurer," "Foreign Insurance Company, etc.," "Foreign Life Insurance Company, etc.," "Foreign Non-Life Insurance Company, etc.," "Foreign Mutual Company," "All Shareholders' Voting Rights, etc.," "Subsidiary Company" and "Subsidiary" "Major Shareholder Threshold," "Insurance Company's Major Shareholder," "Insurance Holding Company," "Low-Cost, Short-Term Insurers," "Life Insurance Agent," "Non-Life Insurance Representative," "Low-Cost, Short-Term Insurance Agent," "Insurance Agent," "Affiliated Insurance Company, etc.," "Insurance Broker," "Insurance Solicitation," and "Method of Public Notice" mean "Insurance Business," "Insurance Company," "Life Insurance Company," Non-Life Insurance Company," "Mutual Company," "Foreign Insurer," "Foreign Insurance Company, etc. ," "Foreign Life Insurance Company, etc. ," "Foreign Non-Life Insurance Company, etc. ," "Foreign Mutual Company," "All Shareholders' Voting Rights, etc. ," "Subsidiary Company" and "Subsidiary" "Major Shareholder Threshold," "Insurance Company's Major Shareholder," "Insurance Holding Company," "Low-Cost, Short-Term Insurers," "Life Insurance Agent," "Non-Life Insurance Representative," "Low-Cost, Short-Term Insurance Agent," "Insurance Agent, "Affiliated Insurance Company, etc.," "Insurance Broker," "Insurance Solicitation," and "Method of Public Notice" as respectively defined in Article 2 of the Insurance Business Act (hereinafter referred to as the "Act").

(Scope of Persons Excluded from the Category of "Company or Other Enterprise")
Article 1-2 (1) The enterprise specified by Cabinet Order, referred to in Article 2, paragraph (1), item (ii), sub-item (b) of the Act, shall be a company (including a foreign company; the same shall apply in item (ii) of the following Article) or any other en-

terprise (excluding an Insurance Company, Foreign Insurance Company, etc., Underwriting Member (meaning an Underwriting Member as defined in Article 219, paragraph (1) of the Act; the same shall apply hereinafter) of a Licensed Specified Juridical Person (meaning a Licensed Specified Juridical Person as defined in Article 223, paragraph (1) of the Act; the same shall apply hereinafter), and also excluding a Low-Cost, Short-Term Insurer) whose sole purpose is for an organization comprising said company or other enterprise or the officers or employees thereof (including persons who formerly held positions as officers or employees; hereinafter the same shall apply in this paragraph and Article 1-3, items (ii) and (iii)) to render underwriting services for the insurance specified in the items of Article 3, paragraph (4) of the Act or in the items of paragraph (5) of that Article with those officers or employees or the relatives thereof (limited to their spouses and their relatives by blood or affinity within the second degree of kinship; the same shall apply hereinafter) as the other parties thereto.

(2) The relatives specified by Cabinet Order, referred to in Article 2, paragraph (1), item (ii), sub-item (b) of the Act, shall be spouses and relatives by blood or affinity within the second degree of kinship.

(Business Excluded from the Definition of Insurance Business)

Article 1-3 The business specified by Cabinet Order, referred to in Article 2, paragraph (1), item (ii), sub-item (g), shall be as follows:
(i) that which a local government undertakes with an enterprise (limited to enterprises located within the district of said local government) or its officers or employees (excluding the business set forth in Article 2, paragraph (1), item (ii), sub-item (a)) as the other party thereto;
(ii) that which a single company (excluding a company (other than an Insurance Company, Foreign Insurance Company, etc., Underwriting Members of a Licensed Specified Juridical Person, and also excluding Low-Cost, Short-Term Insurers) whose sole purpose is for an organization comprising such company or its Consolidated Subsidiary Company, etc. (meaning a Subsidiary Company or other type of company which is required to prepare its financial statements or any other documents on a consolidated basis together with such company pursuant to the provisions of Cabinet Office Ordinance, and including a company which was a Consolidated Subsidiary Company, etc.; hereinafter the same shall apply in this item) and their officers or employees to render underwriting services for the insurance specified in the items of Article 3, paragraph (4) of the Act and in the items of paragraph (5) of that Article with the members of that organization or their relatives as the other parties) or its Consolidated Subsidiary Company, etc. and their officers or employees undertake for its members and their relatives as the other parties (excluding business set forth in Article 2, paragraph (1), item (ii), sub-item (b) or (d));
(iii) that which an organization comprising a single umbrella religious corporation (meaning, where there exists a religious organization as defined in Article 52, paragraph (2), item (iv) of the Religious Corporations Act, (Act No. 126 of 1951), an entity that is the relevant religious organization and that is a religious corporation (meaning a religious corporation as defined in Article 4, paragraph (2) of the same Act); the same shall apply hereinafter in this item), a religious corporation under the control of said umbrella religious corporation, or the officers or employees thereof undertakes with the members of said organization or their relatives as the other parties thereto (excluding business set forth in Article 2, paragraph (1), item (ii), sub-item (b));

(iv) that which an organization comprising members (including persons who formerly were members; hereinafter the same shall apply in this item) of a single National Government Employees' Mutual Aid Association (meaning a National Government Employees' Mutual Aid Association established under Article 3, paragraph (1) or (2) of the National Government Employees' Mutual Aid Association Act (Act No. 128 of 1958)) or members of a Local Government Employees' Mutual Aid Association (meaning a Local Government Employees' Mutual Aid Association established under Article 3, paragraph (1) of the Local Government Employees', etc. Mutual Aid Association Act (Act No. 152 of 1962); hereinafter the same shall apply in this item) (in the case of an organization comprising members of a Local Government Employees' Mutual Aid Association, limited to an organization comprising members appointed by the same appointer) undertakes with the members thereof or their relatives as the other parties thereto;

(v) that which an organization comprising members of the Diet (including persons who were formerly members of the Diet) or by members (including persons who formerly were members) of a single Regional Council Members' Mutual Aid Association (meaning a Regional Council Members' Mutual Aid Association as defined in Article 151, paragraph (1) of the Local Government Employees', etc. Mutual Aid Association Act; and limited to an association comprising members belonging to the council of the same local government) undertakes with the members thereof or their relatives as the other parties thereto;

(vi) that which a single School (meaning a school as defined in Article 1 of the School Education Act (Act No. 26 of 1947); the same shall apply in item (viii)) undertakes with the children or young children thereof as the other parties thereto;

(vii) that which an organization comprising a single Specialized Training College (meaning a Specialized Training College as defined in Article 124 of the School Education Act; hereinafter the same shall apply in this item and the following item), a single School for Specialized Education (limited to a School for Specialized Education as defined in Article 134, paragraph (1) of that Act that is as specified by Cabinet Office Ordinance; hereinafter the same shall apply in this item and the following item) or by students of a single Specialized Training College or School for Specialized Education (for a School for Specialized Education, limited to an institution as specified by Cabinet Office Ordinance; hereinafter the same shall apply in this item and the following item) undertakes with the students thereof as the other parties thereto;

(viii) that which an organization comprising the students of two or more Schools, etc. (meaning Schools, Specialized Training Colleges, and Schools for Specialized Education; the same shall apply in the following item) established by the same founder (excluding the State and local governments; the same shall apply in the following item) undertakes with the Students, etc. (meaning students, children, or young children; the same shall apply in that item) thereof as the other parties thereto; and

(ix) that which an organization comprising the guardians (meaning the persons who exercise parental authority or who are the curators) of the Students, etc. of a single School, etc. , the guardians of the Students, etc. of two or more Schools, etc. established by the same founder, or the teachers and staff members thereof, undertakes with its members or Students, etc. as the other parties thereto.

Article 1-4 (1) The number of persons specified by Cabinet Order, referred to in Article 2, paragraph (1), item (iii) of the Act, shall be one thousand.

(2) The business specified by Cabinet Order, referred to in Article 2, paragraph (1), item

(iii) of the Act, shall be that which falls under any of the following items:
(i) where two or more organizations have entrusted the management of their business and property to the same person, or where two or more organizations are closely related as specified by Cabinet Office Ordinance, business in which the total number other parties for said two or more organizations does not exceed one thousand;
(ii) where two or more organizations have jointly invested of monies or other assets collected as insurance premiums, or where they have jointly reinsured insurance contracts underwritten thereby, business in which the total number of other parties for said two or more organizations does not exceed one thousand;
(iii) the business of underwriting reinsurance; and
(iv) business that includes the underwriting of insurance and in which the total amount of annual insurance premiums (for an insurance contract specified by Cabinet Office Ordinance, meaning insurance premiums as specified by Cabinet Office Ordinance; hereinafter the same shall apply in this item) collected from a single individual exceeds five hundred thousand yen; or business that includes the underwriting of insurance and in which the total amount of annual insurance premiums collected from a single juridical person exceeds ten million yen.

(Terms of Coverage for Insurance under Low-Cost, Short-Term Insurance Services)
Article 1-5 The period specified by Cabinet Order, referred to in Article 2, paragraph (17) of the Act, shall be one year (or two years, for the insurance specified in Article 3, paragraph (5), item (i) of the Act).

(Amounts of Insurance Proceeds for Insurance Connected with Low-Cost, Short-Term Insurance Services)
Article 1-6 The amount specified by Cabinet Order, referred to in Article 2, paragraph (17) of the Act, shall be, per insured person, the amount specified in each of the following items in accordance with the categories of insurance set forth therein:
(i) insurance where the insurer promises to pay a fixed amount of insurance proceeds in connection with a person's death (excluding insurance as specified in item (v)): three million yen
(ii) insurance where the insurer promises to pay a fixed amount of insurance proceeds in connection with any of the events specified in Article 3, paragraph (4), item (ii), sub-item (a), (b), (d) or (e) of the Act, or to compensate the relevant person for damages thereto that arise therefrom (excluding insurance specified in the following item and item (iv)): eight hundred thousand yen
(iii) Critical Illness Insurance (meaning insurance where the insurer promises to pay a fixed amount of insurance proceeds, in connection with a person's critically ill state as specified by Cabinet Office Ordinance from among the events specified in Article 3, paragraph (4), item (ii), sub-item (b) or (d) of the Act; or insurance where the insurer promises to compensate such person for damages thereto that arise therefrom; hereinafter the same shall apply in this item and the following item) that requires that, where any insurance set forth in item (i), the following item, or item (v) has been included in addition to said Critical Illness Insurance in the insurance underwritten for the same insured, the insurance proceeds or damage compensation under the Critical Illness Insurance (hereinafter referred to as "Payment, etc. of Insurance Proceeds" in this Article) will accordingly result in a reduction in the amount of insurance proceeds from the insurance set forth in item (i), the following item, or item (v) by the portion corresponding to the

amount of such Payment, etc. of Insurance Proceeds (excluding insurance as specified in the following item): three million yen
(iv) Specific Critical Illness Insurance (meaning Critical Illness Insurance that covers a person's critically ill state resulting from an injury he/she has received; hereinafter the same shall apply in this item) that requires that, where any insurance set forth in item (i), the preceding item or the following item has been included in addition to said Specific Critical Illness Insurance in the insurance underwritten for the same insured, the Payment, etc. of such Insurance Proceeds will accordingly result in a reduction in the insurance proceeds under the insurance set forth in item (i), the preceding item or the following item by the portion corresponding to the amount of such Payment, etc. of Insurance Proceeds. : six million yen
(v) Accidental Death Insurance (meaning insurance where the insurer promises to pay a fixed amount of insurance proceeds in connection with the event specified in Article 3, paragraph (4), item (ii), sub-item (c) of the Act; or insurance where the insurer promises to compensate the relevant person for damage arising therefrom; hereinafter the same shall apply in this item): three million yen (or six million yen where any insurance set forth in item (i) has been included in addition to said Accidental Death Insurance in the insurance underwritten for the same insured, the Payment, etc. of Insurance Proceeds under the Accidental Death Insurance will accordingly result in a reduction in the amount of insurance proceeds from the insurance set forth in item (i) by the portion corresponding to the amount of such Payment, etc. of Insurance Proceeds); or
(vi) insurance specified in Article 3, paragraph (5), item (i) of the Act: ten million yen

(Insurance Excluded from Insurance Connected with Low-Cost, Short-Term Insurance Services)
Article 1-7 Insurance specified by Cabinet Order, referred to in Article 2, paragraph (17) of the Act, shall be as follows:
(i) insurance where the insurer promises to pay a fixed amount of insurance proceeds, in connection with a person's survival;
(ii) insurance where the insurer promises to pay a maturity refund upon expiration of the term of coverage;
(iii) insurance for which the creation of a Special Account as set forth in Article 118, paragraph (1) is required under that paragraph;
(iv) reinsurance;
(v) insurance for which the amount of insurance premiums, or the amount of benefits such as insurance proceeds or refunds, is denominated in a foreign currency; and
(vi) insurance whose insurance premiums, in whole or in part, are to be paid on a regular basis or by way of installment payments, and where the payment period exceeds one year.

(Special Relationships)
Article 2 The special relationship specified by Cabinet Order, referred to in Article 2-2, paragraph (1), item (vi) of the Act, shall be the relationship of relatives within the third degree of kinship.

Chapter II Insurance Companies, Foreign Insurance Companies, etc. and Low-Cost, Short-Term Insurers

Section 1 Insurance Companies, Foreign Insurance Companies, etc. and Low-Cost, Short-Term Insurers

(Minimum Requirements for the Amount of Stated Capital or Total Amount of Funds)
Article 2-2 The amount specified by Cabinet Order, referred to in Article 6, paragraph (1) of the Act, shall be one billion yen.

(Scope of Insurance Claims, etc.)
Article 3 The rights specified by Cabinet Order, referred to in Article 17, paragraph (5) of the Act, shall be as follows:
(i) insurance claims;
(ii) the right to claim compensation for damages (excluding the claims specified in the preceding item); and
(iii) a right to claim refunds, surplus, Policy Dividends (meaning policy dividends as defined in Article 114, paragraph (1) of the Act; the same shall apply in Article 36-4, item (iv) and Article 37-4-6, item (iv)) or any other type of benefit (excluding insurance proceeds).

Article 4 Insurance Claims, etc. under Article 17, paragraph (6) of the Act shall be limited to the claims that have already arisen as of the time of the public notice given pursuant to paragraph (2) of that Article.

(Replacement of Terms in the Provisions of the Companies Act That Are Applied Mutatis Mutandis to Instances Where There Has Been a Violation of the Restriction on the Distribution of Dividends of Surplus to Shareholders)
Article 4-2 Where, pursuant to the provisions of Article 17-6, paragraph (2) of the Act, the provisions of Article 463, paragraph (2) of the Companies Act (Act No. 86 of 2005) are applied mutatis mutandis to instances where a stock company has engaged in any act specified in the items of Article 17-6, paragraph (1) of the Act, in violation of that paragraph, the technical replacement of terms in connection with the relevant provisions shall be as set forth in the following table:

Provisions of the Companies Act whose terms are to be replaced	Original terms	Terms to replace the original terms
Article 463, paragraph (2)	who are liable pursuant to the provisions of that paragraph	who were delivered monies, etc. due to the relevant act

(Replacement of Terms in the Provisions of the Companies Act That Are Applied Mutatis Mutandis to the Employees, etc. of Mutual Company)
Article 4-3 (1) Where, pursuant to the provisions of Article 21, paragraph (1) of the Act, the provisions of Article 10, Article 12, paragraph (1) and Article 13 of the Companies Act are applied mutatis mutandis to the employees of a Mutual Company, the techni-

cal replacement of terms in connection with these provisions shall be as set forth in the following table:

Provisions of the Companies Act whose terms are to be replaced	Original terms	Terms to replace the original terms
Article 10	head office or branch office	principal office or secondary office
Article 12, paragraph (1), item (iii)	any other Company or merchant (excluding any Company; the same shall apply in Article 24)	a company (including a foreign company; hereinafter the same shall apply in this Part) or other Mutual Company (including a Foreign Mutual Company) or merchant (excluding a merchant that is a company)
Article 12, paragraph (1), item (iv)	a director, executive officer or any member who executes the operation of any other Company	a director, executive officer or any other member who executes the business of a company; or the director or executive officer of any other Mutual Company (including a Foreign Mutual Company)
Article 13	the head office or any branch office	the principal office or any secondary office

(2) Where, pursuant to the provisions of Article 21, paragraph (1) of the Act, the provisions of Article 17, paragraph (1) the Companies Act are applied mutatis mutandis to the person acting as the agent or intermediary for transactions on behalf of a Mutual Company, the technical replacement of terms in connection with the relevant provisions shall be as set forth in the following table:

Provisions of the Companies Act whose terms are to be replaced	Original terms	Terms to replace the original terms
Article 17, paragraph (1), item (ii)	a director, executive officer or any member who executes operation of any other Company	a director, executive officer or any other member who executes the business of a company; or the director or executive officer of any other Mutual Company (including a Foreign Mutual Company)

(3) Where, pursuant to the provisions of Article 21, paragraph (1) of the Act, the provisions of Articles 22 and 23 of the Companies Act are applied mutatis mutandis to instances where a Mutual Company either assigns its business, or takes over any business or operation, the technical replacement of terms in connection with these provisions shall be as set forth in the following table:

Provisions of the Companies Act whose terms are to be replaced	Original terms	Terms to replace the original terms
Article 22, paragraph (1)	Assignee Company	Assignee

Article 22, paragraph (2)	in cases where the Assignee Company registers, at the location of its head office, without delay after it has accepted the assignment of the business, a statement to the effect that it will not be liable for the performance of the obligations of the Assignor Company	where, without delay after it has been assigned the business, an Assignee that is a company or a Mutual Company (including a Foreign Mutual Company) has registered, at the place in which its head office or principal office is located (including a principal branch in Japan (meaning a principal branch in Japan as defined in Article 187, paragraph (1), item (iv) of the Insurance Business Act)) a statement to the effect that it will not be liable to perform the obligations of the Assignor Mutual Company (meaning a Mutual Company that has assigned its business; hereinafter the same shall apply in this paragraph); where, without delay after it has been assigned the business, an Assignee that is a merchant (excluding a merchant that is a company; hereinafter the same shall apply in this paragraph) has registered a statement to the effect that it will not be liable to perform the obligations of the Assignor Mutual Company; or where, without delay after it has been assigned the business, an Assignee that is a Mutual Company has registereds, at the place in which its principal office is located, a statement to the effect that it will not be liable to perform the obligations of the company that has assigned its business thereto or the merchant that has assigned its operations thereto.
	the Assignee Company and	the Assignee and
Article 22, paragraphs (3) and (4), and Article 23	the Assignee Company	the Assignee

(Replacement of Terms in the Provisions of the Commercial Code That Are Applied Mutatis Mutandis to the Activities of Mutual Companies)

Article 4-4 Where, pursuant to the provisions of Article 21, paragraph (2) of the Act, the provisions of Article 522 the Commercial Code (Act No. 48 of 1899) are applied mutatis mutandis to the activities of a Mutual Company, the technical replacement of terms in connection with the relevant provisions shall be as set forth in the following table:

Provisions of the Commercial Code whose terms are to be replaced	Original terms	Terms to replace the original terms
Article 522	this Act	the Insurance Business Act and this Act

(Replacement of Terms in the Provisions of the Companies Act That Are Applied Mutatis Mutandis to an Inspector's Investigation of Particulars Detailed or Recorded in the Articles of Incorporation of a Mutual Company)

Article 4-5 Where, pursuant to the provisions of Article 24, paragraph (2) of the Act, the provisions of Article 33, paragraphs (1) and (11) and Article 870 (limited to the portion involving items (ii) and (v)) of the Companies Act are applied mutatis mutandis to an inspector's investigation of the particulars listed in items of Article 24, paragraph (1) of the Act detailed or recorded in the articles of incorporation of a Mutual Company, if any, the technical replacement of terms in connection with these provisions shall be as set forth in the following table:

Provisions of the Companies Act whose terms are to be replaced	Original terms	Terms to replace the original terms
Article 33, paragraph (1)	Article 30(1)	Article 30, paragraph (1) as applied mutatis mutandis pursuant to Article 23, paragraph (4) of the Insurance Business Act
Article 33, paragraph (11), item (ii)	item (ii) of Article 28	Article 24(1)(i) of the Insurance Business Act
Article 870, item (v)	the person who contributes property other than monies set forth in Article 28(i) and the assignor set forth in item (ii) of that Article	the assignor set forth in Article 24, paragraph (1), item (i) of the Insurance Business Act

(Consent for Particulars That Are Required to Be Included in Written Documents to Be Provided by Electromagnetic Means)

Article 4-6 (1) A person who seeks to provide the information specified in the provisions set forth in the following items by Electromagnetic Means (meaning Electromagnetic Means as defined in Article 16, paragraph (2), item (iv) of the Act; the same shall apply hereinafter; and such person shall be referred to as a the "Sender" in the following paragraph) shall, in advance and pursuant to the provisions of Cabinet Office Ordinance, indicate to the recipient of such information the type and contents of the Electromagnetic Means that the Sender will use and obtain his/her consent in writing or by Electromagnetic Means:

(i) Article 28, paragraph (3) of the Act (including the cases where applied mutatis mutandis pursuant to Article 60-2, paragraph (4) and Article 78, paragraph (3) of the Act);

(ii) Article 30-7, paragraph (3);

(iii) Article 74, paragraph (3) and Article 76, paragraph (1) of the Companies Act as applied mutatis mutandis pursuant to Article 30-8, paragraph (6) of the Act;

(iv) Article 310, paragraph (3) and Article 312, paragraph (1) of the Companies Act as applied mutatis mutandis pursuant to Article 41, paragraph (1) of the Act;

(v) Article 310, paragraph (3) of the Companies Act as applied mutatis mutandis pursuant to Article 44-2, paragraph (3) of the Act (including the cases where applied mutatis mutandis pursuant to Article 77, paragraph (6) of the Act);

(vi) Article 312, paragraph (1) of the Companies Act as applied mutatis mutandis pursuant to Article 49, paragraph (1) of the Act;

(vii) Article 61-2, paragraph (3) of the Act;
(viii) Article 721, paragraph (4), Article 725, paragraph (3), Article 727, paragraph (1) and Article 739, paragraph (2) of the Companies Act as applied mutatis mutandis pursuant to Article 61-8, paragraph (2) of the Act;
(ix) Article 74, paragraph (3) of the Companies Act as applied mutatis mutandis pursuant to Article 74, paragraph (3) of the Act;
(x) Article 76, paragraph (1) of the Companies Act as applied mutatis mutandis pursuant to Article 74, paragraph (3) of the Act (including the cases where applied mutatis mutandis pursuant to Article 77, paragraph (6) of the Act);
(xi) Article 93, paragraph (3) of the Act;
(xii) Article 555, paragraph (3) and Article 557, paragraph (1) of the Companies Act as applied mutatis mutandis pursuant to Article 184 of the Act;
(xiii) Article 555, paragraph (3) and Article 557, paragraph (1) of the Companies Act as applied mutatis mutandis pursuant to Article 212, paragraph (4) of the Act;
(xiv) Article 555, paragraph (3) and Article 557, paragraph (1) of the Companies Act as applied as applied mutatis mutandis pursuant to Article 822, paragraph (3) of that Act as further applied mutatis mutandis pursuant to Article 213 of the Act; and
(xv) Article 555, paragraph (3) and Article 557, paragraph (1) of the Companies Act as applied mutatis mutandis pursuant to Article 235, paragraph (4) of the Act.
(2) When a Sender who has obtained the consent set forth in the preceding paragraph is notified in writing or by Electromagnetic Means to the effect that a recipient refuses to be provided with the information by Electromagnetic Means, the Sender shall not provide the recipient with the relevant information by Electromagnetic Means; provided, however, that this shall not apply where the recipient has given his/her consent under that paragraph again.

(Approval of Notice by Electromagnetic Means)
Article 4-7 (1) A person who, pursuant to the provisions set forth in the following items, seeks to send a notice by Electromagnetic Means (referred to as the "Notifier" in the following paragraph) shall, in advance and pursuant to the provisions of Cabinet Office Ordinance, indicate to the recipient of such notice the type and contents of the Electromagnetic Means the Notifier will use and obtain his/her consent in writing or by Electromagnetic Means:
(i) Article 68, paragraph (3) of the Companies Act as applied mutatis mutandis pursuant to Article 30-8, paragraph (6) of the Act;
(ii) Article 299, paragraph (3) of the Companies Act as applied mutatis mutandis pursuant to Article 41, paragraph (1) of the Act;
(iii) Article 299, paragraph (3) of the Companies Act as applied mutatis mutandis pursuant to Article 49, paragraph (1) of the Act;
(iv) Article 720, paragraph (2) of the Companies Act as applied mutatis mutandis pursuant to Article 61-8, paragraph (2) of the Act;
(v) Article 68, paragraph (3) of the Companies Act as applied mutatis mutandis pursuant to Article 74, paragraph (3) of the Act (including the cases where applied mutatis mutandis pursuant to Article 77, paragraph (6) of the Act);
(vi) Article 549, paragraph (2) of the Companies Act as applied mutatis mutandis pursuant to Article 184 of the Act;
(vii) Article 549, paragraph (2) of the Companies Act as applied mutatis mutandis pursuant to Article 549, paragraph (4) of the Companies Act, as further applied mutatis mutandis pursuant to Article 184 of the Act;
(viii) Article 549, paragraph (2) of the Companies Act as applied mutatis mutandis

pursuant to Article 212, paragraph (4) of the Act;
(ix) Article 549, paragraph (2) of the Companies Act as applied mutatis mutandis pursuant to Article 549, paragraph (4) of the Companies Act, as further applied mutatis mutandis pursuant to Article 212, paragraph (4) of the Act;
(x) Article 549, paragraph (2) of the Companies Act as applied mutatis mutandis pursuant to Article 822, paragraph (3) of the Companies Act, as further applied mutatis mutandis pursuant to Article 213 of the Act;
(xi) Article 549, paragraph (2) of the Companies Act as applied mutatis mutandis pursuant to Article 549, paragraph (4) of the Companies Act, as applied mutatis mutandis pursuant to Article 822, paragraph (3) of the Companies Act, and as further applied mutatis mutandis pursuant to Article 213 of the Act;
(xii) Article 549, paragraph (2) of the Companies Act as applied mutatis mutandis pursuant to Article 235, paragraph (4) of the Act; and
(xiii) Article 549, paragraph (2) of the Companies Act as applied mutatis mutandis pursuant to Article 549, paragraph (4) of the Companies Act, as further applied mutatis mutandis pursuant to Article 235, paragraph (4) of the Act.
(2) Where a Notifier who has obtained the consent set forth in the preceding paragraph is notified in writing or by Electromagnetic Means to the effect that a recipient refuses to be provided with notices by Electromagnetic Means, the Notifier shall not provide said recipient with notices by Electromagnetic Means; provided, however, that this shall not apply where the recipient has given his/her consent under that paragraph again.

(Replacement of Terms in Provisions of the Companies Act That Are Applied Mutatis Mutandis to an Action for a Declaratory Judgment as to the Absence or Invalidity of a Resolution of an Organizational Meeting of a Mutual Company and to an Action to Revoke a Resolution of an Organizational Meeting of a Mutual Company)
Article 4-8 Where, pursuant to the provisions of Article 30-8, paragraph (6) of the Act, the provisions of Article 937, paragraph (1) of the Companies Act (limited to the portion involving sub-item (g) of item (i)) are applied mutatis mutandis to an action for a declaratory judgment as to the absence or invalidity of a resolution of an organizational meeting of a Mutual Company or an action to revoke a resolution of an organizational meeting of a Mutual Company, the technical replacement of terms in connection with the relevant provisions shall be as set forth in the following table:

Provisions of the Companies Act whose terms are to be replaced	Original terms	Terms to replace the original terms
Article 937, paragraph (1) (limited to the portion pertaining to sub-item (g) of item (i))	items of Article 930(2)	items of Article 930, paragraph (2) as applied mutatis mutandis pursuant to Article 64, paragraph (3) of the Insurance Business Act

(Replacement of Terms in Provisions of the Companies Act That Are Applied Mutatis Mutandis to Investigations by the Directors at Incorporation, etc.)
Article 4-9 Where, pursuant to the provisions of Article 30-11, paragraph (2) of the Act, the provisions of Article 93, paragraph (3) of the Companies Act are applied mutatis mutandis to an investigation under Article 30-11, paragraph (1) of the Act, the technical replacement of terms in connection with the relevant provisions shall be as set

[7] Order for Enforcement of the Insurance Business Act, Art.4-10〜5 Chap.II, Sec.1

forth in the following table:

Provisions of the Companies Act whose terms are to be replaced	Original terms	Terms to replace the original terms
Article 93, paragraph (3)	the Shareholders at Incorporation	the persons who seek to become members

(Replacement of Terms in Provisions of the Companies Act That Are Applied Mutatis Mutandis to the Liability of the Incorporators, Directors at Incorporation, and Auditors at Incorporation of a Mutual Company)
Article 4-10 Where, pursuant to the provisions of Article 30-14 of the Act, the provisions of Article 52, paragraph (2) (excluding item (ii)) and Article 55 of the Companies Act are applied mutatis mutandis to the liability of the incorporators, Directors at Incorporation, or Auditors at Incorporation of a Mutual Company, the technical replacement of terms in connection with these provisions shall be as set forth in the following table:

Provisions of the Companies Act whose terms are to be replaced	Original terms	Terms to replace the original terms
Article 52, paragraph (2), item (i)	Article 33(2)	Article 33, paragraph (2) as applied mutatis mutandis pursuant to Article 24, paragraph (2) of that Act
Article 55	all shareholders	all members

(Rights for which a Base Date Cannot be Fixed)
Article 4-11 The rights specified by Cabinet Order, referred to in Article 33, paragraph (3) of the Act, shall be as follows:
(i) rights to receive distributions of surplus; and
(ii) rights to receive distributions of residual assets.

(Replacement of Terms in Provisions of the Companies Act That Are Applied Mutatis Mutandis to the Granting of Benefits in Relation to the Exercise of a Member's or Representative Member's Rights)
Article 5 (1) Where, pursuant to the provisions of Article 33-2, paragraph (2) of the Act, the provisions of Article 120, paragraph (2) of the Companies Act are applied mutatis mutandis to the case set forth in Article 33-2, paragraph (1) of the Act, the technical replacement of terms in connection with the relevant provisions shall be as set forth in the following table:

Provisions of the Companies Act whose terms are to be replaced	Original terms	Terms to replace the original terms
Article 120, paragraph (2)	shareholders' rights	members' rights or Representative Members' rights

(2) Where, pursuant to the provisions of Article 33-2, paragraph (2) of the Act, the provisions of Article 851, paragraph (1) (excluding item (i)) and paragraph (3) of the Companies Act are applied mutatis mutandis to an action for the return of benefits under

Article 120, paragraph (3) of the Companies Act as applied mutatis mutandis pursuant to Article 33-2, paragraph (2) of the Act, the technical replacement of terms in connection with these provisions shall be as set forth in the following table:

Provisions of the Companies Act whose terms are to be replaced	Original terms	Terms to replace the original terms
Article 851, paragraph (1), item (ii)	when such person acquires shares of the Stock Company incorporated through the merger or the Stock Company surviving a merger, or the Wholly Owning Parent Company thereof,	when such person has become a member of the Stock Company incorporated through the merger or the Stock Company surviving the merger,
Article 851, paragraph (3)	the Stock Company incorporated through the merger or the Stock Company surviving a merger, or the Wholly Owning Parent Company thereof	the Mutual Company or the Mutual Company surviving the merger

(Specified Mutual Companies)
Article 5-2 The Mutual Company specified by Cabinet Order, referred to in Article 38, paragraph (1) of the Act, shall be a Mutual Company with fifty thousand or less members in total.

(Number of Members Required to Exercise the Right to Demand That a Meeting of the General Members' Council of a Specified Mutual Company Be Called)
Article 5-2-2 The number of members specified by Cabinet Order, referred to in Article 38, paragraph (1) of the Act, shall three percent of the total number of members or 150 members, whichever is less.

(Number of Members Required to Exercise the Right to Submit a Proposal in Regard to a Specified Mutual Company)
Article 5-2-3 The number of members specified by Cabinet Order, referred to in Article 39, paragraph (1) of the Act, shall be one percent of the total number of members or 50 members, whichever is less.

(Replacement of Terms in Provisions of the Companies Act That Are Applied Mutatis Mutandis to the General Members' Council of a Mutual Company)
Article 5-2-4 Where, pursuant to the provisions of Article 41, paragraph (1) of the Act, the provisions of Article 319, paragraph (5) of the Companies Act are applied mutatis mutandis to the general members' council of a Mutual Company, the technical replacement of terms in connection with the relevant provisions shall be as set forth in the following table:

Provisions of the Companies Act whose terms are to be replaced	Original terms	Terms to replace the original terms

| Article 319, paragraph (5) | the annual shareholders meeting | the annual general meeting of the members |

(Replacement of Terms in Provisions of the Companies Act That Are Applied Mutatis Mutandis to an Action for a Declaratory Judgment as to the Absence or Invalidity of a Resolution of the General Members' Council of a Mutual Company and to an Actions to Revoke a Resolution of the General Members' Council of a Mutual Company)

Article 5-2-5 Where, pursuant to the provisions of Article 41, paragraph (2) of the Act, the provisions of Article 836, paragraph (1) and Article 937, paragraph (1) (limited to the portion involving sub-item (g) of item (i)) of the Companies Act are applied mutatis mutandis to an action for a declaratory judgment as to the absence or invalidity of a resolution of the general members' council of a Mutual Company or an action to revoke a resolution of the general members' council of a Mutual Company, the technical replacement of terms in connection with these provisions shall be as set forth in the following table:

Provisions of the Companies Act whose terms are to be replaced	Original terms	Terms to replace the original terms
Article 836, paragraph (1)	a shareholder or a Shareholder at Incorporation	a member
	provided, however, that this shall not apply when such shareholder is a director, company auditor, executive officer or liquidator or when such Shareholder at Incorporation is a Director at Incorporation or a Company Auditor at Incorporation.	provided, however, that this shall not apply when such a member is a director, company auditor, executive officer or a liquidator.
Article 937, paragraph (1) (limited to the portion pertaining to sub-item (g) of item (i))	head office	principal office
	items of Article 930(2)	items of Article 930, paragraph (2) as applied mutatis mutandis pursuant to Article 64, paragraph (3) of the Insurance Business Act
	branch office	secondary office

(Replacement of Terms in Provisions of the Companies Act That Are Applied Mutatis Mutandis to Proxy Voting)

Article 5-2-6 Where, pursuant to the provisions of Article 44-2, paragraph (3) of the Act, the provisions of Article 310, paragraphs (3), (4), (6) and (7) of the Companies Act are applied mutatis mutandis to the case set forth in paragraph (1) of Article 44-2, paragraph (1) of the Act, the technical replacement of terms in connection with these provisions shall be as set forth in the following table:

Provisions of the Companies Act whose terms are to be replaced	Original terms	Terms to replace the original terms
Article 310, paragraphs (3) and (4)	shareholder	Representative Member
Article 310, paragraph (6)	head office	principal office
Article 310, paragraph (7)	business hours (eigyou jikan)	business hours (jigyou jikan)

(Replacement of Terms in Provisions of the Companies Act That Are Applied Mutatis Mutandis to an Action for a Declaratory Judgment as to the Absence or Invalidity of a Resolution of the General Representative Members' Council of a Mutual Company and to an Action to Revoke a Resolution of the General Representative Members' Council of a Mutual Company)

Article 5-2-7 Where, pursuant to the provisions of Article 49, paragraph (2) of the Act, the provisions of Article 836, paragraph (1) and Article 937, paragraph (1) (limited to the portion involving sub-item (g) of item (i)) of the Companies Act are applied mutatis mutandis to an action for a declaratory judgment as to the absence or invalidity of a resolution of the General Representative Members' Council of a Mutual Company or an action to revoke a resolution of General Representative Members' Council of a Mutual Company, the technical replacement of terms in connection with these provisions shall be as set forth in the following table:

Provisions of the Companies Act whose terms are to be replaced	Original terms	Terms to replace the original terms
Article 836, paragraph (1)	a shareholder or a Shareholder at Incorporation	a member
	provided, however, that this shall not apply when such shareholder is a director, company auditor, executive officer or liquidator or when such Shareholder at Incorporation is a Director at Incorporation or a Company Auditor at Incorporation.	provided, however, that this shall not apply when such a member is a director, company auditor, executive officer or a liquidator.
Article 937, paragraph (1) (limited to the portion pertaining to sub-item (g) of item (i))	head office	principal office
	items of Article 930(2)	items of Article 930, paragraph (2) as applied mutatis mutandis pursuant to Article 64, paragraph(3) of the Insurance Business Act
	branch office	secondary office

(Number of Members Required to Exercise the Right to Demand That a Meeting of the General Representative Members' Council Be Called at a Specified Mutual Company with a General Representative Members' Council)

Article 5-2-8 The number specified by Cabinet Order, referred to in Article 50, paragraph (1) of the Act, shall be five percent of the total number of members or 250 members, whichever is less.

(Replacement of Terms in Provisions of the Companies Act That Are Applied Mutatis Mutandis to the Company Auditors of a Mutual Company)

Article 6 Where, pursuant to the provisions of Article 53-6, paragraph (2) of the Act, the provisions of Article 336, paragraph (4) (limited to the portion involving item (ii)) of the Companies Act are applied mutatis mutandis to the company auditors of a Mutual Company, the technical replacement of terms in connection with the relevant provisions shall be as set forth in the following table:

Provisions of the Companies Act whose terms are to be replaced	Original terms	Terms to replace the original terms
Article 336, paragraph (4) (limited to the portion pertaining to item (ii))	preceding three paragraphs	the preceding paragraph and Article 53-6, paragraph(1) of the Insurance Business Act

(Replacement of Terms in Provisions of the Companies Act That Are Applied Mutatis Mutandis to Statements of Opinions on the Election, Dismissal, or Resignation of the Accounting Advisors, etc. of a Mutual Company)

Article 6-2 Where, pursuant to the provisions of Article 53-11 of the Act, the provisions of Article 345, paragraph (5) of the Companies Act are applied mutatis mutandis to the statement of opinions on the election, dismissal, or resignation of the accounting advisor, company auditor, or accounting auditor of a Mutual Company, the technical replacement of terms in connection with the relevant provisions shall be as set forth in the following table:

Provisions of the Companies Act whose terms are to be replaced	Original terms	Terms to replace the original terms
Article 345, paragraph (5)	Article 340(1)	Article 53-9, paragraph (1) of the Insurance Business Act

(Replacement of Terms in Provisions of the Companies Act That Are Applied Mutatis Mutandis to the Accounting Advisors of a Mutual Company)

Article 7 Where, pursuant to the provisions of Article 53-17 of the Act, the provisions of Article 374, paragraph (1) of the Companies Act are applied mutatis mutandis to the accounting advisors of a Mutual Company, the technical replacement of terms in connection with the relevant provisions shall be as set forth in the following table:

Provisions of the Companies Act whose terms are to be replaced	Original terms	Terms to replace the original terms

| Article 374, paragraph (1) | Article 396(1) | Article 53-22, paragraph (1) of that Act |

(Replacement of Terms in Provisions of the Companies Act That Are Applied Mutatis Mutandis to the Company Auditors of a Mutual Company)

Article 7-2 Where, pursuant to the provisions of Article 53-20 of the Act, the provisions of Article 383, paragraph (1) and Article 388 of the Companies Act are applied mutatis mutandis to the company auditors of a Mutual Company, the technical replacement of terms in connection with these provisions shall be as set forth in the following table:

Provisions of the Companies Act whose terms are to be replaced	Original terms	Terms to replace the original terms
Article 383, paragraph (1)	under paragraph (2) of that Article	Article 373, paragraph(2) as applied mutatis mutandis pursuant to Article 53-16 of that Act
Article 388	a Company with Auditors (including a Stock Company the articles of incorporation of which provide that the scope of the audit by its company auditors shall be limited to an audit related to accounting)	a Company with Auditors

(Replacement of Terms in Provisions of the Companies Act That Are Applied Mutatis Mutandis to Liability for Damages of the Officers, etc. of a Mutual Company)

Article 7-3 Where, pursuant to the provisions of Article 53-36 of the Act, the provisions of Article 425, paragraph (1) (excluding item (ii)) and Article 428, paragraph (1) of the Companies Act are applied mutatis mutandis to the liability for damages of the officers, etc. of a Mutual Company, the technical replacement of terms in connection with these provisions shall be as set forth in the following table:

Provisions of the Companies Act whose terms are to be replaced	Original terms	Terms to replace the original terms
Article 425, paragraph (1) (excluding item (ii))	the preceding Article	Article 53-34 of the Insurance Business Act
Article 428, paragraph (1)	Article 356(1) (including cases of mutatis mutandis application under Article 419(2))	Article 356, paragraph(1), item (ii) of this Act as applied mutatis mutandis pursuant to Article 53-15 of the Insurance Business Act (including the cases where applied mutatis mutandis pursuant to the first sentence of Article 419, paragraph (2) of that Act as further ap

| | | plied mutatis mutandis pursuant to Article 53-32 of that Act) |

(Replacement of Terms in Provisions of the Companies Act That Are Applied Mutatis Mutandis to Liability Actions in a Mutual Company)

Article 7-4 (1) Where, pursuant to the provisions of Article 53-37 of the Act, the provisions of Article 850, paragraph (4) and Article 851, paragraph (1) (excluding item (i)) and paragraph (3) of the Companies Act are applied mutatis mutandis to a liability action in a Mutual Company, the technical replacement of terms in connection with these provisions shall be as set forth in the following table:

Provisions of the Companies Act whose terms are to be replaced	Original terms	Terms to replace the original terms
Article 850, paragraph (4)	The provisions of Article 55, Article 120(5), Article 424 (including the cases where applied mutatis mutandis pursuant to Article 486(4)), Article 462(3) (limited to the portion pertaining to the obligations assumed for the portion not exceeding the Distributable Amount prescribed in the proviso to that paragraph), Article 464(2) and Article 465(2)	The provisions of Article 55 as applied mutatis mutandis pursuant to Article 30-14 of the Insurance Business Act; Article 53-34 of that Act (including the cases where applied mutatis mutandis pursuant to Article 180-11, paragraph(4) of that Act); and Article 55-3, paragraph(3) of that Act (limited to the part related to the obligations assumed for the portion that does not exceed the amount prescribed in the proviso to that paragraph)
Article 851, paragraph (1), item (ii)	when such person acquires shares of the Stock Company incorporated through the merger or the Stock Company surviving a merger, or the Wholly Owning Parent Company thereof,	when such person has become a member of the Stock Company incorporated through the merger or the Stock Company surviving the merger,
Article 851, paragraph (3)	the Stock Company incorporated through the merger or the Stock Company surviving a merger, or the Wholly Owning Parent Company thereof	the Mutual Company or the Mutual Company surviving the merger

(2) Where, pursuant to the provisions of Article 53-37 of the Act, the provisions of Article 854, paragraph (1) (excluding sub-item (a) of item (i) and also excluding item (ii)) of the Companies Act are applied mutatis mutandis to an action to dismiss the officer of a Mutual Company, the technical replacement of terms in connection with the relevant provisions shall be as set forth in the following table:

Provisions of the Companies Act whose terms are to be replaced	Original terms	Terms to replace the original terms

Article 854, paragraph (1) (excluding sub-item (a) of item (i) and also excluding item (ii))	Article 329(1)	Article 52, paragraph(1) of the Insurance Business Act
	the following shareholders	the following members or Representative Members
	excluding the following shareholders	excluding the following members or Representative Members
	a shareholder who is the officer	a member of Representative Member who is an officer

(Replacement of Terms in Provisions of the Insurance Business Act That Are Applied Mutatis Mutandis to Consolidated Financial Statements)

Article 8 Where, pursuant to the provisions of Article 54-10, paragraph (6) of the Act, the provisions of Article 54-5 and Article 54-6, paragraph (1) of the Act are applied mutatis mutandis to consolidated financial statements, the technical replacement of terms in connection with these provisions shall be as set forth in the following table:

Provisions of the Insurance Business Act whose terms are to be replaced	Original terms	Terms to replace the original terms
Article 54-5	paragraph (3) of the preceding Article	Article 54-10, paragraph (5)
Article 54-6, paragraph (1)	Article 54-4, paragraph (3)	Article 54-10, paragraph (5)

(Replacement of Terms in Provisions of the Insurance Business Act That Are Applied Mutatis Mutandis to the Reduction of Reserves for the Redemption of Funds)

Article 8-2 Where, pursuant to the provisions of Article 57, paragraph (4) of the Act, the provisions of Article 16, paragraph (1) (excluding the proviso thereto) and paragraph (2), Article 17, paragraph (1) (excluding the proviso thereto), paragraph (2) and paragraph (4), Article 17-2, paragraph (4) and Article 17-4 of the Act are applied mutatis mutandis to a reduction of the reserves for the redemption of funds under Article 57, paragraph (4) of the Act, the technical replacement of terms in connection with these provisions shall be as set forth in the following table:

Provisions of the Insurance Business Act whose terms are to be replaced	Original terms	Terms to replace the original terms
Article 16, paragraph (1) (excluding the proviso thereto)	each of its business offices	each of its offices
Article 16, paragraph (2)	Stock Company	Mutual Company
	Shareholders	members
	the operating hours	the business hours

Article 17, paragraph (1) (excluding the proviso thereto), paragraph (2) and paragraph (4)	Stock Company	Mutual Company
Article 17-2, paragraph (4)	the preceding Article (or, pursuant to the provisions of that Article and the preceding paragraph for any reduction of the capital)	the preceding Article
Article 17-4, paragraph (1)	Stock Company	Mutual Company
	each of its business offices	each of its offices
Article 17-4, paragraph (2)	Stock Company	Mutual Company
	Shareholders	members
	the operating hours	the business hours

(Scope of Insurance Claims, etc.)
Article 8-3 Insurance Claims, etc. under Article 17, paragraph (6) of the Act as applied mutatis mutandis pursuant to Article 57, paragraph (4) of the Act shall be limited to the claims that have already arisen as of the time of the public notice given pursuant to paragraph (2) of that Article.

(Replacement of Terms in Provisions of the Companies Act That Are Applied Mutatis Mutandis to the Solicitation of Funds)
Article 8-4 Where, pursuant to the provisions of Article 60-2, paragraph (4) of the Act, the provisions of Article 209, item (i) of the Companies Act are applied mutatis mutandis to the solicitation of funds under Article 60, paragraph (1) of the Act, the technical replacement of terms in connection with the relevant provisions shall be as set forth in the following table:

Provisions of the Companies Act whose terms are to be replaced	Original terms	Terms to replace the original terms
Article 209, item (i)	Article 199, paragraph (1), item (iv)	Article 60-2, paragraph (1), item (iii) of the Insurance Business Act

(Replacement of Terms in Provisions of the Companies Act That Are Applied Mutatis Mutandis to Instances Where a Mutual Company Issues Corporate Bonds)
Article 9 Where, pursuant to the provisions of Article 61-5 of the Act, the provisions of Article 697, paragraph (1) of the Companies Act are applied mutatis mutandis to instances where a Mutual Company issues corporate bonds, the technical replacement of terms in connection with the relevant provisions shall be as set forth in the following table:

Provisions of the Companies Act whose terms are to be replaced	Original terms	Terms to replace the original terms

| Article 697, paragraph (1), item (i) | trade name | name |

(Replacement of Terms in Provisions of the Companies Act That Are Applied Mutatis Mutandis to Corporate Bond Administrators)

Article 9-2 Where, pursuant to the provisions of Article 61-7, paragraph (8) of the Act, the provisions of Article 709, paragraph (2) of the Companies Act are applied mutatis mutandis to a Corporate Bond Administrator, the technical replacement of terms in connection with the relevant provisions shall be as set forth in the following table:

Provisions of the Companies Act whose terms are to be replaced	Original terms	Terms to replace the original terms
Article 709, paragraph (2)	Article 705(1)	Article 61-7, paragraph(1) of the Insurance Business Act

(Replacement of Terms in Provisions of the Companies Act That Are Applied Mutatis Mutandis to Instances Where a Mutual Company Issues Corporate Bonds)

Article 9-3 Where, pursuant to the provisions of Article 61-8, paragraph (2) of the Act, the provisions of Article 716, Article 724, paragraph (2), Article 729, paragraph (1), Article 733, Article 740, paragraph (2) and Article 741, paragraph (3) of the Companies Act are applied mutatis mutandis to instances where a Mutual Company issues corporate bonds, the technical replacement of terms in connection with these provisions shall be as set forth in the following table:

Provisions of the Companies Act whose terms are to be replaced	Original terms	Terms to replace the original terms
Article 716	this Act	the Insurance Business Act
Article 724, paragraph (2), item (i)	each item of Article 706	each of the items in Article 61-7, paragraph (4) of the Insurance Business Act
Article 724, paragraph (2), item (ii)	paragraph (1) of Article 706, paragraph (1) of Article 736, the proviso to paragraph (1) of Article 737 and Article 738	Article 736, paragraph (1), the proviso to Article 737, paragraph (1) and Article 738 of this Act, and Article 61-7, paragraph (4) of the Insurance Business Act
Article 729, paragraph (1)	Article 707	Article 707 as applied mutatis mutandis pursuant to Article 61-7(8) of the Insurance Business Act
Article 733, item (i)	Article 676	Article 61 of the Insurance Business Act
Article 740, paragraph (2)	Article 702	Article 61-6 of the Insurance Business Act
Article 741, paragraph (3)	Article 705, paragraph (1)	Article 61-7, paragraph (1) of the Insurance Business Act

(Application of Laws and Regulations Governing the Issuance of Corporate Bonds by a Mutual Company)
Article 9-4 The laws and regulations specified by Cabinet Order, referred to in Article 61-9 of the Act, shall be the Secured Bonds Trust Act (Act No. 52 of 1905), the Enterprise Mortgage Act (Act No. 106 of 1958) and the Order for the Registration of Enterprise Mortgages (Cabinet Order No. 187 of 1958); and, for the purpose of the application of the provisions of these laws and regulations to the corporate bonds set forth in Article 61 of the Act, a Mutual Company, its name, principal office, and members shall be deemed to be a stock company, its trade name, head office, and shareholders as set forth in the provisions of Part II of the Companies Act, respectively. In this case, the term "registry of stock companies" in Article 4, paragraph (1) of the Enterprise Mortgage Act shall be deemed to be replaced with "registry of mutual companies."

(Replacement of Terms in Provisions of the Companies Act That Are Applied Mutatis Mutandis to a Dissolution Order for a Mutual Company)
Article 9-5 Where, pursuant to the provisions of Article 63-2 of the Act, the provisions of Article 824, paragraph (1), item (iii) of the Companies Act are applied mutatis mutandis to a dissolution order for a Mutual Company, the technical replacement of terms in connection with the relevant provisions shall be as set forth in the following table:

Provisions of the Companies Act whose terms are to be replaced	Original terms	Terms to replace the original terms
Article 824, paragraph (1), item (iii)	an executive director, an executive officer or a partner who executes the business	executive director (meaning an executive director as defined in Article 53-24, paragraph (3) of the Insurance Business Act) or executive officer

(Replacement of Terms in Provisions of the Companies Act That Are Applied Mutatis Mutandis to Mutual Companies)
Article 10 Where, pursuant to the provisions of Article 64, paragraph (3) of the Act, the provisions of Article 916 (limited to the portion involving item (i)) and Article 930, paragraphs (1) and (2) of the Companies Act are applied mutatis mutandis to a Mutual Company, the technical replacement of terms in connection with these provisions shall be as set forth in the following table:

Provisions of the Companies Act whose terms are to be replaced	Original terms	Terms to replace the original terms
Article 916, item (i)	the items of Article 911(3)	items of Article 64, paragraph (2) of the Insurance Business Act
Article 930, paragraph (1), item (ii)	in the items of Article 922(1) or in the items of Article 922(2)	in the items of Article 169-5, paragraph (2) of the Insurance Business Act

| Article 930, paragraph (2), item (i) | trade name | name |

(Replacement of Terms in Provisions of the Companies Act That Are and Other Acts Applied Mutatis Mutandis to the Registration of a Mutual Company)

Article 10-2　(1) Where, pursuant to the provisions of Article 67 of the Act, the provisions of Article 908, paragraph (1), Article 909 and Article 910 of the Companies Act are applied mutatis mutandis to the registration of a Mutual Company, the technical replacement of terms in connection with these provisions shall be as set forth in the following table:

Provisions of the Companies Act whose terms are to be replaced	Original terms	Terms to replace the original terms
Article 908, paragraph (1), Article 909 and Article 910	this Act	the Insurance Business Act

(2) Where, pursuant to the provisions of Article 67 of the Act, the provisions of the Commercial Registration Act (Act No. 125 of 1963) are applied mutatis mutandis to the registration of a Mutual Company, the technical replacement of terms in connection with the provisions of such Act (including the provisions of such Act as applied mutatis mutandis to the relevant provisions) shall be as set forth in the following table:

Provisions of the Commercial Registration Act whose terms are to be replaced	Original terms	Terms to replace the original terms
Article 1-3	business office	office
Article 12, paragraph (1)	Corporate Reorganization Act (Act No. 154 of 2002)	Act on Special Treatment of Corporate Reorganization Proceedings and Other Insolvency Proceedings of Financial Institutions (Act No. 95 of 1996)
Article 17, paragraph (3), as applied mutatis mutandis pursuant to Article 15	branch office	secondary office
Article 24, item (i), as applied mutatis mutandis pursuant to Article 15	business office	office
Article 24, items (xiii) to (xv) inclusive, as applied mutatis mutandis pursuant to Article 15	trade name	name
Article 48, paragraph (2), as applied mutatis mutandis pursuant to Article 15	items of paragraph (2) of Article 930 of the Companies Act	items of Article 930, paragraph (2) of the Companies Act as applied mutatis mutandis pursuant to Article 64, paragraph (3) of the Insurance Business Act

Article 78, paragraph (3), as applied mutatis mutandis pursuant to Article 15	items of Article 24	items of Article 24 (including the cases where applied mutatis mutandis pursuant to Article 67 of the Insurance Business Act)
Article 82, paragraph (2), as applied mutatis mutandis pursuant to Article 15	head office	head office or principal office
	the preceding paragraph	the preceding paragraph as applied mutatis mutandis pursuant to Article 170, paragraph (3) of the Insurance Business Act
Article 82, paragraph (3), as applied mutatis mutandis pursuant to Article 15	head office	head office or principal office
	Article 80 or the preceding Article	Article 80 or the preceding Article as applied mutatis mutandis pursuant to Article 170, paragraph (3) of the Insurance Business Act
Article 83, paragraph (1), as applied mutatis mutandis pursuant to Article 15	head office	head office or principal office
	items of Article 24	items of Article 24 (including the cases where applied mutatis mutandis pursuant to Article 67 of the Insurance Business Act)
Article 83, paragraph (2), as applied mutatis mutandis pursuant to Article 15	head office	head office or principal office
Article 17, paragraph (2), item (i)	trade name	name
	head office	principal office
Article 17, paragraph (3) and Article 20, paragraph (3)	branch office	secondary office
Article 21, paragraph (1)	trade name	name
Article 24, item (i)	business office	office
Article 24, items (xiii) to (xv) inclusive	trade name	name
Article 25, paragraph (3)	head office	principal office
Article 31, paragraph (1)	the first sentence of Article 17, paragraph (2) of the Commercial Code and the first sentence of Article 22, paragraph (2) of the Companies Act	the first sentence of Article 22, paragraph (2) of the Companies Act as applied mutatis mutandis pursuant to Article 21, paragraph (1) of the Insurance Business Act
Article 33, paragraph (1)	trade name	name

	business office (or a head office, in case of a company; hereinafter the same shall apply in this Article)	principal office
	business office	principal office
	business office	principal office
Article 33, paragraph (2)	trade name	name
	business office	principal office
Article 44, paragraph (2), item (ii)	business office	office
Article 46, paragraph (1)	all shareholders or class shareholders	all members (or all Representative Members, where General Meetings of the Representative Members have been established)
Article 47, paragraph (3)	the preceding paragraph	Article 64, paragraph (1) of the Insurance Business Act
Article 48, paragraph (2)	items of paragraph (2) of Article 930 of the Companies Act	items of Article 930, paragraph (2) of the Companies Act as applied mutatis mutandis pursuant to Article 64, paragraph (3) of the Insurance Business Act
Article 54, paragraph (2), item (iii)	Article 333, paragraph (1) of the Companies Act	Article 333, paragraph (1) of the Companies Act as applied mutatis mutandis pursuant to Article 53-4 of the Insurance Business Act
	Article 337, paragraph (1) of said Act	Article 337, paragraph (1) of the Companies Act as applied mutatis mutandis pursuant to Article 53-7 of the Insurance Business Act
Article 55, paragraph (1)	Article 346, paragraph (4) of the Companies Act	Article 53-12, paragraph (4) of the Insurance Business Act
Article 138, paragraph (1)	head office	principal office
	branch office	secondary office
Article 138, paragraph (2)	branch office	secondary office
Article 148	in this Act	in the Insurance Business Act
	of this Act	of that Act

(Replacement of Terms in Provisions of the Companies Act That Are Applied Mutatis Mutandis to Instances Where Mutual a Company Gives a Public Notice under the Insurance Business Act and Other Acts by Means of Electronic Public Notice)

Article 10-3 Where, pursuant to the provisions of Article 67-2 of the Act, the provisions of Article 940, paragraph (1) and Article 946, paragraph (3) of the Companies Act are applied mutatis mutandis to instances where a Mutual Company gives a public notice under the Act or any other Act by means of Electronic Public Notice, the technical replacement of terms in connection with these provisions shall be as set forth in the following table:

Provisions of the Companies Act whose terms are to be replaced	Original terms	Terms to replace the original terms
Article 940, paragraph (1), item (i)	this Act	the Insurance Business Act
Article 946, paragraph (3)	trade name	name

(Scope of Insurance Claims, etc.)
Article 11 Insurance Claims, etc. under Article 70, paragraphs (5) to (7) inclusive of the Act shall be limited to the claims that have already arisen as of the time of public notice given pursuant to paragraph (2) of that Article.

(Replacement of Terms in Provisions of the Companies Act That Are Applied Mutatis Mutandis to Instances Where a Converting Stock Company Has Issued Share Options)
Article 11-2 Where, pursuant to the provisions of Article 71 of the Act, the provisions of Article 777, paragraph (3) of the Companies Act are applied mutatis mutandis to instances where a converting stock company has issued share options, the technical replacement of terms in connection with the relevant provisions shall be as set forth in the following table:

Provisions of the Companies Act whose terms are to be replaced	Original terms	Terms to replace the original terms
Article 777, paragraph (3)	Effective Day	Effective Date (meaning the Effective Date as defined in Article 69(4)(v) of the Insurance Business Act; the same shall apply hereinafter)

(Replacement of Terms in Provisions of the Companies Act That Are Applied Mutatis Mutandis to Policyholders' Meetings, etc.)
Article 11-3 (1) Where, pursuant to the provisions of Article 74, paragraph (3) of the Act, the provisions of the Companies Act are applied mutatis mutandis to a Policyholders' Meeting, the technical replacement of terms in connection with the provisions of said Act shall be as set forth in the following table:

Provisions of the Companies Act whose terms are to be replaced	Original terms	Terms to replace the original terms
Article 68, paragraph (1)	no later than two weeks (or one week if the Stock Company to be incorporated is not a Public Company, except in cases where the matters listed in item (iii) or item (iv) of paragraph (1) of the preceding Article are decided, (or if a	no later than two weeks

	shorter period of time is provided for in the articles of incorporation in cases where the Stock Company to be incorporated is a Stock Company other than a Company with Board of Directors, such shorter period of time))	
Article 70, and Article 71, paragraphs (1) and (2)	Organizational Meeting Reference Documents	Policyholders' Meeting Reference Documents
Article 74, paragraph (6)	or the Stock Company after the formation of such Stock Company.	or, after the Entity Conversion takes effect, the Converted Mutual Company (meaning a Converted Mutual Company as defined in Article 69, paragraph (4), item (i) of the Insurance Business Act; hereinafter the same shall apply in this Article and Article 81)
	at a place designated by the incorporators (or at the head office of the Stock Company after the formation of such Stock Company	at the incorporator's head office (or, after the Entity Conversion takes effect, at the head office of the Converted Mutual Company
Article 74, paragraph (7)	or the shareholders of the Stock Company after the formation of such Stock Company	or, after the Entity Conversion takes effect, the shareholders of the Converted Mutual Company
	the hours designated by the incorporators (or during the business hours of the Stock Company after the formation of such Stock Company	the incorporator's business hours (or, after the Entity Conversion takes effect, during the business hours of the Converted Mutual Company)
Article 75, paragraph (3) and Article 76, paragraph (4)	at a place designated by the incorporators	at the incorporator's head office
Article 75, paragraph (4) and Article 76, paragraph (5)	hours designated by the incorporators	incorporator's business hours
Article 81, paragraph (2)	or the Stock Company after the formation of such Stock Company. The same shall apply hereinafter in paragraph (2) of the following Article.	or, after the Entity Conversion takes effect, the Converted Mutual Company
	at a place designated by the incorporators (or at the head office of the Stock Company if after the incorporation of such	at the incorporator's head office (or, after the Entity Conversion takes effect, at the principal office of the Con-

	Stock Company. The same shall apply hereinafter in paragraph (2) of the following Article)	verted Mutual Company)
Article 81, paragraph (3)	(or the shareholders and creditors of the Stock Company after the formation of such Stock Company. The same shall apply hereinafter in paragraph (3) of the following Article.)	and creditors (or, after the Entity Conversion takes effect, the members and creditors of the Converted Mutual Company)
	the hours designated by the incorporators (or during the business hours of such Stock Company if after the incorporation of such Stock Company. The same shall apply hereinafter in such paragraph.)	the incorporator's business hours (or, after the Entity Conversion takes effect, during the business hours of the Converted Mutual Company)

(2) Where, pursuant to the provisions of Article 74, paragraph (3) of the Act, the provisions of Article 836, paragraph (1) and Article 937, paragraph (1) (limited to the portion involving sub-item (g) of item (i)) of the Companies Act are applied mutatis mutandis to an action for a declaratory judgment as to the absence or invalidity of a resolution of a Policyholders' Meeting or an action to revoke a resolution of a Policyholders' Meeting, the technical replacement of terms in connection with these provisions shall be as set forth in the following table:

Provisions of the Companies Act whose terms are to be replaced	Original terms	Terms to replace the original terms
Article 836, paragraph (1)	a shareholder or a Shareholder at Incorporation	Policyholders
	provided, however, that this shall not apply when such shareholder is a director, company auditor, executive officer or liquidator or when such Shareholder at Incorporation is a Director at Incorporation or a Company Auditor at Incorporation.	provided, however, that this shall not apply when such a Policyholder is a director, company auditor, officer or liquidator.
Article 937, paragraph (1) (limited to the portion pertaining to sub-item (g) of item (i))	head office	principal office
	items of Article 930(2)	items of Article 930(2) as applied mutatis mutandis pursuant to Article 64(3) of the Insurance Business Act

	branch office	secondary office

(Replacement of Terms in Provisions of the Insurance Business Act That Are, etc. Applied Mutatis Mutandis to General Representative Policyholders' Council)

Article 11-4 (1) Where, pursuant to the provisions of Article 77, paragraph (6) of the Act, the provisions of Article 44-2, paragraph (1) and Article 74, paragraphs (1) to (3) inclusive and (6) of the Act are applied mutatis mutandis to a General Representative Policyholders' Council, the technical replacement of terms in connection with these provisions shall be as set forth in the following table:

Provisions of the Companies Act whose terms are to be replaced	Original terms	Terms to replace the original terms
Article 44-2, paragraph (1)	the articles of incorporation	the resolution under Article 77, paragraph (1)
Article 74, paragraph (1)	Each Policyholder	Each representative policyholder
Article 74, paragraph (2)	Policyholders	representative policyholders
Article 74, paragraph (3)	those provisions	those provisions (excluding Article 75, paragraphs (3) and (4), Article 76, paragraph (5), Article 78 and Article 81, paragraph (3) of that Act)
Article 74, paragraph (6)	Policyholders	representative policyholders

(2) Where the provisions of the first sentence of Article 44-2, paragraph (3) of the Act are applied mutatis mutandis to a General Representative Policyholders' Council pursuant to the provisions of Article 77, paragraph (6), the technical replacement of terms in connection with the provisions of Article 310, paragraphs (3), (4), (6) and (7) of the Companies Act as applied mutatis mutandis pursuant to the first sentence of the first-mentioned paragraph shall be as set forth in the following table:

Provisions of the Companies Act whose terms are to be replaced	Original terms	Terms to replace the original terms
Article 310, paragraphs (3) and (4)	Shareholders/shareholders	representative policyholders
	Stock Company	converting stock company
Article 310, paragraph (6)	Stock Company	converting stock company (or, after the Entity Conversion takes effect, the Converted Mutual Company (meaning a Converted Mutual Company as defined in Article 69(4)(i) of the Insurance Business Act; hereinafter the same shall apply in this Article))

	head office	head office (or, after the Entity Conversion takes effect, the principal office of the Converted Mutual Company)
Article 310, paragraph (7)	during the business hours of the Stock Company	during the business hours of the converting stock company (or, after the Entity Conversion takes effect, business hours of the Converted Mutual Company,)

(3) Where the provisions of Article 74, paragraph (3) of the Act are applied mutatis mutandis to a General Representative Policyholders' Council pursuant to the provisions of Article 77, paragraph (6), the technical replacement of terms in connection with the provisions Companies Act as applied mutatis mutandis pursuant to the first-mentioned paragraph shall be as set forth in the following table:

Provisions of the Companies Act whose terms are to be replaced	Original terms	Terms to replace the original terms
Article 68, paragraph (1)	no later than two weeks (or one week if the Stock Company to be incorporated is not a Public Company, except in cases where the matters listed in item (iii) or item (iv) of paragraph (1) of the preceding Article are decided, (or if a shorter period of time is provided for in the articles of incorporation in cases where the Stock Company to be incorporated is a Stock Company other than a Company with Board of Directors, such shorter period of time))	no later than two weeks
Article 70, and Article 71, paragraphs (1) and (2)	Organizational Meeting Reference Documents	Reference Documents for the General Meeting of the Representative Policyholders
Article 75, paragraph (3)	The incorporator	The converting stock company (or, after the Entity Conversion takes effect, the Converted Mutual Company (meaning a Converted Mutual Company as defined in Article 69, paragraph (4), item (i) of the Insurance Business Act; hereinafter the same shall apply in this Article); the same shall apply in paragraph (4) of the following

		Article)
	at a place designated by the incorporators	at the head office of the converting stock company (or, after the Entity Conversion takes effect, at the principal office of the Converted Mutual Company; the same shall apply in paragraph (4) of the following Article)
Article 75, paragraph (4)	The Shareholders at Incorporation	The Policyholders (or, after the Entity Conversion takes effect, the members of the Converted Mutual Company; the same shall apply in paragraph (5) of the following Article)
	hours designated by the incorporators	business hours of the converting stock company (or, after the Entity Conversion takes effect, the business hours of the Converted Mutual Company; the same shall apply in paragraph (5) of the following Article)
Article 76, paragraph (4)	at a place designated by the incorporators	at the head office
Article 76, paragraph (5)	The Shareholders at Incorporation	The policyholders
	during the hours designated by the incorporators	during the business hours of the converting Mutual Company
Article 78	incorporators	converting stock company
	by the Shareholders at Incorporation	by the representative policyholders
	of the Shareholders at Incorporation	of the policyholders
Article 81, paragraph (2)	or the Stock Company after the formation of such Stock Company. The same shall apply hereinafter in paragraph (2) of the following Article.	or, after the Entity Conversion takes effect, the Converted Mutual Company (meaning a Converted Mutual Company as defined in Article 69(4)(i) of the Insurance Business Act; hereinafter the same shall apply in this Article)
	at a place designated by the incorporators (or at the head office of the Stock Company if after the incorporation of such Stock Company. The same	at the incorporator's head office (or, after the Entity Conversion take effect, at the principal office of the Converted Mutual Company)

		shall apply hereinafter in paragraph (2) of the following Article.)	
Article 81, paragraph (3)	The Shareholders at Incorporation (or the shareholders and creditors of the Stock Company after the formation of such Stock Company. The same shall apply hereinafter in paragraph (3) of the following Article.)	The policyholders and creditors (or, after the Entity Conversion takes effect, the members and creditors of the Converted Mutual Company)
	the hours designated by the incorporators (or during the business hours of such Stock Company if after the incorporation of such Stock Company. The same shall apply hereinafter in such paragraph.)	the business hours of the converting stock company (or, after the Entity Conversion takes effect, during the business hours of the Converted Mutual Company)
Article 836, paragraph (1)	a shareholder or a Shareholder at Incorporation	representative policyholders
	provided, however, that this shall not apply when such shareholder is a director, company auditor, executive officer or liquidator or when such Shareholder at Incorporation is a Director at Incorporation or a Company Auditor at Incorporation.	provided, however, that this shall not apply when a such representative policyholder is a director, company auditor, executive officer or liquidator.
Article 937, paragraph (1) (limited to the portion pertaining to sub-item (g) of item (i))	head office	principal office
	items of Article 930(2)	items of Article 930(2) as applied mutatis mutandis pursuant to Article 64(3) of the Insurance Business Act
	branch office	secondary office

(Replacement of Terms in Provisions of the Insurance Business Act That Are Applied Mutatis Mutandis to the Solicitation of Funds by a Converted Mutual Company)

Article 11-5 Where, pursuant to the provisions of Article 78, paragraph (3) of the Act, the provisions of Article 30 and Article 30-3, paragraphs (1) and (5) of the Act are applied mutatis mutandis to solicitation under paragraph (1) of the first-mentioned Article, the technical replacement of terms in connection with these provisions shall be as set forth in the following table:

Provisions of the Insurance Business Act whose terms are to be replaced	Original terms	Terms to replace the original terms
Article 30	The provisions of the preceding two Articles	The provisions of the preceding two Articles, and the preceding Article as applied mutatis mutandis pursuant to Article 78, paragraph (3)
Article 30-3, paragraph (1)	without delay following the receipt of the notice under Article 29, paragraph (2), pay the full amount of money pertaining to their contribution to the funds solicited at incorporation, at the place of payment listed in Article 28, paragraph (1), item (iii)	no later than the date specified in Article 78, paragraph (2), item (iii), pay the full amount of money pertaining their contribution to the funds solicited at incorporation, at the place of payment at the place specified in item (iv) of that paragraph
Article 30-3, paragraph (5)	prescribed in that paragraph	prescribed in item (iii), paragraph (2) of that Article

(Replacement of Terms in Provisions of the Commercial Registration Act That Are Applied Mutatis Mutandis to Where a Stock Company Has Effected an Entity Conversion)

Article 11-6 Where, pursuant to the provisions of Article 84, paragraph (3) of the Act, the provisions of Article 78, paragraph (3) of the Commercial Registration Act are applied mutatis mutandis to the case set forth in paragraph (1) of the first-mentioned Article, the technical replacement of terms in connection with the relevant provisions shall be as set forth in the following table:

Provisions of the Commercial Registration Act whose terms are to be replaced	Original terms	Terms to replace the original terms
Article 78, paragraph (3)	items of Article 24	items of Article 24 (including the cases where applied mutatis mutandis pursuant to Article 67 of the Insurance Business Act)

(Replacement of Terms in Provisions of the Companies Act That Are Applied Mutatis Mutandis to Actions to Invalidate an Entity Conversion)

Article 11-7 (1) Where, pursuant to the provisions of Article 84-2, paragraph (4) of the Act, the provisions of Article 836, paragraph (1) and Article 937, paragraph (3) (limited to the portion involving item (i)) of the Companies Act are applied mutatis mutandis pursuant to an action to invalidate an entity conversion, the technical replacement of terms in connection with these provisions shall be as set forth in the following table:

Provisions of the Companies Act whose terms are to be replaced	Original terms	Terms to replace the original terms
Article 836, paragraph (1)	an Action Concerning Organization of Company which may be filed by a shareholder or a Shareholder at Incorporation	an action to invalidate the entity conversion
	the shareholder or the Shareholder at Incorporation who has filed	the person who formerly was a shareholder or the member who has filed
	when such shareholder is a director, company auditor, executive officer or liquidator or when such Shareholder at Incorporation is a Director at Incorporation or a Company Auditor at Incorporation	when such person who formerly was a shareholder, or such member is a director, company auditor, executive officer or liquidator
Article 937, paragraph (3) (limited to the portion pertaining to item (i))	head office	principal office and head office

(2) Where, pursuant to the provisions of Article 84-2, paragraph (4) of the Act, the provisions of Article 840, paragraphs (1) and (2) of the Companies Act are applied mutatis mutandis to a judgment of the invalidity of an entity conversion accompanied by the solicitation of funds as set forth in Article 78, paragraph (1) of the Act, the technical replacement of terms in connection with these provisions shall be as set forth in the following table:

Provisions of the Companies Act whose terms are to be replaced	Original terms	Terms to replace the original terms
the first sentence of paragraph (1) of Article 840	to the shareholders of such shares	to the shareholders of such shares (meaning a member who is a creditor of the fund) or any other creditor of the fund
Article 840, paragraph (2)	shareholders	creditors

(Scope of Insurance Claims, etc.)
Article 12 Insurance Claims, etc. under Article 88, paragraphs (5) to (7) inclusive of the Act shall be limited to the claims that have already arisen as of the time of the public notice given pursuant to paragraph (2) of that Article.

(Replacement of Terms in Provisions of the Companies Act That Are Applied Mutatis Mutandis to Instances Where the Particulars of Contributions in Kind Are Prescribed in an Entity Conversion Plan)
Article 12-2 Where, pursuant to the provisions of Article 96-4 of the Act, the provisions of Article 207, paragraph (8) and Article 213, paragraph (1) (excluding items (i)

and (iii)) of the Companies Act are applied mutatis mutandis to instances where the particulars set forth in Article 92, item (iii) of the Act are prescribed, the technical replacement of terms in connection with these provisions shall be as set forth in the following table:

Provisions of the Companies Act whose terms are to be replaced	Original terms	Terms to replace the original terms
Article 207, paragraph (8)	his/her applications for subscription for Shares for Subscription, or his/her manifestation of intention relating to the contract provided for in Article 205	his/her offer to subscribe for Shares for Subscription
Article 213, paragraph (1), item (ii)	shareholders meeting	general meeting of the members (or General Meeting of the Representative Members, if these have been established)

(Replacement of Terms in Provisions of the Companies Act That Are Applied Mutatis Mutandis to a Mutual Company, etc. Implementing an Entity Conversion Involving a Share Exchange on Entity Conversion)

Article 12-3 (1) Where, pursuant to the provisions of Article 96-5, paragraph (3) of the Act, the provisions of Article 791, paragraph (1) (excluding item (i)) and paragraph (4) of the Companies Act are applied mutatis mutandis to a Mutual Company implementing an Entity Conversion involving a Share Exchange on Entity Conversion, the technical replacement of terms in connection with these provisions shall be as set forth in the following table:

Provisions of the Companies Act whose terms are to be replaced	Original terms	Terms to replace the original terms
Article 791, paragraph (1) (excluding item (i))	the Effective Day	the Effective Date (meaning the Effective Date as defined in Article 86, paragraph (4), item (xii) of the Insurance Business Act; the same shall apply hereinafter)
Article 791, paragraph (1), item (ii)	documents or Electromagnetic Records that state or record the number of shares of the Wholly Owned Subsidiary Company in Share Exchange acquired by the Wholly Owning Parent Company through the Share Exchange and any other matters prescribed by the applicable Ordinance of the	documents or Electromagnetic Records set forth in Article 82, paragraph (2) of the Insurance Business Act as applied mutatis mutandis pursuant to Article 95-15 of that Act

		Ministry of Justice as those concerning a Share Exchange	
Article 791, paragraph (4)	shareholders or holders of Share Options of the Wholly Owned Subsidiary Company in Share Exchange	members of the Mutual Company implementing the Entity Conversion involving a Share Exchange on Entity Conversion

(2) Where, pursuant to the provisions of Article 96-5, paragraph (3) of the Act, the provisions of the Companies Act are applied mutatis mutandis to a Wholly Owning Parent Company in a Share Exchange on Entity Conversion, the technical replacement of terms in connection with the provisions of said Act shall be as set forth in the following table:

Provisions of the Companies Act whose terms are to be replaced	Original terms	Terms to replace the original terms
Article 309, paragraph (2) (excluding each of the items)	Notwithstanding the provisions of the preceding paragraph, the resolutions of the following shareholders meetings	The resolution at the shareholders meeting set forth in Article 795, paragraph(1)
Article 324, paragraph (2) (excluding each of the items)	Notwithstanding the provisions of the preceding paragraph, the resolutions of the following Class Meetings	The resolution at the Class Meeting set forth in Article 795, paragraph(4)
Article 794, paragraph (3)	or, in the case where the Monies, etc. to be delivered to shareholders of the Wholly Owned Subsidiary Company in Share Exchange are limited to shares of the Wholly Owning Parent Stock Company in Share Exchange or those prescribed by the applicable Ordinance of the Ministry of Justice as being equivalent thereto (excluding the case prescribed in Article 768(1)(iv)(c),	or, where the shares or monies to be delivered to members of the converting Mutual Company are limited to shares in the Wholly Owning Parent Company established in a Share Exchange on Entity Conversion or any other shares specified by Cabinet Office Ordinance as being equivalent thereto
Article 795, paragraph (2), item (iii)	the book value of the Monies, etc. (excluding shares, etc. of the Wholly Owning Parent Stock Company in Share Exchange) delivered by the Wholly Owning Parent Stock Company in Share Exchange to shareholders of the Wholly Owned Subsidiary Company in Share Exchange	the amount of money to be delivered by the Wholly Owning Parent Stock Company in the Share Exchange to members of the converting Mutual Company

Article 795, paragraph (4), item (iii)	Monies, etc.	shares or monies
	Article 768(1)(ii)(a)	Article 96-7, item (ii), sub-item (a) of the Insurance Business Act
Article 796, paragraph (1)	Monies, etc.	shares or monies
Article 796, paragraph (2), item (ii)	Article 749(1)(ii) or (iii), Article 758(iv) or Article 768(1)(ii) or (iii)	Article 96-7, item (ii) or (iii) of the Insurance Business Act
Article 796, paragraph (3), item (i), sub-item (c)	the book value of property other than shares, etc. of the Surviving Stock Company, etc.	money
Article 797, paragraph (3)	the trade name and domicile of the Absorbed Company, etc. (or, in the cases prescribed in Article 795(3), the fact that it will effect an Absorption-type Merger, etc., the trade name and domicile of the Absorbed Company, etc. and the matters concerning shares set forth in that paragraph)	the name and address of the converting Mutual Company
Article 799, paragraph (1), item (iii)	other than where the Monies, etc. to be delivered to shareholders of the Wholly Owned Subsidiary Company in Share Exchange are only shares of the Wholly Owning Parent Stock Company in Share Exchange or those prescribed by the applicable Ordinance of the Ministry of Justice as being equivalent thereto, or in the cases prescribed in Article 768(1)(iv)	other than where the shares or monies to be delivered to members of the converting Mutual Company are only shares in the Wholly Owning Parent Company established in a Share Exchange on Entity Conversion or any other shares specified by Cabinet Office Ordinance as being equivalent thereto
Article 799, paragraph (2), item (ii)	the trade name and domicile of the Absorbed Company, etc.	the name and address of the converting Mutual Company
Article 799, paragraph (2), item (iii)	the Surviving Stock Company, etc. and the Absorbed Company, etc. (limited to a Stock Company)	the Wholly Owning Parent Company established in the Share Exchange on Entity Conversion and the converting Mutual Company
Article 801, paragraph (6)	or, in cases where Monies, etc. to be delivered to shareholders of the Wholly Owned Subsidiary Company in Share Exchange are limited to shares of the Wholly Owning Parent Stock Company in Share Ex-	or, where the shares or monies to be delivered to members of a converting Mutual Company are limited to shares in the Wholly Owning Parent Company established in the Share Exchange on Entity Conversion or

| | change or those prescribed by the applicable Ordinance of the Ministry of Justice as being equivalent thereto (excluding the case prescribed in Article 768(1)(iv)(c)), | any other shares specified by Cabinet Office Ordinance as being equivalent thereto |

(Replacement of Terms in Provisions of the Companies Act That Are Applied Mutatis Mutandis to a Mutual Company Implementing an Entity Conversion Involving a Share Transfer on Entity Conversion)

Article 12-4 (1) Where, pursuant to the provisions of Article 96-9, paragraph (4) of the Act, the provisions of Article 811, paragraph (1) (excluding item (i)) and paragraph (4) of the Companies Act are applied mutatis mutandis to a Mutual Company implementing an Entity Conversion involving a Share Transfer on Entity Conversion, the technical replacement of terms in connection with these provisions shall be as set forth in the following table:

Provisions of the Companies Act whose terms are to be replaced	Original terms	Terms to replace the original terms
Article 811, paragraph (1), item (ii)	documents or Electromagnetic Records that state or record the number of shares of the Wholly Owned Subsidiary Company in Share Transfer acquired by the Wholly Owning Parent Company Incorporated through Share Transfer and any other matters prescribed by the applicable Ordinance of the Ministry of Justice as those concerning a Share Transfer.	documents or Electromagnetic Records set forth in Article 82, paragraph (2) of the Insurance Business Act as applied mutatis mutandis pursuant to Article 96-15 of that Act
Article 811, paragraph (4)	shareholders or holders of Share Options of the Wholly Owned Subsidiary Company in Share Transfer as of the day of formation of the Wholly Owning Parent Company Incorporated through Share Transfer.	members of the Mutual Company implementing the Entity Conversion involving a Share Transfer on Entity Conversion as of the day of formation of the Wholly Owning Parent Company established in the Share Exchange on Entity Conversion

(2) Where, pursuant to the provisions of Article 96-9, paragraph (4) of the Act, the provisions of Article 309, paragraph (2) (excluding each of the items), Article 806, paragraph (3), Article 808, paragraph (3) (excluding items (i) and (ii)) and Article 810, paragraph (2) of the Companies Act are applied mutatis mutandis to a stock company as set forth in Article 96-9, paragraph (1), item (ix) of the Act, the technical replacement of terms in connection with these provisions shall be as set forth in the following table:

Provisions of the Companies Act whose terms are to be replaced	Original terms	Terms to replace the original terms
Article 309, paragraph (2) (excluding each of the items)	Notwithstanding the provisions of the preceding paragraph, the resolutions of the following shareholders meetings	The resolutions at shareholders' meetings under Article 804, paragraph (1)
Article 806, paragraph (3)	and the trade names and domiciles of the Companies Consolidated through Consolidation-type Merger, the Splitting Company(ies) in Incorporation-type Company Split or the Wholly Owned Subsidiary Company in Share Transfer (hereinafter referred to as the "Consolidated Company, etc." in this Section) and the Incorporated Company,	as well as the trade name or name of the Mutual Company implementing an Entity Conversion involving a Share Transfer on Entity Conversion, any other stock company set forth in Article 96-9, paragraph(1), item (ix) of the Insurance Business Act, and the Wholly Owning Parent Company established in the Share Exchange on Entity Conversion
Article 808, paragraph (3) (excluding items (i) and (ii)) and Article 810, paragraph (2), item (ii)	and the trade names and domiciles of the Consolidated Company, etc. and the Incorporated Company	as well as the trade name or name of the Mutual Company implementing an Entity Conversion involving a Share Transfer on Entity Conversion, any other stock company set forth in Article 96-9, paragraph (1), item (ix) of the Insurance Business Act, and the Wholly Owning Parent Company established in the Share Exchange on Entity Conversion

(Replacement of Terms in Provisions of the Commercial Registration Act That Are Applied Mutatis Mutandis to Where a Converting Mutual Company Carries Out a Share Exchange on Entity Conversion)

Article 12-5 (1) Where, pursuant to the provisions of Article 96-14, paragraph (2) of the Act, the provisions of Article 89 (limited to the portion involving items (i) to (iv) inclusive) of the Commercial Registration Act are applied mutatis mutandis to a converting Mutual Company implementing a Share Exchange on Entity Conversion, the technical replacement of terms in connection with the relevant provisions shall be as set forth in the following table:

Provisions of the Commercial Registration Act whose terms are to be replaced	Original terms	Terms to replace the original terms

Article 89, item (ii)	in the main clause of paragraph (1) or of paragraph (3) of Article 796 of the Companies Act	in the main clauses of Article 796, paragraphs (1) or paragraph (3) of the Companies Act as applied mutatis mutandis pursuant to Article 96-5, paragraph (3) of the Insurance Business Act
	paragraph (4) of said Article	Article 796, paragraph (4) of the Companies Act as applied mutatis mutandis pursuant to Article 96-5, paragraph (3) of the Insurance Business Act
Article 89, item (iii)	Article 799, paragraph (2) of the Companies Act	Article 796, paragraph (2) of the Companies Act as applied mutatis mutandis pursuant to Article 96-5, paragraph (3) of the Insurance Business Act

(2) Where, pursuant to the provisions of Article 96-14, paragraph (2) of the Act, the provisions of Article 925 (excluding items (ii) and (iv)) of the Companies Act are applied mutatis mutandis to where a converting Mutual Company implements a Share Transfer upon Entity Conversion, the technical replacement of terms in connection with the relevant provisions shall be as set forth in the following table:

Provisions of the Companies Act whose terms are to be replaced	Original terms	Terms to replace the original terms
Article 925 (excluding items (ii) and (iv))	In cases where a Stock Company(ies) effects a Share Transfer,	Where a converting Mutual Company or a stock company set forth in Article 96-9, paragraph (1), item (ix) of the Insurance Business Act implements a Share Transfer on Entity Conversion,
Article 925, item (i)	the shareholders meeting set forth in Article 804(1)	the shareholders' meeting set forth in Article 804(1) as applied mutatis mutandis pursuant to Article 96-9(4) of the Insurance Business Act or a General Meeting of the members as set forth in Article 86(1) of that Act (or a General Meeting of the Representative Members, if these have been established)
Article 925, item (iii)	Article 806(3)	Article 806(3) as applied mutatis mutandis pursuant to Article 96-9 (4) of the Insurance Business Act
Article 925, item (v)	if the procedures under the provisions of Article 810 need to be carried out, the day on which such procedures were completed;	the day on which the procedures under Article 88 of the Insurance Business Act were completed; or if the procedures under the provisions of Article 810 as applied mutatis mutandis pursuant to Article 96-9 (4) of that Act (excluding items (i) and (ii)) of paragraph (1) were completed;

Article 925, item (vi)	or, in cases where two or more Stock Companies	or, in cases where two or more converting Mutual Companies or two or more stock companies set forth in Article 96-9(1)(ix) of the Insurance Business Act
	such two or more Stock Companies effecting the Share Transfer	such two or more converting Mutual Companies or two or more stock companies set forth in Article 96-9 (1)(ix) of the Insurance Business Act

(3) Where, pursuant to the provisions of Article 96-14, paragraph (2) of the Act, the provisions of Article 90 of the Commercial Registration Act are applied mutatis mutandis to where a converting Mutual Company implements a Share Transfer on Entity Conversion, the technical replacement of terms in connection with the relevant provisions shall be as set forth in the following table:

Provisions of the Commercial Registration Act whose terms are to be replaced	Original terms	Terms to replace the original terms
Article 90, item (v)	the stock company effecting the share transfer (hereinafter referred to as a "wholly owned subsidiary company in share transfer")	the Mutual Company implementing the Share Transfer on Entity Conversion or the stock company as set forth in Article 96-9, paragraph (1), item (ix) of the Insurance Business Act
	the wholly owned subsidiary company in share transfer has its head office	the Mutual Company implementing the Share Transfer on Entity Conversion or the stock company as set forth in Article 96-9, paragraph (1), item (ix) of the Insurance Business Act has its principal office or head office
Article 90, item (vi)	the wholly owned subsidiary company in share transfer	the Mutual Company implementing the Share Transfer on Entity Conversion or the stock company as set forth in Article 96-9, paragraph (1), item (ix) of the Insurance Business Act has its principal office or head offices
	Article 804, paragraphs (1) and (3) of the Companies Act	Article 86, paragraph (1) of the Insurance Business Act, or Article 804, paragraphs (1) and (3) of the Companies Act as applied mutatis mutandis pursuant to Article 96-9, paragraph (4) of the Insurance Business Act
Article 90, item (vii)	the wholly owned subsidiary company in share transfer	the Mutual Company implementing the Share Transfer on Entity Conversion or the stock company as set forth in Article 96-9, paragraph (1), item (ix) of the Insurance Business Act has its principal office

		or head office
	the public notice and the notices under Article 810, paragraph (2) of the Companies Act	the public notice under Article 88, paragraph (2) of the Insurance Business Act, or the public notice and the notices under Article 810, paragraph (2) of the Companies Act as applied mutatis mutandis pursuant to Article 96-9, paragraph (4) of the Insurance Business Act
items (viii) and (ix) of Article 90	the wholly owned subsidiary company in share transfer	the stock company as set forth in Article 96-9, paragraph (1) of the Insurance Business Act

(Replacement of Terms in Provisions of the Commercial Registration Act That Are Applied Mutatis Mutandis to the Registration Made by Mutual Company Upon Entity Conversion)

Article 12-6 Where, pursuant to the provisions of Article 96-14, paragraph (6) of the Act, the provisions of Article 76 and Article 78, paragraph (3) of the Commercial Registration Act are applied mutatis mutandis to the case set forth in Article 96-14, paragraph (1) of the Act, the technical replacement of terms in connection with these provisions shall be as set forth in the following table:

Provisions of the Commercial Registration Act whose terms are to be replaced	Original terms	Terms to replace the original terms
Article 76	trade name	name
Article 78, paragraph (3)	items of Article 24	items of Article 24 (including the cases where applied mutatis mutandis pursuant to Article 67 of the Insurance Business Act)

(Replacement of Terms in Provisions of the Insurance Business Act That Are Applied Mutatis Mutandis to an Entity Conversion from a Mutual Company to a Stock Company)

Article 12-7 Where, pursuant to the provisions of Article 96-15 of the Act, the provisions of Article 82, paragraphs (2) and (3) of the Act are applied mutatis mutandis to an Entity Conversion from a Mutual Company to a Stock Company, the technical replacement of terms in connection with these provisions shall be as set forth in the following table:

Provisions of the Insurance Business Act whose terms are to be replaced	Original terms	Terms to replace the original terms
Article 82, paragraph (2)	office	business office (or each business office (excluding headquarters), for a converted stock company that has implemented an Entity Conversion in which there was a Share Exchange on Entity Conversion or a Share Transfer on Entity Conversion)

| Article 82, paragraph (3) | Policyholders | Shareholders and Policyholders |
| | business hours | business hours |

(Replacement of Terms in Provisions of the Companies Act That Are Applied Mutatis Mutandis to Actions to Invalidate an Entity Conversion)

Article 12-8 Where, pursuant to the provision of Article 96-16, paragraph (4) of the Act, the provisions of Article 836, paragraph (1) and Article 937, paragraph (3) (limited to the portion involving item (i)) and paragraph (4) of the Companies Act are applied mutatis mutandis to an action to invalidate an Entity Conversion, the technical replacement of terms in connection with these provisions shall be as set forth in the following table:

Provisions of the Companies Act whose terms are to be replaced	Original terms	Terms to replace the original terms
Article 836, paragraph (1)	an Action Concerning Organization of Company which may be filed by a shareholder or a Shareholder at Incorporation	an action to invalidate the Entity Conversion
	order the shareholder or the Shareholder at Incorporation	order the shareholders, or the persons who formerly were members or shareholders
	provided, however, that this shall not apply when such shareholder is a director, company auditor, executive officer or liquidator or when such Shareholder at Incorporation is a Director at Incorporation or a Company Auditor at Incorporation.	provided, however, that this shall not apply when such a shareholders or the persons who formerly was a members or shareholders is a director, company auditor, executive officer or liquidator
Article 937, paragraph (3) (limited to the portion pertaining to item (i))	head office	head office and principal office
Article 937, paragraph (4)	items of Article 930(2)	items of Article 930, paragraph (2) (including the cases where applied mutatis mutandis pursuant to Article 64, paragraph(3) of the Insurance Business Act)
	branch office	branch office and secondary office

(Application of Laws and Regulations to the Entrustment of Solicitation or Management in Relation to Corporate Bonds, etc.)

Article 13 The laws and regulations specified by Cabinet Order, referred to in Article 99, paragraph (6) of the Act, shall be those prescribed in each of the following items; the application of the provisions of these laws and regulations shall be in accordance with the provisions of the relevant item; and, for the purposes of the application of the provisions of such laws and regulations to the business activities set forth in the items of Article 99, paragraph (2) of the Act, the name, principal office, and business activities of a Mutual Company shall be deemed to be the trade name, head office, and business activities of a Stock Company as set forth in Part II of the Companies Act, respectively.

(i) For the purpose of application of the provisions of the Order for Enforcement of the Local Government Finance Act (Cabinet Order No. 267 of 1948) or any other laws and regulations that contain provisions concerning entrustment of solicitation or management in relation to Corporate Bonds, etc. (meaning municipal bonds, corporate bonds or any other types of debentures; hereinafter the same shall apply in this item) or entrustment of business related to Corporate Bonds, etc. such as the issuance thereof (hereinafter collectively referred to as "Entrustment of Solicitation, etc. in relation to Corporate Bonds" in this item), with regard to the provisions concerning Entrustment of Solicitation, etc. in relation to Corporate Bonds, an Insurance Company that is a stock company shall be deemed to be a Bank (meaning a Bank as defined in Article 2, paragraph (1) (Definitions) of the Banking Act (Act No. 59 of 1981); the same shall apply hereinafter) that is allowed accept Entrustment of Solicitation, etc. in relation to Corporate Bonds, and an Insurance Company that is a Mutual Company shall be deemed to be a company or a Bank that is allowed to accept Entrustment of Solicitation, etc. in relation to Corporate Bonds.

(ii) With regard to the application of the provisions of the Secured Bonds Trust Act (including the cases where applied mutatis mutandis pursuant to any other laws and regulations), a Mutual Company shall be deemed to be a company eligible to obtain a license for trust business in relation to secured bonds as referred to in Article 3 of that Act.

(Amount of Business Deposits for a Life Insurance Company, etc. Engaged in Insurance-Proceed Trust Services)

Article 13-2 The amount specified by Cabinet Order, referred to in Article 11, paragraph (2) of the Trust Business Act (Act No. 154 of 2004) as applied mutatis mutandis pursuant to Article 99, paragraph (8) of the Act (including the cases where applied mutatis mutandis pursuant to Article 199 of the Act (including the cases where applied mutatis mutandis pursuant to Article 240, paragraph (1) of the Act); the same shall apply hereinafter) shall be twenty five million yen.

(Terms and Conditions of a Contract That Replaces a Business Deposit)

Article 13-3 Where a Life Insurance Company, etc. Engaged in Insurance-Proceed Trust Services (the term "Insurance-Proceed Trust Services" shall mean the Insurance-Proceed Trust Services as set forth in Article 99, paragraph (3) of the Act, and the same shall apply hereinafter; and the term "Life Insurance Company, etc. Engaged in Insurance-Proceed Trust Services" means a Life Insurance Company or a Foreign Life Insurance Company, etc. (including an Underwriting Member of a party that has obtained a specified life insurance business license as set forth in Article 219, paragraph (4) of the Act and that is deemed to be a Foreign Life Insurance Company, etc. pursuant to the provisions of Article 240, paragraph (1), item (i) of the Act) that engages in Insurance-Proceed Trust Services; the same shall apply hereinafter) concludes a contract as set forth in Article 11, paragraph (3) of the Trust Business Act as applied mutatis mutandis pursuant to Article 99, paragraph (8) of the Act, it shall have a Bank or other type of financial institution specified by Cabinet Office Or-

dinance as the other party thereto, and the terms and conditions thereunder shall satisfy the following requirements:
(i) that, when an order of the Prime Minister under Article 11, paragraph (4) of the Trust Business Act as applied mutatis mutandis pursuant to Article 99, paragraph (8) of the Act has been issued, the business deposit in the amount so ordered will be deposited without delay on behalf of the Life Insurance Company, etc. Engaged in Insurance-Proceed Trust Services;
(ii) that the contract is effective for a period of one year or longer; and
(iii) that the contract may not be cancelled and that the terms thereof may not be amended, unless this is done with the approval from the Commissioner of the Financial Services Agency.

(Procedures for the Fulfillment of Rights in Connection with Business Deposits)
Article 13-4 (1) A person who holds rights pursuant to Article 11, paragraph (6) of the Trust Business Act as applied mutatis mutandis pursuant to Article 99, paragraph (8) of the Act (hereinafter simply referred to as "Rights" in this Article) may file a petition for the fulfillment of those Rights with the Commissioner of the Financial Services Agency.
(2) Where a petition set forth in the preceding paragraph has been filed and where the Commissioner of the Financial Services Agency finds the petition to have reasonable grounds, he/she shall issue a public notice notifying persons who have a Right to the business deposit that they must report their Rights within a fixed period of time not shorter than sixty days and that they will be excluded from the distribution process if they fail to report their Rights within that period, and he/she shall also notify the person who filed the petition under the preceding paragraph (hereinafter referred to as the "Petitioner" in this Article) and the depositor (where the depositor has deposited the full amount of the business deposit under Article 11, paragraph (1) of the Trust Business Act as applied mutatis mutandis pursuant to Article 99, paragraph (8) of the Act on behalf of a Life Insurance Company, etc. Engaged in Insurance-Proceed Trust Services pursuant to the contract set forth in paragraph (3) of that Article and in response to the order issued under paragraph (4) of that Article, the depositor shall include said Life Insurance Company, etc. Engaged in Insurance-Proceed Trust Services; the same shall apply in paragraphs (4) and (5)) to that effect.
(3) Once the public notice under the preceding paragraph has been given, even in the event that the Petitioner withdraws his/her petition, this shall not prevent the procedures from proceeding.
(4) The Commissioner of the Financial Services Agency shall assess the Rights without delay after the period of time set forth in paragraph (2) has elapsed. In this case, the Commissioner of the Financial Services Agency shall give public notice of the date and place and notify the depositor of such information, in advance, and afford the Petitioner, any person who has reported his/her Rights within the designated period, and the depositor an opportunity to introduce evidence and to express their opinions as to the existence of the Rights and the amount of the claims secured by such Rights.
(5) The Commissioner of the Financial Services Agency shall, without delay, prepare a distribution list based on the results of the assessment under the preceding paragraph, shall put such list on public notice, and shall notify the depositor of such list.
(6) The distribution shall be implemented in accordance with the distribution list set forth in the preceding paragraph, after eighty days have elapsed since the day on which the public notice was given under the preceding paragraph.

(7) Where any securities (including book-entry transfer bonds as defined in Article 278, paragraph (1) of the Act on Transfer of Corporate Bonds, Shares, etc. (Act No. 75 of 2001); the same shall apply hereinafter) have been deposited, and where it is necessary for fulfillment of the Rights, the Commissioner of the Financial Services Agency may realize such securities. In this case, the expenses incurred in relation to the realization of such securities shall be deducted from the proceeds of the realization.

(Recovery of Business Deposits)
Article 13-5 (1) A Life Insurance Company, etc. Engaged in Insurance-Proceed Trust Services, the successor thereof, or the party that has deposited the business deposit on behalf of said Life Insurance Company, etc. Engaged in Insurance-Proceed Trust Services may, when it comes to fall under any of the cases set forth in the following, recover the full amount of the business deposit it has deposited, with the approval of the Commissioner of the Financial Services Agency:
  (i) when the Life Insurance Company, etc. Engaged in Insurance-Proceed Trust Services has relocated its Head Office, etc. (meaning its head office or principal office for an Insurance Company; meaning its principal branch in Japan as defined in Article 187, paragraph (1), item (iv) of the Act for a Foreign Insurance Company, etc.; and meaning its principal branch in Japan as defined in Article 220, paragraph (1), item (v) of the Act for a Licensed Specified Juridical Person and its Underwriting Members; the same shall apply in Article 47, paragraphs (1) to (3) inclusive), thereby resulting in a change to the official depository as set forth in Article 11, paragraph (1) of the Trust Business Act as applied mutatis mutandis pursuant to Article 99, paragraph (8) of the Act, and when the full amount of the business deposit is deposited with the new official depository;
  (ii) when any of the following sub-items applies, and when the transfer of the trust property to the new trustee or assignment of trust property to its right holder is completed:
    (a) when the license under Article 3, paragraph (1) of the Act has been rescinded pursuant to the provisions of Article 133 or 134 of the Act;
    (b) when the license under Article 185, paragraph (1) of the Act has been rescinded pursuant to the provisions of Article 205 or 206 of the Act;
    (c) when the license under Article 219, paragraph (1) of the Act has been rescinded pursuant to the provisions of Article 231 or 232 of the Act;
    (d) when the license under Article 219, paragraph (1) of the Act has ceased to be effective pursuant to the provisions of Article 236 of the Act; or
    (e) when the license under Article 3, paragraph (1) or Article 185, paragraph (1) of the Act has ceased to be effective pursuant to the provisions of Article 273 of the Act.
(2) Where a Life Insurance Company, etc. Engaged in Insurance-Proceed Trust Services has concluded a contract as set forth in Article 11, paragraph (3) of the Trust Business Act as applied mutatis mutandis pursuant to Article 99, paragraph (8) of the Act, or has effected any amendment to the terms and conditions thereunder, and has notified the Commissioner of the Financial Services Agency to that effect, in which case the amount of the business deposit (including the Contract Amount (meaning a Contract Amount as defined in that paragraph; hereinafter the same shall apply in this paragraph)) for said Life Insurance Company, etc. Engaged in Insurance-Proceed Trust Services exceeds the amount required to be deposited under that paragraph, the Life Insurance Company, etc. Engaged in Insurance-Proceed Trust Services or the party that has deposited the business deposit on behalf of said Life Insurance Company, etc. Engaged in Insurance-Proceed Trust Services may recover all or part

of the amount in excess thereof, only to the extent of the amount of the business deposit less the Contract Amount, with the approval of the Commissioner of the Financial Services Agency.

(Persons Closely Related to the Settlor and the Trustee)
Article 13-5-2 (1) The persons specified by Cabinet Order as being closely related to the settler under Article 23, paragraph (2) of the Trust Business Act as applied mutatis mutandis pursuant to Article 99, paragraph (8) of the Act, shall be as follows:
(i) any Officer (meaning a director, executive officer, accounting advisor, or member who performs the duties thereof, or company auditor or any other person in a position similar to any of the aforementioned persons; hereinafter the same shall apply in this Article and Article 13-7) or employee of the settlor;
(ii) any Subsidiary, etc. of the settlor;
(iii) the Parent Juridical Person, etc. that has the settlor as its Subsidiary, etc. ;
(iv) any Subsidiary, etc. of the Parent Juridical Person, etc. that has the relevant settlor as its Subsidiary, etc. (excluding the relevant settler itself, and also excluding juridical persons referred to in the preceding two items);
(v) any Affiliated Juridical Person, etc. of the settlor;
(vi) any Affiliated Juridical Person, etc. of the Parent Juridical Person, etc. that has the relevant settlor as its Subsidiary, etc. (excluding the juridical person set forth in the preceding item);
(vii) any Specified Individual Shareholder, etc. of the relevant settlor; and
(viii) the following company, partnership, or any other business entity equivalent thereto (including the equivalent entities in foreign states, but excluding the settlor; hereinafter referred to as the "Juridical Person, etc." in this item) that is associated with the person set forth in the preceding item.
  (a) a Juridical Person, etc. (including the Subsidiary, etc. and the Affiliated Juridical Person, etc. of such Juridical Person, etc.) in which the person referred to in the preceding item holds voting rights (meaning voting rights as set forth in Article 2, paragraph (11) of the Act; the same shall apply hereinafter) that are greater than fifty percent of All Shareholders' Voting Rights, etc. ; and
  (b) a Juridical Person, etc. in which the person referred to in the preceding item holds voting rights that are at least twenty percent and up to fifty percent of All Shareholders' Voting Rights, etc.
(2) The persons specified by Cabinet Order as being closely related to the trustee set forth in Article 23, paragraph (2) of the Trust Business Act as applied mutatis mutandis pursuant to Article 99, paragraph (8) of the Act shall be as follows:
(i) any Officer or employee of the trustee;
(ii) any Subsidiary, etc. of the trustee;
(iii) the Parent Juridical Person, etc. that holds the trustee as its Subsidiary, etc. ;
(iv) any Subsidiary, etc. of the Parent Juridical Person, etc. that holds such trustee as its Subsidiary, etc. (excluding said trustee, and also excluding the juridical persons set forth in the preceding two items);
(v) any Affiliated Juridical Person, etc. of such trustee;
(vi) any Affiliated Juridical Persons, etc. of the Parent Juridical Person, etc. that holds the trustee as its Subsidiary, etc. (excluding the juridical person set forth in the preceding item);
(vii) any Specified Individual Shareholder, etc. of the trustee; and
(viii) the following company, partnership, or other business entity equivalent thereto (including equivalent entities in foreign states, but excluding the trustee itself; hereinafter referred to as the "Juridical Persons, etc." in this item) that is associ-

ated with the person set forth in the preceding item;
  (a) a Juridical Person, etc. in which the person referred to in the preceding item holds voting rights (meaning voting rights as set forth in Article 2, paragraph (11) of the Act; the same shall apply hereinafter) that are greater than fifty percent of All Shareholders' Voting Rights , etc. ; and
  (b) a Juridical Person, etc. in which the person referred to in the preceding item holds voting rights that are at least twenty percent and up to fifty percent of All Shareholders' Voting Rights, etc.
(3) The term "Parent Juridical Person, etc." as set forth in the preceding two paragraphs means a Juridical Person, etc. (meaning a company, partnership, or any other type of entity similar thereto (including an equivalent entity in a foreign state); hereinafter the same shall apply in this paragraph and the following paragraph) that is specified by Cabinet Office Ordinance as the Juridical Person that controls the mechanism that is responsible for decisions on the financial policies and business or operational policies (meaning shareholders' meetings or any other mechanism equivalent thereto; hereinafter referred to as a "Decision-Making Mechanism" in this paragraph) of any other Juridical Person, etc. ; and the term "Subsidiary, etc." as set forth in the preceding two paragraphs shall mean a Juridical Person, etc. whose Decision-Making Mechanism is controlled by its Parent Juridical Person, etc. In this case, where the a Parent Juridical Person and its Subsidiary, etc. jointly control, or where the Subsidiary, etc. solely controls, any other Juridical Person's Decision-Making Mechanism, such other Juridical Person, etc. shall be deemed to be said Parent Juridical Person's Subsidiary, etc.
(4) The term "Affiliated Juridical Person, etc." as set forth in paragraphs (1) and (2) means a Juridical Person, etc. (including a Subsidiary, etc. (meaning a Subsidiary, etc. as set forth in the preceding paragraph; the same shall apply hereinafter)) that is specified by Cabinet Office Ordinance as a Juridical Person, etc. that may have a material impact on the decision-making of any other Juridical Person, etc. (excluding its Subsidiary, etc.) in terms of financial affairs, operational policies, or business policy, by such means as equity contributions, assumption of the office of director or any other position similar thereto by the present or former officer or employee of the first-mentioned Juridical Person, etc. , financing, guarantees of obligations, the provision of security, the transfer of technology, operational transactions or business transactions, and others.
(5) The term "Specified Individual Shareholder, etc." as set forth in paragraphs (1) and (2) means an individual person who holds Subject Voting Rights (meaning Subject Voting Rights as defined in Article 5, paragraph (5) of the Trust Business Act) in the relevant juridical person greater than fifty percent of All Shareholders' Voting Rights, etc.
(6) Where item (viii) of paragraph (1) or item (viii) of paragraph (2) applies, the voting rights held by a person specified in item (vii) of paragraph (1) or item (vii) of paragraph (2) shall include the voting rights represented by the share or contribution that cannot be asserted against the issuer pursuant to the provisions of Article 147, paragraph (1) or Article 148, paragraph (1) of the Act on Transfer of Corporate Bonds, Shares, etc. (including the cases where applied mutatis mutandis pursuant to Article 228, paragraph (1), Article 235, paragraph (1), Article 239, paragraph (1) and Article 276 (limited to the portion involving item (ii)) of that Act).

(Provision of Information by Use of Information and Communications Technology)
Article 13-5-3 (1) When a Life Insurance Company, etc. Engaged in Insurance-Proceed

Trust Services seeks to provide information set forth in Article 34-2, paragraph (4) of the Financial Instruments and Exchange Act (Act No. 25 of 1948) as applied mutatis mutandis pursuant to Article 24-2 of the Trust Business Act as further applied mutatis mutandis pursuant to Article 99, paragraph (8) of the Act (hereinafter referred to as the "Financial Instruments and Exchange Act as Applied Mutatis Mutandis" in this Article to Article 13-5-5 inclusive), pursuant to the provisions of Article 34-2, paragraph (4) of the Financial Instruments and Exchange Act as applied Mutatis Mutandis (including the cases where applied mutatis mutandis pursuant to Article 34-4, paragraph (3) and Article 37-3, paragraph (2) of the Financial Instruments and Exchange Act as Applied Mutatis Mutandis; hereinafter the same shall apply in this Article), it shall, in advance and pursuant to the provisions of Cabinet Office Ordinance, indicate to the recipient of such information the type and details of the means set forth in Article 34-2, paragraph (4) of the Financial Instruments and Exchange Act as Applied Mutatis Mutandis that it will use (hereinafter referred to as the "Electromagnetic Means" in this Article) and shall obtain consent therefrom in writing or by Electromagnetic Means.

(2) Where a Life Insurance Company, etc. Engaged in Insurance-Proceed Trust Services that has obtained the consent set forth in the preceding paragraph is notified in writing or by Electromagnetic Means to the effect that a recipient refuses to be provided with the information by Electromagnetic Means, it shall not provide the recipient with the information set forth in Article 34-2, paragraph (4) of the Financial Instruments and Exchange Act as Applied Mutatis Mutandis by Electromagnetic Means; provided, however, that this shall not apply where the recipient gives his/her consent under that paragraph again.

(Acquisition of Consent by Use of Information and Communications Technology)

Article 13-5-4 (1) Where, pursuant to the provisions of Article 34-3, paragraph (3) of the Financial Instruments and Exchange Act as Applied Mutatis Mutandis (including the cases where applied mutatis mutandis pursuant to Article 34-4, paragraph (4) of the Financial Instruments and Exchange Act as Applied Mutatis Mutandis; hereinafter the same shall apply in this Article), a Life Insurance Company, etc. Engaged in Insurance-Proceed Trust Services, seeks to obtain another party's agreement by the method specified by Cabinet Office Ordinance that is referred to in Article 34-3, paragraph (3) of the Financial Instruments and Exchange Act as Applied Mutatis Mutandis (hereinafter referred to as "Electromagnetic Means" in this Article) in lieu of the written agreement set forth in paragraph (2) of that Article, it shall, in advance and pursuant to the provisions of Cabinet Office Ordinance, indicate the type and details of the Electromagnetic Means to the other party from whom it seeks to obtain agreement, and shall obtain the consent thereof in writing or by Electromagnetic Means.

(2) Where a Life Insurance Company, etc. Engaged in Insurance-Proceed Trust Services that has obtained the consent set forth in the preceding paragraph is notified in writing or by Electromagnetic Means to the effect that the other party refuses to give his/her agreement by Electromagnetic Means, it shall not obtain the agreement set forth in Article 34-3, paragraph (3) of the Financial Instruments and Exchange Act as Applied Mutatis Mutandis from the other party by Electromagnetic Means; provided, however, that this shall not apply where the other party has given his/her consent under the preceding paragraph again.

(Important Particulars That May Influence a Customer's Judgment)

Article 13-5-5 (1) The particulars specified by Cabinet Order, referred to in Article 37,

paragraph (1), item (iii) of the Financial Instruments and Exchange Act as Applied Mutatis Mutandis shall be as follows;
(i) those related to the fees, remuneration, or any other type of consideration payable by a customer under a Specific Trust Agreement (meaning a Specific Trust Agreement as defined in Article 24-2 of the Trust Business Act as applied mutatis mutandis pursuant to Article 99, paragraph (8) of the Act; hereinafter the same shall apply in this Article), as specified by Cabinet Office Ordinance;
(ii) where, with regard to the conclusion of a Specific Trust Agreement by a customer, there is a risk of losses arising directly from a fluctuation in such indicators as the interest rate, the value of currencies, or quotations on a Financial Instruments Market (meaning a Financial Instruments Market as defined in Article 2, paragraph (14) of the Financial Instruments and Exchange Act; the same shall apply hereinafter), the following particulars:
 (a) the indicators; and
 (b) the fact that there is a risk of losses from fluctuations in the relevant indicators, and the reason therefor.
(iii) particulars specified by Cabinet Office Ordinance as those equivalent to the particulars specified in the preceding two items.
(2) Notwithstanding the provisions of the preceding paragraph, where the conduct specified in Article 37, paragraph (1) of the Financial Instruments and Exchange Act as Applied Mutatis Mutandis is to be implemented by means of broadcasting by the use of the broadcasting facilities of a Private Broadcaster (meaning a Private Broadcaster as prescribed in Article 2, item (iii)-3 of the Broadcast Act (Act No. 132 of 1950); the same shall apply in Article 44-5, paragraph (2)) or any other equivalent means specified by Cabinet Office Ordinance, the particulars specified by Cabinet Order that are referred to in Article 37, paragraph (1), item (iii) of the Financial Instruments and Exchange Act as Applied Mutatis Mutandis shall be as follows:
(i) where, with regard to the conclusion of a Specific Trust Agreement by a customer, there is a risk of losses arising directly from fluctuations in such indicators as the interest rate, the value of currencies, or quotations on a Financial Instruments Market, such fact:
(ii) particulars specified by Cabinet Office Ordinance as the particulars equivalent to those specified in the preceding item.

(Replacement of Terms in Provisions of the Financial Instruments and Exchange Act That Are Applied Mutatis Mutandis Pursuant to Provisions of the Trust Business Act, When Such Provisions are Applied Mutatis Mutandis to Where a Life Insurance Company, etc. Engages in Insurance-Proceed Trust Services)
Article 13-5-6 Where, pursuant to the provisions of Article 99, paragraph (8) of the Act, the provisions of Article 24-2 of the Trust Business Act are applied mutatis mutandis to where a Life Insurance Company, etc. engages in Insurance-Proceed Trust Services, the technical replacement of terms in connection with the provisions of the Financial Instruments and Exchange Act, which are applied mutandis pursuant to Article 24-2 of the Trust Business Act, shall be as set forth in the following table:

Provisions of the Financial Instruments and Exchange Act whose terms are to be replaced	Original terms	Terms to replace the original terms

| Article 34 | item (iv), paragraph (1) of that Article | Article 2, paragraph (31), item (iv) |
| Article 40, item (ii) | what is listed in the preceding item | the situation found to be in violation of the provisions of Article 24, paragraph (2) of the Trust Business Act as applied mutatis mutandis pursuant to Article 99, paragraph (8) of the Insurance Business Act |

(Methods That Use Information and Communications Technology)

Article 13-6 (1) Where, pursuant to the provisions of Article 26, paragraph (2) of the Trust Business Act as applied mutatis mutandis pursuant to Article 99, paragraph (8) of the Act, a Life Insurance Company, etc. Engaged in Insurance-Proceed Trust Services seeks to provide the information set forth in that paragraph, it shall, in advance and pursuant to the provisions of Cabinet Office Ordinance, indicate to the settlor the type and details of the electromagnetic means set forth in that paragraph that it will use (hereinafter referred to as the "Electromagnetic Means" in this Article) and shall obtain consent therefrom in writing or by Electromagnetic Means.

(2) Where a Life Insurance Company, etc. Engaged in Insurance-Proceed Trust Services that has obtained the consent set forth in the preceding paragraph is notified in writing or by Electromagnetic Means to the effect that the settler refuses to receive the information by Electromagnetic Means, it shall not provide the settlor with the information set forth in Article 26, paragraph (2) of the Trust Business Act as applied mutatis mutandis pursuant to Article 99, paragraph (8) of the Act by Electromagnetic Means; provided, however, that this shall not apply where the settlor has given his/her consent under the preceding paragraph again.

(3) The provisions of the preceding two paragraphs shall apply mutatis mutandis to where the provisions of Article 26, paragraph (2) of the Trust Business Act are applied mutatis mutandis pursuant to Article 27, paragraph (2) and Article 29, paragraph (4) of that Act, as further applied mutatis mutandis to Article 99, paragraph (8) of the Act. In such case, the term the "settlor" in these provisions shall be deemed to be replaced with "beneficiary of the trust property."

(Persons Closely Related to a Life Insurance Company, etc. Engaged in Insurance-Proceed Trust Services)

Article 13-7 (1) The persons specified by Cabinet Order, referred to in Article 29, paragraph (2) of the Trust Business Act as applied mutatis mutandis pursuant to Article 99, paragraph (8) of the Act, shall be as follows:

(i) any officer or employee of the Life Insurance Company, etc. Engaged in Insurance-Proceed Trust Services;

(ii) any Subsidiary, etc. of the Life Insurance Company, etc. Engaged in Insurance-Proceed Trust Services;

(iii) the Parent Juridical Person, etc. (meaning a Parent Juridical Person, etc. as defined in Article 13-5-2, paragraph (3); the same shall apply hereinafter) that has the Life Insurance Company, etc. Engaged in Insurance-Proceed Trust Services as its Subsidiary, etc. ;

(iv) any Subsidiary, etc. of the Parent Juridical Person, etc. that has said Life Insurance Company, etc. Engaged in Insurance-Proceed Trust Services as its Subsidiary, etc. (excluding said Life Insurance Company, etc. Engaged in Insurance-Pro-

ceed Trust Services and the juridical persons set forth in the preceding two items);
(v) any Affiliated Juridical Person, etc. (meaning an Affiliated Juridical Person, etc. as defined in Article 13-5-2, paragraph (4); the same shall apply hereinafter) of the Life Insurance Company, etc. Engaged in Insurance-Proceed Trust Services;
(vi) any Affiliated Juridical Person, etc. of the Parent Juridical Person, etc. that has said Life Insurance Company, etc. Engaged in Insurance-Proceed Trust Services as its Subsidiary, etc. (excluding the juridical person set forth in the preceding item);
(vii) a Specified Individual Shareholder, etc. (meaning a Specified Individual Shareholder, etc. as defined in Article 13-5-2, paragraph (5); the same shall apply hereinafter) of the Life Insurance Company, etc. Engaged in Insurance-Proceed Trust Services; and
(viii) the following company, partnership, or other business entity equivalent thereto (including equivalent entities in foreign states, but excluding the Life Insurance Company, etc. Engaged in Insurance-Proceed Trust Services, itself; hereinafter referred to as the "Juridical Person, etc." in this item) that is associated with the person set forth in the preceding item.
  (a) a Juridical Person, etc. in which the person referred to in the preceding item holds voting rights that are greater than fifty percent of All Shareholders' Voting Rights, etc. ; and
  (b) a Juridical Person, etc. in which the person referred to in the preceding item holds voting rights that are at least twenty percent and up to fifty percent of All Shareholders' Voting Rights, etc.
(2) Where a Life Insurance Company, etc. Engaged in Insurance-Proceed Trust Services has entrusted its Insurance-Proceed Trust Services to another party pursuant to the provisions of Article 22, paragraph (1) of the Trust Business Act as applied mutatis mutandis pursuant to Article 99, paragraph (8) of the Act, for the purpose of the application of the provisions of the preceding paragraph to the person who has been entrusted with those Insurance-Proceed Trust Services, the term "Life Insurance Company, etc. Engaged in Insurance-Proceed Trust Services" in that paragraph shall be deemed to be replaced with "person entrusted with Insurance-Proceed Trust Services by the Life Insurance Company, etc. Engaged in Insurance-Proceed Trust Services."
(3) The provisions of Article 13-5-2, paragraph (6) shall apply mutatis mutandis to the voting rights held by the person set forth in item (vii) of paragraph (1), where item (viii) of that paragraph applies.

(Scope of Parent Financial Institutions, etc. and Subsidiary Financial Institutions, etc.)
Article 13-8 (1) The parties specified by Cabinet Order, referred to in Article 100-2-2, paragraph (2) of the Act, shall be as follows:
(i) the Parent Juridical Person, etc. of the Insurance Company;
(ii) any Subsidiary, etc. of the Parent Juridical Person, etc. of the Insurance Company (excluding the Insurance Company itself and juridical persons as set forth in the preceding item and in item (i) of paragraph (3));
(iii) any Affiliated Juridical Person, etc. of the Parent Juridical Person, etc. of such Insurance Company (excluding a juridical person set forth in item (ii) of paragraph (3));
(iv) the following company, partnership, or other business entity equivalent thereto (including equivalent entities in foreign states, and excluding the Insurance Com-

pany itself and juridical persons specified in the preceding three items and in the items of paragraph (3); hereinafter referred to as a "Juridical Person, etc." in this item) that is associated with an individual person who holds voting rights that are greater than fifty percent of All Shareholders' Voting Rights, etc. in the relevant Insurance Company (hereinafter referred to as a "Specified Individual Shareholder" in this item and Article 37-9, paragraph (1), item (iv));
  (a) a Juridical Person, etc. (including its Subsidiary, etc. and Affiliated Juridical Person, etc.) in which a Specified Individual Shareholder holds voting rights that are greater than fifty percent of All Shareholders' Voting Rights, etc. ; or
  (b) a Juridical Person, etc. in which a Specified Individual Shareholder holds voting rights that are at least twenty percent and up to fifty percent of All Shareholders' Voting Rights, etc.
(2) The other persons engaged in financial business specified by Cabinet Order, referred to in Article 100-2-2, paragraph (2) of the Act, shall be as follows:
  (i) Foreign Insurance Companies, etc. ;
  (ii) Low-Cost, Short-Term Insurers;
  (iii) Long Term Credit Banks (meaning Long Term Credit Banks as defined in Article 2 (Definitions) of the Long Term Credit Bank Act (Act No. 187 of 1952); the same shall apply in Article 39, item (ii));
  (iv) Shoko Chukin Bank Limited;
  (v) federations of shinkin banks;
  (vi) federations of labor banks;
  (vii) federations of cooperatives engaged in the business prescribed in Article 9-9, paragraph (1), item (i) (Federation of Cooperatives) of the Small and Medium-Sized Enterprise Cooperatives Act (Act No. 181 of 1949);
  (viii) federations of agricultural cooperatives engaged in the business prescribed in Article 10, paragraph (1), item (x) (Business) of the Agricultural Cooperatives Act (Act No. 132 of 1947);
  (ix) mutual aid federations of fishery cooperatives;
  (x) parties that grant monetary loans or that intermediate therefor in the course of trade (including granting of monies by means of discounted bills, assignments for security or any other means similar thereto, and also including intermediation for the receipt of monies by any of the aforementioned means) (such party shall exclude an Insurance Company, a Bank, a Financial Instruments Transaction Business Operator (meaning a Financial Instruments Transaction Business Operator as defined in Article 2, paragraph (9) (Definitions) of the Financial Instruments and Exchange Act; the same shall apply in the following item); and shall also exclude parties specified in the preceding items);
  (xi) persons engaged in any of the following business in a foreign state, in accordance with the laws and regulations of that State (excluding an Insurance Company, Bank, Financial Instruments Transaction Business Operator and parties specified in the preceding items):
    (a) insurance business;
    (b) Banking Business as defined in Article 2, paragraph (2) (Definitions) of the Banking Act; or
    (c) Financial Instruments Business as defined in Article 2, paragraph (8) of the Financial Instruments and Exchange Act.
(3) The person specified by Cabinet Order, referred to in Article 100-2-2, paragraph (3) of the Act, shall be as follows:
  (i) any Subsidiary, etc. of the relevant Insurance Company; and
  (ii) any Affiliated Juridical Person, etc. of the relevant Insurance Company.

(4) The person conducting financial business which is specified by Cabinet Order, referred to in Article 100-2-2, paragraph (3) of the Act, shall be the persons specified in items (i) to (iii) inclusive and items (x) and (xi) of paragraph (2).

(Specified Related Parties of an Insurance Company)

Article 14 The parties to which an Insurance Company is specially related as specified by Cabinet Order, referred to in the main clause of Article 100-3 of the Act, shall be as follows:
(i) any Subsidiary Company of such Insurance Company;
(ii) the Insurance Company's Major Shareholder who holds a number of voting rights in such Insurance Company equal to or exceeding the Major Shareholder Threshold;
(iii) any Insurance Holding Company whose Subsidiaries include the relevant Insurance Company;
(iv) any Subsidiary Company of the juridical person specified in the preceding item (excluding the relevant Insurance Company and the juridical person specified in item (i));
(v) any Subsidiary, etc. of such Insurance Company (excluding a person set forth in item (i));
(vi) the Parent Juridical Person, etc. whose Subsidiaries, etc. include the relevant Insurance Company (excluding juridical persons set forth in items (ii) and (iii));
(vii) any Subsidiary, etc. of the Parent Juridical Person, etc. whose Subsidiaries, etc. include the relevant Insurance Company, etc. (excluding the relevant Insurance Company itself and the juridical persons set forth in the preceding items);
(viii) any Affiliated Juridical Person, etc. of such Insurance Company;
(ix) any Affiliated Juridical Person, etc. of the Parent Juridical Person, etc. whose Subsidiaries, etc. include the relevant Insurance Company (excluding the juridical person set forth in the preceding item);
(x) the following company, partnership, or other type of business entity equivalent thereto (including an equivalent entity in a foreign state, and excluding the Insurance Company itself; hereinafter referred to as a "Juridical Person, etc." in this item) that is associated with a person who, from among the Insurance Company's Major Shareholders who hold a number of voting rights in said Insurance Company equal to or exceeding the Major Shareholders Threshold, holds voting rights in said Insurance Company that are greater than fifty percent of All Shareholders' Voting Rights in said Insurance Company (limited to an individual person; hereinafter referred to as the "Insurance Company's Specified Individual Major Shareholder" in this item):
 (a) a Juridical Person, etc. (including its Subsidiary, etc. and Affiliated Juridical Person, etc.) in which the Insurance Company's Specified Individual Major Shareholder holds voting rights that are greater than fifty percent of All Shareholders' Voting Rights, etc. ;
 (b) a Juridical Person, etc. in which the Insurance Company's Specified Individual Major Shareholder holds voting rights that are at least twenty percent and up to fifty percent of All Shareholders' Voting Rights, etc.

(Insurance Contracts Excluded from Portfolio Transfers)

Article 15 The insurance contracts specified by Cabinet Order, referred to in Article 135, paragraph (2) of the Act, shall be as follows:
(i) an insurance contract under which an insured event has already occurred as of the time of the public notice under Article 137, paragraph (1) of the Act (referred to as

the "Public Notice" in the following item) (limited to an insurance contract that expires upon the payment of the insurance proceeds in connection with an insured event); and

(ii) an insurance contract whose term of coverage has already ended by the time of the Public Notice (including an insurance contract that has been canceled in the middle of the term of coverage or one under which any other grounds for the termination thereof have occurred as of the time of the Public Notice, and excluding an insurance contract set forth in the preceding item).

(Replacement of Terms in Provisions of the Companies Act That Are Applied Mutatis Mutandis to Causes for the Dissolution of a Mutual Company)

Article 15-2 Where, pursuant to the provisions of Article 152, paragraph (2) of the Act, the provisions of paragraph (1) of that Article are applied mutatis mutandis to a Mutual Company, the technical replacement of terms in connection with the provisions of Article 471, item (vi) of the Companies Act as applied by replacing certain terms pursuant to Article 152, paragraph (1) of the Act, shall be as set forth in the following table:

Provisions of the Companies Act whose terms are to be replaced	Original terms	Terms to replace the original terms
Article 471, item (vi)	Article 824 (1) or Article 833 (1)	Article 824(1) as applied mutatis mutandis pursuant to Article 63-2 of the Insurance Business Act

(Insurance Contracts That Are Not Grounds for Refusing Authorization for a Dissolution, etc.)

Article 16 The insurance contracts specified by Cabinet Order, referred to in Article 153, paragraph (3) shall be as follows:

(i) an insurance contract in which the Policyholder is a member; and

(ii) an insurance contract as specified in the following sub-items, excluding the insurance contract referred to in the preceding item:

  (a) an insurance contract under which an insured event has already occurred as of the date of the application for authorization under Article 153, paragraph (1) of the Act (referred to as an "Application" in sub-item (b)), (limited to a contract to be expired upon the payment of insurance proceeds in connection with an insured event); and

  (b) an insurance contract whose term of coverage has already ended as of the Application date (including an insurance contract that has been canceled in the middle of the term of coverage or one under which any other grounds for the termination thereof have occurred as of the Application date, and excluding an insurance contract set forth in sub-item (a)).

(Replacement of Terms in Provisions of the Companies Act, etc. That Are Applied Mutatis Mutandis to a Mutual Company)

Article 16-2 (1) Where, pursuant to the provisions of Article 158 of the Act, the provisions of Article 926 of the Companies Act are applied mutatis mutandis to a Mutual Company, the technical replacement of terms in connection with the relevant provisions shall be as set forth in the following table:

[7] Order for Enforcement of the Insurance Business Act, Chap.II, Sec.1
Art.17〜17-2

Provisions of the Companies Act whose terms are to be replaced	Original terms	Terms to replace the original terms
Article 926	Article 471(i) to (iii) or Article 641(i) to (iv)	Article 471(iii) of this Act as applied mutatis mutandis pursuant to Article 152(2) of the Insurance Business Act
	head office	principal office

(2) Where, pursuant to the provisions of Article 158 of the Act, the provisions of Article 71, paragraph (3) of the Commercial Registration Act are applied mutatis mutandis to a Mutual Company, the technical replacement of terms in connection with the relevant provisions shall be as set forth in the following table:

Provisions of the Commercial Registration Act whose terms are to be replaced	Original terms	Terms to replace the original terms
Article 71, paragraph (3)	liquidating stock company	liquidating Mutual Company
	Article 483, paragraph (4) of said Act	Article 180-9, paragraph (4) of said Act

(Replacement of Terms in Provisions of the Insurance Business Act That Are Applied Mutatis Mutandis to Absorption-Type Mergers between Stock Companies and Mutual Companies Where the Stock Company Survives)

Article 17 Where, pursuant to the provisions of Article 164, paragraph (3) of the Act, the provisions of Article 90, paragraph (3) of the Act are applied mutatis mutandis to an absorption-type merger under Article 164, paragraph (1) of the Act, the technical replacement of terms in connection with the relevant provisions shall be as set forth in the following table:

Provisions of the Insurance Business Act whose terms are to be replaced	Original terms	Terms to replace the original terms
Article 90, paragraph (3)	converting Mutual Company	Absorbed Mutual Company

(Replacement of Terms in Provisions of the Insurance Business Act That Are Applied Mutatis Mutandis to Consolidation-Type Mergers between Stock Companies and Mutual Companies Where the Stock Company Is Incorporated)

Article 17-2 (1) Where, pursuant to the provisions of Article 165, paragraph (5) of the Act, the provisions of Article 90, paragraph (3) of the Act are applied mutatis mutandis to a consolidation-type merger under Article 165, paragraph (1) of the Act, the technical replacement of terms in connection with the relevant provisions shall be as set forth in the following table:

Provisions of the Insurance Business Act whose terms are to be replaced	Original terms	Terms to replace the original terms
Article 90, paragraph (3)	converting Mutual Company	Consolidated Mutual Company

(2) Where, pursuant to the provisions of Article 165, paragraph (5) of the Act, the provisions of Article 162, paragraph (3) of the Act are applied mutatis mutandis to a Consolidated Mutual Company, the technical replacement of terms in connection with the relevant provisions shall be as set forth in the following table:

Provisions of the Insurance Business Act whose terms are to be replaced	Original terms	Terms to replace the original terms
Article 162, paragraph (3)	absorption-type merger	consolidation-type merger

(Replacement of Terms in Provisions of the Companies Act That Are Applied Mutatis Mutandis to Share Purchase Demand Against an Extinct Stock Company)

Article 17-3 Where, pursuant to the provisions of Article 165-5, paragraph (2) of the Act, the provisions of Article 785, paragraphs (5) and (7) and Article 786, paragraph (1) of the Companies Act are applied mutatis mutandis to the request under Article 165-5, paragraph (1) of the Act, the technical replacement of terms in connection with these provisions shall be as set forth in the following table:

Provisions of the Companies Act whose terms are to be replaced	Original terms	Terms to replace the original terms
Article 785, paragraph (5)	prior to the Effective Day	prior to the Effective Date (meaning the Effective Date as defined in Article 165-2(1) of the Insurance Business Act)
Article 785, paragraph (7)	the Absorption-type Merger, etc.	the Absorption-type Merger, etc. or Consolidation-type Merger
Article 786, paragraph (1)	the Company Surviving Absorption-type Merger;	the Absorbing Mutual Company; or, where a Consolidation-type Merger is to be effected, the Formed Company, after the day of its formation;

(Replacement of Terms in Provisions of the Companies Act That Are Applied Mutatis Mutandis to a Share Option Purchase Demand Against an Extinct Stock Company)

Article 17-4 Where, pursuant to the provisions of Article 165-6, paragraph (2) of the Act, the provisions of Article 787, paragraphs (5) and (7) and Article 788, paragraphs (1) and (5) of the Companies Act are applied mutatis mutandis to a request under Article 165-6, paragraph (1) of the Act, the technical replacement of terms in connection with these provisions shall be as set forth in the following table:

Provisions of the Companies Act whose terms are to be replaced	Original terms	Terms to replace the original terms
Article 787, paragraph (5)	the Effective Day	the Effective Date (meaning the Effective Date as defined in Article 165-2(1) of the Insurance Business Act)
Article 787, paragraph (7)	the Absorption-type Merger, etc.	the Absorption-type Merger or the Consolidation-type Merger
Article 788, paragraph (1)	the Company Surviving Absorption-type Merger;	the Absorbing Mutual Company; or, where a Consolidation-type Merger is to be effected, the Formed Company, after the day of its formation;
Article 788, paragraph (5)	at the times provided for in the following items for the categories of Share Options set forth respectively in those items	on the Effective Date

(Replacement of Terms in Provisions of the Insurance Business Act That Are Applied Mutatis Mutandis to an Objection of the Creditors of an Extinct Stock Company)

Article 17-5 Where, pursuant to the provisions of Article 165-7, paragraph (4) of the Act, the provisions of Article 70, paragraph (4) and paragraphs (6) to (8) inclusive of the Act are applied mutatis mutandis to an objection of the creditors as set forth in Article 165-7, paragraph (1) of the Act, the technical replacement of terms in connection with these provisions shall be as set forth in the following table:

Provisions of the Insurance Business Act whose terms are to be replaced	Original terms	Terms to replace the original terms
Article 70, paragraph (4)	the Entity Conversion	consolidation-type merger or absorption-type merger of the relevant extinct stock company
Article 70, paragraph (6)	Article 69, paragraph (1)	Article 165-3, paragraph (1)
paragraphs (7) and (8) of Article 70	the preceding paragraphs	paragraph (4) to (6) inclusive and Article 165-7, paragraphs (1) to (3) inclusive

(Scope of Insurance Claims, etc.)

Article 17-6 Insurance Claims, etc. under Article 70, paragraphs (5) to (7) inclusive of the Act as applied mutatis mutandis pursuant to Article 165-7, paragraph (4) of the Act shall be limited to the claims that have already arisen as of the time of the public notice given pursuant to Article 165-7, paragraph (2) of the Act.

(Replacement of Terms in Provisions of the Insurance Business Act, etc.

That Are Applied Mutatis Mutandis to an Absorbing Stock Company)

Article 17-7 (1) Where, pursuant to the provisions of Article 165-12 of the Act, the provisions of Article 165-4, paragraph (1), Article 165-5, paragraph (2) and Article 165-7, paragraph (2) of the Act are applied mutatis mutandis to an Absorbing Stock Company, the technical replacement of terms in connection with these provisions shall be as set forth in the following table:

Provisions of the Insurance Business Act whose terms are to be replaced	Original terms	Terms to replace the original terms
Article 165-4, paragraph (1)	its shareholders and the registered pledgees of its shares, and the holders of its share options and the registered pledgees of its share options	its shareholders
	and of the trade name or name and address of the Absorbing Mutual Company, or the Stock Company carrying on the Insurance Business or Mutual Company to be incorporated by the merger (hereinafter referred to as "Formed Company" in this Section)	and of the name and address of the Absorbed Mutual Company
Article 165-4, paragraph (2)	Article 785, paragraph (5)	Article 797, paragraph (5)
	Article 786	Article 798
	the preceding paragraph	Article 797, paragraph (1)
Article 165-7, paragraph (2), item (ii)	The trade names or names and addresses of the Absorbing Mutual Company or other consolidated companies (referring to consolidated stock companies and Consolidated Mutual Companies; the same shall apply in Article 165-17, paragraph (2)) and the Formed Company;	The name and address of the Absorbed Mutual Company

(2) Where, pursuant to the provisions of Article 165-12 of the Act, the provisions of Article 165-5, paragraph (2) of the Act are applied mutatis mutandis to an Absorbing Stock Company, the technical replacement of terms in connection with the provisions of Article 797, paragraphs (5) and (7) of the Companies Act as applied mutatis mutandis pursuant to Article 165-5, paragraph (2) of the Act, shall be as set forth in the following table:

Provisions of the Companies Act whose terms are to be replaced	Original terms	Terms to replace the original terms
Article 797, paragraph (5)	the Effective Day	the Effective Date (meaning the Effective Date as defined in Article 165-

		2, paragraph (1) of the Insurance Business Act; the same shall apply hereinafter)
Article 797, paragraph (7)	the Absorption-type Merger, etc.	the Absorption-type Merger

(3) Where, pursuant to the provisions of Article 165-12 of the Act, the provisions of Article 165-7, paragraph (4) of the Act are applied mutatis mutandis to an Absorbing Stock Company, the technical replacement of terms in connection with the provisions of Article 70, paragraph (4) and paragraphs (6) to (8) inclusive of the Act as applied mutatis mutandis pursuant to Article 165-7, paragraph (4) of the Act shall be as set forth in the following table:

Provisions of the Insurance Business Act whose terms are to be replaced	Original terms	Terms to replace the original terms
Article 70, paragraph (4)	the Entity Conversion	the Absorption-type Merger of the relevant Absorbing Stock Company
Article 70, paragraph (6)	Article 69, paragraph (1)	Article 165-10, paragraph (1)
Article 70, paragraph (7)	pursuant to the provisions of the preceding paragraphs	pursuant to the provisions of the preceding three paragraphs, and Article 165-7, paragraphs (1) to (3) inclusive
	An Entity Conversion	An Absorption-type Merger
Article 70, paragraph (8)	in the preceding paragraphs	in paragraphs (4) to (7) inclusive and Article 165-7, paragraphs (1) to (3) inclusive

(4) Where, pursuant to the provisions of Article 165-12 of the Act, the provisions of Article 797, paragraphs (1) and (2) of the Companies Act are applied mutatis mutandis to an Absorbing Stock Company, the technical replacement of terms in connection with these provisions shall be as set forth in the following table:

Provisions of the Companies Act whose terms are to be replaced	Original terms	Terms to replace the original terms
Article 797, paragraphs (1) and (2)	the Absorption-type Merger, etc.	the Absorption-type Merger

(Scope of Insurance Claims, etc.)
Article 17-8 Insurance Claims, etc. under Article 70, paragraphs (5) to (7) inclusive of the Act as applied mutatis mutandis pursuant to Article 165-7, paragraph (4) of the Act as further applied mutatis mutandis pursuant to Article 165-12 of the Act, shall be limited to the claims that have already arisen as of the time of the public notice given pursuant to Article 165-7, paragraph (2) of the Act as applied mutatis mutandis pursuant to Article 165-12 of the Act.

(Replacement of Terms in Provisions of the Insurance Business Act That Are Applied Mutatis Mutandis to a Stock Company Established by Consolidation-Type Merger)

Article 17-9 Where, pursuant to the provisions of Article 165-14, paragraph (3) of the Act, the provisions of Article 165-13, paragraph (1) of the Act are applied mutatis mutandis to a Stock Company Established by Consolidation-Type Merger, the technical replacement of terms in connection with the relevant provisions shall be as set forth in the following table:

Provisions of the Insurance Business Act whose terms are to be replaced	Original terms	Terms to replace the original terms
Article 165-13, paragraph (1)	as a result of the absorption-type merger	as a result of the consolidation-type merger
	the Absorbed Mutual Company	the Consolidated Mutual Company or the Consolidated Stock Company
	as pertaining to an absorption-type merger	as pertaining to a consolidation-type merger

(Replacement of Terms in Provisions of the Insurance Business Act That Are Applied Mutatis Mutandis to Objections of the Creditors of an Extinct Mutual Company)

Article 17-10 Where, pursuant to the provisions of Article 165-17, paragraph (4) of the Act, the provisions of Article 88, paragraphs (4), (6), (7) and (9) are applied mutatis mutandis to an objection of the creditors as set forth in Article 165-17, paragraph (1) of the Act, the technical replacement of terms in connection with these provisions shall be as set forth in the following table:

Provisions of the Insurance Business Act whose terms are to be replaced	Original terms	Terms to replace the original terms
Article 88, paragraph (4)	the Entity Conversion	the Absorption-type Merger or Consolidation-type Merger of the relevant Absorbed Mutual Company
Article 88, paragraph (6)	Article 86, paragraph (1)	Article 165-16, paragraph (1)
Article 88, paragraph (7)	the preceding paragraphs	the preceding three paragraphs, and Article 165-17, paragraphs (1) to (3) inclusive
Article 88, paragraph (9)	in the preceding paragraphs	in paragraphs (4) to (7) inclusive and Article 165-17, paragraphs (1) to (3) inclusive

(Scope of Insurance Claims, etc.)

Article 17-11 Insurance Claims, etc. under Article 88, paragraphs (5) to (7) inclusive of the Act as applied mutatis mutandis pursuant to Article 165-17, paragraph (4) of the Act shall be limited to the claims that have already arisen as of the time of the public notice given pursuant to Article 165-17, paragraph (2) of the Act.

(Replacement of Terms in Provisions of the Insurance Business Act That Are Applied Mutatis Mutandis to an Absorbing Mutual Company)
Article 17-12 (1) Where, pursuant to the provisions of Article 165-20 of the Act, the provisions of Article 165-17, paragraph (2) of the Act are applied mutatis mutandis to an Absorbing Mutual Company, the technical replacement of terms in connection with the relevant provisions shall be as set forth in the following table:

Provisions of the Insurance Business Act whose terms are to be replaced	Original terms	Terms to replace the original terms
Article 165-17, paragraph (2), item (ii)	the absorbing company (referring to the Absorbing Mutual Company or Absorbing Stock Company; hereinafter the same shall apply in this Section) or other consolidated companies and the Formed Company	the Absorbed Stock Company or the Absorbed Mutual Company

(2) Where, pursuant to the provisions of Article 165-20 of the Act, the provisions of Article 165-17, paragraph (4) of the Act are applied mutatis mutandis to an Absorbing Mutual Company, the technical replacement of terms in connection with the provisions of Article 88, paragraphs (4), (6), (7) and (9) of the Act as applied mutatis mutandis pursuant to Article 165-17, paragraph (4) of the Act, shall be as set forth in the following table:

Provisions of the Insurance Business Act whose terms are to be replaced	Original terms	Terms to replace the original terms
Article 88, paragraph (4)	the Entity Conversion	the absorption-type merger pertaining to such Absorbing Mutual Company
Article 88, paragraph (6)	Article 86, paragraph (1)	Article 165-16, paragraph (1)
Article 88, paragraph (7)	the preceding paragraphs	the preceding three paragraphs, and Article 165-17, paragraphs (1) to (3) inclusive
	the Entity Conversion	the Absorption-type Merger
Article 88, paragraph (9)	in the preceding paragraphs	in paragraphs (4) to (7) inclusive and Article 165-17, paragraphs (1) to (3) inclusive

(Scope of Insurance Claims, etc.)
Article 17-13 Insurance Claims, etc. under Article 88, paragraphs (5) to (7) inclusive of the Act as applied mutatis mutandis pursuant to Article 165-17, paragraph (4) of the Act as further applied mutatis mutandis pursuant to Article 165-20 of the Act, shall be limited to the claims that have already arisen as of the time of the public notice given pursuant to Article 165-17, paragraph (2) of the Act as applied mutatis mutandis pursuant to Article 165-20 of the Act.

(Replacement of Terms in Provisions of the Insurance Business Act That Are Applied Mutatis Mutandis to Formed Mutual Company)

Article 17-14 Where, pursuant to the provisions of Article 165-22, paragraph (3) of the Act, the provisions of Article 165-21, paragraph (1) of the Act are applied mutatis mutandis to a Formed Mutual Company, the technical replacement of terms in connection with the relevant provisions shall be as set forth in the following table:

Provisions of the Insurance Business Act whose terms are to be replaced	Original terms	Terms to replace the original terms
Article 165-21, paragraph (1)	as a result of the absorption-type merger	as a result of the consolidation-type merger
	the Absorbed Mutual Company or Absorbed Stock Company	the Consolidated Mutual Company or the Consolidated Stock Company
	as pertaining to an absorption-type merger	as pertaining to a consolidation-type merger

(Scope of Insurance Claims, etc.)

Article 17-15 Insurance Claims, etc. under Article 165-24, paragraphs (5) to (7) inclusive of the Act, shall be limited to the claims that have already arisen as of the time of the public notice given pursuant to paragraph (2) of that Article.

(Replacement of Terms in Provisions of the Commercial Registration Act That Are Applied Mutatis Mutandis to the Registration of a Mutual Company)

Article 17-16 Where, pursuant to the provisions of Article 170, paragraph (3) of the Act, the provisions of the Commercial Registration Act are applied mutatis mutandis to registrations concerning a Mutual Company, the technical replacement of terms in connection with the provisions of that Act shall be as set forth in the following table:

Provisions of the Commercial Registration Act whose terms are to be replaced	Original terms	Terms to replace the original terms
Article 79	a company absorbed in the absorption-type merger	an Absorbed Company as set forth in Article 169, paragraph (1) of the Insurance Business Act
	a company consolidated through the consolidation-type merger	a Consolidated Company as set forth in Article 165, paragraph (1), item (i) of that Act
	the trade name and head office	the trade name or name, and the head office or principal office
Article 80, item (ii)	n the main clause of paragraph (1) or of paragraph (3) of Article 796 of the Companies Act	the main clause of paragraph (1) of Article 165-11 of the Insurance Business Act

	paragraph (4) of said Article	paragraph (2) of that Article
Article 80, item (iii)	a document evidencing that the public notice and the notices under Article 799, paragraph (2) of the Companies Act (in cases where, in addition to public notice in an official gazette, a public notice has been given by publication in a daily newspaper that publishes matters on current affairs or by means of electronic public notices pursuant to the provision of paragraph (3) of said Article, the public notice by such method) has been given, and, if any creditor has raised an objection,	if any creditor has raised an objection under Article 165-7, paragraph (1) of the Insurance Business Act as applied mutatis mutandis pursuant to Article 165-12 of that Act or an objection under Article 165-17, paragraph (1) of that Act as applied mutatis mutandis pursuant to Article 165-20 of that Act
Article 80, item (v)	head office	head office of principal office
Article 80, item (vi)	a document evidencing the performance of the relevant procedures under Article 783, paragraphs (1) to (4) inclusive of the Companies Act such as obtaining approval for an absorption-type merger agreement (in the cases referred to in the main clause of Article 784, paragraph (1) of said Act, a document evidencing that the case provided for therein is applicable and a document or minutes of a board of directors evidencing that the consent of the majority of directors has been obtained)	a document evidencing the performance of the relevant procedures under Article 165-3, paragraphs (1) and (5) of the Insurance Business Act such as obtaining approval for an absorption-type merger agreement
Article 80, item (vii)	a membership company	a Mutual Company
	the consent of all partners has been obtained (or, in cases where otherwise provided for in its articles of incorporation, that the procedures under such provision have been performed)	approval has been obtained for the absorption-type merger agreement as referred to in Article 165-16, paragraph (1) of the Insurance Business Act
Article 80, item (viii)	a document evidencing that a company absorbed in absorption-type merger has given the public notice and the notices under Article 789, paragraph (2) of the Companies Act (excluding item (iii), and including the cases where applied mutatis mutandis	if any creditor has raised an objection under Article 165-7, paragraph (1) or Article 165-17, paragraph (1) of the Insurance Business Act,

	pursuant to Article 793, paragraph (2) of said Act) (in cases of a stock company or a limited liability company which, in addition to public notice in an official gazette, has given a public notice by publication in a daily newspaper that publishes matters on current affairs or by method of electronic public notices pursuant to the provision of Article 789, paragraph (3) of said Act (including the cases where applied mutatis mutandis pursuant to Article 793, paragraph (2) of said Act), that the public notice was given by such method), and, if any creditor has raised an objection,	
Article 81, item (iii)	items (x) to (xii) inclusive	items (x) to (xii) inclusive or Article 65, items (viii), (ix) and (xi) to (xiii) inclusive of the Insurance Business Act
Article 81, item (v)	head office	head office of principal office
Article 81, item (vi)	Article 804, paragraphs (1) and (3) of the Companies Act	Article 165-3, paragraphs (1) and (5) of the Insurance Business Act
Article 81, item (vii)	a membership company	a Mutual Company
	that the consent of all partners has been obtained (or, in cases where otherwise provided for in its articles of incorporation, that the procedures under said provision have been performed)	that approval has been obtained for the consolidation-type merger agreement as referred to in Article 165-16, paragraph (1) of the Insurance Business Act
Article 81, item (viii)	a document evidencing that a company consolidated through consolidation-type merger has given the public notice and the notices under Article 810, paragraph (2) of the Companies Act (excluding item (iii), and including the cases where applied mutatis mutandis pursuant to Article 813, paragraph (2) of said Act) (with regard to a stock company or a limited liability company which, in addition to public notice in an official gazette, has given a public notice by publication in a daily newspa-	if any creditor has raised an objection under Article 165-7, paragraph (1) of Article 165-17, paragraph (1) of the Insurance Business Act,

	per that publishes matters on current affairs or by method of electronic public notices pursuant to the provision of Article 810, paragraph (3) of said Act (including the cases where applied mutatis mutandis pursuant to Article 813, paragraph (2) of said Act), that the public notice was given by such method), and, if any creditor has raised an objection,	
Article 82, paragraph (1)	a company surviving an absorption-type merger	a Stock Company or Mutual Company surviving an absorption-type merger
	a company incorporated through a consolidation-type merger	a Stock Company or Mutual Company incorporated through a consolidation-type merger
Article 82, paragraphs (2) and (3)	head office	head office of principal office
Article 82, paragraph (4)	paragraph (2)	paragraph (2) (including the cases where applied mutatis mutandis pursuant to Article 67 of the Insurance Business Act)
	head office	head office of principal office
Article 83, paragraph (1)	head office	head office of principal office
	items of Article 24	items of Article 24 (including the cases where applied mutatis mutandis pursuant to Article 67 of the Insurance Business Act)
Article 83, paragraph (2)	head office	head office of principal office

(Replacement of Terms in Provisions of the Companies Act That Are Applied Mutatis Mutandis to Actions to Invalidate a Merger between One Mutual Company and Another Mutual Company, etc.)

Article 17-17 Where, pursuant to the provisions of Article 171 of the Act, the provisions of Article 836, paragraph (1), Article 937, paragraph (3) (limited to the portions involving items (ii) and (iii)) and paragraph (4) of the Companies Act are applied mutatis mutandis to an action to invalidate a merger as set forth in Article 159, paragraph (1) of the Act, the technical replacement of terms in connection with these provisions shall be as set forth in the following table:

Provisions of the Companies Act whose terms are to be replaced	Original terms	Terms to replace the original terms

Article 836, paragraph (1)	a shareholder or a Shareholder at Incorporation	a shareholder or a member
	provided, however, that this shall not apply when such shareholder is a director, company auditor, executive officer or liquidator or when such Shareholder at Incorporation is a Director at Incorporation or a Company Auditor at Incorporation.	provided, however, that this shall not apply when such a shareholder or member is a director, company auditor, executive officer or liquidator.
Article 937, paragraph (3) (limited to the portions pertaining to items (ii) and (iii))	head office	head office of principal office
Article 937, paragraph (4)	items of Article 930(2)	items of Article 930(2) (including the cases where applied mutatis mutandis pursuant to Article 64(3) of the Insurance Business Act)
	branch office	branch office of secondary office

(Insurance Contracts Not Subject to a Company Split)

Article 17-18 The insurance contracts specified by Cabinet Order, referred to in Article 173-2, paragraph (1) of the Act, shall be as follows:

(i) an insurance contract under which an insured event has already occurred as of the time of the public notice under Article 173-4, paragraph (2) of the Act (referred to as the "Public Notice" in the following item and the following Article) (limited to a contract that expires upon the payment of insurance proceeds in connection with the insured event); and

(ii) an insurance contract whose term of coverage has already ended as of the time of the Public Notice (including an insurance contract that has been canceled in the middle of the term of coverage or one under which any other grounds for the termination thereof have occurred as of the time of the Public Notice, and excluding an insurance contract set forth in the preceding item).

(Scope of Insurance Claims, etc.)

Article 17-19 Insurance Claims, etc. under Article 173-4, paragraphs (5) to (7) inclusive of the Act, shall be limited to the claims that have already arisen as of the time of public notice.

(Creditors Not Requiring Separate Demands)

Article 17-20 The creditors specified by Cabinet Order, referred to in Article 173-4, paragraph (11) of the Act, shall be, from among the persons who have rights under an insurance contract, the beneficiaries of a monetary trust in connection with the Insurance-Proceed Trust Services set forth in Article 99, paragraph (3) of the Act, and any other creditors, persons who are other than the known creditors referred to in Article 173-4, paragraph (2) of the Act.

(Replacement of Terms in Provisions of the Commercial Registration Act That Are Applied Mutatis Mutandis to Liquidators Appointed by Prime Minister)

Article 18 Where, pursuant to the provisions of Article 174, paragraph (11) of the Act, the provisions of Article 73, paragraph (3) and Article 74, paragraph (1) of the Commercial Registration Act (including the case where these provisions are applied mutatis mutandis pursuant to Article 183, paragraph (2) of the Act) to a liquidator appointed by the Prime Minister, the technical replacement of terms in connection with these provisions shall be as set forth in the following table:

Provisions of the Commercial Registration Act whose terms are to be replaced	Original terms	Terms to replace the original terms
Article 73, paragraph (3) and Article 74, paragraph (1)	Article 928, paragraph (1), item (ii) of the Companies Act	Article 928, paragraph (1), item (ii) of the Companies Act as applied mutatis mutandis pursuant to Article 183, paragraph (2) of the Insurance Business Act

(Replacement of Terms in Provisions of the Companies Act That Are Applied Mutatis Mutandis to Liquidators of a Mutual Company in Liquidation)

Article 18-2 Where, pursuant to the provisions of Article 180-5, paragraph (4) of the Act, the provisions of Article 937, paragraph (1) (limited to the portions involving sub-items (b) and (c) of item (ii)) of the Companies Act is applied mutatis mutandis to a liquidator as set forth in Article 180-5, paragraph (1) of the Act, the technical replacement of terms in connection with the relevant provisions shall be as set forth in the following table:

Provision of the Companies Act whose terms are to be replaced	Original terms	Terms to replace the original terms
Article 937, paragraph (1), item (ii), sub-item (b)	paragraph (2)(i) of the following Article	item (i), paragraph (2) of the following Article as applied mutatis mutandis pursuant to Article 184 of the Insurance Business Act
Article 937, paragraph (1), item (ii), sub-item (c)	paragraph (2)(ii) of the following Article	item (ii), paragraph (2) of the following Article as applied mutatis mutandis pursuant to Article 184 of the Insurance Business Act

(Replacement of Terms in Provisions of the Companies Act That Are Applied Mutatis Mutandis to Liquidators)

Article 18-3 Where, pursuant to the provisions of Article 180-8, paragraph (4) of the Act, the provisions of Articles 353 to 355 inclusive, Article 356, paragraph (1), Article 357, paragraph (1), Article 360, paragraph (1) and Article 361, paragraph (1) of the Companies Act are applied mutatis mutandis to a liquidator, the technical replacement of terms in connection with these provisions shall be as set forth in the following table:

Provisions of the Companies Act whose terms are to be replaced	Original terms	Terms to replace the original terms
Articles 353 to 355 inclusive, items of paragraph (1) of Article 356, Article 357, paragraph (1), Article 360, paragraph (1) and Article 361, paragraph (1)	Stock Company	Mutual Company Under Liquidation

(Replacement of Terms in Provisions of the Companies Act That Are Applied Mutatis Mutandis to the Representative Liquidator, etc. of a Mutual Company in Liquidation)

Article 18-4 (1) Where, pursuant to the provisions of Article 180-9, paragraph (5) of the Act, the provisions of Article 349, paragraph (4) and Article 351, paragraph (3) of the Companies Act are applied mutatis mutandis to the representative liquidator of a Mutual Company in Liquidation, the technical replacement of terms in connection with these provisions shall be as set forth in the following table:

Provisions of the Companies Act whose terms are to be replaced	Original terms	Terms to replace the original terms
Article 349, paragraph (4) and Article 351, paragraph (3)	Stock Company	Mutual Company Under Liquidation

(2) Where, pursuant to the provisions of Article 180-9, paragraph (5) of the Act, the provisions of Article 352 of the Companies Act are applied mutatis mutandis to the person who is appointed by a provisional disposition order under Article 56 of the Civil Provisional Remedies Act (Act No. 91 of 1989) to perform duties on behalf of the liquidator or the representative liquidator of a Mutual Company in Liquidation, the technical replacement of terms in connection with the relevant provisions shall be as set forth in the following table:

Provisions of the Companies Act whose terms are to be replaced	Original terms	Terms to replace the original terms
Article 352	Stock Company	Mutual Company Under Liquidation

(3) Where, pursuant to the provisions of Article 180-9, paragraph (5) of the Act, the provisions of Article 937, paragraph (1) (limited to the portions involving items (b) and (c) of item (ii)) of the Companies Act is applied mutatis mutandis to a person who is to temporarily perform the duties of the representative liquidator of a Mutual Company in Liquidation, the technical replacement of terms in connection with the relevant provisions shall be as set forth in the following table:

Provisions of the Companies Act whose terms are to be replaced	Original terms	Terms to replace the original terms
Article 937, paragraph (1), item (ii), sub-item (b)	paragraph (2)(i) of the following Article	paragraph (2), item (i) of the following Article as applied mutatis mutandis pursuant to Article 184 of the Insurance Business Act

| Article 937, paragraph (1), item (ii), sub-item (c) | paragraph (2)(ii) of the following Article | paragraph (2), item (ii) of the following Article as applied mutatis mutandis pursuant to Article 184 of the Insurance Business Act |

(Replacement of Terms in Provisions of the Companies Act That Are Applied Mutatis Mutandis to a Mutual Company with a Board of Liquidators)

Article 18-5 Where, pursuant to the provisions of Article 180-14, paragraph (9) of the Act, the provisions of Articles 364 and 365 of the Companies Act are applied mutatis mutandis to a Mutual Company with a board of liquidators, the technical replacement of terms in connection with these provisions shall be as set forth in the following table:

Provisions of the Companies Act whose terms are to be replaced	Original terms	Terms to replace the original terms
Article 364	the board of directors	the board of liquidators
Article 365, paragraph (1)	"board of directors."	"board of liquidators."
Article 365, paragraph (2)	a director	a liquidator
	to the board of directors	to the board of liquidators

(Replacement of Terms in Provisions of the Companies Act That Are Applied Mutatis Mutandis to Administration by the Board of Liquidators in a Mutual Company with a Board of Liquidators)

Article 18-6 Where, pursuant to the provisions of Article 180-15 of the Act, the provisions of Article 366, Article 368, Article 369, paragraphs (1) to (3) inclusive and paragraph (5), Article 370, Article 371, paragraphs (4) and (6) and Article 372, paragraph (1) of the Companies Act are applied mutatis mutandis to administration by the board of liquidators in a Mutual Company with a board of liquidators, the technical replacement of terms in connection with these provisions shall be as set forth in the following table:

Provisions of the Companies Act whose terms are to be replaced	Original terms	Terms to replace the original terms
Article 366, paragraph (1)	director	liquidator
	director	liquidator
Article 366, paragraph (2)	the director designated	the liquidator designated
	directors other than	liquidators other than
Article 366, paragraph (3)	the directors who	the liquidators who
Article 368, paragraph (1)	each director (or, for a Company with Auditors, to each director and each company auditor)	each liquidator and company auditor
Article 368, paragraph (2)	directors (or, for a Company with Auditors, directors and company auditors)	liquidators and company auditors

Article 369, paragraph (1)	the directors	the liquidators
Article 369, paragraph (2)	Directors	Liquidators
Article 369, paragraph (3)	the directors and	the liquidators and
Article 369, paragraph (5)	Directors	Liquidators
Article 370	where directors	where liquidators
	all directors	all liquidators
Article 371, paragraph (4)	Officers or executive officers	liquidators or company auditors
Article 371, paragraph (6)	the requests listed in each item of paragraph (2) applied by the reading of terms under paragraph (3), or a request under paragraph (4) (including the case of the mutatis mutandis application under the preceding paragraph. The same shall apply hereinafter in this paragraph)	the request listed in the items of paragraph (2) or the request set forth in paragraph (4)
	the permission under paragraph (2) applied by the reading of terms under paragraph (3)	the permission under paragraph (2)
Article 372, paragraph (1)	In cases where the directors, accounting advisors, company auditors or accounting auditors have notified all directors (or, for a Company with Auditors, directors and company auditors)	In cases where the liquidators or company auditors have notified all liquidators and company auditors

(Replacement of Terms in Provisions of the Companies Act That Are Applied Mutatis Mutandis to a Mutual Company in Liquidation)

Article 18-7 Where, pursuant to the provisions of Article 180-17 of the Act, the provisions of Article 496, paragraph (1) of the Companies Act are applied mutatis mutandis to a Mutual Company in Liquidation, the technical replacement of terms in connection with the relevant provisions shall be as set forth in the following table:

Provisions of the Companies Act whose terms are to be replaced	Original terms	Terms to replace the original terms
Article 496, paragraph (1)	Article 319(1)	Article 319(1) as applied mutatis mutandis pursuant to Article 41(1) of the Insurance Business Act

(Replacement of Terms in Provisions of the Companies Act, etc. That Are Applied Mutatis Mutandis to the Registration of a Mutual Company's Liquidation)

Article 18-8 (1) Where, pursuant to the provisions of Article 183, paragraph (2) of the Act, the provisions of Article 928, paragraphs (1) and (3) and Article 929 (limited to

Art.18-9　⑦ Order for Enforcement of the Insurance Business Act, Chap.II, Sec.1

the portion involving item (i)) of the Companies Act are applied mutatis mutandis to registration of a Mutual Company's liquidation, the technical replacement of terms in connection with these provisions shall be as set forth in the following table:

Provisions of the Companies Act whose terms are to be replaced	Original terms	Terms to replace the original terms
Article 928, paragraph (1)	Article 478(1)(i)	Article 180-4(1)(i) of the Insurance Business Act
Article 928, paragraph (3)	the matters listed in the items of paragraph (1) shall be registered in the case of a Liquidating Stock Company and the matters listed in the items of the preceding paragraph shall be registered in the case of a Liquidating Membership Company	the matters listed in items of paragraph (1) shall be registered
Article 929, item (i)	Article 507(3)	Article 507(3) as applied mutatis mutandis pursuant to Article 183(1) of the Insurance Business Act

(2) Where, pursuant to the provisions of Article 183, paragraph (2) of the Act, the provisions of Article 73, paragraphs (2) and (3), Article 74, paragraph (1) and Article 75 of the Commercial Registration Act are applied mutatis mutandis to registration of a Mutual Company's liquidation, the technical replacement of terms in connection with these provisions shall be as set forth in the following table:

Provisions of the Commercial Registration Act whose terms are to be replaced	Original terms	Terms to replace the original terms
Article 73, paragraph (2)	Article 478, paragraph (1), item (ii) or (iii) of the Companies Act	Article 180-4, paragraph (1), item (ii) or (iii) of the Insurance Business Act,
Article 73, paragraph (3) and Article 74, paragraph (1)	the court	the Prime Minister or the court
Article 75	Article 507, paragraph (3) of the Companies Act	Article 507, paragraph (3) of the Companies Act as applied mutatis mutandis pursuant to Article 183, paragraph (1) of the Insurance Business Act

(Replacement of Terms in Provisions of the Companies Act That Are Applied Mutatis Mutandis to a Mutual Company in Liquidation)
Article 18-9 Where, pursuant to the provisions of Article 184 of the Act, the provisions of Article 521, Article 522, paragraph (2), Article 536, paragraph (3), Article 542,

paragraph (1) and Article 938, paragraph (2) of the Companies Act are applied mutatis mutandis to a Mutual Company in Liquidation, the technical replacement of terms in connection with these provisions shall be as set forth in the following table:

Provisions of the Companies Act whose terms are to be replaced	Original terms	Terms to replace the original terms
Article 521	Article 492(3)	Article 492, paragraph (3) as applied mutatis mutandis pursuant to Article 180-17 of the Insurance Business Act
Article 522, paragraph (2)	this Act or	the Insurance Business Act, this Act or
Article 536, paragraph (3)	the provisions of paragraph (1)	the provisions of paragraph (1) (excluding item (iv) of paragraph (1))
Article 542, paragraph (1)	Qualified Officers provided for in paragraph (1) of Article 423	Officers, etc. provided for in Article 53-33, paragraph (1) of the Insurance Business Act
Article 938, paragraph (2), item (i)	under the provisions of Article 351(2) as applied mutatis mutandis pursuant to Article 346(2) or Article 483(6) as applied mutatis mutandis pursuant to Article 479(4)	under Article 53-12, paragraph (2) of the Insurance Business Act as applied mutatis mutandis pursuant to Article 180-5, paragraph (4) of that Act or under Article 351, paragraph (2) of this Act as applied mutatis mutandis pursuant to Article 180-9, paragraph (5) of the Insurance Business Act

(Insurance Contracts That May Be Concluded by a Foreign Insurer With No Branch Office, etc. in Japan)

Article 19 The insurance contract specified by Cabinet Order, referred to in the main clause of Article 186, paragraph (1) of the Act, shall be as follows:

(i) a reinsurance contract;

(ii) an insurance contract that covers, in whole or in part, Japanese vessels used for international maritime transportation, cargo being internationally transported by such vessels, and obligations arising from either of these;

(iii) an insurance contract that covers, in whole or in part, Japanese aircrafts used for commercial flights, cargo being internationally transported by such aircrafts, and obligations arising from either of these; and

(iv) any other insurance contract specified by Cabinet Office Ordinance.

(Limited Counterparties to Insurance Underwritten under a Conditional License)

Article 20 The persons specified by Cabinet Order, referred to in Article 188, paragraph (1) of the Act, shall be the members of the United States armed forces, the civilians in the employ thereof, and the dependents thereof provided for in Article 1 of the "Agreement under Article VI of the Treaty of Mutual Cooperation and Security between Japan and the United States of America Regarding Facilities and Areas and the Status of United States Armed Forces in Japan," and any other non-residents as defined in Article 6, paragraph (1), item (vi) of the Foreign Exchange and Foreign Trade Act (Act No. 228 of 1949).

(Provisions Not Applicable to Conditionally Licensed Foreign Life Insurance Company, etc.)
Article 21 The provisions specified by Cabinet Order, referred to in Article 188, paragraph (2) of the Act, shall be Article 192, paragraphs (5) and (6) of the Act; Article 194 of the Act; Article 196 of the Act; Article 197 of the Act; Article 97, paragraph (2), Article 97-2, paragraphs (1) and (2), Article 98, paragraph (1) (limited to the portion involving items (ii) to (xi) inclusive) and paragraphs (3) to (9) inclusive, Article 99, Article 111, paragraph (1) and paragraphs (3) to (6) inclusive, Article 112 and Articles 114 to 122 inclusive of the Act as applied mutatis mutandis pursuant to Article 199 of the Act; and Article 204, paragraph (1) of the Act (limited to the portion involving the submission or modification of the improvement plan).

(Special Provisions on Conditionally Licensed Foreign Life Insurance Companies, etc.)
Article 22 (1) For the purpose of application of the provisions of Article 195 of the Act in relation to a Foreign Insurance Company, etc. licensed pursuant to Article 185, paragraph (1) of the Act under the conditions set forth in Article 188, paragraph (1) of the Act (hereinafter referred to as a "Conditionally Licensed Foreign Life Insurance Company, etc." in this Article and Article 24), the term "for each business year" and "within a reasonable period of time following the end of the business year" in that Article shall be deemed to be replaced with "for each business year designated by the Commissioner of the Financial Services Agency as he/she may find necessary" and "no later than the date designated by the Commissioner of the Financial Services Agency," respectively.
(2) For the purpose of application of the provisions of Article 110, paragraph (1) of the Act as applied mutatis mutandis pursuant to Article 199 of the Act in relation to a Conditionally Licensed Foreign Life Insurance Company, etc. , the term "for each business year in Japan" in that paragraph shall be deemed to be replaced with "for each business year in Japan that is designated by the Commissioner of the Financial Services Agency as he/she may find necessary."
(3) For the purpose of application of the provisions of Article 203 of the Act in relation to a Conditionally Licensed Foreign Life Insurance Company, etc. , the term "Article 187, paragraph (3), items (ii) to (iv) inclusive" in that Article shall be deemed to be replaced with "Article 187, paragraph (3), item (ii)."
(4) For the purpose of application of provisions of Articles 123 to 125 inclusive of the Act as applied mutatis mutandis pursuant to Article 207 of the Act to where a Conditionally Licensed Foreign Insurance Company, etc. seeks to modify the particulars prescribed in the document set forth in Article 187, paragraph (3), item (ii) of the Act, the term "the documents specified in Article 187, paragraph (3), items (ii) to (iv) inclusive" in Article 123, paragraph (1) of the Act as applied mutatis mutandis pursuant to Article 207 of the Act shall be deemed to be replaced with "the documents specified in Article 187, paragraph (3), item (ii)"; the terms "particulars set forth in each of the following items" and "standards prescribed in the relevant item" in Article 124 of the Act as applied mutatis mutandis pursuant to Article 207 of the Act shall be deemed to be replaced with "particulars set forth in item (i)" and "standards prescribed in that item," respectively; the term "the documents specified in Article 187, paragraph (3), items (ii) and (iii)" in item (i) in that Article shall be deemed to be replaced with "the documents specified in Article 187, paragraph (3), item (ii)"; and the

term "the standards listed in Article 5, paragraph (1), item (iii), sub-item (a) to (e) inclusive of or item (iv), sub-item (a) to (c) inclusive" in Article 125 of the Act as applied mutatis mutandis pursuant to Article 207 of the Act shall be deemed to be replaced with "the standards listed in Article 5, paragraph (1), item (iii), sub-item (a) to (e) inclusive".

(Special Provisions on Procedures for Applying for Licenses)
Article 23 (1) Where the provisions of Article 188, paragraph (1) of the Act apply, a Foreign Insurer filing an application for a license under Article 185, paragraph (1) of the Act (hereinafter referred to as "Application for a Conditional License" in this Article) shall, in addition to the particulars listed in the items of Article 187, paragraph (1) of the Act, add a statement in its written application for a license under that paragraph, to the effect that its business will be limited to that related to insurance contracts whose insurance amounts are denominated in foreign currencies and in which the counterparties are the parties specified in Article 20.
(2) For the purpose of application of the provisions of Article 187, paragraph (3) of the Act in relation to a Foreign Insurer filing an Application for a Conditional License, the term "the following documents" in that paragraph shall be deemed to be replaced with "the documents specified in items (i) and (ii)."
(3) For the purpose of application of the provisions of Article 5, paragraph (1) of the Act as applied mutatis mutandis pursuant to Article 187, paragraph (5) of the Act to where an Application for a Conditional License has been filed, the term "the following standards" in the non-itemized part of the items of that paragraph shall be deemed to be replaced with "the standards set forth in items (i) to (iii) inclusive"; and the term "Article 187, paragraph (3), items (ii) and (iii)" in item (iii) of that paragraph shall be deemed to be replaced with "Article 187, paragraph (3), item (ii)."

(Amount to Be Deposited by a Foreign Insurance Company, etc.)
Article 24 The amount specified by Cabinet Order, referred to Article 190, paragraph (1) of the Act, shall be two hundred million yen for a Foreign Insurance Company, etc. (excluding a Conditionally Licensed Foreign Insurance Company, etc.); or ten million yen for a Conditionally Licensed Foreign Insurance Company, etc.

(Terms and Conditions of a Contract That Wholly or Partially Replaces a Deposit)
Article 25 Where a Foreign Insurance Company, etc. concludes a contract as set forth in Article 190, paragraph (3) of the Act, it shall have a Bank or other type of financial institution specified by Cabinet Office Ordinance as the other party to thereto, and the terms and conditions thereunder shall satisfy the following requirements:
(i) that, when an order of the Prime Minister under Article 190, paragraph (4) of the Act has been issued, the amount of deposit so ordered will be deposited without delay on behalf of the Foreign Insurance Company, etc. ;
(ii) that the contract is effective for the period of one year or longer; and
(iii) that the contract may not be cancelled and that the terms and conditions thereof may not be amended, unless this is done with the approval from the Commissioner of the Financial Services Agency.

(Procedures for the Fulfillment of Rights)
Article 26 (1) A person who holds rights as set forth in Article 190, paragraph (6) of the Act (hereinafter simply referred to as the "Rights" in this Article to Article 28 inclusive) may file petition for the fulfillment of those Rights with the Commissioner of

the Financial Services Agency.
(2) Where a petition set forth in the preceding paragraph has been filed and where the Commissioner of the Financial Services Agency finds the petition to have reasonable grounds, he/she shall issue a public notice notifying persons who have a Right to the monies deposited pursuant to the provisions of Article 190, paragraph (1), (2), (4) or (8) of the Act that they must report their Rights within a fixed period of time not shorter than sixty days and that they will be excluded from the distribution process if they fail to report their Rights within that period, and he/she shall also notify the person who filed the petition under the preceding paragraph (hereinafter referred to as the "Petitioner" in the following paragraph and paragraph (4)) and the Foreign Insurance Company, etc. for which the deposit was made (where the Foreign Insurance Company, etc. has concluded a contract under Article 190, paragraph (3) of the Act, including the counterparty to said contract; the same shall apply in paragraphs (4) and (5)) to that effect.
(3) Once the public notice under the preceding paragraph has been given, even in the event that the Petitioner withdraws his/her petition, this shall not prevent the procedures for the fulfillment of the Rights from proceeding.
(4) The Commissioner of the Financial Services Agency shall assess the Rights without delay after the period set forth in paragraph (2) has elapsed. In this case, the Commissioner of the Financial Services Agency shall give public notice of the date and place and notify the Foreign Insurance Company, etc. of such information, in advance, and afford the Petitioner, any person who has reported his/her Rights within the designated period, and the Foreign Insurance Company, etc. an opportunity to introduce evidence and to express their opinions as to the existence of the Rights and the amount of the claims secured by such Rights.
(5) The Commissioner of the Financial Services Agency shall, without delay, prepare a distribution list based on the results of the assessment under the preceding paragraph, shall put such list on public notice, and shall notify the Foreign Insurance Company, etc. thereof.
(6) The distribution shall be implemented in accordance with the distribution list set forth in the preceding paragraph, after eighty days have elapsed since the day that the public notice was given under the preceding paragraph.

(Recovery of Deposits)
Article 27 (1) A person who has deposited monies pursuant to the provisions of Article 190, paragraph (10) of the Act (hereinafter referred to as the "Depositor" in the following paragraph) may, where any of the items of paragraph (10) of that Article applies, file a petition for recovery of the deposit under that paragraph (hereinafter referred to as "Recovery of the Deposit" in this Article) with the Commissioner of the Financial Services Agency; provided, however, that this shall not apply to the period during which the procedures for the fulfillment of Rights under the preceding Article are still pending.
(2) Where a petition under the preceding paragraph has been filed, when, in addition to the Depositor who has filed said petition, there is any other Depositor in connection with the relevant deposit, the petition for Recovery of the Deposit shall be deemed to have been filed by said other Depositor as well.
(3) Where a petition set forth in paragraph (1) has been filed, the Commissioner of the Financial Services Agency shall issue a public notice notifying persons who have a Right to the deposited monies that they must report their Rights within a fixed period of time not shorter than sixty days and that they will be excluded from the distribution process if they fail to report their Rights within that period, and he/she shall

also notify the party that formerly was the Foreign Insurance Company, etc. for which said deposit was made (where that party has concluded a contract under Article 190, paragraph (3) of the Act, the counterparty to said contract shall be included).
(4) Where no Rights have been reported within the period of time specified in the preceding paragraph, the Commissioner of the Financial Services Agency shall approve the Recovery of the Deposit.
(5) The provisions of paragraphs (4) to (6) inclusive of the preceding Article shall apply mutatis mutandis to where Rights have been reported within the period set forth in paragraph (3). In such case, the term "paragraph (2)" in paragraph (4) of the preceding Article shall be deemed to be replaced with "paragraph (3) of the following Article"; the term "notify the Foreign Insurance Company, etc. of such information, and afford the Petitioner" in that paragraph shall be deemed to be replaced with "notify the party who was formerly the Foreign Insurance Company, etc. connected to said deposit (where that party has concluded a contract under Article 190, paragraph (3) of the Act, the counterparty to said contract shall be included; hereinafter referred to as the "Parties Relevant to the Deposit" in paragraph (3) and the following paragraph), and afford"; the term "and the Foreign Insurance Company, etc." shall be deemed to be replaced with "and the Parties Relevant to the Deposit"; and the term "the Foreign Insurance Company, etc." in paragraph (5) of that Article shall be deemed to be replaced with "the Parties Relevant to the Deposit".
(6) Where any Rights have been reported within the period set forth in paragraph (3), the Commissioner of the Financial Services Agency shall grant his/her approval for the Recovery of the Deposit, only to the extent of the amount remaining after completion of the procedures under paragraphs (4) to (6) inclusive of the preceding Article as applied mutatis mutandis pursuant to the preceding paragraphs, if any.

(Realization of Securities Deposited in Lieu of Monies)
Article 28 Where any securities have been deposited pursuant to the provisions of Article 190, paragraph (9) of the Act, and where it is necessary for fulfillment of the Rights, the Commissioner of the Financial Services Agency may realize such securities. In this case, the expenses incurred in relation to the realization of such securities shall be deducted from the proceeds of the realization.

(Scope of Parent Financial Institutions, etc. and Subsidiary Financial Institutions, etc.)
Article 28-2 (1) The persons specified by Cabinet Order, referred to in Article 193-2, paragraph (2) of the Act, shall be as follows:
(i) the Parent Juridical Person, etc. of the relevant Foreign Insurance Company, etc. ;
(ii) any Subsidiary, etc. of the Parent Juridical Person, etc. of the relevant Foreign Insurance Company, etc. (excluding such Foreign Insurance Company, etc. itself and juridical persons set forth in the preceding item and item (i) of paragraph (3));
(iii) any Affiliated Juridical Person, etc. of the Parent Juridical Person, etc. of the relevant Foreign Insurance Company, etc. (excluding a juridical person set forth in item (ii) of paragraph (3));
(iv) the following company, partnership, or other business entity equivalent thereto (including equivalent entities in foreign states, and excluding the Foreign Insurance Company, etc. itself and juridical persons specified in the preceding three items and the items of paragraph (3); hereinafter referred to as a "Juridical Person, etc." in this item) that is associated with an individual who holds voting rights that are greater than fifty percent of All Shareholders' Voting Rights, etc. in the relevant Foreign Insurance Company, etc. (hereinafter referred to as a "Speci-

fied Individual Shareholder, etc." in this item);
  (a) a Juridical Person, etc. (including its Subsidiary, etc. and Affiliated Juridical Person, etc.) in which a Specified Individual Shareholder, etc. holds voting rights that are greater than fifty percent of All Shareholders' Voting Rights, etc. ; or
  (b) a Juridical Person, etc. in which a Specified Individual Shareholder, etc. holds voting rights that are at least twenty percent and up to fifty percent of All Shareholders' Voting Rights, etc.
(2) The persons engaged in financial business specified by Cabinet Order, referred to in Article 193-2, paragraph (2) of the Act, shall be the persons listed in the items of paragraph (2) of Article 13-8 (excluding items (iv), (vi) and (vii)).
(3) The persons specified by Cabinet Order, referred to in Article 193-2, paragraph (3) of the Act, shall be as follows:
  (i) any Subsidiary, etc. of the relevant Foreign Insurance Company, etc. ; and
  (ii) any Affiliated Juridical Person, etc. of the relevant Foreign Insurance Company, etc.
(4) The persons engaged in financial business specified by Cabinet Order, referred to in Article 193-2, paragraph (3) of the Act, shall be the persons specified in Article 13-8, paragraph (2), items (i) to (iii) inclusive and items (x) and (xi).

(Specially Related Parties of a Foreign Insurance Company, etc.)
Article 29 The parties to which a Foreign Insurance Company, etc. is specially related as specified by Cabinet Order, referred to in the main clause of Article 194 of the Act, shall be as follows:
  (i) any Subsidiary, etc. of the relevant Foreign Insurance Company, etc. ;
  (ii) the Parent Juridical Person, etc. whose Subsidiaries, etc. include the relevant Foreign Insurance Company, etc. ;
  (iii) any Subsidiary, etc. of the juridical person specified in the preceding item (excluding the relevant Foreign Insurance Company, etc. itself and the juridical person specified in item (i));
  (iv) any Affiliated Juridical Person, etc. of the relevant Foreign Insurance Company, etc. ; and
  (v) any Affiliated Juridical Person, etc. of the juridical person specified in item (ii) (excluding the juridical person specified in the preceding item).

(Replacement of Terms in Provisions of the Companies Act That Are Applied Mutatis Mutandis to Employees of a Foreign Mutual Company)
Article 29-2 (1) Where, pursuant to the provisions of Article 198, paragraph (1) of the Act, the provisions of Article 10, Article 12, paragraph (1) and Article 13 of the Companies Act are applied mutatis mutandis to the employees of a Foreign Mutual Company, the technical replacement of terms in connection with these provisions shall be as set forth in the following table:

Provisions of the Companies Act whose terms are to be replaced	Original terms	Terms to replace the original terms
Article 10	head office or branch office	office in Japan
Article 12, paragraph (1), item (iii)	any other Company or merchant (excluding any Company; the same shall apply	a company (including a foreign company; the same shall apply hereinafter) or other Mutual

	in Article 24)	Company (including a Foreign Mutual Company) or merchant (excluding a merchant that is incorporated as company)
Article 12, paragraph (1), item (iv)	a director, executive officer or any member who executes the operation of any other Company	a director, executive officer or any other member who administers the business operations of a company; or a director or executive officer of any other Mutual Company (including a Foreign Mutual Company)
Article 13	the head office or any branch office	the office in Japan

(2) Where, pursuant to the provisions of Article 198, paragraph (1) of the Act, the provisions of Article 17, paragraph (1) the Companies Act are applied mutatis mutandis to the person acting as an agent or intermediary in transactions for a Foreign Mutual Company, the technical replacement of terms in connection with the relevant provisions shall be as set forth in the following table:

Provisions of the Companies Act whose terms are to be replaced	Original terms	Terms to replace the original terms
Article 17, paragraph (1), item (ii)	a director, executive officer or any member who executes operation of any other Company	a director, executive officer or any other member who administers the business operations of a company; or a director or executive officer of any other Mutual Company (including a Foreign Mutual Company)

(3) Where, pursuant to the provisions of Article 198, paragraph (1) of the Act, the provisions of Articles 22 and 23 of the Companies Act are applied mutatis mutandis to where a Foreign Mutual Company either transfers its business, or accepts a transfer of business or operations, the technical replacement of terms in connection with these provisions shall be as set forth in the following table:

Provisions of the Companies Act whose terms are to be replaced	Original terms	Terms to replace the original terms
Article 22, paragraph (1)	Assignee Company	Assignee
Article 22, paragraph (2)	in cases where the Assignee Company registers, at the location of its head office, without delay after it has accepted the assignment of the business, a statement to the effect that it	where, without delay after it has been assigned the business, an Assignee that is a company or a Mutual Company (including a Foreign Mutual Company) has registered, at the place in which its head office or principal office is located (including a principal branch in Japan (meaning a

	will not be liable for the performance of the obligations of the Assignor Company	principal branch in Japan as defined in Article 187, paragraph (1), item (iv) of the Insurance Business Act; hereinafter the same shall apply in this paragraph)), a statement to the effect that it will not be liable to perform the obligations of the Assignor Foreign Mutual Company (meaning the Foreign Mutual Company that has assigned its business; hereinafter the same shall apply in this paragraph); where, without delay after it has been assigned the business, an Assignee that is a merchant (excluding a merchant incorporated as a company; hereinafter the same shall apply in this paragraph) has registered a statement to the effect that it will not be liable to perform the obligations of the Assignor Foreign Mutual Company; or where, without delay after it has been assigned the business, an Assignee that is a Mutual Company has registereds, at the place in which its principal branch is located in Japan, a statement to the effect that it will not be liableto perform the obligations of the company that has assigned its business or of the merchant that has assigned its business operations.
	the Assignee Company and	the Assignee and
paragraphs (3) and (4) of Article 22, and Article 23	the Assignee Company	the Assignee

(Insurance Contracts Concluded by Foreign Insurance Companies, etc. in Japan That Are Excluded from Portfolio Transfers)

Article 30 The insurance contracts specified by Cabinet Order, referred to in Article 135, paragraph (2) of the Act as applied mutatis mutandis pursuant to Article 210, paragraph (1) of the Act, shall be as follows:

(i) an insurance contract in Japan under which an insured event has already occurred as of the time of the public notice under Article 137, paragraph (1) of the Act as applied mutatis mutandis pursuant to Article 210, paragraph (1) of the Act (referred to as the "Public Notice" in the following item) (limited to a contract that expires upon the payment of insurance proceeds in connection with insured event); and

(ii) an insurance contract whose term of coverage has already ended as of the time of the Public Notice (including an insurance contract that has been canceled in the middle of the term of coverage or one under which any other grounds for the termination thereof have occurred as of the time of Public Notice, and excluding an insurance contract as set forth in the preceding item).

(Replacement of Terms in Provisions of the Companies Act That Are Applied Mutatis Mutandis to the Registration of a Foreign Mutual Company)

Article 30-2 (1) Where, pursuant to the provisions of Article 215 of the Act, the provisions of Article 933, paragraph (1) (excluding item (i)), paragraph (2) (excluding item (vii)), paragraph (3) and paragraph (4), Article 934, paragraph (2), Article 935, paragraph (2) and Article 936, paragraph (2) of the Companies Act are applied mutatis mutandis to the registration of a Foreign Mutual Company, the technical replacement of terms connection with in these provisions shall be as set forth in the following table:

Provisions of the Companies Act whose terms are to be replaced	Original terms	Terms to replace the original terms
Article 933, paragraph (1) (excluding item (i))	Article 817(1)	Article 193, paragraph (1) of the Insurance Business Act
Article 933, paragraph (1), item (ii)	business office	office
Article 933, paragraph (2) (excluding item (vii))	in the items of Article 911(3) or in the items of Articles 912 to 914	items of Article 64, paragraph (2) of the Insurance Business Act
Article 933, paragraph (2), item (iii)	if the same kind of Company or the most similar Company in Japan is a Stock Company, the method of giving public notice under the provisions of the governing law prescribed in item (i)	the method of giving public notice under the provisions of the governing law prescribed in item (i)
Article 933, paragraph (2), item (iv)	Article 819(3)	Article 819, paragraph (3) as applied mutatis mutandis pursuant to Article 193, paragraph (2) of the Insurance Business Act
Article 933, paragraph (2), item (v)	if there are provisions with regard to the Method of Public Notice under the provisions of Article 939(2), such provisions	the provisions with regard to the Method of Public Notice under Article 217, paragraph (1) of the Insurance Business Act
Article 933, paragraph (2), item (iv), sub-item (b)	the second sentence of Article 939(3)	the second sentence of Article 217, paragraph (2) of the Insurance Business Act
Article 933, paragraph (3)	business office	office
	in Article 911(3)(iii), Article 912(iii), Article 913(iii) or Article 914(iii)	in Article 64, paragraph (2), item (ii) of the Insurance Business Act

[7] Order for Enforcement of the Insurance Business Act,
Art.30-3　　　　　　　　　　Chap.II, Sec.1

	branch office	office
Article 933, paragraph (4)	location(s) of the domicile(s) of its representative(s) in Japan (limited to those whose domicile is in Japan) (or, for a Foreign Company that has established a business office in Japan, the location of such business office).	place in which the office is located
Article 934, paragraph (2), Article 935, paragraph (2) and Article 936, paragraph (2)	business office	office

(2) Where, pursuant to the provisions of Article 215 of the Act, the provisions of Article 933, paragraph (4) of the Companies Act are applied mutatis mutandis to the registration of a Foreign Mutual Company, the technical replacement of terms in connection with the provisions of Article 915, paragraph (1) of that Act as applied mutatis mutandis pursuant to Article 933, paragraph (4) of that Act shall be as set forth in the following table:

Provisions of the Companies Act whose terms are to be replaced	Original terms	Terms to replace the original terms
Article 915, paragraph (1)	the matters listed in the items of Article 911(3) or in the items of the preceding three Articles	matters listed in the items of Article 64, paragraph (2) of the Insurance Business Act

(Replacement of Terms in Provisions of the Commercial Registration Act That Are Applied Mutatis Mutandis to the Registration of a Foreign Mutual Company)

Article 30-3 Where, pursuant to the provisions of Article 216 of the Act, the provisions of the Commercial Registration Act are applied mutatis mutandis to the registration of a Foreign Mutual Company, the technical replacement of terms in connection with the provisions of that Act (including the provisions of that Act as applied mutatis mutandis to such provisions) shall be as set forth in the following table:

Provisions of the Commercial Registration Act whose terms are to be replaced	Original terms	Terms to replace the original terms
Article 1-3	business office	office
Article 12, paragraph (1)	Corporate Reorganization Act (Act No. 154 of 2002)	Act on Special Treatment of Corporate Reorganization Proceedings and Other Insolvency Proceedings of Financial Institutions (Act No.

		95 of 1996)
Article 24, item (ii) as applied mutatis mutandis pursuant to Article 15	business office	office
Article 24, items (xiii) to (xv) inclusive as applied mutatis mutandis pursuant to Article 15	trade name	name
Article 17, paragraph (2), item (i)	its trade name and head office as well as its representative's name and address (in cases where the representative is a juridical person, including the name and address of a person to perform the duties thereof)	its name and principal branch in Japan (meaning the principal branch in Japan as set forth in Article 187, paragraph (1), item (iv) of the Insurance Business Act) as well as the name and address of its Representative Person in Japan
Article 21, paragraph (1)	trade name	name
Article 24, item (i)	business office	office
Article 24, items (xiii) to (xv) inclusive	trade name	name
Article 25, paragraph (3)	head office	principal branch in Japan
Article 27	trade name	trade name or name
	business office (in the case of a company, its head office; hereinafter the same shall apply in this Article)	principal branch in Japan
	such party's business office	such party's principal branch in Japan
Article 33, paragraph (1)	trade name	name
	business office (or a head office, in case of a company; hereinafter the same shall apply in this Article)	principal branch in Japan
	business office	principal branch in Japan
	business office	principal branch in Japan
Article 33, paragraph (2)	trade name	name
	business office	principal branch in Japan
Article 44, paragraph (2), item (ii)	business office	office
Article 129, paragraph (1), item (i)	head office	principal branch in Japan
Article 129, paragraph (1), item (iv)	Article 939, paragraph (2) of the Companies Act	Article 217, paragraph (1) of the Insurance Business Act
Article 138, paragraph (1)	head office	principal branch in Japan
	branch office	secondary office

Article 138, paragraph (2)	branch office	secondary office
Article 148	in this Act	in the Insurance Business Act
	of this Act	of that Act

(Replacement of Terms in Provisions of the Companies Act That Are Applied Mutatis Mutandis to a Foreign Mutual Company, etc. Giving Public Notice under the Insurance Business Act or Other Act by Means of Electronic Public Notice)

Article 30-4 Where, pursuant to the provisions of Article 217, paragraph (3) of the Act, the provisions of Article 946, paragraph (3) of the Companies Act are applied mutatis mutandis to the case where a Foreign Mutual Company, etc. gives a public notice under the Insurance Business Act or any other Act by means of electronic public notice, the technical replacement of terms in connection with the relevant provisions shall be as set forth in the following table:

| Provisions of the Companies Act whose terms are to be replaced | Original terms | Terms to replace the original terms |
| Article 946, paragraph (3) | trade name | trade name or name |

(Amount to Be Deposited by a Licensed Specified Juridical Person)

Article 31 The amount specified by Cabinet Order, referred to in Article 223, paragraph (1) of the Act, shall be two hundred million yen.

(Terms and Conditions of a Contract That Wholly or Partially Replaces a Deposit)

Article 32 Where a Licensed Specified Juridical Person concludes a contract as set forth in Article 223, paragraph (3) of the Act, it shall have a Bank or other type of financial institution specified by Cabinet Office Ordinance as the other party thereto, and the terms and conditions thereunder shall satisfy the following requirements:

(i) that, when an order of the Prime Minister under Article 223, paragraph (4) of the Act has been issued, the amount of deposit so ordered will be deposited without delay on behalf of such Licensed Specified Juridical Person;

(ii) that the contract is effective for the period of one year or longer; and

(iii) that the contract may not be cancelled and the terms and conditions thereof may not be amended, unless this is done with the approval of the Commissioner of the Financial Services Agency.

(Procedure for the Fulfillment of Rights)

Article 33 (1) A person who holds the rights as set forth in Article 223, paragraph (6) of the Act (hereinafter simply referred to as the "Rights" in this Article to Article 35 inclusive) may file a petition for the fulfillment of those Rights with the Commissioner of the Financial Services Agency.

(2) Where a petition set forth in the preceding paragraph has been filed and where the Commissioner of the Financial Services Agency finds the petition to have reasonable grounds, he/she shall issue a public notice notifying persons who have a Right to the monies deposited pursuant to the provisions of Article 223, paragraph (1), (2), (4) or (9) of the Act that they must report their Rights within a fixed period of time not shorter than sixty days and that they will be excluded from the distribution process if

they fail to report their Rights within that period, and he/she shall also notify the person who filed the petition under the preceding paragraph (hereinafter referred to as the "Petitioner" in the following paragraph and paragraph (4)) and the Licensed Specified Juridical Person for which such deposit was made (where the Licensed Specified Juridical Person has concluded a contract under Article 223, paragraph (3) of the Act, including the counterparty to said contract; the same shall apply in paragraphs (4) and (5)) to that effect.
(3) Once the public notice under the preceding paragraph has been given, even in the event that the Petitioner withdraws his/her petition, this shall not prevent the procedures for the fulfillment of the Rights from proceeding.
(4) The Commissioner of the Financial Services Agency shall assess the Rights without delay after the period set forth in paragraph (2) has elapsed. In this case, the Commissioner of the Financial Services Agency shall give public notice of the date and place and notify the Licensed Specified Juridical Person of such information, in advance, and afford the Petitioner, any person who has reported his/her Rights within the designated period, and the Licensed Specified Juridical Person an opportunity to introduce evidence and to express their opinions as to the existence of the Rights and the amount of the claims secured by such Rights.
(5) The Commissioner of the Financial Services Agency shall, without delay, prepare a distribution list based on the results of the assessment under the preceding paragraph, shall put such list on public notice, and shall notify the Licensed Specified Juridical Person thereof.
(6) The distribution shall be implemented in accordance with the distribution list set forth in the preceding paragraph, after eighty days have elapsed since the day that the public notice was given under the preceding paragraph.

(Recovery of Deposits)
Article 34 (1) A person who has deposited monies pursuant to the provisions of Article 223, paragraph (11) of the Act (hereinafter referred to as the "Depositor" in the following paragraph) may, where any of the items of paragraph (11) of that Article applies, file a petition for the recovery of the deposit under that paragraph (hereinafter referred to as the "Recovery of the Deposit" in this Article) with the Commissioner of the Financial Services Agency; provided, however, that this shall not apply during the period when the procedures for fulfillment of the Rights under the preceding Article are still pending.
(2) Where a petition under the preceding paragraph has been filed, when, in addition to the Depositor who has filed said petition, there is any other Depositor in connection to such deposit, the petition for the recovery of said deposit shall be deemed to have been filed by said other Depositor as well.
(3) Where a petition as set forth in paragraph (1) has been filed, the Commissioner of the Financial Services Agency shall issue a public notice notifying persons who have a Right to the deposited monies that they must report their Rights within a fixed period of time not shorter than sixty days and that they will be excluded from the distribution process if they fail to report their Rights within that period, and he/she shall also notify the party that formerly was the Licensed Specified Juridical Person for which said deposit was made (where that party has concluded a contract under Article 223, paragraph (3) of the Act, the counterparty to said contract shall be included).
(4) Where no Rights have been reported within the period of time specified in the preceding paragraph, the Commissioner of the Financial Services Agency shall approve the Recovery of the Deposit.
(5) The provisions of paragraphs (4) to (6) inclusive of the preceding Article shall apply

mutatis mutandis to where any Rights have been reported within the period of time set forth in paragraph (3). In such case, the term "paragraph (2)" in paragraph (4) of the preceding Article shall be deemed to be replaced with "paragraph (3) of the following Article"; the term "notify the Licensed Specified Juridical Person of such information, and afford the Petitioner" in that paragraph shall be deemed to be replaced with "notify the party who was formerly the Licensed Specified Juridical Person for which said deposit was made (where that party has concluded a contract under Article 190, paragraph (3) of the Act, the counterparty to said contract shall be included; hereinafter referred to as the "Parties Relevant to the Deposit" in paragraph (3) and the following paragraph), and afford"; the term "and the Licensed Specified Juridical Person" in that paragraph shall be deemed to be replaced with "and the Parties Relevant to the Deposit"; and the term "the Licensed Specified Juridical Person" in paragraph (5) of that Article shall be deemed to be replaced with "the Parties Relevant to the Deposit."

(6) Where any Rights have been reported within the period set forth in paragraph (3), the Commissioner of the Financial Services Agency shall grant approval for Recovery of the Deposit, to the extent of the amount remaining after completion of the procedures under paragraphs (4) to (6) inclusive of the preceding Article as applied mutatis mutandis pursuant to the preceding paragraph, if any.

(Realization of Securities Deposited in Lieu of Monies)
Article 35 Where any securities have been deposited pursuant to the provisions of Article 223, paragraph (10) of the Act, when it is necessary for fulfillment of the Rights, the Commissioner of the Financial Services Agency may realize such securities. In this case, the expenses incurred in relation to the realization of said securities shall be deducted from the proceeds of the realization.

(Application of Other Laws and Regulations to the Underwriting Members of a Licensed Specified Juridical Person)
Article 36 The laws and regulations specified by Cabinet Order, referred to in Article 240, paragraph (2) of the Act, shall be the Building Lots and Buildings Transactions Business Act (Act No. 176 of 1952), the Act on Compensation for Nuclear Damage (Act No. 147 of 1961), the Act on Contracts for Indemnification of Nuclear Damage (Act No. 148 of 1961), the Act on Prevention of the Transfer of Criminal Proceeds (Act No. 22 of 2007), the Order for Enforcement of the Trade and Investment Insurance Act (Cabinet Order No. 141 of 1953), Order for Enforcement of the Financial Instruments and Exchange Act (Cabinet Order No. 321 of 1965), the Order for Enforcement of the Act on Liability for Oil Pollution Damage (Cabinet Order No. 11 of 1976), the Order for Enforcement of the Act on Limitation of Shipowner Liability (Cabinet Order No. 248 of 1976), the Order for Enforcement of the Act on the Regulation of Membership Contracts concerning Golf Courses and Related Facilities (Cabinet Order No. 19 of 1993), the Order for Enforcement of the Act on Concurrent Engagement, etc. in Trust Business by Financial Institutions (Cabinet Order No. 31 of 1993) and the Order for Enforcement of the Trust Business Act (Cabinet Order No. 427 of 2004); an Underwriting Member of a Licensed Specified Juridical Person shall be deemed to be a Foreign Insurance Company, etc. for the purpose of application of the following provisions: Article 41, paragraph (1) of the Building Lots and Buildings Transaction Business Act (limited to the portion involving item (ii)), Article 2, paragraph (2), item (xvii) of the Act on Prevention of the Transfer of Criminal Proceeds, Article 15-13 of the Order for Enforcement of the Financial Instruments and Exchange Act, the Order for Enforcement of the Act on Limitation of Shipowner Liabili-

ty (limited to the portion involving item (vii)), Article 2 of the Order for Enforcement of the Act on the Regulation of Membership Contracts concerning Golf Courses and Related Facilities, Article 5 of the Order for Enforcement of the Act on Concurrent Engagement, etc. in Trust Business by Financial Institutions and Article 10 of the Order for Enforcement of the Trust Business Act; and the Underwriting Member of a party that has obtained a specified non-life insurance business license shall be deemed to be a Foreign Non-Life Insurance Company, etc. for the purpose of application of the following provisions: Article 8 of the Act on Compensation for Nuclear Damage, Article 18, paragraph (1) of the Act on Contracts for Indemnification of Nuclear Damage, Article 25 of the Order for Enforcement of the Trade and Investment Insurance Act and Article 2, paragraph (1) (limited to the portion involving item (iii)) and paragraph (2) (limited to the portion of item (i) which pertains to item (iii), paragraph (1) of that Article) of the Order for Enforcement of the Act on Liability for Oil Pollution Damage.

(Scope of Insurance Contracts Not Subject to Amendment)
Article 36-2 The insurance contracts specified by Cabinet Order, referred to in Article 240-2, paragraph (4) of the Act, shall be as follows:
(i) an insurance contract under which an insured event has already occurred as of the reference date for amendments to the contract terms and conditions (referred to as the "Base Date" in the following item), (limited to a contract that expires upon the payment of the insurance proceeds in connection with an insured event); and
(ii) an insurance contract whose term of coverage has already ended as of the Base Date (including an insurance contract that has been canceled in the middle of the term of coverage or one under which any other grounds for the termination thereof have occurred as of the Base Date, and excluding an insurance contract set forth in the preceding item).

(Limitation on Changes to Contract Terms and Conditions)
Article 36-3 The rate specified by Cabinet Order, referred to in Article 240-4, paragraph (2) of the Act, shall be three percent per annum.

(Scope of the Right to Claim Covered Insurance Proceeds)
Article 36-4 The rights specified by Cabinet Order, referred to in Article 245, item (i) of the Act, shall be as follows:
(i) insurance claims;
(ii) the right to claim compensation of damages (excluding the claims set forth in the preceding item);
(iii) the right to claim refunds on maturity;
(iv) the right to claim dividends from policyholders' dividends or surplus distributed to members (limited to where the payment claim is filed simultaneously with the claims referred in the preceding three items); and
(v) the right to claim a refund of insurance premiums corresponding to the unfulfilled term (meaning the period of time left in the term of coverage under the insurance contract that has not yet elapsed as of the time of cancellation thereof or as of the time when such contract ceases to be effective; the same shall apply in Article 37-4-6, item (v); and limited to the case where the claim is filed simultaneously with the claims referred to in item (i) or (ii)).

(Scope of Insurance Claims, etc.)
Article 37 The rights specified by Cabinet Order, referred to in Article 88, paragraph

(6) or Article 165-24, paragraph (6) of the Act as applied mutatis mutandis pursuant to Article 70, paragraph (6), Article 165-17, paragraph (4) (including the cases where applied mutatis mutandis pursuant to Article 165-20 of the Act), as further applied mutatis mutandis to Article 165-7, paragraph (4) of the Act as applied by replacing certain terms under Article 255, paragraph (2) of the Act (including the cases where applied mutatis mutandis pursuant to Article 165-12 of the Act), shall be the rights specified in the items of Article 3.

(Insurance Companies Specified by Cabinet Order, Referred to in Article 265-2, Paragraph (1) of the Insurance Business Act)
Article 37-2 The Insurance Companies specified by Cabinet Order, referred to in Article 265-2, paragraph (1) of the Act, shall be as follows:
(i) any Insurance Company (including a Foreign Insurance Company and a Licensed Specified Juridical Person; hereinafter the same shall apply in this Article) engaged solely in business related to reinsurance contracts;
(ii) any Insurance Company engaged solely in business related to underwriting insurance contracts whose insurance proceeds are denominated in foreign currencies and whose counterparties are non-residents as set forth in Article 20; and
(iii) any Insurance Company (excluding an Insurance Company set forth in item (i)) engaged solely in business related to insurance contracts for the expenses and liability of the owners, lessees, or charterers of vessels and any other parties engaged in vessel navigation, incurred in relation to the navigation of a vessel (including reinsurance contracts related to such insurance contracts; referred to as "Shipowners, etc. Liability Insurance Contracts" in item (iii) of the following Article).

(Persons Specified by Cabinet Order, Referred to in Article 265-3, Paragraph (2) of the Insurance Business Act)
Article 37-3 The persons specified by Cabinet Order, referred to in Article 265-3, paragraph (2) of the Act, shall be as follows:
(i) any person who wishes to engage solely in business related to reinsurance contracts;
(ii) any person who wishes to engage solely in business related to underwriting insurance contracts whose insurance proceeds that are denominated in foreign currencies and whose counterparties are non-residents set forth in Article 20; and
(iii) any person who wishes to engage solely in business related to Shipowners, etc. Liability Insurance Contracts (excluding a person who falls under item (i)).

(Maximum Amount of Loans Granted by an Insurance Company or Financial Institution)
Article 37-4 The amount specified by Cabinet Order, referred to in Article 265-42 of the Act, shall be as follows: 460 billion yen for a Life Insurance Policyholders Protection Corporation (meaning a Life Insurance Policyholders Protection Corporation as defined in Article 265-37, paragraph (1) of the Act; the same shall apply hereinafter); or 50 billion yen for a Non-Life Insurance Policyholders Protection Corporation (meaning a Non-Life Insurance Policyholders Protection Corporation as defined in Article 265-37, paragraph (2) of the Act; the same shall apply hereinafter).

(Amount of Losses Incurred by the Successor Insurance Company Under an Agreement)
Article 37-4-2 The amount calculated in accordance with the provisions of Cabinet Or-

der, referred to in Article 270-3-9 of the Act, shall be the lesser of the amounts set forth in item (i) or (ii), calculated for each business year of the Successor Insurance Company Under the Agreement (meaning the Successor Insurance Company Under the Agreement under Article 270-3-6, paragraph (1), item (i); the same shall apply hereinafter).

(i) the amount equivalent to the loss resulting from the transfer of the assets where the assets of the Successor Insurance Company Under the Agreement were purchased pursuant to the provisions of Article 270-3-7 of the Act; and

(ii) the amount calculated in accordance with Cabinet Office Ordinance and Ordinance of Ministry of Finance as the loss resulting from the settlement of profits and losses.

(Replacement of Terms in Provisions of the Insurance Business Act That Are Applied Mutatis Mutandis to the Transfer of Insurance Contracts from a Bankrupt Insurance Company to an Affiliated Corporation)

Article 37-4-3 Where, pursuant to the provisions of Article 270-4, paragraph (9) of the Act, the provisions of Article 136-2, paragraph (1) of the Act are applied mutatis mutandis to transfer of insurance contracts from a Bankrupt Insurance Company to an Affiliated Corporation in relation to the Underwriting of Insurance Contracts, the technical replacement of terms in connection with the relevant provisions shall be as set forth in the following table:

Provisions of the Insurance Business Act whose terms are to be replaced	Original terms	Terms to replace the original terms
Article 137-2, paragraph (1)	Article 135, paragraph (1)	Article 270-4, paragraph (8)

(Amount of Losses in Special Insurance Accounts)

Article 37-4-4 The amount calculated in accordance with Cabinet Order, referred to in Article 270-5, paragraph (4) of the Act, shall be the amount equivalent to the losses in the Special Insurance Account (meaning a Special Insurance Account pursuant to Article 265-40 of the Act; the same shall apply hereinafter) resulting from the settlement of profits and losses, as specified by Cabinet Office Ordinance and Ordinance of Ministry of Finance.

(Application of Other Laws and Regulations to Where a Policyholders Protection Corporation Engages in Insurance Business)

Article 37-4-5 The laws and regulations specified by Cabinet Order, referred to in Article 270-6, paragraph (3) of the Act, shall be as follows: the Temporary Interest Rate Adjustment Act (Act No. 181 of 1947), the Fire and Disaster Management Act (Act No. 186 of 1948), the Act on the Non-Life Insurance Rating Organization of Japan (Act No. 193 of 1948), the Inheritance Tax Act (Act No. 73 of 1950), the Ship Owner's Mutual Insurance Union Act (Act No. 177 of 1950), the Local Tax Act (Act No. 226 of 1950), the Certified Public Tax Accountant Act (Act No. 237 of 1951), the Act on Compensation of Damages Related to Fishing Vessels (Act No. 28 of 1952), the Employees' Pension Insurance Act (Act No. 115 of 1954), the Act Regulating the Receipt of Contributions, Receipt of Deposits and Interest Rates (Act No. 195 of 1954), the Housing Loan Insurance Act (Act No. 63 of 1955), the Automobile Liability Security Act (Act No. 97 of 1955), the Act on the Reserve Requirement System (Act No. 135 of 1957), the National Pension Act (Act No. 141 of 1959), the Act on Compensation for Nuclear Damage, the Income Tax Act (Act No. 33 of 1940), the Act on Earthquake Insurance (Act No. 73 of 1966), the Stamp Tax Act (Act No. 23 of 1967), the Workers' Property Accumulation Promotion Act (Act No. 92 of 1971), the Act on Liability for Oil Pollution Damage (Act No. 95 of 1975), the Defined-Benefit Corporate Pension Act (Act No. 50 of 2001), the Act on the Prevention of the Transfer of Criminal Proceeds, the Order for Budget Settlement and Accounting (Imperial Ordinance No. 165 of 1947), the Order for Enforcement of the Small and Medium-Sized Enterprises' Credit Insurance Act (Cabinet Order No. 350 of 1950), the Order for Enforcement of the Act on Compensation of Damages Related to Fishing Vessels (Cabinet Order No. 68 of 1952), the Order for Enforcement of the Certified Public Accountants Act (Cabinet Order No. 343 of 1952), the Order for Enforcement of the Trade and Investment Insurance Act, the Order for Enforcement of the Customs Act (Cabinet Order No. 150 of 1954), the Order for Enforcement of the Automobile Liability Security Act (Cabinet Order No. 286 of 1955), the Order Providing for the Amount of the Automobile Liability Guarantee Business Levy (Cabinet Order No. 316 of 1955), the Order for Enforcement of the Act on Special Measures Concerning Taxation (Cabinet Order No. 43 of 1957), the Order for Enforcement of the Installment Sales Act (Cabinet Order No. 341 of 1961), the Order for Enforcement of the Income Tax Act (Cabinet Order No. 96 of 1965), the Order for Enforcement of the Corporation Tax Act (Cabinet Order No. 97 of 1965), the Order for Enforcement of the Financial Instruments and Exchange Act, the Order for Enforcement of the Act on Earthquake Insurance (Cabinet Order No. 164 of 1966), the Order for Enforcement of the Stamp Tax Act (Cabinet Order No. 108 or 1967), the Order for Enforcement of the Act on Temporary Measures concerning Interest Subsidies Related to Loans for Building Oceangoing Vessels (Cabinet Order No. 195 of 1969), the Order for Enforcement of the Act on Liability for Oil Pollution Damage, the Order for Enforcement of the Act on Limitation of Shipowner Liability, the Order for Asset Saving Projects for National Government Employees Implemented by National Government Employees' Mutual Aid Associations and Federations of National Government Employees' Mutual Aid Associations (Cabinet Order No. 199 of 1977), the Order for Asset Saving Projects for Local Government Employees Implemented by Local Government Employees' Mutual Aid Associations, etc. (Cabinet Order No. 25 of 1978), the Order for Enforcement of the Act on Regulations, etc. on Advanced Payment Certificates (Cabinet Order No. 193 of 1990), the Order for Enforcement of the Act on the Regulation of Membership Contracts concerning Golf Courses and Related Facilities, the Order for Enforcement of the Act on Concurrent Engagement in Trust Business by Financial Institutions, the Order for Enforcement of the Trust Business Act, and the Order for Enforcement of the Japan Finance Corporation Act (Cabinet Order No. 143 of 2008); a Policyholders Protection Corporation shall be deemed to be an Insurance Company for the purpose of application of the following provisions: Article 1, paragraph (1) of the Temporary Interest Rate Adjustment Act, Article 33 of the Fire and Disaster Management Act, Article 59, paragraph (1), item (i) of the Inheritance Tax Act, Article 5, paragraph (1), item (i), sub-item (c) of the Certified Public Tax Accountant Act, Article 112, paragraph (7) of the Act on Compensation of Damages Related to Fishing Vessels, Article 3 of the Act Regulating the Receipt of Contributions, Receipt of Deposits and Interest Rates. , Article 2, item (iii) of the Housing Loan Insurance Act, Article 14, paragraph (2) and Article 39-5, paragraph (2) of the Act on Liability for Oil Pollution Damage, Article 2, paragraph (2), item (xvi) of the Act on the Prevention of the Transfer of Criminal Proceeds, Article 77, item (i) and Article 100-3, items (i) and (ii) of the Order for Budget Settlement and Accounting, Article 1-2, item (xiv) of the Order for Enforcement of the Small and Medium-Sized Enterprises' Credit Insurance Act, Article 24 of the Order for Enforcement of the Act on Compensation of Damages Related to Fishing Vessels, Article 2, paragraph (1), item (ii) of the Order for Enforcement of the Certified Public Accountants Act, Article 62-7, paragraph (1) and Article 62-21, paragraph (1) of the Order for Enforcement of the Customs Act, the Order for Enforcement of the Automobile Liability Guarantee Act, Article 1 of the Order Providing for the Amount of the Automobile Liability Guarantee Business Levy, Article 7 of Order for Enforcement of the Installment Sales Act, Article 1-9, item (ii) (limited to the portion involving Article 27-28, paragraph (3) of the Financial Instruments and Exchange Act) and Article 15-13 of the Order for Enforcement of the Financial Instruments and Exchange Act, Article 22, item (ii) of the Order for Enforcement of the Stamp Tax Act, Article 1, item (iii) of the Order for Enforcement of the Act on Temporary Measures concerning Interest Subsidies Related to Loans for Building Oceangoing Vessels, item (vi) of the Order for Enforcement of the Act on Limitation of Liability of Shipowners, Article 9, paragraph (2), item (i) of the Order for Enforcement of the Act on Regulation, etc. on Advanced Payment Certificates, Article 2 of the Order for Enforcement of the Act on the Regulation of Membership Contracts concerning Golf Courses and Related Facilities, Article 5 of the Order for Enforcement of the Act Concurrent Engagement in Trust Business by Financial Institutions, Article 10 of the Order for Enforcement of the Trust Business Act and Articles 11 and 13 of the Japan Finance Corporation Act; a Life Insurance Policyholders Protection Corporation shall be deemed to be a Life Insurance Company for the purpose of application of the following provisions: Article 2, paragraph (2) of the Act on the Non-Life Insurance Rating Organization of Japan, Article 34, paragraph (1), item (v) and paragraph (8), and Article 314-2, paragraph (1), item (v) and paragraph (8) of the Local Tax Act, Article 130, paragraph (5) and Article 159, paragraph (7) of the Employees' Pension Insurance Act, Article 2, paragraph (1), item (vii) of the Act on the Reserve Requirement System, Article 128, paragraph (5) and Article 137-15, paragraph (6) of the National Pension Act, Article 76, paragraph (3), items (i) and (iv) of the Income Tax Act, Appended Table No. 3 of the Stamp Tax Act, Article 6, Article 6-2 and Article 12 of the Workers' Property Accumulation Promotion Act, Article 93 of the Defined-Benefit Corporate Pension Act, Article 39-36 of the Order for Enforcement of the Act on Special Measures Concerning Taxation, Article 76, paragraph (2), item (i), Article 209, paragraph (3) and Article 326, paragraph (2), item (i) of the Order for Enforcement of the Income Tax Act, Article 16, paragraph (1), Article 17 and Article 18 of the Supplementary Provisions in the Order for Enforcement of the Corporation Tax Act, Article 4 of the Order for Asset Saving Projects for National Government Employees Implemented by National Government Employees' Mutual Aid Associations and Federations of National Government Employees' Mutual Aid Associations, and Article 4 of the Order for Asset Saving Projects for Local Government Employees Implemented by Local Government Employees' Mutual Aid Associations, etc. ; and a Non-Life Insurance Policyholders Protection Corporation shall be deemed to be a Non-Life Insurance Company for the purpose of application of the following provisions: Article 2, paragraph (1), item (iv), Article 3, paragraphs (1) and (2), Article 6, Article 7 and Article 10, paragraph (1) of the Act on the Non-Life Insurance Rating Organization of Japan, Article 8 of the Ship Owner's Mutual Insurance Union Act, Article 34, paragraph (1), item (v) and paragraph (8) and Article 314-2, paragraph (1), item (v) and paragraph (8) of the Local Tax Act, the Automobile Liability Guarantee Act, Article 8 of the Act on Compensation for Nuclear Damage, Article 76, paragraph (3), item (iv) and Article 77, paragraph (2), item (i) of the Income Tax Act, the Act on Earthquake Insurance, Appended Table No. 3 of the Stamp Tax Act, Article 6, Article 6-2 and Article 12 of the Workers' Property Accumulation Promotion Act, Article 25 of the Order for Enforcement of the Trade and Investment Insurance Act, Article 209, paragraph (3) and Article 326, paragraph (2), item (i) of the Order for Enforcement of the Income Tax Act, Article 3 of the Order for Enforcement of the Act on Earthquake Insurance, Article 2, paragraph (1), item (iii) and Article 2, paragraph (2), item (i) (limited to the portion involving item (iii), paragraph (1) of that Article) of the Order for Enforcement of the Act on Liability for Oil Pollution Damage, Article 4 of the Order for Asset Saving Projects for National Government Employees Implemented by National Government Employees' Mutual Aid Associations and Federations of National Government Employees' Mutual Aid Associations, and Article 4 of the Order for Asset Saving Projects for Local Government Employees Implemented by Local Government Employees' Mutual Aid Associations, etc.

(Scope of Rights That Can Be Purchased)
Article 37-4-6 The rights specified by Cabinet Order, referred to in Article 270-6-8, paragraph (1) of the Act, shall be as follows:
(i) insurance claims;
(ii) the right to claim compensation for damages (excluding the right specified in the preceding item);
(iii) the right to claim refunds at maturity;
(iv) the right to claim dividends from policyholders' dividends, or surplus distributed to members (limited to where the claim is filed simultaneously with the claims referred in the preceding three items);
(v) the right to claim a refund of insurance premiums corresponding to the unfulfilled term (limited to the case where the claim is filed simultaneously with the claims referred to in item (i) or (ii)).

(Special Provisions on the Act on Special Measures Concerning Taxation, Applicable to the Purchase of Insurance Claims, etc.)
Article 37-4-7 (1) For the purpose of application of Article 4-2, paragraphs (2) and (9) of the Act on Special Measures Concerning Taxation (Act No. 26 of 1957), where an event has occurred, in connection with a workers' housing fund savings contract referred to in Article 4-2, paragraph (1) of that Act or in connection with performance of the obligations thereunder, that has rendered any of the requirements set forth in Article 6, paragraph (4), item (ii), sub-item (c) or (d) or in Article 6, paragraph (4), item (c) or (d) of the Workers' Property Accumulation Promotion Act non-applicable, when such event has occurred due to a Purchase of Insurance Claims, etc. (meaning a Purchase of Insurance Claims, etc. as set forth in Article 270-6-8, paragraph (1) of the Act; hereinafter the same shall apply in the following paragraph), such event shall be deemed not to fall under the case specified by Cabinet Order that is referred to in Article 4-2, paragraph (2) of the Act on Special Measures Concerning Taxation or the event set forth in paragraph (9) of that Article.
(2) For the purpose of application of Article 4-3, paragraphs (2) and (10) of the Act on Special Measures Concerning Taxation, where an event has occurred, in connection with a workers' pension savings contract set forth in Article 4-3, paragraph (1) of that Act or in connection with performance of the obligations thereunder, that has rendered any requirement set forth in Article 6, paragraph (2), item (ii), sub-item (b) or (c) or in Article 6, paragraph (2), item (iii), sub-item (b) or (c) of the Workers' Property Accumulation Promotion Act non-applicable, when such an event has occurred due to a Purchase of Insurance Claims, etc. , such event shall be deemed not to fall under the case specified by Cabinet Order that is referred to in Article 4-3, paragraph (2) of the Act on Special Measures Concerning Taxation or the event set forth in

paragraph (10) of that Article.

(Juridical Persons Equivalent to State and Local Governments)
Article 37-5 The juridical persons specified by Cabinet Order as being equivalent to the State and local governments, referred to in Article 271-3, paragraph (1) of the Act, shall be as follows:
(i) Investor Protection Funds under Article 79-21 of the Financial Instruments and Exchange Act;
(ii) The Deposit Insurance Corporation of Japan;
(iii) The Agricultural and Fishery Co-operative Savings Insurance Corporation;
(iv) Policyholders Protection Corporations;
(v) The Government Pension Investment Fund;
(vi) The Banks' Shareholdings Purchase Corporation; and
(vii) the national governments of foreign states.

(Holidays Excluded from Notification Periods)
Article 37-5-2 The holidays specified by Cabinet Order, referred to in Article 271-3, paragraph (1) of the Act, shall be the days (excluding Sundays) specified in the items of Article 1, paragraph (1) of the Act on the Holidays of Administrative Organs (Act No. 91 of 1988).

(Standards for Short-Period, Large Volume Transfers)
Article 37-5-3 The standards specified by Cabinet Order for a case where a large number of voting rights have been transferred within in a short period, referred to in Article 271-4, paragraph (2) of the Act, shall be that the new Proportion of Voting Rights Held (meaning the Proportion of Voting Rights Held as defined in Article 271-3, paragraph (1), item (i) of the Act; hereinafter the same shall apply in this Article) that is to be detailed in the Statement of Changes set forth in that paragraph has come to be less than half of the highest Proportion of Voting Rights Held, among the Proportions of Voting Rights Held (limited to proportions calculated as of a record date that falls on or after the day sixty days prior to the new record date for the calculation of the new Proportion of Voting Rights Held, and proportions calculated as of a record date that falls on or before the day immediately preceding the day sixty days prior to said new record date whose record date is the closest to the sixty days prior to said new record date) that were detailed or was required to have been have been detailed in the Statement of Insurance Company Voting Right Holdings (meaning the Statement of Insurance Company Voting Right Holdings as set forth in Article 271-3, paragraph (1) of Article 271-5, paragraph (1) of the Act) in connection with the relevant Statement of Changes or in any other Statement of Changes (meaning a Statement of Changes as set forth in Article 271-4, paragraph (1) or Article 271-5, paragraph (2) of the Act) in connection with the relevant Statement of Insurance Company Voting Right Holdings, and that it has decreased by greater than five percent from said highest proportion.

(Transactions and Acts That Require Authorization under Article 271-10, Paragraph (1) of the Insurance Business Act)
Article 37-5-4 The transactions or acts specified by Cabinet Order, referred to in Article 271-10, paragraph (1), item (iii) of the Act, shall be as follows:
(i) acquisition of voting rights in Companies, etc. (meaning Companies, etc. as defined in Article 2-2, paragraph (1), item (ii) of the Act) other than Insurance Companies, by a person who wishes to become a holder of said voting rights (exclud-

ing the acquisition of shares or equity interests due to the exercise of a security interest, and also excluding acquisition due to any other grounds specified by Cabinet Office Ordinance);
(ii) a merger to which a company that wishes to become the holder of voting rights (hereinafter referred to as a "Specified Company" in this Article) is a party, in which said Specified Company survives;
(iii) a company split to which a Specified Company is a party (limited to a company split in which the Specified Company causes its business to be succeeded to in part); and
(iv) the transfer of a part of business by such Specified Company.

(Replacement of Terms Concerning the Major Foreign Shareholders of an Insurance Company)
Article 37-5-5 The technical replacement of terms for applying the provisions of the Act to the Major Foreign Shareholders of an Insurance Company (meaning the Major Foreign Shareholders of an Insurance Company under Article 271-17 of the Act; the same shall apply hereinafter) pursuant to the provisions of Article 271-17 of the Act, shall be as set forth in the following table:

Provisions of the Insurance Business Act whose terms are to be replaced	Original terms	Terms to replace the original terms
Article 333, paragraph (1)	the director, executive officer, accounting advisor or the member who carries out the duties thereof, the company auditor, manager, member who administers the business operations, or the liquidator	the director, executive officer, accounting advisor or the member who carries out the duties thereof, the company auditor, representative, manager, member who administers the business operations, or the liquidator, or a person in a position similar to any of these

(Transactions and Acts That Require Authorization under Article 271-18, paragraph (1) of Insurance Business Act)
Article 37-5-6 The transactions and acts specified by Cabinet Order, referred to in Article 271-18, paragraph (1), item (iii) of the Act, shall be as follows:
(i) acquisition by the relevant company or its Subsidiary Company of voting rights in a company other than an Insurance Company (excluding the acquisition of shares or equity interests due to the exercise of a security interest, and also excluding acquisition due to any other grounds specified by Cabinet Office Ordinance);
(ii) a merger to which the relevant company is a party, and in which said company survives;
(iii) a company split to which the relevant company is a party (limited to a company split in which the company causes its business to be succeeded to in part); and
(iv) the transfer of a part of business by the relevant company.

(Company Splits Involving Insurance Holding Companies That Do Not Require Authorization from the Prime Minister)
Article 37-5-7 (1) The types of company split specified by Cabinet Order, referred to in

Article 271-31, paragraph (2) of the Act, shall be the following types of company split (limited to a company split in which the relevant company succeeds to a part of business or causes a part of business to be succeeded to; hereinafter the same shall apply in this Article):

(i) a company split in which the amount of assets or liabilities to be transferred is not more than one-twentieth of the amount of total assets or total liabilities of the relevant Insurance Holding Company; or

(ii) a company split in which the amount of assets or liabilities to be succeeded to is not more than one-twentieth of the amount of total assets or total liabilities of the relevant Insurance Holding Company (excluding the cases specified in the following sub-items).

(a) a company split in which the amount specified by Cabinet Office Ordinance as the amount of obligations of the Splitting Company in an Absorption-type Company Split (meaning a Splitting Company in an Absorption-type Company Split as defined in Article 758, item (i) of the Companies Act; hereinafter the same shall apply in this item) that are to be succeeded to by the relevant Insurance Holding Company (referred to as "Obligations Succeeded to" in item (b)) exceeds the amount specified by Cabinet Office Ordinance as the amount of assets of the Splitting Company in an Absorption-type Company Split that are to be succeeded to by the relevant Insurance Holding Company (referred to as "Assets Succeeded to" in item (b)); or

(b) a company split in which the book value of the monies, etc. to be delivered from the Insurance Holding Company to the Splitting Company in an Absorption-type Company Split (excluding the Shares, etc. (meaning the Shares, etc. as set forth in Article 107, paragraph (2), item (ii), sub-item (e) of the Companies Act) in the relevant Insurance Holding Company) exceeds the Assets Succeeded to less the Obligations Succeeded to.

(2) For the purpose of application of the provisions of the preceding paragraph, the amount of assets (excluding assets as set forth in sub-item (a), item (ii) of that paragraph; hereinafter the same shall apply in this paragraph) or liabilities, or the amount of total assets or total liabilities as referred to in that paragraph shall be based on the book value (for assets or liabilities to be succeeded to in a company split as referred to in item (ii) of that paragraph, meaning the book value to be assigned upon such company split) immediately prior to the company split.

(Transfers and Acquisitions of Business Involving an Insurance Holding Company That Do Not Require Authorization from the Prime Minister)

Article 37-6 (1) The transfers and acquisitions of business specified by Cabinet Order, referred to in Article 271-31, paragraph (3) of the Act, shall be transfers and acquisitions of business specified in the following items:

(i) a transfer of a part of business in which the amount of assets or liabilities to be transferred incidental thereto is not more than one-twentieth of the amount of total assets or total liabilities of the relevant Insurance Holding Company; and

(ii) a transfer of a part of business in which the amount of assets or the liabilities to be acquired incidental thereto is not more than one-twentieth of the amount of total assets or total liabilities of the relevant Insurance Holding Company.

(2) For the purpose of application of the provisions of the preceding paragraph, the amount of assets or liabilities, or the amount of total assets or total liabilities as referred to in that paragraph shall be based on the book value as of the time immediately prior to the implementation of the transfer for a transfer of business referred to in item (i) of that paragraph, or based on the book value (with regard to assets or lia-

bilities to be acquired, meaning the book value to be assigned upon the implementation of the acquisition) as of the time immediately prior to the acquisition for an acquisition of business referred to in item (ii) of that paragraph.

(Replacement of Terms for a Foreign Holding Company Whose Subsidiaries Include an Insurance Company)

Article 37-7 The technical replacement of terms for applying the provisions of the Act to a Holding Company whose Subsidiaries include an Insurance Company and that was incorporated in accordance with the laws and regulations of a foreign state (hereinafter referred to as a "Foreign Holding Company Whose Subsidiaries Include an Insurance Company") pursuant to the provisions of Article 271-17 of the Act as applied mutatis mutandis pursuant to Article 271-20 of that Act, shall be as set forth in the following table:

Provisions of the Insurance Business Act whose terms are to be replaced	Original terms	Terms to replace the original terms
Article 271-30, paragraph (1)	its articles of incorporation	its articles of incorporation or any other provisions equivalent thereto
	its directors, executive officers, accounting advisors or company auditors	its directors, executive officers or company auditors or any person in a position similar to any of the aforementioned positions
Article 271-32, paragraph (2), item (vi)	capital	stated capital or contribution
Article 317, item (vii)	the director, executive officer, accounting advisor, or company auditor	the director, executive officer, accounting advisor, or company auditor or any person in a position similar to any of these
Article 333, paragraph (1)	the director, executive officer, accounting advisor or the member who carries out the duties thereof, the company auditor, manager or liquidator	the director, executive officer, accounting advisor or the member who carries out the duties thereo, the company auditor, manager or liquidator, or any person in a position similar to any of these
	the director, executive officer, accounting advisor or the member who carries out the duties thereof, the company auditor, manager, member who administers the business operations, or the liquidator	the director, executive officer, accounting advisor or the member who carries out the duties thereof, the company auditor, manager, member who administers the business operations, or the liquidator, or any person in a position similar to any of these

(Special Provisions on the Due Date for the Filing of Notifications by a Foreign Specified Holding Company)

Article 37-8 Notwithstanding the provisions of Article 27-18, paragraph (2) of the Act, where a Specified Holding Company as referred to in that paragraph is a Foreign Holding Company Whose Subsidiaries Include an Insurance Company, said Foreign Holding Company Whose Subsidiaries Include an Insurance Company shall, within six months from the end of the business year that includes the day on which the grounds specified in that paragraph have occurred, notify the Commissioner of the Financial Services Agency of the particulars specified in that paragraph; provided, however, that where, due to the laws and regulations or practices of its home state (meaning the State that has enacted the laws and regulations governing the incorporation of the Foreign Holding Company Whose Subsidiaries Include an Insurance Company) that are applicable to the preparation of business accounting books or any other justifiable reasons, it is unable to file the relevant notification within the six-month period, the due date may be extended, subject to the approval of the Commissioner of the Financial Services Agency.

(Scope of a Parent Financial Institution, etc. and Subsidiary Financial Institution, etc.)

Article 37-9 (1) The person specified by Cabinet Order, referred to in Article 271-21-2, paragraph (2) of the Act, shall be as follows:
(i) the Parent Juridical Person, etc. of the relevant Insurance Holding Company;
(ii) any Subsidiary, etc. of the Parent Juridical Person, etc. of the relevant Insurance Holding Company (excluding the Insurance Holding Company itself and juridical persons set forth in the preceding item and item (i) of paragraph (3));
(iii) any Affiliated Juridical Person, etc. of the Parent Juridical Person, etc. of the relevant Insurance Holding Company (excluding a juridical person set forth in item (ii) of paragraph (3));
(iv) the following company, partnership, or other business entity equivalent thereto (including equivalent entities in foreign states, and excluding the Insurance Holding Company itself and the juridical persons specified in the preceding three items and the items of paragraph (3); hereinafter referred to as a "Juridical Person, etc." in this item) that is associated with the Specified Individual Shareholder of the relevant Insurance Holding Company:
  (a) a Juridical Person, etc. (including its Subsidiary, etc. and Affiliated Juridical Person, etc.) in which the relevant Specified Individual Shareholder holds voting rights that are greater than fifty percent of All Shareholders' Voting Rights, etc. ; or
  (b) a Juridical Person, etc. in which the relevant Specified Individual Shareholder holds voting rights that are at least twenty percent and up to fifty percent of All Shareholders' Voting Rights, etc.
(2) The person conducting financial business that is specified by Cabinet Order, referred to in Article 271-21-2, paragraph (2) of the Act, shall be any person specified in the items of paragraph (2) of Article 13-8.
(3) The person specified by Cabinet Order, referred to in Article 271-21-2, paragraph (3) of the Act, shall be as follows:
(i) any Subsidiary, etc. of the relevant Insurance Holding Company; and
(ii) any Affiliated Juridical Person, etc. of the relevant Insurance Holding Company.
(4) The person conducting financial business that is specified by Cabinet Order, referred to in Article 271-21-2, paragraph (3) of the Act, shall be any person specified in Article 13-8, paragraph (2), items (i) to (iii) inclusive, and items (x) and (xi).

Section 2　Special Provisions on Low-Cost, Short-Term Insurers

(Standards for Insurance Premiums Received by Low-Cost, Short-Term Insurers)
Article 38　The standard specified by Cabinet Order, referred to in Article 272, paragraph (2) of the Act, shall be that the amount of Annual Insurance Premiums Collected (meaning the total amount of insurance premiums that have been collected or that it has been determined will be collected in a business year (if the amount of insurance premiums include an amount that already has been or that will be refunded, the amount after deducting such amount; the same shall apply in Article 38-4, item (ii)), reinsurance refunds, and any other amount specified by Cabinet Office Ordinance, less the total of the amounts of reinsurance premiums and cancellation refunds that have been paid or that it has been determined will be paid in the relevant business year) for the previous business year is five billion yen.

(Amount of Stated Capital, etc. of a Low-Cost, Short-Term Insurer That Requires an Accounting Auditor's Audit)
Article 38-2　The amount specified by Cabinet Order, referred to in Article 272-4, paragraph (1), item (i), sub-item (a) of the Act, shall be three hundred million yen.

(Amount of Stated Capital, etc. of a Low-Cost, Short-Term Insurer That Is Required for the Protection of the Policyholders, etc.)
Article 38-3　The amount specified by Cabinet Order, referred to in Article 272-4, paragraph (1), item (ii) of the Act, shall be ten million yen.

(Amount to Be Deposited by Low-Cost, Short-Term Insurers)
Article 38-4　The amount specified by Cabinet Order, referred to in Article 272-5, paragraph (1) of the Act, shall be the amount specified in the following items, in accordance with the categories set forth in each of said items:
(i) for the period from the day on which business commences to the day on which four months have elapsed since the last day of the first business year: ten million yen
(ii) for the period from the day on which four months have elapsed from the day on which each business year begins (excluding the first business year; hereinafter the same shall apply in this item) (such day shall be referred to as the "Reference Date" in the following Article and Article 38-8) to the day on which four months have elapsed since the last day of the relevant business year: ten million yen, plus the product of the amount of the Annual Insurance Premiums Collected (meaning the total of the amount of insurance premiums that have been collected or that it has been determined will be collected in a business year, less the total of the amount of reinsurance premiums and cancellation refunds that have been paid or that it has been determined will be paid in the relevant business year) for the business year immediately prior to the relevant business year and the ratio specified by Cabinet Office Ordinance (if this results in an amount that includes a value of less than one million yen, such a value shall be rounded off).

(Terms and Conditions of a Contract That Wholly or Partially Replaces a Deposit)
Article 38-5　Where a Low-Cost, Short-Term Insurer concludes a contract as set forth in Article 272-5, paragraph (3) of the Act, it shall have a Bank or other type of financial institution specified by Cabinet Office Ordinance as the other party thereto, and

the terms and conditions thereunder shall satisfy the following requirements:
 (i) that, when any of the cases set forth in the following come to apply, the deposit in connection with the order issued by the Prime Minister pursuant to the provisions of Article 272-5, paragraph (4) of the Act (hereinafter simply referred to as the "Order" in this item) will be deposited without delay on behalf of the Low-Cost, Short-Term Insurer;
  (a) where an Order has been issued within the period from the Low-Cost, Short-Term Insurer's business commencement date or the Reference Date, to the day immediately prior to the first Reference Date that falls after either of the aforementioned dates; and
  (b) where the Low-Cost, Short-Term Insurer, even after the first Reference Date that falls after either of the other dates referred to in sub-item (a), has failed to make the deposit under Article 272-5, paragraph (1) of the Act (including conclusion of a contract as set forth in paragraph (3) of that Article), when the other party to said contract has been issued an Order to make the deposit.
 (ii) that the contract will be effective for a period of one year or longer; and
 (iii) that the contract may not be cancelled and the terms and conditions thereunder may not be amended, unless this is done with the approval from the Commissioner of the Financial Services Agency.

(Procedures for the Fulfillment of Rights)
Article 38-6 (1) A person who holds the rights set forth in Article 272-5, paragraph (6) of the Act (hereinafter simply referred to as the "Rights" in this Article and the following Article) may file a petition for the fulfillment of those Rights with the Commissioner of the Financial Services Agency.
(2) Where a petition set forth in the preceding paragraph has been filed and where the Commissioner of the Financial Services Agency finds the petition to have reasonable grounds, he/she shall issue a public notice notifying persons who have a Right to the monies deposited pursuant to the provisions of Article 272-5, paragraph (1), (2), (4) or (8) of the Act that they must report their Rights within a fixed period of time not shorter than sixty days and that they will be excluded from the distribution process if they fail to report their Rights within that period, and he/she shall also notify the person who filed the petition under the preceding paragraph (hereinafter referred to as the "Petitioner" in the following paragraph and paragraph (4)) and the Low-Cost, Short-Term Insurer for which said deposit was made (where the Low-Cost, Short-Term Insurer has concluded a contract under Article 272-5, paragraph (3) of the Act, the counterparty to said contract shall be included; the same shall apply in paragraphs (4) and (5)) to that effect.
(3) Once the public notice under the preceding paragraph has been given, even in the event that the Petitioner withdraws his/her petition, this shall not prevent the procedures for the fulfillment of the Rights from proceeding.
(4) The Commissioner of the Financial Services Agency shall assess the Rights without delay after the period set forth in paragraph (2) has elapsed. In this case, the Commissioner of the Financial Services Agency shall give public notice of the date and place and notify the Low-Cost, Short-Term Insurer of such information, in advance, and afford the Petitioner, any person who has reported his/her Rights within the designated period, and the Low-Cost, Short-Term Insurer an opportunity to introduce evidence and to express their opinions as to the existence of the Rights and the amount of the claims secured by such Rights.
(5) The Commissioner of the Financial Services Agency shall, without delay, prepare a distribution list based on the results of the assessment under the preceding para-

graph, put such list on public notice, and shall notify the Low-Cost, Short-Term Insurer thereof.

(6) Any distribution shall be implemented in accordance with the distribution list set forth in the preceding paragraph, after eighty days have elapsed since the public notice was given under the preceding paragraph.

(7) Where any securities have been deposited pursuant to the provisions of Article 272-5, paragraph (9) of the Act, and where it is necessary for fulfillment of the Rights, the Commissioner of the Financial Services Agency may realize such securities. In this case, the expenses incurred in relation to the realization of such securities shall be deducted from the proceeds of the realization.

(Recovery of Deposits)
Article 38-7 (1) A person who has deposited monies pursuant to the provisions of Article 272-5, paragraph (10) of the Act (hereinafter referred to as the "Depositor" in the following paragraph) may, where any of the items of paragraph (10) of that Article applies, file a petition for the recovery of the deposit under that paragraph (hereinafter referred to as the "Recovery of the Deposit" in this Article) with the Commissioner of the Financial Services Agency; provided, however, that this shall not apply to the period during which the procedures for fulfillment of the Rights under the preceding Article are still pending.

(2) Where the petition under the preceding paragraph has been filed, and where, in addition to the Depositor who has filed said petition, there is any other Depositor in connection to such deposit, the petition for the recovery of the deposit shall be deemed to have been filed by said other Depositor as well.

(3) Where a petition set forth in paragraph (1) has been filed, the Commissioner of the Financial Services Agency shall issue a public notice notifying persons who have a Right to the deposited monies that they must report their Rights within a fixed period of time not shorter than sixty days and that they will be excluded from the distribution process if they fail to report their Rights within that period, and he/she shall also notify the party that formerly was the Low-Cost, Short-Term Insurer for which said deposit was made (where the relevant party has concluded a contract under Article 272-5, paragraph (3) of the Act, the counterparty to said contract shall be included) to that effect.

(4) Where no Rights have been reported within the period specified in the preceding paragraph, the Commissioner of the Financial Services Agency shall approve the Recovery of the Deposit.

(5) The provisions of paragraphs (4) to (6) inclusive of the preceding Article shall apply mutatis mutandis to where any Rights have been within the period specified in paragraph (3). In such case, the terms specified in the middle column of the following table as referred to in the provisions specified in the left column thereof shall be deemed to be replaced with the terms as respectively set forth in the right column thereof.

Article 38-6, paragraph (4)	paragraph (2)	paragraph (3) of the following Article
	notify the Low-Cost, Short-Term Insurance Provider of such information, and, afford the Petitioner, any person	notify the person who formerly was the Low-Cost, Short-Term Insurance Provider for which the deposit was made (where such a person has concluded a contract

		under Article 272-5, paragraph (3) of the Act, the counterparty to said contract shall be included; hereinafter referred to as the "Parties Relevant to the Deposit" in this paragraph and the following paragraph), and afford any person
	and the Low-Cost, Short-Term Insurance Provider	and the Parties Relevant to the Deposit
Article 38-6, paragraph (5)	the Low-Cost, Short-Term Insurance Provider	the Parties Relevant to the Deposit

(6) Where any Rights have been reported within the period set forth in paragraph (3), the Commissioner of the Financial Services Agency shall approve Recovery of the Deposit, only to the extent of the amount remaining after completion of the procedures under paragraphs (4) to (6) inclusive of the preceding Article as applied mutatis mutandis pursuant to the preceding paragraphs, if any.

(Terms and Conditions under a Low-Cost, Short-Term Insurer's Liability Insurance Contract that is Substituted for Part of a Deposit)

Article 38-8 (1) Where a Low-Cost, Short-Term Insurer concludes a Low-Cost, Short-Term Insurers' Liability Insurance Contract as set forth in Article 272-6, paragraph (1) of the Act (hereinafter referred to as the "Liability Insurance Contract" in the following paragraph), it shall have a Non-Life Insurance Company (including a Foreign Non-Life Insurance Company, etc. and also including an Underwriting Member of a juridical person which has obtained a specified non-life insurance business license as referred to in Article 219, paragraph (5) of the Act; the same shall apply in Article 44, paragraph (1)) or any other party specified by Cabinet Office Ordinance as the other party thereto, and the terms and conditions thereunder shall satisfy the following requirements:

(i) the contract promises payment of the amount equivalent to all or part of the insurance proceeds payable by the Low-Cost, Short-Term Insurer, in the event of a shortage in funds to pay insurance proceeds;

(ii) the contract will remain in effect for a period of one year or longer starting from the Low-Cost, Short-Term Insurer's business commencement date or the Reference Date;

(iii) the contract may not be cancelled, and the terms and conditions thereunder may not be modified, unless this is done with the approval from the Commissioner of the Financial Services Agency; and

(iv) any other requirements specified by Cabinet Office Ordinance.

(2) Where a Low-Cost, Short-Term Insurer has concluded a Liability Insurance Contract, the amount that the Prime Minister may approve as the portion of the deposit that it need not deposit under Article 272-6, paragraph (1) of the Act shall have as its limit the amount equivalent to the amount to be deposited less ten million yen.

(Insurance Proceeds Per Policyholder)

Article 38-9 (1) The amount specified by Cabinet Order, referred to in Article 272-13, paragraph (1) of the Act, shall be ten million yen per insured; provided, however, that where the insurance to be underwritten for the insured includes Low-Incidence Insurance (meaning insurance specified in Article 1-6, item (vi) that is designated by the Cabinet Office Ordinance as being projected to have an especially low incidence of insured events; hereinafter the same shall apply in this Article), and where the total amount of the insurance proceeds per insured for said Low-Incidence Insurance and the total amount of the insurance proceeds per insured for any insurance other than the Low-Incidence Insurance is not more than ten million yen, each, such amount shall be twenty million yen.

(2) In the case referred to in the preceding paragraph, the aggregate number of insured persons under a single Policyholder may not exceed one hundred, and the total amount of insurance proceeds per insured, categorized in accordance with the insurance set forth in each of the items of Article 1-6, shall not exceed the amounts set forth in each of those items (where the insurance to be underwritten for the insured contains a Low-Incidence Insurance, item (vi) shall be excluded).

(Specified Related Parties of a Low-Cost, Short-Term Insurer)
Article 38-10 The parties to which the Low-Cost, Short-Term Insurer is specially related as specified by Cabinet Order, referred to in the main clause of Article 100-3 of the Act as applied mutatis mutandis pursuant to Article 272-13, paragraph (2) of the Act, shall be as follows:

(i) any Subsidiary Company of the relevant Low-Cost, Short-Term Insurer;

(ii) the Low-Cost, Short-Term Insurer's Major Shareholder (meaning a Low-Cost, Short-Term Insurer's Major Shareholder as defined in Article 272-34, paragraph (1) of the Act; hereinafter the same shall apply in this Article and Article 47-2, paragraphs (8) to (10) inclusive) who holds a number of voting rights in the relevant Low-Cost, Short-Term Insurer equal to or exceeding the Major Shareholder Threshold;

(iii) the Low-Cost, Short-Term Insurance Holding Company (meaning a Low-Cost, Short-Term Insurance Holding Company as defined in Article 272-37, paragraph (2) of the Act; hereinafter the same shall apply in this Article and Article 47-2, paragraphs (13) and (14)) whose Subsidiaries include the relevant Low-Cost, Short-Term Insurer;

(iv) any Subsidiary Company of the company specified in the preceding item (excluding the Low-Cost, Short-Term Insurer itself and the company specified in item (i));

(v) any Subsidiary, etc. of the relevant Low-Cost, Short-Term Insurer (excluding a company set forth in item (i));

(vi) the Parent Juridical Person, etc. whose Subsidiaries, etc. include the relevant Low-Cost, Short-Term Insurer (excluding persons set forth in items (ii) and (iii));

(vii) any Subsidiary, etc. of the Parent Juridical Person, etc. whose Subsidiaries include the relevant Low-Cost, Short-Term Insurer as its Subsidiary, etc. (excluding such Low-Cost, Short-Term Insurer itself and the persons set forth in the preceding items);

(viii) any Affiliated Juridical Person, etc. of the relevant Low-Cost, Short-Term Insurer;

(ix) any Affiliated Juridical Person, etc. of the Parent Juridical Person, etc. that has the relevant Low-Cost, Short-Term Insurer (excluding the juridical person set forth in the preceding item);

(x) the following company, partnership, or other type of business entity equivalent thereto (including an equivalent entity in a foreign state, and excluding the Low-Cost, Short-Term Insurer itself; hereinafter referred to as a "Juridical Person, etc." in this item) that is associated with a person who, from among the persons specified in item (ii), holds voting rights in the Low-Cost, Short-Term Insurer that

are greater than fifty percent of All Shareholders' Voting Rights in said Low-Cost, Short-Term Insurer (limited to an individual person; hereinafter referred to as a "Low-Cost, Short-Term Insurer's Specified Individual Major Shareholder" in this item):
(a) a Juridical Person, etc. (including its Subsidiary, etc. and Affiliated Juridical Person, etc.) in which the relevant Low-Cost, Short-Term Insurer's Specified Individual Major Shareholder holds voting rights that are greater than fifty percent of All Shareholders' Voting Rights, etc. ; or
(b) a Juridical Person, etc. in which the relevant Low-Cost, Short-Term Insurer's Specified Individual Major Shareholder holds voting rights that are at least twenty percent and up to fifty percent of All Shareholders' Voting Rights, etc.

(Insurance Contracts Concluded by a Low-Cost, Short-Term Insurer That Are Excluded from Portfolio Transfers)
Article 38-11 The insurance contracts specified by Cabinet Order, referred to in Article 135, paragraph (2) of the Act as applied mutatis mutandis pursuant to Article 272-29 of the Act, shall be as follows:
(i) an insurance contract under which an insured event has already occurred as of the time of the public notice under Article 137, paragraph (1) of the Act as applied mutatis mutandis pursuant to Article 272-29 of the Act (referred to as the "Public Notice" in the following item) (limited to a contract that expires upon the payment of insurance proceeds in connection with the insured event); and
(ii) an insurance contract whose term of coverage has already ended as of the time of the Public Notice (including an insurance contract that has been canceled in the middle of the term of coverage or one under which any other grounds for the termination thereof have occurred as of the Public Notice, and excluding an insurance contract set forth in the preceding item).

(Transactions and Acts Requiring Approval in Connection with Holders of a Number of Voting Rights in a Low-Cost, Short-Term Insurer Equal to or Exceeding the Major Shareholder Threshold)
Article 38-12 The transactions and acts specified by Cabinet Order, referred to in Article 272-31, paragraph (1), item (iii) of the Act, shall be as follows:
(i) acquisition of voting rights in a Company, etc. (meaning a Company, etc. as defined in Article 2-2, paragraph (1), item (ii) of the Act) other than a Low-Cost, Short-Term Insurer, by a person who wishes to become the holder of said voting rights (excluding the acquisition of shares or equity interests due to the exercise of a security interest, and also excluding acquisition due to any other grounds specified by Cabinet Office Ordinance);
(ii) a merger to which a company that wishes to become the holder of said voting rights (hereinafter referred to as a "Specified Company" in this Article) is a party, and where said Specified Company survives;
(iii) a company split to which the relevant Specified Company is a party (limited to a company split whereby the Specified Company causes part of its business to be succeeded to); and
(iv) the transfer of a part of business by the relevant Specified Company.

(Transactions and Acts That Require Approval in Connection with a Low-Cost, Short-Term Insurance Holding Company)
Article 38-13 The transactions and acts specified by Cabinet Order, referred to in Article 272-35, paragraph (1), item (iii) of the Act, shall be as follows:

(i) acquisition of voting rights in a company other than a Low-Cost, Short-Term Insurer, by the relevant company or its Subsidiary Company (excluding the acquisition of shares or equity interests due to the exercise of a security interest, and also excluding acquisition due to other grounds specified by Cabinet Office Ordinance);
(ii) a merger to which the relevant company is a party, and where said company survives;
(iii) a company split to which the relevant company is a party (limited to a company split in which said company causes a part of its business to be succeeded to); and
(iv) the transfer of a part of business by the relevant company.

(Replacement of Terms Concerning the Major Shareholder of a Foreign Low-Cost, Short-Term Insurer, etc.)
Article 38-14 The technical replacement of terms for applying the provisions of the Act to the Major Shareholder of a Foreign Low-Cost, Short-Term Insurer, etc. (meaning the Major Shareholder of a Foreign Low-Cost, Short-Term Insurer, etc. provided for in that Article) pursuant to the provisions of Article 272-41 of the Act, shall be as set forth in the following table:

Provisions of the Insurance Business Act whose terms are to be replaced	Original terms	Terms to replace the original terms
Article 272-36, paragraph (1), item (ii)	trade name	trade name or name
Article 272-36, paragraph (1), item (iii)	the amount of capital	the amount of stated capital or contribution
Article 272-36, paragraph (1), item (iv)	directors and company auditors	directors and company auditors, or any person holding position equivalent thereto
	directors and executive officers	directors and executive officers, or any person holding position equivalent thereto
Article 272-36, paragraph (2)	its articles of incorporation	its articles of incorporation or any other rules equivalent thereto
Article 271-30, paragraph (1) as applied mutatis mutandis pursuant to Article 272-40, paragraph (2)	its articles of incorporation	its articles of incorporation or any other rules equivalent thereto
	its directors, executive officers, accounting advisors or company auditors	its directors, executive officers, accounting advisors or company auditors or any person in a position similar to any of these
Article 272-42, paragraph (2), item (vi)	the amount of capital	the amount of stated capital or contribution
Article 317, item (vii)	the director, executive officer, accounting advisor, or company auditor	the director, executive officer, accounting advisor, or company auditor or any person in a posi-

		tion similar to any of these
Article 333, paragraph (1)	the director, executive officer, accounting advisor or the member who carries out the duties thereof, the company auditor, manager, member who administers the business operations, or the liquidator	the director, executive officer, accounting advisor or the member who carries out the duties thereof, the company auditor, representative, manager, member who administers the business operations, or the liquidator, or any person in a position similar to any of these
	the director, executive officer, accounting advisor or the member who carries out the duties thereof, the company auditor, manager or liquidator	the director, executive officer, accounting advisor or the member who carries out the duties thereof, the company auditor, manager or liquidator, or any person in a position similar to any of these
	the director, executive officer, accounting advisor or the member who carries out the duties thereof, a company auditor, manager, member who executes the business or liquidator	the director, executive officer, accounting advisor or the member who carries out the duties thereof, the company auditor, manager, member who administers the business operations, or the liquidator, or any person in a position similar to any of these

(Special Provisions on the Due Date for Notification by a Foreign Specified Low-Cost, Short-Term Insurance Holding Company)

Article 38-15 Notwithstanding the provisions of Article 272-35, paragraph (2) of the Act, where a Specified Low-Cost, Short-Term Insurance Holding Company referred to in that paragraph is a foreign Holding Company whose Subsidiaries include a Low-Cost, Short-Term Insurer, such foreign Holding Company whose Subsidiaries include the Low-Cost, Short-Term Insurer shall, within six months from the end of the business year containing the day on which the grounds specified in that paragraph have occurred, notify the Commissioner of the Financial Services Agency of the particulars specified in that paragraph; provided, however, that where, due to laws and regulations or practices of its own State (meaning the State that has enacted the laws and regulations governing the incorporation of the foreign Holding Company whose Subsidiaries include the relevant Low-Cost, Short-Term Insurer) that are applicable to its business accounting books or for any other justifiable reason, it is unable to file the relevant notification within the six-month period, the Due Date may be extended, subject to approval by the Commissioner of the Financial Services Agency.

Chapter III Insurance Solicitation

(Parties Eligible to Engage in Insurance Solicitation)

Article 39 Parties specified by Cabinet Order, referred to in Article 275, paragraph (1), item (i) of the Act, shall be as follows:

(i) Banks;

(ii) Long Term Credit Banks;
(iii) Shoko Chukin Bank Limited;
(iv) shinkin banks and federations of shinkin banks;
(v) labor banks and federations of labor banks;
(vi) Norinchukin Bank;
(vii) credit cooperatives and any federation of cooperatives that is engaged in business set forth in Article 9-9, paragraph (1), item (i) (Federations of Cooperatives) of the Small and Medium-Sized Enterprise Cooperatives Act;
(viii) agricultural cooperatives and any federation of agricultural cooperatives that is engaged in business set forth in Article 10, paragraph (1), item (iii) (Business) of the Agricultural Cooperatives Act;
(ix) fishery cooperatives engaged in business set forth in Article 11, paragraph (1), item (iv) (Types of Business) of the Fishery Cooperatives Act (Act No. 242 of 1948); federations of fishery cooperatives engaged in business set forth in Article 87, paragraph (1), item (iv) (Types of Business) of that Act; marine products processing cooperatives engaged in business set forth in Article 93, paragraph (1), item (ii) (Types of Business) of that Act; and federations of marine products processing cooperatives engaged in business set forth in Article 97, paragraph (1), item (ii) (Types of Business) of that Act.

(Insurance Contracts with Foreign Insurers Other Than a Foreign Insurance Company, etc., that Insurance Brokers, etc Are Permitted to Engage in Insurance Solicitation)
Article 39-2 The insurance contracts specified by Cabinet Order, referred to in Article 275, paragraph (1), item (iv) of the Act, shall be insurance contracts specified in Article 19, items (i) to (iii) inclusive and any other insurance contracts specified by Cabinet Office Ordinance.

(Registration Fees)
Article 39-3 (1) The amount specified by Cabinet Order, referred to in Article 281 of the Act, shall be as follows: 1,150 yen for a Life Insurance Agent; 1,700 yen for a Non-Life Insurance Representative; and 1,150 yen for a Low-Cost, Short-Term Insurance Agent.
(2) The fees set forth in the preceding paragraph shall be paid through the submission of a revenue stamp equivalent to the amount of the fees, which shall be affixed on the written application for registration; provided, however, that where a registration under Article 276 of the Act is being filed by means of an electromagnetic data processing system as set forth in Article 3, paragraph (1) of the Act on Use of Information and Communications Technology in Administrative Procedure (Act No. 151 of 2002) in accordance with the provisions of that paragraph, payments may be made in cash pursuant to the provisions of Cabinet Office Ordinance.

(Cases Excluded from Restrictions Imposed on Life Insurance Agents)
Article 40 The cases specified by Cabinet Order, referred to in Article 282, paragraph (3) of the Act, shall be as follows:
(i) cases in which, among a Life Insurance Agent and its employees (where the Life Insurance Agent is a juridical person (including an association or a foundation without a juridical personality but for which a representative or administrator has been appointed), this means its officers (including a representative or an administrator of an association or a foundation without a juridical personality) and employees) there is a person who has acquired knowledge, etc. that is required for

carrying out business in connection with Insurance Sales on behalf of two or more Affiliated Insurance Companies, etc. in an accurate and fair manner, or a person who has been specified by the Commissioner of the Financial Services Agency as a person who is qualified to manage such business in an appropriate manner;

(ii) cases in which the relevant Life Insurance Agent comes to have two or more Affiliated Insurance Companies, etc. by making a person specified by the Commissioner of the Financial Services Agency as a Life Insurance Company (including a Foreign Life Insurance Company, etc.) that is closely related to said Life Insurance Agent, its Affiliated Insurance Company, etc. , and where the relevant case has been specified by the Commissioner of the Financial Services Agency as a case in which said Life Insurance Agent is found to be in a position to provide services in connection with Insurance Solicitation it engages in on behalf of the two or more Affiliated Insurance Companies, etc. in an accurate and fair manner.

(Amount of Security Deposits)

Article 41 The amount of security deposit specified by Cabinet Order, referred to in Article 291, paragraph (2) of the Act, shall be forty million yen; provided, however, that on or after the day when three months has elapsed since the last day of an Insurance Broker's first business year, the amount of the security deposit for the period between the day on which three months have elapsed since the last day of the Insurance Broker's first business year (hereinafter referred to as the "Reference Date" in the following Article and Article 44) and the day when three months has elapsed since the day on which each of the relevant business years end shall be the amount equivalent to the total of fees, remuneration and other types of consideration received by the Insurance Broker in connection with brokerage for the conclusion of insurance contracts in the three years prior to the day immediately preceding the day on which each business year begins (if such total amount is less than forty million yen, the amount of the security deposit shall be forty million yen; and if the total amount exceeds eight hundred million yen, the amount of the security deposit shall be eight hundred million yen).

(Terms and Conditions of a Contract That Wholly or Partially Replaces a Deposit)

Article 42 Where an Insurance Broker concludes a contract as set forth in Article 291, paragraph (3) of the Act, it shall have a Bank or other type of financial institution specified by Cabinet Office Ordinance as the other party thereto, and the terms and conditions thereunder shall satisfy the following requirements:

(i) that, when any of the cases set forth in the following come to apply, the deposit in connection with the order issued by the Prime Minister pursuant to the provisions of Article 291, paragraph (4) of the Act (hereinafter simply referred to as the "Order" in this item) will be deposited without delay on behalf of such Insurance Broker:

(a) where an Order has been received within the period of time from the Insurance Broker's business commencement date or the Reference Date, to the date immediately prior to the first Reference Date that falls after either of the aforementioned dates;

(b) where the Insurance Broker, even after the first Reference Date that falls after either of the other dates referred to in sub-item (a), has failed to make the deposit under Article 291, paragraph (1) of the Act (including the conclusion of a contract as set forth in paragraph (3) of that Article), when the other party to said contract has been issued an Order to make the deposit.

(ii) that the contract may not be cancelled and that the terms thereof may not be amended, unless this is done with the approval from the Commissioner of the Financial Services Agency.

(Procedures for the Fulfillment of Rights)
Article 43 (1) A person who holds the rights set forth in Article 291, paragraph (6) of the Act (hereinafter simply referred to as the "Rights" in this Article and the following Article) may file a petition for the fulfillment of those Rights with the Commissioner of the Financial Services Agency.
(2) Where a petition set forth in the preceding paragraph has been filed and where the Commissioner of the Financial Services Agency finds the petition to have reasonable grounds, he/she shall issue a public notice notifying persons who have a Right to the amount deposited pursuant to the provisions of Article 291, paragraph (1), (2), or (8) of the Act that they must report their Rights within a fixed period of time not shorter than sixty days and that they will be excluded from the distribution process if they fail to report their Rights within that period, and he/she shall also notify the person who filed the petition under the preceding paragraph (hereinafter referred to as the "Petitioner" in the following paragraph and paragraph (4)) and the Insurance Broker for which said deposit was made (where the Insurance Broker has concluded a contract under Article 291, paragraph (3) of the Act, including the counterparty to said contract; the same shall apply in paragraphs (4) and (5)) to that effect.
(3) Once the public notice under the preceding paragraph has been given, even in the event that the Petitioner withdraws his/her petition, this shall not prevent the procedures for the fulfillment of the Rights from proceeding.
(4) The Commissioner of the Financial Services Agency shall assess the Rights without delay after the period set forth in paragraph (2) has elapsed. In this case, the Commissioner of the Financial Services Agency shall give public notice of the date and place and notify the Insurance Broker of such information, in advance, and afford the Petitioner, any person who has reported his/her Rights within the designated period, and the Insurance Broker an opportunity to introduce evidence and to express their opinions as to the existence of the Rights and the amount of the claims secured by such Rights.
(5) The Commissioner of the Financial Services Agency shall, without delay, prepare a distribution list based on the results of the assessment under the preceding paragraph, put such list on public notice, and notify the Insurance Broker thereof.
(6) Distribution shall be implemented in accordance with the distribution list set forth in the preceding paragraph, after eighty days have elapsed since the public notice was given under the preceding paragraph.
(7) Where the Commissioner of the Financial Services Agency is unable to locate the office of the Insurance Broker, he/she need not notify said Insurance Broker pursuant to paragraphs (2), (4) and (5).
(8) Where any securities have been deposited pursuant to the provisions of Article 291, paragraph (9) of the Act, and where it is necessary for fulfillment of the Rights, the Commissioner of the Financial Services Agency may realize such securities. In this case, the expenses incurred in connection to such realization of securities shall be deducted from the proceeds of the realization.

(Terms and Conditions of an Insurance Broker Liability Insurance Contract That Partially Replaces a Security Deposit)
Article 44 (1) Where an Insurance Broker concludes an Insurance Broker Liability Insurance Contract as set forth in Article 292, paragraph (1) of the Act (hereinafter re-

ferred to as a "Liability Insurance Contract" in the following paragraph), it shall have a Non-Life Insurance Company or any other party specified by Cabinet Office Ordinance as the other party thereto, and the terms and conditions thereunder shall satisfy the following requirements:

(i) that, where the Insurance Broker has incurred any liability to compensate for damages in connection with its intermediation for the conclusion of insurance contracts, losses it incurs through the compensation of damages that were due to specific grounds (referred to as "Losses Due to Specific Grounds" in the following item) will be covered; and

(ii) that, where the loss that will be covered is limited to where the amount of Loss Due to Specific Grounds exceeds a fixed amount of money and said covered loss will be the portion of the loss that is greater than that fixed amount of money, said fixed amount is not more than the amount specified by the Commissioner of the Financial Services Agency in consideration of the Insurance Broker's business status and the protection of Policyholders, etc. ;

(iii) that the contract will remain in effect for a period of one year or longer starting from the Insurance Broker's business commencement date or the Reference Date; and

(iv) that the contract may not be cancelled, and the terms and conditions thereunder may not be modified, unless this is done with the approval from the Commissioner of the Financial Services Agency; and

(v) any other requirements set forth by the Commissioner of the Financial Services Agency.

(2) Where an Insurance Broker has concluded a Compensation Liability Insurance Contract, the amount that the Prime Minister may approve as the portion of the security deposit that it need not deposit under Article 291, paragraph (1) of the Act shall have as its limit the amount equivalent to the amount to be deposited less forty million yen.

(Ways of Using Information and Communication Technology to Indicate the Name, etc. of an Insurance Broker)

Article 44-2 (1) Where, pursuant to the provisions of Article 296, paragraph (2) of the Act, an Insurance Broker seeks to provide the information set forth in that paragraph, it shall, in advance and pursuant to the provisions of Cabinet Office Ordinance, indicate to the customer the type and details of the means set forth in that paragraph that it will use (hereinafter referred to as "Electromagnetic Means" in this Article) and obtain consent therefrom in writing or by Electromagnetic Means.

(2) Where an Insurance Broker that has obtained the consent set forth in the preceding paragraph is notified in writing or by Electromagnetic Means to the effect that the customer refuses to be provided with the information by Electromagnetic Means, he/she shall not provide said customer with the information set forth in Article 296, paragraph (2) of the Act by Electromagnetic Means; provided, however, that this shall not apply where the customer has given his/her consent under the preceding paragraph again.

(Provision of Information by Use of Information and Communications Technology)

Article 44-3 (1) Where, pursuant to the provisions of Article 34-2, paragraph (4) of the Financial Instruments and Exchange Act as applied mutatis mutandis pursuant to Article 300-2 of the Act (including the cases where applied mutatis mutandis pursuant to Article 34-3, paragraph (3), Article 37-3, paragraph (2) and Article 37-4, paragraph

(2) of the Financial Instruments and Exchange Act; hereinafter the same shall apply in this Article) (such provisions shall be hereinafter referred to as the "Financial Instruments and Exchange Act as Applied Mutatis Mutandis" in this Article to Article 44-5 inclusive), an Insurance Company, etc. (meaning an Insurance Company, etc. as defined in Article 2-2, paragraph (1) of the Act; the same shall apply in the following paragraph, the following Article, Article 45, items (i) and (v) and Article 45-2), a Foreign Insurance Company, etc. , an Insurance Agent, or an Insurance Broker seeks to provide the information set forth in Article 34-2, paragraph (4) of the Financial Instruments and Exchange Act as Applied Mutatis Mutandis, it shall, in advance and pursuant to the provisions of Cabinet Office Ordinance, indicated to the recipient of such information the type and details of the means that it will use (hereinafter referred to as the "Electromagnetic Means") and obtain consent therefrom in writing or by Electromagnetic Means.

(2) Where an Insurance Company, etc. , Foreign Insurance Company, etc. , Insurance Agent or Insurance Broker that has obtained the consent set forth in the preceding paragraph is notified in writing or by Electromagnetic Means to the effect that such recipient refuses to be provided with the information by Electromagnetic Means, it shall not provide the recipient with the information set forth in Article 34-2, paragraph (4) of the Financial Instruments and Exchange Act as Applied Mutatis Mutandis by Electromagnetic Means; provided, however, that this shall not apply where the recipient has given his/her consent under that paragraph again.

(Acquisition of Agreement by Use of Information and Communications Technology)

Article 44-4 (1) Where, pursuant to the provisions of Article 34-3, paragraph (3) of the Financial Instruments and Exchange Act as Applied Mutatis Mutandis (including the cases where applied mutatis mutandis pursuant to Article 34-4, paragraph (4) of the Financial Instruments and Exchange Act as Applied Mutatis Mutandis; hereinafter the same shall apply in this Article), an Insurance Company, etc. , a Foreign Insurance Company, etc. , or an Insurance Broker seeks to obtain agreement by the method specified by Cabinet Office Ordinance that is referred to in Article 34-3, paragraph (3) of the Financial Instruments and Exchange Act as Applied Mutatis Mutandis (hereinafter referred to as "Electromagnetic Means" in this Article) in lieu of via the document set forth in paragraph (2) of that Article, it shall, in advance and pursuant to the provisions of Cabinet Office Ordinance, indicate the type and details of the Electromagnetic Means to the other party from whom it seeks to obtain agreement, and obtain consent therefrom in writing or by Electromagnetic Means.

(2) Where an Insurance Company, etc. , Foreign Insurance Company, etc. or Insurance Broker who has obtained the consent set forth in the preceding paragraph is notified in writing or by Electromagnetic Means to the effect that the other party refuses to give his/her agreement by Electromagnetic Means, it shall not obtain the agreement set forth in Article 34-3, paragraph (3) of the Financial Instruments and Exchange Act as Applied Mutatis Mutandis from the other party by Electromagnetic Means; provided, however, that this shall not apply where the other party has given his/her consent under the preceding paragraph again.

(Important Particulars That May Influence a Customer's Judgment)

Article 44-5 (1) The particulars specified by Cabinet Order, referred to in Article 37, paragraph (1), item (iii) of the Financial Instruments and Exchange Act as Applied Mutatis Mutandis, shall be as follows:

(i) particulars related to the fees, remuneration, or any other type of consideration

payable by a customer under Specified Insurance Contract (meaning a Specified Insurance Contract as defined in Article 300-2 of the Act; the same shall apply hereinafter), as specified by Cabinet Office Ordinance;
(ii) where, with regard to the conclusion of a Specified Insurance Contract by a customer, there is a risk of losses arising directly from a fluctuation in such indicators as the interest rate, the value of currencies, or quotations on a Financial Instruments Market, the following particulars:
 (a) the indicators; and
 (b) the fact that there is a risk of losses from fluctuations in the relevant indicators, and the reason therefor.
(iii) particulars specified by Cabinet Office Ordinance as those equivalent to the particulars specified in the preceding two items.
(2) Notwithstanding the provisions of the preceding paragraph, where the action specified in Article 37, paragraph (1) of the Financial Instruments and Exchange Act as Applied Mutatis Mutandis is to be implemented by means of broadcasting through the use of a Private Broadcaster's broadcasting facilities or by any other means specified by Cabinet Office Ordinance as equivalent thereto, the particulars specified by Cabinet Order that are referred to in Article 37, paragraph (1), item (iii) of the Financial Instruments and Exchange Act as Applied Mutatis Mutandis shall be as follows:
(i) where, with regard to the conclusion of a Specified Insurance Contract by a customer, there is a risk of losses arising directly from a fluctuation in such indicators as the interest rate, the value of currencies, or quotations on a Financial Instruments Market, such risk; and
(ii) particulars specified by Cabinet Office Ordinance as those equivalent to the particulars specified in the preceding item.

(Replacement of Terms in Provisions of the Financial Instruments and Exchange Act That Are Applied Mutatis Mutandis to the Conclusion of Specified Insurance Contracts, etc.)
Article 44-6 (1) Where, pursuant to the provisions of Article 300-2 of the Act, the provisions of Article 34 of the Financial Instruments and Exchange Act are applied mutatis mutandis to the conclusion of a Specified Insurance Contract by an Insurance Company, etc. , a Foreign Insurance Company, etc. , or an Insurance Broker or to the conclusion of a contract that has as its content intermediation for the conclusion of a Specified Insurance Contract thereby on behalf of the customer, the technical replacement of terms in those provisions shall be as set forth in the following table:

Provisions of the Financial Instruments and Exchange Act whose terms are to be replaced	Original terms	Terms to replace the original terms
Article 34	item (iv), paragraph (31) of that Article	Article 2, paragraph (31), item (iv)

(2) Where, pursuant to the provisions of Article 300-2 of the Act, the provisions of Article 37-3, paragraph (1) (excluding items (ii) and (vi)) of the Financial Instruments and Exchange Act are applied mutatis mutandis to the conclusion of a Specified Insurance Contract by an Insurance Company, etc. , a Foreign Insurance Company, etc. , an Insurance Agent, or an Insurance Broker or to its agency or intermediation therefor, the technical replacement of terms in such provision shall be as set forth in the following table:

Provisions of the Financial Instruments and Exchange Act whose terms are to be replaced	Original terms	Terms to replace the original terms
Article 37-3, paragraph (1), item (i)	address	address (for a Foreign Insurance Company, etc., the address of a Branch Office, etc. (meaning Brach Office, as defined in Article 185, paragraph (1) of the Insurance Business Act))

Chapter IV Miscellaneous Provisions

(Cases Where an Application for a Policy under an Insurance Contract May Not Be Withdrawn)
Article 45 The cases specified by Cabinet Order, referred to in Article 309, paragraph (1), item (vi) of the Act, shall be as follows:
(i) where the Applicant, etc. (meaning the Applicant, etc. as defined in Article 309, paragraph (1) of the Act; hereinafter the same shall apply in this Article), upon notifying the relevant Insurance Broker of the day of his/her visit in advance, visited the business office, office or any other facilities similar thereto (hereinafter referred to as the "Business Office, etc." in this item and the following item) of the Insurance Company, etc. , Foreign Insurance Company, etc. (including an Underwriting Member of a licensed specified juridical person; the same shall apply in item (v) and the following Article), Specified Insurance Agent (meaning a Specified Insurance Agent as defined in Article 276 of the Act; the same shall apply in Article 47-3, paragraphs (1) and (4)) or Insurance Broker (hereinafter collectively referred to as the "Insurer" in this Article); where the Applicant, etc. after having expressly indicated in such notice or at such visit that the purpose of his/her visit was to apply for a policy under an insurance contract, the Applicant, etc. applied for such a policy under an insurance contract at the relevant Business Office, etc.;
(ii) where the Applicant, etc. requested to apply for a policy under an insurance contract at a place designated by himself/herself (excluding the Business Office, etc. of the Insurer, and also excluding his/her residence), when he/she has applied for such a policy under an insurance contract;
(iii) where the Applicant, etc. has applied for a policy under an insurance contract by mail or any other means specified by Cabinet Office Ordinance;
(iv) where the Applicant, etc. has paid insurance premiums under an insurance contract or made any other payment equivalent thereto, by means of remittance to the deposit account or savings account of the Insurer (excluding where such Applicant, etc. made such payment at the request of the Insurer that is the other party to the insurance contract, the Insurer that engaged in Insurance Solicitation for the relevant insurance contract, or to the officer or employee thereof);
(v) where the Applicant, etc. applied for a policy under an insurance contract that comes into effect contingent upon a diagnostic examination by a medical doctor designated by the Insurance Company, etc. or a Foreign Insurance Company, etc., when such diagnostic examination has been completed;
(vi) where the insurance contract falls under the category of a workers' asset saving contract, workers' pension saving contract, or workers' housing fund saving con-

tract as defined in Article 6 of the Workers' Property Accumulation Promotion Act;

(vii) where the insurance contract is intended to provide a security for the performance of obligations under a monetary loan agreement, lease agreement, or any other types of agreement; and

(viii) where the insurance contract is intended as the renewal (limited to renewals for the purpose of effecting any change to insurance benefits such as the insurance proceeds or term of coverage) or extension of any insurance contract that has already been concluded (hereinafter referred to as an "Existing Contract" in this item), or for amending the insurance proceeds, term of coverage, or any other terms and conditions under the Existing Contract.

(Ways of Using Information and Communications Technology to Withdraw an Application for a Policy under an Insurance Contract)

Article 45-2 (1) Where, pursuant to the provisions of Article 309, paragraph (2) of the Act, an Insurance Company, etc. or Foreign Insurance Company seeks to provide the information set forth in that paragraph, it shall, in advance and pursuant to the provisions of Cabinet Office Ordinance, indicate to the Applicant, etc. the type and details of the means it will use as set forth in the first sentence of that paragraph (hereinafter referred to as "Electromagnetic Means" in this Article) and obtain consent therefrom in writing or by Electromagnetic Means.

(2) Where an Insurance Company, etc. or a Foreign Insurance Company, etc. that has obtained the consent set forth in the preceding paragraph is notified in writing or by Electromagnetic Means to the effect that the Applicant, etc. refuses to be provided with information by Electromagnetic Means, it shall not provide the Applicant, etc. with the information set forth in Article 309, paragraph (2) of the Act by Electromagnetic Means; provided, however, that this shall not apply where the Applicant, etc. has given his/her consent under the preceding paragraph again.

(Authority Excluded from the Scope of Authority Delegated to the Commissioner of Financial Services Agency)

Article 46 The authority specified by Cabinet Order, referred to in Article 313, paragraph (1) of the Act, shall be as follows:

(i) licensing under Article 3, paragraph (1), Article 185, paragraph (1) and Article 219, paragraph (1) of the Act;

(ii) rescission of licenses granted under Article 3, paragraph (1), Article 185, paragraph (1) and Article 219, paragraph (1) of the Act, as effected pursuant to the provisions of Article 133, Article 134, Article 205, Article 206, Article 231 and Article 232 of the Act;

(iii) authorization under Article 265-9, paragraph (2), Article 271-18, paragraph (1) and the proviso to Article 271-18, paragraph (3) of the Act;

(iv) rescission of authorization under Article 265-9, paragraph (2), Article 271-18, paragraph (1) and the proviso to Article 271-18, paragraph (3) of the Act, as effected pursuant to the provisions of Article 265-47 and Article 271-30, paragraph (1) of the Act;

(v) public notice under the first sentence of Article 189, the first sentence of Article 222, Article 237 (limited to the portion involving item (ii)) and Article 274 (limited to the portion involving items (ii) and (vi)) of the Act; and

(vi) notice under Article 311-3, paragraph (1) of the Act (limited to the portions involving item (i) (excluding the portion involving the registration under Article 272, paragraph (1) of the Act), item (ii) (limited to the portion involving the authorization under Article 271-18, paragraph (1) and the proviso to Article 271-18 of the Act), item (iv) (excluding the portion involving rescission of the registration under Article 272, paragraph (1) of the Act) and item (v) (limited to the portion involving rescission of authorization under Article 271-10, paragraph (1) or the proviso to Article 271-10, paragraph (2) of the Act and rescission of authorization under Article 271-18, paragraph (1) and the proviso to Article 271-18, paragraph (3) of the Act)).

(Delegation of Authority Over Insurance Companies, etc. to the Directors-General of Local Finance Bureaus and Other Officials)
Article 47 (1) Within the authority delegated to the Commissioner of the Financial Services Agency under Article 313, paragraph (1) of the Act and the authority of the Commissioner of the Financial Services Agency conferred under this Cabinet Order (hereinafter referred to as the "Commissioner's Authority"), the following authority may be exercised by the Director-General of the Local Finance Bureau with jurisdiction over the place in which the Head Office, etc. of the Insurance Company, Foreign Insurance Company, etc. , or Licensed Specified Juridical Person or its Underwriting Members (hereinafter referred to as the "Insurance Company, etc." in the following paragraph and paragraph (3)) is located (or by the Director-General of the Fukuoka Local Finance Branch Bureau, where the relevant location is within the district under the jurisdiction of the Fukuoka Local Finance Branch Bureau):
(i) orders for the submission of reports and materials under Article 128, paragraphs (1) and (2), Article 200, paragraphs (1) and (2) and Article 226, paragraphs (1) and (2) of the Act;
(ii) questioning and on-site inspections under Article 129, paragraphs (1) and (2), Article 201, paragraphs (1) and (2) and Article 227, paragraphs (1) and (2) of the Act; and
(iii) orders for the submission of reports and materials, questioning, and on-site inspections as set forth in Article 42, paragraph (1) of the Trust Business Act as applied mutatis mutandis pursuant to Article 99, paragraph (8) of the Act.
(2) The authority referred to in the items of the preceding paragraph in relation to a Business Office, etc. (meaning the business office, office, or any other facilities of an Insurance Company other than its Head Office, etc.; a Subsidiary, etc. (meaning a Subsidiary, etc. as defined in Article 128, paragraph (2) of the Act; and including its facilities) of an Insurance Company; a person that an Insurance Company has entrusted with its business (including its facilities); a Specified Related Party as defined in Article 194 of the Act (including its facilities); a person that a Foreign Insurance Company, etc. has entrusted with business in Japan (including its facilities); a person who a Licensed Specified Juridical Person, etc. as defined in Article 226, paragraph (2) of the Act (including its facilities) has entrusted with its business; a person who conducts business transactions with a Life Insurance Company, etc. Engaged in Insurance-Proceed Trust Services (including its facilities); or a Holding Company (meaning a Holding Company as defined in Article 5, paragraph (2), item (ix) of the Trust Business Act, and including its facilities) whose Subsidiaries include a Life Insurance Company, etc. Engaged in Insurance-Proceed Trust Services; hereinafter the same shall apply in this paragraph and the following paragraph) may, in addition to being exercised by the Director-General of the Local Finance Bureau or the Director-General of the Fukuoka Local Finance Branch Bureau set forth in the preceding paragraph, be exercised by the Director-General of the Local Finance Bureau with jurisdiction over the place in which said Business Office, etc. is located (or over the domicile or residence, where the person who engages in business transactions with a

Life Insurance Company, etc. Engaged in Insurance-Proceed Trust Services is an individual person; hereinafter the same shall apply in this paragraph) (or by the Director-General of the Fukuoka Local Finance Branch Bureau, where the relevant location is within the district under the jurisdiction of the Fukuoka Local Finance Branch Bureau).
(3) When the Director-General of the Local Finance Bureau or the Director-General of the Fukuoka Local Finance Branch Bureau has ordered the Business Office, etc. of an Insurance Company, etc. to submit a report and materials or has conducted questioning or on-site inspections (hereinafter collectively referred to as "Inspection, etc." in this paragraph) at such a Business Office, etc. pursuant to the provisions of the preceding paragraph, and where he/she finds it necessary to conduct an Inspection, etc. at the Head Office, etc. or at any Business Office, etc. other than the first-mentioned Business Office, etc. of such Insurance Company, etc. , he/she may conduct such an Inspection, etc. at the Head Office, etc. or at such other Business Office, etc.
(4) The following Commissioner's Authority shall be delegated to the Director-General of the Local Finance Bureau with jurisdiction over the place in which the principal office (for an individual person, his/her domicile or residence; hereinafter referred to as "Principal Office, etc." in this Article and the following Article) of the Large-Volume Holder of Insurance Company Voting Rights (meaning a Large-Volume Holder of Insurance Company Voting Rights as defined in Article 271-3, paragraph (1) of the Act; hereinafter the same shall apply in this Article) is located (or to the Director-General of the Fukuoka Local Finance Branch Bureau, where the relevant location is within the district under the jurisdiction of the Fukuoka Local Finance Branch Bureau); provided, however, that the foregoing shall not preclude the Commissioner of the Financial Services Agency from exercising the authority specified in items (iii) and (iv), himself/herself, excluding the Commissioner's Authority set forth in items (i) and (ii) in relation to the holder of a number of voting rights in the Insurance Company equal to or exceeding the Major Shareholder Threshold or in relation to a person required to file a notification under Article 271-10, paragraph (3) and Article 271-32, paragraph (1), item (iii) of the Act.
(i) acceptance of documents and notifications under Article 271-3, paragraph (1), Article 271-4, paragraphs (1), (3) and (4), and Article 271-5, paragraphs (1) and (2) of the Act;
(ii) orders for the submission of amended reports under Article 271-6 and Article 271-7 of the Act, and hearings related to such orders;
(iii) orders for the submission of reports and materials under Article 271-8 of the Act; and
(iv) questioning and on-site inspections under Article 271-9, paragraph (1) of the Act.
(5) The authority specified in items (iii) and (iv) of the preceding paragraph may, in addition to being exercised by the Director-General of the Local Finance Bureau or the Director-General of the Fukuoka Local Finance Branch Bureau set forth in the preceding paragraph, be exercised by the Director-General of the Local Finance Bureau with jurisdiction over the place in which the head office or principal office of the Insurance Company or Insurance Holding Company with which the Large-Volume Holder of Insurance Company Voting Rights is connected, is located (or by the Director-General of the Fukuoka Local Finance Branch Bureau, where the relevant location is within the district under the jurisdiction of the Fukuoka Local Finance Branch Bureau).
(6) The authority specified in items (iii) and (iv) of paragraph (4) in relation to an office or other facility other than the Principal Office, etc. of the Large-Volume Holder of

Insurance Company Voting Rights (hereinafter referred to as "Secondary Office, etc." in this paragraph, paragraph (12) of this Article and paragraph (9) of the following Article) may, in addition to being exercised by the Directors-General of the Local Finance Bureaus or the Director-General of the Fukuoka Local Finance Branch Bureau set forth in the preceding two paragraphs, be exercised by the Director-General of the Local Finance Bureau with jurisdiction over the place in which said Secondary Office, etc. is located (or by the Director-General of the Fukuoka Local Finance Branch Bureau, where the relevant location is within the district under the jurisdiction of the Fukuoka Local Finance Branch Bureau).

(7) Notwithstanding the provisions of the preceding three paragraphs, within the Commissioner's Authority that is specified in the items of paragraph (4), that designated by the Commissioner of the Financial Services Agency (referred to as "Commissioner's Specific Authority" in the following paragraph) shall be delegated to the Director-General of the Local Finance Bureau designated by the Commissioner of the Financial Services Agency, or to the Director-General of the Fukuoka Local Finance Branch Bureau.

(8) The provisions of paragraphs (4) to (6) inclusive shall not apply to the Commissioner's Authority specified in the items of paragraph (4) (excluding the Commissioner's Specific Authority) that is designated by the Commissioner of the Financial Services Agency.

(9) When the Commissioner of the Financial Services Agency has made a designation under the preceding two paragraphs, he/she shall issue a public notice to that effect. The same shall apply where he/she has abolished, or effected any amendment to, such designation.

(10) With regard to the Large-Volume Holder of Insurance Company Voting Rights (limited to a holder who is a foreign national or a foreign juridical person; hereinafter the same shall apply in this paragraph) with an office or any other facilities in Japan, its Principal Office, etc. in Japan shall be deemed to be its Principal Office, etc. , and a Large-Volume Holder of Insurance Company Voting Rights that does not have an office or other facilities in Japan, its Principal Office, etc. shall be deemed to be located in the district under the jurisdiction of the Kanto Local Finance Bureau, and the provisions of paragraphs (4) to (9) shall apply.

(11) The Commissioner's Authority as specified in the following items may be exercised by the Director-General of the Local Finance Bureau with jurisdiction over the place in which the Principal Office, etc. of the Insurance Company's Major Shareholder is located (for the authority specified in item (iii), this means the Major Shareholder (meaning a Major Shareholder as defined in Article 5, paragraph (5) of the Trust Business Act; hereinafter the same shall apply in this paragraph) of a Life Insurance Company engaged in Insurance-Proceed Trust Services, or the Major Shareholder of a Holding Company (meaning a Holding Company as defined in Article 5, paragraph (2), item (ix) of the Trust Business Act) whose Subsidiaries include a Life Insurance Company Engaged in Insurance-Proceed Trust Services; hereinafter the same shall apply in this paragraph to paragraph (13) inclusive) or the place in which the head office of the Insurance Company with which said Major Shareholder is connected is located (or by the Director-General of the Fukuoka Local Finance Branch Bureau, where the relevant location is within the district under the jurisdiction of the Fukuoka Local Finance Branch Bureau):

(i) orders for the submission of reports and materials under Article 271-12 of the Act;
(ii) questioning and on-site inspections under Article 271-13, paragraph (1) of the Act; and
(iii) orders for the submission of reports and materials, questioning, and on-site in-

spections under Article 42, paragraph (2) of the Trust Business Act as applied mutatis mutandis pursuant to Article 99, paragraph (8) of the Act.
(12) The authority specified in the items of the preceding paragraph in relation to the Secondary Office, etc. of an Insurance Company's Major Shareholder may, in addition to being exercised by the Director-General of the Local Finance Bureau or the Director-General of the Fukuoka Local Finance Branch Bureau set forth in the preceding paragraph, be exercised by the Director-General of the Local Finance Bureau with jurisdiction over the place in which said Secondary Office, etc. is located (or by the Director-General of the Fukuoka Local Finance Branch Bureau, where the relevant location is within the district under the jurisdiction of the Fukuoka Local Finance Branch Bureau).
(13) With regard to an Insurance Company's Major Shareholder (limited to a foreign national or a foreign juridical person, and including a person who formerly was an Insurance Company's Major Shareholder if said Insurance Company's Major Shareholder has ceased to be the Insurance Company's Major Shareholder; hereinafter the same shall apply in this paragraph) with an office or any other facilities in Japan, its Principal Office, etc. in Japan shall be deemed to be its Principal Office, etc. , and with regard to an Insurance Company's Major Shareholder that does not have an office or other facilities in Japan, its Principal Office, etc. shall be deemed to be located in the district under the jurisdiction of the Kanto Local Finance Bureau, and the provisions of the preceding two paragraphs shall apply.
(14) The Commissioner's Authority specified in the following items may be exercised by the Director-General of the Local Finance Bureau with jurisdiction over the place in which the principal office of the Insurance Holding Company or the head office of the Insurance Company that is the Subsidiary Company of said Insurance Holding Company is located (or by the Director-General of the Fukuoka Local Finance Branch Bureau, where the relevant location is within the district under the jurisdiction of the Fukuoka Local Finance Branch Bureau):
  (i) orders for the submission of reports and materials under Article 271-27, paragraph (1) of the Act; and
  (ii) questioning and on-site inspections under Article 271-28, paragraphs (1) and (2) of the Act.
(15) The authority specified in the items of the preceding paragraph in relation to the Branch Office, etc. (meaning an office or other facilities of an Insurance Holding Company excluding its principal office; a Subsidiary, etc. (meaning a "Subsidiary, etc." as defined in Article 271-27, paragraph (1) of the Act, and including its facilities) or an Insurance Holding Company; or a person that an Insurance Holding Company has entrusted with its business (including its facilities); hereinafter the same shall apply in this paragraph) may, in addition to being exercised by the Director-General of the Local Finance Bureau or the Director-General of the Fukuoka Local Finance Branch Bureau set forth in the preceding paragraph, be exercised by the Director-General of the Local Finance Bureau with jurisdiction over the place in which said Branch Office, etc. is located (or by the Director-General of the Fukuoka Local Finance Branch Bureau, where the relevant location is within the district under the jurisdiction of the Fukuoka Local Finance Branch Bureau).
(16) With regard to a Foreign Holding Company Whose Subsidiaries Include an Insurance Company and that has an office in Japan, its principal office in Japan shall be deemed to be its principal office, and with regard to a Foreign Holding Company Whose Subsidiaries Include an Insurance Company but that does not have an office in Japan, its principal office shall be deemed to be located in the district under the jurisdiction of the Kanto Local Finance Bureau, and the provisions of the preceding two

paragraphs shall apply.

(Delegation of Authority Over Low-Cost, Short-Term Insurers to the Directors-General of Local Finance Bureaus and Other Officials)
Article 47-2 (1) The following Commissioner's Authority (limited to authority over Low-Cost, Short-Term Insurers (excluding the Low-Cost, Short-Term Insurers designated by the Commissioner of the Financial Services Agency)) shall be delegated to the Director-General of the Local Finance Bureau with jurisdiction over the place in which the Head Office, etc. (meaning the head office or a principal office; hereinafter the same shall apply in this Article) of the Low-Cost, Short-Term Insurer is located (or to the Director-General of the Fukuoka Local Finance Branch Bureau, where the relevant location is within the district under the jurisdiction of the Fukuoka Local Finance Branch Bureau); provided, however, that the foregoing shall not preclude the Commissioner of the Financial Services Agency from exercising the authority specified in items (xiii), (xv) and (xvi), himself/herself.

(i) authorization under Article 17-2, paragraph (3), Article 55-2, paragraph (5), Article 57, paragraph (5), Article 80, paragraph (1), Article 96-10, paragraph (1) and Article 153, paragraph (1) of the Act;

(ii) authorization under Article 167, paragraph (1) of the Act (limited to authorization for a merger to which an Insurance Company is not a party);

(iii) authorization under Article 173-6, paragraph (1) of the Act (limited to authorization for a company split to which an Insurance Company is not a party);

(iv) appointment of liquidators under Article 174, paragraphs (1) and (4) of the Act;

(v) acceptance of notifications under Article 174, paragraph (8) of the Act;

(vi) dismissal and appointment of liquidators under Article 174, paragraph (9) of the Act;

(vii) commissioning of registrations under Article 174, paragraph (12) of the Act;

(viii) decisions under Article 175, paragraph (2) of the Act;

(ix) acceptance of documents under Article 176 of the Act;

(x) permission under Article 500, paragraph (2) of the Companies Act (including the cases where applied mutatis mutandis pursuant to Article 181-2 of the Act), as applied by replacing certain terms under Article 178 of the Act;

(xi) orders under Article 179, paragraph (1) of the Act;

(xii) authorization under Article 182, paragraph (6) of the Act;

(xiii) orders under Article 241, paragraph (1) of the Act;

(xiv) acceptance of notifications under Article 241, paragraph (3) of the Act;

(xv) appointment of Insurance Administrators under Article 242, paragraph (2) of the Act;

(xvi) orders under Article 242, paragraph (3) of the Act;

(xvii) appointment and dismissal of Insurance Administrators under Article 242, paragraph (4) of the Act;

(xviii) notices and public notices under Article 242, paragraph (5) of the Act;

(xix) commissioning of a notices and registrations under Article 244, paragraph (1) of the Act (including the cases where applied mutatis mutandis pursuant to Article 248, paragraph (2) of the Act);

(xx) authorization under Article 245 of the Act;

(xxi) orders under Article 246 of the Act;

(xxii) acceptance of reports under Article 246-2 of the Act;

(xxiii) orders under Article 247, paragraphs (1) and (5) of the Act;

(xxiv) approvals under Article 247, paragraphs (2) and (4) of the Act;

(xxv) approvals under Article 247-5, paragraph (1) of the Act;

(xxvi) rescissions under Article 248, paragraph (1) of the Act;
(xxvii) authorization under Article 250, paragraph (5), Article 254, paragraph (4) and Article 255-2, paragraph (3) of the Act;
(xxviii) statements of opinions under Article 271, paragraph (2) of the Act; and
(xxix) approvals under Article 273, paragraph (1), item (v) of the Act.

(2) The Commissioner's Authority specified in the following items shall be delegated to the Director-General of the Local Finance Bureau with jurisdiction over the place in which the Head Office, etc. of the Low-Cost, Short-Term Insurer (including a person who seeks to obtain a registration under Article 272, paragraph (1) of the Act) is located (or to the Director-General of the Fukuoka Local Finance Branch Bureau, where the relevant location is within the district under the jurisdiction of the Fukuoka Local Finance Branch Bureau):

(i) acceptance of written applications for registration under Article 272-2, paragraph (1) of the Act;
(ii) registrations under Article 272-3, paragraph (1) and Article 272-7, paragraph (2) of the Act;
(iii) offering of information for public inspection under Article 272-3, paragraph (2) of the Act; and
(iv) refusal of registrations under Article 272-4, paragraph (1) of the Act.

(3) The Commissioner's Authority specified in the following items (excluding authority of the Low-Cost, Short-Term Insurer designated by the Commissioner of the Financial Services Agency) shall be delegated to the Director-General of the Local Finance Bureau with jurisdiction over the place in which the Head Office, etc. of the Low-Cost, Short-Term Insurer is located (or to the Director-General of the Fukuoka Local Finance Branch Bureau, where the relevant location is within the district under the jurisdiction of the Fukuoka Local Finance Branch Bureau); provided, however, that the foregoing shall not preclude the Commissioner of the Financial Services Agency from exercising the authority specified in items (xvii) to (xx) inclusive and item (xxii), himself/herself.

(i) orders under Article 272-5, paragraphs (2) and (4) of the Act;
(ii) acceptance of notifications under Article 272-5, paragraphs (3), (5) and (8) of the Act;
(iii) approval under Article 272-6, paragraph (1) of the Act;
(iv) orders under Article 272-6, paragraph (2) of the Act;
(v) acceptance of notifications under Article 272-7, paragraph (1) of the Act;
(vi) approval under Article 272-10, paragraph (1) of the Act, Article 272-11, paragraph (1) of the Act, Article 100-3 of the Act as applied mutatis mutandis pursuant to Article 272-13, paragraph (2) of the Act, and Article 272-14, paragraph (2) of the Act;
(vii) acceptance of reports, etc. under Article 272-16, paragraphs (1) and (2) of the Act, and Article 110, paragraph (2) of the Act as applied mutatis mutandis pursuant to paragraph (3) of that Article;
(viii) authorization under Article 115, paragraphs (1) and (2) as applied mutatis mutandis pursuant to Article 272-18 of the Act;
(ix) acceptance of notifications under Article 120, paragraph (3) of the Act as applied mutatis mutandis pursuant to Article 272-18 of the Act;
(x) acceptance of copies of written opinions under Article 121, paragraph (2) of the Act as applied mutatis mutandis pursuant to Article 272-18 of the Act;
(xi) hearings of opinions under Article 121, paragraph (3) of the Act as applied mutatis mutandis pursuant to Article 272-18 of the Act;
(xii) orders under Article 122 of the Act as applied mutatis mutandis pursuant to Ar-

ticle 272-18 of the Act;
(xiii) acceptance of notifications under Article 272-19, paragraph (1) of the Act;
(xiv) notices under Article 272-20, paragraphs (2) and (3) of the Act;
(xv) orders under Article 272-20, paragraph (4) of the Act;
(xvi) acceptance of notifications under Article 272-21, paragraph (1) of the Act;
(xvii) orders for the submission of reports and materials under Article 272-22, paragraph (1) (including the cases where applied mutatis mutandis pursuant to Article 179, paragraph (2) of the Act) and paragraph (2) of the Act;
(xviii) questioning and on-site inspections under Article 272-23, paragraph (1) (including the cases where applied mutatis mutandis pursuant to Article 179, paragraph (2) and Article 271, paragraph (3) of the Act) and paragraph (2) of the Act;
(xix) orders under Article 272-24, paragraphs (1) and (2) and Article 272-25, paragraph (1) of the Act;
(xx) orders for the suspension of business in whole or in part, and rescission of registrations under Article 272-26, paragraph (1) of the Act;
(xxi) orders under Article 272-26, paragraph (2) of the Act;
(xxii) rescission of registrations under Article 272-27 of the Act;
(xxiii) authorization under Article 139, paragraph (1) of the Act as applied mutatis mutandis pursuant to Article 272-29 of the Act (excluding authorization for the transfer of an insurance contract under which an Insurance Company (including a Foreign Insurance Company, etc.; the same shall apply in the following item) is the Transferee Company (meaning a Transferee Company as defined in Article 135, paragraph (1) of the Act));
(xxiv) authorization under Article 142 of the Act as applied mutatis mutandis pursuant to Article 272-30, paragraph (1) of the Act (limited to authorization for the transfer or acquisition of business to which an Insurance Company is not a party);
(xxv) authorization under Article 145, paragraph (1) and Article 149, paragraph (2) of the Act as applied mutatis mutandis pursuant to Article 272-30, paragraph (2) of the Act (excluding authorization for the entrustment of business and property management to which an Insurance Company (including a Foreign Insurance Company, etc. (excluding the companies specified in Cabinet Office Ordinance)) is an Entrusted Company (meaning an Entrusted Company as defined in Article 144, paragraph (1) of the Act as applied mutatis mutandis pursuant to Article 272-30, paragraph (2) of the Act));
(xxvi) approval under Article 38-5, item (iii) and Article 38-8, paragraph (1), item (iii);
(xxvii) acceptance of applications, public notices, notices, assessments, affording of opportunities for presenting opinions, preparation of distribution lists, and realization under Article 38-6; and
(xxviii) acceptance of applications, public notices, notices, approval, assessments, affording of opportunities for presenting opinions, and preparation of distribution lists under Article 38-7, and under Article 38-6 as applied mutatis mutandis pursuant to paragraph (5) of that Article.
(4) The authority specified in items (xvii) and (xviii) of the preceding paragraph in relation to a Business Office, etc. (meaning the business office, office, or any other facilities of a Low-Cost, Short-Term Insurer other than its Head Office, etc., a Subsidiary, etc. (meaning a "Subsidiary, etc." as defined in Article 272-22, paragraph (2) of the Act, and including its facilities) of a Low-Cost, Short-Term Insurer, and a person that a Low-Cost, Short-Term Insurer has entrusted with its business (including its facilities); hereinafter the same shall apply in this paragraph and the following paragraph) may, in addition to being exercised by the Director-General of the Local Finance Bureau or the Director-General of the Fukuoka Local Finance Branch Bureau set forth

in the preceding paragraph, be exercised by the Director-General of the Local Finance Bureau with jurisdiction over the place in which the Business Office, etc. is located (or by the Director-General of the Fukuoka Local Finance Branch Bureau, where its location falls within the district under the jurisdiction of the Fukuoka Local Finance Branch Bureau).
(5) When the Director-General of the Local Finance Bureau or the Director-General of the Fukuoka Local Finance Branch Bureau that has ordered the Business Office, etc. of a Low-Cost, Short-Term Insurer to submit a report and materials or that has conducted questioning or on-site inspections (hereinafter referred to as "Inspection, etc." in this paragraph) pursuant to the provisions of the preceding paragraph finds it necessary to conduct such an Inspection, etc. at the Head Office, etc. or at any Business Office, etc. other than the first-mentioned Business Office, etc. , he/she may conduct said Inspection, etc. at the Head Office, etc. or at such other Business Office, etc.
(6) The Commissioner's Authority specified in the following items shall be delegated to the Director-General of the Local Finance Bureau with jurisdiction over the place in which the head office of the Low-Cost, Short-Term Insurer is located (or to the Director-General of the Fukuoka Local Finance Branch Bureau, where the relevant location is within the district under the jurisdiction of the Fukuoka Local Finance Branch Bureau):
  (i) approval under Article 272-31, paragraph (1) of the Act and the proviso to paragraph (2) of that Article;
  (ii) acceptance of notifications under Article 272-31, paragraph (3) of the Act;
  (iii) acceptance of written applications for approval under Article 272-32, paragraph (1) of the Act;
  (iv) acceptance of notifications under Article 272-42, paragraph (1) of the Act; and
  (v) approval under Article 271-33, paragraph (1), item (i) of the Act as applied mutatis mutandis pursuant to Article 272-43 of the Act.
(7) The Commissioner's Authority specified in the following items (excluding authority in relation to Low-Cost, Short-Term Insurer designated by the Commissioner of the Financial Services Agency) shall be delegated to the Director-General of the Local Finance Bureau with jurisdiction over the place in which the head office of the Low-Cost, Short-Term Insurer is located (or to the Director-General of the Fukuoka Local Finance Branch Bureau, where the relevant location is within the district under the jurisdiction of the Fukuoka Local Finance Branch Bureau); provided, however, that the foregoing shall not preclude the Commissioner of the Financial Services Agency from exercising the authority specified in items (ii) and (iii), himself/herself.
  (i) orders under Article 272-31, paragraph (4) of the Act;
  (ii) orders for the submission of reports and materials under Article 272-12 of the Act as applied mutatis mutandis pursuant to Article 272-34, paragraph (1) of the Act;
  (iii) questioning and on-site inspections under Article 271-13, paragraph (1) of the Act as applied mutatis mutandis pursuant to Article 272-34, paragraph (1) of the Act;
  (iv) orders under Article 271-14 of the Act as applied mutatis mutandis pursuant to Article 272-34, paragraph (1) of the Act; and
  (v) orders and rescissions of approval referred to in Article 271-16, paragraph (1) of the Act as applied mutatis mutandis pursuant to Article 272-34, paragraph (1) of the Act.
(8) The authority specified in items (ii) and (iii) of the preceding paragraph may, in addition to being exercised by the Director-General of the Local Finance Bureau or the Director-General of the Fukuoka Local Finance Branch Bureau set forth in that paragraph, be exercised by the Director-General of the Local Finance Bureau with juris-

Art.47-2   [7] Order for Enforcement of the Insurance Business Act, Chap.IV

diction over the place in which the Principal Office, etc. of the Major Shareholder of a Low-Cost, Short-Term Insurer is located (or by the Director-General of the Fukuoka Local Finance Branch Bureau, where its location falls within the district under the jurisdiction of the Fukuoka Local Finance Branch Bureau).

(9) The authority specified in items (ii) and (iii) of paragraph (7) in relation to the Secondary Office, etc. of the Major Shareholder of a Low-Cost, Short-Term Insurer may, in addition to being exercised by the Directors-General of the Local Finance Bureaus or the Director-General of the Fukuoka Local Finance Branch Bureau set forth in the preceding two paragraphs, be exercised by the Director-General of the Local Finance Bureau with jurisdiction over the place in which said Secondary Office, etc. is located (or by the Director-General of the Fukuoka Local Finance Branch Bureau, where its location falls within the district under the jurisdiction of the Fukuoka Local Finance Branch Bureau).

(10) With regard to a Major Shareholder of a Low-Cost, Short-Term Insurer (including a person who formerly was the Major Shareholder of a Low-Cost, Short-Term Insurer, and limited to a foreign national or a foreign juridical person; hereinafter the same shall apply in this paragraph) with an office or any other facilities in Japan, its Principal Office, etc. in Japan shall be deemed to be its Principal Office, etc. , and with regard to a Major Shareholder of a Low-Cost, Short-Term Insurer that does not have an office or any other facilities in Japan, its Principal Office, etc. shall be deemed to be located in the district under the jurisdiction of the Kanto Local Finance Bureau, and the provisions of the preceding two paragraphs shall apply.

(11) The Commissioner's Authority specified in the following items shall be delegated to the Director-General of the Local Finance Bureau with jurisdiction over the place in which the head office of the Low-Cost, Short-Term Insurer is located (or to the Director-General of the Fukuoka Local Finance Branch Bureau, where the relevant location is within the district under the jurisdiction of the Fukuoka Local Finance Branch Bureau):

(i) approval under Article 272-35, paragraph (1) of the Act and the proviso to paragraph (3) of that Article;
(ii) acceptance of notifications under Article 272-35, paragraphs (2) and (4) of the Act;
(iii) acceptance of written applications for approval under Article 272-36, paragraph (1) of the Act;
(iv) approval under Article 272-39, paragraph (1) of the Act and the proviso to paragraph (4) of that Article;
(v) acceptance of written applications under Article 272-39, paragraph (2) of the Act;
(vi) acceptance of notifications under Article 272-42, paragraph (2) of the Act;
(vii) approval under Article 271-33, paragraph (2), item (i) of the Act as applied mutatis mutandis pursuant to Article 272-43 of the Act; and
(viii) acceptance of notifications under the main clause of Article 38-15 and approval under the proviso to that paragraph.

(12) The Commissioner's Authority specified in the following items (excluding authority in relation to the Low-Cost, Short-Term Insurer designated by the Commissioner of the Financial Services Agency) shall be delegated to the Director-General of the Local Finance Bureau with jurisdiction over the place in which the head office of a Low-Cost, Short-Term Insurer is located (or to the Director-General of the Fukuoka Local Finance Branch Bureau, where the relevant location is within the district under the jurisdiction of the Fukuoka Local Finance Branch Bureau); provided, however, that the foregoing shall not preclude the Commissioner of the Financial Services Agency from exercising the authority specified in items (iii) and (iv), himself/herself.

(i) orders under Article 272-35, paragraph (5) of the Act;

(ii) acceptance of business reports, etc. under Article 271-24 of the Act as applied mutatis mutandis pursuant to Article 272-40, paragraph (2) of the Act;
(iii) orders for the submission of reports and materials under Article 271-27 of the Act as applied mutatis mutandis pursuant to Article 272-40, paragraph (2) of the Act;
(iv) questioning and on-site inspections under Article 271-28, paragraphs (1) and (2) as applied mutatis mutandis pursuant to Article 272-40, paragraph (2) of the Act;
(v) orders under Article 271-29, paragraphs (1) and (2) as applied mutatis mutandis pursuant to Article 272-40, paragraph (2) of the Act; and
(vi) orders and the rescission of approval referred to in Article 271-31, paragraphs (1) and (4) as applied mutatis mutandis pursuant to Article 272-40, paragraph (2) of the Act.
(13) The authority specified in items (iii) and (iv) of the preceding paragraph may, in addition to being exercised by the Director-General of the Local Finance Bureau or the Director-General of the Fukuoka Local Finance Branch Bureau set forth in that paragraph, be exercised by the Director-General of the Local Finance Bureau with jurisdiction over the place in which the principal office of the Low-Cost, Short-Term Insurance Holding Company is located (or by the Director-General of the Fukuoka Local Finance Branch Bureau, where its location falls within the district under the jurisdiction of the Fukuoka Local Finance Branch Bureau).
(14) The authority specified in items (iii) and (iv) of paragraph (12) in relation to the Branch Office, etc. (meaning the office or other facilities of a Low-Cost, Short-Term Insurance Holding Company excluding its principal office, a Subsidiary, etc. (meaning a "Subsidiary, etc." as defined in Article 271-40, paragraph (2) of the Act, and including its facilities) of a Low-Cost, Short-Term Insurance Holding Company or in relation to the person that a Low-Cost, Short-Term Insurance Holding Company has entrusted with its business (including its facilities); hereinafter the same shall apply in this paragraph) may, in addition to being exercised by the Directors-General of the Local Finance Bureaus or the Director-General of the Fukuoka Local Finance Branch Bureau set forth in the preceding two paragraphs, be exercised by the Director-General of the Local Finance Bureau with jurisdiction over the place in which said Branch Office, etc. is located (or by the Director-General of the Fukuoka Local Finance Branch Bureau, where the relevant location is within the district under the jurisdiction of the Fukuoka Local Finance Branch Bureau).
(15) With regard to a foreign Holding Company whose Subsidiaries include a Low-Cost, Short-Term Insurance Holding Company and that has an office in Japan, its principal office in Japan shall be deemed to be its principal office, and with regard to a foreign Holding Company whose Subsidiaries include a Low-Cost, Short-Term Insurance Holding Company and that does not have an office in Japan, its principal office shall be deemed to be located in the district under the jurisdiction of the Kanto Local Finance Bureau, and the provisions of the preceding two paragraphs shall apply.
(16) When the Commissioner of the Financial Services Agency has made a designation under paragraphs (1), (3), (7) and (12), he/she shall issue a public notice to that effect. The same shall apply where the Commissioner of the Financial Services Agency has rescinded such a designation.

(Delegation of Authority Over Insurance Agents, etc. to the Directors-General of Local Finance Bureaus and Other Officials)
Article 47-3 (1) The Commissioner's Authority specified in the following items shall be delegated to the Director-General of the Local Finance Bureau with jurisdiction over the place in which the principal office of the Specified Insurance Agent is located (or

to the Director-General of the Fukuoka Local Finance Branch Bureau, where the relevant location is within the district under the jurisdiction of the Fukuoka Local Finance Branch Bureau); provided, however, that the foregoing shall not preclude the Commissioner of the Financial Services Agency from exercising the authority specified in item (vii), himself/herself.
(i) acceptance of the notifications under Article 127, paragraph (1), item (viii), Article 209, item (ix), Article 234, item (viii) and Article 272-21, paragraph (1), item (vi) of the Act (limited to notifications related to a Specified Insurance Agent or its officers or employees) that are specified by Cabinet Office Ordinance;
(ii) registrations under Article 276, Article 278, paragraph (1) and Article 280, paragraph (2) of the Act, and refusal of registrations pursuant to Article 279, paragraph (1) of the Act;
(iii) acceptance of written applications for registration under Article 277, paragraph (1) of the Act, and acceptance of notifications under Article 280, paragraph (1) and Article 302 of the Act;
(iv) custody of the registry of Life Insurance Agents, the registry of Non-Life Insurance Representatives, and the registry of Low-Cost, Short-Term Insurance Agents under Article 278, paragraph (1) of the Act;
(v) notices under Article 278, paragraph (2), Article 279, paragraphs (2) and (4), Article 280, paragraph (2) and Article 308, paragraph (2) of the Act;
(vi) orders to appear, affording opportunities to present evidence, and hearings of opinions referred to in Article 279, paragraph (2) of the Act;
(vii) orders for the submission of reports and materials under Article 305 of the Act, and implementation of on-site inspections and questioning under that Article;
(viii) orders under Article 306 of the Act;
(ix) rescission of registrations under Article 307, paragraph (1) of the Act, and orders to suspend all or a part of business pursuant to that paragraph;
(x) public notices and rescission of registrations referred to in Article 307, paragraph (2) of the Act; and
(xi) cancellation of registrations pursuant to Article 308, paragraph (1) of the Act.
(2) The Commissioner's Authority specified in the following items shall be delegated to the Director-General of the Local Finance Bureau with jurisdiction over the place in which the principal office of the Insurance Broker is located (or to the Director-General of the Fukuoka Local Finance Branch Bureau, where the relevant location is within the district under the jurisdiction of the Fukuoka Local Finance Branch Bureau); provided, however, that the foregoing shall not preclude the Commissioner of the Financial Services Agency from exercising the authority specified in item (x), himself/herself.
(i) registration under Article 286, Article 288, paragraph (1) and Article 290, paragraph (2) of the Act, and refusal of registrations under Article 289, paragraph (1) of the Act;
(ii) acceptance of documents under Article 287, paragraph (1) and Article 304 of the Act, and acceptance of notifications under Article 290, paragraph (1), Article 291, paragraphs (3), (5) and (8) and Article 302 of the Act;
(iii) custody of the registry of Insurance Brokers under Article 288, paragraph (1) of the Act;
(iv) notices under Article 288, paragraph (1), and Article 289, paragraphs (2) and (4) of the Act;
(v) offering information for public inspection under Article 288, paragraph (3) of the Act;
(vi) orders to appear, affording opportunities to present evidence, and hearings of

opinions referred to in Article 289, paragraph (2) of the Act;
(vii) orders for deposits under Article 291, paragraph (4) and Article 292, paragraph (2) of the Act;
(viii) approval under Article 291, paragraph (10) and Article 292, paragraph (1) of the Act;
(ix) designation under Article 291, paragraph (11) of the Act;
(x) orders for the submission of reports and materials under Article 305 of the Act, and on-site inspections and questioning under that Article;
(xi) orders under Article 306 of the Act;
(xii) rescission of registrations under Article 307, paragraph (1) of the Act, and orders to suspend all or a part of business under that paragraph;
(xiii) public notices and rescission of registrations pursuant to in Article 307, paragraph (2) of the Act; and
(xiv) cancellation of registrations under Article 308, paragraph (1) of the Act.
(3) The authority specified in items (i) and (vii) of paragraph (1) and in item (x) of the preceding paragraph in relation to the offices of a Specified Insurance Agent or Insurance Agent (hereinafter collectively referred to as a "Specified Insurance Agent, etc." in this paragraph and the following paragraph) that are other than its principal office (hereinafter referred to as "Secondary Office(s)" in this paragraph and the following paragraph) may, in addition to being exercised by the Directors-General of the Local Finance Bureaus or the Director-General of the Fukuoka Local Finance Branch Bureau set forth in paragraph (1) and the preceding paragraph, be exercised by the Director-General of the Local Finance Bureau with jurisdiction over the place in which said Secondary Office is located (or by the Director-General of the Fukuoka Local Finance Branch Bureau, where the relevant location is within the district under the jurisdiction of the Fukuoka Local Finance Branch Bureau).
(4) When the Director-General of the Local Finance Bureau or the Director-General of the Fukuoka Local Finance Branch Bureau who, pursuant to the provisions of the preceding paragraph, has ordered the Secondary Office, etc. of a Specified Insurance Agent, etc. to submit reports or materials or has conducted questioning or on-site inspections (hereinafter referred to as "Inspection, etc." in this paragraph) finds it necessary to conduct any Inspection, etc. at the Principal Office or at any Secondary Office other than the first-mentioned Secondary Office, he/she may conduct such Inspection, etc. at the Principal Office or at said other Second Office.
(5) The provisions of each of the preceding paragraphs shall not apply to the Commissioner's Authority set forth in the items of paragraph (1) and the Commissioner's Authority set forth in the items of paragraph (2) that are designated by the Commissioner of the Financial Services Agency.
(6) When the Commissioner of the Financial Services Agency has made a designation under the preceding paragraph, he/she shall issue a public notice to that effect. The same shall apply where the Commissioner of the Financial Services Agency has abolished or effected any amendment to such a designation.

[8] Commercial Registration Act

(Act No. 125 of July 9, 1963)

Chapter I General Provisions (Article 1 and Article 1-2)
Chapter I-II Registry Office and Registrar (Article 1-3 to Article 5)
Chapter II Registry, etc. (Article 6 to Article 13)
Chapter III Registration Procedures
  Section 1 General Rules (Article 14 to Article 26)
  Section 2 Registration of Trade Name (Article 27 to Article 34)
  Section 3 Registration of Minor and Guardian (Article 35 to Article 42)
  Section 4 Registration of Manager (Article 43 to Article 45)
  Section 5 Registration of Stock Company (Article 46 to Article 92)
  Section 6 Registration of General Partnership Company (Article 93 to Article 109)
  Section 7 Registration of Limited Partnership Company (Article 110 to Article 116)
  Section 8 Registration of Limited Liability Company (Article 117 to Article 126)
  Section 9 Registration of Foreign Company (Article 127 to Article 131)
  Section 10 Correction and Cancellation of Registration (Article 132 to Article 138)
Chapter IV Miscellaneous Provisions (Article 139 to Article 148)
  Supplementary Provisions

Chapter I General Provisions

(Purposes)
Article 1 The purpose of this Act is to maintain the credibility of trade names, companies, etc. by establishing a registration system so as to notify the public of the matters to be registered pursuant to the provisions of the Commercial Code (Act No. 48 of 1899), the Companies Act (Act No. 86 of 2005) or any other Act, as well as to contribute to the safe and smooth conduct of transactions.

(Definitions)
Article 1-2 In this Act, the meanings of the terms listed in the following items shall be as prescribed respectively in those items:
  (i) registry: a book in which to record the matters to be registered pursuant to the provisions of the Commercial Code, the Companies Act or any other Act, and which is prepared by means of a magnetic disk (including an object that can record certain matters securely by equivalent means);
  (ii) registration of change: a registration to be made pursuant to the provisions of the Commercial Code, the Companies Act and any other Act, in cases where any of the matters registered has been changed;
  (iii) registration of extinction: a registration to be made pursuant to the provisions of the Commercial Code, the Companies Act or any other Act, in cases where any of the matters registered has extinguished;
  (iv) trade name: a trade name prescribed in Article 11, paragraph (1) of the Commercial Code or in Article 6, paragraph (1) of the Companies Act.

Chapter I-II Registry Office and Registrar

(Registry Office)

Article 1-3 Registration affairs shall be administered by the Legal Affairs Bureau or District Legal Affairs Bureau or the branch bureau thereof or the branch office of any of those bureaus (hereinafter simply referred to as a "registry office"), which has jurisdiction over the location of the business office of the party concerned.

(Delegation of Affairs)
Article 2 The Minister of Justice may delegate affairs that are subject to the jurisdiction of one registry office to another registry office.

(Suspension of Affairs)
Article 3 In the event that a registry office is obliged to suspend its affairs for some reason, the Minister of Justice may specify a period for and order the suspension of the affairs of the registry office.

(Registrar)
Article 4 The affairs of a registry office shall be handled by a registrar (meaning a person appointed by the Director of the Legal Affairs Bureau or District Legal Affairs Bureau from among officials of the Ministry of Justice who work at the registry office; the same shall apply hereinafter).

(Disqualification of Registrar)
Article 5 When a registrar, a registrar's spouse or a relative within the fourth degree of kinship (including a person who was a registrar's spouse or a relative within the fourth degree of kinship; hereinafter the same shall apply in this Article) is the applicant for a registration, such registrar may not make the registration. The same shall apply to cases where a registrar or a registrar's spouse or relative within the fourth degree of kinship files an application for a registration as a representative of the applicants.

Chapter II Registry, etc.

(Commercial Registry)
Article 6 A registry office shall keep the following types of commercial registries:
(i) the trade name registry;
(ii) the minor registry;
(iii) the guardian registry;
(iv) the manager registry;
(v) the stock company registry;
(vi) the general partnership company registry;
(vii) the limited partnership company registry;
(viii) the limited liability company registry; and
(ix) the foreign company registry.

(Prohibition on Carrying Out of Registries and Other Documents)
Article 7 No registry or document annexed thereto (including an electromagnetic record (meaning a record made in an electronic form, a magnetic form, or any other form not recognizable to human perception, which is used in information processing by computers; the same shall apply hereinafter) as prescribed in Article 17, paragraph (4), or electromagnetic record to be attached to a written application for registration as prescribed in Article 19-2 (hereinafter referred to as an "electromagnetic record under Article 19-2"); hereinafter the same shall apply in this Article, Article 9, Article 11-2,

Article 140 and Article 141) may be carried outside of registry offices, except for the cases where it is necessary to do so in order to avoid any contingent circumstance; provided, however, that, with regard to the documents annexed to registries, this shall not apply to the cases where so ordered or commissioned by the court.

(Loss and Restoration of Registries)
Article 8 When the whole or part of a registry has been lost, the Minister of Justice may specify a certain period and issue an order to take the measures necessary for restoration of the registration.

(Prevention of Loss of Registry, etc.)
Article 9 In cases where there is a risk of loss of a registry or any documents annexed thereto, the Minister of Justice may issue an order to take the measures necessary for the prevention thereof.

(Issuance of Certificate of Registered Matters)
Article 10 (1) Any person may, by paying fees, make a request for issuance of a document certifying the matters recorded in the registry (hereinafter referred to as a "certificate of registered matters").
(2) Unless otherwise prescribed in an Ordinance of the Ministry of Justice, a request for issuance of a certificate of registered matters set forth in the preceding paragraph may be filed with the registrar of a registry office of another jurisdiction.
(3) The matters to be specified in a certificate of registered matters shall be prescribed by an Ordinance of the Ministry of Justice.

(Issuance of Documents Specifying Extract of Matters Registered)
Article 11 Any person may, by paying fees, make a request for the issuance of a document stating the summary of the matters recorded in the registry.

(Inspection of Annexed Documents)
Article 11-2 A person who has an interest in the inspection of documents annexed to registries may, by paying fees, make a request for the inspection thereof. In this case, inspection of the information recorded in an electromagnetic record under Article 17, paragraph (4) or information recorded in an electromagnetic record under Article 19-2 shall be conducted by way of inspecting the contents of relevant information made available by the method prescribed by an Ordinance of the Ministry of Justice.

(Certificate of Seal Impression)
Article 12 (1) A person who has submitted to a registry office a seal impression pursuant to the provision of Article 20, or, a manager, a bankruptcy trustee or provisional administrator appointed for a company under the Bankruptcy Act (Act No. 75 of 2004), a trustee or provisional administrator appointed for a company under the Civil Rehabilitation Act (Act No. 225 of 1999), a trustee or provisional administrator appointed for a company under the Corporate Reorganization Act (Act No. 154 of 2002), or a recognition trustee or provisional administrator appointed for a company under the Act on Recognition and Assistance for Foreign Insolvency Proceedings (Act No. 129 of 2000), any one of whom who has submitted his/her seal impression to a registry office, may file a request for issuance of the certificate of such seal impression, subject to the payment of fees.
(2) The provision of Article 10, paragraph (2) shall apply mutatis mutandis to the certifi-

cate set forth in the preceding paragraph.

(Certification of Matters Required for Verification of Measures to Identify the Creator of Electromagnetic Records and Other Matters)
Article 12-2 (1) A person prescribed in paragraph (1) of the preceding Article (hereinafter referred to as a "person submitting a seal impression" in this Article) may, pursuant to the provision of this Article, file a request for a certification of the following matters (with regard to a certification of the period specified in item (ii), limited to that prescribed by an Ordinance of the Ministry of Justice), if the registry office to which such person has submitted its seal impression is the one designated by the Minister of Justice; provided, however, that this shall not apply to a certification of restriction on the authority of representation and any other matter prescribed by an Ordinance of the Ministry of Justice as being unfit for the certification under this paragraph.
  (i) a matter required for verifying that a person submitting a seal impression has taken measures so as to evidence that he/she has prepared information recordable onto electromagnetic records, which measure is prescribed by an Ordinance of the Ministry of Justice as being available for verification as to whether the information has been altered or for otherwise evidencing that said information has been prepared by the person submitting a seal impression himself/herself; and
  (ii) a period of time during which a request for certification under paragraph (8) may be filed, with regard to the matters certified pursuant to the provisions of this paragraph and paragraph (3).
(2) In filing a request for certification pursuant to the provision of the preceding paragraph, the matters specified in each item of said paragraph shall be expressly indicated.
(3) A person submitting a seal impression who has requested a certification pursuant to the provision of paragraph (1) may, together with said request, file a request for certification of the matters registered in relation to such person as prescribed by an Ordinance of the Ministry of Justice.
(4) Unless otherwise provided for in the Cabinet Order, a person submitting a seal impression who requests certification pursuant to the provision of paragraph (1) shall pay the fees.
(5) Certification under paragraphs (1) and (3) shall be issued by a registrar of a registry office designated by the Minister of Justice; provided, however, that a request for certification under these provisions shall be filed via the registry office set forth in paragraph (1).
(6) The designation set forth in paragraph (1) and the preceding paragraph shall be made by means of public notice.
(7) In cases where, during the period of time specified in item (ii) of paragraph (1), the matter specified in item (i) of said paragraph is no longer necessary in order to verify that a person submitting a seal impression himself/herself has taken the measures under said item, the person submitting a seal impression who had requested the certification pursuant to the provision of paragraph (1) may file a notification to that effect with the registry office specified in the main text of paragraph (5) via the registry office set forth in paragraph (1).
(8) Any person may file a request for certification of the following matters with the registry office as set forth in the main text of paragraph (5):
  (i) whether there has been any change to the matters certified pursuant to the provisions of paragraphs (1) and (3) (excluding minor changes prescribed by an Ordinance of the Ministry of Justice);
  (ii) whether the period of time specified in item (ii) of paragraph (1) has elapsed;

(iii) whether the notification set forth in the preceding paragraph has been filed, and if it has been filed, the date of such filing; and
(iv) the matters equivalent to those specified in the preceding three items, which are prescribed by an Ordinance of the Ministry of Justice.
(9) The certification under paragraphs (1) and (3), and the certification under the preceding paragraph and the request therefor shall be made by means of transmission via telecommunication lines connecting a computer to be used by the registrar and a computer to be used by the person who has made the request and any other means, as prescribed by an Ordinance of the Ministry of Justice.
(10) With regard to the certification set forth in the preceding paragraph and the request therefor, the provisions of Article 3 and Article 4 of Act on Use of Information and Communications Technology in Administrative Procedures, etc. (Act No. 151 of 2002; hereinafter referred to as "Act on Use of Information and Communications Technology") shall not apply.

(Fees)
Article 13 (1) The amount of fees set forth in Article 10 to Article 12-2 inclusive shall be specified by a Cabinet Order, taking into consideration any and all relevant circumstances such as commodity price levels, actual costs incurred for issuance of a certificate of registered matters, etc. and others.
(2) The payment of fees set forth in Article 10 to Article 12-2 inclusive shall be made by means of registration revenue stamps; provided however, that, in the case of filing a request for issuance of a certificate of registered matters or a certificate of seal impression by the method prescribed by an Ordinance of the Ministry of Justice, a cash payment of such fees shall be accepted as prescribed by an Ordinance of Ministry of Justice.

Chapter III Registration Procedures

Section 1 General Rules

(Registration Upon Application by Party)
Article 14 Unless otherwise provided for in laws and regulations, no registration may be made without an application filed by a party concerned or a commission issued by a government agency or public office.

(Registration upon Commission)
Article 15 The provisions of Article 5, Article 17 to Article 19-2 inclusive, Article 21, Article 22, Article 23-2, Article 24, Article 48 to Article 50 inclusive (including the cases where applied mutatis mutandis pursuant to Article 95, Article 111 and Article 118), Article 51, paragraphs (1) and (2), Article 52, Article 78, paragraphs (1) and (3), Article 82, paragraphs (2) and (3), Article 83, Article 87, paragraphs (1) and (2), Article 88, Article 91, paragraphs (1) and (2), Article 92, Article 132 and Article 134 shall apply mutatis mutandis to a registration procedure to be performed as commissioned by a government agency or public office.

Article 16 (Deleted)

(Method of Application for Registration)
Article 17 (1) An application for registration shall be filed in writing.
(2) The following matters shall be specified in the form of an application, with the name

and seal of the applicant or its representative (in cases where the representative is a juridical person, a person to perform the duties thereof) or agent affixed thereto:
(i) the name and address of an applicant, or, if an applicant is a company, its trade name and head office as well as its representative's name and address (in cases where the representative is a juridical person, including the name and address of a person to perform the duties thereof);
(ii) if an application is to be filed by an agent, the name and address thereof;
(iii) the grounds for registration;
(iv) the matters to be registered;
(v) if any matter to be registered requires permission from a government agency or public office, the date of the arrival of the permit;
(vi) the amount of registration tax payable, and if there is a tax base amount therefor, including said amount;
(vii) the date of filing; and
(viii) the indication of registry office.
(3) In filing a written application for registration to be made at the location of a branch office of a company, such branch office shall also be specified.
(4) In cases where an electromagnetic record containing the matters listed in item (iv) of paragraph (2), or the matters to be specified in a written application pursuant to the provision of the preceding paragraph (limited to those prescribed by an Ordinance of the Ministry of Justice) has been submitted with a written application, it shall not be required to specify in such written application the matters contained in said electromagnetic record, notwithstanding the provisions of the preceding two paragraphs.

(Document to be Attached to Written Application)
Article 18 In cases where an application for registration is to be filed by an agent, a document evidencing the authority thereof shall be attached to a written application (including an electromagnetic record as prescribed in paragraph (4) of the preceding Article; the same shall apply hereinafter).

Article 19 In filing an application for registration of any matter which requires permission from a government agency or public office, a permit issued by a government agency or public office, or a transcript thereof certified by such agency or office shall be attached to a written application.

(Electromagnetic Records to be Attached to Written Application)
Article 19-2 In cases where the articles of incorporation, minutes or final balance sheet to be attached to a written application for registration has been prepared in the form of an electromagnetic record, or in cases where an electromagnetic record has been prepared in lieu of documents to be attached to a written application for registration, an electromagnetic record (limited to one prescribed by an Ordinance of the Ministry of Justice) containing the contents of the information recorded in the above-mentioned electromagnetic records shall be attached to the written application.

(Submission of Seal Impression)
Article 20 (1) A person who is required to affix a seal to a written application for registration shall submit an impression of such seal to a registry office in advance. The same shall apply to the cases where such person has changed a seal.
(2) In cases where an application for registration is to be filed by a privately appointed agent, the provision of the preceding paragraph shall apply to a person who has appointed said agent or a representative thereof.

(3) The provisions of the preceding two paragraphs shall not apply to an application for registration to be made at the location of a branch office of a company.

(Acceptance of Applications)
Article 21 (1) When a registrar has received a written application for registration, he/she shall enter the type of registration, applicant's name, applicant's trade name (in cases where the applicant is a company), date of acceptance thereof and its acceptance number into an acceptance record book, and shall also enter the date of the acceptance and acceptance number on such written application.
(2) In filing an application for registration pursuant to the provision of Article 3, paragraph (1) of the Act on Use of Information and Communications Technology by use of an electronic data processing system as set forth therein, the portion of the provision of the preceding paragraph referring to an entry on a written application shall not apply.
(3) In cases where a registrar has simultaneously received two or more written applications for registration, or in cases where he/she has received two or more written applications for registration and if the chronological order thereof is uncertain, he/she shall make an entry to that effect into an acceptance record book.

(Receipt)
Article 22 A registrar shall, when he/she has received a written application for registration and any other document (including an electromagnetic record under Article 19-2) and if so requested to do so by an applicant, issue a receipt therefor.

(Order of Registration)
Article 23 A registrar shall make registrations according to the order of the acceptance numbers.

(Identity Confirmation by Registrar)
Article 23-2 (1) Where an application for a registration is filed, and when a registrar finds that there are reasonable grounds to suspect that the application has been filed by a person other than the one who should be the applicant, the registrar shall, except where he/she should dismiss the application pursuant to the provision of the following Article, examine whether or not the applicant has the authority to apply, by requesting the applicant or his/her representative or agent to appear, asking questions of them, or requesting them to present documents or provide any other necessary information.
(2) If the applicant or his/her representative or agent prescribed in the preceding paragraph resides in a remote place or the registrar finds it appropriate for other reasons, the registrar may commission a registrar from another registry office to conduct the examination set forth in said paragraph.

(Dismissal of Application)
Article 24 In cases where there is any ground which falls under any of the following items, a registrar shall dismiss an application for a registration, by a decision stating the reasons therefor; provided, however, that this shall not apply where defects in the application can be corrected, and where the applicant has corrected them within a reasonable period specified by the registrar:
(i) where the location of the business office of the party for which the application is filed is not subject to the jurisdiction of the registry office which has received the application;
(ii) where the purpose of the application is to register matters other than the matters to be registered;

Art.25〜26　⑧ Commercial Registration Act, Chap.III, Sec.1

(iii) where the registration for which the application was filed has already been registered by the same registry office;
(iv) where the application is filed by a person without the authority to apply;
(x) in the case referred to in Article 21, paragraph (3), if, from among two or more written applications referred to in the same paragraph, making a registration based on one application hinders a registration based on any other application;
(vi) where the written application fails to conform to the method specified pursuant to the provisions of an order issued under this Act or of other laws and regulations;
(vii) where the applicant has failed to submit a seal impression pursuant to the provision of Article 20, or in cases where a seal affixed to any of a written application, a document evidencing authority delegated to a privately appointed agent or a transferrer's written approval prescribed in Article 30, paragraph (2) or Article 31, paragraph (2) differs from the seal impression already submitted pursuant to the provision of Article 20;
(viii) where the applicant has failed to attach any document required in relation to a written application (including an electromagnetic record under Article 19-2);
(ix) where any statement or record contained in a written application or documents attached thereto (including an electromagnetic record under Article 19-2; the same shall apply hereinafter) is inconsistent with any statement or record contained in documents attached to a written application or in a registry.
(x) where there exists any ground for the invalidation, revocation or rescission of any matter to be registered;
(xi) where an application has not been filed with the registry office through which the application is required to pass;
(xii) where the applicant has failed to file an application for any other registration to be filed simultaneously therewith;
(xiii) where the purpose of an application is the registration of a trade name which is prohibited from being registered pursuant to the provision of Article 27;
(xiv) where the purpose of an application is to register a trade name which is prohibited from being used pursuant to the provisions of the laws and regulations;
(xv) where a company whose trade name registration has been cancelled has filed an application for any other registration without making a registration of the trade name; or
(xvi) where the applicant has failed to pay the registration tax.

(Registration to be Made After Lapse of Period for Filing Action)
Article 25　(1) In cases where there exists any ground for invalidating, revoking or rescinding a matter to be registered that may only be asserted by filing an action, and if no action has been filed within the period for filing such action, the provision of item (x) of the preceding Article shall not apply.
(2) In filing a written application for registration in the case referred to in the preceding paragraph, a document evidencing that no action set forth in said paragraph had been filed within the period for filing, as well as a document evidencing the existence of the matters to be registered, shall be attached thereto. In this case, no other document except for that set forth in Article 18 needs to be attached thereto.
(3) A company may file with the district court having jurisdiction over the location of its head office a request for issuance of a document evidencing that no action as set forth in paragraph (1) had been filed within the period for filing.

(Change in Administrative Zone, etc.)
Article 26　In cases where there has been any change of administrative zone, county

(gun), ward (ku), cho or aza within a municipality, or the names thereof, a registration shall be deemed to have been made in accordance with the administrative zones, etc. after such change.

Section 2 Registration of Trade Name

(Prohibition on Registration of Identical Trade Name at Same Location)
Article 27 With regard to the registration of a trade name, if a trade name for which a registration was filed is identical to that already registered by any other party and if the location of the applicant's business office (in the case of a company, its head office; hereinafter the same shall apply in this Article) is the same as the location of such other party's business office for which the trade name has been registered, such registration shall not be made.

(Matters to be Registered, etc.)
Article 28 (1) The registration of a trade name shall be made for each business office.
(2) The matters to be registered in relation to the registration of a trade name shall be as follows:
(i) the trade name;
(ii) the type of enterprise;
(iii) the business office; and
(iv) the name and address of a trade name user.

(Registration of Change, etc.)
Article 29 (1) When a person who has registered the trade name has relocated his/her business office to a jurisdictional district of another registry office, such person shall file an application for a registration of the relocation of the business office at the former location, and a registration of the matters listed in items of paragraph (2) of the preceding Article at the new location.
(2) A person who has registered the trade name shall, when any change occurs to the matters listed in items of paragraph (2) of the preceding Article or when it has discontinued the trade name, file a registration to reflect these events.

(Registration of Transfer or Inheritance of Trade Name)
Article 30 (1) A registration of change due to the transfer of a trade name shall be made by the filing of an application by a transferee.
(2) In filing a written application for registration as set forth in the preceding paragraph, a transferrer's written approval as well as a document evidencing that the requirement under Article 15, paragraph (1) of the Commercial Code has been met shall be attached thereto.
(3) In filing an application for a registration of change due to the inheritance of a trade name, a document evidencing such inheritance shall be attached to the written application.

(Registration of Exemption of Liabilities Upon Transfer of Enterprise or Business)
Article 31 (1) A registration under the first sentence of Article 17, paragraph (2) of the Commercial Code and the first sentence of Article 22, paragraph (2) of the Companies Act shall be made by the filing of an application by a transferee.
(2) In filing a written application for a registration as set forth in the preceding paragraph,

a transferrer's written approval shall be attached thereto.

(Registration Filed by Heir)
Article 32 When an heir intends to file an application for a registration under the preceding three Articles, a document evidencing his/her capacity shall be attached to the written application.

(Cancellation of Registration of Trade Name)
Article 33 (1) In cases where any of the following items applies, if a person who has registered a trade name has failed to file a registration prescribed in any of the relevant items, another person who intends to use a trade name identical thereto at the location of the business office (or a head office, in case of a company; hereinafter the same shall apply in this Article) for which such trade name has been registered may file with a registry office an application to cancel the registration of such trade name.
  (i) where use of the registered trade name has been discontinued: registration of the discontinuance of such trade name;
  (ii) where a person who has registered the trade name has failed to use such trade name for two years without any justifiable ground: registration of the discontinuance of such trade name;
  (iii) where a registered trade name has been changed: registration of the change of such trade name; or
  (iv) where a business office for which a trade name has been registered is relocated: registration of the relocation of such business office.
(2) A person who intends to file an application for cancellation of the registration of a trade name pursuant to the provision of the preceding paragraph shall attach to the written application a document evidencing that such person intends to use the identical trade name at the location of the business office for which such trade name has been registered.
(3) The provisions of Article 135 to Article 137 inclusive shall apply mutatis mutandis to the cases where an application set forth in paragraph (1) has been filed.
(4) In cases where a registrar has rendered a decision to the effect that an objection has a reasonable ground pursuant to the provision of Article 136 as applied mutatis mutandis pursuant to the preceding paragraph, he/she shall dismiss the application set forth in paragraph (1).

(Registration of Trade Name of Company)
Article 34 (1) A registration of a company's trade name shall be entered into a company registry.
(2) The provisions of Article 28, Article 29 and Article 30, paragraphs (1) and (2) shall not apply to a company.

Section 3 Registration of Minor and Guardian

(Matters to be Registered, etc. in Relation to Registration of Minor)
Article 35 (1) The matters to be registered in relation to the registration referred to in Article 5 of the Commercial Code shall be as follows:
  (i) the name, date of birth and address of a minor;
  (ii) the type of business; and
  (iii) the business office.
(2) The provision of Article 29 shall apply mutatis mutandis to a registration of a minor.

(Registration Applicant)
Article 36 (1) The registration of a minor shall be made by the filing of an application by the minor.
(2) A registration of extinction due to rescission of the permission for carrying on business or a registration of change due to imposing a limitation on the permission for carrying on business may also be filed by the minor's statutory agent.
(3) A registration of extinction due to a minor's death shall be made by the filing of an application by the minor's statutory agent.
(4) A registrar may, ex officio, make a registration of extinction on the ground of a minor having attained the age of majority.

(Documents to be Attached)
Article 37 (1) In filing a written application for registration referred to in Article 5 of the Commercial Code, a document evidencing the statutory agent's permission shall be attached thereto; provided, however, that this shall not apply to the cases where the statutory agent has affixed his/her name and seal to the written application.
(2) In cases where the guardian of a minor has granted permission on business to be carried out by a minor ward, if no supervisor of the guardian of a minor has been selected, a document evidencing to that effect, or, if a supervisor of the guardian of a minor has been selected, a document evidencing the consent of such supervisor of the guardian of a minor shall be attached to a written application set forth in the preceding paragraph.
(3) The provisions of the preceding two paragraphs shall apply mutatis mutandis to an application for a registration of change due to an increase in the types of business to be carried on.

Article 38 In cases where a minor has relocated his/her business office to a jurisdictional district of another registry office, a document evidencing the registration made at the former location shall be attached to a written application for the registration to be made at the new location.

Article 39 In filing a written application for a registration of extinction due to the death of a minor, a document evidencing the death of the minor shall be attached thereto.

(Matters to be Registered, etc. in Relation to Registration of Guardian)
Article 40 (1) The matters to be registered in relation to the registration referred to in Article 6, paragraph (1) of the Commercial Code shall be as follows:
(i) the name and address of a guardian;
(ii) the name and address of a ward;
(iii) the type of business;
(iv) the business office;
(v) if there is a provision setting forth that two or more guardians of an adult shall exercise their authority jointly, a statement to that effect; and
(v) if there is a provision setting forth that two or more guardians of an adult shall exercise their authority on handling the affairs assigned to each of them separately, a statement to that effect as well as the contents of the affairs to be handled by each of them.
(2) The provision of Article 29 shall apply mutatis mutandis to the registration of a guardian.

(Registration Applicant)

Art.41～43　⑧ Commercial Registration Act, Chap.III, Sec.4

Article 41　(1) The registration of a guardian shall be made by the filing of an application by a guardian.
(2) A registration of extinction to be made on the ground of a minor ward having attained the age of majority may also be filed by such person. The same shall apply to an application for a registration of extinction to be made due to the revocation of an order for the commencement of guardianship with regard to an adult ward.
(3) A registration of extinction due to the retirement of a guardian may also be filed by a new guardian.

(Documents to be Attached)
Article 42　(1) In filing a written application for registration referred to in Article 6, paragraph (1) of the Commercial Code, the following documents shall be attached thereto:
　(i) in cases where no supervisor of a guardian has been selected, a document evidencing to that effect;
　(ii) in cases where a supervisor of a guardian has been selected, a document evidencing that his/her consent has been obtained; and
　(iii) in cases where a guardian is a juridical person, a certificate of the registered matters of said juridical person; provided, however, that this shall not apply to the cases where the juridical person has its head office or principal office within the jurisdictional district of the registry office where the application is to be filed.
(2) In cases where a guardian is a juridical person, a document listed in item (iii) of the preceding paragraph shall be attached to a written application for a registration of change to the matters listed in Article 40, paragraph (1), item (i); provided, however, that this shall not apply to the case where the proviso to such item applies.
(3) The provision of paragraph (1) (limited to the part pertaining to item (i) or (ii)) shall apply mutatis mutandis to a registration of change due to an increase in the types of business to be carried on.
(4) The provision of Article 38 shall apply mutatis mutandis to a registration to be made at a new location, in cases where a guardian has relocated his/her business office to a jurisdictional district of another registry office.
(5) In filing a written application for registration as set forth in paragraph (2) or (3) of the preceding Article, a document evidencing that a minor ward has attained the age of majority, that an order for the commencement of guardianship with regard to an adult ward has been revoked or that a guardian has retired from his/her office shall be attached thereto.

Section 4　Registration of Manager

(Registration of Manager of Merchants Other Than Companies)
Article 43　(1) The matters to be registered in relation to the registration of a manager of a merchant (excluding a company; hereinafter the same shall apply in this paragraph) shall be as follows:
　(i) the name and address of the manager;
　(ii) the name and address of the merchant;
　(iii) in cases where the merchant conducts two or more types of business using two or more trade names, the businesses to be represented by the manager and the trade name to be used; and
　(iv) the business offices where the manager has been stationed.
(2) The provision of Article 29 shall apply mutatis mutandis to the registration set forth in the preceding paragraph.

(Registration of Company's Manager)
Article 44 (1) The registration of a company's manager shall be entered into a company registry.
(2) The matters to be registered in relation to the registration set forth in the preceding paragraph shall be as follows:
(i) the name and address of the manager; and
(ii) the business office where the manager has been stationed.
(3) The provision of Article 29, paragraph (2) shall apply mutatis mutandis to the registration set forth in paragraph (1).

Article 45 (1) In filing a written application for registration of the election of a company's manager, a document evidencing the election thereof shall be attached thereto.
(2) In filing a written application for registration of the extinction of the authority of agent of a company's manager, a document evidencing such extinction shall be attached thereto.

Section 5 Registration of Stock Company

(General Rules on Documents to be Attached)
Article 46 (1) In cases where any matter to be registered requires the consent of all shareholders or class shareholders, or the unanimous consent of specific directors or liquidators, a document evidencing that such consent or unanimous consent has been obtained shall be attached to the written application.
(2) In cases where any matter to be registered requires the resolution of a shareholders meeting, class shareholders meeting, board of directors or board of liquidators, the relevant minutes shall be attached to the written application.
(3) In cases where any matters to be registered are deemed to have been resolved by a shareholders meeting, class shareholders meeting, board of directors or board of liquidators pursuant to the provision of Article 319, paragraph (1) of the Companies Act (including the cases where applied mutatis mutandis pursuant to Article 325 of said Act) or Article 370 of said Act (including cases where applied mutatis mutandis pursuant to Article 490, paragraph (5) of said Act), a document evidencing the case referred to in these provisions is applicable shall, in lieu of the minutes set forth in the preceding paragraph, be attached to the written application.
(4) With regard to any matter to be registered by a company with committees, in cases where an executive officer delegated by resolution of a board of directors pursuant to the provision of Article 416, paragraph (4) of the Companies Act has made any decision, a document evidencing that such decision has been made shall, in addition to the minutes of the relevant board of directors, be attached to the written application.

(Registration of Incorporation)
Article 47 (1) The registration of incorporation of a company shall be made by the filing of an application by a person who shall represent the company.
(2) Unless otherwise provided for in the laws and regulations, the following documents shall be attached to a written application for registration of incorporation:
(i) the articles of incorporation;
(ii) in the case where a solicitation set forth in Article 57, paragraph (1) of the Companies Act has been made, a document evidencing that an application for a subscription for the shares solicited at incorporation as set forth in Article 58, paragraph (1) of said Act has been made or a document evidencing the execution of the contract under Article 61 of said Act;

Art.47　⑧ Commercial Registration Act, Chap.III, Sec.5

(iii) in cases where the articles of incorporation contain any statement or record on the matters listed in items of Article 28 of the Companies Act, the following documents:
(a) a document containing an investigation report prepared by inspectors or directors at incorporation (in cases where a stock company to be incorporated is a company with auditors, directors at incorporation and auditors at incorporation) as well as documents annexed thereto;
(b) in the cases referred to in Article 33, paragraph (10), item (ii) of the Companies Act, a document evidencing the market price of securities (meaning the securities prescribed in said item; the same shall apply hereinafter);
(c) in the cases referred to in Article 33, paragraph (10), item (iii) of the Companies Act, a document containing the verification prescribed in said item as well as documents annexed thereto;
(iv) in the cases where any judicial decision has been rendered in relation to an inspector's report, a transcript of such decision;
(v) a document evidencing the completion of a contribution in money as prescribed in Article 34, paragraph (1) of the Companies Act (in cases where a solicitation set forth in Article 57, paragraph (1) of said Act has been made, a certificate of deposit of the money prescribed in Article 64, paragraph (1) of said Act);
(vi) in cases where there is an administrator of shareholder registry, a document evidencing execution of a contract with such person;
(vii) in cases where a representative director at incorporation has been elected by directors at incorporation, a document relevant thereto;
(viii) in cases where a stock company to be incorporated is a company with committees, a document relevant to the appointment of executive officers at incorporation and a document related to the election of committee members at incorporation and the representative executive officer at incorporation;
(ix) minutes of the organizational meeting and class organizational meeting;
(x) a document evidencing that each of the directors at incorporation, auditors at incorporation and the representative director at incorporation (in cases where the stock company to be incorporated is a company with committees, directors at incorporation, committee members at incorporation, executive officers at incorporation and the representative executive officer at incorporation) appointed or elected pursuant to the provisions of the Companies Act has consented to assume their respective offices;
(xi) in cases where an accounting advisor at incorporation or an accounting auditor at incorporation has been appointed, the following documents:
(a) a document evidencing such person's acceptance of the assumption of office;
(b) in cases where any of these persons is a juridical person, a certificate of registered matters of said juridical person; provided, however, that this shall not apply to cases where the juridical person has its principal office within the jurisdictional district of the registry office where the application is to be filed.
(c) in cases where any of these persons is not a juridical person, a document evidencing that the person appointed as accounting advisor at incorporation falls under any of the persons specified in Article 333, paragraph (1) of the Companies Act, and a document evidencing that the person appointed as accounting advisor at incorporation falls under any of the persons specified in Article 337, paragraph (1) of said Act.
(xii) in cases where there is a provision setting forth that specific matters may be resolved by special directors (meaning special directors as prescribed in Article 373, paragraph (1) of the Companies Act; the same shall apply hereinafter) pursuant to

the provision of said paragraph, a document evidencing the election of such special directors and acceptance of the assumption of office by the persons so elected;
(3) In cases where any matter to be registered requires the consent of all the incorporators or the unanimous consent of specific incorporators, a document evidencing that such consent or unanimous consent has been obtained shall be attached to the written application for registration set forth in the preceding paragraph.
(4) In cases where a resolution of an organizational meeting or class organizational meeting is deemed to have been made pursuant to the provision of Article 82, paragraph (1) of the Companies Act (including the cases where applied mutatis mutandis pursuant to Article 86 of said Act), a document evidencing that such case is applicable shall, in lieu of the minutes specified in item (ix) of paragraph (2), be attached to the written application for registration set forth in said paragraph.

(Registration to be Made at Location of Branch Office)
Article 48 (1) With regard to any matter to be registered at the locations of the head office and branch offices, in filing a written application for registration to be made at the location of a branch office, a document evidencing registration made at the location of the head office shall be attached thereto. In such case, no other document needs to be attached thereto.
(2) With regard to registration of the matters listed in the items of Article 930, paragraph (2) of the Companies Act at the location of a branch office, the date of incorporation of the company, the fact of the establishment or relocation of the branch office and the date of such establishment or relocation shall also be registered.

Article 49 (1) In cases where a company having its head office in the jurisdictional district of a registry office designated by the Minister of Justice intends to file a registration at the location of a branch office with regard to any matter to be registered at the locations of the head office and branch offices, if such branch office is located within the jurisdictional district of other registry office designated by the Minister of Justice, such company may file an application for said registration via the registry office having jurisdiction over the location of its head office.
(2) The designation set forth in the preceding paragraph shall be made by means of public notice.
(3) An application for registration under paragraph (1) and an application for registration to be made at the location of the head office shall be filed simultaneously.
(4) The provisions concerning the documents to be attached to a written application shall not apply to an application for registration under paragraph (1).
(5) A person who intends to file a registration pursuant to the provision of paragraph (1) shall pay the fees.
(6) The amount of fees set forth in the preceding paragraph shall be specified by a Cabinet Order, taking into consideration any and all circumstances such as commodity price levels, actual costs incurred for the notice set forth in paragraphs (2) and (3) of the following Article and others.
(7) The provision of Article 13, paragraph (2) shall apply mutatis mutandis to the payment of fees under paragraph (5).

Article 50 (1) In cases where any of the grounds listed in the items of Article 24 is applicable to an application for registration set forth in paragraph (1) of the preceding Article, a registry office having jurisdiction over the location of the head office shall dismiss said application. The same shall apply to the cases where an applicant has failed to make payment of the fees under paragraph (5) of the preceding Article.

Art.51～53 ⑧ Commercial Registration Act, Chap.III, Sec.5

(2) In the cases referred to in paragraph (1) of the preceding Article, if a registry office having jurisdiction over the location of the head office has made the registration of the matters to be registered at the location of the head office, it shall, without delay, notify the registry office having jurisdiction over the location of the branch office to the effect that the application for registration set forth in said paragraph has been filed; provided, however, that this shall not apply to the cases where the application has been dismissed pursuant to the provision of the preceding paragraph.

(3) In the cases referred to in the main text of the preceding paragraph, if the application for registration set forth paragraph (1) of the preceding Article is an application for registration of incorporation, a registry office having jurisdiction over the location of the head office shall also notify the date of incorporation of the company.

(4) In cases where notice under the preceding two paragraphs has been given, the registrar of a registry office having jurisdiction over the location of the branch office shall be deemed to have received the written application for registration set forth in paragraph (1) of the preceding Article, and the provision of Article 21 shall apply.

(Registration of Relocation of Head Office)
Article 51 (1) In cases of the relocation of a head office to a jurisdictional district of another registry office, an application for registration to be made at the new location shall be filed via the registry office having jurisdiction over the former location. The same shall apply to the submission of a seal impression to a registry office having jurisdiction over the new location pursuant to the provision of Article 20, paragraph (1) or (2).

(2) An application for registration as set forth in the preceding paragraph and an application for registration to be made at the former location shall be filed simultaneously.

(3) In filing a written application for registration as set forth in paragraph (1), no document other than that set forth in Article 18 needs to be attached thereto.

Article 52 (1) In cases where any of the grounds listed in the items of Article 24 is applicable to any of the applications for registration set forth in paragraph (2) of the preceding Article, a registry office having jurisdiction over the former location shall dismiss both of those applications simultaneously.

(2) Except for the case referred to in the preceding paragraph, a registry office having jurisdiction over the former location shall, without delay, send to a registry office having jurisdiction over the new location the written application for registration set forth in paragraph (1) of the preceding Article with its attachments and the seal impression prescribed in said paragraph.

(3) In cases where a registry office having jurisdiction over the new location has received a written application sent under the preceding paragraph, and in cases where it has made the registration set forth in paragraph (1) of the preceding Article or has dismissed such application for registration, it shall, without delay, notify the registry office having jurisdiction over the former location to that effect.

(4) A registry office having jurisdiction over the former location may not make registrations unless and until it has received a notice of completion of registration pursuant to the provision of the preceding paragraph.

(5) In cases where a registry office having jurisdiction over the new location has dismissed an application for registration as set forth in paragraph (1) of the preceding Article, the application for registration filed at the former location shall be deemed to have been dismissed.

Article 53 With regard to the registration to be made at the new location, the date of incorporation of a company, and the fact of the relocation of the head office and the date of the relocation thereof shall also be registered.

(Registration of Change of Directors and Other Officers)
Article 54 (1) In filing an application for a registration of change due to the assumption of office of a director, company auditor, representative director or special director (in the case of a company with committees, a director, committee member, executive officer or representative executive officer), a document evidencing the acceptance of the assumption of each of these offices shall be attached to a written application.
(2) In filing an application for a registration of change due to the assumption of office of an accounting advisor or an accounting auditor, the following documents shall be attached to the written application:
(i) a document evidencing such person's acceptance of the assumption of office;
(ii) in cases where any of those persons is a juridical person, a certificate of registered matters of said juridical person; provided, however, that this shall not apply to cases where the juridical person has its principal office within the jurisdictional district of the registry office where the application is to be filed; and
(iii) in cases where any of those persons is not a juridical person, a document evidencing that the person appointed as an accounting advisor falls under any of the persons specified in Article 333, paragraph (1) of the Companies Act, and a document evidencing that the person appointed as an accounting advisor falls under any of the persons specified in Article 337, paragraph (1) of said Act.
(3) In cases where an accounting advisor or an accounting auditor is a juridical person, the documents listed in item (ii) of the preceding paragraph shall be attached to a written application for a registration of change of name; provided, however, that this shall not apply to the cases where proviso to said item applies.
(4) In filing a written application for a registration of change due to the retirement of a person specified in paragraph (1) or (2), a document evidencing such retirement shall be attached thereto.

(Registration of Change of Person Who is to Temporarily Perform Duties of Accounting Auditor)
Article 55 (1) In filing a written application for a registration of change due to the assumption of office of a person who is to temporarily perform the duties of an accounting auditor as prescribed in Article 346, paragraph (4) of the Companies Act, the following documents shall be attached thereto:
(i) a document relevant to appointment of such person;
(ii) a document evidencing such person's acceptance of the assumption of office;
(iii) in cases where such person is a juridical person, a document listed in item (ii) of paragraph (2) of the preceding Article; provided, however, that this shall not apply to the cases where the proviso to said item applies; and
(iv) in cases where such person is not a juridical person, a document evidencing that he/she is a certified public accountant.
(2) The provisions of paragraphs (3) and (4) of the preceding Article shall apply mutatis mutandis to the registration of a person who is to temporarily perform the duties of an accounting auditor.

(Registration of Change Due to Issues of Shares for Subscription)
Article 56 In filing a written application for a registration of change due to the issue of shares for subscription (meaning shares for subscription as prescribed in Article 199, paragraph (1) of the Companies Act; the same shall apply in item (i)), the following

documents shall be attached thereto:
(i) a document evidencing that an application for subscription for the shares for subscription has been made, or that the contract set forth in Article 205 of the Companies Act has been executed;
(ii) in cases where monies is the subject of a contribution, a document evidencing completion of the payment prescribed in Article 208, paragraph (1) of the Companies Act;
(iii) in cases where a property other than money is the subject of a contribution, the following documents:
   (a) in cases where an inspector has been appointed, a document containing the inspector's investigation report and the documents annexed thereto;
   (b) in the case referred to in Article 207, paragraph (9), item (iii) of the Companies Act, a document evidencing the market price of securities;
   (c) in the case referred to in Article 207, paragraph (9), item (iv) of the Companies Act, a document containing a verification under said item and the documents annexed thereto; and
   (d) in the case referred to in Article 207, paragraph (9), item (v) of the Companies Act, an accounting book containing a statement of the money claim set forth in said item.
(iv) in the cases where any judicial decision has been rendered in relation to an inspector's report, a transcript of such decision.

(Registration of Change due to Exercising of Share Options)
Article 57 In filing a written application for a registration of change due to the exercising of share options, the following documents shall be attached thereto:
(i) a document evidencing that the share options have been exercised;
(ii) in cases where monies are the subject of the contribution to be made on the exercise of share options, a document evidencing completion of the payment under Article 281, paragraph (1) of the Companies Act;
(iii) in cases where any property other than monies is the subject of the contribution to be made on the exercise of share options, the following documents:
   (a) in cases where an inspector has been appointed, a document containing the inspector's investigation report and the documents annexed thereto;
   (b) in the case referred to in Article 284, paragraph (9), item (iii) of the Companies Act, a document evidencing the market price of securities;
   (c) in the case referred to in Article 284, paragraph (9), item (iv) of the Companies Act, a document containing a verification under said item and documents annexed thereto;
   (d) in the case referred to in Article 284, paragraph (9), item (v) of the Companies Act, an accounting book containing a statement on the monetary claim set forth in said item; and
   (e) in the case referred to in the second sentence of Article 281, paragraph (2) of the Companies Act, a document evidencing completion of the payment of monies equivalent to the balance set forth in the second sentence of said paragraph.
(iv) in cases where any judicial decision has been rendered in relation to an inspector's report, a transcript of such decision.

(Registration of Change Due to Delivery of Shares in Exchange for Acquisition of Shares with Put Option)
Article 58 In filing a written application for a registration of change due to the delivery of shares in exchange for the acquisition of shares with put option (limited to those for

which, as a feature of the shares, the matters listed in Article 108, paragraph (2), item (v), sub-item (b) of the Companies Act have been provided), a document evidencing that a demand for the acquisition of such shares with put option has been made shall be attached thereto.

(Registration of Change Due to Delivery of Shares in Exchange for Acquisition of Shares Subject to Call)
Article 59 (1) In filing a written application for a registration of change due to the delivery of shares in exchange for the acquisition of shares subject to call (limited to those for which, as a feature of the shares, the matters listed in Article 108, paragraph (2), item (vi), sub-item (b) of the Companies Act have been provided), the following documents shall be attached thereto:
(i) a document evidencing that the ground set forth in Article 107, paragraph (2), item (iii), sub-item (a) of the Companies Act has arisen; and
(ii) in the case of a company issuing share certificates a document evidencing that such company has given the public notice under the main text of Article 219, paragraph (1) of the Companies Act or that such company has not issued share certificates for any of its shares.
(2) In filing a written application for a registration of change due to the delivery of shares in exchange for the acquisition of share options subject to call (limited to those for which, as a feature of the share options, the matters listed in Article 236, paragraph (1), item (vii), sub-item (d) of the Companies Act have been provided), the following documents shall be attached thereto:
(i) a document evidencing that the ground set forth in Article 236, paragraph (1), item (vii), sub-item (a) of the Companies Act has arisen; and
(ii) a document evidencing that the public notice under Article 293, paragraph (1) of the Companies Act has been given, or that no share option certificate under said paragraph has been issued.

(Registration of Change Due to Delivery of Shares in Exchange for Acquisition of Class Shares Subject to Wholly Call)
Article 60 In filing a written application for a registration of change due to the delivery of shares in exchange for the acquisition of class shares subject to wholly call (meaning class shares subject to wholly call as set forth in Article 171, paragraph (1) of the Companies Act; the same shall apply in Article 68) which has been implemented by a company issuing share certificates, a document listed in item (ii), paragraph (1) of the preceding Article shall be attached thereto.

(Registration of Change due to Consolidation of Shares)
Article 61 With regard to a written application for a registration of change due to the consolidation of shares to be made by a company issuing share certificates, a document listed in Article 59, paragraph (1), item (ii) shall be attached thereto.

(Registration of Change Due to Establishment of Provision of Article of Incorporation Restricting Share Transfer)
Article 62 In filing a written application for a registration of change due to the establishment of a provision of the articles of incorporation providing that the acquisition of shares by transfer requires the company's approval (limited to a registration made by a company issuing share certificates), a document listed in Article 59, paragraph (1), item (ii) shall be attached thereto.

Art.63～67　⑧ Commercial Registration Act, Chap.III, Sec.5

(Registration of Change Due to Abolition of Provisions of Articles of Incorporation that Share Certificates be Issued)
Article 63　In filing a written application for a registration of change due to the abolition of a provision of the articles of incorporation that share certificates be issued, a document evidencing that the company has given public notice under Article 218, paragraph (1) of the Companies Act, or that the company has not issued share certificates for any of its shares shall be attached thereto.

(Registration of Change Due to Appointment of Administrator of Shareholder Registry)
Article 64　In filing a written application for a registration of change due to the appointment of an administrator of a shareholder registry, the articles of incorporation and a document evidencing the execution of a contract with said person shall be attached thereto.

(Registration of Change Due to Share Option Issue)
Article 65　Unless otherwise provided for in the laws and regulations, in filing a written application for a registration of change due to a share option issue, the following documents shall be attached thereto:
(i) a document evidencing that the application for subscription of the share options for subscription (meaning the share options for subscription prescribed in Article 238, paragraph (1) of the Companies Act; the same shall apply in the next item) has been made, or that the contract set forth in Article 244, paragraph (1) of said Act has been executed; and
(ii) in cases where a date for the payment of monies in exchange for the share options for subscription has been prescribed (limited to the cases where such date falls within the day prior to the day of allotment prescribed in Article 238, paragraph (1), item (iv) of the Companies Act), a document evidencing that the payment under Article 246, paragraph (1) of said Act (including the tendering of property other than monies or setting off of claims against the company, as provided for by paragraph (2) of said Article) has been completed.

(Registration of Change Due to Delivery of Share Options in Exchange for Acquisition of Shares with Put Option)
Article 66　In filing a written application for a registration of change due to the delivery of share options in exchange for the acquisition of shares with put option (limited to those for which, as a feature of the shares, the matters listed in Article 107, paragraph (2), item (ii), sub-item (c) or (d) of the Companies Act have been provided), a document evidencing that a demand for the acquisition of such shares with put option has been made shall be attached thereto.

(Registration of Change Due to Delivery of Share Options in Exchange for Acquisition of Shares Subject to Call)
Article 67　(1) In filing a written application for a registration of change due to the delivery of share options in exchange for the acquisition of shares subject to call (limited to those for which, as a feature of the shares, the matters listed in Article 107, paragraph (2), item (iii), sub-item (e) or (f) of the Companies Act have been provided), the documents listed in the items of Article 59, paragraph (1) shall be attached thereto.
(2) In filing a written application for a registration of change due to the delivery of share options in exchange for the acquisition of share options subject to call (limited to those for which, as a feature of the share options, the matters listed in Article 236, paragraph

(1), item (vii), sub-item (f) or (g) of the Companies Act has been provided), the documents listed in the items of Article 59, paragraph (2) shall be attached thereto.

(Registration of Change Due to Delivery of Share Options in Exchange for Acquisition of Class Shares Subject to Wholly Call)
Article 68 In filing a written application for a registration of change due to the delivery of share options in exchange for the acquisition of class shares subject to wholly call which has been implemented by a company issuing share certificates, a document listed in Article 59, paragraph (1), item (ii) shall be attached thereto.

(Registration of Change Due to Increase in Amount of States Capital)
Article 69 In filing a written application for a registration of change due to an increase in the amount of stated capital by reducing the amount of the capital reserve, retained earnings reserve or surplus, a document evidencing that the amount of the capital reserve, retained earnings reserve or surplus pertaining to such reduction have been recorded shall be attached thereto.

(Registration of Change Due to Reduction in Amount of Stated Capital)
Article 70 In filing a written application for a registration of change due to a reduction in the amount of stated capital, a document evidencing that the public notice and the notices under Article 449, paragraph (2) of the Companies Act (in cases where, in addition to public notice in an official gazette, a public notice has been given by publication in a daily newspaper that publishes matters on current affairs or by means of electronic public notices pursuant to the provision of paragraph (3) of said Article, public notice by such method) have been given, and, if any creditor has raised an objection, a document evidencing that the company has made a payment or provided equivalent security to such creditor or has entrusted equivalent property for the purpose of making such creditor receive the payment, or that there is no risk of harm to such creditor by such reduction in the amount of the stated capital, shall be attached thereto.

(Registration of Dissolution)
Article 71 (1) The matters to be registered in relation to a registration of dissolution shall be the fact of dissolution, as well as the grounds and the date therefor.
(2) In filing a written application for a registration of dissolution on any ground for dissolution provided for in the articles of incorporation, a document evidencing that such ground has arisen shall be attached thereto.
(3) In filing a written application for a registration of dissolution filed by a representative liquidator, a document evidencing the capacity of such representative liquidator shall be attached thereto; provided, however, that this shall not apply to the cases where said representative liquidator has assumed the office of liquidator of a liquidating stock company pursuant to the provision of Article 478, paragraph (1), item (i) of the Companies Act (in the cases referred to in Article 483, paragraph (4) of said Act, the cases where said representative liquidator has assumed the office of representative liquidator of a liquidating stock company pursuant to the provision of said paragraph).

(Ex Officio Registration of Dissolution)
Article 72 A registrar shall, ex officio, make a registration of dissolution under the main text of Article 472, paragraph (1) of the Companies Act.

(Registration of Liquidator)
Article 73 (1) In filing a written application for the registration of a liquidator, the articles

of incorporation shall be attached thereto.
(2) In filing a written application for the registration of a liquidator in the cases where a person listed in Article 478, paragraph (1), item (ii) or (iii) of the Companies Act has assumed the office of liquidator, a document evidencing such person's acceptance on the assumption of office shall be attached thereto.
(3) In filing a written application for the registration of a liquidator in the cases where a person appointed by a court has assumed the office of liquidator, a document evidencing the fact of such appointment and the matters listed in Article 928, paragraph (1), item (ii) of the Companies Act shall be attached thereto.

(Registration of Change Related to Liquidator)
Article 74 (1) In filing a written application for a registration of change to any of the matters listed in Article 928, paragraph (1), item (ii) of the Companies Act which relates to a liquidator appointed by a court, a document evidencing the grounds for such change shall be attached thereto.
(2) In filing a written application for a registration of change due to the retirement of a liquidator, a document evidencing such retirement shall be attached thereto.

(Registration of Completion of Liquidation)
Article 75 In filing a written application for a registration of completion of liquidation, a document evidencing that the settlement of accounts has been approved under Article 507, paragraph (3) of the Companies Act shall be attached thereto.

(Registration of Entity Conversion)
Article 76 In filing a registration concerning a membership company after entity conversion in cases where a stock company has effected an entity conversion, the date of incorporation of the company, trade name of the stock company as well as the fact and date of the entity conversion shall also be registered.

Article 77 In filing a written application for the registration set forth in the preceding Article, the following documents shall be attached thereto:
(i) an entity conversion plan;
(ii) the articles of incorporation;
(iii) a document evidencing that the public notice and the notices under Article 779, paragraph (2) of the Companies Act (in cases where, in addition to public notice in an official gazette, a public notice has been given by publication in a daily newspaper that publishes matters on current affairs or by means of electronic public notices pursuant to the provision of paragraph (3) of said Article, the public notice by such method) has been given, and, if any creditor has raised an objection, a document evidencing that the company has made payment or provided equivalent security to such creditor or has entrusted equivalent property for the purpose of making such creditor receive the payment, or that there is no risk of harm to such creditor by such entity conversion;
(iv) in cases where a stock company effecting an entity conversion is a company issuing share certificates, a document listed in Article 59, paragraph (1), item (ii);
(v) in cases where a stock company effecting an entity conversion has issued share options, a document listed in Article 59, paragraph (2), item (ii);
(vi) in cases where a juridical person is to become a partner representing a membership company after entity conversion, the following documents:
　(a) a certificate of registered matters of said juridical person; provided, however, that this shall not apply to cases where the juridical person has its head office or

principal office in the jurisdictional district of the registry office where the application is to be filed;
(b) a document relevant to the appointment of a person who is to perform the duties of the partner; and
(c) a document evidencing that a person who is to perform the duties of the partner has consented to assume his/her office.
(vii) in cases where a juridical person is to become the partner of a membership company after entity conversion (excluding a partner specified in the preceding item, and, with regard to a limited liability company, limited to a partner who executes business), a document listed in sub-item (a) of said item; provided, however, that this shall not apply to the cases where the proviso to sub-item (a) of said item applies; and
(viii) in cases where a stock company intends to effect an entity conversion into a limited partnership company, a document evidencing the value of the contributions already made by the limited partners.

Article 78 (1) In cases where a stock company has effected an entity conversion, an application for registration concerning the stock company and an application for registration concerning the membership company after such entity conversion shall be filed simultaneously.
(2) The provisions on the documents to be attached to a written application shall not apply to an application for registration as set forth in the preceding paragraph concerning a stock company.
(3) In cases where any of the grounds listed in the items of Article 24 is applicable to either of the applications for registration set forth in paragraph (1), a registrar shall dismiss both of those applications simultaneously.

(Registration of Merger)
Article 79 With regard to a registration of change due to an absorption-type merger or a registration of incorporation due to a consolidation-type merger, the fact that the merger has been implemented, as well as the trade name and head office of a company absorbed in the absorption-type merger (hereinafter referred to as a "company absorbed in absorption-type merger") or of a company consolidated through the consolidation-type merger (hereinafter referred to as a "company consolidated through consolidation-type merger") shall also be registered.

Article 80 In filing a written application for a registration of change due to an absorption-type merger, the following documents shall be attached thereto:
(i) an absorption-type merger agreement;
(ii) in the case referred to in the main text of paragraph (1) or of paragraph (3) of Article 796 of the Companies Act, a document evidencing that the case provided for therein is applicable (in cases where any shareholder has notified to the effect that such shareholder dissents from the absorption-type merger pursuant to the provision of paragraph (4) of said Article, including a document evidencing that such absorption-type merger does not fall under the case provided for in said paragraph where approval by a resolution of a shareholders meeting is required);
(iii) a document evidencing that the public notice and the notices under Article 799, paragraph (2) of the Companies Act (in cases where, in addition to public notice in an official gazette, a public notice has been given by publication in a daily newspaper that publishes matters on current affairs or by means of electronic public notices pursuant to the provision of paragraph (3) of said Article, the public notice by

Art.81   ⑧ Commercial Registration Act, Chap.III, Sec.5

such method) has been given, and, if any creditor has raised an objection, a document evidencing that the company has made a payment or provided equivalent security to such creditor or has entrusted equivalent property for the purpose of making such creditor receive the payment, or that there is no risk of harm to such creditor by such absorption-type merger;
(iv) a document evidencing that the amount of stated capital has been recorded pursuant to the provision of Article 445, paragraph (5) of the Companies Act;
(v) a certificate of registered matters of a company absorbed in absorption-type merger; provided, however, that this shall not apply to the cases where the company absorbed in absorption-type merger has its head office in the jurisdictional district of the registry office where the application is to be filed;
(vi) in cases where a company absorbed in absorption-type merger is a stock company, a document evidencing the performance of the relevant procedures under Article 783, paragraphs (1) to (4) inclusive of the Companies Act such as obtaining approval for an absorption-type merger agreement (in the cases referred to in the main text of Article 784, paragraph (1) of said Act, a document evidencing that the case provided for therein is applicable and a document or minutes of a board of directors evidencing that the consent of the majority of directors has been obtained);
(vii) in cases where a company absorbed in absorption-type merger is a membership company, a document evidencing that the consent of all partners has been obtained (or, in cases where otherwise provided for in its articles of incorporation, that the procedures under such provision have been performed);
(viii) a document evidencing that a company absorbed in absorption-type merger has given the public notice and the notices under Article 789, paragraph (2) of the Companies Act (excluding item (iii), and including the cases where applied mutatis mutandis pursuant to Article 793, paragraph (2) of said Act) (in cases of a stock company or a limited liability company which, in addition to public notice in an official gazette, has given a public notice by publication in a daily newspaper that publishes matters on current affairs or by method of electronic public notices pursuant to the provision of Article 789, paragraph (3) of said Act (including the cases where applied mutatis mutandis pursuant to Article 793, paragraph (2) of said Act), that the public notice was given by such method), and, if any creditor has raised an objection, a document evidencing that the company has made a payment or provided equivalent security to such creditor or has entrusted equivalent property for the purpose of making such creditor receive the payment, or that there is no risk of harm to such creditor by such absorption-type merger;
(ix) in cases where a company absorbed in absorption-type merger is a company issuing share certificates, a document listed in Article 59, paragraph (1), item (ii); and
(x) in cases where a company absorbed in absorption-type merger has issued share options, a document listed in Article 59, paragraph (2), item (ii).

Article 81 In filing a written application for the registration of incorporation due to a consolidation-type merger, the following documents shall be attached thereto:
(i) a consolidation-type merger agreement;
(ii) the articles of incorporation;
(iii) the documents listed in items (vi) to (viii) inclusive and items (x) to (xii) inclusive of Article 47, paragraph (2);
(iv) a document listed in item (iv) of the preceding Article;
(v) a certificate of registered matters of a company consolidated through consolidation-type merger; provided, however, that this shall not apply to the cases where the company consolidated through consolidation-type merger has its head office in the

1162   第Ⅰ部 会社法・商法編

jurisdictional district of the registry office where the application is to be filed;
(vi) in cases where a company consolidated through consolidation-type merger is a stock company, a document evidencing the performance of the relevant procedures under Article 804, paragraphs (1) and (3) of the Companies Act such as obtaining approval on the consolidation-type merger agreement;
(vii) in cases where a company consolidated through consolidation-type merger is a membership company, a document evidencing that the consent of all partners has been obtained (or, in cases where otherwise provided for in its articles of incorporation, that the procedures under said provision have been performed);
(viii) a document evidencing that a company consolidated through consolidation-type merger has given the public notice and the notices under Article 810, paragraph (2) of the Companies Act (excluding item (iii), and including the cases where applied mutatis mutandis pursuant to Article 813, paragraph (2) of said Act) (with regard to a stock company or a limited liability company which, in addition to public notice in an official gazette, has given a public notice by publication in a daily newspaper that publishes matters on current affairs or by method of electronic public notices pursuant to the provision of Article 810, paragraph (3) of said Act (including the cases where applied mutatis mutandis pursuant to Article 813, paragraph (2) of said Act), that the public notice was given by such method), and, if any creditor has raised an objection, a document evidencing that the company has made a payment or provided equivalent security to such creditor or has entrusted equivalent property for the purpose of making such creditor receive the payment, or that there is no risk of harm to such creditor by such consolidation-type merger;
(ix) in cases where a company consolidated through consolidation-type merger is a company issuing share certificates, a document listed in Article 59, paragraph (1), item (ii); and
(x) in cases where a company consolidated through consolidation-type merger has issued share options, a document listed in Article 59, paragraph (2), item (ii).

Article 82 (1) In filing an application for a registration of dissolution due to a merger, a person who shall represent a company surviving an absorption-type merger (hereinafter referred to as a "company surviving absorption-type merger") or a company incorporated through a consolidation-type merger (hereinafter referred to as a "company incorporated through consolidation-type merger") shall represent said company surviving absorption-type merger or company incorporated through consolidation-type merger.
(2) With regard to an application for the registration set forth in the preceding paragraph to be made at the location of the head office, if a company surviving absorption-type merger or company incorporated through consolidation-type merger does not have its head office within the jurisdictional district of the registry office where such application is to be filed, such application shall be filed via a registry office having jurisdiction over the location of its head office.
(3) An application for registration as set forth in paragraph (1) to be made at the location of the head office, and an application for registration as set forth in Article 80 or the preceding Article shall be filed simultaneously.
(4) The provisions on the documents to be attached to a written application and the provisions of Article 20, paragraphs (1) and (2) shall not apply to an application for registration as set forth in paragraph (1) to be made at the location of the head office.

Article 83 (1) In cases where any of the grounds listed in the items of Article 24 is applicable to any application for registration set forth in paragraph (3) of the preceding Ar-

ticle, a registry office having jurisdiction over the location of the head office of a company surviving absorption-type merger or company incorporated through consolidation-type merger shall dismiss all of these applications simultaneously.
(2) In the case referred to in paragraph (2) of the preceding Article, if a registry office having jurisdiction over the location of the head office of a company surviving absorption-type merger or company incorporated through consolidation-type merger has made a registration of change due to an absorption-type merger or a registration of incorporation due to a consolidation-type merger, such registry office shall, without delay, enter the date of said registration on the written application for registration set forth in said paragraph and send it to the registry office having jurisdiction over the location of the head office of the company surviving absorption-type merger or company incorporated through consolidation-type merger.

(Registration of Company Split)
Article 84 (1) With regard to a registration of change due to an absorption-type company split to be made by a company which succeeds to all or part of the rights and obligations held by another company implementing an absorption-type company split in connection with its business (hereinafter referred to as a "succeeding company in absorption-type company split"), or with regard to a registration of incorporation due to incorporation-type company split, the fact that the company split has taken place as well as the trade name and head office of a company effecting an absorption-type company split (hereinafter referred to as a "splitting company in absorption-type company split[x8]") or of a company effecting an incorporation-type company split (hereinafter referred to as a "splitting company in incorporation-type company split") shall also be registered.
(2) With regard to a registration of change due to an absorption-type company split or an incorporation-type company split to be made by a splitting company in absorption-type company split or a splitting company in incorporation-type company split, the fact that the company split has taken place as well as the trade name and head office of a succeeding company in absorption-type company split or of a company incorporated through an incorporation-type company split (hereinafter referred to as a "company incorporated through incorporation-type company split") shall also be registered.

Article 85 With regard to a written application for a registration of change due to an absorption-type company split to be made by a succeeding company in absorption-type company split, the following documents shall be attached thereto:
(i) an absorption-type company split agreement;
(ii) in the cases referred to in the main text of paragraph (1) or of paragraph (3) of Article 796 of the Companies Act, a document evidencing that the case provided for therein is applicable (in cases where any shareholder has notified to the effect that such shareholder dissents from an absorption-type company split pursuant to the provision of paragraph (4) of said Article, including a document evidencing that such absorption-type company split does not fall under the case provided for in said paragraph where the approval by a resolution of a shareholders meeting is required;
(iii) a document evidencing that the public notice and the notices under Article 799, paragraph (2) of the Companies Act (in cases where, in addition to the public notice in an official gazette, a public notice has been given by publication in a daily newspaper that publishes matters on current affairs or by means of electronic public notices pursuant to the provision of paragraph (3) of said Article, the public notice by such method) has been given, and, if any creditor has raised an objection, a docu-

ment evidencing that the company has made a payment or provided equivalent security to such creditor or has entrusted equivalent property for the purpose of making such creditor receive the payment, or that there is no risk of harm to such creditor by such absorption-type company split;
(iv) a document evidencing that the amount of stated capital has been recorded pursuant to the provision of Article 445, paragraph (5) of the Companies Act;
(v) a certificate of registered matters of a splitting company in absorption-type company split; provided, however, that this shall not apply to the cases where a splitting company in absorption-type company split has its head office in the jurisdictional district of the registry office where the application is to be filed;
(vi) in cases where a splitting company in absorption-type company split is a stock company, a document evidencing that the absorption-type company split agreement has been approved under Article 783, paragraph (1) of the Companies Act (in the cases referred to in the main text of Article 784, paragraph (1) of the Companies Act or in the provision of paragraph (3) of said Article, a document evidencing that the case provided for therein is applicable and a document or minutes of board of directors evidencing that the consent of the majority of directors has been obtained);
(vii) in cases where a splitting company in absorption-type company split is a limited liability company, a document evidencing that the consent of all the partners has been obtained (or, in cases where otherwise provided for in its articles of incorporation, that the procedures under said provision have been performed)(in cases where said limited liability company intends to have another company succeed to a part of its rights and obligations held in connection with its business, a document evidencing that the consent of the majority of the partners has been obtained);
(viii) a document evidencing that a splitting company in absorption-type company split has given the public notice and the notices under Article 789, paragraph (2) of the Companies Act (excluding item (iii), and including the cases where applied mutatis mutandis pursuant to Article 793, paragraph (2) of said Act) (in cases where, in addition to public notice in an official gazette, a public notice by publication in a daily newspaper that publishes matters on current affairs or by method of electronic public notices pursuant to the provision of Article 789, paragraph (3) of said Act (including the cases where applied mutatis mutandis pursuant to Article 793, paragraph (2) of said Act; hereinafter the same shall apply in this item), that the public notice was given by such method (in the cases excluding where separate notices are not required to be given pursuant to the provision of Article 789, paragraph (3) of the Companies Act, that the public notice and the notices were given)), and, if any creditor has raised an objection, a document evidencing that the company has made a payment or provided equivalent security to such creditor or has entrusted equivalent property for the purpose of making such creditor receive the payment, or that there is no risk of harm to such creditor by such absorption-type company split; and
(ix) in cases where a splitting company in absorption-type company split has issued share options, and where Article 758, item (v) of the Companies Act applies, a document listed in Article 59, paragraph (2), item (ii).

Article 86 In filing a written application for a registration of incorporation due to an incorporation-type company split, the following documents shall be attached thereto:
(i) an incorporation-type company split plan;
(ii) the articles of incorporation;
(iii) the documents listed in items (vi) to (viii) inclusive and items (x) to (xii) inclusive

Art.87   [8] Commercial Registration Act, Chap.III, Sec.5

of Article 47, paragraph (2);
(iv) a document listed in item (iv) of the preceding Article;
(v) a certificate of registered matters of a splitting company in incorporation-type company split; provided, however, that this shall not apply to the cases where a splitting company in incorporation-type company split has its head office in the jurisdictional district of the registry office where the application is to be filed;
(vi) in cases where a splitting company in incorporation-type company split is a stock company, a document evidencing that the incorporation-type company split plan has been approved under Article 804, paragraph (1) of the Companies Act (in the case referred to in Article 805 of said Act, a document evidencing that the case provided for therein is applicable and a document or the minutes of board of directors evidencing that the consent of the majority of the directors has been obtained);
(vii) in cases where a splitting company in incorporation-type company split is a limited liability company, a document evidencing that the consent of all the partners has been obtained (or, in cases where otherwise provided for in its articles of incorporation, that the procedures under said provision have been performed)(in cases where said limited liability company intends to have another company succeed to a part of its rights and obligations held in connection with its business, a document evidencing that the consent of the majority of the partners has been obtained);
(viii) a document evidencing that a splitting company in incorporation-type company split has given the public notice and the notices under Article 810, paragraph (2) of the Companies Act (excluding item (iii), and including the cases where applied mutatis mutandis pursuant to Article 813, paragraph (2) of said Act) (in cases where, in addition to public notice in an official gazette, a public notice has been given by publication in a daily newspaper that publishes matters on current affairs or by means of electronic public notices pursuant to the provision of Article 810, paragraph (3) of said Act (including the cases where applied mutatis mutandis pursuant to Article 813, paragraph (2) of said Act; hereinafter the same shall apply in this item), that the public notice was given by such method (in the cases excluding where separate notices are not required to be given pursuant to the provision of Article 810, paragraph (3) of the Companies Act, that the public notice and the notices were given)), and, if any creditor has raised an objection, a document evidencing that the company has made a payment or provided equivalent security to such creditor or has entrusted equivalent property for the purpose of making such creditor receive the payment, or that there is no risk of harm to such creditor by such incorporation-type company split; and
(ix) in cases where a splitting company in incorporation-type company split has issued share options, and where Article 763, item (x) of the Companies Act applies, a document listed in Article 59, paragraph (2), item (ii).

Article 87 (1) With regard to an application for a registration of change due to absorption-type company split or an incorporation-type company split to be made by a splitting company in absorption-type company split or a splitting company in incorporation-type company split at the location of the head office, if a succeeding company in absorption-type company split or a company incorporated through incorporation-type company split does not have its head office within the jurisdictional district of the registry office where the application is to be filed, such application shall be filed via a registry office having jurisdiction over the location of the head office.
(2) An application for registration as set forth in the preceding paragraph to be made at the location of the head office, and an application for registration as set forth in Article 85 or the preceding Article shall be filed simultaneously.

(3) In filing a written application for registration as set forth in paragraph (1), a certificate of a seal impression of a representative director (in case of a company with committees, a representative executive officer) of a splitting company in absorption-type company split or a splitting company in incorporation-type company split prepared by a registry office. In this case, no other document except for that set forth in Article 18 needs to be attached thereto.

Article 88 (1) In cases where any of the grounds listed in the items of Article 24 is applicable to any of the applications for registration set forth in paragraph (2) of the preceding Article, a registry office having jurisdiction over the location of the head office of a succeeding company in absorption-type company split or a company incorporated through incorporation-type company split shall dismiss both of those applications simultaneously.
(2) In the cases referred to in paragraph (1) of the preceding Article, if a registry office having jurisdiction over the location of the head office of a succeeding company in absorption-type company split or a company incorporated through incorporation-type company split has made a registration of change due to an absorption-type company split or a registration of incorporation due to an incorporation-type company split, such registry office shall, without delay, enter the date of said registration on the written application for registration set forth in said paragraph and send it to the registry office having jurisdiction over the location of the head office of a splitting company in absorption-type company split or a splitting company in incorporation-type company split.

(Registration of Share Exchange)
Article 89 With regard to a written application for a registration of change due to a share exchange to be made by a company acquiring all of the issued shares of a stock company implementing such share exchange (hereinafter referred to as a "wholly owning parent company in a share exchange"), the following documents shall be attached thereto:
(i) a share exchange agreement;
(ii) in the cases referred to in the main text of paragraph (1) or of paragraph (3) of Article 796 of the Companies Act, a document evidencing that the case provided for therein is applicable (in cases where any shareholder has notified to the effect that such shareholder dissents from the share exchange pursuant to the provision of paragraph (4) of said Article, including a document evidencing that such share exchange does not fall under the case provided for in said paragraph where the approval by a resolution of a shareholders meeting is required);
(iii) a document evidencing that the public notice and the notices under Article 799, paragraph (2) of the Companies Act (in cases where, in addition to public notice in an official gazette, a public notice has been given by publication in a daily newspaper that publishes matters on current affairs or by means of electronic public notices pursuant to the provision of paragraph (3) of said Article, the public notice by such method) has been given, and, if any creditor has raised an objection, a document evidencing that the company has made a payment or provided equivalent security to such creditor or has entrusted equivalent property for the purpose of making such creditor receive the payment, or that there is no risk of harm to such creditor by such share exchange;
(iv) a document evidencing that the amount of stated capital has been recorded pursuant to the provision of Article 445, paragraph (5) of the Companies Act;
(v) a certificate of registered matters of a stock company effecting the share exchange (hereinafter referred to as a "wholly owned subsidiary company in share ex-

change"); provided, however, that this shall not apply to the cases where the wholly owned subsidiary company in share exchange has its head office in the jurisdictional district of the registry office where the application is to be filed;
(vi) a document evidencing that the wholly owned subsidiary company in share exchange has performed the relevant procedures under Article 783, paragraphs (1) to (4) inclusive of the Companies Act such as obtaining approval for a share exchange agreement (in the case referred to in the main text of Article 784, paragraph (1) of said Act, a document evidencing that the case provided for therein is applicable and a document or minutes of board of directors evidencing that the consent of the majority of the directors has been obtained);
(vii) a document evidencing that the wholly owned subsidiary company in share exchange has given the public notice and the notices under Article 789, paragraph (2) of the Companies Act (in cases where, in addition to public notice in an official gazette, a public notice has been given by publication in a daily newspaper that publishes matters on current affairs or by means of electronic public notices pursuant to the provision of paragraph (3) of said Article, that the public notice was given by such method), and, if any creditor has raised an objection, a document evidencing that the company has made a payment or provided equivalent security to such creditor or has entrusted equivalent property for the purpose of making such creditor receive the payment, or that there is no risk of harm to such creditor by such share exchange;
(viii) in cases where a wholly owned subsidiary company in share exchange is a company issuing share certificates, a document listed in Article 59, paragraph (1), item (ii); and
(ix) in cases where a wholly owned subsidiary company in share exchange has issued share options, and where Article 768, paragraph (1), item (iv) of the Companies Act applies, a document listed in Article 59, paragraph (2), item (ii).

(Registration of Share Transfer)
Article 90 In filing a written application for a registration of incorporation due to a share transfer, the following documents shall be attached thereto:
(i) a share transfer plan;
(ii) the articles of incorporation;
(iii) the documents listed in items (vi) to (viii) inclusive and items (x) to (xii) inclusive of Article 47, paragraph (2);
(iv) a document listed in item (iv) of the preceding Article;
(v) a certificate of registered matters of the stock company effecting the share transfer (hereinafter referred to as a "wholly owned subsidiary company in share transfer" ; provided, however, that this shall not apply to the cases where the wholly owned subsidiary company in share transfer has its head office in the jurisdictional district of the registry office where the application is to be filed;
(vi) a document evidencing that the wholly owned subsidiary company in share transfer has performed the relevant procedures under Article 804, paragraphs (1) and (3) of the Companies Act such as obtaining approval for the share transfer plan;
(vii) a document evidencing that the wholly owned subsidiary company in share transfer has given the public notice and the notices under Article 810, paragraph (2) of the Companies Act (in cases where, in addition to public notice on in official gazette, a public notice has been given by publication in a daily newspaper that publishes matters on current affairs or by means of electronic public notices pursuant to the provision of paragraph (3) of said Article, that the public notice was given by such method), and, if any creditor has raised an objection, a document evidencing

that the company has made a payment or provided equivalent security to such creditor or has entrusted equivalent property for the purpose of making such creditor receive the payment, or that there is no risk of harm to such creditor by such share transfer;

(viii) in cases where the wholly owned subsidiary company in share transfer is a company issuing share certificates, a document listed in Article 59, paragraph (1), item (ii); and

(ix) in cases where the wholly owned subsidiary company in share transfer has issued share options, and where Article 773, paragraph (1), item (ix) of the Companies Act applies, a document listed in Article 59, paragraph (2), item (ii).

(Applications to be Filed at Same Time)
Article 91 (1) In the case referred to in either of Article 768, paragraph (1), item (iv) or Article 773, paragraph (1), item (ix) of the Companies Act, with regard to an application for a registration of change of share options due to a share exchange or share transfer which shall be made at the location of the head office by a wholly owned subsidiary company in share exchange or a wholly owned subsidiary company in share transfer, if a wholly owning parent company in share exchange or the stock company incorporated through share transfer (hereinafter referred to as a "wholly owning parent company incorporated through share transfer") does not have its head office within the jurisdictional district of the registry office where the application is to be filed, such application shall be filed via a registry office having jurisdiction over the location of its head office.

(2) In the case referred to in either of Article 768, paragraph (1), item (iv) or Article 773, paragraph (1), item (ix) of the Companies Act, an application for registration as set forth in the preceding paragraph to be made at the location of the head office, and an application for registration as set forth in Article 89 or the preceding Article shall be filed simultaneously.

(3) In filing a written application for registration as set forth in paragraph (1), a certificate of a seal impression of a representative director (in the case of a company with committees, a representative executive officer) of a wholly owned subsidiary company in share exchange or a wholly owned subsidiary company in share transfer prepared by a registry office. In this case, no other document except for that set forth in Article 18 needs to be attached thereto.

Article 92 (1) In cases where any of the grounds listed in items of Article 24 is applicable to any of the applications for registration set forth in paragraph (2) of the preceding Article, a registry office having jurisdiction over the location of the head office of the wholly owning parent company in share exchange or the wholly owning parent company incorporated through share transfer shall dismiss all of those applications simultaneously.

(2) In the case referred to in paragraph (1) of the preceding Article, if a registry office having jurisdiction over the location of the head office of the wholly owning parent company in share exchange or the wholly owning parent company incorporated through share transfer has made the registration of change due to a share exchange or the registration of incorporation due to a share transfer, such registry office shall, without delay, enter the date of said registration on the written application for registration set forth in said paragraph and send it to the registry office having jurisdiction over the location of the head office of the wholly owned subsidiary company in share exchange or a wholly owned subsidiary company in share transfer.

Section 6 Registration of General Partnership Company

(General Rule on Documents to be Attached)
Article 93 If any matter to be registered requires the consent of all the partners or the unanimous consent of certain partners or liquidators, a document evidencing that said consent or unanimous consent has been obtained shall be attached to the written application.

(Registration of Incorporation)
Article 94 The following documents shall be attached to a written application for registration of incorporation:
(i) the articles of incorporation;
(ii) in cases where a partner representing the general partnership company is a juridical person, the following documents:
  (a) a certificate of registered matters of said juridical person; provided, however, that this shall not apply to the cases where the juridical person has its head office or principal office in the jurisdictional district of the registry office where the application is to be filed;
  (b) a document relevant to the appointment of a person who is to perform the duties of the partner; and
  (c) a document evidencing that a person who is to perform the duties of the partner has consented to assume his/her office.
(iii) In cases where a partner of a general partnership company (excluding a partner prescribed in the preceding item) is a juridical person, a document listed in sub-item (a) of the preceding item; provided, however, that this shall not apply to the cases where the proviso to sub-item (a) of said item applies.

(Provisions Applied Mutatis Mutandis)
Article 95 The provisions of Articles 47, paragraph (1) and Article 48 to Article 53 inclusive shall apply mutatis mutandis to the registration of a general partnership company.

(Registration of Change Due to Admission or Withdrawal of Partners)
Article 96 (1) In filing a written application for a registration of change due to the admission or withdrawal of the partners of a general partnership company, a document evidencing the fact of such admission or withdrawal (in cases of the admission of a partner which is a juridical person, including the documents listed in Article 94, item (ii) or (iii)) shall be attached thereto.
(2) In cases where a partner of a general partnership company is a juridical person, the documents listed in Article 94, item (ii), sub-item (a) shall be attached to a written application for a registration of change of its trade name or name or relocation of its head office or principal office; provided, however, that this shall not apply to the cases where the proviso to sub-item (a) of said item applies.

(Registration of Change of Person Who is to Perform Duties of Partner Representing General Partnership Company)
Article 97 (1) In cases where a partner representing a general partnership company is a juridical person, in filing a written application for the registration of change due to the assumption of office by a person who is to perform the duties of the partner, a document listed in Article 94, item (ii) shall be attached thereto; provided, however, that in cases where the proviso to sub-item (a) of said item applies, this shall not apply to the documents listed in sub-item (a) of said item.

(2) In filing a written application for a registration of change due to the retirement of a person who is to perform the duties of the partner as prescribed in the preceding paragraph, a document evidencing such retirement shall be attached thereto.

(Registration of Dissolution)
Article 98 (1) The matters to be registered in relation to a registration of dissolution shall be the fact of the dissolution, and the ground and date therefor.
(2) In filing a written application for a registration of dissolution on any ground for dissolution provided for in the articles of incorporation, a document evidencing that said ground has arisen shall be attached thereto.
(3) With regard to a written application for a registration of dissolution filed by a liquidator who represents a liquidating membership company, a document evidencing the capacity of such liquidator shall be attached thereto; provided, however, that this shall not apply to the cases where the liquidator who represents said liquidating membership company has assumed the office of a liquidator of the liquidating membership company pursuant to the provision of Article 647, paragraph (1), item (i) of the Companies Act (in the case referred to in Article 655, paragraph (4) of said Act, the cases where such liquidator has assumed the office of liquidator who represents the liquidating membership company pursuant to the provision of said paragraph).

(Registration of Liquidator)
Article 99 (1) In filing a written application for registration of a liquidator in cases where any of the persons listed in the following items has assumed the office of liquidator of a liquidating membership company, the documents specified in the relevant item shall be attached thereto:
(i) a person listed in Article 647, paragraph (1), item (i) of the Companies Act: the articles of incorporation;
(ii) a person listed in Article 647, paragraph (1), item (ii) of the Companies Act: the articles of incorporation and a document evidencing that said person has consented to assume his/her office;
(iii) a person listed in Article 647, paragraph (1), item (iii) of the Companies Act: a document evidencing that said person has consented to assume his/her office; or
(iv) a person appointed by a court: a document evidencing such appointment and the matters listed in Article 928, paragraph (2), item (ii) of the Companies Act.
(2) The provision of Article 94 (limited to the parts pertaining to item (ii)) shall apply mutatis mutandis to a registration set forth in the preceding paragraph in cases where a liquidator who represents a liquidating membership company (limited to a person listed in item (i) or (iv) of the preceding paragraph) is a juridical person.
(3) The provision of Article 94 (limited to the parts pertaining to item (ii) or (iii)) shall apply mutatis mutandis to a registration set forth in paragraph (1) in cases where a liquidator of a liquidating membership company (limited to a person listed in item (ii) or (iii) of paragraph (1)) is a juridical person.

(Registration of Change Related to Liquidator)
Article 100 (1) In cases where a liquidator of a liquidating membership company is a juridical person, the documents listed in Article 94, item (ii), sub-item (a) shall be attached to a written application for a registration of change of its trade name or name or relocation of its head office or principal office; provided, however, that this shall not apply to the cases where the proviso to sub-item (a) of said item applies.
(2) In filing a written application for a registration of change to any of the matters listed in Article 928, paragraph (2), item (ii) of the Companies Act which relate to a liquidator

appointed by a court, a document evidencing the grounds for such change shall be attached thereto.
(3) In filing a written application for a registration of change due to the retirement of a liquidator, a document evidencing such retirement shall be attached thereto.

(Registration of Change of Person Who is to Perform Duties of Liquidator Who Represents Liquidating Membership Company)
Article 101 The provision of Article 97 shall apply mutatis mutandis to a registration of change due to the assumption of, or resignation from, office of a person who is to perform the duties of liquidator in cases where a liquidator who represents a liquidating membership company is a juridical person.

(Registration of Completion of Liquidation)
Article 102 In filing a written application for a registration of completion of liquidation, a document evidencing that the accounting relating to the liquidation has been approved pursuant to the provision of Article 667 of the Companies Act (in cases where a method for the disposition of assets as set forth in Article 668, paragraph (1) of said Act has been prescribed, a document prepared by all the partners evidencing completion of the disposition of the relevant assets) shall be attached thereto.

(Registration of Continuation)
Article 103 In cases where a judgment upholding a claim relating to an action seeking the invalidation or rescission of the incorporation of a general partnership company has become final and binding, and where the general partnership company continues in existence pursuant to the provision of Article 845 of the Companies Act, a transcript of the judgment shall be attached to a written application for a registration of continuation.

(Registration of Change of Kind of Membership Company)
Article 104 In cases where a general partnership company has become a limited partnership or a limited liability company pursuant to the provision of Article 638, paragraph (1) of the Companies Act, with regard to a registration concerning such limited partnership company or limited liability company, the date of incorporation of the company, trade name of the general partnership company as well as the fact of the change of the kind of membership company and the date of such change shall also be registered.

Article 105 (1) In cases where a general partnership company has become a limited partnership company pursuant to the provision of Article 638, paragraph (1), item (i) or (ii) of the Companies Act, the following documents shall be attached to a written application for registration concerning such limited partnership company:
(i) the articles of incorporation;
(ii) a document evidencing the value of contributions already made by the limited partners; and
(iii) in cases where a limited partner has been admitted, a document evidencing such admission (in cases of the admission of a partner which is a juridical person, including the documents listed in Article 94, item (ii) or (iii)).
(2) In cases where a general partnership company has become a limited liability company pursuant to the provision of Article 638, paragraph (1), item (iii) of the Companies Act, the following documents shall be attached to a written application for registration concerning such limited liability company:

(i) the articles of incorporation; and
(ii) a document evidencing completion of the payment in and delivery relating to the contributions under Article 640, paragraph (1) of the Companies Act.

Article 106 (1) In cases where a general partnership company has become a limited partnership company or a limited liability company pursuant to the provision of Article 638, paragraph (1) of the Companies Act, an application for registration concerning the general partnership company and an application for registration as set forth in paragraph (1) or (2) of the preceding Article shall be filed simultaneously.
(2) The provisions on the documents to be attached to a written application shall not apply to an application for registration as set forth in the preceding paragraph concerning a general partnership company.
(3) In cases where any of the grounds listed in the items of Article 24 is applicable to any application for registration set forth in paragraph (1), a registrar shall dismiss all of these applications simultaneously.

(Registration of Entity Conversion)
Article 107 (1) In filing a registration concerning a stock company after entity conversion in cases where a general partnership company has effected an entity conversion, the following documents shall be attached to a written application for registration concerning the stock company after entity conversion:
(i) an entity conversion plan;
(ii) the articles of incorporation; and
(iii) a document evidencing that each of directors (directors and company auditors, in cases where the stock company after entity conversion is a company with auditors (including a stock company the articles of incorporation of which provide that the scope of the audit by its company auditors shall be limited to an audit related to accounting) of the stock company after entity conversion has consented to assume their respective offices;
(iv) in cases where an accounting advisor or an accounting auditor of a stock company after entity conversion has been appointed, the documents listed in the items of Article 54, paragraph (2);
(v) a document listed in Article 47, paragraph (2), item (vi); and
(vi) a document evidencing that the public notice and the notices under Article 779, paragraph (2) of the Companies Act (excluding item (ii)) as applied mutatis mutandis pursuant to Article 781, paragraph (2) of said Act has been given, and, if any creditor has raised an objection, a document evidencing that the company has made a payment or provided equivalent security to such creditor or has entrusted equivalent property for the purpose of making such creditor receive the payment, or that there is no risk of harm to such creditor by such entity conversion.
(2) The provisions of Article 76 and Article 78 shall apply mutatis mutandis to the cases prescribed in the preceding paragraph.

(Registration of Merger)
Article 108 (1) In filing a written application for a registration of change due to an absorption-type merger, the following documents shall be attached thereto:
(i) an absorption-type merger agreement;
(ii) the documents listed in items (v) to (x) inclusive of Article 80;
(iii) a document evidencing that the public notice and the notices under Article 799, paragraph (2) of the Companies Act (excluding item (iii)) as applied mutatis mutandis pursuant to Article 802, paragraph (2) of said Act (in cases where, in addition to

Art.109

public notice in an official gazette, a public notice has been given by publication in a daily newspaper that publishes matters on current affairs or by means of electronic public notices pursuant to the provision of Article 799, paragraph (3) of said Act as applied mutatis mutandis pursuant to Article 802, paragraph (2) of said Act, the public notice by such method) has been given, and, if any creditor has raised an objection, a document evidencing that the company has made a payment or provided equivalent security to such creditor or has entrusted equivalent property for the purpose of making such creditor receive the payment, or that there is no risk of harm to such creditor by such absorption-type merger; and

(vi) in cases where a juridical person is to become a partner of a company surviving absorption-type merger, the document listed in Article 94, item (ii) or (iii).

(2) In filing a written application for a registration of incorporation due to a consolidation-type merger, the following documents shall be attached thereto:

(i) a consolidation-type merger agreement;

(ii) the articles of incorporation;

(iii) the documents listed in item (v), and items (vii) to (x) inclusive of Article 81;

(iv) in cases where a company consolidated through consolidation-type merger is a stock company, a document evidencing that the consent of all the shareholders has been obtained; and

(v) in cases where a juridical person is to become a partner of a company incorporated through consolidation-type merger, the document listed in Article 94, item (ii) or (iii).

(3) The provisions of Article 79, Article 82 and Article 83 shall apply mutatis mutandis to a registration concerning a general partnership company.

(Registration of Company Split)

Article 109 (1) With regard to a written application for a registration of change due to an absorption-type company split to be made by a succeeding company in absorption-type company split, the following documents shall be attached thereto:

(i) an absorption-type company split agreement;

(ii) the documents listed in items (v) to (viii) inclusive of Article 85;

(iii) a document evidencing that the public notice and the notices under Article 799, paragraph (2) of the Companies Act (excluding item (iii)) as applied mutatis mutandis pursuant to Article 802, paragraph (2) of said Act (in cases where, in addition to the public notice in an official gazette, a public notice has been given by publication in a daily newspaper that publishes matters on current affairs or by method of electronic public notices pursuant to the provision of Article 799, paragraph (3) of said Act as applied mutatis mutandis pursuant to Article 802, paragraph (2) of said Act, the public notice by such method) has been given, and, if any creditor has raised an objection, a document evidencing that the company has made a payment or provided equivalent security to such creditor or has entrusted equivalent property for the purpose of making such creditor receive the payment, or that there is no risk of harm to such creditor by such absorption-type company split; and

(iv) in cases where a juridical person is to become a partner of a succeeding company in absorption-type company split, the document listed in Article 94, item (ii) or (iii).

(2) In filing a written application for a registration of incorporation due to an incorporation-type company split, the following documents shall be attached thereto:

(i) an incorporation-type company split plan;

(ii) the articles of incorporation;

(iii) the documents listed in items (v) to (viii) inclusive of Article 86; and

(iv) in cases where a juridical person is to become a partner of a company incorporated

through an incorporation-type company split, the document listed in Article 94, item (ii) or (iii).
(3) The provisions of Article 84, Article 87 and Article 88 shall apply mutatis mutandis to a registration of a general partnership company.

Section 7 Registration of Limited Partnership Company

(Registration of Incorporation)
Article 110 In filing a written application for a registration of incorporation, a document evidencing the value of contributions already made by limited partners shall be attached thereto.

(Provisions Applied Mutatis Mutandis)
Article 111 The provisions of Article 47, paragraph (1), Article 48 to Article 53 inclusive, Article 93, Article 94 and Article 96 to Article 103 inclusive shall apply mutatis mutandis to a registration of a limited partnership company.

(Registration of Performance of Contributions)
Article 112 In filing a written application for a registration of change due to the performance of the contribution by limited partners, a document evidencing completion of said performance shall be attached thereto.

(Registration of Change of Kind of Membership Company)
Article 113 (1) In cases where a limited partnership company has become a general partnership company pursuant to the provision of Article 638, paragraph (2), item (i) or Article 639, paragraph (1) of the Companies Act, in filing a written application for a registration concerning such general partnership company, the articles of incorporation shall be attached thereto.
(2) In cases where a limited partnership company has become a limited liability company pursuant to the provision of Article 638, paragraph (2), item (ii) or Article 639, paragraph (2) of the Companies Act, in filing a written application for a registration concerning such limited liability company, the following documents shall be attached thereto:
(i) the articles of incorporation; and
(ii) in cases where said company has become a limited liability company pursuant to the provision of Article 638, paragraph (2), item (ii) of the Companies Act, a document evidencing completion of the payment in and delivery relating to the contributions under Article 640, paragraph (1) of said Act.
(3) The provisions of Article 104 and Article 106 shall apply mutatis mutandis to the cases prescribed in the preceding two paragraphs.

(Registration of Entity Conversion)
Article 114 The provision of Article 107 shall apply mutatis mutandis to the cases where a limited partnership company has effected an entity conversion.

(Registration of Merger)
Article 115 (1) The provision of Article 108 shall apply mutatis mutandis to registration of a limited partnership company.
(2) The provision of Article 110 shall apply mutatis mutandis to a registration of change due to absorption-type merger and a registration of incorporation due to consolidation-

type merger.

(Registration of Company Split)
Article 116 (1) The provision of Article 109 shall apply mutatis mutandis to registration of a limited partnership company.
(2) The provision of Article 110 shall apply mutatis mutandis to a registration of change due to absorption-type company split to be made by a succeeding company in absorption-type company split and a registration of incorporation due to incorporation-type company split.

Section 8 Registration of Limited Liability Company

(Registration of Incorporation)
Article 117 Unless otherwise provided for in the laws and regulations, a document evidencing completion of the payment in and delivery relating to the contributions under Article 578 of the Companies Act shall be attached to a written application for a registration of incorporation.

(Provisions Applied Mutatis Mutandis)
Article 118 The provisions of Article 47, paragraph (1), Article 48 to Article 53 inclusive, Article 93, Article 94, Article 96 to Article 101 inclusive and Article 103 shall apply mutatis mutandis to registration of a limited liability company.

(Registration of Change Due to Admission of Partners)
Article 119 In filing a written application for a registration of change due to the admission of partners, a document evidencing completion of the payment in or delivery relating to the contributions under Article 604, paragraph (3) of the Companies Act shall be attached thereto.

(Registration of Change Due to Reduction in Amount of Stated Capital)
Article 120 In filing a written application for a registration of change due to a reduction in the amount of stated capital, a document evidencing that the public notice and the notices under Article 627, paragraph (2) of the Companies Act (in cases where, in addition to public notice in an official gazette, a public notice has been given by publication in a daily newspaper that publishes matters on current affairs or by method of electronic public notices pursuant to the provision of paragraph (3) of said Article, the public notice by such method) has been given, and, if any creditor has raised an objection, a document evidencing that the company has made a payment or provided equivalent security to such creditor or has entrusted equivalent property for the purpose of making such creditor receive the payment, or that there is no risk of harm to such creditor by such reduction in the amount of stated capital.

(Registration of Completion of Liquidation)
Article 121 In filing a written application for a registration of completion of liquidation, a document evidencing that the accounting relating to the liquidation has been approved pursuant to the provision of Article 667 of the Companies Act shall be attached thereto.

(Registration of Change of Kind of Membership Company)
Article 122 (1) In cases where a limited liability company has become a general partner-

ship company pursuant to the provision of Article 638, paragraph (3), item (i) of the Companies Act, in filing a written application for a registration concerning such general partnership company, the articles of incorporation shall be attached thereto.
(2) In cases where a limited liability company has become a limited partnership company pursuant to the provision of Article 638, paragraph (3), item (ii) or (iii) of the Companies Act, in filing a written application for a registration concerning such limited partnership company, the following documents shall be attached thereto:
(i) the articles of incorporation;
(ii) a document evidencing the value of contributions already performed by limited partners; and
(iii) in cases where any unlimited partner has been admitted, a document evidencing such admission (in the case of the admission of a partner which is a juridical person, including a document listed in Article 94, item (ii) or (iii)).
(3) The provisions of Article 104 and Article 106 shall apply mutatis mutandis to the cases prescribed in the preceding two paragraphs.

(Registration of Entity Conversion)
Article 123 The provision of Article 107 shall apply mutatis mutandis to the cases where a limited liability company has effected an entity conversion. In this case, the term "the public notice and the notices" in item (vi), paragraph (1) of said Article shall be deemed to be replaced with "the public notice and the notices (in cases where, in addition to public notice in an official gazette, a public notice has been given by publication in a daily newspaper that publishes matters on current affairs or by method of electronic public notices pursuant to the provision of Article 779, paragraph (3) of said Act as applied mutatis mutandis pursuant to Article 781, paragraph (2) of said Act, the public notice by such method)".

(Registration of Merger)
Article 124 The provision of Article 108 shall apply mutatis mutandis to registration of a limited liability company. In this case, the term "partner" in item (iv) of paragraph (1) and item (v) of paragraph (2) of said Article shall be deemed to be replaced with "partner executing the business".

(Registration of Company Split)
Article 125 The provision of Article 109 shall apply mutatis mutandis to the registration of a limited liability company. In this case, the term "partner" in item (iv) of paragraph (1) and item (iv) of paragraph (2) of said Article shall be deemed to be replaced with "partner executing the business".

(Registration of Share Exchange)
Article 126 (1) With regard to a written application for a registration of change due to a share exchange to be made by a wholly owning parent company in share exchange, the following documents shall be attached thereto:
(i) a share exchange agreement;
(ii) the documents listed in items (v) to (viii) inclusive of Article 89;
(iii) a document evidencing that the public notice and the notices under Article 799, paragraph (2) of the Companies Act (excluding item (iii)) as applied mutatis mutandis pursuant to Article 802, paragraph (2) of said Act (in cases where, in addition to public notice in an official gazette, a public notice has been given by publication in a daily newspaper that publishes matters on current affairs or by method of electronic public notices pursuant to the provision of Article 799, paragraph (3) of said Act

as applied mutatis mutandis pursuant to Article 802, paragraph (2) of said Act, the public notice by such method) has been given, and, if any creditor has raised an objection, a document evidencing that the company has made a payment or provided equivalent security to such creditor or has entrusted equivalent property for the purpose of making such creditor receive the payment, or that there is no risk of harm to such creditor by such share exchange; and
(iv) in cases where a juridical person is to become a partner executing the business of a wholly owning parent company in share exchange, the document listed in Article 94, item (ii) or (iii).
(2) The provisions of Article 91 and Article 92 shall apply mutatis mutandis to registrations of limited liability companies.

Section 9 Registration of Foreign Company

(Special Provision on Jurisdiction)
Article 127 With regard to the application of the provisions of Article 1-3 and Article 24, item (i), the domicile of a representative in Japan (limited to one whose domicile is in Japan; hereinafter the same shall apply in this Section excluding Article 130, paragraph (1)) of a foreign company that has not established a business office in Japan shall be deemed to be the location of the business office.

(Registration Applicant)
Article 128 In filing an application for registration of a foreign company, a representative in Japan shall represent the foreign company.

(Registration of Foreign Company)
Article 129 (1) In filing a written application for registration of a foreign company pursuant to the provision of Article 933, paragraph (1) of the Companies Act, the following documents shall be attached thereto:
(i) a document which sufficiently evidences the existence of the head office;
(ii) a document evidencing the capacity of the representative in Japan;
(iii) the articles of incorporation of the foreign company and any other document sufficiently characterizing the nature of the foreign company; and
(iv) in cases where methods of public notice have been provided pursuant to the provision of Article 939, paragraph (2) of the Companies Act, a document evidencing such provision.
(2) The documents set forth in the preceding paragraph shall be certified by the competent government agency or consul in Japan of the foreign company's own state or any other competent authority.
(3) In cases where an applicant has attached to its written application for registration set forth in paragraph (1) a certificate of registered matters issued by another registry office certifying that the representative in Japan has been specified or that a business office has been established in Japan, no document specified in said paragraph needs to be attached.

(Registration of Change)
Article 130 (1) In filing a written application for a registration of change of representative in Japan or of a change to the registered matters which has arisen in the foreign country, a document evidencing the fact of such change certified by the competent government agency or consul in Japan of the foreign company's own state or any other competent authority shall be attached thereto.

(2) In cases where all of the representatives in Japan intend to resign, in filing a written application for registration due to such resignation, a document evidencing that the public notice and the notices under Article 820, paragraph (1) of the Companies Act has been given, and, if any creditor has raised an objection, a document evidencing that the company has made a payment or provided equivalent security to such creditor or has entrusted equivalent property for the purpose of making such creditor receive the payment, or that there is no risk of harm to such creditor by such resignation shall be attached thereto in addition to the document set forth in the preceding paragraph; provided, however, that this shall not apply to the cases where the foreign company has received an order for the commencement of liquidation pursuant to the provision of Article 822, paragraph (1) of said Act.
(3) In cases where an applicant has attached to its written application for registration set forth in the preceding two paragraphs a document evidencing that the registration under the preceding two paragraphs has already been made by another registry office, no document specified in the preceding two paragraphs needs to be attached.

(Provisions Applied Mutatis Mutandis)
Article 131 (1) The provisions of Article 51 and Article 52 shall apply mutatis mutandis to the cases where a foreign company has relocated all of its business offices to the jurisdictional districts of other registry offices.
(2) The provisions of Article 51 and Article 52 shall apply mutatis mutandis to cases where a foreign company has closed all of its business offices (excluding the cases where all of its representatives in Japan intend to resign). In this case, each of the terms "new location" and "former location" in these provisions shall be deemed to be replaced with, respectively, "domicile of a representative in Japan (limited to one whose domicile is in Japan)" and "location of the final business office to be closed (in cases where there are two or more business offices, either of them)".
(3) The provisions of Article 51 and Article 52 shall apply mutatis mutandis to the cases where all the representatives in Japan of a foreign company that has not established a business office in Japan have relocated their domiciles to the jurisdictional district of other registry offices.
(4) The provisions of Article 51 and Article 52 shall apply mutatis mutandis to the cases where a foreign company that has not established a business office in Japan has established its business office in the jurisdictional district of another registry office. In this case, each of the terms "new location" and "former location" in these provisions shall be deemed to be replaced with, respectively, "location of business office" and "domicile of representative in Japan (limited to one whose domicile is in Japan)".

Section 10 Correction and Cancellation of Registration

(Correction)
Article 132 (1) In cases where a registration contains any error or omission, the party concerned may file an application for the correction of such registration.
(2) In filing a written application for correction, a document evidencing the existence of the error or omission shall be attached thereto; provided, however, that this shall not apply to cases of correction of a surname, name or address.

Article 133 (1) In cases where a registrar has found any error or omission regarding a registration, he/she shall give notice to a person who has made said application to that effect without delay; provided, however, that this shall not apply to the case where the error or omission has been caused by a mistake committed by a registrar.

(2) In the case referred to in the proviso to the preceding paragraph, a registrar shall, without delay, correct the registration with the permission of the Director of the supervisory Legal Affairs Bureau or District Legal Affairs Bureau.

(Application for Cancellation)
Article 134 (1) In cases where a registration falls under any of the following items, the party concerned may file an application for the cancellation of such registration:
  (i) that any of the grounds listed in items (i) to (iii) inclusive or item (v) of Article 24 is applicable; or
  (ii) that any of the registered matters has a ground for invalidation; provided, however, that this shall not apply to the cases where such invalidation may only be asserted by means of filing an action.
(2) The provision of Article 132, paragraph (2) shall apply mutatis mutandis to the case prescribed in item (ii) of the preceding paragraph.

(Ex Officio Cancellation)
Article 135 (1) In cases where a registrar has found that the registration falls under any of the items of paragraph (1) of the preceding Article, he/she shall give notice to the person who has made said registration to the effect that the registration will be cancelled unless said person files an objection in writing within a fixed period not exceeding one month.
(2) In cases where the domicile or residence of any person who has made the registration is unknown, the registrar shall, in lieu of giving notice as set forth in the preceding paragraph, give public notice of the information to be notified.
(3) A registrar may, in addition to publication in an official gazette, post a public notice of the same information in a newspaper as he/she may deem appropriate.

Article 136 In cases where there is a person who has filed an objection, a registrar shall render a decision with regard to such objection.

Article 137 In cases where no person has filed an objection, or where the registrar has dismissed such objection, the registrar shall cancel the registration.

Article 138 (1) With regard to the registration of the matters to be registered at the location of the head office and branch offices, the provisions of the preceding three Articles shall only be applicable to a registration made at the location of the head office; provided, however, that this shall not apply to the cases where only a registration made at the location of a branch office has any ground for cancellation.
(2) In the case referred to in the main text of the preceding paragraph, if a registrar has effected the cancellation of a registration, he/she shall, without delay, notify the registry office to that effect with the location of the branch office.
(3) A registrar shall effect the cancellation of a registration without delay upon receipt of the notice set forth in the preceding paragraph.

Chapter IV Miscellaneous Provisions

(Exclusion from Application of the Administrative Procedure Act)
Article 139 The provisions of Chapter II and Chapter III of the Administrative Procedure Act (Act No. 88 of 1993) shall not apply to a disposition made by a registrar.

(Exclusion from Application of the Act on Access to Information Held by Administrative Organs)

Article 140 The provisions of the Act on Access to Information Held by Administrative Organs (Act No. 42 of 1999) shall not apply to a registry nor the documents annexed thereto.

(Exclusion from Application of the Act on the Protection of Personal Information Held by Administrative Organs)

Article 141 The provisions of Chapter IV of the Act on the Protection of Personal Information Held by Administrative Organs (Act No. 58 of 2003) shall not apply to the retained personal information (meaning the retained personal information prescribed in Article 2, paragraph (3) of said Act) which is recorded in a registry nor the documents annexed thereto.

(Request for Review)

Article 142 A person who considers a disposition made by a registrar to be unjust may make a request for review to the Director of the Legal Affairs Bureau or District Legal Affairs Bureau who supervises said registrar.

Article 143 A request for review shall be filed via the registrar.

(Handling of Request for Review Case)

Article 144 A registrar, when he/she finds a request for review to be well-grounded, shall make a reasonable disposition.

Article 145 A registrar, when he/she finds a request for review to be groundless, shall refer the case to the Director of the Legal Affairs Bureau or District Legal Affairs Bureau set forth in Article 142 within three days from the date of the request, with his/her opinions attached thereto.

Article 146 The Director of the Legal Affairs Bureau or District Legal Affairs Bureau set forth in Article 142, when he/she finds a request for review to be well-grounded, shall order the registrar to make a reasonable disposition, and shall give notice to the requester for the review and any other person who has an interest in the registration to that effect.

(Exclusion from Application of the Administrative Appeal Act)

Article 147 The provisions of Article 14, Article 17, Article 24, the proviso to Article 25, paragraph (1), Article 34, paragraphs (2) to (7) inclusive, Article 37, paragraph (6), Article 40, paragraphs (3) to (6) inclusive and Article 43 of the Administrative Appeal Act (Act No. 160 of 1962) shall not apply to a request for review pertaining to a disposition made by a registrar.

(Delegation to Ordinance of the Ministry)

Article 148 In addition to what is provided for in this Act, matters concerning the preparation of registries, application forms for registration and documents to be attached to the application as well as any other matter necessary for the enforcement of this Act shall be prescribed by the Ordinance of the Ministry of Justice.

Supplementary Provisions

Art.148　⑧ Commercial Registration Act, Chap.IV, Sec.10

(1) This Act shall come into effect as from April 1, 1964.
(2) Transitional measures and other matters necessary for the enforcement of this Act shall be prescribed separately by another act.

9 Cabinet Office Ordinance on Audit Certification of Financial Statements, etc.

(Ordinance of the Ministry of Finance No.12 of March 28, 1957)

Pursuant to the provisions of Article 193-2 of the Securities and Exchange Act (Act No.25 of 1948) and in order to enforce those provisions, we hereby enact a Ministerial Ordinance for the complete revision of the Rules on Audit Certification of Financial Documents (Securities and Exchange Commission Rules No. 4 of 1951) as follows.

(Scope of Documents on Finance and Accounting Subject to Audit Certification)

Article 1 The documents specified by a Cabinet Office Ordinance, referred to in Article 193-2, paragraph (1) of the Financial Instruments and Exchange Act (Act No.25 of 1948, hereinafter referred to as the "Act"), shall be those set forth in the following items (excluding the explanatory notes set forth in Article 8-17, paragraph (1), item (x) of the Ordinance on Terminology, Forms, and Preparation Methods of Financial Statements, etc. (Ordinance of the Ministry of Finance No.59 of 1963; hereinafter referred to as the "Ordinance on Financial Statements, etc.") (including the cases where applied mutatis mutandis pursuant to Article 5-10 of the Ordinance on Terminology, Forms, and Preparation Methods of Interim Financial Statements, etc. (Ordinance of the Ministry of Finance No.38 of 1977; hereinafter referred to as the "Ordinance on Interim Financial Statements , etc."), those set forth in Article 15, paragraph (1), item (vii) of the Ordinance on Terminology, Forms, and Preparation Methods of Quarterly Financial Statements, etc. (Ordinance of the Ministry of Finance No.63 of 2007; hereinafter referred to as the "Ordinance on Quarterly Financial Statements, etc."), those set forth in Article 15-12, paragraph (1), item (xi) of the Ordinance on Terminology, Forms, and Preparation Methods of Consolidated Financial Statements (Ordinance of the Ministry of Finance No.28 of 1976; hereinafter referred to as the "Ordinance on Consolidated Financial Statements") (including the cases where applied mutatis mutandis pursuant to Article 17-4 of the Ordinance on Terminology, Forms, and Preparation Methods of Interim Consolidated Financial Statements (Ordinance of the Ministry of Finance No.24 of 1999; hereinafter referred to as the "Ordinance on Interim Consolidated Financial Statements") and those set forth in Article 20, paragraph (1), item (viii) of the Ordinance on Terminology, Forms, and Preparation Methods of Quarterly Consolidated Financial Statements (Ordinance of the Ministry of Finance No.64 of 2007; hereinafter referred to as the "Ordinance on Quarterly Consolidated Financial Statements")):

(i) from among the Financial Statements (meaning financial statements as set forth in Article 1, paragraph (1) of the Ordinance on Financial Statements, etc. other than those submitted by the designated juridical person set forth in said paragraph (hereinafter referred to as the "Designated Juridical Person") contained in the written notification submitted pursuant to the provision of Article 5, paragraph (1) of the Act; hereinafter the same shall apply in this Article) or the Financial Documents (meaning financial documents submitted by a foreign company as pursuant to the provisions of Article 129 of the Ordinance on Financial Statements, etc.; the same shall apply hereinafter), those for the most recent business year and the immediately preceding business year if they are related to securities other than Regulated Securities (meaning regulated securities as set forth in Article 5, paragraph (1) of that Act; hereinafter the same shall apply in this item) and those for the most recent Specified Period (meaning a specified period as set forth in Article 24, paragraph (1) of the Act as applied mutatis mutandis pursuant to Article 24, paragraph (5) of the Act; hereinafter the same shall apply in this item) and the immediately preceding Specified Period if they are related to Regulated Securities (excluding Financial Statements or the Financial Documents (hereinafter referred to as "Documents" in this item) of the most recent business year or Specified Period (hereinafter referred to as "Business Year, etc." in this Article) and the immediately preceding Business Year, etc. contained in a written notification, which have the same contents as the Documents contained in any of the written notifications or securities reports submitted previously pursuant to the provision of Article 5, paragraph (1) or Article 24, paragraph (1) or (3) of the Act (including the cases where these provisions are applied mutatis mutandis pursuant to paragraph, paragraph (5) of that Article; hereinafter the same shall apply in this Article));

(ii) the Quarterly Financial Statements (meaning quarterly financial statements as set forth in Article 1, paragraph (1) of the Ordinance on Quarterly Financial Statements, excluding those submitted by a Designated Juridical Person; hereinafter the same shall apply in this Article) contained in the written notification submitted pursuant to the provision of Article 5, paragraph (1) (excluding Quarterly Financial Statements contained in a written notification which have the same contents as the Quarterly Financial Statements contained in any of the written notifications or quarterly reports (excluding a quarterly report submitted by a company engaged in any of the businesses set forth in the items of paragraph (2) of Article 17-15 of the Cabinet Office Ordinance on Disclosure of Corporate Affairs, etc. (Ordinance of the Ministry of Finance No.5 of 1973; hereinafter referred to as the "Cabinet Office Ordinance on Disclosure") (such company shall hereinafter be referred to as a "Company Engaged in a Specified Business") for the Quarterly Accounting Period (meaning the quarterly accounting period set forth in Article 3, item (iv) of the Ordinance on Quarterly Financial Statements, etc.; the same shall apply hereinafter) following the first Quarterly Accounting Period in the relevant business year (hereinafter referred to as the "Second Quarterly Report")) submitted previously pursuant to the provision of Article 5, paragraph (1) or Article 24-4-7, paragraph (1) or (2) of the Act (including the cases where these provisions are applied mutatis mutandis pursuant to paragraph (3) of that Article; hereinafter the same shall apply in this Article));

(iii) the Interim Financial Statements (meaning interim financial statements as set forth in Article 1, paragraph (1) of the Ordinance on Interim Financial Statements, etc. excluding those submitted by a Designated Juridical Person; hereinafter the same shall apply in this Article) contained in a written notification submitted pursuant to the provision of Article 5, paragraph (1) of the Act (excluding Interim Financial Statements contained in a written notification which have the same contents as the Interim Financial Statements contained in any of the written notifications, quarterly reports (limited to a Second Quarterly Report submitted by the a Company Engaged in a Specified Business), or interim reports submitted previously pursuant to the provision of Article 5, paragraph (1), Article 24-4-7, paragraph (1) or (2) or Article 24-5, paragraph (1) of the Act (including the cases where applied mutatis mutandis pursuant to paragraph (3) of that Article; hereinafter the same shall apply in this Article);

(iv) the Consolidated Financial Statements (meaning the consolidated financial statements set forth in Article 1, item (xxi) of the Cabinet Office Ordinance on Disclosure excluding those submitted by a Designated Juridical Person; hereinafter the same shall apply in this Article) contained in a written notification submitted pur-

suant to the provision of Article 5, paragraph (1) of the Act (excluding Consolidated Financial Statements contained in a written notification which have the same contents as the Consolidated Financial Statements contained in any of the written notifications or securities reports submitted previously pursuant to the provision of Article 5, paragraph (1) or Article 24, paragraph (1) or (3) of the Act);
(v) the Quarterly Consolidated Financial Statements (meaning quarterly consolidated financial statements as set forth in Article 1, paragraph (1) of the Ordinance on Quarterly Consolidated Financial Statements excluding those submitted by a Designated Juridical Person; hereinafter the same shall apply in this Article) contained in a written notification submitted pursuant to the provision of Article 5, paragraph (1) of the Act (excluding Quarterly Consolidated Financial Statements contained in a written notification which have the same contents as the Quarterly Consolidated Financial Statements contained in any of the written notifications or quarterly reports (excluding a Second Quarterly Report submitted by a Company Engaged in a Specified Business) submitted previously pursuant to the provision of Article 5, paragraph (1) or Article 24-4-7, paragraph (1) or (2) of the Act);
(vi) the Interim Consolidated Financial Statements (meaning interim consolidated financial statements as set forth in Article 1, paragraph (1) of the Ordinance on Interim Consolidated Financial Statements excluding those submitted by a Designated Juridical Person; hereinafter the same shall apply in this Article) contained in a written notification submitted pursuant to the provision of Article 5, paragraph (1) of the Act (excluding Interim Consolidated Financial Statements contained in a written notification which have the same contents as the Interim Consolidated Financial Statements contained in any of the written notifications, quarterly reports (limited to a Second Quarterly Report submitted by a Company Engaged in a Specified Business), or interim reports submitted previously pursuant to the provision of Article 5, paragraph (1), Article 24-4-7, paragraph (1) or (2) or Article 24-5, paragraph (1) of the Act);
(vii) from among the Financial Statements or the Financial Documents (hereinafter referred to as the "Documents" in this item) for the most recent Business Year, etc. and the immediately preceding Business Year, etc. contained in a securities report submitted pursuant to the provision of Article 24, paragraph (1) or (3) of the Act (excluding Documents for the immediately preceding Business Year, etc. contained in a securities report submitted pursuant to the provision of paragraph (1) of that Article which have the same contents as the Documents contained in any of the written notifications or securities reports submitted previously pursuant to the provision of Article 5, paragraph (1) or Article 24, paragraph (1) or (3) of the Act);
(viii) the Consolidated Financial Statements contained in a securities report submitted pursuant to the provision of Article 24, paragraph (1) or (3) of the Act (excluding Consolidated Financial Statements for the Consolidated Fiscal Year (meaning a consolidated fiscal year as set forth in Article 3, paragraph (2) of the Ordinance on Consolidated Financial Statements; the same shall apply hereinafter) immediately preceding the most recent Consolidated Fiscal Year which have the same contents as the Consolidated Financial Statements contained in any of the written notifications or quarterly reports submitted previously pursuant to the provision of Article 5, paragraph (1) or Article 24, paragraph (1) or (3) of the Act);
(ix) the Quarterly Financial Statements contained in a quarterly report (excluding a Second Quarterly Report submitted by a Company Engaged in a Specified Business) submitted pursuant to the provision of Article 24-4-7, paragraph (1) or (2) of the Act (excluding Quarterly Financial Statements for the business year immediately preceding the relevant business year contained in a quarterly report which

Art.1   ⑨ Cabinet Office Ordinance on Audit Certification
of Financial Statements, etc.

have the same contents as the Quarterly Financial Statements contained in any of the written notifications or quarterly reports submitted previously pursuant to the provision of Article 5, paragraph (1) or Article 24-4-7, paragraph (1) or (2) of the Act);
(x) the Interim Financial Statements contained in a quarterly report (limited to a Second Quarterly Report submitted by a Company Engaged in a Specified Business) submitted pursuant to the provision of Article 24-4-7, paragraph (1) or (2) of the Act (excluding Interim Financial Statements for the business year immediately preceding the relevant business year contained in a quarterly report which have the same contents as the Interim Financial Statements contained in any of the written notifications or quarterly reports submitted previously pursuant to the provision of Article 5, paragraph (1) or Article 24-4-7, paragraph (1) or (2) of the Act);
(xi) the Quarterly Consolidated Financial Statements contained in a quarterly report (excluding a Second Quarterly Report submitted by a Company Engaged in a Specified Business) submitted pursuant to the provision of Article 24-4-7, paragraph (1) or (2) of the Act (excluding Quarterly Consolidated Financial Statements for the Consolidated Fiscal Year immediately preceding the relevant Consolidated Fiscal Year contained in a quarterly report which have the same contents as the Quarterly Consolidated Financial Statements contained in any of the written notifications or quarterly reports submitted previously pursuant to the provision of Article 5, paragraph (1) or Article 24-4-7, paragraph (1) or (2) of the Act);
(xi)-2 the Consolidated Financial Statements under the provision of Article 93 of the Ordinance on Consolidated Financial Statements contained in a quarterly report (limited to a First Quarterly Report (meaning a quarterly report pertaining to the first Quarterly Accounting Period)) submitted pursuant to the provision of Article 24-4-7, paragraph (1) of the Act;
(xii) the Interim Consolidated Finance Statements contained in a quarterly report (excluding a Second Quarterly Report submitted by a Company Engaged in a Specified Business) submitted pursuant to the provision of Article 24-4-7, paragraph (1) or (2) of the Act (excluding Interim Consolidated Financial Statements for the Consolidated Fiscal Year immediately preceding the relevant Consolidated Fiscal Year contained in a quarterly report which have the same contents as the Interim Financial Statements contained in any of the written notifications or quarterly reports submitted previously pursuant to the provision of Article 5, paragraph (1) or Article 24-4-7, paragraph (1) or (2) of the Act);
(xiii) the Interim Financial Statements contained in an interim report submitted pursuant to the provision of Article 24-5, paragraph (1) of the Act (excluding Interim Financial Statements for the Business Year, etc. immediately preceding the relevant Business Year, etc. contained in an interim report which have the same contents as the Interim Financial Statements contained in any of the written notifications or interim reports submitted previously pursuant to the provision of Article 5, paragraph (1) or Article 24-5, paragraph (1) of the Act);
(xiv) the Interim Consolidated Financial Statements contained in an interim report submitted pursuant to the provision of Article 24-5, paragraph (1) of the Act (excluding Interim Consolidated Financial Statements for the Consolidated Fiscal Year immediately preceding the relevant Consolidated Fiscal Year contained in an interim report which have the same contents as the Interim Consolidated Financial Statements contained in any of the written notifications or interim reports submitted previously pursuant to the provision of Article 5, paragraph (1) or Article 24-5, paragraph (1) of the Act);
(xv) documents for amending the documents set forth in any of the preceding items,

which are contained in an amendment or an amendment report submitted pursuant to the provision of Article 7, Article 9, paragraph (1) or Article 10, paragraph (1) of the Act (including cases where these provisions are applied mutatis mutandis pursuant to Article 24-2, paragraph (1), Article 24-4-7, pragraph (4) and Article 24-5, paragraph (5) of the Act);

(xvi) the documents set forth in item (i) to item (xiv) inclusive or documents equivalent thereto contained in a written notification submitted pursuant to the provision of Article 5, paragraph (1) of the Act as applied mutatis mutandis pursuant to Article 27 of the Act, in a securities report submitted pursuant to the provision of Article 24, paragraph (1) or (3) of the Act as applied mutatis mutandis pursuant to Article 27 of the Act (including the cases where these provisions are applied mutatis mutandis pursuant to Article 24, paragraph (5) of the Act as applied mutatis mutandis pursuant to Article 27 of the Act), in a quarterly report submitted pursuant to the provision of Article 24-4-7, paragraph (1) or (2) of the Act as applied mutatis mutandis pursuant to Article 27 of the Act (including the cases where these provisions are applied mutatis mutandis pursuant to Article 24-4-7, paragraph (3) of the Act as applied mutatis mutandis pursuant to Article 27 of the Act) and in a semiannual securities report submitted pursuant to the provision of Article 24-5, paragraph (1) of the Act as applied mutatis mutandis pursuant to Article 27 of the Act (including the cases where applied mutatis mutandis pursuant to Article 24-5, paragraph (3) of the Act as applied mutatis mutandis pursuant to Article 27 of the Act); and

(xvii) documents for amending the documents set forth in the preceding item contained in an amendment or an amendment report submitted pursuant to the provision of Article 7 of the Act as applied mutatis mutandis pursuant to Article 27 of the Act (including the cases where applied mutatis mutandis pursuant to Article 24-2, paragraph (1) of the Act as applied mutatis mutandis pursuant to Article 27 of the Act, the cases where applied mutatis mutandis pursuant to Article 24-4-7, paragraph (4) of the Act as applied mutatis mutandis pursuant to Article 27 of the Act and the cases where applied mutatis mutandis pursuant to Article 24-5, paragraph (5) of the Act as applied mutatis mutandis pursuant to Article 27 of the Act), or pursuant to the provision of Article 9, paragraph (1) of the Act as applied mutatis mutandis pursuant to Article 27 of the Act (including the cases where applied mutatis mutandis pursuant to Article 24-2, paragraph (1) of the Act as applied mutatis mutandis pursuant to Article 27 of the Act, the cases where applied mutatis mutandis pursuant to Article 24-4-7, paragraph (4) of the Act as applied mutatis mutandis pursuant to Article 27 of the Act and the cases where applied mutatis mutandis pursuant to Article 24-5, paragraph (5) of the Act as applied mutatis mutandis pursuant to Article 27 of the Act), or pursuant to the provision of Article10, paragraph (1) of the Act as applied mutatis mutandis pursuant to Article 27 of the Act (including the cases where applied mutatis mutandis pursuant to Article 24-2, paragraph (1) of the Act as applied mutatis mutandis pursuant to Article 27 of the Act, the cases where applied mutatis mutandis pursuant to Article 24-4-7, paragraph (4) of the Act as applied mutatis mutandis pursuant to Article 27 of the Act and the cases where applied mutatis mutandis pursuant to Article 24-5, paragraph (5) of the Act as applied mutatis mutandis pursuant to Article 27 of the Act).

(Certification Deemed Equivalent to Audit Certification)

Article 1-2 The case of having received a certification deemed equivalent to an audit certification pursuant to the provisions of the Cabinet Office Ordinance as set forth in Article 193-2, paragraph (1), item (i) of the Act shall be the case of having received a certification deemed equivalent to an audit certification by way of receiving an offer of a service that is deemed to be equivalent to the service set forth in Article 2, paragraph (1) of the Certified Public Accountants Act (Act No. 103 of 1948) from a Foreign Auditing Firm, etc. (meaning a foreign auditing firm, etc. as set forth in Article 1-3, paragraph (7) of that Act) for Financial Documents of a Foreign Company, etc. (meaning financial documents of a foreign company, etc. as set forth in Article 34-35, paragraph (1) of that Act).

(Approval for Not Being Required to Receive an Audit Certification)
Article 1-3 In cases where a company (including a Designated Juridical Person; hereinafter the same shall apply) submitting the documents set forth in items of Article 1 intends to receive the approval set forth in Article 193-2, paragraph (1), item (iii) of the Act, it shall submit a written application for approval for said documents to the Director-General of a Local Finance Bureau, etc. (meaning the Director-General of a Local Finance Bureau or the Director-General of the Fukuoka Local Finance Branch Bureau to whom said documents shall be submitted pursuant to the provisions of Article 20 (excluding paragraph (3)) of the Cabinet Office Ordinance on Disclosure or pursuant to the provisions of Article 30 of the Cabinet Office Ordinance on Disclosure of Contents, etc. of Regulated Securities (Ordinance of the Ministry of Finance No.22 of 1993).

(Special Interest between a Certified Public Accountant or an Auditing Firm and an Audited Company)
Article 2 (1) The interests specified by a Cabinet Office Ordinance concerning a certified public accountant (including a foreign certified public accountant as set forth in Article 16-2, paragraph (5) of the Certified Public Accountants Act; hereinafter the same shall apply) as set forth in Article 193-2, paragraph (4) of the Act shall be the interests in a case that falls under any of the following items; provided, however, that with regard to item (vi), such interests shall be limited to those in a case relating to the audit certification set forth in Article 193-2, paragraph (1) of the Act (hereinafter referred to as the "Audit Certification") for Consolidated Financial Statements, etc. (meaning Consolidated Financial Statements (meaning the consolidated financial statements specified in Article 1, item (xxi) of the Cabinet Office Ordinance on Disclosure; hereinafter the same shall apply), Interim Consolidated Financial Statements (meaning the interim consolidated financial statements specified in Article 1, paragraph (1) of the Ordinance on Interim Consolidated Financial Statements; the same shall apply hereinafter), and Quarterly Consolidated Financial Statements (meaning the quarterly consolidated financial statements specified in Article 1, paragraph (1) of the Ordinance on Quarterly Consolidated Financial Statements; the same shall apply hereinafter); the same shall apply hereinafter):

(i) the case of having the interests set forth in Article 24, paragraph (1) or (3) of the Certified Public Accountants Act (including the cases where these provisions are applied mutatis mutandis pursuant to Article 16-2, paragraph (6) of that Act);

(ii) the cases where, pursuant to the provision of Article 24-2 of the Certified Public Accountants Act (including the cases where applied mutatis mutandis pursuant to Article 16-2, paragraph (6) of that Act), the services set forth in Article 2, paragraph (1) of that Act may not be carried out;

(iii) the cases where, pursuant to the provision of Article 24-3, paragraph (1) of the Certified Public Accountants Act (including the cases where applied mutatis mutandis pursuant to Article 16-2, paragraph (6) of that Act), the audit-related services set forth in Article 24-3, paragraph (3) of that Act may not be carried out;

(iv) the cases where a person who is engaged in the audit of the company which is to receive an Audit Certification (hereinafter referred to as the "Audited Company") as an assistant (hereinafter referred to as an "Assistant") has the interests set forth in Article 24, paragraph (1), item (i) or (ii), or paragraph (3) of the Certified Public Accountants Act, or in Article 7, paragraph (1), items (i), (iv) to (vi) inclusive, (viii) or (ix) of the Order for Enforcement of the Certified Public Accountants Act (Cabinet Order No.343 of 1952);

(v) the cases where any relative within the second degree of kinship with a certified public accountant has any of the interests set forth in Article 24, paragraph (1), item (i) of the Certified Public Accountants Act or in Article 7, paragraph (1), item (i) of the Order for Enforcement of the Certified Public Accountants Act; or

(vi) the cases where a certified public accountant, his/her spouse or an Assistant has any of the interests set forth in Article 24, paragraph (1), item (i) or (ii), or paragraph (3) of the Certified Public Accountants Act, or in Article 7, paragraph (1), item (i) or items (iv) to (vii) inclusive of the Order for Enforcement of the Certified Public Accountants Act (with regard to an Assistant, excluding the interests set forth in item (vii) of that paragraph) with a Consolidated Subsidiary Company (meaning a consolidated subsidiary company as set forth in Article 2, item (iv) of the Ordinance on Consolidated Financial Statements, Article 2, item (iii) of the Ordinance on Interim Consolidated Financial Statements, and Article 2, item (vii) of the Ordinance on Quarterly Consolidated Financial Statements when the Audited Company is a Domestic Company (meaning a domestic company as set forth in Article 1, item (xx)-3 of the Cabinet Office Ordinance on Disclosure; the same shall apply hereinafter) or meaning a company equivalent to a consolidated subsidiary company as set forth in Article 2, item (iv) of the Ordinance on Interim Consolidated Financial Statements, Article 2, item (iii) of the Ordinance on Interim Consolidated Financial Statements, and Article 2, item (vi) of the Ordinance on Quarterly Consolidated Financial Statements when the Audited Company is a Foreign Company (meaning a foreign company as set forth in Article 1, item (xx)-4 of the Cabinet Office Ordinance on Disclosure, the same shall apply hereinafter); the same shall apply hereinafter) or an Equity Method Affiliate (when the Audited Company is a Domestic Company, this shall mean any Non-Consolidated Subsidiary Company (meaning a non-consolidated subsidiary company as set forth in Article 2, item (vi) of the Ordinance on Consolidated Financial Statements, Article 2, item (v) of the Ordinance on Interim Consolidated Financial Statements, and Article 2, item (ix) of the Ordinance on Quarterly Consolidated Financial Statements; the same shall apply hereinafter), and any Affiliated Company (meaning an affiliate as set forth in Article 2, item (vii) of the Ordinance on Consolidated Financial Statements, Article 2, item (vi) of the Ordinance on Interim Consolidated Financial Statements and Article 2, item (x) of the Ordinance on Quarterly Consolidated Financial Statements; the same shall apply hereinafter) to which the equity method set forth in Article 2, item (viii) of the Ordinance on Consolidated Financial Statements, Article 2, item (vii) of the Ordinance on Interim Consolidated Financial Statements and Article 2, item (xi) of the Ordinance on Quarterly Consolidated Financial Statements is applied, and when the Audited Company is a Foreign Company, this shall mean any company equivalent to a Non-Consolidated Subsidiary Company or to an Affiliated Company to which the equity method set forth in Article 2, item (viii) of the Ordinance on Consolidated Financial Statements, Article 2 (vii) of the Ordinance on Interim Consolidated Financial Statements, and Article 2, item (xi) of the Ordinance on Quarterly Consolidated Financial Statements is applied; the same shall apply hereinafter) of the Audited Company.

(2) The interests specified by a Cabinet Office Ordinance concerning auditing firms, re-

ferred to in Article 193-2, paragraph (4) of the Act, shall mean those in the cases which fall under any of the following items; provided, however, that they shall be limited to those in cases concerning the Audit Certification of Consolidated Financial Statements, etc. with regard to item (vi) to item (ix) inclusive:

(i) the case of having the interests set forth in Article 34-11, paragraph (1) of the Certified Public Accountants Act;

(ii) the case where the business set forth in Article 2, paragraph (1) of the Certified Public Accountants Act may not be carried out pursuant to Article 34-11-2 of that Act;

(iii) the case where the partner of the auditing firm who executes the service of the Audit Certification concerning the Audited Company or his/her spouse has the interests set forth in Article 34-11, paragraph (3) of the Certified Public Accountants Act;

(iv) the case where an Assistant has any of the interests set forth in Article 24, paragraph (1), item (i) or (ii) or paragraph (3) of the Certified Public Accountants Act, or in Article 7, paragraph (1), item (i), item (iv) to item (vi) inclusive, item (viii) or (ix) of the Order for Enforcement of the Certified Public Accountants Act;

(v) the case where any relative within the second degree of kinship with the partner who executes the service of the Audit Certification for the Audited Company has any of the interests set forth in Article 24, paragraph (1), item (i) of the Certified Public Accountants Act or in Article 7, paragraph (1), item (i) of the Order for Enforcement of the Certified Public Accountants Act;

(vi) the case where an auditing firm has any of the interests set forth in Article 34-11, paragraph (1), item (i) of the Certified Public Accountants Act or in Article 15, item (i) to item (iii) inclusive of the Order for Enforcement of the Certified Public Accountants Act with a Consolidated Subsidiary Company or an Equity Method Affiliate of the Audited Company;

(vii) the case where the partner of the auditing firm who executes the service of the Audit Certification for the Audited Company or his/her spouse or an Assistant has any of the interests set forth in Article 24, paragraph (1), item (i) or (ii), or paragraph (3) of the Certified Public Accountants Act, or in Article 7, paragraph (1), item (i) or item (iv) to item (vii) inclusive of the Order for Enforcement of the Certified Public Accountants Act (with regard to an Assistant, excluding the interests set forth in item (vii) of that paragraph) with a Consolidated Subsidiary Company or an Equity Method Affiliate of the Audited Company;

(viii) the case where any of the partners of the auditing firm is a person who serves as a director, executive officer, auditor, or employee of an Equity Method Affiliate of the Audited Company, or a person who has any of the interests set forth in Article 15, item (v) of the Order for Enforcement of the Certified Public Accountants Act with a Consolidated Subsidiary Company or an Equity Method Affiliate of the Audited Company; or

(ix) the case where half or more of the partners of the auditing firm have, with regard to themselves or their spouses, the interests set forth in Article 15 (vii) of the Order for Enforcement of the Certified Public Accountants Act with the Audited Company or any of the interests set forth in Article 24, paragraph (1), item (i) or (ii), or paragraph (3) of the Certified Public Accountants Act or in Article 7, paragraph (1), item (i) or item (iv) to item (vii) inclusive of the Order for Enforcement of the Certified Public Accountants Act with a Consolidated Subsidiary Company or an Equity Method Affiliate of the Audited Company.

(Audit Certification Procedure)

Article 3 (1) The Audit Certification of Financial Statements (meaning financial statements as set forth in Article 1, paragraph (1) of the Ordinance on Financial Statements, etc.; the same shall apply hereinafter), Financial Documents or Consolidated Financial Statements (hereinafter collectively referred to as "Financial Statements, etc.") shall be made based on an audit report prepared by the certified public accountant or the auditing firm who has carried out the audit of the Financial Statements, etc. , the Audit Certification of Interim Financial Statements (meaning interim financial statements as set forth in Article 1, paragraph (1) of the Ordinance on Interim Financial Statements, etc.; the same shall apply hereinafter) or Interim Consolidated Financial Statements (hereinafter collectively referred to as "Interim Financial Statements, etc.") shall be made based on an Interim Audit report prepared by the certified public accountant or the auditing firm who has carried out the audit of the Interim Financial Statements, etc. (hereinafter referred to as "Interim Audit"), and the Audit Certification of Quarterly Financial Statements (meaning quarterly financial statements as set forth in Article 1, paragraph (1) of the Ordinance on Quarterly Financial Statements, etc.; the same shall apply hereinafter), or Quarterly Consolidated Financial Statements (hereinafter collectively referred to as "Quarterly Financial Statements, etc.") shall be made based on a Quarterly Review report prepared by the certified public accountant or the auditing firm who has carried out the audit of the Quarterly Financial Statements, etc. (hereinafter referred to as "Quarterly Review").

(2) The audit report, the Interim Audit report, or the Quarterly Review report set forth in the preceding paragraph shall be prepared based on the results of the audit, the Interim Audit or the Quarterly Review that has been conducted in accordance with the standards and the practices concerning auditing that are generally accepted as fair and appropriate.

(3) The standards for the audit made public by the Business Accounting Council as prescribed in Article 24, paragraph (1) of the Cabinet Order for Organization of the Financial Services Agency (Cabinet Order No. 392 of 1998) shall fall under the standards concerning auditing that are generally accepted as fair and appropriate as referred to in the preceding paragraph.

(Matters to Be Stated in the Audit Report, etc.)

Article 4 (1) On the audit report, the Interim Audit report, or the Quarterly Review report set forth in paragraph (1) of the preceding Article, a certified public accountant or a representative of an auditing firm shall concisely and clearly state the matters specified in the following items for the respective categories set forth in those items, and shall state the date of preparation and affix his/her name and seal thereto. In this case, if an auditing firm prepares said audit report, said Interim Audit report, or said Quarterly Review report, in addition to the representative of said auditing firm, the partner who executes the services concerning said Audit Certification (hereinafter referred to as the "Managing Partner") shall affix his/her name and seal thereto; provided, however, that in cases where said Audit Certification is a Designated Certification (meaning a designated certification as set forth in Article34-10-4, paragraph (2) of the Certified Public Accountants Act.) or a Specified Certification (meaning a specified certification as set forth in Article 34-10-5 (2) of that Act), the Managing Partner serving as the Designated Partner (meaning a designated partner as set forth in Article 34-10-4, paragraph (2) of that Act) related to said Designated Certification or as the Designated Limited Partner (meaning a designated limited partner as set forth in Article 34-10-5, paragraph (2) of that Act; the same shall apply hereinafter) related to said Specified Certification shall state the date of preparation and affix his/her name and seal thereto:

(i) an audit report: the following matters:

(a) the subject of the audit;
(b) the outline of the audit that has been conducted;
(c) opinions as to whether the Financial Statements, etc. subject to the audit adequately present all the material points of the financial position, operating results, and conditions of cash flow in the business year (the Consolidated Fiscal Year in the case of Consolidated Financial Statements) pertaining to said Financial Statements, etc. in accordance with the business accounting standards that are generally accepted as fair and appropriate;
(d) additional information; and
(e) the interests which should be clearly indicated pursuant to the provision of Article 25, paragraph (2) of the Certified Public Accountants Act (including the cases where applied mutatis mutandis pursuant to Article 16-2, paragraph (6) and Article 34-12, paragraph (3) of that Act; the same apply hereinafter);
(ii) an Interim Audit report: the following matters:
(a) the subject of the Interim Audit;
(b) the outline of the Interim Audit that has been conducted;
(c) opinions as to whether the Interim Financial Statements, etc. subject to the Interim Audit presents useful information as to the financial position, operating results, and conditions of cash flow in the interim accounting period (the Interim Consolidated Accounting Period (meaning an interim consolidated accounting period as set forth in Article 3, paragraph (2) of the Ordinance on Interim Financial Statements, etc.; the same shall apply hereinafter) in the case of Interim Consolidated Financial Statements) pertaining to said Interim Financial Statements, etc. in accordance with the standards for preparation of Interim Financial Statements, etc. that are generally accepted as fair and appropriate;
(d) additional information; and
(e) the interests which should be clearly indicated pursuant to the provision of Article 25, paragraph (2) of the Certified Public Accountants Act;
(iii) a Quarterly Review report - the following matters:
(a) the subject of the Quarterly Review;
(b) the outline of the Quarterly Review that has been conducted;
(c) a conclusion as to whether the Quarterly Financial Statements, etc. subject to the Quarterly Review were found to contain any matters, in any of the material points, that would lead one to believe that the Quarterly Financial Statements, etc. fail to adequately present the financial position, operating results, and conditions of cash flow in the Quarterly Accounting Period, etc. (meaning a quarterly accounting period and a business year to date as set forth in Article 3, item (vi) of the Ordinance on Quarterly Financial Statements, etc.; the same shall apply hereinafter) pertaining to said Quarterly Financial Statements, etc. (in the case of Quarterly Consolidated Financial Statements, it shall be the Quarterly Consolidated Accounting Period, etc. (meaning a quarterly consolidated accounting period as set forth in Article 3, item (v) of the Ordinance on Interim Financial Statements, etc. and the consolidated accounting year to date set\ forth in item (vii) of that Article); the same shall apply hereinafter), in accordance with the standards for preparation of Quarterly Financial Statements, etc. that are generally accepted as fair and appropriate;
(d) additional information; and
(e) the interests which should be clearly indicated pursuant to the provision of Article 25, paragraph (2) of the Certified Public Accountants Act.
(2) The following matters shall be stated with regard to the subject of the audit specified in sub-item (a) of item (i) of the preceding paragraph:

(i) the scope of the Financial Statements, etc. that were the subject of the audit;
(ii) a statement that the operator has a liability to prepare the Financial Statements, etc. ; and
(iii) a statement that the certified public accountant or the auditing firm conducting the audit has a liability to express their opinions on the Financial Statements, etc. from an independent standpoint.
(3) The following matters shall be stated with regard to the outline of the audit specified in paragraph (1), item (i), sub-item (b); provided, however, that in cases where any important audit procedure could not be implemented, said audit procedure which could not implemented shall be stated:
(i) a statement that the audit was conducted based on the audit standards that are generally accepted as fair and appropriate;
(ii) a statement that the audit standards require the certified public accountant or the auditing firm conducting the audit to reasonably guarantee that there is no material misstatement in the Financial Statements, etc. ;
(iii) a statement that the audit has been conducted based on audit testing;
(iv) a statement that the presentation in the Financial Statements, etc. has been reviewed as a whole, including an evaluation of the accounting policy and the application method thereof adopted by the operator and the estimates made by the operator; and
(v) a statement that a reasonable basis to allow for the expressing of opinions has been gained as a result of the audit.
(4) With regard to the opinions specified in paragraph (1), item (i), sub-item (c), the matters set forth in the following items shall be stated for the respective categories of opinions set forth in those items:
(i) an unqualified opinion: a statement that the Financial Statements, etc. which have been subject to the audit are found to adequately present all the material points of the financial position, operating results and conditions of cash flow in the business year pertaining to said Financial Statements, etc. in accordance with the business accounting standards that are generally accepted as fair and appropriate;
(ii) a qualified opinion with an exceptive item: a statement that, apart from an exceptive item, the Financial Statements, etc. which have been subject to the audit adequately present all the material points of the financial position, operating results, and conditions of cash flow in the business year pertaining to said Financial Statements, etc. in accordance with the business accounting standards that are generally accepted as fair and appropriate, along with said exceptive item and the influence of said exceptive item on said Financial Statements, etc. or the matters on which the fact that some important audit procedure could not be implemented exerts influence; or
(iii) an adverse opinion: a statement that the Financial Statements, etc. which have been subject to the audit are inadequate and the reason therefor.
(5) With regard to the matters set forth in paragraph (1), item (i), sub-item (d), any matters concerning the explanatory notes under the provision of Article 8-27 of the Ordinance on Financial Statements, etc. or Article 15-22 of the Ordinance on Consolidated Financial Statements, any change in the accounting policy on justifiable grounds, any material contingency, and any material post-balance sheet events, which the certified public accountant or the auditing firm conducting the audit determines appropriate to explain or emphasize, shall be stated.
(6) With regard to the subject of the Interim Audit set forth in paragraph (1), item (ii), sub-item (a), the following matters shall be stated:
(i) the scope of the Interim Financial Statements, etc. that were the subject of the In-

Art.4

⑨ Cabinet Office Ordinance on Audit Certification
of Financial Statements, etc.

terim Audit.
(ii) a statement that the operator has a liability to prepare the Interim Financial Statements, etc. ; and
(iii) a statement that the certified public accountant or the auditing firm conducting the Interim Audit has a liability to express their opinions on the Interim Financial Statements, etc. from an independent standpoint.
(7) The following matters shall be stated with regard to the outline of the Interim Audit set forth in paragraph (1), item (ii), sub-item (b); provided, however, that in cases where any important audit procedure could not be implemented, said procedure which could not be implemented shall be stated:
(i) a statement that the Interim Audit was conducted based on Interim Audit standards;
(ii) a statement that the Interim Audit standards require the certified public accountant or the auditing firm conducting the Interim Audit to reasonably guarantee that the Interim Financial Statements, etc. as a whole contain no material misstatement which impairs the decision-making of investors with regard to the useful presentation of the Interim Financial Statements, etc. ;
(iii) a statement that the Interim Audit has been conducted mainly by using analytical procedures and applying additional audit procedures as needed; and
(iv) a statement that a reasonable basis to allow for the expressing of opinions has been gained as a result of the Interim Audit.
(8) With regard to the opinions specified in paragraph (1), item (ii), sub-item (c), the matters set forth in the following items shall be stated for the respective categories of opinions set forth in those items:
(i) an opinion that the Interim Financial Statements, etc. present useful information: the fact that the Interim Financial Statements, etc. subject to the Interim Audit present useful information concerning the financial position, operating results, and conditions of cash flow in the Interim Accounting Period pertaining to said Interim Financial Statements, etc. in accordance with the standards for preparation of Interim Financial Statements, etc. that are generally accepted as fair and appropriate;
(ii) a qualified opinion with an exceptive item: a statement that, apart from an exceptive item, the Interim Financial Statements, etc. which have been subject to the Interim Audit adequately present all the material points of the financial position, operating results, and conditions of cash flow in the Interim Accounting Period pertaining to said Interim Financial Statements, etc. in accordance with the standards for preparing Interim Financial Statements, etc. that are generally accepted as fair and appropriate. , along with said exceptive item and the influence of said exceptive item on said Interim Financial Statements, etc. or the matters on which the fact that some important audit procedure could not be implemented exerts influence; or
(iii) an opinion that the Interim Financial Statements, etc. do not present useful information: a statement that the Interim Financial Statements, etc. which have been subject to the Interim Audit do not present useful information and the reason therefor.
(9) With regard to the matters set forth in paragraph (1), item (ii), sub-item (d), any matters concerning the explanatory notes under the provision of Article 5-18 of the Ordinance on Interim Financial Statements, etc. or Article 17-14 of the Ordinance on Interim Consolidated Financial Statements, any change in the accounting policy on justifiable grounds, any material contingency, and any material post-balance sheet events which the certified public accountant or the auditing firm conducting the Interim Audit determines appropriate to explain or emphasize, shall be stated.
(10) With regard to the subject of the Quarterly Review, the following matters shall be

stated:
(i) the scope of the Quarterly Financial Statements, etc. that were the subject of the Quarterly Review;
(ii) a statement that the operator has a liability to prepare the Quarterly Financial Statements, etc. ; and
(iii) a statement that the certified public accountant or the auditing firm conducting the Quarterly Review is to express their opinions on the Quarterly Financial Statements, etc. from an independent standpoint.
(11) The following matters shall be stated with regard to the outline of the Quarterly Review set forth in paragraph (1), item (iii), sub-item (b); provided, however, that in cases where any important Quarterly Review procedure could not be implemented, said procedure shall be stated:
(i) a statement that the Quarterly Review was conducted based on the Quarterly Review standards that are generally accepted as fair and appropriate;
(ii) a statement that the Quarterly Review was conducted by questioning procedures, analytical procedures, or any other Quarterly Review procedures, and that it was conducted under more limited procedures than the audit of Financial Statements, etc. ;
(12) With regard to the conclusion set forth in paragraph (1), item (iii), sub-item (c), the matters set forth in the following items shall be stated for the respective categories of conclusions set forth in those items:
(i) an unqualified conclusion: a conclusion that the Quarterly Financial Statements, etc. subject to the Quarterly Review were found to contain no matters, in any of the material points, that would lead one to believe that the Quarterly Financial Statements, etc. fail to adequately present the financial position, operating results, and conditions of cash flow in the Quarterly Accounting Period, etc. pertaining to said Quarterly Financial Statements, etc. , in accordance with the standards for preparation of Quarterly Financial Statements, etc. that are generally accepted as fair and appropriate;
(ii) a qualified conclusion with an exceptive item: a conclusion that, apart from an exceptive item, the Quarterly Financial Statements, etc. subject to the Quarterly Review were found to contain no matters that would lead one to believe that the Quarterly Financial Statements, etc. fail to adequately present the financial position, operating results, and conditions of cash flow in the Quarterly Accounting Period, etc. pertaining to said Quarterly Financial Statements, etc. , in accordance with the standards for preparation of Quarterly Financial Statements, etc. that are generally accepted as fair and appropriate, along with said exceptive item and the influence of said exceptive item on said Quarterly Financial Statements, etc. (limited to cases where it is possible to state such influence) or the matters on which the fact that some important Quarterly Review procedures could not be implemented exerts influence; or
(iii) a negative conclusion: a conclusion that the Quarterly Financial Statements, etc. subject to the Quarterly Review were found to contain matters that would lead one to believe that the Quarterly Financial Statements, etc. fail to adequately present the financial position, operating results, and conditions of cash flow in the Quarterly Accounting Period, etc. pertaining to said Quarterly Financial Statements, etc. , in accordance with the standards for preparation of Quarterly Financial Statements, etc. that are generally accepted as fair and appropriate, and the reason therefor.
(13) With regard to the matters set forth in paragraph (1), item (iii), sub-item (d), any matters concerning the explanatory notes under the provisions of Article 21 of the Ordinance on Quarterly Financial Statements, etc. or Article 27 of the Ordinance on Quar-

terly Consolidated Financial Statements, any change in the accounting policy on justifiable grounds, any material contingency, and any material post-balance sheet events, which the certified public accountant or the auditing firm conducting the Quarterly Review determines appropriate to explain or emphasize, shall be stated.

(14) In cases where the certified public accountant or the auditing firm could not gain a reasonable basis to allow for the expression of an opinion as set forth in paragraph (1), item (i), sub-item (c) or paragraph (1), item (ii), sub-item (c) or could not express the conclusion set forth in paragraph (1), item (iii), sub-item (c) because any of the material audit procedures or Quarterly Review procedures were not implemented or due to any other reason, notwithstanding the provision of that paragraph, the certified public accountant or the auditing firm shall include a statement, in the audit report, Interim Audit report, or Quarterly Review Report, that the opinion set forth in item (i), sub-item (c), or item (ii), sub-item (c) of that paragraph or the conclusion set forth in item (iii), sub-item (c) of that paragraph will not be expressed and the reason therefor.

(Submission of a Written Outline of the Audit, etc.)

Article 5 (1) As part of the report or materials to be submitted pursuant to the provision of Article 193-2, paragraph (6) of the Act, a certified public accountant or an auditing firm shall submit, after the termination of the Audit, etc., a written outline containing the names of the persons engaged in the audit, the Interim Audit or the Quarterly Review (hereinafter referred to as the "Audit, etc."), the number of days required for the Audit, etc., and the outline of any other matters concerning the Audit, etc. to the Director-General of a Local Finance Bureau, etc. to whom the documents set forth in the items of Article 1 concerning said Audit, etc. should be submitted.

(2) The written outline set forth in the preceding paragraph shall be prepared by using the forms specified in the following items for the respective categories of Audit, etc. set forth in those items:

(i) the written outline of an audit of Financial Statements, etc. (excluding Financial Statements, etc. concerning the fund specified in Article 1, item (ix) of the Cabinet Office Ordinance on Disclosure of Contents, etc. of Regulated Securities and the trust property specified in item (ix)-4 of that Article (hereinafter referred to as a "Fund or Trust Property" in this paragraph)): Form No. 1;

(ii) the written outline of an Interim Audit of Interim Financial Statements, etc. (excluding Interim Financial Statements, etc. concerning a Fund or Trust Property): Form No. 2;

(iii) the written outline of an audit of Financial Statements, etc. or an Interim Audit of Interim Financial Statements, etc. concerning a Fund or Trust Property: Form No. 3; and

(iv) the written outline of a Quarterly Review: Form No. 4.

(3) The written outline specified in paragraph (1) shall be submitted by the dates specified in the following items for the respective categories of written outlines set forth in those items:

(i) the written outline set forth in items (i), (ii) and (iv) of the preceding paragraph: the last day of the month following the date of preparation of the audit report, the Interim Audit report, or the Quarterly Review report pertaining to said written outline;

(ii) the written outline set forth in item (iii) of the preceding paragraph: the last day of the month in which three months have elapsed from the date of preparation of the audit report or the Interim Audit report pertaining to said written outline.

(Acceptance of Documents Related to Audit Certification by the Director-

General of a Local Finance Bureau, etc.)

Article 5-2 The documents specified by a Cabinet Office Ordinance as set forth in Article 39, paragraph (2), item (i) of the Order for Enforcement of the Financial Instruments and Exchange Act (Cabinet Order No.321 of September 30, 1965) shall be the written outline of the audit, the written outline of the Interim Audit, or the written outline of the Quarterly Review prescribed in paragraph (1) of the preceding Article.

(Preparation and Keeping of the Audit Record)

Article 6 A certified public accountant or an auditing firm shall, without delay after termination of the Audit, etc. , arrange the records and materials concerning said Audit, etc. into an audit record of said Audit, etc. and shall keep it at the office of the certified public accountant or the auditing firm.

(Notification of Violations of Laws and Regulations)

Article 7 A certified public accountant or an auditing firm that has found any Violations of Laws and Regulations (meaning violations of laws and regulations as set forth in Article 193-3, paragraph (1) of the Act) by a Specified Issuer (meaning a specified issuer as set forth in Article 193-2, paragraph (1) of the Act; the same shall apply in the following Article) in conducting an Audit Certification shall give notice to the auditor, the inspector, or a person equivalent thereto of said Specified Issuer (in cases where there is any other appropriate person for taking the appropriate measures set forth in Article 193-3, paragraph (1) of the Act, such a person) by means of a document stating the contents of the violations and the fact that the violations should be corrected or that any other appropriate measures should be taken.

(Procedure for Proposing an Opinion)

Article 8 A certified public accountant or an auditing firm who intends to make the proposal set forth in Article 193-3, paragraph (2) of the Act shall submit a document containing the following matters to the Commissioner of the Financial Services Agency:
(i) the name and address or the location of the principal office of the certified public accountant or the auditing firm;
(ii) the trade name or the name of the Specified Issuer;
(iii) the date that the notice under Article 193-3, paragraph (1) of the Act was given;
(iv) the gist of the opinion; and
(v) the contents of the opinion (the contents shall be stated separately for the matter set forth in Article 193-3, paragraph (2), item (i) of the Act and for the matter set forth in item (ii) of that paragraph).

⑩ Ordinance on Terminology, Forms, and Preparation Methods of Quarterly Financial Statements, etc.

(Cabinet Office Ordinance No. 63 of August 10, 2007)

Pursuant to the provisions of Article 193 of the Financial Instruments and Exchange Act (Act No. 25 of 1948), and for the purpose of enforcement of that Act, the Ordinance on Terminology, Forms, and Preparation Methods of Quarterly Financial Statements, etc. shall be enacted as follows.

Chapter I General Provisions (Articles 1 to 24)
Chapter II Quarterly Balance Sheet
　Section 1 General Provisions (Articles 25 to 27)
　Section 2 Assets (Articles 28 to 41)
　Section 3 Liabilities (Articles 42 to 47-2)
　Section 4 Net Assets (Articles 48 to 52)
　Section 5 Miscellaneous Provisions (Articles 53 to 55)
Chapter III Quarterly Profit and Loss Statement
　Section 1 General Provisions (Articles 56 and 57)
　Section 2 Net Sales and Cost of Sales (Articles 58 to 60)
　Section 3 Selling Expenses and General and Administrative Expenses (Articles 61 and 62)
　Section 4 Non-operating Revenues and Non-operating Expenses (Articles 63 to 65)
　Section 5 Extraordinary Profit and Extraordinary Loss (Articles 66 to 70)
　Section 6 Miscellaneous Provisions (Articles 71 to 73)
Chapter IV Quarterly Cash Flow Statement
　Section 1 General Provisions (Articles 74 and 75)
　Section 2 Method for Presenting a Quarterly Cash Flow Statement (Articles 76 and 77)
Chapter V Notes on Shareholders' Equity, etc. (Articles 78 to 82)
Chapter VI Quarterly Financial Statements of Specified Companies (Articles 83 and 84)
Chapter VII Quarterly Financial Documents of Foreign Companies (Articles 85 to 89)
　Supplementary Provisions

Chapter I General Provisions

(General Principles for Application)
Article 1　(1) From among finance and accounting documents (hereinafter referred to as "Financial Documents") to be submitted pursuant to the provisions of Article 5, Article 7, Article 9, paragraph (1), Article 10, paragraph (1), Article 24-4-7, paragraph (1) or (2) of the Financial Instruments and Exchange Act (hereinafter referred to as the "Act") (including the cases where any of these provisions are applied mutatis mutandis pursuant to paragraph (4) of that Article and cases where these provisions are applied mutatis mutandis, pursuant to Article 27 of the Act, to a juridical person which has been designated by the Commissioner of the Financial Services Agency pursuant to the provision of Article 1, paragraph (1) of the Ordinance on Terminology, Forms, and Preparation Methods of Financial Statements, etc. (Ordinance of the Ministry of Finance No. 59 of 1963; hereinafter referred to as the "Ordinance on Financial Statements, etc.") (such juridical person shall hereinafter be referred to as a "Designated

Juridical Person")), the terminology, forms, and preparation methods of Quarterly Financial Statements (meaning quarterly balance sheets, quarterly profit and loss statements, and quarterly cash flow statements or, in cases where they are prepared pursuant to Designated International Accounting Standards (meaning Designated International Accounting Standards prescribed in Article 93 of the Ordinance on Terminology, Forms and Preparation Methods of Consolidated Financial Statements (Ordinance of the Ministry of Finance No. 28 of 1976; hereinafter referred to as the "Ordinance on Consolidated Financial Statements"); the same shall apply hereinafter) pursuant to the provision of Article 83, paragraph (2), equivalents to quarterly balance sheets, quarterly profit and loss statements and quarterly cash flow statements and statements of changes in equity of which preparation is required pursuant to Designated International Accounting Standards; the same shall apply hereinafter) shall be governed by the provisions of this Chapter to Chapter VI inclusive, excluding Article 2, and any matters that are not provided for under this Ordinance shall be in compliance with business accounting standards that are generally accepted as fair and appropriate.

(2) Business accounting standards published by the Business Accounting Council prescribed in Article 24, paragraph (1) of the Cabinet Order for Organization of the Financial Services Agency (Cabinet Order No. 392 of 1998) shall be regarded as the business accounting standards that are generally accepted as fair and appropriate prescribed in the preceding paragraph.

(3) Business accounting standards specified by the Commissioner of the Financial Services Agency prescribed in Article 1 (3) of the Ordinance on Financial Statements, etc. shall be regarded as the business accounting standards that are generally accepted as fair and appropriate prescribed in paragraph (1).

(Special Provision for Application)

Article 1-2 The terminology, forms, and preparation methods of Quarterly Financial Statements that a company, as one that engages in international financing activities or business activities, which satisfies either of the following requirements (hereinafter referred to as a "Specified Company") submits may be in accordance with the provisions of Chapter VI:

(i) that it should satisfy the requirements set forth in Article 1-2, item (i) of the Ordinance on Financial Statements, etc. ; or

(ii) that it should be a company that prepared Financial Statements, Interim Financial Statements (meaning documents prescribed in Article 1, paragraph (1) of the Ordinance on Terminology, Forms and Preparation Methods of Interim Financial Statements, etc. (Ordinance of the Ministry of Finance No. 38 of 1977)) or Quarterly Financial Statements pertaining to the business year immediately preceding the business year containing the current Quarterly Accounting Period or the Interim Accounting Period immediately preceding or the Quarterly Accounting Period immediately preceding the current Quarterly Accounting Period, whichever is the period of which last day is the closest to the quarterly balance sheet date, pursuant to Designated International Accounting Standards and should satisfy the requirements set forth in Article 1-2, item (i), sub-items (b) and (c) of the Ordinance on Financial Statements, etc.

(Special Provision for Foreign Companies)

Article 2 From among the Financial Documents to be submitted by a Foreign Company (meaning the foreign company defined in Article 1-3 of the Ordinance on Financial Statements, etc.; the same shall apply in Chapter VII), the terminology, forms, and preparation methods of quarterly Financial Documents shall be governed by the provisions of that Chapter.

(Definitions)

Article 3 In this Ordinance, the meanings of the terms set forth in the following items shall be as prescribed respectively in those items:

(i) Company Submitting Quarterly Financial Statements: a company (including a Designated Juridical Person) which is to submit Quarterly Financial Statements pursuant to the provision of Article 24-4-7, paragraph (1) of the Act (including the cases where it is applied mutatis mutandis pursuant to Article 27 of the Act) and a company (including a Designated Juridical Person) which is to submit Quarterly Financial Statements pursuant to the provision of Article 24-4-7, paragraph (2) of the Act (including the cases where it is applied mutatis mutandis pursuant to Article 27 of the Act);

(ii) Financial Statements: the financial statements defined in Article 1, paragraph (1) of the Ordinance on Financial Statements, etc. ;

(iii) Quarterly Consolidated Financial Statements: the quarterly consolidated financial statements defined in Article 1 (1) of the Ordinance on Terminology, Forms, and Preparation Methods of Quarterly Consolidated Financial Statements (Cabinet Office Ordinance No. 64 of 2007);

(iv) Quarterly Accounting Period: in cases where a business year exceeds three months, each three-month period within said business year (excluding the last such period);

(v) Quarterly Consolidated Accounting Period: in cases where a consolidated fiscal year exceeds three months, each three-month period within said consolidated fiscal year (excluding the last such period);

(vi) Year to Date: the period from the day of commencement of a business year to the last day of a Quarterly Accounting Period;

(vii) Consolidated Year to Date: the period from the day of commencement of a consolidated fiscal year to the last day of a Quarterly Consolidated Accounting Period;

(viii) Cash Flow: any increase or decrease in the Funds defined in the following item;

(ix) Funds: the combined total of cash (including any current deposits, ordinary deposits, and other deposits which the depositor is able to withdraw without waiting for a certain period to elapse; the same shall apply in Articles 75 and 77) and Cash Equivalents (meaning short-term investments which can be easily converted into cash and which involve low risk of fluctuations in value; the same shall apply in Articles 75 and 77);

(x) Derivative Transactions: the transactions defined in Article 8, paragraph (14) of the Ordinance on Financial Statements, etc. ;

(xi) Trading Securities: the securities defined in Article 8, paragraph (20) of the Ordinance on Financial Statements, etc. ;

(xii) Bonds Held to Maturity: the bonds defined in Article 8, paragraph (21) of the Ordinance on Financial Statements, etc. ;

(xiii) Other Securities: the securities defined in Article 8, paragraph (22) of the Ordinance on Financial Statements, etc. ;

(xiv) Treasury Shares: shares of a Company Submitting Quarterly Financial Statements held by the Company Submitting Quarterly Financial Statements itself;

(xv) Company's Own Shares: shares of a Company Submitting Quarterly Financial Statements;

(xvi) Options on the Company's Own Shares: the options on the company's own shares defined in Article 8, paragraph (25) of the Ordinance on Financial Statements, etc. ;

(xvii) Stock Options: the stock options defined in Article 8, paragraph (26) of the Ordinance on Financial Statements, etc. ;
(xviii) Business Combination: the business combination defined in Article 8, paragraph (27) of the Ordinance on Financial Statements, etc. ;
(xix) Acquiring Enterprise: the enterprise defined in Article 8, paragraph (28) of the Ordinance on Financial Statements, etc. ;
(xx) Acquired Enterprise: the enterprise defined in Article 8, paragraph (29) of the Ordinance on Financial Statements, etc. ;
(xxi) Combiner: the enterprise defined in Article 8, paragraph (31) of the Ordinance on Financial Statements, etc. ;
(xxii) Combinee: the enterprise defined in Article 8, paragraph (32) of the Ordinance on Financial Statements, etc. ;
(xxiii) Combined Enterprise: the enterprise defined in Article 8, paragraph (33) of the Ordinance on Financial Statements, etc. ;
(xxiv) Constituent Enterprises: the enterprises defined in Article 8, paragraph (34) of the Ordinance on Financial Statements, etc. ;
(xxv) Purchase Method: the method defined in Article 8, paragraph (35) of the Ordinance on Financial Statements, etc. ;
(xxvi) Reverse Acquisition: the Reverse Acquisition defined in Article 8, paragraph (36) of the Ordinance on Financial Statements, etc. ;
(xxvii) Common Control Transaction, etc. : the common control transaction, etc. defined in Article 8, paragraph (37) of the Ordinance on Financial Statements, etc. ;
(xxviii) Business Divestiture: the business divestiture defined in Article 8, paragraph (38) of the Ordinance on Financial Statements, etc. ;
(xxix) Divesting Enterprise: the enterprise defined in Article 8, paragraph (39) of the Ordinance on Financial Statements, etc. ;
(xxx) Successor Enterprise: the enterprise defined in Article 8, paragraph (40) of the Ordinance on Financial Statements, etc. ;
(xxxi) Financial Instruments: the financial instruments defined in Article 8, paragraph (41) of the Ordinance on Financial Statements, etc. ; and
(xxxii) Asset Retirement Obligations: the asset retirement obligations defined in Article 8, paragraph (42) of the Ordinance on Financial Statements, etc.

(General Principles for Preparation of Quarterly Financial Statements)
Article 4 (1) Quarterly Financial Statements shall be prepared in compliance with the accounting principles and procedures adopted for preparing Financial Statements, in principle.
(2) The accounting principles and procedures adopted for preparing Financial Statements for the business year immediately preceding the business year containing the Quarterly Accounting Period pertaining to the Quarterly Financial Statements (such immediately preceding business year shall hereinafter be referred to as the "Previous Business Year") and the accounting principles and procedures adopted for preparing Quarterly Financial Statements for the Year to Date as of the end of the immediately preceding Quarterly Accounting Period or as of the end of the relevant Quarterly Accounting Period shall be applied continuously in the current Quarterly Accounting Period, except in cases of making a change based on justifiable grounds.
(3) The same presentation method of Quarterly Financial Statements shall be applied continuously, except in cases of making a change based on justifiable grounds.

(Statement of Significant Matters That Serve as the Basis for Preparation of Quarterly Financial Statements)

Article 5 (1) In cases where any accounting principles and procedures and presentation methods adopted for preparation of Quarterly Financial Statements or any other Significant Matters That Serve as the Basis for Preparation of Quarterly Financial Statements (meaning significant matters that are applied in an equivalent manner as those applied in preparing Financial Statements) have been changed, the matters set forth in the following items for the respective cases set forth in those items shall be stated immediately after the quarterly cash flow statement:

(i) in cases where any accounting principles or procedures have been changed in the current business year: a statement to that effect, the reason for the change, and the amount of influence of said change on the Quarterly Financial Statements for the Year to Date;

(ii) in cases where any presentation methods of Quarterly Financial Statements have been changed: the details thereof; and

(iii) in cases where the scope of Funds in the quarterly cash flow statement has been changed: a statement to that effect, the reason for the change, and details of the influence of said change on the quarterly cash flow statement.

(2) In cases where any accounting principles or procedures have been changed voluntarily in the current Quarterly Accounting Period (limited to a Quarterly Accounting Period in or after the Second Quarter (meaning the quarter immediately following the first quarter of the business year; hereinafter the same shall apply in this paragraph and Article 22-3, paragraph (3)) of the current business year), the reason for making the change in or after the Second Quarter and the amount of influence of said change on the Quarterly Financial Statements for the Year to Date as of the end of the immediately preceding Quarterly Accounting Period shall be stated in addition to the matters specified in item (i) of the preceding paragraph.

(3) In cases where any accounting principles or procedures have been changed voluntarily in the Previous Business Year, and there is any difference between the accounting principles and procedures adopted for preparing the Quarterly Financial Statements for the corresponding Quarterly Accounting Period in the Previous Business Year and those adopted for preparing the Quarterly Financial Statements for the current Quarterly Accounting Period, a statement to that effect and the amount of influence on the corresponding Quarterly Accounting Period and Year to Date in the Previous Business Year shall be stated.

(4) In the cases set forth in the preceding three paragraphs (excluding paragraph (1), items (ii) and (iii)), if it is difficult to calculate the accurate amount of influence in a timely manner, an estimated amount obtained by an appropriate method may be stated.

(5) Notwithstanding the provisions of the preceding three paragraphs, if it is difficult to calculate the amount of influence in the cases set forth in paragraphs (2) and (3), a statement to that effect and the reason therefor may be stated in lieu of stating the amount of influence.

(Statement on a Simple Accounting Method)

Article 6 In cases where a simple accounting method has been applied, in compliance with business accounting standards that are generally accepted as fair and appropriate, for preparing Quarterly Financial Statements, a statement to that effect and the details thereof shall be stated immediately after the statements under the provisions of the preceding Article; provided, however, that the statements may be omitted in cases where they have little significance.

(Statement on an Accounting Method Specific to Preparation of Quarterly Financial Statements)

Article 7 In cases where an accounting method specific to preparation of Quarterly Financial Statements has been applied in compliance with business accounting standards that are generally accepted as fair and appropriate, a statement to that effect and the details thereof shall be stated immediately after the statements under the provision of the preceding Article; provided, however, that the statements may be omitted in cases where they have little significance.

(Notes on Significant Post-Balance Sheet Events)
Article 8 If any events that exert a significant influence on the financial position, operating results and Cash Flow conditions of a Company Submitting Quarterly Financial Statements in and/or after the business year containing the Quarterly Accounting Period pertaining to the relevant Quarterly Financial Statements (excluding the Year to Date as of the end of the relevant Quarterly Accounting Period) occur after the quarterly balance sheet date (such events shall be referred to as "Significant Post-Balance Sheet Events" in Article 70, paragraph (4)), said events shall be stated in the notes.

(Notes on Financial Instruments)
Article 8-2 (1) For each account title of a quarterly balance sheet concerning Financial Instruments, if said Financial Instruments are significant for the operation of business of the company and there has been a substantial fluctuation in the amount reported on the quarterly balance sheet or any other amount as compared to the last day of the Previous Business Year, the amount reported on the quarterly balance sheet, the market price, and the difference between said amount reported on the quarterly balance sheet and said market price, as of the quarterly balance sheet date, and the calculation method for the market price shall be stated in the notes for each account title of the quarterly balance sheet; provided, however, that in cases where it is difficult to calculate the accurate amount in a timely manner, an estimated amount may be stated.
(2) Notwithstanding the provision of the preceding paragraph, if it is difficult to calculate the market price as of the quarterly balance sheet date, a statement to that effect, the reason therefor, the outline of said Financial Instruments, and the amount reported on the quarterly balance sheet may be stated in lieu of the matters specified in that paragraph.

(Notes on Securities)
Article 9 (1) In addition to the matters specified in the preceding Article, with regard to securities (limited to the securities set forth in the following items), if said securities are significant for the operation of business of the company and there has been a substantial fluctuation in the amount reported on the quarterly balance sheet or any other amount of said securities as compared to the last day of the Previous Business Year, the matters specified in the following items for the respective categories of securities set forth in those items shall be stated in the notes; provided, however, that in cases where it is difficult to calculate the accurate amount in a timely manner, an estimated amount may be stated:
(i) Bonds Held to Maturity that have a market price: the following matters:
  (a) the amount reported on the quarterly balance sheet as of the quarterly balance sheet date;
  (b) the market price as of the quarterly balance sheet date; and
  (c) the difference between the amount reported on the quarterly balance sheet and the market price as of the quarterly balance sheet date; and
(ii) Other Securities that have a market price: the following matters for each class of shares, bonds and any other securities:

(a) the acquisition cost;
(b) the amount reported on the quarterly balance sheet as of the quarterly balance sheet date; and
(c) the difference between the amount reported on the quarterly balance sheet as of the quarterly balance sheet date and the acquisition cost.
(2) In cases where, during the current Quarterly Accounting Period, there has been any significant change or substantial fluctuation in the matters specified in the items of paragraph (3) of Article 8-7 of the Ordinance on Financial Statements, etc. as compared to the last day of the Previous Business Year, the details thereof shall be stated in the notes.

(Notes on Derivative Transactions)
Article 10 (1) In addition to the matters specified in Article 8-2, with regard to Derivative Transactions (those to which Hedge Accounting is applied may be excluded), if said transactions are significant for the operation of business of the company and there has been a substantial fluctuation in the contract amount or any other amount of said transactions as compared to the last day of the Previous Business Year, the contract amount or the principal equivalent amount specified in the contract, the market price, and valuation gain or loss as of the quarterly balance sheet date shall be stated in the notes, by type of currencies, money rates, shares, bonds, commodities and any other subject matter of transactions; provided, however, that in cases where it is difficult to calculate the accurate amount in a timely manner, an estimated amount may be stated.
(2) The matters specified in the preceding paragraph shall be stated by categorizing them into futures transactions, options transactions, forward transactions, swap transactions and any other Derivative Transactions, or any other types of transactions.

(Application of Tax Effect Accounting)
Article 11 With regard to corporation tax and any other taxes that are imposed on amounts related to profits as the tax base (hereinafter referred to as "Corporation Tax, etc."), Quarterly Financial Statements shall be prepared by applying Tax Effect Accounting (meaning an accounting method which, in cases where there are differences between the amounts of assets and liabilities reported on the quarterly balance sheet and the amounts of assets and liabilities derived as a result of calculating the taxable income, reasonably matches the amount of quarterly net profit before deducing the Corporation Tax, etc. with the applicable amount of Corporation Tax, etc. through appropriate interperiod allocation of the amount of Corporation Tax, etc. pertaining to such differences; the same shall apply hereinafter).

(Notes on Profit or Loss, etc. under the Equity Method)
Article 12 (1) In cases where there is any Affiliated Company (meaning an entity that is regarded as an affiliated company of a company submitting Quarterly Consolidated Financial Statements pursuant to the provisions of Article 8, paragraphs (5) and (6) of the Ordinance on Financial Statements, etc.; hereinafter the same shall apply in this paragraph), the amount of investment in the Affiliated Company, the amount of investment in the case where the Equity Method (meaning the method defined in Article 2, item (viii) of the Ordinance on Terminology, Forms, and Preparation Methods of Consolidated Financial Statements (Ordinance of the Ministry of Finance No. 28 of 1976)) is applied to said investment, and the amount of investment return or investment loss shall be stated in the notes; provided, however, that any Affiliated Company that has little significance in terms of the profit or loss and the retained earnings and any other items may be excluded.

(2) In cases where there is any Special Purpose Company Subject to Disclosure (meaning the special purpose company subject to disclosure defined in Article 8-9, item (ii) of the Ordinance on Financial Statements, etc.; hereinafter the same shall apply in this paragraph), if there has been any significant change or substantial fluctuations in the outline of the Special Purpose Company Subject to Disclosure, the outline of transactions with the Special Purpose Company Subject to Disclosure, the transaction amount, and any other significant matters as compared to such statements as of the end of the Previous Business Year, the details thereof shall be stated in the notes.

(Notes on Grant or Issuance of Stock Options, Options on the Company's Own Shares or Company's Own Shares)
Article 13 In cases where Stock Options or Options on the Company's Own Shares have been granted or the Company's Own Shares have been issued, if the amount of influence on the Quarterly Financial Statements is significant, the matters specified in the following items for the respective cases set forth in those items shall be stated in the notes; provided, however, that in cases where it is difficult to calculate the accurate amount in a timely manner, an estimated amount of influence may be stated:
  (i) in the case of having received an offer of service, the amount reported as expenses for the Quarterly Accounting Period and the account title thereof;
  (ii) in the case of having acquired goods, the initial amount reported as assets or amount reported as expenses for such transaction, and the account title thereof; and
  (iii) in cases where unexercised Stock Options have been forfeited, the amount reported as profit.

(Notes on Stock Options)
Article 14 (1) In addition to the provision of the preceding Article, if any Stock Options have been granted during the current Quarterly Accounting Period, the following matters shall be stated in the notes with regard to said Stock Options; provided, however, that the notes may be omitted in cases where they have little significance:
  (i) the number of persons subject to grants, by category such as Officers and workers;
  (ii) the number of Stock Options granted by class of shares:
  (iii) the grant date;
  (iv) vesting conditions (if there are no vesting conditions, a statement to that effect);
  (v) the requisite service period (if there is no requisite service period, a statement to that effect);
  (vi) the exercise period;
  (vii) the exercise price; and
  (viii) the fair unit value as of the grant date.
(2) In cases where the conditions of Stock Options have been changed during the current Quarterly Accounting Period, the details of such change shall be stated in the notes; provided, however, that in cases where the details of such change have little significance, the notes may be omitted.

(Notes in Cases Where a Business Combination through Acquisition Was Implemented)
Article 15 (1) In cases where a Business Combination has been carried out during the current Quarterly Accounting Period (excluding the cases specified in paragraph (1) of the following Article), the following matters shall be stated in the notes; provided, however, that the notes may be omitted in cases where the transaction pertaining to said Business Combination has little significance:

(i) the outline of the Business Combination;
(ii) the period of performance of the Acquired Enterprise or the acquired business included in the Quarterly Financial Statements for the Quarterly Accounting Period and the Year to Date;
(iii) the acquisition cost for the Acquired Enterprise or the acquired business, and the breakdown thereof;
(iv) in cases where shares have been delivered as the consideration for acquisition, the exchange ratio and the calculation method thereof, and the number of shares delivered or to be delivered by class of shares;
(v) the amount of goodwill that occurred, the cause for the occurrence, the amortization method, and the amortization period, or the amount of gain from negative goodwill and the cause for the occurrence;
(vi) in cases where the amount of goodwill that occurred or the amount of gain from negative goodwill set forth in the preceding item is a provisionally calculated amount, a statement to that effect; and
(vii) the estimated amount of influence that would be exerted on the quarterly profit and loss statement for the Year to Date if the Business Combination is assumed to have been completed on the day of commencement of the current business year.
(2) Notwithstanding the provision of the proviso to the preceding paragraph, in cases where, despite the little significance of the transactions pertaining to individual Business Combinations during the current Quarterly Accounting Period, the transactions pertaining to multiple Business Combinations during the current Quarterly Accounting Period have significance as a whole, the matters set forth in item (i) and items (iii) to (vi) inclusive of that paragraph shall be stated in the notes for the transactions pertaining to such Business Combinations as a whole.
(3) In the case set forth in paragraph (1), item (vii), if it is difficult to calculate the estimated amount of influence, a statement to that effect and the reason therefor may be stated in lieu of stating the estimated amount of influence.
(4) In the case set forth in paragraph (1), item (vii), if said notes have yet to receive an audit certification, a statement to that effect shall be made.

(Notes in Cases Where a Business Combination Resulting in Reverse Acquisition Was Implemented)
Article 16 (1) In cases where a Business Combination resulting in Reverse Acquisition has been carried out during the current Quarterly Accounting Period, the matters equivalent to the matters set forth in items (i) to (vi) inclusive of paragraph (1) of the preceding Article and the amount of influence that would be exerted on the quarterly balance sheet and the quarterly profit and loss statement if the Purchase Method is assumed to have been applied to said Business Combination shall be stated in the notes.
(2) In cases where the notes have been made pursuant to the provision of the preceding paragraph, such notes shall continue to be made in and after the Quarterly Accounting Period following the Quarterly Accounting Period in which the Business Combination was carried out unless the estimated amount of influence loses significance.
(3) Notwithstanding the provisions of the preceding two paragraphs, in Business Combinations set forth in Article 8-18, paragraph (3), item (ii) or (iii) of the Ordinance on Financial Statements, etc. , the notes shall not be required to be stated in cases where the enterprise specified in item (ii) or (iii) of that paragraph prepares Consolidated Financial Statements; in this case, a statement to that effect shall be set down in the notes.

(Notes on Common Control Transaction, etc.)

Article 17 (1) In cases where a Common Control Transaction, etc. has been carried out during the current Quarterly Accounting Period, the following matters shall be stated in the notes:
(i) the outline of the transaction;
(ii) the outline of the accounting implemented; and
(iii) in the case of having additionally acquired Subsidiary Company shares, the matters equivalent to those set forth in Article 15 (1), items (iii) to (v) inclusive.
(2) Notwithstanding the provision of the preceding paragraph, the notes may be omitted in cases where the Common Control Transaction, etc. has little significance; provided, however, that in cases where, despite the little significance of individual Common Control Transactions, etc. during the current Quarterly Accounting Period, the multiple Common Control Transactions, etc. during the current Quarterly Accounting Period have significance as a whole, the matters set forth in the items of that paragraph shall be stated in the notes for the transactions pertaining to such Business Combinations as a whole.
(3) In cases where a Subsidiary Company (meaning the subsidiary company defined in Article 8, paragraph (3) of the Ordinance on Financial Statements, etc.; hereinafter the same shall apply in this paragraph) has absorbed its Parent Company (meaning the parent company defined in that paragraph; hereinafter the same shall apply in this paragraph) through an absorption-type merger, if the Subsidiary Company does not prepare Quarterly Consolidated Financial Statements, the estimated amount of influence that would have been exerted on the quarterly balance sheet and the quarterly profit and loss statement for the Year to Date as of the end of the current Quarterly Accounting Period in the case of assuming that the Parent Company has absorbed the Subsidiary Company through an absorption-type merger shall be stated in the notes.
(4) (2) In cases where the notes have been made pursuant to the provision of the preceding paragraph, such notes shall be made in and after the Quarterly Accounting Period following the Quarterly Accounting Period in which the Business Combination was carried out unless the estimated amount of influence loses significance.

(Notes on Formation of Jointly Controlled Enterprises)
Article 18 (1) In cases where a Formation of a Jointly Controlled Enterprise (meaning a Formation of a Jointly Controlled Enterprise defined in Article 8-22, paragraph (1) of the Ordinance on Financial Statements, etc.; hereinafter the same shall apply in this Article and paragraph (1) of the following Article) has been carried out during the current Quarterly Accounting Period, the matters equivalent to those set forth in items (i) and (ii) of paragraph (1) of the preceding Article shall be stated. In this case, if the matters equivalent to the matters set forth in item (i) of that paragraph are stated, the reason for determining said Business Combination to be a Formation of a Jointly Controlled Enterprise shall be stated.
(2) Notwithstanding the provision of the preceding paragraph, the notes may be omitted in cases where the transaction pertaining to the Formation of a Jointly Controlled Enterprise has little significance; provided, however, that in cases where, despite the little significance of the transactions pertaining to individual Formations of a Jointly Controlled Enterprise during the current Quarterly Accounting Period, the transactions pertaining to multiple Formations of a Jointly Controlled Enterprise during the Quarterly Accounting Period have significance as a whole, the matters set forth in that paragraph shall be stated in the notes for the transactions pertaining to such Business Combinations as a whole.

(Notes by Divesting Enterprise in Business Divestitures)

Article 19 (1) In cases where a significant Business Divestiture has been carried out during the current Quarterly Accounting Period, and said Business Divestiture is neither categorized as a Common Control Transaction, etc. nor formation of a Jointly Controlled Enterprise, Divesting Enterprise shall state the following matters in the notes:
(i) the outline of the Business Divestiture;
(ii) the matters specified in sub-item (a) or (b) as the outline of the accounting implemented:
   (a) in the case of having recognized any gain or loss on transfer, the amount thereof, the fair book values of the assets and liabilities pertaining to the transferred business, and the major breakdown thereof; or
   (b) in the case of not having recognized any gain or loss on transfer, a statement to that effect, the type of consideration received, the fair book values of the assets and liabilities pertaining to the transferred business, and the major breakdown thereof;
(iii) the name of the Reporting Segment (meaning a Reporting Segment prescribed in Article 22-3, paragraph (1)) in which the divested business was included;
(iv) the estimated amount of profit or loss pertaining to the divested business, which is reported on the quarterly profit and loss statement for the Quarterly Accounting Period and the Year to Date; and
(v) if, for a Business Divestiture for which a gain or loss on transfer has been recognized, there is any continuing involvement other than holding Successor Enterprise shares as Subsidiary Company shares or Affiliated Company shares, the outline of such continuing involvement.
(2) The notes may be omitted for the matters set forth in item (v) of the preceding paragraph in cases where said continuing involvement is insignificant.
(3) In cases where, despite the little significance of the transactions pertaining to individual Business Divestitures during the current Quarterly Accounting Period, the transactions pertaining to multiple Business Divestitures during the current Quarterly Accounting Period have significance as a whole, the matters set forth in items (i) and (ii) of that paragraph shall, notwithstanding the provision of paragraph (1), be stated in the notes for said transactions pertaining to Business Divestitures as a whole.

(Notes by Successor Enterprise in Business Divestitures)
Article 20 In cases where a Business Divestiture is not categorized as a Business Combination, the Successor Enterprise shall state the following matters in the notes:
(i) the outline of the transaction;
(ii) the outline of the accounting implemented; and
(iii) the breakdown of the assets, liabilities and net assets succeeded from the Divesting Enterprise.

(Notes on Going Concern Assumption)
Article 21 If, in cases where, as of the quarterly balance sheet date, there is an event or circumstance that would raise significant doubt about an assumption that the company will stay in business in the future (hereinafter referred to as the "Going Concern Assumption"), significant uncertainty on the Going Concern Assumption is still recognized even after measures for eliminating or improving said event or circumstance are taken, the following matters shall be stated in the notes; provided, however, that in cases where said significant uncertainty ceases to be recognized after the quarterly balance sheet date, they shall not be required to be stated:
(i) a statement to the effect that said event or circumstance exists, and details thereof;

(ii) the response measures for eliminating or improving said event or circumstance;
(iii) a statement to the effect that said significant uncertainty is recognized and the reason therefor; and
(iv) whether or not the influence of said significant uncertainty is reflected in the Quarterly Financial Statements.

(Notes on Additional Information)
Article 22 In addition to the notes particularly specified under this Ordinance, if there are any matters that are found to be necessary for persons interested in the Company Submitting Quarterly Financial Statements to make adequate judgments on the financial position, operating results and Cash Flow conditions of the company for the business year containing the Quarterly Accounting Period pertaining to the Quarterly Financial Statements, said matters shall be stated in the notes.

(Notes on Asset Retirement Obligations)
Article 22-2 (1) With regard to Asset Retirement Obligations, if said Asset Retirement Obligations are significant for the operation of business of the company and there has been a substantial fluctuation in the amount reported on the quarterly balance sheet or any other amount of said Asset Retirement Obligations as compared to the last day of the Previous Business Year, the following matters shall be stated in the notes:
(i) the details of such fluctuation; and
(ii) the increase or decrease in the total amount of Asset Retirement Obligations during the current Year to Date.
(2) Notwithstanding the provision of the preceding paragraph, in cases where any Asset Retirement Obligations are not reported on the quarterly balance sheet, a statement to that effect, the reason therefor, and the outline of said Asset Retirement Obligations shall be stated in lieu of the matters set forth in the items of that paragraph.

(Notes on Segment Information, etc.)
Article 22-3 (1) With regard to information on a certain unit of an Enterprise (hereinafter referred to as a "Reporting Segment") (such information will hereinafter be referred to as "Segment Information"), the following matters shall be set down in the notes in accordance with Form No. 1:
(i) the amounts of the net sales and profit or loss for each Reporting Segment;
(ii) the difference between the total amount of profits or losses set forth in the preceding item and the amount reported on the quarterly profit and loss statement for each accounting title equivalent to said item and the main contents of said difference; and
(iii) the outline of the event that served as the cause for fluctuations in the amount of assets for each Reporting Segment (limited to cases where a substantial fluctuation is found as compared to the last day of the Previous Business Year).
(2) In cases where there has been any change in Reporting Segments or any significant change in the calculation method of an amount of profit or loss pertaining to Reporting Segments (referred to as the "Calculation Method Pertaining to Reporting Segments" in the following paragraph and paragraph (4)) during the current Quarterly Accounting Period (including any Quarterly Accounting Periods within the relevant business year prior to the current Quarterly Accounting Period), the contents thereof shall be stated in the notes.
(3) In cases where there has been any change in Reporting Segments or any significant change in the Calculation Method Pertaining to Reporting Segments during any Quarterly Accounting Period in or after the Second Quarter of the relevant business year,

the reason for changing it in or after the Second Quarter shall be set down in the notes in addition to the notes made pursuant to the provision of the preceding paragraph.
(4) In cases where there has been any change in Reporting Segments or any significant change in the Calculation Method Pertaining to Reporting Segments during the Previous Business Year and any difference is observed between the Reporting Segments or the Calculation Method Pertaining to Reporting Segments during the corresponding Quarterly Accounting Period in the Previous Business Year and those matters during the current Quarterly Accounting Period, a statement to that effect and the amounts set forth in paragraph (1), items (i) and (ii) pertaining to the corresponding Year to Date in the Previous Business Year (limited to such amounts calculated on the basis of the Reporting Segments and the Calculation Method Pertaining to Reporting Segments during the current Quarterly Accounting Period) shall be stated in the notes.
(5) If, in the cases set forth in the preceding paragraph, it is difficult to calculate an accurate amount, an amount estimated by an appropriate method may be noted in lieu of the amount prescribed in that paragraph; provided, however, that in cases where it is difficult to calculate an amount, a statement to that effect and the reason therefor may be stated in lieu of the amount prescribed in that paragraph.
(6) In cases where a significant impairment loss pertaining to fixed assets has been recognized, where there has been a significant change in the amount of goodwill or where a significant gain from negative goodwill has been recognized during the current Quarterly Accounting Period, the outline thereof shall be stated in the notes for each Reporting Segment.

(Notes on Rental, etc. Real Properties)
Article 22-4 With regard to any Rental, etc. Real Property (meaning a Rental, etc. Real Property prescribed in Article 8-30, paragraph (1) of the Ordinance on Financial Statements, etc.), in cases where a substantial change is found in the amount reported in any quarterly balance sheet or any other amount for said Rental, etc. Real Property as compared to the last day of the Previous Business Year, the market price of said Rental, etc. Real Property as of the quarterly balance sheet date and the amount reported in the quarterly balance sheet shall be stated in the notes.

(Noting Method)
Article 23 (1) The notes to be stated pursuant to the provisions of this Ordinance shall be stated immediately after the statements under the provisions of Articles 5 to 7 inclusive, except for those that are found appropriate to be stated as Footnotes (meaning the stating of notes at the end of the table or account statement contained in the Quarterly Financial Statements in which the matters pertaining to said notes are stated; the same shall apply in Article 87); provided, however, that matters related to the matters that are stated pursuant to the provisions of Articles 5 to 7 may be stated together therewith.
(2) Notwithstanding the provision of the preceding paragraph, the notes under the provision of Article 21 shall be stated immediately after the quarterly cash flow statement. In this case, notwithstanding the provisions of Articles 5 to 7, the matters stated under these provisions shall be stated immediately after the notes under the provision of Article 21.
(3) In the case of stating notes that are related to a specific account title pursuant to the provisions of this Ordinance, the association between said account title and said notes shall be made clear by appending a symbol to said account title or by other similar method.

(Units for Presenting Amounts)
Article 24 The amounts for the account titles and any other matters contained in Quarterly Financial Statements shall be presented in units of million yen or thousand yen.

Chapter II Quarterly Balance Sheet

Section 1 General Provisions

(Method for Presenting a Quarterly Balance Sheet)
Article 25 (1) The method for presenting a quarterly balance sheet shall be in accordance with the provisions of this Chapter.
(2) A quarterly balance sheet shall be presented by using Form No. 2.

(Classification into Assets, Liabilities and Net Assets)
Article 26 Assets, liabilities and net assets shall be stated by respectively classifying them into the assets section, liabilities section, and net assets section.

(Arrangement of Account Titles)
Article 27 The account titles of assets and liabilities shall be arranged by using the method of current arrangement.

Section 2 Assets

(Classification of Assets)
Article 28 Assets shall be stated by classifying them into current assets, fixed assets and deferred assets, and assets categorized as fixed assets shall be further classified into tangible fixed assets, intangible fixed assets, investments, and any other assets.

(Scopes of the Respective Classes of Assets)
Article 29 The provisions of Articles 15 to 16-3 inclusive, 22, 27, 31 to 31-5 inclusive, and 36 of the Ordinance on Financial Statements, etc. shall apply mutatis mutandis to the scopes of current assets, tangible fixed assets, intangible fixed assets, investments and other assets, and deferred assets. In this case, the term "Within One Year" in Articles 15 to 16-3 of the Ordinance on Financial Statements, etc. shall be deemed to be replaced with "on a day within one year from the day following the quarterly balance sheet date," and the term "Company Submitting Financial Statements" in Article 22, item (viii) and Article 27, item (xii) of the Ordinance on Financial Statements, etc. shall be deemed to be replaced with "Company Submitting Quarterly Financial Statements."

(Classified Presentation of Current Assets)
Article 30 (1) Assets categorized as current assets shall be set down under account titles having names that indicate said assets, in accordance with the following classification of items; provided, however, that any assets categorized under said items of which the amounts are not more than one percent of the total amount of assets, which are found appropriate to be presented collectively with assets categorized under another item, may be set down collectively under an account title having an appropriate name:
(i) cash and deposits;
(ii) negotiable instruments receivable and accounts receivable;
(iii) securities;

(iv) merchandise and manufactured goods (including semi-finished goods);
(v) work in progress;
(vi) raw materials and supplies; and
(vii) others.
(2) Where assets categorized under any of the items set forth in the items of the preceding paragraph are found appropriate to be presented separately, the provision of that paragraph shall not preclude one from separately setting down said assets under an account title having a name that indicates said assets.
(3) Among the assets categorized under the item set forth in paragraph (1), item (vii), any asset of which the amount exceeds ten percent of the total amount of assets or any asset of which the amount is not more than ten percent of the total amount of assets but is found appropriate to be presented separately shall be set down separately under an account title having a name that indicates said asset.
(4) Notwithstanding the provision of the main clause of paragraph (1), assets categorized under the items set forth in items (iv) to (vi) inclusive of said paragraph may be set down collectively under the account title of inventory assets. In this case, the account titles of the assets categorized under said items and the amounts thereof shall be stated in the notes.

(Presentation of Allowances pertaining to Current Asset)
Article 31 The provisions of Article 20 of the Ordinance on Financial Statements, etc. shall apply mutatis mutandis to allowances pertaining to assets categorized as current assets.

(Classified Presentation of Tangible Fixed Assets)
Article 32 (1) Assets categorized as tangible fixed assets shall be set down collectively under an account title having a name that indicates tangible fixed assets; provided, however, that this shall not preclude one from classifying assets categorized as tangible fixed assets into an item that is found to be appropriate, and setting it down under an account title having a name that indicates said assets.
(2) Notwithstanding the provision of the preceding paragraph, in cases where assets categorized as tangible fixed assets include any asset of which the amount exceeds ten percent of the total amount of assets or in cases where the amount of any asset is not more than ten percent of the total amount of assets but is found appropriate to be presented separately, said asset shall be separated from other tangible fixed assets and shall be set down under an account title having a name that indicates each of such assets.

(Presentation of the Amounts of Accumulated Depreciation for Tangible Fixed Assets)
Article 33 The provisions of Articles 25 and 26 of the Ordinance on Financial Statements, etc. shall apply mutatis mutandis to the amounts of accumulated depreciation for tangible fixed assets.

(Presentation of the Amounts of Accumulated Impairment Loss)
Article 34 The provisions of Article 26-2 of the Ordinance on Financial Statements, etc. shall apply mutatis mutandis to the amounts of accumulated impairment loss for tangible fixed assets.

(Classified Presentation of Intangible Fixed Assets)
Article 35 (1) Assets categorized as intangible fixed assets shall be collectively set down

under an account title having a name that indicates intangible fixed assets; provided, however, that this shall not preclude one from classifying assets categorized as intangible fixed assets into an item that is found to be appropriate, and setting it down under an account title having a name that indicates said assets.
(2) The provision of Article 32, paragraph (2) shall apply mutatis mutandis to intangible fixed assets.

(Presentation of the Amounts of Accumulated Amortization, etc. for Intangible Fixed Assets)
Article 36 The provision of Article 30 of the Ordinance on Financial Statements, etc. shall apply mutatis mutandis to the amounts of accumulated amortization and the amounts of accumulated impairment loss for intangible fixed assets.

(Classified Presentation of Investments and Other Assets)
Article 37 (1) Assets categorized as investments and other assets shall be collectively set down under an account title having a name that indicates investments and other assets; provided, however, that this shall not preclude one from classifying assets categorized as investments and other assets into an item that is found to be appropriate, and setting it down under an account title having a name that indicates said assets.
(2) The provision of Article 32, paragraph (2) shall apply mutatis mutandis to investments and other assets.

(Presentation of Allowances pertaining to Investments and Other Assets)
Article 38 The provisions of Article 20 of the Ordinance on Financial Statements, etc. as applied mutatis mutandis pursuant to Article 34 of that Ordinance shall apply mutatis mutandis to allowances pertaining to assets categorized as investments and other assets.

(Classified Presentation of Deferred Assets)
Article 39 (1) Assets categorized as deferred assets shall be collectively set down under an account title having a name that indicates deferred assets; provided, however, that this shall not preclude one from classifying assets categorized as deferred assets into an item that is found to be appropriate, and setting it down under an account title having a name that indicates said assets.
(2) The provision of Article 32, paragraph (2) shall apply mutatis mutandis to deferred assets.

(Presentation of the Amounts of Accumulated Amortization for Deferred Assets)
Article 40 The provision of Article 38 of the Ordinance on Financial Statements, etc. shall apply mutatis mutandis to the amounts of accumulated amortization for deferred assets.

(Notes on Collateral Assets)
Article 41 With regard to assets that have been provided as collateral, if said assets are significant for the operation of business of the company and there has been a substantial fluctuation in the amount of said assets as compared to the last day of the Previous Business Year, the details and the amount of the assets that have been provided as collateral shall be stated in the notes; provided, however, that in cases where it is difficult to calculate the accurate amount in a timely manner, an estimated amount may be stated.

Section 3 Liabilities

(Classification of Liabilities)
Article 42 Liabilities shall be stated by classifying them into current liabilities and fixed liabilities.

(Scopes of the Respective Classes of Liabilities)
Article 43 The provisions of Articles 47 to 48-4 inclusive and 51 to 51-5 inclusive of the Ordinance on Financial Statements, etc. shall apply mutatis mutandis to the scopes of current liabilities and fixed liabilities. In this case, the term "Within One Year" in Articles 47 and 48-2 to 48-4 inclusive of the Ordinance on Financial Statements, etc. shall be deemed to be replaced with "on a day within one year from the day following the quarterly balance sheet date."

(Classified Presentation of Current Liabilities)
Article 44 (1) Liabilities categorized as current liabilities shall be set down under account titles having names that indicate said liabilities, in accordance with the following classification of items; provided, however, that any liabilities categorized under items other than that set forth in item (iv) of which the amounts are not more than one percent of the combined total of liabilities and net assets, which are found appropriate to be presented collectively with liabilities categorized under another item, may be set down collectively under an account title having an appropriate name:
(i) negotiable instruments payable and accounts payable;
(ii) short-term borrowings (including finance negotiable instruments and overdrafts, but excluding short-term borrowings from shareholders, officers, or workers);
(iii) accrued Corporation Tax, etc. ;
(iv) allowances;
(v) Asset Retirement Obligations; and
(vi) others.
(2) Where liabilities categorized under any of the items set forth in the items of the preceding paragraph are found appropriate to be presented separately, the provision of that paragraph shall not preclude one from separately setting down said liabilities under an account title having a name that indicates said liabilities.
(3) In cases where the allowances set forth in paragraph (1), item (iv) include any allowance of which the amount exceeds one percent of the combined total of liabilities and net assets, said allowance shall be separately set down under an account title having a name that indicates the purpose of establishment of said allowance.
(4) Among the liabilities categorized under the item set forth in paragraph (1), item (vi), any liability of which the amount exceeds ten percent of the combined total of liabilities and net assets or any liability of which the amount is not more than ten percent of the combined total of liabilities and net assets but are found appropriate to be presented separately shall be set down under an account title having a name that indicates said liability.

(Classified Presentation of Fixed Liabilities)
Article 45 (1) Liabilities categorized as fixed liabilities shall be set down under account titles having names that indicate said liabilities, in accordance with the following classification of items; provided, however, that any liabilities categorized under items other than that set forth in item (iii) of which the amounts are not more than one percent of the combined total of liabilities and net assets, which are found appropriate to be

presented collectively with liabilities categorized under another item, may be set down collectively under an account title having an appropriate name:
(i) company bonds;
(ii) long-term borrowings (including finance negotiable instruments, but excluding long-term borrowings from shareholders, officers, or workers);
(iii) allowances;
(iv) Asset Retirement Obligations; and
(v) others.
(2) The provision of paragraph (2) of the preceding Article shall apply mutatis mutandis to cases under the preceding paragraph.
(3) The provision of paragraph (3) of the preceding Article shall apply mutatis mutandis to the allowances set forth in paragraph (1), item (iii).
(4) The provision of paragraph (4) of the preceding Article shall apply mutatis mutandis to liabilities categorized under the item set forth in paragraph (1), item (v).

(Notes on Contingent Liabilities)
Article 46 The provision of Article 58 of the Ordinance on Financial Statements, etc. shall apply mutatis mutandis to Contingent Liabilities (meaning guarantee of debts (including acts that have the same effect as guarantee of debts), obligations for compensation pertaining to contentious cases, and other liabilities that have not arisen in reality but may be borne by the business in the future).

(Notes on the Amount of Discount on Negotiable Instruments and the Amount of Transfer by Endorsement)
Article 47 (1) The amount of discount on negotiable instruments receivable or the amount of negotiable instruments receivable transferred by endorsement for the purpose of repaying debts shall be stated in the notes by giving the name of the amount of discount on negotiable instruments receivable or the amount of negotiable instruments receivable transferred by endorsement; provided, however, that notes may be omitted for matters having little significance.
(2) The provision of the preceding paragraph shall apply mutatis mutandis to negotiable instruments other than negotiable instruments receivable that have been discounted or that have been transferred by endorsement for the purpose of repaying debts; provided, however, that the notes on the amount of discount or the amount of transfer by endorsement in such case shall be stated by giving a name that indicates the cause for the occurrence of said claims on negotiable instruments.

(Presentation of Inventory Assets and Reserve for Loss on Construction Contracts)
Article 47-2 The provisions of Article 54-4 of the Ordinance on Financial Statements, etc. shall apply mutatis mutandis to presentation of inventory assets and reserve for loss on construction contracts.

Section 4 Net Assets

(Classification of Net Assets)
Article 48 Net assets shall be stated by classifying them into shareholders' equity, valuation and translation adjustments, and share options.

(Classification and Classified Presentation of Shareholders' Equity)
Article 49 (1) Shareholders' equity shall be classified into stated capital, capital surplus,

and retained earnings, and shall be set down under the account titles of stated capital, capital surplus, and retained earnings respectively.
(2) The provision of Article 61 of the Ordinance on Financial Statements, etc. shall apply mutatis mutandis to stated capital.
(3) The provisions of Article 62 of the Ordinance on Financial Statements, etc. shall apply mutatis mutandis to a deposit for subscriptions to shares as after the application date.
(4) The provision of Article 66 of the Ordinance on Financial Statements, etc. shall apply mutatis mutandis to Treasury Shares.
(5) The provision of Article 66-2 of the Ordinance on Financial Statements, etc. shall apply mutatis mutandis to a deposit for subscriptions to Treasury Shares.

(Classification and Classified Presentation of Valuation and Translation Adjustments)
Article 50 The provisions of Article 67 of the Ordinance on Financial Statements, etc. shall apply mutatis mutandis to valuation and translation adjustments.

(Presentation of Share Options)
Article 51 The provisions of Article 68 of the Ordinance on Financial Statements, etc. shall apply mutatis mutandis to share options.

(Notes on the Per Share Amount of Net Assets)
Article 52 The per share amount of net assets as of the end of the current Quarterly Accounting Period and that as of the end of the Previous Business Year shall be stated in the notes.

Section 5 Miscellaneous Provisions

(Reserves, etc. under Special Law)
Article 53 (1) Reserves or allowances that must be reported under the name of reserves or allowances pursuant to the provisions of laws and regulations and that are inappropriate to be reported in the assets section or the liabilities section (hereinafter referred to as "Reserves, etc." in the following paragraph and Article 71) shall be stated under a separate class that has been added immediately after fixed liabilities, notwithstanding the provisions of Articles 27 and 42.
(2) Reserves, etc. set forth in the preceding paragraph shall be set down under an account title having a name that indicates the purpose of establishment of said Reserves, etc.

(Statement of Assets and Liabilities of a Listed Business)
Article 54 (1) In cases where a company engaged in a business set forth in the appended list of the Ordinance on Financial Statements, etc. (hereinafter referred to as a "Listed Business") prepares a quarterly balance sheet, if it is found inappropriate to state its assets and liabilities pursuant to this Ordinance, said company engaged in a Listed Business may state its assets and liabilities in an equivalent manner as under the provisions of a Law, Regulations, or Rules (meaning the law, regulations, or rules prescribed in Article 2 of the Ordinance on Financial Statements, etc.; the same shall apply hereinafter) applicable to its Financial Statements.
(2) In the cases set forth in the preceding paragraph, the standards for setting down the account titles of assets and liabilities collectively or separately shall be equivalent to those provided under this Ordinance.

(Statement of Net Assets of Designated Juridical Persons)

Article 55 In cases where a Designated Juridical Person prepares a quarterly balance sheet, if it is found inappropriate to state its net assets pursuant to this Ordinance, said Designated Juridical Person may state its net assets in an equivalent manner as under the provisions of a Law, Regulations, or Rules applicable to its Financial Statements. In this case, the governing Law, Regulations, or Rules shall be stated in the notes.

Chapter III Quarterly Profit and Loss Statement

Section 1 General Provisions

(Method for Presenting a Quarterly Profit and Loss Statement)

Article 56 (1) The method for presenting a quarterly profit and loss statement shall be in accordance with the provisions of this Chapter.

(2) A quarterly profit and loss statement shall be presented by using Form No. 3 and Form No. 4.

(Classification of Revenues and Expenses)

Article 57 Revenues and expenses shall be stated by classifying them into account titles having names that indicate the following items:

(i) net sales (including revenues from service operations; the same shall apply hereinafter);

(ii) cost of sales (including service costs; the same shall apply hereinafter);

(iii) selling expenses and general and administrative expenses;

(iv) non-operating revenues;

(v) non-operating expenses;

(vi) extraordinary profit; and

(vii) extraordinary loss.

Section 2 Net Sales and Cost of Sales

(Presentation Method for Net Sales)

Article 58 Net sales shall be set down under an account title having a name that indicates net sales.

(Presentation Method for the Cost of Sales)

Article 59 The cost of sales shall be set down under an account title having a name that indicates the cost of sales.

(Presentation of the Gross Profit or Loss on Sales)

Article 60 The amount of difference between net sales and the cost of sales shall be presented as the gross profit on sales or the gross loss on sales.

Section 3 Selling Expenses and General and Administrative Expenses

(Presentation Method for Selling Expenses and General and Administrative Expense)

Article 61 (1) Selling expenses and general and administrative expenses shall be classified into expense items that are found to be appropriate, and be set down under account titles having names that indicate said expenses; provided, however, that this shall not preclude one from setting down said expenses under the account title of selling expenses, the account title of general and administrative expenses, or the account title of selling expenses and general and administrative expenses collectively, and stating the major expense items and amounts thereof in the notes.

(2) The major expense items prescribed in the proviso to the preceding paragraph shall be provision of allowance (excluding such expense items of which the amount is small) and any other expense items of which the amount exceeds 20 percent of the combined total of selling expenses and general and administrative expenses or those of which the amount is not more than 20 percent of the combined total of selling expenses and general and administrative expenses but are found appropriate to be presented separately.

(Presentation of the Amount of Operating Profit and Loss)
Article 62 The amount obtained by adjusting the gross profit on sales or the gross loss on sales by adding or subtracting the total amount of selling expenses and general and administrative expenses shall be stated as the amount of operating profit or the amount of operating loss.

Section 4 Non-operating Revenues and Non-operating Expenses

(Presentation Method for Non-operating Revenues)
Article 63 Revenues categorized as non-operating revenues shall be set down under account titles having names that indicate said revenues, in accordance with the classification of interest income (excluding interest on securities), dividends income, gain on sales of securities, and others; provided, however, that any revenues of which the amounts are not more than 20 percent of the total amount of non-operating revenues, which are found appropriate to be presented collectively, may be set down under an account title having a name that collectively indicates said revenues.

(Presentation Method for Non-operating Expenses)
Article 64 Expenses categorized as non-operating expenses shall be set down under account titles having names that indicate said expenses, in accordance with the classification of interest expenses (including interest on company bonds), loss on sales of securities, and others; provided, however, that any expenses of which the amounts are not more than 20 percent of the total amount of non-operating expenses, which are found appropriate to be presented collectively, may be set down under an account title having a name that collectively indicates said expenses.

(Presentation of the Amount of Ordinary Profit and Loss)
Article 65 The amount obtained by adjusting the amount of operating profit or the amount of operating loss by adding or subtracting the total amount of non-operating revenues or the total amount of non-operating expenses shall be stated as the amount of ordinary profit or the amount of ordinary loss.

Section 5 Extraordinary Profit and Extraordinary Loss

(Presentation Method for Extraordinary Profit)
Article 66 Profits categorized as extraordinary profit shall be set down under account titles having names that indicate said profits, in accordance with the classification of

gain on prior period adjustment, gain on sales of fixed assets, gain from negative goodwill and others; provided, however, that any profits of which the amounts are not more than 20 percent of the total amount of extraordinary profit, which are found appropriate to be presented collectively, may be set down under an account title having a name that collectively indicates said profits.

(Presentation Method for Extraordinary Loss)
Article 67 Losses categorized as extraordinary loss shall be set down under account titles having names that indicate said losses, in accordance with the classification of loss on prior period adjustment, loss on sales of fixed assets, impairment loss, loss on disaster, and others; provided, however, that any losses of which the amounts are not more than 20 percent of the total amount of extraordinary loss, which are found appropriate to be presented collectively, may be set down under an account title having a name that collectively indicates said losses.

(Presentation of the Amount of Quarterly Net Profit or Interim Net Loss)
Article 68 The amount obtained by adjusting the amount of ordinary profit or the amount of ordinary loss by adding or subtracting the total amount of extraordinary profit or the total amount of extraordinary loss shall be presented as the amount of quarterly net profit before taxes or the amount of quarterly net loss before taxes.

Article 69 (1) The amounts of the items set forth in the following items shall be stated under account titles having names that indicate the contents thereof, immediately after the amount of quarterly net profit before taxes or the amount of quarterly net loss before taxes:
  (i) the corporation tax, inhabitants tax, and Enterprise Tax (meaning the enterprise tax imposed on amounts related to profits as the tax base; the same shall apply in the following item) pertaining to the current Quarterly Accounting Period; and
  (ii) the Deferred Corporation Tax, etc. (meaning adjustments on the corporation tax, inhabitants tax, and Enterprise Tax set forth in the preceding item, which are reported through application of Tax Effect Accounting).
(2) The items set forth in the items of the preceding paragraph may be stated collectively; provided, however, that a statement to that effect shall be set down in the notes in such a case.
(3) The amount obtained by adjusting the amount of quarterly net profit before taxes or the amount of quarterly net loss before taxes by adding or subtracting the amounts of the items set forth in the respective items of paragraph (1) shall be stated as the amount of quarterly net profit or the amount of quarterly net loss.
(4) In cases where there are taxes paid or taxed refunded due to correction, determination, etc. of Corporation Tax, etc. , they shall be stated under an account title having a name that indicates the contents thereof, immediately after the item set forth in paragraph (1), item (i); provided, however, that such amounts may be presented by including them in the amount of the item set forth in paragraph (1), item (i) in cases where such amounts have little significance.

(Notes on the Per Share Amount of Quarterly Net Profit or Loss)
Article 70 (1) The per share amount of quarterly net profit or per share amount of quarterly net loss for the current Quarterly Accounting Period and the Year to Date as of the end of said Quarterly Accounting Period, and the basis for calculation of said amount shall be stated in the notes.
(2) The Diluted Per Share Amount of Quarterly Net Profit (meaning per share amount of

quarterly net profit calculated by supposing exercise of rights pertaining to any rights to acquire common shares, rights to request conversion into common shares, or securities or contracts attaching rights equivalent thereto (hereinafter referred to as "Potential Shares"); hereinafter the same shall apply in this Article) pertaining to the current Quarterly Accounting Period and the Year to Date as of the end of said Quarterly Accounting Period, and the basis for calculation of said amount shall be stated immediately after the statement set forth in the preceding paragraph; provided, however, that in cases where no Potential Shares exist, or in cases where the Diluted Per Share Amount of Quarterly Net Profit is not less than the per share amount of quarterly net profit or where such amount constitutes the per share amount of quarterly net loss, a statement to that effect shall be made, and the Diluted Per Share Amount of Quarterly Net Profit shall not be required to be stated.
(3) In cases where any consolidation of shares or share split has been carried out during the current Quarterly Accounting Period, the following matters shall be stated in the notes; provided, however, that in cases where no Potential Shares existed, or in cases where the Diluted Per Share Amount of Quarterly Net Profit was not less than the per share amount of quarterly net profit or where such amount constituted the per share amount of quarterly net loss during the corresponding Quarterly Accounting Period in the Previous Business Year, a statement to that effect shall be made, and the Diluted Per Share Amount of Quarterly Net Profit pertaining to the corresponding Quarterly Accounting Period in the Previous Business Year and the Year to Date as of the end thereof shall not be required to be stated:
(i) the fact that a consolidation of shares or a share split has been carried out; and
(ii) the per share amount of quarterly net profit or the per share amount of quarterly net loss, and the Diluted Per Share Amount of Quarterly Net Profit pertaining to the corresponding Quarterly Accounting Period and Year to Date in the Previous Business Year, in the case of supposing that the consolidation of shares or the share split were carried out on the day of commencement of the Previous Business Year.
(4) In cases where any consolidation of shares or share split has been carried out after the quarterly balance sheet date, the following matters shall be stated in the notes as Significant Post-Balance Sheet Events; provided, however, that in cases where no Potential Shares existed, or in cases where the Diluted Per Share Amount of Quarterly Net Profit was not less than the per share amount of quarterly net profit or where such amount constituted the per share amount of quarterly net loss in the current Quarterly Accounting Period, a statement to that effect shall be made, and the Diluted Per Share Amount of Quarterly Net Profit pertaining to the current Quarterly Accounting Period and the Year to Date as of the end of said Quarterly Accounting Period shall not be required to be stated:
(i) the fact that a consolidation of shares or a share split has been carried out;
(ii) the per share amount of quarterly net profit or the per share amount of quarterly net loss, and the Diluted Per Share Amount of Quarterly Net Profit pertaining to the corresponding Quarterly Accounting Period and Year to Date in the Previous Business Year, in the case of supposing that the consolidation of shares or the share split were carried out on the day of commencement of the Previous Business Year; and
(iii) the per share amount of quarterly net profit or the per share amount of quarterly net loss, and the Diluted Per Share Amount of Quarterly Net Profit pertaining to the current Quarterly Accounting Period and the Year to Date as of the end of said Quarterly Accounting Period, in the case of supposing that the consolidation of shares or the share split were carried out on the day of commencement of the current business year.

Section 6 Miscellaneous Provisions

(Provision or Reversal of Reserves, etc. under Special Laws)
Article 71 If there has been a provision or reversal of a Reserve, etc., the amount of the provision or reversal shall be set down as an extraordinary loss or extraordinary profit under an account title having a name that indicates that the amount results from said provision or reversal.

(Notes in Cases where There Are Substantial Seasonal Fluctuations in Net Sales or Operating Expenses)
Article 72 In cases where there are substantial seasonal fluctuations in net sale or Operating Expenses (meaning the combined total of the cost of sales, selling expenses, and general and administrative expenses) due to the nature of the business, the situation of such fluctuations shall be stated in the notes.

(Statement of Revenues and Expenses Concerning a Listed Business)
Article 73 (1) In cases where a company engaged in a Listed Business prepares a quarterly profit and loss statement, if it is found inappropriate to state its revenues and expenses pursuant to this Ordinance, said company engaged in a Listed Business may state its revenues and expenses in an equivalent manner as under the provisions of a Law, Regulations, or Rules applicable to its Financial Statements.
(2) In the cases set forth in the preceding paragraph, the standards for setting down the account titles of revenues and expenses collectively or separately shall be equivalent to those provided under this Ordinance.

Chapter IV Quarterly Cash Flow Statement

Section 1 General Provisions

(Method for Presenting a Quarterly Cash Flow Statement)
Article 74 (1) The method for presenting a quarterly cash flow statement shall be in accordance with the provisions of this Chapter.
(2) A quarterly cash flow statement shall be presented by using Form No. 5 or Form No. 6.

(Classification for Presenting a Quarterly Cash Flow Statement)
Article 75 In a quarterly cash flow statement, Cash Flow conditions shall be stated for the following classes:
(i) Cash Flows from operating activities;
(ii) Cash Flows from investment activities;
(iii) Cash Flows from financing activities;
(iv) translation adjustments on cash and Cash Equivalents;
(v) increase or decrease in cash and Cash Equivalents;
(vi) the beginning balances of cash and Cash Equivalents; and
(vii) the balances of cash and Cash Equivalents at the end of the quarter.

Section 2 Method for Presenting a Quarterly Cash Flow Statement

(Presentation Method for Cash Flows from Operating Activities)

Article 76 The provisions of Articles 113 to 118 inclusive of the Ordinance on Financial Statements, etc. shall apply mutatis mutandis to the method for presenting a quarterly cash flow statement. In this case, the phrase "the amount of net profit for the period before taxes or the amount of net loss for the period before taxes" in Article 113, item (ii) of the Ordinance on Financial Statements, etc. shall be deemed to be replaced with "the amount of quarterly net profit before taxes or the amount of quarterly net loss before taxes," and the term "profit and loss statement" in sub0-items (a) and (c) of that item shall be deemed to be replaced with "quarterly profit and loss statement."

(Matters to be Stated in the Notes in a Quarterly Cash Flow Statement)
Article 77 In a quarterly cash flow statement, the relationship between the balances of cash and Cash Equivalents at the end of the quarter and the amounts for the account titles set down in the quarterly balance sheet shall be stated in the notes.

Chapter V Notes on Shareholders' Equity, etc.

(Notes on Issued Shares)
Article 78 With regard to the classes and the total number of issued shares, the total number of issued shares at the end of the current Quarterly Accounting Period shall be stated in the notes, for each class of issued shares.

(Notes on Treasury Shares)
Article 79 With regard to the classes and the total number of Treasury Shares, the total number of Treasury Shares at the end of the current Quarterly Accounting Period shall be stated in the notes, for each class of Treasury Shares.

(Notes on Share Options, etc.)
Article 80 (1) With regard to share options, the following matters shall be stated in the notes:
(i) the class(es) of shares subject to the share options;
(ii) the number of shares subject to share options; and
(iii) the balance of share options at the end of the Quarterly Accounting Period.
(2) In cases where share options have been granted as Stock Options or Options on the Company's Own Shares, the matters set forth in items (i) and (ii) of the preceding paragraph shall not be required to be stated.
(3) The number of shares set forth in paragraph (1), item (ii) shall be stated by stating the number of shares subject to the share options as of the last day of the current Quarterly Accounting Period, for each class of shares subject to the share options; provided, however, that the notes may be omitted in cases where the number of shares that will increase when supposing that the share options are exercised constitutes an insignificant proportion of the total number of issued shares (when holding Treasury Shares, the number of shares after deducting the number of said Treasury Shares) as of the last day of the current Quarterly Accounting Period.
(4) The provisions of the preceding three paragraphs shall apply mutatis mutandis to own share options.

(Notes on Dividends)
Article 81 With regard to the dividends during the Year to Date as of the end of the current Quarterly Accounting Period, the following matters shall be stated in the notes:
(i) in cases where the dividend property is money, the total amount of dividend, the

amount of dividend per share, the reference date, and the effective date for each class of shares;
(ii) in cases where the dividend property is property other than money, the type and the book value of the dividend property, the amount of dividend per share, the reference date, and the effective date for each class of shares; and
(iii) with regard to a dividend of which the reference date is contained in the period from the day of commencement of the current business year to the end of the current Quarterly Accounting Period and of which the effective date will be after the last day of the current Quarterly Accounting Period, the matters equivalent to those set forth in the preceding two items.

(Notes in Cases where There Was a Substantial Change in the Amount of Shareholders' Equity)
Article 82 In cases where there was a substantial change in the amount of shareholders' equity as compared to the end of the Previous Business Year, the major cause of the change shall be stated in the notes.

Chapter VI Quarterly Financial Statements of Specified Companies

(Standards for Preparation of Quarterly Financial Statements of Specified Companies)
Article 83 (1) The terminology, forms, and preparation methods of Quarterly Financial Statements that a Specified Company submits shall be subject to the provisions of the preceding Chapters.
(2) A Specified Company may prepare Quarterly Financial Statements pursuant to Designated International Accounting Standards in addition to Quarterly Financial Statements prepared pursuant to the provision of the preceding paragraph.

(Notes on Special Provision for Accounting Standards)
Article 84 The following matters shall be stated in the notes to Quarterly Financial Statements prepared pursuant to Designated International Accounting Standards:
(i) a statement to the effect that Quarterly Financial Statements are prepared pursuant to Designated International Accounting Standards; and
(ii) a statement to the effect that the company is categorized as a Specified Company and the reason therefor.

Chapter VII Quarterly Financial Documents of Foreign Companies

(Standards for Preparation of Quarterly Financial Documents of Foreign Companies)
Article 85 (1) In cases where the Commissioner of the Financial Services Agency approves a Foreign Company to submit the documents on financial calculation disclosed in its home country (including the state or any other region where the company is headquartered; the same shall apply hereinafter) as Quarterly Financial Documents, on finding no risk of impairing the public interest or protection of investors, the terminology, forms, and preparation methods of said Quarterly Financial Documents shall be, except for matters that were found necessary and instructed by the Commissioner of the Financial Services Agency, the terminology, forms, and preparation methods

used in the home country.
(2) In cases where the documents on financial calculation disclosed in the home country by a Foreign Company do not qualify as those approved by the Commissioner of the Financial Services Agency based on the provision of the preceding paragraph, if the Commissioner of the Financial Services Agency approves said Foreign Company to submit the documents on financial calculation disclosed in an area outside Japan other than its home country as Quarterly Financial Documents, on finding no risk of impairing the public interest or protection of investors, the terminology, forms, and preparation methods of said Quarterly Financial Documents shall be, except for matters that were found necessary and instructed by the Commissioner of the Financial Services Agency, the terminology, forms, and preparation methods used in said area outside Japan other than its home country.
(3) In cases where the documents on financial calculation disclosed in the home country or any other area outside Japan by a Foreign Company do not qualify as those approved by the Commissioner of the Financial Services Agency based on the provisions of the preceding two paragraphs, the terminology, forms, and preparation methods of Quarterly Financial Documents to be submitted by such Foreign Company shall be in accordance with the instructions of the Commissioner of the Financial Services Agency.

(Notes on Accounting Standards)
Article 86 In cases where any accounting principles and procedures for preparing Quarterly Financial Documents adopted by the Foreign Company with regard to the Quarterly Financial Documents under the provisions of the preceding Article differ from accounting principles and procedures for preparing Quarterly Financial Documents in Japan, the contents thereof shall be stated in the notes in said Quarterly Financial Documents.

(Presentation Methods)
Article 87 (1) The provisions of Article 4, paragraph (3) and Article 5, paragraph (1), item (ii) shall apply mutatis mutandis to Quarterly Financial Documents to be submitted by a Foreign Company.
(2) In cases where any presentation methods for the Quarterly Financial Documents to be submitted by a Foreign Company differ from presentation methods in Japan, the contents thereof shall be stated in the notes in said Quarterly Financial Documents.

(Presentation of Monetary Amounts)
Article 88 In cases where the account titles and any other matters set down in Quarterly Financial Documents to be submitted by a Foreign Company are presented in monetary amounts in a currency other than Japanese currency, the amounts for major matters shall also be stated in amounts that have been translated into Japanese currency. In this case, the translation standards adopted for the translation into Japanese currency shall be stated in the notes in said Quarterly Financial Documents.

(Noting Method)
Article 89 (1) The notes to be stated pursuant to the provisions of Article 86, Article 87, paragraph (2), and the preceding Article shall be stated as Footnotes; provided, however, that notes that are found inappropriate to be stated as Footnotes may be stated in other appropriate places.
(2) The provision of Article 23, paragraph (3) shall apply mutatis mutandis to the case of stating matters in the notes pursuant to the provisions of Article 86 and Article 87, paragraph (2).

[11] Ordinance on Terminology, Forms, and Preparation Methods of Consolidated Financial Statements

(Ordinance of the Ministry of Finance No. 28 of October 30, 1976)

Pursuant to the provisions of Article 193 of the Securities and Exchange Act (Act No. 25 of 1948), the Ordinance on Terminology, Forms, and Preparation Methods of Consolidated Financial Statements shall be enacted as follows.

Chapter I General Provisions (Articles 1 to 16)
Chapter II Consolidated Balance Sheet
  Section 1 General Provisions (Articles 17 to 20)
  Section 2 Assets (Articles 21 to 34-3)
  Section 3 Liabilities (Articles 35 to 41)
  Section 4 Net Assets (Articles 42 to 44-2)
  Section 5 Miscellaneous Provisions (Articles 45 to 47)
Chapter III Consolidated Profit and Loss Statement
  Section 1 General Provisions (Articles 48 and 50)
  Section 2 Net Sales and Cost of Sales (Articles 51 to 54)
  Section 3 Selling Expenses and General and Administrative Expenses (Articles 55 to 56)
  Section 4 Non-operating Revenues and Non-operating Expenses (Articles 57 to 61)
  Section 5 Extraordinary Profit and Extraordinary Loss (Articles 62 to 64)
  Section 6 Net Profit for the Period or Net Loss for the Period (Articles 65 and 65-2)
  Section 7 Miscellaneous Provisions (Articles 66 to 69)
Chapter IV Consolidated Statement of Changes in Net Assets
  Section 1 General Provisions (Articles 70 and 71)
  Section 2 Shareholders' Equity (Article 72)
  Section 3 Valuation and Translation Adjustments (Articles 73 and 74)
  Section 4 Share Options (Article 75)
  Section 5 Minority Shareholders' Equity (Article 76)
  Section 6 Matters to be Stated in the Notes (Articles 77 to 80)
  Section 7 Miscellaneous Provisions (Article 81)
Chapter V Consolidated Cash Flow Statement
  Section 1 General Provisions (Articles 82 and 83)
  Section 2 Method for Presenting a Consolidated Cash Flow Statement (Articles 84 to 87)
  Section 3 Miscellaneous Provisions (Articles 88 to 90)
Chapter VI Consolidated Supplementary Schedules (Articles 91 to 92-2)
Chapter VII Special Provisions for Business Accounting Standards (Articles 93 and 94)
  Supplementary Provisions

Chapter I General Provisions

(General Principles for Application)
Article 1 (1) From among finance and accounting documents to be submitted pursuant to the provisions of Article 5, Article 7, Article 9, paragraph (1), Article 10, paragraph (1), Article 24, paragraph (1) or (3) of the Financial Instruments and Exchange Act (Act No. 25 of 1948; hereinafter referred to as the "Act") (including the cases where any of

[11] Ordinance on Terminology, Forms, and Preparation Methods of Consolidated Financial Statements, Chap.I

Art.1

these provisions are applied mutatis mutandis pursuant to Article 24-2, paragraph (1) of the Act and cases where these provisions are applied mutatis mutandis, pursuant to Article 27 of the Act, to a juridical person which has been designated by the Commissioner of the Financial Services Agency pursuant to the provision of Article 1, paragraph (1) of the Ordinance on Terminology, Forms, and Preparation Methods of Financial Statements, etc. (Ordinance of the Ministry of Finance No. 59 of 1963; hereinafter referred to as the "Ordinance on Financial Statements, etc.") (such juridical person shall hereinafter be referred to as a "Designated Juridical Person")), the terminology, forms, and preparation methods of Consolidated Financial Statements (meaning consolidated balance sheets, consolidated profit and loss statements, consolidated statements of changes in net assets, consolidated cash flow statements, and consolidated supplementary schedules or, in cases where they are prepared pursuant to Designated International Accounting Standards (meaning Designated International Accounting Standards prescribed in Article 93; the same shall apply in the following Article) pursuant to the provision of Article 93, equivalents to consolidated balance sheets, consolidated profit and loss statements, consolidated statements of changes in net assets and consolidated cash flow statements of which preparation is required pursuant to said Designated International Accounting Standards; the same shall apply hereinafter) shall be governed by the provisions of this Ordinance, except for those subject to the application of the provision of Article 1-3 of the Ordinance on Financial Statements, etc. , and any matters that are not provided for under this Ordinance shall be in compliance with business accounting standards that are generally accepted as fair and appropriate.

(2) Business accounting standards published by the Business Accounting Council prescribed in Article 24, paragraph (1) of the Cabinet Order for Organization of the Financial Services Agency (Cabinet Order No. 392 of 1998) shall be regarded as the business accounting standards that are generally accepted as fair and appropriate prescribed in the preceding paragraph.

(3) From among the business accounting standards prepared and published by organizations that, in the course of trade, conduct research and study concerning, and development of, business accounting standards which satisfy all of the following requirements, those which are specified by the Commissioner of the Financial Services Agency as such that are found to have been prepared and published under fair and appropriate procedures and are expected to be generally accepted as fair and appropriate business accounting standards shall be regarded as the business accounting standards that are generally accepted as fair and appropriate prescribed in paragraph (1):

(i) that it should be a private organization independent from any person with interest;
(ii) that it should be funded continuously by a large number of persons and not disproportionately by any specific person;
(iii) that it should have set up a council organization composed of persons competent to develop business accounting standards from a highly professional viewpoint (referred to as a "Standards Committee" in the following item and item (v));
(iv) that the Standards Committee should be such that it engages in its duties in a fair and sincere manner; and
(v) that the Standards Committee should be such that it continuously conducts reviews from a perspective of proper responses to changes in the business environment surrounding Companies, etc. (meaning a company, Designated Juridical Person, partnership or any other business entity equivalent thereto (including a business entity equivalent thereto in a foreign state); the same shall apply hereinafter) and practice of Companies, etc. and the International Convergence (meaning ensuring the standardization of business accounting standards on an international

scale).

(Special Provision for Application)
Article 1-2 The terminology, forms, and preparation methods of Consolidated Financial Statements that a company, as one that engages in international financing activities or business activities and that satisfies either of the following requirements (hereinafter referred to as a "Specified Company") submits may be in accordance with the provisions of Chapter VII:

(i) that it should satisfy all of the following requirements:
   (a) that shares that it issues are listed on a Financial Instruments Exchange (meaning a Financial Instruments Exchange prescribed in Article 2, paragraph (16) of the Act) or are registered as Over-the-Counter Traded Securities (meaning Over-the-Counter Traded Securities prescribed in sub-item (c) of item (x) of paragraph (8) of that Article) with an Authorized Financial Instruments Firms Association (meaning an Authorized Financial Instruments Firms Association prescribed in paragraph (13) of that Article);
   (b) that in Annual Securities Reports that it submits under the provision of Article 24, paragraph (1) or (3) of the Act, it should give a statement pertaining to special efforts for ensuring appropriateness of the Consolidated Financial Statements;
   (c) that it should have Officers or employees who have sufficient knowledge of Designated International Accounting Standards and have established a system under which Consolidated Financial Statements can be prepared in an appropriate manner under said standards; and
   (d) that the company, its Parent Company, Other Associated Company (meaning an Other Associated Company prescribed in Article 15-4, item (iv)) or the Parent Company of such Other Associated Company should satisfy any of the following requirements:
      1. that it should have disclosed documents concerning corporate affairs and other related matters prepared in accordance with International Accounting Standards (meaning, from among the business accounting standards prepared and published by organizations that, in the course of trade, conduct research and study concerning, and development of, business accounting standards intended to be used as internationally common business accounting standards, which satisfy all of the requirements set forth in the items of paragraph (3) of the preceding Article, those which are specified by the Commissioner of the Financial Services Agency; hereinafter the same shall apply in this item and Article 93) under laws and regulations of a foreign state for each period specified by said laws and regulations;
      2. that it should have disclosed documents concerning corporate affairs and other related matters prepared in accordance with International Accounting Standards under the rules of a Foreign Financial Instruments Market (meaning a Foreign Financial Instruments Market prescribed in Article 2, paragraph (8), item (iii), sub-item (b) of the Act) for each period specified by said rules; or
      3. that it should have a Consolidated Subsidiary Company (limited to such company of which amount of stated capital is two billion yen or more on the consolidated closing date (in the case of a Consolidated Subsidiary Company of such Parent Company, the last day of the latest business year of such Parent Company)) in a foreign state; or
(ii) that it should be a company that prepared Consolidated Financial Statements, Interim Consolidated Financial Statements (meaning documents prescribed in Article

[11] Ordinance on Terminology, Forms, and Preparation Methods of Consolidated Financial Statements, Chap.I

Art.2

1, paragraph (1) of the Ordinance on Terminology, Forms and Preparation Methods of Interim Consolidated Financial Statements (Ordinance of the Ministry of Finance No. 24 of 1999); hereinafter referred to as the "Ordinance on Interim Consolidated Financial Statements") or Quarterly Consolidated Financial Statements (meaning documents prescribed in Article 1, paragraph (1) of the Ordinance on Terminology, Forms and Preparation Methods of Quarterly Consolidated Financial Statements (Cabinet Office Ordinance No. 64 of 2007; hereinafter referred to as the "Ordinance on Quarterly Consolidated Financial Statements")) pertaining to the Consolidated Fiscal Year (meaning a period prescribed in Article 3, paragraph (2); hereinafter the same shall apply in this item) immediately preceding the current Consolidated Fiscal Year, an Interim Consolidated Accounting Period (meaning a period prescribed in Article 3, paragraph (2) of the Ordinance on Interim Consolidated Financial Statements) within the current Consolidated Fiscal Year or a Quarterly Consolidated Accounting Period (meaning a period prescribed in Article 2, item (iii) of the Ordinance on Quarterly Consolidated Financial Statements) within the current Consolidated Fiscal Year, whichever is the period of which the last day is the closest to the consolidated closing date, pursuant to Designated International Accounting Standards and should satisfy the requirements set forth in sub-items (b) and (c) of the preceding item.

(Definitions)
Article 2 In this Ordinance, the meanings of the terms set forth in the following items shall be as prescribed respectively in those items:
(i) Company Submitting Consolidated Financial Statements: a company or Designated Juridical Person which is to submit Consolidated Financial Statements pursuant to the provisions of the Act;
(ii) Parent Company: an entity that is regarded as the parent company of a Company Submitting Consolidated Financial Statements pursuant to the provision of Article 8, paragraph (3) of the Ordinance on Financial Statements, etc. ;
(iii) Subsidiary Company: an entity that is regarded as a subsidiary company of a Company Submitting Consolidated Financial Statements pursuant to the provisions of Article 8, paragraphs (3), (4), and (7) of the Ordinance on Financial Statements, etc. ;
(iv) Consolidated Subsidiary Company: a Subsidiary Company included in the scope of consolidation;
(v) Consolidated Companies: a Company Submitting Consolidated Financial Statements and its Consolidated Subsidiary Companies;
(vi) Non-consolidated Subsidiary Company: a Subsidiary Company excluded from the scope of consolidation;
(vii) Affiliated Company: an entity that is regarded as an affiliated company of a Company Submitting Consolidated Financial Statements pursuant to the provisions of Article 8, paragraphs (5) and (6) of the Ordinance on Financial Statements, etc. ;
(viii) Equity Method: a method whereby an investor company corrects its investment amount each business year according to the changes in the portions of the investee company's net assets, profit and loss which belong to said investor company;
(ix) deleted;
(x) Securities Registration Statement: the securities registration statement defined in Article 2, paragraph (7) of the Act which is provided for under Article 5, paragraph (1) of the Act (including the cases where applied mutatis mutandis pursuant to Article 27 of the Act);
(xi) Annual Securities Report: the annual securities report defined in Article 24, para-

graph (1) of the Act;
(xii) Minority Shareholders' Equity: the portion of a Consolidated Subsidiary Company's capital which is not equity of the Company Submitting Consolidated Financial Statements;
(xiii) Cash Flow: any increase or decrease in the Funds defined in the following item;
(xiv) Funds: the combined total of cash (including any current deposits, ordinary deposits, and other deposits which the depositor is able to withdraw without waiting for a certain period to elapse; the same shall apply in Chapter V) and Cash Equivalents (meaning short-term investments which can be easily converted into cash and which involve low risk of fluctuations in value; the same shall apply in Chapter V);
(xv) Derivative Transactions: the transactions defined in Article 8, paragraph (14) of the Ordinance on Financial Statements, etc. ;
(xvi) Trading Securities: the securities defined in Article 8, paragraph (20) of the Ordinance on Financial Statements, etc. ;
(xvii) Bonds Held to Maturity: the bonds defined in Article 8, paragraph (21) of the Ordinance on Financial Statements, etc. ;
(xviii) Other Securities: the securities defined in Article 8, paragraph (22) of the Ordinance on Financial Statements, etc. ;
(xix) Treasury Shares: a combined total of the shares of a Company Submitting Consolidated Financial Statements held by the Company Submitting Consolidated Financial Statements itself, and shares of the Company Submitting Consolidated Financial Statements held by any Consolidated Subsidiary Company, Non-consolidated Subsidiary Company to which the Equity Method is applied, and Affiliated Company that represent equity of said Company Submitting Consolidated Financial Statements;
(xx) Company's Own Shares: shares of Consolidated Companies;
(xxi) Options on the Company's Own Shares: Call Options (meaning rights for acquiring the Company's Own Shares which are the underlying assets, by paying a certain amount of money) for which underlying assets are the Company's Own Shares;
(xxii) Stock Options: Options on the Company's Own Shares (meaning the Options on the Company's Own Shares defined in the preceding item) which Consolidated Companies grant to their Workers, etc. (meaning employees hired by said Consolidated Companies and Officers (meaning the officers defined in Article 21, paragraph (1), item (i) of the Act (including the cases where it is applied mutatis mutandis pursuant to Article 27 of the Act); the same shall apply hereinafter) of said Consolidated Companies; hereinafter the same shall apply in this item) as Remuneration (meaning what said Consolidated Companies pay or deliver to their Workers, etc. in consideration for labor, execution of business or the like);
(xxiii) Business Combination: the business combination defined in Article 8, paragraph (27) of the Ordinance on Financial Statements, etc. ;
(xxiv) Acquiring Enterprise: the enterprise defined in Article 8, paragraph (28) of the Ordinance on Financial Statements, etc. ;
(xxv) Acquired Enterprise: the enterprise defined in Article 8, paragraph (29) of the Ordinance on Financial Statements, etc. ;
(xxvi) Combiner: the enterprise defined in Article 8, paragraph (31) of the Ordinance on Financial Statements, etc. ;
(xxvii) Combinee: the enterprise defined in Article 8, paragraph (32) of the Ordinance on Financial Statements, etc. ;
(xxviii) Combined Enterprise: the enterprise defined in Article 8, paragraph (33) of the Ordinance on Financial Statements, etc. ;

(xxix) Constituent Enterprises: the enterprises defined in Article 8, paragraph (34) of the Ordinance on Financial Statements, etc. ;
(xxx) Common Control Transaction, etc. : the common control transaction, etc. defined in Article 8, paragraph (37) of the Ordinance on Financial Statements, etc. ;
(xxxi) Business Divestiture: the business divestiture defined in Article 8, paragraph (38) of the Ordinance on Financial Statements, etc. ;
(xxxii) Divesting Enterprise: the enterprise defined in Article 8, paragraph (39) of the Ordinance on Financial Statements, etc. ;
(xxxiii) Successor Enterprise: the enterprise defined in Article 8, paragraph (40) of the Ordinance on Financial Statements, etc. ;
(xxxiv) Financial Instruments: the financial instruments defined in Article 8, paragraph (41) of the Ordinance on Financial Statements, etc. ; and
(xxxv) Asset Retirement Obligations: the asset retirement obligations defined in Article 8 (42) of the Ordinance on Financial Statements, etc.

(Consolidated Closing Date and Consolidated Fiscal Year)
Article 3 (1) A Company Submitting Consolidated Financial Statements shall specify the last day of its business year as its consolidated closing date, and prepare Consolidated Financial Statements based on said date.
(2) In the case set forth in the preceding paragraph, the period for which Consolidated Financial Statements are prepared (hereinafter referred to as the "Consolidated Fiscal Year") shall be the period from the day following the consolidated closing date preceding the relevant consolidated closing date to the relevant consolidated closing date.
(3) In the case where the consolidated closing date has been changed, a statement to that effect, the reason for the change, and the period of the Consolidated Fiscal Year as changed shall be stated in the notes in the Consolidated Financial Statements.

(General Principles for Preparation of Consolidated Financial Statements)
Article 4 (1) The terminology, forms, and preparation methods of Consolidated Financial Statements to be submitted pursuant to the provisions of the Act shall comply with the following standards:
(i) the Consolidated Financial Statements shall present true information concerning the financial position, operating results and conditions of Cash Flow of the Business Group (meaning a Company Submitting Consolidated Financial Statements and its Subsidiary Companies; the same shall apply hereinafter);
(ii) the Consolidated Financial Statements shall be prepared based on financial statements of Consolidated Companies that have been prepared in compliance with business accounting standards that are generally accepted as fair and appropriate;
(iii) the Consolidated Financial Statements shall clearly present the accounting information necessary for preventing persons interested in the Company Submitting Consolidated Financial Statements from making an erroneous determination on the financial position, operating results and Cash Flow conditions of the Business Group; and
(iv) the accounting principles and procedures adopted by the Company Submitting Consolidated Financial Statements for preparing the Consolidated Financial Statements shall be applied continuously throughout each Consolidated Fiscal Year, except in cases of making a change based on justifiable grounds.
(2) For those matters to be stated in Consolidated Financial Statements that have the same contents, the same presentation method shall be adopted throughout each Consolidated Fiscal Year for preparing Consolidated Financial Statements, except in cases of making a change based on justifiable grounds.

(Scope of Consolidation)

Article 5 (1) A Company Submitting Consolidated Financial Statements shall include all of its Subsidiary Companies in the scope of consolidation; provided, however, that it shall not include a Subsidiary Company that falls under either of the following categories in the scope of consolidation:

(i) a Subsidiary Company where the Company Submitting Consolidated Financial Statements is found to only have temporary control over said Subsidiary Company's body which makes decisions on financial and operational or business policies (meaning a shareholders meeting or any body equivalent thereto); and

(ii) a Subsidiary Company where inclusion of said Subsidiary Company in the scope of consolidation is found likely to lead persons interested in the Company Submitting Consolidated Financial Statements to making a substantially erroneous determination.

(2) Where any Subsidiary Company which should be included in the scope of consolidation pursuant to the provision of the preceding paragraph lacks significance in terms of its assets, net sales (including revenues from service operations; the same shall apply hereinafter), profit or loss, retained earnings and Cash Flows and any other items, to the extent that its exclusion from the scope of consolidation would not hinder reasonable determination on the financial position, operating results and Cash Flow conditions of the Business Group, said Subsidiary Company may be excluded from the scope of consolidation.

(3) In cases where there is any significant matter concerning the financial position, operating results or Cash Flow conditions of a Company, etc. set forth as follows, which is found to exert influence on determination on the financial position, operating results and Cash Flow conditions of the Business Group, the details thereof shall be stated in the notes in the Consolidated Financial Statements:

(i) a Subsidiary Company that is excluded from the scope of consolidation pursuant to the provision of the proviso to paragraph (1); or

(ii) among Companies, etc. whose majority of voting rights are held by the Company Submitting Consolidated Financial Statements on its own account, a Company, etc. that has received an order of commencement of rehabilitation proceedings under the provisions of the Civil Rehabilitation Act (Act No. 225 of 1999), a stock company that has received an order of commencement of corporate reorganization proceedings under the provisions of the Corporate Reorganization Act (Act No. 154 of 2002), a Company, etc. that has received an order of commencement of bankruptcy proceedings under the provisions of the Bankruptcy Act (Act No. 75 of 2004), or any other Company, etc. equivalent thereto, which at the same time is not categorized as a Subsidiary Company due to being found to have no effective parent-subsidiary relationship with the Company Submitting Consolidated Financial Statements.

(Consolidated Balance Sheet)

Article 6 A consolidated balance sheet shall be prepared based on the amounts of assets, liabilities, and net assets reported on the balance sheets of Consolidated Companies for the period corresponding to the Consolidated Fiscal Year of the Company Submitting Consolidated Financial Statements (with regard to any relevant Consolidated Subsidiary Company which settles its accounts pursuant to the provision of Article 12, paragraph (1), the balance sheet pertaining to said settlement of accounts).

(Consolidated Profit and Loss Statement)

Article 7 A consolidated balance sheet shall be prepared based on the amounts of revenues, expenses, etc. reported on the profits and loss statements of Consolidated Companies for the period corresponding to the Consolidated Fiscal Year of the Company Submitting Consolidated Financial Statements (with regard to any relevant Consolidated Subsidiary Company which settles its accounts pursuant to the provision of Article 12, paragraph (1), the profit and loss statement pertaining to said settlement of accounts).

(Consolidated Statement of Changes in Net Assets)
Article 8 A consolidated statement of changes in net assets shall be prepared based on the amounts of increases or decreases in net assets of Consolidated Companies for the period corresponding to the Consolidated Fiscal Year of the Company Submitting Consolidated Financial Statements.

(Consolidated Cash Flow Statement)
Article 8-2 A consolidated cash flow statement shall be prepared based on the amounts reported on the cash flow statements of Consolidated Companies for the period corresponding to the Consolidated Fiscal Year of the Company Submitting Consolidated Financial Statements (with regard to any relevant Consolidated Subsidiary Company which settles its accounts pursuant to the provision of Article 12, paragraph (1), the cash flow statement pertaining to said settlement of accounts).

(Valuation of Assets and Liabilities of Consolidated Subsidiary Companies, etc.)
Article 9 When preparing Consolidated Financial Statements, assets and liabilities of Consolidated Subsidiary Companies shall be valued, investments by the Company Submitting Consolidated Financial Statements in Consolidated Subsidiary Companies shall be offset against the corresponding equity of said Consolidated Subsidiary Companies, and any other necessary elimination of items between the Consolidated Companies shall be made.

(Application of the Equity Method)
Article 10 (1) Investments in any Non-consolidated Subsidiary Company or Affiliated Company shall be reported on a consolidated balance sheet by indicating values calculated by the Equity Method; provided, however, that the Equity Method shall not be applied to investments in a company that fall under either of the following categories:
  (i) an Affiliated Company where the Company Submitting Consolidated Financial Statements is found to only exert a temporary influence on said Affiliated Company's decisions on financial and operational or business policies; or
  (ii) a Non-consolidated Subsidiary Company or Affiliated Company where application of the Equity Method to said company is found likely to lead persons interested in the Company Submitting Consolidated Financial Statements to making a substantially erroneous determination.
(2) Where any Non-consolidated Subsidiary Company or Affiliated Company to which the Equity Method should be applied pursuant to the provision of the preceding paragraph does not, in terms of its profit or loss, retained earnings and any other items, exert a significant influence on Consolidated Financial Statements even if said company is excluded from the target of application of the Equity Method, said company may be excluded from the target of application of the Equity Method.

(Application of Tax Effect Accounting)

Article 11 With regard to Consolidated Companies' corporation tax and any other taxes that are imposed on amounts related to profits as the tax base (hereinafter referred to as "Corporation Tax, etc."), Consolidated Financial Statements shall be prepared by applying Tax Effect Accounting (meaning an accounting method which, in cases where there are differences between the amounts of assets and liabilities reported on the consolidated balance sheet and the amounts of assets and liabilities derived as a result of calculating the taxable income, reasonably matches the amount of net profit for the period before deducing the Corporation Tax, etc. with the applicable amount of Corporation Tax, etc. through appropriate interperiod allocation of the amount of Corporation Tax, etc. pertaining to such differences; the same shall apply hereinafter).

(Subsidiary Company with a Different Accounting Period)
Article 12 (1) Any Consolidated Subsidiary Company the last day of whose business year differs from the consolidated closing date shall, on the consolidated closing date, carry out the necessary settlement of accounts for preparing financial statements that serve as the basis for preparation of Consolidated Financial Statements; provided, however, that this shall not apply when the difference between the last day of the business year of said Consolidated Subsidiary Company and the consolidated closing date is not more than three months, and Consolidated Financial Statements are prepared based on financial statements for said fiscal year.
(2) In cases of preparing Consolidated Financial Statements pursuant to the provision of the proviso to the preceding paragraph, adjustment shall be made with regard to any significant inconsistency in accounting records pertaining to transactions between Consolidated Companies that result from the fact that the last day of the business year of the Consolidated Subsidiary Company differs from the consolidated closing date.

(Statement on the Scope of Consolidation, etc.)
Article 13 (1) Matters on the scope of consolidation and other significant matters that serve as the basis for preparing Consolidated Financial Statements shall be stated immediately after the consolidated cash flow statement, by classifying them into the following matters:
(i) matters on the scope of consolidation;
(ii) matters on application of the Equity Method;
(iii) matters on the business year, etc. of Consolidated Subsidiary Companies; and
(iv) matters on accounting standards.
(2) With regard to the matters on the scope of consolidation set forth in item (i) of the preceding paragraph, the following matters shall be stated; provided, however, that, with regard to the matters set forth in item (i), if said matters are stated in the Securities Registration Statement and the Annual Securities Report, in a place other than Consolidated Financial Statements, the statement of said matters may be omitted by making a statement to that effect:
(i) the number of Consolidated Subsidiary Companies and the names of major Consolidated Subsidiary Companies;
(ii) in cases where there are any Non-consolidated Subsidiary Companies, the names of major Non-consolidated Subsidiary Companies and the reason for excluding them from the scope of consolidation;
(iii) in cases where, in spite of the Company Submitting Consolidated Financial Statements holding a majority of the voting rights of another Company, etc. on its own account, said other Company, etc. is not regarded as a Subsidiary Company, the name of said other Company, etc. and the reason for not regarding it as a Subsidiary Company; and

[II] Ordinance on Terminology, Forms, and Preparation Methods
Art.13　　　　　　of Consolidated Financial Statements, Chap.I

(iv) in cases where there is any Special Purpose Company Subject to Disclosure (meaning the special purpose company subject to disclosure defined in Article 8-9, item (ii) of the Ordinance on Financial Statements, etc.; hereinafter the same shall apply in this item), the outline of the Special Purpose Company Subject to Disclosure, the outline and transaction amounts of transactions with the Special Purpose Company Subject to Disclosure, and any other significant matters.

(3) With regard to the matters on application of the Equity Method set forth in paragraph (1) (ii), the following matters shall be stated:

(i) the number of Non-consolidated Subsidiary Companies or Affiliated Companies to which the Equity Method is applied and the names of major Companies among them;

(ii) in cases where there are any Non-consolidated Subsidiary Companies or Affiliated Companies to which the Equity Method is not applied, the names of major Companies among them;

(iii) in cases where there are any Non-consolidated Subsidiary Companies or Affiliated Companies to which the Equity Method is not applied, the reason for not applying the Equity Method;

(iv) in cases where, in spite of the Company Submitting Consolidated Financial Statements holding not less than 20 percent but not more than 50 percent of the voting rights of another Company, etc. on its own account, said other Company, etc. is not regarded as an Affiliated Company, the name of said other Company, etc. and the reason for not regarding it as an Affiliated Company; and

(v) in cases where there are any matters that are found particularly necessary to be stated with regard to the procedure for application of the Equity Method, the details thereof.

(4) With regard to the matters on the business year, etc. of Consolidated Subsidiary Companies set forth in paragraph (1), item (iii), if there is any Consolidated Subsidiary Company the last day of whose business year differs from the consolidated closing date, the details thereof and whether or not said Consolidated Subsidiary Company has carried out settlement of accounts for preparing financial statements that serve as the basis for preparation of Consolidated Financial Statements shall be stated.

(5) With regard to the matters on accounting standards set forth in paragraph (1), item (iv), the following matters shall be stated:

(i) the valuation standards and the valuation method for significant assets;

(ii) the depreciation/amortization method for significant depreciable/amortizable assets;

(iii) the standards for recognition of significant allowances;

(iv) the standards for recognition of significant revenues and expenses;

(v) the standards for translating significant assets or liabilities that are in a foreign currency into Japanese currency, adopted for preparing financial statements of Consolidated Companies that served as the basis for preparation of Consolidated Financial Statements;

(vi) any significant method of Hedge Accounting (meaning the hedge accounting defined in Article 8-2, item (viii) of the Ordinance on Financial Statements, etc.; the same shall apply in Article 15-7, paragraphs (1) and (3));

(vii) the amortization method and amortization period of goodwill;

(viii) the scope of Funds reported on the consolidated cash flow statement; and

(ix) other significant matters for preparing Consolidated Financial Statements.

(Statement on Changes in Significant Matters that Serve as the Basis for Preparation of Consolidated Financial Statements)

Ⅱ Ordinance on Terminology, Forms, and Preparation Methods of Consolidated Financial Statements, Chap.I

Article 14 In cases where any significant matters that serve as the basis for preparation of Consolidated Financial Statements have been changed, the following matters shall be stated immediately after the statements under the preceding Article:
(i) in cases where the scope of consolidation or the scope of application of the Equity Method has been changed, a statement to that effect, and the reason for the change;
(ii) in cases where any accounting principles or procedures have been changed, a statement to that effect, the reason for the change, and details of the influence of said change on the Consolidated Financial Statements;
(iii) in cases where any presentation methods have been changed, the details of such change; and
(iv) in cases where the scope of Funds in the consolidated cash flow statement has been changed, a statement to that effect, the reason for the change, and details of the influence of said change on the consolidated cash flow statement.

(Notes on Significant Post-Balance Sheet Events)
Article 14-2 If any events that exert a significant influence on the financial position, operating results and Cash Flow conditions of Consolidated Companies, as well as Non-consolidated Subsidiary Companies and Affiliated Companies to which the Equity Method is applied, in and/or after the following Consolidated Fiscal Year occur after the consolidated closing date (such events shall hereinafter be referred to as "Significant Post-Balance Sheet Events"), said events shall be stated in the notes; provided, however, that, with regard to any Subsidiary Company or Affiliated Company the last day of whose business year differs from the consolidated closing date, such events that occur after the balance sheet date of said Subsidiary Company or Affiliated Company shall be stated in the notes.

(Notes on Additional Information)
Article 15 In addition to the notes particularly specified under this Ordinance, if there are any matters that are found to be necessary for persons interested in the Company Submitting Consolidated Financial Statements to make adequate judgments on the financial position, operating results and Cash Flow conditions of the Business Group, said matters shall be stated in the notes.

(Notes on Segment Information, etc.)
Article 15-2 (1) With regard to information on a certain unit of an Enterprise (hereinafter referred to as a "Reporting Segment") (such information will hereinafter be referred to as "Segment Information"), the following matters shall be set down in the notes in accordance with Form No. 1:
(i) the outline of any Reporting Segment;
(ii) the amounts of the net sales, profit or loss, assets, liabilities and other items for each Reporting Segment and the methods of calculation of those amounts; and
(iii) the differences between the total amounts of the amounts of the respective items set forth in the preceding item and the amounts reported on the consolidated balance sheet or the amounts reported on the consolidated profit and loss statement for the respective accounting titles equivalent to said items and the main contents of said differences.
(2) With regard to information related to a Reporting Segment (referred to as "Related Information" in Form No. 2), the following matters shall be set down in the notes in accordance with that form:
(i) information for each product and service;

(ii) information for each region; and
(iii) information for each major customer.
(3) In cases where the following items are reported in the consolidated balance sheet or the consolidated profit and loss statement, the outline for each Reporting Segment shall be set down in the notes in accordance with Form No. 3:
(i) the impairment loss on fixed assets;
(ii) the amortization amount of goodwill and the unamortized balance; or
(iii) the gain from negative goodwill.
(4) Notwithstanding the provisions of the preceding three paragraphs, notes may be omitted for matters having little significance.

(Notes on Lease Transactions)
Article 15-3 The provisions of Article 8-6 of the Ordinance on Financial Statements, etc. shall apply mutatis mutandis to lease transactions. In this case, the term "Company Submitting Financial Statements" in paragraphs (1) and (3) of that Article shall be deemed to be replaced with "Consolidated Companies," the term "as of the end of the current business year" in sub-item (a) of item (i) paragraph (1) and item (ii) and paragraph (2) of that Article shall be deemed to be replaced with "as of the end of the current Consolidated Fiscal Year," the term "balance sheet date" in sub-item (b) of item (ii) of paragraph (1) of that Article shall be deemed to be replaced with "consolidated closing date," and the term "balance sheet" in paragraph (3) of that Article shall be deemed to be replaced with "consolidated balance sheet."

(Scope of Related Parties)
Article 15-4 As used in this Ordinance, the term "Related Party" means any of the following persons:
(i) the Parent Company of a Company Submitting Consolidated Financial Statements;
(ii) a Non-consolidated Subsidiary Company of a Company Submitting Consolidated Financial Statements;
(iii) a Company, etc. having the same Parent Company as a Company Submitting Consolidated Financial Statements;
(iv) Any Other Associated Company (meaning, in cases where the Company Submitting Consolidated Financial Statements is an Affiliated Company of another Company, etc., said other Company, etc.; hereinafter the same shall apply in this item) of a Company Submitting Consolidated Financial Statements, and the Parent Company or a Subsidiary Company of Any Other Associated Company;
(v) an Affiliated Company of a Company Submitting Consolidated Financial Statements, and a Subsidiary Company of said Affiliated Company;
(vi) a Major Shareholder (meaning a major shareholder as defined in Article 163, paragraph (1) of the Act) of a Company Submitting Consolidated Financial Statements and a Close Relative (meaning a relative within the second degree of kinship; the same shall apply in the following item to item (ix)) thereof;
(vii) an Officer of a Company Submitting Consolidated Financial Statements and a Close Relative thereof;
(viii) an Officer of the Parent Company of a Company Submitting Consolidated Financial Statements and a Close Relative thereof;
(ix) an Officer of a significant Subsidiary Company of a Company Submitting Consolidated Financial Statements and a Close Relative thereof;
(x) a Company, etc. , whose majority of voting rights are held by any of the persons set forth in the preceding four items, on his/her own account, and a Subsidiary Company of said Company, etc. ; or

(xi) a corporate pension for the workers of a Company Submitting Financial Statements (limited to cases where such corporate pension carries out significant transactions (excluding contribution of premiums) with the Company Submitting Consolidated Financial Statements or a Consolidated Subsidiary Company).

(Notes on Transactions with Related Parties)

Article 15-4-2 (1) In cases where a Company Submitting Consolidated Financial Statements carries out transactions with any Related Party (such transactions include any transactions which said Related Party carries out with the Company Submitting Consolidated Financial Statements for the benefit of a third party and any transactions carried out between the Company Submitting Consolidated Financial Statements and a third party where said Related Party exerts a significant influence on the Company Submitting Consolidated Financial Statements with regard to said transactions), the following matters shall be stated in the notes for each Related Party, in principle, with regard to any of such transactions that are significant:

(i) in cases where said Related Party is a Company, etc. , its name, location, and stated capital or capital contribution, description of its business, and the share of voting rights in said Related Party held by the Company Submitting Consolidated Financial Statements, or the share of voting rights in the Company Submitting Consolidated Financial Statements held by said Related Party;

(ii) in cases where said Related Party is an individual, his/her name and occupation, and the share of voting rights in the Company Submitting Consolidated Financial Statements held by said Related Party;

(iii) the relationship between the Company Submitting Consolidated Financial Statements and said Related Party;

(iv) the details of the transactions;

(v) the transaction amount by type of transactions;

(vi) conditions of transactions and the policy for deciding the conditions of transactions;

(vii) the ending balances of the respective major account titles pertaining to claims and obligations arising from transactions;

(viii) in cases where there have been any changes in the conditions of transactions, a statement to that effect, the details of the change, and the details of the influence of said change on the Consolidated Financial Statements;

(ix) in cases where claims against the Related Party are categorized as Claims with a Possibility of Default (meaning claims with a possibility of default defined in Article 8-10, paragraph (1), item (ix) of the Ordinance on Financial Statements, etc.) or Claims in Bankruptcy, Reorganization, etc. (meaning claims in bankruptcy, rehabilitation, etc. defined in said item; the same shall apply in Article 23, paragraph (1), item (iii)), the following matters:

(a) the balance of allowance for doubtful accounts as of the end of the current Consolidated Fiscal Year;

(b) the provision of allowance for doubtful accounts, etc. reported for the current Consolidated Fiscal Year; and

(c) the bad debt losses, etc. (including any bad debt losses incurred in cases where the claims were categorized as General Claims (meaning general claims defined in Article 8-10, paragraph (1), item (ix), sub-item (c) of the Ordinance on Financial Statements, etc.)) reported for the current Consolidated Fiscal Year; and

(x) in cases where any allowances other than the allowance for doubtful accounts are established with regard to transactions with the Related Party, matters equivalent to those set forth in the preceding items regarding any such allowances that are

found appropriate to be stated in the notes.
(2) Notwithstanding the provision of the preceding paragraph, the matters set forth in items (ix) and (x) of that paragraph may be stated as a combined amount for each type of Related Party set forth in the items of Article 15-4.
(3) The provisions of the preceding two paragraphs shall apply mutatis mutandis to cases where there are transactions between a Consolidated Subsidiary Company and a Related Party.
(4) With regard to any transactions with a Related Party which have been offset when preparing Consolidated Financial Statements, the notes shall not be required.
(5) With regard to any transactions with a Related Party, which are specified in the following items, the notes prescribed in paragraph (1) shall not be required:
(i) transactions by general competitive bidding, receiving of interest on deposits and dividends, and other transactions of which conditions are apparently similar to those of general transactions in light of the nature of the transactions; and
(ii) payment of Remunerations, bonuses and retirement bonuses to Officers.
(6) The matters set forth in paragraph (1) (including the cases where it is applied mutatis mutandis pursuant to paragraph (3)) shall be stated in the notes according to Form No. 1 of the Ordinance on Financial Statements, etc.

(Notes on the Parent Company or any Significant Affiliated Company)
Article 15-4-3 (1) In cases where companies set forth in the following items exist for a Company Submitting Consolidated Financial Statements, the matters respectively specified in those items shall be stated in the notes:
(i) Parent Company: the name of the Parent Company and, in cases where securities issued by the Parent Company are listed on a Financial Instruments Exchange (meaning a financial instruments exchange defined in Article 2, paragraph (16) of the Act, including one established outside Japan which is of the same nature; hereinafter the same shall apply in this item), a statement to that effect and the name of said Financial Instruments Exchange, and in cases where securities issued by the Parent Company are not listed on a Financial Instruments Exchange, a statement to that effect; and
(ii) significant Affiliated Company: the name of any such Affiliated Company and the amounts for the following items on the balance sheet and the profit and loss statement of any such Affiliated Company on which the amount of investment return or investment loss under the Equity Method has been calculated:
(a) Balance Sheet Items (meaning total current assets, total fixed assets, total current liabilities, total fixed liabilities, total net assets, and any other significant items); and
(b) Profit and Loss Statement Items (meaning net sales, the amount of net profit for the period before taxes or the amount of net loss for the period before taxes, the amount of net profit for the period or the amount of net loss for the period, and any other significant items).
(2) The amounts for items set forth in sub-items (a) and (b) of item (ii) of the preceding paragraph may, notwithstanding the provision of said paragraph, be stated by either of the following methods; in this case, a statement to that effect shall be made:
(i) the method of stating the combined amounts for the significant Affiliated Companies; or
(ii) the method of stating the combined amounts for Affiliated Companies on which the amount of investment return or investment loss under the Equity Method has been calculated.

(Notes on Tax Effect Accounting)
Article 15-5 (1) When Tax Effect Accounting is applied pursuant to the provision of Article 11, the matters set forth in the following items shall be stated in the notes:
  (i) breakdown of major causes for the occurrence of Deferred Tax Assets (meaning the amount reported as assets as a result of applying Tax Effect Accounting; the same shall apply hereinafter) and Deferred Tax Liabilities (meaning the amount reported as liabilities as a result of applying Tax Effect Accounting; the same shall apply hereinafter);
  (ii) if there is a difference between the tax rate used for calculating the Corporation Tax, etc. of the Company Submitting Consolidated Financial Statements for the relevant Consolidated Fiscal Year (hereinafter referred to as the "Normal Effective Statutory Tax Rate" in this Article) and the ratio of the Corporation Tax, etc. (including the deferred Corporation Tax, etc. reported as a result of applying Tax Effect Accounting) to the net profit for the period before deducting the Corporation Tax, etc. (hereinafter referred to as the "Burden Ratio of Corporation Tax, etc. after Application of Tax Effect Accounting" in this Article), the breakdown of the cause for said difference, by major item;
  (iii) if the amount of Deferred Tax Assets and the amount of Deferred Tax Liabilities have been revised as a result of a change in the tax rate of any Corporation Tax, etc. , a statement to that effect and the amounts as revised; and
  (iv) in cases where there was a change in the tax rate of any Corporation Tax, etc. after the consolidated closing date, the details of such change and the influence thereof.
(2) In cases where any amount has been deducted from the Deferred Tax Assets when calculating the Deferred Tax Assets, said amount shall be stated in the notes in addition to the matters set forth in item (i) of the preceding paragraph.
(3) With regard to the matters set forth in paragraph (1), item (ii), the notes may be omitted if the difference between the Normal Effective Statutory Tax Rate and the Burden Ratio of Corporation Tax, etc. after Application of Tax Effect Accounting is not more than five percent of the Normal Effective Statutory Tax Rate.

(Notes on Financial Instruments)
Article 15-5-2 (1) With regard to Financial Instruments, the following matters shall be stated in the notes; provided, however, that notes may be omitted for matters having little significance:
  (i) the following matters concerning the conditions of Financial Instruments:
    (a) the policy on dealing in Financial Instruments;
    (b) contents of Financial Instruments and the risks involved in said Financial Instruments; and
    (c) the risk management system for Financial Instruments;
  (ii) the following matters concerning the market prices of Financial Instruments:
    (a) the amounts reported on the consolidated balance sheet for the respective account titles of the consolidated balance sheet as of the consolidated closing date;
    (b) the market prices for the respective account titles of the consolidated balance sheet as of the consolidated closing date;
    (c) the differences between the amounts reported on the consolidated balance sheet for the respective account titles of the consolidated balance sheet as of the consolidated closing date and the market prices for the respective account titles of the consolidated balance sheet as of the consolidated closing date;
    (d) the calculation methods for the market prices for the respective account titles

Art.15-5-2 ⑪ Ordinance on Terminology, Forms, and Preparation Methods of Consolidated Financial Statements, Chap.I

of the consolidated balance sheet; and

(e) explanations on the matters set forth in sub-items (b) to (d) inclusive.

(2) Notwithstanding the provision of the main clause of the preceding paragraph, the matters set forth in item (ii), sub-items (b) to (e) inclusive of that paragraph are not require to be stated in the notes, if it is difficult to identify the market prices. In this case, a statement to that effect and the reason therefor shall be set down in the notes.

(3) With regard to a Consolidated Company for which Financial Assets (meaning the financial assets defined in Article 8, paragraph (41) of the Ordinance on Financial Statements, etc.; hereinafter the same shall apply in this paragraph) and Financial Liabilities (meaning the financial liabilities defined in Article 8, paragraph (41) of the Ordinance on Financial Statements, etc.; hereinafter the same shall apply in this paragraph) respectively constitute most of the total amount of assets and the total amount of liabilities, and at the same time said Financial Assets and Financial Liabilities are important in light of the business purpose of the company, if there is significance in the rates of fluctuations in the values of said Financial Assets and Financial Liabilities against fluctuations in the figures of money rates, values of currencies, quotations on Financial Instruments Markets (meaning the financial instruments markets defined in Article 2, paragraph (14) of the Act; hereinafter the same shall apply in this paragraph and paragraph (3) of the following Article) and any other indicators, which serve as the causes of major Market Risks (meaning risks of losses incurred by fluctuations in said indicators; hereinafter the same shall apply in this paragraph and the following paragraph) associated with said Financial Assets and Financial Liabilities, the matters specified in the following items for the respective categories of Financial Instruments set forth in those items shall be stated in the notes:

(i) Financial Instruments for which quantitative analyses on Market Risks are used in their risk management: the quantitative information based on said analyses and information related thereto; or

(ii) Financial Instruments for which quantitative analyses on Market Risks are not used in their risk management: the matters set forth in sub-items (a) and (b) below:

(a) the fact that quantitative analyses on Market Risks are not used in their risk management; and

(b) increases and decreases in market prices that have been calculated by assuming a reasonable extent of fluctuations in the figures of money rates, values of currencies, quotations on Financial Instruments Markets and any other indicators, which serve as the causes of Market Risks, and information related thereto.

(4) In cases where the matters set forth in sub-item of item (ii) of the preceding paragraph do not appropriately reflect the actual conditions of Market Risks associated with the Consolidated Company, a statement to that effect and the reason therefor shall be set down in the notes.

(5) With regard to monetary claims (excluding those held for the purpose of gaining profits from fluctuations in market price) and securities (excluding Trading Securities) that have maturities, the total amount of such claims or securities to be redeemed within a certain period shall be stated in the notes.

(6) With regard to company bonds, long-term borrowings, lease obligations and any other debts which require payment of interests, the total amount of such debts to be repaid within a certain period shall be stated in the notes; provided, however, that in cases where said amount is stated in a schedule of company bonds or a schedule of borrowings, etc. prescribed in Article 92, paragraph (1), a statement to that effect may be set down in the notes in lieu of stating said amount.

1242 　　　　　第Ⅰ部 会社法・商法編

(Notes on Securities)

Article 15-6 (1) In addition to the matters specified in the preceding Article, with regard to securities, the matters specified in the following items for the respective categories of securities set forth in those items shall be stated in the notes; provided, however, that notes may be omitted for matters having little significance:

(i) Trading Securities: the valuation difference included in the profit or loss for the current Consolidated Fiscal Year;

(ii) Bonds Held to Maturity: by categorizing such bonds into those of which the market price as of the consolidated closing date exceeds the amount reported on the consolidated balance sheet as of the consolidated closing date and those of which such market price does not exceed such amount reported on the consolidated balance sheet, the following matters for each of such categories:

  (a) the amount reported on the consolidated balance sheet as of the consolidated closing date;
  (b) the market price as of the consolidated closing date; and
  (c) the difference between the amount reported on the consolidated balance sheet as of the consolidated closing date and the market price as of the consolidated closing date;

(iii) Other Securities: by categorizing each class of Securities (meaning shares, bonds and any other securities; the same shall apply in item (v)) into those of which the amount reported on the consolidated balance sheet as of the consolidated closing date exceeds the acquisition cost and those of which such amount reported on the consolidated balance sheet does not exceed the acquisition cost, the following matters for each of such categories:

  (a) the amount reported on the consolidated balance sheet as of the consolidated closing date;
  (b) the acquisition cost; and
  (c) the difference between the amount reported on the consolidated balance sheet as of the consolidated closing date and the acquisition cost;

(iv) Bonds Held to Maturity that were sold off during the current Consolidated Fiscal Year: the cost of the bonds sold, the sale price, the profit or loss on sale, and the reason for the sale, by class of bonds; and

(v) Other Securities that were sold off during the current Consolidated Fiscal Year: the sale price, the total amount of profit on sale and the total amount of loss on sale, by class of Securities.

(2) In cases where the holding purpose for Trading Securities, Bonds Held to Maturity, Subsidiary Company shares, Affiliated Company shares, or Other Securities has been changed during the current Consolidated Fiscal Year, a statement to that effect, the reason for the change (limited to the case of having changed the holding purpose for Bonds Held to Maturity), and details of the influence of said change on the Consolidated Financial Statements shall be stated in the notes; provided, however, that notes may be omitted for matters having little significance.

(3) In cases where it is difficult to sell off securities at market prices on Financial Instruments Markets for a considerable period of time due to low liquidity or any other reasons, if Trading Securities have been changed into Bonds Held to Maturity or Other Securities, or Other Securities have been changed into Bonds Held to Maturity during the current Consolidated Fiscal Year, notwithstanding the provision of the preceding paragraph, the matters specified in the following items for the respective categories of cases set forth in those items shall be stated in the notes; provided, however, that notes may be omitted for matters having little significance:

(i) cases where Trading Securities have been changed into Bonds Held to Maturity:

the following matters pertaining to the securities for which the holding purpose has been changed:
(a) the outline thereof;
(b) the date on which the holding purpose was changed, and the reason therefor;
(c) the profit or loss for the current Consolidated Fiscal Year;
(d) the market price and the amount reported on the consolidated balance sheet as of the consolidated closing date; and
(e) the amount of influence that the change in the holding purpose has on the Consolidated Financial Statements;
(ii) cases where Trading Securities have been changed into Other Securities: the following matters pertaining to the securities for which the holding purpose has been changed:
(a) the matters set forth in sub-items (a) to (c) inclusive of the preceding item;
(b) the amount reported on the consolidated balance sheet as of the consolidated closing date; and
(c) the amount of influence that the change in the holding purpose has on the Consolidated Financial Statements; and
(iii) cases where Other Securities have been changed into Bonds Held to Maturity: the following matters pertaining to the securities for which the holding purpose has been changed:
(a) the matters set forth in item (i), sub-items (a) and (b);
(b) the market price and the amount reported on the consolidated balance sheet as of the consolidated closing date; and
(c) the amount of Valuation Difference on Other Securities (meaning the valuation difference on Other Securities defined in Article 8-7, paragraph (3), item (iii), sub-item (c) of the Ordinance on Financial Statements, etc.) reported on the consolidated balance sheet as of the consolidated closing date.
(4) With regard to securities for which the holding purpose has been changed prior to the current Consolidated Fiscal Year, the matters specified in the following items for the respective categories of cases set forth in those items shall be stated in the notes in the current Consolidated Fiscal Year; provided, however, that notes may be omitted for matters having little significance:
(i) the cases set forth in item (i) of the preceding paragraph: the matters set forth in sub-items (d) and (e) of that item;
(ii) the cases set forth in item (ii) of the preceding paragraph: the matters set forth in sub-items (b) and (c) of that item; and
(iii) the cases set forth in item (iii) of the preceding paragraph: the matters set forth in sub-items (b) and (c) of that item.
(5) In cases of having recognized impairment losses on securities during the current Consolidated Fiscal Year, a statement to that effect and the amount of the impairment losses shall be set down in the notes; provided, however, that notes may be omitted for matters having little significance.

(Notes on Derivative Transactions)
Article 15-7 (1) In addition to the matters specified in Article 15-5-2, with regard to Derivative Transactions, the matters specified in the following items for the respective categories of transactions set forth in those items shall be stated in the notes; provided, however, that notes may be omitted for matters having little significance:
(i) Derivative Transactions to which Hedge Accounting is not applied: the following matters by type of the Subject Matter of Transactions (meaning currencies, money rates, shares, bonds, commodities and any other subject matter of transactions; the

same shall apply in the following item):
- (a) the contract amount as of the consolidated closing date or the principal equivalent amount specified in the contract;
- (b) the market price and valuation gain or loss as of the consolidated closing date; and
- (c) the calculation method for the market price; and
  (ii) Derivative Transactions to which Hedge Accounting is applied: the following matters by type of Subject Matter of Transactions:
- (a) the contract amount as of the consolidated closing date or the principal equivalent amount specified in the contract;
- (b) the market price as of the consolidated closing date; and
- (c) the calculation method for the market price.
(2) The matters specified in item (i) of the preceding paragraph shall be stated by categorizing them into the type of Transactions (meaning futures transactions, options transactions, forward transactions, swap transactions and any other Derivative Transactions; the same shall apply in the following paragraph), distinction between Market Transactions (meaning the market transactions defined in Article 8, paragraph (10), item (iii) of the Ordinance on Financial Statements, etc.) and transactions other than Market Transactions, distinction between those pertaining to purchase contracts and those pertaining to sale contracts, the period from the consolidated closing date to the settlement date of the transaction or to the time of termination of the contract, and other matters.
(3) The matters specified in paragraph (1), item (ii) shall be stated by categorizing them into the method of Hedge Accounting, the type of Transactions, the Hedged Items (meaning the hedged items defined in Article 8-2, item (viii) of the Ordinance on Financial Statements, etc.), and other matters.

(Notes on Retirement Benefits)
Article 15-8 The provision of Article 8-13, paragraph (1) of the Ordinance on Financial Statements, etc. shall apply mutatis mutandis to retirement benefits. In this case, the term "Company Submitting Financial Statements" in item (ii) of that paragraph shall be deemed to be replaced with "Company Submitting Consolidated Financial Statements," the term "balance sheet date" in items (ii) and (iii) of that paragraph shall be deemed to be replaced with "consolidated closing date," and the terms "relevant business year" and "end of the immediately preceding business year" in item (iii) of that paragraph shall be deemed to be replaced with "relevant Consolidated Fiscal Year" and "consolidated closing date preceding the relevant consolidated closing date" respectively.

(Notes on Grant or Issuance of Stock Options, Options on the Company's Own Shares or Company's Own Shares)
Article 15-9 The provision of Article 8-14, paragraph (1) of the Ordinance on Financial Statements, etc. shall apply mutatis mutandis to cases where Stock Options or Options on the Company's Own Shares have been granted or the Company's Own Shares have been issued. In this case, the term "business year" in item (i) of that paragraph shall be deemed to be replaced with "Consolidated Fiscal Year."

(Notes on Stock Options)
Article 15-10 The provisions of Article 8-15 (excluding paragraph (9)) of the Ordinance on Financial Statements, etc. shall apply mutatis mutandis to cases where Stock Options have been granted. In this case, the term "in the current business year" in para-

graph (1), item (ii), sub-items (b), (c), (e) and (f), the term "during the current business year" in item (ix) of that paragraph, the term "granted during the current business year" in paragraph (4) of that Article, and the term "during the relevant business year" in paragraph (7) of that Article shall be deemed to be replaced with "in the current Consolidated Fiscal Year," "during the current Consolidated Fiscal Year," "granted during the current Consolidated Fiscal Year," and "during the relevant Consolidated Fiscal Year," respectively, the terms "end of the previous business year" and "end of the current business year" in paragraph (1), item (ii), sub-items (d) and (g) and the term "end of the business year" in paragraph (7) of that Article shall be deemed to be replaced with "end of the previous Consolidated Fiscal Year," "end of the current Consolidated Fiscal Year," and "end of the Consolidated Fiscal Year" respectively, and the term "conditions during the current business year" in paragraph (4) of that Article shall be deemed to be replaced with "conditions during the current Consolidated Fiscal Year."

(Notes on Transactions for which Consideration Consists of Options on the Company's Own Shares or the Company's Own Shares)
Article 15-11 The provisions of Article 8-16 (excluding paragraph (3)) of the Ordinance on Financial Statements, etc. shall apply mutatis mutandis to cases where Options on the Company's Own Shares have been granted or the Company's Own Shares have been delivered in consideration for receipt of service or acquisition of goods.

(Notes in Cases Where a Business Combination through Acquisition Was Implemented)
Article 15-12 (1) In cases where a Business Combination through acquisition of another Enterprise or a business segment of another Enterprise has been carried out during the current Consolidated Fiscal Year, the following matters shall be stated in the notes:
(i) the outline of the Business Combination;
(ii) the period of performance of the Acquired Enterprise or the acquired business included in the Consolidated Financial Statements;
(iii) the acquisition cost for the Acquired Enterprise or the acquired business, and the breakdown thereof;
(iv) in cases where shares have been delivered as the consideration for acquisition, the exchange ratio and the calculation method thereof and the number of shares delivered or to be delivered by class of shares;
(v) in cases where the acquisition has been carried out through multiple transactions, the difference between the acquisition cost of the Acquired Enterprise and the total amount of the acquisition costs of the respective transactions leading to the acquisition;
(vi) the amount of goodwill that occurred, the cause for the occurrence, the amortization method, and the amortization period, or the amount of gain from negative goodwill and the cause for the occurrence;
(vii) the amount of assets accepted and liabilities assumed on the date of the Business Combination, and major breakdown thereof;
(viii) the details of Contingent Consideration (meaning the consideration for acquisition that is additionally delivered or transferred depending on future events or transaction results that occur after the conclusion of the Business Combination, which is specified in the Business Combination contract) provided for in the Business Combination contract and the accounting policy for the current Consolidated Fiscal Year and thereafter;
(ix) in cases where most of the acquisition cost has been allocated to intangible fixed

assets other than goodwill, the amount that has been allocated to intangible fixed assets other than goodwill, the breakdown thereof by major type, and the weighted average amortization period for the entirety thereof and that by major type;
(x) in cases where allocation of the acquisition cost has yet to complete, a statement to that effect, the reason therefor, and if the initial allocation amounts of the acquisition cost were significantly revised in or after the Consolidated Fiscal Year following the Consolidated Fiscal Year in which the Business Combination was carried out, the details of such revision and the amounts as revised; and
(xi) the estimated amount of influence that would be exerted on the consolidated profit and loss statement for the current Consolidated Fiscal Year if the Business Combination is assumed to have been completed on the day of commencement of the Consolidated Fiscal Year, and the calculation method thereof (excluding the cases where said estimated amount of influence has little significance).
(2) Notwithstanding the provision of the preceding paragraph, the notes may be omitted in cases where the transaction pertaining to the Business Combination has little significance; provided, however, that in cases where, despite the little significance of the transactions pertaining to individual Business Combinations during the current Consolidated Fiscal Year, the transactions pertaining to multiple Business Combinations during the current Consolidated Fiscal Year have significance as a whole, the matters set forth in item (i) and items (iii) to (x) inclusive of that paragraph shall be stated in the notes for such Business Combinations as a whole.
(3) The estimated amount of influence set forth in paragraph (1), item (xi) shall be any of the following amounts and, in cases where said notes have yet to receive an audit certification, a statement to that effect shall be made:
(i) the difference between net sales and the profit and loss information calculated by assuming that the Business Combination has been completed on the day of commencement of the Consolidated Fiscal Year and net sales and the profit and loss information on the consolidated profit and loss statement of the Acquiring Enterprise; or
(ii) net sales and the profit and loss information calculated by assuming that the Business Combination has been completed on the day of commencement of the Consolidated Fiscal Year.

Article 15-13 deletion

(Notes on Common Control Transaction, etc.)
Article 15-14 The provisions of Article 8-20 (excluding paragraph (3)) of the Ordinance on Financial Statements, etc. shall apply mutatis mutandis to a Common Control Transaction, etc. In this case, the term "business year" in that Article shall be deemed to be replaced with "Consolidated Fiscal Year."

(Notes on Formation of Jointly Controlled Enterprises)
Article 15-15 The provisions of Article 8-22 (excluding paragraph (3)) of the Ordinance on Financial Statements, etc. shall apply mutatis mutandis to a Formation of Jointly Controlled Enterprises (meaning a Formation of a Jointly Controlled Enterprise prescribed in paragraph (1) of that Article; the same shall apply in paragraph (1) of the following Article). In this case, the term "business year" in Article 8-22 of the Ordinance on Financial Statements, etc. shall be deemed to be replaced with "Consolidated Fiscal Year."

(Notes by Divesting Enterprise in Business Divestitures)

Article 15-16 (1) In cases where a significant Business Divestiture has been carried out during the current Consolidated Fiscal Year, and said Business Divestiture is neither categorized as a Common Control Transaction, etc. nor a Formation of a Jointly Controlled Enterprise, the Divesting Enterprise shall state the following matters in the notes, in the Consolidated Fiscal Year in which the Business Divesture was carried out:
(i) the outline of the Business Divestiture;
(ii) the outline of the accounting implemented;
(iii) the name of the Reporting Segment in which the divested business was included;
(iv) the estimated amount of profit or loss pertaining to the divested business, which is reported on the consolidated profit and loss statement for the current Consolidated Fiscal Year; and
(v) if, for a Business Divestiture for which a gain or loss on transfer has been recognized, there is any continuing involvement other than holding Successor Enterprise shares as Subsidiary Company shares or Affiliated Company shares, the outline of such continuing involvement.
(2) The notes may be omitted for the matters set forth in item (v) of the preceding paragraph in cases where said continuing involvement is insignificant.
(3) In cases where, despite the little significance of the transactions pertaining to individual Business Divestures during the current Consolidated Fiscal Year, the transactions pertaining to multiple Business Divestures during the current Consolidated Fiscal Year have significance as a whole, the matters set forth in items (i) and (ii) of that paragraph shall, notwithstanding the provision of paragraph (1), be stated in the notes for said transactions pertaining to Business Divestures as a whole.

(Notes by Successor Enterprise in Business Divestures)
Article 15-17 The provision of Article 8-24, paragraph (1) of the Ordinance on Financial Statements, etc. shall apply mutatis mutandis to a Business Divesture that is not categorized as a Business Combination.

(Notes on a Business Combination of a Subsidiary Company)
Article 15-18 (1) In cases where a Subsidiary Company is no longer a Subsidiary Company as a result of carrying out a Business Combination, a Company Submitting Consolidated Financial Statements shall state the following matters in the notes, in the Consolidated Fiscal Year in which said Business Combination was carried out:
(i) the outline of the Business Combination carried out by the Subsidiary Company;
(ii) the outline of the accounting implemented:
(iii) the name of the Reporting Segment in which said Subsidiary Company was included;
(iv) the estimated amount of profit or loss pertaining to said Subsidiary Company, which is reported on the consolidated profit and loss statement for the relevant Consolidated Fiscal Year; and
(v) if, for a Business Combination of a Subsidiary Company for which the Parent Company has recognized a gain or loss on exchange of shares, there is any continuing involvement other than holding shares of said Subsidiary Company as Affiliated Company shares, the outline of such continuing involvement.
(2) The notes may be omitted for the matters set forth in item (v) of the preceding paragraph in cases where said continuing involvement is insignificant.
(3) Notwithstanding the provision of paragraph (1), the notes may be omitted in cases where the transaction pertaining to the Business Combination has little significance; provided, however, that in cases where, despite the little significance of the transac-

tions pertaining to individual Business Combinations during the current Consolidated Fiscal Year, the transactions pertaining to multiple Business Combinations during the Consolidated Fiscal Year have significance as a whole, the matters set forth in items (i) and (ii) of that paragraph shall be stated in the notes.

(Notes on Significant Post-Balance Sheet Events, etc. related to Business Combinations)
Article 15-19 The provisions of Article 8-25 (excluding paragraph (3)) of the Ordinance on Financial Statements, etc. shall apply mutatis mutandis to a Significant Post-Balance Sheet Event related to a Business Combination and a Business Combination wherein an agreement has been reached on major conditions by the consolidated closing date and which has not been completed by that date. In this case, the term "balance sheet date" in that Article shall be deemed to be replaced with "consolidated closing date."

(Notes on Significant Post-Balance Sheet Events, etc. related to Business Divestitures)
Article 15-20 The provision of Article 8-26, paragraph (1) of the Ordinance on Financial Statements, etc. shall apply mutatis mutandis to a Significant Post-Balance Sheet Event related to a Business Divestiture and a Business Divesture wherein an agreement has been reached on major conditions by the consolidated closing date and which has not been completed by that date. In this case, the term "balance sheet date" in that paragraph shall be deemed to be replaced with "consolidated closing date."

(Notes on Significant Post-Balance Sheet Events, etc. related to a Business Combination of a Subsidiary Company)
Article 15-21 In cases where a Business Combination of a Subsidiary Company (limited to cases where it is no longer a Subsidiary Company as a result of said Business Combination) is a case set forth in the following items, the matters respectively specified in those items shall be stated in the notes:
(i) cases where a Business Combination of a Subsidiary Company that has been completed after the consolidated closing date is categorized as a Significant Post-Balance Sheet Event: the matters equivalent to the matters set forth in the items of Article 15-18 (1);
(ii) cases where a Business Combination of a Subsidiary Company wherein an agreement has been reached on major conditions after the consolidated closing date is categorized as a Significant Post-Balance Sheet Event: the matters equivalent to the matters set forth in items (i) and (iii) of paragraph (1) of Article 15-18; and
(iii) cases where a Business Combination of a Subsidiary Company wherein an agreement was reached on major conditions before the consolidated closing date has not been completed by that date (excluding the cases set forth in item (i)): the matters equivalent to the matters set forth in items (i) and (iii) of paragraph (1) of Article 15-18.

(Notes on Going Concern Assumption)
Article 15-22 The provision of Article 8-27 of the Ordinance on Financial Statements, etc. shall apply mutatis mutandis to a Company Submitting Consolidated Financial Statements. In this case, the term "balance sheet date" in that Article shall be deemed to be replaced with "consolidated closing date" and the term "Financial Statements" in item (iv) of that Article shall be deemed to be replaced with "Consolidated Financial Statements."

(Notes on Asset Retirement Obligations)
Article 15-23 The provision of Article 8-28 of the Ordinance on Financial Statements, etc. shall apply mutatis mutandis to Asset Retirement Obligations. In this case, the terms "balance sheet" and "the relevant business year" in that Article shall be deemed to be replaced with "consolidated balance sheet" and "the current Consolidated Fiscal Year" respectively.

(Notes on Rental, etc. Real Properties)
Article 15-24 In cases where there is any Rental, etc. Real Property (meaning a real property which is other than a real property classified as an inventory asset and is owned for the purpose of revenues or profits from rental or transfer; hereinafter the same shall apply in this Article), the following matters shall be set down in the notes; provided, however, that in cases where the total amount of Rental, etc. Real Properties has little significance, notes may be omitted:
(i) the outline of any Rental, etc. Real Property;
(ii) the amount of any Rental, etc. Real Property reported in the consolidated balance sheet and any major change during the current Consolidated Fiscal Year;
(iii) the market price of any Rental, etc. Real Property as of the consolidated closing date and the method of calculation of said market price; and
(iv) the profit or loss concerning any Rental, etc. Real Property.

(Noting Method)
Article 16 (1) The notes to be stated pursuant to the provisions of this Ordinance shall be stated immediately after the statements under the provisions of Articles 13 and 14; provided, however, that this shall not apply in the following cases:
(i) in cases where matters related to the matters that are stated pursuant to the provisions of Article 13 are stated together with said notes; or
(ii) in cases where notes that are found appropriate to be stated as Footnotes (meaning the stating of notes at the end of the table or account statement contained in the Consolidated Financial Statements in which the matters pertaining to said notes are stated) are stated as Footnotes.
(2) Notwithstanding the provision of the preceding paragraph, the notes under the provision of Article 15-22 shall be stated immediately after the consolidated cash flow statement. In this case, notwithstanding the provision of Article 13, paragraph (1), the matters stated under the provisions of that Article shall be stated immediately after the notes under the provision of Article 15-22.
(3) In the case of stating notes that are related to a specific account title pursuant to the provisions of this Ordinance, the association between said account title and said notes shall be made clear by appending a symbol to said account title or by other similar method.

(Units for Presenting Amounts)
Article 16-2 The amounts for the account titles and any other matters contained in Consolidated Financial Statements shall be presented in units of million yen or thousand yen.

Chapter II Consolidated Balance Sheet

Section 1 General Provisions

Ordinance on Terminology, Forms, and Preparation Methods of Consolidated Financial Statements, Chap.II, Sec.2　　Art.17～23

(Method for Presenting a Consolidated Balance Sheet)
Article 17　(1) The method for presenting a consolidated balance sheet shall be in accordance with the provisions of this Chapter.
(2) A consolidated balance sheet shall be presented by using Form No. 4.

(Classification into Assets, Liabilities and Net Assets)
Article 18　Assets, liabilities and net assets shall be stated by respectively classifying them into the assets section, liabilities section, and net assets section.

(Classification of Assets and Liabilities by Business)
Article 19　In cases where Consolidated Companies engage in two or more different types of businesses, statements concerning assets and liabilities may be made by categorizing them by type of business.

(Arrangement of Account Titles)
Article 20　The account titles of assets and liabilities shall be arranged by using the method of current arrangement.

Section 2 Assets

(Classification of Assets)
Article 21　Assets shall be stated by classifying them into current assets, fixed assets and deferred assets, and assets categorized as fixed assets shall be further classified into tangible fixed assets, intangible fixed assets, investments, and any other assets.

(Scopes of the Respective Classes of Assets)
Article 22　The provisions of Articles 15 to 16-3 inclusive, 22, 27, 31 to 31-5 inclusive, and 36 of the Ordinance on Financial Statements, etc. shall apply mutatis mutandis to the scopes of current assets, tangible fixed assets, intangible fixed assets, investments and other assets, and deferred assets. In this case, the term "the Company Submitting Financial Statements" in Article 22, item (viii) and Article 27, item (xii) of the Ordinance on Financial Statements, etc. shall be deemed to be replaced with "a Consolidated Company."

(Classified Presentation of Current Assets)
Article 23　(1) Assets categorized as current assets shall be set down under account titles having names that indicate said assets, in accordance with the following classification of items; provided, however, that assets categorized under any of said items of which the amount is not more than one percent of the total amount of assets and which are found appropriate to be presented collectively with assets categorized under another item, may be set down collectively under an account title having an appropriate name:
(i) cash and deposits;
(ii) negotiable instruments receivable and accounts receivable;
(iii) lease receivables and lease investment assets (limited to those that have arisen based on ordinary transactions, and excluding Claims in Bankruptcy, Reorganization, etc. that are clearly not collectible within one year);
(iv) securities;
(v) merchandise and manufactured goods (including semi-finished goods);
(vi) work in progress;

(vii) raw materials and supplies;
(viii) Deferred Tax Assets; and
(ix) others.
(2) Where assets categorized under any of the items set forth in the items of the preceding paragraph are found appropriate to be presented separately, the provision of that paragraph shall not preclude one from separately setting down said assets under an account title having a name that indicates said assets.
(3) Among the assets categorized under the item set forth in paragraph (1), item (ix), any asset of which the amount exceeds five percent of the total amount of assets shall be set down separately under an account title having a name that indicates said asset.
(4) Notwithstanding the provision of the main clause of paragraph (1), assets categorized under the items set forth in items (v) to (vii) inclusive of said paragraph may be set down collectively under the account title of inventory assets. In this case, the account titles of the assets categorized under said items and the amounts thereof shall be stated in the notes.

(Presentation of Allowances pertaining to Current Assets)
Article 24 The provisions of Article 20 of the Ordinance on Financial Statements, etc. shall apply mutatis mutandis to allowances pertaining to assets categorized as current assets.

Article 25 Deleted.

(Classified Presentation of Tangible Fixed Assets)
Article 26 (1) Assets categorized as tangible fixed assets shall be set down under account titles having names that indicate said assets, in accordance with the following classification of items; provided, however, that assets categorized under any of said items of which the amount is not more than one percent of the total amount of assets and which are found appropriate to be presented collectively with assets categorized under another item, may be set down collectively under an account title having an appropriate name:
(i) buildings (including their attached facilities) and structures;
(ii) machinery and equipment (including their attached facilities) and delivery equipment (vessels and water delivery equipment, railway vehicles and any other land delivery equipment, and aircrafts);
(iii) land;
(iv) leased assets (limited to assets for which a Consolidated Company is the lessee of the Leased Property in finance lease transactions, and where said Leased Property is any of the objects set forth in the preceding three items or in item (vi));
(v) construction in progress; and
(vi) others.
(2) The provision of Article 23, paragraph (2) shall apply mutatis mutandis to the cases set forth in the preceding paragraph.
(3) Notwithstanding the provision of paragraph (1), assets categorized as the leased assets set forth in item (iv) of that paragraph may be included in any of the items set forth in the items of that paragraph (excluding items (iv) and (v)).
(4) The provision of Article 23, paragraph (3) shall apply mutatis mutandis to the assets set forth in paragraph (1), item (vi).

(Presentation of the Amounts of Accumulated Depreciation)
Article 27 The provisions of Articles 25 and 26 of the Ordinance on Financial State-

ments, etc. shall apply mutatis mutandis to the amounts of accumulated depreciation for buildings, structures, and any other tangible fixed assets.

(Presentation of the Amounts of Accumulated Impairment Loss)
Article 27-2 The provisions of Article 26-2 of the Ordinance on Financial Statements, etc. shall apply mutatis mutandis to the amounts of accumulated impairment loss for tangible fixed assets.

(Classified Presentation of Intangible Fixed Assets)
Article 28 (1) Assets categorized as intangible fixed assets shall be set down under account titles having names that indicate said assets, in accordance with the following classification of items; provided, however, that assets categorized under the item set forth in item (i) or item (ii) of which the amount is not more than one percent of the total amount of assets may be set down collectively with assets categorized under item (iii):
(i) goodwill;
(ii) leased assets (limited to assets for which a Consolidated Company is the lessee of the Leased Property in finance lease transactions, and where said Leased Property is categorized under the following item); and
(iii) others.
(2) The provision of Article 23, paragraph (2) shall apply mutatis mutandis to the cases set forth in the preceding paragraph.
(3) Notwithstanding the provision of paragraph (1), assets categorized as the leased assets set forth in item (ii) of that paragraph may be included in the item set forth in item (iii) of that paragraph.
(4) The provision of Article 23, paragraph (3) shall apply mutatis mutandis to the assets set forth in paragraph (1), item (iii).
(5) A difference that results from investments by Consolidated Companies being in excess of the amount of corresponding equity of Consolidated Subsidiary Companies shall be presented by including it into goodwill.

Article 29 The provision of Article 30 of the Ordinance on Financial Statements, etc. shall apply mutatis mutandis to the amounts of accumulated amortization and the amounts of accumulated impairment loss for intangible fixed assets.

(Classified Presentation of Investments and Other Assets, etc.)
Article 30 (1) Assets categorized as investments and other assets shall be set down under account titles having names that indicate said assets, in accordance with the following classification of items; provided, however, that assets categorized under any of said items of which the amount is not more than one percent of the total amount of assets and which are found appropriate to be presented collectively with assets categorized under another item, may be set down collectively under an account title having an appropriate name:
(i) investment securities;
(ii) long-term loans;
(iii) Deferred Tax Assets; and
(iv) others.
(2) The amounts of shares and company bonds of Non-consolidated Subsidiary Companies and Affiliated Companies, any Other Securities (meaning securities other than shares and company bonds) issued by Non-consolidated Subsidiary Companies and Affiliated Companies, and investments in capital of Non-consolidated Subsidiary Companies and

Affiliated Companies shall be stated in the notes, respectively.
(3) In the statements set forth in the preceding paragraph, the amount of investments in jointly controlled enterprises shall be stated in the notes as a constituent item of shares, etc. of Affiliated Companies.
(4) The provision of Article 23, paragraph (2) shall apply mutatis mutandis to the cases set forth in paragraph (1).
(5) The provision of Article 23, paragraph (3) shall apply mutatis mutandis to the assets set forth in paragraph (1), item (iv).

Article 30-2 The provision of Article 32-3 of the Ordinance on Financial Statements, etc. shall apply mutatis mutandis to Deferred Tax Assets pertaining to revaluation prescribed in Article 7, paragraph (1) of the Act on Revaluation of Land (Act No. 34 of 1998; hereinafter referred to as the "Land Revaluation Act").

(Presentation of Allowances pertaining to Investments and Other Assets)
Article 31 The provisions of Article 20 of the Ordinance on Financial Statements, etc. as applied mutatis mutandis pursuant to Article 34 of that Ordinance shall apply mutatis mutandis to allowances pertaining to assets categorized as investments and other assets.

(Classified Presentation of Deferred Assets)
Article 32 (1) Assets categorized as deferred assets shall be set down under account titles having names that indicate said assets, in accordance with the following classification of items; provided, however, that assets categorized under any of said items of which the amount is not more than one percent of the total amount of assets and which are found appropriate to be presented collectively with assets categorized under another item, may be set down collectively under an account title having an appropriate name:
(i) deferred organization expenses;
(ii) business commencement expenses;
(iii) stock issuance expenses;
(iv) company bond issuance expenses; and
(v) development expenses.
(2) The provision of Article 23, paragraph (2) shall apply mutatis mutandis to the cases set forth in the preceding paragraph.

Article 33 The provision of Article 38 of the Ordinance on Financial Statements, etc. shall apply mutatis mutandis to the amounts of accumulated amortization for deferred assets.

Article 34 Deleted.

(Notes on Revaluation of Land for Business Use)
Article 34-2 The provisions of Article 42-2 of the Ordinance on Financial Statements, etc. shall apply mutatis mutandis to notes on the revaluation of land for business use under the provisions of the Land Revaluation Act.

(Notes on Collateral Assets)
Article 34-3 The provision of Article 43 of the Ordinance on Financial Statements, etc. shall apply mutatis mutandis to assets that have been provided as collateral.

Section 3 Liabilities

(Classification of Liabilities)

Article 35 Liabilities shall be stated by classifying them into current liabilities and fixed liabilities.

(Scopes of the Respective Classes of Liabilities)

Article 36 The provisions of Articles 47 to 48-4 inclusive and 51 to 51-5 inclusive of the Ordinance on Financial Statements, etc. shall apply mutatis mutandis to the scopes of current liabilities and fixed liabilities.

(Classified Presentation of Current Liabilities)

Article 37 (1) Liabilities categorized as current liabilities shall be set down under account titles having names that indicate said liabilities, in accordance with the following classification of items; provided, however, that liabilities categorized under an item other than that set forth in item (vi) of which the amount is not more than one percent of the combined total of liabilities and net assets and which are found appropriate to be presented collectively with liabilities categorized under another item, may be set down collectively under an account title having an appropriate name:

(i) negotiable instruments payable and accounts payable;
(ii) short-term borrowings (including finance negotiable instruments and overdrafts);
(iii) lease obligations;
(iv) accrued Corporation Tax, etc. ;
(v) Deferred Tax Liabilities;
(vi) allowances;
(vii) Asset Retirement Obligations; and
(viii) others.

(2) Where liabilities categorized under any of the items set forth in the items of the preceding paragraph are found appropriate to be presented separately, the provision of that paragraph shall not preclude one from separately setting down said liabilities under an account title having a name that indicates said liabilities.

(3) The accrued Corporation Tax, etc. set forth in paragraph (1), item (iv) means accrued amounts of corporation tax, Inhabitants Tax (meaning prefectural inhabitants tax and municipal inhabitants tax; the same shall apply hereinafter), and enterprise tax.

(4) The allowances set forth in paragraph (1), item (vi) shall be set down under an account title having a name that indicates the purpose of establishment of said allowance; provided, however, that such allowances of which the amount is small and which are found appropriate to be presented collectively with liabilities categorized under another item may be set down collectively under an account title having an appropriate name.

(5) Among the liabilities categorized under the item set forth in paragraph (1), item (viii), any liability of which the amount exceeds five percent of the combined total of liabilities and net assets shall be set down under an account title having a name that indicates said liability.

(Classified Presentation of Fixed Liabilities)

Article 38 (1) Liabilities categorized as fixed liabilities shall be set down under account titles having names that indicate said liabilities, in accordance with the following classification of items; provided, however, that liabilities categorized under an item other than that set forth in item (v) of which the amount is not more than one percent of the combined total of liabilities and net assets and which are found appropriate to be pre-

sented collectively with liabilities categorized under another item, may be set down collectively under an account title having an appropriate name:
(i) company bonds;
(ii) long-term borrowings (including finance negotiable instruments; the same shall apply hereinafter);
(iii) lease obligations;
(iv) Deferred Tax Liabilities;
(v) allowances;
(vi) Asset Retirement Obligations; and
(vii) others.
(2) The provision of paragraph (2) of the preceding Article shall apply mutatis mutandis to the cases set forth in the preceding paragraph.
(3) The provision of paragraph (4) of the preceding Article shall apply mutatis mutandis to the allowances set forth in paragraph (1), item (v).
(4) The provision of paragraph (5) of the preceding Article shall apply mutatis mutandis to liabilities categorized under the item set forth in paragraph (1), item (vii).

Article 39 The provision of Article 52-2 of the Ordinance on Financial Statements, etc. shall apply mutatis mutandis to Deferred Tax Liabilities pertaining to revaluation prescribed in Article 7, paragraph (1) of the Act on Revaluation of Land.

(Notes on Contingent Liabilities)
Article 39-2 In cases where there are Contingent Liabilities (meaning guarantee of debts (including acts that have the same effect as guarantee of debts), obligations for compensation pertaining to contentious cases, and other liabilities that have not arisen in reality but may be borne by the business in the future) pertaining to any Consolidated Company, the contents and amounts thereof shall be stated in the notes; provided, however, that notes may be omitted for matters having little significance.

(Notes on the Amount of Discount on Negotiable Instruments and the Amount of Transfer by Endorsement)
Article 39-3 The provisions of Article 58-2 of the Ordinance on Financial Statements, etc. shall apply mutatis mutandis to negotiable instruments that have been discounted or that have been transferred by endorsement for the purpose repaying debts.

(Presentation of Inventory Assets and Reserve for Loss on Construction Contracts)
Article 40 The provisions of Article 54-4 of the Ordinance on Financial Statements, etc. shall apply mutatis mutandis to presentation of inventory assets and reserve for loss on construction contracts.

(Notes on Specified Accounts Pertaining to Business Combination)
Article 41 The provision of Article 56 of the Ordinance on Financial Statements, etc. shall apply mutatis mutandis to specified accounts pertaining to a Business Combination.

Section 4 Net Assets

(Classification of Net Assets)
Article 42 Net assets shall be stated by classifying them into shareholders' equity, valu-

ation and translation adjustments, share options, and Minority Shareholders' Equity.

(Classification and Classified Presentation of Shareholders' Equity)

Article 43 (1) Shareholders' equity shall be classified into stated capital, capital surplus, and retained earnings, and shall be set down under the account titles of stated capital, capital surplus, and retained earnings respectively.

(2) The provisions of Article 62, Article 63, paragraph (2), and Article 65, paragraph (2) of the Ordinance on Financial Statements, etc. shall apply mutatis mutandis to a deposit for subscriptions to shares and to any reserve specified by law that is equivalent to capital reserve or retained earnings reserve.

(3) Treasury Shares shall be set down as a deduction corresponding to shareholders' equity, under the account title of Treasury Shares immediately after retained earnings.

(4) Notwithstanding the provision of paragraph (1), a deposit for subscriptions as after the application date, pertaining to disposal of Treasury Shares, shall be set down under the account title of a deposit for subscriptions to Treasury Shares, immediately after Treasury Shares.

(Classification and Classified Presentation of Valuation and Translation Adjustments)

Article 43-2 (1) Valuation and translation adjustments shall be set down in accordance with the following classification of items, under account titles having names that indicate said items:

(i) the valuation difference on other securities defined in Article 67, paragraph (1), item (i) of the Ordinance on Financial Statements, etc. ;

(ii) the deferred gain or loss on hedges defined in Article 67, paragraph (1), item (ii) of the Ordinance on Financial Statements, etc. ;

(iii) the land revaluation difference defined in Article 67, paragraph (1), item (iii) of the Ordinance on Financial Statements, etc. ; and

(iv) Foreign Currency Translation Adjustments (meaning the translation difference that results from the difference between the exchange rate used for translating the assets and liabilities of any Subsidiary Company or Affiliated Company in a foreign state and the exchange rate used for translating the net assets of such company);

(2) In addition to the items set forth in the preceding paragraph, any item that is found appropriate to be reported as an item of valuation and translation adjustments may be set down under an account title having a name that indicates said item.

(Presentation of Share Options)

Article 43-3 (1) Share options shall be set down under the account title of share options.

(2) Share options issued by the Company Submitting Consolidated Financial Statements held by the Company Submitting Consolidated Financial Statements itself and share options issued by any Consolidated Subsidiary Company held by said Consolidated Subsidiary Company itself shall be deducted from share options; provided, however, that this shall not preclude one from setting down such share options under the account title of own share options, immediately after share options, as a deduction corresponding to share options.

(Presentation of Minority Shareholders' Equity)

Article 43-4 Minority Shareholders' Equity shall be set down under the account title of Minority Shareholders' Equity.

(Notes on Reserve Funds under Contracts)

Article 44 In cases where the amount of retained earnings prescribed in Article 43 (1) include a reserve for bond sinking fund or any other reserve funds accumulated for a specific purpose under a contract, etc. with a creditor, the contents and amounts thereof shall be stated in the notes.

(Notes on the Per Share Amount of Net Assets)
Article 44-2 The per share amount of net assets shall be stated in the notes.

Section 5 Miscellaneous Provisions

(Presentation of Deferred Tax Assets or Deferred Tax Liabilities)
Article 45 (1) In cases where there are the Deferred Tax Assets set forth in Article 23, paragraph (1), item (viii) and the Deferred Tax Liabilities set forth in Article 37, paragraph (1), item (v), the difference between them, excluding those pertaining to different taxable entities, shall be presented as Deferred Tax Assets or Deferred Tax Liabilities under current assets or under current liabilities.

(2) In cases where there are the Deferred Tax Assets set forth in Article 30, paragraph (1), item (iii) and the Deferred Tax Liabilities set forth in Article 38, paragraph (1), item (iv), the difference between them, excluding those pertaining to different taxable entities, shall be presented as Deferred Tax Assets or Deferred Tax Liabilities under investments and other assets or under fixed liabilities.

(Reserves, etc. under Special Laws)
Article 45-2 (1) Reserves or allowances that must be reported under the name of reserves or allowances pursuant to the provisions of laws and regulations and that are inappropriate to be reported in the assets section or the liabilities section (hereinafter referred to as "Reserves, etc.") shall be stated under a separate class that has been added immediately after fixed liabilities, notwithstanding the provisions of Articles 20 and 35.

(2) Reserves, etc. shall be set down under an account title having a name that indicates the purpose of establishment of said Reserves, etc. , and the provisions of law or regulations that provide for the reporting thereof shall be stated in the notes.

(3) With regard to Reserves, etc. , the distinction of whether or not they are recognized to be used within one year shall be stated in the notes; provided, however, that this shall not apply when it is difficult to make such distinction.

(Statement of Assets and Liabilities of a Listed Business)
Article 46 In cases where the main business of a Business Group is a business set forth in the appended list of the Ordinance on Financial Statements, etc. (hereinafter referred to as a "Listed Business"), if it is found inappropriate to state its assets and liabilities by the classification under the provisions of Articles 21 and 35, notwithstanding these provisions, said assets and liabilities may be stated by equivalent classification as that specified by a Law, Regulations, or Rules (meaning the law, regulations, or Rules prescribed in Article 2 of the Ordinance on Financial Statements, etc.; the same shall apply hereinafter) applicable to the financial statements of the company(ies) engaged in said Listed Business. In this case, the governing Law, Regulations or Rules shall be stated in the notes.

(Statement of Net Assets of Designated Juridical Persons)
Article 46-2 In cases where a Designated Juridical Person prepares a consolidated balance sheet, if it is found inappropriate to state its net assets pursuant to this Ordi-

nance, said Designated Juridical Person may state its net assets in an equivalent manner as under the provisions of a Law, Regulations, or Rules applicable to its financial statements. In this case, the governing Law, Regulations, or Rules shall be stated in the notes.

(Statement of Account Titles for Assets and Liabilities of a Listed Business)
Article 47 (1) In cases where the businesses conducted by any Consolidated Company include a Listed Business, if it is found inappropriate to state the account titles for assets and liabilities of said Listed Business according to the classification of the items prescribed in Article 23, paragraph (1), Article 26, paragraph (1), Article 28, paragraph (1), Article 30, paragraph (1), Article 37, paragraph (1), and Article 38, paragraph (1), notwithstanding these provisions, said account titles may be stated in an equivalent manner as under the provisions of a Law, Regulations, or Rules applicable to the financial statements of the company engaged in said Listed Business.
(2) In the cases set forth in the preceding paragraph, the standards for setting down the account titles of assets and liabilities collectively or separately shall be equivalent to those provided under this Ordinance.

Chapter III Consolidated Profit and Loss Statement

Section 1 General Provisions

(Method for Presenting a Consolidated Profit and Loss Statement)
Article 48 (1) The method for presenting a consolidated profit and loss statement shall be in accordance with the provisions of this Chapter.
(2) A consolidated profit and loss statement shall be presented by using Form No. 5.

(Classification of Revenues and Expenses)
Article 49 Revenues and expenses shall be stated by classifying them into account titles having names that indicate the following items:
(i) net sales;
(ii) cost of sales (including service costs; the same shall apply hereinafter);
(iii) selling expenses and general and administrative expenses;
(iv) non-operating revenues;
(v) non-operating expenses;
(vi) extraordinary profit; and
(vii) extraordinary loss.

(Statement of Net Sales, etc. by Business)
Article 50 In cases where Consolidated Companies engage in two or more different types of businesses, the statements on revenues and expenses set forth in items (i) to (iii) of the preceding Article may be made by classifying them by type of business.

Section 2 Net Sales and Cost of Sales

(Presentation Method for Net Sales)
Article 51 Net sales shall be set down under an account title having a name that indicates net sales.

(Presentation Method for the Valuation Difference of Inventory Assets)

Article 51-2 The valuation difference of inventory assets held for the purpose of gaining profits through fluctuations in market prices shall be stated by including it under the account title having a name that indicates net sales; provided, however, that in cases where said amount has little significance, said amount may be stated by including it in non-operating revenues or non-operating expenses.

(Presentation Method for the Cost of Sales)
Article 52 The cost of sales shall be set down under an account title having a name that indicates the cost of sales.

(Notes on Provision of Reserve for Loss on Construction Contracts)
Article 52-2 The provision of Article 76-2 of the Ordinance on Financial Statements, etc. shall apply mutatis mutandis to provision of reserve for loss on construction contracts.

(Statement on Write-down of the Book Value of Inventory Assets)
Article 53 (1) In the case of having written-down the book value of inventory assets held for the purpose of ordinary sales due to a decline in profitability, said written-down amount (in cases of returning, in the current Consolidated Fiscal Year, the written-down amount that had been reported at the end of the previous Consolidated Fiscal Year, it shall be the amount obtained by offsetting said returned amount against the written-down amount reported at the end of the current Consolidated Fiscal Year) shall be set down separately under an account title having a name that indicates the contents thereof, as a constituent item of the cost of sales or of any other item; provided, however, that this shall not preclude one from reporting the ending inventory of said inventory assets in the amount as after the write-down of the book value, and setting down a statement to that effect and said written-down amount in the notes.
(2) Notwithstanding the provision of the preceding paragraph, in cases where said written-down amount has little significance, the amount may be omitted from being set down separately or being stated in the notes.

(Presentation of the Gross Profit or Loss on Sales)
Article 54 The amount of difference between net sales and the cost of sales shall be presented as the gross profit on sales or the gross loss on sales.

Section 3 Selling Expenses and General and Administrative Expenses

(Presentation Method for Selling Expenses and General and Administrative Expenses)
Article 55 (1) Selling expenses and general and administrative expenses shall be classified into expense items that are found to be appropriate, and be set down under account titles having names that indicate said expenses; provided, however, that this shall not preclude one from setting down said expenses under the account title of selling expenses, the account title of general and administrative expenses, or the account title of selling expenses and general and administrative expenses collectively, and stating the major expense items and amounts thereof in the notes.
(2) The major expense items prescribed in the proviso to the preceding paragraph shall be provision of allowance (excluding such expense items of which the amount is small) and any other expense items of which the amount exceeds ten percent of the combined total of selling expenses and general and administrative expenses.

(Notes on Research and Development Expenses)
Article 55-2 With regard to the research and development expenses included in the general and administrative expenses and in the manufacturing expenses for the period, the total amount thereof shall be stated in the notes.

(Presentation of the Amount of Operating Profit and Loss)
Article 56 The amount obtained by adjusting the gross profit on sales or the gross loss on sales by adding or subtracting the total amount of selling expenses and general and administrative expenses shall be stated as the amount of operating profit or the amount of operating loss.

Section 4 Non-operating Revenues and Non-operating Expenses

(Presentation Method for Non-operating Revenues)
Article 57 Revenues categorized as non-operating revenues shall be set down under account titles having names that indicate said revenues, in accordance with the classification of interest income (including interest on securities), dividends income, gain on sales of securities, investment return under the Equity Method, and others; provided, however, that any revenues of which the amounts are not more than ten percent of the total amount of non-operating revenues, which are found appropriate to be presented collectively, may be set down under an account title having a name that collectively indicates said revenues.

(Presentation Method for Non-operating Expenses)
Article 58 Expenses categorized as non-operating expenses shall be set down under account titles having names that indicate said expenses, in accordance with the classification of interest expenses (including interest on company bonds), loss on sales of securities, investment loss under the Equity Method, and others; provided, however, that any expenses of which the amounts are not more than ten percent of the total amount of non-operating expenses, which are found appropriate to be presented collectively, may be set down under an account title having a name that collectively indicates said expenses.

Article 59 Deleted.

Article 60 Deleted.

(Presentation of the Amount of Ordinary IProfit and Loss)
Article 61 The amount obtained by adjusting the amount of operating profit or the amount of operating loss by adding or subtracting the total amount of non-operating revenues or the total amount of non-operating expenses shall be stated as the amount of ordinary profit or the amount of ordinary loss.

Section 5 Extraordinary Profit and Extraordinary Loss

(Presentation Method for Extraordinary Profit)
Article 62 Profits categorized as extraordinary profit shall be set down under account titles having names that indicate said profits, in accordance with the classification of gain on prior period adjustment, gain on sales of fixed assets, gain from negative goodwill and others; provided, however, that any profits of which the amounts are not more

than ten percent of the total amount of extraordinary profit, which are found appropriate to be presented collectively, may be set down under an account title having a name that collectively indicates said profits.

(Presentation Method for Extraordinary Loss)
Article 63 Losses categorized as extraordinary loss shall be set down under account titles having names that indicate said losses, in accordance with the classification of loss on prior period adjustment, loss on sales of fixed assets, impairment loss, loss on disaster, and others; provided, however, that any losses of which the amounts are not more than ten percent of the total amount of extraordinary loss, which are found appropriate to be presented collectively, may be set down under an account title having a name that collectively indicates said losses.

(Notes on Impairment Loss)
Article 63-2 The provision of Article 95-3-2 of the Ordinance on Financial Statements, etc. shall apply mutatis mutandis to assets or Asset Groups (meaning the asset groups defined in that Article) for which impairment loss has been recognized.

(Notes on Gain on Reversal of Specified Accounts Pertaining to Business Combination)
Article 63-3 The provision of Article 95-3-3 of the Ordinance on Financial Statements, etc. shall apply mutatis mutandis pursuant to gain on reversal of specified accounts pertaining to Business Combination.

(Presentation of Net Profit or Net Loss for the Period Before Taxes)
Article 64 The amount obtained by adjusting the amount of ordinary profit or the amount of ordinary loss by adding or subtracting the total amount of extraordinary profit or the total amount of extraordinary loss shall be presented as the amount of net profit for the period before taxes or the amount of net loss for the period before taxes.

Section 6 Net Profit for the Period or Net Loss for the Period

(Net Profit for the Period or Net Loss for the Period)
Article 65 (1) The amounts of the following items shall be stated under account titles having names that indicate the contents thereof, immediately after the amount of net profit for the period before taxes or the amount of net loss for the period before taxes:
  (i) the corporation tax, Inhabitants Tax, and Enterprise Tax (meaning the enterprise tax imposed on amounts related to profits as the tax base; the same shall apply in the following item) pertaining to the relevant Consolidated Fiscal Year; and
  (ii) the Deferred Corporation Tax, etc. (meaning adjustments on the corporation tax, Inhabitants Tax, and Enterprise Tax set forth in the preceding item, which are reported through application of Tax Effect Accounting).
(2) The amount obtained by adjusting the amount of net profit for the period before taxes or the amount of net loss for the period before taxes by adding or subtracting the amounts of the items set forth in the respective items of the preceding paragraph shall be stated as the amount of net profit for the period before minority shareholder profit or loss adjustment or the amount of net loss for the period before minority shareholder profit or loss adjustment.
(3) The amount that represents Minority Shareholders' Equity in the amount of net profit for the period before taxes or the amount of net loss for the period before taxes shall

be stated, under an account title having a name that indicates the contents thereof, next to the amount of net profit for the period before minority shareholder profit or loss adjustment or the amount of net loss for the period before minority shareholder profit or loss adjustment.
(4) The amount obtained by adjusting the amount of net profit for the period before minority shareholder profit or loss adjustment or the amount of net loss for the period before minority shareholder profit or loss adjustment by adding or subtracting the amount that represents Minority Shareholders' Equity in the amount of net profit for the period before taxes or the amount of net loss for the period before taxes shall be stated as the amount of net profit for the period or the amount of net loss for the period.
(5) In cases where there are taxes paid or taxed refunded due to correction, determination, etc. of Corporation Tax, etc. , they shall be stated under an account title having a name that indicates the contents thereof, immediately after the item set forth in paragraph (1), item (i); provided, however, that such amounts may be presented by including them in the amount of the item set forth in paragraph (1), item (i) in cases where such amounts have little significance.

(Notes on the Per Share Amount of Net Profit or Loss for the Period)
Article 65-2 (1) The per share amount of net profit for the period or per share amount of net loss for the period, and the basis for calculation of said amount shall be stated in the notes.
(2) The provision of Article 95-5-2, paragraph (2) of the Ordinance on Financial Statements, etc. shall apply mutatis mutandis to the diluted per share amount of net profit for the period.
(3) The provision of Article 95-5-2, paragraph (3) of the Ordinance on Financial Statements, etc. shall apply mutatis mutandis to cases where any reverse stock split or stock split has been carried out during the current Consolidated Fiscal Year. In this case, the term "previous business year" in the proviso to that paragraph and item (ii) of that paragraph shall be deemed to be replaced with "previous Consolidated Fiscal Year."
(4) The provision of Article 95-5-2, paragraph (4) of the Ordinance on Financial Statements, etc. shall apply mutatis mutandis to cases where any reverse stock split or stock split has been carried out after the consolidated balance sheet date. In this case, the term "current business year" in the proviso to that paragraph and item (iii) of that paragraph shall be deemed to be replaced with "current Consolidated Fiscal Year."

Section 7 Miscellaneous Provisions

(Classified Presentation of a Provision of Allowance)
Article 66 (1) A provision of allowance shall be set down separately under an account title having a name that indicates the purpose of establishment thereof and the fact that it is a provision of allowance; provided, however, that in the cases under Article 52-2 and the proviso to paragraph (1) of Article 55, the contents and the amount thereof may be stated in the notes in lieu of setting down the amount separately.
(2) In cases under the provision of the main clause of the preceding paragraph, such provision of allowance of which the amount is small and which are found appropriate to be presented collectively with another account title may be set down collectively under an account title having an appropriate name.

(Presentation of the Investment Return, etc. under the Equity Method)

Article 66-2 In cases where investment return and investment loss under the Equity Method arise, the amount obtained by offsetting one against the other may be presented.

(Provision or Reversal of Reserves, etc. under Special Laws)
Article 67 If there has been a provision or reversal of a Reserve, etc. , the amount of the provision or reversal shall be set down as an extraordinary loss or extraordinary profit under an account title having a name that indicates that the amount results from said provision or reversal.

(Classification of Revenues and Expenses of a Listed Business)
Article 68 In cases where the main business of a Business Group is a Listed Business, if it is found inappropriate to state its revenues and expenses by classifying them into the items prescribed in Article 49, notwithstanding the provision of that Article, said revenues and expenses may be stated in an equivalent manner as under the provisions of a Law, Regulations, or Rules applicable to the financial statements of the company(ies) engaged in said Listed Business. In this case, the governing Law, Regulations or Rules shall be stated in the notes.

(Statement of Account Titles for Revenues and Expenses of a Listed Business)
Article 69 (1) In cases where the businesses conducted by any Consolidated Company include a Listed Business, if it is found inappropriate to state the account titles for revenues and expenses of said Listed Business according to the provisions of Article 51, Article 52, Article 55, Article 57, and Article 58, notwithstanding these provisions, said account titles may be stated in an equivalent manner as under the provisions of a Law, Regulations, or Rules applicable to the Financial Statements of the company engaged in said Listed Business.

(2) In the cases set forth in the preceding paragraph, the standards for setting down the account titles of revenues and expenses collectively or separately shall be equivalent to those provided under this Ordinance.

Chapter IV Consolidated Statement of Changes in Net Assets

Section 1 General Provisions

(Method for Presenting a Consolidated Statement of Changes in Net Assets)
Article 70 (1) The method for presenting a consolidated statement of changes in net assets shall be in accordance with the provisions of this Chapter.

(2) A consolidated statement of changes in net assets shall be presented by using Form No. 6.

(Classified Presentation of a Consolidated Statement of Changes in Net Assets)
Article 71 (1) A consolidated statement of changes in net assets shall be stated by classifying it into shareholders' equity, valuation and translation adjustments, share options, and Minority Shareholders' Equity.

(2) A consolidated statement of changes in net assets shall be classified into appropriate items, and shall be set down under account titles having names that indicate said items. Said items and account titles shall be consistent with the items and account titles in the net asset section of the consolidated balance sheet at the end of the previ-

ous Consolidated Fiscal Year and at the end of the current Consolidated Fiscal Year.

Section 2 Shareholders' Equity

Article 72 (1) Shareholders' equity shall be stated by classifying it into the balance at the end of the previous Consolidated Fiscal Year, the amount of changes during the current Consolidated Fiscal Year, and the balance at the end of the current Consolidated Fiscal Year.
(2) The amount of changes during the current Consolidated Fiscal Year for the account titles stated under shareholders' equity shall be stated for each cause of such changes.
(3) Dividends of surplus shall be presented as a cause of changes in capital surpluses or retained earnings.
(4) The amount of net profit for the period or the amount of net loss for the period shall be presented as a cause of changes in retained earnings.

Section 3 Valuation and Translation Adjustments

Article 73 (1) Valuation and translation adjustments shall be stated by classifying them into the balance at the end of the previous Consolidated Fiscal Year, the amount of changes during the current Consolidated Fiscal Year, and the balance at the end of the current Consolidated Fiscal Year.
(2) With regard to the account titles stated under valuation and translation adjustments, the amount of changes during the current Consolidated Fiscal Year shall be stated collectively; provided, however, that this shall not preclude one from stating or stating in the notes such amount for each major cause of the changes.

Article 74 The provision of Article 104 of the Ordinance on Financial Statements, etc. shall apply mutatis mutandis to valuation and translation adjustments. In this case, the terms "Article 100, paragraph (2)," "the end of the previous business year," "the end of the current business year," and "the amount of changes during the current business year" in that Article shall be deemed to be replaced with "Article 71, paragraph (2)," "the end of the previous Consolidated Fiscal Year," "the end of the current Consolidated Fiscal Year," and "the amount of changes during the current Consolidated Fiscal Year" respectively.

Section 4 Share Options

Article 75 (1) Share options shall be stated by classifying them into the balance at the end of the previous Consolidated Fiscal Year, the amount of changes during the current Consolidated Fiscal Year, and the balance at the end of the current Consolidated Fiscal Year.
(2) The amount of changes during the current Consolidated Fiscal Year for share options shall be stated collectively; provided, however, that this shall not preclude one from stating or stating in the notes such amount for each major cause of the changes.

Section 5 Minority Shareholders' Equity

Article 76 (1) Minority Shareholders' Equity shall be stated by classifying it into the balance at the end of the previous Consolidated Fiscal Year, the amount of changes during the current Consolidated Fiscal Year, and the balance at the end of the current Consoli-

dated Fiscal Year.
(2) The amount of changes during the current Consolidated Fiscal Year for Minority Shareholders' Equity shall be stated collectively; provided, however, that this shall not preclude one from stating or stating in the notes such amount for each major cause of the changes.

Section 6 Matters to be Stated in the Notes

(Notes on Issued Shares)
Article 77 The provision of Article 106, paragraph (1) of the Ordinance on Financial Statements, etc. shall apply mutatis mutandis to issued shares. In this case, the terms "the end of the previous business year," "the end of the current business year" and "during the current business year" in item (i) of paragraph (1) of that Article shall be deemed to be replaced with "the end of the previous Consolidated Fiscal Year," "the end of the current Consolidated Fiscal Year" and "during the current Consolidated Fiscal Year" respectively.

(Notes on Treasury Shares)
Article 78 The provision of Article 107 of the Ordinance on Financial Statements, etc. shall apply mutatis mutandis to Treasury Shares. In this case, the terms "the end of the previous business year," "the end of the current business year" and "during the current business year" in item (i) of that Article shall be deemed to be replaced with "the end of the previous Consolidated Fiscal Year," "the end of the current Consolidated Fiscal Year" and "during the current Consolidated Fiscal Year" respectively.

(Notes on Share Options, etc.)
Article 79 (1) With regard to share options, the following matters shall be stated in the notes:
(i) the class(es) of shares subject to the share options;
(ii) the total number of shares subject to share options; and
(iii) the balance of share options at the end of the Consolidated Fiscal Year.
(2) In cases where share options have been granted as Stock Options or Options on the Company's Own Shares, the matters set forth in items (i) and (ii) of the preceding paragraph shall not be required to be stated.
(3) The number of shares set forth in paragraph (1), item (ii) shall be stated by stating the number of shares subject to the share options at the end of the previous Consolidated Fiscal Year and at the end of the current Consolidated Fiscal Year, the number of shares that increased or decreased during the current Consolidated Fiscal Year, and the outline of the cause for changes, for each class of shares subject to the share option; provided, however, that the notes may be omitted in cases where the number of shares that will increase when supposing that the share options are exercised constitutes an insignificant proportion of the total number of issued shares (when holding Treasury Shares, the number of shares after deducting the number of said Treasury Shares) at the end of the Consolidated Fiscal Year.
(4) The balance of share options at the end of the Consolidated Fiscal Year set forth in paragraph (1), item (iii) shall be stated by classifying it into that of share options of the Company Submitting Consolidated Financial Statements and that of share options of Consolidated Subsidiary Companies.
(5) With regard to own share options, the following matters shall be stated in the notes in order to clarify the corresponding share options:
(i) with regard to share options issued by the Company Submitting Consolidated Fi-

nancial Statements held by the Company Submitting Consolidated Financial Statements itself, the matters set forth in the items of paragraph (1); and
(ii) with regard to share options issued by any Consolidated Subsidiary Company held by said Consolidated Subsidiary Company itself, the matters set forth in paragraph (1), item (iii).

(Notes on Dividends)
Article 80 The provision of Article 109, paragraph (1) of the Ordinance on Financial Statements, etc. shall apply mutatis mutandis to dividends. In this case, the term "business year" in item (iii) of that paragraph shall be deemed to be replaced with "Consolidated Fiscal Year."

Section 7 Miscellaneous Provisions

Article 81 In cases where a Designated Juridical Person prepares a consolidated statement of changes in net assets, if it is found inappropriate to state matters pursuant to this Ordinance, said Designated Juridical Person may state matters in an equivalent manner as under the provisions of a Law, Regulations, or Rules applicable to its Financial Statements.

Chapter V Consolidated Cash Flow Statement

Section 1 General Provisions

(Method for Presenting a Consolidated Cash Flow Statement)
Article 82 (1) The method for presenting a consolidated cash flow statement shall be in accordance with the provisions of this Chapter.
(2) A consolidated cash flow statement shall be presented by using Form No. 7 or Form No. 8.

(Classification for Presenting a Consolidated Cash Flow Statement)
Article 83 In a consolidated cash flow statement, Cash Flow conditions shall be stated for the following classes:
(i) Cash Flows from operating activities;
(ii) Cash Flows from investment activities;
(iii) Cash Flows from financing activities;
(iv) translation adjustments on cash and Cash Equivalents;
(v) increase or decrease in cash and Cash Equivalents;
(vi) the beginning balances of cash and Cash Equivalents; and
(vii) the ending balances of cash and Cash Equivalents.

Section 2 Method for Presenting a Consolidated Cash Flow Statement

(Presentation Method for Cash Flows from Operating Activities)
Article 84 In the class of Cash Flows from operating activities set forth in item (i) of the preceding Article, the Cash Flows pertaining to transactions that were made subject to calculation of operating profit or operating loss and Cash Flows pertaining to transactions other than investment activities and financing activities shall be set down under account titles having names that indicate the contents thereof, by either of the following methods; provided, however, that such Cash Flows of which the amount is small and which are found appropriate to be presented collectively may be set down

collectively under an account title having an appropriate name:
(i) the method of classifying such Cash Flows into operating income, payment for purchases of raw materials or merchandise, payment of personnel expenses, and other items that are found appropriate, and presenting the total amount of Cash Flows for each major transaction; or
(ii) the method of presenting the amount obtained by adding or subtracting the following items to or from the amount of net profit for the period before taxes or the amount of net loss for the period before taxes:
   (a) any items reported as revenues or expenses on a consolidated profit and loss statement that do not involve any increase or decrease of Funds;
   (b) the amount of increase or decrease in notes and accounts receivable, inventory assets, notes and accounts payable, or any other assets or liabilities that have arisen from operating activities; and
   (c) any items reported as revenues or expenses on a consolidated profit and loss statement that are included in the classes of Cash Flows from investment activities and Cash Flows from financing activities.

(Presentation Method for Cash Flows from Investment Activities)
Article 85 In the class of Cash Flows from investment activities set forth in Article 83, item (ii), payment for acquisition of securities (excluding Cash Equivalents, etc.; hereinafter the same shall apply in this Article), proceeds from sales of securities, payment for acquisition of tangible fixed assets, proceeds from sales of tangible fixed assets, payment for acquisition of investment securities, proceeds from sales of investment securities, payments of loans, proceeds from collection of loans, and any other Cash Flows pertaining to investment activities shall be set down under account titles having names that indicate the contents thereof, by the method of presenting the total amount of Cash Flows for each major transaction; provided, however, that such Cash Flows of which the amount is small and which are found appropriate to be presented collectively may be set down collectively under an account title having an appropriate name.

(Presentation Method for Cash Flows from Financing Activities)
Article 86 In the class of Cash Flows from financing activities set forth in Article 83, item (iii), proceeds from short-term borrowings, payment for repayment of short-term borrowings, proceeds from long-term borrowings, payment for repayment of long-term borrowings, proceeds from issuance of company bonds, payment for redemption of company bonds, proceeds from issuance of shares, payment for acquisition of Treasury Shares, and any other Cash Flows pertaining to financing activities shall be set down under account titles having names that indicate the contents thereof, by the method of presenting the total amount of Cash Flows for each major transaction; provided, however, that such Cash Flows of which the amount is small and which are found appropriate to be presented collectively may be set down collectively under an account title having an appropriate name.

(Statement of Translation Adjustments Pertaining to Cash and Cash Equivalents)
Article 87 (1) In the class of translation adjustments pertaining to cash and Cash Equivalents set forth in Article 83, item (iv), the difference that occurs from translation of foreign currency Funds into yen currency shall be stated.
(2) In the class of increase or decrease in cash and Cash Equivalents set forth in Article 83, item (v), the amount obtained by adding or subtracting the difference that occurs from translation of foreign currency Funds into yen currency prescribed in the preced-

ing paragraph to or from the combined total of the balance of income and expenditures of Cash Flows from operating activities, Cash Flows from investment activities, and Cash Flows from financing activities, shall be stated.

Section 3 Miscellaneous Provisions

(Presentation Method for Cash Flows Pertaining to Interests and Dividends)
Article 88 (1) Cash Flows pertaining to interests and dividends shall be stated by either of the following methods:
 (i) the method of stating the amount of interests and dividends received and the amount of interests paid under the class of Cash Flows from operating activities set forth in Article 83, item (i) and stating the amount of dividends paid under the class of Cash Flows from financing activities set forth in item (iii) of that Article; or
 (ii) the method of stating the amount of interests and dividends received under the class of Cash Flows from investment activities set forth in Article 83, item (ii) and stating the amount of interests and dividends paid under the class of Cash Flows from financing activities set forth in item (iii) of that Article.
(2) The amount of dividends paid shall be stated by classifying it into the amount of dividends paid by the Company Submitting Consolidated Financial Statements and the amount of dividends paid to Minority Shareholders (meaning shareholders of Consolidated Subsidiary Companies other than Consolidated Companies).

(Presentation Method for Cash Flows, etc. Pertaining to Acquisition or Sales of Subsidiary Company Shares Involving a Change in the Scope of Consolidation)
Article 89 (1) Cash Flows pertaining to acquisition or sales of Subsidiary Company shares involving a change in the scope of consolidation shall be set down under an account title having a name that indicates the contents thereof under the class of Cash Flows from investment activities set forth in Article 83, item (ii).
(2) The provision of the preceding paragraph shall apply mutatis mutandis to Cash Flows pertaining to a takeover or transfer of a business or a merger, etc. carried out in consideration for cash or Cash Equivalents.

(Matters to be Stated in the Notes in a Consolidated Cash Flow Statement)
Article 90 (1) The following matters shall be stated in the notes in a consolidated cash flow statement; provided, however, that the notes may be omitted for matters set forth in items (ii) to (iv) inclusive in cases where the amount of assets or liabilities prescribed respectively in those items have little significance:
 (i) the relationship between the ending balances of cash and Cash Equivalents and the amounts for the account titles set down in a the consolidated balance sheet;
 (ii) in cases where any company has become a Consolidated Subsidiary Company as a result of acquisition of shares, the major breakdown of assets and liabilities of said company;
 (iii) in cases where any company is no longer a Consolidated Subsidiary Company as a result of sales of shares, the major breakdown of assets and liabilities of said company;
 (iv) in cases where there has been a takeover or transfer of a business or a merger, etc. carried out in consideration for cash or Cash Equivalents, the major breakdown of assets and liabilities that have increased or decreased as a result of such takeover or transfer of a business or such merger, etc. ; and
 (v) the contents of significant non-cash transactions.

(2) The non-cash transactions set forth in item (v) of the preceding paragraph means exercise of share options attached to company bonds with share options in exchange for redemption of the company bonds, acquisition of assets (excluding cash and Cash Equivalents) through issuance, etc. of shares, a merger, or any other transactions that do not involve any increase or decrease of Funds, and that have significant influence on Cash Flows in and/or after the following Consolidated Fiscal Year.

Chapter VI Consolidated Supplementary Schedules

(Method for Presenting Consolidated Supplementary Schedules)
Article 91 The method for presenting consolidated supplementary schedules shall be in accordance with the provisions of this Chapter.

(Types of Supplementary Schedules)
Article 92 (1) The types of consolidated supplementary schedules shall be a schedule of company bonds, a schedule of borrowings, etc. , and a schedule of Asset Retirement Obligations.
(2) The forms for the schedule of company bonds, schedule of borrowings, etc. , and schedule of Asset Retirement Obligations prescribed in the preceding paragraph shall be in accordance with Form No. 9 through Form No. 11.

(Omission of Preparation of Consolidated Supplementary Schedules)
Article 92-2 (1) In cases where the amount of Asset Retirement Obligations at the end of the current Consolidated Fiscal Year and that at the end of the immediately preceding Consolidated Fiscal Year are not more than one percent of the combined total of liabilities and net assets at the end of the respective Consolidated Fiscal Years, the supplementary schedule of Asset Retirement Obligations prescribed in paragraph (1) of the preceding Article may be omitted from being prepared.
(2) In the case of having omitted preparation of a supplementary schedule of Asset Retirement Obligations pursuant to the provision of the preceding paragraph, a statement to that effect shall be set down in the notes.

Chapter VII Special Provisions for Business Accounting Standards

(Special Provision for Accounting Standards)
Article 93 The terminology, forms, and preparation methods of Consolidated Financial Statements that a Specified Company submits may be in compliance with International Accounting Standards (limited to those which are specified by the Commissioner of the Financial Services Agency as such that are found to have been prepared and published under fair and appropriate procedures and are expected to be accepted as fair and appropriate business accounting standards; referred to as "Designated International Accounting Standards" in the following Article).

(Notes on Special Provision for Accounting Standards)
Article 94 The following matters shall be stated in the notes to the Consolidated Financial Statements prepared pursuant to Designated International Accounting Standards:
(i) a statement to the effect that the Consolidated Financial Statements are prepared pursuant to Designated International Accounting Standards; and
(ii) a statement to the effect that the company is categorized as a Specified Company

and the reason therefor.

⑫ Order for Enforcement of the Act on Book-Entry of Company Bonds, Shares, etc.

(Cabinet Order No. 362 of December 6, 2002)

The Cabinet hereby enacts this Cabinet Order revising the entire Order for Enforcement of the Act on Book-entry of Short-term Bonds, etc. (Cabinet Order No. 120 of 2002) pursuant to the provisions of the Act on Book-entry of Bonds, etc. (Act No. 75 of 2001).

Chapter I Book-entry Institution, etc. (Article 1 and Article 2)
Chapter II Participant Protection Trust (Article 3 - Article 6)
Chapter III Book-entry of Company Bonds (Article 7 - Article 14)
Chapter IV Book-entry of National Government Bonds (Article 15)
Chapter V Book-entry of Local Government Bonds, etc. (Article 16 - Article 27)
Chapter V-2 Book-entry of Beneficial Interests in Trusts Issuing Beneficiary Certificates (Article 27-2 - Article 27-12)
Chapter VI Book-entry of Shares (Article 28 - Article 41)
Chapter VII Book-entry of Share Options (Article 42 - Article 50)
Chapter VIII Book-entry of Company Bonds with Share Options (Article 51 - Article 59)
Chapter IX Book-entry of Investment Units, etc. (Article 60 - Article 70)
Chapter X Book-entry Resulting from Entity Conversion, etc. (Article 71 - Article 83)
Chapter XI Miscellaneous Provisions (Article 84 - Article 86)
   Supplementary Provisions

Chapter I Book-entry Institution, etc.

(Minimum Amount of Stated Capital)
Article 1 The amount to be specified by a Cabinet Order as prescribed in Article 5, paragraph (1) of the Act on Book-entry of Company Bonds, Shares, etc. (Act No. 75 of 2001; hereinafter referred to as the "Act") shall be 500,000,000 yen.

(Participants Excluded from Joint Guarantee Requirement)
Article 2 Persons to be specified by a Cabinet Order as prescribed in Article 11, paragraph (2) of the Act shall be the following:
(i) A person listed in Article 44, paragraph (1), item (xiii) of the Act
(ii) A qualified institutional investor as prescribed in Article 2, paragraph (3), item (i) of the Financial Instruments and Exchange Act (Act No. 25 of 1948)
(iii) A juridical person established by the State, a local government or a special Act (excluding those falling under the preceding item)
(iv) A Book-entry Institution, etc. (excluding those falling under the preceding three items)
(v) A foreign government or a person equivalent to those listed in item (ii) or (iii) under the laws and regulations of a foreign state
(vi) In addition to the persons listed in the preceding items, those designated by the Commissioner of the Financial Services Agency, the Minister of Justice and the Minister of Finance

Chapter II Participant Protection Trust

(Matters for Public Notice Pertaining to Payments to Beneficiaries)
Article 3 Matters to be specified by a Cabinet Order as prescribed in Article 59, paragraph (1) of the Act shall be the following:
(i) The method of notification of Claims Subject to Compensation set forth in Article 59, paragraph (1) of the Act
(ii) The period, place and method of payment of the amount set forth in Article 60, paragraph (1) of the Act
(iii) Any materials and other articles which a Participant shall submit or present when making a request set forth in Article 60, paragraph (1) of the Act
(iv) Any other matters that a trustee of a participant protection trust finds necessary

(Reasons for Change to Notification Period)
Article 4 Reasons to be specified by a Cabinet Order as prescribed in Article 59, paragraph (2) of the Act shall be the following:
(i) Public notice of distribution pursuant to the provisions of Article 197, paragraph (1) of the Bankruptcy Act (Act No. 75 of 2004) (including cases where applied mutatis mutandis pursuant to Article 209, paragraph (3) of the same Act) has been given.
(ii) Notice pursuant to the provisions of Article 65-2 of the Act has been given.
(iii) A decision approving a reorganization plan pursuant to the provisions of Article 199, paragraph (1) of the Corporate Reorganization Act (Act No. 154 of 2002) or Article 120, paragraph (1) of the Act on Special Treatment of Corporate Reorganization Proceedings and Other Insolvency Proceedings of Financial Institutions, etc. (Act No. 95 of 1996) has been made.
(iv) A decision approving a rehabilitation plan pursuant to the provisions of Article 174, paragraph (1) of the Civil Rehabilitation Act (Act No. 225 of 1999) has been made.
(v) Any other reason specified by a Cabinet Officer Ordinance, an Ordinance of the Ministry of Justice or an Ordinance of the Ministry of Finance.

(Maximum Amount of Payment to Beneficiaries)
Article 5 The amount to be specified by a Cabinet Order as prescribed in Article 60, paragraph (4) of the Act shall be 10,000,000 yen; provided, however, that if, prior to the payment prescribed in paragraph (1) of the same Article, distribution or repayment (excluding that related to claims with priority rights; hereinafter referred to as "repayment, etc." in this Article) has been made during bankruptcy proceedings, rehabilitation proceedings, reorganization proceedings, special liquidation proceedings, or foreign insolvency proceedings related to the Immediately Superior Institution in Bankruptcy (which means the Immediately Superior Institution in Bankruptcy as prescribed in Article 58 of the Act), the amount specified in the following items based on the case listed therein:
(i) Where the amount of the Claims Subject to Compensation (as prescribed in Article 60, paragraph (1) of the Act; hereinafter the same shall apply in this and the following Article) is 10,000,000 yen or less: The amount obtained by subtracting, from the amount of such Claims Subject to Compensation, the amount of repayment, etc. made to the Participant who holds such Claims Subject to Compensation (or, if such Participant holds other claims related to such repayment, etc. other than such Claims Subject to Compensation, the amount obtained by multiplying the amount of repayment, etc. to such Participant by the ratio obtained by dividing the amount of such Claims Subject to Compensation by the total amount of all claims related to such repayment, etc.; the same shall apply in the following item)

(ii) Where the amount of the Claims Subject to Compensation exceeds 10,000,000 yen: The amount obtained by subtracting, from 10,000,000 yen, the amount obtained by multiplying the amount of repayment, etc. made to the Participant who holds such Claims Subject to Compensation by the ratio obtained by dividing 10,000,000 yen by the amount of such Claims Subject to Compensation

(Special Provisions of the Act on Special Measures Concerning Taxation in the Case of Payment Related to Claims Subject to Compensation)
Article 6 (1) Where any event by which a workers asset accumulation home savings contract as prescribed in Article 4-2, paragraph (1) of the Act on Special Measures Concerning Taxation (Act No. 26 of 1957) or its performance ceases to satisfy the requirements prescribed in Article 6, paragraph (4), item (i), (b) or (c) of the Act on the Promotion of Workers Asset Accumulation (Act No. 92 of 1971) occurs due to a payment (a payment set forth in Article 61-2, paragraph (1) of the Act: the same shall apply in the following paragraph) related to Claims Subject to Compensation, with regard to the application of the provisions of Article 4-2, paragraph (2) and paragraph (9) of the Act on Special Measures Concerning Taxation, such event shall be deemed to be outside the scope of the cases to be specified by a Cabinet Order as prescribed in paragraph (2) or the events prescribed in paragraph (9) of the same Article.
(2) Where any event by which a workers asset accumulation pension savings contract as prescribed in Article 4-3, paragraph (1) of the Act on Special Measures Concerning Taxation or its performance ceases to satisfy the requirements prescribed in Article 6, paragraph (2), item (i), (b) or (c) of the Act on the Promotion of Workers Asset Accumulation occurs due to a payment related to Claims Subject to Compensation, with regard to the application of the provisions of Article 4-3, paragraph (2) and paragraph (10) of the Act on Special Measures Concerning Taxation, such event shall be deemed to be outside the scope of the cases to be specified by a Cabinet Order as prescribed in paragraph (2) of the same Article or the events prescribed in paragraph (10) of the same Article.

Chapter III Book-entry of Company Bonds

(Matters to be Described or Recorded in a Book-entry Account Registry)
Article 7 Matters to be specified by a Cabinet Order as prescribed in Article 68, paragraph (3), item (vi) of the Act shall be those concerning restrictions on the disposition of Book-entry Company Bonds (Book-entry Company Bonds as prescribed in Article 66 of the Act; the same shall apply hereinafter).

(Application for Description or Record of Trust)
Article 8 (1) The description or record in the book-entry account registry (hereinafter referred to as the "description or record of trust" in this Chapter) as prescribed in Article 75, paragraph (1) of the Act shall be made upon application to the Immediately Superior Institution, depending upon the classification of the case under the following items, by the persons prescribed therein:
(i) Where, by transfer or pledge of Book-entry Company Bonds by a settlor of a trust (hereinafter simply referred to as a "settlor") to a trustee of a trust (hereinafter simply referred to as a "trustee"), the rights to such Book-entry Company Bonds come to belong to the trust property: Settlor
(ii) Where, by changing the trustee, the rights to Book-entry Company Bonds belonging to the trust property are transferred to a new trustee (hereinafter simply referred to as a "new trustee") as prescribed in Article 62, paragraph (1) of the Trust

Act (Act No. 108 of 2006): the previous trustee as prescribed in Article 59, paragraph (1) of the same Act (hereinafter simply referred to as the "previous trustee")
(iii) Any cases other than those listed in the preceding two items: Trustee
(2) A person who intends to apply as set forth in the preceding paragraph shall indicate the following matters in the application:
(i) The account of the trustee or new trustee
(ii) The issue and amount of Book-entry Company Bonds related to the application
(iii) Whether the description or record of trust under the account set forth in item (i) is to be made in the Ownership Column (Ownership Column as prescribed in Article 69, paragraph (2), item (i), (a) of the Act; the same shall apply in Article 11, paragraph (2), item (iii)) or the Pledge Column (Pledge Column as prescribed in Article 69, paragraph (2), item (i), (b) of the Act; the same shall apply in Article 11, paragraph (2), item (iii))

(Application by Subrogation)
Article 9 (1) In the cases listed in paragraph (1), item (iii) of the preceding Article, a beneficiary of a trust (hereinafter simply referred to as a "beneficiary") or a settlor may apply for the description or record of trust on behalf of a trustee.
(2) A beneficiary or settlor shall, in applying pursuant to the provisions of the preceding paragraph, indicate in the application the individual or business name and address of the trustee and the cause of subrogation, and submit materials certifying the cause of such subrogation and the fact that the rights to Book-entry Company Bonds related to the application belong to the trust property.

(Simultaneous Application)
Article 10 (1) In the case listed in Article 8, paragraph (1), item (i), an application for a description or record of trust shall be made simultaneously with an application for book-entry related to the transfer or pledge of Book-entry Company Bonds as prescribed in the same item.
(2) In a case under the preceding paragraph, a Book-entry Institution, etc. shall, when it gives notice pursuant to the provisions of Article 70, paragraph (4), item (ii) or item (iv) of the Act, or pursuant to the provisions of paragraph (5), item (ii) or item (iv) (including cases where applied mutatis mutandis pursuant to paragraph (6) of the same Article) or paragraph (7), item (ii) of the same Article (including cases where applied mutatis mutandis pursuant to paragraph (8) of the same Article), simultaneously give notice of the matters listed in each item under Article 8, paragraph (2).
(3) A Book-entry Institution, etc. which has received notice pursuant to the provisions of the preceding paragraph shall simultaneously enter the description or record of trust in the book-entry account registry it maintains in accordance with the contents of the notice given pursuant to the provisions of the preceding paragraph when it enters the description or record pursuant to the provisions of Article 70, paragraph (4), item (iii), paragraph (5), item (iii) (including cases where applied mutatis mutandis pursuant to paragraph (6) of the same Article) or paragraph (7), item (i) (including cases where applied mutatis mutandis pursuant to paragraph (8) of the same Article) of the Act.

(Application for Deletion of Description or Record of Trust)
Article 11 (1) A description or record of trust shall be deleted upon application by a person prescribed under an item below to such person's Immediately Superior Institution (or, in the case listed in item (iii), the trustee's Immediately Superior Institution), depending upon the classification of the case under the respective item:
(i) Where, by transfer of the rights to Book-entry Company Bonds, such rights cease

to belong to the trust property: Trustee
  (ii) Where, by changing a trustee, rights to Book-entry Company Bonds which are trust property are transferred to a new trustee: Previous trustee
  (iii) Where, due to the transfer of the rights to Book-entry Company Bonds to trustee's own property, the rights to such Book-entry Company Bonds cease to belong to the trust property: Trustee and beneficiary
(2) A person who intends to apply as set forth in the preceding paragraph shall include the following in the application:
  (i) The account of the trustee or previous trustee
  (ii) The issue and amount of Book-entry Company Bonds related to the application
  (iii) Whether the description or record of trust is to be deleted from the Ownership or Pledge Column in the account described in item (i)
(3) A beneficiary as prescribed in paragraph (1), item (iii) shall, in applying pursuant to the provisions of the same paragraph, submit materials identifying itself as a beneficiary.

(Simultaneous Application)
Article 12 In the case described in paragraph (1), item (i) of the preceding Article, an application for deletion of the description or record of trust shall be submitted simultaneously with an application for book-entry related to the transfer of rights prescribed in the same item.

(Change of a Trustee)
Article 13 (1) Upon a change in the trustee, the previous trustee shall apply for book-entry (hereinafter referred to as an "application for entry of an increase in the amount, etc." in this Article) and request that the description or record of an increase in the amount of the rights to Book-entry Company Bonds belonging to the trust property be made in the new trustee's account. Simultaneously with such application, an application (hereinafter referred to as an "application for entry of change of a trustee, etc." in this Article) shall be submitted pursuant to the provisions of Article 8, paragraph (1) (limited to the portion related to item (ii)) and Article 11, paragraph (1) (limited to the portion related to item (ii)) for the rights to such Book-entry Company Bonds. In this case, simultaneously with these applications, materials certifying such change shall be submitted.
(2) The provisions of Article 10, paragraphs (2) and (3) shall apply mutatis mutandis to the cases described in the first sentence of the preceding paragraph.
(3) Where the duties of a trustee are terminated or where there is a change in the trustee pursuant to the provisions of Article 56, paragraph (1), items (i) to (iv) or (vi) of the Trust Act or Article 8 of the Act on Charitable Trusts (Act No. 62 of 1922), the new trustee may also apply for the entry of an increase in the amount, etc. and an application for entry of a change in the trustee, etc. In this case, entry of a change in the trustee, etc. shall be applied for simultaneously with an application for entry of an increase in the amount, etc.
(4) In the case described in the preceding paragraph, the provisions of the second sentence of paragraph (1) shall apply mutatis mutandis.

(Provision of Contents of Book-entry Company Bonds)
Article 14 The method to be specified by a Cabinet Order as prescribed in Article 87, paragraph (1) of the Act shall be any of the following:
  (i) A method of delivering or sending a document stating the matters (hereinafter referred to as the "contents of Book-entry Company Bonds" in this Article) listed in Article 69, paragraph (1), item (vii) of the Act (or, if the contents of Book-entry

Company Bonds are recorded in an electromagnetic record (which means an electromagnetic record as prescribed in Article 4, paragraph (3) of the Act; hereinafter the same shall apply in this item), a document prepared by outputting the contents of the information recorded in such electromagnetic record) to the Participant

(ii) A method of providing the contents of Book-entry Company Bonds to a Participant by electromagnetic means (electromagnetic means as prescribed in Article 34, paragraph (3) of the Act; the same shall apply hereinafter) specified by a Cabinet Office Ordinance or an Ordinance of the Ministry of Justice (in the case of a Book-entry Institution which handles national government bonds, a Cabinet Office Ordinance, an Ordinance of the Ministry of Justice or an Ordinance of the Ministry of Finance; the same shall apply in the following item)

(iii) A method of making the contents of Book-entry Company Bonds subject to notice as set forth in Article 69, paragraph (1) of the Act available to many and unspecified persons by electromagnetic means specified by a Cabinet Office Ordinance or an Ordinance of the Ministry of Justice until the day the total amount of such Book-entry Company Bonds described or recorded in the book-entry account registry maintained by the Book-entry Institution is deleted from the book-entry account registry

Chapter IV Book-entry of National Government Bonds

(Mutatis Mutandis Application of Provisions Concerning Company Bonds to National Government Bonds)
Article 15 The provisions of Article 7 shall apply mutatis mutandis to the matters to be specified by a Cabinet Order as prescribed in Article 91, paragraph (3), item (vi) of the Act, and the provisions of Articles 8 to 13 shall apply mutatis mutandis to the description or record prescribed in Article 100, paragraph (1) of the Act. In this case, the terms listed in the middle column of the following table, found in the provisions listed in the left column of said table, shall be deemed to be replaced with the terms listed in the right column of said table.

Article 8, paragraph (2), item (iii)	Article 68, paragraph (3), item (iii) of the Act	Article 91, paragraph (3), item (iii) of the Act
Article 10, paragraph (2)	Article 70, paragraph (4), item (ii) of the Act	Article 95, paragraph (4), item (ii) of the Act
Article 10, paragraph (3)	Article 70, paragraph (4), item (iii) of the Act	Article 95, paragraph (4), item (iii) of the Act
Article 11, paragraph (2), item (iii)	Article 68, paragraph (3), item (iii) of the Act	Article 91, paragraph (3), item (iii) of the Act

Chapter V Book-entry of Local Government Bonds, etc

(Mutatis Mutandis Application of Provisions Concerning Company Bonds to Local Government Bonds)
Article 16 The provisions of Article 7 shall apply mutatis mutandis to the matters to be specified by a Cabinet Order as prescribed in Article 68, paragraph (3), item (vi) of the Act as applied mutatis mutandis pursuant to Article 113 of the Act, the provisions of Article 8 to Article 13 shall apply mutatis mutandis to the description or record pre-

scribed in Article 75, paragraph (1) of the Act as applied mutatis mutandis pursuant to Article 113 of the Act, and the provisions of Article 14 shall apply mutatis mutandis to the methods to be specified by a Cabinet Order as prescribed in Article 87, paragraph (1) of the Act as applied mutatis mutandis pursuant to Article 113 of the Act.

(Mutatis Mutandis Application of Provisions Concerning Company Bonds to Investment Corporation Bonds)

Article 17 The provisions of Article 7 shall apply mutatis mutandis to the matters to be specified by a Cabinet Order as prescribed in Article 68, paragraph (3), item (vi) of the Act as applied mutatis mutandis pursuant to Article 115 of the Act, the provisions of Article 8 to Article 13 shall apply mutatis mutandis to the description or record prescribed in Article 75, paragraph (1) of the Act as applied mutatis mutandis pursuant to Article 115 of the Act, and the provisions of Article 14 shall apply mutatis mutandis to the methods to be specified by a Cabinet Order as prescribed in Article 87, paragraph (1) of the Act as applied mutatis mutandis pursuant to Article 115 of the Act.

(Replacement of Terms in the Provisions of the Act as Applied Mutatis Mutandis to Investment Corporation Bonds)

Article 18 Where, under the provisions of Article 115 of the Act, the provisions of the Act are applied mutatis mutandis to investment corporation bonds as prescribed in the Act on Investment Trusts and Investment Corporations (Act No. 198 of 1951), the technical replacement of terms related to such provisions shall be carried out as prescribed in the following table:

Provision containing the terms to be replaced	Terms to be replaced	Replacement terms
Article 85, paragraph (1)	Article 723, paragraph (1) of the Companies Act	Article 723, paragraph (1) of the Companies Act as applied mutatis mutandis pursuant to Article 139-10, paragraph (2) of the Act on Investment Trusts and Investment Corporations
Article 85, paragraph (2)	Article 718, paragraph (1) and Article 736, paragraph (1) of the Companies Act	Article 718, paragraph (1) and Article 736, paragraph (1) of the Companies Act as applied mutatis mutandis pursuant to Article 139-10, paragraph (2) of the Act on Investment Trusts and Investment Corporations
Article 86, paragraph (1)	Article 718, paragraph (1) of the Companies Act	Article 718, paragraph (1) of the Companies Act as applied mutatis mutandis pursuant to Article 139-10, paragraph (2) of the Act on Investment Trusts and Investment Corporations
	paragraph (3) of the same Article	Article 718, paragraph (3) of the Companies Act as applied mutatis mutandis pursuant to Article 139-10, paragraph (2) of the Act on Investment Trusts and Investment Corporations

(Mutatis Mutandis Application of Provisions Concerning Company Bonds to Mutual Company Bonds)

Article 19 The provisions of Article 7 shall apply mutatis mutandis to the matters to be specified by a Cabinet Order as prescribed in Article 68, paragraph (3), item (vi) of the Act as applied mutatis mutandis pursuant to Article 117 of the Act, the provisions of Article 8 to Article 13 shall apply mutatis mutandis to the description or record prescribed in Article 75, paragraph (1) of the Act as applied mutatis mutandis pursuant to Article 117 of the Act, and the provisions of Article 14 shall apply mutatis mutandis to the methods to be specified by a Cabinet Order as prescribed in Article 87, paragraph (1) of the Act as applied mutatis mutandis pursuant to Article 117 of the Act.

(Replacement of Terms in the Provisions of the Act as Applied Mutatis Mutandis to Mutual Company Bonds)

Article 20 Where, under the provisions of Article 117 of the Act, the provisions of the Act are applied mutatis mutandis to mutual company bonds as prescribed in the Insurance Business Act (Act No. 105 of 1995), the technical replacement of terms related to such provisions shall be carried out as prescribed in the following table:

Provision containing the terms to be replaced	Terms to be replaced	Replacement terms
Article 85, paragraph (1)	Article 723, paragraph (1) of the Companies Act	Article 723, paragraph (1) of the Companies Act as applied mutatis mutandis pursuant to Article 61-8, paragraph (2) of the Insurance Business Act
Article 85, paragraph (2)	Article 718, paragraph (1) and Article 736, paragraph (1) of the Companies Act	Article 718, paragraph (1) and Article 736, paragraph (1) of the Companies Act as applied mutatis mutandis pursuant to Article 61-8, paragraph (2) of the Insurance Business Act
Article 86, paragraph (1)	Article 718, paragraph (1) of the Companies Act	Article 718, paragraph (1) of the Companies Act as applied mutatis mutandis pursuant to Article 61-8, paragraph (2) of the Insurance Business Act
	paragraph (3) of the same Article	Article 718, paragraph (3) of the Companies Act as applied mutatis mutandis pursuant to Article 61-8, paragraph (2) of the Insurance Business Act

(Mutatis Mutandis Application of Provisions Concerning Company Bonds to Specified Company Bonds)

Article 21 The provisions of Article 7 shall apply mutatis mutandis to the matters to be specified by a Cabinet Order as prescribed in Article 68, paragraph (3), item (vi) of the Act as applied mutatis mutandis pursuant to Article 118 of the Act, the provisions of Article 8 to Article 13 shall apply mutatis mutandis to the description or record prescribed in Article 75, paragraph (1) of the Act as applied mutatis mutandis pursuant to

Article 118 of the Act, and the provisions of Article 14 shall apply mutatis mutandis to the methods to be specified by a Cabinet Order as prescribed in Article 87, paragraph (1) of the Act as applied mutatis mutandis pursuant to Article 118 of the Act.

(Replacement of Terms in the Provisions of the Act as Applied Mutatis Mutandis to Specified Company Bonds)
Article 22 Where, under the provisions of Article 118 of the Act, the provisions of the Act are applied mutatis mutandis to specified company bonds (excluding convertible specified company bonds and specified company bonds with subscription rights for new preferred equity investments) as prescribed in the Act on the Securitization of Assets (Act No. 105 of 1998), the technical replacement of terms related to such provisions shall be carried out as prescribed in the following table:

Provision containing the terms to be replaced	Terms to be replaced	Replacement terms
Article 85, paragraph (1)	Article 723, paragraph (1) of the Companies Act	Article 723, paragraph (1) of the Companies Act as applied mutatis mutandis pursuant to Article 129, paragraph (2) of the Act on the Securitization of Assets
Article 85, paragraph (2)	Article 718, paragraph (1) and Article 736, paragraph (1) of the Companies Act	Article 718, paragraph (1) and Article 736, paragraph (1) of the Companies Act as applied mutatis mutandis pursuant to Article 129, paragraph (2) of the Act on the Securitization of Assets
Article 86, paragraph (1)	Article 718, paragraph (1) of the Companies Act	Article 718, paragraph (1) of the Companies Act as applied mutatis mutandis pursuant to Article 129, paragraph (2) of the Act on the Securitization of Assets
	paragraph (3) of the same Article	Article 718, paragraph (3) of the Companies Act as applied mutatis mutandis pursuant to Article 129, paragraph (2) of the Act on the Securitization of Assets

(Mutatis Mutandis Application of Provisions Concerning Company Bonds to Special Corporation Bonds)
Article 23 The provisions of Article 7 shall apply mutatis mutandis to the matters to be specified by a Cabinet Order as prescribed in Article 68, paragraph (3), item (vi) as applied mutatis mutandis pursuant to Article 120 of the Act, the provisions of Article 8 to Article 13 shall apply mutatis mutandis to the description or record prescribed in Article 75, paragraph (1) of the Act as applied mutatis mutandis pursuant to Article 120 of the Act, and the provisions of Article 14 shall apply mutatis mutandis to the methods to be specified by a Cabinet Order as prescribed in Article 87, paragraph (1) of the Act as applied mutatis mutandis pursuant to Article 120 of the Act.

(Mutatis Mutandis Application of Provisions Concerning Company Bonds to

Art.24～26 — Order for Enforcement of the Act on Book-Entry of Company Bonds, Shares, etc., Chap.V

Beneficial Interests in a Domestic or Foreign Investment Trust)
Article 24 The provisions of Article 7 shall apply mutatis mutandis to the matters to be specified by a Cabinet Order as prescribed in Article 68, paragraph (3), item (vi) of the Act as applied mutatis mutandis pursuant to Article 121 of the Act, the provisions of Article 8 to Article 13 shall apply mutatis mutandis to the description or record prescribed in Article 75, paragraph (1) of the Act as applied mutatis mutandis pursuant to Article 121 of the Act, and the provisions of Article 14 shall apply mutatis mutandis to the methods to be specified by a Cabinet Order as prescribed in Article 87, paragraph (1) of the Act as applied mutatis mutandis pursuant to Article 121 of the Act. In this case, the terms listed the middle column of the following table, found in the provisions listed in the left column of said table, shall be deemed to be replaced with the terms listed in the right column of said table.

Article 8, paragraph (2), item (ii) and Article 11, paragraph (2), item (ii)	amount	number of units
Article 13, paragraph (1)	increase in the amount	increase in number of units
Article 14	total amount	total number of units

(Mutatis Mutandis Application of Provisions Concerning Company Bonds to Beneficial Interests in a Loan Trust)
Article 25 The provisions of Article 7 shall apply mutatis mutandis to the matters to be specified by a Cabinet Order as prescribed in Article 68, paragraph (3), item (vi) of the Act as applied mutatis mutandis pursuant to Article 122 of the Act, the provisions of Article 8 to Article 13 shall apply mutatis mutandis to the description or record prescribed in Article 75, paragraph (1) of the Act as applied mutatis mutandis pursuant to Article 122 of the Act, and the provisions of Article 14 shall apply mutatis mutandis to the methods to be specified by a Cabinet Order as prescribed in Article 87, paragraph (1) of the Act as applied mutatis mutandis pursuant to Article 122 of the Act.

(Mutatis Mutandis Application of Provisions Concerning Company Bonds to Beneficial Interests in a Specific Purpose Trust)
Article 26 The provisions of Article 7 shall apply mutatis mutandis to the matters to be specified by a Cabinet Order as prescribed in Article 68, paragraph (3), item (vi) of the Act as applied mutatis mutandis pursuant to Article 124 of the Act, the provisions of Article 8 to Article 13 shall apply mutatis mutandis to the description or record prescribed in Article 75, paragraph (1) of the Act as applied mutatis mutandis pursuant to Article 124 of the Act, and the provisions of Article 14 shall apply mutatis mutandis to the methods to be specified by a Cabinet Order as prescribed in Article 87, paragraph (1) of the Act as applied mutatis mutandis pursuant to Article 124 of the Act. In this case, the terms listed the middle column of the following table, found in the provisions listed in the left column of said table ,l shall be deemed to be replaced with the terms listed in the right column of said table.

Article 8, paragraph (2), item (ii) and Article 11, paragraph (2), item (ii)	amount	number of equity interests
Article 13, paragraph (1)	increase in the amount	increase in the number of equity interests
Article 14	total amount	total number of equity interests

(Mutatis Mutandis Application of Provisions Concerning Company Bonds to Foreign Bonds)

Article 27 The provisions of Article 7 shall apply mutatis mutandis to the matters to be specified by a Cabinet Order as prescribed in Article 68, paragraph (3), item (vi) of the Act as applied mutatis mutandis pursuant to Article 127 of the Act, the provisions of Article 8 to Article 13 shall apply mutatis mutandis to the description or record prescribed in Article 75, paragraph (1) of the Act as applied mutatis mutandis pursuant to Article 127 of the Act, and the provisions of Article 14 shall apply mutatis mutandis to the methods to be specified by a Cabinet Order as prescribed in Article 87, paragraph (1) of the Act as applied mutatis mutandis pursuant to Article 127 of the Act.

Chapter V-2 Book-entry of Beneficial Interests in a Trust Issuing a Beneficiary Certificate

(Matters to be Described or Recorded in a Book-entry Account Registry)

Article 27-2 The matters to be specified by a Cabinet Order as prescribed in Article 127-4, paragraph (3), item (vii) of the Act shall concern restrictions on the disposition of Book-entry Beneficial Interests (which means Book-entry Beneficial Interests as prescribed in Article 127-2, paragraph (1) of the Act; the same shall apply hereinafter).

(Measures and Instructions where Fractions Exist after the Consolidation of Book-entry Beneficial Interests)

Article 27-3 (1) The description or record to be specified by a Cabinet Order as prescribed in Article 127-11, paragraph (5) of the Act shall be as prescribed in the following items depending upon the classification of the Ownership Column, etc. (Ownership Column, etc. prescribed in Article 127-10, paragraph (3) of the Act; hereinafter the same shall apply in this Chapter) under such items:

(i) The Ownership Column (Ownership Column as prescribed in Article 127-5, paragraph (2), item (i), (a) of the Act; hereinafter the same shall apply in this Chapter) on the account of the Participant set forth in Article 127-11, paragraph (5) of the Act: The description or record of a decrease in the number (any fraction of such number of less than one (which shall be referred to as the "fraction in the Ownership Column" in item (iv)) shall be rounded up) that results from multiplying the number of Book-entry Beneficial Interests as set forth in Article 127-11, paragraph (1), item (i) of the Act described or recorded in such Ownership Column by the rate of decrease (the rate of decrease as prescribed in item (ii) of the same paragraph; the same shall apply in the following item)

(ii) The Pledge Column (Pledge Column prescribed in Article 127-5, paragraph (2), item (i), (b) of the Act; hereinafter the same shall apply in this Chapter) on the account of the Participant set forth in Article 127-11, paragraph (5) of the Act: The description or record of a decrease in the number (any fraction less than one in such number (which shall be referred to as the "fraction in the Pledge Column" in item (iv)) shall be rounded up) that results from multiplying the number of Book-entry Beneficial Interests set forth in Article 127-11, paragraph (1), item (i) of the Act described or recorded in such Pledge Column by the rate of decrease

(iii) The customer account that is among the accounts of a Superior Institution of the Participant prescribed in the preceding two items: The description or record of a decrease in the number of Book-entry Beneficial Interests described or recorded as prescribed in the preceding two items

(iv) The Ownership Column on the beneficiary's account, in the book-entry account registry maintained by the Immediately Superior Institution of the Participant who is the beneficiary of the Book-entry Beneficial Interests set forth in Article 127-11, paragraph (1), item (i) of the Act book-entry(if there is more than one such institution, the one specified by the Book-entry Institution) of such beneficiary: The description or record of an increase in the number that results from the totaling of the number obtained by subtracting the fraction in the Ownership Column for the Book-entry Beneficial Interests held by such beneficiary from one and the number obtained by subtracting the fraction in the Pledge Column for the same from one (any fraction of said number of less than one (which shall be referred to as the "fraction for issuer" under item (vi)) shall be discarded)

(v) The customer account that is among the accounts of the Book-entry Institution, etc. at which the account set forth in the preceding item has been opened and its Superior Institution: The description or record of an increase in the number described or recorded as prescribed in the same item

(vi) The Ownership Column of the account set forth in Article 127-11, paragraph (1), item (iv) of the Act: The description or record of an increase in the total (any fraction of the total number of less than one shall be discarded) of the issuer fraction

(vii) The customer account that is among the accounts of the Book-entry Institution, etc. at which the account set forth in the preceding item has been opened and its Superior Institution: The description or record of an increase in the number described or recorded as prescribed in the same item

(2) The instructions to be given by a Book-entry Institution pursuant to the provisions of Article 127-11, paragraph (5) of the Act shall be given to the persons listed in the following items with regard to the matters prescribed therein:

(i) All Subordinate Institutions: Instructions to the effect that the matters necessary for the descriptions or records prescribed in items (iii) to (vii) of the preceding paragraph should be reported

(ii) The Account Management Institution required to enter the description or record prescribed in the preceding item: Matters subject to such description or record

(Measures and Instructions in Cases Where Fractions Result from the Splitting of Book-entry Beneficial Interests)

Article 27-4 (1) The description or record to be specified by a Cabinet Order as prescribed in Article 127-12, paragraph (5) of the Act shall be as prescribed in the following items depending upon the classification of the Ownership Column, etc. under such items:

(i) The Ownership Column on the account of a Participant set forth in Article 127-12, paragraph (5) of the Act: The description or record of an increase in the number (any fraction of such number of less than one (which shall be referred to as the "fraction in the Ownership Column" in item (iv)) shall be discarded) resulting from multiplying the number of Book-entry Beneficial Interests set forth in paragraph (1), item (i) of the same Article described or recorded in such Ownership Column by the rate of increase (which means the rate of increase as prescribed in item (ii) of the same paragraph; the same shall apply in the following item)

(ii) The Pledge Column on the account of a Participant set forth in Article 127-12, paragraph (5) of the Act: The description or record of an increase in the number (any fraction of such number of less than one (which shall be referred to as the "fraction in the Pledge Column" in item (iv)) shall be discarded) resulting from multiplying the number of Book-entry Beneficial Interests set forth in paragraph (1), item (i) of the same Article that are described or recorded in such Pledge Col-

umn by the rate of increase
- (iii) The customer account among the accounts of a Superior Institution to a Participant prescribed in the preceding two items: The description or record of an increase in the number of Book-entry Beneficial Interests described or recorded as prescribed in the preceding two items
- (iv) The Ownership Column on the beneficiary's account, in the book-entry account registry maintained by the Immediately Superior Institution of the Participant who is the beneficiary of Book-entry Beneficial Interests as set forth in Article 127-12, paragraph (1), item (i) of the Act (if there is more than one such institution, the one specified by the Book-entry Institution) of such beneficiary: The description or record of an increase in the number resulting from the totaling of the fraction in the Ownership Column and the fraction in the Pledge Column for the Book-entry Beneficial Interests held by such beneficiary (any fraction of less than one of said number (which shall be referred to as the "issuer fraction" in item (vi)) shall be discarded)
- (v) The customer account that is among the accounts of the Book-entry Institution, etc. with which the account set forth in the preceding item has been opened and its Superior Institution: The description or record of an increase in the number that has been described or recorded as prescribed in the same item
- (vi) The Ownership Column of the account set forth in Article 127-12, paragraph (1), item (iv) of the Act: The description or record of an increase in the total (any fraction less of than one in said total number shall be discarded) of the issuer fraction
- (vii) The customer account that is among the accounts of the Book-entry Institution, etc. with which the account set forth in the preceding item has been opened and its Superior Institution: the description or record of an increase in the number that has been described or recorded as prescribed in the same item

(2) The instructions to be given by a Book-entry Institution pursuant to the provisions of Article 127-12, paragraph (5) of the Act shall be given to the entities listed in the following items with regard to the matters prescribed therein:
- (i) All Subordinate Institutions: Instructions to the effect that matters necessary for the description or record prescribed in items (iii) to (vii) of the preceding paragraph should be reported
- (ii) The Account Management Institution required to enter the description or record prescribed in the preceding item: Matters subject to such description or record

(Measures and Instructions where Fractions Result from the Delivery of Book-entry Beneficial Interests of Other Issues by Consolidation of Trusts)

Article 27-5 (1) The description or record to be specified by a Cabinet Order as prescribed in Article 127-13, paragraph (5) of the Act shall be as prescribed in the following items, depending upon the classification of the Ownership Column, etc. under said items:

(i) The Ownership Column on the account of the Participant set forth in Article 127-13, paragraph (5) of the Act: The description or record of an increase in the number (any fraction of said number of less than one (which shall be referred to as the "fraction in the Ownership Column" in item (iv)) shall be discarded) related to the Book-entry Beneficial Interests set forth in item (i) of the same paragraph resulting from the multiplying of the number of Book-entry Beneficial Interests (hereinafter referred to as "Book-entry Beneficial Interests after consolidation" in this paragraph) set forth in paragraph (1), item (ii) of the same Article that are described or recorded in such Ownership Column by an allotment ratio (an allotment ratio prescribed in item (iii) of the same paragraph; the same shall apply in the fol-

Art.27-5

lowing item)
(ii) The Pledge Column on the account of the Participant set forth in Article 127-13, paragraph (5) of the Act: The description or record of an increase in the number related to Book-entry Beneficial Interests after consolidation (any fraction of said number of less than one (which shall be referred to as the "fraction in the Pledge Column" in item (iv)) shall be discarded) that results from multiplying the number of Book-entry Beneficial Interests set forth in paragraph (1), item (ii) of the same Article that are described or recorded in such Pledge Column by an allotment ratio
(iii) Customer account among the accounts of the Superior Institutions of a Participant prescribed in the preceding two items: The description or record of an increase in the number of Book-entry Beneficial Interests after consolidation that has been described or recorded as prescribed in the preceding two items
(iv) The Ownership Column of an account of a Participant who is a beneficiary of Book-entry Beneficial Interests as set forth in Article 127-13, paragraph (1), item (ii) of the Act in the book-entry account registry maintained by the Immediately Superior Institution (if there are more than one such institution, the one specified by the Book-entry Institution) of such beneficiary: The description or record of an increase in the total (any fraction of such number of less than one (which shall be referred to as the "issuer fraction" in item (vi)) shall be discarded) of the fraction in the Ownership Column and the fraction in the Pledge Column related to the Book-entry Beneficial Interests after consolidation held by such beneficiary
(v) Customer account among the accounts of the Book-entry Institution, etc. at which the account set forth in the preceding item has been opened and its Superior Institution: The description or record of an increase in the number related to the Book-entry Beneficial Interests after consolidation described or recorded as prescribed in the same item
(vi) The Ownership Column of the account set forth in Article 127-13, paragraph (1), item (v) of the Act: The description or record of an increase in the total number related to the Book-entry Beneficial Interests after consolidation (any fraction of such total number of less than one shall be discarded) of the issuer fraction
(vii) The customer account among the accounts of the Book-entry Institution, etc. with which the account set forth in the preceding item has been opened and its Superior Institution: The description or record of an increase in the number related to Book-entry Beneficial Interests after consolidation described or recorded as prescribed in said item
(viii) The Ownership Column or Pledge Column on the account of the Participant set forth in Article 127-13, paragraph (5) of the Act or the customer account among the accounts of the Immediately Superior Institution of such Participant: The deletion of the description or record of all Book-entry Beneficial Interests set forth in paragraph (1), item (ii) of the same Article
(2) The instructions to be given by a Book-entry Institution pursuant to the provisions of Article 127-13, paragraph (5) of the Act shall be given to the persons listed in the following items with regard to the matters prescribed therein:
(i) All Subordinate Institutions: Instructions to the effect that matters necessary for the descriptions or records prescribed in items (iii) to (vii) of the preceding paragraph should be reported
(ii) The Account Management Institution required to enter the description or record prescribed in the preceding item: Matters subject to such description or record

(Measures and Instructions where Fractions Result from the Delivery of Book-entry Beneficial Interests of Other Issues by Split of Trusts)

⑫ **Order for Enforcement of the Act on Book-Entry of Company Bonds, Shares, etc., Chap.V-2**

[2010年11月26日訳]

Art.27-6

Article 27-6 (1) The description or record to be specified by a Cabinet Order as prescribed in Article 127-14, paragraph (5) of the Act shall be as prescribed in the following items depending upon the classification of the Ownership Column, etc. under said items:

(i) The Ownership Column on the account of the Participant set forth in Article 127-14, paragraph (5) of the Act: The description or record of an increase in the number (any fraction of such number of less than one (which shall be referred to as the "fraction in the Ownership Column" in item (iv)) shall be discarded) related to the Book-entry Beneficial Interests (hereinafter referred to as "Book-entry Beneficial Interests after split" in this paragraph) set forth in item (i) of the same paragraph that results from multiplying the number of Book-entry Beneficial Interests set forth in paragraph (1), item (ii) of the same Article that are described or recorded in such Ownership Column by an allotment ratio (which means an allotment ratio prescribed in item (iii) of the same paragraph; the same shall apply in the following item)

(ii) The Pledge Column on the account of the Participant set forth in Article 127-14, paragraph (5) of the Act: The description or record of an increase in the number related to Book-entry Beneficial Interests after a split (any fraction of such number of less than one (which shall be referred to as the "fraction in the Pledge Column" in item (iv)) shall be discarded) that results from multiplying the number of Book-entry Beneficial Interests as set forth in paragraph (1), item (ii) of the same Article that are described or recorded in such Pledge Column by an allotment ratio

(iii) The customer account among the accounts of a Superior Institution of a Participant as prescribed in the preceding two items: The description or record of an increase in the number of Book-entry Beneficial Interests after a split that has been described or recorded as prescribed in the preceding two items

(iv) Ownership Column on the account of the Participant who is a beneficiary of Book-entry Beneficial Interests set forth in Article 127-14, paragraph (1), item (ii) of the Act in the book-entry account registry maintained by the Immediately Superior Institution (if there is more than one such institution, the one specified by the Book-entry Institution) of such beneficiary: The description or record of an increase in the total (any fraction of such total of less than one (which shall be referred to as the "issuer fraction" in item (vi)) shall be discarded) obtained by adding the fractions in the Ownership and Pledge Columns related to the Book-entry Beneficial Interests after a split held by such beneficiary

(v) The customer account among the accounts of the Book-entry Institution, etc. with which the account set forth in the preceding item has been opened and its Superior Institution: The description or record of an increase in the number related to the Book-entry Beneficial Interests after a split that has been described or recorded as prescribed in the same item

(vi) The Ownership Column of the account set forth in Article 127-14, paragraph (1), item (v) of the Act: The description or record of an increase in the total related to the Book-entry Beneficial Interests after a split (any fraction of such total of less than one shall be discarded) of the issuer fraction

(vii) The customer account among the accounts of the Book-entry Institution, etc. at which the account set forth in the preceding item has been opened and its Superior Institution: The description or record of an increase in the number related to Book-entry Beneficial Interests after a split that has been described or recorded as prescribed in the same item

(2) The instructions to be given by a Book-entry Institution pursuant to the provisions of Article 127-14, paragraph (5) of the Act shall be given to the persons listed in the fol-

12 社債，株式等の振替に関する法律施行令

lowing items with regard to the matters prescribed in such items:
(i) All Subordinate Institutions: Instructions to the effect that matters necessary for the description or record prescribed in items (iii) to (vii) of the preceding paragraph should be reported
(ii) The Account Management Institution required to enter the description or record prescribed in the preceding item: Matters subject to such description or record

(Application for Description or Record of a Book-entry Beneficial Interest Trust)
Article 27-7 (1) The description or record in the book-entry account registry (hereinafter referred to as the "description or record of a Book-entry Beneficial Interest Trust") prescribed in Article 127-18, paragraph (1) of the Act shall be entered upon application by a person prescribed in the following items to its Immediately Superior Institution based on the classification of the case under such items:
(i) Where, by transfer or pledge of Book-entry Beneficial Interests by a settlor to a trustee, such Book-entry Beneficial Interests become part of the trust property: Settlor
(ii) Where, by changing a trustee, the Book-entry Beneficial Interests belonging to the trust property are transferred to a new trustee: Previous trustee
(iii) Any cases other than those listed in the preceding two items: Trustee
(2) A person who intends to apply as set forth in the preceding paragraph shall indicate the following matters in the application:
(i) The account of the trustee or new trustee
(ii) The issue and number of Book-entry Beneficial Interests related to the application
(iii) Whether the description or record of the Book-entry Beneficial Interests Trust is to be made in the Ownership or Pledge Column in the account set forth in item (i)

(Application by Subrogation)
Article 27-8 (1) In a cases under paragraph (1), item (iii) of the preceding Article, a beneficiary or a settlor may apply for the description or record of a Book-entry Beneficial Interest Trust on behalf of a trustee.
(2) A beneficiary or settlor shall, in applying pursuant to the provisions of the preceding paragraph, indicate in the application the individual or business name and address of the trustee and the cause of subrogation, and submit materials certifying the cause of such subrogation and the fact that the rights to Book-entry Beneficial Interests related to the application belong to the trust property.

(Simultaneous Application)
Article 27-9 (1) In a case which falls under Article 27-7, paragraph (1), item (i), an application for the description or record of a Book-entry Beneficial Interest trust shall be made simultaneously with an application for book-entry related to the transfer or a pledge of Book-entry Beneficial Interests as prescribed in the same item.
(2) In a case falling under the preceding paragraph, a Book-entry Institution, etc. shall, when it gives notice pursuant to the provisions of Article 127-7, paragraph (4), item (ii) or (iv) of the Act, or pursuant to the provisions of paragraph (5), item (ii) or (iv) of the same Article (including cases where applied mutatis mutandis pursuant to paragraph (6) of the same Article) or the provisions of paragraph (7), item (ii) of the same Article (including cases where applied mutatis mutandis pursuant to paragraph (8) of the same Article),provide simultaneous notice on the matters listed in each item under Article 27-7, paragraph (2).
(3) A Book-entry Institution, etc. which has received notice pursuant to the provisions of

the preceding paragraph shall, when it enters a description or record pursuant to the provisions of Article 127-7, paragraph (4), item (iii), the provisions of paragraph (5), item (iii) of the same Article (including cases where applied mutatis mutandis pursuant to paragraph (6) of the same Article), or the provisions of paragraph (7), item (i) of the same Article (including cases where applied mutatis mutandis pursuant to paragraph (8) of the same Article) of the Act, simultaneously enter a description or record of Book-entry Beneficial Interests in the book-entry account registry it maintains in accordance with the contents of the notice given pursuant to the provisions of the preceding paragraph.

(Application for Deletion of Description or Record of Book-entry Beneficial Interests)

Article 27-10 (1) The description or record of a Book-entry Beneficial Interest Trust shall be deleted upon application by a person prescribed in the following items to its Immediately Superior Institution (or, in the case listed in item (iii), the trustee's Immediately Superior Institution), depending upon the classification of the case under the following items:
  (i) Where Book-entry Beneficial Interests cease to belong to the trust property due to transfer: Trustee
  (ii) Where the Book-entry Beneficial Interests which belong to the trust property are transferred to a new trustee: Previous trustee
  (iii) Where, such Book-entry Beneficial Interests cease to belong to the trust property because Book-entry Beneficial Interests comes to belong to trustee's own property: Trustee and beneficiary
(2) A person who intends to apply as set forth in the preceding paragraph shall indicate the following matters in the application:
  (i) The account of the trustee or previous trustee
  (ii) The issue and number of Book-entry Beneficial Interests in connection with the application
  (iii) Whether the description or record of a Book-entry Beneficial Interest Trust is to be deleted from the Ownership Column or the Pledge Column of the account set forth in item (i)
(3) A beneficiary prescribed in paragraph (1), item (iii) shall, in applying pursuant to the provisions of the same paragraph, submit materials identifying itself as a beneficiary.

(Simultaneous Application)

Article 27-11 In the case listed in paragraph (1), item (i) of the preceding Article, an application for deletion of a description or record of a Book-entry Beneficial Interest Trust shall be made simultaneously with an application for book-entry related to transfer of Book-entry Beneficial Interests prescribed in the same item.

(Change of Trustee)

Article 27-12 (1) When a trustee is changed, the previous trustee shall apply for book-entry (hereinafter referred to as an "application for entry of an increase, etc." in paragraph (3)) requesting that the description or record of an increase for Book-entry Beneficial Interests belonging to the trust property be made in the new trustee's account, and simultaneously with such application, an application (which shall be referred to as an "application for entry of a change of a trustee, etc." in paragraph (3)) pursuant to the provisions of Article 27-7, paragraph (1) (limited to the portion related to item (ii)) and Article 27-10, paragraph (1) (limited to the portion related to item (ii)) for such Book-entry Beneficial Interests. In this case, simultaneously with these applications,

materials certifying the change shall also be submitted.
(2) The provisions of Article 27-9, paragraphs (2) and (3) shall apply mutatis mutandis to cases falling under the first sentence of the preceding paragraph.
(3) Where the termination of a trustee's duties and change of the trustee occur pursuant to the provisions of Article 56, paragraph (1), items (i) to (iv) or (vi) of the Trust Act or Article 8 of the Act on Charitable Trusts, the new trustee may also apply for an entry of an increase, etc. and for an entry of a change of a trustee, etc. In this case, the application for an entry of a change of a trustee, etc. shall be submitted simultaneously with the application for an entry of an increase, etc.
(4) In the case of the preceding paragraph, the provisions of the second sentence of paragraph (1) shall apply mutatis mutandis.

Chapter VI Book-entry of Shares

(Matters to be Described or Recorded in a Book-entry Account Registry)
Article 28 The matters to be specified by a Cabinet Order as prescribed in Article 129, paragraph (3), item (vii) of the Act shall be the following:
(i) Matters concerning restrictions on the disposition of Book-entry Shares (Book-entry Shares as prescribed in Article 128, paragraph (1) of the Act; the same shall apply hereinafter)
(ii) Where the issuer is a person listed in (a) to (c) below and the Participant is a person prescribed therein, language to that effect
  (a) A general broadcaster (excluding one listed in (b) below) as prescribed in Article 52-8, paragraph (1) of the Broadcast Act (Act No. 132 of 1950): A foreign national, etc. prescribed in the same paragraph
  (b) An entrusting broadcaster as prescribed in Article 2, item (iii)-5 of the Broadcast Act: A foreign national, etc. as prescribed in Article 52-8, paragraph (1) of the same Act as applied with replacement of relevant terms pursuant to the provisions of Article 52-28, paragraph (1) of the same Act
  (c) A certified broadcasting holding company as prescribed in Article 52-32, paragraph (1) of the Broadcast Act: A foreign national, etc. prescribed in the same paragraph
(iii) Where an issuer is a domestic air carrier as prescribed in Article 120-2, paragraph (1) of the Civil Aeronautics Act (Act No. 231 of 1952) or its holding company, etc. and a Participant is a foreign national, etc. prescribed in the same paragraph, language to that effect
(iv) Where an issuer is Nippon Telegraph and Telephone Corporation and a Participant is a person listed in one of the items under Article 6, paragraph (1) of the Act on Nippon Telegraph and Telephone Corporation, etc. (Act No. 85 of 1984), language to that effect.

(Matters Requiring Notification under a New Entry or Record Procedure)
Article 29 The matters to be specified by a Cabinet Order as prescribed in Article 130, paragraph (1), item (viii) of the Act shall be those listed in items (ii) to (iv) of the preceding Article.

(Measures and Instructions where Fractions Result from the Consolidation of Book-entry Shares)
Article 30 (1) The description or record to be specified by a Cabinet Order as prescribed in Article 136, paragraph (5) of the Act shall be as prescribed in the following items, depending upon the classification of the Ownership Column, etc. (Ownership Column,

etc. as prescribed in Article 135, paragraph (3) of the Act; hereinafter the same shall apply in this Chapter) under said items:

(i) The Ownership Column (Ownership Column as prescribed in Article 130, paragraph (2), item (i), (a) of the Act; hereinafter the same shall apply in this Chapter) on the account of the Participant set forth in Article 136, paragraph (5) of the Act: The description or record of a decrease in the number (any fraction of less than one in that number (which shall be referred to as the "fraction in the Ownership Column" in item (iv)) shall be rounded up) that results from multiplying the number of Book-entry Shares set forth in Article 136, paragraph (1), item (i) of the Act (or, for Book-entry Shares for which a request (hereinafter referred to as a "special shareholder request") set forth in Article 151, paragraph (2), item (i) of the Act has been made, the number for each special shareholder prescribed in the same item (hereinafter simply referred to as a "special shareholder")) that are described or recorded in such Ownership Column by the rate of decrease (which means the rate of decrease as prescribed in Article 136, paragraph (1), item (ii) of the Act; the same shall apply in the following item)

(ii) The Pledge Column (Pledge Column as prescribed in Article 130, paragraph (2), item (i), (b) of the Act; hereinafter the same shall apply in this Chapter) on the account of the Participant set forth in Article 136, paragraph (5) of the Act: The description or record of the decrease in number for each shareholder, represented by the numbers that result from multiplying each shareholder's number of Book-entry Shares set forth in Article 136, paragraph (1), item (i) of the Act that are described or recorded in the relevant Pledge Column by the rate of decrease (any fraction of such number of less than one (which shall be referred to as the "fraction in the Pledge Column" in item (iv)) shall be rounded up; hereinafter the same shall apply in this item)Book-entry, and the description or record of the decrease in the number of said Book-entry Shares, represented by the sum total of the numbers that result from such multiplication

(iii) The customer account among the accounts of an Superior Institution of a Participant prescribed in the preceding two items: The description or record of a decrease in the number of Book-entry Shares described or recorded as prescribed in the preceding two items

(iv) The Ownership Column of the account of a Participant who is a shareholder (including special shareholders) of Book-entry Shares as set forth in Article 136, paragraph (1), item (i) of the Act in the book-entry account registry maintained by the Immediately Superior Institution (if there is more than one such institution,, the one specified by the Book-entry Institution) of such shareholder: The description or record of an increase in the number that results from totaling the number obtained by subtracting the fraction in the Ownership Column for the Book-entry Shares held by such shareholder from one and the number obtained by subtracting the fraction in the Pledge Column for the same from one (any fraction of the result obtained of less than one (which shall be referred to as the "issuer fraction" in item (vi)) shall be discarded)

(v) The customer account among the accounts of the Book-entry Institution, etc. with which the account set forth in the preceding item has been opened and its Superior Institution: The description or record of an increase in the number that has been described or recorded as prescribed in the same item

(vi) The Ownership Column of the account set forth in Article 136, paragraph (1), item (iv) of the Act: The description or record of an increase in the total (any fraction less than one in that total number shall be discarded) of the issuer fraction

(vii) The customer account among the accounts of the Book-entry Institution, etc.

with which the account set forth in the preceding item has been opened and its Superior Institution: The description or record of an increase in the total that has been described or recorded as prescribed in the same item.
(2) The instructions to be given by a Book-entry Institution pursuant to the provisions of Article 136, paragraph (5) of the Act shall be given to the persons listed in the following items in relation to the matters prescribed therein:
  (i) All Subordinate Institutions: Instructions to the effect that matters necessary for the descriptions or records prescribed in items (iii) to item (vii) of the preceding paragraph should be reported
  (ii) The Account Management Institution required to enter the description or record prescribed in the preceding item: Matters subject to such description or record.

(Measures and Instructions in Cases Where Fractions Result from the Split of Book-entry Shares)
Article 31 (1) The description or record to be specified by a Cabinet Order as prescribed in Article 137, paragraph (5) of the Act shall be as prescribed in the following items depending upon the classification of the Ownership Column, etc. under said items:
  (i) The Ownership Column on the account of the Participant set forth in Article 137, paragraph (5) of the Act: The description or record of an increase in the number (any fraction of such number of less than one (which shall be referred to as the "fraction in the Ownership Column" in item (iv)) shall be discarded) that results from multiplying the number of Book-entry Shares (or, for Book-entry Shares for which a special shareholder request has been made, the number for each special shareholder) set forth in paragraph (1), item (i) of the same Article that are described or recorded in such Ownership Column by the rate of increase (which means the rate of increase as prescribed in item (ii) of the same paragraph; the same shall apply in the following item)
  (ii) The Pledge Column on the account of the Participant set forth in Article 137, paragraph (5) of the Act: The description or record of the increase in number for each shareholder, represented by the numbers that result from multiplying each shareholder's number of Book-entry Shares set forth in paragraph (1), item (i) of the same Article that are described or recorded in the relevant Pledge Column by the rate of increase (any fraction of such number of less than one (which shall be referred to as the "fraction in the Pledge Column" in item (iv)) shall be discarded; hereinafter the same shall apply in this item), and the description or record of the increase in the number of said Book-entry Shares, represented by the sum total of the numbers that result from such multiplication
  (iii) Customer account among the accounts of the Superior Institution of a Participant prescribed in the preceding two items: The description or record of an increase in the number of Book-entry Shares described or recorded as prescribed in the preceding two items
  (iv) The Ownership Column of the account of a Participant who is a shareholder (including special shareholders) of Book-entry Shares as set forth in Article 137, paragraph (1), item (i) of the Act in the book-entry account registry maintained by the Immediately Superior Institution (if there is more than one such institution, the one specified by the Book-entry Institution) of such shareholder: The description or record of an increase in the number that results from totaling the fraction in the Ownership Column and the fraction in the Pledge Column for the Book-entry Shares held by such shareholder (any fraction of such number of less than one (which shall be referred to as the "fraction for issuer" in item (vi)) shall be discarded)

(v) Customer account among the accounts of the Book-entry Institution, etc. with which the account set forth in the preceding item has been opened and its Superior Institution: The description or record of an increase in the number described or recorded as prescribed in the same item
(vi) The Ownership Column of the account as set forth in Article 137, paragraph (1), item (iv) of the Act: The description or record of an increase in the total (any fraction of such number of less than one shall be discarded) of the issuer fraction
(vii) Customer account among the accounts of the Book-entry Institution, etc. with which the account set forth in the preceding item has been opened and its Superior Institution: The description or record of an increase in the number described or recorded as prescribed in the same item.
(2) The instructions to be given by a Book-entry Institution pursuant to the provisions of Article 137, paragraph (5) of the Act shall be given to the persons listed in the following items in relation to the matters prescribed therein:
(i) All Subordinate Institutions: Instructions to the effect that matters necessary for the description or record prescribed in items (iii) to (vii) of the preceding paragraph should be reported
(ii) The Account Management Institution required to enter the description or record prescribed in the preceding item: Matters subject to such description or record.

(Measures and Instructions in Cases Where Fractions Result from the Delivery of Book-entry Shares of Other Issues as the Result of Merger, etc.)

Article 32 (1) The description or record to be specified by a Cabinet Order as prescribed in Article 138, paragraph (5) of the Act shall be as prescribed in the following items depending upon the classification of the Ownership Column, etc. under said items:
(i) The Ownership Column on the account of the Participant set forth in Article 138, paragraph (5) of the Act: The description or record of an increase in the number (any fraction of such number of less than one (which shall be referred to as the "fraction in the Ownership Column" in item (iv)) shall be discarded) that results from multiplying the number of Book-entry Shares set forth in paragraph (1), item (ii) of the same Article (or, for Book-entry Shares for which a special shareholder request has been made, the number for each special shareholder) that are described or recorded in such Ownership Column by an allotment ratio (which means an allotment ratio prescribed in item (iii) of the same paragraph; the same shall apply in the following item), for the Book-entry Shares set forth in item (i) of the same paragraph (hereinafter referred to as "Book-entry Shares of the Surviving Company, etc." in this paragraph)
(ii) The Pledge Column on the account of the Participant set forth in Article 138, paragraph (5) of the Act: The description or record of the increase in the number of each shareholder's Book-entry Shares in the Surviving Company, etc., represented by the numbers that result from multiplying each shareholder's number of Book-entry Shares set forth in paragraph (1), item (ii) of the same Article that are described or recorded in the relevant Pledge Column by the allotment ratio (any fraction of such number of less than one (which shall be referred to as the "fraction in the Pledge Column" in item (iv)) shall be discarded; hereinafter the same shall apply in this item), and the description or record of the increase in the number of said Book-entry Shares in the Surviving Company, etc., represented by the sum total of the numbers that result from such multiplication
(iii) Customer account among the accounts of the Superior Institution of a Participant prescribed in the preceding two items: The description or record of an increase in the number of Book-entry Shares of the Surviving Company, etc. that has been de-

scribed or recorded as prescribed in the preceding two items
- (iv) The Ownership Column of the account of a Participant who is a shareholder (including special shareholders) of Book-entry Shares set forth in Article 138, paragraph (1), item (ii) of the Act in the book-entry account registry maintained by the Immediately Superior Institution (if there is more than one such institution, the one specified by the Book-entry Institution) of such shareholder: The description or record of an increase in the number that results from totaling the fraction in the Ownership Column and the fraction in the Pledge Column for the Book-entry Shares of the Surviving Company, etc. held by such shareholder (any fraction of the number of less than one (which shall be referred to as the "fraction for issuer" in item (vi)) shall be discarded)
- (v) Customer account among the accounts of the Book-entry Institution, etc. with which the account set forth in the preceding item has been opened and its Superior Institution: The description or record of an increase in the number related to the Book-entry Shares of the Surviving Company, etc. that has been described or recorded as prescribed in the same item
- (vi) The Ownership Column of the account set forth in Article 138, paragraph (1), item (v) of the Act: The description or record of an increase in the total number (any fraction of such total number of less than one shall be discarded) of the issuer fraction for the Book-entry Shares of the Surviving Company, etc.
- (vii) Customer account among the accounts of the Book-entry Institution, etc. with which the account set forth in the preceding item has been opened and its Superior Institution: The description or record of an increase in the number related to the Book-entry Shares of the Surviving Company, etc. that has been described or recorded as prescribed in the same item
- (viii) The Ownership Column or Pledge Column on the account of the Participant set forth in Article 138, paragraph (5) of the Act or the customer account among the accounts of the Superior Institution of such Participant: The deletion of a description or record of all Book-entry Shares set forth in paragraph (1), item (ii) of the same Article.

(2) The instructions to be given by a Book-entry Institution pursuant to the provisions of Article 138, paragraph (5) of the Act shall be given to the persons listed in the following items in relation to the matters prescribed therein:
- (i) All Subordinate Institutions: To the effect that matters necessary for the description or record prescribed in items (iii) to (vii) of the preceding paragraph should be reported
- (ii) The Account Management Institutions which are required to enter descriptions or records as prescribed in the preceding item: Matters subject to such description or record.

(Application for Description or Record of Trust)

Article 33 (1) The description or record in the book-entry account registry (hereinafter referred to as the "description or record of trust" in this Chapter) as prescribed in Article 142, paragraph (1) of the Act shall be entered upon application by a person prescribed in the following respective items depending upon the classification of the case under said items to the person's Immediately Superior Institution:
- (i) Where, by transfer or pledge of Book-entry Shares by a settlor to a trustee, such Book-entry Shares come to belong to the trust property: Settlor
- (ii) Where, by changing a trustee, the rights to Book-entry Shares which belong to the trust property are transferred to a new trustee: Previous trustee
- (iii) Any cases other than those listed in the preceding two items: Trustee.

(2) A person who intends to apply as set forth in the preceding paragraph shall indicate the following matters in the application:
  (i) The account of the trustee or new trustee
  (ii) The issue and number of Book-entry Shares related to the application
  (iii) Whether the description or record of trust is to be made in the Ownership Column or Pledge Column in the account set forth in item (i).

(Application by Subrogation)
Article 34 (1) In the cases listed in paragraph (1), item (iii) of the preceding Article, a beneficiary or a settlor may apply for the description or record of trust on behalf of a trustee.
(2) A beneficiary or settlor shall, in applying pursuant to the provisions of the preceding paragraph, indicate in the application the individual or business name and address of the trustee and the reason for the subrogation, and submit materials certifying the reason for such subrogation and the fact that the rights to Book-entry Shares related to the application belong to the trust property.

(Simultaneous Application)
Article 35 (1) In the case listed in Article 33, paragraph (1), item (i), an application for a description or record of trust shall be submitted simultaneously with an application for book-entry related to the transfer or pledge of Book-entry Shares prescribed in the same item.
(2) In the case of the preceding paragraph, a Book-entry Institution, etc. shall, when it provides notice pursuant to the provisions of Article 132, paragraph (4), item (ii) or (v) of the Act, or pursuant to the provisions of paragraph (5), item (ii) or (v) (including cases where applied mutatis mutandis pursuant to paragraph (6) of the same Article) or paragraph (7), item (iii) (including cases where applied mutatis mutandis pursuant to paragraph (8) of the same Article) of the same Article, simultaneously provide notice of the matters listed in each item under Article 33, paragraph (2).
(3) A Book-entry Institution, etc. which has received notice pursuant to the provisions of the preceding paragraph shall, when generating a description or record pursuant to the provisions of Article 132, paragraph (4), item (iii) or (iv) of the Act, or the provisions of paragraph (5), item (iii) or (iv) of the same Article (including cases where applied mutatis mutandis pursuant to paragraph (6) of the same Article), or the provisions of paragraph (7), item (i) or (ii) of the same Article (including cases where applied mutatis mutandis pursuant to paragraph (8) of the same Article), simultaneously enter a description or record of trust in the book-entry account registry it maintains in accordance with the contents of the notice given pursuant to the provisions of the preceding paragraph.

(Application for Deletion of Description or Record of Trust)
Article 36 (1) The description or record of trust shall be deleted upon application by a person prescribed in the following respective items to the person's Immediately Superior Institution (or, in the case listed in item (iii), the trustee's Immediately Superior Institution) depending on the classification of the case under said items:
  (i) Where, by transfer of the rights to Book-entry Shares, the rights to such Book-entry Shares cease to belong to the trust property: Trustee
  (ii) Where, by changing a trustee, the rights to Book-entry Shares belonging to the trust property are transferred to a new trustee: Previous trustee
  (iii) Where, due to the transfer of the rights to Book-entry Shares to trustee's own property, the rights to such Book-entry Shares cease to belong to the trust proper-

ty: Trustee and beneficiary.
(2) A person who intends to apply as set forth in the preceding paragraph shall indicate the following matters in the application:
(i) The account of the trustee or previous trustee
(ii) The issue and number of Book-entry Shares to which the application pertains.
(iii) Whether the description or record of trust is to be deleted from the Ownership Column or the Pledge Column of the account set forth in item (i).
(3) A beneficiary prescribed in paragraph (1), item (iii) shall, in applying pursuant to the provisions of the same paragraph, submit materials identifying itself as a beneficiary.

(Simultaneous Application)
Article 37 In the case listed in paragraph (1), item (i) of the preceding Article, an application for deletion of a description or record of trust shall be submitted simultaneously with an application for book-entry in relation to a transfer of rights prescribed in said item.

(Change of a Trustee)
Article 38 (1) Upon a change of a trustee, the previous trustee shall apply for book-entry (hereinafter referred to as an "application for entry of an increase, etc." in paragraph (3)), requesting that the description or record of an increase for Book-entry Shares that belong to the trust property be entered in the new trustee's account, and simultaneously with such application, an application (which shall be referred to as an "application for entry of a change of a trustee, etc." in paragraph (3)) pursuant to the provisions of Articles 33, paragraph (1) (limited to the portion related to item (ii)) and Article 36, paragraph (1) (limited to the portion related to item (ii)) for such Book-entry Shares. In this case, simultaneously with these applications, materials certifying the change shall also be submitted.
(2) The provisions of Articles 35, paragraph (2) and paragraph (3) shall apply mutatis mutandis to cases under the first sentence of the preceding paragraph.
(3) Where the termination of the duties of a trustee and change of a trustee occur pursuant to the provisions of Article 56, paragraph (1), items (i) to (iv) or (vi) of the Trust Act or Article 8 of the Act on Charitable Trusts, a new trustee may also apply for entry of an increase, etc. and for change of an entry of a trustee, etc. In this case, an application for change of an entry of a trustee, etc. shall be made simultaneously with an application for entry of an increase, etc.
(4) In a case under the preceding paragraph, the provisions of the second sentence of paragraph (1) shall apply mutatis mutandis.

(Notice to All Shareholders)
Article 39 The time to be specified by a Cabinet Order as prescribed in Article 151, paragraph (1), item (vii) of the Act shall be the time at which the court specifies a reference date as prescribed in Article 194, paragraph (1) of the Corporate Reorganization Act, and the date to be specified by a Cabinet Order as prescribed in the same item shall be said reference date.

(Period for Exercise of Minority Shareholders' Rights, etc.)
Article 40 The period to be specified by a Cabinet Order as prescribed in Article 154, paragraph (2) of the Act shall be four weeks.

(Provision of Contents of Book-entry Shares)
Article 41 The method to be specified by a Cabinet Order as prescribed in Article 162,

paragraph (1) of the Act shall be that of making the matters specified in the items under the same paragraph in relation to Book-entry Shares to which the notices listed in such items pertain available to many and unspecified persons, by electromagnetic means specified by a Cabinet Office Ordinance or an Ordinance of the Ministry of Justice, until the day on which all such Book-entry Shares described or recorded in the book-entry account registry maintained by a Book-entry Institution are deleted from the book-entry account registry.

Chapter VII Book-entry of Share Options

(Matters to be Described or Recorded in a Book-entry Account Registry)
Article 42 Matters to be specified by a Cabinet Order as prescribed in Article 165, paragraph (3), item (vi) of the Act shall be the following:
(i) Matters concerning restrictions on the disposal of Book-entry Share Options (Book-entry Share Options as prescribed in Article 163 of the Act; the same shall apply hereinafter)
(ii) Matters listed in Article 28, items (ii) to (iv).

(Matters to be Reported in a New Description or Record Procedure)
Article 43 The matters to be specified by a Cabinet Order as prescribed in Article 166, paragraph (1), item (viii) of the Act shall be those listed in item (ii) of the preceding Article.

(Application for a Description or Record of Trust)
Article 44 (1) The description or record in the book-entry account registry (hereinafter referred to as the "description or record of trust" in this Chapter) prescribed in Article 176, paragraph (1) of the Act shall be entered upon application by a person prescribed in one of the following items depending on the classification of the case under said items to the person's Immediately Superior Institution:
(i) Where, via transfer or pledge of Book-entry Share Options by a settlor to a trustee, such Book-entry Share Options come to belong to the trust property: Settlor
(ii) Where, by a change of a trustee, the rights to Book-entry Share Options which belong to the trust property are transferred to a new trustee: Previous trustee
(iii) Any cases other than those listed in the preceding two items: Trustee.
(2) A person who intends to apply as set forth in the preceding paragraph shall indicate the following matters in the application:
(i) The account of the trustee or new trustee
(ii) The issue and number of Book-entry Share Options to which the application pertains
(iii) Whether the description or record of trust in the account set forth in item (i) is to be entered in the Ownership Column (Ownership Column prescribed in Article 166, paragraph (2), item (i), (a) of the Act; the same shall apply in Article 47, paragraph (2), item (iii)) or the Pledge Column (Pledge Column as prescribed in Article 166, paragraph (2), item (i), (b) of the Act; the same shall apply in Article 47, paragraph (2), item (iii)).

(Application by Subrogation).
Article 45 (1) In the cases listed in paragraph (1), item (iii) of the preceding Article, a beneficiary or a settlor may apply for the description or record of trust on behalf of a trustee.

(2) A beneficiary or settlor shall, in applying pursuant to the provisions of the preceding paragraph, indicate in the application the individual or business name and address of the trustee and the reason for the subrogation, and shall submit materials certifying the reason for such subrogation and the fact that the rights to Book-entry Share Options related to the application belong to the trust property.

(Simultaneous Application)
Article 46 (1) In the case listed in Article 44, paragraph (1), item (i), an application for a description or record of trust shall be made simultaneously with an application for book-entry related to the transfer or pledge of Book-entry Share Options prescribed in the same item.
(2) In the case of the preceding paragraph, a Book-entry Institution, etc. shall, when it gives notice pursuant to the provisions of Article 168, paragraph (4), item (ii) or item (v) of the Act, or pursuant to the provisions of paragraph (5), item (ii) or item (v) (including cases where applied mutatis mutandis pursuant to paragraph (6) of the same Article) or paragraph (7), item (iii) (including the cases where applied mutatis mutandis pursuant to paragraph (8) of the same Article) of the same Article, simultaneously provide notice on the matters listed in each item under Article 44, paragraph (2).
(3) A Book-entry Institution, etc. which has received notice pursuant to the provisions of the preceding paragraph shall, when it enters a description or record pursuant to the provisions of Article 168, paragraph (4), item (iii) or (iv) of the Act, or the provisions of paragraph (5), item (iii) or (iv) of the same Article (including cases where applied mutatis mutandis pursuant to paragraph (6) of the same Article), or the provisions of paragraph (7), item (i) or (ii) of the same Article (including the cases where applied mutatis mutandis pursuant to paragraph (8) of the same Article), simultaneously enter a description or record of trust in the book-entry account registry it maintains in accordance with the contents of the notice given pursuant to the provisions of the preceding paragraph.

(Application for Deletion of Description or Record of Trust)
Article 47 (1) The description or record of trust shall be deleted upon application by a person prescribed in the following items to its Immediately Superior Institution (or, in the case listed in item (iii), the trustee's Immediately Superior Institution) depending upon the classification of the case under said items:
(i) Where, by transfer of the rights to Book-entry Share Options, the rights to such Book-entry Share Options cease to belong to the trust property: Trustee
(ii) Where, by change of a trustee, the rights to Book-entry Share Options which belong to the trust property are transferred to a new trustee: Previous trustee
(iii) Where, due to the transfer of the rights to Book-entry Share Options to trustee's own property, the rights to such Book-entry Share Options cease to belong to the trust property: Trustee and beneficiary.
(2) A person who intends to apply as set forth in the preceding paragraph shall indicate the following matters in the application:
(i) The account of the trustee or previous trustee
(ii) The issue and number of Book-entry Share Options related to the application
(iii) Whether the description or record of trust is to be deleted from the Ownership Column or the Pledge Column of the account set forth in item (i).
(3) A beneficiary prescribed in paragraph (1), item (iii) shall, in applying pursuant to the provisions of the same paragraph, submit materials identifying itself as a beneficiary.

(Simultaneous Application)

Article 48 In the case listed in paragraph (1), item (i) of the preceding Article, an application for deletion of a description or record of trust shall be submitted simultaneously with an application for book-entry related to transfer of rights as prescribed in the same item.

(Change of a Trustee)
Article 49 (1) Upon a change of a trustee, the previous trustee shall apply for book-entry (hereinafter referred to as an "application for entry of an increase, etc." in paragraph (3)), requesting that the description or record of an increase for Book-entry Share Options that belong to the trust property be entered in the new trustee's account, and simultaneously apply (which shall be referred to as an "application for entry of a change of a trustee, etc." in paragraph (3)) pursuant to the provisions of Articles 44, paragraph (1) (limited to the portion related to item (ii)) and Article 47, paragraph (1) (limited to the portion related to item (ii)) for such Book-entry Share Options. In this case, materials certifying the change shall also be submitted simultaneously with these applications.
(2) The provisions of Article 46, paragraphs (2) and (3) shall apply mutatis mutandis to cases under the first sentence of the preceding paragraph.
(3) Where the termination of the duties of a trustee and change of a trustee occur pursuant to the provisions of Article 56, paragraph (1), items (i) to (iv) or (vi) of the Trust Act or Article 8 of the Act on Charitable Trusts, the new trustee may also apply for entry of an increase, etc. and for change of an entry of a trustee, etc. In this case, such applications shall be submitted simultaneously.
(4) In a case under the preceding paragraph, the provisions of the second sentence of paragraph (1) shall apply mutatis mutandis.

(Provision of Contents of Book-entry Transfer Share Options)
Article 50 The method to be specified by a Cabinet Order as prescribed in Article 191, paragraph (1) of the Act shall be that of making the matters listed in Article 166, paragraph (1), item (ix) of the Act pertaining to Book-entry Share Options related to a notice listed in Article 166, paragraph (1) of the Act available to many and unspecified persons using electronic means specified by a Cabinet Office Ordinance or an Ordinance of the Ministry of Justice, until the day all such Book-entry Company Bonds with Share Options described or recorded in the book-entry account registry maintained by a Book-entry Institution are deleted from the book-entry account registry.

Chapter VIII Book-entry of Company Bonds with Share Option

(Matters to be Described or Recorded in Book-entry Account Registry)
Article 51 The matters to be specified by a Cabinet Order as prescribed in Article 194, paragraph (3), item (vi) of the Act shall be the following:
(i) Matters concerning restrictions on the disposal of Book-entry Company Bonds with Share Options (Book-entry Company Bonds with Share Options prescribed in Article 192, paragraph (1) of the Act; the same shall apply hereinafter)
(ii) Matters listed in Article 28, items (ii) to (iv).

(Matters to be Reported in a New Description or Record Procedure)
Article 52 The matters to be specified by a Cabinet Order as prescribed in Article 195, paragraph (1), item (viii) of the Act shall be those listed in item (ii) of the preceding Article.

(Application for Description or Record of Trust)

Article 53 (1) The description or record in the book-entry account registry (hereinafter referred to as the "description or record of trust" in this Chapter) prescribed in Article 207, paragraph (1) of the Act shall be entered upon application, depending upon the classification of the cases listed in the following items, by a person prescribed in the respective item to its Immediately Superior Institution:
  (i) Where, by transfer or pledge of Book-entry Company Bonds with Share Options by a settlor to a trustee, such Book-entry Company Bonds with Share Options come to belong to the trust property: Settlor
  (ii) Where, by change of a trustee, the rights to Book-entry Company Bonds with Share Options which belong to the trust property are transferred to a new trustee: Previous trustee
  (iii) Any cases other than those listed in the preceding two items: Trustee.
(2) A person who intends to apply as set forth in the preceding paragraph shall indicate the following matters in the application:
  (i) The account of the trustee or new trustee
  (ii) The issue and number of Book-entry Company Bonds with Share Options to which the application pertains
  (iii) Whether the description or record of trust of the account set forth in item (i) is to be made in the Ownership Column (Ownership Column as prescribed in Article 195, paragraph (2), item (i), (a) of the Act; the same shall apply in Article 56, paragraph (2), item (iii)) or the Pledge Column (Pledge Column as prescribed in Article 195, paragraph (2), item (i), (b) of the Act; the same shall apply in Article 56, paragraph (2), item (iii)).

(Application by Subrogation)

Article 54 (1) In the cases listed in paragraph (1), item (iii) of the preceding Article, a beneficiary or a settlor may apply for the description or record of trust on behalf of a trustee.
(2) A beneficiary or settlor shall, in applying pursuant to the provisions of the preceding paragraph, indicate in the application the individual or business name and address of the trustee and the reason for the subrogation, and submit materials certifying the cause of the subrogation and the fact that the rights to Book-entry Company Bonds with Share Options related to the application belong to the trust property.

(Simultaneous Application)

Article 55 (1) In the case listed in Article 53, paragraph (1), item (i), an application for description or record of trust shall be submitted simultaneously with an application for book-entry-related to the transfer or pledge of Book-entry Company Bonds with Share Options prescribed in the same item.
(2) In the case of the preceding paragraph, a Book-entry Institution, etc. shall, when it gives a notice pursuant to the provisions of Article 197, paragraph (4), item (ii) or item (v) of the Act, or pursuant to the provisions of paragraph (5), item (ii) or item (v) of the same Article (including the cases where applied mutatis mutandis pursuant to paragraph (6) of the same Article), or the provisions of paragraph (7), item (iii) of the same Article (including cases where applied mutatis mutandis pursuant to paragraph (8) of the same Article), simultaneously give notice on the matters listed in each item under Article 53, paragraph (2).
(3) A Book-entry Institution, etc. which has received notice pursuant to the provisions of the preceding paragraph shall, when it enters the description or record pursuant to the

provisions of Article 197, paragraph (4), items (iii) or (iv) of the Act, or the provisions of paragraph (5), items (iii) or (iv) of the same Article (including cases where applied mutatis mutandis pursuant to paragraph (6) of the same Article), or the provisions of paragraph (7), items (i) or (ii) of the same Article (including cases where applied mutatis mutandis pursuant to paragraph (8) of the same Article), simultaneously enter a description or record of trust in the book-entry account registry it maintain accordance with the contents of the notice given pursuant to the provisions of the preceding paragraph.

(Application for Deletion of Description or Record of Trust)
Article 56 (1) The description or record of trust shall be deleted upon application by a person prescribed in the respective item to its Immediately Superior Institution (or, in the case listed in item (iii), the trustee's Immediately Superior Institution), depending upon the classification of the case under the following items,:
  (i) Where, by transfer of the rights to Book-entry Company Bonds with Share Options, the rights to such Book-entry Company Bonds with Share Options cease to belong to the trust property: Trustee
  (ii) Where, by a change of a trustee, the rights to Book-entry Company Bonds with Share Options belonging to the trust property are transferred to a new trustee: Previous trustee
  (iii) Where, due to the transfer of the rights to Book-entry Company Bonds with Share Options to trustee's own property, the rights to such Book-entry Company Bonds with Share Options cease to belong to the trust property: Trustee and beneficiary.
(2) A person who intends to apply as set forth in the preceding paragraph shall indicate the following matters in the application:
  (i) The account of the trustee or previous trustee
  (ii) The issue and number of Book-entry Company Bonds with Share Options to which the application pertains
  (iii) Whether the description or record of trust is to be deleted from the Ownership Column or the Pledge Column of the account set forth in item (i).
(3) A beneficiary prescribed in paragraph (1), item (iii) shall, in applying pursuant to the provisions of the same paragraph, submit materials identifying itself as a beneficiary.

(Simultaneous Application)
Article 57 In the case described in paragraph (1), item (i) of the preceding Article, an application for deletion of a description or record of trust shall be submitted simultaneously with an application for book-entry related to the transfer of rights prescribed in the same item.

(Change of a Trustee)
Article 58 (1) Upon a change of a trustee, the previous trustee shall apply for book-entry (hereinafter referred to as an "application for entry of an increase, etc." in paragraph (3)) requesting that the description or record of an increase for Book-entry Company Bonds with Share Options that belong to the trust property be entered in the new trustee's account, and simultaneously with such application, an application (which shall be referred to as an "application for entry of a change of a trustee, etc." in paragraph (3)) pursuant to the provisions of Articles 53, paragraph (1) (limited to the portion related to item (ii)) and Article 56, paragraph (1) (limited to the portion related to item (ii)) for such Book-entry Company Bonds with Share Options. In this case, materials certifying the change shall also be submitted simultaneously with these applications.

Art.59～60

(2) The provisions of Article 55, paragraphs (2) and (3) shall apply mutatis mutandis to cases under the first sentence of the preceding paragraph.
(3) Where the termination of the duties of a trustee and change of a trustee occur pursuant to the provisions of Article 56, paragraph (1), items (i) to (iv) or (vi) of the Trust Act or Article 8 of the Act on Charitable Trusts, the new trustee may also apply for entry of an increase, etc. and for change of an entry of a trustee, etc. In this case, an application for a change of an entry of a trustee, etc. shall be made simultaneously with an application for entry of an increase, etc.
(4) In the case of the preceding paragraph, the provisions of the second sentence of paragraph (1) shall apply mutatis mutandis.

(Provision of Contents of Book-entry Company Bonds with Share Options)
Article 59 The method to be specified by a Cabinet Order as prescribed in Article 225, paragraph (1) of the Act shall be that of making the matters specified in each item under said paragraph pertaining to Book-entry Company Bonds with Share Options related to a notice listed in each such item available to many and unspecified persons, by electromagnetic means specified by a Cabinet Office Ordinance or an Ordinance of the Ministry of Justice, until the day all such Book-entry Company Bonds with Share Options described or recorded in the book-entry account registry maintained by a Book-entry Institution are deleted from said book-entry account registry.

Chapter IX Book-entry of Investment Equity, etc.

(Mutatis Mutandis Application of Provisions Concerning Shares to Investment Equity)
Article 60 The provisions of Article 28 (limited to the portion related to item (i)) shall apply mutatis mutandis to the matters to be specified by a Cabinet Order prescribed in Article 129, paragraph (3), item (vii) of the Act as applied mutatis mutandis pursuant to Article 228, paragraph (1) of the Act; the provisions of Article 30, paragraph (1) shall apply mutatis mutandis to the description or record to be specified by a Cabinet Order under Article 136, paragraph (5) of the Act as applied mutatis mutandis pursuant to Article 228, paragraph (1) of the Act; the provisions of Article 30, paragraph (2) shall apply mutatis mutandis to the instructions to be given by a Book-entry Institution pursuant to the provisions of Article 136, paragraph (5) of the Act as applied mutatis mutandis pursuant to Article 228, paragraph (1) of the Act; the provisions of Article 31, paragraph (1) shall apply mutatis mutandis to the description or record to be specified by a Cabinet Order as prescribed in Article 137, paragraph (5) of the Act as applied mutatis mutandis pursuant to Article 228, paragraph (1) of the Act; the provisions of Article 31, paragraph (2) shall apply mutatis mutandis to the instructions to be given to a Book-entry Institution pursuant to the provisions of Article 137, paragraph (5) of the Act as applied mutatis mutandis pursuant to Article 228, paragraph (1) of the Act, the provisions of Article 32, paragraph (1) shall apply mutatis mutandis to the description or record to be specified by a Cabinet Order as prescribed in Article 138, paragraph (5) of the Act as applied mutatis mutandis pursuant to Article 228, paragraph (1) of the Act; the provisions of Article 32, paragraph (2) shall apply mutatis mutandis to the instructions to be given a Book-entry Institution pursuant to the provisions of Article 138, paragraph (5) of the Act as applied mutatis mutandis pursuant to Article 228, paragraph (1) of the Act, the provisions of Articles 33 to 38 shall apply mutatis mutandis to a description or record in the book-entry account registry prescribed in Article 142, paragraph (1) of the Act as applied mutatis mutandis pursuant to Article 228, paragraph (1) of the Act; the provisions of Article 40 shall apply mutatis mutandis to

the period to be specified by a Cabinet Order as prescribed in Article 154, paragraph (2) of the Act as applied mutatis mutandis pursuant to Article 228, paragraph (1) of the Act; and the provisions of Article 41 shall apply mutatis mutandis to the method to be specified by a Cabinet Order as prescribed in Article 162, paragraph (1) of the Act as applied mutatis mutandis pursuant to Article 228, paragraph (1) of the Act. In this case, the terms listed in the middle column of the following table, found in the provisions listed in the left column of the same table shall be deemed to be replaced with the terms listed in the right column of the same table.

Article 30, paragraph (1), item (i)	number of Book-Entry Transfer Shares	number of units of Book-Entry Transfer Investment Equity
	special shareholder request	special investor request
	special shareholder prescribed	special investor prescribed
	special shareholder"	special investor"
	number for each	number of units for each
	multiplying the number	multiplying the number of units
	in that number	in that number of units
Article 30, paragraph (1), item (ii)	number for each	number of units for each
	multiplying the number	multiplying the number of units
	in that number	in that number of units
	number of Book-Entry Transfer Shares	number of units of Book-Entry Transfer Investment Equity
Article 30, paragraph (1), item (iii)	number of Book-Entry Transfer Shares	number of units of Book-Entry Transfer Investment Equity
	number	number of units
Article 30, paragraph (1), item (iv)	special shareholder	special investor
Article 31, paragraph (1), item (i)	number of Book-Entry Transfer Shares	number of units of Book-Entry Transfer Investment Equity
	special shareholder request	special investor request
	number for each such special shareholder	number for each such special investor
	multiplying the number	multiplying the number of units
	in that number	in that number of units
Article 31, paragraph (1), item (ii)	number for each	number of units for each
	multiplying the number	multiplying the number of units
	in that number	in that number of units
	number of Book-Entry Transfer Shares	number of units of Book-Entry Transfer Investment Equity

Article 31, paragraph (1), item (iii)	number of Book-Entry Transfer Shares	number of units of Book-Entry Transfer Investment Equity
	number	number of units
Article 31, paragraph (1), item (iv)	special shareholder	special investor
Article 32, paragraph (1), item (i)	number of Book-Entry Transfer Shares	number of units of Book-Entry Transfer Investment Equity
	special shareholder request	special investor request
	number for each special shareholder	number for each special investor
	multiplying the number	multiplying the number of units
	in that number	in that number of units
	Book-Entry Transfer Shares of the Surviving Company, etc.	Book-Entry Transfer Investment Equity of the surviving investment company
Article 32, paragraph (1), item (ii)	number for each	number of units for each
	multiplying the number	multiplying the number of units
	in that number	in that number of units
	Book-Entry Transfer Shares of the Surviving Company, etc.	Book-Entry Transfer Investment Equity of the surviving investment company
	number of such Book-Entry Transfer Shares of the Surviving Company, etc.	number of units of such Book-Entry Transfer Investment Equity of the surviving investment company
Article 32, paragraph (1), item (iii)	number of such Book-Entry Transfer Shares of the Surviving Company, etc.	number of units of such Book-Entry Transfer Investment Equity of the surviving investment company
	number	number of units
Article 32, paragraph (1), item (iv)	special shareholder	special investor
	Book-Entry Transfer Shares of the Surviving Company, etc.	Book-Entry Transfer Investment Equity of the surviving investment company
Article 32, paragraph (1), items (v) to (vii)	Book-Entry Transfer Shares of the Surviving Company, etc.	Book-Entry Transfer Investment Equity of the surviving investment company
Article 33, paragraph (2), item (ii) and Article 36, paragraph (2), item (ii)	and number	and number of units

(Replacement of Terms in the Provisions of Act as Applied Mutatis Mutandis to Investment Equity)

Article 61　Where the provisions of the Act are applied mutatis mutandis to investment equity as prescribed in the Act on Investment Trusts and Investment Corporations under Article 228, paragraph (1) of the Act, technical replacement of terms related to such provisions shall be made as prescribed in the following table:

Provision containing the terms to be replaced	Terms to be replaced	Replacement terms
Article 153	Article 308, paragraph (1) of the Companies Act	the main text of Article 308, paragraph (1) of the Companies Act as applied mutatis mutandis pursuant to Article 94, paragraph (1) of the Act on Investment Trusts and Investment Corporations

(Mutatis Mutandis Application of Provisions Concerning Shares to Preferred Equity Investments by a Cooperative Financial Institution)

Article 62　The provisions of Article 28 (limited to the portion related to item (i)) shall apply mutatis mutandis to the matters to be specified by a Cabinet Order as prescribed in Article 129, paragraph (3), item (vii) of the Act as applied mutatis mutandis pursuant to Article 235, paragraph (1) of the Act; the provisions of Article 31, paragraph (1) shall apply mutatis mutandis to the description or record to be specified by a Cabinet Order as prescribed in Article 137, paragraph (5) of the Act as applied mutatis mutandis pursuant to Article 235, paragraph (1) of the Act; the provisions of Article 31, paragraph (2) shall apply mutatis mutandis to the instructions to be given by a Book-entry Institution pursuant to the provisions of Article 137, paragraph (5) of the Act as applied mutatis mutandis pursuant to Article 235, paragraph (1) of the Act; the provisions of Article 32, paragraph (1) shall apply mutatis mutandis to the description or record to be specified by a Cabinet Order as prescribed in Article 138, paragraph (5) of the Act as applied mutatis mutandis pursuant to Article 235, paragraph (1) of the Act; the provisions of Article 32, paragraph (2) shall apply mutatis mutandis to the instructions to be given a Book-entry Institution pursuant to the provisions of Article 138, paragraph (5) of the Act as applied mutatis mutandis pursuant to Article 235, paragraph (1) of the Act; the provisions of Articles 33 to 38 shall apply mutatis mutandis to the description or record in the book-entry account registry prescribed in Article 142, paragraph (1) of the Act as applied mutatis mutandis pursuant to Article 235, paragraph (1) of the Act; the provisions of Article 39 shall apply mutatis mutandis to the time to be specified by a Cabinet Order as prescribed in Article 151, paragraph (1), item (vii) of the Act as applied mutatis mutandis pursuant to Article 235, paragraph (1) of the Act and to the date to be specified by a Cabinet Order as prescribed in the same item; the provisions of Article 40 shall apply mutatis mutandis to the period to be specified by a Cabinet Order as prescribed in Article 154, paragraph (2) of the Act as applied mutatis mutandis pursuant to Article 235, paragraph (1) of the Act; and the provisions of Article 41 shall apply mutatis mutandis to the method to be specified by a Cabinet Order as prescribed in Article 162, paragraph (1) of the Act as applied mutatis mutandis pursuant to Article 235, paragraph (1) of the Act. In this case, the terms listed in the middle column of the following table, found in the provisions listed in the left column of the same table, shall be deemed to be replaced with the terms listed in the right column of the same table.

Article 31, paragraph (1)	Ownership Column, etc.	Ownership Column, etc. (which means the Ownership Column, etc. prescribed in Article 135, paragraph (3) of the Act as applied mutatis mutandis by replacing certain terms pursuant to Article 235, paragraph (1) of the Act; hereinafter the same shall apply in this Chapter)
Article 31, paragraph (1), item (i)	Ownership Column of the account	Ownership Column of the account (Ownership Column as prescribed in Article 130, paragraph (2), item (i), (a) of the Act as applied mutatis mutandis by replacing certain terms pursuant to Article 235, paragraph (1) of the Act; hereinafter the same shall apply in this Chapter)
	number of Book-Entry Transfer Shares	number of units of book-entry transfer preferred equity investments
	special shareholder request	request set forth in Article 151, paragraph (2), item (i) of the Act as applied mutatis mutandis by replacing certain terms pursuant to Article 235, paragraph (1) of the Act (which shall be referred to as a "special preferred equity investor request" in paragraph (1), item (i) of the following Article)
	number for each special shareholder	number of units for each special preferred equity investor as prescribed in Article 151, paragraph (2), item (i) of the Act as applied mutatis mutandis by replacing certain terms pursuant to Article 235, paragraph (1) of the Act (hereinafter simply referred to as a "special preferred equity investor" in this paragraph and paragraph (1) of the following Article)
	multiplying the number	multiplying the number of units
	in that number	in that number of units
Article 31, paragraph (1), item (ii)	Pledge Column of the account	Pledge Column of the account (which means the Pledge Column prescribed in Article 130, paragraph (2), item (i), (b) of the Act as applied mutatis mutandis by replacing certain terms pursuant to Article 235, paragraph (1) of the Act; hereinafter the same shall apply in this Chapter)
	number for each	number of units for each
	multiplying the number	multiplying the number of units
	in that number	in that number of units
	number of Book-Entry Transfer Shares	number of units of book-entry transfer preferred equity investments

Article 31, paragraph (1), item (iii)	number of Book-Entry Transfer Shares	number of units of book-entry transfer preferred equity investments
	number	number of units
Article 31, paragraph (1), item (iv)	special shareholder	special preferred equity investor
Article 32, paragraph (1), item (i)	number of Book-Entry Transfer Shares	number of units of book-entry transfer preferred equity investments
	special shareholder request	special preferred equity investor request
	number for each special shareholder	number of units for each special preferred equity investor
	multiplying the number	multiplying the number of units
	in that number	in that number of units
	Book-Entry Transfer Shares of the Surviving Company, etc.	book-entry transfer preferred equity investments of the surviving cooperative structured financial institution
Article 32, paragraph (1), item (ii)	number for each	number of units for each
	multiplying the number	multiplying the number of units
	in that number	in that number of units
	Book-Entry Transfer Shares of the Surviving Company, etc.	book-entry transfer preferred equity investments of the surviving cooperative structured financial institution
	number of such Book-Entry Transfer Shares of the Surviving Company, etc.	number of units of such book-entry transfer preferred equity investments of the surviving cooperative structured financial institution
Article 32, paragraph (1), item (iii)	number of such Book-Entry Transfer Shares of the Surviving Company, etc.	number of units of such book-entry transfer preferred equity investments of the surviving cooperative structured financial institution
	number	number of units
Article 32, paragraph (1), item (iv)	special shareholder	special preferred equity investor
	Book-Entry Transfer Shares of the Surviving Company, etc.	book-entry transfer preferred equity investments of the surviving cooperative structured financial institution
Article 32, paragraph (1), items (v) to (vii)	Book-Entry Transfer Shares of the Surviving Company, etc.	book-entry transfer preferred equity investments of the surviving cooperative financial institution
Article 33, paragraph (2), item (ii) and Article 36, paragraph (2), item (ii)	and number	and number of units

| Article 39 | Article 194, paragraph (1) of the Corporate Reorganization Act | Article 194, paragraph (1) of the Corporate Reorganization Act as applied mutatis mutandis pursuant to Article 116 of the Act on Special Treatment of Corporate Reorganization Proceedings and Other Insolvency Proceedings of Financial Institutions (Act No. 95 of 1996) |

(Replacement of Terms in the Provisions of the Act as Applied Mutatis Mutandis for Preferred Equity Investments by a Cooperative Financial Institution)

Article 63 Where the provisions of the Act are applied mutatis mutandis to preferred equity investments by a cooperative financial institution as prescribed in the Act on Preferred Equity Investment by Cooperative Financial Institutions (Act No. 44 of 1993) pursuant to the provisions of Article 235, paragraph (1) of the Act, the technical replacement of terms related to such provisions shall be carried out as prescribed in the following table:

Provision containing the terms to be replaced	Terms to be replaced	Replacement terms
Article 147, paragraph (3) and paragraph (4) and Article 148, paragraph (3)	Article 124, paragraph (1) of the Companies Act	Article 124, paragraph (1) of the Companies Act as applied mutatis mutandis pursuant to Article 26 of the Act on Preferred Equity Investment by Cooperative Financial Institutions
Article 159, paragraph (1)	Article 230, paragraph (1) of the Companies Act	Article 230, paragraph (1) of the Companies Act as applied mutatis mutandis pursuant to Article 31, paragraph (2) of the Act on Preferred Equity Investment by Cooperative Financial Institutions
Article 159, paragraph (2)	Article 224, paragraph (1) of the Companies Act	Article 224, paragraph (1) of the Companies Act as applied mutatis mutandis by replacing certain terms pursuant to Article 31, paragraph (2) of the Act on Preferred Equity Investment by Cooperative Financial Institutions

(Mutatis Mutandis Application of Provisions Concerning Shares to Preferred Equity Investments by a Special Purpose Company)

Article 64 The provisions of Article 28 (limited to the portion related to item (i)) shall apply mutatis mutandis to the matters to be specified by a Cabinet Order as prescribed in Article 129, paragraph (3), item (vii) of the Act as applied mutatis mutandis pursuant to Article 239, paragraph (1) of the Act; the provisions of Article 30, paragraph (1) shall apply mutatis mutandis to the description or record to be specified by a Cabinet Order as prescribed in Article 136, paragraph (5) of the Act as applied mutatis mutandis pursuant to Article 239, paragraph (1) of the Act; the provisions of Article 30, paragraph (2) shall apply mutatis mutandis to the instructions to be provided by a Book-entry Institution pursuant to the provisions of Article 136, paragraph (5) of the Act as applied mutatis mutandis pursuant to Article 239, paragraph (1) of the Act; the provisions of Articles 33 to 38 shall apply mutatis mutandis to the description or record in the book-entry account registry as prescribed in Article 142, paragraph (1) of the Act as applied mutatis mutandis pursuant to Article 239, paragraph (1) of the Act; the provisions of Article 40 shall apply mutatis mutandis to the period to be specified by a Cabinet Order as prescribed in Article 154, paragraph (2) of the Act as applied mutatis mutandis pursuant to Article 239, paragraph (1) of the Act; and the provisions of Article 41 shall apply mutatis mutandis to the method to be specified by a Cabinet Order as prescribed in Article 162, paragraph (1) of the Act as applied mutatis mutandis pursuant to Article 239, paragraph (1) of the Act. In this case, the terms listed in the middle column of the following table, found in the provisions listed in the left column of the same table, shall be deemed to be replaced with the terms listed in the right column of the same table.

Article 30, paragraph (1), item (i)	number of Book-Entry Transfer Shares	number of units of book-entry transfer preferred equity investments
	request (hereinafter referred to as "special shareholder request")	request
	special shareholder	special preferred equity partner
	number for each	number of units for each
	multiplying the number	multiplying the number of units
	in that number	in that number of units
Article 30, paragraph (1), item (ii)	number for each	number of units for each
	multiplying the number	multiplying the number of units
	in that number	in that number of units
	number of Book-Entry Transfer Shares	number of units of book-entry transfer preferred equity investments
Article 30, paragraph (1), item (iii)	number of Book-Entry Transfer Shares	number of units of book-entry transfer preferred equity investments
	number	number of units
Article 30, paragraph (1), item (iv)	special shareholder	special preferred equity partner
Article 33, paragraph (2), item (ii) and Article 36, paragraph (2), item (ii)	and number	and number of units

(Measures and Instructions where Fractions Result from the Retirement of Book-entry Preferred Equity Investments in Proportion to the Number of Units of Preferred Equity Investments Held)

Article 65 (1) The description or record to be specified by a Cabinet Order as prescribed in Article 242, paragraph (5) of the Act shall be as prescribed in the following items, depending upon the classification of the Ownership Column, etc. (Ownership Column, etc. as prescribed in Article 136, paragraph (3) of the Act as applied mutatis mutandis

Art.65

pursuant to Article 239, paragraph (1) of the Act) as listed in the following items:
(i) The Ownership Column (Ownership Column as prescribed in Article 130, paragraph (2), item (i), (a) of the Act as applied mutatis mutandis pursuant to Article 239, paragraph (1) of the Act; hereinafter the same shall apply in this paragraph) on the account of the Participant set forth in Article 136, paragraph (5) of the Act as applied mutatis mutandis pursuant to Article 239, paragraph (1) of the Act: The description or record of the decrease in the number (any fraction of such number of less than one (which shall be referred to as the "fraction in the Ownership Column" in item (iv)) shall be rounded up) that results from multiplying the number of units of book-entry preferred equity investments (which means book-entry preferred equity investments as prescribed in Article 234, paragraph (1) of the Act; hereinafter the same shall apply in this paragraph) (or, for book-entry preferred equity investments for which a request set forth in Article 151, paragraph (2), item (i) of the Act as applied mutatis mutandis pursuant to Article 239, paragraph (1) of the Act has been made, the number of units of each special preferred equity partner as prescribed in the same item) that are described or recorded in such Ownership Column by the rate of decrease (rate of decrease as prescribed in Article 136, paragraph (1), item (ii) of the Act as applied mutatis mutandis pursuant to Article 239, paragraph (1) of the Act; the same shall apply in the following item)
(ii) The Pledge Column (Pledge Column as prescribed in Article 130, paragraph (2), item (i), (b) of the Act as applied mutatis mutandis pursuant to Article 239, paragraph (1) of the Act) of a Participant's account set forth in Article 136, paragraph (5) of the Act as applied mutatis mutandis in Article 239, paragraph (1) of the Act: The description or record of the decrease in the number of units for each such preferred equity partner, represented by the numbers that result from multiplying each preferred equity partner's number of book-entry preferred equity investments set forth in paragraph (1), item (i) of the same Article that are described or recorded in such Pledge Column by the rate of decrease (any fraction of less than one in that number of units (which shall be referred to as the "fraction in the Pledge Column" in item (iv)) shall be rounded up; hereinafter the same shall apply in this item) book-entry, and the description or record of the decrease in the number of said units of book-entry preferred equity investments, represented by the sum total of the numbers of units that result from such multiplication
(iii) Customer account among the accounts of a Participant's Superior Institution as prescribed in the preceding two items: The description or record of a decrease in the number of units of book-entry preferred equity investments that has been described or recorded as prescribed in the preceding two items
(iv) Ownership Column of the account of a Participant who is a preferred equity partner (including a special preferred equity partner) of book-entry preferred equity investments as set forth in Article 136, paragraph (1), item (i) of the Act as applied mutatis mutandis pursuant to Article 239, paragraph (1) of the Act in the book-entry account registry maintained by the Immediately Superior Institution (if there is more than one such institution, the one specified by the Book-entry Institution) of such preferred equity partner: The description or record of an increase in the number that results from totaling the number obtained by subtracting the fraction in the Ownership Column for the book-entry preferred equity investments held by such preferred equity partner from one and the number obtained by subtracting the fraction in the Pledge Column for the same from one (any fraction of such number of less than one (which shall be referred to as the "issuer fraction" in item (vi)) shall be discarded)
(v) Customer account among the accounts of the Book-entry Institution, etc. with

1310

which the account set forth in the preceding item has been opened and its Superior Institution: The description or record of an increase in the number that has been described or recorded as prescribed in the same item

(vi) The Ownership Column of the account as set forth in Article 136, paragraph (1), item (iv) of the Act as applied mutatis mutandis pursuant to Article 239, paragraph (1) of the Act: The description or record of an increase in the total number (any fraction of such total number of less than one shall be discarded) of the issuer fraction

(vii) Customer account among the accounts of the Book-entry Institution, etc. at which the account set forth in the preceding item has been opened and its Superior Institution: The description or record of an increase in the number that has been described or recorded as prescribed in the same item.

(2) The instructions to be given by a Book-entry Institution pursuant to the provisions of Article 242, paragraph (5) of the Act shall be given to the persons listed in the following items and shall indicate the matters prescribed in the respective items:

(i) All Subordinate Institutions: The fact that matters necessary for the description or record prescribed in items (iii) to (vii) of the preceding paragraph should be reported

(ii) The Account Management Institution which is required to enter the description or record prescribed in the preceding item: Matters subject to such description or record.

(Mutatis Mutandis Application of Provisions Concerning Share Options to Subscription Rights for New Preferred Equity Investments by a Special Purpose Company)

Article 66 The provisions of Article 42 (excluding item (ii)) shall apply mutatis mutandis to the matters to be specified by a Cabinet Order as prescribed in Article 165, paragraph (3), item (vi) of the Act as applied mutatis mutandis pursuant to Article 249, paragraph (1) of the Act; the provisions of Articles 44 to 49 shall apply mutatis mutandis to the description or record in the book-entry account registry as prescribed in Article 176, paragraph (1) of the Act as applied mutatis mutandis pursuant to Article 249, paragraph (1) of the Act, and the provisions of Article 50 shall apply mutatis mutandis to the methods to be specified by a Cabinet Order as prescribed in Article 191, paragraph (1) of the Act as applied mutatis mutandis pursuant to Article 249, paragraph (1) of the Act. In this case, the terms listed in the middle column of the following table, found in the provisions listed in the left column of said table, shall be deemed to be replaced with the terms listed in the right column of the same table.

Article 44, paragraph (2), item (ii) and Article 47, paragraph (2), item (ii)	and number	and amount
Article 49, paragraph (1)	increase	increased amount
	application for entry of an increase, etc.	application for entry of an increase in the amount, etc.
Article 49, paragraph (3)	application for description or an increase, etc.	application for entry of an increase in the amount, etc.

(Mutatis Mutandis Application of Provisions Concerning Company Bonds with Share Options to Convertible Specified Company Bonds by Special Purpose Company)

Article 67 The provisions of Article 51 (excluding item (ii)) shall apply mutatis mutandis to the matters to be specified by a Cabinet Order as prescribed in Article 194, paragraph (3), item (vi) of the Act as applied mutatis mutandis pursuant to Article 251, paragraph (1) of the Act, the provisions of Articles 53 to 58 shall apply mutatis mutandis to the description or record in the book-entry account registry as prescribed in Article 207, paragraph (1) of the Act as applied mutatis mutandis pursuant to Article 251, paragraph (1) of the Act, and the provisions of Article 59 shall apply mutatis mutandis to the methods to be specified by a Cabinet Order as prescribed in Article 225, paragraph (1) of the Act as applied mutatis mutandis pursuant to Article 251, paragraph (1) of the Act. In this case, the terms listed in the middle column of the following table, found in the provisions listed in the left column of said table, shall be deemed to be replaced with the terms listed in the right column of the same table.

Article 53, paragraph (2), item (ii) and Article 56, paragraph (2), item (ii)	and number	and amount
Article 58, paragraph (1)	increase	increased in the amount
	application for entry of an increase, etc.	application for entry of an increase in the amount, etc.
Article 58, paragraph (3)	application for entry of an increase, etc.	application for entry of an increase in the amount, etc.

(Replacement of Terms in the Provisions of the Act as Applied Mutatis Mutandis to Convertible Specified Company Bonds by a Special Purpose Company)

Article 68 Where the provisions of the Act are applied mutatis mutandis to convertible specified company bonds as prescribed in the Act on the Securitization of Assets under the provisions of Article 251, paragraph (1) of the Act, the technical replacement of terms related to such provisions shall be carried out as prescribed in the following table:

Provision containing the terms to be replaced	Terms to be replaced	Replacement Terms
Article 221, paragraph (1)	Article 723, paragraph (1) of the Companies Act	Article 723, paragraph (1) of the Companies Act as applied mutatis mutandis pursuant to Article 129, paragraph (2) of the Act on the Securitization of Assets
Article 221, paragraph (2)	Article 718, paragraph (1) and Article 736, paragraph (1) of the Companies Act	Articles 718, paragraph (1) and Article 736, paragraph (1) of the Companies Act as applied mutatis mutandis pursuant to Article 129, paragraph (2) of the Act on the Securitization of Assets
Article 222, paragraph (1)	Article 718, paragraph (1) of the Companies Act	Article 718, paragraph (1) of the Companies Act as applied mutatis mutandis pursuant to Article 129, paragraph (2) of the Act on the Securitization of Assets

	paragraph (3) of the same Article	Article 718, paragraph (3) of the Companies Act as applied mutatis mutandis pursuant to Article 129, paragraph (2) of the Act on the Securitization of Assets

(Mutatis Mutandis Application of Provisions Concerning Company Bonds with Share Options to Specified Company Bonds with Subscription Rights for New Preferred Equity Investments by a Special Purpose Company)

Article 69 The provisions of Article 51 (excluding item (ii)) shall apply mutatis mutandis to the matters to be specified by a Cabinet Order as prescribed in Article 194, paragraph (3), item (vi) of the Act as applied mutatis mutandis pursuant to Article 254, paragraph (1) of the Act; the provisions of Articles 53 to 58 shall apply mutatis mutandis to the description or record in the book-entry account registry as prescribed in Article 207, paragraph (1) of the Act as applied mutatis mutandis pursuant to Article 254, paragraph (1) of the Act; and the provisions of Article 59 shall apply mutatis mutandis to the methods to be specified by a Cabinet Order as prescribed in Article 225, paragraph (1) of the Act as applied mutatis mutandis pursuant to Article 254, paragraph (1) of the Act. In this case, the terms listed in the middle column of the following table, found in the provisions listed in the left column of the same table, shall be deemed to be replaced with the terms listed in the right column of the same table.

Article 53, paragraph (2), item (ii) and Article 56, paragraph (2), item (ii)	and number	and amount
Article 58, paragraph (1)	increase	increase in the amount
	application for entry of an increase, etc.	application for entry of an increase in the amount, etc.
Article 58, paragraph (3)	application for entry of an increase, etc.	application for entry of an increase in the amount, etc.

(Replacement of Terms in the Provisions of the Act as Applied Mutatis Mutandis to Specified Company Bonds with Subscription Rights for New Preferred Equity Investments by a Special Purpose Company)

Article 70 Where the provisions of the Act are applied mutatis mutandis to specified company bonds with subscription rights for new preferred equity investments as prescribed in the Act on the Securitization of Assets in the provisions of Article 254, paragraph (1) of the Act, technical replacement of terms related to such provisions shall be made as prescribed in the following table:

Provision containing the terms to be replaced	Terms to be replaced	Replacement terms
Article 221, paragraph (1)	Article 723, paragraph (1) of the Companies Act	Article 723, paragraph (1) of the Companies Act as applied mutatis mutandis pursuant to Article 129, paragraph (2) of the Act on the Securitization of Assets

Article 221, paragraph (2)	Article 718, paragraph (1) and Article 736, paragraph (1) of the Companies Act	Articles 718, paragraph (1) and Article 736, paragraph (1) of the Companies Act as applied mutatis mutandis pursuant to Article 129, paragraph (2) of the Act on the Securitization of Assets
Article 222, paragraph (1)	Article 718, paragraph (1) of the Companies Act	Article 718, paragraph (1) of the Companies Act as applied mutatis mutandis pursuant to Article 129, paragraph (2) of the Act on the Securitization of Assets
	paragraph (3) of the same Article	Article 718, paragraph (3) of the Companies Act as applied mutatis mutandis pursuant to Article 129, paragraph (2) of the Act on the Securitization of Assets

Chapter X Book-entry Resulting from Entity Conversion, etc.

(Mutatis Mutandis Application of Provisions Concerning Shares in Cases Where Book-entry Shares of a Bank Established by a Consolidation-Type Merger are Delivered to Shareholders of a Bank Dissolved in a Consolidation-Type Merger)

Article 71 The provisions of Article 32, paragraph (1) shall apply mutatis mutandis to the description or record to be specified by a Cabinet Order as prescribed in Article 138, paragraph (5) of the Act as applied mutatis mutandis pursuant to Article 256, paragraph (1) of the Act, and the provisions of Article 32, paragraph (2) shall apply mutatis mutandis to the instructions to be given by a Book-entry Institution pursuant to the provisions of Article 138, paragraph (5) of the Act as applied mutatis mutandis pursuant to Article 256, paragraph (1) of the Act. In this case, "Book-entry Shares of the Surviving Company, etc." in Article 32, paragraph (1), items (i) to (vii) shall be deemed to be replaced with "Book-entry Shares of the bank established by a consolidation-type merger."

(Mutatis Mutandis Application of Provisions Concerning Shares where Book-entry Shares of a Surviving Bank, etc. in an Absorption-Type Merger are Delivered to Preferred Equity Investors of a Cooperative Financial Institution, etc. Dissolved in an Absorption-Type Merger)

Article 72 The provisions of Article 32, paragraph (1) shall apply mutatis mutandis to the description or record to be specified by a Cabinet Order as prescribed in Article 138, paragraph (5) of the Act as applied mutatis mutandis pursuant to Article 256, paragraph (2) of the Act, and the provisions of Article 32, paragraph (2) shall apply mutatis mutandis to the instructions to be given by a Book-entry Institution pursuant to the provisions of Article 138, paragraph (5) of the Act as applied mutatis mutandis pursuant to Article 256, paragraph (2) of the Act. In this case, the terms listed in the middle column of the following table, found in the provisions listed in the left column of the same table shall be deemed to be replaced with the terms listed in the right column of the same table.

Article 32, paragraph (1), item (i)	the number of Book-Entry Transfer Shares set forth in paragraph (1), item (ii) of the same Article	the number of units of book-entry transfer preferred equity investments of the cooperative financial institution dissolved in an absorption-type merger or of the cooperative financial institution dissolved in a consolidation-type merger (hereinafter referred to as "book-entry transfer preferred equity investments of the dissolved cooperative financial institution" in this paragraph) prescribed in Article 256, paragraph (2) of the Act
	special shareholder request	special preferred equity investor request (meanings a request set forth in Article 151, paragraph (2), item (i) of the Act as applied mutatis mutandis by replacing certain terms pursuant to Article 235, paragraph (1) of the Act)
	number for each special shareholder	number of units for each special preferred equity investor (special preferred equity investor as prescribed in the same item; hereinafter the same shall apply in this paragraph)
	item (iii) of the same paragraph	Article 138, paragraph (1), item (iii) of the Act as applied mutatis mutandis pursuant to Article 256, paragraph (2) of the Act
	multiplying the number	multiplying the number of units
	in that number	in that number of units
	Book-Entry Transfer Shares of the Surviving Company, etc.	Book-Entry Transfer Shares of the bank, etc. established by a consolidation-type merger
Article 32, paragraph (1), item (ii)	Book-Entry Transfer Shares set forth in paragraph (1), item (ii) of the same Article	book-entry transfer preferred equity investments of the dissolved cooperative structured financial institution
	in the number	in the number of units
	multiplying the number	multiplying the number of units
	Book-Entry Transfer Shares of the Surviving Company, etc.	Book-Entry Transfer Shares of the bank, etc. established by a consolidation-type merger
Article 32, paragraph (1), item (iii)	Book-Entry Transfer Shares of the Surviving Company, etc.	Book-Entry Transfer Shares of the bank, etc. established by a consolidation-type merger
	number	number of units
Article 32, paragraph (1), item (iv)	Book-Entry Transfer Shares set forth in Article 138, paragraph (1), item (ii) of the Act	book-entry transfer preferred equity investments of the dissolved cooperative financial institution

	special shareholder	special preferred equity investor
	Book-Entry Transfer Shares of the Surviving Company, etc.	Book-Entry Transfer Shares of the bank, etc. established by a consolidation-type merger
Article 32, paragraph (1), item (v) to item (vii)	Book-Entry Transfer Shares of the Surviving Company, etc.	Book-Entry Transfer Shares of the bank, etc. established by a consolidation-type merger
Article 32, paragraph (1), item (viii)	Book-Entry Transfer Shares set forth in paragraph (1), item (ii) of the same Article	book-entry transfer preferred equity investments of the dissolved cooperative structured financial institution

(Mutatis Mutandis Application of Provisions Concerning Shares where Book-entry Preferred Equity Investments of a Surviving Cooperative Bank, etc. in an Absorption-Type Merger are Delivered to Shareholders of a Bank, etc. Dissolved in an Absorption-Type Merger)

Article 73 The provisions of Article 32, paragraph (1) shall apply mutatis mutandis to the description or record to be specified by a Cabinet Order as prescribed in Article 138, paragraph (5) of the Act as applied mutatis mutandis pursuant to Article 256, paragraph (3) of the Act, and the provisions of Article 32, paragraph (2) shall apply mutatis mutandis to the instructions to be given by a Book-entry Institution pursuant to the provisions of Article 138, paragraph (5) of the Act as applied mutatis mutandis pursuant to Article 256, paragraph (3) of the Act. In this case, the terms listed in the middle column of the following table, found in the provisions listed in the left column of the same table, shall be deemed to be replaced with the terms listed in the right column of the same table.

Article 32, paragraph (1), item (i)	set forth in item (i) of the same paragraph	of the surviving shinkin bank in an absorption-type merger or shinkin bank established by a consolidation-type merger prescribed in Article 256, paragraph (3) of the Act
	Book-Entry Transfer Shares of the Surviving Company, etc.	book-entry transfer preferred equity investments of the surviving shinkin bank, etc.
Article 32, paragraph (1), item (ii)	Book-Entry Transfer Shares of the Surviving Company, etc.	book-entry transfer preferred equity investments of the surviving shinkin bank, etc.
	number for each	number of units for each
Article 32, paragraph (1), item (iii)	number of Book-Entry Transfer Shares of the Surviving Company, etc.	number of units of book-entry transfer preferred equity investments of the surviving shinkin bank, etc.
	number	number of units
Article 32, paragraph (1), items (iv) to (vii)	Book-Entry Transfer Shares of the Surviving Company, etc.	book-entry transfer preferred equity investments of the surviving shinkin bank, etc.

(Mutatis Mutandis Application of Provisions Concerning Shares where Book-

entry Preferred Equity Investments of a Surviving Cooperative Financial Institution, etc. in an Absorption-Type Merger are Delivered to Preferred Equity Investors of a Cooperative Financial Institution, etc. Dissolved in an Absorption-Type Merger)

Article 74　The provisions of Article 32, paragraph (1) shall apply mutatis mutandis to the description or record to be specified by a Cabinet Order as prescribed in Article 138, paragraph (5) of the Act as applied mutatis mutandis pursuant to Article 256, paragraph (4) of the Act, and the provisions of Article 32, paragraph (2) shall apply mutatis mutandis to the instructions to be given by a Book-entry Institution pursuant to the provisions of Article 138, paragraph (5) of the Act as applied mutatis mutandis pursuant to Article 256, paragraph (4) of the Act. In this case, the terms listed in the middle column of the following table, found in the provisions listed in the left column of the same table, shall be deemed to be replaced with the terms listed in the right column of the same table.

Article 32, paragraph (1), item (i)	the number of Book-Entry Transfer Shares set forth in paragraph (1), item (ii) of the same Article	the number of units of book-entry transfer preferred equity investments of the cooperative financial institution dissolved in an absorption-type merger or the cooperative financial institution dissolved in a consolidation-type merger (hereinafter referred to as "book-entry transfer preferred equity investments of the dissolved cooperative financial institution" in this paragraph) prescribed in Article 256, paragraph (4) of the Act
	special shareholder request	special preferred equity investor request (meanings a request set forth in Article 151, paragraph (2), item (i) of the Act as applied mutatis mutandis by replacing certain terms pursuant to Article 235, paragraph (1) of the Act)
	number for each special shareholder	number of units for each special preferred equity investor (a special preferred equity investor as prescribed in the same item; hereinafter the same shall apply in this paragraph)
	item (iii) of the same paragraph	Article 138, paragraph (1), item (iii) of the Act as applied mutatis mutandis pursuant to Article 256, paragraph (4) of the Act
	multiplying the number	multiplying the number of units
	in that number	in that number of units
	set forth in item (i) of the same paragraph	of the surviving cooperative financial institution in an absorption-type merger or the cooperative financial institution established by a consolidation-type merger as prescribed in Article 256, paragraph (4) of the Act

	Book-Entry Transfer Shares of the Surviving Company, etc.	book-entry transfer preferred equity investments of the surviving cooperative financial institution, etc.
Article 32, paragraph (1), item (ii)	Book-Entry Transfer Shares set forth in paragraph (1), item (ii) of the same Article	book-entry transfer preferred equity investments of the dissolved cooperative financial institution
	number for each	number of units for each
	multiplying the number	multiplying the number of units
	in that number	in that number of units
	Book-Entry Transfer Shares of the Surviving Company, etc.	book-entry transfer preferred equity investments of the surviving cooperative financial institution
	number of Book-Entry Transfer Shares of the Surviving Company, etc.	number of units of book-entry transfer preferred equity investments of the surviving cooperative financial institution, etc.
Article 32, paragraph (1), item (iii)	number of Book-Entry Transfer Shares of the Surviving Company, etc.	number of units of book-entry transfer preferred equity investments of the surviving cooperative financial institution, etc.
	number	number of units
Article 32, paragraph (1), item (iv)	Book-Entry Transfer Shares set forth in Article 138, paragraph (1), item (ii) of the Act	book-entry transfer preferred equity investments of the dissolved cooperative financial institution
	special shareholder	special preferred equity investor
	Book-Entry Transfer Shares of the Surviving Company, etc.	book-entry transfer preferred equity investments of the surviving cooperative financial institution, etc.
Article 32, paragraph (1), item (v) to (vii)	Book-Entry Transfer Shares of the Surviving Company, etc.	book-entry transfer preferred equity investments of the surviving cooperative financial institution, etc.
Article 32, paragraph (1), item (viii)	Book-Entry Transfer Shares set forth in paragraph (1), item (ii) of the same Article	book-entry transfer preferred equity investments of the dissolved cooperative financial institution

(Replacement of Terms in the Provisions of the Act as Applied Mutatis Mutandis where Book-entry Preferred Equity Investments of a Surviving Cooperative Bank, etc. in an Absorption-Type Merger are Delivered to Shareholders of a Bank, etc. Dissolved in an Absorption-Type Merger)

Article 75 Where the provisions of Article 160, paragraph (1) of the Act are applied mutatis mutandis to instances under the provisions of Article 257, paragraph (4) of the Act in which the shares of a bank dissolved in an absorption-type or consolidation-type merger are not Book-entry Shares and the surviving cooperative bank in the absorption-type merger or the cooperative bank established by the consolidation-type merger seeks to deliver, at the time of the absorption-type or consolidation-type merger, book-entry preferred equity investments to the shareholders of the bank dissolved in said absorption-type or consolidation-type merger, the technical replacement of terms related to such provisions shall be carried out as prescribed in the following table:

Provision containing the terms to be replaced	Terms to be replaced	Replacement terms
Article 160, paragraph (1)	Article 131, paragraph (1), item (i)	Article 131, paragraph (1), item (i) as applied mutatis mutandis pursuant to Article 235, paragraph (1)
	same paragraph	Article 131, paragraph (1) as applied mutatis mutandis pursuant to Article 235, paragraph (1)

(Replacement of Terms in the Provisions of the Act as Applied Mutatis Mutandis where Book-entry Preferred Equity Investments of a Surviving Cooperative Financial Institution, etc. in an Absorption-Type Merger are Delivered to Members of a Surviving Cooperative Financial Institution, etc. in an Absorption-Type Merger)

Article 76 Where the provisions of Article 160, paragraph (1) of the Act are applied mutatis mutandis to the delivery of book-entry preferred equity investments by a surviving cooperative financial institution in an absorption-type merger or a cooperative financial institution established by a consolidation-type merger, at the time of such merger, book-entry to members, etc. of a cooperative financial institution dissolved in an absorption-type or consolidation-type merger in relation to the provisions of Article 257, paragraph (5) of the Act, technical replacement of terms related to such provisions shall be carried out as prescribed in the following table:

Provision containing the terms to be replaced	Terms to be replaced	Replacement terms
Article 160, paragraph (1)	Article 131, paragraph (1), item (i)	Article 131, paragraph (1), item (i) as applied mutatis mutandis pursuant to Article 235, paragraph (1)
	same paragraph	Article 131, paragraph (1) as applied mutatis mutandis pursuant to Article 235, paragraph (1)

(Replacement of Terms in the Provisions of the Act as Applied Mutatis Mutandis where Book-entry Preferred Equity Investments of a Surviving Cooperative Financial Institution, etc. in an Absorption-Type Merger are Delivered to Preferred Equity Investors of a Cooperative Financial Institution, etc. Dissolved in an Absorption-Type Merger)

Article 77 If preferred equity investments of a cooperative financial institution dissolved in an absorption-type or consolidation-type merger are not book-entry preferred equity investments in relation to the provisions of Article 257, paragraph (6) of the Act, where a surviving cooperative financial institution in an absorption-type merger or a cooperative financial institution established by a consolidation-type merger delivers book-entry preferred equity investments to preferred equity investors of a cooperative financial institution dissolved in an absorption-type or consolidation-type merger at the time of such merger, and where the provisions of Article 160, paragraph (1) of

Art.78～79

the Act are applied mutatis mutandis, technical replacement of terms related to such provisions shall be made as prescribed in the following table:

Provision containing the terms to be replaced	Terms to be replaced	Replacement terms
Article 160, paragraph (1)	Article 131, paragraph (1), item (i)	Article 131, paragraph (1), item (i) as applied mutatis mutandis pursuant to Article 235, paragraph (1)
	same paragraph	Article 131, paragraph (1) as applied mutatis mutandis pursuant to Article 235, paragraph (1)

(Replacement of Terms in the Provisions of the Act as Applied Mutatis Mutandis where Shares, etc. other than Book-entry Shares of a Surviving Bank, etc. in an Absorption-Type Merger are Delivered to Preferred Equity Investors of a Cooperative Financial Institution, etc. Dissolved in an Absorption-Type Merger)

Article 78 Where the provisions of Article 160, paragraph (3) of the Act are applied mutatis mutandis to instances under the provisions of Article 258, paragraph (3) of the Act in which the preferred equity investments of a cooperative financial institution dissolved in an absorption-type or consolidation-type merger are book-entry preferred equity investments and the surviving bank in the absorption-type merger or the bank established by the consolidation-type merger seeks to deliver, at the time of the absorption-type or consolidation-type merger, shares, etc. other than Book-entry Shares to the preferred equity investors of the cooperative financial institution dissolved in the absorption-type or consolidation-type merger, or the surviving bank in an absorption-type merger or the bank established by a consolidation-type merger decides not to allot shares, etc. , at the time of the absorption-type or consolidation-type merger, to preferred equity investors with a certain kind of preferred equity investment in the cooperative financial institution dissolved in the absorption-type or consolidation-type merger, the technical replacement of terms related to such provisions shall be made as prescribed in the following table.

Provision containing the terms to be replaced	Terms to be replaced	Replacement terms
Article 160, paragraph (3)	Article 135, paragraph (1), item (ii)	Article 135, paragraph (1), item (ii) as applied mutatis mutandis pursuant to Article 235, paragraph (1)

(Replacement of Terms in the Provisions of the Act as Applied Mutatis Mutandis where Equity Investments other than Book-entry Preferred Equity Investments of a Surviving Cooperative Financial Institution, etc. in an Absorption-Type Merger are Delivered to Preferred Equity Investors in a Cooperative Financial Institution, etc. Dissolved in an Absorption-Type Merger)

Article 79 Where the provisions of Article 160, paragraph (3) of the Act are applied mutatis mutandis to instances under the provisions of Article 258, paragraph (4) of the Act in which the preferred equity investments of a cooperative financial institution dissolved in an absorption-type or consolidation-type merger are book-entry preferred equity investments and the surviving cooperative financial institution in the absorption-type merger or the cooperative financial institution established by the consolidation-type merger seeks to deliver, at the time of the absorption-type or consolidation-type merger, equity investments, etc. other than book-entry preferred equity investments to the preferred equity investors of the cooperative financial institution dissolved in the absorption-type or consolidation-type merger, or the surviving cooperative financial institution in the absorption-type merger or cooperative financial institution established by the consolidation-type merger decides not to allot equity investments, etc. to preferred equity investors with a certain kind of preferred equity investment in the cooperative financial institution dissolved in the absorption-type or consolidation-type merger, the technical replacement of terms related to such provisions shall be made as prescribed in the following table.

Provision containing the terms to be replaced	Terms to be replaced	Replacement terms
Article 160, paragraph (3)	Article 135, paragraph (1), item (ii)	Article 135, paragraph (1), item (ii) as applied mutatis mutandis pursuant to Article 235, paragraph (1)

(Mutatis Mutandis Application of Provisions Concerning Shares where Book-entry Shares are Delivered to Preferred Equity Investors in a cooperative financial institution that Executes a Conversion Pursuant to the Provisions of Article 4, Item (iii) of the Act on Financial Institution Merger and Conversion)

Article 80 The provisions of Article 32, paragraph (1) shall apply mutatis mutandis to the description or record to be specified by a Cabinet Order as prescribed in Article 138, paragraph (5) of the Act as applied mutatis mutandis pursuant to Article 262, paragraph (1) of the Act, and the provisions of Article 32, paragraph (2) shall apply mutatis mutandis to the instructions to be given by a Book-entry Institution pursuant to the provisions of Article 138, paragraph (5) of the Act as applied mutatis mutandis pursuant to Article 262, paragraph (1) of the Act. In this case, the terms listed in the middle column of the following table, found in the provisions listed in the left column of the same table, shall be deemed to be replaced with the terms listed in the right column of the same table.

Article 32, paragraph (1), item (i)	the number of Book-Entry Transfer Shares set forth in paragraph (1), item (ii) of the same Article	the number of units of book-entry transfer preferred equity investments of the cooperative financial institution (hereinafter referred to as "book-entry transfer preferred equity investments of the converting cooperative financial institution" in this paragraph) that executes the conversion prescribed in Article 262, paragraph (1) of the Act
	special shareholder request	special preferred equity investor request (a request set forth in Article 151, paragraph (2), item (i) of the Act as applied mutatis mutandis by replacing certain terms pursuant to Article 235, paragraph (1) of the Act)

	number for each special shareholder	number of units for each special preferred equity investor (special preferred equity investor as prescribed in the same item; hereinafter the same shall apply in this paragraph)
	item (iii) of the same paragraph	Article 138, paragraph (1), item (iii) of the Act as applied mutatis mutandis pursuant to Article 262, paragraph (1) of the Act
	multiplying the number	multiplying the number of units
	in that number	in that number of units
	Book-Entry Transfer Shares of the Surviving Company, etc.	Book-Entry Transfer Shares of the bank after conversion
Article 32, paragraph (1), item (ii)	Book-Entry Transfer Shares set forth in paragraph (1), item (ii) of the same Article	book-entry transfer preferred equity investments of the converting cooperative financial institution
	in the number	in the number of units
	multiplying the number	multiplying the number of units
	Book-Entry Transfer Shares of the Surviving Company, etc.	Book-Entry Transfer Shares of the bank after conversion
Article 32, paragraph (1), item (iii)	Book-Entry Transfer Shares of the Surviving Company, etc.	Book-Entry Transfer Shares of the bank after conversion
Article 32, paragraph (1), item (iv)	Book-Entry Transfer Shares set forth in Article 138, paragraph (1), item (ii) of the Act	book-entry transfer preferred equity investments of the converting cooperative financial institution
	special shareholder	special preferred equity investor
	Book-Entry Transfer Shares of the Surviving Company, etc.	Book-Entry Transfer Shares of the bank after conversion
Article 32, paragraph (1), items (v) to (vii)	Book-Entry Transfer Shares of the Surviving Company, etc.	Book-Entry Transfer Shares of the bank after conversion
Article 32, paragraph (1), item (viii)	Book-Entry Transfer Shares set forth in paragraph (1), item (ii) of the same Article	book-entry transfer preferred equity investments of the converting cooperative financial institution

(Mutatis Mutandis Application of Provisions Concerning Shares where Book-entry Preferred Equity Investments are Delivered to Shareholders of an Ordinary Bank that Executes a Conversion Pursuant to the Provisions of Article 4, Item (ii) of the Act on Financial Institution Merger and Conversion)

Article 81 The provisions of Article 32, paragraph (1) shall apply mutatis mutandis to the description or record to be specified by a Cabinet Order as prescribed in Article

138, paragraph (5) of the Act as applied mutatis mutandis pursuant to Article 262, paragraph (3) of the Act, and the provisions of Article 32, paragraph (2) shall apply mutatis mutandis to the instructions to be given by a Book-entry Institution pursuant to the provisions of Article 138, paragraph (5) of the Act as applied mutatis mutandis pursuant to Article 262, paragraph (3) of the Act. In this case, the terms listed in the middle column of the following table, found in the provisions listed in the left column of the same table, shall be deemed to be replaced with the terms listed in the right column of the same table.

Article 32, paragraph (1), item (i)	set forth in item (i) of the same paragraph	of the shinkin bank after conversion as prescribed in Article 262, paragraph (3) of the Act
	Book-Entry Transfer Shares of the Surviving Company, etc.	book-entry transfer preferred equity investments of the shinkin bank after conversion
Article 32, paragraph (1), item (ii)	multiplying the number	multiplying the number of units
	Book-Entry Transfer Shares of the Surviving Company, etc.	book-entry transfer preferred equity investments of the shinkin bank after conversion
	number of ... for each	number of units of ... for each
Article 32, paragraph (1), item (iii)	number of Book-Entry Transfer Shares of the Surviving Company, etc.	number of units of book-entry transfer preferred equity investments of the shinkin bank after conversion
	number	number of units
Article 32, paragraph (1), items (iv) to (vii)	Book-Entry Transfer Shares of the Surviving Company, etc.	book-entry transfer preferred equity investments of the shinkin bank after conversion

(Mutatis Mutandis Application of Provisions Concerning Shares in where Book-entry Shares of a Company Established by a Consolidation-Type Merger are Delivered to Shareholders of a Stock Company Dissolved in a Consolidation-Type Merger That Is a Bank)

Article 82 The provisions of Article 32, paragraph (1) shall apply mutatis mutandis to the description or record to be specified by a Cabinet Order as prescribed in Article 138, paragraph (5) of the Act as applied mutatis mutandis pursuant to Article 263 of the Act, and the provisions of Article 32, paragraph (2) shall apply mutatis mutandis to the instructions to be given by a Book-entry Institution pursuant to the provisions of Article 138, paragraph (5) of the Act as applied mutatis mutandis pursuant to Article 263 of the Act. In this case, "Book-entry Shares of the Surviving Company, etc." in Article 32, paragraph (1), items (i) to (vii) shall be deemed to be replaced with "Book-entry Shares of the stock company established by a consolidation-type merger."

(Mutatis Mutandis Application of Provisions Concerning Shares where Book-entry Shares of a Financial Instruments Exchange Established by a Consolidation-Type Merger are Delivered to Shareholders of an Incorporated Financial Instruments Exchange Dissolved in a Consolidation-Type Merger)

Article 83 The provisions of Article 32, paragraph (1) shall apply mutatis mutandis to the description or record to be specified by a Cabinet Order as prescribed in Article

138, paragraph (5) of the Act as applied mutatis mutandis pursuant to Article 270 of the Act, and the provisions of Article 32, paragraph (2) shall apply mutatis mutandis to the instructions to be given by a Book-entry Institution pursuant to the provisions of Article 138, paragraph (5) of the Act as applied mutatis mutandis pursuant to Article 270 of the Act. In this case, "Book-entry Shares of the Surviving Company, etc." in Article 32, paragraph (1), items (i) to (vii) shall be deemed to be replaced with "Book-entry Shares of the financial instruments exchange established by a consolidation-type merger."

Chapter XI Miscellaneous Provisions

(Interested Persons Who May Request Certification of Matters Described or Recorded in a Book-entry Account Registry)
Article 84 An interested person to be specified by a Cabinet Order prescribed in Article 277 (including where applied mutatis mutandis pursuant to Article 48 of the Act) of the Act shall be any person who has the right to manage or dispose of the property of the Participant who holds the relevant account as its own account, and any other person specified by a Cabinet Office Ordinance or an Ordinance of the Ministry of Justice (or, in the case of a Book-entry Institution dealing with national government bonds, a Cabinet Office Ordinance, an Ordinance of the Ministry of Justice or an Ordinance of the Ministry of Finance).

(Powers Excluded from the Authorities Delegated to the Commissioner of the Financial Services Agency)
Article 85 The powers to be specified by a Cabinet Order as prescribed in Article 286, paragraph (1) of the Act shall be the following:
(i) Designation pursuant to the provisions of Article 3, paragraph (1) of the Act
(ii) Public Notice pursuant to the provisions of Article 3, paragraph (2) and Article 22, paragraph (2) of the Act
(iii) Rescission of designation set forth in Article 3, paragraph (1) of the Act pursuant to the provisions of Article 22, paragraph (1) of the Act
(iv) Approval pursuant to the provisions of Article 57 of the Act
(v) Notification pursuant to the provisions of Article 282, paragraph (1) of the Act in relation to the designation set forth in item (i) above or rescission of designation as set forth in item (iii) above.

(Delegation of Power to Conduct Inspections, etc. to the Exchange Surveillance Commission)
Article 86 Of the powers delegated to the Commissioner of the Financial Services Agency pursuant to the provisions of Article 286, paragraph (1) of the Act, the powers pursuant to the provisions of Article 20, paragraph (1) of the Act (including where applied mutatis mutandis pursuant to Article 43, paragraph (3) of the Act and where applied mutatis mutandis pursuant to the provisions of Article 48 of the Act by replacement of terms) shall be delegated to the Exchange Surveillance Commission; provided, however, that this shall not preclude the Commissioner of the Financial Services Agency from himself/herself exercising the authority to order submission of reports or materials.

[13] Cabinet Office Ordinance on the Provision and Publication of Information on Securities

(Cabinet Office Ordinance No. 78 of December 5, 2008)

Pursuant to the provisions of Article 27-31, Article 27-32, and Article 27-34 of the Financial Instruments and Exchange Act (Act No. 25 of 1948), the Cabinet Office Ordinance on the provision and publication of Specified Information, on securities, etc. is hereby established as follows.

Table of Contents
Chapter I General Provisions (Article 1)
Chapter II Provision and Publication of Specified Information on Securities (Articles 2 to 11)
Chapter III Provision and Publication of Information on Foreign Securities Information (Articles 12 to 17)
Supplementary Provisions

Chapter I General Provisions

Article 1 In this Cabinet Office Ordinance, the meanings of the terms listed in the following items are as prescribed in each of the relevant items:
  (i) Securities: meaning Securities as prescribed in Article 2, paragraph (1) of the Financial Instruments and Exchange Act (hereinafter referred to as the "Act") and rights that are deemed to be securities pursuant to the provisions of Article 2, paragraph (2) of the Act;
  (ii) Regulated Securities: meaning Regulated Securities as prescribed in Article 5, paragraph (1) of the Act;
  (iii) Issuer: meaning an Issuer as prescribed in Article 2, paragraph (5) of the Act;
  (iv) Specified Information on Securities: meaning Specified Information on Securities as prescribed in Article 27-31, paragraph (1) of the Act;
  (v) Issuer's Information: meaning Issuer's Information as prescribed in Article 27-32, paragraph (1) of the Act;
  (vi) Business Year: meaning a Business Year as prescribed in Article 27-32, paragraph (1) of the Act;
  (vii) Foreign Securities Information: meaning Foreign Securities Information as prescribed in Article 27-32-2, paragraph (1) of the Act;
  (viii) Secondary Distribution of Foreign Securities: meaning Secondary Distribution of Foreign Securities as prescribed in Article 27-32-2, paragraph (1) of the Act; and
  (ix) Designated Foreign Financial Instruments Exchange: meaning a Designated Foreign Financial Instruments Exchange as prescribed in Article 2-12-3, item (iv), sub-item (b) of the Order for Enforcement of the Financial Instruments and Exchange Act (Cabinet Order No. 321 of 1965; hereinafter referred to as the "Order").

Chapter II Provision and Publication of Specified Information on Securities

(Contents of Specified Information on Securities)
Article 2 (1) The information prescribed by Cabinet Office Ordinance, referred to in Article 27-31, paragraph (1) of the Act, shall be the information prescribed in the follow-

ing items in accordance with the category of Securities listed in each of those items; provided, however, that where it is found to be inappropriate as regards the public interest or protection of investors to provide such information on Securities listed in item (i) or item (ii) as such information, it shall be prescribed by the instructions of the Commissioner of the Financial Services Agency:

(i) Specified Listed Securities (meaning Specified Listed Securities as prescribed in Article 2, paragraph (33) of the Act) or Securities that the Issuer thereof intends to list on a Specified Financial Instruments Exchange Market (meaning a Specified Financial Instruments Exchange Market as prescribed in Article 2, paragraph (32) of the Act; hereinafter the same shall apply in this item) (hereinafter such Securities shall be referred to as "Specified Listed Securities, etc."): the information specified by the rules laid down by the relevant Financial Instruments Exchange (meaning a Financial Instruments Exchange as prescribed in Article 2, paragraph (16) of the Act; the same shall apply hereinafter) that has established the Specified Financial Instruments Exchange Market on which the Issuer has listed or intends to list the Specified Listed Securities, etc. (hereinafter such rules shall be referred to as the "Specified Exchange Rules");

(ii) Specified Over-the-Counter Traded Securities (meaning Specified Over-the-Counter Traded Securities as prescribed in Article 2-12-4, paragraph (3), item (ii) of the Order: hereinafter the same shall apply in this item) or Securities that the Issuer thereof intends to register with an Authorized Financial Instruments Firms Association (meaning an Authorized Financial Instruments Firms Association as prescribed in Article 2, paragraph (13) of the Act; hereinafter the same shall apply in this item) as Specified Over-the-Counter Traded Securities (hereinafter such Securities shall be referred to as "Specified Over-the-Counter Traded Securities, etc."): the information specified by the rules laid down by the Authorized Financial Instruments Firms Association with which the Issuer has registered or intends to register the Specified Over-the-Counter Traded Securities, etc. (hereinafter such rules shall be referred to as the "Specified Association Rules"); or

(iii) Securities other than those listed in the preceding two items: the information designated by the Commissioner of the Financial Services Agency.

(2) The information prescribed in the items of the preceding paragraph shall include the information prescribed in the following items, in accordance with the category of Securities listed in each of those items:

(i) Securities (excluding Securities listed in the following item): the following matters (where the Issuer of the Securities has already submitted an Annual Securities Report as prescribed in Article 9-3, paragraph (2) of the Cabinet Office Ordinance on Disclosure of Corporate Affairs, etc. (Ordinance of the Ministry of Finance No. 5 of 1973) (or where the Securities are foreign bonds, etc. as prescribed in Article 1, item (i) of the Cabinet Office Ordinance on Disclosure of Information, etc. about Issuers of Foreign Government Bonds, etc. (Ordinance of the Ministry of Finance No. 26 of 1972), an Annual Securities Report as prescribed in Article 6-2, paragraph (2) of that Ordinance) continuously for one year, to that effect and the matters listed in sub-items (a) and (b)):

(a) that the information falls under the category of Specified Information on Securities;

(b) matters concerning said Securities;

(c) matters concerning Securities other than said Securities issued by the Issuer of said Securities; and

(d) matters concerning the business and accounting of the Issuer (excluding states and local governments) of said Securities.

(ii) Regulated Securities: the following matters:
   (a) that the information falls under the category of Specified Information on Securities;
   (b) matters concerning said Securities;
   (c) matters concerning any details and investment of Funds (meaning funds as prescribed in Article 1, item (ix) of the Cabinet Office Ordinance on Disclosure of Information of Regulated Securities, etc. (Ordinance of the Ministry of Finance No. 22 of 1993); the same shall apply hereinafter) in relation to said Securities, Collateralized Assets (meaning Collateralized Assets as prescribed in Article 1, item (ix)-2 of that Ordinance), and other equivalent property or assets (referred to as "Assets under Management, etc." in sub-item (d) and Article 7, paragraph (3), item (ii)); and
   (d) matters concerning the person engaged in the investment of the Assets under Management, etc.

(Method of Provision or Publication of Specified Information on Securities)
Article 3 An Issuer that intends to provide or publicize Specified Information on Securities shall do so by the methods prescribed in the following items in accordance with the category of Securities listed in each of those items:
(i) Specified Listed Securities, etc. : the method of publication specified in the Specified Exchange Rules;
(ii) Specified Over-the-Counter Traded Securities, etc. : the method of publication specified in the Specified Association Rules; or
(iii) Securities other than those listed in the preceding two items: the method designated by the Commissioner of the Financial Services Agency.

(Provision or Publication of Specified Information on Securities by the Reference Method)
Article 4 (1) The period specified by Cabinet Office Ordinance, referred to in Article 27-31, paragraph (3) of the Act, shall be one year.
(2) Where an Issuer as prescribed in Article 27-31, paragraph (3) of the Act intends to provide or publicize Specified Information on Securities, he/she shall note in the Specified Information on Securities that reference should be made to the Reference Information (meaning Reference Information as prescribed in Article 27-31, paragraph (3) of the Act) in connection with the Issuer (or where the Securities are Regulated Securities, in connection with the Securities or with the Same Class of Securities (meaning the same class of Securities as referred to in Article 4, paragraph (3), item (iii) of the Act) as those issued by the Issuer of the Securities), by the methods prescribed in the following items in accordance with the category of Securities listed in each of those items:
(i) Specified Listed Securities, etc. : the method specified in the Specified Exchange Rules;
(ii) Specified Over-the-Counter Traded Securities, etc. : the method specified in the Specified Association Rules; or
(iii) Securities other than those listed in the preceding two items: the method designated by the Commissioner of the Financial Services Agency.
(3) The information specified by Cabinet Office Ordinance, referred to in Article 27-31, paragraph (3) of the Act, shall be the information prescribed in the following items in accordance with the category of Securities listed in each of those items:
(i) Securities (excluding Securities listed in the following item): information concerning the matters listed in Article 2, paragraph (2), item (i), sub-items (c) and sub-

item (d); or
(ii) Regulated Securities: information concerning the matters listed in Article 2, paragraph (2), item (ii), sub-item (c) and sub-item (d).

(Amendment of Specified Information on Securities)
Article 5　(1) The cases specified by Cabinet Office Ordinance, referred to in Article 27-31, paragraph (4) of the Act, shall be the cases listed in the following items, and the period specified by Cabinet Office Ordinance, referred to in that paragraph, shall be the period prescribed in each of those items:
(i) cases that fall under the case where disclosures have been made (meaning the case where disclosures have been made as prescribed in Article 4, paragraph (7) of the Act; the same shall apply hereinafter) for the Securities connected with the Specified Information on Securities: the period from the date of the provision or publication of the Specified Information on Securities to the date when the case comes to fall under the case where disclosures have been made; or
(ii) cases where Securities connected with the Specified Information on Securities have ceased to exist due to retirement, redemption, or on any other grounds: the period from the date of the provision or publication of the Specified Information on Securities to the date on which said Securities ceased to exist.
(2) An Issuer who is to provide or publicize Amended Specified Information on Securities (meaning Amended Specified Information on Securities as prescribed in Article 27-31, paragraph (4) of the Act; hereinafter the same shall apply in this paragraph) pursuant to the provisions of that paragraph shall provide or publicize the Amended Specified Information on Securities to the other party to the Specified Solicitation or Offer, etc. (meaning Specified Solicitation or Offer, etc. as prescribed in Article 27-31, paragraph (1) of the Act; the same shall apply in Article 8, paragraph (1), item (ii)) in connection with the Specified Information on Securities to which the Amended Specified Information on Securities is related and to the holder of the Securities under the Specified Solicitation or Offer, etc. , by the method prescribed in the following items, in accordance with the category of Securities listed in each of those items, that is the same as the method that he/she used to provide or publicize such Specified Information on Securities:
(i) Specified Listed Securities, etc. : the method specified in the Specified Exchange Rules;
(ii) Specified Over-the-Counter Traded Securities, etc. : the method specified in the Specified Association Rules; or
(iii) Securities other than those listed in the preceding two items: the method designated by the Commissioner of the Financial Services Agency.
(3) The holder prescribed in the preceding paragraph shall be the person prescribed in the following items in accordance with the category of Securities listed in each of those items:
(i) Securities (excluding the Securities listed in the following item): the person who is listed or recorded as the holder in the shareholder registry (including the preferred equity investor registry prescribed in Article 25, paragraph (1) of the Act on Preferred Equity Investment by Cooperative Structured Financial Institutions (Act No. 44 of 1993), and where the relevant Securities are Securities other than share certificates, the registry of the holders thereof); or
(ii) Securities issued by a foreign state or foreign person: the person who is listed in the registry of the holders of the Securities that are being held by the Financial Instruments Business Operator, etc. (meaning a Financial Instruments Business Operator, etc. as prescribed in Article 34 of the Act; the same shall apply in Article 13,

item (iii), Article 14, and Article 16, item (iii)) who has been entrusted to retain said Securities.

(Period in Which Specified Information on Securities Is to Be Publicized)
Article 6 The provisions of paragraph (1) of the preceding Article shall apply mutatis mutandis to the cases and the period specified by Cabinet Office Ordinance, referred to in Article 27-31, paragraph (5) of the Act; provided, however, that the term "the provision or publication" in paragraph (1) of the preceding Article shall be deemed to be replaced with "the publication."

(Contents of an Issuer's Information)
Article 7 (1) An Issuer who is to provide or publicize Issuer's Information pursuant to the provisions of Article 27-32, paragraph (1) of the Act shall do so by the method prescribed in the following items, in accordance with the category of Securities listed in each of those items:
  (i) Specified Listed Securities, etc. : the method of publication specified in the Specified Exchange Rules;
  (ii) Specified Over-the-Counter Traded Securities, etc. : the method of publication specified in the Specified Association Rules; or
  (iii) Securities other than those listed in the preceding two items: the method designated by the Commissioner of the Financial Services Agency.
(2) The information specified by Cabinet Office Ordinance, referred to in Article 27-32, paragraph (1) of the Act, shall be the information prescribed in the following items in accordance with the category of Securities listed in each of those items; provided, however, that where it is found to be inappropriate as regards the public interest or protection of investors to provide such information on the Securities listed in items (i) or (ii) as such information, it shall be prescribed by the instructions of the Commissioner of the Financial Services Agency:
  (i) Specified Listed Securities, etc. : the information specified in the Specified Exchange Rules;
  (ii) Specified Over-the-Counter Traded Securities, etc. : the information specified in the Specified Association Rules; or
  (iii) Securities other than those listed in the preceding two items: the information designated by the Commissioner of the Financial Services Agency.
(3) The information prescribed in the items of the preceding paragraph shall include the information prescribed in the following items in accordance with the category of Securities listed in each of those items:
  (i) Securities (excluding the Securities listed in the following item): the following matters:
    (a) that the information falls under the category of specified information on securities;
    (b) matters concerning Securities other than said Securities issued by the Issuer of said Securities; and
    (c) matters concerning the business and accounting of the Issuer (excluding states and local governments) of said Securities.
  (ii) Regulated Securities: the following matters:
    (a) that the information falls under the category of Issuer's Information;
    (b) matters concerning the details and investment of the Assets under Management, etc. ; and
    (c) matters concerning the person engaged in investment of the Assets under Management, etc.

(4) The cases prescribed by Cabinet Office Ordinance, referred to in the main clause of Article 27-32, paragraph (1) of the Act, shall be the cases listed in the following items, and the period prescribed by Cabinet Office Ordinance, referred to in that paragraph, shall be the period prescribed in each of those items:
(i) where the Securities issued by the Issuer are Regulated Securities: the Specified Period (meaning the Specified Period prescribed in Article 24, paragraph (1) of the Act as applied mutatis mutandis by replacing certain terms pursuant to paragraph (5) of that Article) designated for the Securities; or
(ii) where the Issuer is a person other than a company (excluding the case prescribed in the preceding item): a Business Year or any other equivalent period.
(5) The cases prescribed by Cabinet Office Ordinance, referred to in the main clause of Article 27-32, paragraph (1) of the Act shall be the cases listed in the following items:
(i) cases that fall under the Case Where Disclosures Have Been Made with regard to the Securities prescribed in the items of Article 27-32, paragraph (1) of the Act or other Securities issued by the Issuer of such Securities;
(ii) cases where the Securities prescribed in Article 27-32, paragraph (1), item (i) of the Act have ceased to fall under the category of Securities for Professional Investors (meaning Securities for Professional Investors as prescribed in Article 4, paragraph (3) of the Act; the same shall apply in Article 8, paragraph (1)) pursuant to the provisions of Article 2-12-4, paragraph (1) of the Order; or
(iii) cases where an Issuer of Securities prescribed in Article 27-32, paragraph (1), item (i) of the Act has applied to the Commissioner of the Financial Services Agency for approval not to provide or publicize the Issuer's Information under the provisions of that paragraph, and where the Commissioner of the Financial Services Agency has found the Issuer to fall under any of the following and has given approval for the Issuer's Information (limited to information pertaining to Business Years from the Business Year that includes the day on which the Issuer filed the application to the Business Year that includes the day on which the Issuer ceases to fall under any of the following) not to be provided or publicized:
(a) a person in liquidation; or
(b) a person who is suspending his/her business for a considerable period of time.
(6) The approval referred to in item (iii) of the preceding paragraph shall be given on the condition that the Issuer prescribed in that item has submitted the written application for approval prescribed in that item, with the documents prescribed in the following items attached thereto, in accordance with the category of Issuers listed in each of those items:
(i) an Issuer of Securities listed in Article 5, paragraph (3), item (i): the following documents:
(a) the articles of incorporation and any other equivalent documents;
(b) where the Issuer is a person listed in item (iii), sub-item (a) of the preceding paragraph, a copy of the minutes of the shareholders meeting (or the general meeting of members or the general meeting of representatives for a mutual company, or the general meeting of members for a medical incorporated association) that resolved on the dissolution and the certificate of registered matters for the dissolution, or any documents equivalent thereto; or
(c) where the Issuer is a person listed in item (iii), sub-item (b) of the preceding paragraph, a document that contains the particulars of the suspension of the business and its future prospects;
(ii) an Issuer other than those listed in the preceding item: the following documents:
(a) the documents prescribed in the preceding item;
(b) a document certifying that the representative person of the Issuer listed in the

written application for approval is a person with due authority for the submission of the written application for approval; and
(c) a document certifying that the Issuer has given a person who has an address in Japan the authority to represent the Issuer with regard to any acts concerning the submission of the written application for approval.

(Cases Where the Provision or Publication of Issuer's Information Is Not Required)

Article 8 (1) The cases prescribed by Cabinet Office Ordinance, referred to in Article 27-32, paragraph (2) of the Act shall be where Securities issued by an Issuer that is excluded from the application of the main clause of paragraph (1) of that Article have come to fall under the category of Securities for Professional Investors, and where this falls under any of the cases listed in the following items (limited to item (i) when such Securities have come to fall under the category of Securities listed in Article 4, paragraph (3), item (iv) of the Act):

(i) cases that fall under the Case Where Disclosures Have Been Made with regard to the Securities or other Securities issued by the Issuer;

(ii) cases where the Securities are subject to the provisions of Article 27-31, paragraph (1) of the Act with regard to a Specified Solicitation or Offer, etc. , and the Specified Information on Securities provided or publicized pursuant to the provisions of paragraph (2) of that Article contains information concerning the matters listed in Article 2, paragraph (2), item (i), sub-item (d) or item (ii), sub-item (c) concerning the Business Year immediately prior to the Business Year that includes the day on which the Specified Information on Securities was provided or publicized; or

(iii) cases where the Securities fall under the category of Securities listed in Article 4, paragraph (3), item (iii) of the Act and have become Securities for Professional Investors.

(2) An Issuer who is to provide or publicize Issuer's Information pursuant to the provisions of Article 27-32, paragraph (2) of the Act shall provide or publicize the Issuer's Information to a Holder (meaning a holder as prescribed in Article 5, paragraph (3); the same shall apply in the following Article) of the Securities by the method prescribed in the following items in accordance with the category of Securities listed in each of those items:

(i) Specified Listed Securities, etc. : the method of publication specified in the Specified Exchange Rules;

(ii) Specified Over-the-Counter Traded Securities, etc. : the method of publication specified in the Specified Association Rules; or

(iii) Securities other than those listed in the preceding two items: the method designated by the Commissioner of the Financial Services Agency.

(Amendment of the Issuer's Information)

Article 9 An Issuer who is to provide or publicize Amended Issuer's Information (meaning Amended Issuer's Information as prescribed in Article 27-32, paragraph (3) of the Act; hereinafter the same shall apply in this Article) pursuant to the provisions of that paragraph shall provide or publicize the Amended Issuer's Information to the other party to whom he/she has provided the Issuer's Information to which the Amended Issuer's Information is related and to the holder of the Securities, by the method prescribed in the following items in accordance with the category of Securities listed in each of those items that is the same as the method that he/she used to provide or publicize such Issuer's Information:

(i) Specified Listed Securities, etc. : the method specified in the Specified Exchange

Rules;
(ii) Specified Over-the-Counter Traded Securities, etc. : the method specified in the Specified Association Rules;
(iii) Securities other than those listed in the preceding two items: the method designated by the Commissioner of the Financial Services Agency.

(Period in Which the Issuer's Information, etc. Is to Be Publicized)
Article 10 The cases prescribed by Cabinet Office Ordinance, referred to in Article 27-32, paragraph (4) of the Act, shall be the cases listed in the following items, and the period prescribed by Cabinet Office Ordinance, referred to in that paragraph, shall be the period prescribed in each of those items:
(i) cases that have come to fall under any of the items of Article 7, paragraph (5): the period from the date of publication to the date on which the case came to fall under the relevant item; or
(ii) cases where Securities pertaining to the Issuer's Information have ceased to exist due to retirement, redemption, or any other grounds: the period from the date of the publication of the Issuer's Information to the date on which the Securities ceased to exist.

(Measures for Making Information Available to a Large Number of Persons)
Article 11 The measures for making information available to a large number of persons, referred to in Article 21-2, paragraph (3) of the Act as applied mutatis mutandis by replacing certain terms pursuant to Article 27-34 of the Act, shall be measures that are taken by the methods prescribed in the following items in accordance with the category of Securities listed in each of those items, or by any other means:
(i) Specified Listed Securities, etc. : the method specified in the Specified Exchange Rules;
(ii) Specified Over-the-Counter Traded Securities, etc. : the method specified in the Specified Association Rules; or
(iii) Securities other than those listed in the preceding two items: the method designated by the Commissioner of the Financial Services Agency.

Chapter III Provision and Publication of Foreign Securities Information

(Contents of Foreign Securities Information)
Article 12 (1) The information prescribed by Cabinet Office Ordinance, referred to in Article 27-32-2, paragraph (1) of the Act, shall be the information listed in the right-hand column of the appended table, in accordance with the category of Securities listed in the left-hand column of the table.
(2) The information prescribed in the preceding paragraph shall be the information related to the most recent Business Year (including the fiscal year or any other equivalent period) that the person who is to provide or publicize Foreign Securities Information can provide or publicize.
(3) Where the contents of the whole or a part of the Foreign Securities Information are included in the information already publicized by the Issuer of the Securities or any other equivalent person (limited to information that satisfies all the requirements listed in the following items; hereinafter referred to as the "Publicized Information" in this paragraph), a statement to the effect that reference should be made to the Publicized Information and information about the address of the website on which the Publicized

Information is available shall be deemed to be the whole or a part of the Foreign Securities Information:
(i) that the Publicized Information is publicized based on laws and regulations or foreign laws and regulations on the issuance of the Securities (including any equivalent rules laid down by international organizations), or the rules laid down by the Financial Instruments Exchange that lists the Securities or by the designated Foreign Financial Instruments Exchange (excluding where the Securities are those listed in Article 2-12-3, items (i) to (iii) inclusive of the Order);
(ii) that the Publicized Information is easily obtained via the Internet in Japan; and
(iii) that the Publicized Information is publicized in Japanese or English.

(Cases Where the Provision or Publication of Foreign Financial Information Is Not Required)
Article 13 The cases prescribed by Cabinet Office Ordinance, referred to in the main clause of Article 27-32-2, paragraph (1) of the Act, shall be those that fall under any of the cases listed in the following items:
(i) cases where an Issuer of Securities that are involved in a Secondary Distribution of Foreign Securities (hereinafter referred to as "Foreign Securities in a Secondary Distribution" in this Article) has submitted the Annual Securities Reports under Article 24, paragraph (1) or paragraph (3) of the Act (including cases where these provisions are applied mutatis mutandis pursuant to Article 24, paragraph (5) of the Act (including cases where it is applied mutatis mutandis pursuant to Article 27 of the Act) and Article 27 of the Act) for other Securities that he/she has issued, and he/she provides or publicizes the relevant information on the Foreign Securities in the Secondary Distribution (meaning the information listed in the right-hand column of the appended table, in accordance with the category of Securities listed in the left-hand column of the table under which the Foreign Securities in the Secondary Distribution fall; the same shall apply in the following item);
(ii) cases where an Issuer of Foreign Securities in a Secondary Distribution has already publicized the Specified Information on Securities or Issuer's Information with regard to the Foreign Securities in the Secondary Distribution, and he/she provides or publicizes the relevant information concerning the Foreign Securities in the Secondary Distribution (limited to cases where such information includes the information prescribed in paragraph (1) of the preceding Article);
(iii) cases where the Foreign Securities in a Secondary Distribution are Securities listed in Article 2-12-3, items (i) to (iii) inclusive of the Order (for Securities listed in those items, limited to those for which a foreign national or local government guarantees the redemption of the principal and the payment of the interest), and the Financial Instruments Business Operator, etc. who intends to carry out the Secondary Distribution of the Foreign Securities in the Secondary Distribution can confirm that the Foreign Securities in the Secondary Distribution or other Securities of the same class that the Issuer of the Foreign Securities in the Secondary Distribution issues are to be sold and purchased continuously by two or more Financial Instruments Business Operators, etc., as prescribed by the rules laid down by an Authorized Financial Instruments Firms Association (limited to a single Authorized Financial Instruments Firms Association designated by the Commissioner of the Financial Services Agency); or
(iv) cases where the other party to a Secondary Distribution of Foreign Securities is a Qualified Institutional Investor (limited to a person who acquires the Foreign Securities in the Secondary Distribution on the condition that he/she will not transfer them other than to a Financial Instruments Business Operator, etc. or a Non-Resi-

dent (meaning Non-Residents as prescribed in Article 6, paragraph (1), item (vi) of the Foreign Exchange and Foreign Trade Act (Act No. 228 of 1949))) (excluding where there has been any request for the provision or publication of the Foreign Securities in the Secondary Distribution from the Qualified Institutional Investor by the time the Foreign Securities in the Secondary Distribution are sold).

(Persons Equivalent to Those Who Have Entrusted the Custody of Securities)
Article 14 The persons prescribed by Cabinet Office Ordinance, referred to in Article 27-32-2, paragraph (2) of the Act, shall be those listed in the following items:
(i) A person who has acquired Securities through a Secondary Distribution of Foreign Securities and who is a Member (meaning a member as prescribed in Article 2, paragraph (3) of the Act on Transfer of Corporate Bonds, Shares, etc. (Act No. 75 of 2001); the same shall apply in item (iii)) in connection with Securities that have made the Financial Instruments Business Operator, etc. that carried out the Secondary Distribution of Foreign Securities the Account Management Institution (meaning an account management institution as prescribed in Article 2, paragraph (4) of that Act: the same shall apply in item (iii)) for said Securities;
(ii) A person who has acquired Securities through a Secondary Distribution of Foreign Securities, and has entrusted the custody of the Securities to the Financial Instruments Business Operator, etc. who has carried out the Secondary Distribution of Foreign Securities, but has entrusted, due to a business transfer carried out by the Financial Instruments Business Operator, etc. or for any other reasons, the custody of the Securities to another Financial Instruments Business Operator, etc. (limited to where said other Financial Instruments Business Operator, etc. carries out Secondary Distributions of Foreign Securities of the Same Class as the relevant Securities (meaning Securities of the same class as prescribed in Article 10-2 of the Cabinet Office Ordinance on Definitions under Article 2 of the Financial Instruments and Exchange Act (Ordinance of the Ministry of Finance No. 14 of 1993))); or
(iii) A person who has acquired Securities through a Secondary Distribution of Foreign Securities, who is a member in connection with Securities that have made the relevant Financial Instruments Business Operator, etc. the Account Management Institution for said Securities, and who is a member in connection with Securities that have made a Financial Instruments Business Operator, etc. other than one who has succeeded to the Account Management Institution's business due to a business transfer by the first Financial Instruments Business Operator, etc. or for any other reason, the Account Management Institution for said Securities.

(Cases Where an Event That May Have a Material Influence on Investors' Investment Judgments Has Occurred)
Article 15 (1) The cases where an event has occurred that is prescribed by Cabinet Office Ordinance as one that may have a material influence on the investors' investment judgments, referred to in Article 27-32-2, paragraph (2) of the Act, shall be as follows:
(i) cases where there has been a merger involving the Issuer of the Securities or the person who guarantees the redemption of the principal or the payment of interest on the Securities (referred to as a "Guarantor" in the following item), or any other similar material change in the business concerning the redemption of the principal or the payment of interest for the Securities, or the performance or guarantee of other obligations; or
(ii) cases where rehabilitation proceedings under the Civil Rehabilitation Act (Act No. 225 of 1999), reorganization proceedings under the Corporate Reorganization Act

(Act No. 154 of 2002), or bankruptcy proceedings under the Bankruptcy Act (Act No. 75 of 2004) for the Issuer or the Guarantor of the Securities have commenced or been terminated, or where any other similar event based on foreign laws and regulations has occurred.
(2) With regard to Foreign Securities Information to be provided or publicized pursuant to the provisions of Article 27-32-2, paragraph (2) of the Act in cases falling under any of those listed in the items of the preceding paragraph, the information listed in the following items may be provided or publicized in lieu of the information prescribed in Article 12, paragraph (1):
  (i) the name of the Issuer of the Securities that are involved in the Secondary Distribution of Foreign Securities;
  (ii) the issue of the Securities that are involved in the Secondary Distribution of Foreign Securities; and
  (iii) the fact that the case falls under any of those listed in the items of the preceding paragraph.

(Cases Deemed to Be Cases Where Protection of Investors Would Not Be Impaired)
Article 16 The cases prescribed by Cabinet Office Ordinance, referred to in the proviso to Article 27-32-2, paragraph (2) of the Act, shall be as follows:
  (i) cases that fall under the Case Where Disclosures Have Been Made (meaning the Case Where Disclosures Have Been Made as prescribed in Article 4, paragraph (7) of the Act) with regard to the Securities;
  (ii) cases listed in Article 13, items (ii) to (iv) inclusive; or
  (iii) cases where the number of holders of the Securities (limited to persons who have entrusted the custody of the Securities to the Financial Instruments Business Operator, etc. who has carried out the Secondary Distribution of Foreign Securities in connection with the Securities and persons listed in Article 14) in Japan is less than 50.

(Method of Provision or Publication of Foreign Securities Information)
Article 17 (1) A Financial Instruments Business Operator, etc. who intends to provide or publicize Foreign Securities Information pursuant to the provisions of Article 27-32-2, paragraph (3) of the Act shall do so in any of the ways listed in the following items:
  (i) delivering a document containing the Foreign Securities Information to the other party to whom he/she wishes to provide or publicize it (hereinafter referred to as the "Recipient of the Foreign Securities Information" in this paragraph);
  (ii) sending the Foreign Securities Information by facsimile to the Recipient of the Foreign Securities Information (limited to where the Foreign Securities Information can be received by the Recipient of the Foreign Securities Information and said Recipient of the Foreign Securities Information has agreed to the Foreign Securities Information being provided in this way);
  (iii) sending the Foreign Securities Information by Electronic Mail (meaning electronic mail as prescribed in Article 2, item (i) of the Act on Regulation of the Transmission of Specified Electronic Mail (Act No. 26 of 2002)), the Internet, or any other telecommunications lines (limited to where the Foreign Securities Information can be converted into a document by the Recipient of the Foreign Securities Information using a computer and said Recipient of the Foreign Securities Information has agreed to the Foreign Securities Information being provided in this way); or
  (iv) providing or publicizing information about a website address at which Foreign Securities Information is available or any other information about ways to inspect the

Foreign Securities Information (limited to cases where the Recipient of the Foreign Securities Information has agreed to the Foreign Securities Information being provided in this way).

(2) A Financial Instruments Business Operator, etc. who wishes to provide or publicize Foreign Securities Information pursuant to the provisions of Article 27-32-2, paragraph (2) of the Act shall, when he/she has received a request as prescribed in that paragraph or when the case has come to fall under any of the cases listed in the items of Article 15, paragraph (1), provide or publicize Foreign Securities Information without delay.

Supplementary Provisions

This Cabinet Office Ordinance shall come into effect as of December 12, 2008.

Supplementary Provisions [Cabinet Office Ordinance No. 78 of December 28, 2009] [Extract]

(Effective Date)
Article 1 This Cabinet Office Ordinance shall come into effect as of the day of the enforcement of the Act for the Partial Revision of the Financial Instruments and Exchange Act (Act No. 58 of 2009; hereinafter referred to as the "Revising Act") (April 1, 2010).

(Transitional Measures Concerning the Application of Penal Provisions)
Article 10 With regard to the application of penal provisions to acts committed prior to the enforcement of this Cabinet Office Ordinance (regarding the provisions listed in the items of Article 1 of the Supplementary Provisions, said provisions; hereinafter the same shall apply in this Article), and acts committed after the enforcement of this Cabinet Office Ordinance in cases where the provisions then in force are to remain applicable pursuant to the Supplementary Provisions, the provisions then in force shall remain applicable.

Appended Table (Re. Art. 12)

Securities	Information
Securities listed in Article 2-12-3, item (i) of the Order	1 Issuer's Information:
	(1) the name of the Issuer;
	(2) an outline of the Issuer; and
	(3) an outline of the finances.
	2 Information on Securities:
	(1) the name of the Securities;
	(2) the place of issuance and whether the Securities are listed or unlisted (when Securities are listed, the Financial Instruments Exchange in a foreign state (meaning the Financial Instruments Exchange in a foreign state as prescribed in Article 2-12-3, item (iv), sub-item (b) of the Order; the same shall apply hereinafter) where the Securities are listed);
	(3) the date of issuance;

	(4) the amount of issuance;
	(5) the interest rates and the method of determining the interest payment;
	(6) the date of the interest payment;
	(7) the due date for redemption;
	(8) the amount of redemption and the method of determining the redemption amount;
	(9) the entrusted company or deposit institution;
	(10) matters concerning collateral or guarantees;
	(11) performance priority with other obligations; and
	(12) matters concerning the rating and the name of the rating organization connected to said rating (limited to where the Securities are rated).
	3 When the case falls under any of the cases listed in the items of Article 15, paragraph (1), to that effect and the details thereof.
Securities listed in Article 2-12-3, item (ii) of the Order	1 Issuer's Information:
	(1) the name of the Issuer;
	(2) an outline of the Issuer; and
	(3) an outline of the finances.
	2 Information on Securities:
	(1) the name of the Securities:
	(2) the place of issuance and whether the Securities are listed or unlisted (when Securities are listed, the Financial Instruments Exchange in a foreign state where the Securities are listed);
	(3) the date of issuance;
	(4) the amount of issuance;
	(5) the interest rates and the method of determining the interest payment;
	(6) the date of the interest payment;
	(7) the due date for redemption;
	(8) the amount of redemption and the method of determining the redemption amount;
	(9) the entrusted company or deposit institution;
	(10) matters concerning collateral or guarantees;
	(11) performance priority compared with other obligations; and
	(12) matters concerning the rating and the name of the rating organization connected to said rating (limited to where the Securities are rated).
	3 When the case falls under any of the cases listed in the items of Article 15, paragraph (1), to that effect and the details thereof.

Securities listed in Article 2-12-3, item (iii) of the Order	1 Issuer's Information:
	(1) the name of the Issuer;
	(2) the location of the Issuer;
	(3) an outline of the Issuer (the governing law for the establishment of the Issuer, the purpose of the establishment, the grounds for the establishment, the legal standing, the year of the establishment, and other matters); and
	(4) an outline of the accounting.
	2 Information on Securities:
	(1) the name of the Securities:
	(2) the place of issuance and whether the Securities are listed or unlisted (when Securities are listed, the Financial Instruments Exchange in a foreign state where the Securities are listed);
	(3) the date of issuance;
	(4) the amount of issuance;
	(5) the interest rates and the method of determining the interest payment;
	(6) the date of the interest payment;
	(7) the due date for redemption;
	(8) the amount of redemption and the method of determining the redemption amount;
	(9) the entrusted company or deposit institution;
	(10) matters concerning collateral or guarantees;
	(11) performance priority compared with other obligations;
	(12) the governing law concerning issuance, payment and redemption; and
	(13) matters concerning the rating and the name of the rating organization connected to said rating (limited to where the Securities are rated).
	3 When the case falls under any of the cases listed in the items of Article 15, paragraph (1), to that effect and the details thereof.
Securities listed in Article 2-12-3, item (iv) of the Order	1 Issuer's Information:
	(1) the name of the Issuer;
	(2) the location of the head office of the Issuer;
	(3) the governing law for the establishment of the Issuer, the legal standing, and the year of the establishment;
	(4) the accounting period;
	(5) the details of the business; and
	(6) the outline of the accounting.

	2 Information on Securities:
	(1) the class and the name of the Securities;
	(2) the place for issuance and whether the Securities are listed or unlisted (when Securities are listed, the Financial Instruments Exchange in a foreign state where the Securities are listed);
	(3) the date of issuance;
	(4) the amount of issuance;
	(5) the details of the shares to be converted:
	(a) the Financial Instruments Exchange in Japan or in a foreign state on which the shares to be converted are listed;
	(b) the Issuer and the class of the shares to be converted;
	(c) the conditions for conversion; and
	(d) the period for requesting conversion.
	(6) the interest rates and the method of determining the interest payment;
	(7) the date of the interest payment;
	(8) the due date for redemption;
	(9) the amount of redemption and the method of determining the redemption amount;
	(10) the entrusted company or deposit institution;
	(11) matters concerning collateral or guarantees;
	(12) performance priority compared with other obligations;
	(13) the governing law concerning issuance, payment and redemption; and
	(14) matters concerning the rating and the name of the rating organization connected to said rating (limited to where the Securities are rated).
	3 When the case falls under any of the cases listed in the items of Article 15, paragraph (1), to that effect and the details thereof.
Securities listed in Article 2-12-3, item (v) of the Order	1 Issuer's Information:
	(1) the name of the Issuer;
	(2) the location of the head office of the Issuer;
	(3) the governing law for the establishment of the Issuer, the Issuer's legal standing, and the year of establishment;
	(4) the accounting period;
	(5) the details of the business; and
	(6) an outline of the accounting.
	2 Information on Securities:

	(1) the class and the name of the Securities;
	(2) the place of issuance and whether the Securities are listed or unlisted (when the Securities are listed, the Financial Instruments Exchange in a foreign state where the Securities are listed);
	(3) the date of issuance;
	(4) the amount of issuance;
	(5) the details of the share options:
	(a) the Financial Instruments Exchange in a foreign state on which the share certificates for shares that will be issued through the exercise of the rights are listed;
	(b) the total amount paid for the shares that will be issued through the exercise of the rights;
	(c) the class of the shares that will be issued through the exercise of the rights;
	(d) the issue price of the shares that will be issued through the exercise of the rights; and
	(e) the period for requesting the exercise of the share options and other conditions for exercising them;
	(6) the interest rates and the method of determining the interest payment;
	(7) the date of the interest payment;
	(8) the due date for redemption;
	(9) the amount of redemption and the method of determining the redemption amount;
	(10) the entrusted company or deposit institution;
	(11) matters concerning collateral or guarantees;
	(12) performance priority compared with other obligations;
	(13) the governing law concerning issuance, payment and redemption; and
	(14) matters concerning the rating and the name of the rating organization connected with said rating (limited to where the Securities are rated).
	3 When the case falls under any of the cases listed in the items of Article 15, paragraph (1), to that effect and the details thereof.
Securities listed in Article 2-12-3, item (vi) of the Order	1 Issuer's Information:
	(1) the name of the Issuer;
	(2) the location of the head office of the Issuer;
	(3) the governing law for the establishment of the Issuer, the Issuer's legal standing, and the year of establishment;
	(4) the accounting period;

	(5) the details of the business; (6) where the information listed in (7) is not stated, an outline of the accounting; (7) the following matters concerning information on the Parent Company (meaning the parent company prescribed in Article 2-12-3, item (vi) of the Order) that provides a guarantee: (a) the name; (b) the location of the head office; (c) the governing law for the establishment of the Issuer, the Issuer's legal standing, and the year of establishment; (d) the accounting period; (e) the details of the business; and (f) an outline of the accounting. 2 Information on Securities: (1) the class and the name of the Securities; (2) the place of issuance and whether the Securities are listed or unlisted (when Securities are listed, the Financial Instruments Exchange in a foreign state where the Securities are listed); (3) the date of issuance; (4) the amount of issuance; (5) the interest rates and the method of determining the interest payment; (6) the date of the interest payment; (7) the due date for redemption; (8) the amount of redemption and the method of determining the redemption amount; (9) the entrusted company or deposit institution; (10) matters concerning collateral or guarantees; (11) performance priority compared with other obligations; (12) the governing law concerning issuance, payment and redemption; and (13) matters concerning the rating and the name of the rating organization connected with said rating (limited to where the Securities are rated). 3 When the case falls under any of the cases listed in the items of Article 15, paragraph (1), to that effect and the details thereof.
Securities listed in Article 2-12-3, item (vii) of the Order	1 Issuer's Information: (1) the name of the Issuer; (2) the location of the head office of the Issuer;

	(3) the governing law for the establishment of the Issuer, the Issuer's legal standing, and the year of establishment;
	(4) the accounting period;
	(5) the number of issued shares;
	(6) the details of the business; and
	(7) an outline of the accounting.
	2 Information on Securities:
	(1) the class and the name of the shares;
	(2) the place of issuance and the Financial Instruments Exchange in a foreign state where the shares are listed;
	(3) the trend of the share prices;
	(4) the trend of the business performance:
	(a) the sales;
	(b) the current net earnings; and
	(c) the amount of shareholders' equity;
	(5) per-share information:
	(a) the current net earnings per share; and
	(b) the amount of a dividend per share.
	3 When the case falls under any of the cases listed in the items of Article 15, paragraph (1), to that effect and the details thereof.
Securities listed in Article 2-12-3, item (viii) of the Order	1 Information on Securities:
	(1) the name of the Securities;
	(2) the form of the fund;
	(3) the class of the Securities;
	(4) the place of issuance;
	(5) the Financial Instruments Exchange in a foreign state where the Securities are listed;
	(6) the date of issuance; and
	(7) the unit of trading.
	2 Issuer's Information:
	(1) the address of the Fund on the registry;
	(2) the governing law for the Fund;
	(3) the purpose and the basic nature of the Fund;
	(4) an outline of the major juridical persons and the amount of equity capital;
	(5) investment targets and investment policies;
	(6) investment restrictions;
	(7) an outline of the assets of the Fund;
	(8) remuneration and costs concerning the Fund;
	(9) risks;

	(10) the accounting period;
	(11) the status of the operation of the Fund; and
	(12) the status of the accounting of the Fund.
	3 When the case falls under any of the cases listed in the items of Article 15, paragraph (1), to that effect and the details thereof.
Securities listed in Article 2-12-3, item (ix) of the Order	1 Issuer's Information:
	(1) the name of the Issuer;
	(2) the location of the head office of the Issuer;
	(3) the governing law for the establishment of the Issuer, the Issuer's legal standing, and the year of establishment;
	(4) the accounting period;
	(5) the details of the business; and
	(6) an outline of the accounting.
	2 Information on Securities:
	(1) the name of the Securities;
	(2) the place for issuance and whether the Securities are listed or unlisted (when Securities are listed, the Financial Instruments Exchange in a foreign state where the Securities are listed);
	(3) the date of issuance;
	(4) the details of the options;
	(5) the method and conditions for exercising the options;
	(6) the method of settlement;
	(7) matters concerning the rating and the name of the rating organization connected with said rating (limited to where the Securities are rated);
	(8) the structure for issuing covered warrants;
	(9) risks;
	(10) other matters that may have a material influence on the investors' judgments regarding the options;
	(11) where the targets for exercising the options are Securities, the following matters:
	(a) an outline of the Securities;
	(b) the corporate information of the Issuer of the Securities; and
	(c) other matters that may have a material influence on the investors' judgments regarding the Securities; and
	(12) information concerning Financial Instruments or Financial Indicators in connection with the covered warrants.

	3 When the case falls under any of the cases listed in the items of Article 15, paragraph (1), to that effect and the details thereof.
Securities listed in Article 2-12-3, item (x) of the Order	1 Issuer's Information: (1) the name of the Issuer; (2) the location of the head office of the Issuer; (3) the governing law for the establishment of the Issuer, the Issuer's legal standing, and the year of establishment; (4) the accounting period of the Issuer; (5) the details of the business of the Issuer; and (6) an outline of the accounting of the Issuer. 2 Information on Securities: (1) the name of the Securities; (2) the place of issuance and the Financial Instruments Exchange in a foreign state where the Securities are listed; (3) dividends and the base date; (4) the details of the rights; (5) the method of and conditions for exercising the rights; (6) matters concerning the rating and the name of the rating organization connected with said rating (limited to where the Securities are rated); (7) the details of the Securities pertaining to the rights indicated on depositary receipts; (8) the structure for issuing depositary receipts; (9) other matters that may have a material influence on the investors' judgments regarding the rights indicated on depositary receipts; and (10) corporate information regarding the a person who receives deposits. 3 When the case falls under any of the cases listed in the items of Article 15, paragraph (1), to that effect and the details thereof.

⑭ Cabinet Office Ordinance on Funds Transfer Service Providers

(Cabinet Office Ordinance No. 4 of March 1, 2010)

The Prime Minister hereby issues the Cabinet Office Ordinance on Funds Transfer Service Providers based on the provisions of and for the purpose of enforcing the Payment Services Act (Act No. 59 of 2009) and the Order for Enforcement of the Payment Services Act (Cabinet Order No. 19 of 2010).

Chapter I General Provisions (Article 1 - Article 10)
Chapter II Business (Article 11 - Article 32)
Chapter III Supervision (Article 33 - Article 36)
Chapter IV Miscellaneous Provisions (Article 37 - Article 42)
    Supplementary Provisions

Chapter I General Provisions

(Definition)

Article 1 The terms "Funds Transfer Service", "Funds Transfer Service Provider", "Foreign Funds Transfer Service Provider", "Certified Association for Payment Service Providers", "Trust Company, etc." and "Deposit-taking Institutions" as used in this Cabinet Office Ordinance mean Funds Transfer Service, Funds Transfer Service Provider, Foreign Funds Transfer Service Provider, Certified Association for Payment Service Providers, Trust Company, etc. and Deposit-taking Institutions as prescribed in Article 2 of the Payment Services Act (hereinafter referred to as the "Act"), respectively.

(Attachment of a Translation)

Article 2 If there is a document to be submitted to the Commissioner of the Financial Services Agency (in the case where the authority of the Commissioner of the Financial Services Agency has been delegated to the Directors-General of Local Finance Bureaus or the Director General of the Fukuoka Local Finance Branch Bureau (hereinafter referred to as the "Directors-General of Local Finance Bureaus, etc.") pursuant to the provisions of Article 29 (1) of the Order for Enforcement of the Payment Services Act (hereinafter referred to as the "Order"), said Directors-General of Local Finance Bureaus, etc.; hereinafter the same shall apply except in Article 12, Article 19 (v), and Article 20) pursuant to the provisions of the Act (limited to Chapter III; the same shall apply in the following Article), the Order (limited to Chapter III; the same shall apply in the following Article), or this Cabinet Office Ordinance that cannot be prepared in Japanese under special circumstances, a Japanese translation shall be attached to said document; provided, however, that if said document is the articles of incorporation prepared in English, it is sufficient to attach a Japanese translation of the summary thereof.

(Foreign Currency Conversion)

Article 3 If a document to be submitted to the Commissioner of the Financial Services Agency pursuant to the provisions of the Act, the Order, or this Cabinet Office Ordinance contains items indicated in a foreign currency, the equivalent amounts converted to Japanese currency and the standard used for the conversion shall be included in the supplementary notes to said document.

(Application for Registration)
Article 4 A person intending to obtain a registration under Article 37 of the Act shall submit to the Commissioner of the Financial Services Agency a written application for registration set forth in Article 38 (1) of the Act prepared using appended Form 1 (in the case of a Foreign Funds Transfer Service Provider, appended Form 2) by attaching two copies of said written application for registration and the documents set forth in paragraph (2) of said Article.

(Other Matters to be Stated in Written Application for Registration)
Article 5 Matters specified by a Cabinet Office Ordinance as prescribed in Article 38 (1) (x) of the Act shall be the following matters:
(i) The time of day at which the amount of outstanding obligations in the process of funds transfer (meaning the amount of outstanding obligations in the process of funds transfer prescribed in Article 43 (2) of the Act) is calculated on each business day and the method for calculation;
(ii) The location and contact address of the business office that will respond to complaints or requests for consultation from the users of the Funds Transfer Service; and
(iii) Name of the Certified Association for Payment Service Providers of which the person who submits the written application for registration is a member.

(Documents to be Attached to Written Application for Registration)
Article 6 Documents specified by a Cabinet Office Ordinance as prescribed in Article 38 (2) of the Act shall be the following documents (in the case of a document certified by a public agency, limited to one issued within three months prior to the date of application):
(i) A document prepared using appended Form 3 pledging to the effect that the applicant does not fall under any of the items of Article 40 (1) of the Act;
(ii) Extract of the certificate of residence of its Directors, etc. (meaning Directors, etc. prescribed in Article 40 (1) (x) of the Act; hereinafter the same shall apply) (in the case where said Directors, etc. are foreign nationals, a copy of an alien registration certificate or a certificate of completion of alien registration) or any substitute thereof;
(iii) A certificate by a public agency proving to the effect that its Directors, etc. do not fall under Article 40 (1) (x) (a) or (b) of the Act (in the case where said Directors, etc. are foreign nationals, a written pledge prepared using appended Form 4) or any substitute thereof;
(iv) A curriculum vitae of Directors, etc. of the applicant or a history of the applicant prepared by using appended Form 5 or Form 6;
(v) The register of shareholders prepared using appended Form 7 and the articles of incorporation and a certificate of registered matters or any substitute thereof;
(vi) In the case of a Foreign Funds Transfer Service Provider, a document proving that it is a person who carries out funds transfer transactions (Kawase transactions) in the course of trade in a foreign state under the registration of the same kind as the registration under Article 37 of the Act pursuant to the provisions of laws and regulations of said foreign state (including permission or other administrative dispositions similar to said registration);
(vii) The latest balance sheet (including the related notes) and profit and loss statement (including the related notes) or any substitute thereof (in the case of a juridi-

cal person established in a business year that includes the date of the application for registration, the balance sheet as of the date of establishment prepared pursuant to the provisions of Article 435 (1) of the Companies Act (Act No. 86 of 2005) or any substitute thereof);

(viii) In the case of a company with accounting auditors, a document containing the contents of the accounting audit report prepared pursuant to the provisions of Article 396 (1) of the Companies Act for the business year immediately preceding the business year that includes the date of the application for registration;

(ix) A document stating the expected income and expenditure from the Funds Transfer Service for the three business years after the commencement of the business;

(x) An organization chart concerning the Funds Transfer Service (including organizations that perform the operations pertaining to internal controls);

(xi) A curriculum vitae of the person responsible for the management of the Funds Transfer Service;

(xii) Internal rules concerning the Funds Transfer Service (meaning internal rules and other documents equivalent thereto; the same shall apply in Article 32);

(xiii) Contract documents used in carrying out funds transfer transactions (Kawase transactions) with the users of the Funds Transfer Service;

(xiv) In the case where the Funds Transfer Service is entrusted to a third party, the contract document pertaining to said entrustment contract; and

(xv) Other documents containing other relevant matters.

(Notice to Applicant)
Article 7 When the Commissioner of the Financial Services Agency gives a notice of registration prescribed in Article 39 (2) of the Act, he/she shall give it by a written notice of completion of registration prepared using appended Form 8.

(Public Inspections of Funds Transfer Service Provider Registry)
Article 8 The Commissioner of the Financial Services Agency shall keep the registry of Funds Transfer Service Providers pertaining to the registered Funds Transfer Service Provider at the Local Finance Bureau or the Fukuoka Local Finance Branch Bureau having jurisdiction over the location of the head office of said Funds Transfer Service Provider (in the case of a Foreign Funds Transfer Service Provider, its principal business office in Japan; hereinafter the same shall apply) and make it available for public inspection.

(Notice of Refusal of Registration)
Article 9 If the Commissioner of the Financial Services Agency gives a notice prescribed in Article 40 (2) of the Act, he/she shall give it by a written notice of refusal of registration prepared using appended Form 9.

(Notification of Changes)
Article 10 (1) If a Funds Transfer Service Provider intends to make a notification pursuant to the provisions of Article 41 (1) of the Act, he/she shall submit to the Commissioner of the Financial Services Agency a written notice of changes prepared using appended Form 10 by attaching two copies of said written notice of changes and documents specified in the following items for the categories of cases respectively prescribed therein (in the case of a document certified by a public agency, limited to one issued within three months prior to the date of notification):

(i) In the case of a change in the trade name: A certificate of registered matters that contains the matters pertaining to said change or any substitute thereof, and a document prepared using appended Form 3 pledging to the effect that the Funds Transfer Service Provider does not fall under any of the items of Article 40 (1) of the Act;

(ii) In the case of a change in the amount of capital: A certificate of registered matters that contains the matters pertaining to said change or any substitute thereof;

(iii) In the case of establishment or abolition of a business office or a change in the location of a business office (excluding cases as listed in item (ix)): A certificate of registered matters that contains the matters pertaining to said change;

(iv) In the case of a change in the Directors, etc. : Documents listed in Article 6 (ii) through (iv) that pertain to the person who newly became a Director, etc. , documents listed in item (v) of said Article that pertain to said change, and a document prepared using appended Form 3 pledging to the effect that the Funds Transfer Service Provider does not fall under any of the items of Article 40 (1) of the Act;

(v) In the case of a change in the major shareholders (meaning a shareholder who holds voting rights exceeding ten percent of the voting rights held by all the Shareholders (excluding the voting rights of the shares which cannot be exercised for all matters that are subject to a resolution at a general meeting of shareholders and including the voting rights of the shares for which the shareholder shall be deemed to have voting rights under the provisions of Article 879 (3) of the Companies Act)): The register of shareholders prepared using appended Form 7;

(vi) In the case of a change in the contents or methods of the Funds Transfer Service: The documents listed in Article 6 (x) through (xiii) that pertain to the matters that have been changed;

(vii) In the case of a change in the contents of business that has been entrusted or a person to whom business is entrusted: The documents listed in Article 6 (xiv) that pertain to the matters that have been changed;

(viii) In the case of a change in the other businesses: A certificate of registered matters that contains the matters pertaining to said change or any substitute thereof;

(ix) In the case where a Funds Transfer Service Provider who has obtained the registration under Article 37 of the Act from the Director-General of a Local Finance Bureau, etc. has changed the location of its head office to an area over which another Directors-General of another Local Finance Bureau, etc. has jurisdiction: The document prescribed in item (iii) and a written notice of completion of registration under Article 7 that was delivered prior to said change; and

(x) In the case where the Funds Transfer Service Provider has become a member of a Certified Association for Payment Service Providers or has withdrawn from one: A document that can demonstrate the fact that the Funds Transfer Service Provider has become a member of a Certified Association for Payment Service Providers or has withdrawn from one.

(2) If a notification is made under the preceding paragraph in the case set forth in item (ix) of said paragraph, the Director-General of a Local Finance Bureau, etc. shall notify the Directors-General of the other Local Finance Bureau, etc. referred to in said item to the effect that said notification has been made.

(3) The Director-General of a Local Finance Bureau, etc. who has received the notification under the preceding paragraph shall register the matters notified of in the registry of Funds Transfer Service Providers and notify the person who made said notification of said registration by the written notice of completion of registration prescribed in Article 7.

Chapter II Business

(Making of Security Deposit for Providing Funds Transfer Services to the Local Deposit Office)

Article 11 (1) The period specified by a Cabinet Office Ordinance as prescribed in Article 43 (1) of the Act shall be one week.

(2) The amount of outstanding obligations in the process of funds transfer prescribed in Article 43 (2) of the Act shall be the amount of obligations borne by said Funds Transfer Service Provider to the users in Japan pertaining to funds transfer transactions (Kawase transactions) (in the case where the amount of obligations borne to the users in Japan cannot be distinguished from those borne to the overseas users, the amount of obligations borne by said Funds Transfer Service Provider to all users pertaining to funds transfer transactions (Kawase transactions)) at the time of calculation of the amount of outstanding obligations in the process of funds transfer on each business day.

(3) In the case where a Funds Transfer Service Provider has claims against users who are creditors pertaining to obligations borne by the Funds Transfer Service Provider in relation to funds transfer transactions (Kawase transactions) that it carries out, the Funds Transfer Service Provider may calculate the amount of outstanding obligations in the process of funds transfer set forth in the preceding paragraph as a total of the amounts calculated for each of said users by deducting the amount of said claims from the amount of said obligations.

(4) In the case where a funds transfer transaction (Kawase transaction) is carried out in an amount indicated in foreign currency, the amount of outstanding obligations in the process of funds transfer set forth in paragraph (2) shall be calculated by converting the amount indicated in foreign currency to an amount indicated in Japanese currency using the foreign exchange rate on each business day.

(5) The amount of costs pertaining to the procedure for the execution of the right as prescribed in Article 43 (2) of the Act shall be the amount calculated in accordance with the methods listed in the following items for the categories respectively prescribed therein:

(i) In the case where the amount of outstanding obligations in the process of funds transfer calculated in accordance with the provisions of paragraph (2) is not more than one hundred million yen: The amount obtained by multiplying said amount of outstanding obligations in the process of funds transfer by five percent; and

(ii) In the case where the amount of outstanding obligations in the process of funds transfer calculated in accordance with the provisions of paragraph (2) is more than one hundred million yen: The amount obtained by adding five million yen to an amount obtained by multiplying the amount remaining after deducting one hundred million yen from said amount of outstanding obligations in the process of funds transfer by one percent.

(6) In the case where succession of the Funds Transfer Service occurs, until the person who has succeeded to said business makes a security deposit for providing Funds Transfer Services to the Local Deposit Office in an amount not less than the Required Amount of Deposit (meaning the Required Amount of Deposit prescribed in Article 43 (1) of the Act; hereinafter the same shall apply) pursuant to the provisions of said paragraph (including the case where said person concludes a guarantee contract of security deposit of providing Funds Transfer Services (meaning the guarantee contract of security deposit of providing Funds Transfer Services prescribed in Article 44 of the Act; hereinafter the same shall apply) in lieu of making of the whole or part of the security deposit for providing Funds Transfer Services to the Local Deposit Office pursuant to the provisions of said Article and notifies the Commissioner of the Financial Services Agency to that effect) or concludes a trust contract of security deposit of providing

Funds Transfer Services (meaning the trust contract of security deposit of providing Funds Transfer Services prescribed in Article 45 (1) of the Act; hereinafter the same shall apply) pursuant to the provisions of said Article by obtaining the approval of the Commissioner of the Financial Services Agency and places trust property in the trust under the trust contract in lieu of making of the whole or part of the security deposit for providing Funds Transfer Services to the Local Deposit Office on the business day of said Funds Transfer Service Provider immediately following the date of approval in an amount not less than the Required Amount as Security for Providing Funds Transfer Services (meaning the Required Amount as Security for Providing Funds Transfer Services prescribed in Article 43 (2) of the Act; hereinafter the same shall apply) on the immediately preceding business day, the security deposit for providing Funds Transfer Services, guarantee contract of security deposit of providing Funds Transfer Services, or trust contract of security deposit of providing Funds Transfer Services that has been made or concluded by the person from whom said business has been succeeded shall be deemed to be made or concluded on behalf of the person who has succeeded to said business.

(Types of Bond Certificates That Can Be Used for Security Deposit for Providing Funds Transfer Services)
Article 12 Bond certificates specified by a Cabinet Office Ordinance as prescribed in Article 43 (3) of the Act shall be the following bond certificates:
(i) National government bond certificates (including those the ownership of the right of which is determined based on the statement or record in the book-entry transfer account registry under the provisions of the Act on Transfer of Bonds, Shares, etc. (Act No. 75 of 2001); the same shall apply in Article 19 (v));
(ii) Local government bond certificates;
(iii) Government guaranteed bond certificates (meaning those securities listed in Article 2 (1) (iii) of the Financial Instruments and Exchange Act (Act No. 25 of 1948) for which the government guarantees payment of the principal and interest; the same shall apply in Article 20 (2) (iii)), and
(iv) Corporate bond certificates or any other bond certificates specified by the Commissioner of the Financial Services Agency.

(Appraised Value of Bond Certificates That Can Be Used for Security Deposit for Providing Funds Transfer Services)
Article 13 (1) The appraised value of bond certificates that are deposited to fulfill the security deposit for providing Funds Transfer Services requirement pursuant to the provisions of Article 43 (3) of the Act shall be the amount specified in the following items for the categories of bond certificates respectively prescribed therein:
(i) Bond certificates specified in item (i) of the preceding Article: The face value (for those the ownership of the right of which is determined based on the statement or record in the book-entry transfer account registry under the provisions of the Act on Transfer of Bonds, Shares, etc., the amount stated or recorded in the book-entry transfer account registry; hereinafter the same shall apply in this Article);
(ii) Bond certificates specified in item (ii) of the preceding Article: The amount calculated by deeming every one hundred yen of the face value to be ninety yen;
(iii) Bond certificates specified in item (iii) of the preceding Article: The amount calculated by deeming every one hundred yen of the face value to be ninety-five yen; and
(iv) Bond certificates specified in item (iv) of the preceding Article: The amount calculated by deeming every one hundred yen of the face value to be eighty yen.

(2) With regard to bond certificates that have been issued on a discount basis, the provisions of the preceding paragraph shall apply by deeming the amount obtained by adding the amount calculated by the following formula to the issue price to be the face value:

((face value - issue price) / number of years from the issue date to the redemption date) x (number of years from the issue date to the deposit date)

(3) In the calculation by the formula set forth in the preceding paragraph, fractions below one year shall be omitted for the number of years from the issue date to the redemption date and the number of years from the issue date to the deposit date, and fractions below one yen shall be omitted for the amount obtained by dividing the difference between the face value and the issue price by the number of years from the issue date to the redemption date.

(Notification of Guarantee Contract of Security Deposit of Providing Funds Transfer Services)

Article 14 A person who makes a notification under Article 44 of the Act shall submit to the Commissioner of the Financial Services Agency a written notice of guarantee contract of security deposit of providing Funds Transfer Services prepared using appended Form 11 by attaching a copy of the guarantee contract of security deposit of providing Funds Transfer Services document.

(Requirements to Be Satisfied by Banks, etc. for Conclusion of a Guarantee Contract of Security Deposit of Providing Funds Transfer Services)

Article 15 (1) The category for one that is determined to have sound equity capital as specified by Cabinet Office Ordinances as prescribed in Article 16 (1) of the Order shall be the category specified in the following items for the type of Deposit-taking Institutions respectively prescribed therein:

(i) Banks (excluding Branch Offices of Foreign Banks (meaning the Branch Offices of Foreign Banks prescribed in Article 47 (2) of the Banking Act (Act No. 59 of 1981); the same shall apply in item (vi)); the same shall apply in the following item), Long-term Credit Banks, or federations of Shinkin Banks that have Overseas Business Locations: The Non-consolidated Capital Adequacy Ratio under the International Uniform Standard included in the latest explanatory document on the status of business and property (in the case where there is a explanatory document pertaining to the interim business year of the business year immediately following the business year pertaining to said explanatory document, said explanatory document) shall be not less than eight percent;

(ii) Banks, Long-term Credit Banks, or federations of Shinkin Banks or Shinkin Banks that do not have Overseas Business Locations: The Non-consolidated Capital Adequacy Ratio under the Domestic Standard included in the latest explanatory document on the status of business and property (in the case where there is a explanatory document pertaining to the interim business year of the business year immediately following the business year pertaining to said explanatory document, said explanatory document) shall be not less than four percent;

(iii) Labor banks, federations of labor banks, credit cooperatives, federations of credit cooperatives engaging in the business prescribed in Article 9-9 (1) (i) of the Small and Medium Sized Enterprises, etc. Cooperatives Act (Act No. 181 of 1949), agricultural cooperative or federations of agricultural cooperative engaging in the business prescribed in Article 10 (1) (iii) of the Agricultural Cooperatives Act (Act No. 132 of 1947), fisheries cooperative engaging in the business prescribed in Article 11 (1) (iv) of the Fisheries Cooperatives Act (Act No. 242 of 1948), federations of fisheries cooperatives engaging in the business prescribed in Article 87 (1) (iv) of said Act, fishery processing cooperative engaging in the business prescribed in Article 93 (1) (ii) of said Act, or federations of fishery processing cooperatives engaging in the business prescribed in Article 97 (1) (ii) of said Act: The Non-consolidated Capital Adequacy Ratio included in the latest explanatory document on the status of business and property shall be not less than four percent;

(iv) Norinchukin Bank: The Non-consolidated Capital Adequacy Ratio included in the latest explanatory document on the status of business and property shall be not less than eight percent;

(v) The Shoko Chukin Bank Limited: The Non-consolidated Capital Adequacy Ratio included in the latest explanatory document on the status of business and property (in the case where there is a explanatory document pertaining to the interim business year of the business year immediately following the business year pertaining to said explanatory document, said explanatory document) shall be not less than eight percent; and

(vi) Branch Offices of Foreign Banks: The Foreign Banks (meaning the Foreign Banks prescribed in Article 10 (2) (viii) of the Banking Act) pertaining to said Branch Offices of Foreign Banks shall satisfy the criteria that are equivalent to the criteria prescribed in Article 14-2 of said Act and apply to said Foreign Banks in their respective foreign states.

(2) The term "Overseas Business Locations" as used in items (i) and (ii) of the preceding paragraph means branches or secondary offices located overseas or foreign companies engaging in the banking business (limited to those more than fifty percent of voting rights held by all the shareholders, members or equity investors of which are held by Banks, Long-term Credit Banks, or federations of Shinkin Banks) that have full-time officers or employees at their location.

(3) The term "International Uniform Standard" as used in paragraph (1) (i) means the standard prescribed in the following paragraph that pertains to Banks, Long-term Credit Banks, or federations of Shinkin Banks that have Overseas Business Locations (meaning the Overseas Business Locations prescribed in the preceding paragraph; the same shall apply in paragraph (5)).

(4) The term "Non-consolidated Capital Adequacy Ratio" as used in paragraph (1) (i) and (ii) means the ratio obtained by the formula pertaining to the standard prescribed in Article 14-2 (i) of the Banking Act (including the cases where it is applied mutatis mutandis pursuant to Article 17 of the Long-term Credit Bank Act (Act No. 187 of 1952) or Article 89 (1) of the Shinkin Bank Act (Act No. 238 of 1951)).

(5) The term "Domestic Standard" as used in paragraph (1) (ii) means the standard prescribed in the preceding paragraph that pertains to Banks, Long-term Credit Banks, or federations of Shinkin Banks or Shinkin Banks that do not have Overseas Business Locations.

(6) The term "Non-consolidated Capital Adequacy Ratio" as used in paragraph (1) (iii) means: for labor banks, federations of labor banks, credit cooperatives, federations of cooperatives engaging in the business prescribed in Article 9-9 (1) (i) of the Small and Medium Sized Enterprises, etc. Cooperatives Act, the ratio obtained by the formula pertaining to the standard prescribed in Article 14-2 (i) of the Banking Act as applied mutatis mutandis pursuant to Article 94 (1) of the Labor Bank Act (Act No. 227 of 1953) or Article 6 (1) of the Act on Financial Businesses by Cooperative (Act No. 183 of 1949); for agricultural cooperative or federations of agricultural cooperative engaging in the business prescribed in Article 10 (1) (iii) of the Agricultural Cooperatives Act, the ratio obtained by the formula pertaining to the standard prescribed in Article 11-2 (1) (i) of said Act, and for fisheries cooperative engaging in the business pre-

scribed in Article 11 (1) (iv) of the Fisheries Cooperatives Act, federations of fisheries cooperatives engaging in the business prescribed in Article 87 (1) (iv) of said Act, fishery processing cooperative engaging in the business prescribed in Article 93 (1) (ii) of said Act, or federations of fishery processing cooperatives engaging in the business prescribed in Article 97 (1) (ii) of said Act, the ratio obtained by the formula pertaining to the standard prescribed in Article 11-6 (1) (i) of said Act (including the cases where it is applied mutatis mutandis pursuant to Article 92 (1), Article 96 (1), or Article 100 (1) of said Act).

(7) The term "Non-consolidated Capital Adequacy Ratio" as used in paragraph (1) (iv) means the ratio obtained by the formula pertaining to the standard prescribed in Article 56 (i) of the Norinchukin Bank Act (Act No. 93 of 2001).

(8) The term "Non-consolidated Capital Adequacy Ratio" as used in paragraph (1) (v) means the ratio obtained by the formula pertaining to the standard prescribed in Article 23 (1) (i) of the Shoko Chukin Bank Limited Act (Act No. 74 of 2007).

(Requirements to Be Satisfied by Persons Other Than Banks, etc. for Conclusion of Guarantee Contract of Security Deposit of Providing Funds Transfer Services, etc.)

Article 16 (1) The category for one that is determined to have a sound status with regard to capital adequacy to support the payment of Insurance Claims, etc. as specified by a Cabinet Office Ordinance as prescribed in Article 16 (2) of the Order shall be for one whose Ratio Indicating the Sound Status with Regard to Capital Adequacy to Support the Payment of Insurance Claims, etc. included in the latest explanatory documents on the status of business and property is not less than two hundred percent.

(2) The term "Ratio Indicating the Sound Status with Regard to Capital Adequacy to Support the Payment of Insurance Claims, etc." as prescribed in the preceding paragraph means the ratio obtained by the formula pertaining to the standard prescribed in Article 130, Article 202, or Article 228 of the Insurance Business Act (Act No. 105 of 1995).

(3) Persons specified by a Cabinet Office Ordinance as prescribed in Article 16 (2) of the Order shall be Insurance Companies prescribed in Article 2 (2) of the Insurance Business Act, Foreign Insurance Companies, etc. prescribed in paragraph (7) of said Article, or Underwriting Members (meaning Underwriting Members prescribed in Article 219 (1) of said Act) who have obtained the license under said paragraph.

(Cancellation of Guarantee Contract of Security Deposit of Providing Funds Transfer Services)

Article 17 (1) If a Funds Transfer Service Provider who has concluded a guarantee contract of security deposit of providing Funds Transfer Services comes to fall under any of the following items, it may cancel the whole or part of the guarantee contract of security deposit of providing Funds Transfer Services respectively prescribed therein by obtaining the approval of the Commissioner of the Financial Services Agency:

(i) In the case where the Required Amount of Deposit on the Record Date is less than the total of the amount of security deposit for providing Funds Transfer Services and the secured amount prescribed in Article 44 of the Act on the immediately preceding Record Date: A guarantee contract of security deposit of providing Funds Transfer Services pertaining to any amount within the limit of the amount of said security deposit for providing Funds Transfer Services up to the amount that would cause said total amount to decrease to said Required Amount of Deposit;

(ii) If the procedure for the execution of the right set forth in Article 59 (1) of the Act has been completed: The whole of the relevant guarantee contract of security de-

posit of providing Funds Transfer Services;
(iii) In cases where, as specified by Article 17 (2) of the Order, the performance of obligations borne in relation to funds transfer transactions (Kawase transactions) has been completed: The whole of the relevant guarantee contract of security deposit of providing Funds Transfer Services; and
(iv) In the case where a Funds Transfer Service Provider has concluded a trust contract of security deposit of providing Funds Transfer Services and has obtained the approval of the Commissioner of the Financial Services Agency, if the Funds Transfer Service Provider has placed trust property in the trust under the trust contract on the business day of said Funds Transfer Service Provider immediately following the date of approval in an amount not less than the Required Amount as Security for Providing Funds Transfer Services on the immediately preceding business day: The whole of the relevant guarantee contract of security deposit of providing Funds Transfer Services.
(2) A Funds Transfer Service Provider intending to obtain the approval under the preceding paragraph shall submit to the Commissioner of the Financial Services Agency a written application for approval of cancellation of guarantee contract of security deposit of providing Funds Transfer Services prepared using appended Form 12 by attaching copies of the books and documents listed in Article 33 (1) (iv) through (vii) (limited to those to prove the facts listed in the preceding paragraph).
(3) If the Commissioner of the Financial Services Agency has granted the approval set forth in paragraph (1), he/she shall notify the Funds Transfer Service Provider to that effect by issuing a written approval of cancellation of the guarantee contract of security deposit of providing Funds Transfer Services prepared using appended Form 13.
(4) If a Funds Transfer Service Provider has cancelled the whole or part of the guarantee contract of security deposit of providing Funds Transfer Services by obtaining the approval under paragraph (1), it shall submit to the Commissioner of the Financial Services Agency a written notice of cancellation of the guarantee contract of security deposit of providing Funds Transfer Services prepared using appended Form 14 by attaching a copy of the guarantee contract of security deposit of providing Funds Transfer Services document reflecting said cancellation.

(Application for Approval of a Trust Contract of Security Deposit of Providing Funds Transfer Services)
Article 18 (1) A Funds Transfer Service Provider intending to obtain the approval under Article 45 (1) of the Act shall submit to the Commissioner of the Financial Services Agency a written application for approval of a trust contract of security deposit of providing Funds Transfer Services prepared using appended Form 15 by attaching two copies of said written application for approval of the trust contract of security deposit of providing Funds Transfer Services and a copy of the security deposit for providing Funds Transfer Services trust contract document.
(2) If the Commissioner of the Financial Services Agency has granted the approval set forth in the preceding paragraph, he/she shall notify the Funds Transfer Service Provider to that effect by issuing a written approval of the trust contract of security deposit of providing Funds Transfer Services prepared using appended Form 16.
(3) If a Funds Transfer Service Provider has placed property in the trust under the trust contract of security deposit of providing Funds Transfer Services for the first time after obtaining the approval under paragraph (1), it shall submit to the Commissioner of the Financial Services Agency a written notice of trust contract of security deposit of providing Funds Transfer Services prepared using appended Form 17 by attaching a document proving the amount of the trust property and the Required Amount as Secu-

rity for Providing Funds Transfer Services on each of the three business days immediately preceding the date of said notice.

(Contents of the Trust contract of Security Deposit of Providing Funds Transfer Services)

Article 19 Matters specified by a Cabinet Office Ordinance as prescribed in Article 45 (2) (vii) of the Act shall be the following matters:
(i) The settlor, the trustee, and the beneficiaries of the principal of the trust property under the trust contract of security deposit of providing Funds Transfer Services shall be a Trust Contract Funds Transfer Service Provider (meaning the Trust Contract Funds Transfer Service Provider prescribed in Article 45 (2) (i) of the Act; hereinafter the same shall apply), a Trust Company, etc. , and the users in Japan of funds transfer transactions (Kawase transactions) carried out by said Trust Contract Funds Transfer Service Provider (in the case where the amount of obligations borne by said Trust Contract Funds Transfer Service Provider to the users in Japan cannot be distinguished from those borne to the overseas users, all users of funds transfer transactions (Kawase transactions) carried out by said Trust Contract Funds Transfer Service Provider), respectively;
(ii) In the case where more than one trust contract of security deposit of providing Funds Transfer Services is concluded, the same person shall be appointed as the agent of the beneficiaries for all of the said contracts;
(iii) In the case where the Trust Contract Funds Transfer Service Provider has come to fall under any of the following conditions, the Trust Contract Funds Transfer Service Provider shall not give any instructions to the Trust Company, etc. regarding investment of trust property:
  (a) If it has had its registration under Article 37 of the Act rescinded pursuant to the provisions of Article 56 (1) or (2) of the Act;
  (b) If a Petition for Commencement of Bankruptcy Proceedings, etc. (meaning the Petition for Commencement of Bankruptcy Proceedings, etc. prescribed in Article 2 (10) of the Act) has been filed against the Trust Contract Funds Transfer Service Provider;
  (c) If it has abolished the Funds Transfer Service (in the case of a Foreign Funds Transfer Service Provider, abolition of the Funds Transfer Service at all business offices in Japan; the same shall apply in (c)) or has given a public notice of the abolition of the Funds Transfer Service pursuant to the provisions of Article 61 (3) of the Act;
  (d) If it has received an order to suspend the whole or part of the Funds Transfer Service under the provisions of Article 56 (1) of the Act (limited to cases falling under item (iii) of said paragraph); or
  (e) If the Commissioner of the Financial Services Agency has issued an order to make a deposit;
(iv) In the case where the Trust Contract Funds Transfer Service Provider has come to fall under any of the conditions listed in the preceding item, the beneficiaries and the agent of the beneficiaries may not exercise beneficial claims against the Trust Company, etc. ;
(v) In the case where the trust property under the trust contract of security deposit of providing Funds Transfer Services (excluding those under which money is placed in the trust with a financial institution engaging in the trust business (meaning a financial institution that has obtained the authorization under Article 1 (1) of the Act on Concurrent Operation of Trust Business by a Financial Institution (Act No. 43 of 1943); hereinafter the same shall apply in this Article) and compensation for the

principal is provided; the same shall apply in the following item) is invested, the investment shall be made in the following manner:
  (a) Holding of government bond certificates and other bond certificates specified by the Commissioner of the Financial Services Agency;
  (b) Bank deposits and savings with a Deposit-taking Institution; or
  (c) In any of the following manners:
    1. Call money lending;
    2. Due from bank accounts of a financial institution engaging in the trust business that is the trustee; or
    3. Money in trust for which compensation for the principal is provided under the terms and conditions of the contract pursuant to the provisions of Article 6 of the Act on Concurrent Operation of Trust Business by a Financial Institution;
(vi) In the case where the Trust Contract Funds Transfer Service Provider maintains the trust property in the form of bond certificates or invests the trust property under the trust contract of security deposit of providing Funds Transfer Services in a manner listed in (a) of the preceding item, the Trust Company, etc. or the Trust Contract Funds Transfer Service Provider shall determine the appraised value thereof in accordance with the method prescribed in Article 21;
(vii) In the case where the trust contract of security deposit of providing Funds Transfer Services is a money in trust contract with a financial institution engaging in the trust business under which compensation for the principal is provided, the appraised value of the principal of the trust property shall be the principal amount of said money in trust contract;
(viii) In the case where more than one trust contract of security deposit of providing Funds Transfer Services is concluded, the Trust Contract Funds Transfer Service Provider shall take necessary measures to enable all Trust Companies, etc. to grasp, on a timely basis, the total amount of trust property that is placed in the trust under said more than one trust contract of security deposit of providing Funds Transfer Services;
(ix) In the cases where the Required Amount as Security for Providing Funds Transfer Services notified to the Trust Company, etc. by the Trust Contract Funds Transfer Service Provider has decreased significantly and rapidly, where the Trust Contract Funds Transfer Service Provider fails to report the Required Amount as Security for Providing Funds Transfer Services, and where it is otherwise determined by the Trust Company, etc. that the Trust Contract Funds Transfer Service Provider has failed or is likely to fail to perform its obligations under the trust contract of security deposit of providing Funds Transfer Services, the Trust Company, etc. shall immediately notify the Commissioner of the Financial Services Agency to that effect;
(x) Except in the following cases, the whole or part of the trust contract of security deposit of providing Funds Transfer Services may not be cancelled;
  (a) In the case where the appraised value of the trust property maintained in the trust on a business day exceeds the Required Amount as Security for Providing Funds Transfer Services on the immediately preceding business day, the whole or part of the trust contract of security deposit of providing Funds Transfer Services may be canceled within the limit of said excess amount;
  (b) In the case where the trust property maintained in the trust under one trust contract of security deposit of providing Funds Transfer Services is intended to be placed in the trust under another trust contract of security deposit of providing Funds Transfer Services, the whole or part of the trust contract of security

deposit of providing Funds Transfer Services may be canceled to the extent of such purpose;
(c) In the case where the total of the amount of security deposit for providing Funds Transfer Services and the secured amount on a Record Date exceeds the Required Amount of Deposit on the immediately preceding Record Date;
(xi) The trust property pertaining to the cancellation of the whole or part of the trust contract of security deposit of providing Funds Transfer Services under the preceding item shall be imputed to the Trust Contract Funds Transfer Service Provider;
(xii) The Trust Company, etc. shall, in response to the order under the provisions of Article 46 of the Act, realize the trust property and deposit the proceeds to the Local Deposit Office specified by the Commissioner of the Financial Services Agency;
(xiii) In the case where the Trust Company, etc. has made a deposit in response to the order under the provisions of Article 46 of the Act, it may terminate said trust contract of security deposit of providing Funds Transfer Services;
(xiv) In the case referred to in the preceding item, any residual property remaining after the termination of the whole of said trust contract of security deposit of providing Funds Transfer Services may be imputed to the Trust Contract Funds Transfer Service Provider; and
(xv) Remuneration and any other costs to be paid by the Trust Contract Funds Transfer Service Provider to the Trust Company, etc. or the agent of the beneficiaries and the costs required for the realization of the trust property by said Trust Company, etc. shall be paid out of property other than the principal of the trust property.

(Types of Bank Deposits and Savings Qualified to Be Trust Property)
Article 20 (1) Bank deposits and savings specified by a Cabinet Office Ordinance as prescribed in Article 45 (3) of the Act shall be bank deposits and savings with a Deposit-taking Institution (in the case where the Trust Contract Funds Transfer Service Provider is a Deposit-taking Institution, excluding bank deposits and savings with oneself).
(2) Bond certificates specified by a Cabinet Office Ordinance as prescribed in Article 45 (3) of the Act shall be the following bond certificates (including those the ownership of the right of which is determined based on the statement or record in the book-entry transfer account registry under the provisions of the Act on Transfer of Bonds, Shares, etc.; hereinafter the same shall apply):
(i) National government bond certificates;
(ii) Local government bond certificates;
(iii) Government guaranteed bond certificates;
(iv) Bond certificates prescribed in Article 2-11 of the Order for Enforcement of the Financial Instruments and Exchange Act (Cabinet Order No. 321 of 1965);
(v) Bond certificates issued by a foreign state (limited to those falling under Article 13 (iii) of the Cabinet Office Ordinance on the Provision or Publication of Securities Information, etc. (Cabinet Office Ordinance No. 78 of 2008)); and
(vi) Corporate bond certificates or any other bond certificates specified by the Commissioner of the Financial Services Agency.

(Appraised Value of Bond Certificates Qualified to be Trust Property)
Article 21 In the case where the trust property is maintained in the form of bond certificates pursuant to the provisions of Article 45 (3) of the Act or is invested in bond certificates pursuant to the provisions of Article 19 (v) (a), the appraised value of said bond certificates shall be an amount not exceeding the amount obtained by multiplying the market value of said bond certificates as of each business day of the Funds Trans-

fer Service Provider by the ratio specified in the following items for the categories of bond certificates respectively prescribed therein:
(i) Bond certificates specified in paragraph (2) (i) of the preceding Article: One hundred percent;
(ii) Bond certificates specified in paragraph (2) (ii) of the preceding Article: Ninety percent;
(iii) Bond certificates specified in paragraph (2) (iii) of the preceding Article: Ninety-five percent;
(iv) Bond certificates specified in paragraph (2) (iv) of the preceding Article: Ninety percent;
(v) Bond certificates specified in paragraph (2) (v) of the preceding Article: Eighty-five percent; and
(vi) Bond certificates specified in paragraph (2) (vi) of the preceding Article: Eighty percent.

(Making of Security Deposit for Providing Funds Transfer Services to the Local Deposit Office Based on the Order of the Commissioner of the Financial Services Agency)
Article 22 (1) In the case where any security deposit for providing Funds Transfer Services is required based on the order under Article 46 of the Act, such deposit shall be made to the Local Deposit Office nearest to the head office of the Funds Transfer Service Provider who concluded the relevant guarantee contract of security deposit of providing Funds Transfer Services or trust contract of security deposit of providing Funds Transfer Services.
(2) The person who made the deposit set forth in the preceding paragraph shall, without delay, submit to the Commissioner of the Financial Services Agency a written notice prepared using appended Form 18 by attaching the authenticated copy of the deposit document pertaining to said deposit.

(Public Notice When Performance of Obligations is Impossible)
Article 23 The public notice prescribed in Article 17 (2) (ii) of the Order shall be published in a daily newspaper that publishes items on current events.

(Measures to Ensure Information Security Management Pertaining to the Funds Transfer Service)
Article 24 A Funds Transfer Service Provider shall, in accordance with the contents and methods of its business, take measures to ensure sufficient control of the electronic data processing system pertaining to the Funds Transfer Service.

(Measures to Ensure Information Security Management Pertaining to Personal Information of Individual Users, etc.)
Article 25 A Funds Transfer Service Provider shall, with regard to information security management pertaining to the personal information of users of the Funds Transfer Service who are individuals, supervision of its employees, and in the case where the handling of said information is entrusted to another person, supervision of said other person, take necessary and appropriate measures for preventing leakage, loss, or damage of said information.

(Handling of Specified Non-public Information)
Article 26 In handling personal information regarding race, creed, family origin, domicile of origin, healthcare, or criminal background of the users of Funds Transfer Service

who are individuals and other specified non-public information (meaning information learned in the course of business that has not yet been publicly disclosed), a Funds Transfer Service Provider shall take measures to ensure that said information is not used for a purpose other than for ensuring the appropriate operation of the business and for other purposes which are determined to be necessary.

(Measures to Ensure Proper and Secure Provision/Conduct of the Entrusted Business)

Article 27 If a Funds Transfer Service Provider entrusts its business to a third party, it shall take the following measures in accordance with the contents of the entrusted business:

(i) Measures to ensure that said business is entrusted to a person who has the ability to perform said business in a proper and secure manner;

(ii) Measures to ensure that necessary and appropriate supervision, etc. is conducted with regard to the person to whom business is entrusted including measures to verify whether said person is performing said business in a proper and secure manner by, among others, checking the status of performance of said business by said person regularly or as necessary and causing said person to make any necessary improvements.

(iii) Necessary measures to ensure proper and prompt processing of complaints from the users of the Funds Transfer Service conducted by the person to whom business is entrusted;

(iv) Measures to prevent the protection of the users of the Funds Transfer Service from being hindered, etc. including measures to ensure that in the case where circumstances have arisen under which the person to whom business has been entrusted is unable to perform the entrusted business appropriately, said business will be promptly entrusted to another appropriate third party; and

(v) Measures to ensure that, if it is necessary for the purpose of ensuring the proper and secure provision/conduct of the business of a Funds Transfer Service Provider and protection of the users pertaining to said business, necessary measures will be taken such as amending or canceling the contract pertaining to the entrustment of said business.

(Prevention of Users from Mistaking Funds Transfer Transactions (Kawase Transactions) Carried Out by a Funds Transfer Service Provider for Those Carried Out by a Deposit-taking Institution)

Article 28 (1) In carrying out a funds transfer transaction (Kawase transaction) with the user of the Funds Transfer Service, a Funds Transfer Service Provider shall provide the user in advance with explanation designed to prevent the user from mistaking such funds transfer transaction (Kawase transaction) for funds transfer transactions (Kawase transactions) carried out by a Deposit-taking Institution by delivering documents or any other appropriate methods.

(2) When a Funds Transfer Service Provider provides the explanation prescribed in the preceding paragraph, it shall explain the following matters:

(i) The fact that such funds transfer transaction (Kawase transaction) is not a funds transfer transaction (Kawase transaction) carried out by a Deposit-taking Institution;

(ii) The fact that such funds transfer transaction (Kawase transaction) does not constitute acceptance of bank deposits or savings or Installment Savings, etc. (meaning the Installment Savings, etc. prescribed in Article 2 (4) of the Banking Act);

(iii) The fact that such funds transfer transaction (Kawase transaction) is not entitled

to the payment of insurance claims under Article 53 of the Deposit Insurance Act (Act No. 34 of 1971) or Article 55 of the Agricultural and Fishery Cooperation Savings Insurance Act (Act No. 53 of 1973);
(iv) Whether the Funds Transfer Service Provider has made a security deposit for providing Funds Transfer Services to the Local Deposit Office or concluded a guarantee contract of security deposit of providing Funds Transfer Services or a trust contract of security deposit of providing Funds Transfer Services on behalf of the user, and in the case where a guarantee contract of security deposit of providing Funds Transfer Services or a trust contract of security deposit of providing Funds Transfer Services has been concluded, the name, trade name or other name of the other party thereto; and
(v) Other matters found to be useful for the prevention of the user from mistaking such funds transfer transaction (Kawase transaction) for funds transfer transactions (Kawase transactions) carried out by a Deposit-taking Institution.
(3) In the case where a Funds Transfer Service Provider carries out funds transfer transactions (Kawase transactions) with the users of the Funds Transfer Service at its business office, it shall post the matters listed in items (i) through (iv) of the preceding paragraph at the service counter in a manner easily seen by said users.

(Provision of Information to Users)
Article 29 (1) In carrying out a funds transfer transaction (Kawase transaction) with the user of the Funds Transfer Service, a Funds Transfer Service Provider shall provide the user with information about the contents of the contract pertaining to said funds transfer transaction (Kawase transaction) by the methods prescribed in the following items for the categories of cases respectively prescribed therein:
(i) In the case where the Funds Transfer Service Provider carries out a funds transfer transactions (Kawase transactions) without concluding a contract under which funds transfer transactions (Kawase transactions) are carried out on an ongoing or recurring basis: Method in which the following matters are clearly indicated to the user who will give the instructions pertaining to the funds transfer transaction (Kawase transaction):
(a) Standard performance period;
(b) The amount or the maximum amount of the fees, remuneration, or costs to be paid by the user or the calculation method thereof;
(c) The location and contact address of the business office that will respond to complaints or requests for consultation from the users;
(d) In the case where the funds transfer transaction (Kawase transaction) is carried out in an amount indicated in foreign currency, the amount in Japanese currency converted from said amount and the standard or the method used for the conversion; and
(e) Other matters found to be relevant to the contents of said funds transfer transaction (Kawase transaction).
(ii) In the case where the Funds Transfer Service Provider concludes a contract under which funds transfer transactions (Kawase transactions) are carried out on an ongoing or recurring basis: Method in which the following matters are clearly indicated to the user who will be the other party to said contact:
(a) The maximum amount of the funds transfer transactions (Kawase transactions) to be carried out;
(b) Matters listed in (a) through (d) of the preceding item;
(c) The contract period;
(d) Handling of the cancellation of contract before the expiration of the contract pe-

riod (including calculation method for fees, remuneration, or costs); and
(e) Other matters found to be relevant to the contents of said contract.
(2) In the case where a Funds Transfer Service Provider carries out funds transfer transactions (Kawase transactions) by issuing an exchange certificate or other instruments representing the rights pertaining to the obligations borne by the Funds Transfer Service Provider in relation to funds transfer transactions (Kawase transactions) that it carries out (hereinafter referred to as "Exchange Certificate, etc."), if the Funds Transfer Service Provider has indicated the following matters on said Exchange Certificate, etc. , the provisions of the preceding paragraph shall not apply:
(i) The amount or the maximum amount pertaining to the rights that can be exercised by said Exchange Certificate, etc. ;
(ii) In the case where a period or expiration date for the exercise of rights by said Exchange Certificate, etc. , said period or expiration date;
(iii) Matters listed in item (i) (b) through (d) of the preceding paragraph;
(iv) The scope of facilities or places where rights can be exercised by said Exchange Certificate, etc. ;
(v) Necessary instructions for the use of said Exchange Certificate, etc. ; and
(vi) In the case of an Exchange Certificate, etc. in which the amount is recorded by electromagnetic means (meaning electronic, magnetic, and other means under which the recorded information cannot directly be recognized by human perception), the balance of the amount or the method by which said balance can be ascertained.

(Delivery of Receipt)
Article 30 (1) When a Funds Transfer Service Provider has received money or other funds from a user of the Funds Transfer Service in relation to the funds transfer transactions (Kawase transactions) that it carries out, it shall deliver a document containing the following matters to said user without delay; provided, however, that this shall not apply if the Funds Transfer Service Provider carries out funds transfer transactions (Kawase transactions) by issuing Exchange Certificates, etc.
(i) The trade name and the registration number of the Funds Transfer Service Provider;
(ii) The amount of the funds received from said user; and
(iii) Date of receipt.
(2) In the case where funds are received by way of transfer of funds to a bank account for bank deposits or savings, the provisions of the preceding paragraph shall apply only if the delivery of said document is requested by said user.
(3) A Funds Transfer Service Provider may, by obtaining the approval of said user pursuant to the provisions of the following paragraph, provide said user with the matters listed in paragraph (1) by electromagnetic means in lieu of the delivery of the document prescribed in said paragraph. In this case, the Funds Transfer Service Provider shall be deemed to have delivered the document prescribed in said paragraph.
(4) A Funds Transfer Service Provider intending to provide the matters listed in paragraph (1) pursuant to the provisions of the preceding paragraph shall indicate to said user the type and contents of the electromagnetic means to be used and obtain the approval of said user in advance in writing or by electromagnetic means.
(5) If a Funds Transfer Service Provider who had received the approval under the preceding paragraph has received a notice from said user in writing or by electromagnetic means to the effect that the user will no longer accept provision of information by electromagnetic means, the Funds Transfer Service Provider shall not provide said user with the matters listed in paragraph (1) by electromagnetic means; provided,

however, that this shall not apply if said user gives another approval under the preceding paragraph again at a later time.
(6) The "electromagnetic means" referred to in the preceding three paragraphs shall be the methods that use an electronic data processing system and other methods that use the information communication technology as prescribed in the following items for the categories of cases respectively prescribed therein:
　(i) In the case where an approval or notice is given indicating either that the user will or will not accept provision of information by electromagnetic means: The following methods;
　　(a) A method in which the approval or notice to that effect is recorded in a file installed in the electronic equipment used by the person who receives such approval or notice or the person who obtains the consent; and
　　(b) A method in which a file containing a record of the approval or notice to that effect that is prepared by using a medium that allows for secure recording of certain information such as a magnetic disk, CD-R, or other method equivalent thereto is delivered to the user; or
　(ii) In cases other than those prescribed in the preceding item: The following methods:
　　(a) The following methods that use an electronic data processing system:
　　　1. A method in which information is transmitted through electric telecommunication lines connecting the electric equipment used by the sender with the electric equipment used by the recipient and recorded in a file installed in the electric equipment used by said recipient;
　　　2. A method in which information recorded in a file installed in the electric equipment used by the sender is made available for inspection by the recipient through electric telecommunication lines and recorded in a file installed in the electric equipment used by said recipient; and
　　(b) A method in which a file containing a record of information that is prepared by using a medium that allows for secure recording of certain information such as magnetic disk, CD-R, or other method equivalent thereto is delivered to the user.
(7) The methods prescribed in the items of the preceding paragraph shall satisfy the following criteria:
　(i) In the case of the method prescribed in item (i) of the preceding paragraph, the person who receive an approval or notice shall notify, in writing or by other appropriate methods, the person who gives an approval or notice of the contents of the approval or notice indicating either that he/she will or will not accept provision of information by electromagnetic means;
　(ii) The method prescribed in item (ii) of the preceding paragraph shall be the one that enables the recipient to create a document by outputting the information recorded in the file (including outputting said recorded information by transmitting it to other electronic equipment or any other method); and
　(iii) In the case of the method prescribed in item (ii) (a) of the preceding paragraph, if a mobile phone or PHS phone is used as the electronic equipment of the recipient, the sender shall, at the request of the recipient, deliver a document pertaining to the matters provided by the sender by electromagnetic means for three months from the day on which the information was transmitted to or made available for inspection by the recipient.
(8) The term "electronic data processing system" as used in paragraph (6) (ii) (a) means an electronic data processing system that connects the electronic device used by the sender with the electronic device used by the recipient through electric telecommunication lines.

(Other Measures to Ensure Protection of Users)
Article 31 A Funds Transfer Service Provider shall take the following measures to ensure the protection of the users of the Funds Transfer Service with regard to funds transfer transactions (Kawase transactions) that it carries out:
 (i) If a Funds Transfer Service Provider finds a possibility that a criminal act has been committed with regard to the funds transfer transactions (Kawase transactions) that it carries out after considering any provision of information by the investigative authority, etc. to the effect that said funds transfer transactions (Kawase transactions) were used for the purpose of committing a fraud or other criminal acts and other circumstances, measures to suspend said funds transfer transactions (Kawase transactions), etc. ;
 (ii) In the case where a Funds Transfer Service Provider carries out funds transfer transactions (Kawase transactions) with the users of the Funds Transfer Service by using a computer connected with electric telecommunication lines, appropriate measures to prevent said users from mistaking said Funds Transfer Service Provider for another person; and
 (iii) In the case where a Funds Transfer Service Provider receives instructions regarding funds transfer transactions (Kawase transactions) from the users of the Funds Transfer Service by using a computer connected with electric telecommunication lines, appropriate measures to enable said users to easily confirm or correct the contents of said instructions when using the computer pertaining to said instructions.

(Internal Rules, etc.)
Article 32 A Funds Transfer Service Provider shall, in accordance with the contents and methods of its business, prescribe internal rules, etc. concerning the measures to ensure the protection of the users of the Funds Transfer Service and the proper and secure provision/conduct of Funds Transfer Services (including the measures to prevent crimes) and establish a system for providing training to employees, a system for providing guidance to the person to whom business is entrusted, and other systems sufficient to ensure that the business is operated based on said internal rules, etc.

Chapter III Supervision

(Preparation and Preservation of Books and Documents Pertaining to the Funds Transfer Service)
Article 33 (1) The books and documents pertaining to the Funds Transfer Service as prescribed in Article 52 of the Act shall be the following books and documents:
 (i) Transaction records pertaining to the Funds Transfer Service;
 (ii) General ledger;
 (iii) Customer ledger (limited to cases where a Funds Transfer Service Provider concludes a contract with the users of the Funds Transfer Service under which funds transfer transactions (Kawase transactions) are carried out on an ongoing or recurring basis);
 (iv) Records of the amount of outstanding obligations in the process of funds transfer and the Required Amount as Security for Providing Funds Transfer Services on each business day;
 (v) Records of the Required Amount of Deposit on each Record Date (excluding Trust Contract Funds Transfer Service Providers);
 (vi) Records of the amount of security deposit for providing funds transfer services on

each Record Date (limited to cases where such deposit is made);
(vii) Records of the amount of trust property on each business day (limited to Trust Contract Funds Transfer Service Providers); and
(viii) For each user of the Funds Transfer Service, records of the amount of obligations borne in relation to funds transfer transactions (Kawase transactions) and the amount of claims held in relation to said funds transfer transactions (Kawase transactions) on each business day (limited to cases where the amount of outstanding obligations in the process of funds transfer is calculated pursuant to the provisions of Article 11 (3)).
(2) A Funds Transfer Service Provider shall preserve the books and documents listed in items (i) through (iii) and item (viii) of the preceding paragraph for at least ten years from the day of the closing of the books and books and documents listed in items (iv) through (vii) of the preceding paragraph for at least five years from the day of the closing of the books.

(Reports on the Funds Transfer Service)
Article 34 (1) The written report on the Funds Transfer Service prescribed in Article 53 (1) of the Act shall be prepared using appended Form 19 (in the case of a Foreign Funds Transfer Service Provider, appended Form 20) by separating it into a business summary and a document containing the status of income and expenditure pertaining to the Funds Transfer Service and submitted to the Commissioner of the Financial Services Agency within three months from the last day of the relevant business year.
(2) A Funds Transfer Service Provider intending to submit the written report set forth in the preceding paragraph shall submit it to the Commissioner of the Financial Services Agency by attaching two copies of said written report and the latest balance sheet (including the related notes) and profit and loss statement (including the related notes).

(Reports on the Amount of Outstanding Obligations in the Process of Funds Transfer, etc.)
Article 35 (1) The written report prescribed in Article 53 (2) of the Act shall be prepared using appended Form 21 and submitted for each day specified in the following items for the categories of cases respectively prescribed therein (hereinafter referred to as "Record Date" in this Article) to the Commissioner of the Financial Services Agency within one month from said Record Date:
(i) A Funds Transfer Service Provider who has concluded a guarantee contract of security deposit of providing Funds Transfer Services in lieu of making of the whole of the security deposit for providing Funds Transfer Services to the Local Deposit Office prescribed in Article 43 (1) of the Act and has notified the Commissioner of the Financial Services Agency to that effect: March 31 and September 30 each year;
(ii) A Funds Transfer Service Provider who makes a security deposit for providing Funds Transfer Services to the Local Deposit Office prescribed in Article 43 (1) of the Act: March 31, June 30, September 30, and December 31 each year; and
(iii) A Trust Contract Funds Transfer Service Provider: Last day of each month.
(2) A Funds Transfer Service Provider intending to submit the written report set forth in the preceding paragraph shall submit it to the Commissioner of the Financial Services Agency by attaching two copies of said written report.
(3) A Funds Transfer Service Provider who has made the deposit under Article 43 (1) of the Act shall submit to the Commissioner of the Financial Services Agency the written report set forth in paragraph (1) by attaching a copy of the authenticated copy of the deposit document pertaining to said deposit.
(4) In the case where a Funds Transfer Service Provider who made a notification pursuant

to the provisions of Article 44 of the Act has subsequently changed the terms and conditions of the guarantee contract of security deposit of providing Funds Transfer Services (excluding the cancellation of part of the said guarantee contract of security deposit of providing Funds Transfer Services) or has renewed the guarantee contract of security deposit of providing Funds Transfer Services, the Funds Transfer Service Provider shall submit to the Commissioner of the Financial Services Agency the written report set forth in paragraph (1) by attaching a copy of the contract document or a document verifying said fact.

(5) A Trust Contract Funds Transfer Service Provider shall submit to the Commissioner of the Financial Services Agency the written report set forth in paragraph (1) by attaching a document issued by a Trust Company, etc. verifying the amount of trust property as of the relevant Record Date.

(6) The Commissioner of the Financial Services Agency may, if he/she finds it necessary, order a Funds Transfer Service Provider to submit the authenticated copy of the deposit document set forth in paragraph (3) or the original of the contract document set forth in paragraph (4).

(Method of Public Notice)
Article 36 The public notice prescribed in Article 56 (2) and Article 58 of the Act shall be given in the official gazette.

Chapter IV Miscellaneous Provisions

(Entrustment to Agents for Local Finance Office in the Distribution Proceedings of Security Deposit to Holders of Prepaid Payment Instruments)
Article 37 The Commissioner of the Financial Services Agency may entrust to the Agents for Local Finance Office in the Distribution Proceedings of Security Deposit to Holders of Prepaid Payment Instruments prescribed in Article 59 (3) of the Act the whole or part of the affairs pertaining to the public notice prescribed in paragraph (2) of said Article, the affairs pertaining to the notification prescribed in Article 19 (2) of the Order, the affairs pertaining to the investigation of the rights prescribed in paragraph (4) of said Article (including the public notice or provision of an opportunity prescribed in said paragraph), the affairs pertaining to preparation, public notice, and notification of the distribution table prescribed in paragraph (5) said Article, the affairs pertaining to the provisional distribution prescribed in paragraphs (10) and (11) of said Article, and other affairs pertaining to the procedure for the execution of the rights.

(Notification of Abolition of Business, etc.)
Article 38 (1) A person intending to make a notification pursuant to the provisions of Article 61 (1) of the Act shall submit to the Commissioner of the Financial Services Agency a written notice prepared using appended Form 22 by attaching two copies of said written notice.

(2) The written notice set forth in the preceding paragraph shall contain the following matters:
(i) Trade name;
(ii) Date of registration and registration number;
(iii) Reason for notification;
(iv) The date on which the Funds Transfer Service Provider came to fall under any of the items of Article 61 (1) of the Act;
(v) In the case where the Funds Transfer Service Provider has abolished the Funds Transfer Service, the reason therefor;

(vi) In the case where the Funds Transfer Service Provider has abolished the Funds Transfer Service by way of assignment of business, merger or company split, or for other reasons, the method for succession of said business and the successor.
(3) The public notice prescribed in Article 61 (3) of the Act shall be published in the official gazette or in a daily newspaper that publishes matters on current events.
(4) The public notice and the posting at business offices prescribed in Article 61 (3) of the Act shall include the method for completing the performance of obligations pursuant to the provisions of paragraph (5) of said Article (excluding cases where a public notice is given due to succession of business by way of assignment of business, merger or company split, or for other reasons).
(5) A Funds Transfer Service Provider who has given a public notice pursuant to the provisions of Article 61 (3) of the Act shall immediately submit to the Commissioner of the Financial Services Agency a written notice prepared using appended Form 23 by attaching a copy of said public notice.
(6) If a Funds Transfer Service Provider has abolished the Funds Transfer Service by way of assignment of business, merger or company split, or for other reasons, a document containing the contents of the contract pertaining to the succession of said business and the method for succession of said business shall be attached to the written notice set forth in the preceding paragraph.

(Notification of Violation of Laws and Regulations)
Article 39 If a Funds Transfer Service Provider comes to know that its Director, etc. or employee has committed violation of laws and regulations with regard to the Funds Transfer Service or an act that hinders the proper and secure provision/conduct of Funds Transfer Services, it shall submit to the Director-General of a Local Finance Bureau, etc. a written notice prepared using appended Form 24 containing the following matters within two weeks from the day on which it came to know said fact:
(i) The name of the business office at which such act occurred;
(ii) The name and the title of the Director, etc. or employee who committed said act; and
(iii) Summary of said act.

(Government Agency Through Which to Submit Written Notice, etc.)
Article 40 In the case where a Funds Transfer Service Provider intends to submit to the Director-General of a Local Finance Bureau, etc. the written application for registration prescribed in Article 4 and other documents prescribed in the Act and this Cabinet Office Ordinance (hereinafter referred to as "Written Application, etc." in this Article and the following Article), if there is an office of a Local Finance Bureau, Otaru Sub-office of Hokkaido Local Finance Bureau, or Kitami Sub-office of Hokkaido Local Finance Bureau having jurisdiction over the location of the head office of said Funds Transfer Service Provider, said Funds Transfer Service Provider shall submit said Written Application, etc. through the head of said office or sub-offices.

(Submission of Written Application, etc. through Certified Association for Payment Service Providers)
Article 41 A Funds Transfer Service Provider intending to submit a Written Application, etc. to the Director-General of a Local Finance Bureau, etc. (including submission through the head of an office or sub-office of a Local Finance Bureau prescribed in the preceding Article) may submit it through a Certified Association for Payment Service Providers.

(Standard Processing Period)

Article 42 (1) The Commissioner of the Financial Services Agency shall endeavor to process any application for registration made pursuant to the provisions of the Act, the Order, or this Cabinet Office Ordinance within two months from the day on which said application has arrived at his/her office.

(2) The Commissioner of the Financial Services Agency shall endeavor to process an application for approval of cancellation of the guarantee contract of security deposit of providing Funds Transfer Services prescribed in Article 17 (1) within twenty days.

(3) The period prescribed in the preceding two paragraphs shall not include the following period:

(i) The period required to amend said application;

(ii) The period required for the applicant to change the contents of said application; and

(iii) The period required for the applicant to add materials that are found to be necessary for the examination pertaining to said application.

1st ed 第 1 版 2014・10
ISBN978-4-7972-1431-4 C3332 ￥19800E
Published in Japan, Shinzansha Publishing Co.
under the title of
"Japanese Statute Book"
supervisor, Kashiwagi Noboru
All rights reserved ©Shinzansha, 2014

Japanese Statute Book, Vol. 1
PART I. Companies Act ; Commercial Law
JSB英文六法 第1巻
I 会社法・商法編

2014(平成26)年10月25日　第1版第1刷発行　1st ed 第 1 版 2014・10
1431-4-01011-025-015

Supervisor	Kashiwagi Noboru
監　修	柏　木　　　昇
発行者	今井 貴 稲葉文子
発行所	株式会社 信 山 社

編集第2部

〒113-0033 東京都文京区本郷6-2-9-102
Tel 03-3818-1019　Fax 03-3818-0344
henshu@shinzansha.co.jp
笠間才木支店 〒309-1611 茨城県笠間市笠間515-3
Tel 0296-71-9081　Fax 0296-71-9082
笠間来栖支店 〒309-1625 茨城県笠間市来栖2345-1
Tel 0296-71-0215　Fax 0296-72-5410
出版契約2014-1431-4-01011 Printed in Japan

2014, ©Kashiwagi Noboru, 信山社
印刷・製本／東洋印刷・渋谷文泉閣　制作・ワイズ書籍
ISBN978-4-7972-1431-4 C3332 ￥19800E　分類320010-c-001
1431-4-01011:p1552　012-025-015

JCOPY 〈(社)出版者著作権管理機構 委託出版物〉
本書の無断複写は著作権法上での例外を除き禁じられています。複写される場合は、
そのつど事前に、(社)出版者著作権管理機構(電話03-3513-6969, FAX 03-3513-6979,
e-mail: info@jcopy.or.jp) の許諾を得てください。

新着情報のお知らせ（五十音順）

法令名	公開・更新	年月日	所管庁
医師法	公開	(2013.04.18)	厚生労働省
意匠法	更新(暫定版)	(2013.09.11)	経済産業省
一般社団法人及び一般財団法人に関する法律	公開(暫定版)	(2013.10.17)	
一般社団法人及び一般財団法人に関する法律施行規則	公開(暫定版)	(2013.10.17)	
一般社団法人及び一般財団法人に関する法律施行令	公開(暫定版)	(2013.10.17)	
移転価格事務運営要領の制定について（事務運営指針）	公開	(2011.09.27)	
医療法	最終版	(2014.04.18)	
医療法	公開(暫定版)	(2013.10.24)	
運輸安全委員会設置法	更新	(2010.09.16)	
エネルギーの使用の合理化に関する法律	公開	(2009.07.03)	
会計法（第四章）	公開	(2013.03.21)	
外国為替及び外国貿易法	更新	(2013.05.14)	
外国為替令	最終版	(2013.11.20)	
外国為替令	更新(暫定版)	(2013.09.11)	
外国為替令	公開	(2009.08.12)	
外国人漁業の規制に関する法律施行規則	最終版	(2014.08.15)	
外国人漁業の規制に関する法律施行規則	公開(暫定版)	(2014.05.15)	
外国人漁業の規制に関する法律施行令	最終版	(2014.08.15)	
外国人漁業の規制に関する法律施行令	公開(暫定版)	(2014.05.15)	
外国倒産処理手続の承認援助に関する法律	公開	(2010.11.24)	
外国等に対する我が国の民事裁判権に関する法律	公開	(2011.01.04)	
会社更生法	公開	(2014.01.27)	
会社法施行令	公開	(2010.11.12)	
海難審判法	公開	(2009.10.30)	
海洋生物資源の保存及び管理に関する法律	公開	(2010.05.19)	
化学物質の審査及び製造等の規制に関する法律	更新	(2011.03.03)	
化学物質の審査及び製造等の規制に関する法律施行令	更新	(2012.06.27)	
核原料物質，核燃料物質及び原子炉の規制に関する法律	公開	(2009.06.16)	

新着情報のお知らせ（五十音順）

法令名	公開・更新	年月日	所管庁
貸金業法	公開	(2011.03.03)	
貸金業法施行令	公開	(2013.04.11)	
ガス事業法	更新(暫定版)	(2013.12.04)	
課徴金の減免に係る報告及び資料の提出に関する規則	公開	(2013.07.16)	
割賦販売法	公開(暫定版)	(2013.11.12)	
割賦販売法施行規則	公開(暫定版)	(2013.08.01)	
割賦販売法施行令	公開	(2012.08.14)	
家庭用品品質表示法	最終版	(2014.06.16)	
家庭用品品質表示法	更新(暫定版)	(2014.05.29)	
貨物自動車運送事業法	公開	(2012.01.18)	
貨物利用運送事業法	公開	(2012.01.18)	
肝炎対策基本法	公開	(2011.12.22)	
企業立地の促進等による地域における産業集積の形成及び活性化に関する法律	公開	(2009.05.20)	
気象業務法	公開	(2011.04.19)	
行政事件訴訟法	公開	(2010.09.17)	
行政書士法	公開(暫定版)	(2013.08.28)	
漁業法	公開	(2009.10.30)	
漁業法第五十二条第一項の指定漁業を定める政令	最終版	(2014.06.16)	
漁業法第五十二条第一項の指定漁業を定める政令	公開(暫定版)	(2013.10.16)	
銀行法	更新(暫定版)	(2014.04.18)	
銀行法	更新	(2011.04.13)	
銀行法	公開	(2009.10.30)	
銀行法第二十六条第二項に規定する区分等を定める命令	公開	(2011.04.13)	
金融機関の信託業務の兼営等に関する法律施行規則	公開	(2013.03.21)	
金融機関の信託業務の兼営等に関する法律施行令	公開	(2013.03.21)	
金融商品取引法	更新(暫定版)	(2014.02.20)	
金融商品取引法	公開	(2010.07.01)	
金融商品取引法第二条に規定する定義に関する内閣府令	公開	(2011.04.13)	
金融商品の販売等に関する法律	更新	(2013.04.11)	
金融商品の販売等に関する法律施行令	公開	(2013.04.11)	
景観法	公開(暫定版)	(2014.04.18)	
経済産業省関係化学物質の審査及び製造等の規制に関する法律施行規則	公開	(2012.05.14)	

新着情報のお知らせ（五十音順）

法令名	公開・更新	年月日	所管庁
警察官職務執行法	最終版	(2014.06.30)	
警察官職務執行法	更新(暫定版)	(2013.08.01)	
刑事施設及び被収容者の処遇に関する規則	最終版	(2014.06.16)	
刑事施設及び被収容者の処遇に関する規則	公開(暫定版)	(2014.02.21)	
刑事訴訟規則	公開	(2011.09.08)	
刑事訴訟法（第三編以降）	公開	(2011.10.21)	
研究開発事業計画の認定等に関する命令	最終版	(2014.08.28)	
研究開発事業計画の認定等に関する命令	公開(暫定版)	(2014.07.28)	
原子力基本法	最終版	(2014.07.08)	
原子力基本法	公開(暫定版)	(2013.09.02)	
原子力損害賠償支援機構法	公開	(2013.06.19)	
原子力損害賠償支援機構法施行令	公開	(2013.06.19)	
建設業法	公開	(2013.10.17)	
高圧ガス保安法	公開	(2009.06.26)	
公害紛争処理法	最終版	(2013.12.02)	
公害紛争処理法	公開(暫定版)	(2013.11.20)	
航空法施行規則	公開	(2011.07.08)	
後見登記等に関する法律	公開(暫定版)	(2014.07.25)	
公正取引委員会の審査に関する規則	公開	(2011.12.22)	
公正取引委員会の審判に関する規則	公開	(2013.07.11)	
公正取引委員会の審判費用等に関する政令	公開	(2011.11.11)	
更生保護事業法	最終版	(2014.02.20)	
更生保護事業法	更新(暫定版)	(2013.08.05)	
更生保護法	公開	(2009.05.15)	
港則法	最終版	(2014.03.14)	
港則法	更新(暫定版)	(2014.01.09)	
公認会計士法	公開	(2010.06.03)	
公認会計士法施行規則	公開	(2012.11.12)	
公認会計士法施行令	公開	(2013.03.21)	
公文書等の管理に関する法律	公開(暫定版)	(2013.09.11)	
高齢者虐待の防止，高齢者の養護者に対する支援等に関する法律	公開	(2013.03.21)	
港湾の施設の技術上の基準を定める省令	公開	(2011.08.05)	
港湾法	公開	(2011.08.05)	
国際受刑者移送法	更新	(2011.12.22)	
国際受刑者移送法	公開	(2009.05.20)	

新着情報のお知らせ（五十音順）

法令名	公開・更新	年月日	所管庁
国際的な子の奪取の民事上の側面に関する条約の実施に関する法律	公開(暫定版)	(2014.01.21)	
国債の振替に関する命令	公開(暫定版)	(2014.05.23)	
国際連合安全保障理事会決議第千八百七十四号等を踏まえ我が国が実施する貨物検査等に関する特別措置法	公開	(2013.04.11)	
国際連合平和維持活動等に対する協力に関する法律	公開	(2014.07.08)	
国税徴収法（抄）	公開	(2010.05.20)	
国税通則法（抄）	更新(暫定版)	(2014.03.14)	
国税通則法（抄）	公開	(2010.12.15)	
国籍法	公開	(2009.07.06)	
国籍法施行規則	公開	(2013.12.20)	
国土利用計画法（概要）	公開	(2011.02.25)	
戸籍法	公開	(2014.01.29)	
戸籍法施行規則	公開	(2014.03.18)	
国家公務員法	最終版	(2014.06.12)	
国家公務員法	更新(暫定版)	(2013.10.28)	
国家賠償法	公開	(2010.11.12)	
雇用対策法	公開	(2014.06.26)	
雇用保険法	公開	(2010.06.29)	
債権管理回収業に関する特別措置法	公開	(2012.04.20)	
債権管理回収業に関する特別措置法施行規則	公開	(2012.10.18)	
債権管理回収業に関する特別措置法施行令	公開(暫定版)	(2013.08.01)	
裁判員の参加する刑事裁判に関する法律	公開(暫定版)	(2014.05.08)	
裁判所法	公開	(2009.07.03)	
財務諸表等の監査証明に関する内閣府令	公開	(2013.04.11)	
産業活力の再生及び産業活動の革新に関する特別措置法	公開(暫定版)	(2013.09.25)	
産業活力の再生及び産業活動の革新に関する特別措置法施行規則	公開	(2013.04.18)	
産業活力の再生及び産業活動の革新に関する特別措置法施行令	公開(暫定版)	(2013.08.05)	
産業技術力強化法	更新(暫定版)	(2013.09.25)	
産業技術力強化法施行規則	公開(暫定版)	(2013.09.27)	
産業技術力強化法施行令	公開(暫定版)	(2013.09.27)	
事業主が講ずべき短時間労働者の雇用管理の改善等に関する措置等についての指針	最終版	(2014.04.14)	

新着情報のお知らせ（五十音順）

法令名	公開・更新	年月日	所管庁
事業主が講ずべき短時間労働者の雇用管理の改善等に関する措置等についての指針	公開（暫定版）	(2013.10.28)	
資金移動業者に関する内閣府令	公開	(2013.03.21)	
資金決済に関する法律	公開（暫定版）	(2014.07.08)	
資産の流動化に関する法律	更新（暫定版）	(2014.04.22)	
資産の流動化に関する法律	公開	(2011.06.14)	
資産の流動化に関する法律施行令（暫定版）	公開（暫定版）	(2014.02.28)	
地震保険に関する法律	公開	(2010.04.20)	
持続的養殖生産確保法	公開	(2010.06.15)	
執行官法	公開	(2012.11.20)	
実用新案法	更新（暫定版）	(2014.05.15)	
指定化学物質等の性状及び取扱いに関する情報の提供の方法等を定める省令	公開	(2012.07.05)	
指定漁業の許可及び取締り等に関する省令	公開	(2014.06.16)	
私的独占の禁止及び公正取引の確保に関する法律	更新	(2013.07.08)	
私的独占の禁止及び公正取引の確保に関する法律第九条から第十六条までの規定による認可の申請，報告及び届出等に関する規則	更新（暫定版）	(2014.02.28)	
私的独占の禁止及び公正取引の確保に関する法律第九条から第十六条までの規定による認可の申請，報告及び届出等に関する規則	更新	(2012.07.05)	
児童虐待の防止等に関する法律	公開	(2014.06.16)	
四半期財務諸表等の用語，様式及び作成方法に関する規則	公開	(2013.04.15)	
司法試験法	公開	(2014.06.25)	
社会福祉法	公開	(2013.01.21)	
借地借家法	更新（暫定版）	(2013.10.17)	
借地借家法	公開	(2010.12.15)	
社債，株式等の振替に関する法律施行令	公開	(2013.04.11)	
宗教法人法	公開	(2013.06.26)	
出資の受入れ，預り金及び金利等の取締りに関する法律	更新	(2012.09.12)	
出資の受入れ，預り金及び金利等の取締りに関する法律	公開	(2010.03.23)	
出入国管理及び難民認定法	更新	(2010.11.12)	
出入国管理及び難民認定法施行規則	更新	(2010.06.09)	

新着情報のお知らせ（五十音順）

法令名	公開・更新	年月日	所管庁
出入国管理及び難民認定法第七条第一項第二号の基準を定める省令	更新	(2010.10.01)	
商業登記法	公開	(2009.09.10)	
証券情報等の提供又は公表に関する内閣府令	公開	(2013.04.11)	
少年法	公開	(2011.08.29)	
消費者安全法	公開	(2012.10.04)	
消費者基本法	公開	(2013.03.13)	
消費者教育の推進に関する法律	最終版	(2014.02.20)	
消費者教育の推進に関する法律	公開(暫定版)	(2013.08.06)	
消費者契約法	更新	(2013.02.14)	
消費者契約法施行規則	公開	(2013.02.14)	
消費生活用製品安全法	更新(暫定版)	(2013.09.25)	
消費生活用製品安全法	公開	(2009.05.20)	
消費生活用製品安全法施行令	公開(暫定版)	(2013.10.24)	
商標法	更新(暫定版)	(2014.06.10)	
商品先物取引法	更新(暫定版)	(2013.10.28)	
商品先物取引法施行規則	更新	(2013.05.21)	
商品取引所法	更新	(2010.06.01)	
商品取引所法施行規則	公開	(2010.04.22)	
商品取引所法施行令	公開	(2009.06.26)	
商法	公開	(2013.10.22)	
消防法	公開	(2010.03.23)	
職業能力開発促進法	公開	(2009.07.03)	
所得税法（非居住者，外国法人関連部分）	最終版	(2014.08.15)	
所得税法（非居住者，外国法人関連部分）	更新(暫定版)	(2013.10.24)	
所得税法施行規則（非居住者，外国法人関連部分）	更新(暫定版)	(2014.04.18)	
所得税法施行規則（非居住者，外国法人関連部分）	公開	(2010.12.13)	
所得税法施行令（非居住者，外国法人関連部分）	更新(暫定版)	(2014.03.14)	
所得税法施行令（非居住者，外国法人関連部分）	公開	(2010.04.09)	
私立学校法	公開(暫定版)	(2013.10.28)	
新エネルギー利用等の促進に関する特別措置法	公開	(2010.05.11)	
新エネルギー利用等の促進に関する特別措置法施行令	公開	(2009.05.20)	
新規化学物質の製造又は輸入に係る届出等に関する省令	公開	(2012.01.25)	

新着情報のお知らせ（五十音順）

法令名	公開・更新	年月日	所管庁
人事訴訟法	公開	(2013.01.21)	
信託業法	公開	(2010.12.28)	
信託業法施行規則	**公開(暫定版)**	**(2014.02.28)**	
信託業法施行令	**公開(暫定版)**	**(2014.02.28)**	
信託法	**更新(暫定版)**	**(2014.03.14)**	
信託法	公開	(2010.11.25)	
生物多様性基本法	公開	(2011.01.28)	
絶滅のおそれのある野生動植物の種の保存に関する法律	更新	(2013.08.08)	
絶滅のおそれのある野生動植物の種の保存に関する法律	更新(暫定版)	(2013.08.05)	
総合科学技術会議令	公開	(2009.07.06)	
総合法律支援法	公開	(2009.05.14)	
測量法（概要）	公開	(2009.09.02)	
租税特別措置法（非居住者，外国法人関連部分）	更新(暫定版)	(2014.02.28)	
租税特別措置法施行規則（非居住者，外国法人関連部分）	公開(暫定版)	(2014.03.14)	
租税特別措置法施行令（非居住者，外国法人関連部分）	**更新(暫定版)**	**(2014.05.01)**	
租税特別措置法施行令（非居住者，外国法人関連部分）	更新	(2011.07.29)	
租税特別措置法施行令（非居住者，外国法人関連部分）	公開	(2010.04.09)	
大学設置基準	公開	(2009.09.10)	
大気汚染防止法	最終版	(2013.11.12)	
大気汚染防止法	公開(暫定版)	(2013.08.27)	
大規模小売店舗立地法	公開	(2009.06.26)	
大規模小売店舗立地法施行規則	公開	(2013.08.05)	
大規模小売店舗立地法施行令	公開	(2013.04.18)	
対内直接投資等に関する政令	更新	(2012.10.04)	
対内直接投資等に関する政令	公開	(2009.08.12)	
対内直接投資等に関する命令	更新	(2012.02.03)	
対内直接投資等に関する命令	公開	(2009.08.12)	
建物の区分所有等に関する法律	公開	(2012.06.20)	
短時間労働者の雇用管理の改善等に関する法律施行規則	公開	(2013.01.21)	
仲裁法	**公開(暫定版)**	**(2014.01.14)**	
地理空間情報活用推進基本法	公開(暫定版)	(2014.03.18)	
強くしなやかな国民生活の実現を図るための防災・減災等に資する国土強靱化基本法	公開(暫定版)	(2014.07.25)	

新着情報のお知らせ（五十音順）

法令名	公開・更新	年月日	所管庁
電気事業者による再生可能エネルギー電気の調達に関する特別措置法	公開(暫定版)	(2014.06.30)	
電気事業者による新エネルギー等の利用に関する特別措置法	公開	(2010.04.22)	
電気事業法	最終版	(2014.06.16)	
電気事業法	更新(暫定版)	(2014.01.16)	
電気用品安全法	更新(暫定版)	(2014.02.20)	
電気用品安全法	更新	(2010.07.30)	
電子記録債権法施行規則	公開	(2013.03.21)	
電子記録債権法施行令	公開	(2013.03.21)	
電子公告規則	公開	(2010.12.03)	
統括事業計画の認定等に関する命令	最終版	(2014.08.28)	
統括事業計画の認定等に関する命令	公開(暫定版)	(2014.07.28)	
動産及び債権の譲渡の対抗要件に関する民法の特例等に関する法律	公開	(2010.03.23)	
投資信託及び投資法人に関する法律	公開	(2010.06.09)	
投資信託及び投資法人に関する法律施行令	公開	(2012.11.12)	
逃亡犯罪人引渡法	公開	(2010.03.23)	
特定化学物質の環境への排出量の把握等及び管理の改善の促進に関する法律施行規則	公開	(2012.05.30)	
特定化学物質の環境への排出量の把握等及び管理の改善の促進に関する法律施行令	公開	(2011.02.17)	
特定商取引に関する法律	更新	(2013.04.11)	
特定商取引に関する法律施行令	更新	(2013.04.11)	
特定商品等の預託等取引契約に関する法律	公開	(2012.03.02)	
特定先端大型研究施設の共用の促進に関する法律	公開	(2011.02.10)	
特定多国籍企業による研究開発事業及び統括事業の促進に関する基本方針	最終版	(2014.08.28)	
特定多国籍企業による研究開発事業及び統括事業の促進に関する基本方針	公開(暫定版)	(2014.07.29)	
特定多国籍企業による研究開発事業等の促進に関する特別措置法	最終版	(2014.08.28)	
特定多国籍企業による研究開発事業等の促進に関する特別措置法	公開(暫定版)	(2014.07.29)	
特定多国籍企業による研究開発事業等の促進に関する特別措置法施行規則	最終版	(2014.08.28)	

新着情報のお知らせ（五十音順）

法令名	公開・更新	年月日	所管庁
特定多国籍企業による研究開発事業等の促進に関する特別措置法施行規則	公開(暫定版)	(2014.07.29)	
特定多国籍企業による研究開発事業等の促進に関する特別措置法施行令	最終版	(2014.08.28)	
特定多国籍企業による研究開発事業等の促進に関する特別措置法施行令	公開(暫定版)	(2014.07.29)	
特定秘密の保護に関する法律	公開(暫定版)	(2014.07.01)	
特定物質の規制等によるオゾン層の保護に関する法律	公開(暫定版)	(2013.10.24)	
独立行政法人産業技術総合研究所法	公開	(2011.02.17)	
独立行政法人新エネルギー・産業技術総合開発機構法	公開	(2010.05.20)	
独立行政法人日本学術振興会法	公開(暫定版)	(2013.08.27)	
都市計画法	公開	(2009.09.10)	
土壌汚染対策法	更新	(2013.03.11)	
日本法令外国語訳データベースシステム	開設	(2009.04.01)	
農業法人に対する投資の円滑化に関する特別措置法	最終版	(2014.06.16)	
農業法人に対する投資の円滑化に関する特別措置法	公開(暫定版)	(2013.10.16)	
農用地の土壌の汚染防止等に関する法律	公開(暫定版)	(2013.10.16)	
農林物資の規格化及び品質表示の適正化に関する法律	公開	(2011.02.17)	
破壊活動防止法	公開	(2011.09.29)	
破産法	公開	(2010.04.14)	
犯罪による収益の移転防止に関する法律	公開(暫定版)	(2013.08.08)	
犯罪による収益の移転防止に関する法律施行規則	公開(暫定版)	(2013.08.01)	
犯罪による収益の移転防止に関する法律施行令	公開(暫定版)	(2013.10.28)	
非訟事件手続法	最終版	(2014.07.11)	
非訟事件手続法	公開(暫定版)	(2014.05.15)	
標準対訳辞書（平成20年3月改訂版, Ver.3.0）	公開	(2009.04.01)	
標準対訳辞書（平成21年3月改訂版, Ver.4.1）	公開	(2010.02.17)	
標準対訳辞書（平成21年3月改訂版, Ver4.0）	公開	(2009.05.22)	
標準対訳辞書（平成22年3月改訂版, Ver.5.0）	公開	(2010.04.28)	

新着情報のお知らせ（五十音順）

法令名	公開・更新	年月日	所管庁
標準対訳辞書（平成23年3月改訂版, Ver.6.0）	公開	(2011.06.02)	
標準対訳辞書（平成24年3月改訂版, Ver.7.0）	公開	(2012.04.10)	
標準対訳辞書（平成25年3月改訂版, Ver.8.0）	公開	(2013.05.08)	
標準対訳辞書（平成26年3月改訂版, Ver.9.0）	公開	(2014.06.26)	
肥料取締法	公開	(2014.06.16)	
不公正な取引方法	更新	(2012.07.13)	
不正アクセス行為の禁止等に関する法律	最終版	(2014.08.15)	
不正アクセス行為の禁止等に関する法律	公開(暫定版)	(2014.02.20)	
不正競争防止法	最終版	(2013.11.20)	
不正競争防止法	更新(暫定版)	(2013.08.05)	
不正競争防止法	更新	(2012.04.20)	
不当景品類及び不当表示防止法	更新(暫定版)	(2014.06.10)	
不動産登記規則	公開	(2012.12.14)	
不動産登記法	公開	(2010.03.08)	
不動産登記令	公開	(2013.03.13)	
扶養義務の準拠法に関する法律	公開	(2012.02.01)	
武力攻撃事態における外国軍用品等の海上輸送の規制に関する法律	公開	(2010.03.18)	
武力攻撃事態における捕虜等の取扱いに関する法律	公開	(2009.10.21)	
平成21年5月21日から裁判員制度がスタート		(2009.05.21)	
平成21年度翻訳整備計画〔改定版〕	公開	(2009.04.22)	
平成22年度翻訳整備計画	公開	(2009.04.22)	
平成22年度翻訳整備計画〔改定版〕	公開	(2010.04.28)	
平成23年度翻訳整備計画	公開	(2010.04.28)	
平成23年度翻訳整備計画〔改定版〕	公開	(2011.04.08)	
平成24年度翻訳整備計画	公開	(2011.04.08)	
平成24年度翻訳整備計画〔改定版〕	公開	(2012.04.03)	
平成25年度翻訳整備計画	公開	(2012.04.03)	
平成25年度翻訳整備計画〔改定版〕	公開	(2013.03.28)	
平成26年度翻訳整備計画	公開	(2013.03.28)	
平成26年度翻訳整備計画〔改定版〕	公開	(2014.03.26)	
平成27年度翻訳整備計画	公開	(2014.03.26)	
弁護士法	公開	(2010.03.23)	
弁理士法	公開	(2010.06.21)	
貿易関係貿易外取引等に関する省令	最終版	(2014.05.08)	

新着情報のお知らせ（五十音順）

法令名	公開・更新	年月日	所管庁
貿易関係貿易外取引等に関する省令	**更新(暫定版)**	(2014.01.16)	
貿易関係貿易外取引等に関する省令	公開	(2010.07.05)	
貿易保険法	公開	(2013.05.14)	
法人税法（外国法人関連部分）	更新(暫定版)	(2014.03.14)	
法人税法施行規則（外国法人関連部分）	更新(暫定版)	(2014.05.08)	
法人税法施行規則（外国法人関連部分）	公開	(2010.12.03)	
法人税法施行令（外国法人関連部分）	更新(暫定版)	(2014.03.14)	
法人税法施行令（非居住者，外国法人関連部分）	公開	(2010.04.09)	
法の適用に関する通則法	公開	(2011.05.26)	
保険業法	更新	(2013.03.25)	
保険業法	公開	(2010.07.14)	
保険業法施行令	公開	(2013.03.25)	
保健師助産師看護師法	公開	(2013.04.19)	
保護司法	更新	(2011.05.26)	
民事再生規則	最終版	(2014.03.14)	
民事再生規則	公開(暫定版)	(2013.10.17)	
民事執行規則	公開(暫定版)	(2013.09.25)	
民事執行法施行令	公開	(2012.01.24)	
民事訴訟規則,「循環型社会形成推進基本法,「労働者派遣事業の適正な運営の確保及び派遣労働者の就業条件の整備等に関する法律施行規則	公開	(2009.06.16)	
民事訴訟費用等に関する法律	公開	(2010.12.03)	
民事訴訟法	**更新(暫定版)**	(2013.08.01)	
民事調停法	**公開(暫定版)**	(2014.01.16)	
民事保全法	更新	(2012.11.13)	
民事保全法	公開	(2010.03.08)	
民事保全法施行令	公開	(2012.01.24)	
民法（第四編第五編）	**更新(暫定版)**	(2014.08.19)	
無差別大量殺人行為を行った団体の規制に関する法律	公開	(2014.08.15)	
遺言の方式の準拠法に関する法律	公開	(2012.01.24)	
優越的地位の濫用に関する独占禁止法上の考え方	公開	(2012.03.21)	
有害物質を含有する家庭用品の規制に関する法律	公開	(2011.01.26)	
輸出貿易管理規則	最終版	(2013.09.12)	
輸出貿易管理規則	更新(暫定版)	(2013.08.05)	
輸出貿易管理規則	公開	(2009.07.06)	

1st ed.2014.10　　　　　xi　　　　　JSB英文六法

新着情報のお知らせ（五十音順）

法令名	公開・更新	年月日	所管庁
輸出貿易管理令	**最終版**	**(2014.06.26)**	
輸出貿易管理令	更新(暫定版)	(2014.05.23)	
輸出貿易管理令	最終版	(2013.11.20)	
輸出貿易管理令	更新(暫定版)	(2013.08.05)	
輸出貿易管理令	公開	(2009.10.30)	
輸出貿易管理令別表第一及び外国為替令別表の規定に基づき貨物又は技術を定める省令	更新	(2013.05.14)	
輸出貿易管理令別表第一及び外国為替令別表の規定に基づき貨物又は技術を定める省令	公開	(2010.06.01)	
預金保険法	公開(暫定版)	(2013.08.08)	
預金保険法施行規則	公開	(2013.04.11)	
預金保険法施行令	公開(暫定版)	(2013.09.25)	
予算決算及び会計令（第七章）	**公開**	**(2014.06.25)**	
利息制限法	最終版	(2013.10.22)	
利息制限法	公開(暫定版)	(2013.10.17)	
連結財務諸表の用語，様式及び作成方法に関する規則	公開	(2013.04.11)	
老人福祉法	公開	(2013.04.11)	
労働安全衛生規則	公開	(2011.10.25)	
労働安全衛生法施行令	**最終版**	**(2014.07.29)**	
労働安全衛生法施行令	公開(暫定版)	(2014.05.16)	
労働関係調整法	公開	(2009.10.30)	
労働基準法	**最終版**	**(2014.07.25)**	
労働基準法	更新(暫定版)	(2014.05.08)	
労働契約法	公開	(2011.12.06)	
労働者災害補償保険法	公開	(2010.09.16)	
労働審判法	**最終版**	**(2014.02.28)**	
労働審判法	公開(暫定版)	(2013.09.02)	
労働保険の保険料の徴収等に関する法律	公開	(2009.06.16)	
翻訳法令164本（他に法令名のみの翻訳1653本）	公開	(2009.04.01)	